ANNOTATED
GUIDE TO THE INSOLVENCY LEGISLATION

TWENTY-FIRST EDITION

VOLUME 1

ANNOTATED GUIDE TO THE INSOLVENCY LEGISLATION

Insolvency Act 1986
Insolvency (England and Wales) Rules 2016
Table of Destinations of the Insolvency Rules 1986
Table of Derivations of the Insolvency (England and Wales) Rules 2016

Twenty-first Edition

Volume 1

Len Sealy MA LLM PhD, Barrister and Solicitor (NZ)
SJ Berwin Professor Emeritus of Corporate Law,
University of Cambridge

David Milman LLB PhD
Professor of Law
Law School
Lancaster University
Professorial Associate at Exchange Chambers

Peter Bailey LLM
In-House Author, Sweet & Maxwell
Part-time teacher in Company Law,
School of Law, University of Reading

SWEET & MAXWELL

THOMSON REUTERS

Disclaimer

The publisher advises that any statutory or other materials issued by the Crown or other relevant bodies and reproduced or quoted in this publication are not the authorised official versions of those statutory or other materials. In their preparation, however, the greatest care has been taken to ensure exact conformity with the law as enacted or other material as issued.

While copyright in all statutory and other materials resides in the Crown or other relevant body, copyright in the remaining material in this publication is vested in the publisher.

Published in 2018 by Thomson Reuters, trading as Sweet & Maxwell.
Thomson Reuters is registered in England & Wales. Company No.1679046.
Registered Office and address for service: 5 Canada Square, Canary Wharf, London E14 5AQ.

For further information on our products and services, visit
www.sweetandmaxwell.co.uk

Typeset by Wright and Round Ltd, Gloucestershire
Printed and bound by CPI Group (UK) Ltd, Croydon, CR0 4YY

No natural forests were destroyed to make this product; only farmed timber was used and replanted.

A CIP catalogue record for this book is available from the British Library

ISBN 9780414067691

PREFACE TO THE TWENTY-FIRST EDITION

One might have imagined that this edition would reflect the calm after the storm; the storm being the wholesale replacement of the Insolvency Rules 1986 (SI 1986/1925) by the Insolvency (England and Wales) Rules 2016 (SI 2016/1024) with effect from 6 April 2017 coinciding with the commencement of further provisions of the Deregulation Act 2015 and, fundamentally, the Small Business, Enterprise and Employment Act 2015. As it happens, the pace of change in insolvency law has remained hectic in the intervening 12 months.

The Insolvency Rules 2016 have required some amendment and this explains the Insolvency (England and Wales) and Insolvency (Scotland) (Miscellaneous and Consequential Amendments) Rules 2017 (SI 2017/1115). Moreover, the changes reflected in the 2016 Rules and the 2015 primary legislation have been carried over to insolvent partnerships and limited liability partnerships and to the administration of estates of deceased persons—see the Insolvency (Miscellaneous Amendments) Regulations 2017 (SI 2017/1119). This process of transition required a new *Practice Direction: Insolvency Proceedings* [2018] B.C.C. 241 to accommodate the 2016 Rules and this finally appeared on, and is in force from, 25 April 2018: we have held production of this edition to include the new Practice Direction.

We also note in this edition the Insolvency Amendment (EU 2015/848) Regulations (SI 2017/702). These amend primary and secondary UK legislation so as to reflect the EU Insolvency Regulation 2015/848 taking effect on 26 June 2017 to replace of the former EC Insolvency Regulation 1346/2000. The changes are for the most part cosmetic rather than substantive. Apart from this, there have been no *major* changes in primary legislation.

Turning to reported case law much of it still features the 1986 Rules, though the judiciary helpfully often note the 2016 counterpart provision. Our advice to retain copies of the 19th edition of the *Guide* still applies.

On the personal insolvency front, the IVA has cemented its dominant position as the premier resolution mode, but has thrown up little in the way of new case law. After 30 years of evolution the basic principles are now clear. The debt relief order has also barely troubled the courts, but that might be due to the lack of money to fund any litigation. Bankruptcy, although statistically the least significant of the personal insolvency procedures, does offer food for thought. So, we have the first reported case on the new adjudication procedure (*Re Budniok* [2017] EWHC 368 (Ch)). There have been significant pronouncements on annulment (*Yang* v *OR* [2017] EWCA Civ 1465 and *Oraki v Bramston* [2017] EWCA Civ 403).

The death of receivership as a corporate insolvency procedure in common use is confirmed by the latest official statistics. Administrative receivership has dropped off the radar with only two incidents in 2017. Although administration is still a disappointment in statistical usage terms, it never fails to throw up interesting jurisprudence. *JCAM Commercial Real Estate Property XV Ltd v Davis Haulage Ltd* [2017] EWCA Civ 267 stands out as an important precedent for practitioners to pay heed to. There have been few authorities of interest dealing with CVAs, but a number of cases to note in the winding up sphere, particularly with regard to applications for directions and also the potential impact of s.127 of the Insolvency Act 1986.

More generally the *Lehman Waterfall* litigation continues to provide regular insights into those rare provisions in the Insolvency Rules detailing the position where a *surplus* has to be distributed, including a complex judgment (including a partial dissenting judgment) by the Supreme Court.

The wrongful trading sanction (s.214 of the Insolvency Act 1986) continues to provide unpromising litigation prospects for insolvency practitioners; witness *Nicholson v Fielding* (unreported, 15 September 2017, decision of Deputy Registrar Prentis). There have been few director disqualification cases of note (by way of exception *Secretary of State for Business, Innovation and Skills v Rahman* [2017] EWHC 2468 (Ch) provided a useful review of the jurisprudence on disqualification periods) and no indications of the new disqualification compensation regime ushered in by the Small Business, Enterprise and Employment Act 2015 being used.

Cross-border insolvency issues offer a more lively perspective with important cases being decided with regard to EU Regulation 2015/848 (or its predecessor) and the Cross-Border Insolvency Regulations

2006 (SI 2006/1030); note in particular *Re Agrokor DD* [2017] EWHC 2791 (Ch) and the *Dalnyaya Step* litigation. The latter measure is likely to grow in importance with Brexit.

This is the first edition where Len Sealy has not co-authored the new annotations. But, even in retirement, he continues to play a constructive role behind the scenes. Our thanks are extended to him and (as always) go to Claire Patient who continues to mastermind processing the material at Sweet & Maxwell. We would also like to acknowledge the continuing support we have received from Robin Waghorn on both the online and print versions and we welcome David Montague as a new member of the online team.

An important milestone in insolvency was achieved in the summer of 2017 with the retirement of our old friend Stephen Baister from the position of Chief Bankruptcy Registrar that he held with distinction for the previous 12 years. He has made a considerable contribution to the subject from the bench and his work in drafting practice directions should not go unnoticed. He will be sadly missed but we respectfully wish Nicholas Briggs the best of fortune as Stephen's successor.

The text states the law as at 28 February 2018, though a few later amendments have been incorporated, including those by the Small Business, Enterprise and Employment Act 2015 (Consequential Amendments, Savings and Transitional Provisions) Regulations 2018 (SI 2018/208).

David Milman
Peter Bailey

28 February 2018

ABOUT THE AUTHORS

Len Sealy MA, LLM, PhD, Barrister and Solicitor (NZ) is SJ Berwin Professor Emeritus of Corporate Law at the University of Cambridge. He is an eminent commentator on company and commercial law, having written and lectured extensively in these areas and was for many years General Editor of *British Company Law and Practice.*

David Milman LLB, PhD is Professor of Law at Lancaster University. He is also Co-General Editor of *Insolvency Intelligence* and a Professorial Associate at Exchange Chambers.

Peter Bailey LLM is an In-House Author in Company Law and Insolvency Law at Sweet & Maxwell where he is the In-House Editor of *British Company Law and Practice*, *British Company Cases* and *Sweet & Maxwell's Company Law Newsletter*, and contributes to several other publications, including Totty & Moss, *Insolvency* and Lightman & Moss, *The Law of Administrators and Receivers of Companies* (6th edn). He teaches Company Law part-time at the School of Law, University of Reading.

ABBREVIATIONS

The following abbreviations are used in this work:

BA 1914	Bankruptcy Act 1914
B(A)A 1926	Bankruptcy (Amendment) Act 1926
BEIS	Department for Business, Energy and Industrial Strategy
BIS	Department for Business, Innovation and Skills
BR 1952	Bankruptcy Rules 1952
BRO	Bankruptcy restrictions order
BRU	Bankruptcy restrictions undertaking
CA	Companies Act (e.g. CA 2006 = Companies Act 2006)
CBIR	Cross-Border Insolvency Regulations 2006
CDDA 1986	Company Directors Disqualification Act 1986
CFCSA 1972	Companies (Floating Charges and Receivers) (Scotland) Act 1972
CDO	Competition Disqualification Order
CDU	Competition Disqualification Undertaking
CJA	Criminal Justice Act (e.g. CJA 1988 = Criminal Justice Act 1988)
CMA	Competition and Markets Authority
COMI	Centre of main interests
Cork Report	*Report of the Review Committee on Insolvency Law and Practice* (Cmnd.8558, 1982)
CPR	Civil Procedure Rules
CRAR	Commercial rent arrears recovery
CVA	Company voluntary arrangement
DA 2015	Deregulation Act 2015
DBEIS	Department for Business, Energy and Industrial Strategy
DBERR	Department for Business, Enterprise and Regulatory Reform
DBIS	Department for Business, Innovation and Skills
DRO	Debt relief order
DRRO	Debt relief restrictions order
DRRU	Debt relief restrictions undertaking
DTI	Department of Trade and Industry
EA 2002	Enterprise Act 2002
EC Regulation	EC Regulation on Insolvency Proceedings 2000 (also ECRIP)
ERRA 2013	Enterprise and Regulatory Reform Act 2013
EU Regulation	EU Regulation on Insolvency Proceedings 2015 (also EURIP)
FA	Finance Act (e.g. FA 1985 = Finance Act 1985)
FCA	Financial Conduct Authority
Finality Regulations	Financial Markets and Insolvency (Settlement Finality) Regulations 1999 (SI 1999/2979)
FSA	Financial Services Authority
FSA 1986	Financial Services Act 1986

FSA 2012	Financial Services Act 2012
FSMA 2000	Financial Services and Markets Act 2000
G to E	Model Law on Cross-Border Insolvency Guide to Enactment
HMRC	Her Majesty's Revenue & Customs
IA	Insolvency Act (e.g. IA 1986 = Insolvency Act 1986)
IPA	Income payments agreement
IPO	Income payments order
IR 1986	Insolvency Rules 1986
IR 2016	Insolvency (England and Wales) Rules 2016
I(A)R	Insolvency (Amendment) Rules (e.g. I(A)R 1993 = Insolvency Amendment Rules 1993)
IVA	Individual voluntary arrangement
Judgments Regulation	Council Regulation (EC) 44/2001 of December 22, 2000 on jurisdiction and the recognition and enforcement of judgments in civil and commercial matters
LLP	Limited liability partnership
LLPA 2000	Limited Liability Partnerships Act 2000
LLPR 2001	Limited Liability Partnerships Regulations 2001 (SI 2001/1090)
LPA 1925	Law of Property Act 1925
LRO 2010	Legislative Reform (Insolvency) (Miscellaneous Amendments) Order 2010
OR	Official receiver
POCA 2002	Proceeds of Crime Act 2002
PRA	Prudential Regulation Authority
RSC	Rules of the Supreme Court
SBEEA 2015	Small Business, Enterprise and Employment Act 2015
TCEA 2007	Tribunals, Courts and Enforcement Act 2007
TLATA 1996	Trusts of Land and Appointment of Trustees Act 1996
TUPE Regulations	Transfer of Undertakings (Protection of Employment) Regulations 2006
White Paper	*A Revised Framework for Insolvency Law* (Cmnd.9175, 1984)

CONTENTS

Case Table

References within square brackets are located in Volume 2.

The following abbreviations are used in the tables to denote the location of entries in all tables:

[CBIR]	Cross-Border Insolvency Regulations 2006
[CDDA]	Company Directors Disqualification Act 1986
[ER]	EU Regulation on Insolvency Proceedings 2015
IA	Insolvency Act 1986
IR	Insolvency (England and Wales) Rules 2016
[UML]	UNCITRAL Model Law on Cross-Border Insolvency

	Provision
19 Entertainment Ltd, Re [2016] EWHC 1545 (Ch); [2017] B.C.C. 347	[CBIR Sch.1 arts 15, 17, 21]
1st Credit (Finance) Ltd v Bartram [2010] EWHC 2910 (Ch); [2011] B.P.I.R. 1	IA 269, 282(1)–(3), IR 10.5
3T Telecom Ltd, Re [2005] EWHC 275 (Ch); [2006] 2 B.C.L.C. 137	IA Sch.B1 para.111(1), (1A), (1B), [ER art.3(1)]
4 Eng Ltd v Harper [2009] EWHC 2633 (Ch); [2010] B.C.C. 746; [2010] B.P.I.R. 1	IA 423(1)–(3), 425(1), 425(2), (3)
A Ltd, Petitioner [2016] SC Edin 77	IA 117
A/Wear UK (In admin.) Ltd, Re [2013] EWCA Civ 1626; [2014] 1 P. & C.R. DG15	IA Sch.B1 para.43(6)
A&BC Chewing Gum Ltd, Re [1975] 1 W.L.R. 579 Ch D	IA 123
A&C Group Services Ltd, Re [1993] B.C.L.C. 1297 Ch D	[CDDA 12C]
A&C Supplies Ltd, Re [1998] B.C.C. 708; [1998] B.P.I.R. 303 Ch D	IA 29(2), 45(1), (2), 172(1), (2)
A&J Fabrications (Batley) Ltd v Grant Thornton (A Firm) (No.1) [1999] B.C.C. 807 Ch D	IA 212(1)
AA Mutual International Insurance Co Ltd, Re [2004] EWHC 2430 (Ch); [2005] 2 B.C.L.C. 8	IA 8, Sch.B1 paras 9, para.11
AA v BA [2015] IESC 102	IA 306
Aabar Block Sarl v Maud [2015] EWHC 3681 (Ch); [2016] B.P.I.R. 227	IA 266(3), (4), 271(3), IR 10.5
Aabar Block Sarl v Maud [2016] EWHC 1016 (Ch); [2016] B.P.I.R. 803	IA 266(3), (4), 271(3), IR 10.5
Aabar Block Sarl v Maud [2016] EWHC 2175 (Ch); [2016] Bus. L.R. 1243; [2016] B.P.I.R. 1486	IA 266(3), (4), IR 10.5
Aaron v Secretary of State for Business, Enterprise and Regulatory Reform. *See* Secretary of State for Business, Enterprise and Regulatory Reform v Aaron	
AB Agri Ltd v Curtis [2016] B.P.I.R. 1297 Cty Ct	IA 262, IR 15.31
Abbey Forwarding Ltd (In liq.) v Revenue and Customs Commissioners [2015] EWHC 225 (Ch); [2015] Bus. L.R. 882	IA 135
Abbey Forwarding Ltd v Hone [2010] EWHC 1644 (Ch); [2010] B.P.I.R. 1053	IA 168(5)
Abbey Leisure Ltd, Re [1990] B.C.C. 60 CA (Civ Div)	IA 125(2)
Abbot (John), Re [1997] B.C.C. 666; [1998] B.P.I.R. 171 Ch D	IA 263(5), (6)

Case	Provision
Abdulla v Whelan; Re Elsom [2017] EWHC 605 (Ch); [2017] B.P.I.R. 791	IA 283(2), (3), 315
Abermeadow Ltd (No.2), Re [2001] B.C.C. 724 Ch D	[CDDA 7(2)]
Abernethy v Hotbed Ltd [2011] EWHC 1476 (Ch); [2011] B.P.I.R. 1547	IR 10.5
Abrahams v Trustee in Bankruptcy of Abrahams [1999] B.P.I.R. 637 Ch D	IA 283(2), (3)
ACAL Underwriting Ltd, Re [2012] EWHC 4336 (Ch)	IA 107
ACC Bank Plc v McCann [2013] NIMaster 1	IA 282(1)–(3)
ACCA v Koumettou. *See* Association of Chartered Certified Accountants v Koumettou	
ACLI Metals (London) Ltd, Re (1989) 5 B.C.C. 749 Ch D (Companies Ct)	IA 168(5)
Adams v Mason Bullock (A Firm) [2004] EWHC 2910 (Ch); [2005] B.P.I.R. 241	IA 271(1), (2), (4)
Adbury Estates Ltd, Re [2003] B.C.C. 696 Ch D (Companies Ct)	[CDDA 4(1)]
Addlestone Linoleum Co, Re (1887) 37 Ch. D. 191 CA	IA 74(2)(f)
Adeosun v Revenue and Customs Commissioners [2011] EWHC 1577 (Ch); [2011] B.P.I.R. 1555	IA Pt IX, 271(1), (2), (4)
Adjei v Law for All [2011] EWHC 2672 (Ch); [2011] B.C.C. 963	IA Sch.B1 paras 13(2), 26(2), (3)
Adlards Motor Group Holding Ltd, Re [1990] B.C.L.C. 68 Ch D	IA 236
Advent Computer Training Ltd, Re [2010] EWHC 1042 (Ch); [2011] B.C.C. 52	IA Sch.B1 para.49
Advent Computer Training Ltd, Re [2010] EWHC 459 (Ch); [2011] B.C.C. 44	IA Sch.B1 paras 26, 46, 49, 107, IR 1.45
AE Farr Ltd, Re [1992] B.C.C. 150 Ch D (Companies Ct)	IA 236
AE Realisations (1985) Ltd, Re [1988] 1 W.L.R. 200; (1987) 3 B.C.C. 136 Ch D (Companies Ct)	IA 179, 181(1)–(3)
Aectra Refining & Marketing Inc v Exmar NV (The New Vanguard and The Pacifica) [1994] 1 W.L.R. 1634 CA (Civ Div)	IA Second Group of Parts
AET v Kermanshahchi. *See* Anglo Eastern Trust Ltd v Kermanshahchi (No.3)	
AG (Manchester) Ltd (formerly Accident Group Ltd) (In liq.), Re [2008] EWHC 64 (Ch); [2008] B.C.C. 497	[CDDA 12C]
Agilo Ltd v Henry [2010] EWHC 2717 (Ch); [2011] B.P.I.R. 297	IA 268, IR 10.5
Agrenco Madeira-Comércio Internacional Lda, Re [2015] B.C.C. 300 Ch D (Companies Ct)	IA 225
Agricultural Mortgage Corp Plc v Woodward [1994] B.C.C. 688 CA (Civ Div)	IA 423(1)–(3)
Agrimarche Ltd (In creditors' voluntary liq.), Re [2010] EWHC 1655 (Ch); [2010] B.C.C. 775	IA Sch.B1 para.5
Agrokor DD, Re [2017] EWHC 2791 (Ch); [2018] B.C.C. 18; [2018] B.P.I.R. 1	[CBIR Sch.1 art.2]
Ahmad v Bank of Scotland [2016] EWCA Civ 602	IA Pt III, 34
Ahmad v Inland Revenue Commissioners [2004] EWHC 2292 (Ch); [2005] B.P.I.R. 541	IA 267(1), (2)
Ahmed v Ingram [2018] EWCA Civ 519	IA 284(1)–(3), (6)
Ahmed v Landstone Leisure Ltd [2009] EWHC 125 (Ch); [2009] B.P.I.R. 227	IR 10.5
Ahmed v Mogul Eastern Foods [2005] EWHC 3532 (Ch); [2007] B.P.I.R. 975	IA 282(1), (3)
AI Levy (Holdings) Ltd, Re [1964] Ch. 19; [1963] 2 W.L.R. 1464 Ch D	IA 127
AIB Finance Ltd v Alsop [1998] 2 All E.R. 929; [1998] B.C.C. 780	IR 10.5
Aidiniantz v Sherlock Holmes International Society Ltd [2015] EWHC 2882 (Ch); [2015] B.P.I.R. 1329	IA 125(1)
Aiglon Ltd v Gau Shan Co Ltd [1993] 1 Lloyd's Rep. 164 QBD (Comm)	IA 425(1)
Ailyan v Smith [2010] EWHC 24 (Ch); [2010] B.P.I.R. 289	IA 238(2), 339(1)–(3), 423(1)–(3), 425(1)
Aim Underwriting Agencies (Ireland) Ltd, Re [2004] EWHC 2114 (Ch); [2005] I.L.Pr. 22	[ER art.3(1)]

Case	Provision
Beverley Group Plc v McClue [1995] B.C.C. 751; [1996] B.P.I.R. 25 Ch D	IA 1(1), 5(2), IR 2.25–2.38
Bezier Acquisitions Ltd, Re [2011] EWHC 3299 (Ch); [2012] 2 All E.R. (Comm) 322; [2012] B.C.C. 219	IA Sch.B1 para.26(2), (3), IR 3.8
BHS Ltd (In admin.), Re [2016] EWHC 1965 (Ch); [2016] B.C.C. 609	IA Sch.B1 para.103
BHT (UK) Ltd, Re [2004] EWHC 201 (Ch); [2004] B.C.C. 301	IA 40(1), (2), 175
Bibby ACF Ltd v Agate [2013] B.P.I.R. 685 Ch D	IA 423(1)–(3)
Bickland Ltd, Re [2012] EWHC 706 (Ch); [2013] B.C.C. 501	IA Sch.B1 para.13(1), (3), IR 3.51
Bieber v Teathers Ltd (In liq.) [2012] EWCA Civ 1466; [2013] 1 B.C.L.C. 248	IA 107
Bill Hennessey Associates Ltd, Re [1992] B.C.C. 386 Ch D (Companies Ct)	IR 7.4–7.12
Bilta (UK) Ltd (In liq.) v Nazir; sub nom. Jetivia SA v Bilta (UK) Ltd (In liq.) [2015] UKSC 23; [2016] A.C. 1; [2015] B.C.C. 343	IA 213, 238, 423(1)–(3)
Birchall (A Bankrupt), Re; sub nom. Bell v Birchall [2015] EWHC 1541 (Ch); [2015] B.P.I.R. 751	IA 305(2), Pt IX, IR 7.108(1)–(4)
Bird v Hadkinson [2000] C.P. Rep. 21; [1999] B.P.I.R. 653 Ch D	IA 366(1)
Birdi v Price [2017] EWHC 1859 (Ch); [2017] B.P.I.R. 1140	IA 283(2), (3)
Bishop v Fox Unreported 9 February 2016	IR 12.1
Bishopsgate Investment Management Ltd (In provisional liq.) v Maxwell; Mirror Group Newspapers Plc v Maxwell [1993] Ch. 1; [1992] B.C.C. 222 CA (Civ Div)	IA 133, 236
Bishopsgate Investment Management Ltd (No.2), Re [1994] B.C.C. 732 Ch D (Companies Ct)	IA 236
Blackburn v Alexander [2015] CSOH 179; 2016 G.W.D. 2–48	IA 242
Blackspur Group Plc (No.2), Re [1998] 1 W.L.R. 422; [1998] B.C.C. 11 CA (Civ Div)	[CDDA 1, 7(1)]
Blackspur Group Plc (No.3), Re; sub nom. Secretary of State for Trade and Industry v Davies (No.3) [2001] EWCA Civ 1595; [2004] B.C.C. 839	[CDDA, 1A]
Blackspur Group Plc, Re; sub nom. Secretary of State for Trade and Industry v Eastaway [2003] B.C.C. 520 Ch D	[CDDA, 7(1)]
Blackspur Group Plc, Re; sub nom. Eastaway v Secretary of State for Trade and Industry [2007] EWCA Civ 425; [2007] B.C.C. 550	IR 12.59, [CDDA, 1A]
Blair Carnegie Nimmo (as Liquidator of St Margaret's School Edinburgh Ltd), Re [2013] CSOH 4; [2013] B.P.I.R. 188	IA 135, IR 18.28
Blavo v Law Society [2017] EWHC 561 (Ch); [2017] 1 W.L.R. 4514; [2017] B.P.I.R. 909	IA 267(1), (2), IR 10.5
Blemain Finance Ltd v Goulding [2013] EWCA Civ 1630; [2014] 1 P. & C.R. DG16	IA 283, 284(1)–(3), (6)
Blight v Brewster [2012] EWHC 165 (Ch); [2012] 1 W.L.R. 2841; [2012] B.P.I.R. 476	IA Pt III, 342A
Blights Builders Ltd, Re [2006] EWHC 3549 (Ch); [2007] 3 All E.R. 776; [2007] B.C.C. 712	IA Sch.B1 paras 25, 104, IR 1.2, 12.64
Block Transfer by Kaye, Re a [2010] EWHC 692 (Ch); [2010] B.P.I.R. 602	IA 263(4), IR Pt 12 Ch.6 sub-div.B
Bloom v Pensions Regulator. *See* Nortel Companies, Re	
Blue Monkey Gaming Ltd v Hudson [2014] 4 All E.R. (D) 222 Ch D	IA Sch.B1 para.67
BLV Realty Organisation Designs Ltd, Re [2010] EWHC 1791 (Ch)	IA 123
BNY Corporate Trustee Services Ltd v Eurosail-UK 2007–3BL Plc [2013] UKSC 28; [2013] 1 W.L.R. 1408; [2013] B.C.C. 397	IA Pt IV, 123(1)
Bolsover DC v Ashfield Nominees Ltd [2010] EWCA Civ 1129; [2012] B.C.C. 803; [2011] B.P.I.R. 7	IA 123, Pt IX Ch.1, 267(1), (2)
Bonney v Mirpuri [2013] B.P.I.R. 412	IA 276(1), 376

	Provision
Bonus Breaks Ltd, Re [1991] B.C.C. 546 Ch D (Companies Ct)	IA 216(3)
Booth v Mond 2010] EWHC 1576 (Ch); [2010] B.P.I.R. 1111	IA Pt VIII, 310A(3), (6), (7), IR 10.115–10.117, 14.2
Border Counties Farmers Ltd, Re [2017] EWHC 2610 (Ch)	IA 250
Borodzicz v Horton [2016] B.P.I.R. 24 Ch D	IA 299(5), 304(2), IR 18.16, [App.IV]
Botleigh Grange Ltd v Revenue and Customs Commissioners [2016] EWHC 3081 (Ch)	IA 123
Bournemouth & Boscombe Athletic Football Club Co Ltd, Re [1998] B.P.I.R. 183 Ch D	IA 6(3), IR 2.25–2.38
Bowe Watts Clargo Ltd [2017] EWHC 7879 (Ch)	IR 14.25
Bowen Travel Ltd, Re [2012] EWHC 3405 (Ch); [2013] B.C.C. 182	IA Sch.B1 paras 3(1), (3), 13(1), (3)
Bower v Marris, 41 E.R. 525; (1841) Cr. & Ph. 351 Ch	IR 14.23
Bowles v Trefilov Unreported 29 April 2016	IA 279(3)–(5), 210
Bowman Power Systems (UK) Ltd, Re Unreported 26 October 2004 Ch D	IA 216(3)
Boyd & Hutchinson v Foenander [2003] EWCA Civ 1516; [2004] B.P.I.R. 20	IA 306
Boyden v Canty (No.2) [2007] EWCA Civ 241; [2007] B.P.I.R. 299	IA 311(1), 363(2), (4)
Boyden v Watson [2004] B.P.I.R. 1131 CC	IA 310(1), (1A), (2)
BPE Solicitors v Gabriel [2015] UKSC 39; [2015] A.C. 1663	IA 306
BPR Ltd, Re [1998] B.C.C. 259 Ch D	[CDDA 22(5)]
Brabon, Re [2000] B.C.C. 1171; [2000] B.P.I.R. 537 Ch D	IA 339(1)–(3), 423(1)–(3)
BRAC Rent-A-Car International Inc, Re [2003] EWHC 128 (Ch); [2003] 1 W.L.R. 1421; [2003] B.C.C. 248	[ER Preamble 25, art.3, 3(1)]
Bradburn v Kaye [2006] B.P.I.R. 605 Ch D	IA 276(1)
Bradcrown Ltd, Re [2002] B.C.C. 428; Ch D (Companies Ct)	[CDDA 12C]
Bradley-Hole (A Bankrupt), Re [1995] 1 W.L.R. 1097; [1995] B.C.C. 418 Ch D	IA 263(5), (6)
Bradley v Secretary of State for Business, Innovation and Skills [2016] CSIH 80; 2017 S.C. 153; 2016 S.L.T. 1097; 2016 G.W.D. 33-587	[CDDA 12C]
Bramble Ex p. (1880) 13 Ch. D. 885 Ch D	IA 236(4)–(6)
Brampton Manor (Leisure) Ltd v McLean [2006] EWHC 2983 (Ch); [2007] B.C.C. 640	IA 34
Bramston and Defty v Oraki [2014] EWHC 4828 (Ch); [2014] EWHC 2982 (Ch); [2014] B.P.I.R. 1374	IA 303(1), 304(2), 305(2)
Bramston v Haut [2012] EWCA Civ 1637; [2013] 1 W.L.R. 1720	IA Pt VIII, 252(1), 279(3)–(5), 303(1), 363(1)
Bramston v Riaz [2014] B.P.I.R. 42 CC	IA 339(1)–(3)
Branchempire Ltd, Re [2010] EWHC 3017 (Ch); [2011] B.P.I.R. 536	IA 236, 236(2)
Branston & Gothard Ltd, Re [1999] 1 All E.R. (Comm) 289	IA 127, 239(4)
Brauch (A Debtor), Ex p. Brittanic Securities & Investments Ltd, Re [1978] Ch. 316 CA (Civ Div)	IA 265
Brazzill v Willoughby [2010] EWCA Civ 561; [2010] 2 B.C.L.C. 259	IA 107
Brehm, Re. *See* Commerzbank AG v Brehm	
Bremner (A Bankrupt), Re [1999] 1 F.L.R. 912; [1999] B.P.I.R. 185 Ch D	IA 336(3)–(5)
Brent LBC v Kane [2014] EWHC 4564 (Ch)	IA 423(1)–(3)
Brian D Pierson (Contractors) Ltd, Re [1999] B.C.C. 26; [1999] B.P.I.R. 18 Ch D (Companies Ct)	IA 214, 214(1), 239(6), [CDDA 10]
Brian Sheridan Cars Ltd, Re [1995] B.C.C. 1035 Ch D (Companies Ct)	IR 12.59, [CDDA 1(1)]
Bridgend Goldsmiths Ltd, Re [1995] B.C.C. 226 Ch D	IA 108, 263(5), (6)
Brightlife Ltd, Re [1987] Ch. 200; (1986) 2 B.C.C. 99359 Ch D (Companies Ct)	IA 40(1), (2), 175(2)(b)

	Provision
Brilliant Independent Media Specialists Ltd, Re [2015] B.C.C. 113; [2014] B.P.I.R. 1395 Ch D (Companies Ct) .	IA Sch.B1 para.59, IR 18.16, 18.28
Brillouet v Hachette Magazines Ltd [1996] B.P.I.R. 522 CA (Civ Div) . . .	IA 375(1)
Brister v Official Receiver [2015] EW Misc B22 (CC); [2015] B.P.I.R. 1008 CC	IA 282(1), (3), 421(1), (1A), (1B), (2)
Bristol & West Building Society v Saunders [1997] Ch. 60; [1997] B.C.C. 83 Ch D	IA 285(3), (4)
Bristol & West Building Society v Trustee of the Property of John Julius Back (A Bankrupt) [1997] B.P.I.R. 358.	IA 285(3), (4)
Bristol Airport Plc v Powdrill; sub nom. Paramount Airways Ltd (No.1), Re [1990] Ch. 744; [1990] B.C.C. 130 CA (Civ Div)	IA 246, 248, 436
Bristol Alliance Nominee (No.1) Ltd v Bennett [2013] EWCA Civ 1626; [2014] 1 P. & C.R. DG15	IA Sch.B1 para.43(6)
Bristol Athenaeum, Re (1889) 43 Ch. D. 236 Ch D	IA 220(1)
Britannia Heat Transfer Ltd (In admin.), Re [2007] B.C.C. 470; [2007] B.P.I.R. 1038 Ch D	IA Pt I, 5
Britannia Homes Centres Ltd, Re [2001] 2 B.C.L.C. 63 Ch D	[CDDA 1(1)]
British & Commonwealth Holdings Plc (Joint Administrators) v Spicer & Oppenheim [1993] A.C. 426; [1992] B.C.C. 977 HL	IA 236
British American Racing (Holdings) Ltd, Re [2004] EWHC 2947 (Ch); [2005] B.C.C. 110	IA Sch.B1 paras 3(1), (3), 12(1), (4)
British Eagle International Airlines Ltd v Compagnie Nationale Air France [1975] 1 W.L.R. 758 HL	IA 107
Brittain v Courtway Estates Holdings SA [2008] EWHC 1791 (Ch); [2008] B.P.I.R. 1229	IA 423(1)–(3)
Brittain v Haghighat [2009] EWHC 934 (Ch); [2009] B.P.I.R. 785	IA 375(1)
Brittain v Haghighat; sub nom. Haghighat (A Bankrupt), Re [2010] EWCA Civ 1521; [2011] B.P.I.R. 328.	IA 336(3)–(5), 337(4)–(6)
Broadside Colours and Chemicals Ltd [2011] EWHC 1034 (Ch); [2011] 2 B.C.L.C. 597	IA 212(1)
Broadside Colours and Chemicals Ltd, Re [2012] EWHC 195 (Ch)	IA 375(1), IR 12.59
Brook Martin & Co (Nominees) Ltd, Re [1993] B.C.L.C. 328 Ch D	IA 236
Brook v Reed [2011] EWCA Civ 331; [2012] 1 W.L.R. 419; [2011] B.C.C. 423.	IR 18.28, [App.IV]
Brooke Marine Ltd, Re [1988] B.C.L.C. 546 Ch D	IA 124, Sch.B1 para.13)]
Brooke v Hewitt, 30 E.R. 997; (1796) 3 Ves. Jr. 253 Ct of Ch	IA 345(1)–(3)
Brooks Transport (Purfleet) Ltd, Re [1993] B.C.C. 766 Ch D (Companies Ct)	[CDDA 1(1)]
Brooks v Armstrong [2015] EWHC 2289 (Ch); [2015] B.C.C. 661	IA 214(3)
Brooks v Armstrong [2016] EWHC 2893 (Ch); [2017] B.C.C. 99	IA 214, 214(3)
Broomfield Developments Ltd, Re Unreported, 19 June 2017	IA 124A, IR 7.108(1)–(4),
Brown Bear Foods Ltd, Re; sub nom. Shaw v Webb [2014] EWHC 1132 (Ch)	IA Sch.B1 para.13(1), (3)
Brown v Beat [2002] B.P.I.R. 421 Ch D	IA 303(1), 304(1)
Brown v City of London Corp; sub nom. Sobam BV, Re [1996] 1 W.L.R. 1070; [1996] B.C.C. 351 Ch D	IA 44(1), (2)
Brown v Stonegale Ltd [2016] UKSC 30; 2016 G.W.D. 20–359	IA 242
Browne v Mavroudis [2014] NI Master 18.	IA 263I
Brownridge Plastics Ltd, Re Unreported	IA Sch.B1, para.111(1), 111(1A), 111(1B)
Brumark Investments Ltd, Re; sub nom. Inland Revenue Commissioner v Agnew; Agnew v Inland Revenue Commissioner [2001] UKPC 28; [2001] 2 A.C. 710; [2001] B.C.C. 259.	IA 40(1), (2)

	Provision
Bruton v Inland Revenue Commissioners [2000] B.P.I.R. 946 Ch D	IA 267(1), (2)
BTI 2014 LLC v Sequana SA [2016] EWHC 1686 (Ch); [2017] Bus. L.R. 82	IA 423(1)–(3)
BTR (UK) Ltd, Re [2012] EWHC 2398 (Ch); [2012] B.C.C. 864	IA 124, Sch.B1 para.55
Buccament Bay Ltd, Re; Harlequin Property (SVG) Ltd, Re [2014] EWHC 4776 (Ch); [2015] 1 B.C.L.C. 646)	IA 220, [ER art.3]
Buchler v Al-Midani (No.2) [2005] EWHC 3183 (Ch); [2006] B.P.I.R. 867	IA 366(1)
Buchler v Al-Midani (No.3) [2006] EWHC 170 (Ch); [2006] B.P.I.R. 881	IA 363(2)(4)
Buchler v Talbot; sub nom. Leyland DAF Ltd, Re [2004] UKHL 9; [2004] 2 A.C. 298; [2004] B.C.C. 214	IA Pt III, 59(1), (2), 107, 115, 175, 176ZA, Sch.B1 paras 65(2), 99, IR 7.108(1)–(4), 7.111–7.116, 18.16
Buckingham International Plc (In liq.) (No.2), Re [1998] B.C.C. 943 CA (Civ Div)	IA 183
Buckley v Secretary of State for Business, Energy and Industrial Strategy [2017] CSOH 105; 2017 G.W.D. 24-404	[CDDA 17]
Budge v AF Budge (Contractors) Ltd (In rec. and liq.) [1997] B.P.I.R. 366 CA (Civ Div)	IR 10.5
Budniok, Re [2017] EWHC 368 (Ch); [2017] B.P.I.R. 521	IA Pt IX Ch.A1, 263I, 263N
Buildlead Ltd (In creditors' voluntary liq.) (No.1), Re [2003] EWHC 1981 (Ch); [2003] 4 All E.R. 864; [2005] B.C.C. 133	IR 7.63–7.66
Buildlead Ltd (In creditors' voluntary liq.) (No.2), Re [2004] EWHC 2443 (Ch); [2005] B.C.C. 138; [2004] B.P.I.R. 1139	IA 108, 4.113–4.120, IR 7.63–7.66, 17.23
Bukhari v Bukhari [1999] B.P.I.R. 157 CA (Civ Div)	IA 305(2)
Bullard & Taplin Ltd, Re [1996] B.C.C. 973; [1996] B.P.I.R. 526 Ch D	IA 263(5), (6)
Bulmer Ex p. Greaves, Re [1937] Ch. 499; [1937] 1 All E.R. 323 CA	IA 301(1), 17.25
Bunting Electric Manufacturing Co Ltd, Re [2005] EWHC 3345 (Ch); [2006] 1 B.C.L.C. 550	[CDDA 12C]
Burford Midland Properties Ltd v Marley Extrusions Ltd [1994] B.C.C. 604 Ch D	IA 1(1), 5(2)
Burgo Group SpA v Illochroma SA (C-327/13) EU:C:2014:2158 [2015] 1 W.L.R. 1046; [2015] B.C.C. 33	[ER Preamble 23, 24, 34–40]
Burke v Chapman & Chubb (A Firm) [2008] EWHC 341 (QB); [2008] 2 F.L.R. 1207; [2008] B.P.I.R. 266	IA 283(5), 284(1)–(3), (6)
Burlington Loan Management Ltd v Lomas. *See* Lehman Bros International (Europe), Re	
Burnden Group Ltd, Re [2017] EWHC 406 (Ch); [2017] B.P.I.R. 585	IR 14.3–14.11
Burnden Group Ltd, Re; Fielding v Hunt [2017] EWHC 247 (Ch); [2017] B.P.I.R. 554	IR 14.3–14.11
Burnden Holdings (UK) Ltd v Fielding [2018] UKSC 14	IA 212(1)
Burnden Holdings (UK) Ltd (In liq.) v Fielding [2017] EWHC 2118 (Ch)	IA 212(3)
Burnett's Trustee v Grainger [2004] UKHL 8; 2004 S.C. (H.L.) 19; 2004 S.L.T. 513	IA Pt IX
Burnham Marketing Services Ltd, Re [1993] B.C.C. 518 CC	[CDDA 12C]
Burton & Deakin Ltd, Re [1977] 1 W.L.R. 390 Ch D	IA 127
Burton v Burton [1986] 2 F.L.R. 419; [1986] Fam. Law 330	IA 284(1)–(3), (6)
Bush v Bank Mandiri (Europe) Ltd [2011] B.P.I.R. 19 Ch D	IR 10.2, 10.5
Business City Express Ltd, Re [1997] B.C.C. 826 Ch D	IA 426(4), (5), (11)
Business Dream Ltd (In liq.), Re [2011] EWHC 2860 (Ch); [2012] B.C.C. 115; [2012] B.P.I.R. 490	IA Sch.B1 para.25, 27
Business Environment Fleet Street Ltd, Re [2014] EWHC 3540 (Ch); [2015] 1 W.L.R. 1167	IA Sch.B1 para.72

	Provision
Busytoday Ltd, Re [1992] 1 W.L.R. 683; [1992] B.C.C. 480 Ch D (Companies Ct)	IR 12.59
Butters v BBC Worldwide Ltd 2011] UKSC 38; [2012] 1 A.C. 383; [2011] B.C.C. 734	IA Pt IV
Butterworth v Soutter [2000] B.P.I.R. 582 Ch D	IA 282(4)
Butts Park Ventures (Coventry) Ltd v Bryant Homes Central Ltd [2003] EWHC 2487 (Ch); [2004] B.C.C. 207	IA 220(1)
Buzzle Operations Pty (In liq.) v Apple Computer Australia Pty Ltd [2011] NSWCA 109	[CDDA 22(5)]
BW Estates Ltd, Re; sub nom. Randhawa v Turpin [2015] EWHC 517 (Ch); [2016] B.C.C. 475; [2016] 1 B.C.L.C. 708	IA Sch.B1 paras 3(1), (3), 29(2), (6), 29(3)
BW Estates Ltd, Re; sub nom. Randhawa v Turpin [2017] EWCA Civ 1201; [2017] B.C.C. 406	IA Sch.B1 paras 3(1), (3), 12(1), (4), 22(1), 22(2)
BXL Services, Re [2012] EWHC 1877 (Ch); [2012] B.C.C. 657	IA Sch.B1 para.26(2), (3)
Byers v Yacht Bull Corp [2010] EWHC 133 (Ch); [2010] B.C.C. 368; [2010] B.P.I.R. 535	IA 423(1)–(3), [ER Preamble 7, art.2(2)]
Byford (Deceased), Re [2003] EWHC 1267 (Ch); [2004] 1 F.L.R. 56; [2003] B.P.I.R. 1089	IA 283A, 335A
C Brooks Thurmond III v Rajapakse [2008] B.P.I.R. 283 Ch D	IA 310
Cabletel Installations Ltd, Re Unreported 20 April 2004	IR 18.28
Cabvision Ltd v Feetum [2005] EWCA Civ 1601; [2006] Ch. 585; [2006] B.C.C. 340	IA 72E(1), (2), Sch.A1 para.45, Sch.2A
Cadbury Schweppes Plc v Somji [2001] 1 W.L.R. 615; [2001] B.P.I.R. 172 CA (Civ Div)	IA 276(1)
Cadlock v Dunn [2015] EWHC 1318 (Ch); [2015] B.P.I.R. 739	IA 335A
Cadogan Estates Ltd v McMahon [2001] 1 A.C. 378; [2001] B.P.I.R. 17 HL	IA 345(1)–(3)
Cadwell v Jackson [2001] B.P.I.R. 966 Ch D	IR 14.2, 14.3–14.11
Cahillane v National Asset Loan Management Ltd [2014] EWHC 1992 (Ch); [2014] B.P.I.R. 1093	IR 10.1, 10.5, 14.15–14.19, 14.41, 15.31
Calahurst Ltd, Re (1989) 5 B.C.C. 318 Ch D (Companies Ct)	IR 12.59
Caldwell, Re Unreported 1998	IA 333(1), (3)
Cale v Assuidoman KPS (Harrow) Ltd [1996] B.P.I.R. 245 Ch D	IR 10.5
Caledonian Ltd, Re [2016] EWHC 2854 (Ch)	IA 124A
Calibre Solicitors Ltd, Re; sub nom. Justice Capital Ltd v Murphy [2014] All E.R. (D) 187 Ch D (Companies Ct)	IR 18.34, Sch.5
Calmex Ltd, Re [1989] 1 All E.R. 485; (1988) 4 B.C.C. 761 Ch D (Companies Ct)	IA 130(1), 147(1), IR 7.14–7.24
Cambridge Gas Transport Corp v Official Committee of Unsecured Creditors of Navigator Holdings Plc [2006] UKPC 26; [2007] 1 A.C. 508; [2006] B.C.C. 962	IA 145(1), 423(1)–(3), 426, [CBIR]
Campbell Coverings Ltd, Re (No.2) [1954] Ch. 225 Ch D	IA 133
Cancol Ltd, Re [1996] 1 All E.R. 37; [1995] B.C.C. 1133 Ch D	IA 1(1), 6(1), IR 2.25–2.38
Canning v Irwin Mitchell LLP [2017] EWHC 718 (Ch); [2017] B.P.I.R. 934	IR 10.1, 10.2, 12.64, [App.IV]
Cannonquest Ltd, Re [1997] B.C.C. 644 CA (Civ Div)	[CDDA 1(1)]
Canty v Boyden [2006] EWCA Civ 194; [2006] B.P.I.R. 624	IA 303(1)
Capewell v Customs and Excise Commissioners [2007] UKHL 2; [2007] 1 W.L.R. 386; [2007] B.P.I.R. 678	IA Pt III
Capital for Enterprise Fund a LP v Bibby Financial Services Ltd [2015] EWHC 2593 (Ch)	IA Sch.B1 para.2
Capital Prime Properties Plc v Worthgate Ltd (In liq.) [2000] B.C.C. 525 Ch D	IA 178(4)

	Provision
Capitol Films Ltd (In admin.), Re [2010] EWHC 3223 (Ch); [2011] B.P.I.R. 334	IA Sch.B1 para.71
Cardona, Re [1997] B.C.C. 697; [1997] B.P.I.R. 604 Ch D (Bankruptcy)	IR 16.7
Care Matters Partnership Ltd (In admin.), Re [2011] EWHC 2543 (Ch); [2011] B.C.C. 957	IA Sch.B1 paras 13(2), 104
Care People Ltd, Re [2013] EWHC 1734 (Ch); [2013] B.C.C. 466	IA Sch.B1 para.14, IR 12.64
Carecraft Construction Co Ltd, Re [1994] 1 W.L.R. 172; [1993] B.C.C. 336 Ch D (Companies Ct)	[CDDA 1, 1A, 7(1), 8(1), 12C, 17]
Cargo Agency Ltd, Re [1992] B.C.C. 388 Ch D	[CDDA 1(1), 6(1), 12C]
Carman v Baron, noted (1996) 12 I.L.&P. 60	IA 310
Carman v Cronos Group SA [2005] EWHC 2403 (Ch); [2006] B.C.C. 451	IA 213(1)
Carman v Letchford; sub nom. Hollier (A Bankrupt), Re [2010] EWHC 3155 (Ch); [2014] B.P.I.R. 927	IA 339(1)–(3), 340(1), (2)
Carreras Rothmans Ltd v Freeman Mathews Treasure Ltd (In liq.) [1985] Ch. 207; [1985] 1 All E.R. 155; (1984) 1 B.C.C. 99210 Ch D	IA 107
Carter Commercial Developments Ltd, Re [2002] B.C.C. 803; [2002] B.P.I.R. 1053 Ch D	IA 246(3), Sch.B1 para.43(6)
Carter-Knight (A Bankrupt) v Peat [2000] B.P.I.R. 268 Ch D	IA 276(1)
Cartesio Oktato es Szolgaltato bt (C-210/06) EU:C:2008:723 [2009] Ch. 354; [2009] B.C.C. 232	[ER art.3(1)]
Cartwright v Cartwright [2002] EWCA Civ 931; [2002] B.P.I.R. 895	IR 14.2
Cartwright v Staffordshire and Moorlands DC [1998] B.P.I.R. 328 CA (Civ Div)	IR 10.1
Cartwright, Re [1975] 1 W.L.R. 573 Ch D	IR 12.64

	Provision
Casa Estates (UK) Ltd (In liq.), Re; sub nom. Bucci v Carman [2014] EWCA Civ 383; [2014] B.C.C. 269	IA 123(1), 240(2)
Cases of Taff's Well Ltd, Re [1992] Ch. 179; [1991] B.C.C. 582 Ch D (Companies Ct)	IA 129
Casson v Law Society [2009] EWHC 1943 (Admin); [2010] B.P.I.R. 49	IA 281(1), 281(2)–(6), (8)
Casterbridge Properties Ltd (No.2), Re; sub nom. Jeeves v Official Receiver [2002] B.C.C. 453; [2002] B.P.I.R. 42 Ch D	IA 133, 236
Castle New Homes Ltd, Re [1979] 1 W.L.R. 1075 Ch D	IA 236
Catch a Ride Ltd v Gardner [2014] EWHC 1220 (Ch)	IA Pt III
Cathie v Secretary of State for Business, Innovation and Skills [2011] EWHC 2234 (Ch); [2011] B.C.C. 685	[CDDA 18]
Cathie v Secretary of State for Business, Innovation and Skills [2012] EWCA Civ 739; [2012] B.C.C. 813	[CDDA 12C]
Cavanagh v Conway [2015] NIQB 69	IA 171
Cavanagh v Dolan. *See* Latlorcan Developments Ltd (In admin.), Re	
CCA v Brecht (1989) 7 A.C.L.C. 40	IA 206(3) [CDDA 1(1)]
Ceart Risk Services Ltd, Re [2012] EWHC 1178 (Ch); [2012] B.C.C. 592	IA Sch.B1 paras 26(2), (3), 104
Cedac Ltd, Re. *See* Secretary of State for Trade and Industry v Langridge	
Cedar Developments Ltd, Re [1995] B.C.C. 220 Ch D	[CDDA 7(2)]
Cedarwood Productions Ltd, Re [2001] EWCA Civ 1083; [2004] B.C.C. 65	[CDDA, 2(1), 1(4)]
Celtic Extraction Ltd (In liq.), Re [2001] Ch. 475; [2000] B.C.C. 487 CA (Civ Div)	IA 178
Centaur Litigation SPC (In liq.) v Terrill [2015] EWHC 3420 (Ch)	IA 426(4)
Central A1 Ltd, Re; sub nom. Rubin & Partners v Cohen [2017] EWHC 220 (Ch); [2017] B.C.C. 69	IA 112(2), IR 6.2–6.9, 7.108(1)–(4)
Centralcrest Engineering Ltd, Re [2000] B.C.C. 727 Ch D (Companies Ct)	IA 212(1)

Case	Provision
Centre Reinsurance International Co v Curzon Insurance Ltd [2006] UKHL 45; [2006] 1 W.L.R. 2863; [2006] B.C.C. 971	IA Pt IV
Centrebind Ltd, Re [1967] 1 W.L.R. 377 Ch D	IA 166
CFL Finance Ltd v Rubin; Re Gertner [2017] EWHC 111 (Ch); [2017] B.P.I.R. 336	IA 262(1)–(3), (8)
Chadwick v Nash [2012] B.P.I.R. 70 Ch D	IA 279(3)–(5), 310(1), (1A), (2), 333(1), (3), IR 10.142
Chamberlin v Revenue and Customs Commissioners [2011] EWCA Civ 271; [2011] B.P.I.R. 691	IA Pt IX Ch.1
Chan Sui v Appasamy [2005] EWHC 3519 (Ch); [2008] B.P.I.R. 18	IR 10.5
Chandler (Terence Norman) v DPP [1964] A.C. 763 HL	IA 214
Chapper v Jackson [2012] EWHC 3897; [2012] B.P.I.R. 257	IA 304(1)
Charalambous v B&C Associates [2009] EWHC 2601 (Ch); [2013] B.C.C. 491	IA 212(3), Sch.B1 para.75
Charit-Email Technology Partnership LLP v Vermillion International Investments Ltd [2009] EWHC 388 (Ch); [2009] B.P.I.R. 762	IA 124(2)–(4A)
Charles Forte Investments Ltd v Amanda [1964] Ch. 240 CA	IA 122(1)
Charnley Davies Business Services Ltd, Re (1987) 3 B.C.C. 408; 1988 P.C.C. 1 Ch D	IA 140
Chartmore Ltd, Re [1990] B.C.L.C. 673 Ch D	[CDDA 1(1), 12C]
Chase Manhattan Bank NA v Israel-British Bank (London) Ltd [1981] Ch. 105; [1979] 3 All E.R. 1025 Ch D	IA 107
Chawda, Re [2014] B.P.I.R. 49	IA 335A
Cherkasov v Olegovich (the official receiver of Dalnyaya Step LLC) [2017] EWHC 3153 (Ch)	[CBIR Sch.1 art.17]
Cherry v Boultbee, 41 E.R. 171; (1839) 4 My. & C. 442 Ch D	IR 14.25
Cheshire West and Chester BC, Petitioners [2010] CSOH 115; [2011] B.C.C. 174	IA Sch.B1 para.74
Chesterfield Catering Co Ltd, Re [1977] Ch. 373 Ch D	IA 124(2)–(4A)
Chesterfield United Inc, Re [2012] EWHC 244 (Ch); [2012] B.C.C. 786	IA 236, [CBIR Sch.1 art.21(1)]
Chesterton International Group Plc v Deka Immobilien Inv GmbH [2005] EWHC 656 (Ch); [2005] B.P.I.R. 1103	IA Pt III, Sch.B1 para.39
Cheung, Re Unreported, 16 May 2017	IA 339(1)–(3)
Cheyne Finance Plc (In rec.), Re [2007] EWHC 2116 (Ch); [2008] 1 B.C.L.C. 732	IA Pt III
Cheyne Finance Plc (In rec.), Re [2007] EWHC 2402 (Ch); [2008] 2 All E.R. 987; [2008] B.C.C. 182	IA Pt III, 35(1), Pt IV, 123(1)
Chief Constable of Greater Manchester v Wright [2015] EWHC 3824 (Ch)	IA 283
Child Maintenance and Enforcement Commission v Beesley [2010] EWCA Civ 1344; [2011] 1 W.L.R. 1704	IA Pt VIII, 257(1), 262, 382(3), (4)
Chinn, Re Unreported 10 November 2015	IA 303(2)
Chohan v Saggar [1994] B.C.C. 134	IA 423(1)–(3), 425(2), (3)
Choudhri v Palta [1992] B.C.C. 787 CA (Civ Div)	IA 37(4)
Choudhury v Inland Revenue Commissioners [2000] B.C.C. 765; [2000] B.P.I.R. 246 CA (Civ Div)	IA 282(4)
Choudhry v Luton BC [2017] EWHC 960 (Ch); [2017] B.P.I.R. 1150	IA 271(5)
Christofi v Barclays Bank Plc [2000] 1 W.L.R. 937; [1999] B.P.I.R. 855 CA (Civ Div)	IA 366(1)
Christophorus 3 Ltd, Re [2014] EWHC 1162 (Ch)	IA Sch.B1 para.2
Church of Scientology Advanced Organisation Saint Hill Europe and South Africa v Scott [1997] B.P.I.R. 418 CA (Civ Div)	IA 306
Churchill v First Independent Factors & Finance Ltd [2006] EWCA Civ 1623; [2007] B.C.C. 45; [2007] B.P.I.R. 14	IR 22.4, 22.5
Ci4Net.com.Inc, Re [2004] EWHC 1941 (Ch); [2005] B.C.C. 277	IA Sch.B1 para.13(1), (3), [ER 3(1)]

Case	Provision
Cohen v Selby; sub nom. Simmon Box (Diamonds) Ltd, Re [2002] B.C.C. 82 CA (Civ Div)	IA 212(3), [CDDA Sch.1 paras 5, 6]
Cohen v TSB Bank Plc [2002] B.P.I.R. 243 Ch D	IA Pt III
Coilcolour Ltd v Camtrex Ltd [2015] EWHC 3202 (Ch); [2016] B.P.I.R. 1129	IR 7.24
Cole v Billington [2013] EWCA Civ 502	IA 423(1)–(3)
Cole v Howlett [2015] EWHC 1697 (Ch); [2015] B.P.I.R. 763	IA 375(1)
Colgate (A Bankrupt), Re [1986] Ch. 439 CA (Civ Div)	IA 363(1)
Colliers International UK Plc (In admin.), Re [2012] EWHC 2942 (Ch); [2013] Ch. 422	IA 130(2), Sch.B1 para.43(6)
Collins & Aikman Corp Group, Re [2005] EWHC 1754 (Ch); [2006] B.C.C. 606	[ER arts 2(6) 3(1)]
Collins & Aikman Europe SA, Re [2006] EWHC 1343 (Ch); [2006] B.C.C. 861	IA Sch.B1 paras 66, [ER art.36]
Collins v Official Receiver [1996] B.P.I.R. 552 HC (Aus)	IA 283(2), (3)
Colt Telecom Group Plc (No.1), Re. *See* Highberry Ltd v Colt Telecom Group Plc (No.1)	
Colt Telecom Group Plc (No.2), Re [2002] EWHC 2815 (Ch); [2003] B.P.I.R. 324	IA Sch.B1 para.11
Comet Group Ltd (In liq.), Re; sub nom. Kahn v Whirlpool (UK) Ltd [2014] EWHC 3477 (Ch); [2015] B.P.I.R. 1	IA 236(3), (3A), IR 12.18
Comite d'entreprise de Nortel Networks SA v Rogeau (C-649/13) EU:C:2015:384; [2016] Q.B. 109; [2015] B.C.C. 490	[ER arts 2(9), 33–40]
Commercial Bank of South Australia, Re (1886) 33 Ch. D. 174 Ch D	IA 221
Commerzbank AG v Brehm [2014] B.P.I.R. 359	IA 263I, 282(1), (3)
Compania Merabello San Nicholas SA, Re [1973] Ch. 75; [1972] 3 W.L.R. 471 Ch D	IA 220
Company CR-2017-000393, Re Unreported, 17 March 2017	IA 172(3)
Company (No.00996 of 1979), Re [1980] Ch. 138 CA (Civ Div)	IA 206(3); [CDDA 1(1)]
Company (No.000359 of 1987), Re; sub nom. Okeanos Maritime Corp [1988] Ch. 210; (1987) 3 B.C.C. 160 Ch D (Companies Ct)	IA 220, 221(5)
Company (No.002567 of 1982), Re [1983] 1 W.L.R. 927; (1983) 1 B.C.C. 98930 Ch D	IA 125(2)
Company (No.003160 of 1986), Re (1986) 2 B.C.C. 99276 Ch D (Companies Ct)	IA 124(2)–(4A)
Company (No.003843 of 1986), Re (1987) 3 B.C.C. 624 Ch D (Companies Ct)	IA 125(2)
Company (No.007523 of 1986), Re (1987) 3 B.C.C. 57 Ch D (Companies Ct)	IA 127
Company (No.00370 of 1987), Ex p. Glossop, Re [1988] 1 W.L.R. 1068; (1988) 4 B.C.C. 506 Ch D (Companies Ct)	IA 122(1)
Company (No.003028 of 1987), Re (1987) 3 B.C.C. 575 Ch D	IA 123, 124(1), 125(2)
Company (No.003096 of 1987), Re (1988) 4 B.C.C. 80 Ch D (Companies Ct)	IA 125(2)
Company (No.003318 of 1987), Re (Oriental Credit Ltd, Re) [1988] Ch. 204; (1987) 3 B.C.C. 564 Ch D	IA 236
Company (No.005009 of 1987) Ex p. Copp, Re (1988) 4 B.C.C. 424 Ch D (Companies Ct)	IA 124(1), 240, 245(3)–(5), 249, [CDDA 22(5)]
Company (No.001363 of 1988), Re (1989) 5 B.C.C. 18 Ch D (Companies Ct)	IA 125(2)
Company (No.004502 of 1988) Ex p. Johnson, Re [1991] B.C.C. 234 Ch D (Companies Ct)	IA 122(1)
Company (No.001448 of 1989), Re (1989) 5 B.C.C. 706 Ch D	IR 7.4–7.12
Company (No.008790 of 1990), Re [1992] B.C.C. 11	IA 123(1)
Company (No.010656 of 1990), Re [1991] B.C.L.C. 464	IA 123

Case	Provision
Company (No.00330 of 1991) Ex p. Holden, Re [1991] B.C.C. 241 Ch D	IA 125(2)
Company (No.000687 of 1991), Re [1991] B.C.C. 210 Ch D (Companies Ct)	IR 7.25–7.32
Company (No.001946 of 1991) Ex p. Fin Soft Holdings SA, Re [1991] B.C.L.C. 737	IA 123
Company (No.003102 of 1991) Ex p. Nyckeln Finance Co, Re [1991] B.C.L.C. 539	IA 220
Company (No.012209 of 1991), Re [1992] 1 W.L.R. 351 Ch D	IA 123
Company (No.006341 of 1992) Ex p. B, Re [1994] 1 B.C.L.C. 225 Ch D	IA 114(4)
Company (No.005374 of 1993), Re [1993] B.C.C. 734 Ch D (Companies Ct)	IA 236
Company (No.007816 of 1994), Re [1997] 2 B.C.L.C. 685 CA (Civ Div)	IA 124A
Company (No.007923 of 1994), Re; Company (No.007924 of 1994), Re [1995] 1 W.L.R. 953; [1995] B.C.C. 634 CA (Civ Div)	IA 124A, IR 7.4–7.12
Company (No.007936 of 1994), Re [1995] B.C.C. 705 Ch D (Companies Ct)	IA 124(2)–(4A)
Company (No.004415 of 1996), Re [1997] 1 B.C.L.C. 479 Ch D	IA 125(2)
Company (No.006685 of 1996), Re [1997] B.C.C. 830 Ch D	IA 123
Company (No.007020 of 1996), Re [1998] 2 B.C.L.C. 54 Ch D	IR 7.25–7.32
Company (No.007130 of 1998), Re [2000] 1 B.C.L.C. 582 Ch D	IA 127
Company (No.2634 of 2002), Re [2002] EWHC 944 (Ch); [2002] 2 B.C.L.C. 591	IA 123
Company (No.1641 of 2003), Re [2003] EWHC 2652 (Ch); [2004] 1 B.C.L.C. 210	IR 14.25
Company (No.2507 of 2003), Re [2003] EWHC 1484 (Ch); [2003] 2 B.C.L.C. 346	IA 123
Company (No.2272 of 2004), Re [2005] EWHC 422 (Ch); [2005] B.P.I.R. 1251	IA 123
Company (No.0254/2015), Re Unreported 27 February 2015	IA 123
Company, Re a [1985] B.C.L.C. 37 Ch D	IA 123(1)
Company, Re a [2010] EWHC 3814 (Ch); [2012] B.C.C. 289	IR 7.4–7.12
Company, Re a [2012] EWHC 4336 (Ch)	IA 123
Company, Re a [2013] EWHC 4291 (Ch)	IA 123
Company, Re a Unreported, 25 August 2016	IA Sch.B1 para.13(2)
Company, Re a Unreported, 26 April 2017	IA 123
Complaint Against Brighton and Hove Council [2010] B.P.I.R. 1407 LGO	IA Pt IX Ch.1
Complaint Against Manchester City Council (07B10432) [2010] B.P.I.R. 476 LGO	IA Pt IX Ch.1
Complaint Against Newham LBC (08019113) [2010] B.P.I.R. 464 LGO	IA Pt IX Ch.1
Complaint Against Thurrock Council (09006694) [2010] B.P.I.R. 1420 LGO	IA Pt IX Ch.1
Concept Oil Services Ltd v EN-GIN Group LLP [2013] EWHC 1897 (Comm)	IA 423(1)–(3)
Conegrade Ltd, Re [2002] EWHC 2411 (Ch); [2003] B.P.I.R. 358	IA 239(6)
Coney (A Bankrupt), Re [1998] B.P.I.R. 333 Ch D	IA 282(1), (3)
Coniston Hotel (Kent) LLP (In liq.), Re [2013] EWHC 93 (Ch); [2015] B.C.C. 1	Sch.B1 paras 74, 75
Coniston Hotel (Kent) LLP (In liq.), Re; sub nom. Berntsen v Tait [2015] EWCA Civ 1001	IA 212(5), Sch.B1 paras 74, 75
Connaught Income Fund Series 1 v Capita Financial Managers Ltd [2014] EWHC 3619 (Comm); [2015] 1 All E.R. (Comm) 751; [2015] 1 B.C.L.C. 241	IA 144(1), Sch.4 para.13
Consolidated Finance Ltd v Collins [2013] EWCA Civ 475; [2013] B.P.I.R. 543	IA 282(1)
Consolidated Finance Ltd v Hunter [2010] B.P.I.R. 1322 CC	IA 282(1), (3)
Consolidated Goldfields of New Zealand, Re [1953] Ch. 689 Ch D	IA 74(1)
Constellation, The [1966] 1 W.L.R. 272 PD&A Div	IA 128
Contex Drouzhba Ltd v Wiseman [2007] EWCA Civ 1201; [2008] B.C.C. 301	IA 213(2)

	Provision
Continental Assurance Co of London Plc (In liq.) (No.1), Re [1996] B.C.C. 888 Ch D (Companies Ct)	[CDDA 1(1), 12C]
Continental Assurance Co of London Plc (In liq.) (No.2), Re [1998] 1 B.C.L.C. 583 Ch D (Companies Ct)	IR 12.64
Continental Assurance Co of London Plc (In liq.) (No.4), Re [2001] B.P.I.R. 733 Ch D	IA 212(1), 212(3), 124, 124(3), 124(4)
Contrarian Funds LLC, Re. *See* Lehman Bros International (Europe) (In admin.), Re	
Cook v Consolidated Finance Ltd [2010] EWCA Civ 369; [2010] B.P.I.R. 1331	IA 282(1), (3)
Cook v Mortgage Debenture Ltd [2016] EWCA Civ 103; [2016] 1 W.L.R. 3048	IA Sch.B1 para.43(6)
Cook v Revenue and Customs Commissioners [2017] B.P.I.R. 1468	IA 282(1), (3)
Cook, Re [1999] B.P.I.R. 881 Ch D	IA 303(1)
Cooke v Dunbar Assets Plc [2016] EWHC 579 (Ch); [2016] B.P.I.R. 576	IA 271(3)
Cooper (A Bankrupt), Re [2005] NICh 1; [2006] N.I. 103; [2007] B.P.I.R. 1206	IA 303(1), 363(1)
Cooper v Fearnley [1997] B.P.I.R. 20 Ch D	IA 255(1), (2)
Cooper v Official Receiver [2002] EWHC 1970 (Ch); [2003] B.P.I.R. 55	IA 276(1)
Cooper v PRG Powerhouse Ltd [2008] EWHC 498 (Ch); [2008] 2 All E.R. (Comm) 964; [2008] B.C.C. 588	IA 107
Cooperative Bank Plc v Phillips [2014] EWHC 2862 (Ch); [2014] B.P.I.R. 1430	IA 42(1), Pt VIII
Co-operative Bank Plc v Phillips [2017] EWHC 1320 (Ch); [2017] B.P.I.R. 1156	IA Pt VIII
Copecrest Ltd, Re [1993] B.C.C. 844 CA (Civ Div)	[CDDA 7(2)]
Copeland & Craddock Ltd, Re [1997] B.C.C. 294 CA (Civ Div)	IA 125(2)
Corbenstoke Ltd (No.2), Re (1989) 5 B.C.C. 767 Ch D (Companies Ct)	IA 172(1), (2)
Cork v Gill [2004] EWHC 2536 (Ch); [2005] B.P.I.R. 272	IA 340(4), (5)
Cork v Rawlins [2001] EWCA Civ 202; [2001] Ch. 792; [2001] B.P.I.R. 222	IA 283(2), (3), 306
Cornelius v Casson [2008] B.P.I.R. 504 Ch D	IA 260(1), (2), (2A)
Cornercare Ltd, Re [2010] EWHC 893 (Ch); [2010] B.C.C. 592	IA Sch.B1 para.28
Cornhill Insurance Plc v Cornhill Financial Services Ltd [1992] B.C.C. 818	IR 12.59
Cornhill Insurance Plc v Improvement Services Ltd [1986] 1 W.L.R. 114; (1986) 2 B.C.C. 98942 Ch D	IA 123(1)
Coroin Ltd (No.2), Re; sub nom. McKillen v Misland (Cyprus) Ltd [2013] EWCA Civ 781; [2014] B.C.C. 14	[CDDA 22(5)]
Corporate Jet Realisations Ltd (In liq.), Re. *See* Green v Chubb	
Corran v Butters [2017] EWHC 2294 (Ch)	IA 307(2), (5), [CDDA 11]
Corvin Construction Ltd, Re Unreported 21 December 2012	IA 124A
Cosco Bulk Carrier Co Ltd v Armada Shipping SA [2011] EWHC 216 (Ch); [2011] 2 All E.R. (Comm) 481; [2011] B.P.I.R. 626	IA 130(2), [CBIR Sch.1 art.21.2]
Cosslett (Contractors) Ltd (In admin.) (No.2), Re. *See* Smith (Administrator of Cosslett (Contractors) Ltd) v Bridgend CBC	
Cosslett (Contractors) Ltd, Re [1998] Ch. 495; [1997] B.C.C. 724 CA (Civ Div)	IA 234(1), (2)
Cosy Seal Insulation Ltd (In admin.), Re [2016] EWHC 1255 (Ch); [2016] 2 B.C.L.C. 319	IA 123(1), 239(6)
Cotswold Co Ltd, Re [2009] EWHC 1151 (Ch); [2010] B.C.C. 812	IA 4(3), 5(2)
Coulter v Chief Constable of Dorset [2004] EWCA Civ 1259; [2005] 1 W.L.R. 130; [2005] B.P.I.R. 62	IA 267(1), (2), 10.5
Coulter v Chief Constable of Dorset [2005] EWCA Civ 1113; [2006] B.P.I.R. 10	IR 10.5
Country Farm Inns Ltd, Re [1997] B.C.C. 801 CA (Civ Div)	[CDDA 6(1)]

	Provision
Debtor (No.544/SD/98), Re [2000] B.C.L.C. 103 CA (Civ Div)	IA 123(1), IR 10.5
Debtor (No.87 of 1999), Re [2000] B.P.I.R. 589 Ch D	IR 10.5
Debtor (No.101 of 1999) (No.2), Re [2001] B.P.I.R. 996 Ch D	IA 262, 262(4)–(7)
Debtor (No.35 of 2000), Re [2002] B.P.I.R. 75 Ch D	IR 10.5
Debtor v Focus Insurance (In liq.); sub nom. Debtor (No.22 of 1993), Re [1994] 1 W.L.R. 46 Ch D	IA 267(1), (2), 270, IR 12.64
Debtors (Nos VA7 and VA8 of 1990) Ex p. Stevens, Re [1996] B.P.I.R. 101 Ch D	IA 375(1)
Delaney v Chen [2010] EWCA Civ 1455; [2011] B.P.I.R. 39	IA 423(1)–(3)
Delberry Ltd, Re [2008] EWHC 925 (Ch); [2008] B.C.C. 653; [2008] B.P.I.R. 1277 Ch D	IA 36(1), 236
Delfin International (SA) Ltd (No.2), Re [2000] 1 B.C.L.C. 71 Ch D (Companies Ct)	IA 124A
Deloitte & Touche AG v Johnson [1999] 1 W.L.R. 1605; [1999] B.C.C. 992 PC (Cayman Islands)	IA 108
Demaglass Holdings Ltd, Re [2001] 2 B.C.L.C. 633 Ch D	IA 125(1), IR 7.108(1)–(4)
Demarco v Bulley Davey (A Firm) [2006] EWCA Civ 188; [2006] B.P.I.R. 645	IA 261(1), 261(2)
Demite Ltd v Protec Health Ltd [1998] B.C.C. 638 Ch D	IA 42(1)
Denis Hilton Ltd, Re [2002] 1 B.C.L.C. 302 Ch D	[CDDA, 1(4), 2(1)]
Dennis (A Bankrupt), Re [1996] Ch. 80 CA (Civ Div)	IA Second Group of Parts
Dennis Rye Ltd v Bolsover DC [2009] EWCA Civ 372; [2009] 4 All E.R. 1140; [2010] B.C.C. 248	IA 123
Dennis, Re [1996] B.P.I.R. 106	IA 283
Densham (A Bankrupt), Re [1975] 1 W.L.R. 1519; [1975] 3 All E.R. 726 Ch D	IA 336(3)–(5)
Dent (A Bankrupt), Re [1994] 1 W.L.R. 956 Ch D	IA Second Group of Parts
Department for Business, Innovation and Skills v Compton [2012] B.P.I.R. 1108 Mags Ct	IA 356(1), 357(1), (3)
Department of Enterprise, Trade and Investment v Black [2012] NIMaster 1	[CDDA 6(1)]
Derfshaw Ltd, Re [2011] EWHC 1565 (Ch); [2011] B.C.C. 631; [2011] B.P.I.R. 1289	IA Sch.B1 para.26(2), (3)
Designer Room Ltd, Re [2004] EWHC 720 (Ch); [2005] 1 W.L.R. 1581; [2004] B.C.C. 904	IA Sch.1
Devon and Somerset Farmers Ltd, Re [1994] Ch. 57; [1993] B.C.C. 410 Ch D	IA First Group of Parts, 29(2), 40(1), (2)
Dewji v Banwaitt [2013] EWHC 3746 (QB); [2014] B.P.I.R. 63	IA 252(2)
Dewrun Ltd, Re [2002] B.C.C. 57 Ch D (Companies Ct)	IA 127
Diamond Computer Systems Ltd, Re [1997] 1 B.C.L.C. 174 Ch D	[CDDA 6(1), 7(1)]
Diamond v Holding Unreported, 2 November 2017	IR 10.5
Dias v Havering LBC [2011] EWHC 172 (Ch); [2011] B.P.I.R. 395	IA 268
Dicetrade Ltd, Re. *See* Secretary of State for Trade and Industry v Worth	
DJ Matthews (Joinery Design) Ltd, Re (1988) 4 B.C.C. 513	[CDDA 1(1), 12C]
DKG Contractors Ltd, Re [1990] B.C.C. 903 Ch D	IA 212(1), 124, 124(4), 239(6), 240(2)
DKLL Solicitors v Revenue and Customs Commissioners [2007] EWHC 2067 (Ch); [2007] B.C.C. 908	IA Sch.B1 para.2
Dobson v Hastings [1992] Ch. 39	[CDDA 7(1)]
Doffman v Wood [2011] EWHC 4008 (Ch); [2012] B.P.I.R. 972	IA 298(1), (2) 311(1)
Doherty v Perrett [2015] NICA 52	IA Pt III
Dollar Land (Feltham) Ltd, Re [1995] B.C.C. 740 Ch D (Companies Ct)	IR 7.14–7.24, 12.59
Dollar Land Holdings Plc, Re [1993] B.C.C. 823 Ch D (Companies Ct)	IA 124(1)

	Provision
Doltable Ltd v Lexi Holdings Plc [2005] EWHC 1804 (Ch); [2006] B.C.C. 918	IA Sch.B1 para.3(1), (3)
Dominion International Group Plc, Re [1995] 1 W.L.R. 649; [1995] B.C.C. 303 Ch D	[CDDA 7(1)]
Dominion International Group Plc (No.2), Re [1996] 1 B.C.L.C. 572 Ch D	[CDDA 6(1), 12C]
Don Basil Williams, Re [2002] EWHC 1393 (Ch); [2003] B.P.I.R. 545	IA 314(1), (2), (6)
Donaldson v O'Sullivan [2008] EWCA Civ 879; [2009] 1 W.L.R. 924; [2009] B.C.C. 99	IA 172(1), (2), 292(1), 303(2), 363(1), IR 10.80, Pt 12 Ch.6 sub-div.B, 12.64
Donohoe v Ingram [2006] EWHC 282 (Ch); [2006] 2 F.L.R. 1084; [2006] B.P.I.R. 417	IA 335A
Dooneen Ltd (t/a McGinnes Associates) v Mond [2016] CSIH 59; 2016 G.W.D. 23–441	IA Pt VIII
Doorbar v Alltime Securities Ltd (Nos 1 and 2) [1996] 1 W.L.R. 456; [1995] B.C.C. 1149 CA (Civ Div)	IA 1(1), 262, 262(1)–(3), (8), IR 2.25–2.38
Dora v Simper [2000] 2 B.C.L.C. 561 CA (Civ Div)	IA 424
Doreen Boards Ltd, Re [1996] 1 B.C.L.C. 501 Ch D	IR 7.25–7.32
Douglas Construction Services Ltd, Re (1988) 4 B.C.C. 553 Ch D (Companies Ct)	[CDDA 1(1), 12C]
Dowland v Architects Registration Board [2013] EWHC 893 (Admin); [2013] B.P.I.R. 566	IA Pt IX, 333(1), (3)
Dowling v Promontoria (Arrow) Ltd [2017] EWHC B25 (Ch); [2017] B.P.I.R. 1477	IR 10.5
Downsview Nominees Ltd v First City Corp Ltd [1993] A.C. 295; [1993] B.C.C. 46 PC (NZ)	IA Pt III, 212(2)
Doyle v James [2010] B.P.I.R. 1063 CC	IA 283A
Doyle v Quinn [2015] B.P.I.R. 226 Ch D	IA 263I
Doyle v Saville [2002] B.P.I.R. 947 Ch D	IA 339(1)–(3)
DPR Futures Ltd, Re [1989] 1 W.L.R. 778; (1989) 5 B.C.C. 603 Ch D (Companies Ct)	IA 155(1)
Drax Holdings Ltd, Re [2003] EWHC 2743 (Ch); [2004] 1 W.L.R. 1049; [2004] B.C.C. 334	IA 220
Drew v HM Advocate, 1996 S.L.T. 1062; 1995 S.C.C.R. 647 HCJ Appeal	IA 206(3), [CDDA 1(1)]
Drivertime Recruitment Ltd, Re [2004] EWHC 1637 (Ch); [2005] 1 B.C.L.C. 411	IA 124A
Dubai Aluminium Co Ltd v Salaam [2007] B.P.I.R. 690 Ch D	IA 267(1), (2), 268, 269
Dubai Bank Ltd v Galadari (1989) 5 B.C.C. 722 Ch D	IA 236
Duke Group Ltd v Carver [2001] B.P.I.R. 459 Ch D	IA 426(4), (5), (11)
Dunbar Assets Plc v Fowler [2013] B.P.I.R. 46 Ch D (Bankruptcy Ct)	IA 266(3), (4), 267(1), (2), 271(3), 363(1)
Dunhill v Hughmans (a firm) [2017] EWHC 2073 (Ch)	IR 10.5
Duomatic Ltd, Re [1969] 2 Ch. 365	IA 212(1)
Dynamics Corp of America (In liq.) (No.2), Re [1976] 1 W.L.R. 757 Ch D	IR 14.21
E-Squared Ltd, Re [2006] EWHC 532 (Ch); [2006] 1 W.L.R. 3414; [2006] B.C.C. 379	IA Sch.B1 para.77(1)
Eastaway v Secretary of State for Trade and Industry. *See* Blackspur Group Plc, Re	
Eastaway v United Kingdom (74976/01) (2005) 40 E.H.R.R. 17 ECHR	[CDDA]
Eastern Capital Futures (In liq.), Re (1989) 5 B.C.C. 223 Ch D (Companies Ct)	IA 115
Ebbvale Ltd v Hosking [2013] UKPC 1; [2013] B.P.I.R. 219	IA 122(1), 123
Eberhardt & Co Ltd v Mair [1995] 1 W.L.R. 1180; [1995] B.C.C. 845 Ch D	IA 268, IR 10.24
Ebrahimi v Westbourne Galleries Ltd [1973] A.C. 360 HL	IA 122(1)
Eck v Zapf [2012] B.P.I.R. 499 Ch D	IA 263I, 265

	Provision
Equiticorp International Plc, Re [1989] 1 W.L.R. 1010; (1989) 5 B.C.C. 599 Ch D	IA 124(1)
Equity & Provident Ltd, Re [2002] EWHC 186 (Ch); [2002] 2 B.C.L.C. 78	IA 124A
Equity Nominees Ltd, Re [2000] B.C.C. 84 Ch D (Companies Ct)	IA 172(1), (2), Sch.B1 para.91, IR 7.63–7.66, 10.77
Erlam v Rahman [2016] EWHC 111 (Ch); [2016] B.P.I.R. 856	IA 335A
ERSTE Bank Hungary Nyrt v Hungary (C-527/10) EU:C:2012:417 [2012] I.L.Pr. 38	[ER]
Erste Group Bank AG (London) v JSC "VMZ Red October" [2015] EWCA Civ 379	IA 423(1)–(3)
Erste Group Bank AG v JSC "VM Red October" [2013] EWHC 2926 (Comm); [2014] B.P.I.R. 81	IA 421A
ESS Production Ltd (In admin.) v Sully [2005] EWCA Civ 554; [2005] B.C.C. 435	IA 216(3), IR 22.7
Estate of Jimmy Savile, Re [2014] EWHC 653 (Ch); [2014] B.P.I.R. 551	IA 284(1)–(3), (6)
Etic Ltd, Re [1928] Ch. 861 Ch D	IA 212(1)
Euro Commercial Leasing Ltd v Cartwright & Lewis [1995] B.C.C. 830 Ch D	IA 234(1), (2), Sch.B1 para.43(6)
Eurocruit Europe Ltd (In liq.), Re [2007] EWHC 1433 (Ch); [2007] B.C.C. 916	IA 212(1)
Eurodis Electron Plc (In admin.), Re [2011] EWHC 1025 (Ch); [2012] B.C.C. 57; [2011] B.P.I.R. 1372	IA 225, Sch.B1 para.8, [ER Preamble 25, 33, arts 3(1), 5]
Eurofood IFSC Ltd (C-341/04) EU:C:2005:579 [2006] E.C.R. I-3813; [2005] B.C.C. 1021 (AG Opinion)	IA 129, [CBIR Sch.1 art.6]
Eurofood IFSC Ltd (C-341/04) EU:C:2006:281 [2006] Ch. 508; [2006] B.C.C. 397	[ER, Preamble 25, arts 2(7), (8), 3(1)]

	Provision
Eurofood IFSC Ltd, Re [2004] B.C.C. 383 HC (Ire)	[ER Preamble 25, art.33]
Eurofood IFSC Ltd, Re [2004] IESC 47; [2005] B.C.C. 999 SC (Ire)	[ER art.33, CBIR Sch.1 art.6]
Euromaster Ltd, Re [2012] EWHC 2356 (Ch); [2013] Bus. L.R. 466; [2012] B.C.C. 754	IA Sch.B1 para.28, IR 12.64
Euromex Ventures Ltd v BNP Paribas Real Estate Advisory and Property Management UK Ltd [2013] EWHC 3007 (Ch)	IA 234(3), (4)
European Directories (DH6) BV, Re [2010] EWHC 3472 (Ch); [2012] B.C.C. 46; [2011] B.P.I.R. 408	IA Sch.B1 para.2, [ER art.3(1)]
Eurostem Maritime, Re [1987] B.C.C. 190	[CDDA 6(1), 22(2)]
Evans v Clarke Wilmott & Clarke [2007] EWHC 852 (Ch); [2008] B.P.I.R. 37	IA 268, 271(3)
Evans v Finance-U-Ltd [2013] EWCA Civ 869; [2013] B.P.I.R. 1001	IA 281(7), 285(3), (4), 322(1), IR 14.3–14.11
Evans v Jones [2016] EWCA Civ 660; [2017] Ch. 1	IA 123(1), 240(2)
Everard v Society of Lloyds [2003] EWHC 1890 (Ch); [2003] B.P.I.R. 1286	IR 10.5
Ex Ced Foods, Re, ANZ National Bank v Sheahan [2012] NZHC 3037; [2013] B.C.C. 321	IA 236, [CBIR Sch.1 art.21.1]
Excalibur Airways Ltd (In liq.), Re [1998] B.P.I.R. 598 Ch D (Companies Ct)	IA 7(4)
Exchange Securities & Commodities Ltd, Re [1983] B.C.L.C. 186	IA 130(2)
Exchange Travel (Holdings) Ltd (No.2), Re [1992] B.C.C. 954 Ch D (Companies Ct)	IA 140(1), (2)
Exchange Travel Agency Ltd v Triton Property Trust Plc [1991] B.C.C. 341 Ch D	IA 248

Case	Provision
Exeter City Council v Bairstow [2007] EWHC 400 (Ch); [2007] 4 All E.R. 437; [2007] B.C.C. 236	IA Sch.B1 para.99(3)–(4), IR 3.51
Express Electrical Distributors Ltd v Beavis [2016] EWCA Civ 765; [2016] 1 W.L.R. 4783; [2016] B.C.C. 566	IA 127
F Options Ltd (In liq.), Re [2011] EWHC 3324 (Ch); [2012] B.P.I.R. 107	IA 239(6), [CDDA 22(5)]
F v F (Divorce: Insolvency: Annulment of Bankruptcy Order) [1994] 1 F.L.R. 359; [1994] 2 F.C.R. 689 Fam Div	IA 282(1), (3)
F-Tex SIA v Lietuvos-Anglijos UAB Jadecloud-Vilma (C-213/10) EU:C:2012:215 [2013] Bus. L.R. 232	IA Sch.4 para.6, [ER art.7(2)(m)]
Fabb v Peters [2013] EWHC 296 (Ch); [2013] B.P.I.R. 264	IA 212(3)
Fagg v Rushton [2007] EWHC 657 (Ch); [2007] B.P.I.R. 1059	IA 383(2)–(4), IR 10.5
Fairway Graphics Ltd, Re [1991] B.C.L.C. 468 Ch D (Companies Ct)	IA 127
Fairway Magazines Ltd, Re [1992] B.C.C. 924 Ch D (Companies Ct)	IA 239(6), 245(2)
Farepak Food and Gifts Ltd (In admin.), Re [2006] EWHC 3272 (Ch); [2008] B.C.C. 22	IA 107
Farepak Food & Gifts Ltd (No.2), Re [2009] EWHC 2580 (Ch); [2010] B.C.C. 735	IA 107
Farmer v Moseley (Holdings) Ltd (Security for Costs) [2002] B.P.I.R. 473 Ch D	IA Sch.4 para.6
Farmizer (Products) Ltd, Re; sub nom. Moore v Gadd [1997] B.C.C. 655 CA (Civ Div)	IA 124
Farnborough Airport Properties Co Ltd v Revenue and Customs Commissioners [2017] UKUT 394 (TCC); [2017] S.T.C. 2293; [2017] B.T.C. 532	IA 44(1), (2)
Farrell v Brien [2016] NICh 9	IA 34
Fashoff (UK) Ltd (t/a Moschino) v Linton [2008] EWHC 537 (Ch); [2008] B.C.C. 542	IA Sch.B1 para.43(6)
Favermead Ltd v FPD Savills Ltd [2005] EWHC 626 (Ch); [2005] B.P.I.R. 715	IA 123
Feakins v Department for Environment, Food and Rural Affairs [2005] EWCA Civ 1513; [2007] B.C.C. 54; [2006] B.P.I.R. 895	IA 423(1)–(3)
Federal-Mogul Aftermarket UK Ltd, Re [2008] EWHC 1099 (Ch); [2008] B.P.I.R. 846	IA 7(4)
Federatie Nederlandse Vakvereniging v Smallsteps BV (C-126/16) EU:C:2017:489; [2017] B.C.C. 540	IA Sch.B1 para.3
Fehily v Atkinson [2016] EWHC 3069 (Ch)	IA Pt VIII
Feldman v Nissim [2010] EWHC 1353 (Ch); [2010] B.P.I.R. 815	IR 10.5
Fender v Inland Revenue Commissioners [2003] EWHC 3543 (Ch); [2003] B.P.I.R. 1304	IA 262, 262(1)–(3), (8)
Fenland DC v Sheppard [2011] EWHC 2829 (Ch); [2012] B.P.I.R. 289	IA 320(1)–(4)
Fern Advisers Ltd v Burford [2014] EWHC 762 (QB); [2014] B.P.I.R. 581	IA 285(1)
Ferris v Meagher [2013] IEHC 380	IA 44(1), (2)
FG Skerritt Ltd v Caledonian Building Systems Ltd [2013] EWHC 1898 (TCC)	IR 14.25
Fieldfisher LLP v Pennyfeathers Ltd [2016] EWHC 566 (Ch); [2016] B.C.C. 697	IA Sch.B1 para.12(1), (4)
Fielding v Seery [2004] B.C.C. 315 Ch D	IA 108
Financial Services Compensation Scheme Ltd v Larnell (Insurances) Ltd (In liq.) [2005] EWCA Civ 1408; [2006] Q.B. 808; [2006] B.C.C. 690	IA 129
Finanzamt Braunschweig-Wilhelmstrasse v Riemann [2015] B.P.I.R. 1405 Ch D	IA 282(1), (3), 375(1)
Finch (UK) Plc, Re [2015] EWHC 2430 (Ch)	IA 212(1), 239(5)
Finelist Ltd, Re [2003] EWHC 1780 (Ch); [2004] B.C.C. 877	[CDDA 7(1), 16]
Firedart Ltd, Re [1994] 2 B.C.L.C. 340 Ch D	[CDDA 12C]
First Express Ltd, Re [1991] B.C.C. 782 Ch D (Companies Ct)	IA Pt III, 234(1), (2)

	Provision
First Independent Factors and Finance Ltd v Mountford [2008] EWHC 835 (Ch); [2008] B.C.C. 598	IA 217(1), 217(3), IR 22.7
Fisher v Raven [1964] A.C. 210 HL	IA 360(2)
Fitch v Official Receiver [1996] 1 W.L.R. 242; [1996] B.C.C. 328	IA 375(1)
Fivestar Properties Ltd, Re; sub nom. West Bromwich Commercial Ltd, Re [2015] EWHC 2782 (Ch); [2016] 1 P. & C.R. DG11	IA Pt IV Ch.IX, Sch.B1 para.84(6), (6A), (6B)
Flack Ex p. Berry, Re [1900] 2 Q.B. 32 QBD	IA 372
Flame SA v Primera Maritime (Hellas) Ltd [2010] EWHC 2053 (Ch)	IA 220, 441
Fletcher v Vooght [2000] B.P.I.R. 435 Ch D	IA 252(1), 256A
Flett v Revenue and Customs Commissioners [2010] EWHC 2662 (Ch); [2010] B.P.I.R. 1075	IA 267(1), (2), 282(1), (3), IR 10.27
Flightline Ltd v Edwards; sub nom. Swissair Schweizerische Luftverkehr AG, Re [2003] EWCA Civ 63; [2003] 1 W.L.R. 1200; [2003] B.C.C. 361	IA 130(2)
Flint (A Bankrupt), Re [1993] Ch. 319 Ch D	IA 284(1)–(3), (6)
Fliptex Ltd v Hogg [2004] EWHC 1280 (Ch); [2004] B.C.C. 870	IA Sch.B1 para.19
Floor Fourteen Ltd, Re; Lewis v Inland Revenue Commissioners [2001] 3 All E.R. 499; [2002] B.C.C. 198 CA (Civ Div)	IA 115, 175(2)(a), 238, Sch.4 para.3A, IR 7.108
FMS Financial Management Services Ltd, Re (1989) 5 B.C.C. 191 Ch D (Companies Ct)	IA 1(1), 7(4)
Focus Insurance Co Ltd, Re [1996] B.C.C. 659 Ch D	IA 426(4), (5), (11)
Foenander v Allan [2006] EWHC 2101 (Ch); [2006] B.P.I.R. 1392	IA 303(1), 335A, 377, IR 12.64, 17.4
Folgate London Market Ltd (formerly Towergate Stafford Knight Co Ltd) v Chaucer Insurance Plc [2011] EWCA Civ 328; [2011] B.C.C. 675; [2011] B.P.I.R. 1001	IA 107
Forcesun Ltd, Re [2002] EWHC 443 (Ch); [2002] 2 B.C.L.C. 302	IA 124A
Ford v Alexander [2012] EWHC 266 (Ch); [2012] B.P.I.R. 528	IA 335A
Ford v Wolverhampton City Council [2008] B.P.I.R. 1304; [2009] R.V.R. 207 LGO	IA Pt IX Ch.1
Forrester & Lamego Ltd, Re [1997] 2 B.C.L.C. 155 Ch D	IA 124A
Forstater, Re [2015] B.P.I.R. 21 Ch D	IA 262(1)–(3), (8), IR 15.27
Forster v Bleasdale [2015] EWHC 1613 (Ch)	IR 12.30
Fortress Value Recovery Fund I LLC v Blue Skye Special Opportunities Fund LP [2013] EWHC 14 (Comm); [2013] 1 All E.R. (Comm) 973	IA 423, [ER arts 7, 18]
Foster v Davenport Lyons [2012] EWHC 275 (Ch); [2012] B.P.I.R. 545	IA 30, Pt IX, 271(3)
Foster v Wilson (1843) 12 M. & W. 191	IA 323
Foster, Re (2012). *See* Foster v Davenport Lyons	
Fourie v Le Roux (Application to Continue Freezing Order) [2004] EWHC 2557 (Ch); [2005] B.P.I.R. 723	IA 426, IR 1.1
Fourie v Le Roux [2005] EWHC 922 (Ch); [2005] B.P.I.R. 779	IA 426
Fourie v Le Roux [2007] UKHL 1; [2007] 1 W.L.R. 320	IA 426
Foxholes Nursing Home Ltd v Accora Ltd [2013] EWHC 3712 (Ch)	IA 123
Foxley v United Kingdom (33274/96) (2001) 31 E.H.R.R. 25; [2000] B.P.I.R. 1009 ECHR	IA 371(1)
Foyle v Turner [2007] B.P.I.R. 43 Ch D	IA Pt IX, 305(2), 335A
France (A Bankrupt), Re; sub nom. Nutting v France [2014] EWHC 2123 (Ch); [2014] B.P.I.R. 1448	IA 433(1)
Francis v Solomon Taylor & Shaw (A Firm) [2013] EWHC 9 (Ch); [2013] B.P.I.R. 314	IA 267(1), (2)
Frank Saul (Fashion) Ltd v HM Revenue and Customs [2012] EWHC 1603 (Ch); [2012] B.P.I.R. 985	IA 123
Frankice (Golders Green) Ltd (In admin.), Re [2010] EWHC 1229 (Ch); [2010] Bus. L.R. 1608	IA Sch.B1 para.43(6)

	Provision
Franses v Hay [2015] EWHC 3468 (Ch); [2016] B.P.I.R. 355	IA Pt VIII
Franses v Oomerjee [2005] B.P.I.R. 1320 Ch D	IA 309
Fraser v Oystertec Plc [2003] EWHC 2787 (Pat); [2004] B.C.C. 233	IA 107
Freakley v Centre Reinsurance International Co [2006] UKHL 45; [2006] 1 W.L.R. 2863; [2006] B.C.C. 971	IA Sch.B1 para.99(3)–(4)
Freeburn v Hunt [2010] B.P.I.R. 325	IA 303(1), IR 18.16
Freeman v Customs and Excise Commissioners [2005] EWHC 582 (Ch); [2005] S.T.C. 610; [2005] B.C.C. 506	IA 107
Freevale Ltd v Metrostore (Holdings) Ltd [1984] Ch. 199 Ch D	IA 37(1), (2), Sch.B1 para.43(6)
French v Barcham [2008] EWHC 1505 (Ch); [2009] 1 W.L.R. 1124	IA 335A
French's (Wine Bar) Ltd, Re (1987) 3 B.C.C. 173 Ch D (Companies Ct)	IA 127
Frontsouth (Witham) Ltd (In admin.), Re 2011] EWHC 1668 (Ch); [2011] B.C.C. 635; [2011] B.P.I.R. 1382	IA Sch.B1 paras 12(1), (4), para.22(1), 77(1), IR 3.4, 12.64
Frosdick v Fox [2017] EWHC 1737 (Ch); [2018] 1 W.L.R. 38; [2017] B.P.I.R. 1194	IA 315, 316
Frost v Unity Trust Bank Plc (No.1) [1998] B.P.I.R. 459 CSIH (1 Div)	IA 252(2)
Fryer v Ewart; sub nom. Ewart v Fryer [1902] A.C. 187 HL	IA 130(1)
FSA Business Software Ltd, Re [1990] B.C.C. 465 Ch D (Companies Ct)	IA 123
Fuller v Cyracuse Ltd [2001] B.C.C. 806 Ch D (Companies Ct)	IA 125(2)
Fulton v AIB Group (UK) Plc [2014] NICh 8; [2014] B.P.I.R. 1169	IA 420(1), Sch.B1 para.43(6)
Funding Corp Block Discounting Ltd v Lexi Holdings Plc (In admin.) [2008] EWHC 985 (Ch); [2008] 2 B.C.L.C. 596	IA Sch.B1 para.43(6)
Funtime Ltd, Re [2000] 1 B.C.L.C. 247 Ch D (Companies Ct)	[CDDA 12C]

	Provision
G-Tech Construction Ltd, Re [2007] B.P.I.R. 1275 Ch D	IA Sch.B1 paras 13(2), 104, IR 12.64
G&M Aldridge Pty Ltd v Walsh [2002] B.P.I.R. 482 HC (Aus)	IA 340(3)
Gaardsoe v Optimal Wealth Management Ltd (In liq.) [2012] EWHC 3266 (Ch); [2013] Ch. 298; [2013] B.C.C. 53	IA 130(2), Sch.B1 para.43(6)
Galeforce Pleating Co Ltd, Re [1999] 2 B.C.L.C. 704 Ch D (Companies Ct)	[CDDA 12C]
Galileo Group Ltd, Re [1999] Ch. 100; [1998] B.C.C. 228 Ch D	IA 236
Gallard, Re [1896] 1 Q.B. 68 CA	IR 17.25
Gallidoro Trawlers Ltd, Re [1991] B.C.C. 691 Ch D (Companies Ct)	IA Sch.B1 para.13(1), (3)
Galloppa v Galloppa [1998] 4 All E.R. 779; [1999] B.P.I.R. 352 Ch D	IA 267(1), (2)
Games Station Ltd, Re. *See* Pillar Denton Ltd v Jervis	
Gardiner v Secretary of State for Business, Enterprise and Regulatory Reform [2009] B.C.C. 742 Ch D	[CDDA 7(2A)]
Garrow v Society of Lloyd's [2000] C.L.C. 241; [1999] B.P.I.R. 885 CA (Civ Div)	IR 10.5
Garwood v Ambrose [2012] EWHC 1494 (Ch); [2012] B.P.I.R. 996	IA 283(2), (3), (4), 339(1)–(3)
Garwood v Bolter [2015] EWHC 3619 (Ch); [2016] B.P.I.R. 367	IA 363(1)
Gas and Electricity Markets Authority v GB Energy Supply Ltd [2016] EWHC 3341 (Ch)	IA 123, Sch.B1
Gate Gourmet Luxembourg IV Sarl v Morby [2015] EWHC 1203 (Ch); [2015] B.P.I.R. 787	IA 265, 269, 413(1), IR 12.64
Gate Gourmet Luxembourg IV Sarl v Morby [2016] EWHC 74 (Ch); [2016] Bus. L.R. 218; [2016] B.P.I.R. 414	IR 10.9, 12.64
Gatnom Capital & Finance Ltd, Re [2010] EWHC 3353 (Ch); [2011] B.P.I.R. 1013	IA 6(1)
Gatnom Capital v Sanders (No.2) [2011] EWHC 3716 (Ch); [2012] B.P.I.R. 299	IA 6(1)
GE Capital Commercial Finance Ltd v Sutton [2004] EWCA Civ 315; [2004] 2 B.C.L.C. 662	IA 234(1), (2)

	Provision
Geddes, Petitioner, 2006 S.L.T. 664; 2007 S.C.L.R. 11 CSOH	IA 172(1), (2)
Gemma Ltd (In liq.) v Davies [2008] EWHC 546 (Ch); [2008] B.C.C. 812	[CDDA 22(5)]
Gendrot v Chadwick [2018] EWHC 48 (Ch)	IA 339(1)–(3)
Genosyis Technology Management Ltd, Re [2006] EWHC 989 (Ch); [2007] 1 B.C.L.C. 208	[CDDA 12C]
Gerald Cooper Chemicals Ltd, Re [1978] Ch. 262 Ch D	IA 213(2)
German Date Coffee Co, Re (1882) 20 Ch. D 169	IA 122(1)
German Graphics Graphische Maschinen GmbH v van der Schee (C-292/08) EU:C:2009:544 [2009] E.C.R. I-8421; [2010] C.E.C. 499	[ER art.6]
Gerrard, Petitioner; sub nom. Hynd's Trustee, Petitioner [2009] CSOH 76; 2009 S.C. 593; [2009] B.P.I.R. 1374	IA 426(4), (5), (11)
Ghadami v Donegan [2014] EWHC 4448 (Ch)	IR 10.5
Ghassemian v Secretary of State for Trade and Industry [2006] EWHC 1715 (Ch); [2007] B.C.C. 229	[CDDA 8(1), 12C]
GHE Realisations Ltd (formerly Gatehouse Estates Ltd), Re [2005] EWHC 2400 (Ch); [2006] 1 W.L.R. 287; [2006] B.C.C. 139	IA Sch.B1 paras 65(3), 84(1), (1A), (1B), (2)
GHLM Trading Ltd v Maroo [2012] EWHC 61 (Ch); [2012] 2 B.C.L.C. 369	IA 212(1), 239
Gibraltar Residential Properties Ltd v Gibralcon 2004 SA [2010] EWHC 2595 (TCC); [2011] B.L.R. 126	[ER Preamble 7]
Gibson Davies Chemists Ltd, Re [1995] B.C.C. 11 Ch D (Companies Ct)	[CDDA 1(1)]
Gibson Dunn & Crutcher v Rio Properties Inc [2004] EWCA Civ 1043; [2004] 1 W.L.R. 2702; [2004] B.P.I.R. 1203	IA 286(1), (2)
Gil v Baygreen Properties Ltd [2004] EWHC 1732 (Ch); [2005] B.P.I.R. 95	IA 423(1)–(3)
Gilbert Deya Ministries v Kashmir Broadcasting Corp Ltd [2010] EWHC 3015 (Ch)	IA 220(1)
Giles v Rhind [2008] EWCA Civ 118; [2009] Ch. 191; [2008] B.P.I.R. 342	IA 423(1)–(3)
Gill v Quinn [2004] EWHC 883 (Ch); [2005] B.P.I.R. 129	IA 282(1), (3)
Gillan v Hec Enterprises Ltd [2016] EWHC 3179 (Ch)	IA 115, Sch.B1 paras 1, 99(3)–(4), IR 18.16
Gillmartin (A Bankrupt), Re [1989] 1 W.L.R. 513 Ch D	IA 271(3)
GL Saunders Ltd (In liq.), Re [1986] 1 W.L.R. 21 Ch D	IA Pt XII
Glasgow (Bankruptcy Trustee) v ELS Law Ltd [2017] EWHC 3004 (Ch); [2018] 1 Costs L.O. 79	IA 183, Pt IX, [CBIR Sch.1 art.21.1]
Glasgow City Council v Craig [2008] CSOH 171; 2009 S.C. 185; 2009 S.L.T. 212; [2010] B.C.C. 235	IA 216(3)
Glatt v Sinclair [2013] EWCA Civ 241; [2013] 1 W.L.R. 3602	IA Pt III
GlaxoSmithKline Export Ltd v UK (Aid) Ltd [2003] EWHC 1383 (Ch); [2004] B.P.I.R. 528	IA 123
Glen Express Ltd, Re [2000] B.P.I.R. 456 Ch D	IR 14.25
Glenister v Rowe [2000] Ch. 76; [1999] B.P.I.R. 674 CA (Civ Div)	IA 262, 382(3), (4), 281(2)–(6), (8)
Global Acquirers Ltd v Laycatelcom Lda Unreported 2 July 2014	IR 7.4–7.12
Global Corporate Ltd v Hale [2017] EWHC 2277 (Ch)	IA 212(1), 239(1)
Global Distressed Alpha Fund 1 Ltd Partnership v PT Bakrie Investindo [2011] EWHC 256 (Comm); [2011] 1 W.L.R. 2038	IA 426, [ER art.32, CBIR Sch.1 art.19]
Global Finance Recoveries Ltd v Jones [2000] B.P.I.R. 1029 Ch D	IA 267(1), (2)
Global Garden Products Italy SpA, Re [2016] EWHC 1884 (Ch); [2017] B.C.C. 637	IA 220
Global Info Ltd, Re [1999] 1 B.C.L.C. 74 Ch D	[CDDA 7(1)]
Global Maritime Investments Cyprus Ltd v OW Supply & Trading A/S (Under Konkurs) [2015] EWHC 2690 (Comm)	[CBIR Sch.1 art.17]
Global Trader Europe Ltd (In liq.), Re [2009] EWHC 699 (Ch); [2010] B.C.C. 729	IA 107, IR 14.14

	Provision
Hagemeister (A Bankrupt), Re [2010] B.P.I.R. 1093 CC	IA 263I, 265, 282(1), (3)
Haghighat (A Bankrupt), Re. *See* Brittain v Haghighat	
Hague v Nam Tai Electronics [2008] UKPC 13; [2008] B.C.C. 295; [2008] B.P.I.R. 363	IA 212(1), 212(3)
Hague v Nam Tai Electronics Inc [2006] UKPC 52; [2007] 2 B.C.L.C. 194	IA 107
Haig v Aitken [2001] Ch. 110; Ch D	IA 283(1), 310(7)
Halabi (In Bankruptcy), Re [2016] B.P.I.R. 373 Ch D	IA 303(2)
Halabi (In Bankruptcy), Re. *See* Revenue and Customs Commissioners v Arie	
Halabi v Camden LBC [2008] EWHC 322 (Ch); [2008] B.P.I.R. 370	IA 282(1), (3), 10.138
Hall v Poolman [2008] B.P.I.R. 892 (Aus)	IA 123
Hall v Van Der Heiden [2010] EWHC 537 (TCC); [2010] B.P.I.R. 585	IA 252(2), 385(1), IR 12.30
Halliwells LLP, Re [2010] EWHC 2036 (Ch); [2011] B.C.C. 57	IA Sch.B1 para.2
Halson Packaging Ltd, Re [1997] B.C.C. 993; [1997] B.P.I.R. 194 Ch D	IA 7(4)
Halt Garage (1964) Ltd, Re [1982] 3 All E.R. 1016 Ch D	IA 238(5)
Hamblin v Field [2000] B.P.I.R. 621 CA (Civ Div)	IA 339(1)–(3)
Hamilton v Brown; sub nom. C&MB Holdings Ltd, Re [2016] EWHC 191 (Ch); [2017] B.C.C. 457; [2016] B.P.I.R. 531	IA 74(1), 124(2)–(4A), 283(4), [CDDA 11]
Hamilton v Naviede. *See* Arrows Ltd, Re	
Hamilton v Official Receiver [1998] B.P.I.R. 602 Ch D	IA 168(5)
Hammonds (A Firm) v Pro-Fit USA Ltd [2007] EWHC 1998 (Ch); [2008] 2 B.C.L.C. 159	IA Sch.B1 paras 11, 12(1), (4)
Hammonds v Thomas Muckle & Sons Ltd [2006] B.P.I.R. 704 Ch D	IA Sch.B1 para.43(6)
Hampton Capital Ltd, Re [2015] EWHC 1905 (Ch)	IA 238(4)
Handelsveem BV v Hill [2011] B.P.I.R. 1024 Hoge Raad (Netherlands)	IA 366(1) [ER arts 21, 22, 32]
Hans Brochier Holdings Ltd v Exner [2006] EWHC 2594 (Ch); [2007] B.C.C. 127	IA Sch.B1 para.21, [ER Preamble 33, art.3(1)]
Hans Place Ltd, Re [1992] B.C.C. 737 Ch D (Companies Ct)	IA 168(5), 178
Hansford v Southampton Magistrates' Court [2008] EWHC 67 (Admin); [2008] 4 All E.R. 432; [2008] B.P.I.R. 379	IA Pt III
Hardy (A Bankrupt) v Buchler [1997] B.C.C. 815; [1997] B.P.I.R. 643 Ch D	IA 363(2), (4)
Hardy v Focus Insurance Co Ltd (In liq.) [1997] B.P.I.R. 77 Ch D	IA 279(3)–(5), 303(1)
Hargreaves v Salt [2010] EWHC 3549 (Fam); [2011] B.P.I.R. 656	IA 339(1)–(3)
Hargreaves, Re. *See* Booth v Mond	
Harlequin Management Services Ltd, Re [2013] EWHC 1926 (Ch)	IA Sch.B1 paras 26(2), (3)
Harlow DC v Hall [2006] EWCA Civ 156; [2006] 1 W.L.R. 2116; [2006] B.P.I.R. 712	IA 285(1)
Harlow v Creative Staging Ltd [2014] EWHC 2787 (Ch)	IA 127, Sch.B1 paras 13(1), (3), 40(1)
Harmony Care Homes Ltd, Re [2009] EWHC 1961 (Ch); [2010] B.C.C. 358	IA 40(1), (2)
Harmony Carpets v Chaffin-Laird [2000] B.C.C. 893; [2000] B.P.I.R. 61 Ch D	IA 263(1), (2)
Harms Offshore AHT Taurus GmbH & Co KG v Bloom [2009] EWCA Civ 632; [2010] Ch. 187; [2010] B.C.C. 822	IA Sch.B1 para.43(6)
Harper v Buchler (No.1) [2004] B.P.I.R. 724 Ch D	IA 282(1), (3)
Harper v Buchler (No.2) [2005] B.P.I.R. 577 Ch D	IA 282(1), (3)
Harper v O'Reilly [1997] B.P.I.R. 656 Ch D	IA 284(1)–(3), (6)

	Provision
Harrington v Bennett [2000] B.P.I.R. 630 Ch D	IA 335A
Harris Simons Construction Ltd, Re [1989] 1 W.L.R. 368; (1989) 5 B.C.C. 11 Ch D	IA 43(1), (2), Sch.A1 para.45, Sch.B1 paras 11, 39
Harris v Gross [2001] B.P.I.R. 586 Ch D	IA 264, 276(1)
Harris v Official Receiver [2016] EWHC 3433 (Ch)	IA 279(3)–(5)
Harris v Secretary of State for Business, Innovation and Skills; sub nom. Clenaware Systems Ltd, Re [2013] EWHC 2514 (Ch); [2015] B.C.C. 283; [2014] 1 B.C.L.C. 447	[CDDA 1(1)]
Harrison v Seggar [2005] EWHC 411 (Ch); [2005] B.P.I.R. 583	IA 271(3)
Harrods (Buenos Aires) Ltd (No.2), Re [1992] Ch. 72; [1991] B.C.C. 249 CA (Civ Div)	IA 125(1)
Hartmayes Ltd, Re, Griffin v Robinson [2013] EWHC 4624 (Ch)	IA 236(3), (3A)
Harvest Finance Ltd, Re [2013] B.P.I.R. 1020	IA 236
Harvest Finance Ltd (In liq.), Re [2014] EWHC 4237 (Ch); [2015] B.P.I.R. 266	IA 236(2), IR 12.20, 12.22
Harvey v Dunbar Assets [2013] EWCA Civ 952; [2013] B.P.I.R. 722	IR 10.5
Harvey v Dunbar Assets Plc [2017] EWCA Civ 60	IA 375(1), IR 10.5
Hawk Insurance Co Ltd, Re [2001] EWCA Civ 241; [2002] B.C.C. 300	IA Sch.4
Hawk Recovery Ltd v Hall [2016] EWHC 1307 (Ch); [2016] B.P.I.R. 1169	IA 335A
Hawkes Hill Publishing Co Ltd (In liq.), Re [2007] B.C.C. 937 Ch D	IA 214(2), 214(3)
Hawking v Hafton House Ltd 1990 S.C. 198; 1990 S.L.T. 496 CSOH	IA 51(1), (2), 55(1), (2)
Haworth, Re; Haworth v Cartmel [2011] EWHC 36 (Ch); [2011] B.P.I.R. 428	IA 268, 282(1), (3), 375(1)
Hayes v Butters [2014] EWHC 4557 (Ch)	IA 306
Hayes v Hayes [2012] EWHC 1240 (Ch); [2012] B.P.I.R. 739	IA 281(2)–(6), (8), IR 14.2
Hayes v Hayes [2014] EWHC 2694 (Ch); [2014] B.P.I.R. 1212	IA 271(1), (2), (4), IR 10.5, 12.1, 12.6
Hayes v Hayes [2017] EWHC 2806 (Ch); [2018] B.P.I.R. 7	IA 307(1)
Hayward (Deceased), Re [1997] Ch. 45 Ch D	IA 314(8)
Headington Investments Ltd Ex. p Maxwell [1993] B.C.C. 500 CA (Civ Div)	IA 236
Healing Research Trustee Co Ltd, Re [1991] B.C.L.C. 716	IA 124(1)
Healthcare Management Services Ltd v Caremark Properties Ltd	IA Sch.B1 para.13(1), (3)
Heath v Tang [1993] 1 W.L.R. 1421 CA (Civ Div)	IA 303(1), 306
Heating Electrical Lighting and Piping Ltd (In liq.) v Ross [2012] EWHC 3764 (Ch); [2012] B.P.I.R. 1122	IA 285(3), (4)
Hedger v Adams [2015] EWHC 2540 (Ch); [2016] B.C.C. 390	IA 212(3)
Helene Plc (In liq.), Re [2000] 2 B.C.L.C. 249	[CDDA, 6(1)]
Hellard and Goldfarb (Joint Supervisors of Pinson Wholesale Ltd), Re [2008] B.C.C. 112; [2007] B.P.I.R. 1322	IA 7(3)
Hellard v Chadwick [2014] EWHC 2158 (Ch); [2014] B.P.I.R. 1234	IA 285(1), 322(1), 339(1)–(3), 340(1), (2), 382(3), (4), IR 14.2
Hellard v Kapoor [2013] EWHC 2204 (Ch); [2013] B.P.I.R. 745	IA 279(3)–(5), 333(1), (3)
Hellard v Kapoor [2013] EWHC 2496 (Ch); [2013] B.P.I.R. 745	IA 333(1), (3)
Hellas Telecommunications (Luxembourg), Re [2017] EWHC 3465 (Ch)	IA Sch.4
Hellas Telecommunications (Luxembourg) II SCA (In admin.), Re [2011] EWHC 3176 (Ch); [2013] 1 B.C.L.C. 426	IA Sch.B1 paras 84(1), (1A), (1B), (2), 98(2)
Hellas Telecommunications (Luxembourg) II SCA, Re [2009] EWHC 3199 (Ch); [2010] B.C.C. 295	IA Sch.B1 paras 2, 111(1), 111(1A),

Case	Provision
	111(1B), [ER art.3(1)]
Hellas Telecommunications (Luxembourg) II SCA, Re [2013] B.P.I.R. 756 Ch D (Companies Ct) . .	IA 236, [ER art.7]
Hellas Telecommunications (Luxembourg) II SCA, Re Unreported 12 November 2013	IR 12.42
Hemming (Deceased), Re [2008] EWHC 8565 (Ch); [2009] B.P.I.R. 50	IA 436
Henderson v Foxworth Investments Ltd [2014] UKSC 41; [2014] 1 W.L.R. 2600	IA 242
Hennelly's Utilities Ltd, Re [2004] EWHC 34 (Ch); [2005] B.C.C. 542 .	[CDDA 1(1)]
Henry, Re; sub nom. Horton v Henry [2014] EWHC 4209 (Ch); [2015] 1 W.L.R. 2488; [2015] B.P.I.R. 313 . . .	IA 310(1), (1A), (2)
Henwood v Barlow Clowes International Ltd (In liq.) [2008] EWCA Civ 577; [2008] B.P.I.R. 778	IA 265
Henwood v Customs and Excise Commissioners [1998] B.P.I.R. 339 .	IA 282(1), (3)
Heritable Bank plc v Winding-up Board of Landsbanki Islands HF. *See* Winding Up Board of Landsbanki Islands HF v Mills	
Heritage Joinery v Krasner [1999] B.P.I.R. 683 Ch D	IA 263(1), (2)
Herry v Dudley MBC [2017] B.P.I.R. 1209	IA Pt IX Ch.I
Hewitt Brannan (Tools) Co Ltd, Re [1990] B.C.C. 354 Ch D (Companies Ct)	IA 124(5)
Hibernia (2005) Ltd, Re [2013] EWHC 2615 (Ch)	IA Sch.B1 paras 3(1), (3), 13(1), (3)
Hibernian Merchants Ltd, Re [1958] Ch. 76 Ch D.	IA 221
Hickling v Baker [2007] EWCA Civ 287; [2007] 1 W.L.R. 2386; [2007] B.P.I.R. 346	IA 364(1), 366(1)
High Street Services v Bank of Credit and Commerce International. *See* MS Fashions Ltd v Bank of Credit and Commerce International SA (In liq.)	
Highberry Ltd v Colt Telecom Group Plc (No.1); sub nom. Colt Telecom Group Plc (No.1), Re [2002] EWHC 2503 (Ch); [2003] B.P.I.R. 311	IR 12.27
Hill Samuel & Co Ltd v Laing, 1989 S.C. 301; 1989 S.L.T. 760 [1991] B.C.C. 665 CSIH (2 Div)	IA 57(2), (4), (5)
Hill v Department for Business, Innovation and Skills [2011] EWHC 3436 (Admin); [2012] B.C.C. 151 . .	[CDDA 13]
Hill v East & West India Dock Co (1884) 9 App. Cas. 448 HL	IA 181(1)–(3)
Hill v Haines; sub nom. Haines v Hill [2007] EWCA Civ 1284; [2008] Ch. 412; [2007] B.P.I.R. 1280	IA 339(1)–(3), 340(4), (5), 382(3), (4)
Hill v Secretary of State for the Environment, Food and Rural Affairs [2005] EWHC 696 (Ch); [2005] B.P.I.R. 1330	IA 283(2), (3), 307(1), [CDDA 11]
Hill v Spread Trustee Co Ltd; sub nom. Nurkowski, Re [2006] EWCA Civ 542; [2007] 1 W.L.R. 2404; [2006] B.C.C. 646; [2006] B.P.I.R. 789	IA 238(4), 423, 423(1)–(3)
Hill v Stokes Plc [2010] EWHC 3726 (Ch); [2011] B.C.C. 473	IA Sch.B1 paras 26(2), (3), 28
Hill v Van Der Merwe [2007] EWHC 1613 (Ch); [2007] B.P.I.R. 1562	IR 12.18
Hills v Alex Lawrie Factors [2001] B.P.I.R. 1038	IA 344(1), (2)
Hindcastle Ltd v Barbara Attenborough Associates Ltd [1997] A.C. 70; [1996] B.C.C. 636 HL	IA 181(1)–(3), 315, 315(3), (5)
Hinton v Wotherspoon [2016] EWHC 621 (Ch); [2016] B.P.I.R. 944	IA 310(1), (1A), (2)
Hirani v Rendle [2003] EWHC 2538 (Ch); [2004] B.P.I.R. 274	IA 282(1), (3)
HJ Tomkins, Re [1990] B.C.L.C. 76 . . .	IA 125(1)
HL Bolton Engineering Co Ltd, Re [1956] Ch. 577 Ch D	IA 82(1), (2)
HLC Environmental Projects Ltd, Re [2013] EWHC 2876 (Ch); [2014] B.C.C. 337	IA 123(1), 212(1)
HM Revenue and Customs Commissioners cases; *See* Revenue and Customs Commissioners	
Hoare v Inland Revenue Commissioners [2002] EWHC 775 (Ch); [2002] B.P.I.R. 986	IA 282(1), (3)

Case	Provision
EWHC 1577 (Ch); [2004] B.C.C. 919; [2003] B.P.I.R. 562	IR 7.33–7.39
Independent Pension Trustee Ltd v LAW Construction Co Ltd, 1997 S.L.T. 1105 CSOH	IA Pt III
India v Taylor [1955] A.C. 491 HL	IR 14.2
Industrial & Commercial Securities Plc, Re (1989) 5 B.C.C. 320 Ch D (Companies Ct)	IR 12.59
Industrial Diseases Compensation Ltd v Marrons [2001] B.P.I.R. 600 Ch D	IA 346(1), (1A), (5)
Inertia Partnership LLP, Re [2007] EWHC 539 (Ch); [2007] B.C.C. 656	IA 124A
Information Governance Ltd, Re [2013] EWHC 2611 (Ch); [2015] B.C.C. 277	IA Sch.B1 para.12(1), (4)
Ing Lease (UK) Ltd v Griswold [1998] B.C.C. 905 Ch D	IA 263(3)
Inland Revenue Commissioners v Adam & Partners Ltd [2002] B.C.C. 247; [2000] B.P.I.R. 986 CA (Civ Div)	IA 1(1)
Inland Revenue Commissioners v Bland [2003] EWHC 1068 (Ch); [2003] B.P.I.R. 1274	IA 262
Inland Revenue Commissioners v Conbeer [1996] 2 All E.R. 345; [1996] B.C.C. 189 Ch D	IR 16.7
Inland Revenue Commissioners v Debtor [1995] B.C.C. 971; [1996] B.P.I.R. 271 Ch D	IA 271(3)
Inland Revenue Commissioners v Duce [1999] B.P.I.R. 189 Ch D	IA 262(1)–(3), (8), 262(4)–(7)
Inland Revenue Commissioners v Goldblatt [1972] Ch. 498 Ch D	IA 40(1), (2)
Inland Revenue Commissioners v Hashmi [2002] EWCA Civ 981; [2002] B.C.C. 943; [2002] B.P.I.R. 974	IA 423(1)–(3)
Inland Revenue Commissioners v Khan [2005] B.P.I.R. 409 Ch D (Bankruptcy)	IR 10.138
Inland Revenue Commissioners v Lee-Phipps [2003] B.P.I.R. 803 Ch D	IA 271(1), (2), (4)
Inland Revenue Commissioners v McEntaggart [2004] EWHC 3431 (Ch); [2007] B.C.C. 260; [2006] B.P.I.R. 750	IA 282(4), 350(1), (2), [CDDA 11, 15]
Inland Revenue Commissioners v Nash [2003] EWHC 686 (Ch); [2004] B.C.C. 150; [2003] B.P.I.R. 1138	IA 217
Inland Revenue Commissioners v Robinson [1999] B.P.I.R. 329 Ch D	IA 282(1), (3)
Inland Revenue Commissioners v Wimbledon Football Club Ltd 2004] EWCA Civ 655; [2004] B.C.C. 638; [2004] B.P.I.R. 700	IA 4(4)
Inquiry into Mirror Group Newspapers Plc, Re [2000] Ch. 194; [2000] B.C.C. 217 Ch D (Companies Ct)	IA 236
INS Realisations Ltd, Re [2006] EWHC 135 (Ch); [2006] 1 W.L.R. 3433; [2006] B.C.C. 307	[CDDA 8A(1), (2)]
Inside Sport Ltd (In liq.), Re [2000] B.C.C. 40 Ch D (Companies Ct)	IA 171
Instant Access Properties Ltd, Re [2011] EWHC 3022 (Ch); [2012] 1 B.C.L.C. 710	[CDDA 7(2)]
Institute of Chartered Accountants in England and Wales v Webb [2009] EWHC 3461 (Ch); [2010] Bus. L.R. D37	IR Pt 12 Ch.6 sub-div.B
Instrumentation Electrical Services Ltd, Re (1988) 4 B.C.C. 301 Ch D (Companies Ct)	IA 124(1)
Integeral Ltd, Re [2013] EWHC 164 (Ch) Ch D (Companies Ct)	IA Sch.B1 para.13(1), (3)
Integrated Medical Solutions Ltd, Re [2012] B.C.C. 215 Ch D (Companies Ct)	IA 426(4), (5), (11), [ER art.46]
Interedil Srl (In liq.) v Fallimento Interedil Srl (C-396/09) EU:C:2011:671 [2012] Bus. L.R. 1582; [2011] E.C.R. I-9915; [2012] B.C.C. 851	[ER art.3(1), (3), (4)]
Interframe Ltd v Brown [2005] EWHC 3527 (Ch); [2008] B.P.I.R. 49	IR 10.5
International Air Transport Association v Ansett Australia Holdings Ltd [2008] HCA 3; [2008] B.P.I.R 57	IA 107
International Brands USA Inc v Goldstein [2005] EWHC 1293 (Ch); [2007] B.C.C. 960; [2005] B.P.I.R. 1455	IR 14.3–14.11, 16.5
International Bulk Commodities Ltd, Re [1993] Ch. 77; [1992] B.C.C. 463 Ch D	IA 29(2), 251

Case	Provision
JSF Finance & Currency Exchange Co Ltd v Akma Solutions Inc [2002] B.P.I.R. 535 Ch D	IA 123
JT Frith Ltd, Re [2012] EWHC 196 (Ch); [2012] B.C.C. 634	IA 176A(2), (6)
Jubilee International Inc v Farlin Timbers Pte Ltd [2005] EWHC 3331 (Ch); [2006] B.P.I.R. 765	IA 123
Judd v Brown [1999] 1 F.L.R. 1191; [1999] B.P.I.R. 517 CA (Civ Div)	IA 305(2), 335A, 336(3)–(5)
Jules v Robertson [2011] EWCA Civ 1322; [2012] B.P.I.R. 126	IA Pt VIII
Jumani v Mortgage Express [2013] EWHC 1571 (Ch)	IA Pt III
Jyske Bank (Gibraltar) Ltd v Spjeldnaes (No.2) [2000] B.C.C. 16; [1999] B.P.I.R. 525 Ch D	IA 423(4), (5), 425(1), IR 1.1
Kaberry v Freethcartwright (A Firm) (formerly Freeth Cartwright Hunt Dickens) (No.2) [2003] EWCA Civ 1077; [2003] B.P.I.R. 1144	IA 306
Kali Ltd v Chawla [2007] EWHC 1989 (Ch); [2008] B.P.I.R. 415	IA 423(1)–(3)
Kam v Kam [2015] HKFCA 91	IA 220
Kane v Revenue Commissioners [2013] NIMaster 17	IA 263I
Kansal v United Kingdom (21413/02) (2004) 39 E.H.R.R. 31; [2004] B.P.I.R. 740 ECHR	IA 236, 433(1)
Kappler v Secretary of State for Trade and Industry [2006] EWHC 3694 (Ch); [2006] B.C.C. 845	[CDDA 7(1), 12C]
Karia (A Bankrupt), Re [2006] B.P.I.R. 1226 Ch D	IA 335A
Karnos Property Co Ltd, Re (1989) 5 B.C.C. 14 Ch D (Companies Ct)	IA 123
Kasumu v Arrow Global (Guernsey) Ltd [2013] EWHC 789 (Ch); [2013] B.P.I.R 1047	IR 10.26, 12.64
Katz v McNally [1997] B.C.C. 784; [1998] B.P.I.R. 30 CA (Civ Div)	IA Sch.4 para.6
Katz v McNally [1999] B.C.C. 291 CA (Civ Div)	IA 239(6)
Katz v Oldham [2016] B.P.I.R. 83 Ch D	IA 304(2)
Kaupthing Capital Partners II Master LP Inc, Re [2010] EWHC 836 (Ch); [2011] B.C.C. 338	IA Sch.B1 paras 29(5), 104
Kaupthing Singer & Friedlander Ltd (In admin.), Re [2010] EWCA Civ 518; [2011] B.C.C. 555; [2010] B.P.I.R. 839	IR 14.24
Kaupthing Singer & Friedlander Ltd (In admin.), Re [2011] UKSC 48; [2012] 1 A.C. 804; [2012] B.C.C. 1	IA Pt IX, IR 14.11, 14.25
Kaupthing Singer & Friedlander Ltd (In admin.), Re [2012] EWHC 2235 (Ch); [2014] 1 B.C.L.C. 13	IA Sch.B1 para.43(6)
Kaupthing Singer & Friedlander Ltd v Coomber [2011] EWHC 3589 (Ch); [2012] B.P.I.R. 774	IA 271(1), (2), (4)
Kaye v Bourne [2004] EWHC 3236 (Ch); [2005] B.P.I.R. 590	IA 276(1)
Kaye v South Oxfordshire District Council [2013] EWHC 4165 (Ch); [2014] B.C.C. 143	IA Pt I, 1(1), 5(2), Sch.B1 para.99(3)–(4), IR 14.1
Kayford Ltd (In liq.), Re [1975] 1 W.L.R. 279 Ch D	IA 107, 239(3)
Kayley Vending Ltd, Re [2009] EWHC 904 (Ch); [2009] B.C.C. 578	IA Sch.B1 para.2
Kaytech International Plc, Re [1999] B.C.C. 390 CA (Civ Div)	[CDDA 12C, 22(5)]
Kean v Lucas [2017] EWHC 250 (Ch); [2017] B.C.C. 311; [2017] B.P.I.R. 702	IA 112(2), 168(2), 171(1), (2), 172(3)
Keely v Ball [2016] EWHC 308 (Ch)	IA 279(3)–(5)
Keenan, Re [1998] B.P.I.R. 205 Ch D	IA 276(1)
Keepers and Governors of the Possessions, Revenues and Goods of the Free Grammar School of John Lyon v Helman [2014] EWCA Civ 17; [2014] 1 P. & C.R. 16	IA 306, 315
Kellar v BBR Graphic Engineers (Yorks) Ltd [2002] B.P.I.R. 544 Ch D	IR 10.5
Kemsley v Barclays Bank Plc [2013] EWHC 1274 (Ch); [2013] B.P.I.R. 839	IA 285(1), [CBIR Sch.1 art.2]
Kent Carpets Ltd v Symes [1996] B.C.C. 137; [1996] B.P.I.R. 169 Ch D (Bankruptcy)	IA 258(1)
Kentish Homes Ltd, Re [1993] B.C.C. 212 Ch D (Companies Ct)	IA 115, IR 14.1

Case	Provision
Key2Law (Surrey) LLP v De'Antiquis [2011] EWCA Civ 1567; [2012] B.C.C. 375	IA Sch.B1 para.3
Keypak Homecare Ltd (No.1), Re (1987) 3 B.C.C. 558 Ch D (Companies Ct)	IA 108
Keypak Homecare Ltd (No.2), Re [1990] B.C.C. 117 Ch D (Companies Ct)	[CDDA 12C]
Khan v Breezevale Sarl [1996] B.P.I.R. 190 Ch D	IR 10.5
Khan v Khan [2015] EWHC 2625 (Ch)	IA 306
Khan v Permayer [2001] B.P.I.R. 95 CA (Civ Div)	IA 258(2)–(5)
Khan v Trident Safeguards Ltd [2004] EWCA Civ 624; [2004] B.P.I.R. 881	IA 306
Khan-Ghauri v Dunbar Bank Plc [2001] B.P.I.R. 618	IA 315(1), (2)
Khan, Re Unreported 5 February 2016	IA 265
Kilvert v Flackett (A Bankrupt) [1998] 2 F.L.R. 806; [1998] B.P.I.R. 721 Ch D	IA 310(1), (1A), (2), 310(7)
King v Anthony [1999] B.P.I.R. 73 CA (Civ Div)	IA 263(3)
King v Inland Revenue Commissioners [1996] B.P.I.R. 414 Ch D	IA 271(3)
Kings v Cleghorn [1998] B.P.I.R. 463 Ch D	IA 263(5), (6)
Kingscroft Insurance Co Ltd, Re [1994] B.C.C. 343 Ch D (Companies Ct)	IA 236
Kinlan v Crimmin [2006] EWHC 779 (Ch); [2007] B.C.C. 106	IA 212(1)
Kirkpatrick v Snoozebox Ltd [2014] B.C.C. 477	IA 87(2), 163, Sch.4 para.6
Kiss Cards Ltd, Re [2016] EWHC 2176 (Ch); [2017] B.C.C. 489; [2016] B.P.I.R. 1450	IA 238(4)
KK v MA [2012] EWHC 788 (Fam); [2012] B.P.I.R. 1137	IA 283(1), 306, 328(4), (5), 330(5)
Klamer v Kyriakides and Braier (a firm) [2005] B.P.I.R. 1115 Ch D	IA 267(1), (2)
Klempka v ISA Daisytek SA [2006] B.C.C. 841 Cour de Cassation (France)	[ER arts 3(1), 33]
Knight v APS Recycling Ltd [2014] EWHC 4620 (Ch)	IR 10.5
Knight v Lawrence [1991] B.C.C. 411 Ch D	IA Pt III
Knight v Rainstorm Pictures Inc Unreported, 5 May 2017	IA 375(1)
Knowles v Coutts & Co [1998] B.P.I.R. 96 Ch D	IA 255(1), (2)
Kolden Holdings Ltd v Rodette Commerce Ltd [2008] EWCA Civ 10; [2008] 3 All E.R. 61	[ER Preamble 25]
Komady Ltd v Ulster Bank Ltd [2015] IEHC 314	IA 34
Kommalage v Sayanthakumar [2014] EWCA Civ 1832; [2015] B.P.I.R. 836	IA Pt IX
Konigsberg (A Bankrupt), Re [1989] 1 W.L.R. 1257 Ch D	IA 311(1)
Kornhaas v Dithmar (C-594/14) EU:C:2015:806; [2016] B.C.C. 116	[ER art.7]
Kotonou v Reeves Unreported 30 October 2015	IA 306
Krasner v Dennison [2001] Ch. 76; [2000] 3 W.L.R. 720 CA (Civ Div)	IA 306
Krasner v McMath [2005] EWCA Civ 1072; [2005] 4 All E.R. 886; [2005] B.C.C. 915	IA Sch.B1 para.99(5)–(6)
Krug International (UK) Ltd, Re [2008] EWHC 2256 (Ch); [2008] B.P.I.R. 1512	IA 212(1), 425(1)
Kubiangha v Ekpenyong [2002] EWHC 1567 (Ch); [2003] B.P.I.R. 623	IA 423(1)–(3)
Kudos Business Solutions Ltd (In liq.), Re [2011] EWHC 1436 (Ch); [2012] 2 B.C.L.C. 65	IA 212(1), 214
Kudos Glass Ltd (In liq.), Re [2002] B.C.C. 416; [2001] B.P.I.R. 517 Ch D	IA 7(4)
Kumar (A Bankrupt), Re [1993] 1 W.L.R. 224 Ch D	IA 339(1)–(3)
Kyrris (No.1), Re [1998] B.P.I.R. 103 Ch D	IA 420(1)
Kyrris (No.2), Re [1998] B.P.I.R. 111 Ch D (Companies Ct)	IA 420(1)
Kyrris v Oldham [2003] EWCA Civ 1506; [2004] B.C.C. 111; [2004] B.P.I.R. 165	IA 212(3)
L v L (School Fees: Maintenance: Enforcement) [1997] 2 F.L.R. 252; [1997] 3 F.C.R. 52	IA Second Group of Parts
La Mutuelles du Mans Assurances IARD, Re [2005] EWHC 1599 (Ch); [2006] B.C.C. 11	IA 220

	Provision
La Senza Ltd, Re; Uniserve Ltd v Croxen [2012] EWHC 1190 (Ch); [2013] B.C.C. 825	IA 233(1), 234(1), (2), Sch.B1 para.43(6)
Lacontha Foundation v GBI Investments Ltd [2010] EWHC 37 (Ch); [2010] B.P.I.R. 356	IA 123
Ladd v Marshall [1954] 1 W.L.R. 1489 CA	IA 282(1), (3), IR 10.5
Lafayette Electronics Europe Ltd, Re [2006] EWHC 1005 (Ch); [2007] B.C.C. 890	IA 124(1), Sch.B1 para.99
Lam v Inland Revenue Commissioners [2005] EWHC 592 (Ch); [2009] B.P.I.R. 301	IA Pt IX Ch.1
Lambeth LBC v Simon [2007] B.P.I.R. 1629 Ch D	IA 268, 271(1), (2), (4), 282(4), IR 10.8, 10.9, 10.24
Lancefield v Lancefield [2002] B.P.I.R. 1108 Ch D	IA 124, 221
Land Rover Group Ltd v UPF (UK) Ltd (In admin. rec.) [2002] EWHC 3183 (QB); [2003] 2 B.C.L.C. 222	IA 37(1), (2)
Landau (A Bankrupt), Re [1998] Ch. 223 Ch D	IA 306, 310, 342A
Landhurst Leasing Plc, Re [1999] 1 B.C.L.C 286 Ch D (Companies Ct)	[CDDA 12C]
Landsman v De Concilio [2005] EWHC 267 (Ch); [2005] B.P.I.R. 829	IA 264
Lang v McKenna [1997] B.P.I.R. 340	IA 283(2), (3), 306
Langley Marketing Services Ltd, Re [1992] B.C.C. 585	IR 12.59
Langreen Ltd (In liq.), Re Unreported 21 October 2011	IA 214(1), 214(2)
Larsen v Navios International Inc [2011] EWHC 878 (Ch); [2012] B.C.C. 353	IR 14.25, [CBIR Sch.1 art.21.1]
Lascomme Ltd v United Dominions Trust (Ireland) [1994] I.L.R.M. 227	IA Pt III
Latlorcan Developments Ltd (In admin.), Re; sub nom. Cavanagh v Dolan [2015] NICh 14	IR 12.64
Latreefers Inc, Re [2000] C.P.L.R. 65; [2001] B.C.C. 174 CA (Civ Div)	IA 123, 135, 220
Laurier v United Overseas Bank Ltd [1996] B.P.I.R. 635 Ch D	IR 10.5
Laverty v British Gas Trading Ltd [2014] EWHC 2721 (Ch); [2014] B.C.C. 701	IA Sch.B1 para.99(3)–(4), IR 3.51, 14.1, 14.2
Law Society v Shah [2007] EWHC 2841 (Ch); [2009] Ch. 223; [2007] B.P.I.R. 1595	IA 281(1), 303(1), 363(1)
Law Society v Southall [2001] EWCA Civ 2001; [2002] B.P.I.R. 336	IA 423
Lazari GP Ltd v Jervis [2012] EWHC 1466 (Ch); [2013] B.C.C. 294	IA Sch.B1 para.43(6)
LB Holdings Intermediate 2 Ltd (In admin.), Re [2017] EWHC 2032 (Ch)	IA Sch.B1 para.60, IR 12.39
LBI hf v Kepler Capita Markets SA (C-85/12, 24 October 2013)	[ER art.1(1)]
LCP Retail Ltd v Segal [2006] EWHC 2087 (Ch); [2007] B.C.C. 584	IR 14.15–14.19
Ledingham-Smith (A Bankrupt), Re [1993] B.C.L.C. 635 Ch D	IA 340(3), 340(4), (5)
Lee Behrens & Co Ltd, Re [1932] 2 Ch. 46 Ch D	IA 238(5)
Lee v Lee (A Bankrupt) [2000] B.C.C. 500; [1999] B.P.I.R. 926 CA (Civ Div)	IA 320(1)–(4)
Leeds United Association Football Club Ltd, Re [2007] EWHC 1761 (Ch); [2008] B.C.C. 11	IA Sch.B1 para.99(5)–(6)
Leeds v Lemos [2017] EWHC 1825 (Ch); [2017] B.P.I.R. 1223	IA 283, 311(1), 423(1)–(3), 436
Legal & Equitable Securities Plc (In liq.), Re [2012] EWHC 910 (Ch); (2012) 109(24) L.S.G. 22	IR 14.3–14.11
Legal and Equitable Securities Plc, Re [2010] EWHC 2046 (Ch); [2011] B.C.C. 354; [2010] B.P.I.R. 1151	IA 376, Sch.5
Legal Services Commission (formerly Legal Aid Board) v Leonard [2002] EWCA Civ 744; [2002] B.P.I.R. 994	IR 10.24
Legal Services Commission v Thipthorpe [2009] B.P.I.R. 1399 CC	IA Pt VIII
Legends Surf Shops Plc (In admin. rec.) v Sun Life Assurance Society Plc [2005] EWHC 1438 (Ch); [2006] B.C.C. 204	IA 44(1), (2)

Case	Provision
Lehman Bros Europe Ltd, Re; Lehman Bros Holdings Plc (In admin.), Re [2017] EWHC 2031 (Ch); [2018] Bus. L.R. 439	IA Sch.B1 paras 64, 65
Lehman Bros International (Europe) (In admin.), Re [2012] UKSC 6; [2012] 3 All E.R. 1	IA 107
Lehman Bros International (Europe) (In admin.), Re Lomas v Burlington Loan Management Ltd [2015] EWHC 2270 (Ch); [2015] B.P.I.R. 1162	IA Sch.B1 para.74
Lehman Bros International (Europe) (In admin.), Re; sub nom. Contrarian Funds LLC v Lomas [2014] EWHC 1687 (Ch); [2014] B.P.I.R. 1259	IR 12.1, 14.3–14.11, Sch.5
Lehman Bros International (Europe) (In admin.), Re; sub nom. Four Private Investment Funds v Lomas [2008] EWHC 2869 (Ch); [2009] B.C.C. 632	IA Sch.B1 para.74
Lehman Bros International (Europe) (In admin.), Re; sub nom. Lomas v Burlington Loan Management Ltd [2015] EWHC 2269 (Ch); [2016] Bus. L.R. 17; [2015] B.P.I.R. 1102	IA 189, IR 14.23
Lehman Bros International (Europe) (In admin.), Re; sub nom. Lomas v Burlington Loan Management Ltd [2016] EWHC 2131 (Ch); [2017] B.C.C. 1	IA 189, IR 14.21, 14.23
Lehman Bros International (Europe) (In admin.), Re. *See* Joint Administrators of LB Holdings Intermediate 2 Ltd v Joint Administrators of Lehman Bros International (Europe)	
Lehman Bros International (Europe) Ltd, Re [2013] EWHC 1664 (Ch); [2014] B.C.C. 132	IA Sch.B1 para.63
Lehman Bros International (Europe), Re; Lomas v Burlington Loan Management Ltd [2017] EWCA Civ 1462; [2017] B.C.C. 759	IA 189, IR 14.23
Lehman Bros Ltd, Re Unreported 15 March 2016	IR 3.62
Leicester v Plumtree Farms Ltd [2003] EWHC 206 (Ch); [2004] B.P.I.R. 296	IA 282(1), (3)
Leicester v Stevenson [2002] EWHC 2831 (Ch); [2003] 2 B.C.L.C. 97	IA 147(1)
Leigh Estates (UK) Ltd, Re [1994] B.C.C. 292 Ch D (Companies Ct)	IA 125(1), Sch.1
Leighton Contracting (Qatar) WLL v Simms [2011] EWHC 1735 (Ch); [2011] B.P.I.R. 1395	IR 15.31
Leisure (Norwich) II Ltd v Luminar Lava Ignite Ltd (In admin.) [2012] EWHC 951 (Ch); [2013] 3 W.L.R. 1132; [2012] B.C.C. 497	IA Sch.B1 para.99(3)–(4), IR 3.51
Leisure Study Group Ltd, Re [1994] 2 B.C.L.C. 65 Ch D	IA 1(2), 7(1), (2), 7(4), Pt III
Lemos v Lemos [2016] EWCA Civ 1181; [2017] 1 P. & C.R. DG11	IA 423(1)–(3)
Lennox Holdings Plc, Re [2009] B.C.C. 155 Ch D	[ER art.3(1)]
Leon v York-o-Matic Ltd [1966] 1 W.L.R. 1450 Ch D	IA 168(5)
Leslie v White [2012] CSOH 124; 2012 G.W.D. 27–563	IA 243(1), (2)
Lesser v Lawrence [2001] Ch. 76; [2000] B.P.I.R. 410 CA (Civ Div)	IA 310
Levy McCallum Ltd v Allen [2007] NI Ch 3	IA 238(4)
Levy v Ellis-Carr [2012] EWHC 63 (Ch); [2012] B.P.I.R. 347	IA 335A, IR 12.24
Levy v Legal Services Commission (formerly Legal Aid Board) [2001] 1 All E.R. 895; [2000] B.P.I.R. 1065 CA (Civ Div)	IA 264, 267(1), (2), 382(3), (4), IR 14.2
Lewis Merthyr Consolidated Collieries Ltd, Re (No.1) [1929] 1 Ch. 498 CA	IA Pt XII
Lewis v Eliades (No.2) [2003] EWCA Civ 1758; [2004] 1 W.L.R. 692	IA 267(1), (2)
Lewis v Hyde [1998] 1 W.L.R. 94; [1997] B.C.C. 976 PC (NZ)	IA 340(3)
Lewis v Kennedy [2010] B.P.I.R. 886 Ch D	IA 282(1), (3)
Lewis v Metropolitan Properties Realizations Ltd [2009] EWCA Civ 448; [2010] Ch. 148	IA 283A
Lewis v Ogwr BC [1996] R.A. 124 QBD	IA 285(1)
Lewis v Secretary of State for Trade and Industry [2003] B.C.C. 567	[CDDA 1(1)]

	Provision
	paras 11, 73(1)(a)
Lombard Natwest Factors Ltd v Koutrouzas [2002] EWHC 1084 (QB); [2003] B.P.I.R. 444	IA 260(1), (2), (2A)
Lombard North Central Plc v Blower [2014] 2267 (Ch); [EWHC 2014] B.P.I.R. 1501	IA 265
Lombard North Central Plc v Brook [1999] B.P.I.R. 701 Ch D	IR 2.25–2.38
Lombard Shipping and Forwarding Ltd, Re [1992] B.C.C. 700 Ch D	[CDDA 7(1), 7(4)]
London and General Bank, Re [1895] 2 Ch. 166 CA	IA 206(3)
London City Corp v Bown, *Times*, 11 October 1989	IA 306, 315(1), (2)
London Flight Centre (Stansted) Ltd v Osprey Aviation Ltd [2002] B.P.I.R. 1115	IA Sch.B1 para.43(6)
London Iron & Steel Co Ltd, Re [1990] B.C.C. 159 Ch D (Companies Ct)	IA 234(1), (2)
London Scottish Finance Ltd (In admin.), Re [2013] EWHC 4047 (Ch); [2014] Bus. L.R. 424	IA Sch.B1 para.49(4)–(8)
Lonergan v Gedling BC [2009] EWCA Civ 1569; [2010] B.P.I.R. 911	IA Pt IX Ch.1
Long v Farrer & Co [2004] EWHC 1774 (Ch); [2004] B.P.I.R. 1218	IA 366(1)
Longmeade Ltd (In admin.), Re [2016] EWHC 356 (Ch); [2017] B.C.C. 203; [2016] B.P.I.R. 666	IA 165(2)
Looe Fish Ltd, Re [1993] B.C.C. 348 Ch D (Companies Ct)	[CDDA 8(1)]
Loquitur Ltd, Re [2003] EWHC 999 (Ch); [2003] S.T.C. 1394	IA 212(3)
Lord (Liquidator of Rosshill Properties Ltd) v Sinai Securities Ltd [2004] EWHC 1764 (Ch); [2004] B.C.C. 986; [2004] B.P.I.R. 1244	IA 238(3)
Lord Advocate v Aero Technologies Ltd (In rec.) 1991 S.L.T. 134 CSOH	IA 57(1)
Lord Advocate v Royal Bank of Scotland Ltd; sub nom. Inland Revenue Commissioners v Royal Bank of Scotland Ltd, 1977 S.C. 155; 1978 S.L.T. 38	IA 60(1)
Lornamead Acquisitions Ltd v Kaupthing Bank HF [2011] EWHC 2611 (Comm); [2013] 1 B.C.L.C. 73	IR 14.3–14.11, [ER art.1(1)]
Lovett v Carson Country Homes Ltd [2009] EWHC 1143 (Ch); [2011] B.C.C. 789	IA Sch.B1 para.14
Lowrie (A Bankrupt), Re [1981] 3 All E.R. 353 Div Ct	IA 336(3)–(5)
Lowston, Re [1991] B.C.L.C. 570 Ch D (Companies Ct)	IA 147(1)
Loy v O'Sullivan [2010] EWHC 3583 (Ch); [2011] B.P.I.R. 181	IA 264, 265, 282(1), (3), 283A, IR 12.64
LSI 2013 Ltd v Solar Panel Co (UK) Ltd [2014] EWHC 248 (Ch)	IA 123
Ludsin Overseas Ltd v Maggs [2014] EWHC 3566 (Ch); [2015] B.P.I.R. 59	IR 10.5
Lummus Agricultural Services Ltd, Re 1999] B.C.C. 953	IA 122(1), 125(1)
Lundy Granite Co, Re (1870–71) L.R. 6 Ch. App. 462 CA in Chancery	IA Sch.B1 para.99(3)–(4), IR 3.51, 7.108(1)–(4)
Lune Metal Products Ltd (In admin.), Re [2006] EWCA Civ 1720; [2007] B.C.C. 217	IA Sch.1
Lutz v Bauerle (C-557/13) EU:C:2015:227; [2015] B.C.C. 413	[ER art.16]
M (Restraint Order), Re [1992] Q.B. 377; [1992] 2 W.L.R. 340 QBD	IA 252(2)
Macari, Re [2017] NICh 5	IA 263I
Mackay Ex p. (1873) L.R. 8 Ch. App. 643	IA 107
MacMillan v T Leith Developments Ltd (In rec. and liq.) [2017] CSIH 23; 2017 S.C. 642; 2017 S.L.T. 415	IA 60(1)
Macpherson v Wise [2011] EWHC 141 (Ch); [2011] B.P.I.R. 47	IR 10.5
Madoff Securities International Ltd v Raven [2013] EWHC 3147 (Comm); [2014] Lloyd's Rep. F.C. 95	IA 212(1)
Magna Alloys & Research Pty Ltd, Re (1975) C.L.C. 40–227	[CDDA 1(1)]
Mahmood v Penrose [2004] EWHC 1500 (Ch; [2005] B.P.I.R. 170	IA 264
Mahomed v Morris (No.2) [2001] B.C.C. 233 CA (Civ Div)	IA 168(5)
Mahon v FBN Bank (UK) Ltd [2011] EWHC 1432 (Ch); [2011] B.P.I.R. 1029	IR 10.5
Majestic Recording Studios Ltd, Re (1988) 4 B.C.C. 519	[CDDA 1(1)]

	Provision
Michael, Re [2009] EWHC 2414 (Ch); [2010] B.P.I.R. 418	IA 303(2)
Micklethwait, Re [2002] EWHC 1123 (Ch); [2003] B.P.I.R. 101	IA 266(3), (4)
Mid East Trading Ltd, Re; sub nom. Phillips v Lehman Brothers [1998] 1 All E.R. 577; [1998] B.C.C. 726 CA (Civ Div)	IA 236
Midland Bank Plc v Wyatt [1995] 1 F.L.R. 697; [1996] B.P.I.R. 288 Ch D	IA 423(1)–(3)
Midland Counties District Bank Ltd v Attwood [1905] 1 Ch. 357 Ch D	IA 91(2)
Midrome Ltd v Shaw [1993] B.C.C. 659 CA (Civ Div)	IA 375(1), IR 12.59
Migration Services International Ltd, Re [2000] B.C.C. 1095 Ch D (Companies Ct)	IA 216(3), [CDDA, 12C]
Mikki v Duncan [2017] EWCA Civ 57; [2017] B.P.I.R. 490	IA 283(2), (3)
Milgate Developments Ltd, Re [1991] B.C.C. 24 Ch D (Companies Ct)	IA 122(1)
Miliangos v George Frank (Textiles) Ltd [1976] A.C. 443 HL	IR 14.21
Millennium Advanced Technology Ltd, Re [2004] EWHC 711 (Ch); [2004] 1 W.L.R. 2177; [2004] 2 B.C.L.C. 77	IA 122(1), 124A
Miller v Bain [2002] B.C.C. 899; [2003] B.P.I.R. 959 Ch D (Companies Ct)	IA 236
Miller v Bayliss [2009] EWHC 2063 (Ch); [2009] B.P.I.R. 1438	IA 303(1)
Miller v McFeely [2012] EWHC 4409 (Ch); [2014] B.P.I.R. 1529	IA 375(1)
Mills v Birchall [2008] EWCA Civ 385; [2008] 1 W.L.R. 1829; [2008] B.C.C. 471; [2008] B.P.I.R. 607	IA Pt III, 37(1), (2)
Mills v Grove Securities Ltd [1997] B.P.I.R. 243; [1996] C.C.L.R. 74 CA (Civ Div)	IA 267(1), (2)
Mineral Resources Ltd, Re [1999] 1 All E.R. 746; [1999] B.C.C. 422 Ch D (Companies Ct)	IA 178
Minmar (929) Ltd v Khalastchi [2011] EWHC 1159 (Ch); [2011] B.C.C. 485	IA Sch.B1 paras 12(1), (4), 22(2), 26(2), (3), 105, IR 3.4
Mireskandari, Re [2014] B.P.I.R. 163	IA 285(1), 285(3), (4), 322(1), 382(3), (4), IR 14.2
Mirror Group (Holdings) Ltd, Re [1992] B.C.C. 972; Ch D	IA Sch.B1 para.63
Mirror Group Newspapers Plc v Maxwell (No.1) [1998] B.C.C. 324 Ch D	IA 35(1), 399(2), IR 18.16
Mistral Finance (In liq.), Re [2001] B.C.C. 27 Ch D (Companies Ct)	IA 238(4), 239(4)
Mitchell v Carter [1997] B.C.C. 907 CA (Civ Div)	IA 183
Mittal v RP Capital Explorer Master Fund [2014] B.P.I.R. 1537 Ch D	IA 267(1), (2)
MK Airlines Ltd (In liq.), Re [2012] EWHC 1018 (Ch); [2012] 3 All E.R. 781; [2014] B.C.C. 87	IA Pt III, Sch.B1 para.99(3)–(4)
MK Airlines Ltd (In liq.), Re [2012] EWHC 2764 (Ch); [2014] B.C.C. 103	IA 178(4), IR 7.108(1)–(4), 14.25
Modern Jet Support Centre Ltd, Re [2005] EWHC 1611 (Ch); [2005] 1 W.L.R. 3880; [2006] B.C.C. 174	IA 183(1)
Mohammed v Southwark LBC [2006] EWCA Civ 765	IR 10.24
Monarch Financial Services Ltd, Re; Cooper v Monarch Financial Services Ltd [2017] EWHC 2324 (Ch); [2017] B.C.C. 570	IA Sch.B1 para.3(1), (3)
Mond v Hammond Suddards (No.2); sub nom. RS&M Engineering Co Ltd, Re [2000] Ch. 40; [2000] B.C.C. 445 CA (Civ Div)	IA 115, 127, 156
Mond v Hyde [1999] Q.B. 1097 CA (Civ Div)	IA 400(2)
Mond v MBNA Europe Bank Ltd [2010] EWHC 1710 (Ch); [2011] Bus. L.R. 513; [2010] B.P.I.R. 1167 Ch D	IA Pt VIII
Mond v United Kingdom (Admissibility) (49606/99) 2003] B.P.I.R. 1347; (2003) 37 E.H.R.R. CD129 ECHR	IA 400(2)
Monecor (London) Ltd v Ahmed [2008] B.P.I.R. 458 Ch D	IA 262, 262(4)–(7)
Money Markets International Stockbrokers Ltd (In liq.) v London	

	Provision
Munro and Rowe, Re; sub nom. Singer v Trustee of the Property of Munro [1981] 1 W.L.R. 1358 Ch D	IA 299(1), (2)
Murjani (A Bankrupt), Re [1996] 1 W.L.R. 1498; [1996] B.C.C. 278 Ch D (Bankruptcy)	IA 366(1)
Murphy v Gooch [2007] EWCA Civ 603; [2007] 2 F.L.R. 934; [2007] B.P.I.R. 1123	IA 335A
Myers v Kestrel Acquisitions Ltd [2015] EWHC 916 (Ch)	IA 123(1)
Myles J Callaghan Ltd (In rec.) v Glasgow DC 1987 S.C. 171; 1988 S.L.T. 227; (1987) 3 B.C.C. 337 CSOH	IA 53(6), (7), 55(1), (2), IR 14.25
N (A Debtor), Re [2002] B.P.I.R. 1024 Ch D (Bankruptcy)	IA 257(1), 262
Naeem (A Bankrupt) (No.18 of 1988), Re [1990] 1 W.L.R. 48 Ch D	IA 4(3), 260(1), (2), (2A), 262
NALM v Cahillane. *See* National Asset Loan Management Ltd v Cahillane	
Namco UK Ltd, Re [2003] EWHC 989 (Ch); [2003] B.P.I.R. 1170	IA 135
Namulas Pension Trustees Ltd v Mouzakis [2011] B.P.I.R. 1724 CC	IA 257(2), (2A), (2B), (3), 260(1), (2), (2A), 262(1)–(3), (8), IR 1.40
Narandas-Girdhar v Bradstock [2016] EWCA Civ 88; [2016] 1 W.L.R. 2366; [2016] B.P.I.R. 428	IA Pt VIII, 257(1), 259, 260(1), (2), (2A), 262
Narinen v Finland (45027/98) [2004] B.P.I.R. 914 ECHR	IA 371(1)
National Asset Loan Management Ltd v Cahillane [2015] EWHC 62 (Ch); [2016] 1 W.L.R. 45; [2015] B.P.I.R. 143	IA 375(1)
National Bank of Kuwait SAK v Menzies [1994] B.C.C. 119 CA (Civ Div)	IA 423(1)–(3)
National Employers Mutual General Insurance Association Ltd (In liq.), Re [1995] B.C.C. 774; Ch D (Companies Ct)	IA 130(2)
National Provincial Bank Ltd v Ainsworth [1965] A.C. 1175 HL	IA 335A
National Union of Flint Glassworkers, Re [2006] B.C.C. 828 Ch D	IA 220(1)
National Westminster Bank Ltd v Halesowen Presswork and Assemblies Ltd [1972] A.C. 785; HL	IA 232, IR 14.25
National Westminster Bank Plc v Jones [2001] EWCA Civ 1541; [2002] B.P.I.R. 361	IA 423(1)–(3)
National Westminster Bank Plc v Kapoor [2011] EWCA Civ 1083; [2012] 1 All E.R. 1201; [2011] B.P.I.R. 1680	IA Pt VIII, 262(1)–(3), (8), IR 15.28
National Westminster Bank Plc v Lucas [2014] EWCA Civ 1632; [2015] B.P.I.R. 450	IA 284(1)–(3), (6)
National Westminster Bank Plc v Msaada Group [2011] EWHC 3423 (Ch); [2012] B.C.C. 226	IA Sch.B1 para.26(2), (3)
National Westminster Bank Plc v Scher [1998] B.P.I.R. 224 Ch D	IA 262
National Westminster Bank Plc v Spectrum Plus Ltd. *See* Spectrum Plus Ltd (In liq.), Re	
National Westminster Bank Plc v Yadgaroff [2011] EWHC 3711 (Ch); [2012] B.P.I.R. 371	IA 262(1)–(3), (8), IR 15.31
Nationwide Building Society v Wright [2009] EWCA Civ 811; [2010] Ch. 318; [2009] B.P.I.R. 1047	IA 346(1), (1A), (5)
Neath Rugby Ltd, Re [2009] EWCA Civ 291; [2010] B.C.C. 597	IA 122(1)
Neath Rugby Ltd, Re; Hawkes v Cuddy [2007] EWHC 2999 (Ch); [2008] B.C.C. 390	IA 216
Neath Rugby Ltd, Re; Hawkes v Cuddy [2007] EWCA Civ 1072; [2008] B.C.C. 125	IA 216, 216(3)
Neath Rugby Ltd, Re; Hawkes v Cuddy [2009] EWCA Civ 291; [2010] B.C.C. 597	IA125(1)
NEF Telecom Co BV, Re [2012] EWHC 2944 (Ch); [2014] B.C.C. 417	IA 221
Nelson v Nelson [1997] 1 W.L.R. 233; [1997] B.P.I.R. 702 CA (Civ Div)	IA 306
Neumans LLP v Andronikou. *See* Portsmouth City Football Club Ltd (In liq.), Re	

Case	Provision
New Bullas Trading Ltd, Re [1994] B.C.C. 36 CA (Civ Div)	IA 40(1), (2)
New Cap Reinsurance Corp Ltd (In liq.) v Grant. *See* Rubin v Eurofinance SA	
New Cap Reinsurance Corp Ltd v HIH Casualty & General Insurance Ltd [2002] EWCA Civ 300; [2002] B.P.I.R. 809	IA 130(2)
New China Hong Kong Capital Ltd, Re [2003] EWHC 1573 (Ch); [2003] B.P.I.R. 1176	IA 236(2)
New Generation Engineers Ltd, Re [1993] B.C.L.C. 435 Ch D (Companies Ct)	[CDDA 12C]
New Hampshire Insurance Co v Rush & Tompkins Group Plc [1998] 2 B.C.L.C. 471 CA (Civ Div)	IA 221
New Millennium Experience Co Ltd, Re [2003] EWHC 1823 (Ch); [2004] 1 All E.R.	IA 89(1)
New Paragon Investments Ltd, Re [2012] B.C.C. 371 Ch D (Companies Ct)	[CBIR Sch.1 arts 2(i), 15]
New Technology Systems Ltd, Re [1997] B.C.C. 810 CA (Civ Div)	[CDDA 1(1)]
Newhart Developments Ltd v Cooperative Commercial Bank Ltd [1978] Q.B. 814 CA (Civ Div)	IA Pt III
Newlands (Seaford) Educational Trust (In admin.), Re [2006] EWHC 1511 (Ch); [2007] B.C.C. 195; [2006] B.P.I.R. 1230	IA 6(1), IR 15.31
Ng (A Bankrupt), Re [1997] B.C.C. 507; [1998] 2 F.L.R. 386 Ch D (Bankruptcy)	IA 305(2)
Ng (A Bankrupt), Re [1998] 2 F.L.R. 38; [1997] B.C.C. 507 Ch D (Bankruptcy)	IA 336(3)–(5)
Niagara Mechanical Services International Ltd (In admin.), Re [2001] B.C.C. 393 Ch D	IA 107
Nicholls v Lan [2006] EWHC 1255 (Ch); [2007] 1 F.L.R. 744; [2006] B.P.I.R. 1243	IA 335A
Nicholson v Fayinka [2014 B.P.I.R. 692	IA 365(1), (2)
Nicholson v Fielding Unreported, 15 September 2017	IA 214(2)
Nickel & Goeldner Spedition GmbH v "Kintra" UAB (C-157/13) EU:C:2014:2145 1 June 2013	[ER Preamble 7]
Nicoll v Cutts (1985) 1 B.C.C. 99427; [1985] P.C.C. 311 CA (Civ Div)	IA 37(1), (2), 44(1), (2)
Nicoll v Steelpress (Supplies) Ltd 1992 S.C. 119; 1993 S.L.T. 533; 1992 S.C.L.R. 332 CSIH (Ex Div)	IA 243(1), (2)
Nike European Operations Netherlands BV v Sportland Oy (C-310/14) EU:C:2015:690; [2015] Bus. L.R. 1547; [2017] B.C.C. 446	[ER art.16]
Nimmo and Fraser, Joint Administrators of Station Properties Ltd [2013] CSOH 120; 2013 G.W.D. 25–504	IA Sch.B1 para.80
Nimmo, Approval of Accounts of Intromissions, Re [2013] CSOH 4	[App.IV]
Noble Trees Ltd, Re [1993] B.C.C. 318 Ch D (Companies Ct)	[CDDA 7(2)]
Nolton Business Centres Ltd, Re [1996] B.C.C. 500 Ch D	IA Sch.B1 para.99(3)–(4), IR 10.148
Norditrack (UK) Ltd, Re [2000] 1 W.L.R. 343; [2000] B.C.C. 441 Ch D (Companies Ct)	IA 84(2A), (2B), 240(1), (3)
Norfolk House Plc (In rec.) v Repsol Petroleum Ltd, 1992 S.L.T. 235 CSOH	IA 72
Norglen Ltd (In liq.) v Reeds Rains Prudential Ltd [1999] 2 A.C. 1; [1998] B.C.C. 44	IA Sch.4 para.6
Norman Holding Co Ltd (In liq.), Re 1991] 1 W.L.R. 10; [1991] B.C.C. 11 Ch D (Companies Ct) Ch D	IR 14.25
Normandy Marketing Ltd, Re [1993] B.C.C. 879 Ch D	IA 220, 225, 441
Normanton Wells Properties Ltd, Re [2011] 1 B.C.L.C. 191 CC	[CDDA 6(2)]
Nortel Companies, Re; sub nom. Bloom v Pensions Regulator [2013] UKSC 52; [2014] 1 A.C. 209; [2013] B.C.C. 624	IA 115, 262, 281(2)–(6), (8), 382(3), (4), Sch.B1 para.5, para.99(3)–(4), IR 3.51, 7.108(1)–(4), 14.1, 14.2

Case	Provision
Nortel Group, Re; sub nom. Nortel Networks UK Ltd, Re [2016] EWHC 2769 (Ch)	IA Sch.B1 para.63
Nortel Networks UK Ltd, Re [2014] EWHC 2614 (Ch)	IA Sch.B1 para.63
Nortel Networks UK Ltd, Re [2017] EWHC 1429 (Ch); [2017] B.C.C. 325	IA Sch.B1 paras 63, 65(3), 99(3)–(4), IR 3.50, 14.2, Sch.2 para.22
Nortel Networks UK Ltd, Re [2017] EWHC 3299 (Ch)	IA Sch.B1 para.76
Nortel Networks SA, Re (No.2) [2009] EWHC 1482 (Ch); [2010] B.C.C. 21	[ER arts 2(6), 36, 37]
Nortel Networks UK Ltd (In admin.), Re; sub nom. Unite the Union v Nortel Networks UK Ltd (In admin.) [2010] EWHC 826 (Ch); [2010] B.C.C. 706; [2010] B.P.I.R. 1003	IA Sch.B1 para.43(6), IR 14.2, 14.3–14.11
Nortel Networks UK Ltd (No.536 of 2009), Re [2015] EWHC 2506 (Ch)	IA Sch.B1 para.65(3)
North Atlantic Insurance Co Ltd v Nationwide General Insurance Co Ltd [2004] EWCA Civ 423; [2004] 2 All E.R. (Comm) 351	IA 107
North Brazilian Sugar Factories, Re (1887) 37 Ch. D. 83 CA	IA 155(1)
North Carolina Estate Co, Re (1889) 5 T.L.R. 328	IA 183
North West Holdings Plc (In liq.), Re [2001] EWCA Civ 67; [2002] B.C.C. 441	IA 124A
Northern Bank Ltd (t/a Danske Bank) v Taylor [2014] NICh 9	IA Sch.B1 para.13(1), (3)
Northsea Base Investment Ltd, Re [2015] EWHC 121 (Ch); [2015] 1 B.C.L.C. 539	IA Sch.B1 para.68(2), (3), [ER art.3(1)]
Nottingham City Council v Pennant [2009] EWHC 2437 (Ch); [2010] B.P.I.R. 430	IA 271(1), (2), (4)
Nowmost Co Ltd, Re [1997] B.C.C. 105 Ch D	IA 125(1)
NRAM Plc v Evans [2015] EWHC 1543 (Ch); [2015] B.P.I.R. 888; [2015] 2 P. & C.R. DG18	IA Pt VIII
NT Gallagher & Son Ltd, Re [2002] EWCA Civ 404; [2002] 1 W.L.R. 2380; [2002] B.C.C. 867	IA 7(4), 263(5), (6)
Nurkowski, Re. *See* Hill v Spread Trustee Co Ltd	
Nutting v Khaliq [2012] EWCA Civ 1726; [2013] B.P.I.R. 340	IR 10.149, 12.1
O'Neill v Ulster Bank Ltd [2015] NICA 64; [2016] B.P.I.R. 126	IR 10.5
O'Callaghan v Clipper Holding II SARL [2017] NICh 29	IA 282(1), (3)
O'Connell v Rollings [2014] EWCA Civ 639	IA Sch.B1 para.71
O'Donnell v Bank of Ireland [2012] EWHC 3749 (Ch); [2013] B.P.I.R. 509	IA 263I
O'Donnell v Governor of the Bank of Ireland [2013] EWHC 489 (Ch); [2013] B.P.I.R. 1078	IA 263I, 375(1)
O'Mahony v National Irish Bank [2012] B.P.I.R. 1174 Ch D	IA 263I, IR 10.24, [ER art.3(1)]
O'Sullivan (Julie), Re [2001] B.P.I.R. 534 Ch D	IA 255(1), (2)
O'Toole v Mitcham (1978) C.L.C. 40–429I	A 236
Oakes v Simms [1997] B.P.I.R. 499 CA (Civ Div)	IA 366(1)
Oakfame Construction Ltd, Re [1996] B.C.C. 67 Ch D	[CDDA 6(1)]
Oakland v Wellswood (Yorkshire) Ltd [2009] EWCA Civ 1094; [2010] B.C.C. 263	IA Sch.B1 para.3
Oakley v Ultra Vehicle Design Ltd (In liq.) [2005] EWHC 872 (Ch); [2006] B.C.C. 57; [2006] B.P.I.R. 115	IA Pt I
Oakrock Ltd v Travelodge Hotels Ltd [2015] EWHC 30 (TCC)	IA Pt 1
Oakwood Storage Services Ltd, Re [2003] EWHC 2807 (Ch); [2004] 2 B.C.L.C. 404	IR 7.4–7.12
Oasis Merchandising Services Ltd (In liq.), Re [1998] Ch. 170; [1997] B.C.C. 282 CA (Civ Div)	IA 212(1), 213(2), 238, Sch.4 para.6

	Provision
Oben v Blackman [1999] B.C.C. 446; [2000] B.P.I.R. 302 Ch D	IR 12.64
OBG Ltd v Allan [2007] UKHL 21; [2008] 1 A.C. 1; [2007] 2 W.L.R. 920	IA 34
Octagon Assets Ltd v Remblance [2009] EWCA Civ 581; [2010] 2 All E.R. 688; [2009] B.P.I.R. 1129	IR 10.5
Office Metro Ltd, Re [2012] EWHC 1191 (Ch); [2012] B.C.C. 829; [2012] B.P.I.R. 1049	[ER arts 3(2)–(4)]
Officeserve Technologies Ltd (In liq.) v Anthony-Mike [2017] EWHC 1920 (Ch); [2017] B.C.C. 574; [2017] B.P.I.R. 1291	IA 127
Official Custodian for Charities v Parway Estates Developments Ltd (In liq.) [1985] Ch. 151; (1984) 1 B.C.C. 99253 CA (Civ Div)	IA 130(1)
Official Receiver (as Liquidator of Celtic Extraction Ltd and Bluestone Chemicals Ltd) v Environment Agency [2001] Ch. 475; [2000] B.C.C. 487; [1999] B.P.I.R. 986 CA (Civ Div)	IA 436
Official Receiver for Northern Ireland v Doyle [2016] NIMaster 7	IA 339(1)–(3)
Official Receiver for Northern Ireland v Gallagher [2013] NIMaster 12	IA 382(1), (2), (5)
Official Receiver for Northern Ireland v Gallagher [2014] NICh 6; [2014] B.P.I.R. 918	IA 284(1)–(3), (6)
Official Receiver for Northern Ireland v Mallon [2013] NIMaster 9; [2013] B.P.I.R. 621	IA 339(1)–(3)
Official Receiver for Northern Ireland v O'Brien [2012] NICh 12; [2012] B.P.I.R. 826	IA 335A, Pt IX
Official Receiver for Northern Ireland v Rooney [2008] NICh 22; [2009] 2 F.L.R. 1437; [2009] B.P.I.R. 536	IA 336(3)–(5)
Official Receiver for Northern Ireland v Sinnamon [2013] NICh 11; [2013] B.P.I.R. 900	IA 304(1)
Official Receiver for Northern Ireland v Snoddon [2014] NI Master 5	IA 337(1), (2)
Official Receiver for Northern Ireland v Stranaghan [2010] NICh 8; [2010] B.P.I.R. 928	IA 339(1)–(3)
Official Receiver for Northern Ireland v Urey [2014] NI Master 16	IA 284(1)–(3), (6)
Official Receiver v B [1994] 2 B.C.L.C. 1 Ch D	[CDDA 7(2)]
Official Receiver v Baars [2009] B.P.I.R. 524 Ch D	IA Sch.4A
Official Receiver v Baker [2013] EWHC 4594 (Ch); [2014] B.P.I.R. 724	IA 310, 310(7)
Official Receiver v Bathurst [2008] EWHC 1724 (Ch); [2008] B.P.I.R. 1548	IA 284, Sch.4A
Official Receiver v Bayliss Unreported, 26 July 2017	IA 281A, Sch.4A, IR 12.28, 12.39
Official Receiver v Becker [2013] B.P.I.R. 352 CC	IA 282(1)
Official Receiver v Brady [1999] B.C.C. 258 Ch D	[CDDA 22(2)]
Official Receiver v Brown [2017] EWHC 2762 (Ch); [2018] B.P.I.R. 98	IA 288(4)
Official Receiver v Brunt [1999] 1 W.L.R. 1129; [1999] B.C.C. 571 CA (Civ Div)	IA 400(2), [CDDA 1(1)]
Official Receiver v Cooksey [2013] B.P.I.R. 526 CC	IA 279(3)–(5), 333(1), (3), 375(1)
Official Receiver v Cummings-John [2000] B.P.I.R. 320 Ch D	IA 363(2), (4)
Official Receiver v Dhaliwall [2006] 1 B.C.L.C. 285	[CDDA 12C]
Official Receiver v Doganci [2007] B.P.I.R. 87 Ch D	IA Sch.4A
Official Receiver v Doshi [2001] 2 B.C.L.C. 235 Ch D	IA 214(2), [CDDA 12C]
Official Receiver v Eichler [2007] B.P.I.R. 1636 Ch D	IA 263I
Official Receiver v Eichler [2011] B.P.I.R. 1293 Ch D	IA 263I, 282(1), (3), [ER art.3(1)]
Official Receiver v Gibson [2015] B.P.I.R. 717	IA Sch.4A
Official Receiver v Going [2011] EWHC 786 (Ch); [2011] B.P.I.R. 1069	IA Sch.4A
Official Receiver v Hollens [2007] EWHC 754 (Ch); [2007] 3 All E.R. 767; [2007] B.P.I.R. 830	IA 303(2A)–(2C)
Official Receiver v Keelan [2012] B.P.I.R. 613 CC	IA 265, 282(1), (3)

	Provision
Official Receiver v Key [2009] B.C.C. 11 CC	[CDDA 6(1)]
Official Receiver v Lloyd [2015] B.P.I.R. 374 CC	IA 283(2), (3), Sch.4A
Official Receiver v May [2008] EWHC 1778 (Ch); [2008] B.P.I.R. 1562	IA Sch.4A
Official Receiver v McKay [2009] EWCA Civ 467; [2010] Ch. 303; [2009] B.P.I.R. 1061	IA Pt IX, 282(1), (3)
Official Receiver v McWilliams [2012] NICh 28	IA 279, 279(3)–(5), 333(1), (3), IR.10.142, 14.3–14.11
Official Receiver v Merchant [2006] B.P.I.R. 1525 Ch D	IA Sch.4A
Official Receiver v Mitterfellner [2009] B.P.I.R. 1075 Ch D	IA 263I, 282(1), (3), [ER art.3(1)]
Official Receiver v Norman Unreported December 5, 2012	IA 310(1), (1A), (2)
Official Receiver v Norriss [2015] EWHC 2697 (Ch); [2015] B.C.C. 906; [2016] B.P.I.R. 188	IA 236, 366(1)
Official Receiver v Pafundo [2000] B.C.C. 164 CA (Civ Div)	[CDDA 6(3)–(3C), 7(1)]
Official Receiver v Pyman [2007] EWHC 2002 (Ch); [2007] B.P.I.R. 1150	IA Sch.4A, [CDDA 1(2)]
Official Receiver v Sahaviriya Steel Industries Public Co Ltd [2015] EWHC 2877 (Ch); [2016] B.C.C. 456	IA 233
Official Receiver v Southey [2009] B.P.I.R. 89 Ch D (Bankruptcy)	IA Sch.4A
Official Receiver v Stern (No.2) [2001] EWCA Civ 1787; [2004] B.C.C. 581 CA (Civ Div)	[CDDA 12C]
Official Receiver v Stojevic [2007] EWHC 1186 (Ch); [2008] Bus. L.R. 641	[CDDA 7(1)]
Official Receiver v Urey [2015] NICh 11	IA 284(1)–(3), (6), 306
Official Receiver v Vass [1999] B.C.C. 516 Ch D	[CDDA 12C, 22(5)]
Official Receiver v Wild [2012] EWHC 4279 (Ch)	[CDDA 12C]
Official Receiver v Wilson [2013] B.P.I.R. 907 Ch D	IA 310(1), (1A), (2)
OGX Petroleo E Gas SA, Re; sub nom. Nordic Trustee ASA v OGX Petroleo E Gas SA [2016] EWHC 25 (Ch); [2016] Bus. L.R. 121	IA 130(2), [CBIR Sch.1 arts 15, 20]
OJSC Ank Yugraneft, Re [2008] EWHC 2614 (Ch); [2010] B.C.C. 475	IA 135, 220
Okon v Lewisham LBC [2016] EWHC 864 (Ch); [2016] B.P.I.R. 958; [2016] R.A. 281	IA 267 (1), (2)
Oldham v Katz [2018] EWHC 540 (Ch)	IA Sch.B1 para.75
Olympic Airlines SA, Re [2015] UKSC 27; [2015] 1 W.L.R. 2399; [2015] B.C.C. 404	[ER art.3(2)–(4), (3), (4)]
Omni Trustees Ltd, Re; Official Receiver v Norriss [2015] EWHC 2697 (Ch); [2015] B.C.C. 906; [2016] B.P.I.R. 188	IA 236, 236(2)
Omokwe v HFC Bank Ltd [2007] B.P.I.R. 1157 HC	IA 267(1), (2), 282(1), (3), IR 10.2
OMP Leisure Ltd, Re [2008] B.C.C. 67 Ch D	IA Sch.B1 para.14(2), (3)
One World Logistics Freight Ltd, Re [2018] EWHC 264 (Ch)	IA Sch.B1 para.13(1), (3)
Oracle (North West) Ltd v Pinnacle Financial Services (UK) Ltd [2009] B.C.C. 159 Ch D	IA Sch.B1 para.13(1), (3)
Oraki v Bramston [2017] EWCA Civ 403; [2017] B.P.I.R. 1021	IA 299(5), 304(1), 305(2), 330(5)
Oraki v Dean & Dean (a firm) [2013] EWCA Civ 1629; [2014] B.P.I.R. 266	IA 282(1), (3), IR 18.16
Oraki v Dean & Dean [2017] EWHC 11 (Ch)	IA 282(1), (3), 375(1), IR 10.132–10.141

	Provision
Ord v Upton [2000] Ch. 352; [2000] B.P.I.R. 104 CA (Civ Div)	IA 306
Orexim Trading Ltd v Mahavir Port and Terminal Private Ltd [2017] EWHC 2663 (Comm); [2018] B.P.I.R. 124	IA 423(1)–(3)
Orient Power Holdings Ltd, Re [2009] B.C.C. 452 HC (HK)	IA 139
Oriental Commercial Bank, Re (1871–72) L.R. 7 Ch. App. 99 CA in Chancery	IR 14.3–14.11
Oriental Inland Steam Co Ex p. Scinde Railway Co, Re (1873–74) L.R. 9 Ch. App. 557 CA (Chancery)	IA 183, Sch.B1 para.43(6)
Orion Media Marketing Ltd v Media Brook Ltd [2003] B.P.I.R. 474 Ch D (Companies Ct)	IA 123
Orleans Motor Co Ltd, Re [1911] 2 Ch. 41 Ch D	IA 245(2)
Orrick, Herrington & Sutcliffe (Europe) LLP v Frohlich [2012] B.P.I.R. 169 Ch D	IA 267(1), (2), 268
Ortega Associates Ltd (In liq.), Re [2007] EWHC 2046 (Ch); [2008] B.C.C. 256	IA 212(3)
Osborn v Cole [1999] B.P.I.R. 251 Ch D	IA 303(1)
OTG Ltd v Barke [2011] B.C.C. 608 EAT	IA Sch.B1 para.3
Ouvaroff (A Bankrupt), Re [1997] B.P.I.R. 712 Ch D	IA 366(1)
Oval 1742 Ltd (In creditors' voluntary liq.), Re; sub nom. Customs and Excise Commissioners v Royal Bank of Scotland Plc [2007] EWCA Civ 1262; [2008] B.C.C. 135	IA 40(1), (2), 175
Ovenden Colbert Printers Ltd, Re [2013] EWCA Civ 1408; [2015] B.C.C. 61; [2014] 1 B.C.L.C. 291; [2014] B.P.I.R. 285	IA 238(4)
Overend Gurney & Co, Re; sub nom. Grissell's Case (1865–66) L.R. 1 Ch. App. 528 CA in Chancery	IA 74(1), IR 14.25
Overnight Ltd (In liq.), Re [2009] EWHC 601 (Ch); [2010] B.C.C. 787	IA 213
Overnight Ltd (In liq.) (No.2), Re [2010] EWHC 613 (Ch); [2010] B.C.C. 796	IA 213(2)
Overnight Ltd (In liq.) (No.3), Re [2010] EWHC 1587 (Ch); [2010] B.C.C. 808	IA 213(2)

	Provision
Owo-Samson v Barclays Bank Plc (No.1) [2003] EWCA Civ 714; [2003] B.P.I.R. 1373	IA 282(1), (3)
Owusu v Jackson (t/a Villa Holidays Bal Inn Villas) (C-281/02) EU:C:2005:120 [2005] Q.B. 801	IA 125(1)
Oxford Pharmaceuticals Ltd, Re [2009] EWHC 1753 (Ch); [2010] B.C.C. 834; [2010] B.P.I.R. 608	IA 127, 239(6), 241(2)
Oxted Financial Services v Gordon [1998] B.P.I.R. 231 Ch D	IA 266(3), (4)
Pace Europe Ltd v Dunham [2012] EWHC 852 (Ch); [2012] B.P.I.R. 836	IA 267(1), (2), IR 10.5
Pacific & General Insurance Co Ltd v Home & Overseas Insurance Co Ltd [1997] L.R.L.R. 65; [1997] B.C.C. 400 QBD (Comm)	IA 135
Packaging Direct Ltd, Re [1994] B.C.C. 213 Ch D (Companies Ct)	[CDDA 7(2)]
PAG Management Services Ltd, Re; sub nom. Secretary of State for Business, Innovation and Skills v PAG Management Services Ltd [2015] EWHC 2404 (Ch); [2015] B.C.C. 720; [2015] R.A. 519	IA 87(1), 91(1), 124A
Paget Ex p. Official Receiver, Re [1927] 2 Ch. 85 CA	IA 290(3), (5)
Painter v Hutchison [2007] EWHC 758 (Ch); [2008] B.P.I.R. 170	IR 14.32
PAL SC Realisations 2007 Ltd (In liq.), Re [2010] EWHC 2850 (Ch); [2011] B.C.C. 93	IA 176A(2), (6), 176A(9), IR 14.15–14.19
Palmer (Gavin) (Deceased) (A Debtor), Re [1994] Ch. 316 CA (Civ Div)	IA 421(1), (1A), (1B), (2), 421A
Pamstock Ltd, Re [1994] B.C.C. 264 Ch D (Companies Ct)	[CDDA 7(1), 12C]
Pan Ocean Co Ltd, Re [2015] EWHC 1500 (Ch)	[CBIR Sch.1 art.21.2]
Pan Ocean Ltd, Re [2014] EWHC 2124 (Ch); [2014] Bus. L.R. 1041	[CBIR Sch.1 art.21.1]
Pannell v Official Receiver [2008] EWHC 736 (Ch); [2008] B.P.I.R. 629	IA 283A
Panter v Rowellian Football Social Club [2011] EWHC 1301 (Ch); [2012] Ch. 125; [2014] B.C.C. 321	IA 220(1), Sch.B1

	Provision
Pearl Maintenance Services Ltd, Re [1995] B.C.C. 657 Ch D	IA 40(1), (2)
Pearson v Lehman Brothers Finance SA [2011] EWCA Civ 1544; [2012] 2 B.C.L.C. 151	IA 107
Pena v Coyne (No.2) [2004] EWHC 2685 (Ch); [2004] B.P.I.R. 1286	IA 423(1)–(3), 425(1)
Penrose v Official Receiver [1996] 1 W.L.R. 482; [1995] B.C.C. 311 Ch D	IA 216(3)
Penwith DC v VP Developments Ltd [2005] EWHC 259 (Ch); [2005] B.C.C. 393; [2005] B.P.I.R. 1010	IA 123
Peoples Phone Ltd v Nicolaou [2011] EWHC 1129 (Ch); [2011] B.P.I.R. 1477	IA Pt VIII
Peoples Restaurant Group Ltd, The, Re Unreported 30 November 2012	IA Pt IV Ch.IX, Sch.B1 paras 84(6), (6A), (6B)
Peppard (A Bankrupt), Re [2009] B.P.I.R. 331	IA 339(1)–(3)
Peppermint Park Ltd, Re [1998] B.C.C. 23 Ch D (Companies Ct)	[CDDA 12C]
Performing Right Society Ltd v Rowland [1997] 3 All E.R. 336; [1998] B.P.I.R. 128 Ch D	IA 306, 436
Permacell Finesse Ltd (In liq.), Re [2007] EWHC 3233 (Ch); [2008] B.C.C. 208	IA 176A(2), (6)
Peterkin v Merton LBC [2011] EWHC 376 (Ch); [2012] B.P.I.R. 388	IA 260(1), (2), (2A)
Pettit v Bradford Bulls (Northern) Ltd [2016] EWHC 3557 (Ch); [2017] B.C.C. 50	IA Sch.B1 para.79(1)
Pettit v Novakovic [2007] B.C.C. 462 Ch D	IA 127, 284, 284(1)–(3), (6)
PFTZM Ltd, Re [1995] B.C.C. 280 Ch D (Companies Ct)	IA 124(1), 236, 240
Philipp and Lion Ltd, Re [1994] B.C.C. 261 Ch D (Companies Ct)	[CDDA 7(2)]
Phillips (Liquidator of AJ Bekhor & Co) v Brewin Dolphin Bell Lawrie Ltd (formerly Brewin Dolphin & Co Ltd) [2001] UKHL 2; [2001] 1 W.L.R. 143; [2001] B.C.C. 864	IA 238(4)
Phillips & Co v Bath Housing Co-operative Ltd [2012] EWCA Civ 1591; [2013] 1 W.L.R. 1479	IA 267(1), (2)
Phillips v McGregor-Paterson [2009] EWHC 2385 (Ch); [2010] B.P.I.R. 239	IA 127, 212(3), 239(6)
Phillips v Symes [2005] EWHC 2867 (Ch); [2006] B.P.I.R. 1430	IA 306, 330(5)
Phillips v Symes [2006] EWHC 2595 (Ch); [2008] B.P.I.R. 212	IA 227
Philpott v Lycee Francais Charles de Gaulle School [2015] EWHC 1065 (Ch); [2016] 1 All E.R. (Comm) 1	IR 14.25
Phoenix Kapitaldienst GmbH, Re [2008] B.P.I.R. 1082 Ch D	IA 426, [CBIR]
Phoenix Kapitaldienst GmbH, Re [2012] EWHC 62 (Ch); [2013] Ch. 61; [2012] B.C.C. 561	IA 423(1)–(3), 426, [ER art.1(1)]
Phoenix Properties Ltd v Wimpole Street Nominees Ltd [1992] B.C.L.C. 737 Ch D	IA Pt III
Picard v FIM Advisers LLP [2010] EWHC 1299 (Ch); [2011] 1 B.C.L.C. 129	[CBIR Sch.1 art.21.1]
Piccadilly Property Management Ltd, Re [2000] B.C.C. 44; [1999] B.P.I.R. 260 Ch D (Companies Ct)	IR 7.14–7.24, 12.59
Pick v Chief Land Registrar [2011] EWHC 206 (Ch); [2012] Ch. 564 [2011] B.P.I.R. 1090	IA 306, IR 10.13
Pick v Goel [2006] EWHC 833 (Ch); [2007] 1 All E.R. 982; [2006] B.P.I.R. 827	IA 340(4), (5)
Pick v Sumpter [2010] EWHC 685 (Ch); [2010] B.P.I.R. 638	IA 335A, 375(1)
Pickard v Constable [2017] EWHC 2475 (Ch); [2018] B.P.I.R. 140	IA 335A
Pickard (Trustee) v Roberts [2016] EWHC 187 (Ch)	IR 1.1
Pickering v Davy [2017] EWCA Civ 30	IA Pt IV Ch.IX
Pike v Cork Gully [1997] B.P.I.R. 723 CA (Civ Div)	IA 307(1), 308(1), (4)
Pillar Denton Ltd v Jervis; Re Games Station Ltd [2014] EWCA Civ 180; [2015] Ch. 87; [2014] B.C.C. 165	IA Sch.B1 para.99(3)–(4), IR 3.51, 7.108(1)–(4)
Pimlico Capital Ltd, Re [2002] EWHC 878 (Ch); [2002] 2 B.C.L.C. 544	IA 124(2)–(4A)

	Provision
Pinecord Ltd (In liq.), Re [1995] B.C.C. 483 Ch D	IR 14.25
Pinemoor Ltd, Re [1997] B.C.C. 708 Ch D (Companies Ct)	[CDDA 6(1), 7(1)]
Pinewood Joinery v Starelm Properties Ltd [1994] B.C.C. 569 Ch D (Companies Ct)	IA 423(1)–(3), 423(4), (5), 424
Pinstripe Farming Co Ltd, Re [1996] B.C.C. 913 Ch D	IA 135
Pioneer Cladding Ltd v John Graham Construction Ltd [2015] EWHC 1314 (QB); [2015] 5 Costs L.R. 781	IA 130(2)
Pitt v Mond [2001] B.P.I.R. 624 Ch D	IA 263(1), (2)
Pittortou, Re [1985] 1 W.L.R. 58 Ch D	IA 335A
PK Airfinance Sarl v Alpstream AG. *See* Alpstream AG v PK Airfinance Sarl	
Platts v Western Trust & Savings Ltd [1996] B.P.I.R. 339 CA (Civ Div)	IR 10.5
Pleatfine Ltd, Re (1983) 1 B.C.C. 98942 Ch D	IA 118
Plummer, Re [2004] B.P.I.R. 767 Ch D (Bankruptcy)	IA 257(1), 260(1), (2), (2A), 262
PNC Telecom Plc (In admin.), Re [2003] EWHC 2220 (Ch); [2004] B.P.I.R. 314	IA 236
PNC Telecom Plc v Thomas [2007] EWHC 2157 (Ch); [2008] 2 B.C.L.C. 95	IA 212(3)
Pollard v Ashurst [2001] Ch. 595; [2001] B.P.I.R. 131 CA (Civ Div)	IA 314(8)
Polly Peck International Ex. P the joint administrators [1994] B.C.C. 15 Ch D (Companies Ct)	IA 235
Polly Peck International Plc (In admin.) (No.2), Re [1993] B.C.C. 890 Ch D (Companies Ct)	[CDDA 6(1), 7(1), 12C]
Polly Peck International Plc (in admin.) (No.4) [1997] 2 B.C.L.C. 630 Ch D	IA Sch.B1 para.43(6)
Polly Peck International Plc (In admin.) (No.4), Re [1996] 2 All E.R. 433; [1996] B.C.C. 486	IR 14.3–14.11
Polymer Vision R&D Ltd v Van Dooren [2011] EWHC 2951 (Comm); [2012] I.L.Pr. 14	[ER Preamble 7]
Popely v Popely [2004] EWCA Civ 463; [2004] B.P.I.R. 778	IR 10.5
Port v Auger [1994] 1 W.L.R. 862 Ch D	IA 303(1)
Portbase Clothing Ltd, Re; sub nom. Mond v Taylor [1993] Ch. 388; [1993] B.C.C. 96 Ch D (Companies Ct)	IA 107, 115, 176ZA, Pt XII, IR 7.108(1)–(4)
Portfolios of Distinction Ltd, Re [2006] EWHC 782 (Ch); [2004] 1 W.L.R. 2177; [2006] 2 B.C.L.C. 261	IA 124A
Portland Place (Historic House) Ltd, Re [2012] EWHC 4199 (Ch); [2013] W.T.L.R. 1049	[CDDA 1(1), 17]
Portman Building Society v Gallwey [1955] 1 W.L.R. 96 Ch D	IA 232
Portsmouth City Football Club Ltd (In admin.), Re [2010] EWHC 2013 (Ch); [2011] B.C.C. 149; [2010] B.P.I.R. 1123	IA Sch.B1 para.74
Portsmouth City Football Club Ltd (In liq.), Re; Neumans LLP v Andronikou [2013] EWCA Civ 916; [2014] 1 All E.R. 12; [2013] B.C.C. 741	IA Sch.B1 paras 40(1), 65, 66, IR 3.51, 7.108(1)–(4)
Potter v Revenue and Customs Commissioners Unreported 2008	IA 271(1), (2), (4)
Potters Oils Ltd, Re (No.2) [1986] 1 W.L.R. 201; (1985) 1 B.C.C. 99593 Ch D	IA 36(1)
Powdrill v Watson; sub nom. Paramount Airways Ltd (No.3), Re; Talbot v Cadge; Leyland DAF Ltd (No.2), Re [1995] 2 A.C. 394; [1995] B.C.C. 319 HL	IA 37(1), (2), 44(1), (2), 57(1A), (2A)–(2C), Sch.B1 para.96
Power v Brown [2009] EWHC 9 (Ch); [2009] B.P.I.R. 340	IA 284(1)–(3), (6), 314(1), (2), (6), Sch.5
Power v Hodges [2015] EWHC 2931 (Ch); [2016] B.P.I.R. 140	IA 236
Power v Sharp Investments Ltd; sub nom. Shoe Lace Ltd, Re [1993] B.C.C. 609 CA (Civ Div)	IA 245(2)
Powertrain Ltd, Re [2015] EWHC 3998 (Ch); [2016] B.C.C. 216; [2016] B.P.I.R. 456	IA 212(3)

	Provision
BV (C-112/10) [2011] E.C.R. I-11525; [2012] B.P.I.R. 438	[ER art.3(3), (4)]
Produce Marketing Consortium Ltd (In liq.) (No.1), Re; sub nom. Halls v David [1989] 1 W.L.R. 745; (1989) 5 B.C.C. 399 Ch D (Companies Ct)	IA 124
Produce Marketing Consortium Ltd (In liq.), Re (No.2) (1989) 5 B.C.C. 569 Ch D (Companies Ct)	IA 214, 214(3), 214(4)
Professional Computer Group Ltd, Re [2008] EWHC 1541 (Ch); [2009] B.C.C. 323	IR 3.12(2)
Promwalk Services Ltd, Re [2002] EWHC 2688 (Ch); [2003] 2 B.C.L.C. 305	[CDDA 22(5)]
Property Professionals - Ltd, Re [2013] EWHC 1903 (Ch); [2013] B.C.C. 606	IA Sch.B1 paras 77(1), 83
Prosser v Castle Sanderson Solicitors [2002] EWCA Civ 1140; [2003] B.C.C. 440; [2002] B.P.I.R. 1163	IA 256(1)
Prudential Assurance Co Ltd v PRG Powerhouse Ltd [2007] EWHC 1002 (Ch); [2007] B.C.C. 500; [2007] B.P.I.R. 839	IA 6(1)
Pudsey Steel Services Ltd, Re [2015] B.P.I.R. 1459	IA Sch.B1 para.55, IR 18.16
Pui-Kwan v Kam-Ho. *See* Melodious Corp, Re	
Pulsford v Devenish [1903] 2 Ch. 625 Ch D	IR 1.37, 7.51
Purewal v Countrywide Residential Lettings Ltd [2015] EWCA Civ 1122; [2016] 4 W.L.R. 31; [2016] B.P.I.R. 177	IA Pt III, 283(1), 306
Purpoint Ltd, Re [1991] B.C.C. 121 Ch D (Companies Ct)	IA 124, 212(1), 215(4), [CDDA 10]
Purvis v Customs and Excise Commissioners [1999] B.P.I.R. 396 Ch D	IA 375(2)
Purvis, Re [1997] 3 All E.R. 663; [1998] B.P.I.R. 153 Ch D	IA 271(5), IR 10.29
Pyke v Law Society [2006] EWHC 3489 (Ch)	IA 267(1), (2)
QMD Hotels Ltd Administrators, Noters [2010] CSOH 168; [2012] B.C.C. 794	IA 176A(3)–(5)
QRS 1 ApS v Frandsen [1999] 1 W.L.R. 2169 CA (Civ Div)	IR 14.2
Quadmost Ltd (In liq.) v Reprotech (Pebsham) Ltd [2001] B.P.I.R. 349 QBD	IA Sch.4 para.6
Quantum Distribution (UK) Ltd (In liq.), Re [2012] CSOH 191; 2013 S.L.T. 211; [2013] B.P.I.R. 117	IA 163
Quickdome Ltd, Re (1988) 4 B.C.C. 296 Ch D (Companies Ct)	IA 124(2)–(4A)
Quinn Finance v Galfis Investments Ltd [2012] NICh 9	IA 423(1)–(3)
Quinn Finance v Lyndhurst Development Trading SA [2012] NICh 15	IA 423(1)–(3)
R. v Appleyard (Gordon Henry) (1985) 81 Cr. App. R. 319; [1985] Crim. L.R. 723 CA (Crim Div)	[CDDA 2(1)]
R. v Austen (Styliano Pierre) (1985) 1 B.C.C. 99528; (1985) 7 Cr. App. R. (S.) 214 CA (Crim Div)	[CDDA 1(1)]
R. v Barnet Magistrates Court Ex p. Philippou [1997] B.P.I.R. 134 QBD	IA 252(2), IR 14.23
R. v Brady (Paul Clement) [2004] EWCA Crim 1763; [2004] 1 W.L.R. 3240; [2005] B.C.C. 357	IA 218(3), 236
R. v Brockley (Frank) [1994] B.C.C. 131; (1994) 99 Cr. App. R. 385 CA (Crim Div)	[CDDA 1, 11, 13]
R. v Cadman (Paul Martin) [2012] EWCA Crim 611; [2012] 2 Cr. App. R. (S.) 88	[CDDA 2(3)]
R. v Campbell [1984] B.C.L.C. 83 CA (Crim Div)	[CDDA 1(1)]
R. v Carass (Clive Louden) [2001] EWCA Crim 2845; [2002] 1 W.L.R. 1714	IA 206(4)
R. v Carr-Briant (Howard Bateman) [1943] K.B. 607 CCA	IA 206(4)
R. v Chandler (Lloyd) [2015] EWCA Crim 1825; [2016] B.C.C. 212	[CDDA 2]
R. v Cole (Philip Francis); R. v Birch (David Brian); R. v Lees (Francis Gerard) [1998] B.C.C. 87 CA (Crim Div)	IA 216(4), [CDDA 1]
R. v Corbin (Nigel Ian Henry) (1984) 6 Cr. App. R. (S.) 17; [1984] Crim. L.R. 302 CA (Crim Div)	[CDDA 2(1)]

	Provision
R. v Creggy (Stuart) [2008] EWCA Crim 394; [2008] 3 All E.R. 91; [2008] B.C.C. 323	[CDDA 1(1)]
R. v Daniel (Anthony Lala) [2002] EWCA Crim 959; [2003] 1 Cr. App. R. 6; [2002] B.P.I.R. 1193	IA 352, 354(1)
R. v Dickson (William Ewing) [1991] B.C.C. 719 CA (Crim Div)	IA 130(2)
R. v Doring (Petra) [2002] EWCA Crim 1695; [2002] B.C.C. 838; [2002] B.P.I.R. 1204	IA 206(3), 216, 216(4), [CDDA 11]
R. v Faryab (Frank) [1999] B.P.I.R. 569 CA (Crim Div)	IA 433(1)
R. v Georgiou (Christakis) (1988) 4 B.C.C. 322; (1988) 87 Cr. App. R. 207 CA (Crim Div)	[CDDA 1(1), 2(1)]
R. v Godwin (Roger Wyatt) (1980) 71 Cr. App. R. 97; [1980] Crim. L.R. 426 CA (Crim Div)	IA 360(1)
R. v Goodman (Ivor Michael) [1993] 2 All E.R. 789; [1992] B.C.C. 625 CA (Crim Div)	[CDDA 1(1), 1(2), 2(2)]
R. v Holmes (David Leonard) [1991] B.C.C. 394; (1992) 13 Cr. App. R. (S.) 29 CA (Crim Div)	[CDDA 1]
R. v Johnstone (Robert Alexander) [2003] UKHL 28; [2003] 3 All E.R. 884	IA 206(4)
R. v Kansal (Yash Pal) [1993] Q.B. 244; [1992] B.C.C. 615 CA (Crim Div)	IA 433(1)
R. v Kansal (Yash Pal) [2001] UKHL 62; [2002] 2 A.C. 69; [2002] B.P.I.R. 370	IA 433(1)
R. v Kearns (Nicholas Gary) [2002] EWCA Crim 748; [2002] 1 W.L.R. 2815; [2002] B.P.I.R. 1213	IA 354(3)
R. v Kemp (Peter David Glanville) [1988] Q.B. 645; (1988) 4 B.C.C. 203 CA (Crim Div)	IA 213
R. v Lyons (Isidore Jack) (No.3) [2002] UKHL 44; [2003] 1 A.C. 976; [2002] B.C.C. 968	IA 236
R. v McCredie (Graeme George) [2000] B.C.C. 617; [2000] B.P.I.R. 1129 CA (Crim Div)	IA 206(1), (2), 216(4)
R. v Millard (Ray) (1994) 15 Cr. App. R. (S.) 445; [1994] Crim. L.R. 146 CA (Crim Div)	[CDDA 1, 1(2), 2(1), 2(3)]
R. v Miller (Simon) [1977] 3 All E.R. 986 CA (Crim Div)	IA 360(2)
R. v Mungroo (Ivan Kimble) [1998] B.P.I.R. 784 CA (Crim Div)	IA 357(1), (3)
R. v Neuberg (Karen) [2016] EWCA Crim 1927	IA 216(4)
R. v Robinson [1990] B.C.C. 656; [1990] Crim. L.R. 804 CA (Crim Div)	IA 206(1), (2)
R. v Seager (Mornington Stafford) [2009] EWCA Crim 1303; [2010] 1 W.L.R. 815; [2012] B.C.C. 124	[CDDA 13]
R. v Secretary of State for Social Security Ex p. Taylor; R. v Secretary of State for Social Security Ex p. Chapman [1997] B.P.I.R. 505 QBD	IA 285(1)
R. v Secretary of State for Trade and Industry Ex p. Lonrho Plc [1992] B.C.C. 325 QBD	[CDDA 1, 8(1)]
R. v Secretary of State for Trade and Industry Ex p. McCormick [1998] B.C.C. 379 CA (Civ Div)	IA 236, [CDDA, 1, 8(1)]
R. v Shacter (Norman) [1960] 2 Q.B. 252 CCA	IA 206(3)
R. v Taylor (George Charles) [2011] EWCA Crim 728; [2011] 1 W.L.R. 1809; [2012] B.C.C. 663	IA 206(1), (2), 210
R. v Teece (Anthony) (1994) 15 Cr. App. R. (S.) 302 CA (Crim Div)	[CDDA 13]
R. v Theivendran (Sundranpillai) (1992) 13 Cr. App. R. (S.) 601 CA (Crim Div)	[CDDA 13]
R. v Ward (Michael Grainger) [2001] EWCA Crim 1648; [2002] B.C.C. 953	[CDDA 1(1)]
R. v Young (Steven Kenneth) [1990] B.C.C. 549 CA (Crim Div)	[CDDA 1]
R. (on the application of Balding) v Secretary of State for Work and Pensions; sub nom. Secretary of State for Work and Pensions v Balding [2007] EWCA Civ 1327; [2008] 1 W.L.R. 564; [2007] B.P.I.R. 1669	IA 382(3), (4)
R. (on the application of Griffin) v Richmond Magistrates' Court [2008] EWHC 84 (Admin); [2008] 1 W.L.R. 1525; [2008] B.C.C. 575	IA 206(4), 208(4), 352
R. (on the application of Hollis) v ACCA [2014] EWHC 2572 (Admin); [2014] B.P.I.R. 1317	IA 6(1)
R. (on the application of Howard) v Official Receiver [2013] EWHC	

	Provision
Revenue and Customs Commissioners v Football League Ltd [2012] EWHC 1372 (Ch); [2013] B.C.C. 60; [2012] B.P.I.R. 686	IA 6(1), 107
Revenue and Customs Commissioners v Garwood [2012] B.P.I.R. 575 Ch D	IA 271(3)
Revenue and Customs Commissioners v Maxwell [2010] EWCA Civ 1379; [2011] Bus. L.R. 707; [2012] B.C.C. 30	IR 15.35
Revenue and Customs Commissioners v Millichap [2011] B.P.I.R. 145	IR 14.25
Revenue and Customs Commissioners v Morris [2007] EWHC 3345 (Ch); [2008] B.P.I.R. 391	IA Pt IX Ch.1
Revenue and Customs Commissioners v Munir [2015] EWHC 1366 (Ch); [2015] B.C.C. 425	IA 135
Revenue and Customs Commissioners v Portsmouth City Football Club Ltd (In admin.) [2010] EWHC 2013 (Ch); [2011] B.C.C. 149; [2010] B.P.I.R. 1123	IA 6(1)
Revenue and Customs Commissioners v Potter [2008] B.P.I.R. 1033 Ch D	IA 271(1), (2), (4)
Revenue and Customs Commissioners v Rochdale Drinks Distributors Ltd [2011] EWCA Civ 1116; [2012] S.T.C. 186; [2013] B.C.C. 419; [2011] B.P.I.R. 1604	IA 127, 135
Revenue and Customs Commissioners v Soor [2005] EWHC 3080 (Ch); [2006] B.P.I.R. 429	IR 10.3, 10.4
Revenue and Customs Commissioners v Walsh [2005] EWCA Civ 1291; [2006] B.C.C. 431	IA 216(3)
Revenue and Customs Commissioners v Winnington Networks Ltd [2014] EWHC 1259 (Ch); [2014] B.C.C. 675	IA 124A, 135
Revenue and Customs Commissioners v Yousef [2008] EWHC 423 (Ch); [2008] B.C.C. 805; [2008] B.P.I.R. 1491	IA 217(2)
Rex Williams Leisure Centre Plc, Re [1994] Ch. 350; [1994] B.C.C. 551 CA (Civ Div)	[CDDA 1(4), 7(1), 16]
Rey v FNCB Ltd [2006] EWHC 1386 (Ch); [2006] B.P.I.R. 1260	IA 258(2)–(5), IR 14.15–14.19
Reynolds Ex p. Reynolds, Re (1882) 21 Ch. D. 601 CA	IA 366(1)

	Provision
Reynolds Porter Chamberlain LLP v Khan [2016] B.P.I.R. 722 Ch D (Bankruptcy Ct)	IA 265(4)
Rica Gold Washing Co Ltd, Re (1879) 11 Ch. D. 36 CA	IA 124(2)–(4A), 124A, 172(1), (2), 212(5)
Rich (A Bankrupt), Re [2008] B.P.I.R. 485 CC	IA 339(1)–(3), 340(4), (5), 382(3), (4)
Richards v Vivendi SA [2017] EWHC 1581 (Ch); [2017] B.P.I.R. 1390	IA 282(1), (3)
Richbell Information Services Inc v Atlantic & General Investment Trust Ltd (Validation of Disposition) [1999] B.C.C. 871 Ch D	IA 123, 127
Richbell Strategic Holdings Ltd (In liq.) (No.2), Re [2001] B.C.C. 409 Ch D	IA 133, IR 7.98–7.107
Richbell Strategic Holdings Ltd (No.1), Re [1997] 2 B.C.L.C. 429 Ch D (Companies Ct)	IA 123
Richborough Furniture Ltd, Re [1996] B.C.C. 155 Ch D	[CDDA 6(1), 22(5)]
Ricketts v Ad Valorem Factors Ltd [2003] EWCA Civ 1706; [2004] 1 All E.R. 894; [2004] B.C.C. 164	IA 216, 216(3), 217
Ridgeway Motors (Isleworth) Ltd v ALTS Ltd [2005] EWCA Civ 92; [2005] 1 W.L.R. 2871; [2005] B.C.C. 496	IA 123, Pt IX Ch.1
Ridsdale v Bowles [2015] B.P.I.R. 1275 CC	IA 267(1), (2), 282(1), (3), 323
Riemann, Re. *See* Finanzamt Braunschweig-Wilhelmstrasse v Riemann	
Rightmatch Ltd (Acting by its LPA Receiver) v Meisels [2014] B.P.I.R. 733	IA 271(1), (2), (4), IR 10.24
Rimar Pty Ltd v Pappas (1986) 60 A.J.L.R. 309	IA 307(4)
Ringinfo Ltd, Re [2002] 1 B.C.L.C. 210 Ch D (Companies Ct)	IA 123
Rio Properties Inc v Al-Midani [2003] B.P.I.R. 128 Ch D	IA 267(1), (2), 284(1)–(3), (6)
Ritchie v Burns 2001 S.L.T. 1383; [2001] B.P.I.R. 666 CSOH	IA 336(3)–(5)

	Provision
RJ Falcon Developments Ltd, Re (1987) 3 B.C.C. 146 Ch D (Companies Ct)	IA 124(5), 195
Robert v Woodall [2016] EWHC 538 (Ch); [2016] B.P.I.R. 643	IA 306
Robert v Woodall [2016] EWHC 2987 (Ch); [2017] 4 W.L.R. 11	IA 306
Roberts v Frohlich [2011] EWHC 257 (Ch); [2012] B.C.C. 407	IA 212(1), 214(2)
Roberts v Nunn [2004] EWHC 114 (Ch); [2004] 1 F.L.R. 1123; [2004] B.P.I.R. 623	IA 283(5)
Roberts v Pinnacle Entertainment Ltd [2003] EWHC 2394 (Ch); [2004] B.P.I.R. 208	IA 262(1)–(3), (8)
Roberts, Re [1900] 1 Q.B. 122 CA	IA 310(1), (1A), (2)
Robertson (A Bankrupt), Re [1989] 1 W.L.R. 1139 Ch D	IA 282(1), (3), IR 10.136
Roches Leisure Services Ltd, Re [2005] EWHC 3148 (Ch); [2006] B.P.I.R. 453 Ch D	IR 12.59
Rocks v Brae Hotel (Shetland) Ltd, 1997 S.L.T. 474; [1997] B.C.C. 670 CSOH (1 Div)	IA 123
Rocksteady Services Ltd, Re [2001] C.P. Rep. 1; [2001] B.C.C. 467 CA (Civ Div)	[CDDA 7(2)]
Rodencroft Ltd, Re [2004] EWHC 862 (Ch); [2004] 1 W.L.R. 1566; [2004] B.C.C. 631	IA 124A
Rodenstock GmbH, Re [2011] EWHC 1104 (Ch); [2012] B.C.C. 459	IA 220, 221, [ER, Preamble 7]
Rolled Steel Products (Holdings) Ltd v British Steel Corp [1986] Ch. 246; (1984) 1 B.C.C. 99158 CA (Civ Div)	IA 232, 238(5)
Rolus Properties Ltd, Re (1988) 4 B.C.C. 446 Ch D (Companies Ct)	[CDDA 12C]
Romar Engineering Co Ltd, Re [2003] B.C.C. 535; [2002] B.P.I.R. 409 Ch D	IR 7.108
Ronelp Marine Ltd v STX Offshore and Shipbuilding Co [2016] EWHC 2228 (Ch)	[CBIR Sch.1 art.21]
Rooney v Cardona (No.1) [1999] 1 W.L.R. 1388; [1999] B.P.I.R. 291 CA (Civ Div)	IA 283(2), (3)
Rooney v Das [1999] B.P.I.R. 404 Ch D	IA 340(4), (5)
Rose v AIB Group (UK) Plc; sub nom. Tain Construction Ltd, Re [2003] EWHC 1737 (Ch); [2003] 1 W.L.R. 2791; [2004] B.C.C. 11	IA 127
Roseoak Investments Ltd v Network Rail Infrastructure Ltd [2009] EWHC 3769 (Ch); [2010] B.P.I.R. 646	IR 10.5
Ross (A Bankrupt) (No.1), Re [1998] B.C.C. 29; [1997] B.P.I.R. 735 CA (Civ Div)	IA Second Group of Parts
Ross (A Bankrupt) (No.2), Re [2000] B.P.I.R. 636 CA (Civ Div)	IA 266(3), (4)
Ross v Revenue and Customs Commissioners [2010] EWHC 13 (Ch); [2010] 2 All E.R. 126; [2010] B.P.I.R. 652	IA 271(1), (2), (4)
Ross v Revenue and Customs Commissioners [2012] EWHC 1054 (Ch); [2012] B.P.I.R. 843	IA 375(1)
Rothschild v Bell (A Bankrupt) [2000] Q.B. 33; [1999] B.P.I.R. 300 CA (Civ Div)	IA 283(3A)
Rottenberg v Monjack [1992] B.C.C. 688 Ch D	IA 37(4)
Rottmann v Official Receiver [2008] EWHC 1794 (Ch); [2009] B.P.I.R. 617	IA 433(1), IR 10.99–10.105
Rottman v Official Receiver [2009] EWCA Civ 473	IA 290(3), (5)
Rowbotham Baxter Ltd, Re [1990] B.C.C. 113 Ch D (Companies Ct)	IA Sch.B1 para.3(1), (3)
Rowbury v Official Receiver [2015] EWHC 2276 (Ch)	IA 262, IR 15.27
Rowbury v Official Receiver [2015] EWHC 2951 (Ch); [2016] B.P.I.R. 500	IR 15.31
Rowe v Sanders [2002] EWCA Civ 242; [2002] 2 All E.R. 800 (Note)	IA 306, 310
Rowntree Ventures Ltd v Oak Property Partners Ltd [2017] EWCA Civ 1944	IA Sch.B1 paras 8, 11, 13
Royal Bank of Canada v Chetty [1997] B.P.I.R. 137 CA (Sask)	IA 306
Royal Bank of Scotland Plc v Binnell [1996] B.P.I.R. 352 Ch D	IR 10.5
Royal Bank of Scotland Plc v Debtor. *See* Debtor (No.68 of 1992), Re	
Royal Bank of Scotland Plc v Etridge (No.2) [2001] UKHL 44; [2002] 2 A.C. 773	IR 10.5

	Provision
Royal Bank of Scotland Plc v Farley [1996] B.P.I.R. 638 CA (Civ Div)	IA 282(1), (3)
Royal British Bank v Turquand [1843–60] All E.R. Rep. 435; 119 E.R. 886; (1856) 6 El. & Bl. 327 Ex Chamber	IA 42(1)
Royscot Spa Leasing Ltd v Lovett [1995] B.C.C. 502 CA (Civ Div)	IA 423(1)–(3)
RS&M Engineering Co Ltd, Re. *See* Mond v Hammond Suddards (No.2)	
Rubin v Coote [2011] EWCA Civ 106; [2011] B.C.C. 596	IA Sch.4 para.6A
Rubin v Dweck [2012] B.P.I.R. 854 Ch D (Bankruptcy)	IA 423(1)–(3), 425(1)
Rubin v Eurofinance SA; New Cap Reinsurance Corp Ltd (In liq.) v Grant [2012] UKSC 46; [2013] 1 A.C. 236; [2013] B.C.C. 1	IA 145(1), 423(1)–(3), 426, 426(4), (5), (11), [ER, CBIR, Sch.1 arts 21, 25.2, 27]
Rubin v Gunner [2004] EWHC 316 (Ch); [2004] B.C.C. 684	IA 214(4)
Ruiz (A Bankrupt), Re [2011] EWHC 913 (Fam); [2011] 2 F.L.R. 1351; [2011] B.P.I.R. 1139	IA 282(1), (3), 336(3)–(5)
Ruiz (A Bankrupt), Re [2011] EWCA Civ 1646; [2012] B.P.I.R. 446	IA 336(3)–(5)
Rusant Ltd v Traxys Far East Ltd [2013] EWHC 4083 (Comm)	IA 123
Rusjon Ltd (In liq.), Re [2007] EWHC 2943 (Ch); [2008] B.P.I.R. 26	IA 115
Russell Cooke Trust Co Ltd v Elliott [2007] EWHC 1443 (Ch); [2007] 2 B.C.L.C. 637	IA 40(1), (2)
Russell v Russell [1998] 1 F.L.R. 936; [1998] B.P.I.R. 259 Ch D	IA 264, 382(3), (4)
Russian & English Bank v Baring Bros & Co Ltd (No.2) [1932] 1 Ch. 663 Ch D	IA 123
Russian & English Bank v Baring Bros & Co Ltd (No.4) [1936] A.C. 405 HL	IA 225
Ruttle Plant Hire Ltd v Secretary of State for the Environment Food and Rural Affairs [2007] EWHC 2870 (TCC); [2008] 2 All E.R. (Comm) 264; [2008] B.C.C. 790	IA Sch.4 para.6
Ruttle Plant Hire Ltd v Secretary of State for the Environment, Food and Rural Affairs [2008] EWHC 238 (TCC); [2009] 1 All E.R. 448	IA Sch.4 para.6
RVB Investments Ltd v Bibby [2013] EWHC 65 (Ch)	IA 181(1)–(3)
Ryan v Tiuta International Ltd [2015] B.P.I.R. 123 Ch D	IR 10.5
S&A Conversions Ltd, Re (1988) 4 B.C.C. 384 CA (Civ Div)	IA 192(2)
SA&D Wright Ltd, Re [1992] B.C.C. 503 CA (Civ Div)	IA 127
Safehosts (London) Ltd, Re [2013] EWHC 2479 (Ch); [2013] B.C.C. 721	IA Sch.B1 para.13(1), (3)
Safier v Wardell [2017] EWHC 20 (Ch)	IA 415(1)–(3)
Sahaviriya Steel Industries UK Ltd v Hewden Stuart Ltd [2015] EWHC 2726 (Ch); [2016] B.C.C. 450	IA 127
Said v Butt [1920] 3 K.B. 497 KBD	IA Sch.B1 para.59
Saini v Petroform Ltd [1997] B.P.I.R. 515 CA (Civ Div)	IA 306
Salcombe Hotel Development Co Ltd, Re (1989) 5 B.C.C. 807 Ch D	IA 166(4), (5)
Salford Estates (No.2) Ltd v Altomart Ltd [2014] EWCA Civ 1575; [2015] Ch. 589; [2015] B.C.C. 306	IA 123, 124
Salliss v Hunt [2014] EWHC 229 (Ch); [2014] 1 W.L.R. 2402	IA 282(4), IR 18.16, [App.IV]
Salter v Wetton; sub nom. Calder (Deceased), Re [2011] EWHC 3192 (Ch); [2012] B.P.I.R. 63	IA 341(2), (3), 435(5)
Salters Hall School Ltd (In liq.), Re [1998] B.C.C. 503 Ch D (Companies Ct)	IR 18.21
Salvage Association, The, Re [2003] EWHC 1028 (Ch); [2004] 1 W.L.R. 174; [2003] B.C.C. 504	IA 1(4)–(6), Sch.B1 para.111(1), 111(1A), 111(1B), [ER art.2(6)]
Salvidge v Hussein [2000] B.C.C. 36; [1999] B.P.I.R. 410 Ch D (Bankruptcy Ct)	IR 10.5
Samsun Logix Corp v DEF [2009] EWHC 576 (Ch); [2010] B.C.C. 556	[CBIR, Sch.1 arts 2(i), 20]

	Provision
Samuel Sherman Plc, Re [1991] 1 W.L.R. 1070; [1991] B.C.C. 699 Ch D (Companies Ct)	[CDDA 8(1)]
Sanders v Donovan [2012] B.P.I.R. 219 Ch D (Bankruptcy)	IA 283(1), 284(1)–(3), (6), 306, 436
Sandford Farm Properties Ltd Unreported 26 June 2015	IA 236
Sandhu (t/a Isher Fashions UK) v Jet Star Retail Ltd (In admin.) [2011] EWCA Civ 459 CA (Civ Div)	IA Sch.B1 para.67
Sands v Clitheroe [2006] B.P.I.R. 1000 Ch D	IA 423(1)–(3)
Sands v Layne [2016] EWCA Civ 1159; [2017] C.P. Rep. 14	IA 271(3), 306, 375(1)
Sands v Monem [2010] EWHC 1972 (Ch); [2010] B.P.I.R. 1431	IA 340(1), (2)
Sands v Singh [2015] EWHC 2219 (Ch); [2015] B.P.I.R. 1293	IA 283A
Sands v Singh [2016] EWHC 636 (Ch); [2016] B.P.I.R. 737	IA 339(1)–(3), 423(1)–(3)
Sands v Wright [2010] B.P.I.R. 1437 Ch D	IA Pt IX, 284(4)
Sandwell Copiers Ltd, Re (1988) 4 B.C.C. 227 Ch D (Companies Ct)	IA 115
Sankey Furniture Ltd Ex p. Harding, Re [1995] 2 B.C.L.C. 594 Ch D	IA 108, 172(1), (2), IR 10.77
Sanko Steamship Co Ltd, Re [2015] EWHC 1031 (Ch)	[CBIR Sch.1 arts 17, 21.2]
Sargent v Customs and Excise Commissioners [1995] 1 W.L.R. 821; [1995] S.T.C. 398 CA (Civ Div)	IA Pt III
SAS Rover France, Re Unreported 19 May 2005	[ER art.33, 36]
Sasea Finance Ltd (In liq.) v KPMG (formerly KPMG Peat Marwick McLintock) (No.1) [1998] B.C.C. 216 Ch D	IA 236, 236(2)
Saunders (A Bankrupt), Re; sub nom. Bristol & West Building Society v Saunders [1997] Ch. 60; [1997] B.C.C. 83 Ch D	IA 130(2)
Saunders v United Kingdom (19187/91) [1997] B.C.C. 872; (1997) 23 E.H.R.R. 313 ECHR	IA 236, 433(1), [CDDA, 8(1)]
Saver Ltd, Re [1999] B.C.C. 221 Ch D (Companies Ct)	[CDDA 1(1)]
Saville v Gerrard [2004] EWHC 1363 (Ch); [2005] B.C.C. 433; [2004] B.P.I.R. 1332	IA 172(1)(2)
SAW (SW) 2010 Ltd v Wilson [2017] EWCA Civ 1001; [2018] 2 W.L.R. 636; [2017] B.C.C. 373	IA 29(2), Sch.B1 para.14(2), (3)
Sayers v Clarke Walker [2002] EWCA Civ 645; [2002] 1 W.L.R. 3095	IR 12.59
SB Corporate Solutions Ltd v Prescott [2012] Bus. L.R. D91 Ch D	IA Sch.B1 para.13(1), (3)
Schmid v Hertel (C-328/12) EU:C:2014:6 [2014] 1 W.L.R. 633; [2015] B.C.C. 25	[ER art.3]
Schmitt v Deichmann. *See* Phoenix Kapitaldienst GmbH	
Schooler v Customs and Excise Commissioners [1996] B.P.I.R. 207 CA (Civ Div)	IA 267(1), (2) 420(1)
Schrade v Sparkasse Ludenscheid [2013] B.P.I.R. 911	IA 263I, [ER art.3(1)]
Schroder Exempt Property Unit Trust v Birmingham City Council [2014] EWHC 2207 (Admin); [2014] B.C.C. 690	IA 178(4), 181(1)–(3)
Schuppan (A Bankrupt) (No.1), Re [1996] 2 All E.R. 664; [1996] B.P.I.R. 486 Ch D	IA Sch.5
Schuppan (A Bankrupt) (No.2), Re [1997] B.P.I.R. 271 Ch D	IA 423(1)–(3)
Schweizerische Lactina Panchaud AG v Germany (C-346/88) [1989] E.C.R. 4579; [1991] 2 C.M.L.R. 283	[ER Preamble]
Schweppe v Harper [2008] EWCA Civ 442; [2008] B.P.I.R. 1090	IA 282(4)
Science and Media LLP, Re [2014] B.P.I.R. 774	IA 183(2)
Scientific Investment Pension Plan, Re [1999] Ch. 53; [1998] B.P.I.R. 410 Ch D	IA 283(2), (3)
SCMLLA Properties Ltd v Gesso Properties (BVI) Ltd [1995] B.C.C. 793 Ch D	IA 178(4)
Scott v Davis [2003] B.P.I.R. 1009 Ch D (Bankruptcy)	IA 310(1), (1A), (2)
Scottish & Newcastle Plc, Petitioners [1993] B.C.C. 634 CSOH	IA 53(6), (7), 60(1)

	Provision
Scottish Widows Plc v Tripipatkul [2003] EWHC 1874 (Ch); [2004] B.C.C. 200; [2003] B.P.I.R. 1413	IA 181(1)–(3)
Screw Conveyor Ltd, Re. *See* Bank Leumi (UK) plc, Petitioner	
SCT Industri AB (In liq.) v Alpenblume AB (C-111/08) EU:C:2009:419 [2010] Bus. L.R. 559; [2009] E.C.R. I-5655	[ER arts 6, 7(2)(m)]
Sea Voyager Maritime Inc v Bielecki (t/a Hughes Hooker & Co) [1999] 1 All E.R. 628; [1999] B.C.C. 924	IA 262(1)–(3), (8)
Seaconsar (Far East) Ltd v Bank Markazi Jomhouri Islami Iran (Service Outside Jurisdiction) [1994] 1 A.C. 438 HL	IA 220
Seagon v Deko Marty Belgium NV (C-339/07) [2009] 1 W.L.R. 2168; [2009] B.C.C. 34	[ER arts 3, 16]
Seagull Manufacturing Co Ltd (In liq.) (No.1), Re [1993] Ch. 345; [1993] B.C.C. 241 CA (Civ Div)	IA 133, 236, 290(1), (2), 366(1)
Seagull Manufacturing Co Ltd (In liq.) (No.2), Re [1994] Ch. 91; [1993] B.C.C. 833 Ch D (Companies Act)	[CDDA 6(1)]
Seagull Manufacturing Co Ltd (No.3), Re [1995] B.C.C. 1088	[CDDA 1(1)]
Seal v Chief Constable of South Wales [2007] UKHL 31; [2007] 1 W.L.R. 1910	IA 285(3), (4)
Seat Pagine Gialle SpA, Re [2012] EWHC 3686 (Ch)	IA 221
Sebry v Companies House [2015] EWHC 115 (QB); [2015] B.C.C. 236	IA 130(1), IR 10.13
Secondus v Atkinson [2013] B.P.I.R. 632 Ch D	IA 282(4), IR 10.134, 18.28
Secretary of State for Business, Energy and Industrial Strategy v Rigil Kent Acquisitions Ltd [2017] EWHC 3636 (Ch)	IA 135
Secretary of State for Business, Enterprise and Regulatory Reform v Aaron [2008] EWCA Civ 1146; [2009] B.C.C. 375	[CDDA 7(1)]
Secretary of State for Business, Enterprise and Regulatory Reform v Amway (UK) Ltd [2009] EWCA Civ 32; [2009] B.C.C. 781	IA 124A
Secretary of State for Business, Enterprise and Regulatory Reform v Art IT Plc [2008] EWHC 258 (Ch); [2009] 1 B.C.L.C. 262	IA 124A
Secretary of State for Business, Enterprise and Regulatory Reform v Charter Financial Solutions Ltd [2009] EWHC 1118 (Ch); [2011] 2 B.C.L.C. 788	IA 124A
Secretary of State for Business, Enterprise and Regulatory Reform v Doffman. *See* Stakefields (Midlands) Ltd, Re	
Secretary of State for Business, Enterprise and Regulatory Reform v Poulter [2009] B.C.C. 608 Ch D	[CDDA 12C, 22(5)]
Secretary of State for Business, Enterprise and Regulatory Reform v Smith, 2010 S.L.T. (Sh Ct) 26; [2009] B.C.C. 497 Sh Ct	[CDDA 16]
Secretary of State for Business, Enterprise and Regulatory Reform v Sullman [2008] EWHC 3179 (Ch); [2010] B.C.C. 500	[CDDA 8(1), 8(2), 12C]
Secretary of State for Business, Innovation and Skills v Akbar [2017] EWHC 2856 (Ch)	[CDDA 12C]
Secretary of State for Business, Innovation and Skills v Atkar Unreported 10 June 2016	[CDDA 1(1)]
Secretary of State for Business, Innovation and Skills v Bloch [2013] CSOH 57; 2013 G.W.D. 13–275	[CDDA 1(2)]
Secretary of State for Business, Innovation and Skills v Broomfield Developments Ltd [2014] EWHC 3925 (Ch)	IA 124A, IR 7.4–7.12
Secretary of State for Business, Innovation and Skills v Chohan [2011] EWHC 1350 (Ch); [2012] 1 B.C.L.C. 138	[CDDA 6(1), 7(1)]
Secretary of State for Business, Innovation and Skills v Chohan, sub nom. Re UKLI Ltd [2013] EWHC 680 (Ch); [2013] Lloyd's Rep. F.C. 351	[CDDA 22(5)]
Secretary of State for Business, Innovation and Skills v Combined Maintenance Services Ltd Unreported 6 November 2014	IA 124A, IR 7.4–7.12

	Provision
Secretary of State for Business, Innovation and Skills v Coward [2011] B.C.C. 712 EAT	IA Pt IV
Secretary of State for Business, Innovation and Skills v Doffman [2010] EWHC 3175 (Ch); [2011] 2 B.C.L.C. 541	[CDDA 12C]
Secretary of State for Business, Innovation and Skills v Harriss [2016] EWHC 794 (Ch)	[CDDA 1(1)]
Secretary of State for Business, Innovation and Skills v Hawkhurst Capital Plc [2013] EWHC 4219 (Ch); [2016] B.C.C. 125	IA 124A, 135
Secretary of State for Business, Innovation and Skills v Jeromson [2013] ScotSC 26	[CDDA 12C]
Secretary of State for Business, Innovation and Skills v KJK Investments Ltd; Secretary of State for Business, Innovation and Skills v G Loans Ltd [2015] EWHC 1589 (Ch)	IA 124A
Secretary of State for Business, Innovation and Skills v Melaris (Re Waterfall Media Ltd) [2013] B.P.I.R. 1109	IA 279(3)–(5)
Secretary of State for Business, Innovation and Skills v New Horizon Energy Ltd [2015] EWHC 2961 (Ch); [2017] B.C.C. 629	IA 124A, 135
Secretary of State for Business, Innovation and Skills v PAG Management Services Ltd. *See* PAG Management Services Ltd, Re	
Secretary of State for Business, Innovation and Skills v Pawson [2015] EWHC 2626 (Ch)	[CDDA 8(1)]
Secretary of State for Business, Innovation and Skills v PGMRS Ltd [2010] EWHC 2983 (Ch); [2011] B.C.C. 368	IA 124A
Secretary of State for Business, Innovation and Skills v Potiwal [2012] EWHC 3723 (Ch); [2013] Lloyd's Rep. F.C. 124	[CDDA 7(1)]
Secretary of State for Business, Innovation and Skills v Rahman [2017] EWHC 2468 (Ch)	[CDDA 1(2), 2(3), 6(4)]
Secretary of State for Business, Innovation and Skills v Reza [2013] CSOH 86; 2013 G.W.D. 19–380	[CDDA 12C]
Secretary of State for Business, Innovation and Skills v Warry [2014] EWHC 1381 (Ch)	[CDDA 1(2)]
Secretary of State for Business, Innovation and Skills v Weston [2014] EWHC 2933 (Ch); [2014] B.C.C. 581	[CDDA 2(1), 4(1), 7]
Secretary of State for Business, Innovation and Skills v World Future Ltd [2013] EWHC 723 (Ch)	IA 124A
Secretary of State for Trade and Industry v Arif [1996] B.C.C. 586 Ch D	[CDDA 1(1), 1(2)]
Secretary of State for Trade and Industry v Arnold [2007] EWHC 1933 (Ch); [2008] B.C.C. 119	[CDDA 6(3)–(3C), 7(1)]
Secretary of State for Trade and Industry v Ashcroft (No.1) [1998] Ch. 71; [1997] B.C.C. 634 CA (Civ Div)	[CDDA 7(1)]
Secretary of State for Trade and Industry v Aurum Marketing Ltd [2002] B.C.C. 31 CA (Civ Div)	IA 124A
Secretary of State for Trade and Industry v Bairstow [2003] EWCA Civ 321; [2004] Ch. 1; [2003] B.C.C. 682	[CDDA 7(1)]
Secretary of State for Trade and Industry v Baker (No.2); sub nom. Barings Plc (No.2), Re [1998] Ch. 356; [1998] B.C.C. 888 Ch D (Companies Ct	[CDDA 1, 7(1)]
Secretary of State for Trade and Industry v Baker (No.5) [2001] B.C.C. 273 CA (Civ Div)	[CDDA 6(1), 12C, 9A(5)–(8)]
Secretary of State for Trade and Industry v Baker (No.5); sub nom. Barings Plc (No.5), Re [2000] 1 W.L.R. 634; [1999] B.C.C. 960 Ch D	[CDDA 1(1)]
Secretary of State for Trade and Industry v Bannister [1996] 1 W.L.R. 118; [1995] B.C.C. 1027 CA (Civ Div)	[CDDA 1(1), 7(1)]
Secretary of State for Trade and Industry v Barnett (Re Harbour Lane Ltd) [1998] 2 B.C.L.C. 64 Ch D (Companies Ct)	[CDDA 1(1)]
Secretary of State for Trade and Industry v Becker [2002] EWHC 2200 (Ch); [2003] 1 B.C.L.C. 555	[CDDA 22(5)]

Case	Provision
Secretary of State for Trade and Industry v Bell Davies Trading Ltd [2004] EWCA Civ 1066; [2005] 1 All E.R. 324 (Note); [2005] B.C.C. 564	IA 124A
Secretary of State for Trade and Industry v Blackwood, 2003 S.L.T. 120; [2005] B.C.C. 366 CSIH (1 Div)	[CDDA 12C]
Secretary of State for Trade and Industry v Blunt [2006] B.C.C. 112 Ch D	[CDDA 6(1), 12C]
Secretary of State for Trade and Industry v Carr [2006] EWHC 2110 (Ch); [2007] B.C.C. 313 Ch D (Companies Ct)	[CDDA 8(1)]
Secretary of State for Trade and Industry v Collins [2000] B.C.C. 998 CA (Civ Div)	[CDDA 1(1)]
Secretary of State for Trade and Industry v Crane (No.2); sub nom. Priority Stainless (UK) Ltd, Re [2004] B.C.C. 825	[CDDA 7(4)]
Secretary of State for Trade and Industry v Creegan [2004] B.C.C. 835	[CDDA 12C]
Secretary of State for Trade and Industry v Davies (No.1) [1996] 4 All E.R. 289; [1997] B.C.C. 235 CA (Civ Div)	[CDDA 7(2)]
Secretary of State for Trade and Industry v Dawes [1997] B.C.C. 121 Ch D	[CDDA 1, 6(1), 7(1), 12C]
Secretary of State for Trade and Industry v Deverell [2001] Ch. 340; [2000] B.C.C. 1057 CA (Civ Div)	[CDDA 1(1), 22(5)]
Secretary of State for Trade and Industry v Frid; sub nom. West End Networks Ltd (In liq.), Re [2004] UKHL 24; [2004] 2 A.C. 506; [2004] B.C.C. 525; [2004] B.P.I.R. 841	IA 323, IR, 14.25
Secretary of State for Trade and Industry v Gill [2004] EWHC 175 (Ch); [2005] B.C.C. 24	[CDDA 7(1), 16]
Secretary of State for Trade and Industry v Goldberg (No.2) [2003] EWHC 2843 (Ch); [2004] 1 B.C.L.C. 597	[CDDA 12C]
Secretary of State for Trade and Industry v Hall [2006] EWHC 1995 (Ch); [2009] B.C.C. 190	[CDDA 22(5)]
Secretary of State for Trade and Industry v Harper [1993] B.C.C. 518 CC	[CDDA 12C]
Secretary of State for Trade and Industry v Hickling [1996] B.C.C. 678 Ch D	[CDDA 7(1), 22(5)]
Secretary of State for Trade and Industry v Hollier [2006] EWHC 1804 (Ch); [2007] B.C.C. 11	[CDDA 8(1), 12C]
Secretary of State for Trade and Industry v Jabble [1998] B.C.C. 39 CA (Civ Div)	IA 34, [CDDA 6(2)]
Secretary of State for Trade and Industry v Joiner [1993] B.C.C. 549 Ch D (Companies Ct)	[CDDA 12C]
Secretary of State for Trade and Industry v Jones [1999] B.C.C. 336 Ch D	[CDDA 1(1), 22(5)]
Secretary of State for Trade and Industry v Key [2004] B.P.I.R. 214 EAT	IA Pt IV
Secretary of State for Trade and Industry v Laing [1996] 2 B.C.L.C. 324 Ch D	[CDDA 22(5)]
Secretary of State for Trade and Industry v Langridge; sub nom. Cedac Ltd, Re [1991] Ch. 402; [1991] B.C.C. 148 CA (Civ Div)	[CDDA 1, 16]
Secretary of State for Trade and Industry v Lewis [2003] B.C.C. 611 Ch D	[CDDA 6(1)]
Secretary of State for Trade and Industry v Leyton Housing Trustees Ltd [2000] 2 B.C.L.C. 808 Ch D	IA 124A
Secretary of State for Trade and Industry v Liquid Acquisitions Ltd [2002] EWHC 180 (Ch); [2003] 1 B.C.L.C. 375	IA 124A
Secretary of State for Trade and Industry v London Citylink Ltd [2005] EWHC 2875 (Ch)	IA 124A
Secretary of State for Trade and Industry v Lubrani (No.2) [1998] B.C.C. 264 Ch D (Companies Ct)	[CDDA 1(1)]
Secretary of State for Trade and Industry v Martin [1998] B.C.C. 184 Ch D	[CDDA 7(2)]
Secretary of State for Trade and Industry v McTighe (No.2) [1997] B.C.C. 224 CA (Civ Div)	[CDDA 1, 1(1), 7(2), 12C]

	Provision
Secretary of State for Trade and Industry v Moffatt [1996] 2 B.C.L.C. 16 Ch D	[CDDA 7(1)]
Secretary of State for Trade and Industry v North West Holdings Plc [1998] B.C.C. 997 CA (Civ Div)	IR 7.4–7.12
Secretary of State for Trade and Industry v Palmer, 1995 S.L.T. 188; [1994] B.C.C. 990 CSIH	[CDDA 7(2), 9(4), (5)]
Secretary of State for Trade and Industry v Paulin [2005] EWHC 888 (Ch); [2005] B.C.C. 927; [2005] B.P.I.R. 968	[CDDA 1(1)]
Secretary of State for Trade and Industry v Queen, 1998 S.L.T. 735; [1998] B.C.C. 678 CSIH (Ex Div)	[CDDA 6(1)]
Secretary of State for Trade and Industry v Rosenfield [1999] B.C.C. 413 Ch D	[CDDA 1(1)]
Secretary of State for Trade and Industry v Slater [2008] B.C.C. 70; [2008] I.C.R. 54 EAT	IA 86
Secretary of State for Trade and Industry v Swan [2005] EWHC 603 (Ch); [2005] B.C.C. 596	[CDDA 12C]
Secretary of State for Trade and Industry v Taylor [1997] 1 W.L.R. 407; [1997] B.C.C. 172 Ch D (Companies Ct)	[CDDA 12C]
Secretary of State for Trade and Industry v Thornbury [2007] EWHC 3202 (Ch); [2008] B.C.C. 768	[CDDA 12C]
Secretary of State for Trade and Industry v Tillman [1999] B.C.C. 703 CA (Civ Div)	[CDDA 6(1), 7(1)]
Secretary of State for Trade and Industry v Tjolle [1998] B.C.C. 282 Ch D	[CDDA 1, 7(2), 22(5)]
Secretary of State for Trade and Industry v Travel Time (UK) Ltd [2000] B.C.C. 792 (Companies Ct)	IA 124A
Secretary of State for Trade and Industry v Van Hengel [1995] B.C.C. 1 Ch D (Companies Ct)	[CDDA 12C]
Secretary of State for Trade and Industry v Vohora [2007] EWHC 2656 (Ch); [2009] B.C.C. 369	[CDDA 7(2)]
Secretary of State for Trade and Industry v Walker [2003] EWHC 175 (Ch); [2003] 1 B.C.L.C. 363	[CDDA 6(1)]
Secretary of State for Trade and Industry v Worth; sub nom. Dicetrade Ltd, Re [1994] B.C.C. 371 CA (Civ Div)	[CDDA 1(1), 17]
Secretary of State for Work and Pensions v Balding [2007] EWCA Civ 1327; [2008] 1 W.L.R. 564; [2007] B.P.I.R. 1669	IA 281(1)
Secretary of State for Work and Pensions v Payne [2011] UKSC 60; [2012] 2 A.C. 1	IA Pt 7A, 251G, 281(1), 285(1), 306, 382(3), (4), IR 9.2
Secure & Provide Plc, Re [1992] B.C.C. 405 Ch D (Companies Ct)	IA 124A
Securum Finance Ltd v Camswell Ltd [1994] B.C.C. 434 Ch D	IA 123
SED Essex Ltd, Re [2013] EWHC 1583 (Ch); [2014] B.C.C. 628	IA 127, 135
Segal v Pasram [2008] EWHC 3448 (Ch); [2008] 1 F.L.R. 271 [2007] B.P.I.R. 881	IA 339(1)–(3)
SEIL Trade Finance Ltd, Re [1992] B.C.C. 538 Ch D	IA 246(3)
Sekhon v Edginton [2015] EWCA Civ 816; [2015] 1 W.L.R. 4435; [2015] B.P.I.R. 1397	IA 271(3), 271(5), IR 10.23
Senator Hanseatische Verwaltungsgesellschaft mbH, Re [1997] 1 W.L.R. 515; [1997] B.C.C. 112 CA (Civ Div)	IA 124A
Sendo Ltd, Re [2005] EWHC 1604 (Ch); [2006] 1 B.C.L.C. 395	IA Sch.B1 para.111(1), 111(1A), 111(1B), [ER art.3(1)]
Sequestrated Estate of William Rose, Re [2013] ScotSC 42; [2013] B.P.I.R. 955	IA 283A(5), (6)
Servaccomm Redhall Ltd, Re [2004] EWHC 760 (Ch); [2006] 1 B.C.L.C. 1	[CDDA 1(1)]
Seven Eight Six Properties Ltd v Ghafoor [1997] B.P.I.R. 519 CA (Civ Div)	IA 306
Sevenoaks Stationers (Retail) Ltd, Re [1991] Ch. 164; [1990] B.C.C. 765 CA (Civ Div)	IA Sch.4A, [CDDA 1, 1(1), 1(2), 2(3), 7(1), 12C]
Shah v Baverstock [2007] B.P.I.R. 1191 CC	IA 339(1)–(3)

	Provision
Shah v Cooper [2003] B.P.I.R. 1018 Ch D	IA 256(1)
Shah v Patel [2008] EWCA Civ 979; [2010] B.P.I.R. 496 CA (Civ Div)	IA 134
Shalson v DF Keane Ltd [2003] EWHC 599 (Ch); [2003] B.P.I.R. 1045	IA 268
Shamash v Inland Revenue Commissioners [2002] B.P.I.R. 189 Ch D	IA 282(1), (3)
Shamji v Johnson Matthey Bankers Ltd (1986) 2 B.C.C. 98910 CA (Civ Div)	IA 34
Shapland Inc, Re [2000] B.C.C. 106; [1999] B.P.I.R. 391 Ch D	IA 238(4), 239(4), 239(6)
Share (Lorraine), Re [2002] 2 F.L.R. 88; [2002] B.P.I.R. 194	IA 339(1)–(3)
Sharp v Thomson; sub nom. Sharp v Joint Receivers of Albyn Construction Ltd; Sharp v Woolwich Building Society 1997 S.C. (H.L.) 66; 1997 S.L.T. 636; [1998] B.C.C. 115 HL	IA 50, 53(6), (7)
Sharp v Woolwich Building Society. *See* Sharp v Thomson	
Sharples v Places for People Ltd. *See* Godfrey v A2 Dominion Homes Ltd	
Shaw v Breish [2017] EWHC 2972 (Comm)	IA Pt III
Shaw v Doleman [2009] EWCA Civ 279; [2009] B.C.C. 730; [2009] B.P.I.R. 945	IA 181(1)–(3)
Shaw v MFP Foundations & Piling Ltd [2010] EWHC 9 (Ch); [2010] B.P.I.R. 397	IR 10.5
Sheldrake v DPP [2004] UKHL 43; [2005] 1 A.C. 264; [2005] 1 All E.R. 237	IA 206(4)
Shepheard v Lamey [2001] B.P.I.R. 939 Ch D	IR 7.63–7.66
Shepherd v Official Receiver [2006] EWHC 2902 (Ch); [2007] B.P.I.R. 101	IA 303(1)
Shepherds Investments Ltd v Walters [2006] EWHC 836 (Ch); [2007] 2 B.C.L.C. 202	[CDDA 22(5)]
Sheppard & Cooper Ltd v TSB Bank Plc (No.2) [1996] 2 All E.R. 654; [1996] B.C.C. 965 Ch D	IA 34
Sherborne Associates Ltd, Re [1995] B.C.C. 40 QBD (Merc)	IA 214(1), 214(2), 214(3)
Sheridan Millennium Ltd, Re; sub nom. Curistan v Keenan [2014] NICA 29	IA Sch.B1 para.75, Sch.1
Sherman, Re [1916] W.N. 26	IA 283(2), (3)
Shettar, Re [2003] EWHC 220 (Ch); [2003] B.P.I.R. 1055	IA 303(1)
Shierson v Rastogi (A Bankrupt) [2007] EWHC 1266 (Ch); [2007] B.P.I.R. 891	IA 279(3)–(5), 333(1), (3)
Shierson v Vlieland-Boddy [2005] EWCA Civ 974; [2005] 1 W.L.R. 3966; [2005] B.C.C. 949	IA 129, [ER art.3(1)]
Shilena Hosiery Co Ltd, Re [1980] Ch. 219 Ch D	IA 423
Shire Court Residents Ltd v Registrar of Companies [1995] B.C.C. 821 Ch D	IA Pt IV Ch.IX
Shlosberg v Avonwick Holdings Ltd; sub nom. Avonwick Holdings Ltd v Shlosberg [2016] EWCA Civ 1138	IA 283(1), 311(1)
Shrimpton v Darbys Solicitors LLP [2011] EWHC 3796 (Ch); [2012] B.P.I.R. 631	IA Pt IX, 271(1), (2), (4), 271(3)
Shruth Ltd (In liq.), Re. *See* International Brands USA Inc v Goldstein	
Shuttleworth v Secretary of State for Trade and Industry [2000] B.C.C. 204 Ch D	[CDDA 1(1)]
Siebe Gorman & Co Ltd v Barclays Bank Ltd [1979] 2 Lloyd's Rep. 142 Ch D	IA 40(1), (2), IR 4.22–4,24
SIG Security Services Ltd, Re [1998] B.C.C. 978 Ch D	[CDDA 7(1)]
Signland, Re [1982] 2 All E.R. 609	IR 7.4–7.12
Silentpride Ltd, Re Unreported 9 October 2014)	IA Sch.B1 para.13(1), (3)
Silven Properties Ltd v Royal Bank of Scotland Plc [2003] EWCA Civ 1409; [2004] 1 W.L.R. 997; [2003] B.C.C. 1002	IA Pt III
Simion v Brown [2007] EWHC 511 (Ch); [2007] B.P.I.R. 412	IR 18.28, [App.IV]
Simmon Box (Diamonds) Ltd, Re. *See* Cohen v Selby	
Simmonds v Pearce [2017] EWHC 35 (QB)	IA 312(4)
Simmonds v Pearce [2017] EWHC 3126 (Admin); [2018] B.P.I.R. 206	IA 333(1), (3), 363(2), (4), 433(1)

	Provision
1527 (Ch); [2016] B.C.C. 485; [2015] B.P.I.R. 1462	IA 163, Sch.B1 para.69
Stevensdrake Ltd (t/a Stevensdrake Solicitors) v Hunt [2017] EWCA Civ 1173; [2017] B.C.C. 611; [2017] B.P.I.R. 1408	IA Sch.B1 para.69
Stichting Shell Pensioenfonds v Krys [2014] UKPC 41; [2015] A.C. 616; [2015] B.C.C. 205	IR 4.3–4.11, [CBIR Sch.1 art.20.3]
Stocznia Gdynia SA, Re; Bud-bank Leasing SP zo o, Re [2010] B.C.C. 255 Ch D (Companies Ct)	[CBIR, Sch.1 arts 2(i), 6]
Stojevic v Official Receiver [2006] EWHC 3447 (Ch); [2007] B.P.I.R. 141	[ER art.3(1)]
Stone v Vallance [2008] B.P.I.R. 236 Ch D	IR 10.5
Stonham v Ramrattan [2011] EWCA Civ 119; [2011] 1 W.L.R. 1617	IA 283A, 283(2), (5), (6), 339 (1)–(3), 342(1)
Storm Funding Ltd, Re [2013] EWHC 4019 (Ch); [2014] Bus. L.R. 454	IA Sch.B1 para.99(3)–(4)
Stow v Stow [2008] EWHC 495 (Ch); [2008] Ch. 461; [2008] B.P.I.R. 673	IA 339(1)–(3), 423(1)–(3)
Strategic Value Master Fund Ltd v Ideal Standard International Acquisition Sarl [2011] EWHC 171 (Ch); [2011] 1 B.C.L.C. 475	IA Pt IV
Strongmaster Ltd v Kaye [2002] EWHC 444 (Ch); [2002] B.P.I.R. 1259 Ch D	IA 263(5), (6)
Structural Concrete Ltd, Re [2001] B.C.C. 578 Ch D	[CDDA 1(1), 12C]
Sugar Properties (Derisley Wood) Ltd, Re (1987) 3 B.C.C. 88 Ch D (Companies Ct)	IA 127
Sun Legend Investments Ltd v Jade Yuk Kuen Ho [2013] B.P.I.R. 533 CC	IA 267(1), (2)
Sunberry Properties Ltd v Innovate Logistics Ltd (In admin.) [2008] EWCA Civ 1321; [2009] B.C.C. 164	IA Sch.B1 paras 2, 43(6)
Sunwing Vacation Inc v E-Clear (UK) Plc [2011] EWHC 1544 (Ch); [2011] B.C.C. 889; [2011] B.P.I.R. 1524	IA 112(2), 155(1)
Super Aguri F1 Ltd, Re; sub nom. Long v Turner [2011] B.C.C. 452; [2011] B.P.I.R. 256 Ch D	IR 18.23, 18.28
Supperstone v Auger [1999] B.P.I.R. 152 Ch D	IA 303(2)
Supperstone v Hurst (No.3) [2006] EWHC 2147 (Ch); [2006] B.P.I.R. 1263	IA 303(1)
Supperstone v Lloyd's Names Association Working Party [1999] B.P.I.R. 832 Ch D	IA 307(2), (5), 310(7)
Supporting Link Alliance Ltd, Re [2004] EWHC 523 (Ch); [2004] 1 W.L.R. 1549; [2004] B.C.C. 764	IA 124A
Surrey Leisure Ltd, Re [1999] B.C.C. 847	[CDDA 6(1), 16]
Sustainable Wealth Investments (UK) Ltd (In liq.), Re; [2015] EWHC 1674 (Ch)	IA 112(2)
Sutton Glassworks Ltd, Re [1996] B.C.C. 174 Ch D (Companies Ct)	[CDDA 7(1)]
Sutton v GE Capital Commercial Finance Ltd [2004] EWCA Civ 315; [2004] 2 B.C.L.C. 662	IA Pt III, 42(1)
Sutton, Re [2014] B.P.I.R. 1349 Ch D (Bankruptcy Ct)	IA 271(1), (2), (4), 271(5)
Sweatfield Ltd, Re [1997] B.C.C. 744; [1998] B.P.I.R. 276 Ch D	IA 1(1), 6(1), 262(1)–(3), (8)
Sweden v Holmqvist (C-310/07) EU:C:2008:573 [2008] E.C.R. I-7871; [2008] I.R.L.R. 970	[ER Preamble 4]
Swift 736 Ltd, Re [1993] B.C.C. 312 CA (Civ Div)	[CDDA 12C]
Swift Advances Plc v Ahmed [2015] EWHC 3265 (Ch); [2016] B.P.I.R. 197	IA 423(1)–(3)
Swift Advances Plc v McKay [2011] NICh 2	IA 306
Swindon Town Properties Ltd v Swindon Town Football Co Ltd [2003] B.P.I.R. 253 Ch D	IA 6
SwissAir Schweizerische Luftverkehr-Aktiengesellschaft, Re [2009] EWHC 2099 (Ch); [2010] B.C.C. 667; [2009] B.P.I.R. 1505	IA 426, [CBIR, Sch.1 art.21.2]

	Provision
Swissport (UK) Ltd (In liq.) v Aer Lingus Ltd [2007] EWHC 1089 (Ch); [2009] B.C.C. 113	IR 14.25
Switch Services Ltd (In admin.), Re [2012] Bus. L.R. D91 Ch D	IR 12.59
Sykes (Butchers) Ltd, Re [1998] B.C.C. 484 Ch D (Companies Ct)	[CDDA 1(1), 12C]
Sykes & Sons Ltd, Re [2012] EWHC 1005 (Ch); [2012] B.P.I.R. 1273	IA 123
Sykes v Shillito [2017] EWHC 3588 (Ch)	IA 375(2)
Synergi Partners Ltd, Re [2015] EWHC 964 (Ch); [2015] B.C.C. 333; [2015] B.P.I.R. 1300	IA Sch.B1 paras 13(2), 104
Syska v Vivendi Universal SA [2009] EWCA Civ 677; [2009] 2 All E.R. (Comm) 891; [2009] Bus. L.R. 1494; [2010] B.C.C. 348	[ER arts 4(2)(e), (f), 18]
T&D Services (Timber Preservation & Damp Proofing Contractors) Ltd, Re [1990] B.C.C. 592 Ch D (Companies Ct)	[CDDA 12C]
T&N Ltd, Re [2004] EWHC 2878 (Ch); [2005] B.C.C. 982	IA 124(1)
T&N Ltd, Re [2005] EWHC 2870 (Ch); [2006] 1 W.L.R. 1728; [2006] B.P.I.R. 532	IA 3(3), 124(1), Pt IX, 382(1), (2), 14.1, 14.2
Tack, Re [2000] B.P.I.R. 164 Ch D	IA 276(1)
Tager v Westpac Banking Corp [1998] B.C.C. 73; [1997] B.P.I.R. 543 Ch D	IA 262(1)–(3), (8), 376
Tagore Investments SA v Official Receiver [2008] EWHC 3495 (Ch); [2009] B.P.I.R. 392	IA 346(6)
Tailby v HSBC Bank Plc, Re Anwar Ul-Haq Rashid [2015] B.P.I.R. 143 Ch D	IA 238(4), 339(1)–(3)
Takavarasha v Newham LBC [2004] EWHC 3232 (Ch); [2006] B.P.I.R. 311	IR 10.2
Talbot v Cadge. *See* Powdrill v Watson	
Tallington Lakes Ltd v Ancasta International Boat Sales Ltd [2012] EWCA Civ 1712; [2014] B.C.C. 327	IA 123
Tambrook Jersey Ltd, Re. *See* HSBC Bank Plc v Tambrook Jersey Ltd	
Tanfern Ltd v Cameron-MacDonald [2000] 1 W.L.R. 1311 CA (Civ Div)	[CDDA 1(1)]

	Provision
Tanner v Everitt [2004] EWHC 1130 (Ch); [2004] B.P.I.R. 1026	IA 262(1)–(3), (8)
Tanner v Millar [2013] EWHC 750 (Ch); [2014] B.P.I.R. 512	IA 339(1)–(3)
Tansoft Ltd, Re [1991] B.C.L.C. 339 Ch D	[CDDA 12C]
Tasarruf Mevduati Sigorta Fonu v Merrill Lynch Bank & Trust Co (Cayman) Ltd [2011] UKPC 17; [2012] 1 W.L.R. 1721	IA Pt III
Tasbian Ltd (No.1), Re [1990] B.C.C. 318 CA (Civ Div)	[CDDA 7(2)]
Tasbian Ltd (No.2), Re [1990] B.C.C. 322 CA (Civ Div)	IR 12.59, [CDDA 21, 22(5)]
Tasbian Ltd (No.3), Re [1992] B.C.C. 358 CA (Civ Div)	IR 12.59, [CDDA 7(2)]
Tate Building Services Ltd v B&M McHugh Ltd [2014] EWHC 2971 (TCC); [2014] B.P.I.R. 1560	IA Pt I
Tay Bok Choon v Tahansan Sdn Bhd [1987] 1 W.L.R. 413; (1987) 3 B.C.C. 132 PC (Malaysia)	IA 122(1)
Taylor (A Bankrupt), Re [2006] EWHC 3029 (Ch); [2007] Ch. 150; [2007] B.P.I.R. 175 Ch D	IA 285(3), (4), 323
Taylor Made Foods Plc Unreported 28 February 2010	IA Sch.B1 para.76, IR 3.54
Taylor Sinclair (Capital) Ltd (In liq.), Re [2002] B.P.I.R. 203 Ch D (Companies Ct)	IA 238(4), 423(1)–(3)
Taylor v Secretary of State for Business, Innovation and Skills [2016] EWHC 1953 (Ch); [2016] 2 B.C.L.C. 350	[CDDA 8A(1), (2)]
Taylor v The Macdonald Partnership [2015] EWCA Civ 921	IA 282(1), (3)
Taylor v Van Dutch Marine Holding Ltd [2017] EWHC 636 (Ch); [2017] 1 W.L.R. 2571	IA Pt III
Taylor v Ziya [2012] B.P.I.R. 1283 Ch D	IA 239(6), 435(2), (8)
Taylor, Noter 1993 S.L.T. 375; [1992] B.C.C. 440	IA Sch.4 paras 2, 3
Taylor's Industrial Flooring Ltd, Re [1990] B.C.C. 44 CA (Civ) Div)	IA 123(1)

Case	Provision
	IR 7.108(1)–(4), 14.1
Total Network SL v Revenue and Customs Commissioners [2008] UKHL 19; [2008] 1 A.C. 1174 [2008] B.P.I.R. 699	IA Pt IX Ch.1
Tottenham Hotspur Plc v Edennote Plc [1994] B.C.C. 681 Ch D	IR 14.1
Tout and Finch Ltd, Re [1954] 1 W.L.R. 178 Ch D	IA 283(2), (3)
Townsend v Biscoe [2010] WL 3166608 Ch D	IA Sch.B1 para.71
Towsey (t/a Towsey Plastering Contractors) v Highgrove Homes Ltd [2013] B.L.R. 45 Ch D (Companies Ct)	IA 123
TPS Investments (UK) Ltd (In admin.), Re [2018] EWHC 360 (Ch)	IA Sch.B1 para.43(6)
Tradegro (UK) Ltd v Wigmore Street Investments Ltd [2011] EWCA Civ 268; [2011] 2 B.C.L.C. 616	IA 107, 130(2)
Trading Partners Ltd, Re. *See* Akers v Lomas	
Tradition (UK) Ltd v Ahmed [2008] EWHC 2946 (Ch); [2009] B.P.I.R. 626	IA 256(1), 262, IR 15.23
Trainfx Ltd, Re; sub nom. Hellenic Capital Investments Ltd v Trainfx Ltd [2015] EWHC 3713 (Ch); [2016] B.C.C. 493	IA Sch.B1 paras 11, 14, 35
Tramway Building & Construction Co Ltd, Re [1988] Ch. 293; (1987) 3 B.C.C. 443 Ch D	IA 127
Transbus International Ltd (In liq.), Re [2004] EWHC 932 (Ch); [2004] 1 W.L.R. 2654; [2004] B.C.C. 401	IA Sch.B1, para.68(2), (3)
Transmetro Corp Ltd v Real Investments Pty Ltd (1999) 17 A.C.L.C. 1314	IA 178(3)
Transocean Equipment Manufacturing & Trading Ltd, Re [2005] EWHC 2603 (Ch); [2006] B.C.C. 184; [2006] B.P.I.R. 594	IA 212(1)
TransTec Automotive (Campsie) Ltd, Re [2001] B.C.C. 403 Ch D (Companies Ct)	IA 37(1), (2)
TransTec Plc, Re [2005] EWHC 1723 (Ch); [2006] B.C.C. 295	[CDDA 1(4)]
TransTec Plc, Re [2006] EWHC 2110 (Ch); [2007] B.C.C. 313	[CDDA 12C]
Transworld Trading Ltd, Re [1999] B.P.I.R. 628 Ch D	IA 239(6)
Travel Mondial (UK) Ltd, Re [1991] B.C.C. 224 Ch D (Companies Ct)	[CDDA 12C]
Treasury Solicitor v Doveton [2008] EWHC 2812 (Ch); [2009] B.P.I.R. 352	IA 423(1)–(3)
Treharne v Forrester [2003] EWHC 2784 (Ch); [2004] B.P.I.R. 338	IA 284(1)–(3), (6)
Trinity Insurance Co Ltd, Re [1990] B.C.C. 235 Ch D (Companies Ct)	IA 123
Trow v Ind Coope (West Midlands) Ltd [1967] 2 Q.B. 899 CA (Civ Div)	IA 86
Trowbridge v Trowbridge [2002] EWHC 3114 (Ch); [2003] 2 F.L.R. 231; [2003] B.P.I.R. 258	IA 423(1)–(3)
Truex v Toll [2009] EWHC 396 (Ch); [2009] 1 W.L.R. 2121; [2009] B.P.I.R. 692	IA 267(1), (2)
Trustee in Bankruptcy of St John Poulton v Ministry of Justice [2010] EWCA Civ 392; [2011] Ch. 1; [2010] B.P.I.R. 775	IA 412(1), (2), (2A), (2B), (6), IR, 10.13
Trustee of the Estate of Bowe (A Bankrupt) v Bowe [1998] 2 F.L.R. 439; [1997] B.P.I.R. 747 Ch D	IA 336(3)–(5)
Trustee of the Property of FC Jones & Sons (A Firm) v Jones [1997] Ch. 159 CA (Civ Div)	IA Second Group of Parts, 283
TS&S Global Ltd v Fithian-Franks [2007] EWHC 1401 (Ch); [2007] B.P.I.R. 424	IA 268, IR 10.5
TSB Bank Plc v Platts (No.1) [1997] B.P.I.R. 151 Ch D	IA 266(3), (4)
TSB Bank Plc v Platts (No.2) [1998] Lloyd's Rep. Bank. 163; [1998] 2 [1998] B.P.I.R. 284 CA (Civ Div)	IA 267(1), (2), 267(4), (5)
TSB Bank v Katz and Katz [1997] B.P.I.R. 147 Ch D	IA 423(4), (5)
TT Industries Ltd, Re [2006] B.C.C. 372; [2006] B.P.I.R. 597 Ch D	IA Sch.B1 para.77(1)
Tucker (A Bankrupt) Ex p. Tucker, Re [1990] Ch. 148 CA (Civ Div)	IA 236, 366(1), 367(3)
Tucker and Spratt v Gold Fields Mining LLC. *See* Gold Fields Mining LLC v Tucker	

Case	Provision
Tucker v Atkins [2013] EWHC 4469 (Ch); [2014] B.P.I.R. 1359	IA 252(2), 279(3)–(5), 303(1)
Tucker v Atkins [2014] EWHC 2260 (Ch); [2014] B.P.I.R. 1569	IA 252(2), 255(1), (2)
Tudor Grange Holdings Ltd v Citibank NA [1992] Ch. 53 Ch D	IA Pt III
Tully (A Bankrupt), Re [2017] NICh 18	IA 303(2)
Tunkers France v Expert France (C-641/16) EU:C:2017:847; [2018] I.L.Pr. 7	[ER art.3]
Turner (A Bankrupt), Re [1974] 1 W.L.R. 1556 Ch D	IA 336(3)–(5)
Turner v Avis [2009] 1 F.L.R. 74; [2008] B.P.I.R. 114 Ch D	IA 335A
Turner v Royal Bank of Scotland Plc (Relitigation) [2000] B.P.I.R. 683 CA (Civ Div)	IR 10.5
Turner v Turner [2006] EWHC 2023 (Ch); [2006] B.P.I.R. 1531	IR 10.5
Turner, Petitioner, 1994 S.L.T. 811; [1993] B.C.C. 299 CSOH	IA 59(1), (2)
Turnstem Ltd, Re [2004] EWHC 1765 (Ch); [2005] 1 B.C.L.C. 388	IA 147(1)
Twinsectra Ltd v Yardley [2002] UKHL 12; [2002] 2 A.C. 164	IA 107
TXU Europe German Finance BV, Re [2005] B.C.C. 90; [2005] B.P.I.R. 209 Ch D (Companies Ct)	IA 221(4), [ER art.3]
TXU Europe Group Plc, Re [2011] EWHC 2072 (Ch); [2012] B.C.C. 363; [2012] B.P.I.R. 463	IA Pt I, 7(4)
TXU UK Ltd (In admin.), Re [2002] EWHC 2784 (Ch); [2003] B.P.I.R. 1062	IA Sch.1
Tymans v Craven [1952] 2 Q.B. 100 CA	IA Pt IV Ch.IX
UIC Insurance Co Ltd (In provisional liq.), Re [2007] B.P.I.R. 589 Ch D	IR 7.33–7.39
UK (Aid) Ltd, Re; GlaxoSmithKline Export Ltd v UK (Aid) Ltd [2003] EWHC 1090 (Ch); [2003] B.P.I.R. 1206	IA 123
UK Coal Operations Ltd, Re [2013] EWHC 2581 (Ch); [2014] 1 B.C.L.C. 471	IA Sch.B1 paras 49, 51
UK Housing Alliance (North West) Ltd, Re; sub nom. Mackay v Kaupthing Singer & Friedlander Ltd [2013] EWHC 2553 (Ch); [2013] B.C.C. 752	IA Sch.B1 para.43
UK Steelfixers Ltd, Re [2012] EWHC 2409 (Ch); [2012] B.C.C. 751	IA Sch.B1 paras 2, 13(1), (3)
UK-Euro Group Plc, Re [2006] EWHC 2102 (Ch); [2007] 1 B.C.L.C. 812	IA 124A
UKLI Ltd, Re; sub nom. Secretary of State for Business, Innovation and Skills v Chohan [2013] EWHC 680 (Ch); [2013] Lloyd's Rep. F.C. 351	[CDDA 22(5)]
Ultimate Invoice Finance Ltd, Petitioner [2017] CSOH 72; 2017 S.L.T. 791; 2017 G.W.D. 15-243	IA Sch.B1 para.17
Ultra Motorhomes International Ltd, Re [2005] EWHC 872 (Ch); [2006] B.C.C. 57; [2006] B.P.I.R. 115	[ER arts 3(1), 6, 84]
Unadkat & Co (Accountants) Ltd v Bhardwaj [2006] EWHC 2785 (Ch); [2007] B.C.C. 452	IR 7.108(1)–(4)
Unidare Plc v Cohen [2005] EWHC 1410 (Ch); [2006] Ch. 489	IA 245(3)–(5), 435(6), (7), (9)–(11), Sch.B1 para.74
Unigreg Ltd, Re [2005] B.P.I.R. 220 Ch D	IA 238(4)
Unit 2 Windows Ltd (In liq.), Re [1985] 1 W.L.R. 1383; [1985] (1985) 1 B.C.C. 99489 Ch D	IA 59(1), (2)
United Drug (UK) Holdings Ltd v Bilcare Singapore Pte Ltd [2013] EWHC 4335 (Ch)	[CBIR Sch.1 art.20.6]
UOC Corp (No.1), Re; sub nom. Alipour v Ary [1997] 1 W.L.R. 534; [1997] B.C.C. 377 CA (Civ Div)	IA 123, 124(1), 135
UOC Corp (No.2), Re; sub nom. Alipour v UOC Corp (No.2) [1998] B.C.C. 191 Ch D (Companies Ct)	IR 7.33–7.39
Upton v Taylor [1999] B.P.I.R. 168 Ch D	IR 18.22
Vadher v Weisgard [1997] B.C.C. 219; [1998] B.P.I.R. 295 Ch D	IA 375(2)
Vaidya v Wijayawardhana [2010] EWHC 716 (Ch); [2010] B.P.I.R. 1016	IR 10.5
Van Buggenhout and Van de Mierop (Liquidators of Grontimmo SA) v Banque Internationale a Luxembourg	

Statutes Table

Provision

Provision

	Provision
(5)	IA 57(1A), (2A)–(2C)
s.4(1)	IA 1(2)
(2)	IA 1(2), 7(1), (2), 230
(3)	IA Sch.B1 paras 49(3), 73
(4)	IA 4, Sch.B1 para.73
(a)	IA 4(4)
(5)	IA Sch.B1 para.73
(6)	IA 5(3), (4), Sch.8 para.6, IR 2.25–2.38
(7)	IA 4, 4(4)
s.4A	IA 4(1), 4A(1), 7(5)
(2)	IA 5
(b)	IA 3
(5)	IA 4A
(6)	IA 4A(2), (3), (4), (6), IR 2.25–2.38
(6A)	IR 2.25–2.38
s.5	IA 3, 6(5)
(2)	IA 4, 5, 6(2)
(a)	IR 2.40, 2.39–2.44, [ER art.2(6)]
(b)	IA 5(2)
(2A)(a)	IA 7B
(3)(a)	IA 5(3), (4)
(b)	IA 5(3), (4)
(4)	IA 6(3)
s.6	IA 5, 5(3), (4), 6(1), 6(2), 6(3), 6(5), 6(7), IR 2.9, 2.25–2.38, 12.27, 15.15
(1)(b)	IA 6, 6(1)
(2)	IA 6
(c)	IA 6
(3)	IA 6, 6(7), 7B
(4)	IA 4, 6(1), 6(5)
(5)	IA 6(4)
(6)	IA 5
(7)	IA 6
s.6A	IA 6, 262A(1), (2)
s.7(2)	IA 1(2), 7(4)
(3)	IA 6
(4)	IA 1(2), 6(4), IR 7.14–7.24
(b)	IA 7(2), 124, Sch.B1 para.12(1), (4)
(5)	IA 230
(b)	IA 7(5)
(6)	IA 1(2), 231
s.7A	IA 7A(1)
(2)	IA 7A(8), (9)
(4)(b)	IA 124
(5)	IA 7A(6)
(7)	IA 7A(6)
Pt II	IA 175, 176ZB, 241, 242, 246ZC, 246ZD, Sch.B1, para.1, Sch.B1 paras 2, 9, 10, 11, 12(2), 13(1), (3), 22, 25, 46(4), (6), 47, 47(1), 47(2), (5), 65(2), 73, 83, 84, 85, 104, Sch.1, IR 3.1, 3.3–3.10, [CDDA Sch.1]
s.8	IA 140, Sch.B1 para.1, para.111, Sch.1, [CDDA 7(2)]
(1)	IA Sch.B1 paras 11, 39, 111(1), 111(1A), 111(1B)
(b)	IA Sch.B1 paras 11, 39
(2)	IA Sch.B1 paras 11, 39, 111(1), 111(1A), 111(1B)
(3)	IA Pt II, 230
(5)(b)	IA Pt II
ss.8–27	IA Pt II
s.9	IA 1(1), 7(4), Pt III, 29(2)
(1)	IA Sch.B1 para.12(1), (4)
(3)	IA Sch.B1 paras 14(2), (3), 39
(4)	[CDDA 7(2)]
s.10	IA 248
(1)	IA 248
s.11	IA 248, 429(2)–(4), Sch.B1 para.43(6)
(3)	IA 246(3), 248, Sch.B1 paras 43
(c)	IA Sch.B1 para.43(6)
(5)	IA 40(1), (2)
s.12	IA 188, Sch.B1 para.45
s.14	IA Sch.1
(1)(a)	IA Sch.1
(2)	IA Sch.1
(3)	IA Sch.B1 para.68(2), (3)
(5)	IA 44(1), (2)
s.15	IA Pt III, 43(1), (2), Sch.1
(2)	IA 248
s.17(1)	IA Sch.B1 para.67
(2)	IA Sch.1
(a)	IA Sch.B1 para.68(2), (3)
s.18	IA 240(1), (3)
(1)	IA Sch.1
(2)	IA Sch.1
s.19	IA 37(1), (2), 44(1), (2), 57(1A), (2A)–(2D), Sch.B1, paras 99(3)–(4), 99(5)–(6)
(1)	IA Sch.B1 para.87
(4)–(10)	IA Sch.B1 para.99, para.99(5), (6)
(10)	IA Sch.B1 para.99(5)–(6)
s.20(2)	IA 174(6)
(3)	IA 174(6)
s.21	IA Sch.B1 para.46
s.22	IA 2(3), 3(2), 131, 131(1)
(5)	IA Sch.B1 para.48(2), (3)
s.23	IA Sch.1
s.25	IA Sch.B1 para.54
s.26	IA 101, 141
s.27	IA 6
Pt III	IA 212(2), 443, [CBIR reg.3, art.2]
s.28	IA 29(2)
ss.28–49	IA 28
s.29	IA 72A
(1)	IA 29(1)
(2)	IA Pt III, 42(1), 251, 388(4), Sch.B1 para.14, IR 4.2
(b)	IA 43(7)
s.30	IA 230, 232, 388(4), 390(1)

	Provision
s.88	IA 127
s.89	IA 73, IR 5.1
(1)	IA 95(1), 97(1)
(2)	IA 89(1)
(3)	IR 5.1
s.90	IA 73, 89
Pt IV Ch.III (ss.91–96)	IA 90
s.91	IA 114(1), (2)
(2)	IA 103, 114(1), (2)
ss.91–92	IA 91(1)
s.92(3)	IA 93
s.92A	IA 93, IR 18.2
(1)	IA 92A
s.93	IA 92A, 105(1)
s.94	IR 18.14
(5)	IA 171(6)
s.95	IA 105(4)
(2)	IA 105(4)
(3)(a)	IA 131
(4)	IA 96
s.96	IA 97(2), 105(4)
Pt IV Ch.IV (ss.97–106)	IA 90, 97(1)
s.97(2)	IA 96
s.98	IA 166
s.99	IA 2(3), 3(2), 95(4), 96, 131
s.100	IA 96, 139, 165(1), 166(2)
(2)	IA 171(1), (2)
(3)	IA 104
(4)	IA 100
s.101	IA 96, 141, Sch.B1 para.57
(1)	IR 17.2
s.102	IA 96
s.103	IA 101, IR 17.2
s.104	IA 108
s.104A	IA 105, IR 18.2
(1)	IA 104A
s.105(1)	IA 105(4)
ss.105–108	IA 77
s.106	IR 18.14
(5)	IA 171(6)
Pt IV Ch.V (ss.107–116)	IA 90
s.107	IA 6(1), 115, 143(1), 148(1), 154, 165(5), Sch.B1 paras 1, 65(1), 67, 74, IR 14.12
s.108	IA 171(3), 171(4)
(2)	IA 171(3)
s.109	IA 130(1), IR1.10–1.15
s.110	IA Pt I, IR 17.2, 18.3–18.13
s.111	IA 110(3), 110(5)
(1)	IA 110, Sch.B1 para.71
s.112	IA 112(2), 130(2), 165(4), 167(3), Sch.B1 paras 99, 99(3)–(4), IR 6.2–6.9, 7.108(1)–(4),18.34
(1)	IA 115, 128
s.114	IA 166, 166(1)
(2)	IA 91(2)
(3)	IA 91(2),166(3)
s.115	IA 107, 156, 238, Sch.B1 para.1, Sch.4 para.3A
s.117	IA 120, 216(5), 220, [CDDA 2(2)]
(7)	IA 120
s.118	IA 120
s.119	IA 120
s.120	IA 117, 216(5), 220, [CDDA 2(2)]
s.121	IA 117
s.122	IA 73, 123(2), 221(5)
(1)(e)	IA 124(2)–(4A)
(fa)	IA 124(2)–(4A)
(g)	IA 122(1), 124(1), IR Pt 7, [ER art.1]
(2)	IA 221(7)
s.123	IA 122(1), 124(1), Pt VI, 163, 240(2), Sch.B1 paras 11, 27(2), (3), IR 7.2–7.3, [CDDA 6(2)]
(1)	[CDDA 6(2)]
(a)	IA 222, IR 7.2–7.3
(b)–(e)	IA 224
(e)	IA 214(6)
(2)	IA 216(6), 123(1), 224(2)
s.124	IA 1(1), 7(4), Sch.B1 paras 13, 13(1), (3), Sch.1, IR 7.4–7.12
(1)	[CBIR Sch.1 art.11]
(2)	IA 125(1), 172(1), (2), 212(5)
(3)	IA 4(6), 172(1), (2), 212(5)
(3A)	IA 122(1)
s.124A	IA 87(1), 91(1), 122(1), 135, 220, 441, IR Pt 7, 7.4–7.12, [ER art.1]
s.125	IA 116, 122(1), 123(2)
(1)	IA 147(1)
s.126	IA 130(2)
(1)	IA 128, 130(2)
s.127	IA 88, 122(1), 125(2), 129, 135, 175(2)(a), 284, Sch.A1, Sch.B1 paras 13(1), (3), 37(3)(a)–(c), 40(1), Sch.4 para.6, [ER 31]
ss.127–129	IA 130(1)
s.128	IA 130(2), 176(1), 176(2), 183(1)
s.129	IA 86, 127, 176(2), 183(1), 214(2), 240(1), (3), 247(2), IR 14.3–14.11, [ER art.2(7), (8)]
(1A)	IA 127, Sch.B1 para.13(1), (3)
(2)	[ER art.2(7), (8)]
s.130(1)	IA 147(1)
(2)	IA 126, 128
(3A)	IA 130
s.131	IA 2(3), 3(2), 95(4), 99, 210, Sch.B1 para.47]
(1)	IA 131(5)
(6)	IA131(3)
s.132	IA 131(2), 133(1)
s.133	IA 134, 198, 235, 236, 290, 366(1), IR 7.98–7.107, Pt 12 Ch.4 sub-div.B
(1)	IA 133(2), (4), 206(3)

	Provision
s.134	IA 133, IR 7.98–7.107, Pt 12 Ch.4 sub-div.B
s.135	IA 286(1), (2), IR 7.33–7.39
(4)	IA Sch.4
s.136	IA 137, 138, 140(1), (2), IR 7.52–7.57, 7.60
(2)	IA 144(2)
(3)	IA 144(2)
(4)	IA 137(1), 141(1), (2)
(5)	IA 131(2)
(c)	IA 137
s.135	IA 131
s.136	IA 137, 139
(5)(c)	IA 136(4), (5)
s.137	IA 136, 138, 139, IR 7.60
(2)	IA 138(5)
(5)	IA 141(1), (2)
s.138(1)	IA 131
s.139	IA 131, 140(1), (2), 141(1), (2), IR 7.60
(4)(a)	IA 172(3)
s.140	IA 131, 131(1), 136(1), 141(1), (2)
(1)	IA 172(3), IR 17.29
(3)	IA 141(1), (2)
s.141	IA 101, 142, IR 7.52–7.57
(3)	IR 17.6
(3A)	IR 17.2
(4)	IR 17.28
(5)	IA 165(6), IR 17.28
ss.141–142	IA Sch.B1 para.57
s.142	IA 101
s.143	IA Sch.B1 para.65(1)
(1)	IA 144(1), IR 7.117–7.118
s.144	IA 107
s.145	IA 306
s.146	IA Sch.B1 paras 65(1), 99(3)–(4), IR 18.14
(2)	IR 7.69–7.72
(6)	IA 146A
(7)	IA 146A
s.147	IA 5(3), (4), 112(1), (2), 125(1), Sch.B1 para.38(2)
s.148	IR 7.76, 7.79–7.80
s.149(1)	IA 149(2)
(2)	IA 149(1), 149(2)
s.150	IA 149(1), IR 7.86–7.91
s.153	IA 160
s.154	IA 150(2), IR 7.117–7.118
s.156	IA 115, 148(1), IR 3.51
s.160	IA 148(1), 165(4), IR 17.2
(1)	IA 150(1), 153
(b)	IR 7.76, 7.79–7.80, 7.117–7.118
(c)	IR 7.78
(d)	IR 7.86–7.91
(d)	IA 161
(2)	IA 148(1), 150(1), 165(4), IR 7.81–7.85, 7.86–7.91, 7.117–7.118
s.162(2)	IA 162
(3)	IA 162
s.164	IR 7.75
s.165	IA 166(2), Sch.4, IR 17.2
(2)	IA 165
(a)	IA 165
(3)	IA 165
(4)(c)	IA 165
ss.165–167	IA Sch.4
s.166	IA 100, 114, 114(1), (2), 165, Sch.4
(1A)	IA 166
(2)	IA 166(3)
s.167	IR 7.77, 17.2
(1)	IA 87(1), 167
(a)	IA 141(4), (5)
(2)	IA 141(4), (5)
s.168	IA 420(1), Sch.4
(5)	IA 167(3)
s.169	IA Sch.4
s.170	IA 192(2), [CDDA 3(3)]
s.171	IA 172(3), IR 7.63–7.66
(1)	IA Sch.B1 para.91(1)
(2)	IA 171(3)
(3)	IA 172(3)
s.172	IA 171, IR 7.63–7.66
(1)	IA 108, 212(5), IR 3.64, 7.63–7.66
(2)	IA 108, 172(3), 172(4), 212(5), IR 3.64
(3)(b)	IA 172(4)
s.173	IA 174(1), 212(4), Sch.B1 para.98(2)
(2)	IA 174(4)
(4)	IA 173(1), 174(6)
s.174	IA 173(1), 212(4), 299(1), (2), Sch.8 paras 12, 14
(3)	IA 146(1)
Pt IV Ch VIII	IA 149(2), Sch.8 paras 12, 14, IR 14.25
s.175	IA 40(1), (2), 107, 115, 149(2), Sch.B1 para.65(2), IR 14.3–14.11, 14.25
(2)(a)	IA Sch.B1 para.65(2)
(b)	IA 107, 175, 251
s.176	IA 115, 128
(2A)	IA176(2)
(3)	IA 107, 176(2)
s.176ZA	IA 107, 115, 175, Sch.B1 para.65(2), IR 7.108–7.110, 7.108(1)–(4), 7.111–7.116
(3)	IR 7.108(1)–(4)
s.176ZB	IA 127, 238, 239, 242, 243, Sch.1, Sch.4 para.6
(2)(b)	IA 214(1)
(3)(a)	IA 213(2)
(g)	IA 244
s.176A	IA 40(1), (2), 107, Pt XII, 420(1), Sch.B1 paras 3, 3(2), (4), 52, 65(2), 65(3), 78(1)–(2A), 98(3), IR 3.50, 4.22–4.24, 7.108(1)–(4), 10.148, 12.14, 12.15, 14.15–14.19, 14.26–14.31, 18.33, [CBIR Sch.1 art.22]

	Provision
s.333	IA 288(4), 363(2), (4)
(2)	IA 307(1), 307(3), IR 6.202, 10.125, 10.126
(4)	IA 349
s.334	IR 10.150–10.153
(3)	IA 334(1)
s.335A	IA 336(3)–(5), 337(4)–(6), 363(2), (4)
(3)	IA 336(3)–(5)
s.336	IA 335A, 421A
(4)	IA 336(2), 337(4)–(6)
(5)	IA 337(4)–(6)
ss.336–338	IA Second Group of Parts, 313
s.337(2)(a)	IA 337(4)–(6)
s.339	IA 238, 238(3), 238(4), 283A, 341(1), 342D(3)–(8), 342E(1), (2), 343(6), 382(3), (4), 423 (1)–(3)
(1)	IA 340(1), (2)
(2)	IA 340(1), (2), 342(1)
(3)	IA 423(1)–(3)
ss.339–341	IA 339
ss.339–342	IA 342D(1), (2)
s.340	IA 238, 239, 341(1), 342D(3)–(8), 342E(1), (2), 382(3), (4), 423
(2)	IA 342(1)
(3)(b)	IA 340(4), (5)
(5)	IA 341(1), 341(2), (3), 435(1), 435(4)
s.341	IA 339(1)–(3)
(1)	IA 341(2), (3)
s.342	IA 241
(1)	IA 425(1)
s.342A	IA 281A, 342B(1), 342B(2), (3), 342C(3), 423(1)–(3)
ss.342A–342C	IA 306, 342A
s.342B	IA 342A(7), (8)
s.342C	IA 342A(7), (8)
ss.342D–342F	IA 342A
s.343	IA 244, 322(2)
s.344(1)	IA 344(3)
s.345	IA 186
s.346	IA 183, 285(1), IR 12.57
s.347	IA 285(1), 328
s.348(2)	IA 348(5), (6)
s.349A	IR 17.2
s.350	IA 353(1), (2), 354(1), 355, 356(2), 357(2), 358, 359(1), 360(1)
(2)	IA 282(4)
s.351	IA 356(2), 358, 359(2)
(a)	IA 353(1), (2), 354(1), 357(1), (3), 359(1)
(b)	IA 354(1), 355(1), (2), 359(1)
(c)	IA 354(1), 355(1), (2), 359(1)
s.352	IA 206(4), 353(3), 354(1), 354(2), 355, 356(1), 357(2), 358, 359(1), 360(1)
ss.352–362	IA 351
s.353	IA 307(1), 351, 352
ss.353–362	IA 352
s.354	IA 351, 418(1)
(1)	IA 354(2)
s.355	IA 251P, 351
s.356	IA 351
(2)	IA 356(1)
s.357	IA 251, 351, 352
(1)	IA 357(2)
s.358	IA 351
s.359	IA 351
(1)	IA 359(2)
(2)	IA 359(1)
s.360	IA 251S, 429(2)–(4), 429(5), Sch.A1
(1)	IA 360(4)
s.361	IA 351
(3)	IA 355
(4)	IA 355
s.362	IA 351
s.363	IA 303(1)
(1)	IA 377
s.364	IA 366(1)
(3)	IA 418(1)
s.365	IA 371(1)
s.366	IA 133, 236, 367(3), 367(4), 368, 369(1), (2), (6), 369(7), IR Pt 12 Ch.4 sub-div.B
ss.366–367	IA 367(3)
s.367	IA 366(1), 368, 369(7), IR Pt 12 Ch.4 sub-div.B
s.368	IA 369(7)
s.369	IA 10.118–10.120
(1)	IA 369(4), (5)
s.370	IA 287(1), (2), IR 10.94–10.98
s.371	IR 10.166
s.372	IA 233, 373(1)
s.372A	IA 233A, 372
s.373	IA 363(1)
(2)	IA 375(3)
s.374	IA 373(3)
s.375	IA 255(1), (2), 263I, 282(1), (3), IR 12.58, 12.59
(1)	IA 282(1), (3), 375(2), 377
(2)	IA 375(1), [CDDA 1(1)]
s.376	IA 262(1)–(3), (8), 283A(5), (6), IR 1.3, Sch.5
s.377	IA Sch.5, IR 17.27
s.379ZA	IA 379ZC, IR 15.1, 15.3, 15.6
s.379ZB	IA 379ZC, IR Pt 15, 15.7
s.379A	IR 15.43
s.379B	IR 1.49
s.379C	IA 383A, IR 1.39
(1)	IR 14.1
(2)	IR 14.1
Pt XI	IA 436
ss.380–385	IR 1.2
ss.381–385	IA 380

Statutory Instruments Table

Provision

(3) . . . IA Sch.6

Deregulation Act 2015 and Small Business, Enterprise and Employment Act 2015 (Consequential Amendments) (Savings) Regulations 2017 (SI 2017/540) . . . IA 421(1), (1A), (1B), (2)

Disqualified Directors Compensation Orders (Fees) (England and Wales) Order 2016 (SI 2016/1047) . . . [CDDA 15A–15C]

Disqualified Directors Compensation Orders (Fees) (Scotland) Order 2016 (2016/1048) . . . [CDDA 15A–15C]

Education (Company Directors Disqualification Act 1986: Amendments to Disqualification Provisions) (England) Regulations 2004 (SI 2004/3264) . . . [CDDA 1]

Education (Disqualification Provisions: Bankruptcy and Mental Health) (England) Regulations 2006 (SI 2006/2198) . . . [CDDA 11]

Education (Student Loans) (Repayment) (Amendment) Regulations 2010 (SI 2010/661) . . . IA 281(2)–(6), (8), 283(6)

Education (Student Loans) (Repayment) Regulations 2009 (SI 2009/470) . . . IA 281(2)–(6), (8)

reg.80 . . . IA 281(2)–(6), (8), 283(6)

Education (Student Support) (No.2) Regulations 2002 (SI 2002/3200)

reg.39 . . . IA 283(6)

Education (Student Support) (No.2) Regulations 2002 (Amendment) (No.3) Regulations 2004 (SI 2004/2041)

reg.5 . . . IA 281(2)–(6), (8), 283(6)

Electricity Act 1989 (Commencement No.2) Order 1990 (SI 1990/117 (C. 4)) . . IA 372(4), (5)

Electricity and Gas (Smart Meters Licensable Activity) Order 2012 (SI 2012/2400)

art.29 . . . IA Sch.2A

Energy Administration Rules 2005 (SI 2005/2483) . . . IA 411(1), (1A), (1B), (2), (2A), (2B), (2C), (2D), (7), Sch.B1

Energy Supply Company Administration Rules 2013 (SI 2013/1046) . . . IA Sch.B1

Energy Supply Company Administration (Scotland) Rules 2013 (SI 2013/1047) . . . IA Sch.B1

Enterprise Act 2002 (Commencement No.3, Transitional and Transitory Provisions and Savings) Order 2003 (SI 2003/1397)

art.1 . . . [CDDA, 8A(1), (2), (2A), 9A, 16, 17, 18(2A)]

art.2(1) . . . [CDDA, 8A(1), (2), (2A), 9A, 16, 17, 18(2A)]

Sch. . . [CDDA, 8A(1), (2), (2A) 9A, 16, 17, 18(2A)]

Provision

Enterprise Act 2002 (Commencement No.4 and Transitional Provisions and Savings) Order 2003 (SI 2003/2093) . . . IA Pt III, Sch.B1 para.1

art.2(1) . . . IA Pt II, Sch.A1, Sch.B1

art.3 . . . IA 212(1), 230, 231, 232, 240(1), (3), 243, 245, Sch.A1

(1) . . . IA Pt II

(2) . . . IA Pt II

(3) . . . IA Pt II, Sch.B1 para.9

art.4 . . . IA Pt XII, Sch.6

Sch.1 . . . IA Pt II, Sch.A1, Sch.B1

Enterprise Act 2002 (Disqualification from Office: General) Order 2006 (SI 2006/1722) . . . [CDDA 11]

Enterprise Act 2002 (Insolvency) Order 2003 (SI 2003/2096) . . . IA 62(6), 84(2A), (2B), 422(1), (1A), [CDDA 21(2)]

art.1 . . . IA Sch.B1 paras 12(5), 43

art.2(1) . . . IA Sch.B1 paras 12(5), 43

(2) . . . IA Sch.B1 para.12(5)

(3) . . . IA Sch.B1 para.43

Enterprise Act 2002 (Insolvency) Order 2004 (SI 2004/2312) . . . IA Sch.A1

Enterprise and Regulatory Reform Act 2013 (Commencement No. 9 and Saving Provisions) Order 2016 (SI 2016/191) . . IA Pt IX

Enterprise and Regulatory Reform Act 2013 (Competition) (Consequential, Transitional and Saving Provisions) Order 2014 (SI 2014/892)

Sch.1 paras 52–54 . . . [CDDA 9A]

para.54 . . . [CDDA 9D]

Enterprise and Regulatory Reform Act 2013 (Consequential Amendments) (Bankruptcy) and the Small Business, Enterprise and Employment Act 2015 (Consequential Amendments) Regulations 2016 (SI 2016/481) . . . IA Pt IX

reg.2 . . . [CDDA 11]

Sch.1 para.8 . . . [CDDA 11]

European Communities (Recognition of Professional Qualifications) Regulations 2007 (SI 2007/2781) . . . IA 390

European Co-operative Society Regulations 2006 (SI 2006/2078) . . . IA

reg.33(1) . . . IA 124C

(2) . . . IA 124(2)–(4A)

European Economic Interest Grouping Regulations 19889 (SI 1989/638)

reg.20 . . . [CDDA, 1]

European Grouping of Territorial Cooperation Regulations 2007 (SI 2007/1949)

reg.7 . . . IA 220

Sch. Pt 2 . . . IA 220

Provision

	Provision
r.7	IR
Pt 1	IR Pt 3, Pt 6, Pt 7
r.1.2	IA 251, IR 1.1, 2.1, 2.10, 2.34, 3.28, 10.80, 10.142, 10.143, 14.3–14.11, Pt 15, 15.13, 15.21, 21.1–21.3
(2)	IR 1.55, 1.57, 3.1, 3.2, 3.16–3.19, 3.20–3.22, 3.23–3.26, 4.3, 4.16, 15.1, 15.17, 15.32, 15.34, 16.3, 16.1–16.7, 17.22, 17.25
(3)	IR 2.34, 15.21
rr.1.2 et seq.	IA Sch.8 paras 12, 14
r.1.5	IR 1.35
r.1.6	IR 1.10–1.15, 1.15–1.18, 1.19–1.27, 1.35
rr.1.10–1.12	IR 3.27, 3.38, 3.56, 4.5, 4.14, 7.4–7.12, 7.14–7.24, 7.33–7.39, 7.59, 7.98–7.107, 20.1–20.7, 22.4, 22.5
rr.1.10–1.13	IR 15.3
rr.1.10–1.18	IR 14.31
r.1.11	IR 18.3–18.13, 20.1–20.7
r.1.13	IR 20.1–20.7
r.1.15	IR 3.35(10), 3.26, 7.59, 7.98–7.107
rr.1.15–1.18	IR 18.3–18.13
r.1.16	IR 3.35(10), 3.26, 7.59, 7.98–7.107
r.1.18	IR 3.35(10), 3.26, 7.59, 7.98–7.107
r.1.19	IR 1.28–1.34, 7.59
rr.1.19–1.22	IR, 7.69–7.72, 18.3–18.13
rr.1.21–1.26	IR 1.28–1.34, 7.59
r.1.22	IR 7.59
r.1.23(2)	IR 1.37
rr.1.28 et seq.	IA Sch.B1 para.46
r.1.35	IR 7.86–7.91
r.1.37(2)(a)	IA 136(4), (5), 246C
rr.1.37–1.39	IA 248A
r.1.38(2)	IR 1.39
r.1.42	IA Sch.B1 para.26
rr.1.42–1.44	IR 1.36
r.1.44	IA Sch.B1 para.26
r.1.45	IA 137(4), (5), Sch.B1 para.46
r.1.47	IA 379B
r.1.48(2)	IA 246B
rr.1.48–149	IA 246B
r.1.49	IA 379B, IR 1.50
r.1.50	IA 137(4)(5), IR 1.49
r.1.52	IR 1.36
Pt 2	IA Pt I
r.2.1	IR 1.2
r.2.3	IA 1(3), 2(3), 3(2)
(i)	IA 2(2)
(h)	IA 2(2)
r.2.4	IA 2(3)
r.2.5	IA 3(2)
r.2.6	IA 2(3), 2.11
r.2.7	IA 2(2)
r.2.9	IA 2(2)
r.2.12	IA 2(2)
r.2.25	IA 3
(1)	IR 2.26
(2)	IR 2.30
(3)	IR 2.26
(6)	IR 1.49
rr.2.25–2.29	IA 3(2)
r.2.26	IR 2.25
r.2.27	IR 2.25, 2.29
r.2.28	IA 5
(2)	IR 2.39–2.44
r.2.29	IA 3, 4(5)
r.2.30	IR 2.25, 2.26
r.2.33	IA 7(1), (2)
r.2.35	IA 5(2)
r.2.36	IA 5(2)
r.2.38	IR 2.25
(3)	IA 4(6), (6A)
(6)	IA Pt I, 4(6), (6A) Sch.8 para.6
r.2.40	IA 6
r.2.44(1)	IA Pt I
(2)	IA Pt I
r.2.45	IA 7(1), (2)
r.2.67	IR 7.108(1)–(4)
Pt 3	IA Pt II, Sch.B1 para.10, IR 3.27
r.3.1	IR Pt 4, 4.1
r.3.2	IR 3.3–3.10
r.3.3	IA Sch.B1 para.12, IR 3.2, Pt 4, 4.1, 4.2
r.3.5	IA Sch.B1 para.12
r.3.6	IA Sch.B1 paras 13, 38, IR 3.52
r.3.7	IA Sch.B1 para.12(2)
r.3.11(1)	IA Sch.B1 para.36
(2)	IA Sch.B1 para.36
r.3.14	IA Sch.B1 paras 37, 38
r.3.15(3)	IA Sch.B1 para.13(1), (3)
r.3.16	IA Sch.B1 paras 14, 18
r.3.18(3)	IA Sch.B1 para.20
r.3.19	IA Sch.B1 para.20
r.3.20	IA Sch.B1 para.19
(9)(d)	IA Sch.B1 para.19
rr.3.20 et seq.	IA Sch.B1 para.18
r.3.23	IA Sch.B1 paras 22, 26(2), (3), 29
(j)	IA Sch.B1 para.22
(4)	IA Sch.B1 para.26(2), (3)
(6)(b)	IA Sch.B1 para.27(2), (3)
r.3.24	IA Sch.B1 para.29, (2), (6)
r.3.26	IA Sch.B1 para.32
r.3.27	IA Sch.B1 para.46
(1)	IA Sch.B1 para.46(2)
(2)	IA Sch.B1 para.46(5)
(3)	IA Sch.B1 para.46(5)
r.3.29(3)	IA Sch.B1 para.47(1)
r.3.31	IA Sch.B1 para.47(2), (5)
r.3.33	IA Sch.B1 para.48
r.3.34	IA Sch.B1 para.47(2), (5)
r.3.35(1)(d)	IA Sch.B1 para.49
(h)	IA Sch.B1 para.49

	Provision
r.7.38	IA 135, IR 18.28
r.7.39	IA Sch.B1 para.17
r.7.40	IA 131
r.7.41	IR 7.47
r.7.43	IR 7.40–7.42
r.7.45	IR 7.43, 7.46, 7.108(1)–(4)
r.7.46	IA 235(5), IR 7.46
r.7.47	IR 7.46
r.7.48	IA 136(4), (5)
r.7.51	IA 147(3)
r.7.52	IA 136(4), (5)
r.7.53	IA 100
rr.7.53 et seq.	IA 139
r.7.56	IA 140
r.7.57	IA 137
r.7.58	IR 4.4
r.7.59	IA 109(1)
r.7.60	IA 136(4), (5), 137
r.7.61	IA 146, 171(5), 172(6)
(7)	IR 7.69–7.72
rr.7.61–7.66	IR 7.67–6.68
r.7.63	IA 174(4)
r.7.65	IA 108, 172(1), (2)
r.7.66	IA 172(4)
r.7.68	IA 172(5)
r.7.69	IR 7.63–7.66
r.7.70	IA 174(2), (3), (4)
r.7.73	IA 171, 172(5), 172(8)
r.7.76	IA 160
r.7.78	IA 160, 234(1), (2)
r.7.79	IA 148(1), 150(1), 160
r.7.86	IA 150(1), 160
r.7.87	IA 150(1)
r.7.88	IR 7.86–7.91
rr.7.93 et seq.	IA 177(5)
r.7.98	IA 133, (2), (3), 134
rr.7.98 et seq.	Pt 12 Ch.4 sub-div.B
r.7.101(4)	IA 133(2), (3)
r.7.105	IA 133(4)
(1)	IA 133
r.7.108	IA 115, 148(1), 156, 176A, Sch.4 para.3A, IR 3.51, 6.42, 6.43
(2)	IA 115, 175(2)(a)
(4)(j)	IR 7.108(1)–(4)
(m)	IR 17.24, 7.108(1)–(4)
r.7.109	IR 7.108(1)–(4)
r.7.110	IA 115
r.7.111	IA 176ZA, (1), (3), Sch.4 para.3A, IR 7.113(2)
rr.7.111–7.116	IR 6.44–6.48, 7.108–7.110, 7.108(1)–(4)
rr.7.111 et seq.	IA 176ZA
rr.7.112–7.116	IR 7.108–7.110
r.7.114(4)(c)	IR 113(2)
r.7.115	IR 7.113(2)

	Provision
r.7.116	IR 7.113(2)
r.7.117	IA154
r.7.119	IA 203(3)–(4), (6), (7)
Pt 8	IR Pt 2, 8.2, 8.3, 8.5, 8.7, 8.8, 8.9, 8.11, 8.13, 8.15, 8.17, 8.18, 8.22, 8.23, 8.24, 8.25, 8.26, 8.27, 8.29, 8.30, 8.31
rr.8.1–8.38	IA Pt VIII
r.8.3	IA256(1)
rr.8.3–8.7	IA 253(1)–(3)
r.8.5	IA 256(2)
r.8.7	IA 256(2)
r.8.8	IA 253(4)
r.8.13	IA 256(5)
r.8.15	IA 256(1)
r.8.17	IA 256(1), (3), (3A), 256(5)
rr.8.19–8.21	IA 256A
r.8.20–8.21	IA 373(1)
r.8.22	IA 257(2), (2A), (2B), (3), 258(6)
r.8.24	IR 1.49
r.8.25	IA 263(5), (6)
r.8.26	IA 263(5), (6)
r.8.27	IA 262
r.8.28	IR 8.29
r.8.29	IA 263(5), (6)
r.8.31	IA 263(5), (6)
r.8.32	IA 261(2)
rr.8.32–8.35	IR 8.36
Pt 9	IA Sch.4ZA
r.9.2	IA 251A, 251G, 382(3), (4)
rr.9.2–9.20	IA Pt 7A
r.9.3	IA 251B
r.9.4	IA 251B
r.9.5	IA 251B
r.9.6	IA 251C, 251D
r.9.7	IA 251C
r.9.8	IA 251C
r.9.9	IA 251C
r.9.10	IA 251E
r.9.11	IA 251E
r.9.12	IA 251E
r.9.13	IA 251C, 251K
r.9.14	IA 251K
r.9.15	IA 251K, IR Pt 9
r.9.16	IA 251K
r.9.17	IA 251L
r.9.18	IA 251L
r.9.19	IA 251J
r.9.20	IA 251H
r.9.21	IA 251M
r.9.22	IA 251M, 251N
r.9.23	IA 251A, 271(3)
r.9.24	IA 251M
rr.10.1–10.5	IA 268
r.10.4	IR 10.5
r.10.5(4)(c)	IA 269

	Provision
r.10.13	IR 10.25
r.10.16	IA 271, 313(2)–(4)
r.10.17	IA 268
r.10.26	IR 12.64
rr.10.21	IA 271
r.10.24	IA 271
rr.10.24–10.56	IA Pt IX, IR 10.26
r.10.25	IA 307(1)
r.10.26	IA 307(1), IR 10.24
r.10.32	IA 278
r.10.35	IR Sch.7
r.10.37	IA 374(2), (3)
r.10.39	IA 263K
r.10.40	IA 263K
rr.10.42–10.44	IA 263N
r.10.43	IA 278
r.10.45	IA 263M
r.10.46	IA 263M
r.10.47	IA 263H
r.10.48	IA 263H, 263N
rr.10.49–10.56	IA 286(1)
rr.10.55–10.61	IA 288(2)
r.10.56	IA 288(1), (2A), (3)
r.10.58	IA 288(1), (2A), (3)
rr.10.59–10.61	IR 10.63–10.65
r.10.64	IA 423
rr.10.67–10.75	IA 292(1)
rr.10.70–10.72	IR 10.73
r.10.72	IA 296(1)–(3), 300(3), (4)
r.10.74	IA 292(4), 296(4), (5)
rr.10.77–10.83	IA 298(9)
r.10.78	IA 298
r.10.85	IA 298(6)
rr.10.86–10.88	IA 299(1), (2)
r.10.93	IA 305(3)
rr.10.94–10.98	IA 370(1), (2)
r.10.99	IA 433(1), Pt 12 Ch.4 sub-div.B
rr.10.100–10.105	IA 290
r.10.105	IA 308, 308(1), (4)
r.10.106	IA 308, 308(1), (4)
r.10.109	IA 310(1), (1A), (2)
rr.10.109–10.114	IA 310(3)–(5)
rr.10.115–10.117	IA 310
rr.10.118–10.120	IA 369(7)
r.10.125	IA 307(3), 310(3)–(5), 333(2)
rr.10.125–10.126	IA 333(2)
r.10.126	IA 307(4)
rr.10.132–10.141	IA 282(1), (3)
r.10.134	IR 18.32–18.37
r.10.136	IR 10.133
r.10.137	IR 10.136
r.10.138	IA 282(1), (3)
(7)	IA 282(1), (3)
r.10.139	IA 282(1), (3)
r.10.142	IA 333(1), (3)

	Provision
rr.10.142–10.146	IA 280(1)
r.10.144	IA 279(3)–(5)
r.10.145	IA 279(3)–(5)
r.10.146	IA 251G, 281(1), (2)–(6), (8)
r.10.149	IA 328, Sch.5
(n)	IR 17.24
r.10.150–10.153	IA 334(3), 335(5), (6)
r.10.153A	IR Pt 20
r.10.155	IA 402(4)
r.10.160–10.161	IR 10.144–10.147
r.10.166	IA 371(1)
r.10.167	IA 283A
r.10.168	IR 10.169
Pt 11	IR Pt 10
rr.11.1–11.12	IA Pt 7A, 251V, Sch.4ZB
r.11.1 et seq.	[CDDA 11]
r.11.6	IR 11.7
r.11.18	IA 251E, Pt 11 Ch.6
rr.11.18–11.21	IA 251W
r.11.19	IA 251L, IR Pt 11 Ch.6
Pt 12	IA 234(1), (2), 303(1), 363(1), IR Pt 3, Pt 6, Pt 7
r.12.1	IR Pt 12
r.12.4	IR 1.1
rr.12.6 et seq.	IA 168, IR Pt 9
rr.12.14–12.16	IR Pt 12
r.12.15	IA 176A(3)–(5)
r.12.16	IR Pt 12
r.12.17	IA 236, IR 7.98–7.107
rr.12.17–12.22	IA 366(1), 367(4)
r.12.18	IA 236
(1)	IR 12.22
(b)	IR 12.22
r.12.20(2)	IA 236
r.12.21(2)	IA 236
(4)	IR 12.22
r.12.22	Pt 12 Ch.4 sub-div.B
(4)	IA 236(2)
r.12.23	IR Pt 12 Ch.4 sub-div.C
rr.12.23–12.26	IR Pt 12
rr.12.30–12.34	IA 373(4)
r.12.31	IA 117
r.12.35	IA 363(1)
rr.12.35–12.38	IA 172, 303(2), IR 7.63–7.66, Pt 12
rr.12.35 et seq.	IR 3.64
r.12.37(6)	IA 172
r.12.41	IA 176A(3)–(5)
r.12.44	IA 184, 346(2)
rr.12.51 et seq.	IA 134
r.12.52	IA 47(3), (5), (6), 131, 235(5), Pt 12 Ch.9
r.12.53	IA 364(2), 365(3), (4), 366(2)–(4)
r.12.54	IA 364(2)
r.12.55	IA 236(4)–(6), 366(2)–(4)
r.12.56	IA 365(3), (4)
r.12.57	IA 346(2), 346(3), (4)

Provision

r.12.58 IR 12.61
r.12.59 IA 130(1), 133(2), (3), 147(1), 375(1), IR 7.14–7.24, 7.33–7.39, Pt 12, Sch.10, [CDDA 1(1), 1A, 21, CBIR Sch.2 para.67]
r.12.60 IA 280(2), (3), 282(1), (3), 375(3)
r.12.64 IA 377, Sch.B1 paras 22(2), 25, 28, IR 10.8, 10.9, Pt 12
Pt 13 IA 399
r.13.1(1) IA 399
r.13.5 IR Pt 13
Pt 14 IA 322(1), 324(1)–(3), IR Pt 3, Pt 6, Pt 7, Pt 10
r.14.1 IA 1(1), 3(3), 115, 123, 124(1), 263G, 281(1), Sch.B1 para.99(3)–(4), (5)–(6), Sch.8 paras 12, 14, IR Pt 14, 14.2, 14.3–14.11, 14.25
(3) IA 86, Sch.B1 para.11, IR 14.3–14.11, 14.26–14.31
r.14.2 IA 1(1), 3(3), 251G(5), 285(3), (4), 322(1), 382(3), (4), 413(1), Pt 14, 14.1, 14.3–14.11
rr.14.3 et seq. IA 107
r.14.5 IA 322(3), (4), IR Pt 14
r.14.8 IR Pt 14, 14.25, 14.33
r.14.12 IA Sch.B1 para.65(1)
(7)(c) IR 14.23
r.14.14 IR 14.25
rr.14.14–14.19 IA 269
rr.14.14 et seq. IA Sch.8 paras 12, 14
rr.14.20–14.23 IA 189
rr.14.21–14.23 IR 14.25
r.14.23 IA 189
(4) IA 189(4)
(5) IA 189(4)
(7) IA 189
(a) IA 189
r.14.24 IR Pt 14, 14.14, 14.21, 14.25, 14.44
(6)(e) IR 14.25
rr.14.25 IA Sch.4 para.6, IR Pt 14, 14.14, 14.24, 14.44, [ER art.9]
rr.14.26 et seq. IA Sch.B1 para.65
r.14.27 IR 14.26–14.31, 14.34
rr.14.27 et seq. IA 107
r.14.28 IA 328
rr.14.28–14.30 IR 14.26–14.31
r.14.29 IR 14.1
r.14.30 IR 14.31, 14.32
r.14.31 IR Pt 14, 14.1
r.14.34 IA 324(4), Sch.B1 para.65(1)
(2) IR 14.33, 14.39
r.14.39 IA 153, IR 14.34
r.14.40 IA 153, 325(2), IR 14.34
r.14.41 IR 14.19
r.14.44 IA 189(1), (2), IR 14.25

Provision

r.14.45 IR 14.36–14.38
Pt 15 IA Pt I, 3, 4(5), 5(2), 246ZE(11), Pt VIII, 257(2), (2A), (2B), (3), 258(6), 259, 379A, IR 2.25–2.38, 3.38, Pt 5, Pt 10, 15.1, 15.39
r.15.2 IA 136(4), (5), IR 18.24–18.27
(1) IR 2.27, 2.34, 2.39–2.44, 15.1
r.15.3 IA 160, 168, IR 15.1, 18.24–18.27
rr.15.3–15.7 IR Pt 3, Pt 6, Pt 7
r.15.7 IA 5(2), 246ZE–246ZG, 379ZB, IR 3.38
(3) IA 171(1), (2)
rr.15.7–15.11 IA 246ZE–246ZG
r.15.8 IA Sch.B1 para.54(2)–(4), IR 3.38
(3)(j) IR 2.25
rr.15.8 et seq. IA Sch.B1 para.53
r.15.11 IA Pt I, 259, IR 3.38
(1) IR 2.25, 2.31
(2) IR 2.25
r.15.12 IR 2.25, 3.38, 15.8
r.15.13 IR 3.38
r.15.14 IA Pt I
(1) IR 2.25–2.38
r.15.18 IA Sch.B1 para.52(2)–(4)
rr.15.20–15.22 IA 195
r.15.21 IA 4(6), (6A)
r.15.24 IR 15.23
r.15.27 IA 262
r.15.28 IR 2.25, 3.38, 15.31
(5) IR 2.25–2.38
rr.15.28–15.35 IR 15.35
r.15.29 IA 5(2)
r.15.31 IA Pt I, 262, IR 2.25, 3.38, 15.28, 15.35
(1) IR 15.35
(d) IR 2.25–2.38
(2) IR 2.25–2.38, 15.35
(3) IR 2.25–2.38, 14.1
(4) IR 2.25–2.38
(5) IR 2.25–2.38
(6)(a) IR 3.38
(b) IR 2.25–2.38
r.15.32 IR 3.38
r.15.33 IA 262
r.15.34 IA Pt I, 258(1), IR 2.25
(1) IR 2.25–2.38, 3.38
(2) IA Sch.B1 para.52, 3.38
(3) IR 2.25–2.38
(4) IR 2.25–2.38
(5) IR 2.25–2.38
r.15.35 IA Pt I, 6, IR 15.33
(1) IR 2.25–2.38
(2) IR 2.25–2.38
(5)(a) IR 2.25–2.38
r.15.36 IR 15.22, 15.44
r.15.37 IR 15.45
r.15.41 IA Sch.B1 para.59(1), (2)

	Provision
Pt 3	IR Pt 4
Pt 4	IR Pt 6, Pt 7, Pt 19
r.4.8(2)	IR 7.4–7.12
r.4.11	IR 7.25–7.32
r.4.90	IR 14.25
r.4.127(1)	IR 18.16
r.4.148A(1)	IR 18.16
r.4.173–4.178	IR 17.29
r.4.192	IR 19.1–19.11
r.4.218	IR 7.108(1)–(4)
(1)	IR 7.108(1)–(4)
(2)	IR 7.77
r.4.218A	IR 7.111
rr.4.218A–4.218E	IR 12.22
rr.4.226–4.230	IR Pt 22
Pt 5	IR Pt 8
r.5.4	IR 8.4
r.5.4A	IR 8.18
r.5.4B(1)–(4)	IR 8.20
(2)	IA 373(1)
(5)–(7)	IR 8.21
r.5.21(3)	IR 15.31
Ch.8	IR 8.32
Ch.9	IR 8.32
r.5.24(4A)	IA 262
r.5.31	IR 8.28
r.5.68	IR 8.6
Pt 5A	IR Pt 9
Pt 6	IR Pt 11, Pt 19
r.6.1	IR 10.1
(5)	IR 10.1
r.6.3	IR 10.2
r.6.5(4)(a)	IR 10.5
(b)	IR 10.5
(d)	IR 10.5
(6)	IR 10.5
r.6.11	IR 10.3
r.6.24A	IR 10.28
r.6.25	IR 24
(2)	IR 10.24
(3)	IR 10.24
r.6.26	IR 10.26, 12.64
r.6.35(1)	IR 10.165
rr.6.37–6.50B	IA Pt IX
rr.6.37–6.50A	IR 10.34–10.48
r.6.132(5)	IR 12.64
r.6.137A	IR 10.88
r.6.138A(1)	IR, 18.16
r.6.145	IR 10.89
r.6.175(6)	IA 433(1)
r.6.184	IR 19.1–19.11
r.6.193B(2)	IR 10.115–10.117
r.6.206(4)	IR 10.132
r.6.211(6)	IA 282(1), (3)
r.6.215	IA 333(1), (3)
(5)	IR 10.142
r.6.235A	IR 10.166
r.6.237	IA 283A
Pt 6A	IR Pt 11, Pt 11 Ch.5
r.6A.6	IR 11.20
r.6A.8(2)	IR 11.23
Pt 7	IR Pt 12
r.7.9	IR 12.28
r.7.11	IR 12.30
r.7.31A(6)	IR 12.39
(8)	IR 12.39
r.7.34	IR 12.42
(4)	IR 12.42
r.7.47	IR Pt 12
r.7.51	IR 12.1
r.7.55	IR 10.5, IR 10.26, Pt 12, 12.64
r.7.62(5)	[ER art.3]
Pt 8	IR Pt 16
r.9.2(1)	IR 12.22
r.9.6(3)	IR 12.22
(4)	IR 12.22
(8)	IR12.22
Pt 10	IR Pt 13
Pt 11	IR Pt 14
r.12.12	IA 426
r.12.20A	IA 426
r.12A.21	IR 15.20
r.12A.22	IR 15.43
r.12A.23	IR 15.36, 15.44
r.12A.24	IR 15.37, 15.45
r.12A.25	IR 15.38, 15.46
r.13.12	IA Pt IX, IR 14.1
Sch.1	IR 15.29
Schs 2A–2C	IR Sch.9
Sch.2B	IR Sch.8
Sch.2C	IR Sch.9
Sch.5	IR Sch.3
Sch.6	IR 18.38
Insolvency Rules (Northern Ireland) 1991 (SR 1991/364)	IA 441, IR 3
Insolvency (Scotland) Amendment Rules 2006 (SI 2006/734)	IA 411(1)–(2D), (7), 411(1), (1A), (1B), (2), (2A), (2B), (2C), (2D), (7)
Insolvency (Scotland) Amendment Rules 2007 (SI 2007/2537)	IA 411(1)–(2D), (7), 411(1), (1A), (1B), (2), (2A), (2B), (2C), (2D), (7)
Insolvency (Scotland) Amendment Rules 2009 (SI 2009/662)	IA 411(1)–(2D), (7), 411(1), (1A), (1B), (2), (2A), (2B), (2C), (2D), (7)
Insolvency (Scotland) Amendment Rules 2014 (SI 2014/114)	IA 411(1), (1A), (2), (2A), (2B), (2C), (2D), (7)

European and Other Legislation Table

Introduction

The insolvency legislation of 1985 and 1986

The Insolvency Act 1985 was a major piece of new legislation, implementing the most comprehensive review of the subjects of bankruptcy and corporate insolvency for over a century. Its provisions were based largely on the recommendations contained in the Cork Report (see below), after publication of a White Paper entitled *A Revised Framework for Insolvency Law*, Cmnd.9175 (1984). Although it received the Royal Assent and became law on 30 October 1985, the Government decided to delay implementation of all but a few of its provisions and to draw up a new Act, consolidating its provisions with those parts of the Companies Act 1985 dealing with receivership and winding up. This became the Insolvency Act 1986. At the same time a separate Bill was prepared to consolidate the law relating to the disqualification of company directors, which became the Company Directors Disqualification Act 1986. The two consolidating Acts received Royal Assent on 25 July 1986 and were brought into force together on 29 December 1986. On the same date the Insolvency Rules 1986 became operative, replacing the Companies (Winding up) Rules 1949 and the Bankruptcy Rules 1952.

The Cork Report

The main inspiration for the reforms made by the Insolvency Act 1985 was the *Report of the Review Committee on Insolvency Law and Practice*, the chairman of which was the late Sir Kenneth Cork ("the Cork Report", Cmnd.8558 (1982)). This committee was appointed in January 1977 with a wide-ranging brief, and its Report, published in June 1982, made proposals for extensive and radical changes in the law and practice of bankruptcy and corporate insolvency, amounting virtually to the introduction of a completely new code.

Later legislation

There have been a number of changes made to the Act of 1986 since it came into force and, in addition, new legislation in related areas. Among these may be noted the following:

Extension to insolvent partnerships
By the Insolvent Partnerships Order 1994 (SI 1994/2421) the 1986 Act was modified so as to make its provisions applicable to insolvent partnerships as from 1 December 1994. This Order has since been extensively amended. For the full text, as amended, see Vol.2 of this *Guide*.

Extension to building societies
The Building Societies Act 1986 was amended in 1989 so as to provide that where a building society is being wound up, the Insolvency Act 1986 (and the corresponding legislation for Northern Ireland) are to apply: see below, Introductory note to Part IV. Other insolvency procedures were made available to building societies by the Building Societies Act 1997 s.39(1).

Disapplication of insolvency legislation to "market contracts" and "market charges"
The Companies Act 1989 Pt VII modified the application of insolvency law and the enforcement of certain rights and remedies in relation to certain contracts on the financial markets. These are contracts connected with "recognised investment exchanges" and "recognised clearing houses" (CA 1989 s.155), with certain overseas investment exchanges and clearing houses (s.170), with certain money market institutions (s.171) and with settlement arrangements provided by the Bank of England (s.172). Part VII

has effect in three principal ways: (1) it gives effect to contractual settlement procedures in the various financial markets, displacing the normal rules of insolvency law, where one of the contracting parties becomes insolvent (see the notes to IA 1986 ss.107 and 328, below); (2) it preserves (and, in some cases, enhances) the priority of a chargee where a charge has been taken to secure obligations and liabilities arising under a market contract (see the notes to ss.10(1), 11(2), 11(3), 15(1), 15(2), 43, 61, 127 and 284, below); and (3) it safeguards rights and remedies in relation to property provided as cover for margin in relation to market contracts and market charges (see CA 1989 ss.177–181, and note in particular s.180(2), which provides that an investment exchange, clearing house or chargee may authorise the commencement or continuation of enforcement proceedings by an unsecured creditor against property held as margin "notwithstanding any provision of IA 1986"). The order-making powers of Pt VII were brought into force on 25 March 1991 and the remaining provisions (except ss.169(4), 170–172, 176, 178 and 181) became operative on 25 April 1991. The Financial Markets and Insolvency Regulations 1991 (SI 1991/880), which contain important modifications to the provisions of Pt VII, also came into force on the latter date. A number of statutory instruments have since amended or extended this legislation: for details, see the relevant parts of CA 1989 reproduced in Vol.2. Amendments have also been made by EA 2002 Sch.17 paras 43–47 to extend the above disapplication provisions to companies entering into administration under the new administration regime established by IA 1986 Sch.B1.

The insolvency legislation is similarly disapplied in relation to payment and securities settlement systems by the Financial Markets and Insolvency (Settlement Finality) Regulations 1999 (SI 1999/2979), discussed below.

Insolvency Act 1994

The ruling of the Court of Appeal in *Powdrill v Watson, Re Paramount Airways Ltd (No.3)* [1995] 2 A.C. 394 (see below, annotations to ss.19 and 44) caused immediate concern amongst insolvency practitioners because of their possible exposure to personal liability in claims brought by former employees of companies which were, or had been, in administration or administrative receivership. The Insolvency Act 1994 was passed to clarify the question of the liability of office-holders in such circumstances, with effect from 15 March 1994 (but not retrospectively). See the note to s.44, below.

Insolvency (No.2) Act 1994

This short Act amending the Insolvency Act 1986 was also passed in 1994, on the initiative of the Law Society, primarily to remove doubts about the position of a person who purchases unregistered land in a transaction which is challenged as a transaction at an undervalue or a preference under IA 1986 ss.238–241 or 339–342 (or the corresponding provisions in the Northern Ireland insolvency legislation). See the notes to ss.241 and 342, below.

Human Rights Act 1998

The United Kingdom has been a party to the European Convention for the Protection of Human Rights and Fundamental Freedoms since its inception in 1950, but the Convention was only given force in UK domestic law by the Human Rights Act 1998, which became fully operative on 2 October 2000. In consequence, issues of human rights may now be raised before our own courts, rather than having to be litigated before the European Court of Human Rights in Strasbourg.

While the Act does not directly amend the insolvency legislation in any way, it is of significance because (a) the courts are directed to have regard to the established case law of the European Court and opinions and decisions of the European Commission of Human Rights and the Committee of Ministers (s.2); (b) domestic legislation must, so far as possible, be construed in a way which is compatible with Convention rights (s.3); (c) it is unlawful for a public authority (e.g. the Secretary of State or the Insolvency Service) to act in a way which is incompatible with a Convention right (s.6); and (d) in the preparation of new legislation, the draftsman is necessarily concerned to ensure that it is compatible with Convention rights. There will therefore be occasion to refer to the Convention and the Act of 1998 at various times in the discussion which follows.

Civil Procedure Rules 1998

These Rules (commonly known as the CPR) came into force on 26 April 1999. On the same date amendments to the Insolvency Rules 1986 were brought into effect, so as to apply all those provisions of the CPR and such practice of the High Court and County Court as is not inconsistent with IR 1986 to insolvency proceedings, and to bring the terminology used in the Rules into line with the CPR.

Disapplication of insolvency legislation to payment and securities settlement systems

The Financial Markets and Insolvency (Settlement Finality) Regulations 1999 (SI 1999/2979) (the "Finality Regulations"), which became operative on 11 December 1999, were enacted in order to implement Directive 98/26 of the European Community ([1998] O.J. L166/45) into the law of the United Kingdom. The object of the Directive is to reduce the risks associated with participation in payment and securities settlement systems by minimising the disruption caused if insolvency proceedings are brought against a participant in such a system. For this purpose, a settlement system must be specifically designated by the Financial Conduct Authority or the Bank of England. These Regulations were extended to Northern Ireland by SI 2006/50.

Regulations 13 to 19 modify the law of insolvency so far as it applies to transfer orders effected through a designated system and to collateral security provided in connection with participation in such a system. But the normal rules of insolvency apply to a transfer order which is entered into a designated system *after* the making of the court order or passing of a winding-up resolution, unless the transfer order is carried out on the same day as the court order or resolution and the relevant person (e.g. the settlement agent or clearing house) does not have notice of the insolvency at the time of settlement (reg.20).

The Regulation was amended from 6 April 2011 by SI 2010/2993, implementing EC Directive 98/26, to make provision for linked or "inoperable" systems, and to ensure that credit claims may be used as financial collateral.

Where a transaction is both a market contract or market charge (as defined for the purposes of Pt VII of the Companies Act 1989 (see above)) and a transfer order or a collateral security charge under the Finality Regulations, certain provisions of the 1989 Act are disapplied, so that the Regulations govern the situation (reg.21). For the text of the Regulations, as amended, see Vol.2.

Insolvency Act 2000

This Act received the Royal Assent on 30 November 2000. The two principal reforms were (a) provision for a moratorium in voluntary arrangements for small companies (s.1 and Sch.1); and (b) the introduction of a formal scheme of disqualification undertakings entered into under an administrative procedure in lieu of disqualification orders made by a court (ss.5–8). Other amendments included: improvements to the procedure for an individual voluntary arrangement (s.3 and Sch.3), new rules relating to the prosecution of delinquent officers and members of a company in a compulsory winding up, designed to bring the law into conformity with the Human Rights Act 1998 (s.11), and a power conferred on the Secretary of State (by s.14) to give effect to the UNCITRAL Model Law on Cross-Border Insolvency.

Section 14 (the enabling provision relating to the Model Law) came into operation with the passing of the Act. Other parts of the Act were brought into force in stages, implementation being finally completed on 1 January 2003.

Extension to limited liability partnerships

The Limited Liability Partnerships Act 2000 introduced a new form of incorporated body, the limited liability partnership (LLP), into the law of Great Britain, and provided for the recognition of similar bodies incorporated or established outside the jurisdiction, which are referred to in the Act as "oversea limited liability partnerships". Section 14 of this Act authorised provision to be made by regulation about the insolvency and winding up of LLPs and oversea LLPs by applying or incorporating, with such modifications as might appear appropriate, Pts I to IV, VI and VII of IA 1986. This was done by the Limited Liability Partnership Regulations 2001 (SI 2001/1090), which are reproduced (as amended) in Vol.2. The Act and Regulations came into force on 6 April 2001.

The EC Regulation on Insolvency Proceedings 2000 and the EU Regulation on Insolvency Proceedings 2015

These two Regulations set out common rules on cross-border insolvency proceedings within the European Union. Regulation 1346/2000, [2000] O.J. L160/1 came into force on 31 May 2002 and was succeeded by Regulation (EU) 2015/848 [2015] O.J. L141/19 on 26 June 2017. As a Regulation, each of them has direct applicability (i.e. they did not need to be implemented by domestic legislation).

The background to this legislation is set out in Vol.2, where the full text of the 2015 Regulation is reproduced with an accompanying commentary. If it is necessary to consult the superseded version, reference should be made to the 19th edition of this work.

Article 46 of the original Regulation required the Commission, after 10 years, to present to the Parliament a report on the application of the Regulation in practice, with any proposal for adaptation. Accordingly, following a consultation exercise earlier in the year, the Commission in December 2012 announced that it had adopted a proposal to amend the Regulation, moving towards a "rescue and recovery" culture with less emphasis on liquidation. The scope of the Regulation would be extended to include pre-insolvency and debt discharge proceedings, and other problems which had been revealed in the first 10 years of the Regulation's operation (e.g. the failure to address issues relating to corporate groups) would be dealt with. Events moved on. In December 2014 it was announced that the Justice Ministers of the Member States had agreed on a draft recast text to replace the original Regulation, incorporating many of the reforms outlined in these proposals. In the event, after the draft had been passed through all the legislative procedures, the Parliament finally approved and signed the text on 20 May 2015, and the new Regulation was published in the Official Journal on 5 June 2015 to enter into force 20 days after publication, i.e. on 26 June 2015. However, under art.84 the Regulation is to apply in practice only after another two years, i.e. to insolvency proceedings opened on or after 26 June 2017.

The operation of EURIP 2015/848 on 26 June 2017 required consequential amendments to domestic legislation from that date, primarily by the Insolvency Amendment (EU 2015/848) Regulations 2017 (SI 2017/702) which amended amongst other things the Insolvency Act 1986, the Insolvency (England and Wales) Rules 2016 (SI 2016/1024) (and their Northern Ireland counterparts) and the Insolvency (Scotland) Rules 1986 (SI 1986/1915), and, purely in relation to Scotland, by the Insolvency (Regulation (EU) 2015/848) (Miscellaneous Amendments) (Scotland) Regulations 2017 (SSI 2017/210).

For further details, see the Introductory note to the Regulation in Vol.2.

Extension of administration procedure to insurance companies

The administration procedure was not available to insurance companies under IA 1986, as originally enacted. However, this has since been made possible by special legislation. See the note to IA 1986 Sch.B1 para.9.

Enterprise Act 2002

This Act followed a number of initiatives and consultations by the DTI and the Treasury between 1999 and 2001 which culminated in the publication of a White Paper published by the Insolvency Service on 31 July 2001, entitled *Productivity and Enterprise: Insolvency—A Second Chance*. Its main proposals concerning corporate insolvency were (a) that the right to appoint an administrative receiver be restricted to holders of floating charges granted in connection with transactions in the capital markets; (b) that the Crown's standing as a preferential creditor be abolished; (c) that the administration procedure be streamlined by reducing its considerable formalities; and (d) to simplify the transition from an administration to a winding up where it was likely that there would be funds available for distribution to unsecured creditors. In regard to bankruptcy law, various reforms which had been outlined in a White Paper of 13 February 2000 would be introduced, together with the abolition of Crown preference in personal insolvencies, and a system of "bankruptcy restriction orders", on analogy with director disqualification orders, would be instituted for the more culpable debtors. It was also proposed to extend the director disqualification regime by adding the disqualification of directors as an additional sanction for breaches of the competition laws.

The ensuing Act, which in a number of respects went further than the White Paper, received Royal Assent as the Enterprise Act 2002 on 7 November 2002. The provisions of this Act relating to corporate insolvency and the abolition of the Crown's preferential status, together with supporting statutory instruments (principally the Insolvency (Amendment) Rules 2003 (SI 2003/1730)), were brought into force on 15 September 2003. The remaining sections dealing with the bankruptcy of individuals became effective from 1 April 2004.

The Enterprise Act 2002 s.255 also gives power to the Treasury, with the concurrence of the Secretary of State, to make orders extending legislative provisions governing CVAs and administrations to bodies such as co-operative societies and friendly societies.

Proceeds of Crime Act 2002

This Act provides for the confiscation of assets of persons convicted of criminal offences. Part 9 of the Act, which became operative on 24 March 2003, deals with the potential conflicts which may arise between the criminal law confiscation rules and the insolvency regimes of bankruptcy, sequestration (in Scotland), winding up and receivership. It also applies in the insolvency of limited liability partnerships. The impact of this legislation, relevant parts of which are reproduced in Vol.2, is discussed at appropriate places in the text which follows.

Financial Collateral Arrangements (No.2) Regulations 2003

These Regulations (SI 2003/3226, revoking and replacing SI 2003/3112, which was not brought into force because of a drafting error) became operative on 26 December 2003. They implement the Directive of the EU Parliament and Council 2002/47, and (inter alia) disapply various provisions of domestic insolvency legislation in relation to financial collateral arrangements, giving priority, for instance, to close-out netting provisions in such an arrangement over the rules which would otherwise prevail in a winding up. The Regulation was amended from 6 April 2011 by SI 2010/2993, implementing EC Directive 98/26, to make provision for linked or "inoperable" systems, and to ensure that credit claims may be used as financial collateral.

Credit Institutions (Reorganisation and Winding Up) Regulations 2004

These Regulations (SI 2004/1945, effective 5 May 2004) implement the Directive of the EU Parliament and Council 2001/24, and provide for the recognition and co-ordination of proceedings for the reorganisation and winding up of banking and other credit institutions throughout the EEA.

Cross-Border Insolvency Regulations 2006

As noted above, the IA 2000 s.14 made provision for the enactment in this country of legislation based on the Model Law on Cross-Border Insolvency, which had been adopted by the United Nations Commission on International Trade Law (UNCITRAL) on 30 May 1997 and later formally agreed by the UN General Assembly on December 15 of the same year. Following the publication by the DTI of a consultation paper and a draft of the proposed legislation in August 2005 the Cross-Border Insolvency Regulations 2006 (SI 2006/1030) were signed into law on 3 April 2006 and came into force on the following day. The Regulations embody (in Sch.1) a modified form of the Model Law, specifically adapted to relate to Great Britain and its existing legislation. The text is reproduced in Vol.2, accompanied by a full annotation. Applied to Northern Ireland by SR 2007/115 as from 12 April 2007.

Companies Act 2006

This Act (the largest ever passed in Parliamentary history) received the Royal Assent on 8 November 2006, and finally came fully into force on 1 October 2009. The legislation both reformed and consolidated much of the preceding Companies Act 1985. Note that the law on investigations by the Department for Business, Energy and Industrial Strategy remains in the 1985 Act for the time being. For the most part its provisions do not directly impact upon insolvency practice in the sense of making real changes. Note also that the Companies Act 2006 applies to Northern Ireland. A number of statutory instruments came into force with the Act on 1 October 2009. In consequence of the Act, extensive amendments were made to the Insolvency Act 1986 and the other legislation which is annotated in this work. All the changes of substance have been noted at the appropriate places, but there are many minor textual changes (e.g. those which simply replace section numbers of CA 1985 with the corresponding numbers of CA 2006, or are purely verbal or cosmetic), and these amendments have been made without annotation. A new Pt 25 of the Act, dealing with the registration of company charges, came into force on 6 April 2013. We have included the new provisions in the text of CA 2006 in Vol.2.

Fraud Act 2006

This Act came into force on 15 January 2007. Among other reforms, it extends the law relating to fraudulent trading (IA 1986 s.213) to sole traders and other persons participating in fraudulent business, and increases the penalties for persons convicted of fraudulent trading.

Demise of the Department of Trade and Industry

In the course of the Cabinet reshuffle following the resignation of Mr Blair as Prime Minister, the Department of Trade and Industry (formerly the longstanding Board of Trade) was replaced by the Department for Business, Enterprise and Regulatory Reform (BERR). In June 2009 it was replaced by the Department for Business, Innovation and Skills (BIS), which in turn was superseded by the Department for Business, Energy and Industrial Strategy (BEIS) in 2016. All matters relating to individual bankruptcy and corporate insolvency remain within the brief of the new Department.

Tribunals, Courts and Enforcement Act 2007

This received the Royal Assent on 19 July 2007. A number of elements of this legislation are relevant to insolvency practitioners, particularly those engaged in personal insolvency work. The most significant development was the introduction of the "NINA" scheme for debtors with "no income and no assets" (see s.108 and Schs 17 and 18 of the Act). This reform, which necessitates the insertion of Pt 7A and new Schs 4ZA and 4ZB into the Insolvency Act 1986, was brought into force by the Tribunals, Courts and Enforcement Act 2007 (Commencement No.7) Order 2009 (SI 2009/382) with effect from 6 April 2009. It provides a bureaucratic means of debt relief outside the parameters of bankruptcy or IVA regimes. Linked to this are debt relief restriction orders and undertakings, which are designed to combat abuse by debtors (Sch.19). These reforms produce consequential amendments in the Insolvency Act 1986 (see Sch.20 to the 2007 Act). Note SI 2012/2404. The 2007 Act also contains many reforms relating to various debt enforcement procedures (Pts 3 and 4); changes are made to the county court administration procedure (s.106); regulations are set in place for debt management schemes (ss.109 et seq.), enforcement restriction orders are introduced (s.107); abolition of the common law right of distress for rent is at last implemented (s.71). In June 2009 the Ministry of Justice announced that Pt 4 of the 2007 Act (relating to attachment of earnings orders, charging orders and information requests and orders) was not to be brought into force. The provisions in Pt 3 dealing with commercial rent arrears recovery came into effect on 6 April 2014—see SI 2013/1894, SI 2014/1 and SI 2014/768 (C. 27) for details, see Fletcher [2014] 27 Insolv. Int. 127. Apart from this, it is understood that the remaining provisions of the Act will not come into force in the near future and therefore the affected legislation in this text has not been changed for this edition, though annotations do in some cases anticipate the reforms on the horizon.

Banking Act 2009

New insolvency and administration regimes for banking companies and building societies were introduced by the Banking Act 2009, which received the Royal Assent on 12 February 2009 and came into force on 21 February. This legislation is intended to strengthen the statutory framework for financial stability and depositor protection when banking companies encounter financial difficulties. Part 1 of the Act introduces the "Special Resolution Regime" (SRR), which provides three stabilisation options: transfer to a purchaser in the private sector, transfer to a bridge bank and transfer to temporary public sector ownership. The SRR may also be applied to building societies, and there is power also to apply it to credit unions. Part 1 of the Act was substantially amended by the Bank Recovery and Resolution Order 2014 (SI 2014/3329) as from 1 January 2015, to implement in part Directive 2014/59 establishing a framework for the recovery and resolution of credit institutions and investment firms; the Directive requires EEA states to have powers to manage the failure of credit institutions and investment firms and their group companies as an alternative to insolvency so that critical functions continue to be performed. Implementation of the Directive was completed on 16 December 2016 by the Bank Recovery and Resolution Order 2016 (SI 2016/1239), which amended the Bank Recovery and Resolution Order 2014 (above). Part 2 of the Act establishes a new insolvency procedure called a "bank insolvency order" based on existing liquidation provisions to provide for the orderly winding up, pursuant to a court order, of a failed bank and to facilitate rapid payments under the Financial Services Compensation Scheme to eligible claimants (or to transfer such accounts to another financial institution). Part 3 establishes a new administration procedure (again following the making of a court order) to deal with the remaining assets where there has been a partial transfer of business from a failing bank. The powers conferred by this legislation have already been used to cope with some recent bank failures. The provisions of the Insolvency Act 1986 and the Insolvency Rules 1986 are modified for the purposes of this legislation by the Act itself and by the swathe of secondary legislation which has followed in its wake. Relevant statutory instruments include the Banking Act 2009 (Bank Administration) (Modification for Application to Banks in Temporary Public Ownership) Regulations 2009 (SI 2009/312); the Banking Act 2009 (Bank Administration) (Modification for Application to Multiple Transfers) Regulations 2009 (SI 2009/313); the Banking Act 2009 (Sharing Information) Regulations 2009 (SI 2009/314); the Banking Act 2009 (Parts 2 and 3 Consequential Amendments) Order 2009 (SI 2009/317); the Banking Act 2009 (Third Party Compensation Arrangements for Partial Property Transfers) Regulations 2009 (SI 2009/319); the Banking Act 2009 (Restriction of Partial Property Transfers) Order 2009 (SI 2009/322); the Bank Insolvency (Scotland) Rules 2009 (SI 2009/351); the Bank Administration (Scotland) Rules 2009 (SI 2009/350); the Bank Insolvency (England and Wales) Rules 2009 (SI 2009/356), the Bank Administration (England and Wales) Rules 2009 (SI 2009/357) and the Scottish and Northern Ireland Banknote Regulations 2009 (SI 2009/3056). This legislation generally came into force on 21 February 2009. As regards building societies, see the Building Societies (Insolvency and Special Administration) Order 2009 (SI 2009/805), effective 29 March 2009. Several of these statutory instruments have been amended by supplementary legislation. The Treasury has published, and updated, "Banking Act 2009: special resolution regime code of practice" to supplement the legislation (March 2017: see *https;//www.gov.uk/government/uploads/system/uploads/attachment_data/file/602948/Special-Resolution-Regime-Code-of-Practice.pdf*).

Similar legislation has been enacted for investment banks: see the Investment Bank Special Administration Regulations 2011 (SI 2011/245), effective 8 February 2011 (following the Bloxham review of 2014 and a Treasury consultation exercise in 2016, the Regulations were amended by the Investment Bank (Amendment of Definition) and Special Administration (Amendment) Regulations 2017 (SI 2017/443) as from 6 April 2017) and, for Scotland, the Investment Bank Special Administration (Scotland) Rules 2011 (SI 2011/2262 (S 3), effective 14 November 2011. The legislation was extended to investment firms by the Bank Recovery and Resolution (No.2) Order 2014 (SI 2014/3348), effective 1 January 2015.

This legislation is too voluminous to be included in the present work and detailed references to the special case of banking insolvencies and administrations will not normally be given.

For an early commentary on this legislation, see R. Tomasic (2009) Insolv. Int. 65, 81.

Revision of the Insolvency Rules and consolidation of secondary legislation

In September 2005 the Insolvency Service began a project to review, consolidate and simplify the Insolvency Rules and nine other statutory instruments:

The Insolvent Partnerships Order 1994 (SI 1994/2421)
The Insolvency Regulations 1994 (SI 1994/2507)
The Insolvency Proceedings (Fees) Order 2004 (SI 2004/593)
The Insolvency Proceedings (Monetary Limits) Order 1986 (SI 1986/1996)
The Administration of Insolvent Estates of Deceased Persons Order 1986 (SI 1986/1999)
The Insolvency Practitioners and Insolvency Services Account (Fees) Order 2003 (SI 2003/3363)

The Insolvent Companies (Disqualification of Unfit Directors) Proceedings Rules 1987 (SI 1987/2023)
The Insolvent Companies (Reports on Conduct of Directors) Rules 1996 (SI 1996/1909)
The Companies (Disqualification Orders) Regulations 2001 (SI 2001/967)

The first landmark in this major exercise was reached with the enactment in February 2010 of the Insolvency (Amendment) Rules 2010 (SI 2010/686) and the Insolvency (Amendment) (No.2) Rules 2010 (SI 2010/734), which came into force on 6 April 2010. The amending rules (which extend to nearly 200 pages) had among their objects the simplification of procedures (for instance abolishing the use of affidavits and the routine filing of copies of documents with the court) and the use of modern techniques for the communication of information (websites and other electronic means) in place of paper documents and for the holding of meetings without personal attendance. For a more detailed account of these changes, see the Introductory note to the Insolvency (England and Wales) Rules 2016 below. In anticipation of this measure Parliament authorised the making on 6 January 2010 by the Secretary of State for Business, Innovation and Skills of a Legislative Reform Order, the Legislative Reform (Insolvency) (Miscellaneous Provisions) Order 2010 (SI 2010/18, operative from 6 April 2010) ("LRO 2010") which made a number of amendments to the Insolvency Act 1986 to pave the way for the making of the amending Rules. The principal amendments made by this Order are described in the Introduction to IA 1986 below.

This was but the first step in the overall revision programme. In the following year it was planned to consolidate the original 1986 Rules with these amendments into a single enactment, to come into force on 6 April 2011, and at the same time to make new statutory instruments replacing those listed in the preceding paragraph. However this timetable was soon acknowledged to be unachievable and in the event it was overtaken by a much more ambitious project. Instead of a simple consolidation, it was proposed that the whole of the Insolvency Rules should be reviewed and redrafted, grouping together the rules on some topics (e.g. "Meetings", so that the same provisions would govern a meeting of creditors whatever the form of insolvency proceeding), and incorporating many other reforms to keep pace with modern developments.

In September 2013 the Insolvency Service commenced a consultation exercise, which included the publication of a draft of the recast rules. Over 1,000 comments and suggestions were received from stakeholders, and on 19 June 2014 in response to these comments a further revised set of draft rules was published, together with an announcement that, after further consultation, a revised set of draft rules would be published for review by the Insolvency Rules Committee in early 2015, with a view to bringing the new rules into force in 2016 (a deadline which has been postponed several times). In the end the referral to the Insolvency Rules Committee finally occurred on 20 July 2015. Finally, on 25 October 2016, the recast Rules were published as the Insolvency (England and Wales) Rules 2016 (SI 2016/1024) and the effective date for them to become operative was confirmed as 6 April 2017. From the latter date the 2016 Rules were amended by the Insolvency (England and Wales) (Amendment) Rules 2017 (SI 2017/366). The commencement also occasioned the Insolvency (England and Wales) Rules 2016 (Consequential Amendments and Savings) Rules 2017 (SI 2017/369) effective from the same date to amend other legislation. The 2016 Rules were further amended by the Insolvency (England and Wales) and Insolvency (Scotland) (Miscellaneous and Consequential Amendments) Rules 2017 (SI 2017/1115) as from 8 December 2017.

See below for further developments.

The Scottish Government is planning to replace the Insolvency (Scotland) Rules 1986 (SI 1986/1915) in a similar exercise to the Insolvency (England and Wales) Rules 2016. The Scottish Government announced on 11 November 2016, that in order for stakeholders to have sufficient time to familiarise themselves with the structure and content of the proposed new rules after publication and before they come into force, it was anticipated that the rules would not commence before October 2017 but after further delay it is now understood that the Rules may be published by April 2018 followed by a six-month familiarisation period for them come into force in October 2018.

Enterprise and Regulatory Reform Act 2013

The Insolvency Service in November 2011 issued a consultation exercise, *Reform of the Process to Apply for Bankruptcy and Compulsory Winding Up*, proposing that undisputed bankruptcy and liquidation cases should no longer require the involvement of the court—a reform which had been considered for some time. The proposals were originally (in October 2007) aimed only at debtor petitions in bankruptcy, but with the November 2011 consultation they were extended to debtor and creditor petitions in both bankruptcy and corporate insolvency where the petition was undisputed. (However, the reform which has since been enacted is confined to debtor applications in bankruptcy.) The recommendation was that these undisputed petitions should be taken away from the court and be determined instead in an out-of-court administrative procedure by an "Adjudicator" appointed by the Secretary of State. This reform reflects the fact that more than 80 per cent of bankruptcies these days involve uncontested bankruptcy petitions presented by debtors themselves. This represents a considerable drain on the court system. In spite of some misgivings (see S. Baister and F. Toube (2012) 25 Insolv. Int. 49) being expressed about the reform proposals, the government decided to introduce a new procedure to deal with such cases, and this was effected (as from 6 April 2016) by bringing into force ERRA 2013 s.71 and Sch.18, which inserted a new Ch.A1 into IA 1986 Pt 9 (ss.263H–263O).

Section 263H outlines the debtor's rights to use this procedure, which involves an application to an adjudicator authorised to act under the new s.398A. Jurisdictional issues are dealt with by s.263I. The procedure cannot be used if there is an extant bankruptcy petition before the court. Various procedural requirements are outlined in s.263J. Sections 263K, 263L and 263M deal with the role of the adjudicator and the ability to make a bankruptcy order. Where the adjudicator refuses to make a bankruptcy order, appeal/review mechanisms are mapped out by s.263N. Criminal offences may be committed under s.263O where the applicant makes false or misleading representations.

The introduction of this new procedure has necessitated a large number of consequential changes in the existing legislation. These changes, insofar as they relate to the primary legislation, are largely of a referential/definitional nature and are mapped out in ERRA 2013 Sch.19. Many other consequential changes have been made also to a wide range of statutory instruments. The text of the Acts and SIs included in the pages which follow has been brought up to date to take account of these changes (in many cases, where the alteration is purely verbal and makes no change of substance, without annotation).

Although, as noted above, it was originally proposed that undisputed winding-up cases should also be dealt with by a similar out-of-court procedure, this suggestion encountered considerable opposition and on 9 October 2012 it was announced that it would not be pursued further. Uncontested creditor petitions were also at one stage proposed for inclusion in the new scheme but this proposal has likewise fallen by the wayside.

The facility of early discharge from bankruptcy before the expiry of the standard 12 months (see IA 1986 s.279(2)) was abolished by ERRA 2013 s.73 and Sch.21 with effect from 1 October 2013. This change required some modification of secondary legislation—see Insolvency (Amendment) Rules 2013 (SI 2013/2135).

The impact of this Act on bankruptcy procedures has been noted above. However, it is now clear as a result of later amendments to the legislation that its footprint has been more significant. Section 92 enables the Secretary of State to amend IA 1986 ss.233 and 372 which prevent suppliers of essential utilities from threatening to cut off supplies to insolvency office holders unless pre-appointment arrears are first paid. The aim of these amendments is to prevent suppliers of a wider range of essential services (for example IT services) from cutting off supplies in such circumstances.

In addition the Secretary of State is given power by ERRA 2013 ss.93 and 94 to make regulations to neutralise insolvency break clauses in contracts for essential supplies. This has been achieved by the Insolvency (Protection of Essential Supplies) Order 2015 (SI 2015/989), inserting new ss.233A and 372A into IA 1986 (for corporate and individual insolvency respectively) with effect from 1 October 2015. Note that this new power can only be exercised in respect of companies undergoing administration or CVA, or individual debtors tied into an IVA. This represents a narrower scope of insolvency scenario than is prescribed in IA 1986 ss.233 and 372. Arrangements to reassure suppliers who have been deprived of contractual rights in this way are specified in the new sections. The court might play a role in this context and provisions are made to ensure prompt payment where a supplier is obliged to continue supplying under this new regime. Also this power to override contractual provisions cannot be used to rewrite existing contracts—it can only apply to supply contracts made after the new legislation has come into force. This reform will be welcomed by R3 and the turnaround lobby, which have campaigned for some time for such a change in the law in order to enhance the prospects for business rescue. For discussion see annotations to IA 1986 ss.233–233A and 372–372A.

The Financial Services Act 2012

This Act transferred overall responsibility for the financial regulatory system in the UK to the Bank of England, and established the Financial Conduct Authority and the Prudential Regulation Authority to take over the functions of the former Financial Services Authority. This was done primarily by amendments to the Financial Services and Markets Act 2000. The Act received the Royal Assent on 19 December 2012. All the amendments made by the new Act and associated statutory instruments to the 1986 Act and Rules, and also to the legislation governing banking and insurance companies and bodies such as building societies and co-operatives, have been incorporated in the text and annotations in the current edition.

Extension of administration and CVA procedures to co-operative and community benefit societies and credit unions

When the Industrial and Provident Societies and Credit Unions (Arrangements, Reconstructions and Administration) Order 2014 (SI 2014/229) came into force on 6 April 2014, the provisions of IA 1986 Pt 1 and Sch.B1 (as modified) were extended to all societies registered under the Industrial and Provident Societies Act 1965, apart from any society which is a private registered provider of social housing or is registered as a social landlord. The bodies concerned are mainly the co-operatives, community benefit societies and credit unions.

Demise of the Competition Commission and the Office of Fair Trading

By ERRA 2013 ss.25–27, the Office of Fair Trading was abolished and merged with the Competition Commission to become the Competition and Markets Authority (CMA), and the functions of the OFT were transferred to the CMA. This change came into effect on 1 April 2014.

Commencement of proceedings: single county court

The Crime and Courts Act 2013 s.17 established the single county court for England and Wales, replacing the former system under which there were numerous county courts, each with its own county court jurisdiction. In consequence, two statutory instruments were enacted to deal with questions of jurisdiction under the new regime.

The London Insolvency District (County Court at Central London) Order 2014 (SI 2014/818) revokes and replaces the 2011 Order of the same name (SI 2011/761) with effect from 22 April 2014. This Order designates the area comprised in the London insolvency district for the purposes of insolvency proceedings.

The Insolvency (Commencement of Proceedings) and Insolvency Rules 1986 (Amendment) Rules 2014 (SI 2014/817), which also took effect on 22 April 2014, identified county court hearing centres for the commencement of insolvency proceedings. Schedule 2 of these Rules amended the Insolvency Rules 1986 to reflect the new regime of hearing centres for the single county court introduced by the Crime and Courts Act 2013. These provisions have since been replaced by IR 2016 Sch.6.

The commentary and statutory text in this edition takes full account of the changes introduced by these reforms, in most cases without annotation.

Protection of depositors with banks and building societies

The Banks and Building Societies (Depositor Preference and Priorities) Order 2014 (SI 2014/3486), implementing in part Directive 2014/39/EU of the European Parliament, alters the priorities for the distribution of assets in the winding up of a bank or building society. In the case of a bank (or other "credit institution"), deposits which are eligible for compensation under the financial services compensation scheme (and certain other deposits) are treated as preferential debts and given a higher priority than other deposits. In regard to a building society, a new category of preferential debts ("secondary preferential debts") is created for the holders of deposits, ranking after the ordinary preferential debts but ahead of the unsecured creditors.

Improved transparency for professional fees

There have been a number of developments in recent years to ensure that fees charged by insolvency office holders are properly regulated and fully transparent. This policy was moved further forward when the Insolvency (Amendment) Rules 2015 (SI 2015/443) took effect on 1 October 2015. This statutory instrument reflects the policy of introducing binding fee estimates as announced by the Government on 3 March 2015 to apply in the case of administration, liquidation and bankruptcy. This policy is informed by the Kempson Report (2013) and the responses received in a follow-up consultation exercise carried out in 2014. It has required amendments to be made to relevant parts of the Insolvency Rules.

Deregulatory proposals—the "Red tape challenge"

Shortly after the Coalition government of 2010–2015 took office, it announced its intention to re-examine the whole gamut of regulatory legislation with a view to reducing unnecessary bureaucracy and, in particular, "burdens on business"; and it invited the public to draw its attention to instances and examples where reforms could be made. This exercise was dubbed the "Red tape challenge" and attracted over 22,000 replies. By 1 July 2013 the government was in a position to unveil a Deregulation Bill, which included one or two provisions in the area of insolvency, in particular dealing with the authorisation of insolvency practitioners and the reporting of director misconduct. But more was to come. Following consultations and a workshop held in September 2012, the Insolvency Service announced that early in 2013 it would produce proposals, for consideration by Ministers, to reduce bureaucratic and other burdens in the administration of insolvency proceedings, and in due course detailed proposals were published on 18 July 2013. Many of the reforms were anticipated by the Red tape exercise and these proposals have now found their way into two major pieces of legislation, which received the Royal Assent on the same day (26 March 2015) as the Deregulation Act 2015 and the Small Business, Enterprise and Employment Act 2015. It is, perhaps, a sad comment that so far as insolvency is concerned, while the new Acts do achieve some simplification and speeding up of decision-making and other procedures, their net effect is to increase the volume of insolvency legislation (and the size of this work!) quite substantially.

Deregulation Act 2015

As noted above, this Act received the Royal Asset and came into force on 26 March 2015. Only a fraction of its provisions impact upon insolvency law.

One significant change is made by s.17. This (finally) allows for the partial authorisation of insolvency practitioners. It is now possible to authorise insolvency practitioners to take up only certain offices. This sort of reform resulting in two-tier authorisation was envisaged by s.4 of the Insolvency Act 2000 but it never materialised. Policymakers have argued that this reform should help to expand the talent pool and may in theory reduce costs by introducing a greater degree of competition into the market. Specialisation may enhance performance. This change has been achieved by amending Pt 13 of the Insolvency Act 1986. New ss.390A and 390B have been introduced into the 1986 Act. A revised s.391 is substituted. It has to be said that the insolvency profession is sceptical about the projected benefits flowing from said reforms.

Section 19 feeds into Sch.6 which makes a number of changes to corporate law and insolvency law. Consequential amendments flow from the new rules on authorisation of insolvency practitioners. Deeds of arrangement are finally abolished with the repeal of the 1914 Act of the same name. A large number of consequential amendments are provided for. There are changes in Sch.6 to liquidation law in that s.151 is to be repealed and s.174 is amended. There are a number of procedural changes spelled out in Sch.6 with respect to director disqualification. The law on company administration is modified. This is particularly so with regard to Sch.B1 para.25 appointments and in terms of release on vacation of office.

As for the bankruptcy changes outlined in Sch.6 it will in future be possible to appoint a private sector insolvency practitioner to act as interim receiver under s.286 of the Act. Changes are made with regard to the bankrupt's obligation under s.288 to provide a statement of affairs. There are technical changes made to s.307 relating to after acquired property. The law on interim receivers as outlined in s.370 is to be modified.

In Sch.6 of the Act we find amendments being made to s.44 of the 1986 Act with regard to the range of liabilities arising on the adoption of contracts of employment by an administrative receiver and an administrator.

Small Business, Enterprise and Employment Act 2015

As noted above, this major piece of legislation received the Royal Assent on 26 March 2015. Insofar as it affects insolvency legislation, it has now been fully implemented via a series of commencement orders.

The reforms introduced by this legislation span the whole range of corporate law and insolvency law (among many other subjects). There are major changes to director disqualification regime effected by Pt 9. For instance, disqualification on the ground of unfitness is extended to include misconduct abroad (s.105) and instructing another person who has been found unfit (s.105). The possibility of compensation orders being linked to disqualification is introduced (s.110). Additional time is given to commence disqualification proceedings (s.108).

Significant reforms have been introduced by Pt 10 to the powers of office-holders. These include extending the fraudulent trading and wrongful trading options to administrators (s.117) and allowing fraudulent and wrongful trading and similar claims to be assigned (s.118).

Insolvency procedures are deregulated in an effort to curb costs. Sanction requirements are relaxed (ss.120–121). Meetings may in certain circumstances be dispensed with (ss.122–123 and Sch.9). Requiring formal proof of small debts is no longer essential (ss.131–132). The regulation of trustees in bankruptcy is modified by Sch.10.

In order to enhance public confidence in the operation of our insolvency system a new regime is created for the regulation of insolvency practitioners (ss.137–143). The recognised professional bodies will come under greater scrutiny by virtue of a regulatory regime that bears more than a passing resemblance to that applied to the legal profession by the Legal Services Act 2007. There is a clear move away from informal self-regulation towards a model where greater transparency and accountability hold sway.

Most of the provisions in the 2015 Act operate as amendments to the Insolvency Act 1986 and the Company Directors Disqualification Act 1986. All of its amendments and the new sections introduced via its provisions that are in force as at 6 April 2017, are incorporated, in the text of the Insolvency Act 1986 and the Company Directors Disqualification Act 1986 which follows, with annotations (except where the amendment is minor or purely verbal and effects no change of substance). Although there are some repeals effected by the 2015 Act (for example the scrapping of the fast track IVA model by s.135) the net effect of this legislation is to further expand the legislative corpus of insolvency law.

It was unclear whether the reforms effected by this Act and the Deregulation Act applied to bodies other than companies, e.g. building societies, insolvent partnerships and LLPs. No guidance was given in the legislation itself. The Deregulation Act 2015, the Small Business, Enterprise and Employment Act 2015 and the Insolvency (Amendment) Act (Northern Ireland) 2016 (Consequential Amendments and Transitional Provisions) Regulations 2017 (SI 2017/400) and the Deregulation Act 2015 and Small Business, Enterprise and Employment Act 2015 (Consequential Amendments) (Savings) Regulations 2017 (SI 2017/540) effected amendments to, amongst others, the Building Societies Act 1986, the Friendly Societies Act 1992, the Administration of Insolvent Estates of Deceased Persons Order 1986 (SI 1986/1999) and the Insolvent Partnerships Order 1994 (SI 1994/2421), but many of the amendments did not apply to LLPs or special administration regimes of railway companies, energy companies, etc. The Insolvency (Miscellaneous Amendments) Regulations 2017 (SI 2017/1119) are in force from 8 December 2017 fully to bring the regimes for LLPs, insolvent partnerships and the administration of insolvent estates of deceased persons into line with the insolvency procedures that apply to companies and other entities. The position is further discussed in the note to IA 1986 s.213.

The process of incorporating the deregulatory reforms made by SBEEA 2015 is ongoing—see the Small Business, Enterprise and Employment Act 2015 (Consequential Amendments, Savings and

Transitional Provisions) Regulations 2018 (SI 2018/208) which introduces changes with necessary modifications to the rules relating to building societies, banks, etc.

Third Parties (Rights against Insurers) Act 2010
This Act received the Royal Assent as long ago as 25 March 2010, but its implementation was delayed because it had been defectively drafted, with references to legislation that was out of date. It was not until the Insurance Bill of 2015 was before Parliament that there was an opportunity to amend it and it was possible to bring it into force from 1 August 2016.

Corporate restructuring agreements
Moves are afoot which may lead to reform of the law in this area, both domestically and in the EU. In the UK there has been pressure for many years to amend the law so as to make provision for a moratorium during the period when a scheme of reconstruction or arrangement under CA 2006 Pt 26 is in preparation, and on 29 September 2016 the Insolvency Service published the responses to a consultation by the Government which showed broad support for proposals towards this end. In a separate initiative, the European Commission on 22 November 2016 put forward a proposal for a directive on insolvency restructuring, addressing this topic (which is expressly not covered by the EU Regulation on Insolvency Proceedings 2015).

Bankruptcy (Scotland) Act 2016
This Act came into force with effect from 30 November 2016. Scottish bankruptcy law is outside the scope of this work, but the new Act has given rise to a mass of consequential legislation amendments by the Bankruptcy (Scotland) Act 2016 (Consequential Provisions and Modifications) Order 2016 (SI 2016/1034). We have endeavoured to incorporate those changes in the law without detailed annotation.

Companies House forms
The Insolvency Rules of 1986 required the use of a large number of prescribed forms, and pro forma models of these forms were published which users could complete. The new Rules, however, do not contain prescribed forms but rather specify the *content* of the information to be included. But Companies House continues to require some insolvency forms to be sent to it in the form prescribed by the Registrar's Rules (made under the Companies Act 2006 s.1117). These are to be differentiated from the existing forms by the provision of insolvency "identifiers", so that company voluntary arrangement forms will be numbered "CVA[number]", administration forms will be "AM[number]", for voluntary liquidation "LIQ[number]" and for compulsory liquidation "WU[number]". A Table of these forms is reproduced in App.VII.

The Insolvency Service surprisingly announced on 20 January 2017, that it would replace a small number of compulsory liquidation and bankruptcy forms containing prescribed content and which have been identified as having an impact upon official receiver work and which would benefit customers, but there will be no legal requirement to use them. They will be available from 6 April 2017. It is also understood that HM Courts and Tribunal Service is preparing some court forms for use under the 2016 Rules.

Director disqualification compensation orders
After a year's delay, Rules were published which set out the procedure for applying for compensation orders under the Company Directors Disqualification Act 1986 s.15A, and for revoking or varying compensation undertakings under s.15C (effective from 1 October 2016).

Introduction of the Business and Property Courts
High Court work in corporate and personal insolvency is usually carried out in specialist courts of the Chancery Division: the Companies Court and the Bankruptcy Court. A reform of the court structure was instituted as from 2 October 2017 with the introduction of the "Business and Property Courts" from that date to act as an umbrella for specialist court work. All High Court insolvency and company work from 2

October 2017 is heard in the Business and Property Courts of England and Wales, which includes the courts of the Chancery Division. This specialist area of work is assigned to the Company and Insolvency List and in London is heard in the Rolls Building. For further details see the Chancery Guide (amended October 2017) at p.113 and Ch.31 (available at *https://www.judiciary.gov.uk/wp-content/uploads/2017/09/chancery-guide-bpcs-amendments-20171002.pdf* but subject to further amendment).

Insolvency and corporate governance

While this 21st edition was at proof, the Insolvency Service and BEIS on 20 March 2018 published a consultation exercise, *Insolvency and Corporate Governance*, seeking comments by 11 June 2018 on proposals for improvements to corporate governance within companies which are in or approaching insolvency. In particular it considers:

- sales of businesses in distress;
- reversal of value extraction (i.e. asset stripping) schemes in a rescue situation;
- investigation into the actions of directors of dissolved companies; and
- strengthening corporate governance in pre-insolvency situations (in relation to group structures, shareholder responsibilities, the payment of dividends, directors' duties and the role of professional advisers, and providing protection for company supply chains in the event of insolvency).

The consultation is available at *https://assets.publishing.service.gov.uk/government/uploads/system/uploads/attachment_data/file/691857/Condoc_-_Insolvency_and_Corporate_Governance_FINAL_.pdf.*

Special note: in order to make space available for the new Rules and the accompanying Tables of Destinations and Derivations, we are no longer able to include Parts 2 of the Insolvency Act 1986 and Insolvency Rules 1986 which deal with administrations under the older law, and for the same reason we cannot continue to reproduce parts of the Insolvency Act 2000 and the Enterprise Act 2002 as formerly. However, it may be necessary at times for readers to make reference to this legislation, and also to the Insolvency Rules 1986 and the original EC Regulation on Insolvency Proceedings 2000, in circumstances where proceedings continue be governed by that earlier law. We therefore strongly recommend that readers should retain copies of the 19th edition of the *Annotated Guide* for future reference.

Insolvency Act 1986

On its enactment, the Insolvency Act 1986 brought into one composite Act the whole of the provisions of the Insolvency Act 1985 (except for ss.12–14, 16, 18 and Sch.2, which were separately consolidated into CDDA 1986) and ss.467–650 and 659–674 of CA 1985, together with certain parts of other ancillary legislation. It deals with both corporate insolvency and the bankruptcy of individuals, but in this context "corporate insolvency" has to be understood in a much wider sense than normal, for the Act is concerned with the winding up and receivership of all companies, whether "solvent" (meaning financially viable) or not, and also with voluntary arrangements, administration and associated matters. Insolvent partnerships are also dealt with by subordinate legislation made under s.420 of the Act, and limited liability partnerships by the Limited Liability Partnerships Regulations 2001 (SI 2001/1090). The Act applies also, with modifications where necessary, in the insolvency of other bodies such as building societies, friendly societies, co-operative and community benefit societies and credit unions, either by virtue of the particular legislation governing them or because they are treated as "unregistered companies" under IA 1986 Pt V. The Act applies to England and Wales and to Scotland in relation to corporate insolvency, but only to England and Wales in regard to the bankruptcy of individuals. (Responsibility for Scottish liquidations and receiverships has been devolved to the Scottish Executive, but other procedures (i.e. administrations and CVAs) remain with the Insolvency Service.) The corresponding bankruptcy provisions for Scotland were revised separately by the Bankruptcy (Scotland) Act 1985 (which has since been repealed and replaced as from 30 November 2016 by the Bankruptcy (Scotland) Act 2016). Only a few sections of IA 1986 apply to Northern Ireland. (See the note to s.441.) The corresponding law for that jurisdiction is to be found in the separate legislation which is listed in the note to s.441, below. However the law in Northern Ireland so closely mirrors that of Great Britain that this annotation should be of assistance to practitioners in that jurisdiction.

The IA 1985, apart from a few sections which had already become operative, was brought into force immediately before the 1986 consolidating legislation, and was then at once repealed by the latter Acts (see SI 1986/1924 (C. 71)). This brief moment of existence was sufficient to activate repeals which swept away many special features of insolvency law that had been familiar for over a century: the doctrine of relation back, acts of bankruptcy, winding up subject to the supervision of the court, and many more. Attention has been drawn to these changes at appropriate points in the discussion which follows.

Most Acts of Parliament, or at least the larger ones, are divided into Parts, and the Parts subdivided into Chapters, with yet further subdivisions marked by italic subheadings. The present Act has one further tier in this hierarchy: the Parts are collected into three "Groups of Parts". The "First Group of Parts" comprises "Company Insolvency" and "Companies Winding Up"—once again, we notice the ambivalence in the use of the word "insolvency"—and is broken into Pts I–VII; the Group has its own definition sections in Pt VII. The Second Group deals with "Insolvency of Individuals" and "Bankruptcy" and contains four Parts, continuing in numerical sequence from VIII to XI, again with separate interpretation provisions. The Third Group, which comprises Pts XII–XIX, is concerned with the administration of the Act and miscellaneous matters affecting all types of insolvency.

The Act has been amended in minor respects by later legislation, and more substantially by IA 2000, which came into force on various dates between 30 November 2000 and 1 January 2003, and the Enterprise Act 2002, which became operative as regards corporate insolvency and the abolition of Crown preference on 15 September 2003, and in relation to the bankruptcy of individuals on 1 April 2004. In January, 2010 the Secretary of State for Business, Innovation and Skills made a Legislative Reform Order, the Legislative Reform (Insolvency) (Miscellaneous Provisions) Order 2010 (SI 2010/18, operative from 6 April 2010) which amended IA 1986 in a number of respects in order to facilitate the making of the amending Rules as described below.

The principal amendments made to IA 1986 by this Order are as follows:

- authorising the holding of meetings without physical attendance (ss.246A, 379A);

- authorising the use of websites as a means of communication (ss.246B, 379B);
- clarifying reference to things "in writing" and "post" to remove uncertainty about the use of electronic communication, subject to some exceptions where hard copy continues to be required (s.436B);
- removal of the use of affidavits (in England and Wales);
- removal of the requirement for annual meetings in voluntary liquidations, and their replacement by progress reports (in England and Wales) (ss.92A, 104A);
- removal of the requirement for certain documents to be filed in court in IVAs;
- removal of the requirement for sanction for certain compromises in a winding up (in England and Wales) (Sch.4) and bankruptcy (Sch.6).

Some of these reforms apply to insolvencies existing prior to 6 April 2010 as well as insolvencies commencing after that date, while others are subject to transitional provisions contained in LRO art.12.

We have endeavoured to draw attention to this aspect of the particular reforms in the commentary.

SBEEA 2015 and DA 2015 have added considerably to this list of deregulatory measures. Most notably we may mention:

- enabling administrators to bring actions for fraudulent and wrongful trading;
- empowering office-holders to assign their statutory right to sue for preferences, undervalue transactions, etc.;
- authorising the use of decision-making procedures other than physical meetings by creditors and contributories, and abolishing altogether the requirement to hold final meetings,
- enabling the use of the "deemed consent" procedure in decision-making;
- allowing creditors to opt out from involvement in decision-making.

Far and away the most significant change in this area of the law in 2017 was the enactment of the new Insolvency Rules, replacing in their entirety the Insolvency Rules 1986 and the many amending statutory instruments made over the previous three decades. At long last the Insolvency (England and Wales) Rules 2016 (SI 2016/1024) were finally laid before Parliament on 25 October 2016, and are in force from 6 April 2017. An Explanatory Memorandum was published at the same time reiterating that the three principal purposes of the recast Rules are: to consolidate the Insolvency Rules 1986 and the 28 amending instruments thereto, to restructure and update the language of the rules, and to modernise and give effect to policy changes made to the Insolvency Act 1986 by the DA 2015 and the SBEEA 2015. Over the course of 2017, a number of refinements have been made to the matrix of provisions contained in the Insolvency Rules 2016. For a detailed summary see Bailey [2018] 31 Insolv. Int. 7 and also the overview by Milman [2018] 31 Insolv. Int. 30. The Rules were amended by the Insolvency (England and Wales) (Amendment) Rules 2017 (SI 2017/366) as from 6 April 2017 and subsequently by, amongst others, the Insolvency Amendment (EU 2015/848) Regulations 2017 (SI 2017/702) as from 26 June 2017 and the Insolvency (England and Wales) and Insolvency (Scotland) (Miscellaneous and Consequential Amendments) Rules 2017 (SI 2017/1115) as from 8 December 2017.

Another important change in 2017 was replacement of the EC Regulation on Insolvency Proceedings 1346/2000 by the Recast EU Regulation 2015/848 as from 26 June 2017. Regulation 2015/848, reproduced in Vol.2 with annotations, is considerably longer than its predecessor and has a wider ambit. Although the Regulation, like Regulation 1346/2000, has direct applicability and direct effect in the UK, it has had a knock-on effect on the Insolvency Act 1986 (and IR 2016) with largely consequential amendments occasioned by the Insolvency Amendment (EU 2015/848) Regulations 2017 (SI 2017/702) from 26 June 2017. The above changes are all covered in this 21st edition.

Given the vast amount of changes to the Insolvency Act 1986 in over 31 years of its operation, one might be forgiven for wondering if there are any plans for its modernisation and consolidation, following the example of the IR 2016. However desirable this might be, it appears extremely unlikely that it will happen in the current Parliament as an enormous amount of legislative time is being dedicated to the process of "Brexit". What effect the latter may have on insolvency law (especially concerning the EU Regulation mentioned above) after March 2019, only time will tell.

Insolvency Act 1986

(1986 Chapter 45)

ARRANGEMENT OF SECTIONS

Part VIII

Individual Voluntary Arrangements

Moratorium for insolvent debtor

Procedure where no interim order made

Creditors' meeting

Consideration and implementation of debtor's proposal

Fast-track voluntary arrangement

Part IX

Bankruptcy

Chapter AI

Adjudicators: Bankruptcy Applications by Debtors and Bankruptcy Orders

Chapter I

The Court: Bankruptcy Petitions; Bankruptcy Orders

Preliminary

Creditor's petition

Debtor's petition

Other cases for special consideration

Chapter IA

Commencement and Duration of Bankruptcy

Chapter II

Protection of Bankrupt's Estate and Investigation of His Affairs

Part 17A

Supplementary Provisions

Part XVIII

Interpretation

Part XIX

Final Provisions

Schedules

Insolvency Act 1986

(1986 Chapter 45)

An Act to consolidate the enactments relating to company insolvency and winding up (including the winding up of companies that are not insolvent, and of unregistered companies); enactments relating to the insolvency and bankruptcy of individuals; and other enactments bearing on those two subject matters, including the functions and qualification of insolvency practitioners, the public administration of insolvency, the penalisation and redress of malpractice and wrongdoing, and the avoidance of certain transactions at an undervalue.

[*25th July 1986*]

The First Group of Parts: Company Insolvency; Companies Winding Up

Introductory note to the First Group of Parts

The First Group of Parts deals with insolvency procedures in relation to companies (including the winding up of solvent companies), while the Second Group is concerned with the bankruptcy of individuals. "Company" is normally defined for this purpose by CA 2006 ss.1(1), 1171 (see the note to s.73, below.) Some Parts of the Act (and, in particular, Pt IV, dealing with winding up) are extended so as to apply to bodies and associations other than "companies", including partnerships: see the Introductory note to Part IV preceding s.73, below. However, in the absence of any provision to this effect, the First Group of Parts applies only to companies within the statutory definition. Accordingly, where a society incorporated under the Co-operative and Community Benefit Societies Act 2014 (formerly the Industrial and Provident Societies Act 1965) is in receivership, the creditors who would be entitled to preferential payment in the case of a company have no priority: *Re Devon & Somerset Farmers Ltd* [1994] Ch. 57; [1993] B.C.C. 410. Exceptionally, the European Regulation on Insolvency Proceedings 2015 may confer jurisdiction under IA 1986 where the body concerned has its centre of main interests within the UK, even though it does not fall within the statutory definition. But note the impact of the Insolvency Act 1986 (Amendment) Regulations 2005 (SI 2005/879) on this issue: see s.1(4) below.

Part I

Company Voluntary Arrangements

Introductory note to Part I

Part I of IA 1986, which replaces IA 1985 ss.20–26, introduced an entirely new procedure into UK company law, the "Company Voluntary Arrangement"—a term which is commonly abbreviated to "CVA".

The original CVA regime as contained in Pt I of IA 1986 has been the subject of major statutory elaboration through the mechanism of ss.1, 2 of, and Schs 1, 2 to, the Insolvency Act 2000. The effect of these changes has been to introduce a new optional CVA model with moratorium for small eligible companies. (For further guidance on eligibility see the Insolvency Act 1986 (Amendment) (No.3) Regulations 2002 (SI 2002/1990).) There are also amendments to the general CVA model.

The Cork Committee (*Report*, paras 400–403) considered it a weakness of the former company law that a company, unlike an individual, could not enter into a binding arrangement with its creditors for the composition of its indebtedness by some relatively simple procedure. Unless it could obtain the separate consent of every creditor, the only options previously available to a company were the formal statutory procedures of:

(1) a scheme of liquidation and reconstruction under CA 1985 s.582 (formerly CA 1948 s.287 (now IA 1986 s.110));

(2) a scheme of compromise or arrangement under CA 1985 ss.425–427 (CA 1948 ss.206–208 (now CA 2006 Pt 26)); and

(3) the little-used "binding arrangement" under CA 1985 s.601 (CA 1948 s.306 (obsolete)).

Each of these methods was too slow, cumbersome and costly to be at all useful in practice.

The present sections introduce a simpler scheme, more or less along the lines recommended by the Cork Committee. The CVA has proved to be of limited utility in practice, however, for two reasons. First, it cannot be made binding upon a secured or preferential creditor without his consent, and secondly, until the enactment of s.1A there was no provision in the Act for obtaining a moratorium while the proposal for an arrangement is being drawn up and considered (contrast the "interim order" available in the case of an insolvent individual: see ss.252–254). However, a moratorium could be achieved if a proposal for a voluntary arrangement is combined with an application to the court for the appointment of an administrator under Sch.B1: this is, of course, a more elaborate and costly procedure.

In view of these considerations, it is not surprising that the CVA procedure has been relatively little used (especially when compared with the much larger number of individual voluntary arrangements). In the first few years after the 1986 Act, the average number was under 100 per year, and although the figure has now crept up somewhat, the overall picture has been disappointing. In the light of this experience the Government suggested modifications to the CVA procedure in order to improve its effectiveness (and appeal). In particular it favoured the introduction of an optional moratorium facility for CVAs involving small eligible companies. This reform was enacted by the Insolvency Act 2000 s.1 with detailed provision being made in the accompanying Sch.A1. Unfortunately, there was a delay in bringing this reform into effect; this delay was apparently caused by concerns in the City over the impact of the new CVA moratorium on certain specialised corporate financing schemes. The new model came into force only on 1 January 2003—see the Insolvency Act 2000 (Commencement No.3 and Transitional Provisions) Order 2002 (SI 2002/2711 (C. 83)). Since 1 December 1994, a voluntary arrangement procedure modelled upon the CVA has been available for an insolvent partnership: see the Insolvent Partnerships Order 1994 (SI 1994/2421) art.5 and Sch.1. It is a prerequisite that the partnership be unable to pay its debts. As with a CVA, there is no provision for an interim order during which a stay of proceedings operates, although this can be achieved by applying at the same time for an administration order. Alternatively, if the partners are individuals, they may enter into individual voluntary arrangements, which will have much the same effect.

The CVA procedure has been extended to building societies by s.90A of the Building Societies Act 1986 (inserted by the Building Societies Act 1997 s.39, effective 1 December 1997). A foreign company may be permitted to use a CVA by exploiting the facility of s.426, IA 1986—*Re Television Trade Rentals Ltd* [2002] EWHC 211 (Ch); [2002] B.C.C. 807. NHS Foundation Trusts can take advantage of the CVA procedure (with or without moratorium)—the Independent Regulator of NHS Foundation Trusts is given power by s.53 of the National Health Service Act 2006 to direct foundation trustees to exploit this recovery procedure. The CVA procedure has been made available to industrial and provident societies by the Industrial and Provident Societies and Credit Unions (Arrangements, Reconstructions and Administration) Order 2014 (SI 2014/229) with effect from 6 April 2014.

The initiative in setting up a CVA is taken by the directors or, if the company is being wound up or is subject to an administration order, by the liquidator or administrator as the case may be. A "proposal" is formulated for consideration by meetings of the company's members and by its creditors using a range of decision processes: if the proposal is accepted at the respective meetings, the scheme becomes operative and binding upon the company and all of its creditors—even those who did not support the proposal. Thereafter, it is administered by a "supervisor" who must be qualified to act as an insolvency practitioner in relation to the company. The arrangement is conducted throughout under the aegis of the court, but the court itself is not involved in a judicial capacity unless there is some difficulty or disagreement.

It is not a prerequisite for the application of this Part of the Act that the company should be "insolvent" or "unable to pay its debts" within the statutory definitions of those terms.

A related reform effected by IA 1985 (see Sch.10 Pt II) was the repeal of CA 1985 s.615(2), a provision of ancient origin which stated that any general assignment by a company of its property for the benefit of its creditors was "void to all intents".

The provision which prohibits a company from giving financial assistance in the acquisition of its own shares (CA 2006 s.678) does not apply to anything done under a voluntary arrangement: see CA 2006 s.681(2)(g). The abolition of the financial assistance bar for private companies will reduce the significance of this point.

CVAs fall within the ambit of the EU Regulation on Insolvency Proceedings (2015/848) and the Cross-Border Insolvency Regulations (SI 2006/1030).

Although the EU Regulation on Insolvency Proceedings (2015/848) does apply to CVA cases it was held by Lloyd LJ (sitting as a Judge of the Chancery Division) in *Oakley v Ultra Vehicle Design Ltd* [2005] EWHC 872 (Ch); [2006] B.C.C. 115 that it did not apply if the CVA had been initiated prior to the coming into effect of the EC Regulation.

A CVA is not an "agreement" for the purposes of s.203 of the Employment Rights Act 1996—*Re Britannia Heat Transfer Ltd* [2007] B.P.I.R. 1038. This is because it was a statutory construct established under a specified procedure. This interpretation by HHJ Norris QC has served to protect CVAs from being avoided under s.203, thereby protecting their value as a reorganisation tool for distressed businesses.

The fact that the successful party under an arbitration award is undergoing a CVA does not deny that party the possibility of enforcing that award by summary judgment—see *Mead General Building Ltd v Dartmoor Properties Ltd* [2009] B.C.C. 510; [2009] B.P.I.R. 516 (Coulson J). Compare *Westshield Ltd v Whitehouse* [2013] EWHC 3576 (TCC) which was concerned with whether an adjudicator's decision could be enforced by a party undergoing a CVA. Akenhead J refused to allow enforcement as the other party had raised a counterclaim which required consideration by the CVA supervisors for a possible set off under the CVA. Further consideration of the issue of enforcement of arbitral awards where one party was undergoing a CVA is to be found in *Tate Building Services Ltd v B&M McHugh Ltd* [2014] EWHC 2971 (TCC); [2014] B.P.I.R. 1560.

On the interpretation of CVA terms see *Appleyard Ltd v Ritecrown Ltd* [2009] B.P.I.R. 235 and *Tucker and Spratt v Gold Fields Mining LLC* [2009] EWCA Civ 173; [2009] B.P.I.R. 704. The latter case is an important precedent dealing with the lodging of late claims. For further consideration see *Re Energy Holdings (No.3) Ltd* [2010] EWHC 788 (Ch); [2010] B.P.I.R. 1339. In *Re TXU Europe Group plc* [2011] EWHC 2072 (Ch) Newey J held that in making any distributions to shareholders once creditor claims had been met in the supervisors must comply with requirements as to return of capital imposed by CA 2006 Pt 23. This would only be permitted if the company went into liquidation.

In *Re Sixty UK Ltd* [2010] B.P.I.R. 1234 the court had to determine whether on the terms of the arrangement a party was entitled to rank as a creditor in a CVA. On the interpretation of the terms of a CVA note also the approach of Edwards-Stuart J in *Oakrock Ltd v Travelodge Hotels Ltd* [2015] EWHC 30 (TCC).

For the issue of whether business rates are capable of being encompassed within a CVA see *Kaye v South Oxfordshire District Council* [2013] EWHC 4165 (Ch).

For the corresponding provisions relating to voluntary arrangements for insolvent individuals, see ss.252–263. There is a close parallel between the two sets of provisions, and so cases decided under the individual voluntary arrangement sections may well be relevant in CVA proceedings, and vice versa.

The Act contemplates that a system will be set up by subordinate legislation for the registration of voluntary arrangements in a register open to public inspection: see Sch.8 para.6. The rules make provision for registration with the registrar of companies: IR 2016 rr.2.38(6), 2.44(1) and 2.44(4).

For the rules relating to CVAs, see IR 2016 Pt 2. The position has been made more complicated by locating a number of key provisions in IR 2016 Pt 15—see for example rr.15.11, 15.14, 15.31, 15.34 and 15.35. Note the role of Statement of Insolvency Practice (SIP) 3 in promoting good practice. A new SIP 3 was introduced in July 2014 with SIP 3.2 being applicable to CVAs.

In 2012 there were 839 CVAs recorded for England and Wales. 767 CVAs were established in England and Wales in 2011. The 2013 figure was 577. In 2014 only 563 CVAs were recorded for England and Wales. This figure fell to 364 in 2015 and 346 in 2016. Only 292 were recorded in 2017.

Previously there were reform proposals in the air. A consultation document, a copy of which is available on the Insolvency Service website, was launched by the Insolvency Service in June 2009. Essentially it is opening up for discussion a number ideas designed to reinvigorate corporate rescue. A number of proposals are relevant to the CVA models. These include: extending the Sch.A1 procedure to larger and medium-sized companies; introducing a court-initiated moratorium for CVAs; and improving the position with regard to securing rescue finance. For a summary of these proposals see (2009) 255 Co. L.N. 1.

A further, unrelated, consultation exercise, *Proposals for a Restructuring Moratorium*, launched by the Insolvency Service on 26 July 2010, proposed a moratorium for companies restructuring their debts. This would apply to any company that could be subject to a CVA or to a scheme of arrangement under Pt 26 of CA 2006, although the company would not need to be so subject at the time of the application. Thus the directors of a company who were considering a CVA might apply for this moratorium to allow the company some breathing space while a CVA proposal was being formulated. Eligibility and qualifying conditions would apply. The moratorium as proposed would be similar to that in a small company CVA under Sch.A1. It contains some specific proposals for where a CVA is in place or where a CVA proposal is under consideration (possible to save a court hearing). For a summary of the proposal see (2010) 269 Co. L.N. 1. The consultation paper is on the Insolvency Service's website. In the end this came to nothing. But in May 2016 this area of law reform was revisited by the Insolvency Service. In its *Review of the Corporate Insolvency Framework* new proposals were put forward for a broad moratorium. These were favourably received. For discussion of this initiative see Bailey (2016) 386 Co. L.N. 1 and Umfreville (2016) 385 Co. L.N. 1. The responses to the consultation published on the Insolvency Service website in September 2016 were summarised by Bailey in (2016) 388 Co. L.N. 1. The government is now considering the responses to this consultation.

The proposal

1 Those who may propose an arrangement

1(1) [Directors] The directors of a company (other than one which is in administration or being wound up) may make a proposal under this Part to the company and to its creditors for a composition in satisfaction of its debts or a scheme of arrangement of its affairs (from here on referred to, in either case, as a "voluntary arrangement").

1(2) [Interpretation] A proposal under this Part is one which provides for some person ("the nominee") to act in relation to the voluntary arrangement either as trustee or otherwise for the purpose of supervising its implementation; and the nominee must be a person who is qualified to act as an insolvency practitioner in relation to the voluntary arrangement.

1(3) [Administrator, liquidator] Such a proposal may also be made–

(a) where the company is in administration, by the administrator, and

(b) where the company is being wound up, by the liquidator.

1(4) ["Company" in Pt 1] In this Part "company" means–

(a) a company registered under the Companies Act 2006 in England and Wales or Scotland;

(b) a company incorporated in an EEA State other than the United Kingdom; or

(c) a company not incorporated in an EEA State but having its centre of main interests in a member State other than Denmark.

1(5) ["Centre of main interests"] In subsection (4), in relation to a company, "centre of main interests" has the same meaning as in Article 3 of the EU Regulation.

1(6) [Northern Ireland] If a company incorporated outside the United Kingdom has a principal place of business in Northern Ireland, no proposal under this Part shall be made in relation to it unless it also has a principal place of business in England and Wales or Scotland (or both in England and Wales or Scotland).

General Note

In any case where the company is not subject to an administration order or being wound up, the initiative in proposing a voluntary arrangement is taken by the directors, and the more elaborate procedure laid down by s.2 applies. An insolvency practitioner who is "qualified" to act in relation to the company must be brought in as "nominee" to report on the directors' proposals and to organise the meetings, etc. by which the scheme is to be implemented. (In practice, the directors will in most cases have consulted the proposed nominee in advance and invoked his help in drawing up the proposal.) Where, however, there is an administrator or liquidator already in office, he will normally himself act as the nominee and may then proceed directly to summon meetings of the company and its creditors under s.3.

Neither creditors nor members of a company have standing to propose a voluntary arrangement. Section 1(2) was modified by s.2 and Sch.2 to IA 2000 to recognise the fact that, under IA 2000, turnaround specialists may act as nominees or supervisors. The language of ss.1(1) and 1(3) was recast by EA 2002 s.248 and Sch.17 to reflect the fact that it is no longer strictly accurate to refer to administration *orders*.

Note amendment by DA 2015 s.19 and Sch.6.

S.1(1)

The directors have power to act only when the company is not in liquidation or subject to administration.

There is no statutory definition of "creditor" for the purposes of this Part of the Act. It would be normal to give the word its dictionary meaning, "one to whom a debt is owing"—a phrase which would exclude a prospective or contingent creditor and a person whose claim was for unliquidated damages (see Roy Goode, *Principles of Corporate Insolvency Law*, 4th edn (2011), at 2–26). This view is reinforced by the fact that the concepts of "debt" and "provable debt" are extended to include these wider categories of claim by IR 2016 rr.14.1 and 14.2; but this provision is confined to the winding up of companies. It is also noteworthy that although contingent and prospective creditors are expressly given the same rights as creditors elsewhere in the Act (see, e.g. ss.9, 124 (standing to present petition for administration or winding-up order)), there is no similar provision here in Pt I. It would therefore be reasonable to assume that the term "creditor" does not have the wider meaning in this section. Fortunately, any doubts that there might have been on this question have now been resolved. In *Doorbar v Alltime Securities Ltd* [1996] 1 W.L.R. 456; [1995] B.C.C. 1,149 the Court of Appeal (affirming Knox J [1994] B.C.C. 994) held that rent under a lease becoming due in the future was capable of being included in an individual voluntary arrangement under s.258 of the Act, and this ruling has since been applied in the context of a CVA in *Re Cancol Ltd* [1996] 1 All E.R. 37; [1995] B.C.C. 1,133; and *Re Sweatfield Ltd* [1997] B.C.C. 744; and in *Beverley Group plc v McClue* [1995] B.C.C. 751 a person with a claim for an unliquidated amount was held entitled to vote as a creditor. Of course, it is possible that the terms of a scheme of voluntary arrangement should be so drawn up as to exclude future or contingent creditors from its operation. This was the case in *Burford Midland Properties Ltd v Marley Extrusions Ltd* [1994] B.C.C. 604 (a case which contains a useful discussion of the terms "future", "contingent" and "prospective" liabilities).

In *Re FMS Financial Management Services Ltd* (1989) 5 B.C.C. 191, former clients of the company who appeared to have good claims against it for damages for misrepresentation were not treated as creditors for the purposes of a CVA; but an order was made by the court, after the scheme had been approved, directing that they should be admitted to prove on the same terms as the company's creditors.

For the issue of whether business rates are capable of being encompassed within a CVA see *Kaye v South Oxfordshire District Council* [2013] EWHC 4165 (Ch).

The terms "composition" and "scheme of arrangement" are not synonymous. The latter involves something less than the release or discharge of a creditor's debts—e.g. a moratorium. Thus, in *Inland Revenue Commissioners v Adam & Partners Ltd* [2000] B.P.I.R. 986 a proposed moratorium which offered nothing to creditors was not sufficient to constitute a "composition" but could amount to a "scheme of arrangement". See also the discussion in *March Estates plc v Gunmark Ltd* [1996] 2 B.C.L.C. 1.

S.1(2)

The Act obviously contemplates that in most cases the "nominee" himself will in due course administer the scheme (e.g. by acting as a trustee for the benefit of the company's creditors), although it is possible in certain circumstances for someone other than the original nominee to be appointed instead (see ss.2(4), 4(2)). When it is finally settled who it is that is to have charge of the scheme, the Act (by s.7(2)) designates him "the supervisor". This tends to obscure the fact that in the great majority of situations "the supervisor" will be the same person as "the nominee" and, where the company is the subject of an administration order or is being wound up, also the same person as the administrator or liquidator. By whatever means he is chosen, however, the "supervisor" must be a person who is qualified to act as an insolvency practitioner in relation to the company; and in this way the legislation ensures that no voluntary scheme can be implemented without independent professional approval and supervision.

The criteria by which a person is deemed to be "qualified" to act as an insolvency practitioner "in relation to" a particular company are laid down in ss.388–398 and 419, below.

The section provides for the nominee or supervisor to act "as trustee or otherwise". In *Re Leisure Study Group Ltd* [1994] 2 B.C.L.C. 65, Harman J held that funds in the hands of a supervisor were held on trust for the company's unsecured creditors, and had been put out of reach of the security conferred by a floating charge; see the note on s.7(4).

Nothing in this Part of the Act gives the supervisor, as such, power to perform any act in the name of the company or makes him an officer of the company: whatever authority he has must come from the terms of the voluntary arrangement itself, or from the fact that he is also the company's administrator or liquidator. It has been assumed by the draftsman that a decision of the company in general meeting under s.4(1) will be competent, as a matter of company law, to give wide powers of management to a supervisor regardless of the terms of the company's articles. We must probably infer from the general tenor of the Act that the terms of a voluntary arrangement are capable of overriding the articles if necessary. The position would have been less uncertain if the supervisor had been given certain statutory powers and a more clearly defined authority.

The nominee (and, later, the supervisor) is referred to throughout in the singular. There is nothing to prevent the appointment of joint nominees or supervisors, however: see the note to s.7(6) below.

S.1(3)

In the two situations referred to in this subsection, the proposal not only may but (by virtue of the bracketed words in s.1(1)) must be made by the administrator or liquidator. In this case, the administrator or liquidator may appoint himself to be the nominee and proceed immediately to summon meetings under s.3. If for any reason he appoints someone else, the more elaborate procedure under s.2 must be followed. A bank liquidator may propose a CVA—see s.113 of the Banking Act 2009.

For the rules which apply when the application is made under this subsection, see IR 2016 rr.2.3 et seq.

S.1(4)–(6)

Subsection (4) was originally inserted by the Insolvency Act 1986 (Amendment) (No.2) Regulations 2002 (SI 2002/1240) as part of the implementation strategy for the EC Regulation on Insolvency Proceedings (1346/2000). However, because of the way the 2002 Regulations had been drafted an unintentional consequence arose in that in *Re Salvage Association* [2003] EWHC 1028 (Ch); [2003] B.C.C. 504 Blackburne J held that CVAs were now available for corporate bodies which did not qualify as "companies" within the meaning of the Companies Act 1985. Apparently this caused concerns in the City of London about the potential impact on niche financing transactions—see G. Moss [2005] 18 Insolv. Int. 92. Accordingly, subs.(4) was replaced and new subs.(5) inserted by the Insolvency Act 1986 (Amendment) Regulations 2005 (SI 2005/879) to neutralise this unintended consequence whilst allowing companies incorporated in EEA states and those having a centre of main interests in Member States (except Denmark) to access the CVA procedure. Subsection (5) was amended by the Insolvency Amendment (EU 2015/848) Regulations 2017 (SI 2017/702) regs 1, 2(1), Sch. paras 1, 2 in relation to proceedings opened on or after 26 June 2017 (see reg.3) when the Recast EU Regulation 2015/848 came into force. Subsection (6) deals with non-UK companies having a principal place of business in Northern Ireland. Note the amendment to subs.(4)(a) introduced by the Companies Act 2006 (Consequential Amendments, Transitional Provisions and Savings) Order 2009 (SI 2009/1941) with effect from 1 October 2009. This clarifies the meaning of the word "company" in the light of the Companies Act 2006.

1A Moratorium

1A(1) [Directors] Where the directors of an eligible company intend to make a proposal for a voluntary arrangement, they may take steps to obtain a moratorium for the company.

1A(2) [Applicability of Sch.A1] The provisions of Schedule A1 to this Act have effect with respect to–

(a) companies eligible for a moratorium under this section,

(b) the procedure for obtaining such a moratorium,

(c) the effects of such a moratorium, and

(d) the procedure applicable (in place of sections 2 to 6 and 7) in relation to the approval and implementation of a voluntary arrangement where such a moratorium is or has been in force.

General Note

This introduces the new Sch.A1 which offers a moratorium facility for the CVA in circumstances where the company is classed as "small" and "eligible". The criteria governing eligibility were added to by Insolvency Act 1986 (Amendment) (No.3) Regulations 2002 (SI 2002/1990—inserting additional paras 4A–4K into Sch.A1). See further the discussion under Sch.A1. Note in particular that a company cannot be regarded as eligible if it has incurred a liability of £10 million or more under an agreement which is part of a capital market arrangement (Sch.A1 para.4C). The new CVA model came into operation on 1 January 2003—see Insolvency Act 2000 (Commencement No.3) and Transitional Provisions Order 2002 (SI 2002/2711).

Full discussion of this CVA variant is to be found at Sch.A1. All indications suggest that it is not being used extensively and, with the advent of the out of court administration entry model, that pattern is likely to persist. Nevertheless substantial amendments have been made to Sch.A1 by SBEEA 2015. These are primarily the result of the introduction of new creditor decision procedures.

2 Procedure where nominee is not the liquidator or administrator

2(1) [Application] This section applies where the nominee under section 1 is not the liquidator or administrator of the company and the directors do not propose to take steps to obtain a moratorium under section 1A for the company.

2(2) [Report to court] The nominee shall, within 28 days (or such longer period as the court may allow) after he is given notice of the proposal for a voluntary arrangement, submit a report to the court stating–

(a) whether, in his opinion, the proposed voluntary arrangement has a reasonable prospect of being approved and implemented,

(b) whether, in his opinion, the proposal should be considered by a meeting of the company and by the company's creditors, and

(c) if in his opinion it should, the date on which, and time and place at which, he proposes a meeting of the company should be held.

2(3) [Information to nominee] For the purposes of enabling the nominee to prepare his report, the person intending to make the proposal shall submit to the nominee–

(a) a document setting out the terms of the proposed voluntary arrangement, and

(b) a statement of the company's affairs containing–

(i) such particulars of its creditors and of its debts and other liabilities and of its assets as may be prescribed, and

(ii) such other information as may be prescribed.

2(4) [Replacement of nominee by court] The court may–

(a) on an application made by the person intending to make the proposal, in a case where the nominee has failed to submit the report required by this section or has died, or

(b) on an application made by that person or the nominee, in a case where it is impracticable or inappropriate for the nominee to continue to act as such,

direct that the nominee be replaced as such by another person qualified to act as an insolvency practitioner, in relation to the voluntary arrangement.

GENERAL NOTE

The wording of s.2(1) and (2) was modified by IA 2000 s.2 and Sch.2. Section 2(4) was also substituted by those provisions.

Note amendment by DA 2015 s.19 and Sch.6.

S.2(1)

Section 2 will necessarily apply where the proposal is made by the directors under s.1(1); and it will also apply when an administrator or liquidator designates someone other than himself as nominee.

S.2(2)

No step towards implementing the proposal can be taken under this section until a report has first been submitted by the nominee to the court. The court's role is, however, primarily an administrative one, and it will not be involved judicially except when there is some dispute or difficulty. The procedure which the section envisages is as follows:

(1) The directors decide to propose an arrangement, and themselves find an insolvency practitioner who is qualified to act as supervisor and who is willing, at least in principle, to do so (see IR 2016 r.2.3(i)(h)). As has been mentioned above, it is likely in most cases that the directors will seek the intended nominee's professional assistance in preparing the proposal in advance. The routine contemplated by the Act will then be largely a formality.

(2) The directors give notice of the proposal for a voluntary arrangement to the nominee, and submit to him a document setting out the terms of the proposed arrangement and a statement of the company's affairs (s.2(3)(a), (b)). (It is not clear from the section itself whether the "notice" referred to in s.2(2) is constituted by the formal submission of the document and statement of affairs specified in s.2(3) or is some separate and earlier notification. The former interpretation is plainly the one intended, since the 28-day period referred to in s.2(2) only starts to run from the receipt of the document.) The court may permit the statement of affairs to be censored—see IR 2016 rr.2.7, 2.12.

(3) The nominee has 28 days (or longer, if the court allows) to prepare and submit a report to the court. This will ensure that a scheme always has the benefit of a preliminary opinion from a professional insolvency practitioner.

(4) If the nominee forms the view that the proposed scheme should go ahead, he reports to the court his opinion that meetings of the company should be summoned and views of its creditors should be sought, and he must

himself fix their date, time and place. (On the formalities for summoning meetings, see the comment to s.3(1) and (2), below.)

(5) Under s.3(1), it will normally then be the nominee's role to engage with the members and creditors.

(6) If the nominee considers that the proposed scheme should not be taken further, s.2(2) appears to suggest that he should submit a negative report to the court, and this is confirmed by IR 2016 r.2.9. However, nothing is made to depend on the filing of such a report, and the company is not barred from seeking a second opinion from another nominee.

(7) Where the initiative is not taken by the directors but by an administrator or liquidator who elects not to nominate himself, the responsibility for selecting the intended nominee and preparing the documentation specified in s.2(3) falls upon that person and not on the directors.

Necessarily, the nominee is heavily reliant on the information provided by the debtor company and there is therefore a consequential need for complete candour on the part of the latter. Where the nominee has doubts about the accuracy and reliability of this information, he has a responsibility to satisfy himself, within the resources available to him, by further inquiries. See the position discussed (in the context of an individual voluntary arrangement) in *Re a Debtor (No.140 IO of 1995)* [1996] 2 B.C.L.C. 429.

Subsection (2) was amended by SBEEA 2015 s.126 and Sch.9 para.2 to reflect a broader range of creditor decision methods.

S.2(3)

This subsection gives details of the two documents on which the nominee is to base his report to the court. On the contents of the proposal see IR 2016 r.2.3.

The "statement of the company's affairs" must be made up to a date no earlier than two weeks before the date of the proposal: IR 2016 rr.2.4, 2.6.

The "statement of the company's affairs" referred to is similar to the statement which must be submitted to an administrator (s.22), an administrative receiver (ss.47, 66) and a liquidator (ss.99, 131). On this topic, see the note to s.131.

S.2(4)

If, after the expiration of the 28 days or longer period provided for by s.2(2), the nominee has not submitted a report either in favour of or against proceeding with the proposal, this subsection allows the directors (or the administrator or liquidator, where appropriate) to invoke the court's help and have an alternative nominee appointed. However, there appears to be no reason why an intended proposal should not be aborted without the court's involvement, for at this stage no creditor will have been affected by the scheme or even have been made aware of it, and the court itself will not yet be in the picture. This course should certainly be permissible if the first intended nominee consents; if he does not, however, a professional code of conduct might possibly inhibit a colleague from replacing him against his wishes, and in that case the court's aid would be necessary.

3 Consideration of proposal

3(1) [Company meeting and creditor decision] Where the nominee under section 1 is not the liquidator or administrator, and it has been reported to the court under section 2(2) that the proposal should be considered by a meeting of the company and by the company's creditors, the person making the report shall (unless the court otherwise directs)–

(a) summon a meeting of the company to consider the proposal for the time, date and place proposed in the report, and

(b) seek a decision from the company's creditors as to whether they approve the proposal.

3(2) [Where nominee liquidator or administrator] Where the nominee is the liquidator or administrator, he shall–

(a) summon a meeting of the company to consider the proposal for such time, date and place as he thinks fit, and

(b) seek a decision from the company's creditors as to whether they approve the proposal.

3(3) [Mode of creditor decision] A decision of the company's creditors as to whether they approve the proposal is to be made by a qualifying decision procedure.

3(4) [Notice of qualifying decision procedure] Notice of the qualifying decision procedure must be given to every creditor of the company of whose claim and address the person seeking the decision is aware.

General Note

A voluntary arrangement comes into effect under s.5 when the proposal has been approved by both a meeting of the company and by its creditors (unless s.4A(2)(b) applies).

Both s.2(2)(b) and s.3(2) appear to leave it to the nominee's discretion to fix such matters as the time and date of the meeting and of the creditor decision, the length of notice which is to be given and the order in which the two decisions are to be made. However such discretion as is given to the nominee by ss.2(2)(b) and 3(2) is exercisable only within the constraints imposed by the rules: see IR 2016 rr.2.25, 2.29 and Pt 15.

There were be several changes made to s.3 made by SBEEA 2015 s.126 and Sch.9. These reflect the move away from meetings as the only way in which the views of creditors may be determined.

S.3(1)

Where the nominee is not the liquidator or administrator, no step can be taken to summon meetings until he has made a favourable report to the court under s.2(2). Once he has done so, it becomes his duty to summon the meetings (without any court order or other formality) in accordance with his own proposals.

No guidance is given by the section as to the basis on which the court might "otherwise direct", or as to who (apart from the nominee himself) might have standing to apply for such a direction.

S.3(2)

Where the nominee is the liquidator or administrator, the procedure outlined in s.2 is bypassed. He himself proceeds straight to the decision making procedure, and at this stage nothing is notified or reported to the court. There appears to be no power under this subsection for the court to "direct otherwise".

A nominee who is himself the liquidator or administrator will have received, or be entitled to receive, a "statement of affairs" under ss.22, 99 or 131.

For the appropriate rules, see IR 2016 rr.2.3, 2.5, 2.25–2.29.

S.3(3)

A nominee who has prepared a report under s.2(2) will have been given particulars of the company's creditors under s.2(3)(b). A liquidator or administrator who has appointed himself as nominee will receive this information with the "statement of affairs". The question of who might be a "creditor" and hence a party to a CVA was considered by David Richards J in one instalment of the *Re T & N Ltd* saga (see *Re T & N Ltd* [2005] EWHC 2870 (Ch); [2006] B.P.I.R. 532). The judge held that individuals who may have suffered latent injury through exposure to asbestos could be treated as creditors for CVA purposes. Such future potential tort claimants as the law then stood would not be regarded as creditors enjoying provable debts on liquidation (see IR 2016 rr.14.1 and 14.2). This significant judgment paved the way for a subsequent relaxation of the aforementioned Insolvency Rules (see annotations thereto).

Consideration and implementation of proposal

4 Decisions of the company and its creditors

4(1) [Decision] This section applies where, under section 3–

(a) a meeting of the company is summoned to consider the proposed voluntary arrangement, and

(b) the company's creditors are asked to decide whether to approve the proposed voluntary arrangement.

4(1A) [Possibility of modifications] The company and its creditors may approve the proposed voluntary arrangement with or without modifications.

4(2) [Modifications] The modifications may include one conferring the functions proposed to be conferred on the nominee on another person qualified to act as an insolvency practitioner in relation to the voluntary arrangement.

But they shall not include any modification by virtue of which the proposal ceases to be a proposal such as is mentioned in section 1.

4(3) [Limitation on approval] Neither the company nor its creditors may approve any proposal or modification which affects the right of a secured creditor of the company to enforce his security, except with the concurrence of the creditor concerned.

4(4) [Further limitation] Subject as follows, neither the company nor its creditors may approve any proposal or modification under which–

(a) any preferential debt of the company is to be paid otherwise than in priority to such of its debts as are not preferential debts,

(aa) any ordinary preferential debt of the company is to be paid otherwise than in priority to any secondary preferential debts that it may have,

(b) a preferential creditor of the company is to be paid an amount in respect of an ordinary preferential debt that bears to that debt a smaller proportion than is borne to another ordinary preferential debt by the amount that is to be paid in respect of that other debt or

(c) a preferential creditor of the company is to be paid an amount in respect of a secondary preferential debt that bears to that debt a smaller proportion than is borne to another secondary preferential debt by the amount that is to be paid in respect of that other debt.

However, such a proposal or modification may be approved with the concurrence of the preferential creditor concerned.

4(5) [Decision in accordance with rules] Subject as above, the meeting of the company and the qualifying decision procedure shall be conducted in accordance with the rules.

4(6) [Report to court, notice: company meeting] After the conclusion of the company meeting in accordance with the rules, the chairman of the meeting shall report the result of the meeting to the court, and, immediately after reporting to the court, shall give notice of the result of the meeting to such persons as may be prescribed.

4(6A) [Report to court, notice: creditors' decision] After the company's creditors have decided whether to approve the proposed voluntary arrangement the person who sought the decision must–

(a) report the creditors' decision to the court, and

(b) immediately after reporting to the court, give notice of the creditors' decision to such persons as may be prescribed.

4(7) [Interpretation] References in this section to preferential debts, ordinary preferential debts, secondary preferential debts and preferential creditors are to be read in accordance with section 386 in Part XII of this Act.

General Note

The terms of the scheme, when approved by the meetings, bind every member and creditor (see s.5(2)).

No provision appears to be made for any subsequent modification of the scheme unless that modification is put forward by the person who made the original proposal (see s.6(4)). The only opportunity, therefore, for any of the company's members or creditors to seek to have the proposal modified will be at the meetings themselves. Note the amendments made to subss.(4) and (7) by the Banks and Building Societies (Depositor Preference and Priorities) Order 2014 (SI 2014/3486) with effect from 1 January 2015. These changes relate to the new classification of preferential debts into ordinary preferential debts and secondary preferential debts.

Note amendment by DA 2015 s.19 and Sch.6.

Section 4 was amended by SBEEA 2015 s.126 and Sch.9 to reflect the move away from the exclusive use of meetings to determine creditor views. This amendment resulted in the addition of subs.(6A).

S.4(1)

The scheme can only go ahead in a modified form if both the members and creditors approve the same modifications (but see the qualification in s.4A).

S.4(2)
The modifications may include the substitution of a different nominee to administer the scheme; but no modification may take the proceedings outside the scope of s.1 altogether (i.e. amount to a wholly different course of action, such as putting the company into liquidation). Note that s.4(2) was modified by IA 2000 s.2 and Sch.2 to reflect the fact that a wider group of professionals can now act as nominees/supervisors.

S.4(3)
No voluntary arrangement can affect the rights of a secured creditor without his consent. In *March Estates plc v Gunmark Ltd* [1996] 2 B.C.L.C. 1 Lightman J held that a landlord's right of forfeiture was to be treated as a security for this purpose, but in the latter case of *Razzaq v Pala* [1998] B.C.C. 66 at 71 the same judge said that this ruling had been given without full argument and that, on reconsideration, he should have held otherwise. In *Thomas v Ken Thomas Ltd* [2006] EWCA Civ 1504; [2007] B.P.I.R. 959 the Court of Appeal held that, on the construction of the particular CVA before it, the landlord's right to forfeit had indeed been surrendered in exchange for rights under the CVA. Neuberger LJ, who read the main judgment, disagreed both with Hoffmann J in *Re Naeem* [1990] 1 W.L.R. 48; and Lightman J in *March Estates v Gunmark plc* [1996] 2 B.C.L.C. 1 on this particular point. This disagreement was not merely based upon the facts of this particular CVA, but was more general in nature. Reference also was made to the importance of the rescue culture which is prioritised over the rights of individual creditors including landlords. See also *Re The Cotswold Co Ltd* [2009] 2 B.C.L.C. 371.

S.4(4)
The rights of preferential creditors (as defined in s.4(7)) are similarly protected, as regards both their priority vis-à-vis all other debts and their right to rank equally with each other. There is no provision which obliges the preferential creditors to accept a decision made by a majority of them, even if it is passed at a separate class meeting (contrast CA 1985 s.425 [CA 2006 s.895]).

Apart from this and the preceding subsection, there is nothing in the Act which restricts the arrangements which a proposal may make, or requires creditors to be given equal treatment. It is thus permissible, e.g. for small creditors to be given more favourable treatment than larger ones.

The meaning of s.4(4)(a) was considered by the Court of Appeal in *Inland Revenue Commissioners v Wimbledon FC* [2004] EWCA Civ 655; [2004] B.C.C. 638. Here it was held that a restructuring scheme designed to save a football club which involved the introduction of third party funds to repay certain creditors ("the football creditors") in full where other preferential creditors merely received a dividend did not contravene this prohibition in s.4(4)(a) because it only applied to restrict the use of the company's assets for repayment purposes under the proposed arrangement and did not encompass use of third party assets outside the arrangement strictly speaking. Having made that distinction, the Court of Appeal added that had there been a breach of s.4 the court would have had no option but to strike down the arrangement.

S.4(5)
Although this subsection refers in terms only to the conduct of the meeting and the creditor decision process (and not, e.g. to their summoning) it is plain that the rules apply to all aspects of such meetings and decisions: see the note to s.3 above.

For the appropriate rules, see IR 2016 r.2.29 and Pt 15 generally.

S.4(6), (6A)
The chairman of the meetings will be appointed or selected in accordance with the rules (see IR 2016 r.15.21). It is perhaps odd that it is the chairman, rather than the nominee, who is required to report to the court, but the report must be filed in court very quickly (within four business days: see IR 2016 r.2.38(3)), and difficulties could arise, if, e.g. the nominee was abroad. IR 2016 r.2.38(6) provides that if the voluntary arrangement is approved by the meetings, the supervisor must send a copy of the chairman's report to the registrar of companies.

The making of the chairman's report to the court and the giving of the prescribed notices have no direct legal consequences (although time is made to run for various purposes, e.g. the stay of a winding-up order, from the date that the report is made to the court). The voluntary arrangement itself takes effect as a result of the decisions alone, and the court plays no active part in the proceedings at any stage.

S.4(7)
"Preferential debts" and "preferential creditors" are defined for the purpose of this Part of the Act by s.386 and Sch.6, below. The list of preferential creditors is settled by reference to a "relevant date", which determines both the existence and the amount of a preferential debt. To ascertain the "relevant date" for the purpose of the present section, see s.387(3A).

The section makes no reference to the possibility that a voluntary arrangement and a receivership might co-exist. In such a case, there would also be a list of preferential creditors who were entitled to rank in priority to the charge-holder in the receivership. There would then be two lists of preferential debts defined by reference to different "relevant dates"; but those relating to the receivership would have no significance for the purposes of this Part of the Act.

4A Approval of arrangement

4A(1) [Application] This section applies to a decision, under section 4, with respect to the approval of a proposed voluntary arrangement.

4A(2) [Decision to be in accordance with rules] The decision has effect if, in accordance with the rules–

(a) it has been taken by the meeting of the company summoned under section 3 and by the company's creditors pursuant to that section, or

(b) (subject to any order made under subsection (4)) it has been taken by the company's creditors pursuant to that section.

4A(3) [Application to court] If the decision taken by the company's creditors differs from that taken by the company meeting, a member of the company may apply to the court.

4A(4) [Application under s.4A(3)] An application under subsection (3) shall not be made after the end of the period of 28 days beginning with–

(a) the day on which the decision was taken by the company's creditors, or

(b) where the decision of the company meeting was taken on a later day, that day.

4A(5) [Regulated companies] Where a member of a regulated company, within the meaning given by paragraph 44 of Schedule A1, applies to the court under subsection (3), the appropriate regulator is entitled to be heard on the application.

4A(5A) [Appropriate regulator] "The appropriate regulator" means–

(a) where the regulated company is a PRA-regulated company within the meaning of paragraph 44 of Schedule A1, the Financial Conduct Authority and the Prudential Regulation Authority, and

(b) in any other case, the Financial Conduct Authority.

4A(6) [Court powers] On an application under subsection (3), the court may–

(a) order the decision of the company meeting to have effect instead of the decision of the company's creditors, or

(b) make such other order as it thinks fit.

General Note

This new section was introduced by s.2 of, and Sch.2 to, the Insolvency Act 2000 with effect from 1 January 2003. It seeks to provide more detailed guidance on the effect of a CVA being approved.

Amendments were made to this provision by the Financial Services Act 2012 Sch.18. These changes include a minor amendment to subs.(5) and the addition of a new subs.(5A).

Note amendments made by SBEEA 2015 s.126 and Sch.9.

S.4A(1)

This identifies the applicability of s.4A.

S.4A(2), (3), (4), (6)

The main point to grasp from these subsections is that, if there is a mismatch between the decisions taken by the creditors and members, the former decision will prevail. In such circumstances a member can apply to the court within 28 days to challenge this effect. On such an application the court enjoys wide powers under subs.(6).

S.4A(5)

This provision is not of general application.

5 Effect of approval

5(1) [Operation] This section applies where a decision approving a voluntary arrangement has effect under section 4A.

5(2) [Effect of composition or scheme] The voluntary arrangement–

(a) takes effect as if made by the company at the time the creditors decided to approve the voluntary arrangement, and

(b) binds every person who in accordance with the rules–

(i) was entitled to vote in the qualifying decision procedure by which the creditors' decision to approve the voluntary arrangement was made, or

(ii) would have been so entitled if he had had notice of it,

as if he were a party to the voluntary arrangement.

5(2A) [Amounts payable upon cessation] If–

(a) when the arrangement ceases to have effect any amount payable under the arrangement to a person bound by virtue of subsection (2)(b)(ii) has not been paid, and

(b) the arrangement did not come to an end prematurely,

the company shall at that time become liable to pay to that person the amount payable under the arrangement.

5(3) [Court powers] Subject as follows, if the company is being wound up or is in administration, the court may do one or both of the following, namely–

(a) by order stay or sist all proceedings in the winding up or provide for the appointment of the administrator to cease to have effect;

(b) give such directions with respect to the conduct of the winding up or the administration as it thinks appropriate for facilitating the implementation of the voluntary arrangement.

5(4) [Limit on s.5(3)(a)] The court shall not make an order under subsection (3)(a)–

(a) at any time before the end of the period of 28 days beginning with the first day on which each of the reports required by section 4(6) and (6A) has been made to the court, or

(b) at any time when an application under the next section or an appeal in respect of such an application is pending, or at any time in the period within which such an appeal may be brought.

General Note

The former regime under which both meetings had to approve the proposal has been mitigated by s.4A(2). Section 5(2), however, quite clearly makes the time of the creditors' decision the critical time for the scheme to take effect, and not that of the later of the two decisions. On timing see IR 2016 r.2.28.

It appears that the scheme takes effect at once and continues to be effective even though a challenge is mounted under s.6; but this is subject to any directions which may be given by the court under s.6(6).

Although the effect of a CVA is to establish a statutory "contract" between the company and its creditors it has been held by HHJ Norris QC in *Re Britannia Heat Transfer Ltd* [2007] B.C.C. 470 that it does not constitute an "agreement" for the purposes of s.203 of the Employment Rights Act 1996.

On the pragmatic correct approach towards the construction of the terms of a CVA see *Simpson v Bowker* [2007] EWCA Civ 772.

Amendments were made to this provision by SBEEA 2015 s.126 and Sch.9.

S.5(2)

The word "approved" was deleted by Sch.5 to IA 2000 by authority of s.15(1). For consideration of the former wording of s.5(2) see *Wood v Heart Hospital* [2009] B.P.I.R. 1538.

For the rules relating to the right to vote and the requisite majorities for decisions of creditors and members, see IR 2016 rr.2.35, 2.36 and Pt 15.

This subsection makes the scheme binding on all the company's creditors entitled to vote, including absentees and dissentients.

"Notice" in the context of s.5(2)(b) was given a broad interpretation in *Beverley Group plc v McClue* [1995] B.C.C. 751: a formal notice which had been sent had not been received by the creditor, but he had learned of the creditors' meeting indirectly and had also attended the members' meeting.

A voluntary arrangement does not bind a person who was not entitled to vote on the creditors' decision, and such a person cannot take advantage of the arrangement: *R A Securities Ltd v Mercantile Credit Co Ltd* [1994] B.C.C. 598. However where a creditor who was entitled to vote assigns the benefit of his contract with the company, the assignee takes that benefit as modified by the arrangement; and where land is leased to the debtor company and the reversion is assigned, the assignee is bound by the arrangement as a matter of property law: *Burford Midland Properties Ltd v Marley Extrusions Ltd* [1994] B.C.C. 604. The position of a landlord on a CVA was further considered in *Re The Cotswold Co Ltd* [2009] 2 B.C.L.C. 371. Claims not brought within the arrangement can still be pursued by a participating creditor—*Alman v Approach Housing Ltd* [2001] B.P.I.R. 203. On the issue of the extent to which a local billing authority is bound in respect of unpaid business rates see *Kaye v South Oxfordshire District Council* [2013] EWHC 4165 (Ch).

On the position of creditors whose claims are future or contingent or for an unliquidated amount, see the note to IR 2016 rr.15.7 and 15.29. See also note to s.3(3) on future tort claimants.

The release of the debtor company from liability under a voluntary arrangement does not also release a solvent co-debtor who is not a party to the arrangement: *March Estates plc v Gunmark Ltd* [1996] 2 B.C.L.C. 1; *Johnson v Davies* [1998] 2 B.C.L.C. 252, although in the latter case the Court of Appeal stated that in principle there is no reason why a term in an agreement could not have the effect of releasing a co-debtor depending on the construction of the agreement, the surrounding circumstances and any terms that could be implied.

Note that the approval of a scheme brings into operation the provisions of s.233, which prevent the suppliers of gas, electricity, etc. from imposing certain terms as to payment as a condition of making a supply available: see s.233(1)(c).

S.5(2)(b)

This was substituted by s.2 of and Sch.2 to IA 2000. It binds in unknown creditors.

S.5(2A)

This was inserted by s.2 of and Sch.2 to IA 2000.

S.5(3), (4)

The word "approved" was removed from s.5(3)(b) by Sch.5 to IA 2000 on the authority of s.15(1). The phraseology used here was modified by s.248 of and Sch.17 to EA 2002 to cater for the change in nature of the administration regime.

If the company is being wound up or is in administration, the court is empowered to stay (or in Scotland, sist) the winding-up order or to terminate the administration, or to give directions short of taking either of these steps which will facilitate the implementation of the scheme; but it may not make an order under s.5(3)(a) until 28 days after the later of the chairman's reports has been made to the court under s.4(6), nor while a hearing or an appeal from a ruling under s.6 is pending. For the interaction of s.5(3) with s.147 see *McGruther v James Scott Ltd* [2004] S.C. 514.

6 Challenge of decisions

6(1) [Application to court] Subject to this section, an application to the court may be made, by any of the persons specified below, on one or both of the following grounds, namely–

(a) that a voluntary arrangement which has effect under section 4A unfairly prejudices the interests of a creditor, member or contributory of the company;

(b) that there has been some material irregularity at or in relation to the meeting of the company, or in relation to the relevant qualifying decision procedure.

6(1A) ["Relevant qualifying decision procedure"] In this section–

(a) the "relevant qualifying decision procedure" means the qualifying decision procedure in which the company's creditors decide whether to approve a voluntary arrangement;

(b) references to a decision made in the relevant qualifying decision procedure include any other decision made in that qualifying decision procedure.

6(2) [Applicants] The persons who may apply under this section are–

(a) a person entitled, in accordance with the rules, to vote at the meeting of the company or in the relevant qualifying decision procedure;

(aa) a person who would have been entitled, in accordance with the rules, to vote in the relevant qualifying decision procedure if he had had notice of it;

(b) the nominee or any person who has replaced him under section 2(4) or 4(2); and

(c) if the company is being wound up or is in administration, the liquidator or administrator.

6(3) [Time for application] An application under this section shall not be made–

(a) after the end of the period of 28 days beginning with the first day on which each of the reports required by section 4(6) and (6A) has been made to the court; or

(b) in the case of a person who was not given notice of the relevant qualifying decision procedure, after the end of the period of 28 days beginning with the day on which he became aware that the relevant qualifying decision procedure had taken place;

but (subject to that) an application made by a person within subsection (2)(aa) on the ground that the voluntary arrangement prejudices his interests may be made after the arrangement has ceased to have effect, unless it came to an end prematurely.

6(4) [Powers of court] Where on such an application the court is satisfied as to either of the grounds mentioned in subsection (1), it may do any of the following, namely–

(a) revoke or suspend any decision approving the voluntary arrangement which has effect under section 4A or, in a case falling within subsection (1)(b) any decision taken by the meeting of the company, or in the relevant qualifying decision procedure which has effect under that section;

(b) give a direction to any person for the summoning of a further company meeting to consider any revised proposal the person who made the original proposal may make or, in a case falling within subsection (1)(b), and relating to the company meeting, a further company meeting to reconsider the original proposal;

(c) direct any person–

(i) to seek a decision from the company's creditors (using a qualifying decision procedure) as to whether they approve any revised proposal the person who made the original proposal may make, or

(ii) in a case falling within subsection (1)(b) and relating to the relevant qualifying decision procedure to seek a decision from the company's creditors (using a qualifying decision procedure) as to whether they approve the original proposal.

6(5) [Revocation or suspension of approval] Where at any time after giving a direction under subsection (4)(b) or (c) in relation to a revised proposal the court is satisfied that the person who made the original proposal does not intend to submit a revised proposal, the court shall revoke the direction and revoke or suspend any decision approving the voluntary arrangement which has effect under section 4A.

6(6) [Supplemental directions] In a case where the court, on an application under this section with respect to any meeting or relevant qualifying decision procedure–

(a) gives a direction under subsection (4)(b) or (c), or

(b) revokes or suspends an approval under subsection (4)(a) or (5), the court may give such supplemental directions as it thinks fit and, in particular, directions with respect to things done under the voluntary arrangement since it took effect.

6(7) [Effect of irregularity] Except in pursuance of the preceding provisions of this section, a decision–

(a) taken at a company meeting summoned under section 3 is not invalidated by any irregularity at or in relation to the meeting, and

(b) a decision of the company's creditors made in the relevant qualifying decision procedure is not invalidated by any irregularity in relation to the relevant qualifying decision procedure.

General Note

Section 6 lays down a procedure whereby the various interested persons who are listed in s.6(2) may apply to the court to challenge the fairness or regularity of a voluntary arrangement which has been approved under the preceding sections and also, it would seem (under s.6(1)(b)), the regularity of a creditors' decision process or members' meeting in the case where such approval was not forthcoming. If a person does not come within any of the categories of applicants listed in s.6(2) (e.g. because he or she was not "a person entitled to vote"), there may be available the alternative possibility of an appeal under IR 2016 r.15.35 see *Re Cranley Mansions Ltd, Saigol v Goldstein* [1994] 1 W.L.R. 1610; [1994] B.C.C. 576. By implication, and in part by the express words of s.6(3) and (7), a scheme of voluntary arrangement, once approved, is probably not open to challenge by any other procedure or on any other grounds than are set out here.

The section is obviously modelled on what is now CA 2006 s.994, a provision which allows the court to grant a remedy to a member of a company who establishes that the company's affairs are being or have been conducted in a manner which is unfairly prejudicial to the interests of some or all of the members or that some act or omission of the company is or would be so prejudicial. Similar language is used also in IA 1986 s.27; but compare Sch.B1 para.74. Decisions under these related provisions may be helpful in the interpretation of s.6.

Section 6 is concerned only with the events leading up to the implementation of an arrangement and not with complaints about the conduct of the scheme of voluntary arrangement by the supervisor: this is dealt with by a different procedure under s.7(3).

The scope of the power of intervention under s.6 was considered by Warren J as part of his lengthy judgment in *Sisu Capital Fund Ltd v Tucker* [2005] EWHC 2170 (Ch); [2005] EWHC 2321 (Ch); [2006] B.P.I.R. 154. This was a complex case involving a group of companies with interlocking CVAs and administrations. Here the proposals under attack contained releases for office holders in respect of possible claims that might have been brought against them. In view of the speculative nature of these claims it was held that this was neither unreasonable nor unfairly prejudicial. It was not the role of the court to impose terms which might have been more advantageous to those accepted by creditors. The court could not say that a CVA was unfair simply because the petitioning creditors might have been better protected under a scheme of arrangement constructed under CA 1985 s.425 (now CA 2006 s.895). Even if the releases were unfairly prejudicial the court would in any event exercise its discretion under s.6 to refuse to make an order. This conclusion is entirely consistent with judicial thinking in the field.

For the procedure on the making of an order under s.6, see IR 2016 r.2.40.

Note that it is an offence for an officer or former officer of a company to make a false representation or commit any other fraud for the purpose of obtaining the approval of the members or creditors to a proposal: IA 1986 s.6A. An officer would also, in principle, be civilly liable to the company or any other person who could prove damage resulting from such a fraud.

The text of s.6 was substantially amended by s.2 of, and Sch.2 to, IA 2000 to cater for changes brought in by that legislation. Minor linguistic changes were made to s.6(2)(c) by s.248 of, and Sch.17 to, EA 2002 to acknowledge the fact that it is no longer accurate to speak of administration *orders*.

For an unsuccessful attempt to invoke s.6 see *Swindon Town Properties v Swindon Town FC* [2003] B.P.I.R. 253.

There were a number of changes made to this provision by SBEEA 2015 s.126 and Sch.9. These reflect the broader decision-making procedures available to creditors.

S.6(1)

Although the word "may" appears to be permissive, it would probably be construed by a court in the sense "may and may only be" so as to make this the only procedure for challenging a scheme once it has been approved.

It may not be unfairly prejudicial to make a differentiation in the treatment of members of the same class (*Re Cancol Ltd* [1996] 1 All E.R. 37; [1995] B.C.C. 1,133). A rare successful challenge under s.6(1)(a) occurred in *Prudential Assurance Co Ltd v PRG Powerhouse Ltd* [2007] EWHC 1002 (Ch); [2007] B.C.C. 500 which was concerned with the common practice of "guarantee stripping" where a guarantor of a tenant company's rent obligations is relieved of liability via a CVA of the tenant company. Here Etherton J, after full consideration of a large number of authorities, concluded that the CVA did relieve the guarantor of its obligations but in so doing unfairly prejudiced the interests of the landlords. For discussion of this important authority see Chalkiadis (2007) 219 Co. L.N. 1; and Swain (2008) 20 Insolv. Int. 123. Another guarantee stripping scheme was struck down in *Mourant v Sixty UK Ltd* [2010] B.C.C. 882; [2010] B.P.I.R. 1264. Here the court was most critical of the scheme contained in the CVA, which offered the landlords far less than would have been the case under any other insolvency regime. The CVA fell foul of both the criteria of material irregularity and unfair prejudice. For subsequent developments in this matter see *R. (on the application of Hollis) v ACCA* [2014] EWHC 2572 (Admin); [2014] B.P.I.R. 1317. Here the court held that findings made by Henderson J could be used as evidence in any subsequent disciplinary proceedings.

A more conventional outcome was recorded in *Revenue and Customs Commissioners v Portsmouth City FC* [2011] B.C.C. 149; [2010] B.P.I.R. 1123. Here Mann J rejected a challenge to a CVA involving a football club. Both in cases of material irregularity and unfair prejudice each element of the grounds for challenge needs to be established. The commercial realities of the situation needed to be borne in mind. The judge refused to be drawn into a decision on the legality of the so-called football creditor rule; that was a matter for another time and place where all interested parties could be properly represented. A more direct challenge to the football creditor rule proved unsuccessful before David Richards J in *Revenue and Customs Commissioners v Football League Ltd* [2012] EWHC 1372 (Ch); [2012] B.P.I.R. 686. See annotation to s.107.

A s.6 challenge succeeded in *Re Gatnom Capital & Finance Ltd* [2010] EWHC 3353 (Ch) because the votes of certain creditors should not have been allowed as the transactions under which debts were said to be due to them were found to be shams. A material irregularity was thus shown to exist to the satisfaction of Roth J and a revocation order under s.6(4) was granted. On the potential non-party costs implications of a failure to successfully resist a challenge to a CVA launched under s.6 see Newey J in *Re Gatnom Capital and Finance Ltd (No.2)* [2011] EWHC 3716 (Ch); [2012] B.P.I.R. 299. On the question of "material irregularity", see the same case and also *Re Cranley Mansions Ltd, Saigol v Goldstein* [1994] 1 W.L.R. 1610; [1994] B.C.C. 576; and *Re Sweatfield Ltd* [1997] B.C.C. 744. In *Re Newlands (Seaford) Educational Trust* [2006] B.C.C. 195 an attempt to challenge under s.6(1)(b) the decision of the chair of the creditors' meeting when valuing a claim was unsuccessful before Sir Andrew Morritt C.

S.6(2)

For the meaning of the phrase "a person entitled, in accordance with the rules, to vote" see the notes to s.5(2). The appropriate regulator can apply or be heard on an application under s.6—Financial Services and Markets Act 2000 s.356 as amended.

S.6(3)

The time limit here specified is the same as that stipulated in s.5(4). On the calculation of this time, see the note to that subsection and *Re Bournemouth and Boscombe AFC Co Ltd* [1998] B.P.I.R. 183 which confirms that this 28-day limit cannot be extended. The 28-day time limit was reasserted in *Wood v Heart Hospital* [2009] B.P.I.R. 1538. The time limit for making applications under s.6 cannot be waived by invoking CPR r.3.2(a)—on this see *Re Beloit Walmsley Ltd* [2008] B.P.I.R. 1445. For discussion of the powers of the court under s.6 and any discretion given to supervisors to accept late claims see *Tucker and Spratt v Gold Fields Mining LLC* [2009] EWCA Civ 173; [2009] B.P.I.R. 704.

S.6(4)

The court may revoke or suspend the approvals given by a meeting, or via creditor decision process, or one of the meetings, with or without giving directions as to the summoning of further meetings or further decision processes. If it decides to revoke but gives no such directions, it is of course always open to any of the persons mentioned in s.1(1) or (3) to put forward a fresh scheme. However, there is probably no power to reopen the original proposal (with or without modifications) otherwise than by direction of the court under s.6(4)(b).

Under s.6(4)(b), the court may direct "any person" (not necessarily the nominee) to summon the further meetings. However, only the person who made the original proposal may draw up a revised one: this will be the liquidator or administrator of the company if s.1(3) applies, and the directors if it does not. (If this person declines to co-operate, s.6(5) applies and the arrangement falls through.)

The court seems to have no power to make any decision other than those set out in this subsection: it cannot, e.g. approve a proposal subject to modifications of its own devising, or even remit a proposal with such modifications to the meetings for reconsideration. (See, however, the note to s.7(4), below.)

S.6(5)

If it appears that the directors, the liquidator or the administrator, as the case may be (see s.6(4)), do not intend to submit a revised scheme, the matter can proceed no further.

S.6(6)
An arrangement is effective as soon as the members and creditors have given their approval (s.5). It is not suspended while an application under s.6 is pending. This subsection empowers the court, in the event of a successful challenge, to give supplemental directions to cover acts done under an arrangement before the court gave its ruling.

S.6(7)
An approval given at a meeting or via a creditors' decision process is not open to challenge as irregular otherwise than by proceeding under s.6 itself. Once the 28 days laid down by s.6(3) have elapsed, therefore, the approval is irrebuttably deemed valid for all purposes.

6A False representations, etc.

6A(1) [Offence] If, for the purpose of obtaining the approval of the members or creditors of a company to a proposal for a voluntary arrangement, a person who is an officer of the company–

(a) makes any false representation, or

(b) fraudulently does, or omits to do, anything,

he commits an offence.

6A(2) [Application of s.6A(1)] Subsection (1) applies even if the proposal is not approved.

6A(3) ["Officer"] For purposes of this section "officer" includes a shadow director.

6A(4) [Penalties] A person guilty of an offence under this section is liable to imprisonment or a fine, or both.

General Note

This addition was introduced via s.2 of, and Sch.2 to, the IA 2000 with effect from 1 January 2003. It seeks to prevent abuse of the CVA mechanism by instilling a degree of integrity reinforced by the criminal law.

S.6A(1)
The bare bones of the offence of seeking to obtain the approval of a CVA by false misrepresentations are outlined.

S.6A(2)
It is no defence that the CVA was voted down by creditors.

S.6A(3)
The offence applies to officers and shadow directors—see the note to s.206(3).

S.6A(4)
This specifies the sanction, though the details are to be found in Sch.10.

7 Implementation of proposal

7(1) [Application] This section applies where a voluntary arrangement has effect under section 4A.

7(2) [Supervisor of composition or scheme] The person who is for the time being carrying out in relation to the voluntary arrangement the functions conferred–

(a) on the nominee by virtue of the approval of the voluntary arrangement by the company or its creditors (or both) pursuant to section 3,

(b) by virtue of section 2(4) or 4(2) on a person other than the nominee,

shall be known as the supervisor of the voluntary arrangement.

7(3) [Application to court] If any of the company's creditors or any other person is dissatisfied by any act, omission or decision of the supervisor, he may apply to the court; and on the application the court may–

(a) confirm, reverse or modify any act or decision of the supervisor,

(b) give him directions, or

(c) make such other order as it thinks fit.

7(4) [Application for directions by supervisor] The supervisor–

(a) may apply to the court for directions in relation to any particular matter arising under the voluntary arrangement, and

(b) is included among the persons who may apply to the court for the winding up of the company or for an administration order to be made in relation to it.

7(5) [Court appointment powers] The court may, whenever–

(a) it is expedient to appoint a person to carry out the functions of the supervisor, and

(b) it is inexpedient, difficult or impracticable for an appointment to be made without the assistance of the court,

make an order appointing a person who is qualified to act as an insolvency practitioner in relation to the voluntary arrangement, either in substitution for the existing supervisor or to fill a vacancy.

7(6) [Limit on s.7(5) power] The power conferred by subsection (5) is exercisable so as to increase the number of persons exercising the functions of supervisor or, where there is more than one person exercising those functions, so as to replace one or more of those persons.

General Note

Amended by DA 2015 s.19 and Sch.6.

Further amendments are made by SBEEA 2015 s.126 and Sch.9.

S.7(1), (2)

The wording of these subsections was modified by IA 2000 s.2 and Sch.2. As soon as a scheme of voluntary arrangement takes effect, the nominee (or his replacement appointed under ss.2(4) or 4(2)) is redesignated the "supervisor". The supervisor holds funds collected by him on trust for the creditors entitled under the arrangement. These funds cannot be seized by a subsequently appointed receiver: *Re Leisure Study Group Ltd* [1994] 2 B.C.L.C. 65. On s.7(2) for the duties of the supervisor see *Appleyard Ltd v Ritecrown Ltd* [2009] B.P.I.R. 235 (duty of supervisor is to carry out terms of CVA, not to act as champion for unsecured creditors). This case is also significant for making the point that a supervisor of a CVA is an officer of the court and therefore in principle subject to the ethical duties imposed by the rule in *Ex p. James* (1873–74) L.R. 9 Ch. App. 609.

For the rules relating to the implementation of the arrangement and the duties of the supervisor, see IR 2016 r.2.33, 1.26A et seq. Note also IR 2016 r.2.45 (time recording).

S.7(3)

The court is given wide—indeed, unlimited—powers to oversee the conduct of the arrangement by the supervisor; and anyone at all (subject, no doubt, to his being able to show that he has some interest in the matter) may invoke the jurisdiction under this section. As to whether a creditor can apply under s.7(3) where the company is also undergoing administration see *Holdenhurst Securities plc v Cohen* [2001] 1 B.C.L.C. 460. The right of application under s.7(3) does not exclude a direct action by a creditor unless the terms of the CVA preclude this—*Alman v Approach Housing Ltd* [2001] 1 B.C.L.C. 530. For an application by the company under s.7(3) see *County Bookshops Ltd v Grove* [2002] EWHC 1160 (Ch); [2002] B.P.I.R. 772. For passing mention of s.7(3) see *Re Hellard and Goldfarb (Joint Supervisors of Pinson Wholesale Ltd)* [2007] B.P.I.R. 1323 (a case concerned with an application for directions with regard to the right of remuneration of CVA supervisors).

S.7(4)

The supervisor (like a liquidator, administrator, trustee, and others discharging comparable functions) may apply to the court for directions. Although the Act nowhere states explicitly that the court may give directions which modify the scheme or extend it to include persons who have not taken part in the meetings, this was in fact done in *Re FMS Financial Management Services Ltd* (1989) 5 B.C.C. 191. Here a voluntary arrangement had been agreed to by both the members and various groups of creditors, but not by another group composed of former clients of the company who appeared to have good claims against the company for damages for misrepresentation. Hoffmann J directed that they should be treated as creditors and be given the benefit of the scheme, with the consequence that the other creditors received a substantially smaller dividend. The power to seek directions does not enable the court to modify the terms of a CVA—*Re Alpa Lighting Ltd* [1997] B.P.I.R. 341. For an important case involving an application for directions under s.7(4) see *Re Federal-Mogul Aftermarket Ltd* [2008] B.P.I.R. 846. An application for directions was made by supervisors in *Re Energy Holdings (No.3) Ltd* [2010] B.P.I.R. 1339 where much of the debate centred on the construction of the terms of the particular CVA. See also *Re TXU Europe Group plc* [2011] EWHC 2072 (Ch) where Newey J gave directions warning that the proposed distribution by the supervisors to shareholders once creditors had been repaid would constitute an unlawful distribution of capital contrary to CA 2006 Pt 23. Such a distribution could only be made if the company went into liquidation.

The supervisor may also apply for an administration order or a winding-up order (para.(b)), but is not listed in either s.9 or s.124 among the categories of persons who are entitled to petition for those orders. This difficulty has to be overcome by having the supervisor petition in the name of the company, on analogy with IR 2016 r.7.7. On winding-up petitions presented by supervisors, see *Re Leisure Study Group Ltd* [1994] 2 B.C.L.C. 65.

A supervisor may apply for a winding-up order under s.7(4)(b) even though he is no longer "carrying out the functions" under the CVA: this wording (in s.7(2)) is descriptive only and not restrictive: *Re Arthur Rathbone Kitchens Ltd* [1998] B.C.C. 450.

Difficult issues arise where a company undergoing the CVA procedure then goes into liquidation. What is the effect of the liquidation on the CVA and what happens to the funds collected by the CVA supervisor? In spite of the relative scarcity of CVAs on the ground we now have a substantial body of case law to grapple with: *Re Halson Packaging Ltd* [1997] B.P.I.R. 194 (HHJ Maddocks); *Re Arthur Rathbone Kitchens Ltd* [1997] 2 B.C.L.C. 280 (Roger Kaye QC); *Re Excalibur Airways Ltd* [1998] 1 B.C.L.C. 436 (Jonathan Parker J); *Re Maple Environmental Services Ltd* [2000] B.C.C. 93 (HHJ Boggis); *Welsby v Brelec Installations* [2000] 2 B.C.L.C. 576 (Blackburne J); and *Re Kudos Glass Ltd* [2000] 1 B.C.L.C. 390 (Richard McCombe QC). This confusing corpus of first-instance case law arguably establishes certain propositions: a CVA can survive subsequent liquidation and the funds collected may be insulated from the residual assets of the company now undergoing the distributional process of winding up. However, whether these twin consequences will apply in an individual case depends to some extent upon the language of the CVA and also upon the circumstances under which the liquidation was commenced. The leading authority now is *Re NT Gallagher & Son Ltd* [2002] EWCA Civ 404; [2002] 1 W.L.R. 2380. Here a civil engineering company had fallen into financial difficulties in 1995 partly because of a substantial contractual dispute which was the subject of litigation initiated by the company ("the Mercury claim"). The CVA was designed to allow the company to continue trading pending the resolution of this substantial claim. Post-CVA creditors were to be paid out of cash flow. Under the CVA monthly payments were to be made by the company to the supervisors for the benefit of participating creditors; the language of "trust" was not used in relation to these payments. As is normal practice the supervisors were *required* to petition for the winding up of the company in the event of failure to comply with the terms of the CVA. By March 1997 the company had failed to keep up with the schedule of payments under the arrangement but the supervisors, after consulting the creditors, decided not to petition for winding up. In so deciding they concluded that they were not subject to an obligation to seek the winding up but were merely vested with a discretionary power; a conclusion, although not contested in the litigation, the correctness of which was viewed as "dubious" by the Court of Appeal (para.20). In any event, the problems of the company grew and in 1997 it was eventually placed into creditors' voluntary winding up with the agreement of the directors and supervisors. The Mercury claim had not been resolved by this date. The mathematics of the insolvency were interesting; the supervisors retained a sum of in excess of £500,000, but the post-CVA liabilities amounted to approximately £2.5 million. Total liabilities exceeded £5 million. The residual assets of the company amounted to £98,000 plus two causes of action (the Mercury claim and one other claim). At first instance (see [2001] B.P.I.R. 1088) HHJ Howarth held that both the sums retained by the supervisors and the Mercury claim were held on trust for the CVA creditors and further concluded that those trusts were not terminated by the subsequent liquidation. The CVA creditors could prove in the liquidation of the company provided they surrendered their "security" in respect of the Mercury claim. The liquidators appealed but the Court of Appeal dismissed this appeal, though it varied part of the order of HHJ Howarth by allowing the CVA creditors to prove in the liquidation after giving credit for any dividends received from the supervisors. Thus, the analogy used by the trial judge under which the Mercury claim was treated as tantamount to a security (which could be surrendered) did not find favour in the Court of Appeal.

In reaching these conclusions, the Court of Appeal, through Peter Gibson LJ, recognised the unsatisfactory nature of the present law, resting as it does on fine distinctions: "It makes little sense for the form of the liquidation to affect the question of the effect of liquidation on trusts created by a CVA" (para.43). Again, Peter Gibson LJ stated:

> "We would question whether the mere fact that a supervisor presents a petition entails that the CVA or IVA creditors have elected to terminate the CVA or IVA trust in their favour. Even if there is evidence that all the CVA or IVA creditors supported the presentation of a petition, it does not follow that they were thereby evincing an

intention that the trust should come to an end and that the trust assets should revert to the company or debtor" (para.43).

The real significance of this ruling from the Court of Appeal lies in the guidelines for future cases. The following principles have now been established (see para.54). These general rules apply equally to cases of voluntary and compulsory liquidation. Moreover, the question of whether the petitioner is the supervisor or not is immaterial; what mattered is the solution specified in the arrangement.

The governing principles are:

1. Funds collected by the supervisor would, provided the terms of the arrangement made this clear, be held on trust exclusively for the benefit of the CVA participants. The fact that the language of "trust" is not employed in the CVA proposal is immaterial (see para.29).

2. The fate of the CVA trust depends upon the terms under which that arrangement was entered into. On this see the later case of *Re Zebra Industrial Products Ltd* [2004] EWHC 549 (Ch); [2005] B.C.C. 104.

3. The stated effect of liquidation on the CVA should be respected. The contractual foundation of voluntary arrangements is thus reiterated.

4. It is perfectly possible for a CVA to come to an end but for the underlying trust to survive. In this context Peter Gibson LJ declared: "We do not therefore accept that to treat a trust created by a CVA as continuing notwithstanding the liquidation of the company is productive of such unfairness that the court should conclude that liquidation brings the trust to an end" (para.49). In the absence of express provision the following default rule will, according to Peter Gibson LJ, operate:

> "Further, as a matter of policy, in the absence of any provision in the CVA as to what should happen to trust assets on liquidation of the company, the court should prefer a default rule which furthers rather than hinders what might be taken to be the statutory purpose of Part I of the Act. Parliament plainly intended to encourage companies and creditors to enter into CVAs so as to provide creditors with a means of recovering what they are owed without recourse to the more expensive means provided by winding up or administration, thereby giving many companies the opportunity to continue to trade" (para.50).

5. CVA creditors who have not been fully reimbursed by the trust moneys can prove for the balance in the liquidation.

It is clear from the approach taken by the Court of Appeal in *Gallagher* that the contractual basis of the CVA is now the dominant perspective and thus CVA documentation should be reviewed. This ruling will prove a considerable boost to company voluntary arrangements by offering strong protection (with a commensurate incentive) to those creditors who choose to participate in the CVA as a way of recovering their debts, albeit over a more protracted timeframe than their original contractual rights provided for. The Court of Appeal has confirmed that at heart CVAs are a matter of contract and that this contract can have a negative impact upon the general creditors outside the scheme by establishing a resilient trust of corporate funds. From the perspective of those counterparties who continue to deal with a company undergoing a CVA the dangers of dealing with such a business are exacerbated; not surprisingly, the extension of credit to such a company will be a matter of some considerable risk requiring prudent countermeasures. At the very least some inquiries as to the financial status of the company would be wise (see here para.49). The problem here is that it is quite possible to deal with a company already undergoing the CVA process without realising it (see paras 45 and 49). The end result, therefore, of *Gallagher* is that it may indeed encourage the setting of a CVA, but may have a negative impact upon the day-to-day operation of such arrangements by obstructing the flow of new credit.

S.7(5)

This is a rather puzzling provision, for none of the preceding sections appears to give the shareholders and creditors, acting either together or independently, a power to fill a vacancy in the office of supervisor or to replace a supervisor once appointed: it seems that once the shareholders and creditors have approved a proposal under s.4A, they have no further role. So the reference in para.(b) to appointing a substitute supervisor "without the assistance of the court" is strange. Since no power appears to be conferred on the meeting of shareholders or on the creditors by the rules, it seems that the only way in which a vacancy can be filled or a replacement supervisor appointed is by invoking the jurisdiction of the court under this subsection. See *Clements v Udal* [2001] B.P.I.R. 454. The wording of s.7(5) was modified by IA 2000 s.2 and Sch.2.

S.7(6)
This is the only reference in the Act to the possibility of appointing several persons as joint supervisors (or as joint nominees), although other "office-holders" are specifically covered by s.231. It appears, however, that the general statutory assumption applies, so that words in the singular include the plural (Interpretation Act 1978 s.6); and this construction may be applied throughout this Part of the Act.

7A Prosecution of delinquent officers of company

7A(1) [Application] This section applies where a moratorium under section 1A has been obtained for a company or the approval of a voluntary arrangement in relation to a company has taken effect under section 4A or paragraph 36 of Schedule A1.

7A(2) [Procedure for reporting offence to "the appropriate authority"] If it appears to the nominee or supervisor that any past or present officer of the company has been guilty of any offence in connection with the moratorium or, as the case may be, voluntary arrangement for which he is criminally liable, the nominee or supervisor shall forthwith–

(a) report the matter to the appropriate authority, and

(b) provide the appropriate authority with such information and give the authority such access to and facilities for inspecting and taking copies of documents (being information or documents in the possession or under the control of the nominee or supervisor and relating to the matter in question) as the authority requires.

In this subsection, "the appropriate authority" means–

(i) in the case of a company registered in England and Wales, the Secretary of State, and

(ii) in the case of a company registered in Scotland, the Lord Advocate.

7A(3) [Powers exercisable by Secretary of State] Where a report is made to the Secretary of State under subsection (2), he may, for the purpose of investigating the matter reported to him and such other matters relating to the affairs of the company as appear to him to require investigation, exercise any of the powers which are exercisable by inspectors appointed under section 431 or 432 of the Companies Act 1985 to investigate a company's affairs.

7A(4) [Obligations to assist Secretary of State] For the purpose of such an investigation any obligation imposed on a person by any provision of the Companies Acts to produce documents or give information to, or otherwise to assist, inspectors so appointed is to be regarded as an obligation similarly to assist the Secretary of State in his investigation.

7A(5) [Answers as evidence in investigation] An answer given by a person to a question put to him in exercise of the powers conferred by subsection (3) may be used in evidence against him.

7A(6) [Answers as evidence in criminal proceedings] However, in criminal proceedings in which that person is charged with an offence to which this subsection applies–

(a) no evidence relating to the answer may be adduced, and

(b) no question relating to it may be asked,

by or on behalf of the prosecution, unless evidence relating to it is adduced, or a question relating to it is asked, in the proceedings by or on behalf of that person.

7A(7) [Offences under s.7A(6)] Subsection (6) applies to any offence other than–

(a) an offence under section 2 or 5 of the Perjury Act 1911 (false statements made on oath otherwise than in judicial proceedings or made otherwise than on oath), or

(b) an offence under section 44(1) or (2) of the Criminal Law (Consolidation) (Scotland) Act 1995 (false statements made on oath or otherwise than on oath).

7A(8) [Assistance to be given to prosecuting authority] Where a prosecuting authority institutes criminal proceedings following any report under subsection (2), the nominee or supervisor, and every officer and agent of the company past and present (other than the defendant or defender), shall give the authority all assistance in connection with the prosecution which he is reasonably able to give.

For this purpose–

"agent" includes any banker or solicitor of the company and any person employed by the company as auditor, whether that person is or is not an officer of the company,

"prosecuting authority" means the Director of Public Prosecutions, the Lord Advocate or the Secretary of State.

7A(9) [Court directions under s.7A(8)] The court may, on the application of the prosecuting authority, direct any person referred to in subsection (8) to comply with that subsection if he has failed to do so.

General Note

Introduced by s.2 of, and Sch.2 to, the Insolvency Act 2000 with effect from 1 January 2003.

S.7A(1)

This defines the circumstances under which s.7A applies—i.e. to both types of CVA.

S.7A(2)

Here we have a formal "whistleblowing" obligation imposed on the nominee/supervisor. This is a significant departure from the previous position with regard to CVAs where insolvency practitioners were not expected to discharge such a public service duty. The absence of such a duty may well have been one of the attractions in the CVA model for company directors. On procedures for reporting suspected criminality see *Dear IP*, Ch.20, 10–11.

S.7A(3), (4), (5)

This explains the powers available to the Secretary of State to follow up any report made under subs.(3). The power of investigation is bolstered by the provisions of subss.(4) and (5). Note the amendment to subs.(3) and (4) by the Companies Act 2006 (Consequential Amendments, Transitional Provisions and Savings) Order 2009 (SI 2009/1941) (effective from 1 October 2009). This takes account of the enactment of the Companies Act 2006.

S.7A(6)

This qualifies subs.(5), though in turn this qualification is limited by subs.(7).

S.7A(8), (9)

These deal with follow up matters resulting from a prosecution instituted as a result of a report made under subs.(2).

7B Arrangements coming to an end prematurely

7B For the purposes of this Part, a voluntary arrangement the approval of which has taken effect under section 4A or paragraph 36 of Schedule A1 comes to an end prematurely if, when it ceases to have effect, it has not been fully implemented in respect of all persons bound by the arrangement by virtue of section 5(2)(b)(i) or, as the case may be, paragraph 37(2)(b)(i) of Schedule A1.

General Note

This is a curious definitional provision which seeks to identify when a CVA comes to an end prematurely. It needs to be read in the light of ss.5(2A)(a) and 6(3).

Part II

Administration

IMPORTANT

There are now two administration regimes, each governed by what is referred to in the legislation as "Part II" of IA 1986. For the "original" Pt II, along with the associated Rules, with annotations, reference should be made to the 19th edition of this work. The "new" Pt II is to be found in

Sch.B1 to the Act. The "new" Pt II applies to all administrations commenced after 15 September 2003, except in the relatively few cases to which EA 2002 s.249 applies. In order to distinguish between the original and the new Parts, the statutory text of the former has been set in italics, and the same distinction is made in the corresponding Rules.

8 Administration

8 Schedule B1 to this Act (which makes provision about the administration of companies) shall have effect.

Introductory note to the new Part II

Part 10 of the EA 2002, the relevant provisions of which were brought into effect from 15 September 2003 by the Enterprise Act 2002 (Commencement No.4 and Transitional Provisions and Savings) Order 2003 (SI 2003/2093 (C. 85)) art.2(1) and Sch.1, introduced a wholly new administration regime for companies. This was done by declaring (in s.248) that a new Pt II, now to be found set out in Sch.B1 to IA 1986, is to be "substituted" for that contained in IA 1986 as originally drafted and since amended. The side-note to s.248 refers to the "replacement" of Pt II. So the natural inference which the reader might have drawn was that the former Pt II had been consigned to oblivion, subject only to whatever transitional provisions might be needed to deal with companies which were in administration when s.248 was brought into force. But this is not so. In the immediately following section (s.249) it is provided that s.248 "shall have no effect" in relation to a number of categories of public-utility company and to building societies. So, so far as concerns these bodies, the former Pt II survives. It survives also where a petition for an administration order was presented to the court before 15 September 2003 (SI 2003/2093 art.3(2)).

In consequence, we now have two versions of Pt II, one in ss.8–27 and another in Sch.B1; and as if that were not confusing enough, we have two different sections each numbered s.8! Section 8 of the "new" Pt II is set out above.

The draftsman has endeavoured to make Sch.B1 largely self-standing, and in doing so has removed references to administration and administrators from many sections in other parts of the Act (e.g. in s.212, the well-known "misfeasance" section). In order to cope with situations involving administrators appointed under the original regime, the former references are reinstated by the Enterprise Act 2002 (Commencement No.4 and Transitional Provisions and Savings) Order 2003 (SI 2003/2093 (C. 85)) arts 3(2), (3). This saving provision applies in cases where a petition for an administration order was presented before 15 September 2003. In the case of building societies and the utility companies mentioned in s.249, the original wording of the Act is preserved because EA 2002 s.249 disapplies Sch.B1 in regard to these bodies.

The administration procedure has been made available to bodies other than companies. Provision was made for building societies by the Building Societies Act 1986 s.90A (inserted by the Building Societies Act 1997 s.39, effective 1 December 1997): as noted above, the original Pt II applies. In the application of Pt II of IA 1986 to Building Societies it is to be read subject to the modifications set out in the Building Societies Act 1986 Sch.15A paras 10 et seq. The original Pt II was also extended to insolvent partnerships by the Insolvent Partnerships Order 1994 (SI 1994/2421) art.6 and Sch.2, which in turn was superseded by the Insolvent Partnerships (Amendment) Order 2005 (SI 2005/1516, effective 1 July 2005), substituting a modified IA 1986 Sch.B1 and so introducing the new Pt II regime. The Limited Liability Partnerships Regulations 2001 (SI 2001/1090) were amended by the Limited Liability Partnerships (Amendment) Regulations 2005 (SI 2005/1989) reg.3 and Sch.3, as from 1 October 2005 so as to make the new Pt II available to LLPs. This regime has now been extended also to most forms of co-operative and community benefit societies and credit unions.

The new administration regime has also been applied with special modifications to various types of company governed by separate legislation, e.g. energy companies, railway companies and the Post Office—the main object being to ensure that supplies and services are not interrupted. However, in regard to other public-utility companies the original Pt II continues to apply (see above).

The administration procedure was formerly not available to insurance companies. However, by the Financial Services and Markets Act 2000 (Administration Orders Relating to Insurers) Order 2002 (SI 2002/1242), which came into force on 31 May 2002, this became possible for the first time. The 2002 Order has now been repealed by the Financial Services and Markets Act 2000 (Administration Orders Relating to Insurers) Order 2010 (SI 2010/3023), effective 1 February 2011. The Schedule to the 2010 instrument lists a series of modifications to IA 1986 Sch.B1 in the application of that regime to insurers. This Order must be read in conjunction with the Insurers (Reorganisation and Winding Up) Regulations 2004 (SI 2004/353), effective 18 February 2004. The 2004 Regulations were enacted in order to take account of the changes to insolvency law brought about by EA 2002. In addition to making provision for the recognition in this country of insolvency proceedings instituted elsewhere in the EEA, the 2004 Regulations make a number of important changes to the substance of the administration regime so far as it affects UK insurers. In particular, such an undertaking may be put into administration only by court order (even under the new Pt II), and preferential status is accorded to insurance debts ahead of all other debts. The 2004 and 2010 Regulations are reproduced in Vol.2. For a case under the 2004 Regulations, see *Re AA Mutual International Insurance Co Ltd* [2004] EWHC 2430 (Ch); [2005] 2 B.C.L.C. 8. Lloyd's was excluded from the provisions of the above legislation, but comparable provision has now brought it within the net: see the Insurers (Reorganisation and Winding Up) (Lloyd's) Regulations 2005 (SI 2005/1998, effective 10 August 2005).

For the same reason, banks and other "authorised institutions" under the banking legislation were excluded by the Act as originally drafted. However, by the Banks (Administration Proceedings) Order 1989 (SI 1989/1276), effective from 23 August 1989, the original Pt II of the Act was extended so as to apply in relation to banks and the other bodies mentioned in the original s.8(5)(b) which were companies within the meaning of CA 1985 s.735 [CA 2006 ss.1(1), 1171]; but this statutory instrument has since been revoked, subject to transitional arrangements, and the new Pt II now applies to these bodies instead (see the Banks (Former Authorised Institutions) (Insolvency) Order 2006 (SI 2006/3107), effective 15 December 2006). The reference to s.8(5)(b) is replaced by a reference to IA 1986 s.422(1). The 2006 Order, art.3 and Sch., provides that certain modifications shall be applied to Pt II in relation to the application of the administration procedure to these institutions. In particular, these modifications confer rights on the Financial Conduct Authority or the Prudential Regulation Authority, as appropriate, to participate in the proceedings. In contrast with the legislation governing insurance companies, these bodies may be put into administration without a court order (but the consent of the FCA or PRA must be obtained and filed in court (Sch. para.5)). The Credit Institutions (Reorganisation and Winding Up) Regulations 2004 (SI 2004/1045, effective 5 May 2004), which are also reproduced in Vol.2, inter alia prohibit courts in the UK from making an administration order in regard to a credit institution based elsewhere in the EEA and require the notification of UK administration proceedings in other EEA jurisdictions, but do not otherwise affect the 1989 Order. On the special administration regime established by the Banking Act 2009 where there has been government intervention in the affairs of a failing bank or building society, see above, p.6.

The Insolvency (Amendment) Rules 2003 (SI 2003/1730), which also came into force on 15 September 2003, supplemented the legislation by providing a new set of Rules which govern administrations under the new regime. See now IR 2016 Pt 3. But the rules in force prior to 15 September 2003 continue to apply to administrations under the original Pt II: see I(A)R 2003 r.5(2)–(4).

Confusingly, both sets of rules are referred to as "Pt 2" of the Rules, and these use similar but not corresponding numbering. In previous editions, we have been able to include the text of the original Pt II of the Act and Rules, with annotations. However, we have had to make space in order to accommodate the new Rules and the Table of Destinations and Derivations, and have decided that we must exclude the original Pt II. We recommend that readers should retain their copies of the 19th edition of the *Guide* in order to have access to this material.

Part III

Receivership

Introductory note to Part III

The Companies Acts have not previously contained many provisions dealing with receivership, at least in relation to England and Wales; matters were left to the general law and the terms of the instrument under or by which the receiver was appointed. The Cork Committee (*Report*, Ch.8) recommended that the law should be amended so that in many respects it was placed on a statutory basis. The recommendations were broadly followed by IA 1985 Ch.IV, which is now consolidated along with a few sections of CA 1985 into the present Act.

Among the principal changes made are the introduction of the new concept of "administrative receiver" (s.29(2)), and the requirement that an administrative receiver be a qualified insolvency practitioner. The date on which a receiver takes office and the extent to which agency rules apply have been clarified, and new provisions ensure that other creditors are kept in the picture regarding the progress of the receivership. The administrative receiver is given the statutory powers set out in Sch.1, and other specific powers including power to dispose of encumbered property (s.43). In many other respects an administrative receivership is placed on a similar footing to a liquidation—e.g. in regard to a statement of affairs, the appointment of a committee of creditors, and the removal of the receiver.

To all intents and purposes these days appointments of receivers to enforce security are effected out of court in pursuance of a contractual power vested in the debenture holder to make such an appointment. The advantage in this course of action is speed and lack of cost. There is, however, always the facility of applying to the court for such an appointment, but this is rare because of the cost and the delay—for an unusual example see *Bank of Credit and*

Commerce International SA v BRS Kumar Bros Ltd [1994] B.C.L.C. 211. A right to appoint a receiver will usually permit the appointment of joint receivers—*Doherty v Perrett* [2015] NICA 52. Cases decided in relation to these other forms of receiver may have a wider value. For an important statement of principle on the right of a receiver to claim remuneration from the receivership assets see *Capewell v Revenue and Customs Commissioners* [2007] UKHL 2; [2007] B.P.I.R. 678. *Capewell* (above) was followed in *Barnes v Eastenders Group* [2014] UKSC 26; [2014] B.P.I.R. 867 where the Supreme Court confirmed that the cost of the receivership falls on the person making an invalid appointment and not on the estate. Concerns were expressed about short notice appointments of receivers under the Proceeds of Crime Act 2002.

On the question of the compatibility of a receivership designed to enforce a confiscation order and the requirements of art.1 of the First Protocol ECHR see also *Hansford v Southampton Magistrates Court* [2006] EWHC 67 (Admin); [2008] B.P.I.R. 379.

On the power of the court to appoint a receiver by way of equitable execution over future receipts from a defined foreign asset—see *Masri v Consolidated Contractors International UK Ltd* [2008] EWCA Civ 303; [2008] B.P.I.R. 531. The use of receivership by way of equitable execution continues to suggest its potential—see the discussion in cases such as *Fonu v Merrill Lynch Bank & Trust Co (Cayman) Ltd* [2011] UKPC 17 and *Blight v Brewster* [2012] EWHC 165 (Ch); [2012] B.P.I.R. 476 where the outcome favoured injunctive relief instead of a receivership by way of equitable execution. On whether it was appropriate to appoint receivers by way of equitable execution over foreign assets see *Cruz City 1 Mauritius Holdings v Unitech Ltd* [2014] EWHC 3131 (Comm); [2015] 1 B.C.L.C. 377.

A court appointed receiver is an officer of the court. For the implications flowing from this status see *Glatt v Sinclair* [2013] EWCA Civ 241; [2013] B.P.I.R. 468. This ruling is significant in terms of the receiver's claim to remuneration and expenses incurred after discharge. *Wood v Gorbunova* [2013] EWHC 1935 (Ch); [2014] 1 B.C.L.C. 487 is worthy of note. Here Morgan J reaffirmed that a receiver appointed by the court is an officer of the court. But Morgan J then went on to consider potential liability of such a receiver in the event of the receiver instituting unsuccessful litigation. Liability for costs may arise in certain circumstances. Gloster J stressed in *Barclay Pharmaceuticals Ltd v Waypharm LP* [2013] EWHC 503 (Comm) that permission is required to sue a court appointed receiver for alleged breach of duty. For another illustration of a court appointment being made in the case of a solvent firm see *BAT Industries plc v Windward Prospects Ltd* [2013] EWHC 3612 (Comm). For the use of the receivership remedy in cases where disputes have arisen as to the conduct of businesses that were solvent see *Catch a Ride Ltd v Gardner* [2014] EWHC 1220 (Ch). The courts are reluctant to appoint a receiver in respect of a solvent company because of the negative connotations associated with the term "receivership"—see Ferris J in *Jaber v Science and Info Tech Ltd* [1992] B.C.L.C. 764 at 789.

Another novel potential usage of receivership was highlighted by the Chancellor, Sir Andrew Morritt in *Re MK Airlines Ltd* [2012] EWHC 1018 (Ch) where it was pointed out at [26] that receivership could be used by administrators to enforce the charge conferred on them in respect of their claim for remuneration and expenses under IA 1986 Sch.B1 para.99.

In *Day v Tiuta International Ltd* [2014] EWCA Civ 1246 the Court of Appeal upheld the appointment of receivers who were appointed out of court to enforce an equitable security interest created by subrogation.

For a case where a receivership order made under the Senior Courts Act 1981 s.37(1) was modified (but not retrospectively) see *Shaw v Breish* [2017] EWHC 2972 (Comm).

It must be remembered that a receiver appointed to enforce a fixed charge may be subject to the old established provisions of LPA 1925. For consideration of this statutory code see *Phoenix Properties v Wimpole Street Nominees Ltd* [1992] 1 B.C.L.C. 737; and *Sargent v C & E Commissioners* [1995] 2 B.C.L.C. 34. Note *Jumani v Mortgage Express* [2013] EWHC 1571 (Ch) (Mark Cawson QC)—an attempt to challenge the appointment of an LPA receiver and the actions of said receiver failed. Specialised statutory regimes also exist for certain types of receivership involving (for example) companies incorporated by statute or as part of statutory insolvency regimes, but these are not our concern in this work.

The enforcement of security is not as a general rule prohibited by the existence of a prior freezing order over a debtor's assets—*Taylor v Van Dutch Marine Holding Ltd* [2017] EWHC 636 (Ch).

The institution of receivership was unknown in Scotland until the enactment of CFCSA 1972. In the present Act the provisions of that legislation are consolidated, incorporating certain modifications made by IA 1985. Comparable provisions dealing with receivers and administrative receivers in Northern Ireland are to be found in the Insolvency (Northern Ireland) Order 1989 (SI 1989/2405) (NI 19) arts 40–59 (as amended).

Receivership enjoyed a renaissance in a niche context as a device to deal with distressed hedge funds—see *Re Cheyne Finance plc (No.1)* [2008] 1 B.C.L.C. 732; *Re Cheyne Finance plc (No.2)* [2008] B.C.C. 182 and *Re Whistlejacket Capital Ltd* [2008] 2 B.C.L.C. 683. Note also Milman (2009) 247 Co. L.N. 1.

Although the following provisions provide some statutory framework for the mechanism of an administrative receivership there is still a substantial body of rules derived from decisions of the courts. These court-derived principles continue to be important.

Part III applies to limited liability partnerships by virtue of the Limited Liability Partnerships Regulations 2001 (SI 2001/1090) reg.5(1)(a) as from 6 April 2001 subject to reg.5(2) and (3).

Many key issues are not addressed by the legislation. For example, what is the effect of the appointment of a receiver on the power of the directors to litigate on behalf of the company? Compare here *Newhart Developments v Cooperative Commercial Bank* [1978] Q.B. 814 with *Tudor Grange Holdings v Citibank* [1992] Ch. 53; the Irish High Court case of *Lascomme Ltd v United Dominions Trust (Ireland)* [1994] I.L.R.M. 227 and *Independent Pension Trustee v LAW Construction, The Times* Scots Law Report, 1 November 1996. For discussion see Doyle (1996) 17 Co Law 131. *Newhart* was followed most recently by the Court of Appeal in *Sutton v GE Capital Commercial Finance* [2004] EWCA Civ 315; [2004] 2 B.C.L.C. 662. The Court of Appeal ruled in *Mills v Birchall* [2008] B.P.I.R. 607 that a receiver who conducts litigation on behalf of a company in receivership as part of the security enforcement process does not normally do so at the risk of personal liability for costs under a third party costs order if the litigation is unsuccessful. The defendant in such proceedings is advised to seek an early security for costs order against the claimant company.

On receivers as agents see *Edenwest Ltd v CMS Cameron McKenna* [2012] EWHC 1258 (Ch) and *Snr Denton v Kirwan* [2012] UKEAT 0158/12/1007. In *Edenwest* (above) the primary duty of the receiver to bring about a situation under which the secured creditor could be repaid was seen as critical. Again, in *International Leisure Ltd v First National Trustee Co UK Ltd* [2012] EWHC 1971 (Ch) Edward Bartley Jones QC sitting in the High Court was at pains to stress that, notwithstanding the agency provision, a receiver's primary duty was to the debenture holder who appointed him. For the meaning of "acting by the receivers" see *TBAC Investments Ltd v Valmar Works Ltd* [2015] EWHC 1213 (Ch).

The duties of a director to his company may be enforced by an administrative receiver and those duties are not discharged on the company entering administrative receivership—on this see *Simtel Communications Ltd v Rebak* [2006] 2 B.C.L.C. 571.

The question of whether a receiver owes a duty of care to the company (and those claiming through it) when managing and realising the assets has also been left for the courts to grapple with. For a generous treatment of receivers' duties by the Privy Council in this scenario see *Downsview Nominees v First City Corporation Ltd* [1993] A.C. 295; [1993] B.C.C. 46. Here it was held that the responsibilities of receivers are essentially equitable in nature and there was no room for superimposing common law duties of care in negligence. This case is difficult to reconcile with earlier authorities such as *Standard Chartered Bank v Walker* [1982] 1 W.L.R. 1410 and *Knight v Lawrence* [1991] B.C.C. 411 and is best viewed as part of a general retreat on the part of the courts in the areas of economic loss and professional liability. See generally Berg [1993] J.B.L. 213 and Fealy [1994] 45 N.I.L.Q. 61. Most commentators have been critical of the approach of the Privy Council but for rare support see Rajak (1997) 21 Insolv. L. 7. Those commentators who have been critical of the aforementioned Privy Council ruling will have welcomed the subsequent clarification of the law by the Court of Appeal in *Medforth v Blake* [2000] Ch. 86; [1999] B.C.C. 771. In this case it was held that a receiver taking control of a farming business had no obligation to continue to operate the farm, but if that course of action was taken, the receiver should take reasonable steps to ensure that the business was conducted as profitably as possible and, in particular, that the customary discounts on bulk purchase of livestock feed be obtained. The Court of Appeal felt able to reconcile *Downsview* by indicating that this duty to take reasonable care could be seen as part of the obligation to act in good faith. This decision is far more in tune with prevailing professional standards. For comment see Frisby (2000) 63 M.L.R. 413. The issue of the duties owed by receivers (or mortgagees) when managing, selling or considering the sale of charged property have continued to trouble the courts over the past two years—see for example *Hadjipanayi v Yeldon* [2001] B.P.I.R. 487; *Worwood v Leisure Merchandising* [2002] 1 B.C.L.C. 249; *Cohen v TSB Bank* [2002] 2 B.C.L.C. 32; and *Silven Properties Ltd v Royal Bank of Scotland* [2003] EWCA Civ 1409. At the end of the day each case does turn on its own peculiar facts and most claims alleging breach of duty tend to fail. Another vexed issue concerns both the timing of a sale and the selection of a purchaser where the mortgagor wishes to buy the property. In *Lloyds Bank v Cassidy* [2002] EWCA Civ 1606; [2003] B.P.I.R. 424 the Court of Appeal felt that these were issues in need of clarification. In *Bell v Long* [2008] B.P.I.R. 1211 the court ruled that a receiver (or a mortgagee) is entitled to choose the timing of sale even if that works to the disadvantage of the debtor. If a duty of care is owed by selling receivers that duty is owed to any party having an interest in the equity of redemption—*Raja v Austin Gray (a firm)* [2002] EWCA Civ 1965; [2003] B.P.I.R. 725. See also *Meah v GE Money Home Finance Ltd* [2013] EWHC 20 (Ch) where there was an attempt to challenge a sale by mortgagee. The challenge failed—although some criticisms could be levelled at the sale process, the standard laid down in *Cuckmere Brick Co v Mutual Finance* [1971] Ch. 949 had not been breached. In *Aodhcon LLP v Bridgeco Ltd* [2014] EWHC 535 (Ch); [2014] 2 B.C.L.C. 237 the High Court reviewed the practicalities involved in applying the test that stated that on a sale by a mortgagee a duty to take reasonable care to obtain the best price reasonably obtainable applied.

Some consideration of the duties of receivers is to be found in the judgment of the court in *Purewal v Countrywide Residential Lettings Ltd* [2015] EWCA Civ 1122. See also *PK Airfinance SARL v Alpstream AG* [2015] EWCA Civ 1318 where the comparable issue of the standard of care owed by mortgagees was revisited together with an analysis of the parties to whom a duty of care may be owed by a mortgagee. The latest review of the duties of receivers is to be found in *Ahmad v Bank of Scotland* [2016] EWCA Civ 602 at [38] of the judgment. The case provides particular analysis of the duties of a receiver when settling legal claims—there must be proof of an egregious error before the court will intervene in the decision to settle.

Other jurisdictions have had the foresight to address this issue through legislation—see Irish Companies Act 2014 s.439 and the New Zealand Receiverships Act 1993 s.19. In both cases a statutory duty of care when selling company assets has been imposed. In Canada s.247 of the Bankruptcy and Insolvency Act 1992 requires receivers to deal with the security in a commercially reasonable manner.

The rules on set-off on receivership are also within the province of common law: *John Dee Group Ltd v W M H (21) Ltd* [1998] B.C.C. 972.

The effect of the appointment of an administrative receiver was considered by Judge Weeks QC in *Chesterton International Group plc v Deka Immobilien Inv GmbH* [2005] EWHC 656 (Ch); [2005] B.P.I.R. 1103. Here it was held that once an administrative receiver had been validly appointed by a debenture holder it would not then be possible to seek the appointment of an administrator unless that debenture holder consented. This was the position as outlined in para.39(1) of Sch.B1 to the IA 1986.

The relationship between the various corporate insolvency regimes is interesting. It has been clear from the earliest of days that the right of a secured creditor to have a receiver appointed would be protected by the law. Thus, although receivership and liquidation can run concurrently, in practice the liquidator must wait in the wings, at least so far as concerns the property covered by the charge, until the receiver has fulfilled his functions. This is so even though the agency character of the receiver's role changes: *Sowman v David Samuel Trust Ltd* [1978] 1 W.L.R. 22 or even if liquidation precedes receivership: *Re First Express Ltd* [1991] B.C.C. 782. The advent of the administration order regime posed little threat to the rights of the secured creditor in that a right of veto was created by IA 1986 s.9 in favour of a person having the power to appoint an administrative receiver (i.e. a creditor whose security includes a general floating charge) see *Re Croftbell Ltd* [1990] B.C.C. 781. However, if this veto was not exercised, the administrator did enjoy the power to interfere with the rights of the secured creditor (see IA 1986 s.15). The new administration regime under EA 2002 offers good protection to the qualifying floating charge holder. A secured creditor who waits for a CVA to be put in place before appointing a receiver may also be in difficulties: *Re Leisure Study Group Ltd* [1994] 2 B.C.L.C. 65.

Where a receiver pursues litigation on behalf of the company as part of the security realisation process and such litigation is unsuccessful it is unlikely that the receiver will be made subject of a third party costs order pursuant to s.51 of the Supreme Court Act 1981, now rebranded Senior Courts Act 1981, according to the Court of Appeal in *Mills v Birchall* [2008] EWCA Civ 385; [2008] B.P.I.R. 607—see annotation to s.37.

Neither receivership nor administrative receivership constitute collective insolvency proceedings for the purposes of either the EU Regulation on Insolvency Proceedings (2015/848) or the UNCITRAL Cross-Border Insolvency Regulations (SI 2006/1030).

Note the limitations imposed upon a receiver's power of realisation where s.430 of POCA 2002 applies.

As an institution the future of receivership is likely to be a diminished one. This is a result of the changes introduced by EA 2002 limiting the option of administrative receivership to pre-commencement floating charges and to other specialised corporate financing situations—see the note to ss.72A et seq. The relevant provisions barring administrative receivership do not apply to floating charges created before 15 September 2003—see the Enterprise Act 2002 (Commencement No.4 and Transitional Provisions and Savings) Order 2003 (SI 2003/2093 (C. 85)). Having said that, the controversial ruling of the House of Lords in *Re Leyland DAF Ltd* [2004] UKHL 9; [2004] B.C.C. 214 to the effect that liquidation expenses could not be made payable out of assets held by receivers for the floating charge holder should maintain a degree of competitive edge for the institution of receivership, in particular when compared to administration. Note also the Crown Statement of June 2005 on this subject—see R3 Technical Bulletin 71.2. *Leyland DAF* (above) was partially reversed when s.1282 of Companies Act 2006 was brought into force in April 2008. This reversal applies only to English law and Northern Ireland—there are no signs of a reversal of *Leyland DAF* in Scots law.

There were 1,222 cases of receivership recorded in England and Wales in 2012. This fell to 917 in 2013. A further decline to 724 receivership appointments was recorded for 2014. For a review of the current status of receivership in English Law see Rajak (2013) 329 Co. L.N. 1. These figures disguise the decline in administrative receivership—there were only 11 in 2015 and just five in 2016. There were two recorded in 2017.

Chapter I

Receivers and Managers (England and Wales)

Preliminary and general provisions

28 Extent of this Chapter

28(1) ["Company" in Pt 3 Ch.1] In this Chapter "company" means a company registered under the Companies Act 2006 in England and Wales or Scotland.

28(2) [Non-application of Pt 3 Ch.2] This Chapter does not apply to receivers appointed under Chapter 2 of this Part (Scotland).

General Note

This emphasises that ss.28–49 only apply to receivers and managers appointed under English law. The Scots have their own rules: see ss.50–71. However, Ch.1 applies to building societies subject to certain modifications: see Sch.15A as inserted by Sch.6 and s.39 of the Building Societies Act 1997.

The changes made to the law relating to receivers and managers by IA 1985 and IA 1986 are not retrospective: see Sch.11 para.2(2).

Note the change made by the Companies Act 2006 (Consequential Amendments, Transitional Provisions and Savings) Order 2009 (SI 2009/1941) with effect from 1 October 2009. This change involves the substitution of a new s.28 in the light of the enactment of the Companies Act 2006.

29 Definitions

29(1) [Interpretation] It is hereby declared that, except where the context otherwise requires–

(a) any reference in this Act to a receiver or manager of the property of a company, or to a receiver of it, includes a receiver or manager, or (as the case may be) a receiver of part only of that property and a receiver only of the income arising from the property or from part of it; and

(b) any reference in this Act to the appointment of a receiver or manager under powers contained in an instrument includes an appointment made under powers which, by virtue of any enactment, are implied in and have effect as if contained in an instrument.

29(2) ["Administrative receiver"] In this Chapter "administrative receiver" means–

(a) a receiver or manager of the whole (or substantially the whole) of a company's property appointed by or on behalf of the holders of any debentures of the company secured by a charge which, as created, was a floating charge, or by such a charge and one or more other securities; or

(b) a person who would be such a receiver or manager but for the appointment of some other person as the receiver of part of the company's property.

S.29(1)

This section defines "receiver and manager" in such a way as to include partial receiverships. Receivers of income appointed under LPA 1925 (see above) are included under the term "receiver". There is a definition of the phrase "receiver and manager" located in s.1170A of the Companies Act 2006. This mirrors the definition used in s.29(1) of the Insolvency Act 1986.

Note the amendment introduced into subs.(1) via the Companies Act 2006 (Consequential Amendments, Transitional Provisions and Savings) Order 2009 (SI 2009/1941) with effect from 1 October 2009.

S.29(2)

This seeks to cast light upon the unhappy term "administrative receiver", a label first introduced in 1985. It is important to distinguish an administrative receiver from his untitled fellows because, inter alia, ss.42–49, the rules on officeholders and the mitigating provisions in s.2 of IA 1994 only apply to administrative receivers. Moreover, it is only a person having the right to appoint an administrative receiver who can veto the appointment of an administrator (see IA 1986 s.9 and *Re Croftbell Ltd* [1990] B.C.C. 781). The idea of a lightweight or strategic floating charge was upheld by the Court of Appeal in *SAW (SW) 2010 Ltd v Wilson* [2017] EWCA Civ 1001; [2017] B.C.C. 373. Here the Court of Appeal supported *Croftbell* (above).

In view of the importance attached to the status of being an administrative receiver it is unfortunate that this provision was not drafted in clearer terms. A number of uncertainties exist:

(1) Can there be multiple concurrent administrative receivers? The better view here would appear to be "no": see Oditah [1991] J.B.L. 49.

(2) Can a court-appointed receiver enjoy this status? The consensus here appears to deny this: see Gordon Stewart, *Administrative Receivers and Administrators* (CCH, 1987), p.13; but compare Schumacher (1993) 9 I.L. & P. 43 for an interesting counter-argument. In *Re A & C Supplies Ltd* [1998] B.C.C. 708 Blackburne J indicated that the court did not enjoy the power to appoint an administrative receiver.

(3) Can an administrative receiver be appointed over the assets of a foreign company? The general rule of interpretation of companies legislation is that the word "company" does not encompass foreign companies; however, this rule can be displaced by the context. Such a displacement was accepted in the context of s.29(2) by Mummery J in *Re International Bulk Commodities Ltd* [1993] Ch. 77; [1992] B.C.C. 463. This ruling has not escaped criticism and the later judgment in *Re Devon and Somerset Farmers Ltd* [1994] Ch. 57; [1993] B.C.C. 410 to the effect that an industrial and provident society cannot go into administrative receivership (because it is not a "company") sits uneasily alongside it. An equally restrictive view was taken in *Re Dairy Farmers of Britain Ltd* [2009] EWHC 1389 (Ch); [2010] B.C.C. 637 where Henderson J indicated that an industrial and provident society fell outside the administrative receivership regime; indeed such a body did not come within the scope of Pts I–III of the IA 1986. The fact that a qualifying floating charge holder cannot initiate an administrative receivership for an industrial and provident society is underlined by the Industrial and Provident Societies and Credit Unions (Arrangements, Reconstructions and Administration) Order 2014 (SI 2014/229) art.17 inserting a new s.43A into the Industrial and Provident Societies Act 1965. The view that it is now not possible to have an administrative receiver appointed over the assets of a foreign company has been reinforced by consequential amendments introduced in the wake of the introduction of the Companies Act 2006. In particular, the new definition of "company" introduced into s.28 of IA 1986 (see above) would appear to rule out this option. For explanation and critique see Moss, Segal and Fletcher [2010] 23 Insolv. Int. 57.

(4) Can an administrative receiver be appointed by a fixed chargee? The answer to this is also negative. Moreover, even if the chargee enjoys a hybrid security comprising fixed and floating charges, the appointment must be made under the floating charge element in order for an administrative receivership to result: *Meadrealm Ltd v Transcontinental Golf Construction* (1991) (Vinelott J, unreported) noted by Marks in (1993) 6 Insolv. Int. 41. See also Marks and Emmett [1994] J.B.L. 1.

30 Disqualification of body corporate from acting as receiver

30 A body corporate is not qualified for appointment as receiver of the property of a company, and any body corporate which acts as such a receiver is liable to a fine.

General Note

This provision continues the rather curious bar on corporate receivers. If a corporate receiver is appointed, a fine will be incurred and the appointment is also invalid. On penalties, see s.430 and Sch.10. Corporations are also barred from being qualified to act as insolvency practitioners: see s.390(1). For comment see *Re Foster* [2012] EWHC 275 (Ch); [2012] B.P.I.R. 545 at [18] per Roth J.

31 Disqualification of bankrupt or person in respect of whom a debt relief order is made

31(1) [Offence] A person commits an offence if he acts as receiver or manager of the property of a company on behalf of debenture holders while–

(a) he is an undischarged bankrupt,

(aa) a moratorium period under a debt relief order applies in relation to him, or

(b) a bankruptcy restrictions order or a debt relief restrictions order is in force in respect of him.

31(2) [Sanction] A person guilty of an offence under subsection (1) shall be liable to imprisonment, a fine or both.

31(3) [Non-application to court appointee] This section does not apply to a receiver or manager acting under an appointment made by the court.

GENERAL NOTE

Schedule 21 to EA 2002 substituted a new s.31 into IA 1986 to cater for the advent of bankruptcy restrictions orders in April 2004.

S.31(1), (3)
Undischarged bankrupts or persons subject to a BRO (or BRU) are prohibited from acting as receivers and managers unless the court makes the appointment—hardly likely! Note amendment by Pt 1 para.2 of Sch.20 to the Tribunals, Courts and Enforcement Act 2007 to cater for advent of debt relief orders.

S.31(2)
This indicates the sanction, full details of which are to be found in Sch.10.

32 Power for court to appoint official receiver

32 Where application is made to the court to appoint a receiver on behalf of the debenture holders or other creditors of a company which is being wound up by the court, the official receiver may be appointed.

GENERAL NOTE

If a company is in liquidation, the court, in those rare cases where debenture holders apply to it to have a receiver appointed, may appoint the official receiver. For further details see ss.399–401.

Receivers and managers appointed out of court

33 Time from which appointment is effective

33(1) [Effect of appointment] The appointment of a person as a receiver or manager of a company's property under powers contained in an instrument–

(a) is of no effect unless it is accepted by that person before the end of the business day next following that on which the instrument of appointment is received by him or on his behalf, and

(b) subject to this, is deemed to be made at the time at which the instrument of appointment is so received.

33(2) [Joint receivers or managers] This section applies to the appointment of two or more persons as joint receivers or managers of a company's property under powers contained in an instrument, subject to such modifications as may be prescribed by the rules.

S.33(1)
The appointment of a receiver and manager out of court takes effect when he receives the letter of appointment, provided that he accepts the office before the end of the next business day. For administrative receivers see also IR 2016 r.4.1.

S.33(2)
The above rule applies to joint receivers, subject to the modifications made by the rules: see also IR 2016 r.4.1.

34 Liability for invalid appointment

34 Where the appointment of a person as the receiver or manager of a company's property under powers contained in an instrument is discovered to be invalid (whether by virtue of the invalidity of the instrument or otherwise), the court may order the person by whom or on whose behalf the appointment was made to indemnify the person appointed against any liability which arises solely by reason of the invalidity of the appointment.

General Note

This permits the court to order that the appointor of a receiver indemnify the latter against liability in trespass, where the appointment turns out to be invalid. Invalidity may be the result of the debenture charge being unregistered or being avoided under IA 1986 s.245. This provision will prove useful because challenges to appointments are becoming more common: see, e.g. *Shamji v Johnson Matthey Bankers Ltd* (1986) 2 B.C.C. 98,910 where the challenge proved unsuccessful. Short notice appointments are permitted under "on demand" debentures: *Sheppard and Cooper Ltd v TSB Bank (No.2)* [1996] B.C.C. 965. The courts will refuse to hear belated complaints about the initiation of the receivership: see *Secretary of State v Jabble* [1998] B.C.C. 39 for an optimistic attempt to challenge the propriety of the receivership in consequential director disqualification proceedings! In *Re Asset Visions Ltd* [2003] B.P.I.R. 305 an attempt to challenge an appointment of a receiver on the grounds that the terms of the debenture governing the appointment were allegedly qualified by a verbal agreement did not appeal to the court. A rare recent authority on the appointment of administrative receivers is *Brampton Manor (Leisure) Ltd v McLean* [2006] EWHC 2983 (Ch) where the point was made by Evans-Lombe J that provided events had occurred justifying the appointment of an administrative receiver the fact that the debenture had relied on other grounds to support the appointment would not induce the court to conclude that the appointment was invalid. The issue of the legal consequences of an appointment of receivers which was found to be invalid was considered by the Court of Appeal in *OBG Ltd v Allan* [2005] EWCA Civ 106. Here it was held (somewhat surprisingly) that the tort of wrongful interference with contractual relations could not be used to render invalidly appointed receivers liable for their acts in terminating a number of the company's contracts in the wake of their appointment. The Court of Appeal was reluctant to extend the scope of this economic tort in circumstances where the receivers had no wilful intention to procure a breach of contract. On the question whether the invalid appointment of the receivers involved the receivers committing the tort of conversion with regard to the contractual rights of the company placed in receivership, it was held that there was no tort of conversion of a chose in action recognised in English law. Mance LJ stressed that counsel had agreed that the actions of an improperly appointed receiver remain valid by virtue of s.232 of the IA 1986. This case proceeded to the House of Lords as part of a joined appeal with two other cases, not concerned with the same subject matter. In its judgment *OBG Ltd v Allan* [2007] UKHL 21; [2007] 2 W.L.R. 920 the House of Lords issued some important guidance on the status of various economic torts in English law. At the end of the day the claim against the receivers failed and the appeal was dismissed. There was unanimity that the receivers did not intend to induce the company in receivership to breach its contractual obligations and therefore the tort of unlawful interference with contractual relations was not established. The House split on the conversion issue but, bearing in mind the strict liability aspect of this tort, the majority ruled that it could only apply to conversion of chattels and not conversion of choses in action. The courts should not take the initiative in extending the parameters of this tort; such action should be for the prerogative of Parliament. Lord Hoffmann, whose judgment was supported by the majority, reiterated that the receivers had not been negligent and that there was no justification for extending the scope of conversion and thereby holding them responsible on a strict liability basis. These comments will reassure the insolvency practitioner profession. Some further insights into this area of law may be gleaned from the judgment of HHJ Purle QC in *Ahmad v Bank of Scotland* [2014] EWHC 4611 (Ch).

For an abortive attempt to challenge the appointment of receivers on various grounds, including lack of good faith, see the Irish case of *Komady Ltd v Ulster Bank Ltd* [2015] IEHC 314. An attempt to challenge the appointment of a receiver also failed in *McCann v Halpin* [2016] IESC 11 and in *Farrell v Brien* [2016] NICh 9. Another attempt to challenge the appointment of receivers on a variety of grounds met with the same fate in *Clydesdale Bank plc v Gough* [2017] EWHC 2230 (Ch).

35 Application to court for directions

35(1) [Application] A receiver or manager of the property of a company appointed under powers contained in an instrument, or the persons by whom or on whose behalf a receiver or manager has been so appointed, may apply to the court for directions in relation to any particular matter arising in connection with the performance of the functions of the receiver or manager.

35(2) [Order, directions by court] On such an application, the court may give such directions, or may make such order declaring the rights of persons before the court or otherwise, as it thinks just.

S.35(1)

This allows a receiver, or his appointor, to apply to the court for directions in the event of legal uncertainty arising. The latter was only given this facility by IA 1985, as a result of the recommendations of the Cork Committee (*Report*, para.828). This provision is to be widely interpreted and enables guidance to be sought on remuneration: *Re Therm-a-Stor Ltd* [1997] B.C.C. 301; and *Munns v Perkins* [2002] B.P.I.R. 120. Such guidance may be welcome in the light of the more stringent regime ushered in by Ferris J in *Mirror Group Newspapers v Maxwell* [1998] B.C.C. 324. For an important commercial precedent delivered in response to a s.35 application for directions see *Re Cheyne Finance plc* [2007] EWHC 2402 (Ch); [2008] B.C.C. 182. Note *Bank of Ireland v Edeneast Ltd* [2013] NIQB 95 where the court took a wide view of the power to give directions. The case is unusual in that it involved a court-appointed receiver and manager.

The Financial Conduct Authority or the Prudential Regulation Authority may, in an appropriate case, be heard on such an application—FSMA 2000 s.363(2).

S.35(2)

The court enjoys general discretion as to any declaration it may make on such an application.

36 Court's power to fix remuneration

36(1) [Remuneration] The court may, on an application made by the liquidator of a company, by order fix the amount to be paid by way of remuneration to a person who, under powers contained in an instrument, has been appointed receiver or manager of the company's property.

36(2) [Extent of court's power] The court's power under subsection (1), where no previous order has been made with respect thereto under the subsection–

(a) extends to fixing the remuneration for any period before the making of the order or the application for it,

(b) is exercisable notwithstanding that the receiver or manager has died or ceased to act before the making of the order or the application, and

(c) where the receiver or manager has been paid or has retained for his remuneration for any period before the making of the order any amount in excess of that so fixed for that period, extends to requiring him or his personal representatives to account for the excess or such part of it as may be specified in the order.

But the power conferred by paragraph (c) shall not be exercised as respects any period before the making of the application for the order under this section, unless in the court's opinion there are special circumstances making it proper for the power to be exercised.

36(3) [Variation, amendment of order] The court may from time to time on an application made either by the liquidator or by the receiver or manager, vary or amend an order made under subsection (1).

S.36(1)

This allows the court to determine the remuneration of a receiver and manager appointed out of court where the liquidator of the company asks for this to be done. Such applications in the past have been rare, if only because of the courtesy that exists between fellow insolvency practitioners. For a recent but unsuccessful application, see *Re Potters Oils Ltd (No.2)* [1986] 1 W.L.R. 201; (1985) 1 B.C.C. 99,593. With a more questioning era looming with regard to professional remuneration levels applications under this provision may become more commonplace. In *Munns v Perkins* [2002] B.P.I.R. 120 a fee amounting to 4.2 per cent of the value of assets realised was deemed reasonable.

The High Court in *Re Delberry Ltd* [2008] B.P.I.R. 1277 indicated that the investigatory mechanism under s.236 could be used to facilitate a s.36 claim by procuring the delivery up of documents relating to the conduct of the receivership.

S.36(2)

This provides further details of the powers of the court where an application has been made to it under s.36(1).

S.36(3)

The court can vary any order it makes fixing remuneration.

37 Liability for contracts, etc.

37(1) [Personal liability, indemnity] A receiver or manager appointed under powers contained in an instrument (other than an administrative receiver) is, to the same extent as if he had been appointed by order of the court–

(a) personally liable on any contract entered into by him in the performance of his functions (except in so far as the contract otherwise provides) and on any contract of employment adopted by him in the performance of those functions, and

(b) entitled in respect of that liability to indemnity out of the assets.

37(2) [Interpretation of s.37(1)(a)] For the purposes of subsection (1)(a), the receiver or manager is not to be taken to have adopted a contract of employment by reason of anything done or omitted to be done within 14 days after his appointment.

37(3) [Extent of s.37(1)] Subsection (1) does not limit any right to indemnity which the receiver or manager would have apart from it, nor limit his liability on contracts entered into without authority, nor confer any right to indemnity in respect of that liability.

37(4) [Vacation of office] Where at any time the receiver or manager so appointed vacates office–

(a) his remuneration and any expenses properly incurred by him, and

(b) any indemnity to which he is entitled out of the assets of the company,

shall be charged on and paid out of any property of the company which is in his custody or under his control at that time in priority to any charge or other security held by the person by or on whose behalf he was appointed.

S.37(1), (2)

Receivers appointed out of court are personally liable on contracts entered into by them (unless they have contracted out), and existing contracts of employment adopted by them, although they have 14 days' grace to decide whether to adopt or not. This latter provision is designed to cope with the problems thrown up by *Nicoll v Cutts* (1985) 1 B.C.C. 99,427. Where a receiver adopts a contract of employment under s.37(1)(a) the case will be caught by the rule in *Re Paramount Airways Ltd (No.3)* [1994] B.C.C. 172 (*Powdrill v Watson* [1995] 2 A.C. 394) and this adoption will impose all accrued employment liabilities on the receiver. (See the notes to ss.19 and 44.) The relief extended by s.2 of IA 1994 to mitigate this rule has (for unconvincing reasons) deliberately not been extended to non-administrative receivers, though the Government was supposed to be reconsidering this matter: see DTI Press Notice P/94/319. Such receivers may have to adopt contracts of employment if they are enforcing a fixed charge over, say, a hotel and they wish to retain staff pending a sale of the hotel as a going concern. It is implicit in s.37(1)(a) that a receiver is entitled not to adopt existing contracts of the company. Where he chooses this option as a rule no injunction will lie against him to enforce observance of the contract: see *Airlines Airspares Ltd v Handley Page Ltd* [1970] Ch. 193. However, in some cases the contract may be enforced: see *Freevale Ltd v Metrostore (Holdings) Ltd* [1984] Ch. 199; *Amec Properties v Planning Research and Systems* [1992] 13 E.G. 109; the discussion in *Astor Chemical Ltd v Synthetic Technology Ltd* [1990] B.C.C. 97; and *Ash & Newman v Creative Devices Research Ltd* [1991] B.C.L.C. 403. The uncertainties in this area have continued through cases like *Transtec Automotive (Campsie) Ltd* [2001] B.C.C. 403; and *Land Rover Group v UPF (UK) Ltd* [2002] EWHC 3183 (QB); [2003] 2 B.C.L.C. 222.

For an abortive attempt to make receivers (and their appointing debenture holder) personally liable in costs in the event of unsuccessful litigation brought in the company's name see *Mills v Birchall* [2008] EWCA Civ 385; [2008] B.P.I.R. 607. The action here was merely to enforce a contractual right forming part of the security—it was properly characterised as an action by the company and neither by the receivers nor the debenture holder. The receivers were the agents of the company as both the debenture and s.109(2) of the Law of Property Act 1925 made clear. The debenture holder did not fund the action which had been financed by the receivers out of realisations. In a normal case like this it would be inappropriate to render either the receivers or the debenture holder personally responsible for the costs of the other side even though the litigation had been unsuccessful.

This provision was held not to apply in *Re Dairy Farmers of Britain Ltd* [2009] EWHC 1389 (Ch); [2010] B.C.C. 637.

S.37(3)
The receiver's statutory indemnity in respect of contractual liability under s.37(1)(b) is not exhaustive. On the other hand, it does not apply to contracts entered into by him without authority.

S.37(4)
This accords high priority status to the receiver's right to remuneration and indemnity. However it is important to remember that this priority only extends to the proceeds of assets caught by the security. The right to remuneration cannot be charged against assets encompassed by a prior security: *Choudhri v Palta* [1992] B.C.C. 787. Furthermore, in cases where the receiver has realised sufficient funds to repay the debenture holder and also (arguably) to satisfy his own claim to remuneration, etc. the court might intervene and offer interlocutory relief to prevent further sales until the quantum of remuneration has been settled: *Rottenberg v Monjack* [1992] B.C.C. 688.

38 Receivership accounts to be delivered to registrar

38(1) [Where appointment under powers in instrument] Except in the case of an administrative receiver, every receiver or manager of a company's property who has been appointed under powers contained in an instrument shall deliver to the registrar of companies for registration the requisite accounts of his receipts and payments.

38(2) [Time for delivering accounts] The accounts shall be delivered within one month (or such longer period as the registrar may allow) after the expiration of 12 months from the date of his appointment and of every subsequent period of 6 months, and also within one month after he ceases to act as receiver or manager.

38(3) [Form of accounts] The requisite accounts shall be an abstract in the prescribed form showing–

(a) receipts and payments during the relevant period of 12 or 6 months, or

(b) where the receiver or manager ceases to act, receipts and payments during the period from the end of the period of 12 or 6 months to which the last preceding abstract related (or, if no preceding abstract has been delivered under this section, from the date of his appointment) up to the date of his so ceasing, and the aggregate amount of receipts and payments during all preceding periods since his appointment.

38(4) ["Prescribed"] In this section "prescribed" means prescribed by regulations made by statutory instrument by the Secretary of State.

38(5) [Penalty on default] A receiver or manager who makes default in complying with this section is liable to a fine and, for continued contravention, to a daily default fine.

S.38(1), (2)
Receivers or managers other than administrative receivers must periodically submit accounts to Cardiff.

S.38(3), (4)
These regulate the form of the accounts. For building societies see para.25 of Sch.15A as inserted by s.39, and Sch.6 to the Building Societies Act 1997.

S.38(5)
Criminal sanctions are imposed on the receiver in the event of default. On penalties, see s.430 and Sch.10. Note also the enforcement procedures laid down in s.41.
For administrative receivers, see IR 2016 r.4.17.

Provisions applicable to every receivership

39 Notification that receiver or manager appointed

39(1) [Statement in invoices etc.] Where a receiver or manager of the property of a company has been appointed–

(a) every invoice, order for goods or services, business letter or order form (whether in hard copy, electronic or any other form) issued by or on behalf of the company or the receiver or manager or the liquidator of the company; and

(b) all the company's websites,

must contain a statement that a receiver or manager has been appointed.

39(2) [Penalty on default] If default is made in complying with this section, the company and any of the following persons, who knowingly and wilfully authorises or permits the default, namely, any officer of the company, any liquidator of the company and any receiver or manager, is liable to a fine.

S.39(1)

Invoices, business letters, etc. must disclose the fact that a receiver and manager has been appointed. A new s.39(1) was substituted by the Companies (Trading Disclosures) (Insolvency) Regulations 2008 (SI 2008/1897) (as amended by SI 2009/218) with effect from 1 October 2008. This change was necessary to comply with EC Directive 2003/58 and seeks to promote disclosure where electronic invoices are used and where the company has a website. Note also that under CA 2006 s.859K the fact of the appointment must be notified to Cardiff, and by virtue of IA 1986 s.46, notice must be given to creditors. Where a secured creditor intends to enforce security in the case of a railway company special advance notification requirements have been imposed by s.62(7) of the Railways Act 1993. For building societies see para.26 of Sch.15A as inserted by s.39 of and Sch.6 to the Building Societies Act 1997.

S.39(2)

Criminal sanctions may be imposed on various named persons in the event of a breach of s.39(1). On penalties, see s.430 and Sch.10.

40 Payment of debts out of assets subject to floating charge

40(1) [Application] The following applies, in the case of a company, where a receiver is appointed on behalf of the holders of any debentures of the company secured by a charge which, as created, was a floating charge.

40(2) [Payment of preferential debts] If the company is not at the time in course of being wound up, its preferential debts (within the meaning given to that expression by section 386 in Part XII) shall be paid out of the assets coming to the hands of the receiver in priority to any claims for principal or interest in respect of the debentures.

40(3) [Recoupment of payments] Payments made under this section shall be recouped, as far as may be, out of the assets of the company available for payment of general creditors.

S.40(1), (2)

These subsections impose an obligation on every receiver appointed to enforce a floating charge to pay preferential claims (see s.386 and Sch.6). However, this obligation does not extend to receivers of industrial and provident societies: *Re Devon and Somerset Farmers Ltd* [1994] Ch. 57; [1993] B.C.C. 410. This is a positive obligation (*IR Commissioners v Goldblatt* [1972] Ch. 498) and a continuing responsibility that is not discharged simply because the debenture holder has been repaid: *Re Pearl Maintenance Services Ltd* [1995] B.C.C. 657. Note that the fact that the charge may have crystallised prior to the appointment of the receiver does not take the case outside the scope of s.40. This follows from the revised definition of "floating charge" which was introduced by IA 1985 (see now IA 1986 s.251), and which is incorporated into the wording of s.40(1). For the significance of this change in the law see *Re Brightlife Ltd* [1987] Ch. 200; (1986) 2 B.C.C. 99,359. The duty imposed by s.40 is limited by s.11(5) but the fact that the company may go into liquidation during the currency of the receivership does not relieve the receiver of his obligation to pay preferential claims: *Re Eisc Teo Ltd* [1991] I.L.R.M. 760. The determination of whether a charge is floating or fixed is clearly of considerable importance for the purposes of s.40—see here *Chalk v Kahn* [2000] 2 B.C.L.C. 361. All authorities on this vexed issue of security characterisation must be read in the light of the advice of the Privy Council in *Agnew v CIR (Re Brumark Investments Ltd)* [2001] UKPC 28; [2001] 2 A.C. 710. For comment see Sealy (2001) 76 Co. L.N. 1. This latter ruling upset established receivership practice and created real worries for practitioners who may have made distributions on the basis of a misinterpretation of the law (relying on the discredited authority of *Re New Bullas Trading Ltd* [1994] 1 B.C.L.C. 485). These concerns were somewhat alleviated by a Crown Departments Statement offering in effect an amnesty for erroneous distributions made prior to 5 June 2001 (i.e. the date when the Privy Council handed down its judgment). For comment see Milman [2002]

Insolv. L. 77. For a further judicial authority in this field see *Re BHT (UK) Ltd* [2004] EWHC 201 (Ch), where an attempt to unwind pre-5 June 2001 distributions under a now "suspect" fixed charge failed. Further confirmation of the vulnerability of "fixed charges" to judicial recharacterisation is provided by the ruling of Sir Andrew Morritt V.C. in *Re Spectrum Plus Ltd* [2004] EWHC 9 (Ch); [2004] B.C.C. 51 where a standard debenture fixed charge modelled upon that upheld by Slade J in *Siebe Gorman & Co Ltd v Barclays Bank* [1979] 2 Lloyd's Rep. 142 was in fact held only to create a floating charge. This decision of Morritt V.C. was surprisingly reversed by the Court of Appeal (see [2004] EWCA Civ 670; [2004] B.C.C. 660) which laid great store on the importance of the contractual relationship between the lending bank and the borrower and also on the fact that as *Siebe Gorman* (above) was an established authority that had stood for two decades legitimate expectations in commercial practice required reassurance. These lines of reasoning were greeted with some scepticism in many quarters—see for example Milman [2004] 17 Insolv. Int. 116; and Smart [2004] 17 Insolv. Int. 118. The issue, which it has been estimated was of relevance to some 500 insolvencies worth at least £200 million collectively, was then referred to the House of Lords which sat as a full panel of seven members. That panel unanimously ruled (*National Westminster Bank v Spectrum Plus Ltd* [2005] UKHL 41; [2005] 3 W.L.R. 58; [2005] B.C.C. 694) that *Siebe Gorman* (above) should be overruled and that the standard bank debenture that was the subject of the litigation in fact created only a floating and not a fixed charge. Moreover, the House of Lords refused to mitigate the potentially dire consequences of this ruling for banks by giving it only prospective effect. One might therefore anticipate a number of challenges by those acting on behalf of preferential creditors to require banks to regurgitate funds which were paid to them under mistake as to the status of the *Siebe Gorman*-type debenture. Equally receivers who have made such distributions in error should look to their indemnity arrangements with debenture holders.

For comment see Berg [2006] J.B.L. 22. Some of the difficulties have been mitigated by the Crown Statement of July 2005. The Crown Departments are still active in dealing with the consequences of *Brumark* (above) and *Spectrum* (above). This is apparent from *Dear IP*, March 2008. The House of Lords ruling in *Spectrum* (above) was applied by the court in *Re Beam Tube Products Ltd* [2006] B.C.C. 615 to recharacterise a charge described as "fixed" to merely floating status. But compare *Russell Cooke Trust Co Ltd v Elliott* [2007] EWHC 1443 (Ch), where, somewhat bizarrely, the opposite conclusion was arrived at (i.e. a "floating charge" judged to be a fixed charge) when the security documentation was deconstructed. Both cases merely confirm the legal adage that labels are to be treated with caution. In *Re Harmony Care Homes Ltd* [2009] EWHC 1961 (Ch); [2010] B.C.C. 358 a charge labelled as "fixed" was found to enjoy that characteristic as there was a sufficient degree of control operated by the security.

For the difficult questions of interpretation posed by s.40 see *Re H & K Medway Ltd* [1997] 1 W.L.R. 1422; [1997] B.C.C. 853; not following *Griffiths v Yorkshire Bank* [1994] 1 W.L.R. 1427 (discussed by Cooke in (1995) 11 I.L. & P. 163). In the former case Neuberger J explains the relationship between s.40 and CA 1985 s.196 [CA 2006 s.754]. See also Waller [1997–98] 3 R.A.L.Q. 131. For a rare discussion of CA 1985 s.196 (now CA 2006 s.754) see *Revenue and Customs Commissioners v Royal Bank of Scotland (Re Oval 1742 Ltd)* [2007] EWCA Civ 1262; [2008] B.C.C. 135, where the relationship with IA 1986 s.175 was also reviewed. Here both the judge at first instance and the Court of Appeal felt justified in adopting a wide view of the concept of "taking possession" and in so doing concentrated upon the substance of the matter under review rather than the form.

The receiver's obligation to cater for preferential claims will be mitigated when the full consequences of the abolition of Crown preferential debt (introduced via EA 2002 s.251) are felt. However, not all preferential debts will disappear. Moreover, receivers will in future have to take account of the special reserve fund for unsecured creditors, which was introduced by EA 2002 s.252 (see IA 1986 s.176A and IR 2016 rr.4.22–4.24). This does not apply to floating charges created before 15 September 2003. Holders of floating charges created before this date thus gain from this package of reforms.

The former prohibition on building societies creating floating charges, which was found in the Building Societies Act 1986 s.9B, was repealed by the Financial Services (Banking Reform) Act 2013, which in turn was commenced by the Financial Services (Banking Reform) Act 2013 (Commencement No.8 and Consequential Provisions) Order 2015 (SI 2015/428 (C. 25)). Further consequential matters are to be dealt with by the Building Societies (Floating Charges and Other Provisions) Order 2016 (SI 2016/679).

S.40(3)

This makes it clear that the real burden of meeting the claims of preferential creditors falls on the unsecured creditors.

41 Enforcement of duty to make returns

41(1) [Court order re defaults] If a receiver or manager of a company's property–

(a) having made default in filing, delivering or making any return, account or other document, or in giving any notice, which a receiver or manager is by law required to file, deliver, make or give, fails to make good the default within 14 days after the service on him of a notice requiring him to do so, or

(b) having been appointed under powers contained in an instrument, has, after being required at any time by the liquidator of the company to do so, failed to render proper accounts of his receipts and payments and to vouch them and pay over to the liquidator the amount properly payable to him,

the court may, on an application made for the purpose, make an order directing the receiver or manager (as the case may be) to make good the default within such time as may be specified in the order.

41(2) [Application for order] In the case of the default mentioned in subsection (1)(a), application to the court may be made by any member or creditor of the company or by the registrar of companies; and in the case of the default mentioned in subsection (1)(b), the application shall be made by the liquidator.

In either case the court's order may provide that all costs of and incidental to the application shall be borne by the receiver or manager, as the case may be.

41(3) [Other enactments] Nothing in this section prejudices the operation of any enactment imposing penalties on receivers in respect of any such default as is mentioned in subsection (1).

S.41(1)
This subsection sets out an enforcement procedure to deal with receivers who fail to submit accounts, returns, etc.

S.41(2)
Applicants to the court for an enforcement order are identified. Applicants may be indemnified against costs thereby arising. The appropriate regulator may apply where appropriate—FSMA 2000 s.363(3).

S.41(3)
Sanctions imposed by individual sections creating obligations to file returns, etc. are not prejudiced by s.41.

Administrative receivers: general

42 General powers

42(1) [Powers in Sch.1] The powers conferred on the administrative receiver of a company by the debentures by virtue of which he was appointed are deemed to include (except in so far as they are inconsistent with any of the provisions of those debentures) the powers specified in Schedule 1 to this Act.

42(2) [Interpretation of Sch.1] In the application of Schedule 1 to the administrative receiver of a company–

(a) the words "he" and "him" refer to the administrative receiver, and

(b) references to the property of the company are to the property of which he is or, but for the appointment of some other person as the receiver of part of the company's property, would be the receiver or manager.

42(3) [Deemed capacity] A person dealing with the administrative receiver in good faith and for value is not concerned to inquire whether the receiver is acting within his powers.

S.42(1)
A model list of 23 implied powers for an administrative receiver (for the definition of this term, see s.29(2)) is set out by Sch.1 to this Act. These are commonly found in most standard commercial debentures. These 23 implied powers would appear to cover almost every eventuality, particularly when one bears in mind the general nature of power number 23. The implied powers are the same as those accorded to an administrator. The exercise of these powers may be subject to constraints imposed by companies legislation: see for example *Demite Ltd v Protec Health Ltd* [1998] B.C.C. 638 where the power to sell was subjected to the restrictions imposed by s.320 of CA 1985 [CA 2006 s.190]. The position here will remain unchanged under the Companies Act 2006. It is clear from the extent of these powers that once a company goes into administrative receivership the control of its management passes from the directors to the receiver. For the implications of this see *Re Joshua Shaw & Sons Ltd* (1989) 5 B.C.C. 188. The powers conferred on an administrative receiver (whether conferred by the debenture or by statutory provision) are given to assist in the

realisation of assets. Powers should not be used to further the interests of the debenture holder in litigation with third parties—*Sutton v GE Capital Commercial Finance* [2004] EWCA Civ 315; [2004] 2 B.C.L.C. 662. On the exercise of realisation powers see *Cooperative Bank plc v Phillips* [2014] EWHC 2862 (Ch); [2014] B.P.I.R. 1430 where Morgan J held that it was *not* a misuse of the power to seek possession by a second chargee where the property was already fully encumbered for the benefit of a first chargee.

For an illustration of judicial support for maximising the powers of a receiver see *McDonald v McDonald* [2014] EWCA Civ 1049; [2014] B.P.I.R. 1270 at [65] per Arden LJ. This case went onto the Supreme Court but not on an issue affecting this point—*McDonald v McDonald* [2016] UKSC 28. The Supreme Court dismissed the appeal.

S.42(2)

This is an interpretation provision designed to smooth out any difficulties in the application of Sch.1.

S.42(3)

This statutory provision is an extension of the basic company law philosophy contained in *Royal British Bank v Turquand* (1856) 6 E. & B. 327; and in CA 2006 s.40.

43 Power to dispose of charged property, etc.

43(1) [Application to court] Where, on an application by the administrative receiver, the court is satisfied that the disposal (with or without other assets) of any relevant property which is subject to a security would be likely to promote a more advantageous realisation of the company's assets than would otherwise be effected, the court may by order authorise the administrative receiver to dispose of the property as if it were not subject to the security.

43(2) [Application of s.43(1)] Subsection (1) does not apply in the case of any security held by the person by or on whose behalf the administrative receiver was appointed, or of any security to which a security so held has priority.

43(3) [Conditions for order] It shall be a condition of an order under this section that–

(a) the net proceeds of the disposal, and

(b) where those proceeds are less than such amount as may be determined by the court to be the net amount which would be realised on a sale of the property in the open market by a willing vendor, such sums as may be required to make good the deficiency,

shall be applied towards discharging the sums secured by the security.

43(4) [Where two or more securities] Where a condition imposed in pursuance of subsection (3) relates to two or more securities, that condition shall require the net proceeds of the disposal and, where paragraph (b) of that subsection applies, the sums mentioned in that paragraph to be applied towards discharging the sums secured by those securities in the order of their priorities.

43(5) [Copy of order to registrar] A copy of an order under this section shall, within 14 days of the making of the order, be sent by the administrative receiver to the registrar of companies.

43(6) [Penalty for non-compliance] If the administrative receiver without reasonable excuse fails to comply with subsection (5), he is liable to a fine and, for continued contravention, to a daily default fine.

43(7) ["Relevant property"] In this section "relevant property", in relation to the administrative receiver, means the property of which he is or, but for the appointment of some other person as the receiver of part of the company's property, would be the receiver or manager.

General Note

This section applies to England and Wales only (see s.440(2)(a)).

Section 43 does not apply in relation to the enforcement of "market charges" (as defined by CA 1989 s.173): see s.175 of that Act (as qualified by the Financial Markets and Insolvency Regulations 1991 (SI 1991/880, amended by SI 1995/586 and SI 1998/27)), and the introductory note at p.3, above.

S.43(1), (2)
These provisions create a novel facility for administrative receivers by allowing them to apply to the court for the disposal of property that is subject to a prior charge (normally a fixed charge). The court must be satisfied that such disposal would promote a more advantageous realisation of the company's assets. The word "likely" in this context would probably be construed by the courts as meaning "a reasonable prospect": see *Re Harris Simons Construction Ltd* [1989] 1 W.L.R. 368; (1989) 5 B.C.C. 11. A similar power is given to an administrator by s.15, but the power under s.15 is wider in that it covers property subject to title retention.

"Relevant property" is defined in s.43(7).

For further details, see IR 2016 r.4.16.

S.43(3), (4)
If the court orders a disposal, the net proceeds are to be paid to discharge the prior security or securities (see s.43(4)). If the court decides that the sale was at an undervalue, the deficiency must be made good.

S.43(5), (6)
A copy of the disposal order must be registered at Cardiff within 14 days or else the administrative receiver may incur criminal sanctions. Note the minor amendment introduced in subs.(5) by the Companies Act 2006 (Consequential Amendments, Transitional Provisions and Savings) Order 2009 (SI 2009/1941) with effect from 1 October 2009.

On penalties, see s.430 and Sch.10.

S.43(7)
This is an interpretation provision and is best understood in relation to s.29(2)(b).

44 Agency and liability for contracts

44(1) [Position of administrative receiver] The administrative receiver of a company–

(a) is deemed to be the company's agent, unless and until the company goes into liquidation;

(b) is personally liable on any contract entered into by him in the carrying out of his functions (except in so far as the contract otherwise provides) and, to the extent of any qualifying liability, on any contract of employment adopted by him in the carrying out of those functions; and

(c) is entitled in respect of that liability to an indemnity out of the assets of the company.

44(2) [Interpretation] For the purposes of subsection (1)(b) the administrative receiver is not to be taken to have adopted a contract of employment by reason of anything done or omitted to be done within 14 days after his appointment.

44(2A) [Interpretation of s.44(1)(b)] For the purposes of subsection (1)(b), a liability under a contract of employment is a qualifying liability if–

(a) it is a liability to pay a sum by way of wages or salary or contribution to an occupational pension scheme,

(b) it is incurred while the administrative receiver is in office, and

(c) it is in respect of services rendered wholly or partly after the adoption of the contract.

44(2B) [Further interpretation of s.44(1)(b)] Where a sum payable in respect of a liability which is a qualifying liability for the purposes of subsection (1)(b) is payable in respect of services rendered partly before and partly after the adoption of the contract, liability under subsection (1)(b) shall only extend to so much of the sum as is payable in respect of services rendered after the adoption of the contract.

44(2C) [Interpretation of s.44(2A), (2B)] For the purposes of subsections (2A) and (2B)–

(a) wages or salary payable in respect of a period of holiday or absence from work through sickness or other good cause are deemed to be wages or (as the case may be) salary in respect of services rendered in that period, and

(b) a sum payable in lieu of holiday is deemed to be wages or (as the case may be) salary in respect of services rendered in the period by reference to which the holiday entitlement arose.

44(2D) [Repealed]

44(3) [Effect on other rights] This section does not limit any right to indemnity which the administrative receiver would have apart from it, nor limit his liability on contracts entered into or adopted without authority, nor confer any right to indemnity in respect of that liability.

S.44(1), (2)

By virtue of s.44(1)(a), an administrative receiver is deemed to be the company's agent, provided that the company has not gone into liquidation, whereupon the agency relationship terminates. This is merely a statutory declaration of the standard agency provision found in most commercial debentures. For the position on winding up, see *Gosling v Gaskell and Grocott* [1897] A.C. 575; and the article by Turing in (1994) 9 I.L. & P. 163. One implication of the agency relationship was illustrated in *Brown v City of London Corp* [1996] 1 W.L.R. 1070 (also reported as *Re Sobam BV* [1996] B.C.C. 351) where it was held that a receiver was not liable for rates during his period of occupation. The termination of this agency relationship does not result in a change of occupation for rating purposes—*Re Beck Foods Ltd* [2001] EWCA Civ 1934; [2002] B.C.C. 495. These developments represent a further blow for local authorities which no longer enjoy preferential status with respect to unpaid rates and who additionally have difficulty in protecting their interests through distress, as was confirmed by *Re ELS Ltd* [1994] B.C.C. 449. But note in *Farnborough Airport Properties Co Ltd v Revenue and Customs Commissioners* [2016] UKFTT 431 (TC) the First Tier Tribunal held in a group relief context that the appointment of a receiver resulted in a change of control. This was confirmed on appeal to the Upper Tribunal—[2017] UKUT 394 (TCC).

Although receivers are agents, they do not count as commercial agents for the purposes of that discrete category—see McGee [2013] J.B.L. 534 for explanation.

The unusual nature of this agency relationship was noted by Birmingham J in Ireland in *Ferris v Meagher* [2013] IEHC 380 at [16].

An agent is not normally liable personally on a contract which he makes for his principal, and in the light of this, para.(b) may seem somewhat surprising—especially when it is contrasted with s.14(5), which deems an administrator to be the company's agent without a similar qualification. The explanation is that a receiver is entitled to stipulate for an indemnity from the charge holder as a term of his accepting office, contracting out of this liability. For a case where such contracting out would have found favour with the courts see *Amec Properties v Planning Research and Systems* [1992] 13 E.G. 109. For the practical significance of this indemnity see *Lipe Ltd v Leyland DAF Ltd* [1993] B.C.C. 385.

Sections 44(1)(a) and 44(2) now need to be read in the light of amendments made by IA 1994. The background to these amendments can be traced back ultimately to the case of *Nicoll v Cutts* (1985) 1 B.C.C. 99,427 where it was held that a receiver who continued to retain the services of company employees during the receivership did not thereby adopt their contracts of employment. This decision was immediately counteracted by an express statutory provision extending the personal contractual liability of administrative receivers to cases of adopted contracts of employment. Insolvency practitioners sought to neutralise this statutory intervention by sending all employees whose services were being retained a letter to the effect that their contracts of employment were not being adopted nor was the administrative receiver undertaking personal liability thereon. This practice drew its support from the unreported ruling of Harman J in *Re Specialised Mouldings Ltd* (13 February 1987). The ability of insolvency practitioners to avoid the effect of the statutory rules imposing liability in cases of adoption was reviewed by the Court of Appeal in *Re Paramount Airways Ltd (No.3)* [1994] B.C.C. 172. Here the Court of Appeal held (confirming the first instance ruling of Evans-Lombe J) that adoption could occur simply by retaining staff without changing the terms of their employment. A transparent ploy such as sending a "*Specialised Mouldings*" letter was of no effect. As a result of this pronouncement from the Court of Appeal administrative receivers who retained staff after the initial 14-day period for reflection did so on the basis that they became personally liable for all accrued and current rights arising under the relevant contracts of employment. Not surprisingly, administrative receivers were reluctant to assume such personal risk, even though it would be covered by their indemnity. Debenture holders would be less willing to wait for their money by allowing the receiver to generate it through a corporate rescue but would instead insist on an immediate sale.

The economic and political consequences of abandoning a corporate rescue strategy were so great that the government was persuaded to legislate immediately. This legislation takes the form of IA 1994 which applies to contracts of employment adopted on or after 15 March 1994 (this legislation is to this extent retrospective as Royal Assent was only given on 24 March 1994). Under s.2 of this Act where a contract of employment is adopted by an administrative receiver he will only become personally responsible for "qualifying liabilities". These are defined in the new ss.44(2A)–(2D) (inserted by IA 1994 s.2(1), (3), (4)) as certain liabilities accruing only after the date when the contract was adopted. The government has indicated that it will not be persuaded to extend the retrospective effect of this legislation beyond 15 March 1994: see DTI Press Notice P/95/282.

Note repeal of subs.(2D) by DA 2015 s.19 and Sch.6 para.26.

The issue was revisited when *Paramount* (and the direct appeals in *Re Leyland DAF* and *Re Ferranti International* [1994] B.C.C. 654) reached the House of Lords (reported sub nom. *Powdrill v Watson* [1995] 2 A.C. 394; [1995] B.C.C. 319). Their Lordships were of course concerned to clarify the law pre-15 March 1994 and in essence they approved of the approach of the Court of Appeal with regard to adoption. However they took a more restrictive view of the extent of liabilities incurred in cases of adoption. For a review of the whole saga see Mudd (1994) 10 I.L. & P. 38 and (1995) 11 I.L. & P. 78. Pre-1994 claims still continue to trouble receivers, as is clear from the Scottish case of *Jamieson, Petitioners*, 1997 S.C. 195; [1997] B.C.C. 682. On whether adoption can occur by error, see *Re Antal International Ltd* [2003] EWHC 1339 (Ch); [2003] 2 B.C.L.C. 406 a case on administration.

In s.44(1)(b) the words ", to the extent of any qualifying liability," were inserted after "provides) and" by IA 1994 s.2(1), (2), (4).

For discussion of what might be viewed as "wages or salary" in the context of administration see *Re Allders Department Stores Ltd* [2005] EWHC 172 (Ch); [2005] B.C.C. 289. See annotation to Sch.B1 para.99.

For further comment on s.44 and the possibility of personal liability of administrative receivers see *Legends Surf Shops plc v Sun Life Assurance Society plc* [2005] EWHC 1438 (Ch); [2006] B.C.C. 204 (Laddie J), a case involving an application for relief against forfeiture brought by administrative receivers of the tenant company.

S.44(3)

This, in effect, merely extends s.37(3) to administrative receivers.

45 Vacation of office

45(1) [Removal by court, resignation] An administrative receiver of a company may at any time be removed from office by order of the court (but not otherwise) and may resign his office by giving notice of his resignation in the prescribed manner to such persons as may be prescribed.

45(2) [Vacation of office] An administrative receiver shall vacate office if he ceases to be qualified to act as an insolvency practitioner in relation to the company.

45(3) [Effect of vacation of office] Where at any time an administrative receiver vacates office–

(a) his remuneration and any expenses properly incurred by him, and

(b) any indemnity to which he is entitled out of the assets of the company,

shall be charged on and paid out of any property of the company which is in his custody or under his control at that time in priority to any security held by the person by or on whose behalf he was appointed.

45(4) [Notice to registrar] Where an administrative receiver vacates office otherwise than by death, he shall, within 14 days after his vacation of office, send a notice to that effect to the registrar of companies.

45(5) [Penalty for non-compliance] If an administrative receiver without reasonable excuse fails to comply with subsection (4), he is liable to a fine and, for continued contravention, to a daily default fine.

S.45(1), (2)

These subsections outline the situations where the tenure of an administrative receiver comes to an end. Note that (as a result of a change in the law made by IA 1985) he can only be removed by debenture holders if they successfully apply to the court. This will make it clear that he is not entirely the minion of the debenture holders who appointed him. If he loses his qualification as an insolvency practitioner (see Pt XIII) he must also vacate office. Although the court has the power to remove an administrative receiver it does not enjoy the consequential power of appointing a replacement: *Re A & C Supplies Ltd* [1998] B.C.C. 708. Such a replacement can only be effected by a debenture holder enjoying a floating charge.

S.45(3)

This subsection protects the priority status of the administrative receiver's right to remuneration and indemnity.

S.45(4), (5)

On vacating office the administrative receiver must notify Cardiff within 14 days or incur a fine. A similar obligation is imposed by CA 1985 s.405(2). Note prospective amendment in s.45(5): the words "and, for continued contravention, to a daily default fine" are to be repealed by CA 1989 Schs 16 and 24 from a day to be appointed.

On penalties, see s.430 and Sch.10.

On payment of unclaimed dividends by a former administrative receiver of a now dissolved company into the Insolvency Services Account see the Insolvency (Amendment) Regulations 2008 (SI 2008/670), which insert a new reg.3C into the Insolvency Regulations 1994 (SI 1994/2507).

For further information, see IR 2016 rr.4.18–4.21.

Administrative receivers: ascertainment and investigation of company's affairs

46 Information to be given by administrative receiver

46(1) [Notices] Where an administrative receiver is appointed, he shall–

(a) forthwith send to the company and publish in the prescribed manner a notice of his appointment, and

(b) within 28 days after his appointment, unless the court otherwise directs, send such a notice to all the creditors of the company (so far as he is aware of their addresses).

46(2) [Non-application] This section and the next do not apply in relation to the appointment of an administrative receiver to act–

(a) with an existing administrative receiver, or

(b) in place of an administrative receiver dying or ceasing to act,

except that, where they apply to an administrative receiver who dies or ceases to act before they have been fully complied with, the references in this section and the next to the administrative receiver include (subject to the next subsection) his successor and any continuing administrative receiver.

46(3) [Where company being wound up] If the company is being wound up, this section and the next apply notwithstanding that the administrative receiver and the liquidator are the same person, but with any necessary modifications arising from that fact.

46(4) [Penalty for non-compliance] If the administrative receiver without reasonable excuse fails to comply with this section, he is liable to a fine and, for continued contravention, to a daily default fine.

S.46(1), (4)

These provisions impose obligations on the administrative receiver to give notice of his appointment to various named parties. Criminal sanctions are imposed in the event of default (on penalties, see s.430 and Sch.10). Note also s.39, and CA 2006 s.871(1) (entry of appointment in register of charges). When the Companies Act 2006 (Amendment of Part 25) Regulations 2013 (SI 2013/600) came into force, s.871 of the 2006 Act was restructured as s.859K with some limited modification.

S.46(2), (3)

Qualifications to the above obligations are imposed. Compliance with s.46(1) is a once and for all requirement. Provision is made for the case where the company is in liquidation and the administrative receiver is also the liquidator.

For further details, see IR 2016 r.4.5.

47 Statement of affairs to be submitted

47(1) [Duty of administrative receiver] Where an administrative receiver is appointed, he shall forthwith require some or all of the persons mentioned below to make out and submit to him a statement in the prescribed form as to the affairs of the company.

47(2) [Contents of statement] A statement submitted under this section shall be verified by a statement of truth by the persons required to submit it and shall show–

(a) particulars of the company's assets, debts and liabilities;

(b) the names and addresses of its creditors;

(c) the securities held by them respectively;

(d) the dates when the securities were respectively given; and

(e) such further or other information as may be prescribed.

47(3) [Persons in s.47(1)] The persons referred to in subsection (1) are–

(a) those who are or have been officers of the company;

(b) those who have taken part in the company's formation at any time within one year before the date of the appointment of the administrative receiver;

(c) those who are in the company's employment, or have been in its employment within that year, and are in the administrative receiver's opinion capable of giving the information required;

(d) those who are or have been within that year officers of or in the employment of a company which is, or within that year was, an officer of the company.

In this subsection "employment" includes employment under a contract for services.

47(4) [Time for statement] Where any persons are required under this section to submit a statement of affairs to the administrative receiver, they shall do so (subject to the next subsection) before the end of the period of 21 days beginning with the day after that on which the prescribed notice of the requirement is given to them by the administrative receiver.

47(5) [Release, extension of time] The administrative receiver, if he thinks fit, may–

(a) at any time release a person from an obligation imposed on him under subsection (1) or (2), or

(b) either when giving notice under subsection (4) or subsequently, extend the period so mentioned;

and where the administrative receiver has refused to exercise a power conferred by this subsection, the court, if it thinks fit, may exercise it.

47(6) [Penalty for non-compliance] If a person without reasonable excuse fails to comply with any obligation imposed under this section, he is liable to a fine and, for continued contravention, to a daily default fine.

S.47(1), (2), (4)

A statement of affairs containing the information outlined in s.47(2) and the rules must be submitted to the administrative receiver within 21 days of his requiring it (or longer, if s.47(5) is activated). Amended by LRO 2010 (SI 2010/18).

S.47(3), (5), (6)

The persons who may be required by the administrative receiver to participate in the submission of the statement of affairs are identified by s.47(3), although they may be excused either by the administrative receiver or the courts. Criminal sanctions are imposed on defaulters. On penalties, see s.430 and Sch.10.

For further information, see IR 2016 rr.4.6–4.11. For enforcement by the administrative receiver, see IR 2016 r.12.52.

48 Report by administrative receiver

48(1) [Duty of administrative receiver] Where an administrative receiver is appointed, he shall, within 3 months (or such longer period as the court may allow) after his appointment, send to the registrar of companies, to any trustees for secured creditors of the company and (so far as he is aware of their addresses) to all such creditors, other than opted-out creditors, a report as to the following matters, namely–

(a) the events leading up to his appointment, so far as he is aware of them;

(b) the disposal or proposed disposal by him of any property of the company and the carrying on or proposed carrying on by him of any business of the company;

(c) the amounts of principal and interest payable to the debenture holders by whom or on whose behalf he was appointed and the amounts payable to preferential creditors; and

(d) the amount (if any) likely to be available for the payment of other creditors.

48(2) [Copies of report] The administrative receiver shall also, within 3 months (or such longer period as the court may allow) after his appointment, either–

(a) send a copy of the report (so far as he is aware of their addresses) to all unsecured creditors of the company, other than opted-out creditors; or

(b) publish in the prescribed manner a notice stating an address to which unsecured creditors of the company should write for copies of the report to be sent to them free of charge.

48(3) [Omitted]

48(4) [Where company in liquidation] Where the company has gone or goes into liquidation, the administrative receiver–

(a) shall, within 7 days after his compliance with subsection (1) or, if later, the nomination or appointment of the liquidator, send a copy of the report to the liquidator, and

(b) where he does so within the time limited for compliance with subsection (2), is not required to comply with that subsection.

48(5) [Report to include summary of statement] A report under this section shall include a summary of the statement of affairs made out and submitted to the administrative receiver under section 47 and of his comments (if any) upon it.

48(6) [Limit on report only] Nothing in this section is to be taken as requiring any such report to include any information the disclosure of which would seriously prejudice the carrying out by the administrative receiver of his functions.

48(7) [Application of s.46(2)] Section 46(2) applies for the purposes of this section also.

48(8) [Penalty for non-compliance] If the administrative receiver without reasonable excuse fails to comply with this section, he is liable to a fine and, for continued contravention, to a daily default fine.

S.48(1), (4), (7)

These subsections require an administrative receiver to submit a report (normally within three months of his appointment) to various named parties, including the liquidator (see s.48(4)) and the FCA where appropriate—FSMA 2000 s.363(4). There is no need to send the report to opted-out creditors. The contents of the report are also detailed. It is clear from s.48(7) that this obligation does not apply to an administrative receiver succeeding another or assisting an incumbent administrative receiver.

Note also the whistleblowing duty imposed by FSMA 2000 s.364.

S.48(2)

More widespread publication of the report is required by s.48(2). Unsecured creditors, in particular, are to be given access to this report. A meeting of unsecured creditors must also be called at which this report is presented.

S.48(5), (6)

These provisions go into further detail on the administrative receiver's report. It should contain a summary of the statement of affairs submitted to him, but need not include "any information, the disclosure of which would seriously prejudice the carrying out by the administrative receiver of his functions". It is not clear whether the test to be applied here is subjective or objective. See also *Gomba Holdings UK Ltd v Homan & Bird* [1986] 1 W.L.R. 1301; (1986) 2 B.C.C. 99,102.

S.48(8)

Again, criminal sanctions are imposed on a defaulting administrative receiver. On penalties, see s.430 and Sch.10.

Section 48 is amplified by IR 2016 rr.4.13 and 4.14.

Editors' note: This provision was amended by SBEEA 2015 s.126 and Sch.9 para.12 to cater for the position of opted-out creditors.

49 Committee of creditors

49(1) [Creditors may establish committee] Where an administrative receiver has sent or published a report as mentioned in section 48(2) the company's unsecured creditors may, in accordance with the rules, establish a committee ("the creditors' committee") to exercise the functions conferred on it by or under this Act.

49(2) [Committee may summon administrative receiver] If such a committee is established, the committee may, on giving not less than 7 days' notice, require the administrative receiver to attend before it at any reasonable time and furnish it with such information relating to the carrying out by him of his functions as it may reasonably require.

S.49(1)

This empowers the unsecured creditors in their decision made under s.48(2) to set up a committee. An FCA representative may attend where appropriate—FSMA 2000 s.363(5).

This provision was amended by SBEEA 2015 s.126 and Sch.9 para.13. This amendment reflects the opting out system for creditors.

S.49(2)

The committee of creditors can request information from the administrative receiver. The test of reasonableness is presumably designed to protect information of the type envisaged by s.48(6).

Further details on the constitution, role and working of this committee are provided by IR 2016 rr.17.3–17.27, and in particular by rr.17.22 and 17.23.

Chapter II

Receivers (Scotland)

50 Extent of this Chapter

50 This Chapter extends to Scotland only.

General Note

Scottish debenture holders were only given the remedy of receivership in 1972 and, since that date, their law of receivership has developed separately from the English counterpart, although on similar lines. There have been problems in fitting this new remedy into the general system of Scottish corporate insolvency law, and problems of statutory interpretation have troubled the Scottish courts on a number of occasions. For the floating charge in Scotland, see Bankruptcy and Diligence etc. (Scotland) Act 2007 Pt 2 (ss.37–49) which repeals Pt XVIII (which includes ss.462–466) of the CA 1985; and the discussion in the House of Lords in *Sharp v Woolwich Building Society* [1998] B.C.C. 115 (often referred to as *Sharp v Thomson* 1997 S.C. (HL) 66). This particular case has caused real difficulties in practice and, as a result, has attracted the attention of both the Scottish Law Commission (see SLC Report No.208, December 2007) and the Scottish Executive (see Scottish Executive Papers No.242). Reference should also be made to the Receivers (Scotland) Regulations 1986 (SI 1986/1917 (S 141)).

The changes made in this area of the law by IA 1985 and IA 1986 do not operate retrospectively; see Sch.11 para.3(2).

Sections 50–71 apply to LLPs with suitable modifications—see Limited Liability Partnerships (Scotland) Regulations 2001 (SI 2001/128) reg.4, Sch.2.

51 Power to appoint receiver

51(1) [Floating charge holder may appoint receiver] It is competent under the law of Scotland for the holder of a floating charge over all or any part of the property (including uncalled capital), which may from time to time be comprised in the property and undertaking of an incorporated company (whether a company registered under the Companies Act 2006 or not)

(a) which the Court of Session has jurisdiction to wind up; or

(b) where paragraph (a) does not apply, in respect of which a court of a member state other than the United Kingdom has under the EU Regulation jurisdiction to open insolvency proceedings,

to appoint a receiver of such part of the property of the company as is subject to the charge.

51(2) [Appointment by court on application] It is competent under the law of Scotland for the court, on the application of the holder of such a floating charge, to appoint a receiver of such part of the property of the company as is subject to the charge.

51(2ZA) [Repealed]

51(2A) [Application of s.51(1), (2)] Subsections (1) and (2) are subject to section 72A.

51(3) [Those disqualified] The following are disqualified from being appointed as receiver–

(a) a body corporate;

(b) an undischarged bankrupt; and

(ba) a person subject to a bankruptcy restrictions order;

(c) a firm according to the law of Scotland.

51(4) [Scottish firm] A body corporate or a firm according to the law of Scotland which acts as a receiver is liable to a fine.

51(5) [Undischarged bankrupt] An undischarged bankrupt or a person subject to a bankruptcy restrictions order who so acts is liable to imprisonment or a fine, or both.

51(6) ["Definitions] In this section, "receiver" includes joint receivers; and

"bankruptcy restrictions order" means–

(a) a bankruptcy restrictions order made under section 155 of the Bankruptcy (Scotland) Act 2016;

(b) [Repealed]

(c) a bankruptcy restrictions order made under paragraph 1 of Schedule 4A to this Act; or

(d) a bankruptcy restrictions undertaking entered into under paragraph 7 of that Schedule.

"the EU Regulation" is Regulation (EU) 2015/848 of the European Parliament and of the Council on insolvency proceedings;

"court" is to be construed in accordance with Article 2(6) of the EU Regulation;

"insolvency proceedings" is to be construed in accordance with Article 2(4) of the EU Regulation.

S.51(1), (2)

These provisions authorise the holder of a floating charge in Scotland (for the meaning of this term, see IA 1986 s.70) to appoint a receiver out of court or to apply to the court for such an appointment. For the meaning of "property" within subs.(1) see *Hawking v Hafton House Ltd*, 1990 S.L.T. 496. A number of technical amendments are made to subsections (3), (5) and (6) of s.51 by the Bankruptcy and Diligence etc. (Scotland) Act 2007. Note the Companies Act 2006 (Consequential Amendments, Transitional Provisions and Savings) Order 2009 (SI 2009/1941) (effective from 1 October 2009) which amends s.51 by introducing a reference to the Companies Act 2006.

The wording in s.51 that the power of appointment applies to a company which the Court of Session has jurisdiction to wind up has caused the Scottish Government concern that it may restrict inward investment from EU Member States into Scotland. On 22 July 2010, the Scottish Government issued a consultation letter asking for comments on the scenario that if a borrowing company has its centre of main interests in an EU Member State (outside the UK) and has no "establishment" in the UK (for jurisdiction purposes of art.3 of the EU Regulation), then the Court of Session may not have jurisdiction to wind up the company, and so receivers could not be appointed to it in Scotland and this may be a disincentive to investment in Scotland. The consultation exercise asks whether a floating charge-holder has power to appoint a receiver to such a company and whether s.51 already provides such a power (and if not, how the power might best be created). It also asks whether powers for floating charge-holders to appoint could be enhanced (e.g. to make an appointment over part only of the company's assets covered by the charge, unless s.51 already provides such a power) and how the efficacy of s.51 may be enhanced generally. The consultation does not seem to consider the position of winding up the company as an unregistered company under s.221(7). For comment with suggestions for reform of s.51 see H. Patrick [2010] Scots Law Times 177. The Scottish Government hopes that the Insolvency Act 1986 Amendment (Appointment of Receivers) (Scotland) Regulations 2011 (SSI 2011/140) which take effect on 17 March 2011 will resolve these difficulties. These regulations amend subs.(1) and (6) and insert a new subs.(2ZA). In a change of direction, subs.(2ZA) was then repealed with effect from 1 April 2016 as a result of the Public Services Reform (Insolvency) (Scotland) Order 2016 (SSI 2016/141). This repeal will increase flexibility with regard to Scottish receiverships by encompassing property located outside Scotland. Consequential amendments to s.51(6) have been made as follows: s.51(6)(a) amended by the Bankruptcy (Scotland) Act 2016 (Consequential Provisions and Modifications) Order 2016 (SI 2016/1034) art.7(1), Sch.1 para.4(1), (2) as from 30 November 2016; s.51(6)(b) repealed by the Bankruptcy and Debt Advice (Scotland) Act 2014 s.56(2) and Sch.4 as from 1 April 2015; s.51(6)(d) amended by the Insolvency (Regulation (EU) 2015/848) (Miscellaneous Amendments) (Scotland) Regulations 2017 (SSI 2017/210) reg.2 as from 26 June 2017.

Note IR 2016 Introductory Rule 3(2).

S.51(2A)

This was inserted by s.248 of and Sch.17 to EA 2002 to reflect the new restrictive approach towards administrative receivership (or receivership in Scotland). See the commentary on s.72A. See Patrick [2003] 16 Insolv. Int. 65 for comment.

S.51(3)–(5)

These subsections deal with the question of disqualification and mirror the English provisions to a large extent. However, note that Scottish partnerships, which possess legal personality, are also disqualified. A Scottish receiver will have to be a qualified insolvency practitioner within the meaning of IA 1986 Pt XIII, if he is an administrative receiver, as will commonly be the case (see IA 1986 s.251). On penalties, see s.430 and Sch.10. See note above on amendments.

S.51(6)

Joint receivers are permissible under Scottish law. See note above on amendments.

52 Circumstances justifying appointment

52(1) [Events for s.51(1) appointment] A receiver may be appointed under section 51(1) by the holder of the floating charge on the occurrence of any event which, by the provisions of the instrument creating the charge, entitles the holder of the charge to make that appointment and, in so far as not otherwise provided for by the instrument, on the occurrence of any of the following events, namely–

(a) the expiry of a period of 21 days after the making of a demand for payment of the whole or any part of the principal sum secured by the charge, without payment having been made;

(b) the expiry of a period of 2 months during the whole of which interest due and payable under the charge has been in arrears;

(c) the making of an order or the passing of a resolution to wind up the company;

(d) the appointment of a receiver by virtue of any other floating charge created by the company.

52(2) [Events for s.51(2) appointment] A receiver may be appointed by the court under section 51(2) on the occurrence of any event which, by the provisions of the instrument creating the floating charge, entitles the holder of the charge to make that appointment and, in so far as not otherwise provided for by the instrument, on the occurrence of any of the following events, namely–

(a) where the court, on the application of the holder of the charge, pronounces itself satisfied that the position of the holder of the charge is likely to be prejudiced if no such appointment is made;

(b) any of the events referred to in paragraphs (a) to (c) of subsection (1).

S.52(1)

This subsection provides a model list of grounds (which can be varied by the debenture) under which a Scots receiver can be appointed out of court by a holder of a floating charge.

S.52(2)
A receiver can be appointed by the court on the occurrence of any of the events specified in s.52(1) or on grounds of prejudice (a Scottish synonym for "jeopardy").

53 Mode of appointment by holder of charge

53(1) [Instrument of appointment] The appointment of a receiver by the holder of the floating charge under section 51(1) shall be by means of an instrument subscribed in accordance with the Requirements of Writing (Scotland) Act 1995 ("the instrument of appointment"), a copy (certified in the prescribed manner to be a correct copy) whereof shall be delivered by or on behalf of the person making the appointment to the registrar of companies for registration within 7 days of its execution and shall be accompanied by a notice in the prescribed form.

53(2) [Penalty on default] If any person without reasonable excuse makes default in complying with the requirements of subsection (1), he is liable to a fine and, for continued contravention, to a daily default fine.

53(3) (Ceased to have effect and repealed by Law Reform (Miscellaneous Provisions) (Scotland) Act 1990 s.74, Sch.8 para.35 and Sch.9 as from 1 December 1990.)

53(4) [Execution on behalf of floating charge holders] If the receiver is to be appointed by the holders of a series of secured debentures, the instrument of appointment may be executed on behalf of the holders of the floating charge by any person authorised by resolution of the debenture-holders to execute the instrument.

53(5) [Entry on register] On receipt of the certified copy of the instrument of appointment in accordance with subsection (1), the registrar shall, on payment of the prescribed fee, enter the particulars of the appointment in the register.

53(6) [Effect of appointment] The appointment of a person as a receiver by an instrument of appointment in accordance with subsection (1)–

(a) is of no effect unless it is accepted by that person before the end of the business day next following that on which the instrument of appointment is received by him or on his behalf, and

(b) subject to paragraph (a), is deemed to be made on the day on and at the time at which the instrument of appointment is so received, as evidenced by a written docquet by that person or on his behalf;

and this subsection applies to the appointment of joint receivers subject to such modifications as may be prescribed.

53(7) [Attachment of charge] On the appointment of a receiver under this section, the floating charge by virtue of which he was appointed attaches to the property then subject to the charge; and such attachment has effect as if the charge was a fixed security over the property to which it has attached.

S.53(1), (2), (5)
Section 53(1) specifies the exclusive method by which a receiver can be appointed out of court. Note that, as in English law (CA 2006 s.871), a notice in proper form of the appointment must be delivered for registration to the Scottish Companies Registry in Edinburgh, whereupon the registrar must register it: see s.53(1). Criminal sanctions are imposed for default. A textual amendment to subs.(1) was made by the Requirements of Writing (Scotland) Act 1995 s.14(1) and Sch.4 para.58(a). Section 53(1) was modified by the Scotland Act 1998 s.125(1) and Sch.8 para.23(1)–(3) so that anything done by the registrar of companies in Scotland or the assistant registrar of friendly societies for Scotland by virtue of s.53(1) as applied in relation to friendly societies, industrial and provident societies or building societies may be done to or by the Accountant in Bankruptcy as from 1 July 1999 (see SI 1998/3178 (C. 79) art.2). Note prospective amendment in s.53(2): the words "and, for continued contravention, to a daily default fine" are to be repealed by CA 1989 Schs 16 and 24 from a day to be appointed. On penalties, see s.430 and Sch.10. For the prescribed form under s.53(1), see the Receivers (Scotland) Regulations 1986 (SI 1986/1917 (S 141)) Form 1 (Scot). Note that s.436B is inapplicable.

Note the minor amendment made to subs.(5) by the Companies Act 2006 (Amendment of Part 25) Regulations 2013 (SI 2013/600) Sch.2 para.2 by changing the former reference to the "register of charges" to the "register".

S.53(3)

This subsection was repealed by the Law Reform (Miscellaneous Provisions) (Scotland) Act 1990 s.74 and Sch.9: see SI 1990/2328 (C. 60) art.3.

S.53(4)

This subsection, which was substituted by s.14(1) and Sch.4 para.58(b) to the Requirements of Writing (Scotland) Act 1995, deals with the way in which the instrument of appointment is executed. For the meaning of "holder of the floating charge" and "series of secured debentures" in s.53(4), see s.70.

S.53(6), (7)

The time of the appointment is fixed (for the English position, see IA 1986 s.33(1)). The appointment of the receiver causes crystallisation by converting the charge into a fixed security, but this does not render it immune from attack under IA 1986 s.245, nor from the preferential claims regime. See the Receivers (Scotland) Regulations 1986 (SI 1986/1917 (S 141)). On s.53(7) see *Myles J Callaghan Ltd (in receivership) v City of Glasgow District Council* (1987) 3 B.C.C. 337; *Scottish and Newcastle plc, Petitioners* [1993] B.C.C. 634; and *Sharp v Woolwich Building Society* [1998] B.C.C. 115.

54 Appointment by court

54(1) [Petition to court] Application for the appointment of a receiver by the court under section 51(2) shall be by petition to the court, which shall be served on the company.

54(2) [Issue of interlocutor] On such an application, the court shall, if it thinks fit, issue an interlocutor making the appointment of the receiver.

54(3) [Copy of interlocutor to registrar, penalty on default] A copy (certified by the clerk of the court to be a correct copy) of the court's interlocutor making the appointment shall be delivered by or on behalf of the petitioner to the registrar of companies for registration, accompanied by a notice in the prescribed form, within 7 days of the date of the interlocutor or such longer period as the court may allow.

If any person without reasonable excuse makes default in complying with the requirements of this subsection, he is liable to a fine and, for continued contravention, to a daily default fine.

54(4) [Entry on register] On receipt of the certified copy interlocutor in accordance with subsection (3), the registrar shall, on payment of the prescribed fee, enter the particulars of the appointment in the register.

54(5) [Date of appointment] The receiver is to be regarded as having been appointed on the date of his being appointed by the court.

54(6) [Attachment of charge] On the appointment of a receiver under this section, the floating charge by virtue of which he was appointed attaches to the property then subject to the charge; and such attachment has effect as if the charge were a fixed security over the property to which it has attached.

54(7) [Rules of court re urgent cases] In making rules of court for the purposes of this section, the Court of Session shall have regard to the need for special provision for cases which appear to the court to require to be dealt with as a matter of urgency.

S.54(1), (2)

These provisions outline the procedure by which a receiver can be appointed by the court in Scotland.

S.54(3), (4)

The court's order (interlocutor) is to be registered at Edinburgh, normally within seven days. Criminal sanctions are imposed for failure to submit the order for registration. Section 54(3) modified by Scotland Act 1998 s.125(1) and Sch.8 para.23(1)–(3) so that anything done by the registrar of companies in Scotland or the assistant registrar of friendly societies for Scotland by virtue of s.54(3) as applied in relation to friendly societies, industrial and provident societies or building societies may be done to or by the Accountant in Bankruptcy as from 1 July 1999 (see SI 1998/3178 (C. 79) art.2). Note prospective amendment in s.54(3): the words "and, for continued contravention, to a daily default fine" are to be repealed by CA 1989 Schs 16 and 24 from a day to be appointed. On penalties, see s.430

and Sch.10. For the notice in prescribed form under s.54(3), see Form 2 (Scot) in the Receivers (Scotland) Regulations 1986 (SI 1986/1917 (S 141)).

Note the minor amendment made to subs.(4) by the Companies Act 2006 (Amendment of Part 25) Regulations 2013 (SI 2013/600) Sch.2 para.2 by changing the former reference to the "register of charges" to the "register".

S.54(5), (6)

These subsections regulate the timing and the effect of the appointment.

S.54(7)

Special rules of court may be devised to expedite urgent cases.

55 Powers of receiver

55(1) [Powers in instrument] Subject to the next subsection, a receiver has in relation to such part of the property of the company as is attached by the floating charge by virtue of which he was appointed, the powers, if any, given to him by the instrument creating that charge.

55(2) [Powers in Sch.2] In addition, the receiver has under this Chapter the powers as respects that property (in so far as these are not inconsistent with any provision contained in that instrument) which are specified in Schedule 2 to this Act.

55(3) [Restriction on powers] Subsections (1) and (2) apply–

(a) subject to the rights of any person who has effectually executed diligence on all or any part of the property of the company prior to the appointment of the receiver, and

(b) subject to the rights of any person who holds over all or any part of the property of the company a fixed security or floating charge having priority over, or ranking pari passu with, the floating charge by virtue of which the receiver was appointed.

55(4) [Enquiry as to authority not necessary] A person dealing with a receiver in good faith and for value is not concerned to enquire whether the receiver is acting within his powers.

S.55(1), (2)

Scottish receivers enjoy the 23 implied powers listed in Sch.2 to the Act. These can be added to by the debenture. For the English position, see s.42 and Sch.1. For a recent authority here, see *Myles J Callaghan Ltd (in receivership) v City of Glasgow District Council* (1987) 3 B.C.C. 337. The powers of the receiver do not extend to assets which cannot be regarded as the "property" of the company: see *Hawking v Hafton House Ltd*, 1990 S.L.T. 496.

S.55(3), (4)

The rights of third parties, such as holders of a fixed security (for definition, see s.70) and execution creditors, vis-à-vis the receiver in the exercise of his powers are regulated. Third parties need not check to see that the receiver is acting within his powers. See *Iona Hotels Ltd, Petitioners*, 1991 S.L.T. 11.

56 Precedence among receivers

56(1) [Order of precedence] Where there are two or more floating charges subsisting over all or any part of the property of the company, a receiver may be appointed under this Chapter by virtue of each such charge; but a receiver appointed by, or on the application of, the holder of a floating charge having priority of ranking over any other floating charge by virtue of which a receiver has been appointed has the powers given to a receiver by section 55 and Schedule 2 to the exclusion of any other receiver.

56(2) [Where floating charges rank equally] Where two or more floating charges rank with one another equally, and two or more receivers have been appointed by virtue of such charges, the receivers so appointed are deemed to have been appointed as joint receivers.

56(3) [Receivers to act jointly] Receivers appointed, or deemed to have been appointed, as joint receivers shall act jointly unless the instrument of appointment or respective instruments of appointment otherwise provide.

56(4) [Suspension of receiver's powers] Subject to subsection (5) below, the powers of a receiver appointed by, or on the application of, the holder of a floating charge are suspended by, and as from the date of, the appointment of a receiver by, or on the application of, the holder of a floating charge having priority of ranking over that charge to such extent as may be necessary to enable the receiver second mentioned to exercise his powers under section 55 and Schedule 2; and any powers so suspended take effect again when the floating charge having priority of ranking ceases to attach to the property then subject to the charge, whether such cessation is by virtue of section 62(6) or otherwise.

56(5) [Effect of suspension] The suspension of the powers of a receiver under subsection (4) does not have the effect of requiring him to release any part of the property (including any letters or documents) of the company from his control until he receives from the receiver superseding him a valid indemnity (subject to the limit of the value of such part of the property of the company as is subject to the charge by virtue of which he was appointed) in respect of any expenses, charges and liabilities he may have incurred in the performance of his functions as receiver.

56(6) [Floating charge remains attached] The suspension of the powers of a receiver under subsection (4) does not cause the floating charge by virtue of which he was appointed to cease to attach to the property to which it attached by virtue of section 53(7) or 54(6).

56(7) [Same receiver by several charges] Nothing in this section prevents the same receiver being appointed by virtue of two or more floating charges.

S.56(1), (2), (3)
Two competing receivers may be appointed over the same company's assets, but only the one with priority can exercise the statutory powers conferred on receivers. In the event of a "tie" they are deemed to have been appointed as joint receivers, and must act jointly.

S.56(4), (5), (6)
These subsections deal with the situation where the receiver who was appointed first has to give way to a receiver appointed subsequently, but enjoying priority. This is a matter not dealt with by any English statutory provision. The first receiver's powers are suspended until the latter has fulfilled his role. However, he should not hand over property to the latter until he has received an indemnity from him. Furthermore, the mere fact that a receiver's powers have been suspended does not cause the floating charge under which he was appointed to refloat.

S.56(7)
To make matters easier, the same receiver can act for competing chargees, although this may produce conflicts of interest.

57 Agency and liability of receiver for contracts

57(1) [Receiver deemed agent] A receiver is deemed to be the agent of the company in relation to such property of the company as is attached by the floating charge by virtue of which he was appointed.

57(1A) [Further qualification re receiver as agent] Without prejudice to subsection (1), a receiver is deemed to be the agent of the company in relation to any contract of employment adopted by him in the carrying out of his functions.

57(2) [Personal liability] A receiver (including a receiver whose powers are subsequently suspended under section 56) is personally liable on any contract entered into by him in the performance of his functions, except in so far as the contract otherwise provides, and, to the extent of any qualifying liability, on any contract of employment adopted by him in the carrying out of those functions.

57(2A) [Interpretation of s.57(2)] For the purposes of subsection (2), a liability under a contract of employment is a qualifying liability if–

(a) it is a liability to pay a sum by way of wages or salary or contribution to an occupational pension scheme,

(b) it is incurred while the receiver is in office, and

(c) it is in respect of services rendered wholly or partly after the adoption of the contract.

57(2B) [Further interpretation of s.57(2)] Where a sum payable in respect of a liability which is a qualifying liability for the purposes of subsection (2) is payable in respect of services rendered partly before and partly after the adoption of the contract, liability under that subsection shall only extend to so much of the sum as is payable in respect of services rendered after the adoption of the contract.

57(2C) [Interpretation of s.57(2A), (2B)] For the purposes of subsections (2A) and (2B)–

(a) wages or salary payable in respect of a period of holiday or absence from work through sickness or other good cause are deemed to be wages or (as the case may be) salary in respect of services rendered in that period, and

(b) a sum payable in lieu of holiday is deemed to be wages or (as the case may be) salary in respect of services rendered in the period by reference to which the holiday entitlement arose.

57(2D) [Repealed]

57(3) [Indemnity] A receiver who is personally liable by virtue of subsection (2) is entitled to be indemnified out of the property in respect of which he was appointed.

57(4) [Contracts before appointment] Any contract entered into by or on behalf of the company prior to the appointment of a receiver continues in force (subject to its terms) notwithstanding that appointment, but the receiver does not by virtue only of his appointment incur any personal liability on any such contract.

57(5) [Interpretation of s.57(2)] For the purposes of subsection (2), a receiver is not to be taken to have adopted a contract of employment by reason of anything done or omitted to be done within 14 days after his appointment.

57(6) [Effect] This section does not limit any right to indemnity which the receiver would have apart from it, nor limit his liability on contracts entered into or adopted without authority, nor confer any right to indemnity in respect of that liability.

57(7) [Continuation of contract] Any contract entered into by a receiver in the performance of his functions continues in force (subject to its terms) although the powers of the receiver are subsequently suspended under section 56.

S.57(1)

As in English law, this subsection makes the receiver the company's agent. Indeed, it goes further, because it would appear to confer such status on court-appointed receivers. In view of this agency relationship there is no change of occupation when a receiver takes possession of the company's premises, and the receiver does not become personally liable for rates accruing on such premises: *McKillop and Watters, Petitioners* [1994] B.C.C. 677. Having said that, it may well be in the case of certain statutory provisions that the court might find a receiver to be in joint occupation. Such a conclusion was arrived at in *Lord Advocate v Aero Technologies Ltd*, 1991 S.L.T. 134 in the context of s.23 of the Explosives Act 1875.

S.57(1A), (2A)–(2C)

These were inserted by IA 1994 (s.3(1), (2), (4), (5)) to counteract the problems posed for Scottish receivers by the ruling of the Court of Appeal in *Re Paramount Airways Ltd (No.3)* [1994] B.C.C. 172; see the discussions on ss.19, 37 and 44 above. A receiver's personal liability under s.57(2) on adoption was distinct from the company's liability under s.60—*Lindop v Stewart Noble & Sons Ltd*, 1999 S.C.L.R. 889 which is discussed by Lewis [1999] Insolv. L. 303. Note the repeal of the former subs.(2D) by the Public Services Reform (Insolvency) (Scotland) Order 2016 (SSI 2016/141). This provision dealt with the range of employee wage rights for payment purposes on adoption of contracts of employment on receivership and has been repealed in the light of changes in the nature of certain employment contracts. A full rationale is provided in the Explanatory Notes to the 2016 Order.

S.57(2), (4), (5)

These provisions reproduce the position in English law by making the receiver personally liable on contracts entered into by him and on existing contracts of employment adopted by him, although the circumstances where adoption will occur are limited by s.57(5). Apart from contracts of employment adopted by the receiver, he is not personally liable on the company's existing contracts. For discussion of s.57(2) see *Hill Samuel & Co Ltd v Laing* [1991] B.C.C. 665. In s.57(2) the words, "to the extent of any qualifying liability," inserted after the words "provides, and" by IA 1994 s.3(1), (3), (5) in relation to contracts of employment adopted on or after 15 March 1994. For judicial support for the policy behind IA 1994 reforms in this area see *Lindop v Stuart Noble & Sons Ltd*, 1999 S.C.L.R. 889.

S.57(3), (6)

These subsections deal with the receiver's indemnity against personal liability, and make it clear that it does not extend to unauthorised contracts.

S.57(7)

If a receiver's powers are suspended under s.56, contracts entered into by the receiver will normally remain in force.

58 Remuneration of receiver

58(1) [Remuneration by agreement] The remuneration to be paid to a receiver is to be determined by agreement between the receiver and the holder of the floating charge by virtue of which he was appointed.

58(2) [Where remuneration not specified or disputed] Where the remuneration to be paid to the receiver has not been determined under subsection (1), or where it has been so determined but is disputed by any of the persons mentioned in paragraphs (a) to (d) below, it may be fixed instead by the Auditor of the Court of Session on application made to him by–

(a) the receiver;

(b) the holder of any floating charge or fixed security over all or any part of the property of the company;

(c) the company; or

(d) the liquidator of the company.

58(3) [Accounting for excess] Where the receiver has been paid or has retained for his remuneration for any period before the remuneration has been fixed by the Auditor of the Court of Session under subsection (2) any amount in excess of the remuneration so fixed for that period, the receiver or his personal representatives shall account for the excess.

S.58(1)

This subsection states the general rule that the receiver's remuneration is to be fixed by agreement with the debenture holder who appointed him.

S.58(2), (3)

This is a fall-back provision, permitting the Auditor of the Court of Session, on the application of any of various named parties, to fix remuneration in cases where there is no agreement within the meaning of s.58(1), or where there is a dispute as to the level of remuneration. It is interesting to note that CA 1985 s.474 fixed a time-limit for such an application and also specified the correct procedure to be followed—this has been omitted in s.58. Presumably this could be dealt with in the rules: see Sch.8 para.15. Section 58(3) deals with the position when a receiver has received remuneration which turns out to be excessive: surplus amounts have to be repaid.

59 Priority of debts

59(1) [Certain debts to be paid in priority out of assets] Where a receiver is appointed and the company is not at the time of the appointment in course of being wound up, the debts which fall under subsection (2) of this section shall be paid out of any assets coming to the hands of the receiver in priority to any claim for principal or interest by the holder of the floating charge by virtue of which the receiver was appointed.

59(2) [Preferential debts] Debts falling under this subsection are preferential debts (within the meaning given by section 386 in Part XII) which, by the end of a period of 6 months after advertisement by the receiver for claims in the *Edinburgh Gazette* and in a newspaper circulating in the district where the company carries on business either–

(i) have been intimated to him, or

(ii) have become known to him.

59(3) [Recoupment of payments] Any payments made under this section shall be recouped as far as may be out of the assets of the company available for payment of ordinary creditors.

S.59(1), (2)

These subsections impose a positive obligation on the receiver to meet the preferential claims listed in Sch.6 to the Act. The position in Scottish law differs from its English counterpart in that claims must be submitted to the receiver within six months of an advertisement being placed in the *Gazette*. A further difference exists between English and Scottish law with regard to preferential debts on receivership. Where the Crown wishes to exercise a set-off and has total debts owed to it which have both unsecured and preferential elements, it can exercise the set-off with respect to the unsecured debts without rateably setting off preferential debts. The effect of this is to enhance its overall priority position by preserving its preferential status: see *Turner, Petitioner* [1993] B.C.C. 299. For the approach in English law see *Re Unit 2 Windows Ltd* (1985) 1 B.C.C. 99,489.

For the potential impact of *Re Leyland DAF Ltd* [2004] UKHL 9; [2004] B.C.C. 214 in Scotland see R3 Technical Bulletin 63.6.5 (April 2004). *Leyland DAF* (ibid.) was reversed by s.1282 in the Companies Act 2006. How that change in the law will be introduced in Scotland is not clear at present.

S.59(3)

As with s.40(3), this makes it clear that the burden of meeting the preferential claims will ultimately fall on the unsecured creditors.

60 Distribution of moneys

60(1) [Payment of moneys by receiver] Subject to the next section, and to the rights of any of the following categories of persons (which rights shall, except to the extent otherwise provided in any instrument, have the following order of priority), namely–

(a) the holder of any fixed security which is over property subject to the floating charge and which ranks prior to, or pari passu with, the floating charge;

(b) all persons who have effectually executed diligence on any part of the property of the company which is subject to the charge by virtue of which the receiver was appointed;

(c) creditors in respect of all liabilities, charges and expenses incurred by or on behalf of the receiver;

(d) the receiver in respect of his liabilities, expenses and remuneration, and any indemnity to which he is entitled out of the property of the company; and

(e) the preferential creditors entitled to payment under section 59,

the receiver shall pay moneys received by him to the holder of the floating charge by virtue of which the receiver was appointed in or towards satisfaction of the debt secured by the floating charge.

60(2) [Balance of moneys] Any balance of moneys remaining after the provisions of subsection (1) and section 61 below have been satisfied shall be paid in accordance with their respective rights and interests to the following persons, as the case may require–

(a) any other receiver;

(b) the holder of a fixed security which is over property subject to the floating charge;

(c) the company or its liquidator, as the case may be.

60(3) [Doubt as to person entitled] Where any question arises as to the person entitled to a payment under this section, or where a receipt or a discharge of a security cannot be obtained in respect of any such payment, the receiver shall consign the amount of such payment in any joint stock bank of issue in Scotland in name of the Accountant of Court for behoof of the person or persons entitled thereto.

S.60(1)
This subsection outlines a priority ranking for claims against the assets of a company which is in receivership. There is no parallel provision in English law. When presented in this way it is not surprising that banks have become uneasy about the protection offered by the floating charge. However, EA 2002 does offer them some comfort in that it radically reduces the categories of preferential claim. For the meaning of "fixed security" in subs.(1)(a), see s.70. The position under subs.(1)(c) was considered by the Court of Session (Inner House) in *Lindop v Stuart Noble & Sons Ltd*, 1999 S.C.L.R. 889 in the context of an employee whose contract of employment had initially been adopted by the receiver and then who had subsequently been dismissed. The claim based upon s.60(1)(c) for preferential treatment in respect of salary in lieu of notice was rejected; only new contracts made by receivers were covered by s.60(1)(c). In rejecting this claim the court was mindful not to allow the policy of IA 1994 limiting a receiver's liabilities to "qualifying liabilities" to be circumvented. See also *Scottish and Newcastle plc, Petitioners* [1993] B.C.C. 634 for further guidance on the operation of s.60.

See recent judgment of the Court of Session Inner House in *MacMillan v T Leith Developments Ltd* [2017] CSIH 23 which deals with priority rights where there has been an arrestment. The Court of Session departed from its previous view in *Lord Advocate v Royal Bank of Scotland Ltd* 1977 S.C. 155 and held that inhibition constitutes effectually executed diligence and could therefore prevail over a later crystallisation of a floating charge. This latest ruling offers valuable insights into policy issues, the interpretation of s.60 and the possibilities for reform. By departing from a much criticised precedent of some 40 years standing, the Court of Session has raised the possibility of completed distributions by receivers being reopened.

S.60(2)
This provision maps out the fate of any surplus moneys in the hands of the receiver, after the claims listed in s.60(1) have been met.

S.60(3)
In the event of a dispute over whether a claim should be met or not, the receiver should pay an appropriate sum of money into a recognised Scottish bank in the name of the Accountant of Court, pending the resolution of the dispute.

61 Disposal of interest in property

61(1) [Application to court] Where the receiver sells or disposes, or is desirous of selling or disposing, of any property or interest in property of the company which is subject to the floating charge by virtue of which the receiver was appointed and which is–

(a) subject to any security or interest of, or burden or encumbrance in favour of, a creditor the ranking of which is prior to, or pari passu with, or postponed to the floating charge, or

(b) property or an interest in property affected or attached by effectual diligence executed by any person,

and the receiver is unable to obtain the consent of such creditor or, as the case may be, such person to such a sale or disposal, the receiver may apply to the court for authority to sell or dispose of the property or interest in property free of such security, interest, burden, encumbrance or diligence.

61(1A) [Inhibition after creation of floating charge] For the purposes of subsection (1) above, an inhibition which takes effect after the creation of the floating charge by virtue of which the receiver was appointed is not an effectual diligence.

61(2) [Authorisation by court] Subject to the next subsection, on such an application the court may, if it thinks fit, authorise the sale or disposal of the property or interest in question free of such security, interest, burden, encumbrance or diligence, and such authorisation may be on such terms or conditions as the court thinks fit.

61(3) [Condition for authorisation] In the case of an application where a fixed security over the property or interest in question which ranks prior to the floating charge has not been met or provided for in full, the court shall not authorise the sale or disposal of the property or interest in question unless it is satisfied that the sale or disposal would be likely to provide a more advantageous realisation of the company's assets than would otherwise be effected.

61(4) [Condition for s.61(3)] It shall be a condition of an authorisation to which subsection (3) applies that–

(a) the net proceeds of the disposal, and

(b) where those proceeds are less than such amount as may be determined by the court to be the net amount which would be realised on a sale of the property or interest in the open market by a willing seller, such sums as may be required to make good the deficiency,

shall be applied towards discharging the sums secured by the fixed security.

61(5) [Where s.61(4) condition re several securities] Where a condition imposed in pursuance of subsection (4) relates to two or more such fixed securities, that condition shall require the net proceeds of the disposal and, where paragraph (b) of that subsection applies, the sums mentioned in that paragraph to be applied towards discharging the sums secured by those fixed securities in the order of their priorities.

61(6) [Copy of authorisation to registrar] A copy of an authorisation under subsection (2) shall, within 14 days of the granting of the authorisation, be sent by the receiver to the registrar of companies.

61(7) [Penalty for non-compliance] If the receiver without reasonable excuse fails to comply with subsection (6), he is liable to a fine and, for continued contravention, to a daily default fine.

61(8) [Receiver to give document to disponee] Where any sale or disposal is effected in accordance with the authorisation of the court under subsection (2), the receiver shall grant to the purchaser or disponee an appropriate document of transfer or conveyance of the property or interest in question, and that document has the effect, or, where recording, intimation or registration of that document is a legal requirement for completion of title to the property or interest, then that recording, intimation or registration (as the case may be) has the effect, of–

(a) disencumbering the property or interest of the security, interest, burden or encumbrance affecting it, and

(b) freeing the property or interest from the diligence executed upon it.

61(9) [Ranking of creditor in winding up] Nothing in this section prejudices the right of any creditor of the company to rank for his debt in the winding up of the company.

S.61(1), (2)

These subsections allow a receiver to apply to the court for the sale of property subject to a fixed charge, or over which diligence has been effectually executed.

Editors' note: a subs.(1A) was inserted by s.155(2) of the Bankruptcy and Diligence etc. (Scotland) Act 2007. A new subs.(1B) will also be inserted by Sch.5 para.14(2) of the Bankruptcy and Diligence etc. (Scotland) Act 2007 from a date yet to be appointed. The purpose of these new subsections is to clarify the meaning of provisions in subs.(1).

Section 61 does not apply in relation to the enforcement of "market charges" (as defined by CA 1989 s.173): see s.175 of that Act (as qualified by the Financial Markets and Insolvency Regulations 1991 (SI 1991/880)) (as amended by SI 1995/2049 and SI 1998/27), and the introductory note at p.1, above.

S.61(3), (4), (5)

If the receiver has not set aside a sufficient sum to meet the claim of the holder of the "fixed security" (for the meaning of this term, see s.70), the court should only assent to the sale if it would promote a more effective realisation of the company's assets. Even where assent is given, the actual net proceeds (or a reasonable amount, if the sale was at an undervalue) must be set aside for the fixed chargee (or chargees).

S.61(6), (7)

If the court permits the sale to go ahead, the receiver must register the fact at Edinburgh, or incur a default fine. On penalties, see s.430 and Sch.10. Section 61(6) modified by Scotland Act 1998 s.125(1) and Sch.8 para.23(1)–(3) so that anything done by the registrar of companies in Scotland or the assistant registrar of friendly societies for Scotland by virtue of s.61(6) as applied in relation to friendly societies, industrial and provident societies or building societies may be done to or by the Accountant in Bankruptcy as from 1 July 1999 (see SI 1998/3178 (C. 79) art.2).

Note the Companies Act 2006 (Consequential Amendments, Transitional Provisions and Savings) Order 2009 (SI 2009/1941) (effective from 1 October 2009) which omits a reference to certification by the clerk of the court.

S.61(8)
This subsection provides a mechanism for assuring the purchaser under the forced sale that he can acquire an effective title from the receiver.

S.61(9)
This is a saving provision allowing a person who has been deprived of his claim against specific property to rank instead as a creditor of the company on winding up.

62 Cessation of appointment of receiver

62(1) [Removal, resignation] A receiver may be removed from office by the court under subsection (3) below and may resign his office by giving notice of his resignation in the prescribed manner to such persons as may be prescribed.

62(2) [Cessation of qualification] A receiver shall vacate office if he ceases to be qualified to act as an insolvency practitioner in relation to the company.

62(3) [Removal on application] Subject to the next subsection, a receiver may, on application to the court by the holder of the floating charge by virtue of which he was appointed, be removed by the court on cause shown.

62(4) [On vacation of office] Where at any time a receiver vacates office–

(a) his remuneration and any expenses properly incurred by him, and

(b) any indemnity to which he is entitled out of the property of the company,

shall be paid out of the property of the company which is subject to the floating charge and shall have priority as provided for in section 60(1).

62(5) [Notice of cessation to registrar, penalty on default] When a receiver ceases to act as such otherwise than by death he shall, and, when a receiver is removed by the court, the holder of the floating charge by virtue of which he was appointed shall, within 14 days of the cessation or removal (as the case may be) give the registrar of companies notice to that effect, and the registrar shall enter the notice in the register.

If the receiver or the holder of the floating charge (as the case may require) makes default in complying with the requirements of this subsection, he is liable to a fine and, for continued contravention, to a daily default fine.

62(6) [Cessation of attachment of charge] If by the expiry of a period of one month following upon the removal of the receiver or his ceasing to act as such no other receiver has been appointed, the floating charge by virtue of which the receiver was appointed–

(a) thereupon ceases to attach to the property then subject to the charge, and

(b) again subsists as a floating charge;

and for the purposes of calculating the period of one month under this subsection no account shall be taken of any period during which the company is in administration under Part II of this Act.

S.62(1)–(3)
These subsections deal with the situations where a receiver will vacate office. Note that he can only be removed by the court on the application of the holder of the floating charge (for the meaning of this term, see s.70), and not out of court by the holder of the floating charge who appointed him. As to the qualification as an insolvency practitioner, see Pt XIII. For the relevant notice of resignation under s.62(1), see the Receivers (Scotland) Regulations 1986 (SI 1986/1917 (S 141)).

S.62(4)
This protects the priority of the receiver's right to indemnity and remuneration.

S.62(5)
Notification must be given to Edinburgh of the receiver leaving office: see Form 3 (Scot) under the Receivers (Scotland) Regulations 1986 (SI 1986/1917 (S 141)). The person responsible for giving notice will incur criminal sanctions in the event of default. On penalties, see s.430 and Sch.10. Section 62(5) was modified by the Scotland Act 1998 s.125(1) and Sch.8 para.23(1)–(3) so that anything done by the registrar of companies in Scotland or the assistant registrar of friendly societies for Scotland by virtue of s.62(5) as applied in relation to friendly societies, industrial and provident societies or building societies may be done to or by the Accountant in Bankruptcy as from 1 July 1999 (see SI 1998/3178 (C. 79) art.2). Note prospective amendment: the words "and, for continued contravention, to a daily default fine" are to be repealed by CA 1989 Schs 16 and 24 from a day to be appointed.

Note the amendment made to subs.(5) by the Companies Act 2006 (Amendment of Part 25) Regulations 2013 (SI 2013/600) Sch.2 para.2 by changing the former reference to the "register of charges" to the "register".

S.62(6)
This provides for the "refloating" of the floating charge on the expiry of one month after the receiver leaves office. Note the semantic change made by the Enterprise Act 2002 (Insolvency) Order 2003 (SI 2003/2096).

63 Powers of court

63(1) [Directions, on application] The court on the application of–

(a) the holder of a floating charge by virtue of which a receiver was appointed, or

(b) a receiver appointed under section 51,

may give directions to the receiver in respect of any matter arising in connection with the performance by him of his functions.

63(2) [Where receiver's appointment invalid] Where the appointment of a person as a receiver by the holder of a floating charge is discovered to be invalid (whether by virtue of the invalidity of the instrument or otherwise), the court may order the holder of the floating charge to indemnify the person appointed against any liability which arises solely by reason of the invalidity of the appointment.

S.63(1)
This provision, like its English counterpart (IA 1986 s.35), allows both the receiver or the holder of the floating charge (for definition, see s.70) under which he was appointed to apply to the court for guidance. Such an application was the basis for the litigation in *McKillop and Watters, Petitioners* [1994] B.C.C. 677. Prior to IA 1985, only the appointor (and not the receiver) could make such an application. The power of the Scottish courts to give directions is more limited than the power of their English counterparts under s.35: see here *Jamieson, Petitioners*, 1997 S.C. 195; [1997] B.C.C. 682.

The appropriate regulator may in an appropriate case be heard on a s.63 application—FSMA 2000 s.363(2).

S.63(2)
This allows the court to excuse a receiver from trespass liability arising out of an invalid appointment, and instead to impose that liability on his appointor. For the English counterpart, see s.34.

64 Notification that receiver appointed

64(1) [Statement in invoices etc.] Where a receiver has been appointed–

(a) every invoice, order for goods or services, business letter or order form (whether in hard copy, electronic or any other form) issued by or on behalf of the company or the receiver or the liquidator of the company; and

(b) all the company's websites,

must contain a statement that a receiver has been appointed.

64(2) [Penalty on default] If default is made in complying with the requirements of this section, the company and any of the following persons who knowingly and wilfully authorises or permits the default, namely any officer of the company, any liquidator of the company and any receiver, is liable to a fine.

S.64(1)
Invoices, business letters, etc. must disclose the fact that a receiver has been appointed. The English equivalent is to be found in s.39. A new s.64(1) was substituted by the Companies (Trading Disclosures) (Insolvency) Regulations 2008 (SI 2008/1897) with effect from 1 October 2008. This substitution was necessary to comply with EC Directive 2003/58. It extends the disclosure requirement to electronic invoices and company websites.

S.64(2)
Criminal sanctions are imposed on various named parties for breach of s.64(1). On penalties, see s.430 and Sch.10.

65 Information to be given by receiver

65(1) [Notification of appointment] Where a receiver is appointed, he shall–

(a) forthwith send to the company and publish notice of his appointment, and

(b) within 28 days after his appointment, unless the court otherwise directs, send such notice to all the creditors of the company (so far as he is aware of their addresses).

65(2) [Restriction] This section and the next do not apply in relation to the appointment of a receiver to act–

(a) with an existing receiver, or

(b) in place of a receiver who has died or ceased to act,

except that, where they apply to a receiver who dies or ceases to act before they have been fully complied with, the references in this section and the next to the receiver include (subject to subsection (3) of this section) his successor and any continuing receiver.

65(3) [If company being wound up] If the company is being wound up, this section and the next apply notwithstanding that the receiver and the liquidator are the same person, but with any necessary modifications arising from that fact.

65(4) [Penalty for non-compliance] If a person without reasonable excuse fails to comply with this section, he is liable to a fine and, for continued contravention, to a daily default fine.

S.65(1), (2), (4)
These subsections provide for a receiver on taking up his appointment to give notice to the company and its creditors. See note to s.62(5). This obligation, once complied with, does not have to be fulfilled by successor receivers, or a later appointed joint receiver. Criminal sanctions are imposed in the event of default. On penalties, see s.430 and Sch.10. For the notice under s.65(1)(a) see Form 4 (Scot) in the Receivers (Scotland) Regulations 1986 (SI 1986/1917 (S 141)).

S.65(3)
This caters for the situation where the receiver and liquidator are the same person. It also applies to s.66.

66 Company's statement of affairs

66(1) [Duty of receiver] Where a receiver of a company is appointed, the receiver shall forthwith require some or all of the persons mentioned in subsection (3) below to make out and submit to him a statement in the prescribed form as to the affairs of the company.

66(2) [Contents of statement] A statement submitted under this section shall be verified by affidavit by the persons required to submit it and shall show–

(a) particulars of the company's assets, debts and liabilities;

(b) the names and addresses of its creditors;

(c) the securities held by them respectively;

(d) the dates when the securities were respectively given; and

(e) such further or other information as may be prescribed.

66(3) [Persons in s.66(1)] The persons referred to in subsection (1) are–

(a) those who are or have been officers of the company;

(b) those who have taken part in the company's formation at any time within one year before the date of the appointment of the receiver;

(c) those who are in the company's employment or have been in its employment within that year, and are in the receiver's opinion capable of giving the information required;

(d) those who are or have been within that year officers of or in the employment of a company which is, or within that year was, an officer of the company.

In this subsection "employment" includes employment under a contract for services.

66(4) [Time for statement] Where any persons are required under this section to submit a statement of affairs to the receiver they shall do so (subject to the next subsection) before the end of the period of 21 days beginning with the day after that on which the prescribed notice of the requirement is given to them by the receiver.

66(5) [Release, extension re statement] The receiver, if he thinks fit, may–

(a) at any time release a person from an obligation imposed on him under subsection (1) or (2), or

(b) either when giving the notice mentioned in subsection (4) or subsequently extend the period so mentioned,

and where the receiver has refused to exercise a power conferred by this subsection, the court, if it thinks fit, may exercise it.

66(6) [Penalty for non-compliance] If a person without reasonable excuse fails to comply with any obligation imposed under this section, he is liable to a fine and, for continued contravention, to a daily default fine.

S.66(1), (2)

These provisions require the receiver to ask persons listed in s.66(3) for a statement of the company's affairs in the prescribed form (see s.70), containing details specified in s.66(2). For the relevant form of the statement, see Form 5 (Scot) in the Receivers (Scotland) Regulations 1986 (SI 1986/1917 (S 141)).

S.66(3)–(6)

Section 66(3) identifies the persons who may be required to contribute towards the submission of the statement of affairs, which must normally be submitted within 21 days of a request for it. Criminal sanctions are imposed to deal with defaults. On penalties, see s.430 and Sch.10.

The receiver enjoys discretion under s.66(5) to release certain persons from their obligations in respect of the statement of affairs or to extend the deadline for submission.

67 Report by receiver

67(1) [Duty of receiver] Where a receiver is appointed under section 51, he shall within 3 months (or such longer period as the court may allow) after his appointment, send to the registrar of companies, to the holder of the floating charge by virtue of which he was appointed and to any trustees for secured creditors of the company and (so far as he is aware of their addresses) to all such creditors, other than opted-out creditors, a report as to the following matters, namely–

(a) the events leading up to his appointment, so far as he is aware of them;

(b) the disposal or proposed disposal by him of any property of the company and the carrying on or proposed carrying on by him of any business of the company;

(c) the amounts of principal and interest payable to the holder of the floating charge by virtue of which he was appointed and the amounts payable to preferential creditors; and

(d) the amount (if any) likely to be available for the payment of other creditors.

67(2) [Copies of report] The receiver shall also, within 3 months (or such longer period as the court may allow) after his appointment, either–

(a) send a copy of the report (so far as he is aware of their addresses) to all unsecured creditors of the company, other than opted-out creditors, or

(b) publish in the prescribed manner a notice stating an address to which unsecured creditors of the company should write for copies of the report to be sent to them free of charge.

67(3) [Omitted]

67(4) [Where company in liquidation] Where the company has gone or goes into liquidation, the receiver–

(a) shall, within 7 days after his compliance with subsection (1) or, if later, the nomination or appointment of the liquidator, send a copy of the report to the liquidator, and

(b) where he does so within the time limited for compliance with subsection (2), is not required to comply with that subsection.

67(5) [Report to involve summary of statement of affairs] A report under this section shall include a summary of the statement of affairs made out and submitted under section 66 and of his comments (if any) on it.

67(6) [Information not to be disclosed] Nothing in this section shall be taken as requiring any such report to include any information the disclosure of which would seriously prejudice the carrying out by the receiver of his functions.

67(7) [Section 65(2)] Section 65(2) applies for the purposes of this section also.

67(8) [Penalty for non-compliance] If a person without reasonable excuse fails to comply with this section, he is liable to a fine and, for continued contravention, to a daily default fine.

67(9) ["Secured creditor"] In this section "secured creditor", in relation to a company, means a creditor of the company who holds in respect of his debt a security over property of the company, and "unsecured creditor" shall be construed accordingly.

S.67(1), (5), (6)

These subsections require the receiver to prepare a report which must be submitted to various named parties (excluding opted-out creditors but including the appropriate regulator in an appropriate case—FSMA 2000 s.363(4), as amended by the Financial Services Act 2012 Sch.14). The report should include certain specified details but need not disclose "prejudicial" information (see s.67(6)). It should also include a summary of the statement of affairs submitted to him under s.66, plus any comments he wishes to make. Section 67(1) was modified by the Scotland Act 1998 s.125(1) and Sch.8 para.23(1)–(3) so that anything done by the registrar of companies in Scotland or the assistant registrar of friendly societies for Scotland by virtue of s.67(1) as applied in relation to friendly societies, industrial and provident societies or building societies may be done to or by the Accountant in Bankruptcy as from 1 July 1999 (see SI 1998/3178 (C. 79) art.2).

S.67(2)–(4)

These provisions relate to the dissemination of the receiver's report to creditors and liquidator (if applicable). The report is to be submitted to a meeting of the company's creditors, unless the court rules to the contrary. With regards to s.67(2) see the Receivers (Scotland) Regulations 1986 (SI 1986/1917 (S 141)). Note that s.436B does not apply.

S.67(7), (9)

These are merely interpretation provisions. Section 65(2) dispenses with the need for a report when an additional receiver is appointed to act with an existing receiver, or a new receiver to replace one who has ceased to act.

S.67(8)

The receiver will incur criminal sanctions for failure to fulfil any of the stated obligations. On penalties, see s.430 and Sch.10.

Editors' note: This provision was amended by SBEEA 2015 Sch.9 para.14. Subsections (1) and (2) were modified and subs.(3) omitted.

68 Committee of creditors

68(1) [Creditors may establish committee] Where a receiver has sent or published a report as mentioned in section 67(2) the company's unsecured creditors may, in accordance with the rules, establish a committee ("the creditors' committee") to exercise the functions conferred on it by or under this Act.

68(2) [Powers of committee] If such a committee is established, the committee may on giving not less than 7 days' notice require the receiver to attend before it at any reasonable time and furnish it with such information relating to the carrying out by him of his functions as it may reasonably require.

S.68(1)

Creditors may set up a committee of creditors. In an appropriate case the appropriate regulator representative can attend—FSMA 2000 s.363(5).

This provision was amended by SBEEA 2015 Sch.9 para.15 to reflect the move away from the use of creditor meetings.

S.68(2)

This committee can make reasonable requests for information from the receiver. It may be unreasonable to request information covered by s.67(6).

69 Enforcement of receiver's duty to make returns, etc.

69(1) [Court order re receiver's default] If any receiver–

(a) having made default in filing, delivering or making any return, account or other document, or in giving any notice, which a receiver is by law required to file, deliver, make or give, fails to make good the default within 14 days after the service on him of a notice requiring him to do so; or

(b) has, after being required at any time by the liquidator of the company so to do, failed to render proper accounts of his receipts and payments and to vouch the same and to pay over to the liquidator the amount properly payable to him,

the court may, on an application made for the purpose, make an order directing the receiver to make good the default within such time as may be specified in the order.

69(2) [Application to court] In the case of any such default as is mentioned in subsection (1)(a), an application for the purposes of this section may be made by any member or creditor of the company or by the registrar of companies; and, in the case of any such default as is mentioned in subsection (1)(b), the application shall be made by the liquidator; and, in either case, the order may provide that all expenses of and incidental to the application shall be borne by the receiver.

69(3) [Other enactments] Nothing in this section prejudices the operation of any enactments imposing penalties on receivers in respect of any such default as is mentioned in subsection (1).

S.69(1)

The court can compel a receiver to submit returns, etc. if he fails to comply with a notice to do so. For the English counterpart, see s.41.

S.69(2)

This subsection identifies the applicants for an enforcement order under s.69(1). The appropriate regulator may apply in an appropriate case—FSMA 2000 s.363(3).

S.69(3)

This enforcement mechanism is in addition to any criminal sanctions that may be imposed by individual provisions.

70 Interpretation for Chapter II

70(1) [Definitions] In this Chapter, unless the contrary intention appears, the following expressions have the following meanings respectively assigned to them–

"company" means an incorporated company (whether or not a company registered under the Companies Act 2006) which the Court of Session has jurisdiction to wind up;

"fixed security", in relation to any property of a company, means any security, other than a floating charge or a charge having the nature of a floating charge, which on the winding up of the company in Scotland would be treated as an effective security over that property, and (without prejudice to that generality) includes a security over that property, being a heritable security within the meaning of the Conveyancing and Feudal Reform (Scotland) Act 1970;

"instrument of appointment" has the meaning given by section 53(1);

"prescribed fee" means the fee prescribed by regulations made under this Chapter by the Secretary of State;

"receiver" means a receiver of such part of the property of the company as is subject to the floating charge by virtue of which he has been appointed under section 51;

"register" has the meaning given by section 1080 of the Companies Act 2006;

"secured debenture" means a bond, debenture, debenture stock or other security which, either itself or by reference to any other instrument, creates a floating charge over all or any part of the property of the company, but does not include a security which creates no charge other than a fixed security; and

"series of secured debentures" means two or more secured debentures created as a series by the company in such a manner that the holders thereof are entitled pari passu to the benefit of the floating charge.

70(2) [Reference to holder of floating charge] Where a floating charge, secured debenture or series of secured debentures has been created by the company, then, except where the context otherwise requires, any reference in this Chapter to the holder of the floating charge shall–

(a) where the floating charge, secured debenture or series of secured debentures provides for a receiver to be appointed by any person or body, be construed as a reference to that person or body;

(b) where, in the case of a series of secured debentures, no such provision has been made therein but–

(i) there are trustees acting for the debenture-holders under and in accordance with a trust deed, be construed as a reference to those trustees, and

(ii) where no such trustees are acting, be construed as a reference to–

(aa) a majority in nominal value of those present or represented by proxy and voting at a meeting of debenture-holders at which the holders of at least one-third in nominal value of the outstanding debentures of the series are present or so represented, or

(bb) where no such meeting is held, the holders of at least one-half in nominal value of the outstanding debentures of the series.

70(3) [Reference to floating charge etc.] Any reference in this Chapter to a floating charge, secured debenture, series of secured debentures or instrument creating a charge includes, except where the context otherwise requires, a reference to that floating charge, debenture, series of debentures or instrument as varied by any instrument.

70(4) [Reference to instrument] References in this Chapter to the instrument by which a floating charge was created are, in the case of a floating charge created by words in a bond or other written acknowledgement, references to the bond or, as the case may be, the other written acknowledgement.

General Note

These are general interpretation provisions for the purposes of ss.50–71 and their main aim is to link these provisions dealing with Scottish receiverships with the sections in CA 1985 regulating the floating charge in Scotland, and also with the general rules of Scots law. Note the Companies Act 2006 (Consequential Amendments, Transitional Provisions and Savings) Order 2009 (SI 2009/1941), which took effect on 1 October 2009). This Order amends s.70 by making reference to the Companies Act 2006. Note that s.436B does not apply.

Note subs.(1) is amended by of the Companies Act 2006 (Amendment of Part 25) Regulations 2013 (SI 2013/600) Sch.2 para.2 by changing the definition of the register of charges to: "'the register' has the meaning given by s.1080 of the Companies Act 2006".

71 Prescription of forms, etc.; regulations

71(1) [Prescribed forms] The notice referred to in section 62(5), and the notice referred to in section 65(1)(a) shall be in such form as may be prescribed.

71(2) [Regulations] Any power conferred by this Chapter on the Secretary of State to make regulations is exercisable by statutory instrument; and a statutory instrument made in the exercise of the power so conferred to prescribe a fee is subject to annulment in pursuance of a resolution of either House of Parliament.

S.71(1)

The notice of a receiver taking office or ceasing to act is in a form prescribed by the Receivers (Scotland) Regulations 1986 (SI 1986/1917 (S 141)). See note to ss.62, 65.

S.71(2)

The Secretary of State may make regulations, but where the power involves the prescribing of a fee it is subject to annulment by either the House of Lords or the Commons. See the regulations referred to above.

Chapter III

Receivers' Powers in Great Britain as a Whole

72 Cross-border operation of receivership provisions

72(1) [Receivers' powers] A receiver appointed under the law of either part of Great Britain in respect of the whole or any part of any property or undertaking of a company and in consequence of the company having created a charge which, as created, was a floating charge may exercise his powers in the other part of Great Britain so far as their exercise is not inconsistent with the law applicable there.

72(2) ["Receiver"] In subsection (1) "receiver" includes a manager and a person who is appointed both receiver and manager.

General Note

This section allows a receiver appointed in England to act in Scotland, and vice versa, in so far as this is not inconsistent with local law. This provision, which can be traced back to 1970, is less important now that the Scots have a system of receivership running along similar lines to the English regime. For the utility of s.72 see *Norfolk House v Repsol Petroleum*, 1992 S.L.T. 235.

Chapter IV

Prohibition of Appointment of Administrative Receiver

72A Floating charge holder not to appoint administrative receiver

72A(1) [Prohibition] The holder of a qualifying floating charge in respect of a company's property may not appoint an administrative receiver of the company.

72A(2) [Scotland] In Scotland, the holder of a qualifying floating charge in respect of a company's property may not appoint or apply to the court for the appointment of a receiver who on appointment would be an administrative receiver of property of the company.

72A(3) [Meanings in s.72A(1), (2)] In subsections (1) and (2)–

"holder of a qualifying floating charge in respect of a company's property" has the same meaning as in paragraph 14 of Schedule B1 to this Act, and

"administrative receiver" has the meaning given by section 251.

72A(4) [Application of section] This section applies–

(a) to a floating charge created on or after a date appointed by the Secretary of State by order made by statutory instrument, and

(b) in spite of any provision of an agreement or instrument which purports to empower a person to appoint an administrative receiver (by whatever name).

72A(5) [Provision in order] An order under subsection (4)(a) may–

(a) make provision which applies generally or only for a specified purpose;

(b) make different provision for different purposes;

(c) make transitional provision.

72A(6) [Exceptions] This section is subject to the exceptions specified in sections 72B to 72GA.

General Note

This new section, and those following, were added by s.250 of EA 2002. That provision was modified by the Insolvency Act 1986 (Amendment) (Administrative Receivership and Urban Regeneration etc.) Order 2003 (SI 2003/1832) to take effect immediately on the coming into force of s.72A on 15 September 2003. Note also the insertion by s.250(2) and Sch.18 of Sch.2A into the 1986 Act to further bolster these provisions. Schedule 2A was also modified by the Insolvency Act 1986 (Amendment) (Administrative Receivership and Capital Market Arrangements) Order 2003 (SI 2003/1468).

Perhaps the most high profile of all of the changes introduced by EA 2002 was the curtailing of the floating charge holder's entitlement to enforce security through the appointment of an "administrative receiver" (see IA 1986 s.29). After some debate the Government was convinced by the argument that administrative receivership was not a rescue procedure in keeping with the spirit of collectivism but rather a selfish and largely unaccountable recovery mechanism. It therefore decided to curtail its usage, though as a concession to the banking community it offered the option of appointing an administrator out of court.

This change was not retrospective—i.e. it does not deprive this option of installing an administrative receiver from those creditors covered by a floating charge created before the operational date. This point was conceded early on in the gestation of the Enterprise Bill—DTI Press Notice P/2001/629). The Government may have been concerned to head off challenges by banks alleging infringement of their property rights under art.1 of the First Protocol of the ECHR. Moreover, administrative receivership is to survive for certain specialised financing arrangements; these mirror the exceptions to the CVA *cum moratorium* procedure in IA 2000.

S.72A(1), (3)

This outlines the basic prohibition—note again that the wording (albeit obtusely) allows existing floating charges to retain this traditional enforcement mode.

S.72A(2), (3)

Administrative receivership is not a term recognised in Scotland; the institution in that jurisdiction uses the clearer denomination of receivership. Hence the need for separate legislative treatment.

On the interface between this provision and s.84(2A) see the comments on HHJ Purle QC in *Bevan v Walker* [2018] EWHC 265 (Ch).

S.72A(4)

This reinforces the prospective-only nature of the reform. However, its restrictive effect cannot be overridden by provision in any debenture. The date appointed under s.72A(4)(a) is 15 September 2003—see the Insolvency Act 1986, Section 72A (Appointed Date) Order 2003 (SI 2003/2095).

S.72A(5), (6)

These rules may be modified by secondary legislation and are qualified by later statutory provisions. Note subs.(6) was modified slightly by the Insolvency Act 1986 (Amendment) (Administrative Receivership and Urban Regeneration etc.) Order 2003 (SI 2003/1832).

72B First exception: capital market

72B(1) [Conditions for capital market arrangement] Section 72A does not prevent the appointment of an administrative receiver in pursuance of an agreement which is or forms part of a capital market arrangement if–

(a) a party incurs or, when the agreement was entered into was expected to incur, a debt of at least £50 million under the arrangement, and

(b) the arrangement involves the issue of a capital market investment.

72B(2) ["Capital market arrangement", "capital market investment"] In subsection (1)–

"capital market arrangement" means an arrangement of a kind described in paragraph 1 of Schedule 2A, and

"capital market investment" means an investment of a kind described in paragraph 2 or 3 of that Schedule.

S.72B(1), (2)

This exception relates to capital market agreements. The exclusion of general insolvency principles from this area of commerce has precedents—witness Companies Act 1989 Pt VII.

72C Second exception: public-private partnership

72C(1) [Requirement of step-in rights] Section 72A does not prevent the appointment of an administrative receiver of a project company of a project which–

(a) is a public-private partnership project, and

(b) includes step-in rights.

72C(2) ["Public-private partnership project"] In this section "public-private partnership project" means a project–

(a) the resources for which are provided partly by one or more public bodies and partly by one or more private persons, or

(b) which is designed wholly or mainly for the purpose of assisting a public body to discharge a function.

72C(3) ["Step-in rights", "project company"] In this section–

"step-in rights" has the meaning given by paragraph 6 of Schedule 2A, and

"project company" has the meaning given by paragraph 7 of that Schedule.

S.72C(1), (2), (3)

These provide the continuance of administrative receivership for certain public finance initiative agreements containing "step in" rights as defined by subs.(3).

72D Third exception: utilities

72D(1) [Requirement of step-in rights] Section 72A does not prevent the appointment of an administrative receiver of a project company of a project which–

(a) is a utility project, and

(b) includes step-in rights.

72D(2) ["Utility project", "regulated business", "Step-in rights", "project company"] In this section–

(a) "utility project" means a project designed wholly or mainly for the purpose of a regulated business,

(b) "regulated business" means a business of a kind listed in paragraph 10 of Schedule 2A,

(c) "step-in rights" has the meaning given by paragraph 6 of that Schedule, and

(d) "project company" has the meaning given by paragraph 7 of that Schedule.

S.72D(1), (2)
The creation of discrete insolvency regimes for utilities is now well established—witness the special administration regime under the Railways Act 1993.

72DA Exception in respect of urban regeneration projects

72DA(1) [Administrative receiver of project company] Section 72A does not prevent the appointment of an administrative receiver of a project company of a project which–

(a) is designed wholly or mainly to develop land which at the commencement of the project is wholly or partly in a designated disadvantaged area outside Northern Ireland, and

(b) includes step-in rights.

72DA(2) ["Develop"] In subsection (1) "develop" means to carry out–

(a) building operations,

(b) any operation for the removal of substances or waste from land and the levelling of the surface of the land, or

(c) engineering operations in connection with the activities mentioned in paragraph (a) or (b).

72DA(3) [Meanings] In this section–

"building" includes any structure or erection, and any part of a building as so defined, but does not include plant and machinery comprised in a building,

"building operations" includes–

(a) demolition of buildings,

(b) filling in of trenches,

(c) rebuilding,

(d) structural alterations of, or additions to, buildings and

(e) other operations normally undertaken by a person carrying on business as a builder,

"designated disadvantaged area" means an area designated as a disadvantaged area under section 92 of the Finance Act 2001,

"engineering operations" includes the formation and laying out of means of access to highways, "project company" has the meaning given by paragraph 7 of Schedule 2A,

"step-in rights" has the meaning given by paragraph 6 of that Schedule,

"substance" means any natural or artificial substance whether in solid or liquid form or in the form of a gas or vapour, and

"waste" includes any waste materials, spoil, refuse or other matter deposited on land.

S.72DA(1)–(3)
This additional exception was created by the Insolvency Act 1986 (Amendment) (Administrative Receivership and Urban Regeneration etc.) Order 2003 (SI 2003/1832) for reasons of social policy.

72E Fourth exception: project finance

72E(1) [Requirement of step-in rights] Section 72A does not prevent the appointment of an administrative receiver of a project company of a project which–

(a) is a financed project, and

(b) includes step-in rights.

72E(2) ["Financed", "project company", "step-in rights"] In this section–

(a) a project is "financed" if under an agreement relating to the project a project company incurs, or when the agreement *is* entered into is expected to incur, a debt of at least £50 million for the purposes of carrying out the project,

(b) "project company" has the meaning given by paragraph 7 of Schedule 2A, and

(c) "step-in rights" has the meaning given by paragraph 6 of that Schedule.

S.72E(1), (2)
This fourth exception deals with certain project finance agreements containing "step in" rights. In *Cabvision Ltd v Feetum* [2005] EWCA Civ 1601; [2006] B.C.C. 340 the Court of Appeal (confirming the first instance decision of Lewison J) rejected a contention that the s.72A bar on the appointment of administrative receivers over the undertaking of an LLP was disapplied by s.72E ("the project finance exception"). On the issue of construction raised in connection with the project finance exception the judge was correct in his interpretation as to whether this was a financed project. The Court of Appeal found that on the facts the critical agreement to consider was the facility agreement and not the earlier software licensing agreement. This project under the terms of the facility agreement did not involve the LLP incurring indebtedness *of at least* £50 million. With regard to the further issue of whether this debenture created step-in rights (within the meaning of Sch.2A para.6) it was inconceivable that Parliament would have intended that the mere right to appoint an administrative receiver under the terms of a debenture constituted step-in rights. Such an interpretation would have the effect of rendering the s.72A bar nugatory. Accordingly, the exception provided for by s.72E did not apply. For comment see Yeowart [2006] 19 Insolv. Int. 36.

72F Fifth exception: financial market

72F Section 72A does not prevent the appointment of an administrative receiver of a company by virtue of–

(a) a market charge within the meaning of section 173 of the Companies Act 1989 (c. 40),

(b) a system-charge within the meaning of the Financial Markets and Insolvency Regulations 1996 (S.I. 1996/1469),

(c) a collateral security charge within the meaning of the Financial Markets and Insolvency (Settlement Finality) Regulations 1999 (S.I. 1999/2979).

General Note

This section deals specifically with the financial markets.

72G Sixth exception: social landlords

72G Section 72A does not prevent the appointment of an administrative receiver of a company which is–

(a) a private registered provider of social housing, or

(b) registered as a social landlord under Part I of the Housing Act 1996 (c. 52) or under Part 2 of the Housing (Scotland) Act 2010 (asp 17).

GENERAL NOTE

This section deals with the possibility of administrative receivership in the case of a registered social landlord.

This provision was reworded by the Housing and Regeneration Act 2008 (Consequential Provisions) Order 2010 (SI 2010/866) Sch.2 para.61(2) and (3) with effect from 1 April 2010.

Note minor referential amendment made to para.(b) by the Housing (Scotland) Act 2010 (Consequential Provisions and Modifications) Order 2012 (SI 2012/700) as from 1 April 2012.

72GA Exception in relation to protected railway companies etc.

72GA Section 72A does not prevent the appointment of an administrative receiver of–

(a) a company holding an appointment under Chapter I of Part II of the Water Industry Act 1991,

(b) a protected railway company within the meaning of section 59 of the Railways Act 1993 (including that section as it has effect by virtue of section 19 of the Channel Tunnel Rail Link Act 1996, or

(c) a licence company within the meaning of section 26 of the Transport Act 2000.

GENERAL NOTE

This further exception relating to "protected companies" was created by the Insolvency Act 1986 (Amendment) (Administrative Receivership and Urban Regeneration etc.) Order 2003 (SI 2003/1832).

72H Sections 72A to 72G: supplementary

72H(1) [Conditions for capital market arrangement] Schedule 2A (which supplements sections 72B to 72G) shall have effect.

72H(2) [Order-making power] The Secretary of State may by order–

(a) insert into this Act provision creating an additional exception to section 72A(1) or (2);

(b) provide for a provision of this Act which creates an exception to section 72A(1) or (2) to cease to have effect;

(c) amend section 72A in consequence of provision made under paragraph (a) or (b);

(d) amend any of sections 72B to 72G;

(e) amend Schedule 2A.

72H(3) [Statutory instrument] An order under subsection (2) must be made by statutory instrument.

72H(4) [Provision in order] An order under subsection (2) may make–

(a) provision which applies generally or only for a specified purpose;

(b) different provision for different purposes;

(c) consequential or supplementary provision;

(d) transitional provision.

72H(5) [Procedure for order] An order under subsection (2)–

(a) in the case of an order under subsection (2)(e), shall be subject to annulment in pursuance of a resolution of either House of Parliament,

(b) in the case of an order under subsection (2)(d) varying the sum specified in section 72B(1)(a) or 72E(2)(a) (whether or not the order also makes consequential or transitional provision), shall be subject to annulment in pursuance of a resolution of either House of Parliament, and

(c) in the case of any other order under subsection (2)(a) to (d), may not be made unless a draft has been laid before and approved by resolution of each House of Parliament.

S.72H(1)
This directs us to Sch.2A.

S.72H(2)–(5)
Subsection (2) creates a power to make delegated rules. This order making power lead to the Insolvency Act 1986 (Amendment) (Administrative Receivership and Capital Market Arrangements) Order 2003 (SI 2003/1468) and the Insolvency Act 1986 (Amendment) (Administrative Receivership and Urban Regeneration) Order 2003 (SI 2003/1832), both of which modify primary provisions inserted by EA 2002—see Sch.2A. For legal aspects of such delegated rules the position is outlined by subss.(3)–(5).

PART IV

WINDING UP OF COMPANIES REGISTERED UNDER THE COMPANIES ACTS

Introductory note to Part IV
This Part of the Act deals with the winding up of all registered companies, whether solvent or insolvent. For this purpose, the term "company" (or "registered company") is defined by the Companies Acts (see the note to s.73(1) below). The winding-up provisions are extended to unregistered companies by Pt V of the Act: for the definition of "unregistered company", see s.220. Insolvent partnerships (including limited partnerships) may be wound up under Pt V of the Act as unregistered companies by virtue of the Insolvent Partnerships Order 1994 (SI 1994/2421): see the note to s.420. But the winding up of limited liability partnerships (LLPs) is governed by IA 1986 Pt IV, by virtue of LLPR 2001 reg.5(1)(a), as modified by reg.5(2) and (3).

Part IV applies generally to Scotland as well as to England and Wales, apart from particular sections which are noted as they occur. However the Rules (IR 2016) apply only in England and Wales.

Where a building society is being wound up under Pt X of the Building Societies Act 1986, Pts IV, VI, VII, XII and XIII of the present Act (and, for Northern Ireland, Pt XX of the Companies (Northern Ireland) Order 1986) apply, subject to the modifications made by Sch.15 to that Act: see Building Societies Act 1986 s.90 and Sch.15, as amended by CA 1989 s.211(1), (2) and Sch.24. Note that the amendments made by CA 1989: (i) require the liquidator of a building society to be a qualified insolvency practitioner under Pt XIII of IA 1986 (s.211(2)(a)); and (ii) extend the concept of "shadow director" to building societies (s.211(2)(b)). Transitional provisions contained in SI 1990/1392 (C. 41) art.7, protect the position of liquidators appointed prior to the commencement of CA 1989 s.211(2)(a), i.e. 31 July 1990.

Special regimes established by the Banking Act 2009 apply where a banking company or building society which is in financial difficulties is the subject of government intervention. See the note on p.6.

The provisions of IA 1986 are made to apply to the winding up of a co-operative society or community benefit society which is a "registered society" (as defined in s.1 of the Act) by the Co-operative and Community Benefit Societies Act 2014 s.123. Other bodies, such as friendly societies, which are not provided for by specific legislation, may be wound up as unregistered companies under Pt V of IA 1986: see *Re Victoria Society, Knottingley* [1913] 1 Ch. 167.

The winding up of insurance undertakings is the subject of a special regime: see the Insurers (Winding Up) Rules 2001 (SI 2001/3635), the Insurers (Reorganisation and Winding up) Regulations 2004 (SI 2004/353) and, as regards Lloyd's, the Insurers (Reorganisation and Winding Up) (Lloyd's) Regulations 2005 (SI 2005/1998). These Regulations introduce special rules for insurers applicable throughout the EEA. Comparable provision is made for banking companies and similar institutions by the Credit Institutions (Reorganisation and Winding Up) Regulations 2004 (SI 2004/1045), effective 5 May 2004.

[**Special note:** SBEEA 2015 Pt 10 and Sch.9 has made a large number of amendments to the sections in this Chapter of the Act, which have all been incorporated into the text which follows. But many of the alterations are only minor verbal changes, or purely consequential on substantive amendments elsewhere, and these have been made without detailed annotation. To a lesser extent, the numerous similar minor changes made by the Bankruptcy (Scotland) Act 2016 (Consequential Provisions and Modifications) Order 2016 (SI 2016/1034) have been incorporated without annotation.]

Chapter I

Preliminary

Introductory

73 Scheme of this Part

73(1) [Application of Pt 4] This Part applies to the winding up of a company registered under the Companies Act 2006 in England and Wales or Scotland.

73(2) [Types of winding up] The winding up may be either–

(a) voluntary (see Chapters 2 to 5), or

(b) by the court (see Chapter 6).

73(3) [Application of Chs 1, 7–10] This Chapter and Chapters 7 to 10 relate to winding up generally, except where otherwise stated.

General Note

This section was substituted by the Companies Act 2006 (Consequential Amendments, Transitional Provisions and Savings) Order 2009 (SI 2009/1941) art.2 and Sch.1 para.75(2) as from 1 October 2009. This makes no change of substance.

Prior to the coming into force of IA 1986, there were three modes of winding up: (1) voluntary; (2) by the court; and (3) subject to the supervision of the court. The last of these methods was little used, and was abolished by IA 1985 s.235(3) and Sch.10 Pt II. A voluntary winding up is commenced by the passing of a resolution (usually a special resolution) by the company in general meeting (see s.84): it may be either a "members' voluntary winding up", conducted under the control of the members, if the directors are able to make a declaration of solvency under s.89, or a "creditors' voluntary winding up", if the directors do not make such a declaration, in which case the creditors have control (see ss.89, 90). A winding up by the court (or "compulsory winding up"), as the name suggests, follows from the making of a court order (see ss.122 et seq.).

The Insolvency Act 1986 contains no definition of "company", either generally or for the purposes of this section (although there are some sections which give the term a particular definition for their own specific purpose). Instead, the expression "a company registered under the Companies Act 2006" is used, as in s.73(1), which in effect directs the reader to that Act and, in particular to ss.1(1) and 1171. There we find that the phrase "registered under this Act" is not limited to companies incorporated under CA 2006 but includes also companies formed and registered under earlier Acts and, indeed, companies which "are to be treated" as if formed and registered under the 2006 Act. The relevant sections read as follows:

1 Companies

1(1) In the Companies Acts, unless the context otherwise requires–

"company" means a company formed and registered under this Act, that is–

(a) a company so formed and registered after the commencement of this Part, or

(b) a company that immediately before the commencement of this Part–

(i) was formed and registered under the Companies Act 1985 (c. 6) or the Companies (Northern Ireland) Order 1986 (S.I. 1986/1032 (N.I. 6)), or

(ii) was an existing company for the purposes of that Act or that Order,

(which is to be treated on commencement as if formed and registered under this Act).

1171 The former Companies Acts

In the Companies Acts–

"the former Companies Acts" means–

(a) the Joint Stock Companies Acts, the Companies Act 1862 (c. 89), the Companies (Consolidation) Act 1908 (c. 69), the Companies Act 1929 (c. 23), the Companies Act (Northern Ireland) 1932 (c. 7 (N.I.)), the Companies Acts 1948 to 1983, the Companies Act (Northern Ireland) 1960 (c. 22 (N.I.)), the Companies (Northern Ireland) Order 1986 (S.I. 1986/1032 (N.I. 6)) and the Companies Consolidation (Consequential Provisions) (Northern Ireland) Order 1986 (S.I. 1986/1035 (N.I. 9)), and

(b) the provisions of the Companies Act 1985 (c. 6) and the Companies Consolidation (Consequential Provisions) Act 1985 (c. 9) that are no longer in force;

"the Joint Stock Companies Acts" means the Joint Stock Companies Act 1856 (c. 47), the Joint Stock Companies Acts 1856, 1857 (20 & 21 Vict. c. 14), the Joint Stock Banking Companies Act 1857 (c. 49), and the Act to enable Joint Stock Banking Companies to be formed on the principle of limited liability (1858 c. 91), but does not include the Joint Stock Companies Act 1844 (c. 110).

The term "existing company", referred to in s.1(1)(b)(ii), was defined by CA 1985 s.735(1)(b), (c) as follows:

(b) "existing company" means a company formed and registered under the former Companies Acts, but does not include a company registered under the Joint Stock Companies Acts, the Companies Act 1862 or the Companies (Consolidation) Act 1908 in what was then Ireland;

(c) "the former Companies Acts" means the Joint Stock Companies Acts, the Companies Act 1862, the Companies (Consolidation) Act 1908, the Companies Act 1929 and the Companies Acts 1948 to 1983.

The definition of "the Joint Stock Companies Acts" (s.735(3)) was identical with that in CA 2006 s.1171.

Contributories

74 Liability as contributories of present and past members

74(1) [Liability to contribute] When a company is wound up, every present and past member is liable to contribute to its assets to any amount sufficient for payment of its debts and liabilities, and the expenses of the winding up, and for the adjustment of the rights of the contributories among themselves.

74(2) [Qualifications to liability] This is subject as follows–

(a) a past member is not liable to contribute if he has ceased to be a member for one year or more before the commencement of the winding up;

(b) a past member is not liable to contribute in respect of any debt or liability of the company contracted after he ceased to be a member;

(c) a past member is not liable to contribute, unless it appears to the court that the existing members are unable to satisfy the contributions required to be made by them;

(d) in the case of a company limited by shares, no contribution is required from any member exceeding the amount (if any) unpaid on the shares in respect of which he is liable as a present or past member;

(e) nothing in the Companies Acts or this Act invalidates any provision contained in a policy of insurance or other contract whereby the liability of individual members on the policy or contract is restricted, or whereby the funds of the company are alone made liable in respect of the policy or contract;

(f) a sum due to any member of the company (in his character of a member) by way of dividends, profits or otherwise is not deemed to be a debt of the company, payable to that member in a case of competition between himself and any other creditor not a member of the company, but any such sum may be taken into account for the purpose of the final adjustment of the rights of the contributories among themselves.

74(3) [Company limited by guarantee] In the case of a company limited by guarantee, no contribution is required from any member exceeding the amount undertaken to be contributed by him to the company's assets in the event of its being wound up; but if it is a company with a share capital, every member of it is liable (in addition to the amount so undertaken to be contributed to the assets), to contribute to the extent of any sums unpaid on shares held by him.

S.74(1)

A "contributory" is a member or past member of the company who is liable to contribute to the assets of the company in a winding up (s.79). This includes a member whose shares are fully paid: *Re Anglesea Colliery Company* (1866) L.R. 1 Ch. 555; and may include a former member: *Re Consolidated Goldfields of New Zealand Ltd* [1953] Ch. 689. A person to whom shares have been transferred but not registered is deemed to be a "member" by virtue of s.250 and accordingly a "contributory" with standing to present a winding-up petition: *Hamilton v Brown; Re C&MB Holdings Ltd* [2016] EWHC 191 (Ch); [2017] B.C.C. 457. However the court has power to order the rectification of the register of members with retrospective effect, where it is satisfied that a person has never been a member: see *Barbor v Middleton* (1988) 4 B.C.C. 681.

"Debts and liabilities" in s.74(1) is to be given a broad meaning and is not confined to provable debts. In *Re Lehman Bros International (Europe)* [2014] EWHC 704 (Ch); [2014] B.C.C. 193 David Richards J held that the term included statutory interest and non-provable debts. This view was upheld on appeal (*Joint Administrators of LB Holdings Intermediate 2 Ltd v Lomas* [2015] EWCA Civ 485; [2016] Ch. 50; [2015] B.C.C. 431), the Court of Appeal confirming, amongst other things, that the payment of subordinated debt was postponed to the payment of statutory interest and the Supreme Court upheld this view: *Joint Administrators of LB Holdings Intermediate 2 Ltd v Joint Administrators of Lehman Brothers International (Europe)* [2017] UKSC 38; [2017] B.C.C. 235 at [56].

It is well established at common law that a contributory who is also a creditor may not recover anything in a liquidation until he has first discharged all of his liabilities as a contributory: *Re Overend Gurney & Co, Grissell's Case* (1865-66) L.R. 1 Ch. App. 528. At first instance and in the Court of Appeal in *Re Lehman Bros* ([2014] EWHC 704 (Ch); [2014] B.C.C. 193 at [179] and [2015] EWCA Civ 485; [2016] Ch. 50; [2015] B.C.C. 431 at [245]) respectively it was agreed that this judge-made "contributory rule" applied only in liquidation and not in a distributing administration. However the Supreme Court disagreed, with Lord Neuberger ([2015] EWCA Civ 485; [2016] Ch. 50; [2015] B.C.C. 431), after warning (at [176]) against laying down new judge-made rules onto the "detailed and coherent nature of the 1986 legislation", concluding (at [178]) that the rule, at least in a modified version, could be extended to a distributing administration to proved claims provided it was effected in a way that was "principled, practical and in harmony with applicable legislative provisions and principles".

S.74(2)

This provision defines the extent to which both present and past members are liable to contribute to the assets. The principle of limited liability will, where appropriate, apply so as to restrict the amount payable (para.(d)). A past member is liable only in the circumstances listed in paras (a)–(c).

Paragraph (f) subordinates any sums payable by the company to any member qua member (e.g. a dividend declared but not paid) to the company's obligations to its general creditors. The member cannot set off these sums directly against his own contribution.

S.74(2)(f)

In *Soden v British & Commonwealth Holdings plc (in admin.)* [1998] A.C. 298; [1997] B.C.C. 952 the House of Lords held that sums due to a member "in his character of a member" were only those sums the right to which was based on a cause of action on the statutory contract contained in s.14 of CA 1985 [now CA 2006 s.33(1)] and other rights imposed by the Companies Acts. The expression did not include damages awarded to a person who had acquired shares in the company by purchase from an existing member in reliance on a misrepresentation by the company. In contrast, damages for misrepresentation or breach of warranty awarded to a person who had obtained the shares by subscription from the company have been held to be within the section (*Re Addlestone Linoleum Co* (1887) 37 Ch. D. 191; *Webb Distributors (Australia) Pty Ltd v State of Victoria* (1993) 11 A.C.L.C. 1178). The question may, however, be open to reargument in view of CA 2006 s.655, which overrides part of the ratio decidendi of the *Addlestone Linoleum* case.

S.74(3)

This states the limit of the liability of a contributory where a company is limited by guarantee.

75 Directors, etc. with unlimited liability

75 [Omitted by the Companies Act 2006 (Consequential Amendments, Transitional Provisions and Savings) Order 2009 (SI 2009/1941) art.2 and Sch.1 para.75(4) from 1 October 2009, subject to savings in art.9(a).]

76 Liability of past directors and shareholders

76(1) [Application] This section applies where a company is being wound up and–

(a) it has under Chapter 5 of Part 18 of the Companies Act 2006 (acquisition by limited company of its own shares: redemption or purchase by private company out of capital) made a payment out of capital in respect of the redemption or purchase of any of its own shares (the payment being referred to below as "the relevant payment"), and

(b) the aggregate amount of the company's assets and the amounts paid by way of contribution to its assets (apart from this section) is not sufficient for payment of its debts and liabilities, and the expenses of the winding up.

76(2) [Contribution of past shareholders, directors] If the winding up commenced within one year of the date on which the relevant payment was made, then–

(a) the person from whom the shares were redeemed or purchased, and

(b) the directors who signed the statement made in accordance with section 714(1) to (3) of the Companies Act 2006 for purposes of the redemption or purchase (except a director who shows that he had reasonable grounds for forming the opinion set out in the statement),

are, so as to enable that insufficiency to be met, liable to contribute to the following extent to the company's assets.

76(3) [Amount payable] A person from whom any of the shares were redeemed or purchased is liable to contribute an amount not exceeding so much of the relevant payment as was made by the company in respect of his shares; and the directors are jointly and severally liable with that person to contribute that amount.

76(4) [Application to court] A person who has contributed any amount to the assets in pursuance of this section may apply to the court for an order directing any other person jointly and severally liable in respect of that amount to pay him such amount as the court thinks just and equitable.

76(5) [Non-application of s.74] Section 74 does not apply in relation to liability accruing by virtue of this section.

76(6) [Omitted by the Companies Act 2006 (Consequential Amendments, Transitional Provisions and Savings) Order 2009 (SI 2009/1941) art.2 and Sch.1 para.73(5)(d).]

General Note

When a payment has been made out of capital by a private company in connection with a redemption or repurchase of shares under CA 2006 s.709, and the company is wound up insolvent within one year of the payment, this section applies so as to make the recipient of the payment liable to refund it in whole or part and, in some circumstances also, the directors jointly and severally liable with him.

Note that although the persons liable under this section fall within the definition of "contributory" for the purposes of this Act, they will not normally be regarded as "contributories" when construing a company's articles (see s.79(3)).

Section 76(2)(b) amended by the Companies Act 2006 (Consequential Amendments and Transitional Provisions) Order 2011 (SI 2011/1265) art.6(1), (3) from 12 May 2011.

77 Limited company formerly unlimited

77(1) [Application] This section applies in the case of a company being wound up which was at some former time registered as unlimited but has re-registered as a limited company.

77(2) [Contribution by past members] Notwithstanding section 74(2)(a) above, a past member of the company who was a member of it at the time of re-registration, if the winding up commences within the period of 3 years beginning with the day on which the company was re-registered, is liable to contribute to the assets of the company in respect of debts and liabilities contracted before that time.

77(3) [If no past members existing members] If no persons who were members of the company at that time are existing members of it, a person who at that time was a present or past member is liable to contribute as above notwithstanding that the existing members have satisfied the contributions required to be made by them.

This applies subject to section 74(2)(a) above and to subsection (2) of this section, but notwithstanding section 74(2)(c).

77(4) [No limitation on contribution] Notwithstanding section 74(2)(d) and (3), there is no limit on the amount which a person who, at that time, was a past or present member of the company is liable to contribute as above.

General Note

Sections 105–108 of CA 2006 enable an unlimited company to re-register as limited, but the unlimited liability of both present and past members continues if a winding up ensues within three years of the date of re-registration. The present section deals with the liability of these persons as contributories.

Section 76(2)(b) amended by the Companies Act 2006 (Consequential Amendments and Transitional Provisions) Order 2011 (SI 2011/1265) art.6(1), (3) from 12 May 2011.

78 Unlimited company formerly limited

78(1) [Application] This section applies in the case of a company being wound up which was at some former time registered as limited but has been re-registered as unlimited.

78(2) [Limitation on contribution] A person who, at the time when the application for the company to be re-registered was lodged, was a past member of the company and did not after that again become a member of it is not liable to contribute to the assets of the company more than he would have been liable to contribute had the company not been re-registered.

General Note

When a limited company is converted to an unlimited company under CA 2006 s.102, the limited liability of past members is preserved by this provision.

79 Meaning of "contributory"

79(1) ["Contributory"] In this Act the expression "contributory" means every person liable to contribute to the assets of a company in the event of its being wound up, and for the purposes of all proceedings for determining, and all proceedings prior to the final determination of, the persons who are to be deemed contributories, includes any person alleged to be a contributory.

79(2) [Qualification] The reference in subsection (1) to persons liable to contribute to the assets does not include a person so liable by virtue of a declaration by the court under section 213 (imputed responsibility for company's fraudulent trading) or section 214 (wrongful trading) in Chapter X of this Part.

79(3) [Reference in articles] A reference in a company's articles to a contributory does not (unless the context requires) include a person who is a contributory only by virtue of section 76.

General Note

This section defines the term "contributory" for the purposes of the present Act. It incorporates (by s.79(2)) an amendment made by IA 1985 Sch.6 para.5 which makes it plain that a person is not deemed a contributory merely because he has been ordered by the court to contribute to the company's assets following a finding of fraudulent or wrongful trading under ss.213, 214.

See also the note to s.74(1).

80 Nature of contributory's liability

80 The liability of a contributory creates a debt (in England and Wales in the nature of an ordinary contract debt) accruing due from him at the time when his liability commenced, but payable at the times when calls are made for enforcing the liability.

General Note

"Due" in this section is equivalent to "owing", or "constituting a debt", in contrast with "payable", which is the relevant date for the purposes of the Statutes of Limitation. The words "an ordinary contract debt" were substituted for the former words "a specialty" with effect from 1 October 2009: see the Companies Act 2006 (Consequential Amendments, Transitional Provisions and Savings) Order 2009 art.2 and Sch.1 para.75(9), subject to savings in art.11. In consequence, the period of limitation is now six years.

81 Contributories in case of death of a member

81(1) [Personal representative liable] If a contributory dies either before or after he has been placed on the list of contributories, his personal representatives, and the heirs and legatees of heritage of his heritable estate in Scotland, are liable in a due course of administration to contribute to the assets of the company in discharge of his liability and are contributories accordingly.

81(2) [Where personal representatives on list of contributories] Where the personal representatives are placed on the list of contributories, the heirs or legatees of heritage need not be added, but they may be added as and when the court thinks fit.

81(3) [Where default in payment] If in England and Wales the personal representatives make default in paying any money ordered to be paid by them, proceedings may be taken for administering the estate of the deceased contributory and for compelling payment out of it of the money due.

General Note

This section provides that on the death of a contributory, his personal representatives (or their Scottish counterparts) are substituted for him as contributories.

82 Effect of contributory's bankruptcy

82(1) [Application] The following applies if a contributory becomes bankrupt, either before or after he has been placed on the list of contributories.

82(2) [Trustee in bankruptcy a contributory] His trustee in bankruptcy represents him for all purposes of the winding up, and is a contributory accordingly.

82(3) [Trustee called on to admit to proof] The trustee may be called on to admit to proof against the bankrupt's estate, or otherwise allow to be paid out of the bankrupt's assets in due course of law, any money due from the bankrupt in respect of his liability to contribute to the company's assets.

82(4) [Estimated value of liability to future calls] There may be proved against the bankrupt's estate the estimated value of his liability to future calls as well as calls already made.

S.82(1), (2)

The trustee in bankruptcy is deemed a contributory and represents the bankrupt for all purposes of the winding up. It was held under the virtually identical wording of CA 1948 s.216 that this section does not empower a contributory's trustee in bankruptcy to present a winding-up petition (unless the trustee has been registered as a member), since its provisions only become effective once a winding up is in place: *Re H L Bolton (Engineering) Co Ltd* [1956] Ch. 577 at 582–583. In Scotland, however, the wording of the Bankruptcy (Scotland) Act 1985 s.31 was held to be sufficiently wide to empower a trustee to petition: *Taylor, Petitioner; Cumming's Trustee v Glenrinnes Farms Ltd* [1993] B.C.C. 829.

S.82(3), (4)

These subsections deal with the proof against the bankrupt's estate of his liability to the company as a contributory.

83 Companies registered but not formed under the Companies Act 2006

83(1) [Application] The following applies in the event of a company being wound up which is registered but not formed under the Companies Act 2006.

83(2) [Contributories re debts and liabilities before registration] Every person is a contributory, in respect of the company's debts and liabilities contracted before registration, who is liable–

(a) to pay, or contribute to the payment of, any debt or liability so contracted, or

(b) to pay, or contribute to the payment of, any sum for the adjustment of the rights of the members among themselves in respect of any such debt or liability, or

(c) to pay, or contribute to the amount of, the expenses of winding up the company, so far as relates to the debts or liabilities above-mentioned.

83(3) [Amounts liable to be contributed] Every contributory is liable to contribute to the assets of the company, in the course of the winding up, all sums due from him in respect of any such liability.

83(4) [Death etc. of contributory] In the event of the death, bankruptcy or insolvency of any contributory, provisions of this Act, with respect to the personal representatives, to the heirs and legatees of heritage of the heritable estate in Scotland of deceased contributories and to the trustees of bankrupt or insolvent contributories respectively, apply.

General Note

As explained in the note to s.73, Pt 4 of the Act is expressed to apply to companies "registered under CA 2006", but that phrase includes some companies formed under certain very early Acts which are "to be treated as if" formed and registered under the 2006 Act (CA 2006 s.1(1)(c)(ii)). This section deals with these rare cases.

Chapter II

Voluntary Winding Up (Introductory and General)

Resolutions for, and commencement of, voluntary winding up

84 Circumstances in which company may be wound up voluntarily

84(1) [Circumstances] A company may be wound up voluntarily–

(a) when the period (if any) fixed for the duration of the company by the articles expires, or the event (if any) occurs, on the occurrence of which the articles provide that the company is to be dissolved, and the company in general meeting has passed a resolution requiring it to be wound up voluntarily;

(b) if the company resolves by special resolution that it be wound up voluntarily;

(c) [Repealed]

84(2) [Definition] In this Act the expression "a resolution for voluntary winding up" means a resolution passed under either of the paragraphs of subsection (1).

84(2A) [Written notice to holder of qualifying floating charge] Before a company passes a resolution for voluntary winding up it must give written notice of the resolution to the holder of any qualifying floating charge to which section 72A applies.

84(2B) [Where written notice given] Where notice is given under subsection (2A) a resolution for voluntary winding up may be passed only–

(a) after the end of the period of five business days beginning with the day on which the notice was given, or

(b) if the person to whom the notice was given has consented in writing to the passing of the resolution.

84(3) [Copy of resolution to registrar] Chapter 3 of Part 3 of the Companies Act 2006 (resolutions affecting a company's constitution) applies to a resolution under paragraph (a) of subsection (1) as well as a special resolution under paragraph (b).

84(4) [Effect of Commonhold and Leasehold Reform Act 2002] This section has effect subject to section 43 of the Commonhold and Leasehold Reform Act 2002.

General Note

A company may be wound up only by following the statutory procedure: it is improper to attempt to do so without appointing an insolvency practitioner: *Re Ipcon Fashions Ltd* (1989) 5 B.C.C. 773. However, in an appropriate case the company may proceed directly to a dissolution under CA 2006 ss.1003–1011: see the note preceding s.201.

An insurance company may be wound up voluntarily, either as a members' or creditors' winding up: see the Insurers (Reorganisation and Winding Up) Regulations 2004 (SI 2004/353) regs 7, 9(4).

S.84(1)

Paragraph (a) calls for a "resolution" (i.e. an *ordinary* resolution) and para.(b) for a *special* resolution. The former para.(c) provided for an *extraordinary* resolution where the company was insolvent, but this category of resolution has not survived the enactment of CA 2006 and a special resolution is now required in such a case. The Companies Act 2006 (Commencement No.3, Consequential Amendments, Transitional Provisions and Savings) Order 2007 (SI 2007/2194) art.10(1) and Sch.4 para.39, effective 1 October 2007 accordingly repeals s.84(1)(c) and amends s.84(2) and (3).

S.84(2A), (2B)

These provisions (inserted by SI 2003/2096 from 15 September 2003) give the charge holder a brief opportunity to appoint an administrator, failing which his right to do so will be lost. Failure to give notice to a qualifying floating charge holder under subs.(2A) does not apparently invalidate the appointment of the liquidator—*Bevan v Walker* [2018] EWHC 265 (Ch); compare *Re Eco Link Resources Ltd* [2012] B.C.C. 731.

A resolution for voluntary winding up cannot be passed conditionally upon the happening of some other event, e.g. the discharge of an administration order: *Re Norditrack (UK) Ltd* [2000] B.C.C. 441.

S.84(3)

Section 29(1)(a) of CA 2006 provides for the registration of all special resolutions, and the requirement to register is extended to resolutions falling within s.84(1)(a) by this provision. The liquidator, for the purposes of these provisions, is deemed to be an officer of the company and liable accordingly to penal sanctions for non-compliance (CA 2006 s.30(4)).

S.84(4)

Section 84(4) inserted by the Commonhold and Leasehold Reform Act 2002 s.68 and Sch.5 para.6 as from 27 September 2004 (in relation to England and Wales only). Section 43 of this Act prescribes additional procedural requirements for the passing of a resolution for the voluntary winding up of a commonhold association.

85 Notice of resolution to wind up

85(1) [Notice in Gazette] When a company has passed a resolution for voluntary winding up, it shall, within 14 days after the passing of the resolution, give notice of the resolution by advertisement in the Gazette.

85(2) [Penalty on default] If default is made in complying with this section, the company and every officer of it who is in default is liable to a fine and, for continued contravention, to a daily default fine.

For purposes of this subsection the liquidator is deemed an officer of the company.

General Note

It is the responsibility of the company and its officers (including the liquidator: s.85(2)) to see that notice of the resolution to wind up is gazetted. The liquidator, when appointed, is under a separate obligation to publish notice of his appointment in the *Gazette*: see s.109.

S.85(2)
On penalties, see s.430 and Sch.10.

86 Commencement of winding up

86 A voluntary winding up is deemed to commence at the time of the passing of the resolution for voluntary winding up.

General Note

The "commencement" of a winding up is significant for many purposes under this Act and, previously, the Companies Acts. For the corresponding provision in relation to a winding up by the court, see s.129.

It should be noted that this section refers to the "time" of commencement, as does s.129. In contrast, s.278, the corresponding provision in bankruptcy, states that a bankruptcy "commences *with the day* on which the order is made"—an expression which clearly relates back to the preceding midnight—while other sections of the Act and provisions in the rules refer to the "date" of an event (see, e.g. s.183(2)(a): "date on which he had notice"; "date of commencement of the winding up"; s.240(3)(e): "date of the commencement of the winding up"; and r.14.1(3)(b), (c): "date when the company went into liquidation"). It must be inferred that the draftsmen used these different wordings deliberately, so that where the word "time" is used the normal convention that "the law takes no account of part of a day" (*Trow v Ind Coope (West Midlands) Ltd* [1967] 2 Q.B. 899) is ousted, and an event is to be pinpointed to the precise time of the day when it occurred. This could be an important consideration in some areas of commerce (e.g. financial dealing rooms), where even seconds can count.

The EU Regulation refers to the "time of the opening" of insolvency proceedings. In the case of a creditors' voluntary winding up, this will be the time of the passing of the shareholders' resolution. See the note to the Regulation art.2(8). See also *Secretary of State for Trade and Industry v Slater* [2008] B.C.C. 70 where the court rejected an argument that, for the purposes of the TUPE Regulations 2006, a creditors' voluntary liquidation had commenced at a date earlier than the meetings of the company and creditors.

Consequences of resolution to wind up

87 Effect on business and status of company

87(1) [Cessation of business] In case of a voluntary winding up, the company shall from the commencement of the winding up cease to carry on its business, except so far as may be required for its beneficial winding up.

87(2) [Continuation of corporate state etc.] However, the corporate state and corporate powers of the company, notwithstanding anything to the contrary in its articles, continue until the company is dissolved.

S.87(1)
In the case of a compulsory winding up, the liquidator may carry on the company's business, "so far as may be necessary for its beneficial winding up" (see s.167(1) and Sch.IV para.5). In a voluntary winding up the question whether it is beneficial to continue the business is a matter for the liquidator's own bona fide judgment.

In *Secretary of State for Business, Innovation and Skills v PAG Management Services Ltd* [2015] EWHC 2404 (Ch) a scheme designed to avoid the payment of business rates involved the formation of special purpose vehicles which took leases of the properties in question and then were immediately wound up without liquidators being appointed. It was held that there was no violation of s.87 because the companies did not carry on any business. However, an order was made for the winding up of the companies on more general public interest grounds: see the note to s.124A.

S.87(2)

The corporate personality of the company in a compulsory winding up also continues until dissolution, although this is not expressly stated in the Act. It follows that acts should normally be done by the liquidator in the name of the company, and not in his own name. In *Kirkpatrick v Snoozebox Ltd* [2014] B.C.C. 477 it was held that a liquidator has no power to institute proceedings in his own name, except where this is authorised by statute. However, where the Act empowers a liquidator (or other office-holder) to institute litigation (e.g. to recover property under s.234 or to have a transaction at an undervalue or a preference set aside under ss.238–239), he should bring the claim in his own name: *Re Cosslett Contractors Ltd (No.2), Smith v Bridgend BC* [2001] UKHL 58; [2002] 1 A.C. 336; [2001] B.C.C. 740 at [32]. Section 212 (misfeasance) permits the liquidator to use either procedure.

88 Avoidance of share transfers, etc. after winding-up resolution

88 Any transfer of shares, not being a transfer made to or with the sanction of the liquidator, and any alteration in the status of the company's members, made after the commencement of a voluntary winding up, is void.

General Note

In a compulsory winding up, a transfer of shares made after the commencement of the winding up is similarly void, but can be validated only by order of the court: see s.127. Section 88 is disapplied in relation to any transfer of shares under a financial collateral arrangement: Financial Collateral Arrangements (No.2) Regulations 2003 (SI 2003/3226) reg.10(2).

Declaration of solvency

89 Statutory declaration of solvency

89(1) [Declaration by directors] Where it is proposed to wind up a company voluntarily, the directors (or, in the case of a company having more than two directors, the majority of them) may at a directors' meeting make a statutory declaration to the effect that they have made a full inquiry into the company's affairs and that, having done so, they have formed the opinion that the company will be able to pay its debts in full, together with interest at the official rate (as defined in section 251), within such period, not exceeding 12 months from the commencement of the winding up, as may be specified in the declaration.

89(2) [Requirements for declaration] Such a declaration by the directors has no effect for purposes of this Act unless–

(a) it is made within the 5 weeks immediately preceding the date of the passing of the resolution for winding up, or on that date but before the passing of the resolution, and

(b) it embodies a statement of the company's assets and liabilities as at the latest practicable date before the making of the declaration.

89(3) [Declaration to registrar] The declaration shall be delivered to the registrar of companies before the expiration of 15 days immediately following the date on which the resolution for winding up is passed.

89(4) [Offence, penalty] A director making a declaration under this section without having reasonable grounds for the opinion that the company will be able to pay its debts in full, together with interest at the official rate, within the period specified is liable to imprisonment or a fine, or both.

89(5) [Presumption] If the company is wound up in pursuance of a resolution passed within 5 weeks after the making of the declaration, and its debts (together with interest at the official rate) are not paid or provided for in full within the period specified, it is to be presumed (unless the contrary is shown) that the director did not have reasonable grounds for his opinion.

89(6) [Penalty for non-compliance with s.89(3)] If a declaration required by subsection (3) to be delivered to the registrar is not so delivered within the time prescribed by that subsection, the company and every officer in default is liable to a fine and, for continued contravention, to a daily default fine.

General Note

The category of a voluntary winding up (members' or creditors': see s.90), and the legal rules which apply to it in consequence, depend on whether a statutory declaration of solvency has been made under this section. The responsibility for assessing the likely solvency of the company is placed squarely on the directors (or a majority of them): if they make the declaration, the matter proceeds as a members' voluntary winding up under the control of the members; if they do not, the creditors take over. The severe penalties and reversed onus of proof prescribed by s.89(4) and (5) provide directors with a strong deterrent against making a declaration of solvency irresponsibly.

There is no obligation upon the directors to make a statutory declaration when the company is insolvent or not believed to be solvent: the matter simply proceeds as a creditors' voluntary winding up.

S.89(1)
A statutory declaration is a formal declaration made before a justice of the peace, solicitor or commissioner for oaths, and is equivalent to an oath for most legal purposes, including the law of perjury. The declaration here required must be made at a directors' meeting, held before the shareholders' meeting at which the resolution for winding up is to be passed, and within the time specified in s.89(2).

The directors must themselves fix the period, not exceeding 12 months from the commencement of the winding up, within which they predict that the company will be able to pay its debts in full. Since the directors' declaration must be made with reference to a future date, they should plainly take into account any prospective and contingent liabilities of which they are aware. On the other hand, it should be noted that they are not required to assert that the company itself is, or will be, "solvent": if the directors have a firm commitment from a third party (such as parent company) that it will meet any liabilities that the company cannot discharge from its own resources, they may well be justified in making a declaration and allowing the liquidation to proceed as a members' voluntary winding up.

Minor inaccuracies in a statement of assets and liabilities on which the directors had relied in making a declaration of solvency were held insufficient to invalidate the declaration in *Re New Millennium Experience Co Ltd* [2003] EWHC 1823 (Ch); [2004] 1 All E.R. 689; [2004] 1 B.C.L.C. 19.

S.89(2)
The five-week period is reckoned back from the date of the winding-up resolution, and the declaration must be based on a financial statement which is as up-to-date as practicable.

S.89(3)
Form 4.70 should be used.

S.89(4)–(6)
The penalties under s.89(4) are stringent—up to two years' imprisonment and an unlimited fine, if the proceedings are on indictment (see Sch.10). If a director's prediction of solvency turns out in the event to be wrong, s.89(5) reverses the normal burden of proof and requires him to show that in fact he had reasonable grounds for making it.

On penalties, see s.430 and Sch.10.

90 Distinction between "members' " and "creditors' " voluntary winding up

90 A winding up in the case of which a directors' statutory declaration under section 89 has been made is a "members' voluntary winding up"; and a winding up in the case of which such a declaration has not been made is a "creditors' voluntary winding up".

General Note

In the sections of the Act which follow, Chapter III (ss.91–96) applies only to a members' voluntary winding up and Chapter IV (ss.97–106) only to a creditors' voluntary winding up, while Chapter V (ss.107–116) applies to a voluntary winding up of either kind.

Chapter III

Members' Voluntary Winding Up

Introductory note to Part IV, Chapter III
Members' voluntary liquidations are discussed in Totty, Moss & Segal, *Insolvency*, paras D1–04 et seq.

91 Appointment of liquidator

91(1) [Appointment by general meeting] In a members' voluntary winding up, the company in general meeting shall appoint one or more liquidators for the purpose of winding up the company's affairs and distributing its assets.

91(2) [Cessation of directors' powers] On the appointment of a liquidator all the powers of the directors cease, except so far as the company in general meeting or the liquidator sanctions their continuance.

S.91(1)

In *Secretary of State for Business, Innovation and Skills v PAG Management Services Ltd* [2015] EWHC 2404 (Ch); [2015] B.C.C. 720 a scheme designed to avoid the payment of business rates involved the formation of special purpose vehicles which took leases of the properties in question and then were immediately wound up without liquidators being appointed. It was held that there was no violation of ss.91–92 because this was only incidental and not fundamental to the scheme. However, an order was made for the winding up of the companies on more general public interest grounds: see the note to s.124A. For the relevant rule, see IR 2016 r.5.2.

S.91(2)

On the making of a winding-up order *by the court* the appointments of all the directors are terminated automatically: *Measures Brothers Ltd v Measures* [1910] 2 Ch. 248. Any act purportedly done in the company's name by the directors is a nullity: *Park Associated Developments Ltd v Kinnear* [2013] EWHC 3617 (Ch) (purported transfers of land owned by company declared void). It appears from this subsection that a resolution for voluntary winding up does not of itself operate to remove the directors from office, for if this were the case it would not be possible to sanction the continuance of their powers. This view is, perhaps, confirmed by some reported cases concerning employees, e.g. *Midland Counties District Bank Ltd v Attwood* [1905] 1 Ch. 357, although there are dicta in other cases to the contrary (e.g. *Reigate v Union Manufacturing Co (Ramsbottom) Ltd* [1918] 1 K.B. 592 at 606). It is also endorsed by s.114(2), (3).

92 Power to fill vacancy in office of liquidator

92(1) [Filling of vacancy] If a vacancy occurs by death, resignation or otherwise in the office of liquidator appointed by the company, the company in general meeting may, subject to any arrangement with its creditors, fill the vacancy.

92(2) [Convening of general meeting] For that purpose a general meeting may be convened by any contributory or, if there were more liquidators than one, by the continuing liquidators.

92(3) [Manner of holding meeting] The meeting shall be held in manner provided by this Act or by the articles, or in such manner as may, on application by any contributory or by the continuing liquidators, be determined by the court.

S.92(3)

The reference to "this Act" is probably a slip: fairly obviously, it should have been to the Companies Act, as was the case in the pre-consolidation provision (CA 1985 s.581(3)). The present Act contains no provisions regulating the holding of meetings in a members' voluntary winding up. The subject is not dealt with in the rules apart from IR 2016 r.5.2, concerning the appointment of the liquidator. In all other respects, the procedure will be the normal one for company meetings laid down by the company's articles and CA 2006 Pt 13.

92A Progress report to company (England and Wales)

92A(1) [Duty of liquidator] Subject to section 96, where the company is registered in England and Wales, the liquidator must–

(a) for each prescribed period produce a progress report relating to the prescribed matters; and

(b) within such period commencing with the end of the period referred to in paragraph (a) as may be prescribed send a copy of the progress report to–

  (i) the members of the company; and

  (ii) such other persons as may be prescribed.

92A(2) [Penalty] A liquidator who fails to comply with this section is liable to a fine.

General Note

Section 92A was inserted by LRO 2010 (SI 2010/18) art.5(2) from 6 April 2010, and the heading and s.92A(1) amended by SBEEA 2015 s.136(1), (2) as from 26 May 2015. The requirement to hold annual meetings has been removed (in England and Wales) by the amendment of s.93. This coincides with the introduction of a provision for the liquidator in that jurisdiction to produce annual progress reports, corresponding to the similar obligation for administrations (where, however, the intervals are six-monthly). For the prescribed matters, see IR 2016 rr.18.3, 18.7.

93 General company meeting at each year's end (Scotland)

93(1) [If winding up for more than one year] Subject to sections 96 and 102, in the event of the winding up of a company registered in Scotland continuing for more than one year, the liquidator shall summon a general meeting of the company at the end of the first year from the commencement of the winding up, and of each succeeding year, or at the first convenient date within 3 months from the end of the year or such longer period as the Secretary of State may allow.

93(2) [Account by liquidator] The liquidator shall lay before the meeting an account of his acts and dealings, and of the conduct of the winding up, during the preceding year.

93(3) [Penalty for non-compliance] If the liquidator fails to comply with this section, he is liable to a fine.

General Note

This section now applies in Scotland only, following amendments made by LRO 2010 (SI 2010/18) art.6(2) as from 6 April 2010. There is no longer a requirement to hold AGMs in England and Wales. See the note to s.92A. On the holding of meetings during a winding up, see the note to s.92(3).

S.93(3)
On penalties, see s.430 and Sch.10.

94 Final account prior to dissolution

94(1) [Liquidator's account of winding up] As soon as the company's affairs are fully wound up the liquidator must make up an account of the winding up, showing how it has been conducted and the company's property has been disposed of.

94(2) [Copy of account to members] The liquidator must send a copy of the account to the members of the company before the end of the period of 14 days beginning with the day on which the account is made up.

94(3) [Copy of account to registrar of companies] The liquidator must send a copy of the account to the registrar of companies before the end of that period (but not before sending it to the members of the company).

94(4) [Penalty for default of s.94(2)] If the liquidator does not comply with subsection (2) the liquidator is liable to a fine.

94(5) [Penalty for default of s.94(3)] If the liquidator does not comply with subsection (3) the liquidator is liable to a fine and, for continued contravention, a daily default fine.

General Note

Section 94 substituted by SBEEA 2015 Sch.9 paras 1, 18 as from 6 April 2017.

This section replaces a provision requiring the liquidator to hold a final meeting prior to dissolution. Instead, he must now make up and distribute a final account. The relevant rules are IR 2016 rr.5.9, 5.10 and 18.14.

When the liquidator has sent to the registrar his final account under this section, dissolution of the company follows automatically three months after the return is registered, unless the court makes an order deferring the date: see s.201(2), (3).

S.94(4), (5)
On penalties, see s.430 and Sch.10.

95 Effect of company's insolvency

95(1) [Application] This section applies where the liquidator is of the opinion that the company will be unable to pay its debts in full (together with interest at the official rate) within the period stated in the directors' declaration under section 89.

95(1A) [Duties of liquidator re statement of affairs] The liquidator must before the end of the period of 7 days beginning with the day after the day on which the liquidator formed that opinion–

(a) make out a statement in the prescribed form as to the affairs of the company, and

(b) send it to the company's creditors.

95(2)–(3) [Omitted]

95(4) [Contents of statement of affairs] The statement as to the affairs of the company shall show–

(a) particulars of the company's assets, debts and liabilities;

(b) the names and addresses of the company's creditors;

(c) the securities held by them respectively;

(d) the dates when the securities were respectively given; and

(e) such further or other information as may be prescribed.

95(4A) [Verification of statement of affairs by liquidator] The statement as to the affairs of the company shall be verified by the liquidator–

(a) in the case of a winding up of a company registered in England and Wales, by a statement of truth; and

(b) in the case of a winding up of a company registered in Scotland, by affidavit.

95(4B) [Power of creditors to nominate liquidator] The company's creditors may in accordance with the rules nominate a person to be liquidator.

95(4C) [Liquidator to seek nomination] The liquidator must in accordance with the rules seek such a nomination from the company's creditors.

95(5)–(7) [Omitted]

95(8) [Penalty for non-compliance with s.95(1)–(4A)] If the liquidator without reasonable excuse fails to comply with subsections (1) to (4A), he is liable to a fine.

General Note

The earlier law had for a long time been criticised as unsatisfactory (see, e.g. the Cork Committee's *Report*, paras 674–676). The repealed section in the Companies Act required the liquidator in a members' voluntary winding up, if he formed the opinion that the company was insolvent, to summon a meeting of the creditors and inform them of the position. However, the Act made no further provision, and so all that the creditors could then do was petition the court for a compulsory winding-up order to replace the voluntary liquidation. The present section empowers the creditors, without applying to the court, to convert the liquidation into a creditors' voluntary winding up and, if they wish, to substitute a liquidator of their own choice.

Section 95(2A)(b) amended by LRO 2010 (SI 2010/18) art.7 as from 6 April 2010; s.95(4) amended and s.95(4A) inserted by LRO 2010 art.5(2) also from 6 April 2010 (the latter amendments with retrospective effect). Section 95(2)–(3), (5)–(7) omitted and s.95(1A), (4B), (4C) inserted by SBEEA 2015 Sch.9 paras 1, 19 as from 6 April 2017.

S.95(1)
The reference is to the directors' statutory declaration of solvency by virtue of which the liquidation proceeded initially as a members' voluntary winding up: see s.89(1).

S.95(4)
The "statement of affairs" provision is parallel to that which applies in a creditors' voluntary winding up (see the comments to s.99 and s.131), except that in the present situation the responsibilities in connection with the statement are imposed on the liquidator and not the directors.
For the relevant rules, see IR 2016 rr.6.2 et seq.

S.95(8)
On penalties, see s.430 and Sch.10.

96 Conversion to creditors' voluntary winding up

96(1) [Date of conversion] The winding up becomes a creditors' voluntary winding up as from the day on which–

(a) the company's creditors under section 95 nominate a person to be liquidator, or

(b) the procedure by which the company's creditors were to have made such a nomination concludes without a nomination having been made.

96(2) [Effect on declaration of solvency] As from that day this Act has effect as if the directors' declaration under section 89 had not been made.

96(3) [Liquidator] The liquidator in the creditors' voluntary winding up is to be the person nominated by the company's creditors under section 95 or, where no person has been so nominated, the existing liquidator.

96(4) [Application where existing liquidator not nominated] In the case of the creditors nominating a person other than the existing liquidator any director, member or creditor of the company may, within 7 days after the date on which the nomination was made by the creditors, apply to the court for an order either–

(a) directing that the existing liquidator is to be liquidator instead of or jointly with the person nominated by the creditors, or

(b) appointing some other person to be liquidator instead of the person nominated by the creditors.

96(4A) [Application by qualifying floating charge holder] The court shall grant an application under subsection (4) made by the holder of a qualifying floating charge in respect of the company's property (within the meaning of paragraph 14 of Schedule B1) unless the court thinks it right to refuse the application because of the particular circumstances of the case.

96(5) ["Existing liquidator"] The "existing liquidator" is the person who is liquidator immediately before the winding up becomes a creditors' voluntary winding up.

General Note

Section 96 substituted by SBEEA 2015 Sch.9 paras 1, 20 as from 6 April 2017.
It will, of course, be competent for the creditors to appoint a liquidator of their own choosing and to establish a liquidation committee under ss.100 and 101, respectively, by virtue of the general provisions of the present section.
Section 97(2) makes it clear that the statement of affairs prepared under s.95(4) is deemed equivalent to the statement required by s.99, so that there is no need to duplicate this exercise. This is also confirmed by s.102.

Chapter IV

Creditors' Voluntary Winding Up

Introductory note to Part IV, Chapter IV
Creditors' voluntary liquidations are discussed in Totty, Moss & Segal, *Insolvency*, paras D1–22 et seq.

97 Application of this Chapter

97(1) [Application] Subject as follows, this Chapter applies in relation to a creditors' voluntary winding up.

97(2) [Non-application of ss.99, 100] Sections 99 and 100 do not apply where, under section 96 in Chapter III, a members' voluntary winding up has become a creditors' voluntary winding up.

S.97(1)

Chapter IV applies in every voluntary winding up where the directors do not make a statutory declaration of solvency under s.89(1).

A creditors' voluntary winding up is a "collective insolvency proceeding" within the scope of the EU Regulation: see the note to the Regulation art.1(1). In order to secure recognition of the winding up in other EU Member States, a certificate of confirmation must be obtained from the court: see Annex A of the Regulation and IR 2016 rr.21.4 et seq.

S.97(2)

See the note to s.96, above.

98 Meeting of creditors [Repealed]

General Note

Section 98 repealed by SBEEA 2015 Sch.9 paras 1, 22 as from 6 April 2017.

99 Directors to lay statement of affairs before creditors

99(1) [Duty of directors] The directors of the company must, before the end of the period of 7 days beginning with the day after the day on which the company passes a resolution for voluntary winding up–

(a) make out a statement in the prescribed form as to the affairs of the company, and

(b) send the statement to the company's creditors.

99(2) [Contents of statement] The statement as to the affairs of the company shall show–

(a) particulars of the company's assets, debts and liabilities;

(b) the names and addresses of the company's creditors;

(c) the securities held by them respectively;

(d) the dates when the securities were respectively given; and

(e) such further or other information as may be prescribed.

99(2A) [Verification of statement of affairs by directors] The statement as to the affairs of the company shall be verified by some or all of the directors–

(a) in the case of a winding up of a company registered in England and Wales, by a statement of truth; and

(b) in the case of a winding up of a company registered in Scotland, by affidavit.

99(3) [Penalty for non-compliance] If the directors without reasonable excuse fail to comply with subsection (1), (2) or (2A), they are guilty of an offence and liable to a fine.

General Note

Section 99(1), (3) substituted by SBEEA 2015 Sch.9 paras 1, 23 as from 6 April 2017.

By this provision the Act imposes an obligation on those who have had control of an insolvent company to make full disclosure of its affairs in a creditors' voluntary winding up. The "statement of affairs" is called for in other situations: for detailed discussion, see the note to s.131.

Section 99(2), (3) was amended and s.99(2A) inserted by LRO 2010 (SI 2010/18) art.5(3) as from 6 April 2010 (with retrospective effect).

For the relevant rules, see IR 2016 rr.6.3 et seq.

S.99(3)
On penalties, see s.430 and Sch.10.

100 Appointment of liquidator

100(1) [Nomination by company] The company may nominate a person to be liquidator at the company meeting at which the resolution for voluntary winding up is passed.

100(1A) [Nomination by creditors] The company's creditors may in accordance with the rules nominate a person to be liquidator.

100(1B) [Directors to seek nomination from creditors] The directors of the company must in accordance with the rules seek such a nomination from the company's creditors.

100(2) [Person who is liquidator] The liquidator shall be the person nominated by the creditors or, where no person has been so nominated, the person (if any) nominated by the company.

100(3) [Where different persons nominated] In the case of different persons being nominated, any director, member or creditor of the company may, within 7 days after the date on which the nomination was made by the creditors, apply to the court for an order either–

(a) directing that the person nominated as liquidator by the company shall be liquidator instead of or jointly with the person nominated by the creditors, or

(b) appointing some other person to be liquidator instead of the person nominated by the creditors.

General Note

Section 100(1)–(1B) substituted by SBEEA 2015 Sch.9 paras 1, 24 as from 6 April 2017.

Although the section uses the word "nominate" rather than "appoint", the nomination is immediately effective in that nothing more is needed to empower the person so chosen to act.

The person nominated must be qualified to act in relation to the company as an insolvency practitioner: see ss.388, 389. A liquidator appointed under this section is not an officer of the court: *Re T H Knitwear (Wholesale) Ltd* [1988] Ch. 275; (1988) 4 B.C.C. 102.

For the relevant rules, see IR 2016 rr.6.20 et seq., 7.53 et seq.; and in regard to the liquidator's remuneration, rr.18.16 et seq.

Note prospective insertion of new s.100(4) by EA 2002 s.248 and Sch.17 para.14. The holder of a "qualifying" floating charge (for definition, see Sch.B1 para.14(2)–(3)) is to be given the power to select the liquidator unless the court thinks the circumstances exceptional.

101 Appointment of liquidation committee

101(1) [Creditors may appoint committee] The creditors may in accordance with the rules appoint a committee ("the liquidation committee") of not more than 5 persons to exercise the functions conferred on it by or under this Act.

101(2) [Members appointed by company] If such a committee is appointed, the company may, either at the meeting at which the resolution for voluntary winding up is passed or at any time subsequently in general meeting, appoint such number of persons as they think fit to act as members of the committee, not exceeding 5.

101(3) [Creditors may object to members appointed by company] However, the creditors may, if they think fit, decide that all or any of the persons so appointed by the company ought not to be members of the liquidation committee; and if the creditors so decide–

(a) the persons mentioned in the resolution are not then, unless the court otherwise directs, qualified to act as members of the committee; and

(b) on any application to the court under this provision the court may, if it thinks fit, appoint other persons to act as such members in place of those persons.

101(4) [Scotland] In Scotland, the liquidation committee has, in addition to the powers and duties conferred and imposed on it by this Act, such of the powers and duties of commissioners on a bankrupt estate as may be conferred and imposed on liquidation committees by the rules.

General Note

Section 101(1) substituted by SBEEA 2015 Sch.9 paras 1, 25 as from 6 April 2017.

Provision is made for comparable committees by s.26 and Sch.B1 para.57 (administration), ss.49, 68 (administrative receivership) and ss.141, 142 (winding up by the court).

S.101(1)

In addition to the functions conferred on the liquidation committee by the Act itself (see, e.g. s.103), further provisions about its functions, membership and proceedings are contained in the rules: see IR 2016 rr.17.3 et seq.

102 Creditors' meeting where winding up converted under s.96 [Repealed]

General Note

Section 102 repealed by SBEEA 2015 Sch.9 paras 1, 26 as from 6 April 2017.

103 Cesser of directors' powers

103 On the appointment of a liquidator, all the powers of the directors cease, except so far as the liquidation committee (or, if there is no such committee, the creditors) sanction their continuance.

General Note

The appointment of a liquidator does not operate of itself to remove the directors from office: see the note to s.91(2).

104 Vacancy in office of liquidator

104 If a vacancy occurs, by death, resignation or otherwise, in the office of a liquidator (other than a liquidator appointed by, or by the direction of, the court), the creditors may fill the vacancy.

General Note

Where the appointment of the previous liquidator was made by or under a court order (see s.100(3)), it appears that a further application to the court is required to fill the vacancy.

104A Progress report to company and creditors (England and Wales)

104A(1) [Duty of liquidator] Where the company is registered in England and Wales the liquidator must–

(a) for each prescribed period produce a progress report relating to the prescribed matters; and

(b) within such period commencing with the end of the period referred to in paragraph (a) as may be prescribed send a copy of the progress report to–

(i) the members and creditors, other than opted-out creditors of the company; and

(ii) such other persons as may be prescribed.

104A(2) [Penalty] A liquidator who fails to comply with this section is liable to a fine.

General Note

Section 104A was inserted by LRO 2010 (SI 2010/18) art.5(3) from 6 April 2010. Heading and s.104A(1) amended by SBEEA 2015 s.136(3) as from 26 May 2015. The requirement to hold annual meetings was removed (in England and Wales) by the amendment of s.105. This coincides with the introduction of a provision for the liquidator in that jurisdiction to produce annual progress reports, corresponding to the similar obligation for administrations (where, however, the intervals are six-monthly). For the prescribed matters, see IR 2016 rr.18.3 et seq.

105 Meetings of company and creditors at each year's end (Scotland)

105(1) [Liquidator to summon meetings] If the winding up of a company registered in Scotland continues for more than one year, the liquidator shall summon a general meeting of the company and a meeting of the creditors at the end of the first year from the commencement of the winding up, and of each succeeding year, or at the first convenient date within 3 months from the end of the year or such longer period as the Secretary of State may allow.

105(2) [Liquidator to lay account] The liquidator shall lay before each of the meetings an account of his acts and dealings and of the conduct of the winding up during the preceding year.

105(3) [Penalty for non-compliance] If the liquidator fails to comply with this section, he is liable to a fine.

105(4) [Qualification to requirement] Where under section 96 a members' voluntary winding up has become a creditors' voluntary winding up, and the liquidator sends a statement of affairs to the company's creditors under section 95(1A)(b) 3 months or less before the end of the first year from the commencement of the winding up, the liquidator is not required by this section to summon a meeting of creditors at the end of that year.

General Note

This section now applies in Scotland only, following amendments made by LRO 2010 (SI 2010/18) art.6(4) as from 6 April 2010. There is no longer a requirement to hold AGMs in England and Wales. See the note to s.104A.

S.105(1)
The corresponding provision in the case of a members' voluntary winding up is s.93; under that section, however, the liquidator is required to report only to the members.

S.105(3)
On penalties, see s.430 and Sch.10.

S.105(4)
This subsection is linked with the procedure prescribed by ss.95, 96 for the situation when a company in a members' voluntary winding up proves to be insolvent. In that case, a creditors' meeting will have been held quite recently, under s.95(2), and there would be little point in summoning a second one so soon afterwards. A general meeting of the company under s.105(1) must, however, still be convened.

106 Final account prior to dissolution

106(1) [Liquidator's account of winding up] As soon as the company's affairs are fully wound up the liquidator must make up an account of the winding up, showing how it has been conducted and the company's property has been disposed of.

106(2) [Duty of liquidator re copy account, etc.] The liquidator must, before the end of the period of 14 days beginning with the day on which the account is made up–

(a) send a copy of the account to the company's members,

(b) send a copy of the account to the company's creditors (other than opted-out creditors), and

(c) give the company's creditors (other than opted-out creditors) a notice explaining the effect of section 173(2)(e) and how they may object to the liquidator's release.

106(3) [Copy account to register of companies and objection to release] The liquidator must during the relevant period send to the registrar of companies–

(a) a copy of the account, and

(b) a statement of whether any of the company's creditors objected to the liquidator's release.

106(4) [Relevant period in s.106(3)] The relevant period is the period of 7 days beginning with the day after the last day of the period prescribed by the rules as the period within which the creditors may object to the liquidator's release.

106(4A) [Application of s.106(4B)] Subsection (4B) applies where, immediately before the liquidator sends a copy of the account of the winding up to the registrar under subsection (3), there are EU insolvency proceedings open in respect of the company in one or more other member States.

106(4B) [Duty of liquidator to send statement to registrar] The liquidator must send to the registrar, with the copy of the account, a statement–

(a) identifying those proceedings,

(b) identifying the member State liquidator appointed in each of those proceedings, and

(c) indicating, in relation to each of those member State liquidators, whether that member State liquidator consents to the company being dissolved.

106(5) [Penalty for non-compliance with s.106(2)] If the liquidator does not comply with subsection (2) the liquidator is liable to a fine.

106(6) [Penalty for non-compliance with s.106(3] If the liquidator does not comply with subsection (3) the liquidator is liable to a fine and, for continued contravention, a daily default fine.

106(7) [Scotland: application of s.106(8)] Subsection (8) applies where, immediately before the liquidator sends a copy of the account of the winding up to the registrar under subsection (3), there are EU insolvency proceedings open in respect of the company in one or more other member States.

106(8) [Scotland: duty of liquidator to send statement to registrar] The liquidator must send to the registrar, with the copy of the account, a statement–

(a) identifying those proceedings,

(b) identifying the member State liquidator appointed in each of those proceedings, and

(c) indicating, in relation to each of those member State liquidators, whether that member State liquidator consents to the company being dissolved.

General Note

Section 106 substituted by SBEEA 2015 Sch.9 paras 1, 29 as from 6 April 2017.

The affairs of a company may be "fully wound up" even though the company continues to hold property, if the liquidator has done all that he can do to wind up the company: *Re Wilmott Trading Ltd* [2000] B.C.C. 321. The property in that case was a waste management licence. Neuberger J held that on the subsequent dissolution of the company the licence would cease to exist.

For the relevant rules, see IR 2016 rr.6.28, 18.14.

On penalties, see s.430 and Sch.10.

Section 106(4A), (4B) inserted by the Insolvency Amendment (EU 2015/848) Regulations 2017 (SI 2017/702) regs 1, 2, Sch. paras 1, 3 in relation to proceedings opened in England and Wales on or after 26 June 2017 (see reg.3) when the Recast EU Regulation 2015/848 came into force.

Section 106(7), (8) inserted in relation to Scotland only by the Insolvency Amendment (EU 2015/848) Regulations 2017 (SI 2017/702) regs 1, 2(2)(b), Sch. paras 55, 56 in relation to proceedings opened on or after 26 June 2017 (see reg.3) when the Recast EU Regulation 2015/848 came into force.

Chapter V

Provisions Applying to both kinds of Voluntary Winding Up

107 Distribution of company's property

107 Subject to the provisions of this Act as to preferential payments, the company's property in a voluntary winding up shall on the winding up be applied in satisfaction of the company's liabilities pari passu and, subject to that application, shall (unless the articles otherwise provide) be distributed among the members according to their rights and interests in the company.

General Note

This section refers to "preferential payments", and not merely to "preferential debts", and thus includes, e.g. the expenses of the winding up (including the liquidator's remuneration) which are given priority by s.115, as well as the preferential debts defined by ss.386, 387.

The company's "property" or "assets" which it is the liquidator's duty to get in and apply under this section (and, in a compulsory liquidation, s.144) is property which is beneficially owned by the company (although where the company holds property on trust, it may also be the duty of the liquidator to see to the due administration of the trust: see the *Berkeley Applegate* cases, discussed in the note to s.115, below). Property which the company does not own beneficially does not form part of the insolvent estate (see, e.g. *Re Global Trader Europe Ltd* [2009] EWHC 602 (Ch); [2010] B.C.C. 729; compare *Re MF Global UK Ltd* [2013] EWHC 92 (Ch); further proceedings [2013] EWHC 1655 (Ch); [2013] 2 B.C.L.C. 426). Similarly, it is not caught by a floating charge in a receivership. In a number of cases (of which the best known are perhaps *Barclays Bank Ltd v Quistclose Investments Ltd* [1970] A.C. 567; *Re Kayford Ltd* [1975] 1 W.L.R. 279; *Chase Manhattan Bank NA v Israel–British Bank (London) Ltd* [1979] 3 All E.R. 1025; and *Carreras Rothmans Ltd v Freeman Matthews Treasure Ltd* [1985] 1 All E.R. 155), sums which might have been thought to be recoverable from the company as a debt or in other common-law proceedings have been held to be subject to a trust in the company's hands, with the consequence that the party beneficially entitled could claim the sum in full rather than be obliged to prove as a creditor. Cases applying these precedents include *Re Japan Leasing (Europe) plc* [1999] B.P.I.R. 911 (since doubted in *Re D&D Wines International Ltd* (below)); *Re Niagara Mechanical Services International Ltd* [2001] B.C.C. 393; *Twinsectra Ltd v Yardley* [2002] UKHL 12; [2002] 2 A.C. 164; and *Re Margaretta Ltd* [2005] EWHC 582 (Ch); [2005] B.C.C. 506. See also *Re Farepak Food and Gifts Ltd* [2006] EWHC 3272 (Ch); [2008] B.C.C. 22; further proceedings *Re Farepak Food and Gifts Ltd (No.2)* [2009] EWHC 2580 (Ch); [2010] B.C.C. 735; *Cooper v PRG Powerhouse Ltd* [2008] EWHC 498 (Ch); [2008] B.C.C. 588. See also *Re Lehman Brothers International (Europe)* [2009] EWCA Civ 1161; [2010] B.C.C. 272; *Re Lehman Brothers International (Europe) (No.2)* [2010] EWCA Civ 917; [2011] 2 B.C.L.C. 184; *Re Lehman Brothers International (Europe), CRC Credit Fund Ltd v GLG Investments plc* [2010] EWCA Civ 917, affirmed on appeal [2012] UKSC 6; [2012] 3 All E.R. 1; [2012] 1 B.C.L.C. 487; *Pearson v Lehman Brothers Finance SA* [2010] EWHC 2914 (Ch); *Brazzill v Willoughby* [2010] EWCA Civ 561; [2010] 2 B.C.L.C. 259 (administration; statutory trust); *Re Equilift Ltd* [2009] EWHC 3104 (Ch); [2010] B.C.C. 860; *Mundy v Brown* [2011] EWHC 377 (Ch); *Re Acal Underwriting* (unreported, 31 July 2013); *Bestrustees plc v Kaupthing Singer & Friedlander Ltd* [2013] EWHC 2407 (Ch); *Green v Eltai* [2015] B.P.I.R. 24; *Re Crown Holdings (London) Ltd* [2015] EWHC 1876 (Ch) (implied trust based on unconscionable receipt (criticised by N. Segal (2016) 29 Insolv. Int. 27)), and contrast *Re BA Peters plc* [2008] EWCA Civ 1604; [2010] 1 B.C.L.C. 142; *Tradegro (UK) Ltd v Wigmore Street Investments Ltd* [2011] EWCA Civ 268; [2011] 2 B.C.L.C. 616; *Re Wedgwood Museum Trust Ltd* [2011] EWHC 3782 (Ch); [2013] B.C.C. 281; *Bieber v Teathers Ltd* [2012] EWCA Civ 1466; *Re D&D Wines International Ltd* [2014] EWCA Civ 215; [2014] 2 B.C.L.C. 129, where the existence of a trust was not established (upheld by the Supreme Court on this point *Bailey v Angove's Pty Ltd* [2016] UKSC 47; [2016] B.C.C. 594). See Kelly [2017] 30 Insolv. Int. 29.

The equitable concepts which were applied in the cases above are not recognised in Scots law: *Clark and Whitehouse, Noters* [2012] CSOH 55.

Note however that an arrangement which is in form a trust may risk being categorised as a floating charge (and accordingly void if unregistered) if the company retains a degree of control over the property affected: *Gray v G-T-P Ltd* [2010] EWHC 1772 (Ch); [2011] B.C.C. 869.

Corresponding issues may arise in an administration: indeed, some of the cases cited above were concerned with the question whether particular assets in the hands of a company fell into the estate for the purposes of an administration.

The order of application of the assets in the hands of the liquidator will be:

(1) the expenses of the winding up, including the liquidator's remuneration (s.115);

(2) the preferential debts, as defined by ss.386, 387 and Sch.6 (s.175);

(3) any preferential charge on goods distrained that arises under s.176(3);

(4) the company's general creditors;

(5) any debts or other sums due from the company to its members qua members (s.74(2)(f));

(6) the members generally, in accordance with their respective rights and interests (s.107).

Secured creditors will, in principle, be entitled to be paid out of the proceeds of their security (so far as it extends) ahead of all other claims. However, where the security is by way of floating charge, the debts which are preferential debts in the liquidation must be paid first (s.175(2)(b)) and, where s.176A applies, the unsecured creditors will rank ahead of the charge holder in respect of the "prescribed part": see the note to that section. In *Re Leyland DAF Ltd, Buchler v Talbot* [2004] UKHL 9; [2004] 2 A.C. 298; [2004] B.C.C. 214 the House of Lords held that a liquidator was not entitled to claim his expenses in priority to the rights of the holder of a floating charge, and that it was immaterial whether or not the charge had crystallised before the commencement of the liquidation. This overruled the decision in *Re Barleycorn Enterprises Ltd* [1970] Ch. 465, which had been followed in a number of cases including *Re Portbase Clothing Ltd, Mond v Taylor* [1993] Ch. 388; [1993] B.C.C. 96. However, the ruling in *Leyland DAF* has since been reversed by statute: see CA 2006 s.1282, inserting new s.176ZA into IA 1986 with effect from 6 April 2008. See the notes to s.176ZA and rr.6.44–6.48.

The statutory order for the application of assets may not be varied by contractual arrangements between the parties concerned, such as a pooling or clearing-house arrangement: *British Eagle International Air Lines Ltd v Cie Nationale Air France* [1975] 1 W.L.R. 758. A pooling arrangement may, however, be structured in a way which does not breach this principle: *North Atlantic Insurance Co Ltd v Nationwide General Insurance Co* [2004] EWCA Civ 423; [2004] 2 All E.R. (Comm) 351. Note that the *British Eagle* case has not been followed, on similar facts, by the High Court of Australia: *International Air Transport Association v Ansett Australia Holdings Ltd* [2008] HCA 3; [2008] B.P.I.R. 57.

The rule in the *British Eagle* case is part of a wider principle, which declares it to be against public policy to displace the insolvency laws by any provision in a contract or other transaction inter partes, e.g. by a term that in the event of one party's bankruptcy a specified asset should become the property of the other (*Ex p. Mackay* (1873) L.R. 8 Ch. App. 643), or by a purported redemption of shares in a company in liquidation by way of a set-off against a judgment debt (*Hague v Nam Tai Electronics Inc* [2006] UKPC 52; [2007] 2 B.C.L.C. 194). But in *Money Markets International Stockbrokers Ltd v London Stock Exchange Ltd* [2001] 2 B.C.L.C. 347 it was held that this principle (commonly known as the "anti-deprivation rule") was not infringed where the rules of a mutual company provided that a member's share should be transferred to a trustee without consideration on his ceasing to be a member, and the member's insolvency was an event leading to the termination of his membership. The share in these circumstances was not a free-standing asset but merely something incidental to his membership rights. The principle in *Ex p. Mackay* was held to apply in *Fraser v Oystertec plc* [2003] EWHC 2787 (Ch); [2004] B.C.C. 233 to an agreement which provided that, in the event of its insolvency, legal ownership of a patent held by a company should pass to a named individual. It was held that such a "divestiture" provision was not merely void as against the company's creditors in any insolvency proceedings which might ensue, but totally void. See also *Folgate London Market Ltd v Chaucer Insurance plc* [2011] EWCA Civ 328; [2011] B.C.C. 675 (clause in agreement purporting to release party from payment obligation, where the principle was applied in favour of an assignee). Contrast *Belmont Park Investments Pty Ltd v BNY Corporate Trustee Services Ltd* [2011] UKSC 38; [2012] 1 A.C. 383; [2011] B.C.C. 734, where a security document provided that monies received by the trustee of the collateral in connection its realisation or enforcement of the security should be applied in a specified order of priority unless an event of default (which included the liquidation of the company concerned) should occur, in which case the defaulting party was to lose its priority. This was construed as the grant of a limited and conditional interest in the property which continued only for so long as the latter party was not in default, and not as a divestiture provision prohibited under the *British Eagle* principle. The Supreme Court held that commercial sense and an absence of intention to evade insolvency laws were highly relevant factors in the application of the rule, and contractual provisions in a complex commercial transaction which had been entered into in good faith should not be invalidated. A plea that the anti-deprivation rule should be reconsidered and discarded altogether was rejected. A similar ruling upholding the transaction was given in *Lomas v JFB Firth Rixson Inc* [2012] EWCA Civ 419; [2013] 1 B.C.L.C. 27 (payment obligations under interest rate swap agreement expressed to be conditional on no "continuing event of default" (defined as including administration)).

The latter two cases and the *British Eagle* principle were considered in the context of the "football creditor" rule in *Revenue & Customs Commissioners v Football League Ltd* [2012] EWHC 1372 (Ch); [2013] B.C.C. 60; [2012] B.P.I.R. 686. Under the articles of association of the Football League, if a company in the League entered administration its membership would be suspended and would be renewed only if debts owing to "football creditors" (i.e. other clubs, players and various football authorities and associations) were paid in full, and the club would be paid it share of receipts from TV rights etc. from the league only if it completed the season. David Richards J held that, on the proceedings in issue before him, the football creditor rule was not in breach of the pari passu principle or anti-deprivation rule. This was because the pari passu principle applied only where a purpose of the insolvency procedure was to effect a distribution and did not apply until the administrator had given notice of a proposed distribution: in a typical case, the provisions of the articles relevant to football creditors would have taken effect at an earlier stage. The purpose of the anti-deprivation rule was to prevent insolvency proceedings from being undermined by dispositions of assets designed to avoid the effects of the proceedings: administration was as much a proceeding for the benefit of creditors as liquidation and would be equally hampered or frustrated by dispositions designed to avoid the administration process, so that the anti-deprivation rule applied when a company went into administration as it did when a company went into liquidation. The Football League's articles made the legal entitlement to payments conditional and the court could not disregard the legal rights and obligations created by the articles, even if they had been drafted to achieve a particular end. If a club had no legal entitlement to payments from the Football League until it had completed the season, it was not deprived of an asset if, as a result of going into administration or liquidation, it could not complete the season. Likewise, there was no asset of the club to which the pari passu principle could be applied. The league's power to require the transfer of a member's share, if it went into administration or liquidation, was not void by reason of the anti-deprivation rule. See further Fletcher (2013) 26 Insolv. Int. 49. (Note that the Football League's rules now provide that a purchaser from the administrator of a club company must make prescribed payments to the club's creditors within a prescribed period, but this does not affect the football creditors' rule so far as the club itself is concerned.)

There are legitimate ways by which creditors of a company may agree that in the event of an insolvency some debts should be subordinated to others, without infringing the principle of the *British Eagle* case, by (for instance) incorporating an undertaking not to prove in respect of the "postponed" debts, and/or a declaration that any moneys received towards payment of such debts should be held on trust for the creditor or creditors having priority, until the latter have been paid in full: *Re SSSL Realisations (2002) Ltd* [2006] EWCA Civ 7; [2006] Ch. 610; [2006] B.C.C. 233. In relation to the priority of repayments involving statutory interest where there are postponed creditors, see the note to s.189.

Moreover, it should be noted that both CA 1989 Pt VII and the Finality Regulations remove various arrangements and transactions altogether from the scope of the insolvency legislation, and specifically disapply particular provisions of the latter legislation in relation to market transactions or payment or settlement systems which come within their ambit. (See also the Financial Collateral Arrangements (No.2) Regulations 2003 (SI 2003/3226), and note the general reversal of the *British Eagle* principle in the Finality Regulations reg.14.) The impact of these provisions is noted at the relevant places in this *Guide*.

Special regimes are made to apply in particular cases by other legislation, e.g. as regards insurance companies (Insurers (Reorganisation and Winding Up) Regulations 2004 (SI 2004/353)) and the "owner" of regulated covered bonds (Regulated Covered Bonds Regulations 2008 (SI 2008/346)).

Property subject to a restraint order or other order under POCA 2002 is also excluded from the assets available for distribution by the liquidator: see s.426 of that Act. But once the company is in liquidation, the powers under the 2002 Act may not be exercised in relation to property which belonged to the company at the time when it went into liquidation (see s.426(4)–(6), (9)).

A creditor or contributory has no legal or equitable interest in the property of the company held by the liquidator, but only a right to have the assets duly administered by him: *Banque Nationelle de Paris plc v Montman Ltd* [2000] 1 B.C.L.C. 576.

There has for several years been some concern that the law may make insufficient protection for customers (and particularly consumers) who make prepayments for the supply of goods and services by a company which goes into insolvency without having fulfilled the order. In consequence, the Law Commission on 18 June 2015 sought comments on proposals for the reform of the law, possibly including limited amendments to insolvency law and the increased use of trust accounts. In July 2016 the Commission published a final report, *Consumer Prepayments on Retailer Insolvency* (Law Com. No.368), in which it makes a number of recommendations for improvements in the law and business practice, but only relatively minor reforms to insolvency law, limited to small prepayments. See Akintola [2018] J.B.L. 1.

Provision is made for the proof and payment of debts by IR 2016 rr.14.3 et seq. and 14.27 et seq.

108 Appointment or removal of liquidator by the court

108(1) [If no liquidator acting] If from any cause whatever there is no liquidator acting, the court may appoint a liquidator.

108(2) [Removal, replacement] The court may, on cause shown, remove a liquidator and appoint another.

General Note

The power of the court supplements the power of the members under s.92 (members' voluntary winding up) and that of the creditors under s.104 (creditors' voluntary winding up) to fill any such vacancy themselves. A liquidator once appointed, however, may be removed only by the court "on cause shown" under s.108(2). The case of *Re Keypak Homecare Ltd* (1987) 3 B.C.C. 558 contains a useful review of the principles upon which the court will act in exercising its power to remove a liquidator under s.108(2). In *Re Bridgend Goldsmiths Ltd* [1995] B.C.C. 226 the court exercised its powers under s.108(1) to appoint a new liquidator when the previous liquidator had ceased to be qualified to act as an insolvency practitioner. An application to remove liquidators was refused in *AMP Music Box Enterprises Ltd v Hoffman* [2002] EWHC 1899 (Ch); [2002] B.C.C. 996, where their conduct had, in the past, been open to the criticism that they had not pursued certain claims very actively but the court considered that they had more recently given the matter more attention. Other cases illustrating the exercise of the court's discretion include *Fielding v Seery* [2004] B.C.C. 315; *Re Buildlead Ltd (No.2)* [2004] EWHC 2443 (Ch); [2005] B.C.C. 138; *Sisu Capital Fund Ltd v Tucker* [2005] EWHC 2170 and 2321 (Ch); [2006] B.C.C. 463; [2006] B.P.I.R. 154 and *Re York Gas Ltd* [2010] EWHC 2275 (Ch); [2011] B.C.C. 447 (appointment of additional liquidator); *Hobbs v Gibson* [2010] EWHC 3676 (Ch); *Beattie v Smailes* [2011] EWHC 1563 (Ch); [2012] B.C.C. 205 (conflict of interest).

In *Re Sankey Furniture Ltd Ex p. Harding* [1995] 2 B.C.L.C. 594 the court declined to use its power under s.108(2) to remove a liquidator (who wished to resign) where this would by-pass the statutory requirement that a meeting of creditors be called to consider whether or not to accept the resignation: the fact that this would save the expense of a meeting was not sufficient to justify the court intervening in a matter which was for the creditors to decide. However, it is now well established that where an insolvency practitioner seeks to resign from multiple offices and be replaced (usually by other members of the same firm), the court is willing to make orders without these statutory formalities: see the note to s.172(1), (2).

An application may be made under s.108 by anyone whom the court considers proper, e.g. a former liquidator who has ceased to be qualified to act in relation to the company (*Re A J Adams (Builders) Ltd* [1991] B.C.C. 62) or the recognised professional body of which such a person was once a member (*Re Stella Metals Ltd (in liq.)* [1997] B.C.C. 626). But the court will not remove the liquidator of an insolvent company on the application of a contributory: *Deloitte & Touche AG v Johnson* [1999] B.C.C. 992.

Save in very exceptional cases, notice of the application should be given to the liquidator whom it is sought to remove, in order to give him an opportunity to be heard: *Clements v Udal* [2001] B.C.C. 658.

For the relevant rules, see IR 2016 rr.5.4, 6.22, 7.56 (appointment), 5.7, 6.27, 7.65 (removal).

109 Notice by liquidator of his appointment

109(1) [Notice in Gazette and to registrar] The liquidator shall, within 14 days after his appointment, publish in the Gazette and deliver to the registrar of companies for registration a notice of his appointment in the form prescribed by statutory instrument made by the Secretary of State.

109(2) [Penalty on default] If the liquidator fails to comply with this section, he is liable to a fine and, for continued contravention, to a daily default fine.

S.109(1)

The duty of the liquidator to give notice of his appointment under this section is additional to his duty to notify creditors under IR 2016 rr.6.22 et seq. and also to the obligation imposed by s.85 on the company and its officers (including the liquidator) to notify the passing of the resolution for voluntary winding up by advertisement in the *Gazette*. Further advertising and registration requirements are imposed by r.7.59.

The gazetting of the liquidator's appointment under this section constitutes an "official notification" of the event for the purposes of CA 2006 ss.1077–1079. If there has not been an official notification, or (in some circumstances) if the official notification is less than 15 days old, s.1079(1) provides that the company "is not entitled to rely against other persons on the happening" of the appointment of the liquidator. This provision has its origin in the EC First Company Law Directive; its meaning and effect (so far as English law is concerned) is obscure. What matters under the Act is the fact that the company has gone into liquidation: nothing turns on the appointment of the liquidator, as such.

The Insolvency Service has confirmed that the requirements of s.109 must be followed where a creditors' voluntary liquidation follows an administration under Sch.B1 para.83: see *Dear IP*, March 2006.

S.109(2)
On penalties, see s.430 and Sch.10.

110 Acceptance of shares, etc., as consideration for sale of company property

110(1) [Application] This section applies, in the case of a company proposed to be, or being, wound up voluntarily, where the whole or part of the company's business or property is proposed to be transferred or sold–

(a) to another company ("the transferee company"), whether or not the latter is a company registered under the Companies Act 2006, or

(b) to a limited liability partnership (the "transferee limited liability partnership").

110(2) [Shares etc. in compensation for transfer] With the requisite sanction, the liquidator of the company being, or proposed to be, wound up ("the transferor company") may receive, in compensation or part compensation for the transfer or sale–

(a) in the case of the transferee company, shares, policies or other like interests in the transferee company for distribution among the members of the transferor company, or

(b) in the case of the transferee limited liability partnership, membership in the transferee limited liability partnership for distribution among the members of the transferor company.

110(3) [Sanction for s.110(2)] The sanction requisite under subsection (2) is–

(a) in the case of a members' voluntary winding up, that of a special resolution of the company, conferring either a general authority on the liquidator or an authority in respect of any particular arrangement, and

(b) in the case of a creditors' voluntary winding up, that of either the court or the liquidation committee.

110(4) [Alternative to s.110(2)] Alternatively to subsection (2), the liquidator may (with that sanction) enter into any other arrangement whereby the members of the transferor company may–

(a) in the case of the transferee company, in lieu of receiving cash, shares, policies or other like interests (or in addition thereto) participate in the profits of, or receive any other benefit from, the transferee company, or

(b) in the case of the transferee limited liability partnership, in lieu of receiving cash or membership (or in addition thereto), participate in some other way in the profits of, or receive any other benefit from, the transferee limited liability partnership.

110(5) [Sale binding on transferors] A sale or arrangement in pursuance of this section is binding on members of the transferor company.

110(6) [Special resolution] A special resolution is not invalid for purposes of this section by reason that it is passed before or concurrently with a resolution for voluntary winding up or for appointing liquidators; but, if an order is made within a year for winding up the company by the court, the special resolution is not valid unless sanctioned by the court.

General Note

This section deals with a corporate "reconstruction", under which the whole or part of the business of a company in liquidation is sold by the liquidator to another company or limited liability partnership and the members of the first company agree to accept shares or other securities in the purchasing company instead of the cash distribution to which they would normally be entitled. Provided that the sanction referred to in s.110(3) is obtained, the scheme is binding on all the members except those who dissent in writing under s.111(1).

Rule 18.11 requires a liquidator who makes a distribution in specie to members in a reconstruction under s.110 to give specified details of the basis of the valuation of the property concerned, in progress reports and in his reports to members and creditors at final meetings and any meeting to receive a liquidator's resignation.

Subsections (1), (2) and (4) were amended by the Limited Liability Partnerships Regulations 2001 (SI 2001/1090, effective 6 April 2001) to make possible the use of a limited liability partnership as the transferee.

S.110(1)

For the definition of "company" referred to, see CA 2006 ss.1(1) and 1171, and the note to s.73 above. The "transferee company" may be a company outside this definition—e.g. a company incorporated overseas.

S.110(2), (4)

The consideration which the members agree to accept normally consists of or includes shares in the transferee company, or corresponding interests in an LLP, but it may take other forms.

S.110(3)

The consolidation has introduced an ambiguity into the section by running together two provisions which were formerly stated separately in CA 1985 s.582(2) and s.593. As it stands, para.(b) of the new subsection appears to read as an *alternative* to para.(a), but it should be an *additional* requirement; i.e. in a members' voluntary winding up, only the sanction in para.(a) is needed, but in a creditors' winding up, *both* para.(a) and para.(b) apply. If this were not so, the members could be obliged to accept shares without their consent, and s.111 would not apply at all!

S.110(5)

This should be read subject to the right of a member to dissent under s.111. In fact, although the arrangement may be "binding" under this provision, in the sense that a dissenting member cannot prevent the deal from going ahead, nothing can oblige him to become a member of the transferee company without his consent. It is necessary in practice therefore for a scheme of reconstruction to make express provision for recalcitrant but inactive shareholders, e.g. by creating a trust to hold the new shares on their behalf.

S.110(6)

The sanction of the court is not required before the liquidator puts a scheme of reconstruction into effect.

111 Dissent from arrangement under s.110

111(1) [Application] This section applies in the case of a voluntary winding up where, for the purposes of section 110(2) or (4), there has been passed a special resolution of the transferor company providing the sanction requisite for the liquidator under that section.

111(2) [Objections by members of transferor company] If a member of the transferor company who did not vote in favour of the special resolution expresses his dissent from it in writing, addressed to the liquidator and left at the company's registered office within 7 days after the passing of the resolution, he may require the liquidator either to abstain from carrying the resolution into effect or to purchase his interest at a price to be determined by agreement or by arbitration under this section.

111(3) [Where liquidator purchases member's interest] If the liquidator elects to purchase the member's interest, the purchase money must be paid before the company is dissolved and be raised by the liquidator in such manner as may be determined by special resolution.

111(4) [Arbitration] For purposes of an arbitration under this section, the provisions of the Companies Clauses Consolidation Act 1845 or, in the case of a winding up in Scotland, the Companies Clauses Consolidation (Scotland) Act 1845 with respect to the settlement of disputes by arbitration are incorporated with this Act, and–

(a) in the construction of those provisions this Act is deemed the special Act and "the company" means the transferor company, and

(b) any appointment by the incorporated provisions directed to be made under the hand of the secretary or any two of the directors may be made in writing by the liquidator (or, if there is more than one liquidator, then any two or more of them).

General Note

This section confers on a dissenting member the right to have his shareholding in the company bought out in cash, provided that he takes the prompt action prescribed by s.111(2). The notice of dissent and (in the case of a company registered in Scotland) the appointment under s.111(4)(b) must be in hard copy (s.436B(2)(d), (e)).

112 Reference of questions to court

112(1) [Application to court] The liquidator or any contributory or creditor may apply to the court to determine any question arising in the winding up of a company, or to exercise, as respects the enforcing of calls or any other matter, all or any of the powers which the court might exercise if the company were being wound up by the court.

112(2) [Court order] The court, if satisfied that the determination of the question or the required exercise of power will be just and beneficial, may accede wholly or partially to the application on such terms and conditions as it thinks fit, or may make such other order on the application as it thinks just.

112(3) [Copy of order to registrar] A copy of an order made by virtue of this section staying the proceedings in the winding up shall forthwith be forwarded by the company, or otherwise as may be prescribed, to the registrar of companies, who shall enter it in his records relating to the company.

S.112(1), (2)

The powers of the court in a winding up by the court are contained in Chapter VI of this Part, and more specifically in ss.147 et seq.

Where a company is an "authorised person" under FSMA 2000, the Financial Conduct Authority may apply to the court or participate in the proceedings: FSMA 2000 s.365.

S.112(2)

The court's powers are discretionary. It may refuse to permit proceedings under this provision where some other procedure is more appropriate: *Re Stetzel Thomson & Co Ltd* (1988) 4 B.C.C. 74, or when the applicant would not have standing to invoke some other, more appropriate, procedure: *Re James McHale Automobiles Ltd* [1997] B.C.C. 202; *MG Rover Dealer Properties Ltd v Hunt* [2013] B.C.C. 698; [2012] B.P.I.R. 590. Contrast *Autobrokers Ltd v Dymond* [2015] EWHC 2691 (Admin); [2017] B.C.C. 291, where the court backed the creditors' right to requisition a meeting and penalised the liquidators (who resisted the application) in costs. In *Kean v Lucas* [2017] EWHC 250 (Ch); [2017] B.C.C. 13 the court refused an application by a liquidator in a creditors' voluntary liquidation for directions that would have prevented a meeting which the requisite number of creditors sought to vote for the liquidator's removal: the liquidator had failed to satisfy the threshold test that it would be "just and beneficial" to the winding up to restrain the removal meeting. However the court confirmed, in *Re Central A1 Ltd; Rubin v Cohen* [2017] EWHC 220 (Ch); [2017] B.C.C. 69, that it had jurisdiction on an application for directions to determine a dispute as to reasonableness or necessity regarding fixed fees charged by accountants for work undertaken in relation to statements of affairs and meetings of creditors of a large number of companies to enable them to be placed into creditors' voluntary liquidation. It is not a complete bar to the exercise of discretion that the applicant is using the procedure to obtain a collateral advantage: *Re Movitex Ltd* [1992] B.C.C. 101. In *Re Sustainable Wealth Investments (UK) Ltd* [2015] EWHC 1674 (Ch) the court ordered pre-action disclosure under s.112 of a settlement agreement by a company, now in liquidation, to facilitate a tracing claim against it, but refused to order disclosure of various other documents. The court's powers under this section were invoked to make various orders facilitating co-operation under the CBIR between the provisional liquidators in a UK liquidation and the US trustee in bankruptcy of an associated company in *Re Bernard L Madoff Investment Securities LLC* [2009] EWHC 442 (Ch); [2010] B.C.C. 328. See also *Sunwing Vacation Inc v E-Clear (UK) plc* [2011] EWHC 1544 (Ch); [2011] B.C.C. 889.

S.112(3)

No rules appear to have been prescribed for the purposes of this section.

113 Court's power to control proceedings (Scotland)

113 If the court, on the application of the liquidator in the winding up of a company registered in Scotland, so directs, no action or proceeding shall be proceeded with or commenced against the company except by leave of the court and subject to such terms as the court may impose.

114 No liquidator appointed or nominated by company

114(1) [Application] This section applies where, in the case of a voluntary winding up, no liquidator has been appointed or nominated by the company.

114(2) [Limit on exercise of directors' powers] The powers of the directors shall not be exercised, except with the sanction of the court or (in the case of a creditors' voluntary winding up) so far as may be necessary to secure compliance with sections 99 (statement of affairs) and 100(1B) (nomination of liquidator by creditors), during the period before the appointment or nomination of a liquidator of the company.

114(3) [Non-application of s.114(2)] Subsection (2) does not apply in relation to the powers of the directors–

(a) to dispose of perishable goods and other goods the value of which is likely to diminish if they are not immediately disposed of, and

(b) to do all such other things as may be necessary for the protection of the company's assets.

114(4) [Penalty for non-compliance] If the directors of the company without reasonable excuse fail to comply with this section, they are liable to a fine.

General Note

This section is designed as a counter to the practice of "centrebinding" which was condemned as unsatisfactory by the Cork Committee (*Report*, paras 666 et seq.), and should be read in conjunction with the notes to s.166 below. The Committee drew attention to the fact that there was in every voluntary liquidation a period of time during which the directors remained in control of the company but, until the necessary meetings had been convened and a liquidator appointed, the company's assets and the interests of creditors were most inadequately protected. This period could be extended if the appointment of the liquidator was not made at the same time as the passing of the resolution for winding up but deferred until a later occasion. The Committee's recommendation was that a voluntary liquidation should commence as soon as the *directors* had decided that, because of its liabilities, the company could not carry on business, and that they should be obliged immediately to appoint a provisional liquidator who would assume effective control and safeguard the position until the appropriate meeting had made a permanent appointment.

The legislature did not accept this recommendation of the Committee, and so it remains the law that a voluntary winding up commences when the company's special resolution is passed. This section does, however, in part curb the abuse to which the report drew attention, by providing that the directors should have only very limited powers, restricted to the preservation of the company's assets, until a liquidator has been appointed. The weakness of the section is, however, that it operates only *after* the voluntary winding up has commenced: the directors will still be in full control during the period which must elapse while the meeting of the company is being convened.

S.114(1), (2)

In a members' voluntary winding up, the liquidator is appointed by the company in general meeting under s.91. These provisions should ensure that an appointment is made promptly, whereupon the powers of the directors will normally cease (see s.91(2)). Section 114(2) should also encourage the members to nominate a liquidator promptly in the case of a creditors' voluntary winding up. In this event, it may be inferred from the wording of s.166 that, once the company has nominated a liquidator, he automatically takes office and is vested with the powers and duties set out in that section.

S.114(3)

The very limited powers which the directors retain are confined to the disposal of perishable goods and the protection of assets. They will not extend to continuing to manage the business in any general sense. (Note that para.(a) is confined in its scope to *goods*. Other property which may be likely to diminish in value (e.g. shares in a bear market) is not covered by this paragraph, although some actions of the directors in relation to such property may be justified under para.(b).)

S.114(4)

A contract entered into in breach of s.114 would, at least prima facie, be illegal and void. However it is possible that a third party who has dealt with the directors in good faith and without knowledge of the resolution could enforce the transaction on the basis of the directors' ostensible authority: *Re a Company (No.006341 of 1992) Ex p. B Ltd* [1994] 1 B.C.L.C. 225.

On penalties, see s.430 and Sch.10.

115 Expenses of voluntary winding up

115 All expenses properly incurred in the winding up, including the remuneration of the liquidator, are payable out of the company's assets in priority to all other claims.

General Note

The expenses of the winding up rank ahead of the claims of the preferential creditors who are given priority by ss.175, 176.

In the case of a creditors' voluntary winding up (including one which has commenced as a members' winding up but later proves to be insolvent), the order of priority as between the different categories of expenses is set out in IR 2016 rr.6.42, 7.108, but the court has power to vary these general rules by virtue of ss.112(1) and 156 and rr.6.43 and 7.110.

The ruling in *Re Barleycorn Enterprises Ltd* [1970] Ch. 465 (which was followed in a number of cases including *Re Portbase Clothing Ltd, Mond v Taylor* [1993] Ch. 388; [1993] B.C.C. 96) that for the purposes of s.115, the company's "assets" include assets covered by a floating charge, was overruled by the House of Lords in *Re Leyland DAF Ltd, Buchler v Talbot* [2004] UKHL 9; [2004] 2 A.C. 298; [2004] B.C.C. 214, but has since been reinstated by legislation: see s.176ZA, below.

This section does not declare that all expenses properly incurred by a liquidator are payable out of the company's assets, but only that expenses which *are* so payable should have priority to other claims.

In a number of cases, e.g. *Re M C Bacon Ltd (No.2)* [1991] Ch. 127; [1990] B.C.C. 430; *Re RS & M Engineering Co Ltd, Mond v Hammond Suddards (a firm)* [2000] Ch. 40; [2000] B.C.C. 445; and *Re Floor Fourteen Ltd, Lewis v Inland Revenue Commissioner* [2001] 3 All E.R. 449; [2002] B.C.C. 198, it was held that a liquidator's costs in pursuing claims under ss.238 (transaction at an undervalue), 239 (preference), or 214 (wrongful trading), however properly the litigation may have been brought, were not payable out of the company's assets. However, the effect of these rulings has been reversed. Rules 6.42(2), 7.108(2) now specify as expenses of the liquidation expenses or costs which are properly chargeable or incurred by the official receiver or liquidator "relating to the conduct of any legal proceedings which he has power to bring or defend whether in his own name or the name of the company". This puts beyond doubt any contention that such expenses do not fall within s.115. However, damages awarded against a liquidator who, in pursuing such a claim, committed a breach of contract were held not to be "costs of the litigation" in *Re SSSL Realisations (2002) Ltd* [2004] EWHC 1760 (Ch); [2005] 1 B.C.L.C. 1. There was no appeal on this point: see [2006] EWCA Civ 7; [2006] Ch. 610; [2006] B.C.C. 233.

Pre-liquidation expenses, other than those specifically incurred for the purpose of enabling the company to pass the winding-up resolution and take other steps required by statute, cannot ordinarily be claimed under this section: *Re AV Sorge & Co Ltd* (1986) 2 B.C.C. 99306; *Re Sandwell Copiers Ltd* (1988) 4 B.C.C. 227; *Re WF Fearman Ltd (No.2)* (1988) 4 B.C.C. 141.

Corporation tax on post-liquidation profits is payable in priority as a liquidation expense, even if the income in question has not been, and never will be, received: *Kahn v Inland Revenue Commissioners, Re Toshoku Finance (UK) plc* [2002] UKHL 6; [2002] 1 W.L.R. 671; [2002] B.C.C. 110. In the same case it was also held that rates and similar local taxes will also come within the definition of liquidation expenses (at paras 34, 40–41, overruling *Re Kentish Homes Ltd* [1993] B.C.C. 212). Contrast *Re Allders Department Stores Ltd* [2005] EWHC 172 (Ch); [2005] B.C.C. 289 (redundancy payments not "necessary disbursements" in an administration); and see Lyons and Birch (2005) 18 Insolv. Int. 150. In *Re Nortel GmbH, Bloom v Pensions Regulator* [2013] UKSC 52; [2014] A.C. 209; [2013] B.C.C. 624 the Supreme Court, reversing the courts below, held that payments which had been made by the administrators in consequence of a financial support direction by the Pensions Regulator were provable debts ranking pari passu with the companies' unsecured creditors and not administration (or, by analogy, liquidation) expenses (distinguishing *Toshoku*, above). See further the notes to Sch.B1 para.99(3) and rr.3.51 et seq., 6.42, 7.108 and 14.1.

In *Re Berkeley Applegate (Investment Consultants) Ltd (No.2)* (1988) 4 B.C.C. 279, a liquidator had done substantial work in relation to assets in which, after investigation, the company proved to have no beneficial interest.

It was held, in the circumstances, that he was entitled to be paid his proper expenses and remuneration as a charge on those assets, even though they were not "the company's assets" within s.115. (See further *Re Berkeley Applegate (Investment Consultants) Ltd (No.3)* (1989) 5 B.C.C. 803; and compare *Re Eastern Capital Futures Ltd* (1989) 5 B.C.C. 223; *Re Rusjon Ltd* [2007] EWHC 2943 (Ch); [2008] 2 B.C.L.C. 234; *Re MF Global UK Ltd* [2013] EWHC 1655 (Ch); [2013] 1 W.L.R. 3874; [2013] 2 B.C.L.C. 426 (court's inherent jurisdiction to make order relating to distribution of trust assets); *Gillan v HEC Enterprises Ltd* [2016] EWHC 3179 (Ch) (claim disallowed).) The grant of a *Berkeley Applegate* order, and its scope, are matters entirely within the court's discretion: *Green v Bramston* [2010] EWHC 3106 (Ch). Although there is room for doubt whether the *Berkeley Applegate* principle applies in Scotland, in *Joint Liquidators of Direct Sharedeal Ltd, Petitioners* [2013] CSOH 45 an order on similar principles allowing liquidators reasonable remuneration was made.

In relation to the financial markets and securities settlement systems, s.175 has effect subject to the priority accorded to the claim of a participant or central bank to collateral security by the Finality Regulations reg.14(5), (6), unless the terms on which the collateral security was provided expressly state that the expenses, remuneration or preferential debts are to have priority: see the note on p.3.

On the general rules regarding the distribution of assets in a voluntary winding up, see the note to s.107.

116 Saving for certain rights

116 The voluntary winding up of a company does not bar the right of any creditor or contributory to have it wound up by the court; but in the case of an application by a contributory the court must be satisfied that the rights of the contributories will be prejudiced by a voluntary winding up.

General Note

The court has, in any case, a discretion under s.125 to refuse a winding-up order, even where the application is made by a creditor. The wishes of a majority of the company's creditors will be taken into account, but will not be regarded as decisive: see *Re Home Remedies Ltd* [1943] Ch. 1; *Re Southard & Co Ltd* [1979] 1 W.L.R. 1198; *Re Medisco Equipment Ltd* (1983) 1 B.C.C. 98,944. In *Re Internet Investment Corp Ltd* [2009] EWHC 2744 (Ch) a compulsory winding up was ordered on the petition of a contributory, where there was concern whether a liquidator appointed by the majority shareholders in a voluntary winding up would be impartial.

Chapter VI

Winding Up by the Court

Introductory note to Part IV, Chapter VI
Winding up by the court is discussed in Totty, Moss & Segal, *Insolvency*, paras D1–71 et seq.

Jurisdiction (England and Wales)

117 High Court and county court jurisdiction

117(1) [High Court] The High Court has jurisdiction to wind up any company registered in England and Wales.

117(2) [County court] Where in the case of a company registered in England and Wales the amount of its share capital paid up or credited as paid up does not exceed £120,000, then (subject to this section) the county court has concurrent jurisdiction with the High Court to wind up the company.

117(2A) [London cases to be commenced in the High Court] Despite subsection (2), proceedings for the exercise of the jurisdiction to wind up a company registered in England and Wales may be commenced only in the High Court if the place which has longest been the company's registered office during the 6 months immediately preceding the presentation of the petition for winding up is in the district that is the London insolvency district for the purposes of the second Group of Parts of this Act.

117(3) [Increase, reduction of s.117(2) sum] The money sum for the time being specified in subsection (2) is subject to increase or reduction by order under section 416 in Part XV.

117(4) [Omitted]

117(5) [Extent of winding-up jurisdiction] Every court in England and Wales having winding-up jurisdiction has for the purposes of that jurisdiction all the powers of the High Court; and every prescribed officer of the court shall perform any duties which an officer of the High Court may discharge by order of a judge of that court or otherwise in relation to winding up.

117(6) [Omitted]

117(7) [Applicability of EU Regulation] This section is subject to Article 3 of the EU Regulation (jurisdiction under EU Regulation).

117(8) [Nomination of judicial office holder] The Lord Chief Justice may nominate a judicial office holder (as defined in section 109(4) of the Constitutional Reform Act 2005) to exercise his functions under this section.

General Note

Section 117(2) amended and s.117(4), (6) omitted by the Crime and Courts Act 2013 s.17 and Sch.9 paras 52, 93(a), (b) as from 22 April 2014. Section 117(2A) inserted by the High Court and County Courts Jurisdiction Order 1991 (SI 1991/724) Sch.1(I) para.1 and the High Court and County Court Jurisdiction (Amendment) Order 2014 (SI 2014/821) art.2(10)(a)(ii) as from 22 April 2014.

For the corresponding provisions relating to Scotland, see ss.120, 121. In *A Ltd, Petitioner* [2016] SC Edin 77 it was held that the Sheriff Court (the equivalent of the County Court in England and Wales) had jurisdiction to wind up a company limited by guarantee, although the point is not dealt with in the legislation which, in s.117(2), only refers to companies limited by shares. On similar reasoning, the County Court would presumably have jurisdiction in England.

In the present Act, the word "court", when used in relation to a company, means the court having jurisdiction to wind up the company: see IA 1986 s.251. [There is a different definition in CA 2006 s.1156(1), but that in IA 1986 is preserved by s.1156(2).] This will be the appropriate court as defined by this section. Where the company's share capital does not exceed £120,000, both the High Court and the county court have jurisdiction. However, where the company's registered office is in the London insolvency district, all cases must be *commenced* in the High Court (s.117(2A)). The relevant date for determining the question of jurisdiction is that when the proceedings in question are commenced (which in some contexts may be a date later than that on which the company in fact went into liquidation): *Re Lichfield Freight Terminal Ltd* [1997] B.C.C. 11 (disqualification proceedings).

Where a matter is already the subject of proceedings in the county court, application should be made to that court and not to the High Court. The latter may, however, allow such an application to continue under IR 2016 r.12.31: *Re Sankey Furniture Ltd Ex p. Harding* [1995] 2 B.C.L.C. 594.

Winding-up proceedings are a form of "suit and legal process", but are not a method of "enforcing a judgment or arbitration award": *Re International Tin Council* [1989] Ch. 309; (1988) 4 B.C.C. 653 CA; affirming [1987] Ch. 419; (1987) 3 B.C.C. 103. A creditor who has presented a winding-up petition is "pursuing a course of action" which confers jurisdiction on the court to grant appropriate interim relief (e.g. a freezing order): *Revenue and Customs Commissioners v Egleton* [2006] EWHC 2313 (Ch); [2007] B.C.C. 78. However where, as in the case itself, the freezing order is sought against third parties it is a provisional liquidator and not the petitioning creditor who should pursue this course.

Where jurisdiction in a matter relating to winding up is conferred on a court by this section, Council Regulation (EC) 44/2001 on the recognition and enforcement of judgments in civil and commercial matters (the Judgments Regulation) cannot be invoked to confer jurisdiction on a court elsewhere in the EU: *Citigate Dewe Rogerson Ltd v Artaban Public Affairs Sprl* [2009] EWHC 1689 (Ch); [2011] 1 B.C.L.C. 625.

Proposals made by the Insolvency Service to replace the court procedure by an administrative process in uncontested cases have been abandoned.

S.117(1)

Although insolvency proceedings in the High Court are normally heard in the Companies Court, an application to the Queen's Bench Division was held competent in *X-Fab Semiconductor Foundries AG v Plessey Semiconductors Ltd* [2014] EWHC 3190 (QB).

S.117(7)

Article 3 of the EU Regulation, which superseded EC Regulation 1346/2000 as from 26 June 2017 (and the subsection was amended by the Insolvency Amendment (EU 2015/848) Regulations 2017 (SI 2017/702) regs 1, 2(1),

Sch. paras 1, 4 in relation to proceedings opened on or after that date), empowers the courts of a Member State to open insolvency proceedings only if the centre of the debtor's main interests (COMI) is situated within its territory (in the case of "main" proceedings) or—subject to certain limitations—if it possesses an establishment within that territory (in the case of "secondary" or "territorial" proceedings). (See the note to the EU Regulation art.3.) Although there is a presumption that a company's COMI is the place of its registered office, there will be some cases where a company incorporated in England and Wales and having its registered office here has its COMI in another Member State. In that event, our courts will have no jurisdiction at all to open main proceedings and will be able to open secondary or territorial proceedings only if the company possesses an establishment here. These questions of jurisdiction are discussed more fully in the note to art.3 referred to above. According to a Scots case the Regulation only applies to jurisdiction between Member States and does not apply in relation to jurisdiction between the countries of the UK as a Member State, so that a company registered in England and Wales but whose COMI it was alleged had moved to Scotland could not be the subject to an administration order by the Court of Session in Scotland: *Bank Leumi (UK) plc, Petitioner* [2017] CSOH 129; [2017] B.C.C. 753.

S.117(8)

Section 117(8) inserted by the Constitutional Reform Act 2005 ss.15(1), 148 and Sch.4 paras 185, 186(1), (3) as from 3 April 2006.

118 Proceedings taken in wrong court

118(1) [Wrong court] Nothing in section 117 invalidates a proceeding by reason of its being taken in the wrong court.

118(2) [Continuation] The winding up of a company by the court in England and Wales, or any proceedings in the winding up, may be retained in the court in which the proceedings were commenced, although it may not be the court in which they ought to have been commenced.

General Note

It would appear that this provision may be invoked to validate proceedings which have been mistakenly brought in a court which has no insolvency jurisdiction at all: *Re Pleatfine Ltd* (1983) 1 B.C.C. 98,942.

119 Proceedings in county court; case stated for High Court

119(1) [Special case] If any question arises in any winding-up proceedings in a county court which all the parties to the proceedings, or which one of them and the judge of the court, desire to have determined in the first instance in the High Court, the judge shall state the facts in the form of a special case for the opinion of the High Court.

119(2) [Transmission] Thereupon the special case and the proceedings (or such of them as may be required) shall be transmitted to the High Court for the purposes of the determination.

Jurisdiction (Scotland)

120 Court of Session and sheriff court jurisdiction

120(1) [Court of Session] The Court of Session has jurisdiction to wind up any company registered in Scotland.

120(2) [Vacation judge] When the Court of Session is in vacation, the jurisdiction conferred on that court by this section may (subject to the provisions of this Part) be exercised by the judge acting as vacation judge.

120(3) [Concurrent jurisdiction of sheriff court] Where the amount of a company's share capital paid up or credited as paid up does not exceed £120,000, the sheriff court of the sheriffdom in which the company's registered office is situated has concurrent jurisdiction with the Court of Session to wind up the company; but–

(a) the Court of Session may, if it thinks expedient having regard to the amount of the company's assets to do so–

(i) remit to a sheriff court any petition presented to the Court of Session for winding up such a company, or

(ii) require such a petition presented to a sheriff court to be remitted to the Court of Session; and

(b) the Court of Session may require any such petition as above-mentioned presented to one sheriff court to be remitted to another sheriff court; and

(c) in a winding up in the sheriff court the sheriff may submit a stated case for the opinion of the Court of Session on any question of law arising in that winding up.

120(4) ["Registered office"] For the purposes of this section, the expression "registered office" means the place which has longest been the company's registered office during the 6 months immediately preceding the presentation of the petition for winding up.

120(5) [Increase, reduction of s.120(3) sum] The money sum for the time being specified in subsection (3) is subject to increase or reduction by order under section 416 in Part XV.

120(6) [Applicability of EU Regulation] This section is subject to Article 3 of the EU Regulation (jurisdiction under EU Regulation).

General Note

This section lays down provisions for Scotland which correspond generally with those made for England and Wales by s.117. There are, however, no Scottish counterparts to ss.118 and 119.

The Sheriff Court has jurisdiction to wind up company limited by guarantee: see the note to s.117.

Section 120(6) is the counterpart for Scotland of s.117(7): see the note to that subsection and note *Bank Leumi (UK) plc, Petitioner* [2017] CSOH 129; [2017] B.C.C. 753 that the EU Regulation only applies to jurisdiction between Member States and not within Member States. Thus the Scottish court does not have jurisdiction under s.120(6) to wind up an English-registered company.

Section 120(6) was amended by the Insolvency Amendment (EU 2015/848) Regulations 2017 (SI 2017/702) regs 1, 2(1), Sch. paras 1, 5 in relation to proceedings opened on or after 26 June 2017 (see reg.3) when the Recast EU Regulation 2015/848 came into force.

121 Power to remit winding up to Lord Ordinary

121(1) [Remission to Lord Ordinary] The Court of Session may, by Act of Sederunt, make provision for the taking of proceedings in a winding up before one of the Lords Ordinary; and, where provision is so made, the Lord Ordinary has, for the purposes of the winding up, all the powers and jurisdiction of the court.

121(2) [Report by Lord Ordinary] However, the Lord Ordinary may report to the Inner House any matter which may arise in the course of a winding up.

Grounds and effect of winding-up petition

122 Circumstances in which company may be wound up by the court

122(1) [Circumstances] A company may be wound up by the court if–

(a) the company has by special resolution resolved that the company be wound up by the court,

(b) being a public company which was registered as such on its original incorporation, the company has not been issued with a trading certificate under section 761 of the Companies Act 2006 (requirement as to minimum share capital) and more than a year has expired since it was so registered,

(c) it is an old public company, within the meaning of Schedule 3 to the Companies Act 2006 (Consequential Amendments, Transitional Provisions and Savings) Order 2009,

(d) the company does not commence its business within a year from its incorporation or suspends its business for a whole year,

(e) [Omitted by the Companies Act 2006 (Consequential Amendments and Transitional Provisions) Order 2011 (SI 2011/1265) art.6(4) as from 12 May 2011.]

(f) the company is unable to pay its debts,

(fa) at the time at which a moratorium for the company under section 1A comes to an end, no voluntary arrangement approved under Part I has effect in relation to the company,

(g) the court is of the opinion that it is just and equitable that the company should be wound up.

122(2) [Scotland] In Scotland, a company which the Court of Session has jurisdiction to wind up may be wound up by the Court if there is subsisting a floating charge over property comprised in the company's property and undertaking, and the court is satisfied that the security of the creditor entitled to the benefit of the floating charge is in jeopardy.

For this purpose a creditor's security is deemed to be in jeopardy if the Court is satisfied that events have occurred or are about to occur which render it unreasonable in the creditor's interests that the company should retain power to dispose of the property which is subject to the floating charge.

S.122(1)

The court has in all cases a discretion whether to make a winding-up order or not. This is implicit in the opening words of the section, and is confirmed by s.125.

Paragraphs (b) and (c) were introduced in conjunction with the redefinition of the public company and the enactment of new statutory rules applicable to such companies by CA 1980. The remaining paragraphs of this subsection are of long standing.

Section 122(1)(e) formerly made it a ground for a winding-up order if a public company had only one member. This is now permitted (CA 2006 s.7).

Paragraph (f) is elaborated by the presumptions set out in s.123. If a creditor establishes that a company is unable to pay its debts, he is normally entitled to have a winding-up order made as of course, unless the court considers that there is some special reason why it should not do so. One consideration which would incline the court to refuse an order would be that a majority of the company's creditors were opposed to the making of an order; but if the opposing creditors are not independent outsiders but are associated with the directors their views are likely to be discounted: *Re Lummus Agricultural Services Ltd* [1999] B.C.C. 953.

Paragraph (fa) was inserted by the Insolvency Act 2000 s.1, Sch.1 paras 1, 6 with effect from 1 January 2003. The addition of this ground will obviate the need to prove insolvency under s.123. But in most cases the alternative of a creditors' voluntary winding up will be preferred. A petition on this ground may be presented only by one or more creditors: s.124(3A).

Paragraph (g) has been the subject of interpretation in a considerable number of cases, among the best known of which are *Re German Date Coffee Company* (1882) 20 Ch. D. 169 (failure of object); *Re T E Brinsmead & Sons* [1897] 1 Ch. 406 (fraud); *Re Yenidje Tobacco Co Ltd* [1916] 2 Ch. 426 (deadlock); *Loch v John Blackwood Ltd* [1924] A.C. 783 (impropriety); and *Ebrahimi v Westbourne Galleries Ltd* [1973] A.C. 360 (breakdown of confidence). The last-mentioned case established that in the exercise of its jurisdiction on the "just and equitable" ground the court is not restricted by the rights and wrongs of the position as a matter of law but may have regard to wider considerations, such as the expectation of a member of a small "quasi-partnership" company that he will have a say in matters of management. For further illustrations on this point, see *Re Zinotty Properties Ltd* [1984] 1 W.L.R. 1249; (1984) 1 B.C.C. 99,139; *Tay Bok Choon v Tahansan Sdn Bhd* [1987] 1 W.L.R. 413; (1987) 3 B.C.C. 132. Failure on the part of the directors to pay reasonable dividends is in theory capable of supporting a winding-up petition on the "just and equitable" ground, although such a case would be extremely difficult to prove: *Re a Company (No.00370 of 1987)* [1988] 1 W.L.R. 1068; (1988) 4 B.C.C. 506.

The jurisdiction under s.122(1)(g) may not be invoked to protect interests of the petitioner other than his interests as a member: *Re J E Cade & Son Ltd* [1991] B.C.C. 360 (petitioner seeking to assert rights as freeholder of land in occupation of company); contrast *Ebbvale Ltd v Hosking* [2013] UKPC 1; [2013] 2 B.C.L.C. 204 (possible advantage to petitioning creditor in related litigation). Nor is it appropriate to rely on s.122(1)(g) to seek to have a company wound up on public interest grounds (even where the petitioner is a local authority who alleges the dishonest misapplication of public money): the intention of Parliament is that all such cases should be brought by the Secretary of State under s.124A: *Re Millennium Advanced Technology Ltd* [2004] EWHC 711 (Ch); [2004] 4 All E.R. 465; [2004] 2 B.C.L.C. 77.

It is not a prerequisite for the application of s.122(1)(g) that the company should be insolvent. However, in *Re ARM Asset Backed Securities SA* [2013] EWHC 3351 (Ch); [2014] B.C.C. 252 an English court was held to have jurisdiction to wind up a Luxembourg-registered company under the EC Regulation on the "just and equitable" ground where it was established that its COMI had moved to England and it was shown on the facts that it was insolvent. The latter was necessary to bring the case within the Regulation.

There is in practice a considerable overlap between the jurisdiction to grant a winding-up order under s.122(1)(g) and that for relief on the ground of unfairly prejudicial conduct under CA 2006 s.994, and it has been common for a petition to seek orders under each of these provisions in the alternative. In *Practice Direction—Order under section 127 Insolvency Act 1986* [2007] B.C.C. 839 (reproduced in App.V to this *Guide* (Vol.2)), attention is drawn to the undesirability of asking as a matter of course for a winding-up order unless that is the relief which the petitioner would prefer or may be the only relief to which he may be entitled. The Practice Direction also requires a person presenting a petition under s.122(1)(g) to state whether he consents to an order under IA 1986 s.127: see the note to that section. However, the jurisdiction under the two provisions does not always overlap; a winding-up order may be justified in circumstances (such as deadlock) which do not constitute unfairly prejudicial conduct (*Re Neath Rugby Ltd* [2009] EWCA Civ 291; [2010] B.C.C. 597).

Where the dispute in a petition for winding up under s.122(1)(g) is essentially one which involves only rival factions of shareholders, it is a misfeasance for those in control of the company to spend its money in the proceedings, except in relation to matters in which the company, as such, is concerned, e.g. in making disclosure of documents in the possession of the company, or in connection with an application under s.127 (below) to validate a disposition of the company's property or sanction the continuance of its business pending the hearing of the petition: *Re Milgate Developments Ltd* [1991] B.C.C. 24; *Re a Company (No.004502 of 1988) Ex p. Johnson* [1991] B.C.C. 234.

It is an abuse of the process of the court to present a winding-up petition for an improper purpose, e.g. to bring pressure on the directors to register share transfers (*Charles Forte Investments Ltd v Amanda* [1964] Ch. 240), but this will not necessarily be the case where the complainant has no other remedy: *CVC/Opportunity Equity Partners Ltd v Demarco Almeida* [2002] UKPC 16; [2002] B.C.C. 684.

S.122(2)

This provision can be traced back to s.4 of the Companies (Floating Charges) (Scotland) Act 1961, the Act which first introduced the floating charge to Scotland, where it was unknown at common law. At that time, however, it was not possible in Scotland to enforce a floating charge by the appointment of a receiver, and so winding up was the only remedy which the law could provide for in a case when the security was in jeopardy. The present subsection is arguably no longer required, now that receivership is available: see s.52(2) above.

123 Definition of inability to pay debts

123(1) [Inability to pay debts] A company is deemed unable to pay its debts–

(a) if a creditor (by assignment or otherwise) to whom the company is indebted in a sum exceeding £750 then due has served on the company, by leaving it at the company's registered office, a written demand (in the prescribed form) requiring the company to pay the sum so due and the company has for 3 weeks thereafter neglected to pay the sum or to secure or compound for it to the reasonable satisfaction of the creditor, or

(b) if, in England and Wales, execution or other process issued on a judgment, decree or order of any court in favour of a creditor of the company is returned unsatisfied in whole or in part, or

(c) if, in Scotland, the induciae of a charge for payment on an extract decree, or an extract registered bond, or an extract registered protest, have expired without payment being made, or

(d) if, in Northern Ireland, a certificate of unenforceability has been granted in respect of a judgment against the company, or

(e) if it is proved to the satisfaction of the court that the company is unable to pay its debts as they fall due.

123(2) [Proof that assets less than liabilities] A company is also deemed unable to pay its debts if it is proved to the satisfaction of the court that the value of the company's assets is less than the amount of its liabilities, taking into account its contingent and prospective liabilities.

123(3) [Increase, reduction of sum in s.123(1)(a)] The money sum for the time being specified in subsection (1)(a) is subject to increase or reduction by order under section 416 in Part XV.

General Note

The question of a company's inability to pay its debts may be determined by the court as a matter of fact (s.123(1)(e)) or settled by the application of a number of presumptions, four of which (s.123(1)(a)–(d)) turn purely on the evidence, while the fifth (s.123(2)) involves a judicial assessment of the position.

The minimum threshold figure of £750 was the same in bankruptcy and has remained unchanged in winding up since the 1986 Act came into force. Following a consultation exercise, the sum has been increased to £5,000 in bankruptcy cases from 1 October 2015 (see the Insolvency Act 1986 (Amendment) Order 2015 (SI 2015/922)), but, perhaps oddly, no comparable change has been made for corporate insolvency.

On the meaning of the term "debt" in the present context, see IR 2016 r.14.1. See also the discussion of the related term "creditor" in the note to s.1(1). It is sufficient to give a creditor standing to petition that he should have a legal title to the debt, even though the beneficial interest may be in another person: *Bell Group Finance (Pty) Ltd (in liq.) v Bell Group (UK) Holdings Ltd* [1996] B.C.C. 505.

A winding-up order will not be made on the basis of a debt which is genuinely disputed: *Re LHF Wools Ltd* [1970] Ch. 27; *Re Trinity Insurance Co Ltd* [1990] B.C.C. 235; *Re Janeash Ltd* [1990] B.C.C. 250; *Re a Company (No.0010656 of 1990)* [1991] B.C.L.C. 464; *Re Richbell Strategic Holdings Ltd* [1997] 2 B.C.L.C. 429; *Re a Company (No.2634 of 2002)* [2002] EWHC 944 (Ch); [2002] 2 B.C.L.C. 591; *Re MCI WorldCom Ltd* [2002] EWHC 2436 (Ch); [2003] 1 B.C.L.C. 330; *Re UK (Aid) Ltd, Glaxosmithkline Export Ltd v UK (Aid) Ltd* [2003] EWHC 1090 (Ch); [2003] 2 B.C.L.C. 351; *Favermead Ltd v FPD Savills Ltd* [2005] EWHC 626 (Ch); [2005] B.P.I.R. 715; *Jubilee International Ltd v Farlin Timbers Pte Ltd* [2005] EWHC 3331 (Ch); [2006] B.P.I.R. 765; contrast *Southern Cross Group plc v Deka Immobilien Investment* [2005] B.P.I.R. 1103 (prior opportunity to litigate not taken); *Tallington Lakes Ltd v Ancasta International Boat Sales Ltd* [2012] EWCA Civ 1712; [2014] B.C.C. 327; *Angel Group Ltd v British Gas Trading Ltd* [2012] EWHC 2702 (Ch); [2013] B.C.C. 265 (debt disputed in part but a sum well in excess of £750 clearly due); see also *Re a Company* [2013] EWHC 4291 (Ch). This is also the case where the company has a genuine and serious cross-claim for an amount which exceeds the petition debt (or which, if successful, would reduce the company's net indebtedness below the statutory minimum of £750): *Re Bayoil SA* [1998] B.C.C. 988; *Richbell Information Services Inc v Atlantic General Investments Trust Ltd* [1999] B.C.C. 871; *Re Latreefers Inc* [1999] 1 B.C.L.C. 271; *Greenacre Publishing Group v The Manson Group* [2000] B.C.C. 11; *Orion Media Marketing Ltd v Media Brook Ltd* [2002] 1 B.C.L.C. 184; *Re Ringinfo Ltd* [2002] 1 B.C.L.C. 210; *Montgomery v Wanda Modes Ltd* [2002] 1 B.C.L.C. 289; *Re VP Developments Ltd* [2005] EWHC 259 (Ch); [2005] B.C.C. 393; *Penwith D.C. v VP Developments Ltd* [2005] EWHC 259 (Ch); [2005] B.P.I.R. 1010; *Re a Company (No.2272 of 2004)* [2005] EWHC 422 (Ch); [2005] B.P.I.R. 1251; *R&S Fire and Security Services Ltd v Fire Defence plc* [2013] EWHC 4222 (Ch); [2013] 2 B.C.L.C. 92 (cross-claim recognised despite "pay now, litigate later" provision in contract).

It was pointed out in *Bayoil* (above) and repeated in *Re a Company* [2013] EWHC 4291 (Ch) that where the petition debt is disputed in good faith on substantial grounds the petitioner is regarded (unless there is an undisputed part of the debt in excess of £750) as not being a creditor of the company and so has no legal standing to present the petition in the first place, rather than the petition being regarded as a matter of the court's discretion; whereas the case of an undisputed debt with a genuine and serious cross-claim is treated differently, in that the dismissal or staying of the petition can only be a matter for the discretion of the court. (On this discretion see *Wilson & Sharp Investments Ltd v Harbourview Developments Ltd* [2015] EWCA Civ 1030; [2015] B.P.I.R. 1496.) A petitioner whose debt is disputed or subject to a cross-claim is not to be regarded as a contingent creditor for the purposes of presenting a winding-up petition (see *LSI 2013 Ltd v Solar Panel Co (UK) Ltd* [2014] EWHC 248 (Ch)). Although the Companies Court when exercising winding-up jurisdiction has repeatedly stated that it is not the forum to resolve parties' disputes as to debts or cross-claims, in *Botleigh Grange Ltd v Revenue and Customs Commissioners* [2016] EWHC 3081 (Ch), the court was prepared to entertain a petition involving a dispute that could be determined on the documents alone, did not require further or oral evidence and was not intricate or complex.

An application to restrain presentation of a petition must be to a court with jurisdiction to wind up the company (IR 2016 r.7.24). In *Re a Company* (unreported, 26 April 2017) Norris J stressed that the petitioner must establish its standing to petition as a creditor and in a complex set of facts adjourned the matter for 14 days to give the creditor time to formulate its response to the company's challenge to the petitioner's standing as such. The threshold for granting an injunction to restrain the presentation of a winding-up petition is low: the court simply has to form a view about whether the challenge to the debt is being put forward in good faith and has sufficient substance to justify it being determined in an ordinary civil action: *Mulalley & Co Ltd v Regent Building Services Ltd* [2017] EWHC 2962 (Ch).

However a petition will not be struck out or dismissed merely because the company alleges that the debt is disputed; the court must be satisfied that there is a genuine dispute founded on substantial grounds: *Re a Company (No.006685 of 1996)* [1997] B.C.C. 830; compare *Re a Company (No.001946 of 1991) Ex p. Fin Soft Holding SA* [1991] B.C.L.C. 737; *Denis Rye Ltd v Bolsover District Council* [2009] EWCA Civ 372; [2009] 4 All E.R. 1140; [2010] B.C.C. 248; *Re City Centre Resources Ltd* [2013] EWHC 4249 (Ch) (dispute whether loan repayable); *Foxholes Nursing Home Ltd v Accora Ltd* [2013] EWHC 3712 (Ch) (petition used as pressure by creditor); *Winnington Networks Communications Ltd v Revenue & Customs Commissioners* [2015] EWHC 1096 (Ch); [2015] B.C.C. 554 (mere unsubstantiated assertion that debt disputed insufficient; company's directors later heavily penalised in costs); *Re Company 0254/2015* (unreported, 27 February 2015) (substantial grounds shown). If the debt is disputed, the court will normally strike out the petition, leaving the question of its validity to be determined in other proceedings. However this is a rule of practice and not of law, and so may be departed from, in the court's discretion, in an appropriate case—e.g. where, in the case of a foreign company, the petitioner would otherwise be without a remedy; *Re Russian & English Bank* [1932] Ch. 663; *Re Claybridge Shipping Co SA* [1981] Com. L.R. 107n; cf. *Re UOC Corp, Alipour v Ary* [1997] 1 W.L.R. 534; [1997] B.C.C. 377; *Jubilee International Ltd v Farlin Timbers Pte Ltd* (above); *Parmalat Capital Finance Ltd v Food Holdings Ltd* [2008] UKPC 23; [2009] 1 B.C.L.C. 274 or the circumstances are for some other reason exceptional (*Lacontha Foundation Ltd v GBI Investments Ltd* [2010] EWHC 37 (Ch); [2010] B.P.I.R. 356). The fact that the debt is based on a cheque does not exclude the court's discretion: *Re a Company* [2012] EWHC 4336. Although it would not normally be appropriate to make a winding-up order on the basis of a judgment debt when an appeal against the judgment is pending, there are rulings to the contrary in *Re A&BC Chewing Gum Ltd* [1975] 1 W.L.R. 579; *El-Ajou v Dollar Land (Manhattan) Ltd* [2005] EWHC 2861 (Ch); [2007] B.C.C. 953 and *Re BLV Realty II Ltd* [2010] EWHC 1791 (Ch). If the parties have agreed that disputes under an agreement should go to arbitration, it has been held not appropriate for the court to decide an issue as to a debt under that agreement on a winding-up petition: the insolvency process is not to be used for debt recovery (*Rusant Ltd v Traxys Far East Ltd* [2013] EWHC 4083 (Ch): the court refused to allow the petition to proceed and the matter was to go to arbitration; compare *Salford Estates (No.2) Ltd v Altomart Ltd* [2014] EWCA Civ 1575; [2015] B.C.C. 306 and *Re Measure Market Exchange Ltd* (unreported, 18 May 2015)). Where the debt is based on the award of an arbitrator or similar adjudicator, it may be appropriate for the court to adopt a similar approach, but if the debtor has the right to appeal against the award the court may direct him to follow that course: *Towsey v Highgrove Homes Ltd* [2013] B.L.R. 45. However, the legislation relating to Value Added Tax, exceptionally, authorises the enforcement of an assessment for VAT by winding-up proceedings even though an appeal against the liability has not been disposed of: *Re D & D Marketing (UK) Ltd* [2002] EWHC 660 (Ch); [2003] B.P.I.R. 539; cf. *Re The Arena Corporation Ltd* [2004] EWCA Civ 371; [2004] B.P.I.R. 415; *Hall v Poolman* [2008] B.P.I.R. 892 (Australia); and contrast *Customs & Excise Commissioners v Anglo Overseas Ltd* [2004] EWHC 2198 (Ch); [2005] B.P.I.R. 137. In *Re Enta Technologies Ltd* [2014] EWHC 548 (Ch); [2014] B.C.C. 683 it was held at first instance that the mere existence of a tax assessment creates a statutory debt, incapable of dispute and remaining extant unless and until any appeal to a tax tribunal is successful. But this view was doubted in *Re Parkwell Investments Ltd* [2014] EWHC 3381 (Ch); [2014] B.C.C. 721, and on appeal the *Enta* decision was reversed (*Revenue & Customs Commissioners v Changtel Solutions UK Ltd* [2015] EWCA Civ 29; [2015] B.C.C. 317). The court's discretion is not completely abrogated by the jurisdiction of the tax tribunal, and the question whether the appeal has a real prospect of success is likely to be a compelling factor in the court's exercise of that discretion. If a petition fails on the basis that the debt is genuinely disputed, the petitioner should pay the costs of that failure save in exceptional circumstances: *Re Sykes & Son Ltd* [2012] EWHC 1005 (Ch); [2012] B.P.I.R. 1273. Where the company is solvent, it is an abuse of the process of the court to present a petition for winding up based on a disputed debt, which the court will restrain by injunction and may penalise in costs, possibly on an indemnity basis: *Re a Company (No.0012209 of 1991)* [1991] 1 W.L.R. 351; *Re a Company (No.2507 of 2003)* [2003] EWHC 1484 (Ch); [2003] 2 B.C.L.C. 346; *Glaxosmithkline v UK (Aid) Ltd* [2003] EWHC 1383 (Ch); [2004] B.P.I.R. 528; *Re Realstar Ltd* [2007] EWHC 2921 (Ch); [2008] B.P.I.R. 1391; contrast *Frank Saul (Fashion) Ltd v Revenue and Customs* [2012] EWHC 1603 (Ch); [2012] B.P.I.R. 985 (fault on both sides; no order as to costs). A winding-up order made on the basis of a debt which might have been disputed at the time remains in force unless and until it is rescinded by a later order: *Wilson v Specter Partnership* [2007] EWHC 133 (Ch); [2007] B.P.I.R. 649. In the case of a prospective debt which has not yet fallen due, the court may take the view that the matter should be resolved when the petition is heard rather than on an application to strike out: *Securum Finance Ltd v Camswell Ltd* [1994] B.C.C. 434. (On petitions by a prospective or contingent creditor, see further *Re a Company (No.003028 of 1987)* (1987) 3 B.C.C. 575 at 585; and *JSF Finance & Currency Exchange Co Ltd v Akma Solutions Inc* [2001] 2 B.C.L.C. 307.)

Where the company has a cross-claim against the petitioner pending in another court, the court has a discretion whether to make a winding-up order or to dismiss the petition: *Re FSA Business Software Ltd* [1990] B.C.C. 465.

A dispute as to the genuineness of a debt may also be relevant to determine the standing of a person claiming to be a creditor who seeks a winding-up order on grounds other than the company's insolvency. In this case the question is necessarily one for the court to determine: *Morrice (or Rocks) v Brae Hotel (Shetland) Ltd* [1997] B.C.C. 670 (but compare *Baker Hughes Ltd v CCG Contracting International Ltd*, 2005 S.C. 65 (petition dismissed as a serious abuse of process where standing as creditor not shown)).

Where a winding-up petition in respect of an undisputed debt is based on collateral motive, the proceedings may amount to abuse of process (i) where the petitioner does not really want to obtain liquidation but issued or threatened to issue the proceedings to put pressure on the company to take action that it was unwilling to take; and (ii) where the petitioner wants to obtain the relief sought but is not acting in the interests of his class of creditors or where the success of his petition would disadvantage the body of creditors (see *Ebbvale Ltd v Hosking* [2013] UKPC 1; [2013] 2 B.C.L.C. 204).

A petition may not be presented based on a statute-barred debt: *Re Karnos Property Co Ltd* (1989) 5 B.C.C. 14; *Bolsover District Council v Ashfield Nominees Ltd* [2010] EWCA Civ 1129; [2012] B.C.C. 803. But a judgment debt is not subject to any statutory limitation: *Ridgeway Motors (Isleworth) Ltd v ALTS Ltd* [2005] EWCA Civ 92; [2005] B.C.C. 496.

Where a company or other body is, or has been, an "authorised person" or "authorised representative" under FSMA 2000, or is or has been carrying on a "regulated activity" in contravention of s.19 of that Act, there is a special provision in s.367(4) of that Act setting out (presumably, additional) circumstances in which such a body is to be deemed unable to pay its debts.

Under the EU Regulation art.34, where "main" insolvency proceedings have been opened in the Member State where the debtor has his centre of main interests, his insolvency is to be taken as conclusively established for the purposes of any secondary proceedings. In such a situation it would not be necessary or, indeed, relevant to invoke the provisions of the present section. In contrast, the CBIR art.31 states that recognition of a foreign main proceeding is, for the purpose of commencing a proceeding under British insolvency law, presumptive (but not conclusive) proof that the debtor is unable to prove his debts (or the Scottish equivalent, "apparently insolvent").

Where the term "unable to pay its debts" occurs elsewhere in the Act (as, e.g. in relation to administration in Sch.B1 para.11(a)), the s.123 tests apply: *Gas and Electricity Markets Authority v GB Energy Supply Ltd* [2016] EWHC 3341 (Ch).

S.123(1)

Paragraphs (a) to (d) correspond with events which would, in the case of an individual, have been acts of bankruptcy prior to the passing of the present Act, and survive as grounds for the making of a bankruptcy order (ss.267, 268). Paragraph (a) was modified by IA 1985 by the addition of the words "in the prescribed form", so that an informal demand will now no longer be sufficient for the purpose of this provision.

In *Re a Debtor (No.544/SD/98)* [2000] 1 B.C.L.C. 103 at 116, Robert Walker LJ drew attention to a significant difference between the function of the statutory demand in the corporate and individual insolvency regimes respectively. In the former, it merely provides one means of establishing a company's inability to pay its debts, but in bankruptcy it is not the debtor's general inability to pay his debts that is crucial but his apparent inability to pay the debt which is the subject of the statutory demand.

Section 123(1)(a) specifies only one method for the service of a statutory demand, viz. by leaving it at the company's registered office. In *Re a Company* [1985] B.C.L.C. 37 Nourse J held that a demand sent by telex was not a good statutory demand; but when Morritt J in *Re a Company (No.008790 of 1990)* [1992] B.C.C. 11 was asked to follow this ruling in relation to a demand which had been sent by registered post, he held that, once it was admitted that the demand had been received at the office (albeit through the post), it had been "left at" the office and therefore properly served. Proof of posting alone, however, would not have been sufficient. It is not clear whether a similar interpretation could be applied to the case of a demand sent by telex, fax or electronic means which had admittedly been received.

Under the previous legislation an inaccuracy in the statutory demand, such as an overstatement of the sum due, was normally regarded as fatal, but there have now been several rulings under s.268 of the present Act which mark a departure from the earlier law, and have not treated a defective statutory demand as invalid: see the notes to that section. It is likely that a similar approach will be taken in regard to a statutory demand under s.123.

For the form and rules relating to the statutory demand, see IR 2016 rr.7.2 et seq. A statutory demand must be in hard copy (s.436B(2)(f)).

Paragraph (e) (as CA 1985 s.518(1)(e)) formerly read: "if it is proved to the satisfaction of the court that the company is unable to pay its debts (and, in determining that question, the court shall take into account the company's contingent and prospective liabilities)". This formula was unhelpful in that it ran together two issues: (1) the question whether current debts could be met as they fell due, i.e. "commercial" solvency; and (2) the question whether the company would ultimately prove solvent if its future as well as its present liabilities were brought into the reckoning. The confusion was resolved by the amendment made by IA 1985: contingent and prospective liabilities are not (at least normally) relevant for the purposes of para.(e), while insolvency calculated on a balance-sheet basis becomes a separate test under s.123(2). However, in Australia (where the statutory definition of insolvency is based on the commercial test), it is well established by the case law that reference may be made to debts which will fall due in the future, and in *Re Cheyne Finance plc* [2007] EWHC 2402 (Ch); [2008] B.C.C. 182, where the term "insolvency event" in a document was defined by reference to the commercial test, this approach was followed. In *BNY Corporate Trustee Services Ltd v Eurosail-UK 2007-3BL plc* [2013] UKSC 28; [2013] 1 W.L.R. 1408; [2013] B.C.C. 397 the Supreme Court examined closely the two definitions of insolvency in s.123(1)(e) and s.123(2) and their relationship to each other. The company Eurosail, part of the Lehman Bros group, had issued loan notes in a securitisation transaction that were enforceable in various "events of default", which included the company "being unable to pay its debts as and when they fall due" and "being deemed unable to pay its debts within the meaning of s.123(1) or (2) of the Insolvency Act 1986" (with the omission of the words "it is proved to the satisfaction of the court"). Following the collapse of the Lehman group Eurosail was in a substantial net liability position, according to its balance sheet, but was not insolvent under the cash-flow test (i.e. it was able to meet its current liabilities). The question for the court was whether it was insolvent under the balance-sheet test as defined by s.123(2). All the courts ruled that it had not been proved, on a balance of probabilities, that the company was or was deemed to be "unable to pay its debts" under the statutory balance-sheet test. The ruling in *Cheyne Finance* was expressly approved, but with the qualification that in introducing a "cash-flow" test for the purposes of s.123(2), only those debts falling due in the reasonably near future are to be taken into account. Once the court has to move beyond the reasonably near future, a comparison of present assets with present and future liabilities (discounted for contingencies and deferment) becomes the only sensible test. The further ahead the liabilities fall due (in *Eurosail* the final redemption date of the notes was 2045), the more speculative the exercise becomes, and other factors such as the movements of currencies and interest rates are incapable of prediction with any confidence. The Supreme Court also decisively rejected the view, which had found favour with the Court of Appeal, that an alternative formulation of the test for determining insolvency might be whether the company's affairs had "reached the point of no return". In *Re Casa Estates (UK) Ltd, Bucci v Carman* [2014] EWCA Civ 383; [2014] B.C.C. 269 the company was able to pay its debts as they fell due, but only by incurring other debts on a longer-term basis. There was no evidence how these liabilities were to be satisfied. The Court of Appeal upheld the judge's finding that the company was insolvent on a balance-sheet basis. See also *Re HLC Environmental Projects Ltd* [2013] EWHC 2876 (Ch); [2014] B.C.C. 337, where it was held that the contingent liability in question, which was likely to materialise in the reasonably near future, should be brought into account at its full value. *Eurosail* was also followed in *Myers v Kestrel Acquisitions Ltd* [2015] EWHC 916 (Ch), and applied in *Evans v Jones* [2016] EWCA Civ 660 where the Court of Appeal held that contingent assets could not be taken into account in determining a company is unable to pay its debts, especially where the contingency was whether the company would become insolvent and a potential claim for a preference would be discovered and pursued. See also *Re Cosy Seal Insulation Ltd* [2016] EWHC 1255 (Ch). For commentary, see Walton (2013) 26 Insolv. Int. 124.

In *R. v Commissioners of HM Treasury* [2009] EWHC 227 (Admin); [2009] B.C.C. 251 the court discussed the question of insolvency in the special case of a banking company. The view was expressed that insolvency in this context referred primarily to balance-sheet, rather than cash-flow, insolvency but that a lack of liquidity on the part of a (balance-sheet) solvent company, if sufficiently serious, could mean that the company was insolvent for the purposes of IA 1986.

It has been held that failure to pay a debt which is due and not disputed is of itself evidence of insolvency under s.123(1)(e), even though there is other evidence showing a substantial surplus of assets over liabilities (*Cornhill Insurance plc v Improvement Services Ltd* [1986] 1 W.L.R. 114; (1986) 2 B.C.C. 98,942), and even though a statutory demand has not been served under s.123(1)(e) (*Re Taylor's Industrial Flooring Ltd* [1990] B.C.C. 44).

S.123(2)

It is not clear from the language of this provision whether the presumption implied by the word "deemed" may be rebutted by proof that the company is in fact able to meet all its current debts. The issue might in any case be resolved by the court deciding in its discretion (see ss.122, 125) not to make a winding-up order.

124 Application for winding up

124(1) [Application to court] Subject to the provisions of this section, an application to the court for the winding up of a company shall be by petition presented either by the company, or the directors, or by any creditor or creditors (including any contingent or prospective creditor or creditors), contributory or contributories, or by a member State liquidator appointed in proceedings by virtue of Article 3(1) of the EU Regulation or a temporary administrator (within the meaning of Article 52 of the EU Regulation) or by the designated officer for a magistrates' court in the exercise of the power conferred by section 87A of the Magistrates' Courts Act 1980 (enforcement of fines imposed on companies), or by all or any of those parties, together or separately.

124(2) [Conditions for contributory to present winding-up petition] Except as mentioned below, a contributory is not entitled to present a winding-up petition unless either–

(a) the number of members is reduced below 2, or

(b) the shares in respect of which he is a contributory, or some of them, either were originally allotted to him, or have been held by him, and registered in his name, for at least 6 months during the 18 months before the commencement of the winding up, or have devolved on him through the death of a former holder.

124(3) [Non-application of s.124(2)] A person who is liable under section 76 to contribute to a company's assets in the event of its being wound up may petition on either of the grounds set out in section 122(1)(f) and (g), and subsection (2) above does not then apply; but unless the person is a contributory otherwise than under section 76, he may not in his character as contributory petition on any other ground.

124(3A) [Petition on s.122(1)(fa) ground] A winding-up petition on the ground set out in section 122(1)(fa) may only be presented by one or more creditors.

124(4) [Petition by Secretary of State] A winding-up petition may be presented by the Secretary of State–

(a) if the ground of the petition is that in section 122(1)(b) or (c), or

(b) in a case falling within section 124A or 124B below.

124(4AA) [Petition by Financial Conduct Authority] A winding up petition may be presented by the Financial Conduct Authority in a case falling within section 124C(1) or (2).

124(4A) [Petition by Regulator of Community Interest Companies] A winding-up petition may be presented by the Regulator of Community Interest Companies in a case falling within section 50 of the Companies (Audit, Investigations and Community Enterprise) Act 2004.

124(5) [Petition by official receiver] Where a company is being wound up voluntarily in England and Wales, a winding-up petition may be presented by the official receiver attached to the court as well as by any other person authorised in that behalf under the other provisions of this section; but the court shall not make a winding-up order on the petition unless it is satisfied that the voluntary winding up cannot be continued with due regard to the interests of the creditors or contributories.

General Note

This section lists the persons who have standing to present a winding-up petition; but it is not exhaustive, for the Attorney-General or the Charity Commission may petition in the case of a charitable company or charitable incorporated organisation (Charities Act 2011 s.113), the Financial Conduct Authority and the Prudential Regulation Authority may do so in the case of various bodies carrying on investment business: FSMA 2000 s.367, and the Director of Public Prosecutions and other prosecuting authorities are empowered to petition to have a company wound up on public interest grounds following a conviction for breach of a serious crime prevention order (Serious Crime Act 2007 s.27).

The Act empowers the supervisor of an IVA (s.7(4)(b)) to apply to the court for a winding-up order and by Sch.1 para.21, states that an administrator and an administrative receiver may present a petition for winding up; but (no doubt as a result of a drafting slip) no mention is made of these office-holders in s.124(1). A partial attempt has been made to overcome this difficulty without amendment of s.124(1) by an alteration made to the rules in 1987 (now IR

2016 r.7.27(1)). This states that a petition by a "relevant office-holder" must be expressed to be the petition of the company by the office-holder. "Relevant office-holder" means an administrator, administrative receiver or the supervisor of a CVA (r.7.4(2)).

The terms "member State liquidator" and "temporary administrator" have special meanings for the purposes of the Recast EU Regulation: see the notes to the Regulation arts 2(5) and 52. In particular, a "member State liquidator" is within the definition of an insolvency practitioner in most forms of insolvency proceeding (apart from receivership). An insolvency practitioner appointed under art.3(1) will have been appointed in "main" proceedings in a Member State other than the UK and, as such, is empowered by art.37(1)(a) to request the opening of secondary proceedings (i.e. apply for a winding-up order) in this jurisdiction if the debtor possesses an establishment here. See generally the notes to the articles referred to. Similarly, the CBIR art.9, provides that a "foreign representative" of an insolvency proceeding abroad is entitled to apply directly to a court in Great Britain (for this or any other purpose). A foreign representative (defined in art.2(j)) includes one appointed on an interim basis and is not restricted to a representative in a "main" proceeding. It is not a precondition that the foreign proceeding should have been recognised under art.15. No special formalities apply (other than a translation, where required). Article 13 of the CBIR accords to foreign creditors (including the tax and social security authorities) the same rights regarding the commencement of, and participation in, a British proceeding as creditors in Great Britain.

As a general rule, a winding-up order may only be made on the basis of a petition presented under this section: *Re Brooke Marine Ltd* [1988] B.C.L.C. 546. However, the court may in a proper case make an order of its own motion (*Lancefield v Lancefield* [2002] B.P.I.R. 1108); *Re BTR (UK) Ltd* [2012] EWHC 2398 (Ch); [2012] B.C.C. 864; *Re Marches Credit Union Ltd* [2013] EWHC 1731 (Ch) (where a petition presented by the directors was potentially defective but it was in the public interest and a matter of urgency to order the winding up), and an exception has now also been made by Sch.B1 para.13(1)(e): on an application for an administration order made under para.12 of that Schedule, the court may treat the application as a winding-up petition and make any order which the court could make under s.125. Further, the court using its wide power under Sch.B1 para.79(4)(d) on ending administration on the administrator's application has made winding-up orders without a petition: see *Re Graico Property Co Ltd* [2016] EWHC 2827 (Ch); [2017] B.C.C. 15; *Re West End Quay Estate Management Ltd* [2018] B.C.C. 1.

For the procedure on an application for winding up, see IR 2016 rr.7.7. A deposit of £1,600 (but £5,000 for a petition under s.124A) is payable on presentation of the petition: Insolvency Proceedings (Fees) Order 2016 (SI 2016/692) art.2(c), (d). Before presenting a winding-up petition a creditor must conduct a search to ensure that no petition is pending. Save in exceptional circumstances a second winding-up petition should not be presented whilst a prior petition is pending. A petitioner who presents his own petition while another petition is pending does so at risk as to costs (see the *Practice Direction: Insolvency Proceedings* [2018] B.C.C. 241 (reproduced as App.IV to this *Guide*) para.9.2).

Although a winding-up petition is a species of legal proceedings, it is not a "claim or counterclaim" within the Arbitration Act 1996 s.9: *Best Beat Ltd v Rossall* [2006] EWHC 1494 (Comm); [2006] B.P.I.R. 1387; *Salford Estates (No.2) Ltd v Altomart Ltd* [2014] EWCA Civ 1575; [2015] B.C.C. 306.

On applications for permission to amend errors in petitions, see the *Practice Direction* [2018] B.C.C. 241, para.9.9.

S.124(1)

The directors are empowered to present a petition for the winding up of their company, as a result of a change made by IA 1985. This has overcome a difficulty revealed in *Re Emmadart Ltd* [1979] Ch. 540, in which the court ruled that the practice of allowing a company to present a petition on the strength of a resolution of the directors, which had been tolerated for many years, was irregular (at least in the absence of an enabling provision in the company's articles). The amendments make it possible in cases of urgency for a petition to be presented without the delay necessarily involved in summoning a general meeting of the company. Where the petition is presented by the directors, they petition in their own names, rather than that of the company; and—at least in the absence of a formal board resolution—they must act unanimously: *Re Instrumentation Electrical Services Ltd* (1988) 4 B.C.C. 301. However, where a proper resolution has been passed by a majority of the directors at a board meeting, it becomes the duty of all its directors, including those who took no part in the meeting and those who voted against the resolution, to implement it; and thereafter any director has authority to present a petition on behalf of all of them: *Re Equiticorp International plc* [1989] 1 W.L.R. 1010; (1989) 5 B.C.C. 599 (a case decided on the similar wording of IA 1986 s.*9(1)*).

Under the former law, a contingent or prospective creditor could not be heard on a petition until he had given security for costs and had established that he had a prima facie case. This requirement was repealed by IA 1985 Sch.10 Pt II. On contingent creditors, see *Re T&N Ltd* [2005] EWHC 2870 (Ch); [2005] B.C.C. 982 and the note to r.14.1. A contingent creditor may present a petition on the "just and equitable" ground (s.122(1)(g)): *Re a Company (No.003028 of 1987)* (1987) 3 B.C.C. 575; compare *Re Dollar Land Holdings plc* [1993] B.C.C. 823. Where there has been an equitable assignment of a debt by way of security, the assignor's equity of redemption gives him sufficient interest as a creditor to petition, and the assignee need not be joined as petitioner: *Parmalat Capital Finance Ltd v Food Holdings Ltd* [2008] UKPC 23; [2008] B.C.C. 371.

On the standing of a person claiming to be a creditor where his debt is disputed by the company, see the note to s.123. Administrators whose remuneration was yet to be paid were held to be creditors entitled to petition in *Re Lafayette Electronics Europe Ltd* [2006] EWHC 1005, 1006 (Ch); [2007] B.C.C. 890.

Where a person has been compelled to pay a debt owed by a company to a third party, the company is under an obligation at common law to reimburse the person who made the payment, and the latter is a prospective creditor of the company with standing to present a petition for its winding up: *Re Healing Research Trustee Co Ltd* [1991] B.C.L.C. 716.

Where a creditor seeks to withdraw a petition, another creditor may apply to be substituted as petitioner. In *Re Wavern Engineering Co Ltd* (1987) 3 B.C.C. 3 leave was given by the court to a creditor to withdraw a petition in the mistaken belief that no other creditor was willing to support the petition. The court rescinded the leave to withdraw and made an order substituting another creditor as petitioner.

Where the petitioner's status as a contributory is in dispute, it was formerly the practice that his standing to petition should be established in separate proceedings: *Re J N 2 Ltd* [1978] 1 W.L.R. 183; but it is now accepted that this is not an inflexible rule and that it may be departed from in the interests of justice: *Re UOC Corp Ltd, Alipour v Ary* [1997] 1 W.L.R. 534; [1997] B.C.C. 377; further proceedings [2002] EWHC 937 (Ch); [2002] 2 B.C.L.C. 770.

Section 124(1) was amended by the Insolvency Amendment (EU 2015/848) Regulations 2017 (SI 2017/702) regs 1, 2, Sch. paras. 1, 6 in relation to proceedings opened on or after 26 June 2017 (see reg.3) when the Recast EU Regulation 2015/848 came into force.

S.124(2)–(4A)

These provisions restrict the circumstances in which winding-up proceedings may be instituted by a contributory: generally speaking, he must have been a member of at least six months' standing. Supplementing this statutory rule is the principle, long settled at common law, under which the court will dismiss a petition brought by a contributory unless he shows that he will have a financial interest in the outcome of the liquidation, so that, e.g. the holder of fully paid shares may not seek an order for the winding up of a wholly insolvent company (*Re Rica Gold Washing Company* (1879) 11 Ch. D. 36; *Re Chesterfield Catering Co Ltd* [1977] Ch. 373; *Re Martin-Coulter Enterprises Ltd* (1988) 4 B.C.C. 210). Exceptionally, where the petition (on the "just and equitable" ground) is based on or alleges a failure to supply accounts, and by reason of the company's default insufficient accounts are available to tell whether there will in fact be a surplus for contributories, the petitioner is not required to prove that he has a tangible interest in the outcome: *Re Wessex Computer Stationers Ltd* [1992] B.C.L.C. 366; *Re a Company (No.007936 of 1994)* [1995] B.C.C. 705. On similar reasoning, a member may not petition for relief under CA 2006 s.994 on the grounds of unfairly prejudicial conduct if the company is insolvent, but an exception is made if he shows that his shares would have had a value but for the wrongdoing of the respondents, and where this is in doubt the court will adopt a flexible approach: *Re Tobian Properties Ltd* [2012] EWCA Civ 998; [2013] B.C.C. 98. The question whether the *Rica Gold* principle applied to LLPs was left open in *Charit-email Technology Partnership LLP v Vermillion International Investments Ltd* [2009] EWHC 388 (Ch); [2009] B.P.I.R. 762. The persons liable under s.76 are (1) former shareholders whose shares have been redeemed or repurchased out of capital by a company which is subsequently wound up insolvent within a year of the transaction; and (2) directors made jointly and severally liable with such former shareholders.

Section 124(2)(a) does not apply where the company has always had only one shareholder (*Re Pimlico Capital Ltd* [2002] EWHC 878 (Ch); [2002] 2 B.C.L.C. 544); indeed, it is likely that the legislators overlooked the obvious case for the repeal of this provision when s.122(1)(e) was deleted.

A person who has agreed to take a transfer of shares but whose name has not been entered on the register of members has no standing as a "contributory" to present a winding-up petition: *Re a Company (No.003160 of 1986)* (1986) 2 B.C.C. 99276, *Re Quickdome Ltd* (1988) 4 B.C.C. 296. However, person to whom shares have been transferred but not registered is deemed to be a "member" by virtue of s.250 and accordingly a "contributory" with standing to present a winding-up petition: *Hamilton v Brown* [2016] EWHC 191 (Ch). On the same reasoning, the trustee in bankruptcy of a contributory was held to have standing.

Section 124(3A) was inserted by IA 2000 s.1, Sch.1 paras 1, 6 with effect from 1 January 2003, when the ground of winding up under s.122(1)(fa) was also introduced. Section 124(4A) was inserted by the Companies (Audit, Investigations and Community Enterprise) Act 2004 s.50(1), (3) as from 1 July 2005. Section 124(3) was amended by the Companies Act 2006 (Consequential Amendments, Transitional Provisions and Savings) Order 2009 (SI 2009/1941) art.2(1) and Sch.1 para.73(13) as from 1 October 2009.

Section 124(4)(b) amended by the European Public Limited-Liability Company Regulations 2004 (SI 2004/2326) reg.73(4)(a) as from 8 October 2004. Section 124(4AA) inserted by the European Cooperative Society Regulations 2006 (SI 2006/2078) reg.33(2) as from 18 August 2006.

S.124(5)

In the exercise of its discretion under this provision the court will normally have regard to the wishes of a majority in value of the company's creditors, where the company is insolvent, but will not necessarily be bound by this: *Re Southard & Co Ltd* [1979] 1 W.L.R. 1198; *Re Medisco Equipment Ltd* (1983) 1 B.C.C. 98,944; *Re Falcon R J Developments Ltd* (1987) 3 B.C.C. 146; *Re M C H Services Ltd* (1987) 3 B.C.C. 179; *Re Hewitt Brannan (Tools) Co Ltd* [1990] B.C.C. 354. The case for a court order will be stronger where there is a suspicion of sharp practice calling for an impartial investigation of the company's affairs: *Re Gordon & Breach Science Publishers Ltd* [1995] B.C.C. 261.

124A Petition for winding up on grounds of public interest

124A(1) [Power of Secretary of State] Where it appears to the Secretary of State from–

(a) any report made or information obtained under Part XIV (except section 448A) of the Companies Act 1985 (company investigations, &c.),

(b) any report made by inspectors under–

  (i) section 167, 168, 169 or 284 of the Financial Services and Markets Act 2000, or

  (ii) where the company is an open-ended investment company (within the meaning of that Act), regulations made as a result of section 262(2)(k) of that Act;

(bb) any information or documents obtained under section 165, 171, 172, 173 or 175 of that Act,

(c) any information obtained under section 2 of the Criminal Justice Act 1987 or section 52 of the Criminal Justice (Scotland) Act 1987 (fraud investigations), or

(d) any information obtained under section 83 of the Companies Act 1989 (powers exercisable for purpose of assisting overseas regulatory authorities),

that it is expedient in the public interest that a company should be wound up, he may present a petition for it to be wound up if the court thinks it just and equitable for it to be so.

124A(2) [Non-application] This section does not apply if the company is already being wound up by the court.

General Note

For examples of the exercise of this jurisdiction, see *Re Walter L Jacob & Co Ltd* (1989) 5 B.C.C. 244; *Re Market Wizard Systems (UK) Ltd* [1998] 2 B.C.L.C. 282; *Secretary of State for Trade & Industry v Leyton Housing Trustees Ltd* [2000] 2 B.C.L.C. 808; *Re Equity & Provident Ltd* [2002] EWHC 188 (Ch); [2002] 2 B.C.L.C. 78; *Re Delfin International (SA) Ltd* [2000] 1 B.C.L.C. 71 (where a foreign company was ordered to be wound up under the section); *Re Drivertime Recruitment Ltd* [2004] EWHC 1637 (Ch); [2005] 1 B.C.L.C. 411; *Re UK-Euro Group plc* [2006] EWHC 2102 (Ch); [2007] 1 B.C.L.C. 812; *Re The Inertia Partnership LLP* [2007] EWHC 539 (Ch); [2007] B.C.C. 656; *Secretary of State for Business, etc. v Art IT plc* [2008] EWHC 258 (Ch); [2009] 1 B.C.L.C. 262; *Re Corvin Construction Ltd* (unreported, 21 December 2012) and of a refusal to exercise it; *Re Secure & Provide plc* [1992] B.C.C. 405; *Re Forrester & Lamego Ltd* [1997] 2 B.C.L.C. 155; *Secretary of State for Trade & Industry v Travel Time (UK) Ltd* [2000] B.C.C. 792 and *Secretary of State for Business, Innovation and Skills v KJK Investments Ltd* [2015] EWHC 1589 (Ch) (investment company with no realistic prospect of returns to investors, lack of commercial probity and of any commercial basis for the business); *Re Caledonian Ltd* [2016] EWHC 2854 (Ch) (deliberate misselling of investment products). See also *Re ForceSun Ltd* [2002] EWHC 443 (Ch); [2002] 2 B.C.L.C. 302; and *Re Alpha Club (UK) Ltd* [2002] EWHC 884 (Ch); [2004] B.C.C. 754, where the court ruled it appropriate to make a winding-up order under s.124A even though the company was already in voluntary liquidation. In *Re a Company (No.007816 of 1994)* [1997] 2 B.C.L.C. 685 and *Re Titan International Inc* [1998] 1 B.C.L.C. 102 the court declined to order the winding up of foreign companies on public interest grounds for want of evidence of a sufficient connection with the jurisdiction or of prejudice to the public interest in this country.

Note that proceedings under s.124A do not fall within the scope of the EU Regulation, even where the company in question is insolvent: *Re Marann Brooks CSV Ltd* [2003] B.C.C. 239; or the Brussels Convention (now the Recast Judgments Regulation 1215/2012): *Re Senator Hanseatische Verwaltungsgesellschaft mbH* [1997] B.C.C. 112.

In an appropriate case, a provisional liquidator may be appointed: *Secretary of State for Business, Innovation and Skills v Hawkhurst Capital plc* [2013] EWHC 4219 (Ch); [2016] B.C.C. 125; *Revenue and Customs Commissioners v Winnington Networks Ltd* [2014] EWHC 1259 (Ch); [2014] B.C.C. 675; *Secretary of State for Business, Innovation and Skills v New Horizon Energy Ltd* [2015] EWHC 2961 (Ch); [2017] B.C.C. 629.

It may be expedient to order that a company should be wound up in the public interest even though it has not acted unlawfully: *Re Senator Hanseatische Verwaltungsgesellschaft mbH* [1997] 1 W.L.R. 515; [1997] B.C.C. 112, or even where it has not acted at all but may potentially be used for an unlawful purpose: *Secretary of State for Business, Innovation and Skills v PGMRS Ltd* [2010] EWHC 2983 (Ch); [2011] B.C.C. 368.

In *Secretary of State for Business, Innovation and Skills v PAG Management Services Ltd* [2015] EWHC 2404 (Ch); [2015] B.C.C. 720 a scheme designed to avoid the payment of business rates involved the formation of special purpose vehicles which took leases of the properties in question and then were immediately wound up without liquidators being appointed. Although he declined to rule that any specific provisions of IA 1986 had been infringed, Norris J held that the use of a company in liquidation as an asset shelter with an inherent bias towards prolongation of the liquidation, subverting the true purpose and function of insolvency law, justified the winding up of the companies concerned in the public interest.

In *Re Portfolios of Distinction Ltd* [2006] EWHC 782 (Ch); [2006] 2 B.C.L.C. 261 it was said that while in some cases the public would be seen to be affected where a company was committing offences, in others it would be expedient in the public interest to protect members of the public who had dealt with a company whose business was "inherently objectionable", i.e. that it caused members of the public inevitable loss, whether that derived from illegal activity or not. On the balance of probabilities it was held that the Secretary of State's case had not been made out.

A petition on public interest grounds may only be brought under this section and only by the Secretary of State: *Re Millennium Advanced Technology Ltd* [2004] EWHC 711 (Ch); [2004] 1 W.L.R. 2177. Where the Secretary of State decided not to pursue a petition on public interest grounds under s.124A, Harman J declined an application by contributories of the company to be substituted as petitioners: the existing evidence, he said, would not be material to the revised petition, which would be on different grounds (*Re Xyllyx plc (No.1)* [1992] B.C.L.C. 376).

A contributory may appear to oppose a public-interest petition and may file evidence in opposition, whether or not the company also appears to oppose it: *Re Rodencroft Ltd* [2004] EWHC 862 (Ch); [2004] B.C.C. 631. If the company does not appear in such a case, the court should be astute to inquire why this is so (ibid.). But the contributory has no standing unless he can show that he would have an interest in the surplus if a winding-up order were made and the company proved to be solvent: *Secretary of State for Business, Innovation and Skills v World Future Ltd* [2013] EWHC 723 (Ch), following *Re Rica Gold Washing Co Ltd* (1879) 11 Ch. D. 36.

The Financial Services and Markets Act 2000 s.367 authorises the Financial Conduct Authority or the Prudential Regulation Authority (as appropriate) to petition for the winding up of a body specified in that section on the ground (inter alia) that it is just and equitable that it should be wound up. This jurisdiction may be exercised analogously with s.124A: *Re Inertia Partnership LLP* (above).

In *Re Supporting Link Ltd* [2004] EWHC 523 (Ch); [2004] B.C.C. 764 the company had offered undertakings which, it contended, would make it unnecessary for the court to make a winding-up order, but it was held that, unless the Secretary of State was content to accept the undertakings, the court should be very slow indeed to accede to such a request, and a winding-up order was duly made. An offer of undertakings was refused in *Re London Citylink Ltd* [2005] EWHC 2875 (Ch); *Secretary of State for Business, Enterprise and Regulatory Reform v Charter Financial Solutions Ltd* [2009] EWHC 1118; [2011] 2 B.C.L.C. 788 and in *Re Corvin Construction Ltd* (unreported, 21 December 2012). In contrast, in *Secretary of State for Business, etc. v Amway (UK) Ltd* [2008] EWHC 1054 (Ch); [2008] B.C.C. 713, where the court held that the company's business was not inherently unlawful or objectionable but its merits had been oversold in its promotional material and it had used improper techniques to recruit customers, a winding-up petition was dismissed on undertakings by the company to adhere to a new business model. This ruling was affirmed on appeal [2009] EWCA Civ 32; [2009] B.C.C. 781.

In *Secretary of State for Trade and Industry v Bell Davies Trading Ltd* [2004] EWCA Civ 1066; [2005] 1 All E.R. 324; [2005] B.C.C. 564 the Court of Appeal (at [110] and [111]) gave the following guidance on the approach to be adopted on this question:

> "[110] A valuable review of the authorities on the proper approach of the court to s 124A public interest petitions, in general, and to the practice relating to the acceptance of undertakings, in particular, was carried out by the Vice-Chancellor in his judgment in *Re Supporting Link Ltd* [2004] EWHC 523 (Ch); [2004] B.C.C. 764; [2004] 1 W.L.R. 1549. The judge has a discretion whether or not to make a winding-up order. As for undertakings, the court has a discretion whether or not to accept them if they are proffered and whether or not to make the giving of them a condition of dismissing the petition. In considering the exercise of his discretion the willingness or otherwise of the Secretary of State to accept undertakings, which have to be policed by the Department of Trade and Industry, is an important factor.

[111] Thus, in the exercise of the discretion, the judge is entitled (a) to dismiss the petition on undertakings if, for example, he is satisfied that the offending business has ceased or if the undertakings are acceptable to the Secretary of State; or (b) to dismiss the petition on undertakings, even if that course is opposed by the Secretary of State, although that will be unusual; or (c) to refuse to accept undertakings and to wind the company up, if, for example, he is not satisfied that those giving the undertakings can be trusted."

A deposit of £5,000 is payable on the filing of the petition. A petition presented under this section on public interest grounds is required to be advertised in the same way as a creditor's petition, unless the court directs otherwise under IR 2016 r.7.10(1). For a discussion of the considerations affecting the exercise of the court's discretion in this respect, see *Re a Company (No.007923 of 1994), Re a Company (No.007924 of 1994)* [1995] B.C.C. 634 and 641; *Secretary of State for Business, Innovation and Skills v Broomfield Developments Ltd* [2014] EWHC 3925 (Ch); *Secretary of State for Business, Innovation and Skills v Combined Maintenance Services Ltd* (unreported, 6 November 2014) (where it was said that the court may be more inclined to dispense with advertising in the case of a petition under s.124A than in a creditors' petition, where there is a need for other creditors to be informed).

In *Secretary of State for Trade and Industry v Aurum Marketing Ltd* [2002] B.C.C. 31, where a company which had operated a swindle was ordered to be wound up on public interest grounds, its sole director was ordered to pay both the applicant's and the company's costs personally. Costs were also awarded against directors personally in *Re North West Holdings plc* [2001] EWCA Civ 67; [2002] B.C.C. 441, where the Court of Appeal held that, although it was the normal rule that directors should not be ordered to pay their company's costs, an exception should be made where the directors had no bona fide belief that the company had an arguable defence and that it was in the interests of the company to advance that defence. A similar order was made against a majority shareholder in *Secretary of State for Trade and Industry v Liquid Acquisitions Ltd* [2002] EWHC 180 (Ch); [2003] 1 B.C.L.C. 375. In *Re Broomfield Developments Ltd* (unreported, 19 June 2017), where the Secretary of State and the company agreed a consent order for dismissal of the petition subject to the company going into creditors' voluntary liquidation, the court did not have jurisdiction (under the Senior Courts Act 1981 s.51) to order the company to pay the Secretary of State's costs from its assets as expenses of liquidation but ordered costs without that priority.

Section 124A(1)(b) was substituted and s.124A(1)(bb) inserted by the Financial Services and Markets Act 2000 (Consequential Amendments and Repeals) Order 2001 (SI 2001/3649) as from 1 December 2001.

Generally on s.124A, see Keay (1999) 20 Co. Law. 296.

124B Petition for winding up of SE

124B(1) [Right to present petition] Where–

(a) an SE whose registered office is in Great Britain is not in compliance with Article 7 of Council Regulation (EC) No 2157/2001 on the Statute for a European company (the "EC Regulation") (location of head office and registered office), and

(b) it appears to the Secretary of State that the SE should be wound up, he may present a petition for it to be wound up if the court thinks it is just and equitable for it to be so.

124B(2) [Disapplication of s.124B] This section does not apply if the SE is already being wound up by the court.

124B(3) ["SE"] In this section "SE" has the same meaning as in the EC Regulation.

General Note

Section 124B was inserted by the European Public Limited-Liability Company Regulations 2004 (SI 2004/2326) reg.73(3), as from 8 October 2004. The EC Regulation 2157/2001 on the *Societas Europaea* requires that an SE should have its head office in the Member State in which its registered office is situated. Where an SE no longer complies with this, the Member State having the registered office is required by art.64 of the Regulation to take appropriate measures to have the SE regularise its position, failing which it must be liquidated.

124C Petition for winding up of SCE

124C(1) [Breach of European Cooperative Society Regulation] Where, in the case of an SCE whose registered office is in Great Britain–

(a) there has been such a breach as is mentioned in Article 73(1) of Council Regulation (EC) No 1435/2003 on the Statute for a European Cooperative Society (SCE) (the "European Cooperative Society Regulation") (winding up by the court or other competent authority), and

(b) it appears to the Financial Conduct Authority that the SCE should be wound up,

the Financial Conduct Authority may present a petition for the SCE to be wound up if the court thinks it is just and equitable for it to be so.

124C(2) [Non-compliance with European Cooperative Society Regulation art.6] Where, in the case of an SCE whose registered office is in Great Britain–

(a) the SCE is not in compliance with Article 6 of the European Cooperative Society Regulation (location of head office and registered office, and

(b) it appears to the Financial Conduct Authority that the SCE should be wound up,

the Financial Conduct Authority may present a petition for the SCE to be wound up if the court thinks it is just and equitable for it to be so.

124C(3) [Non-application of s.124C] This section does not apply if the SCE is already being wound up by the court.

124C(4) ["SCE"] In this section "SCE" has the same meaning as in the European Cooperative Society Regulation.

General Note

Section 124C inserted by the European Cooperative Society Regulations 2006 (SI 2006/2078) reg.33(1) as from 18 August 2006.

125 Powers of court on hearing of petition

125(1) [Extent of powers] On hearing a winding-up petition the court may dismiss it, or adjourn the hearing conditionally or unconditionally, or make an interim order, or any other order that it thinks fit; but the court shall not refuse to make a winding-up order on the ground only that the company's assets have been mortgaged to an amount equal to or in excess of those assets, or that the company has no assets.

125(2) [Just and equitable winding up] If the petition is presented by members of the company as contributories on the ground that it is just and equitable that the company should be wound up, the court, if it is of opinion–

(a) that the petitioners are entitled to relief either by winding up the company or by some other means, and

(b) that in the absence of any other remedy it would be just and equitable that the company should be wound up,

shall make a winding-up order; but this does not apply if the court is also of the opinion both that some other remedy is available to the petitioners and that they are acting unreasonably in seeking to have the company wound up instead of pursuing that other remedy.

S.125(1)

This provision gives the court the widest discretion. For instance, in *Re Internet Investment Corp Ltd* [2009] EWHC 2744 (Ch); [2010] 1 B.C.L.C. 458 a compulsory winding up was preferred to a voluntary liquidation because the director's conduct necessitated a thorough investigation.

There is no established rule, comparable with that applicable in the case of a contributory petitioner (see the note to s.124(2) above), that a creditor's petition will be dismissed unless he can show that he will have a tangible benefit from the liquidation (*Re Crigglestone Coal Co Ltd* [1906] 2 Ch. 327): the court's discretion is unfettered, except by the concluding words of the subsection. For cases in which the court reviewed the authorities and discussed the basis on which the discretion will be exercised, where a petition is opposed by some creditors, see *Re Television Parlour plc* (1988) 4 B.C.C. 95; *Re H J Tomkins & Son Ltd* [1990] B.C.L.C. 76; *Re Leigh Estates (UK) Ltd* [1994] B.C.C. 292; *Re Lummus Agricultural Services Ltd* [1999] B.C.C. 953; and *Re Demaglass Holdings Ltd* [2001] 2 B.C.L.C. 633. In *Bell Group Finance (Pty) Ltd v Bell Group (UK) Holdings Ltd* [1996] B.C.C. 505 it was held to be a good reason for the making of a winding-up order that it would allow an investigation to take place into the affairs of a hopelessly insolvent company. An argument that the only proper procedure in such a case was the Secretary of State petitioning on the grounds of public interest, and not a creditor petitioning on the grounds of insolvency, was rejected by the court.

One basis for the exercise of the court's discretion to dismiss a winding-up petition (or to grant a stay of the winding-up proceedings under s.147) has traditionally been that of *forum non conveniens*, i.e. that it is more appropriate that the matter be dealt with by a court in some other jurisdiction. In *Re Harrods (Buenos Aires) Ltd* [1992] Ch. 72; [1991] B.C.C. 249, a petition was presented for the winding up of an English-registered company which carried on business exclusively in Argentina. The Court of Appeal ruled that the courts of Argentina were the appropriate forum, and ordered a stay of the English proceedings. However, the ECJ has ruled that such a decision is inconsistent with art.2 of the Brussels Convention: *Owusu v Jackson* (C-281/02) [2005] Q.B. 801, and so the *Harrods* case must now be treated as overruled (where the Convention or its successor applies).

For the procedure on the making of a winding-up order, see IR 2016 rr.7.21 et seq.

It is the usual practice, where a creditor's petition is dismissed because the debt on which it is based has been paid in full, for the court in its discretion to order the company to pay the petitioner's costs, whether or not the company appears at the hearing. See this matter discussed fully in *Re Nowmost Co Ltd* [1997] B.C.C. 105. In *Winnington Networks Communications Ltd v HMRC* (unreported, 24 November 2015) the company's directors were ordered to pay personally the petitioning creditor's costs and also the costs of the company's unsuccessful defence, where they were unable to show that they had a genuine belief that the company had a defence.

The court may in its discretion order a company to give security for costs as a condition of granting permission to appeal against a winding-up order. The factors to be taken into account are discussed by Henderson J in *Aidiniantz v Sherlock Holmes International Society Ltd* [2015] EWHC 2882 (Ch).

The jurisdiction conferred by s.125 is confined to the disposal of the petition. The section does not confer on the court jurisdiction to deal with other matters, such as a claim for damages in tort for the malicious institution of proceedings: *Partizan Ltd v O J Kilkenny & Co Ltd* [1998] B.C.C. 912.

S.125(2)

It is not sufficient for the purposes of this provision simply to show that the petitioner has alternative remedies open to him; he must also be acting unreasonably in not pursuing them.

In *Re a Company (No.002567 of 1982)* [1983] 1 W.L.R. 927, this subsection was relied on to refuse relief to a petitioner who had agreed to sell his shares to the majority shareholders at an independent valuation and had then reneged on this arrangement. A similar ruling was given in *Fuller v Cyracuse Ltd* [2001] B.C.C. 806, where the petitioner had refused to accept an offer by the company to buy his shares at an independent valuation. In contrast, it was held not unreasonable to refuse a similar offer in *Re Data Online Transactions (UK) Ltd, Apcar v Aftab* [2003] B.C.C. 510.

This was a minority shareholder's petition on the "just and equitable" ground, where it is common to seek in the alternative an order under CA 2006 s.994 [formerly CA 1985 s.459], on the grounds of "unfair prejudice". In this situation the court is frequently asked to exercise its discretion under s.125(2) on the ground that the petitioner is unreasonably refusing to pursue some other form of relief or to accept some other remedy. On the exercise of the court's discretion, see, e.g. *Re a Company (No.003028 of 1987)* (1987) 3 B.C.C. 575; *Re a Company (No.003843 of 1986)* (1987) 3 B.C.C. 624; *Re a Company (No.003096 of 1987)* (1988) 4 B.C.C. 80; *Re a Company (No.001363 of 1988)* (1989) 5 B.C.C. 18; *Vujnovich v Vujnovich* (1989) 5 B.C.C. 740; *Re Abbey Leisure Ltd* [1990] B.C.C. 60; *Re a Company (No.00330 of 1991) Ex p. Holden* [1991] B.C.C. 241; *Re Copeland & Craddock Ltd* [1997] B.C.C. 294; *Re a Company (No.004415 of 1996)* [1997] 1 B.C.L.C. 479; *CVC/Opportunity Equity Partners Ltd v Demarco Almeida* [2002] UKPC 16; [2002] B.C.C. 684; *Re Woven Rugs Ltd* [2008] B.C.C. 903; *Maresca v Brookfield Development and Construction Ltd* [2013] EWHC 3151 (Ch) (where the court refused a winding-up order and instead, in effect, imposed a settlement on the parties). It was thought that if conduct relied on in an unfairly prejudicial conduct petition was not unfair for the purposes of s.994 it could not found a case for a winding-up order on the just and equitable ground as the winding-up jurisdiction was no wider than the s.994 jurisdiction as a winding-up order was the death sentence for the company (*Re Guidezone Ltd* [2001] B.C.C. 692), but the Court of Appeal has since doubted this and stated there may be cases which satisfied the requirements of one jurisdiction but not the other: *Re Neath Rugby Ltd; Hawkes v Cuddy* [2009] EWCA Civ 291; [2010] B.C.C. 597.

In a Practice Direction (see *Practice Direction—Order under section 127 Insolvency Act 1986* [2007] B.C.C. 839 (reproduced as App.V to this *Guide*)) the attention of practitioners is drawn to the undesirability of including "as a matter of course" a prayer for winding up as an alternative to an order under CA 2006 s.994. It should be included only if that is the relief which the petitioner prefers or if it is considered that it may be the only relief to which he is entitled. This may be seen as an attempt to discourage the use of an alternative prayer for winding up as a tactical device to put pressure on the company and its controllers. (See further the notes to s.127 below.)

126 Power to stay or restrain proceedings against company

126(1) [Exercise of power] At any time after the presentation of a winding-up petition, and before a winding-up order has been made, the company, or any creditor or contributory, may–

(a) where any action or proceeding against the company is pending in the High Court or Court of Appeal in England and Wales or Northern Ireland, apply to the court in which the action or proceeding is pending for a stay of proceedings therein, and

(b) where any other action or proceeding is pending against the company, apply to the court having jurisdiction to wind up the company to restrain further proceedings in the action or proceeding;

and the court to which application is so made may (as the case may be) stay, sist or restrain the proceedings accordingly on such terms as it thinks fit.

126(2) [Where company registered but not formed under CA 2006] In the case of a company registered but not formed under the Companies Act 2006, where the application to stay, sist or restrain is by a creditor, this section extends to actions and proceedings against any contributory of the company.

126(3) [Application of s.126(1) HMRC action for deduction from accounts] Subsection (1) applies in relation to any action being taken in respect of the company under Part 1 of Schedule 8 to the Finance (No. 2) Act 2015 (enforcement by deduction from accounts) as it applies in relation to any action or proceeding mentioned in paragraph (b) of that subsection.

General Note

The making of a winding-up order operates automatically to stay all actions and proceedings against the company, as does also the appointment of a provisional liquidator, unless the court directs otherwise (see s.130(2)). This section empowers the court to make interim orders during the period when the hearing of a winding-up application is pending.

S.126(2)

See the notes to ss.73, 83 regarding these companies.

In relation to the financial markets, nothing in s.126 affects any action taken by an exchange or clearing house for the purpose of its default proceedings: CA 1989 s.161(4).

S.126(3)

Section 126(3) inserted by the Finance (No.2) Act 2015 s.51 and Sch.8 paras 26, 27 as from 28 November 2015. This follows the introduction of HMRC's power to make deductions from accounts held with deposit-takers as a means of enforcing payment.

127 Avoidance of property dispositions, etc.

127(1) [Dispositions etc. void after commencement of winding up] In a winding up by the court, any disposition of the company's property, and any transfer of shares, or alteration in the status of the company's members, made after the commencement of the winding up is, unless the court otherwise orders, void.

127(2) [No effect on administrator while petition suspended] This section has no effect in respect of anything done by an administrator of a company while a winding-up petition is suspended under paragraph 40 of Schedule B1.

General Note

When an order is made for the winding up of a company by the court, it is deemed for various statutory purposes to have commenced from the time of the presentation of the petition or an even earlier time: see s.129. This section accordingly operates with retrospective effect to avoid the property dispositions and other legal events mentioned, unless the court orders otherwise. It is not necessary that the company should be insolvent. There is a good deal of similarity between s.127 and s.284 (which restricts post-petition dispositions of property made by a person who is made bankrupt). But there are differences between the two regimes, so that decisions given under the one section will not necessarily be binding under the other: *Pettit v Novakovic* [2007] B.C.C. 462.

An application may be made to the court under this section for the prospective validation of a transaction before a winding-up order has been made: see, e.g. *Re A I Levy (Holdings) Ltd* [1964] Ch. 19.

Application may be made to the court by the company itself or by any interested person, such as the disponee of the property: *Re Argentum Reductions (UK) Ltd* [1975] 1 W.L.R. 186. The principles upon which the court will act in exercising its discretion under this section are well settled. The leading case is *Re Gray's Inn Construction Co Ltd* [1980] 1 W.L.R. 711. Where the company is insolvent, the primary purpose of the section is to ensure that all creditors are paid pari passu. A transaction which has, or is likely to have, the effect of reducing the assets available to creditors will not be validated; but if there is no serious risk to creditors or if the company is likely to improve the position of its creditors by trading profitably pending the hearing of the petition, the discretion may be exercised. These and other fundamental principles on granting validation orders were summarised and applied in *Wilson v SMC Properties Ltd* [2015] EWHC 870 (Ch), confirmed on appeal [2016] EWHC 444 (Ch); [2016] B.C.C. 504 (where a disposition was validated because there was no loss to creditors). Payments into or out of the company's bank account were held (or in some respects conceded) to be "dispositions of the company's property" for the purposes of this section, both when the account was in credit and when it was overdrawn, in *Re Gray's Inn Construction Co Ltd* (above); and in *Re McGuinness Bros (UK) Ltd* (1987) 3 B.C.C. 571 at 574; and this view was upheld in the case of an overdrawn account in *Re Tain Construction Ltd, Rose v AIB Group (UK) plc* [2003] EWHC 1737 (Ch); [2003] 1 W.L.R. 2791; [2004] B.C.C. 11. But other cases suggest that this view is too wide. In *Re Barn Crown Ltd* [1994] 1 W.L.R. 147; [1994] B.C.C. 381 payments into an account which was in credit were held not to be within the section—a ruling which has been criticised by Professor Goode, *Principles of Corporate Insolvency Law*, 4th edn (2011), at 13–131. Professor Goode (ibid., at 13–133) also considers that *Re Gray's Inn Construction Co Ltd* is wrong (save in certain exceptional cases) in so far as it supports the view that payments out of an account which is overdrawn involve a disposition of the company's property. And in *Bank of Ireland v Hollicourt (Contractors) Ltd* [2001] Ch. 555; [2000] B.C.C. 1210 the Court of Appeal, endorsing the ruling of Lightman J in *Coutts & Co v Stock* [2000] 1 W.L.R. 906; [2000] B.C.C. 247, held that payments made by cheque out of a company's bank account to a third party involve no disposition of the company's property to the bank—which merely acts as the company's agent in making a disposition in favour of the third party—and that this is so whether the account is in credit or overdrawn. Several of the latter cases and Professor Goode's analysis were analysed in detail in *Officeserve Technologies Ltd (in liq.) v Anthony-Mike* [2017] EWHC 1920 (Ch); [2017] B.C.C. 574 which concluded that an agreement not to sue on a debt was the same as the release of a debt and therefore a disposition under s.127 which the court in its discretion refused to validate. [Note that *Hollicourt* was distinguished in *Pettit v Novakovic* (above), a case on s.284 which imposes similar restrictions on post-petition dispositions in bankruptcy.]

For other decisions under the section, see *Re a Company (No.007523 of 1986)* (1987) 3 B.C.C. 57 (order refused—company currently trading at a loss); *Re Sugar Properties (Derisley Wood) Ltd* (1987) 3 B.C.C. 88 (order granted authorising sale of shares in racehorses); *Re French's Wine Bar Ltd* (1987) 3 B.C.C. 173 (completion of agreement to sell leasehold property sanctioned); *Re Tramway Building & Construction Co Ltd* [1988] Ch. 293; (1987) 3 B.C.C. 443 (transfer of land validated: no reduction of assets); *Re Webb Electrical Ltd* (1988) 4 B.C.C. 230 (repayment of advance made by director to company not validated: no benefit to company); *Re Fairway Graphics Ltd* [1991] B.C.L.C. 468 (order refused: benefit to creditors not shown); *Re Rafidain Bank* [1992] B.C.C. 376 (order sought for benefit of one creditor only: refused); *Re S A & D Wright Ltd, Denney v John Hudson & Co Ltd* [1992] B.C.C. 503 (fuel oil supplied to company which enabled it to continue its business; seller's requirement in usual course of trading that payment for previous supplies be made as a condition for delivery of new supplies: held not a preference, and order made validating such payments); *Richbell Information Services Inc v Atlantic General Investments Ltd* [1999] B.C.C. 871 (a funding arrangement to enable litigation to be conducted to pursue a claim to recover assets claimed by the company, which would ultimately involve a disposition of proceeds of the litigation: validating order made); *Re Airfreight Express (UK) Ltd* [2005] B.P.I.R. 250; *Re Albany Building Ltd* [2007] B.C.C. 591 (sales of property on advantageous terms); *RC Brewery Ltd v Revenue and Customs Commissioners* [2013] EWHC 1184 (Ch); [2013] B.C.C. 718 (validation order refused where only reason was attempt to buy time to pay off debt); *Re SED Essex Ltd* [2013] EWHC 1583 (Ch); [2014] B.C.C. 628 (relevance of likelihood of successful s.127 application to appointment of provisional liquidator; cf. *Revenue and Customs Commissioners v Rochdale Drinks Distributors Ltd* [2011] EWCA Civ 1116; [2013] B.C.C. 419; *Wilson v SMC Properties Ltd* [2015] EWHC 870 (Ch) (property sold to a third party in good faith, at arm's length and not at an undervalue: transaction validated as it had not favoured a pre-liquidation creditor and there had been no loss and upheld on appeal: [2016] EWHC 444 (Ch); [2016] B.C.C. 504); *Sahaviriya Steel Industries UK Ltd v Hewden Stuart Ltd* [2015] EWHC 2726 (Ch); [2016]

B.C.C. 450 (partial validation granted; hearing held in private to protect commercial confidentiality); *Express Electrical Distributors Ltd v Beavis* [2016] EWCA Civ 765; [2016] B.C.C. 566 (validation refused: disposition held prejudicial to the interests of unsecured creditors)). In *Re Tain Construction Ltd, Rose v AIB Group* [2003] EWHC 1737 (Ch); [2003] 1 W.L.R. 2791; [2004] B.C.C. 11 it was held to be material, but not decisive, that (i) the petition had not been advertised and the payee bank was unaware that it had been presented; and (ii) the payments had been made in the ordinary course of business. Even where the parties had acted in good faith a validation order might be refused if there were grounds for thinking that the transaction was an attempt to prefer the disponee or a guarantor of the overdraft. The bank in that case also sought to argue that it had changed its position to its detriment. While not ruling out the possibility that this might be a factor going to the exercise of the court's discretion, the judge regarded it as more relevant to the restitutionary claim which followed from the disponee's failure to obtain a validating order; however, in the case itself the defence of change of position failed on the evidence.

Where the company is solvent, the same considerations do not arise. The court will be concerned to avoid paralysing the company's business, and will normally give leave for it to continue trading, the onus being on the person opposing the grant of leave to justify refusal (*Re Burton & Deakin Ltd* [1977] 1 W.L.R. 390). But the fact that the company is solvent is not determinative: in *Re a Company (No.007130 of 1988)* [2000] 1 B.C.L.C. 582 the court refused to authorise payments out of the bank account of a solvent company which was the subject of a petition to wind it up on public interest grounds, there being evidence of irregularities in the conduct of the company's management.

"The company's property", in s.127, means property beneficially owned by the company: *Re Margart Pty Ltd, Hamilton v Westpac Banking Corp* (1984) 2 A.C.L.C. 709; *Re Branston & Gothard Ltd* [1999] B.P.I.R. 466. Where a company has entered into a binding and unconditional contract for the sale of an interest in land (or, probably, any other specifically enforceable contract to alienate property) before the presentation of a winding-up petition against it, it will in most cases already have disposed of the beneficial interest in the property concerned, and so, strictly speaking, the completion of the transaction by the conveyance of the legal title after the presentation of the petition is not a "disposition" within s.127. However, in practice it may be prudent to seek an order from the court that, in so far as the completion may involve any disposition of the property of the company, it should be treated as valid and effective: *Re French's Wine Bar Ltd* (above). The Supreme Court has held that where property held on trust for a company as beneficiary is transferred by the trustee after a winding-up petition is presented against the company, that is not a disposition of the company's property under s.127 since the company's beneficial interest continues, despite the disposal of the legal title even if in breach of trust: *Akers v Samba Financial Group* [2017] UKSC 6; [2017] 2 W.L.R. 713; [2017] B.C.C. 511. In the latter case Lord Collins considered at [96] that the combined effect of s.127 and the definition of "property" in s.436 is that the avoidance provisions of s.127 apply to property "wherever situated" and so it appears that the section can have extra-territorial effect on property situated outside the jurisdiction. In *Officeserve Technologies Ltd (in liq.) v Anthony-Mike* [2017] EWHC 1920 (Ch); [2017] B.C.C. 574 the court took a wide interpretation of property, also invoking s.436.

Where property is recovered by a liquidator under s.127 and the company's assets are subject to a floating charge, the charge attaches to the property, which is deemed to have remained all along the property of the company: *Re RS&M Engineering Co Ltd, Mond v Hammond Suddards* [2000] Ch. 40 at 50; [2000] B.C.C. 445 at 451. However the liquidator cannot assign to a third party the right to bring proceedings to have a disposition declared void under s.127 and to recover the property from the recipient: *Re Ayala Holdings Ltd (No.2)* [1996] 1 B.C.L.C. 467. (This ruling may be open to question (although no doubt correct on the facts of the case itself), for no right to bring proceedings is specifically conferred on the liquidator. It is hard to see why an assignment in favour of a person having a charge over the company's assets should not be effective—or, for that matter, why such a chargee could not institute proceedings in his own right.) Note that there is no mention of s.127 in the new ss.176ZB (recoveries by a liquidator or administrator under specified statutory provisions not caught by a floating charge) and 248ZD (these office-holders empowered to assign the right of action under the specified provisions, and their proceeds, to third parties). This is, no doubt, because the power to institute proceedings under these sections is not conferred specifically (or exclusively) on the liquidator. The relevant questions remain to be determined under the common law.

The section applies in the winding up of a foreign company: *Re Sugar Properties (Derisley Wood) Ltd* (above).

Section 127 does not provide the liquidator with any cause of action against the directors for any loss which the company may have sustained: its only consequence, in the absence of a validation order, is to make the dispositions void. If loss can be shown, an action for misfeasance or breach of duty under s.212 may lie (*Phillips v McGregor-Paterson* [2009] EWHC 2385 (Ch); [2010] 1 B.C.L.C. 72; *Re Oxford Pharmaceuticals Ltd* [2009] EWHC 1753 (Ch); [2010] B.C.C. 834).

It has been common practice for a shareholder petitioning for relief on the grounds of unfair prejudice (CA 2006 s.994) to add an alternative prayer for the winding up of the company. This automatically brings into operation the provisions of s.127 so that, unless the court gives leave, the company's business will be paralysed, usually to the prejudice of all concerned. Accordingly, in a Practice Direction (*Practice Direction—Order under section 127 of the Insolvency Act 1986* [2007] B.C.C. 839) attention is drawn to the undesirability of asking as a matter of course for a winding-up order as an alternative to relief under that provision; and whenever a winding-up order is asked for in any petition by a contributory the petitioner is required to state in advance whether he consents or objects to a s.127 order in the standard form which is appended to the Practice Direction. If he is prepared to consent, the registrar will normally make an order without further inquiry. The Practice Direction (including the standard form of order) is reproduced at App.V of this *Guide*.

Where a winding-up petition has been presented and the company wishes to apply for a validating order under s.127, a further *Practice Direction* [2018] B.C.C. 241 (reproduced as App.IV to this *Guide*) para.9.11 gives directions as to (i) who may hear the application; (ii) to whom notice of the application should be given; (iii) what evidence is required in support of the application; (iv) urgent cases; and (v) the standard of proof.

The court's discretion can extend to validating a transaction to which the company is not a party, but only in special circumstances. In *Re Dewrun Ltd* [2002] B.C.C. 57 the company had transferred freehold property to another company which had given a charge to its bank. An order was made validating the transaction to the limited extent of confirming the bank's charge.

In *Re J Smiths Haulage Ltd* [2007] B.C.C. 135 an administrator was appointed by the holder of a floating charge and immediately disposed of the company's business, unaware that a winding-up petition had been presented some five weeks earlier. It was held that, since the effect of the appointment was to suspend (rather than stay) the winding-up order (IA 1986 Sch.B1 para.40(1)(b)), the petition was without legal effect for the period of the administration and so s.127 did not apply to avoid the disposition. This case was followed in *Harlow v Creative Staging Ltd* [2014] EWHC 2787 (Ch), so that once administration ceased the suspended petition could be heard and a winding up ordered, consequently rendering certain interim dispositions void unless validated by the court.

A provision similar to s.127 is made in relation to a voluntary winding up by s.88, except that it applies only to transfers of shares and alterations in the status of the company's members; and in this case the sanction of the liquidator and not the leave of the court is needed to validate the transaction.

In the context of the financial markets, s.127 does not apply to a market contract or any disposition of property in pursuance of such a contract, the provision of margin in relation to market contracts, a market charge, and certain other transactions: see CA 1989 ss.163(4), 175(3)–(5). A similar dispensation applies in relation to financial and securities settlement systems: s.127 does not apply to a disposition of property as a result of which the property becomes subject to a collateral security charge, or any transactions pursuant to which that transaction is made: Finality Regulations reg.19(3). Section 127 is also disapplied in relation to a transfer order or a contract for the purpose of realising security in such systems: reg.16(1). See the notes on pp.1–3.

In the liquidation of a collateral-taker or collateral-provider under a financial collateral arrangement, s.127 is disapplied (a) in relation to a property or security interest created or otherwise arising under such an arrangement or (b) to prevent a close-out netting provision taking effect in accordance with its terms: Financial Collateral Arrangements (No.2) Regulations 2003 (SI 2003/3226) reg.10(1).

Section 127 continues to apply even although the winding-up order is subsequently discharged (e.g. under Sch.B1 para.37(3)(a)): *Re Albany Building Ltd* [2007] B.C.C. 591, and so any post-petition transactions are avoided unless the court orders otherwise.

Note that there is no scope for the application of s.127 in the case where the court exercises the power (conferred by Sch.B1 para.13(1)(e)) to order a winding up instead of making an administration order, since in that case the winding up is deemed to commence on the making of the order: see s.129(1A).

S.127(2)

This provision was inserted (and the former s.127 renumbered as s.127(1)) by EA 2002 s.248 and Sch.17 para.15, with effect from 15 September 2003. See further the notes to Sch.B1 para.40.

128 Avoidance of attachments, etc.

128(1) [Attachments etc. void] Where a company registered in England and Wales is being wound up by the court, any attachment, sequestration, distress or execution put in force against the estate or effects of the company after the commencement of the winding up is void.

128(2) [Application to Scotland] This section, so far as relates to any estate or effects of the company situated in England and Wales, applies in the case of a company registered in Scotland as it applies in the case of a company registered in England and Wales.

128(3) ["Attachment" in s.128(1) includes HMRC hold notice or deduction notice] In subsection (1) "attachment" includes a hold notice or a deduction notice under Part 1 of Schedule 8 to the Finance (No. 2) Act 2015 (enforcement by deduction from accounts) and, if subsection (1) has effect in relation to a deduction notice, it also has effect in relation to the hold notice to which the deduction notice relates (whenever the hold notice was given).

General Note

In spite of the apparently unqualified wording of s.128, it has been held that the court may override the effect of the section by an order made under s.126(1) or s.130(2): see, e.g. *The Constellation* [1966] 1 W.L.R. 272.

There is no provision in the Act which avoids attachments, etc. in a similar way in a voluntary winding up; but the liquidator may apply to the court under either s.126(1) or s.130(2) to have such a process stayed or set aside, by virtue of the powers conferred on the court by s.112(1).

Further sections of the Act deal with the question of executions, etc. which have been begun but not completed at the time when the winding up of the company is deemed to commence: see ss.183, 184.

Section 176 of the Act is expressed to be without prejudice to this section. Section 176 imposes a charge on goods which have been distrained in the three months before a winding-up order (or their proceeds, if they have been sold) for the benefit of the company's preferential creditors.

In relation to the financial markets, nothing in s.128 affects any action taken by an exchange or clearing house for the purpose of its default proceedings: CA 1989 s.161(4).

S.128(3)

Section 128(3) inserted by the Finance (No.2) Act 2015 s.51 and Sch.8 paras 26, 28 as from 28 November 2015. This follows the introduction of HMRC's power to make deductions from accounts held with deposit-takers as a means of enforcing payment.

Commencement of winding up

129 Commencement of winding up by the court

129(1) [Time of passing of resolution] If, before the presentation of a petition for the winding up of a company by the court, a resolution has been passed by the company for voluntary winding up, the winding up of the company is deemed to have commenced at the time of the passing of the resolution; and unless the court, on proof of fraud or mistake, directs otherwise, all proceedings taken in the voluntary winding up are deemed to have been validly taken.

129(1A) [Winding-up order on administration application] Where the court makes a winding-up order by virtue of paragraph 13(1)(e) of Schedule B1, the winding up is deemed to commence on the making of the order.

129(2) [Time of presentation of petition] In any other case, the winding up of a company by the court is deemed to commence at the time of the presentation of the petition for winding up.

General Note

The effect of s.192(1), (2) is to backdate the operation of the winding-up order (for the operation of certain statutory provisions) to the time when the petition for winding up was presented (or, if the company was then already in voluntary liquidation, to the time when the resolution for voluntary winding up was passed).

On the significance of the word "time", see the note to s.86.

A voluntary liquidation commences at the time of the passing of the resolution for voluntary winding up: see s.86.

The term "commencement of the winding up" is defined differently for the purposes of s.185 (effect of diligence in Scotland): see s.185(3).

Subsection (1A) was inserted by EA 2002 s.248 and Sch.17 para.16, with effect from 15 September 2003. Under Sch.B1 para.13(1)(e) the court is empowered, in hearing an application for an administration order, to treat the application as a winding-up petition and order the company to be wound up. In this case, the commencement of the winding up is not back-dated.

In the application of the EU Regulation, the critical point for many purposes is the "time of the opening of proceedings", which is defined by art.2(8) as "the time at which the judgment opening proceedings becomes effective, regardless of whether it is a final judgment or not". This will (at least prima facie) refer to the time when the court pronounces its order, except in the case where the company is already in creditors' voluntary liquidation, when it would be the time of the passing of the shareholders' resolution. However, where the issue for the court is the determination of the debtor's "centre of main interests" (COMI), it may be necessary to examine the position at some earlier time, e.g. on the hearing of an application to serve the proceedings abroad: see the discussion of *Shierson v Vlieland-Boddy* [2005] EWCA Civ 974; [2005] B.C.C. 949 in the note to art.3(1) of the Regulation. In *Re Eurofood IFSC Ltd* [2005] B.C.C. 1,021 the Advocate General (at para.93) thought that a statutory provision equivalent to s.129, defining the "commencement of the winding up" was conclusive to fix the "time of the opening of the proceedings". However, this is to give too wide a meaning to the former phrase: in practice, the definition is applied only for the purposes of other sections of the Act which use the same expression (e.g. s.127), and not for other purposes such as the proving of debts. Moreover, the Advocate General's opinion overlooks the fact that s.129(c) has effect only if a winding-up order is eventually made. (The EC Court in its judgment [2006] B.C.C. 397 (at para.59) found it unnecessary to examine this question, in the light of its ruling that the appointment of a provisional liquidator (coincidentally on the same day that the petition was presented) settled the matter. But the Court would surely have considered it critical that s.129 on its own does not have the effect of divesting the company of its assets as from the presentation of the petition.)

It has been held that the periods of limitation prescribed by the Limitation Act 1980 cease to run on the making of a winding-up order, and not (except as against the petitioning creditor) at the time when the winding-up petition is presented: *Re Cases of Taff's Well Ltd* [1992] Ch. 179; [1991] B.C.C. 582; and see *Financial Services Compensation Scheme Ltd v Larnell (Insurances) Ltd* [2005] EWCA Civ 1408; [2006] B.C.C. 690. Accordingly, in the case of a six-year period of limitation, the liquidator in a winding up by the court is at liberty to distribute the assets of the company without regard to the claims of creditors which accrued more than six years before the making of the winding-up order. In the same case the judge expressed the view, obiter, that an administration order would not prevent time running against a creditor of the company.

130 Consequences of winding-up order

130(1) [Copy of order to registrar] On the making of a winding-up order, a copy of the order must forthwith be forwarded by the company (or otherwise as may be prescribed) to the registrar of companies, who shall enter it in his records relating to the company.

130(2) [Actions stayed on winding-up order] When a winding-up order has been made or a provisional liquidator has been appointed, no action or proceeding shall be proceeded with or commenced against the company or its property, except by leave of the court and subject to such terms as the court may impose.

130(3) [Actions stayed re companies registered but not formed under CA 2006] When an order has been made for winding up a company registered but not formed under the Companies Act 2006, no action or proceeding shall be commenced or proceeded with against the company or its property or any contributory of the company, in respect of any debt of the company, except by leave of the court, and subject to such terms as the court may impose.

130(3A) [Action or proceeding in s.130(2), (3) includes HMRC deduction from accounts] In subsections (2) and (3), the reference to an action or proceeding includes action in respect of the company under Part 1 of Schedule 8 to the Finance (No. 2) Act 2015 (enforcement by deduction from accounts).

130(4) [Effect of order] An order for winding up a company operates in favour of all the creditors and of all contributories of the company as if made on the joint petition of a creditor and of a contributory.

General Note

Section 130(3A) inserted by the Finance (No.2) Act 2015 s.51 and Sch.8 para.27 as from 28 November 2015. In relation to the financial markets, nothing in s.130 affects any action taken by an exchange or clearing house for the purpose of its default proceedings: CA 1989 s.161(4).

S.130(1)

Under the rules prescribed for the purposes of this provision the court is required to send two copies of the order to the official receiver, who is then charged with the responsibility for serving the company and the registrar and for gazetting and advertising the order: see IR 2016 r.7.22.

Neither the registration of a winding-up order in the Companies Registry nor the gazetting of the fact that a company is in liquidation or of the appointment of a liquidator operates as notice to the world that the company is in liquidation: *Ewart v Fryer* [1901] 1 Ch. 499 (but see more particularly the report in (1900) 82 L.T. 415); affirmed sub nom. *Fryer v Ewart* [1902] A.C. 187; *Official Custodian for Charities v Parway Estates Developments Ltd (in liq.)* [1985] Ch. 151 at 160.

The registrar is required to publish in the *Gazette* notice of the receipt by him of the copy of the winding-up order (CA 2006 s.1078) and this amounts to "official notification" of the making of the winding-up order for the purposes of CA 2006 s.1079. On the effect of "official notification", see the note to s.109, above. It is not easy, however, to reconcile s.1079 with the provisions contained in ss.127–129 above which give a winding-up order retrospective effect: this is a difficult question which awaits judicial determination.

In *Re Calmex Ltd* [1989] 1 All E.R. 485; (1988) 4 B.C.C. 761, a winding-up order had been made against the company in error, and the court exercised its jurisdiction under IR 2016 r.12.59 to rescind it. The registrar of companies took the view that the winding-up order which had been recorded under s.130(1) should remain on his files, but the court ordered it to be removed on the ground that the rescinding order had rendered it a nullity.

In *Sebry v Companies House* [2015] EWHC 115 (QB); [2015] B.C.C. 236 a winding-up order was made against a company (T and Son Ltd) and a copy of the order (without the company's number) was sent as required to Companies House, which inadvertently registered it against an unrelated company (T and Sons Ltd). This had disastrous consequences for the latter company, which was driven out of business. The court held that the Registrar owed a common-law duty when registering a winding-up order to take reasonable care to ensure that it was not registered against the wrong company, which had been broken in this case, and that T and Sons Ltd were entitled to substantial damages. (The court, without deciding the question, also expressed the view that an action for breach of statutory duty would not lie on these facts.)

S.130(2)

The stay provided for by this subsection is automatic, but only where the order is made by a court in this jurisdiction. Where a foreign court has ordered a winding up (including an order in "main" proceedings under the EU Regulation), the court may order a stay, but this is a matter for its discretion: *Mazur Media Ltd v Mazur Media GmbH* [2004] EWHC 1566 (Ch); [2004] 1 W.L.R. 2966; [2004] B.P.I.R. 1253. The recognition of a foreign proceeding as a "main" proceeding under the CBIR art.17.2(a) also triggers a comparable automatic stay: see the CBIR art.20; and note *Re OGX Petroleo e Gás SA* [2016] EWHC 25 (Ch) for a comparison between a stay under CBIR art.20 and under s.130(2). There is also a discretionary power conferred on the court to grant a stay or other relief (whether or not the foreign proceeding is recognised as a main proceeding) by art.21. In *Cosco Bulk Carrier Shipping Co Ltd v Armada Shipping SA* [2011] EWHC 216 (Ch); [2011] B.P.I.R. 626 Briggs J exercised the discretion under art.21 to order the lifting of a stay in a case where the respondent company was in liquidation in Switzerland, on the ground that the issues involved questions of shipping law which could better be considered by expert arbitrators in this country. Noting the procedural nature of art.21 in *Bakhshiyeva v Sberbank of Russia* [2018] EWHC 59 (Ch) the court held that it could not grant discretionary relief that went beyond procedural assistance and affected the substance of parties' rights and obligations.

There is no corresponding moratorium in a voluntary winding up, although the company (and others) may apply for a stay of any proceedings under IA 1986 ss.112 and 126: *Gaardsoe v Optimal Wealth Management Ltd* [2012] EWHC 3266 (Ch); [2013] Ch. 298; [2013] B.C.C. 53.

The power conferred on the court by this subsection complements that provided for in s.126(1), and has been held to qualify the apparently categorical wording of s.128: see the note to that section.

Where the court is asked to give leave to bring an action against a company which is in liquidation, it will seek to do what is right and fair in all the circumstances. In *New Cap Reinsurance Corp Ltd v HIH Casualty & General Insurance Ltd* [2002] EWCA Civ 300; [2002] 2 B.C.L.C. 228 there were issues common to the claim pending against the company and an action between the claimants and third parties, and the hearing of the latter was imminent. The judge's decision to allow the action to proceed was upheld by the Court of Appeal. Leave will be refused if the proposed action raises issues which can with equal convenience and less delay and expense be decided in the liquidation proceedings: *Re Exchange Securities & Commodities Ltd* [1983] B.C.L.C. 186. The court will not undertake any investigation into the merits of the proposed claim or consider the background material to the s.130 application (*Re Bank of Credit and Commerce International SA (No.4)* [1994] 1 B.C.L.C. 419); and accordingly in that case the court declined to make an order for specific discovery of certain documents in favour of the liquidators.

In *Re National Employers' Mutual General Insurance Association* [1995] B.C.C. 774 Rattee J held that the court could not give leave under this section retrospectively; but in the later case of *Re Saunders (a Bankrupt), Bristol & West Building Society v Saunders* [1997] Ch. 60; [1997] B.C.C. 83 Lindsay J (after an exhaustive examination of authorities which had not been cited to Rattee J in the previous case) ruled that this was not so, and that the lack of prior consent was not an absolute bar to the commencement of an action or proceeding. This decision was followed in *Re Linkrealm Ltd* [1998] B.C.C. 478. *Saunders* (above) was followed by Chief Registrar Baister in *Bank of Scotland v Breytenbach* [2012] B.P.I.R. 1, and David Richards J in *Re Colliers International UK plc* [2012] EWHC 2942 (Ch): see note to s.285(3), (4).

Leave is not needed where the applicants are not proceeding against either the company or the company's property: *Re Lineas Navieras Bolivianas SAM* [1995] B.C.C. 666 (a case where the Admiralty Court had made an order for the sale of a ship belonging to the company: the effect of this order was to convert the company's interest in the ship into a right on the part of the applicants to have their claims met from the proceeds of sale).

Leave was also not needed in *Pioneer Cladding Ltd v John Graham Construction Ltd* [2015] 5 Costs L.R. 781, as s.130(2) did not apply to an application for costs consequent upon a judgment on liability given against a company before it went into liquidation.

In *Re Swissair Schweizerische Luftverkehr-Aktiengesellschaft, Flightline Ltd v Edwards* [2003] EWCA Civ 63; [2003] 1 W.L.R. 1200; [2003] B.C.C. 361 an action had been begun against the company and the claimant had obtained a freezing order over assets up to the amount being claimed. The freezing order was later discharged when an equivalent sum was paid into an account in the joint names of the parties' solicitors. Neuberger J, at first instance, took the view that the arrangement gave the claimant a security interest in the funds so held, and in the light of that ruling granted leave for the action to continue. The Court of Appeal decided that no security interest had been created and accordingly that leave should be refused. See also *Tradegro (UK) Ld v Wigmore Street Investments Ltd* [2011] EWCA Civ 268; [2011] 2 B.C.L.C. 616 (moneys deposited to protect a specific claim held not to be as security).

A criminal prosecution against a company is a "proceeding" within the meaning of this subsection. Accordingly, the leave of the court is required before any prosecution may be brought: *R. v Dickson* [1991] B.C.C. 719.

S.130(3)

See the notes to ss.73, 83 regarding these companies.

S.130(3A)

Section 130(3A) inserted by the Finance (No.2) Act 2015 s.51 and Sch.8 paras 26, 29 as from 28 November 2015. This follows the introduction of HMRC's power to make deductions from accounts held with deposit-takers as a means of enforcing payment.

Investigation procedures

131 Company's statement of affairs

131(1) [Powers of official receiver] Where the court has made a winding-up order or appointed a provisional liquidator, the official receiver may require some or all of the persons mentioned in subsection (3) below to make out and submit to him a statement in the prescribed form as to the affairs of the company.

131(2) [Contents of statement] The statement shall show–

(a) particulars of the company's assets, debts and liabilities;

(b) the names and addresses of the company's creditors;

(c) the securities held by them respectively;

(d) the dates when the securities were respectively given; and

(e) such further or other information as may be prescribed or as the official receiver may require.

131(2A) [Verification of statement of affairs] The statement shall be verified by the persons required to submit it–

(a) in the case of an appointment of a provisional liquidator or a winding up by the court in England and Wales, by a statement of truth; and

(b) in the case of an appointment of a provisional liquidator or a winding up by the court in Scotland, by affidavit.

131(3) [Persons in s.131(1)] The persons referred to in subsection (1) are–

(a) those who are or have been officers of the company;

(b) those who have taken part in the formation of the company at any time within one year before the relevant date;

(c) those who are in the company's employment, or have been in its employment within that year, and are in the official receiver's opinion capable of giving the information required;

(d) those who are or have been within that year officers of, or in the employment of, a company which is, or within that year was, an officer of the company.

131(4) [Time for submitting statement] Where any persons are required under this section to submit a statement of affairs to the official receiver, they shall do so (subject to the next subsection) before the end of the period of 21 days beginning with the day after that on which the prescribed notice of the requirement is given to them by the official receiver.

131(5) [Release, extension of time] The official receiver, if he thinks fit, may–

(a) at any time release a person from an obligation imposed on him under subsection (1) or (2) above; or

(b) either when giving the notice mentioned in subsection (4) or subsequently, extend the period so mentioned;

and where the official receiver has refused to exercise a power conferred by this subsection, the court, if it thinks fit, may exercise it.

131(6) [Definitions] In this section–

"employment" includes employment under a contract for services; and

"the relevant date" means–

(a) in a case where a provisional liquidator is appointed, the date of his appointment; and

(b) in a case where no such appointment is made, the date of the winding-up order.

131(7) [Penalty on default] If a person without reasonable excuse fails to comply with any obligation imposed under this section, he is liable to a fine and, for continued contravention, to a daily default fine.

131(8) [Scotland] In the application of this section to Scotland references to the official receiver are to the liquidator or, in a case where a provisional liquidator is appointed, the provisional liquidator.

General Note

On the making of a winding-up order, the official receiver (in England and Wales) normally becomes liquidator of the company, at least on an interim basis until a liquidator is chosen by the creditors and contributories under s.139. (The one exception is where the company is already under the control of an administrator or of the supervisor of a voluntary arrangement: see s.140.) In order to put the official receiver in possession of information about the company so that he may make the decisions and discharge the duties which rest upon him under the provisions of the Act which follow, the officers and employees of the company and others specified are required to complete and submit to him a "statement of affairs" under this section. This has long been a feature of a winding up by the court, and it is not simply continued in the present Act but extended to the analogous cases of a CVA (s.2(3)(b)), an administration (s.22 and Sch.B1 para.47), an administrative receivership (ss.47, 66) and a creditors' voluntary winding up, whether originally so constituted (s.99) or converted from a members' voluntary winding up when the company turns out to be insolvent (s.95(3)(a)). Failure by the officers and others concerned to comply with this requirement is sanctioned by criminal penalties (s.131(7)), and untruthfulness in the answers given is punishable as perjury, since s.131(2) stipulates that the statement shall be verified by a statement of truth or affidavit.

In *Re Wallace Smith Trust Co Ltd* [1992] B.C.C. 707, the respondent director had failed to submit a statement of affairs after being required by the official receiver to do so; and the official receiver had then sought and obtained an order ex parte for his public examination in order to obtain the information which ought to have been furnished in the statement of affairs. Ferris J held that, while this course was not an abuse of the process of the court, it would have been more appropriate for a specific order or orders to have been sought under IR 2016 r.12.52 requiring the director to complete and submit the statement of affairs, and possibly also seeking the order for public examination as an alternative in case the court refused to make the specific orders.

The information given by a person in a statement of affairs may (subject to certain safeguards) be used in evidence in subsequent proceedings against him, and also against any other person who concurs in the making of the statement: see s.433.

Where a provisional liquidator has been appointed by the court under s.135 before a winding-up order has been made, the section also comes into operation and the official receiver may proceed to requisition a statement of affairs in anticipation of the making of a winding-up order which may in due course be made.

The provisions of this and the succeeding sections apply whether or not the company is insolvent.

On the office of official receiver, see ss.399 et seq., below.

In Scotland, where there is no official receiver, the functions of the official receiver under this section are conferred by s.131(8) on the liquidator, who is appointed by the court when the winding-up order is made (s.138(1)).

Section 131(2) was amended and s.131(2A) inserted by LRO 2010 (SI 2010/18) art.5(4) as from 6 April 2010 (with retrospective effect).

For the relevant rules, see IR 2016 rr.7.40 et seq. and on enforcement, r.12.52.

S.131(1)

The Act gives the official receiver a discretion, so that he may dispense with the procedure in any case he considers appropriate. One situation where this would be so is where the winding-up order follows the discharge of an administration order (s.140), and the administrator is appointed liquidator by the court. (No similar discretion is given to the supervisor, administrator, etc. in the analogous cases established by ss.2(3)(b), 22, etc. that are referred to in the general note to this section.)

S.131(2)

The information listed here will be required by the official receiver in order that he may make his report to the court under s.132, and may be relevant to the question whether an application to the court under s.133 should be made or granted. Details of the creditors will be needed e.g. if a decision of, or notice to, creditors is required under s.136(5).

S.131(3)

The terms "employment" and "the relevant date" are defined in s.131(6), below. "Officer" includes a director, manager or secretary: see CA 2006 s.1173(1) and the note to s.206(3).

S.131(5)

The discretion here given to the official receiver supplements the general discretionary terms of s.131(1).

S.131(6)

The inclusion of a person employed under a contract for services gives the section potentially a very wide scope, extending (for example) to an accountant or auditor.

S.131(7)

On penalties, see s.430 and Sch.10.

S.131(8)

As noted above, there is no official receiver in Scotland and so the liquidator or provisional liquidator is empowered to act instead. A liquidator or provisional liquidator will have the full range of discretionary powers conferred by this section on the official receiver.

132 Investigation by official receiver

132(1) [Duty of official receiver] Where a winding-up order is made by the court in England and Wales, it is the duty of the official receiver to investigate–

(a) if the company has failed, the causes of the failure; and

(b) generally, the promotion, formation, business, dealings and affairs of the company,

and to make such report (if any) to the court as he thinks fit.

132(2) [Report prima facie evidence] The report is, in any proceedings, prima facie evidence of the facts stated in it.

S.132(1)

The official receiver has a discretion to decide whether a report to the court is called for, but has a statutory duty to investigate the matters listed in paras (a) and (b), which applies whether or not he is also the liquidator.

The officers of the company (and its employees and other persons who are specified in s.235(3)) are under a duty to co-operate with the official receiver: see s.235, below.

S.132(2)

The evidentiary presumption applies not only for the purpose of any immediate court hearing, but "in any proceedings".

133 Public examination of officers

133(1) [Application to court] Where a company is being wound up by the court, the official receiver or, in Scotland, the liquidator may at any time before the dissolution of the company apply to the court for the public examination of any person who–

(a) is or has been an officer of the company; or

(b) has acted as liquidator or administrator of the company or as receiver or manager or, in Scotland, receiver of its property; or

(c) not being a person falling within paragraph (a) or (b), is or has been concerned, or has taken part, in the promotion, formation or management of the company.

133(2) [Request to make application] Unless the court otherwise orders, the official receiver or, in Scotland, the liquidator shall make an application under subsection (1) if he is requested in accordance with the rules to do so by–

(a) one-half, in value, of the company's creditors; or

(b) three-quarters, in value, of the company's contributories.

133(3) [Court's duties] On an application under subsection (1), the court shall direct that a public examination of the person to whom the application relates shall be held on a day appointed by the court; and that person shall attend on that day and be publicly examined as to the promotion, formation or management of the company or as to the conduct of its business and affairs, or his conduct or dealings in relation to the company.

133(4) [Persons taking part] The following may take part in the public examination of a person under this section and may question that person concerning the matters mentioned in subsection (3), namely–

(a) the official receiver;

(b) the liquidator of the company;

(c) any person who has been appointed as special manager of the company's property or business;

(d) any creditor of the company who has tendered a proof or, in Scotland, submitted a claim in the winding up;

(e) any contributory of the company.

General Note

The Act makes provision for both a public examination under this section and a private examination under s.236.

Although s.133 is by its terms expressed to apply only in a winding up by the court, s.112 can be invoked to make it apply also in a voluntary liquidation: see *Re Campbell Coverings Ltd (No.2)* [1954] Ch. 225; and *Bishopsgate Investment Management Ltd (in provisional liquidation) v Maxwell, Mirror Group Newspapers plc v Maxwell* [1993] Ch. 1 at 24, 46; [1992] B.C.C. 222 at 232, 249; *Re Pantmaenog Timber Co Ltd, Official Receiver v Wadge, Rapps & Hunt (a firm)* [2003] UKHL 49; [2004] 1 A.C. 158; [2003] B.C.C. 659, at para.56.

Under the present section, the court has power to direct the public examination of an officer of a company in compulsory liquidation who is outside the jurisdiction, and to order service of the order of the court or other relevant document to be effected on him outside the jurisdiction: *Re Seagull Manufacturing Co Ltd (in liq.)* [1993] Ch. 345; [1993] B.C.C. 241; *Re Casterbridge Properties Ltd* [2002] B.C.C. 453; upheld (where this point was not in issue) sub nom. *Jeeves v Official Receiver* (below). See also the discussion of *Seagull Manufacturing* in *Masri v Consolidated Contractors International (UK) Ltd* [2009] UKHL 43; [2010] B.C.C. 25, where the House of Lords declined to draw an analogy between s.133 and CPR Pt 71 in a case where the company concerned was not in liquidation. (For the position in a private examination, see the note to s.236, below.)

A person who is subject to examination under s.133 is not entitled to refuse to answer questions on the ground that in doing so he may incriminate himself: this follows by analogy with the cases decided under ss.236, 290 and 366; however, the use that can later be made in criminal proceedings of information obtained under compulsion is now generally prohibited: see *Bishopsgate Investment Management Ltd (in provisional liquidation) v Maxwell* [1993] Ch. 1 at 24, 46, 62; [1992] B.C.C. 222 at 233, 249, 262, and the notes to those sections.

For the rules regarding the procedure for obtaining an order for examination, and the conduct of the examination, see IR 2016 rr.7.98 et seq. The examination is on oath: r.7.105(1). Questions as to the admissibility or otherwise of questions at the examination are a matter for the presiding judge or registrar at the hearing, although the court does have power when ordering the examination to control the form of the examination (as distinct from giving directions as to the conduct of the hearing itself): *Re Richbell Strategic Holdings Ltd* [2001] B.C.C. 409. For the sanctions for nonattendance, see s.134, below.

S.133(1)

The public examination provisions apply also to Scotland (unlike s.132). They may be invoked whether the company is solvent or insolvent.

On the meaning of the term "officer", see the note to s.206(3).

S.133(2), (3)

Section 133(3) appears to give the court no discretion to refuse an order once an application has been made, and this view was upheld, subject to very limited qualification, by the Court of Appeal in *Jeeves v Official Receiver* [2003] EWCA Civ 1246; [2003] B.C.C. 912. Having satisfied itself that the prerequisites of s.133(1) have been met, the court must make an order unless there are no questions which could properly be put to the examinee at the hearing of the examination, or there are no purposes to be served by such an examination. If there are particular questions or areas of inquiry to which objection might be made, this is better raised and debated at the examination itself or, if more convenient, at a preliminary hearing. (The appellant in this case had resisted an order on the ground that if the examination proceeded, he ran the risk of prosecution in another jurisdiction for violation of its confidentiality laws.)

However, under s.133(2) the court is empowered to intervene in order to *prevent* an application from being made to it by the official receiver following a request by the creditors or contributories. The grounds on which the court may make such an order are not stated in the present section, but IR 2016 r.7.101(4) indicates that the official receiver may object that the creditors' request is an unreasonable one. It does, however, appear to be plain from the two subsections, read together, that any other objectors will be out of court if they do not take action before the official receiver does.

In *Jeeves v Official Receiver* it was also noted that, since an application under s.133 would normally be made without notice to the intended examinee, he would have an opportunity to raise matters which he might wish the court to take into account by making an application under r.12.59 to have the order set aside; but this could be done only on one or other of the very limited grounds set out above.

For the procedure, see IR 2016 rr.7.98 et seq.

S.133(4)

It appears that an officer or past officer of the company, though liable himself to be examined under the section, has no right to question those of his colleagues being examined with him unless he falls coincidentally within one of the categories (a)–(e). See further IR 2016 r.7.105.

134 Enforcement of s.133

134(1) [Non-attendance] If a person without reasonable excuse fails at any time to attend his public examination under section 133, he is guilty of a contempt of court and liable to be punished accordingly.

134(2) [Warrant etc. re non-attendance] In a case where a person without reasonable excuse fails at any time to attend his examination under section 133 or there are reasonable grounds for believing that a person has absconded, or is about to abscond, with a view to avoiding or delaying his examination under that section, the court may cause a warrant to be issued to a constable or prescribed officer of the court–

(a) for the arrest of that person; and

(b) for the seizure of any books, papers, records, money or goods in that person's possession.

134(3) [Consequences of warrant] In such a case the court may authorise the person arrested under the warrant to be kept in custody, and anything seized under such a warrant to be held, in accordance with the rules, until such time as the court may order.

General Note

This provision deals with the enforcement of s.133. The respondent in *Shah v Patel and Karia* [2008] EWCA Civ 979; [2010] B.P.I.R. 496 had failed to provide information required under a court order. A sentence of 12 months' imprisonment for contempt was upheld as reasonable. Other details relating to the conduct of the examination and summoning of those required to attend are dealt with in the rules: see IR 2016 rr.7.98 et seq., 12.51 et seq.

S.134(2)

A person who appeals unsuccessfully against an order for his arrest under s.134(2)(a) is "singularly close" to being in contempt of court, and may be ordered to pay the official receiver's costs on an indemnity basis: *Re Avatar Communications Ltd* (1988) 4 B.C.C. 473.

Appointment of liquidator

135 Appointment and powers of provisional liquidator

135(1) [Time of appointment] Subject to the provisions of this section, the court may, at any time after the presentation of a winding-up petition, appoint a liquidator provisionally.

135(2) [Appointment in England, Wales] In England and Wales, the appointment of a provisional liquidator may be made at any time before the making of a winding-up order; and either the official receiver or any other fit person may be appointed.

135(3) [Appointment in Scotland] In Scotland, such an appointment may be made at any time before the first appointment of liquidators.

135(4) [Provisional liquidator] The provisional liquidator shall carry out such functions as the court may confer on him.

135(5) [Powers of provisional liquidator] When a liquidator is provisionally appointed by the court, his powers may be limited by the order appointing him.

General Note

The primary reason for appointing a provisional liquidator is normally to ensure the preservation of the company's assets pending the hearing of the winding-up petition. Since an appointment in such circumstances anticipates the eventual making of a winding-up order virtually as a foregone conclusion, it is usually made only with the consent of the company itself or in a clear case of insolvency. Given the serious (and possibly terminal) effect that an appointment is likely to have on the business of a trading company, the applicant must demonstrate as a threshold test that a winding-up order is likely to be made at the hearing and, if that test is satisfied, it remains a matter of discretion whether the appointment should be made: *Revenue and Customs Commissioners v Rochdale Drinks Distributors Ltd* [2011] EWCA Civ 1116; [2013] B.C.C. 419. The principles to be followed before taking the "serious step" of appointing a provisional liquidator on an ex parte application are summarised in *Revenue and Customs Commissioners v Winnington Networks Ltd* [2014] EWHC 1259 (Ch); [2014] B.C.C. 675. See also *Secretary of State for Business, Innovation and Skills v New Horizon Energy Ltd* [2015] EWHC 2961 (Ch); [2017] B.C.C. 629; *Re Parkwell Investments Ltd* [2014] EWHC 3381 (Ch); [2014] B.C.C. 721. If the application is made ex parte, the same principles apply as in a creditor's winding up petition. It is not sufficient simply to establish a "good prima facie case" for a winding up. But provisional liquidators are also appointed in other situations—as formerly, in the case of an insurance company, when the alternative of administration was not available, as a step towards putting in place a scheme of arrangement under CA 2006 Pt 26 (*Smith v UIC Insurance Co Ltd* [2001] B.C.C. 11 at 20–21); or in order to investigate whether there might be possible claims for fraudulent or wrongful trading under IA 1986 ss.213 or 214 (*Re Latreefers Inc* [2001] B.C.C. 174 at 184–185). A provisional liquidator may be appointed after the presentation of a public interest petition under s.124A: *Secretary of State for Business, Innovation and Skills v Hawkhurst Capital plc* [2013] EWHC 4219 (Ch); [2016] B.C.C. 125. Because of the potentially damaging effect that the appointment of a provisional liquidator may cause to the company (particularly if a winding-up order is not made on the petition), the petitioner may be required to give an undertaking in damages. This was done in *Rochdale Drinks Distributors Ltd* (above) and also in *Abbey Forwarding Ltd v Revenue & Customs Commissioners* [2015] EWHC 225 (Ch), where the court ordered an inquiry as to damages against the Commissioners. A contention that the undertaking automatically terminated on the making of a winding-up order was rejected. In contrast, in *Re Parkwell Investments Ltd* (above) an undertaking was not required.

It is a contempt of court to impede a provisional liquidator in the exercise of his functions. In *Revenue & Customs Commissioners v Munir* [2015] EWHC 1366 (Ch); [2015] B.C.C. 425 the directors and secretary who paid away assets of their company after a provisional liquidator had been appointed received substantial prison sentences.

An application for the appointment of a provisional liquidator must be made to a High Court judge or an Insolvency and Companies Court Judge and, unless otherwise ordered, is held in public. (See *Practice Direction: Insolvency Proceedings* [2018] B.C.C. 241, para.3.4(4) (reproduced as App.IV to this *Guide*).) A person applying ex parte for the appointment of a provisional liquidator owes a duty to the court to make full disclosure of all material facts, and any order obtained in breach of this obligation is liable to be set aside: *Re OJSC Ank Yugraneft* [2008] EWHC 2614 (Ch); [2010] B.C.C. 475. If a provisional liquidator has been appointed on an ex parte application and the company wishes to challenge the appointment, the burden of proof is upon it to show a good arguable case why the order should not have been made, and it is not sufficient for it to assert that it disputes the debt in question or that it intends to appeal: *Revenue and Customs Commissioners v Rochdale Drinks Distributors Ltd* (above). It is not normally within the duties of a provisional liquidator to realise assets: *Ashborder BV v Green Gas Power Ltd* [2005] EWHC 1031 (Ch).

A provisional liquidator must be qualified to act as an insolvency practitioner in relation to the company in question: see s.388(1)(a). In *Re W F Fearman Ltd (No.2)* (1988) 4 B.C.C. 141 it was held to be inappropriate for the court to make an order directly appointing the provisional liquidators, who were already in office, to be the liquidators of the company when the winding-up order was subsequently made, since to do so would deprive the creditors of their say in the selection of a liquidator under s.136. However, a practical solution was found by giving leave to the official receiver to continue to use the services of the former provisional liquidators as special managers.

The court may group together associated companies and appoint the official receiver as liquidator or provisional liquidator where it is in the public interest even though the directors and creditors of some of the companies propose other liquidators: see *Re BBH Property 1 Ltd* [2017] EWHC 2584 (Ch).

The appointment of a provisional liquidator automatically revokes the authority of an agent appointed to act on behalf of the company by or on behalf of the directors: *Pacific & General Insurance Ltd (in liq.) v Home & Overseas Insurance Co Ltd* [1997] B.C.C. 400.

For further examples of the exercise of the jurisdiction under this section see *Re Pinstripe Farming Co Ltd* [1996] B.C.C. 913; *Re UOC Corp, Alipour v Ary* [1997] B.C.C. 377; *Re Goodwill Merchant Financial Services Ltd* [2001] 1 B.C.L.C. 259; *Re Namco UK Ltd* [2003] EWHC 989 (Ch); [2003] 2 B.C.L.C. 78; (which also contains a discussion of the powers under s.135(5) which it is appropriate to include in the form of the court's order); *MHMH Ltd v Carwood Barker Holdings Ltd* [2004] EWHC 3174 (Ch); [2005] B.C.C. 536; and *Re SED Essex Ltd* [2013] EWHC 1583 (Ch); [2014] B.C.C. 628 (relevance of likelihood of successful s.127 application to appointment of provisional liquidator); *Re SED Essex Ltd* (above) (risk if control returned to company's management). In *Equitas Ltd v Jacob* [2005] EWHC 1440 (Ch); [2005] B.P.I.R. 1312 it was held that s.135(4) empowered the court to circulate certain information about some creditors to other creditors. In *Re Daewoo Motor Co Ltd* [2005] EWHC 2799 (Ch); [2006] B.P.I.R. 415 the court authorised the provisional liquidator of a company to remit the proceeds of realisation of its assets to a receiver overseas, without proceeding to a winding up.

For a recent review of this jurisdiction to appoint a provisional liquidator see the ruling of Marcus Smith J in *Secretary of State for Business, Energy and Industrial Strategy v Rigil Kent Acquisitions Ltd* [2017] EWHC 3636 (Ch). The judgment contains useful insights on whether undertakings should be accepted in lieu of appointment and whether an appointment could be made on an interim basis pending the submission of new evidence.

A provisional liquidator is now formally listed in Annex B to the EU Regulation as an "insolvency practitioner" for the purposes of art.2(5) of the Regulation. This puts beyond doubt any question whether such an office-holder comes within the statutory definition, even though it does not of itself resolve other difficulties, such as the time when the proceedings in question are opened and whether such proceedings can be "main" proceedings. (See the discussion in the note to art.2(8).) Under the CBIR a provisional liquidator is within the definition of a "British insolvency officeholder" (CBIR 2006 Sch.1 art.2(b)) and (as "one appointed on an interim basis") also within that of a "foreign representative" (Sch.1 art.2(j)).

On the remuneration and expenses of a provisional liquidator, see the notes to rr.7.38, 6.42 and 18.16, for Scotland, *Re Blair Carnegie Nimmo* [2013] CSOH 4; [2013] B.P.I.R. 188.

For the relevant rules, see IR 2016 rr.7.33 et seq.

136 Functions of official receiver in relation to office of liquidator

136(1) [Application] The following provisions of this section have effect, subject to section 140 below, on a winding-up order being made by the court in England and Wales.

136(2) [Official receiver liquidator] The official receiver, by virtue of his office, becomes the liquidator of the company and continues in office until another person becomes liquidator under the provisions of this Part.

136(3) [Vacancy] The official receiver is, by virtue of his office, the liquidator during any vacancy.

136(4) [Powers of official receiver when liquidator] At any time when he is the liquidator of the company, the official receiver may in accordance with the rules seek nominations from the company's creditors and contributories for the purpose of choosing a person to be liquidator of the company in place of the official receiver.

136(5) [Duty of official receiver] It is the duty of the official receiver–

(a) as soon as practicable in the period of 12 weeks beginning with the day on which the winding-up order was made, to decide whether to exercise his power under subsection (4), and

(b) if in pursuance of paragraph (a) he decides not to exercise that power, to give notice of his decision, before the end of that period, to the court and to the company's creditors and contributories, and

(c) (whether or not he has decided to exercise that power) to exercise his power under subsection (4) if he is at any time requested, in accordance with the rules, to do so by one-quarter, in value, of the company's creditors;

and accordingly, where the duty imposed by paragraph (c) arises before the official receiver has performed a duty imposed by paragraph (a) or (b), he is not required to perform the latter duty.

136(6) [Contents of s.136(5)(b) notice] A notice given under subsection (5)(b) to the company's creditors shall contain an explanation of the creditors' power under subsection (5)(c) to require the official receiver to seek nominations from the company's creditors and contributories.

General Note

The official receiver has a discretion to decide whether or not to seek nominations from creditors and contributories to replace him with a "private" liquidator. He has 12 weeks in which to reach a decision, but the creditors may in any case require him to seek nominations.

If the official receiver decides to not seek nominations, he continues in office as liquidator. His decision not to seek nominations is therefore, in effect, a decision to keep the liquidation in his own hands.

Section 136 should be read in conjunction with s.137, which alternatively gives the Secretary of State power to appoint a liquidator other than the official receiver.

S.136(1)

Section 140 applies when the company is already subject to administration or a voluntary arrangement. The court is then empowered to make an immediate appointment of the insolvency practitioner who has been the administrator or supervisor to be the liquidator in the winding up.

S.136(2)

If the company is already in voluntary liquidation when a winding-up order is made, the existing liquidator is displaced: see IR 2016 rr.5.14 and 6.31.

S.136(4), (5)

The official receiver must make an initial decision, within the first 12 weeks after the making of the winding-up order, whether to seek nominations or not; and if he decides not to, he must give the notices specified by s.136(5(b) (creditors are not expressly stated to be able to opt out of receiving these notices: see effect of IR 2016 r.1.37(2)(a)). However, he is free to seek nominations even after this 12-week period has expired, and the creditors' power to requisition him to do so also continues. This is made clear by the use of the phrase "at any time" in s.136(4) and (5)(c).

Following a consultation exercise, the Insolvency Service announced on 28 October 2010 that it plans to adopt as its policy in all compulsory liquidations the removal of the requirement for the official receiver to issue a notice under s.136(5)(b) to the creditors and to file it in court, but this does not appear to have occurred.

For the rules dealing with decision-making under this section, see IR 2016 rr.7.52, 15.2 et seq. (and note under r.15.18(1) that a decision on nominations sought under s.136(5)(c) is a "requisitioned decision"); and for the official receiver's reporting obligations, see rr.7.48 et seq.: see also r.7.60 (hand-over of assets).

137 Appointment by Secretary of State

137(1) [Application by official receiver] In a winding up by the court in England and Wales the official receiver may, at any time when he is the liquidator of the company, apply to the Secretary of State for the appointment of a person as liquidator in his place.

137(2) [Decision by official receiver] If nominations are sought from the company's creditors and contributories in pursuance of a decision under section 136(5)(a), but no person is chosen to be liquidator as a result, it is the duty of the official receiver to decide whether to refer the need for an appointment to the Secretary of State.

137(3) [Duty of Secretary of State] On an application under subsection (1), or a reference made in pursuance of a decision under subsection (2), the Secretary of State shall either make an appointment or decline to make one.

137(4) [Notice of appointment by liquidator] Where a liquidator has been appointed by the Secretary of State under subsection (3), the liquidator shall give notice of his appointment to the company's creditors or, if the court so allows, shall advertise his appointment in accordance with the directions of the court.

137(5) [Contents of notice or advertisement] In that notice or advertisement the liquidator must explain the procedure for establishing a liquidation committee under section 141.

General Note

If the official receiver forms the opinion that the conduct of the winding up may be handed over to a private liquidator, he may either invite the creditors and contributories to nominate an insolvency practitioner under s.136, or apply under the present section to the Secretary of State to make an appointment. The Secretary of State may decline to do so (s.137(3)), in which case the official receiver is, in effect, directed to continue in office. Since the establishment by the Insolvency Service of the Regional Trustee/Liquidator Units, rather more cases involving a straightforward realisation of assets have been kept within the Service rather than passed over to an insolvency practitioner: see *Dear IP*, June 2007, Ch.3.

There is no provision corresponding to s.136(5)(c) empowering the creditors to require the official receiver to make an application to the Secretary of State under this section, or to apply to him directly themselves.

For the relevant rules, see IR 2016 rr.7.57, 7.60.

S.137(1)

The official receiver may make an application under this section "at any time", and may plainly do so as an alternative to seeking nominations under s.136(4). Once he has sought nominations, however, he is probably bound to go through with that procedure, and could have recourse to his powers under the present section only if the creditors and contributories fail to choose a liquidator.

S.137(2)

If the official receiver's request for nominations does not result in the appointment of a liquidator, it is the duty of the official receiver to make a *decision* under this subsection, but he is under no duty to make a *reference*: he may well decide to stay in office as liquidator himself.

S.137(3)

As has already been observed, a negative decision by the Secretary of State is effectively a direction to the official receiver that he should continue in office himself.

S.137(4), (5)

The court may allow the liquidator to advertise the fact of his appointment rather than notify creditors individually. No guidance is given as to the basis on which the court should exercise this discretion, but fairly obviously it might be used to avoid unjustified expense where there are many creditors, although this could be alleviated by use of email or websites (see IR 2016 rr.1.45, 1.50). The notice or advertisement must explain how to appoint a liquidation committee.

138 Appointment of liquidator in Scotland

138(1) [Appointment] Where a winding-up order is made by the court in Scotland, a liquidator shall be appointed by the court at the time when the order is made.

138(2) [Period of office of interim liquidator] The liquidator so appointed (here referred to as "the interim liquidator") continues in office until another person becomes liquidator in his place under this section or the next.

138(3) [Interim liquidator to seek nominations for liquidator] The interim liquidator shall (subject to the next subsection) as soon as practicable in the period of 28 days beginning with the day on which the winding-up order was made or such longer period as the court may allow, in accordance with the rules seek nominations from the company's creditors and contributories for the purpose of choosing a person (who may be the person who is the interim liquidator) to be liquidator of the company in place of the interim liquidator.

138(4) [Qualification to s.138(3)] If it appears to the interim liquidator, in any case where a company is being wound up on grounds including its inability to pay its debts, that it would be inappropriate to seek a nomination from the company's contributories under subsection (3), he may seek a nomination only from the company's creditors for the purpose mentioned in that subsection.

138(5) [If no person nominated or appointed as liquidator] If a nomination is sought from the company's creditors, or nominations are sought from the company's creditors and contributories, in pursuance of this section but no person is appointed or nominated as a result, the interim liquidator shall make a report to the court which shall appoint either the interim liquidator or some other person to be liquidator of the company.

138(6) [Notification] A person who becomes liquidator of the company in place of the interim liquidator shall, unless he is appointed by the court, forthwith notify the court of that fact.

General Note

There is no official receiver in Scotland, or any equivalent public officer, and so the liquidator in a Scottish winding up is invariably a private insolvency practitioner. This section provides for the appointment of an "interim liquidator", whose duty it is to take custody of the company's property and to seek nominations for liquidator, etc. as in a winding up in England or Wales, but he does not enjoy the discretionary powers entrusted to the official receiver under ss.136, 137, and the court is more closely involved throughout the proceedings. Note under s.138(4) in an insolvent liquidation the interim liquidator does not need to seek nomination from contributories if to do so would appear "inappropriate" to him. The Secretary of State's powers under s.137 do not apply in Scotland.

S.138(5)

In contrast with the position in England and Wales (s.137(2)), the interim liquidator's obligation is mandatory and not discretionary, and the residual power of appointment lies with the court rather than the Secretary of State.

139 Choice of liquidator by creditors and contributories

139(1) [Application] This section applies where a company is being wound up by the court and nominations are sought from the company's creditors and contributories for the purpose of choosing a person to be liquidator of the company.

139(2) [Nomination of liquidator] The creditors and the contributories may in accordance with the rules nominate a person to be liquidator.

139(3) [Liquidator] The liquidator shall be the person nominated by the creditors or, where no person has been so nominated, the person (if any) nominated by the contributories.

139(4) [Where different persons nominated] In the case of different persons being nominated, any contributory or creditor may, within 7 days after the date on which the nomination was made by the creditors, apply to the court for an order either–

(a) appointing the person nominated as liquidator by the contributories to be a liquidator instead of, or jointly with, the person nominated by the creditors; or

(b) appointing some other person to be liquidator instead of the person nominated by the creditors.

General Note

This section lays down the rules and procedure for the appointment of a liquidator in compulsory liquidation when nominations of the creditors and contributories are sought for the purpose. It is very similar in terms to s.100, which governs a creditors' voluntary winding up. Unlike ss.136, 137, it applies in Scotland as well as England and Wales.

The word "nominate" is used in a sense equivalent to "appoint": see the note to s.100.

In *Re Orient Power Holdings Ltd* [2009] B.C.C. 452 (a decision of the High Court of Hong Kong) companies which had been in receivership were ordered to be wound up. The creditors appointed two independent persons together with one of the receivers (S) as liquidators. The official receiver sought the removal of S on the grounds that there was a risk that he might not be impartial, being the appointee of the secured creditors, but the court confirmed the appointment because the liquidation would benefit from the knowledge of the companies' affairs that S had acquired while receiver, leaving it open to any concerned creditor to have recourse to the court should need arise.

For the relevant rules, see IR 2016 rr.7.53 et seq.

140 Appointment by the court following administration or voluntary arrangement

140(1) [Appointment of administrator] Where a winding-up order is made immediately upon the appointment of an administrator ceasing to have effect, the court may appoint as liquidator of the company the person whose appointment as administrator has ceased to have effect.

140(2) [Appointment of supervisor] Where a winding-up order is made at a time when there is a supervisor of a voluntary arrangement approved in relation to the company under Part I, the court may appoint as liquidator of the company the person who is the supervisor at the time when the winding-up order is made.

140(3) [Position of official receiver] Where the court makes an appointment under this section, the official receiver does not become the liquidator as otherwise provided by section 136(2), and section 136(5)(a) or (b) does not apply.

General Note

This section links in with the procedures for the appointment of an administrator (IA 1986 ss.8 et seq. and Sch.B1) and for instituting a scheme of voluntary arrangement (IA 1986 ss.1 et seq.). If a compulsory winding up follows immediately upon the termination of an administration or a voluntary arrangement, an insolvency practitioner who is fully aware of the company's circumstances will already be in office as the administrator or supervisor of the scheme, and it may make good sense to appoint him to the post of liquidator at the time when the winding-up order is made, so that he can get on with the conduct of the liquidation straightaway. Many of the formalities which are necessary in the case of a normal winding-up order can be bypassed in such a case. In *Re Charnley Davies Business Services Ltd* (1987) 3 B.C.C. 408, the court (with some reluctance) appointed the former administrator as liquidator even though litigation was pending in which his conduct while administrator was to be challenged as irregular.

Subsection (1) was reworded by EA 2002 s.248 and Sch.B1 para.17, to reflect the fact that a company may now be put into administration without a court order. The expression "the appointment of an administrator ceases to have effect" means "the administration is terminated": see Sch.B1 para.1(2)(c), (d).

For the relevant rules, see IR 2016 rr.7.56, 6.16. Rule 6.16 deals with the situation where the existence of further creditors becomes known to the insolvency practitioner who becomes liquidator.

S.140(1), (2)

Section 140 does not empower the court to appoint as liquidator a person who has not previously occupied the position of administrator or supervisor, whether alone or as an additional liquidator (*Re Exchange Travel (Holdings) Ltd* [1992] B.C.C. 954). If an appointment is not made under this section, the normal procedure under ss.136 and 139 must be followed.

Liquidation committees

141 Liquidation committee (England and Wales)

141(1) [Application] This section applies where a winding up order has been made by the court in England and Wales.

141(2) [Establishment by creditors and contributories] If both the company's creditors and the company's contributories decide that a liquidation committee should be established, a liquidation committee is to be established in accordance with the rules.

141(3) [Establishment by creditors or contributories] If only the company's creditors, or only the company's contributories, decide that a liquidation committee should be established, a liquidation committee is to be established in accordance with the rules unless the court orders otherwise.

141(3A) ["Liquidation committee"] A "liquidation committee" is a committee having such functions as are conferred on it by or under this Act.

141(3B) [Requisition by one-tenth in value of creditors] The liquidator must seek a decision from the company's creditors and contributories as to whether a liquidation committee should be established if requested, in accordance with the rules, to do so by one-tenth in value of the company's creditors.

141(3C) [Non-application of s.141(3B)] Subsection (3B) does not apply where the liquidator is the official receiver.

141(4) [Committee not to function where official receiver liquidator] The liquidation committee is not to be able or required to carry out its functions at any time when the official receiver is liquidator; but at any such time its functions are vested in the Secretary of State except to the extent that the rules otherwise provide.

141(5) [Where no committee etc.] Where there is for the time being no liquidation committee, and the liquidator is a person other than the official receiver, the functions of such a committee are vested in the Secretary of State except to the extent that the rules otherwise provide.

General Note

Section 141(1)–(3) substituted and s.141(3A)–(3C) inserted by SBEEA 2015 Sch.9 paras 1, 36 as from 6 April 2017.

Prior to the reforms effected by IA 1985, 1986, the "committee of inspection" had been a feature of the law of bankruptcy and company liquidation for over a century. In the present Act, the title "liquidation committee" has been substituted, both here and in relation to a creditors' voluntary winding up (s.101), while for the purposes of an administration (s.26) and an administrative receivership (ss.49, 68), where it is composed entirely of creditors, it is called the "creditors' committee" or "committee of creditors".

In contrast to the detailed provisions of s.101, the present section has nothing to say about the composition of the committee, but this is clarified by the rules. It is stated in IR 2016 r.17.3 that the committee shall consist of between three and five creditors and also (if the company is solvent) up to three contributories. Once the creditors have all been paid in full, the creditor members of the committee cease to be members: r.17.13.

S.141(1), (2)

The liquidation committee has no role to play while the official receiver is liquidator, as is confirmed by later subsections, and so the machinery for establishing a committee comes into operation only when there is a private liquidator, or when the appointment of a private liquidator is contemplated. The present provisions should be read in conjunction with ss.136(4), 137(5), 139 and 140(3).

Where a liquidator has been appointed by court order under s.140, following upon an administration or voluntary arrangement, s.141(2) will apply, so that he or the creditors may take steps to establish a liquidation committee even though the official receiver is released from his duties in this regard by s.140(3).

S.141(4), (5)

A number of provisions in the Act empower the liquidator to act "with the consent of the liquidation committee" (see, e.g. s.167(1)(a)), while others require him to give notice to the committee of what he has done (see, e.g. s.167(2)). By substituting the Secretary of State for the committee in the circumstances set out, the present subsections enable the liquidator to exercise such powers when there is no committee or none competent to act.

The rules which have been made for the purposes of this section are IR 2016 rr.17.3 et seq. and, for s.141(4), (5) r.17.28. For further guidance, see [2001] Insolv. Int. 61.

142 Liquidation committee (Scotland)

142(1) [Application] This section applies where a winding up order has been made by the court in Scotland.

142(2) [Establishment by creditors and contributories] If both the company's creditors and the company's contributories decide that a liquidation committee should be established, a liquidation committee is to be established in accordance with the rules.

142(3) [Establishment by creditors or contributories] If only the company's creditors, or only the company's contributories, decide that a liquidation committee should be established, a liquidation committee is to be established in accordance with the rules unless the court orders otherwise.

142(4) [Requisition by one-tenth in value of creditors] A liquidator appointed by the court other than under section 139(4)(a) must seek a decision from the company's creditors and contributories as to whether a liquidation committee should be established if requested, in accordance with the rules, to do so by one-tenth in value of the company's creditors.

142(5) [Where no committee etc.] Where in the case of any winding up there is for the time being no liquidation committee, the functions of such a committee are vested in the court except to the extent that the rules otherwise provide.

142(6) ["Liquidation committee"] A "liquidation committee" is a committee having the powers and duties conferred and imposed on it by this Act, and of the powers and duties of commissioners in a sequestration as may be conferred and imposed on such committees by the rules.

General Note

Section 142(1)–(4) substituted by SBEEA 2015 Sch.9 paras 1, 37 as from 6 April 2017.

This section contains provisions for Scotland similar to those laid down for England and Wales by s.141, and the notes to that section generally apply here also, apart from the references to the official receiver, who of course has no Scottish counterpart.

The liquidator's functions

143 General functions in winding up by the court

143(1) [Functions] The functions of the liquidator of a company which is being wound up by the court are to secure that the assets of the company are got in, realised and distributed to the company's creditors and, if there is a surplus, to the persons entitled to it.

143(2) [Duty of liquidator not official receiver] It is the duty of the liquidator of a company which is being wound up by the court in England and Wales, if he is not the official receiver–

(a) to furnish the official receiver with such information,

(b) to produce to the official receiver, and permit inspection by the official receiver of, such books, papers and other records, and

(c) to give the official receiver such other assistance,

as the official receiver may reasonably require for the purposes of carrying out his functions in relation to the winding up.

S.143(1)
The functions of a liquidator in a compulsory winding up are expressed in this subsection rather differently from those of a liquidator in a voluntary liquidation, set out in s.107; but in substance their duties are broadly the same; and similar rules apply regarding the application of assets: see the notes to s.107.

S.143(2)
On the liquidator's duties of care, etc. see the note to s.212; and on enforcement of the liquidator's obligations, see IR 2016 r.12.52.

144 Custody of company's property

144(1) [Liquidator to take property into custody] When a winding-up order has been made, or where a provisional liquidator has been appointed, the liquidator or the provisional liquidator (as the case may be) shall take into his custody or under his control all the property and things in action to which the company is or appears to be entitled.

144(2) [In Scotland where no liquidator] In a winding up by the court in Scotland, if and so long as there is no liquidator, all the property of the company is deemed to be in the custody of the court.

S.144(1)
The term "property" has a very comprehensive definition for the purposes of the present Act: see s.436. The "assets of the company" in s.143(1) are not restricted to assets existing at the date of the winding up (*Connaught Income Fund Series 1 v Capita Financial Managers Ltd* [2014] EWHC 3619 (Comm); [2015] B.C.L.C. 241). As regards property not beneficially owned by the company, see the note to s.107. On the nature of the liquidator's duty to get in the company's property, and whether (or when) it may be categorised as fiduciary, see *Re Mama Milla Ltd; Sharma v Top Brands Ltd* [2015] EWCA Civ 1140; [2016] B.C.C. 1.

In *Joint Liquidators of the Scottish Coal Co Ltd, Noters* [2013] CSIH 108 the Inner House of the Court of Session, reversing the court below ([2013] CSOH 124), held that a Scottish liquidator had no power to abandon or otherwise disclaim property. See the note to s.178.

It is also the duty of the liquidator to take control of assets held by the company on trust, although such assets are not available for distribution under the winding up. On the question of the liquidator's right to remuneration and his costs and expenses incurred in performing the company's functions as trustee, see the notes to rr.18.15 et seq.

S.144(2)
There is no equivalent to this provision for England and Wales in view of s.136(2), (3), which ensures that the official receiver holds the office of liquidator if there is any vacancy.

145 Vesting of company property in liquidator

145(1) [Court order] When a company is being wound up by the court, the court may on the application of the liquidator by order direct that all or any part of the property of whatsoever description belonging to the company or held by trustees on its behalf shall vest in the liquidator by his official name; and thereupon the property to which the order relates vests accordingly.

145(2) [Action re property by liquidator] The liquidator may, after giving such indemnity (if any) as the court may direct, bring or defend in his official name any action or other legal proceeding which relates to that property or which it is necessary to bring or defend for the purpose of effectually winding up the company and recovering its property.

General Note

The estate of a bankrupt individual vests automatically in his trustee by operation of law: see s.306. In contrast, the property of a company which is in liquidation remains vested in it unless an order is sought under the present section.

S.145(1)
It is normally unnecessary to have a vesting order made, in view of the wide powers conferred on the liquidator to act in the company's name (see Sch.4). However, an order may be needed in special circumstances: e.g. where the company is a foreign company which has already been wound up or dissolved in its home jurisdiction; or where the body is unincorporated and is being wound up as an "unregistered company" under ss.220 et seq.

When it receives a letter of request from a foreign court, the court has a wide discretionary jurisdiction at common law, including power to make a vesting order in favour of the person or persons nominated in the letter of request: *Cambridge Gas Transport Corp v Official Committee of Unsecured Creditors (of Navigator Holdings plc)* [2006] UKPC 26; [2006] B.C.C. 962. (This case was disapproved on other grounds in *Rubin v Eurofinance SA* [2012] UKSC 46; [2013] B.C.C. 1.)

S.145(2)

The liquidator would normally bring and defend actions in the name of the company: see Sch.4 para.4.

146 Final account

146(1) [Application] This section applies where a company is being wound up by the court and the liquidator is not the official receiver.

146(2) [Liquidator's account of winding up] If it appears to the liquidator that the winding up of the company is for practical purposes complete the liquidator must make up an account of the winding up, showing how it has been conducted and the company's property has been disposed of.

146(3) [Copy account to creditors, etc.] The liquidator must–

(a) send a copy of the account to the company's creditors (other than opted-out creditors), and

(b) give the company's creditors (other than opted-out creditors) a notice explaining the effect of section 174(4)(d) and how they may object to the liquidator's release.

146(4) [Copy account to registrar of companies; objection to liquidator's release] The liquidator must during the relevant period send to the court and the registrar of companies–

(a) a copy of the account, and

(b) a statement of whether any of the company's creditors objected to the liquidator's release.

146(5) [Relevant period in s.146(4)] The relevant period is the period of 7 days beginning with the day after the last day of the period prescribed by the rules as the period within which the creditors may object to the liquidator's release.

146(6) [Application of s.146(7)] Subsection (7) applies where, immediately before the liquidator sends a copy of the account to the registrar under subsection (4) (or, where the liquidator sends a copy of the account to the court and the registrar on different days, immediately before the liquidator sends the first of those copies) there are EU insolvency proceedings open in respect of the company in one or more other member States.

146(7) [Duty of liquidator to send statement to court and registrar of companies] The liquidator must send to the court and the registrar, with the copy of the account, a statement–

(a) identifying those proceedings,

(b) identifying the member State liquidator appointed in each of those proceedings,

(c) indicating, in relation to each of those member State liquidators, whether that member State liquidator consents to the company being dissolved.

General Note

Section 146 substituted by SBEEA 2015 Sch.9 paras 1, 38 as from 6 April 2017.

This section applies only where a company is being wound up by the court and the liquidator is not the official receiver. It replaces a section which required the holding of a final creditors' meeting at which the liquidator submitted his report and sought his release. Under the new rules, this requirement has been abolished and the liquidator prepares a "final account", which is sent to all the creditors (except those who have opted out). He is entitled to his release unless objection is made within the "prescribed period" (normally eight weeks form the sending of the notice): IR 2016 r.7.61.

S.146(1)
Where the official receiver is the liquidator, the question of his release is for the Secretary of State to determine: see s.174(3).

S.146(2), (3)
It is clear that the winding up must in fact be completed and the company's property finally distributed (apart from what needs to be retained under s.146(3)): the creditors cannot grant the liquidator a prospective or conditional release.

S.146(6), (7)
These subsections add a further duty on the liquidator to send a statement to the registrar of companies and the court where there are EU insolvency proceedings open in respect of the company in one or more other Member States. They were inserted by the Insolvency Amendment (EU 2015/848) Regulations 2017 (SI 2017/702) regs 1, 2, Sch. paras 1, 7 in relation to proceedings in England and Wales opened on or after 26 June 2017 (see reg.3) when the Recast EU Regulation 2015/848 came into force.

146A Official receiver's duty to send statement to registrar about other proceedings

146A(1) [Application of section] This section applies where–

(a) the official receiver sends to the registrar of companies a notice that the winding up of a company by the court is complete, and

(b) immediately before the official receiver sends the notice there are EU insolvency proceedings open in respect of the company in one or more other member States.

146A(2) [Duty of official receiver to send statement to registrar of companies] The official receiver must send to the registrar, with the notice, a statement–

(a) identifying those proceedings,

(b) identifying the member State liquidator appointed in each of those proceedings, and

(c) indicating, in relation to each of those member State liquidators, whether that member State liquidator consents to the company being dissolved.

General Note

Section 146A inserted by the Insolvency Amendment (EU 2015/848) Regulations 2017 (SI 2017/702) regs 1, 2, Sch. paras 1, 8 in relation to proceedings opened on or after 26 June 2017 (see reg.3) when the Recast EU Regulation 2015/848 came into force. The section is the equivalent to s.146(6), (7) but where the liquidator is the official receiver.

General powers of court

147 Power to stay or sist winding up

147(1) [Court may order stay on application] The court may at any time after an order for winding up, on the application either of the liquidator or the official receiver or any creditor or contributory, and on proof to the satisfaction of the court that all proceedings in the winding up ought to be stayed or sisted, make an order staying or sisting the proceedings, either altogether or for a limited time, on such terms and conditions as the court thinks fit.

147(2) [Report by official receiver] The court may, before making an order, require the official receiver to furnish to it a report with respect to any facts or matters which are in his opinion relevant to the application.

147(3) [Copy of order to registrar] A copy of every order made under this section shall forthwith be forwarded by the company, or otherwise as may be prescribed, to the registrar of companies, who shall enter it in his records relating to the company.

S.147(1)
An order for the stay (or, in Scotland, sist) of the winding-up proceedings may be made either for a limited time, or "altogether". In the latter case, the order for liquidation is, in effect, terminated; the liquidator will then be entitled to

a discharge and the directors reinstated in control. For the principles on which the court will grant or refuse a stay, see *Re Lowston Ltd* [1991] B.C.L.C. 570; and *McGruther v James Scott Ltd*, 2004 S.C. 514. In exceptional circumstances, the company's auditor was permitted to apply for a stay in *PricewaterhouseCoopers v Saad Investments Co Ltd* [2014] UKPC 35; [2015] B.C.C. 53 (the firm was the target of an application to furnish documents).

Prior to the 1986 legislation, it was not possible to rescind a winding-up order altogether: the nearest possible thing was the grant of a permanent stay. The consequence was that, technically, the company remained subject to the order, although its operation was suspended. In this situation, a copy of the winding-up order remains on the file at Companies House (see IA 1986 s.130(1)), where it can be the source of misunderstanding (e.g. in relation to credit references). It is now possible, however, for the court to rescind a winding-up order under IR 2016 r.12.59 (e.g. on the ground of mistake), and declare it to have been a nullity. The registrar is then bound to remove the order from his files: *Re Calmex Ltd* [1989] 1 All E.R. 485; (1988) 4 B.C.C. 761. However, the jurisdiction to rescind is to be exercised very cautiously, and only to correct an obvious injustice (*Leicester v Stevenson* [2003] 2 B.C.L.C. 97); and see *Re Turnstem Ltd* [2004] EWHC 1765 (Ch); [2005] 1 B.C.L.C. 388. See also the *Practice Direction* [2018] B.C.C. 241 (reproduced as App.IV to this *Guide*), para.9.10. On the question of standing to apply for the rescission of a winding-up order. see r.12.59 and J. Curl [2009] 22 Insolv. Int. 145.

A stay may be granted on the ground of *forum non conveniens*, i.e. that the courts of another jurisdiction are more appropriately placed to deal with the proceedings: see the note to s.125(1). Although it is not the court's normal practice to stay a winding up pending an appeal to another court, the jurisdiction does exist and may be exercised in an appropriate case: *Credit Lucky Ltd v National Crime Agency* [2014] EWHC 83 (Ch) (where the request was refused).

S.147(2)

The officers of the company and its employees and others specified are under a duty to co-operate with the official receiver: see s.235.

S.147(3)

No regulations appear to have been prescribed for the purposes of this section; but IR 2016 r.7.51 empowers the court to impose requirements as to notification.

148 Settlement of list of contributories and application of assets

148(1) [Court's duties] As soon as may be after making a winding-up order, the court shall settle a list of contributories, with power to rectify the register of members in all cases where rectification is required, and shall cause the company's assets to be collected, and applied in discharge of its liabilities.

148(2) [Court may dispense with list] If it appears to the court that it will not be necessary to make calls on or adjust the rights of contributories, the court may dispense with the settlement of a list of contributories.

148(3) [Distinction between types of contributories] In settling the list, the court shall distinguish between persons who are contributories in their own right and persons who are contributories as being representatives of or liable for the debts of others.

S.148(1)

On the meaning of contributories, and their liability, see the note to s.74 above.

The powers conferred by this section have been delegated to the liquidator by rules made under s.160, below; but the power to rectify the register of members may be exercised by the liquidator only with the special leave of the court: s.160(2). For the relevant rules, see IR 2016 rr.7.79 et seq.

The general power of the court to rectify the register of members (e.g. in the case of omission or mistake) is contained in CA 2006 s.125.

The principles governing the application of assets in a voluntary winding up (s.107) and in a winding up by the court under this section are substantially equivalent. See further the note to that section.

On the order of priority of the expenses of a liquidation *inter se*, see IR 2016 rr.6.42, 7.108, and the note to s.156.

S.148(2)

This would apply, in particular, where the shares are fully paid.

S.148(3)

The categories of contributories are known as the "A List" and "B List" contributories. The circumstances in which the latter are liable to contribute are set out in s.74(2); see also ss.75, 76.

149 Debts due from contributory to company

149(1) [Court may order payment from contributory] The court may, at any time after making a winding-up order, make an order on any contributory for the time being on the list of contributories to pay, in manner directed by the order, any money due from him (or from the estate of the person who he represents) to the company, exclusive of any money payable by him or the estate by virtue of any call.

149(2) [Allowances and set-offs] The court in making such an order may–

(a) in the case of an unlimited company, allow to the contributory by way of set-off any money due to him or the estate which he represents from the company on any independent dealing or contract with the company, but not any money due to him as a member of the company in respect of any dividend or profit, and

(b) in the case of a limited company, make to any director or manager whose liability is unlimited or to his estate the like allowance.

149(3) [Money due to contributory may be allowed when creditors paid] In the case of any company, whether limited or unlimited, when all the creditors are paid in full (together with interest at the official rate), any money due on any account whatever to a contributory from the company may be allowed to him by way of set-off against any subsequent call.

S.149(1)
This provision allows the liquidator to recover in a summary way moneys (other than calls, which are dealt with in s.150) due by a member to the company, thus avoiding the formality of a conventional action. However, it is confined to sums owed by the member qua member, e.g. dividends improperly paid to him, and may not be used to claim an ordinary debt: *Re Marlborough Club Co* (1868) L.R. 5 Eq. 365. One consequence of this is that the contributory loses his normal right as a debtor to set off against such a claim any sums due from the company to him (*Re Whitehouse & Co* (1878) 9 Ch. D. 595), apart from the special case where a contributory's liability is unlimited, which is dealt with in s.149(2).

S.149(2)
The right of set-off in the two situations of unlimited liability referred to is not automatic, but rests in the discretion of the court. No set-off lies in any case in regard to dividends or profits payable to the member, in keeping with the principle expressed in s.74(2)(f).

On the question of set-off generally, see the Introductory note to Part IV, Chapter VIII preceding s.175.

S.149(3)
The restrictions as to set-off described in the notes to s.149(1) and (2) no longer apply once the claims of the general creditors have been fully satisfied.

On the entitlement of a creditor to interest, see the note to s.189.

150 Power to make calls

150(1) [Court may make calls to satisfy debts] The court may, at any time after making a winding-up order, and either before or after it has ascertained the sufficiency of the company's assets, make calls on all or any of the contributories for the time being settled on the list of the contributories to the extent of their liability, for payment of any money which the court considers necessary to satisfy the company's debts and liabilities, and the expenses of winding up, and for the adjustment of the rights of the contributories among themselves, and make an order for payment of any calls so made.

150(2) [Matters to be considered] In making a call the court may take into consideration the probability that some of the contributories may partly or wholly fail to pay it.

S.150(1)
This provision authorises the court to settle the liability of contributories to pay calls, and to enforce this liability in a summary way. The powers of the court have been delegated to the liquidator by regulations made under s.160(1): see IR 2016 rr.7.79, 7.86 et seq. In regard to the making of calls, the rules provide for the liquidator to act with the alternative sanction of the liquidation committee: r.7.87. The liquidator may not act without authorisation unless the court gives special leave: s.160(2). In *Administrators of LB Holdings Intermediate 2 Ltd v Joint Administrators of*

Lehman Bros International (Europe) [2017] UKSC 38; [2017] 2 W.L.R. 1497; [2017] B.C.C. 235 Lord Neuberger stressed that moneys paid under a call were paid to the liquidator—not the company—and were held by the liquidator on a statutory fund once the company had gone into liquidation. Thus where a company was seeking to prove future calls and it was not in liquidation, there was no extant debt: the potential creditor was a future liquidator, not the company. Similarly, if a contributory was also a subordinated creditor, its potential liabilities under s.150 could not be set off against claims against it as a subordinated creditor.

S.150(2)
The court may take into account the likelihood that some contributories may default, so saving the need for a further call on the remainder. If the amount thus raised is surplus to the liquidator's needs, it is of course returnable under s.154.

151 Payment into bank of money due to company [Repealed]

General Note

Section 151 was repealed by DA 2015 Sch.6 para.9 as from 1 October 2015.

152 Order on contributory to be conclusive evidence

152(1) [Order evidence that money due] An order made by the court on a contributory is conclusive evidence that the money (if any) thereby appearing to be due or ordered to be paid is due, but subject to any right of appeal.

152(2) [Other matters stated in order] All other pertinent matters stated in the order are to be taken as truly stated as against all persons and in all proceedings except proceedings in Scotland against the heritable estate of a deceased contributory; and in that case the order is only prima facie evidence for the purpose of charging his heritable estate, unless his heirs or legatees of heritage were on the list of contributories at the time of the order being made.

General Note

This section applies only to orders against contributories, but it is not confined to orders for the payment of calls.

153 Power to exclude creditors not proving in time

153 The court may fix a time or times within which creditors are to prove their debts or claims or to be excluded from the benefit of any distribution made before those debts are proved.

General Note

A creditor who does not prove his debt within the time fixed by the court is excluded from participating in any distribution made before he proves, but his right to prove is not itself affected, and he may be paid out of such assets as remain or later become available. See further IR 2016 rr.14.39, 14.40.

The power of the court under this section may be delegated by rules to the liquidator: see s.160(1). There does not appear to have been any specific exercise of this power in IR 2016.

A creditor may, of course, be barred from claiming by the operation of the statutes of limitation. In *Re Joshua Shaw & Sons Ltd* (1989) 5 B.C.C. 188 the debts of all the company's unsecured creditors, apart from the Crown, became statute-barred during the course of a long-running receivership. The ironic consequence was that the surplus which was found to exist at the conclusion of the receivership went to the company's shareholders.

154 Adjustment of rights of contributories

154 The court shall adjust the rights of the contributories among themselves and distribute any surplus among the persons entitled to it.

General Note

For the corresponding provision in a voluntary winding up, see s.107.

For the relevant rules, see IR 2016 rr.7.117 et seq.

155 Inspection of books by creditors, etc.

155(1) [Court may make order for inspection] The court may, at any time after making a winding-up order, make such order for inspection of the company's books and papers by creditors and contributories as the court thinks just; and any books and papers in the company's possession may be inspected by creditors and contributories accordingly, but not further or otherwise.

155(2) [Statutory rights of government department] Nothing in this section excludes or restricts any statutory rights of a government department or person acting under the authority of a government department.

155(3) [Government department includes Scottish Administration] For the purposes of subsection (2) above, references to a government department shall be construed as including references to any part of the Scottish Administration.

S.155(1)
The company's books and papers are not ordinarily accessible even to members while the company is a going concern; and although this section does confer such a right on creditors and contributories in a winding up, subject to the leave of the court, there are dicta which state that the court's leave will in practice be granted only for purposes connected with the liquidation, and only where the exercise of the power would be just and beneficial: *Re North Brazilian Sugar Factories* (1887) 37 Ch. D. 83; *Re D P R Futures Ltd* [1989] 1 W.L.R. 778; (1989) 5 B.C.C. 603; *MG Rover Dealer Properties Ltd v Hunt* [2012] B.P.I.R. 590; *Sunwing Vacation Inc v E-Clear (UK) plc* [2011] EWHC 1544 (Ch); [2011] B.C.C. 889. (An indirect connection may be sufficient: *Sunwing Vacation Inc v E-Clear (UK) plc* [2011] EWHC 1544 (Ch); [2011] B.C.C. 889.) However, it is understood that the court will in fact grant leave in a suitable case, e.g. where a creditor needs to obtain information to defend a claim under a guarantee, or an insurance company to defend a claim made against it, even though the claim in question may not be so connected. The same cases also held that the court's jurisdiction under s.155 extends only to books and papers in the possession of the company: it cannot, for instance, extend to documents formerly in the custody of the company which have been seized by the Serious Fraud Office.

S.155(2)
The statutory rights most obviously referred to here are those of the Secretary of State, and inspectors appointed by him, under CA 1985 ss.431 et seq. [not affected by CA 2006].

S.155(3)
This subsection was inserted by the Scotland Act 1998 (Consequential Modifications) (No.2) Order 1999 (SI 1999/1820) arts 1(2), 4 and Sch.2 Pt 1 para.85, effective 1 July 1999.

156 Payment of expenses of winding up

156 The court may, in the event of the assets being insufficient to satisfy the liabilities, make an order as to the payment out of the assets of the expenses incurred in the winding up in such order of priority as the court thinks just.

General Note

On the meaning of "assets" in the context of the present section, see the note to s.115.

The rules contain provisions dealing with the payment of expenses of a winding up in the normal case, but subject to any order of the court: IR 2016 rr.6.42, 7.108. The present section gives the court the power to make such an order where it is appropriate, but the power is limited to varying the order of priority and does not extend to making an order giving priority to costs that are not within the list contained in the above rules: *Re R S & M Engineering Co Ltd* [2000] Ch. 40; [2000] B.C.C. 445; *Re MT Realisations Ltd* [2003] EWHC 2895 (Ch); [2004] 1 B.C.L.C. 119. The court will only in exceptional circumstances exercise its jurisdiction under this section to confer on the liquidator's remuneration, or any part of it, priority over liquidation expenses which would normally rank before it: *Re Linda Marie Ltd (in liq.)* (1988) 4 B.C.C. 463.

In relation to the financial markets and securities settlement systems, s.156 has effect subject to the priority accorded to the claim of a participant or central bank to collateral security by the Finality Regulations reg.14(5), (6), unless the terms on which the collateral security was provided expressly state that the expenses, remuneration or preferential debts are to have priority: see the note on p.3.

157 Attendance at company meetings (Scotland)

157 In the winding up by the court of a company registered in Scotland, the court has power to require the attendance of any officer of the company at any meeting of creditors or of contributories, or of a liquidation committee, for the purpose of giving information as to the trade, dealings, affairs or property of the company.

General Note

There is no direct counterpart of this provision for England and Wales.

158 Power to arrest absconding contributory

158 The court, at any time either before or after making a winding-up order, on proof of probable cause for believing that a contributory is about to quit the United Kingdom or otherwise to abscond or to remove or conceal any of his property for the purpose of evading payment of calls, may cause the contributory to be arrested and his books and papers and moveable personal property to be seized and him and them to be kept safely until such time as the court may order.

General Note

The former legislation, after the phrase "for the purpose of evading calls" contained the additional words "or of avoiding examination respecting the company's affairs". These words have been deleted; the point is amply covered elsewhere in the Act: see s.236(5).

159 Powers of court to be cumulative

159 Powers conferred on the court by this Act are in addition to, and not in restriction of, any existing powers of instituting proceedings against a contributory or debtor of the company, or the estate of any contributory or debtor, for the recovery of any call or other sums.

160 Delegation of powers to liquidator (England and Wales)

160(1) [Delegation by rules] Provision may be made by rules for enabling or requiring all or any of the powers and duties conferred and imposed on the court in England and Wales in respect of the following matters–

(a) the seeking of decisions on any matter from creditors and contributories,

(b) the settling of lists of contributories and the rectifying of the register of members where required, and the collection and application of the assets,

(c) the payment, delivery, conveyance, surrender or transfer of money, property, books or papers to the liquidator,

(d) the making of calls,

(e) the fixing of a time within which debts and claims must be proved,

to be exercised or performed by the liquidator as an officer of the court, and subject to the court's control.

160(2) [No rectification etc. without special leave] But the liquidator shall not, without the special leave of the court, rectify the register of members, and shall not make any call without either that special leave or the sanction of the liquidation committee.

General Note

For the relevant rules, see IR 2016 rr.15.3 et seq. (meetings, etc.); 7.76 et seq. (assets); 7.78 (surrender of books, etc.); 7.79 et seq. (list of contributories); 7.86 (rectifying register), and see the note to s.153 (time for proving).

Enforcement of, and appeal from, orders

161 Orders for calls on contributories (Scotland)

161(1) [Court may order calls on contributories on receipt of list] In Scotland, where an order, interlocutor or decree has been made for winding up a company by the court, it is competent to the court, on production by the liquidators of a list certified by them of the names of the contributories liable in payment of any calls, and of the amount due by each contributory, and of the date when that amount became due, to pronounce forthwith a decree against those contributories for payment of the sums so certified to be due, with interest from that date until payment (at 5 per cent per annum) in the same way and to the same effect as if they had severally consented to registration for execution, on a charge of 6 days, of a legal obligation to pay those calls and interest.

161(2) [Extraction of decree] The decree may be extracted immediately, and no suspension of it is competent, except on caution or consignation, unless with special leave of the court.

General Note

The procedure for making calls on contributories in a winding up by the court in England and Wales is prescribed in rather different terms by s.160(1)(d) and the rules made thereunder.

162 Appeals from orders in Scotland

162(1) [Appeal from order on winding up] Subject to the provisions of this section and to rules of court, an appeal from any order or decision made or given in the winding up of a company by the court in Scotland under this Act lies in the same manner and subject to the same conditions as an appeal from an order or decision of the court in cases within its ordinary jurisdiction.

162(2) [Orders by judge acting as vacation judge] In regard to orders or judgments pronounced by the judge acting as vacation judge–

(a) none of the orders specified in Part I of Schedule 3 to this Act are subject to review, reduction, suspension or stay of execution, and

(b) every other order or judgment (except as mentioned below) may be submitted to review by the Inner House by reclaiming motion enrolled within 14 days from the date of the order or judgment.

162(3) [Order in Sch.3 Pt II] However, an order being one of those specified in Part II of that Schedule shall, from the date of the order and notwithstanding that it has been submitted to review as above, be carried out and receive effect until the Inner House have disposed of the matter.

162(4) [Orders by Lord Ordinary] In regard to orders or judgments pronounced in Scotland by a Lord Ordinary before whom proceedings in a winding up are being taken, any such order or judgment may be submitted to review by the Inner House by reclaiming motion enrolled within 14 days from its date; but should it not be so submitted to review during session, the provisions of this section in regard to orders or judgments pronounced by the judge acting as vacation judge apply.

162(5) [Decrees for payment of calls in winding up] Nothing in this section affects provisions of the Companies Acts or this Act in reference to decrees in Scotland for payment of calls in the winding up of companies, whether voluntary or by the court.

General Note

This section deals with a number of special points of Scottish procedure. It should be read in conjunction with Sch.3, below, which makes more detailed provisions for the purposes of s.162(2) and (3).

CHAPTER VII

LIQUIDATORS

Preliminary

163 Style and title of liquidators

163 The liquidator of a company shall be described–

(a) where a person other than the official receiver is liquidator, by the style of "the liquidator" of the particular company, or

(b) where the official receiver is liquidator, by the style of "the official receiver and liquidator" of the particular company;

and in neither case shall he be described by an individual name.

GENERAL NOTE

A court-appointed liquidator is an officer of the court and subject to the control of the court, and as such is expected to observe high standards of conduct: *Re Quantum Distribution (UK) Ltd* [2012] CSOH 191. See further the note to Sch.B1 para.5.

On the question whether a liquidator is an "officer" for the purposes of IA 1986 (and perhaps also other statutes), see the note to s.206(3), and compare the Social Security Administration Act 1992 s.121C, under which insolvency practitioners have been held liable as "officers" for unpaid National Insurance contributions. The non-statutory term "office holder" plainly includes a liquidator. It may be important to distinguish between acts or activities performed by a liquidator by virtue of his office, such as adjudicating upon proofs of debt, and acts performed as agent of the company (e.g. entering into a contract in its name: *Stead, Hazel & Co v Cooper* [1933] 1 K.B. 840). In *Re Southern Pacific Personal Loans Ltd* [2013] EWHC 2485 (Ch); [2014] B.C.C. 56 it was ruled that a liquidator who received and processed personal data did so in the latter capacity and accordingly was not personally responsible as a "data controller" for the purposes of the Data Protection Act 1988. In *Stevensdrake Ltd v Hunt* [2015] EWHC 1527 (Ch); [2016] B.C.C. 485 a liquidator was held personally liable to solicitors under a conditional fee agreement on the wording of that document; compare other proceedings at [2017] EWCA Civ 1173; [2017] B.C.C. 611.

It follows from s.123 that a liquidator may not bring a claim in his own name, unless empowered to do so by statute (as, for example, by ss.212, 238, 239): *Kirkpatrick v Snoozebox Ltd* [2014] B.C.C. 477.

164 Corrupt inducement affecting appointment

164 A person who gives, or agrees or offers to give, to any member or creditor of a company any valuable consideration with a view to securing his own appointment or nomination, or to securing or preventing the appointment or nomination of some person other than himself, as the company's liquidator is liable to a fine.

GENERAL NOTE

It is perhaps surprising that this old provision has survived the reforms made by IA 1985, including the requirement that a liquidator must now be a professional insolvency practitioner.

On penalties, see s.430 and Sch.10.

Liquidator's powers and duties

165 Voluntary winding up

165(1) [Application] This section has effect where a company is being wound up voluntarily, but subject to section 166 below in the case of a creditors' voluntary winding up.

165(2) [Powers in Sch.4] The liquidator may exercise any of the powers specified in Parts 1 to 3 of Schedule 4.

165(3) [Deleted]

165(4) [Other powers] The liquidator may–

(a) exercise the court's power of settling a list of contributories (which list is prima facie evidence of the liability of the persons named in it to be contributories),

(b) exercise the court's power of making calls,

(c) summon general meetings of the company for the purpose of obtaining its sanction by special resolution or for any other purpose he may think fit.

165(5) [Duty re payment of debts] The liquidator shall pay the company's debts and adjust the rights of the contributories among themselves.

165(6) [Notice to committee re exercise of powers] Where the liquidator in exercise of the powers conferred on him by this Act disposes of any property of the company to a person who is connected with the company (within the meaning of section 249 in Part VII), he shall, if there is for the time being a liquidation committee, give notice to the committee of that exercise of his powers.

General Note

This section deals with the powers and duties of the liquidator in a voluntary winding up. It is to be read in conjunction with Sch.4, in which some powers are set out in detail. Note the limitation on powers of the liquidator to deal with property covered by s.426 of the POCA 2002 (restraint orders, etc.).

Section 165(4)(c) amended by the Companies Act 2006 (Commencement No.3, Consequential Amendments, Transitional Provisions and Savings) Order 2007 (SI 2007/2194 (C. 84)) art.10(1) and Sch.4 para.41(1), as from 1 October 2007. Section 165(2) substituted and s.165(3) deleted by SBEEA 2015 s.120(1), (2) as from 26 May 2015.

S.165(1)

The relationship between ss.165 and 166 is a little confusing. Section 165 applies to every voluntary winding up, *including* a creditors' voluntary winding up where the liquidator has been nominated by the company; but s.166 supplements s.165 in the latter case by imposing restrictions on the powers exercisable by the liquidator pending a decision of the creditors on the nomination of a liquidator under s.100.

S.165(2)

Until the amendments made by SBEEA 2015, many of the powers conferred on a liquidator by s.165 were exercisable only with the sanction of a special resolution of the company (in the case of a members' voluntary winding up) or (in a creditors' voluntary winding up) of the court, the liquidation committee or a special resolution of the creditors. The 2015 Act has removed the need for sanction in all cases. Schedule 4 was formerly divided into three parts, specifying respectively the powers exercisable in the different situations. Curiously, the division into parts has survived, although it is no longer of any significance.

In the first reported case since the requirement of sanction was abolished, *Re Longmeade Ltd* [2016] EWHC 356 (Ch); [2017] B.C.C. 203, Snowden J has summarised the principles governing the exercise of powers by a liquidator. Primarily, this is a matter for the liquidator's commercial judgment, in what he considers to be in the best interests of the company and all those with an interest in its estate—a decision on which the court will not give him directions or generally interfere. He may, but is not bound to, consult the creditors, and he may discount the views of any creditor who is influenced by extraneous and individual considerations.

S.165(4)

These are matters for which, in the case of a winding up by the court, power is in the first instance conferred by the Act upon the court itself, but then normally delegated to the liquidator by rules made under s.160. Note, however, that under the present section the liquidator in a voluntary winding up may make calls without any sanction (para.(b)), in contrast with s.160(2) which stipulates that in a compulsory winding up he may do so only with the special leave of the court.

Reference should be made also to s.112, which empowers the court to determine questions and exercise powers in a voluntary winding up as if the company were being wound up by the court.

S.165(5)

There is some overlap between this provision and s.107. On the application of assets generally, see the note to that section.

S.165(6)

This provision, first introduced by IA 1985, is designed to ensure that, at least in any voluntary winding up where there is a liquidation committee, no property of the company shall be disposed of to someone "connected with" the company unless it is done with the modest amount of disclosure specified. (The legislators have not gone so far as to stipulate for the *sanction* of the committee.) No doubt this requirement is part of the general package of measures aimed at the abuse known as the "phoenix syndrome" (see the note to s.216, below). If there is no liquidation committee, s.141(5) applies, vesting the relevant powers in the Secretary of State.

The category of persons "connected with" a company is very widely defined, and includes a director, employee or controlling shareholder, a close relative of any of these persons, and a company in the same group. See the notes to ss.249 and 435, below.

166 Creditors' voluntary winding up

166(1) [Application] This section applies where, in the case of a creditors' voluntary winding up, a liquidator has been nominated by the company.

166(1A) [Scottish liquidator's power of sale not challengeable by prior inhibition] The exercise by the liquidator of the power specified in paragraph 6 of Schedule 4 to this Act (power to sell any of the company's property) shall not be challengeable on the ground of any prior inhibition.

166(2) [Non-exercise of s.165 powers] The powers conferred on the liquidator by section 165 shall not be exercised, except with the sanction of the court, before–

(a) the company's creditors under section 100 nominate a person to be liquidator, or

(b) the procedure by which the company's creditors were to have made such a nomination concludes without a nomination having been made.

166(3) [Non-application of s.166(2)] Subsection (2) does not apply in relation to the power of the liquidator–

(a) to take into his custody or under his control all the property to which the company is or appears to be entitled;

(b) to dispose of perishable goods and other goods the value of which is likely to diminish if they are not immediately disposed of; and

(c) to do all such other things as may be necessary for the protection of the company's assets.

166(4) [Omitted]

166(5) [Where default re ss.99, 100] If the directors fail to comply with–

(a) section 99(1), (2) or (2A), or

(b) section 100(1B),

the liquidator shall, within 7 days of the relevant day, apply to the court for directions as to the manner in which that default is to be remedied.

166(6) ["The relevant day"] "The relevant day" means the day on which the liquidator was nominated by the company or the day on which he first became aware of the default, whichever is the later.

166(7) [Penalty for non-compliance] If the liquidator without reasonable excuse fails to comply with this section, he is liable to a fine.

General Note

Section 166(1A) was inserted by the Bankruptcy and Diligence etc. (Scotland) Act 2007 s.155(3) as from 22 April 2009. Section 166(2) substituted and s.166(4) omitted by SBEEA 2015 Sch.9 paras 1, 40 as from 6 April 2017.

This section should be read in conjunction with ss.98 and 114, above. Taken together, they should ensure (as is undoubtedly intended) that the practice which had become notorious under the name of "centrebinding" is totally stamped out. The abuse takes its name from the case of *Re Centrebind Ltd* [1967] 1 W.L.R. 377, where the members of an insolvent company resolved to go into voluntary liquidation and appointed their own liquidator who, before any creditors' meeting had been held, took immediate steps to restrain the Inland Revenue from proceeding with a distress on the company's assets. Plowman J held that the liquidator had power to act until the creditors' meeting had been held.

Although the acts of the company and its liquidator in the *Centrebind* case itself were done entirely in good faith, it was not long before the practice developed of calling only a shareholders' meeting in the first instance to pass a winding-up resolution and, although the company was known to be insolvent, deliberately putting off for some time, or perhaps indefinitely, the holding of the creditors' meeting. This, of course, involved a technical breach of the Companies Act (CA 1985 s.588(2)), which required the latter meeting to be held on the same day as the members' meeting or the very next day and, indeed, was a criminal offence. However, it meant that the controllers of a company, with the aid of an unscrupulous liquidator nominated by them, could effectively sell the assets off at a knock-down price to a purchaser closely connected with themselves (e.g. a new company controlled by them), and the creditors were powerless to prevent it.

The introduction by IA 1985 of a mandatory requirement that liquidators shall be of professional standing is probably in itself sufficient to ensure that "centrebinding" will no longer be part of insolvency practice; but the legislature has made doubly sure of this by provisions such as the present.

S.166(1)

Where no liquidator has been nominated by the company the directors will remain in control of the company's property, but their powers will be limited to protecting the assets and disposing of perishable goods, unless they obtain the sanction of the court (see s.114).

S.166(2)

The provisions of s.166 operate to qualify s.165 only during the interval between the nomination of a liquidator by the company and a decision of the creditors on the nomination of a liquidator under s.100.

S.166(3)

The restricted powers given to the liquidator (unless he has the sanction of the court under s.166(2)) are, as regards paras (b) and (c), the same as those allowed to directors by s.114(3). In addition he has, by para.(a), the power to take over custody and control of the company's property from the directors. The term "property" is widely defined: see s.436.

S.166(4), (5)

The language of s.166(5) is permissive rather than mandatory. There is no obligation on the liquidator to apply for directions where there is no need for them: *Re Salcombe Hotel Development Co Ltd* (1989) 5 B.C.C. 807; contrast *Re WeSellCNC.com Ltd* [2013] EWHC 4577 (Ch), where the liquidation had proceeded as a members' voluntary winding up but no declaration of solvency had been made.

Section 166(5)(a) amended by the Legislative Reform (Insolvency) (Advertising Requirements) Order 2009 art.3(3), as from 6 April 2009, and s.166(5)(b) amended by LRO 2010 (SI 2010/18) art.5(5) from 6 April 2010 (with retrospective effect).

S.166(7)

On penalties, see s.430 and Sch.10.

167 Winding up by the court

167(1) [Powers of liquidator] Where a company is being wound up by the court, the liquidator may exercise any of the powers specified in Parts 1 to 3 of Schedule 4.

167(2) [Duty of liquidator] Where the liquidator (not being the official receiver), in exercise of the powers conferred on him by this Act–

(a) disposes of any property of the company to a person who is connected with the company (within the meaning of section 249 in Part VII), or

(b) employs a solicitor to assist him in the carrying out of his functions,

he shall, if there is for the time being a liquidation committee, give notice to the committee of that exercise of his powers.

167(3) [Control of court] The exercise by the liquidator in a winding up by the court of the powers conferred by this section is subject to the control of the court, and any creditor or contributory may apply to the court with respect to any exercise or proposed exercise of any of those powers.

General Note

Section 167(1) substituted by SBEEA 2015 s.120(1), (3) as from 26 May 2015.

The liquidator, in a winding up by the court, is given specific powers and duties by various other sections of the Act. In addition, the present provision confers on him general powers by reference to Sch.4. Note the limitation on the liquidator's powers with regard to property covered by s.426 of POCA 2002 (restraint orders, etc.).

S.167(1)

SBEEA 2015 has removed the need for sanction in all cases. The division of Sch.4 into parts is now of no significance.

S.167(3)

There is no provision in the Act directly corresponding to this subsection which applies in a voluntary winding up, but the supervisory powers of the court may be invoked in such a case by an application made under s.112.

The court is traditionally reluctant to interfere in the exercise of discretion by a liquidator, and will not do so where it has been exercised in good faith: see the note to s.168(5), below. In *Re Greenhaven Motors Ltd* [1997] B.C.C. 547 at first instance, Harman J thought that a contributory should not be entitled to make an application under this subsection unless there was a real prospect that there would be assets available to yield him a substantial return, but on appeal ([1999] B.C.C. 463 at 466) this point was left open.

168 Supplementary powers (England and Wales)

168(1) [Application] This section applies in the case of a company which is being wound up by the court in England and Wales.

168(2) [Decisions from creditors or contributories] The liquidator may seek a decision on any matter from the company's creditors or contributories; and must seek a decision on a matter–

(a) from the company's creditors, if requested to do so by one-tenth in value of the creditors;

(b) from the company's contributories, if requested to do so by one-tenth in value of the contributories.

168(3) [Liquidator may apply to court for directions] The liquidator may apply to the court (in the prescribed manner) for directions in relation to any particular matter arising in the winding up.

168(4) [Liquidator to use own discretion] Subject to the provisions of this Act, the liquidator shall use his own discretion in the management of the assets and their distribution among the creditors.

168(5) [Application to court re acts of liquidator] If any person is aggrieved by an act or decision of the liquidator, that person may apply to the court; and the court may confirm, reverse or modify the act or decision complained of, and make such order in the case as it thinks just.

168(5A) [Court order re insolvent partnerships] Where at any time after a winding-up petition has been presented to the court against any person (including an insolvent partnership or other body which may be wound up under Part V of the Act as an unregistered company), whether by virtue of the provisions of the Insolvent Partnerships Order 1994 or not, the attention of the court is drawn to the fact that the person in question is a member of an insolvent partnership, the court may make an order as to the future conduct of the insolvency proceedings and any such order may apply any provisions of that Order with any necessary modifications.

168(5B) [Order or directions under s.168(5A)] Any order or directions under subsection (5A) may be made or given on the application of the official receiver, any responsible insolvency practitioner, the trustee of the partnership or any other interested person and may include provisions as to the administration of the joint estate of the partnership, and in particular how it and the separate estate of any member are to be administered.

168(5C) [Sections under which court order made re insolvent partnerships] Where the court makes an order for the winding up of an insolvent partnership under–

(a) section 72(1)(a) of the Financial Services Act 1986;

(b) section 92(1)(a) of the Banking Act 1987; or

(c) section 367(3)(a) of the Financial Services and Markets Act 2000,

the court may make an order as to the future conduct of the winding up proceedings, and any such order may apply any provisions of the Insolvent Partnerships Order 1994 with any necessary modifications.

General Note

Section 168(2) substituted by SBEEA 2015 Sch.9 paras 1, 41 as from 6 April 2017.

This section provides in general terms for consultation between the liquidator and the creditors and contributories, either on his initiative or on requisition by one-tenth in value of those concerned, and also for the court to give directions and to supervise and control the acts and decisions of the liquidator.

For the rules relating to decision proceedings, see IR 2016 rr.15.3 et seq. and as regard applications to the court, rr.12.6 et seq.

S.168(2)

Although this subsection imposes a duty on the liquidator who has received a requisition to seek a decision, the court has jurisdiction to override that duty by directing him not to comply with it: *Re Barings plc, Hamilton v Law Debenture Trustees Ltd* [2001] 2 B.C.L.C. 159. The court would not apply the latter case in *Kean v Lucas* [2017] EWHC 250 (Ch); [2017] B.C.C. 311 in refusing an application by a liquidator in creditors' voluntary liquidation for an order to prevent a meeting which the requisite number of creditors sought to convene to vote for the liquidator's removal.

S.168(5)

Notwithstanding the width of the words "may ... make such order in the case as it thinks just", the court will not normally review the exercise by the liquidator of his powers and discretions in the management and realisation of the corporate property. The court will only interfere with a decision of a liquidator if it was taken in bad faith or if it was so perverse as to demonstrate that no liquidator properly advised could have taken it: *Re a Debtor* [1949] Ch. 236 at 241; *Re Hans Place Ltd* [1992] B.C.C. 737 at 745–746; *Leon v York-o-Matic Ltd* [1966] 1 W.L.R. 1450; *Re Greenhaven Motors Ltd* [1997] B.C.C. 547; *Re Edennote Ltd, Tottenham Hotspur v Ryman* [1996] B.C.C. 718; *Hamilton v Official Receiver* [1998] B.P.I.R. 602; *Re Abbey Forwarding Ltd* [2010] EWHC 1644 (Ch); [2010] B.P.I.R. 1053.

On the meaning of "person aggrieved", see the remarks of Warner J (obiter) in *Re ACLI Metals (London) Ltd (AML Holdings Inc v Auger)* (1989) 5 B.C.C. 749 at 754; and *Re Edennote Ltd* (above) at 721–722. Apart from creditors and contributories, those who may apply are not "any outsider" who is dissatisfied with some act or decision of a liquidator, but rather persons directly affected by a power given specifically to a liquidator, such as a landlord following the disclaimer of a lease: *Mahomed v Morris* [2001] B.C.C. 233.

S.168(5A)–(5C)

These subsections were inserted by the Insolvent Partnerships Order 1994 (SI 1994/2421) arts 1, 14(1) with effect from 1 December 1994. Subsection (5C) was briefly repealed by SI 2001/3649 arts 1, 306 as from 1 December 2001 and then reinstated in revised form by SI 2002/1555 arts 1, 15 as from 3 July 2002. They empower the court to make appropriate orders when a winding-up petition has been presented against any person (including a company, partnership or other body) and it appears that that person is a member of an insolvent partnership. Similar provisions apply in regard to bankruptcy petitions: see s.303(2A)–(2C).

169 Supplementary powers (Scotland)

169(1) [Deleted]

169(2) [Liquidator's powers] In a winding up by the court in Scotland, the liquidator has (subject to the rules) the same powers as a trustee on a bankrupt estate.

S.169(1)

Deleted by SBEEA 2015 s.120(1), (4) as from 26 May 2015.

S.169(2)

For the powers of the trustee on a bankrupt estate in Scotland, see the Bankruptcy (Scotland) Act 2016.

170 Enforcement of liquidator's duty to make returns, etc.

170(1) [Powers of court if liquidator fails to file returns, etc.] If a liquidator who has made any default–

(a) in filing, delivering or making any return, account or other document, or

(b) in giving any notice which he is by law required to file, deliver, make or give,

fails to make good the default within 14 days after the service on him of a notice requiring him to do so, the court has the following powers.

170(2) [On application court may order to make good default] On an application made by any creditor or contributory of the company, or by the registrar of companies, the court may make an order directing the liquidator to make good the default within such time as may be specified in the order.

170(3) [Costs] The court's order may provide that all costs of and incidental to the application shall be borne by the liquidator.

170(4) [Penalties] Nothing in this section prejudices the operation of any enactment imposing penalties on a liquidator in respect of any such default as is mentioned above.

General Note

This section contains provisions parallel to those in CA 2006 s.1113, which deal with the enforcement of such defaults against the company itself and its officers and are, of course, not confined to a winding up. A liquidator is not normally an "officer" for the purposes of the Companies Acts: see the note to s.206(3).

Removal; vacation of office

171 Removal, etc. (voluntary winding up)

171(1) [Application] This section applies with respect to the removal from office and vacation of office of the liquidator of a company which is being wound up voluntarily.

171(2) [Removal from office] Subject to the next subsection, the liquidator may be removed from office only by an order of the court or–

(a) in the case of a members' voluntary winding up, by a general meeting of the company summoned specially for that purpose, or

(b) in the case of a creditors' voluntary winding up, by a decision of the company's creditors made by a qualifying decision procedure instigated specially for that purpose in accordance with the rules.

171(3) [Where liquidator in MVL appointed by court: company meeting] Where the liquidator in a members' voluntary winding up was appointed by the court under section 108, a meeting such as is mentioned in subsection (2)(a) shall be summoned only if–

(a) the liquidator thinks fit,

(b) the court so directs, or

(c) the meeting is requested in accordance with the rules by members representing not less than one-half of the total voting rights of all the members having at the date of the request a right to vote at the meeting.

171(3A) [Liquidator in CVL appointed by court: qualifying decision procedure] Where the liquidator in a creditors' voluntary winding up was appointed by the court under section 108, a qualifying decision procedure such as is mentioned in subsection (2)(b) is to be instigated only if–

(a) the liquidator thinks fit,

(b) the court so directs, or

(c) it is requested in accordance with the rules by not less than one-half in value of the company's creditors.

171(4) [Vacation of office] A liquidator shall vacate office if he ceases to be a person who is qualified to act as an insolvency practitioner in relation to the company.

171(5) [Resignation] A liquidator may, in the prescribed circumstances, resign his office by giving notice of his resignation to the registrar of companies.

171(6) [Vacation after final account sent in MVL] In the case of a members' voluntary winding up where the liquidator has produced an account of the winding up under section 94 (final account), the liquidator vacates office as soon as the liquidator has complied with section 94(3) (requirement to send final account to registrar).

171(7) [Vacation after final account sent in CVL] In the case of a creditors' voluntary winding up where the liquidator has produced an account of the winding up under section 106 (final account), the liquidator vacates office as soon as the liquidator has complied with section 106(3) (requirement to send final account etc. to registrar).

General Note

Section 171(2)(b), (3), (6) substituted and s.171(3A) and (7) inserted by SBEEA 2015 Sch.9 paras 1, 42 as from 6 April 2017.

This section sets out in detail the manner by which a liquidator in a voluntary winding up may be removed or resign from his office, and the circumstances in which he must vacate it. It complements s.172, which applies in a winding up by the court. Together, the two sections set out the legal position comprehensively and in some detail. An important consequence of this is that the power of the company or of the contributories in general meeting to remove the liquidator in a creditors' voluntary winding up—even a liquidator whom they have themselves appointed—is no longer recognised.

On "block transfers", see the note to s.172.

A liquidator cannot voluntarily vacate office and leave the final distribution of assets to a third party: *Cavanagh v Conway* [2015] NIQB 69.

For the liquidator's duties on vacating office, see IR 2016 rr.6.32, 7.73, 5.13. A liquidator who ought to have resigned but instead resists an application for his removal may be ordered to pay costs on an indemnity basis: *Shepheard v Lamey* [2001] B.P.I.R. 939.

On a petition for the compulsory winding up of a company which is already in voluntary liquidation, the court may decline to make an order where a more appropriate course would be to allow the voluntary winding up to continue and apply to the court to have the liquidator removed and replaced: see *Re Inside Sports Ltd* [2000] B.C.C. 40 at 43 (where on the special facts of the case a winding-up order was considered more appropriate).

S.171(1), (2)

The members may remove a liquidator only in a members' voluntary winding up. The creditors alone have this power in a creditors' winding up, even where the liquidator was originally appointed by the members under s.100(2). In *Kean v Lucas* [2017] EWHC 250 (Ch); [2017] B.C.C. 311 the court refused an application by a liquidator for an order preventing a meeting which the requisite number of creditors sought to convene to vote for the liquidator's removal: the wishes of the creditors should prevail.

For the rules prescribed for the purposes of s.171(2)(b), see IR 2016 rr.6.26, 15.7(3).

S.171(3)

Section 108 empowers the court to appoint a liquidator in a voluntary winding up in the circumstances there set out. A liquidator so appointed may be removed:

(1) "on cause shown", by order of the court (s.108(2));

(2) by the members or the creditors under s.171(2), if the liquidator himself thinks it "fit" to summon a meeting for the purpose (s.171(3));

(3) by the members or the creditors under s.171(2) if the court so directs (s.171(3)); or

(4) by the members or the creditors under s.171(2), if a decision procedure is requested by members or creditors, as the case may be, having the necessary 50 per cent-plus majority stipulated for by s.171(3)(c) or (3A)(c).

An application to have a liquidator removed under this section failed in *SISU Capital Fund Ltd v Tucker* [2005] EWHC 2170 and 2321 (Ch); [2006] B.C.C. 463.

For the relevant rules, see IR 2016 r.6.26.

S.171(4)

The terms "act as an insolvency practitioner in relation to" a particular company, and "qualified to act as an insolvency practitioner" are defined respectively in s.388(1) and s.390.

When a liquidator ceases to be qualified to act as an insolvency practitioner in relation to a company, he vacates office ipso facto and automatically, and does not continue in office until he has complied with his obligations under the rules to notify the registrar, etc. However, the former liquidator in a voluntary liquidation who has vacated office on the ground of disqualification is a proper person to make application to the court under s.108 to have another liquidator appointed in his place (*Re A J Adams (Builders) Ltd* [1991] B.C.C. 62).

For the relevant rules, see IR 2016 rr.6.30, 6.33.

S.171(5)

The circumstances in which a liquidator may resign are defined in IR 2016 rr.6.25, 7.61.

S.171(6)

If the meeting in question was inquorate, so that the liquidator's report could not be considered, s.94(5) and s.106(5) respectively state that the liquidator shall be deemed to have complied with the requirements of the section in question. It would seem therefore that the words "whose report was considered at the meeting" in the present subsection should be taken to include such cases of deemed compliance.

172 Removal, etc. (winding up by the court)

172(1) [Application] This section applies with respect to the removal from office and vacation of office of the liquidator of a company which is being wound up by the court, or of a provisional liquidator.

172(2) [Removal from office] Subject as follows, the liquidator may be removed from office only by an order of the court or by a decision of the company's creditors made by a qualifying decision procedure instigated specially for that purpose in accordance with the rules; and a provisional liquidator may be removed from office only by an order of the court.

172(3) [Replacing certain types of liquidator] Where–

(a) the official receiver is liquidator otherwise than in succession under section 136(3) to a person who held office as a result of a nomination by a meeting of the company's creditors or contributories, or

(b) the liquidator was appointed by the court otherwise than under section 139(4)(a) or 140(1), or was appointed by the Secretary of State,

a qualifying decision procedure such as is mentioned in subsection (2) shall be instigated only if the liquidator thinks fit, the court so directs, or it is requested, in accordance with the rules, by not less than one-quarter, in value, of the creditors.

172(4) [If liquidator appointed by Secretary of State] If appointed by the Secretary of State, the liquidator may be removed from office by a direction of the Secretary of State.

172(5) [Vacation of office] A liquidator or provisional liquidator, not being the official receiver, shall vacate office if he ceases to be a person who is qualified to act as an insolvency practitioner in relation to the company.

172(6) [Resignation] A liquidator may, in the prescribed circumstances, resign his office by giving notice of his resignation to the court.

172(7) [Where s.204 order] Where an order is made under section 204 (early dissolution in Scotland) for the dissolution of the company, the liquidator shall vacate office when the dissolution of the company takes effect in accordance with that section.

172(8) [Vacation after final account sent] Where the liquidator has produced an account of the winding up under section 146 (final account), the liquidator vacates office as soon as the liquidator has complied with section 146(4) (requirement to send account etc. to registrar and to court).

172(9) [Scotland: application of s.172(10)] Subsection (10) applies where, immediately before a liquidator gives notice to the court and the registrar under subsection (8) (or, where the liquidator gives notice to the court and the registrar on different days, immediately before the liquidator gives the first of those notices), there are EU insolvency proceedings open in respect of the company in one or more other member States.

172(10) [Scotland: duty of liquidator to send notice to court and registrar] The liquidator must send to the court and the registrar, with the notice, a statement–

(a) identifying those proceedings,

(b) identifying the member State liquidator appointed in each of those proceedings, and

(c) indicating, in relation to each of those member State liquidators, whether that member State liquidator consents to the company being dissolved.

General Note

Section 172(8) substituted by SBEEA 2015 Sch.9 paras 1, 43 as from 6 April 2017.

This section contains provisions, complementary to those in s.171, which apply in a compulsory winding up. The notes to s.171 apply generally to the present section also, subject to the additional points below.

S.172(1), (2)

A provisional liquidator may be removed only by court order.

The exercise by the court of its power to replace the liquidator originally appointed is a matter of discretion for the trial judge, which will not be lightly disturbed on appeal: *Parmalat Capital Finance Ltd v Food Holdings Ltd* [2008] UKPC 23; [2008] B.C.C. 371.

There is nothing in the present section which empowers the shareholders or contributories in general meeting to remove a liquidator, even in cases where the company is demonstrably solvent, and even where the original liquidator was the members' appointee.

Where a liquidator who has been appointed by the creditors wishes to vacate office, the creditors have the right to decide whether to accept his resignation and the court will not exercise its own power to do so without good reason: see *Re Sankey Furniture Ltd Ex p. Harding* [1995] 2 B.C.L.C. 594.

"Block transfer" orders: although rr.6.25(2) and 7.21(2) appear to make it mandatory for the liquidator to send a notice to creditors before resigning his office, the court has an overriding power to by-pass this procedure and make orders for his removal and replacement without the statutory formalities. This course is particularly appropriate where the insolvency practitioner concerned wishes to be relieved from multiple offices by making a single application. The terms on which such orders had been made in the past were examined by Neuberger J in *Re Equity Nominees Ltd* [2000] B.C.C. 84 and a new form of order settled, dealing with the information to be given to creditors and the manner in which the outgoing liquidator should deal with the accounts of his administration. For the relevant rules, see IR 2016 rr.12.35–12.38. The applicant (other than the Secretary of State) is required by r.12.37(6) to give notice of the application to the Secretary of State on or before the date the application is made. In practice this should be sent to the IP Regulation Section of the Insolvency Service: see *Dear IP*, December 2013.

See also *Re Alt Landscapes Ltd* [1999] B.P.I.R. 459; *Re A & C Supplies Ltd* [1998] B.C.C. 708; *Clements v Udal* [2001] B.C.C. 658; *Customs and Excise Commissioners v Allen* [2003] B.P.I.R. 830; and *Re a Licence Holder, Saville v Gerrard* [2004] EWHC 1363 (Ch); [2005] B.C.C. 433. It appears that such an order cannot be back-dated: *Darrell v Miller* [2003] EWHC 2811 (Ch); [2004] B.P.I.R. 470.

The legal authority for the making of block transfer orders was challenged (in relation to the replacement of a trustee in bankruptcy) in *Donaldson v O'Sullivan* [2008] EWHC 387 (Ch); [2008] B.C.C. 328; on appeal [2008] EWCA Civ 879; [2009] B.C.C. 99. The legitimacy of the procedure was upheld, specifically as regards bankruptcy under s.303(2), and more generally in relation to other insolvencies under the general powers of the court.

It was held in *Re Armstrong Brands Ltd* [2015] EWHC 3303 (Ch); [2016] B.C.C. 657 that the making of a block transfer order establishes as a matter of record the validity of the original appointments, so that they are no longer open to challenge.

A similar procedure for block transfers, by-passing the formalities of the Insolvency (Scotland) Rules 1986 rr.4.28–4.29, has received the blessing of the Scottish courts: *Geddes, Petitioner*, 2006 S.L.T. 664.

A contributory holding fully-paid shares in an insolvent company has no standing to apply to the court for an order removing a liquidator, on the analogy of *Re Rica Gold Washing Co* (1879) 11 Ch. D. 36 (see the note to s.124(2), (3) above): *Re Corbenstoke Ltd (No.2)* (1989) 5 B.C.C. 767.

For the rules prescribed for the purposes of s.172(2), see IR 2016 r.7.65.

S.172(3)
The liquidator may be removed by a decision of the creditors without any special formality under s.172(2) above only where:

(1) he was originally appointed by the company's creditors or contributories (s.172(2));

(2) the official receiver is liquidator in succession to a person who was appointed as in (1) (s.172(3)(a));

(3) the liquidator was a nominee of the contributories whom the court appointed liquidator either jointly with, or instead of, a nominee of the creditors (ss.139(4)(a), 172(3)(b)); or

(4) the liquidator was formerly the administrator of the company who was appointed by the court when the winding-up order was made immediately upon the termination of the administration (ss.140(1), 172(3)(b)).

In contrast with s.171(3), the percentage of creditors necessary to request a decision under s.172(2) is one-quarter, rather than "not less than one-half".

The court will not give a direction under s.172(3) unless it is satisfied that it is in the best interests of the liquidation to do so: *Managa Properties Ltd v Brittain* [2009] EWHC 157 (Ch); [2009] B.P.I.R. 306. In *Re a Company CR-2017-000393* (unreported, 17 March 2017), it was held that the court had jurisdiction to direct the liquidators not to hold a creditors' meeting if that would not be conducive to the proper process of the liquidation and do justice between all those interested in it: removing and replacing the liquidators would cause delay and add to the expense of the liquidation and it was a significant factor that the liquidators were seeking to make claims against some of the respondent creditors who sought their removal. (Cf. the creditors' voluntary winding-up case of *Kean v Lucas* [2017] EWHC 250 (Ch); [2017] B.C.C. 311 referred to in the note to s.171.)

S.172(4)
This power is additional to that of the court under s.172(2) and that of the creditors under s.172(3)(b). For the relevant rules, see IR 2016 r.7.66.

S.172(5)
For the relevant rules, see IR 2016 rr.7.68, 7.73.

S.172(6)
The relevant circumstances are prescribed by IR 2016 r.7.61.

S.172(8)
When the liquidator vacates office pursuant to this provision, he must deliver up the company's books and records to the official receiver: see IR 2016 rr.6.32, 7.73.

S.172(9), (10)
Section 172(9), (10) inserted in relation to Scotland only by the Insolvency Amendment (EU 2015/848) Regulations 2017 (SI 2017/702) regs 1, 2(2)(b), Sch. paras 55, 57 in relation to proceedings opened on or after 26 June 2017 (see reg.3) when the Recast EU Regulation 2015/848 came into force.

Release of liquidator

173 Release (voluntary winding up)

173(1) [Application] This section applies with respect to the release of the liquidator of a company which is being wound up voluntarily.

173(2) [Time of release] A person who has ceased to be a liquidator shall have his release with effect from the following time, that is to say–

(a) in the following cases, the time at which notice is given to the registrar of companies in accordance with the rules that the person has ceased to hold office–

(i) the person has been removed from office by a general meeting of the company,

(ii) the person has been removed from office by a decision of the company's creditors and the company's creditors have not decided against his release,

(iii) the person has died;

(b) in the following cases, such time as the Secretary of State may, on the application of the person, determine–

(i) the person has been removed from office by a decision of the company's creditors and the company's creditors have decided against his release,

(ii) the person has been removed from office by the court,

(iii) the person has vacated office under section 171(4);

(c) in the case of a person who has resigned, such time as may be prescribed;

(d) in the case of a person who has vacated office under subsection (6) of section 171, the time at which he vacated office;

(e) in the case of a person who has vacated office under section 171(7)–

(i) if any of the company's creditors objected to the person's release before the end of the period for so objecting prescribed by the rules, such time as the Secretary of State may, on an application by that person, determine, and

(ii) otherwise, the time at which the person vacated office.

173(2A) [Following removal by creditors] Where the person is removed from office by a decision of the company's creditors, any decision of the company's creditors as to whether the person should have his release must be made by a qualifying decision procedure.

173(3) [Application to Scotland] In the application of subsection (2) to the winding up of a company registered in Scotland, the references to a determination by the Secretary of State as to the time from which a person who has ceased to be liquidator shall have his release are to be read as references to such a determination by the Accountant of Court.

173(4) [Effect of release] Where a liquidator has his release under subsection (2), he is, with effect from the time specified in that subsection, discharged from all liability both in respect of acts or omissions of his in the winding up and otherwise in relation to his conduct as liquidator.

But nothing in this section prevents the exercise, in relation to a person who has had his release under subsection (2), of the court's powers under section 212 of this Act (summary remedy against delinquent directors, liquidators, etc.).

GENERAL NOTE

Section 173(2)(a), (b), (e) substituted and s.173(2A) inserted by SBEEA 2015 Sch.9 paras 1, 44 as from 6 April 2017.

S.173(1)

For the corresponding provisions relating to a winding up by the court, see s.174. The effect of a release is stated in s.173(4).

S.173(2), (3)

The times at which the release of a liquidator becomes effective in different circumstances are set out in the various paragraphs of this subsection. For the relevant rules, see IR 2016 rr.6.28, 6.33, 18.14 (creditors' voluntary winding up) and rr.5.9, 5.10 and 18.14 (members' voluntary winding up).

It is open to the members or creditors to resolve against the release of a liquidator in the cases mentioned in paras (b) and (e)(i). The question of a release is then a matter for the Secretary of State (or, in Scotland, the Accountant of Court) to determine.

S.173(4)

When applying to the Secretary of State for release, insolvency practitioners are required to confirm that a period of notice has been given to creditors and that no objections have been received from them (*Dear IP*, September 2014).

174 Release (winding up by the court)

174(1) [Application] This section applies with respect to the release of the liquidator of a company which is being wound up by the court, or of a provisional liquidator.

174(2) [Where official receiver ceases to be liquidator] Where the official receiver has ceased to be liquidator and a person becomes liquidator in his stead, the official receiver has his release with effect from the following time, that is to say–

(a) in a case where that person was nominated by the company's creditors or contributories, or was appointed by the Secretary of State, the time at which the official receiver gives notice to the court that he has been replaced;

(b) in a case where that person is appointed by the court, such time as the court may determine.

174(3) [Where official receiver gives notice to Secretary of State] If the official receiver while he is a liquidator gives notice to the Secretary of State that the winding up is for practical purposes complete, he has his release with effect from such time as the Secretary of State may determine.

174(4) [Person other than official receiver] A person other than the official receiver who has ceased to be a liquidator has his release with effect from the following time, that is to say–

(a) in the following cases, the time at which notice is given to the court in accordance with the rules that the person has ceased to hold office–

   (i) the person has been removed from office by a decision of the company's creditors and the company's creditors have not decided against his release,

   (ii) the person has died;

(b) in the following cases, such time as the Secretary of State may, on the application of the person, determine–

   (i) the person has been removed from office by a decision of the company's creditors and the company's creditors have decided against his release;

   (ii) the person has been removed from office by the court or the Secretary of State;

   (iii) the person has vacated office under section 172(5) or (7);

(c) in the case of a person who has resigned, such time as may be prescribed;

(d) in the case of a person who has vacated office under section 172(8)–

   (i) if any of the company's creditors objected to the person's release before the end of the period for so objecting prescribed by the rules, such time as the Secretary of State may, on an application by that person, determine, and

   (ii) otherwise, the time at which the person vacated office.

174(4ZA) [Following removal by creditors] Where the person is removed from office by a decision of the company's creditors, any decision of the company's creditors as to whether the person should have his release must be made by a qualifying decision procedure.

174(4A) [Where compulsory winding-up order rescinded] Where a winding-up order made by the court in England and Wales is rescinded, the person (whether the official receiver or another person) who is the liquidator of the company at the time the order is rescinded has his release with effect from such time as the court may determine.

174(5) [Provisional liquidator] A person who has ceased to hold office as a provisional liquidator has his release with effect from such time as the court may, on an application by him, determine.

174(6) [Effect of release] Where the official receiver or a liquidator or provisional liquidator has his release under this section, he is, with effect from the time specified in the preceding provisions of this section, discharged from all liability both in respect of acts or omissions of his in the winding up and otherwise in relation to his conduct as liquidator or provisional liquidator.

But nothing in this section prevents the exercise, in relation to a person who has had his release under this section, of the court's powers under section 212 (summary remedy against delinquent directors, liquidators, etc.).

174(7) [Application to Scotland] In the application of this section to a case where the order for winding up has been made by the court in Scotland, the references to a determination by the Secretary of State as to the time from which a person who has ceased to be liquidator has his release are to such a determination by the Accountant of Court.

General Note

Section 174(4)(a), (b), (d) substituted and s.174(4ZA) inserted by SBEEA 2015 Sch.9 paras 1, 45 as from 6 April 2017.

S.174(1)
Section 173 deals with the corresponding questions in a voluntary liquidation.

S.174(2), (3)
These two subsections govern the release of the official receiver as liquidator. Necessarily, of course, they apply only in England and Wales.

For the relevant rules, see IR 2016 r.7.70.

S.174(4)
The provisions of this subsection are broadly parallel to those of s.173(2). For the rules prescribed for the purposes of s.174, see IR 2016 rr.7.63, 7.70.

S.174(4A)
Section 174(4A) inserted by DA 2015 Sch.6 para.10 as from 1 October 2015.

S.174(6)
See the corresponding provisions relating to an administrator (s.20(2), (3)) and a liquidator in a voluntary winding up (s.173(4)).

Chapter VIII

Provisions of General Application in Winding Up

Preferential debts

175 Preferential debts (general provision)

175(1) [Payment in priority] In a winding up the company's preferential debts shall be paid in priority to all other debts.

175(1A) [Priority of ordinary preferential debts] Ordinary preferential debts rank equally among themselves after the expenses of the winding up and shall be paid in full, unless the assets are insufficient to meet them, in which case they abate in equal proportions.

175(1B) [Priority of secondary preferential debts] Secondary preferential debts rank equally among themselves after the ordinary preferential debts and shall be paid in full, unless the assets are insufficient to meet them, in which case they abate in equal proportions.

175(2) [Ranking and priority] Preferential debts–

(a) [Omitted]

(b) so far as the assets of the company available for payment of general creditors are insufficient to meet them, have priority over the claims of holders of debentures secured by, or holders of, any floating charge created by the company, and shall be paid accordingly out of any property comprised in or subject to that charge.

175(3) ["Preferential debts", "ordinary preferential debts", "secondary preferential debts"] In this section "preferential debts", "ordinary preferential debts" and "secondary preferential debts" each has the meaning given in section 386 in Part 12.

General Note

Section 175(1) amended, s.175(2)(a) omitted and s.175(1A), (1B), (3) inserted by the Banks and Building Societies (Depositor Preference and Priorities) Order 2014 (SI 2014/3486) art.5 as from 1 January 2015. The amendments made by the 2014 Order are consequential upon the introduction of the category of "secondary preferential debts", giving preference (after the ordinary preferential debts) to bank and building society depositors. For a full discussion, see the notes to s.386 and Sch.6.

Rules giving certain categories of unsecured debt priority in a bankruptcy or winding up have been a feature of the legislation for over a century. However, the impact of this provision (and the corresponding section in bankruptcy, s.328) has been significantly reduced following the abolition of the Crown's priority in regard to PAYE, NIC contributions and VAT, effected by EA 2002 s.251.

Until *Re Leyland DAF Ltd, Buchler v Talbot* [2004] UKHL 9; [2004] 2 A.C. 298; [2004] B.C.C. 214 it was understood that it was not only the preferential debts, but also the expenses of the liquidation, that had to be paid in priority to the holder of a floating charge; but the *Leyland DAF* decision reversed this ruling. The reversal was, however, only temporary, for the Companies Act 2006 s.1282, has reinstated the former interpretation: see s.176ZA, below. In *Re BHT (UK) Ltd* [2004] EWHC 201 (Ch); [2004] B.C.C. 301 the company was in receivership and realisations of the charged property had been paid to the chargee in the belief that the charge was a fixed charge. The question for the court was whether, if the charge was in fact a floating charge, either the company or its liquidator could claim from the chargee the amounts payable to the preferential creditors. The court ruled to the contrary: any claim which the preferential creditors might wish to make could be done by them in their own right.

A further change made by the insolvency legislation of 1985 was to bring into line, not only the law of company insolvency and individual bankruptcy, but also that of CVAs, receiverships and individual voluntary arrangements, so that the same rules set out in Sch.6 apply to them all.

Note that there was no provision for preferential debts in a company administration under the original IA 1986 Pt II, except where the administration was linked with a voluntary arrangement (s.387(2)) or where a winding-up order immediately followed upon the discharge of the administration order (s.387(3)(a)). However, a new subs.(3A) has been added to s.387, which applies to all administrations commencing on or after 15 September 2003, bringing administrations into line with other insolvency procedures in this respect. See the notes to that provision.

The Companies Act 2006 s.754 makes similar provision for priority to be given to the preferential debts where (if the company is not being wound up) possession is taken by or on behalf of the holder of a floating charge of assets subject to the charge. In *Customs and Excise Commissioners v Royal Bank of Scotland plc, Re Oval 1742 Ltd* [2007] EWCA Civ 1262; [2008] B.C.C. 135 the court adopted a broad approach to the interpretation of this provision, holding that where certain assets were released from the defendant bank's charge and sold by the company, and a substantial part of the proceeds paid to the bank, it had "taken possession" of these proceeds. In substance there had been a realisation of the bank's security. Other proceeds which had been paid to the bank after the company had gone into liquidation were held to rank after the preferential debts in accordance with s.175(2)(b).

In relation to payment and securities settlement systems, where "collateral security" (as defined in the Finality Regulations reg.2(1)) has been provided by a company to which those regulations apply, the claim of a participant or central bank to such security must be paid in priority to the expenses of the winding up, remuneration and preferential debts, unless the terms on which the security was provided expressly state that the expenses, remuneration and preferential debts shall have priority (Finality Regulations reg.14(5), (6)). (See the introductory note at p.3 above.)

S.175(2)(a)

Expenses incurred by a liquidator in pursuing claims under ss.127 (post-petition dispositions), 214 (wrongful trading), 238 (transactions at an undervalue) and 239 (preferences) were held not to be "expenses of the liquidation" in a number of cases, culminating with *Re Floor Fourteen Ltd, Lewis v Inland Revenue Commissioners* [2001] 3 All E.R. 499; [2002] B.C.C. 198. But an amendment to the rules has reversed these rulings: see rr.6.42(2), 7.108(2).

S.175(2)(b)
This important provision continues the rule, laid down in successive Companies Acts, which subordinates the claims of a secured creditor holding a floating charge (but not a fixed charge) to those of the preferential creditors. A similar rule applies in a receivership (ss.40, 59).

However, the application of the rule is now different because the statutory definition of a floating charge has been reworded, so that it includes any charge which, *as created*, was a floating charge (see s.251). In consequence, any charge which was originally a floating charge but has become a fixed charge (e.g. by crystallisation, or by a notice of conversion) before the "relevant date" defined by s.387 will now be subordinated to the preferential debts under the present section. The decisions in *Re Woodroffes (Musical Instruments) Ltd* [1986] Ch. 366; *Re Brightlife Ltd* [1987] Ch. 200; (1986) 2 B.C.C. 99,359; *Stein v Saywell* (1969) 121 C.L.R. 529; and *Re Griffin Hotel Co Ltd* [1941] Ch. 129, which were previously authorities to the contrary, are accordingly no longer good law.

176 Preferential charge on goods distrained, etc

176(1) [Application] This section applies where a company is being wound up by the court in England and Wales, and is without prejudice to section 128 (avoidance of attachments, etc.).

176(2) [Application of s.176(2A)] Subsection (2A) applies where–

(a) any person (whether or not a landlord or person entitled to rent) has distrained upon the goods or effects of the company, or

(b) Her Majesty's Revenue and Customs has been paid any amount from an account of the company under Part 1 of Schedule 8 to the Finance (No. 2) Act 2015 (enforcement by deduction from accounts),

in the period of 3 months ending with the date of the winding-up order.

176(2A) [Effect of person distraining or HMRC deduction from accounts] Where this subsection applies–

(a) in a case within subsection (2)(a), the goods or effects, or the proceeds of their sale, and

(b) in a case within subsection (2)(b), the amount in question,

is charged for the benefit of the company with the preferential debts of the company to the extent that the company's property is for the time being insufficient for meeting those debts.

176(3) [Surrender of goods under s.176(2A)] Where by virtue of a charge under subsection (2A) any person surrenders any goods or effects to a company or makes a payment to a company, that person ranks, in respect of the amount of the proceeds of sale of those goods or effects by the liquidator or (as the case may be) the amount of the payment, as a preferential creditor of the company, except as against so much of the company's property as is available for the payment of preferential creditors by virtue of the surrender or payment.

General Note

Heading amended by the Finance (No.2) Act 2015 s.51 and Sch.8 paras 26, 30(4) as from 28 November 2015.

S.176(1)
The present section does not apply in the case of a voluntary liquidation; and it will apply only if the distress is not void, under the provisions of s.128, as having been put in force after the commencement of the winding up.

S.176(2)–(3)
Section 176(2), (3) amended and s.176(2A) inserted by the Finance (No.2) Act 2015 s.51 and Sch.8 paras 26, 30 as from 28 November 2015. This follows the introduction of HMRC's power to make deductions from accounts held with deposit-takers as a means of enforcing payment.

The effect of subs.(2) is to make the claims of the preferential creditors a first charge on the goods distrained or their proceeds. Note that the significant date for reckoning the three-month period is that of the winding-up *order*, and not (as in s.128) the date of commencement of the winding up, which will be earlier (see s.129).

S.176(3)
The effect of subss.(2) and (3), taken together, is as follows:

(1) To the extent that there is property of the company (independently of the proceeds of sale or payment) available for payment of the preferential debts, the preferential creditors participate pari passu.

(2) In regard to the proceeds of sale or payment, the person who has surrendered the goods or made the payment and the preferential creditors together rank pari passu.

Accordingly, that person is not a "postponed" preferential creditor except as regards the property referred to in para.(1) above: *Re Memco Engineering Ltd* [1986] Ch. 86; (1985) 1 B.C.C. 99,460 (a case on the repealed CA 1985 s.319(7)).

Property subject to floating charge

176ZA Payment of expenses of winding up (England and Wales)

176ZA(1) [Priority over floating charge assets] The expenses of winding up in England and Wales, so far as the assets of the company available for payment of general creditors are insufficient to meet them, have priority over any claims to property comprised in or subject to any floating charge created by the company and shall be paid out of any such property accordingly.

176ZA(2) [Reference in s.176ZA(1) to assets of company, claims to property] In subsection (1)–

(a) the reference to assets of the company available for payment of general creditors does not include any amount made available under section 176A(2)(a);

(b) the reference to claims to property comprised in or subject to a floating charge is to the claims of–

(i) the holders of debentures secured by, or holders of, the floating charge, and

(ii) any preferential creditors entitled to be paid out of that property in priority to them.

176ZA(3) [Rules may restrict s.176ZA(1)] Provision may be made by rules restricting the application of subsection (1), in such circumstances as may be prescribed, to expenses authorised or approved–

(a) by the holders of debentures secured by, or holders of, the floating charge and by any preferential creditors entitled to be paid in priority to them, or

(b) by the court.

176ZA(4) [References to the expenses of the winding up] References in this section to the expenses of the winding up are to all expenses properly incurred in the winding up, including the remuneration of the liquidator.

General Note

Section 176ZA was inserted by the Companies Act 2006 s.1282 with effect from 6 April 2008: see the Companies Act 2006 (Commencement No.5, Transitional Provisions and Savings) Order 2007 (SI 2007/3495 (C. 150)) art.3(1)(v) and, for transitional provisions, the Companies Act 2006 (Commencement No.6, Saving and Commencement Nos 3 and 5 (Amendment)) Order 2008 (SI 2008/674 (C. 26)) art.5 and Sch.3 para.6(5).

This section reverses the decision of the House of Lords in *Re Leyland DAF Ltd, Buchler v Talbot* [2004] UKHL 9; [2004] 2 A.C. 298; [2004] B.C.C. 214, in which it was held that a liquidator was not entitled to claim his expenses in priority to the rights of the holder of a floating charge, and that it was immaterial whether or not the charge had crystallised before the commencement of the liquidation. This ruling overruled the decision in *Re Barleycorn Enterprises Ltd* [1970] Ch. 465, which had stood for many years and had been followed in a number of cases including *Re Portbase Clothing Ltd, Mond v Taylor* [1993] Ch. 388; [1993] B.C.C. 96. The priority rule established by *Re Barleycorn* is thus reinstated. Section 1282 was added to the Companies Bill at a late stage and before it was brought into force the Insolvency Service instituted a consultation exercise in August 2007 with a view to introducing rules to restrict the application of s.176ZA in order to provide a better balance between the various stakeholders in a liquidation. The resulting rules are rr.6.44 et seq., 7.111 et seq.

S.176ZA(1), (3)

The scope of s.176ZA(1) is limited by the rules referred to above, which require that the liquidator should have obtained authorisation in advance, or subsequent approval, by the floating charge holder and any preferential creditor, for the incurring of expense in certain specified categories of litigation, in order to be entitled to the priority conferred by the section. The court has back-up powers to sanction the incurring of litigation expenses where authorisation or approval has not been given or where the creditor concerned is or is intended to be a defendant in the litigation (rr.6.48, 7.116). The rules do not apply to litigation expenses which do not exceed £5,000 (r.6.44(1), 7.111). For further details and the procedure and transitional provisions, see the notes to the above rules.

176ZB Application of proceeds of office-holder claims

176ZB(1) [Application of section] This section applies where–

(a) there is a floating charge (whether created before or after the coming into force of this section) which relates to property of a company which–

(i) is in administration, or

(ii) has gone into liquidation; and

(b) the administrator or the liquidator (referred to in this section as "the office-holder") has–

(i) brought a claim under any provision mentioned in subsection (3), or

(ii) made an assignment (or, in Scotland, assignation) in relation to a right of action under any such provision under section 246ZD.

176ZB(2) [Proceeds not part of company's property for floating charge holder] The proceeds of the claim or assignment (or, in Scotland, assignation) are not to be treated as part of the company's net property, that is to say the amount of its property which would be available for satisfaction of claims of holders of debentures secured by, or holders of, any floating charge created by the company.

176ZB(3) [Relevant provisions] The provisions are–

(a) section 213 or 246ZA (fraudulent trading);

(b) section 214 or 246ZB (wrongful trading);

(c) section 238 (transactions at an undervalue (England and Wales));

(d) section 239 (preferences (England and Wales));

(e) section 242 (gratuitous alienations (Scotland));

(f) section 243 (unfair preferences (Scotland));

(g) section 244 (extortionate credit transactions).

176ZB(4) [Disapplication of s.176ZB(2) by CVA or scheme of arrangement] Subsection (2) does not apply to a company if or in so far as it is disapplied by–

(a) a voluntary arrangement in respect of the company, or

(b) a compromise or arrangement agreed under Part 26 of the Companies Act 2006 (arrangements and reconstructions).

General Note

Section 176ZB inserted by SBEEA 2015 s.119 as from 1 October 2015. Whatever the position at common law (on which there may have been some controversy: see, e.g. *ANC Ltd v Clark Goldring & Page Ltd* [2001] B.C.C. 479 at 485), it confirms beyond doubt that the recoveries by an office-holder under the statutory provisions listed form part of the insolvent estate and are not to be treated as part of the company's assets covered by a floating charge. Note that sums recovered under the misfeasance section (s.212) are not included in this list: they will be subject to any such security.

The section does not apply to proceedings that commenced before 6 April 2017 in relation to bank or building society insolvency under Pt 2 of the Banking Act 2009, building society and certain other relevant societies administration under Pt 2 of IA 1986, building society special administration under Pt 3 of the Banking Act 2009 or special administrations under the Investment Bank Special Administration Regulations 2011 (SI 2011/245): see the Deregulation Act 2015, Small Business, Enterprise and Employment Act 2015 and the Insolvency (Amendment) Act (Northern Ireland) 2016 (Consequential Amendments and Transitional Provisions) Regulations 2017 (SI 2017/400) regs 1, 13, 14.

176A Share of assets for unsecured creditors

176A(1) [Application of section] This section applies where a floating charge relates to property of a company–

(a) which has gone into liquidation,

(b) which is in administration,

(c) of which there is a provisional liquidator, or

(d) of which there is a receiver.

176A(2) [Prescribed part for unsecured debts] The liquidator, administrator or receiver–

(a) shall make a prescribed part of the company's net property available for the satisfaction of unsecured debts, and

(b) shall not distribute that part to the proprietor of a floating charge except in so far as it exceeds the amount required for the satisfaction of unsecured debts.

176A(3) [Non-application of s.176A(2)] Subsection (2) shall not apply to a company if–

(a) the company's net property is less than the prescribed minimum, and

(b) the liquidator, administrator or receiver thinks that the cost of making a distribution to unsecured creditors would be disproportionate to the benefits.

176A(4) [Disapplication of s.176A(2)] Subsection (2) shall also not apply to a company if or in so far as it is disapplied by–

(a) a voluntary arrangement in respect of the company, or

(b) a compromise or arrangement agreed under Part 26 of the Companies Act 2006 (arrangements and reconstructions).

176A(5) [Non-application by court order] Subsection (2) shall also not apply to a company if–

(a) the liquidator, administrator or receiver applies to the court for an order under this subsection on the ground that the cost of making a distribution to unsecured creditors would be disproportionate to the benefits, and

(b) the court orders that subsection (2) shall not apply.

176A(6) [Net property in s.176A(2), (3)] In subsections (2) and (3) a company's net property is the amount of its property which would, but for this section, be available for satisfaction of claims of holders of debentures secured by, or holders of, any floating charge created by the company.

176A(7) [Provision in order] An order under subsection (2) prescribing part of a company's net property may, in particular, provide for its calculation–

(a) as a percentage of the company's net property, or

(b) as an aggregate of different percentages of different parts of the company's net property.

176A(8) [Procedure for order] An order under this section–

(a) must be made by statutory instrument, and

(b) shall be subject to annulment pursuant to a resolution of either House of Parliament.

176A(9) ["Floating charge", "prescribed"] In this section–

"floating charge" means a charge which is a floating charge on its creation and which is created after the first order under subsection (2)(a) comes into force, and

"prescribed" means prescribed by order by the Secretary of State.

176A(10) [Transitional or incidental provision] An order under this section may include transitional or incidental provision.

General Note

This section, introduced by EA 2002 s.252 with effect from 15 September 2003, is one of the major innovations made by the 2002 Act. The measure has some parallel with a recommendation of the Cork Committee (Cmnd.8558 (1982), at para.1538) that a "10 per cent fund" should be set aside out of the net realisations of property subject to a floating charge and that this fund be made available to unsecured creditors upon the insolvency of the company. This is seen by some as a quid pro quo for the abolition of the Crown's preferential status as a creditor: without such a provision, there would simply be a windfall for the charge holder. The "prescribed part" (also referred to as the "special reserved fund" or "ring-fenced sum" for the unsecured creditors) is calculated on the net realisations of property subject to any floating (but not fixed) charge.

The amount of the prescribed part has been fixed as follows:

Where the net property does not exceed £10,000:	50% of that property
Where the net property exceeds £10,000:	50% of the first £10,000, plus 20% of the property which exceeds £10,000, up to a maximum prescribed part of £600,000.

(See the Insolvency Act 1986 (Prescribed Part) Order 2003 (SI 2003/2097), effective 15 September 2003.)

Subsections (3)–(5) set out various situations in which the obligation to set aside a prescribed part does not apply.

Rule 3.50(2) states that the costs associated with the prescribed part shall be paid out of that part. For other relevant rules, see rr.6.42(3), 7.108(3), 4.22–4.24, 7.3A et seq.

Section 176A is disapplied in relation to any charge created or otherwise arising under a financial collateral arrangement: Financial Collateral Arrangements (No.2) Regulations 2003 (SI 2003/3226) reg.10(3).

On the application of this provision to insolvent partnerships, see the Insolvent Partnerships (Amendment) Order 2006 (SI 2006/622, effective 6 April 2006), which corrects errors contained in earlier legislation.

For analysis see Akintola [2017] 30 Insolv. Int. 55.

S.176A(1)

The section only applies where there is a floating charge. Paragraph (d) would therefore not apply to a fixed-charge receivership, but it would apply to any other kind of receivership, including a court-appointed receivership (for confirmation, see r.4.22). A crystallised floating charge would not be within this exception. An administrative receiver is excluded from r.4.22 only because he already has reporting obligations under s.48.

There is no obligation to set aside a prescribed part where a charge holder, instead of appointing a receiver, enters into possession (personally or through an agent) under CA 2006 s.754.

S.176A(2), (6)

The office-holder is required by s.176A only to set the prescribed part aside: this section does not authorise him to make a distribution (for which the consent of the court may be required: see, e.g. Sch.B1 para.65(3)). Where there are preferential creditors, the prescribed part is reckoned by reference to net property remaining after their claims have been satisfied, i.e. out of the property which is available to be paid to the floating charge holder.

Section 176A(2)(b) does not make any specific provision for the case where a floating charge secures only part of the debt owed to the charge holder, leaving the remainder of the debt unsecured. Two judicial decisions now make it clear that the charge holder is not entitled to claim any part of the prescribed part in respect of his unsecured surplus: *Re Permacell Finesse Ltd* [2007] EWHC 3233 (Ch); [2008] B.C.C. 208; and *Re Airbase Services (UK) Ltd* [2008] EWHC 124 (Ch); [2008] 1 W.L.R. 1516; [2008] B.C.C. 213. In the latter case Patten J held that the section applied to all charge holders, whether their charge was floating or fixed, so as to prohibit them from participating in the prescribed part in respect of an unsecured surplus. Both categories of charge holder will, of course, continue to be entitled to prove in the liquidation for the unsecured part of their debt, but this will be of value only in those cases where both the prescribed part and the secured part of the floating charge holder's debt have been fully met and there are still funds available for distribution.

However, a floating charge holder who has elected to surrender his security (whether at the beginning of the administration or liquidation or at a later time) is to be treated as an unsecured creditor for all purposes, and is accordingly entitled to share in the prescribed part: *Re PAL SC Realisations 2007 Ltd* [2010] EWHC 2850 (Ch); [2011] B.C.C. 93. See also *Re JT Frith Ltd* [2012] EWHC 196 (Ch) (creditor deemed to have surrendered his security because he omitted to mention it in his submission of proof: entitled to share in prescribed part).

S.176A(3)–(5)

These provisions can be invoked in order to excuse the office-holder from his obligation to set aside the prescribed part in the following situations:

- where the net property is less than the prescribed minimum (fixed by SI 2003/2097 art.2 at £10,000) and he thinks that the cost of making a distribution to the unsecured creditors would be disproportionate to the benefits (for examples of the exercise of this jurisdiction, see *Re Hydroserve Ltd* [2007] EWHC 3026 (Ch); [2008] B.C.C. 175; *Re Courts plc* [2008] EWHC 2339 (Ch); [2009] 1 W.L.R. 1499; [2008] B.C.C. 917; *Re International Sections Ltd* [2009] EWHC 137 (Ch); [2009] B.C.C. 574; *QMD Hotels Ltd Administrators, Noters* [2010] CSOH 168; [2012] B.C.C. 794);
- where the net property is £10,000 or more and the office-holder applies to the court for an order disapplying subs.(2) on the same ground; or
- where it is disapplied by the terms of a CVA or scheme of compromise or arrangement under CA 2006 Pt 26.

In *Re Courts plc* (above) it was held that there could be no selective disapplication of s.176A(2): the provision must be applied in its entirety to all creditors, or not at all (even if, in the case of smaller creditors, the cost of distribution would exceed what they would receive). In *Re International Sections Ltd* (above), where the distribution would have been under 1.5 pence in the pound, it was said that dispensation under s.176A(5) should be the exception rather than the rule. Permission was refused: it was held that regard should be had to the position of the unsecured creditors as a body and not to the fact that the dividend for each creditor would be small. It was also held that "costs" (now "expenses") in IR 2016 r.3.50(2) included the liquidator's charges for making the distribution. See further *Joint Administrators of Castlebridge Plant Ltd, Noters* [2015] CSOH 165; [2017] B.C.C. 87 in which the Scottish court, in dismissing an application under s.176A(5), stressed that disapplication of the prescribed part should be the exception and not the rule.

Rules 12.41 and 12.15 deal with the procedure where application is made to the court under s.176A(5).

S.176A(9)

This section applies only in relation to floating charges that are *created* after the section is brought into force (i.e. on or after 15 September 2003). Where the relevant insolvency proceedings are instituted on or after that date but the charge was created on an earlier date, the charge holder will get the best of both worlds, enjoying the benefit of the abolition of the Crown's preference but not being subject to the deduction of the prescribed part.

The subsection uses the present tense (which *is* a floating charge on its creation), in contrast with s.251, which uses *was*, but there is no material distinction between the two (*Re PAL SC Realisations 2007 Ltd* (above)).

Special managers

177 Power to appoint special manager

177(1) [Power of court] Where a company has gone into liquidation or a provisional liquidator has been appointed, the court may, on an application under this section, appoint any person to be the special manager of the business or property of the company.

177(2) [Application to court] The application may be made by the liquidator or provisional liquidator in any case where it appears to him that the nature of the business or property of the company, or the interests of the company's creditors or contributories or members generally, require the appointment of another person to manage the company's business or property.

177(3) [Powers of special manager] The special manager has such powers as may be entrusted to him by the court.

177(4) [Extent of s.177(3) powers] The court's power to entrust powers to the special manager includes power to direct that any provision of this Act that has effect in relation to the provisional liquidator or liquidator of a company shall have the like effect in relation to the special manager for the purposes of the carrying out by him of any of the functions of the provisional liquidator or liquidator.

177(5) [Duties of special manager] The special manager shall–

(a) give such security or, in Scotland, caution as may be prescribed;

(b) prepare and keep such accounts as may be prescribed; and

(c) produce those accounts in accordance with the rules to the Secretary of State or to such other persons as may be prescribed.

General Note

The former CA 1985 s.556 provided for the appointment of a special manager when the official receiver became the liquidator or provisional liquidator of a company. The present section extends this facility to all liquidators, and now applies also to Scotland. The appointment of a special manager allows a liquidator to have assistance from someone with particular managerial or commercial expertise that he may not have himself.

A special manager is not required to be qualified to act as an insolvency practitioner: indeed, there may be a particular need to invoke the present section when the skills in question are those which an insolvency practitioner does not normally have. (There is no longer the option of bringing in such an expert in the role of liquidator, or joint liquidator, unless by chance he is also qualified under this Act for appointment.)

In *Re W F Fearman Ltd (No.2)* (1988) 4 B.C.C. 141 the court gave leave to the official receiver to use the services of the outgoing provisional liquidators as special managers, in order to maintain continuity in the administration of the insolvency pending the choice by a creditors' meeting of liquidators on a permanent basis.

S.177(1), (2)

The appointment must in all cases be made by the court, on the application of the liquidator or provisional liquidator himself.

S.177(3), (4)

The powers of a special manager are determined in each case by the court, and they may be made subject to any statutory provision that applies to a liquidator—e.g. an obligation to obtain the consent of the liquidation committee on particular matters.

S.177(5)

The rules prescribed for the purposes of this section are to be found in IR 2016 rr.5.17 et seq., 6.37 et seq., 7.93 et seq.

Disclaimer (England and Wales only)

178 Power to disclaim onerous property

178(1) [Application] This and the next two sections apply to a company that is being wound up in England and Wales.

178(2) [Disclaimer by liquidator] Subject as follows, the liquidator may, by the giving of the prescribed notice, disclaim any onerous property and may do so notwithstanding that he has taken possession of it, endeavoured to sell it, or otherwise exercised rights of ownership in relation to it.

178(3) [Onerous property] The following is onerous property for the purposes of this section–

(a) any unprofitable contract, and

(b) any other property of the company which is unsaleable or not readily saleable or is such that it may give rise to a liability to pay money or perform any other onerous act.

178(4) [Effect of disclaimer] A disclaimer under this section–

(a) operates so as to determine, as from the date of the disclaimer, the rights, interests and liabilities of the company in or in respect of the property disclaimed; but

(b) does not, except so far as is necessary for the purpose of releasing the company from any liability, affect the rights or liabilities of any other person.

178(5) [Where notice of disclaimer not to be given] A notice of disclaimer shall not be given under this section in respect of any property if–

(a) a person interested in the property has applied in writing to the liquidator or one of his predecessors as liquidator requiring the liquidator or that predecessor to decide whether he will disclaim or not, and

(b) the period of 28 days beginning with the day on which that application was made, or such longer period as the court may allow, has expired without a notice of disclaimer having been given under this section in respect of that property.

178(6) [Persons sustaining loss etc.] Any person sustaining loss or damage in consequence of the operation of a disclaimer under this section is deemed a creditor of the company to the extent of the loss or damage and accordingly may prove for the loss or damage in the winding up.

General Note

Sections 178–182 enlarge and, in some respects, modify the law regarding disclaimer which was formerly contained in CA 1985 ss.618, 619 and 629. These provisions, which correspond to the bankruptcy rules set out in ss.315 et seq. below, apply in England and Wales only. Scots law has no statutory equivalent. It was held in *Joint Liquidators of the Scottish Coal Co Ltd, Noters* [2013] CSIH 108, reversing the court below, that a liquidator in Scotland has no power to abandon or otherwise disclaim property (certain open cast mining sites) or the associated statutory licences. In regard to a matter of pure contract, where no question of the ownership of property was in issue, it had earlier been held that, without formally disclaiming, a liquidator or administrator could repudiate or decline to perform a contract if this was in the interests of the creditors as a whole: *Joint Administrators of Rangers Football Club, Noters* [2012] CSOH 55.

In the context of the financial markets, s.178 does not apply in relation to a market contract or a contract effected by an exchange or clearing house for the purpose of realising property provided as margin in relation to market contracts: see CA 1989 s.164(1). The section is also disapplied by the Finality Regulations reg.16(1) in relation to a transfer order or a contract for the purpose of realising security in payment and securities settlement systems. (See the notes on pp.1–3 above.) It (and any equivalent Scottish rule of law) is also disapplied in the liquidation of a collateral-taker or collateral-provider under a financial collateral arrangement: Financial Collateral Arrangements (No.2) Regulations 2003 (SI 2003/3226) reg.10(4).

A waste management licence is "property", or alternatively an interest incidental to property, which may be disclaimed under the section: *Celtic Extraction Ltd & Bluestone Chemicals Ltd v Environment Agency* [2001] Ch. 475; [2000] B.C.C. 487 (overruling *Re Mineral Resources Ltd* [1999] B.C.C. 422, in which Neuberger J had held that a licence could not be disclaimed because that would be inconsistent with the Environmental Protection Act 1990).

In *Environment Agency v Hillridge Ltd* [2003] EWHC 3023 (Ch); [2004] 2 B.C.L.C. 358 the company had created a trust fund to cover the cost of remedial work at its landfill site after waste tipping ceased. It was held, following the *Celtic Extraction* decision, that the disclaimer of the lease of the site put an end to the company's waste management licence, but that the trusts were not terminated. However, the trust fund did not become repayable to the company or pass to the control of the Environmental Agency: as bona vacantia it reverted to the Crown.

S.178(2)

Under the former law as contained in CA 1985, only the official receiver was empowered to disclaim property on his own authority; any other liquidator was required to obtain the leave of the court. Every liquidator may now exercise the power to disclaim without leave. It is left to the person affected by the proposed disclaimer to take his objection to the court, if he has one. However, the effect of the change in the law removing the requirement of leave is to make the liquidator's decision to disclaim primarily a matter for his discretion, similar to his other powers in the management and realisation of the company's property, which will normally be reviewed by the court only if it has been exercised mala fide or perversely. Cases relating to the granting of leave under the former law are now irrelevant (*Re Hans Place Ltd* [1992] B.C.C. 737).

For the rules regulating disclaimer generally, see IR 2016 Pt 19.

The 12-month time limit which was formerly imposed by CA 1985 s.618(3) has been abolished.

S.178(3)

This is a new and wider definition of "onerous property". The previous specific references in CA 1985 s.618(1) to "land (of any tenure) burdened with onerous covenants" and "shares or stock in companies" have been dropped—though such items are clearly within the wider terms of the new definition—and the former requirement that, to be "onerous", property had to be "unsaleable, or not readily saleable, by reason of its binding its possessor to the performance of any onerous act or to the payment of any sum of money" has now been replaced by s.178(3)(b), in which these attributes are expressed as alternatives.

The term "property" is itself widely defined for the purposes of the present Act by s.436, below. Both this term and the expression "onerous contract" were closely examined by the Court of Appeal in *Re SSSL Realisations (2002) Ltd* [2006] EWCA Civ 7; [2006] Ch. 610; [2006] B.C.C. 233, where the court was concerned with a deed of indemnity which the insolvent company had given as part consideration for a bond provided by the respondents. " 'Property' ", it was said (at [35]), "must involve some element of benefit or entitlement for the person holding it"—a proposition that appears to be confirmed by the descriptive words "unsaleable or not readily saleable". The deed of indemnity did not give rise to a liability to pay money or perform any other onerous act: it simply imposed on the company a disability, preventing it from collecting an asset. This could not be described as "property". On the phrase "onerous contract", Chadwick LJ adopted five principles derived from a number of Australian authorities and summed up as follows by Chesterman J in *Transmetro Corp Ltd v Real Investments Pty Ltd* (1999) 17 A.C.L.C. 1314 at 1320:

- A contract is unprofitable … if it imposes on the company continuing financial obligations which may be regarded as detrimental to the creditors, which presumably means that the contract confers no sufficient reciprocal benefit.
- Before a contract may be unprofitable … it must give rise to prospective liabilities.
- Contracts which will delay the winding up of the company's affairs because they are to be performed over a substantial period of time and will involve expenditure that may not be recovered are unprofitable.
- No case has decided that a contract is unprofitable merely because it is financially disadvantageous. The cases focus on the nature and cause of the disadvantage.
- A contract is not unprofitable merely because the company could have made, or could make, a better bargain.

The critical feature, Chadwick LJ concluded, is that "performance of the future obligations will prejudice the liquidator's obligation to realise the company's property and pay a dividend to creditors within a reasonable time" (at [36]–[54]). Accordingly, the liquidators could not disclaim the deed of indemnity, because it failed to meet these criteria.

S.178(4)

The effect of a disclaimer is, apart from the operation of any vesting order made by the court under the succeeding sections, that the disclaimed property vests in the Crown as bona vacantia (or, in the case of land held in fee simple, by escheat). In *Scmlla Properties Ltd v Gesso Properties (BVI) Ltd* [1995] B.C.C. 793 it was held that a legal charge over a freehold interest in land, and the leases of tenants created out of the freehold, survived a disclaimer of the freehold interest.

A disclaimer should be construed so as to interfere with the rights of third parties as little as possible: thus, although the effect of the disclaimer of a contract is to release the company from its obligations, it does not undo the contract in so far as it has been performed and other parties have acquired rights and interests under it: *Capital Prime Properties plc v Worthgate Ltd* [2000] B.C.C. 525. See also *Groveholt Ltd v Hughes* [2005] EWCA Civ 897; [2005] 2 B.C.L.C. 421.

The disclaimer of a lease does not terminate the liability of a guarantor (including a predecessor who has assigned the lease to the company). See the note to s.181. The Act does not require the company, when disclaiming, to intend to vacate the property immediately (although it may become liable, e.g. as a trespasser): *Re MK Airlines Ltd (No.2)* [2012] EWHC 2764 (Ch); [2014] B.C.C. 103. Where the liquidator of a tenant company has disclaimed the lease, the landlord becomes the "owner" of unoccupied property (with the right to immediate possession) for the purpose of liability for non-domestic rates. If there is a guarantor, s.178(4)(b) preserves his rights and liabilities, but those rights are contractual in nature and do not give him a right to immediate possession: *Schroder Exempt Property Unit Trust v Birmingham City Council* [2014] EWHC 2207 (Admin); [2014] B.C.C. 690.

S.178(5)

This corresponds with the repealed CA 1985 s.619(2), with the necessary modification that in para.(b) the liquidator must now give an actual notice of disclaimer within the 28-day period, instead of a notice that he intends to apply to the court for leave to disclaim. For the procedure under this subsection, see IR 2016 r.19.9.

S.178(6)

This is the same as the former CA 1985 s.619(8), with the substitution of the words "sustaining loss or damage" for the less precise term "injured". A sum due to a party under the terms of a contract does not come within this expression: *Groveholt Ltd v Hughes* (above). *Re Park Air Services plc* [2000] 2 A.C. 172; [1999] B.C.C. 135 gives guidance on the method of calculating the loss or damage suffered by a landlord in consequence of the disclaimer of a lease. The company in this case was solvent. The House of Lords held that, following disclaimer, the landlord could not prove in the winding up for future rent but instead had a statutory right to compensation, to be reckoned on the same basis as if he were claiming damages for breach of a contract that had been wrongfully terminated (with an allowance or discount for the accelerated receipt of sums falling due in the future). Interest under s.189 was also allowed.

179 Disclaimer of leaseholds

179(1) [Requirement for disclaimer to take effect] The disclaimer under section 178 of any property of a leasehold nature does not take effect unless a copy of the disclaimer has been served (so far as the liquidator is aware of their addresses) on every person claiming under the company as underlessee or mortgagee and either–

(a) no application under section 181 below is made with respect to that property before the end of the period of 14 days beginning with the day on which the last notice served under this subsection was served; or

(b) where such an application has been made, the court directs that the disclaimer shall take effect.

179(2) [Court's directions or orders] Where the court gives a direction under subsection (1)(b) it may also, instead of or in addition to any order it makes under section 181, make such orders with respect to fixtures, tenant's improvements and other matters arising out of the lease as it thinks fit.

General Note

Under the former law, when leave to disclaim had to be sought in every case, the court could require such notices to be given to persons interested as it thought appropriate. The present section, now that the court is no longer involved, makes express provision for notice to be given to underlessees and mortgagees of leasehold property, at least 14 days before the disclaimer can take effect.

The disclaimer of a lease has the effect of destroying any underlease; but the underlessee has the right, if he chooses, to remain in occupation for the term of the underlease, paying the rent reserved by the lease and performing the covenants contained in it: *Re A E Realisations (1985) Ltd* [1988] 1 W.L.R. 200; (1987) 3 B.C.C. 136.

There is no jurisdiction to make a vesting order in favour of a landlord on terms that it shall be subject to and with the benefit of existing subleases: *Re I T M Corp Ltd (in liq.)* [1997] B.C.C. 554.

The statutory provisions perhaps tacitly assume that it is the tenant who will seek the disclaimer of a lease, but the Australian High Court in *Willmott Growers Group Inc v Willmott Forests Ltd* [2013] HCA 51 allowed a landlord to disclaim, partly on the basis that a lease is a species of contract.

S.179(1)

An underlessee or mortgagee has 14 days after receiving notice of the proposed disclaimer in which to apply to the court to have a vesting order made in his favour, or such other relief as the court thinks fit.

S.179(2)

This provision confers on the court additional powers to those prescribed by ss.181, 182.

180 Land subject to rentcharge

180(1) [Application] The following applies where, in consequence of the disclaimer under section 178 of any land subject to a rentcharge, that land vests by operation of law in the Crown or any other person (referred to in the next subsection as "the proprietor").

180(2) [Liability of proprietor et al.] The proprietor and the successors in title of the proprietor are not subject to any personal liability in respect of any sums becoming due under the rentcharge except sums becoming due after the proprietor, or some person claiming under or through the proprietor, has taken possession or control of the land or has entered into occupation of it.

General Note

The purpose of this section is to ensure that the Crown or any other person in whom land vests as a result of a disclaimer (see the note to s.178(4)) is not made personally liable in respect of the rentcharge unless it (or he) takes possession or control of the land.

181 Powers of court (general)

181(1) [Application] This section and the next apply where the liquidator has disclaimed property under section 178.

181(2) [Application to court] An application under this section may be made to the court by–

(a) any person who claims an interest in the disclaimed property, or

(b) any person who is under any liability in respect of the disclaimed property, not being a liability discharged by the disclaimer.

181(3) [Powers of court] Subject as follows, the court may on the application make an order, on such terms as it thinks fit, for the vesting of the disclaimed property in, or for its delivery to–

(a) a person entitled to it or a trustee for such a person, or

(b) a person subject to such a liability as is mentioned in subsection (2)(b) or a trustee for such a person.

181(4) [Limit on court's powers] The court shall not make an order under subsection (3)(b) except where it appears to the court that it would be just to do so for the purpose of compensating the person subject to the liability in respect of the disclaimer.

181(5) [Relationship with s.178(6)] The effect of any order under this section shall be taken into account in assessing for the purpose of section 178(6) the extent of any loss or damage sustained by any person in consequence of the disclaimer.

181(6) [Effect of vesting order] An order under this section vesting property in any person need not be completed by conveyance, assignment or transfer.

S.181(1)–(3)

As has been explained above, the liquidator's power to disclaim no longer requires the leave of the court, and so the court becomes involved only if an application is made to it by a person who is interested in the property or otherwise affected by the disclaimer. These subsections deal with the right to make such an application, and set out the general powers of the court in such proceedings. The relevant procedure is laid down by IR 2016 r.19.11. (In regard to vesting orders affecting leasehold property, the provisions of s.182 apply in addition.)

In *Re Vedmay Ltd* [1994] 1 B.C.L.C. 676 it was held that the term "interest" in s.181(2) is not confined to a proprietary interest, and that a subtenant of premises who was in occupation as a statutory tenant had no proprietary interest in the premises, but merely a "status of irremovability"; but even so, since he had a financial interest in the subsistence of the head-lease, he had a sufficient interest for the purpose of s.181. However in *Lloyds Bank SF Nominees v Aladdin Ltd (in liq.)* [1996] 1 B.C.L.C. 720 it was held that a proprietary interest of some kind was essential, so that, if the *Vedmay* decision is to stand, it must be because of the finding that the tenant had a "status of irremovability". The guarantor of a debt secured by a charge over a company's assets similarly has only a financial and not a proprietary interest in those assets: *Re Spirit Motorsport Ltd (in liq.)* [1996] 1 B.C.L.C. 684. See also *Re Ballast plc, St Paul Travelers Insurance Co Ltd v Dargan* [2006] EWHC 3189 (Ch); [2007] B.C.C. 620; [2007] B.P.I.R. 117.

In *Stacey v Hill* [1991] 1 K.B. 660 it was held that the disclaimer of a lease brought to an end the obligations of a guarantor or surety in respect of future liabilities under the lease. This ruling was in stark contrast with *Hill v East & West India Dock Co* (1884) 9 App. Cas. 448, in which the House of Lords had held that the disclaimer of a lease which has been assigned does not determine the continuing liability of the original lessee on the covenants in the lease, or the liability of any surety for the original lessee. The anomaly has now been rectified. In *Hindcastle Ltd v Barbara Attenborough Associates Ltd* [1997] A.C. 70; [1996] B.C.C. 636 the House of Lords decided that the two could not stand together and that *Stacey v Hill* should be overruled. It follows that both a guarantor of a lease and an original or former lessee of a lease which has been assigned are "persons under a liability in respect of the disclaimed property, not being a liability discharged by the disclaimer" under s.181(2)(b), and that accordingly they have standing to apply for a vesting order under the present section. See also *Shaw v Doleman* [2009] EWCA Civ 279; [2009] B.C.C. 730, where the assignor argued that her liability had been terminated by the disclaimer on the construction of the wording of the assignment, but the *Hindcastle* ruling was followed; and note *RVB Investments Ltd v Bibby* [2013] EWHC 65 (Ch), where it was held that the wording of the covenants in the lease did not prevent *Hindcastle* being applied, and an order for specific performance was made against the guarantor requiring him to take a new lease. In consequence, the surety and not the landlord was responsible for the payment of business rates. Contrast *Schroder Exempt Property Unit Trust v Birmingham City Council* [2014] EWHC 2207 (Admin); [2014] B.C.C. 690, where the guarantor had not called for the lease and the liability for business rates was held to fall on the landlord.

In *Scottish Widows plc v Tripipatkul* [2004] EWHC 1874 (Ch); [2004] B.C.C. 200 the landlord, after the lessee company's liquidator had disclaimed the lease, sold the reversion of the leased property to the claimant. It was held that the benefit of covenants which had been given by the appellant and which survived the disclaimer had been assigned along with the reversion.

The terms of a guarantee sometimes provide that in the event of the lease being disclaimed the guarantor will take a new lease from the landlord for the residue of the term at the same rent. In *Re A E Realisations (1985) Ltd* [1988] 1 W.L.R. 200; (1987) 3 B.C.C. 136, the court declined to make a vesting order in favour of a guarantor because it would have achieved nothing that would not be brought about by the grant of a new lease under the agreement.

Section 1012 of the Companies Act 2006 provides that, when a company is dissolved, all property and rights vested in or held on trust for the company are deemed to be bona vacantia and vest in the Crown (or, where appropriate, the Duchy of Lancaster or the Duke of Cornwall), subject to the possible restoration of the company to the register under ss.1024 et seq. However, the Crown or another appropriate entity may disclaim the property (s.1013). The corresponding sections of the 1985 Act which these provisions replace (CA 1985 ss.656–657) went on to state that ss.178(4) and 179–182 of IA 1986 should apply to such property as if it had been disclaimed by a liquidator; but the 2006 Act makes self-standing provision to essentially the same effect in ss.1015 (for England and Wales and Northern Ireland) and ss.1020–1022 (for Scotland). In *RVB Investments Ltd v Bibby* (above) it was held that the law derived from s.182 applied to cases under s.1012.

S.181(3)

"The disclaimed property" should be read as including part only of the disclaimed property: see *Hunt v Conwy County Borough Council* [2013] EWHC 1154 (Ch); [2014] 1 W.L.R. 254 (a decision on the analogous s.320(2)(a)).

S.181(4)

If a vesting order is made under s.181(3)(b), the beneficiary will not be someone "entitled" to the property in question (compare s.181(3)(a)), but someone who is under a liability in respect of it. A vesting order allows the court to do rough justice by allowing the applicant to take over the property in exchange for the extinction of his liability, provided that the condition in this subsection is met.

S.181(5)

The beneficiary under a vesting order proves in the winding up under s.178(6) for any loss or damage which he may have sustained overall, after bringing into account the effect of the order, which may in itself have left him better or worse off.

S.181(6)

The vesting order operates itself as a conveyance of the property without the need for any other legal act.

182 Powers of court (leaseholds)

182(1) [Limit on court's power] The court shall not make an order under section 181 vesting property of a leasehold nature in any person claiming under the company as underlessee or mortgagee except on terms making that person–

(a) subject to the same liabilities and obligations as the company was subject to under the lease at the commencement of the winding up, or

(b) if the court thinks fit, subject to the same liabilities and obligations as that person would be subject to if the lease had been assigned to him at the commencement of the winding up.

182(2) [Where order re part of property in lease] For the purposes of an order under section 181 relating to only part of any property comprised in a lease, the requirements of subsection (1) apply as if the lease comprised only the property to which the order relates.

182(3) [Court may vest estate in someone else] Where subsection (1) applies and no person claiming under the company as underlessee or mortgagee is willing to accept an order under section 181 on the terms required by virtue of that subsection, the court may, by order under that section, vest the company's estate or interest in the property in any person who is liable (whether personally or in a representative capacity, and whether alone or jointly with the company) to perform the lessee's covenants in the lease.

The court may vest that estate and interest in such a person freed and discharged from all estates, incumbrances and interests created by the company.

182(4) [Where s.182(1) applies] Where subsection (1) applies and a person claiming under the company as underlessee or mortgagee declines to accept an order under section 181, that person is excluded from all interest in the property.

General Note

This provision is designed to ensure that persons who have a subordinate interest in leasehold property owned by the company have an opportunity to take over the property itself on the same terms, in effect, as those upon which the company formerly held it.

In *Re I T M Corp Ltd (in liq.)* [1997] B.C.C. 554, a vesting order had been made in favour of a landlord on terms that it should be subject to and with the benefit of existing subleases. On appeal, it was held (1) that the court had no jurisdiction to make an order in favour of a landlord until the interests of all the other relevant parties who could obtain an interest in the property under the statutory mechanism had been cleared away; and (2) that a vesting order in favour of a landlord could only be made freed of the sublessees' interests.

S.182(4)

This provision is limited in its application to persons who have a proprietary interest in the property. It cannot be invoked to determine a statutory tenancy: *Re Vedmay Ltd* [1994] 1 B.C.L.C. 676.

Execution, attachment and the Scottish equivalents

183 Effect of execution or attachment (England and Wales)

183(1) [Where creditor seeking benefit of execution or attachment] Where a creditor has issued execution against the goods or land of a company or has attached any debt due to it, and the company is subsequently wound up, he is not entitled to retain the benefit of the execution or attachment against the liquidator unless he has completed the execution or attachment before the commencement of the winding up.

183(2) [Qualifications] However–

(a) if a creditor has had notice of a meeting having been called at which a resolution for voluntary winding up is to be proposed, the date on which he had notice is substituted, for the purpose of subsection (1), for the date of commencement of the winding up;

(b) a person who purchases in good faith under a sale by the enforcement officer, or other officer charged with the execution of the writ any goods of a company on which execution has been levied in all cases acquires a good title to them against the liquidator; and

(c) the rights conferred by subsection (1) on the liquidator may be set aside by the court in favour of the creditor to such extent and subject to such terms as the court thinks fit.

183(3) [Execution, attachment] For purposes of this Act–

(a) an execution against goods is completed by seizure and sale, or by the making of a charging order under section 1 of the Charging Orders Act 1979;

(b) an attachment of a debt is completed by receipt of the debt; and

(c) an execution against land is completed by seizure, by the appointment of a receiver, or by the making of a charging order under section 1 of the Act above mentioned.

183(4) [Definitions] In this section "goods" includes all chattels personal; and "enforcement officer" means an individual who is authorised to act as an enforcement officer under the Courts Act 2003.

183(4A) [Attachment by HMRC deduction from accounts] For the purposes of this section, Her Majesty's Revenue and Customs is to be regarded as having attached a debt due to a company if it has taken action under Part 1 of Schedule 8 to the Finance (No. 2) Act 2015 (enforcement by deduction for accounts) as a result of which an amount standing to the credit of an account held by the company is–

(a) subject to arrangements made under paragraph 6(3) of that Schedule, or

(b) the subject of a deduction notice under paragraph 13 of that Schedule.

183(5) [Scotland] This section does not apply in the case of a winding up in Scotland.

General Note

Note: The Tribunals, Courts and Enforcement Act 2007 (Commencement No.11) Order 2014 (SI 2014/768 (C. 27)) art.2(1), effective 6 April 2014 brings into force the new system for the recovery of rent etc., replacing (or in addition to) the traditional law of distress. However, s.62(1) and Sch.12 para.69 of the 2007 Act specifically provide that Sch.12 (Taking control of goods) is subject to IA 1986 ss.183, 184 and 346, so that these sections (which deal with the situation where the owner of goods become subject to winding-up or bankruptcy proceedings) remain unaffected by any changes effected by the 2007 Act.

Section 183 does not have extra-territorial effect, so as to deprive a creditor who has completed an execution process abroad of the assets which he has successfully seized. However the court has a discretion (at least where the creditor in question is amenable to the jurisdiction) to restrain a creditor from bringing or continuing a foreign execution process (*Re Oriental Inland Steam Co Ex p. Scinde Railway Co* (1874) 9 Ch. App. 557; *Re North Carolina Estate Co* (1889) 5 T.L.R. 328; *Re Vocalion (Foreign) Ltd* [1932] 2 Ch. 196); and it also has authority to direct a liquidator to intervene in foreign garnishment proceedings, or to direct him not to do so: *Mitchell v Carter* [1997] B.C.C. 907. Accordingly, it has jurisdiction to decide whether a creditor may retain the fruits of a current or future foreign execution process. (However, in later proceedings (reported as *Re Buckingham International plc (No.2)* [1998] B.C.C. 943) the court declined to make such an order, holding that the circumstances did not justify disturbing the statutory pari passu principle. Also see *Glasgow (Bankruptcy Trustee) v ELS Law Ltd* [2017] EWHC 3004 (Ch) where it held that it was not for the courts to extend a solicitor's lien to an insurer as this would alter the priority of creditors which was a matter for the legislature.)

S.183(1)

This section deals with the situation where a creditor has levied execution against the property of a company which then goes into liquidation. Its effect is to deprive him of the benefit of the execution unless it has been "completed" (as that term is defined in s.183(3)) before the commencement of the winding up. Since a winding up may commence at a time earlier than the date of a winding-up order, an execution which has in fact then been completed may be avoided retrospectively.

On the "commencement" of a winding up, see ss.86 and 129. The section may operate even earlier than this time: see s.182(3)(a).

The present provisions are complementary to s.128, which avoids all executions and attachments put in force *after* the commencement of a winding up, but whereas s.128 is restricted to a winding up by the court, s.183 applies to all categories of winding up.

Distress levied against goods by the Revenue for unpaid taxes is not "execution" within s.183: *Re Modern Jet Support Centre Ltd* [2005] EWHC 1611 (Ch); [2005] 1 W.L.R. 3880; [2006] B.C.C. 174.

S.183(2)
Notice of the summoning of a meeting is here, in effect, treated as equivalent to the now discarded "notice of an act of bankruptcy" formerly applicable in the case of an insolvent individual.

The present provision causes the execution creditor to lose the benefit of his execution, but a bona fide purchaser of goods from the enforcement officer is protected by para.(b).

On the significance of the word "date", see the note to s.86.

The court has an overriding jurisdiction: see para.(c). An order was granted in favour of an execution creditor under this provision in *Re Science and Media LLP* [2014] B.P.I.R. 774, but Chief Register Baister emphasised that only "weighty, special or exceptional circumstances" would justify disturbing the pari passu principle.

S.183(3)
These provisions define with precision the point at which an execution or attachment is "completed".

S.183(4)
The definition of "goods" is much wider than, e.g. that in the Sale of Goods Act 1979, and extends to intangible property such as choses in action.

This subsection and parts of s.184 were amended by the Courts Act 2003 s.109(1) and Sch.8 paras 295–296, to reflect the redesignation of the court officers referred to.

S.183(4A)
Section 183(4A) inserted by the Finance (No.2) Act 2015 s.51 and Sch.8 paras 26, 31 as from 28 November 2015. This follows the introduction of HMRC's power to make deductions from accounts held with deposit-takers as a means of enforcing payment.

S.183(5)
For the position governing the winding up of a company in Scotland, see s.185. Note, however, that where a company registered in England or Wales has assets in Scotland, the provisions of s.185 will apply, presumably to the exclusion of the present section: see s.185(4).

184 Duties of officers charged with execution of writs and other processes (England and Wales)

184(1) [Application] The following applies where a company's goods are taken in execution and, before their sale or the completion of the execution (by the receipt or recovery of the full amount of the levy), notice is served on the enforcement officer, or other officer, charged with execution of the writ or other process, that a provisional liquidator has been appointed or that a winding-up order has been made, or that a resolution for voluntary winding up has been passed.

184(2) [Enforcement officer to deliver goods and money to liquidator] The enforcement officer or other officer shall, on being so required, deliver the goods and any money seized or received in part satisfaction of the execution to the liquidator; but the costs of execution are a first charge on the goods or money so delivered, and the liquidator may sell the goods, or a sufficient part of them, for the purpose of satisfying the charge.

184(3) [Costs where goods sold etc.] If under an execution in respect of a judgment for a sum exceeding £500 a company's goods are sold or money is paid in order to avoid sale, the enforcement officer or other officer shall deduct the costs of the execution from the proceeds of sale or the money paid and retain the balance for 14 days.

184(4) [If within time notice is served] If within that time notice is served on the enforcement officer or other officer of a petition for the winding up of the company having been presented, or of a meeting having been called at which there is to be proposed a resolution for voluntary winding up, and an order is made or a resolution passed (as the case may be), the enforcement officer or other officer shall pay the balance to the liquidator who is entitled to retain it as against the execution creditor.

184(5) [Liquidator's rights may be set aside by court] The rights conferred by this section on the liquidator may be set aside by the court in favour of the creditor to such extent and subject to such terms as the court thinks fit.

184(6) [Definitions] In this section, "goods" includes all chattels personal; and "enforcement officer" means an individual who is authorised to act as an enforcement officer under the Courts Act 2003.

184(7) [Increase, reduction of s.184(3) sum] The money sum for the time being specified in subsection (3) is subject to increase or reduction by order under section 416 in Part XV.

184(8) [Scotland] This section does not apply in the case of a winding up in Scotland.

General Note

This section defines the obligations of an enforcement officer where a company's goods are taken in execution, thus facilitating the operation of s.184. For the rules as regards costs, see r.12.44. (See also the note to s.183.)

S.184(1), (2)
These subsections apply where a notice is served on the officer that the company in question is either actually in liquidation or in the hands of a provisional liquidator. The benefit of the execution must be surrendered to the liquidator, subject to payment of the officer's costs.

S.184(3)–(5)
These provisions deal with the duties of an officer enforcing a judgment debt of over £500. He is required to retain in his hands the net proceeds of the sale, or any money paid to him in order to avoid sale, for 14 days; and if within that time he receives notice that a winding-up petition has been presented or a meeting called to consider a resolution for voluntary winding up, he must continue to hold the money until he learns whether a liquidation has in fact resulted and, if so, hand it to the liquidator (unless the court orders otherwise under s.184(5)).

S.184(6)
The definitions are identical with those in s.183(4).

185 Effect of diligence (Scotland)

185(1) [Application of Bankruptcy (Scotland) Act] In the winding up of a company registered in Scotland, the following provisions of the Bankruptcy (Scotland) Act 2016–

(a) subsections (3) to (10) of section 23A (effect of sequestration on land attachment) and section 24 (effect of sequestration on diligence generally); and

(b) subsections (6), (7), (10) and (11) of section 109 (management and realisation of estate),

apply, so far as consistent with this Act, in like manner as they apply in the sequestration of a debtor's estate, with the substitutions specified below and with any other necessary modifications.

185(2) [Substitutions] The substitutions to be made in those sections of the Act of 2016 are as follows–

(a) for references to the debtor, substitute references to the company;

(b) for references to the sequestration, substitute references to the winding up;

(c) for references to the date of sequestration, substitute references to the commencement of the winding up of the company; and

(d) for references to the trustee, substitute references to the liquidator.

185(3) [Definition] In this section, "the commencement of the winding up of the company" means, where it is being wound up by the court, the day on which the winding-up order is made.

185(4) [English company with estate in Scotland] This section, so far as relating to any estate or effects of the company situated in Scotland, applies in the case of a company registered in England and Wales as in the case of one registered in Scotland.

General Note

Section 185(2)(d) was amended (by deletion of the word "permanent" before "trustee") by the Bankruptcy and Diligence etc. (Scotland) Act 2007 s.226(2) and Sch.6 as from 1 April 2008. Note prospective amendment of s.185(1)(a) by s.226(1) and Sch.5 para.14 of the same Act. Section 185(1) and (2) amended by the Bankruptcy (Scotland) Act 2016 (Consequential Provisions and Modifications) Order 2016 (SI 2016/1034) art.7(1), Sch.1 para.4(1), (3) as from 30 November 2016.

In relation to the financial markets, nothing in s.185 affects any action taken by an exchange or clearing house for the purpose of its default proceedings: see the note on pp.1–2, and CA 1989 s.161(4).

S.185(1)–(3)

These provisions apply to the winding up of a company in Scotland the rules relating to diligence, etc. (the Scottish equivalent of execution and attachment) in the bankruptcy of an individual. (Note, particularly, the special definition of the term "the commencement of the winding up" for this purpose.)

S.185(4)

It is plain from ss.183(5) and 184(8) that the converse to s.185(4) does not apply: i.e. a company registered in Scotland which has assets in England and Wales will be governed in relation to such property by s.185, and not by those sections.

Miscellaneous matters

186 Rescission of contracts by the court

186(1) [Power of court] The court may, on the application of a person who is, as against the liquidator, entitled to the benefit or subject to the burden of a contract made with the company, make an order rescinding the contract on such terms as to payment by or to either party of damages for the non-performance of the contract, or otherwise as the court thinks just.

186(2) [Damages] Any damages payable under the order to such a person may be proved by him as a debt in the winding up.

General Note

This provision can be traced back to the Bankruptcy Act 1883 and was extended to companies by the Companies Act 1929. It was formerly included as part of the section on disclaimer but is now treated separately. The corresponding provision for bankruptcy is IA 1986 s.345. It is concerned with contracts entered into by the company which are still wholly or partly at an executory stage on the date of liquidation. If the company at that date, or the liquidator subsequently, has committed a repudiatory breach then, on ordinary contractual principles, the other party will be entitled to terminate the contract and claim damages without recourse to the court. Alternatively, s.186 entitles him to achieve the same result by court order, which will overcome any doubt as to his right to repudiate and quantify the sum for which he can prove in the liquidation.

In the context of the financial markets, s.186 does not apply in relation to a market contract or a contract effected by an exchange or clearing house for the purpose of realising property provided as margin in relation to market contracts: see CA 1989 s.164(1). The section is also disapplied by the Finality Regulations reg.16(1) in relation to a transfer order or a contract for the purpose of realising security in payment and securities settlement systems. (See the notes on pp.1–3 above.)

187 Power to make over assets to employees

187(1) [CA 2006 s.247 payment on winding up] On the winding up of a company (whether by the court or voluntarily), the liquidator may, subject to the following provisions of this section, make any payment which the company has, before the commencement of the winding up, decided to make under section 247 of the Companies Act 2006 (power to provide for employees or former employees on cessation or transfer of business).

187(2) [Power exercisable by liquidator] The liquidator may, after the winding up has commenced, make any such provision as is mentioned in section 247(1) if–

(a) the company's liabilities have been fully satisfied and provision has been made for the expenses of the winding up,

(b) the exercise of the power has been sanctioned by a resolution of the company, and

(c) any requirements of the company's articles as to the exercise of the power conferred by section 247(1) are complied with.

187(3) [Source of payment] Any payment which may be made by a company under this section (that is, a payment after the commencement of its winding up) may be made out of the company's assets which are available to the members on the winding up.

187(4) [Control by court] On a winding up by the court, the exercise by the liquidator of his powers under this section is subject to the court's control, and any creditor or contributory may apply to the court with respect to any exercise or proposed exercise of the power.

187(5) [Effect] Subsections (1) and (2) above have effect notwithstanding anything in any rule of law or in section 107 of this Act (property of company after satisfaction of liabilities to be distributed among members).

General Note

The provisions of this section and of CA 2006 s.247 were first introduced (as CA 1980 s.74) to negate the common law ruling in *Parke v Daily News Ltd* [1962] Ch. 927. Section 247 applies when the company is a going concern, and the present section when it is being wound up. In *Parke's* case, it was held to be ultra vires for a company which had sold its business to a third party to make substantial ex gratia payments to the employees who were thereby made redundant. Both s.247 and the present section are framed in wide terms, so as not merely to negative any question of ultra vires (abolished by CA 1989 s.108 from 4 February 1991), but to ensure that such payments will not be invalidated on any other grounds.

Section 187(1) amended, and s.187(2) substituted, by the Companies Act 2006 (Commencement No.3, Consequential Amendments, Transitional Provisions and Savings) Order 2007 (SI 2007/2194 (C. 84)) art.10(1) and Sch.4 para.42(2), (3), as from 1 October 2007.

S.187(1)

This subsection applies where the company has already resolved under CA 2006 s.247(4), before the commencement of the winding up, to make a payment to the employees: the liquidator is authorised to implement the resolution and make that payment. This may be made only out of profits of the company which are available for dividend (s.247(7)(b)).

S.187(2)

Once the winding up has commenced, it is still permissible for a company's shareholders to agree to make over assets to the employees, but the restriction to profits available for dividend no longer applies, and instead the payment must be made out of the surplus in the hands of the liquidator after all the company's debts and the costs of the winding up have been met. An ordinary resolution of the shareholders is required or, if the company's articles so stipulate, a resolution passed by a larger majority. However, a payment cannot be made on the basis of a decision of the directors alone, even if the articles authorise this course, since CA 2006 s.247(4)(b), which permits this prior to the commencement of winding up, is nullified by the present provision.

S.187(3)

This provision is not permissive (as it appears to be), but mandatory: the payment cannot be made out of any assets other than those available to the members.

S.187(4), (5)

The grounds on which the court might interfere to set aside a resolution of the members are not set out. It may be assumed that a plea of ultra vires would not succeed, or an objection that the exercise of power by the majority was not in the best interests of the company (see CA 2006 s.247(2) ("to promote the success of the company")). However, there are clearly circumstances where a minority shareholder might claim that the majority was acting oppressively or mala fide or in a discriminatory way—e.g. perhaps if the majority shareholders were themselves the employees who stood to benefit.

188 Notification that company is in liquidation

188(1) [Statement in invoices etc.] When a company is being wound up, whether by the court or voluntarily–

(a) every invoice, order for goods or services, business letter or order form (whether in hard copy, electronic or any other form) issued by or on behalf of the company, or a liquidator of the company or a receiver or manager of the company's property, and

(b) all the company's websites,

must contain a statement that the company is being wound up.

188(2) [Penalty on default] If default is made in complying with this section, the company and any of the following persons who knowingly and wilfully authorises or permits the default, namely, any officer of the company, any liquidator of the company and any receiver or manager, is liable to a fine.

General Note

This section has its counterpart in the provisions relating to administration (s.*12* and Sch.B1 para.45) and receivership (ss.39, 64). Section 188(1) was substituted by the Companies (Registrar, Languages and Trading Disclosures) Regulations 2006 (SI 2006/3429) reg.7(1), as from 1 January 2007. Section 188(1)(a) was amended by the Companies (Trading Disclosures) (Insolvency) Regulations 2008 (SI 2008/1897) reg.5(1), as from 1 October 2008.

S.188(2)
On penalties, see s.430 and Sch.10.

189 Interest on debts

189(1) [Payment of interest] In a winding up interest is payable in accordance with this section on any debt proved in the winding up, including so much of any such debt as represents interest on the remainder.

189(2) [Surplus after payment of debts] Any surplus remaining after the payment of the debts proved in a winding up shall, before being applied for any other purpose, be applied in paying interest on those debts in respect of the periods during which they have been outstanding since the company went into liquidation.

189(3) [Ranking of interest] All interest under this section ranks equally, whether or not the debts on which it is payable rank equally.

189(4) [Rate of interest] The rate of interest payable under this section in respect of any debt ("the official rate" for the purposes of any provision of this Act in which that expression is used) is whichever is the greater of–

(a) the rate specified in section 17 of the Judgments Act 1838 on the day on which the company went into liquidation, and

(b) the rate applicable to that debt apart from the winding up.

189(5) [Scotland] In the application of this section to Scotland–

(a) references to a debt proved in a winding up have effect as references to a claim accepted in a winding up, and

(b) the reference to section 17 of the Judgments Act 1838 has effect as a reference to the rules.

General Note

Before the reform of insolvency legislation in 1985, the legal rules governing the entitlement to interest on debts in a winding up were confused and unsatisfactory (see the Cork Committee's *Report*, Ch.31). On the recommendation of the Committee, all these old rules and the associated anomalies have been done away with and replaced by new provisions. Note that the new law applies in both solvent and insolvent liquidations.

The judgment of David Richards J in *Re Lehman Bros International (Europe)* [2014] EWHC 704 (Ch); [2014] B.C.C. 193 contains a detailed discussion of the entitlement to interest (i) under a contractual provision, (ii) by statute, in an administration, (iii) by statute, where a liquidation immediately follows the administration and (iv) independently of any of these provisions, and their respective priority in a distribution to creditors. This judgment was largely upheld on appeal (*Joint Administrators of LB Holdings Intermediate 2 Ltd v Lomas* [2015] EWCA Civ 485; [2015] 3 W.L.R. 1205; [2015] B.C.C. 431), but some elements of it were overturned by the Supreme Court in *Joint Administrators of LB Holdings Intermediate 2 Ltd v Joint Administrators of Lehman Bros International (Europe)* [2017] UKSC 38; [2017] 2 W.L.R. 1497; [2017] B.C.C. 235. The topic was explored further in a later judgment of David Richards J (*Re Lehman Bros International (Europe); Lomas v Burlington Loan Management Ltd* [2015] EWHC 2269 (Ch)); [2016] B.C.C. 239, later proceedings [2016] EWHC 2131 (Ch)). A judgment of Hildyard J ([2016] EWHC 2417 (Ch)) considered issues arising from the distribution of a substantial surplus in the Lehman Bros group administration (including payment of interest under an ISDA master agreement on early termination amounts) and was affirmed at [2017] EWCA Civ 1462; [2017] B.C.C. 759. Further directions were given in *Re Lehman Bros International (Europe), Lomas v HMRC* [2016] EWHC 2492 (Ch) (a tax issue) but later reversed on appeal: [2017] EWCA Civ 2124. This series of rulings has come to be known as the "Waterfall" proceedings.

Among the points established by the first case (at first instance and on appeal) we may list:

- The Supreme Court primary point on interest that s.189 (supplemented by what is now IR 2016 r.14.23) provides a complete statutory code for the recovery of interest on proved debts (in administration and liquidation), so that there is no room for judge-made law as to contractual rights in the event of a surplus or to fill gaps created by a lacuna.
- The right to interest under r.14.23(7) ("statutory interest") on the transmission from administration to liquidation continues into the liquidation and the obligation to pay it passes to the liquidator along with the surplus as enunciated by David Richards J and by the Court of Appeal was overruled by the Supreme Court: interest under r.14.23(7)(a) could not be claimed from a subsequent liquidator as the rule was a direction to the administrator while he was in office—not a direction to a subsequent liquidator—so that when the administration ended, r.14.23(7) no longer applied (that appeared to be an oversight in the statutory scheme, but it was not appropriate for a judge to rewrite a statutory provision to correct it).
- Claims for losses incurred on the conversion of foreign debts into sterling rank as non-provable debts, payable after provable debts but in priority to subordinated debts, but the Supreme Court overruled the principle that currency conversion losses can be claimed as non-provable debts (see the note to rr.14.20–14.23).
- Subordinated debt must be valued taking into account the contingency that all non-provable debts be paid.

The second hearing before David Richards J was concerned with a detailed examination of the rules relation to statutory interest in an administration and a winding up (and upheld by the Court of Appeal: [2017] EWCA Civ 1462; [2017] B.C.C. 759), and is discussed below in the note to IR 2016 r.14.23.

In *Re Empire Paper Ltd* [1999] B.C.C. 406, X Ltd had guaranteed the debt of E Ltd. Both companies were in liquidation. X Ltd had been called upon to pay the debt and, since it was solvent, the debt had been paid with statutory interest under s.189. E Ltd, however, was insolvent, and it was held that this fact prevented X Ltd from proving in the liquidation for the sum which it had paid as interest.

S.189(1), (2)

No interest is payable on debts in the course of a winding up except in accordance with this section, which applies only if there is a surplus remaining after the payment in full of all proved debts (s.189(2)). The relevant date for the purposes of s.189 is normally the date when the company "went into liquidation", which will be, in a compulsory winding up, the date of the winding-up order and, in a voluntary liquidation, that of the winding-up resolution (see *Re Lines Bros Ltd* [1983] Ch. 1, and compare s.247(2)). However, where a creditor proves for loss or damage following a disclaimer by the liquidator, interest runs from the date of the disclaimer: *Re Park Air Services plc* [2000] 2 A.C. 172; [1999] B.C.C. 135.

Where interest is payable under this section, it runs on all debts and liabilities proved in the winding up, including any debts representing interest due up to the date of liquidation, and it runs on each individual debt until the creditor is paid either in whole or in part. In the latter case, interest will cease to be payable on the part of the debt that has been paid. If a final dividend is declared in consequence of which any of the creditors receive in total less than 100p in the £, no creditor (whether preferential or not) is entitled to interest. If interest is due, it is payable before any money is returned to shareholders (s.189(2)).

In regard to debts payable at a future time, see IR 2016 r.14.44.

S.189(3)

The preferential and non-preferential debts are entitled to interest at the same rate: the former have no priority. If the preferential creditors have been paid earlier in time than the other creditors, the period over which interest is due to them will be correspondingly shorter.

S.189(4)

The rate of interest payable under the Judgments Act 1838 s.17, is currently 8 per cent (SI 1993/564). If the debt itself carries interest at a higher rate, the latter is payable; but a creditor cannot merely by giving notice impose an obligation to pay interest at a rate higher than that specified in s.189(4)(a): see IR 2016 r.14.23(4), (5).

S.189(5)

A rate of 15 per cent is specified in the Insolvency (Scotland) Rules 1986 (SI 1986/1915 (S 139)) r.4.66(2)(b).

190 Documents exempt from stamp duty

190(1) [Application] In the case of a winding up by the court, or of a creditors' voluntary winding up, the following has effect as regards exemption from duties chargeable under the enactments relating to stamp duties.

190(2) [Exempt documents of company registered in England and Wales] If the company is registered in England and Wales, the following documents are exempt from stamp duty–

(a) every assurance relating solely to freehold or leasehold property, or to any estate, right or interest in, any real or personal property, which forms part of the company's assets and which, after the execution of the assurance, either at law or in equity, is or remains part of those assets, and

(b) every writ, order, certificate, or other instrument or writing relating solely to the property of any company which is being wound up as mentioned in subsection (1), or to any proceeding under such a winding up.

"Assurance" here includes deed, conveyance, assignment and surrender.

190(3) [Exempt document of company registered in Scotland] If the company is registered in Scotland, the following documents are exempt from stamp duty–

(a) every conveyance relating solely to property, which forms part of the company's assets and which, after the execution of the conveyance, is or remains the company's property for the benefit of its creditors,

(b) any articles of roup or sale, submission and every other instrument and writing whatsoever relating solely to the company's property, and

(c) every deed or writing forming part of the proceedings in the winding up.

"Conveyance" here includes assignation, instrument, discharge, writing and deed.

General Note

This section applies only in the case of a winding up by the court or a creditors' voluntary winding up. It exempts from stamp duty all conveyances, etc. which are made to facilitate the winding up and which do not beneficially transfer assets out the hands of the liquidator.

191 Company's books to be evidence

191 Where a company is being wound up, all books and papers of the company and of the liquidators are, as between the contributories of the company, prima facie evidence of the truth of all matters purporting to be recorded in them.

General Note

The presumption which this provision creates applies only "as between the contributories of the company", and is rebuttable.

192 Information as to pending liquidations

192(1) [Statement to registrar] If the winding up of a company is not concluded within one year after its commencement, the liquidator shall, at such intervals as may be prescribed, until the winding up is concluded, send to the registrar of companies a statement in the prescribed form and containing the prescribed particulars with respect to the proceedings in, and position of, the liquidation.

192(2) [Penalty on default] If a liquidator fails to comply with this section, he is liable to a fine and, for continued contravention, to a daily default fine.

General Note

The relevant rules are rr.18.3, 18.7, 18.8.

S.192(2)

On penalties, see s.430 and Sch.10.

The liquidator's obligations may also be enforced by seeking an order for compliance under s.170. If a liquidator fails to comply with such an order, he will be in contempt of court and liable to imprisonment: *Re S & A Conversions Ltd* (1988) 4 B.C.C. 384; *Re Allan Ellis (Transport & Packing) Services Ltd* (1989) 5 B.C.C. 835.

193 Unclaimed dividends (Scotland)

193(1) [Application] The following applies where a company registered in Scotland has been wound up, and is about to be dissolved.

193(2) [Liquidator to lodge unclaimed money in bank] The liquidator shall lodge in an appropriate bank or institution as defined in section 228(1) of the Bankruptcy (Scotland) Act 2016 (not being a bank or institution in or of which the liquidator is acting partner, manager, agent or cashier) in the name of the Accountant of Court the whole unclaimed dividends and unapplied or undistributable balances, and the deposit receipts shall be transmitted to the Accountant of Court.

193(3) [Application of Bankruptcy (Scotland) Act] The provisions of section 150 of the Bankruptcy (Scotland) Act 2016 (so far as consistent with this Act and the Companies Acts) apply with any necessary modifications to sums lodged in a bank or institution under this section as they apply to sums deposited under section 148 of the Act first mentioned.

General Note

Section 150 of the Bankruptcy (Scotland) Act 2016 provides that unclaimed dividends in an individual bankruptcy shall be held in a bank in the name of the Accountant in Bankruptcy for a period of seven years, during which they may be claimed by those entitled. After the seven years, the money passes to the Scottish Ministers who may thereafter pay undisputed claims in his discretion.

The present section applies the same rules to a company liquidation in Scotland. The Insolvency (Scotland) Rules 1986 r.4.68(1) is to the same effect.

Section 193(2), (3) amended by the Bankruptcy (Scotland) Act 2016 (Consequential Provisions and Modifications) Order 2016 (SI 2016/1034 art.7(1), Sch.1 para.4(1), (4) as from 30 November 2016.

194 Resolutions passed at adjourned meetings [Repealed]

General Note

Section 194 repealed by SBEEA 2015 Sch.9 paras 1, 46 as from 6 April 2017.

195 Court's powers to ascertain wishes of creditors or contributories

195(1) [Power of court] The court may–

(a) as to all matters relating to the winding up of a company, have regard to the wishes of the creditors or contributories (as proved to it by any sufficient evidence), and

(b) if it thinks fit, for the purpose of ascertaining those wishes, direct qualifying decision procedures to be instigated or the deemed consent procedure to be used in accordance with any directions given by the court, and appoint a person to report the result to the court.

195(2) [Creditors] In the case of creditors, regard shall be had to the value of each creditor's debt.

195(3) [Contributories] In the case of contributories, regard shall be had to the number of votes conferred on each contributory.

General Note

The use of "may", rather than "shall", in the opening words of the section gives the court a residuary discretion to act without having regard to the wishes of the creditors (or contributories) where there are "special circumstances"—e.g. where it is not practicable to hold meetings because of the complexities of the case and the difficulty of identifying who the creditors are: *Re Bank of Credit & Commerce International SA (No.2)* [1992] B.C.C. 715. However, the court will not lightly disregard or overrule the views of the majority creditors whose interests are at stake: *Re Falcon R J Developments Ltd* (1987) 3 B.C.C. 146: *Re William Thorpe & Son Ltd* (1989) 5 B.C.C. 156. See also the note to s.125(1), above.

The conduct of any decision procedures directed by the court to be called is dealt with by the rules, as well as being covered in part by the terms of the section itself. For the relevant rules, see IR 2016 rr.15.20–15.22.

196 Judicial notice of court documents

196 In all proceedings under this Part, all courts, judges and persons judicially acting, and all officers, judicial or ministerial, of any court, or employed in enforcing the process of any court shall take judicial notice–

(a) of the signature of any officer of the High Court or of the county court in England and Wales, or of the Court of Session or a sheriff court in Scotland, or of the High Court in Northern Ireland, and also

(b) of the official seal or stamp of the several offices of the High Court in England and Wales or Northern Ireland, or of the Court of Session, appended to or impressed on any document made, issued or signed under the provisions of this Act or the Companies Acts, or any official copy of such a document.

197 Commission for receiving evidence

197(1) [Courts for examination of witnesses] When a company is wound up in England and Wales or in Scotland, the court may refer the whole or any part of the examination of witnesses–

(a) to the county court in England and Wales, or

(b) to the sheriff principal for a specified sheriffdom in Scotland, or

(c) to the High Court in Northern Ireland or a specified Northern Ireland County Court,

("specified" meaning specified in the order of the winding-up court).

197(2) [Commissioners for taking evidence] Any person exercising jurisdiction as a judge of the court to which the reference is made (or, in Scotland, the sheriff principal to whom it is made) shall then, by virtue of this section, be a commissioner for the purpose of taking the evidence of those witnesses.

197(3) [Power of judge or sheriff principal] The judge or sheriff principal has in the matter referred the same power of summoning and examining witnesses, of requiring the production and delivery of documents, of punishing defaults by witnesses, and of allowing costs and expenses to witnesses, as the court which made the winding-up order.

These powers are in addition to any which the judge or sheriff principal might lawfully exercise apart from this section.

197(4) [Return or report re examination] The examination so taken shall be returned or reported to the court which made the order in such manner as that court requests.

197(5) [Northern Ireland] This section extends to Northern Ireland.

198 Court order for examination of persons in Scotland

198(1) [Examination of any person on affairs of company] The court may direct the examination in Scotland of any person for the time being in Scotland (whether a contributory of the company or not), in regard to the trade, dealings, affairs or property of any company in course of being wound up, or of any person being a contributory of the company, so far as the company may be interested by reason of his being a contributory.

198(2) [Directions to take examination] The order or commission to take the examination shall be directed to the sheriff principal of the sheriffdom in which the person to be examined is residing or happens to be for the time; and the sheriff principal shall summon the person to appear before him at a time and place to be specified in the summons for examination on oath as a witness or as a haver, and to produce any books or papers called for which are in his possession or power.

198(3) [Duties of sheriff principal re examination] The sheriff principal may take the examination either orally or on written interrogatories, and shall report the same in writing in the usual form to the court, and shall transmit with the report the books and papers produced, if the originals are required and specified by the order or commission, or otherwise copies or extracts authenticated by the sheriff.

198(4) [Where person fails to appear for examination] If a person so summoned fails to appear at the time and place specified, or refuses to be examined or to make the production required, the sheriff principal shall proceed against him as a witness or haver duly cited; and failing to appear or refusing to give evidence or make production may be proceeded against by the law of Scotland.

198(5) [Fees and allowances] The sheriff principal is entitled to such fees, and the witness is entitled to such allowances, as sheriffs principal when acting as commissioners under appointment from the Court of Session and as witnesses and havers are entitled to in the like cases according to the law and practice of Scotland.

198(6) [Objection by witness] If any objection is stated to the sheriff principal by the witness, either on the ground of his incompetency as a witness, or as to the production required, or on any other ground, the sheriff principal may, if he thinks fit, report the objection to the court, and suspend the examination of the witness until it has been disposed of by the court.

General Note

This section applies in Scotland in addition to ss.133 and 236, which also provide for the judicial examination of persons who have been connected with a company that is in liquidation. There appears to be a considerable degree of overlap. The report to the court under s.198(3) must be in hard copy (LRO 2010 (SI 2010/18) art.4(2)(g)).

199 Costs of application for leave to proceed (Scottish companies)

199 Where a petition or application for leave to proceed with an action or proceeding against a company which is being wound up in Scotland is unopposed and is granted by the court, the costs of the petition or application shall, unless the court otherwise directs, be added to the amount of the petitioner's or applicant's claim against the company.

200 Affidavits etc. in United Kingdom and overseas

200(1) [Swearing of affidavit] An affidavit required to be sworn under or for the purposes of this Part may be sworn in the United Kingdom, or elsewhere in Her Majesty's dominions, before any court, judge or person lawfully authorised to take and receive affidavits, or before any of Her Majesty's consuls or vice-consuls in any place outside Her dominions.

200(2) [Judicial notice of signatures etc.] All courts, judges, justices, commissioners and persons acting judicially shall take judicial notice of the seal or stamp or signature (as the case may be) of any such court, judge, person, consul or vice-consul attached, appended or subscribed to any such affidavit, or to any other document to be used for the purposes of this Part.

General Note

This provision is designed to simplify the normal requirements for the taking of evidence abroad, for use in winding-up proceedings.

Chapter IX

Dissolution of Companies After Winding Up

Introductory note to Part IV, Chapter IX

The dissolution of a company extinguishes its legal personality, so that it goes out of existence for all purposes. Any property and rights formerly vested in it are deemed to belong to the Crown, as bona vacantia (CA 2006 s.1013). (Note, however, that in *Re Wilmott Trading Ltd* [2000] B.C.C. 321 Neuberger J held that the particular "property" in that case—a waste management licence—did not revert to the Crown on the dissolution of the company, but ceased to exist.)

Under the former provisions of the Companies Acts, different rules regarding dissolution applied in a compulsory winding up and a voluntary winding up, a court order being always required in the former case. The reforms in the law of insolvency which were introduced by IA 1985 dispensed with this need for a court order and so brought the various types of winding up into line. A further innovation was the provision for early dissolution now contained in s.202 below. This enables the official receiver, in a winding up by the court, to apply to the registrar of companies to have the company dissolved at an early stage in the liquidation, when the company is so hopelessly insolvent that it is pointless to proceed further. In Scotland, the liquidator is empowered to make a similar application to the court (s.204). It is possible also for a company which is in administration under IA 1986 Sch.B1 to move directly from administration to dissolution, if the administrator thinks that the company has no property which might permit a distribution to its creditors (Sch.B1 para.84).

In addition to these procedures, a company may be dissolved by having its name struck off the register under CA 2006 ss.1000–1011, on the ground that it has ceased to carry on business. The initiative may be taken by the registrar under ss.1000–1002, which provides that after he has made a preliminary inquiry and followed the prescribed procedure (including sending formal notice to the company of his intention to strike off and gazetting the notice) he may strike the company's name off the register after two (formerly three) months. Alternatively, the company itself may apply to have its name struck off (ss.1003–1011). This procedure is now available to all companies (under CA 1985 only private companies could apply). The directors who are making the application must make a declaration that neither s.1004 nor s.1005 prevents the application from being made (see the Registrar of Companies and Applications for Striking Off Regulations 2009 (SI 2009/1803, effective 1 October 2009) reg.2). Section 1004 bans a company from making an application if (inter alia) it has changed its name or carried on business within the previous three months; and s.1005 prevents an application if a scheme of arrangement under CA 2006 Pt 26 or an insolvency proceeding or moratorium is current. The registrar must first publish a notice in the *Gazette* inviting any person to show cause why the name should not be struck off and if there is no response he may then do so after two months. In either case, the company is dissolved by the publication in the *Gazette* of a further notice that the name has been struck off. The striking-off procedure is available also to LLPs (Limited Liability Partnerships (Application of Companies Act 2006) Regulations 2009 (SI 2009/1804) regs 50, 51).

The Companies (Striking Off) (Electronic Communications) Order 2014 (SI 2014/1602) authorises the use of electronic means for the sending of notices and other communications in the striking off procedure.

A company which has been dissolved may be restored to the register under CA 2006 ss.1024 et seq. Under the former legislation a court order was always needed for this purpose and separate procedures with different time limits applied. The 2006 Act, following a recommendation of the Company Law Review, institutes a simpler mechanism enabling a company which has been struck off (whether or not it has also been dissolved) to be reinstated in many cases by an administrative procedure without the involvement of the court. Application must be made to the registrar by a former member or former director within six years of the dissolution (s.1024). It must be shown that:

- the company was carrying on business at the date when it was struck off,
- if any property or right has vested in the Crown as bona vacantia, the Crown representative has given his written consent to the restoration,
- the applicant has delivered to the registrar such documents as are necessary to bring up to date the records kept by the registrar and paid any outstanding penalties (s.1025).

The general effect of restoration (whether effected administratively or by the court) is that the company is deemed to have continued in existence as if it had not been dissolved or struck off (ss.1028(1), 1032(1)). In other words, reinstatement is retrospective in its effect, so that everything that has been done in the company's name while the company was struck off is automatically validated. So, in *Peaktone Ltd v Joddrell* [2012] EWCA Civ 1035; [2013] B.C.C. 112 proceedings which had been commenced against a company during the period when it was dissolved were deemed to have been effective after the company was restored to the register. This reflects the position under CA 1985 s.653 as decided in *Tyman's Ltd v Craven* [1952] 2 Q.B. 100. See also *Re Fivestar Properties Ltd* [2015] EWHC 2782 (Ch) (freehold property which had vested in the Crown as bona vacantia and subsequently been disclaimed revested in the company on restoration), and contrast *ELB Securities Ltd v Love* [2015] CSIH 67 (lease of premises disclaimed by Crown: disclaimer had the effect of bringing company's rights under the lease to an end; rights not revived by reinstatement of company). The court may give such directions and make such provision (on an application to be made within three years from the date of restoration) as seems just for placing the company and all other persons in the same position (as nearly as may be) as if the company had not been dissolved or struck off (s.1028(3)). The court's discretion under this provision is very wide—it may, for example, extend to overriding a limitation period which would normally apply: *Davy v Pickering* [2015] EWHC 380 (Ch); [2016] B.C.C. 50. (But this discretion should be sparingly exercised: *Barclays Bank plc v Registrar of Companies* [2015] EWHC 2806 (Ch); [2016] B.C.C. 64; *County Leasing Management Ltd v Hawkes* [2015] EWCA Civ 1251; [2016] B.C.C. 102 and, indeed, the Court of Appeal in *Pickering v Davy* [2017] EWCA Civ 30; [2017] B.C.C. 171 has since allowed an appeal in that case. Use of the discretion was also refused in *Housemaker Services Ltd v Cole* [2017] EWHC 753 (Ch), where the latter three cases were followed.) However, the power to grant ancillary relief may have limitations: see *Re The Peoples' Restaurant Group Ltd* (unreported, 30 November 2012), where an order was made reinstating the company but the applicant was unsuccessful in seeking to have the company placed in liquidation with backdated effect. In the *Barclays Bank* case (above) it was stressed that, although asset recovery might be the normal purpose of seeking reinstatement, there might well be other objectives, e.g. the investigation of transactions meriting examination.

For the difficult position of joinder of third parties to an application for restoration, see *Welsh Minsters v Price* [2017] EWCA Civ 1768; [2018] B.C.C. 93: the court had power under CPR r.19.2(2) to join a third party to proceedings to restore a company to the register to enable that party to complain that the court was misled when making a restoration order or that there had been a breach of undertakings. Alternatively, a company that has been struck off (or dissolved or is deemed to have been dissolved) may be restored to the register by court order (s.1029(1)). Section 1029(2) lists the persons who may apply. The six-year time limit also applies here, but there is no limit where the purpose of the application is to bring proceedings against the company for damages for personal injury (s.1030(1)); and if the application is made where the company has been struck off and the registrar has refused reinstatement under s.1024, application may be made within 28 days from the registrar's refusal even if the six-year period has expired (s.1030(5)). The effect and consequences of the restoration are broadly the same as under s.1028 above. Sections 1033 and 1034 contain supplementary provisions dealing with problems which may arise in relation to the company's name (e.g. if another company with the same or a similar name has been registered after it was struck off) or property which was vested in the Crown as bona vacantia has been disposed of. Guidance notes on administrative striking off and restoration are available on the Companies House website.

Provision is made by the Co-operative and Community Benefit Societies Act 2014 for the dissolution of a registered co-operative or community benefit society (as defined by s.1 of that Act), either by an instrument of dissolution (ss.119–122) or, on its being wound up, in pursuance of an order or resolution made as is directed in the case of companies (s.122). A society may also be dissolved under Sch.B1 para.84 following an administration (s.125).

201 Dissolution (voluntary winding up)

201(1) [Application] This section applies, in the case of a company wound up voluntarily, where the liquidator has sent to the registrar of companies his final account and return under section 94 (members' voluntary) or his final account and statement under section 106 (creditors' voluntary).

201(2) [Duty of registrar] The registrar on receiving the account, or the account and statement and any statement under section 106(4B), shall forthwith register it or them; and on the expiration of 3 months from the registration of the account the company is deemed to be dissolved (except where subsection (2A) applies).

201(2A) [Application of s.201(2A)] This subsection applies where a statement sent to the registrar under section 106(4B) indicates that a member State liquidator does not consent to the company being dissolved.

201(2B) [Deemed dissolution following EU proceedings] Where subsection (2A) applies, the company is deemed to be dissolved at the end of the period of 3 months beginning with the date (if any) recorded in the register as the date on which the registrar was notified that–

(a) all proceedings identified in the statement sent under section 106(4B) were closed, or

(b) every member State liquidator appointed in those proceedings consented to the company being dissolved.

201(3) [Power of court re deferring date] However, the court may, on the application of the liquidator or any other person who appears to the court to be interested, make an order deferring the date at which the dissolution of the company is to take effect for such time as the court thinks fit.

201(4) [Copy of order to registrar] It is the duty of the person on whose application an order of the court under this section is made within 7 days after the making of the order to deliver to the registrar a copy of the order for registration; and if that person fails to do so he is liable to a fine and, for continued contravention, to a daily default fine.

General Note

The company is automatically dissolved under this section on the expiration of three months from the filing of the liquidator's final return: no further formality is needed. Note the provision in s.201(2A), (2B) where a Member State liquidator does not consent to dissolution.

S.201(2), (2A), (2B)

Section 201(2) amended and s.201(2A), (2B) inserted by the Insolvency Amendment (EU 2015/848) Regulations 2017 (SI 2017/702) regs 1, 2(1), Sch. paras 1, 9 in relation to proceedings in England and Wales only opened on or after 26 June 2017 (see reg.3) when the Recast EU Regulation 2015/848 came into force.

Note that there are equivalent amendments to s.201(2) and insertion of equivalent s.201(2A), (2B) in relation to Scotland only by the Insolvency Amendment (EU 2015/848) Regulations 2017 (SI 2017/702) regs 1, 2(2)(b), Sch. paras 55, 58 in relation to proceedings opened on or after 26 June 2017 (see reg.3) when the Recast EU Regulation 2015/848 came into force.

S.201(3), (4)

The power of the court under subs.(3) is limited to extending the three-month period. "A copy" was substituted for "an office copy" in s.201(4) by the Companies (Registrar, Languages and Trading Disclosures) Regulations 2006 (SI 2006/3429) reg.3(1)(d) as from 1 January 2007.

On penalties, see s.430 and Sch.10.

202 Early dissolution (England and Wales)

202(1) [Application] This section applies where an order for the winding up of a company has been made by the court in England and Wales.

202(2) [Official receiver may apply for dissolution] The official receiver, if–

(a) he is the liquidator of the company, and

(b) it appears to him–

(i) that the realisable assets of the company are insufficient to cover the expenses of the winding up, and

(ii) that the affairs of the company do not require any further investigation,

may at any time apply to the registrar of companies for the early dissolution of the company.

202(2A) [Application of s.202(2B) following s.202(2) application] Subsection (2B) applies where, immediately before the official receiver makes an application under subsection (2), there are EU insolvency proceedings open in respect of the company in one or more other member States.

202(2B) [Duty of official receiver to send statement to registrar] The official receiver must send to the registrar, with the application, a statement–

(a) identifying those proceedings,

(b) identifying the member State liquidator appointed in each of those proceedings, and

(c) indicating, in relation to each of those member State liquidators, whether that member State liquidator consents to the company being dissolved.

202(3) [Notice by official receiver] Before making an application under section (2), the official receiver shall give not less than 28 days' notice of his intention to do so to the company's creditors, other than opted-out creditors, and contributories and, if there is an administrative receiver of the company, to that receiver.

202(4) [Effect of notice on official receiver] With the giving of that notice the official receiver ceases (subject to any directions under the next section) to be required to perform any duties imposed on him in relation to the company, its creditors or contributories by virtue of any provision of this Act, apart from a duty to make an application under subsection (2) and send any statement under subsection (2B).

202(5) [Duty of registrar] On the receipt of the official receiver's application under subsection (2) and any statement under subsection (2B) the registrar shall forthwith register it or them and, at the end of the period of 3 months beginning with the day of the registration of the application, the company shall be dissolved (except where subsection (6) applies).

202(6) [Where member State liquidator does not consent to dissolution] This subsection applies where a statement under subsection (2B) indicates that a member State liquidator does not consent to the company being dissolved.

202(7) [Deemed dissolution following EU proceedings] Where subsection (6) applies, the company is deemed to be dissolved at the end of the period of 3 months beginning with the date (if any) recorded in the register as the date on which the registrar was notified that–

(a) all proceedings identified in the statement under subsection (2B) were closed, or

(b) every member State liquidator appointed in those proceedings consented to the company being dissolved.

202(8) [Power of Secretary of State to give directions] However, the Secretary of State may, on the application of the official receiver or any other person who appears to the Secretary of State to be interested, give directions under section 203 at any time before the end of the period in subsection (5) or (7).

General Note

The Cork Committee (*Report*, paras 649–651) recommended that a procedure should be introduced to enable the official receiver to apply to the court for the early dissolution of a company which was in compulsory liquidation and hopelessly insolvent. The legislature has gone one better and dispensed with the need for a court order: the official receiver's application is sent to the registrar of companies and takes effect automatically after three months, unless the Secretary of State intervenes in the meantime. The official receiver (and the taxpayer) is thus spared the pointless expense of completing the winding up. A similar procedure is now available where a company in administration has no property which might permit a distribution to creditors: see Sch.B1 para.84.

Section 202(2A), (2B), (6), (7) inserted, (8) amended and renumbered from s.202(5) and s.202(3)–(5) amended by the Insolvency Amendment (EU 2015/848) Regulations 2017 (SI 2017/702) regs 1, 2(1), Sch. paras 1, 10 in relation to proceedings opened on or after 26 June 2017 (see reg.3) when the Recast EU Regulation 2015/848 came into force.

S.202(1)

For the corresponding provision for Scotland, see s.204.

S.202(2), (2A), (2B)

The powers under this section may be exercised only by the official receiver, and only if he is the liquidator. Special provision applies where there are EU proceedings.

Paragraph (2)(b)(ii) leaves it to the judgment of the official receiver to decide that the circumstances of the insolvency do not create any suspicion of impropriety, and perhaps even to consider such policy questions as whether the circumstances, though dubious, really justify the expenditure of public money which would be involved in investigating the company's affairs further.

S.202(3), (4)

The official receiver's duties (as liquidator or otherwise) cease as soon as he gives the notice, i.e. even while the 28-day period referred to in s.202(3) and the three-month period in s.202(5) are running, he has no obligation to take further steps in the liquidation.

It seems that the liquidator comes under a *duty* to apply for a dissolution once he has given a notice under s.202(3): if he starts the dissolution process, he must go through with it, and if he has second thoughts he must invoke the powers of the Secretary of State under s.203.

S.202(5), (6), (7)

The dissolution takes effect automatically on the expiry of the three-month period, unless the Secretary of State has directed that a longer period than three months be substituted. Special provision applies where there are EU proceedings and the Member State liquidator does not consent to the company's dissolution.

203 Consequence of notice under s.202

203(1) [Application for directions] Where a notice has been given under section 202(3), the official receiver or any creditor or contributory of the company, or the administrative receiver of the company (if there is one) may apply to the Secretary of State for directions under this section.

203(2) [Grounds for application] The grounds on which that application may be made are–

(a) that the realisable assets of the company are sufficient to cover the expenses of the winding up;

(b) that the affairs of the company do require further investigation; or

(c) that for any other reason the early dissolution of the company is inappropriate.

203(3) [Scope of directions] Directions under this section–

(a) are directions making such provision as the Secretary of State thinks fit for enabling the winding up of the company to proceed as if no notice had been given under section 202(3), and

(b) may, in the case of an application under section 202(8), include a direction deferring the date at which the dissolution of the company is to take effect for such period as the Secretary of State thinks fit.

203(4) [Appeal to court] An appeal to the court lies from any decision of the Secretary of State on an application for directions under this section.

203(5) [Copy of directions etc. to registrar] It is the duty of the person on whose application any directions are given under this section, or in whose favour an appeal with respect to an application for such directions is determined, within 7 days after the giving of the directions or the determination of the appeal, to deliver to the registrar of companies for registration such a copy of the directions or determination as is prescribed.

203(6) [Penalty on default re s.203(5)] If a person without reasonable excuse fails to deliver a copy as required by subsection (5), he is liable to a fine and, for continued contravention, to a daily default fine.

S.203(1)–(3)

The Secretary of State is empowered by this section to override the official receiver's notice under s.202(3) which initiated the dissolution process, so that the winding up proceeds as before. It also appears from s.203(3)(b) that the Secretary of State may confirm the effect of the notice but delay the dissolution by substituting a longer period than three months for the operation of s.202(5). Subsection (3)(b) amended by the Insolvency Amendment (EU 2015/848) Regulations 2017 (SI 2017/702) regs 1, 2(1), Sch. paras 1, 11 in relation to proceedings opened on or after 26 June 2017 (reg.3) when the Recast EU Regulation 2015/848 came into force.

S.203(4)

The use of the term "appeal" is significant, since it makes it clear that the court may substitute its own decision on the merits of the case for that of the Secretary of State. For the relevant procedure, see IR 2016 r.7.119.

S.203(5)

The seven-day period is extremely short, especially since it runs from the date of the giving of the directions or determination of the appeal, and not from the day when the applicant is notified of the outcome of his application.

It does not appear that there is any obligation to register a decision on the part of the Secretary of State to give no "directions". (However, there is equally no machinery provided to warn the registrar that an application to the Secretary of State has been made: time will continue to run for the purposes of s.202(5) while such an application is under consideration.)

S.203(6)

On penalties, see s.430 and Sch.10.

204 Early dissolution (Scotland)

204(1) [Application] This section applies where a winding-up order has been made by the court in Scotland.

204(2) [Application by liquidator] If after a liquidator has been appointed under section 138 (appointment of liquidator in Scotland) it appears to the liquidator that the realisable assets of the company are insufficient to cover the expenses of the winding up, he may apply to the court for an order that the company be dissolved.

204(3) [Court order] Where the liquidator makes that application, if the court is satisfied that the realisable assets of the company are insufficient to cover the expenses of the winding up and it appears to the court appropriate to do so, the court shall make an order that the company be dissolved in accordance with this section.

204(4) [Copy of order to registrar etc.] A copy of the order shall within 14 days from its date be forwarded by the liquidator to the registrar of companies, who shall forthwith register it; and, at the end of the period of 3 months beginning with the day of the registration of the order, the company shall be dissolved.

204(4A) [Application of s.204(4B): EU insolvency proceedings] Subsection (4B) applies where immediately before the liquidator makes an application under subsection (2), there are EU insolvency proceedings open in respect of the company in one or more other member States.

204(4B) [Duty of liquidator to send statement to registrar] The liquidator must send to the registrar with the copy of the order forwarded under subsection (4) a statement–

(a) identifying those proceedings,

(b) identifying the member State liquidator appointed in each of those proceedings, and

(c) indicating, in relation to each of those member State liquidators, whether that member State liquidator consents to the company being dissolved.

204(4C) [Registrar to register statement] The registrar must forthwith register a statement received under subsection (4B).

204(4D) [Application of s.204(4E)] Subsection (4E) applies where–

(a) the court makes an order under subsection (3) that the company be dissolved in accordance with this section, but

(b) a statement under subsection (4B) indicates that a member State liquidator does not consent to the company being dissolved.

204(4E) [Deemed dissolution] The company is deemed to be dissolved at the end of the period of 3 months beginning with the date (if any) recorded in the register as the date on which the registrar was notified that–

(a) all proceedings identified in the statement under subsection (4B) were closed, or

(b) every member State liquidator appointed in those proceedings consented to the company being dissolved.

204(5) [Court may defer dissolution] The court may, on an application by any person who appears to the court to have an interest, order that the date at which the dissolution of the company is to take effect shall be deferred for such period as the court thinks fit.

204(6) [Copy of s.204(5) order to registrar] It is the duty of the person on whose application an order is made under subsection (5), within 7 days after the making of the order, to deliver to the registrar of companies such a copy of the order as is prescribed.

204(7) [Penalty for non-compliance with s.204(4)] If the liquidator without reasonable excuse fails to comply with the requirements of subsection (4), he is liable to a fine and, for continued contravention, to a daily default fine.

204(8) [Penalty for non-compliance with s.204(6)] If a person without reasonable excuse fails to deliver a copy as required by subsection (6), he is liable to a fine and, for continued contravention, to a daily default fine.

General Note

There is no official receiver in Scotland, so that a private liquidator will be in office in every winding up by the court. In the absence of a public officer comparable with the official receiver, it is necessary in Scotland to refer to the court for decision the question whether an early dissolution of the company is justified. This section accordingly modifies the procedure of ss.202, 203 to meet the different circumstances in Scotland.

S.204(2)

There is no obligation in Scotland to give the company's creditors and contributories the 28-day notice required in England and Wales by s.202(3). In Scotland, on the other hand, the liquidator cannot set any steps in motion to bring about an early dissolution until after the meetings of creditors and contributories have been held. It is reasonable to assume that they will have been made aware of the company's hopeless insolvency at the statutory meetings.

S.204(3)–(8)

The whole of the proceedings in an application for early dissolution in Scotland are dealt with by the court. There is no involvement of the Secretary of State at any stage. Apart from this, the comments to ss.202, 203 apply to the present section.

Provision for EU insolvency proceedings is contained in s.204(4A)–(4E) inserted in relation to Scotland only by the Insolvency Amendment (EU 2015/848) Regulations 2017 (SI 2017/702) regs 1, 2(2)(b), Sch. paras 55, 59 in relation to proceedings opened on or after 26 June 2017 (see reg.3) when the Recast EU Regulation 2015/848 came into force.

On penalties, see s.430 and Sch.10.

205 Dissolution otherwise than under ss.202–204

205(1) [Application] This section applies where the registrar of companies receives–

(a) a final account and statement sent under section 146(4) (final account);

(b) a notice from the official receiver that the winding up of a company by the court is complete.

205(2) [Duty of registrar etc.] The registrar shall, on receipt of the final account and statement or the notice and any statement under section 146(7) or 146A(2), forthwith register them or it; and, subject as follows, at the end of the period of 3 months beginning with the day of the registration of the final account or notice, the company shall be dissolved.

205(2A) [Application of s.202(2B)] Subsection (2B) applies where a statement sent to the registrar under section 146(7) or 146A(2) indicates that a member State liquidator does not consent to the company being dissolved.

205(2B) [Dissolution following EU proceedings] The company is not dissolved at the end of the period mentioned in subsection (2) but is instead dissolved at the end of the period of 3 months beginning with the date (if any) recorded in the register as the date on which the registrar was notified that–

(a) all proceedings identified in the statement under section 146(7) or 146A(2) were closed, or

(b) every member State liquidator appointed in those proceedings consented to the company being dissolved.

205(3) [Deferral by Secretary of State] The Secretary of State may, on the application of the official receiver or any other person who appears to the Secretary of State to be interested, give a direction deferring the date at which the dissolution of the company is to take effect for such period as the Secretary of State thinks fit.

205(4) [Appeal to court] An appeal to the court lies from any decision of the Secretary of State on an application for a direction under subsection (3).

205(5) [Non-application of s.205(3) in Scotland] Subsection (3) does not apply in a case where the winding-up order was made by the court in Scotland, but in such a case the court may, on an application by any person appearing to the court to have an interest, order that the date at which the dissolution of the company is to take effect shall be deferred for such period as the court thinks fit.

205(6) [Copy of direction etc. to registrar] It is the duty of the person–

(a) on whose application a direction is given under subsection (3);

(b) in whose favour an appeal with respect to an application for such a direction is determined; or

(c) on whose application an order is made under subsection (5),

within 7 days after the giving of the direction, the determination of the appeal or the making of the order, to deliver to the registrar for registration such a copy of the direction, determination or order as is prescribed.

205(7) [Penalty for non-compliance with s.205(6)] If a person without reasonable excuse fails to deliver a copy as required by subsection (6), he is liable to a fine and, for continued contravention, to a daily default fine.

S.205(1), (2), (2A), (2B)

Dissolution takes place automatically three months after the registrar has been given the notification by the liquidator or the official receiver required by this section: no court order is required. Special provision is made following EU proceedings. Section 205(2) amended and subss.(2A), (2B) inserted by the Insolvency Amendment (EU 2015/848) Regulations 2017 (SI 2017/702) regs 1, 2, Sch. paras 1, 12 in relation to proceedings opened in England and Wales on or after 26 June 2017 (see reg.3) when the Recast EU Regulation 2015/848 came into force.

Note that there are equivalent amendments to s.205(2) and insertion of equivalent s.205(2A), (2B) in relation to Scotland only by the Insolvency Amendment (EU 2015/848) Regulations 2017 (SI 2017/702) regs 1, 2(2)(b), Sch. paras 55, 60 in relation to proceedings opened on or after 26 June 2017 (see reg.3) when the Recast EU Regulation 2015/848 came into force.

S.205(3)–(4)
The Secretary of State, in England and Wales, and the court are given roles under the present section comparable with those which they discharge in relation to the early liquidation procedure under ss.202(5), 203(3)(b) and 203(4): see, further, the notes to those provisions, and for the relevant procedure, see IR 2016 r.7.119.

S.205(5)
Compare s.204(5), and see the notes to that subsection.

S.205(6), (7)
Compare ss.203(5), (6) and 204(6), (8), and for the relevant rule, see IR 2016 r.7.119.
On penalties, see s.430 and Sch.10.

Chapter X

Malpractice before and during Liquidation; Penalisation of Companies and Company Officers; Investigations and Prosecutions

Offences of fraud, deception, etc.

206 Fraud, etc. in anticipation of winding up

206(1) [Offences by officers] When a company is ordered to be wound up by the court, or passes a resolution for voluntary winding up, any person, being a past or present officer of the company, is deemed to have committed an offence if, within the 12 months immediately preceding the commencement of the winding up, he has–

- (a) concealed any part of the company's property to the value of £500 or more, or concealed any debt due to or from the company, or
- (b) fraudulently removed any part of the company's property to the value of £500 or more, or
- (c) concealed, destroyed, mutilated or falsified any book or paper affecting or relating to the company's property or affairs, or
- (d) made any false entry in any book or paper affecting or relating to the company's property or affairs, or
- (e) fraudulently parted with, altered or made any omission in any document affecting or relating to the company's property or affairs, or
- (f) pawned, pledged or disposed of any property of the company which has been obtained on credit and has not been paid for (unless the pawning, pledging or disposal was in the ordinary way of the company's business).

206(2) [Further offences] Such a person is deemed to have committed an offence if within the period above mentioned he has been privy to the doing by others of any of the things mentioned in paragraphs (c), (d) and (e) of subsection (1); and he commits an offence if, at any time after the commencement of the winding up, he does any of the things mentioned in paragraphs (a) to (f) of that subsection, or is privy to the doing by others of any of the things mentioned in paragraphs (c) to (e) of it.

206(3) ["Officer"] For purposes of this section, "officer" includes a shadow director.

206(4) [Defences] It is a defence–

(a) for a person charged under paragraph (a) or (f) of subsection (1) (or under subsection (2) in respect of the things mentioned in either of those two paragraphs) to prove that he had no intent to defraud, and

(b) for a person charged under paragraph (c) or (d) of subsection (1) (or under subsection (2) in respect of the things mentioned in either of those two paragraphs) to prove that he had no intent to conceal the state of affairs of the company or to defeat the law.

206(5) [Offence re person pawning property etc. as in s.206(1)(f)] Where a person pawns, pledges or disposes of any property in circumstances which amount to an offence under subsection (1)(f), every person who takes in pawn or pledge, or otherwise receives, the property knowing it to be pawned, pledged or disposed of in such circumstances, is guilty of an offence.

206(6) [Penalty] A person guilty of an offence under this section is liable to imprisonment or a fine, or both.

206(7) [Increase, reduction of sums in s.206(1)(a), (b)] The money sums specified in paragraphs (a) and (b) of subsection (1) are subject to increase or reduction by order under section 416 in Part XV.

S.206(1), (2)

This section makes it an offence for an officer of a company to conceal or remove property, falsify entries in the company's books or perpetrate other similar acts after the commencement of a winding up (s.206(2)), and "deems" an officer or past officer to have committed an offence if he has been guilty of any of these acts and a winding up ensues within the next 12 months (s.206(1)). "Book or paper" in s.206(1)(d) was given an extended meaning so as to include computer records in *R. v Taylor* [2011] EWCA Crim 728; [2011] 1 W.L.R. 1809.

The diversion of a debt due to a company into the account of the accused or a third party is equivalent to the "removal" of property for the purposes of s.206(1)(b): *R. v Robinson* [1990] B.C.C. 656.

It may be a defence to a charge under s.206(1) that the liquidator has abandoned the property in question, but this will not be established without proof that the liquidator is aware of its existence—which it will be the duty of the officers of the company (in most cases, the defendants themselves) to declare and deliver up under s.208: *R. v McCredie* [2000] B.C.C. 617.

S.206(3)

The term "officer" is not defined with precision: the definition in IA 1986 s.251 merely states that "officer, in relation to a body corporate, *includes* a director, manager or secretary". A director "includes any person occupying the position of director, by whatever name called" (ibid.). A director (in this extended sense) and a secretary plainly will always be "officers". Shadow directors (for definition, see s.251) are frequently declared to be officers for the purposes of a particular provision, as in the present subsection, and so it is reasonable to infer that where there is no such statement (e.g. as in s.207) the opposite is the case. The same argument would apply in the case of a liquidator: the fact that he is declared to be an officer for the purposes of s.85(2), for example, suggests that he is ordinarily not to be deemed one. This is confirmed by the distinction that appears to be drawn between "officers" on the one hand and liquidators, administrators and receivers on the other (e.g. by ss.133(1) and 212(1), and compare also s.219(3)).

The word "manager", used in CA 2006 s.1173, could well be a source of difficulty. It is not clear whether a person would need to have been appointed to a post carrying managerial responsibilities to come within this concept, or whether it is sufficient that he has taken some part in the management of the company's business, even at a relatively humble level. In *Re a Company (No.00996 of 1979)* [1980] Ch. 138 at 144, Shaw LJ said:

> "The expression 'manager' should not be too narrowly construed. It is not to be equated with a managing or other director or a general manager … [Any] person who in the affairs of the company exercises a supervisory control which reflects the general policy of the company for the time being or which is related to the general administration of the company is in the sphere of management. He need not be a member of the board of directors. He need not be subject to specific instructions from the board".

A number of provisions in the legislation (e.g. IA 1986 ss.212(1)(c), 216(3), 217(4) and CDDA 1986 ss.1(1)(d), 11, 15(4)) refer to a person "taking part in the management" of a company (and compare "involved in the management": IA 1986 s.217(1), CDDA 1986 ss.2, 15(1)). It would not necessarily follow that a person coming within such a formula was a "manager" for the purposes of the present section, but cases decided under these provisions may be of some relevance: see, e.g. *CCA v Brecht* (1987) 7 A.C.L.C. 40; *Re Clasper Group Services Ltd*

(1988) 4 B.C.C. 673; *Drew v Lord Advocate* [1996] S.L.T. 1062; *Re a Company* [1980] Ch. 138; *Re Market Wizard Systems (UK) Ltd* [1998] 2 B.C.L.C. 282; and *R. v Doring* [2002] EWCA Crim 1695; [2002] B.C.C. 838.

Both an administrator and a receiver and manager (including an administrative receiver) discharge functions which can only be described as managerial, but in the leading case of *Re B Johnson & Co (Builders) Ltd* [1955] Ch. 634 a receiver and manager appointed by a debenture-holder was held not to be an "officer" for the purposes of what is now s.212. (The point is now covered by s.212(1)(b).) An administrator has been held to be an "officer" who may be granted relief under the court's discretionary jurisdiction conferred by CA 2006 s.1157: *Re Home Treat Ltd* [1991] B.C.C. 165.

An auditor has been held to be an officer for the purposes of s.212 in a number of cases, e.g. *Re London and General Bank* [1895] 2 Ch. 166; *Re Thomas Gerrard & Son Ltd* [1968] Ch. 455 at 473; and also under other statutory provisions similar to s.206: *R. v Shacter* [1960] 2 Q.B. 252; but the question is not free from doubt: compare CA 2006 s.1157 ("whether or not he is an officer of the company").

Bankers and solicitors and other professional advisers are not, as such, "officers" of the company (*Re Imperial Land Co of Marseilles, Re National Bank* (1870) L.R. 10 Eq. 298), as appears to be confirmed by s.219(3).

S.206(4)

The onus of proof with respect to mens rea is, unusually, put on the defendant. In such a case, the burden of proof on the accused is less than that required at the hands of the prosecution, which must prove the case "beyond reasonable doubt": instead, the burden may be discharged by evidence which satisfies the court on a balance of probabilities: *R. v Carr-Briant* [1943] K.B. 607; *Morton v Confer* [1963] 1 W.L.R. 763; [1963] 2 All E.R. 765. This, at least, was the view taken before the enactment of the Human Rights Act 1986. In *R. v Carass* [2001] EWCA Crim 2845; [2002] 1 W.L.R. 1714, the Court of Appeal took the view that s.206 imposed only an evidentiary, as opposed to a legal, burden of proof on the defendant and that, on this ground, there was no incompatibility with the Human Rights Act. But in *R. (Griffin) v Richmond Magistrates' Court* [2008] EWHC 84 (Admin); [2008] 1 W.L.R. 1525; [2008] 1 B.C.L.C. 681 (a case on s.208, below) the Divisional Court reviewed the authorities, including the House of Lords' rulings in *Sheldrake v DPP* [2005] 1 All E.R. 237; and *R. v Johnstone* [2003] 3 All E.R. 884, and concluded that *R. v Carass* was wrongly decided: the burden of proof under both ss.206 and 208 is a legal burden and, because of the seriousness of these offences, this is compatible with the Human Rights Act on the grounds of reasonableness and proportionality. The issue has also been considered by the Court of Appeal in relation to the corresponding bankruptcy offences in *Re Attorney General's Reference (No.1 of 2004)* [2004] EWCA Crim 1025; [2004] B.P.I.R. 1073, discussed in the note to s.352, below.

S.206(5)

In regard to the offence created by this provision, the normal rule as to onus of proof will apply.

S.206(6)

The sanctions fixed by Sch.10 for these offences and the other offences involving dishonesty defined in the following sections are severe: up to seven years' imprisonment; but the maximum has not been increased in line with changes made to other legislation by the Fraud Act 2006.

On penalties, see s.430 and Sch.10.

S.206(7)

See the note to s.206(1), (2) above.

207 Transactions in fraud of creditors

207(1) [Offences by officers] When a company is ordered to be wound up by the court or passes a resolution for voluntary winding up, a person is deemed to have committed an offence if he, being at the time an officer of the company–

(a) has made or caused to be made any gift or transfer of, or charge on, or has caused or connived at the levying of any execution against, the company's property, or

(b) has concealed or removed any part of the company's property since, or within 2 months before, the date of any unsatisfied judgment or order for the payment of money obtained against the company.

207(2) [Exception] A person is not guilty of an offence under this section–

(a) by reason of conduct constituting an offence under subsection (1)(a) which occurred more than 5 years before the commencement of the winding up, or

211 False representations to creditors

211(1) [Offences by past or present officer] When a company is being wound up, whether by the court or voluntarily, any person, being a past or present officer of the company–

(a) commits an offence if he makes any false representation or commits any other fraud for the purpose of obtaining the consent of the company's creditors or any of them to an agreement with reference to the company's affairs or to the winding up, and

(b) is deemed to have committed that offence if, prior to the winding up, he has made any false representation, or committed any other fraud, for that purpose.

211(2) ["Officer"] For purposes of this section, "officer" includes a shadow director.

211(3) [Penalty] A person guilty of an offence under this section is liable to imprisonment or a fine, or both.

General Note

This section applies only to past and present officers (including shadow directors). The notes to s.206 apply generally to s.211; but the onus of establishing fraud is here placed on the prosecution.

Penalisation of directors and officers

212 Summary remedy against delinquent directors, liquidators, etc.

212(1) [Application] This section applies if in the course of the winding up of a company it appears that a person who–

(a) is or has been an officer of the company,

(b) has acted as liquidator or administrative receiver of the company, or

(c) not being a person falling within paragraph (a) or (b), is or has been concerned, or has taken part, in the promotion, formation or management of the company,

has misapplied or retained, or become accountable for, any money or other property of the company, or been guilty of any misfeasance or breach of any fiduciary or other duty in relation to the company.

212(2) [Interpretation] The reference in subsection (1) to any misfeasance or breach of any fiduciary or other duty in relation to the company includes, in the case of a person who has acted as liquidator of the company, any misfeasance or breach of any fiduciary or other duty in connection with the carrying out of his functions as liquidator of the company.

212(3) [Examination, orders] The court may, on the application of the official receiver or the liquidator, or of any creditor or contributory, examine into the conduct of the person falling within subsection (1) and compel him–

(a) to repay, restore or account for the money or property or any part of it, with interest at such rate as the court thinks just, or

(b) to contribute such sum to the company's assets by way of compensation in respect of the misfeasance or breach of fiduciary or other duty as the court thinks just.

212(4) [Limit on s.212(3) application] The power to make an application under subsection (3) in relation to a person who has acted as liquidator of the company is not exercisable, except with the leave of the court, after he has had his release.

212(5) [Exercise of s.212(3) power] The power of a contributory to make an application under subsection (3) is not exercisable except with the leave of the court, but is exercisable notwithstanding that he will not benefit from any order the court may make on the application.

S.212(1)

This re-enacts, with some amendments introduced by IA 1985, the traditional "misfeasance" section of successive Companies Acts, providing a summary remedy in the liquidation of a company for the restoration of property and the assessment of compensation or damages for breach of duty against its former officers and others. (On the meaning of the term "officer", see the note to s.206(3).) The section applies to de facto directors: *Holland v Revenue and Customs, Re Paycheck Services 3 Ltd* [2010] UKSC 51; [2011] B.C.C. 1. There has been some uncertainty whether shadow directors are within s.212, but the better view (now supported by Lords Hope and Collins in *Re Paycheck Services 3 Ltd*) is that they do not, since other provisions in the Act state specifically that shadow directors are included and this is not so in s.212. (See also *Mumtaz Properties Ltd v Saeed Ahmed* [2011] EWCA Civ 610; *Re Idessa (UK) Ltd* [2011] EWHC 804 (Ch); [2012] B.C.C. 315; *Re Snelling House Ltd* [2012] EWHC 440 (Ch).)

As originally enacted, the section applied to administrators as well as those listed, but all references to administrators were removed by EA 2002 Sch.17 para.18, which came into effect on 15 September 2003. At the same time a separate provision dealing with misfeasance by administrators was enacted in EA 2002 Sch.16, which is now to be found in IA 1986 Sch.B1 para.75, and a saving provision, reinstating s.212 as formerly worded, came into effect under the Enterprise Act 2002 (Commencement No.4 and Transitional Provisions and Savings) Order 2003 (SI 2003/2093 (C. 85)) art.3. This saving provision applies in cases where a petition for an administration order was presented before 15 September 2003, and also in the administration of insolvent partnerships commencing prior to 1 July 2005, limited liability partnerships and bodies which are insurers under FSMA 2000 and SI 2001/2634. There is no mention in the Order of building societies and the public utility companies listed in EA 2002 s.249, but in these cases the original s.212 will continue to apply because s.249 disapplies the new s.8(3) in regard to such bodies. There is also no mention of the supervisor of a CVA, but subs.(2)(c) could no doubt be invoked. The words "breach of trust" in CA 1985 have been replaced by "breach of any fiduciary or other duty", and this also has the effect of extending the coverage of the remedy, for although "breach of trust" and "breach of fiduciary duty" may be regarded as synonymous, it had been held that the former wording did not include claims based on negligence (*Re B Johnson & Co (Builders) Ltd* [1955] Ch. 634). However in *Re D'Jan of London Ltd* [1993] B.C.C. 646 Hoffmann LJ clearly accepted that the section now covers "breaches of any duty including the duty of care", and applied it in a straightforward case of negligence brought against a director. See also *Re Centralcrest Engineering Ltd* [2000] B.C.C. 727 (where a liquidator was held liable); *Re Westlowe Storage & Distribution Ltd* [2000] B.C.C. 851; *Re Pantone 485 Ltd* (below); *Re Continental Assurance Co of London plc* [2001] B.P.I.R. 733 (a lengthy judgment in which it was held that the case in misfeasance against both the executive and the non-executive directors of the company had not been made out); *Re Transocean Equipment Manufacturing & Trading Ltd* [2005] EWHC 2603 (Ch); [2006] B.C.C. 184 (where the acts of misfeasance took place while the company was dissolved); and *Kinlan v Crimmin* [2006] EWHC 779 (Ch); [2007] B.C.C. 106 (where a repurchase of shares had been carried out under professional advice but without complying with all the statutory formal requirements); *Re Idessa (UK) Ltd* [2011] EWHC 804 (Ch); [2012] B.C.C. 315 (director as a fiduciary obliged to account for propriety of payments made); *Re HLC Environmental Projects Ltd* [2013] EWHC 2876 (Ch); [2014] B.C.C. 337 (payments made in breach of fiduciary and statutory duties when director should have been aware that company was insolvent); *Madoff Securities International Ltd v Raven* [2013] EWHC 3147 (Comm) (a wide-ranging review of the duties owed by the director of a solvent company); *Re Mama Milla Ltd; Sharma v Top Brands Ltd* [2015] EWCA Civ 1140; [2016] B.C.C. 1 (nature of the duties owed by a liquidator, and whether fiduciary: liquidator held liable for negligence and failure to get in company's property; plea based on illegality rejected); *Goldtrail Travel Ltd v Aydin* [2014] EWHC 1587 (Ch) (co-defendants held liable for dishonest assistance in director's breach of fiduciary duty; plea of ex turpi causa rejected). See also *Re Snelling House Ltd* [2012] EWHC 440 (Ch).

In *Base Metal Trading Ltd v Shamurin* [2004] EWCA Civ 1316; [2005] 1 W.L.R. 1157; [2005] B.C.C. 325, Arden LJ observed that, in the case of a company incorporated abroad which is being wound up in this country, the content of the duties of directors will be determined by the law of the jurisdiction of incorporation, but s.212 may be invoked to enforce such duties. In *Hague v Nam Tai Electronics Inc* [2008] UKPC 13; [2008] B.C.C. 295 (a misfeasance claim alleging wrongdoing by a liquidator) the Privy Council ruled that, having accepted appointment as liquidator in the jurisdiction of the company's incorporation, it was not open to him to contest the competence of the courts of that jurisdiction to hear the case.

It is well settled that the section creates no new liabilities, but only provides a simpler procedure for the recovery of property or compensation in a winding up. Even here, there are limitations on its use—e.g. it is not available to enforce a contractual debt (*Re Etic Ltd* [1928] Ch. 861), and in *Re Continental Assurance Co of London plc* (above), at 855 it was said to be improper to use it to circumvent the difficulties of establishing a preference claim. Note, however, that the fact that s.212 provides a statutory remedy against a company officer does not in any way exclude the pursuit of common-law remedies in contract and tort against the same person: *A & J Fabrications (Batley) Ltd v*

Grant Thornton [1999] B.C.C. 807. Necessarily, if the company is not in liquidation, neither s.212 nor any of the later sections establishing liability for wrongful trading, preference, etc. can be invoked, but such wrongdoing will normally be actionable at common law at the suit of the company (*GHLM Trading Ltd v Maroo* [2012] EWHC 61 (Ch)). While the company is solvent, breaches of this nature may be condoned by the shareholders under what is usually referred to as the *Duomatic* principle ([1969] 2 Ch. 365), but this plea is not available if the company is insolvent or approaching insolvency: *Re Finch (UK) plc* [2015] EWHC 2430 (Ch). See also *Ball (Liquidator of PV Solar Solutions Ltd) v Hughes* [2017] EWHC 3228 (Ch) where the *Duomatic* principle above was rendered inapplicable in an insolvency case where directors' duty to have regard to the interests of creditors was also a major issue because of the company's insolvency (see CA 2006 s.172(3)).

Where a claim is brought under s.212 against directors alleging negligence and/or breach of duty, it is open to them to claim contribution from professional advisers on whose advice they acted, e.g. insolvency practitioners who had advised that they could continue trading before the company went into liquidation: *Re International Championship Management Ltd* [2006] EWHC 768 (Ch); [2007] B.C.C. 95. Contrast the position where the claim is brought under ss.214, 238 or 239, or where the claim is vested by statute in the liquidator (ibid.).

The question whether a claim under s.212 is statute-barred is determined on the same basis as for other claims. So, in *Re Pantone 485 Ltd* [2002] 1 B.C.L.C. 266, where a director used the company's money for his own benefit in a way which rendered him accountable to it as trustee, the claim was held to be within s.21(1)(b) of the Limitation Act 1980 and accordingly not statute-barred. See also *Re Eurocruit Ltd* [2007] EWHC 1433 (Ch); [2007] B.C.C. 916; *Re Broadside Colours and Chemicals Ltd* [2011] EWHC 1034 (Ch); [2011] 2 B.C.L.C. 597; *Burnden Holdings (UK) Ltd v Fielding* [2018] UKSC 14.

Sums or property recovered under this section are the product of a chose in action vested in the company prior to the liquidation and are accordingly "assets of the company" which are capable of being made the subject of a charge (*Re Anglo-Austrian Printing & Publishing Union* [1895] 2 Ch. 891), or of being assigned by it or the liquidator: *Re Oasis Merchandising Services Ltd* [1998] Ch. 170; [1997] B.C.C. 282.

Where directors make payments in breach of duty to one or more of their number, there may be concurrent liability under this section and under such other provisions as s.214 (wrongful trading) (see, for example, *Roberts v Frohlich* [2011] EWHC 257 (Ch); [2012] B.C.C. 407) and s.239 (preference). In one such case, *Re DKG Contractors Ltd* [1990] B.C.C. 903, it was ordered that liability under the various heads should not be cumulative but that payments made under ss.212 and 239 should go to satisfy the liability under s.214. However, in a later case, *Re Purpoint Ltd* [1991] B.C.C. 121, Vinelott J made orders against the respondent for the payment of separate sums under ss.212 and 214, being satisfied that there was no injustice in the nature of overlap or "double counting" in making the orders cumulative. More recently, in *Re Idessa (UK) Ltd* [2011] EWHC 804 (Ch); [2012] B.C.C. 315, and *Re Kudos Business Solutions Ltd* [2011] EWHC 1436 (Ch), *Re DKG Contractors* has been followed in preference to *Re Purpoint* in order to obviate any risk of double counting. See also the calculations in *Re MDA Investment Management Ltd* [2003] EWHC 2277 (Ch) and [2004] EWHC 42 (Ch); [2005] B.C.C. 783. For a comprehensive discussion of this and related questions, see Roy Goode, *Principles of Corporate Insolvency Law*, 4th edn (2011), at 14–48—14–50. See also *Re Krug International (UK) Ltd* [2008] EWHC 2256 (Ch); [2008] B.P.I.R. 1512 (s.423 claim against foreign third party held properly joined with s.212 proceedings against directors).

A sum awarded against a misfeasant officer under s.212 cannot be set off against a debt due to him from the company: *Re Anglo-French Co-operative Society Ex p. Pelly* (1882) 21 Ch. D. 492; *Manson v Smith (liquidator of Thomas Christy Ltd)* [1997] 2 B.C.L.C. 161. Both cases are discussed in *Global Corporate Ltd v Hale* [2017] EWHC 2277 (Ch) at [58]–[64].

The provisions of s.212 apply to directors of building societies: see Building Societies Act 1986 s.90 and Sch.15.

S.212(2)

This provision is probably intended to remove any doubts on the question whether all the duties of a liquidator or administrator are owed to the company. It is curious, but at the same time it may well be significant, that there is no mention of an administrative receiver in this subsection, even though he is mentioned in s.212(1)(b). *Johnson's* case (above) held that a receiver and manager at common law was not concerned to manage the business for the benefit of the company, but only to realise his creditor's security, and that he was under no duty to the company or its contributories to preserve the goodwill and business of the company. This view was confirmed by the Privy Council in *Downsview Nominees Ltd v First City Corporation Ltd* [1993] A.C. 295; [1993] B.C.C. 46, where it was held that a receiver and manager owes no general duty in negligence to, inter alios, the debtor company to use reasonable care in the exercise of his powers. However, it was also stated in the latter case that equity imposes specific duties on such a receiver, including a duty to exercise his powers in good faith; and that, if a receiver decides to sell the charged property, he must take reasonable care to obtain a proper price. (See also *Medforth v Blake* [2000] Ch. 86; [1999] B.C.C. 771, and the Introductory note to Part III.) There is thus potentially scope (albeit of a limited nature) for s.212 to be invoked against an administrative receiver or a receiver and manager.

S.212(3)

Although a creditor has standing to bring proceedings under s.212, the court can only make an order in favour of the company, and not the individual applicant (*Oldham v Kyrris* [2003] EWCA Civ 1506; [2004] B.C.C. 111). A liquidator owes no duty at common law (in the absence of special circumstances) to an individual creditor: *Fabb v Peters* [2013] EWHC 296 (Ch); [2013] B.P.I.R. 264. This is so even though it may well be arguable, where the defendant is a liquidator, that the duties owed by a liquidator in an insolvent liquidation are owed to the creditors as a class as well as to the company (*Hague v Nam Tai Electronics Inc* (above)). See also *Charalambous v B&C Associates* [2009] EWHC 2601 (Ch); [2013] B.C.C. 491 (no duty in tort owed by administrator to unsecured creditor). An assignee of a creditor's claim has standing: *Mullarkey v Broad* [2007] EWHC 3400 (Ch); [2008] 1 B.C.L.C. 638. A contributory's right to make an application is qualified by s.212(5). An administrator is not given standing by s.212(3), but he may initiate proceedings in the name of the company: *Irwin v Lynch* [2010] EWCA Civ 1153; [2011] 1 W.L.R. 1364.

The court has a discretion under para.(a) to order the respondent to make restitution in whole or in part, and under para.(b) to order payment of "such sum … as the court thinks just". Clearly, in relation to para.(b), the question of quantum is a matter for the discretion of the court (but even so, it does not extend to enabling the court to disregard the need to establish causation: *Re Simmon Box (Diamonds) Ltd, Cohen v Selby* [2002] B.C.C. 82). In *Re D'Jan of London Ltd* (above) the respondent was ordered to pay a sum which was less than the company's actual loss. However under para.(a) the court (although empowered to order restoration of "all or any part" of the misapplied money or property) does not have a discretion which is similarly unfettered: in particular, it will not reopen a decision as to quantum which has already been settled in the course of the liquidation or in other proceedings: *Re AMF International Ltd* [1996] B.C.C. 335.

Section 1157 of the Companies Act 2006 (formerly CA 1985 s.727) empowers the court, in any proceedings against an officer or auditor of a company for (inter alia) negligence, breach of duty or breach of trust, to relieve the defendant either wholly or partly from liability if he has acted honestly and reasonably and ought, in the circumstances, fairly to be excused. This provision has been invoked in many cases brought under IA 1986 s.212 (and, indeed, it was on this provision that Hoffmann LJ relied in the *D'Jan* case). Directors who continued trading on professional advice were held not to be liable either for misfeasance under s.212 or wrongful trading under s.214 (*Re Continental Assurance Co of London plc (No.4)* [2007] B.C.L.C. 289); and in *Re Ortega Associates* Ltd [2007] EWHC 2046 (Ch); [2008] B.C.C. 256 a director was held not liable under s.212 for the dishonesty of a fellow director when he had been advised by his solicitor to take no action; the deputy judge went on to hold that even if there had been any breach of duty he should be wholly relieved from liability under s.727. Note also *Hedger v Adams* [2015] EWHC 2540 (Ch); [2016] B.C.C. 390 (director held not negligent but would in any case have been granted relief). In *Re Marini Ltd* [2003] EWHC 234 (Ch); [2004] B.C.C. 172 it was said that the court would have the greatest difficulty in thinking it ever likely that a defaulting director should be granted relief if the consequence of doing so would be to leave the director enjoying benefits at the expense of creditors which he would never have received but for the default; and in *Re Loquitur Ltd* [2003] EWHC 999 (Ch); [2003] 2 B.C.L.C. 442 Etherton J said that in view of the terms of CA 1985 s.270 [now CA 2006 s.836] he had no jurisdiction to grant relief under this provision from liability for the wrongful payment of a dividend if the consequence was to leave the company insolvent or potentially so. However, rather paradoxically, his Lordship went on to observe that the court's discretion under s.212 was additional to that under the present section and was not subject to a similar limitation, and in exercise of the former thought it appropriate to limit the amount that the respondents were ordered to pay. In *Burnden Holdings (UK) Ltd (in liq.) v Fielding* [2017] EWHC 2118 (Ch) at [84] it was considered (also in a case on distributions under what is now CA 2006 s.836) that there was no invariable rule that relief should not be granted to the detriment of creditors of an insolvent company: everything depended on all the circumstances, including the nature of the breach of duty which gave rise to the claim against the directors. See also *Re MDA Investment Management Ltd* [2003] EWHC 227 (Ch) and [2004] EWHC 42 (Ch); [2005] B.C.C. 783, where relief was refused to a director who had acted honestly but not reasonably (reasonableness being an issue to be determined on an objective basis); *PNC Telecom plc v Thomas (No.2)* [2007] EWHC 2157 (Ch); [2008] 2 B.C.L.C. 95. See also *Holland v Revenue and Customs, Re Paycheck Services 3 Ltd* [2010] UKSC 51; [2011] B.C.C. 1, where the Supreme Court ruled that the discretion conferred by s.212 empowers the court to reduce the amount that the defendant has to pay, but not to exonerate him altogether from liability. However, there is no similar limitation under the additional discretion conferred by CA 2006 s.1157, if the court finds that he has acted honestly and reasonably and ought fairly to be excused.

The question whether a defendant should be granted relief under s.1157 is fact-sensitive and not suitable for summary determination: *Rawnsley v Weatherall Green & Smith North Ltd* [2010] B.C.C. 406; *Phillips v McGregor-Paterson* [2009] EWHC 2385 (Ch); [2010] 1 B.C.L.C. 72 and reiterated in *Burnden Holdings (UK) Ltd (in liq.) v Fielding* [2017] EWHC 2118 (Ch). In *Rawnsley* HHJ Behrens also expressed the view that it was "seriously arguable" that a liquidator was not within the ambit of s.1157. However, in *Re Powertrain Ltd* [2015] EWHC 3998 (Ch); [2016] B.C.C. 216 when the matter was more fully argued, Newey J concluded that a liquidator was an "officer" and accordingly entitled to relief.

A defendant who wishes to apply for relief under s.1157 should give notice of the intention to do so at the earliest opportunity to avoid adjournment and further evidence: *Cullen Investments Ltd v Brown* [2017] EWHC 2793 (Ch).

S.212(4)

For the release of a liquidator, see ss.173, 174, and an administrator, Sch.B1 para.98. In *Parkinson Engineering Services plc v Swan* [2009] EWCA Civ 1366; [2010] 1 B.C.L.C. 163 a claim in negligence had originally been brought by the liquidator in the company's name against the company's former administrators, but the administration order was discharged when the company was ordered to be wound up, and the administrators had been granted their release. The Court allowed an application brought by the liquidator to amend the proceedings by substituting himself as claimant and granting him leave under s.212(5) to proceed notwithstanding their release. This approach was followed in *Irwin v Lynch* [2010] EWCA Civ 1153.

S.212(5)

Formerly, a contributory had standing to apply without the leave of the court, but only when he could show that he had an interest in the outcome of the proceedings. The subsection in its present form runs counter to the approach reflected in such decisions as *Re Rica Gold Washing Co* (1879) 11 Ch. D. 36: see the notes to ss.124(2), (3), 172(1), (2) above. There is no comparable statutory provision where a creditor is the applicant, but it has been held (in relation to Sch.B1 para.75) that in order to have standing an unsecured creditor must show that he will have a pecuniary interest in the relief sought: *Re Coniston Hotel (Kent) LLP, Berntsen v Tait* [2014] EWHC 1100 (Ch).

A contributory may not apply for leave unless the company is in liquidation: he must instead use the derivative action procedure: *Wightman v Bennett* [2005] B.P.I.R. 470.

213 Fraudulent trading

213(1) [Application] If in the course of the winding up of a company it appears that any business of the company has been carried on with intent to defraud creditors of the company or creditors of any other person, or for any fraudulent purpose, the following has effect.

213(2) [Court may hold persons liable] The court, on the application of the liquidator may declare that any persons who were knowingly parties to the carrying on of the business in the manner above-mentioned are to be liable to make such contributions (if any) to the company's assets as the court thinks proper.

General Note

The Companies Acts have for a long time contained provisions dealing with "fraudulent trading", making it both a criminal offence (CA 2006 s.993) and a ground for imposing personal liability upon those concerned (CA 1985 s.630, now replaced by the present section). Originally, both the criminal and the civil sanctions could be invoked only in a winding up, but the criminal provision has for some years applied without this limitation.

As enacted, the fraudulent trading provision applied only in a liquidation, but SBBEA 2015 by s.117(1), (2), with effect from 1 October 2015, has extended its scope so as to apply also in an administration. This has been done, not by an amendment to s.213, but by inserting a new s.246ZA into IA 1986. As the wording of s.246ZA is virtually identical to that of s.213, the commentary which follows applies to both regimes.

The Cork Committee (*Report*, Ch.44) considered that the previous law in this area was inadequate to deal with irresponsible trading, mainly because the courts have always insisted on the very strict standards of pleading and proof which are invariably applied in cases of fraud. It is not enough, for "fraudulent trading", to show that the company continued to run up debts when the directors knew that it was insolvent; there has to be "actual dishonesty, involving real moral blame" (*Re Patrick and Lyon Ltd* [1933] Ch. 786). (See also *Aktieselskabet Dansk Skibsfinansiering v Brothers* [2001] 2 B.C.L.C. 324; and *Bernasconi v Nicholas Bennett & Co* [2000] B.C.C. 921.)

The Committee recommended that while this should continue to be the approach in criminal proceedings for fraudulent trading, civil liability to pay compensation could arise where loss was suffered as a result of "unreasonable" conduct, which they proposed should be termed "wrongful trading", and that for this purpose the more relaxed standard of proof appropriate to civil proceedings should apply. The former provision creating civil liability for fraudulent trading (CA 1985 s.630) could be subsumed into the new law of wrongful trading.

In the event, the legislators adopted the Committee's recommendations on wrongful trading in broad terms, but they did so by creating an *additional* new provision (s.214, below) and left the former law on fraudulent trading intact, with one or two minor amendments (the present section). There is, however, now less reason for liquidators to invoke it, since the concept of wrongful trading, with its less onerous standard of proof, is wide enough to include all cases of fraudulent trading perpetrated by directors, and for all practical purposes the consequences will be the same. However, s.213 continues to have a role to play where allegations of fraudulent trading are made against other parties, as is dramatically illustrated by the number of cases brought by the liquidators of BCCI: see *Re BCCI, Morris v State Bank of India* [1999] B.C.C. 943; further proceedings [2003] EWHC 1868 (Ch); [2003] B.C.C. 735; and *Morris v Bank of India* [2004] EWHC 528 (Ch); [2004] B.C.C. 404 (and, on appeal, [2005] EWCA Civ 693; [2005] B.C.C. 739); *Morris v Bank of America National Trust* [2000] B.C.C. 1076; *Re BCCI, Banque Arabe Internationale d'Investissement SA v Morris* [2002] B.C.C. 407.

In *Re Overnight Ltd* [2009] EWHC 601 (Ch); [2010] B.C.C. 787 it was ruled that for the purposes of the Statutes of Limitation a cause of action under s.213 arises when the winding-up order is made and not at any earlier date, because the appointment of a liquidator (and not a provisional liquidator) is necessary since only he is authorised to issue proceedings. It would follow that a cause of action under s.246ZA arises on the commencement of the administration.

The Supreme Court has confirmed that s.213 has extra-territorial effect, so that "any persons" resident outside the jurisdiction who are knowingly parties to the fraudulent trading may be liable, and the section is directed to recovering assets wherever they might be: *Jetivia SA v Bilta (UK) Ltd* [2015] UKSC 23; [2015] B.C.C. 343.

At common law, the defence *ex turpi causa non oritur actio* prevents a person from benefiting from a fraud to which he was a party. It was held in *Jetivia SA v Bilta* (above) that this defence did not apply to a claim under s.213 where the company which (through its directors) was allegedly a party to the fraud was a victim rather than a wrongdoer. The scope of the illegality defence is the subject of some controversy and awaits further consideration by the Supreme Court: see S. Griffin (2015) 374 Co. L.N. 1.

The Fraud Act 2006, which came into force on 15 January 2007, increased the maximum penalty for contravention of CA 2006 s.993 from seven to ten years' imprisonment (s.10(1)). It also redefined various offences involving fraud or dishonesty, and in particular extended the scope of the fraudulent trading offence (CA 2006 s.993) so as to include being a party to the fraudulent carrying on of a business by a sole trader or other person who is outside the reach of s.993 (s.9).

In an action under s.213 or s.246ZA it is necessary for the liquidator to plead and prove dishonesty. In *Atkinson v Corcoran* [2011] EWHC 3484 (Ch) Bean J contrasted this position with that in a claim to recover preferences under s.239, where it is sufficient for the liquidator to list the disputed payments and thereby impose the onus of justifying them on to the defendant directors.

The extension of the fraudulent and wrongful trading provisions so as to include administrations as from 1 October 2015 did not appear on the face of the legislation to apply to bodies other than companies, such as LLPs, insolvent partnerships and building societies. There was no clue to this poser in SBEEA 2015 itself, but eventually the Insolvency (Miscellaneous Amendments) Regulations 2017 (SI 2017/1119) from 8 December 2017 brought the regime for LLPs (by amendments to the Limited Liability Partnerships Regulations 2001 (SI 2001/1090)) and insolvent partnerships (by amendments to the Insolvent Partnerships Order 1994 (SI 1994/2421)) into line with the insolvency procedures that apply to companies. Fraudulent and wrongful trading were applied to building societies in administration by the Deregulation Act 2015, the Small Business, Enterprise and Employment Act 2015 and the Insolvency (Amendment) Act (Northern Ireland) 2016 (Consequential Amendments and Transitional Provisions) Regulations 2017 (SI 2017/400) as from 6 April 2017.

S.213(1)

The section, unlike the equivalent criminal provision (see above), applies only in a winding up (or, following SBEEA 2015 reform, an administration).

The words "or for any fraudulent purpose" could not be wider, and should not be construed in any limiting way. The wording is certainly wide enough to include frauds committed against potential creditors: see *R. v Kemp* [1988] Q.B. 645; (1988) 4 B.C.C. 203. See also *Re L Todd (Swanscombe) Ltd* [1990] B.C.C. 125 (fraudulent evasion of value added tax). However, in *Morphitis v Bernasconi* [2002] EWCA Civ 289; [2003] Ch. 552; [2003] B.C.C. 540 the Court of Appeal ruled that, although a business may be found to have been carried on with intent to defraud creditors even where only one creditor is shown to have been defrauded, it does not necessarily follow that this is the case whenever a fraud on a creditor has been perpetrated. In such a situation the appropriate remedy may be for the creditor to pursue his own remedy under the general law, and not for the liquidator to seek a contribution to the general assets of the company in the winding up.

In *Bank of India v Morris* [2005] EWCA Civ 693; [2005] B.C.C. 739, the Bank of India was held liable under s.213 on the ground that it had knowingly been a party to frauds committed by officers of BCCI. The Court of Appeal held that it was not necessary to show that any members of the board of the Bank of India had knowledge of the fraud: the appropriate rule of attribution for the purposes of s.213 and its policy was to fix the bank with the knowledge of the employee who had authority to conclude the transactions in question; and it was immaterial that he had acted dishonestly and in breach of his duty to his employer.

A company cannot be treated as "carrying on business" after the date on which a winding-up petition was presented if a winding-up order is subsequently made, and so any transactions made after that date are incapable of constituting fraudulent trading: *Carman v Cronos Group SA* [2005] EWHC 2403 (Ch); [2006] B.C.C. 451. This case is also authority for the following: (a) that the period of fraudulent trading is not interrupted during the time when the company concerned has been struck off but later reinstated, and (b) that where money has been taken from the defendant and wrongfully paid to third parties without resulting in any loss to the company concerned, this does not come within s.213.

S.213(2)

Two changes are made from the former law.

First, it is only the liquidator or administrator who has standing to apply for relief. Previously, an individual creditor or contributory could also apply, but this was thought undesirable because it might encourage a creditor to put improper pressure upon directors to settle his claim personally.

Secondly, the order which the court may make declares the wrongdoers "liable to make such contributions (if any) to the company's assets as the court thinks proper". This makes it clear that any sums ordered to be paid must go into the general funds in the hands of the liquidator or administrator and be held for the benefit of the whole body of creditors. Under the previous wording, the court had power to order that a defendant should directly reimburse a particular creditor (*Re Cyona Distributors Ltd* [1967] Ch. 889; *Re Gerald Cooper Chemicals Ltd (in liq.)* [1978] Ch. 262). However, a creditor may have a claim for damages directly against a director (e.g. for fraud), independently of s.213: *Contex Drouzhba Ltd v Wiseman* [2007] EWCA Civ 1201; [2008] B.C.C. 301.

In other respects, the law remains the same. Thus, those who may be made liable are "any persons who were knowingly parties" to the fraudulent trading (who need not have any connection with the company itself: *Re BCCI, Banque Arabe Internationale d'Investissement SA v Morris* (above)). This may be contrasted with the wrongful trading provision (s.214) which is limited in its scope to directors and former directors, but pointedly avoids the words "parties to" (and, indeed, "business" or "trading").

In certain cases under the former law it was held appropriate to include a punitive as well as a compensatory element in the court's order, but in *Morphitis v Bernasconi* (above) the Court of Appeal has denied that there is any such power: to make such an award would be foreign to the principle underlying s.213. This was reiterated in *Re Mavisat Ltd* (unreported, 11 December 2017), in which the court went on to mention that s.213(2) did not use the language of loss or causation; prior to the 1986 Act the court's primary power was to declare that any person who was knowingly a party to fraudulent trading should be "personally responsible, without any limitation of liability, for all or any of the debts or other liabilities of the company" but the changed wording in s.213(2) remained relatively new with little established jurisprudence to draw on in relation to the point.

The right to bring proceedings under s.213, and the fruits of any such proceeding, were incapable of assignment at common law (*Re Oasis Merchandising Services Ltd* [1998] Ch. 170; [1997] B.C.C. 282) but this has been reversed by statute (s.246ZD: see the notes to that section and Sch.4 para.6). The proceeds of any action brought under s.213 fall into the general assets in the hands of the liquidator or administrator and are not caught by any floating charge (s.176ZB(3)(a)).

In *Re Overnight Ltd (No.2)* [2010] EWHC 613 (Ch); [2010] B.C.C. 796 it was held that where liability is established against more than one defendant, the liability of each should be fixed separately, that the contribution need not be the same for each defendant and that it was open to the court to declare that liability should be joint and several. On the facts, one defendant was held fully liable for the company's loss, but a second liable, on a joint and several basis, for only 50 per cent of that loss. In further proceedings (*Re Overnight Ltd (No.3)* [2010] EWHC 1587 (Ch); [2010] B.C.C. 808) it was contended that the liquidator's delay in commencing proceedings had been unreasonable with the result that interest forming part of the loss had unnecessarily increased, but Roth J declined to exercise discretion to reduce the sum payable.

Further provisions relating to proceedings for fraudulent trading are contained in s.215, below.

In addition to the civil liability to pay compensation under this section and the criminal sanctions of CA 2006 s.993, a person who is guilty of fraudulent trading may be made the subject of a disqualification order: see CDDA 1986 ss.4, 10.

214 Wrongful trading

214(1) [Declaration by court, on application] Subject to subsection (3) below, if in the course of the winding up of a company it appears that subsection (2) of this section applies in relation to a person who is or has been a director of the company, the court, on the application of the liquidator, may declare that

that person is to be liable to make such contribution (if any) to the company's assets as the court thinks proper.

214(2) [Application] This subsection applies in relation to a person if–

(a) the company has gone into insolvent liquidation,

(b) at some time before the commencement of the winding up of the company, that person knew or ought to have concluded that there was no reasonable prospect that the company would avoid going into insolvent liquidation or entering insolvent administration, and

(c) that person was a director of the company at that time;

but the court shall not make a declaration under this section in any case where the time mentioned in paragraph (b) above was before 28th April 1986.

214(3) [Limit on declaration] The court shall not make a declaration under this section with respect to any person if it is satisfied that after the condition specified in subsection (2)(b) was first satisfied in relation to him that person took every step with a view to minimising the potential loss to the company's creditors as (on the assumption that he had knowledge of the matter mentioned in subsection (2)(b)) he ought to have taken.

214(4) [Interpretation of s.214(2), (3)] For the purposes of subsections (2) and (3), the facts which a director of a company ought to know or ascertain, the conclusions which he ought to reach and the steps which he ought to take are those which would be known or ascertained, or reached or taken, by a reasonably diligent person having both–

(a) the general knowledge, skill and experience that may reasonably be expected of a person carrying out the same functions as are carried out by that director in relation to the company, and

(b) the general knowledge, skill and experience that that director has.

214(5) [Interpretation of s.214(4)] The reference in subsection (4) to the functions carried out in relation to a company by a director of the company includes any functions which he does not carry out but which have been entrusted to him.

214(6) [Interpretation re insolvent liquidation] For the purposes of this section a company goes into insolvent liquidation if it goes into liquidation at a time when its assets are insufficient for the payment of its debts and other liabilities and the expenses of the winding up.

214(6A) [Interpretation of insolvent administration] For the purposes of this section a company enters insolvent administration if it enters administration at a time when its assets are insufficient for the payment of its debts and other liabilities and the expenses of the administration.

214(7) ["Director"] In this section "director" includes a shadow director.

214(8) [Section 213] This section is without prejudice to section 213.

General Note

For the background to this provision, see the note to s.213 above. As enacted, the wrongful trading provision applied only in a liquidation, but SBBEA by s.117(1), (2), with effect from 1 October 2015, has extended its scope so as to apply also in an administration. This has been done, not by an amendment to s.214, but by inserting a new s.246ZB into IA 1986. As the wording of s.246ZB corresponds closely to that of s.214, the commentary which follows applies to both regimes. For additional commentary on some minor points, see also the note to s.246ZB. Consequential amendments were made to s.214(2)(b) and (3), and s.214(6A) inserted, by SBEEA s.117(3) as from 1 October 2015.

On the question whether the new provision applies to bodies other than companies, such as insolvent partnerships and LLPs, see the note to s.213.

The section, according to the marginal note, is concerned with "wrongful trading"; but it is notable that the word "trading" is not used in the text of the Act. (The marginal note may not normally be used as an aid for the construction of the text: *Chandler v Director of Public Prosecutions* [1964] A.C. 763 (but some exceptions are noted in Halsbury, *Laws of England*, 5th edn, Vol.96, para.1113).) The section itself is singularly imprecise in defining just what conduct on the part of a director will bring him within its scope.

The Cork Committee (*Report*, para.1806) did put forward its own draft definition of "wrongful trading", the essential part of which read: "... at any time when the company is insolvent or unable to pay its debts as they fall due it incurs further debts or other liabilities to other persons without a reasonable prospect of meeting them in full". However, this definition was explicitly rejected by Parliament when an attempt was made to introduce it as an amendment to the Insolvency Bill 1985, and so it would be wrong to refer to it for guidance on the meaning of the present section. In particular, there may be wrongful trading under s.214 even though the company does not incur further debts: one example mentioned during the parliamentary debate was the case where a company allows its assets to be depleted, e.g. by the payment of excessive directors' fees. It was, presumably, a concern to ensure that this kind of conduct was caught that led the draftsman to omit the word "trading" from his formulation. In *Paton v Martin* [2016] SC Air 57 it was held that selling some of the company's main assets and paying the proceeds into the personal account of one of the directors was "trading" for the purposes of the section.

The amount of contribution to be ordered is left entirely to the court's discretion, and is not related by the terms of the Act either to any particular period of trading or to the loss suffered by the company or creditors. However, in *Re Produce Marketing Consortium Ltd* (1989) 5 B.C.C. 569 at 597, Knox J said:

> "In my judgment the jurisdiction under sec. 214 is primarily compensatory rather than penal. Prime facie the appropriate amount that a director is declared to be liable to contribute is the amount by which the company's assets can be discerned to have been depleted by the director's conduct which caused the discretion under sec. 214(1) to arise. However Parliament has indeed chosen very wide words of discretion and it would be undesirable to seek to spell out limits on that discretion... The fact that there was no fraudulent intent is not of itself a reason for fixing the amount at a nominal or low figure, for that would amount to frustrating what I discern as Parliament's intention in adding sec. 214 to sec. 213 in the *Insolvency Act* 1986, but I am not persuaded that it is right to ignore that fact totally".

In *Re Purpoint Ltd* [1991] B.C.C. 121 and *Re Kudos Business Solutions Ltd* [2011] EWHC 1436 (Ch), where the company's accounts were in disarray so that it was difficult to assess its net asset position at the relevant dates, the respondents were ordered to pay a sum equal to the aggregate of debts incurred after the date on which they ought to have concluded that insolvent liquidation was inevitable.

Although the section is silent on the question of causation, it must be shown that if the defendant had complied with his duties to the requisite standard the loss in question would not have resulted (as a matter of probability): *Lexi Holdings plc v Luqman* [2008] EWHC 1639 (Ch); [2008] 2 B.C.L.C. 725 at [40]. In that case the company's managing director, S, had defrauded it of some £60 million. The defendant non-executive directors had remained inactive and (inter alia) had not disclosed to the other directors their knowledge that S had a criminal record. They were held not liable for the loss because the likely result of disclosing this would have been nothing more than the resignation of the other directors. In *Re Ralls Builders Ltd, Grant v Ralls* [2016] EWHC 243 (Ch); [2016] B.C.C. 293 the company's financial situation had deteriorated to a position where the directors should have concluded that insolvent liquidation was inevitable, but they were excused from making a contribution under s.214 because it was held that the company had suffered no loss caused by their continuing to trade and that had not worsened the position of the creditors as a whole. The liquidators were later unsuccessful in an application for a contribution order against the directors in relation to the liquidators' increased costs by the company continuing to trade [2016] EWHC 1812 (Ch); [2016] B.C.C. 581. For critique see Moss [2017] 30 Insolv. Int. 49 and 88. This point as to a need for a casual connection between the amount of a contribution order under s.214 and the continuation of trading was also adopted in *Brooks v Armstrong* [2016] EWHC 2893 (Ch); [2017] B.C.C. 99.

In *Re Marini Ltd* [2003] EWHC 334 (Ch); [2004] B.C.C. 172, HHJ Seymour thought that the powers of the court under s.214 could not arise unless it was demonstrated that the company was, at the date of the actual liquidation, worse off than it would have been if it had ceased trading at the date when the director(s) ought to have realised that insolvent liquidation was inevitable. With respect, this view ignores the relevance of the causation factor. If this can be brought into account in order to reduce the director's liability (see *Re Brian D Pierson (Contractors) Ltd* [1999] B.C.C. 26), it must be just as relevant if the company receives an unexpected windfall which leaves it better off despite the continued wrongful trading.

For a highly critical article on the denial of contribution liability for wrongful trading where there has been no increase in the net deficiency as evinced in several of the above cases, see Moss (2017) 30 (4) Insol. Int. 49–53.

In the light of the ruling of the Court of Appeal in *Morphitis v Bernasconi* [2002] EWCA Civ 289; [2003] Ch. 552; [2003] B.C.C. 540, it will not be appropriate to include a punitive element in the amount of contribution awarded (and it was repeated in *Brooks v Armstrong* that the award is compensatory rather than punitive): see the note to s.213(2), above.

Summary judgment on a s.214 claim was awarded in *Re Bangla Television Ltd* [2009] EWHC 1632 (Ch); [2010] B.C.C. 143. In *Re Nine Miles Down UK Ltd, Singla v Hedman* [2009] EWHC 3510 (Ch); [2010] B.C.C. 674, summary judgment was refused but a contribution order for wrongful trading was later made by Peter Smith J at the full trial (*Singla v Hedman (No.2)* [2010] EWHC 902 (Ch); [2010] B.C.C. 684).

Where a claim under s.214 is brought against a number of directors, liability is several and not joint and several, that is to say that the position of each individual has to be separately assessed, and payment by one does not discharge the liability of any other: *Re Continental Assurance Co of London plc* [2001] B.P.I.R. 733 at 846–848. However, it was also said in this case that the court may, in its discretion, order that the liability of any two or more directors should be joint and several for the whole or part of the sum which the court has assessed for contribution to the company's assets. In *Paton v Martin* [2016] SC Air 57 one of several directors who was not directly involved in the wrongful trading was held jointly and severally liable with the other directors because he was in breach of his more general responsibilities as a director.

In an appropriate case, an application may be made under s.214 against the foreign directors of a foreign company which is being wound up in this jurisdiction as an unregistered company: *Re Howard Holdings Ltd* [1998] B.C.C. 549.

There will plainly be cases in which claims will be made against the former director of a company both under this section and under some other provisions of the Act, e.g. s.212 (misfeasance) or s.239 (preference). In such a case there may be no injustice in making orders which impose cumulative liability on the defendant: *Re Purpoint Ltd* [1991] B.C.C. 121. However, in *Re DKG Contractors Ltd* [1990] B.C.C. 903 the court ruled that payments made under ss.212 and 239 should go to satisfy the liability under s.214, and that enforcement should be limited to what was necessary to pay the company's creditors and the costs and expenses of the liquidation. (See also *Re Idessa (UK) Ltd* [2011] EWHC 804 (Ch); *Re Kudos Business Solutions Ltd* [2011] EWHC 1436 (Ch).) On this and related questions, see the note to s.212(1).

It has been ruled that, as a matter of law, CA 2006 s.1157 [formerly CA 1985 s.727] (which empowers the court to relieve a director from liability for breach of duty where he has acted honestly and reasonably and ought fairly to be excused) is not available to a director in s.214 proceedings: *Re Produce Marketing Consortium Ltd (Halls v David)* [1989] 1 W.L.R. 745; (1989) 5 B.C.C. 399.

A claim under s.214 (and, similarly, a claim under s.213) is a "claim for the recovery of a sum recoverable under any enactment" within s.9(1) of the Limitation Act 1980, and the appropriate limitation period is six years, reckoned from the date when the company went into insolvent liquidation or administration: *Re Farmizer (Products) Ltd, Moore v Gadd* [1997] B.C.C. 655. However even if proceedings are commenced within the limitation period, unreasonable delay in prosecuting the claim may justify a striking-out order (ibid.).

The provisions of ss.214–217 and 246ZB apply to the directors of building societies (Building Societies Act 1986 Sch.15 para.1(b)). In regard to limited liability partnerships, see the note preceding s.215 below.

S.214(1)

Four points may be noted:

(1) The section applies only to present and past directors (including shadow directors: s.214(7)). In *Re a Company (No.005009 of 1987)* (1988) 4 B.C.C. 424 (interlocutory proceedings in the saga of *Re M C Bacon Ltd*: see [1990] B.C.C. 78 at 79G) Knox J ruled that a company's bank which, on becoming apprised of the fact that its client company is in financial difficulties, makes recommendations to its directors as to the future conduct of its business could, in principle, incur liability under the section as a "shadow director"—or, at least, that on the evidence before him the case was not so obviously unsustainable that an allegation to that effect should be struck out without proceeding to trial. A bank would not, however (it is submitted), risk liability as a shadow director if its requirements were expressed as conditions of extending loan facilities to the company rather than as instructions. (Compare the views expressed in *Re PFTZM Ltd (in liq.)* [1995] B.C.C. 280.) In *Re Hydrodan (Corby) Ltd* [1994] B.C.C. 161, Millett J accepted as correct a concession by counsel that s.214 applies also to de facto directors. (See further on this point the notes to s.251, below.) On the question whether a non-executive director may be liable for wrongful trading, see *Re Langreen Ltd* (unreported, 21 October 2011), where the substance of what the director did was held to be the determining factor. Proceedings may be brought against the estate of a deceased director: *Re Sherborne Associates Ltd* [1995] B.C.C. 40.

(2) The remedy is available only in a winding up or administration.

(3) Only the liquidator or administrator has standing to bring proceedings.

(4) Any sum paid by a defendant goes into the general assets in the hands of the liquidator or administrator. Accordingly, it will not be caught by a charge over the assets of the company (as is now confirmed by

s.176ZB(2)(b)). Both the right to bring proceedings and the fruits of any such litigation may be assigned to a third party (s.264ZD, reversing the position at common law). See the note to Sch.4 paras 6, 13.

The comments to s.213 on these points are also relevant for this subsection.

A person held liable under this section may also have a disqualification order made against him: see CDDA 1986 s.10, although the power appears to be used sparingly (see *Re Brian D Pierson (Contractors) Ltd* [1999] B.C.C. 26). Alternatively, an application under this section may be consolidated with proceedings for a disqualification order, as was done in *Official Receiver v Doshi* [2001] 2 B.C.L.C. 235.

S.214(2)

On the meaning of "has gone into insolvent liquidation" see s.214(6); and for "the commencement of the winding up" see ss.86 and 129.

28 April 1986 was the date when this provision (as IA 1985 s.15) was first brought into force (SI 1986/463).

The words "knew or ought to have concluded" are to be read in conjunction with s.214(4). See the note to that provision, below.

Note that a director does not contravene the section simply by allowing the company to continue to trade when it is insolvent, or when he knows or ought to know that it is insolvent (on either a balance-sheet or cash-flow test): the question is whether he knows or ought to have concluded that there is no reasonable prospect of avoiding insolvent liquidation: *Re Hawkes Hill Publishing Co Ltd* [2007] B.C.C. 937. See also *Roberts v Frohlich* [2011] EWHC 257 (Ch); [2012] B.C.C. 407; *Re Langreen Ltd* (above); *Re Ralls Builders Ltd, Grant v Ralls* [2016] EWHC 243 (Ch); [2016] B.C.C. 293. Where the liquidator alleges that a respondent knew or ought to have concluded that there was no reasonable prospect of avoiding insolvent liquidation by reference to specific dates, but fails to make out his case as to the dates pleaded, he is not entitled to substitute later dates: *Re Sherborne Associates Ltd* [1995] B.C.C. 40. In *Nicholson v Fielding* (unreported, 15 September 2017) the directors of a company in the car transportation business were held to have acted reasonably in the circumstances in continuing to trade despite apparent balance sheet insolvency: the question of wrongful trading could not be addressed by looking at the company's business in an economic vacuum, particularly given the uncertain contractual arrangements of the car logistics industry and the effect of the global financial crisis on that market at the time, so that an objective director would not have concluded at the relevant date that the company was doomed. This appears to give the courts a broad remit but, it seems likely that not every judge would appear so lenient.

S.214(3)

The section, as has been noted, pointedly avoids giving any concrete meaning to the concept of "wrongful trading" or any positive guidance as to the types of conduct which will lead to liability. There is thus a major gap in the law, as framed, which is having to be filled by decisions of the courts in test cases. The only objective facts that need to be established are those relating to the winding up of the company, its insolvency, and that the director held office at the material time (s.214(2)); beyond that, liability turns on his knowledge or imputed knowledge (s.214(2)(b)) and his failure to take "every step with a view to minimising the potential loss to the company's creditors as … he ought to have taken". What a director knows, or must be taken to know, for these purposes is assessed by a mixture of subjective and objective tests (see the note to s.214(4) below).

The phrases "took *every* step" and "*minimising* the potential loss to creditors" seem, at first sight, rather overstated. However, there is no doubt that the use of "every step" was deliberate: a proposed amendment to "every reasonable step" was expressly rejected in Parliament; and on similar reasoning, we must assume that "minimise" was fully intended, rather than, say, "reduce" or "avert".

The bracketed words in the subsection credit a director, for the purpose of determining what he "ought" to have done, with an awareness of the company's financial position and (by virtue of s.214(4)) with a degree of general knowledge, skill and experience which in reality he may not have had. These fictitious assumptions as to the directors' state of mind were invoked against the defendants in *Re Produce Marketing Consortium Ltd* (1989) 5 B.C.C. 569. The company had kept inadequate accounting records, and in consequence the directors were in breach of their statutory duty to prepare accounts for the financial year ending 30 September 1985, which should have been laid before the shareholders and delivered to the registrar of companies by the end of July 1986. Knox J held that he should assume, for the purposes of s.214, that these financial results were known to the directors at the latter date, at least to the extent of the size of the deficiency of assets over liabilities.

The Act gives no affirmative guidance as to the steps which a director "ought" to take when insolvency is threatening. It was plainly assumed in the Government's White Paper (Cmnd.9175, para.12) that a conscientious director would seek to have the company put into receivership, administration, or voluntary liquidation as soon as possible. There is a clear risk that this may seem the safest course for directors, faced as they are with the threat of personal liability and possible disqualification, even when in their own business judgment there is a good case for carrying on. It is clear that any decision to do so ought to be fully reasoned and documented and, where necessary, made with the benefit of outside professional advice, in order that the requirements of the present subsection can be met if a charge of wrongful trading is brought. It is significant that in *Re Continental Assurance Co of London plc* [2001] B.P.I.R. 733, in which all of the directors concerned were held not to be liable for wrongful trading, management accounts had been prepared (albeit that they may not have been wholly accurate) and two licensed insolvency practitioners were advising the company at the material time. See also *Re Hawkes Hill Publishing Co Ltd* (above) and *Re Ralls Builders Ltd, Grant v Ralls* [2016] EWHC 243 (Ch); [2016] B.C.C. 293.

In *Brooks v Armstrong* [2015] EWHC 2289 (Ch) Mr Registrar Jones ruled that, once it has been established that the director knew or ought to have concluded that there was no reasonable prospect that the company would avoid going into insolvent liquidation, the onus is on the director to establish that he had taken every step to minimise the possible loss—a view which, if taken literally, leaves the court with very little discretion. However, in the case itself, the learned registrar was prepared to give the directors the benefit of the doubt, holding that liability under s.214 did not accrue until the insolvent trading had continued for quite some time. (The liquidators' appeal ([2016] EWHC 2893 (Ch); [2017] B.C.C. 99) was dismissed as there had been no increase in the net deficiency to creditors caused by the decision to continue trading, following *Re Ralls Builders Ltd* [2016] EWHC 243 (Ch); [2016] B.C.C. 293.) In *Re Sherborne Associates Ltd* (above) it was emphasised that the court should be aware of the danger of making assumptions with the benefit of hindsight, and in the case of a claim against the estate of a deceased director should be particularly astute to recognise the possibility of explanations for his conduct which he might have been able to give had he lived.

S.214(4)

The tests to be applied under this subsection combine both subjective and objective criteria. The director is thus to be judged by the standards of the "reasonable" director, even though he himself is lacking or below average in knowledge, skill or experience, but by his own higher standards if these are above average. In *Re DKG Contractors Ltd* [1990] B.C.C. 903 it was observed: "Patently, [the directors'] own knowledge, skill and experience were hopelessly inadequate for the task they undertook. That is not sufficient to protect them". However, it should be noted that in the *Produce Marketing* case (above), Knox J accepted a submission that the objective standards fixed by the section do require the court to have regard to the particular company and its business, so that the general knowledge, skill and experience postulated will be much less extensive in a small company in a modest way of business, with simple accounting procedures and equipment, than it will be in a large company with sophisticated procedures. This approach could also give scope for the courts to make some allowances in the case of non-executive and part-time directors. (*Re Continental Assurance Co of London plc* (above) contains an important analysis of the position of non-executive directors in this context.) In *Singla v Hedman (No.2)* [2010] EWHC 902 (Ch); [2010] B.C.C. 684 the court refused to accept the defendant's argument that there was a lower standard of responsibility in an inherently risky trade such as the film industry, and stressed the objective part of the test. For a detailed examination of the standards prescribed by s.214(4), see *Rubin v Gunner* [2004] EWHC 316 (Ch); [2004] B.C.C. 684.

In applying objective standards to the conduct of company directors in this way, the Act broke new ground, for the case law had traditionally emphasised the need for honesty and conscientiousness but had not demanded that directors should exercise any particular degree of competence or diligence or skill. However, in *Re D'Jan of London Ltd* [1993] B.C.C. 646, Hoffmann LJ expressed the view that "the duty of care owed by a director at common law is accurately stated in s.214 of the Insolvency Act 1986", and this view has not only been accepted in later cases but adopted in the statutory statement of directors' duties in the Companies Act 2006.

S.214(5)

The remarks made in the preceding paragraph are underlined by the present subsection, which puts sins of omission into the same category as sins of commission. This, too, is a departure from the common law, which has never had effective sanctions to penalise passive defaults such as non-attendance at board meetings.

S.214(6)

Section 214 applies only in a liquidation (but it is immaterial whether this is a compulsory or voluntary liquidation), or an administration. The phrase "goes into insolvent liquidation" is defined in those definitions and again in s.246ZB(6)(a) and the phrase "enters insolvent administration" in s.246ZB(6)(b). The test of insolvency applied by these definitions is on a "balance sheet" rather than a "liquidity" or "commercial" basis. (The recommendation of the Cork Committee was that *either* should be sufficient.) The definition of "inability to pay debts" in s.123(1)(e) and (2) may be contrasted.

The Act gives no indication whether the company's assets are to be valued for the purpose of s.214 on a "going concern" rather than a "break-up" basis, or whether contingent and future liabilities are to be brought into the reckoning. It is submitted that it would be wrong to judge these matters with the wisdom of hindsight, if it does happen that, e.g. the assets have had to be sold up piecemeal in the winding up which has resulted. The reference to "going into insolvent liquidation" in relation to the making of business judgments in s.214(2)(b) and the corresponding expressions in s.246ZB(2) surely indicates that the question of solvency is to be assessed on the basis of going-concern assumptions for all the purposes of the present section.

On the problems of valuation for the purposes of determining "insolvency" under the present section, see the comments of Professor Roy Goode, *Principles of Corporate Insolvency Law*, 4th edn (2011), at 4–22—4–39.

S.214(7)

For the definition of these terms, see the note to s.206.

S.214(8)

In view of the heavier onus of proof required by s.213, it is unlikely that that section will be invoked in future where a liquidator has a choice of proceeding under either section. The one respect in which the two sections do not overlap, however, is that s.213 applies also to persons other than directors and shadow directors, provided that they are knowingly parties to the fraudulent trading.

Special note re limited liability partnerships. The members of limited liability partnerships are subject to the wrongful trading regime established by s.214, and an additional provision is made for them by IA 1986 s.214A, inserted (but applicable only to LLPs) by the LLP Regulations 2001 (SI 2001/1090) Sch.3. This section empowers the court to order a member of a limited partnership to make such contribution to the assets of an insolvent limited partnership as it thinks proper where withdrawals of property have been made at a time when the partnership was likely to be unable to pay its debts in a winding up. The full text of s.214A is reproduced in Vol.2.

215 Proceedings under ss.213, 214

215(1) [Evidence by liquidator] On the hearing of an application under section 213 or 214, the liquidator may himself give evidence or call witnesses.

215(2) [Further court directions] Where under either section the court makes a declaration, it may give such further directions as it thinks proper for giving effect to the declaration; and in particular, the court may–

(a) provide for the liability of any person under the declaration to be a charge on any debt or obligation due from the company to him, or on any mortgage or charge or any interest in a mortgage or charge on assets of the company held by or vested in him, or any person on his behalf, or any person claiming as assignee from or through the person liable or any person acting on his behalf, and

(b) from time to time make such further order as may be necessary for enforcing any charge imposed under this subsection.

215(3) ["Assignee"] For the purposes of subsection (2), "assignee"–

(a) includes a person to whom or in whose favour, by the directions of the person made liable, the debt, obligation, mortgage or charge was created, issued or transferred or the interest created, but

(b) does not include an assignee for valuable consideration (not including consideration by way of marriage or the formation of a civil partnership) given in good faith and without notice of any of the matters on the ground of which the declaration is made.

215(4) [Directions re priority of debts] Where the court makes a declaration under either section in relation to a person who is a creditor of the company, it may direct that the whole or any part of any debt owed by the company to that person and any interest thereon shall rank in priority after all other debts owed by the company and after any interest on those debts.

215(5) [Sections 213, 214] Sections 213 and 214 have effect notwithstanding that the person concerned may be criminally liable in respect of matters on the ground of which the declaration under the section is to be made.

General Note

Corresponding provision for administrations is made by s.246ZC.

S.215(3)

In s.215(3)(b) the words "or the formation of a civil partnership" inserted by the Civil Partnership Act 2004 s.261(1) and Sch.27 para.112 as from 5 December 2005.

S.215(4)

The court is empowered to make a declaration, ancillary to an order for contribution, subordinating any debt owed by the company to a respondent so that it ranks after the company's other debts. Such a declaration was made in *Re Purpoint Ltd* [1991] B.C.C. 121.

216 Restriction on re-use of company names

216(1) [Application] This section applies to a person where a company ("the liquidating company") has gone into insolvent liquidation on or after the appointed day and he was a director or shadow director of the company at any time in the period of 12 months ending with the day before it went into liquidation.

216(2) [Prohibited name] For the purposes of this section, a name is a prohibited name in relation to such a person if–

(a) it is a name by which the liquidating company was known at any time in that period of 12 months, or

(b) it is a name which is so similar to a name falling within paragraph (a) as to suggest an association with that company.

216(3) [Restriction] Except with leave of the court or in such circumstances as may be prescribed, a person to whom this section applies shall not at any time in the period of 5 years beginning with the day on which the liquidating company went into liquidation–

(a) be a director of any other company that is known by a prohibited name, or

(b) in any way, whether directly or indirectly, be concerned or take part in the promotion, formation or management of any such company, or

(c) in any way, whether directly or indirectly, be concerned or take part in the carrying on of a business carried on (otherwise than by a company) under a prohibited name.

216(4) [Penalty] If a person acts in contravention of this section, he is liable to imprisonment or a fine, or both.

216(5) ["The court"] In subsection (3) "the court" means any court having jurisdiction to wind up companies; and on an application for leave under that subsection, the Secretary of State or the official receiver may appear and call the attention of the court to any matters which seem to him to be relevant.

216(6) [Interpretation re name] References in this section, in relation to any time, to a name by which a company is known are to the name of the company at that time or to any name under which the company carries on business at that time.

216(7) [Interpretation re insolvent liquidation] For the purposes of this section a company goes into insolvent liquidation if it goes into liquidation at a time when its assets are insufficient for the payment of its debts and other liabilities and the expenses of the winding up.

216(8) ["Company"] In this section "company" includes a company which may be wound up under Part V of this Act.

General Note

This is one of a number of innovations made by IA 1985 which together form a package designed to strike down the "phoenix" phenomenon. This term was used to describe an abuse of the privilege of limited liability which, perhaps more than anything else, showed the inadequacies of the former insolvency law in the corporate sector. A company would be put into receivership (or voluntary liquidation) at a time when it owed large sums to its unsecured creditors. Frequently, the receiver was appointed by a controlling shareholder who had himself taken a floating charge over the whole of the company's undertaking, and there was nothing to stop him from appointing a receiver with whom he could act in collusion. The receiver would sell the entire business as a going concern at a knock-down price to a new company incorporated by the former controllers of the defunct company. As a result, what was essentially the same business would be carried on by the same people in disregard of the claims of the creditors of the first company, who in effect subsidised the launch of the new company debt-free. It was not unknown for the procedure to be repeated several times. The use of nominees or "front men" could add to the confusion and help to deceive future creditors: on the other hand, advantage could sometimes be gained from using a new company name similar to that of the old company, and cashing in on what was left of its goodwill. (On phoenix companies, see the comments of Jacob J in *Western Intelligence Ltd v KDO Label Printing Machines Ltd* [1998] B.C.C. 472.) The present section is aimed to counter both of these latter aspects of the "phoenix syndrome", but it is so widely drawn that it extends to situations well beyond the phoenix scenario. It is not based on any of the Cork Committee's recommendations, and was introduced at a late stage during the passage of the Insolvency Bill through Parliament in 1985. It simply makes the re-use of the name of a company which has been wound up insolvent a criminal offence in the circumstances defined; but it is not based on any requirement that there should be an attempt to exploit the goodwill of the liquidating company (see the comments of Peter Gibson LJ in *Thorne v Silverleaf* [1994] B.C.C. 113). It is rather surprisingly confined in its scope to directors and shadow directors of the extinct company, but it is not necessary that the person concerned should hold such a position in the second company (*R. v Doring* [2002] EWCA Crim 1695; [2002] B.C.C. 838). In addition, any such person and any nominee or "front man" through whom he conducts the second business may incur personal liability, without limitation, under s.217. The conditions for liability are stringently drawn, the penalties draconian and both criminal and civil liability are automatic: if they are met, the court has no discretion to absolve the defendant or limit his liability (*Ricketts v Ad Valorem Factors Ltd* [2003] EWCA Civ 1706; [2004] B.C.C. 164).

The civil consequences of a breach of s.216 are spelt out in s.217, and it is usually in proceedings brought under that section by a creditor that such proceedings will be instituted. But a shareholder may plead a breach of s.216 in proceedings under CA 2006 s.994 (unfairly prejudicial conduct): *Re Neath Rugby Club Ltd, Hawkes v Cuddy* [2007] EWHC 1789 (Ch); [2007] B.C.C. 671; on appeal [2007] EWCA Civ 1072; [2008] B.C.C. 125; further proceedings [2008] B.C.C. 390. The subject is discussed by C. Werner (2009) 22 Insolv. Int. 105.

S.216(1)

Many phrases in this subsection have special meanings. "Company" and "gone into insolvent liquidation" are defined in ss.216(8) and 216(7) respectively; the "appointed day" is the day on which the present Act came into force (29 December 1986: see ss.436, 443); "director" and "shadow director" have the meanings ascribed to them by s.251.

The prohibition applies to anyone who has been a director or shadow director of the old company within the 12 months prior to its liquidation, and lasts for the period of five years that follows that event (s.216(3)).

S.216(2)

The ban applies to the use of the same name or a similar name: see, further, the note to s.216(6).

It should be emphasised that the present section is not directed against the reuse of an insolvent company's name in itself: there will be no ban on this practice provided that no director of the former company is associated with the second business. It is only directors who can contravene the section, and only directors who are liable to punishment. This explains the phrase "a prohibited name *in relation* to such a person".

S.216(3)

The ban is not restricted to the use of a prohibited name by a newly formed company: an established company (perhaps a member of the same group as the defunct company) may well have a "similar" name already, or may change its name to a "prohibited" name, with the result that its directors may be caught by this section. (Note that IR 2016 r.22.7, may give a director an exemption in the former of these cases.) In *Ricketts v Ad Valorem Factors Ltd* (above), the Court of Appeal drew attention to the hazards which ss.216–217 might pose where one company in a group went into liquidation. (It is understood that in practice Official Receivers allow a three month "period of grace" in order to allow "associated" companies to change their names before taking action for breach of the section.) In *ESS Production Ltd v Sully* [2005] EWCA Civ 554; [2005] B.C.C. 435 the acronym "ESS" had been used informally as a shorthand expression to refer to various companies in which the respondent "S" was a principal shareholder and director. One of these companies had been registered under the name "Electronic Sales Services Ltd" throughout the 12-month qualifying period but had changed its name to "ESS Solutions Ltd" some seven months later. The Court of Appeal held that the informal use of the acronym was sufficient reason to hold that this company had been "known by" a name which linked it to the company that had gone into liquidation, with the result that S was liable for its debts. The test of "similarity" is not to be applied in the abstract, simply by looking at the names in question without regard to the context, but in relation to the circumstances in which they were actually used or likely to be used:

Ricketts v Ad Valorem Factors Ltd (above); *Revenue and Customs Commissioners v Walsh* [2005] EWHC 1304 (Ch); [2005] EWCA Civ 1291; [2006] B.C.C. 431. The fact that the names of the companies contain a name or surname that is common or well-known (e.g. "Walsh", "William" or "Williams") is irrelevant: *Walsh* (above); *Revenue and Customs Commissioners v Benton-Diggins* [2006] EWHC 793 (Ch); [2006] B.C.C. 769.

Section 216 is infringed where the second company carries on only part of its business under a prohibited name, but in that case civil liability under s.217 is restricted to debts incurred in carrying on that part of the business: *Glasgow City Council v Craig* [2008] CSOH 171; [2010] B.C.C. 235.

The court is given power to grant dispensations from the prohibition imposed by this section, which it is likely to do when the insolvency is not linked with any blameworthy conduct on the part of the director concerned. *Re Bonus Breaks Ltd* [1991] B.C.C. 546 is an illustration of such a case. There, the applicant had been a director of a company which had gone into insolvent liquidation, but she had not behaved culpably and had lost substantial sums of her own money. A new company was set up with a capital of £50,000, including £49,000 in redeemable shares. Morritt J gave leave for her to be a director of the new company against undertakings offered by the applicant that its capital base would be maintained and that it would not redeem any redeemable shares nor purchase its own shares out of distributable profits for a period of two years, unless such action was approved by a director independent of the company's founders. However, in *Penrose v Official Receiver* [1996] 1 W.L.R. 482; [1996] B.C.C. 311, Chadwick J held that neither the fact that the new company was undercapitalised nor that the applicant was inexperienced and lacked management skills were relevant factors: the object of the section is to prevent abuses of the "phoenix" variety, and therefore the appropriate questions are whether there is any risk to the creditors of the new company beyond that permitted under the law relating to the incorporation of limited liability companies, or any substantial risk that people would be confused by the similarity of names. (See also *Re Lightning Electrical Contractors Ltd* [1996] B.C.C. 950 and *Re Bowman Power Systems Ltd*, 26 October 2004, *British Company Law and Practice New Developments*, para.96–031.) In this case it was also held that it is wrong in principle to treat an applicant for leave under s.216 as if he were a person who has been disqualified on the grounds of unfitness from acting as a director under CDDA 1986—at least without evidence of misconduct. (However, a contravention of s.216 may be evidence of "unfitness" justifying disqualification: *Re Migration Services International Ltd* [2000] B.C.C. 1095.) Leave may be granted in respect of "dormant" companies, provided that they are specified; but the court will not give a blanket permission to use the prohibited name in respect of any company to be formed in the future: *Re Lightning Electrical Contractors Ltd* [1996] B.C.C. 950.

The court's leave could not be granted retrospectively, since this would have the effect of decriminalising the director's past conduct: see the notes to CDDA 1986 s.1. But a person who has been acting as a director in breach of s.216 could seek leave for the future, as was accepted by both courts in *Re Neath Rugby Club Ltd* (above).

The rules also specify three sets of circumstances where the section will not apply: see IR 2016 rr.22.4 et seq. These are (1) where the whole, or substantially the whole, of the business of an insolvent company is acquired by a successor company and the liquidator (or equivalent office-holder) of the insolvent company gives notice to its creditors under r.22.4; (2) for an interim period, where an application is made to the court within seven days of the liquidation and the court grants leave not later than six weeks from that date (r.22.6); and (3) where the second company has been known by the name in question for at least 12 months prior to the liquidation and has not been a dormant company (r.22.7). All other cases will have to go to the court for authorisation: the relevant rules are rr.22.1, 22.3.

Paragraphs (b) and (c), by the use of the term "indirectly", will be effective to stop a person from controlling another company or carrying on a new business through others as "front" men. In addition, para.(c) makes it clear that it will be an offence to use a prohibited name even where no second company is involved, but in this case the civil consequences prescribed by s.217 will not be applicable.

The phrase "be concerned or take part in the management of a company" is not defined, but the note to s.217 is relevant in this context.

S.216(4)

Note that it is only a person who was a director or shadow director of the liquidating company who can be convicted of an offence under this section. In contrast, the civil liability imposed by s.217 extends also to persons who act on the instructions of such ex-directors.

The offence under this section is one of strict liability: mens rea need not be shown; *R. v Cole, Lees & Birch* [1998] B.C.C. 87. In the same case it was held that a sentence of community service is not inappropriate in this context. (See also *R. v McCredie* [2000] B.C.C. 617; and *R. v Doring* (above).)

Conviction of the offence may also expose a person who has benefited to a criminal compensation order: see *R. v Neuberg* [2016] EWCA Crim 1927.

On penalties, see s.430 and Sch.10.

S.216(5)
For the courts having jurisdiction to wind up companies, see ss.117 and 120. It is clear that "the court" need not be the same court as that which may have been involved in the liquidation of the old company.

S.216(6)
This provision should be read with s.216(2) above. In addition to forbidding the use of an identical name, the section bans a name "so similar as to suggest an association with" the former company. It is likely that this will catch the common and, in many ways, convenient practice of calling a new company by a name such as "John Smith (2014) Ltd", after the original John Smith Ltd has gone out of business. (There will, of course, be no objection to this so long as the first company was wound up solvent.)

The offence is not confined to the use of a prohibited name by a company: an unincorporated business is caught as well (s.216(3)(c)). Further, the prohibition is not confined to a company's registered name. A company may carry on business under another name. Thus, for example, John Smith Ltd, before it went into solvent liquidation, may have used the trade name of "City Autos". It will be an offence for a former director of the company to take part in the management of any business using the name "John Smith", or "City Autos", or any name similar to either. It will also be an offence for him to be a director of any company having the registered name "John Smith Ltd" or "City Autos Ltd" and also of any other company, X Ltd, if it trades under the name "John Smith" or "City Autos"—or a similar name in each case.

It is the last of these possibilities that it is most likely to mislead creditors and members of the public generally, i.e. the use of the same trade name by a succession of limited companies.

S.216(7)
This subsection defines "goes into insolvent liquidation" in terms identical to s.214(6). See the note to that provision and, for the meaning of "goes into liquidation", s.247(2).

S.216(8)
The effect of this provision is to include "unregistered" as well as registered companies within the section. See the note to s.220. Section 216 does not apply to partners in a partnership: *Re Newton Coaches Ltd* [2016] EWHC 3068 (Ch).

217 Personal liability for debts, following contravention of s.216

217(1) [Personal liability] A person is personally responsible for all the relevant debts of a company if at any time–

(a) in a contravention of section 216, he is involved in the management of the company, or

(b) as a person who is involved in the management of the company, he acts or is willing to act on instructions given (without the leave of the court) by a person whom he knows at that time to be in contravention in relation to the company of section 216.

217(2) [Joint and several liability] Where a person is personally responsible under this section for the relevant debts of a company, he is jointly and severally liable in respect of those debts with the company and any other person who, whether under this section or otherwise, is so liable.

217(3) [Relevant debts of company] For the purposes of this section the relevant debts of a company are–

(a) in relation to a person who is personally responsible under paragraph (a) of subsection (1), such debts and other liabilities of the company as are incurred at a time when that person was involved in the management of the company, and

(b) in relation to a person who is personally responsible under paragraph (b) of that subsection, such debts and other liabilities of the company as are incurred at a time when that person was acting or was willing to act on instructions given as mentioned in that paragraph.

217(4) [Person involved in management] For the purposes of this section, a person is involved in the management of a company if he is a director of the company or if he is concerned, whether directly or indirectly, or takes part, in the management of the company.

217(5) [Interpretation] For the purposes of this section a person who, as a person involved in the management of a company, has at any time acted on instructions given (without the leave of the court) by a person whom he knew at that time to be in contravention in relation to the company of section 216 is presumed, unless the contrary is shown, to have been willing at any time thereafter to act on any instructions given by that person.

217(6) ["Company"] In this section "company" includes a company which may be wound up under Part V.

General Note

This section imposes personal liability on a person who contravenes s.216 by reusing a prohibited company name. In addition, it makes similarly liable anyone who allows himself to be used as a "front" man or nominee in breach of that section. Since the criminal liability prescribed by s.216 affects only directors and shadow directors, the category of those who are potentially liable on a civil basis is wider than those who may be convicted of the statutory offence.

In *Thorne v Silverleaf* [1994] B.C.C. 109, summary judgment was given in favour of the plaintiff against a director who had infringed s.216. The Court of Appeal held that it was irrelevant that the plaintiff had allegedly aided and abetted the director in the commission of this offence. It was immaterial that he was aware of the facts, and even that he was aware both of the facts and that they constituted a contravention of s.216. It was also held on the evidence that the plaintiff had not waived his right to seek recovery against the director under s.217.

Inland Revenue Commissioners v Nash [2003] EWHC 686 (Ch); [2004] B.C.C. 150; *Archer Structures Ltd v Griffiths* [2003] EWHC 957 (Ch); [2004] B.C.C. 156; and *Ricketts v Ad Valorem Factors Ltd* [2003] EWCA Civ 1706; [2004] B.C.C. 164 suggest that regular use is being made of this remedy (not least by the Revenue). See further Milman (2005) 17 Co. L.N. 2. There is some parallel with CDDA 1986 ss.11, 15.

The right conferred by s.217 is (on analogy with CDDA 1986 s.15) a right conferred on the creditors concerned, and not on the company or its liquidator (*Re Prestige Grindings Ltd* [2006] B.C.C. 421, and see Duncan [2012] N.L.J. 1175). It is inappropriate to appoint the liquidator to represent those creditors by an order under CPR r.19.6. However, the company will be entitled to a contribution order in respect of any sums recovered by a creditor (s.217(2)).

S.217(1)

Many of the terms used in this provision are defined or explained in the following subsections, and in particular "relevant debts", "involved in the management of a company", "is willing to act" and "company".

For a person to be made liable under para.(b), it will be necessary to show that he knew all the facts which are relevant to a contravention of s.216.

Liability under the section is automatic, not requiring a special application to the court or court order of any sort and, for a case coming within para.(a), not requiring a prior conviction of the director concerned. The court has no power under CA 2006 s.1157 to relieve a director from liability under s.217: *First Independent Factors & Finance Ltd v Mountford* [2008] EWHC 835 (Ch); [2008] B.C.C. 598.

S.217(2)

A person liable under this section is primarily liable, jointly and severally with the company and others concerned, and not in any secondary way. In *Revenue and Customs v Yousef* [2008] EWHC 423 (Ch); [2008] B.C.C. 805 it was held that there was no right of indemnity as between persons liable for the company's debts under s.217, or as between them and the company, either by reason of s.217 itself or under the Civil Liability (Contribution) Act 1978.

S.217(3)

Liability extends not only to debts in the narrow sense but also to all other obligations, such as claims for damages; and it applies to all debts and obligations arising during the relevant time and not merely those incurred *by* the acts of the person in question. The assignee of a debt has standing to sue a director under s.217: *First Independent Factors & Finance Ltd v Mountford* (above).

The phrase "willing to act" is explained in s.217(5).

S.217(4)

A director is irrebuttably presumed to be "involved in the management" of the company.

In regard to other persons, the best guide to the meaning of the phrase may be found in cases where the courts have construed closely similar, but not identical, provisions such as "take part in" or "be concerned in" the management of a company. For a full discussion, see the note to s.206(3).

S.217(5)
This provision creates a presumption against a person who is proved at any one time to have acted on the instructions of another whom he then knew to be contravening s.216. Once this is shown, he is rebuttably presumed to have been "willing to act" on the other's instructions at any time afterwards.

S.217(6)
"Unregistered" companies are included by this formula. See the note to s.220.

Investigation and prosecution of malpractice

218 Prosecution of delinquent officers and members of company

218(1) [Court may direct matter to be referred for prosecution] If it appears to the court in the course of a winding up by the court that any past or present officer, or any member, of the company has been guilty of any offence in relation to the company for which he is criminally liable, the court may (either on the application of a person interested in the winding up or of its own motion) direct the liquidator to refer the matter–

(a) in the case of a winding up in England and Wales, to the Secretary of State, and

(b) in the case of a winding up in Scotland, to the Lord Advocate.

218(2) [Deleted]

218(3) [Report—winding up by court] If in the case of a winding up by the court in England and Wales it appears to the liquidator, not being the official receiver, that any past or present officer of the company, or any member of it, has been guilty of an offence in relation to the company for which he is criminally liable, the liquidator shall report the matter to the official receiver.

218(4) [Report—voluntary winding up] If it appears to the liquidator in the course of a voluntary winding up that any past or present officer of the company, or any member of it, has been guilty of an offence in relation to the company for which he is criminally liable, he shall forthwith report the matter–

(a) in the case of a winding up in England and Wales, to the Secretary of State, and

(b) in the case of a winding up in Scotland, to the Lord Advocate,

and shall furnish to the Secretary of State or (as the case may be) the Lord Advocate such information and give to him such access to and facilities for inspecting and taking copies of documents (being information or documents in the possession or under the control of the liquidator and relating to the matter in question) as the Secretary of State or (as the case may be) the Lord Advocate requires.

218(5) [Reference to Secretary of State] Where a report is made to the Secretary of State under subsection (4) he may, for the purpose of investigating the matter reported to him and such other matters relating to the affairs of the company as appear to him to require investigation, exercise any of the powers which are exercisable by inspectors appointed under section 431 or 432 of the Companies Act 1985 to investigate a company's affairs.

218(6) [Court may direct liquidator to make report] If it appears to the court in the course of a voluntary winding up that–

(a) any past or present officer of the company, or any member of it, has been guilty as above-mentioned, and

(b) no report with respect to the matter has been made by the liquidator under subsection (4),

the court may (on the application of any person interested in the winding up or of its own motion) direct the liquidator to make such a report.

On a report being made accordingly, this section has effect as though the report had been made in pursuance of subsection (4).

General Note

This provision establishes a reporting chain through which suspected criminal offences uncovered in the course of a winding up may be referred to the appropriate persons for investigation and, where appropriate, prosecution. This section and s.219 were amended by IA 2000 s.10 as from 2 April 2001 as a streamlining measure. Reports in England and Wales now go directly to the Secretary of State and not as previously in the first instance to the Director of Public Prosecutions. (For transitional provisions, see the Insolvency Act 2000 (Commencement No.1 and Transitional Provisions) Order 2001 (SI 2001/766) art.3(4).) The former s.218(2) became redundant and was accordingly repealed.

Guidance on the duty of practitioners to report potential criminal offences is given by the Insolvency Service in *Dear IP* Ch.20.10, December 2012 and in an article in (2013) 26 Insolv. Int. 33. There is no similar obligation to report suspected criminality imposed by the Act on administrators and receivers, but the Insolvency Service has indicated that such reports are both encouraged and welcomed. If there is suspicion of money laundering or terrorist financing, there is an additional statutory obligation on the practitioner to report it to the Serious Organised Crime Agency.

S.218(1)

In a winding up by the court, the court is empowered to take the initial step when an offence is suspected, by directing the liquidator to refer the matter to the Secretary of State or the Lord Advocate. The court may act of its own motion or on the application of "a person interested in the winding up". In England and Wales, if the liquidator (not being the official receiver) himself suspects wrongdoing, he is obliged to report the matter to the official receiver (s.218(3)); but it is unclear whether that provision by implication debars him from making an application to the court on his own initiative under s.218(1). In Scotland, where s.218(3) does not apply, it would seem to be clear that the liquidator should make application to the court in all cases.

On the meaning of "officer", see the note to s.206(3).

S.218(3)

The section is oddly silent as to what the official receiver should do, both in the case when he is not the liquidator and receives a report of a suspected offence, and in the case where, as liquidator, he suspects an offence himself. It must be intended that he shall (either with or without conducting his own investigation into the matter) refer the case to the prosecuting authority without the need for any intervention by the court. This is confirmed by *R. v Brady* [2004] EWCA Crim 1763; [2005] B.C.C. 357. In this case it was also observed that s.218 is not exhaustive: it says nothing about assisting criminal investigators or prosecutors who might approach the official receiver or liquidator directly, or what he is to do if he becomes aware of apparent criminal behaviour himself; but here, too it would seem that he is entitled to pass on information which he holds to the relevant prosecuting authority.

S.218(4), (6)

In a voluntary winding up, the liquidator's duty is to report the matter himself directly to the Secretary of State or the Lord Advocate, and thereafter to co-operate with the authority as described, and also give the further assistance referred to in s.219(3). The court has, under s.218(6), a further power to give the liquidator directions to this effect.

S.218(5)

The Secretary of State's powers of investigation under CA 1985 ss.431, 432, are far-reaching, and under those sections are not restricted to pursuing inquiries in connection with suspected criminal offences. [These sections are not affected by CA 2006.] Additional provisions governing an investigation by the Secretary of State under the present subsection are laid down by s.219 below.

219 Obligations arising under s.218

219(1) [Assistance to investigation by Secretary of State] For the purpose of an investigation by the Secretary of State in consequence of a report made to him under section 218(4), any obligation imposed on a person by any provision of the Companies Act 1985 to produce documents or give information to, or otherwise to assist, inspectors appointed as mentioned in section 218(5) is to be regarded as an obligation similarly to assist the Secretary of State in his investigation.

219(2) [Answer may be used as evidence] An answer given by a person to a question put to him in exercise of the powers conferred by section 218(5) may be used in evidence against him.

219(2A) [Use of evidence in criminal proceedings] However, in criminal proceedings in which that person is charged with an offence to which this subsection applies–

(a) no evidence relating to the answer may be adduced, and

(b) no question relating to it may be asked,

by or on behalf of the prosecution, unless evidence relating to it is adduced, or a question relating to it is asked, in the proceedings by or on behalf of that person.

219(2B) [Offences to which s.219(2A) not applicable] Subsection (2A) applies to any offence other than–

(a) an offence under section 2 or 5 of the Perjury Act 1911 (false statements made on oath otherwise than in judicial proceedings or made otherwise than on oath), or

(b) an offence under section 44(1) or (2) of the Criminal Law (Consolidation) (Scotland) Act 1995 (false statements made on oath or otherwise than on oath).

219(3) [Liquidator and officer to assist, where criminal proceedings instituted] Where criminal proceedings are instituted by the Director of Public Prosecutions, the Lord Advocate or the Secretary of State following any report or reference under section 218, it is the duty of the liquidator and every officer and agent of the company past and present (other than the defendant or defender) to give to the Director of Public Prosecutions, the Lord Advocate or the Secretary of State (as the case may be) all assistance in connection with the prosecution which he is reasonably able to give.

For this purpose "agent" includes any banker or solicitor of the company and any person employed by the company as auditor, whether that person is or is not an officer of the company.

219(4) [Direction by court re assistance] If a person fails or neglects to give assistance in the manner required by subsection (3), the court may, on the application of the Director of Public Prosecutions, the Lord Advocate or the Secretary of State (as the case may be) direct the person to comply with that subsection; and if the application is made with respect to a liquidator, the court may (unless it appears that the failure or neglect to comply was due to the liquidator not having in his hands sufficient assets of the company to enable him to do so) direct that the costs shall be borne by the liquidator personally.

General Note

The provisions of this section are designed to facilitate the investigations which may be made by the various officials and authorities when a suspected criminal offence is reported to them under the preceding section. The company's bankers, solicitors and auditors are specifically included among those obliged to assist (s.219(3)).

Changes were made to the wording of s.219(1), (3) and (4) by IA 2000 s.10(7) with effect from 2 April 2001 consequentially upon the reform of s.218: see the note to that section.

Section 11 of the same Act inserted the new subss.(2A) and (2B) as from the same date. These provisions limit the use of evidence obtained under compulsion in subsequent criminal prosecutions. A similar reform was made by the Youth Justice and Criminal Evidence Act 1999 s.55 and Sch.3, covering most of the provisions in the companies and insolvency legislation dealing with the use of such evidence, but this provision did not include s.219. See further the notes to ss.236 and 433.

Part V

Winding Up of Unregistered Companies

220 Meaning of "unregistered company"

220(1) ["Unregistered company"] For the purposes of this Part, "unregistered company" includes any association and any company, with the exception of a company registered under the Companies Act 2006 in any part of the United Kingdom.

220(2) [Former references to trustee savings banks, now repealed.]

General Note

This section was replaced as from 1 October 2009, but without any change of substance, by the Companies Act 2006 (Consequential Amendments, Transitional Provisions and Savings) Order 2009 Sch.1 para.76.

The earliest companies legislation that enabled companies to acquire corporate status by registration was accompanied by Winding-up Acts which provided machinery for the winding up of companies which had not registered. Part V of the present Act, which consolidates CA 1985 Pt XXI, is what survives today of that legislation. There are almost certainly, however, no "unregistered companies" in the old sense still around; and for practical purposes it is probably true to say that Pt V will be applied to two or three other types of "unregistered" company—(1) statutory companies incorporated by private Act of Parliament; (2) foreign companies which have been carrying on business in Great Britain or have some other relevant connection with this jurisdiction; and (3) other bodies, such as unregistered friendly societies, for which provision for winding up is not made by specific legislation. Obsolete references to partnerships and limited partnerships contained in CA 1985 s.665, were repealed by IA 1985 Sch.10 Pt II; but paradoxically this Part of the Act is now made to apply to the winding up of insolvent partnerships: see the note to s.420. (Limited liability partnerships, in contrast, are wound up under Pt IV.)

English courts have exercised jurisdiction to wind up foreign companies under the present section or its predecessors for a very long period: s.225, which expressly refers to companies incorporated outside Great Britain but applies in limited circumstances only, is a relative newcomer which has rarely, if ever, been invoked.

Sections 220 and 221 give no guidance as to the criteria which will justify an English court in assuming jurisdiction. The matter has been left to the discretion of the courts. In practice, it is normally considered a sufficient nexus for the company to have, or have had, a place of business or branch office within the jurisdiction, or to have assets here (*Banque des Marchands de Moscou (Koupetschesky) v Kindersley* [1951] Ch. 112; [1950] 2 All E.R. 549), but other factors may also be regarded as relevant, e.g. the fact that a claim may be brought by the company against an insurer in England (*Re Compania Merabello San Nicholas SA* [1973] Ch. 75; [1972] 3 All E.R. 448), that a winding-up order will entitle former employees of the company to claim statutory redundancy payments (*Re Eloc Electro-Optieck and Communicatie BV* [1982] Ch. 43; [1981] 2 All E.R. 1111), or that the debt upon which the petition is founded was incurred here (*Re a Company (No.00359 of 1987)* [1988] Ch. 210; (1987) 3 B.C.C. 160 (also known as *Re Okeanos Maritime Corp*)). It is not necessary that the company should have assets within the jurisdiction: *Re a Company (No.003102 of 1991) Ex p. Nyckeln Finance Co Ltd* [1991] B.C.L.C. 539. However the court must be satisfied that there is a reasonable possibility that the winding-up order will benefit those applying for it, and the court must be able to exercise jurisdiction over one or more persons interested in the distribution of the company's assets: *Re Real Estate Development Co* [1991] B.C.L.C. 210; *Atlantic & General Investment Trust Ltd v Richbell Information Services Inc* [2000] B.C.C. 111; *Re Latreefers Inc* [2001] B.C.C. 174; *Re Westminster Property Management Ltd, Official Receiver v Stern (No.2)* [2001] B.C.C. 305; *Re OJSC Ank Yugraneft* [2008] EWHC 2614 (Ch); [2010] B.C.C. 475. These cases may be contrasted with *Banco Nacional de Cuba v Cosmos Trading Corp* [2000] B.C.C. 910 (where an order was refused because the connection with the UK was minimal and no benefit to the creditors could realistically be expected) and *Re Buccament Bay Ltd* [2014] EWHC 4776 (Ch); [2015] 1 B.C.L.C. 646 (no potential benefit to UK creditors). The "presence of assets" factor is more relevant where the petition is brought by a creditor on the ground of insolvency. In contrast, in *Kam v Kam* [2015] HKFCA 91 the petitioner sought winding up on the just and equitable ground, where the dispute was essentially between the shareholders. The Hong Kong Court of Final Appeal held that the presence of shareholders was sufficient to give the court jurisdiction.

Everything in the preceding paragraph must now be reconsidered in the light of the Recast EU Regulation, so far as concerns companies which have their "centre of main interests" (COMI) in another EU Member State. The Regulation confers exclusive jurisdiction to open "main" insolvency proceedings upon the State where the COMI is situated—which is rebuttably presumed to be the place of its registered office (art.3(1)). In regard to "secondary" and "territorial" proceedings—where the COMI is in another Member State—art.3(2) stipulates that the local courts have jurisdiction only if the debtor "possesses an establishment" within the territory of the latter. The effect of secondary or territorial proceedings is restricted to the assets of the debtor situated in that territory. If main proceedings have already been opened, the ancillary proceedings are termed "secondary", and they must be winding-up proceedings. If main proceedings have not yet been opened, the proceedings are "territorial", and another Member State has jurisdiction in only two cases: (a) where main proceedings cannot be opened because of conditions laid down by the law of the "main" State; or (b) where the opening of territorial proceedings is requested by a creditor who has his domicile, habitual residence or registered office within the territory in question, or whose claim arises from the operation of that establishment. These questions of jurisdiction are discussed more fully in the note to the EU Regulation art.3; but it will be apparent that where the Regulation applies, the UK courts' jurisdiction under s.220 is more limited than that described above.

The CBIR do not impose similar jurisdictional limitations where the COMI is in a foreign state. Schedule 1 art.28 does state that, after the formal recognition by a British court of a foreign proceeding as a main proceeding, the *effects* of a proceeding under British insolvency law in relation to the debtor shall, in so far as the assets of that debtor are concerned, be restricted to assets that are located in Great Britain (and to other assets for certain purposes), but this wording does not restrict the jurisdiction of the court as such.

The court, having exercised its discretion to hold that it has jurisdiction in respect of the particular company, has a further discretion whether or not to make an order, and if so upon what terms: see the notes to s.221.

The object of s.220(1)(b) appears fairly plainly to be to ensure that a company registered in one part of the UK may be wound up only in that jurisdiction, e.g. a company registered in England and Wales may only be wound up by the High Court or the county court (s.117), and a company registered in Scotland only by the Court of Session or a sheriff court (s.120). However this is not the case so far as concerns a company registered in Northern Ireland. In *Re Normandy Marketing Ltd* [1993] B.C.C. 879 Morritt J held that by virtue of s.220 and s.441, read together, the court in England had jurisdiction to wind up a company registered in Northern Ireland, on the petition of the Secretary of State under s.124A, provided that it had a principal place of business in England or Wales. In an appropriate case, s.225 could also be invoked to give a court in Great Britain jurisdiction over a Northern Ireland company. Otherwise, the allocation of jurisdiction over a foreign company as between the different parts of the UK is dealt with by s.221(2), (3).

The Judgments Regulation (Regulation (EU) 1215/2012 of 20 December 2012, effective 10 January 2015 (superseding Council Regulation (EC) 44/2001 of 22 December 2000) on jurisdiction and the enforcement of judgments in civil and commercial matters), which largely supersedes the Brussels Convention of 1968, does not apply to the winding up of insolvent companies (art.2(b)). In regard to solvent foreign companies, art.22(2) has the effect of denying a British court jurisdiction where the company has its "seat" in a contracting state other than the UK. However, conversely, a solvent company which is incorporated abroad in a contracting state will be subject to jurisdiction here under Pt V of IA 1986 if it has its "seat" in this country. On the question of jurisdiction in relation to schemes of arrangement, and the possible overlap between the present section, the Judgments Regulation and the EU Insolvency Regulation, see *Re Rodenstock GmbH* [2011] EWHC 1104 (Ch); [2012] B.C.C. 459; *Re Van Gansewinkel Groep BV* [2015] EWHC 2151 (Ch); [2016] B.C.C. 172 and *Re Global Garden Products Italy SpA* [2016] EWHC 1884 (Ch); [2017] B.C.C. 637.

Similar considerations may also arise in an application to the court for permission to serve a winding-up petition out of the jurisdiction. Here the relevant questions are (1) whether the applicant can establish a good arguable case that the court has jurisdiction and, if so, (2) whether there is a serious issue to be tried as to whether the court ought to exercise its jurisdiction to make a winding-up order: *Flame SA v Primera Maritime (Hellas) Ltd* [2010] EWHC 2053 (Ch), applying *Seaconsar Far East Ltd v Bank Markazi Jomhouri Islami Iran* [1994] 1 A.C. 438.

An unregistered company can be wound up only by order of the court: s.221(4)—except where the EU Regulation applies: see the note to s.221(4).

Various other statutory provisions refer to "a company liable to be wound up under the Insolvency Act 1986". For example, CA 2006 s.895 uses this definition in relation to the scope of its provisions relating to reconstructions and arrangements. In such a context it may not always be appropriate to apply the case law which has been established for the purposes of the court's winding-up jurisdiction. In *Re Drax Holdings Ltd* [2003] EWHC 2743 (Ch); [2004] B.C.C. 334, the judgment of Lawrence Collins J discusses the principles which will guide the court in the exercise of its discretion to assume jurisdiction in such a case. It is necessary that there should be a sufficient connection with the jurisdiction, but other preconditions which would apply in an insolvency (e.g. likelihood of benefit to those applying for a winding-up order) might not be relevant. The *Drax Holdings* judgment was followed in *Re La Mutuelles du Mans Assurances IARD* [2005] EWHC 1599 (Ch); [2006] B.C.C. 11; and in *Re DAP Holding NV* [2005] EWHC 2092 (Ch); [2006] B.C.C. 48 and *Re Sovereign Marine and General Insurance Co Ltd* [2006] EWHC 1335 (Ch); [2006] B.C.C. 774, in which it was held that the UK court had jurisdiction to sanction schemes of arrangement involving insurance companies based elsewhere in the EU, in the light of the construction of the relevant EC legislation. See further the note to s.221.

A European grouping of territorial cooperation ("EGTC") which has its registered office in the United Kingdom is to be wound up as an unregistered company under Pt V of the Act (or the Northern Ireland equivalent): European Grouping of Territorial Cooperation Regulations 2007 (SI 2007/1949, effective 1 August 2007) reg.7; and IR 2016 will apply with the modifications set out in Pts 2 and 3 of the Schedule to those Regulations.

S.220(1)

The term "association" has been held to mean only an association formed for gain or profit: *Re St James's Club* (1852) 2 De G.M. & G. 383; *Re The Bristol Athenaeum* (1889) 43 Ch. D. 236; *Panter v Rowellian Football Social Club* [2011] EWHC 1301 (Ch); [2012] Ch. 125; [2014] B.C.C. 321. These decisions may have turned, in part, upon the special wording of the earlier legislation; but the ruling in the former case was given renewed authority when it was endorsed by the Court of Appeal in *Re International Tin Council* [1989] Ch. 309; (1988) 4 B.C.C. 653. The Council was an organisation formed by international treaty with the legal character, status and capacities of a corporate body. In holding that it was not within CA 1985 s.665 (the precursor of the present section), the court adopted the broad test laid down in *Re St James's Club* (above): was the association one which Parliament could reasonably have intended should be subject to the winding-up process? If any state, whether a member of the Council or not, could subject that enterprise to its own domestic law, the independence and international character of the organisation would be fragmented and destroyed. Accordingly, an English court would not assume jurisdiction under s.665. The ruling in *Re St James's Club* was applied to a professional football club in *Re Witney Town Football and Social Club* [1993] B.C.C. 874. For the same reason s.220 does not confer jurisdiction to wind up a trade union: *Re National Union of Flint Glassworkers* [2006] B.C.C. 828, or an unincorporated charitable trust (*Gilbert Deya Ministries v Kashmir Broadcasting Corp Ltd* [2010] EWHC 3015 (Ch), or an unincorporated social club (*Baker v West Reading Social Club* [2014] EWHC 3033 (Ch); [2014] B.C.C. 575).

Note, however, that the court also has power under its general equitable jurisdiction to order the winding up of an unincorporated association, independently of this Part of IA 1986, and to give powers to those administering the winding up similar to those conferred on liquidators by Sch.4: *Butts Park Ventures (Coventry) Ltd v Bryant Homes Central Ltd* [2003] EWHC 2487 (Ch); [2004] B.C.C. 207 and *Baker v West Reading Social Club* (above). In the latter case the powers conferred on the liquidator were restricted to those the court considered sufficient. In *National Union of Flint Glassworkers* (above) an order was made in the exercise of this jurisdiction for the dissolution of the union concerned.

221 Winding up of unregistered companies

221(1) [Application of winding-up provisions] Subject to the provisions of this Part, any unregistered company may be wound up under this Act; and all the provisions of Regulation (EC) No 1082/2006 of the European Parliament and of the Council and of this Act about winding up apply to an unregistered company with the exceptions and additions mentioned in the following subsections.

221(2) [Principal place of business in Northern Ireland] If an unregistered company has a principal place of business situated in Northern Ireland, it shall not be wound up under this Part unless it has a principal place of business situated in England and Wales or Scotland, or in both England and Wales and Scotland.

221(3) [Deemed registration, registered office] For the purpose of determining a court's winding-up jurisdiction, an unregistered company is deemed–

(a) to be registered in England and Wales or Scotland, according as its principal place of business is situated in England and Wales or Scotland, or

(b) if it has a principal place of business situated in both countries, to be registered in both countries;

and the principal place of business situated in that part of Great Britain in which proceedings are being instituted is, for all purposes of the winding up, deemed to be the registered office of the company.

221(4) [No voluntary winding up] No unregistered company shall be wound up under this Act voluntarily, except in accordance with the EU Regulation.

221(5) [Circumstances for winding up] The circumstances in which an unregistered company may be wound up are as follows–

(a) if the company is dissolved, or has ceased to carry on business, or is carrying on business only for the purpose of winding up its affairs;

(b) if the company is unable to pay its debts;

(c) if the court is of opinion that it is just and equitable that the company should be wound up.

221(6) [Repealed as from 21 July 1986—Trustee Savings Banks Act 1985 s.4(3) and SI 1986/1223 (C. 36).]

221(7) [Scotland] In Scotland, an unregistered company which the Court of Session has jurisdiction to wind up may be wound up by the court if there is subsisting a floating charge over property comprised in the company's property and undertaking, and the court is satisfied that the security of the creditor entitled to the benefit of the floating charge is in jeopardy.

For this purpose a creditor's security is deemed to be in jeopardy if the court is satisfied that events have occurred or are about to occur which render it unreasonable in the creditor's interests that the company should retain power to dispose of the property which is subject to the floating charge.

General Note

On the question when the court will exercise jurisdiction to wind up a foreign company, see the note to s.220.

The court has an unrestricted discretion to make or refuse an order, or to make an order subject to conditions. Thus, in the case of an overseas company, it may decline to order a winding up, or grant a stay of proceedings here, on the ground that insolvency proceedings already instituted in another jurisdiction are capable of dealing with the matter (*New Hampshire Insurance Co v Rush & Tompkins Group plc* [1998] 2 B.C.L.C. 471). Alternatively, it may direct that the local winding up be conducted on a basis ancillary to a principal liquidation elsewhere (see *Re Commercial Bank of South Australia* (1886) 33 Ch. D. 174; *Re Hibernian Merchants Ltd* [1958] Ch. 76). (Note also in this connection the CBIR Sch.1 art.28, on the effect of the recognition of a foreign proceeding as a "main" proceeding.) In *Lancefield v Lancefield* [2002] B.P.I.R. 1108 it was held that the court could of its own motion make a winding-up order under s.220 even though no petition had been presented.

Under CA 2006 s.895(2)(b), a "company", for the purposes of schemes of arrangement under Pt 26 of that Act means "any company liable to be wound up under IA 1986". In *Re Rodenstock GmbH* [2011] EWHC 1104 (Ch); [2012] B.C.C. 459 it was held that, for the purposes of this definition, nothing in (what is now) the Judgments Regulation 2012/1215 or the EU Regulation should be taken as intended to impact restrictively upon the scope of the court's traditional jurisdiction in this country to sanction schemes of arrangement. The fact that, on the particular facts of the case, it would not be possible to have the company put into liquidation did not prevent it being "a company liable to be wound up" within the definition.

Re Rodenstock has been followed in a number of other cases where a procedure comparable to a Pt 26 scheme of arrangement is not available to the company in question in its home jurisdiction: see, e.g. *Primacom Holdings GmbH v Credit Agricole* [2012] EWHC 164 (Ch); [2013] B.C.C. 201; *Re Seat Pagine Gialle SpA* [2012] EWHC 3686 (Ch); *Re NEF Telecom Co BV* [2012] EWHC 2944 (Ch); *Re Cortefiel SA and MEP II Sarl* [2012] EWHC 4192 (Ch). There was some concern that, under the proposals for the reform of the EC Regulation, schemes of arrangement and similar procedures would be brought within its scope, so making it impossible for companies which have their COMI within another EU jurisdiction to avail themselves of the Pt 26 procedure in this country, but happily, under the recast Regulation which came into force on 26 June 2017, express provision is made for the exclusion of such proceedings. (The topic is now the subject of a separate EU initiative.)

Section 221(1) amended by European Grouping of Territorial Cooperation Regulations 2007 (SI 2007//1949) Sch.1 para.7 as from 1 August 2007.

S.221(4)

Section 221(4) amended by the Insolvency Amendment (EU 2015/848) Regulations 2017 (SI 2017/702) regs 1, 2, Sch. paras 1, 13 in relation to proceedings opened in England and Wales on or after 26 June 2017 (see reg.3) when the Recast EU Regulation 2015/848 came into force.

Previously the words "except in accordance with the EC Regulation" were added by the Insolvency Act 1986 (Amendment) (No.2) Regulations 2002 (SI 2002/1240, effective 31 May 2002). It is thus now possible for a company incorporated elsewhere in the EU which has its centre of main interests in England to be wound up in England under a creditors' voluntary winding up: see *Re TXU Europe German Finance BV* [2005] B.C.C. 90. The administration of such a liquidation will be governed by English law.

S.221(5)

The grounds for the winding up of an unregistered company which are set out in this subsection are more restricted than those for registered companies: see s.122.

The court has jurisdiction to wind up a foreign company under this subsection even though it has no assets here, provided that a sufficiently close connection can be shown, e.g. that the debt upon which the petition is founded was incurred here: *Re a Company (No.00359 of 1987)* [1988] Ch. 210; (1987) 3 B.C.C. 160. However, this will not be the case where the EU Regulation applies.

S.221(6)

This was repealed as from 21 July 1986—Trustee Savings Banks Act 1985 s.4(3) and SI 1986/1223 (C. 36).

S.221(7)

See the note to s.122(2).

222 Inability to pay debts: unpaid creditor for £750 or more

222(1) [Deemed inability to pay debts] An unregistered company is deemed (for the purposes of section 221) unable to pay its debts if there is a creditor, by assignment or otherwise, to whom the company is indebted in a sum exceeding £750 then due and–

(a) the creditor has served on the company, by leaving at its principal place of business, or by delivering to the secretary or some director, manager or principal officer of the company, or by otherwise serving in such manner as the court may approve or direct, a written demand in the prescribed form requiring the company to pay the sum due, and

(b) the company has for 3 weeks after the service of the demand neglected to pay the sum or to secure or compound for it to the creditor's satisfaction.

222(2) [Increase or reduction of s.222(1) sum] The money sum for the time being specified in subsection (1) is subject to increase or reduction by regulations under section 417 in Part XV; but no increase in the sum so specified affects any case in which the winding-up petition was presented before the coming into force of the increase.

General Note

This provision modifies the definition of "inability to pay debts" contained in s.123(1)(a) above to meet the case of an unregistered company. See further the notes to that section.

S.222(1)(a)

The demand must be "in the prescribed form", and also in hard copy (LRO 2010 (SI 2010/18) art.4(2)(h)). For details, see IR 2016 rr.7.3 et seq.

223 Inability to pay debts: debt remaining unsatisfied after action brought

223 An unregistered company is deemed (for the purposes of section 221) unable to pay its debts if an action or other proceeding has been instituted against any member for any debt or demand due, or claimed to be due, from the company, or from him in his character of member, and–

(a) notice in writing of the institution of the action or proceeding has been served on the company by leaving it at the company's principal place of business (or by delivering it to the secretary, or some director, manager or principal officer of the company, or by otherwise serving it in such manner as the court may approve or direct), and

(b) the company has not within 3 weeks after service of the notice paid, secured or compounded for the debt or demand, or procured the action or proceeding to be stayed or sisted, or indemnified the defendant or defender to his reasonable satisfaction against the action or proceeding, and against all costs, damages and expenses to be incurred by him because of it.

General Note

There is no provision corresponding directly to this section in the case of a registered company. The notice under s.223(a) must be in hard copy (LRO 2010 (SI 2010/18) art.4(2)(i)).

224 Inability to pay debts: other cases

224(1) [Deemed inability to pay debts] An unregistered company is deemed (for purposes of section 221) unable to pay its debts–

(a) if in England and Wales execution or other process issued on a judgment, decree or order obtained in any court in favour of a creditor against the company, or any member of it as such, or any person authorised to be sued as nominal defendant on behalf of the company, is returned unsatisfied;

(b) if in Scotland the inducíae of a charge for payment on an extract decree, or an extract registered bond, or an extract registered protest, have expired without payment being made;

(c) if in Northern Ireland a certificate of unenforceability has been granted in respect of any judgment, decree or order obtained as mentioned in paragraph (a);

(d) if it is otherwise proved to the satisfaction of the court that the company is unable to pay its debts as they fall due.

224(2) [Deemed inability—another situation] An unregistered company is also deemed unable to pay its debts if it is proved to the satisfaction of the court that the value of the company's assets is less than the amount of its liabilities, taking into account its contingent and prospective liabilities.

General Note

The provisions of this section correspond with those of s.123(1)(b)–(e), (2): see the notes to that section.

225 Company incorporated outside Great Britain may be wound up though dissolved

225(1) [Extent] Where a company incorporated outside Great Britain which has been carrying on business in Great Britain ceases to carry on business in Great Britain, it may be wound up as an unregistered company under this Act, notwithstanding that it has been dissolved or otherwise ceased to exist as a company under or by virtue of the laws of the country under which it was incorporated.

225(2) [Applicability of EU Regulation] This section is subject to the EU Regulation.

General Note

The jurisdiction of the court to wind up a foreign company is not, of course, limited to the circumstances set out in this section. In practice, the more widely drawn provisions of s.221 are normally relied on: s.225 derives originally from CA 1928 s.91, which was enacted to remove a doubt as to the court's jurisdiction which arose in connection with the dissolution of Russian banks following the revolution of 1917 (see the explanation by Lord Atkin in *Russian and English Bank v Baring Bros & Co Ltd* [1936] A.C. 405 at 423–425); it did not confer any new power to wind up companies (per Megarry J in *Re Compania Merabello San Nicholas SA* [1973] Ch. 75 at 85, 86; and per Morritt J in *Re Normandy Marketing Ltd* [1993] B.C.C. 879 at 883). In *Re Eurodis Electron plc* [2011] EWHC 1025 (Ch); [2012] B.C.C. 57 a Belgian company which had been put into administration in this country was later ordered to be wound up by a Belgian court and subsequently dissolved. The Belgian proceedings had been wrongly brought because the company's COMI was in England and the existing English proceedings were main proceedings, but it was held that an English court had no jurisdiction to overrule the Belgian court's decisions and must respect the fact that the company had been dissolved. The administration could not be continued but it was appropriate to make a winding-up order. In *Re Agrenco Madeira-Comércio Internacional Lda* [2015] B.C.C. 300 the court held that an ongoing winding up in England would survive the subsequent dissolution of a Portuguese company in its home jurisdiction.

S.225(2)

This subsection was added by the Insolvency Act 1986 (Amendment) (No.2) Regulations 2002 (SI 2002/1240, effective 31 May 2002), in parallel with the amendment to s.221(4) and amended by the Insolvency Amendment (EU 2015/848) Regulations 2017 (SI 2017/702) regs 1, 2(1), Sch. paras 1, 13 in relation to proceedings opened on or after 26 June 2017 (see reg.3) when the Recast EU Regulation 2015/848 came into force. See the note to s.221(4).

226 Contributories in winding up of unregistered company

226(1) [Deemed contributory] In the event of an unregistered company being wound up, every person is deemed a contributory who is liable to pay or contribute to the payment of any debt or liability of the company, or to pay or contribute to the payment of any sum for the adjustment of the rights of members among themselves, or to pay or contribute to the payment of the expenses of winding up the company.

226(2) [Liability for contribution] Every contributory is liable to contribute to the company's assets all sums due from him in respect of any such liability as is mentioned above.

226(3) [Unregistered company re mines in stannaries] In the case of an unregistered company engaged in or formed for working mines within the stannaries, a past member is not liable to contribute to the assets if he has ceased to be a member for 2 years or more either before the mine ceased to be worked or before the date of the winding-up order.

226(4) [Omitted by the Companies Act 2006 (Consequential Amendments, Transitional Provisions and Savings) Order 2009 Sch.1 para.76(5).]

General Note

The reference in s.226(3) to "the stannaries" is to certain Cornish tin-mining companies, which were formerly governed by separate legislation.

227 Power of court to stay, sist or restrain proceedings

227 The provisions of this Part with respect to staying, sisting or restraining actions and proceedings against a company at any time after the presentation of a petition for winding up and before the making of a winding-up order extend, in the case of an unregistered company, where the application to stay, sist or restrain is presented by a creditor, to actions and proceedings against any contributory of the company.

General Note

Compare *Phillips & Harland v Symes* [2006] EWHC 2595 (Ch); [2008] B.P.I.R. 212.

228 Actions stayed on winding-up order

228 Where an order has been made for winding up an unregistered company, no action or proceeding shall be proceeded with or commenced against any contributory of the company in respect of any debt of the company, except by leave of the court, and subject to such terms as the court may impose.

229 Provisions of this Part to be cumulative

229(1) [Part V in addition to Pt IV] The provisions of this Part with respect to unregistered companies are in addition to and not in restriction of any provisions in Part IV with respect to winding up companies by the court; and the court or liquidator may exercise any powers or do any act in the case of unregistered companies which might be exercised or done by it or him in winding up companies registered under the Companies Act 2006 in England and Wales or Scotland.

229(2) [Omitted by the Companies Act 2006 (Consequential Amendments, Transitional Provisions and Savings) Order 2009 Sch.1 para.76(6)(b).]

Part VI

Miscellaneous Provisions Applying to Companies which are Insolvent or in Liquidation

Introductory note to Part VI

The heading to this Part is likely to give rise to confusion, because of the phrase "companies which are insolvent". The natural inference to be drawn from this would be that nothing in ss.230–246 applies to a company which is solvent (in a financial sense) so that, for instance, an officer of a company is not under a duty to co-operate with an administrative receiver if the company in question is in fact solvent. The possible confusion is made worse by the absence of any statutory definition of "insolvent" company, though there is a definition of "insolvency" in s.247(1) (and of "onset of insolvency" in ss.240(3) and 245(5), of "goes into insolvent liquidation" in ss.214(6) and 216(7), and of "becomes insolvent" in CDDA 1986 s.6(2)). "Insolvency" in ss.247(1), 240(3) and 245(5) plainly refers to the various types of insolvency *proceedings* (liquidation, administration, administrative receivership, etc.) while "insolvent" in ss.214(6), 214(7) and CDDA 1986 s.6(2) is concerned with the company's financial state.

In the heading to this Part, the words "which are insolvent" should probably be taken as meaning "which are the subject of insolvency proceedings"; and "insolvency" could then be construed in accordance with the definition in s.247(1). This may violate to a degree the more natural connotation of the word "insolvent"; but it does mean that the whole of Pt VI can be applied without qualification. The alternative is to take "insolvent" as meaning "not financially viable", which raises serious problems because (1) no definition of "insolvent" is given in the body of this Part, and the word admits of many interpretations (see the note to s.123); and (2) the whole of Pt VI would be subject to limitations which the text of the Act does not specify.

It is generally understood that headings within a statute may be looked at to resolve an ambiguity in the sections that are grouped under them (Halsbury, *Laws of England*, 5th edn, Vol.96, para.1112); but it would be unusual to import into the text of an Act qualifications (and ambiguities) which appear only from the words of a heading.

It is therefore submitted that Pt VI applies to *all* companies, whether financially "solvent" or "insolvent", and that "insolvent" must be read analogously with the definition of "insolvency" in s.247(1)—that is, as meaning "which are the subject of insolvency proceedings".

On the scope of the EU Regulation on Insolvency Proceedings 2015, see the Introductory note to the Regulation in Vol.2.

Insolvency cannot be inferred from the mere fact that a company has been dissolved: *Secretary of State for Business, Innovation and Skills v Coward* [2011] B.C.C. 712.

Various definitions of insolvency are found in other legislation: see, e.g. Sale of Goods Act 1979 s.61(4); Employment Rights Act 1996 s.183 (on which, see *Secretary of State for Trade and Industry v Key* [2004] B.P.I.R. 214). The term may also call for construction when used in a document (e.g. "insolvency event"), as in *Martyn Rose Ltd v AKG Group Ltd* [2003] EWCA Civ 375; [2003] 2 B.C.L.C. 102; and *Centre Reinsurance International Co v Curzon Insurance Ltd* [2004] EWHC 200 (Ch); [2006] 1 B.C.L.C. 187. (Note that this case went to appeal, ultimately to the House of Lords ([2006] 1 W.L.R. 2863; [2006] UKHL 45; [2006] B.C.C. 971), but there was no appeal on this point.) See also *Re Cheyne Finance plc* [2007] EWHC 2402 (Ch); [2008] B.C.C. 182; *Merrill Lynch International Bank Ltd v Winterthur Swiss Insurance Co* [2007] EWHC 893 (Comm); [2008] B.P.I.R.129; *Butters v BBC Worldwide Ltd* [2009] EWHC 1954 (Ch); [2009] B.P.I.R. 1315; *BNY Corporate Trustee Services Ltd v Eurosail-UK 2007-3BL plc* [2013] UKSC 28; [2013] 1 W.L.R. 1408; [2013] B.C.C. 397; *Re MF Global UK Ltd* [2012] EWHC 3068 (Ch); [2013] 1 W.L.R. 903; and see the note to s.123.

However, the test for "insolvency" in a document must be determined by the law applicable to the particular debtor so that (e.g. in the case of a foreign company) definitions under English law will be irrelevant: *Strategic Value Master Fund Ltd v Idea Standard International Acquisition Sarl* [2011] EWHC 171 (Ch); [2011] 1 B.C.L.C. 475.

Office-holders

230 Holders of office to be qualified insolvency practitioners

230(1) (Section 230(1) ceased to have effect and repealed by the Enterprise Act 2002 s.248(3), Sch.17 para.9, 19 and s.278(2), Sch.26 as from 15 September 2003.)

230(2) [Administrative receiver] Where an administrative receiver of a company is appointed, he must be a person who is so qualified.

230(3) [Liquidator] Where a company goes into liquidation, the liquidator must be a person who is so qualified.

230(4) [Provisional liquidator] Where a provisional liquidator is appointed, he must be a person who is so qualified.

230(5) [Official receiver] Subsections (3) and (4) are without prejudice to any enactment under which the official receiver is to be, or may be, liquidator or provisional liquidator.

General Note

This section requires that a person appointed to any of the various offices mentioned shall be qualified to act as an insolvency practitioner in relation to the company in question. The term "act as an insolvency practitioner" (in relation to a company) is defined by s.388(1), and "qualified" and "qualified … in relation to" by s.390(2) and s.390(3) respectively. It is an offence under s.389 for a person to act as an insolvency practitioner in relation to a company at a time when he is not qualified to do so.

Section 230(1), which required an administrator to be qualified to act as an insolvency practitioner in relation to the company, was repealed by EA 2002 Sch.17 para.19 with effect from 15 September 2003. The point, so far as concerns administrators appointed under IA 1986 Sch.B1, is now covered by para.6 of the latter Schedule. At the same time a separate provision dealing with this category of administrators was enacted in EA 2002 Sch.16, which is now to be found in IA 1986 Sch.B1 para.75, and a saving provision, reinstating s.230(1), came into effect under the Enterprise Act 2002 (Commencement No.4 and Transitional Provisions and Savings) Order 2003 (SI 2003/2093 (C. 85)) art.3. This saving provision applies in cases where a petition for an administration order was presented before 15 September 2003, and also in the administration of insolvent partnerships commencing prior to 1 July 2005, limited liability partnerships and bodies which are insurers under FSMA 2000 and SI 2001/2634. There is no mention in the Order of the public utility companies listed in EA 2002 s.249 but in these cases the original s.230 will continue to apply because s.249 disapplies the new s.8(3) in regard to such bodies.

See also the note to s.212(1).

There is no reference in s.230 to the nominee or the supervisor of a voluntary arrangement under Pt I of the Act, which is a little odd since each of these is required also to be a "qualified" insolvency practitioner (see ss.1(2), 2(4), 4(2), 7(5)).

A receiver who is not an administrative receiver is not required to be a qualified insolvency practitioner, but there are specific prohibitions in ss.30, 31, 51(3) on the appointment of corporate bodies and undischarged bankrupts as receivers.

Section 388 defines the expression "acts as an insolvency practitioner", and (in s.388(6)) disapplies that section in relation to insolvency proceedings under the EU Regulation in a Member State other than the UK. The CBIR reg.8 similarly disapplies s.388 as regards anything done by a foreign representative under or by virtue of the CBIR or in relation to relief granted or co-operation or co-ordination provided under those Regulations.

S.230(5)

The official receiver is an officer of the court and is responsible directly to it and to the Secretary of State (see s.400(2)). He is not subject to the regulatory regime introduced by this Act for private insolvency practitioners.

231 Appointment to office of two or more persons

231(1) [Application] This section applies if an appointment or nomination of any person to the office of administrative receiver, liquidator or provisional liquidator–

(a) relates to more than one person, or

(b) has the effect that the office is to be held by more than one person.

231(2) [Declaration in appointment or nomination] The appointment or nomination shall declare whether any act required or authorised under any enactment to be done by the administrative receiver, liquidator or provisional liquidator is to be done by all or any one or more of the persons for the time being holding the office in question.

General Note

There are very few references in the present Act to joint appointments, but under the normal rules of statutory interpretation words in the singular may be taken to include the plural (Interpretation Act 1978 s.6(c)), and (if it were needed) this section adds further confirmation.

Section 231 makes no reference to the possibility of making a joint appointment to the post of nominee or supervisor of a voluntary arrangement, but it appears from s.7(6) that this, too, is contemplated by the Act: see the note to that provision.

The word "administrator" has been omitted from subss.(1) and (2) by EA 2002 Sch.17 para.20. The point is now covered by IA 1986 Sch.B1 paras 100 et seq. for administrators appointed under that Schedule, and in other cases by s.249 and the Enterprise Act 2002 (Commencement No.4 and Transitional Provisions and Savings) Order 2003 (SI 2003/2093 (C. 85)) art.3. See the notes to ss.212(1) and 230.

232 Validity of office-holder's acts

232 The acts of an individual as administrative receiver, liquidator or provisional liquidator of a company are valid notwithstanding any defect in his appointment, nomination or qualifications.

General Note

This is a standard-form provision, similar to that applicable to directors (CA 2006 s.161). It could not operate, however, to protect acts done where there was no power to appoint at all—e.g. where an administrative receiver is purportedly appointed under an invalid instrument. (See, on this latter point, s.34 above, and on void appointments generally, *Morris v Kanssen* [1946] A.C. 459; *Rolled Steel Products (Holdings) Ltd v British Steel Corporation* [1986] Ch. 246; (1984) 1 B.C.C. 99,158.)

The protection conferred by s.232 is confined to acts done by an *individual*. A body corporate is not qualified to act as an insolvency practitioner (s.390(1)), and it is extremely unlikely that in future there would ever be an attempt to appoint one to hold any of the offices listed in s.232. It is probably correct to infer from the express limitation of s.232 to individuals that any act done by such a corporate appointee would be wholly void. In the case of a receiver (not necessarily an administrative receiver), s.30 adds a further statutory ban on corporate appointments, and it is established that acts done by a receiver appointed in breach of this provision are totally ineffective: see *Portman Building Society v Gallwey* [1955] 1 W.L.R. 96.

The word "administrator" has been omitted from s.232 by EA 2002 Sch.17 para.21. The point is now covered by IA 1986 Sch.B1 para.104 for administrators appointed under that Schedule, and in other cases by EA 2002 s.249 and the Enterprise Act 2002 (Commencement No.4 and Transitional Provisions and Savings) Order 2003 (SI 2003/2093 (C. 85)) art.3. See the notes to ss.212(1) and 230.

There is again no reference in this section to the acts of a person as the nominee or supervisor of a voluntary arrangement. The explanation must be that such a person's role and functions are not statutory, but depend in each case upon the terms of the arrangement.

Management by administrators, liquidators, etc.

233 Supplies of gas, water, electricity, etc.

233(1) [Application] This section applies in the case of a company where–

(a) the company enters administration, or

(b) an administrative receiver is appointed, or

(ba) a moratorium under section 1A is in force, or

(c) a voluntary arrangement approved under Part I, has taken effect, or

(d) the company goes into liquidation, or

(e) a provisional liquidator is appointed;

and "the office-holder" means the administrator, the administrative receiver, the nominee, the supervisor of the voluntary arrangement, the liquidator or the provisional liquidator, as the case may be.

233(2) [If request by office-holder] If a request is made by or with the concurrence of the office-holder for the giving, after the effective date, of any of the supplies mentioned in the next subsection, the supplier–

(a) may make it a condition of the giving of the supply that the office-holder personally guarantees the payment of any charges in respect of the supply, but

(b) shall not make it a condition of the giving of the supply, or do anything which has the effect of making it a condition of the giving of the supply, that any outstanding charges in respect of a supply given to the company before the effective date are paid.

233(3) [Supplies in s.233(2)] The supplies referred to in subsection (2) are–

(a) a supply of gas by a gas supplier within the meaning of Part I of the Gas Act 1986,

(aa) a supply of gas by a person within paragraph 1 of Schedule 2A to the Gas Act 1986 (supply by landlords etc.),

(b) a supply of electricity by an electricity supplier within the meaning of Part I of the Electricity Act 1989,

(ba) a supply of electricity by a class of person within Class A (small suppliers) or Class B (resale) of Schedule 4 to the Electricity (Class Exemptions from the Requirement for a Licence) Order 2001 (S.I. 2001/3270),

(c) a supply of water by a water undertaker or, in Scotland, Scottish Water,

(ca) a supply of water by a water supply licensee within the meaning of the Water Industry Act 1991, (cb) a supply of water by a water services provider within the meaning of the Water Services etc. (Scotland) Act 2005,

(cc) a supply of water by a person who has an interest in the premises to which the supply is given,

(d) a supply of communications services by a provider of a public electronic communications service,

(e) a supply of communications services by a person who carries on a business which includes giving such supplies,

(f) a supply of goods or services mentioned in subsection (3A) by a person who carries on a business which includes giving such supplies, where the supply is for the purpose of enabling or facilitating anything to be done by electronic means.

233(3A) [Goods and services in s.233(3)(f)] The goods and services referred to in subsection (3)(f) are–

(a) point of sale terminals;

(b) computer hardware and software;

(c) information, advice and technical assistance in connection with the use of information technology;

(d) data storage and processing;

(e) website hosting.

233(4) [Effective date] "The effective date" for the purposes of this section is whichever is applicable of the following dates–

(a) the date on which the company entered administration,

(b) the date on which the administrative receiver was appointed (or, if he was appointed in succession to another administrative receiver, the date on which the first of his predecessors was appointed),

(ba) the date on which the moratorium came into force,

(c) the date on which the voluntary arrangement took effect,

(d) the date on which the company went into liquidation,

(e) the date on which the provisional liquidator was appointed.

233(5) [Definitions] The following applies to expressions used in subsection (3)–

(a) [Repealed]

(b) [Repealed]

(c) [Repealed]

(d) "communications services" do not include electronic communications services to the extent that they are used to broadcast or otherwise transmit programme services (within the meaning of the Communications Act 2003).

General Note

Section 233 was extensively amended by the Insolvency (Protection of Essential Supplies) Order 2015 (SI 2015/989) art.2 as from 1 October 2015, implementing the Enterprise and Regulatory Reform Act 2013 s.92.

This section (and its counterpart in bankruptcy, s.372 below) implements a recommendation of the Cork Committee (*Report*, para.1462). Prior to the present Act, a supplier of goods like gas or water or services such as the telephone was able, by virtue of its monopoly position, to compel the payment of an account incurred before the commencement of a liquidation or receivership by threatening to cut off the connection unless the arrears were paid in full or payment was personally guaranteed by the liquidator or receiver. If the supply was essential for the preservation of the company's assets (e.g. livestock or frozen food), there was little choice but to pay, and so the supplier could have its debt paid in priority even to the statutory preferential creditors. The legality of this practice was upheld in *Wellworth Cash & Carry (North Shields) Ltd v North Eastern Electricity Board* (1986) 2 B.C.C. 99,265. This section prohibits further resort to this practice. The supplier may require the "office-holder" to undertake personal responsibility for payment for any new supply, but may not make the provision of a new supply conditional upon receiving payment or security for the old. The scope of s.233 was extended by the 2015 Order so as to add to the supplies specified in the original Act the categories of supply listed in s.233(2)(aa), (ba), (ca)–(cc) and (e) and the supply of the goods and services specified in s.233(3A) where it is for the purpose of enabling or facilitating anything to be done by electronic means (s.233(2)(f)). The protection now includes the supply of utilities by a landlord to a tenant. Note that until the commencement of the Water Act 2014 s.1 the words "licensed water supplier" are to be substituted for the words "water supply licensee" in s.233(2)(ca): see art.2(4) of the Order.

In *Official Receiver v Sahaviriya Steel Industries UK Ltd* [2015] EWHC 2877 (Ch); [2016] B.C.C. 456 the court was asked for the first time as to the extra-territorial effect of s.233. The official receiver as liquidator wished to make a request for an ongoing IT system supply from the company's parent company in Thailand and applied for permission for service out of the jurisdiction on the parent for that request. The circumstances leading to the making of the application were of such potential gravity that justice required that permission be granted as access to the IT system was necessary so that the UK plant could be managed safely. The order was granted without notice as there was already a high risk of damage to the plant which would be heightened if the system access was not restored.

For a valuable analysis of this provision and s.233A see Hodgson and Sidle [2017] Recovery (Winter).

S.233(1)

The section extends to a CVA, provided that it has taken effect, as well as to the other situations listed, and "office-holder" is accordingly defined to include the supervisor of such a scheme. Formerly, there was no equivalent protection during the period prior to the holding of the statutory meetings, but amendments made by IA 2000 s.1 and Sch.1 paras 1, 8(1), (2) as from 1 January 2003 (by the insertion of para.(ba) into subss.(1) and (4)) now meet that need for companies which are eligible for a moratorium. Other companies may be well advised to consider the alternative of administration.

S.233(2)

The "effective date" is defined by s.233(4).

S.233(3)

Some of the terms used in this subsection are explained in s.233(5). The scope of the section is confined to statutory undertakers and similar bodies which are under a legal obligation to provide a service to the public: a private supplier of, e.g. gas or water is not affected. Section 233(3)(c) amended and s.233(5)(c) repealed by the Water Industry (Scotland) Act 2002 (Consequential Modifications) Order 2004 (SI 2004/1822) art.1(2) and Sch. para.14 as from 14 July 2004.

S.233(4)

The phrase "go into liquidation" is defined in s.247(2): see the note to that subsection.

S.233(5)(a), (b), (c)

The definitions formerly set out here became redundant when s.233(3)(a), (b) was reworded by the Gas Act 1995 s.16(1) and Sch.4 para.14(1), as from 1 March 1996, the Utilities Act 2000 s.108 and Sch.6 para.47(1), (2)(a) as from 1 October 2001 and the Water Industry (Scotland) Act 2002 (Consequential Modifications) Order 2004 (SI 2004/1822) art.1(2) and Sch. para.14 as from 14 July 2004, respectively. The substance of s.233 is unchanged.

233A Further protection of essential supplies

233A(1) [Cessation of insolvency-related term of contract for supply] An insolvency-related term of a contract for the supply of essential goods or services to a company ceases to have effect if–

(a) the company enters administration, or

(b) a voluntary arrangement approved under Part 1 takes effect in relation to the company.

233A(2) [Non-cessation of insolvency-related term] An insolvency-related term of a contract does not cease to have effect by virtue of subsection (1) to the extent that–

(a) it provides for the contract or the supply to terminate, or any other thing to take place, because the company becomes subject to an insolvency procedure other than administration or a voluntary arrangement;

(b) it entitles a supplier to terminate the contract or the supply, or do any other thing, because the company becomes subject to an insolvency procedure other than administration or a voluntary arrangement; or

(c) it entitles a supplier to terminate the contract or the supply because of an event that occurs, or may occur, after the company enters administration or the voluntary arrangement takes effect.

233A(3) [Power of supplier to terminate contract or supply] Where an insolvency-related term of a contract ceases to have effect under this section the supplier may–

(a) terminate the contract, if the condition in subsection (4) is met;

(b) terminate the supply, if the condition in subsection (5) is met.

233A(4) [Condition for terminating contract under s.233A(3)(a)] The condition in this subsection is that–

(a) the insolvency office-holder consents to the termination of the contract,

(b) the court grants permission for the termination of the contract, or

(c) any charges in respect of the supply that are incurred after the company entered administration or the voluntary arrangement took effect are not paid within the period of 28 days beginning with the day on which payment is due.

The court may grant permission under paragraph (b) only if satisfied that the continuation of the contract would cause the supplier hardship.

233A(5) [Condition for terminating contract under s.233A(3)(b)] The condition in this subsection is that–

(a) the supplier gives written notice to the insolvency office-holder that the supply will be terminated unless the office-holder personally guarantees the payment of any charges in respect of the continuation of the supply after the company entered administration or the voluntary arrangement took effect, and

(b) the insolvency office-holder does not give that guarantee within the period of 14 days beginning with the day the notice is received.

233A(6) [Securing protection of interests of suppliers] For the purposes of securing that the interests of suppliers are protected, where–

(a) an insolvency-related term of a contract (the "original term") ceases to have effect by virtue of subsection (1), and

(b) the company subsequently enters administration, or a voluntary arrangement subsequently has effect in relation to it,

the contract is treated for the purposes of subsections (1) to (5) as if, immediately before the subsequent administration is entered into or the subsequent voluntary arrangement takes effect, it included an insolvency-related term identical to the original term.

233A(7) [Contract for supply of essential goods or services] A contract for the supply of essential goods or services is a contract for a supply mentioned in section 233(3).

233A(8) [Insolvency-related term of contract for supply of essential goods or services] An insolvency-related term of a contract for the supply of essential goods or services to a company is a provision of the contract under which–

(a) the contract or the supply would terminate, or any other thing would take place, because the company enters administration or the voluntary arrangement takes effect,

(b) the supplier would be entitled to terminate the contract or the supply, or to do any other thing, because the company enters administration or the voluntary arrangement takes effect, or

(c) the supplier would be entitled to terminate the contract or the supply because of an event that occurred before the company enters administration or the voluntary arrangement takes effect.

233A(9) ["Insolvency office-holder"] In this section "insolvency office-holder" means–

(a) in a case where a company enters administration, the administrator;

(b) in a case where a voluntary arrangement under Part 1 takes effect in relation to a company, the supervisor of the voluntary arrangement.

233A(10) [No effect before 1 October 2015] Subsection (1) does not have effect in relation to a contract entered into before 1st October 2015.

General Note

This section was inserted by the Insolvency (Protection of Essential Supplies) Order 2015 (SI 2015/989) art.4 as from 1 October 2015, implementing the Enterprise and Regulatory Reform Act 2013 s.93. It provides that certain "insolvency-related terms" in contracts cease to have effect, so preventing a supplier from terminating a supply, terminating a contract, altering the terms of a contract or compelling higher payments for the supply, when a company enters administration or a CVA is approved. It affects only those contracts for the supplies listed under s.233. It does not apply, however in a winding up: the supplier is free to terminate a contract (etc.) when a company goes into liquidation. Corresponding provision is made for an IVA by s.372A.

S.233A(2)
In so far as a contract entitles the supplier to terminate the contract (etc.) in the event of a liquidation or an insolvency procedure other than an administration or CVA, it is not affected by s.233A. A similar exemption applies where the contract empowers the supplier to take such action on the happening of an event subsequent to the commencement of an administration or CVA.

S.233A(3)–(5)
Note these exceptions to the operation of s.233A.

234 Getting in the company's property

234(1) [Application] This section applies in the case of a company where–

(a) the company enters administration,

(b) an administrative receiver is appointed, or

(c) the company goes into liquidation, or

(d) a provisional liquidator is appointed;

and "the office-holder" means the administrator, the administrative receiver, the liquidator or the provisional liquidator, as the case may be.

234(2) [Court's powers] Where any person has in his possession or control any property, books, papers or records to which the company appears to be entitled, the court may require that person forthwith (or within such period as the court may direct) to pay, deliver, convey, surrender or transfer the property, books, papers or records to the office-holder.

234(3) [Application of s.234(4)] Where the office-holder–

(a) seizes or disposes of any property which is not property of the company, and

(b) at the time of seizure or disposal believes, and has reasonable grounds for believing, that he is entitled (whether in pursuance of an order of the court or otherwise) to seize or dispose of that property,

the next subsection has effect.

234(4) [Liability of office-holder] In that case the office-holder–

(a) is not liable to any person in respect of any loss or damage resulting from the seizure or disposal except in so far as that loss or damage is caused by the office-holder's own negligence, and

(b) has a lien on the property, or the proceeds of its sale, for such expenses as were incurred in connection with the seizure or disposal.

S.234(1), (2)

The present section replaces CA 1985 s.551, which applied only to a winding up by the court, and extends its provisions to every kind of winding up and to all other "insolvency" procedures except a voluntary arrangement. The office-holder may invoke the assistance of the court to get possession of the company's property and records. However, the powers conferred by ss.234–236 may be used only for the due exercise of the office-holder's statutory functions (and, in the case of an administrative receiver, such additional functions as are given to him by the charge instrument): *Sutton v GE Capital Commercial Finance Ltd* [2004] EWCA Civ 315; [2004] 2 B.C.L.C. 662. In that case an administrative receiver had requested a firm of solicitors to deliver up documents in order to assist the debenture holder in an action against a third party. The Court of Appeal ruled that this was beyond his statutory powers, which were limited to enabling him to get in, protect and realise the mortgaged property for the benefit of the debtor company and its creditors. The judgment in *Re Corporate Jet Realisations Ltd* [2015] EWHC 221 (Ch); [2015] B.C.C. 625 contains a detailed discussion of the relative rights of the office-holder and the person against whom the order for delivery up is sought, weighing on the one hand the office-holder's need and on the other hand considerations of oppression, privacy and confidentiality.

An order under s.234 should not be sought ex parte, except perhaps in very exceptional circumstances: *Re First Express Ltd* [1991] B.C.C. 782. The application should be brought in the name of the office-holder, rather than that of the company: *Re Cosslett (Contractors) Ltd (No.2), Smith v Bridgend County Borough Council* [2001] UKHL 58; [2002] 1 A.C. 336; [2001] B.C.C. 740 at [32].

Under earlier provisions corresponding to the present section, the courts had held that its procedure was not appropriate to determine questions of disputed ownership, but in *Re London Iron & Steel Co Ltd* [1990] B.C.C. 159 Warner J held that the words "to which the company appears to be entitled", coupled with the comprehensive rules laid down in IR 2016 Pt 12, are of sufficient scope to enable the court to settle such matters; and it now seems that the courts entertain such questions as a matter of course: see *Euro Commercial Leasing Ltd v Cartwright & Lewis* [1995] B.C.C. 830 (solicitor's lien); *Re Cosslett (Contractors) Ltd* [1998] Ch. 495; [1997] B.C.C. 724 (plant on construction site). However the court has no such power where the question of ownership falls to be determined by a foreign court: *Re Leyland DAF Ltd, Talbot v Edcrest Ltd* [1994] B.C.C. 166.

In *Re La Senza Ltd, Uniserve Ltd v Croxon* [2012] EWHC 1190 (Ch); [2013] B.C.C. 825 the company was in administration. The claimants sought an order under Sch.B1 para.43(3)(b) allowing them to sell goods which they held under a contractual lien; the administrators, however, had agreed to sell the goods to a third party and requested the court to order the claimants under s.234 to deliver the goods to them. The court in its discretion ruled in favour of the claimants: the terms on which the administrators intended to sell the goods did not adequately protect the claimants' rights under their lien.

Section 234(2) provides a procedure under which the court may order the delivery up of books or other documents to the office-holder. Under s.236(2), in contrast, an order may be sought directing the delivery up of such documents to the court (although, in practice, delivery directly to the office-holder is commonly made). The factors relevant to the exercise of the court's discretion are essentially the same in both cases, and so reference should be made to the more detailed discussion on this point in the note to s.236. In *Walker Morris v Khalastchi* [2001] 1 B.C.L.C. 1 the applicants, who had been requested by the liquidator to hand over files of documents relating to the company, wished to impose conditions that the liquidator should not release any of the documents or disclose their contents to the Revenue without an order of the court, but it was ruled that, since the files were the property of the company, the liquidator was entitled to possession of them and that it was for the liquidator to decide whether to make voluntary disclosure of the documents.

In a winding up by the court, the powers conferred on the court by this section are exercisable by the liquidator or provisional liquidator: see IR 2016 r.7.78. The liquidator is thus empowered to impose the requirement on his own authority.

No sanction is spelt out either in the Act or in the rules for a failure to comply with a requirement imposed under this subsection. No doubt such a failure could be dealt with under the inherent powers of the court, even in the case where the requirement is imposed by a liquidator.

S.234(3), (4)
These provisions give an immunity to the office-holder (and a lien for his expenses) where he mistakenly but bona fide seizes or disposes of property which does not belong to the company. The protection is given whether or not he has acted in pursuance of a court order granted under s.234(2)—although such an order would go a long way towards establishing his good faith.

The immunity is "in respect of any loss or damage resulting from the seizure or sale" (negligence apart). It does not appear to extend to liability for the wrongful interference per se, and so the owner would not be prevented from suing to establish his right to the return of the property itself or the proceeds of its sale.

It was held in *Welsh Development Agency Ltd v Export Finance Co* [1992] B.C.C. 270 that (notwithstanding the wide definition of "property" in s.436) the protection given to office-holders by these subsections extends only to the seizure and disposal of tangible property, and that they do not apply to wrongful dealings with choses in action. Liquidators who had sold equipment justifiably believing that it belonged to the company were held to be entitled to the protection of s.234 in *Euromex Ventures Ltd v BNP Paribas Real Estate Advisory and Property Management UK Ltd* [2013] EWHC 3007 (Ch).

On the liability of an administrator or other office holder where this statutory defence does not apply, see E. Goodwin (2009) 22 Insolv. Int. 4.

235 Duty to co-operate with office-holder

235(1) [Application] This section applies as does section 234; and it also applies, in the case of a company in respect of which a winding-up order has been made by the court in England and Wales, as if references to the office-holder included the official receiver, whether or not he is the liquidator.

235(2) [Duty to give information etc.] Each of the persons mentioned in the next subsection shall–

(a) give to the office-holder such information concerning the company and its promotion, formation, business, dealings, affairs or property as the office-holder may at any time after the effective date reasonably require, and

(b) attend on the office-holder at such times as the latter may reasonably require.

235(3) [Persons in s.235(2)] The persons referred to above are–

(a) those who are or have at any time been officers of the company,

(b) those who have taken part in the formation of the company at any time within one year before the effective date,

(c) those who are in the employment of the company, or have been in its employment (including employment under a contract for services) within that year, and are in the office-holder's opinion capable of giving information which he requires,

(d) those who are, or have within that year been, officers of, or in the employment (including employment under a contract for services) of, another company which is, or within that year was, an officer of the company in question, and

(e) in the case of a company being wound up by the court, any person who has acted as administrator, administrative receiver or liquidator of the company.

235(4) ["The effective date"] For the purposes of subsections (2) and (3), "the effective date" is whichever is applicable of the following dates–

(a) the date on which the company entered administration,

(b) the date on which the administrative receiver was appointed or, if he was appointed in succession to another administrative receiver, the date on which the first of his predecessors was appointed,

(c) the date on which the provisional liquidator was appointed, and

(d) the date on which the company went into liquidation.

235(5) [Penalty for non-compliance] If a person without reasonable excuse fails to comply with any obligation imposed by this section, he is liable to a fine and, for continued contravention, to a daily default fine.

General Note

In imposing on the former officers and employees of the company, and others, a statutory duty to co-operate with the liquidator or other office-holder by giving him such information as he may reasonably require (and to attend for this purpose on the office-holder), this section supplements the traditional powers to have such persons examined either publicly (s.133) or privately (s.236) before the court. No court order is required under the present provisions.

Information and documents obtained by the office-holder pursuant to this section may properly be disclosed to the Secretary of State so that he may determine whether director disqualification proceedings should be brought. This is so even though the office-holder has given an assurance that the information or documents will be used only for the purposes of the administration, since such disclosure is within "the purposes of the administration" (*Re Polly Peck International plc Ex p. the joint administrators* [1994] B.C.C. 15). The use of statements obtained under s.235 in disqualification proceedings does not in itself involve a breach of the European Convention on Human Rights (or, by inference, of the Human Rights Act 1998): *Re Westminster Property Management Ltd, Official Receiver v Stern* [2000] 1 W.L.R. 2230; [2001] B.C.C. 121. The question whether the use of such statements is unfair is to be determined by the trial judge.

In *Re Bernard L Madoff Investment Securities LLC* [2009] EWHC 442 (Ch); [2010] B.C.C. 328 a US company and an associated English company were both in liquidation and the court granted an application for an order under the Data Protection Act 1998 authorising in the public interest the transfer by the English liquidator to his American counterpart of certain specified information; but it declined to make an order under s.235 authorising the US trustee to ask questions about the American company because the section could not be used as a shortcut to an application by him under art.21 of the CBIR. It also directed that the s.235 interview should be restricted to questions about the English company.

S.235(1)

The situations to which the section applies, and the consequent definition of "office-holder", are the same as are described in s.234(1). A voluntary arrangement is excluded. Where the liquidator in a winding up by the court in England and Wales is not the official receiver, the official receiver as well as the private liquidator has the powers conferred by the section.

S.235(2), (3)

The "effective date" is defined in s.235(4) below.

For the meaning of the term "officer", see the note to s.206(3).

The extension of "employment" to include employment under a contract for services is wide enough to include solicitors, accountants and others who have rendered professional services to the company. A bank or financial institution which provided services to the company (as distinct from being simply a lender) could well fall within the definition.

The phrases "as the office-holder may reasonably require" and "in the office-holder's opinion" are matters left by the statute to the office-holder's discretion, but would no doubt be subject to the general powers of the court to control an office-holder if he were acting unreasonably; and in any event the question of reasonableness could be raised as a defence if a prosecution were brought.

S.235(4)

A company "goes into liquidation" at the times described in s.247(2): see the note to that subsection.

S.235(5)

On penalties, see s.430 and Sch.10.

The duty imposed by this section may also be enforced by court order—e.g. where a director has failed to submit a statement of affairs when required by an office-holder to do so: see IR 2016 r.12.52, and *Re Wallace Smith Trust Co Ltd* [1992] B.C.C. 707. For other relevant rules, see rr.7.46 et seq.

236 Inquiry into company's dealings, etc.

236(1) [Application] This section applies as does section 234; and it also applies in the case of a company in respect of which a winding-up order has been made by the court in England and Wales as if references to the office-holder included the official receiver, whether or not he is the liquidator.

236(2) [Court's powers] The court may, on the application of the office-holder, summon to appear before it–

(a) any officer of the company,

(b) any person known or suspected to have in his possession any property of the company or supposed to be indebted to the company, or

(c) any person whom the court thinks capable of giving information concerning the promotion, formation, business, dealings, affairs or property of the company.

236(3) [Powers re account, production] The court may require any such person as is mentioned in subsection (2)(a) to (c) to submit to the court an account of his dealings with the company or to produce any books, papers or other records in his possession or under his control relating to the company or the matters mentioned in paragraph (c) of the subsection.

236(3A) [Where s.236(3) account to be contained] An account submitted to the court under subsection (3) must be contained in–

(a) a witness statement verified by a statement of truth (in England and Wales), and

(b) an affidavit (in Scotland).

236(4) [Application of s.236(5)] The following applies in a case where–

(a) a person without reasonable excuse fails to appear before the court when he is summoned to do so under this section, or

(b) there are reasonable grounds for believing that a person has absconded, or is about to abscond, with a view to avoiding his appearance before the court under this section.

236(5) [Court's power re warrant] The court may, for the purpose of bringing that person and anything in his possession before the court, cause a warrant to be issued to a constable or prescribed officer of the court–

(a) for the arrest of that person, and

(b) for the seizure of any books, papers, records, money or goods in that person's possession.

236(6) [Court authorisation re custody] The court may authorise a person arrested under such a warrant to be kept in custody, and anything seized under such a warrant to be held, in accordance with the rules, until that person is brought before the court under the warrant or until such other time as the court may order.

General Note

This power of the court to summon persons to appear before it for examination was formerly provided for by CA 1985 s.561, but that section was confined in its scope to a winding up by the court. It is now extended to other forms of corporate "insolvency" proceedings, although not to a voluntary arrangement. An examination conducted under this section is private, in contrast to the public examination of officers and others which may be ordered under s.133.

The court's discretion under this section is unfettered, although it is generally exercised along fairly well-settled lines. There are overriding requirements that the examination should be necessary in the interests of the winding up, and that it should not be oppressive or unfair to the respondent (*Re Embassy Art Products Ltd* (1987) 3 B.C.C. 292; *Re Adlards Motor Group Holding Ltd* [1990] B.C.L.C. 68; and see also *British & Commonwealth Holdings plc (Joint Administrators) v Spicer & Oppenheim, Re British & Commonwealth Holdings plc (No.2)* [1993] A.C. 426; [1992]

B.C.C. 977). The onus of establishing a case is on the office-holder, but the views of office-holders that an examination should be ordered "are normally entitled to a good deal of weight" (*Joint Liquidators of Sasea Finance Ltd v KPMG* [1998] B.C.C. 216 at 220; contrast *Re XL Communications Group plc* [2005] EWHC 2413 (Ch)). The section is not to be used just to give the office-holder special advantages in ordinary litigation: *Re Atlantic Computers plc* [1998] B.C.C. 200; *Re Sasea Finance Ltd* [1999] B.C.C. 103; *Re Ex Ced Foods, ANZ National Bank v Sheahan* [2012] NZHC 3037; [2013] B.C.C. 321. In the latter case it was held that the court had jurisdiction (under the equivalent provision in the New Zealand legislation) to order an examination even though the company had proved solvent and there was a surplus after all the creditors had been paid in full, but in such circumstances the factors weighing against the making of an order would necessarily be very strong. As a general (but not invariable) rule, an office-holder may not apply for examination if he has made a firm decision to commence proceedings against the respondent (*Re Castle New Homes Ltd* [1979] 1 W.L.R. 1075; [1979] 2 All E.R. 775; as explained in *Cloverbay Ltd (Joint Administrators) v Bank of Credit and Commerce International SA (Re Cloverbay Ltd (No.2))* [1991] Ch. 90; [1990] B.C.C. 414); *Re Alocasia Ltd, Jackson v Baker Tilly* (unreported, 10 April 2014); and see *Re RBG Resources plc* [2002] EWCA Civ 1624; [2002] B.C.C. 1005. However even the fact that criminal charges have already been brought against the respondent does not constitute an absolute bar to the making of an order (*Re Arrows Ltd (No.2)* [1992] B.C.C. 446). The court has to balance the importance to the office-holder of obtaining the information against the degree of oppression to the person sought to be examined, bearing in mind that the office-holder's views should be afforded great weight but are not determinative. The fact that proceedings are pending against the respondent including very serious allegations of fraud and dishonesty could make it oppressive to order his examination in advance of the trial, but this consideration may be outweighed by the liquidator's need for information to enable him to get on with his primary function of identifying and getting in the company's assets; and an examination may nevertheless be ordered: *Daltel Europe Ltd v Makki* [2004] EWHC 726 (Ch); [2005] 1 B.C.L.C. 594. The case for making an order against an officer or former officer of the company will usually be stronger than it would be against a third party (see *Re Westmead Consultants Ltd* [2002] 1 B.C.L.C. 384); and an order for oral examination is much more likely to be oppressive than an order for the production of documents (*Cloverbay Ltd*, above). However (even in the case of a third party) an application is not necessarily unreasonable because it is inconvenient for the respondent or may cause him considerable work, or may make him vulnerable to future claims (*British & Commonwealth Holdings*, above). In *Re Trading Partners Ltd* [2002] 1 B.C.L.C. 655 an order was made in favour of liquidators against receivers for the production of material which had been collected by the receivers at their debenture-holders' expense, despite objections based on a possible conflict of interest, the only restriction placed by the court being on documents which might disclose the strategy proposed to be adopted for the receivership. It may be oppressive to seek an order for examination without prior notice to the respondents or without first having asked for the information by letter or some similar means, although such a course of action would be justified in some exceptional cases (*Re Embassy Art Products Ltd*, above). In *Re an Inquiry into Mirror Group Newspapers plc* [2000] B.C.C. 217 inspectors appointed under CA 1985 ss.432 and 442 wished to put extensive questions to the respondent on matters on which he had already been questioned at length under (inter alia) s.236, and had been questioned in cross-examination in a criminal trial: in all, he had undergone interrogations over a total of 61 days. The court directed the inspectors to do their best to avoid questioning him on topics on which he had been questioned before, and so far as possible to rely on the answers which he had already given in the course of the earlier procedures.

In *Re Bank of Credit & Commerce International SA* [1997] B.C.C. 561, where the office-holders in the BCCI liquidation applied to have the production by members of the Bank of America Group of an extensive list of books and documents set out under 12 heads, the court ordered disclosure subject to staging periods spread out between 14 and 84 days, and expressed the tentative view that the costs of compliance with the order (involving, inter alia, air freighting 100 boxes of documents from San Francisco to London) should be costs in the liquidation.

In *Re Delberry Ltd* [2008] EWHC 925 (Ch); [2008] B.C.C. 653 administrative receivers had sold the company's business within a few days of their appointment pursuant to a "pre-pack" agreement. In a subsequent liquidation the liquidator applied to the court to have the receivers produce documents relating to their receivership and their pre-receivership work in order to see whether the remuneration which they had been paid was open to challenge and also whether they might be liable for breach of duty or misfeasance. The court held that these objects were within the scope of s.236.

Any doubts which there might have been on the question whether a respondent could be excused from complying with an order under s.236 on the ground of self-incrimination were set at rest by a series of cases in 1992—at least in the case where he is an officer or former officer of the insolvent company. The relevant cases are: *Re Jeffrey S Levitt Ltd* [1992] Ch. 457; [1992] B.C.C. 137; not following *Re Barlow Clowes (Gilt Managers) Ltd (No.2)* (Ferris J, unreported, 31 July 1990); *Re A E Farr Ltd* [1992] B.C.C. 150 (where Ferris J decided not to follow his earlier judgment); and *Bishopsgate Investment Management Ltd (in provisional liquidation) v Maxwell (Re Bishopsgate Investment Management Ltd, Mirror Group Newspapers plc v Maxwell)* [1993] Ch. 1; [1992] B.C.C. 222. It has been confirmed that the position is the same in Scotland: *Liquidator of Tay Square Properties Ltd, Noter*, 2005 S.L.T. 469. However, the fact that the privilege against self-incrimination has been impliedly abrogated by statute is a factor which can be taken into account when the court exercises its discretion whether or not to make an order ([1993] Ch. 1 at 63; [1992] B.C.C. 222 at 262). Where the person concerned is not an officer or former officer, the plea of self-incrimination may be available (see the Australian case *O'Toole v Mitcham* (1978) C.L.C. para.40–429). However, it should be noted that these cases were decided before the ruling, discussed below, in *Saunders v United Kingdom* (1997) 23 E.H.R.R. 313; [1997] B.C.C. 872 in which it was held that the *use* in later criminal proceedings of statements obtained under compulsion was contrary to the European Convention on Human Rights, and in practice the use of such statements was discontinued and is now banned by law. This development would suggest that an objection on the ground of self-incrimination is now even less likely to be upheld. For further proceedings, see *R. v Lyons* [2002] UKHL 44; [2003] 1 A.C. 976; [2002] B.C.C. 968.

The ruling in *Saunders v UK* (above) was followed in *Kansal v United Kingdom* [2004] B.P.I.R. 740.

In *Re Pantmaenog Timber Co Ltd, Official Receiver v Wadge Rapps & Hunt (a firm)* [2003] UKHL 49; [2004] 1 A.C. 158; [2003] B.C.C. 659 the House of Lords, reversing the Court of Appeal, ruled that the Official Receiver could make an application under s.236 even when his sole purpose was to obtain information for the purposes of instituting disqualification proceedings against a director on the ground of unfitness under CDDA 1986 s.6. The Court of Appeal had held that the Official Receiver's powers in this regard were limited to those conferred by CDDA 1986 s.7(4), but the House of Lords said that the two provisions should be seen as complementary to each other. It was also open to an office-holder, such as a liquidator, to invoke s.236 for the same purpose—his functions were not confined to the administration of the insolvent company's estate—and the Official Receiver could do so whether or not he was the company's liquidator.

Although information collected under s.236 is confidential (because obtained through a process of compulsion), the confidentiality is not absolute and may be outweighed by considerations of public interest, so that (for instance) if it reveals evidence of tax fraud it may be passed to the Revenue's prosecuting authority: *R. v Brady* [2004] EWCA Crim 1763; [2005] B.C.C. 357. The decision whether or not to disclose is, however, for the official receiver and not for the court. An office-holder should similarly, it appears, take his own advice about the use of information obtained under s.236 rather than ask the court for directions: *Re PNC Telecom plc* [2003] EWHC 2220 (Ch); [2004] B.P.I.R. 314.

On the other side of the coin, it was held in *Re ABC Ltd; XYZ (liquidator of ABC Ltd) v Revenue & Customs Commissioners* [2010] EWHC 1645 (Ch); [2010] B.P.I.R.1297 that information obtained by Revenue & Customs under a letter of request under the Crime (International Co-operation) Act 2003 to Dutch prosecuting authorities investigating a VAT fraud could be disclosed in a s.236 examination in the UK and was not precluded by s.9 of the 2003 Act (which restricted the use of such information in criminal investigations and proceedings but had no application in civil proceedings).

In *Bellmex International Ltd v Green* [2001] B.C.C. 253 it was said that the s.236 power should not normally be used to deal with factual issues arising on a proof of debt.

In *Re Brook Martin & Co (Nominees) Ltd* [1993] B.C.L.C. 328, the directors of the company against whom a s.236 order was sought were also the company's solicitors, and they raised a plea of professional privilege. Vinelott J held that no privilege could be asserted in respect of documents which belonged to the company itself. In regard to documents where the privilege arose through acts done on behalf of other clients, he left open the question whether it could, in exceptional circumstances, be overridden by an order under s.236. A claim of privilege was held to be outweighed in the public interest where there was evidence that the documents in question were relevant to an investigation of fraud in *Re Harvest Finance Ltd* [2013] B.P.I.R. 1020 (unreported, 27 September 2013). Where proceedings have been opened in this country in respect of a foreign-registered company which are "main proceedings" under the EC Regulation, the question whether documents are protected by legal professional privilege is to be determined by English law. However, the law of the company of incorporation may be relevant in relation to the question whether the court's discretion should be exercised in regard to documents which are not so protected (*Re Hellas Telecommunications (Luxembourg) II SCA* [2013] B.P.I.R. 756). In *Re Galileo Group Ltd* [1998] B.C.C. 228 an order was refused where the information which was being sought had been given in confidence.

The transcripts of the examination of a person under this section attract legal professional privilege (*Dubai Bank Ltd v Galadari* (1989) 5 B.C.C. 722), but this is subject to the powers of the court to allow inspection under r.12.21(2).

The object of an order under s.236 was said by Browne-Wilkinson V.C. in the *Cloverbay Ltd* case ([1991] Ch. 90 at 102; [1990] B.C.C. 415 at 419–420) to be limited to enabling the office-holder "to get sufficient information to reconstitute the state of knowledge that the company should possess. In my judgment its purpose is not to put the company in a better position than it would have enjoyed if liquidation or administration had not supervened". However, in *British & Commonwealth Holdings plc (Joint Administrators) v Spicer & Oppenheim (Re British & Commonwealth Holdings plc (No.2))* [1993] A.C. 426; [1992] B.C.C. 977, the House of Lords rejected this narrow approach, holding that an order could properly be made extending to all documents (and, it would appear, all information) which the office-holder reasonably required to have to carry out his functions. In *Re Webinvest Ltd* [2017] EWHC 2446 (Ch) the court commented that the principal purpose of the powers to compel third parties to provide material to office-holders under s.236 (and ss.235 and 366) was to assist with the beneficial winding up of the company (or a bankruptcy) but that it was not necessary to show that the disclosure of the material to the liquidators would actually benefit the insolvent estate of a parent company.

In some early cases decided under the section, an order was made on terms that the record should not be used in subsequent criminal proceedings, or disclosed to the Serious Fraud Office (e.g. *Re Arrows Ltd (No.2)* [1992] B.C.C. 125; and *Re Arrows Ltd (No.4)* (at first instance) [1992] B.C.C. 987). However, in the light of the rulings in *Rank Film Distributors Ltd v Video Information Centre* [1982] A.C. 380; and *AT & T Istel Ltd v Tully* [1992] Q.B. 315 (cases decided on analogous statutory provisions), it was later accepted that the civil courts have no jurisdiction to impose a condition on the use by prosecuting authorities in criminal proceedings of evidence given in the civil proceedings, such as a condition of the kind described: see the *Bishopsgate Investment Management Ltd* case [1992] Ch. 1 at 19; [1992] B.C.C. 222 at 228; and *Re Arrows Ltd (No.4); Hamilton v Naviede* in the House of Lords [1995] 2 A.C. 75; [1994] B.C.C. 641. However, these rulings must now be reconsidered in the light of the decision of the European Court of Human Rights in *Saunders v United Kingdom* (1997) 23 E.H.R.R. 313; [1997] B.C.C. 872, which held that the use of self-incriminating statements obtained under compulsion (in that case, by DTI inspectors acting under CA 1985 s.432) in subsequent criminal proceedings was unfair and a breach of art.6(1) of the European Convention on Human Rights. In the light of this ruling, the practice of using such statements in criminal proceedings was discontinued, and the Youth Justice and Criminal Evidence Act 1999 s.59 and Sch.3 now forbids prosecutors from doing so by statute. (But such statements may be used in disqualification proceedings: *R. v Secretary of State for Trade and Industry Ex p. McCormick* [1998] B.C.C. 379.) Moreover, the Convention has since been incorporated into the domestic law of the United Kingdom by the Human Rights Act 1998.

In *Re Headington Investments Ltd Ex p. Maxwell* [1993] B.C.C. 500, the Court of Appeal held that there was no public interest immunity to prevent the disclosure of s.236 transcripts to the prosecution or regulatory authorities and that, if such disclosure is made, a person facing actual or potential prosecution was not entitled to have simultaneous disclosure made to him: the material would in due course be made available to him in the criminal proceedings, and any question of unfairness or prejudice was a matter for the judge at trial.

For the rules and procedure governing the examinations, see IR 2016 rr.12.17 et seq. Application is made to the court by the office-holder. Although in many, if not most, cases it may be appropriate for the application to be made ex parte, Vinelott J in *Re Maxwell Communications Corporation plc, Homan v Vogel* [1994] B.C.C. 741 said that some good reason must be shown to justify this course: if the person affected is given notice it may enable the scope of the order to be clarified and in this and in other ways save time and expense. See also on this issue *Re Embassy Art Products Ltd* (1987) 3 B.C.C. 292; and *Re PFTZM Ltd (in liq.)* [1995] B.C.C. 280 (where an order obtained ex parte was set aside on the ground that it was oppressive). In *Miller v Bain* [2002] B.C.C. 899 the respondent director had failed to co-operate with the liquidator by attending for interview and proposed to absent himself for over a year. The liquidator applied ex parte for an order requiring him to attend for a private examination, and was awarded costs of the ex parte application in view of the respondent's recalcitrant attitude. Costs were also awarded in *Hunt v Renzland* [2008] B.P.I.R. 1380.

The application to the court must be in writing, specifying the grounds on which it is being made (r.12.18). This document is confidential, and may not be inspected by anyone, without an order of the court, other than the persons mentioned in r.12.21(2). It had been the invariable practice since *Re Gold Co* (1879) 12 Ch. D. 77 that this document should not be disclosed to the person against whom the order was sought—i.e. that the court would never exercise its discretion to allow inspection by such a person. However, in *Re British & Commonwealth Holdings plc (No.1)* [1992] Ch. 342; [1992] B.C.C. 165, the Court of Appeal decided to depart from this practice, and ruled instead that where an application has been made to have the order set aside, inspection of the document should prima facie be allowed if the court is of the opinion that otherwise it might be unable fairly or properly to dispose of the application. It is for the office-holder to satisfy the court that confidentiality in whole or in part would nevertheless be appropriate. See further on this question *Re Bishopsgate Investment Management Ltd (No.2)* [1994] B.C.C. 732.

In *Re Seagull Manufacturing Co Ltd (in liq.)* [1993] Ch. 345; [1993] B.C.C. 241 the Court of Appeal, affirming Mummery J [1992] Ch. 128; [1991] B.C.C. 550, held that the public examination provisions of s.133 have extra-territorial effect, and Mummery J in particular contrasted s.133 with the powers under ss.236, 237 which, he said, did not extend beyond the jurisdiction. However, the Court of Session in *McIsaac, Petitioners; Joint Liquidators of First Tokyo Index Trust Ltd* [1994] B.C.C. 410, rejected a submission that a s.236 order could not be made against a person resident in New York. (See also *Miller v Bain* [2003] B.P.I.R. 959.) The issue is examined in detail by Burton J in *Re Casterbridge Properties Ltd* [2002] B.C.C. 453 at 475 et seq. Here, it was held that while s.236 undoubtedly has extra-territorial effect to the extent that the court may order the private examination of a person based in a foreign country if the examination is to be held abroad, the question whether an order may be made for such a person to be examined within the UK remained unresolved. In *Re Anglo American Insurance Co Ltd* [2002] B.C.C. 715 the alternative course was adopted of applying for letters of request to courts in Bermuda and the United States, and Neuberger J held that for this purpose the rules governing the exercise of the s.236 jurisdiction, set out in IR 2016 rr.12.17 et seq., reflected the way in which the court would exercise its inherent jurisdiction where an application is made for letters of request. In *Re Mid East Trading Ltd, Phillips v Lehman Brothers* [1998] B.C.C. 726, the Court of Appeal held that an order could be made under s.236 in respect of documents situated abroad, where the company in question was being wound up as an unregistered company under IA 1986 Pt V. However, it was emphasised in that case that the court's power extended only to order the production of documents relating to the particular company which was in liquidation. In *Re MF Global UK Ltd* [2015] EWHC 2319 (Ch) David Richards J concluded, following the bankruptcy case of *Re Tucker* [1990] Ch. 148, that he did not have jurisdiction to make a s.236 order against a French company to produce documents to the English court. However, this decision must now be contrasted with *Re Omni Trustees Ltd; Official Receiver v Norriss* [2015] EWHC 2697 (Ch); [2015] B.C.C. 906 in which the court distinguished *Re Tucker* as it considered that s.236 was structured differently from the provision of the Bankruptcy Act 1914 on which the ruling in the latter case was based: the power in the bankruptcy section to order the production of documents was merely ancillary to, and dependent upon, the principal power to summon a respondent to attend for examination before the court, whereas s.236(3) was considered to confer a freestanding power, independent of the power to summon a person to appear before the court, to require a person to submit to the court an account of dealings and to produce books, papers and records. The court in *Omni Trustees* concluded that s.236 has extra-territorial effect so as to empower the court to order a person outside the jurisdiction to produce documents. But the question whether a person outside the jurisdiction can be ordered to attend before the English court under s.236 remains open. In *Re a Company (No.003318 of 1987) (Oriental Credit Ltd)* [1988] Ch. 204; (1987) 3 B.C.C. 564 it was held that the court has the power to grant an order restraining a person from leaving the jurisdiction pending the holding of an examination under this section.

It has been held that where a foreign court seeks the co-operation of a court in the United Kingdom to have a person who is resident here examined for the purposes of an insolvency proceeding in the foreign jurisdiction, the considerations which might inhibit an English court from making an order under s.236 should not be taken into account: see the notes to s.426, below.

In *Re Barlow Clowes Gilt Managers Ltd* [1992] Ch. 208; [1991] B.C.C. 608, statements had been given voluntarily by various persons to a representative of the liquidators of a company under the threat, express or implicit, that if they did not do so voluntarily the liquidators would have recourse to their powers under ss.236, 237. Other persons, who had been charged with criminal offences in connection with the affairs of the company, sought to have access to the transcripts of these interviews; but Millett J held that the information contained in the transcripts could be used only for purposes connected with the liquidation. The liquidators had, in this instance, given the interviewees assurances of confidentiality which would not have been needed had the information been obtained under s.236; but even so, information obtained in a private examination under the statute could also have been disclosed only to the extent that it was for the benefit of the liquidation. (On the giving of undertakings by office-holders, see further *McIsaac, Petitioners* [1994] B.C.C. 410.)

Information or documents obtained by an office-holder pursuant to s.236 are subject to an obligation of confidentiality, but this may in an appropriate case be waived by the court: *Re a Company (No.005374 of 1993)* [1993] B.C.C. 734. In that case administrative receivers were allowed to disclose information to the bank which had appointed them. Information may also be disclosed to the Secretary of State for the purpose of considering whether to bring disqualification proceedings: see the notes to s.235, above.

The order may permit the liquidator to disclose the information produced by the examination to a third party, e.g. the assignee of a claim vested in the company, provided that he undertakes to use the information for the benefit of the company: *Re Sandford Farm Properties Ltd* (unreported, 26 June 2015).

The court has no jurisdiction to authorise anyone other than the applicant (or a solicitor or counsel instructed by him) to examine the witness, except in the rare case where there are two office-holders and IR 2016 r.12.20(2) applies: *Re Maxwell Communications Corporation plc, Homan v Vogel* [1994] B.C.C. 741.

An order under s.236 becomes inoperative if the office-holder in whose favour it has been granted ceases to hold office: *Re Kingscroft Insurance Co Ltd* [1994] B.C.C. 343.

In *Re Galileo Group Ltd* [1998] B.C.C. 228, Lightman J expressed the view that s.236 was, at least primarily, designed to protect the interests of creditors in an insolvent liquidation: it was not intended to gain a windfall for shareholders in a solvent liquidation. This was a factor that the court might take into account in deciding whether, in its discretion, to grant an order under s.236.

The CBIR Sch.1 art.21(1)(g) permits the foreign representative in an overseas liquidation to obtain an order under s.236 for the disclosure of documents: *Re Chesterfield United Inc* [2012] EWHC 244 (Ch); [2012] B.C.C. 786.

CPR r.31.17 may not be used by a creditor to obtain disclosure of information which a liquidator might have obtained under s.236 but has chosen not to do so: *Re Branchempire Ltd* [2010] EWHC 3017 (Ch); [2011] B.P.I.R. 536.

Section 236 binds the Crown, so that it may be ordered to disclose information obtained in the form of transcripts of evidence under the powers of investigation conferred by CA 1985 s.432, subject to prior disclosure to the witnesses whose evidence was covered by the order and subject also to any application by them to have the order set aside: *Soden v Burns* [1996] 1 W.L.R. 1512; [1997] B.C.C. 308.

Failure to comply with a s.236 order is a serious contempt of court, which may justify a custodial sentence: *Power v Hodges* [2015] EWHC 2931 (Ch).

S.236(1)

This provision is identical with s.235(1): see the note to that subsection.

S.236(2)

Only the office-holder has standing to make application to the court: *Re James McHale Automobiles Ltd* [1997] B.C.C. 202. The former legislation was not so restricted and other persons, such as contributories, were commonly allowed to apply. If a liquidator has not exercised his power to obtain disclosure of information under s.236 it is not open to a third party to seek to do so by other means, e.g. under CPR r.31.17: *Re Branchempire Ltd* [2010] EWHC 3017 (Ch); [2011] B.P.I.R. 536.

"Property of the company" extends to property not beneficially owned by the company but held by it on trust: *Re Omni Trustees Ltd* [2015] EWHC 2122 (Ch).

The list of persons who may be summoned is shorter than that in s.235(2), but it is potentially of wider scope in view of the discretion given to the court by para.(c). In *Joint Liquidators of Sasea Finance Ltd v KPMG* [1998] B.C.C. 216 at 222 it was said that a company's auditors were "most probably" officers within s.236(2)(a). In *Re Trading Partners Ltd, Akers v Lomas* [2002] 1 B.C.L.C. 655 an order was made for the inspection of working papers and litigation documents held by the administrative receivers of companies related to the company in liquidation.

Although the court has power in its discretion (under r.12.22(4)) to award costs in favour of a person who complies with an order under s.236(2) or (3), the court declined to make such an award in *Re Harvest Finance Ltd* [2014] EWHC 4237 (Ch); [2015] 2 B.C.L.C. 240, taking the view that such compliance was a public duty. The question whether costs awarded against an office-holder (e.g. for delay in proceeding with an application) should be on an indemnity basis is discussed in *Re New China Hong Kong Capital Ltd* [2003] EWHC 1573 (Ch); [2003] B.P.I.R. 1176.

S.236(3), (3A)

Although any person whom the court thinks capable of giving "information" may be summoned under s.236(2)(c), s.236(3) refers to the production of "books, papers or other records". In *Re Comet Group Ltd; Kahn v Whirlpool (UK) Ltd* [2014] EWHC 3477 (Ch) the court considered that if "information" was sought, the court could only order it to be provided by summoning a person to answer questions, ordering interrogatories, or ordering affidavits. If the applicant did not know the identity of the particular documents he wished to see but adequately described them, e.g. by reference to the subject matter they contained, that could be sufficient. The case also confirmed that "books, papers or other records" include documents in electronic form.

Section 236(3) refers to the production of books, etc. "relating to the company". In *Re Corporate Jet Realisations Ltd* [2015] EWHC 221 (Ch); [2015] 2 B.C.L.C. 95, where a liquidation followed a receivership the court, on the application of the liquidator, was prepared to order production of a range of records and files created by the receivers, except those subject to privilege, confidentiality or the receivers' strategic considerations.

Failure to comply with an order under this section is a contempt of court which may be sanctioned by imprisonment: *Re Hartmayes Ltd, Griffin v Robinson* (unreported, 6 December 2013).

Section 236(3) was amended and s.236(3A) inserted by LRO 2010 (SI 2010/18) art.5(6) from 6 April 2010 (with retrospective effect).

S.236(4)–(6)

These provisions, especially when read in conjunction with s.237, are more extensive and detailed than the former CA 1985 s.561(4), which was confined to the apprehension of the person summoned, and also stipulated that he had to be tendered a reasonable sum for his expenses. The repealed section also stated (s.561(3)) that if a person (e.g. a solicitor) who was ordered to produce a document relating to the company claimed a lien on it, such production should be without prejudice to the lien. The present section does not reproduce this provision. In many cases the lien will now be unenforceable by virtue of s.246, which will allow the office-holder to demand possession of the document and so make the need for an order for its production superfluous. However even in those cases where s.246 does not apply (e.g. where the office-holder is an administrative receiver, or where the document gives a title to property and is held as such (s.246(3)), an order for production under s.236 will not affect the lien: *Ex p. Bramble* (1880) 13 Ch. D. 885; *Re Aveling Barford Ltd* [1989] 1 W.L.R. 360; (1988) 4 B.C.C. 548).

In *Re Bank of Credit & Commerce International (No.7)* [1994] 1 B.C.L.C. 455 an order made under s.236 against a person domiciled abroad was buttressed by a requirement that he should give security in the sum of £500,000 as a condition of being allowed to leave the country.

For relevant rule, see IR 2016 r.12.55.

237 Court's enforcement powers under s.236

237(1) [Order to deliver property] If it appears to the court, on consideration of any evidence obtained under section 236 or this section, that any person has in his possession any property of the company, the court may, on the application of the office-holder, order that person to deliver the whole or any part of the property to the office-holder at such time, in such manner and on such terms as the court thinks fit.

237(2) [Order to pay money due] If it appears to the court, on consideration of any evidence so obtained, that any person is indebted to the company, the court may, on the application of the office-holder, order that person to pay to the office-holder, at such time and in such manner as the court may direct, the whole or any part of the amount due, whether in full discharge of the debt or otherwise, as the court thinks fit.

237(3) [Order re examination of persons] The court may, if it thinks fit, order that any person who if within the jurisdiction of the court would be liable to be summoned to appear before it under section 236 or this section shall be examined in any part of the United Kingdom where he may for the time being be, or in a place outside the United Kingdom.

237(4) [Examination on oath etc.] Any person who appears or is brought before the court under section 236 or this section may be examined on oath, either orally or (except in Scotland) by interrogatories, concerning the company or the matters mentioned in section 236(2)(c).

General Note

Most of these detailed provisions supplementing s.236 had no counterpart in earlier legislation. There is some overlap with s.234.

S.237(3)

In *Re MF Global UK Ltd* [2015] EWHC 2319 (Ch); [2016] Ch. 325; [2015] B.C.C. 891 David Richards J held that this provision is independent of s.236 and has extra-territorial effect, but only where the case is covered by available procedural machinery by which the person concerned could be compelled to comply with the court's order.

Adjustment of prior transactions (administration and liquidation)

General Note

The topic of antecedent transactions is discussed in Totty, Moss and Segal, *Insolvency*, Ch.F2.

238 Transactions at an undervalue (England and Wales)

238(1) [Application] This section applies in the case of a company where–

(a) the company enters administration, or

(b) the company goes into liquidation;

and "the office-holder" means the administrator or the liquidator, as the case may be.

238(2) [Application to court by office-holder] Where the company has at a relevant time (defined in section 240) entered into a transaction with any person at an undervalue, the office-holder may apply to the court for an order under this section.

238(3) [Court order] Subject as follows, the court shall, on such an application, make such order as it thinks fit for restoring the position to what it would have been if the company had not entered into that transaction.

238(4) [Interpretation] For the purposes of this section and section 241, a company enters into a transaction with a person at an undervalue if–

(a) the company makes a gift to that person or otherwise enters into a transaction with that person on terms that provide for the company to receive no consideration, or

(b) the company enters into a transaction with that person for a consideration the value of which, in money or money's worth, is significantly less than the value, in money or money's worth, of the consideration provided by the company.

238(5) [Restriction on court order] The court shall not make an order under this section in respect of a transaction at an undervalue if it is satisfied–

(a) that the company which entered into the transaction did so in good faith and for the purpose of carrying on its business, and

(b) that at the time it did so there were reasonable grounds for believing that the transaction would benefit the company.

General Note

To put the present section into context, it is necessary to discuss briefly the reforms made by IA 1985 in response to the recommendations made in Ch.28 of the Cork Committee's *Report*, which appear in the present Act under the headings "transactions at an undervalue"; "preferences"; and "provisions against debt avoidance" (see respectively ss.238 and 339; ss.239 and 340; and ss.423 et seq.). The concern of the Committee was to state the law more logically and accurately and remove doubts as to its scope, to make the law relating to corporate insolvency and individual bankruptcy broadly the same, and to remove the former emphasis on fraud which was implicit in the traditional terms "fraudulent conveyance" and "fraudulent preference".

The new concept of "transactions at an undervalue" is based on the former BA 1914 s.42, which declared void against the trustee in bankruptcy settlements of property made by a person who became bankrupt within a stated period thereafter. This section has been replaced, in the case of an individual bankrupt, by the broader provisions of IA 1986 s.339, and (in accordance with the recommendations of the Cork Committee (*Report*, para.1237)) applied to corporate insolvency as well as bankruptcy by the present section.

The former rules relating to "fraudulent preferences" (BA 1914 s.44; CA 1985 s.615) are redefined (under the neutral title of "preferences") by IA 1986 s.239 for company insolvencies and s.340 for bankruptcies. As is indicated by the new designation, the law has been changed so that it is no longer necessary to show a dominant and improper intention to give the creditor in question a preference over creditors generally.

Finally, the law governing "fraudulent conveyances", which can be traced back to a statute of Elizabeth I, has been brought up to date and appears in IA 1986 as ss.423 et seq., which apply to both companies and individuals. Once again, the word "fraudulent" has been pointedly dropped from the present statutory provision.

There is a considerable overlap between the three topics here discussed, and particularly, as regards transactions at an undervalue, between ss.238 and 423 et seq. The distinguishing features of the latter sections are: (1) they are not confined to situations where a company is in liquidation or subject to an administration order, or an individual is bankrupt; (2) there is no time limit; and (3) application may be made to the court by any "victim" of the transaction, and not merely the "office-holder" or trustee in bankruptcy; but (4) the requisite intention to put assets out of reach of creditors or prejudice their interests must be shown.

Sections 238–241 deal with transactions at an undervalue and preferences involving companies incorporated in England and Wales: see s.440(2)(a). Equivalent provision is made for Scotland, with the distinctive labels "gratuitous alienations" and "unfair preferences", by ss.242, 243; but these sections follow in detail the rather different bankruptcy law of Scotland.

The provisions of ss.238–243 do not operate retrospectively so as to invalidate a transaction which occurred before the present Act came into force, unless it could have been invalidated under the corresponding provisions of the former law: see Sch.11 para.9.

For the purposes of the Limitation Act 1980, applications to set aside transactions under ss.238–241 are generally actions on a speciality within s.8(1) of that Act, to which a 12-year period of limitation applies, but where the substance of the claim is not to set aside a transaction but to recover a sum by virtue of these sections the period is six years: *Re Priory Garage (Walthamstow) Ltd* [2001] B.P.I.R. 144.

Sections 238 and 239 (and also ss.423 et seq.) are to be construed as having extraterritorial effect, so that an order may be made against a person who is outside the jurisdiction: *Re Paramount Airways Ltd (in admin.)* [1993] Ch. 223; [1992] B.C.C. 416. There are, however, two safeguards: first, the court has a discretion under the sections as to the order which it may make. If a foreign element is involved, it will have to be satisfied that, in respect of the relief sought against him, the respondent is a person sufficiently connected with this jurisdiction for it to be just and proper to make the order. Secondly, a person who wishes to serve the proceedings has to obtain the leave of the court to do so.

Whether a company is to be regarded as the victim of a wrongful act committed by a director or is, by the rules of attribution, to be considered one of the perpetrators depends on the circumstances: *Jetivia SA v Bilta (UK) Ltd* [2015] UKSC 23; [2015] B.C.C. 343. If the claim is to have the transaction set aside for the benefit of the company, it is likely to fall into the former category.

At common law, the right of a liquidator or administrator to institute proceedings to set aside a transaction at an undervalue or a preference under ss.238 and 239 did not form part of the company's property at the commencement of the insolvency so as to be capable of being charged by the company or of being sold by him: *Re Yagerphone Ltd* [1935] Ch. 392; *Re Oasis Merchandising Services Ltd* [1998] Ch. 170; [1997] B.C.C. 282. However, both of these restrictions have been superseded by statute. Section 176ZB confirms that the proceeds of an action brought by an office-holder under s.238 or 239 fall into the insolvent estate and are not subject to any floating charge over the assets of the company while, in contrast, s.246ZD(2) reverses the common-law position and empowers a liquidator or administrator to assign the right of action under these sections, and the fruits of any such action, to a third party. See the notes to those sections. It had also been held that a liquidator could not recoup the costs of such litigation out of the general assets in the liquidation: *Re Floor Fourteen Ltd, Lewis v Inland Revenue Commissioners* [2001] 3 All E.R. 499; [2002] B.C.C. 198, but this ruling has been nullified as a result of legislative changes: see the note to s.115.

In the context of the financial markets, no order may be made under s.238 in relation to a market contract to which a recognised investment exchange or clearing house is a party or which is entered into under its default rules, or a disposition of property in pursuance of such a market contract: see CA 1989 s.165. It is also disapplied in relation to payment and securities settlement systems by the Finality Regulations 1999 reg.17. (See the introductory notes at pp.1–3 above.)

A transaction may be the subject of a challenge under ss.238–243 and at the same time open to objection as a "tainted gift" under POCA 2002. In that case, s.427 of the latter Act provides that no order or decree may be made under ss.238, 239, 242, 243 or 423 at a time when the recipient of the tainted gift is the subject of a restraint order or confiscation order under the 2002 Act, and any order or decree made under the above sections after the POCA order is discharged shall take into account any realisation made of property held by the recipient.

S.238(1)

This and the next three sections apply in a narrower range of situations than do earlier sections in this Part, i.e. only to company administrations and liquidations, and "office-holder" means the administrator or liquidator. It does not appear that the official receiver, where he is not the liquidator, is given standing also, as he is by s.235.

For the meaning of "goes into liquidation", see s.247(2).

S.238(2)

Only the office-holder, as defined in s.238(1), may make application. This may be contrasted with the wider category permitted to apply for an order under s.423: see s.424(1).

A "relevant time" for the purposes of this section is defined by reference not only to the calendar but also to the company's solvency: see s.240. On the meaning of "transaction", see *Ailyan and Fry v Smith* [2010] EWHC 24 (Ch); [2010] B.P.I.R. 289, discussed in the note to s.339, below.

S.238(3)

This subsection (and the corresponding s.239(3) relating to preferences) is curiously worded. On the face of it, the use of the word "shall" and the concluding phrase "for restoring the position to what it would have been if the company had not entered into that transaction" would appear to tie the court's hands, so that (subject only to s.238(5)) it *must* make an order, and then only an order which restores the status quo. However the words "as it thinks fit" and the many and varied examples of possible orders (set out in s.241) which it is open to the court to make clearly indicate that the applicant is not entitled to demand any particular form of order as of right, and this consideration, coupled with the fact that the court's jurisdiction in this sphere is equitable in origin, must lead to the conclusion that the court may in its discretion decline to make any order at all. In *Re Paramount Airways Ltd (in admin.)* [1993] Ch. 223 at 239; [1992] B.C.C. 416 at 425, Nicholls V.C. endorsed this view, and in relation to the corresponding provision in bankruptcy (s.339), the court in *Singla v Brown* [2007] EWHC 405; [2008] Ch. 357

declined to make any order even though the conditions for the application of that section had been satisfied. In the case of *Re MDA Investment Management Ltd* [2003] EWHC 2277 (Ch) and [2004] EWHC 42 (Ch); [2005] B.C.C. 783 the court declined to make an order because the company had been on the verge of collapse at the time that the company entered into the transaction and to restore it to that position would have conferred no benefit on it. See also *Re Parkside International Ltd* [2008] EWHC 3554 (Ch); [2010] B.C.C. 309. The exercise of the discretion in regard to third parties may have to be even more flexible. In *Lord v Sinai Securities Ltd* [2004] EWHC 1764 (Ch); [2004] B.C.C. 986 Hart J said that the primary concern under s.238(3) is with the restoration of the company's position, and indicated that the remedy of any other party would necessarily have to be subordinated to that.

S.238(4)

A "transaction at an undervalue" may include an outright gift (para.(a)), but otherwise must involve some form of dealing between the parties (*Re Taylor Sinclair (Capital) Ltd* [2001] 2 B.C.L.C. 176), and where consideration is given, the discrepancy in value must be "significant" (para.(b)). If there has not been any transaction to which the company was a party, s.238 cannot apply: *Re Ovenden Colbert Printers Ltd* [2013] EWCA Civ 1408; [2014] B.C.L.C. 291. Compare *Re Hampton Capital Ltd* [2015] EWHC 1905 (Ch) (payment held not to be within s.238 because neither a gift nor involving any "transaction", but defendant held liable on grounds of unjust enrichment). See also *Re Kiss Cards Ltd* [2016] EWHC 2176 (Ch); [2017] B.C.C. 489 (payment into joint account of director and his wife: "gift" or "transaction"?).

In the leading case of *Re M C Bacon Ltd* [1990] B.C.C. 78 Millett J held that the creation of security over a company's assets was not a transaction at an undervalue. Section 238(4)(b), he said, requires a comparison to be made between the value obtained by the company for the transaction and the value of the consideration provided by the company. Both values have to be measurable in money or money's worth and have to be considered from the company's point of view. The mere creation of security over the company's assets does not deplete them or diminish their value. Loss by the company of the ability to apply the proceeds of the assets otherwise than in satisfaction of the secured debt is not capable of valuation in money terms, nor is the consideration received by the company in return. The ruling in *Re Mistral Finance Ltd* [2001] B.C.C. 27 is to the same effect. But this aspect of the ruling in *Re M C Bacon Ltd* has been questioned. In *Hill v Spread Trustee Co Ltd* [2006] EWCA Civ 542; [2006] B.C.C. 646 (a case on s.423) Arden LJ thought that the value to the creditor of the right to have recourse to his security should not invariably be left out of account when assessing the respective considerations given by the parties.

Similar reasoning would very possibly be applicable to a guarantee given by a company of another's indebtedness. In the Northern Ireland case of *Levy McCallum Ltd v Allen* [2007] NICh 3 Treacy J declined to hold that a guarantee provided by a company to another company in the same group was liable to be set aside as a transaction at an undervalue under the corresponding section in that jurisdiction. In *Tailby v HSBC Bank plc* (unreported, 28 July 2014), a case on s.339, it was held that a personal guarantee given by a debtor to secure a company's bank overdraft, but only made after the overdraft facility had been fully drawn, was not a transaction at an undervalue by the debtor.

In *Phillips v Brewin Dolphin Bell Lawrie Ltd* [2001] 1 W.L.R. 143; [2001] B.C.C. 864 the House of Lords was concerned with a complex series of linked transactions, in one of which the company had sold its business, worth £1.05 million, to B Ltd for a nominal consideration of £1 and the assumption by B Ltd of redundancy costs of £325,000, and by a contract executed contemporaneously B Ltd's parent company had agreed to lease computers from the company for four quarterly payments of £312,500. The Court of Appeal had considered that the only "transaction" to be considered under s.238 was that for the sale of the business and that no account should be taken of the related contracts; but the House of Lords held that there was no reason why the consideration for a transaction should not be provided by a third party and that, on the facts, the agreement for the sale of the business had been entered into for a consideration which included the benefit of the leasing agreement. The leasing agreement turned out to be worthless but one payment of £312,500 had been made in advance. It followed that credit ought to be given both for this sum and for the £325,000 in determining the amount which the court should order to be repaid to the company's liquidator under s.238.

In *Barber v CI Ltd* [2006] B.C.C. 927 it was held that a payment which is itself open to challenge as a preference cannot constitute valuable consideration so as to take a transaction outside the scope of s.238. The decision is the subject of criticism by Look Chan Ho and Mokal in (2006) 22 I.L. & P. 183. This article was drawn to the attention of the court when the case went to appeal (*Re Sonatacus Ltd* [2007] EWCA Civ 31; [2007] B.C.C. 186) where the point was left open because a decision on the basis of preference (s.239) was sufficient to conclude the case.

In *Re Lewis's of Leicester Ltd* [1995] B.C.C. 514 a company trading as a department store, in anticipation of closing down its operations, had segregated moneys received from several of its concessionaires and placed them in separate bank accounts in circumstances which, the court held, established a trust in their favour. It was further held that the creation of a trust in this way was not a transaction at an undervalue, since the company's assets were not diminished by what was in substance an arrangement for accelerated payment of sums which would in any event become due to the concessionaires in the future.

See also *Re Barton Manufacturing Co Ltd* [1998] B.C.C. 827 (alleged loans to directors held to be gratuitous payments); *Re Shapland Inc* [2000] B.C.C. 106 (retrospective conversion of interest-free loan to interest-bearing loan); and *Re Thoars (decd)* [2002] EWHC 2416 (Ch); [2003] 1 B.C.L.C. 499 (possibility of taking into account events after the transaction in assessing the value of property or consideration). For later proceedings—sub nom. *Ramlort Ltd v Reid*—see [2004] EWCA Civ 800; [2004] B.P.I.R. 985. See further *Re Bangla Television Ltd* [2006] EWHC 2292 (Ch); [2007] 1 B.C.L.C. 609 (past consideration disregarded); *Re Unigreg Ltd* [2005] B.P.I.R. 220 (summary judgment given against foreign defendants); *Clements v Henry Hadaway Organisation Ltd* [2007] EWHC 2953 (Ch); [2008] 1 B.C.L.C. 223 (excessive management charges); *Singla v Hedman (No.2)* [2010] EWHC 902 (Ch); [2010] B.C.C. 684 (gratuitous transfer of film licence declared void); *Stanley v TMK Finance Ltd* [2010] EWHC 3349 (Ch); [2011] B.P.I.R. 876 (sale of freehold property); *Mann Aviation Group (Engineering) Ltd v Longmint Aviation Ltd* [2011] EWHC 2238 (Ch); [2012] B.P.I.R. 1405 (inter-company book transfer which depleted debtor company's assets); *Re Sofra Bakery Ltd* [2013] EWHC 1499 (Ch); [2015] 1 B.C.L.C. 338 (dispute as to whether goodwill included in sale transaction).

S.238(5)

These provisions bear a distinct resemblance to the "three-fold test" of Eve J in *Re Lee, Behrens and Co Ltd* [1932] 2 Ch. 46, which had a chequered history in the context of the doctrine of ultra vires (and, in that context, was later declared to be largely inappropriate: see *Rolled Steel Products (Holdings) Ltd v British Steel Corporation* [1986] Ch. 246; (1984) 1 B.C.C. 99,158). It may well be that s.238(5) will prove most difficult to apply in relation to the very types of transaction illustrated by the facts of the two cases mentioned: the payment of gratuities and pensions to employees and their dependants, and the giving of guarantees (especially within corporate groups). There may be problems, too, with regard to the "genuineness" of directors' remuneration (compare *Re Halt Garage (1964) Ltd* [1982] 3 All E.R. 1016), but it is very likely that the present section will make it easier to impeach such transactions.

239 Preferences (England and Wales)

239(1) [Application] This section applies as does section 238.

239(2) [Application to court by office-holder] Where the company has at a relevant time (defined in the next section) given a preference to any person, the office-holder may apply to the court for an order under this section.

239(3) [Court order] Subject as follows, the court shall, on such an application, make such order as it thinks fit for restoring the position to what it would have been if the company had not given that preference.

239(4) [Interpretation] For the purposes of this section and section 241, a company gives a preference to a person if–

(a) that person is one of the company's creditors or a surety or guarantor for any of the company's debts or other liabilities, and

(b) the company does anything or suffers anything to be done which (in either case) has the effect of putting that person into a position which, in the event of the company going into insolvent liquidation, will be better than the position he would have been in if that thing had not been done.

239(5) [Restriction on court order] The court shall not make an order under this section in respect of a preference given to any person unless the company which gave the preference was influenced in deciding to give it by a desire to produce in relation to that person the effect mentioned in subsection (4)(b).

239(6) [Presumption] A company which has given a preference to a person connected with the company (otherwise than by reason only of being its employee) at the time the preference was given is presumed, unless the contrary is shown, to have been influenced in deciding to give it by such a desire as is mentioned in subsection (5).

239(7) [Interpretation re preference] The fact that something has been done in pursuance of the order of a court does not, without more, prevent the doing or suffering of that thing from constituting the giving of a preference.

General Note

The former law relating to "fraudulent preferences", as contained in CA 1985 s.615 and earlier Companies Acts, had long been thought unsatisfactory and, in particular, as the Cork Committee pointed out (*Report*, para.1244), the word "fraudulent" was both inaccurate and misleading. The Committee recommended that the term "fraudulent preference" should be replaced by "voidable preference". The draftsman, however, has rejected this suggestion (and the expression "undue preference", which is common in Australia) in favour of simply "preference", except in Scotland, for which "unfair preference" has been chosen. These differences over terminology are unimportant. The object of the change, at least in regard to England and Wales, is to remove the implication that an improper motive approaching fraud must be shown (and proved to the high standard which that charge requires), and to reflect the fact that under the redefined law it is not necessary for the liquidator even to show that the *dominant* intention of the company was to give the one creditor a preference. It need now only be established that the company was "influenced by a desire" to bring about a preference, and in some cases the burden of proof on this point is reversed (see s.239(5), (6)). The liquidator's burden may therefore be lighter than it would be if proceedings were brought under s.213 (or, arguably, s.214): *Atkinson v Corcoran* [2011] EWHC 3484 (Ch).

In the first reported case under the new section, *Re M C Bacon Ltd* [1990] B.C.C. 78, Millett J "emphatically protested" against the citation of cases decided under the old law: these, he said, could not be of any assistance in construing the language of the new statute, which had been so completely and deliberately changed.

Two new provisions inserted into IA 1986 by SBEEA 2015 have resolved certain points which were the subject of some uncertainty at common law. First, s.176ZB confirms that the proceeds of an action brought by an office-holder under s.238 or 239 fall into the insolvent estate and are not subject to any floating charge over the assets of the company. Secondly, s.246ZD(2) reverses the common-law position and empowers a liquidator or administrator to assign the right of action under these sections, and the fruits of any such action, to a third party. See the notes to those sections. On the question whether the costs of litigation under the section may be recouped from the general assets in the liquidation, see the general note to s.238.

In the context of the financial markets, no order may be made under s.239 in relation to a market contract to which a recognised investment exchange or clearing house is a party or which is entered into under its default rules, or a disposition of property in pursuance of such a market contract: see CA 1989 s.165. It is also disapplied in relation to payment and securities settlement systems by the Finality Regulations 1999 reg.17. (See the introductory notes at pp.1–3 above.) Note again the potential impact of s.427 of the POCA 2002.

For the corresponding provisions in bankruptcy, see s.340; and for the position in Scotland, see s.243.

A company may also seek redress at common law where a director has acted in breach of duty (by, e.g. advancing the interests of a particular creditor) in circumstances analogous to a preference which do not fall within the scope of s.239: *GHLM Trading Ltd v Maroo* [2012] EWHC 61 (Ch); [2012] 2 B.C.L.C. 369. It is likely that the company will need to show (a) that it had suffered loss, (b) that the director had profited, and (c) that the transaction was not binding on the company (ibid.).

In *Re Parkside International Ltd* [2008] EWHC 3554 (Ch); [2010] B.C.C. 309 the insolvent company A and two other companies, B and C, were members of the same group. Shortly before A was put into administration B had assigned to C a debt owed to it by A. It was held that this was not a transaction "suffered" by A, being an act over which A had no control, and that this was so even though the three companies had common directors and, further, that although there may have been a desire to improve the position of the group as a whole, this was not the same as a desire to prefer one set of creditors over others.

S.239(1)

Section 238, which is referred to, restricts the jurisdiction to cases where a company is in administration or liquidation, and defines "office-holder" accordingly. Only a relevant office-holder may apply, and so an application under s.239 by a creditor did not need to be considered: the applicant needed to join the liquidators as parties to the application: *Global Corporate Ltd v Hale* [2017] EWHC 2277 (Ch).

S.239(2)

"Relevant time" refers both to the period within which the preference is given and to the company's solvency: see s.240(2). This is the time when the decision to enter into the transaction is taken, and not the time when the transaction is effected (see *Re M C Bacon Ltd* (above) at 88, followed in *Re Stealth Construction Ltd* [2011] EWHC 1305 (Ch); [2012] 1 B.C.L.C. 297). The terms "preference" and "any person" are explained in s.239(4).

S.239(3)

The court's powers are similar to those conferred by s.238(3) and include the power to decline to make any order: see the note to that subsection and *Re Parkside International Ltd* [2008] EWHC 3554 (Ch); [2009] B.P.I.R. 549. In *Re Kayford Ltd* [1975] 1 W.L.R. 279 a mail-order company in anticipation of possible insolvency had placed money sent as prepayments by its customers into a special bank account, and it was held that these sums were impressed with a trust which took them out of the insolvent estate when the company was later wound up. Under the law as it then stood, no question of fraudulent preference arose, but such an arrangement could now fall within s.239. If this were so, the circumstances might well justify the court in refusing to make an order. In *Re Lewis's of Leicester Ltd* [1995] B.C.C. 514 a somewhat similar arrangement in favour of certain concessionaires was made by a department store in anticipation of closing down its trading operations; but the court held that the company's desire was not to give the concessionaires a preference but to prevent the store from looking "more like a morgue than a market during its final weeks of trading".

S.239(4)

Examples of a preference given by the Cork Committee in its *Report* (para.1208) were: paying the whole or part of a debt, providing security or further security for an existing debt, and returning goods which have been delivered but not paid for. In *Re Mistral Finance Ltd* [2001] B.C.C. 27 the giving of security to secure an existing debt was struck down as a preference, but a clause which accelerated the obligations of both parties in the event of a liquidation, in consequence of which the creditor acquired a right of set-off, was held not to be open to challenge.

The phrase "going into insolvent liquidation" is not expressly defined for the purposes of the present section as it is for ss.214 and 216. That may, however, be a more helpful definition than anything that can be inferred from ss.240 and 247.

In *Re Thirty-Eight Building Ltd* [1999] B.C.C. 260 the transaction which was challenged was a transfer of the beneficial interest in certain assets to the trustees of a pension fund. It was held that the "creditor" who had to be identified under s.239(4) was the person who was the transferee in law (in this case the trustees and not the beneficiaries under the trust), and it was that person who had to receive a preference. The question was left open whether different considerations would apply where the trustees and the beneficiaries were the same individuals.

A transfer of funds held by the company on trust does not amount to a preference: *Re Branston & Gothard Ltd* [1999] B.P.I.R. 466.

In *Re Shapland Inc* [2000] B.C.C. 106 it was argued that even if the transaction in question was a preference, no order should be made because it would result in advantage to a secured creditor, rather than the company's unsecured creditors whose interests it was understood the legislation was intended to benefit. The court, although holding that the submission was not borne out by the facts of the case, thought it very doubtful that it was correct.

S.239(5)

The phrase "was influenced … by a desire to produce" replaces language contained in BA 1914 s.44(1) which had been construed as requiring the person who sought to have the payment or other transaction avoided to show that it had been made "with the dominant intention to prefer" the particular creditor. The Cork Committee (*Report*, paras 1248–1258), by a majority, took the view that the requirement of an intention (or dominant intention) to prefer should be retained, and rejected the alternative (established in Australia and the US and adopted in Scotland: see s.243) that it should be sufficient that the conduct in question had the *effect* of giving a preference.

In *Re M C Bacon Ltd* [1990] B.C.C. 78 at 87, Millett J held that it is no longer necessary to establish a dominant intention to prefer, nor is it sufficient to establish an *intention*: there must be a desire to produce the effect mentioned in the section. "Intention is objective, desire is subjective. A man can choose the lesser of two evils without desiring either … A man is not to be taken as *desiring* all the necessary consequences of his actions … It will still be possible to provide assistance to a company in financial difficulties provided that the company is actuated only by proper commercial considerations. Under the new regime a transaction will not be set aside as a voidable preference unless the company positively wished to improve the creditor's position in the event of its own insolvent liquidation." Accordingly, in that case, it was held that a decision by a company to give its bank a charge to secure existing borrowings (when the only alternative, if the bank withdrew its support, was liquidation) was not voidable as a preference under the present section.

The Cork Committee (*Report*, para.1256) took the view that pressure for payment by the creditor should continue, as under the former law, to afford a defence to a claim for the avoidance of a preference. The decision in *Re M C Bacon Ltd* (above) suggests that the new section will be so interpreted "unless the company positively wished to improve the creditor's position in the event of its own insolvency".

The "*Duomatic*" principle, which might in normal circumstances be invoked to allow a breach of duty by the directors to be condoned by the unanimous consent of all the shareholders, does not apply to a preferential transaction when insolvency is imminent: *Re Finch (UK) plc* [2015] EWHC 2430 (Ch).

S.239(6)

This important change, introduced on the recommendation of the Cork Committee, reverses the burden of proof in regard to intention when the beneficiary of the preference is a person "connected with" the company. This phrase is defined by s.249 and is fully discussed in the note to that section (but the special exception of employees in the present provision should be noted). The effect of s.239(6)—not least when s.240(2) is also taken into account—will make it very difficult for directors and controlling shareholders and their relatives, and other companies in the same group (all of which are "connected persons"), to retain the benefit of a preferential payment under the new legislation. For cases where the statutory presumption against connected persons was held to have been rebutted on the evidence, see *Re Beacon Leisure Ltd* [1991] B.C.C. 213; and *Re Fairway Magazines Ltd* [1992] B.C.C. 924. These may be contrasted with *Re DKG Contractors Ltd* [1990] B.C.C. 903; *Weisgard v Pilkington* [1995] B.C.C. 1,108; *Re Brian D Pierson (Contractors) Ltd* [1999] B.C.C. 26; *Wills v Corfe Joinery Ltd (in liq.)* [1997] B.C.C. 511; *Re Transworld Trading Ltd* [1999] B.P.I.R. 628; *Katz v McNally* [1999] B.C.C. 291; *Re Shapland Inc* [2000] B.C.C. 106; *Re Conegrade Ltd* [2002] EWHC 2411 (Ch); [2003] B.P.I.R. 358; *Barber v C.I. Ltd* [2006] B.C.C. 927 (affirmed on appeal sub nom. *Re Sonatacus Ltd* [2007] EWCA Civ 31; [2007] B.C.C. 186); *Re Cityspan Ltd* [2007] EWHC 751 (Ch); [2008] B.C.C. 60; *Re Stealth Construction Ltd* [2011] EWHC 1305 (Ch); [2012] 1 B.C.L.C. 297; *Re F Options Ltd* [2011] EWHC 3324 (Ch); *Taylor v Ziya* [2012] B.P.I.R. 1283; *Re Cosy Seal Insulation Ltd* [2016] EWHC 1255 (Ch), where the presumption was applied. In *Re Oxford Pharmaceuticals Ltd* [2009] EWHC 1753; [2010] B.C.C. 834 (order made against third party but not against director) the respondent succeeded in rebutting the presumption as regards some payments but not others. The judgment also contains a discussion of the overlap between preference and misfeasance proceedings. In *Phillips v McGregor-Paterson* [2009] EWHC 2385 (Ch) it was ruled that it was not appropriate to dispose of a s.239 claim on a summary basis because it was necessary to hear evidence in order to determine issues such as the company's insolvency and a desire to prefer.

240 "Relevant time" under ss.238, 239

240(1) [Relevant time] Subject to the next subsection, the time at which a company enters into a transaction at an undervalue or gives a preference is a relevant time if the transaction is entered into, or the preference given–

(a) in the case of a transaction at an undervalue or of a preference which is given to a person who is connected with the company (otherwise than by reason only of being its employee), at a time in the period of 2 years ending with the onset of insolvency (which expression is defined below),

(b) in the case of a preference which is not such a transaction and is not so given, at a time in the period of 6 months ending with the onset of insolvency,

(c) in either case, at a time between the making of an administration application in respect of the company and the making of an administration order on that application, and

(d) in either case, at a time between the filing with the court of a copy of notice of intention to appoint an administrator under paragraph 14 or 22 of Schedule B1 and the making of an appointment under that paragraph.

240(2) [Where not relevant time] Where a company enters into a transaction at an undervalue or gives a preference at a time mentioned in subsection (1)(a) or (b), that time is not a relevant time for the purposes of section 238 or 239 unless the company–

(a) is at that time unable to pay its debts within the meaning of section 123 in Chapter VI of Part IV, or

(b) becomes unable to pay its debts within the meaning of that section in consequence of the transaction or preference;

but the requirements of this subsection are presumed to be satisfied, unless the contrary is shown, in relation to any transaction at an undervalue which is entered into by a company with a person who is connected with the company.

240(3) [Onset of insolvency] For the purposes of subsection (1), the onset of insolvency is–

(a) in a case where section 238 or 239 applies by reason of an administrator of a company being appointed by administration order, the date on which the administration application is made,

(b) in a case where section 238 or 239 applies by reason of an administrator of a company being appointed under paragraph 14 or 22 of Schedule B1 following filing with the court of a copy of a notice of intention to appoint under that paragraph, the date on which the copy of the notice is filed,

(c) in a case where section 238 or 239 applies by reason of an administrator of a company being appointed otherwise than as mentioned in paragraph (a) or (b), the date on which the appointment takes effect,

(d) in a case where section 238 or 239 applies by reason of a company going into liquidation either following conversion of administration into winding up by virtue of Article 51 of the EU Regulation or at the time when the appointment of an administrator ceases to have effect, the date on which the company entered administration (or, if relevant, the date on which the application for the administration order was made or a copy of the notice of intention to appoint was filed), and

(e) in a case where section 238 or 239 applies by reason of a company going into liquidation at any other time, the date of the commencement of the winding up.

General Note

Both ss.238 and 239 apply only to a transaction or preference which takes place at a "relevant time". This section explains that term. Two factors may be in issue in determining the question whether a time is a "relevant time": (1) whether the transaction takes place within one of the four periods set out in s.240(1); and (2) whether the company is, at that time, insolvent, or becomes insolvent as a result of the transaction.

Once again, as with s.239(6), the burden of proof (this time, of "insolvency") varies with the position of the other party to the transaction: it is on the liquidator or administrator in the normal case, but on that other party if he is a person "connected with" the company (s.240(2)). Moreover, in the case of a preference, the period by reference to which a "relevant time" is reckoned is increased from six months to two years if the other party is a "connected person" (s.240(1)(a), (b)). In regard to a transaction at an undervalue, the period is two years in all cases (s.240(1)(a)).

On the meaning of "connected person", see the notes to ss.249 and 435. It is, in principle, possible for a company's bank to come within the definition of a "connected person" for the purposes of the present group of sections, if its involvement in the company's affairs is such as to make it a "shadow director": see *Re a Company (No.005009 of 1987)* (1988) 4 B.C.C. 424 and ss.249(a), 251. However where a bank or other creditor of a company simply makes terms for the continuation of credit in the light of threatened default, the court will not infer that its directors are accustomed to act in accordance with its directions so as to make it a shadow director: *Re PFTZM Ltd (in liq.)* [1995] B.C.C. 280.

Section 240 is disapplied in relation to payment and securities settlement systems by the Finality Regulations reg.17. (See the introductory note at p.3 above.)

S.240(1), (3)

The periods for the purposes of ss.238, 239 are determined by reference to a date which is defined by s.240(3) and is very misleadingly called "the onset of insolvency". This has nothing whatever to do with the company's inability to pay its debts (although, to add to the confusion, that issue does matter for the wholly unrelated questions raised by s.240(2)). The "onset of insolvency" is to be determined by reference to the various dates set out in s.240(3).

(On the "commencement" of a winding up, see the notes to ss.86 and 129, where the reference is, more precisely, to the "time" rather than the "date" of commencement. It must be assumed that this variation in language is deliberate: see the note to s.86.)

The requirement that the company should go into liquidation *immediately* upon the discharge of an administration order for s.240(3)(a) to apply calls for a measure of procedural ingenuity if it is proposed that the winding up should be a voluntary winding up, where the order was made under the original Pt II. See *Re Norditrack (UK) Ltd* [2000] 1 W.L.R. 343; [2000] B.C.C. 441.

Subsection (1)(c) was reworded and subs.(1)(d) added, and subs.(3)(a)–(e) substituted for the former subs.(3)(a)–(b) by EA 2002 Sch.17 para.26, with effect from 15 September 2003, to take account of the fact that applications for an administration order under IA 1986 Sch.B1 are not made by petition and that appointments may also be made out of court. However, the former wording (which referred to the time or date of the presentation of a petition for an administration order), has been reinstated for cases not coming within Sch.B1 by EA 2002 s.249 and the Enterprise Act 2002 (Commencement No.4 and Transitional Provisions and Savings) Order 2003 (SI 2003/2093 (C. 85)), art.3. See the notes to ss.212 and 230(1).

Section 240(3)(d) (as the former s.240(3)(aa)) was inserted by the Insolvency Act 1986 (Amendment) (No.2) Regulations 2002 (SI 2002/1240, effective 31 May 2002) and amended by the Insolvency Amendment (EU 2015/848) Regulations 2017 (SI 2017/702) regs 1, 2(1), Sch. paras 1, 15 in relation to proceedings opened on or after 26 June 2017 (see reg.3) when the Recast EU Regulation 2015/848 came into force. Article 51 of the EU Regulation empowers the insolvency practitioner in "main" insolvency proceedings in one Member State to apply to have an administration in another Member State (which will be "secondary" or "territorial" proceedings) converted into another type of insolvency proceeding. For the meaning of these technical terms, see the notes to the Regulation arts 2, 3.

The "relevant time" is a time within the six-month or two-year period ending with the "onset of insolvency" as defined in s.240(3). The period will be two years for all undervalue-transactions (s.240(1)(a)); in the case of a preference, it will be two years if the recipient of the preference is a "connected person", and six months if he is not; but employees are again not treated as "connected persons" for this purpose (s.240(1)(a), (b)).

S.240(2)

Section 240(1) and (3) are concerned only with the calculation of time, in the ordinary sense. However, s.240(2) introduces a further factor: a "time" will not be a "relevant" time (and therefore a transaction at an undervalue or a preference will not be liable to be set aside) unless the company is then unable to pay its debts, or becomes unable to pay its debts as a result of the impugned transaction. In other words, a company may enter into any transaction at an undervalue that it chooses or give any creditor a preference without violating ss.238 or 239, so long as it is solvent or so long as the event takes place outside the period leading up to its being put into administration or liquidation that is specified in s.240(1): only if both these conditions are satisfied will the transaction have occurred at a "relevant time" so as to bring those sections into play. (Note, however, that s.423 may be applicable if the necessary intent can be proved.)

The definition of "unable to pay its debts", for the purpose of s.240(2), is the same as in s.123, that is, either (1) deemed unable to pay because of an unpaid statutory demand for over £750 or an unsatisfied execution; or (2) proved unable in either a "commercial" or a "balance-sheet" sense. Assets and liabilities must be valued at the relevant time and on a "break-up" and not a "going concern" basis, but hindsight may be used by the court to determine the value of potential liabilities: *Watchorn v Jupiter Industries Ltd* [2014] EWHC 3003 (Ch); [2015] B.P.I.R. 184. A company may be insolvent even though it is currently able to pay its debts as they fall due: *Re Casa Estates (UK) Ltd, Bucci v Carman* [2014] EWCA Civ 383; [2014] B.C.C. 269 (payment funded by incurring future indebtedness, with no evidence as to how these liabilities would be satisfied). Inability may also be inferred from the fact that the company has invoices which it has not paid: *Re DKG Contractors Ltd* [1990] B.C.C. 903. See also *Evans v Jones* [2016] EWCA Civ 660, where the Court of Appeal refused to include a contingent claim in determining whether a company was unable to pay its debts, on the ground that the contingency was too remote. For further discussion, see the note to s.123.

Finally, as regards inability to pay debts, there is the question of the burden of proof. This, in relation to a transaction at an undervalue, lies on the liquidator or administrator when the other party is not a "connected person", but on that other party if he is. (There is no similar provision in relation to a preference, but the question of the company's solvency will be relevant, at least indirectly, to the question of intention for which s.239(6) places the burden of proof on the "connected person".) On the meaning of "connected person", see the note to s.249; but note that s.240(2) rather oddly does not repeat the exception for employees which appears in ss.239(6) and 240(1)(a). (This may be a drafting error, in that the former provision corresponding to ss.238–240, IA 1985 s.101, applied the employee exception to all connected persons in the provision: see IA 1985 s.101(11).)

241 Orders under ss.238, 239

241(1) [Extent of orders] Without prejudice to the generality of sections 238(3) and 239(3), an order under either of those sections with respect to a transaction or preference entered into or given by a company may (subject to the next subsection)–

(a) require any property transferred as part of the transaction, or in connection with the giving of the preference, to be vested in the company,

(b) require any property to be so vested if it represents in any person's hands the application either of the proceeds of sale of property so transferred or of money so transferred,

(c) release or discharge (in whole or in part) any security given by the company,

(d) require any person to pay, in respect of benefits received by him from the company, such sums to the office-holder as the court may direct,

(e) provide for any surety or guarantor whose obligations to any person were released or discharged (in whole or in part) under the transaction, or by the giving of the preference, to be under such new or revived obligations to that person as the court thinks appropriate,

(f) provide for security to be provided for the discharge of any obligation imposed by or arising under the order, for such an obligation to be charged on any property and for the security or charge to have the same priority as a security or charge released or discharged (in whole or in part) under the transaction or by the giving of the preference, and

(g) provide for the extent to which any person whose property is vested by the order in the company, or on whom obligations are imposed by the order, is to be able to prove in the winding up of the company for debts or other liabilities which arose from, or were released or discharged (in whole or in part) under or by, the transaction or the giving of the preference.

241(2) [Restriction on orders] An order under section 238 or 239 may affect the property of, or impose any obligation on, any person whether or not he is the person with whom the company in question entered into the transaction or (as the case may be) the person to whom the preference was given; but such an order–

(a) shall not prejudice any interest in property which was acquired from a person other than the company and was acquired in good faith and for value, or prejudice any interest deriving from such an interest, and

(b) shall not require a person who received a benefit from the transaction or preference in good faith and for value to pay a sum to the office-holder, except where that person was a party to the transaction or the payment is to be in respect of a preference given to that person at a time when he was a creditor of the company.

241(2A) [Presumption re good faith in s.241(2)] Where a person has acquired an interest in property from a person other than the company in question, or has received a benefit from the transaction or preference, and at the time of that acquisition or receipt–

(a) he had notice of the relevant surrounding circumstances and of the relevant proceedings, or

(b) he was connected with, or was an associate of, either the company in question or the person with whom that company entered into the transaction or to whom that company gave the preference,

then, unless the contrary is shown, it shall be presumed for the purposes of paragraph (a) or (as the case may be) paragraph (b) of subsection (2) that the interest was acquired or the benefit was received otherwise than in good faith.

241(3) [Relevant surrounding circumstances in s.241(2A)(a)] For the purposes of subsection (2A)(a), the relevant surrounding circumstances are (as the case may require)–

(a) the fact that the company in question entered into the transaction at an undervalue; or

(b) the circumstances which amounted to the giving of the preference by the company in question;

and subsections (3A) to (3C) have effect to determine whether, for those purposes, a person has notice of the relevant proceedings.

241(3A) [Notice of administration proceedings] Where section 238 or 239 applies by reason of a company's entering administration, a person has notice of the relevant proceedings if he has notice that–

(a) an administration application has been made,

(b) an administration order has been made,

(c) a copy of a notice of intention to appoint an administrator under paragraph 14 or 22 of Schedule B1 has been filed, or

(d) notice of the appointment of an administrator has been filed under paragraph 18 or 29 of that Schedule.

241(3B) [Notice of liquidation following administration] Where section 238 or 239 applies by reason of a company's going into liquidation at the time when the appointment of an administrator of the company ceases to have effect, a person has notice of the relevant proceedings if he has notice that–

(a) an administration application has been made,

(b) an administration order has been made,

(c) a copy of a notice of intention to appoint an administrator under paragraph 14 or 22 of Schedule B1 has been filed,

(d) notice of the appointment of an administrator has been filed under paragraph 18 or 29 of that Schedule, or

(e) the company has gone into liquidation.

241(3C) [Notice where liquidation at other times] In a case where section 238 or 239 applies by reason of the company in question going into liquidation at any other time, a person has notice of the relevant proceedings if he has notice–

(a) where the company goes into liquidation on the making of a winding-up order, of the fact that the petition on which the winding-up order is made has been presented or of the fact that the company has gone into liquidation;

(b) in any other case, of the fact that the company has gone into liquidation.

241(4) [Application of ss.238–241] The provisions of sections 238 to 241 apply without prejudice to the availability of any other remedy, even in relation to a transaction or preference which the company had no power to enter into or give.

General Note

The present section sets out in detail various orders which the court is empowered to make when avoiding a preference or a transaction at an undervalue under ss.238, 239, although it is not intended to limit the general powers of the court. It is designed in part to meet defects in the former law which the Cork Committee (*Report*, paras 1270–1276) identified as likely to arise when a company's obligation is backed by a surety or guarantor. For example, a payment may have been made to a creditor with a view to releasing the surety or guarantor rather than preferring the creditor, and the creditor may have released the guarantee and returned any security given before the payment is struck down as a preference. The creditor would then in all probability have had no remedy against the guarantor.

Section 241 was amended by the Insolvency (No.2) Act 1994 ss.1(1) and 6, with effect from 26 July 1994, as follows:

(1) in s.241(2), in both para.(a) and para.(b), the words "in good faith and for value" were substituted for the former wording, "in good faith, for value and without notice of the relevant circumstances";

(2) new subs.(2A) was inserted; and

(3) new subss.(3), (3A), (3B) and (3C) were substituted for the former subs.(3).

The amendments have effect only in relation to interests acquired and benefits received after the 1994 Act came into force (s.6(3)). For the corresponding provisions in relation to bankruptcy, see s.342 below (as amended).

The amendment, which stems from a recommendation of the Law Society, was designed to get over a perceived difficulty in relation to unregistered land, where a bona fide purchaser might have been taken to have had notice of a transaction that was liable to be set aside under either ss.238 or 239 in the event of a later insolvency. By removing the references to notice from s.241(2), a buyer of unregistered land is put into the same position as a buyer of registered land.

In subss.(3A) and (3B) the reference was formerly to the making of an administration order. The new wording was substituted by EA 2002 Sch.17 para.26, with effect from 15 September 2003, to take account of the fact that applications are no longer made by petition, and that appointments may also be made out of court. However, orders under the original IA 1986 Pt II are made on a petition, and where that regime continues to apply the original wording of the two subsections remains effective.

S.241(1)

Section 241(1) is "subject to the next subsection", which protects bona fide purchasers for value.

In *Re Husky Group Ltd* [2014] EWHC 3003 (Ch) the company had assigned valuable trade marks for a nominal consideration to its parent in anticipation of winding down its business (in fact it went into insolvent liquidation). The parent, who was privy to the wrongdoing, was ordered under s.241(1)(d) to pay the full value of the patents, with costs on an indemnity basis and interest at the highest allowable rate.

The court's discretion extends to refusing to make any order: see the note to s.238(3). In an appropriate case it may appoint a receiver and manager pending trial: *Walker v WA Personnel Ltd* [2002] B.P.I.R. 621. On the question whether the discretion may be exercised so as to benefit the holder of a security, rather than the company's unsecured creditors, see the remarks of Neuberger J, obiter, in *Ciro Citterio Menswear plc v Thakrar* (10 July 2002, referred to by P. Fleming, in [2003] Insolv. Int. 33 at 34).

Paragraphs (e) and (f) will empower the court to impose revived or new obligations on a guarantor or surety if his former obligations were released or discharged by the transaction which is later impugned, and to reinstate a security with the same priority as a former security or charge.

S.241(2)

This subsection allows third parties to be brought into the proceedings and orders to be made against them or their property instead of, or as well as, against the party with whom the company has dealt in the transaction under challenge. In particular, it will enable an order for repayment to be made directly against a surety or guarantor when the real object of a payment made by the company to a particular creditor was to release the guarantee rather than prefer the creditor. Bona fide third parties acquiring property or benefits for value will, however, be protected. Nevertheless, the concluding words of para.(b) indicate that the person who was the actual counterparty to a transaction at an undervalue or who himself, as a creditor, received the benefit of a preference will not be protected merely because he acted in good faith and for value. (This is in keeping with the traditional view taken in relation to fraudulent preferences, that it is the intention of the company to give an improper preference which is crucial, and that the state of mind of the creditor himself is immaterial.) Although s.241(2) does specifically envisage the making of orders against third parties (i.e. parties who have not in fact been preferred themselves), this is only appropriate if such an order is required as part of the process of restoring the position to what it would otherwise have been: *Re Oxford Pharmaceuticals Ltd* [2009] EWHC 1753; [2010] B.C.C. 834.

S.241(2A)–(3C)

These subsections, which were substituted for the former s.241(3) as described above, relate to two categories of person who have acquired an interest in property otherwise than from the company itself: (1) one who had notice of the "relevant surrounding circumstances" *and* of the "relevant proceedings" at the material time; and (2) one who was "connected with" or an "associate" of the company or the counterparty to the transaction. (For the meaning of the terms "connected with" and "associate", see ss.249 and 435, below.) As against such a person, there is a (rebuttable) statutory presumption of a lack of good faith. (In *Re Sonatacus Ltd* [2007] EWCA Civ 31; [2007] B.C.C. 186 the Court of Appeal said that "it was obvious" that the onus of proving good faith lay on the third party in any event.) The requirement in s.241(2A)(a) that the person (if not a "connected person" or "associate") should have notice of the insolvency proceedings as well as of the relevant surrounding circumstances is the major change effected by the 1994 reform.

Sections 241(3)–(3C) clarify the meaning of the terms "the relevant surrounding circumstances" and "notice of the relevant proceedings" used in s.241(2A).

S.241(4)

The phrase "a transaction which the company had no power to enter into or give" is, no doubt, a reference to the common-law doctrine of ultra vires, which was abolished for almost all purposes by CA 1989 s.108 (which inserted a revised s.35(1) into CA 1985 with effect from 4 February 1991 (see SI 1991/2569 (C. 68) art.4(a), 7) [and see now CA 2006 s.39]). However, the question of corporate capacity still has some relevance in relation to charitable companies (see CA 2006 ss.39(2), 42), and so the doctrine of ultra vires could apply in this restricted area. It is possible also that s.241(1) could be construed as extending to illegal transactions, e.g. those in contravention of the "financial assistance" provisions contained in CA 2006 ss.678 et seq. This subsection will allow the court to override the general law by, e.g. ordering the recipient of an ultra vires loan or gift to give security for its due repayment (s.241(1)(f)).

242 Gratuitous alienations (Scotland)

242(1) [Challenge to alienations] Where this subsection applies and–

(a) the winding up of a company has commenced, an alienation by the company is challengeable by–

(i) any creditor who is a creditor by virtue of a debt incurred on or before the date of such commencement, or

(ii) the liquidator;

(b) a company enters administration, an alienation by the company is challengeable by the administrator.

242(2) [Application of s.242(1)] Subsection (1) applies where–

(a) by the alienation, whether before or after 1st April 1986 (the coming into force of section 75 of the Bankruptcy (Scotland) Act 1985), any part of the company's property is transferred or any claim or right of the company is discharged or renounced, and

(b) the alienation takes place on a relevant day.

242(3) [Interpretation of s.242(2)(b)] For the purposes of subsection (2)(b), the day on which an alienation takes place is the day on which it becomes completely effectual; and in that subsection "relevant day" means, if the alienation has the effect of favouring–

(a) a person who is an associate (within the meaning of the Bankruptcy (Scotland) Act 2016) of the company, a day not earlier than 5 years before the date on which–

(i) the winding up of the company commences, or

(ii) as the case may be, the company enters administration; or

(b) any other person, a day not earlier than 2 years before that date.

242(4) [Duties of court on challenge under s.242(1)] On a challenge being brought under subsection (1), the court shall grant decree of reduction or for such restoration of property to the company's assets or other redress as may be appropriate; but the court shall not grant such a decree if the person seeking to uphold the alienation establishes–

(a) that immediately, or at any other time, after the alienation the company's assets were greater than its liabilities, or

(b) that the alienation was made for adequate consideration, or

(c) that the alienation–

(i) was a birthday, Christmas or other conventional gift, or

(ii) was a gift made, for a charitable purpose, to a person who is not an associate of the company,

which, having regard to all the circumstances, it was reasonable for the company to make:

Provided that this subsection is without prejudice to any right or interest acquired in good faith and for value from or through the transferee in the alienation.

242(5) ["Charitable purpose" in s.242(4)] In subsection (4) above, "charitable purpose" means any charitable, benevolent or philanthropic purpose, whether or not it is charitable within the meaning of any rule of law.

242(6) [Interpretation] For the purposes of the foregoing provisions of this section, an alienation in implementation of a prior obligation is deemed to be one for which there was no consideration or no adequate consideration to the extent that the prior obligation was undertaken for no consideration or no adequate consideration.

242(7) [Rights of challenge] A liquidator and an administrator have the same right as a creditor has under any rule of law to challenge an alienation of a company made for no consideration or no adequate consideration.

242(8) [Scotland only] This section applies to Scotland only.

General Note

This section deals with the setting aside of transactions at an undervalue (or the granting of "other redress": s.242(4)) in Scotland. It differs on a number of points of substance from s.238, following in these respects the Bankruptcy (Scotland) Act 1985 s.34 (now the Bankruptcy (Scotland) Act 2016 s.98).

The rights of creditors under Scots common law, including the right to challenge a debtor's action as a gratuitous alienation, survive the present legislation: see *Bank of Scotland v Pacific Shelf (Sixty Two) Ltd* (1988) 4 B.C.C. 457. On the present section, see *Henderson v Foxworth Investments Ltd* [2014] UKSC 41; [2014] 1 W.L.R. 2600 (where the trial judge's finding that a standard security had been made for adequate consideration was upheld by the Supreme Court, and contrast *Brown Ltd v Stonegale Ltd* [2016] UKSC 30 and *Blackburn v Alexander* [2015] CSOH 179, where a contention that the transactions in question were for adequate consideration was not established).

For a detailed analysis of the section including principles dating back to the Paulian action in Roman law and the (Scottish) Bankruptcy Act 1621 see *Grampian MacLennan's Distribution Services Ltd (Liquidators of) v Carnbroe Estates Ltd* [2018] CSIH 7 in which the court evinced three critical features of this area of law: (i) once a debtor is insolvent, his assets must be managed in such a way as to protect the interests of his creditors; (ii) it followed from that that, if a debtor alienates property once he is insolvent, he must obtain full consideration for the property alienated; and (iii) under the relevant statutes a series of presumptions operate whereby it is the person who receives the debtor's property who must establish that full consideration was given. The appellate court went on to overturn the earlier decision that sale of a company's property with an open market value of £1,200,000 (£800,000 if a restricted marketing period were assumed) for £550,000 was not a gratuitous alienation in the circumstances of an off-market sale under financial pressure.

In subss.(1)(b) and (3)(a)(ii) the reference was formerly to the making of an administration order. The new wording was substituted by EA 2002 Sch.17 para.28, with effect from 15 September 2003, to take account of the fact that applications are no longer made by petition, and that appointments may also be made out of court. However, orders under the original IA 1986 Pt II are made on a petition, and where that regime continues to apply the original wording of the two subsections remains effective.

Two new provisions inserted into IA 1986 by SBEEA 2015 have resolved certain points which were the subject of some uncertainty at common law. First, s.176ZB confirms that the proceeds of an action brought by an office-holder under s.242 fall into the insolvent estate and are not subject to any floating charge over the assets of the company. Secondly, s.246ZD(2) reverses the common-law position and empowers a liquidator or administrator to assign the right of action under this section, and the fruits of any such action, to a third party. See the notes to those sections.

In the context of the financial markets, no decree may be granted under s.242 in relation to a market contract to which a recognised investment exchange or clearing house is a party or which is entered into under its default rules, or a disposition of property in pursuance of such a market contract: see CA 1989 s.165. Section 242 is also disapplied in relation to payment and securities settlement systems by the Finality Regulations reg.17. (See the introductory notes at pp.1–3 above.)

An application under s.242 formed the backdrop to the litigation reported as *Henderson v 3052775 Nova Scotia Ltd* [2006] UKHL 21, though the proceedings reported are concerned with procedural aspects of Scottish law rather than substantive consideration of s.242.

S.242(1)

In the case of a liquidation, a creditor is given standing to challenge under para.(a)(i), in contrast with s.238(2), which restricts the right to the "office-holder".

S.242(2), (3)

The periods of five years and two years fixed by s.242(3) are different from those prescribed for England and Wales by s.240(1), but correspond with those that apply in the bankruptcy of an individual in Scotland: see the Bankruptcy (Scotland) Act 2016 s.98(4). The meaning of "associate" under the Bankruptcy (Scotland) Act 2016 s.229, is similar to, but not co-extensive with, that of "associate" as defined for the purposes of this Act: see s.435 and the note to that section. For a case where an associate was held liable under s.242(3)(a) see *Stak Realty Group Co Ltd v McKenna*

[2010] CSOH 29. For England and Wales, the term used by s.240(1) is "connected person", which is slightly wider in scope: see s.249.

Section 242(3)(a) amended by the Bankruptcy (Scotland) Act 2016 (Consequential Provisions and Modifications) Order 2016 (SI 2016/1034) art.7(1), Sch.1 para.4(1), (5) as from 30 November 2016.

S.242(4)

"Gratuitous alienation" includes a transaction for consideration at an undervalue (para.(b)); "reasonable" gifts and charitable donations may be justified (para.(c)). The requirement as to solvency is here more logically placed with the substantive aspects of the statutory provision, rather than linked to the definition of "relevant day": contrast s.240(2). See *McLuckie Bros Ltd v Newhouse Contracts Ltd*, 1993 S.L.T. 641. On s.242(4) see the comments of Lord Glennie in *Stak Realty Group Co Ltd v McKenna* [2010] CSOH 29.

243 Unfair preferences (Scotland)

243(1) [Application of s.243(4)] Subject to subsection (2) below, subsection (4) below applies to a transaction entered into by a company, whether before or after 1st April 1986, which has the effect of creating a preference in favour of a creditor to the prejudice of the general body of creditors, being a preference created not earlier than 6 months before the commencement of the winding up of the company or the company enters administration.

243(2) [Non-application of s.243(4)] Subsection (4) below does not apply to any of the following transactions–

(a) a transaction in the ordinary course of trade or business;

(b) a payment in cash for a debt which when it was paid had become payable, unless the transaction was collusive with the purpose of prejudicing the general body of creditors;

(c) a transaction whereby the parties to it undertake reciprocal obligations (whether the performance by the parties of their respective obligations occurs at the same time or at different times) unless the transaction was collusive as aforesaid;

(d) the granting of a mandate by a company authorising an arrestee to pay over the arrested funds or part thereof to the arrester where–

  (i) there has been a decree for payment or a warrant for summary diligence, and

  (ii) the decree or warrant has been preceded by an arrestment on the dependence of the action or followed by an arrestment in execution.

243(3) [Interpretation of s.243(1)] For the purposes of subsection (1) above, the day on which a preference was created is the day on which the preference became completely effectual.

243(4) [Persons who may challenge] A transaction to which this subsection applies is challengeable by–

(a) in the case of a winding up–

  (i) any creditor who is a creditor by virtue of a debt incurred on or before the date of commencement of the winding up, or

  (ii) the liquidator; and

(b) where the company has entered administration, the administrator.

243(5) [Duties of court on s.243(4) challenge] On a challenge being brought under subsection (4) above, the court, if satisfied that the transaction challenged is a transaction to which this section applies, shall grant decree of reduction or for such restoration of property to the company's assets or other redress as may be appropriate:

Provided that this subsection is without prejudice to any right or interest acquired in good faith and for value from or through the creditor in whose favour the preference was created.

243(6) [Rights of challenge] A liquidator and an administrator have the same right as a creditor has under any rule of law to challenge a preference created by a debtor.

243(7) [Scotland only] This section applies to Scotland only.

General Note

The law relating to unfair preferences in the bankruptcy of individuals is contained in the Bankruptcy (Scotland) Act 1985 s.36. The present section substantially follows that provision and differs in material respects from s.239—most notably in not requiring any proof of a desire to prefer. For the survival of the common law, see *Bank of Scotland v Pacific Shelf (Sixty Two) Ltd* (1988) 4 B.C.C. 457.

In subss.(1) and (4)(b) the reference was formerly to the making of an administration order. The new wording was substituted by EA 2002 Sch.17 para.29, with effect from 15 September 2003, to take account of the fact that applications are no longer made by petition, and that appointments may also be made out of court. However, the former wording has been reinstated for cases not coming within Sch.B1 by EA 2002 s.249 and by the Enterprise Act 2002 (Commencement No.4 and Transitional Provisions and Savings) Order 2003 (SI 2003/2093 (C. 85)) art.3. See the notes to ss.212 and 230(1).

Two new provisions inserted into IA 1986 by SBEEA 2015 have resolved certain points which were the subject of some uncertainty at common law. First, s.176ZB confirms that the proceeds of an action brought by an office-holder under s.243 fall into the insolvent estate and are not subject to any floating charge over the assets of the company. Secondly, s.246ZD(2) reverses the common-law position and empowers a liquidator or administrator to assign the right of action under this section, and the fruits of any such action, to a third party. See the notes to those sections.

A payment made by a company is not within the section unless it has completely divested itself of the funds within the relevant period: *Craiglaw Developments Ltd v Wilson* [1998] B.C.C. 530.

In the context of the financial markets, no decree may be granted under s.243 in relation to a market contract to which a recognised investment exchange or clearing house is a party or which is entered into under its default rules, or a disposition of property in pursuance of such a market contract. Section 243 is also disapplied in relation to payment and securities settlement systems by the Finality Regulations reg.17. (See the introductory notes at pp.1–3 above.)

S.243(1), (2)

The vital factor, in contrast with the subjective requirement regarding intent in s.239(1), (5), is whether the transaction has the effect of creating a preference: the intention of the parties is not relevant, unless there is collusion (s.243(2)(b), (c)). An attempt to invoke s.243(2)(b) was rejected by the court in *Leslie v White* [2012] CSOH 124. For the purposes of s.243(2)(c) there must be a strict equivalence of reciprocal obligations: *Nicoll v Steelpress (Supplies) Ltd*, 1993 S.L.T. 533.

S.243(4)

As with s.242, a creditor has standing to bring proceedings in the case of a winding up.

244 Extortionate credit transactions

244(1) [Application] This section applies as does section 238, and where the company is, or has been, a party to a transaction for, or involving, the provision of credit to the company.

244(2) [Court order re extortionate transaction] The court may, on the application of the office-holder, make an order with respect to the transaction if the transaction is or was extortionate and was entered into in the period of 3 years ending with the day on which the company entered administration or went into liquidation.

244(3) [Extortionate transaction—interpretation] For the purposes of this section a transaction is extortionate if, having regard to the risk accepted by the person providing the credit–

(a) the terms of it are or were such as to require grossly exorbitant payments to be made (whether unconditionally or in certain contingencies) in respect of the provision of the credit, or

(b) it otherwise grossly contravened ordinary principles of fair dealing;

and it shall be presumed, unless the contrary is proved, that a transaction with respect to which an application is made under this section is or, as the case may be, was extortionate.

244(4) [Extent of court order] An order under this section with respect to any transaction may contain such one or more of the following as the court thinks fit, that is to say–

(a) provision setting aside the whole or part of any obligation created by the transaction,

(b) provision otherwise varying the terms of the transaction or varying the terms on which any security for the purposes of the transaction is held,

(c) provision requiring any person who is or was a party to the transaction to pay to the office-holder any sums paid to that person, by virtue of the transaction, by the company,

(d) provision requiring any person to surrender to the office-holder any property held by him as security for the purposes of the transaction,

(e) provision directing accounts to be taken between any persons.

244(5) [Exercise of powers] The powers conferred by this section are exercisable in relation to any transaction concurrently with any powers exercisable in relation to that transaction as a transaction at an undervalue or under section 242 (gratuitous alienations in Scotland).

General Note

Section 66 of BA 1914, which was formerly applied in the winding up of insolvent companies by CA 1985 s.612, restricted the rate of interest that could be proved for in a liquidation, in the case of a debt carrying interest, to five per cent p.a. In keeping with the recommendations of the Cork Committee (*Report*, para.1380), s.66 has now been repealed (see the note to s.189). The removal of s.66, without more, would allow proofs in a winding up to include sums representing exorbitant rates of interest; and accordingly the court is given power by this section to reopen credit agreements on the application of a liquidator or administrator. This is in keeping with a recommendation of the Cork Committee (*Report*, para.1381). The section is modelled on ss.137–140 of the Consumer Credit Act 1974 (now superseded).

The proceeds of an action brought by an office-holder under s.244 fall into the insolvent estate and are not subject to any floating charge over the assets of the company (s.176ZB(3)(g)). The liquidator or administrator may assign the right of action under this section, and the fruits of any such action, to a third party (s.246ZD(2)(g)). See the notes to those sections.

For the corresponding provision in bankruptcy, see s.343.

S.244(1)

Section 238 applies to companies that are in liquidation or administration. Although s.238 is confined to England and Wales, it is submitted that the present section extends also to Scotland, for otherwise the reference to Scotland in s.244(5) would be pointless. This means that the word "applies" in s.244(1) must be construed with reference only to the different forms of insolvency proceedings and not to questions of geography or jurisdiction (even though the wording of s.245(1) would suggest the contrary). This interpretation is supported by s.440(2).

"Credit" is not defined.

S.244(2)

There is a three-year time limit for the retrospective re-opening of transactions under this section. (Note, however, that the time is reckoned from the date when the company "went into liquidation", in the case of a liquidation, and not from the "commencement of the winding up".)

S.244(3)

The test for "extortionate", in a commercial transaction where the interest rates were spelled out at the outset, is a very stringent one: *White v Davenham Trust Ltd* [2010] EWHC 2748 (Ch); [2011] B.C.C. 77. The onus of proof that a transaction was not extortionate is put in every case on to the person who gave the credit.

S.244(4)

The orders which the court is empowered to make include orders affecting third parties, e.g. sureties.

S.244(5)

On transactions at an undervalue, see ss.238, 240, 241.

245 Avoidance of certain floating charges

245(1) [Application] This section applies as does section 238, but applies to Scotland as well as to England and Wales.

245(2) [Invalidity of floating charge] Subject as follows, a floating charge on the company's undertaking or property created at a relevant time is invalid except to the extent of the aggregate of–

(a) the value of so much of the consideration for the creation of the charge as consists of money paid, or goods or services supplied, to the company at the same time as, or after, the creation of the charge,

(b) the value of so much of that consideration as consists of the discharge or reduction, at the same time as, or after, the creation of the charge, of any debt of the company, and

(c) the amount of such interest (if any) as is payable on the amount falling within paragraph (a) or (b) in pursuance of any agreement under which the money was so paid, the goods or services were so supplied or the debt was so discharged or reduced.

245(3) [Relevant time] Subject to the next subsection, the time at which a floating charge is created by a company is a relevant time for the purposes of this section if the charge is created–

(a) in the case of a charge which is created in favour of a person who is connected with the company, at a time in the period of 2 years ending with the onset of insolvency,

(b) in the case of a charge which is created in favour of any other person, at a time in the period of 12 months ending with the onset of insolvency,

(c) in either case, at a time between the making of an administration application in respect of the company and the making of an administration order on that application, or

(d) in either case, at a time between the filing with the court of a copy of notice of intention to appoint an administrator under paragraph 14 or 22 of Schedule B1 and the making of an appointment under that paragraph.

245(4) [Qualification to s.245(3)(b)] Where a company creates a floating charge at a time mentioned in subsection (3)(b) and the person in favour of whom the charge is created is not connected with the company, that time is not a relevant time for the purposes of this section unless the company–

(a) is at that time unable to pay its debts within the meaning of section 123 in Chapter VI of Part IV, or

(b) becomes unable to pay its debts within the meaning of that section in consequence of the transaction under which the charge is created.

245(5) [Onset of insolvency in s.245(3)] For the purposes of subsection (3), the onset of insolvency is–

(a) in a case where this section applies by reason of an administrator of a company being appointed by administration order, the date on which the administration application is made,

(b) in a case where this section applies by reason of an administrator of a company being appointed under paragraph 14 or 22 of Schedule B1 following filing with the court of a copy of notice of intention to appoint under that paragraph, the date on which the copy of the notice is filed,

(c) in a case where this section applies by reason of an administrator of a company being appointed otherwise than as mentioned in paragraph (a) or (b), the date on which the appointment takes effect, and

(d) in a case where this section applies by reason of a company going into liquidation, the date of the commencement of the winding up.

245(6) [Value of goods, services etc. in s.245(2)(a)] For the purposes of subsection (2)(a) the value of any goods or services supplied by way of consideration for a floating charge is the amount in money which at the time they were supplied could reasonably have been expected to be obtained for supplying the goods or services in the ordinary course of business and on the same terms (apart from the consideration) as those on which they were supplied to the company.

General Note

Under CA 1985 s.617, which this section replaces, a floating charge was declared invalid if it was created within 12 months of the commencement of a winding up (unless it could be proved that the company, immediately after the creation of the charge, was solvent), except to the amount of any cash paid to the company at the time of, or subsequently to the creation of, and in consideration for, the charge. In other words, a floating charge could not be created within that time to secure past indebtedness, but only an advance of "new money".

The present Act not only formulates more elaborate provisions to apply in such circumstances, but introduces several major changes:

(1) "floating charge" is redefined so as to include any charge which was originally created as a floating charge but has since become a fixed charge (s.251);

(2) the provisions apply in an administration as well as a liquidation;

(3) the section expressly covers some benefits conferred on the company otherwise than by the payment of "cash";

(4) the 12-month period is extended to two years if the chargee is a person "connected with" the company; and

(5) the exception where the company is proved at the material time to have been solvent will not be available to a chargee who is a person "connected with" the company.

The provisions of s.245 do not apply to invalidate a charge created before the Act came into force, except to the extent that it could have been invalidated under the previous law: see Sch.11 para.9. If a charge is created or otherwise arises under a financial collateral arrangement, s.245 is disapplied and it will not be avoided for non-registration: Financial Collateral Arrangements (No.2) Regulations 2003 (SI 2003/3226) regs 4(4), 10(5). In *Gray v G-T-P Group Ltd* [2010] EWHC 1772 (Ch); [2011] B.C.C. 869 the company failed to prove that the charge in question came within this exception.

In *Crumpler v Candey Ltd* [2017] EWHC 1511 (Ch) an issue was whether the relevant charge was floating or fixed: the court concluded that it was floating so that the section could apply (and that the other conditions of the section were met).

In subss.(3) and (5) the references were formerly to the presentation of a petition for an administration order and the making of such an order. The new wording was substituted by EA 2002 Sch.17 para.31, with effect from 15 September 2003, to take account of the fact that the procedure is now by application and appointments may be made out of court. However, the former wording has been reinstated for cases not coming within Sch.B1 by EA 2002 s.249 and the Enterprise Act 2002 (Commencement No.4 and Transitional Provisions and Savings) Order 2003 (SI 2003/2093 (C. 85)) art.3. See the notes to ss.212 and 230(1).

S.245(1)
The section applies where a company is in liquidation or is in administration.

S.245(2)
A charge will not be invalidated by this section to the extent that the chargee has increased the company's assets in any of the ways described. The extended wording removes doubts about the scope of the former phrase "cash paid to the company" by stipulating that goods or services supplied to the company or the release of a debt in whole or part will be as good as "new money". Whether paras (a) and (b) will themselves be open to a restrictive interpretation is unclear: it is hard to see why other forms of valuable consideration (e.g. the transfer of land or shares) were not included within the reform that was made.

The question whether the payment of money or the supply of goods or services is made "at the same time as" the execution of a charge is one of fact and degree—*Re Shoe Lace Ltd, Power v Sharp Investments Ltd* [1993] B.C.C. 609. In that case, money was advanced in four payments on different dates in April, May, June and on 16 July following a resolution of the company's directors to grant the debenture in March; but the debenture was not executed until 24 July. The Court of Appeal, affirming Hoffmann J [1992] B.C.C. 367, held that the payments could not be said to have been made at the same time as the execution of the debenture. Sir Christopher Slade, giving the leading judgment, said (at 620):

"In a case where no presently existing charge has been created by any agreement or company resolution preceding the execution of the formal debenture, then … no moneys paid before the execution of the debenture will qualify for exemption under the subsection, unless the interval between payment and execution is so short that it can be regarded as minimal and payment and execution can be regarded as contemporaneous".

However, where a promise to execute a debenture creates a present equitable right to a security, and moneys are advanced in reliance on it, any delay between the advances and the execution of the formal instrument of charge is immaterial: the charge has already been "created" and is immediately registrable, so that other creditors of the company will have had the opportunity to learn of its existence (ibid. at 619). In *Rehman v Chamberlain* [2011] EWHC 2318 (Ch) an argument that a charge had been "created" on this equitable basis failed on the facts.

In *Re Fairway Magazines Ltd* [1992] B.C.C. 924 it was held, following *Re Orleans Motor Co Ltd* [1911] 2 Ch. 41, that payments made by the lender directly to the company's bank which reduced its overdraft (and consequently the lender's liability under a personal guarantee) were not payments made "to the company" within the meaning of the section: the money never became available to the company to be used as it liked.

Interest was allowable under the repealed CA 1985 s.617, as it is under para.(c).

S.245(3)–(5)

These provisions are similar to s.240, both in their effect and in the very confusing language which is used. For more detailed comment, see the notes to that section: it is necessary to give the reminder that the phrase "the onset of insolvency" is not used with reference to the company's financial state but only with the question whether an administration or liquidation is deemed to have "commenced"; the issue of its financial well-being (or otherwise) is separately dealt with in s.245(4) in language which avoids the words "solvent" and "insolvent".

To sum up these provisions:

- a floating charge can be retrospectively invalidated within a two-year period for a "connected" chargee, and a 12-month period in other cases; further, if there is, or has been, an administration order in force, the period is extended to include the time between the making of an application for an administration order and the administration order, or the filing of a notice of intention to appoint an administrator and the making of an appointment under Sch.B1 paras 14 or 22;
- the "new consideration" exception applies whether the chargee is a connected person or not; and
- the "solvency" exception will now apply only where the chargee is not a connected person (using the term "solvency" in its everyday sense). The burden of establishing "solvency" under CA 1985 s.617, was put on the person seeking to uphold the charge. This is presumably still the case, although the section does not make the point clear.

The various technical expressions which appear in these provisions are discussed in more detail in the note to s.240.

On the meaning of "connected person", see the notes to ss.249 and 435. It is, in principle, possible for a company's bank to come within the definition of a "connected person" for the purposes of the present section, if its involvement in the company's affairs is such as to make it a "shadow director": see *Re a Company (No.005009 of 1987)* (1988) 4 B.C.C. 424 and ss.249(a), 251. See also *Unidare plc v Cohen* [2005] EWHC 1410 (Ch); [2006] Ch. 489; [2006] 2 B.C.L.C. 140 (discussed in the note to s.435).

All the references to time in s.245(2) are to the time of creation of the charge. So it would seem that a floating charge created in favour of A will attract all the disadvantages associated with "connected" chargees if A was a "connected person" at that time, and it will be immaterial that he has since ceased to be so connected. Conversely, if A was not a connected person at the time of creation, but becomes "connected" within the two-year period, his charge will have the more favourable treatment accorded by s.245(3)(b) and (4). [See *Unidare plc v Cohen* (above).] Again, if a floating charge is created in favour of A and is later assigned to B, the only relevant question will be whether A was, at the time of creation, a "connected person": it will not matter whether B was then, or was at the time of the assignment, or has since become, a "connected person". There are clearly advantages, if one is a "connected person", of taking a charge by assignment rather than directly and, if one is not, of re-financing with a new charge rather than taking an assignment of a charge from a "connected" chargee—unless in either case the whole arrangement could be challenged as evasive.

S.245(6)

This subsection deals with the position where goods or services, rather than "new money", is the consideration provided for a charge. It is made clear that it is the true value of the goods or services that counts, and not the price or valuation that the parties themselves have agreed on as the consideration for the supply. The chargee cannot defeat the object of the Act by having the company credit him with an unrealistic sum.

In *Crumpler v Candey Ltd* [2017] EWHC 1511 (Ch) HHJ Davis-White QC, having determined that a disputed charge was a floating charge in nature, then considered the potential impact of s.245. But he was not able to determine the matter at this stage of proceedings as the value of services supplied by the chargee to the company after the creation of the charge required valuation.

246 Unenforceability of liens on books, etc.

246(1) [Application] This section applies in the case of a company where–

(a) the company enters administration, or

(b) the company goes into liquidation, or

(c) a provisional liquidator is appointed;

and "the office-holder" means the administrator, the liquidator or the provisional liquidator, as the case may be.

246(2) [Lien etc. unenforceable] Subject as follows, a lien or other right to retain possession of any of the books, papers or other records of the company is unenforceable to the extent that its enforcement would deny possession of any books, papers or other records to the office-holder.

246(3) [Non-application] This does not apply to a lien on documents which give a title to property and are held as such.

General Note

This section ensures that a liquidator or administrator is not prevented from taking possession of any of the company's books, etc. because a lien is claimed over them (e.g. by a solicitor or accountant for outstanding fees). It relates only to liens on "books, papers and other records" and not to liens on other categories of goods, and operates to extinguish the lien (or, at the least, to render it unenforceable to the extent specified in s.246(2)). Liens not caught by the section remain valid, but in the case of an administration will not be enforceable without the leave of the court under para.43(6) of Sch.B1 or s.11(3): *Bristol Airport plc v Powdrill* [1990] Ch. 744 at 762 (reported as *Re Paramount Airways Ltd* [1990] B.C.C. 130 at 150).

In subs.(1)(a) the reference was formerly to the making of an administration order. The new wording was substituted by EA 2002 Sch.17 para.32, with effect from 15 September 2003, to take account of appointments made out of court.

Note that s.246 does not apply in favour of an administrative receiver or the supervisor of a voluntary arrangement.

Section 246 does not apply to Scotland (see s.440(2)(a)); but the corresponding provisions of the Bankruptcy (Scotland) Act 1985 s.38(4), which are more limited in scope, have been extended to company liquidations by the rules: see the Insolvency (Scotland) Rules 1986 (SI 1986/1915 (S 139)) r.4.22(1).

S.246(3)

The exception created by s.246(3) is not limited to the case where the person claiming the lien does so by reason of the fact that the documents in question confer "a title to property" upon him. The words "as such" mean "in circumstances which are such as to give rise to a lien". In other words, it is sufficient that the person has a lien over the documents, and the documents are of a kind which give a title to property to somebody: *Re SEIL Trade Finance Ltd* [1992] B.C.C. 538. See also the case of *Re Carter Commercial Developments Ltd* [2002] B.C.C. 803; [2002] B.P.I.R. 1053, noted by S. Unwin in [2003] Insolv. Int. 4.

Administration: penalisation of directors etc

246ZA Fraudulent trading: administration

246ZA(1) [Application] If while a company is in administration it appears that any business of the company has been carried on with intent to defraud creditors of the company or creditors of any other person, or for any fraudulent purpose, the following has effect.

246ZA(2) [Court may declare any persons liable] The court, on the application of the administrator, may declare that any persons who were knowingly parties to the carrying on of the business in the manner mentioned in subsection (1) are to be liable to make such contributions (if any) to the company's assets as the court thinks proper.

General Note

This and ss.246ZB and 246ZC were inserted by the SBBEA s.117(1), (2)–(3) with effect from 1 October 2015, so that the liability for fraudulent trading and wrongful trading is extended from liquidations to include also administrations. For commentary, see the note to s.213. See also note after s.246ZC.

246ZB Wrongful trading: administration

246ZB(1) [Declaration of court on application by administrator] Subject to subsection (3), if while a company is in administration it appears that subsection (2) applies in relation to a person who is or has been a director of the company, the court, on the application of the administrator, may declare that that person is to be liable to make such contribution (if any) to the company's assets as the court thinks proper.

246ZB(2) [Application] This subsection applies in relation to a person if–

(a) the company has entered insolvent administration,

(b) at some time before the company entered administration, that person knew or ought to have concluded that there was no reasonable prospect that the company would avoid entering insolvent administration or going into insolvent liquidation, and

(c) the person was a director of the company at that time.

246ZB(3) [No declaration where person minimised loss to creditors] The court must not make a declaration under this section with respect to any person if it is satisfied that, after the condition specified in subsection (2)(b) was first satisfied in relation to the person, the person took every step with a view to minimising the potential loss to the company's creditors as (on the assumption that the person had knowledge of the matter mentioned in subsection (2)(b)) the person ought to have taken.

246ZB(4) [Test for facts known in s.214(2), (3)] For the purposes of subsections (2) and (3), the facts which a director of a company ought to know or ascertain, the conclusions which the director ought to reach and the steps which the director ought to take are those which would be known or ascertained, or reached or taken, by a reasonably diligent person having both–

(a) the general knowledge, skill and experience that may reasonably be expected of a person carrying out the same functions as are carried out by that director in relation to the company, and

(b) the general knowledge, skill and experience that that director has.

246ZB(5) [Interpretation of functions in s.214(4)] The reference in subsection (4) to the functions carried out in relation to a company by a director of the company includes any functions which the director does not carry out but which have been entrusted to the director.

246ZB(6) [Interpretation of insolvent administration/liquidation] For the purposes of this section–

(a) a company enters insolvent administration if it enters administration at a time when its assets are insufficient for the payment of its debts and other liabilities and the expenses of the administration;

(b) a company goes into insolvent liquidation if it goes into liquidation at a time when its assets are insufficient for the payment of its debts and other liabilities and the expenses of the winding up.

246ZB(7) ["Director"] In this section "director" includes shadow director.

246ZB(8) [Section 246ZA] This section is without prejudice to section 246ZA.

GENERAL NOTE

As noted above, this section was inserted by SBBEA by s.117(1), (2) with effect from 1 October 2015, so that the liability for wrongful trading is extended from liquidations to include also administrations. For commentary, see the note to ss.213 and 214. See also the note after s.246ZC.

S.246ZB(2), (6)
Note that the expressions "insolvent administration" and "insolvent liquidation" are defined on a "balance sheet" and not a "cash-flow" basis. (See the note to s.214(6).) If insolvency has been alleged or established at the initiation of the insolvency procedure purely on a cash-flow reckoning it will be necessary to adduce further evidence to satisfy the present requirement. If the company has been put into administration by or on the application of the holder of a floating charge, it may not have been necessary to allege or prove insolvency at all, and in that case proof of insolvency will be required *de novo.*

246ZC Proceedings under section 246ZA or 246ZB

246ZC Section 215 applies for the purposes of an application under section 246ZA or 246ZB as it applies for the purposes of an application under section 213 but as if the reference in subsection (1) of section 215 to the liquidator was a reference to the administrator.

GENERAL NOTE

See the note to s.215.

Note that s.246ZA–246ZC do not apply to proceedings that commenced before 6 April 2017 in relation to building society administration under Pt 2 of IA 1986, to bank or building society insolvency under Pt 2 of the Banking Act 2009 or to any bank administration or building society special administration under Pt 3 of the Banking Act 2009: see the Deregulation Act 2015, Small Business, Enterprise and Employment Act 2015 and the Insolvency (Amendment) Act (Northern Ireland) 2016 (Consequential Amendments and Transitional Provisions) Regulations 2017 (SI 2017/400) regs 1, 13, 15.

Power to assign certain causes of action

246ZD Power to assign

246ZD(1) [Application] This section applies in the case of a company where–

(a) the company enters administration, or

(b) the company goes into liquidation;

and "the office-holder" means the administrator or the liquidator, as the case may be.

246ZD(2) [Power of office-holder to assign right of action/proceeds] The office-holder may assign a right of action (including the proceeds of an action) arising under any of the following–

(a) section 213 or 246ZA (fraudulent trading);

(b) section 214 or 246ZB (wrongful trading);

(c) section 238 (transactions at an undervalue (England and Wales));

(d) section 239 (preferences (England and Wales));

(e) section 242 (gratuitous alienations (Scotland));

(f) section 243 (unfair preferences (Scotland));

(g) section 244 (extortionate credit transactions).

GENERAL NOTE

Section 246ZD was inserted by SBEEA 2015 s.118 with effect from 1 October 2015. It removes any doubt which may have existed at common law as to the power of office-holders to assign these statutory rights of action and their proceeds. Note that s.246ZD does not apply to proceedings that commenced before 6 April 2017 in relation to bank or building society insolvency under Pt 2 of the Banking Act 2009, building society administration under Pt 2 of IA 1986, building society special administration under Pt 3 of the Banking Act 2009 or special administrations under the Investment Bank Special Administration Regulations 2011 (SI 2011/245) and winding up of a relevant collective investment scheme: see the Deregulation Act 2015, Small Business, Enterprise and Employment Act 2015 and the Insolvency (Amendment) Act (Northern Ireland) 2016 (Consequential Amendments and Transitional Provisions) Regulations 2017 (SI 2017/400) regs 1, 13, 16.

Decisions by creditors and contributories

246ZE Decisions by creditors and contributories: general

246ZE(1) [Application] This section applies where, for the purposes of this Group of Parts, a person ("P") seeks a decision about any matter from a company's creditors or contributories.

246ZE(2) [Qualifying decision procedure] The decision may be made by any qualifying decision procedure P thinks fit, except that it may not be made by a creditors' meeting or (as the case may be) a contributories' meeting unless subsection (3) applies.

246ZE(3) [Requisition for creditors'/contributories' meeting] This subsection applies if at least the minimum number of creditors or (as the case may be) contributories make a request to P in writing that the decision be made by a creditors' meeting or (as the case may be) a contributories' meeting.

246ZE(4) [Meeting to be summoned] If subsection (3) applies P must summon a creditors' meeting or (as the case may be) a contributories' meeting.

246ZE(5) [Section 246ZE(2) subject to qualifying decision procedure/meeting] Subsection (2) is subject to any provision of this Act, the rules or any other legislation, or any order of the court–

(a) requiring a decision to be made, or prohibiting a decision from being made, by a particular qualifying decision procedure (other than a creditors' meeting or a contributories' meeting);

(b) permitting or requiring a decision to be made by a creditors' meeting or a contributories' meeting.

246ZE(6) [Deemed consent procedure under s.246ZF] Section 246ZF provides that in certain cases the deemed consent procedure may be used instead of a qualifying decision procedure.

246ZE(7) ["Minimum number" in s.246ZE(3)] For the purposes of subsection (3) the "minimum number" of creditors or contributories is any of the following–

(a) 10% in value of the creditors or contributories;

(b) 10% in number of the creditors or contributories;

(c) 10 creditors or contributories.

246ZE(8) [Creditors in s.246ZE(7)] The references in subsection (7) to creditors are to creditors of any class, even where a decision is sought only from creditors of a particular class.

246ZE(9) [References to a meeting] In this section references to a meeting are to a meeting where the creditors or (as the case may be) contributories are invited to be present together at the same place (whether or not it is possible to attend the meeting without being present at that place).

246ZE(10) [Creditors except in s.246ZE(8)] Except as provided by subsection (8), references in this section to creditors include creditors of a particular class.

246ZE(11) ["Qualifying decision procedure"] In this Group of Parts "qualifying decision procedure" means a procedure prescribed or authorised under paragraph 8A of Schedule 8.

(See General Note after s.246ZG.)

246ZF Deemed consent procedure

246ZF(1) [When may be used instead of qualifying decision procedure] The deemed consent procedure may be used instead of a qualifying decision procedure where a company's creditors or contributories are to make a decision about any matter, unless–

(a) a decision about the matter is required by virtue of this Act, the rules, or any other legislation to be made by a qualifying decision procedure, or

(b) the court orders that a decision about the matter is to be made by a qualifying decision procedure.

246ZF(2) [Rules re remuneration to be by qualifying decision procedure] If the rules provide for a company's creditors or contributories to make a decision about the remuneration of any person, they must provide that the decision is to be made by a qualifying decision procedure.

246ZF(3) [Notice for deemed consent procedure] The deemed consent procedure is that the relevant creditors (other than opted-out creditors) or (as the case may be) the relevant contributories are given notice of–

(a) the matter about which they are to make a decision,

(b) the decision that the person giving the notice proposes should be made (the "proposed decision"),

(c) the effect of subsections (4) and (5), and

(d) the procedure for objecting to the proposed decision.

246ZF(4) [Deemed consent if appropriate number do not object] If less than the appropriate number of relevant creditors or (as the case may be) relevant contributories object to the proposed decision in accordance with the procedure set out in the notice, the creditors or (as the case may be) the contributories are to be treated as having made the proposed decision.

246ZF(5) [Where appropriate number object] Otherwise–

(a) the creditors or (as the case may be) the contributories are to be treated as not having made a decision about the matter in question, and

(b) if a decision about that matter is again sought from the creditors or (as the case may be) the contributories, it must be sought using a qualifying decision procedure.

246ZF(6) ["Appropriate number" in s.246ZF(4)] For the purposes of subsection (4) the "appropriate number" of relevant creditors or relevant contributories is 10% in value of those creditors or contributories.

246ZF(7) ["Relevant creditors" in s.246ZF(3), (4)] "Relevant creditors" means the creditors who, if the decision were to be made by a qualifying decision procedure, would be entitled to vote in the procedure.

246ZF(8) ["Relevant contributories" in s.246ZF(3), (4)] means the contributories who, if the decision were to be made by a qualifying decision procedure, would be entitled to vote in the procedure.

246ZF(9) [Creditors in s.246ZF] In this section references to creditors include creditors of a particular class.

246ZF(10) [Further provision by rules] The rules may make further provision about the deemed consent procedure.

(See General Note after s.246ZG.)

246ZG Power to amend sections 246ZE and 246ZF

246ZG(1) [Power re minimum number of creditors/contributories] The Secretary of State may by regulations amend section 246ZE so as to change the definition of–

(a) the minimum number of creditors;

(b) the minimum number of contributories.

246ZG(2) [Power re appropriate number of relevant creditors/contributories] The Secretary of State may by regulations amend section 246ZF so as to change the definition of–

(a) the appropriate number of relevant creditors;

(b) the appropriate number of relevant contributories.

246ZG(3) [Defining minimum number or appropriate number] Regulations under this section may define the minimum number or the appropriate number by reference to any one or more of–

(a) a proportion in value,

(b) a proportion in number,

(c) an absolute number,

and the definition may include alternative, cumulative or relative requirements.

246ZG(4) [Power in s.246ZG(1)] Regulations under subsection (1) may define the minimum number of creditors or contributories by reference to all creditors or contributories, or by reference to creditors or contributories of a particular description.

246ZG(5) [Different definitions for different cases in ss.246ZE, 246ZF] Regulations under this section may make provision that will result in section 246ZE or 246ZF having different definitions for different cases, including–

(a) for creditors and for contributories,

(b) for different kinds of decisions.

246ZG(6) [Transitional provisions] Regulations under this section may make transitional provision.

246ZG(7) [Power exercisable by statutory instrument] The power of the Secretary of State to make regulations under this section is exercisable by statutory instrument.

246ZG(8) [Approval of statutory instrument] A statutory instrument containing regulations under this section may not be made unless a draft of the instrument has been laid before, and approved by a resolution of, each House of Parliament.

General Note to ss.246ZE–246ZG

Sections 246ZE–246ZG were inserted by SBEEA 2015 s.122(1), (2) from 6 April 2017. Reference should also be made to Sch.8A and r.15.7.

These provisions introduce the "deemed consent procedure", which allows decisions which would ordinarily be made by the contributories or creditors at a meeting to be made without a physical meeting (or other equivalent procedure), simply by giving notice of the proposed decision and deeming consent to have been given unless a specified proportion (generally 10 per cent) or 10 in number of the contributories or creditors object within a specified time. For further details, see rr.15.7–15.11. The deemed consent procedure may not be used to make a decision on remuneration, or where its use is prohibited by the Act, the Rules or any other legislation, or court order (s.246ZF(1), (2)).

S.246ZE(11)

The meaning of the phrase "qualifying decision procedure" has to be tracked down through Sch.8 para.8A to IR 2016 Pt 15. Essentially it refers to a decision reached by the company's contributories or creditors by correspondence, electronic voting, virtual meeting or physical meeting (as appropriate in the circumstances) and achieved by whatever majority (and in accordance with any conditions as to notice, eligibility to vote, etc.) that is prescribed by the remaining rules of Pt 15. If the procedure ticks all the boxes in that Part, it "qualifies".

246A Remote attendance at meetings

246A(1) [Application of section] Subject to subsection (2), this section applies to–

(a) any meeting of the creditors of a company summoned under this Act or the rules, or

(b) any meeting of the members or contributories of a company summoned by the office-holder under this Act or the rules, other than a meeting of the members of a company in a members' voluntary winding up.

246A(2) [Non-application to appointment of receiver, Scottish winding up] This section does not apply where–

(a) a company is being wound up in Scotland, or

(b) a receiver is appointed under section 51 in Chapter 2 of Part 3.

246A(3) [Attendance at meeting by persons not present together] Where the person summoning a meeting ("the convener") considers it appropriate, the meeting may be conducted and held in such a way that persons who are not present together at the same place may attend it.

246A(4) [Attendance at meeting by exercise of right to speak and vote] Where a meeting is conducted and held in the manner referred to in subsection (3), a person attends the meeting if that person is able to exercise any rights which that person may have to speak and vote at the meeting.

246A(5) [When exercising right to speak and vote] For the purposes of this section–

(a) a person is able to exercise the right to speak at a meeting when that person is in a position to communicate to all those attending the meeting, during the meeting, any information or opinions which that person has on the business of the meeting; and

(b) a person is able to exercise the right to vote at a meeting when–

(i) that person is able to vote, during the meeting, on resolutions put to the vote at the meeting, and

(ii) that person's vote can be taken into account in determining whether or not such resolutions are passed at the same time as the votes of all the other persons attending the meeting.

246A(6) [Duty of convener to make arrangements] The convener of a meeting which is to be conducted and held in the manner referred to in subsection (3) shall make whatever arrangements the convener considers appropriate to–

(a) enable those attending the meeting to exercise their rights to speak or vote, and

(b) ensure the identification of those attending the meeting and the security of any electronic means used to enable attendance.

246A(7) [Where unnecessary or inexpedient to specify place for meeting] Where in the reasonable opinion of the convener–

(a) a meeting will be attended by persons who will not be present together at the same place, and

(b) it is unnecessary or inexpedient to specify a place for the meeting, any requirement under this Act or the rules to specify a place for the meeting may be satisfied by specifying the arrangements the convener proposes to enable persons to exercise their rights to speak or vote.

246A(8) [Convener to regard legitimate interests of the creditors etc. for s.246A(6), (7)(b)] In making the arrangements referred to in subsection (6) and in forming the opinion referred to in subsection

(7)(b), the convener must have regard to the legitimate interests of the creditors, members or contributories and others attending the meeting in the efficient despatch of the business of the meeting.

246A(9) [Request for convener to specify place for meeting] If–

(a) the notice of a meeting does not specify a place for the meeting,

(b) the convener is requested in accordance with the rules to specify a place for the meeting, and

(c) that request is made–

(i) in the case of a meeting of creditors or contributories, by not less than ten percent in value of the creditors or contributories, or

(ii) in the case of a meeting of members, by members representing not less than ten percent of the total voting rights of all the members having at the date of the request a right to vote at the meeting,

it shall be the duty of the convener to specify a place for the meeting.

246A(10) ["The office-holder"] In this section, "the office-holder", in relation to a company, means–

(a) its liquidator, provisional liquidator, administrator, or administrative receiver, or

(b) where a voluntary arrangement in relation to the company is proposed or has taken effect under Part 1, the nominee or the supervisor of the voluntary arrangement.

General Note

Section 246A was inserted by LRO 2010 (SI 2010/18) art.3(1) as from 6 April 2010 (with retrospective effect). It applies with the limitations set out in subsection (2). The section removes any doubt that a "meeting" under the Act or the Rules may be held without the participants being physically present, whether it takes place by video-link, telephone conference or electronic means. It is no longer necessary to specify any place where the meeting is to be held.

Giving of notices etc by office-holders

246B Use of websites

246B(1) [Provision of notice by website] Subject to subsection (2), where any provision of this Act or the rules requires the office-holder to give, deliver, furnish or send a notice or other document or information to any person, that requirement is satisfied by making the notice, document or information available on a website–

(a) in accordance with the rules, and

(b) in such circumstances as may be prescribed.

246B(2) [Non-application to appointment of receiver, Scottish winding up] This section does not apply where–

(a) a company is being wound up in Scotland, or

(b) a receiver is appointed under section 51 in Chapter 2 of Part 3.

246B(3) ["The office-holder"] In this section, "the office-holder" means–

(a) the liquidator, provisional liquidator, administrator, or administrative receiver of a company, or

(b) where a voluntary arrangement in relation to a company is proposed or has taken effect under Part 1, the nominee or the supervisor of the voluntary arrangement.

GENERAL NOTE

Section 246B was inserted by LRO 2010 (SI 2010/18) art.3(1) as from 6 April 2010 (with retrospective effect). It applies with the limitations set out in subsection (2). The section allows an office-holder who is required by the Act to give notice or send any document to any person to do so by means of a website (unless personal service is required). The rules which have been made for the purpose are rr.1.48–1.49. The person must be notified that the document is available for viewing and downloading and be given details for accessing the website, and is entitled to request a hard copy. This must be sent within five business days (r.1.48(2)).

246C Creditors' ability to opt out of receiving certain notices

246C(1) [Non-application of rules re notice to creditors] Any provision of the rules which requires an office-holder of a company to give a notice to creditors of the company does not apply, in circumstances prescribed by the rules, in relation to opted-out creditors.

246C(2) [Non-application of s.246C(1)] Subsection (1)–

(a) does not apply in relation to a notice of a distribution or proposed distribution to creditors;

(b) is subject to any order of the court requiring a notice to be given to all creditors (or all creditors of a particular category).

246C(3) [Participation of opted-out creditors] Except as provided by the rules, a creditor may participate and vote in a qualifying decision procedure or a deemed consent procedure even though, by virtue of being an opted-out creditor, the creditor does not receive notice of it.

246C(4) ["Give", "notice", "office-holder" in s.246C] In this section–

"give" includes deliver, furnish or send;

"notice" includes any document or information in any other form;

"office-holder", in relation to a company, means–

(a) a liquidator, provisional liquidator, administrator or administrative receiver of the company,

(b) a receiver appointed under section 51 in relation to any property of the company, or

(c) the supervisor of a voluntary arrangement which has taken effect under Part 1 in relation to the company.

GENERAL NOTE

Section 246C inserted by SBEEA 2015 s.124(3) from 6 April 2017. On opted-out creditors, see the note to s.248A. If a creditor has opted out, he must still be sent notice of a distribution, and otherwise if a court so orders (s.246C(2)). He may still participate in a decision even though he does not receive notice of it (s.246C(3)). If a creditor has opted out, he must still be sent any notice which the Act requires to be delivered to all creditors without expressly excluding opted-out creditors: IR 2016 r.1.37(2)(a).

PART VII

INTERPRETATION FOR FIRST GROUP OF PARTS

247 "Insolvency" and "go into liquidation"

247(1) ["Insolvency"] In this Group of Parts, except in so far as the context otherwise requires, "insolvency", in relation to a company, includes the approval of a voluntary arrangement under Part I, or the appointment of an administrator or administrative receiver.

247(2) [Company in liquidation] For the purposes of any provision in this Group of Parts, a company goes into liquidation if it passes a resolution for voluntary winding up or an order for its winding up is made by the court at a time when it has not already gone into liquidation by passing such a resolution.

247(3) [Resolution following administration or voluntary arrangement] The reference to a resolution for voluntary winding up in subsection (2) includes a reference to a resolution which is deemed to occur by virtue of–

(a) paragraph 83(6)(b) of Schedule B1, or

(b) an order made following conversion of administration or a voluntary arrangement into winding up by virtue of Article 51 of the EU Regulation.

S.247(1)

This meaning of "insolvency" is discussed in the Introductory note to Part VI, preceding s.230, above, where attention is drawn to the fact that the Act uses the term to describe the various *proceedings*, such as winding up, administration and receivership, which are the subject of the present Act, and not to describe a company's adverse financial situation. The related word "insolvent" is not defined by this section, and at times it appears to be used in the Act in the everyday sense (e.g. "goes into insolvent liquidation": s.214(6)) rather than analogously with the definition of "insolvency" in the present section.

S.247(2)

The time when a company "goes into liquidation" is to be distinguished from the time when its winding up *commences*: see the notes to ss.86 and 129. The phrase was the subject of judicial consideration (in connection with the construction of a trust deed) in *Mettoy Pension Trustees Ltd v Evans* [1991] 2 All E.R. 513, where a meaning in conformity with the definition in the present subsection was approved.

S.247(3)

This subsection was amended by EA 2002 Sch.17 para.33(3), with effect from 15 September 2003, by the insertion of the reference to para.83(6)(b).

Section 247(3), in its original form, was inserted by the Insolvency Act 1986 (Amendment) (No.2) Regulations 2002 (SI 2002/1240, effective 31 May 2002) and s.243(3)(b) was amended by the Insolvency Amendment (EU 2015/848) Regulations 2017 (SI 2017/702) regs 1, 2(1), Sch. paras 1, 16 in relation to proceedings opened on or after 26 June 2017 (see reg.3) when the Recast EU Regulation 2015/848 came into force. Where "main" insolvency proceedings have been opened in the Member State where the company in question has its centre of main interests, and the company is already subject to a CVA or administration in "territorial" proceedings in this country, art.51 empowers its insolvency practitioner to apply to a UK court to have these proceedings converted to another proceeding. The intention behind s.247(3) might have been thought to be to back-date the time of "going into liquidation" to that when the CVA or administration took effect, but even so the reference to a "resolution" which is "deemed to occur" is, at first sight, baffling, particularly as regards a company in administration. For elucidation, we must look to IR 2016 rr.21.2 et seq. This rules out any question of back-dating. The court making an order for conversion under these rules may (inter alia) order that the company be wound up "as if a resolution for a voluntary winding up under s.184 were passed on the day on which the order was made". Unless, therefore, the court were to assume jurisdiction to make an order to the contrary, the time of "going into liquidation" will not be retrospective.

248 "Secured creditor", etc.

248(1) In this Group of Parts, except in so far as the context otherwise requires–

(a) "secured creditor", in relation to a company, means a creditor of the company who holds in respect of his debt a security over property of the company, and "unsecured creditor" is to be read accordingly; and

(b) "security" means–

  (i) in relation to England and Wales, any mortgage, charge, lien or other security, and

  (ii) in relation to Scotland, any security (whether heritable or moveable), any floating charge and any right of lien or preference and any right of retention (other than a right of compensation or set off).

General Note

The term "security" as here defined does not include the owner's rights under a hire-purchase, conditional sale, chattel leasing or retention of title agreement, although for some purposes (e.g. Sch.B1 para.72) these rights are treated analogously with security interests.

In *Bristol Airport plc v Powdrill* [1990] Ch. 744 (reported as *Re Paramount Airways Ltd* [1990] B.C.C. 130) it was held that the statutory right of an airport under the Civil Aviation Act 1982 s.88, to detain an aircraft for failure to pay outstanding aircraft charges was a "lien or other security" within s.248(b)(i). In *Exchange Travel Agency Ltd v Triton Property Trust plc* [1991] B.C.C. 341 a landlord's right of re-entry on non-payment of rent was held to be a "security", and this ruling was followed by Lightman J in *March Estates plc v Gunmark Ltd* [1996] 2 B.C.L.C. 1; but in *Razzaq v Pala* [1998] B.C.C. 66 the same judge, after hearing full argument, said that he had been wrong to do so, and this was confirmed by the House of Lords on appeal (sub nom. *Re Park Air Services plc* [2000] 2 A.C. 172 at 186; [1999] B.C.C. 135 at 142). Later cases (notably *Re Lomax Leisure Ltd* [2000] B.C.C. 352) have endorsed the latter ruling. The position thus appears to be settled as a matter of general law, but for practical purposes the agreed view has been reversed as regards IA 1986 ss.*10* and *11* by the amendments made to those sections by IA 2000 s.9. Corresponding provisions now also apply in CVAs (see Sch.A1 para.12(1)(f)), administrations under the new Pt II (Sch.B1 paras 43(4), 44(5)) and IVAs (s.252(2)(aa)).

248A "Opted-out creditor"

248A(1) [Meaning] For the purposes of this Group of Parts "opted-out creditor", in relation to an office-holder of a company, means a person who–

(a) is a creditor of the company, and

(b) in accordance with the rules has elected (or is deemed to have elected) to be (and not to cease to be) an opted-out creditor in relation to the office-holder.

248A(2) ["Office-holder" in s.248] In this section, "office-holder", in relation to a company, means–

(a) a liquidator, provisional liquidator, administrator or administrative receiver of the company,

(b) a receiver appointed under section 51 in relation to any property of the company, or

(c) the supervisor of a voluntary arrangement which has taken effect under Part 1 in relation to the company.

General Note

Section 248A inserted by SBEEA 2015 s.124(4) from 6 April 2017. The relevant rules are rr.1.37–1.39.

249 "Connected" with a company

249 For the purposes of any provision in this Group of Parts, a person is connected with a company if–

(a) he is a director or shadow director of the company or an associate of such a director or shadow director, or

(b) he is an associate of the company;

and "associate" has the meaning given by section 435 in Part XVIII of this Act.

General Note

The meaning of "associate" (a term which the Act applies in the bankruptcy of individuals as well as in the winding up, etc. of companies) is defined at length in s.435. The phrase "connected with" a company is used largely to put it beyond doubt that a director or shadow director is always included for the purposes of the statutory provision in question. So, also, will be the "associates" of such a director or shadow director.

It is, in principle, possible for a company's bank to come within the definition of a "connected person", if its involvement in the company's affairs is such as to make it a "shadow director": see *Re a Company (No.005009 of 1987)* (1988) 4 B.C.C. 424.

For the meaning of "associate", see the note to s.435; and for "director" and "shadow director", see s.251. The concepts of "connected person" and "associate" are examined in detail by D. Pollard in (2009) 22 Insolv. Int. 33.

250 "Member" of a company

250 For the purposes of any provision in this Group of Parts, a person who is not a member of a company but to whom shares in the company have been transferred, or transmitted by operation of law, is to be regarded as a member of the company, and references to a member or members are to be read accordingly.

General Note

"Member" is defined for the purposes of the Companies Acts by CA 2006 s.112, and under that definition the term is confined to (1) the subscribers to the memorandum; and (2) those who have agreed to become members and whose names are entered in the register of members. The present provision is designed to include the transferees of shares under unregistered transfers, and the personal representatives of deceased members and others to whom shares have been transmitted by operation of law. It is wide enough, however, to include other categories of person, e.g. holders of share warrants to bearer.

This section was no doubt inserted with the benign intention of ensuring that an unregistered transferee of shares should enjoy the same rights as a member—for instance, to petition for a winding-up order and to vote at meetings of contributories. It appears to be wide enough, however, to impose burdens upon an unregistered transferee as well—for instance, if the shares are not fully paid, to render him directly liable to the company as a contributory for calls on the shares under s.74. Whether the legislators intended to effect such a radical change in the law by a side-wind must be open to question.

This provision cannot apply to companies limited by guarantee—*Re Border Counties Farmers Ltd* [2017] EWHC 2610 (Ch).

251 Expressions used generally

251 In this Group of Parts, except in so far as the context otherwise requires–

"administrative receiver" means–

(a) an administrative receiver as defined by section 29(2) in Chapter I of Part III, or

(b) a receiver appointed under section 51 in Chapter II of that Part in a case where the whole (or substantially the whole) of the company's property is attached by the floating charge;

"agent" does not include a person's counsel acting as such;

"books and papers" and "books or papers" includes accounts, deeds, writing and documents;

"business day" means any day other than a Saturday, a Sunday, Christmas Day, Good Friday or a day which is a bank holiday in any part of Great Britain;

"chattel leasing agreement" means an agreement for the bailment or, in Scotland, the hiring of goods which is capable of subsisting for more than 3 months;

"contributory" has the meaning given by section 79;

"the court", in relation to a company, means a court having jurisdiction to wind up the company;

"deemed consent procedure" means the deemed consent procedure provided for by section 246ZF;

"director" includes any person occupying the position of director, by whatever name called;

"document" includes summons, notice, order and other legal process, and registers;

"EU insolvency proceedings" means insolvency proceedings as defined in Article 2(4) of the EU Regulation;

"floating charge" means a charge which, as created, was a floating charge and includes a floating charge within section 462 of the Companies Act (Scottish floating charges);

"the Gazette" means–

(a) as respects companies registered in England and Wales, the London Gazette;

(b) as respects companies registered in Scotland, the Edinburgh Gazette;

"member State liquidator" means a person falling within the definition of "insolvency practitioner" in Article 2(5) of the EU Regulation appointed in insolvency proceedings listed in Annex A to the EU Regulation;

"officer", in relation to a body corporate, includes a director, manager or secretary;

"the official rate", in relation to interest, means the rate payable under section 189(4);

"prescribed" means prescribed by the rules;

"qualifying decision procedure" has the meaning given by section 246ZE(11);

"receiver", in the expression "receiver or manager", does not include a receiver appointed under section 51 in Chapter II of Part III;

"retention of title agreement" means an agreement for the sale of goods to a company, being an agreement–

(a) which does not constitute a charge on the goods, but

(b) under which, if the seller is not paid and the company is wound up, the seller will have priority over all other creditors of the company as respects the goods or any property representing the goods;

"the rules" means rules under section 411 in Part XV; and

"shadow director", in relation to a company, means a person in accordance with whose directions or instructions the directors of the company are accustomed to act but so that a person is not deemed a shadow director by reason only that the directors act–

(a) on advice given by that person in a professional capacity;

(b) in accordance with instructions, a direction, guidance or advice given by that person in the exercise of a function conferred by or under an enactment (within the meaning given by section 1293 of the Companies Act 2006);

(c) in accordance with guidance or advice given by that person in that person's capacity as a Minister of the Crown (within the meaning of the Ministers of the Crown Act 1975).

General Note

Most of the definitions listed here are self-explanatory. For a discussion of terms defined by reference to other sections, see the notes to those sections. Section 251 formerly ended with a general provision declaring that any expression which was defined in the Companies Acts but not in the list of terms set out above should have the same meaning for the purposes of the present Group of Parts, but this was repealed by the Companies Act 2006 (Consequential Amendments, Transitional Provisions and Savings) Order 2009 (SI 2009/1941) Sch.1 para.77(4) as from 1 October 2009.

The term "administrative receiver" may include a receiver of the property of a foreign company: see *Re International Bulk Commodities Ltd* [1993] Ch. 77; [1992] B.C.C. 463 and the notes to s.29(2), above.

The definition of "business day" in the Act differs from that in the rules, at least in some contexts. See the note to IR 2016 r.1.2.

The definition of "floating charge" was introduced by the 1986 Act. The change is discussed in the notes to ss.175(2)(b) and 245.

The definition of "shadow director" was amended by SBEEA 2015 s.90(1) as from 26 May 2015.

A shadow director is to be distinguished from a de facto director. A de facto director is a person who assumes to act as a director and is held out as such by the company, and who claims and purports to be a director, although never actually or validly appointed as such. A shadow director, in contrast, claims not to be a director but claims that others are the directors to the exclusion of himself. The two concepts, and the leading ruling of the Supreme Court in *Holland v Revenue and Customs, Re Paycheck Services 3 Ltd* [2010] UKSC 51; [2011] B.C.C. 1, are discussed in detail in the note to CDDA 1986 s.22(5).

Note insertion of new definitions of "agent", "books and papers", "court", "document" and "the Gazette" by Companies Act 2006 (Consequential Amendments, Transitional Provisions and Savings) Order 2009 (2009/1941) Sch.1 para.77(1), (2) as from 1 October 2009, and of "deemed consent procedure" and "qualifying decision procedure" inserted by SBEEA 2015 s.122(1), (4) from 6 April 2017.

The definitions of "EU insolvency proceedings" and "member State liquidator" were inserted by the Insolvency Amendment (EU 2015/848) Regulations 2017 (SI 2017/702) regs 1, 2(1), Sch. paras 1, 17 in relation to proceedings opened on or after 26 June 2017 (see reg.3) when the Recast EU Regulation 2015/848 came into force.

The Second Group of Parts: Insolvency of Individuals; Bankruptcy

Introductory note to the Second Group of Parts

Bankruptcy legislation in England can be traced back to 1542, and the system with which practitioners will be familiar was contained in BA 1914 (as amended in 1926 and 1976). This system was the product of the 1883 reforms pushed through by Gladstone and Joseph Chamberlain. For a superb historical review outlining the violent policy swings in the nineteenth century see Lester, *Victorian Insolvency* (1995). In view of the changed social conditions and altered political economy in the twentieth century it is not surprising that both the Blagden Committee (Cmnd.221) in 1957 and the Cork Committee (Cmnd.8558) in 1982 felt that major revision was long overdue. Part III of IA 1985 did put the law on a modern footing, although its changes were less radical than the Cork Committee had hoped for. IA 1986 ss.252–385 remodel the 1985 legislation mainly by fragmenting its more cumbersome provisions into several sections. Most of the provisions in the 1985 Act relating to bankruptcy never came into force. Cases under the 1914 Act still came before the courts for many years after 1986—see for example *Re Dent* [1994] 1 W.L.R. 956; *Re Dennis* [1996] Ch. 80, discussed by Tee in (1996) 55 C.L.J. 21; *Trustee of F C Jones v Jones* [1996] B.P.I.R. 644; *Re Ross* [1998] B.C.C. 29.

What were the most obvious reforms introduced by the 1985 Act and now found in the 1986 Act? The bankruptcy procedure was greatly simplified, with the abolition of the concept of the act of bankruptcy and the intermediate stage of the receiving order. An attempt was made wherever possible to harmonise bankruptcy procedures with those of company liquidations, although unlike many jurisdictions there is still a distinction between corporate and personal insolvency law. Another reform which is more symbolic than significant in practice was the abolition of the concept of reputed ownership in bankruptcy law (it did not operate on corporate insolvency). Other changes worthy of mention were the rules giving increased protection to the family home (see ss.336–338), the attempt to produce a viable alternative to bankruptcy via voluntary arrangements (ss.252–263), plus a host of minor measures designed to streamline and improve the effectiveness of bankruptcy procedures. The liberalising trend dating back to the Justice Report of 1975 and IA 1976 is again apparent, particularly with the provisions on discharge (ss.279 and 280). This trend has continued with EA 2002.

Criticisms can be made of the 1986 Act. It was heavily dependent on IR 1986. On the other hand it must be conceded that the 1914 Act was considerably supplemented by BR 1952. The drafting of the provisions of Pt III of the 1985 Act left much to be desired, and Muir Hunter QC, a leading commentator on bankruptcy law, predicted that this deficiency would lead to an increase in litigation. The drafting of the 1986 Act was much improved. In its 1994 Report entitled *Insolvency Law: An Agenda for Reform* Justice identified a number of weaknesses with the post-1986 bankruptcy regime. Concerns were expressed about the increasing use of bankruptcy to recover small debts and the considerable amount of litigation surrounding the use of statutory demands. Many of these problems could be traced back to the failure of government to implement the changes to the county court administration order procedure which were enacted in 1990.

Finally, it should be noted that ss.252–385 of IA 1986 are not the sole source of law on debt and personal insolvency. Parts XII and XIX of the Act also contain provisions that will be important in practice. Criminal bankruptcy (so far as concerns orders which are still in force: see the notes to ss.264 and 277) is dealt with by the Powers of the Criminal Courts Act 1973. The Deeds of Arrangement Act 1914 survived until repealed by DA 2015. Administration orders against judgment debtors remain governed by the County Courts Act 1984 (as amended). Indeed there are still provisions of the Debtors Act 1869 which may return to haunt debtors—see for example s.13 (offence to make a gift to defeat creditors). Thus in *Woodley v Woodley (No.2)* [1994] 1 W.L.R. 1167 a debtor (who subsequently became bankrupt on his own petition) was threatened with imprisonment by a judge under s.5 of the 1869 Act for wilfully refusing to pay a judgment debt where he had the means to do so prior to his bankruptcy. On appeal, the committal order was quashed by the Court of Appeal because there was a sufficient degree of doubt as to whether he was deliberately defying the law or had been confused as to his obligations. For a more recent case involving s.5 of the Debtors Act 1869 see *L v L* [1997] 2 F.L.R. 252. For the continued relevance of s.5 of the 1869 Act see *Prest v Prest* [2014] EWHC 3722 (Fam) which featured an application by a judgment creditor to have a judgment debtor committed for contempt. For later appeal proceedings see *Prest v Prest* [2015] EWCA Civ 714. Note also Insolvent Debtors Relief Act 1729 as discussed in *Aectra Refining v Exmar, The Times*, 15 August 1994.

The personal insolvency provisions in the 1986 legislation have been amended considerably by IA 2000 and EA 2002.

The law on personal insolvency in Scotland (or sequestration, as it is termed) was formerly found in the Bankruptcy (Scotland) Act 1985 (as amended by the Bankruptcy (Scotland) Act 1993) and associated delegated legislation. The Scottish Law Commission considered the possibility of consolidating the 1985 Act. A Consultation Paper to that effect was published in August 2011. The personal insolvency reforms in EA 2002 were not made applicable to Scotland—for reform in Scotland see McKenzie-Skene [2004] J.B.L. 171 and our Introduction. In November 2012 the Scottish government announced that it was planning significant reforms in personal insolvency law as applied in its jurisdiction. These reforms would include measures designed to take debtor induced bankruptcies out of the court system in Scotland. Scotland also has a procedure called the protected trust deed—the rules here were reconstituted by the Protected Trust Deeds (Scotland) Regulations 2013 (SSI 2013/318) which revoked the former 2008 rules. In addition to specific insolvency measures in Scotland readers should note related legislation such as the Home Owner and Debtor Protection (Scotland) Act 2010 (asp 6) which constrained the rights of secured creditors wishing to take action against the debtor's family home by introducing safeguards for debtors. The above legislative framework (including the 1985 Act) has recently been reconsolidated by the Bankruptcy (Scotland) Act 2016.

Comparable provisions dealing with personal insolvency in Northern Ireland are now contained in the Insolvency (Northern Ireland) Order 1989 (SI 1989/2405) (NI 19) arts 226–345 in particular. The EA 2002 reforms were introduced into the Province by SI 2005/1455 (NI 10). See note to s.441. Latest reforms to personal insolvency law in Ireland are explained by Bennett in [2014] 27 Insolv. Int. 24.

For a general review of the subject see Milman, *Personal Insolvency Law, Regulation and Policy* (2005). For a perceptive analysis of the live issues and reform options in consumer bankruptcy law in Britain (covering both English and Scots law) see McKenzie-Skene and Walters (2006) 80 Am. Banky Law Jo. 477. Further illuminating insights into the broad policy issues raised by personal insolvency can be found in Ramsay (2012) 75 M.L.R. 212 and Spooner [2013] Euro Rev. of Priv. Law 747. Note also Milman [2015] 28 Insolv. Int. 37 and [2017] J.B.L. 617.

In January 2014 R3 produced an impressive overview on personal insolvency regimes entitled "The Personal Insolvency Landscape". This report represents an exemplary illustration of "joined-up" thinking in this field in which the competing interests of creditors and debtors are finely balanced.

Part 7A

Debt Relief Orders

Introductory note to Part 7A

These new debt relief provisions are introduced by Pt 5 of the Tribunals, Courts and Enforcement Act 2007. Part 7A (ss.251A–251X) inserted by the Tribunals, Courts and Enforcement Act 2007 s.108(1) and Sch.17 as from 24 February 2009, for the purpose of making rules, regulations and orders and from 6 April 2009, for all other purposes (see Tribunals, Courts and Enforcement Act 2007 (Commencement No.7) Order 2009 (SI 2009/382) art.2).

The debt relief order (DRO) mechanism was introduced into Northern Ireland by the Debt Relief Act (Northern Ireland) 2010—this legislation, which passed by the Assembly, will not become fully operational until 30 June 2011—see the Debt Relief (2010 Act) (Commencement) Order (Northern Ireland) 2011 (SR 2011/13 (C. 2)). See also the Debt Relief Orders (Designation of Competent Authorities) Regulations (Northern Ireland) 2011 (SR 2011/15) as amended by the Debt Relief Orders (Designation of Competent Authorities) (Amendment) Regulations (Northern Ireland) 2011 (SR 2011/367).

The background to this reform lies in the fact that existing regimes for dealing with personal insolvency are unable to cater efficiently for the small-scale insolvent with debts of less than £15k. The problem has been made worse by the lack of usage of the county court administration order procedure, which itself is remodelled by the 2007 Act (see s.106 and Sch.16). Accordingly, it was felt that there was a need for a new low cost procedure designed to enable small debtors to clear their debts. Proposals to this effect first appeared in 2004. The proposals were labelled "NINA"—"no income, no assets"—and were specifically designed for debtors with few realisable possessions and little in the way of surplus income. Such individuals could not be effectively dealt with either through bankruptcy or an IVA. The proposals were firmed up in 2005/2006 and then included in the Tribunals, Courts and Enforcement Bill. Similar reforms were introduced in New Zealand via the "No Assets Procedure". Debt relief schemes of a similar ilk have been operating in parts of Europe for some time. Ireland has introduced a comparable mechanism (the debt relief notice) via Pt 3 of its Personal Insolvency Act 2012, as amended by the Land and Conveyancing Law Reform Act 2013 s.2. In *Back v Finland* [2005] B.P.I.R. 1 the European Court of Human Rights upheld a similar debt adjustment scheme, concluding that it did not unfairly diminish the rights of creditors in a manner contrary to art.1 of the First Protocol ECHR.

Section 108(1) of the 2007 Act directs us to Sch.17, which inserts a new Pt 7A into IA 1986. This Part comprises ss.251A–251X, a substantial corpus of law. Part 7A is also be supported by Schs 4ZA and 4ZB (as amended), which are inserted by Schs 18 and 19 of the 2007 Act. These provisions inserted into the 1986 Act were in turn supplemented by new provisions added to IR 1986 by the Insolvency (Amendment) Rules 2009 (SI 2009/642). Note now in particular IR 2016 rr.9.2–9.20. Supplementary provisions on debt relief restriction orders and undertakings are found in IR 2016 rr.11.1–11.12.

The introduction of DROs and associated paraphernalia has also required a number of discrete statutory instruments—see the Insolvency Proceedings (Monetary Limits) (Amendment) Order 2009 (SI 2009/465) which provides financial criteria for the purposes of obtaining a DRO. For an overview see Milman (2009) 22 Insolv. Int. 153.

In August 2014 the Insolvency Service launched a consultation on the future of the debt relief order procedure. The outcome of this exercise is the increase in various financial criteria in order to make the procedure more widely available. So, the maximum debt level went up from £15k to £20k and the maximum asset level is increased from £300 to £1k (with exceptions). The monthly surplus income figure remains unchanged at £50. These changes were implemented for applications made after 1 October 2015—see Insolvency Proceedings (Monetary Limits) (Amendment) Order 2015 (SI 2015/26).

For consequential provisions dealing with a range of disqualifications imposed upon persons who become subject to the DRO procedure see the Tribunals, Courts and Enforcement Act 2007 (Consequential Amendments) Order 2012 (SI 2012/2404).

For a detailed review of the DRO regime with useful comparisons being drawn with bankruptcy see *Secretary of State for Work and Pensions v Payne and Cooper* [2011] UKSC 60 but note I(A)R 2012 (SI 2012/469). For a detailed analysis of the role of the OR in connection with the making and revocation of DROs see *R. (the application of Howard) v Official Receiver* [2013] EWHC 1839 (Admin).

There were 31,027 DROs granted in England and Wales in 2012. This fell to 27,546 in 2013. The comparable figure for 2014 was 26,688. In 2015 24,175 DROs were recorded. Figures for 2016 suggest that DROs were on the rise again to 26,196, largely as a result of the increase of the maximum debt limit from £15k to £20k. They fell back in 2017 to 24,894.

Preliminary

251A Debt relief orders

251A(1) [Application re qualifying debts] An individual who is unable to pay his debts may apply for an order under this Part ("a debt relief order") to be made in respect of his qualifying debts.

251A(2) ["Qualifying debt" in Pt 7A] In this Part "qualifying debt" means (subject to subsection (3)) a debt which–

(a) is for a liquidated sum payable either immediately or at some certain future time; and

(b) is not an excluded debt.

251A(3) [Secured debt not qualifying debt] A debt is not a qualifying debt to the extent that it is secured.

251A(4) ["Excluded debt" in Pt 7A] In this Part "excluded debt" means a debt of any description prescribed for the purposes of this subsection.

General Note

This describes the concept of a debt relief order (DRO). A DRO is potentially available to a debtor with qualifying debts. It cannot be used to wipe the slate clean of secured debt (s.251A(3)) or debts which are viewed as "excluded"—see s.251A(4)) and IR 2016 r.9.2 here. It follows from Sch.4ZA that a debtor cannot take advantage of this procedure if an undischarged bankrupt, or subject to an IVA or if subject to a bankruptcy petition (but see IR 2016 r.9.23 here).

Applications for a debt relief order

251B Making of application

251B(1) [Application to official receiver through approved intermediary] An application for a debt relief order must be made to the official receiver through an approved intermediary.

251B(2) [Contents of application] The application must include–

(a) a list of the debts to which the debtor is subject at the date of the application, specifying the amount of each debt (including any interest, penalty or other sum that has become payable in relation to that debt on or before that date) and the creditor to whom it is owed;

(b) details of any security held in respect of any of those debts; and

(c) such other information about the debtor's affairs (including his creditors, debts and liabilities and his income and assets) as may be prescribed.

251B(3) [Further provision in rules] The rules may make further provision as to–

(a) the form of an application for a debt relief order;

(b) the manner in which an application is to be made; and

(c) information and documents to be supplied in support of an application.

251B(4) [When application made] For the purposes of this Part an application is not to be regarded as having been made until–

(a) the application has been submitted to the official receiver; and

(b) any fee required in connection with the application by an order under section 415 has been paid to such person as the order may specify.

General Note

The procedure for applying for a DRO is explained. Electronic submission is *required*—IR 2016 r.9.4. The debtor must apply to the official receiver via an approved intermediary—see s.251U and IR 2016 r.9.5. For further detail on the contents of the application see IR 2016 r.9.3.

251C Duty of official receiver to consider and determine application

251C(1) [Application of s.251C] This section applies where an application for a debt relief order is made.

251C(2) [Stay of application] The official receiver may stay consideration of the application until he has received answers to any queries raised with the debtor in relation to anything connected with the application.

251C(3) [Determination of application] The official receiver must determine the application by–

(a) deciding whether to refuse the application;

(b) if he does not refuse it, by making a debt relief order in relation to the specified debts he is satisfied were qualifying debts of the debtor at the application date;

but he may only refuse the application if he is authorised or required to do so by any of the following provisions of this section.

251C(4) [Discretionary refusal] The official receiver may refuse the application if he considers that–

(a) the application does not meet all the requirements imposed by or under section 251B;

(b) any queries raised with the debtor have not been answered to the satisfaction of the official receiver within such time as he may specify when they are raised;

(c) the debtor has made any false representation or omission in making the application or on supplying any information or documents in support of it.

251C(5) [Mandatory refusal] The official receiver must refuse the application if he is not satisfied that–

(a) the debtor is an individual who is unable to pay his debts;

(b) at least one of the specified debts was a qualifying debt of the debtor at the application date;

(c) each of the conditions set out in Part 1 of Schedule 4ZA is met.

251C(6) [Requirement for Sch.4ZA Pt 2 conditions] The official receiver may refuse the application if he is not satisfied that each condition specified in Part 2 of Schedule 4ZA is met.

251C(7) [Notification of reasons for refusal] If the official receiver refuses an application he must give reasons for his refusal to the debtor in the prescribed manner.

251C(8) ["Specified debt"] In this section "specified debt" means a debt specified in the application.

General Note

The role of the official receiver on an application for a DRO is outlined. The important point to note is that the official receiver is not to be seen as a rubber stamp. The official receiver should adopt a questioning approach (but see s.251D). The official receiver must be satisfied that the conditions laid down in Sch.4ZA have been met. On verification checks see IR 2016 r.9.6. Note also the financial criteria mapped out in the Insolvency Proceedings (Monetary Limits) (Amendment) Order 2009 (SI 2009/465). See also IR 2016 r.9.13. The geographical link must be established. There must have been no preferences or transactions at an undervalue within the previous two years. The debts must not exceed the prescribed amount (£15k). The debtor's monthly surplus income must not exceed the prescribed amount (£50)—see IR 2016 r.9.7. The debtor must not have property in excess of the prescribed maximum amount (£300)—see IR 2016 rr.9.8 and 9.9 (which deal with excluded items). Note that domestic vehicles with a realisable value of less than £1k are excluded—IR 2016 r.9.9. Note that the financial criteria are changed by the Insolvency Proceedings (Monetary Limits) (Amendment) Order 2015 (SI 2015/26). So the maximum debt level for applications after 1 October 2015 is £20k and the maximum asset value (subject to a limited motor vehicle exemption) is raised to £1k. The surplus income figure remains unchanged.

The Insolvency Service announced on 9 November 2010, that following a consultation in March 2010 the DRO regime would be amended to provide access to debtors with an approved pension, thereby removing a perceived disadvantage as even those with small-value pension rights, not receivable for many years, are currently excluded. See I(A)R 2011 (SI 2011/785); see now IR 2016 r.9.9.

251D Presumptions applicable to the determination of an application

251D(1) [Presumptions] The following presumptions are to apply to the determination of an application for a debt relief order.

251D(2) [Debtor an individual unable to pay debts] The official receiver must presume that the debtor is an individual who is unable to pay his debts at the determination date if–

(a) that appears to the official receiver to be the case at the application date from the information supplied in the application and he has no reason to believe that the information supplied is incomplete or inaccurate; and

(b) he has no reason to believe that, by virtue of a change in the debtor's financial circumstances since the application date, the debtor may be able to pay his debts.

251D(3) [Specified debt a qualifying debt] The official receiver must presume that a specified debt (of the amount specified in the application and owed to the creditor so specified) is a qualifying debt at the application date if–

(a) that appears to him to be the case from the information supplied in the application; and

(b) he has no reason to believe that the information supplied is incomplete or inaccurate.

251D(4) [Schedule 4ZA para.1 condition of domiciled or resident] The official receiver must presume that the condition specified in paragraph 1 of Schedule 4ZA is met if–

(a) that appears to him to be the case from the information supplied in the application;

(b) any prescribed verification checks relating to the condition have been made; and

(c) he has no reason to believe that the information supplied is incomplete or inaccurate.

251D(5) [Other Sch.4ZA conditions] The official receiver must presume that any other condition specified in Part 1 or 2 of Schedule 4ZA is met if–

(a) that appears to him to have been the case as at the application date from the information supplied in the application and he has no reason to believe that the information supplied is incomplete or inaccurate;

(b) any prescribed verification checks relating to the condition have been made; and

(c) he has no reason to believe that, by virtue of a change in circumstances since the application date, the condition may no longer be met.

251D(6) [References to information supplied] References in this section to information supplied in the application include information supplied to the official receiver in support of the application.

251D(7) ["Specified debt" in s.251D] In this section "specified debt" means a debt specified in the application.

General Note

This explains presumptions which the official receiver should make use of when dealing with an application for a DRO. The effect of these presumptions is to water down the questioning approach to be taken by the official receiver when dealing with an application for a DRO. See IR 2016 r.9.6. In effect one might characterise the official receiver as a watchdog and not a bloodhound when performing this role. In view of the potential numbers of applications for DROs, this is inevitable.

Making and effect of debt relief order

251E Making of debt relief orders

251E(1) [Application of s.251C] This section applies where the official receiver makes a debt relief order on determining an application under section 251C.

251E(2) [Order in prescribed form] The order must be made in the prescribed form.

251E(3) [Contents of order] The order must include a list of the debts which the official receiver is satisfied were qualifying debts of the debtor at the application date, specifying the amount of the debt at that time and the creditor to whom it was then owed.

251E(4) [Duty of official receiver re order] The official receiver must–

(a) give a copy of the order to the debtor; and

(b) make an entry for the order in the register containing the prescribed information about the order or the debtor.

251E(5) [Provision in rules] The rules may make provision as to other steps to be taken by the official receiver or the debtor on the making of the order.

251E(6) [Notification to creditors in rules] Those steps may include in particular notifying each creditor to whom a qualifying debt specified in the order is owed of–

(a) the making of the order and its effect,

(b) the grounds on which a creditor may object under section 251K, and

(c) any other prescribed information.

251E(7) ["The effective date"] In this Part the date on which an entry relating to the making of a debt relief order is first made in the register is referred to as "the effective date".

General Note

This describes the effect of a DRO made by an official receiver. For form of DRO see IR 2016 r.9.10. On notification see IR 2016 rr.9.11 and 9.12. For entry on the individual insolvency register see IR 2016 r.11.18.

251F Effect of debt relief order on other debt management arrangements

251F(1) [Application of s.251F] This section applies if–

(a) a debt relief order is made, and

(b) immediately before the order is made, other debt management arrangements are in force in respect of the debtor.

251F(2) [Other debt management arrangements to cease] The other debt management arrangements cease to be in force when the debt relief order is made.

251F(3) ["Other debt management arrangements"] In this section "other debt management arrangements" means–

(a) an administration order under Part 6 of the County Courts Act 1984;

(b) an enforcement restriction order under Part 6A of that Act;

(c) a debt repayment plan arranged in accordance with a debt management scheme that is approved under Chapter 4 of Part 5 of the Tribunals, Courts and Enforcement Act 2007.

General Note

This details the effect of a DRO on other debt management arrangements, such as an administration order, an enforcement restrictions order and a debt repayment plan. Basically a DRO will trump these.

251G Moratorium from qualifying debts

251G(1) [Moratorium on specified qualifying debts] A moratorium commences on the effective date for a debt relief order in relation to each qualifying debt specified in the order ("a specified qualifying debt").

251G(2) [Effect of moratorium] During the moratorium, the creditor to whom a specified qualifying debt is owed–

(a) has no remedy in respect of the debt, and

(b) may not–

(i) commence a creditor's petition in respect of the debt, or

(ii) otherwise commence any action or other legal proceedings against the debtor for the debt,

except with the permission of the court and on such terms as the court may impose.

251G(3) [Effect on existing petition, action or proceeding] If on the effective date a creditor to whom a specified qualifying debt is owed has any such petition, action or other proceeding as mentioned in subsection (2)(b) pending in any court, the court may–

(a) stay the proceedings on the petition, action or other proceedings (as the case may be), or

(b) allow them to continue on such terms as the court thinks fit.

251G(4) [Debt in s.251G(2)(a), (b) to include] In subsection (2)(a) and (b) references to the debt include a reference to any interest, penalty or other sum that becomes payable in relation to that debt after the application date.

251G(5) [Right of secured creditor to enforce] Nothing in this section affects the right of a secured creditor of the debtor to enforce his security.

General Note

The moratorium associated with the DRO is explained. The moratorium will only have effect as against those creditors owed qualifying debts. Once the DRO is in place leave will be required to enforce a qualifying debt. There is an exception provided for in the case of the moratorium being terminated early by the official receiver under s.251H or by the court under s.251M.

The moratorium was given strong support by the Supreme Court in *Secretary of State for Work and Pensions v Payne* [2011] UKSC 60 where a pragmatic interpretation of the exercise of a "remedy" was adopted. But in spite of this steer from the Supreme Court it has been held that s.251G(2) does not preclude the making of a possession order for rent arrears—*Sharples v Places for People Homes Ltd; Godfrey v A2 Dominion Homes Ltd* [2011] EWCA Civ 813; [2011] B.P.I.R. 1488. For discussion of these authorities and the light they throw upon judicial attitudes towards the DRO regime see D. Milman [2012] 25 Insolv. Int. 104. Both of these decisions depend very much upon judicial interpretation of perceived social policy. In *Payne* (above) the Supreme Court indicated that, if Parliament did not like the consequences of its interpretation of the law, then the solution lay in its hands through amending legislation. This suggestion has been acted on to some extent. See Insolvency (Amendment) Rules 2012 (SI 2012/469), which came into force on 19 March 2012 for applications for DROs and also bankruptcy petitions presented on or after that date. Under this amendment the list of excluded debts in IR 2016 r.9.2 is supplemented by inclusion of a reference to any obligation arising from a payment out of the Social Fund under s.138(1)(b) of the Social Security Contributions and Benefits Act 1992 by way of crisis loan and budgeting loan. Comparable amendments have been made in bankruptcy law by adding the aforementioned to the list of debts surviving discharge in IR 2016 r.10.146 and amending the list of provable debts found in IR 2016 r.14.2 through the exclusion of this item. It is clear from the Explanatory Memorandum para.7.3 that the aim of this amendment is to protect the Social Fund from bad debts. From a more positive perspective this should help the Social Fund to continue to make provision for needy applicants (para.10.2).

A further authority of note on the effect of the moratorium is *Irwell Valley Housing Ltd v Docherty* [2012] EWCA Civ 704. Here the question related to its impact upon the enforcement of a valid conditional order for possession granted in favour of a landlord *prior* to the tenant obtaining a DRO. The order was not enforceable if the tenant continued to pay current rent plus arrears at a specified rate. The Court of Appeal construed this as meaning that once the DRO had come to an end only those rent arrears which were in existence at the time of the DRO were discharged—rent arrears accruing thereafter were not discharged and the possession order could be enforced. Permission to appeal against the enforcement of the possession order was accordingly refused.

251H The moratorium period

251H(1) [Duration of moratorium] The moratorium relating to the qualifying debts specified in a debt relief order continues for the period of one year beginning with the effective date for the order, unless–

(a) the moratorium terminates early; or

(b) the moratorium period is extended by the official receiver under this section or by the court under section 251M.

251H(2) [Grounds for extension of moratorium period] The official receiver may only extend the moratorium period for the purpose of–

(a) carrying out or completing an investigation under section 251K;

(b) taking any action he considers necessary (whether as a result of an investigation or otherwise) in relation to the order; or

(c) in a case where he has decided to revoke the order, providing the debtor with the opportunity to make arrangements for making payments towards his debts.

251H(3) [Permission of court for s.251G(2)(a) extension] The official receiver may not extend the moratorium period for the purpose mentioned in subsection (2)(a) without the permission of the court.

251H(4) [Extension no to exceed three months] The official receiver may not extend the moratorium period beyond the end of the period of three months beginning after the end of the initial period of one year mentioned in subsection (1).

251H(5) [Extensions to be made before end of moratorium] The moratorium period may be extended more than once, but any extension (whether by the official receiver or by the court) must be made before the moratorium would otherwise end.

251H(6) [Moratorium terminating early] References in this Part to a moratorium terminating early are to its terminating before the end of what would otherwise be the moratorium period, whether on the revocation of the order or by virtue of any other enactment.

General Note

This details the duration of the DRO moratorium. The moratorium is to last for one year subject to extension or early termination. On the effect of the death of the debtor during the moratorium period see IR 2016 r.9.20.

251I Discharge from qualifying debts

251I(1) [Discharge at end of moratorium] Subject as follows, at the end of the moratorium applicable to a debt relief order the debtor is discharged from all the qualifying debts specified in the order (including all interest, penalties and other sums which may have become payable in relation to those debts since the application date).

251I(2) [No discharge if early termination] Subsection (1) does not apply if the moratorium terminates early.

251I(3) [No discharge for fraud] Subsection (1) does not apply in relation to any qualifying debt which the debtor incurred in respect of any fraud or fraudulent breach of trust to which the debtor was a party.

251I(4) [Other persons not released] The discharge of the debtor under subsection (1) does not release any other person from–

(a) any liability (whether as partner or co-trustee of the debtor or otherwise) from which the debtor is released by the discharge; or

(b) any liability as surety for the debtor or as a person in the nature of such a surety.

251I(5) [No discharge on s.251M revocation of order] If the order is revoked by the court under section 251M after the end of the moratorium period, the qualifying debts specified in the order shall (so far as practicable) be treated as though subsection (1) had never applied to them.

General Note

The DRO regime does not envisage any distribution being made to creditors. At the end of the DRO moratorium period the debtor is relieved from liability to pay for qualifying debts. This discharge effect does not apply in cases of early termination. Sureties of the debtor are not relieved from liability.

Duties of debtor

251J Providing assistance to official receiver etc

251J(1) [When s.251J duties apply] The duties in this section apply to a debtor at any time after the making of an application by him for a debt relief order.

251J(2) [Scope of debtor's duty] The debtor must–

(a) give to the official receiver such information as to his affairs,

(b) attend on the official receiver at such times, and

(c) do all such other things,

as the official receiver may reasonably require for the purpose of carrying out his functions in relation to the application or, as the case may be, the debt relief order made as a result of the application.

251J(3) [Debtor's duty to notify official receiver] The debtor must notify the official receiver as soon as reasonably practicable if he becomes aware of–

(a) any error in, or omission from, the information supplied to the official receiver in, or in support of, the application;

(b) any change in his circumstances between the application date and the determination date that would affect (or would have affected) the determination of the application.

251J(4) [Duration of s.251J duties] The duties under subsections (2) and (3) apply after (as well as before) the determination of the application, for as long as the official receiver is able to exercise functions of the kind mentioned in subsection (2).

251J(5) [Further duty to notify official receiver] If a debt relief order is made as a result of the application, the debtor must notify the official receiver as soon as reasonably practicable if–

(a) there is an increase in his income during the moratorium period applicable to the order;

(b) he acquires any property or any property is devolved upon him during that period;

(c) he becomes aware of any error in or omission from any information supplied by him to the official receiver after the determination date.

251J(6) [Prescribed particulars of s.251J(3), (5) notification] A notification under subsection (3) or (5) must give the prescribed particulars (if any) of the matter being notified.

General Note

A debtor who obtains a DRO has certain duties to provide assistance to the official receiver. These duties are similar to those owed by a bankrupt to the official receiver/trustee in bankruptcy. Note also IR 2016 r.9.19 and the duty to notify OR of an increase in income or acquisition of property.

Objections, investigations and revocation

251K Objections and investigations

251K(1) [Creditors' right to object] Any person specified in a debt relief order as a creditor to whom a specified qualifying debt is owed may object to–

(a) the making of the order;

(b) the inclusion of the debt in the list of the debtor's qualifying debts; or

(c) the details of the debt specified in the order.

251K(2) [Conditions for objection] An objection under subsection (1) must be–

(a) made during the moratorium period relating to the order and within the prescribed period for objections;

(b) made to the official receiver in the prescribed manner;

(c) based on a prescribed ground;

(d) supported by any information and documents as may be prescribed;

and the prescribed period mentioned in paragraph (a) must not be less than 28 days after the creditor in question has been notified of the making of the order.

251K(3) [Official receiver to consider objections] The official receiver must consider every objection made to him under this section.

251K(4) [Official receiver's power of investigation] The official receiver may–

(a) as part of his consideration of an objection, or

(b) on his own initiative,

carry out an investigation of any matter that appears to the official receiver to be relevant to the making of any decision mentioned in subsection (5) in relation to a debt relief order or the debtor.

251K(5) [Purpose of investigation] The decisions to which an investigation may be directed are–

(a) whether the order should be revoked or amended under section 251L;

(b) whether an application should be made to the court under section 251M; or

(c) whether any other steps should be taken in relation to the debtor.

251K(6) [Duration of investigation power] The power to carry out an investigation under this section is exercisable after (as well as during) the moratorium relating to the order.

251K(7) [Official receiver's power to require information] The official receiver may require any person to give him such information and assistance as he may reasonably require in connection with an investigation under this section.

251K(8) [Investigation as official receiver thinks fit] Subject to anything prescribed in the rules as to the procedure to be followed in carrying out an investigation under this section, an investigation may be carried out by the official receiver in such manner as he thinks fit.

General Note

This is an important quality control mechanism in that it allows creditors with qualifying debts to object to the DRO, whereupon the official receiver must investigate. In certain circumstances the official receiver may investigate on his own initiative. See IR 2016 rr.9.13, 9.14 and 9.16. The right of objection is available during the moratorium period but must be made within 30 days of notification of the DRO—IR 2016 r.9.15. On the response options of the OR see IR 2016 r.9.16.

251L Power of official receiver to revoke or amend a debt relief order

251L(1) [Power exercisable during moratorium] The official receiver may revoke or amend a debt relief order during the applicable moratorium period in the circumstances provided for by this section.

251L(2) [Grounds for revocation] The official receiver may revoke the order on the ground that–

(a) any information supplied to him by the debtor–

(i) in, or in support of, the application, or

(ii) after the determination date,

was incomplete, incorrect or otherwise misleading;

(b) the debtor has failed to comply with a duty under section 251J;

(c) a bankruptcy order has been made in relation to the debtor; or

(d) the debtor has made a proposal under Part 8 (or has notified the official receiver of his intention to do so).

251L(3) [Revocation where official receiver should not have been satisfied] The official receiver may revoke the order on the ground that he should not have been satisfied–

(a) that the debts specified in the order were qualifying debts of the debtor as at the application date;

(b) that the conditions specified in Part 1 of Schedule 4ZA were met;

(c) that the conditions specified in Part 2 of that Schedule were met or that any failure to meet such a condition did not prevent his making the order.

251L(4) [Revocation where Sch.4ZA paras 1 and 8 conditions not met] The official receiver may revoke the order on the ground that either or both of the conditions in paragraphs 7 and 8 of Schedule 4ZA (monthly surplus income and property) are not met at any time after the order was made.

For this purpose those paragraphs are to be read as if references to the determination date were references to the time in question.

251L(5) [Date revocation takes effect] Where the official receiver decides to revoke the order, he may revoke it either–

(a) with immediate effect, or

(b) with effect from such date (not more than three months after the date of the decision) as he may specify.

251L(6) [Duty of official receiver to consider] In considering when the revocation should take effect the official receiver must consider (in the light of the grounds on which the decision to revoke was made and all the other circumstances of the case) whether the debtor ought to be given the opportunity to make arrangements for making payments towards his debts.

251L(7) [Revocation may be changed immediate effect] If the order has been revoked with effect from a specified date the official receiver may, if he thinks it appropriate to do so at any time before that date, revoke the order with immediate effect.

251L(8) [Power to amend to correct error or omission] The official receiver may amend a debt relief order for the purpose of correcting an error in or omission from anything specified in the order.

251L(9) [Amending power cannot add to qualifying debts] But subsection (8) does not permit the official receiver to add any debts that were not specified in the application for the debt relief order to the list of qualifying debts.

251L(10) [Provision in rules] The rules may make further provision as to the procedure to be followed by the official receiver in the exercise of his powers under this section.

General Note

An official may revoke or amend a DRO. See further IR 2016 rr.9.17, 9.18. Various grounds for revocation are identified—these include provision of incomplete/misleading information, failure to cooperate, the making of a bankruptcy order or the making of a proposal for an IVA. On registration see IR 2016 r.11.19. For an explanation of the procedure required to revoke a DRO see Stadlen J in *R. (on the application of Howard) v Official Receiver* [2013] EWHC 1839 (Admin); [2014] B.P.I.R. 204. On the revocation of a DRO see *The Mayor and Burgesses of the London Borough of Islington v C and the Official Receiver* [2012] B.P.I.R. 363, a helpful clarification of the law by District Judge Hart. The case is useful for its consideration of Sch.4ZA and the discussion of what is relevant for calculating monthly surplus income (para.7) and what is required before it can be established that the debtor has given a preference (para.10).

Role of the court

251M Powers of court in relation to debt relief orders

251M(1) [Application to court by any person] Any person may make an application to the court if he is dissatisfied by any act, omission or decision of the official receiver in connection with a debt relief order or an application for such an order.

251M(2) [Application for directions, or order re any matter] The official receiver may make an application to the court for directions or an order in relation to any matter arising in connection with a debt relief order or an application for such an order.

251M(3) [Section 251M(2) matters include compliance with s.251J duty] The matters referred to in subsection (2) include, among other things, matters relating to the debtor's compliance with any duty arising under section 251J.

251M(4) [Application at any time] An application under this section may, subject to anything in the rules, be made at any time.

251M(5) [Power of court to extend moratorium period] The court may extend the moratorium period applicable to a debt relief order for the purposes of determining an application under this section.

251M(6) [Power of court on application] On an application under this section the court may dismiss the application or do one or more of the following–

(a) quash the whole or part of any act or decision of the official receiver;

(b) give the official receiver directions (including a direction that he reconsider any matter in relation to which his act or decision has been quashed under paragraph (a));

(c) make an order for the enforcement of any obligation on the debtor arising by virtue of a duty under section 251J;

(d) extend the moratorium period applicable to the debt relief order;

(e) make an order revoking or amending the debt relief order;

(f) make an order under section 251N; or

(g) make such other order as the court thinks fit.

251M(7) [Section 251M(6)(e) revocation order] An order under subsection (6)(e) for the revocation of a debt relief order–

(a) may be made during the moratorium period applicable to the debt relief order or at any time after that period has ended;

(b) may be made on the court's own motion if the court has made a bankruptcy order in relation to the debtor during that period;

(c) may provide for the revocation of the order to take effect on such terms and at such a time as the court may specify.

251M(8) [Section 251M(6)(e) amendment order] An order under subsection (6)(e) for the amendment of a debt relief order may not add any debts that were not specified in the application for the debt relief order to the list of qualifying debts.

General Note

Another safety mechanism lies in the fact that a dissatisfied person may apply to court for it to overrule the official receiver. See IR 2016 r.9.21. By comparing the counterpart provision in bankruptcy law one would imagine that most challenges will fail. The official receiver can also apply if the debtor fails to cooperate. Under IR 2016 r.9.24 the court can extend the moratorium period whilst considering such an application. For the appropriate court for the application see IR 2016 r.9.22.

251N Inquiry into debtor's dealings and property

251N(1) [Application by official receiver] An order under this section may be made by the court on the application of the official receiver.

251N(2) [Persons who may be summoned to appear] An order under this section is an order summoning any of the following persons to appear before the court–

(a) the debtor;

(b) the debtor's spouse or former spouse or the debtor's civil partner or former civil partner;

(c) any person appearing to the court to be able to give information or assistance concerning the debtor or his dealings, affairs and property.

251N(3) [Requirement for persons in s.251N(2)(c)] The court may require a person falling within subsection (2)(c)–

(a) to provide a written account of his dealings with the debtor; or

(b) to produce any documents in his possession or under his control relating to the debtor or to the debtor's dealings, affairs or property.

251N(4) [Application of s.251N(5)] Subsection (5) applies where a person fails without reasonable excuse to appear before the court when he is summoned to do so by an order under this section.

251N(5) [Warrant for arrest or seizure] The court may cause a warrant to be issued to a constable or prescribed officer of the court–

(a) for the arrest of that person, and

(b) for the seizure of any records or other documents in that person's possession.

251N(6) [Custody of person or holding of records etc.] The court may authorise a person arrested under such a warrant to be kept in custody, and anything seized under such a warrant to be held, in accordance with the rules, until that person is brought before the court under the warrant or until such other time as the court may order.

General Note

The court (see IR 2016 r.9.22 here) can order an investigation into the debtor's dealings or property. Third parties can be ordered to provide information. The court enjoys power to order arrest for non co-operation.

Offences

251O False representations and omissions

251O(1) [Applicant knowingly or recklessly making representation or omission] A person who makes an application for a debt relief order is guilty of an offence if he knowingly or recklessly makes any false representation or omission in making the application or providing any information or documents to the official receiver in support of the application.

251O(2) [Applicant intentionally failing to comply with s.251J(3) duty] A person who makes an application for a debt relief order is guilty of an offence if–

(a) he intentionally fails to comply with a duty under section 251J(3) in connection with the application; or

(b) he knowingly or recklessly makes any false representation or omission in providing any information to the official receiver in connection with such a duty or otherwise in connection with the application.

251O(3) [Immaterial for s.251O(3) offence whether order made] It is immaterial for the purposes of an offence under subsection (1) or (2) whether or not a debt relief order is made as a result of the application.

251O(4) [Intentionally failing to comply with s.251J(5) duty after order] A person in respect of whom a debt relief order is made is guilty of an offence if–

(a) he intentionally fails to comply with a duty under section 251J(5) in connection with the order; or

(b) he knowingly or recklessly makes any false representation or omission in providing information to the official receiver in connection with such a duty or otherwise in connection with the performance by the official receiver of functions in relation to the order.

251O(5) [Immaterial matters for s.251O(4) offence] It is immaterial for the purposes of an offence under subsection (4)–

(a) whether the offence is committed during or after the moratorium period; and

(b) whether or not the order is revoked after the conduct constituting the offence takes place.

General Note

This offence is similar to that found with regard to those who falsely procure IVAs (see IA 1986 s.262A). The offence may still be committed even if the DRO is never obtained.

251P Concealment or falsification of documents

251P(1) [Offence] A person in respect of whom a debt relief order is made is guilty of an offence if, during the moratorium period in relation to that order–

(a) he does not provide, at the request of the official receiver, all his books, papers and other records of which he has possession or control and which relate to his affairs;

(b) he prevents the production to the official receiver of any books, papers or other records relating to his affairs;

(c) he conceals, destroys, mutilates or falsifies, or causes or permits the concealment, destruction, mutilation or falsification of, any books, papers or other records relating his affairs;

(d) he makes, or causes or permits the making of, any false entries in any book, document or record relating to his affairs; or

(e) he disposes of, or alters or makes any omission in, or causes or permits the disposal, altering or making of any omission in, any book, document or record relating to his affairs.

251P(2) [Effective dates for s.251P(1)(b)–(e) offences] A person in respect of whom a debt relief order is made is guilty of an offence if–

(a) he did anything falling within paragraphs (c) to (e) of subsection (1) during the period of 12 months ending with the application date; or

(b) he did anything falling within paragraphs (b) to (e) of subsection (1) after that date but before the effective date.

251P(3) [Defence if no intent to defraud or conceal] A person is not guilty of an offence under this section if he proves that, in respect of the conduct constituting the offence, he had no intent to defraud or to conceal the state of his affairs.

251P(4) [Application of s.251P(2)(a) to trading record] In its application to a trading record subsection (2)(a) has effect as if the reference to 12 months were a reference to two years.

251P(5) ["Trading record"] In subsection (4) "trading record" means a book, document or record which shows or explains the transactions or financial position of a person's business, including–

(a) a periodic record of cash paid and received,

(b) a statement of periodic stock-taking, and

(c) except in the case of goods sold by way of retail trade, a record of goods sold and purchased which identifies the buyer and seller or enables them to be identified.

251P(6) [Immaterial to offence if order revoked after conduct] It is immaterial for the purposes of an offence under this section whether or not the debt relief order in question is revoked after the conduct constituting the offence takes place (but no offence is committed under this section by virtue of conduct occurring after the order is revoked).

General Note

There are some parallels here with bankrupts who conceal/falsify information (see IA 1986 s.355). The offence applies to activities occurring within the moratorium period.

251Q Fraudulent disposal of property

251Q(1) [Offence] A person in respect of whom a debt relief order is made is guilty of an offence if he made or caused to be made any gift or transfer of his property during the period between–

(a) the start of the period of two years ending with the application date; and

(b) the end of the moratorium period.

251Q(2) [Transfer of property includes execution against it] The reference in subsection (1) to making a transfer of any property includes causing or conniving at the levying of any execution against that property.

251Q(3) [Defence if no intent to defraud or conceal] A person is not guilty of an offence under this section if he proves that, in respect of the conduct constituting the offence, he had no intent to defraud or to conceal the state of his affairs.

251Q(4) [Proof of lack of intention] For the purposes of subsection (3) a person is to be taken to have proved that he had no such intent if–

(a) sufficient evidence is adduced to raise an issue as to whether he had such intent; and

(b) the contrary is not proved beyond reasonable doubt.

251Q(5) [Immaterial to offence if order revoked after conduct] It is immaterial for the purposes of this section whether or not the debt relief order in question is revoked after the conduct constituting an offence takes place (but no offence is committed by virtue of conduct occurring after the order is revoked).

General Note

Again the parallel here is to be found in bankruptcy law, notably IA 1986 s.357. The court will look at events occurring within the two-year period prior to the making of the application for the DRO. Presumably, the law is seeking here to combat the practice whereby a would-be DRO applicant seeks to reduce assets in order to qualify for a DRO.

251R Fraudulent dealing with property obtained on credit

251R(1) [Offence] A person in respect of whom a debt relief order is made is guilty of an offence if during the relevant period he disposed of any property which he had obtained on credit and, at the time he disposed of it, had not paid for it.

251R(2) [Offence by person acquiring or receiving property] Any other person is guilty of an offence if during the relevant period he acquired or received property from a person in respect of whom a debt relief order was made (the "debtor") knowing or believing–

(a) that the debtor owed money in respect of the property, and

(b) that the debtor did not intend, or was unlikely to be able, to pay the money he so owed.

251R(3) ["Relevant period"] In subsections (1) and (2) "relevant period" means the period between–

(a) the start of the period of two years ending with the application date; and

(b) the determination date.

251R(4) [Defence of ordinary course of business] A person is not guilty of an offence under subsection (1) or (2) if the disposal, acquisition or receipt of the property was in the ordinary course of a business carried on by the debtor at the time of the disposal, acquisition or receipt.

251R(5) [Regard to price in ordinary course of business] In determining for the purposes of subsection (4) whether any property is disposed of, acquired or received in the ordinary course of a business carried on by the debtor, regard may be had, in particular, to the price paid for the property.

251R(6) [Defence if no intent to defraud or conceal] A person is not guilty of an offence under subsection (1) if he proves that, in respect of the conduct constituting the offence, he had no intent to defraud or to conceal the state of his affairs.

251R(7) [Disposing or acquiring include pawning or pledging] In this section references to disposing of property include pawning or pledging it; and references to acquiring or receiving property shall be read accordingly.

251R(8) [Immaterial to offence if order revoked after conduct] It is immaterial for the purposes of this section whether or not the debt relief order in question is revoked after the conduct constituting an offence takes place (but no offence is committed by virtue of conduct occurring after the order is revoked).

General Note

The disposition of goods acquired on credit where those goods have not be paid for is a practice that should not be facilitated by the obtaining of a DRO. The disposal must have occurred within the two-year period prior to the application for the DRO even if the goods were obtained earlier than that period. Note the disponee might incur criminal liability under subs.(2). Of the defences, note the trading defence where the disposal is in the ordinary course of business.

251S Obtaining credit or engaging in business

251S(1) [Offence] A person in respect of whom a debt relief order is made is guilty of an offence if, during the relevant period–

(a) he obtains credit (either alone or jointly with any other person) without giving the person from whom he obtains the credit the relevant information about his status; or

(b) he engages directly or indirectly in any business under a name other than that in which the order was made without disclosing to all persons with whom he enters into any business transaction the name in which the order was made.

251S(2) [Relevant information as to status in s.251S(1)(a)] For the purposes of subsection (1)(a) the relevant information about a person's status is the information that–

(a) a moratorium is in force in relation to the debt relief order,

(b) a debt relief restrictions order is in force in respect of him, or

(c) both a moratorium and a debt relief restrictions order is in force,

as the case may be.

251S(3) ["Relevant period"] In subsection (1) "relevant period" means–

(a) the moratorium period relating to the debt relief order, or

(b) the period for which a debt relief restrictions order is in force in respect of the person in respect of whom the debt relief order is made,

as the case may be.

251S(4) [Disapplication of s.251S(1)(a) if credit below prescribed amount] Subsection (1)(a) does not apply if the amount of the credit is less than the prescribed amount (if any).

251S(5) [Further examples of obtaining credit] The reference in subsection (1)(a) to a person obtaining credit includes the following cases–

(a) where goods are bailed to him under a hire-purchase agreement, or agreed to be sold to him under a conditional sale agreement;

(b) where he is paid in advance (in money or otherwise) for the supply of goods or services.

General Note

This duty of disclosure applies to a person who is subject to a DRO or a DRRO. The figure for the purposes of subs.(4) is £500—see the Insolvency Proceedings (Monetary Limits) (Amendment) Order 2009 (SI 2009/465). For a comparable restriction on obtaining credit, see IA 1986 s.360.

251T Offences: supplementary

251T(1) [Proceedings instituted by Secretary of State for DPP] Proceedings for an offence under this Part may only be instituted by the Secretary of State or by or with the consent of the Director of Public Prosecutions.

251T(2) [Conduct outside jurisdiction not a defence] It is not a defence in proceedings for an offence under this Part that anything relied on, in whole or in part, as constituting the offence was done outside England and Wales.

251T(3) [Penalty] A person guilty of an offence under this Part is liable to imprisonment or a fine, or both (but see section 430).

General Note

This is a supplementary provision. Note the extraterritorial aspect in subs.(2).

Supplementary

251U Approved intermediaries

251U(1) ["Approved intermediary"] In this Part "approved intermediary" means an individual for the time being approved by a competent authority to act as an intermediary between a person wishing to make an application for a debt relief order and the official receiver.

251U(2) ["Competent authority"] In this section "competent authority" means a person or body for the time being designated by the Secretary of State for the purposes of granting approvals under this section.

251U(3) [Limitation of competent authority] Designation as a competent authority may be limited so as to permit the authority only to approve persons of a particular description.

251U(4) [Power to make regulations] The Secretary of State may by regulations make provision as to–

(a) the procedure for designating persons or bodies as competent authorities;

(b) descriptions of individuals who are ineligible to be approved under this section;

(c) the procedure for granting approvals under this section;

(d) the withdrawal of designations or approvals under this section;

and provision made under paragraph (a) or (c) may include provision requiring the payment of fees.

251U(5) [Provision in rules] The rules may make provision about the activities to be carried out by an approved intermediary in connection with an application for a debt relief order, which may in particular include–

(a) assisting the debtor in making the application;

(b) checking that the application has been properly completed;

(c) sending the application to the official receiver.

251U(6) [Provision about other activities in rules] The rules may also make provision about other activities to be carried out by approved intermediaries.

251U(7) [No fee for approved intermediary] An approved intermediary may not charge a debtor any fee in connection with an application for a debt relief order.

251U(8) [No liability in damages for approved intermediary] An approved intermediary is not liable to any person in damages for anything done or omitted to be done when acting (or purporting to act) as an approved intermediary in connection with a particular application by a debtor for a debt relief order.

251U(9) [Non-application of s.251U(8)] Subsection (8) does not apply if the act or omission was in bad faith.

251U(10) [Regulations under s.251U(4)] Regulations under subsection (4) shall be made by statutory instrument subject to annulment in pursuance of a resolution of either House of Parliament.

General Note

This framework section deals with matters of relevance to the key operational feature of the DRO scheme, namely the channelling of applications though approved intermediaries. There is no direct right of access to a DRO—instead applications will in effect be filtered by professionals including insolvency practitioners.

For the rules relating to the designation of competent authorities see the Debt Relief Orders (Designation of Competent Authorities) Regulations 2009 (SI 2009/457). These regulations (amended by SI 2009/1553) also provide information on how the designated authorities should approve intermediaries.

Note the linkage with s.415A(A1).

251V Debt relief restrictions orders and undertakings

251V Schedule 4ZB (which makes provision about debt relief restrictions orders and debt relief restrictions undertakings) has effect.

General Note

This keys in Sch.4ZB which deals with DRRO and DRRU and interim orders. Further detail is provided by IR 2016 rr.11.1–11.12. The grounds on which a DRRO may be obtained are identified in para.2(2) of the Schedule. If a debtor was an undischarged bankrupt within the previous six years he may come in for special attention.

251W Register of debt relief orders etc

251W The Secretary of State must maintain a register of matters relating to–

(a) debt relief orders;

(b) debt relief restrictions orders; and

(c) debt relief restrictions undertakings.

General Note

DROs, DRROs, and DRRUs, like bankruptcies and IVAs, will be in the public domain. For the public register (entries and deletion of entries) see IR 2016 rr.11.18–11.21. But note the privacy concession in IR 2016 rr.20.1, 20.4 and 20.6.

251X Interpretation

251X(1) [Definitions in Pt 7A] In this Part–

"the application date", in relation to a debt relief order or an application for a debt relief order, means the date on which the application for the order is made to the official receiver;

"approved intermediary" has the meaning given in section 251U(1);

"debt relief order" means an order made by the official receiver under this Part;

"debtor" means–

(a) in relation to an application for a debt relief order, the applicant; and

(b) in relation to a debt relief order, the person in relation to whom the order is made;

"debt relief restrictions order" and "debt relief restrictions undertaking" means an order made, or an undertaking accepted, under Schedule 4ZB;

"the determination date", in relation to a debt relief order or an application for a debt relief order, means the date on which the application for the order is determined by the official receiver;

"the effective date" has the meaning given in section 251E(7);

"excluded debt" is to be construed in accordance with section 251A;

"moratorium" and "moratorium period" are to be construed in accordance with sections 251G and 251H;

"qualifying debt", in relation to a debtor, has the meaning given in section 251A(2);

"the register" means the register maintained under section 251W;

"specified qualifying debt" has the meaning given in section 251G(1).

251X(2) [Creditor in debt relief order] In this Part references to a creditor specified in a debt relief order as the person to whom a qualifying debt is owed by the debtor include a reference to any person to whom the right to claim the whole or any part of the debt has passed, by assignment or operation of law, after the date of the application for the order.

General Note

This is a general interpretation division.

Part VIII

Individual Voluntary Arrangements

Introductory note to Part VIII

The provisions of Pt VIII deal with voluntary arrangements entered into by debtors as an alternative to bankruptcy. A debtor can select a "nominee" to put his proposals into effect. Prior to 1985, a debtor who wished to make an arrangement with his creditors to avoid the consequences of bankruptcy could use the Deeds of Arrangement Act 1914 much of which has survived IA 1986. The problem with a deed of arrangement made under this 1914 legislation was that it could easily be frustrated by a dissenting creditor petitioning for bankruptcy, especially as the mere execution of a deed of arrangement was construed as an act of bankruptcy. Consequently, such deeds of arrangement came to be increasingly under-employed (there were only 51 in 1984). Deeds of arrangement were not abolished immediately, but rather have been left to wither on the vine. Deeds of arrangement and individual voluntary arrangements are mutually exclusive: see s.260(3) below. There were two deeds of arrangement entered into in 1992, though this figure had leaped to four for 1997. Since then the deed of arrangement has become extinct. The annual report of the Secretary of State made under s.379 must disclose statistics concerning the Deeds of Arrangement Act 1914. Under BA 1914 ss.16, 17, and 21 there was provision for schemes of composition or arrangement once bankruptcy proceedings had started (and even after adjudication). These provisions were little used and have now been supplanted by the more flexible system of voluntary arrangements established by the 1985 Act, and now to be found in the 1986 legislation. The Cork Committee (*Report*, para.399) called for the introduction of a more effective system of voluntary arrangements. Although IA 1986 has not adopted the specific Cork proposal for debts arrangement orders, the general policy of the Cork Committee has been followed. DA 2015 at last repealed the Deeds of Arrangement Act 1914.

The original IVA regime as set forth in Pt VIII of IA 1986 has been the subject of significant changes introduced through the medium of s.3 of and Sch.3 to the Insolvency Act 2000. The IVA regime has undergone change as a result of IA 2000. Procedural modifications have been introduced, including the decoupling of the IVA institution from the interim order. An IVA can come into being without the need for an interim order in an appropriate case. These reforms took effect on 1 January 2003.

A number of further changes were also introduced into the IVA mechanism via the provisions of EA 2002. These latter reforms, which included the "fast-track IVA", did not take effect until April 2004. Fast track IVAs have now been abolished.

Individual voluntary arrangements have proved popular with debtors. For background discussion see Williams (1986) 2 I.L. & P. 11. The impact of the new system of individual voluntary arrangements is covered by Pond in (1988) 4 I.L. & P. 66, 104; (1989) 5 I.L. & P. 73; [1995] J.B.L. 118. There were 44,332 IVAs entered into in 2006 (as compared to 62,956 bankruptcies). This increasing popularity may be attributed to a number of factors. The moratorium initiated by the interim order does allow a period of calm during which a debtor can seek to come to a mutually beneficial arrangement with his creditors without fear of an impatient creditor throwing a spanner in the works by petitioning for bankruptcy. Statistics do show that creditors achieve a higher rate of return under an IVA because the administration costs are so much lower—rates of return double those found in bankruptcy cases are sometimes cited. An increasingly important advantage for the debtor is that in avoiding bankruptcy he also avoids the attendant restrictions and disqualifications—e.g. the bar on becoming a company director. For the impact of an IVA on a debtor's right to litigate see *Envis v Thakkar* [1997] B.P.I.R. 189. For general discussion see Mullarkey (1993) 137 S.J. 192; Oditah [1994] L.M.C.L.Q. 210; and Pond (1993) 9 Insolv. L. 9; (1994) 10 Insolv. L. 2. See Tonge [2006] 19 Insolv. Int. 53. For a review of recent developments in IVA law and practice see Milman [2014] 27 Insolv. Int. 1. A practical overview is provided by Frieze in [2015] 28 Insolv. Int. 85.

Although the IVA has proved a statistical success there are concerns with regard to its operation. It can be relatively expensive to operate (though not so expensive as bankruptcy). Critics have said that it is over-legalistic. R3 has responded by introducing model IVA terms but these are not compulsory. In *Cooperative Bank plc v Phillips* [2014] EWHC 2862 (Ch); [2014] B.P.I.R. 1430 we are provided with some judicial illumination from Morgan J on the proper interpretation of cl.7 of the R3 Standard IVA Conditions (set off rights). The IVA does also have a high failure rate, which might suggest that it is inefficient or being used in unsuitable cases. For a review of these operational and wider policy issues see the report by Michael Green, *Individual Voluntary Arrangements: Over-indebtedness and the Insolvency Regime* (November 2002) (short report mounted on Insolvency Service website). At the end of the day Green concludes that if the IVA is reformed to neutralise its deficiencies it should become the premier model for dealing with personal insolvency, thereby relegating bankruptcy to a secondary role. As a result of concerns about potential misselling of IVAs the IVA Forum agreed an IVA Protocol in January 2008. This is essentially a guide to best practice. Details of the background to this initiative and associated document can be accessed via *Dear IP*, March 2008. The Insolvency Service produced proposals in 2005 for a deregulated IVA model (or models) denominated SIVA 1 and SIVA 2 (simplified IVAs). The intention behind these is to cut down on bureaucracy and thereby to reduce costs. Essentially SIVAs would not permit modifications of proposals which would be offered to creditors on a "take it, or leave it" basis. The thinking on the SIVA proposals was contained in an Insolvency Service consultative document (posted on its website) which was published in March 2006. See generally Barc (2005) 21 I.L. & P. 168. The move towards the introduction of simplified IVAs took a step forward with the publication of a consultative document by the Insolvency Service in May 2007 (see Insolvency Service Press Notice 4 May 2007). Under these proposals simplified IVAs would be available to those debtors owing less than £75k. A simplified IVA can be entered into by procuring the support of only a simple majority of creditors. Meetings as such are not to be held; voting will be by post. Creditors claims are to be filed with the IP within 90 days. Many of the more formal procedural/filing/reporting rules relating to IVAs will be waived. Turnaround specialists would be able to supervise IVAs and s.389A will be amended to make this clear. There will also be a general restructuring of Pt VIII to make it easier to understand. It was intended to introduce the SIVA and these other reforms via a legislative reform order under the Legislative and Regulatory Reform Act 2006 with the changes to be introduced at some stage in 2008. For discussion of these proposals see Pond [2007] 20 Insolv. Int. 9. In December 2008 the Government suddenly announced that it was abandoning plans to introduce the SIVA model through a legislative reform order. The reason given for this policy change was the success of the IVA Protocol, which had been agreed earlier that year between IPs, major creditors and the Insolvency Service. This Protocol had reduced costs associated with IVAs, one of the main reasons behind the introduction of SIVAs. The IVA Protocol is not justiciable, but the court will take note of its provisions—*Mond v MBNA Europe Bank Ltd* [2010] EWHC 1710 (Ch); [2010] B.P.I.R. 1167. That said, a creditor may still be entitled to reject a Protocol-compliant IVA. The latest version of the IVA Protocol was published on the Insolvency Service website on 20 June 2016.

In *Co-operative Bank plc v Phillips* [2017] EWHC 1320 (Ch); [2017] B.P.I.R. 1156 HHJ Paul Matthews was required to consider whether an IVA could be supplemented by implied terms; he answered this in the affirmative. The implied term in this case related to the suspension of time running for limitation purposes. He also took the opportunity to explain the nature of an IVA. It was not an unconditional composition of debt. It was conditional upon the supervisor confirming that the debtor had fulfilled obligations under the IVA. If that was not the case a certificate of termination would enable creditors to pursue the debtor for what was owed.

Statement of Insolvency Practice 3 was revised with effect from July 2014. IVAs are dealt with by SIP 3.1.

The IVA procedure does not apply in Scotland (see s.440(2)). However, a somewhat comparable procedure, known as the debt arrangement scheme, was introduced via the Debt Arrangement and Attachment (Scotland) Act 2002. This Scottish Act has spawned a considerable quantity of secondary legislation including the Debt Arrangement Scheme (Scotland) Regulations 2004 (SSI 2004/468) (as amended by SSI 2004/470); The Debt Arrangement and Attachment (Scotland) Act 2002 (Transfer of Functions to the Accountant in Bankruptcy) Order 2004 (SSI 2004/448); Act of Sederunt (Debt Arrangement and Attachment (Scotland) Act 2002) Amendment (The Debt Arrangement Scheme (Scotland) Regulations 2004) 2004 (SSI 2004/505); and the Act of Sederunt (Sheriff Court Bankruptcy Rules) 1996 Amendment 2004 (SSI 2004/534). Further amendments to the debt arrangements scheme in

Scotland will be made by the Debt Arrangement Scheme (Scotland) Regulations 2011 (SSI 2011/141) and the Debt Arrangement Scheme (Interest, Fees, Penalties and Other Charges) (Scotland) Regulations 2011 (SSI 2011/238). These changes were consolidated in the Bankruptcy (Scotland) Act 2016.

Note *Bank of Ireland Mortgage Bank v Sheridan* [2015] NICh 12; [2015] B.P.I.R. 1001 where an IVA was declared a nullity on the grounds of procedural irregularity. The irregularity here involved a jurisdictional error.

Part VIII of the Act is supplemented by IR 2016 rr.8.1–8.38 and by IR 2016 Pt 15 which deals with decision-making. Note in particular that it is a crime fraudulently to procure a voluntary arrangement: IA 1986 s.262A. Although IVAs are provided with a statutory framework, the fact that they are at heart contracts must not be forgotten—*Raja v Rubin* [1999] B.P.I.R. 575. As to who might qualify as a creditor for the purposes of an IVA see *Legal Services Commission v Thipthorpe* [2009] B.P.I.R. 1399. A recurrent theme in IVA litigation concerns the question whether a party can be treated as a creditor for the purposes of participating in an IVA—see for instance *Re Hargreaves (Booth v Mond)* [2010] EWHC 1576 (Ch); [2010] B.P.I.R. 1111 (creditor status confirmed) and *CMEC v Beesley* [2010] EWCA Civ 1344 (creditor status rejected). On the interpretation of termination provisions in an IVA see *Franses v Hay* [2015] EWHC 3468 (Ch); [2016] B.P.I.R. 355.

On whether, as a matter of linguistics, debts that are not fully repaid can be said to be "satisfied" as a result of an IVA see *NRAM plc v Evans* [2015] EWHC 1543 (Ch).

For the wider impact of an IVA see *Jules v Robertson* [2011] EWCA Civ 1322; [2012] B.P.I.R. 126. For the impact of an IVA on third parties see *Jones v FCA* [2013] EWHC 2731 (Ch); [2013] B.P.I.R. 1030 where HHJ Roger Kaye QC dismissed the appeal from the ruling of District Judge Giles (which had been reported in [2013] B.P.I.R. 589). Co obligors were not released from their commitments by virtue of one debtor entering into an IVA with his creditors.

Note also the curious case of *Peoples Phone Ltd v Nicolaou* [2011] EWHC 1129 (Ch); [2011] B.P.I.R. 1477 where the status of a party who had mistakenly surrendered a claim, which was now the subject of rectification proceedings, had to be considered by HHJ Behrens when deciding whether to delay distributions to known IVA creditors. For interpretation of the terms of an IVA with regard to procedures to be followed to bring an IVA to an end see the approach of Registrar Briggs in *Franses v Hay* [2015] EWHC 3468 (Ch).

For the underlying principles applicable to IVAs see *Kapoor v National Westminster Bank plc* [2011] EWCA Civ 1083; [2011] B.P.I.R. 1680. For a purposive interpretation of the IVA statutory provisions see the approach of HHJ Purle QC in *Smith-Evans v Smailes* [2013] EWHC 3199 (Ch). The purposive approach towards the interpretation of Pt VIII was favoured by the High Court in *Narandas-Girdhar v Bradstock* [2014] EWHC 1321(Ch); [2014] B.P.I.R. 1014. Although on the facts the evidence indicated that the debtor had approved modifications and the creditors supported the actions of the chair, had that not been the case the court would not have found the IVA a complete nullity. This liberal approach is not without its critics—see the article by Barber on what are described as "involuntary arrangements" [2014] 27 Insolv. Int. 113. In spite of these views being expressed, the Court of Appeal in *Narandas-Girdhar v Bradstock* [2016] EWCA Civ 88 upheld the purposive approach adopted at first instance in that case.

Lack of mental capacity on the part of a debtor entering an IVA does not render the IVA void, according to Stephen Jourdan QC (sitting as a Deputy Judge of the High Court) in *Fehily v Atkinson* [2016] EWHC 3069 (Ch) at [126]. The judge indicated that where such a lack of capacity is established to the satisfaction of the court it might render the IVA voidable but that conclusion was expressed obiter dicta and in a very tentative fashion.

A number of elements in the IVA procedure were examined by the Court of Appeal in *Bramston v Haut* [2012] EWCA Civ 1637 where a debtor (unusually) sought a suspension of his discharge from bankruptcy in order to promote an IVA. The Court of Appeal refused to overrule the opposition of the trustee in bankruptcy to this strategy.

Note *Green v Wright* [2015] EWHC 993 (Ch); [2015] B.P.I.R. 806 where HHJ Hodge QC ruled that sums received after a certificate of completion has been signed will revert to the debtor and not to the supervisor on behalf of the IVA creditors. On appeal ([2017] EWCA Civ 111) the Court of Appeal took a different view, holding that, notwithstanding the issue of a certificate of completion, the IVA trusts continued to apply to receipts arising after completion. The case did turn very much upon the wording of the particular IVA and on the fact that the PPI claim was admittedly part of the IVA assets. The Scottish decision in *Dooneen (t/a McGinnes Associates) v Mond* [2016] CSIH 59 on receipts from PPI compensation after final dividends had been paid out under protected trust deeds comes to the opposite conclusion.

The provision of insolvency practitioner services in connection with a consumer IVA is VAT exempt—*Paymex Ltd v Revenue and Customs Commissioners* [2011] UKFTT 350 (TC); [2012] B.P.I.R. 178.

The Insolvency Service estimates that only 3 per cent of IVAs are post bankruptcy IVAs including fast track IVAs—see Insolvency Service Consultative Document May 2007 para.30.

There were 46,694 IVAs recorded for England and Wales in 2012. This figure increased to 48,967 in 2013. In 2014 this figure had increased to 52,190, clearly establishing the IVA as the most popular regime for the resolution of personal debt through an established legal procedure. With the general decline in personal insolvency this figure fell to 39,993 in 2015. This figure for 2016 was 49,417. The 2017 total was 59,220.

Moratorium for insolvent debtor

252 Interim order of court

252(1) [Power of court] In the circumstances specified below, the court may in the case of a debtor (being an individual) make an interim order under this section.

252(2) [Effect of interim order] An interim order has the effect that, during the period for which it is in force–

(a) no bankruptcy petition relating to the debtor may be presented or proceeded with,

(aa) no landlord or other person to whom rent is payable may exercise any right of forfeiture by peaceable re-entry in relation to premises let to the debtor in respect of a failure by the debtor to comply with any term or condition of his tenancy of such premises, except with the leave of the court, and

(b) no other proceedings, and no execution or other legal process, may be commenced or continued and no distress may be levied against the debtor or his property except with the leave of the court.

S.252(1)

In effect, this section allows for an application for an interim order in circumstances described in s.253. On the exercise of discretion see s.255. Prior to the coming into force of the Insolvency Act 2000 the making of an interim order was an essential prerequisite to any valid IVA—*Fletcher v Vooght* [2000] B.P.I.R. 435. On one set of circumstances where s.252 might be used see *Bramston v Haut* [2012] EWCA Civ 1637.

S.252(2)

The effect of an interim order is to impose a moratorium on proceedings *against* an insolvent debtor (see *Frost v Unity Trust Bank* [1998] B.P.I.R. 459). The aim of this provision is to prevent a viable proposal being destroyed by a selfish creditor. For an early illustration of an interim order being used to prevent a sheriff acting on behalf of judgment creditors from completing the execution process, see *Re Peake* [1987] C.L.Y. 215 (Blackburn County Court). An attempt to use an interim order to continually block bankruptcy proceedings proved unsuccessful before Scott J in *Re a Debtor (No.83 of 1988)* [1990] 1 W.L.R. 708 (this case is reported as *Re Cove (a Debtor)* in [1990] 1 All E.R. 949).

In *Re M (Restraint Order)* [1992] 2 W.L.R. 340 Otton J held that the making of an interim order under s.252 did not affect the right of the prosecution to make an application for a receiver of realisable property of a person against whom a restraint order had already been made under s.8 of the Drug Trafficking Offences Act 1986. The effect of the interim order was only to protect assets not already covered by the restraint order. Assets covered by the restraint order could no longer be considered as part of the debtor's estate until the defendant was either acquitted, in which case the restraint order would be discharged, or convicted whereupon the restraint order would be converted into a confiscation order. See also *R. v Barnet Justices Ex p. Phillippou* [1997] B.P.I.R. 134, where the court concluded that an interim order did not offer protection against the enforcement of a criminal compensation order which was viewed as being akin to a fine.

The effect of the interim order moratorium came under further scrutiny in *Hall and Shivers v Van Der Heiden* [2010] EWHC 537 (TCC); [2010] B.P.I.R. 585. Here the court granted leave for legal proceedings to continue notwithstanding the interim order because the circumstances under which the interim order had been obtained were open to question.

This provision came in for further scrutiny from Andrews J in *Dewji v Banwaitt* [2013] EWHC 3746 (QB). Here Andrews J upheld the decision below to grant leave under s.252(2)(b) to a judgment creditor to continue the charging order execution process notwithstanding the grant of an interim order in favour of the judgment debtor. Andrews J made the point that an appellate court would be reluctant to interfere with the exercise of discretion on a matter of granting such leave.

In *Tucker v Atkins* [2013] EWHC 4469 (Ch); [2014] B.P.I.R. 1359 Barling J held that for a debtor who wishes to pursue an IVA notwithstanding the fact that bankruptcy has already occurred an application under s.252 is the way forward rather than seeking to suspend automatic discharge under s.279. In later proceedings in *Tucker v Atkins* [2014] EWHC 2260 (Ch); [2014] B.P.I.R. 1569 the IVA proposal was allowed by Asplin J to proceed to creditor vote as it was deemed serious and viable. In *Singh v Singh* [2013] EWHC 4783 (Ch); [2014] B.P.I.R. 1555 the question facing the court again was whether the IVA proposal was serious and viable? Proudman J held that it was, and therefore the creditors should have the final say on it, rather than have it blocked by the court. There was also some uncertainty as to the respective voting power of potential opponents and again Proudman J felt that this uncertainty was best resolved by allowing the proposal to be put to creditors.

Note also *Stella v Harris* [2014] EWHC 4492 (Ch); [2015] B.P.I.R. 926. Here Mann J allowed a party to have judgment entered against the debtor in order to establish his position as a creditor. The judgment was not being enforced and this was not seen as stealing a march upon other creditors.

The wording of s.252(2) was modified by s.3 of and Sch.3 to IA 2000 to strengthen the moratorium by the amendment of subs.(2)(b). Note the addition of subpara.2(2)(aa) covering forfeiture by a landlord and the inclusion of distress within the moratorium. Thus *Re A Debtor (No.13A IO and 14A IO of 1994)* [1995] 1 W.L.R. 1127; [1996] B.C.C. 57 is no longer representative of the law. The latter amendment of subs.(2)(b) counteracts *McMullen & Sons v Cerrone* [1994] B.C.C. 25.

For the consequences of non-compliance with s.252(2) see *Clarke v Coutts & Co (a firm)* [2002] EWCA Civ 943; [2002] B.P.I.R. 916.

253 Application for interim order

253(1) [Where application made] Application to the court for an interim order may be made where the debtor intends to make a proposal under this Part, that is, a proposal to his creditors for a composition in satisfaction of his debts or a scheme of arrangement of his affairs (from here on referred to, in either case, as a "voluntary arrangement").

253(2) [Nominee] The proposal must provide for some person ("the nominee") to act in relation to the voluntary arrangement either as trustee or otherwise for the purpose of supervising its implementation and the nominee must be a person who is qualified to act as an insolvency practitioner, or authorised to act as nominee, in relation to the voluntary arrangement.

253(3) [Applicants] Subject as follows, the application may be made–

(a) if the debtor is an undischarged bankrupt, by the debtor, the trustee of his estate, or the official receiver, and

(b) in any other case, by the debtor.

253(4) [Notice for s.253(3)(a)] An application shall not be made under subsection (3)(a) unless the debtor has given notice of the proposal to the official receiver and, if there is one, the trustee of his estate.

253(5) [Omitted]

General Note

A number of relatively minor textual amendments were made to s.253(1), (2) and (4) by s.3 of and Sch.3 to IA 2000. The amendment to subs.(2) reflects the fact that in future a wider category of professionals may be permitted to act as nominees/supervisors of voluntary arrangements.

S.253(1)–(3)

These provisions define the essence of the proposal for a voluntary arrangement, to implement which the interim order is sought, and they identify who may apply for an interim order. In an appropriate case the appropriate regulator may be heard on such an application—FSMA 2000 s.357(1). For further details, see IR 2016 rr.8.3–8.7. It seems that an interim order may be sought in respect of partnership debts: *Re Cupit (Note)* [1996] B.P.I.R. 560. A discharged bankrupt cannot access the IVA procedure by seeking an interim order—*Wright v Official Receiver* [2001] B.P.I.R. 196. Compare *Re Ravichandran* [2004] B.P.I.R. 814—same result where discharge came *after* interim order but *before* IVA agreed.

S.253(4)

Where the debtor is an undischarged bankrupt two business days' notice is required: see IR 2016 r.8.8.

S.253(5)

Subsection (5) was omitted by ERRA 2013 Sch.19 para.2.

254 Effect of application

254(1) [Stay pending interim order] At any time when an application under section 253 for an interim order is pending–

(a) no landlord or other person to whom rent is payable may exercise any right of forfeiture by peaceable re-entry in relation to premises let to the debtor in respect of a failure by the debtor to comply with any term or condition of his tenancy of such premises, except with the leave of the court, and

(b) the court may forbid the levying of any distress on the debtor's property or its subsequent sale, or both, and stay any action, execution or other legal process against the property or person of the debtor.

254(2) [Stay or continuance] Any court in which proceedings are pending against an individual may, on proof that an application under that section has been made in respect of that individual, either stay the proceedings or allow them to continue on such terms as it thinks fit.

General Note

Where an application for an interim order is pending, the court can take immediate steps to protect the debtor and his assets from legal action. (For the meaning of "the court", see s.385(1).) Indeed, any court in which proceedings are pending can also take such protective steps. The effect of the application has been broadened by s.3 of and Sch.3 to IA 2000 to enable the court to place restrictions on forfeiture and distress.

255 Cases in which interim order can be made

255(1) [Conditions for order] The court shall not make an interim order on an application under section 253 unless it is satisfied–

(a) that the debtor intends to make a proposal under this Part;

(b) that on the day of the making of the application the debtor was an undischarged bankrupt or was able to make a bankruptcy application;

(c) that no previous application has been made by the debtor for an interim order in the period of 12 months ending with that day; and

(d) that the nominee under the debtor's proposal is willing to act in relation to the proposal.

255(2) [Order to facilitate consideration and implementation of proposal] The court may make an order if it thinks that it would be appropriate to do so for the purpose of facilitating the consideration and implementation of the debtor's proposal.

255(3) [Where debtor is undischarged bankrupt] Where the debtor is an undischarged bankrupt, the interim order may contain provision as to the conduct of the bankruptcy, and the administration of the bankrupt's estate, during the period for which the order is in force.

255(4) [Extent of s.255(3) provision] Subject as follows, the provision contained in an interim order by virtue of subsection (3) may include provision staying proceedings in the bankruptcy or modifying any provision in this Group of Parts, and any provision of the rules in their application to the debtor's bankruptcy.

255(5) [Limit to interim order] An interim order shall not, in relation to a bankrupt, make provision relaxing or removing any of the requirements of provisions in this Group of Parts, or of the rules, unless the court is satisfied that that provision is unlikely to result in any significant diminution in, or in the value of, the debtor's estate for the purposes of the bankruptcy.

255(6) [When order ceases to have effect] Subject to the following provisions of this Part, an interim order made on an application under section 253 ceases to have effect at the end of the period of 14 days beginning with the day after the making of the order.

S.255(1), (2)

These subsections deal with the circumstances under which the court may make an interim order. Note the minor textual change to subs.(1) by IA 2000 s.3 and Sch.3. Section 255(2) gives general discretion provided the order would facilitate the consideration and implementation of the proposals. Section 255(1) cuts down this discretion by establishing a series of pre-conditions. For the criteria applied by the court when exercising its discretion under s.255(2) of IA 1986 see *Davidson v Stanley* [2004] EWHC 2595 (Ch); [2005] B.P.I.R. 279. Here an interim order was refused as the debtor's proposal was wholly unrealistic. The reference in s.255(1)(d) to the nominee being qualified was removed by Sch.5 to IA 2000 on the authority of s.15(1). The debtor must not have applied for a similar order within the previous 12 months. This restriction cannot be circumvented by an application under s.375—*Hurst v Bennett (No.2)* [2002] B.P.I.R. 102.

The proposal must be viable: *Cooper v Fearnley* [1997] B.P.I.R. 20; *Hook v Jewson Ltd* [1997] B.C.C. 752; *Knowles v Coutts & Co* [1998] B.P.I.R. 96. It appears that this "viability" requirement permits the court to review the proposed fee for the nominee—*Re Julie O'Sullivan* [2001] B.P.I.R. 534.

Note *Tucker v Atkins* [2014] EWHC 2260 (Ch); [2014] B.P.I.R. 1569 where the viability threshold was just crossed. Asplin J allowed the proposal to go to creditors in circumstances where an undertaking had been given to pay certain creditors in full from third party funding. In *Singh v Singh* [2013] EWHC 4783 (Ch); [2014] B.P.I.R. 1555 Proudman J allowed a proposal to go to the creditors' meeting in circumstances where the level of opposition debt was disputed. The court felt that rather than blocking the proposal the better course of action was for the creditors to determine the fate of the proposal.

Note amendment made to subs.(1)(b) by ERRA 2013 Sch.19 para.3.

S.255(3)–(5)

These provisions deal with supplementary matters that may be included in the interim order where the applicant is an undischarged bankrupt—but such a provision in an interim order must not reduce the value of the debtor's estate.

S.255(6)

The interim order will normally expire within 14 days of the order. Unfortunately, the wording of s.255(6) is not reflected in the old Form 5.2. The Insolvency Service has picked up this error (see *Dear IP*, March 2008) but the Form could not be changed until the Insolvency Rules were themselves amended and we have now moved into an era where official forms have been discarded.

256 Nominee's report on debtor's proposal

256(1) [Report to court] Where an interim order has been made on an application under section 253, the nominee shall, before the order ceases to have effect, submit a report to the court stating–

(a) whether, in his opinion, the voluntary arrangement which the debtor is proposing has a reasonable prospect of being approved and implemented, and

(aa) whether, in his opinion, the debtor's creditors should consider the debtor's proposal.

256(2) [Information to nominee] For the purpose of enabling the nominee to prepare his report the debtor shall submit to the nominee–

(a) a document setting out the terms of the voluntary arrangement which the debtor is proposing, and

(b) a statement of his affairs containing–

(i) such particulars of his creditors and of his debts and other liabilities and of his assets as may be prescribed, and

(ii) such other information as may be prescribed.

256(3) [Directions by court] The court may–

(a) on an application made by the debtor in a case where the nominee has failed to submit the report required by this section or has died, or

(b) on an application made by the debtor or the nominee in a case where it is impracticable or inappropriate for the nominee to continue to act as such, direct that the nominee shall be replaced as such by another person qualified to act as an insolvency practitioner, or authorised to act as nominee, in relation to the voluntary arrangement.

256(3A) [Further directions] The court may, on an application made by the debtor in a case where the nominee has failed to submit the report required by this section, direct that the interim order shall continue, or (if it has ceased to have effect) be renewed, for such further period as the court may specify in the direction.

256(4) [Extension of period of interim order] The court may, on the application of the nominee, extend the period for which the interim order has effect so as to enable the nominee to have more time to prepare his report.

256(5) [Extension for consideration by creditors] If the court is satisfied on receiving the nominee's report that the debtor's creditors should consider the debtor's proposal, the court shall direct that the period for which the interim order has effect shall be extended, for such further period as it may specify in the direction, for the purpose of enabling the debtor's proposal to be considered by his creditors in accordance with the following provisions of this Part.

256(6) [Discharge of interim order] The court may discharge the interim order if it is satisfied, on the application of the nominee–

(a) that the debtor has failed to comply with his obligations under subsection (2), or

(b) that for any other reason it would be inappropriate for the debtor's creditors to consider the debtor's proposal.

General Note

Amendments are made by SBEEA 2015 s.126 and Sch.9 para.61. These changes reflect the new creditors' decision procedure.

S.256(1)

The nominee of the debtor must, before the interim order has expired (see s.255(6)), report to the court whether in his opinion it is worth initiating a creditors' decision process to consider the debtor's proposal. For the nominee's responsibilities when evaluating the proposal see *Greystoke v Hamilton-Smith* [1997] B.P.I.R. 24; and *Shah v Cooper* [2003] B.P.I.R. 1018. The wording of subs.(1) was subsequently amended by IA 2000 s.3 and Sch.3 by the insertion of a new sub-para.(a) requiring the nominee to attest to the viability of the proposal, thus reflecting the standards previously developed at common law. For general discussion of the responsibilities of nominees, see *Prosser v Castle Sanderson (a firm)* [2002] EWCA Civ 1140; [2003] B.C.C. 440. This provision was considered in *Tradition (UK) Ltd v Ahmed* [2009] B.P.I.R. 626. See in general IR 2016 rr.8.3, 8.15 and 8.17.

S.256(2)

To facilitate the nominee making his report, the debtor must submit to him details of his proposal and statement of affairs. See IR 2016 rr.8.5, 8.7.

S.256(3), (3A)

Subsection (3) has been replaced and subs.(3A) inserted by s.3 of and Sch.3 to IA 2000. If the nominee fails to submit a report the debtor can apply to the court to have him replaced, and the interim order may be extended in such a situation. See IR 2016 r.8.17.

S.256(4)

This also allows for the extension of the order where the nominee requires more time to prepare his report.

S.256(5)

If, after receiving the nominee's report, the court is satisfied that a decision of creditors should be sought, the court can again extend the interim order. Note also IR 2016 rr.8.13, 8.17. Several such extensions can be granted but the patience of the court is not limitless: *Re a Debtor (No.83 of 1988)* [1990] 1 W.L.R. 708.

S.256(6)

The interim order can be discharged by the court if the debtor has failed to play his part or if it would be inappropriate to call a creditors' meeting.

Procedure where no interim order made

256A Debtor's proposal and nominee's report

256A(1) [Application] This section applies where a debtor (being an individual)–

(a) intends to make a proposal under this Part (but an interim order has not been made in relation to the proposal and no application for such an order is pending), and

(b) if he is an undischarged bankrupt, has given notice of the proposal to the official receiver and, if there is one, the trustee of his estate.

256A(2) [Duty of debtor] For the purpose of enabling the nominee to prepare a report under subsection (3), the debtor shall submit to the nominee–

(a) a document setting out the terms of the voluntary arrangement which the debtor is proposing, and

(b) a statement of his affairs containing–

(i) such particulars of his creditors and of his debts and other liabilities and of his assets as may be prescribed, and

(ii) such other information as may be prescribed.

256A(3) [Report of nominee] If the nominee is of the opinion that the debtor is an undischarged bankrupt, or is able to make a bankruptcy application, the nominee shall, within 14 days (or such longer period as the court may allow) after receiving the document and statement mentioned in subsection (2), submit a report to the debtor's creditors stating–

(a) whether, in his opinion, the voluntary arrangement which the debtor is proposing has a reasonable prospect of being approved and implemented, and

(b) whether, in his opinion, the debtor's creditors should consider the debtor's proposal.

256A(4) [Court response] The court may–

(a) on an application made by the debtor in a case where the nominee has failed to submit the report required by this section or has died, or

(b) on an application made by the debtor or the nominee in a case where it is impracticable or inappropriate for the nominee to continue to act as such,

direct that the nominee shall be replaced as such by another person qualified to act as an insolvency practitioner, or authorised to act as nominee, in relation to the voluntary arrangement.

256A(5) [Time limit extended] The court may, on an application made by the nominee, extend the period within which the nominee is to submit his report.

General Note

This new provision was introduced by IA 2000 s.3 and Sch.3 with effect from 1 January 2003. It is designed to decouple the IVA procedure from the need to have an interim order. Under the original model a purported IVA constructed without an interim order was a nullity—*Fletcher v Vooght* [2000] B.P.I.R. 435. See IR 2016 rr.8.19–8.21. Note amendments made to subs.(1) and (3) by ERRA 2013 Sch.19 para.4.

Amendments were made to this section by SBEEA 2015 s.126 and Sch.9 para.62.

S.256A(1)
This defines where s.256A applies.

S.256A(2)
This indicates the information required of the debtor.

S.256A(3), (5)
Note that the reporting obligation was amended by LRO 2010 (SI 2010/18). Where the nominee reaches certain conclusions on the documentation furnished to him he makes a report to creditors on whether an IVA is suitable. The 14-day period may be extended—subs.(5).

S.256A(4)
This provides a protective mechanism for the debtor where the nominee has failed to act in accordance with subs.(4).

S.256A(5)
The court can extend the time-limit specified in subs.(3).

Creditors' decisions

257 Consideration of debtor's proposal by creditors

257(1) [Application] This section applies where it has been reported to the court under section 256 or to the debtor's creditors under section 256A that the debtor's creditors should consider the debtor's proposal.

257(2) [Decision sought] The nominee (or the nominee's replacement under section 256(3) or 256A(4)) must seek a decision from the debtor's creditors as to whether they approve the proposed voluntary arrangement (unless, in the case of a report to which section 256 applies, the court otherwise directs).

257(2A) [Creditors' decision procedure] The decision is to be made by a creditors' decision procedure.

257(2B) [Notice] Notice of the creditors' decision procedure must be given to every creditor of the debtor whose claim and address the nominee (or the nominee's replacement) is aware.

257(3) [Creditors of debtor] For this purpose the creditors of a debtor who is an undischarged bankrupt include–

(a) every person who is a creditor of the bankrupt in respect of a bankruptcy debt, and

(b) every person who would be such a creditor if the bankruptcy had commenced on the day on which notice of the creditors' decision procedure is given.

General Note

Amendments were to be made to this provision by SBEEA 2015 s.126 and Sch.9 paras 63 and 64. New subss.(2A) and (2B) were added.

S.257(1)
Subsection (1) was substituted by LRO 2010 (SI 2010/18). This deals with reporting obligations. This provision requires the nominee to seek a decision from creditors in accordance with his report, unless the court has directed otherwise. In *Re a Debtor (No.83 of 1988)* [1990] 1 W.L.R. 708, Scott J held that this provision (in appropriate circumstances) enables the court to discharge any previous order directing that a creditors' meeting be convened. In order for the approval of the IVA to be binding the meeting must be summoned strictly in accordance with the report to the court—*Re N (a Debtor)* [2002] B.P.I.R. 1024. Minor textual changes were made by IA 2000 s.3 and Sch.3 to cater for the advent of s.256A.

In *Vlieland-Boddy v Dexter Ltd* [2003] EWHC 2592 (Ch); [2004] B.P.I.R. 235 the High Court indicated that if the registrar was not satisfied that a creditors' meeting under s.257 should be called then any such meeting that was held could not be regarded as a valid meeting for the purposes of Pt VIII of IA 1986.

In *Re Plummer* [2004] B.P.I.R. 767 it was held by Registrar Baister that for IVA modifications to become binding it must be proved that the debtor assented to them. Therefore a report by the chairman of the creditors' meeting held under s.257 that an IVA had been proved was inaccurate and the purported IVA was a total nullity. The status of *Re Plummer* (above) is in some doubt at the moment in view of the comments of HHJ Purle QC in *Smith-Evans v Smailes* [2013] EWHC 3199 (Ch). These doubts have been reinforced by the view taken of *Re Plummer* (above) by Briggs LJ in *Narandas-Girdhar v Bradstock* [2016] EWCA Civ 88.

See *CMEC v Beesley* [2010] EWCA Civ 1344. See also *Price v Davis* [2014] EWCA Civ 26 for linkage with ss.260 and 264.

S.257(2), (2A), (2B), (3)

These subsections identify which creditors are to participate in the decision—this will depend on whether the debtor is an undischarged bankrupt or not. An FCA representative may attend in an appropriate case—FSMA 2000 s.357(3). On the importance of compliance with s.257(2) see *Namulas Pension Trustees Ltd v Mouzakis* [2011] B.P.I.R. 1724.

For further information, reference should be made to IR 2016 r.8.22 and Pt 15.

Consideration and implementation of debtor's proposal

258 Approval of debtor's proposal

258(1) [Decision re approval] This section applies where under section 257 the debtor's creditors are asked to decide whether to approve the proposed voluntary arrangement.

258(2) [Approval with modifications] The creditors may approve the proposed voluntary arrangement with or without modifications, but shall not approve it with modifications unless the debtor consents to each modification.

258(3) [Extent of modifications] The modifications subject to which the proposed voluntary arrangement may be approved may include one conferring the functions proposed to be conferred on the nominee on another person qualified to act as an insolvency practitioner or authorised to act as nominee, in relation to the voluntary arrangement.

But they shall not include any modification by virtue of which the proposal ceases to be a proposal under this Part.

258(4) [Certain modifications not to be approved] The creditors shall not approve any proposal or modification which affects the right of a secured creditor of the debtor to enforce his security, except with the concurrence of the creditor concerned.

258(5) [Other modifications not to be approved] Subject as follows, the creditors shall not approve any proposal or modification under which–

(a) any preferential debt of the debtor is to be paid otherwise than in priority to such of his debts as are not preferential debts,

(aa) any ordinary preferential debt of the debtor is to be paid otherwise than in priority to any secondary preferential debts that the debtor may have,

(b) a preferential creditor of the debtor is to be paid an amount in respect of an ordinary preferential debt that bears to that debt a smaller proportion than is borne to another ordinary preferential debt by the amount that is to be paid in respect of that other debt, or

(c) a preferential creditor of the debtor is to be paid an amount in respect of a secondary preferential debt that bears to that debt a smaller proportion than is borne to another secondary preferential debt by the amount that is to be paid in respect of that other debt.

However, the creditors may approve such a proposal or modification with the concurrence of the preferential creditor concerned.

258(6) [Omitted]

258(7) [Definitions] In this section "preferential debt", "ordinary preferential debt" and "secondary preferential debt" each has the meaning given by section 386 in Part XII; and "preferential creditor" is to be construed accordingly.

S.258(1)

The creditors can either approve or reject the composition which is being put to them. No mention is made of any required majority—under BA 1914 ss.16(2) and 21(1) it was three-fourths in value of the debtor's creditors: IR 2016 r.15.34 essentially retains the position, although it actually specifies a majority *in excess of* three-quarters. The decision of the meeting is final: *Kent Carpets Ltd v Symes* [1996] B.C.C. 137.

S.258(2)–(5)

These provisions deal with modifications to the proposed scheme. Textual changes were made to subs.(3) by s.3 of, and Sch.3 to, IA 2000. The debtor must assent to any modification and the modification may involve a change of nominee, but the basic proposal must still fall within s.253. A modified IVA that does not have the support of the debtor is void—*Reid v Hamblin* [2001] B.P.I.R. 929. Changes affecting the rights of secured creditors are only permitted in so far as the secured creditors agree, see *Khan v Permayer* [2001] B.P.I.R. 95 where the secured creditor waived his security in favour of a dividend. See also *Rey v FNCB Ltd* [2006] EWHC 1386 (Ch). Section 258(4) was considered in *Webb v MacDonald* [2010] B.P.I.R. 503, where the protection of secured creditors under the IVA was emphasised. On who is a secured creditor for these purposes see *Re a Debtor (No.10 of 1992)* [1995] Ch. 525, reported as *Peck v Craighead* [1995] B.C.C. 525. Similar protection is available to consolidate the priority enjoyed by preferential creditors on bankruptcy. This confirms the position under BA 1914 s.16(19).

Note amendments made to subs.(5) by the Banks and Building Societies (Depositor Preference and Priorities) Order 2014 (SI 2014/3486) with effect from 1 January 2015. These changes result from the new recategorisation of the different types of preferential debts.

S.258(6)

The meeting must be conducted according to the rules: see IR 2016 r.8.22 and Pt 15.

S.258(7)

This defines preferential debts, etc. for the purposes of this provision. Note amendments made to subs.(7) by the Banks and Building Societies (Depositor Preference and Priorities) Order 2014 (SI 2014/3486) with effect from 1 January 2015. These changes result from the new recategorisation of the different types of preferential debts.

Editors' note: Note amendment by SBEEA 2015 s.126 and Sch.9 para.65.

259 Report of decisions to court

259(1) [Notice] When pursuant to section 257 the debtor's creditors have decided whether to approve the debtor's proposal (with or without modifications) the nominee (or the nominee's replacement under section 256(3) or 256A(4) must–

(a) give notice of the creditors' decision to such persons as may be prescribed, and

(b) where the creditors considered the debtor's proposal pursuant to a report to the court under section 256(1)(aa), report the creditors' decision to the court.

259(2) [Discharge of interim order] If the report is that the creditors have declined (with or without modifications) to approve the voluntary arrangement proposed under section 256, the court may discharge any interim order which is in force in relation to the debtor.

General Note

Subsection (1) was substituted and subs.(2) amended by LRO 2010 (SI 2010/18). The change relates to reporting obligations. The nominee must report any decision to the court and give notice to prescribed persons. If the creditors have completely rejected the debtor's proposals, the court may discharge any interim order.

For further obligations imposed on the nominee, see IR 2016 Pt 15 (especially r.15.11).

This provision was amended by SBEEA 2015 s.126 and Sch.9 para.66.

260 Effect of approval

260(1) [Effect] This section has effect where pursuant to section 257 the debtor's creditors decide to approve the proposed voluntary arrangement (with or without modifications).

260(2) [Effect of approved composition or scheme] The approved arrangement–

(a) takes effect as if made by the debtor at the time the creditors decided to approve the proposal, and

(b) binds every person who in accordance with the rules–

(i) was entitled to vote in the creditors' decision procedure by which the decision to approve the proposal was made, or

(ii) would have been so entitled if he had had notice of it,

as if he were a party to the arrangement.

260(2A) [Amounts payable under s.260(2)(b)(ii)] If–

(a) when the arrangement ceases to have effect any amount payable under the arrangement to a person bound by virtue of subsection (2)(b)(ii) has not been paid, and

(b) the arrangement did not come to an end prematurely, the debtor shall at that time become liable to pay to that person the amount payable under the arrangement.

260(3) [Omitted]

260(4) [Certain interim orders to cease] Any interim order in force in relation to the debtor immediately before the end of the period of 28 days beginning with the day on which the report with respect to the creditors' decision was made to the court under section 259 ceases to have effect at the end of that period.

This subsection applies except to such extent as the court may direct for the purposes of any application under section 262 below.

260(5) [Bankruptcy petition stayed by s.260(4) interim order] Where proceedings on a bankruptcy petition have been stayed by an interim order which ceases to have effect under subsection (4), that petition is deemed, unless the court otherwise orders, to have been dismissed.

General Note

This provision was amended by SBEEA 2015 s.126 and Sch.9 para.67.

S.260(1), (2), (2A)

HHJ Purle QC considered this provision in *Smith-Evans v Smailes* [2013] EWHC 3199 (Ch). HHJ Purle QC adopted a purposive interpretation to the meaning of the s.257 meeting as mentioned in subs.(1). In *Narandas-Girdhar v Bradstock* [2014] EWHC 1321 (Ch); [2014] B.P.I.R. 1014 the more liberal approach of HHJ Purle QC in *Smailes* (above) was preferred to the more technical stance towards modifications and procedural departures adopted by Registrar Baister in *Re Plummer* [2014] B.P.I.R. 767. This liberal approach was also preferred on appeal in *Narandas-Girdhar v Bradstock* [2016] EWCA Civ 88. Accordingly, errors as to voting entitlements or the failure to secure the consent of the debtor to variations did not render an IVA void. These flaws might constitute material irregularity for s.262 purposes but did not nullify the IVA. Such lapses were capable of ratification. For a critique of this liberal approach and the rise of the phenomenon of "involuntary arrangements" see Barber [2014] 27 Insolv. Int. 113. But see the perspective of Briggs LJ in *Narandas-Girdhar v Bradstock* [2016] EWCA Civ 88.

Subsection 2(b) was replaced and subs.(2A) was inserted by IA 2000 s.3 and Sch.3. These modifications deal with the position of unknown creditors and their rights in cesser of the arrangement in circumstances where they have still not been paid. Where the creditors' meeting approves the debtor's proposal (whether modified or not), this will bind every person falling within s.260(2)(b). A creditor can split a debt and be bound by the IVA only in respect of part of the sums owing: *Re Hoare* [1997] B.P.I.R. 683. The legislation does not fully bring out the contractual foundation of a voluntary arrangement. That has been illustrated by court decisions. For example, in *Welburn v Dibb Lupton Broomhead* [2002] EWCA Civ 1601; [2003] B.P.I.R. 768, the court indicated that whether a cause of action had become one of the "trust assets" was essentially a matter of contractual construction. On the interpretation of IVAs see *Golstein v Bishop* [2013] EWHC 1706 (Ch); [2013] B.P.I.R. 708. The contract nature of an IVA can be reinforced by granting the supervisors a power of attorney—see for example *Masters v Furber* [2013] EWHC 3023 (Ch).

A secured creditor who accepts a dividend on a voluntary arrangement does not necessarily waive rights of security—*Whitehead v Household Mortgage Corp* [2002] EWCA Civ 1657.

Note that court approval is not required to make the scheme binding, unlike under s.16 of the 1914 Act. Notwithstanding approval of a scheme by creditors under s.260, an aggrieved creditor may apply to the court under s.262 if the scheme unfairly prejudices him in his capacity as a creditor: see here *Re Naeem (a Bankrupt) (No.18 of 1988)* [1990] 1 W.L.R. 48.

For the effect of s.260 in releasing old debts and creating new obligations see *Re Wisepark Ltd* [1994] B.C.C. 221 at 223. On the effect of an IVA on sureties see *Johnson v Davies* [1998] 1 B.C.L.C. 580; *Greene King plc v Stanley* [2001] EWCA Civ 1966; [2002] B.P.I.R. 491; *Lombard Natwest Factors Ltd v Koutrouzas* [2002] EWHC 1084 (QB); [2003] B.P.I.R. 444; and *Lloyds Bank v Ellicott* [2002] EWCA Civ 1333; [2003] B.P.I.R. 632. A creditor with a non-provable matrimonial debt can be bound by an IVA—*JP v A Debtor* [1999] B.P.I.R. 206. On future tort claims see annotation to s.3 above.

On whether a post-IVA creditor can become bound see *Re Goldspan Ltd* [2003] B.P.I.R. 93.

On what debts are covered by an IVA see *Cornelius v Casson* [2008] B.P.I.R. 504, which confirms that each case turns upon the individual terms of the particular IVA.

This section featured in the judgment in the county court in *Namulas Pension Trustees Ltd v Mouzakis* [2011] B.P.I.R. 1724. Here District Judge Stark set aside an IVA because the proper notice requirements had not been satisfied. The binding effect under s.260 only applied to those who had been given proper notice of the meeting such as would have enabled them to vote.

In *Peterkin v Merton LBC* [2011] EWHC 376 (Ch) Vos J indicated that the binding effect of the IVA scheme was not intended to cover future debts arising after the IVA was agreed. Thus a creditor who had debts within the IVA was not precluded from using enforcement procedures such as charging orders to recover debts outside the IVA even though they arose during the currency of the IVA. The appeal in *Peterkin* was dismissed—[2013] EWCA Civ 121.

A minor case management point arose in *Grimme Landmaschinenfabrik GmbH v Scott* [2009] B.P.I.R. 506 where the fact that the defendant was undergoing an IVA was deemed by Kitchin J to be a relevant consideration in determining the time required to prepare a defence in patent proceedings.

For the binding effect of s.260 see *Price v Davis* [2014] EWCA Civ 26.

S.260(4), (5)

Interim orders automatically lapse within 28 days of the report to the court. One effect of this is that if the interim order has "blocked" a bankruptcy petition, the petition is now to be treated as having been dismissed.

Note amendment by DA 2015 s.19 and Sch.6. This omits subs.(3).

261 Additional effect on undischarged bankrupt

261(1) [Application of section] This section applies where–

(a) pursuant to section 257, the debtor's creditors decide to approve the proposed voluntary arrangement (with or without modifications), and

(b) the debtor is an undischarged bankrupt.

261(2) [Annulment of bankruptcy order] Where this section applies the court shall annul the bankruptcy order on an application made–

(a) by the bankrupt, or

(b) where the bankrupt has not made an application within the prescribed period, by the official receiver.

261(3) [When application for annulment not to be made] An application under subsection (2) may not be made–

(a) during the period specified in section 262(3)(a) during which the creditors' decision can be challenged by application under section 262,

(b) while an application under that section is pending, or

(c) while an appeal in respect of an application under that section is pending or may be brought.

261(4) [Court to give directions] Where this section applies the court may give such directions about the conduct of the bankruptcy and the administration of the bankrupt's estate as it thinks appropriate for facilitating the implementation of the approved voluntary arrangement.

General Note

This was replaced and reconstituted by EA 2002 s.264 and Sch.22. This provision was then amended by SBEEA 2015 s.126 and Sch.9 para.68.

S.261(1)
This explains the ambit of this section. The Court of Appeal considered the issue of an IVA post bankruptcy in *Demarco v Perkins and Bulley Davey* [2006] EWCA Civ 188; [2006] B.P.I.R. 645. This case involved allegations of professional negligence in that insolvency advisers had failed to get a bankruptcy annulled pursuant to s.261(1)(a) before the debtor was automatically discharged from bankruptcy with the result that a valid IVA could not then be embarked upon. The Court of Appeal gave guidance on the quantum of liability in such cases.

S.261(2)
If an IVA is made under this provision the court should annul the extant bankruptcy order. See IR 2016 rr.8.32 et seq. In *Re Johnson* [2006] B.P.I.R. 987 (HHJ Roger Kaye QC sitting in the Leeds County Court) a question arose as to whether a discharged bankrupt who previously had had an IVA approved could seek an annulment under s.261 of the IA 1986. It was held that a person whose bankruptcy had been automatically discharged could still be regarded as a "bankrupt" for the purposes of seeking an annulment under this provision. The term "bankrupt" when used in s.261 could include a former bankrupt. This conclusion is plausible because it is clear from s.282(3) that a discharged bankrupt could seek an annulment under s.282 but it is difficult to square with the heading of s.261 which is "Additional Effect on Undischarged Bankrupt". Having raised that doubt, it is possible to square this conclusion with the assumptions made in *Demarco v Perkins and Bulley Davey* [2006] EWCA Civ 188 (IVA not possible because bankruptcy had already been discharged), because in *Re Johnson* (above) the IVA was agreed *before* the discharge occurred.

S.261(3)
This explains when an application can be made under this provision.

S.261(4)
This outlines the wide consequential powers of the court.

262 Challenge of creditors' decision

262(1) [Application to court] Subject to this section, an application to the court may be made, by any of the persons specified below, on one or both of the following grounds, namely–

(a) that a voluntary arrangement approved by a decision of the debtor's creditors pursuant to section 257 unfairly prejudices the interests of a creditor of the debtor;

(b) that there has been some material irregularity in relation to a creditors' decision procedure instigated under that section.

262(2) [Applicants] The persons who may apply under this section are–

(a) the debtor;

(b) a person who–

(i) was entitled, in accordance with the rules, to vote in the creditors' decision procedure, or

(ii) would have been so entitled if he had had notice of it;

(c) the nominee (or his replacement under section 256(3), 256A(4) or 258(3)); and

(d) if the debtor is an undischarged bankrupt, the trustee of his estate or the official receiver.

262(3) [Time for application] An application under this section shall not be made–

(a) after the end of the period of 28 days beginning with the day on which the creditors decided whether to approve the proposed voluntary arrangement or, where a report was required to be made to the court under section 259(1)(b), the day on which the report was made; or

(b) in the case of a person who was not given notice of the creditors' decision procedure, after the end of the period of 28 days beginning with the day on which he became aware that a decision as to whether to approve the proposed voluntary arrangement had been made, but (subject to that) an application made by a person within subsection (2)(b)(ii) on the ground that the arrangement prejudices his interests may be made after the arrangement has ceased to have effect, unless it has come to an end prematurely.

262(4) [Court's powers] Where on an application under this section the court is satisfied as to either of the grounds mentioned in subsection (1), it may do one or both of the following, namely–

(a) revoke or suspend any approval given by a decision of the debtor's creditors;

(b) direct any person to seek a decision from the debtor's creditors (using a creditors' decision procedure) as to whether they approve–

(i) any revised proposal the debtor may make, or

(ii) in a case falling within subsection (1)(b), the debtor's original proposal.

262(5) [Revocation of direction, approval] Where at any time after giving a direction under subsection (4)(b) in relation to a revised proposal the court is satisfied that the debtor does not intend to submit such a proposal, the court shall revoke the direction and revoke or suspend any approval previously given by the debtor's creditors.

262(6) [Further direction] Where the court gives a direction under subsection (4)(b), it may also give a direction continuing or, as the case may require, renewing, for such period as may be specified in the direction, the effect in relation to the debtor of any interim order.

262(7) [Supplemental directions] In any case where the court, on an application made under this section with respect to a creditors' decision, gives a direction under subsection (4)(b) or revokes or suspends an approval under subsection (4)(a) or (5), the court may give such supplemental directions as it thinks fit, and, in particular, directions with respect to–

(a) things done since the decision under any voluntary arrangement approved by the decision, and

(b) such things done since the decision as could not have been done if an interim order had been in force in relation to the debtor when they were done.

262(8) [Effects of irregularity at meeting] Except in pursuance of the preceding provisions of this section, the approval of a voluntary arrangement by a decision of the debtor's creditors pursuant to section 257 is not invalidated by any irregularity in relation to the creditors' decision procedure by which the decision was made.

General Note

This provision was amended by SBEEA 2015 s.126 and Sch.9 para.69. Note also amendment made by SBEEA 2015 s.134. In particular note the move away from the exclusive use of meetings as the forum in which creditor decisions are reached.

Modifications to s.262 were made by IA 2000 s.3 and Sch.3. Of these modifications the provisions dealing with unidentified (and therefore unnotified) creditors are the most significant. Under s.16 of BA 1914, it was the task of the court to approve the scheme, and it had to consider whether it was reasonable and for the benefit of the general creditors. Under the 1986 Act, the court's role is reduced and it will assume such a paternal posture only if the decision of the majority of creditors is challenged under s.262. The court will consider whether the interests of some creditors have been unfairly prejudiced and will be less concerned with an overview of the scheme—it will assume that it is beneficial to the creditors if the majority support it. It is important to grasp that the remedy is only available to protect the complainant's interests as a creditor and not ulterior interests, a point confirmed in *Doorbar v Alltime Securities Ltd (No.2)* [1995] B.C.C. 1,149. Furthermore, the court has more discretion under s.262 to secure the revision of the scheme to meet any objections. In *Re Naeem (a Bankrupt) (No.18 of 1988)* [1990] 1 W.L.R. 48 a landlord successfully exploited s.262 before a registrar to block a scheme on the ground that it unfairly prejudiced his interests, but on appeal to Hoffmann J the scheme was reinstated as no unfair prejudice to his interests as a creditor could be established. This case is also instructive on the question of who pays the costs of a s.262 application. See also *March Estates v Gunmark* [1996] B.P.I.R. 439.

Challenges under the s.262 procedure are only required where an IVA has come into existence (albeit with some irregularity). Where the flaw (whether it be procedural or substantive) is so serious as to render the purported IVA a nullity the time limits specified in s.262(3) become irrelevant—*Inland Revenue Commissioners v Bland and Sargent* [2003] EWHC 1068 (Ch); [2003] B.P.I.R. 1274; *Vlieland-Boddy v Dexter Ltd* [2003] EWHC 2592 (Ch); [2004] B.P.I.R. 235; *Re Plummer* [2004] B.P.I.R. 767. See *Smith-Evans v Smailes* [2013] EWHC 3199 (Ch) where HHJ Purle QC cast doubt upon *Re Plummer*. These doubts were reinforced by the comments of Briggs LJ in *Narandas-Girdhar v Bradstock* [2016] EWCA Civ 88.

A success for s.262 was notched up in *Re a Debtor (No.222 of 1990) Ex p. Bank of Ireland (No.2)* [1993] B.C.L.C. 233 where Harman J found that as the nominee/chairman had conducted the IVA meeting in a materially irregular way by denying certain creditors a vote (see the earlier proceedings reported in [1992] B.C.L.C. 137) he should be personally liable for the costs of the IVA which had to be set aside. It is difficult not to feel some sympathy for the unfortunate insolvency practitioner here as the right to vote on an IVA in certain contentious cases is less than clear. See also *Fender v Inland Revenue Commissioners* [2003] B.P.I.R. 1304. For another s.262 application that resulted in difficulties for the insolvency practitioner concerned, see *Re N (a Debtor)* [2002] B.P.I.R. 1024. For a successful application by a creditor resulting in the insolvency practitioner being held partly responsible in costs see *AB Agri Ltd v Curtis* [2016] B.P.I.R. 1297. A s.262 application on the grounds of unfair prejudice also succeeded in *Re A Debtor (No.1 of 1999)* [2000] B.P.I.R. 998.

By way of comparison a s.262 application failed in *Re a Debtor (No.259 of 1990)* [1992] 1 W.L.R. 226 where the court made the point that the alleged unfairness must emanate from the scheme itself. For another unsuccessful petition alleging unfair prejudice see *National Westminster Bank v Scher* [1998] B.P.I.R. 224.

For consequential procedural aspects of an application under s.262, see IR 2016 r.8.27. Note also *Re a Debtor (No.87 of 1993) (No.1)* [1996] B.C.C. 74 (hearsay evidence not admissible).

A challenge by a creditor under s.262 provided the basis for the complex litigation reported as *Smurthwaite v Simpson-Smith* [2006] EWCA Civ 1183. The report in question throws little light on the substantive aspects of the provision in that it deals with preliminary issues linked to disclosure of documents and costs incurred in respect of applications to seek disclosure, though once again it does show the difficulties faced by the chairman of the creditors meeting in dealing with disputed debts.

In *Coutts & Co v Passey* [2007] B.P.I.R. 323 the issue was whether a material irregularity had occurred in that the applicant creditor had not been allowed to vote for the full amount which it claimed was due. The disputed element in the debt related to legal costs incurred by the applicant bank in seeking to recover its lending to a client. Under the terms of the lending agreement there was an express provision that the client would be liable for recovery costs. The court felt that this fact provided sufficient grounds to distinguish *Glenister v Rowe* [2000] Ch. 76. *Glenister v Rowe* [2000] Ch 76 was overruled in *Re the Nortel Companies* [2013] UKSC 52; [2013] B.C.C. 624.

For further consideration of s.262 and its relationship with IR r.5.22 (now IR 2016 rr.15.31 and 15.33) see *Monecor (London) Ltd v Ahmed* [2008] B.P.I.R. 458. This case provides an up to date interpretation of the concept of material irregularity and considers the options open to the court under s.262(4). A number of aspects of IVA procedure were reviewed by the court in *Tradition (UK) Ltd v Ahmed* [2009] B.P.I.R. 626.

For a case where material irregularity was established see *Golstein v Bishop* [2016] EWHC 2187 (Ch). For later proceedings in this long running litigation see *Golstein v Bishop* [2016] EWHC 2804 (Ch).

See *Rowbury v Official Receiver* [2015] EWHC 2276 (Ch) where an IVA was revoked because of a material irregularity occurring at the creditors' meeting. This irregularity was the result of a failure to suspend the meeting under the then IR 1986 r.5.24(4A) for one hour pending the clarification of a proxy vote. See now IR 2016 r.15.27.

In *CMEC v Beesley* [2010] EWCA Civ 1344 the question was whether CMEC was a creditor for the purposes of the IVA. The Court of Appeal, rejecting the view taken at first instance, held that CMEC was not a creditor and therefore could not be bound by the terms of the IVA.

The flexibility offered by s.262 was noted in *Narandas-Girdhar v Bradstock* [2016] EWCA Civ 88. So procedural errors which might constitute material irregularity could be resolved under s.262 without rendering an IVA a complete nullity.

Note *Linfoot v Adamson* [2012] EWHC Misc 16 (CC); [2012] B.P.I.R. 1033 at [53] for the difference between an application made under s.262 and one brought on the basis of s.263(3).

S.262(1)–(3), (8)

Within 28 days of the chairman's report to the court a dissenter may apply to the court to challenge the scheme. Section 262(2) allows the debtor, creditors, nominee, trustee or official receiver to make such an application. As to who is a creditor, see *Sea Voyager Maritime Inc v Bielecki* [1999] 1 All E.R. 628. An appropriate regulator may apply (and be heard on the application of another) in an appropriate case—FSMA 2000 s.357(5) and (6). The grounds for the challenge are that the scheme unfairly prejudices the interests of a creditor, or that there has been some *material* irregularity in relation to the meeting. The test for material irregularity is the same under the Act and the Rules: *Re Sweatfield Ltd* [1997] B.C.C. 744. Irregularity will not be regarded as material unless it would be likely to affect the outcome of the vote: *Doorbar v Alltime Securities* [1995] B.C.C. 1,149. The irregularity need not be at the meeting as such but may occur in the preparatory documentation: *Re a Debtor (No.87 of 1993) (No.2)* [1996] B.C.C. 80. In *Fender v Inland Revenue Commissioners* [2003] B.P.I.R. 1304 the court indicated that a material irregularity might occur in the proposal, the statement of affairs the nominee's report or in the nominee's chairmanship of the creditors' meeting. See also *Inland Revenue Commissioners v Duce* [1999] B.P.I.R. 189. In *Roberts v Pinnacle Entertainment Ltd* [2003] EWHC 2394 (Ch); [2004] B.P.I.R. 208 a misguided refusal by the chair of the creditors' meeting to admit a major creditor to voting was held to be a material irregularity within s.262(1)(b). Material irregularity can arise even though no party can be said to be at blame: *Great Yarmouth BC v Alterman* (unreported county court ruling noted in *Current Law Week*, 17 April 1998). An IVA was set aside for material irregularity in *Namulas Pension Trustees Ltd v Mouzakis* [2011] B.P.I.R. 1724 where there had been failure to comply with notice requirements so as to enable the exercise of voting rights.

In *Kapoor v National Westminster Bank plc* [2011] EWCA Civ 1083; [2011] B.P.I.R. 1680 the Court of Appeal indicated that material irregularity could be understood in a wide sense and could encompass an uncommercial equitable assignment of a debt in order to generate artificial voting rights. That said, there was no rule as such banning an equitable assignee of a debt from exercising voting rights. For discussion of the assignment issue in this case see Turner [2012] 71 C.L.J. 270.

In *Revenue and Customs Commissioners v Earley* [2011] EWHC 1783 (Ch); [2011] B.P.I.R. 1590 the High Court set aside an IVA approval where the revenue authorities, who were owed more than 50 per cent of the debt, had been prevented from exercising their proper voting rights—this was found to be a material irregularity.

For a successful challenge to an IVA on the basis of s.262(1)(b) see *National Westminster Bank plc v Yadgaroff* [2011] EWHC 3711 (Ch) where Norris J held that there had been a material irregularity in that a creditor with an unascertained claim had been allowed to vote for too high a sum.

In *CFL Finance Ltd v Rubin; Re Gertner* [2017] EWHC 111 (Ch); [2017] B.P.I.R. 336 an IVA approval was revoked on the grounds of material irregularity in terms of determination of entitlement to voting rights. The duty of good faith between IVA creditors was stressed. HHJ Keyser QC rejected an argument based upon unfair prejudice.

Unless there has been a successful challenge under this section, irregularities will not invalidate the scheme—see s.262(8).

The 28-day time limit for applications under s.262 arguably only applied where the IVA is preceded by an interim order. The 28-day limit is applied more generally by amendment of subs.(3) by SBEEA 2015 s.134.

The 28-day period for challenge can be extended: *Tager v Westpac Banking Corp* [1998] B.C.C. 73. In *Tanner v Everitt* [2004] EWHC 1130 (Ch); [2004] B.P.I.R. 1026 the court indicated that there might be some flexibility with regard to challenges outside the 28 day limit but that did not extend to an attempt to use s.262 some 13 years after the event!

Warren J considered various aspects of the s.262 jurisdiction in *Re Timothy* [2005] EWHC (Ch); [2005] B.P.I.R. 329. An application made under s.376 of the IA 1986 to extend time for a s.262 application was rejected because of an unjustifiable 9 month delay after the IVA was agreed. It was important that parties to an IVA feel reassured that it not be set aside out of time. Moreover, the underlying complaint of unfair prejudice, although arguable, was not bound to succeed.

For the effect of s.262(8) see *Re Forstater* [2015] B.P.I.R. 21 where the point was made by Registrar Derrett that this subsection can only operate if there was a valid meeting in existence.

S.262(4)–(7)

These provisions outline what the court may do where a scheme is challenged. It may revoke or suspend the approval or call for further meetings to be held—i.e. to reconsider the proposals or to consider revised proposals. If the debtor does not intend to put revised proposals the court can simply revoke or suspend its support for the scheme, although it can direct the interim relief to continue and also make supplementary directions. The court refused to give a direction under s.262(4)(b) for a further meeting in *Re A Debtor (No.101 of 1999) (No.2)* [2001] B.P.I.R. 996. See also *Monecor (London) Ltd v Ahmed* [2008] B.P.I.R. 458. Note also the unusual case of *Davis v Price* [2013] EWHC 323 (Ch); [2013] B.P.I.R. 200 (David Richards J). On appeal (*Price v Davis* [2014] EWCA Civ 26) the Court of Appeal upheld the ruling of David Richards J in his interpretation of the binding effect of an IVA which had been suspended and then reinstated by a further vote. Creditors whose rights crystallised after the first vote were entitled to vote at the later meeting and if they chose not to vote they would be bound by the IVA.

On the meaning of "further meeting" within s.262(4)(b) see the comments of Arden LJ in *Price v Davis* [2014] EWCA Civ 26 at [44]. On directions under s.262(7) see *Inland Revenue Commissioners v Duce* [1999] B.P.I.R. 189. For the scope of the jurisdiction under s.262(7) see *Re a Debtor (No.83 of 1988)* [1990] 1 W.L.R. 708. On revoking see *Re Cardona* [1997] B.C.C. 697.

On s.262 and the possibility of freestanding claims outside the provision see the discussion in *Zelouf v Khanna* [2016] B.P.I.R. 1288.

262A False representations etc.

262A(1) [Offence] If for the purpose of obtaining the approval of his creditors to a proposal for a voluntary arrangement, the debtor–

(a) makes any false representation, or

(b) fraudulently does, or omits to do, anything,

he commits an offence.

262A(2) [Unapproved proposal] Subsection (1) applies even if the proposal is not approved.

262A(3) [Penalty] A person guilty of an offence under this section is liable to imprisonment or a fine, or both.

General Note

Introduced by IA 2000 s.3 and Sch.3 with effect from 1 January 2003, this new provision seeks to introduce a new sanction for those debtors who make false representations to seek creditor approval for a voluntary arrangement. Debtors do need to take this provision seriously as prosecutions have been recorded.

S.262A(1), (2)
These define the extent of the offence—the fact that the IVA is voted down by creditors is immaterial. See the note to s.6A.

S.262A(3)
The sanction is hereby specified, though details of this can only be discovered by reference to Sch.10.

262B Prosecution of delinquent debtors

262B(1) [Application] This section applies where a voluntary arrangement approved by a decision of the debtor's creditors pursuant to section 257 has taken effect.

262B(2) [Whistleblowing obligation] If it appears to the nominee or supervisor that the debtor has been guilty of any offence in connection with the arrangement for which he is criminally liable, he shall forthwith–

(a) report the matter to the Secretary of State, and

(b) provide the Secretary of State with such information and give the Secretary of State such access to and facilities for inspecting and taking copies of documents (being information or documents in his possession or under his control and relating to the matter in question) as the Secretary of State requires.

262B(3) [Consequences] Where a prosecuting authority institutes criminal proceedings following any report under subsection (2), the nominee or, as the case may be, supervisor shall give the authority all assistance in connection with the prosecution which he is reasonably able to give.

For this purpose, "prosecuting authority" means the Director of Public Prosecutions or the Secretary of State.

262B(4) [Power of court] The court may, on the application of the prosecuting authority, direct a nominee or supervisor to comply with subsection (3) if he has failed to do so.

General Note

This again reflects a desire to combat IVA abuse by imposing a "whistleblowing" obligation on the nominee/supervisor.

Note amendment made by SBEEA 2015 s.126 and Sch.9 para.70 to reflect broader creditor decision procedures.

S.262B(1)
This indicates the applicability of this section.

S.262B(2)

The details of the whistleblowing obligation are specified. For procedures on reporting suspected criminality see *Dear IP*, December 2007.

S.262B(3), (4)

These deal with consequential matters where a prosecution of a debtor is instituted in the wake of a report made under subs.(2).

262C Arrangements coming to an end prematurely

262C For the purposes of this Part, a voluntary arrangement approved by a decision of the debtor's creditors pursuant to section 257 comes to an end prematurely if, when it ceases to have effect, it has not been fully implemented in respect of all persons bound by the arrangement by virtue of section 260(2)(b)(i).

General Note

This explains when an IVA can be said to come to an end prematurely. This new provision was inserted by IA 2000 s.3 and Sch.3 with effect from 1 January 2003. Its importance can be gleaned by reference to s.260(2A).

This provision was subject to amendment by SBEEA 2015 s.126 and Sch.9 para.71.

263 Implementation and supervision of approved voluntary arrangement

263(1) [Application] This section applies where a voluntary arrangement approved by a decision of the debtor's creditors pursuant to section 257 has taken effect.

263(2) [Supervisor of voluntary arrangement] The person who is for the time being carrying out, in relation to the voluntary arrangement, the functions conferred by virtue of the approval on the nominee (or his replacement under section 256(3), 256A(4) or 258(3)) shall be known as the supervisor of the voluntary arrangement.

263(3) [Application to court re actions of supervisor] If the debtor, any of his creditors or any other person is dissatisfied by any act, omission or decision of the supervisor, he may apply to the court; and on such an application the court may–

(a) confirm, reverse or modify any act or decision of the supervisor,

(b) give him directions, or

(c) make such other order as it thinks fit.

263(4) [Application for directions] The supervisor may apply to the court for directions in relation to any particular matter arising under the voluntary arrangement.

263(5) [Court may fill supervisor vacancy etc.] The court may, whenever–

(a) it is expedient to appoint a person to carry out the functions of the supervisor, and

(b) it is inexpedient, difficult or impracticable for an appointment to be made without the assistance of the court,

make an order appointing a person who is qualified to act as an insolvency practitioner or authorised to act as supervisor, in relation to the voluntary arrangement, either in substitution for the existing supervisor or to fill a vacancy.

263(6) [Exercise of s.263(5) power] The power conferred by subsection (5) is exercisable so as to increase the number of persons exercising the functions of the supervisor or, where there is more than one person exercising those functions, so as to replace one or more of those persons.

General Note

Minor textual amendments were made to s.263(3) and (5) by IA 2000 s.3 and Sch.3. In s.263(5) the amendment reflects the possibility of non-IPs in future acting as nominees/supervisors. Note amendment by DA 2015 s.19 and Sch.6.

An amendment will be made to subs.(1) by SBEEA 2015 s.126 and Sch.9 para.72.

S.263(1), (2)

Once the scheme has taken effect the "nominee" will be transformed into the "supervisor" of the composition or scheme. On the standards of competence expected of the nominee/supervisor see *Heritage Joinery v Krasner* [1999] B.P.I.R. 683; and *Pitt v Mond* [2001] B.P.I.R. 624. Compare *Harmony Carpets v Chaffin-Laird* [2000] B.P.I.R. 61. On the need for the insolvency practitioner to maintain independence see the comments of Jacob LJ in *Smurthwaite v Simpson-Smith* [2006] B.P.I.R. 1504 at 1524 ([33]).

An IVA supervisor is not technically an officer of the court—*Masters v Furber* [2013] EWHC 3023 (Ch) at [11] per HHJ Purle QC.

S.263(3)

This allows for the court to interfere with decisions of the supervisor which have been objected to. Compare IA 1986 s.303(1). For an application that failed largely on procedural grounds see *Timmins v Conn* [2004] EWCA Civ 1761; [2005] B.P.I.R. 647. For a direction under para.(b) see *Ing Lease (UK) Ltd v Griswold* [1998] B.C.C. 905. Creditors have no private rights of action outside s.263 to enforce a supervisor's duties—*King v Anthony* [1999] B.P.I.R. 73. In *Timmins v Conn* [2004] EWCA Civ 1761; [2005] B.P.I.R. 647 the Court of Appeal on an application by a creditor under s.263(3) had to grapple with the difficulties in interpreting IVA terms, and in particular with whether certain assets (the debtor's interest in the family home) had been excluded from the IVA. The Court of Appeal concluded that the debtor's share in the family home had formed part of the IVA assets from the outset. The suggestion that it had been formally excluded by the supervisor did not stand up. As this share in the family home had not been realised it could not be said that the IVA had been successfully completed. However, the court could not grant the applicant a declaration to the above effect as it would impact upon the debtor who was not a party to the proceedings. The case is therefore of some procedural significance. The court felt unable to make a compensation order against the supervisor partly because it would be impossible to quantify damage as the unrealised asset in question might still be traceable.

See the comments of the court in *Linfoot v Adamson* [2012] EWHC Misc 16 (CC); [2012] B.P.I.R. 1033 as to the reluctance of the court to interfere with the actions of a supervisor on an application under s.263. HHJ Behrens made the connection with the judicial approach to challenges to the conduct of a trustee in bankruptcy launched under s.303.

See *Stericker v Horner* [2012] B.P.I.R. 645 at [38] on the potential limitations of the jurisdiction under s.263(3).

S.263(4)

The supervisor may apply to the court for directions, as can a trustee in bankruptcy under IA 1986 s.303(2). For an example see *Re a Debtor (No.638 IO of 1994), The Times*, 3 December 1998; and *Horrocks v Broome* [1999] B.P.I.R. 66. This power to seek directions does not authorise the court to vary the IVA—*Re Alpa Lighting Ltd* [1997] B.P.I.R. 341; *Raja v Rubin* [1999] B.P.I.R. 575. On s.263(4) see *Re A Block Transfer by Kaye and Morgan* [2010] B.P.I.R. 602. On an application for directions the court has no power to vary the terms of an IVA.

S.263(5), (6)

The court can fill vacancies, appoint substitutes or increase the number of supervisors. On this jurisdiction see *Re Bridgend Goldsmiths* [1995] B.C.C. 226 (a questionable authority); *Re Bullard & Taplin* [1996] B.C.C. 973; *Re Stella Metals Ltd* [1997] B.C.C. 626 (professional body can apply for replacement where original appointee ceases to be qualified); *Re Abbott* [1997] B.C.C. 666 (original appointment made by county court therefore case had to be transferred High Court to enable it to replace); and *Clements v Udal* [2001] B.P.I.R. 454.

For further provisions on the implementation of the voluntary arrangement and the role of the supervisor, see IR 2016 rr.8.25, 8.26, 8.29 and 8.31. Note that an IVA may expire automatically by effluxion of time—*Strongmaster Ltd v Kaye* [2002] EWHC 444 (Ch); [2002] B.P.I.R. 1259.

It is disappointing that the IVA legislation does not address the scenario where an IVA established under Pt VIII of IA 1986 fails and the debtor is declared bankrupt. We are told by s.264(1)(c) that a supervisor may present a bankruptcy petition but bankruptcy may occur in other circumstances—e.g. by default towards post-IVA creditors. What is the impact of bankruptcy upon the earlier IVA? More importantly, what happens to the funds collected by the IVA supervisor—are they reserved exclusively for the IVA participants or can they be claimed by the trustee in bankruptcy for the benefit of the creditors at large? The case law here is voluminous: *Re McKeen* [1995] B.C.C. 412 (Morritt J); *Re Bradley-Hole* [1995] 1 W.L.R. 1097 (Rimer J); *Davis v Martin-Sklan* [1995] 2 B.C.L.C. 483 (Blackburne J); *Kings v Cleghorn* [1998] B.P.I.R. 463 (HHJ Behrens); and *Re Coath* [2000] B.P.I.R. 981 (DJ Field). A useful analysis of some of the earlier of these authorities is provided by Bailey in [1995–96] 2 R.A.L.Q. 87 and

Walton [1997–98] 3 R.A.L.Q. 277. Some clarity in the law has now been introduced by the Court of Appeal ruling in *Re N.T. Gallagher & Son Ltd* [2002] EWCA Civ 404. Although this case is concerned with CVAs the principles developed in that case were expressly intended to apply mutatis mutandis to IVAs. In short it is clear that an IVA may survive subsequent bankruptcy and that funds collected by the supervisor may be retained and kept out of the hands of the trustee in bankruptcy. The IVA documentation will be important here. For a full discussion of these principles see note to s.7 above.

Fast-track voluntary arrangement

263A Availability [Omitted]

263B Decision [Omitted]

263C Result [Omitted]

263D Approval of voluntary arrangement [Omitted]

263E Implementation [Omitted]

263F Revocation [Omitted]

263G Offences [Omitted]

Editors' note: Sections 263A–263G were omitted by SBEEA 2015 s.135. The fast track IVA scheme provided for by these provisions was misconceived and little used.

Part IX

Bankruptcy

Introductory note to Part IX
Before embarking upon the analysis of the provisions of IA 1986 with regard to bankruptcy a caveat ought to be issued with regard to usage of statutory predecessors. Where this is appropriate the legislative origins of particular provisions are identified in the following text. However, care must be taken in handling these former provisions (which are largely from BA 1914) for it is now clear that the courts are minded to interpret the bankruptcy sections of IA 1986 in their own light and are not necessarily going to take advantage of earlier interpretations of similar provisions in the 1914 Act. Thus in *Re a Debtor (No.1 of 1987)* [1989] 1 W.L.R. 271, a leading case on statutory demands, Nicholls LJ declared:

> "I do not think that on this the new bankruptcy code simply incorporates and adopts the same approach as the old code. The new code has made many changes in the law of bankruptcy, and the court's task, with regard to the new code, must be to construe the new statutory provisions in accordance with the ordinary canons of construction, unfettered by previous authorities." (ibid., at 276.)

More recently in the House of Lords' ruling in *Smith v Braintree District Council* [1990] 2 A.C. 215, which was concerned with the interpretation of IA 1986 s.285, Lord Jauncey (at 237–238) reinforced this view on the modus operandi of interpretation:

> "… the Act of 1986, although re-enacting many provisions from earlier statutes, contains a good deal of fresh material derived from the Insolvency Act 1985. In particular, the legislation now emphasises the importance of the rehabilitation of the individual insolvent, it provides for automatic discharge from bankruptcy in many cases, and it abolishes mandatory public examinations as well as enabling a bankrupt to be discharged without public examination. Thus not only has the legislative approach to individual bankruptcy altered since the mid-19th century, but social views as to what conduct involves delinquency, as to punishment and as to the desirability of

imprisonment have drastically changed … In these circumstances, I feel justified in construing section 285 of the Act of 1986 as a piece of new legislation without regard to 19th century authorities or similar provisions of repealed Bankruptcy Acts …".

See also *Official Receiver v McKay* [2009] B.P.I.R. 1061 where the Court of Appeal discarded an old precedent on annulment. See also *Sands and Treharne v Wright* [2010] B.P.I.R. 1437 where the dangers of placing reliance on old precedents were again highlighted. The fact that the new bankruptcy regime differs from the 1914 model in terms of the initiation procedure is so obvious that there is no need for the court to use *Hansard* to elucidate the point—*Shrimpton v Darbys Solicitors LLP* [2011] EWHC 3796 (Ch) at [38].

These are important statements of principle that should be borne in mind when trying to attach meaning to the new statutory provisions in bankruptcy law. Having said that, there are instances where pre-1985 law has been important and therefore generalisations must be treated with caution.

It should also be borne in mind that there are significant principles of common law in bankruptcy which have never been embodied in legislation. For example the rule against double proof and the curious duty imposed on trustees to act honourably as devised in *Ex p. James* (1874) L.R. 9 Ch. App. 609, which for once was applied in *Patel v Jones* [2001] B.P.I.R. 919. However, increasingly courts permit trustees to act so as to maximise returns to creditors even where they may be viewed as taking advantage—see the comparable Scottish authority of *Burnett's Trustee v Grainger* [2004] UKHL 8; [2004] S.L.T. 513. For recent discussion of the rule in *Ex p. James* (1873–74) L.R. 9 Ch. App. 609 and its application to trustees in bankruptcy see *Bank of Baroda v Patel* [2009] B.P.I.R. 255. For an up to date review of the principle in *Ex p. James* (above) see *Re Young* [2017] B.P.I.R. 1116. The rule in *Ex p. James* cannot be applied to a court officer appointed by a foreign court—*Glasgow (Bankruptcy Trustee of Harlequin Property Svg) v ELS Law Ltd* [2017] EWHC 3004 (Ch). Presumably, such application is however possible if the foreign court requests it. On the rule against double proof see *Re Kaupthing Singer & Freidlander Ltd* [2011] UKSC 48. Another example of a common law rule that applies to both bankruptcy and corporate insolvency is the anti-avoidance principle designed to protect the insolvent estate—see the full discussion of the current status of this rule in *Belmont Park Investments Pty Ltd v BNY Corporate Trustee Services Ltd* [2011] UKSC 38; [2011] B.P.I.R. 1223.

The similarities/differences between governing principles of personal and corporate insolvency law are well illuminated by the judgment of David Richards J in *Re T & N Ltd* [2005] EWHC 2870 (Ch); [2006] B.P.I.R. 532. In discussing the different rules relating to proof of debt by future tort claimants (for bankrupts s.382 of the Act and for companies IR 1986 r.13.12) the judge concluded that the principle of disallowing proof was the same for both cases, but for companies the social consequences of applying the principle were more serious by virtue of the fact that for an insolvent company liquidation was the end of the matter, whereas for an individual the possibility of pursuing the claim after discharge of the bankrupt was real. At the end of the day IR 1986 r.13.12 was amended by SI 2006/1272 to allow future tort claims to be proved on corporate insolvency whereas s.382 has remained unamended for the present. In IR 2016 the comparable provision is located in r.14.1. A substantive difference has thus emerged, though in view of the point made by David Richards J that difference may in this instance be justified. There are still significant differences between the bankruptcy and winding up procedures; for instance, bankruptcy petitions are not advertised as such.

It should be remembered that in addition to the Act and the Rules and the underlying common law, there are a number of relevant practice directions governing bankruptcy cases. Some of these are referred to in connection with the relevant legislative provisions. Most, however, have now been overtaken by the *Practice Direction: Insolvency Proceedings* [2018] B.C.C. 241 (reproduced as App.IV to this *Guide*). A case of general significance in bankruptcy litigation is *Hocking v Walker* [1997] B.P.I.R. 93, where the Court of Appeal held that a bankrupt may be required to give security for costs when appealing against a bankruptcy order. CPR Practice Direction 70 can apply to bankruptcy proceedings—*Kommalage v Sayanthakumar* [2015] EWCA Civ 1832; [2015] B.P.I.R. 836.

The provisions in Pt IX of IA 1986 have been substantially amended by Pt 10 of EA 2002. Most of these changes took effect in April 2004. Transitional provisions are contained in s.256 of and Sch.19 to EA 2002. The purpose of these amending provisions was to liberalise bankruptcy law in this country. The thinking behind this reform was that by removing some of the unpleasantness associated with business failure individuals would be more inclined to undertake entrepreneurial risk. The problem with this reasoning is that the majority of bankrupts these days are consumer debtors taking no part whatsoever in the risks associated with trade. Having said that, consumer credit is now a key feature of our economy and any government is naturally concerned with the downside of such an economic facility deemed so vital to the health of the national economy. The 2002 Act changes bankruptcy topography in a number of ways. First, automatic discharge is now available after a maximum of one year (EA 2002 s.256). Official receivers will no longer be subject to a statutory obligation to investigate the causes of every bankruptcy (EA 2002 s.258). Disqualifications imposed on bankrupts are relaxed in a variety of ways (see EA 2002 ss.265–268). Certain bankruptcy offences are decriminalised (EA 2002 s.263). The rights of bankrupts and their families over the home are further strengthened by requiring a trustee to take firm action within three years or lose entitlement to this major asset (s.261). To compensate for these changes the concept of a bankruptcy restriction order (or undertaking) is introduced to deal with those bankrupts whose conduct is not beyond reproach (s.257 and Schs 20, 21). Other changes introduced by the 2002 Act include reforms to the income payments regime (ss.259, 260). Further changes have been made by ERRA 2013, DA 2015 and SBEEA 2015. Each of these reforms will be considered below at the appropriate statutory point in the amended 1986 Act.

Illuminating details of the profile of the modern bankrupt are contained in an Insolvency Service report, *The Characteristics of a Bankrupt* (March 2006—see IS Press Notice, 27 March 2006 for a summary). From this we learn that the average age of a bankrupt is falling (to age 41 at present). Male bankrupts still predominate, but the female population of bankrupts is growing. The proportion of bankrupts aged under 30 is nearly 19 per cent and rising. Another recommended source of data and insights is the *Bankruptcy Courts Survey*, a pilot study carried out in 2005 for the Insolvency Service by John Tribe of the Centre for Insolvency Law and Policy at Kingston University, details of which are available on the Insolvency Service website under "Insolvency Research" (personal research resources) section—for comment see editorial, (2006) 22 I.L. & P. 1.

The long term future of bankruptcy as the premier legal institution for dealing with personal insolvency is in question. Apart from the increasing significance of IVAs (which now comprise the majority of all personal insolvencies) the advent of debt relief orders and other debt-related procedures under the Tribunals, Courts and Enforcement Act 2007 is likely to have a significant impact on bankruptcy usage, though the precise timescale for the introduction of these new procedures is still unpredictable.

The huge increase in self generated bankruptcies by means of debtor petitions has led to a rethink on whether such largely uncontested cases should be taken out of the court system—see Insolvency Service Consultative Document (October 2007) entitled "*Bankruptcy: Proposals for Reform of the Debtor Petition Process*". In November 2011 the Insolvency Service repeated this proposal and extended it to undisputed *creditor* petitions. The original suggestion that the new out of court adjudication procedure should also be extended to uncontested creditor petitions attracted a fierce response—see S. Baister and F. Toube [2012] 25 Insolv. Int. 49. As a result in October 2012 the government agreed upon a more limited reform and the reforms outlined in ERRA 2013 are restricted to debtor petitions in bankruptcy. These changes took effect in April 2016.

The Scottish Government on 24 February 2012, commenced an exercise, Consultation on Bankruptcy Law Reform, including proposals for debt relief and also removing the court from non-contentious creditor bankruptcy petitions, seeking comments by 18 May 2012. In a response to this consultation exercise the Scottish government announced in November 2012 announced that it was planning significant reforms in Scottish personal insolvency law, including reforms designed to take debtor petitions in bankruptcy out of the court system. We await the formal tabling of legislation to this effect. The Scottish Law Commission published its proposals for bankruptcy reform in May 2013. See Scottish Law Commission Report No.232—"Report on the Consolidation of Bankruptcy Legislation in Scotland". The Bankruptcy (Scotland) Act 2016 represents a significant step forward. This major piece of legislation consisting of 238 sections and 9 schedules reconsolidates personal insolvency law in Scotland by replacing provisions scattered in a number of Acts (including the Bankruptcy (Scotland) Act 1985 and the discrete statutes dealing with debt arrangements and home owner protection) with a single statute laid down in user-friendly fashion.

For a general overview of modern developments in bankruptcy and personal insolvency law in the context of an enterprise-driven economy see Milman (2008) 20 Singapore Academy of Law Journal 438.

The English courts have said that art.6 ECHR has no relevance to delay in the completion of the bankruptcy process by the trustee as that administrative process does not itself determine the civil rights of the bankrupt—*Holtham v Kelmanson* [2006] EWHC 2588 (Ch); [2006] B.P.I.R. 1422, *Foyle v Turner* [2007] B.P.I.R. 43. But one interpretation of *Skurcak v Slovakia* [2007] B.P.I.R. 440 might be to suggest that the matter is not entirely free of doubt. Much may depend upon the operation of the particular bankruptcy regime operating in each adhering State. In *Adeosun v Revenue and Customs Commissioners* [2011] EWHC 1577 (Ch); [2011] B.P.I.R. 1555—an attempt to challenge bankruptcy under ECHR art.6 failed as the court (Vos J) held it was a proportionate remedy in the circumstances of the case. A challenge based upon ECHR art.1 of the First Protocol failed in *Shrimpton v Darbys Solicitors LLP* [2011] EWHC 3796 (Ch) at [40].

A properly made bankruptcy order does not infringe art.1 of the First Protocol of ECHR—see David Richards J in *Shrimpton v Darbys Solicitors LLP* [2011] EWHC 3796 (Ch); [2012] B.P.I.R. 631 at [40]. An art.6 argument also failed in *Re Foster* [2012] EWHC 275 (Ch); [2012] B.P.I.R. 545. The potential impact of a number of provisions in ECHR was considered by Deeny J in *Official Receiver for Northern Ireland v O'Brien* [2012] NICh 12; [2012] B.P.I.R. 826. The provisions in arts 6, 8 and 1 of the First Protocol could not be considered in isolation. In sales of family property the rights of the non bankrupt spouse under art.8 were particularly important.

Professional stigma can still attach to bankruptcy—see *Dowland v Architects Registration Board* [2013] EWHC 893 (Admin); [2013] B.P.I.R. 566. See also *Moseley v SRA* [2013] EWHC 2108 (Admin); [2013] B.P.I.R. 855. For the impact of bankruptcy on the professional responsibilities of a solicitor see *Bell v Bircham* [2015] EWHC 1541 (Ch); [2015] B.P.I.R. 751.

As IVAs and DROs grow in popularity, bankruptcy is now the least popular of the three formal personal insolvency regimes.

Chapter AI

Adjudicators: Bankruptcy Applications by Debtors and Bankruptcy Orders

Introductory note to Chapter A1

Activated by of ERRA 2013 s.71 and brought into force from 6 April 2016 by Commencement Order No.9 (SI 2016/191), this introduces a new bankruptcy procedure for debtors. It avoids the waste of resources involved in requiring debtors to present a petition to court to procure their own bankruptcy where in most cases the petition will be unopposed, and instead substitutes an out of court adjudication procedure operated by a new cadre of "adjudicators" appointed by the Secretary of State under s.398A. Official receivers are debarred from holding office as an adjudicator. The new procedure will not apply to bankruptcy proceedings commenced by debtors prior to 6 April 2016—practitioners would be well advised to retain their copies of the 18th edition of the *Annotated Guide to Insolvency Legislation* for the immediate future.

New ss.263H–263O are introduced into the Insolvency Act 1986. These sections deal with jurisdictional matters, the adjudication procedure and appeal rights. Other sections in the 1986 Act are deleted as redundant. Many other sections of the 1986 Act suffer consequential amendment—these are itemised in ERRA 2013 Sch.19. Other legislation will experience consequential amendment in the light of the advent of this new procedure—see the Enterprise and Regulatory Reform Act 2013 (Consequential Amendments) (Bankruptcy) and the Small Business, Enterprise and Employment Act 2015 (Consequential Amendments) Regulations 2016 (SI 2016/481).

As part of this package of reforms we have to take account of the Insolvency (Amendment) Rules 2016 (SI 2016/187). These introduced new rr.6.37–6.50B into IR 1986 and also made many consequential reforms. These Amendment Rules were purely interim in nature: they were superseded when the general reconsolidation of the Insolvency Rules 1986 took place via the Insolvency (England and Wales) Rules 2016 (SI 2016/1024) (see IR 2016 rr.10.24–10.56). Financial matters relating to this new bankruptcy adjudication procedure are covered by the Insolvency Proceedings (Fees) Order 2016 (SI 2016/692). The adjudicator's administration fee is £130. The administration fee of the official receiver is £1,990.

See *Re Budniok* [2017] B.P.I.R. 521.

263H Bankruptcy applications to an adjudicator

263H(1) [Application by individual] An individual may make an application to an adjudicator in accordance with this Chapter for a bankruptcy order to be made against him or her.

263H(2) [Ground for application inability to pay debts] An individual may make a bankruptcy application only on the ground that the individual is unable to pay his or her debts.

General Note

This identifies the new adjudication procedure to be used by debtors who are unable to pay their debts. Note the procedure for the opening of a file on the application—see IR 2016 r.10.47. The debtor intending to make an application can apply to the court to protect his privacy in respect of his home address—see the procedure mapped out in IR 2016 r.20.5. On the appropriate court see IR 2016 r.10.48.

263I Debtors against whom an adjudicator may make a bankruptcy order

263I(1) [Jurisdiction] An adjudicator has jurisdiction to determine a bankruptcy application only if–

(a) the centre of the debtor's main interests is in England and Wales, or

(b) the centre of the debtor's main interests is not in a member state of the European Union which has adopted the EU Regulation, but the test in subsection (2) is met.

263I(2) [Test for jurisdiction] The test is that–

(a) the debtor is domiciled in England and Wales, or

(b) at any time in the period of three years ending with the day on which the application is made to the adjudicator, the debtor–

(i) has been ordinarily resident, or has had a place of residence, in England and Wales, or

(ii) has carried on business in England and Wales.

263I(3) [Debtor carrying on business] The reference in subsection (2) to the debtor carrying on business includes–

(a) the carrying on of business by a firm or partnership of which the debtor is a member, and

(b) the carrying on of business by an agent or manager for the debtor or for such a firm or partnership.

263I(4) [Meaning of centre of main interests] In this section, references to the centre of the debtor's main interests have the same meaning as in Article 3 of the EU Regulation.

General Note

This determines jurisdictional criteria for the use of the adjudication procedure. Note the linkage with the revised s.265, which in future will only apply to creditor petitions. In *Re Budniok* [2017] EWHC 368 (Ch); [2017] B.P.I.R. 521 the adjudicator said COMI not established on the evidence to found bankruptcy but on appeal Chief Registrar Baister came to a different conclusion. It is interesting that the "personally present" qualification found in the former s.265(1)(b) and used to access bankruptcy is no longer available. This might affect bankruptcy tourism.

Many of the cases on COMI determined under the now repealed s.272 will retain some value for the purposes of s.263I—they are therefore noted below. Section 263I(1)(b), (4) amended by the Insolvency Amendment (EU 2015/848) Regulations 2017 (SI 2017/702) regs 1, 2(1), Sch. paras 1, 18 in relation to proceedings opened on or after 26 June 2017 (see reg.3) when the Recast EU Regulation 2015/848 came into force.

For further indications of caution on the part of the courts towards debtor petitions presented by debtors who have recently arrived on our shores see *OR v Mitterfellner* [2009] B.P.I.R. 1075 and *Re Hagemeister* [2010] B.P.I.R. 1093. The courts will only accede to such self-generated bankruptcies if there has been a genuine transfer of the centre of main interests for the purposes of EC Regulation 1346/2000. Chief Registrar Baister reviewed this group of authorities in *Re Eichler (No.2)* [2011] B.P.I.R. 1293 and once again set aside a bankruptcy order that had been obtained by a German debtor several years previously in 2007 (see [2007] B.P.I.R. 1636). The evidence did not show that the debtor had COMI within the jurisdiction at the relevant time. Chief Registrar Baister explained how the English courts were dealing with the issue of what might loosely be termed as "bankruptcy tourists".

In *Irish Bank Resolution Corp Ltd v Quinn* [2012] NICh 1 the bankruptcy of a high profile figure was set aside on the grounds that the evidence did not show the presence of COMI in Northern Ireland. Deeny J in an obiter part of the judgment also made comments about possible non-disclosure of information pertaining to the COMI of that individual at the relevant time when the bankruptcy order was made in Northern Ireland. For a contested debtor's petition see *O'Mahony v National Irish Bank* [2012] B.P.I.R. 1174 where the challenge to the debtor's petition, alleging a lack of jurisdiction, failed, as the evidence supported the debtor's contention that his COMI was located within the English jurisdiction. But see also *Eck v Zapf* [2012] B.P.I.R. 499—petition dismissed as debtor had failed to discharge burden of proof that his COMI was within the jurisdiction.

Note *O'Donnell v Bank of Ireland* [2012] EWHC 3749 (Ch); [2013] B.P.I.R. 509 where Newey J held after a seven day trial of contested debtors' petitions that the debtors did not have COMI within the jurisdiction. This conclusion was reinforced when Newey J dismissed the subsequent s.375 application seeking a review of his earlier decision—see [2013] EWHC 489 (Ch); [2013] B.P.I.R. 1078. The point was made that the prospects of succeeding under s.375 in the wake of a contested hearing with cross examination were slim. See also *Schrade v Sparkasse Ludenscheid* [2013] B.P.I.R. 911 where Chief Registrar Baister refused to make a bankruptcy order on the grounds of lack of jurisdiction (COMI was in Germany) and the failure to make full disclosure in the petition. An appeal from this refusal of a bankruptcy order was dismissed by Alan Steinfeld QC (sitting as a judge of the High Court) ([2014] B.P.I.R. 1058). The Chief Registrar could not be shown to have erred in determining COMI and was correct in not adjourning the hearing to allow the debtor petitioner to correct deficiencies in the paperwork submitted by the debtor. A contested debtor's petition was also dismissed in *Kane v Revenue Commissioners* [2013] NIMaster 17 both on the grounds of a lack of COMI and because it was viewed as an abuse of process. Compare *Re Brehm* [2014] B.P.I.R. 359

where Chief Registrar Baister concluded that the balance of the evidence supported the view that the debtor had COMI in England at the date of the bankruptcy petition. COMI was established by the petitioning debtor in *Doyle v Quinn* [2015] B.P.I.R. 226. Chief Registrar Baister noted that a debtor could only have one COMI and that COMI could be relocated—the critical question was the location of COMI at the date of the bankruptcy petition. A debtor petition was successfully resisted by a creditor in *Browne v Mavroudis* [2014] NIMaster 18 on grounds of lack of COMI and of non-disclosure. For a useful case decided under the previous statutory provision see *Re Muldoon* [2016] NIMaster 5. Here a debtor petition in bankruptcy was unsuccessful because of the lack of COMI in Northern Ireland. See *Re Macari* [2017] NICh 5 where the evidence suggested that the debtor's COMI was now in Northern Ireland and not in the Republic of Ireland, where the debtor had previously been based.

263J Conditions applying to bankruptcy application

263J(1) [Contents of application] A bankruptcy application must include–

(a) such particulars of the debtor's creditors, debts and other liabilities, and assets, as may be prescribed, and

(b) such other information as may be prescribed.

263J(2) [Fee or deposit payable] A bankruptcy application is not to be regarded as having been made unless any fee or deposit required in connection with the application by an order under section 415 has been paid to such person, and within such period, as may be prescribed.

263J(3) [No withdrawal] A bankruptcy application may not be withdrawn.

263J(4) [Debtor duty of notification to adjudicator] A debtor must notify the adjudicator if, at any time before a bankruptcy order is made against the debtor or the adjudicator refuses to make such an order–

(a) the debtor becomes able to pay his or her debts, or

(b) a bankruptcy petition has been presented to the court in relation to the debtor.

General Note

This section identifies preconditions, particularly with regard to information requirements. Details of fee and deposit are to be found in the Insolvency Proceedings Fees Order 2016 (SI 2016/692). Note that once made the application cannot be withdrawn (subs.(3)). If a creditor petitions for the bankruptcy of the debtor the onus is on the debtor to notify the adjudicator (subs.(4)).

263K Determination of bankruptcy application

263K(1) [Requirements for adjudicator's determination] After receiving a bankruptcy application, an adjudicator must determine whether the following requirements are met–

(a) the adjudicator had jurisdiction under section 263I to determine the application on the date the application was made,

(b) the debtor is unable to pay his or her debts at the date of the determination,

(c) no bankruptcy petition is pending in relation to the debtor at the date of the determination, and

(d) no bankruptcy order has been made in respect of any of the debts which are the subject of the application at the date of the determination.

263K(2) [Duty of adjudicator to make bankruptcy order] If the adjudicator is satisfied that each of the requirements in subsection (1) are met, the adjudicator must make a bankruptcy order against the debtor.

263K(3) [Duty of adjudicator to refuse bankruptcy order] If the adjudicator is not so satisfied, the adjudicator must refuse to make a bankruptcy order against the debtor.

263K(4) [Prescribed period for determination] The adjudicator must make a bankruptcy order against the debtor or refuse to make such an order before the end of the prescribed period ("the determination period").

General Note

This details the modus operandi of the adjudication process. It is a black and white decision process with very little discretion available to the adjudicator. The adjudicator has 28 days to reach a decision—IR 2016 rr.10.39, 10.40.

263L Adjudicator's requests for further information

263L(1) [Power of adjudicator to request necessary information] An adjudicator may at any time during the determination period request from the debtor information that the adjudicator considers necessary for the purpose of determining whether a bankruptcy order must be made.

263L(2) [Specified date for information] The adjudicator may specify a date before which information requested under subsection (1) must be provided; but that date must not be after the end of the determination period.

263L(3) [Information may be given orally under rules] If the rules so prescribe, a request under subsection (1) may include a request for information to be given orally.

263L(4) [Rules may prescribe persons and circumstances for information] The rules may make provision enabling or requiring an adjudicator to request information from persons of a prescribed description in prescribed circumstances.

General Note

This is a pragmatic provision enabling the adjudicator to be better informed. Doubly important in view of the mechanistic nature of the decision-making process.

263M Making of bankruptcy order

263M(1) [Where bankruptcy order made] This section applies where an adjudicator makes a bankruptcy order as a result of a bankruptcy application.

263M(2) [Prescribed form] The order must be made in the prescribed form.

263M(3) [Copy order to debtor and notice to others] The adjudicator must–

(a) give a copy of the order to the debtor, and

(b) give notice of the order to persons of such description as may be prescribed.

General Note

This formalises one outcome of the adjudication process—the making of the bankruptcy order. For consequential matters see IR 2016 rr.10.45, 10.46.

263N Refusal to make a bankruptcy order: review and appeal etc.

263N(1) [Adjudicator to give notice of reasons for refusal, etc.] Where an adjudicator refuses to make a bankruptcy order on a bankruptcy application, the adjudicator must give notice to the debtor–

(a) giving the reasons for the refusal, and

(b) explaining the effect of subsections (2) to (5).

263N(2) [Debtor may request adjudicator to review information] If requested by the debtor before the end of the prescribed period, the adjudicator must review the information which was available to the adjudicator when the determination that resulted in the refusal was made.

263N(3) [Duty to confirm refusal or make bankruptcy order] Following a review under subsection (2) the adjudicator must–

(a) confirm the refusal to make a bankruptcy order, or

(b) make a bankruptcy order against the debtor.

263N(4) [Adjudicator duty on confirming refusal] Where the adjudicator confirms a refusal under subsection (3), the adjudicator must give notice to the debtor–

(a) giving the reasons for the confirmation, and

(b) explaining the effect of subsection (5).

263N(5) [Debtor right of appeal against confirmed refusal] If the refusal is confirmed under subsection (3), the debtor may appeal against the refusal to the court before the end of the prescribed period.

General Note

If the adjudicator refuses to make a bankruptcy order, the debtor can ask for a review. If on review the adjudicator maintains his position, there is an appeal route to the court. Note IR 2016 rr.10.42–10.44. The relevant court is identified by IR 2016 r.10.48.

On s.263N(5) see the test case of *Re Budniok* [2017] EWHC 368 (Ch); [2017] B.P.I.R. 521 where Chief Registrar Baister overturned a negative COMI determination by the adjudicator. The case provides an excellent review of the new adjudicator system and how it links to the courts. See Watson [2017] 30 Insol. Int. 89 for comment.

263O False representations and omissions

263O(1) [Offence re application or information] It is an offence knowingly or recklessly to make any false representation or omission in–

(a) making a bankruptcy application to an adjudicator, or

(b) providing any information to an adjudicator in connection with a bankruptcy application.

263O(2) [Offence of failure to notify adjudicator as required] It is an offence knowingly or recklessly to fail to notify an adjudicator of a matter in accordance with a requirement imposed by or under this Part.

263O(3) [Immaterial to offence if bankruptcy order made or not] It is immaterial for the purposes of an offence under this section whether or not a bankruptcy order is made as a result of the application.

263O(4) [No defence if anything done outside jurisdiction] It is not a defence in proceedings for an offence under this section that anything relied on, in whole or in part, as constituting the offence was done outside England and Wales.

263O(5) [Proceedings only by Secretary of State or DPP] Proceedings for an offence under this section may only be instituted–

(a) by the Secretary of State, or

(b) by or with the consent of the Director of Public Prosecutions.

General Note

This is a necessary provision designed to protect the integrity of this new insolvency procedure. It has parallels in other insolvency regimes. Note the extraterritorial nature of subs.(4). This could be relevant to bankruptcy tourists.

Chapter I

The Court: Bankruptcy Petitions and Bankruptcy Orders

Introductory note to Part IX, Chapter I

The 1985 Act implemented the recommendation of Cork (*Report*, para.529), that acts of bankruptcy should be abolished. The presentation of a bankruptcy petition is not "an action on a judgment" for the purposes of s.24 of the Limitation Act 1980—*Ridgeway Motors (Isleworth) Ltd v ALTS Ltd* [2005] EWCA Civ 92; [2005] 2 All E.R. 304. But see also *Revenue and Customs Commissioners v Morris* [2007] EWHC 3345 (Ch); [2008] B.P.I.R. 391 where the court held that a bankruptcy petition is an available method of enforcement of obligations arising under EC Council Directive 76/308 (which deals with European agricultural levies and customs).

HMRC can use bankruptcy petitions to recover tax arrears, even though it has no explicit statutory authorisation to do so—see the comments of Lord Walker in *Total Network SL v Revenue and Customs Commissioners* [2008] B.P.I.R. 699. Bankruptcy proceedings cannot be used to unpick tax assessments as there are dedicated procedures to achieve that goal—*Lam v Inland Revenue Commissioners* [2009] B.P.I.R. 301. The same applies to VAT assessments—*Revenue and Customs Commissioners v Chamberlin* [2011] EWCA Civ 271; [2011] B.P.I.R. 691 and *Revenue and Customs Commissioners v Earley* [2011] EWHC 1783 (Ch); [2011] B.P.I.R. 1590. *Lam v Inland Revenue Commissioners* (above) and *Revenue and Customs Commissioners v Chamberlin* (above) were followed in *Vieira v Revenue and Customs Commissioners* [2017] EWHC 936 (Ch); [2017] B.P.I.R. 1062. The court will not go behind a tax assessment even if it is under appeal. See para.11.4.4 of the *Practice Direction: Insolvency Proceedings* [2018] B.C.C. 241. That said, the court does enjoy some limited discretion to adjourn proceedings until the First Tier Tribunal has resolved the appeal. Note also *Hope v Ireland* [2014] EWHC 3854 (Ch) where, albeit in the context of a disputed vote on an IVA, the court upheld the validity of an extant and unappealed VAT assessment, notwithstanding its withdrawal at a much later date.

In a growing number of cases local government ombudsmen have ruled that the mechanistic use of bankruptcy proceedings to collect council tax arrears without regard to the personal circumstances of the debtor or the possibility of using alternative recovery methods could constitute maladministration—see *Ford v Wolverhampton CC* [2008] B.P.I.R. 1304; *Re An Investigation into Complaint 07/A/12661 Against Camden LBC* [2008] B.P.I.R. 1572 and *Report of an Investigation into Complaint 08 002 300 v Exeter CC* [2009] B.P.I.R. 598. These rulings are beginning to have an impact on bankruptcy litigation—see *Hunt v Fylde BC* [2008] B.P.I.R. 1368.

In *Complaint Against Newham LBC* [2010] B.P.I.R. 464 the ombudsman stressed the need for the various departments in the council to talk to each other about vulnerable debtors. In *Complaint 07B10432 Against Manchester City Council* [2010] B.P.I.R. 476 the desirability of having a written policy evaluating the appropriateness of bankruptcy as against alternative debt recovery methods was stressed.

For further significant ombudsman rulings see *Complaint 08014087 Against Brighton and Hove Council* [2010] B.P.I.R. 1407 (lack of communication between different local authority departments) and *Complaint 09006694 Against Thurrock Council* [2010] B.P.I.R. 1420, where the local authority, having come up with an alternative to bankruptcy, was criticised for charging an entry fee for that alternative as there was no legal authority for the levying of such a charge. A further finding of maladministration was made in *Report of an Investigation into Complaint (No.10 002 564) Against Torbay Council* [2011] B.P.I.R. 1098 where it was found that bankruptcy proceedings had been pursued without adequate thought being given to the health of the debtor.

The courts tend to take a more traditional approach towards the question of the use of the bankruptcy procedure to collect council tax arrears. So in *Lonergan v Gedling BC* [2010] B.P.I.R. 911 the Court of Appeal held that there was legal power under the 1992 Regulations to take such action. It also rejected attempts to place reliance upon the European Convention on Human Rights to challenge the use of the bankruptcy jurisdiction by local authorities. See also *Bolsover DC v Ashfield Nominees Ltd* [2010] EWCA Civ 1129; [2011] B.P.I.R. 7.

On costs where the local authority withdraws a bankruptcy petition at the hearing of the petition see *Banfield v Harrow LBC* [2010] EWHC 2707 (Ch); [2011] B.P.I.R. 4 (Lewison J).

For interesting discussion in the EAT on whether bankruptcy proceedings are an appropriate solution towards recovery of unpaid costs incurred in employment tribunal proceedings see *Herry v Dudley Metropolitan Borough Council* [2017] B.P.I.R. 1209. Here there were doubts as to whether the successful employer would recover anything from bankrupting the impecunious employee.

The courts are becoming increasingly irritated by parties to a divorce seeking to use the bankruptcy procedure as a tactical tool—see the comments of the court in *Ella v Ella* [2009] B.P.I.R. 441.

For a useful discussion of the dissemination of information about bankruptcy see *Smeaton v Equifax plc* [2013] EWCA Civ 108.

For a discussion on whether bankruptcy is a natural result of a breach of contract see *Willett v Economy Power Ltd* [2012] EWCA Civ 1164.

The total recorded number of bankruptcies in England and Wales in 2012 was 31,756. This fell to 24,536 in 2013. This figure dropped to 20,318 in 2014, further indicating the decline in usage of bankruptcy. The 2015 total was down to 15,797. The figure for 2016 was 15,044. There is some evidence that the new bankruptcy application procedure may have stabilised the seemingly unstoppable decline in decline in bankruptcy. The 2017 total was 15,082.

Preliminary

264 Who may present a bankruptcy petition

264(1) [Presentation of petition] A petition for a bankruptcy order to be made against an individual may be presented to the court in accordance with the following provisions of this Part–

(a) by one of the individual's creditors or jointly by more than one of them,

(ba) by a temporary administrator (within the meaning of Article 52 of the EU Regulation),

(bb) by an insolvency practitioner (within the meaning of Article 2(5) of the EU Regulation) appointed in proceedings by virtue of Article 3(1) of the EU Regulation,

(c) by the supervisor of, or any person (other than the individual) who is for the time being bound by, a voluntary arrangement proposed by the individual and approved under Part VIII, or

(d) where a criminal bankruptcy order has been made against the individual, by the Official Petitioner or by any person specified in the order in pursuance of section 39(3)(b) of the Powers of Criminal Courts Act 1973.

264(2) [Power of court to make order] Subject to those provisions, the court may make a bankruptcy order on any such petition.

General Note

This section describes the persons who may present a bankruptcy petition and authorises the court to make an order on such a petition. In *Mahmood v Penrose* [2005] B.P.I.R. 170 a petitioner in whose favour a costs award had been made jointly was held to have locus standi for the purposes of s.264(1)(a). Sub-subsections (1)(ba) and (bb) were introduced to cater for the advent of EC Council Regulation 1346/2000 with effect from 31 May 2002 and were amended by the Insolvency Amendment (EU 2015/848) Regulations 2017 (SI 2017/702) regs 1, 2(1), Sch. paras 1, 19 in relation to proceedings opened on or after 26 June 2017 (see reg.3) when the Recast EU Regulation 2015/848 came into force. See also Insolvency Proceedings (Fees) Amendment Order 2005 (SI 2005/544). For the "Official Petitioner" in s.264(1)(d) see s.402. The FCA and the PRA may petition in an appropriate case—for the position here see s.372 of FSMA 2000. See Peat (2006) 22 I.L. & P. 7. It may also be heard on a s.264 petition presented by any other party—see FSMA 2000 s.374(2). Creditors with separate debts can join together and present a single bankruptcy petition: *Re Allen (Re a Debtor 367 of 1992)* [1998] B.P.I.R. 319. A creditor with a non-provable bankruptcy debt is entitled to present a petition, though the court is unlikely to accede to it unless there are exceptional circumstances—*Russell v Russell* [1998] B.P.I.R. 259. Such exceptional circumstances were present in *Wheatley v Wheatley* [1999] B.P.I.R. 431. On the general issue of petitions and non-provable debts see *Levy v Legal Services Commission* [2000] B.P.I.R. 1065.

On the jurisdiction of the English courts to hear default petitions by IVA supervisors see *Loy v O'Sullivan* [2010] EWHC 3583 (Ch); [2011] B.P.I.R. 181. A default petition can be presented under s.264(1)(c) even though the specified duration for the IVA has expired—*Harris v Gross* [2001] B.P.I.R. 586. In *Clarke v Birkin* [2006] EWHC 340 (Ch); [2006] B.P.I.R. 632 Evans-Lombe J upheld a bankruptcy ruling made by a Registrar on a petition by IVA-participating creditors for the bankruptcy of the applicant pursuant to s.264(1)(c) of the IA 1986 on the grounds that the debtor had failed to comply with his obligations under the arrangement. The debtor did not deny that he had been in default in making payments, but he argued that it was not a material default. Evans-Lombe J held that as the Registrar had properly considered all relevant factors in this case when making the bankruptcy order there were no grounds for interfering with that order which was a proper exercise of his discretion. Indeed there was a term in the IVA making it clear that failure to pay instalments on time could not be remedied by subsequent payment. As to who should be appointed trustee on such a petition see *Landsman v de Concilio* [2005] EWHC 267 (Ch); [2005] B.P.I.R. 829. For a case where a bankruptcy order was made on a petition under s.264(1)(c) as a result of a failed IVA see *Varden Nuttall Ltd v Baker* (unreported, 6 May 2016, Proudman J).

Chief Registrar Baister accepted in *Re Akaydin* [2013] B.P.I.R. 539 that for a debtor to petition within the English jurisdiction all that needed to be shown was ordinary residence at some time within the three years immediately preceding the petition.

Note prospective amendment: s.264(1)(d) and the word "or" immediately preceding it are to be repealed by CJA 1988 s.170(2) and Sch.16 as from a day to be appointed. (The power to make criminal bankruptcy orders has been abolished by s.101 of this Act, with effect from 3 April 1989 (see SI 1989/264 (C. 8)), but this and other provisions of IA 1986 and IR 2016 remain in force for the time being to govern orders already existing: see further the note to s.277.)

In the future, once s.115 of the Tribunals, Courts and Enforcement Act 2007 is commenced, the right of an unsecured creditor with a qualifying debt to petition will be restricted if the debtor has entered a debt repayment scheme under the 2007 Act. In such circumstances the creditor cannot petition for bankruptcy during the currency of such a scheme.

Note amendment made to subs.(1) involving the omission of para.(b) by ERRA 2013 Sch.19 para.6.

The fee for a creditor's petition is now £280, with a debtor's petition costing £180: see the Civil Proceedings Fees Order 2008 (SI 2008/1053 (L. 5)) as amended by the Civil Proceedings Fees (Amendment) Order 2014 (SI 2014/874 (L. 17)). The relevant deposits for petitions presented under s.264(1) are £900 for petitions presented under para.(a), (c) and (d) and £550 for petitions presented by debtors under para.(b) (from 6 April 2010—see the Insolvency Proceedings (Fees) Order 2016 (SI 2016/692). The official receiver's administration fee is £2,775. Bankruptcy petitions (unlike winding up petitions) do not have to be advertised. See generally on the advertisement and gazetting of bankruptcy proceedings *Smeaton v Equifax plc* [2013] EWCA Civ 108.

After June 2017 the EC Regulation on Insolvency Proceedings (1346/2000) will be superseded by the Recast EU Insolvency Regulation (2015/848).

265 Creditor's petition: debtors against whom the court may make a bankruptcy order

265(1) [Conditions for presentation of creditor's petition] A bankruptcy petition may be presented to the court under section 264(1)(a) only if–

(a) the centre of the debtor's main interests is in England and Wales, or

(b) the centre of the debtor's main interests is not in a member state of the European Union which has adopted the EU Regulation, but the test in subsection (2) is met.

265(2) [Test for s.265(1)(b)] The test is that–

(a) the debtor is domiciled in England and Wales, or

(b) at any time in the period of three years ending with the day on which the petition is presented, the debtor–

(i) has been ordinarily resident, or has had a place of residence, in England and Wales, or

(ii) has carried on business in England and Wales.

265(3) [Debtor carrying on business] The reference in subsection (2) to the debtor carrying on business includes–

(a) the carrying on of business by a firm or partnership of which the debtor is a member, and

(b) the carrying on of business by an agent or manager for the debtor or for such a firm or partnership.

265(4) [Centre of main interests] In this section, references to the centre of the debtor's main interests have the same meaning as in Article 3 of the EU Regulation.

General Note

A new version of s.265 was substituted by ERRA 2013 Sch.19 para.7. This reflects the fact that it will only be relevant in future to *creditor* petitions in bankruptcy. Debtor petitions ceased to be an option after 6 April 2016 with the coming into force of ERRA 2013 s.71. Jurisdictional issues on the new debtor adjudication procedure are covered by IA 1986 s.263I.

Note that the "personally present" qualification to enable a debtor to use English bankruptcy procedures found in the former s.265(1)(b) appears to have been dropped. Old cases on the personally present requirement in the former s.265(1)(b) will still have some value for the short term.

The purpose of these provisions is to establish a geographic connection between the debtor and the English bankruptcy system. For an instructive authority here, see *Re Brauch* [1978] Ch. 316. In *Re Thulin* [1995] 1 W.L.R. 165 a non-resident Swede was bankrupted by the English courts to facilitate the international collection of his assets. For the purposes of s.265(2)(b)(ii) a person does not cease to carry on business until arrangements have been made to settle business debts: see *Re a Debtor (No.784 of 1991)* [1992] Ch. 554 where Hoffmann J followed *Theophile v Solicitor General* [1950] A.C. 186. Note also *Wilkinson v Inland Revenue Commissioners* [1998] B.P.I.R. 418. The issue of the jurisdiction of the English courts under s.265 was considered in *Barlow Clowes International Ltd v Henwood* [2008] EWCA Civ 577. At first instance it was held that there was a lack of jurisdiction because the domicile of origin had been replaced first by a domicile of choice in the Isle of Man and then by a domicile of choice in Mauritius. This latter conclusion was disputed on the facts. On appeal, the Court of Appeal ruled that where the debtor had abandoned his domicile of choice in the Isle of Man without acquiring a new domicile of choice in Mauritius then the original domicile of origin was revived. This judgment contains an excellent review of the rules on domicile insofar as they may be relevant for the purposes of s.265.

On service outside the jurisdiction see *Anglo Irish Bank Corp Ltd v Flannery* [2013] B.P.I.R. 1 (Chief Registrar Baister)—for the dismissal of the appeal by Newey J see [2012] EWHC 4090 (Ch); [2013] B.P.I.R. 165. Here a creditor petition failed on the grounds that the debtor was not carrying on business within the jurisdiction. The evidence put forward by the creditor citing the alleged commercial activities of the debtor was too tenuous. Similarly, in *Masters v Barclays Bank plc* [2013] EWHC 2166 (Ch); [2013] B.P.I.R. 1058 Norris J held that a creditor petition should be dismissed for lack of jurisdiction. The debtor could not be shown to be carrying on business within the jurisdiction simply by remaining liable under a guarantee. It was however accepted in principle that performing a single act might constitute the carrying out of business.

In *Re Akaydin* [2013] B.P.I.R. 539 debtor petitions were held by Chief Registrar Baister to satisfy the jurisdictional test as the debtors had been ordinarily resident within the jurisdiction *at some time* within the previous three years. This interpretation may be viewed by some commentators as offering the potential for bankruptcy tourism by debtors based outside the EU provided they can satisfy the ordinary residence test (which is stricter than the test for establishing COMI under EURIP 2015/848). But in this case the debtors (who hailed from Turkey and New Zealand) had lived for several years in England and so they could hardly be described as opportunistic bankruptcy tourists.

Where a domicile of choice is abandoned the domicile of origin is revived unless a new domicile of choice is selected—*Gate Gourmet Luxembourg IV SARL v Morby* [2015] EWHC 1203 (Ch). The unsuccessful appeal by the debtor/bankrupt (see [2016] EWHC 74 (Ch)) did not relate to this jurisdictional finding.

A person does not cease to carry on business in the jurisdiction until all business obligations are resolved—*Gate Gourmet Luxembourg IV SARL v Morby* (above). This observation was not questioned on the abortive appeal by the debtor/bankrupt.

A debtor was found to be present at the date of the presentation of the bankruptcy petition in *Gate Gourmet Luxembourg IV SARL v Morby* (above). Again this conclusion was not challenged on appeal.

In *Re Khan, Reynolds Porter Chamberlain v Khan* [2016] B.P.I.R. 722 Chief Registrar Baister found that the debtor was within the jurisdiction on the basis of having a place of residence here. Chief Registrar Baister undertakes a full analysis of the concepts of ordinary residence and place of residence for bankruptcy purposes in the context of a creditor petition.

Section 265(1)(b) in its previous form was considered in *Re Kekhman, JSC Bank of Moscow v Kekhman* [2014] B.P.I.R. 959. Here Chief Registrar Baister found that a foreign debtor had qualified to seek his own bankruptcy by being present in the jurisdiction at the date of his petition. Chief Registrar Baister, accordingly refused an annulment application. On appeal ([2015] EWHC 396 (Ch)) Morgan J confirmed the jurisdiction to make the bankruptcy order and dismissed the application to annul it (albeit on different grounds to those put forward by Chief Registrar Baister). The judgment of Morgan J contains a useful account of the requirement of "benefit" and "sufficient connection" when the court is exercising its jurisdiction. The existence of a liability under guarantees governed by English law helped to establish a connection with the English jurisdiction. There are doubts as to the future relevance of this case to debtor-induced bankruptcies in the light of s.263I.

Subsection (1) is derived from Insolvency Act 1986 (Amendment) (No.2) Regulations 2002 (SI 2002/1240) reg.14 with effect from 31 May 2002. The EU Regulation overrides s.265(1) where the debtor has his centre of main interests in another EU Member State—our local courts enjoy only limited jurisdiction to open a local bankruptcy. On when COMI is to be determined—*Shierson v Vlieland-Boddy* [2005] EWCA Civ 974. Where there is no COMI within an EU Member State, s.265 retains its importance to found jurisdiction—*Geveran Trading Co v Skjevesland* [2003] B.C.C. 209 (confirmed on appeal [2002] EWHC 2898 (Ch); [2003] B.C.C. 391). See also the approach taken by Lewison J in *Cross Construction (Sussex) Ltd v Tseliki* [2006] EWHC 1056 (Ch). See also *Re Hagemeister* [2010] B.P.I.R. 1093. A debtor's petition was dismissed in *Eck v Zapf* [2012] B.P.I.R. 499 for lack of jurisdiction. The burden of proof was on the debtor/petitioner to establish COMI and not on the objecting creditor to disprove it. This issue of locating COMI was to be determined at the date of the presentation of the petition.

A bankruptcy was annulled in *Official Receiver v Keelan* [2012] B.P.I.R. 613 on the basis of lack of COMI. See also *Sparkasse Hilden Ratingen Velbert v Benk* [2012] EWHC 2432 (Ch); [2012] B.P.I.R. 1258 where a bankruptcy order was annulled because the debtor did not have COMI in the jurisdiction at the relevant time.

See also *Anglo Irish Bank Corp v Flannery* [2012] EWHC 4090 (Ch); [2013] B.P.I.R. 165 where Newey J confirmed a ruling of Chief Registrar Baister, who had refused jurisdiction on a creditor petition on the grounds that the debtor was not carrying on business. The suggested link with the English jurisdiction was far too tenuous.

On s.265 jurisdiction and default petitions by IVA supervisors see *Loy v O'Sullivan* [2010] EWHC 3583 (Ch); [2011] B.P.I.R. 181.

Jurisdictional issues in relation to a creditor petition also surfaced in *Lombard North Central plc v Blower* [2014] EWHC 2267 (Ch); [2014] B.P.I.R. 1501.

Section 265(1)(b) and (4) were amended by the Insolvency Amendment (EU 2015/848) Regulations 2017 (SI 2017/702) regs 1, 2(1), Sch. paras 1, 20 in relation to proceedings opened on or after 26 June 2017 (see reg.3) when the Recast EU Regulation 2015/848 came into force.

266 Other preliminary conditions

266(1) [Treatment of petition] Where a bankruptcy petition relating to an individual is presented by a person who is entitled to present a petition under two or more paragraphs of section 264(1), the petition is to be treated for the purposes of this Part as a petition under such one of those paragraphs as may be specified in the petition.

266(2) [Limit on withdrawal of petition] A bankruptcy petition shall not be withdrawn without the leave of the court.

266(3) [Power of dismissal or stay] The court has a general power, if it appears to it appropriate to do so on the grounds that there has been a contravention of the rules or for any other reason, to dismiss a bankruptcy petition or to stay proceedings on such a petition; and, where it stays proceedings on a petition, it may do so on such terms and conditions as it thinks fit.

266(4) [Where criminal bankruptcy order] Without prejudice to subsection (3), where a petition under section 264(1)(a) or (c) in respect of an individual is pending at a time when a criminal bankruptcy order is made against him, or is presented after such an order has been so made, the court may on the application of the Official Petitioner dismiss the petition if it appears to it appropriate to do so.

S.266(1)

A person may be entitled to present a petition under two or more paragraphs of s.264(1), but he must specify which paragraph he is relying on.

S.266(2)

The leave of the court is required before a petition can be withdrawn. This repeats BA 1914 ss.5(7) and 6(2).

S.266(3), (4)

The court has general discretion to stay or dismiss petitions, as was the case under BA 1914 s.113. This discretion is to be kept flexible: *TSB Bank v Platts* [1997] B.P.I.R. 151. See also *Oxted Financial Services v Gordon* [1998] B.P.I.R. 231; and *Re Micklethwait* [2002] EWHC 1123 (Ch); [2003] B.P.I.R. 101 where the court refused to invoke s.266(3). Compare *Re Ross (No.2)* [2000] B.P.I.R. 636. See also *Westminster CC v Parkin* [2001] B.P.I.R. 1156, where the court refused to intervene even where the petition debt was subject to appeal because it did not believe that the appeal had a reasonable prospect of success. Note *Shepherd v LSC* [2003] B.P.I.R. 140 where a bankruptcy order was made notwithstanding the fact that it was conceded by all sides that there were no assets to realise. In *John Lewis v Pearson Burton* [2004] B.P.I.R. 70 Pumfrey J held that it had been incorrect for a district judge to have dismissed a bankruptcy petition by using discretion vested by s.266(3) because the creditor had been entitled to refuse an offer from the debtor to repay the debt over a seven year period. Furthermore, the fact that the creditor had not exhausted all other remedies instead of bankruptcy was immaterial. The case was remitted for reconsideration. Section 266(3) was considered by Rimer J in *Revenue and Customs Commissioners v Crossman* [2007] EWHC 1585 (Ch); [2007] B.P.I.R. 1068. Here the court refused to exercise its discretion to dismiss the petition. On the potential usage of s.266(3) see *Dunbar Assets plc v Fowler* [2013] B.P.I.R. 46 at [37] per Chief Registrar Baister. For the exercise of discretion under s.266(3) see *Aabar Block SARL v Maud* [2015] EWHC 3681 (Ch) where the petition was adjourned for a second time. For later proceedings see *Aabar Block SARL v Maud* [2016] EWHC 1016 (Ch); [2016] B.P.I.R. 803, where, after two adjournments of the petition, judicial patience was exhausted and a bankruptcy order was made by Registrar Briggs. But this bankruptcy order was appealed and Snowden J quashed the bankruptcy order remitting the case for yet further consideration—see [2016] EWHC 2175 (Ch) and discussed by Najib in [2016] 9 CRI 214.

Section 266(4) ensures that if there is a possibility of a petition based on a criminal bankruptcy order, that should receive priority treatment. For the role of the official petitioner, see s.402.

Note minor amendment made to subs.(4) by ERRA 2013 Sch.19 para.8.

Note prospective amendment: s.266(4) is to be repealed by CJA 1988 s.170(2) and Sch.16 as from a day to be appointed: see the note to s.264.

Creditor's petition

267 Grounds of creditor's petition

267(1) [Requirements] A creditor's petition must be in respect of one or more debts owed by the debtor, and the petitioning creditor or each of the petitioning creditors must be a person to whom the debt or (as the case may be) at least one of the debts is owed.

267(2) [Conditions for presentation of petition] Subject to the next three sections, a creditor's petition may be presented to the court in respect of a debt or debts only if, at the time the petition is presented–

(a) the amount of the debt, or the aggregate amount of the debts, is equal to or exceeds the bankruptcy level,

(b) the debt, or each of the debts, is for a liquidated sum payable to the petitioning creditor, or one or more of the petitioning creditors, either immediately or at some certain, future time, and is unsecured,

(c) the debt, or each of the debts, is a debt which the debtor appears either to be unable to pay or to have no reasonable prospect of being able to pay, and

(d) there is no outstanding application to set aside a statutory demand served (under section 268 below) in respect of the debt or any of the debts.

267(3) [Interpretation] A debt is not to be regarded for the purposes of subsection (2) as a debt for a liquidated sum by reason only that the amount of the debt is specified in a criminal bankruptcy order.

267(4) ["The bankruptcy level"] "The bankruptcy level" is £5,000; but the Secretary of State may by order in a statutory instrument substitute any amount specified in the order for that amount or (as the case may be) for the amount which by virtue of such an order is for the time being the amount of the bankruptcy level.

267(5) [Approval of order by Parliament] An order shall not be made under subsection (4) unless a draft of it has been laid before, and approved by a resolution of, each House of Parliament.

S.267(1), (2)

These provisions explain what debts can be used as the basis of a creditor's petition. Basically, the debt must be undisputed and for a liquidated sum in excess of the bankruptcy level (see s.267(4)). The Kempson Review of IP Fees (July 2013) suggested that the figure of £750 should now be raised to a realistic level. No specific figure was identified but we may have been talking here of an increase to something like £3,000. In *Coulter v Chief of Dorset Police* [2004] EWCA Civ 1259; [2005] B.P.I.R. 62 the Court of Appeal reiterated that for the purposes of s.267 a petitioner must be a creditor who must have a debt which is payable immediately or at some future time. An unliquidated claim cannot provide the basis for a petition—*Hope v Premierpace (Europe) Ltd* [1999] B.P.I.R. 695. On whether a debt is unliquidated or disputed see *TSB v Platts (No.2)* [1998] B.P.I.R. 284. In *Dubai Aluminium Co*

Ltd v Salaam [2007] B.P.I.R. 690 Registrar Simmonds held that the reference to "debt" in s.267 must be taken to mean unsecured debt. Here it was held that where the debtor had paid the debt cited in the petition it would be wrong to allow that petition to be amended to include some other debt. The proper approach in such cases was to present a new statutory demand. The debtor must appear to be unable to pay or have no reasonable prospect of paying this debt. If an application is pending to set aside the statutory demand for payment of this debt, it falls outside the category of qualifying debts. For what constitutes an outstanding set-aside application see *Ariyo v Sovereign Leasing* [1998] B.P.I.R. 177. A statute-barred debt cannot form the basis for a statutory demand: *Jelly v All Type Roofing* [1997] B.C.C. 465; *Bruton v Inland Revenue Commissioners* [2000] B.P.I.R. 946. Compare *Times Newspapers Ltd v Chohan* [2001] B.P.I.R. 943; *Global Finance Recoveries Ltd v Jones* [2000] B.P.I.R. 1029; and *West Bromwich Building Society v Crammer* [2002] EWHC 2618 (Ch); [2003] B.P.I.R. 783. Note also *Phillips & Co v Bath Housing* [2012] EWCA Civ 1591 for a consideration of limitation issues in a non-bankruptcy case but which contains a discussion of some of the bankruptcy authorities. Note *Mittal v RP Capital Explorer Master Fund* [2014] B.P.I.R. 1537 where Deputy Registrar Briggs found that the debt was statute-barred and accordingly set aside the statutory demand.

On the difference between a petition debt and a bankruptcy debt see the observations of Master Kelly in *ORNI v Gallagher* [2013] NIMaster 12 at [13].

In *Howell v Lerwick Commercial Mortgage Corp* [2015] EWHC 1177 (Ch); [2015] B.P.I.R. 821 Nugee J sought to clarify what was meant by a petitionable debt for the purposes of s.267(2)(c). It seems that a petition can be presented where there is a counterclaim that might reduce the debt balance to below the minimum debt—but in such a case the petition is likely to fail.

In *Regis Direct Ltd v Hakeem* (unreported, 3 October 2012) Norris J upheld a bankruptcy order notwithstanding the fact that the petition had been inadvertently presented whilst there was an extant set aside application in respect of the statutory demand. This set aside application was in fact dismissed some three days after the bankruptcy order was made; in those circumstances there was no point in setting aside the bankruptcy order. There was no injustice to the debtor.

Where the petitioner has mixed motives in presenting the petition, that fact may not necessarily be fatal to the petition—see *Ridsdale v Bowles* [2015] B.P.I.R. 1275.

For full consideration of the requirements that must be established for the tort of malicious presentation of a bankruptcy petition see *Jacob v Vockrodt* [2007] EWHC 2403 (QB); [2007] B.P.I.R. 1568.

See also *Rio Properties Inc v Al-Midani* [2003] B.P.I.R. 128 where the court held that a foreign gaming debt which had apparently been settled via an English law compromise could form the basis of a bankruptcy petition.

See *Pace Europe Ltd v Dunham* [2012] B.P.I.R. 836 on the enforceability of foreign judgments via statutory demands in bankruptcy. Here HHJ Purle QC provides a careful analysis of the significance of the principles laid down in *Lewis v Eliades* [2003] EWCA Civ 1758. A novel point arose before District Judge Musgrave in *Sun Legend Investments Ltd v Jade Yuk Kuen Ho* [2013] B.P.I.R. 533. Here the point at issue was whether a statutory demand could be presented in respect of a foreign judgment debt. The creditor was not as such seeking to enforce the foreign judgment debt, but was using it as evidence of an inability to pay debts. The court held that the statutory demand procedure could be used.

In *Klamer v Kyriakides and Braier (a firm)* [2005] B.P.I.R. 1115 Mr Registrar Simmonds held that a solicitor's bill that had not been assessed was not a liquidated debt capable of forming the basis of a statutory demand/bankruptcy petition for the purposes of s.267(2)(b) of the IA 1986. In *Truex v Toll* [2009] EWHC 396 (Ch); [2009] B.P.I.R. 692 Proudman J ruled that an untaxed solicitor's bill was not a liquidated debt for the purposes of s.267. Here it could not be said that the client had admitted liability to pay the invoice because the alleged admission was not unequivocal and was not supported by consideration. The courts have reiterated that an unassessed solicitors' bill is not a liquidated sum—*Wallace LLP v Yates* [2010] B.P.I.R. 1041. It will only become a liquidated sum if the client has accepted it or otherwise is estopped from challenging it—see *Moseley v Else Solicitors LLP* [2010] B.P.I.R. 1192. An estoppel argument failed in *Wallace LLP v Yates* (above). *Truex* was considered in the Northern Irish case of *Moore and Grimley v Williamson* [2011] NICh 20. Deputy Registrar Schaffer gave further consideration to the position where solicitors use the bankruptcy procedure to recover fees in *Orrick, Herrington and Sutcliffe (Europe) LLP v Frohlich* [2012] B.P.I.R. 169. The amount due to the solicitors must be a liquidated sum at the date of the statutory demand—the fact that it becomes liquidated by the date of the petition does not prevent the bankruptcy procedure from being defective.

As to what is a liquidated sum see the decision of HHJ Klein in *Blavo v Law Society* [2017] EWHC 561 (Ch); [2017] B.P.I.R. 909 (intervention costs not viewed as liquidated sum). In so deciding, the court refused to follow *Pyke v Law Society* [2006] EWHC 3489 (Ch).

A sum due under an interim payments order made under CPR r.25.6 is a "debt" for these purposes: *Maxwell v Bishopsgate Investment Management Ltd* [1993] T.L.R. 67. In so deciding Chadwick J noted that the abolition of acts of bankruptcy had produced this change in the law—a final judgment was not necessary under the new bankruptcy code to justify a statutory demand. A taxed costs order can found a statutory demand—*Galloppa v Galloppa* [1999] B.P.I.R. 352. A debt arising under a regulated hire purchase agreement can found the basis for a statutory demand: *Mills v Grove Securities Ltd* [1997] B.P.I.R. 243. A joint debt owed by a partner also falls within s.267(1) according to *Schooler v Customs and Excise Commissioners* [1996] B.P.I.R. 207. Non-provable bankruptcy debts can provide the basis for a petition—*Levy v Legal Services Commission* [2000] B.P.I.R. 1065. On the status of unpaid community charge see *Re Wood* [1994] 1 C.L. 257 (1993, Tamworth County Court). The debt can be a sum due in a foreign currency according to Morritt J in *Re a Debtor (51/SD/1991)* [1992] 1 W.L.R. 1294. In *McGuinness v Norwich & Peterborough Building Society* [2011] EWCA Civ 1286; [2012] B.P.I.R. 145 (upholding the earlier ruling of Briggs J) the Court of Appeal held on the wording of the guarantee in question the guarantor could be regarded as a principal debtor—that liability could therefore be characterised as a liquidated sum for the purposes of s.267. See also *Sofaer v Anglo Irish Asset Finance plc* [2011] EWHC 1480 (Ch); [2011] B.P.I.R. 1736 where Lewison J came to a similar conclusion. The wording of guarantees appears to be evolving to improve their enforceability and to enable the creditor to pursue the guarantor without first seeking to recover from the principal borrower. An argument that a guarantee liability was not for a liquidated sum was rejected by Chief Registrar Baister in *Dunbar Assets plc v Fowler* [2013] B.P.I.R. 46. On construction of this particular guarantee a conditional payment obligation arose, rather than generating a claim in damages. In *Francis v Solomon Taylor & Shaw* [2013] EWHC 9 (Ch) the High Court ruled that, under the terms of the guarantee under review in that case, the liability of the guarantor was for a liquidated sum within the meaning of s.267.

In *Hurley v The Darjan Estate Co plc* [2012] EWHC 189 (Ch); [2012] 1 W.L.R. 1782; [2012] B.P.I.R. 1021 sums in rent due under a lease that was defective in some respects were held to constitute contingent debts and liquidated sums.

Presumably the rule in *Re McGreavy* [1950] Ch. 269, that an unpaid rates demand is a "debt" for the purposes of a bankruptcy petition, is preserved by s.267. For confirmation that unpaid council tax arrears constitute a debt for the purposes of s.267 even if no liability order has been made see *Bolsover DC v Ashfield Nominees Ltd* [2010] EWCA Civ 1129; [2011] B.P.I.R. 7. For discussion of the position with regard to unpaid community charges see *Preston BC v Riley* [1999] B.P.I.R. 284 (an authority on county court administration orders).

The refusal of the courts to allow bankruptcy proceedings to be used to unpick tax assessments was again to the fore in *Flett v Revenue and Customs Commissioners* [2010] EWHC 2662 (Ch); [2010] B.P.I.R. 1075.

A council tax liability order is a "debt" for the purposes of s.267—see Peter Smith J in *Smolen v Tower Hamlets LBC* [2007] B.P.I.R. 448. A reduction in the amount of liability (provided the reduction does not take the liability to a sum under £750) does not affect that position. In *Yang v Official Receiver* [2013] EWHC 3577 (Ch); [2014] B.P.I.R. 826 it was confirmed by HHJ Hodge QC that a liability order made in respect of an alleged unpaid council tax bill was a liability for s.267 purposes, even if it was subsequently successfully challenged. For an example of a local council seeking to enforce a liability order via bankruptcy proceedings see *Okon v London Borough of Lewisham* [2016] EWHC 864 (Ch); [2016] B.P.I.R. 958. Here the proceedings were adjourned conditionally pending clarification of issues relating to the underlying liability order. The court gave guidance on the approach to be adopted by the parties where an appeal to the Valuation Tribunal challenging the liability as assessed was an option.

A statutory demand can be issued in respect of a consumer credit debt notwithstanding the provisions of s.141 of the Consumer Credit Act 1974—*Omokwe v HFC Bank Ltd* [2007] B.P.I.R. 1157.

For guidance on preparing the petition see *Practice Direction: Insolvency Proceedings* [2018] B.C.C. 241 (see App.IV).

The criteria in s.267(2)(a) and (b) were *not* satisfied in *Dean & Dean v Angel Airlines SA* [2009] EWHC 447 (Ch) [2009] B.P.I.R. 409.

For the scope of s.267(2)(d) see *Ahmad v Commissioners of Inland Revenue* [2004] EWHC 2292 (Ch); [2005] B.P.I.R. 541. Section 267(2)(d) must, in the opinion of Mummery J, be read as being subject to s.270: see *Re a Debtor (No.22 of 1993)* [1994] 1 W.L.R. 46 (sometimes cited as *Focus Insurance v A Debtor*).

S.267(3)

This narrows the definition of a liquidated sum to exclude amounts of debts specified in criminal bankruptcy orders.

Note prospective amendment: s.267(3) is to be repealed by CJA 1988 s.170(2) and Sch.16 as from a day to be appointed: see the note to s.264.

S.267(4), (5)

The current bankruptcy level is now £5,000, although the Secretary of State can increase it. On whether this amount must still be outstanding at the date of the hearing: *Re Patel* [1986] 1 W.L.R. 221 (a case decided under the 1914 Act). Whether this case would be followed under the new regime is questionable—*Lilley v American Express (Europe) Ltd* [2000] B.P.I.R. 70. The courts are not favourably disposed to bankruptcy proceedings brought to recover debts slightly in excess of the minimum debt: *City Electrical Factors Ltd v Hardingham* [1996] B.P.I.R. 541. The Kempson Review of IP Fees (July 2013) suggested that the then figure of £750 should be raised to a realistic level. No specific figure was identified but many observers assumed an increase to something like £3,000. The figure of £750 formerly specified in subs.(4) for creditor petitions was raised to £5,000 when the Insolvency Act 1986 (Amendment) Order 2015 (SI 2015/922) came into force on 1 October 2015. This was a substantial uplift, though it is unlikely that a creditor would consider bankruptcy for a level of debt anywhere near the old level of £750; other options would be pursued. Creditors would be well advised to take note of this change and respond accordingly. The minimum debt figure of £750 remains in place for debtor applications. Where there is an undisputed debt clearly in excess of the statutory minimum but a balance that is disputed the petition can proceed: *TSB Bank v Platts (No.2)* [1998] B.P.I.R. 284.

268 Definition of "inability to pay", etc.; the statutory demand

268(1) [Interpretation of s.267(2)(c)] For the purposes of section 267(2)(c), the debtor appears to be unable to pay a debt if, but only if, the debt is payable immediately and either–

(a) the petitioning creditor to whom the debt is owed has served on the debtor a demand (known as "the statutory demand") in the prescribed form requiring him to pay the debt or to secure or compound for it to the satisfaction of the creditor, at least 3 weeks have elapsed since the demand was served and the demand has been neither complied with nor set aside in accordance with the rules, or

(b) execution or other process issued in respect of the debt on a judgment or order of any court in favour of the petitioning creditor, or one or more of the petitioning creditors to whom the debt is owed, has been returned unsatisfied in whole or in part.

268(2) [Further interpretation] For the purposes of section 267(2)(c) the debtor appears to have no reasonable prospect of being able to pay a debt if, but only if, the debt is not immediately payable and–

(a) the petitioning creditor to whom it is owed has served on the debtor a demand (also known as "the statutory demand") in the prescribed form requiring him to establish to the satisfaction of the creditor that there is a reasonable prospect that the debtor will be able to pay the debt when it falls due,

(b) at least 3 weeks have elapsed since the demand was served, and

(c) the demand has been neither complied with nor set aside in accordance with the rules.

General Note

This section defines "inability to pay" and "statutory demand", terms featuring in s.267. A debtor will be deemed unable to pay a debt if he fails to meet a demand in the prescribed form served on him within three weeks—under the previous law the debtor was given only 10 days' grace—or an execution for a judgment debt has been returned unsatisfied. In *Re a Debtor (No.1 of 1987)* [1989] 1 W.L.R. 271 the Court of Appeal, confirming a ruling of Warner J, took a relaxed view of a statutory demand that contained errors as to the amount owed. The Court of Appeal refused to set aside this demand as no injustice had been done to the debtor. In so deciding the Court of Appeal departed from the position under the pre-1985 bankruptcy law and indicated that the new provisions had to be interpreted in their own context. This case is a watershed authority marking a fundamental change in attitude on the part of the courts to procedural errors in the bankruptcy process. Formerly, in the case of a defect in a bankruptcy notice the whole proceedings would be invalidated. Now that bankruptcy is viewed as a more user-friendly regime for the debtor the courts feel justified in adopting a more pragmatic stance. For a full discussion of this relaxation of judicial attitudes see Milman [1994] Conv. 289–298. Thus if the debt mentioned in the demand is overstated this will not invalidate the demand (provided the undisputed element exceeds the minimum bankruptcy level): see here *Re a Debtor (490/SD/1991)* [1992] 1 W.L.R. 507 where Hoffmann J disclaimed his earlier contrary view in *Re a Debtor (No.10 of 1988)* [1989] 1 W.L.R. 405. Similar principles would appear to apply if part of the debt is disputed but there is an undisputed balance—failure to highlight the dispute may not be critical (*Re a Debtor (657/SD/1991)* [1993] B.C.L.C. 1280, per Ferris J). Equally errors as to the degree of security enjoyed by the creditor might be overlooked: see *Re a*

Debtor (No.106 of 1992), The Independent, 20 April 1992. But it should be emphasised that there is a world of difference between a defective statutory demand (which may be excused) and a document that cannot be construed as a statutory demand—*Agilo Ltd v Henry* [2010] EWHC 2717 (Ch) per Newey J.

Bankruptcy proceedings cannot be used to go behind a determination of the Revenue General Commissioners—*Cullinane v Inland Revenue Commissioners* [2000] B.P.I.R. 996. But the HMRC should note its obligations to citizens under the Disability Discrimination Act 1995 in the light of the protection offered by the Mental Capacity Act 2005—*Re Haworth* [2011] EWHC 36 (Ch).

An important point to note is that a statutory demand is a document issued by a creditor. Unlike the old bankruptcy notice it is not issued by the court and does not form part of court proceedings. This can have implications. Thus in *Re a Debtor (No.190 of 1987), The Times*, 21 May 1988 Vinelott J held that the relieving jurisdiction in the then r.7.55 was inapplicable—but in view of the more liberal attitude of the courts to procedural irregularities this hardly matters. Equally it was held in *Re a Debtor (No.88 of 1991)* [1993] Ch. 286 that the presentation of a statutory demand is not an "action" within the meaning of s.69 of the Solicitors Act 1974 and so the one month moratorium imposed on solicitors seeking to recover fees from debtor clients does not apply (though the moratorium would extend to the presentation of the petition). For discussion see Start (1992) 142 N.L.J. 1121 and Simmonds (1992) 26 Law. Soc. Gaz. 18. See also *Shalson v DF Keane Ltd* [2003] EWHC 599 (Ch); [2003] B.P.I.R. 1045 where it was held that the mere service of a statutory demand did not constitute the commencement of legal proceedings so as to trigger the stay on such proceedings under the terms of s.9 of the Arbitration Act 1996.

The requirements of s.268 were reviewed in *Orrick, Herrington & Sutcliffe (Europe) LLP v Frohlich* [2012] B.P.I.R. 169. For clarification of the import of this provision see the comments of Nugee J in *Howell v Lerwick Commercial Mortgage Corp* [2015] EWHC 1177 (Ch); [2015] B.P.I.R. 821.

On issue estoppel and failed set-aside applications note *Eberhardt & Co v Mair* [1995] B.C.C. 845.

On what constitutes an unsatisfied execution within s.268(1)(b) see *Re a Debtor (No.340 of 1992)* [1996] 2 All E.R. 211; and *Skarzynski v Chalford Property Co Ltd* [2001] B.P.I.R. 673.

In *Dubai Aluminium v Salaam* [2007] B.P.I.R. 690 Registrar Simmonds ruled that where a bankruptcy petition referred to unsecured and secured debts and the unsecured debts had been paid off the creditor could not then amend its petition and revalue its security to create a new unsecured debt. In such a case the requirements of s.268 were not satisfied and a new statutory demand would have to be served.

Where council tax arrears liability orders are relied upon by local authorities to form the basis of a statutory demand the amounts in question should be precise and itemised—the courts have expressed their irritation at being asked to accede to a bankruptcy petition on the basis of imprecise information about the debtor's status with regard to council tax arrears—*London Borough of Lambeth v Simon* [2007] B.P.I.R. 1629. Indeed on 31 March 2008 a local government ombudsman has gone so far as to suggest that for a local authority (in this case Wolverhampton City Council) to present a bankruptcy petition for council tax arrears of £1,105 without fully considering other options (such as a charging order) could amount to maladministration. Other local authorities have been criticised for similar practices—see above. That said, the courts are resistant to invitations to go behind liability orders—see the comments of Henderson J in *Dias v Havering LBC* [2011] EWHC 172 (Ch).

If the requirements of s.268 are satisfied it is no defence for the debtor to establish that he was solvent at the time. A solvent debtor can be made subject to a bankruptcy order—*Johnson v Tandrige DC* [2008] B.P.I.R. 405. See also the discussion in *Evans v Clarke Willmott & Clarke* [2007] EWHC 852 (Ch); [2008] B.P.I.R. 37.

A statutory demand does not constitute a formal demand under a guarantee—rather it is a prescribed form solely designed for the purposes of bankruptcy law—*TS & S Global Ltd v Fithian-Franks* [2007] EWHC 1401 (Ch); [2007] B.P.I.R. 424. For the purposes of s.268 the debt must be both liquidated and payable immediately—*Wallace LLP v Yates* [2010] B.P.I.R. 1041.

For further details on the statutory demand, see IR 2016 rr.10.1–10.5 and *Practice Direction: Insolvency Proceedings* [2018] B.C.C. 241, para.11, which is included as App.IV.

For security as to costs where s.268(2) is relied upon see IR 2016 rr.10.17.

269 Creditor with security

269(1) [Where debt not unsecured] A debt which is the debt, or one of the debts, in respect of which a creditor's petition is presented need not be unsecured if either–

(a) the petition contains a statement by the person having the right to enforce the security that he is willing, in the event of a bankruptcy order being made, to give up his security for the benefit of all the bankrupt's creditors, or

(b) the petition is expressed not to be made in respect of the secured part of the debt and contains a statement by that person of the estimated value at the date of the petition of the security for the secured part of the debt.

269(2) [Debt in s.269(1)(b)] In a case falling within subsection (1)(b) the secured and unsecured parts of the debt are to be treated for the purposes of sections 267 to 270 as separate debts.

General Note

Secured debts can form the basis of a creditor's petition, provided the creditor is willing to give up his security or if the petition is in respect of an unsecured part of the same debt. See *Zandfarid v BCCI* [1996] B.P.I.R. 501. In *Barclays Bank v Mogg* [2003] EWHC 2645 (Ch); [2004] B.P.I.R. 259 David Richards J held that a failure to comply with the requirements of s.269, although a serious procedural flaw, might not be fatal to the success of the petition where the debtor was not misled and had suffered no prejudice. Drawing on authorities dealing with the 1914 Act it was held that the court retained discretion to permit the petition to be amended. The fact that a creditor with security can use the bankruptcy procedure was reiterated by Roth J in *1st Credit (Finance) Ltd v Bartram* [2010] EWHC 2910 (Ch); [2011] B.P.I.R. 1. See also *Gate Gourmet Luxembourg IV SARL v Morby* [2015] EWHC 1203 (Ch); [2015] B.P.I.R. 787—the unsuccessful appeal (reported as [2016] EWHC 74 (Ch)) did not relate to this issue. The security must be disclosed together with a willingness to waive it in the bankruptcy process. Note the overlap with IR 2016 r.10.5(4)(c). Note also s.383(3) here. For the linkage between s.269 and ss.267 and 268 see *Dubai Aluminium v Salaam* [2007] B.P.I.R. 690.

See also IR 2016 rr.14.15–14.19.

270 Expedited petition

270 In the case of a creditor's petition presented wholly or partly in respect of a debt which is the subject of a statutory demand under section 268, the petition may be presented before the end of the 3-week period there mentioned if there is a serious possibility that the debtor's property or the value of any of his property will be significantly diminished during that period and the petition contains a statement to that effect.

General Note

The three weeks' grace given to the debtor by s.268 can be cut short and the petition presented prematurely if the petition alleges that there is a serious possibility of a significant fall in value of the debtor's assets. The power to expedite the petition under s.270 can only be invoked if the statutory demand has been served—*Wehmeyer v Wehmeyer* [2001] B.P.I.R. 548. This procedure can still be invoked even though there is an extant set-aside application with respect to the statutory demand: see the ruling of Mummery J in *Re a Debtor (No.22 of 1993)* [1994] 1 W.L.R. 46 (sometimes cited as *Focus Insurance v A Debtor*). However, should the set-aside application succeed at the end of the day the creditor might be exposed to some sort of personal claim by the debtor, a point considered by Mummery J.

271 Proceedings on creditor's petition

271(1) [Conditions for bankruptcy order] The court shall not make a bankruptcy order on a creditor's petition unless it is satisfied that the debt, or one of the debts, in respect of which the petition was presented is either–

(a) a debt which, having been payable at the date of the petition or having since become payable, has been neither paid nor secured or compounded for, or

(b) a debt which the debtor has no reasonable prospect of being able to pay when it falls due.

271(2) [Where petition contains s.270 statement] In a case in which the petition contains such a statement as is required by section 270, the court shall not make a bankruptcy order until at least 3 weeks have elapsed since the service of any statutory demand under section 268.

271(3) [Dismissal of petition] The court may dismiss the petition if it is satisfied that the debtor is able to pay all his debts or is satisfied–

(a) that the debtor has made an offer to secure or compound for a debt in respect of which the petition is presented,

(b) that the acceptance of that offer would have required the dismissal of the petition, and

(c) that the offer has been unreasonably refused;

and, in determining for the purposes of this subsection whether the debtor is able to pay all his debts, the court shall take into account his contingent and prospective liabilities.

271(4) [Interpretation] In determining for the purposes of this section what constitutes a reasonable prospect that a debtor will be able to pay a debt when it falls due, it is to be assumed that the prospect given by the facts and other matters known to the creditor at the time he entered into the transaction resulting in the debt was a reasonable prospect.

271(5) [Powers of court to amend etc.] Nothing in sections 267 to 271 prejudices the power of the court, in accordance with the rules, to authorise a creditor's petition to be amended by the omission of any creditor or debt and to be proceeded with as if things done for the purposes of those sections had been done only by or in relation to the remaining creditors or debts.

General Note

If a petition is granted under IA 1986 it is followed by a bankruptcy order. The previous intermediate stage of a receiving order (BA 1914 s.3) has been abolished. Note IR 2016 rr.10.21, 10.16 and 10.24. Note that bankruptcy petitions, unlike winding up petitions, are not advertised. If the court makes a bankruptcy order it can of course be appealed. Where this happens and a trustee has been installed in the interim it is important that any successful appeal addresses the issue of the trustee's remuneration and expenses for the period in which he was in office—*Appleyard v Wewelwala* [2012] EWHC 3302 (Ch).

S.271(1), (2), (4)

The power of the court to make a bankruptcy order is qualified by these provisions. See *Marquis de Louville de Toucy v Bonhams 1793 Ltd* [2011] EWHC 3809 (Ch); [2012] B.P.I.R. 793 on the evidence required by the court in order to satisfy its function under s.271. For an explicit assertion of the jurisdiction of the court under s.271 see *Potter v Revenue and Customs Commissioners* (unreported 2008). Where the bankruptcy petition is contested the court should consider whether the defence raises a genuinely triable issue (even if it is improbable)—*Markham v Karsten* [2007] EWHC 1509 (Ch); [2007] B.P.I.R. 1109. See also *Kaupthing Singer & Friedlander Ltd v Coomber* [2011] EWHC 3589 (Ch) where the attempts by the debtors to forestall the making of bankruptcy orders were also unsuccessful. See *Lambeth LBC v Simon* [2007] B.P.I.R. 1629 for a strong assertion by the bankruptcy court of its right (and in some cases its duty) to go behind judgments triggering bankruptcy proceedings. For an abortive attempt to challenge the judgment upon which a bankruptcy petition was based see: *Hope v Revenue and Customs Commissioners* [2017] EWHC 812 (Ch); [2017] B.P.I.R. 992 (Registrar Briggs). The attempt to impugn the judgment and the underlying tax assessments would not be permitted in this case—the decision on whether the bankruptcy petition should be granted was to be determined later. In *Smolen v Tower Hamlets LBC* [2007] B.P.I.R. 448 Peter Smith J confirmed that ss.271(1)(a) and 271(1)(b) are alternatives and not cumulative. Note that in the event of a petition presented prematurely the court must wait until the three weeks have elapsed before making the order. Unsuccessful arguments which have been run on a failed set aside application with regard to the statutory demand should not generally be revisited when the petition is being heard—on this see *Adams v Mason Bullock (a firm)* [2005] B.P.I.R. 241. However, if the argument was not considered on its merits at that earlier stage it can be raised when the petition is being heard—see *Inland Revenue Commissioners v Lee-Phipps* [2003] B.P.I.R. 803. Moreover in *Barnes v Whitehead* [2004] B.P.I.R. 693 the court ruled that an earlier failure by the debtor to raise a dispute as to the existence of the debt by seeking to have the statutory demand set aside did not preclude the debtor from raising this very issue at a later date when the petition was being heard. The court had to be satisfied under s.271 that an undisputed debt existed. In *Hayes v Hayes* [2014] EWHC 2694 (Ch); [2014] B.P.I.R. 1212 Nugee J dismissed the appeal from the Registrar who had refused to grant a bankruptcy order on a creditor petition. The petition was dismissed because of a serious and substantial cross claim that had been firmed up since the abortive set aside application. Nugee J reviewed the position with regard to cross claims that had not been asserted on a timely basis. Any significant delay might undermine the supposed genuineness of a cross claim. Nugee J also offered important guidance on when arguments used in a failed set aside application might be revisited at petition stage. See also further discussion of these issues in *Adams v Mason Bullock (a firm)* (above). In *Rightmatch Ltd (Acting by its LPA Receiver) v Meisels* [2014] B.P.I.R. 733 Registrar Jones considered the role of the court in determining whether to grant a bankruptcy petition in relation to arguments used (and dismissed) on a set aside application and arguments that could have been deployed on such an application. This provides useful case management guidance. The definition of when a debtor has a "reasonable prospect" of paying a debt certainly leaves a lot to be desired. On s.271(1)(a) see *Artman v Artman* [1996] B.P.I.R. 511. On s.271(1)(a) see *Kaupthing Singer & Friedlander Ltd v Coomber* [2011] EWHC 3589 (Ch); [2012] B.P.I.R. 774. On whether joint debts have been compounded see *Re a Bankrupt (No.622 of 1995), The Times*, 27 June 1996.

The existence of discretion under s.271 was emphasised in *Revenue and Customs Commissioners v Potter* [2008] B.P.I.R. 1033, where the court was not satisfied that the petition debt was owed by the defendant—the debt may have been owed by a company which she controlled. The petition was therefore dismissed.

Again in *Dean & Dean v Angel Airlines SA* [2009] EWHC 447 (Ch); [2009] B.P.I.R. 409 Patten J refused to make a bankruptcy order against a party because he was not satisfied that a debt was owing within the terms of s.267(2)(a) and (b). See also *Hayes v Hayes* [2014] EWHC 2694 (Ch); [2014] B.P.I.R. 1212 where Nugee J indicated that a bankruptcy petition will not be granted if there exists a serious and genuine cross claim that may exceed the petition debt.

Further consideration was given to the discretion of the court under s.271 in *Ross v Revenue and Customs Commissioners* [2010] B.P.I.R. 652 where the court again ruled that the rejection by HMRC of an offer of security was not unreasonable. It did however caution the Revenue against adopting a blanket policy in favour of rejecting security in every case. The court did indicate that the courts should be reluctant to agree to an adjournment of the petition hearing. See also *Re Bance* [2016] EWHC 1028 (Ch) where as a matter of discretion a bankruptcy order was refused. This was an unusual case in which a second petition had been presented in respect of a judgment debt linked to an allegation of fraud.

In *Nottingham City Council v Pennant* [2010] B.P.I.R. 430 HHJ Purle QC held that a local authority was entitled to reject the offer to pay in instalments by a debtor with whom there had been difficulties in collecting debt from in the past. In such a case it was not appropriate to stay the making of a bankruptcy order just to see that the debtor was keeping up with the repayment schedule. Allowing bankruptcy to remain in limbo could cause problems because of the potential impact of provisions such as s.284.

An attempt to challenge the refusal by a creditor to accept the debtor's offer to pay based upon a speculative future income stream was rejected by David Richards J in *Shrimpton v Darbys Solicitors LLP* [2011] EWHC 3796 (Ch). For another abortive attempt to challenge a refusal to accept a debtor's offer see *Adeosun v Revenue and Customs Commissioners* [2011] EWHC 1577 (Ch); [2011] B.P.I.R. 1555.

The bankruptcy petition was dismissed in *Re Sutton* [2014] B.P.I.R. 1349 (Chief Registrar Baister).

It would appear from *Howell v Lerwick Commercial Mortgage Corp* [2015] EWHC 1177 (Ch); [2015] B.P.I.R. 821 that if a petition has been allowed to proceed where the minimum debt is likely to be less than the minimum required amount then its prospects of success are slim.

S.271(3)

This provision states that the court may dismiss the petition if the debtor is able to meet his debts, or has made a proposal to the creditor to secure or compound the debt and it has been unreasonably refused. For discussion of the operation of this provision see *Re Gilmartin (a Bankrupt)* [1989] 1 W.L.R. 513 where Harman J concluded that the registrar had been correct in deciding that an offer had not been unreasonably refused by the petitioner and the supporting creditors. In *Re a Debtor (No.32 of 1993)* [1994] 1 W.L.R. 899; [1994] B.C.C. 438 it was held by Timothy Lloyd QC (sitting as a deputy High Court judge) that a debtor can offer to secure or compound within the meaning of s.271(3) where there is just a single creditor involved. However, in determining whether the creditor's refusal of the offer was unreasonable it must be established to the satisfaction of the court that no reasonable hypothetical creditor would have rejected the debtor's offer; the fact that some creditors might have accepted it is not conclusive. In *Inland Revenue Commissioners v A Debtor* [1995] B.C.C. 971 the court could not be persuaded that the refusal of tax officers to accept security for a debt was unreasonable. In *Evans v Clarke, Willmott & Clarke* [2007] EWHC 852 (Ch); [2008] B.P.I.R. 37 the creditor was held not to have behaved unreasonably in rejecting the debtor's offer as no clear and satisfactory offer had in fact been made. In *Revenue and Customs Commissioners v Garwood* [2012] B.P.I.R. 575 Chief Registrar Baister emphasised that the court enjoys wide discretion under s.271(3). The judgment contains a comprehensive analysis of the considerations that the court should take into account for the purposes of s.271. Some 10 points are highlighted. A mechanistic response by a creditor in the face of attempts by the debtor to settle matters does not go down well with the court; the creditor should reflect upon what is being offered. An objective test should be applied. In this case (unusually) the court held that the creditor had acted unreasonably in its response to the debtor's offers.

Shrimpton v Darby's Solicitors LLP [2011] EWHC 3796 (Ch); [2012] B.P.I.R. 631 is but one further example of an abortive attempt to argue that a creditor was acting unreasonably in rejecting the debtor's offer.

In *Dunbar Assets plc v Fowler* [2013] B.P.I.R. 46 Chief Registrar Baister ruled that the creditor had not unreasonably refused the debtor's offer of security/deferred consideration. It could not be said that refusal was beyond the range of possible actions that a reasonable creditor would take. For yet another unsuccessful attempt to challenge a creditor's refusal to accept the offer put forward by the debtor on the grounds of unreasonableness see *Cooke v Dunbar Assets plc* [2016] EWHC 579 (Ch); [2016] B.P.I.R. 576.

The creditor's refusal to compound was found not to be unreasonable by Registrar Briggs in *Barclays Bank v Atay* [2015] EWHC 3198 (Ch). The creditor was not obliged to accept an offer by the debtor involving payments by instalments over a long period of time.

On s.271(3) generally see *Re a Debtor (No.415/SD/1993)* [1994] 1 W.L.R. 917; and *King v Inland Revenue Commissioners* [1996] B.P.I.R. 414. In *Re a Debtor (No.2389 of 1989)* [1991] Ch. 326 Vinelott J held that the proposal of a voluntary arrangement by the debtor under Pt VIII of the Act cannot be regarded as an "offer" for the purposes of s.271(3) in that the decision on acceptance is not solely a matter for the petitioning creditor. The consequences of acceptance or refusal of such a proposal are dealt with exclusively by Pt VIII. For discussion, see Griffiths (1991) 135 S.J. 598.

On s.271(3) see *Sands v Layne* [2014] EWHC 3665 (Ch).

The court also has discretion to adjourn the petition but this discretion must be carefully watched—*Harrison v Seggar* [2005] EWHC 411 (Ch); [2005] B.P.I.R. 583. On the jurisdiction to adjourn under CPR r.3.1(2)(b) see *Sekhon v Edginton* [2015] EWCA Civ 816; [2015] 1 W.L.R. 4435. The later the debtor leaves any request to adjourn the less likely it is to be granted by the court. A last minute offer to pay is unlikely to persuade the court to adjourn, unless there is clear evidence that the debtor can pay. The jurisdiction to adjourn is governed by the principles in CPR r.3.1(2)(b). This important procedural authority was applied by HHJ Behrens in *Day v Refulgent Ltd* [2016] EWHC 7 (Ch); [2016] B.P.I.R. 594. It is clear from the latter case that any appeal against a refusal by a first instance judge to adjourn faces an uphill struggle. For an unusual instance where the hearing of the petition was adjourned for a second time see *Aabar Block SARL v Maud* [2015] EWHC 3681 (Ch). A bankruptcy order was eventually made (after two adjournments of the petition) by Registrar Briggs in *Aabar Block SARL v Maud* [2016] EWHC 1016 (Ch). But on appeal ([2016] EWHC 2175 (Ch)) that bankruptcy order was quashed by Snowden J and this complex case was remitted for yet another hearing of the bankruptcy petition.

Having made a bankruptcy order under s.271 the court has jurisdiction to stay the order if appropriate—*Emap Active Ltd v Hill* [2007] EWHC 1592 (Ch); [2007] B.P.I.R. 1228. But care must be taken when interpreting this case as its facts were very unusual. Rather it should be seen as an example of an exception proving the rule (that a stay will not normally be granted). The general reluctance of the court to grant stays save in exceptional circumstances is apparent in *Re Foster* [2012] B.P.I.R. 545—see comments of Roth J at [24] citing David Richards J.

Putative bankrupts frequently fail to turn up for the hearing of the petition against them. Provided they have been served with the petition and given appropriate notice the mere fact that the judge decides to hear the petition in their absence does not necessarily involve a contravention of art.6 ECHR—*Manyan v Dewar Hogan* [2004] EWHC 3107 (Ch); [2006] B.P.I.R. 71.

Note also IR 2016 r.9.23—possibility of a debt relief order.

S.271(5)

This protects the discretion of the court to amend petitions, etc. Presumably this would permit consolidation of petitions or changes in the carriage of proceedings (compare the repealed BA 1914 ss.110 and 111). See *Re Purvis* [1998] B.P.I.R. 153. The bankruptcy petition was dismissed in *Re Sutton* [2014] B.P.I.R. 1349 by Chief Registrar Baister after a detailed analysis of *Re Purvis* (above).

For the possible impact on s.271(3) of the EU Mortgage Credit Directive (2014/17/EU) see the intriguing piece by J. Williams in [2017] 10 CRI 131.

On adjournment and s.271(3) see the approach of Newey J in *Choudhry v Luton BC* [2017] EWHC 960 (Ch); [2017] B.P.I.R. 1150 where *Sekhon* (above) is discussed but an adjournment of the petition (which was founded upon council tax liability orders) was refused on the facts.

272 Grounds of debtor's petition [Omitted]

273 Appointment of insolvency practitioner by the court [Omitted]

274 Action on report of insolvency practitioner [Omitted]

274A Debtor who meets conditions for a debt relief order [Omitted]

275 Summary administration [Repealed]

General Note to ss.272–275

Editors' note—summary administration was repealed from 1 April 2004—see s.269 of and Sch.23 to EA 2002. Subsequently ss.272 and 273 were omitted in the wake of the changes made to debtor-induced bankruptcies by ERRA 2013 (effective from 6 April 2016). But ss.272 and 273 retain an existence in the discrete context of petitions for the administration of deceased insolvents and in the context of insolvent partnerships—see Enterprise and Regulatory Reform Act 2013 (Commencement No.9 and Saving Provisions) Order 2016 (SI 2016/191).

Other cases for special consideration

276 Default in connection with voluntary arrangement

276(1) [Conditions for s.264(1)(c) bankruptcy order] The court shall not make a bankruptcy order on a petition under section 264(1)(c) (supervisor of, or person bound by, voluntary arrangement proposed and approved) unless it is satisfied–

(a) that the debtor has failed to comply with his obligations under the voluntary arrangement, or

(b) that information which was false or misleading in any material particular or which contained material omissions–

  (i) was contained in any statement of affairs or other document supplied by the debtor under Part VIII to any person, or

  (ii) was otherwise made available by the debtor to his creditors in connection with a creditors' decision procedure instigated under that Part, or

(c) that the debtor has failed to do all such things as may for the purposes of the voluntary arrangement have been reasonably required of him by the supervisor of the arrangement.

276(2) [Expenses] Where a bankruptcy order is made on a petition under section 264(1)(c), any expenses properly incurred as expenses of the administration of the voluntary arrangement in question shall be a first charge on the bankrupt's estate.

General Note

This provision was subject to minor amendment by SBEEA 2015 s.126 and Sch.9 para.73 to reflect new creditor decision procedures.

S.276(1)

This allows the court to make a bankruptcy order where a debtor has failed to fulfil his obligations under a voluntary arrangement set up by virtue of ss.252–263. The jurisdiction here is discretionary and if appropriate the court may permit the IVA to continue—*Kaye v Bourne* [2004] EWHC 3236 (Ch); [2005] B.P.I.R. 590. In *Bonney and Hughes-Holland v Mirpuri* [2013] B.P.I.R. 412 Registrar Jones confirmed the wide discretion enjoyed by the court in dealing with s.276 applications but stressed that the prime concern is what is in the best interests of creditors. Material omissions in the proposal, etc. may also justify this course of action—*Re Tack* [2000] B.P.I.R. 164. On s.276(1)(b) and the continuing duty of disclosure see *Somji v Cadbury Schweppes plc* [2001] B.P.I.R. 172. The fact that the debtor is not to blame for the failure of the IVA is irrelevant: *Re Keenan* [1998] B.P.I.R. 205. Nor indeed is it a bar to a s.276 petition that the debtor has remedied the default by the time the petition is heard—*Carter-Knight v Peat* [2000] B.P.I.R. 268. A default petition can be presented by the supervisor even though the time period specified in the IVA has expired—*Harris v Gross* [2001] B.P.I.R. 586. In *Bradburn v Kaye* [2006] B.P.I.R. 605 Mr Recorder Hodge QC (sitting as a Deputy Judge of the High Court) held that an IVA could be set aside under s.276(1)(b) of the IA 1986 and a bankruptcy order substituted on the grounds of non disclosure of the full extent of potential liabilities to the Revenue. It was material non disclosure because had the Revenue been treated as a creditor for the full amount it would have been in a position to block the IVA. There was no need to show that the non disclosure was culpable. Moreover, the existence of a waiver provision in the IVA terms excusing default or non disclosure could not override the statutory jurisdiction under s.276. On the other hand, the alternative grounds put forward by the supervisor (i.e. failure to obtain consent before incurring further credit contrary to the IVA terms) for setting aside were rejected. Although in engaging the services of accountants the debtor technically had incurred further credit in breach of the IVA that alone would not have persuaded this court to exercise its jurisdiction under s.276(1)(a) to set aside the IVA because this was a technical breach and the IVA was delivering the promised payments on time to creditors. Where an IVA is set aside under s.276 it is not a nullity ab initio—see *Cooper v Official Receiver* [2002] EWHC 1970 (Ch); [2003] B.P.I.R. 55.

S.276(2)

Where the court takes this drastic step, the expenses already incurred in connection with the scheme become a first charge on the bankrupt's estate.

277 Petition based on criminal bankruptcy order

277(1) [Duty of court] Subject to section 266(3), the court shall make a bankruptcy order on a petition under section 264(1)(d) on production of a copy of the criminal bankruptcy order on which the petition is based.

This does not apply if it appears to the court that the criminal bankruptcy order has been rescinded on appeal.

277(2) [Effect of appeal pending] Subject to the provisions of this Part, the fact that an appeal is pending against any conviction by virtue of which a criminal bankruptcy order was made does not affect any proceedings on a petition under section 264(1)(d) based on that order.

277(3) [When appeal is pending] For the purposes of this section, an appeal against a conviction is pending–

(a) in any case, until the expiration of the period of 28 days beginning with the date of conviction;

(b) if notice of appeal to the Court of Appeal is given during that period and during that period the appellant notifies the official receiver of it, until the determination of the appeal and thereafter for so long as an appeal to the Supreme Court is pending within the meaning of subsection (4).

277(4) [When appeal to Supreme Court pending] For the purposes of subsection (3)(b) an appeal to the Supreme Court shall be treated as pending until any application for leave to appeal is disposed of and, if leave to appeal is granted, until the appeal is disposed of; and for the purposes of this subsection an application for leave to appeal shall be treated as disposed of at the expiration of the time within which it may be made, if it is not made within that time.

General Note

This section deals with petitions arising out of criminal bankruptcy orders. Criminal bankruptcy orders were first introduced in 1972, and the legislation currently in force is the Powers of the Criminal Courts Act 1973 ss.39, 40. However, the power to make such orders was abolished by CJA 1988 s.101, with effect from 3 April 1989 (see SI 1989/264 (C. 8)), and so it is most unlikely that there will be any occasion to invoke the provisions of s.264(1)(d) or s.277 in the future.

Chapter IA

Commencement and Duration of Bankruptcy

278 Commencement and continuance

278 The bankruptcy of an individual against whom a bankruptcy order has been made–

(a) commences with the day on which the order is made, and

(b) continues until the individual is discharged under this Chapter.

General Note

Bankruptcy commences at the date of the order (and not when the petition was presented), and lasts until discharge.

See IR 2016 rr.10.32 and 10.43.

Note amendment to para.(b) made by ERRA 2013 Sch.19 para.11.

279 Duration

279(1) [Discharge from bankruptcy in one year] A bankrupt is discharged from bankruptcy at the end of the period of one year beginning with the date on which the bankruptcy commences.

279(2) [Repealed]

279(3) [Order that discharge period ceases to run] On the application of the official receiver or the trustee of a bankrupt's estate, the court may order that the period specified in subsection (1) shall cease to run until–

(a) the end of a specified period, or

(b) the fulfilment of a specified condition.

279(4) [When order may be made] The court may make an order under subsection (3) only if satisfied that the bankrupt has failed or is failing to comply with an obligation under this Part.

279(5) ["Condition" in s.279(3)(b)] In subsection (3)(b) "condition" includes a condition requiring that the court be satisfied of something.

279(6) [Non-application of s.279(1)–(5)] In the case of an individual who is made bankrupt on a petition under section 264(1)(d)–

(a) subsections (1) to (5) shall not apply, and

(b) the bankrupt is discharged from bankruptcy by an order of the court under section 280.

279(7) [Power of court to annul bankruptcy order] This section is without prejudice to any power of the court to annul a bankruptcy order.

General Note

These new provisions on discharge, which were introduced by s.256 of EA 2002, came into effect in April 2004. These provisions must be read in the light of Sch.19 to EA 2002 which makes transitional provisions.

Automatic discharge, which was pioneered in 1976 is now widely accepted as a feature of bankruptcy regulation, in spite of concerns raised by the Cork Committee (Cmnd.8558, para.607). A lucid historical survey of discharge in bankruptcy is provided by J Tribe in a three part article published in [2012] 25 Insolv. Int. 108 and 117 and [2013] 26 Insolv. Int. 1.

For further provisions on discharge see IR 2016 rr.10.142–10.146.

For discussion of the equivalent provision in Northern Ireland (art.253 of the 1989 Insolvency Order) see *Official Receiver v McWilliams* [2012] NICh 28.

The Official Receiver obtained 1,213 suspensions in 2011/2012. There were 711 suspension of discharge orders granted in 2015/2016. This drop in numbers merely reflects the decline of bankruptcy.

S.279(1)

This introduces the new one-year maximum period before discharge takes effect. It is a significant reduction on the existing three-year period, though not as great as the government intended when it initially proposed six months! When assessing this discharge period it must be borne in mind that discharge does not for the most part mean that the powers of the trustee vis-à-vis the estate have come to an end. Realisation powers and income payments matters can continue for some time thereafter.

S.279(2)

Subsection (2) was repealed by ERRA 2013 s.73 and Sch.21 Pt 3. Early discharge before the standard 12-month period has elapsed has not worked in practice and is not cost effective. This repeal necessitated amendments to the connecting Insolvency Rules and these were made by Insolvency (Amendment) Rules 2013 (SI 2013/2135) with effect from 1 October 2013.

S.279(3)–(5)

These deal with the converse situation where the trustee or official receiver wish to extend the one-year period for a specified period or until a condition is satisfied. This will only happen if the bankrupt has failed to fulfil his obligations. Cases decided under the former s.279(3) will continue to be instructive—see here *Hardy v Focus Insurance Co Ltd* [1997] B.P.I.R. 77; *Holmes v Official Receiver* [1996] B.C.C. 246; *Jacobs v Official Receiver*

[1999] 1 W.L.R. 619; and *Bagnall v Official Receiver* [2004] EWCA Civ 1925; [2004] B.P.I.R. 445 where the Court of Appeal adopted a purposive view on whether interim orders could in principle be made suspending discharge pending a full hearing. Late applications for such an order were not to be encouraged and the lateness of any application might persuade the court not to grant the order sought. On s.279(3) see *Hafiz v Ingram* [2012] EWHC 274 (Ch); [2012] B.P.I.R. 1116. A 12-month suspension of discharge was upheld on appeal by Norris J in *Keely v Bell* [2016] EWHC 308 (Ch); [2016] B.P.I.R. 653. The bankrupt had failed to discharge his obligations under s.291 and the suspension had been granted notwithstanding that the application by the trustee was in some respects late. Norris J considered the nature of the obligation of the bankrupt to cooperate so as to ensure that a suspension of discharge was lifted. Essentially the trustee wishing to have a suspension imposed needed to show that the bankrupt had not done all that was reasonable to comply with requests to cooperate. Late application for suspension should be avoided but the court could still grant a suspension of discharge on a late application. A conditional suspension might be appropriate if there were specific things that the bankrupt should be required to do. In the case of general non-compliance a fixed term suspension of discharge was more appropriate.

On circumstances where suspension of automatic discharge might be appropriate see *Shierson v Rastogi* [2007] EWHC 1266 (Ch); [2007] B.P.I.R. 864. For an unsuccessful application for suspension of discharge see *Chadwick v Nash* [2012] B.P.I.R. 70 (Mr Registrar Nicholls). The application was refused because the evidence suggested that the bankrupt had done all he could reasonably do in terms of co-operation and to impose conditions on the grant of automatic discharge so late in the day was seen as unacceptable. One possible reason behind the application was the desire to secure an income payments agreement before discharge—but the court indicated that the matters raised on the suspension application were more appropriate for an income payments order application and no such application had been made. In *Bramston v Haut* [2012] EWHC 1279 (Ch); [2012] B.P.I.R. 672 the bankrupt (unusually) wanted the discharge suspended so as to be able to put forward an IVA to his creditors. The trustee was opposed to this course of action. At first instance the bankrupt was successful in challenging the approach of the trustee; Arnold J held that, even if the *Wednesbury* test was applied to review the actions of the trustee, that test had become more relaxed with modern developments in Public Law. But a more conservative approach was adopted in the Court of Appeal [2012] EWCA Civ 1637 where the court indicated that something amounting to perversity must be established before the court would intervene. The views of the trustee on this matter therefore prevailed. Barling J confirmed in *Tucker v Atkins* [2013] EWHC 4469 (Ch); [2014] B.P.I.R. 1359 that it was not possible for an undischarged bankrupt to invoke s.279 to obtain suspension of discharge to promote an IVA. The correct procedure was to seek an interim order under s.252 and to obtain suspension of discharge through that route. Discharge was suspended in *Hellard v Kapoor* [2013] EWHC 2204 (Ch); [2013] B.P.I.R. 745—for the costs implications see [2013] EWHC 2496 (Ch); [2013] B.P.I.R. 745 at 753. In *Mawer v Bland* [2013] EWHC 3122 (Ch) Rose J granted a suspension from discharge until the trustee could confirm full co-operation from the bankrupt. On s.279(3) see *Wilson v Williams* [2015] EWHC 1841 (Ch); [2015] B.P.I.R. 1319. Here HHJ Behrens upheld a first instance decision to suspend discharge until co-operation with the trustee could be confirmed. For the appropriate form of any order that may be made under s.279(3) see the comments of Nugee J in *Weir v Hilsdon* [2017] EWHC 983 (Ch); [2017] B.P.I.R. 1088. Nugee J stressed the importance of customising the order so as to make it appropriate to the facts of each individual case. The need to take into account the desirability of certainty had to be balanced with the necessity of supporting the trustee in securing the bankrupt's cooperation. For critique of this area of practice see Patterson [2016] 29 Insolv. Int. 22 and [2017] 30 Insolv. Int. 85. For critique of this area of practice see Patterson [2016] 29 Insolv. Int. 22 and [2017] 30 Insol. Int. 85. *OR v Cooksey* [2013] B.P.I.R. 526 is a curious case. Here an automatic discharge had been suspended for non-co-operation. The bankrupt having mended his ways was then successful in persuading the courts that he should be granted a certificate of discharge pursuant to what is now IR 2016 r.10.144/10.145.

Chief Registrar Baister refused to suspend discharge in *Bowles v Trefilov* (unreported, 29 April 2016) as the evidence before the court did not justify suspension.

On the submission of evidence where suspension is sought see *ORNI v McWilliams* [2012] NICh 28 where Deeny J deals with the equivalent provision in Northern Ireland.

For a curious case where the bankrupt was (for good reason) unaware that his discharge had been suspended see *Secretary of State for Business, Innovation and Skills v Melaris* (*Re Waterfall Media Ltd*) [2013] B.P.I.R. 1109 (Registrar Barber).

Note *Harris v Official Receiver* (unreported, 4 November 2016, Andrew Simmonds QC)—when a fixed term suspension order has expired that does not preclude a further indefinite suspension order being sought if cooperation is not forthcoming.

S.279(6)

This deals with a special (and extremely rare) case involving criminal bankruptcy.

Note linguistic change made to subs (6) by ERRA 2013 Sch.19 para.12 to reflect the new out of court debtor adjudication bankruptcy procedure.

S.279(7)
This provision governing discharge does not affect the power of the court to annul a bankruptcy order—see s.282.

280 Discharge by order of the court

280(1) [Application to court] An application for an order of the court discharging an individual from bankruptcy in a case falling within section 279(6) may be made by the bankrupt at any time after the end of the period of 5 years beginning with the date on which the bankruptcy commences.

280(2) [Powers of court] On an application under this section the court may–

(a) refuse to discharge the bankrupt from bankruptcy,

(b) make an order discharging him absolutely, or

(c) make an order discharging him subject to such conditions with respect to any income which may subsequently become due to him, or with respect to property devolving upon him, or acquired by him, after his discharge, as may be specified in the order.

280(3) [Commencement of effect of order] The court may provide for an order falling within subsection (2)(b) or (c) to have immediate effect or to have its effect suspended for such period, or until the fulfilment of such conditions (including a condition requiring the court to be satisfied as to any matter), as may be specified in the order.

General Note

Tracking back through s.279(6) and 264(1)(d) it becomes apparent on closer examination that s.280 only applies to cases of criminal bankruptcy. The headnote could be more explicit here. Minor textual changes were made by s.269 of and Sch.23 to EA 2002.

S.280(1)
This provision deals with the situation where an undischarged bankrupt applies to the court for his discharge. Automatic discharge is not available where a person was made bankrupt as a result of a criminal bankruptcy order (the other previous exclusion from automatic discharge, where the debtor had been made bankrupt within the 15 years prior to the commencement of the present bankruptcy, was removed from 1 April 2004 as a result of the EA 2002 changes coming into effect). In the case of a person subject to a criminal bankruptcy order he must wait for five years after the commencement of the bankruptcy to elapse before applying to the court for his discharge. See also IR 2016 rr.10.142–10.146.

There is no provision in the present Act for the automatic review of cases every five years by the official receiver, as was required by IA 1976 s.8. However, this is immaterial, as automatic discharge under s.279 is now the general rule.

S.280(2), (3)
On such an application the court has a variety of options open to it, including the grant of conditional or suspended discharges. The Secretary of State can appeal against a discharge order, see IR 2016 r.12.60.

281 Effect of discharge

281(1) [Discharge qualified release] Subject as follows, where a bankrupt is discharged, the discharge releases him from all the bankruptcy debts, but has no effect–

(a) on the functions (so far as they remain to be carried out) of the trustee of his estate, or

(b) on the operation, for the purposes of the carrying out of those functions, of the provisions of this Part;

and, in particular, discharge does not affect the right of any creditor of the bankrupt to prove in the bankruptcy for any debt from which the bankrupt is released.

281(2) [Enforcement of security] Discharge does not affect the right of any secured creditor of the bankrupt to enforce his security for the payment of a debt from which the bankrupt is released.

281(3) [Fraud etc.] Discharge does not release the bankrupt from any bankruptcy debt which he incurred in respect of, or forbearance in respect of which was secured by means of, any fraud or fraudulent breach of trust to which he was a party.

281(4) [Fines, other penalties] Discharge does not release the bankrupt from any liability in respect of a fine imposed for an offence or from any liability under a recognisance except, in the case of a penalty imposed for an offence under an enactment relating to the public revenue or of a recognisance, with the consent of the Treasury.

281(4A) [Confiscation order] In subsection (4) the reference to a fine imposed for an offence includes a reference to–

(a) a charge ordered to be paid under section 21A of the Prosecution of Offences Act 1985 (criminal courts charge), whether on conviction or otherwise:

(b) a confiscation order under Part 2, 3 or 4 of the Proceeds of Crime Act 2002.

281(5) [Debts re damages etc.] Discharge does not, except to such extent and on such conditions as the court may direct, release the bankrupt from any bankruptcy debt which–

(a) consists in a liability to pay damages for negligence, nuisance or breach of a statutory, contractual or other duty, or to pay damages by virtue of Part I of the Consumer Protection Act 1987, being in either case damages in respect of personal injuries to any person, or

(b) arises under any order made in family proceedings or under a maintenance calculation made under the Child Support Act 1991.

281(6) [Other bankruptcy debts] Discharge does not release the bankrupt from such other bankruptcy debts, not being debts provable in his bankruptcy, as are prescribed.

281(7) [Liability as surety] Discharge does not release any person other than the bankrupt from any liability (whether as partner or co-trustee of the bankrupt or otherwise) from which the bankrupt is released by the discharge, or from any liability as surety for the bankrupt or as a person in the nature of such a surety.

281(8) [Definitions] In this section–

"family proceedings" means–

(a) proceedings in the family court; and

(b) family proceedings within the meaning of Part V of the Matrimonial and Family Proceedings Act 1984.

"fine" means the same as in the Magistrates' Courts Act 1980; and

"personal injuries" includes death and any disease or other impairment of a person's physical or mental condition.

S.281(1)

As a general rule, discharge releases the bankrupt from liability in respect of "bankruptcy debts" (see s.382). However, any residual functions of the trustee are not to be affected, and creditors in respect of whose debts the bankrupt has been released by the discharge may still prove in the bankruptcy. See further IR 2016 r.10.146. A discharged bankrupt cannot escape the attentions of a trustee by seeking an IVA as at this stage he is no longer a "debtor" for the purposes of s.253—see *Wright v Official Receiver* [2001] B.P.I.R. 196.

Note also the effect of discharge on disqualifications, see for example s.427(2)(a).

As to what constitutes a bankruptcy debt for the purposes of a s.281 discharge see *Secretary of State for Work and Pensions v Balding* [2007] EWCA Civ 1327; [2007] B.P.I.R. 1669. *Balding* (above) was approved by the Supreme Court in *Secretary of State for Work and Pensions v Payne* [2011] UKSC 60. See also *Casson and Wales v Law*

Society [2009] EWHC 1943 (Admin)—liability not discharged by bankruptcy because it did not qualify as a contingent liability at time of bankruptcy order and so was not a bankruptcy debt. See also s.382 and the note to IR 2016 r.14.1.

Discharge prevents a creditor from pursuing a debtor who is now a discharged bankrupt, but it does not destroy any underlying cause of action—see *Law Society v OR and Shah* [2007] EWHC 2841 (Ch); [2007] B.P.I.R. 1595. This can have consequences in relation to the Third Parties (Rights Against Insurers) Act 2010, which came into force in August 2016.

Note also *Arnold v Williams* [2008] EWHC 218 (Ch); [2008] B.P.I.R. 247.

For a comparative overview of the position on discharge in Europe see Baister [2015] 28 Insolv. Int. 65.

S.281(2)–(6), (8)

In s.281(5)(a) the words "or to pay damages by virtue of Part I of the Consumer Protection Act 1987, being in either case" have been substituted by the Consumer Protection Act 1987. Subsection (5) has been amended by the Children Act 1989 which removed the words "or in domestic proceedings" from the original text. Subsection (8) now has a new definition of "family proceedings" provided by the Children Act 1989.

These provisions deal with the exceptions to the general release in s.281(1). Note especially IR 2016 r.10.146 to explain the word "prescribed" in s.281(6). Security enforcement rights are preserved notwithstanding the release of the debt. Debts connected with fraud or breach of trust survive, as does liability in respect of a fine (see s.281(8)) or similar penalty (note the exception for fines, etc. in respect of public revenue offences). On the meaning of "fraud" for the purposes of s.281(3) see *Masters v Leaver* [2000] B.P.I.R. 284; *Mander v Evans* [2001] B.P.I.R. 902; and *Woodland Ferrari v UCL Group Retirement Benefits Scheme* [2002] B.P.I.R. 1270. Note here *Anglo Manx Group Ltd v Aitken* [2002] B.P.I.R. 215 where the significance of limitation periods continuing to run throughout the period of bankruptcy was emphasised. Liability to pay damages in respect of personal injuries (see s.281(8)), or liability arising from family or domestic proceedings (see s.281(8)) is not released unless the court so directs. There is also no release in respect of debts not provable in bankruptcy. Note that the list of exceptions in BA 1914 s.28 has been widened. The Cork Committee recommended that there should be no release of fines on discharge, but by a majority voted against allowing claims for personal injury to survive—see the *Report*, paras 1330 and 1333 respectively. Both items, however, have been added to the list of exceptions. Liability in respect of student loans is not discharged—Higher Education Act 2004 s.42 and reg.5 of the Education (Student Support) (No.2) Regulations 2002 (Amendment) (No.3) Regulations 2004 (SI 2004/2041). The current rules relating to student loans are detailed in reg.80 of the Education (Student Loans) (Repayment) Regulations 2009 (SI 2009/470) as amended by Education (Student Loans) (Repayment) (Amendment) Regulations 2010 (SI 2010/661).

Section 281(4) has effect as if the reference to a fine included a reference to a confiscation order (an extended meaning introduced by CJA 1988). Section 281(4A) was inserted by POCA 2002 Sch.11 para.16(2).

In *Soutzos v Asombang* [2010] B.P.I.R. 960 an attempt to establish that a debt fell within s.281(3), and so was not discharged, failed. On s.281(3) see *ECO Quest plc v GFI Consultants Ltd* [2014] EWHC 4329 (QB); [2015] B.P.I.R. 244.

On debts being preserved under s.281(3) see the ruling of Registrar Jones in *Re Bance* [2016] EWHC 1028 (Ch). This was an unusual case of a second bankruptcy petition being based upon an earlier judgment alleging fraud. As a matter of discretion a second bankruptcy order was refused by Registrar Jones as at that time it appeared to serve no purpose.

As there was no contingent liability found to be present in *Casson and Wales v The Law Society* [2009] EWHC 1943 (Admin); [2010] B.P.I.R. 49 there was no discharge of that item. One wonders about the status of this case in the wake of *Nortel* [2013] UKSC 52; [2013] B.C.C. 624, which has widened the concept of what might constitute a provable debt and has rejected the narrow view taken in cases such as *Glenister v Rowe* [2000] Ch. 76.

On s.281(5) see *Hayes v Hayes* [2012] EWHC 1240 (Ch); [2012] B.P.I.R. 739. The court noted the lack of clarity on the issue of whether the court should order release from a debt under s.281. At the end of the day, this was a matter for judicial discretion but the importance of family orders not being frustrated through exploitation of a bankruptcy process was particularly important. Note also *McRoberts v McRoberts* [2012] EWHC 2966 (Ch); [2013] B.P.I.R. 77 where further consideration was given to this matter by Hildyard J and broad approval was given to the views expressed in *Hayes v Hayes* (above). See also on s.281(5) the case of *Re Tovey (decd), Berry v Child Support Agency* [2016] EWHC 1418 (Ch); [2016] B.P.I.R. 1256.

S.281(7)

Although the bankrupt may be released from liability for a debt, any co-obligor (e.g. a partner of the bankrupt, or co-trustee, etc.) and any person liable as surety for him is not so released. On s.281(7) see *Evans v Finance-U-Ltd* [2013] EWCA Civ 869; [2013] B.P.I.R. 1001.

281A Post-discharge restrictions

281A Schedule 4A to this Act (bankruptcy restrictions order and bankruptcy restrictions undertaking) shall have effect.

General Note

This new provision is introduced via s.257 of EA 2002 with effect from April 2004. It directs our attention to the new Sch.4A. In order to reassure the public concerned about the risks posed by early discharge the Government introduced a degree of balance in the form of a bankruptcy restriction order which will be applied to those bankrupts deemed not to be "honest" or, more accurately, those whose conduct falls within subparas (a)–(m) of para.2(2) in Sch.4A. We thus have a return to a former manifestation in bankruptcy law under which legal distinctions were drawn between types of bankrupt. Looking at (a)–(m) there are some predictable *indiciae* of misbehaviour—note the reappearance of now decriminalised conduct in (a) and (j). Of the other *indiciae* one can envisage a flood of litigation clarifying the ambit of these provisions—para.(k) looks a prime candidate. Subparagraph (e) will raise many concerns and guidance may have to be drawn from any jurisprudence under s.342A. Serial bankrupts will fall foul of para.2(3).

For procedural aspects see *OR v Bayliss* (unreported, 26 July 2017, E. Johnson QC).

Applications for a BRO must normally be made within one year of the bankruptcy, though the court can grant an extension. The possibility of an interim order is provided for by para.5 for extreme cases.

Where the court grants a BRO against a bankrupt a series of restrictions will be applied for a period of not less than 2 years and up to 15 years after the grant of the order (see Sch.21 to the 2002 Act). In anticipation of a flood of cases disabling the courts the possibility of securing restrictions via an undertakings procedure is provided for by para.7. Actually very few BROs (or BRUs for that matter) were made in the first year of operation of the new scheme but the numbers are steadily increasing.

All BROs and BRUs should be listed in a public register—Sch.4A para.12.

In 2011/2012 some 873 new BROs/BRUs were secured with some 83 per cent of this combined total consisting of BRUs.

282 Court's power to annul bankruptcy order

282(1) [Power of annulment] The court may annul a bankruptcy order if it at any time appears to the court–

(a) that, on any grounds existing at the time the order was made, the order ought not to have been made, or

(b) that, to the extent required by the rules, the bankruptcy debts and the expenses of the bankruptcy have all, since the making of the order, been either paid or secured for to the satisfaction of the court.

282(2) [Where petition under s.264(1)(a), (b), (c)] The court may annul a bankruptcy order made against an individual on a petition under paragraph (a) or (c) of section 264(1) or on a bankruptcy application if it at any time appears to the court, on an application by the Official Petitioner–

(a) that the petition was pending or the application was ongoing at a time when a criminal bankruptcy order was made against the individual or was presented after such an order was so made, and

(b) no appeal is pending (within the meaning of section 277) against the individual's conviction of any offence by virtue of which the criminal bankruptcy order was made;

and the court shall annul a bankruptcy order made on a petition under section 264(1)(d) if it at any time appears to the court that the criminal bankruptcy order on which the petition was based has been rescinded in consequence of an appeal.

282(3) [Annulment whether or not discharged] The court may annul a bankruptcy order whether or not the bankrupt has been discharged from the bankruptcy.

282(4) [Effect of annulment] Where the court annuls a bankruptcy order (whether under this section or under section 261 in Part VIII)–

(a) any sale or other disposition of property, payment made or other thing duly done, under any provision in this Group of Parts, by or under the authority of the official receiver or a trustee of the bankrupt's estate or by the court is valid, but

(b) if any of the bankrupt's estate is then vested, under any such provision, in such a trustee, it shall vest in such person as the court may appoint or, in default of any such appointment, revert to the bankrupt on such terms (if any) as the court may direct;

and the court may include in its order such supplemental provisions as may be authorised by the rules.

282(5) [Repealed from 1 April 2004.]

S.282(1), (3)

The court can annul a bankruptcy order if it should never have been made (compare here *Re a Bankrupt (No.622 of 1995), The Times*, 27 June 1996; *Henwood v Customs and Excise Commissioners* [1998] B.P.I.R. 339; and *Hope v Premierpace (Europe) Ltd* [1999] B.P.I.R. 695) and also if the bankrupt has paid all his debts and bankruptcy expenses to the extent required by the rules: see IR 2016 r.10.138. Conditional annulment is frowned upon—*Re Hagemeister* [2010] B.P.I.R. 1093. If a conditional annulment is ordered the bankruptcy remains in place until the conditions for annulment are met—*Oraki v Dean & Dean* [2017] EWHC 11 (Ch). In *Paulin v Paulin* [2009] B.P.I.R. 572 the Court of Appeal stressed that, where a wife applies for the annulment of her husband's bankruptcy and alleges that he procured his own bankruptcy as a tactic in a divorce dispute, the onus is on her to show that he was not insolvent at the time the bankruptcy order was made. The burden of proof is the ordinary burden expected in civil cases but, if she can establish he was not insolvent in terms of his balance sheet, then he falls under an evidential burden to show that he was insolvent on a commercial basis. This case is also significant with regard to the question as to whether the court can revisit its own judgment on the question of annulment. *Arif v Zar* [2012] EWCA Civ 986; [2012] B.P.I.R. 948 examines procedural aspects of the linkage between annulment proceedings and proceedings dealing with ancillary relief on divorce. The court needs to be alert to the potential abuse of annulment proceedings. The question of annulment rests upon the discretion of the court: *Askew v Peter Dominic Ltd* [1997] B.P.I.R. 163; *Re Coney* [1998] B.P.I.R. 333; *Skarzynski v Chalford Property Co Ltd* [2001] B.P.I.R. 673. Annulment is discretionary and therefore establishing grounds for annulment is no guarantee that the court will annul—*Omokwe v HFC Bank* [2007] B.P.I.R. 1157 (per Chief Registrar Baister). But the court stressed in *Royal Bank of Scotland v The Debtor* [1996] B.P.I.R. 478 that there is no inherent power of annulment beyond the statutory power. The discretion enjoyed by the court under s.282 does not permit it to refuse to annul a bankruptcy order in circumstances where it was clear that the order should not have been made in the first place due to a lack of jurisdiction—*Re Meyden* [2016] EWHC 414 (Ch); [2016] B.P.I.R. 697 per Nugee J.

Moreover the s.375 review jurisdiction cannot be used to circumvent the stringent conditions of s.282—*Inland Revenue Commissioners v Robinson* [1999] B.P.I.R. 329. For the distinction between rescission and annulment see *Hoare v Inland Revenue Commissioners* [2002] EWHC 755 (Ch); [2002] B.P.I.R. 986. The views of Peter Smith J expressed in *Hoare* (above) were questioned in the Court of Appeal in *Yang v Official Receiver* [2017] EWCA Civ 1465. For discussion of the role of the court under these distinct jurisdictions see *Hunt v Peasegood* [2001] B.P.I.R. 76. The relationship between ss.282 and 375 was further reviewed in *Ahmed v Mogul Eastern Foods* [2005] EWHC 3532 (Ch) by Patten J. Points of similarity and areas of difference in these two jurisdictions were highlighted. In particular Patten J was disinclined to allow the rule in *Ladd v Marshall* [1954] 1 W.L.R. 1489 to intrude into the s.282 jurisdiction. For the wide power of the court under s.282(1) and its relationship with the s.375 review jurisdiction see *Snopek v Urang Ltd* [2008] B.P.I.R. 1416. On s.282 and its relationship with the s.375 review jurisdiction see also *Revenue and Customs Commissioners v Cassells* [2009] B.P.I.R. 284. On the facts here an annulment was not a realistic possibility. Another aspect of the annulment jurisdiction was considered by HHJ Hodge QC in *Yang v Official Receiver* [2013] EWHC 3577 (Ch). Once again the distinction between annulment under s.282 and rescission under s.375 was judicially reviewed. A bankruptcy order made upon the basis of liability orders which were subsequently set aside could not be annulled under s.282(1)(a) as it could not be said that the bankruptcy order was invalid when it was made. The proper course of action in such cases was a rescission granted under s.375(1). The Court of Appeal held that liability orders remain valid until set aside. If such orders are set aside the appropriate response is to rescind the bankruptcy order and not to annul it as this would imply that the liability orders never existed. The Court of Appeal explained the difference between annulment and rescission. On dissemination of information about annulment see *Smeaton v Equifax plc* [2013] EWCA Civ 108. Annulment can be granted even though discharge has occurred—though it may not be in the interests of the former bankrupt in such a case to seek annulment—*Owo-Samson v Barclays Bank (No.1)* [2003] EWCA Civ 714; [2003] B.P.I.R. 1373. The Secretary of State can appeal against an annulment order, see IR 2016 r.12.60. An annulment of a bankruptcy order was refused by Warner J in *Re Robertson (a Bankrupt)* [1989] 1 W.L.R. 1139 where there had been failure to prove all debts. See also *Artman v Artman* [1996] B.P.I.R. 511 (annulment refused). The court can annul conditionally—*Engel v Peri* [2002] EWHC 799 (Ch); [2002] B.P.I.R. 961; *Hirani v Rendle* [2004] B.P.I.R. 274; *Thornhill v Atherton* [2004] EWCA Civ 1858; [2005] B.P.I.R. 437. For general analysis of annulment see Brockman and French [2006] 19 Insolv. Int. 62 and 93.

Harman J considered the nature of the jurisdiction to annul in *Re a Debtor (No.68 of 1992)* [1993] T.L.R. 69. Here the point was made that on an annulment hearing under s.282 it was not possible for the court to consider evidence which had been unavailable to the court which had made the bankruptcy in the first place. Relevant considerations on an annulment application were discussed in *Lloyds v Waters* [2001] B.P.I.R. 698. For an unsuccessful s.282 application see *Shamash v Inland Revenue Commissioners* [2002] B.P.I.R. 189. In dealing with an annulment application the court should take into account material events occurring after the date of the bankruptcy order—see *Watts v Newham LBC* [2009] B.P.I.R. 718.

Bankruptcy is a class remedy and the court should not annul without a proper investigation of the facts—*Housiaux v Customs and Excise Commissioners* [2003] EWCA Civ 257; [2003] B.P.I.R. 858; *Leicester v Plumtree Farms* [2004] B.P.I.R. 296.

The Court of Appeal ruling in *Oraki v Dean & Dean (a firm)* [2013] EWCA Civ 1629 provides an important illustration of the annulment jurisdiction at work. Here a party was successful in having a bankruptcy annulled under s.282(1)(a) on the grounds that the bankruptcy order should not have been made. But the Court of Appeal ruled that the judge at first instance was correct in making such annulment conditional on payment of the claim for remuneration and costs submitted by the trustee in bankruptcy. There was a presumption that the trustee was entitled to be paid for work properly completed notwithstanding the later annulment. The Court of Appeal stressed the discretion enjoyed by judges at first instance in dealing with such difficult cases and underlined its reluctance to interfere with their decisions. Each case must turn on its own facts. For ongoing litigation in this case see *Oraki v Dean & Dean* [2017] EWHC 11 (Ch). In this latter stage of proceedings the judge made the important point that a bankruptcy order made without jurisdiction remains valid until annulled, as do acts performed under said order. For the latest proceedings in this difficult case see *Oraki v Bramston* [2017] EWCA Civ 403 where the Court of Appeal dismissed the appeal from Proudman J and rejected claims that the trustees in bankruptcy had failed to bring the bankruptcies to an end expeditiously. See also *1st Credit (Finance) Ltd v Carr* [2013] EWHC 2318 (Ch); [2013] B.P.I.R. 1012 for comparable judicial thinking.

On going behind a default judgment for the purposes of s.282(1)(a) see *Royal Bank of Scotland v Farley* [1996] B.P.I.R. 638; and *Hunter v Lex Vehicle Finance* [2005] EWHC 223 (Ch); [2005] B.P.I.R. 586. In *Re a Debtor (No.169 of 1997)* (unreported but noted in *Current Law Week*, 14 August 1998) a county court judge annulled a bankruptcy order under s.282(1)(a) because the consent order upon which the petition has been based should never have been made. In *Ridsdale v Bowles* [2015] B.P.I.R. 1275 the county court observed that although the court can look behind a judgment on an annulment application it would not do so if the applicant had delayed unreasonably in challenging said judgment. The court also accepted the possibility of mixed motives on the part of a petitioner. The court will be unlikely to exercise its discretion to annul a bankruptcy in cases of hopeless insolvency.

An annulment application under s.282(1)(a) was allowed on appeal in *Mowbray v Sanders* [2015] EWHC 296 (Ch) because it appeared that the petition debt may have been statute-barred. The annulment was conditional on payment of certain sums by the applicant. On costs see *Mowbray v Sanders* [2015] EWHC 2317 (Ch).

In *Whig v Whig* [2007] EWHC 1856 (Fam); [2007] B.P.I.R. 1418 Munby J on the application of a wife refused to annul a bankruptcy order made against her insolvent husband on his own petition. The effect of that bankruptcy order had been to frustrate the wife's claims to ancillary relief, but the court held that, as the husband was insolvent and bad faith on his part could not be established, annulment under s.282(1)(a) was not justified. In the light of *Paulin v Paulin* [2009] EWCA Civ 221 this authority must be treated with some caution.

In *Re Ruiz* [2011] EWHC 913 (Fam); [2011] B.P.I.R. 1139 an attempt by a wife to secure the annulment of her husband's bankruptcy failed before Peter Jackson J. One reason for this failure to obtain annulment may have been that the application was made 18 months after the bankruptcy order was granted, though the wife did not become aware of the bankruptcy order immediately. The evidence indicated that the husband was insolvent and it was noted that the statutory rights of the wife under family law (and any rights under ECHR art.8) did not confer cast iron guarantees that the family home would not be sold if the husband became bankrupt. A balance had to be maintained between family rights and the rights of creditors. Leave to appeal this judgment was dismissed—see [2011] EWCA Civ 1646. The bankruptcy court is under no obligation to delay its decision on a bankruptcy petition simply because ancillary relief proceedings were ongoing.

Note *Taylor v The Macdonald Partnership* [2015] EWCA Civ 921 which shows that protracted delay in making an annulment application can prove fatal. This was an abortive application for permission to appeal against a refusal by HHJ Hodge to annul a disputed bankruptcy nine years after discharge.

On liability for the trustee's costs of the bankruptcy on an annulment application see *Tetteh v Lambeth LBC* [2008] B.P.I.R. 241. Where the annulment is made pursuant to s.282(1)(a) the starting point is that the petitioning creditor is liable for the bankruptcy costs but that presumption may be rebutted on the facts of each case. In *Redbridge LBC v Mustafa* [2010] EWHC 1105 (Ch); [2010] B.P.I.R. 893 the court reviewed the question of liability for costs on annulment under s.282(1)(a). Further consideration of this issue was provided by HHJ Pelling in the difficult case of *Re Haworth* [2011] EWHC 36 (Ch). On costs in the wake of an annulment see *Willett v Economy Power Ltd* [2012] EWCA Civ 1164; [2012] B.P.I.R. 1298.

In order to succeed in an annulment application under s.282(1)(a) there should be new evidence that was not before the court making the bankruptcy order—but see the flexible approach adopted by Roth J in the unusual case of *1st Credit (Finance) Ltd v Carr* [2013] EWHC 2318 (Ch); [2013] B.P.I.R. 1012.

In *Hunt v Fylde BC* [2008] B.P.I.R. 1368 the court ordered annulment under s.282(1)(a) because it uncovered circumstances not apparent at the time when the bankruptcy order was made. The bankruptcy was annulled under s.282(1)(a) in *Official Receiver v Mitterfellner* [2009] B.P.I.R. 1075 because the debtor did not have a genuine COMI in the jurisdiction so as to justify the making of the bankruptcy order by the English court. See also *Re Hagemeister* [2010] B.P.I.R. 1093. In cases such as *Re Eichler (No.2)* [2011] B.P.I.R. 1293 and *Irish Bank Resolution Corp Ltd v Quinn* [2012] NICh 1 bankruptcies were annulled because the evidence suggested that the petitioning debtors did not have their COMI within the jurisdiction at the relevant time. See *Sparkasse Hilden Ratingen Velbert v Benk* [2012] EWHC 2432 (Ch); [2012] B.P.I.R. 1258 where a bankruptcy was annulled by HHJ Purle QC on an application by a German creditor as the evidence showed that the debtor did not have COMI in the jurisdiction at the relevant time. The applicant creditor had discharged the burden of proof that on the balance of probability COMI was not within the jurisdiction at the date of the petition.

Official Receiver v Keelan [2012] B.P.I.R. 613 was another case where the bankruptcy of a debtor with foreign links was annulled under s.282(1)(a) for lack of jurisdiction. *Die Sparkasse Bremen AG v Armutcu* [2012] EWHC 4026 (Ch); [2013] B.P.I.R. 10 provides another example of a debtor-induced bankruptcy being annulled on the grounds of a lack of COMI. The annulment here was granted by Proudman J *after* discharge from bankruptcy had been obtained, as s.282(3) envisaged. The application was made by a *secured* creditor. See also *OR v Becker* [2013] B.P.I.R. 352 where District Judge Dancey reviewed the law on such applications. The case is interesting because of the use of an intermediary by the German debtor and the spotlight placed upon that feature by the court. A bankruptcy obtained by a debtor on an ex parte application was also annulled on the application of a creditor in *ACC Bank plc v McCann* [2013] NIMaster 1.

In *Commerzbank AG v Brehm* [2014] B.P.I.R. 359 Chief Registrar Baister dismissed an annulment application by a German creditor of a German debtor who had successfully petitioned for bankruptcy in the English courts. The case was marginal but the creditor had failed to convince the court that the debtor did not have COMI in the jurisdiction. For an annulment application by a German creditor in a COMI case see Registrar Briggs' ruling in *Re Riemann* [2015] B.P.I.R. 1405. The application failed because COMI within the English jurisdiction had been established and, in any case, several years had elapsed since discharge. The bankrupt had fully co-operated with the official receiver.

An annulment application was dismissed in *JSC Bank of Moscow v Kekhman* [2014] B.P.I.R. 959 by Chief Registrar Baister. Although there were some errors in the information provided by the debtor to the court these did not justify annulment. On appeal ([2015] EWHC 396 (Ch)) Morgan J, whilst rejecting some of the reasoning used by Chief Registrar Baister, nevertheless confirmed that, on balance and in the exercise of discretion, this application to annul the bankruptcy should be dismissed. It clearly was a very borderline case. The judgment of Morgan J contains detailed discussion of the approach that should be taken by the court to the issues of connection to the jurisdiction and any potential benefit flowing from the order when considering any annulment application on jurisdictional grounds. See notes to ss.265 and 272.

As to what must be established by the bankrupt in order to procure an annulment under s.282(1)(a) see *Flett v Revenue and Customs Commissioners* [2010] B.P.I.R. 1075. It is not sufficient to merely raise the possibility that there may have been a defence to the debt. See *Parveen v Manchester City Council* [2010] B.P.I.R. 152 for a case of annulment under s.282(1)(a)—the bankruptcy order should not have been made as it represented a disproportionate response to council tax arrears. An application to annul pursuant to s.282(1)(a) failed in *Loy v O'Sullivan* [2010] EWHC 3583 (Ch); [2011] B.P.I.R. 181.

Although there is no fixed limitation period in which annulment must be sought the longer the bankrupt waits the more difficult it may be to ensure that the creditors can be contacted to enable them to be repaid in full for the purposes of s.282(1)(b)—*Gill v Quinn* [2004] EWHC 883 (Ch); [2005] B.P.I.R. 129. For the general principles relevant when considering whether to annul see *Harper v Buchler* [2004] B.P.I.R. 724. For later proceedings in this case see *Harper v Buchler (No.2)* [2005] B.P.I.R. 577 where the court indicated that it would be unlikely to exercise its discretion to annul a bankruptcy order made a decade ago unless statutory interest was paid. For further consideration of whether (and to what extent) statutory interest should be paid see *Wilcock v Duckworth* [2005] B.P.I.R. 682. On the issue of whether statutory interest is payable where a bankruptcy is annulled under s.282(1)(b) see *Lewis v Kennedy* [2010] B.P.I.R. 886. Registrar Jacques indicated that where there is a surplus in the estate that would be the normal expectation unless special circumstances were present (as in this case). The issue of payment of statutory interest on an annulment under s.282(1)(b) is addressed by IR 2016 r.10.138 which was derived from I(A)R 2010 (SI 2010/686). For an instructive review of these questions see Pomeroy [2005] 18 Insolv. Int. 90. On the question of solicitors' undertakings and s.282(1)(b) annulments see *Halabi v Camden LBC* [2008] EWHC 322 (Ch); [2008] B.P.I.R. 370. Here the county court practice of granting an annulment by reference to a solicitors' undertaking was ruled to be undesirable and should in future by replaced by a practice involving annulment orders conditional upon certain events occurring to the satisfaction of the official receiver. The inconvenient ruling in *Halabi* was neutralised by I(A)R 2010 (SI 2010/686) through amendments to IR 1986 and by the insertion of r.6.211(6) (now IR 2016 r.10.138(7)). There was no prospect of an annulment under s.282(1)(b) in *Dadourian Group v Simms* [2008] B.P.I.R. 508.

In *Webster v Mackay* [2013] EWHC 2571 (Ch); [2013] B.P.I.R. 1136 HHJ Purle QC dismissed an appeal from Chief Registrar Baister who had ruled that there were no grounds for annulment under s.282(1)(a) nor the exceptional circumstances required for a rescission of the bankruptcy order under s.375. The point was made that the older the order the less likely it is that the court will set it aside.

In *OR v McKay* [2009] B.P.I.R. 1061 the Court of Appeal departed from an old precedent when seeking to give a modern meaning to s.282(1)(b).

An annulment application cannot be used to relitigate issues determined in the bankruptcy proceedings—*Balendran v Law Society* [2004] EWHC 495 (Ch); [2004] B.P.I.R. 859. In *Crammer v West Bromwich Building Society* [2012] EWCA Civ 517; [2012] B.P.I.R. 963 the Court of Appeal confirmed that the annulment jurisdiction is not to be used to revisit points which had been the subject of adjudication during the bankruptcy proceedings unless there are exceptional circumstances. But there was discretion to take account of matters that were available to the bankrupt in the earlier stage of the proceedings, but which were not raised by him. In comparison, the power of rescission under s.375 only applied to new material. See *Ahmed v Mogul Eastern Foods* [2005] EWHC 3532 (Ch).

On annulment and disputed debts see *Guinan III v Caldwell Associates Ltd* [2004] EWHC 3348 (Ch); [2004] B.P.I.R. 531. The test for whether a debt is disputed is the same on an annulment application as it is on a set aside application—*Woolsey v Payne* [2015] EWHC 968 (Ch); [2015] B.P.I.R. 933. *Guinan* (above) was applied in Northern Ireland in *O'Callaghan v Clipper Holding II SARL* [2017] NICh 29.

For a case where the bankruptcy was annulled because the petitioner should have done more to explain the frailty of the debtor to the court see *Brister v Official Receiver* [2015] EW Misc B22 (CC); [2015] B.P.I.R. 1008. Here the debtor had in fact died before the bankruptcy order was made, though the creditor and court were unaware of this.

An annulment application alleging procedural unfairness was rejected in *Simmons v Mole Valley* [2004] EWHC 475 (Ch); [2004] B.P.I.R. 1022 because the bankrupt had not bothered to attend the hearing of the bankruptcy petition.

In *Smith v 1st Credit (Finance) Ltd* [2012] EWHC 2600 (Ch); [2013] B.P.I.R. 129 the High Court dismissed an appeal from the county court which had refused an application to annul by a person who had been bankrupted by the assignee of the original debt. The evidence showed that the debtor had been given due notice of this assignment.

In *Richards v Vivendi SA* [2017] EWHC 1581 (Ch); [2017] B.P.I.R. 1390 Morgan J quashed a decision on an annulment application and remitted it for rehearing by the High Court. The reason given was that the district judge hearing the annulment application had not given proper consideration to the fresh evidence submitted by the bankrupt who was applying for annulment.

There is no provision in s.282 requiring the annulment order to be gazetted and published in a local paper, as was necessary under BA 1914 s.29(3): now see IR 2016 r.10.139. Formerly an application for annulment had to be supplemented with a request for rescission of the receiving order under what is now s.375(1). With the abolition of receiving orders this is no longer necessary. For a Court of Appeal authority on rescission of receiving orders, which might have some impact on judicial practice in cases of annulment of bankruptcy orders, see *Re a Debtor (No.707 of 1985), The Times*, 21 January 1988.

In *Cook v Revenue and Customs Commissioners* [2017] B.P.I.R. 1468 an annulment was granted by Deputy Registrar Garwood. Although it was not the case that every failure to put the full facts before the court would result in an annulment, in this instance the court making the bankruptcy order was not apprised of the full position with regard to the tax position. In granting an annulment the court should consider the interests of all creditors and not just the petitioning creditors. Here there were no other creditors. Any non-cooperation by the bankrupt could be taken into account when dealing with expenses on annulment.

Under BA 1914 s.29, the application for annulment had to be made by "any person interested". This requirement, which caused problems in *Re Beesley Ex p. Beesley v The Official Receiver* [1975] 1 All E.R. 385, has been dropped. See here *F v F* [1994] 1 F.L.R. 359 (application by wife of debtor). For discussion, see Miller (1994) 10 I.L. & P. 66. A similar change has been made with regard to s.375. A secured creditor may in certain circumstances be able to apply for annulment—see the comments of Proudman J in *Die Sparkasse Bremen AG v Armutcu* [2012] EWHC 4026 (Ch).

For further provisions on annulment, see IR 2016 rr.10.132–10.141. In *Howard v Savage* [2006] EWHC 3693 (Ch); [2007] B.P.I.R. 1097 Lewison J stressed the link between the requirements of s.282(1)(b) and the Insolvency Rules. For an illuminating review of this jurisdiction see Briggs and Sims [2002] Insolv. L. 2.

Local authorities which through maladministration have improperly sought the bankruptcy of a council tax defaulter are increasingly being called upon to seek a remedial annulment in the wake of an adverse ruling from local government ombudsmen.

Annulment funding agreements are generating a substantial body of case law in their own right—*Annulment Funding Co Ltd v Cowey* [2010] EWCA Civ 711; [2010] B.P.I.R. 1304; *Consolidated Finance Ltd v Hunter* [2010] B.P.I.R. 1322; *Cook v Consolidated Finance Ltd* [2010] EWCA Civ 369; [2010] B.P.I.R. 1331. On regulatory issues linked to annulment funding agreements see *Consolidated Finance Ltd v Collins* [2013] EWCA Civ 475; [2013] B.P.I.R. 543.

S.282(2)

This provision confirms the supremacy of the system of criminal bankruptcy over ordinary bankruptcy cases. The subsection also allows the court to annul a bankruptcy order which was granted on a petition based on a criminal bankruptcy order if that latter order has been rescinded on appeal.

Note prospective amendment: s.282(2) is to be repealed by CJA 1988 s.170(2) and Sch.16 as from a day to be appointed; see the note to s.264.

This provision is subject to amendment by ERRA 2013 Sch.19.

S.282(4)

This deals with the practical effects of annulment—dispositions of property, etc. carried out by a trustee are valid. On annulment, the court can order the revesting of the property in the former bankrupt or some other person. For the rules on liability for costs of the trustee where the bankruptcy is annulled see *Butterworth v Soutter* [2000] B.P.I.R. 582. Where a bankruptcy is annulled under s.282(1)(a) the trustee is entitled to claim payment of costs and expenses where the annulment is postponed pending payment of such items—*Thornhill v Atherton (No.2)* [2008] B.P.I.R. 691. In such a case the trustee can realise estate assets to recover payment. For the effect of annulment on prosecutions for bankruptcy offices, see s.350(2). However, in the case of offences not covered by s.350(2) annulment of a bankruptcy order does not "whitewash" any crimes that may have been committed whilst the individual was bankrupt, for example, the offence of acting as a director whilst being an undischarged bankrupt contrary to s.11 of the CDDA 1986—for discussion see *Inland Revenue Commissioners v McEntaggart* [2004] EWHC 3431 (Ch); [2006] B.P.I.R. 750. On annulment a bankruptcy petition does not necessarily lapse—*Choudhury v Inland Revenue Commissioners* [2000] B.P.I.R. 246. This conclusion was reached notwithstanding the terms of the then r.6.213.

For the effect of annulment upon unknown debts see *London Borough of Lambeth v Simon* [2007] B.P.I.R. 1629. On the interpretation of agreements between bankrupts and third parties designed to facilitate the obtaining of an annulment see *Schweppe v Harper* [2008] B.P.I.R. 1090.

On the consequences of annulment for any claim by trustees for remuneration and costs see *Ella v Ella* [2009] B.P.I.R. 441. On the issue of a trustee's claim for remuneration and expenses in comparable circumstances see the decision of Briggs J in *Appleyard v Wewelwala* [2012] EWHC 3302 (Ch). This case did not feature an annulment but rather a successful appeal against the bankruptcy order in circumstance where the trustee had no notice of such appeal. In such circumstances the court should use its discretion to ensure that the trustee was not left out of pocket. The problem arose because there was no provision in the legislation for the trustee to be notified of an appeal against the bankruptcy order (as opposed to an application to annul).

On the financial aspects of seeking an annulment under s.282(1)(b) in connection with the trustee's entitlement to remuneration during the period of bankruptcy see the approach of Registrar Jones in *Secondus v Atkinson* [2013] B.P.I.R. 632. As to which debts have to be paid in order for s.282(1)(b) to come into play see *Salliss v Hunt* [2014] EWHC 229 (Ch); [2014] 1 W.L.R. 2402.

On s.282(4) see *Redbridge LBC v Mustafa* [2010] B.P.I.R. 893.

S.282(5)
This provision (which dealt with the implications of annulment) was repealed by EA 2002 s.269 and Sch.23 with effect from 1 April 2004.

Chapter II

Protection of Bankrupt's Estate and Investigation of His Affairs

283 Definition of bankrupt's estate

283(1) [Bankrupt's estate] Subject as follows, a bankrupt's estate for the purposes of any of this Group of Parts comprises–

(a) all property belonging to or vested in the bankrupt at the commencement of the bankruptcy, and

(b) any property which by virtue of any of the following provisions of this Part is comprised in that estate or is treated as falling within the preceding paragraph.

283(2) [Non-application of s.283(1)] Subsection (1) does not apply to–

(a) such tools, books, vehicles and other items of equipment as are necessary to the bankrupt for use personally by him in his employment, business or vocation;

(b) such clothing, bedding, furniture, household equipment and provisions as are necessary for satisfying the basic domestic needs of the bankrupt and his family.

This subsection is subject to section 308 in Chapter IV (certain excluded property reclaimable by trustee).

283(3) [Further non-application of s.283(1)] Subsection (1) does not apply to–

(a) property held by the bankrupt on trust for any other person, or

(b) the right of nomination to a vacant ecclesiastical benefice.

283(3A) [Further non-application of s.283(1)] Subject to section 308A in Chapter IV, subsection (1) does not apply to–

(a) a tenancy which is an assured tenancy or an assured agricultural occupancy, within the meaning of Part I of the Housing Act 1988, and the terms of which inhibit an assignment as mentioned in section 127(5) of the Rent Act 1977, or

(b) a protected tenancy, within the meaning of the Rent Act 1977, in respect of which, by virtue of any provision of Part IX of that Act, no premium can lawfully be required as a condition of assignment, or

(c) a tenancy of a dwelling-house by virtue of which the bankrupt is, within the meaning of the Rent (Agriculture) Act 1976, a protected occupier of the dwelling-house, and the terms of which inhibit an assignment as mentioned in section 127(5) of the Rent Act 1977, or

(d) a secure tenancy, within the meaning of Part IV of the Housing Act 1985, which is not capable of being assigned, except in the cases mentioned in section 91(3) of that Act.

283(4) [References to property] References in any of this Group of Parts to property, in relation to a bankrupt, include references to any power exercisable by him over or in respect of property except in so far as the power is exercisable over or in respect of property not for the time being comprised in the bankrupt's estate and–

(a) is so exercisable at a time after either the official receiver has had his release in respect of that estate under section 299(2) in Chapter III or the trustee of that estate has vacated office under section 298(8), or

(b) cannot be so exercised for the benefit of the bankrupt;

and a power exercisable over or in respect of property is deemed for the purposes of any of this Group of Parts to vest in the person entitled to exercise it at the time of the transaction or event by virtue of which it is exercisable by that person (whether or not it becomes so exercisable at that time).

283(5) [Property in bankrupt's estate] For the purposes of any such provision in this Group of Parts, property comprised in a bankrupt's estate is so comprised subject to the rights of any person other than the bankrupt (whether as a secured creditor of the bankrupt or otherwise) in relation thereto, but disregarding–

(a) any rights in relation to which a statement such as is required by section 269(1)(a) was made in the petition on which the bankrupt was made bankrupt, and

(b) any rights which have been otherwise given up in accordance with the rules.

283(6) [Other enactments] This section has effect subject to the provisions of any enactment not contained in this Act under which any property is to be excluded from a bankrupt's estate.

General Note

The major change effected by this provision is the abolition of the doctrine of reputed ownership. This doctrine, which could trace its origins back to 1623, stated that if the debtor appeared to be in possession of property which secretly belonged to another, that would boost his creditworthiness, and therefore his creditors should be entitled to treat that property as part of the bankrupt's estate. The rationale of this doctrine, which applied only to traders who became bankrupt, was criticised by Parke B. long ago in *Belcher v Bellamy* (1848) 2 Exch. 303. It did not reflect commercial practices and it appeared particularly inappropriate with the growth of hire-purchase and consumer credit in the twentieth century. Both the courts and Parliament began to curtail the scope of the doctrine: see, e.g. Consumer Credit Act 1974 s.192(3) and Sch.4 para.6. The doctrine did not apply in Ireland and many Commonwealth jurisdictions. Accordingly, calls for abolition were made by the Cork Committee (*Report*, 1093) and the White Paper, para.116. Incidentally, the abolition of the doctrine may throw up difficulties—the problem of title retention clauses which has troubled corporate insolvency law over the past decade might now raise its ugly head. The doctrine of reputed ownership which applied only to personal and not corporate insolvency law at least served to keep that problem at bay in the law of bankruptcy. The doctrine of "relation back" of the trustee's title to the date of the act of bankruptcy has also been abandoned in the wake of the new procedures for bankruptcy. See *Re Dennis* [1996] B.P.I.R. 106 for the significance of this change. For general discussion of the new rules on the bankrupt's estate see Milman (1988) 4 I.L. & P. 71. For a general analysis of the bankruptcy estate see Brown (2007) 11 Jo of S. Pacific Law 89. On the entitlement of the estate to claim windfalls see *Trustee of F C Jones v Jones* [1996] B.P.I.R. 644. Note that property subject to a restraint, etc. order under the Proceeds of Crime Act 2002 is also excluded from the estate—POCA 2002 s.417. On the interface between the rules governing the bankruptcy estate and the issues relating to the Proceeds of Crime Act 2002 see *Chief Constable of Greater Manchester v Wright* [2015] EWHC 3824 (Ch).

On a potential clash between this section and the provisions in the Land Registration Act 2002 ss.23, 58 and 86(5) see *Blemain Finance Ltd v Goulding* [2013] EWCA Civ 1630 where the primacy of the 2002 Act was stressed.

The estate does not include property that is subject to a recovery claim under s.423—see HHJ Hodge QC's judgment in *Leeds v Lemos* [2017] EWHC 1825 (Ch); [2017] B.P.I.R. 1223.

S.283(1)

This section identifies the bankrupt's estate. Note the possible impact of ss.307–309 here and the general definition of "property" in s.436. Notwithstanding the wide terms of s.283(1)(a) personal correspondence of the debtor does not vest in the trustee—*Haig v Aitken* [2000] B.P.I.R. 462. In *Malcolm v Benedict Mackenzie* [2004] EWCA Civ 1748; [2005] B.P.I.R. 176 the Court of Appeal reaffirmed that the rules relating to the vesting of personal pension rights in the estate did not infringe the European Convention on Human Rights. In particular in this case the bankrupt fell under the old rules applying to bankruptcies commenced pre-29 May 2000 and the fact that his position was materially worse than a later bankrupt did not constitute an infringement of art.14 of the Convention. A right to challenge a tax assessment was held to be property in *R. (Singh) v Revenue and Customs Commissioners* [2010] B.P.I.R. 933. For the linkage between s.283 and powers of attorney see *Sanders v Donovan* [2012] B.P.I.R. 219.

See also *KK v MA* [2012] EWHC 788 (Fam); [2012] B.P.I.R. 1137 at [27] for the link with s.306.

Clearly the estate would include a bankrupt's bank account. This poses problems for such individuals and in December 2012 the Insolvency Service announced that reforms would be made in banking practices to facilitate continued usage by undischarged bankrupts of banking accounts whilst at the same time protecting the estate.

In *Shlosberg v Avonwick Holdings Ltd* [2016] EWHC 1001 (Ch) Arnold J had to consider whether a right to legal privilege was "property". He decided that it was not to be regarded as property. The appeal from the decision of Arnold J was dismissed by the Court of Appeal in *Avonwick Holdings Ltd v Schlosberg* [2016] EWCA Civ 1138.

In the curious cases of *Young v Hamilton* [2010] B.P.I.R. 1468 and *Young v OR* [2010] B.P.I.R. 1477 both the Northern Irish and English courts ruled that bankruptcy deprived a bankrupt the right to commence/continue proceedings in his own name. The loss of control of litigation did not infringe the requirements of the European Convention on Human Rights. The possibility of foreign property vesting in the estate was also considered in *Thornhill v Atherton (No.2)* [2008] B.P.I.R. 691.

In *Walden v Atkins* [2013] EWHC 1387 (Ch); [2013] B.P.I.R. 943 rights arising under a proprietary estoppel were held to constitute "property" within the meaning of s.436 and so formed part of the estate. Note also *Purewal v Countrywide Residential Lettings Ltd* [2015] EWCA Civ 1122 (inclusion of mortgaged property within estate).

For the commencement of the bankruptcy, see s.278(a).

S.283(2), (3)

These provisions list those items that are excluded from the estate. Section 283(2) again reflects a change in the law. See *Hill v Secretary of State* [2005] EWHC 696 (Ch); [2006] 1 B.C.L.C. 601. It was felt that a bankrupt ought to be allowed to keep a greater range of personal possessions than BA 1914 permitted—see the Cork *Report*, para.1113. Thus, the £250 limit has been dropped. It had been overtaken by inflation and discriminated against debtors with capital-intensive businesses. Vehicles are now included among the exceptions, as are general items of business equipment. Thus the old restrictive authorities on "tools" such as *Re Sherman* [1916] W.N. 26 have lost much of their importance. On tools of trade see *Official Receiver v Lloyd* [2015] B.P.I.R. 374. In *Mikki v Duncan* [2017] EWCA Civ 57; [2017] B.P.I.R. 490 the Court of Appeal ruled that the benefit of a contract under which the bankrupt had a vehicle on hire purchase could not, as it was a chose in action, itself be a tool of the trade. It therefore vested in the estate. The trustee was therefore entitled to agree to the sale of the car with the finance provider and to treat any surplus proceeds of sale as part of the estate. On the other hand, such property may now be "replaced" by the trustee under s.308. For an unusual case which involved the court being asked to rule on whether a large number of individual items fell within the estate see *Wood v Lowe* [2015] EWHC 2634 (Ch); [2015] B.P.I.R. 1537. On the "tools of the trade" issue HHJ Saffman made the point that the bankrupt did not have to be using them at the time the question was being determined in order for them to qualify as tools of the trade. On s.283(2) and tools of the trade see Newey J in *Birdi v Price* [2017] EWHC 1859 (Ch); [2017] B.P.I.R. 1140. Trust property is not included in the estate: see *Re Tout & Finch Ltd* [1954] 1 W.L.R. 178; and *Re McKeown* [1974] N.I. 226. Funds held on trust for IVA creditors all come within this exception—*Re Coath* [2000] B.P.I.R. 981. See also *Abrahams v Trustee of Property of Abrahams* [1999] B.P.I.R. 637 (bankrupt holds lottery win on resulting trust for ticket purchaser). For a more complex question relating to a possible trust see *Rooney v Cardona* [1999] B.P.I.R. 291. Where the trustee in bankruptcy realises trust property with the consent of the beneficiary he may be entitled to realisation costs out of the trust fund—*Re Sobey* [1999] B.P.I.R. 1009. Section 283(3) repeats BA 1914 s.38(b).

With regard to the trust exception note that the onus of proof is on the person asserting so to establish that a trust has been created—see *Thandi v Sands* [2014] EWHC 2378 (Ch); [2015] B.P.I.R. 162 where HHJ David Cooke was not persuaded that several properties apparently comprised in the estate were subject to a trust. See also *Bennett v Daci* [2014] EWHC 4479 (Ch). On the scope of the s.283(3) exemption see *Abdulla v Whelan; Re Elsom* [2017] EWHC 605 (Ch); [2017] B.P.I.R. 791. The trust exemption applies even in cases where the bankrupt is one of the trust beneficiaries. For comment see Williamson [2017] 10 CRI 167.

Although the estate does not encompass trust property, in reality such property may be intermingled with the bankrupt's assets. Accordingly, if the trustee incurs expense in identifying and protecting the trust property there may be the possibility of an allowance under the *Berkeley Applegate* principle (*Re Berkeley Applegate Ltd (No.2)* [1989] Ch. 32). But that principle has its limitations—see *Credit and Mercantile plc v Kaymuu Ltd* [2014] EWHC 1746 (Ch); [2014] B.P.I.R. 1127.

Certain "personal" claims may also be excluded from the estate—for discussion see *Collins v Official Receiver* [1996] B.P.I.R. 552; *Lang v McKenna* [1997] B.P.I.R. 340; *Re Bell* [1998] B.P.I.R. 26. Compare *Cork v Rawlins* [2001] B.P.I.R. 222.

Note that pensions benefits can be excluded from the estate if they have been lawfully forfeited. For the position at common law see *Aitchison and Tuivaiti v NZI Life Superannuation Nominees* [1996] B.P.I.R. 215; and *Re The Trusts of the Scientific Investment Pension Plan* [1998] B.P.I.R. 410. The position here is now governed by the Pensions Act 1995 and the Welfare Reform and Pensions Act 1999. See note to s.306.

S.283(3A)

Subsection (3A) was introduced into s.283 by s.117(1) of the Housing Act 1988. Its effect is to add assured tenancies, protected tenancies, protected occupancies of dwelling houses and secure tenancies to the list of exclusions from the bankrupt's estate. Continuation tenancies are outside this exclusion—*Rothschild v Bell* [1999] B.P.I.R. 300. This provision has to be read however in the light of the newly introduced s.308A which enables the trustee to claim such tenancies by giving notice to the bankrupt.

S.283(4)

This deals with rights to exercise powers over the property of others. Note *Clarkson v Clarkson* [1994] B.C.C. 921. On s.283(4) see the discussion in *Hamilton v Brown* [2016] EWHC 191 (Ch). An amendment was made to subs.(4)(a) by SBEEA 2015 s.126 and Sch.9 para.74. On s.283(4) see *Hamilton v Brown* [2016] B.P.I.R. 531.

S.283(5)

Third-party rights over the bankrupt's property are preserved, unless those rights have been surrendered. Rights in this context means property rights (including equitable interests)—*Mountney v Treharne* [2002] EWCA Civ 1174. On the potential impact of the s.283(5) exclusion see *Roberts v Nunn and Tiffany* [2004] EWHC 114 (Ch); [2004] B.P.I.R. 623 (consent order had it been made with jurisdiction would have excluded pension rights from estate). For an abortive attempt to rely on s.283(5) see *Avis v Turner* [2007] EWCA Civ 748; [2007] B.P.I.R. 663. On s.283(5) see also *Burke v Chapman and Chubb* [2008] B.P.I.R. 266. Note linguistic change made to subs.(5)(a) by ERRA 2013 Sch.19 para.14. Note *Wood v Lowe* [2016] EWHC 1010 (Ch) where the court held that a beneficial interest in property held by a third party, which in fact was held by that third party as nominee for the bankrupt, vested in the estate.

S.283(6)

Property may be excluded from the estate by other statutes. For example statute now provides that student loans are specifically excluded from the estate—Higher Education Act 2004 s.42 and reg.5 of the Education (Student Support) (No.2) Regulations 2002 (Amendment No.3) Regulations 2004 (SI 2004/2041)—these provisions amend s.22 of the Teaching and Higher Education Act 1998 and reg.39 of the Education (Student Support) (No.2) Regulations 2002 (SI 2002/3200) with 1 September 2004 being specified as the cut off date for the new regime. The current rules are detailed in reg.80 of the Education (Student Loans) (Repayment) Regulations 2009 (SI 2009/470) as amended by Education (Student Loans) (Repayment) (Amendment) Regulations 2010 (SI 2010/661). For student loans made under earlier regimes, e.g. the Education (Student Loans) Act 1990 Sch.2 para.5(1) transitional provision apply.

283A Bankrupt's home ceasing to form part of estate

283A(1) [Application of section] This section applies where property comprised in the bankrupt's estate consists of an interest in a dwelling-house which at the date of the bankruptcy was the sole or principal residence of–

(a) the bankrupt,

(b) the bankrupt's spouse or civil partner, or

(c) a former spouse or former civil partner of the bankrupt.

283A(2) [Interest to vest in bankrupt] At the end of the period of three years beginning with the date of the bankruptcy the interest mentioned in subsection (1) shall–

(a) cease to be comprised in the bankrupt's estate, and

(b) vest in the bankrupt (without conveyance, assignment or transfer).

283A(3) [Non-application of s.283A(2)] Subsection (2) shall not apply if during the period mentioned in that subsection–

(a) the trustee realises the interest mentioned in subsection (1),

(b) the trustee applies for an order for sale in respect of the dwelling-house,

(c) the trustee applies for an order for possession of the dwelling-house,

(d) the trustee applies for an order under section 313 in Chapter IV in respect of that interest, or

(e) the trustee and the bankrupt agree that the bankrupt shall incur a specified liability to his estate (with or without the addition of interest from the date of the agreement) in consideration of which the interest mentioned in subsection (1) shall cease to form part of the estate.

283A(4) [Where application for order dismissed] Where an application of a kind described in subsection (3)(b) to (d) is made during the period mentioned in subsection (2) and is dismissed, unless the court orders otherwise the interest to which the application relates shall on the dismissal of the application–

(a) cease to be comprised in the bankrupt's estate, and

(b) vest in the bankrupt (without conveyance, assignment or transfer).

283A(5) [Effect of late notification of interest] If the bankrupt does not inform the trustee or the official receiver of his interest in a property before the end of the period of three months beginning with the date of the bankruptcy, the period of three years mentioned in subsection (2)–

(a) shall not begin with the date of the bankruptcy, but

(b) shall begin with the date on which the trustee or official receiver becomes aware of the bankrupt's interest.

283A(6) [Power of court to substitute longer period] The court may substitute for the period of three years mentioned in subsection (2) a longer period–

(a) in prescribed circumstances, and

(b) in such other circumstances as the court thinks appropriate.

283A(7) [Provision in rules for shorter period] The rules may make provision for this section to have effect with the substitution of a shorter period for the period of three years mentioned in subsection (2) in specified circumstances (which may be described by reference to action to be taken by a trustee in bankruptcy).

283A(8) [Other provision in rules] The rules may also, in particular, make provision–

(a) requiring or enabling the trustee of a bankrupt's estate to give notice that this section applies or does not apply;

(b) about the effect of a notice under paragraph (a);

(c) requiring the trustee of a bankrupt's estate to make an application to the Chief Land Registrar.

283A(9) [Rules concerning notice of disapplication of section] Rules under subsection (8)(b) may, in particular–

(a) disapply this section;

(b) enable a court to disapply this section;

(c) make provision in consequence of a disapplication of this section;

(d) enable a court to make provision in consequence of a disapplication of this section;

(e) make provision (which may include provision conferring jurisdiction on a court or tribunal) about compensation.

General Note

This important reform is introduced by s.261 of EA 2002. In the debate on the powers of a trustee in bankruptcy concerns were expressed about the practice adopted by certain trustees of not realising family homes immediately but allowing the matter to lie dormant, only acting many years after discharge where the value of the property had increased due to inflation. This was seen as unjust, a criticism accepted by the Government, which permitted a late amendment of the Bill. For judicial comment on the thinking behind the new policy here see Lawrence Collins J in *Re Byford (decd)* [2003] EWHC 1267 (Ch); [2003] B.P.I.R. 1089. We thus move over to a regime under which the trustee in dealing with the bankrupt's home must "use it or lose it".

For a useful comparison between s.283A and the Scottish counterpart see *McKinnon v Graham* [2013] EWHC 2870 (Ch); [2013] B.P.I.R. 1070. It is clear from this case that differences of substance, and not merely nuance, do exist. A similar "use it or lose it" provision has been introduced into Ireland by the Bankruptcy (Amendment) Act 2015 s.10.

The three-year time limit imposed on trustees wishing to realise the family home did not apply retrospectively to bankruptcies commencing before s.283A took effect—*Vidyarthi v Clifford* [2005] B.P.I.R. 233. For other transitional matters see EA 2002 s.261 and *Dear IP* Issue 25 (December 2005). On the transitional provisions applying to s.283A see *Stonham v Ramrattan* [2011] EWCA Civ 119.

For consideration of whether the application by the trustee was made within the three-year deadline see *Sands v Singh* [2015] EWHC 2219 (Ch); [2015] B.P.I.R. 1293.

Section 283A does not apply to an asset vested in a third party at the commencement of the bankruptcy but which might be recovered by the trustee through the use of the s.339 avoidance tool—*Stonham v Ramrattan* [2011] EWCA Civ 119.

In *Lewis v Metropolitan Property Realizations Ltd* [2009] B.P.I.R. 79 Proudman J took a flexible view on the word "realisation" by holding that a property was realised where the trustee took a deferred consideration. On appeal ([2009] EWCA Civ 448), however, the Court of Appeal preferred a more traditional construction of the word and ruled that the taking of deferred consideration did not constitute "realisation". Although this interpretation may accord with a literal approach, it will do nothing to aid the position of a trustee in bankruptcy when considering the best options to convert the estate interest in the debtor's property.

In *Pannell v Official Receiver* [2008] B.P.I.R. 629 the court concluded that the three year "use it or lose it" rule only applied to bankruptcies occurring after 29 December 1986 based upon petitions presented on or after that date. That said one would imagine difficulties with ECHR in the case of realisations of property of individuals declared bankrupt prior to that date.

In *Re Byford* [2003] EWHC 1267 (Ch); [2003] B.P.I.R. 1089 Lawrence Collins J made the point that s.283A does not oblige the trustee to go for an immediate sale of the family home; rather he has a three year window of opportunity in which to act.

One trend that is beginning to emerge is the tendency of former bankrupts to seek to have the "use it or lose it" provision applied in contexts for which it was not perhaps intended. This pattern is manifested in cases such as *Stonham v Ramrattan* [2011] EWCA Civ 119; *Doyle v James* [2010] B.P.I.R. 1063; *Young v OR* [2010] B.P.I.R. 1477; *Loy v O'Sullivan* [2010] EWHC 3583 (Ch); [2011] B.P.I.R. 181. The refusal of the courts to be drawn into this approach is to be welcomed.

The Insolvency Service has offered guidance on the interaction between s.283A, the former IR 1986 r.6.237 (now IR 2016 r.10.167) and the old Form 6.83—see *Dear IP*, September 2007.

The Land Registry has issued a guide explaining the position with regard to the trustee's dealings with the Chief Land Registrar—see Land Registry Practice Guide 34.

The interface between this provision and the rules on disclaimer was reviewed by Sir William Blackburne in *Hunt v Conwy CBC* [2013] EWHC 1154 (Ch); [2013] B.P.I.R. 790. Note also *Hunt v Withinshaw* [2015] EWHC 3072 (Ch) where the court examined the interaction of this provision with the rules on disclaimer.

S.283A(1)

This defines the type of property covered by this new restrictive provision. The interest must be in a dwelling house (see s.385) that is the sole or principal residence of the bankrupt, the bankrupt's spouse or former spouse. Note the additional reference to civil partners by Sch.27 to the Civil Partnership Act 2004. Thus the provision does not protect interests in second homes purchased for investment or recreation purposes. However, one could envisage a situation where two or even three properties were caught by this provision if for example the bankrupt was divorced and was also living apart from a second spouse. Thus, low value dwelling 1 was occupied by the bankrupt, low value dwelling 2 was occupied by current (but separated) spouse, and low value property 3 was occupied by former spouse.

S.283A(2), (3), (4)

If the trustee fails to take the specified action within three years the property will revest in the bankrupt. The specified courses of action which the trustee must take are identified in subs.(3). Note the qualification dealt with by subs.(4)—early unsuccessful action by the trustee might result in the *immediate* revesting of the dwelling in the bankrupt. For comment on s.283A(4) see *Garwood v Ambrose* [2012] EWHC 1494 (Ch); [2012] B.P.I.R. 996 at [5].

S.283A(5), (6)

The three-year period does not begin to run until the trustee has been informed of the bankrupt's interest where notification has not occurred within the initial three months. This provision suggests that if a bankrupt waits until the three months are nearly expired before notifying the interest then the trustee in effect has only two years and nine months to take action. Generally, the three-year period may be extended according to subs.(6) and one would imagine that this power might be used in cases where the bankrupt is seen as trying to exploit this potential loophole. A trustee cannot seek to exploit the extension facility in the Bankruptcy Scotland Act 1985 s.39A(7) (the equivalent of s.283A(6)) once the standard three year period has expired—see *Re Sequestrated Estate of William Rose* [2013] ScotsSC 42; [2013] B.P.I.R. 955. For discussion of the Scottish counterpart provision see *Cleghorn v Cooper Watson Ltd* [2017] CSOH 74. Lord Tyre makes the point at [30] that the three year period runs from the time the trustee is aware of the debtor's interest in the property. Time is not suspended until the debtor later notifies the trustee that it is a family home. In *Lismore v Davey* [2013] NIMaster 5; [2015] B.P.I.R. 1425 Master Kelly also ruled that the provision in s.283A(6) could not be invoked once the three-year period had expired. On appeal the High Court in Northern Ireland agreed and opted for a purposive interpretation of this provision see *Lismore v Davey* [2014] NICh 2; [2015] B.P.I.R. 1425.

Moreover, there was no scope for applying the Northern Irish equivalent provision to s.376. For detailed discussion of the import of s.283A(5) see *Stonham v Ramrattan* [2011] EWCA Civ 119.

S.283A(7)–(9)

These deal with the potential content of secondary rules.

284 Restrictions on dispositions of property

284(1) [Where person made bankrupt] Where a person is made bankrupt, any disposition of property made by that person in the period to which this section applies is void except to the extent that it is or was made with the consent of the court, or is or was subsequently ratified by the court.

284(2) [Application of s.284(1) to payment] Subsection (1) applies to a payment (whether in cash or otherwise) as it applies to a disposition of property and, accordingly, where any payment is void by virtue of that subsection, the person paid shall hold the sum paid for the bankrupt as part of his estate.

284(3) [Relevant period] This section applies to the period beginning with the day of the making of the bankruptcy application or (as the case may be) the presentation of the bankruptcy petition and ending with the vesting, under Chapter IV of this Part, of the bankrupt's estate in a trustee.

284(4) [Limit to effect of s.284(1)–(3)] The preceding provisions of this section do not give a remedy against any person–

(a) in respect of any property or payment which he received before the commencement of the bankruptcy in good faith, for value and without notice that the bankruptcy application had been made or (as the case may be) that the bankruptcy petition had been presented, or

(b) in respect of any interest in property which derives from an interest in respect of which there is, by virtue of this subsection, no remedy.

284(5) [Debt after commencement of bankruptcy] Where after the commencement of his bankruptcy the bankrupt has incurred a debt to a banker or other person by reason of the making of a payment which is void under this section, that debt is deemed for the purposes of any of this Group of Parts to have been incurred before the commencement of the bankruptcy unless–

(a) that banker or person had notice of the bankruptcy before the debt was incurred, or

(b) it is not reasonably practicable for the amount of the payment to be recovered from the person to whom it was made.

284(6) [Property not in bankrupt's estate] A disposition of property is void under this section notwithstanding that the property is not or, as the case may be, would not be comprised in the bankrupt's estate; but nothing in this section affects any disposition made by a person of property held by him on trust for any other person.

General Note

In the context of the financial markets, s.284 does not apply to a market contract or any disposition of property in pursuance of such a contract, the provision of margin in relation to market contracts, a market charge, and certain other transactions: see CA 1989 ss.163(4), 175(3)–(5), and the note on p.3.

A new set of guidelines is contained in *Practice Direction: Insolvency Proceedings* [2018] B.C.C. 241 at para.12.8. The effect of this new judicial guidance is to clarify procedures where leave is sought.

Although authorities decided under s.127 may be of assistance in interpreting s.284 the point has been made by HHJ Norris QC in *Pettit v Novakovic* [2007] B.C.C. 462 that authorities cannot automatically be transposed as the statutory language may differ and the purposes of the two provisions had subtle differences.

Some consideration was given to this provision by the court in *OR v Bathurst* [2008] B.P.I.R. 1548.

See also *Tomlinson v Bridging Finance Ltd* [2010] B.P.I.R. 759 where the point was made that once property has vested in the trustee in bankruptcy any subsequent disposition of the property by the debtor will clearly infringe s.284.

In *Governor of the Bank of Ireland v Gill* [2013] EWHC 2996 (Ch) the court made the point that the potential problems posed by s.284 provide a good reason for the judicial reluctance to stay or adjourn bankruptcy petitions. In *Revenue and Customs Commissioners v de Freitas* [2016] EWHC 1433 (Ch); [2016] B.P.I.R. 1179 Asplin J ruled that the potentially damaging impact of s.284 justified dismissing the petition presented by HMRC and not adjourning it.

Note linguistic changes made to subss.(1), (3) and (4) by ERRA 2013 Sch.19 para.15. These changes reflect the new bankruptcy adjudication procedure for debtors.

S.284(1)–(3), (6)

Any disposition of property or payment of money by the debtor after the date of the petition will be void unless approved by the court, either at the time or subsequently. This is so even if the property would not have formed part of the bankrupt's estate under s.283. Moreover, it would appear that a transfer of an interest in the matrimonial home pursuant to a consent order made under s.24 of the Matrimonial Causes Act 1973 constitutes a "disposition" for these purposes and is therefore void. This startling conclusion was arrived at by Nicholas Stewart QC (sitting as a deputy judge of the High Court) in *Re Flint* [1993] Ch. 319. This case once again illustrates that where a conflict occurs between rules of family law and principles of bankruptcy law the latter are often victorious. This critical view of the law is reinforced by *Woodley v Woodley (No.2)* [1994] 1 W.L.R. 1167 where the Court of Appeal held that the presentation of a bankruptcy petition by a debtor husband is not a disposition for the purposes of s.37 of the Matrimonial Causes Act 1973 and cannot be challenged as an attempt to avoid an order for matrimonial relief. *Re Flint* (above) is inconsistent with *Burton v Burton* [1986] 2 F.L.R. 419 and was not followed by Jonathan Parker J in *Beer v Higham* [1997] B.P.I.R. 349. However, see *Harper v O'Reilly* [1997] B.P.I.R. 656; and *Mountney v Treharne* [2002] EWCA Civ 1174; [2002] B.P.I.R. 1126 for continuing problems of uncertainty on the interface between matrimonial law and insolvency law. *Beer v Higham* (above) is no longer good law. For comment on the unpredictability of *Mountney v Treharne* (above) see *Burke v Chapman & Chubb* [2008] EWHC 341 (QB); [2008] B.P.I.R. 266 at [57]. In spite of the criticism levelled at *Re Flint* (above) it was followed by Lindsay J in *Treharne and Sand v Forrester* [2004] EWHC 2784 (Ch); [2004] B.P.I.R. 338. Thus a matrimonial property transfer order made after the presentation of the bankruptcy petition could be viewed as a void disposition by the debtor for the purposes of s.284. The argument that the court might be viewed as the disponor was specifically rejected.

Warwick v Trustee in Bankruptcy of Yarwood [2010] EWHC 2272 (Ch); [2010] B.P.I.R. 1443 is an authority of some significance. Here a matrimonial settlement by ex spouses, which had not been finalised by the time a creditor petitioned for the bankruptcy of the husband, was struck down by HHJ Cooke because it constituted a disposition of the husband's property contrary to s.284. The continuing difficulties posed by this provision and its interface with matrimonial ancillary relief were discussed by the court in *ORNI v Gallagher* [2014] NICh 6; [2014] B.P.I.R. 918. Here Deeny J refused to allow the bankruptcy provision to be used to avoid an order for matrimonial property settlement. Although the case outcome may be linked to the structure of the court system in Northern Ireland there is no doubt that it favours matrimonial property rights over the bankruptcy regime. But compare *ORNI v Urey* [2014] NIMaster 16 where the chronology was different and therefore Master Kelly concluded that *Gallagher* (above) could be distinguished. On appeal *Urey v OR* [2015] NICh 11—not a breach of s.284 as no disposition possible. Note *Re Elichaoff, Robert v Woodall* [2016] EWHC 538 (Ch); [2016] B.P.I.R. 643, a decision of Registrar Jones on interface between insolvency law and matrimonial property rules. For the appeal see [2016] EWHC 2987 (Ch) where the court held inter alia that claims under the Matrimonial Causes Act 1973 do not vest in a trustee in bankruptcy.

The application of IA 1986 s.284 in a case involving a deceased insolvent was considered by HHJ David Cooke in *Williams v Lawrence* [2011] EWHC 2001 (Ch); [2011] B.P.I.R. 1761. For the impact of s.284 in a case of a deceased insolvent see further the judgment of Arnold J in *Gorbunova v The Estate of Berezovsky* [2016] EWHC 1829 (Ch). Note also *Re Shirtcliffe (decd)* [2016] EWHC 726 (Ch); [2016] B.P.I.R. 1218 (HHJ Kaye QC). The estate here was being administered *outside bankruptcy* pursuant to the Administration and Insolvent Estates of Deceased Persons Order 1986 art.4. See note to s.421 below.

Section 284 impacted upon a power of attorney in *Sanders v Donovan* [2012] B.P.I.R. 219.

This provision compensates for the abolition of the doctrine of "relation back" of title and the end of the protection offered by receiving orders.

Note that s.284 allows the court some discretion with regard to avoidance—the provision in BA 1914 allowed no such flexibility. Leave was granted in *Rio Properties Inc v Al-Midani* [2003] B.P.I.R. 128 to enable funds to be used as payment for legal advice. On s.284(6) and sums akin to trust moneys see *Re Mordant* [1996] B.P.I.R. 302.

In *Pathania v Adedeji* [2014] EWCA Civ 681 the power of the court to ratify transactions which might otherwise contravene s.284 was highlighted. The judgment is interesting for the discussion of whether the conversion of a claim into a favourable judgment by a litigating bankrupt, who has pursued the claim notwithstanding his bankruptcy, might be regarded as a disposition falling within the ambit of s.284.

Re The Estate of Jimmy Savile [2014] EWHC 653 (Ch); [2014] B.P.I.R. 551 Sales J made validation order pursuant to s.284 for payment of professional expenses out of an insolvent estate—but he qualified this validation by allowing for the possibility of a later challenge by interested parties. The approach of Sales J to this ratification point was upheld on appeal—see *National Westminster Bank plc v Lucas* [2014] EWCA Civ 1632. Warren J made ratification orders *ex abundanti cautela* under s.284 in *National Westminster Bank plc v Lucas* [2016] EWHC 1934 (Ch).

As to what constitutes a "payment" for the purposes of s.284(2) see *Pettit v Novakovic* [2007] B.C.C. 462.

On s.284(6) see *Power v Brown* [2009] B.P.I.R. 340, where the court ruled that the provision did not apply on the facts of the case. Master Matthews made some useful observations on the potential of s.284(6) in *Goldcrest Distribution Ltd v McCole* [2016] EWHC 1571 (Ch) at paras [24]–[26].

A transaction in breach of s.284 is void and not merely voidable—see *Bateman v Hyde* [2009] B.P.I.R. 737. In this case the court found that s.284(6) was not applicable.

As the section is silent as to remedies, the general law applies, and the Court of Appeal in *Ahmed v Ingram* [2018] EWCA Civ 519 approved previous authorities stating that restitutionary principles should be applied, so that trust property actually lost as a result of the breach of trust is restored to the estate. In that case a transfer of property (shares), rather than a cash payment, was void under s.284 and the court explained in detail the principles to be applied in assessing the loss to the estate in such a situation.

S.284(4)

This offers protection to third parties, especially bona fide purchasers for value without notice of the petition. In *Sands and Treharne v Wright* [2010] B.P.I.R. 1437 an attempt by the recipient of the disposition to build a defence on the back of the good faith provision in s.284(4) proved unsuccessful.

Note also *Weir v Area Estates Ltd* [2010] EWCA Civ 801; [2010] B.P.I.R. 1459, where the s.284(4) point was not pursued at the appeal.

Note also *Blemain Finance Ltd v Goulding* [2013] EWCA Civ 1630 for comment on the interface with the Land Registration Act 2002 s.86(5).

S.284(5)

This provision deals with payments by the bankrupt avoided under this section, thus leaving the bankrupt indebted to the payee. If the sum of money can be recovered from the payee he will be treated as a pre-bankruptcy creditor unless he had notice of the petition at the time the debt was incurred.

285 Restriction on proceedings and remedies

285(1) [Court's power to stay] At any time when proceedings on a bankruptcy application are ongoing or proceedings on a bankruptcy petition are pending or an individual has been made bankrupt the court may stay any action, execution or other legal process against the property or person of the debtor or, as the case may be, of the bankrupt.

285(2) [Where proceedings pending against individual] Any court in which proceedings are pending against any individual may, on proof that a bankruptcy application has been made or a bankruptcy petition has been presented in respect of that individual or that he is an undischarged bankrupt, either stay the proceedings or allow them to continue on such terms as it thinks fit.

285(3) [Limit on creditors' actions] After the making of a bankruptcy order no person who is a creditor of the bankrupt in respect of a debt provable in the bankruptcy shall–

(a) have any remedy against the property or person of the bankrupt in respect of that debt, or

(b) before the discharge of the bankrupt, commence any action or other legal proceedings against the bankrupt except with the leave of the court and on such terms as the court may impose.

This is subject to sections 346 (enforcement procedures) and 347 (limited right to distress).

285(4) [Right of secured creditor] Subject as follows, subsection (3) does not affect the right of a secured creditor of the bankrupt to enforce his security.

285(5) [Where goods of undischarged bankrupt held by pledge etc.] Where any goods of an undischarged bankrupt are held by any person by way of pledge, pawn or other security, the official receiver may, after giving notice in writing of his intention to do so, inspect the goods.

Where such a notice has been given to any person, that person is not entitled, without leave of the court, to realise his security unless he has given the trustee of the bankrupt's estate a reasonable opportunity of inspecting the goods and of exercising the bankrupt's right of redemption.

285(6) [Interpretation] References in this section to the property or goods of the bankrupt are to any of his property or goods, whether or not comprised in his estate.

General Note

In relation to the financial markets, nothing in s.285 affects any action taken by an exchange or clearing house for the purpose of its default proceedings: CA 1989 s.161(4). Note amendments made to subss.(1) and (2) by ERRA 2013 Sch.19 para.16.

S.285(1)

This provision authorises the court (for definition, see s.385) to stay actions, executions, etc. where a bankruptcy petition is pending or, indeed, after the grant of the order. The Blagden Committee (Cmnd.221 (1957)), paras 19–20, called for the insertion of a provision *ex abundanti cautela* to the effect that High Court proceedings could be stayed under this provision. This has not been done, presumably because the existing language was deemed sufficiently wide. In *Re Smith (a Bankrupt) Ex p. Braintree District Council* [1990] 2 A.C. 215, the House of Lords held that this provision did enable it to stay proceedings for committal for non-payment of rates. There was no justification for excluding such proceedings from the scope of s.285. See also *Lewis v Ogwr BC* [1996] Rating Appeals 124. Compare *R. v Secretary of State for Social Security Ex p. Taylor* [1997] B.P.I.R. 505 (authorities' right to deduct benefits at source not prejudiced by s.285(3)). But *R. v Secretary of State for Social Security Ex p. Taylor and Chapman* was overruled by the Supreme Court in *Secretary of State for Work and Pensions v Payne* [2011] UKSC 60. In *Harlow District Council v Hall* [2006] EWCA Civ 156; [2006] B.P.I.R. 712 the Court of Appeal (Civil Division) held that there was no breach of s.285 of the IA 1986 where the court had ordered the surrender of a secure tenancy pursuant to s.79 of the Housing Act 1985, such surrender of possession to be completed the day before the bankruptcy petition was presented by the debtor. At the commencement of the bankruptcy the local authority were not seeking to enforce a remedy against the property of the bankrupt under the terms of s.285. The remedy had already been granted. The court also expressed the view that the same result would probably have been arrived at had the bankruptcy order predated the ending of possession. This view seems to have been taken because it was common ground between the parties that the secure tenancy would not have vested in the trustee on bankruptcy and so there was no estate to be protected within the spirit of s.285. Roth J indicated (at [22]) in *Kemsley v Barclays Bank plc* [2013] EWHC 1274 (Ch); [2013] B.P.I.R. 839 that this provision does not apply to obstruct foreign enforcement proceedings, though the English courts can use the Senior Courts Act 1981 s.37 to achieve the same effect. The court refused to stay an application for summary judgment against a bankrupt in *Fern Advisers Ltd v Burford* [2014] EWHC 762 (QB); [2014] B.P.I.R. 581.

Registrar Barber gave detailed consideration to the exercise of discretion under s.285(1) in *Re Mireskandari* [2014] B.P.I.R. 163. Here leave was refused after a full consideration of all of the relevant factors. The decision of Registrar Barber in *Re Mireskandari* [2014] B.P.I.R. 163 went to appeal—although the appeal was dismissed (see *Hellard v Chadwick* [2014] EWHC 2158 (Ch); [2014] B.P.I.R. 1234) Charles Hollander QC appeared to take a more expansive view as to what was caught by s.285. The need to support the protective policy underpinning s.285 was emphasised.

On various aspects of s.285 see also *Arnold v Williams* [2008] EWHC 218 (Ch); [2008] B.P.I.R. 247.

S.285(2)

Any court may exercise such staying powers on proof that a bankruptcy petition is pending. On this see *Re Eileen Davies* [1997] B.P.I.R. 619 and *Godfrey v Torpy*, *The Times*, 16 May 2007. For discussion on s.285(2) as to whether a freezing order can be maintained notwithstanding bankruptcy see the judgment of Richard Salter QC in *Eco Quest plc v GFI Consultants Ltd* [2014] EWHC 4329 (QB) at [84] et seq.

S.285(3), (4)

This compels unsecured creditors of the bankrupt to look solely to bankruptcy procedures as a remedy to secure payment of their debts once the bankruptcy order has been made. This general rule is qualified by ss.346, 347. Secured creditors do not suffer such a disability, unless s.285(5) below applies. Subsection (3) only protects against the enforcement of provable debts—*Re X* [1996] B.P.I.R. 494. As to which debts are provable see IR 2016 r.14.2. Landlords exercising powers of re-entry are also not hindered by this provision: *Razzaq v Pala* [1998] B.C.C. 66.

One view is that s.285(3) is to be interpreted in a purposive manner: *Bristol and West Building Society v Saunders* [1997] Ch. 60; [1997] B.C.C. 83 and leave can therefore be granted retrospectively. For factors relevant to the grant of leave *nunc pro tunc* see *Bristol and West Building Society v Back and Melinek* [1997] B.P.I.R. 358. This liberal approach was questioned. *Saunders* (above) was not followed by HHJ Kershaw in *Re Taylor* [2007] B.P.I.R. 175; [2007] 1 Ch. 150 and the court therefore refused to grant a retrospective validation under s.285(3)(c). Proceedings instituted without leave were *void* and could not retrospectively be validated. This latter, more draconian, interpretation appeared to be in line with the approach of the majority of the House of Lords in *Seal v Chief Constable of South Wales Police* [2007] UKHL 31; [2007] 1 W.L.R. 1910 to this issue in general in civil procedure. *Re Saunders* (above) was, however, followed by Chief Registrar Baister in *Bank of Scotland plc v Breytenbach* [2012] B.P.I.R. 1 in preference to *Re Taylor* (above). This must now be taken as confirming the possibility that retrospective leave is available. See also David Richards J in *Bank of Ireland v Colliers International UK plc* [2012] EWHC 2942 (Ch); [2012] B.P.I.R. 1099 where the authority of *Re Saunders* (above) was reaffirmed in preference to *Re Taylor* (above). On s.285(3) see *Sharples v Places for People Homes Ltd* [2011] EWCA Civ 813; [2011] B.P.I.R. 1488 which assimilates the law of bankruptcy with that applicable to DROs (see *Godfrey v A2 Dominion Homes Ltd* also reported at [2011] EWCA Civ 813; [2011] B.P.I.R. 1488). There was a full discussion of the issue of leave (in the context of derivative proceedings featuring a solvent company) by HHJ Davis-White in *Wilton UK Ltd v Shuttleworth* [2017] EWHC 2195 (Ch).

On the operation of s.285(3) see *Dadourian Group International v Simms* [2008] EWHC 723 (Ch); [2008] B.P.I.R. 508. The court here stressed that creditors with provable debts cannot lay claim to particular assets—they merely have a right of proof in the bankruptcy and must look to the general pool of realised assets to satisfy that right.

For the scope of the bar imposed by s.285(3) see *Re Heating and Electrical Piping Ltd* [2012] B.P.I.R. 1122 where HHJ Peter Langan QC stressed that s.285(3)(a) does not debar the handing down of a judgment, merely the enforcement thereof. In considering the meaning of "remedy" in s.285(3)(a) in *Re Mireskandari* ([2014] B.P.L.R. 163 22 November 2013) Registrar Barber followed *Heating Electrical and Piping Ltd v Ross* [2012] B.P.I.R. 1122—an application to seek a declaration could not be regarded as a pursuit of a remedy. Only if the declaration was enforced would the concept of remedy be engaged. On appeal (see [2014] B.P.I.R. 1234) Charles Hollander QC adopted a wider view of what might be caught by the s.285 moratorium. We await further clarification on this issue.

Subsection (3) was discussed in *Evans v Finance-U-Ltd* [2013] EWCA Civ 869; [2013] B.P.I.R. 1001.

A council tax liability order was quashed in *R. (Mohammed) v Southwark LBC* [2009] B.P.I.R. 882 in view of the failure of the local authority to obtain permission under s.285.

S.285(5)

This allows the official receiver to inspect any of the bankrupt's goods which have been used as security and to redeem them if necessary. The person holding the goods cannot enforce his security without the leave of the court.

S.285(6)

This gives the words "property" and "goods" a meaning that is not restricted by s.283.

286 Power to appoint interim receiver

286(1) [Court's power] The court may, if it is shown to be necessary for the protection of the debtor's property, at any time after the presentation of a bankruptcy petition and before making a bankruptcy order, appoint the official receiver or an insolvency practitioner to be interim receiver of the debtor's property.

286(2) [Omitted]

286(3) [Rights, powers etc. of interim receiver] The court may by an order appointing any person to be an interim receiver direct that his powers shall be limited or restricted in any respect; but, save as so directed, an interim receiver has, in relation to the debtor's property, all the rights, powers, duties and immunities given by the next section.

286(4) [Contents of court order] An order of the court appointing any person to be an interim receiver shall require that person to take immediate possession of the debtor's property or, as the case may be, the part of it to which his powers as interim receiver are limited.

286(5) [Duties of debtor] Where an interim receiver has been appointed, the debtor shall give him such inventory of his property and such other information, and shall attend on the interim receiver at such times, as the latter may for the purpose of carrying out his functions under this section reasonably require.

286(6) [Application of s.285(3)] Where an interim receiver is appointed, section 285(3) applies for the period between the appointment and the making of a bankruptcy order on the petition, or the dismissal of the petition, as if the appointment were the making of such an order.

286(7) [Ceasing to be interim receiver] A person ceases to be interim receiver of a debtor's property if the bankruptcy petition relating to the debtor is dismissed, if a bankruptcy order is made on the petition or if the court by order otherwise terminates the appointment.

286(8) [Interpretation] References in this section to the debtor's property are to all his property, whether or not it would be comprised in his estate if he were made bankrupt.

General Note

Subsection (2) is omitted and subs.(8) is amended by ERRA 2013 Sch.19 para.17.

S.286(1)

The court may appoint the official receiver as an interim receiver or a private insolvency practitioner after the presentation of the bankruptcy petition if such an appointment is necessary to protect the debtor's property. In *Gibson Dunn & Crutcher v Rio Properties Inc* [2004] EWCA Civ 1043; [2004] B.P.I.R. 1203 the Court of Appeal indicated that it was possible to appoint some other suitably qualified person apart from the official receiver to act as an interim receiver pursuant to s.286. The interim receiver has a company law counterpart in the provisional liquidator (IA 1986 s.135). As an alternative to the official receiver, the person appointed on a debtor's petition under s.273(2) to make a report on the possibility of a rescue plan can be given the role of interim receiver. For the powers and role of an interim receiver vis-à-vis the debtor see *Re Baars* [2002] EWHC 2159 (Ch); [2003] B.P.I.R. 523.

The law on interim receivers can be expanded by the rules—see Sch.9 paras 9, 30. The key provisions are IR 2016 rr.10.49–10.56.

There were amendments to this provision made by DA 2015 s.19 and Sch.6.

S.286(3)

This describes the role of such an interim receiver—note the degree of control over him exercised by the court. Subsection (3) was amended by SBEEA 2015 s.133 and Sch.10 para.2.

S.286(4), (8)

The interim receiver should normally take immediate possession of the debtor's assets—even those assets which would not subsequently form part of the bankrupt's estate.

S.286(5)

This requires the debtor to accede to the interim receiver's demands for assistance.

S.286(6)

During this interim receivership the debtor's assets enjoy the same protection as if a bankruptcy order had been made.

S.286(7)

This deals with termination of the interim receivership.

287 Powers of interim receiver

287(1) [Interim receiver is receiver and manager] An interim receiver appointed under section 286 is the receiver and (subject to section 370 (special manager)) the manager of the debtor's property and is under a duty to act as such.

287(2) [Function and powers of interim receiver] The function of an interim receiver while acting as receiver or manager of the debtor's property under this section is to protect the property; and for this purpose–

(a) he has the same powers as if he were a receiver or manager appointed by the High Court, and

(b) he is entitled to sell or otherwise dispose of any perishable goods comprised in the property and any other goods so comprised the value of which is likely to diminish if they are not disposed of.

287(3) [Steps re protecting property] An interim receiver while acting as receiver or manager of the debtor's property under this section–

(a) shall take all such steps as he thinks fit for protecting the debtor's property,

(b) is not required to do anything that involves his incurring expenditure, except in pursuance of directions given by–

  (i) the Secretary of State, where the official receiver is the interim receiver, or

  (ii) the court, in any other case,

(c) may, if he thinks fit (and shall, if so directed by the court) at any time seek a decision on a matter from the debtor's creditors.

287(4) [Liability of interim receiver] Where–

(a) an interim receiver acting as receiver or manager of the debtor's property under this section seizes or disposes of any property which is not the debtor's property, and

(b) at the time of the seizure or disposal the interim receiver believes, and has reasonable grounds for believing, that he is entitled (whether in pursuance of an order of the court or otherwise) to seize or dispose of that property,

the interim receiver is not to be liable to any person in respect of any loss or damage resulting from the seizure or disposal except in so far as that loss or damage is caused by his negligence; and he has a lien on the property, or the proceeds of its sale, for such of the expenses of the interim receivership as were incurred in connection with the seizure or disposal.

287(5) [Omitted]

General Note

Note amendment by SBEEA 2015 s.126 and Sch.19 para.75. Further amendments are to be made by SBEEA 2015 Sch.10 para.3. Subsection (5) is omitted. These reflect the possibility of the interim receiver being a private practitioner and the fact that the debtor is not technically bankrupt at this stage.

S.287(1), (2)

The official receiver (or a private practitioner) is to act as receiver and manager of the debtor's property between the date of the bankruptcy petition and when the trustee takes control. If the estate has vested immediately in the trustee by virtue of s.297, then s.287 does not apply. His role is of a caretaker nature (like a court-appointed receiver and manager), although he may sell perishables, etc. For the nature of the receivership in the hands of the official receiver operating under s.287(1) see *Dadourian Group International v Simms* [2008] EWHC 723 (Ch); [2008] B.P.I.R. 508. For discussion of the relationship between this provision and the automatic vesting of the bankrupt's property in the trustee pursuant to s.306 note *Pathania v Adedeji* [2014] EWCA Civ 681.

Under BA 1914 s.10, the official receiver could, in the period before the receiving order and the trustee taking over, appoint a manager—under s.287 it seems that the official receiver must fulfil this role himself. The court can, however, appoint a special manager under s.370 instead of the official receiver.

For the relevance of s.287 on an application for a BRO see *Michael v Official Receiver* [2013] EWHC 4286 (Ch); [2014] B.P.I.R. 666 (Roth J). Permission to appeal has been granted—see [2014] EWCA Civ 534.

Further details on the role of the official receiver as receiver and manager may be provided by regulations which may be made by the Secretary of State under the rules: see Sch.9 paras 10, 30 and IR 2016 Introductory Rule 5.

S.287(3)
These paragraphs detail further the obligations of the interim receiver while acting as receiver and manager. His duty to protect the assets is stressed, although he cannot incur expenditure unless directed to do so by the Secretary of State. He may, and, if directed by the court, must, call meetings of creditors.

S.287(4)
This offers protection from liability for wrongful seizure of assets where the interim receiver has acted reasonably and without negligence. Moreover, he has a lien over any proceeds of the wrongful sale to cover his expenses.

288 Statement of affairs

288(1) [Submission of statement to official receiver] Where a bankruptcy order has been made otherwise than on a bankruptcy application, the official receiver may at any time before the discharge of the bankrupt require the bankrupt to submit to the official receiver a statement of affairs.

288(2) [Contents of statement] The statement of affairs shall contain–

(a) such particulars of the bankrupt's creditors and of his debts and other liabilities and of his assets as may be prescribed, and

(b) such other information as may be prescribed.

288(2A) [Response period] Where a bankrupt is required under subsection (1) to submit a statement of affairs to the official receiver, the bankrupt shall do so (subject to subsection (3)) before the end of the period of 21 days beginning with the day after that on which the prescribed notice of the requirement is given to the bankrupt by the official receiver.

288(3) [Powers of official receiver] The official receiver may, if he thinks fit–

(a) release a bankrupt from an obligation imposed on the bankrupt under subsection (1), or

(b) either when giving notice mentioned in subsection (2A) or subsequently, extend the period mention in that subsection;

and where the official receiver has refused to exercise a power conferred by this section, the court, if it thinks fit, may exercise it.

288(4) [Penalty for non-compliance] A bankrupt who–

(a) without reasonable excuse fails to comply with an obligation imposed under this section, or

(b) without reasonable excuse submits a statement of affairs that does not comply with the prescribed requirements,

is guilty of a contempt of court and liable to be punished accordingly (in addition to any other punishment to which he may be subject).

S.288(1), (2A), (3)
Where a bankruptcy order has been made on the initiative of a creditor, the bankrupt normally has 21 days to submit a statement of affairs to the official receiver. A bankrupt may be released from this obligation by the official receiver (see IR 2016 rr.10.58 and 10.56), who may also extend the 21-day period. If the official receiver refuses to exercise his discretion the court may intervene. This provision differs from its predecessor in a number of respects. The time period mentioned in BA 1914 s.14 was seven days. Furthermore, under the 1914 Act a statement of affairs was required within three days where the debtor had petitioned for his own bankruptcy: the position now is governed by s.272(2).

Subsection (1) is amended by ERRA 2013 Sch.19 para.18.

S.288(2)
This specifies the contents of the statement of affairs. The rules amplify these requirements: see IR 2016 rr.10.55–10.61.

For the evidential status of such a statement, see s.433.

S.288(4)
Non-compliance can result in liability for contempt of court. A bankrupt who fails to meet his obligations under this provision may be subject to punishment for contempt—for discussion see *Official Receiver v Brown* [2017] EWHC 2762 (Ch). For certification by the Official Receiver of the bankrupt's breach of s.288 obligations (and obligations under ss.291, 312 and 333) see the earlier proceedings reported in [2017] EWHC 2728 (Ch).

Amendments to this provision are made by DA 2015 s.19 and Sch.6.

289 Investigatory duties of official receiver

289(1) [Investigation and report] The official receiver shall–

(a) investigate the conduct and affairs of each bankrupt (including his conduct and affairs before the making of the bankruptcy order), and

(b) make such report (if any) to the court as the official receiver thinks fit.

289(2) [Non-application of s.289(1)] Subsection (1) shall not apply to a case in which the official receiver thinks an investigation under that subsection unnecessary.

289(3) [Where application for discharge] Where a bankrupt makes an application for discharge under section 280–

(a) the official receiver shall make a report to the court about such matters as may be prescribed, and

(b) the court shall consider the report before determining the application.

289(4) [Report prima facie evidence of facts] A report by the official receiver under this section shall in any proceedings be prima facie evidence of the facts stated in it.

General Note

This substituted provision was introduced by s.258 of EA 2002 with effect from April 2004.

S.289(1)
This in effect repeats the current position suggesting that all bankrupts should be investigated by the OR.

S.289(2)
This is the key change, removing the mandatory obligation to investigate in circumstances where the OR deems this "unnecessary". No criteria are given for the making of this judgment, but reference to the grounds for the making of a BRO in Sch.4A might provide a useful pointer. One would imagine that the Insolvency Service would produce its own internal guidelines for official receivers. One effect of not having an investigation would be the reduction in bankruptcy administration costs.

S.289(3)
This deals with reports to the court where the bankrupt makes a discharge application under s.280.

S.289(4)
This outlines the evidential status of any report made by the OR.

290 Public examination of bankrupt

290(1) [Application to court] Where a bankruptcy order has been made, the official receiver may at any time before the discharge of the bankrupt apply to the court for the public examination of the bankrupt.

290(2) [Duty of official receiver to make application] Unless the court otherwise orders, the official receiver shall make an application under subsection (1) if notice requiring him to do so is given to him, in accordance with the rules, by one of the bankrupt's creditors with the concurrence of not less than one-half, in value, of those creditors (including the creditor giving notice).

290(3) [Direction re public examination] On an application under subsection (1), the court shall direct that a public examination of the bankrupt shall be held on a day appointed by the court; and the bankrupt shall attend on that day and be publicly examined as to his affairs, dealings and property.

290(4) [Persons taking part in examination] The following may take part in the public examination of the bankrupt and may question him concerning his affairs, dealings and property and the causes of his failure, namely–

(a) the official receiver and, in the case of an individual made bankrupt on a petition under section 264(1)(d), the Official Petitioner,

(b) the trustee of the bankrupt's estate, if his appointment has taken effect,

(c) any person who has been appointed as special manager of the bankrupt's estate or business,

(d) any creditor of the bankrupt who has tendered a proof in the bankruptcy.

290(5) [Penalty re non-attendance] If a bankrupt without reasonable excuse fails at any time to attend his public examination under this section he is guilty of a contempt of court and liable to be punished accordingly (in addition to any other punishment to which he may be subject).

General Note

Under BA 1914 s.15, a public examination was required in every case of bankruptcy. This was unfortunate because it seemed unnecessary to ask every bankrupt to undergo such an ordeal and, in some cases, public examinations caused embarrassment to third parties not directly concerned with the bankruptcy. The most notorious example of this was provided by the public examination of John Poulson in 1972. Accordingly, IA 1976 s.6 permitted the official receiver to ask the court to relieve certain bankrupts of this onerous procedure.

The Bankruptcy Rules 1952 rr.188–196 contained additional material on public examinations and the relevant provisions are now IR 2016 rr.10.100–10.105.

S.290(1), (2)

The position now is that a public examination will only be held where the official receiver asks for one. However, his hand can be forced by a majority of the bankrupt's creditors. It was held by the Court of Appeal in *Re Seagull Manufacturing Co Ltd* [1993] Ch. 345; [1993] B.C.C. 241 that the court has jurisdiction in the case of a public examination under s.133 to order a person resident outside the jurisdiction to attend for examination. (For the position in a private examination, see the notes to s.236, above.)

S.290(3), (5)

The court fixes the date of the public examination and the bankrupt must attend or face liability for contempt. Self-incrimination is no excuse for refusal to answer questions (*Re Paget* [1927] 2 Ch. 85). That said, the use of information gleaned from a public examination in criminal proceedings in English law is tightly controlled as a result of the requirements of the ECHR. Indeed, the court can adjourn a public examination and direct that further proceedings be conducted in private where there are real concerns that the transcript of a public examination might jeopardise the position of the bankrupt with regard to foreign criminal proceedings—for discussion on this point see *Rottmann v Official Receiver* [2009] B.P.I.R. 617—confirmed in [2009] EWCA Civ 473.

S.290(4)

This determines who may attend and participate in the public examination. This means that the authority of *Re Stern (a Bankrupt)* [1982] 1 W.L.R. 860 has been superseded.

Subsection (4) is amended by ERRA 2013 Sch.19 para.19.

291 Duties of bankrupt in relation to official receiver

291(1) [Omitted]

291(2) [Omitted]

291(3) [Omitted]

291(4) [Bankrupt to give information] The bankrupt shall give the official receiver such inventory of his estate and such other information, and shall attend on the official receiver at such times, as the official receiver may reasonably require–

(a) for a purpose of this Chapter, or

(b) in connection with the making of a bankruptcy restrictions order.

291(5) [Application of s.291(4)] Subsection (4) applies to a bankrupt after his discharge.

291(6) [Penalty for non-compliance] If the bankrupt without reasonable excuse fails to comply with any obligation imposed by this section, he is guilty of a contempt of court and liable to be punished accordingly (in addition to any other punishment to which he may be subject).

S.291(1)–(3)
These were omitted by SBEEA 2015 s.133 and Sch.10 para.4.

S.291(4), (5)
Subsection (4) was reconstituted by EA 2002 s.269 and Sch.23 with effect from 1 April 2004. This imposes an additional obligation on the bankrupt to provide information and be prepared to assist the official receiver where this is reasonably requested. The obligation continues to apply after discharge.

S.291(6)
Failure to comply with the above obligations results in liability for contempt of court.

Chapter III

Trustees In Bankruptcy

Tenure of office as trustee

291A First trustee in bankruptcy

291A(1) [Official receiver as first trustee] On the making of a bankruptcy order the official receiver becomes trustee of the bankrupt's estate, unless the court appoints another person under subsection (2).

291A(2) [Voluntary arrangement] If when the order is made there is a supervisor of a voluntary arrangement approved in relation to the bankrupt under Part 8, the court may on making the order appoint the supervisor of the arrangement as the trustee.

291A(3) [Notice] Where a person becomes trustee of a bankrupt's estate under this section, the person must give notice of that fact to the bankrupt's creditors (or, if the court so allows, advertise it in accordance with the court's directions).

291A(4) [Creditors' committee] A notice or advertisement given by a trustee appointed under subsection (2) must explain the procedure for establishing a creditors' committee under section 301.

General Note

A new s.291A is introduced before s.292 by SBEEA 2015 s. 133. This new section effects a change in bankruptcy procedure in that it makes the OR the first trustee in bankruptcy pending the possible appointment of a private practitioner as trustee at a later date. Although it is a new section, it draws upon former existing provisions in some cases: for example, s.291A(2) clearly based upon the now superseded s.297(5).

292 Appointment of trustees: general provision

292(1) [Scope] This section applies to any appointment of a person (other than the official receiver) as trustee of a bankrupt's estate.

292(2) [Qualification for trustee] No person may be appointed as trustee of a bankrupt's estate unless he is, at the time of the appointment, qualified to act as an insolvency practitioner in relation to the bankrupt.

292(3) [Joint trustees] Any power to appoint a person as trustee of a bankrupt's estate includes power to appoint two or more persons as joint trustees; but such an appointment must make provision as to the circumstances in which the trustees must act together and the circumstances in which one or more of them may act for the others.

292(4) [Requirement of acceptance of appointment] The appointment of any person as trustee takes effect only if that person accepts the appointment in accordance with the rules. Subject to this, the appointment of any person as trustee takes effect at the time specified in his certificate of appointment.

292(5) [Omitted]

S.292(1)

This relates to the appointment of a trustee in bankruptcy. Normally it will be a decision for the creditors, although there are situations whether the Secretary of State, or the court, may assume responsibility for the appointment. Section 292 is not exhaustive of the circumstances in which a trustee in bankruptcy may be appointed—*Donaldson v O'Sullivan* [2008] EWHC 387 (Ch); [2008] B.P.I.R. 288 which was confirmed in [2008] EWCA Civ 879. A reference to summary administration was deleted by EA 2002 s.269 and Sch.23 with effect from 1 April 2004. See generally IR 2016 rr.10.67–10.75.

SBEEA 2015 s.133 and Sch.10 para.5 makes changes to subs.(1).

S.292(2)

Under BA 1914 s.19 the trustee had to be a "fit person"—now he must be properly qualified under Pt XIII.

S.292(3)

This restates BA 1914 s.77 which permitted the appointment of joint trustees.

S.292(4)

For the appointment to take effect the trustee must accept the post in accordance with the rules (see IR 2016 r.10.74).

The date of the appointment is specified in the certificate of appointment.

S.292(5)

The aforementioned provisions do not apply where the official receiver acts as trustee: see ss.293(3), 295(4), 297 and 300(2).

SBEEA 2015 s.133 and Sch.10 para.5 makes changes to subs.(5).

293 Summoning of meeting to appoint first trustee [Omitted]

General Note

This section was omitted by SBEEA 2015 s.133 and Sch.10 para.6.

294 Power of creditors to requisition meeting [Omitted]

General Note

This section was omitted by SBEEA 2015 s.133 and Sch.10 para.6.

295 Failure of meeting to appoint trustee [Omitted]

General Note

This section was omitted by SBEEA 2015 s.133 and Sch.10 para.6.

296 Appointment of trustee by Secretary of State

296(1) [Application for appointment instead of official receiver] At any time when the official receiver is the trustee of a bankrupt's estate by virtue of any provision of this Chapter he may apply to the Secretary of State for the appointment of a person as trustee instead of the official receiver.

296(2) [Duty of Secretary of State] On an application under subsection (1) the Secretary of State shall either make an appointment or decline to make one.

296(3) [Making of application] Such an application may be made notwithstanding that the Secretary of State has declined to make an appointment either on a previous application under subsection (1) or under section 300(4) below.

296(4) [Notice etc., re appointment] Where the trustee of a bankrupt's estate has been appointed by the Secretary of State (whether under this section or otherwise), the trustee shall give notice to the bankrupt's creditors of his appointment or, if the court so allows, shall advertise his appointment in accordance with the court's directions.

296(5) [Contents of notice] In that notice or advertisement the trustee shall explain the procedure for establishing a creditors' committee under section 301.

S.296(1)–(3)

This permits the official receiver when acting as a trustee to seek another appointment in his stead. He cannot do this where he is acting as a trustee in case of summary administration or a bankruptcy initiated as the result of a criminal bankruptcy order. On the other hand, he is not precluded from making such an application by the fact that he has previously made unsuccessful applications under ss.295, 296(1) or 300(4). On an application by the official receiver the Secretary of State has discretion whether to appoint a trustee or not. See also IR 2016 s.10.72.

Subsections (1) and (3) were amended by SBEEA 2015 s.133 and Sch.10 para.7.

S.296(4), (5)

Any appointment of a trustee by the Secretary of State must be notified to the creditors by the trustee or, if the court permits, be advertised with a view to informing the creditors whether a committee should be set up under s.301. See also IR 2016 r.10.74 for the advertisement of the appointment.

Subsection (5) was amended by SBEEA 2015 s.126 and Sch.9 para.76.

297 Special cases [Omitted]

General Note

This section was omitted by SBEEA 2015 s.133 and Sch.10 para.8.

298 Removal of trustee; vacation of office

298(1) [Removal by court order or by creditors' decision] Subject as follows, the trustee of a bankrupt's estate may be removed from office only by an order of the court or by a decision of the bankrupt's creditors made by a creditors' decision procedure instigated specially for that purpose in accordance with the rules.

298(2) [Omitted]

298(3) [Deleted]

298(4) [Where official receiver trustee under s.291A] Where the official receiver is trustee by virtue of section 291A(1) or a trustee is appointed by the Secretary of State or (otherwise than under section 291A(2)) by the court, a creditors' decision procedure may be instigated for the purpose of removing the trustee only if–

(a) the trustee thinks fit, or

(b) the court so directs, or

(c) one of the bankrupt's creditors so requests with the concurrence of not less than one-quarter, in value, of the creditors (including the creditor making the request).

298(4A) [Removal of trustee by creditors] Where the bankrupt's creditors decide to remove a trustee, they may in accordance with the rules appoint another person as trustee in his place.

298(4B) [Time of removal] Where the decision to remove a trustee is made under subsection (4), the decision does not take effect until the bankrupt's creditors appoint another person as trustee in his place.

298(5) [Where trustee appointed by Secretary of State] If the trustee was appointed by the Secretary of State, he may be removed by a direction of the Secretary of State.

298(6) [Vacation of office] The trustee (not being the official receiver) shall vacate office if he ceases to be a person who is for the time being qualified to act as an insolvency practitioner in relation to the bankrupt.

298(7) [Resignation] The trustee may, in the prescribed circumstances, resign his office by giving notice of his resignation to the prescribed person.

298(8) [Vacation on s.331 notice] The trustee shall vacate office on giving notice to the prescribed person that the trustee has given notice under section 331(2).

298(8A) [Notice contents and timing] A notice under subsection (8)–

(a) must not be given before the end of the period prescribed by the rules as the period within which the bankrupt's creditors may object to the trustee's release, and

(b) must state whether any of the bankrupt's creditors objected to the trustee's release.

298(9) [When bankruptcy order annulled] The trustee shall vacate office if the bankruptcy order is annulled.

General Note

A number of amendments were made by SBEEA 2015 s.126 and Sch.9 para.77 and by SBEEA 2015 s.133 and Sch.10 para.9. These provide further detail on removal of a trustee and reflect the wider decision-taking procedures available to creditors.

S.298(1), (2)
Trustees may as a general rule only be removed by the court or by creditors. However, this does not apply where the official receiver is trustee. See also IR 2016 r.10.78. There has been a lack of guidance on the principles to be applied in the context of this provision—see *Smedley v Brittain* [2008] B.P.I.R. 219. Removal was refused in *Doffman and Isaacs v Wood and Hellard* [2011] EWHC 4008 (Ch); [2012] B.P.I.R. 972 in circumstances where a conflict of interest was alleged. Proudman J concluded that the potential conflict could be addressed in a way that did not involve removal and thus dismissed the application on terms.

S.298(3)
This was deleted by s.269 of and Sch.23 to EA 2002 as from 1 April 2004. It covered summary administration.

S.298(4), (4A), (4B)
The drafting of this provision is complex. It covers the official receiver acting as trustee by virtue of s.291A, and trustees appointed by the Secretary of State, or by the court (but not under s.297(5)). This allows a creditors' decision process to be instigated to dismiss the trustee—either the trustee himself, the court or creditors owed 25 per cent of the bankrupt's debts can call for this. This was reduced from 50 per cent in the original 1985 Bill.

S.298(5)
The Secretary of State can remove his own appointees.

S.298(6)
A trustee must vacate office if he ceases to be qualified to act: see Pt XIII and IR 2016 r.10.85.

S.298(7)
Resignation in the circumstances prescribed is permitted. See IR 2016 r.10.77. Note amendments to subss.(7) and (8) by ERRA 2013 Sch.19 para.23.

S.298(8), (8A)
The trustee shall vacate office after giving notice to the court of the outcome of the final communication with creditors (see s.331). This provision was subject to amendment by ERRA 2013 Sch.19.

S.298(9)
Annulment of the bankruptcy order will cause the trustee to vacate office.
For further details on removal and vacation of office, see IR 2016 rr.10.77–10.83.

299 Release of trustee

299(1) [Time of release for official receiver] Where the official receiver has ceased to be the trustee of a bankrupt's estate and a person is appointed in his stead, the official receiver shall have his release with effect from the following time, that is to say–

(a) where that person is appointed by the bankrupt's creditors or by the Secretary of State, the time at which the official receiver gives notice under this paragraph to the prescribed person that he has been replaced, and

(b) where that person is appointed by the court, such time as the court may determine.

299(2) [Time of release if notice given by official receiver] If the official receiver while he is the trustee gives notice to the Secretary of State that the administration of the bankrupt's estate in accordance with Chapter IV of this Part is for practical purposes complete, he shall have his release with effect from such time as the Secretary of State may determine.

299(3) [Time of release for person not official receiver] A person other than the official receiver who has ceased to be the trustee shall have his release with effect from the following time, that is to say–

(a) in the following cases, the time at which notice is given to the prescribed person in accordance with the rules that that person has ceased to hold office–

(i) the person has been removed from office by a decision of the bankrupt's creditors and the creditors have not decided against his release,

(ii) the person has died;

(b) in the following cases, such time as the Secretary of State may, on an application by the person, determine–

(i) the person has been removed from office by a decision of the bankrupt's creditors and the creditors have decided against his release,

(ii) the person has been removed from office by the court or by the Secretary of State,

(iii) the person has vacated office under section 298(6);

(c) in the case of a person who has resigned, such time as may be prescribed;

(d) in the case of a person who has vacated office under section 298(8)–

(i) if any of the bankrupt's creditors objected to the person's release before the end of the period for so objecting prescribed by the rules, such time as the Secretary of State may, on an application by that person, determine, and

(ii) otherwise, the time at which the person vacated office.

299(3A) [Creditors to determine release] Where the person is removed from office by a decision of the bankrupt's creditors, any decision of the bankrupt's creditors as to whether the person should have his release must be made by a creditors' decision procedure.

299(4) [Time of release where bankruptcy order annulled] Where a bankruptcy order is annulled, the trustee at the time of the annulment has his release with effect from such time as the court may determine.

299(5) [Effect of release] Where the official receiver or the trustee has his release under this section, he shall, with effect from the time specified in the preceding provisions of this section, be discharged from all liability both in respect of acts or omissions of his in the administration of the estate and otherwise in relation to his conduct as trustee.

But nothing in this section prevents the exercise, in relation to a person who has had his release under this section, of the court's powers under section 304.

General Note

A number of amendments were made by SBEEA 2015 s.126 and Sch.9 para.78 to reflect new creditor decision procedures.

S.299(1), (2)
These provisions deal with the release of an official receiver who has been acting as trustee. The procedure to be followed depends on whether he is being replaced or whether he has simply completed the administration of the estate.

For the equivalent provision for the release of liquidators, see s.174. As to the possibility of a release being set aside, see *Re Munro Ex p. Singer v Trustee in Bankruptcy* [1981] 1 W.L.R. 1358. Release is also dealt with by IR 2016 rr.10.86–10.88.

This provision was subject to amendment by ERRA 2013 Sch.19.

S.299(3), (3A)
This fixes the date of release for trustees other than the official receiver. Again, the date will vary according to the circumstances of the case—a comprehensive list of possibilities is provided for. This provision was subject to amendment by ERRA 2013 Sch.19. The creditors decide on release—subs.(3A).

S.299(4)
Where release is the result of the annulment of the bankruptcy order the court will fix the date of release. See *Dear IP* Issue 26 (March 2006).

S.299(5)
This is a general provision dealing with the *effect* of a release: it serves as a discharge of liabilities, unless an action is subsequently brought under s.304. Note the observations of Proudman J in *Oraki v Bramston* [2015] EWHC 2046 (Ch); [2015] B.P.I.R. 1238 on the extent of the release under s.299(5) and the relationship with s.304 at [158]–[162]. In *Oraki v Bramston* [2017] EWCA Civ 403; [2017] B.P.I.R. 1021 David Richards LJ raised doubts about the interpretation of the relationship between s.299(5) and s.304 put forward by Proudman J but he did not elaborate further as it was not necessary to do so for the purposes of reaching a decision in the case. For comment see Milman [2017] 30 Insolv. Int. 91 at 92.

Note also *Re Borodzicz* [2016] B.P.I.R. 24 where Chief Registrar Baister provides a lucid explanation of the importance of release under s.299 in wiping the slate clean for the office-holder.

300 Vacancy in office of trustee

300(1) [Application] This section applies where the appointment of any person as trustee of a bankrupt's estate fails to take effect or, such an appointment having taken effect, there is otherwise a vacancy in the office of trustee.

300(2) [Official receiver trustee] The official receiver shall be trustee until the vacancy is filled.

300(3) [Appointment of trustee] The official receiver may ask the bankrupt's creditors to appoint a person as trustee, and must do so if so requested by not less than one tenth in value of the bankrupt's creditors.

300(3A) [Appointment by creditors] If the official receiver makes such a request the bankrupt's creditors may in accordance with the rules appoint a person as trustee.

300(4) [If vacancy not filled] If at the end of the period of 28 days beginning with the day on which the vacancy first came to the official receiver's attention he has not asked, and is not proposing to ask the bankrupt's creditors to appoint a person as trustee, he shall refer the need for an appointment to the Secretary of State.

300(5) [Deleted]

300(6) [Duty of Secretary of State re s.300(4), (5)] On a reference to the Secretary of State under subsection (4) the Secretary of State shall either make an appointment or decline to make one.

300(7) [If no appointment on s.300(4), (5) reference] If on a reference under subsection (4) no appointment is made, the official receiver shall continue to be trustee of the bankrupt's estate, but without prejudice to his power to make a further reference.

300(8) [Interpretation] References in this section to a vacancy include a case where it is necessary, in relation to any property which is or may be comprised in a bankrupt's estate, to revive the trusteeship of that estate after the vacation of office by the trustee under section 298(8) or the giving by the official receiver of notice under section 299(2).

General Note

A number of amendments were made by SBEEA 2015 s.126 and Sch.9 para.79 to reflect the wider decision-making procedures available to creditors.

S.300(1), (2)
Where the appointment of a trustee fails to take effect (e.g. because he refuses the appointment) or a casual vacancy occurs, the official receiver must act as trustee during the interregnum.

S.300(3), (4)
The official receiver may (and, in cases under s.314(7), must) ask creditors to fill this vacancy. If he fails to act within 28 days he must refer the matter to the Secretary of State. See IR 2016 r.10.72.

S.300(5)
This was deleted by s.269 of and Sch.23 to EA 2002 with effect from 1 April 2004. It dealt with summary administration.

S.300(6), (7)
Where a casual vacancy has been referred to the Secretary of State he has discretion whether to fill it or not. If the vacancy is not filled the official receiver must act as trustee pending the resolution of the matter.

S.300(8)
This defines what is meant by a "vacancy" for the purposes of the present section.

Control of trustee

301 Creditors' committee

301(1) [Meeting may establish committee] Subject as follows, a bankrupt's creditors may, in accordance with the rules, establish a committee (known as "the creditors' committee") to exercise the functions conferred on it by or under this Act.

301(2) [Exception] The bankrupt's creditors shall not establish such a committee, or confer any functions on such a committee, at any time when the official receiver is the trustee of the bankrupt's estate, except in connection with the appointment of a person to be trustee instead of the official receiver.

General Note

Amendments were made to this provision by SBEEA 2015 s.126 and Sch.9 para.80.

S.301(1)
This enables the general meeting of creditors to establish a committee to supervise the trustee. Under the 1914 Act this committee was known as a "committee of inspection" but this title has now been dropped on the recommendation of the Cork Committee (*Report*, para.932). The role and general position of the committee is now governed by the Rules—see now IR 2016 rr.17.3–17.26. Under BA 1914 many of these details were spelled out in the provisions of the Act itself. Under BA 1914 s.79(1) the committee had general power to give directions to the trustee. This power was not re-enacted in the 1986 Act and therefore the role of the committee is more limited. Members of this committee occupy a fiduciary position vis-à-vis the bankrupt's estate: *Re Bulmer Ex p. Greaves* [1937] Ch. 499.

A representative of the appropriate regulator can attend where appropriate—FSMA 2000 s.374(4).

S.301(2)
The committee has no role where the official receiver is trustee—he is supervised by the Secretary of State under s.302.

This could apply to cases of criminal bankruptcy.

302 Exercise by Secretary of State of functions of creditors' committee

302(1) [Where official receiver trustee] The creditors' committee is not to be able or required to carry out its functions at any time when the official receiver is trustee of the bankrupt's estate; but at any such time the functions of the committee under this Act shall be vested in the Secretary of State, except to the extent that the rules otherwise provide.

302(2) [Where no committee] Where in the case of any bankruptcy there is for the time being no creditors' committee and the trustee of the bankrupt's estate is a person other than the official receiver, the functions of such a committee shall be vested in the Secretary of State, except to the extent that the rules otherwise provide.

S.302(1)
This reiterates that the committee established under s.301 cannot exercise any control functions when the official receiver is acting as trustee. Instead, control in such cases must be exercised by the Secretary of State. See IR 2016 r.17.26.

S.302(2)
For the relevant rules, see IR 2016 r.17.26.

303 General control of trustee by the court

303(1) [Application to court] If a bankrupt or any of his creditors or any other person is dissatisfied by any act, omission or decision of a trustee of the bankrupt's estate, he may apply to the court; and on such an application the court may confirm, reverse or modify any act or decision of the trustee, may give him directions or may make such other order as it thinks fit.

303(2) [Application by trustee for directions] The trustee of a bankrupt's estate may apply to the court for directions in relation to any particular matter arising under the bankruptcy.

303(2A) [Insolvent partnerships] Where at any time after a bankruptcy petition has been presented to the court against any person, whether under the provisions of the Insolvent Partnerships Order 1994 or not, the attention of the court is drawn to the fact that the person in question is a member of an insolvent partnership, the court may make an order as to the future conduct of the insolvency proceedings and any such order may apply any provisions of that Order with any necessary modifications.

303(2B) [Court power to consolidate s.303(2A) proceedings] Where a bankruptcy petition has been presented against more than one individual in the circumstances mentioned in subsection (2A) above, the court may give such directions for consolidating the proceedings, or any of them, as it thinks just.

303(2C) [Order or directions under s.303(2A), (2B)] Any order or directions under subsection (2A) or (2B) may be made or given on the application of the official receiver, any responsible insolvency practitioner, the trustee of the partnership or any other interested person and may include provisions as to the administration of the joint estate of the partnership, and in particular how it and the separate estate of any member are to be administered.

S.303(1)
This permits any person (including a discharged bankrupt—*Osborn v Cole* [1999] B.P.I.R. 251 or a person whose bankruptcy has been annulled—*Engel v Peri* [2002] EWHC 799 (Ch); [2002] B.P.I.R. 961) who is dissatisfied with a decision of a trustee in bankruptcy to apply to the court for relief. On such an application the court enjoys general discretion to deal with the matter. This is a useful reserve control power, but in practice, as the Cork Committee observed (*Report*, para.779), such applications rarely succeed: see, for an example of an unsuccessful application, *Re a Debtor Ex p. The Debtor v Dodwell (The Trustee)* [1949] Ch. 236. See also *Canty v Boyden* [2006] EWCA Civ 194; [2006] B.P.I.R. 624. In *Osborn v Cole* (above) this difficulty was exemplified by requiring proof that the trustee was

acting in a manner in which no reasonable trustee would act. On the appropriate test to be applied by the court under s.303 see *Bank of Baroda v Patel* [2009] B.P.I.R. 255, a case where *Osborne v Cole* (above) was followed. In *Supperstone v Hurst (No.3)* [2006] EWHC 2147 (Ch); [2006] B.P.I.R. 1263 the strict test for interference with the actions of the trustee was applied by Warren J. In effect we are looking at *Wednesbury* unreasonableness. It was not surprising therefore that the application under s.303 was dismissed. *Miller v Bayliss* [2009] B.P.I.R. 1438 provides yet another example of the reluctance of the court to intervene in respect of the actions of the trustee. This case is also significant for casting light upon the issue of locus standi under s.303. Certainly this provision cannot be used to challenge the exercise of public law functions by an official receiver: *Hardy v Focus Insurance Co Ltd* [1997] B.P.I.R. 77. The fact that the courts are reluctant to direct a trustee to engage in speculative litigation is apparent from the comments of the Court of Appeal in *James v Rutherford-Hodge* [2005] EWCA Civ 1580; [2006] B.P.I.R. 973. In *Shepherd v Official Receiver* [2007] B.P.I.R. 101 Gabriel Moss QC refused to exercise the s.303 jurisdiction to order an official receiver to investigate further the possibility of a claim being brought against the Legal Services Commission. See *Law Society v OR and Shah* [2007] EWHC 2841 (Ch); [2007] B.P.I.R. 1595 for an example of a case where usage of s.303 was deemed not to be appropriate because the conduct of the trustees did not amount to *Wednesbury* unreasonableness. Interestingly, the jurisdiction of the court under s.363 was held not to be so limited.

A leading authority on this provision now is *Bramston v Haut* [2012] EWHC 1279 (Ch); [2012] B.P.I.R. 672 where at first instance Arnold J proposed an approach that had the potential to be more interventionist. This approach was based on the view that the application of the *Wednesbury* test was becoming more flexible in recent years. On appeal, the Court of Appeal ([2012] EWCA Civ 1637) reverted to orthodoxy holding that the court should only intervene with the trustee's decisions if they are "perverse". This criterion was said to be more strict than the *Wednesbury* test, but in practice this may make little difference as both tests will mean that intervention by the court will be limited to wholly exceptional cases. That said, one advantage in the perversity test is that it does sever the link with trends in Public Law which may not always be appropriate to apply to the actions of a trustee in bankruptcy. *Bramston v Haut* (above) was followed by Barling J in *Tucker v Atkins* [2013] EWHC 4469 (Ch); [2014] B.P.I.R. 1359. The difficulty involved in challenging a trustee's actions are once again clearly illustrated by the comments of Newey J in *Aslam v Finn & Field* [2013] EWHC 3405 (Ch).

It is uncertain whether the change from "aggrieved" in BA 1914 to "dissatisfied" will produce any practical differences. In *Osborn v Cole* (above) the old law was found to be of some value. Note also IR 2016 Pt 12. Section 303 is not an appropriate tool to use to fix the trustee's remuneration—*Engel v Peri* [2002] EWHC 799 (Ch); [2002] B.P.I.R. 961. In *Woodbridge v Smith* [2004] B.P.I.R. 247 Registrar Baister held that the wife of a bankrupt had standing s.303 to apply to the court to extract information from the trustee giving a breakdown on his claim for fees and expenses. Although s.303 could not be used to fix the remuneration and charges of the trustee it could be used in this indirect fashion to facilitate that goal. There is still dispute as to whether the court can utilise s.303 to determine the remuneration and expenses of the trustee—*Re Cooper* [2005] NICh 1; [2007] B.P.I.R. 1206 (a case involving the equivalent statutory provision in Northern Ireland). On the use of s.303 as a means of challenging the remuneration of a trustee see *Barker v Bajjon* [2008] B.P.I.R. 771. The potential usage of s.303 by a bankrupt disgruntled at the composition of a creditors' committee was noted by Nicholas Strauss QC in *Foenander v Allan* [2006] B.P.I.R. 1392. See also *Freeburn v Hunt* [2010] B.P.I.R. 325 (another remuneration case).

For another possible use of s.303 see the discussion in *R. (Singh) v Revenue and Customs Commissioners* [2010] B.P.I.R. 933, where the court refused to interfere with the decision by the trustee to accept a proof of unassessed tax liability from the revenue authorities. In *McNulty v Revenue and Customs Commissioners* [2010] UKFTT 509 (TC); [2011] B.P.I.R. 1051 it was confirmed that a bankrupt's right to appeal a tax assessment vested in his trustee. If the bankrupt was dissatisfied with the trustee's approach towards such an appeal the solution lay in the application to the court under s.303.

Those lawyers looking for a more liberal use of this control facility will have been disappointed by the comments of Harman J in *Port v Auger* [1994] 1 W.L.R. 862 at 873–874. Although Harman J appeared to accept that the change in terminology from "aggrieved" to "dissatisfied" may have indicated an intention on the part of the legislature to widen access to the court he expressed the view that the applicant must have some substantial interest that has been adversely affected and then went on to suggest that the s.303 jurisdiction should not be invoked lightly by the court for fear of inflicting unnecessary expense on the insolvent estate. For a case which pushed the s.303 jurisdiction to the limit see *Re Cook* [1999] B.P.I.R. 881. In *Re Shettar* [2003] B.P.I.R. 1055 Park J on an application under s.303 refused to direct the trustee to assign a statute-barred cause of action back to the bankrupt because in so doing the trustee might expose himself to potential liability for costs if the bankrupt unsuccessfully pursued that claim. Further consideration to this matter was given by the court in *Hunt v Harb* [2011] EWCA Civ 1239; [2012] B.P.I.R. 117.

In *Heath v Tang* [1993] 1 W.L.R. 1421 it was suggested by the court that this provision might prove useful if the trustee refuses to pursue a claim of action belonging to the debtor but now vested in the estate. On this see also the notes on ss.285(3) and 306.

In *Skeete v Pick* [2007] EWHC 2211 (Ch) the court indicated that in principle s.303 might be engaged where a trustee acknowledged a third party interest in the bankrupt's property which the bankrupt disputed.

There is a good account of the case law governing the s.303 jurisdiction in *Smedley v Brittain* [2008] B.P.I.R. 219. See also *Bramston and Defty v Oraki* [2014] EWHC 4828 (Ch); [2014] EWHC 2982 (Ch) and [2014] B.P.I.R. 1374.

On the interface between s.303 and s.304 see *Brown v Beat* [2002] B.P.I.R. 421.

See also *Linfoot v Adamson* [2012] EWHC Misc 16 (CC); [2012] B.P.I.R. 1033 on the link with the comparable provision in IVA law (s.263(3)).

S.303(2)

This is a useful facility in that it allows a trustee in bankruptcy to apply to the court for guidance on a difficult matter. For an illustration of the court giving such directions see *Re a Debtor (No.26A of 1975)* [1985] 1 W.L.R. 6. Other interested parties may also apply—*Supperstone v Auger* [1999] B.P.I.R. 152. Subsection (2) of this provision has provided the jurisdiction to appoint a trustee in bankruptcy under a block transfer order—*Donaldson v O'Sullivan* [2008] EWCA Civ 879 but see now IR 2016 rr.12.35–12.38.

Re Michael [2010] B.P.I.R. 418 holds that it does not matter whether the case is covered by s.303(1) or s.303(2)—the same test governing judicial intervention applies. The courts are most reluctant to double guess a matter of professional judgment on the part of a trustee in bankruptcy.

For an application for directions under s.303(2) see the decision of Registrar Derrett in *Ariel v Revenue and Customs Commissioners, Re Halabi* [2016] B.P.I.R. 373. The litigation was concerned with the respective jurisdictions of the bankruptcy court and the First Tier Tax Tribunal. But the directions given in this case by Registrar Derrett under s.303(2) were then quashed on appeal by Mann J in *Revenue and Customs Commissioners v Ariel* [2016] EWHC 1674 (Ch); [2016] B.P.I.R. 1144—the Tax Tribunal enjoyed primacy. In *Re Chinn* (unreported, 10 November 2015) Registrar Barber refused to give directions to a trustee on what was characterised as a "bomb shelter" application. The application related to proof of debt: in the view of Registrar Barber the trustee should first adjudicate on this, and then appeal rights could come into play if that adjudication was challenged. Such precautionary applications to the court should be discouraged. For the costs arising on an application for directions under s.303(2) see *Re Tully* [2017] NICh 18—costs borne by estate not trustee personally.

S.303(2A)–(2C)

For insolvent partners there are modifications in the form of subss.(2A)–(2C) inserted by the Insolvent Partnerships Order 1994 (SI 1994/2421) art.14. These are reproduced in Vol.2. On the usage of s.303(2A)–(2C) in the context of an insolvent partnership see *Official Receiver v Hollens* [2007] EWHC 754 (Ch); [2007] B.P.I.R. 830 where the court gave directions to facilitate the appropriate handling of the partnership assets.

On subs.(2A) see *McLean v Trustees of the Bankrupt Estates of Dent* [2016] EWHC 2650 (Ch).

304 Liability of trustee

304(1) [Powers of court on application] Where on an application under this section the court is satisfied–

(a) that the trustee of a bankrupt's estate has misapplied or retained, or become accountable for, any money or other property comprised in the bankrupt's estate, or

(b) that a bankrupt's estate has suffered any loss in consequence of any misfeasance or breach of fiduciary or other duty by a trustee of the estate in the carrying out of his functions,

the court may order the trustee, for the benefit of the estate, to repay, restore or account for money or other property (together with interest at such rate as the court thinks just) or, as the case may require, to pay such sum by way of compensation in respect of the misfeasance or breach of fiduciary or other duty as the court thinks just.

This is without prejudice to any liability arising apart from this section.

304(2) [Applicants] An application under this section may be made by the official receiver, the Secretary of State, a creditor of the bankrupt or (whether or not there is, or is likely to be, a surplus for the purposes of section 330(5) (final distribution)) the bankrupt himself.

But the leave of the court is required for the making of an application if it is to be made by the bankrupt or if it is to be made after the trustee has had his release under section 299.

304(3) [Limit on liability] Where–

(a) the trustee seizes or disposes of any property which is not comprised in the bankrupt's estate, and

(b) at the time of the seizure or disposal the trustee believes, and has reasonable grounds for believing, that he is entitled (whether in pursuance of an order of the court or otherwise) to seize or dispose of that property,

the trustee is not liable to any person (whether under this section or otherwise) in respect of any loss or damage resulting from the seizure or disposal except in so far as that loss or damage is caused by the negligence of the trustee; and he has a lien on the property, or the proceeds of its sale, for such of the expenses of the bankruptcy as were incurred in connection with the seizure or disposal.

General Note

The Cork Committee (*Report*, paras 777–788) called for the introduction of a statutory duty of care imposed on trustees. This section goes some way towards this, and towards rationalising the law on the liability of trustees.

S.304(1)

This allows the court to impose liability on the trustee for misfeasance or misapplication of money belonging to the estate, etc. The remedy is at the discretion of the court, and it is worth noting that interest can be awarded against the trustee. The comparable provision in company law is to be found in s.212. See *Green v Satsangi* [1998] B.P.I.R. 55 where an order made against a trustee under s.304 was quashed on appeal. A claim under s.304 will be unlikely to succeed where the trustee can show that his actions are merely the result of carrying out a court order—by analogy with *Chapper v Jackson* [2012] EWHC 3897 (Ch).

Proudman J rejected the notion of additional liability at common law in her decision in *Oraki v Bramston* [2015] EWHC 2046 (Ch); [2015] B.P.I.R. 1238. In *Oraki v Bramston* [2017] EWCA Civ 403; [2017] B.P.I.R. 1021 David Richards LJ disagreed with Proudman J's view of the exclusive nature of the s.304 duty—but he refused to elaborate on this matter as it was not required to reach a decision in the case. See Milman [2017] 30 Insolv. Int. 91 at 92 for discussion.

In *McAteer v Lismore* [2012] NICh 7; [2012] B.P.I.R. 812 Deeny J, when dealing with the comparable provision in art.277 of the Northern Ireland Insolvency Order 1989, found that a trustee had breached his duty of care by failing to advertise a property belonging to the estate on more than one occasion over a period of several years and by eventually selling at a price that was deemed to be an undervalue. See also *Official Receiver for Northern Ireland v Sinnamon* [2013] NICh 11; [2013] B.P.I.R. 900—this deals with art.277 of the NI Order and features an unsuccessful attempt to invoke this provision.

S.304(2)

This determines who can apply for relief under s.304(1). Note that if the bankrupt applies, or the application is made after the date of the trustee's release, the leave of the court must first be obtained. See here *Brown v Beat* [2002] B.P.I.R. 421. In *McGuire v Rose* [2013] EWCA Civ 429 the Court of Appeal confirmed that the provision could in principle be invoked by a bankrupt notwithstanding the lack of a prospective surplus in the estate (as subs.(2) indicates). In that particular case the s.304 application proved abortive. On s.304(2) note also *Re Borodzicz* [2016] B.P.I.R. 24 (Chief Registrar Baister). In this case the court explained the criteria for the granting of leave once a trustee had been discharged pursuant to s.299. The court will be influenced by the policy underpinning s.299 and by its natural reluctance to micro-manage the administration of the estate by the trustee. On the test to be applied in order to obtain leave to proceed see further the comments in *Katz v Oldham* [2016] B.P.I.R. 83. Here Registrar Derrett held that the test to be applied under s.304(2) is the same as for the pursuit of misfeasance proceedings against liquidators or administrators.

Note also *Bramston and Defty v Oraki* [2014] EWHC 4828 (Ch); [2014] EWHC 2982 (Ch) and [2014] B.P.I.R. 1374 for discussion by Nicholas Strauss QC in the High Court of the nature of any duty owed to a bankrupt by a trustee not to act negligently. Note that any such duty must be subject to the overriding s.305(2) obligation to realise the estate and that the failure of a bankrupt who anticipates a surplus to launch a s.303 complaint does not necessarily debar the bankrupt from later suing for negligence if the circumstances dictate.

S.304(3)

This is not a new provision, but rather a reformulation of BA 1914 s.61. It is designed to protect a trustee who innocently seizes or disposes of property belonging to a third party. Note that this protection is lost if he acts negligently. The problem of a trustee seizing property which does not belong to the bankrupt may arise more frequently in the future with the abolition of the concept of reputed ownership.

Chapter IV

Administration by Trustee

Preliminary

305 General functions of trustee

305(1) [Application of Ch.IV] This Chapter applies in relation to any bankruptcy where either–

(a) the appointment of a person as trustee of a bankrupt's estate takes effect, or

(b) the official receiver becomes trustee of a bankrupt's estate.

305(2) [Function of trustee] The function of the trustee is to get in, realise and distribute the bankrupt's estate in accordance with the following provisions of this Chapter; and in the carrying out of that function and in the management of the bankrupt's estate the trustee is entitled, subject to those provisions, to use his own discretion.

305(3) [Duties of trustee] It is the duty of the trustee, if he is not the official receiver–

(a) to furnish the official receiver with such information,

(b) to produce to the official receiver, and permit inspection by the official receiver of, such books, papers and other records, and

(c) to give the official receiver such other assistance,

as the official receiver may reasonably require for the purpose of enabling him to carry out his functions in relation to the bankruptcy.

305(4) [Official name of trustee] The official name of the trustee shall be "the trustee of the estate of..., a bankrupt" (inserting the name of the bankrupt); but he may be referred to as "the trustee in bankruptcy" of the particular bankrupt.

S.305(1)
Sections 305–335 apply to cases where the trustee's appointment is effective or where the official receiver is acting as trustee.

S.305(2)
This describes the general role of the trustee and confers considerable residual discretion upon him. On the implications of s.305(2) see *Foyle v Turner* [2007] B.P.I.R. 43. The courts are minded to maximise his room for manoeuvre: *Judd v Brown* [1997] B.P.I.R. 470 at 476–477. It is important that the trustee retains professional independence and is not seen to be acting as a hired gun for a major creditor—*Re Ng* [1997] B.C.C. 507, per Lightman J, a comment which was approved by the Court of Appeal in *Trustee in Bankruptcy of Bukhari v Bukhari* [1999] B.P.I.R. 157. With regard to s.305(2) note the comments of the court in *Thornhill v Atherton (No.2)* [2008] B.P.I.R. 691 to the effect that it was not a misuse of the power of realisation for a trustee to carry out that role simply to generate funds to repay his claim for remuneration and costs.

On s.305(2) see the discussion in *Bramston and Defty v Oraki* [2014] EWHC 4828 (Ch); [2014] EWHC 2982 (Ch) and [2014] B.P.I.R. 1374.

On the role of a trustee in bankruptcy of a bankrupt solicitor where the SRA has not intervened in the practice see *Bell v Birchall* [2015] EWHC 1541 (Ch); [2015] B.P.I.R. 751. Here the court refused to deploy the *Berkeley Applegate* principle to support the trustee in dealing with the issue of client funds.

Note also *Oraki v Bramston* [2015] EWHC 2046 (Ch); [2015] B.P.I.R. 1238 (Proudman J).

Note the new whistleblowing duty imposed in appropriate cases by s.373 of FSMA 2000 as amended by Financial Services Act 2012 Sch.14.

S.305(3)
This provision makes the trustee subordinate to the official receiver. Further details of the relationship can be seen in IR 2016 r.10.93.

S.305(4)
This describes the official name of the trustee and repeats BA 1914 s.76, although his powers are not mentioned in the new provision.

Acquisition, control and realisation of bankrupt's estate

306 Vesting of bankrupt's estate in trustee

306(1) [Time of vesting] The bankrupt's estate shall vest in the trustee immediately on his appointment taking effect or, in the case of the official receiver, on his becoming trustee.

306(2) [Mode of vesting] Where any property which is, or is to be, comprised in the bankrupt's estate vests in the trustee (whether under this section or under any other provision of this Part), it shall so vest without any conveyance, assignment or transfer.

General Note

This section provides that the bankrupt's property shall vest in the trustee, on his appointment taking effect, or in the official receiver where he becomes trustee. No conveyance, etc. is required. On automatic vesting see *Urey v Official Receiver* [2015] NICh 11. A trustee takes assets subject to equities—*Avis v Turner* [2007] B.P.I.R. 663. For the interaction between the automatic vesting under s.306 and the Land Registration Act 2002 see the explanation given by Proudman J in *Pick v Chief Land Registrar* [2011] EWHC 206 (Ch); [2011] B.P.I.R. 1090; [2012] 3 W.L.R. 3. On the vesting of property in the estate see also *Bennett v Daci* [2014] EWHC 4479 (Ch) and *Khan v Khan* [2015] EWHC 2625 (Ch), where the official receiver became the trustee.

In *Re D'Eye* [2016] B.P.I.R. 883 Chief Registrar Baister noted the link with s.284.

In *Dadourian Group International v Simms* [2008] EWHC 723 (Ch); [2008] B.P.I.R. 508 Warren J made the point that automatic vesting under s.306 only applied on the appointment of a trustee in bankruptcy, whether it be a private trustee or the official receiver—until that happened the estate remained vested in the bankrupt.

This automatic vesting is to be compared with the position under s.145 where the court may direct that some or all of the company's property shall vest in the liquidator in a compulsory liquidation. The bankrupt retains no immediate beneficial interest in this property until a surplus has been determined—*Ram v Ram (No.2)* [2004] EWCA Civ 1684; [2005] B.P.I.R. 628. Once the estate has vested in the trustee the bankrupt merely has a contingent right to participate in any eventual surplus that might materialise; that did not confer an immediate beneficial right—on this see *James v Rutherford-Hodge* [2005] EWCA Civ 1580; [2006] B.P.I.R. 973. The earlier decision of Peter Smith J in *Phillips v Symes* [2005] EWHC 2867 (Ch); [2006] B.P.I.R. 1430 (on the meaning of s.330(5)) is difficult to reconcile with this view.

The property does not have to be located within the jurisdiction to vest: *Singh v Official Receiver* [1997] B.P.I.R. 530; *Pollard v Ashurst* [2001] B.P.I.R. 131. It follows from *Thornhill v Atherton (No.2)* [2008] B.P.I.R. 691 that foreign assets form part of the estate. For automatic vesting and foreign property see *Sanders v Donovan* [2012] B.P.I.R. 219.

For the impact of s.306 on claims pursued by a claimant who becomes bankrupt but who continues the litigation in spite of the bankruptcy see *Pathania v Adedeji* [2014] EWCA Civ 681. The case is also of interest for its discussion of the linkage between s.306 and s.287.

For the meaning of "property" within s.306(2) see *London City Corp v Bown, The Times*, 11 October 1989, where it was held by the Court of Appeal that a non-assignable secure periodic tenancy within the meaning of the Housing Act 1985 confers only personal rights and therefore could not be regarded as "property" for these purposes. Similarly in *Re Rae* [1995] B.C.C. 102; and *Griffiths v Civil Aviation Authority* [1997] B.P.I.R. 50 personal and non-transferable rights to hold a licence did not vest in the trustee. Compare *Cork v Rawlins* [2001] B.P.I.R. 222 (insurance policies). See *Re Pritchard* [2007] B.P.I.R. 1385 (automatic vesting of interests under a life policy). See *Ward v Official Receiver* [2012] B.P.I.R. 1073 (interest incidental to property—see s.436). Note also *KK v MA* [2012] EWHC 788 (Fam); [2012] B.P.I.R. 1137. Transferable licences of value may on the other hand be regarded as property: *Environment Agency v Stout* [1998] B.P.I.R. 576. Personal injury compensation also cannot be claimed by the trustee for the estate: *Lang v McKenna* [1996] B.P.I.R. 419; and [1997] B.P.I.R. 340; and *Rahall v McLennan* [2000] B.P.I.R. 140. The generality of this latter statement was questioned in *Re Bell* [1998] B.P.I.R. 26 where it was held that compensation for personal injury leading to damage to assets of economic value might form part of the estate; see also *Davis v Trustee in Bankruptcy of Davis* [1998] B.P.I.R. 572. If the claim is hybrid (i.e. contains an element relating to an allegation of damage to assets of the bankrupt coupled with a personal claim) the claim vests in the trustee, but any proceeds of action relating to the personal element are held on trust for the bankrupt—see here *Ord v Upton* [2000] 2 W.L.R. 755. The difficulty in distinguishing these issues was reflected by *Mulkerrins v PricewaterhouseCoopers* [2003] UKHL 41; [2003] 1 W.L.R. 1937. In *Grady v Prison Service* [2003] EWCA Civ 527 a claim for unfair dismissal was held to be "personal" and therefore did not vest within the estate. For further consideration of the difficulties posed by the issue of hybrid claims see *Kaberry v Freethcartwright* [2003] EWCA Civ 1077; [2003] B.P.I.R. 1144. In the curious decision in *Khan v Trident Safeguards Ltd* [2004] EWCA Civ 624; [2004] B.P.I.R. 881 the Court of Appeal held that a bankrupt could recharacterise claims alleging racial discrimination by restricting the remedy sought to a declaration and compensation for injured feelings, thereby removing such claims from the category of "hybrid" claims to be pursued by the trustee in bankruptcy. This decision will cause many practical difficulties and is undoubtedly influenced by the laudable desire to see that claims of discrimination are not stifled by the technicalities of bankruptcy law. Ironically, the court indicated that the proceeds of such a claim might be treated as being encompassed within that estate. By way of contrast in *Saini v Petroform Ltd* [1997] B.P.I.R. 515 the right to seek a new business tenancy under the Landlord and Tenant Act 1954 was held to be property. Again in *Performing Rights Society v Rowland* [1998] B.P.I.R. 128 the personal right to receive royalties from the PRS vested in the trustee as property as did the right of a lawyer to receive professional fees under a contingency fee agreement in *Royal Bank of Canada and Burlingham Associates v Chetty* [1997] B.P.I.R. 137. Note also *Johnson v Official Receiver* [2014] EWHC 2609 (Ch); [2014] B.P.I.R. 1245 where Proudman J confirmed that a hybrid claim vests in the trustee subject to any personal injury compensation being paid out by the trustee to the bankrupt when such compensation is received. In *Grant v Hayes* [2014] EWHC 2646 (Ch); [2014] B.P.I.R. 1455 the court was faced with the question as to whether a claim in tort for harassment under the Protection from Harassment Act 1997 fell within the bankruptcy estate. The harassment was said to have occurred both before the commencement of the bankruptcy and continued until after discharge. Nugee J held it did not become entirely vested in the estate because of the continuing nature of the claim—the cause of action continued after the discharge from bankruptcy and was therefore capable of being pursued by the former bankrupt. Note also the related case of *Hayes v Butters* [2014] EWHC 4557 (Ch). Here Nugee J held that a hybrid claim for harassment seeking compensation for personal and non-personal loss vested in the estate, but a claim relating to alleged harassment post bankruptcy did not so vest but could be pursued by the former bankrupt and could not be struck out on the application of the trustee. The case provides valuable discussion of the nature of so-called hybrid claims. One can only conclude that the dividing line between personal rights which are outside the estate and property rights which the trustee can lay claim to is unclear. On current trends the courts are inclined to treat assets of value as being proprietorial and therefore caught by s.306. This would appear to be confirmed by the approach of the Irish Supreme Court in *AA v BA* [2015] IESC 102. Compare *Bank of Ireland v O'Donnell* [2016] IECA 227 where the right of residence was held to be a personal right. See also *Robert v Woodall* [2016] EWHC 538 (Ch) and [2016] EWHC 2897 (Ch)—claims under Matrimonial Causes Act 1973 held to be "personal".

The rights of action possessed by the debtor at the time of his bankruptcy form part of the estate under the control of the trustee: see *Heath v Tang* [1993] 1 W.L.R. 1421; *Nelson v Nelson* [1997] B.P.I.R. 702. *Heath v Tang* (above) was applied in *Dadourian Group International Inc v Simms* [2008] EWHC 723 (Ch); [2008] B.P.I.R. 508. *Heath v Tang* (above) and the issue of "personal" claims was discussed in the Northern Irish case of *Swift Advances plc v McKay* [2011] NICh 2. The issue of whether rights of appeal pass to the trustee or are retained by the bankrupt has generated much controversy but again the courts are inclined to treat these as forming part of the estate: *Wordsworth v Dixon* [1997] B.P.I.R. 337; *Church of Scientology v Scott* [1997] B.P.I.R. 418; *Cummings and Fuller v Claremont Petroleum* [1998] B.P.I.R. 187; and see *Boyd and Hutchinson v Foenander* [2003] EWCA Civ 1516; [2004] B.P.I.R. 20. A right to challenge a tax assessment was held to be property in *R. (Singh) v Revenue and Customs Commissioners* [2010] B.P.I.R. 933. In *McNulty v Revenue and Customs Commissioners* [2012] S.T.C. 2110 Arnold J. sitting in the Upper Tribunal (Tax and Chancery Chamber) reaffirmed that a right to appeal in tax cases vests automatically in the trustee under s.306 and therefore the taxpayer has no locus standi to pursue an appeal. For confirmation that appeal rights are vested in the estate see *Cowey v Insol Funding Ltd* [2012] EWHC 2421 (Ch); [2012] B.P.I.R. 958. In *Muhammed v Robert* (unreported, 18 June 2014) the High Court confirmed that a right to apply to set aside a default judgment vests in trustee in bankruptcy. See also *Seven Eight Six Properties Ltd v Ghafoor* B.P.I.R. 519 (right to resist possession proceedings forms part of estate); *Hunt v Peasegood* [2001] B.P.I.R. 76. See also *Young v Hamilton* [2010] B.P.I.R. 1468 and *Young v OR* [2010] B.P.I.R. 1477, where the courts in Northern Ireland and England upheld the automatic vesting provisions with regard to the right to continue to pursue a cause of action in the face of a challenge from the bankrupt citing the European Convention on Human Rights. Note also *Thames Chambers Solicitors v Miah* [2013] EWHC 1245 (QB); [2013] B.P.I.R. 650 where Tugendhat J held that the cause of action had vested in the trustee. A case which bucks the trend is *Re GP Aviation Group International Ltd* [2013] EWHC 1447 (Ch); [2013] B.P.I.R. 576 where HHJ Pelling held (after some detailed research) that a bare right of appeal was not a chose in action and did not constitute property.

Note the comments of Birss J in *Lilley v Financial Times Ltd* [2017] EWHC 1916 (Ch) to the effect that where a bankrupt pursues a claim properly vested in his trustee the best course of action for the court is to stay the action rather than strike it out as an abuse of process. The striking out option should only be used if the bankrupt is pursuing the claim with knowledge that he lacked locus standi.

The right to appeal tax assessments and penalties automatically vests in the trustee—see *Ali v Revenue and Customs Commissioners* [2015] UKFTT 464 (TC); [2015] B.P.I.R. 1348. Here the Tribunal also confirmed that the bankrupt has no standing to apply for permission to appeal out of time in respect of assessments and penalties. See also *Bank of Ireland v O'Donnell* [2015] IESC 89 where the Supreme Court in Ireland determined that proceedings were blocked because the applicant lacked locus standi in view of his bankruptcy. The vesting of appeal rights in the trustee extends to any rights of appeal which the bankrupt might have in respect of the judgment forming the basis of the petition debt—see *Re Muhammed* [2014] EWHC 4800 (Ch). However, the right to appeal the bankruptcy order itself does not as a matter of practice and commonsense vest in the estate; it can be pursued by the bankrupt—*Sands v Layne* [2016] EWCA Civ 1159.

Although an appeal may vest in the trustee, the trustee will have to consider carefully whether to pursue such an appeal. Potential liability for costs will be an issue—helpful guidance on the position here has been provided by the Supreme Court in *BPE Solicitors v Gabriel* [2015] UKSC 39. Here the Supreme Court ruled that any personal liability for costs of the trustee in bankruptcy would not extend to costs incurred prior to the adoption of the appeal by him.

The position with regard to pension benefits has undergone considerable change in recent years. For bankruptcies commencing prior to 29 May 2000 personal and occupational pension benefits automatically vest in the estate—*Re Landau* [1998] Ch. 223; *Krasner v Dennison* [2001] Ch. 76; *Patel v Jones* [2001] B.P.I.R. 919; and *Rowe v Sanders* [2002] EWCA Civ 242; [2002] B.P.I.R. 847. In the latter case the Court of Appeal has confirmed that there is no infringement of fundamental rights expectations as a result of this automatic vesting. Moreover, in view of this vesting there is no need to seek an income payments order in respect of pension benefits. For bankruptcies commencing after 29 May 2000 the position is governed by ss.11 and 12 of the Welfare Reform and Pensions Act 1999 which seeks to exclude certain specified pensions from the estate, subject to the clawback provisions in ss.342A–342C of the 1986 Act. More detailed legislative provision on the new scheme is found in the Occupational and Personal Pension Schemes (Bankruptcy) Regulations 2002 (SI 2002/427). This establishes machinery to enable a bankrupt to seek a court order to exclude pension benefits from his estate or to facilitate agreements between the trustee and the bankrupt as to pension rights. In *Malcolm v Benedict Mackenzie* [2004] EWCA Civ 1748; [2005] B.P.I.R. 176 the Court of Appeal held that the differential treatment for vesting purposes of personal pensions of pre- and post-29 May 2000 bankrupts did not infringe art.14 ECHR.

Note also *Purewal v Countrywide Residential Lettings Ltd* [2015] EWCA Civ 1122 (mortgaged property forms part of estate).

Provisions seeking to forfeit personal pension rights on bankruptcy (and thereby to circumvent bankruptcy law) are ineffective—Welfare Reform and Pensions Act 1999 s.14 (which inserts a new s.159A into the Pension Schemes Act 1993).

The anti-deprivation principle may come into play to defeat attempts to deny assets to the estate—see *Kotonou v Reeves* (unreported, 30 October 2015) (Mann J).

Income-related social security benefits do not form part of the estate: *Mulvey v Secretary of State for Social Security* [1997] B.P.I.R. 696. For comment on this Scottish authority see *Secretary of State for Work and Pensions v Payne* [2011] UKSC 60.

See also *Keepers and Governors of the Possessions, Revenues and Goods of the Free Grammar School of John Lyon v Helman* [2014] EWCA Civ 17 for passing comment on s.306.

306A Property subject to restraint order

306A(1) [Application] This section applies where–

(a) property is excluded from the bankrupt's estate by virtue of section 417(2)(a) of the Proceeds of Crime Act 2002 (property subject to a restraint order),

(b) an order under section 50, 67A, 128, 131A, 198 or 215A of that Act has not been made in respect of the property,

(c) the restraint order is discharged, and

(d) immediately after the discharge of the restraint order the property is not detained under or by virtue of section 44A, 47J, 122A, 127J, 193A or 195J of that Act.

306A(2) [Vesting] The property vests in the trustee as part of the bankrupt's estate.

306A(3) [Non-application of s.306A(2)] But subsection (2) does not apply to the proceeds of property realised by a management receiver under section 49(2)(d) or 197(2)(d) of that Act (realisation of property to meet receiver's remuneration and expenses).

306AA Property released from detention

306AA(1) [Application] This section applies where–

(a) property is excluded from the bankrupt's estate by virtue of section 417(2)(b) of the Proceeds of Crime Act 2002 (property detained under certain provisions),

(b) no order is in force in respect of the property under section 41, 50, 120, 128, 190 or 198 of that Act, and

(c) the property is released.

306AA(2) [Vesting] The property vests in the trustee as part of the bankrupt's estate.

306B Property in respect of which receivership or administration order made

306B(1) [Application] This section applies where–

(a) property is excluded from the bankrupt's estate by virtue of section 417(2), (c) of the Proceeds of Crime Act 2002 (property in respect of which an order for the appointment of a receiver or administrator under certain provisions of that Act is in force),

(b) a confiscation order is made under section 6, 92 or 156 of that Act,

(c) the amount payable under the confiscation order is fully paid, and

(d) any of the property remains in the hands of the receiver or administrator (as the case may be).

306B(2) [Vesting] The property vests in the trustee as part of the bankrupt's estate.

306BA Property in respect of which realisation order made

306BA(1) [Application] This section applies where–

(a) property is excluded from the bankrupt's estate by virtue of section 417(2)(d) of the Proceeds of Crime Act 2002 (property in respect of which an order has been made authorising realisation of the property by an appropriate officer),

(b) a confiscation order is made under section 6, 92 or 156 of that Act,

(c) the amount payable under the confiscation order is fully paid, and

(d) any of the property remains in the hands of the appropriate officer.

306BA(2) [Vesting] The property vests in the trustee as part of the bankrupt's estate.

306C Property subject to certain orders where confiscation order discharged or quashed

306C(1) [Application] This section applies where–

(a) property is excluded from the bankrupt's estate by virtue of section 417(2)(a), (b), (c) or (d) of the Proceeds of Crime Act 2002 (property excluded from bankrupt's estate),

(b) a confiscation order is made under section 6, 92 or 156 of that Act, and

(c) the confiscation order is discharged under section 30, 114 or 180 of that Act (as the case may be) or quashed under that Act or in pursuance of any enactment relating to appeals against conviction or sentence.

306C(2) [Vesting] Any such property vests in the trustee as part of the bankrupt's estate if it is in the hands of–

(a) a receiver appointed under Part 2 or 4 of that Act,

(b) an administrator appointed under Part 3 of that Act,

(c) an appropriate officer (within the meaning of section 41A, 120A or 190A of that Act).

306C(3) [Non-application of s.306C] But subsection (2) does not apply to the proceeds of property realised by a management receiver under section 49(2)(d) or 197(2)(d) of that Act (realisation of property to meet receiver's remuneration and expenses).

General Note to ss.306A–306C

Note insertion of ss.306A, 306B and 306C by Sch.11 to the Proceeds of Crime Act 2002. The 2002 Act deals with the interface between insolvency law and criminal proceeds recovery proceedings. Generally speaking, a bankrupt's estate will not include assets which are the subject of a criminal recovery action (s.417 of the 2002 Act) but the three new prospective sections deal with the return to the estate of such assets if the relevant criminal proceedings order is discharged, or liability extinguished through the confiscation process or the order quashed. In such circumstances the excluded assets are returned to the estate. Amendments were made to ss.306A and 306C and ss.306AA and 306BA inserted by Policing and Crime Act 2009 Sch.7 paras 54–58.

307 After-acquired property

307(1) [Power of trustee] Subject to this section and section 309, the trustee may by notice in writing claim for the bankrupt's estate any property which has been acquired by, or has devolved upon, the bankrupt since the commencement of the bankruptcy.

307(2) [Limit on s.307(1) notice] A notice under this section shall not be served in respect of–

(a) any property falling within subsection (2) or (3) of section 283 in Chapter II,

(aa) any property vesting in the bankrupt by virtue of section 283A in Chapter II,

(b) any property which by virtue of any other enactment is excluded from the bankrupt's estate, or

(c) without prejudice to section 280(2)(c) (order of court on application for discharge), any property which is acquired by, or devolves upon, the bankrupt after his discharge.

307(3) [Vesting on service of notice] Subject to subsections (4) and (4A), upon the service on the bankrupt of a notice under this section the property to which the notice relates shall vest in the trustee as part of the bankrupt's estate; and the trustee's title to that property has relation back to the time at which the property was acquired by, or devolved upon, the bankrupt.

307(4) [Outsiders] Where, whether before or after service on the bankrupt of a notice under this section–

(a) a person acquires property in good faith, for value and without notice of the bankruptcy,

(b) [Repealed]

the trustee is not in respect of that property entitled by virtue of this section to any remedy against that person or any person whose title to any property derives from that person.

307(4A) [No remedy against banker by trustee] Where a banker enters into a transaction before service on the banker of a notice under this section (and whether before or after service on the bankrupt of a notice under this section) the trustee is not in respect of that transaction entitled by virtue of this section to any remedy against the banker.

This subsection applies whether or not the banker has notice of the bankruptcy.

307(5) [Interpretation] References in this section to property do not include any property which, as part of the bankrupt's income, may be the subject of an income payments order under section 310.

S.307(1)

This enables the trustee to take the initiative and claim property vesting in the bankrupt after the commencement of the bankruptcy (as defined in s.278(a)). Under BA 1914 s.28(a) such property *automatically* vested in the trustee: see *Re Pascoe* [1944] Ch. 219. Prior to 1944 it was generally believed that positive intervention by the trustee was required. The Cork Committee (*Report*, para.1152) felt that it would be more flexible if the trustee could be allowed to choose whether the estate wanted such property. The advantage in such a change is highlighted by the White Paper, para.112—it saves the trustee from wasting his time in having to disclaim onerous after-acquired property. See also IR 2016 rr.10.25 and 10.26. The operation of this provision does depend on the bankrupt being honest with his trustee, as he is required to be by ss.333(2) and 353. The bankrupt must tell the trustee within 21 days of the acquisition of the property: see IR 2016 r.10.125.

For s.307 at work see *Pike v Cork Gully* [1997] B.P.I.R. 723; and *Re Mathew* (unreported, but noted in *Current Law Week*, 20 September 1996). This latter case involved a trustee laying claim to a legacy where the bankrupt had not kept the trustee fully informed. See also *Hill v Secretary of State* [2005] EWHC 696 (Ch); [2006] 1 B.C.L.C. 601. Note also *Hayes v Hayes* [2017] EWHC 2806 (Ch)—the latest instalment in long-running litigation. This merely makes the point that after-acquired property must be acquired within the prescribed timescale.

This provision might become necessary for the estate to claim appeal/review rights arising after the commencement of the bankruptcy—see the discussion in *R. (Singh) v Revenue and Customs Commissioners* [2010] B.P.I.R. 933. On protective measures designed to safeguard a potential s.307 claim see *Wood v Baker* [2015] EWHC 2536 (Ch); [2015] B.P.I.R. 1524.

S.307(2), (5)

Certain after-acquired property cannot be claimed by the trustee: property which would not be included in the estate in any case, and property acquired after the date of discharge. Section 307(2)(aa) was inserted by s.261 of EA 2002 with effect from 1 April 2004. Note also that income which may be caught by s.310 cannot fall under s.307. See *Supperstone v Lloyds Names Working Party* [1999] B.P.I.R. 832. On the link between the rules on after-acquired property and income flowing into the estate from an income payments order see *Official Receiver v Negus* [2011] EWHC 3719 (Ch). In *Arnold v Williams* [2008] EWHC 218 (Ch); [2008] B.P.I.R. 247 it was confirmed that s.307(2)(c) does not apply after discharge. This case provides an interesting discussion as to whether a trustee can use s.307 to compel a bankrupt to appeal post-bankruptcy tax assessments made in the period before discharge. On s.307(2)(c) note the comments of HHJ Matthews in *Corran v Butters* [2017] EWHC 2294 (Ch) at [126].

See *ECO Quest plc v GFI Consultants Ltd* [2014] EWHC 4329 (QB); [2015] B.P.I.R. 244 on the potential linkage with s.310.

S.307(3)

On service of the trustee's notice the property vests in the trustee. The trustee has 42 days to claim the property after receiving notice of it from the bankrupt, see IA 1986 s.309(1)(a), or else it can be disposed of by the bankrupt. For a clear explanation of the rationale and operation of this and related provisions see *Viscount St Davids v Lewis* [2015] EWHC 2826 (Ch); [2015] B.P.I.R. 1471 where Henderson J dismissed the appeal from the first instance ruling reported in [2015] EWHC 831 (Ch); [2015] B.P.I.R. 907. The court will err in favour of the trustee where the evidence is unclear as to his/her state of knowledge as to the acquisition of the after-acquired property by the bankrupt. Note linkage with ss.309, 333(2) and IR 2016 r.10.125.

S.307(4)

This protects bona fide purchasers (for value, without notice…) of after-acquired property from the bankrupt. It is based on BA 1914 s.47 which, in turn, confirmed the rule in *Cohen v Mitchell* (1890) 25 Q.B.D. 262. For a comparable Australian authority see *Rimar Pty Ltd v Pappas* (1986) 60 A.L.J.R. 309. However, the third party loses his protection if he has notice of the bankruptcy order: thus, *Hunt v Fripp* [1898] 1 Ch. 675 is reversed. If the disponee is not protected the trustee can recover the property under IR 2016 r.10.126.

Editors' note: Note amendments to subss.(3) and (4) and insertion of subs.(4A) by DA 2015 s.19 and Sch.6 para.16. The aim of this change is to protect bona fide banking transactions.

308 Vesting in trustee of certain items of excess value

308(1) [Claim by trustee in writing] Subject to section 309, where–

(a) property is excluded by virtue of section 283(2) (tools of trade, household effects, etc.) from the bankrupt's estate, and

(b) it appears to the trustee that the realisable value of the whole or any part of that property exceeds the cost of a reasonable replacement for that property or that part of it,

the trustee may by notice in writing claim that property or, as the case may be, that part of it for the bankrupt's estate.

308(2) [Vesting on service of s.308(1) notice] Upon the service on the bankrupt of a notice under this section, the property to which the notice relates vests in the trustee as part of the bankrupt's estate; and, except against a purchaser in good faith, for value and without notice of the bankruptcy, the trustee's title to that property has relation back to the commencement of the bankruptcy.

308(3) [Application of funds by trustee] The trustee shall apply funds comprised in the estate to the purchase by or on behalf of the bankrupt of a reasonable replacement for any property vested in the trustee under this section; and the duty imposed by this subsection has priority over the obligation of the trustee to distribute the estate.

308(4) [Reasonable replacement] For the purposes of this section property is a reasonable replacement for other property if it is reasonably adequate for meeting the needs met by the other property.

General Note

This is a new provision which implements the recommendations of the Cork Committee (*Report*, para.1101). This section is supplemented by IR 2016 rr.10.105, 10.106.

S.308(1), (4)

The trustee is allowed to claim certain property, which would normally not be included in the bankrupt's estate by virtue of s.283(2), if that property can be reasonably replaced (as defined in s.308(4), producing a surplus for the estate. See *Pike v Cork Gully* [1997] B.P.I.R. 723. Note the 42-day limit in s.309. The provision is designed to prevent bankrupts with large debts from continuing to live a life of luxury surrounded by expensive cars and consumer durables. A bankrupt who objects to replacement can complain to the court under s.303. A third party can pay off the trustee to avert replacement: IR 2016 r.10.105. A minor change has been made to subs.(1) to accommodate the insertion of s.308A: see Housing Act 1988 Sch.17 para.73.

S.308(2)

Once the trustee has given notice, the property in question will vest in the trustee, subject to the rights of any bona fide purchaser.

S.308(3)

The cost of the replacement is to be met out of the estate funds and the defrayment of this cost takes priority over the trustee's obligation to distribute. The replacement may occur before or after the sale of the original item, see IR 2016 r.10.106.

S.308(4)

It would appear from the link with subs.(1) that the test as to what is "reasonable" is likely to be applied subjectively, i.e. does the trustee believe it is reasonable? Provided his decision is not totally erratic, the court would not intervene.

308A Vesting in trustee of certain tenancies

308A Upon the service on the bankrupt by the trustee of a notice in writing under this section, any tenancy–

(a) which is excluded by virtue of section 283(3A) from the bankrupt's estate, and

(b) to which the notice relates,

vests in the trustee as part of the bankrupt's estate; and, except against a purchaser in good faith, for value and without notice of the bankruptcy, the trustee's title to that tenancy has relation back to the commencement of the bankruptcy.

309 Time-limit for notice under s.307 or 308

309(1) [Timing of notice] Except with the leave of the court, a notice shall not be served–

(a) under section 307, after the end of the period of 42 days beginning with the day on which it first came to the knowledge of the trustee that the property in question had been acquired by, or had devolved upon, the bankrupt;

(b) under section 308 or section 308A, after the end of the period of 42 days beginning with the day on which the property or tenancy in question first came to the knowledge of the trustee.

309(2) [Deemed knowledge] For the purposes of this section–

(a) anything which comes to the knowledge of the trustee is deemed in relation to any successor of his as trustee to have come to the knowledge of the successor at the same time; and

(b) anything which comes (otherwise than under paragraph (a)) to the knowledge of a person before he is the trustee is deemed to come to his knowledge on his appointment taking effect or, in the case of the official receiver, on his becoming trustee.

General Note

The trustee must claim the property or seek replacement (under ss.307, 308 or 308A) within 42 days after it has come to his notice, as defined by s.309(2). In *Viscount St Davids v Lewis* [2015] EWHC 2826 (Ch); [2015] B.P.I.R. 1471 Henderson J indicated that the court would require a high degree of certainty on the part of the trustee to found knowledge and to start the 42 day clock running. The court refused to permit a s.307 notice to be served out of time in *Solomons v Williams* [2001] B.P.I.R. 1123. In *Franses v Oomerjee* [2005] B.P.I.R. 1320 the court refused to accept a notice given under s.307 in view of the delays involved. The notice was given by a trustee in bankruptcy some 15 weeks after his appointment, that appointment having been made in November 2004 with respect to a bankruptcy commencing as long ago as 1991. The bankrupt had notified the official receiver in 1997 of the after acquired-property but no action was taken. No explanation could be given for the delays in serving the s.307 notice in this case and in view of the prejudice to the bankrupt permission to claim the after-acquired property was refused. Note the minor changes made to subs.1(b) by s.117(3) of the Housing Act 1988.

310 Income payments orders

310(1) [Order by court] The court may, make an order ("an income payments order") claiming for the bankrupt's estate so much of the income of the bankrupt during the period for which the order is in force as may be specified in the order.

310(1A) [Applicant for order] An income payments order may be made only on an application instituted–

(a) by the trustee, and

(b) before the discharge of the bankrupt.

310(2) [Limit on order] The court shall not make an income payments order the effect of which would be to reduce the income of the bankrupt when taken together with any payments to which subsection (8) applies below what appears to the court to be necessary for meeting the reasonable domestic needs of the bankrupt and his family.

310(3) [Extent of order] An income payments order shall, in respect of any payment of income to which it is to apply, either–

(a) require the bankrupt to pay the trustee an amount equal to so much of that payment as is claimed by the order, or

(b) require the person making the payment to pay so much of it as is so claimed to the trustee, instead of to the bankrupt.

310(4) [Power to discharge or vary attachment of earnings] Where the court makes an income payments order it may, if it thinks fit, discharge or vary any attachment of earnings order that is for the time being in force to secure payments by the bankrupt.

310(5) [Sums part of estate] Sums received by the trustee under an income payments order form part of the bankrupt's estate.

310(6) [Period of order] An income payments order must specify the period during which it is to have effect; and that period–

(a) may end after the discharge of the bankrupt, but

(b) may not end after the period of three years beginning with the date on which the order is made.

310(6A) [Variation of order] An income payments order may (subject to subsection (6)(b)) be varied on the application of the trustee or the bankrupt (whether before or after discharge).

310(7) [Income of the bankrupt] For the purposes of this section the income of the bankrupt comprises every payment in the nature of income which is from time to time made to him or to which he from time to time becomes entitled, including any payment in respect of the carrying on of any business or in respect of any office or employment and (despite anything in section 11 or 12 of the Welfare Reform and Pensions Act 1999) any payment under a pension scheme but excluding any payment to which subsection (8) applies.

310(8) [Application] This subsection applies to–

(a) payments by way of guaranteed minimum pension.

310(9) [Definitions] In this section–

"guaranteed minimum pension" has the same meaning given in the Pension Schemes Act 1993.

General Note

One of the defects in BA 1914 was that it did not have an effective mechanism to enable the trustee to appropriate the income of the bankrupt for the benefit of the estate. BA 1914 s.51 was largely ineffective, especially where the bankrupt was self-employed. The Cork Committee (*Report*, paras 591–598) recommended a change in the law which would enable creditors to be paid off out of future income rather than the proceeds of a forced sale. Although s.310 introduces such a mechanism the evidence is that income payment orders have not been widely used: see Justice, *Insolvency Law: An Agenda for Reform* (1994) at para.4.30.

For the relationship with s.306 see *Re Landau* [1998] Ch. 223, a case of major significance on pension rights and the unreported 1994 county court case of *Carman v Baron*, which is noted by Greenstreet in (1996) 12 I.L. & P. 60. Section 310 does not apply to a pension which has automatically vested in the trustee—*Lesser v Lawrence* [2000] B.P.I.R. 410; and *Rowe v Sanders* [2002] EWCA Civ 242; [2002] B.P.I.R. 847. In the context of income payments orders and pensions note also s.91 of the Pensions Act 1995 and the amendments effected by Sch.3 para.15. On the role of s.310 in matrimonial proceedings note *Albert v Albert* [1996] B.P.I.R. 232; and *Re X* [1996] B.P.I.R. 494.

In *Official Receiver v Baker* [2013] EWHC 4594 (Ch); [2014] B.P.I.R. 724 Warren J emphasised that it is possible to obtain an IPO against income generated (in this case gambling winnings) after the making of a bankruptcy order.

Thomas v Edmondson [2014] EWHC 1494 (Ch); [2014] B.P.I.R. 1070 (Asplin J) decides that there is no bar preventing the making of an IPO in circumstances where the bankrupt has already entered an IPA (which is due to expire). There is no rule restricting income payments to three years, though this may be a factor when determining the ambit of the IPO.

For an application for an income payments order in a cross border insolvency see *C Brooks Thurmond III v Rajapakse* [2008] B.P.I.R. 283. This case is interesting in that it confirms that lump sums may be made subject to an income payments order and considers the susceptibility of pensions to the income payments regime. An income payments order was made by Chief Registrar Baister in the curious case of *Bowles v Trefilov* (unreported, 29 April 2016).

In 2011/2012 the official receiver obtained 10,158 new IPOs/IPAs. The Insolvency Service estimates that IPOs/IPAs are now used in about 14 per cent of all bankruptcies and typically they run for three years. A fee of £150 is payable.

S.310(1), (1A), (2)

In subs.(1) the phrase "on the application of the trustee" was deleted by EA 2002 s.259 with effect from April 2004. Subsection (1A) was added by that same provision. Section 310 permits an application to court for an income payments order, but the court cannot appropriate so great a proportion of the bankrupt's income as to reduce him and his family to penury. This restriction existed at common law: *Re Roberts* [1900] 1 Q.B. 122. Note the amendment introduced into subs.(2) by Sch.3 para.15 to the Pensions Act 1995. The bankrupt must be given 28 days' notice of the application, see IR 2016 r.10.109. Reasonable domestic need is to be determined by reference to the circumstances of each case and may include private school fees where removal from a school might be detrimental to the children: *Re Rayatt* [1998] B.P.I.R. 495. In *Scott v Davis* [2003] B.P.I.R. 1009 the issue of private school fees was revisited and the court stressed the importance of there being evidence that on the facts of the particular case that they were a reasonable domestic need. For further discussion of this subsection see *Kilvert v Flackett* [1998] B.P.I.R. 721; and *Malcolm v Official Receiver* [1999] B.P.I.R. 97. In *Boyden v Watson* [2004] B.P.I.R. 1131 the court rejected an application for an income payments order in the most scathing of terms. The bankrupt had insufficient funds once his reasonable domestic needs had been met. On a detailed analysis of reasonable domestic needs, albeit in a different context, see *Official Receiver v Norman* (unreported, 5 December 2012, Milton Keynes County Court, District Judge Rand). See also *Official Receiver v Wilson* [2013] B.P.I.R. 907 where the point is also touched upon.

Chadwick v Nash [2012] B.P.I.R. 70 highlights the fact that an income payments order cannot be applied for after discharge. The courts are not receptive to late applications to suspend discharge to facilitate some sort of income payments arrangement where the circumstances are such that there should have been a much earlier application for an income payments order.

An important authority to note here is *Raithatha v Williamson* [2012] EWHC 909 (Ch); [2012] B.P.I.R. 621; [2012] 1 W.L.R. 3559, where the issue of pension rights was once again the subject of discussion before Bernard Livesey QC (sitting in the High Court). Here an expansive view of what is income for the purposes of s.310 was adopted. Where the bankrupt had not made an election prior to his bankruptcy to take up his rights under a pension scheme the payments that the bankrupt was entitled to receive could be treated as income for the purposes of s.310. Lump sum payments to a bankrupt may count as income as there was no requirement of periodic payments. For a perceptive critique of this ruling see Briggs (2012) 25 Insolv. Int. 65.

In *Re X (Application for an income payments order)* [2014] B.P.I.R. 1081 District Judge Smith ruled that the court cannot direct a bankrupt to make an election to draw down pension benefits in a way that would prevent the bankrupt from having sufficient funds to cover long term reasonable domestic needs. *Raithatha v Williamson* (above) was distinguished. But one might ask whether this is a correct interpretation of s.310? For instance what do we mean by the reasonable domestic needs of the "bankrupt"? Clearly it cannot be restricted to the undischarged bankrupt as an IPO can run beyond bankruptcy—but how far forward can you project things when providing for the reasonable domestic needs of a former bankrupt? In spite of these uncertainties Robert Englehart QC (sitting in the High Court) has adopted a similar stance in *Re Henry, Horton v Henry* [2014] EWHC 4209 (Ch); [2015] 1 W.L.R. 2488 and has refused to direct a bankrupt to draw down an uncrystallised capital sum not yet in payment from his pension pot in order to service an IPO. In *Re Wotherspoon* [2016] EWHC 621 (Ch); [2016] B.P.I.R. 944 Registrar Jones expressed a preference for the decision of Robert Englehart QC in *Re Henry* (above) mainly because of the perceived pensions protective policy in this area of law application of strict rules of judicial precedent. That was a wise preference because the Court of Appeal subsequently upheld that first instance ruling in *Re Henry* in its long-awaited judgment in *Horton v Henry* [2016] EWCA Civ 989. The Court of Appeal concluded that there was indeed a clear policy developed in the Welfare Reform and Pensions Act 1999 to protect pension entitlements and that *Raithatha* (above) had not given sufficient weight to that policy when deciding whether there was power to compel a bankrupt to elect to draw down a pension entitlement. A purposive approach was required when interpreting s.310. It is to be noted that *Horton v Henry* dealt with the position before the advent of "pensions' freedom" in 2015; its impact will in fact be greater in the light of the post-2015 landscape. This unanimous ruling from the Court of Appeal with come as a disappointment to trustees looking to maximise asset realisation potential. There is an argument that the protection given to pension entitlements should be reviewed in the light of social/economic developments since 1999. For full analysis see Cawson [2017] 30 Insolv. Int. 5.

S.310(3)–(5)

These provisions deal with the effect of an income payments order. Either the bankrupt or some third party can be directed to make payments to the trustee, the sums thereby received forming part of the estate. On making such an order the court can modify any attachment of earnings order relating to the bankrupt's income. Note that s.310(3) is amplified by the Rules: see Sch.9 para.15 and IR 2016 rr.10.109–10.114. The order may be reviewed on the application of either party or varied on the application of the trustee. The latter might occur where the bankrupt's income increases. Note here the obligation to notify the trustee within 21 days (s.332(2) and r.10.125).

In *Official Receiver v Negus* [2011] EWHC 3719 (Ch) Newey J held that the court can still grant an IPO even though the creditors will receive no direct benefit from such order. There was nothing improper in making an IPO to ensure that the costs of the official receiver were met.

S.310(6), (6A)
Subsection (6) was reconstituted by s.259 of EA 2002 with effect from April 2004.

Subsection (6A), which deals with variation of IPOs, was inserted by s.259 of EA 2002 with effect from April 2004.

S.310(7)
This defines "income" in wide terms and emphasises that it covers the income of a self-employed person. Presumably payments in the nature of capital are not covered by s.310 unless such payments could be treated as a single surge of income, as was the subject of discussion in the case of *Kilvert v Flackett* (above). See also *Supperstone v Lloyds Names Working Party* [1999] B.P.I.R. 832. Further consideration was given to the meaning of "income" in *Official Receiver v Baker* [2014] B.P.I.R. 724. In allowing an appeal by the Official Receiver against refusal of an IPO Warren J held that money standing to the credit of a bankrupt in an account before the IPO was sought, but representing post-bankruptcy income, could be regarded as income for the purposes of s.310. This broad interpretation was necessary to prevent a lacuna opening up in the law. Again the text of this subsection has been supplemented by Sch.3 para.15 to the Pensions Act 1995 and s.18 coupled with Sch.2 to the Welfare Reform and Pensions Act 1999 with effect from 29 May 2000 (see Welfare Reform and Pensions Act 1999 (Commencement No.7) Order 2000 (SI 2000/1382 (C. 41))). Note the limitation on income identified in *Dear IP* Issue 24 (September 2005).

S.310(8), (9)
These completely new subsections were introduced by the Pensions Act 1995 (Sch.3 para.15). Subsection (9) was amended by the Pensions Act 2008 (Abolition of Protected Rights) (Consequential Amendments) (No.2) Order 2011 (SI 2011/1730) art.3 with effect from 6 April 2012. Note in s.310(8), para.(b) was removed by the Pensions Act 2008 (Abolition of Protected Rights) (Consequential Amendments) (No.2) Order 2011 (SI 2011/1730).

310A Income payments agreement

310A(1) ["Income payments agreement"] In this section "income payments agreement" means a written agreement between a bankrupt and his trustee or between a bankrupt and the official receiver which provides–

(a) that the bankrupt is to pay to the trustee or the official receiver an amount equal to a specified part or proportion of the bankrupt's income for a specified period, or

(b) that a third person is to pay to the trustee or the official receiver a specified proportion of money due to the bankrupt by way of income for a specified period.

310A(2) [Enforceability of agreement] A provision of an income payments agreement of a kind specified in subsection (1)(a) or (b) may be enforced as if it were a provision of an income payments order.

310A(3) [Discharge or variation of attachment of earnings order] While an income payments agreement is in force the court may, on the application of the bankrupt, his trustee or the official receiver, discharge or vary an attachment of earnings order that is for the time being in force to secure payments by the bankrupt.

310A(4) [Application of s.310(5), (7)–(9)] The following provisions of section 310 shall apply to an income payments agreement as they apply to an income payments order–

(a) subsection (5) (receipts to form part of estate), and

(b) subsections (7) to (9) (meaning of income).

310A(5) [Period of agreement] An income payments agreement must specify the period during which it is to have effect; and that period–

(a) may end after the discharge of the bankrupt, but

(b) may not end after the period of three years beginning with the date on which the agreement is made.

310A(6) [Variation of agreement] An income payments agreement may (subject to subsection (5)(b)) be varied–

(a) by written agreement between the parties, or

(b) by the court on an application made by the bankrupt, the trustee or the official receiver.

310A(7) [Power to vary] The court–

(a) may not vary an income payments agreement so as to include provision of a kind which could not be included in an income payments order, and

(b) shall grant an application to vary an income payments agreement if and to the extent that the court thinks variation necessary to avoid the effect mentioned in section 310(2).

General Note

This innovation (which took effect in April 2004) came about as a result of the enactment of s.260 of EA 2002. The aim is to put in place a legally binding income payments scheme without the need for a formal court order. Once again the underlying policy goal is to reduce administration costs, a particularly important consideration bearing in mind the inefficiencies involved in the IPO procedure. A fee of £150 is payable. Further provision for IPAs is to be found in IR 2016 rr.10.115–10.117.

S.310A(1)
This defines what is meant by an income payments agreement (IPA). The agreement must be in writing. IPAs can be used to divert sums due to the bankrupt from a third party.

S.310A(2), (4)
The effect of an IPA is equivalent to that of an IPO. This is reinforced by subs.(4).

S.310A(3), (6), (7)
Variation and discharge of IPAs is hereby provided for. Note also the variation possibilities covered by subs.(6), including variation by agreement in writing and the limitations on the court imposed by subs.(7).

In *Re Hargreaves (Booth v Mond)* [2010] B.P.I.R. 1111 the question was whether arrears due under an income payments agreement could rank as debts in the subsequent IVA of the former bankrupt. The court held that they could be so regarded. Under s.310A(6) the terms of the IPA could be varied and so the trustee in bankruptcy could compromise the sums due under an individual voluntary arrangement.

S.310A(5)
This regulates the duration of an IPA. It can last beyond the date of discharge but cannot persist for more than three years after the agreement date. Note *Thomas v Edmondson* [2014] EWHC 1494 (Ch); [2014] B.P.I.R. 1070 where Asplin J held that there is no rule precluding the grant of an income payments order once an income payments agreement has expired. This should assist trustees who might wish to get the bankrupt to agree to a varied IPA.

311 Acquisition by trustee of control

311(1) [Trustee to take possession] The trustee shall take possession of all books, papers and other records which relate to the bankrupt's estate or affairs and which belong to him or are in his possession or under his control (including any which would be privileged from disclosure in any proceedings).

311(2) [Trustee like receiver] In relation to, and for the purpose of acquiring or retaining possession of, the bankrupt's estate, the trustee is in the same position as if he were a receiver of property appointed by the High Court; and the court may, on his application, enforce such acquisition or retention accordingly.

311(3) [Where estate includes transferable property] Where any part of the bankrupt's estate consists of stock or shares in a company, shares in a ship or any other property transferable in the books of a company, office or person, the trustee may exercise the right to transfer the property to the same extent as the bankrupt might have exercised it if he had not become bankrupt.

311(4) [Where estate includes things in action] Where any part of the estate consists of things in action, they are deemed to have been assigned to the trustee; but notice of the deemed assignment need not be given except in so far as it is necessary, in a case where the deemed assignment is from the bankrupt himself, for protecting the priority of the trustee.

311(5) [Where goods held by pledge] Where any goods comprised in the estate are held by any person by way of pledge, pawn or other security and no notice has been served in respect of those goods by the official receiver under subsection (5) of section 285 (restriction on realising security), the trustee may serve such a notice in respect of the goods; and whether or not a notice has been served under this subsection or that subsection, the trustee may, if he thinks fit, exercise the bankrupt's right of redemption in respect of any such goods.

311(6) [Effect of s.311(5) notice] A notice served by the trustee under subsection (5) has the same effect as a notice served by the official receiver under section 285(5).

S.311(1)
This describes the most basic duty of a trustee, which is to collect the bankrupt's property together. For the impact of this provision on privileged documents see *Re Konigsberg (a Bankrupt)* [1989] 1 W.L.R. 1257. *Scholsberg v Avonwick Holdings Ltd* [2016] EWHC 1001 (Ch) provides a good discussion by Arnold J of the implications of *Re Konigsberg* (above). The appeal from the decision of Arnold J was dismissed—*Avonwick Holdings Ltd v Schlosberg* [2016] EWCA Civ 1138. The implications of *Avonwick* (above) were discussed by HHJ Hodge QC in *Leeds v Lemos* [2017] EWHC 1825 (Ch); [2017] B.P.I.R. 1223. In *Avonwick* the Court of Appeal had decided that privilege was not property that automatically vested in the trustee. This later decision of HHJ Hodge further protects privilege. It decides that the *Crescent Farm* principle ([1972] Ch. 553) does not apply in bankruptcy cases—[242]. *Re Konigsberg* (above) is therefore a weakened authority. The right to take papers is limited to business or financial records and does not include personal correspondence even if it has an economic value—see *Haig v Aitken* [2000] B.P.I.R. 462 where the possibility that seizure of such documents might infringe art.8 ECHR (right of privacy) was also considered by the court. In *Boyden v Canty (No.2)* [2007] EWCA Civ 241; [2007] B.P.I.R. 299 the court indicated that failure to comply with obligations under s.311 could be regarded as contempt justifying committal.

See also the comments of Proudman J in *Doffman and Isaacs v Wood and Hellard* [2011] EWHC 4008 (Ch); [2012] B.P.I.R. 972 at [30].

On the limitations of the scope of legal privilege and its non-availability to accountants see the approach of the Supreme Court in *R. (on the application of Prudential plc) v Special Commissioner of Income Tax* [2013] UKSC 1.

S.311(2)
While carrying out the above function the trustee will be treated as if he were a court-appointed receiver and will, for example, enjoy the protection of the law of contempt.

S.311(3), (4)
These provisions deal with the trustee's rights in respect of certain intangible forms of property, such as shares or choses in action. This provision was considered in *Hunt v Harb* [2011] EWCA Civ 1239; [2012] B.P.I.R. 117.

S.311(5), (6)
These provisions, based on BA 1914 s.59 deal with the situation where the bankrupt's goods have been given as security to some other person. The trustee may (if the official receiver has not already done so) serve a notice on the third party in order to redeem the goods. Such a notice has the same effect as a notice served by the official receiver under s.285(5).

312 Obligation to surrender control to trustee

312(1) [Bankrupt to surrender property] The bankrupt shall deliver up to the trustee possession of any property, books, papers or other records of which he has possession or control and of which the trustee is required to take possession.

This is without prejudice to the general duties of the bankrupt under section 333 in this Chapter.

312(2) [Other persons in possession] If any of the following is in possession of any property, books, papers or other records of which the trustee is required to take possession, namely–

(a) the official receiver,

(b) a person who has ceased to be trustee of the bankrupt's estate, or

(c) a person who has been the supervisor of a voluntary arrangement approved in relation to the bankrupt under Part VIII,

the official receiver or, as the case may be, that person shall deliver up possession of the property, books, papers or records to the trustee.

312(3) [Bankers, agents et al. of bankrupt] Any banker or agent of the bankrupt or any other person who holds any property to the account of, or for, the bankrupt shall pay or deliver to the trustee all property in his possession or under his control which forms part of the bankrupt's estate and which he is not by law entitled to retain as against the bankrupt or trustee.

312(4) [Penalty for non-compliance] If any person without reasonable excuse fails to comply with any obligation imposed by this section, he is guilty of a contempt of court and liable to be punished accordingly (in addition to any other punishment to which he may be subject).

S.312(1)

This provision obliges the bankrupt, in addition to his general duty to assist the trustee, to hand over possession of his property, books, etc. to the trustee.

S.312(2), (3)

This obligation extends to official receivers, former trustees, supervisors of a voluntary arrangement, bankers and agents of the bankrupt, although the latter two groups may have certain rights of retention as against the trustee.

S.312(4)

The above obligations are reinforced by the law of contempt. In *Simmonds v Pearce* [2017] EWHC 35 (QB) the Divisional Court found that the debtor had not breached his obligations under this provision and therefore there was no contempt.

313 Charge on bankrupt's home

313(1) [Application to court by trustee] Where any property consisting of an interest in a dwelling house which is occupied by the bankrupt or by his spouse or former spouse or by his civil partner or former civil partner is comprised in the bankrupt's estate and the trustee is, for any reason, unable for the time being to realise that property, the trustee may apply to the court for an order imposing a charge on the property for the benefit of the bankrupt's estate.

313(2) [Benefit of charge] If on an application under this section the court imposes a charge on any property, the benefit of that charge shall be comprised in the bankrupt's estate and is enforceable, up to the charged value from time to time, for the payment of any amount which is payable otherwise than to the bankrupt out of the estate and of interest on that amount at the prescribed rate.

313(2A) [Meaning of charged value in s.313(2)] In subsection (2) the charged value means–

(a) the amount specified in the charging order as the value of the bankrupt's interest in the property at the date of the order, plus

(b) interest on that amount from the date of the charging order at the prescribed rate.

313(2B) [Court's duty in valuing interest] In determining the value of an interest for the purposes of this section the court shall disregard any matter which it is required to disregard by the rules.

313(3) [Provision in order] An order under this section made in respect of property vested in the trustee shall provide, in accordance with the rules, for the property to cease to be comprised in the bankrupt's estate and, subject to the charge (and any prior charge), to vest in the bankrupt.

313(4) [Effect of Charging Orders Act] Subsection (1), (2), (4), (5) and (6) of section 3 of the Charging Orders Act 1979 (supplemental provisions with respect to charging orders) have effect in relation to orders under this section as in relation to charging orders under that Act.

313(5) [No power to vary a charged value] But an order under section 3(5) of that Act may not vary a charged value.

General Note

This is a new provision which would probably be better located next to ss.336–338, which also deal with the matrimonial home. This new package of provisions, which was recommended by the Cork Committee (*Report*, paras 1114–1131), is designed to tilt the balance more in favour of the bankrupt and his family when it comes to selling the family home. This provision, unlike the others dealing with the matrimonial home, was included in the original Insolvency Bill of 1985. For a general view of the operation of s.313 in practice see Hill (1990) 6 I.L. & P. 12. Section 313 is amended with effect from 1 April 2004 by s.260 of EA 2002. The effect is to improve the rights of bankrupts where orders under s.313 are utilised. An important issue of principle was determined in *Gotham v Doodes* [2006] EWCA Civ 1080. Here it had been held by Lindsay J (reluctantly overturning a ruling of Chief Registrar Baister) that a trustee was prevented from enforcing a charging order through sale because of the expiry of a limitation period of 12 years running from the date when the charging order had been granted. In so deciding the judge had felt compelled to follow an obscure Court of Appeal precedent dealing, arguably, with an analogous situation. However, in this case the Court of Appeal held that the limitation period under s.20 of the Limitation Act 1980 only began to run from the order permitting sale and not from when the charging order originally had been granted. Only when sale was permitted did the right to receive the income from the charged property arise. This ruling will reassure trustees who use charging orders as a mode of protecting the interest of the estate in the family home.

S.313(1)

If the trustee cannot sell the bankrupt's interest in the "dwelling house" (for the definition, see s.385) occupied by him or his family he may apply to a court for a charging order on that interest. A novel issue arose before Chief Registrar Baister in *Re Parkins* [2014] B.P.I.R. 1054. Here the issue was whether a charging order should be granted as it was "impracticable" to sell the property—the court held that this term could be liberally construed to cover situations where it would be unwise to sell the property because the underlying debt on which the bankruptcy was based was still under challenged. This is a sensible interpretation. Note also the link with s.332. Note the insertion of the reference to civil partners by the Civil Partnership Act 2004 Sch.27.

S.313(2)–(4)

These provisions deal with the effect of the court granting such a charging order. It attaches to the property in question until enforced, although the property ceases to vest in the trustee and will revert to the bankrupt (subject to the charge). Certain parts of s.3 of the Charging Orders Act 1979 will apply to such an order made by the court under s.313(1).

Amendments to ss.313(2), 313(2A) and 313(2B) here are designed to ensure that where the value of the charged property increases over time the benefit accrues to the bankrupt and not to the estate. This in effect is achieved by providing for the value of the bankrupt's interest in the charged property to be identified on application; that charged value then gets the benefit of any inflationary uplift.

A minor amendment is made to s.313(4) by the Tribunals, Courts and Enforcement Act 2007 s.93(5) which was brought into force on 1 October 2012 by the Tribunals, Courts and Enforcement Act 2007 (Commencement No.8) Order 2012 (SI 2012/1312).

The rules provide more details of the conditions which may be attached to such a charge: see IR 2016 r.10.16.

S.313(5)

Inserted by s.260 of EA 2002 with effect from 1 April 2004 this prevents a charging order from undermining the protective effect of s.313(2A).

313A Low value home: application for sale, possession or charge

313A(1) [Application of section] This section applies where–

(a) property comprised in the bankrupt's estate consists of an interest in a dwelling-house which at the date of the bankruptcy was the sole or principal residence of–

(i) the bankrupt,

(ii) the bankrupt's spouse or civil partner, or

(iii) a former spouse or former civil partner of the bankrupt, and

(b) the trustee applies for an order for the sale of the property, for an order for possession of the property or for an order under section 313 in respect of the property.

313A(2) [Court's duty to dismiss application] The court shall dismiss the application if the value of the interest is below the amount prescribed for the purposes of this subsection.

313A(3) [Court's duty to disregard matters prescribed by order] In determining the value of an interest for the purposes of this section the court shall disregard any matter which it is required to disregard by the order which prescribes the amount for the purposes of subsection (2).

General Note

Again introduced by s.261(3) of EA 2002 this deals with the realisation of low value properties. The feeling is that the marginal benefit to creditors from realising such an asset is outweighed by the disproportionate suffering imposed upon the bankrupt by the loss of his home. This provision came into effect on 1 April 2004.

S.313A(1)
This seeks to identify what is meant by an interest in a low value home for the purposes of this section. Note s.385. The problem of multiple low value homes might have to be addressed—see the comments on s.283A. Note the insertion of the reference to civil partners by the Civil Partnership Act 2004 Sch.27.

S.313A(2)
The trustee is hereby in effect debarred from taking specified realisation action in respect of an interest in a dwelling covered by subs.(1). The minimum amount prescribed is £1,000 (Insolvency Proceedings (Monetary Limits) (Amendment) Order 2004 (SI 2004/547)), though that valuation figure is then qualified by art.3 of that Order.

S.313(A)(3)
This deals further with the question of valuation and inclusion within this restrictive mechanism.

314 Powers of trustee

314(1) [Powers in Sch.5 Pt I and II] The trustee may exercise any of the powers specified in Parts 1 and 2 of Schedule 5.

314(2) [Powers of appointment re bankrupt] The trustee may appoint the bankrupt–

(a) to superintend the management of his estate or any part of it,

(b) to carry on his business (if any) for the benefit of his creditors, or

(c) in any other respect to assist in administering the estate in such manner and on such terms as the trustee may direct.

314(3) [Omitted]

314(4) [Omitted]

314(5) [Powers in Sch.5 Pt III] Part III of Schedule 5 to this Act has effect with respect to the things which the trustee is able to do for the purposes of, or in connection with, the exercise of any of his powers under any of this Group of Parts.

314(6) [Notice to committee] Where the trustee (not being the official receiver) in exercise of the powers conferred on him by any provision in this Group of Parts–

(a) disposes of any property comprised in the bankrupt's estate to an associate of the bankrupt, or

(b) employs a solicitor,

he shall, if there is for the time being a creditors' committee, give notice to the committee of that exercise of his powers.

314(7) [Power to seek a decision from creditors] Without prejudice to the generality of subsection (5) and Part III of Schedule 5, the trustee may, if he thinks fit, at any time seek a decision on a matter from bankrupt's creditors.

Subject to the preceding provisions in this Group of Parts, he shall seek a decision on a matter if he is requested to do so by a creditor of the bankrupt and the request is made with the concurrence of not less than one-tenth, in value, of the bankrupt's creditors (including the creditor making the request).

314(8) [Capacity of trustee] Nothing in this Act is to be construed as restricting the capacity of the trustee to exercise any of his powers outside England and Wales.

S.314(1), (2), (6)

A trustee may exercise the powers listed in Pt II of Sch.5 without obtaining permission of the committee of creditors (see s.301). This list of powers is derived from BA 1914 s.55. No major changes have been made to these basic powers. Note, however, that if property is disposed of to an "associate" of the bankrupt (for the meaning of this term see s.435), the committee of creditors must be told. Section 314(2) refers to Pt I of Sch.5, which describes powers which the trustee may exercise only with the consent of the committee of creditors. These powers are based on BA 1914 ss.56, 57. The sanction requirement is to protect the bankrupt's estate, see *Re a Debtor (No.26A of 1975)* [1985] 1 W.L.R. 6. See *Re Don Basil Williams* [2002] EWHC 1393 (Ch); [2003] B.P.I.R. 545 where the court sanctioned a compromise favoured by the trustee. The requirement that the trustee should obtain permission before employing a solicitor or agent, contained formerly in s.56(3), has been dropped—but if he does this he must now give notice to the committee according to s.314(6)(b). The meaning of "compromise" and "sale" within the meaning of paras 7 and 9 of Sch.5 was considered in by the court in *Power v Brown* [2009] B.P.I.R. 340.

On the sanction requirement under s.314 see *Grant v Hayes* [2014] EWHC 2646 (Ch); [2014] B.P.I.R. 1455 where the application to the court by the trustee for sanction was dismissed by Nugee J.

Subsections (1) and (2) were amended by SBEEA 2015 s.121 to give trustees greater flexibility in the exercise of powers. As a result of these changes subss.(3) and (4) became redundant and were repealed.

S.314(5)

This provision refers to Pt III of Sch.5, which gives a general account of the trustee's powers (e.g. to hold property and make contracts) that may be exercised in his "official name" (see s.305(4)).

S.314(7)

This deals with the seeking of the views of creditors by the trustee. Note that he must take such a step if asked to do so by creditors owed one-tenth of the bankrupt's total debts. The figure fixed by BA 1914 s.79(2) was one-sixth in value of the total debts. There were amendments to subs.(7) made by SBEEA 2015 s.126 and Sch.9 para.81 to reflect wider creditor decision procedures.

S.314(8)

The trustee may exercise his powers outside England and Wales. This is increasingly important as the problems of cross-border insolvency increase. See here *Re Hayward* [1997] Ch. 45 where the trustee was required by virtue of the European Convention on Jurisdiction and Enforcement of Judgments in Civil Matters to pursue a claim to Spanish real estate in Spain and not in England. Rattee J concluded that the claim was not primarily concerned with insolvency, but with title to immoveable property, and therefore the Spanish courts enjoyed exclusive jurisdiction under the Convention. See also *Pollard v Ashurst* [2001] B.P.I.R. 131. The entry into effect of the EC Regulation on Insolvency Proceedings did improve matters considerably. See now EURIP 2015.

Disclaimer of onerous property

315 Disclaimer (general power)

315(1) [Power of trustee to disclaim] Subject as follows, the trustee may, by the giving of the prescribed notice, disclaim any onerous property and may do so notwithstanding that he has taken possession of it, endeavoured to sell it or otherwise exercised rights of ownership in relation to it.

315(2) [Onerous property] The following is onerous property for the purposes of this section, that is to say–

(a) any unprofitable contract, and

(b) any other property comprised in the bankrupt's estate which is unsaleable or not readily saleable, or is such that it may give rise to a liability to pay money or perform any other onerous act.

315(3) [Effect of disclaimer] A disclaimer under this section–

(a) operates so as to determine, as from the date of the disclaimer, the rights, interests and liabilities of the bankrupt and his estate in or in respect of the property disclaimed, and

(b) discharges the trustee from all personal liability in respect of that property as from the commencement of his trusteeship,

but does not, except so far as is necessary for the purpose of releasing the bankrupt, the bankrupt's estate and the trustee from any liability, affect the rights or liabilities of any other person.

315(4) [Where notice of disclaimer not to be given] A notice of disclaimer shall not be given under this section in respect of any property that has been claimed for the estate under section 307 (after-acquired property) or 308 (personal property of bankrupt exceeding reasonable replacement value) or 308A, except with the leave of the court.

315(5) [Persons sustaining loss or damage] Any person sustaining loss or damage in consequence of the operation of a disclaimer under this section is deemed to be a creditor of the bankrupt to the extent of the loss or damage and accordingly may prove for the loss or damage as a bankruptcy debt.

General Note

This section, and the ones immediately following it, deal with the power of the trustee to disclaim onerous property, and the role of the court in the event of disclaimer. The Cork Committee (*Report*, paras 1182–1199) felt that this power, which has existed since 1869, should be modified to enable the trustee to utilise it more effectively. The comparable provisions relating to disclaimers by liquidators are to be found in ss.178–182. A disclaimer is deemed to have been validly exercised unless the contrary is established: see IR 2016 r.19.10. For historical background see *Hindcastle v Barbara Attenborough Associates* [1997] A.C. 70; [1996] B.C.C. 636.

A lessor can disclaim an onerous lease—for discussion see *Willmott Growers Group Inc v Willmott Forests Ltd* [2013] HCA 51; [2014] B.P.I.R. 785. This ruling from the High Court of Australia might cast doubt on the old English authority of *Re Bastable* [1901] 2 K.B. 518. For a perceptive survey of this and other recent disclaimer cases see Cranston [2014] CRI 3.

Some interesting disclaimer related issues were discussed in *Young v Hamilton* [2010] B.P.I.R. 1468 and *Young v OR* [2010] B.P.I.R. 1477. This provision was mentioned in passing in *Keepers and Governors of the Possessions, Revenues and Goods of the Free Grammar School of John Lyon v Helman* [2014] EWCA Civ 17; [2014] 1 W.L.R. 2451.

See *Abdulla v Whelan* [2017] EWHC 605 (Ch); [2017] B.P.I.R. 791. Trust property (even where the bankrupt is one of the beneficiaries of the trust) cannot be disclaimed because it does not form part of the estate.

Frosdick v Fox [2017] EWHC 1737 (Ch); [2017] B.P.I.R. 1194 confirms that a cause of action which has been vested in the estate could be disclaimed by the trustee, as to pursue the claim (unsuccessfully) might result in a liability in costs.

In the context of the financial markets, s.315 does not apply in relation to a market contract or a contract effected by an exchange or clearing house for the purpose of realising property provided as margin in relation to market contracts: see CA 1989 s.164(1), and the note on p.2.

S.315(1), (2)

This authorises disclaimer of onerous property even though the trustee may have already tried to sell it. As to what is an unprofitable contract see *Re SSSL Realisations (2002) Ltd*, sub nom. *Squires v AIG Europe (UK) Ltd* [2006] EWCA Civ 7; [2006] B.C.C. 233. For the form of the notice see IR 2016 rr.19.1 and 19.2 and Form NDISC. Communication of this notice is covered by IR 2016 rr.19.3–19.6. Property which may be so disclaimed is defined in s.315(2). For the meaning of "property" here see *London City Corporation v Bown, The Times*, 11 October 1989 where a secure periodic tenancy was not so regarded. A cause of action may be disclaimed—*Khan-Ghauri v Dunbar Bank plc* [2001] B.P.I.R. 618. Note that the 12-month cut-off period for disclaimer in BA 1914 s.54(1) has been dropped, against the wishes of the Cork Committee (*Report*, para.1195).

S.315(3), (5)

The effect of disclaimer is explained here. Note that third-party rights are only to be prejudiced in so far as that is absolutely necessary, and anyone suffering losses as a result of a disclaimer can prove in the bankruptcy in respect of it (but see s.320(5) here). On the effect of disclaimer see *MEPC plc v Scottish Amicable Life Assurance Society* [1996] B.P.I.R. 447; and *Hindcastle v Barbara Attenborough Associates* [1997] A.C. 70; [1996] B.C.C. 636.

S.315(4)

Notices of disclaimer are restricted by this provision. Leave of the court is required before the trustee may disclaim after-acquired property which has already been claimed for the estate (s.307), or property claimed under ss.308 or 308A (added by the Housing Act 1988 s.117(3)) with a view to replacement. For the leave procedure, see IR 2016 r.19.8.

These rules on disclaimer are supplemented by IR 2016 rr.19.1–19.11.

316 Notice requiring trustee's decision

316(1) [Where notice not to be given] Notice of disclaimer shall not be given under section 315 in respect of any property if–

(a) a person interested in the property has applied in writing to the trustee or one of his predecessors as trustee requiring the trustee or that predecessor to decide whether he will disclaim or not, and

(b) the period of 28 days beginning with the day on which that application was made has expired without a notice of disclaimer having been given under section 315 in respect of that property.

316(2) [Deemed adoption] The trustee is deemed to have adopted any contract which by virtue of this section he is not entitled to disclaim.

General Note

If the trustee, having been required to make a choice, decides not to disclaim, he cannot later change his mind. Failure to disclaim constitutes adoption. The 28-day period during which the trustee must make his decision has been retained from BA 1914 s.54(4). For the form of a s.316 application see IR 2016 r.19.9. Formerly, the trustee could force a person to declare his interest in disclaimable property by using IR 1986 r.6.184. There appears to be no direct comparator to this provision in the 2016 Rules.

See *Frosdick v Fox* [2017] EWHC 1737 (Ch); [2017] B.P.I.R. 1194 where Birss J held that a bankrupt could not make an application under s.316 in respect of an asset which the trustee wished to disclaim. Section 316 was not intended to protect the bankrupt. If a bankrupt wished to challenge a disclaimer other options should be considered, such as challenging the actions of the trustee under s.304(2), though the prospects of success with such a challenge would be slim and the court would be reluctant to grant leave.

317 Disclaimer of leaseholds

317(1) [Disclaimer of leasehold property] The disclaimer of any property of a leasehold nature does not take effect unless a copy of the disclaimer has been served (so far as the trustee is aware of their addresses) on every person claiming under the bankrupt as underlessee or mortgagee and either–

(a) no application under section 320 below is made with respect to the property before the end of the period of 14 days beginning with the day on which the last notice served under this subsection was served, or

(b) where such an application has been made, the court directs that the disclaimer is to take effect.

317(2) [Where court gives s.317(1)(b) direction] Where the court gives a direction under subsection (1)(b) it may also, instead of or in addition to any order it makes under section 320, make such orders with respect to fixtures, tenant's improvements and other matters arising out of the lease as it thinks fit.

General Note

These provisions deal with disclaimers in respect of onerous land. In the case of leasehold property, both underlessees and mortgagees must be served with notices of disclaimer. Note here on leasehold disclaimer IR 2016 r.19.4.

Formerly, disclaimers of leases required the consent of the court: BA 1914 s.54(3). Now the court will only be involved if an application is made to it within 14 days under s.320. The trustee, after serving notice, must wait for the 14 days to elapse before the disclaimer can take effect. If application to the court has been made, obviously the trustee must wait for the outcome of the application.

The court, if it permits disclaimer, can make special provision for fixtures, etc.

318 Disclaimer of dwelling house

318 Without prejudice to section 317, the disclaimer of any property in a dwelling house does not take effect unless a copy of the disclaimer has been served (so far as the trustee is aware of their addresses) on every person in occupation of or claiming a right to occupy the dwelling house and either–

(a) no application under section 320 is made with respect to the property before the end of the period of 14 days beginning with the day on which the last notice served under this section was served, or

(b) where such an application has been made, the court directs that the disclaimer is to take effect.

General Note

In the case of dwelling houses (for definition, see s.385), all occupiers must be notified. This is a new provision, which substantially mirrors s.317 in many procedural respects.

319 Disclaimer of land subject to rentcharge

319(1) [Application] The following applies where, in consequence of the disclaimer under section 315 of any land subject to a rentcharge, that land vests by operation of law in the Crown or any other person (referred to in the next subsection as "the proprietor").

319(2) [Limit on liability] The proprietor, and the successors in title of the proprietor, are not subject to any personal liability in respect of any sums becoming due under the rentcharge, except sums becoming due after the proprietor, or some person claiming under or through the proprietor, has taken possession or control of the land or has entered into occupation of it.

General Note

These are highly specialised provisions relating to disclaimers of land subject to a rentcharge. The person in whom the land vests subsequently is not subject to the normal rentcharge obligations.

320 Court order vesting disclaimed property

320(1) [Application] This section and the next apply where the trustee has disclaimed property under section 315.

320(2) [Application to court] An application may be made to the court under this section by–

(a) any person who claims an interest in the disclaimed property,

(b) any person who is under any liability in respect of the disclaimed property, not being a liability discharged by the disclaimer, or

(c) where the disclaimed property is property in a dwelling house, any person who at the time when the bankruptcy application was made or (as the case may be) the bankruptcy petition was presented was in occupation of or entitled to occupy the dwelling house.

320(3) [Order by court] Subject as follows in this section and the next, the court may, on an application under this section, make an order on such terms as it thinks fit for the vesting of the disclaimed property in, or for its delivery to–

(a) a person entitled to it or a trustee for such a person,

(b) a person subject to such a liability as is mentioned in subsection (2)(b) or a trustee for such a person, or

(c) where the disclaimed property is property in a dwelling house, any person who at the time when the bankruptcy application was made or (as the case may be) the bankruptcy petition was presented was in occupation of or entitled to occupy the dwelling house.

320(4) [Limit to s.320(3)(b)] The court shall not make an order by virtue of subsection (3)(b) except where it appears to the court that it would be just to do so for the purpose of compensating the person subject to the liability in respect of the disclaimer.

320(5) [Effect of order in s.315(5) assessment] The effect of any order under this section shall be taken into account in assessing for the purposes of section 315(5) the extent of any loss or damage sustained by any person in consequence of the disclaimer.

320(6) [Mode of vesting re order] An order under this section vesting property in any person need not be completed by any conveyance, assignment or transfer.

S.320(1)–(4)

Where a trustee has disclaimed onerous property, certain persons have the right to apply to the court for relief. Note the three-month time limit for applications, see IR 2016 r.19.11. Note that occupiers of dwelling houses have now been given this right. The type of relief which the court may grant is described by these provisions. Vesting and delivery orders may be made according to the general discretion of the court. See *Lee v Lee* [1999] B.P.I.R. 926 for an unusual case. On s.320(2)(a) see *Hackney LBC v Crown Estates Commissioners* [1996] B.P.I.R. 428. This case was distinguished by Roth J in *Fenland DC v Sheppard* [2011] EWHC 2829 (Ch).

Sir William Blackburne gave full consideration to this provision in *Hunt v Conwy CBC* [2013] EWHC 1154 (Ch); [2013] B.P.I.R. 790. See *Hunt v Withinshaw* [2015] EWHC 3072 (Ch).

In Liggett v Northern Bank Ltd [2013] NIMaster 10; [2013] B.P.I.R. 595 the court refused a vesting order as the applicant had no qualifying interest in the disclaimed property. The point was also made that the court lacked the power to grant a vesting order as a form of compensation for any loss caused by a disclaimer.

Note amendments to subss.(2) and (3) made by ERRA 2013 Sch.19 para.25.

S.320(5), (6)

Where a vesting order is made, no conveyance, etc. is required to effect it. If disclaimed property is vested in a person who has suffered loss as a result of the disclaimer, that vesting is to be taken into account when assessing compensation.

Note here IR 2016 r.19.11.

321 Order under s.320 in respect of leaseholds

321(1) [Terms of order re leasehold property] The court shall not make an order under section 320 vesting property of a leasehold nature in any person, except on terms making that person–

(a) subject to the same liabilities and obligations as the bankrupt was subject to under the lease on the day the bankruptcy application was made or (as the case may be) the bankruptcy petition was presented, or

(b) if the court thinks fit, subject to the same liabilities and obligations as that person would be subject to if the lease had been assigned to him on that day.

321(2) [Where order re part of property in lease] For the purposes of an order under section 320 relating to only part of any property comprised in a lease, the requirements of subsection (1) apply as if the lease comprised only the property to which the order relates.

321(3) [Where no person accepts order in s.320 case] Where subsection (1) applies and no person is willing to accept an order under section 320 on the terms required by that subsection, the court may (by order under section 320) vest the estate or interest of the bankrupt in the property in any person who is liable (whether personally or in a representative capacity and whether alone or jointly with the bankrupt) to perform the lessee's covenants in the lease.

The court may by virtue of this subsection vest that estate and interest in such a person freed and discharged from all estates, incumbrances and interests created by the bankrupt.

321(4) [Exclusion from interest in property] Where subsection (1) applies and a person declines to accept any order under section 320, that person shall be excluded from all interest in the property.

General Note

Section 321(1) deals with applications in respect of leasehold property—the person in whom the leasehold property is vested must assume the same obligations as the lessee was subject to prior to his bankruptcy. If only part of the leasehold property is so vested, the order must take this into account when determining the obligations to impose. Section 321(2) and (3) deal with cases where persons decline to accept orders made under s.320—the court may make adjustments to interests in the property concerned. This includes exclusion from all interest in the property in question (s.321(4)).

Note amendment to subs.(1) made by ERRA 2013 Sch.19 para.26.

Distribution of bankrupt's estate

322 Proof of debts

322(1) [Proof in accordance with rules] Subject to this section and the next, the proof of any bankruptcy debt by a secured or unsecured creditor of the bankrupt and the admission or rejection of any proof shall take place in accordance with the rules.

322(2) [Where bankruptcy debt bears interest] Where a bankruptcy debt bears interest, that interest is provable as part of the debt except in so far as it is payable in respect of any period after the commencement of the bankruptcy.

322(3) [Estimation of debt] The trustee shall estimate the value of any bankruptcy debt which, by reason of its being subject to any contingency or contingencies or for any other reason, does not bear a certain value.

322(4) [Where estimate under s.303, 322(3)] Where the value of a bankruptcy debt is estimated by the trustee under subsection (3) or, by virtue of section 303 in Chapter III, by the court, the amount provable in the bankruptcy in respect of the debt is the amount of the estimate.

S.322(1)

The procedure governing proof of "bankruptcy debts" (see s.382) is governed by the rules: see in particular IR 2016 Pt 14. For further discussion see *Arnold v Williams* [2008] EWHC 218 (Ch); [2008] B.P.I.R. 247. For the relationship between this provision and s.267 see *McGuinness v Norwich and Peterborough Building Society* [2011] EWCA Civ 1286; [2012] B.P.I.R. 145. See *Evans v Finance-U-Ltd* [2013] EWCA Civ 869; [2013] B.P.I.R. 1001.

For the question of proof by secured creditors see s.383. For a case where contingent tax penalties were held provable, see *Re Hurren (a Bankrupt)* [1983] 1 W.L.R. 183. Fines were provable debts under the old law: *Re Pascoe Ex p. Trustee of the Bankrupt v Lords Commissioners of His Majesty's Treasury* [1944] Ch. 310. It is not clear from the Act itself whether the recommendation of the Cork Committee (*Report*, para.1330), that this rule should be reversed, has been implemented. However, the fact that fines are not provable is apparent from IR 2016 r.14.2.

On bankruptcy debts note *Hellard v Chadwick* [2014] EWHC 2158 (Ch); [2014] B.P.I.R. 1234.

S.322(2)

Under BA 1914 s.66 there were severe restrictions on proving in respect of interest. These restrictions, which were heavily criticised by the Cork Committee (*Report*, para.1381), have been largely removed except with regard to interest accruing after the commencement of the bankruptcy. It should also be remembered that s.343 may be relevant here.

S.322(3), (4)

This allows the trustee to estimate the value of contingent or uncertain debts. For the costs of the trustee see IR 2016 r.14.5. Under BA 1914 s.30 there was a facility allowing a creditor to appeal against any estimate made by a trustee. This is not specifically recreated by s.322 but possibly a disappointed creditor could make use of s.303. This provision for estimates will be doubly useful now that the old restriction, formerly contained in BA 1914 s.30(1), banning proof in respect of unliquidated claims, has been abolished: see s.382(3). The Cork Committee (*Report*, para.1318) favoured this change partly because the restriction did not apply to a corporate insolvency: *Re Berkeley Securities (Property) Ltd* [1980] 1 W.L.R. 1589—but this had been the subject of some uncertainty. The change in bankruptcy law will be welcomed if it avoids such confusion.

323 Mutual credit and set-off

323(1) [Application] This section applies where before the commencement of the bankruptcy there have been mutual credits, mutual debts or other mutual dealings between the bankrupt and any creditor of the bankrupt proving or claiming to prove for a bankruptcy debt.

323(2) [Account to be taken] An account shall be taken of what is due from each party to the other in respect of the mutual dealings and the sums due from one party shall be set off against the sums due from the other.

323(3) [Qualification to s.323(2)] Sums due from the bankrupt to another party shall not be included in the account taken under subsection (2) if that other party had notice at the time they became due that proceedings on a bankruptcy application relating to the bankrupt were ongoing or that a bankruptcy petition relating to the bankrupt was pending.

323(4) [Balance to trustee] Only the balance (if any) of the account taken under subsection (2) is provable as a bankruptcy debt or, as the case may be, to be paid to the trustee as part of the bankrupt's estate.

General Note

There is little change here. The rules are those in BA 1914 s.31, which in turn reflected common-law authorities such as *Foster v Wilson* (1843) 12 M. & W. 191. The only changes in s.323 are of a terminological or consequential nature reflecting the demise of concepts such as acts of bankruptcy and receiving orders. Notwithstanding the apparent desire of the legislature to reaffirm the old rules on set-off, in *Stein v Blake* [1996] A.C. 243; [1995] B.C.C. 543 the House of Lords concluded that it was possible for a trustee in bankruptcy to assign the net balance of a claim vested in the estate once a self-executing right of set off has been accounted for. This decision of the House of Lords can be seen as one of a number of recent authorities favouring an "estate maximisation" policy on the part of the judiciary. *Stein v Blake* (above) was followed in Australia in *Re Bankrupt Estate of Cirillo* [1997] B.P.I.R. 574. For a review of insolvency set off which involved the House of Lords taking a wide view of its availability see *Secretary of State for Trade and Industry v Frid* [2004] UKHL 24; [2004] B.P.I.R. 841. Note minor amendment to subs.(3) made by ERRA 2013 Sch.19 para.27.

It is worth noting that s.323 does not implement the recommendation of the Cork Committee (*Report*, para.1342) that the decision in *National Westminster Bank Ltd v Halesowen Presswork & Assemblies Ltd* [1972] A.C. 785, banning contracting out of the statutory rules, be reversed. However, there is a special exception allowing contracting out on the financial markets: see CA 1989 ss.159, 163, and the note on p.2, above.

For interpretation of the statutory set off provision see the comments of HHJ Kershaw in *Re Taylor (a Bankrupt)* [2007] B.P.I.R. 175 at [67]–[68].

For an instance where s.323 was held to be inapplicable see *Bateman v Williams* [2009] B.P.I.R. 973.

This section was the subject of passing comment in *Ridsdale v Bowles* [2015] B.P.I.R. 1275. See also *Lockston Group Inc v Wood* [2015] EWHC 2962 (Ch); [2016] B.P.I.R. 94 for the interaction with the Administration of Insolvent Estates of Deceased Persons Order 1986.

For the exclusion of set-off in respect of post-insolvency VAT credits, see Value Added Tax Act 1994 s.81(3)–(5).

On s.323(3) see *Coe v Ashurst* [1999] B.P.I.R. 662.

324 Distribution by means of dividend

324(1) [Duty to declare and distribute] Whenever the trustee has sufficient funds in hand for the purpose he shall, subject to the retention of such sums as may be necessary for the expenses of the bankruptcy, declare and distribute dividends among the creditors in respect of the bankruptcy debts which they have respectively proved.

324(2) [Notice of intention to declare and distribute] The trustee shall give notice of his intention to declare and distribute a dividend.

324(3) [Notice of dividend etc.] Where the trustee has declared a dividend, he shall give notice of the dividend and of how it is proposed to distribute it; and a notice given under this subsection shall contain the prescribed particulars of the bankrupt's estate.

324(4) [Calculation and distribution of dividend] In the calculation and distribution of a dividend the trustee shall make provision–

(a) for any bankruptcy debts which appear to him to be due to persons who, by reason of the distance of their place of residence, may not have had sufficient time to tender and establish their proofs,

(b) for any bankruptcy debts which are the subject of claims which have not yet been determined, and

(c) for disputed proofs and claims.

S.324(1)–(3)

These provide for the declaration of dividends to creditors when the trustee has sufficient funds at his disposal for that purpose, once expenses have been taken into account. Notice of the dividend must be given to creditors. Under BA 1914 s.62(2) the trustee had, as a general rule, to declare the first dividend within four months of the first meeting of creditors; this specific deadline has been dropped.

For further details on declaration of dividends, see IR 2016 Pt 14. For the mechanics of payment, see the Insolvency Regulations 1994 (SI 1994/2507) reg.23.

S.324(4)

This is a good housekeeping provision. The trustee should set aside funds to cover disputed claims or claims by persons who have not yet lodged proofs.

If the trustee proposes to pay an interim dividend at a time when an application to the court to challenge the admission or rejection of a proof is outstanding, the leave of the court is required under IR 2016 r.14.34.

325 Claims by unsatisfied creditors

325(1) [Entitlements of creditors] A creditor who has not proved his debt before the declaration of any dividend is not entitled to disturb, by reason that he has not participated in it, the distribution of that dividend or any other dividend declared before his debt was proved, but–

(a) when he has proved that debt he is entitled to be paid, out of any money for the time being available for the payment of any further dividend, any dividend or dividends which he has failed to receive; and

(b) any dividend or dividends payable under paragraph (a) shall be paid before that money is applied to the payment of any such further dividend.

325(2) [Order re payment of dividend] No action lies against the trustee for a dividend, but if the trustee refuses to pay a dividend the court may, if it thinks fit, order him to pay it and also to pay, out of his own money–

(a) interest on the dividend, at the rate for the time being specified in section 17 of the Judgments Act 1838, from the time it was withheld, and

(b) the costs of the proceedings in which the order to pay is made.

S.325(1)

Late claimants cannot upset properly declared dividends, but they may make a claim on any surplus available.

S.325(2)

This curiously worded provision is derived from BA 1914 s.68. On the one hand, it states that no action shall lie against a trustee for a dividend, but then it permits the court to order the trustee to pay one, and, indeed, to pay interest and costs out of his own pocket.

Compare IR 2016 r.14.40.

326 Distribution of property in specie

326(1) [Division of unsaleable property] Without prejudice to sections 315 to 319 (disclaimer), the trustee may, with the permission of the creditors' committee, divide in its existing form amongst the bankrupt's creditors, according to its estimated value, any property which from its peculiar nature or other special circumstances cannot be readily or advantageously sold.

326(2) [Permission under s.326(1)] A permission given for the purposes of subsection (1) shall not be a general permission but shall relate to a particular proposed exercise of the power in question; and a person dealing with the trustee in good faith and for value is not to be concerned to enquire whether any permission required by subsection (1) has been given.

326(3) [Where no permission under s.326(1)] Where the trustee has done anything without the permission required by subsection (1), the court or the creditors' committee may, for the purpose of enabling him to meet his expenses out of the bankrupt's estate, ratify what the trustee has done.

But the committee shall not do so unless it is satisfied that the trustee acted in a case of urgency and has sought its ratification without undue delay.

S.326(1)

This authorises the trustee to make distributions in specie of the property which is difficult to realise. This is a new facility without precedent in the 1914 Act.

S.326(2), (3)

The trustee must obtain specific permission to exercise his power to make an in specie distribution under s.326(1) above. Unauthorised distributions may, in certain circumstances, be ratified by the creditors' committee.

327 Distribution in criminal bankruptcy

327 Where the bankruptcy order was made on a petition under section 264(1)(d) (criminal bankruptcy), no distribution shall be made under sections 324 to 326 so long as an appeal is pending (within the meaning of section 277) against the bankrupt's conviction of any offence by virtue of which the criminal bankruptcy order on which the petition was based was made.

General Note

In cases of criminal bankruptcy no distribution is to be made until the final appeal in the criminal case is heard.

Note prospective amendment: s.327 is to be repealed by CJA 1988 s.170(2) and Sch.16 as from a day to be appointed; see the note to s.264.

328 Priority of debts

328(1) [Preferential debts to be paid first] In the distribution of the bankrupt's estate, his preferential debts shall be paid in priority to other debts.

328(1A) [Priority of ordinary preferential debts] Ordinary preferential debts rank equally among themselves after the expenses of the bankruptcy and shall be paid in full, unless the bankrupt's estate is insufficient to meet them, in which case they abate in equal proportions between themselves.

328(1B) [Priority of secondary preferential debts] Secondary preferential debts rank equally among themselves after the ordinary preferential debts and shall be paid in full, unless the bankrupt's estate is insufficient to meet them, in which case they abate in equal proportions between themselves.

328(2) [Repealed]

328(3) [Debts neither preferential nor under s.329] Debts which are neither preferential debts nor debts to which the next section applies also rank equally between themselves and, after the preferential debts, shall be paid in full unless the bankrupt's estate is insufficient for meeting them, in which case they abate in equal proportions between themselves.

328(4) [Surplus after payment] Any surplus remaining after the payment of the debts that are preferential or rank equally under subsection (3) shall be applied in paying interest on those debts in respect of the periods during which they have been outstanding since the commencement of the bankruptcy; and interest on preferential debts ranks equally with interest on debts other than preferential debts.

328(5) [Rate of interest under s.328(4)] The rate of interest payable under subsection (4) in respect of any debt is whichever is the greater of the following–

(a) the rate specified in section 17 of the Judgments Act 1838 at the commencement of the bankruptcy, and

(b) the rate applicable to that debt apart from the bankruptcy.

328(6) [Other enactments] This section and the next are without prejudice to any provision of this Act or any other Act under which the payment of any debt or the making of any other payment is, in the event of bankruptcy, to have a particular priority or to be postponed.

328(7) ["Preferential debts", "ordinary preferential debts", "secondary preferential debts"] In this section "preferential debts", "ordinary preferential debts" and "secondary preferential debts" each has the meaning given in section 386 in Part 12.

General Note

This section has dropped what was formerly BA 1914 s.33(6), dealing with payment of debts in the case of partnership insolvency: see s.420 now. The provision relating to insolvent estates of deceased persons has also not been retained—see s.421. The text of BA 1914 s.33(4) is now included in s.347. See also IR 2016 rr.10.149 and 14.28 in this context.

Note significant amendments involving the insertion of new subss.(1A), (1B) and (7) by the Banks and Building Societies (Depositor Preference and Priorities) Order 2014 (SI 2014/3486) with effect from 1 January 2015. These changes reflect the new classification of the different types of preferential debt.

S.328(1), (2)

These provisions deal with preferential debts. Those debts described as preferential by ss.386, 387 and by Sch.6 to this Act are to be paid in priority to other debts (but not the expenses of the bankruptcy: see Sch.9 para.22). In the event of a shortfall they are to abate in equal proportions. Note that the list of preferential debts has been pruned radically by Sch.6 after considerable pressure had been exerted on the government. This issue is considered fully in the note to s.386 below.

S.328(3)

Ordinary debts—i.e. those which are neither preferential nor deferred—rank equally between themselves and abate rateably in the event of a shortfall.

S.328(4), (5)

These provisions deal with the payment of interest on debts which has accrued since the commencement of the bankruptcy (for the meaning of this phrase, see s.278). It is to be paid only after both the preferential and ordinary creditors have been satisfied in full. Interest on preferential debts receives no special treatment. Section 328(5) specifies the maximum rate of interest allowed (currently 8 per cent (see SI 1993/564)). Note the use of the contract interest rate alternative in subs.(5)—this does not appear to have featured in the statutory predecessor (BA 1914 s.33(8))—for discussion see Cork Committee (Cmnd.8558 paras 1383 et seq.). See *KK v MA* [2012] EWHC 788 (Fam); [2012] B.P.I.R. 1137 at [79] for reference to s.328(5)(a).

S.328(6)

The general law on deferred creditors is preserved—for example, a creditor whose case falls within s.3 of the Partnership Act 1890.

329 Debts to spouse

329(1) [Application] This section applies to bankruptcy debts owed in respect of credit provided by a person who (whether or not the bankrupt's spouse or civil partner at the time the credit was provided) was the bankrupt's spouse or civil partner at the commencement of the bankruptcy.

329(2) [Ranking, payment] Such debts–

(a) rank in priority after the debts and interest required to be paid in pursuance of section 328(3) and (4), and

(b) are payable with interest at the rate specified in section 328(5) in respect of the period during which they have been outstanding since the commencement of the bankruptcy;

and the interest payable under paragraph (b) has the same priority as the debts on which it is payable.

General Note

This section differs from its predecessor in the 1914 Act in a number of respects. For example, BA 1914 s.36 related only to a loan in connection with a business or trade carried on by the bankrupt (where the lender was a husband), but not if it was lent by a wife. Note the insertion of the reference to civil partners by the Civil Partnership Act 2004 Sch.27.

330 Final distribution

330(1) [Notice re dividend, etc.] When the trustee has realised all the bankrupt's estate or so much of it as can, in the trustee's opinion, be realised without needlessly protracting the trusteeship, he shall give notice in the prescribed manner either–

(a) of his intention to declare a final dividend, or

(b) that no dividend, or further dividend, will be declared.

330(1A) [Opted-out creditors] A notice under subsection (1)(b) need not be given to opted-out creditors.

330(2) [Contents of notice] The notice under subsection (1) shall contain the prescribed particulars and shall require claims against the bankrupt's estate to be established by a date ("the final date") specified in the notice.

330(3) [Postponement of final date] The court may, on the application of any person, postpone the final date.

330(4) [Trustee's duties after final date] After the final date, the trustee shall–

(a) defray any outstanding expenses of the bankruptcy out of the bankrupt's estate, and

(b) if he intends to declare a final dividend, declare and distribute that dividend without regard to the claim of any person in respect of a debt not already proved in the bankruptcy.

330(5) [Where surplus] If a surplus remains after payment in full and with interest of all the bankrupt's creditors and the payment of the expenses of the bankruptcy, the bankrupt is entitled to the surplus.

330(6) [Applicability of EU Regulation] Subsection (5) is subject to Article 49 of the EU Regulation (surplus in secondary proceedings to be transferred to main proceedings).

S.330(1)–(3)

Where the trustee has realised all that can be converted into money he should notify the creditors (other than opted-out creditors) whether he is in a position to declare a final dividend. This notice must indicate a final date for claims. This final date can be extended by the court. A new subs.(1A) was introduced by SBEEA 2015 s.126 and Sch.9 para.82 to deal with opted-out creditors.

S.330(4)

Once the final date is passed the trustee should pay his final dividend, but not before the costs of the bankruptcy (which often represent a considerable figure) have been defrayed out of the proceeds of realisation.

There appears to be no provision dealing with unclaimed dividends to replace BA 1914 s.153. Generally see IR 1986 Pt 11.

S.330(5)

Any surplus goes to the bankrupt. Subsection (5) was considered in *Phillips v Symes* [2005] EWHC 2867 (Ch); [2006] B.P.I.R. 1430. Here Peter Smith J made the point that the trustee holds the estate on trust for the bankrupt against the possibility of a surplus arising at the end of the day. That being so, an immediate charging order could be granted against the bankrupt's interest in the potential surplus even before such surplus was ascertained. This case may need to be viewed in the light of the later Court of Appeal ruling in *James v Rutherford-Hodge* [2005] EWCA Civ 1580; [2006] B.P.I.R. 973 (mentioned in the annotation to s.306 above). On s.330(5) see the judgment of Charles J in *KK v MA* [2012] EWHC 788 (Fam); [2012] B.P.I.R. 1137 at [28]. On s.330(5) and the link with s.304 see

McGuire v Rose [2013] EWCA Civ 429. For comment on s.330(5) see the views expressed by Proudman J in *Oraki v Bramston* [2015] EWHC 2046 (Ch); [2015] B.P.I.R. 1238.

S.330(6)
This was inserted by Insolvency Act 1986 (Amendment) (No.2) Regulations 2002 (SI 2002/1240) reg.15 with effect from 31 May 2002 and amended by the Insolvency Amendment (EU 2015/848) Regulations 2017 (SI 2017/702) regs 1, 2(1), Sch. paras 1, 21 in relation to proceedings opened on or after 26 June 2017 (see reg.3) when the Recast EU Regulation 2015/848 came into force.

331 Final report

331(1) [Application] Subject as follows in this section and the next, this section applies where–

(a) it appears to the trustee that the administration of the bankrupt's estate in accordance with this Chapter is for practical purposes complete, and

(b) the trustee is not the official receiver.

331(2) [Duty to give notice] The trustee must give the bankrupt's creditors (other than opted-out creditors) notice that it appears to the trustee that the administration of the bankrupt's estate is for practical purposes complete.

331(2A) [Details of notice] The notice must–

(a) be accompanied by a report of the trustee's administration of the bankrupt's estate;

(b) explain the effect of section 299(3)(d) and how the creditors may object to the trustee's release.

331(3) [Omitted]

331(4) [Omitted]

S.331(1), (2), (2A)
These provisions require a trustee (but not an official receiver) to issue a final report to creditors (other than opted-out creditors) on how things went. The final creditors' meeting was scrapped by SBEEA 2015 s.126 and Sch.9 para.83 as part of the attack on red tape. This change rendered otiose subss.(3) and (4) which were omitted.

332 Saving for bankrupt's home

332(1) [Application] This section applies where–

(a) there is comprised in the bankrupt's estate property consisting of an interest in a dwelling house which is occupied by the bankrupt or by his spouse or former spouse or by his civil partner or former civil partner, and

(b) the trustee has been unable for any reason to realise that property.

332(2) [Conditions for s.331 meeting] The trustee shall not give notice under section 331(2) unless either–

(a) the court has made an order under section 313 imposing a charge on that property for the benefit of the bankrupt's estate, or

(b) the court has declined, on an application under that section, to make such an order, or

(c) the Secretary of State has issued a certificate to the trustee stating that it would be inappropriate or inexpedient for such an application to be made in the case in question.

General Note

This again is a new provision. It states that as a general rule there should be no summoning of a final meeting where the bankrupt's interest in a "dwelling house" (for definition, see s.385) has not been realised. Exceptions to this general rule are: (1) where a s.313 charge has been imposed on the property; (2) where the court has refused to grant a s.313 charge; or (3) where the Secretary of State has certified that it would be inappropriate for the trustee to apply for a s.313 charge. Note the insertion of the reference to civil partners by Sch.27 to the Civil Partnership Act 2004. On s.332(2)(c) see *Dear IP* Issue 26 (March 2006).

Note the link with s.313—*Re Parkins* [2014] B.P.I.R. 1054.

A minor amendment has been made to subs.(2) by SBEEA 2015 s.126 and Sch.9 para.84.

Supplemental

333 Duties of bankrupt in relation to trustee

333(1) [Duties] The bankrupt shall–

(a) give to the trustee such information as to his affairs,

(b) attend on the trustee at such times, and

(c) do all such other things,

as the trustee may for the purposes of carrying out his functions under any of this Group of Parts reasonably require.

333(2) [Notice re after-acquired property] Where at any time after the commencement of the bankruptcy any property is acquired by, or devolves upon, the bankrupt or there is an increase of the bankrupt's income, the bankrupt shall, within the prescribed period, give the trustee notice of the property or, as the case may be, of the increase.

333(3) [Application of s.333(1)] Subsection (1) applies to a bankrupt after his discharge.

333(4) [Penalty for non-compliance] If the bankrupt without reasonable excuse fails to comply with any obligation imposed by this section, he is guilty of a contempt of court and liable to be punished accordingly (in addition to any other punishment to which he may be subject).

S.333(1), (3)

These provisions impose duties on a bankrupt, up to and after the date of his discharge, to provide information and assistance to enable the *trustee* to carry out his duties. The comparable provision describing the bankrupt's duties towards the *official receiver* is to be found in s.291. On the nature of the respective duties of bankrupt and trustee see *Morris v Murjani* [1996] B.P.I.R. 458. A bankrupt who fails to comply with his obligations under s.333 runs the risk of having his automatic discharge suspended—*Shierson v Rastogi* [2007] EWHC 1266 (Ch); [2007] B.P.I.R. 891. In *Hellard v Kapoor* [2013] EWHC 2204 (Ch); [2013] B.P.I.R. 745 automatic discharge was suspended for failure to comply with the obligations imposed by s.333. This sanction was applied notwithstanding a failure by the Official Receiver to observe strictly the requirements of IR 1986 r.6.215 (now IR 2016 r.10.142). For the costs implications of this litigation see [2013] EWHC 2496 (Ch); [2013] B.P.I.R. 745 at 753. In *Re Caldwell* (unreported decision of registrar, 1998) the court felt able to bolster this duty to co-operate by exercising its powers under s.39(1) of the Senior Courts Act 1981 and authorising the trustee to execute a power of attorney on behalf of the bankrupt in order to gain access to financial information from foreign authorities: see Archer (1998) 142 S.J. 596. In *OR v Cooksey* [2013] B.P.I.R. 526 the co-operation of the bankrupt was established and a certificate of discharge was then granted. For passing comment on s.333 see *Arnold v Williams* [2008] EWHC 218 (Ch); [2008] B.P.I.R. 247. See also *R. (Singh) v Revenue and Customs Commissioners* [2010] B.P.I.R. 933. See *OR v McWilliams* [2012] NICh 28 for issues relating to the filing of evidence.

In *Williams v Mohammed* [2011] EWHC 3293 (Ch); [2011] B.P.I.R. 1787 the interface between this provision and the rules on professional legal privilege were considered.

For the limitations of this provision see *Horton v Henry* [2016] EWCA Civ 989: s.333 cannot be used to compel a bankrupt to draw down pension funds to enable them to be used to support an income payments order.

On the duty to co-operate and the fact that it survives discharge see the comments of Mr Registrar Nicholls in *Chadwick v Nash* [2012] B.P.I.R. 70.

Note also the bankrupt's more specific duties in regard to property, records, etc. under s.312. In addition to the duties that a bankrupt owes to his trustee he may also owe responsibilities to any professional association of which he is a member—*Moseley v SRA* [2013] EWHC 2108 (Admin); [2013] B.P.I.R. 855 (Lewis J) and *Dowland v Architects Registration Board* [2013] EWHC 893 (Admin); [2013] B.P.I.R. 566.

There was found to be a breach of the provision by the bankrupt in *Simmonds v Pearce* [2017] EWHC 3126 (Admin). This was a test case before the Divisional Court on how the courts would deal with allegations of breach of duty in contempt cases. Andrews J indicated at [28] that the matter should be referred to the Insolvency Rules Committee to enable it to produce guidelines to promote greater clarity on the issue of which judges should deal with contempt issues in bankruptcy cases.

S.333(2)

The obligation to provide information about the property and income is a continuing one. Such an obligation is essential for the operation of ss.307 and 310. The prescribed period is 21 days: see IR 2016 r.10.125. On s.333(2) see *Viscount St Davids v Lewis* [2015] EWHC 2826 (Ch); [2015] B.P.I.R. 1471. Note the link with IR 2016 rr.10.125–10.126. For the unintended consequences that might flow from a bankrupt failing to comply with the obligation of disclosure under s.333(2) see *Barrett v Barrett* [2008] EWHC 1061 (Ch).

S.333(4)

A bankrupt may be held liable for contempt if he breaches any of the above obligations.

334 Stay of distribution in case of second bankruptcy

334(1) [Application, definitions] This section and the next apply where a bankruptcy order is made against an undischarged bankrupt; and in both sections–

(a) "the later bankruptcy" means the bankruptcy arising from that order,

(b) "the earlier bankruptcy" means the bankruptcy (or, as the case may be, most recent bankruptcy) from which the bankrupt has not been discharged at the commencement of the later bankruptcy, and

(c) "the existing trustee" means the trustee (if any) of the bankrupt's estate for the purposes of the earlier bankruptcy.

334(2) [Certain distributions void] Where the existing trustee has been given the prescribed notice of the making of the application or (as the case may be) the presentation of the petition for the later bankruptcy, any distribution or other disposition by him of anything to which the next subsection applies, if made after the giving of the notice, is void except to the extent that it was made with the consent of the court or is or was subsequently ratified by the court.

This is without prejudice to section 284 (restrictions on dispositions of property following bankruptcy order).

334(3) [Application of s.334(2)] This subsection applies to–

(a) any property which is vested in the existing trustee under section 307(3) (after-acquired property);

(b) any money paid to the existing trustee in pursuance of an income payments order under section 310; and

(c) any property or money which is, or in the hands of the existing trustee represents, the proceeds of sale or application of property or money falling within paragraph (a) or (b) of this subsection.

General Note

This provision is, of necessity, more sophisticated than its predecessor as a result of the advent of the new rules on after-acquired property and income payments orders. Note amendment to subs.(2) made by ERRA 2013 Sch.19 para.28.

S.334(1)

Where a petition for bankruptcy is issued against an undischarged bankrupt who is already undergoing the bankruptcy process, his existing trustee, on receiving notice of the petition, must not make any further distributions or dispositions without the consent of the court. However, this only applies to property covered by s.334(3).

S.334(3)
Section 334(3) applies to after-acquired property or money from any income payments order, or the proceeds thereof. Note also IR 2016 rr.10.150–10.153.

335 Adjustment between earlier and later bankruptcy estates

335(1) [Matters in bankrupt's estate] With effect from the commencement of the later bankruptcy anything to which section 334(3) applies which, immediately before the commencement of that bankruptcy, is comprised in the bankrupt's estate for the purposes of the earlier bankruptcy is to be treated as comprised in the bankrupt's estate for the purposes of the later bankruptcy and, until there is a trustee of that estate, is to be dealt with by the existing trustee in accordance with the rules.

335(2) [Sums paid under s.310] Any sums which in pursuance of an income payments order under section 310 are payable after the commencement of the later bankruptcy to the existing trustee shall form part of the bankrupt's estate for the purposes of the later bankruptcy; and the court may give such consequential directions for the modification of the order as it thinks fit.

335(3) [Charge re bankruptcy expenses] Anything comprised in a bankrupt's estate by virtue of subsection (1) or (2) is so comprised subject to a first charge in favour of the existing trustee for any bankruptcy expenses incurred by him in relation thereto.

335(4) [Property not in estate] Except as provided above and in section 334, property which is, or by virtue of section 308 (personal property of bankrupt exceeding reasonable replacement value) or section 308A (vesting in trustee of certain tenancies) is capable of being, comprised in the bankrupt's estate for the purposes of the earlier bankruptcy, or of any bankruptcy prior to it, shall not be comprised in his estate for the purposes of the later bankruptcy.

335(5) [Creditors of earlier bankruptcies] The creditors of the bankrupt in the earlier bankruptcy and the creditors of the bankrupt in any bankruptcy prior to the earlier one, are not to be creditors of his in the later bankruptcy in respect of the same debts; but the existing trustee may prove in the later bankruptcy for–

(a) the unsatisfied balance of the debts (including any debt under this subsection) provable against the bankrupt's estate in the earlier bankruptcy;

(b) any interest payable on that balance; and

(c) any unpaid expenses of the earlier bankruptcy.

335(6) [Priority of amounts in s.335(5)] Any amount provable under subsection (5) ranks in priority after all the other debts provable in the later bankruptcy and after interest on those debts and, accordingly, shall not be paid unless those debts and that interest have first been paid in full.

S.335(1)–(3)
Such items, on the commencement of the second bankruptcy, must be treated as part of the estate for the purpose of that second bankruptcy. The same is true of any money paid to the first trustee under an income payments order after the date of the commencement of the second bankruptcy. Indeed, the income payments order can be modified. However, the first trustee may be entitled to a charge over such property to cover any expenses incurred in relation to it.

S.335(4)
Other property comprised in the bankrupt's estate in the first bankruptcy does not pass to the estate on the second bankruptcy. A minor insertion has been made by the Housing Act 1988 Sch.17 para.74.

S.335(5), (6)
These provisions deal with the status of creditors in the first bankruptcy vis-à-vis the second bankruptcy: any residual claims they may have can be proved for in the second bankruptcy, but they only enjoy deferred status in this respect. This implements the recommendation of the Blagden Committee (Cmnd.221, para.114). Note also IR 2016 rr.10.150–10.153.

CHAPTER V

EFFECT OF BANKRUPTCY ON CERTAIN RIGHTS, TRANSACTIONS, ETC.

Rights under trusts of land

335A Rights under trusts of land

335A(1) [Application for order for sale of land] Any application by a trustee of a bankrupt's estate under section 14 of the Trusts of Land and Appointment of Trustees Act 1996 (powers of court in relation to trusts of land) for an order under that section for the sale of land shall be made to the court having jurisdiction in relation to the bankruptcy.

335A(2) [Interests considered before order] On such an application the court shall make such order as it thinks just and reasonable having regard to–

(a) the interests of the bankrupt's creditors;

(b) where the application is made in respect of land which includes a dwelling house which is or has been the home of the bankrupt or the bankrupt's spouse or civil partner or former spouse or former civil partner–

   (i) the conduct of the spouse, civil partner, former spouse or former civil partner, so far as contributing to the bankruptcy,

   (ii) the needs and financial resources of the spouse, civil partner, former spouse or former civil partner, and

   (iii) the needs of any children; and

(c) all the circumstances of the case other than the needs of the bankrupt.

335A(3) [Assumption by court re interests of creditors] Where such an application is made after the end of the period of one year beginning with the first vesting under Chapter IV of this Part of the bankrupt's estate in a trustee, the court shall assume, unless the circumstances of the case are exceptional, that the interests of the bankrupt's creditors outweigh all other considerations.

335A(4) [Exercise of powers conferred on court] The powers conferred on the court by this section are exercisable on an application whether it is made before or after the commencement of this section.

GENERAL NOTE

This and the following three sections are part of a package to redress the balance of rights between the trustee, on the one hand, and the bankrupt and his family on the other hand, over what will probably represent the bankrupt's most valuable asset, his family home. This is a problem that has troubled the law for many years—witness the decision in *Bendall v McWhirter* [1952] 2 Q.B. 466, which created a "deserted wife's equity" capable of prevailing over the trustee's rights, and its rejection by the House of Lords in *National Provincial Bank Ltd v Ainsworth* [1965] A.C. 1175. This decision, in turn, was reversed by the Matrimonial Homes Act 1967, a piece of legislation consolidated by the Matrimonial Homes Act 1983 which in turn was replaced by the Family Law Act 1996. Notwithstanding this, it was felt that the family's right to a roof over its head required greater protection in the event of the breadwinner becoming bankrupt: see the Cork *Report*, paras 1114–1131. These provisions on the family home were a late insertion in the Insolvency Bill 1985. For the background to this legislation, see Miller (1986) 50 Conv. 393; and Cretney (1991) 107 L.Q.R. 177. For further discussion of this area see Creasey and Doyle (1992) 136 S.J. 920. For a summary of the Joint Insolvency Committee Insolvency Guidance Paper on the family home (2005) see [2006] 19 Insolv. Int. 42.

Where a trustee in bankruptcy makes an application for sale under these provisions an issue will frequently arise as to the allocation of proceeds between the estate and the non-bankrupt party. In such a scenario general equitable principles governing the determination of beneficial interests will be applied, as explained by the House of Lords in *Stack v Dowden* [2007] UKHL 17; [2007] 2 W.L.R. 831—applied in *Kernott v Jones* [2010] EWCA Civ 578. For the view of the Supreme Court on the determination of relative beneficial interests see *Jones v Kernott* [2011] UKSC 53;

[2011] 3 W.L.R. 1121 where the appeal was allowed and the conclusions reached at first instance were upheld. For further discussion of the principles operating in this area see the ruling of Chief Master Marsh in *Erlam v Rahman* [2016] EWHC 111 (Ch) where the issue of determination of beneficial interests in property was a central issue.

In addition, questions may arise as to whether the trustee can invoke equitable accounting principles and charge an "occupation rent" to be paid by the non-bankrupt party. There is a body of precedent governing this scenario—see *Re Gorman* [1990] 1 W.L.R. 616; *Re Pavlou* [1993] 1 W.L.R. 1046; *Re Byford* [2003] B.P.I.R. 1089; and *French v Barcham* [2008] EWHC 1505 (Ch). Uncertainty has crept in as a result of *Murphy v Gooch* [2007] EWCA Civ 603; [2007] B.P.I.R. 1123 where the view was taken that the common law principles of equitable accounting have been replaced by the statutory criteria listed in ss.12–15 of the TLATA 1996, but this view was questioned by Blackburne J in *French v Barcham* (above), where the residual discretion enjoyed by the court was championed. Blackburne J ruled that the principles of equitable accounting were not displaced by the House of Lords precedent of *Stack v Dowden* [2007] UKHL 17. This question is likely to be revisited in the years to come. *French v Barcham* (above) was considered in *Levy v Ellis-Carr* [2012] EWHC 63 (Ch). On equitable accounting in cases of bankruptcy where properties are co-owned or jointly owned see *Davis v Jackson* [2017] EWHC 698 (Ch); [2017] 1 W.L.R. 4005; [2017] B.P.I.R. 950 where Snowden J undertook a comprehensive review of the position.

Another incidental property-related issue that can crop up in bankruptcy cases is related to the so-called "equity of exoneration"—*Re Pittortou* [1985] 1 W.L.R. 58. *Pittortou* (above) was followed by Chief Registrar Baister in *Re Chawda* [2014] B.P.I.R. 49 where the claim by a wife of a bankrupt for an equity of exoneration was dismissed. On *Pittortou* (above) and the equity of exoneration in general in non-bankruptcy situations see the analysis of Morgan J in *Day v Shaw* [2014] EWHC 36 (Ch) at [23]. Further consideration of the equity of exoneration is to be found in *Cadlock v Dunn* [2015] EWHC 1318 (Ch). The Court of Appeal gave support to the equity of exoneration in *Armstrong v Onyearu* [2017] EWCA Civ 268; [2017] B.P.I.R. 869. The judgment of the Court of Appeal contains a comprehensive review of English and Commonwealth authorities. The court stressed that equitable accounting forms part of the law of sureties and, as the term suggests, is to be governed by principles of equity. It is not to be excluded simply because indirect benefit might accrue as a result of its application. For a valuable overview of the treatment of this consideration in the courts see Gardiner [2016] 29 Insolv. Int. 17.

Section 335A was inserted by s.25(1) of and Sch.3 para.23 to the Trusts of Land and Appointment of Trustees Act 1996 with effect from 1 January 1997. For its significance see the note to s.336 below. Early interpretation on the meaning of s.335A is provided by the Court of Appeal in *Judd v Brown* [1999] B.P.I.R. 517 where the point was made that it may be proper to order a sale even if the prime beneficiary would be a secured creditor. In *Re Raval* [1998] B.P.I.R. 389 Blackburne J was faced with the question of whether exceptional circumstances existed for the purposes of s.335A(3). Again the issue centred upon the ill-health of the wife. The registrar had decided that this did constitute an exceptional circumstance but was only prepared to delay the sale of the family home for six months to enable arrangements to be made in the light of the wife's condition. Although Blackburne J agreed with the interpretation of the registrar on whether this was an exceptional circumstance he did not feel that appropriate weight had been given to it when making the order and therefore postponed the sale for just over one year. General principles governing the s.335A jurisdiction were laid down by the High Court in *Harrington v Bennett* [2000] B.P.I.R. 630. Exceptional circumstances within s.335A(3) were present in *Claughton v Charalamabous* [1998] B.P.I.R. 558. In *Barca v Mears* [2005] B.P.I.R. 15 the High Court reluctantly followed *Re Citro* [1991] Ch. 142 but questioned whether the narrow approach used for determining "exceptional circumstances" for the purposes of s.335A(3) was consistent with the requirements of the European Convention on Human Rights and, in particular, with art.8 (right to family life).

A lucid exposition of the principles to be applied under s.335A(ii) and (iii) was provided by Lawrence Collins J in *Dean v Stout* [2005] EWHC 3315 (Ch); [2005] B.P.I.R. 1113. In particular the flexible and open-ended nature of the concept of exceptional circumstances was stressed. The fact that a wife and children will lose the family home is a normal incidence of many bankruptcies and therefore not exceptional. Simply because the proceeds of sale will be swallowed up by bankruptcy expenses does not make the circumstances exceptional. This judgment very much reflects traditional judicial attitudes.

In *Awoyemi v Bowell* [2005] EWHC 2138 (Ch); [2006] B.P.I.R. 1, yet another case on s.335A, Evans-Lombe J stressed that it was very much a matter of discretion as to whether the trustee decided to enforce a possession order granted under s.335A and the court would be reluctant to interfere with that discretion.

In *Donohoe v Ingram* [2006] B.P.I.R. 417 Stuart Isaacs QC (sitting as a Deputy Judge in the High Court) supported a ruling from the District Judge that a sale should be ordered under s.335A notwithstanding the fact that there were still children in the house. A suggestion that sale should be delayed until the youngest child reached 16 was rejected. As more than a year had elapsed since the commencement of the bankruptcy the presumption favoured sale and the mere presence of children in the family home did not constitute exceptional circumstances. Once again the issue whether a narrow construction of "exceptional circumstances" does involve an infringement of the right to family life as conferred by art.8 ECHR was left open. As a small crumb of comfort in the interests of common humanity sale was deferred for three months. An attack on the position in English law based upon ECHR art.8 was rejected by Peter Smith J in *Ford v Alexander* [2012] EWHC 266 (Ch); [2012] B.P.I.R. 528 where it was held that the exceptional circumstances test, if properly applied, maintains an appropriate balance between the competing interests of the parties so as to be consistent with art.8. But compare *Official Receiver for Northern Ireland v O'Brien* [2012] NICh 12; [2012] B.P.I.R. 826 where Deeny J felt that a long delayed sale could be resisted by combined application of arts 6 and 8 of the ECHR. See also the comments of the court in *Hawk Recovery Ltd v Hall* [2016] EWHC 1307 (Ch); [2016] B.P.I.R. 1169 on the general relevance of art.8 of the ECHR.

This continues to be the most litigated aspect of bankruptcy.

The case of *Re Karia* [2006] B.P.I.R. 1226 (which was decided in 2001) shows that the courts will not infer exceptional circumstances exist simply because the proceeds of sale will be swallowed up in meeting the expenses of the bankruptcy. Rights conferred by art.8 had to be balanced against the rights of creditors; that balance here favoured sale.

Again in *Nicholls v Lan* [2006] B.P.I.R. 1243 the High Court held that s.335A was consistent with art.8 ECHR because it sought to balance family interests against those of creditors. The order of the district judge in this case clearly did that to the extent of deferring a sale for 18 months and therefore on appeal the High Court would not interfere. For discussion see Pawlowski [2007] Conv. 78.

In *Foenander v Allan* [2006] B.P.I.R. 1392 the court took the view that even if art.8 had shifted the goalposts for the purposes of s.335A the registrar had been correct in finding no exceptional circumstances on the facts of the case. Ill-health on the part of the brother of the bankrupt who had an interest in and lived in the property did not justify a delay in the realisation of what was the estate's only real asset.

The court in *Foyle v Turner* [2007] B.P.I.R. 43 felt that there was no inconsistency between art.8 and s.335A. According to Judge Norris exceptional circumstances might arise out of prolonged and inordinate delay between initial vesting and application for sale; but in this case a delay of some 13 years was not inordinate. The point was made that the application was made within the new three year period introduced by s.283A which came into effect on 1 April 2004.

The court in *Turner v Avis* [2008] B.P.I.R. 1143 undertook a significant review of the authorities in order to explain what was meant by "exceptional circumstances". In *Everitt v Budhram* [2010] B.P.I.R. 567 Mr Justice Henderson indicated that the word "needs" in s.335A(2) was to be widely interpreted and could encompass financial, medical, emotional and mental needs. See *Grant v Baker* [2016] EWHC 1782 (Ch) where Henderson J agreed with a District Judge's ruling that the presence of a disabled adult in the property constituted an exceptional circumstance, but disagreed on the length of the sale postponement. The District Judge had imposed an indefinite period of suspension, but Henderson J felt that 12 months grace from the date of his ruling was appropriate. There was no reason why a disabled person could not live in private rented accommodation.

Avis v Turner [2007] EWCA Civ 748 confirms the point that s.335A applies where s.14 of Trusts of Land and Appointment of Trustees Act 1996 would operate. Whereas in *Holtham v Kelmanson* [2006] B.P.I.R. 1422 it was held that s.335A did not apply if the applicant trustee was solely interested in the property.

The presumption in s.335A(3) was applied in *Avis v Turner* [2007] EWCA Civ 748; [2007] B.P.I.R. 663. See also *Pick v Sumpter* [2010] B.P.I.R. 638. For the latest review of this provision see the judgment of Warren J in *Pickard v Constable* [2017] EWHC 2475 (Ch). For discussion of this area see Davey [2001] Insolv. L. 2 at 12.

These provisions must be read in the light of s.283A (inserted by EA 2002 from 1 April 2004).

S.335A(2)
Note the amendments introduced by the Civil Partnership Act 2004 Sch.27.

Rights of occupation

336 Rights of occupation etc. of bankrupt's spouse or civil partner

336(1) [Family Law Act 1996] Nothing occurring in the initial period of the bankruptcy (that is to say, the period beginning with the day of the making of the bankruptcy application or (as the case may be) the presentation of the bankruptcy petition and ending with the vesting of the bankrupt's estate in a trustee) is to be taken as having given rise to any home rights under Part IV of the Family Law Act 1996 in relation to a dwelling house comprised in the bankrupt's estate.

336(2) [Where spouse or civil partner's home rights charge on estate] Where a spouse's or civil partner's home rights under the Act of 1996 are a charge on the estate or interest of the other spouse or civil partner, or of trustees for the other spouse or civil partner, and the other spouse or civil partner is made bankrupt–

(a) the charge continues to subsist notwithstanding the bankruptcy and, subject to the provisions of that Act, binds the trustee of the bankrupt's estate and persons deriving title under that trustee, and

(b) any application for an order under section 33 of that Act shall be made to the court having jurisdiction in relation to the bankruptcy.

336(3) [Repealed by Trusts of Land and Appointment of Trustees Act 1996 Pt III s.25(2), 27 and Sch. 4 as from 1 January 1997.]

336(4) [Court orders] On such an application as is mentioned in subsection (2) the court shall make such order under section 33 of the Act of 1996 as it thinks just and reasonable having regard to–

(a) the interests of the bankrupt's creditors,

(b) the conduct of the spouse or former spouse or civil partner or former civil partner, so far as contributing to the bankruptcy,

(c) the needs and financial resources of the spouse or former spouse or civil partner or former civil partner,

(d) the needs of any children, and

(e) all the circumstances of the case other than the needs of the bankrupt.

336(5) [Assumption by court re interests of creditors] Where such an application is made after the end of the period of one year beginning with the first vesting under Chapter IV of this Part of the bankrupt's estate in a trustee, the court shall assume, unless the circumstances of the case are exceptional, that the interests of the bankrupt's creditors outweigh all other considerations.

General Note

For the definitions of "family" and "dwelling house", see s.385. Note amendments made to subss.(1) and (2) by ERRA 2013 Sch.19 para.29.

S.336(1)

This prevents a spouse's matrimonial home rights under the Family Law Act 1996 arising during the period after the date of the petition and up to the time when the property vests in the trustee.

S.336(2)

Where the spouse of a bankrupt has acquired statutory rights of occupation representing a charge on the house owned by the bankrupt, that charge is effective as against the trustee. Any applications made under s.33 of the Family Law Act 1996 (i.e. to have the spouse evicted or to enable him or her to regain possession), however, must be made to the appropriate bankruptcy court. Note that s.336(4), commented on below, applies to such an application.

S.336(3)–(5)

These provisions cover the situation where the spouses or former spouses are joint owners of the property, and a trust for sale has arisen. Any application under s.30 of LPA 1925 or s.14 of the Trusts of Land and Appointment of Trustees Act 1996 (which substantially remodelled the provision in the 1925 Act) to the court by the trustee in bankruptcy of one of the spouses or ex-spouses for an enforced sale is to be made to the relevant bankruptcy court. In the past in cases under s.30 of the 1925 Act, the courts have normally acceded to the trustee's request for sale, although the family interests have been considered: see *Re Solomon* [1967] Ch. 573; *Re Turner* [1974] 1 W.L.R. 1556; *Re Densham* [1975] 1 W.L.R. 1519; *Re Bailey* [1977] 1 W.L.R. 278; *Re Lowrie* [1981] 3 All E.R. 353; *Re Citro (a Bankrupt)* [1991] Ch. 142; *Zandfarid v BCCI* [1996] 1 W.L.R. 1420; and *Re Ng* [1997] B.C.C. 507. A decision which went against the grain and resulted in the sale of the matrimonial home being postponed for several years until the children had finished their education was *Re Holliday* [1981] Ch. 405. A similar more "caring" approach was taken by Hoffmann J in the poorly reported *Re Mott* [1987] C.L.Y. 212 where the sick mother of the bankrupt was allowed to postpone the sale of the house until after her death. In *Re Bremner* [1999] B.P.I.R. 185 a sale was postponed for a short period to allow a terminally ill bankrupt the dignity of dying in his own home. For a comparable problem posed by novel facts see *Re Gorman (a Bankrupt)* [1990] 1 All E.R. 717. In *Re Haghighat*

[2009] B.P.I.R. 268 the court found the presence of exceptional circumstances because the property was occupied by a disabled child. As a result of these exceptional circumstances a three-year maximum period of postponement of sale was ordered. In spite of this leeway, the bankrupt appealed, but the appeal was unsuccessful—*Brittain v Haghighat* [2010] EWCA Civ 1521.

The extent to which the case law under LPA 1925 s.30 retains value is unclear because in future cases where an application is made under s.14 of the Trusts of Land and Appointment of Trustees Act 1996 the factors which the court shall have regard to in non-bankruptcy cases include the intentions of the settlor, the purposes of the trust, the welfare of minors in occupation and the interests of secured creditors of the beneficiary (s.15 of the Trusts of Land and Appointment of Trustees Act 1996). Where the application for sale is by the trustee in bankruptcy the matter is governed by IA 1986 s.335A, which identifies relevant considerations. In spite of this statutory intrusion one suspects that the courts will be reluctant to cast aside all previous jurisprudence on this difficult subject.

Now, if such an application is made, the court has general discretion and can consider all the circumstances (including the interests of the family and creditors and the contribution of either party towards the bankruptcy); but if it is made more than one year after the vesting of the property in the trustee in bankruptcy, it will be the interests of the creditors which will prevail unless there are exceptional counterbalancing factors: see s.335A(3). There is a question as to when the one period presumption in favour of the spouse begins to run. Does it run from the date of the bankruptcy order or from when the estate vests in the trustee? This issue may require clarification through litigation.

There is some discussion of s.336(5) in *Re Citro (a Bankrupt)* (above) where the point is made that many of the old bankruptcy cases (which are discussed above) will be relevant to its interpretation. It is also stressed that this provision will only operate within the context of a marriage (and not to cohabitees). Exceptional circumstances were found to be present in *Judd v Brown* [1997] B.P.I.R. 470 where the illness of the wife was sufficient to persuade the court to refuse an application for sale. Further discussion of s.336(5) is to be found in *Trustee of the Estate of Bowe v Bowe* [1997] B.P.I.R. 747 where Jonathan Parker J found that there was an absence of exceptional circumstances. The fact that the sale of the property might produce no immediate benefit for creditors because the proceeds were to be used to defray the costs of the bankruptcy was not in itself a reason to block the sale. See also *Barca v Mears* [2005] B.P.I.R. 15 and the discussion on s.335A above. The "exceptional circumstances" test used in s.336 has been held not to be inconsistent with the protection offered by art.8 ECHR—*Hosking v Michaelides* [2006] B.P.I.R. 1192. The court in this case ruled that under s.336(4) the voice of creditors should now prevail and the exceptional circumstances as such only justified a postponement of six months in the sale. Section 336(5) does not apply where the spouse has a proprietary interest in the property—*Avis v Turner* [2007] B.P.I.R. 663.

The fact that the wife's rights under this provision are not absolutely guaranteed against the legitimate claims of creditors was underlined in *Re Ruiz* [2011] EWHC 913 (Fam); [2011] B.P.I.R. 1139—the appeal was dismissed [2011] EWCA Civ 1646 also reported in [2012] B.P.I.R. 446 (but note the revised version of this report appended to issue Number 5 of [2014] B.P.I.R.). See note to s.282 above.

In *Official Receiver for Northern Ireland v Rooney and Paulson* [2009] B.P.I.R. 536 the importance of the ECHR requirements was stressed by Weir J in a case of protracted realisation. Here there had been a 12-year hiatus between the start of the bankruptcy and the request of the official receiver to sell the family home. The court cited both arts 6 and 8 ECHR to deny this application as there was evidence that the wives of the bankrupts had been lulled into a false sense of security by the inactivity of the authorities.

For similar problems of social priority encountered under s.40 of the Bankruptcy (Scotland) Act 1985 see *Gourlay's Trustee v Gourlay*, 1995 S.L.T. (Sh Ct) 7; *Hunt's Trustee v Hunt*, 1995 S.C.L.R. 969; *McMahon's Trustee, The Times*, 26 March 1997, and *Ritchie v Burns* [2001] B.P.I.R. 666.

Note the textual amendments made to s.336 by s.66(1) of and Sch.8 para.57 to the Family Law Act 1996 and the repeal in its entirety of subs.(3) and minor repeal in subs.(4) effected by Sch.4 to the Trusts of Land and Appointment of Trustees Act 1996.

337 Rights of occupation of bankrupt

337(1) [Application] This section applies where–

(a) a person who is entitled to occupy a dwelling house by virtue of a beneficial estate or interest is made bankrupt, and

(b) any persons under the age of 18 with whom that person had at some time occupied that dwelling house had their home with that person at the time when the bankruptcy application was made or (as the case may be) the bankruptcy petition was presented and at the commencement of the bankruptcy.

337(2) [Rights of occupation, etc.] Whether or not the bankrupt's spouse or civil partner (if any) has home rights under Part IV of the Family Law Act 1996–

(a) the bankrupt has the following rights as against the trustee of his estate–

(i) if in occupation, a right not to be evicted or excluded from the dwelling house or any part of it, except with the leave of the court,

(ii) if not in occupation, a right with the leave of the court to enter into and occupy the dwelling house, and

(b) the bankrupt's rights are a charge, having the like priority as an equitable interest created immediately before the commencement of the bankruptcy, on so much of his estate or interest in the dwelling house as vests in the trustee.

337(3) [Application of Family Law Act] The Act of 1996 has effect, with the necessary modification, as if–

(a) the rights conferred by paragraph (a) of subsection (2) were home rights under that Act,

(b) any application for such leave as is mentioned in that paragraph were an application for an order under section 33 of that Act, and

(c) any charge under paragraph (b) of that subsection on the estate or interest of the trustee were a charge under that Act on the estate or interest of a spouse or civil partner.

337(4) [Application to court] Any application for leave such as is mentioned in subsection (2)(a) or otherwise by virtue of this section for an order under section 33 of the Act of 1996 shall be made to the court having jurisdiction in relation to the bankruptcy.

337(5) [Court order under s.337(4)] On such an application the court shall make such order under section 33 of the Act of 1996 as it thinks just and reasonable having regard to the interests of the creditors, to the bankrupt's financial resources, to the needs of the children and to all the circumstances of the case other than the needs of the bankrupt.

337(6) [Assumption re interests of creditors] Where such an application is made after the end of the period of one year beginning with the first vesting (under Chapter IV of this Part) of the bankrupt's estate in a trustee, the court shall assume, unless the circumstances of the case are exceptional, that the interests of the bankrupt's creditors outweigh all other considerations.

S.337(1), (2)

These provisions protect the rights of occupation of the bankrupt who has dependent children living with him: he cannot be evicted from the family home without a court order and can apply to the court to regain entry if out of possession. His rights under these provisions are in the nature of an equitable interest binding on the trustee. A number of textual changes have been introduced by the Family Law Act 1996 (see Sch.8 para.58).

For discussion of the comparable provision in Northern Ireland (art.310 of the 1989 Order) see *ORNI v Snoddon* [2014] NIMaster 5.

Note amendments made to subs.(1) by ERRA 2013 Sch.19 para.30.

S.337(3)

This extends certain provisions in the Family Law Act 1996 relating to matrimonial home rights to bankruptcy situations. The substitution of the original subs.(3) was effected by Sch.8 para.58 to the 1996 Act with effect from 1 October 1997.

S.337(4)–(6)

Applications for leave under s.337(2)(a) must be made to the relevant bankruptcy court. On such an application the court should adopt a similar approach to that specified in s.336(4) and (5) above (although the criteria are different), with the creditors' interests having priority where the application is made more than a year after the property has vested in the trustee. On "exceptional circumstances" in s.337(6) see *Barca v Mears* [2005] B.P.I.R. 15 and the discussion on s.335A above. Subsection (6) was the focus of consideration in *Martin-Sklan v White* [2007] B.P.I.R. 76. Exceptional circumstances were found to exist in this case—those circumstances consisted of the fact that there were children of the bankrupt in the house who needed the support network of neighbours, family and local schools because of the ill health/frequent absence of their mother. A postponement of the sale until a date when the youngest

See also *Re Hollier, Carman v Letchford* [2010] EWHC 3155 (Ch); [2014] B.P.I.R. 927 where HHJ Hodge QC undertook a comprehensive review of the requirement of s.339. On valuation a commonsense perspective was recommended.

A TUV finding was made on the facts of *Green v Austin* [2014] B.P.I.R. 1176 (Kingston County Court). District Judge Smart stressed that for a divorcing couple to embark upon informal property transfers outside the judicially sanctioned ancillary relief proceedings runs the risk of subsequent avoidance if one of the parties later becomes bankrupt.

For discussion of the recent judicial pronouncements in this field and critique of *Haines v Hill* (above) see Briggs [2008] 21 Insolv. Int. 90; Daniels [2008] 1 Corp. Res. and Insolv. 82. Note *Re Cheung* (unreported, 16 May 2017, Asplin J).

For general discussion of s.339 see *Re Share* [2002] B.P.I.R. 194. See also *Stow v Stow* [2008] EWHC 495 (Ch); [2008] B.P.I.R. 673—possibility of a trustee challenging a family trust settlement by using s.339 considered in passing. In *Garwood v Ambrose* [2012] EWHC 1494 (Ch) the court held that purported declaration of a trust in favour of wife could in principle breach IA 1986 s.339.

On the difficult issue of valuation of consideration where the transferee has benefited from a statutory discount made only available to the bankrupt see *Pozzuto v Iacovides* [2003] EWHC 431 (Ch); [2003] B.P.I.R. 999. When working out the differences in value/consideration provided there is no need for exact figures—*Ailyan and Fry v Smith* [2010] B.P.I.R. 289.

In *Tailby v HSBC Bank plc, Re Anwar Ul-Haq Rashid* [2015] B.P.I.R. 143 Registrar Derrett rejected an application under s.339 which sought to challenge a guarantee given by a director of a small company in return for business finance for that company. Difficulties were caused by the fact that the guarantee was signed some months after the finance had been provided though the court got around this potential problem by viewing the transaction as a whole. The court was cautious about this TUV claim because the debtor was solvent at the time and gained some benefit in having his company supported. There would also have been difficulties in valuing the commitments which he undertook under said guarantee. The decision will prove reassuring to those involved in small business lending.

Mr Justice Fancourt undertook a review of a number of aspects of this provision in *Gendrot v Chadwick* [2018] EWHC 48 (Ch). In particular there was an informative analysis of when giving up a claim might constitute valuable consideration to be accounted for when assessing undervalue. The factors which the court might take account of when exercising discretion under subs.(2) were also reviewed.

A s.339 claim must be brought within the appropriate limitation period (see *Re Priory Garage (Walthamstow) Ltd* [2001] B.P.I.R. 144) and even then can be struck out for want of prosecution—*Hamblin v Field* [2000] B.P.I.R. 621. Further consideration of the limitation issue is to be found in *Re Yates* [2005] B.P.I.R. 476. A 12-year limitation period applies to claims under s.339—*Segal v Pasram* (above).

The ruling of Thomas Ivory QC in *Singla v Brown* [2007] B.P.I.R. 424 confirms the view taken in *Re Paramount Airways Ltd (No.2)* [1993] Ch. 223 that the court has discretion in exceptional cases to make "no order", even though it has found that a breach of s.339 has occurred. The court in *Trustee in Bankruptcy of Claridge v Claridge* [2011] EWHC 2047 (Ch); [2011] B.P.I.R. 1529 indicated that, although there may technically have been a transaction at an undervalue, it retained discretion in exceptional circumstances not to make a remedial order. The circumstances of the case were seen as exceptional. In *OR for NI v Mallon* [2013] NIMaster 9; [2013] B.P.I.R. 621 Master Kelly upheld a TUV claim by a trustee in bankruptcy notwithstanding the harsh consequences that would be visited upon the transferee of the property in question. An attempt to argue a proprietary estoppel as a defence was dismissed on the facts. The court observed that the trustee could not be criticised for carrying out his statutory functions in the interests of creditors.

See *Hargreaves v Salt* [2010] EWHC 3549 (Fam); [2011] B.P.I.R. 656 for the potential overlaps between s.339 and s.37 of the Matrimonial Causes Act 1973.

In s.339(3)(b) note the insertion of the reference to civil partners by the Civil Partnership Act 2004 Sch.27.

On s.339(3)(c) see *Bramston v Riaz* [2014] B.P.I.R. 42—a payment under an uncommercial contract fell within the meaning of this provision.

On the potential for a TUV claim to be a bankruptcy debt see *Hellard v Chadwick* [2014] EWHC 2158 (Ch); [2014] B.P.I.R. 1234.

340 Preferences

340(1) [Application to court] Subject as follows in this and the next two sections, where an individual is made bankrupt and he has at a relevant time (defined in section 341) given a preference to any person, the trustee of the bankrupt's estate may apply to the court for an order under this section.

341(3) [Insolvent individual under s.341(2)] For the purposes of subsection (2), an individual is insolvent if–

(a) he is unable to pay his debts as they fall due, or

(b) the value of his assets is less than the amount of his liabilities, taking into account his contingent and prospective liabilities.

341(4) [Where person later bankrupt under s.264(1)(d)] A transaction entered into or preference given by a person who is subsequently adjudged bankrupt on a petition under section 264(1)(d) (criminal bankruptcy) is to be treated as having been entered into or given at a relevant time for the purposes of sections 339 and 340 if it was entered into or given at any time on or after the date specified for the purposes of this subsection in the criminal bankruptcy order on which the petition was based.

341(5) [Where appeal pending] No order shall be made under section 339 or 340 by virtue of subsection (4) of this section where an appeal is pending (within the meaning of section 277) against the individual's conviction of any offence by virtue of which the criminal bankruptcy order was made.

S.341(1)

This provides a general definition of "relevant time", for the purposes of ss.339, 340 above. In the case of transactions at an undervalue, it covers a five-year period prior to the presentation of the petition. Formerly, a ten-year period was prescribed. For preferences, it is six months (this was favoured by the Cork Committee: *Report*, para.1260), but this period is extended to two years prior to the petition where the beneficiary is an "associate" of the bankrupt (as defined by s.435, although note the qualification in s.340(5)). See *Re Marsh* [2009] B.P.I.R. 834 (discussed in annotation to s.339).

See *Green v Austin* [2014] B.P.I.R. 1176.

Note amendment made to subs.(1)(a) by ERRA 2013 Sch.19 para.33.

S.341(2), (3)

The time periods given in s.341(1) are qualified by the fact that in most cases (but not a transaction at an undervalue within two years of the petition), it is necessary that the person entering the transaction should either have been insolvent at the time or reduced to insolvency by the transaction. Normally the onus of proving insolvency is on the trustee, but this is not so where the beneficiary of the transaction is an "associate" (see s.435 as qualified by s.340(5)). On s.341(2) see the comments of Briggs J in *Re Calder, Salter v Wetton* [2011] EWHC 3192 (Ch); [2012] B.P.I.R. 63. Note the special definition of insolvency in s.341(3) which now also covers balance-sheet insolvency—this was a late amendment at the Report Stage of the 1985 Bill.

S.341(4), (5)

These provisions modify the above rules where a person was made bankrupt as a result of a petition based on a criminal bankruptcy order. Special provision is made where an appeal is pending against the criminal conviction.

Note prospective amendment: s.341(4) and (5) are to be repealed by CJA 1988 s.170(2) and Sch.16 as from a day to be appointed; see the note to s.264.

342 Orders under ss.339, 340

342(1) [Extent of order] Without prejudice to the generality of section 339(2) or 340(2), an order under either of those sections with respect to a transaction or preference entered into or given by an individual who is subsequently made bankrupt may (subject as follows)–

(a) require any property transferred as part of the transaction, or in connection with the giving of the preference, to be vested in the trustee of the bankrupt's estate as part of that estate;

(b) require any property to be so vested if it represents in any person's hands the application either of the proceeds of sale of property so transferred or of money so transferred;

(c) release or discharge (in whole or in part) any security given by the individual;

(d) require any person to pay, in respect of benefits received by him from the individual, such sums to the trustee of his estate as the court may direct;

(e) provide for any surety or guarantor whose obligations to any person were released or discharged (in whole or in part) under the transaction or by the giving of the preference to be under such new or revived obligations to that person as the court thinks appropriate;

(f) provide for security to be provided for the discharge of any obligation imposed by or arising under the order, for such an obligation to be charged on any property and for the security or charge to have the same priority as a security or charge released or discharged (in whole or in part) under the transaction or by the giving of the preference; and

(g) provide for the extent to which any person whose property is vested by the order in the trustee of the bankrupt's estate, or on whom obligations are imposed by the order, is to be able to prove in the bankruptcy for debts or other liabilities which arose from, or were released or discharged (in whole or in part) under or by, the transaction or the giving of the preference.

342(2) [Effect of order] An order under section 339 or 340 may affect the property of, or impose any obligation on, any person whether or not he is the person with whom the individual in question entered into the transaction or, as the case may be, the person to whom the preference was given; but such an order–

(a) shall not prejudice any interest in property which was acquired from a person other than that individual and was acquired in good faith and for value, or prejudice any interest deriving from such an interest, and

(b) shall not require a person who received a benefit from the transaction or preference in good faith and for value to pay a sum to the trustee of the bankrupt's estate, except where he was a party to the transaction or the payment is to be in respect of a preference given to that person at a time when he was a creditor of that individual.

342(2A) [Presumption re good faith in s.342(2)] Where a person has acquired an interest in property from a person other than the individual in question, or has received a benefit from the transaction or preference, and at the time of that acquisition or receipt–

(a) he had notice of the relevant surrounding circumstances and of the relevant proceedings, or

(b) he was an associate of, or was connected with, either the individual in question or the person with whom that individual entered into the transaction or to whom that individual gave the preference,

then, unless the contrary is shown, it shall be presumed for the purposes of paragraph (a) or (as the case may be) paragraph (b) of subsection (2) that the interest was acquired or the benefit was received otherwise than in good faith.

342(3) [Sums to be paid to trustee] Any sums required to be paid to the trustee in accordance with an order under section 339 or 340 shall be comprised in the bankrupt's estate.

342(4) [Relevant surrounding circumstances in s.342(2A)(a)] For the purposes of subsection (2A)(a), the relevant surrounding circumstances are (as the case may require)–

(a) the fact that the individual in question entered into the transaction at an undervalue; or

(b) the circumstances which amounted to the giving of the preference by the individual in question.

342(5) [Notice of relevant proceedings in s.342(2A)(a)] For the purposes of subsection (2A)(a), a person has notice of the relevant proceedings if he has notice–

(a) of the fact that the bankruptcy application as a result of which, or (as the case may be) the bankruptcy petition on which, the individual in question is made bankrupt has been made or presented; or

(b) of the fact that the individual in question has been made bankrupt.

342(6) [Application of s.249] Section 249 in Part VII of this Act shall apply for the purposes of subsection (2A)(b) as it applies for the purposes of the first Group of Parts.

General Note

Note amendments made to subss.(1) and (5) by ERRA 2013 Sch.19 para.34 consequent upon the new out of court bankruptcy procedure made available to debtors.

S.342(1)

Sections 339(2) and 340(2) confer general discretion on the court where the trustee applies for relief. However, we are here given a non-exhaustive list of the possible forms of relief which the court may grant. On how the claim for relief can affect limitation periods see *Re Priory Garage (Walthamstow) Ltd* [2001] B.P.I.R. 144; and *Re Yates* [2005] B.P.I.R. 476. Note the limitations imposed by s.419 of POCA 2002.

On orders under s.342 see *Stonham v Ramrattan* [2011] EWCA Civ 119, where the point was made that in exercising discretion under s.342 (where a family home is involved) the policy underpinning s.283A is a relevant consideration. In this case the Court of Appeal undertook a useful analysis of s.342 in general.

This provision was considered in *Green v Austin* [2014] B.P.I.R. 1176. District Judge Smart ruled that it would only be in exceptional circumstances for relief to be refused where a TUV had been proven. It was not exceptional simply because the ultimate beneficiary of such relief would be the trustee in bankruptcy seeking to recover professional fees to which he was entitled.

S.342(2)

This subsection was amended by s.2(1) of the Insolvency (No.2) Act 1994 to clarify the degree of protection offered to third parties. Comparable changes have been made in the corporate context: see the annotations to s.241. The Bill leading to this Act was sponsored by the Law Society which was concerned by the uncertainty created by the original version of s.342 in the context of property purchases of unregistered land. Later purchasers in a chain started off by an undervalue transfer might theoretically be prejudiced and therefore be reluctant to transact with that risk in mind until the five-year limitation period had expired. This was creating further problems in the already depressed domestic property market by generating delays or additional cost caused by the necessity of taking out title insurance. For general discussion see Potterton and Cullen (1994) 138 S.J. 710.

Thus the words "in good faith, for value and without notice of the relevant circumstances" have been replaced by "in good faith and for value" with the question of notice now being dealt with by a new subs.(2A). Note that these changes only apply to interests acquired and benefits received after the coming into force of the 1994 Act—i.e. 26 July 1994 (see s.6 (ibid.)). Transactions occurring before that date will be governed by the original wording of s.342.

S.342(2A)

This subsection was introduced by s.2(2) of the Insolvency (No.2) Act 1994 and seeks to provide guidance on what is "good faith" for the purposes of the amended subs.(2) above. The burden of proving good faith switches to the person acquiring an interest in the property if he knows of the relevant surrounding circumstances *and* of the relevant proceedings. A similar reversal of the onus of proof occurs where the acquirer is an associate or connected person (see subs.(6) below). Further guidance on the relevant surrounding circumstances and notice of the relevant proceedings is provided by new subss.(4) and (5), also introduced by the 1994 Act.

S.342(3)

This is unaffected by the 1994 changes.

S.342(4), (5)

See the note to subs.(2A) above.

S.342(6)

This was inserted by s.2(3) of the Insolvency (No.2) Act 1994 and merely renders applicable the standard definitions of associates and connected persons as found in IA 1986.

342A Recovery of excessive pension contributions

342A(1) [Trustee to apply for order] Where an individual who is made bankrupt–

(a) has rights under an approved pension arrangement, or

(b) has excluded rights under an unapproved pension arrangement,

the trustee of the bankrupt's estate may apply to the court for an order under this section.

342A(2) [Court Order] If the court is satisfied–

(a) that the rights under the arrangement are to any extent, and whether directly or indirectly, the fruits of relevant contributions, and

(b) that the making of any of the relevant contributions ("the excessive contributions") has unfairly prejudiced the individual's creditors,

the court may make such order as it thinks fit for restoring the position to what it would have been had the excessive contributions not been made.

342A(3) [Application of s.342A(4)] Subsection (4) applies where the court is satisfied that the value of the rights under the arrangement is, as a result of rights of the individual under the arrangement or any other pension arrangement having at any time become subject to a debit under section 29(1)(a) of the Welfare Reform and Pensions Act 1999 (debits giving effect to pension-sharing), less than it would otherwise have been.

342A(4) [Extent of contributions] Where this subsection applies–

(a) any relevant contributions which were represented by the rights which became subject to the debit shall, for the purposes of subsection (2), be taken to be contributions of which the rights under the arrangement are the fruits, and

(b) where the relevant contributions represented by the rights under the arrangement (including those so represented by virtue of paragraph (a)) are not all excessive contributions, relevant contributions which are represented by the rights under the arrangement otherwise than by virtue of paragraph (a) shall be treated as excessive contributions before any which are so represented by virtue of that paragraph.

342A(5) ["Relevant contributions"] In subsections (2) to (4) "relevant contributions" means contributions to the arrangement or any other pension arrangement–

(a) which the individual has at any time made on his own behalf, or

(b) which have at any time been made on his behalf.

342A(6) [Court considerations in determination] The court shall, in determining whether it is satisfied under subsection (2)(b), consider in particular–

(a) whether any of the contributions were made for the purpose of putting assets beyond the reach of the individual's creditors or any of them, and

(b) whether the total amount of any contributions–

(i) made by or on behalf of the individual to pension arrangements, and

(ii) represented (whether directly or indirectly) by rights under approved pension arrangements or excluded rights under unapproved pension arrangements,

is an amount which is excessive in view of the individual's circumstances when those contributions were made.

342A(7) [Excluded rights] For the purposes of this section and sections 342B and 342C ("the recovery provisions"), rights of an individual under an unapproved pension arrangement are excluded rights if they are rights which are excluded from his estate by virtue of regulations under section 12 of the Welfare Reform and Pensions Act 1999.

342A(8) ["Approved pension arrangement", "unapproved pension arrangement"] In the recovery provisions—"approved pension arrangement" has the same meaning as in section 11 of the Welfare

Reform and Pensions Act 1999; "unapproved pension arrangement" has the same meaning as in section 12 of that Act.

General Note

These clawback provisions originated in s.95 of the Pensions Act 1995, which in turn sought to implement the recommendations of the Goode Committee on Pension Law Review. The 1995 Act provisions were never brought into force. In view of the criticisms generated by cases like *Re Landau* [1998] Ch. 223 and with the advent of the policy in favour of pensions sharing between spouses, Parliament took the opportunity to revisit the area of interface between pensions law and bankruptcy law (see ss.342D–342F below for the new provisions on pensions sharing). As part of an overall package ss.342A–342C were reformulated by s.15 of the Welfare Reform and Pensions Act 1999. This amended provision was designed to balance up the reforms in 1999 designed to give protection to pension pots in the event of bankruptcy. Unfortunately, its wording is restrictive and this may have produced an imbalance in the law meaning that a bankrupt's pension entitlements are excessively protected. This is apparent when one looks at the position on an IVA or even prior to bankruptcy—see *Blight v Brewster* [2012] EWHC 165 (Ch) (availability of a third party debt order). These provisions were brought into force with effect from 29 May 2000—Welfare Reform and Pensions Act 1999 (Commencement No.7) Order 2000 (SI 2000/1382). Comparable provisions have been made for Scotland by ss.13 and 16 of the 1999 Act.

Sections 342A–342C must be read in the light of other changes made by the 1999 Act, namely the reversal of *Re Landau* (above) by ss.11 and 12 of that Act (which enables the Secretary of State to make regulations to exclude pension rights from the bankrupt's estate) and s.14 which prevents personal pension rights being forfeited in the event of the pensioner becoming bankrupt.

The current position on bankruptcy and pensions is explained by Frieze in [2014] 27 Insolv. Int. 24.

Note the minor amendment made by ERRA 2013 Sch.19 para.35.

S.342A(1), (2), (5)

This enables the trustee to apply to the court to claw back for the benefit of the estate excessive contributions to pension schemes which unfairly prejudice creditors. Subsection (5) is a definition provision. For a very rare case on this provision see *Stanley v Wilson* (unreported, 5 August 2016, HHJ Raeside QC). Here the court stated that there is no definition of what was to be regarded as an "excessive" contribution; that would depend upon the facts of each case. A version of the judgment in *Stanley v Wilson* was published in [2017] B.P.I.R. 227 but it appears that a revised version exists—see the Erratum note at the commencement of Issue 4 of 2017 B.P.I.R.

S.342A(3), (4)

These deal with the interface between the clawback and pension-sharing arrangements introduced also by the 1999 Act.

S.342A(6)

This is an important provision which seeks to assist the court in exercising its discretion under subs.2 in determining whether contributions were excessive in the circumstances.

S.342A(7), (8)

These are further definition provisions linked to ss.342B and 342C.

342B Orders under section 342A

342B(1) [Contents of order] Without prejudice to the generality of section 342A(2), an order under section 342A may include provision–

(a) requiring the person responsible for the arrangement to pay an amount to the individual's trustee in bankruptcy,

(b) adjusting the liabilities of the arrangement in respect of the individual,

(c) adjusting any liabilities of the arrangement in respect of any other person that derive, directly or indirectly, from rights of the individual under the arrangement,

(d) for the recovery by the person responsible for the arrangement (whether by deduction from any amount which that person is ordered to pay or otherwise) of costs incurred by that person in complying in the bankrupt's case with any requirement under section 342C(1) or in giving effect to the order.

342B(2) [Adjusting liabilities in s.342B(1)] In subsection (1), references to adjusting the liabilities of the arrangement in respect of a person include (in particular) reducing the amount of any benefit or future benefit to which that person is entitled under the arrangement.

342B(3) [Liabilities in s.342B(1)(c)] In subsection (1)(c), the reference to liabilities of the arrangement does not include liabilities in respect of a person which result from giving effect to an order or provision falling within section 28(1) of the Welfare Reform and Pensions Act 1999 (pension sharing orders and agreements).

342B(4) [Maximum amount payable] The maximum amount which the person responsible for an arrangement may be required to pay by an order under section 342A is the lesser of–

(a) the amount of the excessive contributions, and

(b) the value of the individual's rights under the arrangement (if the arrangement is an approved pension arrangement) or of his excluded rights under the arrangement (if the arrangement is an unapproved pension arrangement).

342B(5) [Provisions in "restoration amount"] An order under section 342A which requires the person responsible for an arrangement to pay an amount ("the restoration amount") to the individual's trustee in bankruptcy must provide for the liabilities of the arrangement to be correspondingly reduced.

342B(6) [Liabilities in s.342B(5)] For the purposes of subsection (5), liabilities are correspondingly reduced if the difference between–

(a) the amount of the liabilities immediately before the reduction, and

(b) the amount of the liabilities immediately after the reduction,

is equal to the restoration amount.

342B(7) [Effect of s.342A order] An order under section 342A in respect of an arrangement–

(a) shall be binding on the person responsible for the arrangement, and

(b) overrides provisions of the arrangement to the extent that they conflict with the provisions of the order.

General Note

This was introduced by s.15 of the Welfare Reform and Pensions Act 1999 with effect from 29 May 2000.

S.342B(1)
This identifies examples of the type of order the court may make under s.342A.

S.342B(2), (3)
These provide further clarification on the precise effect of certain s.342A orders.

S.342B(4)
This caps the maximum amount of an order.

S.342B(5)–(7)
These deal with pension-sharing arrangements.

342C Orders under section 342A: supplementary

342C(1) [Provision of information under s.342A] The person responsible for–

(a) an approved pension arrangement under which a bankrupt has rights,

(b) an unapproved pension arrangement under which a bankrupt has excluded rights, or

(c) a pension arrangement under which a bankrupt has at any time had rights, shall, on the bankrupt's trustee in bankruptcy making a written request, provide the trustee with such information about the arrangement and rights as the trustee may reasonably require for, or in connection with, the making of applications under section 342A.

342C(2) [Non-applicable provisions] Nothing in–

(a) any provision of section 159 of the Pension Schemes Act 1993 or section 91 of the Pensions Act 1995 (which prevent assignment and the making of orders that restrain a person from receiving anything which he is prevented from assigning),

(b) any provision of any enactment (whether passed or made before or after the passing of the Welfare Reform and Pensions Act 1999) corresponding to any of the provisions mentioned in paragraph (a), or

(c) any provision of the arrangement in question corresponding to any of those provisions,

applies to a court exercising its powers under section 342A.

342C(3) [Bankrupt's estate] Where any sum is required by an order under section 342A to be paid to the trustee in bankruptcy, that sum shall be comprised in the bankrupt's estate.

342C(4) [Provisions re calculation and verification etc.] Regulations may, for the purposes of the recovery provisions, make provision about the calculation and verification of–

(a) any such value as is mentioned in section 342B(4)(b);

(b) any such amounts as are mentioned in section 342B(6)(a) and (b).

342C(5) [Powers conferred by s.342A] The power conferred by subsection (4) includes power to provide for calculation or verification–

(a) in such manner as may, in the particular case, be approved by a prescribed person; or

(b) in accordance with guidance from time to time prepared by a prescribed person.

342C(6) [Persons responsible for pension arrangements] References in the recovery provisions to the person responsible for a pension arrangement are to–

(a) the trustees, managers or provider of the arrangement, or

(b) the person having functions in relation to the arrangement corresponding to those of a trustee, manager or provider.

342C(7) [Meaning in ss.342A, 342B and 342C] In this section and sections 342A and 342B–

"prescribed" means prescribed by regulations;

"the recovery provisions" means this section and sections 342A and 342B;

"regulations" means regulations made by the Secretary of State.

342C(8) [Scope of regulations] Regulations under the recovery provisions may–

(a) make different provision for different cases;

(b) contain such incidental, supplemental and transitional provisions as appear to the Secretary of State necessary or expedient.

342C(9) [Making of regulations] Regulations under the recovery provisions shall be made by statutory instrument subject to annulment in pursuance of a resolution of either House of Parliament.

General Note

This was introduced by s.15 of the Welfare Reform and Pensions Act 1999 with effect from 29 May 2000.

S.342C(1), (6)
This is an important provision enabling the trustee in bankruptcy to gain access to the full details of the bankrupt's pension arrangement. Subsection (6) clarifies who is responsible for the provision of such information.

S.342C(2)
This is a saving provision.

S.342C(3)
Any sums clawed back under s.342A form part of the estate.

S.342C(4), (5), (8), (9)
These deal with the power of the Secretary of State to make delegated legislation. See now the Occupational and Personal Pension Schemes (Bankruptcy) (No.2) Regulations 2002 (SI 2002/836) which repealed the similarly-named SI 2002/427 and came into force on 6 April 2002.

342D Recovery of excessive contributions in pension-sharing cases

342D(1) [Meaning of pension-sharing transaction] For the purposes of sections 339, 341 and 342, a pension-sharing transaction shall be taken–

(a) to be a transaction, entered into by the transferor with the transferee, by which the appropriate amount is transferred by the transferor to the transferee; and

(b) to be capable of being a transaction entered into at an undervalue only so far as it is a transfer of so much of the appropriate amount as is recoverable.

342D(2) [Further meaning] For the purposes of sections 340 to 342, a pension-sharing transaction shall be taken–

(a) to be something (namely a transfer of the appropriate amount to the transferee) done by the transferor; and

(b) to be capable of being a preference given to the transferee only so far as it is a transfer of so much of the appropriate amount as is recoverable.

342D(3) [Determination of recoverability] If on an application under section 339 or 340 any question arises as to whether, or the extent to which, the appropriate amount in the case of a pension-sharing transaction is recoverable, the question shall be determined in accordance with subsections (4) to (8).

342D(4) ["Personal contributions"] The court shall first determine the extent (if any) to which the transferor's rights under the shared arrangement at the time of the transaction appear to have been (whether directly or indirectly) the fruits of contributions ("personal contributions")–

(a) which the transferor has at any time made on his own behalf, or

(b) which have at any time been made on the transferor's behalf,

to the shared arrangement or any other pension arrangement.

342D(5) ["The unfair contributions"] Where it appears that those rights were to any extent the fruits of personal contributions, the court shall then determine the extent (if any) to which those rights appear to have been the fruits of personal contributions whose making has unfairly prejudiced the transferor's creditors ("the unfair contributions").

342D(6) [Circumstances where not recoverable] If it appears to the court that the extent to which those rights were the fruits of the unfair contributions is such that the transfer of the appropriate amount could have been made out of rights under the shared arrangement which were not the fruits of the unfair contributions, then the appropriate amount is not recoverable.

342D(7) [Circumstances where recoverable] If it appears to the court that the transfer could not have been wholly so made, then the appropriate amount is recoverable to the extent to which it appears to the court that the transfer could not have been so made.

342D(8) [Court considerations in determination] In making the determination mentioned in subsection (5) the court shall consider in particular–

(a) whether any of the personal contributions were made for the purpose of putting assets beyond the reach of the transferor's creditors or any of them, and

(b) whether the total amount of any personal contributions represented, at the time the pension-sharing transaction was made, by rights under pension arrangements is an amount which is excessive in view of the transferor's circumstances when those contributions were made.

342D(9) [Definitions] In this section and sections 342E and 342F–

"appropriate amount", in relation to a pension-sharing transaction, means the appropriate amount in relation to that transaction for the purposes of section 29(1) of the Welfare Reform and Pensions Act 1999 (creation of pension credits and debits);

"pension-sharing transaction" means an order or provision falling within section 28(1) of the Welfare Reform and Pensions Act 1999 (orders and agreements which activate pension-sharing);

"shared arrangement", in relation to a pension-sharing transaction, means the pension arrangement to which the transaction relates;

"transferee", in relation to a pension-sharing transaction, means the person for whose benefit the transaction is made;

"transferor", in relation to a pension-sharing transaction, means the person to whose rights the transaction relates.

General Note

This was inserted by para.71 of Sch.12 to the Welfare Reform and Pensions Act 1999.

S.342D(1) and (2)
These define a pension-sharing transaction for the purposes of ss.339–342.

S.342D(3)–(8)
These provisions explain what is the appropriate amount recoverable on applications under ss.339 or 340 of the 1986 Act. Essentially the law is seeking to create some sort of balance between the rights of the parties to the pension-sharing arrangement but not at the expense of unfairness to the bankrupt transferor's creditors. The critical issue is the quantum of personal contributions by the transferor and whether the making of those contributions unfairly prejudiced his creditors.

S.342D(9)
This is a definition provision.

342E Orders under section 339 or 340 in respect of pension-sharing transactions

342E(1) [Application] This section and section 342F apply if the court is making an order under section 339 or 340 in a case where–

(a) the transaction or preference is, or is any part of, a pension-sharing transaction, and

(b) the transferee has rights under a pension arrangement ("the destination arrangement", which may be the shared arrangement or any other pension arrangement) that are derived, directly or indirectly, from the pension-sharing transaction.

342E(2) [Contents of order] Without prejudice to the generality of section 339(2) or 340(2), or of section 342, the order may include provision–

(a) requiring the person responsible for the destination arrangement to pay an amount to the transferor's trustee in bankruptcy,

(b) adjusting the liabilities of the destination arrangement in respect of the transferee,

(c) adjusting any liabilities of the destination arrangement in respect of any other person that derive, directly or indirectly, from rights of the transferee under the destination arrangement,

(d) for the recovery by the person responsible for the destination arrangement (whether by deduction from any amount which that person is ordered to pay or otherwise) of costs incurred by that person in complying in the transferor's case with any requirement under section 342F(1) or in giving effect to the order,

(e) for the recovery, from the transferor's trustee in bankruptcy, by the person responsible for a pension arrangement, of costs incurred by that person in complying in the transferor's case with any requirement under section 342F(2) or (3).

342E(3) [Adjusting liabilities in s.342E(2)] In subsection (2), references to adjusting the liabilities of the destination arrangement in respect of a person include (in particular) reducing the amount of any benefit or future benefit to which that person is entitled under the arrangement.

342E(4) [Maximum amount payable] The maximum amount which the person responsible for the destination arrangement may be required to pay by the order is the smallest of–

(a) so much of the appropriate amount as, in accordance with section 342D, is recoverable,

(b) so much (if any) of the amount of the unfair contributions (within the meaning given by section 342D(5)) as is not recoverable by way of an order under section 342A containing provision such as is mentioned in section 342B(1)(a), and

(c) the value of the transferee's rights under the destination arrangement so far as they are derived, directly or indirectly, from the pension-sharing transaction.

342E(5) [Provision on "restoration amount"] If the order requires the person responsible for the destination arrangement to pay an amount ("the restoration amount") to the transferor's trustee in bankruptcy it must provide for the liabilities of the arrangement to be correspondingly reduced.

342E(6) [Liabilities in s.342E(5)] For the purposes of subsection (5), liabilities are correspondingly reduced if the difference between–

(a) the amount of the liabilities immediately before the reduction, and

(b) the amount of the liabilities immediately after the reduction,

is equal to the restoration amount.

342E(7) [Effect of order] The order–

(a) shall be binding on the person responsible for the destination arrangement, and

(b) overrides provisions of the destination arrangement to the extent that they conflict with the provisions of the order.

General Note

This was inserted by para.71 of Sch.12 to the Welfare Reform and Pensions Act 1999.

S.342E(1) and (2)
These explain the remedial powers of the court in pension-sharing cases where ss.339 or 340 have been successfully invoked. Subsection (1) defines the parameters of the provision. The provisions in subs.(2) are not intended to prejudice the flexibility enjoyed by the court.

S.342E(3)–(6)
These are technical provisions explaining various mechanics involving in a remedial order where there is a pension-sharing scenario.

S.342E(7)
This makes is clear that the provisions of any remedial court order prevail over the terms of a pension-sharing agreement.

342F Orders under section 339 or 340 in pension-sharing cases: supplementary

342F(1) [Provision of information: destination arrangement] On the transferor's trustee in bankruptcy making a written request to the person responsible for the destination arrangement, that person shall provide the trustee with such information about–

(a) the arrangement,

(b) the transferee's rights under it, and

(c) where the destination arrangement is the shared arrangement, the transferor's rights under it,

as the trustee may reasonably require for, or in connection with, the making of applications under sections 339 and 340.

342F(2) [Provision of information: no destination arrangement] Where the shared arrangement is not the destination arrangement, the person responsible for the shared arrangement shall, on the transferor's trustee in bankruptcy making a written request to that person, provide the trustee with such information about–

(a) the arrangement, and

(b) the transferor's rights under it,

as the trustee may reasonably require for, or in connection with, the making of applications under sections 339 and 340.

342F(3) [Provision of information: no immediate arrangement] On the transferor's trustee in bankruptcy making a written request to the person responsible for any intermediate arrangement, that person shall provide the trustee with such information about–

(a) the arrangement, and

(b) the transferee's rights under it,

as the trustee may reasonably require for, or in connection with, the making of applications under sections 339 and 340.

342F(4) ["Intermediate arrangement"] In subsection (3) "intermediate arrangement" means a pension arrangement, other than the shared arrangement or the destination arrangement, in relation to which the following conditions are fulfilled–

(a) there was a time when the transferee had rights under the arrangement that were derived (directly or indirectly) from the pension-sharing transaction, and

(b) the transferee's rights under the destination arrangement (so far as derived from the pension-sharing transaction) are to any extent derived (directly or indirectly) from the rights mentioned in paragraph (a).

342F(5) [Non-applicable provisions] Nothing in–

(a) any provision of section 159 of the Pension Schemes Act 1993 or section 91 of the Pensions Act 1995 (which prevent assignment and the making of orders which restrain a person from receiving anything which he is prevented from assigning),

(b) any provision of any enactment (whether passed or made before or after the passing of the Welfare Reform and Pensions Act 1999) corresponding to any of the provisions mentioned in paragraph (a), or

(c) any provision of the destination arrangement corresponding to any of those provisions,

applies to a court exercising its powers under section 339 or 340.

342F(6) [Provisions for calculation and verification etc.] Regulations may, for the purposes of sections 339 to 342, sections 342D and 342E and this section, make provision about the calculation and verification of–

(a) any such value as is mentioned in section 342E(4)(c);

(b) any such amounts as are mentioned in section 342E(6)(a) and (b).

342F(7) [Powers conferred by s.342F(6)] The power conferred by subsection (6) includes power to provide for calculation or verification–

(a) in such manner as may, in the particular case, be approved by a prescribed person; or

(b) in accordance with guidance from time to time prepared by a prescribed person.

342F(8) [Persons responsible for pension arrangements] In section 342E and this section, references to the person responsible for a pension arrangement are to–

(a) the trustees, managers or provider of the arrangement, or

(b) the person having functions in relation to the arrangement corresponding to those of a trustee, manager or provider.

342F(9) [Meanings in s.342F] In this section–

"prescribed" means prescribed by regulations;

"regulations" means regulations made by the Secretary of State.

342F(10) [Scope of regulations] Regulations under this section may–

(a) make different provision for different cases;

(b) contain such incidental, supplemental and transitional provisions as appear to the Secretary of State necessary or expedient.

342F(11) [Making of regulations] Regulations under this section shall be made by statutory instrument subject to annulment in pursuance of a resolution of either House of Parliament.

GENERAL NOTE

This was inserted by para.71 of Sch.12 to the Welfare Reform and Pensions Act 1999.

S.342F(1)–(3)
These provisions enable a trustee in bankruptcy to secure information about pensions where there is a pensions-sharing arrangement. This is a prelude to the exercise of avoidance powers.

S.342F(4)
This is a technical definition provision explaining a concept central to subs.(3).

S.342F(5)
This is a saving provision preserving the powers of the court notwithstanding an apparent conflict with other legislative provisions under pensions law.

S.342F(6), (7), (10) and (11)
These deal with the making of secondary rules.

S.342F(8) and (9)
These again are interpretation provisions.

343 Extortionate credit transactions

343(1) [Application] This section applies where a person is made bankrupt who is or has been a party to a transaction for, or involving, the provision to him of credit.

343(2) [Order by court] The court may, on the application of the trustee of the bankrupt's estate, make an order with respect to the transaction if the transaction is or was extortionate and was not entered into more than 3 years before the commencement of the bankruptcy.

343(3) [Extortionate transaction] For the purposes of this section a transaction is extortionate if, having regard to the risk accepted by the person providing the credit–

(a) the terms of it are or were such as to require grossly exorbitant payments to be made (whether unconditionally or in certain contingencies) in respect of the provision of the credit, or

(b) it otherwise grossly contravened ordinary principles of fair dealing;

and it shall be presumed, unless the contrary is proved, that a transaction with respect to which an application is made under this section is or, as the case may be, was extortionate.

343(4) [Extent of order] An order under this section with respect to any transaction may contain such one or more of the following as the court thinks fit, that is to say–

(a) provision setting aside the whole or part of any obligation created by the transaction;

(b) provision otherwise varying the terms of the transaction or varying the terms on which any security for the purposes of the transaction is held;

(c) provision requiring any person who is or was party to the transaction to pay to the trustee any sums paid to that person, by virtue of the transaction, by the bankrupt;

(d) provision requiring any person to surrender to the trustee any property held by him as security for the purposes of the transaction;

(e) provision directing accounts to be taken between any persons.

343(5) [Sums to trustee] Any sums or property required to be paid or surrendered to the trustee in accordance with an order under this section shall be comprised in the bankrupt's estate.

343(6) [Application under Consumer Credit Act] The powers conferred by this section are exercisable in relation to any transaction concurrently with any powers exercisable under this Act in relation to that transaction as a transaction at an undervalue.

General Note

This is a new provision enabling the trustee in bankruptcy to reopen a credit bargain made by a bankrupt, on the grounds that it was extortionate vis-à-vis the bankrupt. The Cork Committee (*Report*, para.1381) called for such a provision, and its introduction in some senses can be viewed as a quid pro quo for the repeal of BA 1914 s.66, which placed restrictions on a lender proving for interest: see the White Paper, para.87.

A corresponding provision has been introduced for corporate insolvency: see s.244.

Note minor amendment made by ERRA 2013 Sch.19 para.36 to reflect the new out of court bankruptcy procedure for debtors.

S.343(1), (2)

These permit the trustee to reopen extortionate credit bargains entered into by the bankrupt for the provision of credit to him within three years of the commencement of his bankruptcy (see s.278).

S.343(3)

The onus is on the other party to show that the bargain was not "extortionate" within the meaning of this subsection.

S.343(4)

This explains what the court may do if the bargain is extortionate—again this provision has been borrowed from the Consumer Credit Act 1974.

S.343(5)

Any "proceeds" of such an action become part of the bankrupt's estate.

S.343(6)
Formerly this subsection contained in its first paragraph reference to s.139(1)(a) of the Consumer Credit Act 1974 in that it denied a trustee in bankruptcy/undischarged bankrupt access to that particular transactional avoidance mechanism. That particular section in the 1974 Act was repealed and replaced by a new regime governing unfair consumer credit relationships which is contained in the Consumer Credit Act 2006 ss.19–22. Hence the repeal of the first paragraph of s.343(6) by Sch.4 to the 2006 Act. Subsection 6 still reminds us, however, that the transaction may also be challenged under s.339.

344 Avoidance of general assignment of book debts

344(1) [Application] The following applies where a person engaged in any business makes a general assignment to another person of his existing or future book debts, or any class of them, and is subsequently made bankrupt.

344(2) [Certain assignments void against trustee] The assignment is void against the trustee of the bankrupt's estate as regards book debts which were not paid before the making of the bankruptcy application or (as the case may be) the presentation of the bankruptcy petition, unless the assignment has been registered under the Bills of Sale Act 1878.

344(3) [Definitions] For the purposes of subsections (1) and (2)–

(a) "assignment" includes an assignment by way of security or charge on book debts, and

(b) "general assignment" does not include–

  (i) an assignment of book debts due at the date of the assignment from specified debtors or of debts becoming due under specified contracts, or

  (ii) an assignment of book debts included either in a transfer of a business made in good faith and for value or in an assignment of assets for the benefit of creditors generally.

344(4) [Registration under Bills of Sales Act] For the purposes of registration under the Act of 1878 an assignment of book debts is to be treated as if it were a bill of sale given otherwise than by way of security for the payment of a sum of money; and the provisions of that Act with respect to the registration of bills of sale apply accordingly with such necessary modifications as may be made by rules under that Act.

S.344(1), (2)
This provides that a general assignment of book debts by a trader shall be void on bankruptcy unless registered under the Bills of Sale Act 1878. Note the word "general" is now used in the text of subs.(1)—in s.43 of the 1914 Act this word merely appeared in the marginal note. For a rare authority on the effect of s.344(2) see *Hills v Alex Lawrie Factors* [2001] B.P.I.R. 1038.

Amendments were made to subss.(1) and (2) by ERRA 2013 Sch.19 para.37.

S.344(3)
This provision clarifies s.344(1) by stressing that assignments by way of security are covered but not specific assignments of specific book debts, nor assignments connected with a bona fide transfer of a business for value, nor a general assignment of assets for the benefit of creditors generally.

S.344(4)
This provision describes the mechanics of registration under the 1878 Act.

345 Contracts to which bankrupt is a party

345(1) [Application] The following applies where a contract has been made with a person who is subsequently made bankrupt.

345(2) [Court order on application] The court may, on the application of any other party to the contract, make an order discharging obligations under the contract on such terms as to payment by the applicant or the bankrupt of damages for non-performance or otherwise as appear to the court to be equitable.

345(3) [Damages as bankruptcy debt] Any damages payable by the bankrupt by virtue of an order of the court under this section are provable as a bankruptcy debt.

345(4) [Where joint contract] Where an undischarged bankrupt is a contractor in respect of any contract jointly with any person, that person may sue or be sued in respect of the contract without the joinder of the bankrupt.

GENERAL NOTE

In the context of the financial markets, s.345 does not apply in relation to a market contract or a contract effected by an exchange or clearing house for the purpose of realising property provided as margin in relation to market contracts: see CA 1989 s.164(1), and the note on p.2.

Note amendment was made to subs.(1) by ERRA 2013 Sch.19 para.38.

S.345(1)–(3)

At common law the general rule, as laid down in *Brooke v Hewitt* (1796) 3 Ves. 253, was that the bankruptcy of a party to a contract did not terminate that contract. Hence the need to confer on trustees a power to disclaim onerous contracts. There is no need to have recourse to s.345 if the contract provides that bankruptcy is a terminating event—on this common provision and the consequences of bankruptcy in general see *Cadogan Estates v McMahon* [2001] B.P.I.R. 17. Section 345(2) in effect redresses the balance as far as the other contracting party is concerned. He can now apply to the court to have contractual obligations discharged. The court enjoys general discretion and can order compensation payments to be paid by either party. If the bankrupt is ordered to pay compensation, that sum constitutes a provable debt.

S.345(4)

This repeats BA 1914 s.118 and allows a person who has entered into a contract jointly with a bankrupt to sue the other party to the contract without the joinder of the bankrupt to the proceedings.

346 Enforcement procedures

346(1) [Creditor's execution against bankrupt] Subject to section 285 in Chapter II (restrictions on proceedings and remedies) and to the following provisions of this section, where the creditor of any person who is made bankrupt has, before the commencement of the bankruptcy–

(a) issued execution against the goods or land of that person, or

(b) attached a debt due to that person from another person,

that creditor is not entitled, as against the official receiver or trustee of the bankrupt's estate, to retain the benefit of the execution or attachment, or any sums paid to avoid it, unless the execution or attachment was completed, or the sums were paid, before the commencement of the bankruptcy.

346(1A) [Attachment by HMRC deduction from accounts] For the purposes of this section, Her Majesty's Revenue and Customs is to be regarded as having attached a debt due to a person if it has taken action under Part 1 of Schedule 8 to the Finance (No. 2) Act 2015 (enforcement by deduction from accounts) as a result of which an amount standing to the credit of an account held by that person is–

(a) subject to arrangements made under paragraph 6(3) of that Schedule, or

(b) the subject of a deduction notice under paragraph 13 of that Schedule

346(2) [Where goods taken in execution] Subject as follows, where any goods of a person have been taken in execution, then, if before the completion of the execution notice is given to the enforcement officer or other officer charged with the execution that that person has been made bankrupt–

(a) the enforcement officer or other officer shall on request deliver to the official receiver or trustee of the bankrupt's estate the goods and any money seized or recovered in part satisfaction of the execution, but

(b) the costs of the execution are a first charge on the goods or money so delivered and the official receiver or trustee may sell the goods or a sufficient part of them for the purpose of satisfying the charge.

346(3) [Balance of sale proceeds] Subject to subsection (6) below, where–

(a) under an execution in respect of a judgment for a sum exceeding such sum as may be prescribed for the purposes of this subsection, the goods of any person are sold or money is paid in order to avoid a sale, and

(b) before the end of the period of 14 days beginning with the day of the sale or payment the enforcement officer or other officer charged with the execution is given notice that a bankruptcy application has been made or a bankruptcy petition has been presented in relation to that person, and

(c) a bankruptcy order is or has been made as a result of that application or on that petition,

the balance of the proceeds of sale or money paid, after deducting the costs of execution, shall (in priority to the claim of the execution creditor) be comprised in the bankrupt's estate.

346(4) [Duty of enforcement officer re sum in s.346(3)] Accordingly, in the case of an execution in respect of a judgment for a sum exceeding the sum prescribed for the purposes of subsection (3), the enforcement officer or other officer charged with the execution–

(a) shall not dispose of the balance mentioned in subsection (3) at any time within the period of 14 days so mentioned or while proceedings on a bankruptcy application are ongoing or (as the case may be) there is pending a bankruptcy petition of which he has been given notice under that subsection, and

(b) shall pay that balance, where by virtue of that subsection it is comprised in the bankrupt's estate, to the official receiver or (if there is one) to the trustee of that estate.

346(5) [Completion of execution or attachment] For the purposes of this section–

(a) an execution against goods is completed by seizure and sale or by the making of a charging order under section 1 of the Charging Orders Act 1979;

(b) an execution against land is completed by seizure, by the appointment of a receiver or by the making of a charging order under that section;

(c) an attachment of a debt is completed by the receipt of the debt.

346(6) [Setting aside of s.346(1)–(3) rights by court] The rights conferred by subsections (1) to (3) on the official receiver or the trustee may, to such extent and on such terms as it thinks fit, be set aside by the court in favour of the creditor who has issued the execution or attached the debt.

346(7) [Acquisition in good faith] Nothing in this section entitles the trustee of a bankrupt's estate to claim goods from a person who has acquired them in good faith under a sale by an enforcement officer or other officer charged with an execution.

346(8) [Non-application of s.346(2), (3)] Neither subsection (2) nor subsection (3) applies in relation to any execution against property which has been acquired by or has devolved upon the bankrupt since the commencement of the bankruptcy, unless, at the time the execution is issued or before it is completed–

(a) the property has been or is claimed for the bankrupt's estate under section 307 (after-acquired property), and

(b) a copy of the notice given under that section has been or is served on the enforcement officer or other officer charged with the execution.

346(9) ["Enforcement officer"] In this section "enforcement officer" means an individual who is authorised to act as an enforcement officer under the Courts Act 2003.

General Note

The former references to the "sheriff" were replaced by "enforcement officer" by Sch.8 to the Courts Act 2003.

Note amendments were made to subss.(1)–(4) by ERRA 2013 Sch.19 para.39.

S.346(1), (1A), (5)

Where a creditor has begun an execution process before the commencement of the bankruptcy (see s.278(a)), but has failed to complete before that date, he will not be allowed to proceed further and any proceeds received after the commencement of the bankruptcy must be handed over to the estate. The stages at which the various execution processes are deemed to be completed are described by s.346(5). In *Nationwide Building Society v Wright* [2009] B.P.I.R. 1047 the Court of Appeal held that it was not the intention of s.346 to defeat a creditor who had obtained a final charging order prior to the making of the bankruptcy order. For comment on this case see D. Capper [2010] C.J.Q. 150.

Executions may also be restrained under s.285. The court retains the power to set aside a garnishee order notwithstanding the provisions of s.346—*Industrial Diseases Compensation Ltd v Marrons* [2001] B.P.I.R. 600.

Note the insertion of subs.(1A) to cater for the new HMRC power to deduct directly from accounts. This amendment was introduced by Finance (No.2) Act 2015 s.51 and Sch.8 para.32.

S.346(2)

This deals with the position of an enforcement officer who has seized goods in execution. The goods must be handed over to the estate, although the enforcement officer's costs are a first charge on such goods. Note also IR 2016 r.12.57. For the enforcement officer's costs see r.12.44.

S.346(3), (4)

These provisions deal with the situation where the enforcement officer has received the proceeds of sale of goods seized in execution of a judgment for a "prescribed amount" (see s.418), or has been paid not to sell them. The amount is £1,000 under the Insolvency Proceedings (Monetary Limits) (Amendment) Order 2004 (SI 2004/547) operating from 1 April 2004. If, within 14 days thereafter, the sheriff is given notice of the bankruptcy petition, the balance of the proceeds after deducting costs must be paid to the estate if the petition succeeds. The enforcement officer therefore under a duty to retain proceeds for the required period, just in case this obligation is activated.

On s.346(3)(b) see IR 2016 r.12.57.

S.346(6)

The court has discretion to set aside the rights of the estate in favour of the execution creditor. On the exercise of discretion under s.346(6) see *Tagore Investments v Official Receiver* [2009] B.P.I.R. 392. In this case the unusual circumstances justified the court departing from the pari passu rule and allowing the execution to proceed.

S.346(7)

Bona fide purchasers from the enforcement officer are protected.

S.346(8)

This provision lays down special rules for execution against property acquired by the bankrupt after the commencement of the bankruptcy.

347 Distress, etc.

347(1) [Limit on statutory CRAR] CRAR (the power of commercial rent arrears recovery under section 72(1) of the Tribunals, Courts and Enforcement Act 2007) is exercisable where the tenant is an undischarged bankrupt (subject to sections 252(2)(b) and 254(1) above and subsection (5) below) against goods and effects comprised in the bankrupt's estate, but only for 6 months' rent accrued due before the commencement of the bankruptcy.

347(2) [CRAR where bankruptcy order later made] Where CRAR has been exercised to recover rent from an individual to whom a bankruptcy application or a bankruptcy petition relates and a bankruptcy order is subsequently made as a result of that application or on that petition, any amount recovered by way of CRAR which–

(a) is in excess of the amount which by virtue of subsection (1) would have been recoverable after the commencement of the bankruptcy, or

(b) is in respect of rent for a period or part of a period after goods were taken control of under CRAR, shall be held for the bankrupt as part of his estate.

347(3) [Application of s.347(3A)] Subsection (3A) applies where–

(a) any person (whether or not a landlord or person entitled to rent) has distrained upon the goods or effects of an individual who is made bankrupt before the end of the period of 3 months beginning with the distraint, or

(b) Her Majesty's Revenue and Customs has been paid any amount from an account of an individual under Part 1 of Schedule 8 to the Finance (No. 2) Act 2015 (enforcement by deduction from accounts) and the individual is made bankrupt before the end of the period of 3 months beginning with the payment.

347(3A) [Effect of person distraining or HMRC deduction from accounts] Where this subsection applies–

(a) in a case within subsection (3)(a), the goods or effects, or the proceeds of their sale, and

(b) in a case within subsection (3)(b), the amount in question,

is charged for the benefit of the bankrupt's estate with the preferential debts of the bankrupt to the extent that the bankrupt's estate is for the time being insufficient for meeting them.

347(4) [Where surrender under s.347(3)] Where by virtue of any charge under subsection (3A) any person surrenders any goods or effects to the trustee of a bankrupt's estate or makes a payment to such a trustee, that person ranks, in respect of the amount of the proceeds of the sale of those goods or effects by the trustee or, as the case may be, the amount of the payment, as a preferential creditor of the bankrupt, except as against so much of the bankrupt's estate as is available for the payment of preferential creditors by virtue of the surrender or payment.

347(5) [CRAR not exercisable after discharge from bankruptcy] CRAR is not exercisable at any time after the discharge of a bankrupt against any goods or effects comprised in the bankrupt's estate.

347(6) [Repealed]

347(7) [Repealed]

347(8) [Rights to distrain other than for rent] Subject to sections 252(2)(b) and 254(1) above nothing in this Group of Parts affects any right to distrain otherwise than for rent; and any such right is at any time exercisable without restriction against property comprised in a bankrupt's estate, even if that right is expressed by any enactment to be exercisable in like manner as a right to distrain for rent.

347(9) [Exercise of right] Any right to distrain against property comprised in a bankrupt's estate is exercisable notwithstanding that the property has vested in the trustee.

347(10) [Landlord's right to prove] The provisions of this section are without prejudice to a landlord's right in a bankruptcy to prove for any bankruptcy debt in respect of rent.

347(11) [Repealed]

Editors' note: Note amendments to subss.(1), (2) and (5) made by Sch.14 para.44 of the Tribunals, Courts and Enforcement Act 2007 and the repeal of subs.(6), (7) and (11) by Sch.23 Pt 4. These changes took effect on 6 April 2014 through the Tribunals, Courts and Enforcement Act 2007 (Commencement No.11) Order 2014 (SI 2014/768 (C. 27)). The changes relate to the abolition of distress and the introduction of commercial rent arrears recovery.

General Note

Subsections (1)–(3) were amended by ERRA 2013 Sch.19 para.40.

S.347(1), (2), (5), (9)
This continues the favoured treatment of landlords. A landlord may still exercise CRAR on the goods of an undischarged bankrupt (even if they have vested in the trustee—s.347(9)), but only for a maximum of six months' rent accruing before the commencement of the bankruptcy. There is a similar rule where an administration order is in

force: see County Courts Act 1984 s.116. Where CRAR is levied after the petition but before the order, the landlord must hand over any proceeds in excess of the amount of rent referred to in s.347(1). CRAR cannot be levied after the discharge of the bankrupt. Subsection (1) was subject to minor amendment by IA 2000 Sch.3.

S.347(3), (3A), (4)
These make special provision out of the proceeds of a distress for the preferential creditors (see s.328) in so far as the estate is insufficient to meet their claims. However, the landlord who loses out as a result of this provision is then subrogated to the claims of the preferential creditors against the general estate of the bankrupt.

This provision was subject to amendment by ERRA 2013 Sch.19.

Note subss.(3) and (4) were amended, and a new subs.(3A) was introduced by Finance (No.2) Act 2015 s.51 and Sch.8 para.33 as a consequence of the giving of power to HMRC to deduct directly from accounts.

S.347(6), (7)
These provisions deal with special forms of distress. Although normally 12 months' rent can be claimed, this is reduced to six months' rent in the event of bankruptcy. Special protection is offered to enforcement officers who inadvertently breach this provision, but the landlord himself may still incur liability. The ancient title of sheriff was replaced by enforcement officer by Sch.8 to the Courts Act 2003 with effect from 1 September 2004.

S.347(8)
Distress otherwise than for rent is not hampered by bankruptcy. Again, note amendment by IA 2000 Sch.3.

S.347(10)
As an alternative to levying distress for rent, a landlord can of course prove for the unpaid amount in the bankruptcy.

348 Apprenticeships, etc.

348(1) [Application] This section applies where–

(a) a bankruptcy order is made in respect of an individual to whom another individual was an apprentice or articled clerk at the time when the application for the order was made or (as the case may be) the petition for the order was presented, and

(b) the bankrupt or the apprentice or clerk gives notice to the trustee terminating the apprenticeship or articles.

348(2) [Discharge etc.] Subject to subsection (6) below, the indenture of apprenticeship or, as the case may be, the articles of agreement shall be discharged with effect from the commencement of the bankruptcy.

348(3) [If money paid] If any money has been paid by or on behalf of the apprentice or clerk to the bankrupt as a fee, the trustee may, on an application made by or on behalf of the apprentice or clerk, pay such sum to the apprentice or clerk as the trustee thinks reasonable, having regard to–

(a) the amount of the fee,

(b) the proportion of the period in respect of which the fee was paid that has been served by the apprentice or clerk before the commencement of the bankruptcy, and

(c) the other circumstances of the case.

348(4) [Priority of s.348(3) power] The power of the trustee to make a payment under subsection (3) has priority over his obligation to distribute the bankrupt's estate.

348(5) [Instead of s.348(3) payment] Instead of making a payment under subsection (3), the trustee may, if it appears to him expedient to do so on an application made by or on behalf of the apprentice or clerk, transfer the indenture or articles to a person other than the bankrupt.

348(6) [Where s.348(5) transfer] Where a transfer is made under subsection (5), subsection (2) has effect only as between the apprentice or clerk and the bankrupt.

S.348(1)
This section applies where a principal is declared bankrupt and notice is given to terminate a contract of apprenticeship or articled clerkship. Either party can give notice to terminate.
Note amendment to subs.(1)(a) made by ERRA 2013 Sch.19 para.41.

S.348(2)
The effect of such notice is to discharge the contract from the date of the commencement of the bankruptcy (for the meaning of this term, see s.278(a)).

S.348(3), (4)
The trustee can repay any fee paid by the apprentice or articled clerk in whole or in part. Factors such as the duration of the apprenticeship which is unexpired and the general circumstances of the case are relevant here. The approach will be similar to that taken with regard to premiums under s.40 of the Partnership Act 1890. The sum of money repaid under s.348(3) ranks as a pre-preferential debt.

S.348(5), (6)
As an alternative, the trustee can transfer the apprenticeship, etc. to another principal if the apprentice, etc. so wishes. The continuity of the apprenticeship in such a case will not be disrupted by s.348(2). This latter provision clarifies the former law under BA 1914 s.34.

349 Unenforceability of liens on books, etc.

349(1) [Unenforceability] Subject as follows, a lien or other right to retain possession of any of the books, papers or other records of a bankrupt is unenforceable to the extent that its enforcement would deny possession of any books, papers or other records to the official receiver or the trustee of the bankrupt's estate.

349(2) [Non-application of s.349(1)] Subsection (1) does not apply to a lien on documents which give a title to property and are held as such.

General Note

This section renders ineffective liens, etc. on the books and records of a bankrupt in so far as they would deny possession of them to the official receiver or trustee. Liens on documents of title are not affected. Here the public interest is accorded priority over private security rights.
See also s.333(4) for another indication of how liens on books require special treatment from the law. Regulations made by the Secretary of State pursuant to the rules may allow the trustee wide powers to deal with, and dispose of, the bankrupt's books: see IR 2016 Introductory Rule 5. Note also the Insolvency Regulations 1994 (SI 1994/2507) reg.30.

S.349(2)
On the interpretation of this provision, see the note to s.246(3).

349A Arbitration agreements to which bankrupt is party

349A(1) [Application of section] This section applies where a bankrupt had become party to a contract containing an arbitration agreement before the commencement of his bankruptcy.

349A(2) [If contract adopted by trustee] If the trustee in bankruptcy adopts the contract, the arbitration agreement is enforceable by or against the trustee in relation to matters arising from or connected with the contract.

349A(3) [If contract not adopted by trustee] If the trustee in bankruptcy does not adopt the contract and a matter to which the arbitration agreement applies requires to be determined in connection with or for the purposes of the bankruptcy proceedings–

(a) the trustee with the consent of the creditors' committee, or

(b) any other party to the agreement,

may apply to the court which may, if it thinks fit in all the circumstances of the case, order that the matter be referred to arbitration in accordance with the arbitration agreement.

349A(4) ["Arbitration agreement", "the court"] In this section–

"arbitration agreement" has the same meaning as in Part I of the Arbitration Act 1996; and

"the court" means the court which has jurisdiction in the bankruptcy proceedings.

General Note

This customised provision was introduced by the Arbitration Act 1996 s.107(1) and Sch.3 para.46 with effect from 31 January 1997. With increased usage/recourse to arbitration it is a valuable addition to insolvency legislation.

Note *Bannai v Erez (Trustee in Bankruptcy of Reifman)* [2013] EWHC 3689 (Comm) for the application of this provision in an international cross border recognition context.

Chapter VI

Bankruptcy Offences

Preliminary

350 Scheme of this Chapter

350(1) [Application] Subject to section 360(3) below, this Chapter applies–

(a) where an adjudicator has made a bankruptcy order as a result of a bankruptcy application, or

(b) where the court has made a bankruptcy order on a bankruptcy petition.

350(2) [Effect of annulment of bankruptcy] This Chapter applies whether or not the bankruptcy order is annulled, but proceedings for an offence under this Chapter shall not be instituted after the annulment.

350(3) [Liability of bankrupt after discharge] Without prejudice to his liability in respect of a subsequent bankruptcy, the bankrupt is not guilty of an offence under this Chapter in respect of anything done after his discharge; but nothing in this Group of Parts prevents the institution of proceedings against a discharged bankrupt for an offence committed before his discharge.

350(3A) [Effect of bankruptcy restrictions order] Subsection (3) is without prejudice to any provision of this Chapter which applies to a person in respect of whom a bankruptcy restrictions order is in force.

350(4) [Where not defence] It is not a defence in proceedings for an offence under this Chapter that anything relied on, in whole or in part, as constituting that offence was done outside England and Wales.

350(5) [Institution of proceedings for offence] Proceedings for an offence under this Chapter or under the rules shall not be instituted except by the Secretary of State or by or with the consent of the Director of Public Prosecutions.

350(6) [Penalty] A person guilty of any offence under this Chapter is liable to imprisonment or a fine, or both.

General Note

The Cork Committee (*Report*, para.1900) called for greater use to be made of the criminal law in controlling fraud in bankruptcy. In addition, it recommended a cautious tidying up of the offences (para.1883), and this has been to some extent implemented by the following provisions in the Act. Incidentally, the Blagden Committee (Cmnd.221 (1957) paras 206–213) also suggested that the criminal law should be applied more strictly to control fraudulent bankrupts. Note that the rules themselves create several offences, the punishments for which are prescribed by Sch.3 to the Rules. For an analysis of the new regime of bankruptcy offences see Griffiths (1986) 2 I.L. & P. 73.

S.350(1), (2)

These are new provisions dealing with bankruptcy offences in general. In particular, s.350(2) makes it clear that the subsequent annulment of the bankruptcy is relevant only in so far as a prosecution cannot be instituted after this date. But see *Inland Revenue Commissioners v McEntaggart* [2004] EWHC 3431 (Ch); [2006] B.P.I.R. 750.

Note amendment to subs.(1) made by ERRA 2013 Sch.19 para.42.

S.350(3)

This repeats the provision under the 1914 Act—the bankrupt cannot be guilty for acts done after his discharge, but he can be prosecuted after his discharge for earlier misconduct.

S.350(3A)

This was inserted by EA 2002 s.257 and Sch.21 with effect from 1 April 2004 to deal with the effect of BROs.

S.350(4)

By way of contrast, it is not a defence to show that the conduct complained of was done outside England and Wales.

S.350(5)

This is a new general provision replacing the fragmentary approach of the 1914 Act. Prosecutions now require the consent of the Director of Public Prosecutions or the Secretary of State. Formerly, the court's consent was needed for certain prosecutions.

S.350(6)

For details of penalties, see s.430 and Sch.10.

351 Definitions

351 In the following provisions of this Chapter–

(a) references to property comprised in the bankrupt's estate or to property possession of which is required to be delivered up to the official receiver or the trustee of the bankrupt's estate include any property which would be such property if a notice in respect of it were given under section 307 (after-acquired property), section 308 (personal property and effects of bankrupt having more than replacement value) or section 308A (vesting in trustee of certain tenancies);

(b) "the initial period" means the period between the making of the bankruptcy application or (as the case may be) the presentation of the bankruptcy petition and the commencement of the bankruptcy.

General Note

This section contains definitions of three concepts and phrases which recur throughout ss.352–362:

(a) "property": see ss.353, 354, 356, 357, 358, 359, 362;

(b) "initial period": see ss.354, 355, 356, 358, 359, 362 (for further explanation, see s.278(a));

(c) "before petition": see ss.354, 355, 356, 358, 359, 361, 362.

In s.351(a) the words relating to s.308A inserted and consequential amendment made by the Housing Act 1988 Sch.17 para.75.

Note amendments made by ERRA 2013 Sch.19 para.43.

352 Defence of innocent intention

352 Where in the case of an offence under any provision of this Chapter it is stated that this section applies, a person is not guilty of the offence if he proves that, at the time of the conduct constituting the offence, he had no intent to defraud or to conceal the state of his affairs.

General Note

This is an important new general defence. If the bankrupt is charged with certain offences in ss.353–362, he has a defence if he can prove that he had not intended to defraud or conceal his affairs. The provisions creating the offences state whether s.352 applies. On the burden of proof see *R. v Daniel* [2002] EWCA Crim 959; [2002] B.P.I.R. 1193.

In *Attorney General's Reference (No.1 of 2004)* [2004] EWCA Crim 1025; [2004] B.P.I.R. 1074 the Court of Appeal sought to explain the relationship between ss.352, 353 and 357 in the context of the requirements of art.6 of the European Convention on Human Rights. According to the court only an evidential burden of proof (as opposed to a legal burden) is generated by the interaction of the statutory provisions in ss.352 and 357 and accordingly there is no breach of art.6. When s.352 is read with s.353 even if a legal burden is created there is no breach of art.6. See also *R. (Griffin) v Richmond Magistrates Court* [2008] B.P.I.R. 468 (a case on s.208).

Wrongdoing by the bankrupt before and after bankruptcy

353 Non-disclosure

353(1) [Offence] The bankrupt is guilty of an offence if–

(a) he does not to the best of his knowledge and belief disclose all the property comprised in his estate to the official receiver or the trustee, or

(b) he does not inform the official receiver or the trustee of any disposal of any property which but for the disposal would be so comprised, stating how, when, to whom and for what consideration the property was disposed of.

353(2) [Exception to s.353(1)(b)] Subsection (1)(b) does not apply to any disposal in the ordinary course of a business carried on by the bankrupt or to any payment of the ordinary expenses of the bankrupt or his family.

353(3) [Application of s.352] Section 352 applies to this offence.

S.353(1), (2)

This makes it an offence for the bankrupt to fail to disclose items of "property" (for definition, see s.351(a)) to his trustee or official receiver. Moreover, certain disposals of property which have resulted in a diminution of the estate must also be revealed. Note the positive nature of the obligations imposed here. There is a defence for bona fide business and domestic transactions. Note *Williams v Mohammed* [2011] B.P.I.R. 1787.

For the appropriate penalty, see ss.350, 430 and Sch.10.

S.353(3)

The general defence in s.352 applies here. See the note to s.352.

354 Concealment of property

354(1) [Offence of concealment etc.] The bankrupt is guilty of an offence if–

(a) he does not deliver up possession to the official receiver or trustee, or as the official receiver or trustee may direct, of such part of the property comprised in his estate as is in his possession or under his control and possession of which he is required by law so to deliver up,

(b) he conceals any debt due to or from him or conceals any property the value of which is not less than the prescribed amount and possession of which he is required to deliver up to the official receiver or trustee, or

(c) in the 12 months before the making of the bankruptcy application or (as the case may be) the presentation of the bankruptcy petition, or in the initial period, he did anything which would have been an offence under paragraph (b) above if the bankruptcy order had been made immediately before he did it.

Section 352 applies to this offence.

354(2) [Offence re removal of property] The bankrupt is guilty of an offence if he removes, or in the initial period removed, any property the value of which was not less than the prescribed amount and possession of which he has or would have been required to deliver up to the official receiver or the trustee.

Section 352 applies to this offence.

354(3) [Offence re failure to account for loss] The bankrupt is guilty of an offence if he without reasonable excuse fails, on being required to do so by the official receiver, the trustee or the court–

(a) to account for the loss of any substantial part of his property incurred in the 12 months before the making of the bankruptcy application or (as the case may be) the presentation of the bankruptcy petition or in the initial period, or

(b) to give a satisfactory explanation of the manner in which such a loss was incurred.

General Note

Note amendment to subss.(1) and (3) by ERRA 2013 Sch.19 para.44.

S.354(1)

This is a related offence of failing to hand over "property" (for definition, see s.351(a)), or concealing debts or property which is not less than the "prescribed amount" (see s.418). The amount is £1,000 under the Insolvency Proceedings (Monetary Limits) (Amendment) Order 2004 (SI 2004/547) (which operates from 1 April 2004). Note that, in the case of concealment, conduct in the "initial period" (i.e. between the petition and order: see s.351(b)) and, indeed, in the 12 months "before petition" (see s.351(c)), is covered.

The general defence in s.352 applies. See *R. v Daniel* [2002] EWCA Crim 959; [2002] B.P.I.R. 1193. See also *Williams v Mohammed* [2011] B.P.I.R. 1787.

For penalties, see ss.350, 430 and Sch.10.

S.354(2)

Removal of "property" from the estate after the order or in the "initial period" is unlawful where the property exceeds the "prescribed amount" (£1,000—see the note to s.354(1)). The general defence in s.352 applies. Settling a non-provable debt during the period in question is an offence under s.354: *Woodley v Woodley (No.2)* [1994] 1 W.L.R. 1167.

S.354(3)

Failure to provide explanations for substantial losses of "property" dating back to 12 months "before petition", or in the "initial period", is unlawful, unless there is a reasonable excuse for this. The words ", the trustee" were inserted by s.269 of and Sch.23 to EA 2002 with effect from 1 April 2004. The existence of the offence under s.354(3)(a) does not infringe fundamental human rights expectations—*R. v Kearns (Nicholas Gary)* [2002] EWCA Crim 748; [2002] B.P.I.R. 1213. The time limit referred to in s.354(3) is the same as that in BA 1914, in spite of recommendations from the Cork Committee (*Report*, para.1888) that it should be extended to two years.

355 Concealment of books and papers; falsification

355(1) [Offence re non-delivery of books etc.] The bankrupt is guilty of an offence if he does not deliver up possession to the official receiver or the trustee, or as the official receiver or trustee may direct, of all books, papers and other records of which he has possession or control and which relate to his estate or his affairs.

Section 352 applies to this offence.

355(2) [Offence re destruction, concealment etc.] The bankrupt is guilty of an offence if–

(a) he prevents, or in the initial period prevented, the production of any books, papers or records relating to his estate or affairs;

(b) he conceals, destroys, mutilates or falsifies, or causes or permits the concealment, destruction, mutilation or falsification of, any books, papers or other records relating to his estate or affairs;

(c) he makes, or causes or permits the making of, any false entries in any book, document or record relating to his estate or affairs; or

(d) in the 12 months before the making of the bankruptcy application or (as the case may be) the presentation of the bankruptcy petition, or in the initial period, he did anything which would have been an offence under paragraph (b) or (c) above if the bankruptcy order had been made before he did it.

Section 352 applies to this offence.

355(3) [Offence re disposal, alteration etc.] The bankrupt is guilty of an offence if–

(a) he disposes of, or alters or makes any omission in, or causes or permits the disposal, altering or making of any omission in, any book, document or record relating to his estate or affairs, or

(b) in the 12 months before the making of the bankruptcy application or (as the case may be) the presentation of the bankruptcy petition, or in the initial period, he did anything which would have been an offence under paragraph (a) if the bankruptcy order had been made before he did it.

Section 352 applies to this offence.

355(4) [Application of s.355(2)(d), (3)(b)] In their application to a trading record subsections (2)(d) and (3)(b) shall have effect as if the reference to 12 months were a reference to two years.

355(5) ["Trading record"] In subsection (4) "trading record" means a book, document or record which shows or explains the transactions or financial position of a person's business, including–

(a) a periodic record of cash paid and received,

(b) a statement of periodic stock-taking, and

(c) except in the case of goods sold by way of retail trade, a record of goods sold and purchased which identifies the buyer and seller or enables them to be identified.

General Note

This involved provision is somewhat tautological.

For penalties, see ss.350, 430 and Sch.10, and for defences, see s.352. Note that, in the case of those basic records described by s.361(3), the 12-month periods referred to in s.355 are extended to two years: see s.361(4).

Note amendments made to subss.(2) and (3) by ERRA 2013 Sch.19 para.45.

S.355(1), (2)

Failure to deliver up books and records is an offence. Moreover, if one prevents such books and records being produced, or conceals, destroys or falsifies them, this will also be unlawful. Note that for concealment and falsification, the relevant period is extended to 12 months "before petition" (see s.351(c)), plus the "initial period" (see s.351(b)).

S.355(3)

It is unlawful for a bankrupt to dispose of or alter books or records—this again extends to the 12 months "before petition" and the "initial period".

S.355(4), (5)

These were added by EA 2002 s.269 and Sch.23 with effect from 1 April 2004. They clarify the position.

356 False statements

356(1) [Offence re material omission] The bankrupt is guilty of an offence if he makes or has made any material omission in any statement made under any provision in this Group of Parts and relating to his affairs.

Section 352 applies to this offence.

356(2) [Offence re failing to inform etc.] The bankrupt is guilty of an offence if–

(a) knowing or believing that a false debt has been proved by any person under the bankruptcy, he fails to inform the trustee as soon as practicable; or

(b) he attempts to account for any part of his property by fictitious losses or expenses; or

(c) in connection with any creditors' decision procedure or deemed consent procedure in the 12 months before the making of the bankruptcy application or (as the case may be) the presentation of the bankruptcy petition or (whether or not in connection with such a procedure) at any time in the initial period, he did anything which would have been an offence under paragraph (b) if the bankruptcy order had been made before he did it; or

(d) he is, or at any time has been, guilty of any false representation or other fraud for the purpose of obtaining the consent of his creditors, or any of them, to an agreement with reference to his affairs or to his bankruptcy.

S.356(1)

This is a general offence derived from BA 1914 s.154(6), prohibiting the bankrupt from making false statements by omission. The statement must relate to his "affairs" (for definition, see s.385(2)).

See also *DBIS v Compton* [2012] B.P.I.R. 1108 (Davison DJ sitting in the magistrates court) for a useful illustration of how charges under this provision are dealt with by the court (and dismissed).

Section 356(1) (unlike s.356(2)) does not, on its face, require any intent to cheat or defraud, but of course the general defence under s.352 can be utilised to offer a defence to the innocent bankrupt.

S.356(2)

This provision specifies certain prohibited forms of conduct involving falsehoods. Such behaviour was an offence under BA 1914 s.154(1), (7), (12), and (16). For definitions of "property", "before petition" and "initial period", see the note to s.351.

The penalties for the above offences are dealt with by ss.350, 430 and Sch.10.

Note insertion in subs.(2)(c) made by ERRA 2013 Sch.19 para.46.

Minor changes were introduced by SBEEA 2015 s.126 and Sch.9 para.85 to deal with new creditor decision procedures.

357 Fraudulent disposal of property

357(1) [Offence re transfer] The bankrupt is guilty of an offence if he makes or causes to be made, or has in the period of 5 years ending with the commencement of the bankruptcy made or caused to be made, any gift or transfer of, or any charge on, his property.

Section 352 applies to this offence.

357(2) [Interpretation] The reference to making a transfer of or charge on any property includes causing or conniving at the levying of any execution against that property.

357(3) [Offence re concealment or removal of property] The bankrupt is guilty of an offence if he conceals or removes, or has at any time before the commencement of the bankruptcy concealed or removed, any part of his property after, or within 2 months before, the date on which a judgment or order for the payment of money has been obtained against him, being a judgment or order which was not satisfied before the commencement of the bankruptcy.

Section 352 applies to this offence.

S.357(1), (3)

Based partly on BA 1914 s.156 and partly on s.6 of the 1926 Act, this provision prohibits fraudulent disposal by the bankrupt of any "property" (see s.351(a)) within five years of his bankruptcy commencing (for the definition of "commencement", see s.278(a)). It also covers attempts to defeat judgments by concealment of property. For sanctions see *R. v Mungroo* [1998] B.P.I.R. 784.

See also the ruling of Davison DJ sitting in the magistrates court in *DBIS v Compton* [2012] B.P.I.R. 1108, where charges brought under s.357 were dismissed.

S.357(2)

This is a supplementary provision, based partly on s.6 of the 1926 Act. It indicates that the bankrupt commits an offence under s.357(1) if he causes or connives at the levying of execution on his "property".

A bankrupt charged with offences under this section can rely on the general defence in s.352. For the issue of reverse burdens of proof and compliance with ECHR see *Attorney General's Reference (No.1 of 2004)* [2004] EWCA Crim 1025; [2004] B.P.I.R. 1074 and the annotation to s.352 above. The relevant penalties are specified by ss.350, 430 and Sch.10.

358 Absconding

358 The bankrupt is guilty of an offence if–

(a) he leaves, or attempts or makes preparations to leave, England and Wales with any property the value of which is not less than the prescribed amount and possession of which he is required to deliver up to the official receiver or the trustee, or

(b) in the 6 months before the making of the bankruptcy application or (as the case may be) the presentation of the bankruptcy petition, or in the initial period, he did anything which would have been an offence under paragraph (a) if the bankruptcy order had been made immediately before he did it.

Section 352 applies to this offence.

General Note

This largely repeats BA 1914 s.159, although the previous arbitrary figure of £250 has been dropped—unfortunately, in favour of another arbitrary figure to be fixed under s.418. The figure from 1 April 2004 is £1,000: see the Insolvency Proceedings (Monetary Limits) (Amendment) Order 2004 (SI 2004/547). For a critique of this, see the Cork *Report*, para.1889. Note that the offence covers absconding, etc. within the six months prior to the petition.

The s.352 defence applies here. For penalties, see ss.350, 430 and Sch.10. The terms "property", "before petition" and "initial period" are all defined in s.351.

Note amendment made by ERRA 2013 Sch.19 para.47 by the insertion of additional words into para.(b).

359 Fraudulent dealing with property obtained on credit

359(1) [Offence re disposal of property obtained on credit] The bankrupt is guilty of an offence if, in the 12 months before the making of the bankruptcy application or (as the case may be) the presentation of the bankruptcy petition, or in the initial period, he disposed of any property which he had obtained on credit and, at the time he disposed of it, had not paid for.

Section 352 applies to this offence.

359(2) [Offence re knowingly dealing with bankrupt] A person is guilty of an offence if, in the 12 months before the making of the bankruptcy application or (as the case may be) the presentation of the bankruptcy petition or in the initial period, he acquired or received property from the bankrupt knowing or believing–

(a) that the bankrupt owed money in respect of the property, and

(b) that the bankrupt did not intend, or was unlikely to be able, to pay the money he so owed.

359(3) [Disposals etc. in ordinary course of business] A person is not guilty of an offence under subsection (1) or (2) if the disposal, acquisition or receipt of the property was in the ordinary course of a business carried on by the bankrupt at the time of the disposal, acquisition or receipt.

359(4) [Ordinary course of business] In determining for the purposes of this section whether any property is disposed of, acquired or received in the ordinary course of a business carried on by the bankrupt, regard may be had, in particular, to the price paid for the property.

359(5) [Interpretation] In this section references to disposing of property include pawning or pledging it; and references to acquiring or receiving property shall be read accordingly.

S.359(1)

Based on BA 1914 s.154(1), (15), this provision prohibits a bankrupt from disposing of "property" (for definition, see s.351(a)) obtained on credit, where the disposal occurs within 12 months "before petition" (see s.351(c)), or in the "initial period" (see s.351(b)).

The s.352 defence applies here.

On penalties for the offences in this and the following subsections, see ss.350, 430 and Sch.10.

Note amendments to subss.(1) and (2) made by ERRA 2013 Sch.19 para.48.

S.359(2)

Derived from s.154(3), this penalises the knowing recipient of property obtained on credit and unlawfully disposed of under s.359(1). Note again the definitions in s.351.

A defence for the innocent recipient is built into this subsection.

S.359(3), (4)

These are saving provisions for disposals and receipts of "property" in the ordinary course of business. In determining whether this saving facility can operate, the price paid for the property is clearly relevant.

S.359(5)

This provision defines disposal of "property" so as to include pawns and pledges.

360 Obtaining credit; engaging in business

360(1) [Offence re credit, non-disclosure of bankruptcy] The bankrupt is guilty of an offence if–

(a) either alone or jointly with any other person, he obtains credit to the extent of the prescribed amount or more without giving the person from whom he obtains it the relevant information about his status; or

(b) he engages (whether directly or indirectly) in any business under a name other than that in which he was made bankrupt without disclosing to all persons with whom he enters into any business transaction the name in which he was so made.

360(2) [Cases of bankrupt obtaining credit] The reference to the bankrupt obtaining credit includes the following cases–

(a) where goods are bailed to him under a hire-purchase agreement, or agreed to be sold to him under a conditional sale agreement, and

(b) where he is paid in advance (whether in money or otherwise) for the supply of goods or services.

360(3) [Scotland or Northern Ireland] A person whose estate has been sequestrated in Scotland, or who has been adjudged bankrupt in Northern Ireland, is guilty of an offence if, before his discharge, he does anything in England and Wales which would be an offence under subsection (1) if he were an undischarged bankrupt and the sequestration of his estate or the adjudication in Northern Ireland were an adjudication under this Part.

360(4) [Information for s.360(1)(a)] For the purposes of subsection (1)(a), the relevant information about the status of the person in question is the information that he is an undischarged bankrupt or, as the case may be, that his estate has been sequestrated in Scotland and that he has not been discharged.

360(5) [Application of section] This section applies to the bankrupt after discharge while a bankruptcy restrictions order is in force in respect of him.

360(6) [Relevant information] For the purposes of subsection (1)(a) as it applies by virtue of subsection (5), the relevant information about the status of the person in question is the information that a bankruptcy restrictions order is in force in respect of him.

S.360(1)

This prevents an undischarged bankrupt from obtaining credit to the extent of the prescribed amount, either solely or jointly, without disclosing the relevant information about his status. It also prohibits him from carrying on a business under a name which was not the name by which he was declared bankrupt. Note that a person who enters into an individual voluntary arrangement is not subject to these disabilities. The figure from 1 April 2004 is £500 under the Insolvency Proceedings (Monetary Limits) (Amendment) Order 2004 (SI 2004/547) made under s.418. The offence under s.360(1) is one of strict liability (see *R. v Scott* [1998] B.P.I.R. 471) and the general defence under s.352 does not apply, although the offence would not operate where credit is obtained for an independent third person: *R. v Godwin* (1980) 71 Cr. App. Rep. 97.

The sanction for breach of s.360 is specified by ss.350, 430 and Sch.10.

Note amendments to subs.(1)(b) made by ERRA 2013 Sch.19 para.49.

S.360(2)
This represents a change in the law by extending the meaning of "obtaining credit" to cover receipt of goods under a hire-purchase agreement and receiving payment in advance for goods or services. Thus, authorities such as *R. v Miller* [1977] 3 All E.R. 986; and *Fisher v Raven* [1964] A.C. 210 are no longer good law on this point.

S.360(3)
This applies the above offence to a person whose estate is sequestrated in Scotland or who is declared bankrupt in Northern Ireland and who obtains credit in England and Wales.

S.360(4)
This provision defines the "relevant information" for the purposes of s.360(1).

S.360(5), (6)
This was inserted by s.257 of and Sch.21 to EA 2002 with effect from 1 April 2004 to deal with the effect of BROs.

361 Failure to keep proper accounts of business [Repealed]

General Note

This offence of failing to keep accounts was repealed by EA 2002 s.263 with effect from 1 April 2004. However such conduct might justify a BRO. The continued relevance of this now defunct provision was highlighted in *Michael v Official Receiver* [2013] EWHC 4286 (Ch); [2014] B.P.I.R. 666 where Roth J in reducing a BRO from 8 years to 6.5 years indicated that although it was no longer an offence to fail to keep books such a failure was a relevant consideration in determining whether to grant a BRO—see Sch.4A para.2(2)(a). Permission to appeal this ruling has been given—[2014] EWCA Civ 534.

362 Gambling [Repealed]

General Note

This offence of gambling, etc., was repealed by s.263 of EA 2002 with effect from April 2004. Such behaviour is, however, still frowned upon and may form the basis for a bankruptcy restrictions order.

Chapter VII

Powers of Court in Bankruptcy

363 General control of court

363(1) [Power of court] Every bankruptcy is under the general control of the court and, subject to the provisions in this Group of Parts, the court has full power to decide all questions of priorities and all other questions, whether of law or fact, arising in any bankruptcy.

363(2) [Bankrupt to do as directed] Without prejudice to any other provision in this Group of Parts, an undischarged bankrupt or a discharged bankrupt whose estate is still being administered under Chapter IV of this Part shall do all such things as he may be directed to do by the court for the purposes of his bankruptcy or, as the case may be, the administration of that estate.

363(3) [Application for directions] The official receiver or the trustee of a bankrupt's estate may at any time apply to the court for a direction under subsection (2).

363(4) [Contempt of court] If any person without reasonable excuse fails to comply with any obligation imposed on him by subsection (2), he is guilty of a contempt of court and liable to be punished accordingly (in addition to any other punishment to which he may be subject).

S.363(1)
This confers on "the court" (see ss.373 and 385) the power to resolve all disputes in bankruptcy matters. The breadth of the jurisdiction of the court under s.363 was underlined in *Law Society v Shah* [2007] EWHC 2841 (Ch); [2007] B.P.I.R. 1595. See also *Engel v Peri* [2002] EWHC 799 (Ch); [2002] B.P.I.R. 961 where the point was made that the s.363 jurisdiction is still available notwithstanding the fact that the bankruptcy may already have been annulled. For

the use of s.363(1) in the context of an annulment see *Howard v Savage* [2006] EWHC 3693 (Ch); [2007] B.P.I.R. 1097. In *Re Colgate* [1986] Ch. 439, the court used the predecessor of this provision to fix the remuneration of a trustee where this was in dispute. Section 363 may also be of use in fixing the remuneration of the trustee—*Re Cooper* [2005] NICh 1; [2007] B.P.I.R. 1206 (Weatherup J in High Court of Northern Ireland dealing with the equivalent statutory provision in that jurisdiction). Note also *Woodbridge v Smith* [2004] B.P.I.R. 247. For the wide power of the court under s.363 see *Re Gonsalves* [2011] B.P.I.R. 419 (discretion whether to suspend an order for possession of bankrupt's home where Housing Act 1980 applied). Appointment of an additional trustee might also be a suitable use of this power—*Clements v Udal* [2001] B.P.I.R. 454. This provision may be utilised to appoint a trustee in bankruptcy pursuant to a block transfer order—*Donaldson v O'Sullivan* [2008] EWCA Civ 879. On block transfer orders generally see IR 2016 rr.12.35 et seq. There is some discussion of this provision in passing in *Bramston v Haut* [2012] EWCA Civ 1637.

On the potential usage of the control power in s.363(1) see the comments of Chief Registrar Baister in *Dunbar Assets plc v Fowler* [2013] B.P.I.R. 46 at [37]. See also *Barker v Bajjon* [2008] B.P.I.R. 771. The rules are also relevant here: see IR 2016 r.18.23 and Pt 12.

In *Garwood v Bolter* [2015] EWHC 3619 (Ch); [2016] B.P.I.R. 367 HHJ Behrens opined at [25] that this section may in principle confer jurisdiction on the court to make a possession order under the Housing Act 1988.

See *Re Halabi, Ariel v Revenue and Customs Commissioners* [2016] B.P.I.R. 1144 where Mann J notes at [54]–[55] the limitations of s.363.

S.363(2), (4)

This places an undischarged bankrupt squarely under the thumb of the court: see *Hardy v Buchler* [1997] B.P.I.R. 643. If he unreasonably fails to obey its instructions he could be liable for contempt; see *Official Receiver v Cummings-John* [2000] B.P.I.R. 320. In *Boyden v Canty (No.2)* [2007] EWCA Civ 241; [2007] B.P.I.R. 299 failure to comply with s.363 (and other obligations) justified the bankrupt being committed to prison for six months.

See *Simmonds v Pearce* [2017] EWHC 3126 (Admin) for consideration of contempt liability for breach of this provision. In this case the Divisional Court reviewed procedural aspects of contempt liability and also the evidential value of information obtained in a public examination in the light of s.433. The bankrupt was found to be in breach of obligations under ss.363(2) and 333.

An order was made under s.363(2) in *Buchler v Al Midani (No.3)* [2006] EWHC 170 (Ch); [2006] B.P.I.R. 881 to prevent a bankrupt from frustrating the realisation of assets located in Spain by interfering in legal proceedings taking place in that jurisdiction.

Subsection (2) was at issue in *Holtham v Kelmanson* [2006] B.P.I.R. 1422. Here Evans-Lombe J indicated that a former bankrupt who was the absolute owner of land could be ordered under this provision to deliver up property to a trustee and that it was not necessary to consider an application under s.335A or s.14 of the Trusts of Land and Appointment of Trustees Act 1996.

S.363(3)

The trustee or official receiver may apply to the court for a direction that the undischarged bankrupt behave in a certain way. This must not be confused with the power to apply for directions under s.303(2). See *McGrath v Finnegan* [2009] NIMaster 74 where the point was made that official receivers are subject to the rule of honour laid down by the court in *Ex p. James* (1873–74) L.R. 9 Ch. App. 609.

364 Power of arrest

364(1) [Court's power re warrant] In the cases specified in the next subsection the court may cause a warrant to be issued to a constable or prescribed officer of the court–

(a) for the arrest of a debtor to whom a bankruptcy application or a bankruptcy petition relates or of an undischarged bankrupt, or of a discharged bankrupt whose estate is still being administered under Chapter IV of this Part, and

(b) for the seizure of any books, papers, records, money or goods in the possession of a person arrested under the warrant,

and may authorise a person arrested under such a warrant to be kept in custody, and anything seized under such a warrant to be held, in accordance with the rules, until such time as the court may order.

364(2) [Where s.364(1) powers exercisable] The powers conferred by subsection (1) are exercisable in relation to a debtor or undischarged or discharged bankrupt if, at any time after the making of the bankruptcy application or the presentation of the bankruptcy petition relating to him or the making of the bankruptcy order against him, it appears to the court–

(a) that there are reasonable grounds for believing that he has absconded, or is about to abscond, with a view to avoiding or delaying the payment of any of his debts or his appearance to a bankruptcy petition or to avoiding, delaying or disrupting any proceedings in bankruptcy against him or any examination of his affairs, or

(b) that he is about to remove his goods with a view to preventing or delaying possession being taken of them by the official receiver or the trustee of his estate, or

(c) that there are reasonable grounds for believing that he has concealed or destroyed, or is about to conceal or destroy, any of his goods or any books, papers or records which might be of use to his creditors in the course of his bankruptcy or in connection with the administration of his estate, or

(d) that he has, without the leave of the official receiver or the trustee of his estate, removed any goods in his possession which exceed in value such sum as may be prescribed for the purposes of this paragraph, or

(e) that he has failed, without reasonable excuse, to attend any examination ordered by the court.

General Note

Note amendments made to subss.(1) and (2) by ERRA 2013 Sch.19 para.50.

S.364(1)

This provides for the issue of warrants for the arrest of debtors or undischarged bankrupts and for seizure of their books. In *Hickling v Baker* [2007] EWCA Civ 287; [2007] B.P.I.R. 346, the Court of Appeal stressed that in exercising jurisdiction to commit under s.364 the court should seek to conform with the protections guaranteed by art.5 ECHR. The purpose of s.364 was not to punish as such, but to compel a bankrupt to comply with his legal obligations. Although notice of the application was not essential under s.364 it would be normal to expect notice of the application to be given to the bankrupt. Where an application is made without notice the application should explain why that is so. Where a person is arrested under s.364 he should be brought before the court as soon as possible. This case is highly significant in outlining good practice with regard to s.364 committals so as to ensure that there is no breach of art.5 ECHR.

S.364(2)

The court can issue such a warrant if any of the five facts listed in (a)–(e) appear to it to be present. Under BA 1914 s.23 there were only four paras ((a)–(d)), but in substance the grounds have not been added to. The grounds are aimed at debtors who are likely to abscond, avoid public examination or hide assets. What is now para.(d) used to include an arbitrary minimum amount of £60 but this has been scrapped, as the Blagden Committee recommended; but alas in favour of another random figure fixed under s.418. From 1 April 2004 under the Insolvency Proceedings (Monetary Limits) (Amendment) Order 2004 (SI 2004/547) the figure is £1,000.

Note also IR 2016 rr.12.53, 12.54.

365 Seizure of bankrupt's property

365(1) [Court's power re warrant] At any time after a bankruptcy order has been made, the court may, on the application of the official receiver or the trustee of the bankrupt's estate, issue a warrant authorising the person to whom it is directed to seize any property comprised in the bankrupt's estate which is, or any books, papers or records relating to the bankrupt's estate or affairs which are, in the possession or under the control of the bankrupt or any other person who is required to deliver the property, books, papers or records to the official receiver or trustee.

365(2) [Power to break open premises etc.] Any person executing a warrant under this section may, for the purpose of seizing any property comprised in the bankrupt's estate or any books, papers or records relating to the bankrupt's estate or affairs, break open any premises where the bankrupt or anything that may be seized under the warrant is or is believed to be and any receptacle of the bankrupt which contains or is believed to contain anything that may be so seized.

365(3) [Power of court re search] If, after a bankruptcy order has been made, the court is satisfied that any property comprised in the bankrupt's estate is, or any books, papers or records relating to the bankrupt's estate or affairs are, concealed in any premises not belonging to him, it may issue a warrant authorising any constable or prescribed officer of the court to search those premises for the property, books, papers or records.

365(4) [Execution of s.365(3) warrant] A warrant under subsection (3) shall not be executed except in the prescribed manner and in accordance with its terms.

S.365(1), (2)
These provisions allow the court to issue a warrant for the seizure of the bankrupt's property even though it may be in the possession of a third party. Forcing entry into premises or breaking open "receptacles" is permitted when executing such a warrant. For an example of an order being made under s.365 see *Williams v Mohammed (No.2)* [2012] B.P.I.R. 238. A s.365 order was granted by Chief Registrar Baister in *Re A Bankrupt* [2012] B.P.I.R. 469 in favour of a German insolvency administrator by applying the recognition principle in art.25 of the EC Regulation on Insolvency Proceedings 1346/2000. Chief Registrar Baister also made a s.365 order in *Nicholson v Fayinka* [2014] B.P.I.R. 692.

S.365(3), (4)
A search warrant (in the prescribed form) for a third party's premises may also be obtained under this section, although the court must be satisfied that the bankrupt's property, etc. is concealed there. Fishing expeditions will not be permitted.

Note also IR 2016 rr.12.53, 12.56.

366 Inquiry into bankrupt's dealings and property

366(1) [Power of court to summon bankrupt to appear] At any time after a bankruptcy order has been made the court may, on the application of the official receiver or the trustee of the bankrupt's estate, summon to appear before it–

(a) the bankrupt or the bankrupt's spouse or former spouse or civil partner or former civil partner,

(b) any person known or believed to have any property comprised in the bankrupt's estate in his possession or to be indebted to the bankrupt,

(c) any person appearing to the court to be able to give information concerning the bankrupt or the bankrupt's dealings, affairs or property.

The court may require any such person as is mentioned in paragraph (b) or (c) to submit a witness statement verified by a statement of truth to the court containing an account of his dealings with the bankrupt or to produce any documents in his possession or under his control relating to the bankrupt or the bankrupt's dealings, affairs or property.

366(2) [Application of s.366(3)] Without prejudice to section 364, the following applies in a case where–

(a) a person without reasonable excuse fails to appear before the court when he is summoned to do so under this section, or

(b) there are reasonable grounds for believing that a person has absconded, or is about to abscond, with a view to avoiding his appearance before the court under this section.

366(3) [Issue of warrant re non-appearance] The court may, for the purpose of bringing that person and anything in his possession before the court, cause a warrant to be issued to a constable or prescribed officer of the court–

(a) for the arrest of that person, and

(b) for the seizure of any books, papers, records, money or goods in that person's possession.

366(4) [Power re custody etc.] The court may authorise a person arrested under such a warrant to be kept in custody, and anything seized under such a warrant to be held, in accordance with the rules, until that person is brought before the court under the warrant or until such other time as the court may order.

S.366(1)
Amended by LRO 2010 (SI 2010/18). This permits the trustee or official receiver to ask the court to examine the bankrupt privately (or his spouse, or former spouse, or third parties believed to be in possession of the bankrupt's property or of information about his affairs). Civil partners and former civil partners fall within this section by virtue of Sch.27 to the Civil Partnership Act 2004. On the meaning of "affairs", see s.385(2). The power to direct the bankrupt to attend for examination survives discharge: *Oakes v Simms* [1997] B.P.I.R. 499. On the linkage between ss.366 and 364 see *Hickling v Baker* [2007] EWCA Civ 287; [2007] B.P.I.R. 346.

This changes the previous law in a number of respects. The BA 1914 provision referred to the bankrupt's "wife", which made an assumption which can no longer be justified in an age of sexual equality. The new provision also allows the court to require affidavits from the persons mentioned in para.(a) and (b). This reform, which was recommended by the Cork *Report*, para.903, reverses the rule in *Ex p. Reynolds* (1882) 21 Ch. D. 601.

On the relationship between s.366 and professional privilege see *Re Murjani* [1996] 1 W.L.R. 1498; [1996] B.C.C. 278; and *Re Ouvaroff* [1997] B.P.I.R. 712. Where inquiries are made of a bank concerning a client's affairs, major issues of confidentiality can arise—*Christofi v Barclays Bank plc* [1999] B.P.I.R. 855.

It was held in *Re Tucker (a Bankrupt) Ex p. Tucker* [1990] Ch. 148 that the court had no jurisdiction under s.25(6) of BA 1914 (the precursor of the present section) over British subjects resident abroad. In *Re Seagull Manufacturing Co Ltd* [1992] Ch. 128 at 137; [1991] B.C.C. 550 at 555 Mummery J expressed the view that there was little doubt that, on the authority of *Re Tucker*, the court would construe ss.366 and 367 as subject to the same territorial limitation. In the Court of Appeal in the same case, [1993] Ch. 345; [1993] B.C.C. 241, no opinion was expressed on this point. The potential extraterritorial effect of s.366 was considered by Patten J in *Buchler v Al Midani (No.2)* [2005] EWHC 3183 (Ch); [2006] B.P.I.R. 867. The English courts would take note of the attitude of foreign courts before exercising discretion under s.366 to make a disclosure order against a party based abroad. Contrast the position in regard to a public examination under s.133: see the notes to that section and to s.236. *Re Tucker* (above) was followed by David Richards J in *Re MF Global UK Ltd* [2015] EWHC 2319 (Ch). But *MF Global* was not followed by HHJ Hodge QC in *Official Receiver v Norriss* [2015] EWHC 2697 (Ch). This difference of opinion on a matter of the scope of the provision will have to be resolved at some later date in a case taken to the Court of Appeal. The position may be different where s.426 can be called into aid: *McIsaac, Petitioners* [1994] B.C.C. 410. Note also *Handelsveem BV v Hill* [2011] B.P.I.R. 1024 (enforcement of a s.366 order of English court by a Dutch Supreme Court using EC Regulation (1346/2000) procedures).

For the principles governing the exercise of discretion under s.366 see the comments of Rimer J in *Long v Farrer & Co* [2004] EWHC 1774 (Ch); [2004] B.P.I.R. 1218.

The case of *Hooper v Duncan Lewis (Solicitors) Ltd* [2010] B.P.I.R. 591 should be noted in this context. Here the court acceded to an application for the provision of information under s.366. The order covered disclosure of client files and an examination of the chief executive of the firm of solicitors.

For the permitted use of material obtained by compulsion under this provision see the judgment of Arnold J in *Willmont v Shlosberg; Re Webinvest Ltd* [2017] EWHC 2446 (Ch).

On s.366 generally see *Albert v Albert* [1996] B.P.I.R. 232; and *Bird v Hadkinson* [1999] B.P.I.R. 653. Further provisions on s.366 examinations are contained in the rules: see IR 2016 rr.12.17–12.22. For an illuminating review see Frith (2005) 21 I.L. & P. 141.

S.366(2)–(4)
The court can order the arrest of absconders, plus the seizure of property. Note also IR 2016 rr.12.53 and 12.55.

367 Court's enforcement powers under s.366

367(1) [Power to order delivery] If it appears to the court, on consideration of any evidence obtained under section 366 or this section, that any person has in his possession any property comprised in the bankrupt's estate, the court may, on the application of the official receiver or the trustee of the bankrupt's estate, order that person to deliver the whole or any part of the property to the official receiver or the trustee at such time, in such manner and on such terms as the court thinks fit.

367(2) [Power to order payment from bankrupt debtor] If it appears to the court, on consideration of any evidence obtained under section 366 or this section, that any person is indebted to the bankrupt, the court may, on the application of the official receiver or the trustee of the bankrupt's estate, order that person to pay to the official receiver or trustee, at such time and in such manner as the court may direct, the whole or part of the amount due, whether in full discharge of the debt or otherwise as the court thinks fit.

367(3) [Place of examination] The court may, if it thinks fit, order that any person who if within the jurisdiction of the court would be liable to be summoned to appear before it under section 366 shall be examined in any part of the United Kingdom where he may be for the time being, or in any place outside the United Kingdom.

367(4) [Examination on oath] Any person who appears or is brought before the court under section 366 or this section may be examined on oath, either orally or by interrogatories, concerning the bankrupt or the bankrupt's dealings, affairs and property.

S.367(1), (2)
If, as a result of information gleaned from the examination, it appears that the bankrupt's property is in the possession of a third party, the court can order it to be handed over. Debts owing to the bankrupt can also be ordered to be paid.

S.367(3)
Examinations under s.366 do not have to be held in the UK. In *Re Tucker (a Bankrupt) Ex p. Tucker* [1990] Ch. 148 (decided under BA 1914 s.25(6)), the Court of Appeal refused to exercise its discretion to allow examination of a witness in Belgium, since it was not possible to compel him to attend such examination. On the question whether ss.366–367 extend to the examinations of witnesses abroad, see the notes to s.366.

S.367(4)
This deals with the form of the examination under s.366. Note also IR 2016 rr.12.17–12.22.

368 Provision corresponding to s.366, where interim receiver appointed

368 Sections 366 and 367 apply where an interim receiver has been appointed under section 286 as they apply where a bankruptcy order has been made, as if–

(a) references to the official receiver or the trustee were to the interim receiver, and

(b) references to the bankrupt and to his estate were (respectively) to the debtor and his property.

General Note

This extends ss.366 and 367 to situations where the debtor has not yet been declared bankrupt, but an interim receiver has been appointed after presentation of the petition under s.286.

369 Order for production of documents by inland revenue

369(1) [Power of court] For the purposes of an examination under section 290 (public examination of bankrupt) or proceedings under sections 366 to 368, the court may, on the application of the official receiver or the trustee of the bankrupt's estate, order an inland revenue official to produce to the court–

(a) any return, account or accounts submitted (whether before or after the commencement of the bankruptcy) by the bankrupt to any inland revenue official,

(b) any assessment or determination made (whether before or after the commencement of the bankruptcy) in relation to the bankrupt by any inland revenue official, or

(c) any correspondence (whether before or after the commencement of the bankruptcy) between the bankrupt and any inland revenue official.

369(2) [Order re disclosure of document] Where the court has made an order under subsection (1) for the purposes of any examination or proceedings, the court may, at any time after the document to which the order relates is produced to it, by order authorise the disclosure of the document, or of any part of its contents, to the official receiver, the trustee of the bankrupt's estate or the bankrupt's creditors.

369(3) [Condition for s.369(1) order] The court shall not address an order under subsection (1) to an inland revenue official unless it is satisfied that that official is dealing, or has dealt, with the affairs of the bankrupt.

369(4) [Where s.369(1) document not in official's possession] Where any document to which an order under subsection (1) relates is not in the possession of the official to whom the order is addressed, it is the duty of that official to take all reasonable steps to secure possession of it and, if he fails to do so, to report the reasons for his failure to the court.

369(5) [Where document held by another official] Where any document to which an order under subsection (1) relates is in the possession of an inland revenue official other than the one to whom the order is addressed, it is the duty of the official in possession of the document, at the request of the official to whom the order is addressed, to deliver it to the official making the request.

369(6) ["Inland revenue official"] In this section "inland revenue official" means any inspector or collector of taxes appointed by the Commissioners of Inland Revenue or any person appointed by the Commissioners to serve in any other capacity.

369(7) [Non-application] This section does not apply for the purposes of an examination under sections 366 and 367 which takes place by virtue of section 368 (interim receiver).

S.369(1), (3), (6)
The court can order Inland Revenue officials (as defined by s.369(6)) to hand over tax documents relating to the bankrupt's financial affairs to assist examinations under ss.290 or 366. Only officials dealing with the bankrupt can be so directed.

S.369(2)
The court can order the disclosure of any document ordered to be produced under s.369(1) to the official receiver or the trustee.

S.369(4), (5)
Where the court makes an order under s.369(1), an Inland Revenue official must use his best efforts to obtain the documents in question, and this may involve securing possession of them from another Inland Revenue official.

S.369(7)
This states that s.369 does not apply where the debtor has not been declared bankrupt and where there is merely an examination under ss.366, 367 at the request of his interim receiver under s.368.

For further information, see IR 2016 rr.10.118–10.120.

370 Power to appoint special manager

370(1) [Power of court] The court may, on an application under this section, appoint any person to be the special manager–

(a) of a bankrupt's estate, or

(b) of the business of an undischarged bankrupt, or

(c) of the property or business of a debtor in whose case an interim receiver has been appointed under section 286.

370(2) [Application to court] An application under this section may be made by the interim receiver or the trustee of the bankrupt's estate in any case where it appears to the interim receiver or trustee that the nature of the estate, property or business, or the interests of the creditors generally, require the appointment of another person to manage the estate, property or business.

370(3) [Powers of special manager] A special manager appointed under this section has such powers as may be entrusted to him by the court.

370(4) [Powers included in s.370(3)] The power of the court under subsection (3) to entrust powers to a special manager includes power to direct that any provision in this Group of Parts that has effect in relation to the official receiver, interim receiver or trustee shall have the like effect in relation to the special manager for the purposes of the carrying out by the special manager of any of the functions of the official receiver, interim receiver or trustee.

370(5) [Duties of special manager] A special manager appointed under this section shall–

(a) give such security as may be prescribed,

(b) prepare and keep such accounts as may be prescribed, and

(c) produce those accounts in accordance with the rules to the Secretary of State or to such other persons as may be prescribed.

S.370(1), (2)

The court can appoint a special manager of the bankrupt's estate or business, or indeed of a debtor's estate or business where an interim receiver has been installed. The application may be made by the official receiver or trustee where it appears that it is in the interests of the creditors that such an appointment be made. Under s.10 of the 1914 Act the official receiver made the appointment. Note amendments to this provision made by DA 2015 s.19 and Sch.6 para.14 to reflect the fact that a private insolvency practitioner may now act as interim receiver.

For the question of remuneration see Sch.9 para.20.

This section should be read in conjunction with s.287 and IR 2016 rr.10.94–10.98.

371 Re-direction of bankrupt's letters, etc.

371(1) [Power of court] Where a bankruptcy order has been made, the court may from time to time, on the application of the official receiver or the trustee of the bankrupt's estate, order a postal operator (within the meaning of Part 3 of the Postal Services Act 2011) to re-direct and send or deliver to the official receiver or trustee or otherwise any postal packet (within the meaning of that Act) which would otherwise be sent or delivered by the operator concerned to the bankrupt at such place or places as may be specified in the order.

371(2) [Duration of court order] An order under this section has effect for such period, not exceeding 3 months, as may be specified in the order.

S.371(1)

This provision allows the court on an application from the official receiver or trustee to order a postal operator to redirect the bankrupt's mail after a bankruptcy order has been made. The mail can then be opened by the official receiver or trustee (see s.365). This provision dates back to s.85 of the Debtors Act 1869. Unfortunately there are questions as to its legality in the light of art.8 ECHR and its relationship with the Interception of Communications Act 1985: see Jaconelli [1994] Conv. 370 on these intriguing issues. In *Foxley v UK* [2000] B.P.I.R. 1009 the European Court of Human Rights held that a s.371 order does not per se breach art.8 ECHR provided its terms are strictly observed and it is not used in a disproportionate manner. Interception of communications between a bankrupt and his lawyers is not acceptable. Further consideration to the issue of redirection of post was given by the European Court of Human Rights in *Narinen v Finland* [2004] B.P.I.R. 914. Here it was stressed that any interference with a debtor's correspondence would only be permitted under a precise legal authority. For authoritative advice on the correct procedure to be adopted see *Singh v Official Receiver* [1997] B.P.I.R. 530. Note also the newly introduced IR 2016 r.10.166. For a recent analysis of this provision see *Smedley v Brittain* [2008] B.P.I.R. 219, where the question of compliance with art.8 of the ECHR was fully considered.

See *Re A Bankrupt* [2012] B.P.I.R. 469 where Chief Registrar Baister made such an order in favour of a German insolvency administrator on an application that was founded upon the co-operation mechanisms embodied in art.25 of the EC Regulation on Insolvency Proceedings (1346/2000).

Note that the power to open the bankrupt's mail does not extend to outgoing mail. Moreover, a debtor who enters into an individual voluntary arrangement to settle his debts cannot have his mail opened under this provision.

In s.371(1) the words "a postal operator (within the meaning of the Postal Services Act 2000)" substituted for the words "the Post Office", the words "that Act" substituted for the words "the Post Office Act 1953" and the words "the operator concerned" substituted for the word "them" by the Postal Services Act 2000 s.127(4), Sch.8 para.20 as from 26 March 2001 (see the Postal Service Act 2000 (Commencement No.4 and Transitional and Savings Provisions) Order 2001 (SI 2001/1148 (C. 37)) art.2(2), Sch. Note that the commencement date of 26 March 2001 had previously been set by the Postal Services Act 2000 (Commencement No.1 and Transitional Provisions) Order 2000 (SI

2000/2957 (C. 88)) art.2(3), Sch.3, but that implementation was revoked by art.43 of SI 2001/1148 (C. 37). Further amendment to subs.(1) was made by the Postal Services Act 2011 Sch.12 para.125 which substituted the words for "the Postal Services Act 2000" with "Part 3 of the Postal Services Act 2011" with effect from 1 October 2011 (see the Postal Services Act 2011 (Commencement No.1 and Transitional Provisions) Order 2011 (SI 2011/2329 (C. 82)) art.3).

S.371(2)
The maximum period of interference permitted by the order is three months, as was the case previously.

Part X

Individual Insolvency: General Provisions

372 Supplies of gas, water, electricity, etc.

372(1) [Application] This section applies where on any day ("the relevant day")–

(a) a bankruptcy order is made against an individual or an interim receiver of an individual's property is appointed, or

(b) a voluntary arrangement proposed by an individual is approved under Part VIII,

and in this section "the office-holder" means the official receiver, the trustee in bankruptcy, the interim receiver or the supervisor of the voluntary arrangement, as the case may be.

372(2) [Where s.372(3) request] If a request falling within the next subsection is made for the giving after the relevant day of any of the supplies mentioned in subsection (4), the supplier–

(a) may make it a condition of the giving of the supply that the office-holder personally guarantees the payment of any charges in respect of the supply, but

(b) shall not make it a condition of the giving of the supply, or do anything which has the effect of making it a condition of the giving of the supply, that any outstanding charges in respect of a supply given to the individual before the relevant day are paid.

372(3) [Type of request] A request falls within this subsection if it is made–

(a) by or with the concurrence of the office-holder, and

(b) for the purposes of any business which is or has been carried on by the individual, by a firm or partnership of which the individual is or was a member, or by an agent or manager for the individual or for such a firm or partnership.

372(4) [Supplies in s.372(2)] The supplies referred to in subsection (2) are–

(a) a supply of gas by a gas supplier within the meaning of Part I of the Gas Act 1986;

(aa) a supply of gas by a person within paragraph 1 of Schedule 2A to the Gas Act 1986 (supply by landlords etc.);

(b) a supply of electricity by an electricity supplier within the meaning of Part I of the Electricity Act 1989,

(ba) a supply of electricity by a class of person within Class A (small suppliers) or Class B (resale) of Schedule 4 to the Electricity (Class Exemptions from the Requirement for a Licence) Order 2001 (S.I. 2001/3270);

(c) a supply of water by a water undertaker,

(ca) a supply of water by a licensed water supplier within the meaning of the Water Industry Act 1991;

(cb) a supply of water by a person who has an interest in the premises to which the supply is given;

(d) a supply of communications services by a provider of a public electronic communications service;

(e) a supply of communications services by a person who carries on a business which includes giving such supplies;

(f) a supply of goods or services mentioned in subsection (4A) by a person who carries on a business which includes giving such supplies, where the supply is for the purpose of enabling or facilitating anything to be done by electronic means.

372(4A) [Goods and services in s.372(4)(f)] The goods and services referred to in subsection (4)(f) are–

(a) point of sale terminals;

(b) computer hardware and software;

(c) information, advice and technical assistance in connection with the use of information technology;

(d) data storage and processing;

(e) website hosting.

372(5) [Definitions] The following applies to expressions used in subsection (4)–

(a) Repealed]

(b) [Repealed]

(c) "communications services" do not include electronic communications services to the extent that they are used to broadcast or otherwise transmit programme services (within the meaning of the Communications Act 2003).

General Note

This section represents a late change of mind by the government in that it did not appear in the early forms of the 1985 Bill. It is designed to stop public utilities "blackmailing" the trustee in bankruptcy, etc. of an insolvent individual into paying arrears in respect of public utility supplies as a precondition to receiving supplies in the future. It was not clear at common law whether a public utility could behave in such a way: see *Re Flack* [1900] 2 Q.B. 32—but the Cork Committee (*Report*, para.1466) favoured legislation to outlaw expressly such "priority gaining".

For the corresponding provisions in corporate insolvencies, see s.233.

ERRA 2013 s.92(2) enables the Secretary of State to extend the potential scope of this provision. Note also ss.94 and 95 of the 2013 Act for further details and information on potential supplementary orders. These powers have now been exercised. On 9 February 2015 the government announced through Written Statement (HCWS265) that continuity of essential IT and utility supplies will be protected from termination, subject to a range of measures designed to avoid hardship to suppliers. Section 372 will be amended in subs.(4) and by the addition of subs.(4A) as part of this rescue friendly strategy and a new s.372A will be inserted to protect against the operation of termination clauses against a customer undergoing a voluntary arrangement. A number of protective mechanisms are in turn offered to suppliers to maintain a balance of fairness. These will include the possibility of an application to court to terminate supplies and the ability to seek personal guarantees from insolvency practitioners. Insolvency practitioners will be encouraged to contact suppliers to discuss their needs. A statutory instrument has been laid before Parliament with a view to effecting these changes, which will apply to contracts made after 1 October 2015. See the Insolvency (Protection of Essential Supplies) Order 2015 (SI 2015/989).

Note also amendments made by DA 2015 s.19 and Sch.6 to remove all references to deeds of arrangement.

S.372(1)–(3)

These provisions enable an office-holder (as defined by s.372(1)) to request a supply from a public utility. The supplier, although he may require the office-holder to guarantee future payments personally, cannot require arrears to be paid as a precondition to the making of the supply.

S.372(4), (5)

These provisions list the public utilities that are covered by this section—gas, electricity, water and telecommunications (but not cable services). Subsections (4) and (5) have been amended to cope with utility privatisation legislation. Section 372(4)(d) substituted by the Communications Act 2003 Sch.17 para.82(3)(a) as from 25 July 2003 (see Communications Act 2003 (Commencement No.1) Order 2003 (SI 2003/1900 (C. 77)) art.2(1) and Sch.1). Previously in s.372(4) para.(a) substituted by the Gas Act 1995 s.16(1), Sch.4 para.14(3) as from 1 March 1996 (see Gas Act 1995 (Appointed Day and Commencement) Order 1996 (SI 1996/218 (C. 4)) art.2).

Paragraph (b) substituted by the Utilities Act 2000 s.108 Sch.6 Pt III para.47(3)(b) as from 1 October 2001 (see Utilities Act 2000 (Commencement No.6 and Transitional Provisions) Order 2001 (SI 2001/3266 (C. 106)) arts 1 and 2 and Sch.), subject to transitional provisions. Previously para.(b) substituted by the Electricity Act 1989 s.112(1) and Sch.16 para.35(1), (3)(a) as from 31 March 1990 (see Electricity Act 1989 s.113(2) and SI 1990/117 (C. 4)).

372A Further protection of essential supplies

372A(1) [Cessation of insolvency-related term of contract of supply] An insolvency-related term of a contract for the supply of essential goods or services to an individual ceases to have effect if–

(a) a voluntary arrangement proposed by the individual is approved under Part 8, and

(b) the supply is for the purpose of a business which is or has been carried on by the individual, by a firm or partnership of which the individual is or was a member, or by an agent or manager for the individual or for such a firm or partnership.

372A(2) [Non-cessation of insolvency-related term] An insolvency-related term of a contract does not cease to have effect by virtue of subsection (1) to the extent that–

(a) it provides for the contract or the supply to terminate, or any other thing to take place, because the individual becomes subject to an insolvency procedure other than a voluntary arrangement;

(b) it entitles a supplier to terminate the contract or the supply, or do any other thing, because the individual becomes subject to an insolvency procedure other than a voluntary arrangement; or

(c) it entitles a supplier to terminate the contract or the supply because of an event that occurs, or may occur, after the voluntary arrangement proposed by the individual is approved.

372A(3) [Power of supplier to terminate contract or supply] Where an insolvency-related term of a contract ceases to have effect under this section the supplier may–

(a) terminate the contract, if the condition in subsection (4) is met;

(b) terminate the supply, if the condition in subsection (5) is met.

372A(4) [Condition for terminating contract under s.372A(3)(a)] The condition in this subsection is that–

(a) the supervisor of the voluntary arrangement consents to the termination of the contract,

(b) the court grants permission for the termination of the contract, or

(c) any charges in respect of the supply that are incurred after the voluntary arrangement is approved are not paid within the period of 28 days beginning with the day on which payment is due.

The court may grant permission under paragraph (b) only if satisfied that the continuation of the contract would cause the supplier hardship.

372A(5) [Condition for terminating supply under s.372A(3)(b)] The condition in this subsection is that–

(a) the supplier gives written notice to the supervisor of the voluntary arrangement that the supply will be terminated unless the supervisor personally guarantees the payment of any charges in respect of the continuation of the supply after the arrangement was approved, and

(b) the supervisor does not give that guarantee within the period of 14 days beginning with the day the notice is received.

372A(6) [Securing protection of interests of suppliers] For the purposes of securing that the interests of suppliers are protected, where–

(a) an insolvency-related term of a contract (the "original term") ceases to have effect by virtue of subsection (1), and

(b) a subsequent voluntary arrangement proposed by the individual is approved,

the contract is treated for the purposes of subsections (1) to (5) as if, immediately before the subsequent voluntary arrangement proposed by the individual is approved, it included an insolvency-related term identical to the original term.

372A(7) [Contract for supply of essential goods or services] A contract for the supply of essential goods or services is a contract for a supply mentioned in section 372(4).

372A(8) [Insolvency-related term of contract for supply of essential goods or services] An insolvency-related term of a contract for the supply of essential goods or services to an individual is a provision of the contract under which–

(a) the contract or the supply would terminate, or any other thing would take place, because the voluntary arrangement proposed by the individual is approved,

(b) the supplier would be entitled to terminate the contract or the supply, or to do any other thing, because the voluntary arrangement proposed by the individual is approved, or

(c) the supplier would be entitled to terminate the contract or the supply because of an event that occurred before the voluntary arrangement proposed by the individual is approved.

372A(9) [No effect before 1 October 2015] Subsection (1) does not have effect in relation to a contract entered into before 1st October 2015.

General Note

This was inserted with effect from 1 October 2015 by the Insolvency (Protection of Essential Supplies) Order 2015 (SI 2015/989). This applies only in the case of an IVA and will neutralise termination provisions in contracts made on or after 1 October 2015. There are exceptions to this restriction on the right of termination: if the supplies remain unpaid for after 20 days or the supervisor fails within 14 days to give a personal guarantee as requested.

373 Jurisdiction in relation to insolvent individuals

373(1) [High Court and county courts] The High Court and the county court have jurisdiction throughout England and Wales for the purposes of the Parts in this Group.

373(2) [Powers of county court] For the purposes of those Parts, the county court has, in addition to its ordinary jurisdiction, all the powers and jurisdiction of the High Court; and the orders of the court may be enforced accordingly in the prescribed manner.

373(3) [Exercise of jurisdiction] Jurisdiction for the purposes of those Parts is exercised–

(a) by the High Court or the county court in relation to the proceedings which, in accordance with the rules, are allocated to the London insolvency district, and

(b) by the county court in relation to the proceedings which are so allocated to any other insolvency district.

373(4) [Operation of s.373(3)] Subsection (3) is without prejudice to the transfer of proceedings from one court to another in the manner prescribed by the rules; and nothing in that subsection invalidates any proceedings on the grounds that they were initiated or continued in the wrong court.

S.373(1)

This vests bankruptcy jurisdiction in the High Court and the county courts in the case of England and Wales. See also Pt 7 of the rules here. For the fees in county court proceedings see the County Court Fees (Amendment No.2) Order

1986 (SI 1986/2143). See the ruling of Morritt C in *Revenue and Customs Commissioners v Earley* [2011] EWHC 1783 (Ch) on the jurisdiction of the High Court notwithstanding the terms of IR r.5.14B(2) (now IR 2016 rr.8.20–8.21). Note amendments made by Sch.9 of the Crime and Courts Act 2013 reflecting general reforms to the county court system.

S.373(2)

In bankruptcy matters county courts are to have all the powers of the High Court. This was the case under BA 1914 s.103. See here *Re a Debtor (No.2A of 1980)* [1981] Ch. 148.

S.373(3)

This provision allocates cases between the High Court and county courts—much will depend upon the "insolvency districts" which are described in s.374. Note amendment by the London Insolvency District (Central London County Court) Order 2011 (SI 2011/761). Note amendments made by Sch.9 of the Crime and Courts Act 2013 reflecting general reforms to the county court system.

S.373(4)

The transfer of proceedings from one court to another is permitted. Note IR 2016 rr.12.30–12.34. See also IR 2016 Sch.6, for insolvency courts.

374 Insolvency districts

374(1) [Order by Lord Chancellor] The Lord Chancellor may, with the concurrence of the Lord Chief Justice, by order designate the areas which are for the time being to be comprised, for the purposes of the Parts in this Group, in the London insolvency district and the insolvency district, or districts of the county court.

374(2) [Incidental provisions etc.] An order under this section may contain such incidental, supplemental and transitional provisions as may appear to the Lord Chancellor and the Lord Chief Justice necessary or expedient.

374(3) [Order by statutory instrument] An order under this section shall be made by statutory instrument and, after being made, shall be laid before each House of Parliament.

374(4) [Relevant districts] Subject to any order under this section–

(a) the district which, immediately before the appointed day, is the London bankruptcy district becomes, on that day, the London insolvency district;

(b) any district which immediately before that day is the bankruptcy district of a county court becomes, on that day, the insolvency district of that court, and

(c) any county court which immediately before that day is excluded from having jurisdiction in bankruptcy is excluded, on and after that day, from having jurisdiction for the purposes of the Parts in this Group.

374(5) [LCJ nominee] The Lord Chief Justice may nominate a judicial office holder (as defined in section 109(4) of the Constitutional Reform Act 2005) to exercise his functions under this section.

S.374(1), (4), (5)

The Lord Chancellor may by order designate the insolvency districts—certain county courts can be prevented from handling bankruptcy matters, whereas others may be given this jurisdiction for the first time. See for example the Civil Courts (Amendment No.3) Order 1992 (SI 1992/1810), the Civil Courts (Amendment) Order 1998 (SI 1998/1880), the Civil Courts (Amendment) (No.2) Order 1998 (SI 1998/2910) and the Civil Courts (Amendment) Order 2006 (SI 2006/1542). Subject to this power, existing jurisdictional patterns are to be retained. For alternative county courts see IR 2016 Sch.6. See the London Insolvency District (Central London County Court) Order 2011 (SI 2011/761).

Subsections (1) and (2) were amended and a new subs.(5) inserted by the Constitutional Reform Act 2005 s.15 and Sch.4 Pt I para.187.

Note amendments made by Sch.9 of the Crime and Courts Act 2013 reflecting general reforms to the county court system.

S.374(2), (3)
These provisions permit any order by the Lord Chancellor to deal with ancillary matters and regulate the mode by which such orders are to be made.

See IR 2016 r.10.37 and Sch.6.

375 Appeals etc. from courts exercising insolvency jurisdiction

375(1) [Review, rescission etc.] Every court having jurisdiction for the purposes of the Parts in this Group may review, rescind or vary any order made by it in the exercise of that jurisdiction.

375(2) [Appeals] An appeal from a decision made in the exercise of jurisdiction for the purposes of those Parts by the county court or by an insolvency and companies court judge lies to a single judge of the High Court; and an appeal from a decision of that judge on such an appeal lies to the Court of Appeal.

375(3) [No other appeals] The county court is not, in the exercise of its jurisdiction for the purposes of those Parts, to be subject to be restrained by the order of any other court, and no appeal lies from its decision in the exercise of that jurisdiction except as provided by this section.

S.375(1)
This confers a general "safety valve" power on the courts to review, rescind or vary orders on bankruptcy matters. The equivalent in corporate insolvency law is IR 2016 r.12.59 and broadly speaking similar principles should be applied: *Midrome Ltd v Shaw* [1993] B.C.C. 659. See also the comments of the court in *Re Broadside Colours and Chemicals Ltd* [2012] EWHC 195 (Ch)—noted in the annotation to IR 2016 r.12.59. A rescission of a bankruptcy order granted under this provision does not have to be gazetted—*Smeaton v Equifax plc* [2013] EWCA Civ 108; [2013] B.P.I.R. 231. This review jurisdiction must be kept flexible but must not be allowed to become a gateway for late appeals or to undermine the principle of *res judicata: Re Debtors (No.VA7 and VA8) Ex p. Stevens* [1996] B.P.I.R. 101; and *Brillouet v Hachette Magazines* [1996] B.P.I.R. 518 or to avoid other restrictions on applications to the court—*Hurst v Bennett (No.2)* [2002] B.P.I.R. 102. It is not appropriate to allow s.375 to be used as a further appeal mechanism where the bankrupt has exhausted his appeal rights—*Egleton v Inland Revenue Commissioners* [2003] EWHC 3226 (Ch); [2004] B.P.I.R. 476. The comments of HHJ Kaye QC in *Harvey v Dunbar Assets plc* [2015] EWHC 3355 (Ch); [2016] B.P.I.R. 48 about not allowing arguments that have been dismissed at an earlier hearing to be rerun are apposite to the s.375 jurisdiction. If a bankrupt persists in making applications under s.375 to reopen issues finally determined the court might be prepared to grant a civil restraint order—*Hurst v Bennett* [2004] EWCA Civ 230; [2004] B.P.I.R. 732. For a successful attempt to invoke the jurisdiction see *Fitch v Official Receiver* [1996] 1 W.L.R. 242, CA; [1996] B.C.C. 328. For a very unusual case where the s.375 jurisdiction was used to procure an annulment see *Amihyia v Official Receiver* [2005] B.P.I.R. 264. The recurring issue of the relationship between annulment under s.282 and rescission under s.375 is reviewed in *Webster v Mackay* [2013] EWHC 2571 (Ch); [2013] B.P.I.R. 1136. Rescission might be resorted to more frequently in view of *Yang v Official Receiver* [2017] EWCA Civ 1465. In this latter case we find a rare example of the jurisdiction to rescind being used.

A comprehensive review of the s.375 review mechanism was conducted by Laddie J in *Papanicola (as trustee in bankruptcy for Mak) v Humphreys* [2005] EWHC 335 (Ch); [2005] 2 All E.R. 418. Key points to emerge from the judgment include:

- discretionary nature of the jurisdiction;
- onus on applicant to persuade court to exercise this exceptional discretion;
- ability of court to weigh up wide range of circumstances including events occurring after original court order and facts not brought to the attention of the court (subject to satisfactory explanation);
- a better presentation of matters put before the original hearing was not something that the review jurisdiction was intended to encourage;
- CPR 39.3(3)–(5), although not formally engaged by s.375, was relevant when exercising the review jurisdiction.

See *Cole v Howlett* [2015] EWHC 1697 (Ch); [2015] B.P.I.R. 763 where Peter Smith J examined the analogous jurisdiction under the CPR and explained the linkage with s.375. This provision was considered by Registrar Briggs in *Re Riemann* [2015] B.P.I.R. 1405 where the court found no justification for rescinding a bankruptcy order where the bankrupt had since been discharged.

In *Ross v Revenue and Customs Commissioners* [2012] EWHC 1054 (Ch); [2012] B.P.I.R. 843 Norris J stressed the wide discretion given to the court under s.375 and made the point that on review the court could consider new material that had come to light since the original order was made. That said, the onus was on the applicant to show the presence of exceptional circumstances justifying the quashing of the original order. Guidance was given on what new material might be relevant for these purposes. The mere reduction in the petition debt was not in itself sufficient to justify a rescission of the bankruptcy order. On the facts of this case, an order under s.375 was not justified. In *Arif v Zar* [2012] EWCA Civ 986; [2012] B.P.I.R. 948 the requirement of fresh evidence was again noted.

In *Crammer v West Bromwich Building Society* [2012] EWCA Civ 517; [2012] B.P.I.R. 963 the Court of Appeal undertakes a useful comparison between annulment and rescission.

In *Skeete v Pick* [2007] EWHC 2211 (Ch) the court identified circumstances in which the bankrupt might consider invoking the s.375 jurisdiction (though it was careful to stress that it was not indicating whether such an application would succeed).

In *Hurst v Supperstone (No.2)* [2007] EWHC 865 (Ch); [2007] B.P.I.R. 1104 the court refused to permit the s.375 jurisdiction to be used to review a costs order. This refusal was based on the facts but it was accepted in principle that costs orders fell within the s.375 purview if a cogent case could established for a costs order review.

In *Snopek v Urang* [2008] B.P.I.R. 1416 the court indicated that on a s.375 review it could consider evidence that had materialised after the date of the making of the bankruptcy order which was under review.

On the right of a trustee in bankruptcy to be present at a s.375 application hearing see *Oraki v Dean & Dean* [2017] EWHC 11 (Ch).

On the exercise of discretion under s.375 see *Revenue and Customs Commissioners v Cassells* [2009] B.P.I.R. 284.

An application under s.375 also failed in *Re Haghighat (No.2)* [2009] B.P.I.R. 785 where the difficulty of the burden of proof facing the applicant was emphasised. In *OR v Cooksey* [2013] B.P.I.R. 526 an attempt to use s.375 to challenge the issue of a certificate of discharge also met with no success.

A further illustration of an unsuccessful attempt to invoke s.375 is provided by *Raguz v Scottish & Newcastle Ltd* [2010] B.P.I.R. 945. Compare the curious case of *Pick v Sumpter* [2010] B.P.I.R. 638. In *Miller v McFeely* [2012] EWHC 4409 (Ch); [2014] B.P.I.R. 1529 Proudman J refused to review a rescission of a bankruptcy.

In *O'Donnell v Governor of the Bank of Ireland* [2013] EWHC 489 (Ch); [2013] B.P.I.R. 1078 another s.375 application failed. Newey J refused to revisit his earlier decision on whether the debtors had their COMI within the jurisdiction (see note to s.272) as it had been arrived at after a seven day contested hearing with full evidence. The so-called new evidence added little and there were no good grounds put forward to explain why it was not put before the court when the bankruptcy petition was being heard.

The case of *Re Haworth* [2011] EWHC 36 (Ch) identifies the type of exceptional circumstances where the power of rescission of a bankruptcy order might be used.

Appleyard v Wewelwala [2012] EWHC 3302 (Ch) dealt with a novel point relating to the remuneration of a trustee in bankruptcy where the bankruptcy order was successfully appealed. But during the course of his judgment Briggs J noted one limitation on the s.375 jurisdiction—it only enables the court to review the first instance ruling and not an appellate ruling. The narrow view expressed by Briggs J in *Appleyard v Wewelwala* (above) to the effect that s.375 cannot be invoked to challenge appellate decisions was followed by David Donaldson QC in the High Court in *Sands v Layne* [2014] EWHC 3665 (Ch); [2015] B.P.I.R. 134, but only after considerable wavering—see [15]. But it was directly questioned by Kevin Prosser QC (sitting in the High Court) in *NALM v Cahillane* [2015] EWHC 62 (Ch); [2015] B.P.I.R. 1433. This difference of opinion has now been resolved. In the appeal in *Sands v Layne* [2016] EWCA Civ 1159 the Court of Appeal reviewed the jurisdiction of the court under s.375. A wide view of this jurisdiction was adopted so as to enable judges to review decisions they had made when exercising appellate jurisdiction. The views of the court as expressed in *NALM v Cahillane* (above) were preferred over the approach taken in *Appleyard v Wewelwala* (above). Thus, in principle, a registrar (from 26 February 2018 known as an Insolvency and Companies Court Judge: see the note to s.375(2) below) might have jurisdiction to review a decision of a High Court judge, though it might be politic to assign the review to another High Court judge—see the comments of McCombe LJ at [63].

In *Knight v Rainstorm Pictures Inc* (unreported, 5 May 2017, Barling J) the court refused to set aside a bankruptcy order as there was insufficient evidence that it had been obtained through fraud.

S.375(2)

In s.375(2) the words, "with the leave of the judge or of the Court of Appeal," formerly appearing after the words "on such an appeal lies" repealed by Access to Justice Act 1999 ss.106, 108(3)(f), Sch.15 Pt III as from 27 September 1999.

This provision deals with the question of appeals, whether against a decision of the county court or High Court. Under s.55 of the Access to Justice Act 1999 a "second appeal" to the Court of Appeal is only permitted with the leave of the Court of Appeal and on restricted grounds.

In *Re a Debtor (No.32/SD/1991)* [1993] 1 W.L.R. 314 Millett J indicated that in a s.375(1) review the court can hear fresh evidence not available at the original hearing. Such a review therefore differs fundamentally from a simple appeal where this would not be permitted. By way of contrast a case brought under s.375(2) is a true appeal: *Vadher v Weisgard* [1997] B.C.C. 219. For the inconsistencies on the admission of fresh evidence see *Purvis v Customs and Excise Commissioners* [1999] B.P.I.R. 396 at 398, per Hazel Williamson QC. Vinelott J further considered the nature of the court's jurisdiction under s.375 in later proceedings in *Re a Debtor (No.32/SD/1991) (No.2)* [1994] B.C.C. 524. According to his Lordship (at 528G) it was an exceptional reserve jurisdiction only to be resorted to in the most extreme of cases. It existed to prevent "miscarriages of justice" in the field of bankruptcy law where a person's reputation and freedom of action was at stake.

Section 375(2) and its relationship with insolvency appeals procedures was reviewed in *Bailey v Dargue* [2009] B.P.I.R. 1. For the differences between an appeal and a review under s.375 see *Raguz v Scottish & Newcastle Ltd* [2010] B.P.I.R. 945. On s.375(2) and appeals in personal insolvency proceedings see *Sykes v Shillito* [2017] EWHC 3588 (Ch).

Section 375(2) was amended by the Alteration of Judicial Titles (Registrar in Bankruptcy of the High Court) Order 2018 (SI 2018/130) arts 1, 3 Sch. para.7(a) as from 26 February 2018.

Note also *Practice Direction: Insolvency Proceedings* [2018] B.C.C. 241, Pt 4.

S.375(3)

This complements s.373(2) by conferring jurisdictional integrity on the county courts.

See further IR 2016 r.12.60.

376 Time-limits

376 Where by any provision in this Group of Parts or by the rules the time for doing anything (including anything in relation to a bankruptcy application) is limited, the court may extend the time, either before or after it has expired, on such terms, if any, as it thinks fit.

General Note

This provision once again emphasises the general control of the court over bankruptcy proceedings by allowing it to extend time-limits. For the primacy of s.376 see *Tager v Westpac Banking Corporation* [1998] B.C.C. 73. For guidance on how the discretion under s.376 should be exercised see *Warley Continental Services v Johal* [2004] B.P.I.R. 353 (extension of time refused where time limit under IA 1986 s.262 had expired) and *Legal and Equitable Securities plc v Linton* [2010] EWHC 2046 (Ch); [2011] B.C.C. 354. Registrar Jones undertook a detailed consideration of this provision in *Bonney v Mirpuri* [2013] B.P.I.R. 412. The application to invoke s.376 was rejected and the court stressed the link with CPR r.3.9. An attempt to use the Northern Irish equivalent of s.376 to circumvent retrospectively the three year time limit in s.283A was rejected in *Lismore v Davey* [2013] NIMaster 5. The time for making an application to set aside a statutory demand was extended by Rose J in *Maud v Libyan Investment Authority* [2015] EWHC 1625 (Ch); [2015] B.P.I.R. 858. In taking this decision Rose J took account of the public interest considerations raised by the case.

Note minor amendment made by ERRA 2013 Sch.19 para.51.

377 Formal defects

377 The acts of a person as the trustee of a bankrupt's estate or as a special manager, and the acts of the creditors' committee established for any bankruptcy, are valid notwithstanding any defect in the appointment, election or qualifications of the trustee or manager or, as the case may be, of any member of the committee.

General Note

This provision displays a liberal attitude towards procedural defects in the appointment or qualifications of the trustee, etc. Corresponding sections in the case of company officers and office-holders are s.232 above and CA 2006 s.161. It is necessary to instil confidence in third parties and to preclude the need to investigate that correct procedures have been followed. Note that the predecessor of s.377 only covered situations where the trustee, etc. acted in good faith, but this is not mentioned in s.377. Under BA 1914 s.147(1), which is not specifically repeated in IA 1986, other defects in bankruptcy proceedings could be excused by the court unless substantial and irreparable injustice has been caused by the irregularity. Presumably such cases could now be dealt with under ss.363(1) and 375(1). Finally it should be remembered that the question of a trustee's qualifications must be viewed in the light of the requirements of Pt XIII. This section was considered in *Foenander v Allan* [2006] B.P.I.R. 1392, where it was held that alleged defects in the membership of the creditors' committee which had appointed a trustee could not invalidate the actions of said trustee.

Schedule 9 para.32 states that non-compliance with the rules may be made a criminal offence.

Compare also IR 2016 r.12.64.

378 Exemption from stamp duty

378 Stamp duty shall not be charged on–

(a) any document, being a deed, conveyance, assignment, surrender, admission or other assurance relating solely to property which is comprised in a bankrupt's estate and which, after the execution of that document, is or remains at law or in equity the property of the bankrupt or of the trustee of that estate,

(b) any writ, order, certificate or other instrument relating solely to the property of a bankrupt or to any bankruptcy proceedings.

General Note

This section offers welcome relief from the operation of stamp duty on documents connected with bankruptcy matters.

379 Annual report

379 As soon as practicable after the end of 1986 and each subsequent calendar year, the Secretary of State shall prepare and lay before each House of Parliament a report about the operation during that year of so much of this Act as is comprised in this Group of Parts.

General Note

This section requires the Secretary of State to lay before Parliament an annual report on the working of IA 1986. This is not a new obligation. The 1984 annual report (published in November 1985) is a mine of statistical information on the working of the old bankruptcy legislation.

This provision, unlike its predecessor, makes no mention of the obligation imposed on bankruptcy officers to provide the raw statistics to the Department of Trade and Industry to facilitate the preparation of this report.

Change is made by DA 2015.

Creditors' decisions

379ZA Creditors' decisions: general

379ZA(1) [Application] This section applies where, for the purposes of this Group of Parts, a person ("P") seeks a decision from an individual's creditors about any matter.

379ZA(2) [Creditors' decision procedure] The decision may be made by any creditors' decision procedure P thinks fit, except that it may not be made by a creditors' meeting unless subsection (3) applies.

379ZA(3) [Request for creditors' meeting] This subsection applies if at least the minimum number of creditors request in writing that the decision be made by a creditors' meeting.

379ZA(4) [Meeting to be summoned] If subsection (3) applies, P must summon a creditors' meeting.

379ZA(5) [Section 379ZA(2) subject to creditors' decision procedure/meeting] Subsection (2) is subject to any provision of this Act, the rules or any other legislation, or any order of the court–

(a) requiring a decision to be made, or prohibiting a decision from being made, by a particular creditors' decision procedure (other than a creditors' meeting);

(b) permitting or requiring a decision to be made by a creditors' meeting.

379ZA(6) [Deemed consent procedure under s.379ZB] Section 379ZB provides that in certain cases the deemed consent procedure may be used instead of a creditors' decision procedure.

379ZA(7) ["Minimum number" in s.379ZA(3)] For the purposes of subsection (3) the "minimum number" of creditors is any of the following–

(a) 10% in value of the creditors;

(b) 10% in number of the creditors;

(c) 10 creditors.

379ZA(8) [Creditors in s.379ZA(7)] The references in subsection (7) to creditors are to creditors of any class, even where a decision is sought only from creditors of a particular class.

379ZA(9) [References to a meeting] In this section references to a meeting are to a meeting where the creditors are invited to be present together at the same place (whether or not it is possible to attend the meeting without being present at that place).

379ZA(10) [References to creditors except in s.379ZA(8)] Except as provided by subsection (8), references in this section to creditors include creditors of a particular class.

379ZA(11) ["Creditors' decision procedure"] In this Group of Parts "creditors' decision procedure" means a procedure prescribed or authorised under paragraph 11A of Schedule 9.

General Note

Inserted by SBEEA 2015 s.123. This facilitates the taking of decisions by creditors by removing the need for a formal meeting to be held in every instance. In view of creditor apathy and the cost of arranging meetings this is a sensible strategy. Creditors holding 10% of the debt or 10% in number or 10 creditors can in writing request that a meeting be held—see subs.(7). The creditors' decision procedure is mapped out by Sch.9 para.11A.

379ZB Deemed consent procedure

379ZB(1) [When may be used instead of creditors' decision procedure] The deemed consent procedure may be used instead of a creditors' decision procedure where an individual's creditors are to make a decision about any matter, unless–

(a) a decision about the matter is required by virtue of this Act, the rules or any other legislation to be made by a creditors' decision procedure, or

(b) the court orders that a decision about the matter is to be made by a creditors' decision procedure.

379ZB(2) [Rules re remuneration to be by creditors' decision procedure] If the rules provide for an individual's creditors to make a decision about the remuneration of any person, they must provide that the decision is to be made by a creditors' decision procedure.

379ZB(3) [Notice for deemed consent procedure] The deemed consent procedure is that the relevant creditors (other than opted-out creditors) are given notice of–

(a) the matter about which the creditors are to make a decision,

(b) the decision the person giving the notice proposes should be made (the "proposed decision"),

(c) the effect of subsections (4) and (5), and

(d) the procedure for objecting to the proposed decision.

379ZB(4) [Deemed consent if appropriate number do not object] If less than the appropriate number of relevant creditors object to the proposed decision in accordance with the procedure set out in the notice, the creditors are to be treated as having made the proposed decision.

379ZB(5) [Where appropriate number object] Otherwise–

(a) the creditors are to be treated as not having made a decision about the matter in question, and

(b) if a decision about that matter is again sought from the creditors, it must be sought using a creditors' decision procedure.

379ZB(6) ["Appropriate number" in s.379ZB(4)] For the purposes of subsection (4) the "appropriate number" of relevant creditors is 10% in value of those creditors.

379ZB(7) ["Relevant creditors" in s.379ZB(3), (4)] "Relevant creditors" means the creditors who, if the decision were to be made by a creditors' decision procedure, would be entitled to vote in the procedure.

379ZB(8) [Creditors in s.379ZB] In this section references to creditors include creditors of a particular class.

379ZB(9) [Further provision by rules] The rules may make further provision about the deemed consent procedure.

General Note

Inserted by SBEEA 2015 s.123. This specifies a new procedure (the deemed consent procedure) by which creditors can express their views in an individual insolvency scenario. Essentially it involves the giving of notice by the office-holder of a proposed course of action and if the required number of creditors (10% in value) fail to object, then the course of action is deemed approved. Note the limitations preventing this procedure being used in certain instances—e.g. in fixing remuneration. For further details see IR 2016 r.15.7.

379ZC Power to amend sections 379ZA and 379ZB

379ZC(1) [Power re minimum number of creditors] The Secretary of State may by regulations amend section 379ZA so as to change the definition of the minimum number of creditors.

379ZC(2) [Power re appropriate number of relevant creditors] The Secretary of State may by regulations amend section 379ZB so as to change the definition of the appropriate number of relevant creditors.

379ZC(3) [Defining minimum number or appropriate number] Regulations under this section may define the minimum number or the appropriate number by reference to any one or more of–

(a) a proportion in value,

(b) a proportion in number,

(c) an absolute number,

and the definition may include alternative, cumulative or relative requirements.

379ZC(4) [Power in s.379ZC(1)] Regulations under subsection (1) may define the minimum number of creditors by reference to all creditors, or by reference to creditors of a particular description.

379ZC(5) [Different definitions for different cases in ss.379ZA, 379ZB] Regulations under this section may make provision that will result in section 379ZA or 379ZB having different definitions for different cases, including for different kinds of decisions.

379ZC(6) [Transitional provisions] Regulations under this section may make transitional provision.

379ZC(7) [Power exercisable by statutory instrument] The power of the Secretary of state to make regulations under this section is exercisable by statutory instrument.

379ZC(8) [Approval of statutory instrument] A statutory instrument containing regulations under this section may not be made unless a draft of the instrument has been laid before, and approved by a resolution of, each House of Parliament.

General Note

Inserted by SBEEA 2015 s.123, this section imports flexibility into the new decision-taking mechanisms installed by ss.379ZA and 379ZB. Virtually all possibilities for modification are covered. In view of the novelty of these procedures, this is a sensible precaution.

379A Remote attendance at meetings [Omitted]

General Note

Introduced by LRO 2010 (SI 2010/18). This provision was designed to give the convener of a creditors' meeting (whether in bankruptcy or an IVA) discretion as to whether it should be held remotely using advances in communications technology. It mirrored s.246A.

This provision was omitted by SBEEA 2015 s.126 and Sch.9 para.88 in the wake of changes made to creditor decision procedures reducing the significance of meetings. See now IR 2016 Pt 15.

Giving of notices etc by office-holders

379B Use of websites

379B(1) [Application of section; meaning of "the office-holder"] This section applies where–

(a) a bankruptcy order is made against an individual or an interim receiver of an individual's property is appointed, or

(b) a voluntary arrangement in relation to an individual is proposed or is approved under Part 8, and "the office-holder" means the official receiver, the trustee in bankruptcy, the interim receiver, the nominee or the supervisor of the voluntary arrangement, as the case may be.

379B(2) [Provision of notice by website] Where any provision of this Act or the rules requires the office-holder to give, deliver, furnish or send a notice or other document or information to any person, that requirement is satisfied by making the notice, document or information available on a website–

(a) in accordance with the rules, and

(b) in such circumstances as may be prescribed.

General Note

Introduced by LRO 2010 (SI 2010/18) this allows the office-holder to make use of a website in communications with stakeholders. It mirrors s.246B. See IR 2016 rr.1.47 and 1.49.

New ss.379ZA and 379ZB was introduced when SBEEA 2015 s.123 was brought into force. These new provisions deal with creditor decisions without the need for a formal meeting. Note also proposed new s.379C, which deals with the right of creditors to opt out of receiving notices. This provision will be explained further by proposed new s.383A—see SBEEA 2015 s.125.

379C Creditors' ability to opt out of receiving certain notices

379C(1) [Non-application of rules re notice to creditors] Any provision of the rules which requires an office-holder to give a notice to creditors of an individual does not apply, in circumstances prescribed by the rules, in relation to opted-out creditors.

379C(2) [Non-application of s.379C(1)] Subsection (1)–

(a) does not apply in relation to a notice of a distribution or proposed distribution to creditors;

(b) is subject to any order of the court requiring a notice to be given to all creditors (or all creditors of a particular category).

379C(3) [Participation of opted-out creditors] Except as provided by the rules, a creditor may participate and vote in a creditors' decision procedure or a deemed consent procedure even though, by virtue of being an opted-out creditor, the creditor does not receive notice of it.

379C(4) [“Give”, “notice”, “office-holder”] In this section–

“give” includes deliver, furnish or send;

“notice” includes any document or information in any other form;

“office-holder”, in relation to an individual, means–

(a) where a bankruptcy order is made against the individual, the official receiver or the trustee in bankruptcy;

(b) where an interim receiver of the individual’s property is appointed, the interim receiver;

(c) the supervisor of a voluntary arrangement approved under Part 8 in relation to the individual.

General Note

This provision was inserted by SBEEA 2015 s.125(3) as part of a strategy of cutting costs in the face of creditor apathy. The critical point to grasp is that by opting out of receiving notices a creditor does not disenfranchise himself. Note link with s.383A.

Part XI

Interpretation for Second Group of Parts

380 Introductory

380 The next five sections have effect for the interpretation of the provisions of this Act which are comprised in this Group of Parts; and where a definition is provided for a particular expression, it applies except so far as the context otherwise requires.

General Note

This introduces the bankruptcy interpretation sections. Meanings attributed in ss.381–385 can be excluded by the context. Note also Pt XVIII of the Act and IR 2016 Pt 1.

381 “Bankrupt” and associated terminology

381(1) [“Bankrupt”] “Bankrupt” means an individual who has been made bankrupt and, in relation to a bankruptcy order, it means the individual made bankrupt by that order.

381(1A) [“Bankruptcy application”] “Bankruptcy application” means an application to an adjudicator for a bankruptcy order.

381(2) [“Bankruptcy order”] “Bankruptcy order” means an order making an individual bankrupt.

381(3) [“Bankruptcy petition”] “Bankruptcy petition” means a petition to the court for a bankruptcy order.

General Note

These common phrases are hereby defined.

Note amendment of subss.(1) and (2) plus insertion of subs.(1A) by ERRA 2013 Sch.19 para.52.

382 “Bankruptcy debt”, “liability”, etc.

382(1) [“Bankruptcy debt”] “Bankruptcy debt”, in relation to a bankrupt, means (subject to the next subsection) any of the following–

(a) any debt or liability to which he is subject at the commencement of the bankruptcy,

(b) any debt or liability to which he may become subject after the commencement of the bankruptcy (including after his discharge from bankruptcy) by reason of any obligation incurred before the commencement of the bankruptcy,

(c) any amount specified in pursuance of section 39(3)(c) of the Powers of Criminal Courts Act 1973 in any criminal bankruptcy order made against him before the commencement of the bankruptcy, and

(d) any interest provable as mentioned in section 322(2) in Chapter IV of Part IX.

382(2) [Liability in tort] In determining for the purposes of any provision in this Group of Parts whether any liability in tort is a bankruptcy debt, the bankrupt is deemed to become subject to that liability by reason of an obligation incurred at the time when the cause of action accrued.

382(3) [References to debtor liability] For the purposes of references in this Group of Parts to a debt or liability, it is immaterial whether the debt or liability is present or future, whether it is certain or contingent or whether its amount is fixed or liquidated, or is capable of being ascertained by fixed rules or as a matter of opinion; and references in this Group of Parts to owing a debt are to be read accordingly.

382(4) ["Liability"] In this Group of Parts, except in so far as the context otherwise requires, "liability" means (subject to subsection (3) above) a liability to pay money or money's worth, including any liability under an enactment, any liability for breach of trust, any liability in contract, tort or bailment and any liability arising out of an obligation to make restitution.

382(5) [Child support] Liability under the Child Support Act 1991 to pay child support maintenance to any person is not a debt or liability for the purposes of Part 8.

S.382(1), (2), (5)

These provisions define a bankruptcy debt. The section heading was amended by the Welfare Reform Act 2012 s.142 and a new subs.(5) was also added by this legislation to clarify the position with regard to child support. It would appear from the comments of David Richards J in *Re T & N Ltd* [2005] EWHC 2870 (Ch); [2006] B.P.I.R. 532 that future tort claims would not rank as bankruptcy debts under s.382 of the IA 1986. Having said that, the judge made the point that after discharge such claimants could still pursue the erstwhile bankrupt. On the difference between a bankruptcy debt and a petition debt see Master Kelly in *OR for NI v Gallagher* [2013] NIMaster 12 at [13].

In *McGuinness v Norwich and Peterborough Building Society* [2011] EWCA Civ 1286; [2012] B.P.I.R. 145 the court examined the relationship between the provisions in ss.382 and 267.

On the meaning of "obligation" in s. 382(1)(b) see the comments of Irwin J in *Soor v Redbridge LBC* [2016] EWHC 77 (Admin); [2016] B.P.I.R. 766. Irwin J considered whether obligations incurred by a person acting as a trustee (who subsequently became bankrupt) could be regarded as bankruptcy debts. He decided that as a general rule they were not bankruptcy debts, though each case rested on its own facts and individual circumstances needed to be investigated to determine this matter. Irwin J indicated that it was arguable that a liability to council tax incurred by virtue of one's position as a trustee under a trust in the period before (or during) the bankruptcy might be so regarded.

A new class of bankruptcy debt will be created by SBEEA 2015 s.110, which inserts a new s.15B(5) into the Company Directors Disqualification Act 1986. Sums directed to be paid under a compensation order or undertaking given in connection with disqualification proceedings rank as bankruptcy debts.

Note prospective amendment: s.382(1)(c) is to be repealed by CJA 1988 s.170(2) and Sch.16 as from a day to be appointed; see the note to s.264.

S.382(3), (4)

These provisions make liability in tort a bankruptcy debt and make it clear that both contingent and unliquidated liabilities are capable of forming the basis of a bankruptcy debt. On the latter point, this is a change in the law, which the Cork Committee (*Report*, para.1318) called for. The concept of what is a bankruptcy debt has changed in recent times. The former view, as exemplified by cases like *Glenister v Rowe* [2000] Ch. 76 and *R. (Steele) v Birmingham City Council* [2005] EWCA Civ 1824, was that the mere *risk* of liability (for example, as to adverse costs in litigation) could not qualify as a contingent liability and so could not stand as a bankruptcy or provable debt. This appeared to be so even if the risk was a genuine likelihood or stronger possibility. This narrow interpretation caused problems and ran counter to the idea that an insolvency process should be as inclusive as possible. Accordingly, *Glenister v Rowe* (above) was overruled in *Re Nortel Companies* [2013] UKSC 52; [2013] B.C.C. 624. For discussion see Moss [2013] 26 Insolv. Int. 108. The precise scope of this Supreme Court ruling on a number of authorities which drew support from *Glenister v Rowe* (above) remains to be determined. See also *Re Mireskandari* (unreported, 22 November 2013, Registrar Barber) where a wide view was taken of the concept of a provable debt. Subsection (4) was mentioned in *R. (Balding) v Secretary of State for Work and Pensions* [2007] EWHC 759 (Admin). Here the Divisional Court ruled that the liability to repay overpaid social security benefit where that liability had been determined prior to bankruptcy was to be regarded as a bankruptcy debt. As such, on discharge from bankruptcy of the recipient that liability was extinguished and deductions could not be made in respect of it from future benefit payments. On appeal the Court of Appeal upheld this ruling and confirmed that the liability to repay the overpayment (which had been adjudicated prior to bankruptcy) was a bankruptcy debt which was released on discharge from bankruptcy—see *Secretary of State for Work and Pensions v Balding* [2007] EWCA Civ 1327; [2007] B.P.I.R. 1669. Mummery LJ sympathised with the difficulties that this conclusion would cause for the public exchequer, but the solution lay in the hands of Parliament by introducing amending legislation. See I(A)R 2012 (SI 2012/469)—see now IR 2016 r.9.2. *Balding* was approved by the Supreme Court in *Secretary of State for Work and Pensions v Payne* [2011] UKSC 60. In *Re Argent, Tester v Long* [2016] B.P.I.R. 1120 Deputy Registrar Garwood gave further consideration to the meaning of this provision in the context of a possible tort claim and noted that the provision applied both as to debts/obligations to which the debtor was subject to, plus those which he may become subject to. The Deputy Registrar confirmed that the *Nortel* (above) precedent applied in bankruptcy cases.

In *Secretary of State for Work and Pensions v Payne* [2011] UKSC 60 Lord Mance suggested that there may be a need for reform here by excluding recoupment liability from the list of bankruptcy debts. See also *CMEC v Beesley* [2010] EWCA Civ 1344 where it was held that the Child Maintenance and Enforcement Commission was not capable of being regarded as a creditor for IVA purposes in respect of maintenance arrears of a non-resident parent. Although this sum of arrears could be seen as a bankruptcy debt it was not a provable debt. There was no contingent liability found to exist in *Casson and Wales v The Law Society* [2009] EWHC 1943 (Admin); [2010] B.P.I.R. 49 as again we were faced with mere possibilities. The fact that there was an "accident of timing" did not persuade the court to conclude otherwise. A debt arising in respect of a lump sum payable under matrimonial proceedings is a bankruptcy debt (*Russell v Russell* [1998] B.P.I.R. 259) but until recently was not a provable debt. On the significance of this see *Woodley v Woodley (No.2)* [1994] 1 W.L.R. 1167; and *Levy v LSC* [2000] B.P.I.R. 1065. The court will only grant a bankruptcy order on the basis of a non-provable debt if the circumstances are exceptional—*Wehmeyer v Weymeyer* [2001] B.P.I.R. 548. Lump sums in matrimonial proceedings were made provable debts by the Insolvency (Amendment) Rules 2005 (SI 2005/527). As to whether a wife's putative claims to ancillary relief on divorce are contingent debts compare *Re Rich* [2008] B.P.I.R. 485 with *Re Jones* [2008] B.P.I.R. 1051. It is submitted that the latter decision is more likely to be representative of the law in the wake of *Haines v Hill* [2007] EWCA Civ 1284; [2007] B.P.I.R. 1280.

Hellard v Chadwick, Re Mireskandari [2014] EWHC 2158 (Ch); [2014] B.P.I.R. 1234 makes it clear that claims under ss.339 and 340 may constitute bankruptcy debts.

In *Smurthwaite v Simpson-Smith and Mond (No.2)* [2006] B.P.I.R. 1483 the court considered the application of s.382—but comments here need to be viewed in the context of the appeal in this complex litigation see *Smurthwaite v Simpson-Smith and Mond (No.2)* [2006] B.P.I.R. 1504. In *El Ajou v Stern* [2006] EWHC 3067 (Ch); [2007] B.P.I.R. 693 (an IVA case) there was further consideration of what constitutes a bankruptcy debt for the purposes of s.382.

For the corresponding definitions in corporate insolvency, see the note to Sch.8 paras 12, 14.

Note that bankruptcy debts are not always provable: see the note to IR 2016 r.14.2.

383 "Creditor", "security", etc.

383(1) ["Creditor"] "Creditor"–

(a) in relation to a bankrupt, means a person to whom any of the bankruptcy debts is owed (being, in the case of an amount falling within paragraph (c) of the definition in section 382(1) of "bankruptcy debt", the person in respect of whom that amount is specified in the criminal bankruptcy order in question), and

(b) in relation to an individual to whom a bankruptcy application or bankruptcy petition relates, means a person who would be a creditor in the bankruptcy if a bankruptcy order were made on that application or petition.

383(2) [Securing of debt] Subject to the next two subsections and any provision of the rules requiring a creditor to give up his security for the purposes of proving a debt, a debt is secured for the purposes of this Group of Parts to the extent that the person to whom the debt is owed holds any security for the debt (whether a mortgage, charge, lien or other security) over any property of the person by whom the debt is owed.

383(3) [Where s.269(1)(a) statement made] Where a statement such as is mentioned in section 269(1)(a) in Chapter I of Part IX has been made by a secured creditor for the purposes of any bankruptcy petition and a bankruptcy order is subsequently made on that petition, the creditor is deemed for the purposes of the Parts in this Group to have given up the security specified in the statement.

383(4) [Qualification to s.383(2)] In subsection (2) the reference to a security does not include a lien on books, papers or other records, except to the extent that they consist of documents which give a title to property and are held as such.

S.383(1)

This defines "creditor".

Note prospective amendment: in s.383(1)(a) the words from "(being," to "question)" are to be repealed by CJA 1988 s.170(2) and Sch.16 as from a day to be appointed; see the note to s.264.

This provision was subject to amendment by ERRA 2013 Sch.19.

S.383(2)–(4)

These provisions deal with the security and secured creditors. Section 383(2) defines "security", but this must be read in the light of s.383(4), excluding liens over books, etc. As to what constitutes "security" for the purposes of s.383(2) see *Fagg v Rushton* [2007] EWHC 657 (Ch); [2007] B.P.I.R. 1059. In *Sofaer v Anglo Irish Finance plc* [2011] EWHC 1480 (Ch); [2011] B.P.I.R. 1736 the definition of security in s.383(2) was applied—it did not apply to a creditor with security over the assets of some third party (as opposed to the assets of the debtor). A landlord's right of re-entry is not regarded as security for these purposes: *Razzaq v Pala* [1998] B.C.C. 66. See also *Re a Debtor (No.310 of 1988)* [1989] 1 W.L.R. 452. Section 383(3) would be better located in s.269, to which it relates.

Section 383 was also considered in *Re Jones* [2008] B.P.I.R. 1051.

383A "Opted-out creditor"

383A(1) [Meaning] For the purposes of this Group of Parts "opted-out creditor" in relation to an office-holder for an individual means a person who–

(a) is a creditor of the individual, and

(b) in accordance with the rules has elected (or is deemed to have elected) to be (and not to cease to be) an opted out creditor in relation to the office-holder.

383A(2) ["Office-holder"] In this section, "office-holder", in relation to an individual, means–

(a) where a bankruptcy order is made against the individual, the official receiver or the trustee in bankruptcy;

(b) where an interim receiver of the individual's property is appointed, the interim receiver;

(c) the supervisor of a voluntary arrangement approved under Part 8 in relation to the individual.

General Note

Inserted by SBEEA 2015 s.125(4). This defines an opted-out creditor for the purposes of s.379C for example. Not that opting out relates to the receipt of notices. Opting out does not disenfranchise a creditor.

384 "Prescribed" and "the rules"

384(1) [Definitions] Subject to the next subsection and sections 342C(7) and 342F(9) in Chapter V of Part IX, "prescribed" means prescribed by the rules; and "the rules" means rules made under section 412 in Part XV.

384(2) [Interpretation] References in this Group of Parts to the amount prescribed for the purposes of any of the following provisions–

section 251S(4);

section 313A;

section 346(3);

section 354(1) and (2);

section 358;

section 360(1);

section 361(2);

section 364(2)(d),

paragraphs 6 to 8 of Schedule 4ZA,

and references in those provisions to the prescribed amount are to be read in accordance with section 418 in Part XV and orders made under that section.

General Note

This section defines "prescribed" and "the rules" and must be read in the light of ss.418 and 412 respectively. A textual modification to s.384(1) was made by para.71 of Sch.12 to the Welfare Reform and Pensions Act 1999. The reference to s.313A was introduced by EA 2002 s.261(4).

Note amendment by Pt 1 para.4 of Sch.20 to the Tribunals, Courts and Enforcement Act 2007.

Note amendment by ERRA 2013 Sch.19 para.54.

385 Miscellaneous definitions

385(1) [Definitions] The following definitions have effect–

"adjudicator" means a person appointed by the Secretary of State under section 398A;

"the court", in relation to any matter, means the court to which, in accordance with section 373 in Part X and the rules, proceedings with respect to that matter are allocated or transferred;

"creditors' decision procedure" has the meaning given by section 379ZA(11);

"creditor's petition" means a bankruptcy petition under section 264(1)(a);

"criminal bankruptcy order" means an order under section 39(1) of the Powers of Criminal Courts Act 1973;

"debt" is to be construed in accordance with section 382(3);

"the debtor"–

(za) in relation to a debt relief order or an application for such an order, has the same meaning as in Part 7A,

(a) in relation to a proposal for the purposes of Part VIII, means the individual making or intending to make that proposal, and

(b) in relation to a bankruptcy application or a bankruptcy petition, means the individual to whom the application or petition relates;

"debt relief order" means an order made by the official receiver under Part 7A;

"deemed consent procedure" means the deemed consent procedure provided for by section 379ZB;

"determination period" has the meaning given in section 263K(4);

"dwelling house" includes any building or part of a building which is occupied as a dwelling and any yard, garden, garage or outhouse belonging to the dwelling house and occupied with it;

"estate", in relation to a bankrupt is to be construed in accordance with section 283 in Chapter II of Part IX;

"family", in relation to a bankrupt, means the persons (if any) who are living with him and are dependent on him;

"insolvency administration order" means an order for the administration in bankruptcy of the insolvent estate of a deceased debtor (being an individual at the date of his death);

"insolvency administration petition" means a petition for an insolvency administration order;

"the Rules" means the Insolvency (England and Wales) Rules 2016;

"secured" and related expressions are to be construed in accordance with section 383; and

"the trustee", in relation to a bankruptcy and the bankrupt, means the trustee of the bankrupt's estate.

385(2) [Interpretation] References in this Group of Parts to a person's affairs include his business, if any.

S.385(1)
This provides general definitions of words commonly appearing in the Second Group of Parts. There are differences from its statutory predecessor. Thus, for example, references to resolutions passed at creditors' meetings have been omitted, as have other terms which have become obsolete. On the other hand, new terms have been included, such as "dwelling house" and "family" (note its extended meaning). Note the discussion of "the court" and its jurisdiction in *Hall and Shivers v Van Der Heiden* [2010] B.P.I.R. 585. Note also ss.382 and 383, and ss.435, 436.

Note prospective amendment: in s.385(1) the definition of "criminal bankruptcy order" is to be repealed by CJA 1988 s.170(2) and Sch.16 as from a day to be appointed; see the note to s.264.

Note that a number of the terms were given revised definitions by ERRA 2013 Sch.19 para.55. New definitions were added by SBEEA 2015 s.123(4).

Definition of "the Rules" substituted by Insolvency (England and Wales) Rules 2016 (Consequential Amendments and Savings) Rules 2017 (SI 2017/369) r.2(1), Sch.1 para.3 as from 6 April 2017.

S.385(2)
This is inserted *ex abundanti cautela*—a person's "affairs" would cover his business.

Note amendment by Pt 1 para.5 of Sch.20 to the Tribunals, Courts and Enforcement Act 2007.

The Third Group of Parts: Miscellaneous Matters Bearing on both Company and Individual Insolvency; General Interpretation; Final Provisions

Introductory note to the Third Group of Parts
Parts XII–XIX of IA 1986 consist of a great variety of matters. Apart from the usual "mechanical" provisions (interpretation, short title, commencement, etc.), there is a group of sections, namely ss.386–387, which substantially reduce the significance of preferential claims in insolvency law. EA 2002 s.251 further reduces these by removing preferential status from Crown debts. The provisions on the qualification of insolvency practitioners are to be found in Pt XIII. There is also reference to official receivers (happily retained for corporate and personal insolvencies), the official petitioner, the Insolvency Rules Committee, insolvency service finance, insolvent estates of deceased persons and insolvent partnerships. The connection of other sections within Pt XVII with insolvency law is more indirect—thus there are provisions dealing with Parliamentary disqualification and restrictive trade practices.

Scholars of legislative history should note ss.423–425, which revamp s.172 of LPA 1925, a provision which can trace its own ancestry back to 1571!

Part XII

Preferential Debts in Company and Individual Insolvency

Introductory note to Part XII
Preferential claims have been a part of insolvency law for nearly a hundred years. A preferential claim is essentially an unsecured one that is given especially favourable treatment by the legislature. Although the legislature is at liberty to create new preferential claims it seems clear that the courts will not do so on their own initiative: see here *Re*

Rafidain Bank [1992] B.C.C. 376. It is not surprising, therefore, that the state has been the main preferential claimant. In the context of corporate insolvency law, this means that preferential claims are to be satisfied out of a company's assets subject to a floating charge in priority to the debenture holder enjoying that charge. They do not rank ahead of the claims of a debenture holder secured by a fixed charge: *Re Lewis Merthyr Consolidated Collieries Ltd* [1929] 1 Ch. 498; *Re G L Saunders Ltd* [1986] 1 W.L.R. 215. Although preferential claims enjoy no inherent priority over a fixed charge, such a priority can arise if the fixed chargee surrenders priority in respect of the charged asset to a floating chargee and fails to do so via a subrogation mechanism. A simple postponement agreement can lead to the fixed chargee inadvertently also surrendering priority to preferential claims: see *Re Portbase (Clothing) Ltd* [1993] Ch. 388; [1993] B.C.C. 96.

The proliferation of preferential claims since 1945 has worried banks enjoying the security of a floating charge and has led them to seek increased security in the form of the highly artificial fixed charge over future assets. The end result of these trends has been to make the position of unsecured creditors even more unhappy.

After reviewing the evidence, the Cork Committee (*Report*, para.1450) called for a radical reduction in the number of preferential claims:

> "We unhesitatingly reject the argument that debts owed to the community ought to be paid in priority to debts owed to private creditors. A bad debt owed to the State is likely to be insignificant, in terms of total Government receipts; the loss of a similar sum by a private creditor may cause substantial hardship, and bring further insolvencies in its train" (para.1410).

In the early drafts of the Insolvency Bill 1985, the Government refused to act on this proposal because of the implications for the public exchequer. Reluctantly, however, it included provisions in IA 1985 (s.89 and Sch.4) which did reduce its own preferential position, and it is these provisions which have found their way into IA 1986.

The continued survival of preferential claims under English law was the subject of constant debate. It is interesting to note that the Crown's preferential rights have been entirely swept away in Australia by the 1992 amendments to the Corporations Law and in Canada have been significantly reduced by the Bankruptcy and Insolvency Act 1992. In view of these developments in other jurisdictions it came as no surprise when the Government indicated that it was intending to abolish Crown preferential debt. That process of abolition was completed by s.251 of EA 2002 with effect from 15 September 2003. Thus a number of preferential items are removed from the list in Sch.6. The underlying intention was that this sacrifice on the part of the state would compensate floating charge holders for the new burden created by the reserved fund for unsecured creditors (see s.176A). Although this is a significant change its impact must not be overestimated; other preferential claims will continue to survive for the foreseeable future.

In September 2015 the Government rejected calls to extend preferential status to self-employed "workers" who are owed money when the firm for which they are providing services collapses—see Government Response to the Joint House of Commons Committees' Report on the Impact of the Closure of City Link on Employment (Cm.9123) paras 27–30.

In July 2016 the Law Commission in its report on *Consumer Prepayments on Retailer Insolvency* (LC 368) urged the government to consider creating a new class of preferential claim (ranking after employee preferential status) on out of pocket consumers who had prepaid £250 or more for goods or services in the six months prior to the retail insolvency. An official response to this recommendation is awaited. For comment on this Law Commission Report, see Akintola [2018] J.B.L. 1.

Part XII applies to limited liability partnerships by virtue of the Limited Liability Partnerships Regulations 2001 (SI 2001/1090) reg.5(1)(b) as from 6 April 2001 subject to reg.5(2) and (3). For transitional provision see SI 2003/2093 (C. 85) art.4 and SI 2003/2332. Note also *Jackson and Long, Noters* [2004] S.C. 474.

Re application of Pt XII to insolvent partnerships, see the Insolvent Partnerships Order 1994 (SI 1994/2421), especially arts 10, 11, Sch.7.

386 Categories of preferential debts

386(1) [Debts listed in Sch.6] A reference in this Act to the preferential debts of a company or an individual is to the debts listed in Schedule 6 to this Act (contributions to occupational pension schemes; remuneration, &c. of employees; levies on coal and steel production; debts owed to the Financial Services Compensation Scheme; deposits covered by Financial Services Compensation Scheme; other deposits); and references to preferential creditors are to be read accordingly.

386(1A) [References to "ordinary preferential debts"] A reference in this Act to the "ordinary preferential debts" of a company or an individual is to the preferential debts listed in any of paragraphs 8 to 15B of Schedule 6 to this Act.

386(1B) [References to "secondary preferential debts"] A reference in this Act to the "secondary preferential debts" of a company or an individual is to the preferential debts listed in paragraph 15BA or 15BB of Schedule 6 to this Act.

386(2) ["The debtor"] In Schedule 6 "the debtor" means the company or the individual concerned.

386(3) [Interpretation of Sch.6] Schedule 6 is to be read with Schedule 4 to the Pension Schemes Act 1993 (occupational pension scheme contributions).

General Note

These provisions, allied to Sch.6, reduce the number of preferential claims to a bare minimum. Note Banking Act 2009 ss.103 and 145. Note changes made to subs.(1) and insertion of subss.(1A) and (1B) by the Financial Services (Banking Reform) Act 2013 s.13(2) with effect from 31 December 2014 as amended and commenced by the Banks and Building Societies (Depositor Preference and Priorities) Order 2014 (SI 2014/3486) on 1 January 2015 and further amendment of subs.(1) by the Deposit Guarantee Scheme Regulations 2015 (SI 2015/486) reg.14(1), (2) as from 26 March 2015. Note the distinction between "ordinary preferential debts" and "secondary preferential debts" introduced by subss.(1A) and (1B).

S.386(3)
The reference to Sch.4 to the Pension Schemes Act 1993 was substituted for the former reference to Sch.3 to the Social Security Pensions Act 1975 by s.190 of and Sch.8 para.18 to the 1993 Act.

387 "The relevant date"

387(1) [Explanation of Sch.6] This section explains references in Schedule 6 to the relevant date (being the date which determines the existence and amount of a preferential debt).

387(2) [Part I s.4] For the purposes of section 4 in Part I (consideration of company voluntary arrangement), the relevant date in relation to a company which is not being wound up is–

(a) if the company is in administration, the date on which it entered administration, and

(b) if the company is not in administration, the date on which the voluntary arrangement takes effect.

387(2A) [Schedule A1 para.31] For the purposes of paragraph 31 of Schedule A1 (consideration of company voluntary arrangement where a moratorium under section 1A is in force), the relevant date in relation to a company is the date of filing.

387(3) [Company being wound up] In relation to a company which is being wound up, the following applies–

(a) if the winding up is by the court, and the winding-up order was made immediately upon the discharge of an administration order, the relevant date is the date on which the company entered administration;

(aa) if the winding up is by the court and the winding-up order was made following conversion of administration into winding up by virtue of Article 51 of the EU Regulation, the relevant date is the date on which the company entered administration;

(ab) if the company is deemed to have passed a resolution for voluntary winding up by virtue of an order following conversion of administration into winding up under Article 51 of the EU Regulation, the relevant date is the date on which the company entered administration;

(b) if the case does not fall within paragraph (a), (aa) or (ab) and the company–

  (i) is being wound up by the court, and

  (ii) had not commenced to be wound up voluntarily before the date of the making of the winding-up order,

  the relevant date is the date of the appointment (or first appointment) of a provisional liquidator or, if no such appointment has been made, the date of the winding-up order;

(ba) if the case does not fall within paragraph (a), (aa), (ab) or (b) and the company is being wound up following administration pursuant to paragraph 83 of Schedule B1, the relevant date is the date on which the company entered administration;

(c) if the case does not fall within paragraph (a), (aa), (ab), (b) or (ba), the relevant date is the date of the passing of the resolution for the winding up of the company.

387(3A) [Company in administration] In relation to a company which is in administration (and to which no other provision of this section applies) the relevant date is the date on which the company enters administration.

387(4) [Company in receivership] In relation to a company in receivership (where section 40 or, as the case may be, section 59 applies), the relevant date is–

(a) in England and Wales, the date of the appointment of the receiver by debenture-holders, and

(b) in Scotland, the date of the appointment of the receiver under section 53(6) or (as the case may be) 54(5).

387(5) [Part VIII s.258] For the purposes of section 258 in Part VIII (individual voluntary arrangements), the relevant date is, in relation to a debtor who is not an undischarged bankrupt–

(a) where an interim order has been made under section 252 with respect to his proposal, the date of that order, and

(b) in any other case, the date on which the voluntary arrangement takes effect.

387(6) [Bankrupt] In relation to a bankrupt, the following applies–

(a) where at the time the bankruptcy order was made there was an interim receiver appointed under section 286, the relevant date is the date on which the interim receiver was first appointed after the making of the bankruptcy application or (as the case may be) the presentation of the bankruptcy petition;

(b) otherwise, the relevant date is the date of the making of the bankruptcy order.

General Note

The purpose of these provisions is to explain the meaning of the phrase "the relevant date", used extensively in Sch.6. The timing for assessment of preferential claims depends on the particular insolvency regime involved, and whether corporate or individual.

Paragraphs (aa) and (ab) were inserted into subs.(3) by the Insolvency Act 1986 (Amendment) (No.2) Regulations 2002 (SI 2002/1240) reg.16 with effect from 31 May 2002. This insertion made necessary consequential amendments in the remainder of this subsection. The provisions were amended by the Insolvency Amendment (EU 2015/848) Regulations 2017 (SI 2017/702) regs 1, 2(1), Sch. paras 1, 22 in relation to proceedings opened on or after 26 June 2017 (see reg.3) when the Recast EU Regulation 2015/848 came into force.

Subsection (2) was replaced, subs.(3) amended and subs.(3A) inserted by Sch.17 to EA 2002. Subsection (2A) was inserted by IA 2000 Sch.1. Subsection (6)(a) was amended by ERRA 2013 Sch.19 para.56. Subsections (2) and (2A) were then amended in minor fashion by SBEEA 2015 to reflect wider decision procedures available to creditors.

Note Banking Act 2009 ss.103 and 145.

Part XIII

Insolvency Practitioners and their Qualification

Introductory note to Part XIII

A major recommendation of the Cork Committee (*Report*, Chs 15–17) was that every insolvency practitioner should be a member of a recognised professional body, or at least have some minimum professional qualification, and that all practitioners should be subject to compulsory bonding to secure the due performance of their obligations. This, it was hoped, would curb the abuses associated in the past with "cowboy" liquidators, often people with no practical experience or relevant qualifications, who engaged in dubious practices to the detriment of creditors, sometimes in league with the controllers of the defunct company whose irresponsibility (and perhaps fraud) had brought about its collapse.

These proposals were accepted by the government in its White Paper (paras 8–11), and the framework for the new professional regime was set up by IA 1985 ss.1–11, now Pt XIII of the present Act. Much of its detail, however, has been left to be prescribed in the form of rules: see the Insolvency Practitioners Regulations 2005 (SI 2005/524). The 2005 Regulations repeal the 1990 Regulations (SI 1990/439) of the same name. The law now requires every insolvency practitioner either to be a member of a recognised professional body, or to be personally authorised to act by the Secretary of State (s.390(2)).

The Committee accepted that some concessionary arrangements would need to be made for established practitioners with substantial experience and a good record who lacked a professional qualification. However, since 1 April 1990 (the date when the now repealed 1990 Regulations referred to above came into effect), it has been necessary for persons applying to the Secretary of State for authorisation to have passed the examination set by the Joint Insolvency Examination Board or to have a similar overseas qualification, unless they already hold a current authorisation.

The introduction of professional standards for all insolvency practitioners has allowed some relaxation of the law, e.g. in such matters as the need to obtain the consent of the court before action is taken; and many of the functions which were formerly entrusted only to the official receiver have now been devolved upon private insolvency practitioners.

The policy towards insisting on a compulsory professional qualification limited to insolvency practitioners took a strange turn with the enactment and implementation of s.4 of IA 2000, which permitted other authorised persons to act as nominees or supervisors of voluntary arrangement. For background comment, see the note to s.389A below.

When the winding-up provisions of IA 1986 were extended to apply to building societies by the Building Societies Act 1986 Pt XIII was not specifically included. This oversight has since been corrected by CA 1989 s.211(2)(a). See the general note to Pt IV, preceding s.73, above. Part XIII applies to limited liability partnerships by virtue of the Limited Liability Partnerships Regulations 2001 (SI 2001/1090) reg.5(1)(b) as from 6 April 2001 subject to reg.5(2) and (3).

On the application of Pt XIII to insolvent partnerships, see the Insolvent Partnerships Order 1994 (SI 1994/2421), especially arts 10, 11, Sch.7.

In November 1996, the DTI Insolvency Service and the recognised professional bodies established a Working Party with terms of reference to review the state of regulation of the insolvency profession and to consider whether the regulation could be made more efficient and effective. The Working Party in December 1997 issued a consultation document inviting comments on such matters as the qualifications for entry into the profession, the scope and effectiveness of the regulatory regime, and its complaints procedures, and published its report on 24 February 1999. The report recommended the establishment of a new Insolvency Practices Council, to consist of a majority of lay members together with representatives from the professions to provide expertise and informed comment. The Council's remit includes to set professional and ethical standards and to promote efficiency, transparency and independence while at the same time assisting insolvency practice to respond to changing demands. The first chairman of the Council was appointed on 21 December 1999. The IPC funds strategic research. For example, it funded an empirical study produced by Adrian Walters and Mary Seneviratne of Nottingham Trent University in 2008 into Complaints Handling Procedures—see IPC *2007 Annual Report* at p.9 for full details. Unfortunately, in a letter to stakeholders dated 8 March 2012 the IPC announced that it was to disband. For an explanation of this decision see *Dear IP* Issue 53 (March 2012).

In October 2001 the Insolvency Service issued a publication giving guidance on the making of complaints about insolvency practitioners. On insolvency practitioners generally see Milman [2012] (92) Amicus Curiae 2.

The market for insolvency services in the UK corporate sector was the subject of an economic study carried out by the Office of Fair Trading in 2009–2010—see "The Market for Corporate Insolvency Practitioners" (OFT, June 2010). For follow up action by the Insolvency Service see the consultation launched on 10 February 2011 with views being sought on the pros and cons of an Independent Complaints Body (which could look at issues such as fees) and other regulatory reforms. The profession and regulators have agreed to make complaints procedures more transparent and consistent with the introduction of a single gateway which will come into operation from Spring 2013.

For an incisive analysis of how the complaints Gateway is working see Wood [2017] 30 Insolv. Int. 106.

A further review of IP fees was announced by the Minister of Business on behalf of the government on 20 December 2012 with a statement to the effect that Professor Elaine Kempson would be undertaking this review. The Kempson Report was published in June 2013. This made a number of suggestions for future reform in order to further regulate arrangements for payment of IP fees and expenses. The government took forward these proposals in

February 2014 with a consultation paper entitled "Strengthening the Regulatory Regime and Fee Structure for Insolvency Practitioners". The consultation period ended on 28 March 2014.

The Insolvency Service carries out annual reviews of insolvency practitioner regulations. For a summary of the 2013 Annual Review of Insolvency Practitioner Regulation see [2014] 27 Insolv. Int. 65.

Major changes to the rules governing the authorisation of and responsibilities owed by insolvency practitioners were made by the Insolvency Practitioners Regulations 2005 (SI 2005/524). These regulations, which took effect on 1 April 2005, repeal and replace the existing regulatory matrix founded upon the 1990 Regulations. In particular SI 1990/439, SI 1993/221, SI 2002/2710, SI 2002/2748 and SI 2004/473 are all repealed. Under the 2005 Regulations, broadly speaking, an insolvency practitioner must be an authorised person within the meaning of Pt 2 of the 2005 Regulations. Regulation 6 deals with the criteria for determining whether a candidate for authorisation is a fit and proper person. Apart from issues of personal integrity, there are detailed requirements mapped out in reg.7 as to requisite experience and training. Continuing professional development is compulsory (reg.9). Details on annual returns by authorised persons to the Secretary of State are outlined in reg.11.

Insolvency practitioners must lodge a bond in the form of a security or caution to cover potential liabilities to the insolvent estate in cases where duties are not properly performed (see Pt 3 of the 2005 Regulations which refers to Sch.2). The terms of the bond, amount of cover and penalties thereunder are dealt with by Sch.2.

Responsibilities with regard to maintaining records are dealt with by Pt 4 of the 2005 Regulations with the details of the minimum information required being specified in Sch.3 to those Regulations. Provision is made for identifying the location of such records (reg.14) and inspection procedures (regs 15–17). These records should contain information on the insolvency practitioner, the insolvent, details of bonding, information on meetings of creditors, the basis upon which remuneration is to be calculated and details on distributions.

The form and content of Pt 13 in the years to come will change significantly.

Firstly, we have significant reforms introduced by DA 2015 being enacted. Essentially we are looking at a move away from general authorisation of insolvency practitioners enabling a person so authorised to take on any insolvency office towards a system in which insolvency practitioners may be authorised to hold certain types of insolvency office. Under the detailed provisions found in DA 2015 s.17 and Sch.6 there will be amendments to s.389(1A) and a repeal of s.389A. New ss.390A and 390B will be introduced. A revised s.391 will be substituted. Sections 392–398 plus Sch.7 will be replaced. It is believed that this raft of changes will reduce costs, encourage the development of expertise and increase the number of professionals working in certain areas of insolvency thus increasing competition. These are laudable aims but it remains to be seen if this reform will achieve those goals.

A more fundamental change to the regulatory systems affecting insolvency practitioners will be made by SBEEA 2015 Pt 10. The essence of this reform is to improve regulatory structures and to move to a system of regulation akin to that applying to other professionals, such as the legal profession. The changes are widespread and will also include changes made by DA 2015. There will be a further substitution of a revised s.391. A new s.391A will appear. Both of these provisions deal with the recognition of recognised professional bodies and will lay down for the future the procedures that should be followed to secure recognition. Recognised professional bodies will have regulatory objectives laid down by ss.391B and 391C. A system of oversight (including a penalty regime) of recognised professional bodies by the Secretary of State will be established by ss.391D–391N. Penalties may be of a financial nature or involve a reprimand or ultimately removal of recognition from an RPB. A system of direct sanctions orders granted by the courts on the application of the Secretary of State against individual insolvency practitioners where this is deemed to be in the public interest will be established under ss.391O–391Q. As an alternative the Secretary of State may under new s.391R give a direct sanctions direction to the relevant RPB instructing them to act against an insolvency practitioner. A *single* regulator may be established by the Secretary of State in due course if the aforementioned reforms do not enhance public confidence in the regulation of insolvency practitioners (see below). Finally, provision will be made to facilitate information gathering by the Secretary of State (s.391S) with the backup of compliance orders (s.391T). The Explanatory Notes to SBEEA 2015 Pt 10 are particularly helpful in offering insights into these reforms. Note also SBEEA 2015 ss.144–146. These self-standing provisions, supported by SBEEA 2015 Sch.11, enable the Secretary of State to designate a single regulator for insolvency practitioners. There is a seven year cut-off period for the excise of this power. These provisions are to be found in Vol.2 of this work.

The current position relating to the stewardship responsibilities of IPs working in the personal insolvency context is reviewed by Milman in [2017] J.B.L. 617.

Restrictions on unqualified persons acting as liquidator, trustee in bankruptcy, etc.

388 Meaning of "act as insolvency practitioner"

388(1) [Acting as insolvency practitioner re company] A person acts as an insolvency practitioner in relation to a company by acting–

(a) as its liquidator, provisional liquidator, administrator or administrative receiver, or

(b) where a voluntary arrangement in relation to the company is proposed or approved under Part I, as nominee or supervisor.

388(2) [Acting as insolvency practitioner re individual] A person acts as an insolvency practitioner in relation to an individual by acting–

(a) as his trustee in bankruptcy or interim receiver of his property or as trustee (or interim trustee) in the sequestration of his estate; or

(b) as trustee under a deed which is in Scotland, a trust deed for his creditors; or

(c) where a voluntary arrangement in relation to the individual is proposed or approved under Part VIII, as nominee or supervisor;

(d) in the case of a deceased individual to the administration of whose estate this section applies by virtue of an order under section 421 (application of provisions of this Act to insolvent estates of deceased persons), as administrator of that estate.

388(2A) [Acting as insolvency practitioner re insolvent partnership] A person acts as an insolvency practitioner in relation to an insolvent partnership by acting–

(a) as its liquidator, provisional liquidator or administrator, or

(b) as trustee of the partnership under article 11 of the Insolvent Partnerships Order 1994, or

(c) where a voluntary arrangement in relation to the insolvent partnership is proposed or approved under Part I of the Act, as nominee or supervisor.

388(2B) [Acting as nominee re voluntary arrangement] In relation to a voluntary arrangement proposed under Part I or VIII, a person acts as nominee if he performs any of the functions conferred on nominees under the Part in question.

388(3) [Interpretation] References in this section to an individual include, except in so far as the context otherwise requires, references to any debtor within the meaning of the Bankruptcy (Scotland) Act 2016.

388(4) [Definitions] In this section–

"administrative receiver" has the meaning given by section 251 in Part VII;

"company" means–

(a) a company registered under the Companies Act 2006 in England and Wales or Scotland, or

(b) a company that may be wound up under Part 5 of this Act (unregistered companies); and

"sequestration" means sequestration under the Bankruptcy (Scotland) Act 2016.

388(5) [Application] Nothing in this section applies to anything done by–

(a) the official receiver; or

(b) the Accountant in Bankruptcy (within the meaning of the Bankruptcy (Scotland) Act 2016).

388(6) [Applicability of EU Regulation] Nothing in this section applies to anything done (whether in the United Kingdom or elsewhere) in relation to insolvency proceedings under the EU Regulation in a member State other than the United Kingdom.

General Note

The first step in establishing the statutory requirement that every insolvency practitioner should be professionally qualified is taken in this section, which defines the phrase "acts as an insolvency practitioner". This is not a *general* definition describing the work or activities of such a practitioner in the abstract, but a *specific* definition of what amounts to acting as an insolvency practitioner *in relation to* a particular company or individual. The Act does not make it an offence to carry on an insolvency practitioner's business without the requisite qualification, but rather to act "in relation to" a company or individual when the statutory requirements are not met (s.389).

An important point to bear in mind is that it is possible to "act as an insolvency practitioner" in relation to a person who is not insolvent—and to do so in breach of the Act will be just as much an offence as in a case of actual insolvency. Thus, the liquidator appointed by a company in a members' voluntary winding up "acts as an insolvency practitioner" even where the company has a large cash surplus and has never been in trading difficulties.

Most of the expressions used in this section are defined or explained either in the section itself or elsewhere in the Act.

Section 388 is disapplied to a limited extent by the Cross-Border Insolvency Regulations 2006 (SI 2006/1030).

There were various amendments to s.388(2)(a), (3), (4), (5)(b) by the Bankruptcy (Scotland) Act 2016 (Consequential Provisions and Modifications) Order 2016 (SI 2016/1034) art.7(1), Sch.1 para.4(1), (6) as from 30 November 2016.

S.388(1), (2)

Note the amendments by IA 2000 s.4.

Note amendment by DA 2015 s.19 and Sch.6.

S.388(2A)

Section 388(2A) was inserted and the words "to a partnership and" in s.388(3) were omitted for the purposes of the Insolvent Partnerships Order 1994 (SI 1994/2421) art.15 as from 1 December 1994. Section 388(2A)(c) was amended by the Insolvent Partnerships (Amendment) (No.2) Order 2002 (SI 2002/2708) art.3 as from 1 January 2003.

S.388(2B)

This was inserted by IA 2000 s.4.

S.388(4)

A receiver who is not an administrative receiver (i.e. a receiver of less than a "substantial" part of the company's property (ss.29(2), 251)) is not required to be qualified to act, but certain categories of person are disqualified from acting by ss.30, 31, 51(3).

Note the amendment made to subs.(4) by the Companies Act 2006 (Consequential Amendments, Transitional Provisions and Savings) Order 2009 (SI 2009/1941), which took effect on 1 October 2009. This amendment provides a new definition of "company". For the meaning of "company", see further the note to s.73(1). On "unregistered companies", see s.220. An insolvent partnership is treated as an unregistered company for the purposes of Pt V: see subs.(2A) above and the note to s.420.

Part XIII of IA 1986 was extended to apply to the winding up of building societies by CA 1989 s.211(2)(a) with effect from 31 July 1990, thus remedying an omission made when building societies were first made subject to the winding-up provisions by the Building Societies Act 1986.

S.388(5)

The official receiver, as the holder of a public office, is not required to be qualified to act as an insolvency practitioner. This will include a deputy official receiver (see s.401).

S.388(6)

This was added by Insolvency Act 1986 (Amendment) (No.2) Regulations 2002 (SI 2002/1240) reg.17 with effect from 31 May 2002 and amended by the Insolvency Amendment (EU 2015/848) Regulations 2017 (SI 2017/702) regs 1, 2(1), Sch. paras 1, 23 in relation to proceedings opened on or after 26 June 2017 (see reg.3) when the Recast EU Regulation 2015/848 came into force.

389 Acting without qualification an offence

389(1) [Penalty] A person who acts as an insolvency practitioner in relation to a company or an individual at a time when he is not qualified to do so is liable to imprisonment or a fine, or to both.

389(1A) [Omitted]

389(2) [Non-application to official receiver] This section does not apply to the official receiver or the Accountant in Bankruptcy (within the meaning of the Bankruptcy (Scotland) Act 2016).

S.389(1)
The word "qualified" refers not simply to a professional qualification (which may or may not be required: see s.390(2)(b)), but to a complex set of requirements, some of them specifically related to the company or individual concerned.

On penalties, see s.430 and Sch.10. Note Banking Act 2009 ss.103 and 145.

S.389(1A)
Inserted by IA 2000 s.4.

Subsection (1A) is repealed by DA 2015.

S.389(2)
Amended by the Bankruptcy (Scotland) Act 2016 (Consequential Provisions and Modifications) Order 2016 (SI 2016/1034) art.7(1), Sch.1 para.4(1), (7) as from 30 November 2016.

389A Authorisation of nominees and supervisors [Repealed]

General Note

This new section was added by s.4 of IA 2000. It allowed a wider range of practitioners to service voluntary arrangements, and in particular those turnaround specialists who may be authorised by the Secretary of State. For discussion of the role of turnaround practitioners see Finch [2005] J.B.L. 690. According to an Insolvency Service Consultative Document on Proposed Changes to the IVA Regime (issued in May 2007) this provision is likely to be modified by legislative reform order to make it absolutely clear that non-IPs can apply to operate IVAs, CVAs or both. This is a recognition that the wording of s.389A was unclear.

This provision is repealed by DA 2015.

389B Official receiver as nominee or supervisor

389B(1) [Voluntary arrangement where debtor undischarged bankrupt] The official receiver is authorised to act as nominee or supervisor in relation to a voluntary arrangement approved under Part VIII provided that the debtor is an undischarged bankrupt when the arrangement is proposed.

389B(2) [Power of Secretary of State] The Secretary of State may by order repeal the proviso in subsection (1).

389B(3) [Procedure for s.389B(2) order] An order under subsection (2)–

(a) must be made by statutory instrument, and

(b) shall be subject to annulment in pursuance of a resolution of either House of Parliament.

S.389B(1)
Introduced by EA 2002 s.264 and Sch.22, this enables the official receiver to acts as nominee/supervisor of a "fast track IVA" agreed under s.263A. This is an innovation—previously the role of servicing IVAs was restricted to private insolvency practitioners.

S.389B(2), (3)
These provide future flexibility for the Secretary of State.

The requisite qualification, and the means of obtaining it

390 Persons not qualified to act as insolvency practitioners

390(1) [Must be individual] A person who is not an individual is not qualified to act as an insolvency practitioner.

390(2) [Authorisation necessary under s.390A] A person is not qualified to act as an insolvency practitioner at any time unless at that time the person is appropriately authorised under section 390A.

390(3) [Security as condition required] A person is not qualified to act as an insolvency practitioner in relation to another person at any time unless–

(a) there is in force at that time security or, in Scotland, caution for the proper performance of his functions, and

(b) that security or caution meets the prescribed requirements with respect to his so acting in relation to that other person.

390(4) [Disqualification] A person is not qualified to act as an insolvency practitioner at any time if at that time–

(a) he has been made bankrupt under this Act or the Insolvency (Northern Ireland) Order 1989 or sequestration of his estate has been awarded and (in either case) he has not been discharged,

(aa) a moratorium period under a debt relief order under this Act or the Insolvency (Northern Ireland) Order 1989 applies in relation of him,

(b) he is subject to a disqualification order made or a disqualification undertaking accepted under the Company Directors Disqualification Act 1986 or the Company Directors Disqualification (Northern Ireland) Order 2002,

(c) he is a patient within the meaning of section 329(1) of the Mental Health (Care and Treatment) (Scotland) Act 2003 or has had a guardian appointed to him under the Adults with Incapacity (Scotland) Act 2000 (asp 4), or

(d) he lacks capacity (within the meaning of the Mental Capacity Act 2005) to act as an insolvency practitioner.

390(5) [Disqualification where bankruptcy/debt relief restrictions order] A person is not qualified to act as an insolvency practitioner while there is in force in respect of that person–

(a) a bankruptcy restrictions order under this Act, the Bankruptcy (Scotland) Act 1985 or the Bankruptcy (Scotland) Act 2016 or the Insolvency (Northern Ireland) Order 1989, or

(b) a debt relief restrictions order under this Act or that Order.

General Note

As explained above, the Act uses the one term "qualified" with reference both to the general eligibility of the person to act as a practitioner and also to his specific eligibility to act vis-à-vis a particular company or individual. This section deals mainly with the general requirement, except for the statement in s.390(3)(b) that the practitioner's bonding obligation must relate to the person or company whose affairs he is administering. However, the subject of "qualification" is further dealt with in subordinate legislation made under s.419(2)(b). Reference should be made to the Insolvency Practitioners Regulations 2005 (SI 2005/524), which consolidate and replace earlier regulations dating from 1990.

Each of the regulatory bodies (see the note to s.391(1)), and also the Insolvency Practitioners' Association and the Association of Business Recovery Professionals publishes a guide to professional conduct and ethics, which sets out guiding principles relating to the conduct of insolvency practitioners in regard to accepting appointment as a trustee or office-holder, etc.

For the potential effect of EU Directive 2005/36 on the recognition of professional qualifications of insolvency practitioners who had qualified outside the UK see *Dear IP*, September 2007. This Directive is implemented in the UK by the EC (Recognition of Professional Qualifications) Regulations 2007 (SI 2007/2781).

Note Banking Act 2009 ss.103 and 145.

S.390(1)

The disqualification of corporate bodies is an extension of the prohibition that formerly applied in the case of a liquidator (CA 1985 s.634) and still applies to a receiver (not necessarily an administrative receiver): see ss.30 and 51(3)(a), (c). An act purportedly done by a corporate receiver has been held to be a nullity: see the note to s.232.

On the question of joint appointments, see s.231.

S.390(2)

The Cork Committee recommended (*Report*, para.758) that an insolvency practitioner should be required in all cases to be a member of an "approved" professional body and to have been in general practice for five years before being eligible to act. (Transitional arrangements would have allowed experienced individuals who were not professionally qualified to obtain direct authorisation to act from the Secretary of State.) The Government in its White Paper (para.43) broadly endorsed this view, but in the Insolvency Bill as originally published in 1984 went further, and provided that every insolvency practitioner, whether a member of a profession or not, should be required to hold a certificate issued to him personally by the Secretary of State before he was eligible to act. The legislation in its final form, however, returns to a compromise position: those who are under the supervision of a recognised professional body are to be permitted or authorised to act by that body, and will not be directly licensed or controlled by the Secretary of State, while others may be authorised as individuals to act, either by the Secretary of State or by a "competent authority" to which this function may be delegated (s.392). The "direct licensing" provisions of the Act do not appear, however, to have been purely a transitional arrangement as the Cork Committee envisaged.

Schedule 11 para.21 provides that a person who was already in office (e.g. as a liquidator) when the Act came into force could continue to discharge the functions of that particular office, and so complete the liquidation, etc. without the need for acquiring a qualification under s.390(2) or (3).

S.390(3)

This subsection provides for the bonding of insolvency practitioners, which is a mandatory requirement for all officeholders. The security may be provided either generally or specially for a particular insolvency, and provides a safeguard for creditors and other interested persons who may suffer loss as a result of breach by the insolvency practitioner of the duties and obligations imposed on him by the legislation. The surety's liability is limited to a sum equivalent to the losses caused by the fraud or dishonesty of the practitioner, whether acting alone or in collusion with others; for the maximum amount for which any bond must be given see the Insolvency Practitioners Regulations 2005 (SI 2005/524). On the practicalities associated with insolvency bonds see Hunt and Tribe [2014] 27 Insolv. Int. 17.

On the question of transitional provisions for persons holding office when the Act came into force, see the note to s.390(2) above.

S.390(4)

In s.390(4)(c) the words "or has had a guardian appointed to him under the Adults with Incapacity (Scotland) Act 2000 (asp 4)" inserted at the end by the Adults with Incapacity (Scotland) Act 2000 s.88(2), Sch.5 para.18 as from 1 April 2002 (Adults with Incapacity (Scotland) Act 2000 (Commencement No.1) Order 2001 (SI 2001/81 (C. 2)) art.3, Sch.2). Further amendments were made by the Mental Health (Care and Treatment) (Scotland) Act 2003 (Consequential Provisions) Order 2005 (SI 2005/2078) Sch.1 para.3(3). Subsection (4) was amended by Sch.6 to the Mental Capacity Act 2005 and by the Tribunals, Courts and Enforcement Act 2007.

Note the amendment made to subs.(4)(b) by the Companies Act 2006 (Consequential Amendments, Transitional Provisions and Savings) Order 2009 (SI 2009/1941), which came into effect on 1 October 2009.

If a person comes under any of the disabilities mentioned, his disqualification is automatic, and does not depend upon the withdrawal of his authorisation under s.393. Acts done by a disqualified person may, however, be valid by virtue of s.232: see the note to that section.

Subsection (4)(a) was amended by ERRA 2013 Sch.19 para.58.

S.390(5)

This was inserted by EA 2002 Sch.21 to respond to the advent of BROs from April 2004.

Section 390(5) substituted by the Small Business, Enterprise and Employment Act 2015 s.115(b) as from 1 October 2015 and amended by the Bankruptcy (Scotland) Act 2016 (Consequential Provisions and Modifications) Order 2016 (SI 2016/1034) art.7(1), Sch.1 para.4(1), (8) as from 30 November 2016.

390A Authorisation

390A(1) [Types of authorisation] In this Part–

"partial authorisation" means authorisation to act as an insolvency practitioner–

(a) only in relation to companies, or

(b) only in relation to individuals;

"full authorisation" means authorisation to act as an insolvency practitioner in relation to companies, individuals and insolvent partnerships;

"partially authorised" and "fully authorised" are to be construed accordingly.

390A(2) [Full authorisation] A person is fully authorised under this section to act as an insolvency practitioner–

(a) by virtue of being a member of a professional body recognised under section 391(1) and being permitted to act as an insolvency practitioner for all purposes by or under the rules of that body, or

(b) by holding an authorisation granted by the Department of Enterprise, Trade and Investment in Northern Ireland under Article 352 of the Insolvency (Northern Ireland) Order 1989.

390A(3) [Partial authorisation] A person is partially authorised under this section to act as an insolvency practitioner–

(a) by virtue of being a member of a professional body recognised under section 391(1) and being permitted to act as an insolvency practitioner in relation only to companies or only to individuals by or under the rules of that body, or

(b) by virtue of being a member of a professional body recognised under section 391(2) and being permitted to act as an insolvency practitioner by or under the rules of that body.

General Note

Inserted by DA 2015 s.17. This provision deals with the long-awaited regime for the partial authorisation of insolvency practitioners, which it is hoped will enhance competition in the market for insolvency services.

390B Partial authorisation: acting in relation to partnerships

390B(1) [Authorisation for companies: prohibition if partnership connection] A person who is partially authorised to act as an insolvency practitioner in relation to companies may nonetheless not accept an appointment to act in relation to a company if at the time of the appointment the person is aware that the company–

(a) is or was a member of a partnership, and

(b) has outstanding liabilities in relation to the partnership.

390B(2) [Authorisation for individuals: prohibition if partnership connection] A person who is partially authorised to act as an insolvency practitioner in relation to individuals may nonetheless not accept an appointment to act in relation to an individual if at the time of the appointment the person is aware that the individual–

(a) is or was a member of a partnership other than a Scottish partnership, and

(b) has outstanding liabilities in relation to the partnership.

390B(3) [Authorisation for companies: becoming aware of partnership connection] Subject to subsection (9), a person who is partially authorised to act as an insolvency practitioner in relation to companies may nonetheless not continue to act in relation to a company if the person becomes aware that the company–

(a) is or was a member of a partnership, and

(b) has outstanding liabilities in relation to the partnership,

unless the person is granted permission to continue to act by the court.

390B(4) [Authorisation for individuals: becoming aware partnership connection] Subject to subsection (9), a person who is partially authorised to act as an insolvency practitioner in relation to individuals may nonetheless not continue to act in relation to an individual if the person becomes aware that the individual–

(a) is or was a member of a partnership other than a Scottish partnership, and

(b) has outstanding liabilities in relation to the partnership,

unless the person is granted permission to continue to act by the court.

390B(5) [Permission of court re s.390B(3), (4)] The court may grant a person permission to continue to act for the purposes of subsection (3) or (4) if it is satisfied that the person is competent to do so.

390B(6) [Application for replacement order for fully authorised IP] A person who is partially authorised and becomes aware as mentioned in subsection (3) or (4) may alternatively apply to the court for an order (a "replacement order") appointing in his or her place a person who is fully authorised to act as an insolvency practitioner in relation to the company or (as the case may be) the individual.

390B(7) [Application for permission to continue or replacement order] A person may apply to the court for permission to continue to act or for a replacement order under–

(a) where acting in relation to a company, this section or, if it applies, section 168(5B) (member of insolvent partnership: England and Wales);

(b) where acting in relation to an individual, this section or, if it applies, section 303(2C) (member of insolvent partnership: England and Wales).

390B(8) [Offence] A person who acts as an insolvency practitioner in contravention of any of subsections (1) to (4) is guilty of an offence under section 389 (acting without qualification).

390B(9) [No offence if application for permission or replacement order] A person does not contravene subsection (3) or (4) by continuing to act as an insolvency practitioner during the permitted period if, within the period of 7 business days beginning with the day after the day on which the person becomes aware as mentioned in the subsection, the person–

(a) applies to the court for permission to continue to act, or

(b) applies to the court for a replacement order.

390B(10) ["Business day", "permitted period", "replacement order" in s.390B(9)] For the purposes of subsection (9)–

"business day" means any day other than a Saturday, a Sunday, Christmas Day, Good Friday or a day which is a bank holiday in any part of Great Britain;

"permitted period" means the period beginning with the day on which the person became aware as mentioned in subsection (3) or (4) and ending on the earlier of–

(a) the expiry of the period of 6 weeks beginning with the day on which the person applies to the court as mentioned in subsection (9)(a) or (b), and

(b) the day on which the court disposes of the application (by granting or refusing it);

"replacement order" has the meaning given by subsection (6).

General Note

Inserted by DA 2015 s.17. This provides practical guidance on how the partial authorisation regime will operate where the appointment relates to a company or individual which is linked to a partnership.

391 Recognised professional bodies

391(1) [Order by Secretary of State: full or partial authorisation] The Secretary of State may by order, if satisfied that a body meets the requirements of subsection (4), declare the body to be a recognised professional body which is capable of providing its insolvency specialist members with full authorisation or partial authorisation.

391(2) [Order by Secretary of State: partial authorisation] The Secretary of State may by order, if satisfied that a body meets the requirements of subsection (4), declare the body to be a recognised professional body which is capable of providing its insolvency specialist members with partial authorisation only of the kind specified in the order (as to which, see section 390A(1)).

391(3) [Application under s.391A] Section 391A makes provision about the making by a body of an application to the Secretary of State for an order under this section.

391(4) [Requirements for order] The requirements are that–

(a) the body regulates (or is going to regulate) the practice of a profession,

(b) the body has rules which it is going to maintain and enforce for securing that its insolvency specialist members–

(i) are fit and proper persons to act as insolvency practitioners, and

(ii) meet acceptable requirements as to education and practical training and experience, and

(c) the body's rules and practices for or in connection with authorising persons to act as insolvency practitioners, and its rules and practices for or in connection with regulating persons acting as such, are designed to ensure that the regulatory objectives are met (as to which, see section 391C).

391(5) [Date order takes effect] An order of the Secretary of State under this section has effect from such date as is specified in the order.

391(6) [Revocation of order] An order under this section may be revoked by an order under section 391L or 391N (and see section 415A(1)(b)).

391(7) [Interpretation of RPB members, insolvency specialist members] In this Part–

(a) references to members of a recognised professional body are to persons who, whether members of that body or not, are subject to its rules in the practice of the profession in question;

(b) references to insolvency specialist members of a professional body are to members who are permitted by or under the rules of the body to act as insolvency practitioners.

391(8) [Recognised professional body] A reference in this Part to a recognised professional body is to a body recognised under this section (and see sections 391L(6) and 391N(5)).

General Note

A new s.391 was substituted by DA 2015. In a legislative masterstroke this was then immediately replaced by a further iteration of s.391 courtesy of SBEEA 2015 s.137. This provision deals with the recognition and regulation of recognised professional bodies (RPBs) by the secretary of state. Provision is made for those RPBs having members who only enjoy partial authorisation status.

391A Application for recognition as recognised professional body

391A(1) [Requirements for application] An application for an order under section 391(1) or (2) must–

(a) be made to the Secretary of State in such form and manner as the Secretary of State may require,

(b) be accompanied by such information as the Secretary of State may require, and

(c) be supplemented by such additional information as the Secretary of State may require at any time between receiving the application and determining it.

391A(2) [Requirements may differ] The requirements which may be imposed under subsection (1) may differ as between different applications.

391A(3) [Form and verification of information] The Secretary of State may require information provided under this section to be in such form, and verified in such manner, as the Secretary of State may specify.

391A(4) [Accompanying documents to application] An application for an order under section 391(1) or (2) must be accompanied by–

(a) a copy of the applicant's rules,

(b) a copy of the applicant's policies and practices, and

(c) a copy of any guidance issued by the applicant in writing.

391A(5) [Guidance] The reference in subsection (4)(c) to guidance issued by the applicant is a reference to guidance or recommendations which are–

(a) issued or made by it which will apply to its insolvency specialist members or to persons seeking to become such members,

(b) relevant for the purposes of this Part, and

(c) intended to have continuing effect,

including guidance or recommendations relating to the admission or expulsion of members.

391A(6) [Power of refusal where recognition unnecessary] The Secretary of State may refuse an application for an order under section 391(1) or (2) if the Secretary of State considers that recognition of the body concerned is unnecessary having regard to the existence of one or more other bodies which have been or are likely to be recognised under section 391.

391A(7) [Application of s.39A(8)] Subsection (8) applies where the Secretary of State refuses an application for an order under section 391(1) or (2); and it applies regardless of whether the application is refused on the ground mentioned in subsection (6), because the Secretary of State is not satisfied as mentioned in section 391(1) or (2) or because a fee has not been paid (see section 415A(1)(b)).

391A(8) [Written notice by Secretary of State of decision] The Secretary of State must give the applicant a written notice of the Secretary of State's decision; and the notice must set out the reasons for refusing the application.

General Note

This deals with the application procedure for recognition of an aspiring RPB. The provision was inserted by SBEEA 2015 s.137.

Regulatory objectives

391B Application of regulatory objectives

391B(1) [Duty of RPB] In discharging regulatory functions, a recognised professional body must, so far as is reasonably practicable, act in a way–

(a) which is compatible with the regulatory objectives, and

(b) which the body considers most appropriate for the purpose of meeting those objectives.

391B(2) [Duty of Secretary of State] In discharging functions under this Part, the Secretary of State must have regard to the regulatory objectives.

General Note

This statement of regulatory objectives, which is imported via SBEEA 2015 s.138, represents an important step forward in the regulation of insolvency practitioners by imposing obligations upon RPBs when carrying out their allocated tasks.

391C Meaning of "regulatory functions" and "regulatory objectives"

391C(1) [Application] This section has effect for the purposes of this Part.

391C(2) ["Regulatory functions"] "Regulatory functions", in relation to a recognised professional body, means any functions the body has–

(a) under or in relation to its arrangements for or in connection with–

(i) authorising persons to act as insolvency practitioners, or

(ii) regulating persons acting as insolvency practitioners, or

(b) in connection with the making or alteration of those arrangements.

391C(3) ["Regulatory objectives"] "Regulatory objectives" means the objectives of–

(a) having a system of regulating persons acting as insolvency practitioners that–

(i) secures fair treatment for persons affected by their acts and omissions,

(ii) reflects the regulatory principles, and

(iii) ensures consistent outcomes,

(b) encouraging an independent and competitive insolvency practitioner profession whose members–

(i) provide high quality services at a cost to the recipient which is fair and reasonable,

(ii) act transparently and with integrity, and

(iii) consider the interests of all creditors in any particular case,

(c) promoting the maximisation of the value of returns to creditors and promptness in making those returns, and

(d) protecting and promoting the public interest.

391C(4) ["Regulatory principles"] In subsection (3)(a), "regulatory principles" means–

(a) the principles that regulatory activities should be transparent, accountable, proportionate, consistent and targeted only at cases in which action is needed, and

(b) any other principle appearing to the body concerned (in the case of the duty under section 391B(1)), or to the Secretary of State (in the case of the duty under section 391B(2)), to lead to best regulatory practice.

General Note

This in effect is an interpretation provision designed to put flesh on the bare bones of s.391B. Standing back from the precise definitions, we see the need for RPBs to act fairly and consistently. The requirements of transparency and proportionality are also highlighted.

Oversight of recognised professional bodies

391D Directions

391D(1) [Application] This section applies if the Secretary of State is satisfied that an act or omission of a recognised professional body (or a series of such acts or omissions) in discharging one or more of its regulatory functions has had, or is likely to have, an adverse impact on the achievement of one or more of the regulatory objectives.

391D(2) [Direction of Secretary of State] The Secretary of State may, if in all the circumstances of the case satisfied that it is appropriate to do so, direct the body to take such steps as the Secretary of State considers will counter the adverse impact, mitigate its effect or prevent its occurrence or recurrence.

391D(3) [Requirement of direction re regulatory arrangements] A direction under this section may require a recognised professional body–

(a) to take only such steps as it has power to take under its regulatory arrangements;

(b) to take steps with a view to the modification of any part of its regulatory arrangements.

391D(4) [Requirement of direction re regulatory proceedings] A direction under this section may require a recognised professional body–

(a) to take steps with a view to the institution of, or otherwise in respect of, specific regulatory proceedings;

(b) to take steps in respect of all, or a specified class of, such proceedings.

391D(5) [Direction to take steps] For the purposes of this section, a direction to take steps includes a direction which requires a recognised professional body to refrain from taking a particular course of action.

391D(6) ["Regulatory arrangements"] In this section "regulatory arrangements", in relation to a recognised professional body, means the arrangements that the body has for or in connection with–

(a) authorising persons to act as insolvency practitioners, or

(b) regulating persons acting as insolvency practitioners.

General Note

This provision was introduced by SBEEA 2015 s.139. If the Secretary of State believes that the conduct of an RPB is not consistent with the regulatory objectives as specified in ss.391B and 391C a direction can be given to require it to get back into line. This is an important policing mechanism.

391E Directions: procedure

391E(1) [Notice and draft] Before giving a recognised professional body a direction under section 391D, the Secretary of State must give the body a notice accompanied by a draft of the proposed direction.

391E(2) [Contents of s.391E(1) notice] The notice under subsection (1) must–

(a) state that the Secretary of State proposes to give the body a direction in the form of the accompanying draft,

(b) specify why the Secretary of State has reached the conclusions mentioned in section 391D(1) and (2), and

(c) specify a period within which the body may make written representations with respect to the proposal.

391E(3) [Period for representations in s.391E(2)(c)] The period specified under subsection (2)(c)–

(a) must begin with the date on which the notice is given to the body, and

(b) must not be less than 28 days.

391E(4) [Duty of Secretary of State to decide] On the expiry of that period, the Secretary of State must decide whether to give the body the proposed direction.

391E(5) [Notice of decision to RPB] The Secretary of State must give notice of that decision to the body.

391E(6) [Contents of s.391E(5) notice] Where the Secretary of State decides to give the proposed direction, the notice under subsection (5) must–

(a) contain the direction,

(b) state the time at which the direction is to take effect, and

(c) specify the Secretary of State's reasons for the decision to give the direction.

391E(7) [Publication of 391E] Where the Secretary of State decides to give the proposed direction, the Secretary of State must publish the notice under subsection (5); but this subsection does not apply to a direction to take any step with a view to the institution of, or otherwise in respect of, regulatory proceedings against an individual.

391E(8) [Revocation of direction] The Secretary of State may revoke a direction under section 391D; and, where doing so, the Secretary of State–

(a) must give the body to which the direction was given notice of the revocation, and

(b) must publish the notice and, if the notice under subsection (5) was published under subsection (7), must do so (if possible) in the same manner as that in which that notice was published.

General Note

This provides procedural safeguards for an RPB which might be subjected to a regulatory direction under s.391D. Essentially we have an early warning mechanism and formal requirements for the content of any direction.

391F Financial penalty

391F(1) [Application of section] This section applies if the Secretary of State is satisfied–

(a) that a recognised professional body has failed to comply with a requirement to which this section applies, and

(b) that, in all the circumstances of the case, it is appropriate to impose a financial penalty on the body.

391F(2) [Application to requirement on RPB] This section applies to a requirement imposed on the recognised professional body–

(a) by a direction given under section 391D, or

(b) by a provision of this Act or of subordinate legislation under this Act.

391F(3) [Amount of penalty] The Secretary of State may impose a financial penalty, in respect of the failure, of such amount as the Secretary of State considers appropriate.

391F(4) [Matters Secretary of State to have regard to] In deciding what amount is appropriate, the Secretary of State–

(a) must have regard to the nature of the requirement which has not been complied with, and

(b) must not take into account the Secretary of State's costs in discharging functions under this Part.

391F(5) [To whom penalty payable] A financial penalty under this section is payable to the Secretary of State; and sums received by the Secretary of State in respect of a financial penalty under this section (including by way of interest) are to be paid into the Consolidated Fund.

391F(6) ["Penalty" in ss.391G–391I] In sections 391G to 391I, "penalty" means a financial penalty under this section.

General Note

If an RPB fails to comply with a regulatory direction given under s.391D a financial penalty may be imposed by the Secretary of State. Any money received goes into the Consolidated Fund.

391G Financial penalty: procedure

391G(1) [Notice] Before imposing a penalty on a recognised professional body, the Secretary of State must give notice to the body–

(a) stating that the Secretary of State proposes to impose a penalty and the amount of the proposed penalty,

(b) specifying the requirement in question,

(c) stating why the Secretary of State is satisfied as mentioned in section 391F(1), and

(d) specifying a period within which the body may make written representations with respect to the proposal.

391G(2) [Period for representations] The period specified under subsection (1)(d)–

(a) must begin with the date on which the notice is given to the body, and

(b) must not be less than 28 days.

391G(3) [Duty of Secretary of State on expiry of period] On the expiry of that period, the Secretary of State must decide–

(a) whether to impose a penalty, and

(b) whether the penalty should be the amount stated in the notice or a reduced amount.

391G(4) [Notice of decision] The Secretary of State must give notice of the decision to the body.

391G(5) [Content of notice imposing penalty] Where the Secretary of State decides to impose a penalty, the notice under subsection (4) must–

(a) state that the Secretary of State has imposed a penalty on the body and its amount,

(b) specify the requirement in question and state–

(i) why it appears to the Secretary of State that the requirement has not been complied with, or

(ii) where, by that time, the requirement has been complied with, why it appeared to the Secretary of State when giving the notice under subsection (1) that the requirement had not been complied with, and

(c) specify a time by which the penalty is required to be paid.

391G(6) [Period for payment] The time specified under subsection (5)(c) must be at least three months after the date on which the notice under subsection (4) is given to the body.

391G(7) [Publication of penalty] Where the Secretary of State decides to impose a penalty, the Secretary of State must publish the notice under subsection (4).

391G(8) [Rescission or reduction of penalty] The Secretary of State may rescind or reduce a penalty imposed on a recognised professional body; and, where doing so, the Secretary of State–

(a) must give the body notice that the penalty has been rescinded or reduced to the amount stated in the notice, and

(b) must publish the notice; and it must (if possible) be published in the same manner as that in which the notice under subsection (4) was published.

General Note

This maps out procedural safeguards to be complied with before a financial penalty can be imposed under the previous section. Advance notice is required. The Secretary of State can under subs.(8) rescind or reduce any penalty that has been imposed.

391H Appeal against financial penalty

391H(1) [Right of appeal] A recognised professional body on which a penalty is imposed may appeal to the court on one or more of the appeal grounds.

391H(2) [Appeal grounds] The appeal grounds are–

(a) that the imposition of the penalty was not within the Secretary of State's power under section 391F;

(b) that the requirement in respect of which the penalty was imposed had been complied with before the notice under section 391G(1) was given;

(c) that the requirements of section 391G have not been complied with in relation to the imposition of the penalty and the interests of the body have been substantially prejudiced as a result;

(d) that the amount of the penalty is unreasonable;

(e) that it was unreasonable of the Secretary of State to require the penalty imposed to be paid by the time specified in the notice under section 391G(5)(c).

391H(3) [Period for appeal] An appeal under this section must be made within the period of three months beginning with the day on which the notice under section 391G(4) in respect of the penalty is given to the body.

391H(4) [Power of court] On an appeal under this section the court may–

(a) quash the penalty,

(b) substitute a penalty of such lesser amount as the court considers appropriate, or

(c) in the case of the appeal ground in subsection (2)(e), substitute for the time imposed by the Secretary of State a different time.

391H(5) [Interest where lesser sum substituted] Where the court substitutes a penalty of a lesser amount, it may require the payment of interest on the substituted penalty from such time, and at such rate, as it considers just and equitable.

391H(6) [Interest where later time for payment substituted] Where the court substitutes a later time for the time specified in the notice under section 391G(5)(c), it may require the payment of interest on the penalty from the substituted time at such rate as it considers just and equitable.

391H(7) [Interest where appeal dismissed] Where the court dismisses the appeal, it may require the payment of interest on the penalty from the time specified in the notice under section 391G(5)(c) at such rate as it considers just and equitable.

391H(8) ["The court"] In this section, "the court" means the High Court or, in Scotland, the Court of Session.

General Note

This provision spells out the appeal right of any RPB facing a financial penalty imposed under s.391F. The appeal lies to the court (as defined by subs.(8)). The court has wide powers of disposal of any such appeal—see subs.(4).

391I Recovery of financial penalties

391I(1) [Interest under Judgments Act 1838 s.17] If the whole or part of a penalty is not paid by the time by which it is required to be paid, the unpaid balance from time to time carries interest at the rate for the time being specified in section 17 of the Judgments Act 1838 (but this is subject to any requirement imposed by the court under section 391H(5), (6) or (7)).

391I(2) [Penalty where appeal] If an appeal is made under section 391H in relation to a penalty, the penalty is not required to be paid until the appeal has been determined or withdrawn.

391I(3) [Application of s.391I(4)] Subsection (4) applies where the whole or part of a penalty has not been paid by the time it is required to be paid and–

(a) no appeal relating to the penalty has been made under section 391H during the period within which an appeal may be made under that section, or

(b) an appeal has been made under that section and determined or withdrawn.

391I(4) [Penalty and interest a debt due] The Secretary of State may recover from the recognised professional body in question, as a debt due to the Secretary of State, any of the penalty and any interest which has not been paid.

General Note

This deals with the practicalities of recovery of any penalty imposed on an RPB. Hopefully this provision should not be required. But note that the rate of interest imposed by the Judgments Act 1838 applies.

391J Reprimand

391J(1) [Application of section] This section applies if the Secretary of State is satisfied that an act or omission of a recognised professional body (or a series of such acts or omissions) in discharging one or more of its regulatory functions has had, or is likely to have, an adverse impact on the achievement of one or more of the regulatory objectives.

391J(2) [Power of Secretary of State to publish reprimand] The Secretary of State may, if in all the circumstances of the case satisfied that it is appropriate to do so, publish a statement reprimanding the body for the act or omission (or series of acts or omissions).

General Note

This specifies the lesser sanction of a public reprimand where an RPB is deemed to have fallen short of its responsibilities.

391K Reprimand: procedure

391K(1) [Notice] If the Secretary of State proposes to publish a statement under section 391J in respect of a recognised professional body, it must give the body a notice–

(a) stating that the Secretary of State proposes to publish such a statement and setting out the terms of the proposed statement,

(b) specifying the acts or omissions to which the proposed statement relates, and

(c) specifying a period within which the body may make written representations with respect to the proposal.

391K(2) [Period for representations] The period specified under subsection (1)(c)–

(a) must begin with the date on which the notice is given to the body, and

(b) must not be less than 28 days.

391K(3) [Duty of Secretary of State to make decision] On the expiry of that period, the Secretary of State must decide whether to publish the statement.

391K(4) [Notice of variation of proposed statement] The Secretary of State may vary the proposed statement; but before doing so, the Secretary of State must give the body notice–

(a) setting out the proposed variation and the reasons for it, and

(b) specifying a period within which the body may make written representations with respect to the proposed variation.

391K(5) [Period for representations re variation] The period specified under subsection (4)(b)–

(a) must begin with the date on which the notice is given to the body, and

(b) must not be less than 28 days.

391K(6) [Publication of varied statement] On the expiry of that period, the Secretary of State must decide whether to publish the statement as varied.

GENERAL NOTE

As with other sanctions imposed on RPBs, there is a system of safeguards designed to protect an RPB facing a public reprimand under s.391J.

Revocation etc of recognition

391L Revocation of recognition at instigation of Secretary of State

391L(1) [Power of revocation] An order under section 391(1) or (2) in relation to a recognised professional body may be revoked by the Secretary of State by order if the Secretary of State is satisfied that–

(a) an act or omission of the body (or a series of such acts or omissions) in discharging one or more of its regulatory functions has had, or is likely to have, an adverse impact on the achievement of one or more of the regulatory objectives, and

(b) it is appropriate in all the circumstances of the case to revoke the body's recognition under section 391.

391L(2) [Partial authorisation] If the condition set out in subsection (3) is met, an order under section 391(1) in relation to a recognised professional body may be revoked by the Secretary of State by an order which also declares the body concerned to be a recognised professional body which is capable of providing its insolvency specialist members with partial authorisation only of the kind specified in the order (see section 390A(1)).

391L(3) [Condition for partial authorisation] The condition is that the Secretary of State is satisfied–

(a) as mentioned in subsection (1)(a), and

(b) that it is appropriate in all the circumstances of the case for the body to be declared to be a recognised professional body which is capable of providing its insolvency specialist members with partial authorisation only of the kind specified in the order.

391L(4) ["Revocation order", "partial revocation order"] In this Part–

(a) an order under subsection (1) is referred to as a "revocation order";

(b) an order under subsection (2) is referred to as a "partial revocation order".

391L(5) [Effect of revocation order, partial revocation] A revocation order or partial revocation order–

(a) has effect from such date as is specified in the order, and

(b) may make provision for members of the body in question to continue to be treated as fully or partially authorised (as the case may be) to act as insolvency practitioners for a specified period after the order takes effect.

391L(6) [Partial revocation order] A partial revocation order has effect as if it were an order made under section 391(2).

GENERAL NOTE

This provision (introduced by SBEEA 2015 s.140), deals with the revocation of recognition of an RPB. Revocation may be partial. Provision is made to safeguard the position of the members of the RPB in question.

391M Orders under section 391L: procedure

391M(1) [Notice] Before making a revocation order or partial revocation order in relation to a recognised professional body, the Secretary of State must give notice to the body–

(a) stating that the Secretary of State proposes to make the order and the terms of the proposed order,

(b) specifying the Secretary of State's reasons for proposing to make the order, and

(c) specifying a period within which the body, members of the body or other persons likely to be affected by the proposal may make written representations with respect to it.

391M(2) [Publication of notice] Where the Secretary of State gives a notice under subsection (1), the Secretary of State must publish the notice on the same day.

391M(3) [Period for representations] The period specified under subsection (1)(c)–

(a) must begin with the date on which the notice is given to the body, and

(b) must not be less than 28 days.

391M(4) [Duty of Secretary of State to make decision] On the expiry of that period, the Secretary of State must decide whether to make the revocation order or (as the case may be) partial revocation order in relation to the body.

391M(5) [Notice of decision] The Secretary of State must give notice of the decision to the body.

391M(6) [Content of decision notice for order] Where the Secretary of State decides to make the order, the notice under subsection (5) must specify–

(a) when the order is to take effect, and

(b) the Secretary of State's reasons for making the order.

391M(7) [Publication of notice of decision] A notice under subsection (5) must be published; and it must (if possible) be published in the same manner as that in which the notice under subsection (1) was published.

General Note

This deals with procedural matters associated with a revocation pursuant to s.391L. Essentially the RPB must be put on notice of the concerns of the Secretary of State to allow it to respond.

391N Revocation of recognition at request of body

391N(1) [Power of Secretary of State] An order under section 391(1) or (2) in relation to a recognised professional body may be revoked by the Secretary of State by order if–

(a) the body has requested that an order be made under this subsection, and

(b) the Secretary of State is satisfied that it is appropriate in all the circumstances of the case to revoke the body's recognition under section 391.

391N(2) [Partial authorisation] An order under section 391(1) in relation to a recognised professional body may be revoked by the Secretary of State by an order which also declares the body concerned to be a recognised professional body which is capable of providing its insolvency specialist members with partial authorisation only of the kind specified in the order (see section 390A(1)) if–

(a) the body has requested that an order be made under this subsection, and

(b) the Secretary of State is satisfied that it is appropriate in all the circumstances of the case for the body to be declared to be a recognised professional body which is capable of providing its insolvency specialist members with partial authorisation only of the kind specified in the order.

391N(3) [Publication of notice to make order] Where the Secretary of State decides to make an order under this section the Secretary of State must publish a notice specifying–

(a) when the order is to take effect, and

(b) the Secretary of State's reasons for making the order.

391N(4) [Effect of order] An order under this section–

(a) has effect from such date as is specified in the order, and

(b) may make provision for members of the body in question to continue to be treated as fully or partially authorised (as the case may be) to act as insolvency practitioners for a specified period after the order takes effect.

391N(5) [Effect of order for partial authorisation] An order under subsection (2) has effect as if it were an order made under section 391(2).

General Note

An RPB can in effect fall on its sword and seek de-recognition. For an example of this happening see the Insolvency Practitioners (Recognised Professional Bodies) (Revocation of Recognition) Order 2015 (SI 2015/2067) which removes the Law Society of Scotland from RPB recognition with effect from 18 January 2016. The Law Society also secured its own de-recognition by the Insolvency Practitioners (Recognised Professional Bodies) (Revocation of Recognition) Order 2016 (SI 2016/403).

Court sanction of insolvency practitioners in public interest cases

391O Direct sanctions orders

391O(1) ["Direct sanctions order"] For the purposes of this Part a "direct sanctions order" is an order made by the court against a person who is acting as an insolvency practitioner which–

(a) declares that the person is no longer authorised (whether fully or partially) to act as an insolvency practitioner;

(b) declares that the person is no longer fully authorised to act as an insolvency practitioner but remains partially authorised to act as such either in relation to companies or individuals, as specified in the order;

(c) declares that the person's authorisation to act as an insolvency practitioner is suspended for the period specified in the order or until such time as the requirements so specified are complied with;

(d) requires the person to comply with such other requirements as may be specified in the order while acting as an insolvency practitioner;

(e) requires the person to make such contribution as may be specified in the order to one or more creditors of a company, individual or insolvent partnership in relation to which the person is acting or has acted as an insolvency practitioner.

391O(2) [Relevant RPB to take steps] Where the court makes a direct sanctions order, the relevant recognised professional body must take all necessary steps to give effect to the order.

391O(3) [Where no order] A direct sanctions order must not be made against a person whose authorisation to act as an insolvency practitioner was granted by the Department of Enterprise, Trade and Investment in Northern Ireland (see section 390A(2)(b)).

391O(4) [Maximum contribution in order] A direct sanctions order must not specify a contribution as mentioned in subsection (1)(e) which is more than the remuneration that the person has received or will receive in respect of acting as an insolvency practitioner in the case.

391O(5) ["The court", "relevant recognised professional body"] In this section and section 391P–

"the court" means the High Court or, in Scotland, the Court of Session;

"relevant recognised professional body", in relation to a person who is acting as an insolvency practitioner, means the recognised professional body by virtue of which the person is authorised so to act.

General Note

This section, and the two sections immediately following it deal with the sanctioning of errant insolvency practitioners. Section 391O covers direct sanctions made by the court. Such sanctions can extend to complete exclusion from insolvency practice. Note the possibility under subs.(1)(d) of direct financial contributions to creditors being required—presumably this would cover instances of misfeasance by an office holder. Such a contribution is capped by subs.(4).

See note after s.391R.

391P Application for, and power to make, direct sanctions order

391P(1) [Power of Secretary of State to apply to court] The Secretary of State may apply to the court for a direct sanctions order to be made against a person if it appears to the Secretary of State that it would be in the public interest for the order to be made.

391P(2) [Copy of application to RPB] The Secretary of State must send a copy of the application to the relevant recognised professional body.

391P(3) [Power of court where conditions satisfied] The court may make a direct sanctions order against a person where, on an application under this section, the court is satisfied that condition 1 and at least one of conditions 2, 3, 4 and 5 are met in relation to the person.

391P(4) [Conditions in s.391Q] The conditions are set out in section 391Q.

391P(5) [Matters court must have regard to] In deciding whether to make a direct sanctions order against a person the court must have regard to the extent to which–

(a) the relevant recognised professional body has taken action against the person in respect of the failure mentioned in condition 1, and

(b) that action is sufficient to address the failure.

General Note

Introduced by SBEEA 2015 s.141 this section details the procedure and requirements for an application to be made to the court for a direct sanctions order under s.391O. The circumstances under which the court can make the order are mapped out. It seems to be a jurisdiction of last resort with the hope being that the RPB can deal with the issue before court action is required.

See note after s.391R.

391Q Direct sanctions order: conditions

391Q(1) [Condition 1] Condition 1 is that the person, in acting as an insolvency practitioner or in connection with any appointment as such, has failed to comply with–

(a) a requirement imposed by the rules of the relevant recognised professional body;

(b) any standards, or code of ethics, for the insolvency-practitioner profession adopted from time to time by the relevant recognised professional body.

391Q(2) [Condition 2] Condition 2 is that the person–

(a) is not a fit and proper person to act as an insolvency practitioner;

(b) is a fit and proper person to act as an insolvency practitioner only in relation to companies, but the person's authorisation is not so limited; or

(c) is a fit and proper person to act as an insolvency practitioner only in relation to individuals, but the person's authorisation is not so limited.

391Q(3) [Condition 3] Condition 3 is that it is appropriate for the person's authorisation to act as an insolvency practitioner to be suspended for a period or until one or more requirements are complied with.

391Q(4) [Condition 4] Condition 4 is that it is appropriate to impose other restrictions on the person acting as an insolvency practitioner.

391Q(5) [Condition 5] Condition 5 is that loss has been suffered as a result of the failure mentioned in condition 1 by one or more creditors of a company, individual or insolvent partnership in relation to which the person is acting or has acted as an insolvency practitioner.

391Q(6) ["Relevant recognised professional body"] In this section "relevant recognised professional body" has the same meaning as in section 391O.

General Note

This provision, which again was inserted by SBEEA 2015 s.141, details the conditions that must be met before the court can impose a direct sanctions order. They are cumulative. Note the significance given to failure to observe professional codes and the need for the practitioner concerned to be deemed not to be a fit and proper person. There is also a requirement to prove loss has resulted from the misbehaviour.

See note after s.391R.

391R Direct sanctions direction instead of order

391R(1) ["Direct sanctions direction"] The Secretary of State may give a direction (a "direct sanctions direction") in relation to a person acting as an insolvency practitioner to the relevant recognised professional body (instead of applying, or continuing with an application, for a direct sanctions order against the person) if the Secretary of State is satisfied that–

(a) condition 1 and at least one of conditions 2, 3, 4 and 5 are met in relation to the person (see section 391Q), and

(b) it is in the public interest for the direction to be given.

391R(2) [Consent] But the Secretary of State may not give a direct sanctions direction in relation to a person without that person's consent.

391R(3) [Direction may require relevant RPB to take steps] A direct sanctions direction may require the relevant recognised professional body to take all necessary steps to secure that–

(a) the person is no longer authorised (whether fully or partially) to act as an insolvency practitioner;

(b) the person is no longer fully authorised to act as an insolvency practitioner but remains partially authorised to act as such either in relation to companies or individuals, as specified in the direction;

(c) the person's authorisation to act as an insolvency practitioner is suspended for the period specified in the direction or until such time as the requirements so specified are complied with;

(d) the person must comply with such other requirements as may be specified in the direction while acting as an insolvency practitioner;

(e) the person makes such contribution as may be specified in the direction to one or more creditors of a company, individual or insolvent partnership in relation to which the person is acting or has acted as an insolvency practitioner.

391R(4) [Where no direction] A direct sanctions direction must not be given in relation to a person whose authorisation to act as an insolvency practitioner was granted by the Department of Enterprise, Trade and Investment in Northern Ireland (see section 390A(2)(b)).

391R(5) [Maximum contribution in direction] A direct sanctions direction must not specify a contribution as mentioned in subsection (3)(e) which is more than the remuneration that the person has received or will receive in respect of acting as an insolvency practitioner in the case.

391R(6) ["Relevant recognised professional body"] In this section "relevant recognised professional body" has the same meaning as in section 391O.

General Note

This is best seen as an alternative to a direct sanctions order imposed by the court on an errant insolvency practitioner. It allows for a practitioner to agree to be subjected to a direct sanctions direction by the Secretary of State instead of being hauled before the court. Fewer conditions need to be met for such a direction to be given. The direction is given to the relevant RPB of which the insolvency practitioner is a member. Again note that financial contributions may be required as part of this directions regime.

Note that ss.391O–391R are not affected by certain Banking Act 2009 and Investment Bank Special Administration Regulations 2011 (SI 2011/245) provisions in relation to proceedings that commenced before 6 April 2017: see the Deregulation Act 2015, Small Business, Enterprise and Employment Act 2015 and the Insolvency (Amendment) Act (Northern Ireland) 2016 (Consequential Amendments and Transitional Provisions) Regulations 2017 (SI 2017/400) regs 1, 13, 17.

General

391S Power for Secretary of State to obtain information

391S(1) [Duty of person in s.391S(2) to give information] A person mentioned in subsection (2) must give the Secretary of State such information as the Secretary of State may by notice in writing require for the exercise of the Secretary of State's functions under this Part.

391S(2) [Persons under s.391S(1) duty] Those persons are–

(a) a recognised professional body;

(b) any individual who is or has been authorised under section 390A to act as an insolvency practitioner;

(c) any person who is connected to such an individual.

391S(3) [Connected person] A person is connected to an individual who is or has been authorised to act as an insolvency practitioner if, at any time during the authorisation–

(a) the person was an employee of the individual;

(b) the person acted on behalf of the individual in any other way;

(c) the person employed the individual;

(d) the person was a fellow employee of the individual's employer;

(e) in a case where the individual was employed by a firm, partnership or company, the person was a member of the firm or partnership or (as the case may be) a director of the company.

391S(4) [Time for and verification of information] In imposing a requirement under subsection (1) the Secretary of State may specify–

(a) the time period within which the information in question is to be given, and

(b) the manner in which it is to be verified.

General Note

This provision, inserted by SBEEA 2015 s.142, enables the Secretary of State to obtain information about insolvency practitioners and RPBs before exercising statutory powers.

391T Compliance orders

391T(1) [Power of Secretary of State to application to court] If at any time it appears to the Secretary of State that–

(a) a recognised professional body has failed to comply with a requirement imposed on it by or by virtue of this Part, or

(b) any other person has failed to comply with a requirement imposed on the person by virtue of section 391S,

the Secretary of State may make an application to the court.

391T(2) [Power of court to make order] If, on an application under this section, the court decides that the body or other person has failed to comply with the requirement in question, it may order the body or person to take such steps as the court considers will secure that the requirement is complied with.

391T(3) ["The court"] In this section, "the court" means the High Court or, in Scotland, the Court of Session.

General Note

Introduced by SBEEA 2015 s.143 this gives muscle to the regulatory oversight of the Secretary of State in respect of insolvency practitioners and their RPBs.

392 Authorisation by competent authority [Omitted]

393 Grant, refusal and withdrawal of authorisation [Omitted]

394 Notices [Omitted]

395 Right to make representations [Omitted]

396 Reference to Tribunal [Omitted]

397 Action of Tribunal on reference [Omitted]

398 Refusal or withdrawal without reference to Tribunal [Omitted]

Part XIV

Public Administration (England and Wales)

Adjudicators

398A Appointment etc of adjudicators and assistants

398A(1) [Power of Secretary of State to appoint] The Secretary of State may appoint persons to the office of adjudicator.

398A(2) [Salary, terms, removal determined by Secretary of State] A person appointed under subsection (1)–

(a) is to be paid out of money provided by Parliament such salary as the Secretary of State may direct,

(b) holds office on such other terms and conditions as the Secretary of State may direct, and

(c) may be removed from office by a direction of the Secretary of State.

398A(3) [Official receiver may not be adjudicator] A person who is authorised to act as an official receiver may not be appointed under subsection (1).

398A(4) [Secretary of State may appoint assistants to adjudicator] The Secretary of State may appoint officers of the Secretary of State's department to assist adjudicators in the carrying out of their functions.

General Note

Section 398A was inserted by ERRA 2013 s.71(1). This provision provides for the new cohort of Adjudicators who will deal with debtor petitions in bankruptcy (instead of such petitions being processed through the courts). Official receivers will not be taking on this role. Further details on the operation of this novel regime and on consequential amendments are contained in Schs 18 and 19 of the 2013 Act.

Subsection (1) of this provision authorises the Secretary of State to appoint adjudicators to operate the new out of court bankruptcy procedure to be used by debtors. The financing and tenure of such appointees is explained by subs.(2). Note that under subs.(3) official receivers are debarred. Officers of the Secretary of State's own department may be made available to assist adjudicators (subs.(4)).

Official Receivers

399 Appointment, etc. of official receivers

399(1) [Official receiver] For the purposes of this Act the official receiver, in relation to any bankruptcy, winding up, individual voluntary arrangement, debt relief order or application for such an order, is any person who by virtue of the following provisions of this section or section 401 below is authorised to act as the official receiver in relation to that bankruptcy, winding up, individual voluntary arrangement, debt relief order or application for such an order

399(2) [Power of appointment by Secretary of State] The Secretary of State may (subject to the approval of the Treasury as to numbers) appoint persons to the office of official receiver, and a person appointed to that office (whether under this section or section 70 of the Bankruptcy Act 1914)–

(a) shall be paid out of money provided by Parliament such salary as the Secretary of State may with the concurrence of the Treasury direct,

(b) shall hold office on such other terms and conditions as the Secretary of State may with the concurrence of the Treasury direct, and

(c) may be removed from office by a direction of the Secretary of State.

399(3) [Attachment to particular court] Where a person holds the office of official receiver, the Secretary of State shall from time to time attach him either to the High Court or to the county court.

399(4) [Person authorised to act as official receiver] Subject to any directions under subsection (6) below, an official receiver attached to a particular court is the person authorised to act as the official receiver in relation to every bankruptcy, winding up, individual voluntary arrangement, debt relief order or application for such an order falling within the jurisdiction of that court.

399(5) [Each court to have official receiver] The Secretary of State shall ensure that there is, at all times, at least one official receiver attached to the High Court and at least one attached to the county court; but he may attach the same official receiver to both courts.

399(6) [Directions by Secretary of State] The Secretary of State may give directions with respect to the disposal of the business of official receivers, and such directions may, in particular–

(a) authorise an official receiver attached to one court to act as the official receiver in relation to any case or description of cases falling within the jurisdiction of the other court;

(b) provide, where there is more than one official receiver authorised to act as the official receiver in relation to cases falling within the jurisdiction of any court, for the distribution of their business between or among themselves.

399(7) [Continuation of official receiver] A person who at the coming into force of section 222 of the Insolvency Act 1985 (replaced by this section) is an official receiver attached to a court shall continue in office after the coming into force of that section as an official receiver attached to that court under this section.

General Note

The government in its zeal for public expenditure economies originally wanted to remove official receivers from personal insolvency law and to hive off their functions to the private sector—see its Green Paper on Bankruptcy (Cmnd.7967 (July 1980)), para.8. The outcry that this proposal attracted, not least from the Cork Committee (*Report*, para.723), was sufficient to force a rethink. The IA 1986 retains the role of the official receivers in bankruptcy law, although their involvement is now restricted to the more serious cases. For further guidance on official receivers, see IR 2016 Pt 13 and r.13.1(2) (rights of audience). Note amendment to subss.(1) and (4) by para.7 of Pt 1 to Sch.20 of the Tribunals, Courts and Enforcement Act 2007. On the funding of official receivers see Sixth Report of the House of Commons Business, Innovation and Skills Committee (2012–13) (HC 675).

Note amendments made by Sch.9 of the Crime and Courts Act 2013 reflecting general reforms to the county court system.

S.399(1)

This confirms that official receivers will continue to act both in individual and corporate insolvency cases. Reference to IVAs was inserted by EA 2002 Sch.23. A similar change was also made in subs.(4).

S.399(2)

The question of appointment, remuneration and tenure is to be determined by the Secretary of State. For the remuneration of the official receiver, see the Insolvency Regulations 1994 (SI 1994/2507) reg.35 as inserted by the Insolvency (Amendment) Regulations 2005 (SI 2005/512). The present position is reviewed by Ferris J in *Mirror Group Newspapers v Maxwell* [1998] B.C.C. 324 at 337 and in the Working Party chaired by Ferris J which reported in 1998—see Ferris [1999] Ins. Law. 48.

S.399(3)–(5)

It is the responsibility of the Secretary of State to attach official receivers to the various courts having insolvency jurisdiction. Every court must have at least one official receiver attached to it, although that court may not be his sole responsibility.

S.399(6)

This provision authorises the Secretary of State to give directions to facilitate the disposal of business by official receivers.

S.399(7)

This is a transitional provision designed to ensure continuity.

400 Functions and status of official receivers

400(1) [Functions] In addition to any functions conferred on him by this Act, a person holding the office of official receiver shall carry out such other functions as may from time to time be conferred on him by the Secretary of State.

400(2) [Status] In the exercise of the functions of his office a person holding the office of official receiver shall act under the general directions of the Secretary of State and shall also be an officer of the court in relation to which he exercises those functions.

400(3) [Death or ceasing to hold office] Any property vested in his official capacity in a person holding the office of official receiver shall, on his dying, ceasing to hold office or being otherwise succeeded in relation to the bankruptcy or winding up in question by another official receiver, vest in his successor without any conveyance, assignment or transfer.

S.400(1)

The persons holding office as official receivers will have their functions governed either by the 1986 Act or by directions from the Secretary of State.

S.400(2)

This provision confirms that the Secretary of State has general control over official receivers although, as was the case under BA 1914 s.70(1), it is emphasised that they are also officers of the court. The effect of this is that any wrongful interference with them will constitute contempt of court. For the legal position relating to immunity for actions see *Mond v Hyde* [1999] Q.B. 1097. The immunity from suit of the official receiver was upheld by the European Court of Human Rights in *Mond v UK* [2003] B.P.I.R. 1347 where it was held that by maintaining this immunity English law did not breach the rights of the injured party under ECHR art.6. In *R. (Howard) v Official Receiver* [2013] EWHC 1839 (Admin); [2014] B.P.I.R. 204 Stadlen J confirmed that in granting or revoking a DRO the Official Receiver could be said to be acting judicially and so fell outwith the equality duty imposed by the Equality Act 2010 s.149.

An official receiver can be a litigant in person—*Official Receiver v Brunt* [1999] B.P.I.R. 560 where the Court of Appeal gives detailed consideration to the nature of the office.

S.400(3)

The aim of this provision is to secure continuity of property ownership if an official receiver leaves office prematurely.

401 Deputy official receivers and staff

401(1) [Deputy official receiver] The Secretary of State may, if he thinks it expedient to do so in order to facilitate the disposal of the business of the official receiver attached to any court, appoint an officer of his department to act as deputy to that official receiver.

401(2) [Same status and functions] Subject to any directions given by the Secretary of State under section 399 or 400, a person appointed to act as deputy to an official receiver has, on such conditions and for such period as may be specified in the terms of his appointment, the same status and functions as the official receiver to whom he is appointed deputy.

Accordingly, references in this Act (except section 399(1) to (5)) to an official receiver include a person appointed to act as his deputy.

401(3) [Termination of appointment] An appointment made under subsection (1) may be terminated at any time by the Secretary of State.

401(4) [Staff] The Secretary of State may, subject to the approval of the Treasury as to numbers and remuneration and as to the other terms and conditions of the appointments, appoint officers of his department to assist official receivers in the carrying out of their functions.

S.401(1)

To facilitate the despatch of business by official receivers, the Secretary of State may appoint deputy official receivers.

Under BA 1914 s.71, the deputy could be appointed on application from an official receiver but only for a two-month period at most. The present Act appears to be more flexible on this matter.

S.401(2), (3)

A deputy enjoys the same status as an official receiver, fulfils the same functions and can be dismissed in the same way by the Secretary of State. References in IA 1986 to official receivers include references to deputies.

S.401(4)

The Secretary of State may also appoint civil servants from his department to assist official receivers, although the consent of the Treasury must first be obtained.

The Official Petitioner

402 Official Petitioner

402(1) [Continuation of officer] There continues to be an officer known as the Official Petitioner for the purpose of discharging, in relation to cases in which a criminal bankruptcy order is made, the functions assigned to him by or under this Act; and the Director of Public Prosecutions continues, by virtue of his office, to be the Official Petitioner.

402(2) [Functions] The functions of the Official Petitioner include the following–

(a) to consider whether, in a case in which a criminal bankruptcy order is made, it is in the public interest that he should himself present a petition under section 264(1)(d) of this Act;

(b) to present such a petition in any case where he determines that it is in the public interest for him to do so;

(c) to make payments, in such cases as he may determine, towards expenses incurred by other persons in connection with proceedings in pursuance of such a petition; and

(d) to exercise, so far as he considers it in the public interest to do so, any of the powers conferred on him by or under this Act.

402(3) [Discharge of functions on authority] Any functions of the Official Petitioner may be discharged on his behalf by any person acting with his authority.

402(4) [Inability] Neither the Official Petitioner nor any person acting with his authority is liable to any action or proceeding in respect of anything done or omitted to be done in the discharge, or purported discharge, of the functions of the Official Petitioner.

402(5) ["Criminal bankruptcy order"] In this section "criminal bankruptcy order" means an order under section 39(1) of the Powers of Criminal Courts Act 1973.

S.402(1), (3)
This section preserves the post of official petitioner which will continue to be held by the Director of Public Prosecutions. The DPP can authorise junior officials to act in his stead.

S.402(2), (5)
These provisions describe his functions, the most obvious of which is to present a petition under s.264(1)(d) where a criminal bankruptcy order (as defined by s.402(5)) has been made, although he does have discretion to present petitions in the public interest in other cases.

S.402(4)
This confers immunity on the official petitioner for acts done in the discharge of his duties.

See also IR 2016 r.10.155.

Note prospective amendment: s.402 is to be repealed by CJA 1988 s.170(2) and Sch.16 as from a day to be appointed; see the note to s.264.

Insolvency Service finance, accounting and investment

403 Insolvency Services Account

403(1) [Payment into Account] All money received by the Secretary of State in respect of proceedings under this Act as it applies to England and Wales shall be paid into the Insolvency Services Account kept by the Secretary of State with the Bank of England; and all payments out of money standing to the credit of the Secretary of State in that account shall be made by the Bank of England in such manner as he may direct.

403(2) [Where excess amount] Whenever the cash balance standing to the credit of the Insolvency Services Account is in excess of the amount which in the opinion of the Secretary of State is required for the time being to answer demands in respect of bankrupts' estates or companies' estates, the Secretary of State shall–

(a) notify the excess to the National Debt Commissioners, and

(b) pay into the Insolvency Services Investment Account ("the Investment Account") kept by the Commissioners with the Bank of England the whole or any part of the excess as the Commissioners may require for investment in accordance with the following provisions of this Part.

403(3) [Where invested money required] Whenever any part of the money so invested is, in the opinion of the Secretary of State, required to answer any demand in respect of bankrupts' estates or companies' estates, he shall notify to the National Debt Commissioners the amount so required and the Commissioners–

(a) shall thereupon repay to the Secretary of State such sum as may be required to the credit of the Insolvency Services Account, and

(b) for that purpose may direct the sale of such part of the securities in which the money has been invested as may be necessary.

S.403(1)

Fees, etc. collected in England and Wales by the Secretary of State in respect of proceedings under this Act (see ss.414, 415) are to be paid into the Insolvency Services Account at the Bank of England. The Insolvency Services Account must be used by the liquidators in all compulsory liquidations unless they are authorised by the Secretary of State to use a local bank account to carry on the company's business (see the Insolvency Regulations 1994 (SI 1994/2507) regs 5, 7. Liquidators in voluntary liquidations were also required to use the Insolvency Services Account, but this became optional by virtue of changes to the Insolvency Regulations 1994 made by the Insolvency (Amendment) Regulations 2004 (SI 2004/472) as from 6 April 2004. There has been a large drop in usage of the Insolvency Services Account by liquidators in voluntary liquidations since that date to the extent that the Insolvency Service, in a consultation letter in September 2010, called into question whether the Insolvency Services Account should continue to be used at all for voluntary liquidations as the administrative effort involved may be disproportionate to the benefit. The Insolvency Service thus asked for comments on whether the optional facility for voluntary liquidators to use the Insolvency Services Account needs to be retained and whether removal of the facility would result in extra costs and, if so, what those costs would be. As a result of the Insolvency (Amendment) Regulations 2011 (SI 2011/2203) the payment of moneys into the ISA is not permitted in relation to a voluntary winding up after 1 October 2011.

S.403(2), (3)

These subsections regulate investment of surplus moneys from the above Account in the Investment Account at the Bank of England. See also the Insolvency Regulations 1994 (SI 1994/2507), as amended by SI 2004/472 and SI 2005/512.

404 Investment Account

404 Any money standing to the credit of the Investment Account (including any money received by the National Debt Commissioners by way of interest on or proceeds of any investment under this section) may be invested by the Commissioners, in accordance with such directions as may be given by the Treasury, in any manner for the time being specified in Part II of Schedule 1 to the Trustee Investments Act 1961.

General Note

This section restricts investment of money placed in the Investment Account under s.403(2).

405 Application of income in Investment Account; adjustment of balances [Repealed]

General Note

These provisions provided for the transfer of sums to the Consolidated Fund from the Investment Account and vice versa, where it is appropriate to adjust balances. They were repealed by EA 2002 s.272 with effect from 1 April 2004.

406 Interest on money received by liquidators or trustees in bankruptcy and invested

406 Where under rules made by virtue of paragraph 16 of Schedule 8 to this Act (investment of money received by company liquidators) or paragraph 21 of Schedule 9 to this Act (investment of money received by trustee in bankruptcy) a company or a bankrupt's estate has become entitled to any sum by way of interest, the Secretary of State shall certify that sum and the amount of tax payable on it to the National Debt Commissioners; and the Commissioners shall pay, out of the Investment Account–

(a) into the Insolvency Services Account, the sum so certified less the amount of tax so certified, and

(b) to the Commissioners of Inland Revenue, the amount of tax so certified.

General Note

Where a liquidator or trustee has paid sums into the Insolvency Services Account which have been invested, and these sums have earned interest, s.406 provides a mechanism for allocating these sums between those entitled, including the Revenue in respect of tax payable on the interest. In s.406 the words "or paragraph 21 of Schedule 9 to this Act (investment of money received by trustee in bankruptcy) a company or a bankrupt's estate" substituted for the words "a company" and the sidenote substituted for the former sidenote "Interest on money received by liquidators and invested" by IA 2000 s.13(2) as from 2 April 2001 (see SI 2001/766 (C. 27) arts 1, 2(1)(b)). This change was part of a package to benefit estates of bankrupts, which were otherwise providing an unjustified source of income for the State—a fact deplored by the Cork Committee (Cmnd.8558, para.857).

407 Unclaimed dividends and undistributed balances

407(1) [Duty of Secretary of State] The Secretary of State shall from time to time pay into the Consolidated Fund out of the Insolvency Services Account so much of the sums standing to the credit of that Account as represents–

(a) dividends which were declared before such date as the Treasury may from time to time determine and have not been claimed, and

(b) balances ascertained before that date which are too small to be divided among the persons entitled to them.

407(2) [Sums to credit of Insolvency Services Account] For the purposes of this section the sums standing to the credit of the Insolvency Services Account are deemed to include any sums paid out of that Account and represented by any sums or securities standing to the credit of the Investment Account.

407(3) [Power of Secretary of State] The Secretary of State may require the National Debt Commissioners to pay out of the Investment Account into the Insolvency Services Account the whole or part of any sum which he is required to pay out of that account under subsection (1); and the Commissioners may direct the sale of such securities standing to the credit of the Investment Account as may be necessary for that purpose.

General Note

This section states that unclaimed dividends, etc. are to be moved periodically by the Secretary of State from the Insolvency Services Account (or the Investment Account, where appropriate) to the Consolidated Fund. Investments in securities may need to be realised to achieve this end.

408 Adjustment of balances

408(1) [Payments by Treasury out of Consolidated Fund] The Treasury may direct the payment out of the Consolidated Fund of sums into–

(a) the Insolvency Services Account;

(b) the Investment Account.

408(2) [Certification of reason for payment] The Treasury shall certify to the House of Commons the reason for any payment under subsection (1).

408(3) [Payments by Secretary of State into Consolidated Fund] The Secretary of State may pay sums out of the Insolvency Services Account into the Consolidated Fund.

408(4) [Payments by National Debt Commissioners into Consolidated Fund] The National Debt Commissioners may pay sums out of the Investment Account into the Consolidated Fund.

General Note

This provision was introduced by s.272(2) of the Enterprise Act 2002 in substitution for the original s.408, which dealt with recourse to the Consolidated Fund. This substitution took place on 1 April 2004.

S.408(1)
This permits the Treasury to direct an adjustment of balances from the Consolidated Fund into the Insolvency Services Account and Investment Account. With regard to the Investment Account note the repeal of s.405 by s.272(1) of EA 2002.

S.408(2)
Directions given under subs.(1) must be reasoned.

S.408(3)
This permits payments out of the Insolvency Services Account into the Consolidated Fund.

S.408(4)
Payments from the Investment Fund into the Consolidated Account are hereby authorised.

409 Annual financial statement and audit

409(1) [Preparation of statement] The National Debt Commissioners shall for each year ending on 31st March prepare a statement of the sums credited and debited to the Investment Account in such form and manner as the Treasury may direct and shall transmit it to the Comptroller and Auditor General before the end of November next following the year.

409(2) [Duty of Secretary of State] The Secretary of State shall for each year ending 31st March prepare a statement of the sums received or paid by him under section 403 above in such form and manner as the Treasury may direct and shall transmit each statement to the Comptroller and Auditor General before the end of November next following the year.

409(3) [Additional information] Every such statement shall include such additional information as the Treasury may direct.

409(4) [Examination etc. of statement] The Comptroller and Auditor General shall examine, certify and report on every such statement and shall lay copies of it, and of his report, before Parliament.

General Note

This section lays down a framework for annual financial statements in respect of the Investment Account and the Insolvency Services Account, and the auditing thereof.

Supplementary

410 Extent of this Part

410 This Part of this Act extends to England and Wales only.

General Note

Sections 399–409 do not apply in Scotland, nor in Northern Ireland. This is confirmed by ss.440 and 441.

PART XV

SUBORDINATE LEGISLATION

General insolvency rules

411 Company insolvency rules

411(1) [Rules re Pts 1–7 or EC Regulation] Rules may be made–

(a) in relation to England and Wales, by the Lord Chancellor with the concurrence of the Secretary of State and, in the case of rules that affect court procedure, with the concurrence of the Lord Chief Justice, or

(b) in relation to Scotland, by the Secretary of State,

for the purpose of giving effect to Parts I to VII of this Act or the EU Regulation.

411(1A) [Rules re Banking Act 2009 Pt 2] Rules may also be made for the purpose of giving effect to Part 2 of the Banking Act 2009 (bank insolvency orders); and rules for that purpose shall be made–

(a) in relation to England and Wales, by the Lord Chancellor with the concurrence of–

(i) the Treasury, and

(ii) in the case of rules that affect court procedure, the Lord Chief Justice, or

(b) in relation to Scotland, by the Treasury.

411(1B) [Rules re Banking Act 2009 Pt 3] Rules may also be made for the purpose of giving effect to Part 3 of the Banking Act 2009 (bank administration); and rules for that purpose shall be made–

(a) in relation to England and Wales, by the Lord Chancellor with the concurrence of–

(i) the Treasury, and

(ii) in the case of rules that affect court procedure, the Lord Chief Justice, or

(b) in relation to Scotland, by the Treasury.

411(2) [Contents of rules] Without prejudice to the generality of subsection (1), (1A) or (1B) or to any provision of those Parts by virtue of which rules under this section may be made with respect to any matter, rules under this section may contain–

(a) any such provision as is specified in Schedule 8 to this Act or corresponds to provision contained immediately before the coming into force of section 106 of the Insolvency Act 1985 in rules made, or having effect as if made, under section 663(1) or (2) of the Companies Act 1985 (old winding-up rules), and

(b) such incidental, supplemental and transitional provisions as may appear to the Lord Chancellor or, as the case may be, the Secretary of State or the Treasury necessary or expedient.

411(2A) [Applicability of EU Regulation] For the purposes of subsection (2), a reference in Schedule 8 to this Act to doing anything under or for the purposes of a provision of this Act includes a reference to doing anything under or for the purposes of the EU Regulation (in so far as the provision of this Act relates to a matter to which the EU Regulation applies).

411(2B) [Rules not to create an offence] Rules under this section for the purpose of giving effect to the EU Regulation may not create an offence of a kind referred to in paragraph 1(1)(d) of Schedule 2 to the European Communities Act 1972.

411(2C) [Section 411(2) purposes: Sch.8 reference includes Banking Act 2009 Pt 2] For the purposes of subsection (2), a reference in Schedule 8 to this Act to doing anything under or for the purposes of a provision of this Act includes a reference to doing anything under or for the purposes of Part 2 of the Banking Act 2009.

411(2D) [Section 411(2) purposes: Sch.8 reference includes Banking Act 2009 Pt 3] For the purposes of subsection (2), a reference in Schedule 8 to this Act to doing anything under or for the purposes of a provision of this Act includes a reference to doing anything under or for the purposes of Part 3 of the Banking Act 2009.

411(3) [Interpretation of Sch.8] In Schedule 8 to this Act "liquidator" includes a provisional liquidator or bank liquidator or administrator; and references above in this section to Parts I to VII of this Act or Part 2 or 3 of the Banking Act 2009 are to be read as including the Companies Acts so far as relating to, and to matters connected with or arising out of, the insolvency or winding up of companies.

411(3A) [References in s.411 to Banking Act 2009] In this section references to Part 2 or 3 of the Banking Act 2009 include references to those Parts as applied to building societies (see section 90C of the Building Societies Act 1986).

411(4) [Rules by statutory instrument etc.] Rules under this section shall be made by statutory instrument subject to annulment in pursuance of a resolution of either House of Parliament.

411(5) [Regulations] Regulations made by the Secretary of State or the Treasury under a power conferred by rules under this section shall be made by statutory instrument and, after being made, shall be laid before each House of Parliament.

411(6) [Rules of court] Nothing in this section prejudices any power to make rules of court.

411(7) [LCJ nominee] The Lord Chief Justice may nominate a judicial office holder (as defined in section 109(4) of the Constitutional Reform Act 2005) to exercise his functions under this section.

S.411(1), (1A), (1B), (2), (2A), (2B), (2C), (2D), (7)

These subsections provide for the making of company insolvency rules which may include, for example, the matters specified in Sch.8 to this Act, or former corresponding matters. Note Banking Act 2009 s.100(7). Subsection (1) was amended and subss.(2A) and (2B) added by the Insolvency Act 1986 (Amendment) Regulations 2002 (SI 2002/1037) reg.3 with effect from 3 May 2002 and amended by the Insolvency Amendment (EU 2015/848) Regulations 2017 (SI 2017/702) regs 1, 2(1), Sch. paras 1, 24 in relation to proceedings opened on or after 26 June 2017 (see reg.3) when the Recast EU Regulation 2015/848 came into force. See the Insolvency (Amendment) Regulations 2008 (SI 2008/670). The Insolvency (England and Wales) Rules 2016 (IR 2016) (SI 2016/1024), are to be found below in this Volume. Subsection (1)(a) was amended and subs.(7) inserted by the Constitutional Reform Act 2005 s.15 and Sch.4 Pt I para.188. The Banking Act 2009 ss.125 and 160 makes a number of amendments including the insertion of subss.(1A), (1B), (2C) and (2D).

Note the change to subs.(2)(a) by the Companies Act 2006 (Consequential Amendments, Transitional Provisions and Savings) Order 2009 (SI 2009/1941) (effective from 1 October 2009). This is in consequence of the enactment of the Companies Act 2006.

For recent secondary rules made under s.411 see for example the Energy Administration Rules 2005 (SI 2005/2483), the Energy Administration (Scotland) Rules 2006 (SI 2006/772 (S 8)), the Insolvency (Scotland) Amendment Rules 2006 (SI 2006/734 (S 6)), the Insolvency (Scotland) Amendment Rules 2007 (SI 2007/2537 (S 5)), the PPI Administration Order Rules 2007 (SI 2007/3141), the Insolvency (Scotland) Amendment Rules 2009 (SI 2009/662 (S 1)) and the Insolvency (Scotland) (Amendment) Rules 2014 (SI 2014/114).

The Scotland Act 1998 (Insolvency Functions) Order 2018 (SI 2018/174) enables Scottish Ministers and Ministers of the Crown to bring forward winding up rules or regulations for Scotland in relation to companies, incorporated friendly societies and limited liability partnerships.

S.411(3)

This is an interpretation provision, amplifying terms used in Sch.8 and s.411(1) and (2). Amendment by the Companies Act 2006 (Commencement No.3, Consequential Amendments, Transitional Provisions and Savings) Order 2007 (SI 2007/2194 (C. 84)) art.10 and Sch.4 para.44 as from 1 October 2007, recognises the Companies Act 2006. Note amendments by ss.125 and 160 of the Banking Act 2009.

S.411(4), (5)
These provisions explain how company insolvency rules and regulations may be made. The regulations are the Insolvency Regulations 1994 (SI 1994/2507) as amended, most recently by SI 2004/472. Note amendments by ss.125 and 160 of the Banking Act 2009.

S.411(6)
This is a saving provision mirrored by s.412(5).

412 Individual insolvency rules (England and Wales)

412(1) [Rules by Lord Chancellor] The Lord Chancellor may, with the concurrence of the Secretary of State and, in the case of rules that affect court procedure, with the concurrence of the Lord Chief Justice, make rules for the purpose of giving effect to Parts 7A to 11 of this Act or the EU Regulation.

412(2) [Contents of rules] Without prejudice to the generality of subsection (1), or to any provision of those Parts by virtue of which rules under this section may be made with respect to any matter, rules under this section may contain–

(a) any such provision as is specified in Schedule 9 to this Act or corresponds to provision contained immediately before the appointed day in rules made under section 132 of the Bankruptcy Act 1914; and

(b) such incidental, supplemental and transitional provisions as may appear to the Lord Chancellor necessary or expedient.

412(2A) [Applicability of EU Regulation] For the purposes of subsection (2), a reference in Schedule 9 to this Act to doing anything under or for the purposes of a provision of this Act includes a reference to doing anything under or for the purposes of the EU Regulation (in so far as the provision of this Act relates to a matter to which the EU Regulation applies).

412(2B) [Rules not to create an offence] Rules under this section for the purpose of giving effect to the EU Regulation may not create an offence of a kind referred to in paragraph 1(1)(d) of Schedule 2 to the European Communities Act 1972.

412(3) [Rules to be made by statutory instrument] Rules under this section shall be made by statutory instrument subject to annulment in pursuance of a resolution of either House of Parliament.

412(4) [Regulations] Regulations made by the Secretary of State under a power conferred by rules under this section shall be made by statutory instrument and, after being made, shall be laid before each House of Parliament.

412(5) [Rules of court] Nothing in this section prejudices any power to make rules of court.

412(6) [LCJ nominee] The Lord Chief Justice may nominate a judicial office holder (as defined in section 109(4) of the Constitutional Reform Act 2005) to exercise his functions under this section.

S.412(1), (2), (2A), (2B), (6)
These subsections give authority to the Lord Chancellor, with the agreement of the Secretary of State, to make new rules which replace the 1952 rules. The current rules are the Insolvency (England and Wales) Rules 1986 (SI 2016/1024) (see below) which superseded the Insolvency Rules 1986 (SI 1986/1925). Schedule 9 to the Act (as amended) provides guidelines on the matters which may be dealt with by the rules—e.g. role of the insolvency courts; notices; registration of voluntary arrangements; role of interim receivers and receivers and managers; meetings of creditors; other matters concerned with the administration of the bankrupt's estate; financial provisions; information and records; powers of the court; and miscellaneous and supplementary matters. Subsection (1) was amended and subss.(2A) and (2B) were added by the Insolvency Act 1986 (Amendment) Regulations 2002 (SI 2002/1037) reg.3 with effect from 3 May 2002 and amended by the Insolvency Amendment (EU 2015/848) Regulations 2017 (SI 2017/702) regs 1, 2(1), Sch. paras 1, 25 in relation to proceedings opened on or after 26 June 2017 (see reg.3) when the Recast EU Regulation 2015/848 came into force. Subsection (1) was amended and subs.(6) inserted by the Constitutional Reform Act 2005 s.15 and Sch.4 Pt I para.189.

Note amendment to subs.(1) by para.8 of Pt 1 of Sch.20 to the Tribunals, Courts and Enforcement Act 2007.

The scope of the Lord Chancellor's rule making power under this provision was considered in *Trustee in Bankruptcy of St John Poulton v Ministry of Justice* [2009] B.P.I.R. 1512—but see now [2010] EWCA Civ 392.

S.412(3), (4)
These provisions govern how the Lord Chancellor may make rules under s.412 and how the Secretary of State may exercise powers by regulations under the said rules (see the Insolvency Regulations 1994 (SI 1994/2507). See also the Insolvency (Amendment) Regulations 2004 (SI 2004/472), Insolvency (Amendment) Regulations 2005 (SI 2005/512) and the Insolvency (Amendment) Regulations 2009 (SI 2009/482).

S.412(5)
The power of the court to make its own rules is not to be prejudiced by this provision.

413 Insolvency Rules Committee

413(1) [Continuation of committee] The committee established under section 10 of the Insolvency Act 1976 (advisory committee on bankruptcy and winding-up rules) continues to exist for the purpose of being consulted under this section.

413(2) [Consultation by Lord Chancellor] The Lord Chancellor shall consult the committee before making any rules under section 411 or 412 other than rules which contain a statement that the only provision made by the rules is provision applying rules made under section 411, with or without modifications, for the purposes of provision made by any of sections 23 to 26 of the Water Industry Act 1991 or Schedule 3 to that Act or by any of sections 59 to 65 of, or Schedule 6 or 7 to, the Railways Act 1993.

413(3) [Members of committee] Subject to the next subsection, the committee shall consist of–

(a) a judge of the High Court attached to the Chancery Division;

(b) a circuit judge;

(c) an insolvency and companies court judge;

(d) a district judge;

(e) a practising barrister;

(f) a practising solicitor; and

(g) a practising accountant;

and the appointment of any person as a member of the committee shall be made in accordance with subsection (3A) or (3B).

413(3A) [LCJ consults] The Lord Chief Justice must appoint the persons referred to in paragraphs (a) to (d) of subsection (3), after consulting the Lord Chancellor.

413(3B) [LC consults] The Lord Chancellor must appoint the persons referred to in paragraphs (e) to (g) of subsection (3), after consulting the Lord Chief Justice.

413(4) [Additional members] The Lord Chancellor may appoint as additional members of the committee any persons appearing to him to have qualifications or experience that would be of value to the committee in considering any matter with which it is concerned.

413(5) [LCJ nominee] The Lord Chief Justice may nominate a judicial office holder (as defined in section 109(4) of the Constitutional Reform Act 2005) to exercise his functions under this section.

S.413(1)
This provides for the continuance of the Insolvency Rules Committee established under IA 1976 s.10. This is not to be confused with the Insolvency Court Users' Committee set up by the Vice Chancellor, Sir Nicolas Browne-Wilkinson, in April 1987 to advise on improvements to court practices: see *The Times*, 8 April 1987. In *Woodley v Woodley (No.2)* [1994] 1 W.L.R. 1167 Balcombe LJ (at 1179D) formally invited the Insolvency Rules Committee to consider whether lump sum payments arising out of matrimonial proceedings should be made provable debts under

the then r.12.3 of the Insolvency Rules and so restore the pre-1986 position. A similar, more successful, request was made in *Ram v Ram* [2004] EWCA Civ 1452; [2005] B.P.I.R. 396. See note to IR 2016 r.14.2. See also *Re Austintel Ltd* [1997] B.C.C. 362. A further example of the type of issue that might go to the Insolvency Rules Committee is illustrated by the lacuna noted by Briggs J in *Appleyard v Wewelwala* [2012] EWHC 3302 (Ch) at [37]. The IRC was invited by Registrar Briggs to look at the issue that arose in *Gate Gourmet Luxembourg IV SARL v Morby* [2015] EWHC 1203 (Ch). An appeal against the ruling at first instance failed—see [2016] EWHC 74 (Ch).

For an excellent review of the role and constitution of the Insolvency Rules Committee see Davis [2007] 20 Insolv. Int. 65. This Committee, whose secretariat is provided by the Insolvency Service, fortunately survived the "bonfire of the quangos" announced by the government on 14 October 2010. The Insolvency Rules Committee played a significant role in reviewing the draft version of the Insolvency (England and Wales) Rules 2016 (SI 2016/1024).

S.413(2)

This Committee must normally be consulted before the Lord Chancellor makes any insolvency rules under s.411 or under s.412. Note the provisions in Banking Act 2009 ss.125(8) and 160(6).

S.413(3), (3A), (3B), (4) and (5)

These provisions regulate the composition of the Committee. Like s.413(1) and (2) they represent no real change in the law. Note the amendment to subs.(3) and the insertion of subss.(3A), (3B) and (5) by the Constitutional Reform Act 2005 s.15 and Sch.4 Pt I para.190.

Note amendments made by Sch.9 of the Crime and Courts Act 2013 reflecting general reforms in the county court system.

Section 413(3)(c) amended by the Alteration of Judicial Titles (Registrar in Bankruptcy of the High Court) Order 2018 (SI 2018/130) arts 1, 3 Sch. para.7(b) as from 26 February 2018.

Fees orders

414 Fees orders (company insolvency proceedings)

414(1) [Fees] There shall be paid in respect of–

(a) proceedings under any of Parts I to VII of this Act, and

(b) the performance by the official receiver or the Secretary of State of functions under those Parts,

such fees as the competent authority may with the sanction of the Treasury by order direct.

414(2) [Security for fees] That authority is–

(a) in relation to England and Wales, the Lord Chancellor, and

(b) in relation to Scotland, the Secretary of State.

414(3) [Order by Treasury] The Treasury may by order direct by whom and in what manner the fees are to be collected and accounted for.

414(4) [Security for fees] The Lord Chancellor may, with the sanction of the Treasury, by order provide for sums to be deposited, by such persons, in such manner and in such circumstances as may be specified in the order, by way of security for fees payable by virtue of this section.

414(5) [Incidental matter under order] An order under this section may contain such incidental, supplemental and transitional provisions as may appear to the Lord Chancellor, the Secretary of State or (as the case may be) the Treasury necessary or expedient.

414(6) [Order by statutory instrument etc.] An order under this section shall be made by statutory instrument and, after being made, shall be laid before each House of Parliament.

414(7) [Payment into Consolidated Fund] Fees payable by virtue of this section shall be paid into the Consolidated Fund.

414(8) [Interpretation] References in subsection (1) to Parts I to VII of this Act are to be read as including the Companies Acts so far as relating to, and to matters connected with or arising out of, the insolvency or winding up of companies.

414(8A) [Application to Banking Act 2009 Pt 2] This section applies in relation to Part 2 of the Banking Act 2009 (bank insolvency) as in relation to Parts I to VII of this Act.

414(8B) [Application to Banking Act 2009 Pt 3] This section applies in relation to Part 3 of the Banking Act 2009 (bank administration) as in relation to Parts I to VII of this Act.

414(8C) [References in s.414(8A), (8B) to Banking Act 2009] In subsections (8A) and (8B) the reference to Parts 2 and 3 of the Banking Act 2009 include references to those Parts as applied to building societies (see section 90C of the Building Societies Act 1986).

414(9) [Repealed]

S.414(1), (2)
These subsections govern the fixing of company insolvency fees in England and Wales, and in Scotland. Note the role of the Treasury in such matters. A completely new fees and deposit regime was introduced by the Insolvency Proceedings (Fees) Order 2016 (SI 2016/692). This repeals the 2004 Fees Order and all subsequent amendments. The 2016 Fees Order has attracted Parliamentary criticism for certain aspects of its drafting—see Joint Committee on Statutory Instruments, Ninth Report of Session 2016/17, 12 October 2016 (HL Paper 47/HC 93-ix). On fees generally, see also the Civil Proceedings Fees Order 2008 (SI 2008/1053 (L. 5)) as amended by the Civil Proceedings Fees (Amendment) Order 2014 (SI 2014/874 (L. 17)).

S.414(3), (7)
These provisions deal with the manner of collection and payment into the Consolidated Fund.

S.414(4)
Deposits by way of security may also be provided for.

S.414(5)
This is a safety valve mechanism designed to build flexibility into the system.

S.414(6)
This describes the parliamentary procedure to be used for orders fixing company insolvency fees.

S.414(8), (8A), (8B), (9)
These subsections provide an interpretation facility and a saving mechanism. Amendment of subs.(8) by the Companies Act 2006 (Commencement No.3, Consequential Amendments, Transitional Provisions and Savings) Order 2007 (SI 2007/2194 (C. 84)) art.10 and Sch.4 para.44 as from 1 October 2007, recognises the Companies Act 2006. Subsection (8A) was inserted by ss.126 of the Banking Act 2009. Subsection (8B) was inserted by s.161 of the Banking Act 2009. Subsection (9) was repealed by Courts Reform (Scotland) Act 2014 (Consequential Provisions) Order 2015 (Scottish SI 2015/150) Sch.1 para.4 as from 1 April 2015.

415 Fees orders (individual insolvency proceedings in England and Wales)

415(1) [Payment of fees] There shall be paid in respect of–

(za) the costs of persons acting as approved intermediaries under Part 7A,

(a) proceedings under Parts 7A to 11 of this Act,

(b) the performance by the official receiver or the Secretary of State of functions under those Parts, and

(c) the performance by an adjudicator of functions under Part 9 of this Act,

such fees as the Lord Chancellor may with the sanction of the Treasury by order direct.

415(1A) [Provision by order under s.415(1)] An order under subsection (1) may make different provision for different purposes, including by reference to the manner or form in which proceedings are commenced.

415(2) [Order by Treasury] The Treasury may by order direct by whom and in what manner the fees are to be collected and accounted for.

415(3) [Security for fees] The Lord Chancellor may, with the sanction of the Treasury, by order provide for sums to be deposited, by such persons, in such manner and in such circumstances as may be specified in the order, by way of security for–

(a) fees payable by virtue of this section, and

(b) fees payable to any person who has prepared an insolvency practitioner's report under section 274 in Chapter I of Part IX.

415(4) [Incidental provisions etc. of order] An order under this section may contain such incidental, supplemental and transitional provisions as may appear to the Lord Chancellor or, as the case may be, the Treasury, necessary or expedient.

415(5) [Order by statutory instrument etc.] An order under this section shall be made by statutory instrument and, after being made, shall be laid before each House of Parliament.

415(6) [Payment into Consolidated Fund] Fees payable by virtue of this section shall be paid into the Consolidated Fund.

415(7) [Rules of court] Nothing in this section prejudices any power to make rules of court.

S.415(1)–(3)

These subsections permit the Lord Chancellor, with the assent of the Treasury, to fix fees for bankruptcy proceedings and for tasks carried out by the official receiver or Secretary of State. Deposits which, e.g. represent advance payment of fees may also be similarly prescribed. See also the Civil Proceedings Fees Order 2008 (SI 2008/1053 (L. 5)) (as amended by the Civil Proceedings Fees (Amendment) Order 2014 (SI 2014/874 (L. 17))). See the Insolvency Proceedings (Fees) (Amendment) Order 2004 (SI 2004/593) (as amended by the Insolvency Proceedings (Fees) (Amendment) Order 2011 (SI 2011/1167), the Insolvency Proceedings (Fees) (Amendment) Order 2014 (SI 2014/583)) and the Insolvency Proceedings (Fees) Order 2016 (SI 2016/692). For the rationale and impact of this major reformation of insolvency fees and deposits post-July 2016 see the annotation to s.414. For the company law counterpart, see s.414. The decision in *Safier v Wardell* [2017] EWHC 20 (Ch) will be of interest to practitioners. Although it deals with the fee position pre-July 2016, it will continue to retain some relevance in determining which fees are payable where an annulment is funded via third party finance. For further details, see Sch.9.

Note amendment by Sch.20 to the Tribunals, Courts and Enforcement Act 2007 Pt 1 para.9. Note amendments made to subs.(1) and insertion of subs.(1A) by ERRA 2013 Sch.19 para.59.

S.415(4), (5)

These provisions deal with the procedural prerequisites of such an order from the Lord Chancellor and with supplementary matters which may be included therein.

S.415(6)

Fees collected under this provision are paid into the Consolidated Fund.

S.415(7)

This preserves the inherent power of the court to make rules of court.

415A Fees orders (general)

415A(A1) [Fee by competent authority under s.251U re debt relief orders] The Secretary of State–

(a) may by order require a person or body to pay a fee in connection with the grant or maintenance of a designation of that person or body as a competent authority under section 251U, and

(b) may refuse to grant, or may withdraw, any such designation where a fee is not paid.

415A(1) [Fee by recognised professional bodies] The Secretary of State–

(a) may by order require a body to pay a fee in connection with the grant or maintenance of recognition of the body under section 391, and

(b) may refuse recognition, or revoke an order of recognition under section 391(1) or (2) by a further order, where a fee is not paid.

415A(1A) [Varied fees for full and/or partial authorisation] Fees under subsection (1) may vary according to whether the body is recognised under section 391(1) (body providing full and partial authorisation) or under section 391(2) (body providing partial authorisation).

415A(1B) [Matters Secretary of State regard in setting s.415A(1) fee] In setting under subsection (1) the amount of a fee in connection with maintenance of recognition, the matters to which the Secretary of State may have regard include, in particular, the costs of the Secretary of State in connection with any functions under sections 391D, 391E, 391J, 391K and 391N.

415A(2) [Repealed]

415A(3) [Insolvency Services Account] The Secretary of State may by order require the payment of fees in respect of–

(a) the operation of the Insolvency Services Account;

(b) payments into and out of that Account.

415A(4) [Application of s.414(3), (5)–(7), (9)] The following provisions of section 414 apply to fees under this section as they apply to fees under that section–

(a) subsection (3) (manner of payment),

(b) subsection (5) (additional provision),

(c) subsection (6) (statutory instrument),

(d) subsection (7) (payment into Consolidated Fund), and

(e) subsection (9) (saving for rules of court).

415A(5) [Application of s.391M] Section 391M applies for the purposes of an order under subsection (1)(b) as it applies for the purposes of a revocation order made under section 391L.

General Note

This additional provision was introduced by s.270 of EA 2002. The Secretary of State has made the following order under s.415A—the Insolvency Practitioners and Insolvency Services Account (Fees) Order 2003 (SI 2003/3363) as amended by SI 2004/476, SI 2005/523, SI 2005/3524, SI 2007/133 and SI 2009/487. This Order provides for payment of fees in connection with the authorisation of insolvency practitioners and the recognition of bodies under ss.391, 392, 393. Payment of fees in connection with transactions with the ISA is also prescribed.

The Insolvency Practitioners and Insolvency Services Account (Fees) (Amendment) Order 2007 (SI 2007/133) which amends SI 2003/3363 came into effect on 1 April 2007. See also the Insolvency Practitioners and Insolvency Services Account (Fees) (Amendment) Order 2008 (SI 2008/3), the Insolvency Practitioners and Insolvency Services Account (Fees) (Amendment) (No.2) Order 2008 (SI 2008/672) and the Insolvency Practitioners and Insolvency Services Account (Fees) (Amendment) Order 2012 (SI 2012/2264) effective from 1 October 2012. A recent use of the power to make secondary legislation under s.415A is provided by the Insolvency Practitioners and Insolvency Services Account (Fees) (Amendment) Order 2015 (SI 2015/1977). This increases the fees payable by a body wishing to be recognised as an RPB.

Note amendment by Sch.20 to the Tribunals, Courts and Enforcement Act 2007 Pt 1 para.10.

S.415A(1), (1A), (1B), (2)

The Secretary of State may charge a fee for recognising certain bodies under s.391 or persons under s.393 and may remove recognition if the appropriate fee is not paid. Subsection (2) was repealed by DA 2015 Sch.6 para.22. Note amendment made to subs.(1) by DA 2015 s.17. This provision also introduces a new subs.(1A). New subss.(1B) and (5) were inserted by SBEEA 2015 ss.139(2) and 140(2) respectively.

S.415A(3)

Fees may be charged in respect of the operation of the Insolvency Services Account. On s.415A(3) see the Insolvency Practitioners and Insolvency Services Account (Fees) (Amendment) Order 2012 (SI 2012/2264) effective from 1 October 2012.

S.415A(4)
This extends various provisions in s.414 to s.415A.

S.415A(5)
This is a link with s.391M.

Specification, increase and reduction of money sums relevant in the operation of this Act

416 Monetary limits (companies winding up)

416(1) [Increase or reduction of certain provisions] The Secretary of State may by order in a statutory instrument increase or reduce any of the money sums for the time being specified in the following provisions in the first Group of Parts–

section 117(2) (amount of company's share capital determining whether county court has jurisdiction to wind it up);

section 120(3) (the equivalent as respects sheriff court jurisdiction in Scotland);

section 123(1)(a) (minimum debt for service of demand on company by unpaid creditor);

section 184(3) (minimum value of judgment, affecting sheriff's duties on levying execution);

section 206(1)(a) and (b) (minimum value of company property concealed or fraudulently removed, affecting criminal liability of company's officer).

416(2) [Transitional provisions] An order under this section may contain such transitional provisions as may appear to the Secretary of State necessary or expedient.

416(3) [Approval by Parliament] No order under this section increasing or reducing any of the money sums for the time being specified in section 117(2), 120(3) or 123(1)(a) shall be made unless a draft of the order has been laid before and approved by a resolution of each House of Parliament.

416(4) [Annulment of statutory instrument] A statutory instrument containing an order under this section, other than an order to which subsection (3) applies, is subject to annulment in pursuance of a resolution of either House of Parliament.

S.416(1)
This provision allows the Secretary of State to use statutory instruments to increase or reduce various figures specified in the First Group of Parts without recourse to primary legislation.

In relation to Scotland, s.416(1) applies (with modifications) to limited liability partnerships by virtue of the Limited Liability Partnerships (Scotland) Regulations 2001 (SI 2001/128) reg.4(1), (2) and Sch.2 as from 6 April 2001.

S.416(2)
The statutory instrument may provide for transitional matters.

S.416(3), (4)
The basic parliamentary procedure to be used is mapped out by s.416(4), although this is qualified by s.416(3) in respect of the variation of certain figures. In relation to Scotland, s.416(4) applies (with modifications) to limited liability partnerships by virtue of the Limited Liability Partnerships (Scotland) Regulations 2001 (SI 2001/128) reg.4(1), (2) and Sch.2 as from 6 April 2001.

417 Money sum in s.222

417 The Secretary of State may by regulations in a statutory instrument increase or reduce the money sum for the time being specified in section 222(1) (minimum debt for service of demand on unregistered company by unpaid creditor); but such regulations shall not be made unless a draft of the statutory instrument containing them has been approved by resolution of each House of Parliament.

General Note

This section provides a procedure for modifying the minimum debt for a statutory demand (currently £750).

417A Money sums (company moratorium)

417A(1) [Change of sums] The Secretary of State may by order increase or reduce any of the money sums for the time being specified in the following provisions of Schedule A1 to this Act–

paragraph 17(1) (maximum amount of credit which company may obtain without disclosure of moratorium);

paragraph 41(4) (minimum value of company property concealed or fraudulently removed, affecting criminal liability of company's officer).

417A(2) [Transitional matters] An order under this section may contain such transitional provisions as may appear to the Secretary of State necessary or expedient.

417A(3) [Procedure] An order under this section shall be made by statutory instrument subject to annulment in pursuance of a resolution of either House of Parliament.

General Note

This was introduced by Sch.1 to IA 2000 with effect from 1 January 2003. It enables monetary figures mentioned in connection with the new CVA moratorium procedure to be modified by the Secretary of State.

418 Monetary limits (bankruptcy)

418(1) [Powers of Secretary of State] The Secretary of State may by order prescribe amounts for the purposes of the following provisions in the second Group of Parts–

section 251S(4) (maximum amount of credit which a person in respect of whom a debt relief order is made may obtain without disclosure of his status);

section 273 (minimum value of debtor's estate determining whether immediate bankruptcy order should be made; small bankruptcies level);

section 313A (value of property below which application for sale, possession or charge to be dismissed);

section 346(3) (minimum amount of judgment, determining whether amount recovered on sale of debtor's goods is to be treated as part of his estate in bankruptcy);

section 354(1) and (2) (minimum amount of concealed debt, or value of property concealed or removed, determining criminal liability under the section);

section 358 (minimum value of property taken by a bankrupt out of England and Wales, determining his criminal liability);

section 360(1) (maximum amount of credit which bankrupt may obtain without disclosure of his status);

section 361(2) (exemption of bankrupt from criminal liability for failure to keep proper accounts, if unsecured debts not more than the prescribed minimum);

section 364(2)(d) (minimum value of goods removed by the bankrupt, determining his liability to arrest);

paragraphs 6 to 8 of Schedule 4ZA (maximum amount of a person's debts, monthly surplus income and property for purposes of obtaining a debt relief order);

and references in the second Group of Parts to the amount prescribed for the purposes of any of those provisions, and references in those provisions to the prescribed amount, are to be construed accordingly.

418(2) [Transitional provisions] An order under this section may contain such transitional provisions as may appear to the Secretary of State necessary or expedient.

NICh 8; [2014] B.P.I.R. 1169. Here an insolvent partnership entered administration. The court held that this prevented the service of a statutory demand against the partnership as such action was caught by the moratorium. As it happened the administrators granted leave and the court indicated that such leave could have retrospective effect. For further judicial comment on the 1994 Order see the observations of Norris J in *McLean v Trustees of the Bankrupt Estates of Dent* [2016] EWHC 2650 (Ch).

The 1986 Order replaced the provisions in BA 1914 which dealt with insolvent partnerships: e.g. ss.114, 116, 119 and 127, plus rr.279–297 of BR 1952. For analysis of art.15(3) of the original 1986 Order see *Schooler v Customs and Excise Commissioners* [1996] B.P.I.R. 207. The 1986 Order in turn has been completely replaced by the 1994 Order. There were a number of factors which led to the introduction of the new Order. Amongst these were:

(1) a desire to promote rescue procedures for insolvent partnerships;

(2) the need to enhance the presentation of the relevant provisions to enable practitioners to interpret them more easily;

(3) the necessity of dealing with the problems of conflict between the Act and the 1986 Order as revealed by the case of *Re Marr* [1990] Ch. 773;

(4) the desirability of implementing the recommendations of the Cork Committee on distribution of assets of joint and several estates (see *Report*, paras 1685–1690);

(5) the attractions of streamlining unnecessary procedures in order to reduce running costs.

For a fuller insight into the motivation leading to the introduction of the 1994 Order, see the Insolvency Service's Consultation Document of November 1992.

Under the 1994 Order a partnership continues to be treated as an unregistered company and therefore the provisions of Pt V of IA 1986 are made applicable (with necessary modifications). The purpose of the new rules is to facilitate combined insolvency proceedings against both the firm and its members, where the business is insolvent. If the business is solvent, but an individual partner is in financial difficulties, then the general procedures relating to personal or corporate insolvency, as contained in the 1986 Act, must be used instead. Note that amendments have been made to the Insolvent Partnerships Order 1994 by the Banks and Building Societies (Depositor Preference and Priorities) Order 2014 (SI 2014/3486).

The 1994 Order (in force from 1 December 1994) deals with a number of distinct insolvency situations:

A voluntary arrangement in respect of the firm (a partnership voluntary arrangement or PVA) (art.4). Full details of how Pt I of the Act is to be modified to deal with such a case are provided by Sch.1 to the Order. For analysis of a PVA see Bacon (1994) 10 I.L. & P. 166.

A voluntary arrangement in respect of the members of an insolvent partnership (art.5). This was already a possibility before 1994, but art.5 clarifies the position (especially where both the firm and the partners are participating in voluntary arrangements).

An administration order in respect of the firm (art.6). Details of the modus operandi here are found in Sch.2 to the Order. See *Re Kyrris (No.1)* [1998] B.P.I.R. 103 and *Re Kyrris (No.2)* [1998] B.P.I.R. 111.

The winding up of the partnership firm (arts 7 and 9). Here, the partnership is treated as an unregistered company with the effect that the procedures contained in Pt V of the Act relating to the winding up of such companies are made applicable. The main ground for a winding-up petition is that the firm is unable to pay its debts. Such a petition may be presented by a creditor, or, where the firm consists of not less than eight partners by any member of the partnership. Separate provision is made for petitions presented by creditors (art.7 and Sch.3) and by members (art.9 and Sch.5).

The 1994 Order extends the availability of this winding-up procedure to the case of the winding up by creditor's petition of insolvent partnerships where the partnership has a place of business in England or Wales—it is not necessary that the principal place of business be so located. Thus certain overseas partnerships can now be brought within this regime.

Concurrent insolvency proceedings against the firm and individual partners (arts 8 and 10). Here, it is possible to present consolidated petitions against both the partnership firm and one or more partners in that firm (whether they be individuals or companies). The petitions will be presented to and heard by the same court. The petition against the firm is treated as the principal petition. A creditor can present a petition in such a case on the ground that the partnership is unable to pay its debts. The aim of this procedure is to facilitate the concurrent insolvency regimes—thus normally a single insolvency practitioner will handle the winding up of the firm and the insolvency proceedings against the individual members. A single public examination may be used to kill two birds with one stone. The partnership assets are to be used primarily to settle partnership liabilities; the old bankruptcy rule that the separate estates of the individual partners must first be utilised towards satisfying the claims of their own individual creditors has given way to a system under which creditors of the firm who have not been able to obtain satisfaction out of the firm's assets are entitled to equal treatment in any distribution of the separate estates. Thus the rule in s.33(6) of BA 1914 is abolished and English law is brought into line with Scottish law.

The other main changes introduced by the 1994 Order in this hybrid scenario are as follows:

- this procedure can be used where only one of the members (as opposed to the previous requirement of two) is facing insolvency proceedings concurrently with the partnership;
- special amendments are made to s.271 of the Act to reduce the difficulties encountered in *Re Marr* (above);
- procedural changes are made to cut costs (e.g. by removing the requirement for meetings that may be deemed to be unnecessary).

A joint bankruptcy petition covering all of the partners (art.11). It is possible for all of the partners to petition jointly for their own bankruptcy, or alternatively for some of the partners with the concurrence of the others to do this. In such a case, the trustee acting for the insolvent partners has authority to wind up the partnership firm even though no petition has been presented against it. This form of proceedings can only be initiated by the partners themselves, on the ground that the firm is unable to meet its debts, and it cannot be used if there are corporate partners or partners who dissent from this course of action.

Winding up an unregistered company where an insolvent partnership is a member (art.12). Here the insolvent partnership is treated as if it were a corporate member of the unregistered company.

In addition to the above procedural changes the 1994 Order also makes changes, for the purposes of the Order, to ss.168 and 303 of the Act (supplemental powers of court) and to s.388 (meaning of "act as insolvency practitioner"): see the notes to those sections.

A further amendment to the discrete insolvency regime for partnerships was introduced by the Insolvent Partnerships (Amendment) Order 1996 (SI 1996/1308). The main effect of this amendment was to allow the Bank of England and the Securities and Investments Board (now the PRA) to present winding up petitions in certain circumstances.

The Insolvent Partnerships (Amendment) Order 2001 (SI 2001/767) applies additional provisions inserted into CDDA 1986 to insolvent partnerships where appropriate.

The Insolvent Partnerships (Amendment) Order 2002 (SI 2002/1308) makes further changes into the legal regime governing insolvent partnerships. Essentially this Order catered for the introduction of the EC Regulation (1346/2000) by amending various procedural requirements relating to petitions and providing new forms which must be used for petitions presented after 31 May 2002. Note also SI 2002/2708. See now EURIP 2015.

The Insolvent Partnerships (Amendment) Order 2005 (SI 2005/1516) makes a number of significant changes to the regime for insolvent partnerships as based in the 1994 Order. These changes are introduced to cater for general reforms both to personal and corporate insolvency law made by the Enterprise Act 2002. Amongst the more significant reforms introduced by the 1995 Order are the application of the new administration procedure laid down in Sch.B1 to the 1986 Act to insolvent partnerships (see art.3). The new financial criteria governing Sch.A1 CVAs are now applied to insolvent partnerships (art.6(4)). The abolition of summary administration in bankruptcy law is also carried over to insolvent partnerships (art.5). However the rules on the prescribed part (see s.176A) are explicitly *not* extended to insolvent partnerships (art.4).

Note further changes have been made by the Insolvent Partnerships (Amendment) Order 2006 (SI 2006/622). Minor amendments to the 1994 Order were also made by the Lord Chancellor (Transfer of Functions and Supplementary Provisions) Order 2006 (SI 2006/680).

For technical provisions in the area of pensions see the Pension Protection Fund (Insolvent Partnerships) (Amendment of Insolvency Events) Order 2005 (SI 2005/2893).

S.420(2), (3), (4)

These subsections provide for flexibility of application, transitional matters and the procedure by which delegated legislation is to be made under this section. Subsection (2) was amended and subs.(4) inserted by the Constitutional Reform Act 2005 s.15 and Sch.4 Pt I para.191.

421 Insolvent estates of deceased persons

421(1) [Order by Lord Chancellor] The Lord Chancellor may, by order made with the concurrence of the Secretary of State and the Lord Chief Justice, provide that such provisions of this Act as may be specified in the order shall apply in relation to the administration of the insolvent estates of deceased persons with such modifications as may be so specified.

421(1A) [Provision re EU Regulation] An order under this section may make provision in relation to the EU Regulation.

421(1B) [Provision must not create an offence] But provision made by virtue of this section in relation to the EU Regulation may not create an offence of a kind referred to in paragraph 1(1)(d) of Schedule 2 to the European Communities Act 1972.

421(2) [Incidental provisions etc.] An order under this section may make different provision for different cases and may contain such incidental, supplemental and transitional provisions as may appear to the Lord Chancellor and the Lord Chief Justice necessary or expedient.

421(3) [Order by statutory instrument] An order under this section shall be made by statutory instrument subject to annulment in pursuance of a resolution of either House of Parliament.

421(4) [Interpretation] For the purposes of this section the estate of a deceased person is insolvent if, when realised, it will be insufficient to meet in full all the debts and other liabilities to which it is subject.

421(5) [LCJ nominee] The Lord Chief Justice may nominate a judicial office holder (as defined in section 109(4) of the Constitutional Reform Act 2005) to exercise his functions under this section.

S.421(1), (1A), (1B), (2)

This authorises the Lord Chancellor, with the agreement of the Secretary of State and Lord Chief Justice—see Constitutional Reform Act 2005 s.15 and Sch.4 Pt I para.192—to extend the provisions of IA 1986 to the insolvent estates of deceased persons, subject to any modifications deemed necessary. A minor textual change was made by s.12(2) IA 2000 with effect from 2 April 2001. See SI 2001/766 (C. 27). Subsections (1A) and (1B) were inserted by the Insolvency Act 1986 (Amendment) Regulations 2002 (SI 2002/1037) with effect from 3 May 2002 and amended by the Insolvency Amendment (EU 2015/848) Regulations 2017 (SI 2017/702) regs 1, 2(1), Sch. paras 1, 27 in relation to proceedings opened on or after 26 June 2017 (see reg.3) when the Recast EU Regulation 2015/848 came into force.

The BA 1914 laid down considerable detail on the administration of estates of deceased insolvents, whereas the present Act clearly leaves much to the rules in delegated legislation: see Sch.9 para.19 and the Administration of Insolvent Estates of Deceased Persons Order 1986 (SI 1986/1999).

Orders granted under s.421 and the 1986 Order are extremely rare. The relationship between the Act, the Order and certain common law presumptions was the subject of judicial comment in *Re Palmer* [1994] Ch. 316. Here it was held by the Court of Appeal that the general legal presumption that a judicial act is deemed to have occurred at the earliest moment from the day on which it was done cannot be used to provide an interpretation of the Order that would make it inconsistent with the Act or make the Order ultra vires s.421. Thus an administration order made by the court in respect of the estate of a deceased insolvent could not by using judicial fictions be deemed to have been made during the lifetime of that person. In so deciding the Court of Appeal rejected the approach adopted by Vinelott J at first instance: see [1994] Ch. 316.

For discussion of the meaning of Administration of Insolvent Estates of Deceased Persons Order 1986 art.5 see *Brister v Official Receiver* [2015] EW Misc B22 (CC); [2015] B.P.I.R. 1008.

Another case where this regime was considered, albeit in a Northern Irish context, was *McAteer v Lismore (No.1)* [2002] B.P.I.R. 804. Here Girvan J held that the modus operandi of various transactional avoidance provisions which sought to avoid transactions from the date of the death rather than from the actual date of the commencement of the insolvency administration would have to be reviewed by the court in the light of the right to peaceable enjoyment of one's property as conferred by art.1 of the First Protocol of the European Convention on Human Rights.

In *Re Vos (decd)* [2006] B.P.I.R. 348 Registrar Baister was confronted with another case involving the administration of the estate of deceased insolvent. The issue at stake here was whether payment for professional services rendered to the estate of the deceased insolvent before insolvency was declared could be treated as automatically void by virtue of the operation of s.284 of the IA 1986 (as modified by the Administration of Insolvent Estates of Deceased Persons Order 1986 so as to apply to dispositions on behalf of deceased insolvents with effect from the date of the death). The professional firm involved contended that this provision did not apply and that, even if it did, such payments should be ratified by the court as they were made bona fide in return for beneficial services rendered to the estate. Registrar Baister held that by adopting a purposive approach to interpretation the modified s.284 applied so as to render automatically void any payments made out of the estate of the deceased from the date of the death up to the date of the insolvency order, notwithstanding the fact that the insolvency order was not made until many years after the death. The protective provisions of the Human Rights Act 1998 relating to expropriation of property were not engaged so as to protect the position of the payee. However, the court enjoyed the power to ratify certain payments made prior to any realisation that the estate might be insolvent and would do so here to mitigate to a limited extent the liability to reimburse the estate. This is a cautionary tale. For further insights into the impact of s.284 in this context see *Gorbunova v The Estate of Berezovsky* [2016] EWHC 1829 (Ch).

A rare instance where the administration of the assets of a deceased insolvent has come before the courts is provided by *Hounslow LBC v Ballard* [2010] B.P.I.R. 149. Here the court, declining to follow a pre-1986 precedent, ruled that the court could grant an insolvency order in respect of the estate of a deceased insolvent without requiring service of the petition on the personal representatives. The rules contained in the 1986 Order represented a clean break from the past.

Further consideration was given to the 1986 Order by David Richards J in *Lockston Group Inc v Wood* [2015] EWHC 2962 (Ch). The important point made in this ruling is that it is the date of the death and not the date of the insolvency administration order that is to be used when quantifying provable debts and any voting rights of creditors. This date is also the benchmark for converting foreign debts into sterling and in calculating interest accrual which only counts as a provable debt up to the date of death. Interest accruing after that debt can only be claimed if there is a surplus in the estate. This case is discussed by N. Wood [2016] 9 CRI 16.

Re Tovey (decd), Berry v Child Support Agency [2016] EWHC 1418 (Ch); [2016] B.P.I.R. 1256 makes the point that there is no issue of debt discharge in the case of a deceased insolvent and therefore no need to distinguish provable and non-provable debts.

The regime governing the administration of estates of deceased insolvents was modified with effect from 31 May 2002 by the Administration of Insolvent Estates of Deceased Persons (Amendment) Order 2002 (SI 2002/1309). This piece of delegated legislation owes its existence to EC Council Regulation 1346/2000 on Insolvency Proceedings. The effect of these changes is to facilitate cross-border insolvency administration by providing new forms (instead of those found in the 1986 Order) which are to be used where the EC Regulation applied. See now EURIP 2015/848.

Note amendments made to the 1986 Order by Deregulation Act 2015 and Small Business, Enterprise and Employment Act 2015 (Consequential Amendments) (Savings) Regulations (SI 2017/540) and the Insolvency (Miscellaneous Amendments) Regulations 2017 (SI 2017/1119) Sch.3.

For a recent overview see Lewis and Curl [2018] 11 CRI 26.

S.421(3)

This describes the modus operandi of such extension.

S.421(4)

This determines when the estate of a deceased person is insolvent.

S.421(5)

This was inserted by para.192 of Sch.4 Pt I of the Constitutional Reform Act 2005.

421A Insolvent estates: joint tenancies

421A(1) [Application] This section applies where–

(a) an insolvency administration order has been made in respect of the insolvent estate of a deceased person,

(b) the petition for the order was presented after the commencement of this section and within the period of five years beginning with the day on which he died, and

(c) immediately before his death he was beneficially entitled to an interest in any property as joint tenant.

421A(2) [Power of court] For the purpose of securing that debts and other liabilities to which the estate is subject are met, the court may, on an application by the trustee appointed pursuant to the insolvency administration order, make an order under this section requiring the survivor to pay to the trustee an amount not exceeding the value lost to the estate.

421A(3) [Duty of court] In determining whether to make an order under this section, and the terms of such an order, the court must have regard to all the circumstances of the case, including the interests of the deceased's creditors and of the survivor; but, unless the circumstances are exceptional, the court must assume that the interests of the deceased's creditors outweigh all other considerations.

421A(4) [Terms, etc. of order] The order may be made on such terms and conditions as the court thinks fit.

421A(5) [Sums to be comprised in the estate] Any sums required to be paid to the trustee in accordance with an order under this section shall be comprised in the estate.

421A(6) [Section 421 modifications] The modifications of this Act which may be made by an order under section 421 include any modifications which are necessary or expedient in consequence of this section.

421A(7) ["Survivor"] In this section, "survivor" means the person who, immediately before the death, was beneficially entitled as joint tenant with the deceased or, if the person who was so entitled dies after the making of the insolvency administration order, his personal representatives.

421A(8) [Multiple survivors] If there is more than one survivor–

(a) an order under this section may be made against all or any of them, but

(b) no survivor shall be required to pay more than so much of the value lost to the estate as is properly attributable to him.

421A(9) [Definitions] In this section–

"insolvency administration order" has the same meaning as in any order under section 421 having effect for the time being,

"value lost to the estate" means the amount which, if paid to the trustee, would in the court's opinion restore the position to what it would have been if the deceased had been made bankrupt immediately before his death.

General Note

Introduced by s.12 of IA 2000 with effect from 2 April 2001, this introduces a new s.421A whose effect is to reverse the inconvenient decision of the Court of Appeal in *Re Palmer (decd)* [1994] Ch. 316 which cast doubt upon the effectiveness of secondary legislation made under s.421. Here the Court of Appeal ruled that the Administration of Insolvent Estates of Deceased Persons Order 1986 (SI 1986/1999) did not have the effect that it was apparently intended to have and in particular where a joint tenant of property died insolvent his or her interest in the property passed automatically to the other joint tenant and did not form part of the insolvent estate for distribution amongst creditors. This ruling was seen to favour spouses in particular at the expense of creditors. There are admittedly very few cases where an administration of an estate of a deceased insolvent is required, but the problem was deemed sufficiently serious to require legislative correction. The original clause in the Bill had to be rewritten to counteract unintended consequences with regard to the marketability of property and the final provision arose out of the work of HC Standing Committee B (for explanation see *Hansard*, HL Vol.619, cols 1345–1350).

Under s.421A the survivor can be ordered to pay value to the estate; there is no transfer of property rights as such. The court enjoys discretion to deal with the matter, but as in insolvency generally the interests of creditors prevail unless the case is exceptional. The jurisprudence under s.336 of IA 1986 is likely to be influential here. Subsections (7) and (9) of the new s.421A are definitional.

Concerns were raised as to whether this provision would have retrospective effect. This was eventually conceded by the government, who argued that the limited degree of retroactivity struck the right balance—see *Hansard*, HL Vol.619, cols 1348–9. On closer examination of s.421A(1) the position is that this new provision can only operate if the petition for the administration order was brought within five years of the death and after the coming into force of the section. Therefore there may be some retrospectivity at work depending on commencement dates though the danger here looks to be more theoretical than real.

A recent authority dealing with s.421A is *Wicks v Russell and Parkes* [2009] B.P.I.R. 194, which looks at the interaction between the regime set up by s.421A and the meaning of ss.267(2) and 382.

Note amendment made to subs.(1) by ERRA 2013 Sch.19 para.60.

422 Formerly authorised banks

422(1) [Order by Secretary of State] The Secretary of State may by order made with the concurrence of the Treasury and after consultation with the Financial Conduct Authority and the Prudential Regulation Authority provide that specified provisions in the first Group of Parts shall apply with specified modifications in relation to any person who–

(a) has a liability in respect of a deposit which he accepted in accordance with the Banking Act 1979 (c. 37) or 1987 (c. 22), but

(b) does not have permission under Part 4A of the Financial Services and Markets Act 2000 (c. 8) (regulated activities) to accept deposits.

422(1A) [Where no permission under Financial Services and Markets Act 2000] Subsection (1)(b) shall be construed in accordance with–

(a) section 22 of the Financial Services and Markets Act 2000 (classes of regulated activity and categories of investment),

(b) any relevant order under that section, and

(c) Schedule 2 to that Act (regulated activities).

422(2) [Incidental provisions etc.] An order under this section may make different provision for different cases and may contain such incidental, supplemental and transitional provisions as may appear to the Secretary of State necessary or expedient.

422(3) [Order by statutory instrument etc.] An order under this section shall be made by statutory instrument subject to annulment in pursuance of a resolution of either House of Parliament.

S.422(1), (1A)
Subsection (1) was replaced by EA 2002 s.248 and Sch.17. Subsection (1A) was also inserted in this manner. It replaces an earlier version of subs.(1A) inserted by SI 2002/1555 which was then omitted by the Enterprise Act 2002 (Insolvency) Order 2003 (SI 2003/2096). Subsection (1) was amended by the Financial Services Act 2012 Sch.18.

S.422(2), (3)
These provisions regulate procedural and transitional matters.

Part XVI

Provisions Against Debt Avoidance (England and Wales Only)

423 Transactions defrauding creditors

423(1) [Transaction at undervalue] This section relates to transactions entered into at an undervalue; and a person enters into such a transaction with another person if–

(a) he makes a gift to the other person or he otherwise enters into a transaction with the other on terms that provide for him to receive no consideration;

(b) he enters into a transaction with the other in consideration of marriage or the formation of a civil partnership; or

(c) he enters into a transaction with the other for a consideration the value of which, in money or money's worth, is significantly less than the value, in money or money's worth, of the consideration provided by himself.

423(2) [Order by court] Where a person has entered into such a transaction, the court may, if satisfied under the next subsection, make such order as it thinks fit for–

(a) restoring the position to what it would have been if the transaction had not been entered into, and

(b) protecting the interests of persons who are victims of the transaction.

423(3) [Conditions for court order] In the case of a person entering into such a transaction, an order shall only be made if the court is satisfied that it was entered into by him for the purpose–

(a) of putting assets beyond the reach of a person who is making, or may at some time make, a claim against him, or

(b) of otherwise prejudicing the interests of such a person in relation to the claim which he is making or may make.

423(4) ["The court"] In this section "the court" means the High Court or–

(a) if the person entering into the transaction is an individual, any other court which would have jurisdiction in relation to a bankruptcy petition relating to him;

(b) if that person is a body capable of being wound up under Part IV or V of this Act, any other court having jurisdiction to wind it up.

423(5) [Interpretation] In relation to a transaction at an undervalue, references here and below to a victim of the transaction are to a person who is, or is capable of being, prejudiced by it; and in the following two sections the person entering into the transaction is referred to as "the debtor".

General Note

The purpose of this section and those immediately following it is to revamp s.172 of LPA 1925, which was used to avoid fraudulent conveyances. The Cork Committee wanted this provision widened, and, in particular, to cover payments of money: see the *Report*, para.1238. This has been done. There has been a provision along these lines in English law since 1571, and ultimately it can trace its ancestry back to the Paulian action of Roman law. This provision applies to both individuals and companies alike: *Re Shilena Hosiery Co Ltd* [1980] Ch. 219. The great utility of this provision lies in the fact that no time-limit for avoidance is fixed, in contrast with the case of ss.238, 239 and 339, 340. However, this advantage may be more illusory than real in that the courts are reluctant to reopen transactions going back many years—*The Law Society v Southall* [2001] EWCA Civ 2001; [2002] B.P.I.R. 336. There may also be limitation considerations—see *Re Yates* [2005] B.P.I.R. 476 and now *Re Nurkowski* [2006] EWCA Civ 542; [2006] B.P.I.R. 789 (which is discussed below). (For further points of comparison, see the note to s.238.) See generally Milman and Parry (1997) 48 N.I.L.Q. 24; and Keay [1998] J.B.L. 515.

For guidance on various procedural aspects of a s.423 application see *Godfrey v Torpy*, *The Times*, 16 May 2007. In *Re Baillies Ltd* [2012] EWHC 285 (Ch); [2012] B.P.I.R. 665 HHJ Purle QC discussed further the proposition that proceedings under s.423 are not insolvency proceedings and so, for example, they do not come within the curative provision in IR 2016 r.10.64. At the end of the day the case turned on the fact that the EC Service Regulation (1393/2007) prevailed over IR 2016 r.10.64.

On the potential use of s.423 in commercial litigation generally see *Fortress Value Recovery Fund v Blue Skye Special Opportunities Fund* [2013] EWHC 14 (Comm). Here Flaux J took an expansive view of the potential range of the provision by widely defining victim and making the point that the applicant need not be the person whom the debtor had in mind when entering the disputed transaction. The extra territorial scope of s.423 was also confirmed.

Flaux J confirmed the extraterritorial potential of s.423 in *Erste Group Bank AG v JSC "VMZ Red October"* [2013] EWHC 2926 (Comm).

Flaux J was emphatic in *Erste Group Bank AG v JSC "VMZ Red October"* [2013] EWHC 2926 (Comm) that s.423 does not create a statutory tort and cannot be characterised as such.

In *Anglo-German Breweries Ltd v Chelsea Corp Inc* [2012] EWHC 1481 (Ch) instead of invoking s.423 the court decided to lift the veil of separate corporate personality in order to unravel a disputed transaction.

Note Banking Act 2009 ss.103 and 145.

S.423(1)–(3)

These provisions allow the court to set aside transactions at an undervalue designed to put assets out of reach of creditors. They explain what a transaction at an undervalue is. The definition is similar to that in ss.238(4) and 339(3). Section 423(1)(b) was amended by the Civil Partnership Act 2004 Sch.27. On identification of the relevant "transaction" see *National Westminster Bank v Jones* [2001] EWCA Civ 1541; [2002] B.P.I.R. 361. As to what is a "transaction" for s.423 purposes see *Ailyan and Fry v Smith* [2010] B.P.I.R. 289. The broad remedy which the court should have in mind is stated in s.423(2), although the specifics are detailed in s.425. Section 423(3) makes it clear that the transaction must have been intended to have a prejudicial effect.

Section 423 was the basis of a successful application by a creditor in *Arbuthnot Leasing International Ltd v Havelet Leasing Ltd (No.2)* [1990] B.C.C. 636. In acceding to the application Scott J held that the fact that the debtor had acted on legal advice did not exclude the debtor having the purpose specified in s.423(3)(a). Where there is a prima facie breach of s.423 the court may lift the veil of professional privilege to ascertain motives: *Barclays Bank v Eustice* [1995] 1 W.L.R. 1238; [1995] B.C.C. 978. The status of this authority in providing an exception to the protection of legal privilege was affirmed in *Brent LBC v Kane* [2014] EWHC 4564 (Ch). See also *Re Schuppan* [1997] B.P.I.R. 271.

In *Chohan v Saggar* [1992] B.C.C. 306 (on appeal, [1994] B.C.C. 134) it was held that the requirements of subs.(3) are satisfied provided the dominant purpose of the debtor was to achieve one of the prohibited aims. This analysis sits uneasily alongside the approach the courts have taken to s.238 (see above). Indeed, in *Royscot Spa Leasing Ltd v Lovett* [1995] B.C.C. 502 the Court of Appeal was prepared to accept a test based upon substantial (rather than dominant) purpose, though it did stress that it was important to distinguish between the purpose behind a transaction and the result of it. The dominant purpose test was favoured by Lightman J in *Banca Carige v Banco Nacional de Cuba* [2001] B.P.I.R. 407. The opposite view was taken by the Court of Appeal in *Hashmi v Inland Revenue Commissioners* [2002] EWCA Civ 981 and that now represents the accepted view—*Kubiangha v Ekpenyong* [2002] EWHC 1567 (Ch); [2002] 2 B.C.L.C. 597. A further instance of s.423 being judicially considered is found in *4Eng Ltd v Harper* [2010] B.P.I.R. 1. Here the "substantial purpose" test was again reaffirmed. The mental state of the recipient is not relevant when trying to determine the purpose of the debtor when entering into the transaction: *Moon v Franklin* [1996] B.P.I.R. 196. The court stressed the importance of *purpose* in *Papanicola v Fagan* [2009] B.P.I.R. 320. Here it was clear that the *result* of the transaction would be to defeat creditors but the *purpose* of the transaction was to help to preserve the debtor's marriage. A detailed consideration of this provision is found in the judgment of Sales J in *4Eng Ltd v Harper* [2009] EWHC 2633 (Ch). Amongst the various points made was the support for the substantial purpose test. Some consideration was also given to the relevance of the state of mind of the transferee. In *JSC Mezhdunarodniy Promyshlenniy Bank v Pugachev* [2017] EWHC 2426 (Ch) there is to be found at [443] a short comment by Birss J distinguishing purpose and result and identifying the appropriate timing of purpose.

In *Agricultural Mortgage Corp plc v Woodward* [1994] B.C.C. 688 a transaction falling within s.423(1)(c) was encountered. Here the Court of Appeal found that a grant of an agricultural tenancy by a farmer to his wife just before the mortgagee of the farm was intending to enforce the security was a transaction at an undervalue and should be set aside. Although a fair market rent had been charged by the husband, that rent did not take into account the fact that the wife as tenant could effectively hold the mortgagee to ransom by denying it vacant possession and thus preventing it enforcing its security. Looking at the transaction as a whole the arrangement was designed to defeat the interests of the mortgagee and the wife received real benefits outside the formal tenancy agreement that had not been paid for. In *Midland Bank v Wyatt* [1996] B.P.I.R. 288 a sham family trust established to protect assets in the event of business failure was avoided under s.423. Note also *Re Schuppan* [1997] B.P.I.R. 271 where an attempt by a wife to argue that nothing of value had been transferred was unsuccessful. A successful s.423 case was found in *Trowbridge v Trowbridge* [2003] B.P.I.R. 258. A s.423 application succeeded in *Beckenham MC Ltd v Centralex Ltd* [2004] EWHC 1287 (Ch); [2004] B.P.I.R. 1112 where a property transfer had been carried out in order to defeat the possible grant of a charging order against that property. Another successful s.423 application was exemplified by *Gil v Baygreen Properties Ltd* [2004] EWHC 1732 (Ch); [2005] B.P.I.R. 95. See also *AET v Kermanshahchi* [2003] EWHC 1939 (Ch); [2003] B.P.I.R. 1229; and *Pena v Coyne* [2004] B.P.I.R. 1286. Section 423 was successfully invoked in *Swift Advances plc v Ahmed* [2015] EWHC 3265 (Ch). A s.423 application had succeeded at first instance in *Cole v Billington* [2013] EWCA Civ 502 and the appeal by the defendant was dismissed. For cases falling on the other side of the line see *Menzies v National Bank of Kuwait SAK* [1994] B.C.C. 119; *Pinewood Joinery v Starelm Properties Ltd* [1994] B.C.C. 569; *Re Brabon* [2000] B.P.I.R. 537; *Re Taylor Sinclair (Capital) Ltd* [2002] B.P.I.R. 203. On s.423 note also *Ashe v Mumford* [2001] B.P.I.R. 1. See *Simon Carves Ltd v Hussain* [2013] EWHC 685 (Ch) (Sir William Blackburne) for another abortive attempt to exploit s.423 in a commercial context.

In *Feakins v DEFRA* [2005] EWCA Civ 1513; [2006] B.P.I.R. 895 the jurisdiction under s.423 came under the judicial microscope in the Court of Appeal. As is now consistent with modern authority a wide view of these provisions was adopted. In particular the concept of a "transaction" was applied flexibly to include any arrangement whether it be a formal agreement or informal understanding. The court also adopted a "commercial" view when determining any differential in consideration exchanged between the parties as part of the transaction. On the use of s.423 in commercial litigation generally see *Concept Oil Services Ltd v EN-GIN Group LLP* [2013] EWHC 1897 (Comm). Here Flaux J indicated that the word "transaction" when used in a s.423 context was capable of wide interpretation. It could in principle cover the transfer or continuation of an English company in a foreign jurisdiction. This restructuring would amount to an arrangement which constituted a transaction for s.423 purposes. This interpretation echoes that adopted by Jonathan Parker LJ in *Feakins v DEFRA* (above).

Furthermore, the Court of Appeal in *Re Nurkowski (Hill v Spread Trustee Co Ltd)* [2006] EWCA Civ 542; [2006] B.P.I.R. 789 made a number of important observations on ss.423–425. First, the Inland Revenue could be a "victim" for the purposes of these provisions where property transactions had occurred with the substantial purpose of misleading the tax authorities as to potential capital gains tax liability. The concept should be interpreted flexibly; a party could be a potential victim at one date, cease to be a victim at another and then revert to victim status at some later time. A claim under s.423 that involved a settlement of property being set aside was subject to a 12-year limitation period with time running from the date of the bankruptcy order. The Court of Appeal also took the opportunity to express the view (without finally determining the matter) that the grant of security might constitute a transaction at an undervalue, thereby doubting *Re M C Bacon Ltd* [1991] Ch. 127 on this point. This is interesting as a somewhat differently constituted Court of Appeal in *Feakins v DEFRA* (above) did not express such doubts. This issue is likely to be revisited in future litigation.

In *Sands v Clitheroe* [2006] B.P.I.R. 1000 further consideration was given to the question of who might invoke s.423. Here Registrar Jaques held that a party could in principle invoke s.423 to challenge a transaction entered into many years previously if the substantive requirements of the section were met. The fact that the particular claimant was not in the contemplation of the transferor at the time of the transaction was immaterial. All that was required was that the claimant was prejudiced by the transaction albeit at some later date. This, along with other rulings noted above, will expand the potential of transaction avoidance under s.423.

When assessing differences in the value of consideration the court is concerned with real economic benefits and not artificial book values—*Pena v Coyne (No.1)* [2004] EWHC 2684 (Ch); [2004] 2 B.C.L.C. 703. The curious case of *Delaney v Chen* [2010] EWCA Civ 1455; [2011] B.P.I.R. 39 should be noted with regard to the question of the burden of proving that a transaction was at an undervalue. Here it was found that there was no undervalue on the facts. The Court of Appeal judgment contains a useful discussion of the valuation rules.

Further consideration of s.423 is to be found in *Kali Ltd v Chawla* [2007] EWHC 1989 (Ch); [2007] EWHC 2357 (Ch); [2008] B.P.I.R. 415. Section 423 was invoked successfully in *Griffin v Awoderu* [2008] B.P.I.R. 877, where the court (D. Phillips QC) reviewed its options in redressing the position. A s.423 claim brought on behalf of the Crown succeeded in *HM Treasury Solicitor v Doveton* [2009] B.P.I.R. 352. Here a will was found to be forged and as a result dispositions made under it were avoided and property became bona vacantia. *Barnett v Semenyuk* [2008] B.P.I.R. 1427 provides another illustration of a successful s.423 claim.

For further consideration of the interface between s.423 and the Limitation Act 1980 see *Giles v Rhind* [2008] EWCA Civ 118; [2008] B.P.I.R. 342 where the Court of Appeal indicated that a s.423 claim involved an allegation of "breach of duty" for the purposes of s.32(2) of the Limitation Act 1980.

Note also *Stow v Stow* [2008] EWHC 495 (Ch); [2008] B.P.I.R. 673 where the potential utility of s.423 to the HMRC was commented upon. See also *Revenue and Customs Commissioners v Begum* [2010] EWHC 1799 (Ch); [2011] B.P.I.R. 59. On the potential for a s.423 claim see *Brittain v Courtway Estates* [2008] B.P.I.R. 1229.

In *Soutzos v Asombang* [2010] B.P.I.R. 960 an attempt to challenge a transaction under s.423 failed. The court also made the point that, even if the s.423 claim had been upheld, no relief could have been granted. Another abortive s.423 application featured in *Williams v Taylor* [2012] EWCA Civ 1443. Here although there were elements suggesting that the transaction was at an undervalue the court preferred to accept the evidence of the bankrupt and his wife offering an alternative explanation. A s.423 application was also dismissed by Registrar Jones in *Rubin v Dweck* [2012] B.P.I.R. 854. A number of key points were stressed in the judgment. The limitation period runs from the date of the bankruptcy order. Giving up potential rights in matrimonial proceedings could constitute valuable consideration. In *Bibby ACF Ltd v Agate* [2013] B.P.I.R. 685 Master Bowles refused to follow *Rubin v Dweck* (above) on the question of the valuation of consideration. Master Bowles found that there had been a transaction at an undervalue but the requirement of an intention to defeat creditors had not been established. The s.423 claim therefore failed. For yet another failed s.423 claim see *Withers LLP v Harrison-Welch* [2012] EWHC 3077 (QB) where the grant of security over the property had the effect of defeating a charging order granted in favour of creditor. The court held that on the evidence the grant of the security was not for the purpose of defeating the claim of the creditor.

A speculative s.423 argument failed in *Westbrook Dolphin Square Ltd v Friends Life Ltd* [2014] EWHC 2433 (Ch). The case is valuable for the in depth study of the requirements of s.423 carried out by Mann J. On the other hand, in *Re Husky Group Ltd, Watchorn v Jupiter Industries Ltd* [2014] EWHC 3003 (Ch) an assignment of a trademark was set aside by HHJ Purle QC under s.423. In *B v IB* [2013] EWHC 3755 (Fam); [2014] B.P.I.R. 331 Parker J refused to dismiss a s.423 application which sought to challenge various intra family property transfers. The wide potential usage of s.423 in non-bankruptcy situations was emphasised. A trust deed was found not to be a sham in *Ali v Bashir* [2014] EWHC 3853 (Ch) but nevertheless set aside as a contravention of s.423. An attempt to invoke s.423 was dismissed by Newey J in *Sands v Singh* [2016] EWHC 636 (Ch); [2016] B.P.I.R. 737 because as the alternative claim under s.339 was rejected there was no prospect of a successful claim under s.423. See the General Note to s.339 for further information. A TUV claim failed in *Vasdev v Bellnorth Ltd* [2017] EWHC 1395 (Ch).

In *4Eng Ltd v Harper* [2009] EWHC 2633 (Ch); [2010] B.C.C. 746 some consideration was given to the relevance of the state of mind of the transferee. By way of contrast, in *Moon v Franklin* [1996] B.P.I.R. 196 this was regarded as an irrelevant consideration.

This provision is capable of having extraterritorial effect—*Revenue and Customs Commissioners v Begum* [2010] EWHC 1799 (Ch). This point was confirmed obiter by Sir Andrew Morritt in *Bilta (UK) Ltd v Nazir* [2012] EWHC

2163 (Ch) at [41]. It seems that this interpretation favouring extraterritorial application was implicitly supported on appeal sub nomine *Jetivia SA v Bilta (UK) Ltd* [2013] EWCA Civ 968; [2013] B.C.C. 655 especially at [90] per Patten LJ. Although the s.423 point was not specifically addressed when the case reached the Supreme Court (see [2015] UKSC 23) it is implicit in all of the judgments that s.423 would have extraterritorial effect. To give it such effect is to respond to the reality of modern global commerce. See also *Revenue and Customs Commissioners v Ben Nevis (Holdings) Ltd* [2012] EWHC 1807 (Ch); [2012] S.T.C. 2157 at paras [61]–[68] per HHJ Pelling QC for further consideration of the extra-territorial effect and other jurisdictional issues arising in connection with a s.423 claim. In *Erste Group Bank AG v JSC "VMZ Red October"* [2015] EWCA Civ 379 the Court of Appeal allowed an appeal from the first instance ruling of Flaux J but confirmed the extraterritorial application of s.423 (see [116]). That said, the Court of Appeal declined jurisdiction to allow the s.423 claim to be heard in England as there was no significant connection with the English jurisdiction—see [126]. The alleged tort had been committed in Russia and practicality suggested that the proper forum for resolution of the issue was in Russia. The question of CPR "gateways" and service outside jurisdiction were issues considered by HHJ Waksman QC in *Orexim Trading Ltd v Mahavir Port and Terminal Private Ltd* [2017] EWHC 2663 (Comm). Here the court at [36] questioned the views of Flaux J in *ERSTE* (above) on these issues.

On s.423 applications and the EC Regulation on Insolvency Proceedings (1346/2000) see *Byers v Yacht Bull Corp* [2010] B.P.I.R. 535. Note *Re Phoenix Kapitaldienst GmbH* [2012] EWHC 62 (Ch); [2012] 3 W.L.R. 681 (availability of s.423 to a foreign office holder via use of comity principle at common law). One wonders about the authority of this ruling (which placed heavy reliance upon the views expressed by Lord Hoffmann in *Cambridge Gas* [2006] UKPC 26) in the light of the more restrictive approach towards the comity principle in international insolvency law taken by the majority of the Supreme Court in *Rubin v Eurofinance* [2012] UKSC 46. In *Singularis Holdings Ltd v PricewaterhouseCoopers (Bermuda)* [2014] UKPC 36 Lord Collins (at [98]) went so far as to say that *Phoenix* (above) had been wrongly decided.

Applications under the Northern Irish counterpart provision (art.367 of the 1989 Insolvency Order) featured in two cases which came before McCloskey J, namely *Quinn Finance v Galfis Overseas Ltd* [2012] NICh 9 and *Quinn Finance v Lyndhurst Development Trading SA* [2012] NICh 15.

Section 423 can, in appropriate circumstances, be used to challenge the payment of a dividend to company shareholders—see Rose J in *BTI 2014 LLC v Sequana SA* [2016] EWHC 1686 (Ch). Note also *Stanley v Wilson* (unreported, 5 August 2016, HHJ Raeside QC) for possible linkage with s.342A. For the interface between a potential s.423 application and the freezing order jurisdiction see *Lemos v Lemos* [2016] EWCA Civ 1181.

Aspects of this provision were discussed by HHJ Hodge QC in *Leeds v Lemos* [2017] EWHC 1825 (Ch); [2017] B.P.I.R. 1223. The point was made that a claim to recover property under s.423 does not mean that said property is at the time of the claim property within the estate for the purposes of s.436.

S.423(4), (5)

These provisions define "court" and "victim" (see ss.423(2)(b), 424(1)(a)–(c), 424(2)). The latter term was not used in IA 1985. In *Moon v Franklin* (above) the victims were persons who were suing the debtor for professional negligence. See also *Pinewood Joinery v Starelm Properties* (above); and *Jyske Bank (Gibraltar) v Spjeldnaes (No.2)* [1999] B.P.I.R. 525. A disputed pre-pack was at the heart of the s.423 claim in *Clydesdale v Smailes* [2009] EWHC 3190 (Ch); [2010] B.P.I.R. 77. The court made the point that the concept of a "victim" was much wider than that of a party simply enjoying creditor status.

For a s.423 application that met with some success see *Bataillon v Shone* [2016] EWHC 1174 (QB); [2016] B.P.I.R. 829. Judgment creditors of the debtor were found to be victims. The court observed that a spouse's forbearance in not seeking a divorce/property settlement could constitute consideration when determining whether a TUV had occurred.

Section 423 can be invoked by a plaintiff in any part of the High Court provided the claim does not form part of proceedings being conducted in the Bankruptcy Court or the Companies Court: *TSB Bank plc v Katz* [1997] B.P.I.R. 147. On extraterritoriality see *Jyske Bank (Gibraltar) Ltd v Spjeldnaes (No.2)* (above). In *Banca Carige v Banco Nacional de Cuba* [2001] B.P.I.R. 407 Lightman J stressed that leave is required in order to serve a s.423 claim abroad.

424 Those who may apply for an order under s.423

424(1) [Conditions for s.423 application] An application for an order under section 423 shall not be made in relation to a transaction except–

(a) in a case where the debtor has been made bankrupt or is a body corporate which is being wound up or is in administration, by the official receiver, by the trustee of the bankrupt's estate or the liquidator or administrator of the body corporate or (with the leave of the court) by a victim of the transaction;

(b) in a case where a victim of the transaction is bound by a voluntary arrangement approved under Part I or Part VIII of this Act, by the supervisor of the voluntary arrangement or by any person who (whether or not so bound) is such a victim; or

(c) in any other case, by a victim of the transaction.

424(2) [Treatment of application] An application made under any of the paragraphs of subsection (1) is to be treated as made on behalf of every victim of the transaction.

General Note

These provisions explain who may make a s.423 application (see the annotation to s.423 above for further analysis). A minor textual change to subs.(1)(a) was made by Sch.17 to EA 2002. Note the leave requirement is s.424(1)(a). As to whether leave can be granted retrospectively see the discussion in *Dora v Simper* [2000] 2 B.C.L.C. 561. In *Godfrey v Torpy (No.2)* [2007] EWHC 919 (Ch); [2007] B.P.I.R. 1538 the court held that retrospective leave could be granted where a victim commences a s.423 action without leave. This view is consistent with the approach of Chief Registrar Baister in *Bank of Scotland v Breytenbach* [2012] B.P.I.R. 1. If the person entering into the transaction was a company, then it may be challenged under this provision by the liquidator or administrator. If it was an individual, then the official receiver or trustee may bring the proceedings. Supervisors of voluntary arrangements may also apply in certain cases (most avoidance provisions are not available in the cases of a company or individual voluntary arrangement), as may "victims" (for definition see s.423(5)), who may bring an action either individually or in a representative capacity. See *Moon v Franklin* [1996] B.P.I.R. 196 for an example of a victim making the application. A creditor of an insolvent company can be a victim: *Re Ayala Holdings Ltd* [1993] B.C.L.C. 256. See also *Pinewood Joinery v Starelm Properties Ltd* [1994] B.C.C. 569. For an example of a "victim" see *Ali v Bashir* [2014] EWHC 3853 (Ch).

Note that the FCA or the PRA may apply in an appropriate case—FSMA 2000 s.375, as amended by the Financial Services Act 2012. The Pensions Regulator may also invoke s.423—see Pensions Act 2004 s.58.

Note amendment made to subs.(1)(a) by ERRA 2013 Sch.19 para.61.

425 Provision which may be made by order under s.423

425(1) [Scope of order] Without prejudice to the generality of section 423, an order made under that section with respect to a transaction may (subject as follows)–

(a) require any property transferred as part of the transaction to be vested in any person, either absolutely or for the benefit of all the persons on whose behalf the application for the order is treated as made;

(b) require any property to be so vested if it represents, in any person's hands, the application either of the proceeds of sale of property so transferred or of money so transferred;

(c) release or discharge (in whole or in part) any security given by the debtor;

(d) require any person to pay to any other person in respect of benefits received from the debtor such sums as the court may direct;

(e) provide for any surety or guarantor whose obligations to any person were released or discharged (in whole or in part) under the transaction to be under such new or revived obligations as the court thinks appropriate;

(f) provide for security to be provided for the discharge of any obligation imposed by or arising under the order, for such an obligation to be charged on any property and for such security or charge to have the same priority as a security or charge released or discharged (in whole or in part) under the transaction.

425(2) [Limit to order] An order under section 423 may affect the property of, or impose any obligation on, any person whether or not he is the person with whom the debtor entered into the transaction; but such an order–

(a) shall not prejudice any interest in property which was acquired from a person other than the debtor and was acquired in good faith, for value and without notice of the relevant circumstances, or prejudice any interest deriving from such an interest, and

(b) shall not require a person who received a benefit from the transaction in good faith, for value and without notice of the relevant circumstances to pay any sum unless he was a party to the transaction.

425(3) [Relevant circumstances] For the purposes of this section the relevant circumstances in relation to a transaction are the circumstances by virtue of which an order under section 423 may be made in respect of the transaction.

425(4) ["Security"] In this section "security" means any mortgage, charge, lien or other security.

S.425(1)

This gives illustrations of the types of order the court may make under s.423. This is similar to ss.241(1) and 342(1), but with the omission of para.(g). A declaration was the basis of the relief granted in *Moon v Franklin* [1996] B.P.I.R. 196. Interim relief may be available: *Aiglon Ltd v Gau Shan Co Ltd* [1993] 1 Lloyd's Rep. 164. In *Re Krug International (UK) Ltd* [2008] B.P.I.R. 1512 HHJ Purle QC indicated the scope of potential remedies under s.423 were the avoidance claim to prove successful. For an example of monetary compensation being the preferred remedy under s.425 on the particular facts of the case see *Pena v Coyne (No.2)* [2004] EWHC 2685 (Ch); [2004] 2 B.C.L.C. 730. The remedial jurisdiction of the court when acceding to a s.423 application was considered by Sales J in *4Eng Ltd v Harper* [2009] EWHC 2633 (Ch); [2010] B.P.I.R. 1. Here the judge made the point that the court was under no obligation to seek to maintain the standard of living of the transferee where a breach of s.423 had been established. The broad discretion enjoyed by the court in dealing with questions of relief was stressed by Registrar Jones in *Rubin v Dweck* [2012] B.P.I.R. 854 (where no breach of s.423 was established). On the remedial jurisdiction see *Ailyan and Fry v Smith* [2010] B.P.I.R. 289. For an order given extraterritorial effect see *Jyske Bank (Gibraltar) Ltd v Spjeldnaes (No.2)* [1999] B.P.I.R. 525. Note the limitation imposed on any relief by POCA 2002 s.419.

S.425(2), (3)

Although third-party rights may be affected, there is protection for bona fide purchasers, for value and without notice, who have taken without notice of the relevant circumstances, as defined by s.425(3). The relief granted in *Arbuthnot Leasing International Ltd v Havelet Leasing Ltd (No.2)* [1990] B.C.C. 636 (see the note to s.423, above) took the form of an order that the assets improperly transferred should be held on trust for the transferor, but without prejudice to the claims of those who had become creditors of the transferee since the date of the transfer. In *Chohan v Saggar* [1994] B.C.C. 134 the Court of Appeal considered the aim of an order under s.425. Although the order should seek to restore the original pre-transaction position, sometimes the need to protect third parties may prevent a complete restoration. Partial invalidation of transactions may therefore be the best answer to the problem of balancing the competing interests of creditors and bona fide third parties. There is a useful discussion of the aim of the remedy under s.425 in *4Eng Ltd v Harper* [2010] B.P.I.R. 1. The aim is to restore the parties to the pre-transaction position. The point was also made by Sales J that the transferee under a transaction that is liable to be set aside *may* have available a change of position defence. The comments of Sales J on the potential availability of change of position as a defence to an avoidance claim was criticised by Davenport in an article in [2011] 24 Insolv. Int. 91. Change of position as a defence was also considered by Sales J again in *Trustee in Bankruptcy of Claridge v Claridge* [2011] EWHC 2047 (Ch); [2011] B.P.I.R. 1529. This potential usage of a general doctrine which is not part of the transactional avoidance tradition was in turn questioned by the ILA (see Technical Bulletin No.360) on the grounds that this doctrine should have no place in the context of the transactional provisions in insolvency law. We may expect this contentious issue to be revisited in future litigation.

For the difficult balancing exercise that often arises when determining the precise scope of an order under s.425 see *Griffin v Awoderu* [2008] EWHC 349 (Ch). For further consideration of the remedial jurisdiction under s.425 see the county court case of *Green v Austin* [2014] B.P.I.R. 1176.

The court enjoys discretion in granting relief. For an example of this discretion at work see *Bataillon v Shone* [2016] EWHC 1174 (QB); [2016] B.P.I.R. 829 where some protection was offered to an innocent third party.

S.425(4)
This is an interpretation provision relevant to s.425(1)(c) and (f).

Part XVII

Miscellaneous and General

426 Co-operation between courts exercising jurisdiction in relation to insolvency

426(1) [Enforcement in other parts of UK] An order made by a court in any part of the United Kingdom in the exercise of jurisdiction in relation to insolvency law shall be enforced in any other part of the United Kingdom as if it were made by a court exercising the corresponding jurisdiction in that other part.

426(2) [Limit to s.426(1)] However, without prejudice to the following provisions of this section, nothing in subsection (1) requires a court in any part of the United Kingdom to enforce, in relation to property situated in that part, any order made by a court in any other part of the United Kingdom.

426(3) [Order by Secretary of State] The Secretary of State, with the concurrence in relation to property situated in England and Wales of the Lord Chancellor, may by order make provision for securing that a trustee or assignee under the insolvency law of any part of the United Kingdom has, with such modifications as may be specified in the order, the same rights in relation to any property situated in another part of the United Kingdom as he would have in the corresponding circumstances if he were a trustee or assignee under the insolvency law of that other part.

426(4) [Assistance between courts] The courts having jurisdiction in relation to insolvency law in any part of the United Kingdom shall assist the courts having the corresponding jurisdiction in any other part of the United Kingdom or any relevant country or territory.

426(5) [Request under s.426(4)] For the purposes of subsection (4) a request made to a court in any part of the United Kingdom by a court in any other part of the United Kingdom or in a relevant country or territory is authority for the court to which the request is made to apply, in relation to any matters specified in the request, the insolvency law which is applicable by either court in relation to comparable matters falling within its jurisdiction.

In exercising its discretion under this subsection, a court shall have regard in particular to the rules of private international law.

426(6) [Claim by trustee or assignee] Where a person who is a trustee or assignee under the insolvency law of any part of the United Kingdom claims property situated in any other part of the United Kingdom (whether by virtue of an order under subsection (3) or otherwise), the submission of that claim to the court exercising jurisdiction in relation to insolvency law in that other part shall be treated in the same manner as a request made by a court for the purpose of subsection (4).

426(7) [Application of Criminal Law Act] Section 38 of the Criminal Law Act 1977 (execution of warrant of arrest throughout the United Kingdom) applies to a warrant which, in exercise of any jurisdiction in relation to insolvency law, is issued in any part of the United Kingdom for the arrest of a person as it applies to a warrant issued in that part of the United Kingdom for the arrest of a person charged with an offence.

426(8) [Powers in subordinate legislation] Without prejudice to any power to make rules of court, any power to make provision by subordinate legislation for the purpose of giving effect in relation to companies or individuals to the insolvency law of any part of the United Kingdom includes power to make provision for the purpose of giving effect in that part to any provision made by or under the preceding provisions of this section.

426(9) [Section 426(3) order by statutory instrument etc.] An order under subsection (3) shall be made by statutory instrument subject to annulment in pursuance of a resolution of either House of Parliament.

426(10) ["Insolvency law"] In this section "insolvency law" means–

(a) in relation to England and Wales, provision extending to England and Wales and made by or under this Act or sections 1A, 6 to 10, 12 to 15, 19(c) and 20 (with Schedule 1) of the Company Directors Disqualification Act 1986 and sections 1 to 17 of that Act as they apply for the purposes of those provisions of that Act;

(b) in relation to Scotland, provision extending to Scotland and made by or under this Act, sections 1A, 6 to 10, 12 to 15, 19(c) and 20 (with Schedule 1) of the Company Directors Disqualification Act 1986 and sections 1 to 17 of that Act as they apply for the purposes of those provisions of that Act, Part XVIII of the Companies Act or the Bankruptcy (Scotland) Act 2016;

(c) in relation to Northern Ireland, provision made by or under the Insolvency (Northern Ireland) Order 1989 or the Company Directors Disqualification (Northern Ireland) Order 2002;

(d) in relation to any relevant country or territory, so much of the law of that country or territory as corresponds to provisions falling within any of the foregoing paragraphs;

and references in this subsection to any enactment include, in relation to any time before the coming into force of that enactment the corresponding enactment in force at that time.

426(11) ["Relevant country or territory"] In this section "relevant country or territory" means–

(a) any of the Channel Islands or the Isle of Man, or

(b) any country or territory designated for the purposes of this section by the Secretary of State by order made by statutory instrument.

426(12) [Application to Northern Ireland] In the application of this section to Northern Ireland–

(a) for any reference to the Secretary of State there is substituted a reference to the Department of Economic Development in Northern Ireland;

(b) in subsection (3) for the words "another part of the United Kingdom" and the words "that other part" there is substituted the words "Northern Ireland";

(c) for subsection (9) there is substituted the following subsection–

"(9) An order made under subsection (3) by the Department of Economic Development in Northern Ireland shall be a statutory rule for the purposes of the Statutory Rules (Northern Ireland) Order 1979 and shall be subject to negative resolution within the meaning of section 41(6) of the Interpretation Act (Northern Ireland) 1954."

426(13) [Bank insolvency in Banking Act 2009 s.129 as "insolvency law"] Section 129 of the Banking Act 2009 provides for provisions of that Act about bank insolvency to be "insolvency law" for the purposes of this section.

426(14) [Banking administration in Banking Act 2009 s.165 as "insolvency law"] Section 165 of the Banking Act 2009 provides for provisions of that Act about bank administration to be "insolvency law" for the purposes of this section.

General Note

Section 426 bears some resemblance to s.122 of the Bankruptcy Act 1914, which dealt with co-operation in bankruptcy matters between the courts of the UK and colonial territories. This former provision in English law has been held by the Privy Council in *Al Sabah v Grupo Torras SA* [2005] UKPC 1; [2005] 2 W.L.R. 904 to have continuing effect vis-à-vis the Cayman Islands as it had never been repealed with respect to that jurisdiction. The advice of the Privy Council contains a useful historical perspective on s.426. The Cork *Report*, Ch.49, called for the rationalisation and improvement of co-operation between the insolvency courts in the UK. This section represents a step in that direction. However there are problems of interpretation particularly concerned with the freedom of action enjoyed by the English courts and these have troubled the judiciary in a number of recent cases discussed below.

Various aspects of the s.426 jurisdiction were considered by the courts in the *Fourie v Le Roux* sequence of cases. Blackburne J held in *Fourie v Le Roux* [2004] EWHC 2557 (Ch); [2005] B.P.I.R. 723 that under s.426(5) of the IA 1986 the co-operative jurisdiction under s.426 could only be engaged if the foreign requesting court (here a South African court) specified what assistance it was seeking from the English court. In *Fourie v Le Roux* [2005] EWCA Civ 204; [2005] B.P.I.R. 756 the Court of Appeal had nothing to add on the narrow s.426 point and an appeal from this ruling was dismissed by the House of Lords in *Fourie v Le Roux* [2007] UKHL 1. But when the case came back before Blackburne J in *Fourie v Le Roux* [2004] EWHC 2557 (Ch); [2005] B.P.I.R. 779 a new letter of request from the South African courts fell to be considered. In this latest instalment Blackburne J held that jurisdiction to assist the foreign court existed under s.426 to assist the foreign court even if the assistance would impact upon a party outside the jurisdiction of the requesting court. However this fact was relevant to the question as to whether the English court should exercise its discretion to assist. Moreover, the procedure for serving claims outside the jurisdiction as specified in the then IR 1986 r.12.12 (which was replaced by IR 1986 r.12.20A) did not apply to requests for assistance made under s.426. Service in such cases was governed by CPR Pt 6.20. See now IR 2016 Sch.4 para.1(8). For general discussion in this area see Jerrum [2016] 29 Insolv. Int. 109.

A number of countries and territories were designated for the purposes of s.426 by the Co-operation of Insolvency Courts (Designation of Relevant Countries and Territories) Order 1986 (SI 1986/2123), effective 29 December 1986. These were: Anguilla, Australia, the Bahamas, Bermuda, Botswana, Canada, Cayman Islands, Falkland Islands, Gibraltar, Hong Kong, the Republic of Ireland, Montserrat, New Zealand, St Helena, Turks and Caicos Islands, Tuvalu and the Virgin Islands. Malaysia and South Africa were added by SI 1996/253. Brunei was included by SI 1998/2766. In consequence, the courts of these countries and territories have the right to request assistance in matters of insolvency from courts having jurisdiction in insolvency in any part of the UK. Switzerland is not a designated jurisdiction therefore assistance under s.426 is not available—*Re SwissAir Schweizerische Luftverkehr-Aktiengesellschaft* [2010] B.C.C. 667. The court in *Schmitt v Deichmann* [2012] EWHC 62 (Ch) made it clear that it cannot extend the list of designated countries for the purposes of s.426 but that the growing common law principle of comity might produce the same beneficial effect.

Subsections (4), (5), (10) and (11) of s.426 were extended to the Bailiwick of Guernsey by the Insolvency Act 1986 (Guernsey) Order 1989 (SI 1989/2409), with the modifications specified in the Schedule to that Order, as from 1 February 1990. Accordingly, a co-operative insolvency regime is now established between Guernsey (including Alderney and Sark) and the UK. Note the modifications to s.426(10) by para.16(3) of Sch.4 to the IA 2000.

In relation to the financial markets (see the note on p.2), the provisions of s.426 are subject to the limitations set out in CA 1989 s.183. Part XVII applies to limited liability partnerships by virtue of the Limited Liability Partnerships Regulations 2001 (SI 2001/1090) reg.5(1)(b) as from 6 April 2001 subject to reg.5(2) and (3).

In future s.426 will have to be read alongside s.14 of IA 2000 and regulations made thereunder. Section 14 permits the Secretary of State to adopt the UNICITRAL Model Law on Cross-Border Insolvency Proceedings and to modify existing rules (including s.426) and this was achieved by SI 2006/1030. On an EU level judicial comity in insolvency matters is to be promoted by EU Regulation 2015/848 on insolvency proceedings.

Readers should note that there is always the possibility of judicial comity operating via the common law—on this see *Cambridge Gas Transport Corp v The Official Committee of Unsecured Creditors of Navigator Holdings* [2006] UKPC 26; [2006] B.C.C. 962. *Cambridge Gas* (above) was followed by Registrar Jaques in *Re Phoenix Kapitaldienst GmbH* [2008] B.P.I.R. 1082. The debate over whether English law should commit itself to a position in favour of universalism continues to engage judicial thought. This issue was revisited in a different context by Teare J in *Global Distressed Alpha Fund 1 Ltd Partnership v PT Bakrie Investindo* [2011] EWHC 256 (Comm); [2011] B.P.I.R. 644. The issue here was whether the English courts should accept the proposition that a guarantee which had been discharged under a foreign bankruptcy law could be treated as discharged under English law (which was the proper law of the contract). Although Teare J was, on the basis of a universalist approach, minded to accept such a view, he felt compelled by the Court of Appeal precedent of *Anthony Gibbs & Sons v La Société Industrielle et Commerciale des Métaux* (1890) 25 QBD 399 to reject it in this specific context. There is no doubt, however, that Teare J's sympathies lie with the idea of universalism of bankruptcy at common law. A similar conclusion might also be drawn from a reading of Proudman J's judgment in *Schmitt v Deichmann* [2012] EWHC 62 (Ch). The status of *Cambridge Gas* has been undermined by the ruling of the Supreme Court in *Rubin v Eurofinance* (in a joined appeal with *New Cap Reinsurance Corp v Grant*) [2012] UKSC 46; [2012] B.P.I.R. 1204 where the majority of the Supreme Court disapproved of it. This represented a major blow for those advocating universalism in cross-border insolvency law and has raised concerns on the part of insolvency practitioners that it will increase the costs of administering cross-border insolvency cases. The issue of the current status the common law jurisdiction of modified universalism was revisited in *Singularis Holdings Ltd v PricewaterhouseCoopers* [2014] UKPC 36 where the majority view was that there were a number of limitations on what the court could do to offer comity under private international law in the face of countervailing statutory provisions in the requesting jurisdiction. *Cambridge Gas* was questioned on a number of points and *Al Sabah v Grupo Torras* was confirmed. Lord Collins indicated that the order made in *Phoenix Kapitaldienst* [2013] Ch. 61 could not be supported. *Singularis* (above) raises many questions of interpretation for commentators as there were multiple judgments delivered by the Privy Council and considerable differences of opinion expressed by the Board. For perceptive critique see Rajak (2015) 367 Co. L.N. 1. For the approach of the Scottish courts to modified universalism see *Hooley Ltd v Victoria Jute Co Ltd* [2016] CSOH 141.

S.426(1), (2)
This allows for general enforcement of court orders throughout the UK, although there are limitations expressed with regard to enforcement of court orders against property in different parts of the UK.

S.426(3), (9)
Assimilation of the powers of a trustee, etc. in the different UK jurisdictions is provided for here. The Secretary of State may use statutory instruments to do this.

S.426(4), (5), (11)
The UK courts must on a matter of insolvency law co-operate with each other, and indeed with courts from the Isle of Man, Channel Isles or from any jurisdiction specified by the Secretary of State. These provisions permit the court to offer assistance to courts in other parts of the UK or in other "relevant" countries, as defined in s.426(11). With the increased incidence of cross-border insolvency in recent years the UK courts have increasingly been faced with requests for assistance. For a review of this jurisdiction see Smart (1996) 112 L.Q.R. 397; (1998) 114 L.Q.R. 46; and Fletcher [1997] J.B.L. 470.

In *Re Gerrard (Trustee in the Bankruptcy of Hynd)* [2009] B.P.I.R. 1374 the Scottish courts offered assistance to an English trustee by invoking its jurisdiction under s.426(4). Lord Glennie noted that the Cross-Border Insolvency Regulations 2006 (SI 2006/1030) were not applicable to this scenario.

In spite of the apparent statutory obligation to lend assistance the Court of Appeal confirmed in *Hughes v Hannover-Rucksversicherungs AG* [1997] B.C.C. 921 that the court continues to enjoy discretion in such applications and may think it appropriate to reject the request for assistance. Indeed it chose this course of action in that particular case because the circumstances had changed materially since the date of the request. In *Re Focus Insurance Co Ltd* [1996] B.C.C. 659 Scott V.C. refused assistance to foreign liquidators who had successfully petitioned for the respondent to be bankrupted in England. To offer the assistance sought would involve complicating and possibly undermining the English bankruptcy which the applicants themselves had initiated. Again in *Re J N Taylor Pty Ltd* [1998] B.P.I.R. 347 the primary request for assistance was also rejected because to have acceded to it would result in company officers being subjected to examination by an Australian liquidator in circumstances where no such examination would have been permitted under English law. This decision must be of questionable authority in view of the later Court of Appeal ruling in *England v Smith (Re Southern Equities Corp)* [2001] Ch. 419; [2000] B.P.I.R. 28. Here it was held that the policy of judicial comity was the starting point on any s.426 request. Thus it was possible for the English courts to accede to a request to interview a party under the machinery of Australian insolvency law even though such an interview would not have been allowed had this been an entirely domestic case. Differences in the substantive law between nations on individual statutory provisions did not necessarily mean that one system was fairer than another. The whole picture required consideration. Subsequently, a similar approach was taken by Jonathan Parker J in *Duke Group Ltd v Carver* [2001] B.P.I.R. 459 where an Australian judge was permitted to examine a witness in England pursuant to Australian law. The point was made that it would require something extraordinary to refuse a request for assistance and it was not for the English courts to water down the assistance requested. In *Re Trading Partners Ltd* [2002] B.P.I.R. 606 Patten J acceded to a request from the courts of the British Virgin Islands to allow liquidators of a company to take advantage of s.236 of IA 1986 in order to gain access to documents in the possession of administrative receivers of a related company. In *Re Television Trade Rentals Ltd* [2002] EWHC 211 (Ch); [2002] B.C.C. 807 s.426 was used to apply the CVA procedure to companies incorporated in the Isle of Man. A request to do this retrospectively was refused.

When considering whether to offer assistance the court has a range of options available. According to the Court of Appeal in *Hughes v Hannover-Rucksversicherungs AG* (above) the courts can apply their own inherent general jurisdiction, substantive English insolvency law or the substantive insolvency law of the foreign jurisdiction. Flexibility is the order of the day.

In *Re New Cap Reinsurance Corp Ltd* [2011] EWCA Civ 971; [2011] B.P.I.R. 1428 the Court of Appeal noted a potential limitation on s.426 assistance to enforce a judgment in cases where the Foreign Judgments (Reciprocal

Enforcement) Act 1933 applied. On appeal (see [2012] UKSC 46) the Supreme Court considered further the relevance of the 1933 Act in the context of insolvency proceedings and indicated that on the facts of that case the way forward was via registration of the judgment under the 1933 Act and not by application under s.426.

In *Re Integrated Medical Solutions Ltd* [2012] B.C.C. 215 Chief Registrar Baister indicated that the English courts should wherever possible lend support to a letter of request.

The Court of Appeal took a wide view of the scope of this provision in *HSBC Bank plc v Tambrook Jersey Ltd* [2013] EWCA Civ 576; [2013] B.P.I.R. 484. The Court of Appeal (rejecting the approach taken by Mann J at first instance) held that a court from a scheduled jurisdiction could apply for insolvency assistance, even though no formal insolvency proceedings had been commenced in that jurisdiction. This decision came as a relief to City practitioners engaged in restructuring distressed Jersey companies by using the English administration procedure.

For a request for assistance from the Scottish courts see *McKinnon v Graham* [2013] EWHC 2870 (Ch); [2013] B.P.I.R. 1070. The request was made here by a Scottish trustee in a sequestration of a Scottish debtor, who sought the application of the English "use it or lose it" rules to property located in England, as those rules were to the advantage of the estate as compared to the counterpart rules in Scotland. The English court held that this application was not contrary to public policy.

An order was made under s.426(4) in the case of *Re Dallhold Estates (UK) Pty Ltd* [1992] B.C.C. 394. Here the courts of Western Australia sought help from the English courts to protect the assets of an Australian company having property in this jurisdiction. Although it seems that it is not possible for the English courts to grant an administration order in respect of a foreign company on their own initiative they can in effect do this if they receive a request under s.426. Accordingly the administration order was granted. In *Re Bank of Credit and Commerce International SA* [1993] B.C.C. 787 Rattee J held that when faced with a request for assistance (in this case from the Grand Court of the Cayman Islands) the English courts were not restricted to rendering applicable procedural facilities of English law but could also declare principles of substantive English insolvency law applicable in the particular case. In *Re Business City Express Ltd* [1997] B.C.C. 826 relief was offered by Rattee J to facilitate a rescue plan mounted by the examiner of an Irish company. Although the request involved some departure from normal distribution rules on insolvency the circumstances were such as to justify this on utilitarian grounds.

In the major case of *McGrath v Riddell* [2008] UKHL 21; [2008] B.C.C. 349 the House of Lords on an application under s.426 authorised English provisional liquidators to hand over assets collected in an ancillary winding up in this country to Australian liquidators. This was in spite of the fact that there existed a difference between Australian and English law on pari passu distribution. Although all of their Lordships agreed with this outcome there was an unresolved disagreement between Lord Hoffmann, who argued that there was inherent jurisdiction to do this, and Lord Scott, who maintained that this could only be done within the terms of s.426. This disagreement might have implications in the case of liquidations conducted in jurisdictions not recognised under s.426. What is apparent from this case is that there is an emerging common law principle of international comity in cross border insolvency developing outside the confines of s.426. The restrictive view of Lord Scott appears to have attracted the support of Newey J in *Re Alitalia Linee Aeree Italiane SpA* [2011] EWHC 15 (Ch) and of the majority of the Supreme Court in *Rubin v Eurofinance SA* [2012] UKSC 46.

Norris J granted relief under this provision in *Centaur Litigation SPC v Terrill* [2015] EWHC 3420 (Ch) in the form of a declaration that official liquidators should represent certain companies in litigation. In exercising discretion whether to grant relief Norris J made the point that the fact that the requesting Cayman court had agreed to the letter of request being sent to the English court was a significant but not determinative factor.

S.426(6)

This subsection allows trustees, etc. to claim property situated in other parts of the UK by calling on the assistance of the courts where the property is situated.

S.426(7)

This applies s.38 of the Criminal Law Act 1977 to warrants for arrest in connection with insolvency law matters.

S.426(8)

Delegated legislation can be used to achieve the aim of co-operation as contained in s.426: see the Co-operation of Insolvency Courts (Designation of Relevant Countries and Territories) Order 1986 (SI 1986/2123).

S.426(10), (11), (12)

These provisions define "insolvency law" and "relevant country or territory" for the purposes of this section and these definitions are exhaustive: see *Hughes v Hannover-Rucksversicherungs AG* [1997] B.C.C. 921 here. Provision is also made for Northern Ireland. Subsection (10) was amended and subs.(12) added by Sch.9 to the Insolvency (Northern Ireland) Order 1989 (SI 1989/2405 (NI 19)). Subsection (10)(b) was amended by the Bankruptcy

(Scotland) Act 2016 (Consequential Provisions and Modifications) Order 2016 (SI 2016/1034) art.7(1), Sch.1 para.4(1), (9) as from 30 November 2016.

S.426(13), (14)
Inserted by the Banking Act 2009.

426A Disqualification from Parliament (England and Wales and Northern Ireland)

426A(1) [Bankruptcy restrictions or debt relief restrictions orders] A person in respect of whom a bankruptcy restrictions order or a debt relief restrictions order has effect shall be disqualified–

(a) from membership of the House of Commons,

(b) from sitting or voting in the House of Lords, and

(c) from sitting or voting in a committee of the House of Lords or a joint committee of both Houses.

426A(2) [MP to vacate seat] If a member of the House of Commons becomes disqualified under this section, his seat shall be vacated.

426A(3) [Election return void] If a person who is disqualified under this section is returned as a member of the House of Commons, his return shall be void.

426A(4) [No writ to member of House of Lords] No writ of summons shall be issued to a member of the House of Lords who is disqualified under this section.

426A(5) [Notification of Speaker of various orders] If a court makes a bankruptcy restrictions order or interim order, or a debt relief restrictions order or an interim debt relief restrictions order, in respect of a member of the House of Commons or the House of Lords the court shall notify the Speaker of that House.

426A(6) [Notification of Speaker of various undertakings] If the Secretary of State accepts a bankruptcy restrictions undertaking or a debt relief restrictions undertaking made by a member of the House of Commons or the House of Lords, the Secretary of State shall notify the Speaker of that House.

426A(7) [Notice to Speaker re Northern Ireland BRU] If the Department of Enterprise, Trade and Investment for Northern Ireland accepts a bankruptcy restrictions undertaking made by a member of the House of Commons or the House of Lords under Schedule 2A to the Insolvency (Northern Ireland) Order 1989, the Department shall notify the Speaker of that House.

426A(8) [References re Northern Ireland BRO or interim order] In this section a reference to a bankruptcy restrictions order or an interim order includes a reference to a bankruptcy restrictions order or an interim order made under Schedule 2A to the Insolvency (Northern Ireland) Order 1989.

General Note

Sections 426A–C were introduced by s.266 of EA 2002 as part of a policy of removing automatic restrictions from the shoulders of bankrupts. This policy has lead to the removal of the automatic bar on being a JP (see EA 2002 s.265), a local government member (EA 2002 s.267) and to the introduction of a general power to relax such disqualifications (EA 2002 s.268). Section 426A addresses specifically the position of MPs and members of the House of Lords. Mere bankruptcy does not disqualify a person from holding office as an MP. It appears that a similar principle applies to MEPs. These sections took effect in April 2004. See Insolvency Act 1986 (Disqualification from Parliament) Order 2012 (SI 2012/1544) for further changes in this area. This Order renders s.426A applicable to BRROs and BRRUs made in Northern Ireland and inserts new subs.(7) and (8) with effect from 14 June 2012.

Note amendment to subss.(1), (5) and (6) by para.12 of Pt 1 of Sch.20 to the Tribunals, Courts and Enforcement Act 2007.

For an excellent historical overview see Tribe [2014] 25 K.C.L.J. 79.

S.426A(1)
Those individuals who are the subject of a BRO or BRU are disqualified from Parliament.

S.426A(2)–(4)
These provisions amplify the consequences of disqualification.

S.426A(5), (6)
This imposes an additional obligation on a court making a BRO or interim order or on the Secretary of State accepting a BRU. It is unlikely to be onerous in view of the rarity of the situation.

426B Devolution

426B(1) [Various orders in Scotland, Northern Ireland, Wales] If a court in England and Wales makes a bankruptcy restrictions order or interim order in respect of a member of the Scottish Parliament, the Northern Ireland Assembly or the National Assembly for Wales, or makes a debt relief restrictions order or interim debt relief restrictions order in respect of such a member, the court shall notify the presiding officer of that body.

426B(1A) [Notice of BRO or interim order by Northern Ireland High Court] If the High Court in Northern Ireland makes a bankruptcy restrictions order or interim order under Schedule 2A to the Insolvency (Northern Ireland) Order 1989 in respect of a member of the Scottish Parliament or the National Assembly for Wales, the Court shall notify the presiding officer of that body.

426B(2) [Various undertakings in Scotland, Northern Ireland, Wales] If the Secretary of State accepts a bankruptcy restrictions undertaking or a debt relief restrictions undertaking made by a member of the Scottish Parliament, the Northern Ireland Assembly or the National Assembly for Wales, the Secretary of State shall notify the presiding officer of that body.

426B(3) [Notice of Northern Ireland BRUs] If the Department of Enterprise, Trade and Investment for Northern Ireland accepts a bankruptcy restrictions undertaking made by a member of the Scottish Parliament or the National Assembly for Wales under Schedule 2A to the Insolvency (Northern Ireland) Order 1989, the Department shall notify the presiding officer of that body.

S.426B(1), (1A), (2), (3)
These make special provision for disqualification attendant upon a BRO or BRU or interim order granted in respect of a member of a dissolved assembly. See Insolvency Act (Disqualification from Parliament) Order 2012 (SI 2012/1544) which introduces new subs.(1A) and (3) to address further the position in Northern Ireland.

Note amendment to subss.(1) and (2) by para.13 of Pt 1 of Sch.20 to the Tribunals, Courts and Enforcement Act 2007.

426C Irrelevance of privilege

426C(1) [No effect of Parliamentary privilege on insolvency enactment] An enactment about insolvency applies in relation to a member of the House of Commons or the House of Lords irrespective of any Parliamentary privilege.

426C(2) ["Enactment"] In this section "enactment" includes a provision made by or under–

(a) an Act of the Scottish Parliament, or

(b) Northern Ireland legislation.

S.426C(1), (2)
Parliamentary privilege does not protect Members of Parliament, etc. from the consequences of insolvency prescribed by legislation.

427 Disqualification from Parliament (Scotland)

427(1) [Disqualification of bankrupt] Where a court in Scotland awards sequestration of an individual's estate, the individual is disqualified–

(a) for sitting or voting in the House of Lords,

(b) for being elected to, or sitting or voting in, the House of Commons, and

(c) for sitting or voting in a committee of either House.

427(2) [When disqualification ceases] Where an individual is disqualified under this section, the disqualification ceases–

(a) except where the award is recalled or reduced without the individual having been first discharged, on the discharge of the individual, and

(b) in the excepted case, on the recall or reduction, as the case may be.

427(3) [Disqualified peer] No writ of summons shall be issued to any lord of Parliament who is for the time being disqualified under this section for sitting and voting in the House of Lords.

427(4) [Disqualified MP] Where a member of the House of Commons who is disqualified under this section continues to be so disqualified until the end of the period of 6 months beginning with the day of the award, his seat shall be vacated at the end of that period.

427(5) [Certification of s.427(1) award etc.] A court which makes an award such as is mentioned in subsection (1) in relation to any lord of Parliament or member of the House of Commons shall forthwith certify the award to the Speaker of the House of Lords or, as the case may be, to the Speaker of the House of Commons.

427(6) [Further certification after s.427(5)] Where a court has certified an award to the Speaker of the House of Commons under subsection (5), then immediately after it becomes apparent which of the following certificates is applicable, the court shall certify to the Speaker of the House of Commons–

(a) that the period of 6 months beginning with the day of the award has expired without the award having been recalled or reduced, or

(b) that the award has been recalled or reduced before the end of that period.

427(6A) [Members of the Scottish Parliament] Subsections (4) to (6) have effect in relation to a member of the Scottish Parliament but as if–

(a) references to the House of Commons were to the Parliament and references to the Speaker were to the Presiding Officer, and

(b) in subsection (4), for "under this section" there were substituted "under section 15(1)(b) of the Scotland Act 1998 by virtue of this section".

427(6B) [Members of the National Assembly for Wales] Subsections (4) to (6) have effect in relation to a member of the National Assembly for Wales but as if–

(a) references to the House of Commons were to the Assembly and references to the Speaker were to the presiding officer, and

(b) in subsection (4), for "under this section" there were substituted "under section 16(2) of the Government of Wales Act 2006 by virtue of this section".

427(6C) [Members of the Northern Ireland Assembly] Subsections (4) to (6) have effect in relation to a member of the Northern Ireland Assembly but as if–

(a) references to the House of Commons were to the Assembly and references to the Speaker were to the Presiding Officer; and

(b) in subsection (4), for "under this section" there were substituted "under section 36(4) of the Northern Ireland Act 1998 by virtue of this section".

427(7) [Repealed by EA 2002 s.266(2) with effect from 1 April 2004.]

General Note

See Insolvency Act (Disqualification from Parliament) Order 2012 (SI 2012/1544), which amends the section heading and a number of the subsections in this provision with effect from 14 June 2012 to modify the way in which the legislation addresses the position in Northern Ireland.

S.427(1), (2)
Where a person has been adjudged bankrupt in Scotland or Northern Ireland he is disqualified from both Houses of Parliament until he is discharged or the order is annulled. Similar provision is made for Scotland and Northern Ireland. Local government councillors face a similar bar: Local Government Act 1972 s.80. The former reference to England and Wales was dropped by EA 2002 s.266(2).

S.427(3)
A writ of summons must not be issued in respect of any person so disqualified who is a member of the House of Lords.

S.427(4)
A Member of Parliament who is so disqualified has six months to vacate his seat.

S.427(5), (6)
Where a court makes a bankruptcy order, etc. the Speaker of the appropriate House of Parliament must be notified. Further, the court must notify the Speaker of the Commons of the elapse of the six-month period mentioned in s.427(4) or of any annulment in the meantime.

S.427(6A), (6B), (6C)
These subsections were inserted respectively by the Scotland Act 1998 s.125(1) and Sch.8 para.23 as from 19 November 1998, the Government of Wales Act 2006 s.160 as of 3 May 2007 and the Northern Ireland Act, in order to take account of the devolution of legislative powers to the regional assemblies.

S.427(7)
Repealed by EA 2002 s.266(2).

428 Exemptions from Restrictive Trade Practices Act

428(1), (2) [Repealed]

428(3) ["Insolvency services"] In this section "insolvency services" means the services of persons acting as insolvency practitioners or carrying out under the law of Northern Ireland functions corresponding to those mentioned in section 388(1) or (2) in Part XIII, in their capacity as such.

General Note

Formerly s.428 sought to exclude agreements relating to fees charged for insolvency services, etc. being made subject to the Restrictive Trade Practices Act 1976, especially Pt III of that Act. Schedule 14 also adds insolvency services to the list of exempt services described in Sch.1 to the Restrictive Trade Practices Act 1976, such as legal services, medical services, accountancy services and many other professional services. This is in accord with the general policy of the Act, and in particular Pt XIII, which requires insolvency practitioners to be professionals. The Restrictive Trade Practices Act was repealed by the Competition Act 1998 which introduced a new competition regime on the intended date of 1 March 2000. Subsection (1) was removed by the Competition Act 1998 (Transitional, Consequential and Supplementary Provisions) Order 2000 (SI 2000/311), which sought to implement the policy in the Competition Act 1998 Sch.4 para.19. The effect of this is that the insolvency practitioner profession is excluded from many of the restrictions imposed by competition law.

429 Disabilities on revocation of administration order against an individual

429(1) [Application] The following applies where a person fails to make any payment which he is required to make by virtue of an administration order under Part VI of the County Courts Act 1984.

429(2) [Power of court] The court which is administering that person's estate under the order may, if it thinks fit–

(a) revoke the administration order, and

(b) make an order directing that this section and section 12 of the Company Directors Disqualification Act 1986 shall apply to the person for such period, not exceeding one year, as may be specified in the order.

429(3) [Restrictions] A person to whom this section so applies shall not–

(a) either alone or jointly with another person, obtain credit to the extent of the amount prescribed for the purposes of section 360(1)(a) or more, or

(b) enter into any transaction in the course of or for the purposes of any business in which he is directly or indirectly engaged,

without disclosing to the person from whom he obtains the credit, or (as the case may be) with whom the transaction is entered into, the fact that this section applies to him.

429(4) [Person obtaining credit] The reference in subsection (3) to a person obtaining credit includes–

(a) a case where goods are bailed or hired to him under a hire-purchase agreement or agreed to be sold to him under a conditional sale agreement, and

(b) a case where he is paid in advance (whether in money or otherwise) for the supply of goods or services.

429(5) [Penalty] A person who contravenes this section is guilty of an offence and liable to imprisonment or a fine, or both.

S.429(1)

This section applies where a debtor has failed to comply with his obligations under an administration order granted under Pt VI of the County Courts Act 1984 (as amended by s.13 of the Courts and Legal Services Act 1990).

S.429(2)–(4)

The court has discretion to revoke the administration order and instead apply the following restrictions for a maximum period of one year—subs.(2)(b) was changed by Sch.23 to EA 2002 by the substitution of one year for two years. Prior to IA 1985 there was a similar provision in IA 1976 s.11, allowing for the revocation of administration orders and substitution of receiving orders. The new restrictions are more flexible.

The restrictions that may be imposed by the court where an administration order is revoked are then outlined. Thus, the debtor can be banned from acting as company director, liquidator or promoter, etc. (see CDDA 1986 s.12(2)). Furthermore, he can be made subject to restrictions which are similar to the s.360 curbs—e.g. restrictions on obtaining credit (widely defined by s.429(4)), or, indeed, entering into business transactions without disclosing his true status. The Cork Committee (*Report*, para.317) was in favour of such restrictions.

S.429(5)

The sanctions for the breach of this provision are the same as for contravening s.360: see s.430 and Sch.10.

Editors' note: amendments are to be made to s.429 by Sch.16 para.3 to the Tribunals, Courts and Enforcement Act 2007 from a date yet to be determined.

430 Provision introducing Schedule of punishments

430(1) [Schedule 10] Schedule 10 to this Act has effect with respect to the way in which offences under this Act are punishable on conviction.

430(2) [First, second and third columns of Schedule] In relation to an offence under a provision of this Act specified in the first column of the Schedule (the general nature of the offence being described in the second column), the third column shows whether the offence is punishable on conviction on indictment, or on summary conviction, or either in the one way or the other.

430(3) [Fourth column] The fourth column of the Schedule shows, in relation to an offence, the maximum punishment by way of fine or imprisonment under this Act which may be imposed on a person convicted of the offence in the way specified in relation to it in the third column (that is to say, on indictment or summarily) a reference to a period of years or months being to a term of imprisonment of that duration.

430(4) [Fifth column] The fifth column shows (in relation to an offence for which there is an entry in that column) that a person convicted of the offence after continued contravention is liable to a daily default fine; that is to say, he is liable on a second or subsequent conviction of the offence to the fine specified in that column for each day on which the contravention is continued (instead of the penalty specified for the offence in the fourth column of the Schedule).

430(5) ["Officer who is in default"] For the purpose of any enactment in this Act whereby an officer of a company who is in default is liable to a fine or penalty, the expression "officer who is in default" means any officer of the company who knowingly and wilfully authorises or permits the default, refusal or contravention mentioned in the enactment.

S.430(1)

This directs the reader to Sch.10 for a comprehensive list of punishments for offences created by the Act. For offences under the rules and their punishment see IR 2016 Introductory Rule 6 and Sch.3.

Note Banking Act 2009 ss.103 and 145.

S.430(2)–(4)

These subsections provide a guide to the use of Sch.10.

S.430(5)

This defines the common phrase "officer who is in default". See CA 2006 s.1121(3).

431 Summary proceedings

431(1) [Taking of summary proceedings] Summary proceedings for any offence under any of Parts I to VII of this Act may (without prejudice to any jurisdiction exercisable apart from this subsection) be taken against a body corporate at any place at which the body has a place of business, and against any other person at any place at which he is for the time being.

431(2) [Time for laying information] Notwithstanding anything in section 127(1) of the Magistrates' Courts Act 1980, an information relating to such an offence which is triable by a magistrates' court in England and Wales may be so tried if it is laid at any time within 3 years after the commission of the offence and within 12 months after the date on which evidence sufficient in the opinion of the Director of Public Prosecutions or the Secretary of State (as the case may be) to justify the proceedings comes to his knowledge.

431(3) [Time for commencement of summary proceedings in Scotland] Summary proceedings in Scotland for such an offence shall not be commenced after the expiration of 3 years from the commission of the offence. Subject to this (and notwithstanding anything in section 136 of the Criminal Procedure (Scotland) Act 1995), such proceedings may (in Scotland) be commenced at any time within 12 months after the date on which evidence sufficient in the Lord Advocate's opinion to justify the proceedings came to his knowledge or, where such evidence was reported to him by the Secretary of State, within 12 months after the date on which it came to the knowledge of the latter; and subsection (3) of that section applies for the purpose of this subsection as it applies for the purpose of that section.

431(4) [Certificate by DPP et al. conclusive evidence] For purposes of this section, a certificate of the Director of Public Prosecutions, the Lord Advocate or the Secretary of State (as the case may be) as to the date on which such evidence as is referred to above came to his knowledge is conclusive evidence.

S.431(1), (2), (4)

These subsections regulate summary proceedings under this Act in England and Wales.

Note Banking Act 2009 ss.103 and 145.

S.431(3), (4)

Summary proceedings in Scotland are provided for.

432 Offences by bodies corporate

432(1) [Application] This section applies to offences under this Act other than those excepted by subsection (4).

432(2) [Consent or connivance of various persons] Where a body corporate is guilty of an offence to which this section applies and the offence is proved to have been committed with the consent or connivance of, or to be attributable to any neglect on the part of, any director, manager, secretary or other similar officer of the body corporate or any person who was purporting to act in any such capacity he, as well as the body corporate, is guilty of the offence and liable to be proceeded against and punished accordingly.

432(3) [Where affairs managed by members] Where the affairs of a body corporate are managed by its members, subsection (2) applies in relation to the acts and defaults of a member in connection with his functions of management as if he were a director of the body corporate.

432(4) [Offences excepted] The offences excepted from this section are those under sections 30, 39, 51, 53, 54, 62, 64, 66, 85, 89, 164, 188, 201, 206, 207, 208, 209, 210 and 211 and those under paragraphs 16(2), 17(3)(a), 18(3)(a), 19(3)(a), 22(1) and 23(1)(a) of Schedule A1.

S.432(1)–(3)

Here there is a repetition of CA 1985 s.733. Where an offence under this Act has been committed by a body corporate, any officer who was a party to or responsible for the offence is subject to criminal liability, as well as the body corporate. De facto officers are similarly liable. "Body corporate" is not defined for the purposes of this Part of IA 1986; the definition contained in CA 2006 s.1173(1) applies only to Pts I–VII (see s.251). It is therefore likely that a Scottish firm and a foreign corporation would be within the scope of this provision, even though they are not within s.740.

Note Banking Act 2009 ss.103 and 145.

S.432(3)

Some corporations, and in particular some incorporated by Royal Charter, have no body equivalent to a board of directors and are managed by their members. This is also true of a Scottish firm, if it is within the present provision. In such cases the members may incur personal liability under this section.

S.432(4)

Offences under certain named sections of the Act are excluded from the operation of s.432. Note the addition made by IA 2000 Sch.1.

433 Admissibility in evidence of statements of affairs, etc.

433(1) [General rule on admissibility of statements] In any proceedings (whether or not under this Act)–

(a) a statement of affairs prepared for the purposes of any provision of this Act which is derived from the Insolvency Act 1985,

(aa) a statement made in pursuance of a requirement imposed by or under Part 2 of the Banking Act 2009 (bank insolvency),

(ab) a statement made in pursuance of a requirement imposed by or under Part 3 of that Act (bank administration), and

(b) any other statement made in pursuance of a requirement imposed by or under any such provision or by or under rules made under this Act,

may be used in evidence against any person making or concurring in making the statement.

433(2) [Limits on use of statement in criminal proceedings] However, in criminal proceedings in which any such person is charged with an offence to which this subsection applies–

(a) no evidence relating to the statement may be adduced, and

(b) no question relating to it may be asked,

by or on behalf of the prosecution, unless evidence relating to it is adduced, or a question relating to it is asked, in the proceedings by or on behalf of that person.

433(3) [Offences to which s.433(2) applies] Subsection (2) applies to any offence other than–

(a) an offence under section 22(6), 47(6), 48(8), 66(6), 67(8), 95(8), 99(3), 131(7), 192(2), 208(1)(a) or (d) or (2), 210, 235(5), 353(1), 354(1)(b) or (3) or 356(1) or (2)(a) or (b) or paragraph 4(3)(a) of Schedule 7;

(b) an offence which is–

(i) created by rules made under this Act, and

(ii) designated for the purposes of this subsection by such rules or by regulations made by the Secretary of State;

(c) an offence which is–

(i) created by regulations made under any such rules, and

(ii) designated for the purposes of this subsection by such regulations;

(d) an offence under section 1, 2 or 5 of the Perjury Act 1911 (false statements made on oath or made otherwise than on oath); or

(e) an offence under section 44(1) or (2) of the Criminal Law (Consolidation) (Scotland) Act 1995 (false statements made on oath or otherwise than on oath).

433(4) [Procedure for making regulations] Regulations under subsection (3)(b)(ii) shall be made by statutory instrument and, after being made, shall be laid before each House of Parliament.

General Note

Section 433 was expanded considerably by the addition of three new subss.(2)–(4) via the Youth Justice and Criminal Evidence Act 1999 (ss.59, 68(3) and Sch.3 para.7(2) and (3)) with effect from 14 April 2000. Note Banking Act 2009 ss.103 and 145.

S.433(1)

Amended by ss.128 and 162 of the Banking Act 2009. It declares that any statement of affairs or other statement made in pursuance of a requirement under the insolvency legislation may be used in evidence against the person making it. See *R. v Kansal* [1993] Q.B. 244; [1992] B.C.C. 615; and *Hamilton v Naviede (Re Arrows Ltd (No.4))* [1995] 2 A.C. 75; [1994] B.C.C. 641. On the meaning of what is now s.433(1)(b) see *R. v Sawtell* [2001] B.P.I.R. 381. This wide evidential provision became suspect in view of the ruling of the European Court of Human Rights in *Saunders v UK* (1997) 23 E.H.R.R. 313 on the oppressive usage of compelled evidence in criminal prosecutions. Hence the need for modification by the introduction of subss.(2)–(4) in the Youth Justice and Criminal Evidence Act 1999. Note also *R. v Faryab* [1999] B.P.I.R. 569. On reopening "safe" convictions see *R. v Kansal* [2001] UKHL 62; [2002] B.P.I.R. 370—eventually this particular case proceeded to the European Court of Human Rights where it was held in *Kansal v UK* [2004] B.P.I.R. 740 that the use in a prosecution of transcripts obtained from an interrogation where the suspect was denied the right of silence did infringe the right to a fair trial under art.6 ECHR.

In *Rottmann v Official Receiver* [2009] B.P.I.R. 617 the bankrupt applied under the then IR 1986 r.6.175(6) (see now IR 2016 rr.10.99 et seq.) for the public examination to be suspended lest it prejudice his position with respect to criminal proceedings against him in Germany. The court noted that s.433 only protected the bankrupt's right to silence with respect to proceedings under English law. However, it was observed that the guarantees under ECHR might operate in a protective fashion in the German proceedings. In the circumstances, the court felt that justice would be best served by suspending the public examination and substituting a private examination.

There was discussion of the current provision by HHJ Roger Kaye QC in *Re France, Nutting v France* [2014] EWHC 2123 (Ch); [2014] B.P.I.R. 1448.

There was consideration by the Divisional Court of this provision and in particular the admissibility of matters derived from a public examination of a bankrupt in *Simmonds v Pearce* [2017] EWHC 3126 (Admin).

S.433(2)–(4)

Significant limitations are placed by the new provisions introduced via the 1999 Act upon the use by the prosecution of evidence made available pursuant to subs.(1) in a whole range of prosecutions unless the offence falls within the list prescribed by subs.(3). This list may, according to subs.(4), be modified by delegated legislation. See *Attorney General's Reference (No.7 of 2000)* [2001] EWCA Civ 888; [2001] 1 W.L.R. 1879.

434 Crown application

434 For the avoidance of doubt it is hereby declared that provisions of this Act which derive from the Insolvency Act 1985 bind the Crown so far as affecting or relating to the following matters, namely–

(a) remedies against, or against the property of, companies or individuals;

(b) priorities of debts;

(c) transactions at an undervalue or preferences;

(d) voluntary arrangements approved under Part I or Part VIII, and

(e) discharge from bankruptcy.

General Note

This section makes it clear that specified provisions of the Act, whether they relate to companies or individuals, bind the Crown. Indeed, certain sections are specifically designed to take away Crown privileges—e.g. s.386 and Sch.6.

Part 17A

Supplementary Provisions

434A Introductory

434A The provisions of this Part have effect for the purposes of–

(a) the First Group of Parts, and

(b) sections 411, 413, 414, 416 and 417 in Part 15.

434B Representation of corporations in decision procedures and at meetings

434B(1) [Authorisation of representative] If a corporation is a creditor or debenture-holder, it may by resolution of its directors or other governing body authorise a person or persons to act as its representative or representatives–

(a) in a qualifying decision procedure, held in pursuance of this Act or of rules made under it, by which a decision is sought from the creditors of a company, or

(b) at any meeting of a company held in pursuance of the provisions contained in a debenture or trust deed.

434B(2) [Power exercised by one person] Where the corporation authorises only one person, that person is entitled to exercise the same powers on behalf of the corporation as the corporation could exercise if it were an individual creditor or debenture-holder.

434B(3) [Power exercised by more than one person] Where the corporation authorises more than one person, any one of them is entitled to exercise the same powers on behalf of the corporation as the corporation could exercise if it were an individual creditor or debenture-holder.

434B(4) [Section 434B(3) power exercised differently] Where the corporation authorises more than one person and more than one of them purport to exercise a power under subsection (3)–

(a) if they purport to exercise the power in the same way, the power is treated as exercised in that way;

(b) if they do not purport to exercise the power in the same way, the power is treated as not exercised.

434C Legal professional privilege

434C In proceedings against a person for an offence under this Act nothing in this Act is to be taken to require any person to disclose any information that he is entitled to refuse to disclose on grounds of legal professional privilege (in Scotland, confidentiality of communications).

434D Enforcement of company's filing obligations

434D(1) [Application of s.434D] This section applies where a company has made default in complying with any obligation under this Act–

(a) to deliver a document to the registrar, or

(b) to give notice to the registrar of any matter.

434D(2) [Power to notify company to comply with requirement] The registrar, or any member or creditor of the company, may give notice to the company requiring it to comply with the obligation.

434D(3) [Power to apply to court for failure to comply] If the company fails to make good the default within 14 days after service of the notice, the registrar, or any member or creditor of the company, may apply to the court for an order directing the company, and any specified officer of it, to make good the default within a specified time.

434D(4) [Court order re costs (Scotland: expenses)] The court's order may provide that all costs (in Scotland, expenses) of or incidental to the application are to be borne by the company or by any officers of it responsible for the default.

434D(5) [Section not to affect statutory penalties] This section does not affect the operation of any enactment imposing penalties on a company or its officers in respect of any such default.

434E Application of filing obligations to overseas companies

434E The provisions of this Act requiring documents to be forwarded or delivered to, or filed with, the registrar of companies apply in relation to an overseas company that is required to register particulars under section 1046 of the Companies Act 2006 as they apply in relation to a company registered under that Act in England and Wales or Scotland.

General Note to Part 17A

This additional Part was inserted by the Companies Act (Consequential Amendments etc.) Order 2008 (SI 2008/948). Section 434B deals with the representation of companies and other corporations in decision taking procedures or at meetings of creditors, etc. This provision reflects general provisions operating in corporate law. Section 434C protects legal professional privilege in proceedings for an alleged offence under this Act.

S.434D

This new transparency enforcement provision was inserted by the Companies Act 2006 (Consequential Amendments, Transitional Provisions and Savings) Order 2009 (SI 2009/1941) (operational from 1 October 2009). Its intention is to enable creditors, etc. to gain access to information, which should have been filed. Note that directors may be required personally to meet the costs of an application to secure such information.

S.434E

This new provision, which is specifically applicable to overseas companies, was inserted by the Companies Act 2006 (Consequential Amendments, Transitional Provisions and Savings) Order 2009 (SI 2009/1941) with effect from 1 October 2009.

PART XVIII

INTERPRETATION

435 Meaning of "associate"

435(1) [Determination of whether associate] For the purposes of this Act any question whether a person is an associate of another person is to be determined in accordance with the following provisions of this section (any provision that a person is an associate of another person being taken to mean that they are associates of each other).

435(2) [Associate of individual] A person is an associate of an individual if that person is–

(a) the individual's husband or wife or civil partner,

(b) a relative of–

(i) the individual, or

(ii) the individual's husband or wife or civil partner, or

(c) the husband or wife or civil partner of a relative of–

(i) the individual, or

(ii) the individual's husband or wife or civil partner.

435(3) [Associate of partner] A person is an associate of any person with whom he is in partnership, and of the husband or wife or civil partner or a relative of any individual with whom he is in partnership; and a Scottish firm is an associate of any person who is a member of the firm.

435(4) [Associate of employee, employer] A person is an associate of any person whom he employs or by whom he is employed.

435(5) [Associate of trustee] A person in his capacity as trustee of a trust other than–

(a) a trust arising under any of the second Group of Parts or the Bankruptcy (Scotland) Act 2016, or

(b) a pension scheme or an employees' share scheme,

is an associate of another person if the beneficiaries of the trust include, or the terms of the trust confer a power that may be exercised for the benefit of, that other person or an associate of that other person.

435(6) [Company associate of another company] A company is an associate of another company–

(a) if the same person has control of both, or a person has control of one and persons who are his associates, or he and persons who are his associates, have control of the other, or

(b) if a group of two or more persons has control of each company, and the groups either consist of the same persons or could be regarded as consisting of the same persons by treating (in one or more cases) a member of either group as replaced by a person of whom he is an associate.

435(7) [Company associate of another person] A company is an associate of another person if that person has control of it or if that person and persons who are his associates together have control of it.

435(8) [Person relative of individual] For the purposes of this section a person is a relative of an individual if he is that individual's brother, sister, uncle, aunt, nephew, niece, lineal ancestor or lineal descendant, treating–

(a) any relationship of the half blood as a relationship of the whole blood and the stepchild or adopted child of any person as his child, and

(b) an illegitimate child as the legitimate child of his mother and reputed father;

and references in this section to a husband or wife include a former husband or wife and a reputed husband or wife and references to a civil partner include a former civil partner and a reputed civil partner.

435(9) [Director employee] For the purposes of this section any director or other officer of a company is to be treated as employed by that company.

435(10) [Person with control] For the purposes of this section a person is to be taken as having control of a company if–

(a) the directors of the company or of another company which has control of it (or any of them) are accustomed to act in accordance with his directions or instructions, or

(b) he is entitled to exercise, or control the exercise of, one third or more of the voting power at any general meeting of the company or of another company which has control of it;

and where two or more persons together satisfy either of the above conditions, they are to be taken as having control of the company.

435(11) ["Company"] In this section "company" includes any body corporate (whether incorporated in Great Britain or elsewhere); and references to directors and other officers of a company and to voting power at any general meeting of a company have effect with any necessary modifications.

General Note

Part XVIII applies to limited liability partnerships by virtue of the Limited Liability Partnerships Regulations 2001 (SI 2001/1090) reg.5(1)(b) as from 6 April 2001 subject to reg.5(2) and (3).

Re application of Pt XVIII to insolvent partnerships, see the Insolvent Partnerships Order 1994 (SI 1994/2121), especially arts 10, 11, Sch.7.

S.435(1)

This is a new and complex provision defining the word "associate" for the purposes of the Act. It will be particularly relevant to ss.314(6) and 340(5), and to the definition of "connected person" (s.249), a term extensively used in Pts I–VII. In *Re James Dolman & Co Ltd* [2010] EWHC 3950 (Ch) the mother of a director was held by HHJ David Cooke to be an "associate" for the purposes of a s.238 claim.

S.435(2), (8)

Close family connections are sufficient to make one person an associate of another. On s.435(2) note *Taylor v Ziya* [2012] B.P.I.R. 1283.

S.435(3)

Partnership links with an individual, or his close family, are sufficient to give rise to an "associate" relationship.

S.435(4)

Employers and employees are associates. However, see ss.239(6), 240(1)(a), 340(5).

S.435(5)

Certain trust relationships are caught by the net, where the insolvent or his or its associates could benefit from the trust. Note the change to subs.(5)(b) by the Companies Act 2006 (Consequential Amendments, Transitional Provisions and Savings) Order 2009 (SI 2009/1941) (with effect from 1 October 2009). This reflects the coming into force of CA 2006. On s.435(5) see *Re Calder, Salter v Wetton* [2011] EWHC 3192 (Ch); [2012] B.P.I.R. 63. Section 435(5)(a) was amended by the Bankruptcy (Scotland) Act 2016 (Consequential Provisions and Modifications) Order 2016 (SI 2016/1034) art.7(1), Sch.1 para.4(1), (10) as from 30 November 2016.

S.435(6), (7), (9)–(11)

These deal with the concept of "associate" in relation to companies (including companies incorporated outside Great Britain: see s.435(11)). A company can become an associate if it is controlled by the person in question or by his associate. Control can be determined by reference to a third of voting power at shareholders' meetings or by whether the directors normally act in accordance with his instructions. In *Unidare plc v Cohen* [2005] EWHC 1410 (Ch); [2005] 3 All E.R. 730, it was held that where shares are held on a bare trust it is the beneficiary and not the registered shareholder who has voting "power" for the purposes of s.435(10). Directors and officers are to be treated as being employed by their companies—this will be relevant in connection with s.435(4). In *Smurthwaite v Simpson-Smith and Mond (No.2)* [2006] B.P.I.R. 1483 there was consideration at first instance of what was meant by the term "reputed wife" for the purposes of s.435(8). But these comments need to be viewed in the light of the appeal in this case reported sub nom. *Smurthwaite v Simpson-Smith and Mond (No.2)* [2006] B.P.I.R. 1504 (where s.435(8) does not appear to have been at issue).

436 Expressions used generally

436(1) [Definitions] In this Act, except in so far as the context otherwise requires (and subject to Parts VII and XI)–

"the appointed day" means the day on which this Act comes into force under section 443;

"associate" has the meaning given by section 435;

"body corporate" includes a body incorporated outside Great Britain, but does not include–

(a) a corporation sole, or

(b) a partnership that, whether or not a legal person, is not regarded as a body corporate under the law by which it is governed;

"business" includes a trade or profession;

"the Companies Acts" means the Companies Acts (as defined in section 2 of the Companies Act 2006) as they have effect in Great Britain;

"conditional sale agreement" and "hire-purchase agreement" have the same meanings as in the Consumer Credit Act 1974;

"distress" includes use of the procedure in Schedule 12 to the Tribunals, Courts and Enforcement Act 2007, and references to levying distress, seizing goods and related expressions shall be construed accordingly;

"EEA State" means a state that is a Contracting Party to the Agreement on the European Economic Area signed at Oporto on 2nd May 1992 as adjusted by the Protocol signed at Brussels on 17th March 1993;

"employees' share scheme" means a scheme for encouraging or facilitating the holding of shares in or debentures of a company by or for the benefit of–

(a) the bona fide employees or former employees of–

  (i) the company,

  (ii) any subsidiary of the company, or

  (iii) the company's holding company or any subsidiary of the company's holding company, or

(b) the spouses, civil partners, surviving spouses, surviving civil partners, or minor children or step-children of such employees or former employees.

"the EU Regulation" means Regulation (EU) 2015/848 of the European Parliament and of the Council of 20 May 2015 on insolvency proceedings;

"modifications" includes additions, alterations and omissions and cognate expressions shall be construed accordingly;

"property" includes money, goods, things in action, land and every description of property wherever situated and also obligations and every description of interest, whether present or future or vested or contingent, arising out of, or incidental to, property;

"records" includes computer records and other non-documentary records;

"subordinate legislation" has the same meaning as in the Interpretation Act 1978; and

"transaction" includes a gift, agreement or arrangement, and references to entering into a transaction shall be construed accordingly.

436(2) [Definitions in Companies Acts] The following expressions have the same meaning in this Act as in the Companies Acts–

"articles", in relation to a company (see section 18 of the Companies Act 2006);

"debenture" (see section 738 of that Act);

"holding company" (see sections 1159 and 1160 of, and Schedule 6 to, that Act);

"the Joint Stock Companies Acts" (see section 1171 of that Act);

"overseas company"(see section 1044 of that Act);

"paid up" (see section 583 of that Act);

"private company" and "public company" (see section 4 of that Act);

"registrar of companies" (see section 1060 of that Act);

"share" (see section 540 of that Act);

"subsidiary" (see sections 1159 and 1160 of, and Schedule 6 to, that Act).

General Note

This is general interpretation provision for the Act. It should be read in the light of Pts VII, XI and s.435. Note that the general meaning given to words by s.436 can be excluded where the context demands this.

The "appointed day" was 29 December 1986: see the note to s.443.

The EEA State definition was inserted by the Insolvency Act 1986 (Amendment) Regulations 2005 (SI 2005/879). Note amendment by the Companies Act 2006 (Consequential Amendments, Transitional Provisions and Savings) Order 2009 (SI 2009/1941) (effective from 1 October 2009). This makes a number of changes, some of which result from the enactment of the Companies Act 2006.

Revised definition of "the Companies Acts" by the Companies Act 2006 (Commencement No.3, Consequential Amendments, Transitional Provisions and Savings) Order 2007 (SI 2007/2194 (C. 84)) art.10 and Sch.4 para.45 as from 1 October 2007, recognises the Companies Act 2006.

A definition of "distress" was added by Sch.13 para.85 of the Tribunals, Courts and Enforcement Act 2007 as activated by the Tribunals, Courts and Enforcement Act 2007 (Commencement No.11) Order 2014 (SI 2014/768 (C. 27)) and the Tribunals, Courts and Enforcement Act 2007 (Consequential, Transitional and Saving Provisions) Order 2014 (SI 2014/600). This change took effect on 6 April 2014.

The definition of "EU Regulation" was inserted (replacing former definition to "EC Regulation") by the Insolvency Amendment (EU 2015/848) Regulations 2017 (SI 2017/702) regs 1, 2(1), Sch. paras 1, 28 in relation to proceedings opened on or after 26 June 2017 (see reg.3) when the Recast EU Regulation 2015/848 came into force.

A company's interest as lessee under a lease of a chattel (an aircraft) was held to be "property" within the statutory definition contained in this section in *Bristol Airport plc v Powdrill; Re Paramount Airways Ltd* [1990] Ch. 744; [1990] B.C.C. 130. An expectation to receive a payment from the Criminal Injuries Compensation Board is not property: *Re a Bankrupt (No.145 of 1995)* [1996] B.P.I.R. 238. Compare *Re Rae* [1995] B.C.C. 102; and *Performing Rights Society v Rowland* [1998] B.P.I.R. 128. In *Official Receiver v Environment Agency* [1999] B.P.I.R. 986 the Court of Appeal held that a waste management licence was property for the purposes of s.436. In *Dear v Reeves* [2001] EWCA Civ 277; [2001] B.P.I.R. 577 a right of pre-emption was held to constitute "property" as were occupational benefits in *Patel v Jones* [2001] B.P.I.R. 919. In *Re Hemming (decd)* [2009] B.P.I.R. 50 the court (Richard Snowden QC) held that the right of a residuary legatee (who had become bankrupt) to have the estate of the deceased properly administered was "property" for the purposes of s.436. This again is consistent with a broad interpretation of this pivotal concept in bankruptcy law.

In *Webster v Ashcroft* [2011] EWHC 3848 (Ch); [2012] 1 W.L.R. 1309 rights arising under a proprietary estoppel were held to be property within the meaning of s.436. In *Walden v Atkins* [2013] EWHC 1387 (Ch); [2013] B.P.I.R. 943 the court confirmed that rights arising under an estoppel could be viewed as falling within the definition of property for the purposes of insolvency legislation.

See also *Ward v Official Receiver* [2012] B.P.I.R. 1073 where a wide view of what might constitute property was adopted by Khan DJ in the context of sums received after the making of PPI misselling complaints.

Appeal rights in tax cases may be property rights within the meaning of s.436—*McNulty v Revenue and Customs Commissioners* [2012] S.T.C. 2110. Note the surprising conclusion reached by HHJ Pelling in *Re GP Aviation Group International Ltd* [2013] EWHC 1447 (Ch); [2013] B.P.I.R. 576 to the effect that a bare right of appeal would not normally constitute property. This conclusion was arrived at after a careful review of the underlying authorities. That said, it does go against the general flow of authorities in this area where an expansive view has been taken as to what could be regarded as "property". *Schlosberg v Avonwick Holdings Ltd* [2016] EWHC 1001 (Ch) raised the issue of whether a right to legal privilege constituted "property". Arnold J ruled that it was not to be so regarded. The appeal from the decision of Arnold J was dismissed in *Avonwick Holdings Ltd v Schlosberg* [2016] EWCA Civ 1138.

See *Thornhill v Atherton (No.2)* [2008] B.P.I.R. 691 (foreign property). For confirmation that foreign property is covered see *Sanders v Donovan* [2012] B.P.I.R. 219 (Chief Registrar Baister).

A piece of property that is subject to a recovery claim under s.423 is not to be regarded as "property" for the purposes of s.436—*Leeds v Lemos* [2017] EWHC 1825 (Ch); [2017] B.P.I.R. 1223.

436A Proceedings under EU Regulation: modified definition of property

436A In the application of this Act to proceedings by virtue of Article 3 of the EU Regulation, a reference to property is a reference to property which may be dealt with in the proceedings.

General Note

Section 436A was inserted by Insolvency Act 1986 (Amendment) (No.2) Regulations 2002 (SI 2002/1240) reg.18 with effect from 31 May 2002 and amended by the Insolvency Amendment (EU 2015/848) Regulations 2017 (SI 2017/702) regs 1, 2(1), Sch. paras 1, 29 in relation to proceedings opened on or after 26 June 2017 (see reg.3) when the Recast EU Regulation 2015/848 came into force. This limitation is needed to comply with the EU Regulation on Insolvency Proceedings, where the jurisdiction is sometimes restricted to local assets.

436B References to things in writing

436B(1) [References include things in electronic form] A reference in this Act to a thing in writing includes that thing in electronic form.

436B(2) [Non-application of s.436B(1)] Subsection (1) does not apply to the following provisions–

(a) section 53 (mode of appointment by holder of charge),

(b) section 67(2) (report by receiver),

(c) section 70(4) (reference to instrument creating a charge),

(d) section 111(2) (dissent from arrangement under s. 110),

(e) in the case of a winding up of a company registered in Scotland, section 111(4),

(f) section 123(1) (definition of inability to pay debts),

(g) section 198(3) (duties of sheriff principal as regards examination),

(h) section 222(1) (inability to pay debts: unpaid creditor for £750 or more), and

(i) section 223 (inability to pay debts: debt remaining unsatisfied after action brought).

General Note

Introduced by LRO 2010 (SI 2010/18). This provides (subject to exceptions specified in subs.(2)), that, where the Act requires something to be done in writing, it can now be done via electronic communication. Paragraph (e) in s.436B(2) would have been omitted if Sch.2 of the recent Scotland Bill had been enacted.

Part XIX

Final Provisions

437 Transitional provisions, and savings

437 The transitional provisions and savings set out in Schedule 11 to this Act shall have effect, the Schedule comprising the following Parts–

Part I: company insolvency and winding up (matters arising before appointed day, and continuance of proceedings in certain cases as before that day);

Part II: individual insolvency (matters so arising, and continuance of bankruptcy proceedings in certain cases as before that day);

Part III: transactions entered into before the appointed day and capable of being affected by orders of the court under Part XVI of this Act;

Part IV: insolvency practitioners acting as such before the appointed day; and

Part V: general transitional provisions and savings required consequentially on, and in connection with, the repeal and replacement by this Act and the Company Directors Disqualification Act 1986 of provisions of the Companies Act 1985, the greater part of the Insolvency Act 1985 and other enactments.

General Note

This, coupled with Sch.11, makes transitional provisions and savings.

The significant transitional provisions have been noted at the relevant places in the text. Note the amendment by the Companies Act 2006 (Consequential Amendments, Transitional Provisions and Savings) Order 2009 (SI 2009/1941) with effect from 1 October 2009). This merely recognises the fact that there are now multiple Companies Acts.

438 Repeals

438 The enactments specified in the second column of Schedule 12 to this Act are repealed to the extent specified in the third column of that Schedule.

General Note

This section refers the reader to Sch.12, which lists the provisions repealed by IA 1986. Included amongst the repeals are a large number of provisions in CA 1985, plus virtually the entirety of IA 1985. See also Sch.4 to CDDA 1986.

439 Amendment of enactments

439(1) [Amendment of Companies Act] The Companies Act is amended as shown in Parts I and II of Schedule 13 to this Act, being amendments consequential on this Act and the Company Directors Disqualification Act 1986.

439(2) [Enactments in Sch.14] The enactments specified in the first column of Schedule 14 to this Act (being enactments which refer, or otherwise relate, to those which are repealed and replaced by this Act or the Company Directors Disqualification Act 1986) are amended as shown in the second column of that Schedule.

439(3) [Consequential modifications of subordinate legislation] The Lord Chancellor may by order make such consequential modifications of any provision contained in any subordinate legislation made before the appointed day and such transitional provisions in connection with those modifications as appear to him necessary or expedient in respect of–

(a) any reference in that subordinate legislation to the Bankruptcy Act 1914;

(b) any reference in that subordinate legislation to any enactment repealed by Part III or IV of Schedule 10 to the Insolvency Act 1985; or

(c) any reference in that subordinate legislation to any matter provided for under the Act of 1914 or under any enactment so repealed.

439(4) [Order by statutory instrument etc.] An order under this section shall be made by statutory instrument subject to annulment in pursuance of a resolution of either House of Parliament.

S.439(1), (2)

These subsections refer to Schs 13 and 14 which respectively make consequential amendments to CA 1985 and other legislation. Most of the consequential amendments of CA 1985 are purely minor textual changes. A new s.196 of CA

1985 is enacted to apply the new preferential claims regime to the situation where the holder of a floating charge, instead of putting in a receiver, takes possession of the charged property. The consequential amendments effected by Sch.14 are also of a minor nature.

440 Extent (Scotland)

440(1) [Extension to Scotland except where stated] Subject to the next subsection, provisions of this Act contained in the first Group of Parts extend to Scotland except where otherwise stated.

440(2) [Provisions not extending to Scotland] The following provisions of this Act do not extend to Scotland–

(a) in the first Group of Parts–

section 43;

sections 238 to 241; and

section 246;

(b) the second Group of Parts;

(c) in the third Group of Parts–

sections 399 to 402,

sections 412, 413, 415, 415A(3), 418, 420 and 421,

sections 423 to 425, and

section 429(1) and (2); and

(d) in the Schedules–

Parts II and III of Schedule 11; and

Schedules 12 and 14 so far as they repeal or amend enactments which extend to England and Wales only.

General Note

This section identifies those provisions in IA 1986 which apply to Scotland. Most of the provisions on corporate insolvency apply equally to Scotland, except for certain receivership provisions (Scotland has its own receivership system in ss.50–71), the rules on preferences and transactions at an undervalue (again the Scots have their own rules in ss.242, 243 and also s.246). The rules on personal insolvency do not apply to Scotland, which has its own system contained in the Bankruptcy (Scotland) Act 1985. Note also the Debt Arrangement and Attachment (Scotland) Act 2002. Bearing in mind this point, it is not surprising that certain named miscellaneous provisions in the Third Group of Parts and the Schedules do not operate north of the border. The reference to s.415A(3) in subs.(2)(c) was added by EA 2002 s.270(4).

The mooted return of the jurisdiction to regulate the winding up of companies in Scotland will not change the position on the devolved right to legislate on personal insolvency in Scotland. In addition to specific insolvency measures in Scotland readers should note related legislation such as the Home Owner and Debtor Protection (Scotland) Act 2010 (asp 6) which constrains the rights of secured creditors wishing to take action against the debtor's family home by introducing safeguards for debtors.

441 Extent (Northern Ireland)

441(1) [Provisions extending to Northern Ireland] The following provisions of this Act extend to Northern Ireland–

(a) sections 197, 426, 426A, 426B, 427 and 428; and

(b) so much of section 439 and Schedule 14 as relates to enactments which extend to Northern Ireland.

441(2) [Most of provisions not extending to Northern Ireland] Subject as above, and to any provision expressly relating to companies incorporated elsewhere than in Great Britain, nothing in this Act extends to Northern Ireland or applies to or in relation to companies registered or incorporated in Northern Ireland.

General Note

The Act, generally speaking, does not apply to Northern Ireland, which has its own distinct systems of corporate and personal insolvency law. Certain exceptional provisions do apply in Northern Ireland, however—e.g. s.426, which provides for co-operation between the various UK insolvency courts and s.427, which deals with parliamentary disqualification. See Insolvency Act (Disqualification from Parliament) Order 2012 (SI 2012/1544), which amends s.441(1)(a) to include reference to ss.426A and 426B.

However, legislation has since been enacted which has made the insolvency law of Northern Ireland broadly similar to that of England and Wales. New rules relating to the disqualification of company directors were introduced with effect from 24 September 1986 by the Companies (Northern Ireland) Order 1986 (SI 1986/1032 (NI 6)); and these have since been re-enacted and extended by Pt II of the Companies (Northern Ireland) Order 1989 (SI 1989/2404 (NI 18)). In consequence, legislation equivalent to CDDA 1986 is now in place in Northern Ireland. The 1989 Order was brought into force with effect from 1 October 1991 by the Companies Act (1989 Order) (Commencement No.2) Order (Northern Ireland) 1991 (SR 1991/410 (C. 19)). The Insolvency (Northern Ireland) Order 1989 (SI 1989/2405 (NI 19)) is the counterpart for Northern Ireland of IA 1986. The object of the order is to bring the insolvency legislation, both personal and corporate, of that jurisdiction into line with that of England and Wales. This order was made on 19 December 1989, and was brought into operation in full on 1 October 1991 by the Insolvency (1989 Order) (Commencement No.4) Order (Northern Ireland) 1991 (SR 1991/411 (C. 20)). Previous Commencement Orders were of minimal impact. Note also SI 2002/3152 (NI 6) (SR 2003/545 and SR 2003/546). Other provisions which have been put into force as part of the new insolvency regime in Northern Ireland include the Insolvency Practitioners (Recognised Practitioners Regulations (Northern Ireland) 1991 (SR 1991/302 as amended by SR 2003/547); the Insolvency Rules (Northern Ireland) 1991 (SR 1991/364 as amended by SR 2000/247, SR 2003/549 and SR 2008/118); the Insolvency (Deposits) Order (Northern Ireland) 1991 (SR 1991/384); the Insolvency (Monetary Limits) Order (Northern Ireland) 1991 (SR 1991/386); the Insolvency (Fees) Order (Northern Ireland) 1991 (SR 1991/385); the Insolvency Regulations (Northern Ireland) 1991 (SR 1991/388); the Financial Markets and Insolvency Regulations (Northern Ireland) 1991 (SR 1991/443); and the Insolvency Practitioners Order (Northern Ireland) 1995 (SR 1995/225 (as amended by SR 1996/472)). Note also Occupational and Personal Pension Schemes (Bankruptcy) Regulations (Northern Ireland) 2002 (SR 2002/127); the Insolvency Regulations (Northern Ireland) 1996 (Electronic Communications) Order (Northern Ireland) 2006 (SR 2006/461) which amends SR 1996/574.

The IA 1994, which amended the law relating to the "adoption" of contracts of employment by administrators and administrative receivers, also amends the law applicable in Northern Ireland: see s.4 of and Sch.1 to that Act. There is also an Insolvent Partnerships (Northern Ireland) Order 1991 (SR 1991/366 most recently amended by SI 2003/144 and SR 2003/550) and specific regulations dealing with proceedings and reports arising out of the disqualification of directors (see SR 1991/367, 1991/368, 1991/413 and 2003/345–347). Administration of estates of deceased insolvents in Northern Ireland is covered by SR 1991/365 as amended by SR 2003/103. Many of these provisions have since been the subject of amending legislation: see, e.g. SR 1992/398, 1993/302, 1993/454, 1994/26, 1995/291, 1996/471, 1996/574–577, 1997/1072, 2002/334.

The reforms introduced in English law by the EA 2002 were incorporated into Northern Ireland by the Insolvency (Northern Ireland) Order 2005 (SI 2005/1455 (NI 10)). For commencement see the Insolvency (2005 Order) (Commencement No.1) Order (Northern Ireland) 2006 (SI 2006/21 (C. 1)). Associated measures linked to the advent of the 2005 Order are contained in the Insolvency (2005 Order) (Transitional Provision and Savings) Order (Northern Ireland) 2006 (SR 2006/22); the Insolvency (Amendment) Regulations (Northern Ireland) 2005 (SR 2006/23); the Insolvency (Northern Ireland) Order 1989 Article 59A (Appointed Date) Order (Northern Ireland) 2006 (SR 2006/24); the Insolvency (Northern Ireland) Order 1989 (Prescribed Part) Order (Northern Ireland) 2006 (SR 2006/25); the Insolvency (Monetary Limits) (Amendment) Order (Northern Ireland) 2006 (SR 2006/26); the Insolvency Practitioners Regulations (Northern Ireland) 2006 (SR 2006/33); the Insolvency (Northern Ireland) Order 2005 (Minor and Consequential Amendments) Order (Northern Ireland) 2006 (SR 2006/61). The advent of the 2005 Order has made it necessary to amend the Credit Institutions (Reorganisation and Winding Up) Regulations 2004 (SI

2004/1045) to cater for the new administration procedure now operating in Northern Ireland—see SI 2007/830; the Insolvent Partnerships (Amendment) Order (Northern Ireland) 2006 (SR 2006/515). For further instances of recent secondary legislation see the Insolvency Practitioners and Insolvency Account (Fees) Order (Northern Ireland) 2006 (SR 2006/53) as amended by the Insolvency Practitioners and Insolvency Account (Fees) (Amendment) Order (Northern Ireland) 2011 (SR 2011/389); the Insolvency (Fees) Order (Northern Ireland) 2006 (SR 2006/54) as amended by the Insolvency (Fees) (Amendment) Order (Northern Ireland) 2011 (SR 2011/14); the Insolvency (Fees) (Amendment No.2) Order (Northern Ireland) (SR 2011/390); and the Insolvency (Deposits) Order (Northern Ireland) 2006 (SR 2006/55) as amended by the Insolvency (Deposits) (Amendment) Order (Northern Ireland) 2011 (SR 2011/391). On director disqualification note the Insolvent Companies (Disqualification of Unfit Directors) Proceedings (Amendment) Rules (Northern Ireland) 2005 (SI 2005/517); the Company Directors Disqualification (Amendment) (Northern Ireland) Order 2005 (SI 2005/1454 (NI 9)). See also the Insolvency (Disqualification from Office: General) Order (Northern Ireland) 2008 (SR 2008/94). Note also the Financial Markets and Insolvency (Settlement Finality) (Amendment) Regulations 2006 (SI 2006/50) which extend SI 1999/2979 to Northern Ireland. These regulations were amended by SI 2007/832.

Changes to Northern Irish insolvency laws can be made via UK statutory instruments—see for example the Companies (Trading Disclosures) (Insolvency) Regulations 2008 (SI 2008/1897) which were introduced to ensure compliance with EC Directive 2003/58. These regulations amend art.49, art.159, Sch.A1 para.27 and Sch.B1 para.46 to the 1989 Order with effect from 1 October 2008. Note the Companies Act 2006 (Consequential Amendments, Transitional Provisions and Savings) Order 2009 (SI 2009/1941) (effective from 1 October 2009), which made a number of amendments to Northern Irish insolvency law.

Further changes to insolvency law in Northern Ireland have been made through the Insolvency (Amendment) Rules (Northern Ireland) 2008 (SR 2008/118); the Insolvency (Fees) (Amendment) Order (Northern Ireland) 2009 (SR 2009/201); the Insolvency (Amendment) Regulations (Northern Ireland) 2009 (SR 2009/202); the Insolvency (Deposits) (Amendment) Order (Northern Ireland) 2009 (SR 2009/203); the Insolvency Practitioners and Insolvency Account (Fees) (Amendment) Order (Northern Ireland) 2009 (SR 2009/204); and the Insolvency (Fees) (Amendment) Order (Northern Ireland) 2011 (SR 2011/14).

The debt relief order mechanism was introduced into Northern Ireland by the Debt Relief Act (Northern Ireland) 2010—this legislation, which passed by the Assembly, will not become fully operational until 30 June 2011—see the Debt Relief (2010 Act) (Commencement) Order (Northern Ireland) 2011 (SR 2011/13 (C. 2)). See also the Debt Relief Orders (Designation of Competent Authorities) Regulations (Northern Ireland) 2011 (SR 2011/15) as amended by the Debt Relief Orders (Designation of Competent Authorities) (Amendment) Regulations (Northern Ireland) 2011 (SR 2011/367).

Note the statement in para.84 of the Companies Act 2006 (Consequential Amendments, Transitional Provisions and Savings) Order 2009 (SI 2009/1941) which is reproduced below. This is effective from 1 October 2009.

> "Nothing in the amendments of the Insolvency Act 1986 made by this Schedule is to be read as qualifying the generality of section 441(2) of that Act (which provides that, with certain exceptions, nothing in the Act extends to Northern Ireland or applies to or in relation to companies registered or incorporated in Northern Ireland)."

Section 441(2) was considered by the court in *Re Normandy Marketing Ltd* [1993] B.C.C. 879. Here it was held that s.221 was wide enough to cover Northern Ireland companies and therefore such a company could be wound up under English law under s.124A of IA 1986 on the grounds that it was in the public interest to do so.

There has been some suggestion that debtors based in Ireland are seeking to bankrupt themselves in Northern Ireland as a result of the more liberal rules applicable in the Province. Such a strategy can only succeed if the debtor can establish COMI in Northern Ireland at the time of the petition—see *Irish Bank Resolution Corp v Quinn* [2012] NICh 1. One result of this alleged bankruptcy tourism has been recent reform to liberalise bankruptcy law (and in particular the earlier availability of discharge) in Ireland. This reform has been introduced in Ireland via the Personal Insolvency Act 2012. For background see Spooner [2012] 25 Insolv. Int. 97 and Spooner [2012] 86 Am. Bank. L.J. 243. Latest reforms to personal insolvency law in Ireland are explained in Bennett in [2014] 27 Insolv. Int. 24.

For the distinctive nature of the IVA regime in Northern Ireland see *Bank of Ireland Mortgage Bank v Sheridan* [2015] NICh 12; [2015] B.P.I.R. 1001.

For a review of insolvency litigation in the Province see Capper [2001] Ins. Law 119; [2003] Ins. Law 132; [2005] 18 Insolv. Int. 81; and [2008] 21 Insolv. Int. 59.

In Northern Ireland in 2011 there were approximately 1,650 new bankruptcies and some 1,076 new IVAs recorded. There were 112 DROs.

Editors' note: Major changes are to be made in insolvency law in Northern Ireland by the Insolvency (Amendment) Act (Northern Ireland) 2016. Broadly speaking, these will reflect the changes made in Great Britain by SBEEA 2015.

442 Extent (other territories)

442 Her Majesty may, by Order in Council, direct that such of the provisions of this Act as are specified in the Order, being provisions formerly contained in the Insolvency Act 1985, shall extend to any of the Channel Islands or any colony with such modifications as may be so specified.

General Note

This provides for the extension of the Act by Order in Council to any of the Channel Islands or any colony. The Isle of Man is not included. Note *Re Television Trade Rentals Ltd* [2002] EWHC 211 (Ch); [2002] B.C.C. 807 where s.426 of IA 1986 was used to extend the CVA provisions in Pt I of the Act to companies incorporated in the Isle of Man.

The Insolvency Act 1986 (Guernsey) Order 1989 (SI 1989/2409) makes provision for co-operation between the courts of the Bailiwick of Guernsey (including Alderney and Sark) and the courts of the UK: see the note to s.426.

443 Commencement

443 This Act comes into force on the day appointed under section 236(2) of the Insolvency Act 1985 for the coming into force of Part III of that Act (individual insolvency and bankruptcy), immediately after that Part of that Act comes into force for England and Wales.

General Note

This odd formula ties the commencement date of IA 1986 to the commencement date of Pt III of IA 1985: see SI 1986/1924 (C. 71) and the general note to s.439 above. The date was 29 December 1986. Certain other provisions in the 1985 Act, relating to corporate insolvency and the licensing of insolvency practitioners, had already been put into force (and now form part of the 1986 consolidation).

444 Citation

444 This Act may be cited as the Insolvency Act 1986.

Schedule A1

Moratorium where directors propose voluntary arrangement

Part I

Introductory

Interpretation

1 In this Schedule–

"the beginning of the moratorium" has the meaning given by paragraph 8(1),

"the date of filing" means the date on which the documents for the time being referred to in paragraph 7(1) are filed or lodged with the court,

"hire-purchase agreement" includes a conditional sale agreement, a chattel leasing agreement and a retention of title agreement,

"market contract" and "market charge" have the meanings given by Part VII of the Companies Act 1989,

"moratorium" means a moratorium under section 1A,

"the nominee" includes any person for the time being carrying out the functions of a nominee under this Schedule,

"the settlement finality regulations" means the Financial Markets and Insolvency (Settlement Finality) Regulations 1999, "system-charge" has the meaning given by the Financial Markets and Insolvency Regulations 1996.

Eligible companies

2(1) A company is eligible for a moratorium if it meets the requirements of paragraph 3, unless–

(a) it is excluded from being eligible by virtue of paragraph 4, or

(b) it falls within sub-paragraph (2).

2(2) A company falls within this sub-paragraph if–

(a) it effects or carries out contracts of insurance, but is not exempt from the general prohibition, within the meaning of section 19 of the Financial Services and Markets Act 2000, in relation to that activity,

(b) it has permission under Part IV of that Act to accept deposits,

(bb) it has a liability in respect of a deposit which it accepted in accordance with the Banking Act 1979 (c. 37) or 1987 (c. 22),

(c) it is a party to a market contract or any of its property is subject to a market charge or a system-charge, or

(d) it is a participant (within the meaning of the settlement finality regulations) or any of its property is subject to a collateral security charge (within the meaning of those regulations).

2(3) Paragraphs (a), (b) and (bb) of sub-paragraph (2) must be read with–

(a) section 22 of the Financial Services and Markets Act 2000;

(b) any relevant order under that section; and

(c) Schedule 2 to that Act.

3(1) A company meets the requirements of this paragraph if the qualifying conditions are met–

(a) in the year ending with the date of filing, or

(b) in the financial year of the company which ended last before that date.

3(2) For the purposes of sub-paragraph (1)–

(a) the qualifying conditions are met by a company in a period if, in that period, it satisfies two or more of the requirements for being a small company specified for the time being in section 382(3) of the Companies Act 2006, and

(b) a company's financial year is to be determined in accordance with that Act.

3(3) Section 382(4), (5) and (6) of that Act apply for the purposes of this paragraph as they apply for the purposes of that section.

3(4) A company does not meet the requirements of this paragraph if it is a parent company of a group of companies which does not qualify as a small group or a medium-sized group in relation to the financial year of the company which ended last before the date of filing.

3(5) For the purposes of sub-paragraph (4)–

(a) "group" has the same meaning as in Part 15 of the Companies Act 2006 (see section 474(1) of that Act); and

(b) a group qualifies as small in relation to a financial year if it so qualifies under section 383(2) to (7) of that Act, and qualifies as medium-sized in relation to a financial year if it so qualifies under section 466(2) to (7) of that Act.

3(6) Expressions used in this paragraph that are defined expressions in Part 15 of the Companies Act 2006 (accounts and reports) have the same meaning in this paragraph as in that Part.

4(1) A company is excluded from being eligible for a moratorium if, on the date of filing–

(a) the company is in administration,

(b) the company is being wound up,

(c) there is an administrative receiver of the company,

(d) a voluntary arrangement has effect in relation to the company,

(e) there is a provisional liquidator of the company,

(f) a moratorium has been in force for the company at any time during the period of 12 months ending with the date of filing and–

  (i) no voluntary arrangement had effect at the time at which the moratorium came to an end, or

  (ii) a voluntary arrangement which had effect at any time in that period has come to an end prematurely,

(fa) an administrator appointed under paragraph 22 of Schedule B1 has held office in the period of 12 months ending with the date of filing, or

(g) a voluntary arrangement in relation to the company which had effect in pursuance of a proposal under section 1(3) has come to an end prematurely and, during the period of 12 months ending with the date of filing, an order under section 5(3)(a) has been made.

4(2) Sub-paragraph (1)(b) does not apply to a company which, by reason of a winding-up order made after the date of filing, is treated as being wound up on that date.

Capital market arrangement

4A A company is also excluded from being eligible for a moratorium if, on the date of filing, it is a party to an agreement which is or forms part of a capital market arrangement under which–

(i) a party has incurred, or when the agreement was entered into was expected to incur, a debt of at least £10 million under the arrangement, and

(ii) the arrangement involves the issue of a capital market investment.

Public private partnership

4B A company is also excluded from being eligible for a moratorium if, on the date of filing, it is a project company of a project which–

(i) is a public-private partnership project, and

(ii) includes step-in rights.

Liability under an arrangement

4C(1) A company is also excluded from being eligible for a moratorium if, on the date of filing, it has incurred a liability under an agreement of £10 million or more.

4C(2) Where the liability in sub-paragraph (1) is a contingent liability under or by virtue of a guarantee or an indemnity or security provided on behalf of another person, the amount of that liability is the full amount of the liability in relation to which the guarantee, indemnity or security is provided.

4C(3) In this paragraph–

(a) the reference to "liability" includes a present or future liability whether, in either case, it is certain or contingent,

(b) the reference to "liability" includes a reference to a liability to be paid wholly or partly in foreign currency (in which case the sterling equivalent shall be calculated as at the time when the liability is incurred).

Interpretation of capital market arrangement

4D(1) For the purposes of paragraph 4A an arrangement is a capital market arrangement if–

(a) it involves a grant of security to a person holding it as trustee for a person who holds a capital market investment issued by a party to the arrangement, or

(b) at least one party guarantees the performance of obligations of another party, or

(c) at least one party provides security in respect of the performance of obligations of another party, or

(d) the arrangement involves an investment of a kind described in articles 83 to 85 of the Financial Services and Markets Act 2000 (Regulated Activities) Order 2001 (S.I. 2001/544) (options, futures and contracts for differences).

4D(2) For the purposes of sub-paragraph (1)–

(a) a reference to holding as trustee includes a reference to holding as nominee or agent,

(b) a reference to holding for a person who holds a capital market investment includes a reference to holding for a number of persons at least one of whom holds a capital market investment, and

(c) a person holds a capital market investment if he has a legal or beneficial interest in it.

4D(3) In paragraph 4A, 4C, 4J and this paragraph–

"agreement" includes an agreement or undertaking effected by–

(a) contract,

(b) deed, or

(c) any other instrument intended to have effect in accordance with the law of England and Wales, Scotland or another jurisdiction, and

"party" to an arrangement includes a party to an agreement which–

(a) forms part of the arrangement,

(b) provides for the raising of finance as part of the arrangement, or

(c) is necessary for the purposes of implementing the arrangement.

Capital market investment

4E(1) For the purposes of paragraphs 4A and 4D, an investment is a capital market investment if–

(a) it is within article 77 or 77A of the Financial Services and Markets Act 2000 (Regulated Activities) Order 2001 (S.I. 2001/544) (debt instruments) and

(b) it is rated, listed or traded or designed to be rated, listed or traded.

4E(2) In sub-paragraph (1)–

"listed" means admitted to the official list within the meaning given by section 103(1) of the Financial Services and Markets Act 2000 (c. 8) (interpretation),

"rated" means rated for the purposes of investment by an internationally recognised rating agency,

"traded" means admitted to trading on a market established under the rules of a recognised investment exchange or on a foreign market.

4E(3) In sub-paragraph (2)–

"foreign market" has the same meaning as "relevant market" in article 67(2) of the Financial Services and Markets Act 2000 (Financial Promotion) Order 2001 (S.I. 2001/1335) (foreign markets),

"recognised investment exchange" has the meaning given by section 285 of the Financial Services and Markets Act 2000 (recognised investment exchange).

4F(1) For the purposes of paragraphs 4A and 4D an investment is also a capital market investment if it consists of a bond or commercial paper issued to one or more of the following–

(a) an investment professional within the meaning of article 19(5) of the Financial Services and Markets Act 2000 (Financial Promotion) Order 2001,

(b) a person who is, when the agreement mentioned in paragraph 4A is entered into, a certified high net worth individual in relation to a communication within the meaning of article 48(2) of that order,

(c) a person to whom article 49(2) of that order applies (high net worth company, &c),

(d) a person who is, when the agreement mentioned in paragraph 4A is entered into, a certified sophisticated investor in relation to a communication within the meaning of article 50(1) of that order, and

(e) a person in a State other than the United Kingdom who under the law of that State is not prohibited from investing in bonds or commercial paper.

4F(2) For the purposes of sub-paragraph (1)–

(a) in applying article 19(5) of the Financial Services and Markets Act 2000 (Financial Promotion) Order 2001 for the purposes of sub-paragraph (1)(a)–

  (i) in article 19(5)(b), ignore the words after "exempt person",

  (ii) in article 19(5)(c)(i), for the words from "the controlled activity" to the end substitute "a controlled activity", and

  (iii) in article 19(5)(e) ignore the words from "where the communication" to the end, and

(b) in applying article 49(2) of that order for the purposes of sub-paragraph (1)(c), ignore article 49(2)(e).

4F(3) In sub-paragraph (1)–

"bond" shall be construed in accordance with article 77 of the Financial Services and Markets Act 2000 (Regulated Activities) Order 2001 (S.I. 2001/544), and includes any instrument falling within article 77A of that Order, and

"commercial paper" has the meaning given by article 9(3) of that order.

Debt

4G The debt of at least £10 million referred to in paragraph 4A–

(a) may be incurred at any time during the life of the capital market arrangement, and

(b) may be expressed wholly or partly in a foreign currency (in which case the sterling equivalent shall be calculated as at the time when the arrangement is entered into).

Interpretation of project company

4H(1) For the purposes of paragraph 4B a company is a "project company" of a project if–

(a) it holds property for the purpose of the project,

(b) it has sole or principal responsibility under an agreement for carrying out all or part of the project,

(c) it is one of a number of companies which together carry out the project,

(d) it has the purpose of supplying finance to enable the project to be carried out, or

(e) it is the holding company of a company within any of paragraphs (a) to (d).

4H(2) But a company is not a "project company" of a project if–

(a) it performs a function within sub-paragraph (1)(a) to (d) or is within sub-paragraph (1)(e), but

(b) it also performs a function which is not–

(i) within sub-paragraph (1)(a) to (d),

(ii) related to a function within sub-paragraph (1)(a) to (d), or

(iii) related to the project.

4H(3) For the purposes of this paragraph a company carries out all or part of a project whether or not it acts wholly or partly through agents.

Public-private partnership project

4I(1) In paragraph 4B "public-private partnership project" means a project–

(a) the resources for which are provided partly by one or more public bodies and partly by one or more private persons, or

(b) which is designed wholly or mainly for the purpose of assisting a public body to discharge a function.

4I(2) In sub-paragraph (1) "resources" includes–

(a) funds (including payment for the provision of services or facilities),

(b) assets,

(c) professional skill,

(d) the grant of a concession or franchise, and

(e) any other commercial resource.

4I(3) In sub-paragraph (1) "public body" means–

(a) a body which exercises public functions,

(b) a body specified for the purposes of this paragraph by the Secretary of State, and

(c) a body within a class specified for the purposes of this paragraph by the Secretary of State.

4I(4) A specification under sub-paragraph (3) may be–

(a) general, or

(b) for the purpose of the application of paragraph 4B to a specified case.

Step-in rights

4J(1) For the purposes of paragraph 4B a project has “step-in rights” if a person who provides finance in connection with the project has a conditional entitlement under an agreement to–

(i) assume sole or principal responsibility under an agreement for carrying out all or part of the project, or

(ii) make arrangements for carrying out all or part of the project.

4J(2) In sub-paragraph (1) a reference to the provision of finance includes a reference to the provision of an indemnity.

Person

4K For the purposes of paragraphs 4A to 4J, a reference to a person includes a reference to a partnership or another unincorporated group of persons.

5 The Secretary of State may by regulations modify the qualifications for eligibility of a company for a moratorium.

Part II

Obtaining a moratorium

Nominee's statement

6(1) Where the directors of a company wish to obtain a moratorium, they shall submit to the nominee–

(a) a document setting out the terms of the proposed voluntary arrangement,

(b) a statement of the company's affairs containing–

(i) such particulars of its creditors and of its debts and other liabilities and of its assets as may be prescribed, and

(ii) such other information as may be prescribed, and

(c) any other information necessary to enable the nominee to comply with sub-paragraph (2) which he requests from them.

6(2) The nominee shall submit to the directors a statement in the prescribed form indicating whether or not, in his opinion–

(a) the proposed voluntary arrangement has a reasonable prospect of being approved and implemented,

(b) the company is likely to have sufficient funds available to it during the proposed moratorium to enable it to carry on its business, and

(c) the proposed voluntary arrangement should be considered by a meeting of the company and by the company's creditors.

6(3) In forming his opinion on the matters mentioned in sub-paragraph (2), the nominee is entitled to rely on the information submitted to him under sub-paragraph (1) unless he has reason to doubt its accuracy.

6(4) The reference in sub-paragraph (2)(b) to the company's business is to that business as the company proposes to carry it on during the moratorium.

Documents to be submitted to court

7(1) To obtain a moratorium the directors of a company must file (in Scotland, lodge) with the court–

(a) a document setting out the terms of the proposed voluntary arrangement,

(b) a statement of the company's affairs containing–

(i) such particulars of its creditors and of its debts and other liabilities and of its assets as may be prescribed, and

(ii) such other information as may be prescribed,

(c) a statement that the company is eligible for a moratorium,

(d) a statement from the nominee that he has given his consent to act, and

(e) a statement from the nominee that, in his opinion–

(i) the proposed voluntary arrangement has a reasonable prospect of being approved and implemented,

(ii) the company is likely to have sufficient funds available to it during the proposed moratorium to enable it to carry on its business, and

(iii) the proposed voluntary arrangement should be considered by a meeting of the company and by the company's creditors.

7(2) Each of the statements mentioned in sub-paragraph (1)(b) to (e), except so far as it contains the particulars referred to in paragraph (b)(i), must be in the prescribed form.

7(3) The reference in sub-paragraph (1)(e)(ii) to the company's business is to that business as the company proposes to carry it on during the moratorium.

7(4) The Secretary of State may by regulations modify the requirements of this paragraph as to the documents required to be filed (in Scotland, lodged) with the court in order to obtain a moratorium.

Duration of moratorium

8(1) A moratorium comes into force when the documents for the time being referred to in paragraph 7(1) are filed or lodged with the court and references in this Schedule to "the beginning of the moratorium" shall be construed accordingly.

8(2) A moratorium ends with the later of–

(a) the day on which the company meeting summoned under paragraph 29 is first held, and

(b) the day on which the company's creditors decide whether to approve the proposed voluntary arrangement,

unless it is extended under paragraph 32, but this is subject to the rest of this paragraph.

8(3) In this paragraph the "initial period" means the period of 28 days beginning with the day on which the moratorium comes into force.

8(3A) If the company meeting has not first met before the end of the initial period the moratorium ends at the end of that period, unless before the end of that period it is extended under paragraph 32.

8(3B) If the company's creditors have not decided whether to approve the proposed voluntary arrangement before the end of the initial period the moratorium ends at the end of that period, unless before the end of that period–

(a) the moratorium is extended under paragraph 32, or

(b) a meeting of the company's creditors is summoned in accordance with section 246ZE.

8(3C) Where sub-paragraph (3B)(b) applies, the moratorium ends with the day on which the meeting of the company's creditors is first held, unless it is extended under paragraph 32.

8(4) The moratorium ends at the end of the initial period if the nominee has not before the end of that period–

(a) summoned a meeting of the company, and

(b) sought a decision from the company's creditors,

as required by paragraph 29(1).

8(5) If the moratorium is extended (or further extended) under paragraph 32, it ends at the end of the day to which it is extended (or further extended).

8(6) Sub-paragraphs (2) to (5) do not apply if the moratorium comes to an end before the time concerned by virtue of–

(a) paragraph 25(4) (effect of withdrawal by nominee of consent to act),

(b) an order under paragraph 26(3), 27(3) or 40 (challenge of actions of nominee or directors), or

(c) a decision of one or both of–

(i) the meeting of the company summoned under paragraph 29, or

(ii) the company's creditors.

8(7) If the moratorium has not previously come to an end in accordance with sub-paragraphs (2) to (6), it ends at the end of the day on which a decision under paragraph 31 to approve a voluntary arrangement takes effect under paragraph 36.

8(8) The Secretary of State may by order increase or reduce the period for the time being specified in sub-paragraph (3).

Notification of beginning of moratorium

9(1) When a moratorium comes into force, the directors shall notify the nominee of that fact forthwith.

9(2) If the directors without reasonable excuse fail to comply with sub-paragraph (1), each of them is liable to imprisonment or a fine, or both.

10(1) When a moratorium comes into force, the nominee shall, in accordance with the rules–

(a) advertise that fact forthwith, and

(b) notify the registrar of companies, the company and any petitioning creditor of the company of whose claim he is aware of that fact.

10(2) In sub-paragraph (1)(b), "petitioning creditor" means a creditor by whom a winding-up petition has been presented before the beginning of the moratorium, as long as the petition has not been dismissed or withdrawn.

10(3) If the nominee without reasonable excuse fails to comply with sub-paragraph (1)(a) or (b), he is liable to a fine.

Notification of end of moratorium

11(1) When a moratorium comes to an end, the nominee shall, in accordance with the rules–

(a) advertise that fact forthwith, and

(b) notify the court, the registrar of companies, the company and any creditor of the company of whose claim he is aware of that fact.

11(2) If the nominee without reasonable excuse fails to comply with sub-paragraph (1)(a) or (b), he is liable to a fine.

PART III

EFFECTS OF MORATORIUM

Effect on creditors, etc.

12(1) During the period for which a moratorium is in force for a company–

(a) no petition may be presented for the winding up of the company,

(b) no meeting of the company may be called or requisitioned except with the consent of the nominee or the leave of the court and subject (where the court gives leave) to such terms as the court may impose,

(c) no resolution may be passed or order made for the winding up of the company,

(d) no administration application may be made in respect of the company,

(da) no administrator of the company may be appointed under paragraph 14 or 22 of Schedule B1,

(e) no administrative receiver of the company may be appointed,

(f) no landlord or other person to whom rent is payable may exercise any right of forfeiture by peaceable re-entry in relation to premises let to the company in respect of a failure by the company to comply with any term or condition of its tenancy of such premises, except with the leave of the court and subject to such terms as the court may impose,

(g) no other steps may be taken to enforce any security over the company's property, or to repossess goods in the company's possession under any hire-purchase agreement, except with the leave of the court and subject to such terms as the court may impose, and

(h) no other proceedings and no execution or other legal process may be commenced or continued, and no distress may be levied, against the company or its property except with the leave of the court and subject to such terms as the court may impose.

12(2) Where a petition, other than an excepted petition, for the winding up of the company has been presented before the beginning of the moratorium, section 127 shall not apply in relation to any disposition of property, transfer of shares or alteration in status made during the moratorium or at a time mentioned in paragraph 37(5)(a).

12(3) In the application of sub-paragraph (1)(h) to Scotland, the reference to execution being commenced or continued includes a reference to diligence being carried out or continued, and the reference to distress being levied is omitted.

12(4) Paragraph (a) of sub-paragraph (1) does not apply to an excepted petition and, where such a petition has been presented before the beginning of the moratorium or is presented during the moratorium, paragraphs (b) and (c) of that sub-paragraph do not apply in relation to proceedings on the petition.

12(5) For the purposes of this paragraph, "excepted petition" means a petition under–

(a) section 124A or 124B of this Act,

(b) section 72 of the Financial Services Act 1986 on the ground mentioned in subsection (1)(b) of that section, or

(c) section 92 of the Banking Act 1987 on the ground mentioned in subsection (1)(b) of that section.

(d) section 367 of the Financial Services and Markets Act 2000 on the ground mentioned in subsection (3)(b) of that section.

13(1) This paragraph applies where there is an uncrystallised floating charge on the property of a company for which a moratorium is in force.

13(2) If the conditions for the holder of the charge to give a notice having the effect mentioned in sub-paragraph (4) are met at any time, the notice may not be given at that time but may instead be given as soon as practicable after the moratorium has come to an end.

13(3) If any other event occurs at any time which (apart from this sub-paragraph) would have the effect mentioned in sub-paragraph (4), then–

(a) the event shall not have the effect in question at that time, but

(b) if notice of the event is given to the company by the holder of the charge as soon as is practicable after the moratorium has come to an end, the event is to be treated as if it had occurred when the notice was given.

13(4) The effect referred to in sub-paragraphs (2) and (3) is–

(a) causing the crystallisation of the floating charge, or

(b) causing the imposition, by virtue of provision in the instrument creating the charge, of any restriction on the disposal of any property of the company.

13(5) Application may not be made for leave under paragraph 12(1)(g) or (h) with a view to obtaining–

(a) the crystallisation of the floating charge, or

(b) the imposition, by virtue of provision in the instrument creating the charge, of any restriction on the disposal of any property of the company.

14 Security granted by a company at a time when a moratorium is in force in relation to the company may only be enforced if, at that time, there were reasonable grounds for believing that it would benefit the company.

Effect on company

15(1) Paragraphs 16 to 23 apply in relation to a company for which a moratorium is in force.

15(2) The fact that a company enters into a transaction in contravention of any of paragraphs 16 to 22 does not–

(a) make the transaction void, or

(b) make it to any extent unenforceable against the company.

Company invoices, etc.

16(1) Every invoice, order for goods or services, business letter or order form (whether in hard copy, electronic or any other form) issued by or on behalf of the company, and all the company's websites, must also contain the nominee's name and a statement that the moratorium is in force for the company.

16(2) If default is made in complying with sub-paragraph (1), the company and (subject to sub-paragraph (3)) any officer of the company is liable to a fine.

16(3) An officer of the company is only liable under sub-paragraph (2) if, without reasonable excuse, he authorises or permits the default.

Obtaining credit during moratorium

17(1) The company may not obtain credit to the extent of £250 or more from a person who has not been informed that a moratorium is in force in relation to the company.

17(2) The reference to the company obtaining credit includes the following cases–

(a) where goods are bailed (in Scotland, hired) to the company under a hire-purchase agreement, or agreed to be sold to the company under a conditional sale agreement, and

(b) where the company is paid in advance (whether in money or otherwise) for the supply of goods or services.

17(3) Where the company obtains credit in contravention of sub-paragraph (1)–

(a) the company is liable to a fine, and

(b) if any officer of the company knowingly and wilfully authorised or permitted the contravention, he is liable to imprisonment or a fine, or both.

17(4) The money sum specified in sub-paragraph (1) is subject to increase or reduction by order under section 417A in Part XV.

Disposals and payments

18(1) Subject to sub-paragraph (2), the company may only dispose of any of its property if–

(a) there are reasonable grounds for believing that the disposal will benefit the company, and

(b) the disposal is approved by the committee established under paragraph 35(1) or, where there is no such committee, by the nominee.

18(2) Sub-paragraph (1) does not apply to a disposal made in the ordinary way of the company's business.

18(3) If the company makes a disposal in contravention of sub-paragraph (1) otherwise than in pursuance of an order of the court–

(a) the company is liable to a fine, and

(b) if any officer of the company authorised or permitted the contravention, without reasonable excuse, he is liable to imprisonment or a fine, or both.

19(1) Subject to sub-paragraph (2), the company may only make any payment in respect of any debt or other liability of the company in existence before the beginning of the moratorium if–

(a) there are reasonable grounds for believing that the payment will benefit the company, and

(b) the payment is approved by the committee established under paragraph 35(1) or, where there is no such committee, by the nominee.

19(2) Sub-paragraph (1) does not apply to a payment required by paragraph 20(6).

19(3) If the company makes a payment in contravention of sub-paragraph (1) otherwise than in pursuance of an order of the court–

(a) the company is liable to a fine, and

(b) if any officer of the company authorised or permitted the contravention, without reasonable excuse, he is liable to imprisonment or a fine, or both.

Disposal of charged property, etc.

20(1) This paragraph applies where–

(a) any property of the company is subject to a security, or

(b) any goods are in the possession of the company under a hire-purchase agreement.

20(2) If the holder of the security consents, or the court gives leave, the company may dispose of the property as if it were not subject to the security.

20(3) If the owner of the goods consents, or the court gives leave, the company may dispose of the goods as if all rights of the owner under the hire-purchase agreement were vested in the company.

20(4) Where property subject to a security which, as created, was a floating charge is disposed of under sub-paragraph (2), the holder of the security has the same priority in respect of any property of the company directly or indirectly representing the property disposed of as he would have had in respect of the property subject to the security.

20(5) Sub-paragraph (6) applies to the disposal under sub-paragraph (2) or (as the case may be) sub-paragraph (3) of–

(a) any property subject to a security other than a security which, as created, was a floating charge, or

(b) any goods in the possession of the company under a hire-purchase agreement.

20(6) It shall be a condition of any consent or leave under sub-paragraph (2) or (as the case may be) sub-paragraph (3) that–

(a) the net proceeds of the disposal, and

(b) where those proceeds are less than such amount as may be agreed, or determined by the court, to be the net amount which would be realised on a sale of the property or goods in the open market by a willing vendor, such sums as may be required to make good the deficiency,

shall be applied towards discharging the sums secured by the security or payable under the hire-purchase agreement.

20(7) Where a condition imposed in pursuance of sub-paragraph (6) relates to two or more securities, that condition requires–

(a) the net proceeds of the disposal, and

(b) where paragraph (b) of sub-paragraph (6) applies, the sums mentioned in that paragraph,

to be applied towards discharging the sums secured by those securities in the order of their priorities.

20(8) Where the court gives leave for a disposal under sub-paragraph (2) or (3), the directors shall, within 14 days after leave is given, send a copy of the order giving leave to the registrar of companies.

20(9) If the directors without reasonable excuse fail to comply with sub-paragraph (8), they are liable to a fine.

21(1) Where property is disposed of under paragraph 20 in its application to Scotland, the company shall grant to the disponee an appropriate document of transfer or conveyance of the property, and

(a) that document, or

(b) where any recording, intimation or registration of the document is a legal requirement for completion of title to the property, that recording, intimation or registration,

has the effect of disencumbering the property of, or (as the case may be) freeing the property from, the security.

21(2) Where goods in the possession of the company under a hire-purchase agreement are disposed of under paragraph 20 in its application to Scotland, the disposal has the effect of extinguishing, as against the disponee, all rights of the owner of the goods under the agreement.

22(1) If the company–

(a) without any consent or leave under paragraph 20, disposes of any of its property which is subject to a security otherwise than in accordance with the terms of the security,

(b) without any consent or leave under paragraph 20, disposes of any goods in the possession of the company under a hire-purchase agreement otherwise than in accordance with the terms of the agreement, or

(c) fails to comply with any requirement imposed by paragraph 20 or 21,

it is liable to a fine.

22(2) If any officer of the company, without reasonable excuse, authorises or permits any such disposal or failure to comply, he is liable to imprisonment or a fine, or both.

Market contracts, etc.

23(1) If the company enters into any transaction to which this paragraph applies–

(a) the company is liable to a fine, and

(b) if any officer of the company, without reasonable excuse, authorised or permitted the company to enter into the transaction, he is liable to imprisonment or a fine, or both.

23(2) A company enters into a transaction to which this paragraph applies if it–

(a) enters into a market contract,

(b) gives a transfer order,

(c) grants a market charge or a system-charge, or

(d) provides any collateral security.

23(3) The fact that a company enters into a transaction in contravention of this paragraph does not–

(a) make the transaction void, or

(b) make it to any extent unenforceable by or against the company.

23(4) Where during the moratorium a company enters into a transaction to which this paragraph applies, nothing done by or in pursuance of the transaction is to be treated as done in contravention of paragraphs 12(1)(g), 14 or 16 to 22.

23(5) Paragraph 20 does not apply in relation to any property which is subject to a market charge, a system-charge or a collateral security charge.

23(6) In this paragraph, "transfer order", "collateral security" and "collateral security charge" have the same meanings as in the settlement finality regulations.

Part IV

Nominees

Monitoring of company's activities

24(1) During a moratorium, the nominee shall monitor the company's affairs for the purpose of forming an opinion as to whether–

(a) the proposed voluntary arrangement or, if he has received notice of proposed modifications under paragraph 31(7), the proposed arrangement with those modifications has a reasonable prospect of being approved and implemented, and

(b) the company is likely to have sufficient funds available to it during the remainder of the moratorium to enable it to continue to carry on its business.

24(2) The directors shall submit to the nominee any information necessary to enable him to comply with sub-paragraph (1) which he requests from them.

24(3) In forming his opinion on the matters mentioned in sub-paragraph (1), the nominee is entitled to rely on the information submitted to him under sub-paragraph (2) unless he has reason to doubt its accuracy.

24(4) The reference in sub-paragraph (1)(b) to the company's business is to that business as the company proposes to carry it on during the remainder of the moratorium.

Withdrawal of consent to act

25(1) The nominee may only withdraw his consent to act in the circumstances mentioned in this paragraph.

25(2) The nominee must withdraw his consent to act if, at any time during a moratorium–

(a) he forms the opinion that–

(i) the proposed voluntary arrangement or, if he has received notice of proposed modifications under paragraph 31(7), the proposed arrangement with those modifications no longer has a reasonable prospect of being approved or implemented, or

(ii) the company will not have sufficient funds available to it during the remainder of the moratorium to enable it to continue to carry on its business,

(b) he becomes aware that, on the date of filing, the company was not eligible for a moratorium, or

(c) the directors fail to comply with their duty under paragraph 24(2).

25(3) The reference in sub-paragraph (2)(a)(ii) to the company's business is to that business as the company proposes to carry it on during the remainder of the moratorium.

25(4) If the nominee withdraws his consent to act, the moratorium comes to an end.

25(5) If the nominee withdraws his consent to act he must, in accordance with the rules, notify the court, the registrar of companies, the company and any creditor of the company of whose claim he is aware of his withdrawal and the reason for it.

25(6) If the nominee without reasonable excuse fails to comply with sub-paragraph (5), he is liable to a fine.

Challenge of nominee's actions, etc.

26(1) If any creditor, director or member of the company, or any other person affected by a moratorium, is dissatisfied by any act, omission or decision of the nominee during the moratorium, he may apply to the court.

26(2) An application under sub-paragraph (1) may be made during the moratorium or after it has ended.

26(3) On an application under sub-paragraph (1) the court may–

(a) confirm, reverse or modify any act or decision of the nominee,

(b) give him directions, or

(c) make such other order as it thinks fit.

26(4) An order under sub-paragraph (3) may (among other things) bring the moratorium to an end and make such consequential provision as the court thinks fit.

27(1) Where there are reasonable grounds for believing that–

(a) as a result of any act, omission or decision of the nominee during the moratorium, the company has suffered loss, but

(b) the company does not intend to pursue any claim it may have against the nominee,

any creditor of the company may apply to the court.

27(2) An application under sub-paragraph (1) may be made during the moratorium or after it has ended.

27(3) On an application under sub-paragraph (1) the court may–

(a) order the company to pursue any claim against the nominee,

(b) authorise any creditor to pursue such a claim in the name of the company, or

(c) make such other order with respect to such a claim as it thinks fit,

unless the court is satisfied that the act, omission or decision of the nominee was in all the circumstances reasonable.

27(4) An order under sub-paragraph (3) may (among other things)–

(a) impose conditions on any authority given to pursue a claim,

(b) direct the company to assist in the pursuit of a claim,

(c) make directions with respect to the distribution of anything received as a result of the pursuit of a claim,

(d) bring the moratorium to an end and make such consequential provision as the court thinks fit.

27(5) On an application under sub-paragraph (1) the court shall have regard to the interests of the members and creditors of the company generally.

Replacement of nominee by court

28(1) The court may–

(a) on an application made by the directors in a case where the nominee has failed to comply with any duty imposed on him under this Schedule or has died, or

(b) on an application made by the directors or the nominee in a case where it is impracticable or inappropriate for the nominee to continue to act as such, direct that the nominee be replaced as such by another person qualified to act as an insolvency practitioner in relation to the voluntary arrangement.

28(2) A person may only be appointed as a replacement nominee under this paragraph if he submits to the court a statement indicating his consent to act.

Part V

Consideration and implementation of voluntary arrangement

Duty to summon company meeting and seek a creditors' decision

29(1) Where a moratorium is in force, the nominee shall–

(a) summon a meeting of the company to consider the proposed voluntary arrangement for such a time, date (within the period of time for the time being specified in paragraph 8(3)) and place as he thinks fit, and

(b) seek a decision from the company's creditors as to whether they approve of the proposed voluntary arrangement.

29(2) The decision of the company's creditors is to be made by a qualifying decision procedure.

29(3) Notice of the qualifying decision procedure must be given to every creditor of the company of whose claim the nominee is aware.

Conduct of company meeting and qualifying decision procedure

30(1) Subject to the provisions of paragraphs 31 to 35, the company meeting summoned under paragraph 29 and the qualifying decision procedure instigated under that paragraph shall be conducted in accordance with the rules.

30(2) The company meeting summoned under paragraph 29 may resolve that it be adjourned (or further adjourned).

30(3) After the conclusion of the company meeting in accordance with the rules, the chairman of the meeting shall report the result of the meeting to the court, and, immediately after reporting to the court, shall give notice of the result of the meeting to such persons as may be prescribed.

30(4) After the company's creditors have decided whether to approve the proposed voluntary arrangement the nominee must–

(a) report the decision to the court, and

(b) immediately after reporting to the court, give notice of the decision to such persons as may be prescribed.

Approval of voluntary arrangement

31(1) This paragraph applies where under paragraph 29–

(a) a meeting of the company is summoned to consider the proposed voluntary arrangement, and

(b) the nominee seeks a decision from the company's creditors as to whether they approve the proposed voluntary arrangement.

31(1A) The company and its creditors may approve the proposed voluntary arrangement with or without modifications.

31(2) The modifications may include one conferring the functions proposed to be conferred on the nominee on another person qualified to act as an insolvency practitioner in relation to the voluntary arrangement.

31(3) The modifications shall not include one by virtue of which the proposal ceases to be a proposal such as is mentioned in section 1.

31(4) Neither the company nor its creditors may approve any proposal or modification which affects the right of a secured creditor of the company to enforce his security, except with the concurrence of the creditor concerned..

31(5) Subject to sub-paragraph (6), neither the company nor its creditors may approve any proposal or modification under which–

(a) any preferential debt of the company is to be paid otherwise than in priority to such of its debts as are not preferential debts,

(aa) any ordinary preferential debt of the company is to be paid otherwise than in priority to any secondary preferential debts that it may have,

(b) a preferential creditor of the company is to be paid an amount in respect of an ordinary preferential debt that bears to that debt a smaller proportion than is borne to another preferential debt by the amount that is to be paid in respect of that other debt, or

(c) a preferential creditor of the company is to be paid an amount in respect of a secondary preferential debt that bears to that debt a smaller proportion than is borne to another secondary preferential debt by the amount that is to be paid in respect of that other debt.

31(6) Such a proposal or modification may be approved with the concurrence of the preferential creditor concerned.

31(7) The directors of the company may, before the beginning of the relevant period, give notice to the nominee of any modifications of the proposal for which the directors intend to seek the approval of the company and its creditors.

31(7A) The "relevant period" is–

(a) in relation to the company, the period of seven days ending with the company meeting summoned under paragraph 29 being held;

(b) in relation to the company's creditors, the period of 14 days ending with the end of the period mentioned in paragraph 8(3).

31(7B) Where under sub-paragraph (7) the nominee is given notice of proposed modifications, the nominee must seek a decision from the company's creditors (using a qualifying decision procedure) as to whether the proposed voluntary arrangement should be approved with those modifications.

31(8) References in this paragraph to preferential debts, ordinary preferential debts, secondary preferential debts and preferential creditors are to be read in accordance with section 386 in Part XII of this Act.

Extension of moratorium

32(1) Subject to sub-paragraph (2), a company meeting summoned under paragraph 29 which resolves that it be adjourned (or further adjourned) may resolve that the moratorium be extended (or further extended), with or without conditions.

32(1A) Subject to sub-paragraph (2) the company's creditors may, by a qualifying decision procedure, decide to extend (or further extend) the moratorium, with or without conditions.

32(2) The moratorium may not be extended (or further extended) to a day later than the end of the period of two months beginning with the day after the last day of the period mentioned in paragraph 8(3).

32(3) Where it is proposed to extend (or further extend) the moratorium, before a decision is taken with respect to that proposal, the nominee shall inform the meeting of the company or (as the case may be) inform the company's creditors–

(a) of what he has done in order to comply with his duty under paragraph 24 and the cost of his actions for the company, and

(b) of what he intends to do to continue to comply with that duty if the moratorium is extended (or further extended) and the expected cost of his actions for the company.

32(4) Where, in accordance with sub-paragraph (3)(b), the nominee informs a meeting of the company or informs the company's creditors of the expected cost of his intended actions, the meeting shall resolve or (as the case may be) the creditors by a qualifying decision procedure shall decide whether or not to approve that expected cost.

32(5) If a decision not to approve the expected cost of the nominee's intended actions has effect under paragraph 36, the moratorium comes to an end.

32(6) A meeting of the company may resolve, and the creditors by a qualifying decision procedure may decide that a moratorium which has been extended (or further extended) be brought to an end before the end of the period of the extension (or further extension).

32(7) The Secretary of State may by order increase or reduce the period for the time being specified in sub-paragraph (2).

33(1) The conditions which may be imposed when a moratorium is extended (or further extended) include a requirement that the nominee be replaced as such by another person qualified to act as an insolvency practitioner in relation to the voluntary arrangement.

33(2) A person may only be appointed as a replacement nominee by virtue of sub-paragraph (1) if he submits to the court a statement indicating his consent to act.

33(3) Where it is proposed to appoint a replacement nominee as a condition of extending (or further extending) the moratorium–

(a) the duty imposed by paragraph 32(3)(b) on the nominee shall instead be imposed on the person proposed as the replacement nominee, and

(b) paragraphs 32(4) and (5) and 36(1)(e) apply as if the references to the nominee were to that person.

34(1) If a decision to extend, or further extend, the moratorium takes effect under paragraph 36, the nominee shall, in accordance with the rules, notify the registrar of companies and the court.

34(2) If the moratorium is extended, or further extended, by virtue of an order under paragraph 36(5), the nominee shall, in accordance with the rules, send a copy of the order to the registrar of companies.

34(3) If the nominee without reasonable excuse fails to comply with this paragraph, he is liable to a fine.

Moratorium committee

35(1) This paragraph applies where in accordance with paragraph 32 a meeting of the company resolves, or the company's creditors decide, that the moratorium be extended (or further extended).

35(1A) The meeting may resolve, and the company's creditors may by qualifying decision procedure decide, that a committee be established to exercise the functions conferred on it by the meeting or (as the case may be) by the company's creditors.

35(2) The meeting may resolve that such a committee be established only if–

(a) the nominee consents, and

(b) the meeting approves an estimate of the expenses to be incurred by the committee in the exercise of the proposed functions.

35(2A) A decision of the company's creditors that such a committee be established is to be taken as made only if–

(a) the nominee consents, and

(b) the creditors by a qualifying decision procedure approve an estimate of the expenses to be incurred by the committee in the exercise of the proposed functions.

35(3) Any expenses, not exceeding the amount of the estimate, incurred by the committee in the exercise of its functions shall be reimbursed by the nominee.

35(4) The committee shall cease to exist when the moratorium comes to an end.

Effectiveness of decisions

36(1) Sub-paragraph (2) applies to references to one of the following decisions having effect, that is, a decision, under paragraph 31, 32 or 35, with respect to–

(a) the approval of a proposed voluntary arrangement,

(b) the extension (or further extension) of a moratorium,

(c) the bringing of a moratorium to an end,

(d) the establishment of a committee, or

(e) the approval of the expected cost of a nominee's intended actions.

36(2) The decision has effect if, in accordance with the rules–

(a) it has been taken by the meeting of the company summoned under paragraph 29 and by the company's creditors, or

(b) (subject to any order made under sub-paragraph (5)) it has been taken by the company's creditors.

36(3) If a decision taken by the company's creditors under any of paragraphs 31, 32 or 35 with respect to any of the matters mentioned in sub-paragraph (1) differs from one so taken by the company meeting with respect to that matter, a member of the company may apply to the court.

36(4) An application under sub-paragraph (3) shall not be made after the end of the period of 28 days beginning with–

(a) the day on which the decision was taken by the company's creditors, or

(b) where the decision of the company meeting was taken on a later day, that day.

36(5) On an application under sub-paragraph (3), the court may–

(a) order the decision of the company meeting to have effect instead of the decision of the company's creditors, or

(b) make such other order as it thinks fit.

Effect of approval of voluntary arrangement

37(1) This paragraph applies where a decision approving a voluntary arrangement has effect under paragraph 36.

37(2) The approved voluntary arrangement–

(a) takes effect as if made by the company at the time the creditors decided to approve the voluntary arrangement, and

(b) binds every person who in accordance with the rules–

(i) was entitled to vote in the qualifying decision procedure by which the creditors' decision to approve the voluntary arrangement was made, or

(ii) would have been so entitled if he had had notice of it,

as if he were a party to the voluntary arrangement.

37(3) If–

(a) when the arrangement ceases to have effect any amount payable under the arrangement to a person bound by virtue of sub-paragraph (2)(b)(ii) has not been paid, and

(b) the arrangement did not come to an end prematurely,

the company shall at that time become liable to pay to that person the amount payable under the arrangement.

37(4) Where a petition for the winding up of the company, other than an excepted petition within the meaning of paragraph 12, was presented before the beginning of the moratorium, the court shall dismiss the petition.

37(5) The court shall not dismiss a petition under sub-paragraph (4)–

(a) at any time before the end of the period of 28 days beginning with the first day on which each of the reports required by paragraph 30(3) and (4) has been made to the court, or

(b) at any time when an application under paragraph 38 or an appeal in respect of such an application is pending, or at any time in the period within which such an appeal may be brought.

Challenge of decisions

38(1) Subject to the following provisions of this paragraph, any of the persons mentioned in sub-paragraph (2) may apply to the court on one or both of the following grounds–

(a) that a voluntary arrangement which has taken effect under paragraph 37 unfairly prejudices the interests of a creditor, member or contributory of the company,

(b) that there has been some material irregularity at or in relation to the meeting of the company summoned under paragraph 29, or in relation to the relevant qualifying decision procedure.

38(1A) In this paragraph–

(a) the "relevant qualifying decision procedure" means the qualifying decision procedure in which the creditors decided whether to approve the voluntary arrangement;

(b) references to a decision made in the relevant qualifying decision procedure include any other decision made in that qualifying decision procedure.

38(2) The persons who may apply under this paragraph are–

(a) a person entitled, in accordance with the rules, to vote at the meeting of the company or in the relevant qualifying decision procedure,

(b) a person who would have been entitled, in accordance with the rules, to vote in the relevant qualifying decision procedure if he had had notice of it, and

(c) the nominee.

38(3) An application under this paragraph shall not be made–

(a) after the end of the period of 28 days beginning with the first day on which each of the reports required by paragraph 30(3) and (4) has been made to the court, or

(b) in the case of a person who was not given notice of the relevant qualifying decision procedure, after the end of the period of 28 days beginning with the day on which he became aware that the relevant qualifying decision procedure had taken place,

but (subject to that) an application made by a person within sub-paragraph (2)(b) on the ground that the arrangement prejudices his interests may be made after the arrangement has ceased to have effect, unless it came to an end prematurely.

38(4) Where on an application under this paragraph the court is satisfied as to either of the grounds mentioned in sub-paragraph (1), it may do any of the following–

(a) revoke or suspend–

(i) any decision approving the voluntary arrangement which has effect under paragraph 36, or

(ii) in a case falling within sub-paragraph (1)(b) any decision taken by the meeting of the company, or in the relevant qualifying decision procedure, which has effect under that paragraph,

(b) give a direction to any person–

(i) for the summoning of a further company meeting to consider any revised proposal for a voluntary arrangement which the directors may make, or

(ii) in a case falling within sub-paragraph (1)(b) and relating to the company meeting for the summoning of a further company meeting to reconsider the original proposal.

(c) direct any person–

(i) to seek a decision from the company's creditors (using a qualifying decision procedure) as to whether they approve any revised proposal for a voluntary arrangement which the directors may make, or

(ii) in a case falling within sub-paragraph (1)(b) and relating to the relevant qualifying decision procedure, to seek a decision from the company's creditors (using a qualifying decision procedure) as to whether they approve the original proposal.

38(5) Where at any time after giving a direction under sub-paragraph (4)(b)(i) or (c)(i) the court is satisfied that the directors do not intend to submit a revised proposal, the court shall revoke the direction and revoke or suspend any decision approving the voluntary arrangement which has effect under paragraph 36.

38(6) Where the court gives a direction under sub-paragraph (4)(b) or (c), it may also give a direction continuing or, as the case may require, renewing, for such period as may be specified in the direction, the effect of the moratorium.

38(7) Sub-paragraph (8) applies in a case where the court, on an application under this paragraph–

(a) gives a direction under sub-paragraph (4)(b) or (c), or

(b) revokes or suspends a decision under sub-paragraph (4)(a) or (5).

38(8) In such a case, the court may give such supplemental directions as it thinks fit and, in particular, directions with respect to–

(a) things done under the voluntary arrangement since it took effect, and

(b) such things done since that time as could not have been done if a moratorium had been in force in relation to the company when they were done.

38(9) Except in pursuance of the preceding provisions of this paragraph,

(a) a decision taken at a meeting summoned under paragraph 29 is not invalidated by any irregularity at or in relation to the meeting, and

(b) a decision of the company's creditors made in the relevant qualifying decision procedure is not invalidated by any irregularity in relation to the relevant qualifying decision procedure.

Implementation of voluntary arrangement

39(1) This paragraph applies where a voluntary arrangement has taken effect under paragraph 37.

39(2) The person who is for the time being carrying out in relation to the voluntary arrangement the functions conferred–

(a) by virtue of the approval of the arrangement, on the nominee, or

(b) by virtue of paragraph 31(2), on a person other than the nominee,

shall be known as the supervisor of the voluntary arrangement.

39(3) If any of the company's creditors or any other person is dissatisfied by any act, omission or decision of the supervisor, he may apply to the court.

39(4) On an application under sub-paragraph (3) the court may–

(a) confirm, reverse or modify any act or decision of the supervisor,

(b) give him directions, or

(c) make such other order as it thinks fit.

39(5) The supervisor–

(a) may apply to the court for directions in relation to any particular matter arising under the voluntary arrangement, and

(b) is included among the persons who may apply to the court for the winding up of the company or for an administration order to be made in relation to it.

39(6) The court may, whenever–

(a) it is expedient to appoint a person to carry out the functions of the supervisor, and

(b) it is inexpedient, difficult or impracticable for an appointment to be made without the assistance of the court,

make an order appointing a person who is qualified to act as an insolvency practitioner in relation to the voluntary arrangement, either in substitution for the existing supervisor or to fill a vacancy.

39(7) The power conferred by sub-paragraph (6) is exercisable so as to increase the number of persons exercising the functions of supervisor or, where there is more than one person exercising those functions, so as to replace one or more of those persons.

Part VI

Miscellaneous

Challenge of directors' actions

40(1) This paragraph applies in relation to acts or omissions of the directors of a company during a moratorium.

40(2) A creditor or member of the company may apply to the court for an order under this paragraph on the ground–

(a) that the company's affairs, business and property are being or have been managed by the directors in a manner which is unfairly prejudicial to the interests of its creditors or members generally, or of some part of its creditors or members (including at least the petitioner), or

(b) that any actual or proposed act or omission of the directors is or would be so prejudicial.

40(3) An application for an order under this paragraph may be made during or after the moratorium.

40(4) On an application for an order under this paragraph the court may–

(a) make such order as it thinks fit for giving relief in respect of the matters complained of,

(b) adjourn the hearing conditionally or unconditionally, or

(c) make an interim order or any other order that it thinks fit.

40(5) An order under this paragraph may in particular–

(a) regulate the management by the directors of the company's affairs, business and property during the remainder of the moratorium,

(b) require the directors to refrain from doing or continuing an act complained of by the petitioner, or to do an act which the petitioner has complained they have omitted to do,

(c) require the summoning of a meeting of members for the purpose of considering such matters as the court may direct,

(ca) require a decision of the company's creditors to be sought (using a qualifying decision procedure) on such matters as the court may direct,

(d) bring the moratorium to an end and make such consequential provision as the court thinks fit.

40(6) In making an order under this paragraph the court shall have regard to the need to safeguard the interests of persons who have dealt with the company in good faith and for value.

40(7) Sub-paragraph (8) applies where–

(a) the appointment of an administrator has effect in relation to the company and that appointment was in pursuance of–

(i) an administration application made, or

(ii) a notice of intention to appoint filed,

before the moratorium came into force, or

(b) the company is being wound up in pursuance of a petition presented before the moratorium came into force.

40(8) No application for an order under this paragraph may be made by a creditor or member of the company; but such an application may be made instead by the administrator or (as the case may be) the liquidator.

Offences

41(1) This paragraph applies where a moratorium has been obtained for a company.

41(2) If, within the period of 12 months ending with the day on which the moratorium came into force, a person who was at the time an officer of the company–

(a) did any of the things mentioned in paragraphs (a) to (f) of sub-paragraph (4), or

(b) was privy to the doing by others of any of the things mentioned in paragraphs (c), (d) and (e) of that sub-paragraph,

he is to be treated as having committed an offence at that time.

41(3) If, at any time during the moratorium, a person who is an officer of the company–

(a) does any of the things mentioned in paragraphs (a) to (f) of sub-paragraph (4), or

(b) is privy to the doing by others of any of the things mentioned in paragraphs (c), (d) and (e) of that sub-paragraph,

he commits an offence.

41(4) Those things are–

(a) concealing any part of the company's property to the value of £500 or more, or concealing any debt due to or from the company, or

(b) fraudulently removing any part of the company's property to the value of £500 or more, or

(c) concealing, destroying, mutilating or falsifying any book or paper affecting or relating to the company's property or affairs, or

(d) making any false entry in any book or paper affecting or relating to the company's property or affairs, or

(e) fraudulently parting with, altering or making any omission in any document affecting or relating to the company's property or affairs, or

(f) pawning, pledging or disposing of any property of the company which has been obtained on credit and has not been paid for (unless the pawning, pledging or disposal was in the ordinary way of the company's business).

41(5) For the purposes of this paragraph, "officer" includes a shadow director.

41(6) It is a defence–

(a) for a person charged under sub-paragraph (2) or (3) in respect of the things mentioned in paragraph (a) or (f) of sub-paragraph (4) to prove that he had no intent to defraud, and

(b) for a person charged under sub-paragraph (2) or (3) in respect of the things mentioned in paragraph (c) or (d) of sub-paragraph (4) to prove that he had no intent to conceal the state of affairs of the company or to defeat the law.

41(7) Where a person pawns, pledges or disposes of any property of a company in circumstances which amount to an offence under sub-paragraph (2) or (3), every person who takes in pawn or pledge, or otherwise receives, the property knowing it to be pawned, pledged or disposed of in circumstances which–

(a) would, if a moratorium were obtained for the company within the period of 12 months beginning with the day on which the pawning, pledging or disposal took place, amount to an offence under sub-paragraph (2), or

(b) amount to an offence under sub-paragraph (3),

commits an offence.

41(8) A person guilty of an offence under this paragraph is liable to imprisonment or a fine, or both.

41(9) The money sums specified in paragraphs (a) and (b) of sub-paragraph (4) are subject to increase or reduction by order under section 417A in Part XV.

42(1) If, for the purpose of obtaining a moratorium, or an extension of a moratorium, for a company, a person who is an officer of the company–

(a) makes any false representation, or

(b) fraudulently does, or omits to do, anything,

he commits an offence.

42(2) Sub-paragraph (1) applies even if no moratorium or extension is obtained.

42(3) For the purposes of this paragraph, "officer" includes a shadow director.

42(4) A person guilty of an offence under this paragraph is liable to imprisonment or a fine, or both.

Void provisions in floating charge documents

43(1) A provision in an instrument creating a floating charge is void if it provides for–

(a) obtaining a moratorium, or

(b) anything done with a view to obtaining a moratorium (including any preliminary decision or investigation),

to be an event causing the floating charge to crystallise or causing restrictions which would not otherwise apply to be imposed on the disposal of property by the company or a ground for the appointment of a receiver.

43(2) In sub-paragraph (1), "receiver" includes a manager and a person who is appointed both receiver and manager.

Functions of the Financial Conduct Authority and Prudential Regulation Authority

44(1) This Schedule has effect in relation to a moratorium for a regulated company with the modifications in sub-paragraphs (2) to (16) below.

44(2) Any notice or other document required by virtue of this Schedule to be sent to a creditor of a regulated company must also be sent to the appropriate regulator.

44(3) The appropriate regulator is entitled to be heard on any application to the court for leave under paragraph 20(2) or 20(3) (disposal of charged property, etc.).

44(4) Where paragraph 26(1) (challenge of nominee's actions, etc.) applies, the persons who may apply to the court include the appropriate regulator.

44(5) If a person other than a regulator applies to the court under that paragraph, the appropriate regulator is entitled to be heard on the application.

44(6) Where paragraph 27(1) (challenge of nominee's actions, etc.) applies, the persons who may apply to the court include the appropriate regulator.

44(7) If a person other than a regulator applies to the court under that paragraph, the appropriate regulator is entitled to be heard on the application.

44(8) The appropriate regulator must be given notice of any qualifying decision procedure by which a decision of the company's creditors is sought for the purposes of this Schedule.

44(8A) The appropriate regulator, or a person appointed by the appropriate regulator, may in the way provided for by the rules participate in (but not vote in) any qualifying decision procedure by which a decision of the company's creditors is sought for the purposes of this Schedule.

44(9) A person appointed for the purpose by the appropriate regulator is entitled to attend and participate in (but not to vote at)–

(a) any creditors' meeting summoned under that paragraph,

(b) any meeting of a committee established under paragraph 35 (moratorium committee).

44(10) The appropriate regulator is entitled to be heard on any application under paragraph 36(3) (effectiveness of decisions).

44(11) Where paragraph 38(1) (challenge of decisions) applies, the persons who may apply to the court include the appropriate regulator.

44(12) If a person other than a regulator applies to the court under that paragraph, the appropriate regulator is entitled to be heard on the application.

44(13) Where paragraph 39(3) (implementation of voluntary arrangement) applies, the persons who may apply to the court include the appropriate regulator.

44(14) If a person other than a regulator applies to the court under that paragraph, the appropriate regulator is entitled to be heard on the application.

44(15) Where paragraph 40(2) (challenge of directors' actions) applies, the persons who may apply to the court include the appropriate regulator.

44(16) If a person other than a regulator applies to the court under that paragraph, the appropriate regulator is entitled to be heard on the application.

44(16A) If either regulator makes an application to the court under any of the provisions mentioned in sub-paragraphs (5), (7), (12), (14) or (16) in relation to a PRA-regulated company, the other regulator is entitled to be heard on the application.

44(17) This paragraph does not prejudice any right the appropriate regulator has (apart from this paragraph) as a creditor of a regulated company.

44(17A) "The appropriate regulator" means–

(a) for the purposes of sub-paragraphs (2) to (8) and (10) to (17)–

(i) where the regulated company is a PRA-regulated company, each of the Financial Conduct Authority and the Prudential Regulation Authority, and

(ii) in any other case, the Financial Conduct Authority;

(b) for the purposes of sub-paragraphs (8A) and (9)–

(i) where the regulated company is a PRA-regulated company, the Financial Conduct Authority or the Prudential Regulation Authority, and

(ii) in any other case, the Financial Conduct Authority.

44(18) In this paragraph–

"PRA-authorised person" has the meaning given by section 2B(5) of the Financial Services and Markets Act 2000;

"PRA-regulated activity" has the meaning given by section 22A of the Financial Services and Markets Act 2000;

"PRA-regulated company" means a regulated company which–

(a) is, or has been, a PRA-authorised person,

(b) is, or has been, an appointed representative within the meaning given by section 39 of the Financial Services and Markets Act 2000, whose principal (or one of whose principals) is, or was, a PRA-authorised person, or

(c) is carrying on, or has carried on, a PRA-regulated activity in contravention of the general prohibition;

"regulated company" means a company which–

(a) is, or has been, an authorised person within the meaning given by section 31 of the Financial Services and Markets Act 2000,

(b) is, or has been, an appointed representative within the meaning given by section 39 of that Act, or

(c) is carrying on, or has carried on, a regulated activity, within the meaning given by section 22 of that Act, in contravention of the general prohibition within the meaning given by section 19 of that Act.

"regulator" means the Financial Conduct Authority or the Prudential Regulation Authority.

Subordinate legislation

45(1) Regulations or an order made by the Secretary of State under this Schedule may make different provision for different cases.

45(2) Regulations so made may make such consequential, incidental, supplemental and transitional provision as may appear to the Secretary of State necessary or expedient.

45(3) Any power of the Secretary of State to make regulations under this Schedule may be exercised by amending or repealing any enactment contained in this Act (including one contained in this Schedule) or contained in the Company Directors Disqualification Act 1986.

45(4) Regulations (except regulations under paragraph 5) or an order made by the Secretary of State under this Schedule shall be made by statutory instrument subject to annulment in pursuance of a resolution of either House of Parliament.

45(5) Regulations under paragraph 5 of this Schedule are to be made by statutory instrument and shall only be made if a draft containing the regulations has been laid before and approved by resolution of each House of Parliament.

General Note

On close examination of Sch.A1, we find that this moratorium facility is restricted to "eligible" companies, i.e. small companies, excluding companies such as banks, insurance companies, companies involved with the performance of market contracts. A small company is defined by s.382(3) of CA 2006 as one which fulfils two of the following three conditions:

(a) turnover not more than £6.5 million;

(b) balance sheet total not more than £3.26 million; and

(c) having not more than 50 employees.

These criteria (which apply to any filing after 6 April 2008) may be changed in the future through delegated legislation. The new criteria are specified in the Companies Act 2006 (Amendment) (Account and Reports) Regulations 2008 (SI 2008/393). Possible changes in eligibility might bring larger companies within the catchment and deal with the technical issue of "special purpose vehicle companies" for whom this reform has posed difficulties (see Livingston (2000) 16 I.L. & P. 189). This latter problem has been recognised by the Government (see *Hansard*, HC Vol.355, cols 163–4)—note the further exceptions introduced via paras 4A–4K (see note to s.1A). For consideration of step in rights (para.4K) see *Cabvision Ltd v Feetum* [2005] EWCA Civ 1601; [2006] B.C.C. 340 (a ruling on s.72E).

The new CVA with moratorium also cannot operate where the company is already undergoing administration, administrative receivership or liquidation (including provisional liquidation). The moratorium is also denied to a company currently undergoing a CVA and also to one which has already had recourse to such protection in the previous 12 months. It is estimated that some 38 per cent of all companies may access this new CVA moratorium model. Notwithstanding this potential constituency the procedure has hardly been used.

In order to obtain the CVA moratorium the directors must prepare documents and submit these to the nominee. Subsequently, these documents, accompanied by the nominee's statement, must be submitted by the directors to the court. The nominee must state whether there is a reasonable prospect of the purpose being approved and implemented. The test of "reasonable prospect" for these purposes will presumably be the same as that laid down in administration order cases in *Re Harris Simons Construction Ltd* [1989] 1 W.L.R. 368. The nominee in promoting the proposal is entitled to rely on information provided by the directors and it is an offence for company officers to seek to obtain a moratorium by false representations (para.42). The filing of these documents triggers an initial moratorium (para.8) that will last 28 days or until the creditors' meeting is held. Extensions for a further two months are possible under para.32. No court order as such is required to initiate the moratorium. The moratorium is to be advertised and any creditor who has petitioned for winding up must be personally notified.

The moratorium has the standard incidents found in corporate insolvency law of excluding most hostile actions against the company (see para.12). Proceedings on extant winding-up petitions are stayed and the disabling effect of s.127 of IA 1986 does not operate, though certain restrictions are imposed on the directors' freedom of action during the currency of the moratorium. However, petitions presented to wind up a company in the public interest are not to be obstructed. The effect of the moratorium upon the rights of the floating-charge holder is dealt with in some detail by para.13. Debenture provisions allowing a floating charge to crystallise on the taking of preparatory steps to obtain a moratorium are void (para.43). In this sense this legislation is to have retrospective effect. There is an interesting contrast with administration where the floating charge holder has a right of veto—see *Re Croftbell Ltd* [1990] B.C.C. 781. The exclusion of traditional remedies exercised by secured creditors in the new CVA moratorium has aroused concern, but in practice banks often choose not to exercise such remedies. See Milman and Chittenden, *Corporate Rescue—CVAs and the Challenge of Small Companies*, ACCA Research Report No.44 (1995). This abstinence has become even more noticeable since the advent of the Bankers' Code of Practice in July 1997 under which banks undertake to support business rescues. In any case, banks may still exert considerable influence because they are not obliged to offer continued funding; if the funding for the rescue is not available the nominee must terminate the moratorium (see *Hansard*, HL Vol.613, CWH 13). In addition to the curbs on security enforcement, one effect of the moratorium is that security rights may be overridden with the leave of the court (see para.20). Section 233 of IA 1986 is extended forward to prevent "blackmail" by utility suppliers during the preliminary moratorium period (this prohibition already operates once the CVA has been agreed).

The directors may provide additional security during the moratorium but this will only be enforceable if it is for the benefit of the company (e.g. it has produced rescue funding).

An interesting feature of the moratorium is that it constrains managerial actions on obtaining credit of more than £250 (unless the credit provider has been informed of the moratorium) and also when disposing of property. With regard to the obtaining of credit the case law under IA 1986 s.360 may be relevant. There must be reasonable grounds for believing that the disposal will benefit the company and the nominee (or creditors' committee appointed under para.35) must give approval. Where the directors exceed their limited powers during this period the transaction is not rendered unenforceable (see para.15), though the directors may incur penalties (para.18(3)). Certain other prejudicial conduct by directors in the 12 months prior to the moratorium may be subject to criminal sanction (para.41). The figure of £500 in para.41(4) has been the subject of much parliamentary debate and has been criticised for being arbitrary. Although the Government has stoutly defended its usage, it has nevertheless indicated that the figure could be revised if a problem arose (*Hansard*, HC Standing Committee B, 2 November 2000, col.75). The actions of directors may be challenged by creditors on the grounds of unfair prejudice (para.40). These provisions are clearly designed to prevent abuse of the moratorium facility. Moreover, the nominee is expected to assume a monitoring role during this critical period (para.24).

The actions of the nominee during the moratorium are open to challenge (paras 26 and 27). Nominees must withdraw their consent to act under certain conditions set out in para.25. The court can also replace the nominee.

Part V deals with the consideration and implementation of the proposed CVA. These provisions mirror those found in Pt I of IA 1986.

Paragraph 3(2) was amended in 2008 to drop the reference to s.247 of the Companies Act 1985 and instead to substitute a reference to s.382 of the Companies Act 2006—see the Companies Act 2006 (Consequential Amendments, etc.) Order 2008 (SI 2008/948).

Note the Companies Act 2006 (Consequential Amendments, Transitional Provisions and Savings) Order 2009 (SI 2009/1941) amended para.3(6) to cater for the enactment of the Companies Act 2006. Effective from 1 October 2009.

Minor amendments were made to paras 4E(1) and 4F(3) by the Financial Services and Markets Act 2000 (Regulated Activities) (Amendment) Order 2010 (SI 2010/86).

Paragraph 12(1)(d), (da) substituted for the former para.12(1)(d) by the Enterprise Act 2002 s.248(3) Sch.17 paras 9, 37(1), (3) as from 15 September 2003 (see the Enterprise Act 2003 (Commencement No.4 and Transitional

Provisions and Savings) Order 2003 (SI 2003/2093 (C. 85)) art.2(1), Sch.1), subject to transitional provisions in SI 2003/2093 (C. 85), art.3. The amendment has no effect in relation to certain companies by virtue of the Enterprise Act 2002 s.249(1).

Paragraph 12(1)(b) modified as from 26 December 2003 by the Financial Collateral Arrangements (No.2) Regulations 2003 (SI 2003/3226) reg.8(5).

In para.12(5)(a) the words "or 124B" inserted by the European Public Limited-Liability Company Regulations (SI 2004/2326) reg.73(4)(b) as from 8 October 2004.

Paragraph 12(5)(d) inserted by the Financial Services and Markets Act 2000 (Consequential Amendments) Order 2002 (SI 2002/1555) arts 1, 30 as from 3 July 2002.

Paragraph 16(1) was replaced by the Companies (Trading Disclosures) (Insolvency) Regulations 2008 with effect from 1 October 2008. This substitution was necessary to ensure compliance with EC Directive 2003/58 and is intended to promote disclosure where invoices are in electronic form and where the company has a website.

Paragraphs 20(8) and 34(2) were subject to a minor amendment by the Companies Act 2006 (Consequential Amendments, Transitional Provisions and Savings) Order 2009 (SI 2009/1941). Effective from 1 October 2009.

Paragraph 31 was amended by the Banks and Building Societies (Depositor Preference and Priorities) Order 2014 (SI 2014/3486) with effect from 1 January 2015. The amendment relates to the new categorisation of the different types of preferential debt.

Paragraph 40(7)(a) was amended by the Enterprise Act 2002 (Insolvency) Order 2004 (SI 2004/2312) from 15 October 2004 to reflect the new administration procedure.

A number of minor amendments (including the addition of a new subparas (16A) and (17A)) are made to para.44 by the Financial Services Act 2012 Sch.18.

Note amendment made to paras 28, 31, 33 and 39 by DA 2015 s.19 and Sch.6.

Numerous changes were made to this Schedule when SBEEA 2015 s.126 and Sch.9 took effect. These changes reflect the broader range of creditor decision procedures.

Schedule B1

Administration

Introductory note to Schedule B1

Schedule B1 was inserted into IA 1986 by EA 2002 s.248, (1), (2), with effect from 15 September 2003 (see the Enterprise Act 2002 (Commencement No.4 and Transitional Provisions and Savings) Order 2003 (SI 2003/2093 (C. 85)) art.2(1) and Sch.(1), introducing a new Pt II and inaugurating a wholly new corporate administration regime. Section 248 states that the new Pt II shall "be substituted" for the original Pt II, but this does not mean that the original Pt II is repealed, for s.249, immediately following, reinstates the latter for many purposes. (See the Introductory note to the new Part II.) The original Pt II and the accompanying rules, with annotations, are to be found in the 19th edition of this *Guide*, Vol.2.

The Insolvency (Amendment) Rules 2003 (SI 2003/1730, also effective 15 September 2003) r.5 complements Sch.B1 by substituting a new Pt 2 of the Rules for the original Pt 2 of IR 1986. However, as with Pt II of the Act, the original Pt 2 of the Rules is preserved for those cases where a company or other body is put into administration under the original Pt II. There are thus two sets of rules governing corporate administrations; and, confusingly, the rules of each Pt 2 were similarly (but not correspondingly) numbered. All references to the rules in this annotation to Sch.B1 are to the substituted rules as now consolidated into the Insolvency (England and Wales) Rules 2016, unless otherwise stated.

Although Sch.B1 applies both in England and Wales and in Scotland, a company can only enter administration, by any of the statutory procedures, in the jurisdiction of its incorporation (i.e. a Scottish company must do so in Scotland): *Re Brownridge Plastics Ltd* (unreported), referred to in *Dear IP*, December 2005, and now see *Bank Leumi (UK) plc, Petitioner* [2017] CSOH 129; [2017] B.C.C. 753.

Schedule B1 applies (with modifications) to insurance companies, except that the appointment of an administrator can only be made by court order: see the Financial Services and Markets Act 2000 (Administration Orders Relating to Insurers) Order 2010 (SI 2010/3023) art.2 (replacing as from 1 February 2011 the Financial Services and Markets Act 2000 (Administration Orders Relating to Insurers) Order 2002 (SI 2002/1242) art.3) and the note to para.9.

The Insolvency Service early in 2003 issued a consultation paper proposing that the new Pt II regime should be extended to insolvent partnerships, and this was done by the Insolvent Partnerships (Amendment) Order 2005 (SI 2005/1516), operative from 1 July 2005; the Insolvent Partnerships Order 1994 (SI 1994/2421) was further amended by the Insolvency (Miscellaneous Amendments) Regulations 2017 (SI 2017/1119) as from 8 December 2017.

Similar amendments to the Limited Liability Partnerships Regulations 2001 were made by SI 2005/1989 with effect from 1 October 2005 and again by SI 2017/1119 as from 8 December 2017. Thus from 8 December 2017 the relevant provisions of IR 2016 (as modified) apply to insolvent partnerships and LLPs. Building society administrations continue to be regulated by the original Pt II.

Banks and the other bodies mentioned in IA 1986 s.422(1) which are companies within the meaning of CA 2006 ss.1(1), 1171 have also been brought within the new Pt II (see the Banks (Former Authorised Institutions) (Insolvency) Order 2006 (SI 2006/3107), effective 15 December 2006). Previously the original Pt II had governed administrations relating to these bodies by virtue of the Banks (Administration Proceedings) Order 1989 (SI 1989/1276, as amended). The 2006 Order art.3 and Sch., provides that certain modifications shall be applied to Pt II in relation to the application of the administration procedure to these institutions. In particular, these modifications confer rights on the Financial Conduct Authority or the Prudential Regulation Authority (as appropriate) to participate in the proceedings. In contrast with the legislation governing insurance companies, these bodies may be put into administration without a court order (but the consent of the FCA and the PRA must be obtained and filed in court (Sch. para.5)). The Banking Act 2009 introduces a special form of administration where a bank or building society encounters financial difficulties leading to government intervention, and similar provision has been made for investment banks by the Investment Bank Special Administration Regulations 2011 (SI 2011/245). This new procedure may be put in place by court order to deal with the remaining assets where there has been a partial transfer of business from a failing bank. The Act and the Rules are extensively modified for the purposes of this legislation. See further p.6 above.

The Financial Services (Banking Reform) Act 2013 Pt 6 (when in force from a day to be appointed) will introduce a "financial market infrastructure (FMI) administration" in relation to infrastructure companies. Such a company is defined as a company which is the operator of a recognised inter-bank payment system (unless excluded) which is approved under regulations under CA 2006 s.785 as the operator of a securities settlement system, or a company designated as such by the Treasury.

The Energy Act 2004 s.159 and Schs 20, 21, as extended and modified by the Energy Act 2011 ss.93–102, establishes a special administration regime for bodies licensed to supply energy under that Act, and applies the provisions of Sch.B1 (with modifications) to such bodies. This regime is designed to ensure that energy supplies are maintained where a licensee becomes insolvent. For an interesting decision on this point, involving an urgent Chancery Division hearing conducted by telephone on a Saturday evening, see *Gas and Electricity Markets Authority v GB Energy Supply Ltd* [2016] EWHC 3341 (Ch). For the relevant rules, see the Energy Administration Rules 2005 (SI 2005/2483), effective 1 October 2005 and the Energy Supply Company Administration Rules 2013 (SI 2013/1046), effective 7 June 2013. For Scotland, see the Energy Supply Company Administration (Scotland) Rules 2013 (SI 2013/1047), also effective 7 June 2013. A special insolvency regime for companies that are designated under the Postal Services Act 2011 s.35 as universal postal service providers is in force as from 31 January 2014, under the Postal Administration Rules 2013 (SI 2013/3208). The main features of postal administration are that the company enters the procedure only by a court order on application by the Secretary of State or (with his consent) by OFCOM; the order appoints a postal administrator; the objective is to secure that a universal postal service is provided in accordance with the standards set out in the universal postal service order; and in other respects the process is the same as for normal administration under IA 1986, subject to certain modifications. A modified administration regime has also been introduced to cater for public–private partnerships: see the PPP Administration Order Rules 2007 (SI 2007/3141), effective 30 November 2007 and, for a case not brought under these rules but under the Greater London Authority Act 1999 Sch.15, *Re Metronet Rail BCV Ltd* [2008] 1 B.C.L.C. 760.

The administration regime did not formerly apply to Industrial and Provident Societies: *Re Dairy Farmers of Britain Ltd* [2009] EWHC 1389 (Ch); [2010] Ch. 63; [2010] B.C.C. 637, but by the Industrial and Provident Societies and Credit Unions (Arrangements, Reconstructions and Administration) Order 2014 (SI 2014/229), which came into force on 6 April 2014, the provisions of Sch.B1 (as modified) were extended to all societies registered under the Industrial and Provident Societies Act 1965, apart from any society which was a private registered provider of social housing or registered as a social landlord. (Note that the 1965 Act was superseded by the Co-operative and Community Benefit Societies Act 2014 as from 1 August 2014, and from that date SI 2014/229 was renamed the Co-operative and Community Benefit Societies and Credit Unions (Arrangements, Reconstructions and Administration) Order. Extensive changes have been made to the wording of SI 2014/229 by the Co-operative and Community Benefit Societies and Credit Unions (Arrangements, Reconstructions and Administration) (Amendment) Order 2014 (SI 2014/1822) as from 1 August 2014.)

The new administration regime has not only succeeded in displacing administrative receivership as the primary method available to a floating charge holder to enforce his security, but is also proving to be a popular alternative to a creditors' voluntary winding up in the insolvency of smaller companies, because of its flexibility and informality. The latest (estimated) figure available for 2017 indicate that there were 1,289 administrations compared with only 292

CVAs, and a paltry two administrative receiverships.

As was to be expected when a new and complex regime was introduced, Sch.B1 has encountered a number of teething problems. These have been met, and generally resolved, by judges adopting a bold and purposive approach, as (for instance) by Blackburne J in *Re Ballast plc* [2004] EWHC 2356 (Ch); [2005] B.C.C. 96; by Lawrence Collins J in *Re Transbus International Ltd* [2004] EWHC 932 (Ch); [2004] B.C.C. 401; and by rulings on paras 83–84.

A considerable number of changes have been made to the law governing administrations by SBEEA 2015, which received the Royal Assent on 26 March 2015. The first tranche of reforms, which came into effect in time to be incorporated into the 19th edition of this work, included the following:

- empowering an administrator to bring an action for fraudulent or wrongful trading;
- authorising an administrator to assign a cause of action (such as for fraudulent trading) vested in him by statute;
- debarring a floating charge holder from making a claim against the proceeds of an action brought by an administrator (or assignee) in exercise of specified statutory powers;
- imposing restrictions or conditions on the sale of the company's business by an administrator to connected persons;
- abolition of the requirement to hold creditors' meetings;
- allowing creditors to opt not to receive notices;
- excusing creditors with small debts from the need to submit a proof;
- increasing the period for which an administration may be extended without a court order from six months to one year.

The remaining provisions of SBEEA 2015 dealing with administrations were brought into effect by the Small Business, Enterprise and Employment Act 2015 (Commencement No.6 and Transitional and Savings Provisions) Regulations 2016 (SI 2016/1020) as from 1 October 2016. Further changes are introduced by new IR 2016, operative from 6 April 2017. These reforms include the following:

- abandoning the use of physical meetings of contributories and creditors (in most cases) and substituting other "decision procedures";
- abolition of the requirement to hold final meetings;
- enabling creditors to opt not to receive notices;
- discontinuing the use of prescribed forms.

As well as these more substantive changes, SBEEA 2015 has made consequential and minor amendments, mostly of a purely verbal nature, to very many sections in this part of the Act. Such alterations have been made in the text which follows without detailed annotation.

These reforms do not affect administrations established under the original Pt II. Whether the changes apply to bodies other than companies (e.g. building societies) is uncertain. Curiously, although IR 2016 were originally declared not to apply to LLPs (see the Insolvency (England and Wales) Rules 2016 (Consequential Amendments and Savings) Rules 2017 (SI 2017/369) r.3(b)), although there was no similar exclusion of LLPs in the Insolvency Act itself and it was not made clear in SBEEA 2015 itself. However what may have originally been an oversight was eventually cured by SI 2017/1119 mentioned above extending IR 2016 to LLPs as from 8 December 2017.

Overview of Schedule B1

NATURE OF ADMINISTRATION

Administration

1. [Definitions of "administrator", "in administration", "enters administration" etc.]
2. [How administrator may be appointed]

Purpose of administration

3. [Specified objectives]
4. [Duty of administrator]

Status of administrator

5.

General restrictions

6. [Qualification of administrator]
7. [No appointment where company already in administration]
8. [No appointment if company in liquidation]
9. [Banking and insurance companies]

APPOINTMENT OF ADMINISTRATOR BY COURT

Administration order

10.

Conditions for making order

11.

Administration application

12.

Powers of court

13.

APPOINTMENT OF ADMINISTRATOR BY HOLDER OF FLOATING CHARGE

Power to appoint

14.

Restrictions on power to appoint

15. [Notice to prior floating charge holder]
16. [No appointment if floating charge unenforceable]
17. [No appointment where provisional liquidator of administrative receiver]

Notice of appointment

18.

Commencement of appointment

19. [Commencement under notice in para.18]
20. [Appointor to notify administrator]

Invalid appointment: indemnity

21.

APPOINTMENT OF ADMINISTRATOR BY COMPANY OR DIRECTORS

Power to appoint

22.

Restrictions on power to appoint

23. [No appointment within 12 months of previous administration]
24. [No appointment within 12 months of Sch.A1 moratorium]
25. [No appointment if winding-up petition or administration application undisposed or where administrative receiver]

25A. [Exception to para.25 where petition already presented]

Notice of intention to appoint

26. [Length of notice and to whom to be given]
27. [Copy of notice to court with statutory declaration]
28. [Time limit for notice]

Notice of appointment

29. [Notice and other documents to court]
30. [Statutory declaration where no notice under para.26(1)]

Commencement of appointment

31. [Appointment effective when notice and documents filed in court]
32. [Appointor to notify administrator para.29 satisfied]
33. [Appointment ineffective if prior administration order or floating charge holder appointment]

Invalid appointment: indemnity

34.

ADMINISTRATION APPLICATION—SPECIAL CASES

Application by holder of floating charge

35.

Intervention by holder of floating charge

36.

Application where company in liquidation

37. [Administration superseding compulsory liquidation on application of floating charge holder]
38. [Power of liquidator to make administration application]

ENDING ADMINISTRATION

Automatic end of administration

76. [Appointment to cease after one year subject to extension]
77. [Extension by court order during administration]
78. [Extension by consent]

Court ending administration on application of administrator

79.

Termination of administration where objective achieved

80.

Court ending administration on application of creditor

81.

Public interest winding-up

82.

Moving from administration to creditors' voluntary liquidation

83.

Moving from administration to dissolution

84.

Discharge of administration order where administration ends

85.

Notice to Companies Registrar where administration ends

86.

REPLACING ADMINISTRATOR

Resignation of administrator

87.

Removal of administrator from office

88.

Administrator ceasing to be qualified

89.

Supplying vacancy in office of administrator

90. [Vacancy by death resignation, removal or vacation of office]
91. [Replacement by the court]
92. [Replacement by floating charge holder]
93. [Replacement by company]
94. [Replacement by directors]
95. [When court may make replacement]

Substitution of administrator: competing floating charge-holder

96.

Substitution of administrator appointed by company or directors: creditors' decision

97.

Vacation of office: discharge from liability

98.

Vacation of office: charges and liabilities

99.

GENERAL

Joint and concurrent administrators

100. [General reference]
101. [Reference to persons appointed to act jointly]
102. [Reference to persons appointed to act concurrently]
103. [Who may make joint or concurrent appointment]

Presumption of validity

104.

Majority decision of directors

105.

Penalties

106.

Extension of time limit

107. [Extension by the court]
108. [Extension by administrator with consent]
109. [Reference to period as extended]

Amendment of provision about time

110.

Interpretation

111.

Non-UK companies

111A.

Scotland

112. [References to filing with the court and to charge]
113. [Duty of administrator disposing of property under paras 70 or 71]
114. [Disposal of goods under hire purchase]
115. [Certain payments by administrator]
116. [Priority of certain rights over payment by administrator]

Nature of Administration

Administration

1(1) For the purposes of this Act "administrator" of a company means a person appointed under this Schedule to manage the company's affairs, business and property.

1(2) For the purposes of this Act–

(a) a company is "in administration" while the appointment of an administrator of the company has effect,

(b) a company "enters administration" when the appointment of an administrator takes effect,

(c) a company ceases to be in administration when the appointment of an administrator of the company ceases to have effect in accordance with this Schedule, and

(d) a company does not cease to be in administration merely because an administrator vacates office (by reason of resignation, death or otherwise) or is removed from office.

General Note

The original legislation, s.*8(2)* contains definitions of "administration order" and "administrator" ("an administration order is an order directing that … the affairs, business and property of the company shall be managed by a person ('the administrator') appointed for the purpose by the court"). While the definition of "administrator" remains essentially the same, the new definitions introduced by subpara.(2) are necessary because an administrator can in many cases be appointed under the present Schedule without a court order.

It is only assets beneficially owned by the company which are "property" for the purposes of this definition. Anything held on trust or to which another person is beneficially entitled does not fall within the estate to be managed by the administrator. The same distinction applies in a liquidation, and for convenience the two forms of insolvency proceeding are discussed together in the note to s.107. If the administrator has dealt with property which is not beneficially owned by the company, he may be entitled to be paid his proper expenses and remuneration on the principle established in *Re Berkeley Applegate (Investment Consultants) Ltd (No.2)* [1989] Ch. 32; (1988) 4 B.C.C. 279, discussed in the note to s.115. The principle was applied (in part) in relation to administrators in *Gillan v HEC Enterprises Ltd* [2016] EWHC 3179 (Ch).

These definitions are confined to administrators "appointed under this Schedule". In other cases, the original definitions of "administration order" and "administrator" will continue to apply, by virtue of EA 2002 s.249 and the saving provisions of the Enterprise Act 2002 (Commencement No.4 and Transitional Provisions and Savings) Order 2003 (SI 2003/2093 (C. 85)). See the Introductory note to the new Part II preceding s.8.

Para.1(2)(c), (d)

It is particularly important to note the use of this wording in later provisions of the Schedule, since it is likely to be the source of confusion. The draftsman has throughout chosen to avoid terms such as the "termination" of an administration, or an administration "coming to an end", or a company "ceasing to be in administration" (except in the marginal notes). Instead, in subpara.(2)(c), the circumlocution "the appointment of an administrator ceases to have effect" has been preferred. As is explained in subpara.(2)(d), this does not refer to the ending of the appointment of the particular individual as administrator, but to the ending of the administration itself: in contrast, in the former case, the *office* of administrator continues in being, even though it may for the time being be unoccupied.

2 A person may be appointed as administrator of a company–

(a) by administration order of the court under paragraph 10,

(b) by the holder of a floating charge under paragraph 14, or

(c) by the company or its directors under paragraph 22.

General Note

Under the original legislation, an administrator could only be appointed by court order. The alternative of a direct appointment without application to the court under paras 14 and 22 (sometimes referred to as the "self-certifying route") clearly saves time and expense and has become the norm in the great majority of cases. However, where the administration has a cross-border element there may be uncertainty whether an administrator appointed out of court will be recognised in a foreign jurisdiction, and if there is doubt in this respect it may be thought prudent to obtain a court appointment. But there should no longer be any such doubts in regard to jurisdictions governed by the EC Regulation, since Annexes A and B have been amended to make it clear that out-of-court appointments are included. The same is true of out-of-court appointments under the CBIR, with this difference: whereas other EU Member States are bound under the EC Regulation to accord recognition to such appointments, nothing in the CBIR imposes any equivalent obligation on a foreign court (unless the country concerned has also enacted the Model Law). It may be helpful in these circumstances to take a course similar to that followed in *Re MG Rover España SA* [2005] B.P.I.R. 1162, and have the court make a supplemental order summarising the effect of an administration order and the administrator's responsibilities and powers.

The Enterprise Act 2002 Sch.17 provides (para.1) that in any instrument made before 1 January 2003 a reference to the making of an administration order shall be read so as to include the appointment of an administrator out of court (and correspondingly with a reference to an application for an administration order by petition). In *William Hare Ltd v Shepherd Construction Ltd* [2009] EWHC 1603 (TCC); [2010] B.C.C. 332 (upheld on appeal [2010] EWCA Civ 283) Coulson J declined to give a similar interpretation to a clause in a construction contract concluded in December 2008 which referred to the making of an administration order under IA 1986 Pt II, and held that it did not apply to an out-of-court appointment.

A practice has developed which is not expressly sanctioned by the legislation and, indeed, might have been regarded as of doubtful legitimacy—the "pre-pack" administration. The pre-pack is not altogether a new concept, since it had regularly been used in receiverships for some time prior to the Enterprise Act. In a pre-pack, the insolvency practitioner who, it is intended, is to become the administrator is involved in planning in advance an arrangement under which the business of the company is to be sold immediately after his appointment, bypassing the statutory procedure of a creditors' meeting, and without any direction from the court. The pre-pack is most appropriate where the insolvency is such that there will be no surplus available for distribution to the company's unsecured creditors and the proposed sale is likely to be advantageous by comparison with what might be yielded if all the statutory formalities were followed.

The main advantage of the procedure is the saving of time and expense and the avoidance of possibly adverse publicity which the statutory formalities would involve. The continuity of the business may preserve goodwill and save jobs, and for this reason may enable the business to be sold for a better price. However, two aspects of the pre-pack have given rise to a degree of concern: in most cases, the company's unsecured creditors are likely to receive no dividend and, secondly, they will usually have had no advance notice of the pre-arranged sale and no opportunity to have a say in the decision-making process. These circumstances are all the more likely to arouse suspicion where, as in many cases, the sale is to the existing management or other "connected" persons. Despite these objections, the pre-pack is now regarded as firmly established. Its legitimacy has been upheld in (inter alia) *DKLL Solicitors v Revenue and Customs* [2007] EWHC 2067 (Ch); [2007] B.C.C. 908, *Innovate Logistics Ltd v Sunberry Properties Ltd* [2008] EWCA Civ 1321; [2009] B.C.C. 164; *Re Kayley Vending Ltd* [2009] EWHC 904 (Ch); [2009] B.C.C. 578; *Re Hellas Telecommunications (Luxembourg) II SCA* [2009] EWHC 3199 (Ch); [2010] B.C.C. 295; *Re Halliwells LLP* [2010] EWHC 2036 (Ch); [2011] B.C.C. 57; *Re Christophorus 3 Ltd* [2014] EWHC 1162 (Ch) (where the judge gave an urgent ruling on the construction of a security document in order to facilitate the pre-pack sale); *Capital for Enterprise Fund A LP v Bibby Financial Services Ltd* [2015] EWHC 2593 (Ch) (challenge to pre-pack sale unsuccessful).

In January 2009 the Insolvency Service sought to address these concerns, which had begun to attract adverse public comment, by issuing a Statement of Insolvency Practice (SIP 16, since republished in revised form, as noted below) which requires insolvency practitioners to adhere to an extra-statutory scheme for the regulation of pre-packs. (The SIP applies only to administration pre-packs.) The principal criticisms were that the process did not allow for the business to be fully marketed, that the directors of a failing company might be influenced to put the company into administration by a desire to purchase the business themselves, free of existing debts, and that there was a lack of transparency, especially so far as creditors were concerned. The SIP obliges the company's administrator to send detailed information to creditors at the earliest opportunity (normally when notifying them of the administration). The document also gives directions to practitioners as to the manner in which the work preparatory to their appointment should be conducted (and if the directors are to acquire an interest under the pre-pack sale, requires the directors to be encouraged to take independent advice); and it reminds them of their statutory duties and general legal liabilities. In *Re Hellas Telecommunications (Luxembourg) II SCA* (above) Lewison J required, as a matter of good practice, that the court should be given the same information (or as much of it as possible) when it was considering an application for the making of an administration order in the context of a pre-pack sale, and it is now virtually obligatory for the initiator of a pre-pack to have complied with SIP 16 if the administration is to have the court's blessing: contrast *Re Hellas Communications Ltd* (above) with (for example) *Clydesdale Financial Services Ltd v Smailes* [2009] EWHC 1745; [2009] B.C.C. 810; and see *Re European Directories (DH6) BV* [2010] EWHC 3472 (Ch); [2012] B.C.C. 46. Even so, compliance with SIP 16 is not necessarily sufficient: *Re UK Steelfixers Ltd* [2012] EWHC 2409 (Ch); [2012] B.C.C. 751.

The Insolvency Service monitored the operation of SIP 16 and published a succession of Reports. In March 2010 it commenced a consultation exercise, with a view to introducing legislative controls if this were thought necessary. However, on 26 January 2012 it was announced in a Ministerial Statement that the Government had decided against seeking to do so, stating that while concerns remain about pre-pack sales, particularly in smaller-value asset sales, the benefit of new controls did not outweigh the overall benefit to business of adhering to the moratorium on regulations affecting micro-business. In March 2013, the Government announced during a Parliamentary debate that an independent review would be launched in the late spring of that year to assemble further evidence on how pre-packs are working in practice and to determine whether further regulatory steps are needed. Details of the review were announced on 15 July 2013. The review was undertaken by Ms Teresa Graham CBE, and her report was published on 16 June 2014. The review identified the need to improve public confidence in the pre-pack procedure and found that, while pre-pack sales are an important tool for rescuing struggling businesses, important changes were needed to increase transparency, boost the survival rates of the new business and improve financial returns.

The recommendations made by the review include:

- Creating a "pre-pack pool" where details of a proposed sale to a connected party can be reviewed by an independent person prior to the sale taking place.
- Requesting connected parties to complete a "viability review" for the new company to improve its chances of success.
- Requiring valuations to be carried out by a professional valuer to increase confidence that the sale is at a fair price.
- Ensuring proper marketing is undertaken in order to maximise sale proceeds.

It was not contemplated that these recommendations will be implemented by legislation, at least initially, but rather be introduced on a "comply or explain" basis. However the review suggested a "back-stop" power to regulate disposal of property to connected persons and this was inserted into Sch.B1 para.60A by SBEEA 2015 s.129(1), (4) as from 29 May 2015 to run for five years from that date, although no regulations have yet been made.

The Graham Review is available at *https://www.gov.uk/government/publications/graham-review-into-pre-pack-administration.*

The Joint Insolvency Committee in January 2015 published a revised draft SIP 16 incorporating the Graham recommendations and launched a consultation exercise seeking views and comments. In due course a revised version of SIP 16 came into force on 1 November 2015 affecting all administration appointments starting on or after that date. This version requires considerably more disclosure of information to creditors and increases the compliance obligations for administrators. On the following day the Pre-pack Pool was launched, comprised of experienced business people able to scrutinise independently pre-pack transactions where the sale is to a connected party. Compliance is on a voluntary basis, and although a negative opinion will not prevent the transaction from proceeding, detailed explanation in the SIP report is required.

The observance of the system under SIP 16 by insolvency practitioners was closely monitored from the outset by the Insolvency Service, which required them to send copies of all SIP notices to it. This monitoring role was handed over to the Recognised Professional Bodies in relation to administrators appointed on or after 1 November 2015, who should send a copy of their SIP 16 disclosures to their own professional body.

The text of SIP 16 is available at *http://www.icaew.com/search?text=SIP+16.*

Running in parallel with SIP 16, and to a degree overlapping with it, is SIP 13, which sets standards for the acquisition of assets by connected persons other than directors. A revised version of SIP 13 was published to come into force on 1 December 2016.

As recommended in the Graham report, compliance with SIP 16 (and in particular those parts dealing with sales to connected persons) has for the time being been established on a voluntary basis, but the government has reserved the power (by para.60A) to impose the recommendations by legislation. See the note to para.60A.

In light of the above developments, the Pension Protection Fund (PPF) on 27 July 2015, published guidance on pre-packs and the PPF's concerns on the potential use of pre-packs, particularly in a "phoenix" situation, to "dump" the company's pension liabilities. *PPF Restructuring and insolvency team: Guidance note 2: Pre-packaged administrations* is available at *http://www.pensionprotectionfund.org.uk/DocumentLibrary/Documents/prepack_guidance_note_jul2015.pdf.*

On 12 December 2017 the Insolvency Service announced that the Government was undertaking an assessment of the impact of the voluntary measures introduced from November 2015 mentioned above to improve the transparency of connected party pre-pack sales in administration and would be contacting a variety of interested parties to seek their views. The assessment will look at the impact of reforms on all connected party sales in administration and will help to inform decisions on whether further regulation is needed when the "sunset" regulation-making power in Sch.B1 para.60A expires on 26 May 2020.

The Rules now make provision for the remuneration and expenses incurred by an insolvency practitioner prior to the appointment of an administrator to be paid as an expense of the administration which follows, if approved by the creditors or creditors' committee (r.3.52). In *Re Kayley Vending Ltd* (above) such a payment was authorised by the court under Sch.B1 para.13; but in *Re Johnson Machine and Tool Co Ltd* [2010] EWHC 582 (Ch); [2010] B.C.C. 382 HHJ Purle QC disallowed similar claims and ruled that the court should authorise payment only if the balance of advantage in putting the company into administration was in the creditors' favour.

The Insolvency Service (*Dear IP*, July 2011, p.1.39) draws attention to the potential breach of the Ethical Code where an administrator's pre-administration expenses are paid to him directly by the purchaser of the insolvent business. Such an arrangement circumvents the protective provisions of IR 2016 r.3.52 and it is recommended that a practitioner who is considering entering into such an arrangement should ensure that appropriate safeguards are put in place to reduce any perceived or actual threat to his objectivity.

In *DKLL Solicitors v Revenue and Customs Commissioners* [2007] EWHC 2067 (Ch); [2007] B.C.C. 908 an insolvent firm of solicitors was faced with a winding-up petition issued by the Revenue, its largest creditor. Two partners in the firm applied to the court for an administration order under para.11 of Sch.B1 which, if made by the court, would involve the dismissal of the Revenue's petition. It had been arranged in advance that, immediately on their appointment, the business of the firm would be sold by the administrators to a newly incorporated limited liability partnership for a consideration which would enable the business to be continued without further funding (which would otherwise not be available). The court approved the proposal and made an administration order, notwithstanding the opposition of the Revenue, which had indicated that if a creditors' meeting were held it would use its votes as the majority creditor to defeat the proposed sale.

Where the company which is the subject of a pre-pack is the lessee of premises there may be difficulties, or at least delay, in transferring the lease to the purchaser of the property. In practice, the latter is commonly allowed to occupy the property under a licence. If, as is likely to be the case, this is a breach of the terms of the lease, the lessor cannot enforce his rights without the consent of the administrator or the leave of the court under para.43(6). See further the note to that provision.

In a further effort to allay concerns, the Insolvency Service has established a hotline which can be used to report instances of suspected abuse: *enforcement.hotline@insolvency.gsi.gov.uk*, tel. 0845 601 3546.

On pre-pack administrations, see further S. Frisby (2007) 23 I.L. & P. 152 and (2008) 227 Co. L.N. 1; (2009) 246 Co. L.N. 1, (2008) 21 Insolv. Int. 154 and (2009) 259 Co. L.N. 1.

Para.2(b)
The power of the holder of a floating charge to appoint an administrative receiver has generally been abrogated by IA 1986 s.72A as from 15 September 2003 (but not with retrospective effect): see the note to that section. Charges created after that date will normally be enforced by the appointment of an administrator under para.14.

Purpose of administration

3(1) The administrator of a company must perform his functions with the objective of–

(a) rescuing the company as a going concern, or

(b) achieving a better result for the company's creditors as a whole than would be likely if the company were wound up (without first being in administration), or

(c) realising property in order to make a distribution to one or more secured or preferential creditors.

3(2) Subject to sub-paragraph (4), the administrator of a company must perform his functions in the interests of the company's creditors as a whole.

3(3) The administrator must perform his functions with the objective specified in sub-paragraph (1)(a) unless he thinks either–

(a) that it is not reasonably practicable to achieve that objective, or

(b) that the objective specified in sub-paragraph (1)(b) would achieve a better result for the company's creditors as a whole.

3(4) The administrator may perform his functions with the objective specified in sub-paragraph (1)(c) only if–

(a) he thinks that it is not reasonably practicable to achieve either of the objectives specified in sub-paragraph (1)(a) and (b), and

(b) he does not unnecessarily harm the interests of the creditors of the company as a whole.

General Note

This paragraph contains one of the major changes introduced by the new administration regime. Under the original regime an order may specify one or more of four alternatives: (a) the survival of the company, and the whole or any part of its undertaking, as a going concern; (b) the approval of a voluntary arrangement under IA 1986 Pt I; (c) the sanctioning of a scheme of arrangement or compromise under CA 1985 s.425 [now CA 2006 Pt 26]; and (d) a more advantageous realisation of the company's assets than would be effected on a winding up. For the new regime this formulation has been entirely replaced, and the new wording is significant in a number of respects. First, and most importantly, there is no longer a choice of alternative purposes but a single hierarchy of objects. All administrations, whether instituted by court order or out of court, and regardless of the purpose of the person seeking or making the appointment of the administrator, are to have the same statutory objectives. The rescue of the company is made a matter of priority, and it is only if the administrator is of the opinion that this is not reasonably practicable or that a better result can be achieved for the company's creditors by pursuing some other course that he is permitted to disregard that primary objective. Paragraph 11(b) of Sch.B1 makes it conditional for the making of an administration order that it is reasonably likely to achieve the "purpose of administration". That purpose is the objectives in para.3(1). Rimer LJ pointed out in *Key2 Law (Surrey) LLP v De'Antiquis* [2011] EWCA Civ 1567; [2012] B.C.C. 375 at [98] that an order may be made where one of the objectives is reasonably likely to be achieved, but "it is fallacious to proceed from that to the conclusion that the purpose of the administration order … is to enable the achieving of that particular objective and that alone. It is not. The order is made for the purpose of administration explained in para.3, which keeps all the administrator's options open; and … an administrator who assumes his office with the thought that he might be able to achieve the purpose of administration in one particular way may quickly find that circumstances compel him to change tack and seek to achieve it in another way". This approach was applied by the Court of Appeal in *R. (on the application of Monarch Airlines Ltd (in admin.)) v Airport Coordination Ltd* [2017] EWCA Civ 1892 at [56].

Next, there is a repeated emphasis in all four subparagraphs on the interests of "the company's creditors as a whole". The purpose of this is not so much to make any change in the law governing administrations as to underline the contrast between administration and receivership, and particularly administrative receivership. It is well established that a receiver's duties are owed primarily to the secured creditor who has appointed him, and that all other interests are subordinated to the obligation to safeguard and enforce that security. Subject only to the statutory rights of the company's preferential creditors, his obligations in respect of the "prescribed part" under s.176A and a duty to act in good faith, a receiver is generally free to realise sufficient assets to pay off the secured debt without any concern for the interests of the company itself or its other creditors. Moreover, the holder of a floating charge over all, or substantially all, of the company's assets has the power under the original law to veto the appointment of an administrator and appoint an administrative receiver instead. EA 2002 no longer gives these secured creditors the whip hand: not only does it remove this power of veto (subject to certain specific exceptions and some transitional provisions: see the note to IA 1986 s.72A), so obliging the holder of a floating charge to appoint an administrator rather than a receiver if he wishes to enforce his security, but it lumps the company's secured and preferential creditors together with all the other creditors and requires the administrator to act in the interests of them all. It is only if the requirements of subpara.(4)(a) can be met that the administrator is permitted to realise assets in order to pay off the preferential and secured creditors (para.(1)(c)), and even then only on condition that he does not unnecessarily harm the interests of the creditors as a whole. The priority traditionally attaching to receivership is thus virtually stood on its head.

Under the TUPE Regulations 2006, the statutory protection accorded to employees who continue to work in the business after a sale of the concern in an insolvency depends on whether or not the proceedings in question have been "instituted with a view to the liquidation of the assets of the transferor" (reg.8(7)). The question whether an administration would fall within this phrase was initially held in *Oakland v Wellswood (Yorkshire) Ltd* [2009] EWCA Civ 1094; [2010] B.C.C. 263 to depend on the facts of the case: if the purpose of the administration was the rescue of the company as a going concern (para.3(1)(a)) it would not, but if it was instituted with a view to the liquidation of the company's assets it would—a "fact-based approach". However, in *OTG Ltd v Barke* [2011] B.C.C. 608 the EAT rejected this approach and ruled that, in all administrations where employees were transferred, reg.8(7) should not apply, as a matter of law. In consequence the employees were entitled to the statutory protection. The Court of Appeal has confirmed that this approach is correct: *Key2 Law (Surrey) LLP v De'Antiquis* [2011] EWCA Civ 1567; [2012] B.C.C. 375. (See also *Pressure Coolers Ltd v Molloy* [2011] B.C.C. 894 (EAT); *Spaceright Europe Ltd v Baillavoine* [2011] EWCA Civ 1565; [2012] I.C.R. 520 and *Crystal Palace FC Ltd v Kavanagh* [2013] EWCA Civ 1410; [2014] B.C.C. 664.) The CJEU has held that Directive 2001/23 (implemented in the UK by the TUPE Regulations) must apply for the benefit of employees in the event of a transfer of an undertaking as part of a pre-pack administration: *Federatie Nederlandse Vakvereniging v Smallsteps BV* (C-126/16).

Para.3(1), (3)

The formula "rescuing the company as a going concern" may be contrasted with the wording under the original legislation, "the survival of *the company, and* the whole or any part of its undertaking, as a going concern". The emphasis placed on the rescue or survival of the company (as distinct from its business or undertaking) is rather curious, for the Cork Committee was firmly of the view that it was only the latter that really mattered. In *Re Rowbotham Baxter Ltd* [1990] B.C.C. 113 at 115, Harman J stated that a proposal involving the sale of a "hived down" company formed to take over part of a company's business could not be brought within the original wording, in view of the words which have been italicised above; and even more plainly it could not come within the new formulation. However, this may in fact make it easier for an administrator to conclude that it is not reasonably practicable to achieve a rescue of the company and so move on to the second statutory objective (achieving a better result for the company's creditors as a whole than would be likely under an immediate winding up).

Paragraph 3(1)(b) was relied on in *Re Logitext UK Ltd* [2004] EWHC 2899 (Ch); [2005] 1 B.C.L.C. 326, where the company had no tangible assets but stood a chance of recovering funds by pursuing claims against alleged wrongdoers. The applicant was an unsecured creditor who was prepared to put up funding to enable the administrator to investigate the case and undertake the litigation, but no similar source of funding was likely if the company were put into liquidation. In *Doltable Ltd v Lexi Holdings plc* [2005] EWHC 1804 (Ch); [2006] B.C.C. 918 the company sought an administration order with a view to preventing a secured creditor from selling the secured property (allegedly) at an undervalue. Any surplus would benefit the members. It was held that this was outside the statutory purposes and an order was refused. In *Re British American Racing (Holdings) Ltd* [2004] EWHC 2947 (Ch); [2005] B.C.C. 110 it was argued that a petition presented by a creditor which also held 89 per cent of the company's issued share capital was an abuse of the process of the court because administration would lead to the exclusion of the minority shareholders. This contention was rejected: the applicant, as a creditor, was entitled to proceed on the basis that the company's shares were valueless and a sale of its assets by administrators was likely to achieve a better result for the company's creditors as a whole (in which the applicant would participate in the same way as any other creditor). In *Bank of Scotland plc v Targetfollow Properties Holdings Ltd* [2010] EWHC 3606 (Ch); [2013] B.C.C. 817 a floating charge holder (who had chosen to make an application to the court rather than make an out-of-court appointment) satisfied the court that it should make an order in its discretion under para.3(1) and (b): a restructuring was impracticable and there was no prospect that the business could be rescued as a going concern. In *Re Bowen Travel Ltd* [2012] EWHC 3405 (Ch); [2013] B.C.C. 182, where the supporting evidence was considered to be unreliable and misleading, the court declined to make an administration order and instead ordered the company to be wound up, so that its affairs could be properly investigated for the benefit of creditors. See also *Data Power Systems Ltd v Safehosts (London) Ltd* [2013] EWHC 2479 (Ch); [2013] B.C.C. 721 (company had not traded and was hopelessly insolvent: administration order refused); *Re Hibernia (2005) Ltd* [2013] EWHC 2615 (Ch) (order granted to avoid losing best prospect of achieving a sale); *Re Monarch Financial Services Ltd; Cooper v Monarch Financial Services Ltd* [2017] EWHC 2324 (Ch); [2017] B.C.C. 570 (order where para.3(1)(b) recovery of substantial debt owed to company was more likely to be achieved by administration than in winding up and time of the essence as others at risk of depositing money with the unregulated financial services company).

In considering whether the statutory purpose of administration can be achieved, the potential administrator does not have to consider the directors' motives in appointing him: *Re BW Estates Ltd* [2015] EWHC 517 (Ch); [2016] B.C.C. 475 (overruled on other grounds: [2017] EWCA Civ 1201; [2017] B.C.C. 406).

Para.3(2), (4)

As noted above, the administrator, unlike a receiver, is not subject to an overriding obligation to have regard to the interests of the company's secured and preferential creditors: he must have regard to the interests of the company's creditors as a whole. Once a receiver has paid off the secured charge, his functions are completed: he must hand over control of the company's property to its directors or liquidator. Apart from the statutory obligations to pay the preferential creditors and set aside the prescribed part under s.176A, it is not his concern to see that any of the other creditors' debts are paid, and he owes them no duties either at law or in equity. An administrator, in contrast, is now by these subparagraphs bound to perform his functions in the interests of the company's creditors as a whole: paying off the secured creditors ranks last in the statutory objectives, and in doing so he is under a positive duty not to harm the company's other creditors. A creditor has standing to complain of a breach of this duty under para.74. If the administrator is satisfied on reasonable grounds that the continued performance of a contract would not be in the interests of the creditors and would impede the achievement of the objectives of the administration, he may refuse to perform it (*Joint Administrators of Rangers Football Club plc, Noters* [2012] CSOH 55; [2013] 2 B.C.L.C. 436.

4 The administrator of a company must perform his functions as quickly and efficiently as is reasonably practicable.

General Note

This provision may be thought rather too vague to establish a positive legal duty remediable in damages: the most obvious sanction would be an application to the court to have the defaulting administrator removed and replaced, and for this purpose para.74(2) may help to smooth the path.

Status of administrator

5 An administrator is an officer of the court (whether or not he is appointed by the court).

General Note

As an officer of the court (like the liquidator in a compulsory liquidation), an administrator is bound by the rule in *Ex p. James* (1874) L.R. 9 Ch. App. 609, which imposes a rather ill-defined obligation to act honourably and fairly. But this supposed obligation cannot override the claims of legitimate creditors: *Re Wedgwood Museum Trust Ltd* [2011] EWHC 3782 (Ch); [2013] B.C.C. 281. The Supreme Court has confirmed this view in categorical terms in *Re Nortel GmbH, Bloom v Pensions Regulator* [2013] UKSC 52; [2014] A.C. 209; [2013] B.C.C. 624. He also enjoys the protection of the law of contempt of court if there is any interference with the performance of his duties. The rule does not apply to the liquidator in a voluntary liquidation, although there may be a case for extending it to the situation where an administration is succeeded by a creditors' voluntary winding up and the administrator continues in office as liquidator (a point left open in *Re Agrimarche Ltd* [2010] EWHC 1655 (Ch); [2010] B.C.C. 775).

General restrictions

6 A person may be appointed as administrator of a company only if he is qualified to act as an insolvency practitioner in relation to the company.

General Note

The expression "qualified to act as an insolvency practitioner in relation to the company" refers not only to the requirement that the individual concerned should have the appropriate professional qualification but also to his specific eligibility to act vis-à-vis the particular company. See the note to s.390.

7 A person may not be appointed as administrator of a company which is in administration (subject to the provisions of paragraphs 90 to 97 and 100 to 103 about replacement and additional administrators).

General Note

There cannot be two administrations simultaneously in existence, e.g. one appointed on the initiative of the directors and another by the holder of a floating charge. But it is possible to have administrators representing such different interests appointed to act jointly or concurrently in the same administration: see the notes to paras 90–97 and 100–103.

8(1) A person may not be appointed as administrator of a company which is in liquidation by virtue of–

(a) a resolution for voluntary winding up, or

(b) a winding-up order.

8(2) Sub-paragraph (1)(a) is subject to paragraph 38.

8(3) Sub-paragraph (1)(b) is subject to paragraphs 37 and 38.

General Note

A company which is in liquidation cannot at the same time be put into administration (see e.g. *Rowntree Ventures Ltd v Oak Property Partners Ltd* [2017] EWCA Civ 1944). But paras 37 and 38 empower the court, on the application respectively of a floating charge holder or the liquidator, to order that administration be substituted for a winding up. And in the special case where a winding-up order is made on public interest grounds in relation to a company which is already in administration, the court may order the administration to continue under para.82. See further the notes to those paragraphs.

If there is no company, it cannot be put into, or remain, in administration. In *Re Eurodis Electron plc* [2011] EWHC 1025 (Ch); [2012] B.C.C. 57 the company had been in administration in this country for three years when it was purportedly dissolved by an order of a court in Belgium, although that court lacked jurisdiction because the company's COMI was in England and the English administration was "main" proceedings. There being no way to have the Belgian ruling set aside, it was held that it had to be respected, and consequently the court ordered that the administration should cease and the proceedings should continue as a winding up.

9(1) A person may not be appointed as administrator of a company which–

(a) has a liability in respect of a deposit which it accepted in accordance with the Banking Act 1979 (c. 37) or 1987 (c. 22), but

(b) is not an authorised deposit taker.

9(2) A person may not be appointed as administrator of a company which effects or carries out contracts of insurance.

9(3) But sub-paragraph (2) does not apply to a company which–

(a) is exempt from the general prohibition in relation to effecting or carrying out contracts of insurance, or

(b) is an authorised deposit taker effecting or carrying out contracts of insurance in the course of a banking business.

9(4) In this paragraph–

"authorised deposit taker" means a person with permission under Part IV of the Financial Services and Markets Act 2000 (c. 8) to accept deposits, and

"the general prohibition" has the meaning given by section 19 of that Act.

9(5) This paragraph shall be construed in accordance with–

(a) section 22 of the Financial Services and Markets Act 2000 (classes of regulated activity and categories of investment),

(b) any relevant order under that section, and

(c) Schedule 2 to that Act (regulated activities).

General Note

Under IA 1986 as originally enacted, banking and insurance companies were excluded from the administration regime. But Pt II of the Act was extended to apply (with certain modifications) to banks and the other bodies mentioned in para.9(1)(a), if they were companies within the meaning of CA 1985 s.735, by the Banks (Administration Proceedings) Order 1989 (SI 1989/1276) with effect from 23 August 1989; and similarly the administration procedure was made available to insurance companies by the Financial Services and Markets Act 2000 (Administration Orders Relating to Insurers) Order 2002 (SI 2002/1242) from 31 May 2002 (now superseded by the Financial Services and Markets Act 2000 (Administration Orders Relating to Insurers) Order 2010 (SI 2010/3023) as from 1 February 2011). This paragraph brings forward those provisions so that the categories of banking and insurance companies identified may be made subject to the new administration regime. However, the Enterprise Act 2002 (Commencement No.4 and Transitional Provisions and Savings) Order 2003 (SI 2003/2093, effective 15 September 2003) art.3(3) provided that the original IA 1986 Pt II would continue to apply insofar as was necessary to give effect to the above order of 2002, so that, for administrations already current on that date, it is the provisions of the original Pt II and not the present Schedule that govern the position. The 2002 Order has since been replaced by the Financial Services and Markets Act 2000 (Administration Orders Relating to Insurers) Order 2010 (SI 2010/3023), effective 1 February 2011. Note that, in regard to insurance companies, a company can only be put into administration by court order: see art.2 of the 2010 Order. In regard to Northern Ireland, see the Financial Services and Markets Act 2000 (Administration Orders Relating to Insurers) (Northern Ireland) Order 2007 (SI 2007/846), effective 6 April 2007.

The Banks (Administration Proceedings) Order 1989, referred to above, has been revoked and replaced by the Banks (Former Authorised Institutions) (Insolvency) Order 2006 (SI 2006/3107, effective 15 December 2006): see the note preceding para.1. This Order makes the administration regime under Sch.B1 available to banks and analogous institutions. These orders are supplemented by the Credit Institutions (Reorganisation and Winding Up) Regulations 2004 (SI 2004/1045, effective 5 May 2004), which deny our courts jurisdiction in respect of credit institutions based elsewhere in the EEA and impose certain requirements where the administration involves creditors in other EEA States. On the special administration regime established by the Banking Act 2009 where there has been government intervention in the affairs of a failing bank or building society, see above, p.6.

In regard to insurers, SI 2010/3023 is supplemented by the Insurers (Reorganisation and Winding Up) Regulations 2004 (SI 2004/353, effective 18 February 2004). These latter Regulations apply to all UK insurers except Lloyd's and, as regards Lloyd's, the Insurers (Reorganisation and Winding Up) (Lloyd's) Regulations 2005 (SI 2005/1998), effective 10 August 2005, equivalent provision has since been made. An administration order was made against an insurer in *Re AA Mutual International Insurance Co Ltd* [2004] EWHC 2430 (Ch); [2005] 2 B.C.L.C. 8.

Appointment of Administrator by Court

Administration order

10 An administration order is an order appointing a person as the administrator of a company.

General Note

Under the original Pt II regime, a company can be put into administration only by court order. Paragraphs 14–34 now authorise the alternative of making an appointment extra-judicially, which will be the procedure used in the great majority of cases because of the saving in time, formality and expense. It is only in cases where the initiative is taken by a person other than the company or its directors or the holder of a "qualifying" floating charge (see the note to para.14(2)) that it will be obligatory to use the court procedure. (Note also that for the categories of company mentioned in EA 2002 s.249 and the bodies mentioned in para.11, the only way to have the company put into administration is by court order, but in this case it is the regime under the unamended IA 1986 Pt II which will apply.)

For appointments under the new regime, the relevant rules are to be found in Pt 3 of IR 2016. For appointments under the original regime (including all applications under EA 2002 s.249(2), the Insolvent Partnerships Order 1994 made prior to 1 July 2005, and the Financial Services and Markets Act 2000 (Administration Orders relating to Insurers) Order 2002), the original Pt 2 of the rules applies: reference should be made to Vol.2 of the 19th edition of this work. The Insolvent Partnerships (Amendment) Order 2005 (SI 2005/1516) introduced a modified regime based on Sch.B1 for administrations of insolvent partnerships as from 1 July 2005 and the Insolvent Partnerships Order 1994 (SI 1994/2421) was further amended by the Insolvency (Miscellaneous Amendments) Regulations 2017 (SI 2017/1119) as from 8 December 2017.

Conditions for making order

11 The court may make an administration order in relation to a company only if satisfied–

(a) that the company is or is likely to become unable to pay its debts, and

(b) that the administration order is reasonably likely to achieve the purpose of administration.

General Note

As under the original IA 1986 s.*8(1)*, there are here two preconditions for the making of an administration order: (a) actual or likely insolvency; and (b) the likely achievement of the purpose of the administration. But under that section there was for a time considerable judicial disagreement as to the degree of probability and the appropriate standard of proof to be applied in construing such expressions as "satisfied" and "likely". The decisions under that provision are no doubt apt to give guidance in the construction of the present paragraph, but a note of caution must be expressed because the wording of the two statutory provisions is not identical.

So far as concerns the phrase "satisfied … that the company is or is likely to become unable to pay its debts", however, the language is the same. In *Re COLT Telecom Group plc* [2002] EWHC 2815 (Ch); [2003] B.P.I.R. 324 Jacob J ruled that "likely" in this context meant "more probable than not". It was not enough for the petitioner to give evidence sufficient to satisfy some lesser test, e.g. that there was a "real prospect" of insolvency (as had been held to be the case in regard to the same word, "likely" where it appeared later in the original subsection: see below). "Satisfied" thus means "satisfied on a balance of probabilities". The term "unable to pay its debts" has the meaning given by IA 1986 s.123, i.e. insolvent on either a "cash-flow" or a "balance-sheet" basis: see para.111(1) and the notes to s.123.

There is a slight change in the wording used in para.11(b): the court must now be "satisfied" that "the administration order is reasonably likely to achieve the purpose of the administration", whereas the original s.*8(1)(b)* reads "considers that the making of an order under this section would be likely to achieve one or more of the purposes mentioned below". Thus "is satisfied" replaces "considers" and "likely" becomes "reasonably likely". In *Re Harris Simons Construction Ltd* [1989] 1 W.L.R. 368; (1989) 5 B.C.C. 11, Hoffmann J held that it was sufficient that the court should consider that there was "a real prospect" that one or more of the statutory purposes might be achieved, and later cases (e.g. *Re Lomax Leisure Ltd* [2000] B.C.C. 352 at 363) have consistently applied the "real prospect" test. In construing the new provision, the phrase "is satisfied" might be thought to impose a more stringent standard than "considers", but this appears to be balanced by the insertion of the word "reasonably" before "likely". In *Re AA Mutual International Insurance Co Ltd* [2004] EWHC 2430 (Ch); [2005] 2 B.C.L.C. 8 Lewison J confirmed that the new wording replicates the distinction made under the original Pt II: that under para.11(a) the test is "more probable than not", while for para.11(b) it is "a real prospect". In *Auto Management Services Ltd v Oracle Fleet UK Ltd* [2007] EWHC 392 (Ch); [2008] B.C.C. 761 Warren J said that if an administration could be shown in all but the most unlikely circumstances to produce a result no worse than a liquidation and there were reasonably likely circumstances where the result would be better, that would be significant in influencing the court towards making an order and, in the light of an impression that an administration would be more cost-effective than a liquidation, decided in favour of an administration. In *Rowntree Ventures Ltd v Oak Property Partners Ltd* [2017] EWCA Civ 1944 the Court of Appeal upheld an appeal against a decision where, although the para.11 preconditions were satisfied, the judge had decided against making an order on the basis that the company might fare better in the future, Vos C commenting that it was fallacious for the judge to exercise his discretion against making an administration order on that basis and it would not normally be appropriate to attach great weight to the speculative possibility of turnaround after deeming the insolvency precondition to be satisfied.

An order will be refused if the application is not made for a proper purpose (i.e. not within the statutory definition): see the note to para.3(1), (3). However, it is not necessary for the applicant to identify which of the statutory purposes it is intended should be attained: *Hammonds v Pro-Fit USA Ltd* [2007] EWHC 1998 (Ch); [2008] 2 B.C.L.C. 159.

On the meaning of "debts", see IR 2016 r.14.1(3).

It should be noted that para.11(a) does not apply—i.e. insolvency or near-insolvency is not a prerequisite—where the applicant is the holder of a "qualifying" floating charge and satisfies the court that it is in a position to appoint an administrator under para.14 (see para.35). This reflects the fact that there is no similar prerequisite where the charge holder makes an out-of-court appointment. However, if the charge-holder does choose to seek an appointment by court order, the question of insolvency may be a factor influencing the court in the exercise of its overall discretion: *Re Trainfx Ltd* [2015] EWHC 3713 (Ch); [2016] B.C.C. 493.

Administration application

12(1) An application to the court for an administration order in respect of a company (an "administration application") may be made only by–

(a) the company,

(b) the directors of the company,

(c) one or more creditors of the company,

(d) the designated officer for a magistrates' court in the exercise of the power conferred by section 87A of the Magistrates' Courts Act 1980 (c. 43) (fine imposed on company), or

(e) a combination of persons listed in paragraphs (a) to (d).

12(2) As soon as is reasonably practicable after the making of an administration application the applicant shall notify–

(a) any person who has appointed an administrative receiver of the company,

(b) any person who is or may be entitled to appoint an administrative receiver of the company,

(c) any person who is or may be entitled to appoint an administrator of the company under paragraph 14, and

(d) such other persons as may be prescribed.

12(3) An administration application may not be withdrawn without the permission of the court.

12(4) In sub-paragraph (1) "creditor" includes a contingent creditor and a prospective creditor.

12(5) Sub-paragraph (1) is without prejudice to section 7(4)(b).

General Note

The former procedure, involving a petition to the court, has been replaced by an "administration application". For the relevant rules, see IR 2016 r.3.3.

The court can only make an administration order on an application made under this provision. An application for an administration order must always be listed before a High Court judge or an Insolvency and Companies Court Judge: see the *Practice Direction: Insolvency Proceedings* [2018] B.C.C. 241 (reproduced as App.IV to this *Guide*) para.3.4(1).

Para.12(1), (4)

These subparagraphs cover essentially the same ground as the original s.*9(1)*. It should be noted that, in addition to those listed in this subparagraph, the following (inter alios) also have standing to apply:

- the liquidator of the company (see para.38);
- the supervisor of a CVA (see para.12(5) and s.7(4)(b));
- the Financial Conduct Authority and the Prudential Regulation Authority, under FSMA 2000 s.359 (as amended).

An application by the supervisor of a CVA is treated as if it were an application by the company: see r.3.5. Although the holder of a floating charge has power under Sch.B1 para.14 to appoint an administrator out of court, there may be good reason to seek a court order—e.g. to remove any doubt that the criteria for making the appointment have been met (cf. *Bank of Scotland plc v Targetfollow Properties Holdings Ltd* [2010] EWHC 3606 (Ch)).

Under the original s.*9(1)*, there was uncertainty for a time regarding an application made by "the directors": could they act informally, and must they be unanimous? It is now settled that for that provision they may act informally, if unanimous, but by a majority only if their decision is taken formally at a board meeting. It might have been thought that para.105 of this Schedule, which states that the directors may act by a majority and imposes no formal requirement, was intended to relax this rule, but in *Minmar (929) Ltd v Khalastchi* [2011] EWHC 1159 (Ch); [2011] B.C.C. 486 Morritt C held that notwithstanding para.105, a decision of a majority of the directors is only competent for the purposes of para.12(1)(b) if the company's rules of internal management have been complied with (which will normally mean by passing a resolution at a properly convened directors' meeting). The requirements of the articles also prevailed (and *Minmar* followed) in *Randhawa v Turpin; Re BW Estates Ltd* [2017] EWCA Civ 1201; [2017] B.C.C. 406. In *Re Information Governance Ltd* [2013] EWHC 2611 (Ch); [2015] B.C.C. 277 an application for an administration order had been made by the company's sole director, but two additional directors appointed subsequently opposed the application. David Richards J declined to make an order in the circumstances. In a partnership case, *Re Brake (t/a Stay in Style); Patley Wood Farm LLP v Brake* [2016] EWHC 1688 (Ch); [2017] 1 W.L.R. 343, the unanimous agreement of the partners was required.

The ruling in *Re Frontsouth (Witham) Ltd* [2011] EWHC 1668 (Ch); [2011] B.C.C. 635 goes further, and makes the point (obiter) that where a company's articles confer the exclusive power to manage the company's business on the directors (as do the Model Articles of Association (SI 2008/3229) art.3), the members have no power to act in the name of the company, at least where there is a functioning (or potentially functioning) board of directors, from which the conclusion is drawn that "the company" for the purposes of para.22(1) (and, presumably, para.12(1)(a)) may act only through the board of directors. On this view para.12(1)(a) is virtually redundant. See further the note to para.22(1).

In the case of a petition for a winding-up order, the court will not normally entertain an application by a creditor whose debt is the subject of a genuine dispute or cross-claim. The validity of the debt must first be established in separate proceedings. In *Re Simoco Digital UK Ltd* [2004] EWHC 209 (Ch); [2004] 1 B.C.L.C. 541 it was accepted by counsel and the court that this rule would apply also to applications for an administration order. However, in *Hammonds v Pro-Fit USA Ltd* [2007] EWHC 1998; [2008] 2 B.C.L.C. 159 Warren J took a different view: in an administration application the court could make an order if it was "likely" that the company would become insolvent in the future even if it was not shown to be currently insolvent, and in this situation the court could in its discretion make an order on the basis of a disputed debt. See also *Fieldfisher LLP v Pennyfeathers Ltd* [2016] EWHC 566 (Ch); [2016] B.C.C. 697 (applicants' status as creditors; effect of arbitration clause). A contingent or prospective creditor has standing (para.12(4)). In *Re British American Racing (Holdings) Ltd* [2004] EWHC 2947 (Ch); [2005] B.C.C. 110 objection was taken that the debt was not presently payable, but this argument failed on the facts. See also *El Ajou v Dollar Land (Manhattan) Ltd* [2005] EWHC 2861 (Ch); [2007] B.C.C. 953 (judgment debt not a disputed debt even though appeal pending).

Para.12(2)

The list of persons who must be given notice has been extended by the inclusion of subpara.(2)(c): this is now necessary because EA 2002 s.250, inserting new s.72A into IA 1986, means that the holder of a floating charge can no longer prevent the appointment of an administrator by putting the company into administrative receivership. But, even so, the holder of such a charge may wish to take action under para.14 or para.36 in order to ensure that, if the company is to be put into administration, the administrator will be a person of whom he approves. However, since s.250 is not retrospective, and is also subject to the exceptions set out in ss.72B–72H, it has been necessary to continue to include subparas (a) and (b).

For the persons prescribed for the purposes of sub-para.(2)(d), see r.3.7 and Sch.4 para.3.

Para.12(5)

This subparagraph was inserted by the Enterprise Act 2002 (Insolvency) Order 2003 (SI 2003/2096) arts 1, 2(1), (2), effective 15 September 2003.

Powers of court

13(1) On hearing an administration application the court may–

(a) make the administration order sought;

(b) dismiss the application;

(c) adjourn the hearing conditionally or unconditionally;

(d) make an interim order;

(e) treat the application as a winding-up petition and make any order which the court could make under section 125;

(f) make any other order which the court thinks appropriate.

13(2) An appointment of an administrator by administration order takes effect–

(a) at a time appointed by the order, or

(b) where no time is appointed by the order, when the order is made.

13(3) An interim order under sub-paragraph (1)(d) may, in particular–

(a) restrict the exercise of a power of the directors or the company;

(b) make provision conferring a discretion on the court or on a person qualified to act as an insolvency practitioner in relation to the company.

13(4) This paragraph is subject to paragraph 39.

General Note

The power conferred by subpara.(1)(e) to make a winding-up order in lieu of an administration order is new: previously, in *Re Brooke Marine Ltd* [1988] B.C.L.C. 546 it was ruled that a winding-up order could only be made on a petition presented under s.124.

For the rules and prescribed forms governing an application for an administration order and the supporting documents which must be filed with the application, see rr.3.6 et seq. Among these documents is a statement by the proposed administrator that he consents to act, and that in his opinion the purpose of the administration is reasonably likely to be achieved.

Para.13(1), (3)

As noted above, the power conferred on the court by subpara.(1)(e) to make a winding-up order in lieu of an administration order had no counterpart in the former legislation. A winding-up order was made under this provision against a Delaware corporation in *Re Ci4net.com Inc* [2004] EWHC 1941 (Ch); [2005] B.C.C. 277; while in *Re UK Steelfixers Ltd* [2012] EWHC 2409 (Ch); [2012] B.C.C. 751; *Re Bowen Travel Ltd* [2012] EWHC 3405 (Ch); [2013] B.C.C. 182; *Re Integral Ltd* [2013] EWHC 164 (Ch) and *Re Safehosts (London) Ltd* [2013] EWHC 2479 (Ch) the court on an application for an administration order rejected the supporting evidence as unreliable and misleading and instead ordered the company to be wound up. Alternatively, there may be a petition for winding up already on the file on the basis of which the court may order a liquidation rather than an administration (e.g. because some dispositions of property may be open to challenge under s.127): *Re Brown Bear Foods Ltd, Shaw v Webb* [2014] EWHC 1132 (Ch); *Harlow v Creative Staging Ltd* [2014] EWHC 2787 (Ch). But power to treat an application for an administration order as a winding-up petition does not extended the court's jurisdiction to the making of a winding-up order on any grounds, so that in *Re One World Logistics Freight Ltd* [2018] EWHC 264 (Ch) the court refused a contributory's application since he would not be able to demonstrate that there was likely to be a surplus in a winding up from which he could benefit and the remedy in the context of contributories was an exceptional one which the court would refuse where some other remedy (administration) was available. These cases confirm that the court's power to make an administration order is discretionary and that an application may be refused even though the evidence meets the requirements for making an administration order. However, in *Rowntree Ventures Ltd v Oak Property Partners Ltd* [2017] EWCA Civ 1944 where that was the position, the Court of Appeal considered that the judge had approached the exercise of his discretion on the wrong basis in attaching too much weight to the possibility of turning the company around outside administration and set aside the refusal to make an order (but could not make an administration order as the company had by then entered creditors' voluntary winding up). The court may also, exceptionally, make a winding-up order of its own motion: see the notes to s.124 and para.55 below.

The court's powers under para.13 are wide. In *SB Corporate Solutions Ltd v Prescott* [2012] Bus. L.R. D91, insolvency practitioners were appointed interim managers of the company's affairs after an application for an administration order had been made orally, pending the making of a formal application. (Compare *Re Gallidoro Trawlers Ltd* [1991] B.C.C. 691, decided under the original Pt II.)

In *GP Noble Trustees Ltd v Directors of Berkeley Berry Birch plc* [2006] EWHC 982 (Ch); [2007] B.P.I.R. 1271, the applicant's choice of administrators was disputed by the company's directors but was upheld by the court. In *Oracle (North West) Ltd v Pinnacle Services (UK) Ltd* [2008] EWHC 1920 (Ch); [2009] B.C.C. 159, where there was a dispute as to the choice of an administrator, the creditors' nominee was preferred by the court.

In *Bank of Scotland plc v Targetfollow Properties Holdings Ltd* [2010] EWHC 3606 (Ch); [2013] B.C.C. 817 the company objected to the appointment as administrators of insolvency practitioners who had previously been advising the bank which had applied for the order, but the court made the appointment, observing that remedies would be available if the administrators failed to act impartially. See also *Stanley International Betting Ltd v Stanleybet UK Investments Ltd* [2011] EWHC 1732 (Ch); [2011] B.C.C. 691; *Med-Gourmet Restaurants Ltd v Ostuni Investments Ltd* [2010] EWHC 2834 (Ch); [2013] B.C.C. 47; *Re Hibernia (2005) Ltd* [2013] EWHC 2615 (Ch); *Healthcare Management Services Ltd v Caremark Properties Ltd* [2012] EWHC 1693 (Ch); [2013] B.C.C. 484; *Northern Bank Ltd (t/a Danske Bank) v Taylor* [2014] NICh 9.

Where the court makes an order under para.13(1)(d) or (f), it must give directions regarding the giving of notice of the order under r.3.15(3).

In *Re Bickland Ltd* [2012] EWHC 706 (Ch); [2013] B.C.C. 501 considerable costs had been run up on an application for an order when it was overtaken by an out-of-court appointment made by a secured creditor. The court ordered that these costs be treated as if they were expenses in the ensuing administration.

On the "commencement" of a winding up under para.13(1)(e), see IA 1986 s.129(1A).

Para.13(2)

There was no counterpart to this provision in the former legislation: it makes clear that the court has power to fix a time other than that of the order for it to take effect.

Where the court fixes a time later than that of its order, the interim moratorium which will have been in place under para.44(1)(a) is continued under para.44(1)(b).

An order may be made with retrospective effect (*Re G-Tech Construction Ltd* [2007] B.P.I.R. 1275), but only if the conditions in para.11 are satisfied at the time when the order is made: it is not sufficient that they were met at the earlier date: *Re Care Matters Partnership Ltd* [2011] EWHC 2543 (Ch); [2011] B.C.C. 957; *Re Silentpride Ltd* (unreported, 9 October 2014); *Re a Company* (unreported, 25 August 2016—further appointment made after original administration had expired). Despite considerable disquiet (see *Re Care Matters Partnership Ltd* at [4], [9] and [19]), extensive use has been made of this course in recent cases where the initial appointment of administrators has proved to have been defective (e.g. *Endersby v Astrosoccer 4 U Ltd* (unreported, 7 December 2017)). The order takes effect from the date of the original purported appointment. In *Adjei v Law For All* [2011] EWHC 2672 (Ch); [2011] B.C.C. 963 Norris J stated that there was no need for the court, in addition, to ratify or confirm as valid the acts of the administrators or to declare that they were entitled to remuneration for their services and, indeed, said that the court should decline to do so, as this would risk giving judicial blessing (without proper evidence) to matters which might be the subject of subsequent challenge. See further the note to para.26. In *Re Synergi Partners Ltd* [2015] EWHC 964 (Ch); [2015] B.C.C. 333 the court was asked to make a retrospective appointment back-dated for more than four years. Without deciding whether an order could be made retrospectively for a period of more than one year, HH Judge Hodge QC questioned whether in any case such an order could achieve any purpose and instead ordered the company to be wound up. See also *Re Elgin Legal Ltd* [2016] EWHC 2523 (Ch); [2017] B.C.C. 43.

A defectively appointed administrator will have no standing to apply for this relief, since his appointment was a nullity. Application should be made by the company or the directors.

Para.13(4)

Paragraph 39 preserves the position under the former law, viz. that an administration cannot co-exist with an administrative receivership. It follows that where the holder of a floating charge continues to have the power to appoint an administrative receiver (see the note to IA 1986 s.72A), he can effectively veto the appointment of an administrator. See further the note to para.39.

Appointment of Administrator by Holder of Floating Charge

Power to appoint

14(1) The holder of a qualifying floating charge in respect of a company's property may appoint an administrator of the company.

14(2) For the purposes of sub-paragraph (1) a floating charge qualifies if created by an instrument which–

(a) states that this paragraph applies to the floating charge,

(b) purports to empower the holder of the floating charge to appoint an administrator of the company,

(c) purports to empower the holder of the floating charge to make an appointment which would be the appointment of an administrative receiver within the meaning given by section 29(2), or

(d) purports to empower the holder of a floating charge in Scotland to appoint a receiver who on appointment would be an administrative receiver.

14(3) For the purposes of sub-paragraph (1) a person is the holder of a qualifying floating charge in respect of a company's property if he holds one or more debentures of the company secured–

(a) by a qualifying floating charge which relates to the whole or substantially the whole of the company's property,

(b) by a number of qualifying floating charges which together relate to the whole or substantially the whole of the company's property, or

(c) by charges and other forms of security which together relate to the whole or substantially the whole of the company's property and at least one of which is a qualifying floating charge.

General Note

The power which the holder of a floating charge has enjoyed in the past to appoint an administrative receiver has been abrogated by EA 2002 s.250 (although not with retrospective effect, and subject to the exceptions set out in IA

1986 ss.72B–72H: see the notes to ss.72A–72H, EA 2002 s.250 and para.39, below). The legislature now contemplates that a charge holder will normally enforce his security by putting the company into administration, and in consequence (a) the objective of an administration now expressly includes "realising property in order to make a distribution to one or more secured or preferential creditors" (para.3(1)(c) above); and (b) the holder of a "qualifying" floating charge, as defined in para.14(2), is now given the power to appoint an administrator directly, without the need to apply to the court for an order. However, from the charge holder's point of view, his position is considerably less advantageous than would be the case in a receivership: first, because the administrator has to act in the interests of the company's creditors as a whole (para.3(2)), rather than primarily in the interests of the charge holder; secondly, because satisfying the charge holder's security ranks last in the hierarchy of objectives of an administration—even when the charge holder has appointed the administrator under this paragraph; and thirdly because, even under the new administration regime, the procedure is more formal and elaborate than a receivership, and consequently slower and more expensive. In an appropriate case, however, it may be possible to use a "pre-pack" arrangement (see the note to para.2) to streamline the procedure.

If the charge is enforceable, the holder has a prima facie right to an order unless there are countervailing considerations: *Re St John Spencer Estates & Development Ltd* [2012] EWHC 2317 (Ch); [2013] 1 B.C.L.C. 718.

The holder of a floating charge may still enforce his security by appointing a non-administrative receiver (i.e. a receiver of less than a substantial part of the company's assets), but if the company is then put into administration on the initiative of some other party the receiver may be required to vacate office under para.41(2).

The charge instrument must, of course, have been validly executed: *Re Armstrong Brands Ltd* [2015] EWHC 3303 (Ch); [2016] B.C.C. 657. However, a company may be estopped from denying that a charge instrument has been validly executed if the director (or other person) purporting to act on its behalf had ostensible authority, or if the chargee is entitled to assume that it has been validly executed by virtue of the CA 2006 s.44: *Lovett v Carson Country Homes Ltd* [2009] EWHC 1143 (Ch); [2011] B.C.C. 789 (where the document was in fact a forgery).

For a charge holder to be able to make an appointment under para.14, it is necessary that a default or other event should have occurred which entitles him to enforce the charge (para.16); but it is not a prerequisite that the company should be, or be likely to become, insolvent. In *Re Care People Ltd* [2013] EWHC 1734 (Ch); [2013] B.C.C. 466 the company objected that the appointment was premature or irregular, in that it had been given insufficient time to satisfy a demand made by the charge holder. The court ruled that although this was probably the case, no injustice had been caused by the irregularity because the company could not have met the demand even if proper time had been given, and upheld the appointment as valid. See also *Closegate Hotel Development (Durham) Ltd v McLean* [2013] EWHC 3237 (Ch) (bank not estopped by alleged promises in correspondence from making immediate demand).

If the holder of a qualifying floating charge considers it advisable to have an administrator appointed by order of the court instead of proceeding under para.14, para.35 makes special provision so that insolvency need not be proved. (However, if the charge-holder does choose to seek an appointment by court order, the question of insolvency may be a factor influencing the court in the exercise of its overall discretion: *Hellenic Capital Investments Ltd v Trainfx Ltd* [2015] EWHC 3713 (Ch); [2017] B.C.C. 43.)

Where the appointment of an administrator is to be made under para.14, there will be an interim moratorium only if the charge holder files a notice of intention to appoint an administrator under para.44(2), (3): see the note to those provisions.

For the relevant, see rr.3.16 et seq.

Para.14(2), (3)

It is only if the charge is a "qualifying" floating charge that the holder has the power to appoint an administrator under this paragraph: the holder of any other charge (e.g. a floating charge over part only of the company's assets) will have to apply for a court order. The essential characteristics of a qualifying floating charge, elaborated in more detail in these subparagraphs, are: (a) that the charge must by its terms give the holder power to appoint an administrator (or an administrative receiver); and (b) the charge (or that and other charges taken together) must relate to the whole or substantially the whole of the company's property. So far as concerns characteristic (a), there is a variety of terminology which may be used in the charge instrument: subparas (2)(a)–(d) are alternatives (*Stephen, Petitioner* [2011] CSOH 119; [2012] B.C.C. 537). In the first place, the draftsman may simply refer to para.14 or he may expressly give the charge holder power to appoint an administrator. Alternatively, if he has not brought his precedents up to date to take account of EA 2002 s.250 or (more realistically) if the document was executed before that Act came into force, and the powers conferred on the charge holder include a power to appoint a receiver who would be an administrative receiver as defined by IA 1986 s.29(2), this also will enable the chargee to appoint an administrator directly under this provision. See also *Hooley Ltd v Victoria Jute Co Ltd* [2016] CSOH 141; [2016] B.C.C. 826 (floating charge created abroad over assets in foreign jurisdiction: question whether a "qualifying" floating charge not dependent on whether practically enforceable in that jurisdiction).

Paragraph 14(3)(c) will cover the common case where a chargee takes security by way of a fixed charge over parts of a company's property and a floating charge over all or substantially all of the remainder, and this will be so whether there is one charge instrument or several. It would also seem, at least tacitly, to affirm the effectiveness of what is commonly referred to as a "lightweight" floating charge, which was upheld in *Re Croftbell Ltd* [1990] B.C.C. 781 (see the note to IA 1986 s.9(3)): the holder of such a charge will be able to appoint an administrator directly if it is in his interests to do so. However, it may well make more sense to enforce the fixed-charge elements of the security by other means. Alternatively it may be regarded that a prior fixed charge over all or part of a company's assets left a subsequent floating charge to attach to the company's equity of redemption under the fixed charge, on the basis that the prior charge might be redeemed in due course by repayment of the prior lender, leaving the subsequent floating charge as valuable security. This point, derived from *Croftbell* (above), was applied in *SAW (SW) 2010 Ltd v Wilson* [2017] EWCA Civ 1001; [2017] B.C.C. 373 where the Court of Appeal rejected a contention that the validity of an instrument as a floating charge, at the time of its creation, depended on the existence of uncharged assets of the company creating it, or on a power in the company to acquire assets in the future, free from any fixed charge arising from the crystallisation of a prior floating charge. Rather, the classification of a charge as fixed or as floating was by reference simply to the construction of the relevant instrument creating the charge (applying *National Westminster Bank plc v Spectrum Plus Ltd* [2005] UKHL 41; [2005] 2 A.C. 680; [2005] B.C.C. 694). In the *SAW* case (above), a debenture created an enforceable qualifying floating charge over the company's property within the meaning of para.14 notwithstanding the crystallisation of an earlier charge over the property, and so the appointment of administrators by the subsequent chargee creditor was valid.

The position where there is more than one floating charge over a company's property is dealt with in para.15.

Restrictions on power to appoint

15(1) A person may not appoint an administrator under paragraph 14 unless–

(a) he has given at least two business days' written notice to the holder of any prior floating charge which satisfies paragraph 14(2), or

(b) the holder of any prior floating charge which satisfies paragraph 14(2) has consented in writing to the making of the appointment.

15(2) One floating charge is prior to another for the purposes of this paragraph if–

(a) it was created first, or

(b) it is to be treated as having priority in accordance with an agreement to which the holder of each floating charge was party.

15(3) Sub-paragraph (2) shall have effect in relation to Scotland as if the following were substituted for paragraph (a)–

"(a) it has priority of ranking in accordance with section 464(4)(b) of the Companies Act 1985 (c. 6),".

General Note

This paragraph deals with the position where there are two or more charges, each being or including a floating charge, over the company's property: a junior-ranking chargee who wishes to appoint an administrator must give at least two days' notice to those having priority, or alternatively secure their written consent. Priority is determined by reference to the time of creation, or any agreement between the charge holders (para.15(2)). Curiously, the obligation to give notice is imposed only by reference to the criteria set out in para.14(2), and not also to those in para.14(3): what matters is whether there is a power to appoint an administrator directly conferred on the senior chargee by his charge instrument rather than whether his charge is over the whole or substantially the whole of the company's property. From one point of view, this is unimportant, for there will effectively be no power to make an appointment unless the charge is "substantial". But from another viewpoint para.15((1) poses a problem for a junior chargee, since it may be difficult for him to find out whether the instrument creating the senior-ranking charge contains any of the clauses referred to in para.14(2). The particulars registered in Companies House will not include them unless the company has gratuitously volunteered to file the information, and while in theory he has a right under CA 2006 s.877 to inspect the charge instrument itself at the company's registered office, it is a notorious fact that few companies bother to comply with these particular statutory obligations. The best advice for the holder of a junior-ranking charge is that he should give notice to his superior counterparts in any case, without concerning himself whether or not para.14(2) applies.

The omission by a junior charge holder to give notice to the holder of a prior ranking charge is fatal (unless the latter consents): the purported appointment is invalid from the beginning and cannot be cured retrospectively: *Re Eco Link Resources Ltd* [2012] B.C.C. 731.

Note that notice must be given to a senior chargee even if his charge is not currently enforceable. This view has been confirmed in *Re OMP Leisure Ltd* [2008] B.C.C. 67, where notice had not been given to a senior charge holder but it was probable that that charge had been discharged—in which case it would never be enforceable. Because there was doubt on this point the appointment of the administrators was made subject to the condition that notice should be given to the senior chargee, but HHJ Hodge QC expressed the view that there was no obligation to notify a senior chargee whose charge would never become enforceable. On the "giving" of notice, see the note to para.26.

The options available to a senior chargee who receives such a notice are limited. He would have no right to prevent the holder of the later charge from enforcing his security unless he could persuade the court to intervene on the ground that the appointment was being sought mala fide or for an improper purpose. Most obviously, he could take steps (either by negotiation or by making an appointment himself) to ensure that the proposed administrator was a practitioner of his own choosing, or that such a person should be appointed an additional administrator to act jointly or concurrently with the junior chargee's nominee.

Para.15(1)

In contrast with the position under paras 26–27, there is no obligation to file a copy of the notice with the court, although if this is done the charge holder will enjoy the benefit of a five-day moratorium under para.44(2).

Para.15(2)

Oddly, there is no mention of the case where a number of charges rank pari passu. Prudence would dictate that notice should be given anyway, and also to the trustee of any trust deed.

Section 464(4)(b) of CA 1985 remains in force, but note prospective replacement by the Bankruptcy and Diligence etc (Scotland) Act 2007 s.40(2)(a).

16 An administrator may not be appointed under paragraph 14 while a floating charge on which the appointment relies is not enforceable.

General Note

The power of a floating charge holder to appoint an administrator out of court arises only if a default or other event has occurred which entitles him to enforce the charge. If this is not so, he would still have standing, as a creditor, to apply or to join with other creditors in applying to the court for an order under para.12. On the meaning of "enforceable", see the note to para.35.

This paragraph can also be read as confirming the obvious point that if the charge is invalid or void (e.g. because the charge instrument was not properly executed or particulars of the charge have not been duly registered) it cannot confer any powers on the holder. If the holder purports to appoint an administrator without the power to do so, the administrator will be liable to the company as a trespasser but will be entitled to an indemnity under para.21.

17 An administrator of a company may not be appointed under paragraph 14 if–

(a) a provisional liquidator of the company has been appointed under section 135, or

(b) an administrative receiver of the company is in office.

General Note

It would obviously create difficulties to have two office-holders in post at the same time administering the company's affairs with conflicting objectives. It would, of course, be open to the charge holder to apply to the court under r.7.39 to have the appointment of a provisional liquidator terminated and the company put into administration instead, e.g. with a view to rescuing the company as a going concern. (See the exceptional Scottish case of *Ultimate Invoice Finance Ltd, Petitioner* [2017] CSOH 72 where the court was prepared to take this approach after noting differences in the procedural rules between Scotland and England on appointment of administrators, but cautiously reserved certain ancillary matters.)

This paragraph may be contrasted with para.25, which (unless para.25A applies) bars a company or its directors from appointing an administrator out of court while a petition for a winding-up order or an application to the court for the appointment of an administrator is pending. Neither of these limitations applies to an appointment by the holder of a floating charge under para.14. If an appointment is made under para.14, any petition for winding up is suspended while the company is in administration, unless it is a petition based on public interest grounds (para.40(1)(b), (2)).

Although IA 1986 s.72A now generally prevents a charge holder from appointing an administrative receiver, this provision is not retrospective so as to apply to charges already created before 15 September 2003, and so there will continue to be cases where para.17(b) will apply.

Notice of appointment

18(1) A person who appoints an administrator of a company under paragraph 14 shall file with the court–

(a) a notice of appointment, and

(b) such other documents as may be prescribed.

18(2) The notice of appointment must include a statutory declaration by or on behalf of the person who makes the appointment–

(a) that the person is the holder of a qualifying floating charge in respect of the company's property,

(b) that each floating charge relied on in making the appointment is (or was) enforceable on the date of the appointment, and

(c) that the appointment is in accordance with this Schedule.

18(3) The notice of appointment must identify the administrator and must be accompanied by a statement by the administrator–

(a) that he consents to the appointment,

(b) that in his opinion the purpose of administration is reasonably likely to be achieved, and

(c) giving such other information and opinions as may be prescribed.

18(4) For the purpose of a statement under sub-paragraph (3) an administrator may rely on information supplied by directors of the company (unless he has reason to doubt its accuracy).

18(5) The notice of appointment and any document accompanying it must be in the prescribed form.

18(6) A statutory declaration under sub-paragraph (2) must be made during the prescribed period.

18(7) A person commits an offence if in a statutory declaration under sub-paragraph (2) he makes a statement–

(a) which is false, and

(b) which he does not reasonably believe to be true.

GENERAL NOTE

The appointment of the administrator under para.14 takes effect only when the requirements of this paragraph have been satisfied (para.19). The completion of all the necessary formalities, even with the co-operation of everyone concerned, is bound to take some time—a situation which may be thought disadvantageous from the viewpoint of the floating charge holder in comparison with the speed and simplicity of appointing a receiver. The legislators have taken some steps to meet concerns on this score: first, it is possible at least in some circumstances for the charge holder to secure an interim moratorium for up to five business days by filing a notice of intention to appoint with the court under para.44(2) and, secondly, provision has been made by rr.3.20 et seq. for the appointment of an administrator under para.14 to take effect even when the court is closed, by allowing notice of the appointment to be sent by fax or email: see the note to that rule.

In an appropriate case, it may be possible to use a "pre-pack" arrangement (see the note to para.2) to streamline the procedure.

For the relevant rules, see rr.3.16 et seq.

Para.18(7)

On penalties, see s.430 and Sch.10. The same penalties are prescribed by the Perjury Act 1911 s.5.

Commencement of appointment

19 The appointment of an administrator under paragraph 14 takes effect when the requirements of paragraph 18 are satisfied.

General Note

This provision may be contrasted with the appointment of an administrator by the court, which takes effect from or under the court's order (para.13(2)), and with the appointment of a receiver, where the court is not involved in any way and s.33 applies.

The requirements of para.18 are not satisfied until the relevant documents are filed with the court. The fact that the statutory declaration was made on an earlier date is irrelevant: *Fliptex Ltd v Hogg* [2004] EWHC 1280 (Ch); [2004] B.C.C. 870.

At any time when the court is closed (but not otherwise), IR 2016 r.3.20 allows a notice of appointment to be filed by fax or (in England and Wales) email. The notice must be either faxed to a designated telephone number or sent as an attachment to a designated email address, provided by the Court Service for that purpose. For the relevant telephone number and addresses, see the note to r.3.20. If sent by email, a hard copy of the email must be created detailing its time and date and the address to which it was sent, and containing a copy of the document sent as an attachment. The appointor must retain the report or hard copy. The copy of the faxed notice of appointment, or the email (or a hard copy of the email) containing the notice of appointment, as (in either case) received by the Court Service must be forwarded as soon as reasonably practicable to the court specified in the notice as the court having jurisdiction in the case, to be placed on the relevant court file. The appointment takes effect from the date and time of sending the fax or email, and this is rebuttably presumed to be the date and time shown on the transmission report or hard copy. The appointor must notify the administrator, as soon as reasonably practicable, that the notice has been filed. He must also take three copies of the notice, together with the transmission report or hard copy of the email, and all the necessary supporting documents, to the court on the next day that it is open for business. (If he fails to so within that time, the administrator's appointment ceases to have effect.) There must be delivered with these documents a statement providing, inter alia, "reasons for the out of hours filing of the notice of appointment, including why it would have been damaging to the company and/or its creditors not to have so acted" (r.3.20(9)(d)). While the point, and indeed the legitimacy, of this last requirement may be questioned, it should not be too difficult to find a suitable form of words to meet the case. The court seals the copy notices, endorsed with the date and time when the notice was faxed or sent (according to the report or hard copy) and also with the date when the notice and accompanying documents were delivered to the court. It then issues two of the sealed copies of the notice to the person making the appointment, who must as soon as reasonably practicable send one sealed copy to the administrator.

On the possibility of putting an interim moratorium in place pending compliance with para.19, see the note to para.44(2).

20 A person who appoints an administrator under paragraph 14–

(a) shall notify the administrator and such other persons as may be prescribed as soon as is reasonably practicable after the requirements of paragraph 18 are satisfied, and

(b) commits an offence if he fails without reasonable excuse to comply with paragraph (a).

General Note

It will be in the interests of all concerned (and not least the administrator himself) for para.18 to be complied with expeditiously, since until this is done he will have no power or authority to act. However, it is immaterial for this purpose whether he has been given the notice required by para.20(a).

Rule 3.18(3) requires that the administrator should be sent a copy of the notice of appointment bearing the seal of the court and endorsed with the date and time of filing. It is no doubt intended that this should be the way in which the administrator should be "notified" under para.20(a), although this is not stated in specific terms.

For the "other persons" prescribed by para.20(a), see r.3.19: if the charge holder appoints an administrator in reliance on para.14 after he has received notice that an application has been made to the court for the appointment of an administrator, he must send a copy of the notice of appointment to the applicant and to the court in which the application has been made.

The administrator himself has obligations to give various notices under para.46(2).

On penalties, see s.430, Sch.10 and Sch.B1 para.106(2).

Invalid appointment: indemnity

21(1) This paragraph applies where–

(a) a person purports to appoint an administrator under paragraph 14, and

(b) the appointment is discovered to be invalid.

21(2) The court may order the person who purported to make the appointment to indemnify the person appointed against liability which arises solely by reason of the appointment's invalidity.

General Note

The purported appointment of an administrator may be invalid for any number of reasons: for instance, the charge instrument may be void, e.g. for want of due execution or registration under CA 2006 Pt 25; the charge may not come within the definition of a "qualifying" floating charge under para.14 above; or the conditions rendering the charge enforceable may not have been met. The court has a discretionary power under this provision to order the charge holder (or, indeed, any person) who made the purported appointment to indemnify the appointee against any liability in trespass, etc. that he may have incurred. But there is no power conferred on the court to validate the appointment. There is a parallel with s.34, which deals with the invalid appointment of a receiver. Of course, the parties may in any case have entered into a contract of indemnity, in which case no question of the court's discretion will arise.

In *Hans Brochier Holdings Ltd v Exner* [2006] EWHC 2594 (Ch); [2007] B.C.C. 127 the directors had appointed administrators in England in the belief, reasonably held, that the company's COMI was in England. Shortly afterwards insolvency proceedings were commenced in Germany and on further inquiry it was accepted that the COMI was in Germany. This meant that no main proceedings could be instituted in England and the administrators' appointment (at least as it stood) was invalid. However, it was arguable that the English administration might be continued as territorial proceedings. In that event para.21(2) would not be applicable.

Appointment of Administrator by Company or Directors

Power to appoint

22(1) A company may appoint an administrator.

22(2) The directors of a company may appoint an administrator.

General Note

As has been noted, under IA 1986 Pt II as originally enacted, a company could be put into administration only by order of the court. The reforms made by EA 2002 not only empower the holder of a floating charge to appoint an administrator without the involvement of the court, but confer a similar power on the company itself or its directors. These innovations obviate the need for the involvement of the court (except as a repository of documents) in the great majority of cases.

For the relevant rules, see rr.3.23 et seq.

Para.22(1)

It is submitted that the company should be able to take this step by resolution of the shareholders passed at a general meeting (or a unanimous informal agreement which is equivalent to such a resolution either at common law or under CA 2006 ss.288–289). An ordinary resolution would appear to be sufficient. However, in *Re Frontsouth (Witham) Ltd* [2011] EWHC 1668 (Ch); [2011] B.C.C. 635 Henderson J expressed the view that where a company's articles are in the form of art.70 of the 1985 Table A (which states that "the business of the company shall be managed by the directors"—compare art.3 of the 2008 Model Articles (SI 2008/3229)), the directors alone have competence to decide whether or not to place the company into administration, at least where there is a functioning (or potentially functioning) board of directors. While it may be doubted whether the draftsman intended para.22(1) to be so understood (since it would appear to rob para.22(1) of virtually all substance), the learned judge was plainly concerned to discourage the involvement of the company's shareholders in administration appointments. The court in *Re Eiffel Steelworks Ltd* (unreported, 15 January 2005) took the view that para.22(1) empowered the members to make an appointment, without reference to these remarks. The new rules (r.3.23(j)) continue to support a view that runs contrary to the analysis of Henderson J.

In *Re BW Estates Ltd* [2016] EWHC 2156 (Ch); [2016] B.C.C. 475; further proceedings [2016] B.C.C. 814 an out-of-court appointment had purportedly been made by the company on the strength of a decision made by an inquorate board of directors. The appointment was upheld by the court, applying the well-known "Duomatic" principle, because the shareholders had unanimously consented to the decision, but the decision was overturned on appeal (*Randhawa v Turpin* [2017] EWCA Civ 1201; [2017] B.C.C. 406) as the Duomatic principle had been incorrectly applied.

Para.22(2)
In *Minmar (929) Ltd v Khalastchi* [2011] EWHC 1159 (Ch); [2011] B.C.C. 485 Sir Andrew Morritt C held that for the purpose of para.22(2) (and incidentally, also para.12(1)(b)) the decision of the directors must either be passed formally at a duly constituted board meeting, or otherwise unanimously. In this context he ruled that para.105, which appears to allow the directors to act informally by a majority, does not apply. See further the notes to paras 12(1) and 105. A purported appointment of an administrator by an inquorate meeting is a nullity, incapable of validation under r.12.64: *Re Melodious Corp* [2015] EWHC 621 (Ch); [2016] B.C.C. 727. Thus in *Re BW Estates Ltd; Randhawa v Turpin* (above) a sole director of the company was held on appeal unable to appoint administrators as the company's articles required a quorum at board meetings of two directors.

Restrictions on power to appoint

23(1) This paragraph applies where an administrator of a company is appointed–

(a) under paragraph 22, or

(b) on an administration application made by the company or its directors.

23(2) An administrator of the company may not be appointed under paragraph 22 during the period of 12 months beginning with the date on which the appointment referred to in sub-paragraph (1) ceases to have effect.

General Note

If a company has already been put into administration on the initiative of the company itself or its directors (either out of court under para.22 or by a court order made on its or their application), this provision places a ban on the company being put into administration for a second time under para.22 unless a 12-month period has elapsed since the first appointment "ceased to have effect" (i.e. the administration terminated: see para.1(2)(c)). We may see a parallel here with the similar ban imposed upon a company from entering into a second CVA less than 12 months after it has had the benefit of a moratorium following a proposal for an earlier CVA: see Sch.A1 para.4(1)(f), (g). Note, however, that this restriction only applies to a second appointment made under para.22, i.e. out of court: there is no prohibition on the company or its directors making an application to the court for the appointment of a second administrator within the 12-month period.

24(1) If a moratorium for a company under Schedule A1 ends on a date when no voluntary arrangement is in force in respect of the company, this paragraph applies for the period of 12 months beginning with that date.

24(2) This paragraph also applies for the period of 12 months beginning with the date on which a voluntary arrangement in respect of a company ends if–

(a) the arrangement was made during a moratorium for the company under Schedule A1, and

(b) the arrangement ends prematurely (within the meaning of section 7B).

24(3) While this paragraph applies, an administrator of the company may not be appointed under paragraph 22.

General Note

As noted above, the legislation imposes a ban upon a company from entering into a second CVA less than 12 months after it has had the benefit of a moratorium following a proposal for an earlier CVA (Sch.A1 para.4(1)(f), (g)). This paragraph similarly prohibits the company or its directors from appointing an administrator out of court within that period—although they are not prevented from making an application to the court for an administration order.

See further the note to Sch.A1 para.4(1).

25 An administrator of a company may not be appointed under paragraph 22 if–

(a) a petition for the winding up of the company has been presented and is not yet disposed of,

(b) an administration application has been made and is not yet disposed of, or

(c) an administrative receiver of the company is in office.

General Note

These limitations are more extensive than those which apply where an out-of-court appointment is made by the holder of a floating charge under para.14: see para.17. Once again, the restrictions imposed by this paragraph apply only to the appointment of an administrator by a company or its directors out of court: there is nothing to prevent them from making an application to the court for an appointment, although if there is an administrative receiver in office, para.39 will apply.

A petition is "presented" when it is delivered to the court, and not when it is later sealed and issued: *Re Blights Builders Ltd* [2006] EWHC 3549 (Ch); [2007] B.C.C. 712. A purported appointment of an administrator made after that time is a nullity and cannot be rectified under IR 2016 r.12.64. On the difficulties which may arise where a winding-up petition has been presented to the court but not yet served on the company, see (2009) 22 Insolv. Int. 31.

If notice of intention to appoint an administrator by the company or directors has been given under para.26 and accordingly an interim moratorium has come into operation pursuant to para.46, the appointment of an administrator may proceed notwithstanding the fact that a petition for winding up has been presented (in ignorance of the moratorium) in the meantime: *Re Ramora UK Ltd* [2011] EWHC 3959 (Ch); [2012] B.C.C. 672; compare *Re Business Dream Ltd* [2011] EWHC 2860 (Ch); [2012] B.C.C. 115.

The reference in subpara.(b) to the making of an application, taken literally, would arguably not cover proceedings instituted by petition under the original Pt II. But it would be within the court's powers to restrain the making of an appointment under para.22.

25A(1) Paragraph 25(a) does not prevent the appointment of an administrator of a company if the petition for the winding up of the company was presented after the person proposing to make the appointment filed the notice of intention to appoint with the court under paragraph 27.

25A(2) But sub-paragraph (1) does not apply if the petition was presented under a provision mentioned in paragraph 42(4).

General Note

This paragraph was inserted by DA 2015 Sch.6 para.5 as from 26 May 2015. The ban on making an appointment if a winding-up petition has been presented (imposed by para.25(a)) does not apply if a notice of intention to appoint has been filed. Note the exception of public interest, etc. petitions (para.42(4)).

Notice of intention to appoint

26(1) A person who proposes to make an appointment under paragraph 22 shall give at least five business days' written notice to–

(a) any person who is or may be entitled to appoint an administrative receiver of the company, and

(b) any person who is or may be entitled to appoint an administrator of the company under paragraph 14.

26(2) A person who gives notice of intention to appoint under sub-paragraph (1) shall also give such notice as may be prescribed to such other persons as may be prescribed.

26(3) A notice under this paragraph must–

(a) identify the proposed administrator, and

(b) be in the prescribed form.

General Note

Paragraph 26(2) was amended by DA 2015 Sch.6 para.6 as from 1 October 2015.

This provision gave rise to much controversy in practice and was identified under the Red Tape Challenge as being in need of radical reform. The response to this, effected by DA 2015 amendment referred to above, has been to remove the requirement to give notice to the prescribed persons (including the company itself) where there is no qualifying floating charge holder entitled to notice.

The position now is as follows.

(1) If there is no secured creditor who has, or might have, the right to appoint an administrator under para.14 or an administrative receiver, the company or directors may proceed to make an appointment out of court without giving notice of intention to appoint to anyone, or being required to file such a notice with the court. In this situation there is no interim moratorium. It would be reasonable to suppose that a moratorium could be secured for a few days by filing with the court a notice of intention to appoint even though it there is no person to whom it is obligatory to give notice: see the note to para.44(2); but para.27(1) seems to apply only if a notice of intention has been given under para.26, i.e. only if there are persons entitled to be given such notice.

(2) If there is a secured creditor with a "qualifying" floating charge (whether or not it is currently enforceable), five business days' notice under para.26(1) must be given before an appointment can be made, and a moratorium comes into force under para.44(4) from the time when a copy of the notice is filed with the court. Any appointment must be made within ten business days after the specified documents have been filed. In this situation a copy of the notice must also be given to the persons prescribed under para.26(2), including (in the usual case, where the appointment is made by the directors) to the company itself (para.26(2)).

The giving of notice is dealt with by the Rules. Personal delivery of a document is always permissible (r.1.44), and unless the Act provides otherwise, the use of the post is authorised as an alternative (r.1.42)). A document sent by first class post is deemed to have been served no later than the second day after posting (or the first day after that if it is not a business day). However, the requirement in para.26(1) that the recipient should be given "at least five business days' written notice" may be intended to mean that the notice should be actual notice, without regard to any presumption if the post is used. The decision in *Re Sporting Options plc* [2004] EWHC 3128 (Ch); [2005] B.C.C. 88 appeared to rule out the use of email, but more recently in *Re Advent Computer Training Ltd* [2010] EWHC 459 (Ch); [2011] B.C.C. 44 the use of email communications was permitted in the circumstances of that case: see the note to para.46.

Note that the heading to paras 26–28 and the wording in para.26(2) use the word "intention" to appoint whilst para.26(1) uses the word "proposes" to make an appointment. In this context the words "intention" and "proposes" are synonymous: notice is to be given only if the company or its directors have a settled intention to appoint an administrator (*JCAM Commercial Real Estate Property XV Ltd v Davis Haulage Ltd* [2017] EWCA Civ 267; [2018] 1 W.L.R. 24; [2017] B.C.C. 222). This is because the purpose of giving the notice is to enable other persons to exercise their prior right to appoint an administrator and the purpose of filing a copy in court under para.27 is to trigger an interim moratorium to protect the company and its assets while a decision to appoint is made. The purpose of giving notice is limited and specific so that a settled intention is necessary and a conditional proposal to appoint (e.g. pending other options) is not sufficient for this purpose, otherwise repeated notices given as the effect of the previous one expired could result in ongoing interim moratoria merely as a delaying tactic.

Para.26(1)

This provision enables the charge holder, if he is not content for the administration to proceed under the control of the person proposed by the company or the directors, to appoint an insolvency practitioner of his own choice as administrative receiver or administrator, or negotiate to have such a person appointed instead of or in addition to the company's or directors' nominee. The charge holder would have time, also, to apply to the court to have the latter restrained from proceeding with their application, if he could show that this was inappropriate or for an improper purpose.

The use of the phrase "is or may be" makes it plain that notice must be given even though the charge is not currently enforceable.

Para.26(2), (3)

The new Rules no longer require the use of a statutory "Form", but instead prescribe the contents of the notice—in this case in r.3.23.

The question whether the failure to comply with the notice requirements of para.26 inevitably invalidates the appointment of the administrator has been much debated in recent cases at first instance, and remains the subject of controversy. Only a ruling of a higher court can resolve the current impasse.

It is necessary to consider separately the failure to give notice (i) to a charge holder under para.26(1), (ii) to the persons prescribed under para.26(2) other than the company, and (iii) to the company. In the first case there is a fixed period within which notice must be given (at least five business days), and the reason for this requirement is obviously to give the chargee an opportunity to intervene, as described above. It is not perhaps surprising that in *Adjei v Law for All* [2011] EWHC 2672 (Ch); [2011] B.C.C. 963 the failure to give notice was regarded as fatal (and the directors refused their costs), even though the charge had been paid off. The law was construed strictly; the notice obligation was fundamental.

In the second case, the background considerations are different. None of the persons prescribed has any statutory right to intervene in the appointment process, and there is no time limit. The object of the provision is rather to alert the recipient to the fact that the company is about to be, or has been, put into administration, so that he will not take the execution or other process further in breach of the statutory moratorium. On the basis of this reasoning it is arguably not necessary that the failure to give such notice should automatically invalidate the administrator's appointment in all cases. Paragraph 26(2) could be construed as directory rather than mandatory so that the judge would have a discretion to waive the breach and uphold the appointment (together with any other appropriate remedy, e.g. as regards costs). This was the view taken by HHJ McCahill QC (sitting as a judge of the High Court) in *Hill v Stokes plc* [2010] EWHC 3726; [2011] B.C.C. 473, where notice had not been given to landlords who had distrained on various properties of the company.

In the third case, where it is the company itself that has not been notified, the reasoning adopted by the learned judge in *Hill v Stokes* does not apply, as indeed he himself acknowledged. However, in a series of cases beginning with *Minmar (929) Ltd v Khalastchi* [2011] EWHC 1159 (Ch); [2011] B.C.C. 485, it was accepted that a failure to notify the company means that the purported appointment was defective (and, in *Minmar* itself and *National Westminster Bank plc v Msaada Group* [2011] EWHC 3423 (Ch); [2012] B.C.C. 226, not capable of correction). In contrast, in *Re Virtualpurple Professional Services Ltd* [2011] EWHC 3487 (Ch); [2012] B.C.C. 254 Norris J followed *Hill v Stokes* and stated in his view the obligation to give notice to the company was merely directory and not mandatory. (In *Re Derfshaw Ltd* [2011] EWHC 1565 (Ch); [2011] B.C.C. 631 this issue was raised but not pursued.) In *Re Bezier Acquisitions Ltd* [2011] EWHC 3299 (Ch); [2012] B.C.C. 219 it was by-passed because the judge was able to hold that service of a notice on the company's solicitor (who was present when the directors met) was equivalent to service on the company. Other cases in which the obligation to give notice has been held to be directory and not mandatory include *Re Assured Logistics Solutions Ltd* [2011] EWHC 3029 (Ch); [2012] B.C.C. 541 and *Re BXL Services* [2012] EWHC 1877 (Ch); [2012] B.C.C. 657. In the latter case HHJ Purle QC endeavoured to lay matters to rest by declaring that, unless and until the question was dealt with by a higher court, "the law must now to be taken as settled at first instance" that failure to give notice to one or more of the persons prescribed under para.26(2) was not fatal to the appointment, which accordingly was capable of retrospective validation. See also *Re Eiffel Steelworks Ltd* [2015] EWHC 511 (Ch); [2015] 2 B.C.L.C. 57.

A case decided along similar lines is *Re Ceart Risk Services Ltd* [2012] EWHC 1178 (Ch); [2012] B.C.C. 592, where the appointment of administrators to a financial services company was made without obtaining the prior consent of the FSA as required by FSMA 2000 s.362A, the necessary consent having however been given subsequently. Arnold J held that the requirement of prior notice was directory and not mandatory and could be cured by the later consent. (See also *Re Harlequin Management Services Ltd* [2013] EWHC 1926 (Ch).) This ruling may be contrasted with an earlier ruling, *Re M.T.B. Motors Ltd* [2010] EWHC 3751; [2012] B.C.C. 601, where the judge took the view that s.362A was mandatory, so that the purported appointment was a nullity, but made an administration order with retrospective effect and validating the activities of the administrators in the meantime.

These cases are closely examined by J. Anderson in Co. L.N. 304 (November 2011), 309 (February 2012) and 320 (August 2012).

For the relevant rules, see rr.3.23 et seq. A copy of the notice of intention to appoint must be filed with the court (para.27), and if there is any person to whom notice must be given under para.26(1), written notice must be given also to the following persons:

- any enforcement officer who is known to be charged with execution or other legal process against the company;
- any person who is known to have distrained against the company or its property;
- any supervisor of a CVA;
- the company, if it is not the company that is intending to make the appointment (r.3.23(4)).

It would appear that the amendment made by DA 2015 to para.26(2) (above) does not affect the discussion in the preceding paragraphs, although the occasions when the issues in question will arise will be less frequent.

27(1) A person who gives notice of intention to appoint under paragraph 26 shall file with the court as soon as is reasonably practicable a copy of–

(a) the notice, and

(b) any document accompanying it.

27(2) The copy filed under sub-paragraph (1) must be accompanied by a statutory declaration made by or on behalf of the person who proposes to make the appointment–

(a) that the company is or is likely to become unable to pay its debts,

(b) that the company is not in liquidation, and

(c) that, so far as the person making the statement is able to ascertain, the appointment is not prevented by paragraphs 23 to 25, and

(d) to such additional effect, and giving such information, as may be prescribed.

27(3) A statutory declaration under sub-paragraph (2) must–

(a) be in the prescribed form, and

(b) be made during the prescribed period.

27(4) A person commits an offence if in a statutory declaration under sub-paragraph (2) he makes a statement–

(a) which is false, and

(b) which he does not reasonably believe to be true.

General Note

Where there is a "qualifying" floating charge holder, compliance with this paragraph is a prerequisite to the making of an effective appointment, and the appointment must be made within the following ten business days: see para.28. Where there is no such charge holder, the company or directors may proceed to an immediate appointment: see the note to para.26.

Filing the notice triggers an interim moratorium: see para.44(4). In *Re Business Dream Ltd* [2011] EWHC 2860 (Ch); [2012] B.C.C. 115 the directors had given notice of their intention to appoint an administrator but then changed their mind and resolved to put the company into creditors' voluntary liquidation. It was held that the latter resolution was invalid and incapable of retrospective validation because it was passed during the currency of the moratorium.

Para.27(1)
As well as the statutory declaration referred to in para.27(2), the notice must be accompanied by one or other of the documents referred to in r.3.23(2).

Para.27(2), (3)
An appointment by the company or its directors may only be made if the company is insolvent, or nearly so. For the definition of "unable to pay its debts", see the notes to paras 11, 111(1) and s.123.

The prescribed period is five business days (r.3.23(6)(b)).

Para.27(4)
See the note to para.18(7).

28(1) An appointment may not be made under paragraph 22 unless the person who makes the appointment has complied with any requirement of paragraphs 26 and 27 and–

(a) the period of notice specified in paragraph 26(1) has expired, or

(b) each person to whom notice has been given under paragraph 26(1) has consented in writing to the making of the appointment.

28(2) An appointment may not be made under paragraph 22 after the period of ten business days beginning with the date on which the notice of intention to appoint is filed under paragraph 27(1).

General Note

Paragraph 28(1) only applies where there are persons who must be given notice under para.26(1): if not, an immediate appointment may be made. The reference to para.26 in the second line of para.28(1) is to be taken as a reference to para.26(1) only: *Hill v Stokes plc* [2010] EWHC 3726 (Ch); [2011] B.C.C. 473; *Re Virtualpurple Professional Services Ltd* [2011] EWHC 3487 (Ch); [2012] B.C.C. 254.

If the 10-day period specified in para.28(2) has expired, an appointment cannot be made pursuant to that particular notice, but this does not prevent the directors or company from giving a fresh notice and making a later out-of-court appointment, or applying to the court to make an appointment: *Re Cornercare Ltd* [2010] EWHC 893 (Ch); [2010] B.C.C. 592. Alternatively, the court may be asked (in its discretion) to make an order under r.12.64 validating the appointment retrospectively, since an inadvertent omission to give notice within the 10-day period is not fatal but a mere irregularity (*Re Euromaster Ltd* [2012] EWHC 2356 (Ch); [2012] B.C.C. 754).

Notice of appointment

29(1) A person who appoints an administrator of a company under paragraph 22 shall file with the court–

(a) a notice of appointment, and

(b) such other documents as may be prescribed.

29(2) The notice of appointment must include a statutory declaration by or on behalf of the person who makes the appointment–

(a) that the person is entitled to make an appointment under paragraph 22,

(b) that the appointment is in accordance with this Schedule, and

(c) that, so far as the person making the statement is able to ascertain, the statements made and information given in the statutory declaration filed with the notice of intention to appoint remain accurate.

29(3) The notice of appointment must identify the administrator and must be accompanied by a statement by the administrator–

(a) that he consents to the appointment,

(b) that in his opinion the purpose of administration is reasonably likely to be achieved, and

(c) giving such other information and opinions as may be prescribed.

29(4) For the purpose of a statement under sub-paragraph (3) an administrator may rely on information supplied by directors of the company (unless he has reason to doubt its accuracy).

29(5) The notice of appointment and any document accompanying it must be in the prescribed form.

29(6) A statutory declaration under sub-paragraph (2) must be made during the prescribed period.

29(7) A person commits an offence if in a statutory declaration under sub-paragraph (2) he makes a statement–

(a) which is false, and

(b) which he does not reasonably believe to be true.

General Note

The requirements of this paragraph closely parallel those of para.18: see the note to that provision. The appointment of the administrator takes effect from the time of the filing of the notice of appointment under this provision (para.31).

For the relevant rules, see rr.3.23 et seq.

Para.29(2), (6)

Note that this statutory declaration is additional to that required by para.27(2) to accompany a notice of intention to appoint. The prescribed period is not more than five business days before the notice is filed with the court (r.3.24).

Para.29(3)

In considering whether the statutory purpose of administration can be achieved, the potential administrator does not have to consider the directors' motives in appointing him: *Re BW Estates Ltd* [2015] EWHC 517 (Ch); [2016] B.C.C. 475.

Para.29(5)

In *Re Kaupthing Capital Partners II Master LP Inc* [2010] EWHC 836 (Ch); [2011] B.C.C. 338 the wrong prescribed form was used. The appointment was held to be invalid and incapable of being cured.

Para.29(7)

See the note to para.18(7).

30 In a case in which no person is entitled to notice of intention to appoint under paragraph 26(1) (and paragraph 28 therefore does not apply)–

(a) the statutory declaration accompanying the notice of appointment must include the statements and information required under paragraph 27(2), and

(b) paragraph 29(2)(c) shall not apply.

General Note

Where there is no floating charge holder entitled to notice of intention to appoint under para.26(1), the various time limits set out in paras 26–28(1) do not apply; but the statements and information which would otherwise have accompanied the notice of intention must be given with the notice of appointment, and the filing and notification obligations imposed by para.29 (except for para.29(2)(c)) must still be complied with. Although the words in brackets indicate that para.28 does not apply where the only persons entitled to notice of intention to appoint fall within para.26(2), this is contradicted by paras 27(1) and 28(2), read together, from which it would follow that the ten-day time limit imposed by para.28(2) applies in such a case.

Commencement of appointment

31 The appointment of an administrator under paragraph 22 takes effect when the requirements of paragraph 29 are satisfied.

General Note

As is the case with an out-of-court appointment by a floating charge holder (see para.19), the administrator cannot exercise any powers until the statutory filing and notification requirements have been complied with.

32 A person who appoints an administrator under paragraph 22–

(a) shall notify the administrator and such other persons as may be prescribed as soon as is reasonably practicable after the requirements of paragraph 29 are satisfied, and

(b) commits an offence if he fails without reasonable excuse to comply with paragraph (a).

General Note

A copy of the notice of appointment sealed by the court must be sent to the administrator as soon as reasonably practicable (r.3.26(4)). No other persons appear to have been prescribed under para.32(a).

On penalties, see s.430, Sch.B1 para.106 and Sch.10.

33 If before the requirements of paragraph 29 are satisfied the company enters administration by virtue of an administration order or an appointment under paragraph 14–

(a) the appointment under paragraph 22 shall not take effect, and

(b) paragraph 32 shall not apply.

General Note

An appointment by the court or an out-of-court appointment made by a floating charge holder has preference over one made by the company or its directors, but only if the charge in either of the former categories "takes effect" first: see the definition of "enters administration" in para.1(2). In any event, the company or directors will not have been free to proceed to an appointment if an application is before the court and has not yet been disposed of (para.25(b)).

Invalid appointment: indemnity

34(1) This paragraph applies where–

(a) a person purports to appoint an administrator under paragraph 22, and

(b) the appointment is discovered to be invalid.

34(2) The court may order the person who purported to make the appointment to indemnify the person appointed against liability which arises solely by reason of the appointment's invalidity.

General Note

This paragraph is in identical terms to para.20. See the note to that paragraph.

Administration Application—Special Cases

Application by holder of floating charge

35(1) This paragraph applies where an administration application in respect of a company–

(a) is made by the holder of a qualifying floating charge in respect of the company's property, and

(b) includes a statement that the application is made in reliance on this paragraph.

35(2) The court may make an administration order–

(a) whether or not satisfied that the company is or is likely to become unable to pay its debts, but

(b) only if satisfied that the applicant could appoint an administrator under paragraph 14.

General Note

It is generally a prerequisite for the making of an administration order that the company should be, or be likely to become, insolvent (para.11); but an appointment may be made out of court by the holder of a qualifying floating charge even in the case of a solvent company: see the note to para.14. The present provision enables the holder to apply to the court for an order as an alternative (perhaps if it is thought advisable to clarify that the statutory conditions have been met), and makes an exception to para.11 if the following conditions are satisfied:

- the applicant for the order must be the holder of a qualifying floating charge, as defined in para.14(2);
- the application must expressly state that it is made in reliance on para.35; and
- an event must have occurred or a condition been met which would entitle the charge holder to make an out-of-court appointment under para.14.

If these conditions cannot all be met, the holder of a floating charge may still apply to the court for an administration order, but the company must be shown to be insolvent or nearly so.

For examples of an application under this provision, see *Re St John Spencer Estate & Developments Ltd* [2012] EWHC 2317 (Ch); [2013] 1 B.C.L.C. 718; *Baker v London Bar Co Ltd* [2011] EWHC 3398 (Ch); [2012] B.C.C. 69; *Hellenic Capital Investments Ltd v Trainfx Ltd* [2015] EWHC 3713 (Ch); [2016] B.C.C. 493. The fact that the company has a valid cross-claim against the floating charge holder in excess of the debt charged does not detract from the enforceability of the charge: *Barclays Bank plc v Choicezone Ltd* [2011] EWHC 1303 (Ch); [2012] B.C.C. 767 (and in any case the loan facility may expressly exclude set-off or counterclaim in calculating the debt payable).

Intervention by holder of floating charge

36(1) This paragraph applies where–

(a) an administration application in respect of a company is made by a person who is not the holder of a qualifying floating charge in respect of the company's property, and

(b) the holder of a qualifying floating charge in respect of the company's property applies to the court to have a specified person appointed as administrator (and not the person specified by the administration applicant).

36(2) The court shall grant an application under sub-paragraph (1)(b) unless the court thinks it right to refuse the application because of the particular circumstances of the case.

General Note

This provision enables the holder of a qualifying floating charge to intervene, where an application to the court for an administration order has been made by someone else and he would prefer a different person to be appointed as administrator from the one who has been nominated. The charge holder must produce to the court:

- the written consent of all holders of any prior qualifying floating charge;
- the proposed administrator's consent to act; and
- sufficient evidence to satisfy the court that he is entitled to appoint an administrator under para.14 (r.3.11(1)).

This last requirement no doubt requires proof that the charge is immediately enforceable (para.16).

The court is required to accede to the charge holder's request unless the particular circumstances of the case dictate otherwise. Costs will normally be an expense of the administration (r.3.11(2)).

Where it is proposed to make an out-of-court appointment of an administrator who does not have the approval of the charge holder, he may take his own steps under para.14: see the note to para.26.

Application where company in liquidation

37(1) This paragraph applies where the holder of a qualifying floating charge in respect of a company's property could appoint an administrator under paragraph 14 but for paragraph 8(1)(b).

37(2) The holder of the qualifying floating charge may make an administration application.

37(3) If the court makes an administration order on hearing an application made by virtue of sub-paragraph (2)–

(a) the court shall discharge the winding-up order,

(b) the court shall make provision for such matters as may be prescribed,

(c) the court may make other consequential provision,

(d) the court shall specify which of the powers under this Schedule are to be exercisable by the administrator, and

(e) this Schedule shall have effect with such modifications as the court may specify.

General Note

Paragraph 8(1) imposes a general ban on the appointment of an administrator while a company is being wound up. However, the present provision empowers the court to substitute an administration for the liquidation where (a) the winding up is by court order; and (b) application is made by the holder of a "qualifying" floating charge who would, but for the winding up, be in a position to appoint an administrator out of court under para.14. Paragraph 37(3) ("If the court makes an administration order…") makes it plain that the court is not bound to accede to the application.

Note the court's discretionary powers under para.37(3)(c)–(e). The matters prescribed for the purposes of para.37(3)(b) appear in r.3.14.

Para.37(3)(a)–(c)
An order for the discharge of a winding-up order is not the same as a rescission of the order and does not operate retrospectively, and so a disposition of the company's property after the winding-up petition was presented comes within s.127 and is void unless the court orders otherwise. An administrator has standing to apply under s.127 for the validation of the disposition. (*Re Albany Building Ltd* [2007] B.C.C. 591.) Alternatively, this may be done in exercise of the discretion under para.37(3)(b), (c).

38(1) The liquidator of a company may make an administration application.

38(2) If the court makes an administration order on hearing an application made by virtue of sub-paragraph (1)–

(a) the court shall discharge any winding-up order in respect of the company,

(b) the court shall make provision for such matters as may be prescribed,

(c) the court may make other consequential provision,

(d) the court shall specify which of the powers under this Schedule are to be exercisable by the administrator, and

(e) this Schedule shall have effect with such modifications as the court may specify.

General Note

Paragraph 8, which bans the appointment of the administrator of a company which is in liquidation, is made subject to this paragraph when the company is in voluntary or compulsory liquidation (para.8(2), (3)). The administration can only be instituted by court order, and only the liquidator may make the application.

Para.38(2)
This subparagraph is in similar terms to para.37(3): the court has a discretion whether to make an order or not. But if it does decide to make an order, it must discharge any winding-up order. If the company is in voluntary liquidation, it would be open to the court to grant a stay of the proceedings under s.147.

Rule 3.6 applies, specifying the matters which must be contained in the witness statement in support of the application. The matters prescribed for the purposes of para.38(2)(b) appear in r.3.14.

Effect of administrative receivership

39(1) Where there is an administrative receiver of a company the court must dismiss an administration application in respect of the company unless–

(a) the person by or on behalf of whom the receiver was appointed consents to the making of the administration order,

(b) the court thinks that the security by virtue of which the receiver was appointed would be liable to be released or discharged under sections 238 to 240 (transaction at undervalue and preference) if an administration order were made,

(c) the court thinks that the security by virtue of which the receiver was appointed would be avoided under section 245 (avoidance of floating charge) if an administration order were made, or

(d) the court thinks that the security by virtue of which the receiver was appointed would be challengeable under section 242 (gratuitous alienations) or 243 (unfair preferences) or under any rule of law in Scotland.

39(2) Sub-paragraph (1) applies whether the administrative receiver is appointed before or after the making of the administration application.

General Note

This provision is in similar terms to s.*9(3)*, which applies in the original administration regime. But in some respects the drafting is different: under that section the court was not to dismiss the petition unless it was "*satisfied* … that, if an administration order were made, any security by virtue of which the receiver was appointed would be liable to be released or discharged" under IA 1986 ss.238–240 (or be avoided under s.245 or be challengeable under s.242). It is open to debate whether the phrase "the court thinks" is intended to set a lower standard of proof than "satisfied". (Compare the construction put on the words "if the court … *considers* that the making of an order under this section would be likely…" in the original s.*8(1)(b)* in *Re Harris Simons Construction Ltd* [1989] 1 W.L.R. 368; (1989) 5 B.C.C. 11: see s.*8(1), (2)*.) In *Chesterton International Group plc v Deka Immobilien Inv GmbH* [2005] EWHC 656 (Ch); [2005] B.P.I.R. 1103 administrative receivers were already in post when an application was made to the court for an order. The judge held that, without the consent of the receivers and in the absence of circumstances rendering the security suspect, the court lacked jurisdiction.

Effect of Administration

Dismissal of pending winding-up petition

40(1) A petition for the winding up of a company–

(a) shall be dismissed on the making of an administration order in respect of the company, and

(b) shall be suspended while the company is in administration following an appointment under paragraph 14.

40(2) Sub-paragraph (1)(b) does not apply to a petition presented under–

(a) section 124A (public interest),

(aa) section 124B (SEs), or

(b) section 367 of the Financial Services and Markets Act 2000 (c. 8) (petition by Financial Conduct Authority or Prudential Regulation Authority).

40(3) Where an administrator becomes aware that a petition was presented under a provision referred to in sub-paragraph (2) before his appointment, he shall apply to the court for directions under paragraph 63.

Para.40(1)

Where a petition for winding up has been made to the court but not yet heard or disposed of, it is to be dismissed if the company is put into administration by order of the court, and suspended if an administrator is appointed out of court by a floating charge holder. (An out-of-court appointment cannot be made by the company or its directors at such a time: see para.25(a).) When a winding-up petition is "suspended", it is without legal effect for the period of the administration, and so provisions such as s.127 do not apply: *Re J Smiths Haulage Ltd* [2007] B.C.C. 135; however, once the "suspension" is over (i.e. after the administration has ceased), the winding-up petition is resurrected and s.127 can apply: *Harlow v Creative Staging Ltd* [2014] EWHC 2787 (Ch). In *Re Portsmouth City Football Club Ltd, Neumans LLP v Andronikou* [2013] EWCA Civ 916; [2013] B.C.C. 741 a winding-up petition was suspended when an administrator was appointed out of court. The administration was eventually terminated and a winding-up order made on the original petition. Solicitors who had earlier advised the company in defending the petition sought to claim their fees either as an expense in the administration or as an expense of the liquidation, but were unsuccessful.

Para.40(2)

Although the Act does not generally allow a company to be in administration and in liquidation at the same time (see paras 8, 37, 38 and 42(4)), the possibility is recognised in the case of a winding up on public-interest grounds. If a winding-up order is made in respect of a company which is already in administration, para.82(3)(b) empowers the court to direct that the administration shall continue to have effect, and to give consequential directions.

Paragraph 40(2)(aa) was inserted by the European Public Limited-Liability Company Regulations 2004 (SI 2004/2326) reg.73(4)(c), as from 8 October 2004.

Dismissal of administrative or other receiver

41(1) When an administration order takes effect in respect of a company any administrative receiver of the company shall vacate office.

41(2) Where a company is in administration, any receiver of part of the company's property shall vacate office if the administrator requires him to.

41(3) Where an administrative receiver or receiver vacates office under sub-paragraph (1) or (2)–

(a) his remuneration shall be charged on and paid out of any property of the company which was in his custody or under his control immediately before he vacated office, and

(b) he need not take any further steps under section 40 or 59.

41(4) In the application of sub-paragraph (3)(a)–

(a) "remuneration" includes expenses properly incurred and any indemnity to which the administrative receiver or receiver is entitled out of the assets of the company,

(b) the charge imposed takes priority over security held by the person by whom or on whose behalf the administrative receiver or receiver was appointed, and

(c) the provision for payment is subject to paragraph 43.

General Note

Paragraph 41(1) necessarily applies only where the company is put into administration by court order, but para.41(2) applies in all administrations. (An out-of-court appointment cannot be made if an administrative receiver is already in office: see paras 17(b) and 25(c).)

On para.41 see *Promontoria (Chestnut) Ltd v Craig* [2017] EWHC 2405 (Ch).

Para.41(2)

Paragraph 41(2) does not apply to a receiver appointed under a charge created or otherwise arising under a financial collateral arrangement: Financial Collateral Arrangements (No.2) Regulations 2003 (SI 2003/3226) reg.8(2).

Para.41(4)(c)

Although the legislation makes special provision to secure payment of the outgoing receiver's remuneration and expenses, the moratorium imposed by para.43 will prevent him from enforcing payment during the currency of the administration except with the consent of the administrator or the court.

Moratorium on insolvency proceedings

42(1) This paragraph applies to a company in administration.

42(2) No resolution may be passed for the winding up of the company.

42(3) No order may be made for the winding up of the company.

42(4) Sub-paragraph (3) does not apply to an order made on a petition presented under–

(a) section 124A (public interest),

(aa) section 124B (SEs), or

(b) section 367 of the Financial Services and Markets Act 2000 (c. 8) (petition by Financial Conduct Authority or Prudential Regulation Authority).

42(5) If a petition presented under a provision referred to in sub-paragraph (4) comes to the attention of the administrator, he shall apply to the court for directions under paragraph 63.

Para.42(1)–(3)

Unless para.42(4) applies, a company cannot be put into liquidation either voluntarily or compulsorily while it is in administration. If winding up is to supersede an administration, it is necessary for the administration to be terminated either before or simultaneously with the transition. Voluntary liquidation is likely to be preferred in most cases because it can be carried out more cheaply and quickly and with less formality. The legislation makes express provision for this in para.83 below, so avoiding many of the difficulties experienced under the original regime. Alternatively, the court may make an order under para.79, bringing the administration to an end.

Paragraph 42(4)(aa) was inserted by the European Public Limited-Liability Company Regulations 2004 (SI 2004/2326) reg.73(4)(c), as from 8 October 2004.

Para.42(4), (5)
Once again, winding up on public interest grounds is made an exception, mirroring para.40(2), (3). If the court is satisfied that a winding-up order should be made, it is not required that the administration should be immediately terminated. There might be a case for leaving the administrator in post for a brief period, for instance, if he was in the process of realising security for the benefit of a charge holder. Paragraph 82(3)(b) makes provision for this to be done.

Moratorium on other legal process

43(1) This paragraph applies to a company in administration.

43(2) No step may be taken to enforce security over the company's property except–

(a) with the consent of the administrator, or

(b) with the permission of the court.

43(3) No step may be taken to repossess goods in the company's possession under a hire-purchase agreement except–

(a) with the consent of the administrator, or

(b) with the permission of the court.

43(4) A landlord may not exercise a right of forfeiture by peaceable re-entry in relation to premises let to the company except–

(a) with the consent of the administrator, or

(b) with the permission of the court.

43(5) In Scotland, a landlord may not exercise a right of irritancy in relation to premises let to the company except–

(a) with the consent of the administrator, or

(b) with the permission of the court.

43(6) No legal process (including legal proceedings, execution, distress and diligence) may be instituted or continued against the company or property of the company except–

(a) with the consent of the administrator, or

(b) with the permission of the court.

43(6A) An administrative receiver of the company may not be appointed.

43(7) Where the court gives permission for a transaction under this paragraph it may impose a condition on or a requirement in connection with the transaction.

43(8) In this paragraph "landlord" includes a person to whom rent is payable.

General Note

The provisions of the present paragraph correspond to parts of s.*11(3)* of the original administration regime. They apply once the appointment of an administrator has taken effect: see para.1(2)(a). An interim moratorium may already be in place under para.44 below.

Paragraph 43(6A) was inserted by the Enterprise Act 2002 (Insolvency) Order 2003 (SI 2003/2096 arts 1, 2(1), (3)) as from 15 September 2003.

Para.43(2)
Paragraph 43(2) does not apply to the enforcement of a security interest under a financial collateral arrangement: Financial Collateral Arrangements (No.2) Regulations 2003 (SI 2003/3226) reg.8(1)(a).

The court gave permission to enforce a security to the applicant, an insolvent bank, in *Re UK Housing Alliance (North West) Ltd, Mackay v Kaupthing Singer & Friedlander Ltd* [2013] EWHC 2553 (Ch) to enable it to realise assets for the benefit of its own creditors. The court stated that permission would normally be granted in such cases if a refusal would cause significant loss.

Para.43(6)
The forerunner to this provision is IA 1986 s.*11* (part of the original Pt 2, which of course remains in force for some administrations). In the landmark case of *Re Atlantic Computer Systems plc* [1992] Ch. 505; [1990] B.C.C. 859, decided under that provision, the Court of Appeal made a number of important rulings on the interpretation of the section and gave guidance on the principles governing the exercise of the court's discretion under the section. The company's business was leasing computers, a substantial number of which it held on hire-purchase or long lease from banks and other financial institutions (referred to in the judgment as "the funders"). Two funders applied to the court contending that the administrators, having received payments from the sub-lessees, were obliged to pay the rentals due under the head leases. Alternatively, the funders sought leave under s.*11* to repossess the computer equipment. The trial judge, applying an analogy from winding-up law, held that where leased property was used for the purposes of an administration, the rent or hire charges due to the lessor should rank as an expense of the administration and as such be payable in priority to the company's other creditors; but the Court of Appeal considered that a more appropriate analogy was with administrative receivership, where such charges would not have the same priority. The court expressed the view that, in any case, the discretionary jurisdiction conferred by s.*11* should be exercised on the broadest basis and should not be allowed to become fettered by rigid rules of automatic application. However, it went on to hold that the computers remained "goods in the company's possession", notwithstanding the sub-leases, so that the discretionary powers conferred by s.*11(3)(c)* could be invoked; that lessors and other owners of property in the position of the funders should not be compelled to leave it in the company's hands against their will but should ordinarily be allowed to repossess it; and that this should normally be a matter where the administrator would be expected to give his consent, thus obviating the need to make application to the court for leave.
The judgment concludes with a statement giving guidance on the principles to be applied on applications for the grant of leave under s.*11*. These principles, which are set out at length (see [1992] Ch. 505 at 542–544; [1990] B.C.C. 859 at 879–882), also serve as guidelines to an administrator in determining whether to grant consent, and may be summarised as follows:

(1) The person seeking leave has always to make out a case.

(2) If granting leave to an owner of land or goods to exercise his proprietary rights as lessor and repossess his land or goods is unlikely to impede the achievement of the purpose of the administration, leave should normally be given.

(3) In other cases where a lessor seeks possession, the court has to carry out a balancing exercise, weighing the legitimate interests of the lessor against those of the company's other creditors.

(4) In carrying out the balancing exercise, great importance is normally to be given to the lessor's proprietary interests: an administration for the benefit of unsecured creditors should not be conducted at the expense of those who have proprietary rights.

(5) It will normally be a sufficient ground for the grant of leave that significant loss would be caused to the lessor by a refusal. However if substantially greater loss would be caused to others by the grant of leave, that may outweigh the loss to the lessor caused by a refusal.

(6)–(8) These paragraphs list the various factors to which the court will have regard in assessing the respective losses under heading (5). These include: the financial position of the company, its ability to pay the interest, rentals or other charges (both arrears and continuing charges), the administrator's proposals and the end result sought to be achieved by the administration, the period for which the administration has already been in force and that for which it is expected to continue, the prospects of success of the administration, the likely loss to the applicant if leave is refused, and the conduct of the parties.

(9) The above considerations may be relevant not only to the decision whether or not to grant leave, but also to a decision to impose terms if leave is granted.

(10) The court may, in effect, impose conditions if leave is refused (for instance, by giving directions to the administrator), in which case the above considerations will also be applicable.

(11) A broadly similar approach will apply in many applications for leave to enforce a security.

(c) the appointment of an administrative receiver of the company, or

(d) the carrying out by an administrative receiver (whenever appointed) of his functions.

General Note

This provision gives protection in the case where the appointment of an administrator is sought by court order under para.10, and also establishes a brief moratorium pending the taking effect of an out-of-court appointment. During the interim moratorium the court may give leave for proceedings to continue on the same principles as apply under para.43: *South Coast Construction Ltd v Iverson Road Ltd* [2017] EWHC 61 (TCC). In *Bernhards Sports Surfaces Ltd v Astrosoccer 4 U Ltd* [2017] EWHC 2425 (TCC) the same judge gave permission for debt proceedings to continue against a company, strongly criticising its directors' conduct in giving notice of intention to appoint an administrator as "entirely bogus" and intended to misuse the administration proceedings in an attempt to allow the company to avoid paying a due debt.

Para.44(1)
Under the original regime there is no provision corresponding to that in para.13(2)(a) which expressly empowers the court to specify a time other than that of the order from which the appointment of an administrator is to take effect. Paragraph 44(1)(b) ensures that the interim moratorium continues where a time later that that of the order is fixed by the court. In an appropriate case the court has power under paras 13(1)(f) or 43(7) to modify the terms of the moratorium.

The interim moratorium protects the company (and indirectly, the creditors) from proceedings pending the hearing of the administration application. To protect creditors from dissipation of the company's assets before the hearing, a creditor may apply for a freezing order over the company's assets. The terms of such an order conventionally allow the company to spend a reasonable sum on obtaining legal representation and advice for the freezing-order hearing. For consideration of what is a reasonable amount in such circumstances, see *Appleyard v Reflex Recordings Ltd* [2013] EWHC 4514 (Ch).

Paras 44(2)–(4)
Where the appointment of an administrator is being made out of court, it does not take effect until the filing and notice requirements of paras 18 or 26 have been complied with (see paras 19, 31). Paragraph 44(2) applies where a floating charge holder intending to appoint an administrator files a notice of intention to appoint with the court. Paragraph 44(4) establishes a moratorium where it is the company or its directors who make an out-of-court appointment, for a period which at a maximum cannot exceed ten days. The main difference between paras 44(2) and 44(4) is that the filing of a notice of intention to appoint is optional in the former case but obligatory in the latter—at least where there is a holder of a qualifying floating charge or other person to whom notice must be given under para.26(1). It does not appear that a moratorium could be obtained in either case simply by filing a notice of intention to appoint with the court when there is nobody who is required by the Act to be given notice: the general tenor of the Act, rules and prescribed forms (and especially the requirement that it is in every case a *copy* of the notice that is to be filed) suggests otherwise. In some circumstances the charge holder or the company or its directors may proceed to make an immediate appointment, in which case there will be no interim moratorium: see the note to paras 14 and 26. The position where an appointment is made by the company or its directors and the only persons entitled to notice of intention to appoint are those specified under para.26(2) is unclear.

Importantly, the person filing notice of intention to appoint under para.44(4) must have a settled intention to appoint: to keep filing notices every 10 days merely to obtain a continuous moratorium without having such a settled intention would almost inevitably constitute an abuse of process of the court: *JCAM Commercial Real Estate Property XV Ltd v Davis Haulage Ltd* [2017] EWCA Civ 267; [2017] B.C.C. 222 (although David Richards LJ declined so to order on the facts, he gave a clear warning (at [64]) against any such practice for the future).

Para.44(5)
Under paras 42 and 43 a dispensation from a restriction imposed by the (permanent) statutory moratorium may be granted by either the administrator or the court. Since the appointment of the administrator will not have taken effect when para.44 applies, it is only the court which will have power to grant the necessary leave.

Para.44(6)
This subparagraph refers to an "administration application", and so applies only where an appointment is sought by court order. Paragraph 39 gives the person who has appointed an administrative receiver a veto over a court appointment unless he is willing to consent to an order under para.39(1(a). If an administrative receiver is in office when an application for an administration order is made to the court, the interim moratorium will not take effect unless and until the charge holder decides to give his consent.

Para.44(7)
This subparagraph applies only during an interim moratorium. Paragraph 43 will normally prevent similar action being taken against a company once a permanent moratorium has come into effect. Paragraph 44(7)(d) would allow the administrative receiver to continue to act until the court order is made, even where the charge-holder has signified his intention to consent to the order.

Publicity

45(1) While a company is in administration, every business document issued by or on behalf of the company or the administrator, and all the company's websites, must state–

(a) the name of the administrator, and

(b) that the affairs, business and property of the company are being managed by the administrator.

45(2) Any of the following persons commits an offence if without reasonable excuse the person authorises or permits a contravention of sub-paragraph (1)–

(a) the administrator,

(b) an officer of the company, and

(c) the company.

45(3) In sub-paragraph (1) "business document" means–

(a) an invoice,

(b) an order for goods or services,

(c) a business letter, and

(d) an order form,

whether in hard copy, electronic or any other form.

General Note

This is a parallel provision to those requiring notification of the appointment of a receiver (ss.39, 64) and notification that the company is in liquidation (s.188). Paragraph 45 was amended by the Companies (Trading Disclosures) (Insolvency) Regulations 2008 (SI 2008/1897) reg.4(1), as from 1 October 2008.

On penalties, see s.430 and Sch.10.

Process of Administration

Announcement of administrator's appointment

46(1) This paragraph applies where a person becomes the administrator of a company.

46(2) As soon as is reasonably practicable the administrator shall–

(a) send a notice of his appointment to the company, and

(b) publish a notice of his appointment in the prescribed manner.

46(3) As soon as is reasonably practicable the administrator shall–

(a) obtain a list of the company's creditors, and

(b) send a notice of his appointment to each creditor of whose claim and address he is aware.

46(4) The administrator shall send a notice of his appointment to the registrar of companies before the end of the period of 7 days beginning with the date specified in sub-paragraph (6).

46(5) The administrator shall send a notice of his appointment to such persons as may be prescribed before the end of the prescribed period beginning with the date specified in sub-paragraph (6).

46(6) The date for the purpose of sub-paragraphs (4) and (5) is–

(a) in the case of an administrator appointed by administration order, the date of the order,

(b) in the case of an administrator appointed under paragraph 14, the date on which he receives notice under paragraph 20, and

(c) in the case of an administrator appointed under paragraph 22, the date on which he receives notice under paragraph 32.

46(7) The court may direct that sub-paragraph (3)(b) or (5)–

(a) shall not apply, or

(b) shall apply with the substitution of a different period.

46(8) A notice under this paragraph must–

(a) contain the prescribed information, and

(b) be in the prescribed form.

46(9) An administrator commits an offence if he fails without reasonable excuse to comply with a requirement of this paragraph.

General Note

This is an extended version of the original s.*21*, adjusted to take account of cases where the administrator is appointed out of court. However, the time limits have been altered as noted below. For the relevant rules for the purposes of this paragraph, see r.3.27. On the giving of notice, see IR 2016 rr.1.28 et seq. In *Re Sporting Options plc* [2004] EWHC 3128 (Ch); [2005] B.C.C. 88 Mann J refused to allow the notice of appointment to be sent by email, largely because of possible problems with firewalls. However, in order to save expense, he allowed the administrator to send by post a short indication of the website at which his proposals could be found and indicated that this would be regarded as sufficient service of the proposals. It has subsequently been held that Mann J in *Sporting Options* was not laying down a general rule excluding the sending of notices of appointment by email, but rested his decision on the particular facts that the sending of notices by email was not an appropriate form of communication since emails to many customer-creditors had been kicked back and email addresses might change. Thus email was allowed in *Re Advent Computer Training Ltd* [2010] EWHC 459 (Ch); [2011] B.C.C. 44 where students were required to use email with the company and keep it immediately notified of any change in email address. HHJ Purle QC also noted that emails were commonly in use in the case before him, almost five years after the *Sporting Options* decision, with fewer problems with firewalls. He added that if there was significant incidence of emails being kicked back, then the administrators should seek further directions. The same judge applied his approach in *Advent Computer Training* (above) in *Re All Leisure Holidays Ltd* [2017] EWHC 870 (Ch); [2017] B.C.C. 354 to allow administrators to give notices by email to tour company customer creditors who had previously been receiving information from the companies by email. (For the rules on electronic delivery of documents in insolvency proceedings see IR 2016 rr.1.45 et seq. and note in particular the requirement for consent to electronic delivery by recipients in r.1.45.)

Para.46(2)
The notice must be published in the *Gazette* and may be advertised in such other manner as the administrator thinks fit (r.3.27(1)). Where the appointment has been made by the company under para.22, para.46(2)(a) would seem superfluous, since the company will already have sent a notice to him under para.32(a)!

Para.46(3)
"As soon as reasonably practicable" has been substituted for "within 28 days after the making of the order" under the original regime.

Para.46(4), (6)
The period under the original Pt II is 14 days from the making of the order. Note that subpara.(a) refers to the date of the order, not the date when the order takes effect (so placing a duty on the administrator before his appointment is effective).

Para.46(5)
The prescribed persons are:

- any receiver or administrative receiver;
- the petitioner under any pending winding-up petition, and any provisional liquidator;
- any enforcement officer or agent charged with execution or other legal process against the company;
- any person who has distrained against the company or its property;
- the supervisor of any CVA (r.3.27(2)).

No specific period is prescribed: r.3.27(3) simply states that notice shall be given "as soon as reasonably practicable".

Para.46(9)
On penalties, see s.430, Sch.B1 para.106(2) and Sch.10.

Statement of company's affairs

47(1) As soon as is reasonably practicable after appointment the administrator of a company shall by notice in the prescribed form require one or more relevant persons to provide the administrator with a statement of the affairs of the company.

47(2) The statement must–

(a) be verified by a statement of truth in accordance with Civil Procedure Rules,

(b) be in the prescribed form,

(c) give particulars of the company's property, debts and liabilities,

(d) give the names and addresses of the company's creditors,

(e) specify the security held by each creditor,

(f) give the date on which each security was granted, and

(g) contain such other information as may be prescribed.

47(3) In sub-paragraph (1) "relevant person" means–

(a) a person who is or has been an officer of the company,

(b) a person who took part in the formation of the company during the period of one year ending with the date on which the company enters administration,

(c) a person employed by the company during that period, and

(d) a person who is or has been during that period an officer or employee of a company which is or has been during that year an officer of the company.

47(4) For the purpose of sub-paragraph (3) a reference to employment is a reference to employment through a contract of employment or a contract for services.

47(5) In Scotland, a statement of affairs under sub-paragraph (1) must be a statutory declaration made in accordance with the Statutory Declarations Act 1835 (c. 62) (and sub-paragraph (2)(a) shall not apply).

General Note

The "statement of affairs", which had long been a feature of the liquidation procedure in a compulsory winding up (see s.131), was made a requirement by IA 1986 in administration and a number of other insolvency proceedings. For further comment, see the notes to s.131.

For the relevant rules, forms and other matters prescribed for the purposes of this paragraph, see rr.3.29 et seq.

Para.47(1)
The notice must contain the information specified in r.3.29(3). In addition, the administrator must inform each recipient that a document for the preparation of the statement of affairs will be supplied if requested (r.3.29(3)).

Para.47(2), (5)
The administrator may require any "relevant person" to submit a statement of concurrence stating that he concurs in the statement of affairs (r.3.31). In this event:

- the person making the statement of affairs must be informed;
- that person must deliver a copy of the statement of affairs to the other "relevant person (or persons)";
- the latter then has five business days to submit the statement of concurrence to the administrator;
- a statement of concurrence may be qualified in certain events;
- every statement of concurrence is to be verified by a statement of truth;
- every statement of concurrence is to be filed together with the statement of affairs with the court and sent to the registrar of companies (rr.3.31 et seq.).

There is provision in rr.3.44 et seq. for the court to order that limited disclosure only should be made, or no disclosure at all, where the administrator thinks that disclosure would prejudice the conduct of the administration, and a right given to a creditor by r.3.44 to apply for an order that the administrator should disclose the statement or part of it notwithstanding such an order.

A person making a statement of affairs may be reimbursed expenses which he has incurred (r.3.34).

Para.47(3), (4)
The expression "officer", in relation to a company, includes a director, manager or secretary (CA 2006 s.1121), and at least in some contexts may extend to the holders of other offices: see the note to s.206(3). The wide definition of "employment" used here could include professionals such as the company's auditors and bankers.

48(1) A person required to submit a statement of affairs must do so before the end of the period of 11 days beginning with the day on which he receives notice of the requirement.

48(2) The administrator may–

(a) revoke a requirement under paragraph 47(1), or

(b) extend the period specified in sub-paragraph (1) (whether before or after expiry).

48(3) If the administrator refuses a request to act under sub-paragraph (2)–

(a) the person whose request is refused may apply to the court, and

(b) the court may take action of a kind specified in sub-paragraph (2).

48(4) A person commits an offence if he fails without reasonable excuse to comply with a requirement under paragraph 47(1).

General Note

For the relevant rules, see rr.3.33 et seq.

Para.48(1)
Note that the period is 11 days, not 11 business days.

Para.48(2), (3)
The language used in para.48(2)(a) is rather less clear than that in s.*22(5)*, although the meaning is no doubt meant to be the same. Section *22(5)* empowers the administrator to "release a person from an obligation imposed on him" to submit a statement of affairs, and also to extend the period, and continues: "where the administrator has refused to exercise a power conferred by this subsection, the court, if it thinks fit, may exercise it". Rule 3.37 (which uses similar language) sets out the procedure as regards both the grant of a release and an extension of time.

Para.48(4)
On penalties, see s.430, Sch.B1 para.106(2) and Sch.10.

Administrator's proposals

49(1) The administrator of a company shall make a statement setting out proposals for achieving the purpose of administration.

49(2) A statement under sub-paragraph (1) must, in particular–

(a) deal with such matters as may be prescribed, and

(b) where applicable, explain why the administrator thinks that the objective mentioned in paragraph 3(1)(a) or (b) cannot be achieved.

49(3) Proposals under this paragraph may include–

(a) a proposal for a voluntary arrangement under Part I of this Act (although this paragraph is without prejudice to section 4(3));

(b) a proposal for a compromise or arrangement to be sanctioned under Part 26 of the Companies Act 2006 (arrangements and reconstructions).

49(4) The administrator shall send a copy of the statement of his proposals–

(a) to the registrar of companies,

(b) to every creditor of the company, other than an opted-out creditor, of whose claim and address he is aware, and

(c) to every member of the company of whose address he is aware.

49(5) The administrator shall comply with sub-paragraph (4)–

(a) as soon as is reasonably practicable after the company enters administration, and

(b) in any event, before the end of the period of eight weeks beginning with the day on which the company enters administration.

49(6) The administrator shall be taken to comply with sub-paragraph (4)(c) if he publishes in the prescribed manner a notice undertaking to provide a copy of the statement of proposals free of charge to any member of the company who applies in writing to a specified address.

49(7) An administrator commits an offence if he fails without reasonable excuse to comply with sub-paragraph (5).

49(8) A period specified in this paragraph may be varied in accordance with paragraph 107.

General Note

Rule 3.35 sets out in considerable detail the matters required to be dealt with (in addition to those prescribed by para.49) in the statement of proposals, which must be sent as directed by para.49(4). Note that the copy notice to creditors under para.49(4)(b) may in suitable circumstances be sent by email: see *Re Advent Computer Training Ltd* [2010] EWHC 459 (Ch); [2011] B.C.C. 44 and the General Note to para.46 above.

In the special circumstances of *Re UK Coal Operations Ltd* [2013] EWHC 2581 (Ch); [2014] 1 B.C.L.C. 471 HHJ Purle QC granted an order dispensing altogether with the requirements of formulating proposals and calling a creditors' meeting under para.51. Plans were already in place to move from administration to a CVL within a few days, and to comply with the statutory formalities would involve needless delay and expense.

One of the matters to be included in the proposals is, under r.3.35(1)(d), an account of the circumstances giving rise to the appointment of the administrator. In light of the collapse into administration of delivery company City Link at Christmas 2014, a parliamentary report in March 2015 contained criticism of the administration system, especially in relation to the lack of information to employees and sub-contractors. The Government responded on 17 September 2015, in particular to a recommendation in the report that the Government should work with insolvency professionals to agree a short initial statement to be made publicly available "no later than a week after an administration order has been made setting out a high level summary of the events leading up to the administration". The Government has responded that it intends to consider how this recommendation might work in practice.

Rule 3.45 empowers the administrator to apply to the court for an order authorising him to make limited disclosure of any specified part of the para.49 statement where he thinks that it would prejudice the conduct of the administration or be prejudicial to the interests of a creditor to disclose all the matters specified in r.3.35(l)(h) and (i). Such an order directs that some or all of the specified part must not be sent to the registrar of companies and the members and creditors. The persons listed in para.49(4) must then be sent the para.49 statement to the extent provided by the order and an indication of the nature of the matter in relation to which the order was made. A creditor may apply to the court for an order requiring disclosure of a part of the statement covered by the order and the court on such an application may make the order subject to conditions as to confidentiality, etc. as it sees fit. If there is a material change of circumstances after an order for limited disclosure has been made which renders the limit unnecessary the administrator must apply to the court for the order to be rescinded in whole or in part. For an elaborate example of directions authorising limited disclosure, see *Re Advent Computer Training Ltd (No.2)* [2010] EWHC 1042 (Ch); [2011] B.C.C. 52.

Para.49(2)
Paragraph 3 of Sch.B1 ranks the statutory objectives of an administration in a definite sequence: (1) corporate rescue; (2) a better result for the creditors as a whole than would be likely in a winding up without prior administration; and (3) satisfying the claims of preferential and secured creditors. Subparagraph (2)(b) is a reminder that the administrator cannot lightly disregard this hierarchy, e.g. by treating the administration as in effect a receivership and proceeding immediately to discharge the claims in category (3).

Para.49(3)
These are two of the statutory purposes for which an administration order can be sought under the original regime. Although they have been given no place in the structured "objectives" of the new regime (see above), this is an indication that they have not been wholly forgotten. There will now be less occasion to have recourse to the former practice of combining an administration with a CVA in order to obtain a moratorium, in view of the enactment of Sch.A1, but of course a moratorium is available only for "eligible" companies; and in any case there may sometimes be advantages in a CVA which administration alone could not secure—e.g. if it is desired to involve the members as well as the creditors in the proposals.

Section 4(3) preserves the rights of secured creditors to enforce their security, unless they agree otherwise. (Note also the protection given to secured and preferential creditors by para.73.)

There is at present no statutory provision for a moratorium for the period in which a scheme of arrangement under CA 2006 Pt 26 is formulated and sanctioned, but this can be achieved by putting a scheme together under the protective umbrella of an administration. Again, this may make it possible to achieve rather more than under administration alone, e.g. a restructuring involving more than one company of which some are not insolvent.

Para.49(4)–(8)
Under para.107, the court (or the administrator with the "consent" of the creditors, as there defined) may vary this period: see the note to that paragraph. If the court grants an extension of time, the persons referred to in para.49(4) must be notified (r.3.37(2)).

An administrator is not normally under an obligation to notify any person that he may have a claim against the company, but in the special circumstances of *Re London Scottish Finance Ltd* [2013] EWHC 4047 (Ch) the administrators were directed to notify previous and existing debtors of the company of potential claims that they might have under credit agreements which were unenforceable under the Consumer Credit Act 1974.

The court may make an order limiting disclosure of any specified part of the statement (e.g. because disclosure would prejudice the conduct of the administration (r.3.45)), and such an order may be made with retrospective effect after an unredacted statement has been placed on the register: *Registrar of Companies v Swarbrick* [2014] EWHC 1466 (Ch).

Rule 3.38(4)–(7) deals with the situations where the administrator thinks that he need not seek approval from the creditors (para.52), where he thinks that the purpose of the administration has been sufficiently achieved before he has sent a statement of his proposals to creditors (para.80) and where he chooses the alternative course of publishing a notice relating to the proposals under para.49(6) rather than sending a statement to every member.

On penalties, see s.430, Sch.B1 para.106(2) and Sch.10.

50 [Repealed by SBEEA 2015 Sch.9 paras 1, 10(3) as from 6 April 2017]

Consideration of administrator's proposals by creditors

51(1) The administrator must seek a decision from the company's creditors as to whether they approve the proposals set out in the statement made under paragraph 49(1).

51(2) The initial decision date for that decision must be within the period of 10 weeks beginning with the day on which the company enters administration.

51(3) The "initial decision date" for that decision–

(a) if the decision is initially sought using the deemed consent procedure, is the date on which a decision will be made if the creditors by that procedure approve the proposals, and

(b) if the decision is initially sought using a qualifying decision procedure, is the date on or before which a decision will be made if it is made by that qualifying decision procedure (assuming that date does not change after the procedure is instigated).

51(4) A period specified in this paragraph may be varied in accordance with paragraph 107.

51(5) An administrator commits an offence if he fails without reasonable excuse to comply with a requirement of this paragraph.

General Note

Paragraph 51(1)–(3) and the heading substituted by SBEEA 2015 Sch.9 paras 1, 10(4), (5) as from 6 April 2017.

Under the former rules, the administrator was required to hold an "initial creditors' meeting" in order to determine whether the creditors approved his proposals. This has been replaced by an obligation to seek a decision from the creditors without holding a physical meeting (although this may be requested by the statutory percentage or number of creditors in accordance with s.246ZE).

The administrator is relieved from this obligation in the various circumstances listed in para.52.

The ten-week limit here specified may be varied by the court under para.107 or the administrator with the consent of the creditors under para.108: see the notes to those provisions. Note also that the administrator may dispense with the need to seek a decision from the creditors where he thinks that the purpose of the administration has already been sufficiently achieved (see para.80) or if he decides that the company should move from administration to dissolution under para.84. In *Re UK Coal Operations Ltd* [2013] EWHC 2581 (Ch); [2014] 1 B.C.L.C. 471 it was held that an administrator could in special circumstances decide not to call a creditors' meeting as a matter of commercial necessity.

Para.51(5)

On penalties, see s.430, Sch.B1 para.106(2) and Sch.10.

52(1) Paragraph 51(1) shall not apply where the statement of proposals states that the administrator thinks–

(a) that the company has sufficient property to enable each creditor of the company to be paid in full,

(b) that the company has insufficient property to enable a distribution to be made to unsecured creditors other than by virtue of section 176A(2)(a), or

(c) that neither of the objectives specified in paragraph 3(1)(a) and (b) can be achieved.

52(2) But the administrator shall seek a decision from the company's creditors as to whether they approve the proposals set out in the statement made under paragraph 49(1) if requested to do so–

(a) by creditors of the company whose debts amount to at least 10% of the total debts of the company,

(b) in the prescribed manner, and

(c) in the prescribed period.

52(3) Where a decision is sought by virtue of sub-paragraph (2) the initial decision date (as defined in paragraph 51(3)) must be within the prescribed period.

52(4) The period prescribed under sub-paragraph (3) may be varied in accordance with paragraph 107.

General Note

Paragraph 52(2) amended and para.52(3) substituted by SBEEA 2015 Sch.9 paras 1, 10(6), (7) as from 6 April 2017.

Paragraph 52(1) in essence applies in circumstances where there is likely to be nothing of substance that creditors could decide. These circumstances are:

- that there are sufficient assets to enable all the company's creditors to be paid in full;
- that there will be insufficient assets to enable anything to be paid to the unsecured creditors (apart from anything that may come to them from the "prescribed part", set aside following the realisation of assets subject to a floating charge: see the notes to s.176A); or
- that the only objective of the administration which the administrator thinks is capable of achievement is "realising property in order to make a distribution to one or more secured or preferential creditors" (para.3(1)(c)).

There is obviously an overlap between the latter two situations, but the third would apply and not the second where there was no floating charge or where there are only sufficient assets to make a part payment to the secured or preferential creditors.

Para.52(2)–(4)
Rule 15.18 applies. The period prescribed is 8 business days from the date on which the administrator's proposals are sent out, and the meeting (or alternative) must be held within 28 days of the request being received by the administrator. Security must be given for the expenses of summoning and holding the meeting. The 8-day period may be varied by the court under para.107.

Creditors' decision

53(1) The company's creditors may approve the administrator's proposals–

(a) without modification, or

(b) with modification to which the administrator consents.

53(2) The administrator shall as soon as is reasonably practicable report any decision taken by the company's creditors to–

(a) the court,

(b) the registrar of companies, and

(c) such other persons as may be prescribed.

53(3) An administrator commits an offence if he fails without reasonable excuse to comply with sub-paragraph (2).

General Note

Paragraph 53(1) substituted by SBEEA 2015 Sch.9 paras 1, 10(9), as from 6 April 2017.

The administrator's freedom to act in the exercise of his functions is limited by the scope of the proposals, once approved (see para.68(1))—apart from "insubstantial" deviations (para.54(1)(c)); and so it is important, from his point of view, that they should not be too restrictively drawn. Indeed, in *Re Dana (UK) Ltd* [1999] 2 B.C.L.C. 239 Neuberger J thought that it would make good sense for the proposals put before an initial meeting to include a mechanism empowering the largest and/or representative creditors to approve future decisions or variations of decisions of the administrator. In any event the court may, in exceptional circumstances, authorise the administrator to depart from the approved scheme: see the note to para.54, below.

For the rules governing the decision procedure, see rr.15.8 et seq. Note that the rules invalidate any resolution of the creditors which is opposed by a majority of the creditors who are not "connected with" the company: see r.15.34(2) and, on the meaning of "connected with", s.249.

On the persons prescribed for the purposes of para.53(2)(c), see r.3.41.

On penalties, see s.430, Sch.B1 para.106(2) and Sch.10.

Revision of administrator's proposals

54(1) This paragraph applies where–

(a) an administrator's proposals have been approved (with or without modification) by the company's creditors,

(b) the administrator proposes a revision to the proposals, and

(c) the administrator thinks that the proposed revision is substantial.

54(2) The administrator shall–

(a) [Omitted]

(b) send a statement in the prescribed form of the proposed revision to each creditor who is not an opted-out creditor,

(c) send a copy of the statement, within the prescribed period, to each member of the company of whose address he is aware, and

(d) seek a decision from the company's creditors as to whether they approve the proposed revision.

54(3) The administrator shall be taken to have complied with sub-paragraph (2)(c) if he publishes a notice undertaking to provide a copy of the statement free of charge to any member of the company who applies in writing to a specified address.

54(4) A notice under sub-paragraph (3) must be published–

(a) in the prescribed manner, and

(b) within the prescribed period.

54(5) The company's creditors may approve the proposed revision–

(a) without modification, or

(b) with modification to which the administrator consents.

54(6) The administrator shall as soon as is reasonably practicable report any decision taken by the company's creditors to–

(a) the court,

(b) the registrar of companies, and

(c) such other persons as may be prescribed.

54(7) An administrator commits an offence if he fails without reasonable excuse to comply with sub-paragraph (6).

General Note

Paragraph 54(2)(a) omitted, para.54(2)(b) amended and para.54(2)(d), (5) substituted by SBEEA 2015 Sch.9 paras 1, 10(12)–(15) as from 6 April 2017.

This paragraph often repeats provisions to be found elsewhere, e.g. in paras 49, 51 and 53, and it may be helpful to refer to the notes to those provisions.

The administrator is bound to adhere to the course of action agreed to by the creditors (except that he may, apparently, make "insubstantial" deviations: see para.54(1)(c)). If he wishes to work to a different strategy, he must go back to the creditors for approval of revised proposals. However, in exceptional circumstances (e.g. where the delay involved in considering a revised scheme could cause substantial loss) the court has power under para.68(3)(c)) to authorise an administrator to depart from an approved scheme: cf. *Re Smallman Construction Ltd* (1988) 4 B.C.C. 784; and *Re Dana (UK) Ltd* [1999] 2 B.C.L.C. 239.

Para.54(2)–(4)
Rules 15.8 et seq. and more particularly r.3.42 apply. Members must be sent copies of the statement within five days of sending the statement to creditors, unless s.54(3) applies, when the administrator must publish a notice in accordance with r.3.42(5).

Para.54(7)
On penalties, see s.430, Sch.B1 para.106(2) and Sch.10.

Failure to obtain approval of administrator's proposals

55(1) This paragraph applies where an administrator–

(a) reports to the court under paragraph 53 that a company's creditors have failed to approve the administrator's proposals, or

(b) reports to the court under paragraph 54 that a company's creditors have failed to approve a revision of the administrator's proposals.

55(2) The court may–

(a) provide that the appointment of an administrator shall cease to have effect from a specified time;

(b) adjourn the hearing conditionally or unconditionally;

(c) make an interim order;

(d) make an order on a petition for winding up suspended by virtue of paragraph 40(1)(b);

(e) make any other order (including an order making consequential provision) that the court thinks appropriate.

General Note

Paragraph 55(1) substituted by SBEEA 2015 Sch.9 paras 1, 10(17) as from 6 April 2017.

This provision gives discretionary powers to the court in the event that proposals or revised proposals are not approved by the creditors. Although para.55 does not expressly require the administrator to apply to the court for directions when he reports that his proposals have been rejected, HHJ Behrens in *Re BTR (UK) Ltd, Lavin v Swindell* [2012] EWHC 2398 (Ch) and *Re Pudsey Steel Services Ltd* [2015] B.P.I.R.1459 held that this was implicit in the language of para.55(2). This should normally be done by the administrator, but if he does not, there is no reason why an application should not be made by a creditor. In contrast, in *Re Parmeko Holdings Ltd* [2014] B.C.C. 159 the administrator's proposals were not approved because no creditor attended the meeting. The court ruled that the report to the court should not be accompanied by an application for directions when no effective purpose would be served by any directions the court could give. The administrators should continue to manage the affairs of the company at their discretion, which they were able to do without the backing of a court order. Despite the wide wording of para.(2)(e), the court's powers must be of a limited nature: it could not, for example, impose on the creditors a set of proposals to which they have not agreed. Even so, in *Re BTR (UK) Ltd* (above), the court of its own motion went on to make a winding-up order (and in *Re Pudsey Steel Services Ltd* (above) the court directed the date on which the exit from administration to a creditors' voluntary liquidation should take effect).

In *Re Stanleybet UK Investments Ltd* [2011] EWHC 2820 (Ch); [2012] B.C.C. 550 the administrators had proposed to sell certain shares, but majority creditors had refused to approve the proposal at a creditors' meeting. Faced with these opposing views the administrators applied under para.55(2) for an order that the administration should be terminated in favour of a voluntary liquidation and the court made the order sought, observing that considerable weight should be given to the considered approach of responsible administrators.

Further creditors' decisions

56(1) The administrator of a company shall seek a decision from the company's creditors on a matter if–

(a) it is requested in the prescribed manner by creditors of the company whose debts amount to at least 10% of the total debts of the company, or

(b) he is directed by the court to do so.

56(2) An administrator commits an offence if he fails without reasonable excuse to seek a decision from the company's creditors on a matter as required by this paragraph.

General Note

There appears to be no restriction on the circumstances in which the creditors may exercise this power, or on their reasons or motivation.

Para.56(2)
On penalties, see s.430, Sch.B1 para.106(2) and Sch.10.

Creditors' committee

57(1) The company's creditors may, in accordance with the rules, establish a creditors' committee.

57(2) A creditors' committee shall carry out functions conferred on it by or under this Act.

57(3) A creditors' committee may require the administrator–

(a) to attend on the committee at any reasonable time of which he is given at least seven days' notice, and

(b) to provide the committee with information about the exercise of his functions.

General Note

The appointment of a creditors' or liquidation committee is a feature of most insolvency proceedings: see, e.g. ss.49, 68, 101 and 141–142. For the rules relating to the creditors' committee, see rr.17.1 et seq. The business of the committee may be conducted otherwise than at a meeting (rr.17.19 et seq.).

58 [Repealed by SBEEA 2015 Sch.9 paras 1, 22 as from 6 April 2017]

Functions of Administrator

General powers

59(1) The administrator of a company may do anything necessary or expedient for the management of the affairs, business and property of the company.

59(2) A provision of this Schedule which expressly permits the administrator to do a specified thing is without prejudice to the generality of sub-paragraph (1).

59(3) A person who deals with the administrator of a company in good faith and for value need not inquire whether the administrator is acting within his powers.

General Note

The court will not readily give directions to the administrator in regard to matters which it is his responsibility to deal with: *RAB Capital plc v Lehman Brothers (International) Europe* [2008] EWHC 2335 (Ch); [2008] B.C.C. 915. It is thus for the administrator, and not the creditors' committee, to determine how the administration should be conducted and to assess how best to achieve the purpose of the administration (*Re Brilliant Independent Media Specialists Ltd, Maxwell v Brookes* [2015] B.C.C. 113. The court will not order the removal of an administrator who has made a commercial judgment that a creditor considers to be unfair to him: *Re Zegna III Holdings Inc* [2009] EWHC 2994 (Ch).

An administrator who causes the company to commit a breach of a pre-administration contract is not liable for the tort of procuring a breach of contract, if he acts in good faith: *Lictor Anstalt v MIR Steel UK Ltd* [2011] EWHC 3310 (Ch) (appeal dismissed [2012] EWCA Civ 1397), following *Said v Butt* [1920] 3 K.B. 497. However in later proceedings (*Lictor Anstalt v MIR Steel UK Ltd* [2014] EWHC 3316 (Ch)) it was held that a buyer from an administrator may be liable for the tort of procuring a breach of contract where he knew of the existence or potential existence of a third party's rights and proceeded to purchase the assets in circumstances where this would prevent the company in administration from fulfilling its obligations to the third party. The defence of justification in relation to the tort of inducing a breach of contract could apply to an administrator acting in good faith in accordance with his powers and as necessary to further the objectives of the administration where performance of the contract would not be in the interests of the creditors, but that defence was not available to the purchaser.

Para.59(1), (2)

The powers are here conferred in the widest terms. These powers are not, however, restricted to the management of the company's business (as is normally the case with the board of directors). This is indicated by the use of the word "affairs", and appears also from some of the particular matters mentioned in this Schedule and in Sch.1, e.g. the power to remove a director (para.61). The administrator may summon a meeting of shareholders: see para.6.2 and r.15.41(3).

Para.59(3)

This provision is probably only inserted out of caution, since a third party would almost certainly be protected by the ordinary rules of agency.

60(1) The administrator of a company has the powers specified in Schedule 1 to this Act.

60(2) But the power to sell, hire out or otherwise dispose of property is subject to any regulations that may be made under paragraph 60A.

General Note

The powers conferred by Sch.1, which are common to both administrators and administrative receivers, also apply under the original regime. Paragraph 60(2) inserted by SBEEA 2015 s.129(1), (3) as from 26 May 2015. In *Re LB Holdings Intermediate 2 Ltd (in admin.)* [2017] EWHC 2032 (Ch) where administrators sought directions to use powers under para.60 and Sch.1 para.18 to effect the complicated settlement of a series of inter-company loans in a group, for the benefit of the companies and their creditors, the court stressed that it was not its function to become involved in the merits of the decision or to determine whether a proposed settlement was the best available, but that any proposed settlement had to be rational and free from conflicts of interest (see also note to Sch.B1 para.63 on the court's attitude to directions for settlements).

60A(1) The Secretary of State may by regulations make provision for–

(a) prohibiting, or

(b) imposing requirements or conditions in relation to,

the disposal, hiring out or sale of property of a company by the administrator to a connected person in circumstances specified in the regulations.

60A(2) Regulations under this paragraph may in particular require the approval of, or provide for the imposition of requirements or conditions by–

(a) creditors of the company,

(b) the court, or

(c) a person of a description specified in the regulations.

60A(3) In sub-paragraph (1), "connected person", in relation to a company, means–

(a) a relevant person in relation to the company, or

(b) a company connected with the company.

60A(4) For the purposes of sub-paragraph (3)–

(a) "relevant person", in relation to a company, means–

(i) a director or other officer, or shadow director, of the company;

(ii) a non-employee associate of such a person;

(iii) a non-employee associate of the company;

(b) a company is connected with another if any relevant person of one is or has been a relevant person of the other.

60A(5) In sub-paragraph (4), "non-employee associate" of a person means a person who is an associate of that person otherwise than by virtue of employing or being employed by that person.

60A(6) Subsection (10) of section 435 (extended definition of company) applies for the purposes of sub-paragraphs (3) to (5) as it applies for the purposes of that section.

60A(7) Regulations under this paragraph may–

(a) make different provision for different purposes;

(b) make incidental, consequential, supplemental and transitional provision.

60A(8) Regulations under this paragraph are to be made by statutory instrument.

60A(9) Regulations under this paragraph may not be made unless a draft of the statutory instrument containing the regulations has been laid before Parliament and approved by a resolution of each House of Parliament.

60A(10) This paragraph expires at the end of the period of 5 years beginning with the day on which it comes into force unless the power conferred by it is exercised during that period.

General Note

Paragraph 60A inserted by SBEEA 2015 s.129(1), (4) as from 26 May 2015. A number of the recommendations in the Graham Report on pre-pack administrations (see the note to para.2) which are particularly concerned with sales to connected persons have been adopted in the first instance on the basis that compliance is to be voluntary, but the report also recommended that the Government should take a reserve power to impose the recommendation by legislation. This paragraph authorises the creation of such a power by statutory instrument. No regulations have so far been made. The Insolvency Service from 12 December 2017 began assessing how voluntary measures (SIP 16 etc.) have improved the transparency of connected party pre-pack sales to help decide whether further regulation is needed when the para.60A regulation-making power expires at the end of its five-year period on 26 May 2020.

61 The administrator of a company–

(a) may remove a director of the company, and

(b) may appoint a director of the company (whether or not to fill a vacancy).

62 The administrator of a company may–

(a) call a meeting of members of the company;

(b) seek a decision on any matter from the company's creditors.

63 The administrator of a company may apply to the court for directions in connection with his functions.

General Note

An unusual direction was made under this paragraph in *Re Lehman Brothers International (Europe) Ltd* [2013] EWHC 1664 (Ch); [2014] B.C.C. 132 to reassure the trustee in liquidation of the American arm of the Lehman group that the European company would perform its obligations under a settlement agreement. In *Re Nortel Networks UK Ltd* [2014] EWHC 2614 (Ch) the court approved a complex settlement (and directed that the costs of the application should be paid as an expense of the administration), but at the same time emphasised the limited extent of its role. The court must be careful in giving its blessing to a transaction clearly within the administrator's powers to ensure that the administrator was not surrendering his discretion. At the same time, the court was not a mere rubber stamp: full and frank disclosure of all material facts and circumstances was required for the court to give its approval. (A global settlement was eventually reached and approved by the court: *Re Nortel Networks UK Ltd* [2016] EWHC 2769 (Ch).)

Although this provision confers standing only on an administrator, it is possible that a creditor may also apply for directions under the court's general power to exercise control over administrators as officers of the court: see *Re Mirror Group Holdings Ltd* [1993] B.C.L.C. 538 at 543.

In *Re Allanfield Property Insurance Services Ltd* [2015] EWHC 3721 (Ch) it was held that the court has power under para.63 to give directions to administrators in respect of funds held by them even though they do not form part of the company's assets (e.g. trust funds). Compare *Re Worldspreads Ltd* [2015] EWHC 1719 (Ch), where the court was asked to approve a distribution of client money held on trust by a banking company which was in special administration. Although he was uncertain whether para.63 extended to companies under the special administration regime, Birss J held that he had power to authorise the payments under the court's inherent jurisdiction in relation to trusts.

In *Re Nortel Networks UK Ltd* [2017] EWHC 1429 (Ch); [2017] B.C.C. 325 the court gave an order on an application for directions that administrators could inform potential claimants for expense claims in the administration to notify the administrators by a specified "bar date" of their claim: late expense claims after that date would not be extinguished, but would only be paid to the extent that the administrators had any unreserved funds available after making distributions to unsecured creditors.

64(1) A company in administration or an officer of a company in administration may not exercise a management power without the consent of the administrator.

64(2) For the purpose of sub-paragraph (1)–

(a) "management power" means a power which could be exercised so as to interfere with the exercise of the administrator's powers,

(b) it is immaterial whether the power is conferred by an enactment or an instrument, and

(c) consent may be general or specific.

General Note

The definition of "management power" extends to functions which are wider than those usually associated with management—e.g. the appointment of directors by the company in general meeting.

In *McTear v Engelhard* [2014] EWHC 1056 (Ch) directors who had acted in breach of their fiduciary duties and duties of care were also held to have acted in breach of para.64(1), from which it may be inferred that the usual remedies for breach of duty will lie where there has been a violation of this provision.

Paragraph 64 does not prevent the directors from taking action to challenge the appointment of an administrator: *Stephen, Petitioner* [2011] CSOH 119; [2012] B.C.C. 537; *Closegate Hotel Development (Durham) Ltd v McLean* [2013] EWHC 3237 (Ch).

It is clear that the proposals, or the administrator himself, may leave some functions in the hands of the company's directors or other officers, but not of course so as to absolve the administrator from his own responsibilities.

In *Re Lehman Bros Europe Ltd (in admin.)* [2017] EWHC 2031 (Ch), where administrators wished to make a distribution to the company's sole member but had no power under insolvency legislation to do so, they obtained directions from the court to appoint a director who would exercise "management powers" under para.64 to effect a reduction of capital under the Companies Act 2006 to achieve the desired result.

Distribution

65(1) The administrator of a company may make a distribution to a creditor of the company.

65(2) Section 175 shall apply in relation to a distribution under this paragraph as it applies in relation to a winding up.

65(3) A payment may not be made by way of distribution under this paragraph to a creditor of the company who is neither secured nor preferential unless–

(a) the distribution is made by virtue of section 176A (2)(a), or

(b) the court gives permission.

General Note

Paragraph 65(3) amended by SBEEA 2015 s.128(2) as from 26 May 2015.

Insolvency is a pre-requisite for administration and so it is hardly surprising that this paragraph only relates to distributions to creditors: there is no provision for distributions to members. For an unusual example of an application for directions in the latter regard, particularly in respect of a substantial surplus, see *Re Lehman Bros Europe Ltd (in admin.)* [2017] EWHC 2031 (Ch).

It is left to the proposals as approved by the creditors to determine when and how payments are to be made to those entitled. Rules 14.26 et seq. deal in detail with the making of distributions to creditors, with the proving of debts, quantification of claims, mutual credit and set-off, interest, proof by secured creditors, etc. These provisions apply in a winding up also. Under corresponding provisions in the investment bank special administration rules the court approved a distribution of client assets in *Re Hume Capital Securities plc* (unreported, 20 November 2015).

In *Re Portsmouth City Football Club Ltd, Neumans LLP v Andronikou* [2013] EWCA Civ 916; [2013] B.C.C. 741, affirming Morgan J [2012] EWHC 3088 (Ch), the company had been involved in potential winding-up proceedings before it was put into administration and later into liquidation. The applicants were solicitors who had acted for the company in relation to the earlier winding-up proceedings, and sought an order, either that their fees should be treated as an expense of the administration or liquidation or a necessary disbursement, or that the payment of the fees was a distribution under para.65 or to be treated as such under para.66 below. The application was refused on all grounds. There was no reason connected with the administration or liquidation which would justify treating as a distribution the payment of these debts, which had been incurred prior to the commencement of the administration and were not likely to assist the achievement of the purpose of the administration.

Para.65(1)

Under the general rules of statutory interpretation, "a creditor" includes the plural "creditors". The term "distribution" is not defined for the purposes of this Schedule or for the Act as a whole, although it is used also in the context of liquidations (ss.107, 143, 146, etc.) and personal bankruptcy (ss.324, 330, etc.). The term necessarily relates only to pre-administration creditors. Unsecured creditors rank *inter se* on a pari passu basis (r.14.12). The rules regarding the declaration and payment of a dividend are rr.14.34 et seq.

Note that the rule in a winding up, that a contributory cannot recover anything in respect of any claims he may have as a creditor until he has fully discharged his obligations as a contributory to the company, was thought not to apply in an administration: *Re Lehman Bros International (Europe) Ltd* [2014] EWHC 704 (Ch); [2014] B.C.C. 193; confirmed by the Court of Appeal *Joint Administrators of LB Holdings Intermediate 2 Ltd v Lomas* [2015] EWCA Civ 485; [2015] 3 W.L.R. 1205; [2015] B.C.C. 431, but the Supreme Court has perhaps surprisingly disagreed with this, to allow a "slightly modified" version of the contributory rule in administration: *Joint Administrators of LB Holdings Intermediate 2 Ltd v Joint Administrators of Lehman Bros International (Europe)* [2017] UKSC 38; [2017] 2 W.L.R. 1497; [2017] B.C.C. 235. The reasoning was that although the contributory rule was not provided for in the insolvency legislation, it was regarded as one of the surviving judge-made rules of the insolvency code and as an aspect of a general equitable principle which acted as a qualification to the rules regarding distribution in liquidations was needed to ensure compliance with the rules—and so could be extended, as modified, to administration provided it could be effected in a practical and principled way. It thus filled the gap otherwise left by the disapplication of set-off. Lord Neuberger at [179]–[180] countered the earlier conclusions in the case that the rule could not apply in administration since administrators have no power to make calls on contributories, by deciding that a modified version of the rule would require administrators to retain any sum which, if the rule had not applied, would otherwise have been distributed to a contributory in his capacity as a creditor. This, with respect, seems a somewhat artificial reasoning and may only apply in highly unusual cases such as the instant (solvent) administration.

However, the term "distribution" is capable of a wider construction, and is not applicable only to payments to be made on a rateable basis to the unsecured creditors as a whole. In *Re HPJ UK Ltd* [2007] B.C.C. 284 the company's administrators were authorised under para.65 to make a single payment to the Revenue, reached as a compromise in settlement of a disputed claim. This cleared the way for the administrators to attend to the interests of the remaining creditors (who had approved the settlement). In *Re WW Realisation 1 Ltd* [2010] EWHC 3604 (Ch); [2011] B.C.C. 382 the company was moving from administration to liquidation and the administrators successfully sought an order that they could make a distribution to a secured creditor without making any provision for claims for rent or rates to be paid as expenses of the administration unless such claims were received by a specified date.

Para.65(2)

Section 175 gives priority to the company's preferential creditors ahead of the claims of any floating charge holder (but not the holder of a fixed charge). Note also that s.176A directs that a "prescribed part" of the company's net property shall be made available for the satisfaction of its unsecured debts and paid in priority to the holder of a floating charge. Under IA 1986 Pt II, as originally drafted, there was no statutory category of preferential debts in an administration, unless the administration was followed immediately by a winding up. The new regime introduced by Sch.B1, and in particular this subparagraph, now makes provision for preferential debts to have priority, and s.387 has been amended so as to make the date on which the company enters into administration the relevant date to determine the existence and amount of such debts. The categories of preferential debts are the same as those in other insolvency proceedings, as defined in Sch.6.

Section 175(2)(a) also states that the preferential debts shall rank after the expenses of a winding up. By analogy, the same priority is accorded to the expenses of the administration (including the administrator's remuneration), and those expenses (amplified by the debts referred to in para.99(4) and (5)) will be given priority over the claim of any floating charge holder—or at least those to which para.70 applies (see para.99(3)(b)).

Paragraph 65(2) has not been amended to include a reference to the new s.176ZA, which (reversing the decision of the House of Lords in *Re Leyland DAF Ltd, Buchler v Talbot* [2004] UKHL 9; [2004] 2 A.C. 298; [2004] B.C.C. 214) directs that the expenses of a winding up shall have priority over claims to property comprised in or subject to a floating charge. The corresponding position in an administration under Sch.B1 was not referred to in the judgments in *Leyland DAF* (although paras 69 and 95 were mentioned in argument), and it is probable that the draftsman of s.176ZA took the view that these two paragraphs already gave the expenses of an administration the same priority as s.176ZA now does. Although an argument might still be advanced that in some circumstances the *Leyland DAF* reasoning survives despite paras 69 and 95, it is unlikely to find favour at a time when the "rescue culture" holds sway.

Para.65(3)

This provision applies even though the claims of the secured and preferential creditors have been fully met, but not (by virtue of the insertion of para.65(3)(b) by SBEEA 2015 s.128(2) as from 26 May 2015) in relation to the "prescribed part" to which unsecured creditors are entitled under s.176A. Note, however, the special power given to the administrator by para.66. The section gives no guidance as to the criteria that the court should apply in considering whether or not to grant permission. In *Re GHE Realisations Ltd* [2005] EWHC 2400 (Ch); [2006] 1 W.L.R. 287; [2006] B.C.C. 139 Rimer J said that the principal consideration which should ultimately govern the matter was "the interests of the company's creditors as a whole". In *Re MG Rover Belux SA/NV* [2007] B.C.C. 446 HHJ Norris QC listed a number of further factors which he considered material, including (i) that the proposed distribution should be conducive to the achievement of the then current objectives of the administration; (ii) that proper provision has been made for secured and preferential creditors; (iii) what realistic alternatives there might be; (iv) the basis on which the administration has been conducted so far as the creditors were concerned, and whether they had approved (or not objected to) any proposal concerning the relevant distribution; and (v) the impact of the distribution on any proposed exit route from the distribution. Leave to make a distribution to unsecured, non-preferential creditors of certain UK subsidiary companies was granted in *Re Nortel Networks UK Ltd* [2015] EWHC 2506 (Ch) in keeping with a global protocol approved by the courts in Canada and the US where the parent company and other subsidiaries were based. In later proceedings the court made an order under para.65(3)(b) for the administrators to pay certain creditors where it was in the creditors' interests as a whole, consistent with the general functions and duties of the administrators to utilise the most cost-effective means of paying these creditors (a CVA was inappropriate) and the unsecured creditors would be paid in full later (*Re Nortel Networks UK Ltd* [2017] EWHC 1429 (Ch); [2017] B.C.C. 325).

66 The administrator of a company may make a payment otherwise than in accordance with paragraph 65 or paragraph 13 of Schedule 1 if he thinks it likely to assist achievement of the purpose of administration.

General Note

This provision would, for example, allow the administrator, without reference to the court, to pay off arrears owed to a creditor who made such a payment a condition of making further essential supplies, e.g. of fuel or raw materials. So far as concerns para.13 of Sch.1, it is not easy to think of a payment "likely to assist achievement of the purpose of administration" which is not also "necessary or incidental to the performance of his functions". See also *Re Portsmouth City Football Club Ltd, Neumans LLP v Andronikou*, discussed in the note to para.65.

In *Re MG Rover España SA* [2006] B.C.C. 599 the view was expressed that para.66 could be invoked to empower administrators to make payments to employees under the national laws of EU Member States over and above their entitlement under English law, so avoiding the need to open secondary proceedings (which would necessarily be winding-up proceedings) in each national territory where employee rights were greater than under English law. A similar point was made by Lindsay J in *Re Collins & Aikman Europe SA* [2006] EWHC 1343 (Ch); [2006] B.C.C. 861, where the relationship between paras 65 and 66, IA 1986 Sch.1 para.13 and the court's inherent jurisdiction to authorise payments by an administrator (as an officer of the court) is examined in some detail. See also *Re MG Rover*

Belux SA/NV [2007] B.C.C. 446, where the court approved payments to Belgian creditors of a Belgian-registered company which was in administration in England, so indirectly applying rules of Belgian insolvency law.

General duties

67 The administrator of a company shall on his appointment take custody or control of all the property to which he thinks the company is entitled.

General Note

This provision corresponds to IA 1986 s.*17(1)*, which applies under the original regime, but the phrase "to which he thinks the company is entitled" has been substituted for "to which the company is or appears to be entitled", so making the administrator's subjective belief the critical factor. "Entitled" means "beneficially entitled": as regards property to which the company is not beneficially entitled, see the note to s.107. In *Sandhu v Jet Star Retail Ltd* [2011] EWCA Civ 459 the administrators had taken possession of property which the company had contracted to buy subject to a retention of title agreement. It was held that this was within their powers, as the sellers had given it authority to deal with the property and had not withdrawn that authority. The judgment in *Blue Monkey Gaming Ltd v Hudson* [2014] 4 All E.R. (D) 222 contains a useful summary of the position where goods in the possession of an administrator which are subject to a retention of title provision are claimed by the person alleging ownership. It is not the obligation of the administrator to identify the claimant's assets and it is the responsibility of the latter to be clear and specific as to which goods it claims as its own.

68(1) Subject to sub-paragraph (2), the administrator of a company shall manage its affairs, business and property in accordance with–

(a) any proposals approved under paragraph 53,

(b) any revision of those proposals which is made by him and which he does not consider substantial, and

(c) any revision of those proposals approved under paragraph 54.

68(2) If the court gives directions to the administrator of a company in connection with any aspect of his management of the company's affairs, business or property, the administrator shall comply with the directions.

68(3) The court may give directions under sub-paragraph (2) only if–

(a) no proposals have been approved under paragraph 53,

(b) the directions are consistent with any proposals or revision approved under paragraph 53 or 54,

(c) the court thinks the directions are required in order to reflect a change in circumstances since the approval of proposals or a revision under paragraph 53 or 54, or

(d) the court thinks the directions are desirable because of a misunderstanding about proposals or a revision approved under paragraph 53 or 54.

Para.68(1)

The Act gives few directions as to the functions of an administrator: it is the proposals approved by the creditors which instruct him what he is to do. He may depart from these proposals only in a respect which he does not consider substantial (subpara.(1)(b)), and even the court's power to depart from the approved proposals appears to be strictly limited by para.68(3).

Para.68(2), (3)

The apparent breadth of para.68(2) is misleading: it is severely cut down by para.68(3).

The Act sets out an elaborate procedure which an administrator must follow before his terms of reference are eventually settled by the creditors' approval of the proposals which he has drawn up on the basis of the statement of affairs which he has obtained from the company's officers. This process will necessarily take the best part of two or three months—hence the need to give him interim powers to act under subpara.(3)(a), under the direction of the court. But the Act does not expressly authorise him to set about his task of seeking the rehabilitation of the company at once, on his own initiative.

However the legislation, as worded for the original regime (IA 1986 s.*17(2)(a)*), which has a slightly different emphasis, has been interpreted by the courts as empowering an administrator to take immediate steps, in advance of consulting the creditors and without reference to the court, if he considers that to do so is in the best interests of the company and its creditors. Although the language of para.68(2)–(3) is not the same as that of s.*17(2)(a)*, and arguably leaves less scope for an interpretation similar to that of Vinelott J (discussed in the note to s.*17(2)(a)*), it was held by Lawrence Collins J in *Re Transbus International Ltd* [2004] EWHC 932 (Ch); [2004] 1 W.L.R. 2654; [2004] B.C.C. 401 that a similar meaning is to be given to the new wording: there are many cases in which an administrator will be justified in by-passing the statutory procedure and proceeding to an immediate sale, without the direction of the court—e.g. where the unsecured creditors are likely to be paid in full, or (on the other hand) to receive no payment, or where neither of the first two objectives set out in para.3(1) can be achieved.

These factors have led to the development of the practice known as "pre-pack" administrations where, prior to the company or its directors taking steps to make an out-of-court appointment of an administrator or to apply to the court for an appointment, detailed plans are worked out on the advice and with the co-operation of the insolvency practitioner concerned for the prompt sale of the business soon after he takes office, without the formalities of meetings, etc. contemplated by the Act. This is likely to be practicable only when the assets will not permit any distribution to unsecured creditors. See further on this topic the general note to para.2.

Paragraph 68(2) was relied on by the court in *Re Northsea Base Investment Ltd* [2015] EWHC 121 (Ch) when it was asked to make a direction confirming that the COMI of certain foreign-incorporated companies was in England.

Where proposals have been put to the creditors but rejected, para.55 gives the court extensive powers.

Paragraph 68(3)(c) and (d) expressly give the court power to act in circumstances which might have given rise to doubts under the former legislation, although in *Re Smallman Construction Ltd* (1988) 4 B.C.C. 784; and *Re Dana (UK) Ltd* [1999] 2 B.C.L.C. 239 the court considered that the general power conferred by s.*14(3)* (now para.63) was sufficiently wide to enable it to authorise the departure from an approved scheme. In view of the new statutory language, it is uncertain whether the court could still act in this way, relying on the residual jurisdiction conferred by para.63.

Administrator as agent of company

69 In exercising his functions under this Schedule the administrator of a company acts as its agent.

General Note

It does not follow from this provision that every action taken by an administrator should be treated as having been taken as the company's agent. See, for example, *SNR Denton UK LLP v Kirwan* [2012] UKEAT 0158/12/1007, where solicitors were held to have been retained by the administrators personally and not by the company. In *Wright Hassall LLP v Morris* [2012] EWCA Civ 1472; [2013] B.C.C. 192 the defendant, who was administrator of two companies, had sought advice from solicitors with a view to reclaiming sums on the companies' behalf. Proceedings were later instituted by the solicitors against the defendant "as administrator" of the companies (which were not themselves named as parties), claiming payment of fees which had been incurred. The trial judge held that he was not personally liable, but this was reversed by the Court of Appeal: the mere fact that he had been described "as administrator" did not make him the company's agent. (Compare *Stevensdrake Ltd v Hunt* [2015] EWHC 1527 (Ch); [2016] B.C.C. 485; further proceedings [2016] EWHC 342 (Ch); [2016] B.C.C. 515 (liquidator held personally liable, but appeal allowed in part: [2017] EWCA Civ 1173; [2017] B.C.C. 611).) The question of an administrator's liability in tort was briefly (but inconclusively) raised in *John Smith & Co (Edinburgh) Ltd v Hill* [2010] EWHC 1016 (Ch); [2010] 2 B.C.L.C. 556. A buyer from administrators who knowingly bought property in breach of a third party's rights was held liable for the tort of procuring a breach of contract in *Lictor Anstalt v MIR Steel UK Ltd* [2014] EWHC 3316 (Ch).

Charged property: floating charge

70(1) The administrator of a company may dispose of or take action relating to property which is subject to a floating charge as if it were not subject to the charge.

70(2) Where property is disposed of in reliance on sub-paragraph (1) the holder of the floating charge shall have the same priority in respect of acquired property as he had in respect of the property disposed of.

70(3) In sub-paragraph (2) "acquired property" means property of the company which directly or indirectly represents the property disposed of.

General Note

This provision does not apply in relation to the enforcement of "market charges" (as defined by CA 1989 s.173), to payment and securities settlement systems under the Finality Regulations (reg.19) or to the enforcement of a security interest under a financial collateral arrangement: Financial Collateral Arrangements (No.2) Regulations 2003 (SI 2003/3226) reg.8(1)(b).

Charged property: non-floating charge

71(1) The court may by order enable the administrator of a company to dispose of property which is subject to a security (other than a floating charge) as if it were not subject to the security.

71(2) An order under sub-paragraph (1) may be made only–

(a) on the application of the administrator, and

(b) where the court thinks that disposal of the property would be likely to promote the purpose of administration in respect of the company.

71(3) An order under this paragraph is subject to the condition that there be applied towards discharging the sums secured by the security–

(a) the net proceeds of disposal of the property, and

(b) any additional money required to be added to the net proceeds so as to produce the amount determined by the court as the net amount which would be realised on a sale of the property at market value.

71(4) If an order under this paragraph relates to more than one security, application of money under sub-paragraph (3) shall be in the order of the priorities of the securities.

71(5) An administrator who makes a successful application for an order under this paragraph shall send a copy of the order to the registrar of companies before the end of the period of 14 days starting with the date of the order.

71(6) An administrator commits an offence if he fails to comply with sub-paragraph (5) without reasonable excuse.

General Note

The disapplication provisions referred to in the note to para.70 apply also to this paragraph.

Administrators were granted an order under this provision for the sale of property subject to a fixed charge, in order to facilitate the sale of the company's business as a going concern, in *O'Connell v Rollings* [2014] EWCA Civ 639.

All proper costs, charges and expenses reasonably incurred in the preservation and realisation of the property (including the administrator's remuneration) may be deducted before payment of the realisation proceeds to the charge holder: *Townsend v Biscoe* [2010] WL 3166608. An administrator who acts unreasonably in applying for an order to sell property subject to a fixed charge may be ordered to pay the charge holder's costs personally and on an indemnity basis: *Re Capitol Films Ltd, Rubin v Cobalt Pictures Ltd* [2010] EWHC 3223 (Ch); [2011] B.P.I.R. 334.

Rule 3.49 governs the application to the court. "Market value" is defined in para.111(1).

Para.71(6)

On penalties, see s.430, Sch.B1 para.106(2) and Sch.10.

Hire-purchase property

72(1) The court may by order enable the administrator of a company to dispose of goods which are in the possession of the company under a hire-purchase agreement as if all the rights of the owner under the agreement were vested in the company.

72(2) An order under sub-paragraph (1) may be made only–

(a) on the application of the administrator, and

(b) where the court thinks that disposal of the goods would be likely to promote the purpose of administration in respect of the company.

72(3) An order under this paragraph is subject to the condition that there be applied towards discharging the sums payable under the hire-purchase agreement–

(a) the net proceeds of disposal of the goods, and

(b) any additional money required to be added to the net proceeds so as to produce the amount determined by the court as the net amount which would be realised on a sale of the goods at market value.

72(4) An administrator who makes a successful application for an order under this paragraph shall send a copy of the order to the registrar of companies before the end of the period of 14 days starting with the date of the order.

72(5) An administrator commits an offence if he fails without reasonable excuse to comply with sub-paragraph (4).

General Note

Rule 3.49 governs the application to the court. "Hire-purchase agreement" extends to retention of title, etc. transactions by virtue of the definition in para.111(1), where "market value" is also defined.

Before the court can authorise a sale under this provision it must be satisfied that the property was "in the possession" of the company: *Re Business Environment Fleet Street Ltd* [2014] EWHC 3540 (Ch) (property was subject to leasing agreement with another company in the same group).

On the role of the judge in assessing the market value, see *Stanley J Holmes & Sons Ltd v Davenham Trust plc* [2006] EWCA Civ 1568; [2007] B.C.C. 485.

Para.72(5)

On penalties, see s.430, Sch.B1 para.106(2) and Sch.10.

Protection for secured or preferential creditor

73(1) An administrator's statement of proposals under paragraph 49 may not include any action which–

(a) affects the right of a secured creditor of the company to enforce his security,

(b) would result in a preferential debt of the company being paid otherwise than in priority to its non-preferential debts,

(bb) would result in an ordinary preferential debt of the company being paid otherwise than in priority to any secondary preferential debts that it may have,

(c) would result in one preferential creditor of the company being paid a smaller proportion of an ordinary preferential debt than another, or

(d) would result in one preferential creditor of the company being paid a smaller proportion of a secondary preferential debt than another.

73(2) Sub-paragraph (1) does not apply to–

(a) action to which the relevant creditor consents,

(b) a proposal for a voluntary arrangement under Part I of this Act (although this sub-paragraph is without prejudice to section 4(3)),

(c) a proposal for a compromise or arrangement to be sanctioned under Part 26 of the Companies Act 2006 (arrangements and reconstructions), or

(d) a proposal for a cross-border merger within the meaning of regulation 2 of the Companies (Cross-Border Mergers) Regulations 2007.

73(3) The reference to a statement of proposals in sub-paragraph (1) includes a reference to a statement as revised or modified.

General Note

There was no provision corresponding to this paragraph in the Pt II regime, as originally drafted. There were no preferential creditors. This paragraph is modelled on s.4(3), (4) and Sch.A1 para.31(4), (5), which apply in a CVA, and the notes to those provisions may be relevant here.

Paragraph 73(2)(b) and (c) amended and para.73(2)(d) inserted by the Companies (Cross-Border Mergers) Regulations 2007 (SI 2007/2974) reg.65, as from 15 December 2007. Paragraph 73(1)(bb), (d) inserted and para.73(1)(c) amended by the Banks and Building Societies (Depositor Preference and Priorities) Order 2014 (SI 2014/3486) art.10(2)–(5) as from 1 January 2015. These changes are consequential upon the introduction of the new regime giving priority (after the ordinary preferential creditors) to depositors in the insolvency of banks and building societies.

Para.73(1)(a)
The question whether a landlord seeking to exercise rights of forfeiture, etc. for non-payment of rent is a secured creditor has been the subject of much debate: see the cases discussed by Neuberger J in *Re Lomax Leisure Ltd* [2000] B.C.C. 352. Although the issue has been resolved for the purposes of the present Act by legislation (see s.43(4)), the cases referred to in judgment remain relevant generally.

Para.73(2)(b)
It is surprising that there is no reference to the corresponding provisions in Sch.A1 para.31(4)–(6). The intention may be to pass the consideration of all the issues that may arise to the CVA for decision.

Para.73(2)(c)
A scheme under CA 2006 Pt 26 may involve the variation or abrogation of the rights of secured and preferential creditors, and will be effective (and binding on minorities) if carried at the relevant class meetings and confirmed by the court. Paragraph 73(1) is not to affect this well-sanctioned procedure.

Challenge to administrator's conduct of company

74(1) A creditor or member of a company in administration may apply to the court claiming that–

(a) the administrator is acting or has acted so as unfairly to harm the interests of the applicant (whether alone or in common with some or all other members or creditors), or

(b) the administrator proposes to act in a way which would unfairly harm the interests of the applicant (whether alone or in common with some or all other members or creditors).

74(2) A creditor or member of a company in administration may apply to the court claiming that the administrator is not performing his functions as quickly or as efficiently as is reasonably practicable.

74(3) The court may–

(a) grant relief;

(b) dismiss the application;

(c) adjourn the hearing conditionally or unconditionally;

(d) make an interim order;

(e) make any other order it thinks appropriate.

74(4) In particular, an order under this paragraph may–

(a) regulate the administrator's exercise of his functions;

(b) require the administrator to do or not do a specified thing;

(c) require a decision of the company's creditors to be sought on a matter;

(d) provide for the appointment of an administrator to cease to have effect;

(e) make consequential provision.

74(5) An order may be made on a claim under sub-paragraph (1) whether or not the action complained of–

(a) is within the administrator's powers under this Schedule;

(b) was taken in reliance on an order under paragraph 71 or 72.

74(6) An order may not be made under this paragraph if it would impede or prevent the implementation of–

(a) a voluntary arrangement approved under Part I,

(b) a compromise or arrangement sanctioned under Part 26 of the Companies Act 2006 (arrangements and reconstructions),

(ba) a cross-border merger within the meaning of regulation 2 of the Companies (Cross-Border Mergers) Regulations 2007, or

(c) proposals or a revision approved under paragraph 53 or 54 more than 28 days before the day on which the application for the order under this paragraph is made.

General Note

An application under this provision to have the administrators replaced was unsuccessful in *SISU Capital Fund Ltd v Tucker* [2005] EWHC 2170 and 2371 (Ch); [2006] B.C.C. 463. In *Cheshire West and Chester BC, Petitioners* [2010] CSOH 115; [2011] B.C.C. 174 it was held that a landlord had suffered harm within this section because the administrators had deprived it of rent by granting a third party a licence to occupy the premises. In *Re Meem SL Ltd; Goel v Grant* [2017] EWHC 2688 (Ch) the court described the paradigm case for unfair harm to a creditor as where the administrator treated the applicant less favourably than other creditors which could not be justified by reference to the creditors' interests as a whole or to achieving the administration objective. The concept was not limited to differential treatment but could also include an administrator's decision to sell an asset at an undervalue, thereby causing loss to all creditors, but the court would not interfere with that decision unless it did not withstand logical analysis, which probably meant the same as perversity. The court went on to refuse a para.74 application against the administrators' decision to auction the company's potential claim against its former directors rather than assign it to creditors, as the auction would produce a fixed price without delay for an asset whose value was difficult to assess.

The procedure under para.74 is not appropriate to review a reasonable decision of administrators, even if influenced by a mistake (to convert the administration into a creditors' voluntary liquidation), or a decision to reject a proof: *Unidare plc v Cohen* [2005] EWHC 1410 (Ch); [2006] Ch. 489; [2006] 2 B.C.L.C. 140. Nor will the court use its powers, either under this section or more generally, to give directions to an administrator in the day-to-day management of the administration, e.g. to require him to direct resources to provide information sought by one particular group of creditors: *Four Private Investment Funds v Lomas* [2008] EWHC 2869 (Ch); [2009] 1 B.C.L.C. 161. In *Re Lehman Brothers International (Europe)* [2009] EWHC 2869 (Ch); [2009] B.C.C. 632 a group of creditors applied under para.74 for an order requiring the administrators to disclose more information than had already been given to them in respect of securities held by them. The administrators were carrying out their functions in accordance with the Act and with proposals which had been approved by a meeting of creditors. The court refused relief, holding that the administrators should not be required to devote more time and resources in order to answer the applicants' questions than they had already done, and that any harm alleged by the applicants could not be said to be "unfair".

In later proceedings, *Re Lehman Brothers International (Europe)* [2015] EWHC 2270 (Ch), where there was a dispute whether certain claims had been released by a "claims resolution agreement", the court held on construction of the agreement that they had not, but expressed the view that if this were not the case, relief would have been granted under para.74 on the grounds of unfairness (or, alternatively, in reliance on the principle laid down in *Ex parte James* (1873–74) L.R. 9 Ch. App. 609).

A court may grant relief for a claim brought under para.74 even after the administration has come to an end: *Re Coniston Hotel (Kent) LLP* [2013] EWHC 93 (Ch); [2015] B.C.C. 1; further proceedings [2014] EWHC 1100 (Ch); [2015] EWCA Civ 1001. It may also, arguably, grant relief to an individual creditor if it is established that the administrator has acted unfairly to harm the interests of that creditor alone, but if the alleged harm has affected the creditors generally the appropriate remedy is a claim under para.75 (ibid., and see *Hockin v Marsden* [2014] EWHC 763 (Ch); [2017] B.C.C. 433 (where the court also declined to adopt a different test in place of the statutory test of unfair harm)).

Action taken by administrators in the interests of the creditors as a whole is not open to challenge simply because it affects an individual creditor differently: *Re Zegna III Holdings Inc* [2009] EWHC 2994 (Ch); [2010] B.P.I.R. 277. (Compare *Re Portsmouth City Football Club Ltd* [2010] EWHC 2013 (Ch); [2011] B.C.C. 149, where a football club had exited administration by an approved CVA: the fact that certain "football creditors" (see the note to s.107) had been treated preferentially was not a ground to challenge the approval of the CVA).

Paragraph 74(6)(b) amended and para.74(6)(ba) inserted by the Companies (Cross-Border Mergers) Regulations 2007 (SI 2007/2974) reg.65, as from 15 December 2007.

Para.74(1)
Surprisingly, the draftsman has chosen to abandon the time-honoured expression "unfairly prejudicial to the interests" (familiar to company lawyers from its use in CA 2006 s.994) in favour of "unfairly to harm the interests". It will be a matter for judicial interpretation whether any different meaning is intended.

Para.74(2)
This provision reflects the duty to act expeditiously specifically imposed on an administrator by para.4.

Para.74(5)(a)
As with s.994, the fact that an act is lawful and within the actor's powers does not prevent the court from having regard to wider considerations of an equitable nature in determining whether it is unfairly harmful.

Misfeasance

75(1) The court may examine the conduct of a person who–

(a) is or purports to be the administrator of a company, or

(b) has been or has purported to be the administrator of a company.

75(2) An examination under this paragraph may be held only on the application of–

(a) the official receiver,

(b) the administrator of the company,

(c) the liquidator of the company,

(d) a creditor of the company, or

(e) a contributory of the company.

75(3) An application under sub-paragraph (2) must allege that the administrator–

(a) has misapplied or retained money or other property of the company,

(b) has become accountable for money or other property of the company,

(c) has breached a fiduciary or other duty in relation to the company, or

(d) has been guilty of misfeasance.

75(4) On an examination under this paragraph into a person's conduct the court may order him–

(a) to repay, restore or account for money or property;

(b) to pay interest;

(c) to contribute a sum to the company's property by way of compensation for breach of duty or misfeasance.

75(5) In sub-paragraph (3) "administrator" includes a person who purports or has purported to be a company's administrator.

75(6) An application under sub-paragraph (2) may be made in respect of an administrator who has been discharged under paragraph 98 only with the permission of the court.

General Note

The "misfeasance" section applicable generally in corporate insolvency proceedings is s.212. In the Act as originally drafted, an administrator was listed in s.212(1)(b) as an office-holder who could be made accountable under the section. All references to an administrator have been removed from s.212 by EA 2002 s.278 and Sch.26, and the present paragraph will now apply instead to an administrator appointed under the new regime. The main difference from s.212 is that it is not necessary that the company should be in liquidation. The only other change of significance appears to be the inclusion of a person who has purported to be an administrator. In other respects, the notes to s.212 may be treated as applicable.

The court will not order an administrator under this section to pay compensation to an individual creditor (although arguably a remedy may lie under para.74: see the note to that provision): any payment under para.75 must be for the benefit of the creditors as a class: *Re Coniston Hotel (Kent) LLP* [2013] EWHC 93 (Ch); [2015] B.C.C. 1. In later proceedings (*Re Coniston Hotel (Kent) LLP, Berntsen v Tait* [2014] EWHC 1100 (Ch); on appeal [2015] EWCA Civ 1001) the court ruled that a creditor had standing to make an application under para.75 only if he would have a pecuniary interest in the relief sought. An administrator does not owe any duty of care to an unsecured creditor of the company, unless it can be shown that a special relationship existed between them: *Charalambous v B&C Associates* [2009] EWHC 2601 (Ch); [2013] B.C.C. 491.

For the position of misfeasance liability of joint administrators, see *Oldham v Katz* [2018] EWHC 540 (Ch) under which proof of individual liability may be necessary.

Ending Administration

Automatic end of administration

76(1) The appointment of an administrator shall cease to have effect at the end of the period of one year beginning with the date on which it takes effect.

76(2) But–

(a) on the application of an administrator the court may by order extend his term of office for a specified period, and

(b) an administrator's term of office may be extended for a specified period not exceeding one year by consent.

General Note

Paragraphs 76–86 deal with the ending, or termination, of an administration. However, in these provisions the draftsman prefers to refer to "the appointment of an administrator ceasing to have effect", in keeping with the definition in para.1(2). The period specified in para.76(2)(b) was extended from six months to one year by SBEEA 2015 s.127 from 26 May 2015.

The automatic termination of an administration after one year is a novel feature introduced by the 2002 reforms, emphasising the legislature's concern that matters should be dealt with expeditiously that is also reflected in para.4. The administration may, however, be extended by court order or (subject to a limit of one year) by consent of the creditors in accordance with para.78. The factors relied on by the court in granting an extension of the administration are discussed by Ridgway (2005) Insolv. Int. 25 at 28. An extension was granted in *Re Top Marques Car Rental* [2006] EWHC 746 (Ch); [2006] B.P.I.R. 1328. In *Re Taylor Made Foods plc* (unreported, 28 February 2010) the term of office of the administrators had terminated at a weekend. Henderson J allowed an application for an extension under paras 76 and 77(1)(b) to be made on the Monday, the next day that the Court Office was open. In *Re Nortel Networks UK Ltd* [2017] EWHC 3299 (Ch) the court granted a fourth extension to the complex pan-European Nortel administrations (which commenced almost nine years before) to allow CVA implementations and distributions to be made, but only up to 29 March 2019 to coincide with the "Brexit" date as European matters thereafter were uncertain as at the date of the order.

The Scottish courts have been unwilling to grant an extension if creditors have not been provided with an opportunity to object. The Insolvency Service considers that this may impose an unnecessary burden and has given advice on ways of dealing with the problem: see *Dear IP*, October 2010, Ch.1.16.

In *Dear IP* (October 2008, Ch.1.12) attention is drawn to the practice of including among the administrator's proposals a "blanket resolution" authorising the administrator to extend the period of the administration without calling a further meeting. The Insolvency Service expresses the view that this practice is questionable and that such a provision should only be included in cases where it is "necessary" (within r.3.35(1)(n)). This could be so where it is reasonably foreseeable that the administration may need to run for more than 12 months, e.g. where there are large book debt collections which cannot realistically be completed within a year.

Rules 3.54–3.56 apply in regard to paras 76–78.

77(1) An order of the court under paragraph 76–

(a) may be made in respect of an administrator whose term of office has already been extended by order or by consent, but

(b) may not be made after the expiry of the administrator's term of office.

77(2) Where an order is made under paragraph 76 the administrator shall as soon as is reasonably practicable notify the registrar of companies.

77(3) An administrator who fails without reasonable excuse to comply with sub-paragraph (2) commits an offence.

Para.77(1)

The maximum period for which an administration may be extended out of court is one year (para.76(2)(b)), and there can be only one such an extension (para.78(4)). However, the court may grant a further extension without regard to these restrictions. Even so, there can be no retrospective extension once an administrator's term of office has expired. Exceptionally, in *Re TT Industries Ltd* [2006] B.C.C. 372, HHJ Norris QC, sitting as a deputy judge of the High Court at Birmingham, held that an extension of the administration could be ordered, notwithstanding the lapse of the administrator's appointment, where an application for extension had been made before the administration expired and there were grounds to indicate that the delay was at least in part due to the way the application had been handled by the court staff. In *Re Frontsouth (Witham) Ltd* [2011] EWHC 1668 (Ch); [2011] B.C.C. 635 Henderson J solved the problem by making a fresh appointment of the administrators with retrospective effect, followed by a further order pursuant to para.76(2) extending the administrators' term of office for a specified future period. If the administrator proposes to convert the administration into a creditor's voluntary winding up and files with the registrar of companies a notice of conversion under para.83, the conversion does not take effect on the date of filing but only when it is registered: *Re Globespan Airways Ltd* [2012] EWCA Civ 1159; [2013] 1 W.L.R. 1122; [2013] B.C.C. 252 (followed in *Re Property Professionals + Ltd* [2013] EWHC 1903 (Ch); [2013] B.C.C. 606). If the administration is due to terminate on a date between the filing and the registration (because one-year period prescribed by para.82(1) expires on that date), the life of the administration is extended by implication until the registration takes effect (ibid.). See also *Re E-Squared Ltd* [2006] EWHC 532 (Ch); [2006] B.C.C. 379, noted below, para.83.

An application for the extension of an administration should be made (in the absence of special circumstances) not less than six weeks before the end of the administration. Costs may be disallowed if this deadline is not observed. (The *Practice Direction* [2018] B.C.C. 241 (reproduced as App.IV to this *Guide*) para.8.3 fixes the period at "one month", but it is understood that in practice it is now required that application should be made at least six weeks before the date of expiration.)

Para.77(2), (3)

On penalties, see s.430, Sch.B1 para.106(2) and Sch.10.

78(1) In paragraph 76(2)(b) "consent" means consent of–

(a) each secured creditor of the company, and

(b) if the company has unsecured debts, the unsecured creditors of the company.

78(2) But where the administrator has made a statement under paragraph 52(1)(b) "consent" means–

(a) consent of each secured creditor of the company, or

(b) if the administrator thinks that a distribution may be made to preferential creditors, consent of–

(i) each secured creditor of the company, and

(ii) the preferential creditors of the company.

78(2A) Whether the company's unsecured creditors or preferential creditors consent is to be determined by the administrator seeking a decision from those creditors as to whether they consent.

78(3) [Omitted]

78(4) An administrator's term of office–

(a) may be extended by consent only once,

(b) may not be extended by consent after extension by order of the court, and

(c) may not be extended by consent after expiry.

78(5) Where an administrator's term of office is extended by consent he shall as soon as is reasonably practicable–

(a) file notice of the extension with the court, and

(b) notify the registrar of companies.

78(6) An administrator who fails without reasonable excuse to comply with sub-paragraph (5) commits an offence.

Para.78(1)–(2A)

Paragraph 78(1)(b), (2)(b) substituted, para.78(3) omitted and para.78(2A) inserted by SBEEA 2015 Sch.9 paras 1, 10(25)–(27) as from 6 April 2017.

Paragraph 78 defines "consent" in various ways for the purposes of the one-off extension of an administration which can be made out of court under para.76(2)(b). The alternatives depend on whether the administrator has included in his proposals a statement under para.52(1)(b) that he thinks that the company has insufficient property to enable a distribution to be made to unsecured creditors (other than what they might be entitled to under the "prescribed part" provisions of s.176A). If he has not, and the company has unsecured creditors, the consent must be that of each secured creditor of the company and over 50 per cent in value of the company's unsecured creditors. If he has made such a statement, the consent must be *either* that of each secured creditor of the company *or*, if the administrator thinks that a distribution may be made to the company's preferential creditors, the consent of each secured creditor and over 50 per cent in value of the preferential creditors. There are thus three possible scenarios. The debts of creditors who abstain or choose not to respond are ignored.

Para.78(4)

Note these further limitations on the power to extend an administration by consent.

Para.78(5), (6)

On penalties, see s.430, Sch.B1 para.106(2) and Sch.10.

Court ending administration on application of administrator

79(1) On the application of the administrator of a company the court may provide for the appointment of an administrator of the company to cease to have effect from a specified time.

79(2) The administrator of a company shall make an application under this paragraph if–

(a) he thinks the purpose of administration cannot be achieved in relation to the company,

(b) he thinks the company should not have entered administration, or

(c) the company's creditors decide that he must make an application under this paragraph.

79(3) The administrator of a company shall make an application under this paragraph if–

(a) the administration is pursuant to an administration order, and

(b) the administrator thinks that the purpose of administration has been sufficiently achieved in relation to the company.

79(4) On an application under this paragraph the court may–

(a) adjourn the hearing conditionally or unconditionally;

(b) dismiss the application;

(c) make an interim order;

(d) make any order it thinks appropriate (whether in addition to, in consequence of or instead of the order applied for).

General Note

This paragraph deals with the ending of the administration by order of the court. Paragraph 79(2) applies in all administrations, while para.79(3) is applicable only where the administrator was appointed by the court.

Rules 3.57 and 3.59 apply in this case.

Para.79(1)
Mann J in *Pettit v Bradford Bulls (Northern) Ltd* [2016] EWHC 3557 (Ch); [2017] B.C.C. 50 used this power to make an appointment of administrators with retrospective effect.

Para.79(2)
It appears that in these three situations the administrator *must* make an application. But he may also do so in other circumstances, e.g. where the administration is to be replaced by a compulsory liquidation, as in *Re J Smiths Haulage Ltd* [2007] B.C.C. 135. *Re TM Kingdom Ltd* [2007] B.C.C. 480 confirms that the jurisdiction under para.79(1) is not confined to the situations listed in para.79(2), (3). One reason why a company might fall within para.79(2)(b) would be if it is proved to have been solvent all along.

Para.79(3)
If the administrator was appointed by the court, the administration can only be terminated under this paragraph. If he was appointed out of court and he thinks that the purpose of the administration has been sufficiently achieved, he may follow the alternative procedure under para.80.

Para.79(4)
In *Re Graico Property Ltd* [2016] EWHC 2827 (Ch) the court used the wide power in para.79(4)(d) to make a winding-up order, without a petition, as it ended the administration; followed in *Re West End Quay Estate Management Ltd* [2017] EWHC 958 (Ch); [2018] B.C.C. 1 where it was considered not right to return the company to the control of its directors and so the administrators were discharged, a winding-up order made and it would save time and costs to appoint the administrators as liquidators as they understood the complexities of the case.

Termination of administration where objective achieved

80(1) This paragraph applies where an administrator of a company is appointed under paragraph 14 or 22.

80(2) If the administrator thinks that the purpose of administration has been sufficiently achieved in relation to the company he may file a notice in the prescribed form–

(a) with the court, and

(b) with the registrar of companies.

80(3) The administrator's appointment shall cease to have effect when the requirements of sub-paragraph (2) are satisfied.

80(4) Where the administrator files a notice he shall within the prescribed period send a copy to every creditor of the company, other than an opted-out creditor, of whose claim and address he is aware.

80(5) The rules may provide that the administrator is taken to have complied with sub-paragraph (4) if before the end of the prescribed period he publishes in the prescribed manner a notice undertaking to provide a copy of the notice under sub-paragraph (2) to any creditor of the company who applies in writing to a specified address.

80(6) An administrator who fails without reasonable excuse to comply with sub-paragraph (4) commits an offence.

General Note

Where the administrator has been appointed out of court and he thinks that he has sufficiently achieved the objective of the administration, this paragraph provides a simple and informal way for him to sign off and bring the administration to an end.

In *Nimmo and Fraser, Joint Administrators of Station Properties Ltd* [2013] CSOH 120 the company had been put into administration for the purpose of realising property in order to make a distribution to secured and preferential creditors. In the event, sufficient money was realised to pay all the creditors in full and return control of the company to its directors. The court held that the administrators could terminate the administration under para.80 without seeking the leave of the court, but must first convene a meeting under para.54 to get the creditors' approval for a change of purpose, namely "rescuing the company as a going concern". The judgment gives some detailed directions on the obligations of directors in reaching the conclusion that the company is in a position to be restored as a going concern.

Rule 3.56 applies.

Para.80(1)–(5)
The notice must be sent to creditors (or published under para.80(5)) within five business days (IR 2016 r.3.56(7)). The obligation to notify creditors ensures that any of them who disagree with the administrator's decision may take appropriate action, but this will necessarily only happen after the administration has been terminated pursuant to para.80(3) and it would appear that the court has no power to reinstate the administration.

Para.80(6)
On penalties, see s.430, Sch.B1 para.106(2) and Sch.10.

Court ending administration on application of creditor

81(1) On the application of a creditor of a company the court may provide for the appointment of an administrator of the company to cease to have effect at a specified time.

81(2) An application under this paragraph must allege an improper motive–

(a) in the case of an administrator appointed by administration order, on the part of the applicant for the order, or

(b) in any other case, on the part of the person who appointed the administrator.

81(3) On an application under this paragraph the court may–

(a) adjourn the hearing conditionally or unconditionally;

(b) dismiss the application;

(c) make an interim order;

(d) make any order it thinks appropriate (whether in addition to, in consequence of or instead of the order applied for).

General Note

A creditor may apply to the court to have the administration terminated, but only on the limited grounds set out in para.81(2). Rule 3.58 applies. A challenge to an appointment on the basis of improper motive failed in *Thomas v Frogmore Real Estate Partners GP1 Ltd* [2017] EWHC 25 (Ch).

Public interest winding-up

82(1) This paragraph applies where a winding-up order is made for the winding up of a company in administration on a petition presented under–

(a) section 124A (public interest),

(aa) section 124B (SEs), or

(b) section 367 of the Financial Services and Markets Act 2000 (c. 8) (petition by Financial Conduct Authority or Prudential Regulation Authority).

82(2) This paragraph also applies where a provisional liquidator of a company in administration is appointed following the presentation of a petition under any of the provisions listed in sub-paragraph (1).

82(3) The court shall order–

(a) that the appointment of the administrator shall cease to have effect, or

(b) that the appointment of the administrator shall continue to have effect.

82(4) If the court makes an order under sub-paragraph (3)(b) it may also–

(a) specify which of the powers under this Schedule are to be exercisable by the administrator, and

(b) order that this Schedule shall have effect in relation to the administrator with specified modifications.

General Note

It is only where a winding-up order is made, or a provisional liquidator appointed, on public interest grounds under one of the provisions mentioned in para.82(1) that an administrator can hold office concurrently with a liquidator or provisional liquidator: see para.40(2). The court is here given power either to terminate the administration or to allow it to continue and allocate responsibilities between the two office-holders.

Paragraph 82(1)(aa) was inserted by the European Public Limited-Liability Company Regulations 2004 (SI 2004/2326) reg.73(4)(c), as from 8 October 2004.

Moving from administration to creditors' voluntary liquidation

83(1) This paragraph applies in England and Wales where the administrator of a company thinks–

(a) that the total amount which each secured creditor of the company is likely to receive has been paid to him or set aside for him, and

(b) that a distribution will be made to unsecured creditors of the company (if there are any) which is not a distribution by virtue of section 176A(2)(a).

83(2) This paragraph applies in Scotland where the administrator of a company thinks–

(a) that each secured creditor of the company will receive payment in respect of his debt, and

(b) that a distribution will be made to unsecured creditors (if there are any) which is not a distribution by virtue of section 176A(2)(a).

83(3) The administrator may send to the registrar of companies a notice that this paragraph applies.

83(4) On receipt of a notice under sub-paragraph (3) the registrar shall register it.

83(5) If an administrator sends a notice under sub-paragraph (3) he shall as soon as is reasonably practicable–

(a) file a copy of the notice with the court, and

(b) send a copy of the notice to each creditor, other than an opted-out creditor, of whose claim and address he is aware.

83(6) On the registration of a notice under sub-paragraph (3)–

(a) the appointment of an administrator in respect of the company shall cease to have effect, and

(b) the company shall be wound up as if a resolution for voluntary winding up under section 84 were passed on the day on which the notice is registered.

83(7) The liquidator for the purposes of the winding up shall be–

(a) a person nominated by the creditors of the company in the prescribed manner and within the prescribed period, or

(b) if no person is nominated under paragraph (a), the administrator.

83(8) In the application of Part IV to a winding up by virtue of this paragraph–

(a) section 85 shall not apply,

(b) section 86 shall apply as if the reference to the time of the passing of the resolution for voluntary winding up were a reference to the beginning of the date of registration of the notice under sub-paragraph (3),

(c) section 89 does not apply,

(d) sections 99 and 100 shall not apply,

(e) section 129 shall apply as if the reference to the time of the passing of the resolution for voluntary winding up were a reference to the beginning of the date of registration of the notice under sub-paragraph (3), and

(f) any creditors' committee which is in existence immediately before the company ceases to be in administration shall continue in existence after that time as if appointed as a liquidation committee under section 101.

General Note

Under the original Pt II of IA 1986 it is possible for a company to move more or less seamlessly from administration to compulsory winding up, but various obstacles stand in the way of a move to voluntary liquidation, which have only been overcome with some difficulty. In the present regime these obstacles are eliminated, and a straightforward procedure is laid down by this paragraph to facilitate such a move. Paragraph 83(1), (2) lays down preconditions: first, provision must have been made to ensure that all secured creditors will be paid off and secondly, after that, there must be something remaining available for the unsecured creditors. The simple act of filing a notice with the registrar of companies is then all that is needed to transform the administration into a creditors' voluntary winding up, with an insolvency practitioner chosen by the creditors or the former administrator as liquidator (para.83(6)(a), (7)). Necessarily, a certain amount of "deeming" is required to take account of the fact that this creditors' voluntary liquidation has not come into being by the usual procedure.

The change from administration to liquidation takes effect on registration: it is not sufficient that the notice has been sent to the registrar or received by him. In *Re E-Squared Ltd* [2006] EWHC 532 (Ch); [2006] 1 W.L.R. 3414; [2006] B.C.C. 379 the administrators had sent the notices under para.83 to the registrar while they were still in office but the notices were not registered until after a date when their appointments had ceased to have effect. It was held that the companies had been wound up on the date of registration and that the (by then) former administrators were its liquidators. In *Re Globespan Airways Ltd* [2012] EWCA Civ 1159; [2013] 1 W.L.R. 1122; [2013] B.C.C. 252 the facts were similar. At first instance ([2012] EWHC 359 (Ch); [2012] B.C.C. 479) the trial judge had held that the conversion should be deemed to have taken effect on the date of filing rather than the actual registration, but on appeal this ruling was reversed: the effective date was that of the actual registration, and if before then the administration would ordinarily have terminated under para.76(1) (one year after its commencement), it should be extended until the registration date by implication from the language of para.83. *Re Globespan* was followed in *Re Property Professionals + Ltd* [2013] EWHC 1903 (Ch); [2013] B.C.C. 606, where the court also held that the one-year period referred to in para.76(1) should be reckoned from the actual time of day when the administrators had been appointed, so that the administration will not have lapsed so long as the notice of conversion is received by the registrar before the same time on the anniversary date. In contrast, in *Re Melodious Corp* [2015] EWHC 621 (Ch); [2016] B.C.C. 727, Sir Terence Etherton C was able to distinguish these rulings on the facts and hold that where a conversion notice was sent before the date on which the administrator's office was due to expire, the administration was converted into a winding up on the sending of the notice even if the notice was not received by the registrar until after that date.

Companies House, in a notice dated 21 June 2013, has directed that the filing of a notice of conversion under para.83 must be supplemented by a notice of appointment of liquidator (and subsequently gazetted). The fact that the name of the intended liquidator appears on the notice of conversion is not in itself sufficient. This direction applies only in England and Wales.

This procedure is available whether the administrator has been appointed by the court or out of court. It is not necessary for a court-appointed administrator to seek any order of the court (e.g. under para.79) beforehand: the decision to send a notice under para.83(3) rests entirely at his discretion (*Re Ballast plc* [2004] EWHC 2356 (Ch); [2005] B.C.C. 96). Where the administrator was appointed by court order, he must, however, seek an order if he wishes to obtain his discharge.

Where a company has entered administration before 6 April 2010 and is converted into a creditors' voluntary liquidation on or after that date the amendments to IR 1986 made by I(A)R 2010 will apply, providing for progress reports and removing the requirements to hold annual meetings: see I(A)R (No.2) 2010 r.13. Rule 3.60 applies.

Paragraph 83(1)(b), (2)(b) amended by SBEEA 2015 s.128(3) as from 26 May 2015.

Para.83(6)(b)

The draftsman has used the phrase "on the day" rather than "at the time" (as in s.86). The winding up will therefore be deemed to have commenced as from the preceding midnight: see the note to s.86.

Para.83(7)

The appointment, if made by the creditors, takes effect by the creditors approving the administrator's proposals or revised proposals (r.3.60(6)). If the prescribed procedure for a creditors' appointment is not followed, the administrator(s) (perhaps unwittingly) become liquidators by default: *Hobbs v Gibson* [2010] EWHC 3676 (Ch). In this situation the paragraph does not give the court power to appoint a new liquidator, but a way of achieving this result was found in *Re Angel Group Ltd* [2015] EWHC 3624 (Ch). This paragraph does not deal with the question of joint liquidators, and in particular whether they may act singly. If the creditors make the appointment, this may be authorised by them at the time (s.231(2)), but if (as is more usual) the persons who have been joint administrators become liquidators by virtue of para.83(7)(b), neither the Act nor the Rules appear to give guidance.

Moving from administration to dissolution

84(1) If the administrator of a company thinks that the company has no property which might permit a distribution to its creditors, he shall send a notice to that effect to the registrar of companies.

84(1A) Sub-paragraph (1B) applies where, immediately before the administrator sends the notice, there are EU insolvency proceedings open in respect of the company in one or more other member States.

84(1B) The administrator must send to the registrar, with the notice, a statement–

(a) identifying those proceedings,

(b) identifying the member State liquidator appointed in each of those proceedings, and

(c) indicating, in relation to each of those member State liquidators, whether that member State liquidator consents to the company being dissolved.

84(2) The court may on the application of the administrator of a company disapply sub-paragraph (1) in respect of the company.

84(3) On receipt of a notice under sub-paragraph (1) and any statement under sub-paragraph (1B) the registrar shall register it or them.

84(4) On the registration of a notice in respect of a company under sub-paragraph (1) the appointment of an administrator of the company shall cease to have effect.

84(5) If an administrator sends a notice under sub-paragraph (1) he shall as soon as is reasonably practicable–

(a) file a copy of the notice with the court, and

(b) send a copy of the notice to each creditor, other than an opted-out creditor, of whose claim and address he is aware.

84(6) At the end of the period of three months beginning with the date of registration of a notice in respect of a company under sub-paragraph (1) the company is deemed to be dissolved (except where sub-paragraph (6A) applies).

84(6A) This sub-paragraph applies where a statement under sub-paragraph (1B) indicates that a member State liquidator does not consent to the company being dissolved.

84(6B) Where sub-paragraph (6A) applies, the company is deemed to be dissolved at the end of the period of three months beginning with the date (if any) recorded in the register as the date on which the registrar was notified that–

(a) all proceedings identified in the statement under sub-paragraph (1B) were closed, or

(b) every member State liquidator appointed in those proceedings consented to the company being dissolved.

84(7) On an application in respect of a company by the administrator or another interested person the court may–

(a) extend the period specified in sub-paragraph (6) or (6B),

(b) suspend that period, or

(c) disapply sub-paragraph (6) or (6B).

84(8) Where an order is made under sub-paragraph (7) in respect of a company the administrator shall as soon as is reasonably practicable notify the registrar of companies.

84(9) An administrator commits an offence if he fails without reasonable excuse to comply with sub-paragraph (5).

General Note

This is a new provision which has no counterpart in the original IA 1986 Pt II. It is modelled on the "early dissolution" procedure (ss.202–204) that enables a company in compulsory liquidation to move to dissolution without further formality if it has no assets worth realising. All that is required is for the administrator to send the requisite notice to the registrar of companies and notify the court and the creditors. Unless the court orders otherwise under para.84(7), dissolution follows automatically three months later.

Paragraph 84(1A), (1B), (6A), (6B) inserted and (3), (7) amended by the Insolvency Amendment (EU 2015/848) Regulations 2017 (SI 2017/702) regs 1, 2(1), Sch. paras 1, 30 in relation to proceedings opened on or after 26 June 2017 (see reg.3) when the Recast EU Regulation 2015/848 came into force, to cater for where EU insolvency proceedings are open in respect of the company in one or more other Member States and e.g. consent to dissolution by a Member State liquidator is needed.

Para.84(1), (1A), (1B), (2)

It would appear from the wording of these subparagraphs, taken together and subject to any EU proceedings, that once the administrator has reached a conclusion that the property is insufficient he has no discretion to do otherwise than proceed to a dissolution: only the court can determine that the administration should continue. One situation where this might be appropriate would be where there are circumstances suggesting misconduct which require investigation.

Although on a first reading para.84(1) would appear to apply only in the case where there never has been property of the company in the hands of the administrator which would permit a distribution to its creditors, it has come to be used in practice as a convenient exit route from administration after the administrator has distributed such assets as he has been able to and there is nothing more in his hands—in other words, para.84(1) is read as if it included the words "or no remaining property which might permit a further distribution to its creditors". This practice has received the blessing of the Insolvency Service: see *Dear IP*, March 2005, Ch.1.6 and endorsement by the courts: *Re Preston & Duckworth Ltd* [2006] B.C.C. 133; *Re GHE Realisations Ltd* [2005] EWHC 2400 (Ch); [2006] 1 W.L.R. 287; [2006] B.C.C. 139.

In *Re Hellas Telecommunications (Luxembourg) II SCA* [2011] EWHC 3176 (Ch); [2013] 1 B.C.L.C. 426 the court ruled that the company could not be dissolved under para.84 and directed instead that it should be wound up, in the light of a finding that it had assets available for distribution to creditors, and also because a liquidator would be better placed to pursue inquiries into the company's affairs.

Paragraph 84 applies to both court-appointed and out-of-court administrations, and no court order is necessary at any stage (*Re Ballast plc* [2004] EWHC 2356 (Ch); [2005] B.C.C. 96).

Rule 3.61 applies.

Para.84(4)

The administration comes to an end on registration. There would appear to be no power to reinstate the administration once this has been done.

Para.84(6), (6A), (6B)

Deemed dissolution occurs after three months unless there are EU insolvency proceedings open in respect of the company in one or more other Member States and a Member State liquidator does not consent to the company being dissolved; para.84(6B) may then apply for dissolution. Should it be necessary to revive the company (e.g. if unknown assets belonging to the company come to light), CA 2006 ss.1029 et seq. empowers the court to declare the dissolution void and restore the company to the register if application is made within the ensuing six years. However, the court's powers in making such an order are limited by the terms of s.1032: the company is deemed by the order to have continued in existence as if it had not been dissolved, but it is not possible to grant additional relief such as retrospectively extending the administration period (*Re The Peoples' Restaurant Group Ltd* (unreported, 30 November 2012)). See also *Re Fivestar Properties Ltd* [2015] EWHC 2782 (Ch); [2016] 1 W.L.R. 1104 (property vested in the Crown as bona vacantia and subsequently disclaimed; freehold retrospectively recreated on restoration of company to register). See further the note to s.200.

Para.84(7)

The powers of the court under this subparagraph apply only to para.84(6) or (6B), i.e. to the anticipated dissolution of the company, and not to the ending of the administration under para.84(4).

Para.84(8), (9)

The obligation continues to apply to an administrator even after he has ceased to hold office (para.111(1)). On penalties, see s.430, Sch.B1 para.106(2) and Sch.10.

Discharge of administration order where administration ends

85(1) This paragraph applies where–

(a) the court makes an order under this Schedule providing for the appointment of an administrator of a company to cease to have effect, and

(b) the administrator was appointed by administration order.

85(2) The court shall discharge the administration order.

General Note

This paragraph applies only where the administrator was appointed by court order. Under the original Pt II, it is the discharge of the order which brings the administration to an end. Under Sch.B1, the sequence is reversed.

Notice to Companies Registrar where administration ends

86(1) This paragraph applies where the court makes an order under this Schedule providing for the appointment of an administrator to cease to have effect.

86(2) The administrator shall send a copy of the order to the registrar of companies within the period of 14 days beginning with the date of the order.

86(3) An administrator who fails without reasonable excuse to comply with sub-paragraph (2) commits an offence.

General Note

This provision, again, is not concerned with the situation where an individual administrator ceases to hold office, but with the termination of the administration itself. In contrast with para.85, it is not confined to the case of an administrator appointed by the court: there are other provisions (e.g. para.81) empowering the court to order that an administration should come to an end.

Rule 3.59 applies.

Para.86(3)

On penalties, see s.430, Sch.B1 para.106(2) and Sch.10.

Replacing Administrator

Resignation of administrator

87(1) An administrator may resign only in prescribed circumstances.

87(2) Where an administrator may resign he may do so only–

(a) in the case of an administrator appointed by administration order, by notice in writing to the court,

(b) in the case of an administrator appointed under paragraph 14, by notice in writing to the holder of the floating charge by virtue of which the appointment was made,

(c) in the case of an administrator appointed under paragraph 22(1), by notice in writing to the company, or

(d) in the case of an administrator appointed under paragraph 22(2), by notice in writing to the directors of the company.

General Note

The circumstances in which an administrator may resign his office are prescribed by rr.3.62–3.64, which give further details regarding the giving of notice and its filing with the court and the registrar of companies.

On the question when a notice of resignation takes effect, see the note to s.19(1). For resignation procedures under para 87 see *VE Vegas Investors IV LLC v Shinners* [2018] EWHC 186 (Ch).

Removal of administrator from office

88 The court may by order remove an administrator from office.

General Note

This provision applies to any administrator under the new regime, however appointed. Both the administration itself, and the office of administrator, continue in being: see para.1(2)(d). An application under this provision and para.74 succeeded in *Clydesdale Financial Services Ltd v Smailes* [2009] EWHC 1745 (Ch); [2009] B.C.C. 810 but failed in *SISU Capital Fund Ltd v Tucker* [2005] EWHC 2170 and 2321 (Ch); [2006] B.C.C. 463. See also *Re St Georges Property Services (London) Ltd, Finnerty v Clark* [2011] EWCA Civ 858; [2011] B.C.C. 702. For consideration of the factors the court should take into account when faced with an application under para 88 to remove administrators see the judgment of Registrar Jones in *VE Vegas Investors IV LLC v Shinners* [2018] EWHC 186 (Ch). Costs may be awarded against the administrator: *Coyne v DRC Distribution Ltd* [2008] EWCA Civ 488; [2008] B.C.C. 612. Rule 3.65 applies.

Administrator ceasing to be qualified

89(1) The administrator of a company shall vacate office if he ceases to be qualified to act as an insolvency practitioner in relation to the company.

89(2) Where an administrator vacates office by virtue of sub-paragraph (1) he shall give notice in writing–

(a) in the case of an administrator appointed by administration order, to the court,

(b) in the case of an administrator appointed under paragraph 14, to the holder of the floating charge by virtue of which the appointment was made,

(c) in the case of an administrator appointed under paragraph 22(1), to the company, or

(d) in the case of an administrator appointed under paragraph 22(2), to the directors of the company.

89(3) An administrator who fails without reasonable excuse to comply with sub-paragraph (2) commits an offence.

General Note

An administrator will "cease to be qualified to act" in relation to the company if at any time he fails to meet the criteria set out in s.390. "Shall vacate office" may be read as meaning either something that happens automatically or something which depends on the administrator taking action to step aside. It is probably the former that is intended, the giving of notice under para.89(2) being merely consequential.

Notice must also be given to the registrar of companies (r.3.66).

Para.89(3)
On penalties, see s.390, Sch.B1 para.106(2) and Sch.10.

Supplying vacancy in office of administrator

90 Paragraphs 91 to 95 apply where an administrator–

(a) dies,

(b) resigns,

(c) is removed from office under paragraph 88, or

(d) vacates office under paragraph 89.

General Note

Paragraphs 91–95 apply only if the office of administrator has become vacant. The substitution of one administrator by another is dealt with in paras 96–97, and the appointment of one or more additional administrators in paras 100–103.

Rules 3.62 et seq. apply in these cases.

91(1) Where the administrator was appointed by administration order, the court may replace the administrator on an application under this sub-paragraph made by–

(a) a creditors' committee of the company,

(b) the company,

(c) the directors of the company,

(d) one or more creditors of the company, or

(e) where more than one person was appointed to act jointly or concurrently as the administrator, any of those persons who remains in office.

91(2) But an application may be made in reliance on sub-paragraph (1)(b) to (d) only where–

(a) there is no creditors' committee of the company,

(b) the court is satisfied that the creditors' committee or a remaining administrator is not taking reasonable steps to make a replacement, or

(c) the court is satisfied that for another reason it is right for the application to be made.

General Note

This paragraph applies only where the administrator who has vacated office was appointed by the court. Where the administrator was appointed out of court, a replacement will normally be appointed out of court under paras 92–94, but the court has back-up and, where appropriate, overriding powers in the circumstances set out in para.95.

Rules 3.67 et seq. give details of the procedure and notification requirements.

Para.91(1)
It does not appear that the outgoing administrator may make an application under this provision. But there are situations where this would be appropriate, perhaps particularly where it is sought to replace an insolvency practitioner who holds multiple offices in a single application and appoint replacements, e.g. one or more members of the same firm, as in *Re Equity Nominees Ltd* [2000] B.C.C. 84. (On "block" transfer orders, see the note to s.171(1), (2).) The court would no doubt allow the application to be made under some other provision, e.g. para.63.

Para.91(2)
The persons listed in subparas (1)(b)–(d) must stand aside and allow the creditors' committee, if there is one, or a remaining administrator where there were joint or concurrent appointments, to have first bite at the cherry (not necessarily by applying to the court), subject to the court's discretion under para.91(2)(c).

92 Where the administrator was appointed under paragraph 14 the holder of the floating charge by virtue of which the appointment was made may replace the administrator.

General Note

This provision applies only where the office of administrator has become vacant: for the replacement of an administrator currently in office, see paras 87–97. The right of the holder of the floating charge to replace his own appointee is unqualified, although no doubt this could be challenged under para.95(b) if good reason could be shown.

Rules 3.69, 3.70 apply.

93(1) Where the administrator was appointed under paragraph 22(1) by the company it may replace the administrator.

93(2) A replacement under this paragraph may be made only–

(a) with the consent of each person who is the holder of a qualifying floating charge in respect of the company's property, or

(b) where consent is withheld, with the permission of the court.

General Note

The initial appointment of an administrator by the company under para.22(1) may be made only after giving five days' notice to the holder of a qualifying floating charge under para.26, so enabling the latter to make his own appointment instead. The present paragraph to some extent echoes para.26, giving the charge holder an opportunity to have some say in the choice of a replacement, but stops short of giving him an outright veto.

Rules 3.69, 3.70 apply.

94(1) Where the administrator was appointed under paragraph 22(2) the directors of the company may replace the administrator.

94(2) A replacement under this paragraph may be made only–

(a) with the consent of each person who is the holder of a qualifying floating charge in respect of the company's property, or

(b) where consent is withheld, with the permission of the court.

General Note

This provision is in similar terms to para.93. See the comment to that paragraph.

95 The court may replace an administrator on the application of a person listed in paragraph 91(1) if the court–

(a) is satisfied that a person who is entitled to replace the administrator under any of paragraphs 92 to 94 is not taking reasonable steps to make a replacement, or

(b) that for another reason it is right for the court to make the replacement.

General Note

This provision gives the court back-up powers to deal with situations of inertia or dispute. Only those persons listed in para.91(1) have standing to apply. If anyone else (e.g. an outgoing administrator) wishes to have the court make a replacement, application would have to be made under some other provision, such as para.63. Rule 3.68 applies to the application. See the note to para.91(1).

Rules 3.69, 3.70 apply.

Substitution of administrator: competing floating charge-holder

96(1) This paragraph applies where an administrator of a company is appointed under paragraph 14 by the holder of a qualifying floating charge in respect of the company's property.

96(2) The holder of a prior qualifying floating charge in respect of the company's property may apply to the court for the administrator to be replaced by an administrator nominated by the holder of the prior floating charge.

96(3) One floating charge is prior to another for the purposes of this paragraph if–

(a) it was created first, or

(b) it is to be treated as having priority in accordance with an agreement to which the holder of each floating charge was party.

96(4) Sub-paragraph (3) shall have effect in relation to Scotland as if the following were substituted for paragraph (a)–

"(a) it has priority of ranking in accordance with section 464(4)(b) of the Companies Act 1985 (c. 6) [CA 2006, no equivalent],".

General Note

In contrast with paras 87–95, this provision appears to apply whether or not there is a vacancy in the office of administrator. It deals with the situation where an administrator is or has been in office who has been appointed by the holder of a junior-ranking floating charge. When the initial appointment was made, the charge holder making the appointment would have been required to notify or secure the consent of any senior-ranking charge holder(s) under para.15(1), and it is assumed that the latter took no steps at that time to block the appointment. The present provision allows the holder of a senior-ranking charge to apply to the court subsequently to request that a different person be appointed administrator in place of the junior charge-holder's appointee. No guidance is given to the court as to the basis on which it should exercise its discretion to accede to such a request, although prima facie the holder of a senior-ranking charge would expect the court to support his choice of nominee.

On the meaning of "qualifying" floating charge, see para.14(2). The court would surely also require the senior-ranking charge to be enforceable at the time the application is made, in keeping with para.16, although this is not stated in para.96.

Rules 3.69, 3.70 apply.

Substitution of administrator appointed by company or directors: creditors' decision

97(1) This paragraph applies where–

(a) an administrator of a company is appointed by a company or directors under paragraph 22, and

(b) there is no holder of a qualifying floating charge in respect of the company's property.

97(2) The administrator may be replaced by a decision of the creditors made by a qualifying decision procedure.

97(3) The decision has effect only if, before the decision is made, the new administrator has consented to act in writing.

General Note

Paragraph 97(2), (3) substituted by SBEEA 2015 Sch.9 paras 1, 10(35) as from 6 April 2017.

As with para.96, this provision appears to apply whether or not there is a vacancy in the office of administrator but, in contrast with that paragraph, no application to the court is needed. If there is a vacancy, the company or the directors (as the case may be) will also have the power to appoint a replacement under paras 93 or 94, but it would make no sense for either of them to do so if there is opposition from the creditors' committee, since it could use its power under the present paragraph to override their appointment.

Rules 3.69, 3.70 apply.

Vacation of office: discharge from liability

98(1) Where a person ceases to be the administrator of a company (whether because he vacates office by reason of resignation, death or otherwise, because he is removed from office or because his appointment ceases to have effect) he is discharged from liability in respect of any action of his as administrator.

98(2) The discharge provided by sub-paragraph (1) takes effect–

(a) in the case of an administrator who dies, on the filing with the court of notice of his death,

(b) in the case of an administrator appointed under paragraph 14 or 22 who has not made a statement under paragraph 52(1)(b), at a time appointed by resolution of the creditors' committee or, if there is no committee, by decision of the creditors,

(ba) in the case of an administrator appointed under paragraph 14 or 22 who has made a statement under paragraph 52(1)(b), at a time decided by the relevant creditors, or

(c) in any case, at a time specified by the court.

98(3) For the purposes of sub-paragraph (2)(ba), the "relevant creditors" of a company are–

(a) each secured creditor of the company, or

(b) if the administrator has made a distribution to preferential creditors or thinks that a distribution may be made to preferential creditors–

(i) each secured creditor of the company, and

(ii) the preferential creditors of the company.

98(3A) In a case where the administrator is removed from office, a decision of the creditors for the purposes of sub-paragraph (2)(b), or of the preferential creditors for the purposes of sub-paragraph (2)(ba), must be made by a qualifying decision procedure.

98(4) Discharge–

(a) applies to liability accrued before the discharge takes effect, and

(b) does not prevent the exercise of the court's powers under paragraph 75.

General Note

Paragraph 98(2)(b) and (3)(a), (b) were amended and para.98(2)(ba) inserted by DA 2015 Sch.6 para.7 as from 1 October 2015; para.98(2)(b), (3)(b)(ii) amended and sub-para.(3A) inserted by SBEEA 2015 Sch.9 paras 1, 10(36)–(38) as from 6 April 2017.

The phrase "the appointment of an administrator ceases to have effect" is used by the draftsman as equivalent to "the administration comes to an end" or "is terminated": see, e.g. paras 76, 80, 81. The present provision thus applies both in the case where an administrator is replaced and also where the administration has come to an end.

Para.98(1)

The discharge is not automatic, but takes effect only from the time specified in subpara.(2).

Para.98(2)

It is conceivable that the court could fix a time other than those mentioned in subpara.(2)(a) and (b), although the court would not normally be involved in either of these cases. The court's usual practice is to fix a date 28 days after the administrator has filed his final report. In *Re Hellas Telecommunications (Luxembourg) II SCA* [2011] EWHC 3176 (Ch); [2013] 1 B.C.L.C. 426 the court made such an order despite opposition by certain creditors: it remained open to them to seek the leave of the court to pursue misfeasance proceedings under para.75 if they had a good arguable case. For a similar ruling, see *Re Angel Group Ltd* [2015] EWHC 3624 (Ch).

Where the administrator in question was appointed out of court under paras 14 or 22, it is left to the creditors' committee or creditors to decide when the discharge should take effect. There is some parallel with s.173, which deals with the release of a liquidator in a voluntary winding up, but there is no provision in the present paragraph for the committee or creditors to resolve against a discharge. If they are unwilling to set a date from which the discharge is to take effect, and the contention above is correct, recourse could be had to the court to resolve the matter.

Para.98(3)

Paragraph 52(1)(b) applies where the administrator thinks that the company has insufficient property to enable a distribution to be made to the company's unsecured creditors (apart from anything they may get through the "prescribed part" provisions of s.176A). In such circumstances it is inappropriate that the decision on the administrator's discharge should be in the hands of the creditors' committee or the creditors at large, most of whom will have no interest in the outcome of the administration: hence the need for the consents required by this sub-paragraph.

Vacation of office: charges and liabilities

99(1) This paragraph applies where a person ceases to be the administrator of a company (whether because he vacates office by reason of resignation, death or otherwise, because he is removed from office or because his appointment ceases to have effect).

99(2) In this paragraph–

"the former administrator" means the person referred to in sub-paragraph (1), and

"cessation" means the time when he ceases to be the company's administrator.

99(3) The former administrator's remuneration and expenses shall be–

(a) charged on and payable out of property of which he had custody or control immediately before cessation, and

(b) payable in priority to any security to which paragraph 70 applies.

99(4) A sum payable in respect of a debt or liability arising out of a contract entered into by the former administrator or a predecessor before cessation shall be–

(a) charged on and payable out of property of which the former administrator had custody or control immediately before cessation, and

(b) payable in priority to any charge arising under sub-paragraph (3).

99(5) Sub-paragraph (4) shall apply to a liability arising under a contract of employment which was adopted by the former administrator or a predecessor before cessation; and for that purpose–

(a) action taken within the period of 14 days after an administrator's appointment shall not be taken to amount or contribute to the adoption of a contract,

(b) no account shall be taken of a liability which arises, or in so far as it arises, by reference to anything which is done or which occurs before the adoption of the contract of employment, and

(c) no account shall be taken of a liability to make a payment other than wages or salary.

99(6) In sub-paragraph (5)(c) "wages or salary" includes–

(a) a sum payable in respect of a period of holiday (for which purpose the sum shall be treated as relating to the period by reference to which the entitlement to holiday accrued),

(b) a sum payable in respect of a period of absence through illness or other good cause,

(c) a sum payable in lieu of holiday,

(d) [Omitted]

(e) a contribution to an occupational pension scheme.

General Note

This provision broadly corresponds to s.*19(4)–(10)*, including the reforms made by IA 1994 in consequence of the ruling of the Court of Appeal in *Powdrill v Watson; Re Paramount Airways Ltd (No.3)* [1994] 2 All E.R. 513; [1994] B.C.C. 172. Note that although the paragraph is expressed to apply only where a person ceases to be the administrator, it is well recognised that many of the payments referred to will, in the ordinary case, be paid in the course of the administration.

In *Re Lafayette Electronics Europe Ltd* [2006] EWHC 1005, 1006 (Ch); [2007] B.C.C. 890 the administration had, by an oversight, been allowed to expire at a time when the administrators' fees were outstanding. HHJ Norris QC approved an application by the administrators for them to be appointed provisional liquidators pending the hearing of a winding-up petition which they had presented as creditors in respect of the petition. The only qualification made was that they should have no power to sanction their own fees and to decide upon their own release.

On the effect in this context of the ruling of the House of Lords in *Re Leyland DAF Ltd, Buchler v Talbot* [2004] UKHL 9; [2004] 2 A.C. 298; [2004] B.C.C. 214 and its reversal by statute, see the note to para.65.

Paragraph 99(6)(d) omitted by DA 2015 Sch.6 paras 24, 27 as from 29 May 2015.

Para.99(3)–(4)

In *Exeter City Council v Bairstow* [2007] EWHC 400 (Ch); [2007] B.C.C. 236 (the "*Trident Fashions*" case) David Richards J drew attention to the differences between the provisions governing an administrator's expenses and disbursements under s.*19* and those in the new regime, to which the present paragraph and r.3.51 apply. (There is no corresponding rule where s.*19* applies.) In particular, an administrator's liability to defray non-domestic rates levied against the company were held to be necessary disbursements (and thus entitled to priority), in contrast with the position under s.*19*. The rates with which that case was concerned had been levied in respect of premises occupied by the company while in administration. The decision has left the question regarding the priority accorded to such rates in a somewhat paradoxical situation. Rates accruing on premises occupied by a company while in liquidation are payable as an expense of the liquidation: *Re Toshoku Finance (UK) plc* [2002] UKHL 6; [2002] 1 W.L.R. 671; [2002] B.C.C. 110. See also *Re Nolton Business Centres Ltd* [1996] B.C.C. 500 and *Kaye v South Oxfordshire DC* [2013] EWHC 4165 (Ch); [2014] B.C.C. 143. If the company is in administration under the original Pt II, the rates were not payable as an expense of the administration: *Freakley v Centre Reinsurance International Co* [2006] UKHL 45; [2006] 1 W.L.R. 2863; [2006] B.C.C. 971. If, however, the company is in administration under Sch.B1, the position is the same as in a liquidation and the rates rank as an expense of the administration by virtue of r.3.51. But, following the decision, the position was less clear in relation to rates payable on unoccupied property. These were not payable in a liquidation by virtue of the special exemption conferred by the Non-Domestic Rating (Unoccupied Property) Regulations 1989 (SI 1989/2261). In the absence of any comparable legislative exemption, David Richards J in *Exeter City Council v Bairstow* expressed the view that these also had priority as an expense of a Sch.B1 administration. This observation gave rise to considerable concern and has led to a change in the law, bringing administration into line with liquidation. By the Non-Domestic Rating (Unoccupied Property) (England) Regulations

2008 (SI 2008/386, effective 1 April 2008) the 1989 Regulations are revoked (in their application to England) and a new exemption regime has been introduced which applies both in a liquidation (reg.4(k)) and an administration (whether under the original Pt II or Sch.B1) (reg.4(l)). (There is also a curious reference to IA 1986 ss.112 and 146 in reg.4(m).) For Scotland, the exemption has been extended to both administration regimes by the Non-Domestic Rating (Unoccupied Property) (Scotland) Amendment Regulations 2008 (SSI 2008/83) as from 1 April 2008 and, for Wales, by the Non-Domestic Rating (Unoccupied Property) (Wales) Regulations 2008 (SI 2008/2499 (W 217) as from 1 November 2008. See further the note to r.3.51.

It is possible that some of the cases discussed in this paragraph may be open to review in the light of the decision in *Pillar Denton* (below).

Rent of premises occupied wholly or partly by a company in administration were held to be payable as an administration expense by the Court of Appeal in *Pillar Denton Ltd v Jervis, Re Games Station Ltd* [2014] EWCA Civ 180; [2014] B.C.C. 165 (overruling the first instance decisions *Goldacre (Offices) Ltd v Nortel Networks UK Ltd* [2009] EWHC 3389 (Ch); [2010] Ch. 455; [2010] B.C.C. 299 and *Leisure (Norwich) II Ltd v Luminar Lava Ignite Ltd* [2012] EWHC 951 (Ch); [2012] B.C.C. 497). Applying the "salvage" principle laid down in *Re Lundy Granite Co* (1870–71) L.R. 6 Ch. App. 462, the court held that the rule applied irrespective of the question whether the rent day occurred prior to or during the administration: the determining factor was whether the administrator retained possession of the property for the benefit of the administration; the rent was to be treated as accruing from day to day and ranked as an expense of the administration and not simply a provable debt. Moreover, applying the same principle, if the administrator vacated the premises, leaving the landlord free to re-let, rent ceased to be payable, irrespective of the terms of the lease. These principles apply also in a liquidation.

See also *Re Nortel GmbH, Bloom v Pensions Regulator* [2013] UKSC 52; [2014] A.C. 209; [2013] B.C.C. 624, where money payable under a financial support direction (FSD) imposed by the Pensions Regulator on a company in administration was held by the Supreme Court to be a provable debt ranking pari passu with the company's unsecured creditors. In so ruling the court allowed an appeal from the Court of Appeal ([2012] EWCA Civ 1124; [2012] B.C.C. 83) where it had been held that the payment was a necessary disbursement and accordingly entitled to super-priority as an expense of the administration. In *Re Storm Funding Ltd* [2013] EWHC 4019 (Ch) David Richards J considered the situation where there were multiple insolvencies in a corporate group and contribution notices might be issued to a number of the companies, possibly resulting in an aggregate exceeding the overall shortfall.

Nortel was followed in *Laverty v British Gas Trading Ltd* [2014] EWHC 2721 (Ch); [2014] B.C.C. 701, where the charge for a continued supply of energy to a company in administration (under a deemed contract, after the original supply had been terminated by the provider) was held to be a provable debt, but not an administration expense. See further the notes to rr.3.51 and 14.1.

Pre-administration costs approved under r.3.52 now rank along with the administrator's remuneration (r.3.51(2)(i)).

Remuneration can be paid under para.99(3) only out of property that is beneficially owned by the company, and not property held by it on trust for others: *Gillan v HEC Enterprises Ltd* [2016] EWHC 3179 (Ch).

In *Re MK Airlines Ltd* [2012] EWHC 1018 (Ch); [2012] 3 All E.R. 781; [2014] B.C.C. 87 Morritt C said that the test whether a former administrator had had "custody or control" of company property immediately before he ceased to hold office was entitlement to that property (or to the property from which it was derived): it was not necessary for him to have taken any steps to obtain custody or control of it.

In *Amble Assets LLP v Longbenton Foods Ltd* [2011] EWHC 3774 (Ch) property had been sold by administrators on terms which included the payment by the seller of a deposit, and included a provision in the sale contract to the effect that any successful claim for the return of the deposit should not constitute an administration expense but rank as an unsecured claim. It was held that this was not invalid as an attempt to contract out of the statutory order of priority and should be given contractual effect.

Paragraph 99(3) provides for a "charge" on the company's property for payment of the former administrator's remuneration and expenses (see also para.99(4) in relation to payment for liability on the administrator's contracts). HHJ Purle pointed out in *Re Hotel Company 42 The Calls Ltd; Whitfield v Al Jaber* [2013] EWHC 3925 (Ch); [2014] B.C.C. 136 that although the Act did not provide any machinery for enforcement of the charge, the court had inherent power to enforce any charge, for example by the appointment of a receiver, an order for sale, or both (applying *Re MK Airlines Ltd* (above)). A sale would be subject to the court's directions and the court would order a sale of the company's main asset, a hotel, if and when remuneration was established to be due and remained unpaid. He further noted that the statutory charge amounted to an interest affecting the registered estate, which would be registrable as an agreed notice that would protect the administrator's priority under the Land Registration Act 2002. In *Walker v National Westminster Bank plc* [2016] EWHC 315 (Ch); [2016] B.C.C. 355 it was held that the charge could only be enforced by an order of the court. The nature of the charge was also considered in *Re Nortel Networks UK Ltd* [2017]

EWHC 1429 (Ch) where Snowden J discerned that administration expense claimants have no express statutory right to payment of their claims out of any particular assets or at any particular time: the legal entitlement of an expense creditor under Sch.B1 para.99(3) was simply that his debt would be charged on and payable out of the property of which the administrator had custody or control immediately before the time when he ceased to be the administrator. In those circumstances, the court had jurisdiction to give directions under para.63 for a distribution to unsecured creditors under para.65(3), even though it carried a risk that at the end of the administration insufficient assets might have been retained to enable a late expense claimant to be paid under para.99(3).

Para.99(4)

The estate for the purpose of ascertaining the respective entitlements of the creditors under the statutory charge created by this provision consists only of the property of which the former administrator had control on the date of his cessation of office. Payments already made to creditors coming within the para.99(4) description prior to that date remain undisturbed and should not be brought into account. (*Re Sports Betting Media Ltd* [2007] EWHC 2085 (Ch); [2008] B.C.C. 177.) In the case where there has been a change of administrator, the creditors entitled to the benefit of the charge under the prior administrator's term of office must pay the new administrator the reasonable cost of realising the assets constituting the fund. On "custody or control", see the note to para.99(3) above.

The statutory charge can be enforced by the appointment of a receiver: *Re MK Airlines Ltd* (above).

Para.99(5)–(6)

The liabilities which are payable by virtue of para.99 in priority to the administrator's expenses are those liabilities which have been adopted after 14 days of appointment and which are "wages or salary". These do not include redundancy payments or unfair dismissal payments of employees who have not been kept on: *Re Allders Department Stores Ltd* [2005] EWHC 172 (Ch); [2005] B.C.C. 289 (discussed by Lyons and Birch (2005) 18 Insolv. Int. 150); *Re Leeds United Association Football Club Ltd* [2007] EWHC 1761 (Ch); [2008] B.C.C. 11. Nor are such payments entitled to priority under r.3.51(2)(e)–(f): see the note to r.3.51.

Although the drafting of para.99 follows a different style from that of s.*19(6)–(10)*, it might have been assumed that no change of substance was intended to be made in the law, and indeed that view was confirmed by statements made in Parliament. However, in *Krasner v McMath* [2005] EWHC 1682 (Ch); [2005] B.C.C. 896, Peter Smith J held that payments in lieu of notice and protective awards made in a redundancy situation under the Trade Union and Labour Relations (Consolidation) Act 1992 s.188 were entitled to priority over the administrator's remuneration and expenses, in effect reversing the amendments made to s.*19* in 1994. This view was based in part on the fact that para.99(6)(d) omits the words "payable in respect of a period of holiday" which are to be found in s.*19(10)*. Happily, when the case was taken to appeal (in a joined appeal with another from the decision in *Re Ferrotech Ltd and Re Granville Technology Group Ltd* [2005] EWHC 1848 (Ch); [2005] B.C.C. 905, in which Etherton J had declined to follow this ruling), the Court of Appeal held that (subject to a minor exception where the employee is required to take "garden leave") neither payments in lieu of notice nor protective awards have such priority: see *Re Huddersfield Fine Worsteds Ltd, Re Ferrotech Ltd and Re Granville Technology Group Ltd* [2005] EWCA Civ 1072; [2005] B.C.C. 915. In particular, protective awards are excluded because they arise under statute and not under the contract of employment. (On protective awards, see also *Haine v Day* [2008] EWCA Civ 626; [2008] B.C.C. 845 and the note to r.14.1.)

General

Joint and concurrent administrators

100(1) In this Schedule–

(a) a reference to the appointment of an administrator of a company includes a reference to the appointment of a number of persons to act jointly or concurrently as the administrator of a company, and

(b) a reference to the appointment of a person as administrator of a company includes a reference to the appointment of a person as one of a number of persons to act jointly or concurrently as the administrator of a company.

100(2) The appointment of a number of persons to act as administrator of a company must specify–

(a) which functions (if any) are to be exercised by the persons appointed acting jointly, and

(b) which functions (if any) are to be exercised by any or all of the persons appointed.

General Note

It is well established that expressions in the singular in legislation are to be read as including the plural (Interpretation Act 1978 s.6), but this and the ensuing paragraphs go further, providing that where an appointment is made of more than one person as administrators, they may empowered to act either jointly or concurrently, identifying the functions which each may exercise. Note that the Act does not require the appointment, as such, to be of administrators empowered to act either jointly or concurrently in everything that they do—although these options are permitted. Rather, the appointment must name the persons as administrators and then specify which functions are to be exercised jointly and which may be exercised by any or all (or fewer than all, e.g. authorising cheques to be signed by any two): para.100(2).

Rule 3.69 applies where a joint administrator is appointed.

101(1) This paragraph applies where two or more persons are appointed to act jointly as the administrator of a company.

101(2) A reference to the administrator of the company is a reference to those persons acting jointly.

101(3) But a reference to the administrator of a company in paragraphs 87 to 99 of this Schedule is a reference to any or all of the persons appointed to act jointly.

101(4) Where an offence of omission is committed by the administrator, each of the persons appointed to act jointly–

(a) commits the offence, and

(b) may be proceeded against and punished individually.

101(5) The reference in paragraph 45(1)(a) to the name of the administrator is a reference to the name of each of the persons appointed to act jointly.

101(6) Where persons are appointed to act jointly in respect of only some of the functions of the administrator of a company, this paragraph applies only in relation to those functions.

General Note

It would be an affront to the intelligence of the reader to add any comment to the astonishing verbosity of this paragraph.

102(1) This paragraph applies where two or more persons are appointed to act concurrently as the administrator of a company.

102(2) A reference to the administrator of a company in this Schedule is a reference to any of the persons appointed (or any combination of them).

General Note

For the position where administrators are appointed to act jointly, see para.101.

103(1) Where a company is in administration, a person may be appointed to act as administrator jointly or concurrently with the person or persons acting as the administrator of the company.

103(2) Where a company entered administration by administration order, an appointment under sub-paragraph (1) must be made by the court on the application of–

(a) a person or group listed in paragraph 12(1)(a) to (e), or

(b) the person or persons acting as the administrator of the company.

103(3) Where a company entered administration by virtue of an appointment under paragraph 14, an appointment under sub-paragraph (1) must be made by–

(a) the holder of the floating charge by virtue of which the appointment was made, or

(b) the court on the application of the person or persons acting as the administrator of the company.

103(4) Where a company entered administration by virtue of an appointment under paragraph 22(1), an appointment under sub-paragraph (1) above must be made either by the court on the application of the person or persons acting as the administrator of the company or–

(a) by the company, and

(b) with the consent of each person who is the holder of a qualifying floating charge in respect of the company's property or, where consent is withheld, with the permission of the court.

103(5) Where a company entered administration by virtue of an appointment under paragraph 22(2), an appointment under sub-paragraph (1) must be made either by the court on the application of the person or persons acting as the administrator of the company or–

(a) by the directors of the company, and

(b) with the consent of each person who is the holder of a qualifying floating charge in respect of the company's property or, where consent is withheld, with the permission of the court.

103(6) An appointment under sub-paragraph (1) may be made only with the consent of the person or persons acting as the administrator of the company.

General Note

There may be situations in which it is thought advisable or necessary to appoint one or more additional administrators to act jointly or concurrently with the administrator(s) already in office: the task may call for more manpower than was originally envisaged, or a creditor who holds a "qualifying" floating charge may feel happier if his own appointee joins the person or persons already in office who have been appointed by somebody else. In *Re BHS Ltd* [2016] EWHC 1965 (Ch); [2016] B.C.C. 609 the court, on the application of the original administrators, appointed a second set of administrators to act concurrently with them, each with separate responsibilities in terms of a protocol delineating their respective roles. This paragraph spells out the procedure to be followed. The court has overall control but, subject to that, deference must be shown to floating charge holders. Since the administrator currently in office may have an interest in what is proposed, he is given standing to apply to the court and also a veto on the proposed appointment.

Para.103(6)
This provision applies in each of the cases covered by para.103(2)–(5). It ensures that anyone already in office is not to have wished on to him a newcomer that he does not feel happy to work with—even where the new appointment is made by the court.

Presumption of validity

104 An act of the administrator of a company is valid in spite of a defect in his appointment or qualification.

General Note

This is a standard provision. However, it may not be relied on where the appointment was a nullity (e.g. because the correct procedure had not been followed, as in *Re Kaupthing Capital Partners II Master LP Inc* [2010] EWHC 836 (Ch); [2011] B.C.C. 338, where the wrong form of appointment had been used; and see *Re Synergi Partners Ltd* [2015] EWHC 964 (Ch); [2015] B.C.C. 333); but the difficulty may be overcome if the court makes an order for the administrator to be appointed with retrospective effect: *Re G-Tech Construction Ltd* [2007] B.P.I.R. 1275. In *Re Blights Builders Ltd* [2006] EWHC 3549; [2007] B.C.C. 712 Norris J relied on para.104 to declare that the acts of administrators who had been defectively appointed should be treated as valid, in a situation where it was at least arguable that their appointment was a nullity. Later, in *Re Care Matters Partnership Ltd* [2011] EWHC 2543 (Ch); [2011] B.C.C. 957, after referring to *G-Tech*, he stated that he adhered to his view "that para.104 may supply the answer in many cases", indicating fairly clearly that defective appointments should in many cases be regarded as such, rather than nullities incapable of being validated. In *Re Ceart Risk Services Ltd* [2012] EWHC 1178 (Ch);

[2012] B.C.C. 592 Arnold J held that para.104 was effective to validate acts of an administrator whose appointment, although defective, was curable, but not those where the purported appointment of an administrator was a nullity.

Majority decision of directors

105 A reference in this Schedule to something done by the directors of a company includes a reference to the same thing done by a majority of the directors of a company.

GENERAL NOTE

Although this provision would appear to be of general application, empowering the directors to act by a majority informally and without a meeting, its scope has been severely curtailed as a result of the decision in *Minmar (929) Ltd v Khalastchi* [2011] EWHC 1159 (Ch); [2011] B.C.C. 485. The only provisions of the Act to which it is now likely to apply are paras 18(4) and 29(4) (provision of information to administrator). It does not apply to paras 12(1)(b) (application for an administration order), 22(2) (out-of-court appointment of administrator by the directors), 91(1)(c) and 94(1) (replacement of administrators). In these cases the directors may act by a majority only at a duly constituted board meeting, notwithstanding the apparent general wording of para.105. *Minmar* was followed on this point in *Baker v London Bar Co Ltd* [2011] EWHC 3398 (Ch); [2012] B.C.C. 69 and in the context of a partnership in relation to para.12(1)(b) see also *Re Brake (t/a/ Stay in Style); Patley Wood Farm LLP v Brake* [2016] EWHC 1688 (Ch).

Penalties

106(1) A person who is guilty of an offence under this Schedule is liable to a fine (in accordance with section 430 and Schedule 10).

106(2) A person who is guilty of an offence under any of the following paragraphs of this Schedule is liable to a daily default fine (in accordance with section 430 and Schedule 10)–

(a) paragraph 20,

(b) paragraph 32,

(c) paragraph 46,

(d) paragraph 48,

(e) paragraph 49,

(f) paragraph 51,

(g) paragraph 53,

(h) paragraph 54,

(i) paragraph 56,

(j) paragraph 71,

(k) paragraph 72,

(l) paragraph 77,

(m) paragraph 78,

(n) paragraph 80,

(o) paragraph 84,

(p) paragraph 86, and

(q) paragraph 89.

General Note

For the amounts payable as fines for each of these offences, see Sch.10 and comments.

Extension of time limit

107(1) Where a provision of this Schedule provides that a period may be varied in accordance with this paragraph, the period may be varied in respect of a company–

(a) by the court, and

(b) on the application of the administrator.

107(2) A time period may be extended in respect of a company under this paragraph–

(a) more than once, and

(b) after expiry.

General Note

The scope of this paragraph is limited by the words "varied in accordance with this paragraph". Those paragraphs which refer to para.107 are paras 49, 50, 51, However, it is unlikely that this limitation would override the court's powers under more general provisions such as para.55(2)(e). Note that the period may be varied in relation to some only of the prescribed matters: *Re Advent Computer Training Ltd* [2010] EWHC 459 (Ch); [2011] B.C.C. 44.

Some of the statutory time periods may also be varied by the administrator with the creditors' consent under para.108.

108(1) A period specified in paragraph 49(5) or 51(2) may be varied in respect of a company by the administrator with consent.

108(2) In sub-paragraph (1) "consent" means consent of–

(a) each secured creditor of the company, and

(b) if the company has unsecured debts, the unsecured creditors of the company.

108(3) But where the administrator has made a statement under paragraph 52(1)(b) "consent" means–

(a) consent of each secured creditor of the company, or

(b) if the administrator thinks that a distribution may be made to preferential creditors, consent of–

(i) each secured creditor of the company, and

(ii) the preferential creditors of the company.

108(3A) Whether the company's unsecured creditors or preferential creditors consent is to be determined by the administrator seeking a decision from those creditors as to whether they consent.

108(4) [Omitted]

108(5) The power to extend under sub-paragraph (1)–

(a) may be exercised in respect of a period only once,

(b) may not be used to extend a period by more than 28 days,

(c) may not be used to extend a period which has been extended by the court, and

(d) may not be used to extend a period after expiry.

General Note

Paragraph 108(2)(b), (3)(b)(ii) substituted and para.108(3A) inserted by SBEEA 2015 Sch.9 paras 1, 10(40)–(42) as from 6 April 2017.

The time limits prescribed by the two paragraphs referred to may be varied by the administrator without a court order if the consent of the secured and unsecured creditors is obtained in accordance with this provision. Note the limitations imposed by para.108(5): in these cases there is no alternative but to apply to the court under para.107. Reference may be made also to the notes to paras 76–78, which are drafted in similar language.

Para.108(4)
"Written" includes the use of electronic means: s.436B.

109 Where a period is extended under paragraph 107 or 108, a reference to the period shall be taken as a reference to the period as extended.

Amendment of provision about time

110(1) The Secretary of State may by order amend a provision of this Schedule which–

(a) requires anything to be done within a specified period of time,

(b) prevents anything from being done after a specified time, or

(c) requires a specified minimum period of notice to be given.

110(2) An order under this paragraph–

(a) must be made by statutory instrument, and

(b) shall be subject to annulment in pursuance of a resolution of either House of Parliament.

General Note

The power conferred by this paragraph will allow for adjustments to be made to time provisions specified for the new regime if they prove to be inconvenient in practice, or if it is decided as a matter of policy to set shorter time-limits in order to speed up the rescue process.

Interpretation

111(1) In this Schedule–

"administrative receiver" has the meaning given by section 251,

"administrator" has the meaning given by paragraph 1 and, where the context requires, includes a reference to a former administrator,

"enters administration" has the meaning given by paragraph 1,

"floating charge" means a charge which is a floating charge on its creation,

"in administration" has the meaning given by paragraph 1,

"hire-purchase agreement" includes a conditional sale agreement, a chattel leasing agreement and a retention of title agreement,

"holder of a qualifying floating charge" in respect of a company's property has the meaning given by paragraph 14,

"market value" means the amount which would be realised on a sale of property in the open market by a willing vendor,

"the purpose of administration" means an objective specified in paragraph 3, and

"unable to pay its debts" has the meaning given by section 123.

111(1A) In this Schedule, "company" means–

(a) a company registered under the Companies Act 2006 in England and Wales or Scotland,

(b) a company incorporated in an EEA State other than the United Kingdom, or

(c) a company not incorporated in an EEA State but having its centre of main interests in a member State other than Denmark.

111(1B) In sub-paragraph (1A), in relation to a company, "centre of main interests" has the same meaning as in Article 3 of the EU Regulation.

111(2) [Repealed by LRO 2010 (SI 2010/18) art.4(2) (with retrospective effect).]

111(3) In this Schedule a reference to action includes a reference to inaction.

GENERAL NOTE

Definitions of "correspondence" and "creditors' meeting" deleted by SBEEA 2015 Sch.9 paras 1, 10(44) as from 6 April 2017.

The definitions here set out apply only for the purposes of the present Schedule. This limitation may create some difficulties—for instance, the word "administrator" will have one meaning for the purposes of the Schedule and another where the original s.*8* applies. By way of example, does the term "a former administrator" in the definition in para.111(1) include an administrator who was appointed under s.*8*?

Other definitions may be found in ss.247 et seq. and 435 et seq.

Para.111(1), 111(1A), 111(1B)

Note the rather surprising extension of the scope of para.111(1A)(b) to the whole of the EEA rather than those EU Member States that are within the EU Regulation. The "additional" countries (including Denmark) are thus brought within the jurisdiction of Sch.B1, but without any need to have regard to the provisions of the EU Regulation: questions as to the COMI, whether proceedings are "main", "secondary" or "territorial", etc. do not arise. In sub-para.(c), in contrast, "member State" must refer to countries within the EU.

In *Re Hellas Telecommunications (Luxembourg) II SCA* [2009] EWHC 3199 (Ch); [2010] B.C.C. 295 Lewison J held that an entity incorporated under the laws of Luxembourg that was a combination of a joint stock company and limited partnership was a "company" for the purposes of Sch.B1.

Paragraph 111(1) formerly contained a definition of "company" which read: " 'Company' includes a company which may enter administration by virtue of Article 3 of the EC Regulation". This definition was revoked, and paras 111(1A) and 111(1B) inserted, by the Insolvency Act 1986 (Amendment) Regulations 2005 (SI 2005/879) regs 2(1), 4(a), as from 13 April 2005, in order to reverse the effect of the ruling in *Re The Salvage Association* [2003] EWHC 1028 (Ch); [2004] 1 W.L.R. 174; [2003] B.C.C. 504 (see the note to s.*8(1), (2)*.) It follows that a company incorporated in this jurisdiction by Royal Charter may not be put into administration under Sch.B1. In *Re Dairy Farmers of Britain Ltd* [2009] EWHC 1389 (Ch); [2010] Ch. 63; [2010] B.C.C. 637 it was held that Industrial and Provident Societies [co-operative societies] were not "companies" within this definition, but the administration regime has now been extended to these bodies by statute: see the Industrial and Provident Societies and Credit Unions (Arrangements, Reconstructions and Administration) Order 2014 (SI 2014/229). In *Panter v Rowellian Football Social Club* [2011] EWHC 1301 (Ch); [2012] Ch. 125; [2014] B.C.C. 321 an unincorporated social club was held not to be an "association" within s.220(1) and so not capable of being wound up or put into administration under the Act. On Northern Ireland, see Moss (2005) 18 Insolv. Int. 107; but quaere whether this view is consistent with *Re Brownridge Plastics Ltd*, referred to in the Introductory note to Schedule B1?

For a case on the repealed para.111(1) (but which would now come within s.111(1A)), see *Re Sendo Ltd* [2005] EWHC 1604 (Ch); [2006] 1 B.C.L.C. 395. On para.111(1A) and (1B) see *Bank Leumi (UK) plc, Petitioner* [2017] CSOH 129; [2017] B.C.C. 753 (Scottish court had no jurisdiction to grant administration order in relation to company registered in England and Wales even if its COMI was in Scotland) which is to be preferred to *Re 3T Telecom Ltd* [2005] EWHC 275 (Ch); [2006] 2 B.C.L.C. 137 (English court held to have jurisdiction to make an administration order in relation to a company incorporated in Northern Ireland but whose COMI was in England) where the latter case was decided under the former para.111(1).

"Floating charge": compare the definition in IA 1986 s.251. It is not obvious why different wording has been used.

Paragraph 111(1B) was amended by the Insolvency Amendment (EU 2015/848) Regulations 2017 (SI 2017/702) regs 1, 2(1), Sch. paras 1, 31 in relation to proceedings opened on or after 26 June 2017 (see reg.3) when the Recast EU Regulation 2015/848 came into force.

Paragraph 111(2), which provided that "a reference to a thing in writing includes a reference to a thing in electronic form" is now superseded by the more general provisions of s.436B.

Non-UK companies

111A A company incorporated outside the United Kingdom that has a principal place of business in Northern Ireland may not enter administration under this Schedule unless it also has a principal place of business in England and Wales or Scotland (or both in England and Wales and in Scotland).

General Note

Paragraph 111A was inserted, by the Insolvency Act 1986 (Amendment) Regulations 2005 (SI 2005/879) regs 2(1), 4(c), as from 13 April 2005.

Scotland

112 In the application of this Schedule to Scotland–

(a) a reference to filing with the court is a reference to lodging in court, and

(b) a reference to a charge is a reference to a right in security.

(See General Note after para.116.)

113 Where property in Scotland is disposed of under paragraph 70 or 71, the administrator shall grant to the disponee an appropriate document of transfer or conveyance of the property, and–

(a) that document, or

(b) recording, intimation or registration of that document (where recording, intimation or registration of the document is a legal requirement for completion of title to the property),

has the effect of disencumbering the property of or, as the case may be, freeing the property from, the security.

(See General Note after para.116.)

114 In Scotland, where goods in the possession of a company under a hire-purchase agreement are disposed of under paragraph 72, the disposal has the effect of extinguishing as against the disponee all rights of the owner of the goods under the agreement.

(See General Note after para.116.)

115(1) In Scotland, the administrator of a company may make, in or towards the satisfaction of the debt secured by the floating charge, a payment to the holder of a floating charge which has attached to the property subject to the charge.

115(1A) In Scotland, sub-paragraph (1B) applies in connection with the giving by the court of permission as provided for in paragraph 65(3)(b).

115(1B) On the giving by the court of such permission, any floating charge granted by the company shall, unless it has already so attached, attach to the property which is subject to the charge.

115(2) In Scotland, where the administrator thinks that the company has insufficient property to enable a distribution to be made to unsecured creditors other than by virtue of section 176A(2)(a), he may file a notice to that effect with the registrar of companies.

115(3) On delivery of the notice to the registrar of companies, any floating charge granted by the company shall, unless it has already so attached, attach to the property which is subject to the charge.

115(4) Attachment of a floating charge under sub-paragraph (1B) or (3) has effect as if the charge is a fixed security over the property to which it has attached.

(See General Note after para.116.)

116 In Scotland, the administrator in making any payment in accordance with paragraph 115 shall make such payment subject to the rights of any of the following categories of persons (which rights shall, except to the extent provided in any instrument, have the following order of priority)–

(a) the holder of any fixed security which is over property subject to the floating charge and which ranks prior to, or pari passu with, the floating charge,

(b) creditors in respect of all liabilities and expenses incurred by or on behalf of the administrator,

(c) the administrator in respect of his liabilities, expenses and remuneration and any indemnity to which he is entitled out of the property of the company,

(d) the preferential creditors entitled to payment in accordance with paragraph 65,

(e) the holder of the floating charge in accordance with the priority of that charge in relation to any other floating charge which has attached, and

(f) the holder of a fixed security, other than one referred to in paragraph (a), which is over property subject to the floating charge.

General Note to Paras 112–116

These paragraphs make minor modifications to the provisions of Sch.B1 in its application to Scotland. Some of these are purely terminological. Others reflect differences in conveyancing practice and property law, and the fact that the floating charge is based on statute rather than common law in Scots law.

Paragraphs 115–116 supplement para.99. Paragraph 115(1A), (1B), (4) inserted by SBEEA 2015 s.130 as from 26 May 2015.

Schedule 1

Powers of Administrator or Administrative Receiver

Sections 14, 42

1 Power to take possession of, collect and get in the property of the company and, for that purpose, to take such proceedings as may seem to him expedient.

2 Power to sell or otherwise dispose of the property of the company by public auction or private contract or, in Scotland, to sell, hire out or otherwise dispose of the property of the company by public roup or private bargain.

3 Power to raise or borrow money and grant security therefor over the property of the company.

4 Power to appoint a solicitor or accountant or other professionally qualified person to assist him in the performance of his functions.

5 Power to bring or defend any action or other legal proceedings in the name and on behalf of the company.

6 Power to refer to arbitration any question affecting the company.

7 Power to effect and maintain insurances in respect of the business and property of the company.

8 Power to use the company's seal.

9 Power to do all acts and to execute in the name and on behalf of the company any deed, receipt or other document.

10 Power to draw, accept, make and endorse any bill of exchange or promissory note in the name and on behalf of the company.

11 Power to appoint any agent to do any business which he is unable to do himself or which can more conveniently be done by an agent and power to employ and dismiss employees.

12 Power to do all such things (including the carrying out of works) as may be necessary for the realisation of the property of the company.

13 Power to make any payment which is necessary or incidental to the performance of his functions.

14 Power to carry on the business of the company.

15 Power to establish subsidiaries of the company.

16 Power to transfer to subsidiaries of the company the whole or any part of the business and property of the company.

17 Power to grant or accept a surrender of a lease or tenancy of any of the property of the company, and to take a lease or tenancy of any property required or convenient for the business of the company.

18 Power to make any arrangement or compromise on behalf of the company.

19 Power to call up any uncalled capital of the company.

20 Power to rank and claim in the bankruptcy, insolvency, sequestration or liquidation of any person indebted to the company and to receive dividends, and to accede to trust deeds for the creditors of any such person.

21 Power to present or defend a petition for the winding up of the company.

22 Power to change the situation of the company's registered office.

23 Power to do all other things incidental to the exercise of the foregoing powers.

General Note

This Schedule applies to all administrators, whether appointed under the original Pt II or under Sch.B1, and to administrative receivers.

Under CA 1985, the powers of a receiver (or receiver and manager) appointed out of court were left to be settled almost entirely by the provisions of the instrument under which he was appointed and the terms of the appointment itself. The Cork Committee (*Report*, para.494) recommended that the general powers of a receiver should be set out in a statute, so that it would not be necessary for a person dealing with him to refer to the particular debenture to find out what powers he could exercise in the circumstances. (This was, in fact, already the case in Scotland under Companies (Floating Charges and Receivers) (Scotland) Act 1972 s.15.) The present Schedule and IA 1986 s.42 implement those recommendations, which apply in every *administrative* receivership, and—no doubt reflecting the fact that the administration order regime set up by ss.*8* et seq. was modelled on the institution of receivership—the Schedule is made by s.14 and Sch.B1 para.60 to apply to an administrator as well. An administrator has, in addition, the general statutory powers set out in s.14(1)(a) and para.59, and the specific powers given by ss.14(2) and 15 and paras 70–72.

SBEEA 2015 ss.118–119, introducing new ss.246ZD and 176ZB into IA 1986 as from 1 October 2015, gives statutory power to liquidators and administrators to assign a right of action, and the proceeds of an action, arising under ss.213 or 246ZA (fraudulent trading), 214 or 246ZB (wrongful trading), 238 (transactions at an undervalue), 236 (preferences, 242 (gratuitous alienations (Scotland)), unfair preferences (Scotland)) and 244 (extortionate credit transactions). No similar power is accorded to receivers, since the rights of action in question are not vested in them by the relevant statutory provisions.

The disposal of a "substantial property" by an administrator does not require approval by the company's members under CA 2006 s.190: see s.193(1)(b) of that Act. The administrator may require a proposed equitable assignee of a cause of action to provide an indemnity for costs: *Re Sheridan Millennium Ltd* [2014] NICA 29. On the power of an administrator to sell the business or its property prior to the holding of a creditors' meeting, see the notes to s.17(2) and Sch.B1 para.68.

The powers of an administrative receiver listed in this Schedule may be overridden by the terms of the debenture under which he is appointed, but a person dealing with him in good faith and for value is not concerned to inquire whether he is acting within his powers (s.42(3)). The Act, by s.43, also confers special powers on an administrative receiver to dispose of charged property, etc.

A receiver who is not an administrative receiver is not affected by the provisions described above, and Sch.1 does not apply in such a case.

The Schedule applies in Scotland in the case of an administrator, but not an administrative receiver; all Scottish receivers, however, have the powers set out in s.55 and Sch.2.

The specific powers listed in Sch.1 do not, on the whole, call for detailed comment, apart from para.21 (power to present or defend a winding-up petition), which has clarified doubts regarding a receiver's ability to present such a petition at common law, and removes the limitations upon such powers as he may have had: compare *Re Emmadart Ltd* [1979] Ch. 540. A petition by an administrator or administrative receiver is presented in the name of the company: see the note to s.124. The power of a receiver to present a winding-up petition was also the subject of comment in *Re Anvil Estates Ltd* (unreported, 1993)—discussed by Pugh and Ede in (1994) 10 I.L. & P. 48. The case was actually decided on the basis of the right of the secured creditor (as opposed to the receiver) to petition but there is some useful general discussion in the judgment. The power of an administrative receiver to oppose a winding-up petition presented by another creditor was considered in *Re Leigh Estates (UK) Ltd* [1994] B.C.C. 292.

In some earlier cases under the original Pt II, it was held that para.13 is expressed in sufficiently wide terms as to permit a distribution of assets to be made on the same basis as would have applied if the company had been put into liquidation on the date of the administration order, so giving priority to those creditors whose debts would have been preferential on a winding up: *Re WBSL Realisations 1992 Ltd* [1995] B.C.L.C. 576, and also to authorise an administrator to pay all the company's pre-administration creditors in full: *Re John Slack Ltd* [1995] B.C.C. 1,116. However, in *Re The Designer Room Ltd* [2004] B.C.C. 904 Rimer J held that para.13 could only be construed as giving such powers if, on the particular facts, the making of such payments was necessary or incidental to the performance by the administrators of their functions as such. The mere fact that to do so would achieve the distribution of the assets in question more cheaply did not satisfy this test. Nor could the court authorise the administrators to make such payments in exercise of its inherent jurisdiction. These decisions must now be reconsidered in the light of the ruling of the Court of Appeal in *Re Lune Metal Products Ltd* [2006] EWCA Civ 1720; [2007] B.C.C. 217, where Neuberger LJ drew attention to the differences between Sch.1 and Sch.4 (powers of liquidators), and in particular to the absence in Sch.1 of any power for an administrator to make distributions. Such payments can now only be made where a discharge of the administration is to be followed by a striking off of the companies concerned. For distributions and other payments by administrators under Sch.B1 see paras 65 and 66.

In *Re TXU UK Ltd* [2002] EWHC 2784 (Ch); [2003] 2 B.C.L.C. 341 para.13 was relied on to authorise administrators to compromise certain future claims (so giving them a priority which they would not receive if the company later went into liquidation), on the ground that this course would achieve a benefit to the administration as a whole.

As noted below (see the note to Sch.4 para.6) the statutory authority given to a liquidator to sell any of the company's property enables him to assign a cause of action vested in the company without infringing the common-law rule which declares transactions involving maintenance or champerty to be illegal. A similar protection is given to a trustee in bankruptcy by Sch.6 para.9, and to an administrator by s.14 and para.1 of this Schedule. However, the position as regards an administrative receiver may be different, for the power is derived from s.42, which does not confer the power by virtue of the statute itself but instead by deeming it to have been included in the charge instrument under which the receiver has been appointed. As a mere term in a contract it would not be sufficient to displace the common-law rule.

Schedule 2

Powers of a Scottish Receiver (Additional to Those Conferred on him by the Instrument of Charge)

Section 55

1 Power to take possession of, collect and get in the property from the company or a liquidator thereof or any other person, and for that purpose, to take such proceedings as may seem to him expedient.

2 Power to sell, hire out or otherwise dispose of the property by public roup or private bargain and with or without advertisement.

3 Power to raise or borrow money and grant security therefor over the property.

4 Power to appoint a solicitor or accountant or other professionally qualified person to assist him in the performance of his functions.

5 Power to bring or defend any action or other legal proceedings in the name and on behalf of the company.

6 Power to refer to arbitration all questions affecting the company.

7 Power to effect and maintain insurances in respect of the business and property of the company.

8 Power to use the company's seal.

9 Power to do all acts and to execute in the name and on behalf of the company any deed, receipt or other document.

10 Power to draw, accept, make and endorse any bill of exchange or promissory note in the name and on behalf of the company.

11 Power to appoint any agent to do any business which he is unable to do himself or which can more conveniently be done by an agent, and power to employ and dismiss employees.

12 Power to do all such things (including the carrying out of works), as may be necessary for the realisation of the property.

13 Power to make any payment which is necessary or incidental to the performance of his functions.

14 Power to carry on the business of the company or any part of it.

15 Power to grant or accept a surrender of a lease or tenancy of any of the property, and to take a lease or tenancy of any property required or convenient for the business of the company.

16 Power to make any arrangement or compromise on behalf of the company.

17 Power to call up any uncalled capital of the company.

18 Power to establish subsidiaries of the company.

19 Power to transfer to subsidiaries of the company the business of the company or any part of it and any of the property.

20 Power to rank and claim in the bankruptcy, insolvency, sequestration or liquidation of any person or company indebted to the company and to receive dividends, and to accede to trust deeds for creditors of any such person.

21 Power to present or defend a petition for the winding up of the company.

22 Power to change the situation of the company's registered office.

23 Power to do all other things incidental to the exercise of the powers mentioned in section 55(1) of this Act or above in this Schedule.

General Note

This Schedule provides a model list of powers for a Scottish receiver appointed by a holder of a floating charge. The list, although modified, dates back to the introduction of receivership in Scotland in 1972. The 23 implied powers mirror those of an English administrative receiver set out in Sch.1, with only slight changes in the order. For further comment, see s.55.

Schedule 2A

Exceptions to Prohibition on Appointment of Administrative Receiver: Supplementary Provisions

1 Capital market arrangement

1(1) For the purposes of section 72B an arrangement is a capital market arrangement if–

(a) it involves a grant of security to a person holding it as trustee for a person who holds a capital market investment issued by a party to the arrangement, or (aa) it involves a grant of security to–

(i) a party to the arrangement who issues a capital market investment, or

(ii) a person who holds the security as trustee for a party to the arrangement in connection with the issue of a capital market investment, or

(ab) it involves a grant of security to a person who holds the security as trustee for a party to the arrangement who agrees to provide finance to another party, or

(b) at least one party guarantees the performance of obligations of another party, or

(c) at least one party provides security in respect of the performance of obligations of another party, or

(d) the arrangement involves an investment of a kind described in articles 83 to 85 of the Financial Services and Markets Act 2000 (Regulated Activities) Order 2001 (S.I. 2001/544) (options, futures and contracts for differences).

1(2) For the purposes of sub-paragraph (1)–

(a) a reference to holding as trustee includes a reference to holding as nominee or agent,

(b) a reference to holding for a person who holds a capital market investment includes a reference to holding for a number of persons at least one of whom holds a capital market investment, and

(c) a person holds a capital market investment if he has a legal or beneficial interest in it, and

(d) the reference to the provision of finance includes the provision of an indemnity.

1(3) In section 72B(1) and this paragraph "party" to an arrangement includes a party to an agreement which–

(a) forms part of the arrangement,

(b) provides for the raising of finance as part of the arrangement, or

(c) is necessary for the purposes of implementing the arrangement.

2 Capital market investment

2(1) For the purposes of section 72B an investment is a capital market investment if it–

(a) is within article 77 or 77A of the Financial Services and Markets Act 2000 (Regulated Activities) Order 2001 (S.I. 2001/544) (debt instruments), and

(b) is rated, listed or traded or designed to be rated, listed or traded.

2(2) In sub-paragraph (1)–

"rated" means rated for the purposes of investment by an internationally recognised rating agency,

"listed" means admitted to the official list within the meaning given by section 103(1) of the Financial Services and Markets Act 2000 (c. 8) (interpretation), and

"traded" means admitted to trading on a market established under the rules of a recognised investment exchange or on a foreign market.

2(3) In sub-paragraph (2)–

"recognised investment exchange" has the meaning given by section 285 of the Financial Services and Markets Act 2000 (recognised investment exchange), and

"foreign market" has the same meaning as "relevant market" in article 67(2) of the Financial Services and Markets Act 2000 (Financial Promotion) Order 2001 (S.I. 2001/1335) (foreign markets).

3(1) An investment is also a capital market investment for the purposes of section 72B if it consists of a bond or commercial paper issued to one or more of the following–

(a) an investment professional within the meaning of article 19(5) of the Financial Services and Markets Act 2000 (Financial Promotion) Order 2001,

(b) a person who is, when the agreement mentioned in section 72B(1) is entered into, a certified high net worth individual in relation to a communication within the meaning of article 48(2) of that order,

(c) a person to whom article 49(2) of that order applies (high net worth company, &c.),

(d) a person who is, when the agreement mentioned in section 72B(1) is entered into, a certified sophisticated investor in relation to a communication within the meaning of article 50(1) of that order, and

(e) a person in a State other than the United Kingdom who under the law of that State is not prohibited from investing in bonds or commercial paper.

3(2) In sub-paragraph (1)–

"bond" shall be construed in accordance with article 77 of the Financial Services and Markets Act 2000 (Regulated Activities) Order 2001 (SI 2001/544), and includes any instrument falling within article 77A of that Order, and

"commercial paper" has the meaning given by article 9(3) of that order.

3(3) For the purposes of sub-paragraph (1)–

(a) in applying article 19(5) of the Financial Promotion Order for the purposes of sub-paragraph (1)(a)–

(i) in article 19(5)(b), ignore the words after "exempt person",

(ii) in article 19(5)(c)(i), for the words from "the controlled activity" to the end substitute "a controlled activity", and

(iii) in article 19(5)(e) ignore the words from "where the communication" to the end, and

(b) in applying article 49(2) of that order for the purposes of sub-paragraph (1)(c), ignore article 49(2)(e).

4 "Agreement"

4 For the purposes of sections 72B and 72E and this Schedule "agreement" includes an agreement or undertaking effected by–

(a) contract,

(b) deed, or

(c) any other instrument intended to have effect in accordance with the law of England and Wales, Scotland or another jurisdiction.

5 Debt

5 The debt of at least £50 million referred to in section 72B(1)(a) or 72E(2)(a)–

(a) may be incurred at any time during the life of the capital market arrangement or financed project, and

(b) may be expressed wholly or partly in foreign currency (in which case the sterling equivalent shall be calculated as at the time when the arrangement is entered into or the project begins).

6 Step-in rights

6(1) For the purposes of sections 72C to 72E a project has "step-in rights" if a person who provides finance in connection with the project has a conditional entitlement under an agreement to–

(a) assume sole or principal responsibility under an agreement for carrying out all or part of the project, or

(b) make arrangements for carrying out all or part of the project.

6(2) In sub-paragraph (1) a reference to the provision of finance includes a reference to the provision of an indemnity.

7 Project company

7(1) For the purposes of sections 72C to 72E a company is a "project company" of a project if–

(a) it holds property for the purpose of the project,

(b) it has sole or principal responsibility under an agreement for carrying out all or part of the project,

(c) it is one of a number of companies which together carry out the project,

(d) it has the purpose of supplying finance to enable the project to be carried out, or

(e) it is the holding company of a company within any of paragraphs (a) to (d).

7(2) But a company is not a "project company" of a project if–

(a) it performs a function within sub-paragraph (1)(a) to (d) or is within sub-paragraph (1)(e), but

(b) it also performs a function which is not–

(i) within sub-paragraph (1)(a) to (d),

(ii) related to a function within sub-paragraph (1)(a) to (d), or

(iii) related to the project.

7(3) For the purposes of this paragraph a company carries out all or part of a project whether or not it acts wholly or partly through agents.

8 "Resources"

8 In section 72C "resources" includes–

(a) funds (including payment for the provision of services or facilities),

(b) assets,

(c) professional skill,

(d) the grant of a concession or franchise, and

(e) any other commercial resource.

9 "Public body"

9(1) In section 72C "public body" means–

(a) a body which exercises public functions,

(b) a body specified for the purposes of this paragraph by the Secretary of State, and

(c) a body within a class specified for the purposes of this paragraph by the Secretary of State.

9(2) A specification under sub-paragraph (1) may be–

(a) general, or

(b) for the purpose of the application of section 72C to a specified case.

10 Regulated business

10(1) For the purposes of section 72D a business is regulated if it is carried on–

(a) [Repealed]

(b) in reliance on a licence under section 7, 7A or 7B of the Gas Act 1986 (c. 44) (transport and supply of gas),

(c) in reliance on a licence granted by virtue of section 41C of that Act (power to prescribe additional licensable activity),

(d) in reliance on a licence under section 6 of the Electricity Act 1989 (c. 29) (supply of electricity),

(e) by a water undertaker,

(f) by a sewerage undertaker,

(g) by a universal service provider within the meaning of Part 3 of the Postal Services Act 2011,

(h) by a Post Office company within the meaning of Part 1 of that Act,

(i) [omitted]

(j) in reliance on a licence under section 8 of the Railways Act 1993 (c. 43) (railway services),

(k) in reliance on a licence exemption under section 7 of that Act (subject to sub-paragraph (2) below),

(l) by the operator of a system of transport which is deemed to be a railway for a purpose of Part I of that Act by virtue of section 81(2) of that Act (tramways, &c.),

(m) by the operator of a vehicle carried on flanged wheels along a system within paragraph (l), or

(n) in reliance on a European licence granted pursuant to–

(i) a provision contained in any instrument made for the purpose of implementing Council Directive 1995/18/EC dated 19th June 1995 on the licensing of railway undertakings or Chapter III of Directive 2012/34/EU of the European Parliament and of the Council of 21st November 2012 establishing a single European railway area (recast), or

(ii) any action taken by an EEA State for that purpose.

10(2) Sub-paragraph (1)(k) does not apply to the operator of a railway asset on a railway unless on some part of the railway there is a permitted line speed exceeding 40 kilometres per hour.

10(2A) For the purposes of section 72D a business is also regulated to the extent that it consists in the provision of a public electronic communications network or a public electronic communications service.

10(2B) In sub-paragraph (1)(n), an "EEA State" means a member State, Norway, Iceland or Liechtenstein.

11 "Person"

11 A reference to a person in this Schedule includes a reference to a partnership or another unincorporated group of persons.

General Note

This was inserted by EA 2002 s.250(2) and Sch.8 to further supplement the provisions in ss.72A–H with particular reference to those exceptional situations where the appointment of an administrative receiver is still possible notwithstanding the general bar on that remedy. Before the provisions of Sch.2A came into force they were then modified by the Insolvency Act 1986 (Amendment) (Administrative Receivership and Capital Market Arrangements)

Order 2003 (SI 2003/1468) by the addition of paras 1(1)(aa), 1(1)(ab) and 1(2)(d). Essentially, Sch.2A serves as a complex interpretation provision. These provisions took effect on 15 September 2003. Curiously para.10(1)(a) was omitted and 10(2A) inserted by the Communications Act 2003 with effect from 25 July 2003. On "step in" rights under para.6 see *Cabvision Ltd v Feetum* [2005] EWCA Civ 1601; [2006] B.C.C. 340. Minor amendments were made to paras 2(1) and 3(2) by the Financial Services and Markets Act 2000 (Regulated Activities) (Amendment) Order 2010 (SI 2010/86).

Paragraph 10 was amended by the Postal Services Act 2011 Sch.12 para.126 which amended subparas (g) and (h) and omitted subpara.(i) with effect from 1 October 2011 (see the Postal Services Act 2011 (Commencement No.1 and Transitional Provisions) Order 2011 (SI 2011/2329 (C. 82)) art.3).

Note para.10(1)(b) was amended by the Electricity and Gas (Smart Meters Licensable Activity) Order 2012 (SI 2012/2400) art.29 with effect from 18 September 2012.

Paragraph 10(1)(n) substituted by the Railways (Access, Management and Licensing of Railway Undertakings) Regulations 2016 (SI 2016/645) Sch.1 para.2 as from 29 July 2016.

Schedule 3

Orders in Course of Winding Up Pronounced in Vacation (Scotland)

Section 162

Part I

Orders Which are to be Final

Orders under section 153, as to the time for proving debts and claims.

Orders under section 195 as to meetings for ascertaining wishes of creditors or contributories.

Orders under section 198, as to the examination of witnesses in regard to the property or affairs of a company.

Part II

Orders Which are to take Effect until Matter Disposed of by Inner House

Orders under section 126(1), 130(2) or (3), 147, 227 or 228, restraining or permitting the commencement or the continuance of legal proceedings.

Orders under section 135(5), limiting the powers of provisional liquidators.

Orders under section 108, appointing a liquidator to fill a vacancy.

[Deleted by SBEEA 2015 s.120(5) as from 26 May 2015.]

Orders under section 158, as to the arrest and detention of an absconding contributory and his property.

Schedule 4

Powers of Liquidator in a Winding Up

Sections 165, 167

Part I

1 Power to pay any class of creditors in full.

2 Power to make any compromise or arrangement with creditors or persons claiming to be creditors, or having or alleging themselves to have any claim (present or future, certain or contingent, ascertained or sounding only in damages) against the company, or whereby the company may be rendered liable.

3 Power to compromise, on such terms as may be agreed–

(a) all calls and liabilities to calls, all debts and liabilities capable of resulting in debts, and all claims (present or future, certain or contingent, ascertained or sounding only in damages) subsisting or supposed to subsist between the company and a contributory or alleged contributory or other debtor or person apprehending liability to the company, and

(b) all questions in any way relating to or affecting the assets or the winding up of the company,

and take any security for the discharge of any such call, debt, liability or claim and give a complete discharge in respect of it.

3A Power to bring legal proceedings under section 213, 214, 238, 239, 242, 243 or 423.

Part II

4 Power to bring or defend any action or other legal proceeding in the name and on behalf of the company.

5 Power to carry on the business of the company so far as may be necessary for its beneficial winding up.

Part III

6 Power to sell any of the company's property by public auction or private contract, with power to transfer the whole of it to any person or to sell the same in parcels.

7 Power to do all acts and execute, in the name and on behalf of the company, all deeds, receipts and other documents and for that purpose to use, when necessary, the company's seal.

8 Power to prove, rank and claim in the bankruptcy, insolvency or sequestration of any contributory for any balance against his estate, and to receive dividends in the bankruptcy, insolvency or sequestration in respect of that balance, as a separate debt due from the bankrupt or insolvent, and rateably with the other separate creditors.

9 Power to draw, accept, make and indorse any bill of exchange or promissory note in the name and on behalf of the company, with the same effect with respect to the company's liability as if the bill or note had been drawn, accepted, made or indorsed by or on behalf of the company in the course of its business.

10 Power to raise on the security of the assets of the company any money requisite.

11 Power to take out in his official name letters of administration to any deceased contributory, and to do in his official name any other act necessary for obtaining payment of any money due from a contributory or his estate which cannot conveniently be done in the name of the company.

In all such cases the money due is deemed, for the purpose of enabling the liquidator to take out the letters of administration or recover the money, to be due to the liquidator himself.

12 Power to appoint an agent to do any business which the liquidator is unable to do himself.

13 Power to do all such other things as may be necessary for winding up the company's affairs and distributing its assets.

General Note

The powers of a liquidator in a winding up by the court were formerly set out in CA 1985 s.539(1), (2), and those in a voluntary winding up in CA 1985 s.598(1), (2). Many of these powers are conveniently collected together and arranged in tabulated form in this Schedule, which applies both in England and Wales and in Scotland.

The Schedule formerly divided the different powers into three categories. The powers listed in Pt I (paras 1–3A) could be exercised only with the sanction:

- in a members' voluntary liquidation, of a special resolution of the company,

- in a creditors' voluntary liquidation, of the court or the liquidation committee (or, if there was no such committee, a resolution of the creditors),
- in a winding up by the court, of the court or the liquidation committee.

Exercise of the powers in Pt II (paras 4 and 5) required the same sanction in a winding up by the court but no sanction in a voluntary winding up, while the powers in Pt III (paras 6–13) could be exercised without sanction in all liquidations. SBEEA 2015 s.120, with effect from 26 May 2015, has amended the Act so as to remove the requirement for sanction in all cases, deleting the headings to the three Parts: see the notes to ss.165–167. (However, the division into Parts is now of no significance.) A former para.6A, which made separate provision for the power to compromise claims for England and Wales on the one hand, and Scotland on the other, has been deleted, so that para.3 now applies to both jurisdictions (SBEEA 2015 s.120(6)(a), (b)).

A liquidator in a winding up by the court has also the supplementary powers listed in s.168 (England and Wales) and s.169 (Scotland); and further powers are given to a voluntary liquidator by ss.165, 166.

Schedule 4 does not apply in the case of a provisional liquidator. However, the court has jurisdiction under s.135(4) to confer powers on a provisional liquidator which may include powers corresponding to those set out in Sch.4: *Re Hawk Insurance Co Ltd* [2001] B.C.C. 57.

There may be circumstances where the powers of a liquidator are constrained by agreement—see for example *Re Angel Group Ltd* [2015] EWHC 3624 (Ch).

It was held in *Taylor, Noter* [1992] B.C.C. 440 that the corresponding provisions of CA 1948 empowered the liquidator of a company to enter into any compromise or arrangement that might have been entered into by the company itself. In that case the affairs of a number of companies controlled by the same person had been treated as one, and the liquidator had found it impossible to determine which creditors had claims against the particular companies and which had claims against the individual controller, who was now bankrupt. A scheme was agreed for a single scheme of ranking and division of all the assets and creditors. This case was followed by the Court of Appeal in England in somewhat similar circumstances in *Re Bank of Credit & Commerce International SA (No.2)* [1992] B.C.C. 715. The compromise powers include power to depart from the general rule that creditors are entitled to participate in the estate on a pari passu basis (above).

Where liquidators use their powers to bring litigation under funding agreements, the defendants may seek disclosure of the identity of non-party funders and details of the funding arrangements so as to enable an effective application for security for costs against a non-party to be made: *Re Hellas Telecommunications (Luxembourg)* [2017] EWHC 3465 (Ch).

Para.3A

This paragraph was inserted by EA 2002 s.253, with effect from 15 September 2003. It is part of the package of reforms designed to reverse the effect of decisions such as *Re Floor Fourteen Ltd, Lewis v Inland Revenue Commissioners* [2001] 3 All E.R. 499; [2002] B.C.C. 198, which held that a liquidator pursuing claims under the sections referred to could not claim his costs as expenses of the liquidation. This has now been rectified by an amendment to the Rules (now IR 2016 rr.6.42 and 7.108) but, in order to ensure that liquidators do not make such claims at the expense of the creditors, they may not do so without their approval (or, alternatively, the leave of the court). See the notes to s.115 and rr.6.44 et seq., 7111 et seq.

Para.6

The liquidator's power to sell "any of the company's property" enables him to assign any causes of action which were vested in the company at the time of the winding up, including the right to bring misfeasance proceedings under IA 1986 s.212. The rule of law which would normally prohibit such an assignment—at least an assignment to a third party who had no interest otherwise in the litigation—on the ground that it would be champertous and illegal is displaced by this statutory authority: *Re Park Gate Waggon Works Co* (1881) 17 Ch. D. 234. Such a sale may be made for any consideration, including a share of any proceeds of the action if it is successful. The fact that the company (or the liquidator) is not eligible for legal aid but the assignee may be entitled to it is not a ground for the court to declare the assignment unlawful, but a matter for consideration by the Legal Aid Board (*Norglen Ltd (in liq.) v Reeds Rains Prudential Ltd* [1999] 2 A.C. 1; [1998] B.C.C. 44).

However, if the assignee has a genuine interest in the outcome of the litigation (e.g. as a creditor of the company), an assignment of the "fruits" of such litigation may not be unlawful at common law, at least if the liquidator is left free to conduct the litigation without interference by the assignee; and there is certainly no objection to such a creditor simply putting the liquidator in funds to conduct the litigation on terms that any proceeds shall go in the first instance towards reimbursing him (*Katz v McNally* [1997] B.C.C. 784). See also *Empire Resolution Ltd v MPW Insurance Brokers Ltd* [1999] B.P.I.R. 486; *Farmer v Moseley (Holdings) Ltd* [2001] 2 B.C.L.C. 572 and the analysis of the present state of the law put forward by counsel and approved by the Court of Appeal (as "a valuable aid to clarification of the position") in *ANC Ltd v Clark Goldring & Page Ltd* [2001] B.C.C. 479. The ruling of Lightman J in *Grovewood Holdings plc v James Capel & Co Ltd* [1995] Ch. 80; [1995] B.C.C. 760, that a sale for a consideration which included a provision for the purchaser to finance the litigation was champertous has been much criticised and is probably open to reconsideration: see the *Oasis* judgment [1998] Ch. 170 at 179; [1997] B.C.C. 282 at 288; and *Farmer v Moseley (Holdings) Ltd* [2002] B.P.I.R. 473. Further consideration of this vexed issue is to be found in the judgment of HHJ Behrens in *Rawnsley v Weatherall Green & Smith North Ltd* [2010] B.C.C. 406—sale of cause of action vested in the company and sale of fruits of action permissible but no right to assign cause of action vested personally in liquidator. Fruits of a claim could be assigned but not if linked with conduct of the action. See also *Ruttle Plant Hire Ltd v DEFRA (No.2)* [2008] EWHC 238 (TCC); [2009] 1 All E.R. 448; [2008] B.P.I.R. 1395.

In *Re Oasis Merchandising Services Ltd* [1998] Ch. 170; [1997] B.C.C. 282 and *Re Ayala Holdings Ltd (No.2)* [1996] 1 B.C.L.C. 467 it was held that the power to sell "the company's property" conferred by this paragraph did not extend to empower the liquidator to assign a right of action which arises only in the event of a liquidation and is vested in him by statute, e.g. the right to bring proceedings to recover a preference (IA 1986 s.239) or compensation for fraudulent or wrongful trading (ss.213, 214). Although it was possible to some extent to assign the "fruits" of such litigation under the common-law principles outlined above, the courts insisted that the right of action itself and the control of the litigation were inalienable. However, this has now all been changed by legislation. SBEEA 2015 ss.118–119, introducing new ss.246ZD and 176ZB into IA 1986 as from 1 October 2015, gives statutory power to liquidators (and also administrators) to assign a right of action, and the proceeds of an action, arising under ss.213 or 246ZA (fraudulent trading), 214 or 246ZB (wrongful trading), 238 (transactions at an undervalue), 236 (preferences), 242 (gratuitous alienations (Scotland), unfair preferences (Scotland)) and 244 (extortionate credit transactions). Section 212 is not included in this list because, as noted above, it is well established that the right to bring such proceedings is assignable by virtue of the present statutory provision. Other sections of IA 1986 which are sometimes mentioned in the cases as possibly being unassignable have (it is submitted, rightly) been omitted: to have a post-petition disposition of property declared void under s.127, or a floating charge declared void under s.245.

The right to appeal against tax assessments was held not to be "property" capable of being assigned by the liquidator in *Re GP Aviation Group International Ltd* [2013] EWHC 1447 (Ch); [2014] 1 B.C.L.C. 474.

The Legal Aid, Sentencing and Punishment of Offenders Act 2012 (ss.44, 46), which generally restricts the use of conditional fee agreements and "after the event" insurance in litigation (the "Jackson reforms"), severely impedes the bringing of recovery claims by liquidators and other office-holders. Initially, a two-year exemption (from April 2013) was granted in respect of insolvency proceedings, and on 26 February 2015 this was extended "for the time being", giving rise to hopes that the concession might be continued indefinitely—and to much lobbying to that end. However, on 17 December 2015 the Government announced that it would expire in April 2016, and so ss.44 and 46 now apply to all proceedings—see Legal Aid, Sentencing and Punishment of Offenders Act 2012 (Commencement No.12) Order 2016 (SI 2016/345), effective 6 April 2016. The consequences of this change are unclear at present, but the fear is that recovery litigation may be stifled.

In principle, where a liquidator brings a claim to recover property on behalf of the company, he should institute the claim in the name of the company (see the note to s.87(2)). In this situation, the company may be required to give security for costs under CPR rr.25.12, 25.13. In order to circumvent this, proceedings were sometimes in the past brought by the liquidator in his own name, thus throwing the potential costs burden on the practitioner himself, who had to look to the insolvency assets (or, where available, insurance) for reimbursement. However, in *Kirkpatrick v Snoozebox Ltd* [2014] B.C.C. 477 Master Leslie stated categorically that a liquidator does not have power to bring corporate claims in his own name except where this is authorised by statute. If the proceedings are brought under s.212 (misfeasance), he may sue either in the name of the company or in his own name.

The disposal of a "substantial property" by a liquidator does not require approval by the company's members under CA 2006 s.190 (except in a members' voluntary liquidation): see s.193(1)(a) of that Act.

On the liquidator's power to assign where contractual restrictions have been imposed see *Ruttle Plant Ltd v DEFRA* [2007] EWHC 2870 (TCC); [2008] B.C.C. 790. (See also later proceedings sub nom. *Ruttle Plant Ltd v DEFRA (No.2)* [2008] EWHC 238 (TCC); [2009] 1 All E.R. 448; [2008] B.P.I.R. 1395).

A prohibition on assignment by a company of a claim arising out of a contract is binding on its liquidator: *Quadmost Ltd v Reprotech (Pebsham) Ltd* [2001] B.P.I.R. 349. The fact that the intended defendant has a cross-claim for a larger amount, which can be set off in the liquidation under IR 2016 r.14.25, is also effectively a bar to the assignment of a cause of action by a liquidator: *Craig v Humberclyde Industrial Finance Group Ltd* [1999] B.C.C. 378.

Where the office-holder lawfully assigns a right of action, this has the effect of removing the claim from the insolvency exception under the Judgments Regulation, so that the Judgments Regulation applies to the exclusion of the EC Regulation and the court where the intended defendant is based alone has jurisdiction: *F-Tex SIA v Lietuvos-*

Anglijos UAB "Jadecloud" (C-213/10, 19 April 2012): see the notes to the EU Recast Insolvency Regulation in Vol.2.

In an article in *Company Law Newsletter* (31 October 2005), Sir Gavin Lightman draws attention to the risks inherent in the giving or taking of an assignment of a cause of action by an insolvency office-holder. See also *Hopkins v TL Dallas Group Ltd* [2005] 1 B.C.L.C. 543 at [105].

Para.6A

A compromise was upheld by the court in *Coote v Rubin* [2011] EWCA Civ 106; [2011] B.C.C. 596, despite the opposition of the principal creditor.

Para.13

This power is self-standing, and not merely ancillary to the preceding powers: *Connaught Income Fund Series 1 v Capita Financial Managers Ltd* [2014] EWHC 3619 (Comm); [2015] 1 B.C.L.C. 241.

Schedule 4ZA

Conditions for Making a Debt Relief Order

Part 1

Conditions Which Must be Met

Connection with England and Wales

1(1) The debtor–

(a) is domiciled in England and Wales on the application date; or

(b) at any time during the period of three years ending with that date–

(i) was ordinarily resident, or had a place of residence, in England and Wales; or

(ii) carried on business in England and Wales.

1(2) The reference in sub-paragraph (1)(b)(ii) to the debtor carrying on business includes–

(a) the carrying on of business by a firm or partnership of which he is a member;

(b) the carrying on of business by an agent or manager for him or for such a firm or partnership.

Debtor's previous insolvency history

2 The debtor is not, on the determination date–

(a) an undischarged bankrupt;

(b) subject to an interim order or voluntary arrangement under Part 8; or

(c) subject to a bankruptcy restrictions order or a debt relief restrictions order.

3 A bankruptcy application under Part 9–

(a) has not been made before the determination date; or

(b) has been so made, but proceedings on the application have been finally disposed of before that date.

4 A creditor's petition for the debtor's bankruptcy under Part 9–

(a) has not been presented against the debtor at any time before the determination date;

(b) has been so presented, but proceedings on the petition have been finally disposed of before that date; or

(c) has been so presented and proceedings in relation to the petition remain before the court at that date, but the person who presented the petition has consented to the making of an application for a debt relief order.

5 A debt relief order has not been made in relation to the debtor in the period of six years ending with the determination date.

Limit on debtor's overall indebtedness

6(1) The total amount of the debtor's debts on the determination date, other than unliquidated debts and excluded debts, does not exceed the prescribed amount.

6(2) For this purpose an unliquidated debt is a debt that is not for a liquidated sum payable to a creditor either immediately or at some future certain time.

Limit on debtor's monthly surplus income

7(1) The debtor's monthly surplus income (if any) on the determination date does not exceed the prescribed amount.

7(2) For this purpose "monthly surplus income" is the amount by which a person's monthly income exceeds the amount necessary for the reasonable domestic needs of himself and his family.

7(3) The rules may–

(a) make provision as to how the debtor's monthly surplus income is to be determined;

(b) provide that particular descriptions of income are to be excluded for the purposes of this paragraph.

Limit on value of debtor's property

8(1) The total value of the debtor's property on the determination date does not exceed the prescribed amount.

8(2) The rules may–

(a) make provision as to how the value of a person's property is to be determined;

(b) provide that particular descriptions of property are to be excluded for the purposes of this paragraph.

Part 2

Other Conditions

9(1) The debtor has not entered into a transaction with any person at an undervalue during the period between–

(a) the start of the period of two years ending with the application date; and

(b) the determination date.

9(2) For this purpose a debtor enters into a transaction with a person at an undervalue if–

(a) he makes a gift to that person or he otherwise enters into a transaction with that person on terms that provide for him to receive no consideration;

(b) he enters into a transaction with that person in consideration of marriage or the formation of a civil partnership; or

(c) he enters into a transaction with that person for a consideration the value of which, in money or money's worth, is significantly less than the value, in money or money's worth, of the consideration provided by the individual.

10(1) The debtor has not given a preference to any person during the period between–

(a) the start of the period of two years ending with the application date; and

(b) the determination date.

10(2) For this purpose a debtor gives a preference to a person if–

(a) that person is one of the debtor's creditors to whom a qualifying debt is owed or is a surety or guarantor for any such debt, and

(b) the debtor does anything or suffers anything to be done which (in either case) has the effect of putting that person into a position which, in the event that a debt relief order is made in relation to the debtor, will be better than the position he would have been in if that thing had not been done.

GENERAL NOTE

Introduced by s.108(2) of, and Sch.18 to, the Tribunals, Courts and Enforcement Act 2007 with effect from 6 April 2009, this is an important set of preconditions that must be met before a debtor can qualify for a DRO. These criteria are supplemented by the Insolvency Proceedings (Monetary Limits) (Amendment) Order 2009 (SI 2009/465) which specified maximum indebtedness of £15k, maximum monthly surplus income of £50 and maximum property value of £300. From 1 October 2015 these figures were changed in that the maximum debt was increased to £20k and the maximum asset level went up to £1k. There is no change to the monthly income figure—see Insolvency Proceedings (Monetary Limits) (Amendment) Order 2015 (SI 2015/26). The jurisdiction boxes that must be ticked are the same as those traditionally applied to would be bankrupts under IA 1986 s.265. A DRO is not available to a debtor already undergoing a personal insolvency procedure. Financial criteria are mapped out by paras 6, 7 and 8 subject to clarification by secondary legislation. A DRO is not available to a person who has undertaken a transaction at an undervalue or a preference within the past two years. See IA 1986 Pt 7A and IR 2016 Pt 9.

Note also *The Mayor and Burgesses of the London Borough of Islington v C and the Official Receiver* [2012] B.P.I.R. 363 where conditions 7 and 10 are analysed by District Judge Hart. See note to s.251L.

Note the replacement of para.3 by ERRA 2013 Sch.19 para.62.

SCHEDULE 4ZB

DEBT RELIEF RESTRICTIONS ORDERS AND UNDERTAKINGS

Debt relief restrictions order

1(1) A debt relief restrictions order may be made by the court in relation to a person in respect of whom a debt relief order has been made.

1(2) An order may be made only on the application of–

(a) the Secretary of State, or

(b) the official receiver acting on a direction of the Secretary of State.

Grounds for making order

2(1) The court shall grant an application for a debt relief restrictions order if it thinks it appropriate to do so having regard to the conduct of the debtor (whether before or after the making of the debt relief order).

2(2) The court shall, in particular, take into account any of the following kinds of behaviour on the part of the debtor–

(a) failing to keep records which account for a loss of property by the debtor, or by a business carried on by him, where the loss occurred in the period beginning two years before the application date for the debt relief order and ending with the date of the application for the debt relief restrictions order;

(b) failing to produce records of that kind on demand by the official receiver;

(c) entering into a transaction at an undervalue in the period beginning two years before the application date for the debt relief order and ending with the date of the determination of that application;

(d) giving a preference in the period beginning two years before the application date for the debt relief order and ending with the date of the determination of that application;

(e) making an excessive pension contribution;

(f) a failure to supply goods or services that were wholly or partly paid for;

(g) trading at a time, before the date of the determination of the application for the debt relief order, when the debtor knew or ought to have known that he was himself to be unable to pay his debts;

(h) incurring, before the date of the determination of the application for the debt relief order, a debt which the debtor had no reasonable expectation of being able to pay;

(i) failing to account satisfactorily to the court or the official receiver for a loss of property or for an insufficiency of property to meet his debts;

(j) carrying on any gambling, rash and hazardous speculation or unreasonable extravagance which may have materially contributed to or increased the extent of his inability to pay his debts before the application date for the debt relief order or which took place between that date and the date of the determination of the application for the debt relief order;

(k) neglect of business affairs of a kind which may have materially contributed to or increased the extent of his inability to pay his debts;

(l) fraud or fraudulent breach of trust;

(m) failing to co-operate with the official receiver.

2(3) The court shall also, in particular, consider whether the debtor was an undischarged bankrupt at some time during the period of six years ending with the date of the application for the debt relief order.

2(4) For the purposes of sub-paragraph (2)–

"excessive pension contribution" shall be construed in accordance with section 342A;

"preference" shall be construed in accordance with paragraph 10(2) of Schedule 4ZA;

"undervalue" shall be construed in accordance with paragraph 9(2) of that Schedule.

Timing of application for order

3 An application for a debt relief restrictions order in respect of a debtor may be made–

(a) at any time during the moratorium period relating to the debt relief order in question, or

(b) after the end of that period, but only with the permission of the court.

Duration of order

4(1) A debt relief restrictions order–

(a) comes into force when it is made, and

(b) ceases to have effect at the end of a date specified in the order.

4(2) The date specified in a debt relief restrictions order under sub-paragraph (1)(b) must not be–

(a) before the end of the period of two years beginning with the date on which the order is made, or

(b) after the end of the period of 15 years beginning with that date.

Interim debt relief restrictions order

5(1) This paragraph applies at any time between–

(a) the institution of an application for a debt relief restrictions order, and

(b) the determination of the application.

5(2) The court may make an interim debt relief restrictions order if the court thinks that–

(a) there are prima facie grounds to suggest that the application for the debt relief restrictions order will be successful, and

(b) it is in the public interest to make an interim debt relief restrictions order.

5(3) An interim debt relief restrictions order may only be made on the application of–

(a) the Secretary of State, or

(b) the official receiver acting on a direction of the Secretary of State.

5(4) An interim debt relief restrictions order–

(a) has the same effect as a debt relief restrictions order, and

(b) comes into force when it is made.

5(5) An interim debt relief restrictions order ceases to have effect–

(a) on the determination of the application for the debt relief restrictions order,

(b) on the acceptance of a debt relief restrictions undertaking made by the debtor, or

(c) if the court discharges the interim debt relief restrictions order on the application of the person who applied for it or of the debtor.

6(1) This paragraph applies to a case in which both an interim debt relief restrictions order and a debt relief restrictions order are made.

6(2) Paragraph 4(2) has effect in relation to the debt relief restrictions order as if a reference to the date of that order were a reference to the date of the interim debt relief restrictions order.

Debt relief restrictions undertaking

7(1) A debtor may offer a debt relief restrictions undertaking to the Secretary of State.

7(2) In determining whether to accept a debt relief restrictions undertaking the Secretary of State shall have regard to the matters specified in paragraph 2(2) and (3).

8 A reference in an enactment to a person in respect of whom a debt relief restrictions order has effect (or who is "the subject of" a debt relief restrictions order) includes a reference to a person in respect of whom a debt relief restrictions undertaking has effect.

9(1) A debt relief restrictions undertaking–

(a) comes into force on being accepted by the Secretary of State, and

(b) ceases to have effect at the end of a date specified in the undertaking.

9(2) The date specified under sub-paragraph (1)(b) must not be–

(a) before the end of the period of two years beginning with the date on which the undertaking is accepted, or

(b) after the end of the period of 15 years beginning with that date.

9(3) On an application by the debtor the court may–

(a) annul a debt relief restrictions undertaking;

(b) provide for a debt relief restrictions undertaking to cease to have effect before the date specified under sub-paragraph (1)(b).

Effect of revocation of debt relief order

10 Unless the court directs otherwise, the revocation at any time of a debt relief order does not–

(a) affect the validity of any debt relief restrictions order, interim debt relief restrictions order or debt relief restrictions undertaking which is in force in respect of the debtor;

(b) prevent the determination of any application for a debt relief restrictions order, or an interim debt relief restrictions order, in relation to the debtor that was instituted before that time;

(c) prevent the acceptance of a debt relief restrictions undertaking that was offered before that time; or

(d) prevent the institution of an application for a debt relief restrictions order or interim debt relief restrictions order in respect of the debtor, or the offer or acceptance of a debt relief restrictions undertaking by the debtor, after that time.

General Note

Introduced by s.108(2) to, and Sch.19 of, the Tribunals, Courts and Enforcement Act 2007 with effect from 6 April 2009, these provisions, which are anticipated by s.251V, clarify what is a debt relief restrictions order (DRRO) and the grounds for the making of such an order. The criteria that the court should have regard to mirror those relevant for a bankruptcy restrictions order. DRROs can run for a maximum of 15 years. Interim DRROs are a possibility and there is the predictable alternative of a debt relief restrictions undertaking (DRRU). Most debt relief restrictions (and there are not many) come via the undertakings mode. Note that both DRROs and DRRUs should appear on a public register (s.251W). Further relevant provisions are to be found in IR 2016 rr.11.1–11.12.

SCHEDULE 4A

BANKRUPTCY RESTRICTIONS ORDER AND UNDERTAKING

1 Bankruptcy restrictions order

1(1) A bankruptcy restrictions order may be made by the court.

1(2) An order may be made only on the application of–

(a) the Secretary of State, or

(b) the official receiver acting on a direction of the Secretary of State.

2 Grounds for making order

2(1) The court shall grant an application for a bankruptcy restrictions order if it thinks it appropriate having regard to the conduct of the bankrupt (whether before or after the making of the bankruptcy order).

2(2) The court shall, in particular, take into account any of the following kinds of behaviour on the part of the bankrupt–

(a) failing to keep records which account for a loss of property by the bankrupt, or by a business carried on by him, where the loss occurred in the period beginning 2 years before the making of the bankruptcy application or (as the case may be) the presentation of the bankruptcy petition and ending with the date of the application for the bankruptcy restrictions order;

(b) failing to produce records of that kind on demand by the official receiver or the trustee;

(c) entering into a transaction at an undervalue;

(d) giving a preference;

(e) making an excessive pension contribution;

(f) a failure to supply goods or services which were wholly or partly paid for which gave rise to a claim provable in the bankruptcy;

(g) trading at a time before commencement of the bankruptcy when the bankrupt knew or ought to have known that he was himself to be unable to pay his debts;

(h) incurring, before commencement of the bankruptcy, a debt which the bankrupt had no reasonable expectation of being able to pay;

(i) failing to account satisfactorily to the court, the official receiver or the trustee for a loss of property or for an insufficiency of property to meet bankruptcy debts;

(j) carrying on any gambling, rash and hazardous speculation or unreasonable extravagance which may have materially contributed to or increased the extent of the bankruptcy or which took place between the making of the bankruptcy application or (as the case may be) the presentation of the bankruptcy petition and commencement of the bankruptcy;

(k) neglect of business affairs of a kind which may have materially contributed to or increased the extent of the bankruptcy;

(l) fraud or fraudulent breach of trust;

(m) failing to cooperate with the official receiver or the trustee.

2(3) The court shall also, in particular, consider whether the bankrupt was an undischarged bankrupt at some time during the period of six years ending with the date of the bankruptcy to which the application relates.

2(4) For the purpose of sub-paragraph (2)–

"excessive pension contribution" shall be construed in accordance with section 342A,

"preference" shall be construed in accordance with section 340, and

"undervalue" shall be construed in accordance with section 339.

3 Timing of application for order

3(1) An application for a bankruptcy restrictions order in respect of a bankrupt must be made–

(a) before the end of the period of one year beginning with the date on which the bankruptcy commences, or

(b) with the permission of the court.

3(2) The period specified in sub-paragraph (1)(a) shall cease to run in respect of a bankrupt while the period set for his discharge is suspended under section 279(3).

4 Duration of order

4(1) A bankruptcy restrictions order–

(a) shall come into force when it is made, and

(b) shall cease to have effect at the end of a date specified in the order.

4(2) The date specified in a bankruptcy restrictions order under sub-paragraph (1)(b) must not be–

(a) before the end of the period of two years beginning with the date on which the order is made, or

(b) after the end of the period of 15 years beginning with that date.

5 Interim bankruptcy restrictions order

5(1) This paragraph applies at any time between–

(a) the institution of an application for a bankruptcy restrictions order, and

(b) the determination of the application.

5(2) The court may make an interim bankruptcy restrictions order if the court thinks that–

(a) there are prima facie grounds to suggest that the application for the bankruptcy restrictions order will be successful, and

(b) it is in the public interest to make an interim order.

5(3) An interim order may be made only on the application of–

(a) the Secretary of State, or

(b) the official receiver acting on a direction of the Secretary of State.

5(4) An interim order–

(a) shall have the same effect as a bankruptcy restrictions order, and

(b) shall come into force when it is made.

5(5) An interim order shall cease to have effect–

(a) on the determination of the application for the bankruptcy restrictions order,

(b) on the acceptance of a bankruptcy restrictions undertaking made by the bankrupt, or

(c) if the court discharges the interim order on the application of the person who applied for it or of the bankrupt.

6(1) This paragraph applies to a case in which both an interim bankruptcy restrictions order and a bankruptcy restrictions order are made.

6(2) Paragraph 4(2) shall have effect in relation to the bankruptcy restrictions order as if a reference to the date of that order were a reference to the date of the interim order.

7 Bankruptcy restrictions undertaking

7(1) A bankrupt may offer a bankruptcy restrictions undertaking to the Secretary of State.

7(2) In determining whether to accept a bankruptcy restrictions undertaking the Secretary of State shall have regard to the matters specified in paragraph 2(2) and (3).

8 A reference in an enactment to a person in respect of whom a bankruptcy restrictions order has effect (or who is "the subject of" a bankruptcy restrictions order) includes a reference to a person in respect of whom a bankruptcy restrictions undertaking has effect.

9(1) A bankruptcy restrictions undertaking–

(a) shall come into force on being accepted by the Secretary of State, and

(b) shall cease to have effect at the end of a date specified in the undertaking.

9(2) The date specified under sub-paragraph (1)(b) must not be–

(a) before the end of the period of two years beginning with the date on which the undertaking is accepted, or

(b) after the end of the period of 15 years beginning with that date.

9(3) On an application by the bankrupt the court may–

(a) annul a bankruptcy restrictions undertaking;

(b) provide for a bankruptcy restrictions undertaking to cease to have effect before the date specified under sub-paragraph (1)(b).

10 Effect of annulment of bankruptcy order

10 Where a bankruptcy order is annulled under section 282(1)(a) or (2)–

(a) any bankruptcy restrictions order, interim order or undertaking which is in force in respect of the bankrupt shall be annulled,

(b) no new bankruptcy restrictions order or interim order may be made in respect of the bankrupt, and

(c) no new bankruptcy restrictions undertaking by the bankrupt may be accepted.

11 Where a bankruptcy order is annulled under section 261 or 282(1)(b)–

(a) the annulment shall not affect any bankruptcy restrictions order, interim order or undertaking in respect of the bankrupt,

(b) the court may make a bankruptcy restrictions order in relation to the bankrupt on an application instituted before the annulment,

(c) the Secretary of State may accept a bankruptcy restrictions undertaking offered before the annulment, and

(d) an application for a bankruptcy restrictions order or interim order in respect of the bankrupt may not be instituted after the annulment.

12 Registration

12 The Secretary of State shall maintain a register of–

(a) bankruptcy restrictions orders,

(b) interim bankruptcy restrictions orders, and

(c) bankruptcy restrictions undertakings.

General Note

This was inserted by EA 2002 s.257 and Sch.20 to further supplement the rules on BROs and BRUs. See the notes to s.281A above. Details of the use of BROs and BRUs in practice are mounted on the Insolvency Service website under Press Notices. In 2015/2016 according to Insolvency Service Outcomes there were 432 cases of BROs/DRROs/BRUs/DRRUs recorded, with the vast majority being through the undertakings mode. The figures comprise both bankruptcy and debt relief restrictions, though were are informed that there are very few debt relief restrictions recorded. What is clear is that the number of restrictions, however imposed has fallen by 25 per cent on the previous year. The average restriction lasts 5.1 years.

Cases involving bankruptcy restrictions orders are beginning to be reported. In *Randhawa v Official Receiver* [2006] B.P.I.R. 1435 the court was at pains to stress the common heritage of the BRO regime with the director disqualification procedure. Once the court had concluded that the conduct in question merited a BRO it was obliged to make such an order; this was consistent with the approach taken by the court in the director disqualification case of *Re Grayan Building Services Ltd* [1995] Ch. 241. BROs were intended both to protect the public and also to have a deterrent effect. The three-tier classification in *Re Sevenoaks Stationers Ltd* [1991] Ch. 164 governing the duration of a director disqualification could be adopted for determining the length of the BRO. The three year BRO was upheld. In concluding his judgment Launcelot Henderson QC expressed disquiet that nowhere in Sch.4A was there any indication of the consequences that would ensue if a BRO were breached. If the conduct of the bankrupt is found to fall below the required standard the court *must* impose a BRO at least for the minimum two-year period—*Official Receiver v May* [2008] B.P.I.R. 1562.

Another reported case is *Official Receiver v Merchant* [2006] B.P.I.R. 1525 where Chief Registrar Baister dismissed an application for an interim BRO. The point was made that different considerations applied to the making of an interim order. General guidance was given on procedural aspects where an application for an interim BRO was sought.

In *Official Receiver v Doganci* [2007] B.P.I.R. 87 Chief Registrar Baister refused to grant a BRO because it could not be said that the bankrupt's explanation for the loss of property, although implausible, was untruthful. The bankrupt deserved the benefit of the doubt.

In *OR v Pyman* [2007] EWHC 1150; [2007] B.P.I.R. 1150 on appeal a bankruptcy restrictions order was doubled to seven years because the trial judge had underestimated the degree of culpability of the individual concerned (who had been bankrupted previously). The fact of a previous bankruptcy experience should have alerted the defendant to his responsibilities under bankruptcy law. The advanced age of the defendant was not relevant, unless there was evidence of infirmity.

Where a bankruptcy has been annulled under s.282(1)(b) on the ground that all debts have been paid the court can still grant a BRO provided the application was made before the annulment and within a year of the commencement of the bankruptcy—*Jenkins v OR* [2007] EWHC 1402 (Ch); [2007] B.P.I.R. 740. In this case it was held that in considering whether to make a BRO the court could take into account the fact that the individual whilst an undischarged bankrupt was continuing to act as a company director without leave.

A BRO was refused in *Official Receiver v Southey* [2009] B.P.I.R. 89 because the court was not satisfied that the bankrupt when incurring the debt in question had no reasonable prospect of repaying it. It took this generous view because the bankrupt had lived a precarious financial existence in the past and had always managed to repay his credit.

The issue of the cut off period for applications for a BRO was examined in *Official Receiver v Baars* [2009] B.P.I.R. 524. Here the bankruptcy had been discharged in late 2005 but the application for the BRO was not made to the court for more than two years after that date. The justification for the late application was the allegation that the former bankrupt had not disclosed his assets and this non-disclosure had not come to light until seven months before the application. In the light of these circumstances the court allowed the application to proceed.

A further consideration of the BRO regime is to be found in the judgment of HHJ Pelling in *Official Receiver v Going* [2011] EWHC 786 (Ch); [2011] B.P.I.R. 1069. Here the bankrupt successfully appealed against a eight-year BRO on the basis that the evidence did not support the making of a BRO. The limitations of a court hearing an appeal were noted—the appellate court could not uphold a BRO on evidence that was not presented at first instance. Any evidence used to justify a BRO has to be put before the court considering the matter at first instance.

A nine-year BRO was imposed by the court in *Official Receiver v Bathurst* [2008] B.P.I.R. 1548. Here the court at first instance had imposed a three-year restriction, but this was substantially increased by Sir Andrew Morritt CVO on appeal.

In *Michael v Official Receiver* [2010] EWHC 2246 (Ch) an attempt to challenge the interim BRO procedure on the grounds that it infringed art.6 of the ECHR failed. Arnold J refused to make a declaration of incompatibility under the Human Rights Act 1998. The judgment contains a useful analysis of the interim BRO procedure.

For recent authority considering the BRO regime see *Michael v Official Receiver* [2013] EWHC 4286 (Ch); [2014] B.P.I.R. 666 where Roth J, in spite of rejecting the criticisms of the handling of the case by Chief Registrar Baister, reduced the BRO period from 8 years to 6.5 years. The litigation continues to rumble on—this case went to the Court of Appeal [2014] EWCA Civ 534 where permission to appeal the decision of Roth J was given.

A BRO was made on the facts disclosed in *OR v Lloyd* [2015] B.P.I.R. 374. For a BRO granted under the law in Northern Ireland see *OR v Gibson* [2015] NIMaster 4; [2015] B.P.I.R. 717. An attempt by the bankrupt to raise a "bucket list" defence to justify expenditure met with short shrift.

See *OR v Bayliss* (unreported, 26 July 2017, E Johnson QC).

For comment see Taylor [2007] 20 Insolv. Int. 90. For a comprehensive review see Moser [2013] J.B.L. 679.

Note a number of amendments are made to para.2 by ERRA 2013 Sch.19 para.63.

Schedule 5

Powers of Trustee in Bankruptcy

Section 314

Part I

1 Power to carry on any business of the bankrupt so far as may be necessary for winding it up beneficially and so far as the trustee is able to do so without contravening any requirement imposed by or under any enactment.

2 Power to bring, institute or defend any action or legal proceedings relating to the property comprised in the bankrupt's estate.

2A Power to bring legal proceedings under section 339, 340 or 423.

3 Power to accept as the consideration for the sale of any property comprised in the bankrupt's estate a sum of money payable at a future time subject to such stipulations as to security or otherwise as the creditors' committee or the court thinks fit.

4 Power to mortgage or pledge any part of the property comprised in the bankrupt's estate for the purpose of raising money for the payment of his debts.

5 Power, where any right, option or other power forms part of the bankrupt's estate, to make payments or incur liabilities with a view to obtaining, for the benefit of the creditors, any property which is the subject of the right, option or power.

6 [Deleted]

7 Power to make such compromise or other arrangement as may be thought expedient with creditors, or persons claiming to be creditors, in respect of bankruptcy debts.

8 Power to make such compromise or other arrangement as may be thought expedient with respect to any claim arising out of or incidental to the bankrupt's estate made or capable of being made on the trustee by any person.

Part II

9 Power to sell any part of the property for the time being comprised in the bankrupt's estate, including the goodwill and book debts of any business.

9A Power to refer to arbitration, or compromise on such terms as may be agreed, any debts, claims or liabilities subsisting or supposed to subsist between the bankrupt and any person who may have incurred any liability to the bankrupt.

9B Power to make such compromise or other arrangement as may be thought expedient with respect to any claim arising out of or incidental to the bankrupt's estate made or capable of being made by the trustee on any person.

10 Power to give receipts for any money received by him, being receipts which effectually discharge the person paying the money from all responsibility in respect of its application.

11 Power to prove, rank, claim and draw a dividend in respect of such debts due to the bankrupt as are comprised in his estate.

12 Power to exercise in relation to any property comprised in the bankrupt's estate any powers the capacity to exercise which is vested in him under Parts VIII to XI of this Act.

13 Power to deal with any property comprised in the estate to which the bankrupt is beneficially entitled as tenant in tail in the same manner as the bankrupt might have dealt with it.

Part III

14 For the purposes of, or in connection with, the exercise of any of his powers under Parts VIII to XI of this Act, the trustee may, by his official name–

(a) hold property of every description,

(b) make contracts,

(c) sue and be sued,

(d) enter into engagements binding on himself and, in respect of the bankrupt's estate, on his successors in office,

(e) employ an agent,

(f) execute any power of attorney, deed or other instrument;

and he may do any other act which is necessary or expedient for the purposes of or in connection with the exercise of those powers.

General Note

This schedule, allied to s.314, lists the powers of a trustee in bankruptcy. Like Sch.2, it has been hived off from the mainstream of the legislation. The crucial distinguishing factor used to be the need to obtain the sanction of the committee of creditors (see s.301) before the powers listed in Pt I could be exercised. That sanction requirement was removed by SBEEA 2015 s.121. Paragraph 2A was inserted by s.262 of EA 2002 to ensure that recovery actions were properly sanctioned as the costs of such actions can now be treated as a winding-up expense, see IR 2016 r.10.149.

For a recent decision on the effect of the power now contained in Sch.5 para.3, see *Weddell v Pearce (JA) & Major* [1988] Ch. 26. This case involved the assignment of a cause of action by the trustee for future consideration without obtaining the requisite sanction. It was held by Scott J that notwithstanding this failure to obtain sanction, the assignment took effect in equity. This ruling is in line with the philosophy now expressed in ss.314(3) and 377 of IA 1986. The power to assign was also reviewed by the Australian courts in *Re Cirillo* [1997] B.P.I.R. 166. On the power to assign and the potential dangers where it is agreed that the estate will receive a share of the proceeds of a successful assigned claim see *Hunt v Harb* [2011] EWCA Civ 1239. On the power to employ a solicitor see *Re Schuppan* [1996] B.P.I.R. 486. On the meaning of "compromise" and "sale" within paras 7 and 9 respectively see the judgment of Gabriel Moss QC in *Power v Brown* [2009] B.P.I.R. 340.

Note the deletion of para.6, amendment of para.8 and the insertion of paras 9A and 9B by LRO 2010 (SI 2010/18). The net effect of this is to extend the powers of the trustee by removing the need to obtain sanction before exercising the specified powers.

For further guidance on this Schedule see the note to s.314. Note in particular the impact of SBEEA 2015 in removing the need for sanction in the exercise of powers.

Schedule 6

The Categories of Preferential Debts

Section 386

Category 1: Debts due to Inland Revenue

[Deleted]

Category 2: Debts due to Customs and Excise

[Deleted]

Category 3: Social Security Contributions

[Deleted]

Category 4: Contributions to Occupational Pension Schemes, etc.

8 Any sum which is owed by the debtor and is a sum to which Schedule 4 to the Pension Schemes Act 1993 applies (contributions to occupational pension schemes and state scheme premiums).

Category 5: Remuneration, etc., of Employees

9 So much of any amount which–

(a) is owed by the debtor to a person who is or has been an employee of the debtor, and

(b) is payable by way of remuneration in respect of the whole or any part of the period of 4 months next before the relevant date,

as does not exceed so much as may be prescribed by order made by the Secretary of State.

10 An amount owed by way of accrued holiday remuneration, in respect of any period of employment before the relevant date, to a person whose employment by the debtor has been terminated, whether before, on or after that date.

11 So much of any sum owed in respect of money advanced for the purpose as has been applied for the payment of a debt which, if it had not been paid, would have been a debt falling within paragraph 9 or 10.

12 So much of any amount which–

(a) is ordered (whether before or after the relevant date) to be paid by the debtor under the Reserve Forces (Safeguard of Employment) Act 1985, and

(b) is so ordered in respect of a default made by the debtor before that date in the discharge of his obligations under that Act,

as does not exceed such amount as may be prescribed by order made by the Secretary of State.

Interpretation for Category 5

13(1) For the purposes of paragraphs 9 to 12, a sum is payable by the debtor to a person by way of remuneration in respect of any period if–

(a) it is paid as wages or salary (whether payable for time or for piece work or earned wholly or partly by way of commission) in respect of services rendered to the debtor in that period, or

(b) it is an amount falling within the following sub-paragraph and is payable by the debtor in respect of that period.

13(2) An amount falls within this sub-paragraph if it is–

(a) a guarantee payment under Part III of the Employment Rights Act 1996 (employee without work to do);

(b) any payment for time off under section 53 (time off to look for work or arrange training) or section 56 (time off for ante-natal care) of that Act or under section 169 of the Trade Union and Labour Relations (Consolidation) Act 1992 (time off for carrying out trade union duties etc.);

(c) remuneration on suspension on medical grounds, or on maternity grounds, under Part VII of the Employment Rights Act 1996; or

(d) remuneration under a protective award under section 189 of the Trade Union and Labour Relations (Consolidation) Act 1992 (redundancy dismissal with compensation).

14(1) This paragraph relates to a case in which a person's employment has been terminated by or in consequence of his employer going into liquidation or being made bankrupt or (his employer being a company not in liquidation) by or in consequence of–

(a) a receiver being appointed as mentioned in section 40 of this Act (debenture-holders secured by floating charge), or

(b) the appointment of a receiver under section 53(6) or 54(5) of this Act (Scottish company with property subject to floating charge), or

(c) the taking of possession by debenture-holders (so secured), as mentioned in section 754 of the Companies Act 2006.

14(2) For the purposes of paragraphs 9 to 12, holiday remuneration is deemed to have accrued to that person in respect of any period of employment if, by virtue of his contract of employment or of any enactment, that remuneration would have accrued in respect of that period if his employment had continued until he became entitled to be allowed the holiday.

14(3) The reference in sub-paragraph (2) to any enactment includes an order or direction made under an enactment.

15 Without prejudice to paragraphs 13 and 14–

(a) any remuneration payable by the debtor to a person in respect of a period of holiday or of absence from work through sickness or other good cause is deemed to be wages or (as the case may be) salary in respect of services rendered to the debtor in that period.

Category 6: Levies on Coal and Steel Production

15A Any sums due at the relevant date from the debtor in respect of–

(a) the levies on the production of coal and steel referred to in Articles 49 and 50 of the E.C.S.C. Treaty, or

(b) any surcharge for delay provided for in Article 50(3) of that Treaty and Article 6 of Decision 3/52 of the High Authority of the Coal and Steel Community.

Category 6A: Debts owed to the Financial Services Compensation Scheme

15AA Any debt owed by the debtor to the scheme manager of the Financial Services Compensation Scheme under section 215(2A) of the Financial Services and Markets Act 2000.

Category 7: Deposits covered by Financial Services Compensation Scheme

15B So much of any amount owed at the relevant date by the debtor in respect of an eligible deposit as does not exceed the compensation that would be payable in respect of the deposit under the Financial Services Compensation Scheme to the person or persons to whom the amount is owed.

Category 8: Other deposits

15BA So much of any amount owed at the relevant date by the debtor to one or more eligible persons in respect of an eligible deposit as exceeds any compensation that would be payable in respect of the deposit under the Financial Services Compensation Scheme to that person or those persons.

15BB An amount owed at the relevant date by the debtor to one or more eligible persons in respect of a deposit that–

(a) was made through a non-EEA branch of a credit institution authorised by the competent authority of an EEA state, and

(b) would have been an eligible deposit if it had been made through an EEA branch of that credit institution.

Interpretation for Categories 6A, 7 and 8

15C(A1) In paragraph 15AA "the scheme manager" has the meaning given in section 212(1) of the Financial Services and Markets Act 2000.

15C(1) In paragraphs 15B to 15BB "eligible deposit" means a deposit in respect of which the person, or any of the persons, to whom it is owed would be eligible for compensation under the Financial Services Compensation Scheme.

15C(2) For the purposes of those paragraphs and this paragraph a "deposit" means rights of the kind described in–

(a) paragraph 22 of Schedule 2 to the Financial Services and Markets Act 2000 (deposits), or

(b) section 1(2)(b) of the Dormant Bank and Building Society Accounts Act 2008 (balances transferred under that Act to authorised reclaim fund).

15C(3) In paragraphs 15BA and 15BB, "eligible person" means–

(a) an individual, or

(b) a micro-enterprise, a small enterprise or a medium-sized enterprise, each of those terms having the meaning given in Article 2.1(107) of Directive 2014/59/EU of 15th May 2014 establishing a framework for the recovery and resolution of credit institutions and investment firms.

15C(4) In paragraph 15BB–

(a) "credit institution" has the meaning given in Article 4.1(1) of the capital requirements regulation;

(b) "EEA branch" means a branch, as defined in Article 4.1(17) of the capital requirements regulation, which is established in an EEA state;

(c) "non-EEA branch" means a branch, as so defined, which is established in a country which is not an EEA state;

and for this purpose "the capital requirements regulation" means Regulation (EU) No 575/2013 of the European Parliament and of the Council of 26th June 2013 on prudential requirements for credit institutions and investment firms and amending Regulation (EU) No 648/2012.

Orders

16 An order under paragraph 9 or 12–

(a) may contain such transitional provisions as may appear to the Secretary of State necessary or expedient;

(b) shall be made by statutory instrument subject to annulment in pursuance of a resolution of either House of Parliament.

General Note

This Schedule, which is brought into play by s.386, largely reflects the preferential claims regime as suggested by the Cork Committee (Cmnd.8558, para.1450) and further pruned by EA 2002. Categories 1, 2 and 3 (Crown debts) were abolished by s.251 of EA 2002 effective 15 September 2003. (For transitional provisions, see SI 2003/2093 art.4.)

For the meaning of the phrase "the relevant date", see s.387. For further comment, see the general note to Pt XII. The amount for paras 9 and 12 is fixed at £800: see the Insolvency Proceedings (Monetary Limits) Order 1986 (SI 1986/1996) art.4.

This Schedule has been added to over recent years. New paras 15B and 15C were inserted with effect from 31 December 2014 by s.13 of the Financial Services (Banking Reform) Act 2013 by virtue of its Commencement No.7 Order (SI 2014/3160 (C. 138)). To complicate matters further a category of "secondary preferential debts" was added for insolvencies commencing after 1 January 2015 by the insertion of new paras 15BA and 15BB by the Banks and Building Societies (Depositor Preference and Priorities) Order 2014 (SI 2014/3486). This has become necessary to implement EC Directive 2014/59. One hoped that it was not setting a precedent to expand the range of preferential debts but a new Category 6A (para.15AA) and para.15C(A1) were inserted by the Deposit Guarantee Scheme Regulations 2015 (SI 2015/486) reg.14(1), (3) as from 26 March 2015 to introduce as preferential debts owed by the debtor to the FSCS scheme manager, also part implementing Directive 2014/49, while para.15B concerns deposits covered by the scheme. Debts under paras 8–15B are "ordinary preferential debts" while those listed in paras 15BA and 15BB are "secondary preferential debts" (see s.386(1A) and (1B)).

Amended by DA 2015 s.19 and Sch.6.

Para.8

A minor textual amendment was made here by the Pension Schemes Act 1993 Sch.8 para.18.

Para.13

A new subpara.(2) was added by para.29 of Sch.1 to the Employment Rights Act 1996 to facilitate the recent changes in employment legislation.

Para.14

A minor change was made to para.14(1) by the Companies Act 2006 (Consequential Amendments) Order 2008 (SI 2008/948) to convert references in the Companies Act 1985 into their counterparts in the Companies Act 2006. Paragraph 14(1) was amended by ERRA 2013 Sch.19 para.64.

Schedule 7 [Omitted]

Schedule 8

Provisions Capable of Inclusion in Company Insolvency Rules

Section 411

Courts

1 Provision for supplementing, in relation to the insolvency or winding up of companies, any provision made by or under section 117 of this Act (jurisdiction in relation to winding up).

2(1) Provision for regulating the practice and procedure of any court exercising jurisdiction for the purposes of Parts I to VII of this Act or the Companies Acts so far as relating to, and to matters connected with or arising out of, the insolvency or winding up of companies, being any provision that could be made by rules of court.

2(2) Rules made by virtue of this paragraph about the consequence of failure to comply with practice or procedure may, in particular, include provision about the termination of administration.

Notices, etc.

3 Provision requiring notice of any proceedings in connection with or arising out of the insolvency or winding up of a company to be given or published in the manner prescribed by the rules.

4 Provision with respect to the form, manner of serving, contents and proof of any petition, application, order, notice, statement or other document required to be presented, made, given, published or prepared under any enactment or subordinate legislation relating to, or to matters connected with or arising out of, the insolvency or winding up of companies.

5 Provision specifying the persons to whom any notice is to be given.

5A Provision for enabling a creditor of a company to elect to be, or to cease to be, an opted-out creditor in relation to an office-holder of the company (within the meaning of section 248A), including, in particular, provision–

(a) for requiring an office-holder to provide information to creditors about how they may elect to be, or cease to be, opted-out creditors;

(b) for deeming an election to be, or cease to be, an opted-out creditor in relation to a particular office-holder of a company to be such an election also in relation to any other officeholder of the company.

Registration of Voluntary Arrangements

6 Provision for the registration of voluntary arrangements approved under Part I of this Act, including provision for the keeping and inspection of a register.

Provisional Liquidator

7 Provision as to the manner in which a provisional liquidator appointed under section 135 is to carry out his functions.

Conduct of Insolvency

8 Provision with respect to the certification of any person as, and as to the proof that a person is, the liquidator, administrator or administrative receiver of a company.

8A(1) Provision about the making of decisions by creditors and contributories, including provision–

(a) prescribing particular procedures by which creditors and contributories may make decisions;

(b) authorising the use of other procedures for creditors and contributories to make decisions, if those procedures comply with prescribed requirements.

8A(2) Provision under sub-paragraph (1) may in particular include provision about–

(a) how creditors and contributories may request that a creditors' meeting or a contributories' meeting be held,

(b) the rights of creditors, contributories and others to be given notice of, and participate in, procedures,

(c) creditors' and contributories' rights to vote in procedures,

(d) the period within which any right to participate or vote is to be exercised,

(e) the proportion of creditors or contributories that must vote for a proposal for it to be approved,

(f) how the value of any debt or contribution should be determined,

(g) the time at which decisions taken by a procedure are to be treated as having been made.

9 The following provision with respect to meetings of a company's creditors, contributories or members–

(a) provision as to the manner of summoning a meeting (including provision as to how any power to require a meeting is to be exercised, provision as to the manner of determining the value of any debt or contribution for the purposes of any such power and provision making the exercise of any such power subject to the deposit of a sum sufficient to cover the expenses likely to be incurred in summoning and holding a meeting);

(b) provision specifying the time and place at which a meeting may be held and the period of notice required for a meeting;

(c) provision as to the procedure to be followed at a meeting (including the manner in which decisions may be reached by a meeting and the manner in which the value of any vote at a meeting is to be determined);

(d) provision for requiring a person who is or has been an officer of the company to attend a meeting;

(e) provision creating, in the prescribed circumstances, a presumption that a meeting has been duly summoned and held;

(f) provision as to the manner of proving the decisions of a meeting.

9A Provision about how a company's creditors may nominate a person to be liquidator, including in the case of a voluntary winding up provision conferring functions on the directors of the company.

10(1) Provision as to the establishment, functions, membership and proceedings of a committee provided for by section 49, 68, 101, 141 or 142 of, or paragraph 57 of Schedule B1 to, this Act.

10(2) The following provision with respect to the establishment of a committee under section 101, 141 or 142 of this Act, that is to say–

(a) provision for resolving differences between the company's creditors and its contributories or members;

(b) provision authorising the establishment of the committee without seeking a decision from contributories in a case where a company is being wound up on grounds including its inability to pay its debts; and

(c) provision modifying the requirements of this Act with respect to the establishment of the committee in a case where a winding-up order has been made immediately upon the discharge of an administration order.

11 Provision as to the manner in which any requirement that may be imposed on a person under any of Parts I to VII of this Act by the official receiver, the liquidator, administrator or administrative receiver of a company or a special manager appointed under section 177 is to be so imposed.

12 Provision as to the debts that may be proved in a winding up, as to the manner and conditions of proving a debt and as to the manner and expenses of establishing the value of any debt or security.

13 Provision with respect to the manner of the distribution of the property of a company that is being wound up, including provision with respect to unclaimed funds and dividends.

13A Provision for a creditor who has not proved a small debt to be treated as having done so for purposes relating to the distribution of a company's property (and for provisions of, or contained in legislation made under, this Act to apply accordingly).

"Small debt" means a debt not exceeding an amount prescribed by the rules.

14 Provision which, with or without modifications, applies in relation to the winding up of companies any enactment contained in Parts VIII to XI of this Act or in the Bankruptcy (Scotland) Act 2016.

14A Provision about the application of section 176A of this Act which may include, in particular–

(a) provision enabling a receiver to institute winding-up proceedings;

(b) provision requiring a receiver to institute winding-up proceedings.

Administration

14B Provision which–

(a) applies in relation to administration, with or without modifications, a provision of Parts IV to VII of this Act, or

(b) serves a purpose in relation to administration similar to a purpose that may be served by the rules in relation to winding up by virtue of a provision of this Schedule.

Financial Provisions

15 Provision as to the amount, or manner of determining the amount, payable to the liquidator, administrator or administrative receiver of a company or a special manager appointed under section 177, by way of remuneration for the carrying out of functions in connection with or arising out of the insolvency or winding up of a company.

16 Provision with respect to the manner in which moneys received by the liquidator of a company in the course of carrying out his functions as such are to be invested or otherwise handled and with respect to the payment of interest on sums which, in pursuance of rules made by virtue of this paragraph, have been paid into the Insolvency Services Account.

16A Provision enabling the Secretary of State to set the rate of interest paid on sums which have been paid into the Insolvency Services Account.

17 Provision as to the fees, costs, charges and other expenses that may be treated as the expenses of a winding up.

18 Provision as to the fees, costs, charges and other expenses that may be treated as properly incurred by the administrator or administrative receiver of a company.

19 Provision as to the fees, costs, charges and other expenses that may be incurred for any of the purposes of Part I of this Act or in the administration of any voluntary arrangement approved under that Part.

Information and Records

20 Provision requiring registrars and other officers of courts having jurisdiction in England and Wales in relation to, or to matters connected with or arising out of, the insolvency or winding up of companies–

(a) to keep books and other records with respect to the exercise of that jurisdiction, and

(b) to make returns to the Secretary of State of the business of those courts.

21 Provision requiring a creditor, member or contributory, or such a committee as is mentioned in paragraph 10 above, to be supplied (on payment in prescribed cases of the prescribed fee) with such information and with copies of such documents as may be prescribed.

22 Provision as to the manner in which public examinations under sections 133 and 134 of this Act and proceedings under sections 236 and 237 are to be conducted, as to the circumstances in which records of such examinations or proceedings are to be made available to prescribed persons and as to the costs of such examinations and proceedings.

23 Provision imposing requirements with respect to–

(a) the preparation and keeping by the liquidator, administrator or administrative receiver of a company, or by the supervisor of a voluntary arrangement approved under Part I of this Act, of prescribed books, accounts and other records;

(b) the production of those books, accounts and records for inspection by prescribed persons;

(c) the auditing of accounts kept by the liquidator, administrator or administrative receiver of a company, or the supervisor of such a voluntary arrangement; and

(d) the issue by the administrator or administrative receiver of a company of such a certificate as is mentioned in section 22(3)(b) of the Value Added Tax Act 1983 (refund of tax in cases of bad debts) and the supply of copies of the certificate to creditors of the company.

24 Provision requiring the person who is the supervisor of a voluntary arrangement approved under Part I, when it appears to him that the voluntary arrangement has been fully implemented and that nothing remains to be done by him under the arrangement–

(a) to give notice of that fact to persons bound by the voluntary arrangement, and

(b) to report to those persons on the carrying out of the functions conferred on the supervisor of the arrangement.

25 Provision as to the manner in which the liquidator of a company is to act in relation to the books, papers and other records of the company, including provision authorising their disposal.

26 Provision imposing requirements in connection with the carrying out of functions under section 7A of the Company Directors Disqualification Act 1986 (including, in particular, requirements with respect to the making of periodic returns).

General

27 Provision conferring power on the Secretary of State or the Treasury to make regulations with respect to so much of any matter that may be provided for in the rules as relates to the carrying out of the functions of the liquidator, administrator or administrative receiver of a company.

28 Provision conferring a discretion on the court.

29 Provision conferring power on the court to make orders for the purpose of securing compliance with obligations imposed by or under section 47, 66, 131, 143(2) or 235 of, or paragraph 47 of Schedule B1 to, this Act or section 7(4) of the Company Directors Disqualification Act 1986.

30 Provision making non-compliance with any of the rules a criminal offence.

31 Provision making different provision for different cases or descriptions of cases, including different provisions for different areas.

General Note

Much of the detail of the insolvency regime which IA 1985 introduced and IA 1986 consolidated was left to be spelt out in subordinate legislation by regulations made under ss.411 et seq. This Schedule outlines some of the matters which may be the subject of rules relating to company insolvency. The Companies (Winding-Up) Rules 1949 were superseded by IR 1986, which were brought into force contemporaneously with the commencement of the Act itself; but the Schedule is by no means confined in scope to matters which have traditionally been part of winding-up rules. The IR 1986 have now been replaced by the IR 2016.

Numerous amendments to this Schedule were made by EA 2002. Note that in this Schedule, "liquidator" includes a provisional liquidator (s.411(3)). Attention should also be drawn to IR 2016 Introductory Rule 5, which authorises the Secretary of State (pursuant to Sch.8 para.27 and Sch.9 para.30) to make regulations in regard to various matters, supplementary to the Insolvency Rules made under s.411.

Among the items listed which cannot be regarded as purely procedural or are not self-explanatory the following may be noted.

Para.2

Amendment by the Companies Act 2006 (Commencement No.3, Consequential Amendments, Transitional Provisions and Savings) Order 2007 (SI 2007/2194 (C. 84)) art.10(1) and Sch.4 para.44, as from 1 October 2007, recognises the Companies Act 2006.

Para.5A

Para.5A inserted by SBEEA 2015 s.124(1), (5) from 6 April 2017.

Para.6

There is no mention in the body of the Act of any registration procedure for a CVA, although certain matters must be reported to the court (see, e.g. ss.2(2), 4(6)). The present paragraph has been implemented by IR 2016 r.2.38(6), which provides for registration with the registrar of companies.

Para.8A

Para.8A inserted by SBEEA 2015 s.122(1), (3) from 6 April 2017.

Paras 9A, 10

Para.9A was inserted by SBEEA 2015 Sch.9 paras 58 and 59 from 6 April 2017. Amendments were also made to para.10. These changes reflect new creditor decision procedures.

Paras 12, 14

The Parts of the Act dealing with company insolvency contain no definition of "debts" and no provisions relating to proofs of debts, in marked contrast to those relating to the bankruptcy of individuals (see ss.322, 382), and, indeed, to the repealed CA 1985 s.611. It is only by subordinate legislation made under these paragraphs of the present Schedule that such important matters as the nature of provable debts, the quantification of such debts, allowances for mutual credit and set-off, etc. are established for company liquidations and some (but not all) analogous proceedings. This has been done by IR 2016 rr.1.2 et seq., 14.14 et seq.

For further discussion of the term "debts", see the notes to s.1(1) and IR 2016 r.14.1.

The Companies Acts prior to the present legislation always included a substantive provision (e.g. CA 1985 s.612) which incorporated specified aspects of bankruptcy law into the law governing the winding up of *insolvent* companies. Paragraph 14 of this Schedule is potentially of wider scope, since it applies to solvent liquidations as well.

See further the introductory note to Pt IV, Ch.VIII, following s.174.

Paragraph 14 was amended by the Bankruptcy (Scotland) Act 2016 (Consequential Provisions and Modifications) Order 2016 (SI 2016/1034) art.7(1), Sch.1 para.4(1), (11) as from 30 November 2016.

Para.13A

Paragraph 13A inserted by SBEEA 2015 s.131 as from 26 May 2015.

Para.27

For the relevant regulations see the Insolvency Regulations 1994 (SI 1994/2507, operative 24 October 1994, as amended by SI 2000/485, effective 31 March 2000 and SI 2001/762, effective 2 April 2001); SI 2004/472 (effective 1 April 2004); SI 2005/512 (effective 1 April 2005); and SI 2008/670 (effective 6 April 2008). Paragraph 27 was amended by the Banking Act 2009 s.125(7) as from 21 February 2009.

SCHEDULE 9

PROVISIONS CAPABLE OF INCLUSION IN INDIVIDUAL INSOLVENCY RULES

Section 412

Courts

1 Provision with respect to the arrangement and disposition of the business under Parts 7A to 11 of this Act of courts having jurisdiction for the purpose of those Parts, including provision for the allocation of proceedings under those Parts to particular courts and for the transfer of such proceedings from one court to another.

2 Provision for enabling an insolvency and companies court judge to exercise such of the jurisdiction conferred for those purposes on the High Court as may be prescribed.

3 Provision for regulating the practice and procedure of any court exercising jurisdiction for the purposes of those Parts, being any provision that could be made by rules of court.

4 Provision conferring rights of audience, in courts exercising jurisdiction for the purposes of those Parts, on the official receiver and on solicitors.

Adjudicators

4A Provision for regulating the practice and procedure of adjudicators in the discharge of functions for the purposes of Part 9 of this Act.

4B Provision about the form and content of a bankruptcy application (including an application for a review of an adjudicator's determination).

Appeals against determinations by adjudicators

4C Provision about the making and determining of appeals to the court against a determination by an adjudicator, including provision–

(a) enabling the court to make a bankruptcy order on such an appeal, and

(b) about where such appeals lie.

Notices etc.

5 Provision requiring notice of any proceedings under Parts 7A to 11 of this Act or of any matter relating to or arising out of a proposal under Part VIII or a bankruptcy to be given or published in the prescribed manner.

6 Provision with respect to the form, manner of serving, contents and proof of any petition, application, order, notice, statement or other document required to be presented, made, given, published or prepared under any enactment contained in Parts 7A to 11 or subordinate legislation under those Parts or Part XV (including provision requiring prescribed matters to be verified by affidavit).

7 Provision specifying the persons to whom any notice under Parts VIII to XI is to be given.

7A Provision for enabling a creditor of an individual to elect to be, or to cease to be, an opted-out creditor in relation to an office-holder for the individual (within the meaning of section 383A), including, in particular, provision–

(a) for requiring an office holder to provide information to creditors about how they may elect to be, or cease to be, opted-out creditors;

(b) for deeming an election to be, or cease to be, an opted-out creditor in relation to a particular office-holder for an individual to be such an election also in relation to any other office-holder for the individual.

Debt relief orders

7A Provision as to the manner in which the official receiver is to carry out his functions under Part 7A.

7B Provision as to the manner in which any requirement that may be imposed by the official receiver on a person under Part 7A is to take effect.

7C Provision modifying the application of Part 7A in relation to an individual who has died at a time when a moratorium period under a debt relief order applies in relation to him.

Debt relief restrictions orders and undertakings

7D Provision about debt relief restrictions orders, interim orders and undertakings, including provision about evidence.

Register of debt relief orders and debt relief restrictions orders etc

7E Provision about the register required to be maintained by section 251W and the information to be contained in it, including provision–

(a) enabling the amalgamation of the register with another register;

(b) enabling inspection of the register by the public.

Registration of Voluntary Arrangements

8 Provision for the registration of voluntary arrangements approved under Part VIII of this Act, including provision for the keeping and inspection of a register.

Official Receiver Acting on Voluntary Arrangement

8A Provision about the official receiver acting as nominee or supervisor in relation to a voluntary arrangement under Part VIII of this Act, including–

(a) provision requiring the official receiver to act in specified circumstances;

(b) provision about remuneration;

(c) provision prescribing terms or conditions to be treated as forming part of a voluntary arrangement in relation to which the official receiver acts as nominee or supervisor;

(d) provision enabling those terms or conditions to be varied or excluded, in specified circumstances or subject to specified conditions, by express provision in an arrangement.

Interim Receiver

9 Provision as to the manner in which an interim receiver appointed under section 286 is to carry out his functions, including any such provision as is specified in relation to the trustee of a bankrupt's estate in paragraph 21 or 27 below.

Receiver or Manager

10 [Omitted]

11 Provision with respect to the certification of the appointment of any person as trustee of a bankrupt's estate and as to the proof of that appointment.

11A(1) Provision about the making of decisions by creditors, including provision–

(a) prescribing particular procedures by which creditors may make decisions;

(b) authorising the use of other procedures for creditors to make decisions, if those procedures comply with prescribed requirements.

11A(2) Provision under sub-paragraph (1) may in particular include provision about–

(a) how creditors may request that a creditors' meeting be held,

(b) the rights of creditors and others to be given notice of, and participate in, procedures,

(c) creditors' rights to vote in procedures,

(d) the period within which any right to participate or vote is to be exercised,

(e) the proportion of creditors that must vote for a proposal for it to be approved,

(f) how the value of any debt should be determined,

(g) the time at which decisions taken by a procedure are to be treated as having been made.

12 The following provision with respect to meetings of creditors–

(a) provision as to the manner of summoning a meeting (including provision as to how any power to require a meeting is to be exercised, provision as to the manner of determining the value of any debt for the purposes of any such power and provision making the exercise of any such power subject to the deposit of a sum sufficient to cover the expenses likely to be incurred in summoning and holding a meeting);

(b) provision specifying the time and place at which a meeting may be held and the period of notice required for a meeting;

(c) provision as to the procedure to be followed at such a meeting (including the manner in which decisions may be reached by a meeting and the manner in which the value of any vote at a meeting is to be determined);

(d) provision for requiring a bankrupt or debtor to attend a meeting;

(e) provision creating, in the prescribed circumstances, a presumption that a meeting has been duly summoned and held; and

(f) provision as to the manner of proving the decisions of a meeting.

12A Provision about how a bankrupt's creditors may appoint a person as trustee.

13 Provision as to the establishment, functions, membership and proceedings of a creditors' committee provided for by section 301.

14 Provision as to the manner in which any requirement that may be imposed on a person under Parts VIII to XI of this Act by the official receiver, the trustee of a bankrupt's estate or a special manager appointed under section 370 is to be so imposed and, in the case of any requirement imposed under section 305(3) (information etc. to be given by the trustee to the official receiver), provision conferring power on the court to make orders for the purpose of securing compliance with that requirement.

15 Provision as to the manner in which any requirement imposed by virtue of section 310(3) (compliance with income payments order) is to take effect.

16 Provision as to the terms and conditions that may be included in a charge under section 313 (dwelling house forming part of bankrupt's estate).

17 Provision as to the debts that may be proved in any bankruptcy, as to the manner and conditions of proving a debt and as to the manner and expenses of establishing the value of any debt or security.

18 Provision with respect to the manner of the distribution of a bankrupt's estate, including provision with respect to unclaimed funds and dividends.

18A Provision for a creditor who has not proved a small debt to be treated as having done so for purposes relating to the distribution of a bankrupt's estate (and for provisions of, or contained in legislation made under, this Act to apply accordingly).

"Small debt" means a bankruptcy debt not exceeding an amount prescribed by the rules.

19 Provision modifying the application of Parts VIII to XI of this Act in relation to a debtor or bankrupt who has died.

Financial Provisions

20 Provision as to the amount, or manner of determining the amount, payable to an interim receiver, the trustee of a bankrupt's estate or a special manager appointed under section 370 by way of remuneration for the performance of functions in connection with or arising out of the bankruptcy of any person.

21 Provision with respect to the manner in which moneys received by the trustee of a bankrupt's estate in the course of carrying out his functions as such are to be invested or otherwise handled and with respect to the payment of interest on sums which, in pursuance of rules made by virtue of this paragraph, have been paid into the Insolvency Services Account.

21A Provision enabling the Secretary of State to set the rate of interest paid on sums which have been paid into the Insolvency Services Account.

22 Provision as to the fees, costs, charges and other expenses that may be treated as the expenses of a bankruptcy.

23 Provision as to the fees, costs, charges and other expenses that may be incurred for any of the purposes of Part VIII of this Act or in the administration of any voluntary arrangement approved under that Part.

Information and Records

24 Provision requiring registrars and other officers of courts having jurisdiction for the purposes of Parts VIII to XI–

(a) to keep books and other records with respect to the exercise of that jurisdiction, and

(b) to make returns to the Secretary of State of the business of those courts.

24A Provision requiring adjudicators–

(a) to keep files and other records relating to bankruptcy applications and bankruptcies resulting from bankruptcy applications,

(b) to make files and records available for inspection by persons of a prescribed description, and

(c) to provide files and records, or copies of them, to persons of a prescribed description.

24B Provision requiring an adjudicator to make returns to the Secretary of State of the adjudicator's business under Part 9 of this Act.

24C Provision requiring official receivers–

(a) to keep files and other records relating to bankruptcy applications and bankruptcies resulting from bankruptcy applications, and

(b) to make files and records available for inspection by persons of a prescribed description.

24D Provision requiring a person to whom notice is given under section 293(2), 295(3), 298(7) or (8) or section 299(1)(a) or (3)(a)–

(a) to keep files and other records of notices given under the section in question, and

(b) to make files and records available for inspection by persons of a prescribed description.

25 Provision requiring a creditor or a committee established under section 301 to be supplied (on payment in prescribed cases of the prescribed fee) with such information and with copies of such documents as may be prescribed.

26 Provision as to the manner in which public examinations under section 290 and proceedings under sections 366 to 368 are to be conducted, as to the circumstances in which records of such examinations and proceedings are to be made available to prescribed persons and as to the costs of such examinations and proceedings.

27 Provision imposing requirements with respect to–

(a) the preparation and keeping by the trustee of a bankrupt's estate, or the supervisor of a voluntary arrangement approved under Part VIII, of prescribed books, accounts and other records;

(b) the production of those books, accounts and records for inspection by prescribed persons; and

(c) the auditing of accounts kept by the trustee of a bankrupt's estate or the supervisor of such a voluntary arrangement.

28 Provision requiring the person who is the supervisor of a voluntary arrangement approved under Part VIII, when it appears to him that the voluntary arrangement has been fully implemented and that nothing remains to be done by him under it–

(a) to give notice of that fact to persons bound by the voluntary arrangement, and

(b) to report to those persons on the carrying out of the functions conferred on the supervisor of it.

29 Provision as to the manner in which the trustee of a bankrupt's estate is to act in relation to the books, papers and other records of the bankrupt, including provision authorising their disposal.

Bankruptcy Restrictions Orders and Undertakings

29A Provision about bankruptcy restrictions orders, interim orders and undertakings, including–

(a) provision about evidence;

(b) provision enabling the amalgamation of the register mentioned in paragraph 12 of Schedule 4A with another register;

(c) provision enabling inspection of that register by the public.

General

30 Provision conferring power on the Secretary of State to make regulations with respect to so much of any matter that may be provided for in the rules as relates to the carrying out of the functions of an interim receiver appointed under section 286 or of a trustee of a bankrupt's estate.

31 Provision conferring a discretion on the court.

32 Provision making non-compliance with any of the rules a criminal offence.

33 Provision making different provision for different cases, including different provision for different areas.

General Note to Sch.9

This provides a useful guide to the matters which may be provided for by the rules. Authority to make these rules is given by s.412, and the note on that section should be referred to. Paragraphs 8A and 29A were inserted by EA 2002 s.269 and Sch.23 to deal with the advent of fast-track IVAs and BROs. The utility of para.17 was illustrated in *Woodley v Woodley (No.2)* [1994] 1 W.L.R. 1167. For the regulations referred to in para.30 see the Insolvency Regulations 1994 (SI 1994/2507), operative 24 October 1994, replacing the original Insolvency Regulations 1986 (SI 1986/1994), as amended.

Note amendments made by Sch.9 of the Crime and Courts Act 2013 reflecting general reforms to the county court system.

In para.21 the words "invested or otherwise handled and with respect to the payment of interest on sums which, in pursuance of rules made by virtue of this paragraph, have been paid into the Insolvency Services Account" substituted for the word "handled" by the Insolvency Act 2000 (s.13(1) as from 2 April 2001 (see SI 2001/766 (C. 27) arts 1, 2(1)(b)). See note to s.406.

Note amendment of various paras in Sch.9 by para.14 of Pt 1 of Sch.20 to the Tribunals, Courts and Enforcement Act 2007. Paragraphs 7A to 7E have been inserted.

Amended by DA 2015 s.19 and Sch.6. Further amendments are made by ERRA 2013 Sch.19 para.65. These include the insertion of new paras 4A, 4B, 4C, and 24A–24D. Paragraph 18A was inserted in pursuance of SBEEA 2015 s.132.

SBEEA 2015 s.126 and Sch.9 paras 86 and 87 made further changes to this Schedule. In addition amendments are made by SBEEA 2015 s.133 and Sch.10 paras 10 and 11 from 6 April 2017. Note further amendments made by SBEEA 2015 s.123. These changes include the insertion of new paras 7A, 11A and 12A.

We now appear to have two different paras 7A.

Paragraph 2 amended by the Alteration of Judicial Titles (Registrar in Bankruptcy of the High Court) Order 2018 (SI 2018/130) arts 1, 3 Sch. para.7(c) as from 26 February 2018.

Schedule 10

Punishment of Offences under this Act

Section 430

Note: In the fourth and fifth columns of this Schedule, "the statutory maximum" means–

(a) in England and Wales, the prescribed sum under section 32 of the Magistrates' Courts Act 1980 (c. 43), and

(b) in Scotland, the prescribed sum under section 289B of the Criminal Procedure (Scotland) Act 1975 (c. 21).

Section of Act creating offence	General nature of offence	Mode of prosecution	Punishment	Daily default fine (where applicable)
6A(1)	False representation or fraud for purpose of obtaining members' or creditors' approval of proposed voluntary arrangement.	1. On indictment. 2. Summary.	7 years or a fine, or both. 6 months or the statutory maximum, or both.	
12(2)	Company and others failing to state in correspondence etc. that administrator appointed.	Summary.	One-fifth of the statutory maximum.	
15(8)	Failure of administrator to register office copy of court order permitting disposal of charged property.	Summary.	One-fifth of the statutory maximum.	One-fiftieth of the statutory maximum.
18(5)	Failure of administrator to register office copy of court order varying or discharging administration order.	Summary.	One-fifth of the statutory maximum.	One-fiftieth of the statutory maximum.
21(3)	Administrator failing to register administration order and give notice of appointment.	Summary.	One-fifth of the statutory maximum.	One-fiftieth of the statutory maximum.
22(6)	Failure to comply with provisions relating to statement of affairs, where administrator appointed.	1. On indictment. 2. Summary.	A fine. The statutory maximum.	One-tenth of the statutory maximum.
23(3)	Administrator failing to send out, register and lay before creditors statement of his proposals.	Summary.	One-fifth of the statutory maximum.	One-fiftieth of the statutory maximum.
24(7)	Administrator failing to file court order discharging administration order under s.24.	Summary.	One-fifth of the statutory maximum.	One-fiftieth of the statutory maximum.
27(6)	Administrator failing to file court order discharging administration order under s.27.	Summary.	One-fifth of the statutory maximum.	One-fiftieth of the statutory maximum.
30	Body corporate acting as receiver.	1. On indictment. 2. Summary.	A fine. The statutory maximum.	
31	Bankrupt or person in respect of whom a debt relief order is made acting as receiver or manager.	1. On indictment. 2. Summary.	2 years or a fine, or both. 6 months or the statutory maximum, or both.	
38(5)	Receiver failing to deliver accounts to registrar.	Summary.	One-fifth of the statutory maximum.	One-fiftieth of the statutory maximum.
39(2)	Company and others failing to state in correspondence that receiver appointed.	Summary.	One-fifth of the statutory maximum.	
43(6)	Administrative receiver failing to file copy of order permitting disposal of charged property.	Summary.	One-fifth of the statutory maximum.	One-fiftieth of the statutory maximum.
45(5)	Administrative receiver failing to file notice of vacation of office.	Summary.	One-fifth of the statutory maximum.	One-fiftieth of the statutory maximum.

Section of Act creating offence	General nature of offence	Mode of prosecution	Punishment	Daily default fine (where applicable)
46(4)......................	Administrative receiver failing to give notice of his appointment.	Summary.	One-fifth of the statutory maximum.	One-fiftieth of the statutory maximum.
47(6)......................	Failure to comply with provisions relating to statement of affairs where administrative receiver appointed.	1. On indictment. 2. Summary.	A fine. The statutory maximum.	One-tenth of the statutory maximum.
48(8)......................	Administrative receiver failing to comply with requirements as to his report.	Summary.	One-fifth of the statutory maximum.	One-fiftieth of the statutory maximum.
51(4)......................	Body corporate or Scottish firm acting as receiver.	1. On indictment. 2. Summary.	A fine. The statutory maximum.	
51(5)......................	Undischarged bankrupt acting as receiver (Scotland).	1. On indictment. 2. Summary.	2 years or a fine, or both. 6 months or the statutory maximum, or both.	
53(2)......................	Failing to deliver to registrar copy of instrument of appointment of receiver	Summary.	One-fifth of the statutory maximum.	One-fiftieth of the statutory maximum.
54(3)......................	Failing to deliver to registrar the court's interlocutor appointing receiver.	Summary.	One-fifth of the statutory maximum.	One-fiftieth of the statutory maximum.
61(7)......................	Receiver failing to send to registrar certified copy of court order authorising disposal of charged property.	Summary.	One-fifth of the statutory maximum.	One-fiftieth of the statutory maximum.
62(5)......................	Failing to give notice to registrar of cessation or removal of receiver.	Summary.	One-fifth of the statutory maximum.	One-fiftieth of the statutory maximum.
64(2)......................	Company and others failing to state on correspondence etc. that receiver appointed.	Summary.	One-fifth of the statutory maximum.	
65(4)......................	Receiver failing to send or publish notice of his appointment.	Summary.	One-fifth of the statutory maximum.	One-fiftieth of the statutory maximum.
66(6)......................	Failing to comply with provisions concerning statement of affairs where receiver appointed.	1. On indictment. 2. Summary.	A fine. The statutory maximum.	One-tenth of the statutory maximum.
67(8)......................	Receiver failing to comply with requirements as to his report.	Summary.	One-fifth of the statutory maximum.	One-fiftieth of the statutory maximum.
85(2)......................	Company failing to give notice in Gazette of resolution for voluntary winding up.	Summary.	One-fifth of the statutory maximum.	One-fiftieth of the statutory maximum.
89(4)......................	Director making statutory declaration of company's solvency without reasonable grounds for his opinion.	1. On indictment. 2. Summary.	2 years or a fine, or both. 6 months or the statutory maximum, or both.	

Section of Act creating offence	General nature of offence	Mode of prosecution	Punishment	Daily default fine (where applicable)
89(6)	Declaration under section 89 not delivered to registrar within prescribed time.	Summary.	One-fifth of the statutory maximum.	One-fiftieth of the statutory maximum.
92A(2)	Liquidator failing to send progress report to members.	Summary.	Level 3 on the standard scale.	
93(3)	Liquidator failing to summon general meeting of company at each year's end.	Summary.	One-fifth of the statutory maximum.	
94(4)	Liquidator failing to send to company members a copy of account of winding up.	Summary.	Level 3 on the standard scale.	
94(5)	Liquidator failing to send to registrar a copy of account of winding up.	Summary.	Level 3 on the standard scale.	One tenth of level 3 on the standard scale.
95(8)	Liquidator failing to comply with s.95(1) to (4A), where company insolvent.	Summary.	The statutory maximum.	
99(3)	Directors failing to send statement in prescribed form to creditors.	1. On indictment. 2. Summary.	A fine. The statutory maximum.	
104A(2)	Liquidator failing to send progress report to members and creditors.	Summary.	Level 3 on the standard scale.	
105(3)	Liquidator failing to summon company general meeting and creditors' meeting at each year's end.	Summary.	One-fifth of the statutory maximum.	
106(5)	Liquidator failing to send to company members and creditors a copy of account of winding up.	Summary.	Level 3 on the standard scale.	
106(6)	Liquidator failing to send to registrar a copy of account of winding up.	Summary.	Level 3 on the standard scale.	One tenth of level 3 on the standard scale.
109(2)	Liquidator failing to publish notice of his appointment.	Summary.	One-fifth of the statutory maximum.	One-fiftieth of the statutory maximum.
114(4)	Directors exercising powers in breach of s.114, where no liquidator.	Summary.	The statutory maximum.	
131(7)	Failing to comply with requirements as to statement of affairs, where liquidator appointed.	1. On indictment. 2. Summary.	A fine. The statutory maximum.	One-tenth of the statutory maximum.
164	Giving, offering etc. corrupt inducement affecting appointment of liquidator.	1. On indictment. 2. Summary.	A fine. The statutory maximum.	
166(7)	Liquidator failing to comply with requirements of s.166 in creditors' voluntary winding up.	Summary.	The statutory maximum.	
188(2)	Default in compliance with s.188 as to notification that company being wound up.	Summary.	One-fifth of the statutory maximum.	

Section of Act creating offence	General nature of offence	Mode of prosecution	Punishment	Daily default fine (where applicable)
192(2)	Liquidator failing to notify registrar as to progress of winding up.	Summary.	One-fifth of the statutory maximum.	One-fiftieth of the statutory maximum.
201(4)	Failing to deliver to registrar copy of court order deferring dissolution.	Summary.	One-fifth of the statutory maximum.	One-fiftieth of the statutory maximum.
203(6)	Failing to deliver to registrar copy of directions or result of appeal under s.203.	Summary.	One-fifth of the statutory maximum.	One-fiftieth of the statutory maximum.
204(7)	Liquidator failing to deliver to registrar copy of court order for early dissolution.	Summary.	One-fifth of the statutory maximum.	One-fiftieth of the statutory maximum.
204(8)	Failing to deliver to registrar copy of court order deferring early dissolution.	Summary.	One-fifth of the statutory maximum.	One-fiftieth of the statutory maximum.
205(7)	Failing to deliver to registrar copy of Secretary of State's directions or court order deferring dissolution.	Summary.	One-fifth of the statutory maximum.	One-fiftieth of the statutory maximum.
206(1)	Fraud etc. in anticipation of winding up.	1. On indictment. 2. Summary.	7 years or a fine, or both. 6 months or the statutory maximum, or both.	
206(2)	Privity to fraud in anticipation of winding up; fraud or privity to fraud, after commencement of winding up.	1. On indictment. 2. Summary.	7 years or a fine, or both. 6 months or the statutory maximum, or both.	
206(5)	Knowingly taking in pawn or pledge, or otherwise receiving, company property.	1. On indictment. 2. Summary.	7 years or a fine, or both. 6 months or the statutory maximum, or both.	
207	Officer of company entering into transaction in fraud of company's creditors.	1. On indictment. 2. Summary.	2 years or a fine, or both. 6 months or the statutory maximum, or both.	
208	Officer of company misconducting himself in course of winding up.	1. On indictment. 2. Summary.	7 years or a fine, or both. 6 months or the statutory maximum, or both.	
209	Officer or contributory destroying, falsifying, etc. company's books.	1. On indictment. 2. Summary.	7 years or a fine, or both. 6 months or the statutory maximum, or both.	
210	Officer of company making material omission from statement relating to company's affairs.	1. On indictment. 2. Summary.	7 years or a fine, or both. 6 months or the statutory maximum, or both.	

Section of Act creating offence	General nature of offence	Mode of prosecution	Punishment	Daily default fine (where applicable)
211..........................	False representation or fraud for purpose of obtaining creditors' consent to an agreement in connection with winding up.	1. On indictment. 2. Summary.	7 years or a fine, or both. 6 months or the statutory maximum, or both.	
216(4).....................	Contravening restrictions on re-use of name of company in insolvent liquidation.	1. On indictment. 2. Summary.	2 years or a fine, or both. 6 months or the statutory maximum, or both.	
235(5).....................	Failing to co-operate with office-holder.	1. On indictment. 2. Summary.	A fine. The statutory maximum.	One-tenth of the statutory maximum.
251O(1)..................	False representations or omissions in making an application for a debt relief order.	1. On indictment 2. Summary	7 years or a fine, or both. 12 months or the statutory maximum, or both.	
251O(2)(a).............	Failing to comply with duty in connection with an application for a debt relief order.	1. On indictment 2. Summary	2 years or a fine, or both. 12 months or the statutory maximum, or both.	
251O(2)(b)	False representations or omissions in connection with duty in relation to an application for a debt relief order.	1. On indictment 2. Summary	7 years or a fine, or both. 12 months or the statutory maximum, or both.	
251O(4)(a).............	Failing to comply with duty in connection with a debt relief order.	1. On indictment 2. Summary	2 years or a fine, or both. 12 months or the statutory maximum, or both.	
251O(4)(b)	False representations or omissions in connection with a duty in relation to a debt relief order.	1. On indictment 2. Summary	7 years or a fine, or both. 12 months or the statutory maximum, or both.	
251P(1)..................	Failing to deliver books, records and papers to official receiver, concealing or destroying them or making false entries in them by person in respect of whom a debt relief order is made.	1. On indictment 2. Summary	7 years or a fine, or both. 12 months or the statutory maximum, or both.	
251P(2)..................	Person in respect of whom debt relief order is made doing anything falling within paragraphs (c) to (e) of section 251P(1) during the period of 12 months ending with the application date or doing anything falling within paragraphs (b) to (e) of section 251P(1) after that date but before the effective date.	1. On indictment 2. Summary	7 years or a fine, or both. 12 months or the statutory maximum, or both.	
251Q(1).................	Fraudulent disposal of property by person in respect of whom a debt relief order is made.	1. On indictment 2. Summary	2 years or a fine, or both. 12 months or the statutory maximum, or both.	

Section of Act creating offence	General nature of offence	Mode of prosecution	Punishment	Daily default fine (where applicable)
251R(1)	Disposal of property that is not paid for by person in respect of whom a debt relief order is made.	1. On indictment 2. Summary	7 years or a fine, or both. 12 months or the statutory maximum, or both.	
251R(2)	Obtaining property in respect of which money is owed by a person in respect of whom a debt relief order is made.	1. On indictment 2. Summary	7 years or a fine, or both. 12 months or the statutory maximum, or both.	
251S(1)..................	Person in respect of whom a debt relief order is made obtaining credit or engaging in business without disclosing his status or name.	1. On indictment 2. Summary	2 years or a fine, or both. 12 months or the statutory maximum, or both.	
262A(1).................	False representation or fraud for purpose of obtaining creditors' approval of proposed voluntary arrangement.	1. On indictment. 2. Summary.	7 years or a fine, or both. 6 months or the statutory maximum, or both.	
263O......................	False representations or omissions in connection with a bankruptcy application.	1. On indictment 2. Summary	1. 7 years or a fine, or both. 2. 12 months or the statutory maximum, or both.	
353(1)....................	Bankrupt failing to disclose property or disposals to official receiver or trustee.	1. On indictment. 2. Summary.	7 years or a fine, or both. 6 months or the statutory maximum, or both.	
354(1)....................	Bankrupt failing to deliver property to, or concealing property from, official receiver or trustee.	1. On indictment. 2. Summary.	7 years or a fine, or both. 6 months or the statutory maximum, or both.	
354(2)....................	Bankrupt removing property which he is required to deliver to official receiver or trustee.	1. On indictment. 2. Summary.	7 years or a fine, or both. 6 months or the statutory maximum, or both.	
354(3)....................	Bankrupt failing to account for loss of substantial part of property.	1. On indictment. 2. Summary.	2 years or a fine, or both. 6 months or the statutory maximum, or both.	
355(1)....................	Bankrupt failing to deliver books, papers and records to official receiver or trustee.	1. On indictment. 2. Summary.	7 years or a fine, or both. 6 months or the statutory maximum, or both.	
355(2)....................	Bankrupt concealing, destroying etc. books, papers or records, or making false entries in them.	1. On indictment. 2. Summary.	7 years or a fine, or both. 6 months or the statutory maximum, or both.	
355(3)....................	Bankrupt disposing of, or altering, books, papers or records relating to his estate or affairs.	1. On indictment. 2. Summary.	7 years or a fine, or both. 6 months or the statutory maximum, or both.	

Section of Act creating offence	General nature of offence	Mode of prosecution	Punishment	Daily default fine (where applicable)
356(1)	Bankrupt making material omission in statement relating to his affairs.	1. On indictment. 2. Summary.	7 years or a fine, or both. 6 months or the statutory maximum, or both.	
356(2)	Bankrupt making false statement, or failing to inform trustee, where false debt proved.	1. On indictment. 2. Summary.	7 years or a fine, or both. 6 months or the statutory maximum, or both.	
357	Bankrupt fraudulently disposing of property.	1. On indictment. 2. Summary.	2 years or a fine, or both. 6 months or the statutory maximum, or both.	
358	Bankrupt absconding with property he is required to deliver to official receiver or trustee.	1. On indictment. 2. Summary.	2 years or a fine, or both. 6 months or the statutory maximum, or both.	
359(1)	Bankrupt disposing of property obtained on credit and not paid for.	1. On indictment. 2. Summary.	7 years or a fine, or both. 6 months or the statutory maximum, or both.	
359(2)	Obtaining property in respect of which money is owed by a bankrupt.	1. On indictment. 2. Summary.	7 years or a fine, or both. 6 months or the statutory maximum, or both.	
360(1)	Bankrupt obtaining credit or engaging in business without disclosing his status or name in which he was made bankrupt.	1. On indictment. 2. Summary.	2 years or a fine, or both. 6 months or the statutory maximum, or both.	
360(3)	Person made bankrupt in Scotland or Northern Ireland obtaining credit, etc. in England and Wales.	1. On indictment. 2. Summary.	2 years or a fine, or both. 6 months or the statutory maximum, or both.	
389	Acting as insolvency practitioner when not qualified.	1. On indictment. 2. Summary.	2 years or a fine, or both. 6 months or the statutory maximum, or both.	
429(5)	Contravening s.429 in respect of disabilities imposed by county court on revocation of administration order.	1. On indictment. 2. Summary.	2 years or a fine, or both. 6 months or the statutory maximum, or both.	
Sch.A1, para.9(2)	Directors failing to notify nominee of beginning of moratorium.	1. On indictment. 2. Summary.	2 years or a fine, or both. 6 months or the statutory maximum, or both.	
Sch.A1, para.10(3)	Nominee failing to advertise or notify beginning of moratorium.	Summary.	One-fifth of the statutory maximum.	
Sch.A1, para.11(2)	Nominee failing to advertise or notify end of moratorium.	Summary.	One-fifth of the statutory maximum.	

Section of Act creating offence	General nature of offence	Mode of prosecution	Punishment	Daily default fine (where applicable)
Sch.A1, para.16(2)	Company and officers failing to state in correspondence etc. that moratorium in force.	Summary.	One-fifth of the statutory maximum.	
Sch.A1, para.17(3)(a)..........	Company obtaining credit without disclosing existence of moratorium.	1. On indictment. 2. Summary.	A fine. The statutory maximum.	
Sch.A1, para.17(3)(b)	Obtaining credit for company without disclosing existence of moratorium.	1. On indictment. 2. Summary.	2 years or a fine, or both. 6 months or the statutory maximum, or both.	
Sch.A1, para.18(3)(a)..........	Company disposing of property otherwise than in ordinary way of business.	1. On indictment. 2. Summary.	A fine. The statutory maximum.	
Sch.A1, para.18(3)(b)	Authorising or permitting disposal of company property.	1. On indictment. 2. Summary.	2 years or a fine, or both. 6 months or the statutory maximum, or both.	
Sch.A1, para.19(3)(a)..........	Company making payments in respect of liabilities existing before beginning of moratorium.	1. On indictment. 2. Summary.	A fine. The statutory maximum.	
Sch.A1, para.19(3)(b)	Authorising or permitting such a payment.	1. On indictment. 2. Summary.	2 years or a fine, or both. 6 months or the statutory maximum, or both.	
Sch.A1, para.20(9)	Directors failing to send to registrar copy of court order permitting disposal of charged property.	Summary.	One-fifth of the statutory maximum.	
Sch.A1, para.22(1)	Company disposing of charged property.	1. On indictment. 2. Summary.	A fine. The statutory maximum.	
Sch.A1, para.22(2)	Authorising or permitting such a disposal.	1. On indictment. 2. Summary.	2 years or a fine, or both. 6 months or the statutory maximum, or both.	
Sch.A1, para.23(1)(a)..........	Company entering into market contract, etc.	1. On indictment. 2. Summary.	A fine. The statutory maximum.	
Sch.A1, para.23(1)(b)	Authorising or permitting company to do so.	1. On indictment. 2. Summary.	2 years or a fine, or both. 6 months or the statutory maximum, or both.	
Sch.A1, para.25(6)	Nominee failing to give notice of withdrawal of consent to act.	Summary.	One-fifth of the statutory maximum.	
Sch.A1, para.34(3)	Nominee failing to give notice of extension of moratorium.	Summary.	One-fifth of the statutory maximum.	
Sch.A1, para.41(2)	Fraud or privity to fraud in anticipation of moratorium.	1. On indictment. 2. Summary.	7 years or a fine, or both. 6 months or the statutory maximum, or both.	

Section of Act creating offence	General nature of offence	Mode of prosecution	Punishment	Daily default fine (where applicable)
Sch.A1, para.41(3)	Fraud or privity to fraud during moratorium.	1. On indictment. 2. Summary.	7 years or a fine, or both. 6 months or the statutory maximum, or both.	
Sch.A1, para.41(7)	Knowingly taking in pawn or pledge, or otherwise receiving, company property.	1. On indictment. 2. Summary.	7 years or a fine, or both. 6 months or the statutory maximum, or both.	
Sch.A1, para.42(1)	False representation or fraud for purpose of obtaining or extending moratorium.	1. On indictment. 2. Summary.	7 years or a fine, or both. 6 months or the statutory maximum, or both.	
Sch.B1, para.18(7)	Making false statement in statutory declaration where administrator appointed by holder of floating charge.	1. On indictment. 2. Summary.	2 years, or a fine or both. 6 months, or the statutory maximum or both.	
Sch.B1, para.20....................	Holder of floating charge failing to notify administrator or others of commencement of appointment.	1. On indictment. 2. Summary.	2 years, or a fine or both. 6 months, or the statutory maximum or both.	One-tenth of the statutory maximum.
Sch.B1, para.27(4)	Making false statement in statutory declaration where appointment of administrator proposed by company or directors.	1. On indictment. 2. Summary.	2 years, or a fine or both. 6 months, or the statutory maximum or both.	
Sch.B1, para.29(7)	Making false statement in statutory declaration where administrator appointed by company or directors.	1. On indictment. 2. Summary.	2 years, or a fine or both. 6 months, or the statutory maximum or both.	
Sch.B1, para.32....................	Company or directors failing to notify administrator or others of commencement of appointment.	1. On indictment. 2. Summary.	2 years, or a fine or both. 6 months, or the statutory maximum or both.	One-tenth of the statutory maximum.
Sch.B1, para.45(2)	Administrator, company or officer failing to state in business document that administrator appointed.	Summary.	One-fifth of the statutory maximum.	
Sch.B1, para.46(9)	Administrator failing to give notice of his appointment.	Summary.	One-fifth of the statutory maximum.	One-fiftieth of the statutory maximum.
Sch.B1, para.48(4)	Failing to comply with provisions about statement of affairs where administrator appointed.	1. On indictment. 2. Summary.	A fine. The statutory maximum.	One-tenth of the statutory maximum.
Sch.B1, para.49(7)	Administrator failing to send out statement of his proposals.	Summary.	One-fifth of the statutory maximum.	One-fiftieth of the statutory maximum.
Sch.B1, para.51(5)	Administrator failing to seek creditors' decision.	Summary.	One-fifth of the statutory maximum.	One-fiftieth of the statutory maximum.

Section of Act creating offence	General nature of offence	Mode of prosecution	Punishment	Daily default fine (where applicable)
Sch.B1, para.53(3)	Administrator failing to report decision taken by creditors.	Summary.	One-fifth of the statutory maximum.	One-fiftieth of the statutory maximum.
Sch.B1, para.54(7)	Administrator failing to report creditors' decision on revised proposal.	Summary.	One-fifth of the statutory maximum.	One-fiftieth of the statutory maximum.
Sch.B1, para.56(2)	Administrator failing to seek creditors' decision.	Summary.	One-fifth of the statutory maximum.	One-fiftieth of the statutory maximum.
Sch.B1, para.71(6)	Administrator failing to file court order enabling disposal of charged property.	Summary.	One-fifth of the statutory maximum.	One-fiftieth of the statutory maximum.
Sch.B1, para.72(5)	Administrator failing to file court order enabling disposal of hire-purchase property.	Summary.	One-fifth of the statutory maximum.	One-fiftieth of the statutory maximum.
Sch.B1, para.77(3)	Administrator failing to notify Registrar of Companies of automatic end of administration.	Summary.	One-fifth of the statutory maximum.	One-fiftieth of the statutory maximum.
Sch.B1, para.78(6)	Administrator failing to give notice of extension by consent of term of office.	Summary.	One-fifth of the statutory maximum.	One-fiftieth of the statutory maximum.
Sch.B1, para.80(6)	Administrator failing to give notice of termination of administration where objective achieved.	Summary.	One-fifth of the statutory maximum.	One-fiftieth of the statutory maximum.
Sch.B1, para.84(9)	Administrator failing to comply with provisions where company moves to dissolution.	Summary.	One-fifth of the statutory maximum.	One-fiftieth of the statutory maximum.
Sch.B1, para.86(3)	Administrator failing to notify Registrar of Companies where court terminates administration.	Summary.	One-fifth of the statutory maximum.	One-fiftieth of the statutory maximum.
Sch.B1, para.89(3)	Administrator failing to give notice on ceasing to be qualified.	Summary.	One-fifth of the statutory maximum.	One-fiftieth of the statutory maximum.

GENERAL NOTE

This technique of using a Schedule of punishments is used by CA 1985 and CA 2006, but not by IA 1985. Guidance on the use of Sch.10 is provided by s.430. Sections 431 and 432 are also of assistance when applying Sch.10.

The "statutory maximum" referred to in the introductory note to the Schedule and in cols 4 and 5 is at present £5,000 (but £2,000 in respect of offences committed before 1 October 1992): see CJA 1991 s.17 and SI 1992/333, SI 1993/2118. In the application of those entries in relation to offences committed before the commencement of s.154(1) of the CJA 2003 (C. 44) (limit on magistrates' court powers to impose imprisonment), the references in the fourth column to "12 months" are to be read as references to "6 months".

Schedule 10 was substantially modified by IA 2000 and EA 2002 Sch.17.

Note amendments by para.15 of Pt 1 of Sch.20 to the Tribunals, Courts and Enforcement Act 2007. Note amendments made by LRO 2010 (SI 2010/18).

An amendment is made by ERRA 2013 Sch.19 para.66 by inserting a sanction for breach of s.263O. For offences under this provision committed before the entry into force of CJA 2003 s.154 the maximum is six months.

The entry for Sch.7 para.4(3) was removed by DA 2015 Sch.6 para.22. Further numerous amendments were made to this Schedule by SBEEA 2015 Sch.9.

SCHEDULE 11

TRANSITIONAL PROVISIONS AND SAVINGS

SCHEDULE 12

ENACTMENTS REPEALED

SCHEDULE 13

CONSEQUENTIAL AMENDMENTS OF COMPANIES ACT 1985

SCHEDULE 14

CONSEQUENTIAL AMENDMENTS OF OTHER ENACTMENTS

[Schedules 11–14 have not been reproduced in the present edition of the *Guide*. The full text may be found in *British Companies Legislation*, pp.56,601 et seq., or in the official version of IA 1986 published by The Stationery Office.

Editors' note: Changes are made to Sch.14 by DA 2015 in the wake of the demise of deeds of arrangement.]

Insolvency (England and Wales) Rules 2016

(SI 2016/1024)

These Rules were finally published on 25 October 2016, having been scrutinised by the Insolvency Rules Committee. We have been waiting for these Rules (hereafter "the 2016 Rules" or "IR 2016") for more than a decade—see Bailey (2013) 343 Co. L.N. 1 for background to the history and policy underpinning this elephantine gestation. They entirely replace the Insolvency Rules 1986 (SI 1986/1925), which had been amended on at least 28 occasions—see Sch.1 to the 2016 Rules for the full list of amendment rules. They thus represent a fresh start in some respects, particularly so as they embody a number of reforms to the Insolvency Act 1986 generated by the Small Business, Enterprise and Employment Act 2015 which also take final effect on 6 April 2017. Modern linguistics are employed to give the terminology a contemporary feel. That said, in many respects they merely consolidate and reorder the latest version of the 1986 Rules. This reality is reflected in the fact that the Insolvency Service has produced Tables of Destination and Derivation (which we have reproduced in Appendix I and II of this *Guide*). So we have to analyse a mixture of the old and the new.

As their full title suggests, these 2016 Rules are not applicable in Scotland or in Northern Ireland. The Scots will have their own upgraded Rules shortly, and a similar solution will presumably be applied to Northern Ireland. The non-application of the 1986 Rules to Scotland was confirmed in *Secretary of State for Trade and Industry v Frid* [2004] UKHL 24; [2004] 2 A.C. 506; [2004] B.C.C. 525 at [31].

On the basis of *St John Poulton's Trustee in Bankruptcy v Ministry of Justice* [2010] EWCA Civ 392; [2011] Ch. 1 it would seem that the 2016 Rules will not be capable of generating a private law claim for breach of statutory duty as no common law claim for breach of the Rules is recognised.

Taking an overview of the 2016 Rules *two* features stand out. Firstly, the introduction of the so-called "common Parts". This methodology makes sense in that it does avoid the duplication of similar Rules across different insolvency procedures. But in some respects it does mean that a practitioner will no longer find the Parts as self-contained as they were previously, and some lateral research will be required to find the solution to a legal question. It remains to be seen whether this will cause problems for practitioners. Secondly, the 2016 Rules were meant to signal a move away from the use of prescribed Forms and instead provide more required information detail in the Rules themselves. But that break with formality has been less than complete. Companies House has issued its own prescribed Forms for a number of situations and some "templates" particularly relevant to the activities of the Official Receiver have been produced by the Insolvency Service. HM Courts and Tribunal Service has also provided a number of court forms for use in insolvency proceedings. See Appendix VII for a list of these forms and templates.

The 2016 Rules are generally prospective in effect, with 6 April 2017 being the key operational date. The 1986 Rules continue to apply to some extant insolvency procedures (particularly with regard to meetings) and ongoing legal proceedings—see Sch.2 to the 2016 Rules for a detailed explanation of the transitional complexities. The 19th edition of this *Guide* therefore retains some value during the transition.

Some changes to the Rules were made at the operational date of 6 April 2017. This was particularly so as several of the Rules had attracted Parliamentary criticism—see Joint Committee on Statutory Instruments, 16th Report of Session 2016/17, HL Paper 80, HC 93-xvi. The text of the legislation below contains the amendments introduced via the Insolvency (England and Wales) (Amendment) Rules 2017 (SI 2017/366) and also operational as from 6 April 2017, together with those from a correction slip. For further analysis of the 2016 Rules see Jones and Black [2016] 9 CRI 221. There is also a brief but useful Explanatory Memorandum to the Rules themselves produced by the Insolvency Service.

Another important point concerning the 2016 Rules lies in the fact that they operate to supplement other secondary insolvency legislation that has been upgraded some time since the operational date—such as the Administration of Insolvent Estates of Deceased Persons Order 1986 (SI 1986/1999), the Insolvent Partnerships Order 1994 (SI 1994/2421) and the Limited Liability Partnerships Regulations 2001 (SI 2001/1090) (and see below).

Over the course of 2017, a number of refinements have been made to the matrix of provisions contained in IR 2016. For a detailed summary see Bailey [2018] 31 Insolv. Int. 7 and also the overview by Milman [2018] 31 Insolv. Int. 30.

Looking at the more important measures, firstly, there have been a number of tidying up measures. These are to be found in the Insolvency (England and Wales) and Insolvency (Scotland) (Miscellaneous and Consequential Amendments) Rules 2017 (SI 2017/1115).

Secondly, the 2016 Rules (and primary legislation) have had to take account of the arrival of the EU Recast Insolvency Regulation (2015/848). Consequential changes are thus made by the Insolvency Amendment (EU 2015/848) Regulations 2017 (SI 2017/702).

Finally, the 2016 Rules did not extend to insolvent partnerships, insolvent LLPs or deceased insolvents. The necessary modified provisions have now been provided by the Insolvency (Miscellaneous Amendment) Regulations 2017 (SI 2017/1119).

The Insolvency Service in November 2016 set up a Blog for technical comments on the 2016 Rules. The Rules are required to be reviewed within five years of the commencement date of 6 April 2017 (see IR 2016 r.7). The Explanatory Memorandum para.3.1 mentions as an innovation of the 2016 Rules the use of non-legislative notes intended to assist users of the Rules: they are contained in square brackets and labelled "[Note]". These occur in the text of the Rules themselves and should not be confused with our annotations at the end of a note or a series of notes, or the bold sub-rule square bracket headings that we have inserted at the beginning of each sub-rule to assist in identification of the meaning of that sub-rule as part of the value-added process of the *Guide*.

Insolvency (England and Wales) Rules 2016

(SI 2016/1024)

Made on 18 October 2016 by the Lord Chancellor under ss.411 and 412 of the Insolvency Act 1986, after consultation with the Insolvency Rules Committee under s.413 of the Act, with the concurrence of the Chancellor of the High Court (by authority of the Lord Chief Justice under ss.411(7) and 412(6) of the Act) and with the concurrence of the Secretary of State. Laid before Parliament on 25 October 2016. Operative from 6 April 2017.

[**Note:** These Rules are amended by the Insolvency (England and Wales) (Amendment) Rules 2017 (SI 2017/366) as from 6 April 2017, the Insolvency Amendment (EU 2015/848) Regulations 2017 (SI 2017/702) as from 26 June 2017 and the Insolvency (England and Wales) and Insolvency (Scotland) (Miscellaneous and Consequential Amendments) Rules 2017 (SI 2017/1115) as from 8 December 2017.]

Contents

CHAPTER 6

STATEMENT OF AFFAIRS

CHAPTER 7

ADMINISTRATOR'S PROPOSALS

CHAPTER 8

LIMITED DISCLOSURE OF STATEMENTS OF AFFAIRS AND PROPOSALS

CHAPTER 9

DISPOSAL OF CHARGED PROPERTY

CHAPTER 10

EXPENSES OF THE ADMINISTRATION

CHAPTER 11

EXTENSION AND ENDING OF ADMINISTRATION

CHAPTER 12

REPLACING THE ADMINISTRATOR

PART 4

RECEIVERSHIP

CHAPTER 1

APPOINTMENT OF JOINT RECEIVERS OR MANAGERS TO WHOM PART 3 OF THE ACT APPLIES (OTHER THAN THOSE APPOINTED UNDER SECTION 51 (SCOTTISH RECEIVERSHIPS))

CHAPTER 2

ADMINISTRATIVE RECEIVERS (OTHER THAN IN SCOTTISH RECEIVERSHIPS)

PART 22

PERMISSION TO ACT AS DIRECTOR ETC. OF COMPANY WITH A PROHIBITED NAME (SECTION 216)

SCHEDULES

Introductory Rules

Introductory note to Introductory Rules

These rules deal with preliminary matters. In particular r.4 deals with the question of transitional issues, the details of which are fleshed out in some detail in Sch.2. We are informed by R3 that IR 2016 only apply in England and Wales. Although these IR 2016 represent the main form of secondary legislation, the Secretary of State retains a power to make regulations (r.5). Indeed, it is clear by process of elimination from Sch.1 that numerous pre-2016 Regulations remain in place. Rule 7 requires the Secretary of State to review these Rules within five years. That said, we may expect amendments on an annual basis in much the same way as operated with IR 1986.

1 Citation and commencement

1 These Rules may be cited as the Insolvency (England and Wales) Rules 2016 and come into force on 6th April 2017.

General Note

This rule shows a different nomenclature to the "Insolvency Rules 1986".

In relation to the commencement date, see r.4 and Sch.2 for transitional and savings provisions.

2 Revocations

2 The Rules listed in Schedule 1 are revoked.

General Note

IR 1986 and all the amendment rules thereto are revoked.

3 Extent and application

3(1) [England and Wales] These Rules extend to England and Wales only.

3(2) [Application to CVA, administration, winding up] These Rules as they relate to company voluntary arrangements under Part 1 of the Act, administration under Part 2 of the Act and winding up under Parts 4 and 5 of the Act apply in relation to companies which the courts in England and Wales have jurisdiction to wind up.

3(3) [No application to Scottish receivership] These Rules do not apply to receivers appointed under section 51 (Scottish receivership).

General Note

Corresponding subordinate legislation has been enacted for Scotland, principally by the Insolvency (Scotland) Rules 1986 (SI 1986/1915 (S 139)) (as amended) which are expected to be replaced, possibly in October 2017. Interestingly, there is no mention in r.3 of personal insolvency, presumably as the Scottish equivalent is not contained in the Insolvency (Scotland) Rules 1986 and so there is no confusion between the two sets of rules in this regard.

For the position in Northern Ireland see the Insolvency Rules (Northern Ireland) 1991 (SR 1991/364), (as amended) and the note to IA 1986 s.441.

4 Transitional and savings provisions

4 The transitional and savings provisions set out in Schedule 2 have effect.

General Note

See Sch.2.

5 Power of the Secretary of State to regulate certain matters

5(1) [Regulations in relation to functions of specified office-holders] Under paragraph 27 of Schedule 8 and paragraph 30 of Schedule 9 to the Act, the Secretary of State may, subject to the Act and the Rules made under it, make regulations with respect to any matter provided for in the Rules relating to the carrying out of the functions of–

(a) a liquidator, provisional liquidator, administrator or administrative receiver of a company;

(b) an interim receiver appointed under section 286; and

(c) a trustee of a bankrupt's estate.

5(2) [Specific matters re winding up and bankruptcy] The regulations that may be made may include, without prejudice to the generality of paragraph (1), provision with respect to the following matters arising in companies winding up and individual bankruptcy–

(a) the preparation and keeping by liquidators, trustees, provisional liquidators, interim receivers and the official receiver, of books, accounts and other records, and their production to such persons as may be authorised or required to inspect them;

(b) the auditing of liquidators' and trustees' accounts;

(c) the manner in which liquidators and trustees are to act in relation to the insolvent company's or bankrupt's books, papers and other records, and the manner of their disposal by the responsible office-holder or others;

(d) the supply of copies of documents relating to the insolvency and the affairs of the insolvent company or individual (on payment, in such cases as may be specified by the regulations, of the specified fee)–

  (i) by the liquidator in company insolvency to creditors and members of the company, contributories in its winding up and the liquidation committee; and

  (ii) by the trustee in bankruptcy to creditors and the creditors' committee;

(e) the manner in which insolvent estates are to be distributed by liquidators and trustees, including provision with respect to unclaimed funds and dividends;

(f) the manner in which moneys coming into the hands of a liquidator or trustee in the course of the administration of the proceedings are to be handled and invested, and the payment of interest on sums which have been paid into the Insolvency Services Account under regulations made by virtue of this sub-paragraph;

(g) the amount (or the manner of determining the amount) to be paid to the official receiver as remuneration when acting as provisional liquidator, liquidator, interim receiver or trustee.

5(3) [Other aspects of regulations] Regulations made under this rule may–

(a) confer a discretion on the court;

(b) make non-compliance with any of the regulations a criminal offence;

(c) make different provision for different cases, including different provision for different areas; and

(d) contain such incidental, supplemental and transitional provisions as may appear to the Secretary of State necessary or expedient.

General Note

This clarifies the power of the Secretary of State to make regulations to supplement the existing framework.

It seems that r.5(1) does not authorise regulations to be made with regard to nominees and supervisors of voluntary arrangements as they are not specifically mentioned therein—for background on this lacuna in relation to the predecessor provision see R3 Technical Bulletin 73.2.

6 Punishment of offences

6 Schedule 3 sets out the punishments for certain contraventions of these Rules.

General Note

Unlike its predecessor, r.6 does not attempt to explain the fairly self-explanatory nature of Sch.3.
Note s.431 on summary proceedings.

7 Review

7(1) [Report by Secretary of State] The Secretary of State must from time to time–

(a) carry out a review of these Rules;

(b) set out the conclusions of the review in a report; and

(c) publish the report.

7(2) [Contents of report]The report must in particular–

(a) set out the objectives intended to be achieved by the regulatory system established by these Rules;

(b) assess the extent to which those objectives are achieved; and

(c) assess whether those objectives remain appropriate and, if so, the extent to which they could be achieved with a system that imposes less regulation.

7(3) [First report within five years of commencement] The first report under this rule must be published before the end of the period of five years beginning with the day on which these Rules come into force.

7(4) [Succeeding reports within five-year intervals] Reports under this rule are afterwards to be published at intervals not exceeding five years.

General Note

This rule had no counterpart in IR 1986 but follows a modern legislative drafting practice for extensive legislation.

Part 1

Scope, Interpretation, Time and Rules about Documents

Chapter 1

Scope of these Rules

1.1 Scope

1.1(1) [IA 1986 Pts 1–11, EU Regulation] These Rules are made to give effect to Parts 1 to 11 of the Insolvency Act 1986 and to the EU Regulation.

1.1(2) [References to insolvency proceedings] Consequently references to insolvency proceedings and requirements relating to such proceedings are, unless the context requires otherwise, limited to proceedings in respect of Parts 1 to 11 of the Act and the EU Regulation (whether or not court proceedings).

General Note

Recast EU Regulation 2015/848 as from 26 June 2017 replaced EC Regulation 1346/2000.

See *Jyske Bank (Gibraltar) Ltd v Spjeldnaes* [2000] B.C.C. 16—s.423 proceedings not insolvency proceedings. See also *Fourie v Le Roux* [2004] EWHC 2557 (Ch); [2005] B.P.I.R. 779 which proceeds along the same line of thought. See the note to r.12.64. Some discussion of what might amount to "insolvency proceedings" is to be found in *Pickard v Roberts* [2016] EWHC 187 (Ch) at [37].

Rule 1(1), (2) amended by the Insolvency (England and Wales) and Insolvency (Scotland) (Miscellaneous and Consequential Amendments) Rules 2017 (SI 2017/1115) rr.1(1), (2), 22, 23(1) as from 8 December 2017.

Chapter 2

Interpretation

[Note: the terms which are defined in rule 1.2 include some terms defined by the Act for limited purposes which are applied generally by these Rules. Such terms have the meaning given by the Act for those limited purposes.]

1.2 Defined terms

1.2(1) [Reference to Part, Schedule] In these Rules, unless otherwise stated, a reference to a Part or a Schedule is to a Part of, or Schedule to, these Rules.

1.2(2) [Definitions] In these Rules–

"the Act" means the Insolvency Act 1986, and–

(a) a reference to a numbered section without mention of another Act is to that section of the Act; and

(b) a reference to Schedule A1, B1, 4ZA, 4ZB or 4A is to that Schedule to the Act;

"appointed person" means a person as described in paragraph (3) who is appointed by an office-holder (other than the official receiver);

"Article 1.2 undertaking" means one of the following within the meaning of Article 1.2 of Regulation (EU) 2015/848 of the European Parliament and of the Council ("the EU Regulation")–

(a) an insurance undertaking;

(b) a credit institution;

(c) an investment undertaking which provides services involving the holding of funds or securities for third parties;

(d) a collective investment undertaking;

[Note: "associate" is defined by section 435];

"attendance" and "attend" a person attends, or is in attendance at, a meeting who is present or attends remotely in accordance with section 246A or rule 15.6, or who participates in a virtual meeting, whether that person attends the meeting or virtual meeting in person, by proxy, or by corporate representative (in accordance with section 434B or section 323 of the Companies Act, as applicable);

"authenticate" means to authenticate in accordance with rule 1.5;

"authorised deposit-taker" means a person with permission under Part 4A of the Financial Services and Markets Act 2000 to accept deposits; this definition must be read with–

(a) section 22 of that Act and any relevant order under that section; and

(b) Schedule 2 to that Act;

[Note: "bankrupt's estate" is defined in section 283];

"bankruptcy application" means the bankruptcy application submitted by the debtor to the adjudicator requesting the making of a bankruptcy order against the debtor;

"bankruptcy file" means the file opened by the adjudicator in accordance with rule 10.47;

"bankruptcy restrictions register" means the register referred to in rule 11.13(2) of matters relating to bankruptcy restrictions orders, interim bankruptcy restrictions orders and bankruptcy restrictions undertakings;

"business day" means, for the purposes of these Rules as they relate to Parts 7A to 10 of the Act (insolvency of individuals; bankruptcy), any day other than a Saturday, a Sunday, Christmas Day, Good Friday or a day which is a bank holiday in England and Wales [Note: for the purposes of these Rules as they relate to Parts 1 to 7 of the Act (company insolvency; company winding up) section 251 defines "business day" as including additionally a day which is a bank holiday in Scotland];

"centre of main interests" has the same meaning as in the EU Regulation;

"certificate of service" means a certificate of service which complies with the requirements in Schedule 4;

"Companies Act" means the Companies Act 2006;

[Note: the term "connected" used of a person in relation to a company is defined in section 249 of the Act];

"consumer" means an individual acting for purposes that are wholly or mainly outside that individual's trade, business, craft or profession;

[Note: "contributory" is defined by section 79];

"convener" means an office-holder or other person who seeks a decision in accordance with Part 15 of these Rules;

[Note: "the court" is defined by section 251 for the purposes of these Rules as they relate to Parts 1 to 7 of the Act (company insolvency; company winding up) and by section 385(1) for the purposes of these Rules as they relate to Parts 7A to 10 of the Act (insolvency of individuals; bankruptcy);

"CPR" means the Civil Procedure Rules 1998;

"credit reference agency" means a person authorised or permitted by the Financial Conduct Authority to carry on the regulated activity of providing credit references;

"CVA" means a voluntary arrangement in relation to a company under Part 1 of the Act;

"debt" is defined in rule 14.1(3) for the purposes of administration and winding up and "small debt" is also defined in rule 14.1(3) for administration, winding up and bankruptcy [Note: debt is defined in section 385(1) for the purposes of these Rules as they relate to Parts 7A to 10 of the Act (insolvency of individuals; bankruptcy)];

"debt relief restrictions register" means the register referred to in rule 11.13(2) of matters relating to debt relief restrictions orders and debt relief restrictions undertakings;

"decision date" and "decision procedure" are to be interpreted in accordance with rule 15.2 and Part 15;

"decision procedure" means a decision procedure prescribed by rule 15.3;

[Note: "deemed consent procedure" is defined in section 246ZF for corporate insolvency and 379ZB for individual insolvency; rule 15.7 makes further provision about deemed consent];

"deliver" and "delivery" are to be interpreted in accordance with Chapter 9 of Part 1;

"deliver to the creditors" and similar expressions in these Rules and the Act are to be interpreted in accordance with rule 1.37;

[Note: "distress" is defined in section 436 as including the procedure in Schedule 12 to the Tribunals, Courts and Enforcement Act 2007 (c.15), and references to levying distress, seizing goods and related expressions are to be construed accordingly];

"document" includes a written notice or statement or anything else in writing capable of being delivered to a recipient;

[Note: EU Regulation is defined for the purposes of these Rules by section 436 of the Act as Regulation (EU) 2015/848 of the European Parliament and of the Council.]

"enforcement agent" means a person authorised by section 63(2) of the Tribunals, Courts and Enforcement Act 2007 to act as an enforcement agent;

"enforcement officer" means an individual who is authorised to act as an enforcement officer under the Courts Act 2003(b);

"fees estimate" means a written estimate that specifies–

(a) details of the work the insolvency practitioner ("the IP") and the IP's staff propose to undertake;

(b) the hourly rate or rates the IP and the IP's staff propose to charge for each part of that work;

(c) the time the IP anticipates each part of that work will take;

(d) whether the IP anticipates it will be necessary to seek approval or further approval under Chapter 4 of Part 18; and

(e) the reasons it will be necessary to seek such approval under these Rules;

"file with the court" and similar expressions in these Rules means deliver to the court for filing and such references are to be read as including "submit" and "submission" to the court in the Act (except in sections 236 and 366);

"the Gazette", which has the meaning given in section 251 for the purposes of these Rules as they relate to Parts 1 to 7 of the Act (company insolvency; company winding up), has that meaning for the purposes of these Rules as they relate to Parts 7A to 10 of the Act;

"Gazette notice" means a notice which is, has been or is to be gazetted; "to gazette" means to advertise once in the Gazette;

"general regulations" means regulations made by the Secretary of State under introductory rule 5;

"hearing centre" means a hearing centre of the County Court;

[Note: "Hire purchase agreement" is defined by section 436(1) as having the same meaning as in the Consumer Credit Act 1974 for the purposes of the Act and by paragraph 1 of Schedule A1 (company voluntary arrangement) for the purposes of that Schedule and by paragraph 111(1) of Schedule B1 (administration) for the purposes of that Schedule];

"identification details" and similar references to information identifying persons, proceedings, etc. are to be interpreted in accordance with rule 1.6;

"individual insolvency register" means the register referred to in rule 11.13(1) of matters relating to bankruptcies, debt relief orders and IVAs;

"individual register" has the meaning given by rule 217(1) of the Land Registration Rules 2003;

"insolvent estate" means–

(a) in relation to a company insolvency, the company's assets;

(b) in relation to a bankruptcy, a petition or an application for bankruptcy, the bankrupt's estate (as defined in section 283);

(c) or otherwise the debtor's property;

"IP number" means the number assigned to an office-holder as an insolvency practitioner by the Secretary of State;

"IVA" means a voluntary arrangement in relation to an individual under Part 8 of the Act;

"judge" includes an Insolvency and Companies Court Judge unless the context otherwise requires;

"London Insolvency District" has the meaning given by section 374 of the Act and the London Insolvency District (County Court at Central London) Order 2014;

"main proceedings" means proceedings opened in accordance with Article 3(1) of the EU Regulation and falling within the definition of insolvency proceedings in Article 2(4) of the EU Regulation and which–

(a) in relation to England and Wales, are set out in Annex A to that Regulation under the heading "United Kingdom"; and

(b) in relation to another member State, are set out under the heading relating to that member State;

"meeting" in relation to a person's creditors or contributories means either a "physical meeting" or a "virtual meeting" as defined in rule 15.2, unless the contrary intention is given;

"member State liquidator" means a person falling within the definition of "insolvency practitioner" in Article 2(5) of the EU Regulation appointed in proceedings to which the EU Regulation applies in a member State other than the United Kingdom;

"nominated person" means a person who has been required under section 47 or 131 to make out and submit a statement as to the affairs of a company in administrative receivership or being wound up by the court;

[Note: "nominee" is defined in section 1(2) in relation to company voluntary arrangements and section 253(2) in relation to individual voluntary arrangements];

"non-EU proceedings" means insolvency proceedings which are not main, secondary or territorial proceedings;

"office-holder" means a person who under the Act or these Rules holds an office in relation to insolvency proceedings and includes a nominee;

"permission" of the court is to be read as including "leave of the court" in the Act and in the Company Directors' Disqualification Act 1986;

"petitioner" or "petitioning creditor" includes a person who has been substituted as such or has been given carriage of the petition;

"physical meeting" means a meeting as described in section 246ZE(9) or 379ZA(9);

"Practice Direction" means a direction as to the practice and procedure of a court within the scope of the CPR;

"prescribed order of priority" means the order of priority of payments of expenses set out in–

(a) Chapter 10 of Part 3 for administration proceedings;

(b) Chapter 6 of Part 6 for creditors' voluntary winding up proceedings;

(c) Chapter 14 of Part 7 for winding up by the court proceedings; and

(d) Chapter 18 of Part 10 for bankruptcy proceedings;

"prescribed part" has the same meaning as in section 176A(2)(a) and the Insolvency Act 1986 (Prescribed Part) Order 2003;

"progress report" means a report which complies with Chapter 2 of Part 18;

[Note: "property" is defined by section 436(1) of the Act];

"prove" and "proof" have the following meaning–

(a) a creditor who claims for a debt in writing is referred to as proving that debt;

(b) the document by which the creditor makes the claim is referred to as that creditor's proof; and

(c) for the purpose of voting, or objecting to a deemed consent, in an administration, an administrative receivership, a creditors' voluntary winding up, a CVA or an IVA, the requirements for a proof are satisfied by the convener or chair having been notified by the creditor in writing of a debt;

"proxy" and "blank proxy" are to be interpreted in accordance with Part 16;

"qualified to act as an insolvency practitioner" in relation to a company, debtor or bankrupt has the meaning given by section 390 of the Act;

[Note: "records" are defined in section 436(1) of the Act]

"registered land" has the meaning given by section 132(1) of the Land Registration Act 2002;

"registrar" means an Insolvency and Companies Court Judge and unless the context requires otherwise includes a District Judge–

(a) in a District Registry of the High Court; and

(b) in a hearing centre with relevant insolvency jurisdiction;

"residential address" means the current residential address of an individual or, if that is not known, the last known residential address;

"secondary proceedings" means proceedings opened in accordance with Articles 3(2) and 3(3) of the EU Regulation and falling within the definition of winding-up proceedings in Article 2(4) of that Regulation and which–

(a) in relation to England and Wales, are set out in Annex A to that Regulation under the heading "United Kingdom";

(b) and in relation to another member State are set out under the heading relating to that member State;

"serve" and "service" are to be interpreted in respect of a particular document by reference to Schedule 4;

"solicitor" means a solicitor of the Senior Courts and, in relation to England and Wales, includes any other person who, for the purpose of the Legal Services Act 2007 is an authorised person in relation to an activity which constitutes the conduct of litigation (within the meaning of that Act);

"standard contents" means–

(a) for a Gazette notice, the standard contents set out in Chapter 4 of this Part;

(b) for a notice to be advertised other than in the Gazette, the standard contents set out in Chapter 5 of Part 1;

(c) for a document to be delivered to the registrar of companies, the standard contents set out in Chapter 6 of Part 1;

(d) for notices to be delivered to other persons, the standard contents set out in Chapter 7 of Part 1;

(e) for applications to the court the standard contents set out in Chapter 8 of Part 1;

"standard fee for copies" means 15 pence per A4 or A5 page or 30 pence per A3 page;

"statement of proposals" means a statement made by an administrator under paragraph 49 of Schedule B1 setting out proposals for achieving the purpose of an administration;

"statement of truth" means a statement of truth made in accordance with Part 22 of the CPR;

"temporary administrator" means a temporary administrator referred to in Article 52 of the EU Regulation;

"territorial proceedings" means proceedings opened in accordance with Articles 3(2) and (4) of the EU Regulation and falling within the definition of insolvency proceedings in Article 2(4) of that Regulation and which–

(a) in relation to England and Wales, are set out in Annex A to the EU Regulation under the heading "United Kingdom"; and

(b) in relation to another member State, are set out under the heading relating to that member State;

"trustee" has the same meaning throughout these Rules as they relate to the insolvency of individuals as it has for bankruptcy in section 385(1)(f);

"venue" in relation to any proceedings, attendance before the court, decision procedure or meeting means the time, date and place or platform for the proceedings, attendance, decision procedure or meeting;

"virtual meeting" has the meaning given by rule 15.2(2);

"winding up by the court" means a winding up under section 122(1), 124A or 221;

"witness statement" means a witness statement verified by a statement of truth made in accordance with Part 32 of the CPR;

[Note: "writing": section 436B(1) of the Act provides that a reference to a thing in writing includes that thing in electronic form; subsection (2) excludes certain documents from the application of subsection (1); and

"written resolution" in respect of a private company refers to a written resolution passed in accordance with Chapter 2 of Part 13 of the Companies Act].

1.2(3) **[Appointed person]** An appointed person in relation to a company, debtor or bankrupt must be–

(a) qualified to act as an insolvency practitioner in relation to that company, debtor or bankrupt; or

(b) a person experienced in insolvency matters who is–

(i) a member or employee of the office-holder's firm, or

(ii) an employee of the office-holder.

1.2(4) **[Fee or remuneration]** A fee or remuneration is charged when the work to which it relates is done.

General Note

This interpretation rule should be viewed in the light of IA 1986 interpretation provisions, especially ss.247–251, 380–385, and 435–436: many of these IA 1986 provisions are referred to in the official square bracketed [Notes] to r.1.2(2). The list is not exhaustive and some terms are defined in their relevant Part (e.g. "nominee", "supervisor" and "proposal" in relation to company voluntary arrangements are defined in r.2.1). There is some duplication, especially with definitions for Pt 15, but "qualifying decision procedure" is not included here (see note to r.15.1).

On "file with the court" (or "file in court") see *Re Blights Builders Ltd* [2006] EWHC 3549 (Ch); [2007] B.C.C. 712. Following an Electronic Working Pilot Scheme from November 2015, the use of the electronic filing system

"CE-File" is mandatory from 25 April 2017 for insolvency proceedings in the courts in the Rolls Building in London (where the Bankruptcy Court and Companies Court sit). A practice direction to succeed PD 51O on the Electronic Working Pilot Scheme is anticipated.

On service of documents see Sch.4.

The definitions of "main proceedings", "secondary proceedings" and "territorial proceedings" substituted, and the definitions of "Article 1.2 undertaking", "member State liquidator" and "non-EU proceedings" amended by the Insolvency Amendment (EU 2015/848) Regulations 2017 (SI 2017/702) regs 1, 2(1), Sch. paras 32, 33 in relation to proceedings opened on or after 26 June 2017 (see reg.3) when the Recast EU Regulation 2015/848 came into force.

The definitions of "centre of main interests" and "temporary administrator" amended by the Insolvency (England and Wales) and Insolvency (Scotland) (Miscellaneous and Consequential Amendments) Rules 2017 (SI 2017/1115) rr.1(1), (2), 22, 23(2), 24 as from 8 December 2017.

The definitions of "judge" and "registrar" amended by the Alteration of Judicial Titles (Registrar in Bankruptcy of the High Court) Order 2018 (SI 2018/130) arts 1, 3 Sch. para.14(a)(i) as from 26 February 2018.

1.3 Calculation of time periods

1.3 The rules set out in Schedule 5 apply to the calculation of the beginning and end of time periods under these Rules.

General Note

See Sch.5 which applies CPR r.2.8. On the power of extension of time periods in personal insolvency see IA 1986 s.376.

Chapter 3

Form and content of documents

1.4 Requirement for writing and form of documents

1.4(1) [Requirement for writing] A notice or statement must be in writing unless the Act or these Rules provide otherwise.

1.4(2) [Electronic form] A document in electronic form must be capable of being–

(a) read by the recipient in electronic form; and

(b) reproduced by the recipient in hard-copy form.

General Note

This deals with format issues. Legibility is the critical requirement.

1.5 Authentication

1.5(1) [Electronic form] A document in electronic form is sufficiently authenticated–

(a) if the identity of the sender is confirmed in a manner specified by the recipient; or

(b) where the recipient has not so specified, if the communication contains or is accompanied by a statement of the identity of the sender and the recipient has no reason to doubt the truth of that statement.

1.5(2) [Hard-copy form] A document in hard-copy form is sufficiently authenticated if it is signed.

1.5(3) [Signature by representative] If a document is authenticated by the signature of an individual on behalf of–

(a) a body of persons, the document must also state the position of that individual in relation to the body;

(b) a body corporate of which the individual is the sole member, the document must also state that fact.

General Note

This rule covers modes of authentication. In the modern age, electronic authentication is vital.

1.6 Information required to identify persons and proceedings etc.

1.6(1) [Identification information] Where the Act or these Rules require a document to identify, or to contain identification details in respect of, a person or proceedings, or to provide contact details for an office-holder, the information set out in the table must be given.

1.6(2) [Information re office-holder] Where a requirement relates to a proposed office-holder, the information set out in the table in respect of an office-holder must be given with any necessary adaptations.

Bankrupt	(a) full name; and (b) residential address (subject to any order for limited disclosure made under Part 20).
Company where it is the subject of the proceedings	In the case of a registered company– (c) the registered name; (d) for a company incorporated in England and Wales under the Companies Act or a previous Companies Act, its registered number; (e) for a company incorporated outside the United Kingdom– (i) the country or territory in which it is incorporated, (ii) the number, if any, under which it is registered, and (iii) the number, if any, under which it is registered as an overseas company under Part 34 of the Companies Act. In the case of an unregistered company– (f) its name; and (g) the postal address of any principal place of business.
Company other than one which is the subject of the proceedings	In the case of a registered company– (h) the registered name; (i) for a company incorporated in any part of the United Kingdom under the Companies Act or a previous Companies Act, its registered number; (j) for a company incorporated outside the United Kingdom– (i) the country or territory in which it is incorporated,

Debtor	(m) full name; and (ii) the number, if any, under which it is registered; and (k) the number, if any, under which it is registered as an overseas company under Part 34 of the Companies Act; (l) In the case of an unregistered company– (i) its name, and (ii) the postal address of any principal place of business. (n) residential address (subject to any order for limited disclosure made under Part 20).
Office-holder	(o) the name of the office-holder; and (p) the nature of the appointment held by the office-holder.
Contact details for an office-holder	(q) a postal address for the office-holder; and (r) either an email address, or a telephone number, through which the office-holder may be contacted.
Proceedings	(s) for proceedings relating to a company, the information identifying the company; (t) for proceedings relating to an individual, the full name of the bankrupt or debtor; (u) the full name of the court or hearing centre in which the proceedings are, or are to be, conducted or where documents relating to the proceedings have been or will be filed; and, if applicable, (v) any number assigned to those proceedings by the court, the hearing centre or the adjudicator.

General Note

This rule had no counterpart in IR 1986 but it is innovative and user-friendly.

1.7 Reasons for stating that proceedings are or will be main, secondary etc. under the EU Regulation

1.7 Where these Rules require reasons to be given for a statement that proceedings are or will be main, secondary or territorial or non-EU proceedings, the reasons must include–

(a) for a company–

(i) the centre of main interests,

(ii) the place of the registered office within the meaning of Article 3(1) of the EU Regulation and where appropriate an explanation why this is not the same as the centre of main interests, or

(iii) that there is no registered office if that be the case in non-EU proceedings;

(b) for a debtor, the centre of main interests.

General Note

EC Regulation 1346/2000 was replaced by Recast EU Regulation 2015/848 as from 26 June 2017 and art.3(1) of the Recast Regulation applied to international jurisdiction and COMI.

Title to r.1.7 and r.1.7(a)(ii) amended, and opening words to r.1.7 and r.1.7(a)(iii) amended, by the Insolvency (England and Wales) and Insolvency (Scotland) (Miscellaneous and Consequential Amendments) Rules 2017 (SI 2017/1115) rr.1(1), (2), 22, 23(3), (4), and 30(1), (2), as from 8 December 2017.

1.8 Prescribed format of documents

1.8(1) [Title] Where a rule sets out requirements as to the contents of a document any title required by the rule must appear at the beginning of the document.

1.8(2) [Other contents in order] Any other contents required by the rule (or rules where more than one apply to a particular document) must be provided in the order listed in the rule (or rules) or in another order which the maker of the document considers would be convenient for the intended recipient.

General Note

This rule should help in the light of the absence of prescribed forms in IR 2016 now that only content is prescribed.

1.9 Variations from prescribed contents

1.9(1) [Conditions for departure] Where a rule sets out the required contents of a document, the document may depart from the required contents if–

(a) the circumstances require such a departure (including where the requirement is not applicable in the particular case); or

(b) the departure (whether or not intentional) is immaterial.

1.9(2) [No departure in statutory demand] However this rule does not apply to the required content of a statutory demand on a company set out in rule 7.3 and on an individual set out in rule 10.1.

General Note

Some variations seem inevitable and it is to be hoped that the new system does not cause chaos. Note the sensible standardisation for statutory demands, which feature in insolvency litigation so much.

Chapter 4

Standard contents of Gazette notices and the Gazette as evidence etc.

[Note: (1) the requirements in Chapter 4 must be read with rule 1.6 which sets out the information required to identify an office-holder, a company etc.]

(2) this Chapter does not apply to the notice of a liquidator's appointment prescribed under section 109 by SI 1987/752.]

1.10 Contents of notices to be gazetted under the Act or Rules

1.10(1) [Standard contents] Where the Act or these Rules require or permit a notice to be gazetted, the notice must also contain the standard contents set out in this Chapter in addition to any content specifically required by the Act or any other provision of these Rules.

1.10(2) [Omission of information] Information which this Chapter requires to be included in a Gazette notice may be omitted if it is not reasonably practicable to obtain it.

(See General Note after r.1.14.)

1.11 Standard contents of all notices

1.11(1) [Identification of proceedings, office-holder] A notice must identify the proceedings, if it is relevant to the particular notice, identify the office-holder and state–

(a) the office-holder's contact details;

(b) the office-holder's IP number (except for the official receiver);

(c) the name of any person other than the office-holder who may be contacted about the proceedings; and

(d) the date of the office-holder's appointment.

1.11(2) [Non-application of rule] This rule does not apply to a notice under rule 22.4(3) (Permission to act as a director: first excepted case).

(See General Note after r.1.14.)

1.12 Gazette notices relating to a company

1.12(1) [Information relating to registered company] A notice relating to a registered company must also state–

(a) its registered office;

(b) any principal trading address if this is different from its registered office;

(c) any name under which it was registered in the period of 12 months before the date of the commencement of the proceedings which are the subject of the Gazette notice; and

(d) any other name or style (not being a registered name)–

(i) under which the company carried on business, and

(ii) in which any debt owed to a creditor was incurred.

1.12(2) [Information relating to unregistered company] A notice relating to an unregistered company must also identify the company and specify any name or style–

(a) under which the company carried on business; and

(b) in which any debt owed to a creditor was incurred.

(See General Note after r.1.14.)

1.13 Gazette notices relating to a bankruptcy

1.13 A notice relating to a bankruptcy must also identify the bankrupt and state–

(a) any other address at which the bankrupt has resided in the period of 12 months before the making of the bankruptcy order;

(b) any principal trading address if different from the bankrupt's residential address;

(c) the bankrupt's date of birth;

(d) the bankrupt's occupation;

(e) any other name by which the bankrupt has been known; and

(f) any name or style (other than the bankrupt's own name) under which–

(i) the bankrupt carried on business, and

(ii) any debt owed to a creditor was incurred.

(See General Note after r.1.14.)

1.14 The Gazette: evidence, variations and errors

1.14(1) [Evidence of facts in notice] A copy of the Gazette containing a notice required or permitted by the Act or these Rules to be gazetted is evidence of any facts stated in the notice.

1.14(2) [Conclusive evidence of notice of date of court order] Where the Act or these Rules require an order of the court or of the adjudicator to be gazetted, a copy of the Gazette containing the notice may be produced in any proceedings as conclusive evidence that the order was made on the date specified in the notice.

1.14(3) [Variation of court order to be gazetted] Where an order of the court or of the adjudicator which is gazetted has been varied, or any matter has been erroneously or inaccurately gazetted, the person whose responsibility it was to gazette the order or other matter must as soon as is reasonably practicable cause the variation to be gazetted or a further entry to be made in the Gazette for the purpose of correcting the error or inaccuracy.

General Note to rr.1.10–1.14

These rules dictate the standard content of notices required or permitted in the *Gazette* under IA 1986 or IR 2016, with differentiation between all notices and those for corporate insolvency and for bankruptcy. Note the additional identification requirements in r.1.6 and the caveat that the rules do not apply to the notice of appointment of a liquidator in voluntary winding up under IA 1986 s.109 as per the Companies (Forms) (Amendment) Regulations 1987 (SI 1987/752) reg.5(3) which prescribed Form 600 and 600a: Companies House is to continue use of Form 600.

Note the relaxation to omit information if it is not reasonably practicable to obtain it (r.1.10(2)).

Rule 1.14 explains the significance of the *Gazette*, and in particular issues of evidential status.

Chapter 5

Standard contents of notices advertised otherwise than in the Gazette

[Note: the requirements in Chapter 5 must be read with rule 1.6 which sets out the information required to identify an office-holder, a company etc.]

1.15 Standard contents of notices advertised otherwise than in the Gazette

1.15(1) [Standard content of notice] Where the Act or these Rules provide that a notice may be advertised otherwise than in the Gazette the notice must contain the standard contents set out in this Chapter (in addition to any content specifically required by the Act or any other provision of these Rules).

1.15(2) [Notice to identify office-holder] A notice must, if it is relevant to the particular notice, identify the office-holder and specify the office-holder's contact details.

1.15(3) [Omission of information] Information which this Chapter requires to be included in a notice may be omitted if it is not reasonably practicable to obtain it.

(See General Note after r.1.18.)

1.16 Non-Gazette notices relating to a company

1.16 A notice relating to a company must also identify the proceedings and state–

(a) the company's principal trading address;

(b) any name under which the company was registered in the 12 months before the date of the commencement of the proceedings which are the subject of the notice; and

(c) any name or style (not being a registered name) under which–

(i) the company carried on business, and

(ii) any debt owed to a creditor was incurred.

(See General Note after r.1.18.)

1.17 Non-Gazette notices relating to a bankruptcy

1.17 A notice relating to a bankruptcy must also identify the proceedings, identify the bankrupt and state–

(a) any other address at which the bankrupt has resided in the period of 12 months before the making of the bankruptcy order;

(b) any principal trading address if different from the bankrupt's residential address;

(c) the bankrupt's date of birth;

(d) the bankrupt's occupation;

(e) any other name by which the bankrupt has been known; and

(f) any name or style (other than the bankrupt's own name) under which–

(i) the bankrupt carried on business, and

(ii) any debt owed to a creditor was incurred.

(See General Note after r.1.18.)

1.18 Non-Gazette notices: other provisions

1.18 Information which this Chapter requires to be stated in a notice must be included in an advertisement of that notice in a way that is clear and comprehensible.

General Note to rr.1.15–1.18

This rules cover the use of notices and their contents where the *Gazette* is not involved in relation to corporate insolvency and bankruptcy. Note the additional identification requirements in r.1.6 and relaxation to omit information if it is not reasonably practicable to obtain it (r.1.15(3)).

Chapter 6

Standard contents of documents to be delivered to the registrar of companies

[Note: the requirements in Chapter 6 must be read with rule 1.6 which sets out the information required to identify an office-holder, a company etc.]

1.19 Standard contents of documents delivered to the registrar of companies

1.19(1) Where the Act or these Rules require a document to be delivered to the registrar of companies the document must contain the standard contents set out in this Chapter (in addition to any content specifically required by the Act or any other provision of these Rules).

1.19(2) A document of more than one type must satisfy the requirements which apply to each.

1.19(3) However requirements as to the contents of a document which is to be delivered to another person at the same time as the registrar of companies may be satisfied by delivering to that other person a copy of the document delivered to the registrar.

(See General Note after r.1.27.)

1.20 Registrar of companies: covering notices

1.20(1) [Documents involved] This rule applies where the Act or these Rules require an office-holder to deliver any of the following documents to the registrar of companies–

- (a) an account (including a final report) or a summary of receipts and payments;
- (b) an administrative receiver's report under section 48(1);
- (c) a court order;
- (d) a declaration of solvency;
- (e) a direction of the Secretary of State under section 203 or 205;
- (f) a notice of disclaimer;
- (g) a statement of administrator's proposals (including a statement of revised proposals);
- (h) a statement of affairs;
- (i) a statement of concurrence;
- (j) a notice of an administrator's resignation under paragraph 87(2) of Schedule B1;
- (k) a notice of a liquidator's death which the official receiver is required to deliver under rule 7.67(3)(b);
- (l) a notice that a liquidator has vacated office on loss of qualification to act which the official receiver is required to deliver under rule 7.68(4)(b);
- (m) any report including–
  - (i) a final report,
  - (ii) a progress report (including a final progress report),
  - (iii) a report of a creditors' decision under paragraph 53(2) or 54(6) of Schedule B1, and
  - (iv) a report of a decision approving a CVA under section 4(6) and (6A) or paragraph 30(3) and (4) of Schedule A1 to the Act;
- (n) a copy of the notice that a CVA has been fully implemented or terminated that the supervisor is required to deliver under rule 2.44(3);
- (o) an undertaking given under Article 36 of the EU Regulation.

1.20(2) [Duty of office-holder] The office-holder must deliver to the registrar of companies with a document mentioned in paragraph (1) a notice containing the standard contents required by this Part.

1.20(3) [Notice re multiple documents] Such a notice may relate to more than one document where those documents relate to the same proceedings and are delivered together to the registrar of companies.

(See General Note after r.1.27.)

1.21 Standard contents of all documents

1.21(1) [Contents] A document to be delivered to the registrar of companies must–

- (a) identify the company;
- (b) state–
  - (i) the nature of the document,
  - (ii) the section of the Act, the paragraph of Schedule A1 or B1 or the rule under which the document is delivered,

(iii) the date of the document,

(iv) the name and address of the person delivering the document, and

(v) the capacity in which that person is acting in relation to the company; and

(c) be authenticated by the person delivering the document.

1.21(2) [Omission of office-holder's address] Where the person delivering the document is the office-holder, the address may be omitted if it has previously been notified to the registrar of companies in the proceedings and is unchanged.

(See General Note after r.1.27.)

1.22 Standard contents of documents relating to the office of office-holders

1.22(1) [Identification of office-holder] A document relating to the office of the office-holder must also identify the office-holder and state–

(a) the date of the event of which notice is delivered or of the notice (as applicable);

(b) where the document relates to an appointment, the person, body or court making the appointment;

(c) where the document relates to the termination of an appointment, the reason for that termination; and

(d) the contact details for the office-holder.

1.22(2) [Omission of office-holder's address] Where the person delivering the document is the office-holder, the address may be omitted if it has previously been notified to the registrar of companies in the proceedings and is unchanged.

(See General Note after r.1.27.)

1.23 Standard contents of documents relating to other documents

1.23 A document relating to another document must also state–

(a) the nature of the other document;

(b) the date of the other document; and

(c) where the other document relates to a period of time, the period of time to which it relates.

(See General Note after r.1.27.)

1.24 Standard contents of documents relating to court orders

1.24 A document relating to a court order must also specify–

(a) the nature of the order; and

(b) the date of the order.

(See General Note after r.1.27.)

1.25 Standard contents of returns or reports of decisions

1.25 A return or report of a decision procedure, deemed consent procedure or meeting must also state–

(a) the purpose of the procedure or meeting;

(b) a description of the procedure or meeting used;

(c) in the case of a decision procedure or meeting, the venue;

(d) whether, in the case of a meeting, the required quorum was in place;

(e) the outcome (including any decisions made or resolutions passed); and

(f) the date of any decision made or resolution passed.

(See General Note after r.1.27.)

1.26 Standard contents of returns or reports of matters considered by company members by correspondence

1.26 A return or report of a matter, consideration of which has been sought from the members of a company by correspondence, must also state–

(a) the purpose of the consideration; and

(b) the outcome of the consideration (including any resolutions passed or deemed to be passed).

(See General Note after r.1.27.)

1.27 Standard contents of documents relating to other events

1.27 A document relating to any other event must also state–

(a) the nature of the event, including the section of the Act, the paragraph of Schedule A1 or B1 or the rule under which it took place; and

(b) the date on which the event occurred

General Note to rr.1.19–1.27

These rules cover the content of documents required to be sent to Companies House (multiple notifications may be required for documents of more than one type although multiple party notifications may be effected by copying a notice delivered to Companies House).

Rule 1.20 covers notices that must accompany prescribed documents. Rule 1.22 makes special provision for notifications concerning office-holders. Note the overlap between the r.1.20 requirement in relation to court orders (under r.1.20(1)(c)) and r.1.24. Rules 1.25 and 1.26 cover required details in cases where the notification relates to reports of decisions. Rule 1.27 covers details required in other notifications.

Note the additional identification requirements in r.1.6.

For standard contents of notices to be delivered to persons other than to Companies House see Ch.7 below.

Rule 1.20(1)(o) inserted by the Insolvency Amendment (EU 2015/848) Regulations 2017 (SI 2017/702) regs 1, 2(1), Sch. paras 32, 34 in relation to proceedings opened on or after 26 June 2017 (see reg.3) when the Recast EU Regulation 2015/848 came into force.

Chapter 7

Standard contents of notices for delivery to other persons etc.

[Note: the requirements in Chapter 7 must be read with rule 1.6 which sets out the information required to identify an office-holder, a company etc.]

1.28 Standard contents of notices to be delivered to persons other than the registrar of companies

1.28(1) [Standard contents] Where the Act or these Rules require a notice to be delivered to a person other than the registrar of companies in respect of proceedings under Parts 1 to 11 of the Act or the EU Regulation, the notice must contain the standard contents set out in this Chapter (in addition to any content specifically required by the Act or another provision of these Rules).

1.28(2) [More than one type of notice] A notice of more than one type must satisfy the requirements which apply to each.

1.28(3) [Copy document to other persons] However, the requirements in respect of a document which is to be delivered to another person at the same time as the registrar of companies may be satisfied by delivering to that other person a copy of the document delivered to the registrar.

(See General Note after r.1.34.)

1.29 Standard contents of all notices

1.29 A notice must–

(a) state the nature of the notice;

(b) identify the proceedings;

(c) in the case of proceedings relating to an individual, identify the bankrupt or debtor;

(d) state the section of the Act, the paragraph of Schedule A1 or B1 or the rule under which the notice is given; and

(e) in the case of a notice delivered by the office-holder, state the contact details for the office-holder.

(See General Note after r.1.34.)

1.30 Standard contents of notices relating to the office of office-holders

1.30 A notice relating to the office of the office-holder must also identify the office-holder and state–

(a) the date of the event of which notice is delivered;

(b) where the notice relates to an appointment, the person, body or court making the appointment; and

(c) where the notice relates to the termination of an appointment, the reason for that termination.

(See General Note after r.1.34.)

1.31 Standard contents of notices relating to documents

1.31 A notice relating to a document must also state–

(a) the nature of the document;

(b) the date of the document; and

(c) where the document relates to a period of time the period of time to which the document relates.

(See General Note after r.1.34.)

1.32 Standard contents of notices relating to court proceedings or orders

1.32 A notice relating to court proceedings must also identify those proceedings and if the notice relates to a court order state–

(a) the nature of the order; and

(b) the date of the order.

(See General Note after r.1.34.)

1.33 Standard contents of notices of the results of decisions

1.33 A notice of the result of a decision procedure, deemed consent procedure or meeting must also state–

(a) the purpose of the procedure or meeting;

(b) a description of the procedure or meeting used;

(c) in the case of a decision procedure or meeting, the venue;

(d) whether, in the case of a meeting, the required quorum was in place; and

(e) the outcome (including any decisions made or resolutions passed).

(See General Note after r.1.34.)

1.34 Standard contents of returns or reports of matters considered by company members by correspondence

1.34 A return or report of a matter, consideration of which has been sought from the members of a company by correspondence, must also specify–

(a) the purpose of the consideration; and

(b) the outcome of the consideration (including any resolutions passed or deemed to be passed).

General Note to rr.1.28–1.34

These rules had no direct counterpart in IR 1986 but prescribe extra requirements for standard contents of notices under IA 1986, IR 2016 and the Recast EU Regulation 2015/848 to be delivered to persons other than to Companies House. They are roughly equivalent in nature to the requirements in rr.1.19, 1.21–1.26.

Rule 1.28(1) amended by the Insolvency (England and Wales) and Insolvency (Scotland) (Miscellaneous and Consequential Amendments) Rules 2017 (SI 2017/1115) rr.1(1), (2), 22, 23(5) as from 8 December 2017.

Chapter 8

Applications to the court

[Note: the requirements in Chapter 8 must be read with rule 1.6 which sets out the information required to identify an office-holder, a company etc.]

1.35 Standard contents and authentication of applications to the court under Parts 1 to 11 of the Act

1.35(1) [Application of rule] This rule applies to applications to court under Parts 1 to 11 of the Act (other than an application for an administration order, a winding up petition or a bankruptcy petition).

1.35(2) [Standard contents] The application must state–

(a) that the application is made under the Act or these Rules (as applicable);

(b) the section of the Act or paragraph of a Schedule to the Act or the number of the rule under which it is made;

(c) the names of the parties;

(d) the name of the bankrupt, debtor or company which is the subject of the insolvency proceedings to which the application relates;

(e) the court (and where applicable, the division or district registry of that court) or hearing centre in which the application is made;

(f) where the court has previously allocated a number to the insolvency proceedings within which the application is made, that number;

(g) the nature of the remedy or order applied for or the directions sought from the court;

(h) the names and addresses of the persons on whom it is intended to serve the application or that no person is intended to be served;

(i) where the Act or Rules require that notice of the application is to be delivered to specified persons, the names and addresses of all those persons (so far as known to the applicant); and

(j) the applicant's address for service.

1.35(3) [Authentication] The application must be authenticated by or on behalf of the applicant or the applicant's solicitor.

General Note

This covers the standard contents of court applications excluding those for administration orders and bankruptcy and winding-up petitions. On authentication in r.1.35(3) see r.1.5. Again the identification requirements in r.1.6 apply.

Chapter 9

Delivery of documents and opting out (sections 246C, 248A(a), 379C and 383A(b))

1.36 Application of Chapter

[Note: the registrar's rules include provision for the electronic delivery of documents.]

1.36(1) [Application] This Chapter applies where a document is required under the Act or these Rules to be delivered, filed, forwarded, furnished, given, sent, or submitted in respect of proceedings under Parts 1 to 11 of the Act or the EU Regulation unless the Act, a rule or an order of the court makes different provision including one requiring service of the document.

1.36(2) [Delivery to registrar of companies] However in respect of delivery of a document to the registrar of companies–

(a) subject to sub-paragraph (b) only the following rules in this Chapter apply: rules 1.42 (postal delivery of documents), 1.43 (delivery by document exchange), 1.44 (personal delivery) and 1.52 (proof of delivery of documents);

(b) the registrar's rules made under sections 1068 and 1117 of the Companies Act apply to determine the date when any document is received by the registrar of companies.

General Note

Chapter 9 generally covers delivery of documents under IA 1986 and the Recast EU Regulation 2015/848. Only rr.1.42–1.44 and 1.52 apply to delivery of documents to Companies House.

Rule 1.36(1) amended by the Insolvency (England and Wales) and Insolvency (Scotland) (Miscellaneous and Consequential Amendments) Rules 2017 (SI 2017/1115) rr.1(1), (2), 22, 23(6) as from 8 December 2017.

1.37 Delivery to the creditors and opting out

1.37(1) [No delivery to opted-out creditors] Where the Act or a rule requires an office-holder to deliver a document to the creditors, or the creditors in a class, the requirement is satisfied by the delivery of the document to all such creditors of whose address the office-holder is aware other than opted-out creditors unless the opt out does not apply.

1.37(2) [Notices excluded from opt out] Where a creditor has opted out from receiving documents, the opt out does not apply to–

(a) a notice which the Act requires to be delivered to all creditors without expressly excluding opted-out creditors;

(b) a notice of a change in the office-holder or the contact details for the office-holder;

(c) a notice as provided for by sections 246C(2) or 379C(2) (notices of distributions, intended distributions and notices required to be given by court order); or

(d) a document which these Rules requires to accompany a notice within sub-paragraphs (a) to (c).

1.37(3) [When opt out commences] The office-holder must begin to treat a creditor as an opted-out creditor as soon as reasonably practicable after delivery of the creditor's election to opt out.

1.37(4) [Opt out in consecutive proceedings] An office-holder in any consecutive insolvency proceedings of a different kind under Parts 1 to 11 of the Act in respect of the same company or individual who is aware that a creditor was an opted-out creditor in the earlier proceedings must treat the creditor as an opted out creditor in the consecutive proceedings.

GENERAL NOTE

Delivery of documents by office-holders to creditors. Note the requirement is restricted to only those creditors of whose address the office-holder is aware (r.1.37(1)). It has been a rule at common law for over a century that a liquidator is under a duty to find out from the books and papers of the company and the statement of affairs who the creditors of the company are, and that he may be liable in damages to any creditors who have been overlooked: *Pulsford v Devenish* [1903] 2 Ch. 625. It is unlikely that r.1.37 would be construed as being intended to restrict this duty to creditors of whom the liquidator has actual knowledge. From 6 April 2017 we have the further restriction of the office-holder not being required to sent notices to creditors who have "opted out" except as required by r.1.23(2).

1.38 Creditor's election to opt out

1.38(1) [Election at any time] A creditor may at any time elect to be an opted-out creditor.

1.38(2) [Authenticated notice in writing] The creditor's election to opt out must be by a notice in writing authenticated and dated by the creditor.

1.38(3) [Delivery to office-holder] The creditor must deliver the notice to the office-holder.

1.38(4) [When notice effective] A creditor becomes an opted-out creditor when the notice is delivered to the office-holder.

1.38(5) [Duration of opt out; consecutive proceedings] An opted-out creditor–

(a) will remain an opted-out creditor for the duration of the proceedings unless the opt out is revoked; and

(b) is deemed to be an opted-out creditor in respect of any consecutive insolvency proceedings under Parts 1 to 11 of the Act of a different kind relating to the same company or individual.

1.38(6) [Revocation of opt out] The creditor may at any time revoke the election to opt out by a further notice in writing, authenticated and dated by the creditor and delivered to the office-holder.

1.38(7) [Date of cessation of opt out] The creditor ceases to be an opted-out creditor from the date the notice is received by the office-holder.

(See General Note after 1.39.)

1.39 Office-holder to provide information to creditors on opting-out

1.39(1) [Information on opting out] The office-holder must, in the first communication with a creditor, inform the creditor in writing that the creditor may elect to opt out of receiving further documents relating to the proceedings.

1.39(2) [Contents of communication] The communication must contain–

(a) identification and contact details for the office-holder;

(b) a statement that the creditor has the right to elect to opt out of receiving further documents about the proceedings unless–

(i) the Act requires a document to be delivered to all creditors without expressly excluding opted-out creditors,

(ii) it is a notice relating to a change in the office-holder or the office-holder's contact details, or

(iii) it is a notice of a dividend or proposed dividend or a notice which the court orders to be sent to all creditors or all creditors of a particular category to which the creditor belongs;

(c) a statement that opting-out will not affect the creditor's entitlement to receive dividends should any be paid to creditors;

(d) a statement that unless these Rules provide to the contrary opting-out will not affect any right the creditor may have to vote in a decision procedure or a participate in a deemed consent procedure in the proceedings although the creditor will not receive notice of it;

(e) a statement that a creditor who opts out will be treated as having opted out in respect of any consecutive insolvency proceedings of a different kind in respect of the same company or individual; and

(f) information about how the creditor may elect to be or cease to be an opted-out creditor.

General Note to 1.38–1.39

Creditors' right to opt out from receiving notices was introduced by IA 1986 ss.246C and 379C (inserted by SBEEA 2015 ss.124 and 125) as from 6 April 2017. These rules place a duty on office-holders to inform creditors of their right to opt out and how to cease being opted out (r.1.39) and provide how creditors become opted out or cease being so. On authentication in r.1.38(2) see r.1.5.

1.40 Delivery of documents to authorised recipients

1.40 Where under the Act or these Rules a document is to be delivered to a person (other than by being served on that person), it may be delivered instead to any other person authorised in writing to accept delivery on behalf of the first-mentioned person.

General Note

This covers delivery to another authorised person except in relation to service. This provision must be complied with notwithstanding more flexible provisions in the CPR: *Namulas Pension Trustees Ltd v Mouzakis* [2011] B.P.I.R. 1724 (county court).

1.41 Delivery of documents to joint office-holders

1.41 Where there are joint office-holders in insolvency proceedings, delivery of a document to one of them is to be treated as delivery to all of them.

General Note

The position of joint office-holders is addressed.

1.42 Postal delivery of documents

1.42(1) [Document delivered] A document is delivered if it is sent by post in accordance with the provisions of this rule.

1.42(2) [Type of post] First class or second class post may be used to deliver a document except where these Rules require first class post to be used.

1.42(3) [When document treated as delivered] Unless the contrary is shown–

(a) a document sent by first class post is treated as delivered on the second business day after the day on which it is posted;

(b) a document sent by second class post is treated as delivered on the fourth business day after the day on which it is posted;

(c) where a post-mark appears on the envelope in which a document was posted, the date of that post-mark is to be treated as the date on which the document was posted.

1.42(4) ["Post-mark"] In this rule "post-mark" means a mark applied by a postal operator which records the date on which a letter entered the postal system of the postal operator.

General Note

This explains postal delivery with first and second class post and determination of timing from a post mark.

1.43 Delivery by document exchange

1.43(1) [Delivery to DX] A document is delivered to a member of a document exchange if it is delivered to that document exchange.

1.43(2) [When document treated as delivered] Unless the contrary is shown, a document is treated as delivered–

(a) one business day after the day it is delivered to the document exchange where the sender and the intended recipient are members of the same document exchange; or

(b) two business days after the day it is delivered to the departure facility of the sender's document exchange where the sender and the intended recipient are members of different document exchanges.

General Note

The DX was not recognised in IR 1986 but r.1.43 now directly does so and describes the timing.

1.44 Personal delivery of documents

1.44 A document is delivered if it is personally delivered in accordance with the rules for personal service in CPR Part 6.

General Note

See CPR Pt 6.

1.45 Electronic delivery of documents

1.45(1) [Delivery by electronic means] A document is delivered if it is sent by electronic means and the following conditions apply.

1.45(2) [Conditions] The conditions are that the intended recipient of the document has–

(a) given actual or deemed consent for the electronic delivery of the document;

(b) not revoked that consent before the document is sent; and

(c) provided an electronic address for the delivery of the document.

1.45(3) [Type of consent] Consent may relate to a specific case or generally.

1.45(4) [Deemed consent] For the purposes of paragraph (2)(a) an intended recipient is deemed to have consented to the electronic delivery of a document by the office-holder where the intended recipient and the person who is the subject of the insolvency proceedings had customarily communicated with each other by electronic means before the proceedings commenced.

1.45(5) [Treated as delivered by electronic means] Unless the contrary is shown, a document is to be treated as delivered by electronic means to an electronic address where the sender can produce a copy of the electronic communication which–

(a) contains the document; and

(b) shows the time and date the communication was sent and the electronic address to which it was sent.

1.45(6) [Time when treated as delivered] Unless the contrary is shown, a document sent electronically is treated as delivered to the electronic address to which it is sent at 9.00 am on the next business day after it was sent.

General Note

This identifies where electronic delivery is acceptable and the timing thereof. The courts have moved with the times in relation to consent for electronic communications, from *Re Sporting Options plc* [2004] EWHC 3128 (Ch); [2005] B.C.C. 88, where email was considered not an appropriate form of communication (emails to many customer-creditors had been kicked back and the court was concerned that email addresses might change) but over five years later in *Re Advent Computer Training Ltd* [2010] EWHC 459 (Ch); [2011] B.C.C. 44 email was allowed, partly as by then more commonly in use. The latter case was applied in *Re All Leisure Holidays Ltd* [2017] EWHC 870 (Ch); [2017] B.C.C. 354 where the majority of customers of tour companies had previously provided an email address to receive information from the companies and that was enough to amount to sufficient consent for email as the means of communication to receive notices from administrators of the companies. The reference in r.1.45(3) to consent being given "generally" was considered to be of wide application and would lose much of its practical utility if interpreted in a restrictive way.

1.46 Electronic delivery of documents to the court

1.46(1) [Express permission required] A document may not be delivered to a court by electronic means unless this is expressly permitted by the CPR, a Practice Direction, or these Rules.

1.46(2) [Time when treated as delivered] A document delivered by electronic means is to be treated as delivered to the court at the time it is recorded by the court as having been received or otherwise as the CPR, a Practice Direction or these Rules provide.

General Note

This reflects the limits of electronic delivery where the court is involved.

1.47 Electronic delivery of notices to enforcement officers

1.47 Where anything in the Act or these Rules provides for the delivery of a notice to an enforcement officer or enforcement agent, it may be delivered by electronic means to a person who has been authorised to receive such a notice on behalf of a specified enforcement officer or enforcement agent or on behalf of enforcement officers or enforcement agents generally.

General Note

This rule allows the electronic delivery of notices to enforcement officers and persons authorised by them.

1.48 Electronic delivery by office-holders

1.48(1) [Statement for request for hard copy] Where an office-holder delivers a document by electronic means, the document must contain, or be accompanied by, a statement that the recipient may request a hard copy of the document and a telephone number, email address and postal address that may be used to make that request.

1.48(2) [Duty of to deliver hard copy] An office-holder who receives such a request must deliver a hard copy of the document to the recipient free of charge within five business days of receipt of the request.

General Note

The office-holder may be requested to provide hard copies of documents sent by electronic means by office-holders.

1.49 Use of website by office-holder to deliver a particular document (sections 246B and 379B)

[Note: rule 3.54(3) allows notice of an extension to an administration to be given on a website, and rules 2.25(6) and 8.22(5) do likewise in respect of notice of the result of the consideration of a proposal for a CVA and an IVA respectively.]

1.49(1) [Application for IA 1986 ss.246B, 379B] This rule applies for the purposes of sections 246B and 379B (use of websites).

1.49(2) [Delivery of notice re website] An office-holder who is required to deliver a document to any person may (except where personal delivery is required) satisfy that requirement by delivering a notice to that person which contains–

(a) a statement that the document is available for viewing and downloading on a website;

(b) the website's address and any password necessary to view and download the document; and

(c) a statement that the person to whom the notice is delivered may request a hard copy of the document with a telephone number, email address and postal address which may be used to make that request.

1.49(3) [Duty to deliver hard copy] An office-holder who receives such a request must deliver a hard copy of the document to the recipient free of charge within five business days of receipt of the request.

1.49(4) [Document on website] A document to which a notice under paragraph (2) relates must–

(a) remain available on the website for the period required by rule 1.51; and

(b) be in a format that enables it to be downloaded within a reasonable time of an electronic request being made for it to be downloaded.

1.49(5) [Deemed delivery by website] A document which is delivered to a person by means of a website in accordance with this rule, is deemed to have been delivered–

(a) when the document is first made available on the website; or

(b) when the notice under paragraph (2) is delivered to that person, if that is later.

General Note

Website use by office-holders for the delivery of documents is hereby covered in relation to nominating particular documents—note the linkage with website usage under IA 1986 ss.246B and 379B first introduced by LRO 2010. The official "[Note]" also refers to the specific instances in rr.3.54(3) in administration and 2.25(6) and 8.24 in voluntary arrangement proposals. The recipient may request a hard copy of the relevant document. In *Re All Leisure Holidays Ltd* [2017] EWHC 870 (Ch); [2017] B.C.C. 354 it was held appropriate for administrators to send a single notice to all creditors together with a link to relevant documents. Compare r.1.50 for more general use of websites for delivery of documents.

1.50 General use of website to deliver documents

1.50(1) [Notice] The office-holder may deliver a notice to each person to whom a document will be required to be delivered in the insolvency proceedings which contains–

(a) a statement that future documents in the proceedings other than those mentioned in paragraph (2) will be made available for viewing and downloading on a website without notice to the recipient and that the office-holder will not be obliged to deliver any such documents to the recipient of the notice unless it is requested by that person;

(b) a telephone number, email address and postal address which may be used to make a request for a hard copy of a document;

(c) a statement that the recipient of the notice may at any time request a hard copy of any or all of the following–

(i) all documents currently available for viewing on the website,

(ii) all future documents which may be made available there, and

(d) the address of the website, any password required to view and download a relevant document from that site.

1.50(2) [Documents excluded from website delivery] A statement under paragraph (1)(a) does not apply to the following documents–

(a) a document for which personal delivery is required;

(b) a notice under rule 14.29 of intention to declare a dividend; and

(c) a document which is not delivered generally.

1.50(3) [Document delivered generally] A document is delivered generally if it is delivered to some or all of the following classes of persons–

(a) members,

(b) contributories,

(c) creditors;

(d) any class of members, contributories or creditors.

1.50(4) [No further obligation for notice or hard copy] An office-holder who has delivered a notice under paragraph (1) is under no obligation–

(a) to notify a person to whom the notice has been delivered when a document to which the notice applies has been made available on the website; or

(b) to deliver a hard copy of such a document unless a request is received under paragraph (1)(c).

1.50(5) [Hard copy request] An office-holder who receives such a request–

(a) in respect of a document which is already available on the website must deliver a hard copy of the document to the recipient free of charge within five business days of receipt of the request; and

(b) in respect of all future documents must deliver each such document in accordance with the requirements for delivery of such a document in the Act and these Rules.

1.50(6) [Document to remain in website] A document to which a statement under paragraph (1)(a) applies must–

(a) remain available on the website for the period required by rule 1.51; and

(b) must be in such a format as to enable it to be downloaded within a reasonable time of an electronic request being made for it to be downloaded.

1.50(7) [Deemed delivery by website] A document which is delivered to a person by means of a website in accordance with this rule, is deemed to have been delivered–

(a) when the relevant document was first made available on the website; or

(b) if later, when the notice under paragraph (1) was delivered to that person.

1.50(8) [Non-application of r.1.50(7) re future hard copy request] Paragraph (7) does not apply in respect of a person who has made a request under paragraph (1)(c)(ii) for hard copies of all future documents.

General Note

This provides more general website use for delivery of notices rather than specific nomination in r.1.49. The recipient may request a copies of documents on the website.

1.51 Retention period for documents made available on websites

1.51(1) [Application re rr.1.49, 1.50, 2.25(6), 3.54(3), 8.22(4)] This rule applies to a document which is made available on a website under rules 1.49, 1.50, 2.25(6) (notice of the result of the consideration of a proposal for a CVA), 3.54(3) (notice of an extension to an administration) and 8.22(4) (notice of the result of the consideration of a proposal for an IVA).

1.51(2) [Documents to remain available on website] Such a document must continue to be made available on the website until two months after the end of the particular insolvency proceedings or the release of the last person to hold office as the office-holder in those proceedings.

General Note

Time limit for documents to be available on website.

1.52 Proof of delivery of documents

1.52(1) [Certificate of compliance] A certificate complying with this rule is proof that a document has been duly delivered to the recipient in accordance with this Chapter unless the contrary is shown.

1.52(2) [Content of certificate] A certificate must state the method of delivery and the date of the sending, posting or delivery (as the case may be).

1.52(3) [Certificate by official receiver or adjudicator] In the case of the official receiver or the adjudicator the certificate must be given by–

(a) the official receiver or the adjudicator; or

(b) a member of the official receiver's or adjudicator's staff.

1.52(4) [Certificate by office-holder] In the case of an office-holder other than the official receiver or the adjudicator the certificate must be given by–

(a) the office-holder;

(b) the office-holder's solicitor; or

(c) a partner or an employee of either of them.

1.52(5) [Certificate by other persons] In the case of a person other than an office-holder the certificate must be given by that person and must state–

(a) that the document was delivered by that person; or

(b) that another person (named in the certificate) was instructed to deliver it.

1.52(6) [Certificate endorsed on copy document] A certificate under this rule may be endorsed on a copy of the document to which it relates.

General Note

Proof of delivery by certificate is dealt with.

1.53 Delivery of proofs and details of claims

1.53(1) [No further delivery of proof] Once a proof has, or details of a claim have, been delivered to an office-holder in accordance with these Rules that proof or those details need not be delivered again; and accordingly, where a provision of these Rules requires delivery of a proof or details of a claim by a certain time, that requirement is satisfied if the proof has or the details have already been delivered.

1.53(2) [Application of r.1.53(1) to r.14.3(2)(a), (b) consecutive proceedings] Paragraph (1) also applies to those cases set out in rule 14.3(2)(a) and (b) where a creditor who has proved in insolvency proceedings is deemed to have proved in an insolvency proceedings which immediately follows that proceeding.

General Note

This is a special rule for delivery of proofs confirming that delivery is required once only.

Chapter 10

Inspection of documents, copies and provision of information

1.54 Right to copies of documents

1.54 Where the Act, in relation to proceedings under Parts 1 to 11 of the Act, or these Rules give a person the right to inspect documents, that person has a right to be supplied on request with copies of those documents on payment of the standard fee for copies.

General Note

This indicates that a right to inspect embraces a right to seek copies of documents.

1.55 Charges for copies of documents provided by the office-holder

1.55 Except where prohibited by these Rules, an office-holder is entitled to require the payment of the standard fee for copies of documents requested by a creditor, member, contributory or member of a liquidation or creditors' committee.

General Note

The office-holder can charge for the cost of supplying documents. For the "standard fee" see r.1.2(2).

1.56 Offence in relation to inspection of documents

1.56(1) [Offence] It is an offence for a person who does not have a right under these Rules to inspect a relevant document falsely to claim to be a creditor, a member of a company or a contributory of a company with the intention of gaining sight of the document.

1.56(2) [Relevant document] A relevant document is one which is on the court file, the bankruptcy file or held by the office-holder or any other person and which a creditor, a member of a company or a contributory of a company has the right to inspect under these Rules.

1.56(3) [Penalty] A person guilty of an offence under this rule is liable to imprisonment or a fine, or both.

General Note

This is a useful deterrent to restrict bogus claims to inspect. For the appropriate penalty, see Sch.3.

1.57 Right to list of creditors

1.57(1) [Application of rule] This rule applies to–

(a) administration;

(b) creditors' voluntary winding up;

(c) winding up by the court; and

(d) bankruptcy.

1.57(2) [When right does not apply] A creditor has the right to require the office-holder to provide a list of the names and addresses of the creditors and the amounts of their respective debts unless–

(a) a statement of affairs has been filed with the court or delivered to the registrar of companies; or

(b) the information is available for inspection on the bankruptcy file.

1.57(3) [Duty of office-holder] The office-holder on being required to provide such a list–

(a) must deliver it to the person requiring the list as soon as reasonably practicable; and

(b) may charge the standard fee for copies for a hard copy.

1.57(4) [Omission on creditor details] The office-holder may omit the name and address of a creditor if the office-holder thinks its disclosure would be prejudicial to the conduct of the proceedings or might reasonably be expected to lead to violence against any person.

1.57(5) [Information when creditors details omitted] In such a case the list must include–

(a) the amount of that creditor's debt; and

(b) a statement that the name and address of the creditor has been omitted for that debt.

General Note

Lists of creditors must be available to creditors unless already publicly available, subject to the protective measure in r.1.57(4). For the "standard fee" in r.1.57(3)(b) see r.1.2(2).

1.58 Confidentiality of documents: grounds for refusing inspection

1.58(1) [Power of office-holder to decline inspection] Where an office-holder considers that a document forming part of the records of the insolvency proceedings–

(a) should be treated as confidential; or

(b) is of such a nature that its disclosure would be prejudicial to the conduct of the proceedings or might reasonably be expected to lead to violence against any person;

the office-holder may decline to allow it to be inspected by a person who would otherwise be entitled to inspect it.

1.58(2) [Persons who may be refused inspection] The persons to whom the office-holder may refuse inspection include members of a liquidation committee or a creditors' committee.

1.58(3) [Application to court] Where the office-holder refuses inspection of a document, the person wishing to inspect it may apply to the court which may reconsider the office-holder's decision.

1.58(4) [Conditions in court decision] The court's decision may be subject to such conditions (if any) as it thinks just.

General Note

This explains where an office-holder may decline to disclose information on grounds of confidentiality or because of a threat to personal safety.

Part 2

Company Voluntary Arrangements (CVA)

Introductory note to Part 2
The topic of CVAs to which these rules relate is dealt with in IA 1986 ss.1–7B. On voluntary arrangements for individual debtors, see IA 1986 ss.252 et seq., and IR 2016 Pt 8. Companies House has provided some Forms—those headed "VAM" relate to the moratorium and those designated "CVA" have more general application.

Chapter 1

Preliminary

2.1 Interpretation

2.1 In this Part–

"nominee" and "supervisor" include the proposed nominee or supervisor in relation to a proposal for a CVA; and

"proposal" means a proposal for a CVA.

General Note

These terms are defined here rather than in general definitions in r.1.2.

Chapter 2

The proposal for a CVA (section 1)

[Note: (1) section 1 of the Act sets out who may propose a CVA;

(2) a document required by the Act or these Rules must also contain the standard contents set out in Part 1.]

2.2 Proposal for a CVA: general principles and amendment

2.2(1) [General principles] A proposal must–

(a) contain identification details for the company;

(b) explain why the proposer thinks a CVA is desirable;

(c) explain why the creditors are expected to agree to a CVA; and

(d) be authenticated and dated by the proposer.

2.2(2) [Amendment of proposal] The proposal may be amended with the nominee's agreement in writing in the following cases.

2.2(3) [First case for amendment] The first case is where–

(a) no steps have been taken to obtain a moratorium;

(b) the nominee is not the liquidator or administrator of the company; and

(c) the nominee's report has not been filed with the court under section 2(2).

2.2(4) [Second case for amendment] The second case is where–

(a) the proposal is made with a view to obtaining a moratorium; and

(b) the nominee's statement under paragraph 6(2) of Schedule A1 (nominee's opinion on prospects of CVA being approved etc.) has not yet been submitted to the directors.

(See General Note after r.2.3.)

2.3 Proposal: contents

2.3(1) [Contents as known to proposer] The proposal must set out the following so far as known to the proposer–

Assets	(a) the company's assets, with an estimate of their respective values; (b) which assets are charged and the extent of the charge; (c) which assets are to be excluded from the CVA; and (d) particulars of any property to be included in the CVA which is not owned by the company, including details of who owns such property, and the terms on which it will be available for inclusion;
Liabilities	(e) the nature and amount of the company's liabilities; (f) how the company's liabilities will be met, modified, postponed or otherwise dealt with by means of the CVA and in particular— (i) how preferential creditors and creditors who are, or claim to be, secured will be dealt with, (ii) how creditors who are connected with the company will be dealt with, (iii) if the company is not in administration or liquidation whether, if the company did go into administration or liquidation, there are circumstances which might give rise to claims under section 238 (transactions at an undervalue), section 239 (preferences), section 244 (extortionate credit transactions), or section 245 (floating charges invalid), and (iv) where there are circumstances that might give rise to such claims, whether, and if so what, provision will be made to indemnify the company in respect of them;
Nominee's fees and expenses	(g) the amount proposed to be paid to the nominee by way of fees and expenses;
Supervisor	(h) identification and contact details for the supervisor; (i) confirmation that the supervisor is qualified to act as an insolvency practitioner in relation to the company and the name of the relevant recognised professional body which is the source of the supervisor's authorisation; (j) how the fees and expenses of the supervisor will be determined and paid; (k) the functions to be performed by the supervisor; (l) where it is proposed that two or more supervisors be appointed a statement whether acts done in connection with the CVA may be done by any one or more of them or must be done by all of them;

Guarantees and proposed guarantees	(m) whether any, and if so what, guarantees have been given in respect of the company's debts, specifying which of the guarantors are persons connected with the company; (n) whether any, and if so what, guarantees are proposed to be offered for the purposes of the CVA and, if so, by whom and whether security is to be given or sought;
Timing	(o) the proposed duration of the CVA; (p) the proposed dates of distributions to creditors, with estimates of their amounts;
Type of proceedings	(q) whether the proceedings will be main, territorial or non-EU proceedings with reasons;
Conduct of the business	(r) how the business of the company will be conducted during the CVA;
Further credit facilities	(s) details of any further proposed credit facilities for the company, and how the debts so arising are to be paid;
Handling of funds arising	(t) the manner in which funds held for the purposes of the CVA are to be banked, invested or otherwise dealt with pending distribution to creditors; (u) how funds held for the purpose of payment to creditors, and not so paid on the termination of the CVA, will be dealt with; (v) how the claim of any person bound by the CVA by virtue of section 5(2)(b)(ii) or paragraph 37(2)(b)(ii) of Schedule A1 will be dealt with;
Address (where moratorium proposed)	(w) where the proposal is made in relation to a company that is eligible for a moratorium (in accordance with paragraphs 2 and 3 of Schedule A1) with a view to obtaining a moratorium under Schedule A1, the address to which the documents referred to in paragraph 6(1) of that Schedule must be delivered; and
Other matters	(x) any other matters that the proposer considers appropriate to enable members and creditors to reach an informed decision on the proposal.

2.3(2) [Where proposal made by directors] Where the proposal is made by the directors, an estimate so far as known to them of–

(a) the value of the prescribed part if the proposal for the CVA is not accepted and the company goes into liquidation (whether or not the liquidator might be required under section 176A to make the prescribed part available for the satisfaction of unsecured debts); and

(b) the value of the company's net property (as defined by section 176A(6)) on the date that the estimate is made.

2.3(3) [Where the proposal made by the administrator or liquidator] Where the proposal is made by the administrator or liquidator the following so far as known to the office-holder–

(a) an estimate of–

(i) the value of the prescribed part (whether or not the administrator or liquidator might be required under section 176A to make the prescribed part available for the satisfaction of unsecured debts), and

(ii) the value of the company's net property (as defined by section 176A(6)); and

(b) a statement as to whether the administrator or liquidator proposes to make an application to the court under section 176A(5) and if so the reasons for the application; and

(c) details of the nature and amount of the company's preferential creditors.

2.3(4) [Exclusion of information from estimate under r.2.3(2), (3)(a)] Information may be excluded from an estimate under paragraph (2) or (3)(a) if the inclusion of the information could seriously prejudice the commercial interests of the company.

2.3(5) [Where exclusion affects calculation of estimate] If the exclusion of such information affects the calculation of the estimate, the proposal must include a statement to that effect.

General Note to rr.2.2–2.3

These rules provide measures on the proposal for *all* CVAs.

In r.2.3(1) table, the entry for "Type of proceedings" amended by the Insolvency (England and Wales) and Insolvency (Scotland) (Miscellaneous and Consequential Amendments) Rules 2017 (SI 2017/1115) rr.1(1), (2), 22, 30(3) as from 8 December 2017.

Chapter 3

Procedure for a CVA without a moratorium

[Note: a document required by the Act or these Rules must also contain the standard contents set out in Part 1.]

2.4 Procedure for proposal where the nominee is not the liquidator or the administrator (section 2)

2.4(1) [Application] This rule applies where the nominee is not the same person as the liquidator or the administrator.

2.4(2) [Nominee to deliver notice of consent to act] A nominee who consents to act must deliver a notice of that consent to the proposer as soon as reasonably practicable after the proposal has been submitted to the nominee under section 2(3).

2.4(3) [Notice to state date proposal received] The notice must state the date the nominee received the proposal.

2.4(4) [Period for nominee to submit report] The period of 28 days in which the nominee must submit a report to the court under section 2(2) begins on the date the nominee received the proposal as stated in the notice.

(See General Note after r.2.8.)

2.5 Information for the official receiver

2.5 Where the company is being wound up by the court, the liquidator must deliver to the official receiver–

(a) a copy of the proposal; and

(b) the name and address of the nominee (if the nominee is not the liquidator).

(See General Note after r.2.8.)

2.6 Statement of affairs (section 2(3))

2.6(1) [Contents] The statement of the company's affairs required by section 2(3) must contain the following–

(a) a list of the company's assets, divided into such categories as are appropriate for easy identification, and with each category given an estimated value;

(b) in the case of any property on which a claim against the company is wholly or partly secured, particulars of the claim, and of how and when the security was created;

(c) the names and addresses of the preferential creditors, with the amounts of their respective claims;

(d) the names and addresses of the unsecured creditors with the amounts of their respective claims;

(e) particulars of any debts owed by the company to persons connected with it;

(f) particulars of any debts owed to the company by persons connected with it;

(g) the names and addresses of the company's members, with details of their respective shareholdings; and

(h) any other particulars that the nominee in writing requires to be provided for the purposes of making the nominee's report on the proposal to the court.

2.6(2) [Date to be made up to] The statement must be made up to a date not earlier than two weeks before the date of the proposal.

2.6(3) [Earlier date allowed] However the nominee may allow the statement to be made up to an earlier date (but not more than two months before the date of the proposal) where that is more practicable.

2.6(4) [Explanation for earlier date] Where the statement is made up to an earlier date, the nominee's report to the court on the proposal must explain why.

2.6(5) [Verification] The statement of affairs must be verified by a statement of truth made by the proposer.

2.6(6) [Directors' statement of truth by single director] Where the proposal is made by the directors, only one director need make the statement of truth.

(See General Note after r.2.8.)

2.7 Application to omit information from statement of affairs delivered to creditors

2.7 The nominee, the directors or any person appearing to the court to have an interest, may apply to the court for a direction that specified information be omitted from the statement of affairs as delivered to the creditors where disclosure of that information would be likely to prejudice the conduct of the CVA or might reasonably be expected to lead to violence against any person.

(See General Note after r.2.8.)

2.8 Additional disclosure for assistance of nominee where the nominee is not the liquidator or administrator

2.8(1) [Application] This rule applies where the nominee is not the administrator or the liquidator of the company.

2.8(2) [Nominee may request further information] If it appears to the nominee that the nominee's report to the court cannot properly be prepared on the basis of information in the proposal and statement of affairs, the nominee may require the proposer to provide–

(a) more information about the circumstances in which, and the reasons why, a CVA is being proposed;

(b) particulars of any previous proposals which have been made in relation to the company under Part 1 of the Act; and

(c) any further information relating to the company's affairs which the nominee thinks necessary for the purposes of the report.

2.8(3) [Nominee may require information re directors] The nominee may require the proposer to inform the nominee whether, and if so in what circumstances, any person who is, or has been at any time in the two years before the date the nominee received the proposal, a director or officer of the company has–

(a) been concerned in the affairs of any other company (whether or not incorporated in England and Wales) or limited liability partnership which has been the subject of insolvency proceedings;

(b) been made bankrupt;

(c) been the subject of a debt relief order; or

(d) entered into an arrangement with creditors.

2.8(4) [Access to company's accounts and records] The proposer must give the nominee such access to the company's accounts and records as the nominee may require to enable the nominee to consider the proposal and prepare the nominee's report.

General Note to rr.2.4–2.8

The proposal and the statement of affairs will be relied on by the nominee in the preparation of his report to the court under IA 1986 s.2 and by the meeting of the company and by its creditors in their decision procedure in due course if the proposal goes ahead. These rules seek to ensure that the decisions will be made on a basis of adequate evidence. Note r.2.7 allows applications to the court to omit information from the statement of affairs sent to creditors to protect commercially sensitive information and to protect personal safety.

2.9 Nominee's report on proposal where the nominee is not the liquidator or administrator (section 2(2))

2.9(1) [Accompanying documents] The nominee's report must be filed with the court under section 2(2) accompanied by–

(a) a copy of the report;

(b) a copy of the proposal (as amended under rule 2.2(2), if that is the case); and

(c) a copy of the statement of the company's affairs or a summary of it.

2.9(2) [Nominee's opinions] The report must state–

(a) why the nominee considers the proposal does or does not have a reasonable prospect of being approved and implemented; and

(b) why the members and the creditors should or should not be invited to consider the proposal.

2.9(3) [Court to endorse report and delivery to nominee] The court must endorse the nominee's report and the copy of it with the date of filing and deliver the copy to the nominee.

2.9(4) [Copy to company] The nominee must deliver a copy of the report to the company.

General Note

The court's role is purely an administrative one, unless a challenge is mounted under IA 1986 s.6. Despite this, it is interesting that the nominee must both file the report and provide a copy of it to the court: this might be thought of as overkill.

Rule 2.9(2) appears to go almost further than s.2(2) which merely requires the nominee to report whether, in his opinion, the proposed CVA has a reasonable prospect of being approved and implemented and whether the proposal should be considered by a meeting of the company and by the company's creditors; whereas r.2.9(2) requires the nominee to state why the proposal does *or does not* have that prospect and why the members and creditors should *or should not* be asked to consider it. This may reflect the policy for promoting greater quality controls on CVAs as pursued since IA 2000.

2.10 Replacement of nominee (section 2(4))

2.10(1) [Application by person other than nominee] A person (other than the nominee) who intends to apply to the court under section 2(4) for the nominee to be replaced must deliver a notice that such an application is intended to be made to the nominee at least five business days before filing the application with the court.

2.10(2) [Application by nominee] A nominee who intends to apply under that section to be replaced must deliver a notice that such an application is intended to be made to the person intending to make the proposal, or the proposer, at least five business days before filing the application with the court.

2.10(3) [Statement of replacement nominee] The court must not appoint a replacement nominee unless a statement by the replacement nominee has been filed with the court confirming that person–

(a) consents to act; and

(b) is qualified to act as an insolvency practitioner, in relation to the company.

General Note

This sets out the notice required for applications to court to replace a nominee. The idea of using "turnaround specialists" rather than fully qualified IPs did not work (with no regulatory body for them ever being recognised re CVAs and IVAs) and so the nominee must be qualified to act as an IP in relation to the company (under r.1.2 an "office-holder" includes a nominee). Things may change in the future in the wake of the changes made by DA 2015 and SBEEA 2015.

Chapter 4

Procedure for a CVA with a moratorium

[Note: a document required by the Act or these Rules must also contain the standard contents set out in Part 1.]

2.11 Statement of affairs (paragraph 6(1)(b) of Schedule A1)

2.11(1) [Contents as r.2.6] The statement of affairs required by paragraph 6(1)(b) of Schedule A1 must contain the same information as is required by rule 2.6.

2.11(2) [Date made up to] The statement must be made up to a date not earlier than two weeks before the date of the proposal.

2.11(3) [Earlier date allowed] However the nominee may allow the statement to be made up to an earlier date (but not more than two months before the proposal) where that is more practicable.

2.11(4) [Explanation of earlier date]Where the statement is made up to an earlier date, the nominee's statement to the directors on the proposal must explain why.

2.11(5) [Verification] The statement of affairs must be verified by a statement of truth made by at least one director.

General Note

It is the directors who apply for a CVA with a moratorium and so they who must prepare the statement of affairs which contains the same content and within the same time frame as that by the proposer under r.2.6 where a moratorium is not sought.

2.12 Application to omit information from a statement of affairs

2.12 The nominee, the directors or any person appearing to the court to have an interest, may apply to the court for a direction that specified information be omitted from the statement of affairs as delivered to the creditors where disclosure of that information would be likely to prejudice the conduct of the CVA or might reasonably be expected to lead to violence against any person.

General Note

This allows applications to the court to omit information from the statement of affairs sent to creditors to protect commercially sensitive information and to protect personal safety.

2.13 The nominee's statement (paragraph 6(2) of Schedule A1)

2.13(1) [Submission of statement to directors] The nominee must submit to the directors the statement required by paragraph 6(2) of Schedule A1 within 28 days of the submission to the nominee of the proposal.

2.13(2) [Nominee name and address, authentication] The statement must–

(a) include the name and address of the nominee; and

(b) be authenticated and dated by the nominee.

2.13(3) [Opinion in IA 1986 Sch.A1 para.6(2)] A statement which contains an opinion on all the matters referred to in paragraph 6(2) must–

(a) explain why the nominee has formed that opinion; and

(b) if the nominee is willing to act, be accompanied by a statement of the nominee's consent to act in relation to the proposed CVA.

2.13(4) [Statement of consent to act] The statement of the nominee's consent must–

(a) include the name and address of the nominee;

(b) state that the nominee is qualified to act as an insolvency practitioner in relation to the company; and

(c) be authenticated and dated by the nominee.

General Note

The nominee's response to the directors is explained.

2.14 Documents filed with court to obtain a moratorium (paragraph 7(1) of Schedule A1)

2.14(1) [Statement of affairs] The statement of the company's affairs which the directors file with the court under paragraph 7(1)(b) of Schedule A1 must be the same as the statement they submit to the nominee under paragraph 6(1)(b) of that Schedule.

2.14(2) [Statement of eligibility for moratorium] The statement required by paragraph 7(1)(c) of that Schedule that the company is eligible for a moratorium must–

(a) be made by the directors;

(b) state that the company meets the requirements of paragraph 3 of Schedule A1 and is not a company which falls within paragraph 2(2) of that Schedule;

(c) confirm that the company is not ineligible for a moratorium under paragraph 4 of that Schedule; and

(d) be authenticated and dated by the directors.

2.14(2A) [Statement as to EU or non-EU proceedings] A statement from the nominee whether the proceedings will be main, secondary, territorial or non-EU proceedings with the reasons for so stating must also be filed with the court.

2.14(3) [Statement of nominee's consent to act] The statement required by paragraph 7(1)(d) of that Schedule that the nominee has consented to act must be in the same terms as the statement referred to in rule 2.13(3)(b) and (4).

2.14(4) [Statement of nominee's opinion under IA 1986 Sch.A1 para.7(1)(e)] The statement of the nominee's opinion required by paragraph 7(1)(e) of that Schedule–

(a) must be the same as the statement of opinion required by paragraph 6(2) of that Schedule; and

(b) must be filed with the court not later than ten business days after it was submitted to the directors.

2.14(5) [Copies of schedule indentifying company and listing documents filed] The documents filed with the court under paragraph 7(1) of that Schedule must be accompanied by four copies of a schedule, authenticated and dated by the directors, identifying the company and listing all the documents filed.

2.14(6) [Court to endorse schedule copies; delivery to directors] The court must endorse the copies of the schedule with the date on which the documents were filed and deliver three copies of the endorsed schedule to the directors.

General Note

The documents that need to be authenticated and filed in court to obtain the moratorium are explained along with the filing procedure. The rule provides greater detail than its predecessor as Forms are no longer prescribed for this purpose. Rule 2.14(2A) inserted by the Insolvency Amendment (EU 2015/848) Regulations 2017 (SI 2017/702) regs 1, 2(1), Sch. paras 32, 35 in relation to proceedings opened on or after 26 June 2017 (see reg.3) when the Recast EU Regulation 2015/848 came into force and further amended by the Insolvency (England and Wales) and Insolvency (Scotland) (Miscellaneous and Consequential Amendments) Rules 2017 (SI 2017/1115) rr.1(1), (2), 22, 30(4) as from 8 December 2017.

2.15 Notice and advertisement of beginning of a moratorium

2.15(1) [Directors to deliver endorsed copies to nominee and company] The directors must as soon as reasonably practicable after delivery to them of the endorsed copies of the schedule deliver two copies of the schedule to the nominee and one to the company.

2.15(2) [Nominee to gazette and advertise notice of moratorium] After delivery of the copies of the schedule, the nominee–

(a) must as soon as reasonably practicable gazette a notice of the coming into force of the moratorium; and

(b) may advertise the notice in such other manner as the nominee thinks fit.

2.15(3) [Contents of notice] The notice must specify–

(a) the nature of the business of the company;

(b) that a moratorium under section 1A has come into force; and

(c) the date on which it came into force.

2.15(4) [Delivery of notice] The nominee must as soon as reasonably practicable deliver a notice of the coming into force of the moratorium to–

(a) the registrar of companies;

(b) the company; and

(c) any petitioning creditor of whose address the nominee is aware.

2.15(5) [Contents of notice] The notice must specify–

(a) the date on which the moratorium came into force; and

(b) the court with which the documents to obtain the moratorium were filed.

2.15(6) [Further notice requirements] The nominee must deliver a notice of the coming into force of the moratorium and the date on which it came into force to–

(a) any enforcement agent or other officer who to the knowledge of the nominee is charged with distress or other legal process, against the company or its property; and

(b) any person who to the nominee's knowledge has distrained against the company or its property.

General Note

The fact that the moratorium has started needs to be advertised. This CVA model is not as discreet as the original CVA alternative. See Form VAM1.

2.16 Notice of continuation of a moratorium where physical meeting of creditors is summoned (paragraph 8(3B) of Schedule A1)

2.16(1) [Application] This rule applies where under paragraph 8(3B)(b) and (3C) of Schedule A1 the moratorium continues after the initial period of 28 days referred to in paragraph 8(3) of that Schedule because a physical meeting of the company's creditors is first summoned to take place after the end of that period.

2.16(2) [Nominee to file and deliver notice] The nominee must file with the court and deliver to the registrar of companies a notice of the continuation as soon as reasonably practicable after summoning such a meeting of the company's creditors.

2.16(3) [Content of notice] The notice must–

(a) identify the company;

(b) give the name and address of the nominee;

(c) state the date on which the notice of the meeting was sent to the creditors under rule 15.6;

(d) state the date for which the meeting is summoned;

(e) state that under paragraph 8(3B)(b) and (3C) of Schedule A1 the moratorium will be continued to that date; and

(f) be authenticated and dated by the nominee.

General Note

This rule on notice to the court and registrar of companies of continuation of a moratorium beyond the initial 28-day period had no counterpart before 2017. The creditors' meeting is summoned in accordance with s.246ZE(3). See Form VAM2.

2.17 Notice of decision extending or further extending a moratorium (paragraph 36 of Schedule A1)

2.17(1) [Application] This rule applies where the moratorium is extended, or further extended by a decision which takes effect under paragraph 36 of Schedule A1.

2.17(2) [Filing and delivery of notice] The nominee must, as soon as reasonably practicable, file with the court and deliver to the registrar of companies a notice of the decision.

2.17(3) [Content of notice] The notice must–

(a) identify the company;

(b) give the name and address of the nominee;

(c) state the date on which the moratorium was extended or further extended;

(d) state the new expiry date of the moratorium; and

(e) be authenticated and dated by the nominee.

(See General Note after r.2.18.) See Form VAM3.

2.18 Notice of court order extending or further extending or continuing or renewing a moratorium (paragraph 34(2) of Schedule A1)

2.18 Where the court makes an order extending, further extending, renewing or continuing a moratorium, the nominee must, as soon as reasonably practicable, deliver to the registrar of companies a notice stating the new expiry date of the moratorium.

General Note to rr.2.17, 2.18

The registrar and court need to be informed if the moratorium has been extended or further extended. See Form VAM4.

2.19 Advertisement of end of a moratorium (paragraph 11(1) of Schedule A1)

2.19(1) [Nominee to gazette and advertise notice] After the moratorium ends, the nominee–

(a) must, as soon as reasonably practicable, gazette a notice of its coming to an end; and

(b) may advertise the notice in such other manner as the nominee thinks fit.

2.19(2) [Content of notice] The notice must state–

(a) the nature of the company's business;

(b) that a moratorium under section 1A has ended; and

(c) the date on which it came to an end.

2.19(3) [Nominee to file and deliver notice] The nominee must, as soon as reasonably practicable–

(a) file with the court a notice specifying the date on which the moratorium ended; and

(b) deliver such a notice to–

(i) the registrar of companies,

(ii) the company, and

(iii) the creditors.

2.19(4) [Content of notice to court] The notice to the court must–

(a) identify the company;

(b) give the name and address of the nominee; and

(c) be authenticated and dated by the nominee.

General Note

Where the moratorium has come to an end that fact must be advertised. Note FormVAM7.

2.20 Disposal of charged property etc. during a moratorium

2.20(1) [Application] This rule applies where the company applies to the court under paragraph 20 of Schedule A1 for permission to dispose of–

(a) property subject to a security; or

(b) goods under a hire-purchase agreement.

2.20(2) [Court to fix venue for hearing] The court must fix a venue for hearing the application.

2.20(3) [Notice of venue to security holder] The company must as soon as reasonably practicable deliver a notice of the venue to the holder of the security or the owner of the goods under the agreement.

2.20(4) [Sealed copies of order] If an order is made, the court must deliver two sealed copies of the order to the company and the company must deliver one of them to the holder or owner as soon as reasonably practicable.

General Note

If directors wish to obtain permission to dispose of company property during the course of the moratorium the requirements of this rule must be met.

2.21 Withdrawal of nominee's consent to act (paragraph 25(5) of Schedule A1)

2.21(1) [Nominee to file and deliver notice] A nominee who withdraws consent to act, must file with the court and otherwise deliver a notice under paragraph 25(5) of Schedule A1 as soon as reasonably practicable.

2.21(2) [Content of notice filed in court] The notice filed with the court must–

(a) identify the company;

(b) give the name and address of the nominee;

(c) specify the date on which the nominee withdrew consent;

(d) state, with reference to the reasons at paragraph 25(2) of that Schedule, why the nominee withdrew consent; and

(e) be authenticated and dated by the nominee.

General Note

This outlines formal requirements where a nominee withdraws consent to act. See Form VAM5.

2.22 Application to the court to replace the nominee (paragraph 28 of Schedule A1)

2.22(1) [Notice of directors' application] Directors who intend to make an application under paragraph 28 of Schedule A1 for the nominee to be replaced must deliver a notice of the intention to make the application to the nominee at least five business days before filing the application with the court.

2.22(2) [Notice of nominee's application] A nominee who intends to make an application under that paragraph to be replaced must deliver notice of the intention to make the application to the directors at least five business days before filing the application with the court.

2.22(3) [Replacement nominee's consent and qualification to act] The court must not appoint a replacement nominee unless a statement by the replacement nominee has been filed with the court confirming that person–

(a) consents to act; and

(b) is qualified to act as an insolvency practitioner in relation to the company.

General Note

Procedures governing the replacement of the nominee by the court are explained.

2.23 Notice of appointment of replacement nominee

2.23(1) [Notice to registrar of companies, former nominee, etc.] A person appointed as a replacement nominee must as soon as reasonably practicable deliver a notice of the appointment to the registrar of companies and the former nominee and, where the appointment is not by the court, file a notice of the appointment with the court.

2.23(2) [Content of notice filed in court] The notice filed with the court must–

(a) identify the company;

(b) give the name and address of the replacement nominee;

(c) specify the date on which the replacement nominee was appointed to act; and

(d) be authenticated and dated by the replacement nominee.

General Note

Where a replacement nominee is installed that fact needs to be notified. See Form VAM6

2.24 Applications to court to challenge nominee's actions etc. (paragraphs 26 and 27 of Schedule A1)

2.24 A person intending to make an application to the court under paragraph 26 or 27 of Schedule A1 must deliver a notice of the intention to make the application to the nominee at least five business days before filing the application with the court.

General Note

This explains procedures on applications pursuant to challenge the acts and omissions of the nominee.

Chapter 5

Consideration of the proposal by the company members and creditors

[Note: a document required by the Act or these Rules must also contain the standard contents set out in Part 1.]

2.25 Consideration of proposal: common requirements (section 3)

2.25(1) [Nominee to summon company meeting] The nominee must invite the members of the company to consider a proposal by summoning a meeting of the company as required by section 3.

2.25(2) [Nominee to invite members] The nominee must invite the creditors to consider the proposal by way of a decision procedure.

2.25(2A) [Jurisdiction to open proceedings] The nominee must examine whether there is jurisdiction to open the proceedings and must specify in the nominee's comments on the proposal required by paragraphs (3)(d)(iii) and (5)(a)(iii) whether the proceedings will be main, secondary, territorial or non-EU proceedings with the reasons for so stating.

2.25(3) [Notice to members] In the case of the members, the nominee must deliver to every person whom the nominee believes to be a member a notice which must–

(a) identify the proceedings;

(b) state the venue for the meeting;

(c) state the effect of the following–

(i) rule 2.35 about members' voting rights,

(ii) rule 2.36 about the requisite majority of members for passing resolutions, and

(iii) rule 15.35 about rights of appeal; and

(d) be accompanied by–

(i) a copy of the proposal,

(ii) a copy of the statement of affairs, or if the nominee thinks fit a summary including a list of creditors with the amounts of their debts,

(iii) the nominee's comments on the proposal, unless the nominee is the administrator or liquidator in which case the comments required are limited to stating whether the proceedings will be main, secondary, territorial or non-EU proceedings with the reasons for so stating, and

(iv) details of each resolution to be voted on.

2.25(4) [Notice to creditors] In the case of the creditors, the nominee must deliver to each creditor a notice in respect of the decision procedure which complies with rule 15.8 so far as is relevant.

2.25(5) [Contents of proposal to creditors] The notice must also–

(a) be accompanied by–

(i) a copy of the proposal,

(ii) a copy of the statement of affairs, or if the nominee thinks fit a summary including a list of creditors with the amounts of their debts, and

(iii) the nominee's comments on the proposal, unless the nominee is the administrator or liquidator, and

(b) state how a creditor may propose a modification to the proposal, and how the nominee will deal with such a proposal for a modification.

2.25(6) [Notice may refer to website] The notice may also state that the results of the consideration of the proposal will be made available for viewing and downloading on a website and that no other notice will be delivered to the creditors or members (as the case may be).

2.25(7) [Nominee to comply with requirements for website use] Where the results of the consideration of the proposal are to be made available for viewing and downloading on a website the nominee must comply with the requirements for use of a website to deliver a document set out in rule 1.49(2)(a) to (c), (3) and (4) with any necessary adaptations and rule 1.49(5)(a) applies to determine the time of delivery of the document.

General Note

The members and creditors now consider the proposal, by a meeting in the case of members and a "decision procedure" in the case of creditors: see r.2.27 below. This rule describes how the nominee must invite their respective consideration and the use of websites for making the results available. On the members' meeting see also rr.2.26 and 2.30. The detailed rules on the creditors' decision procedure appear in Pt 15 of these Rules. In particular the minimum notice for decision procedures and notices seeking deemed consent in relation to proposed CVAs is 14 days except for decisions on proposed modifications to the proposal from the directors under Sch.A1 para.31(7) where a moratorium is sought or considerations at physical meetings, where it is seven days (r.15.11(1)); the court may order notice by advertisement (r.15.11(2), 15.12). Under r.15.8(3)(j) for proposed CVAs the notice from the convener to the creditors of the decision procedure must contain a statement of the effects of rr.15.28, 15.31 and 15.34 (voting rights, calculation thereof and the requisite majorities: see note after r.2.38).

Rule 2.25(2A) inserted and r.2.25(3)(d)(iii) amended by the Insolvency Amendment (EU 2015/848) Regulations 2017 (SI 2017/702) regs 1, 2(1), Sch. paras 32, 36 in relation to proceedings opened on or after 26 June 2017 (see reg.3) when the Recast EU Regulation 2015/848 came into force.

2.26 Members' consideration at a meeting

2.26(1) [Notice to consider proposal] Where the nominee invites the members to consider the proposal at a meeting the notice to members under rule 2.25(3) must also–

(a) specify the purpose of and venue for the meeting; and

(b) be accompanied by a blank proxy.

2.26(2) [Convenience of venue] The nominee must have regard to the convenience of those invited to attend when fixing the venue for a meeting (including the resumption of an adjourned meeting).

2.26(3) [Date of meeting] The date of the meeting (except where the nominee is the administrator or liquidator of the company) must not be more than 28 days from the date on which–

(a) the nominee's report is filed with the court under rule 2.9; or

(b) the moratorium came into force.

General Note

The Act is largely silent about the summoning of members' meetings, but this rule, r.2.25(1) and (3) and r.2.30 make plain that a fairly strict procedure must be followed.

2.27 Creditors' consideration by a decision procedure

2.27 Where the nominee is inviting the creditors to consider the proposal by a decision procedure, the decision date must be not less than 14 days from the date of delivery of the notice and not more than 28 days from the date–

(a) the nominee's report is filed with the court under rule 2.9; or

(b) the moratorium came into force.

General Note

The timetable for the creditors' decision. The "decision date" in the case of a decision at a meeting is the date thereof; in the case of decision by a procedure other than a meeting or by the deemed consent procedure, it is the date the decision is made or deemed to be made and is treated as made at 23:59 on that date: r.15.2(1).

The "decision procedure", in light of amendments to IA 1986 by SBEEA 2015 as from 6 April 2017, will normally not involve a physical meeting unless requisitioned by the required threshold under s.246ZE(3). Decision procedures are detailed in Pt 15 of these Rules.

2.28 Timing of decisions on proposal

2.28(1) [Creditors' decision and company meeting] The decision date for the creditors' decision procedure may be on the same day as, or on a different day to, the meeting of the company.

2.28(2) [Creditors' decision first] But the creditors' decision on the proposal must be made before the members' decision.

2.28(3) [Members' decision] The members' decision must be made not later than five business days after the creditors' decision.

2.28(4) [Timing of the members' decision] For the purpose of this rule, the timing of the members' decision is either the date and time of the meeting of the company or, where the nominee invites members to consider the proposal by correspondence, the deadline for receipt of members' votes.

General Note

This allows a maximum of five business days for the members' decision after the creditors' decision but also recognises the fact that there is no point of having a meeting of members if the creditors have voted down the proposal.

2.29 Creditors' approval of modified proposal

2.29(1) [Application] This rule applies where a decision is sought from the creditors following notice to the nominee of proposed modifications to the proposal from the company's directors under paragraph 31(7) of Schedule A1.

2.29(2) [Date for decision procedure] The decision must be sought by a decision procedure with a decision date within 14 days of the date on which the directors gave notice to the nominee of the modifications.

2.29(3) [Creditor notice of the decision date] The creditors must be given at least seven days' notice of the decision date.

General Note

In relation to r.2.29(1) note Sch.A1 para.31(7A) and (7B).

See note to r.2.27 on the "decision date" and decision procedure.

2.30 Notice of members' meeting and attendance of officers

2.30(1) [Date for meeting] A notice under rule 2.25(3) summoning a meeting of the company must be delivered at least 14 days before the day fixed for the meeting to all the members and to–

(a) every officer or former officer of the company whose presence the nominee thinks is required; and

(b) all other directors of the company.

2.30(2) [Officers notified to attend] Every officer or former officer who receives such a notice stating that the nominee thinks that person's attendance is required is required to attend the meeting.

General Note

This rule provides the time limit for notice of the members' meeting called under r.2.25(2).

The nominee is given a wide discretion, on the one hand to insist on the attendance of a director whose presence he may consider helpful and, on the other, to exclude any director who may be thought to hinder the proceedings. Former officers no longer appear limited only to those who were in office within two years of the notice.

Rule 2.30(1) amended by the Insolvency (England and Wales) and Insolvency (Scotland) (Miscellaneous and Consequential Amendments) Rules 2017 (SI 2017/1115) rr.1(1), (2), 2, 3 as from 8 December 2017.

2.31 Requisition of physical meeting by creditors

2.31(1) [Application] This rule applies where the creditors requisition a physical meeting to consider a proposal (with or without modifications) in accordance with section 246ZE and rule 15.6.

2.31(2) [Date for meeting] The meeting must take place within 14 days of the date on which the prescribed proportion of creditors have required the meeting to take place.

2.31(3) [Notice for meeting] A notice summoning a meeting of the creditors must be delivered to the creditors at least seven days before the day fixed for the meeting.

General Note

In case the required threshold (see s.246ZE(7)) of creditors requisition a physical meeting rather than the decision procedure without a meeting, this rule provides the time limit for notice of (and see r.15.11(1)), and holding, the meeting.

2.32 Non-receipt of notice by members

2.32 Where in accordance with the Act or these Rules the members are invited to consider a proposal, the consideration is presumed to have duly taken place even if not everyone to whom the notice is to be delivered receives it.

General Note

This is a useful concession. There are sufficient safety valves in the system in the event of a material irregularity.

2.33 Proposal for alternative supervisor

2.33(1) [Proposed supervisor's consent and qualification to act to nominee] If in response to a notice inviting–

(a) members to consider the proposal by correspondence; or

(b) creditors to consider the proposal other than at a meeting,

a member or creditor proposes that a person other than the nominee be appointed as supervisor, that person's consent to act and confirmation of being qualified to act as an insolvency practitioner in relation to the company must be delivered to the nominee by the deadline in the notice of the decision by correspondence or by the decision date (as the case may be).

2.33(2) [Confirmation of consent and qualification to act to meeting chair] If, at either a meeting of the company or the creditors to consider the proposal, a resolution is moved for the appointment of a person other than the nominee to be supervisor, the person moving the resolution must produce to the chair at or before the meeting–

(a) confirmation that the person proposed as supervisor is qualified to act as an insolvency practitioner in relation to the company; and

(b) that person's written consent to act (unless that person is present at the meeting and there signifies consent to act).

General Note

The procedure in relation to consent and qualification to act on the occurrence that a person other than the nominee is proposed and becomes the supervisor.

2.34 Chair at meetings

2.34 The chair of a meeting under this Part must be the nominee or an appointed person.

General Note

Here we see the modern drafting of the Rules preferring "chair" to the previous "chairman".

An "appointed person" is a person described in r.1.2(3) appointed by the nominee.

A "meeting" for these purposes includes a "virtual meeting" (defined in r.15.2(1)) as well as a physical meeting (r.1.2).

2.35 Members' voting rights

2.35(1) [In accordance with articles] A member is entitled to vote according to the rights attaching to the member's shares in accordance with the articles of the company.

2.35(2) [Shares include any other member's interest] A member's shares include any other interest that person may have as a member of the company.

2.35(3) [Valuation for voting purposes] The value of a member for the purposes of voting is determined by reference to the number of votes conferred on that member by the company's articles.

General Note

Unsurprisingly, the company's articles determine members' voting right.

2.36 Requisite majorities of members

2.36(1) [Majority in value in favour] A resolution is passed by members by correspondence or at a meeting of the company when a majority (in value) of those voting have voted in favour of it.

2.36(2) [Subject to articles] This is subject to any express provision to the contrary in the articles.

2.36(3) [Resolution by correspondence] A resolution is not passed by correspondence unless at least one member has voted in favour of it.

General Note

A majority in value is needed subject to the articles. Rule 2.36(3) appears perplexing but presumably means that there cannot be a resolution without at least one vote in favour.

2.37 Notice of order made under section 4A(6) or paragraph 36(5) of Schedule A1

2.37(1) [Application] This rule applies where the court makes an order under section 4A(6) or paragraph 36(5) of Schedule A1.

2.37(2) [Sealed copy] The member who applied for the order must deliver a sealed copy of it to–

(a) the proposer; and

(b) the supervisor (if there is one different to the proposer).

2.37(3) [Copy to company] If the directors are the proposer a single copy may be delivered to the company at its registered office.

2.37(4) [Notice of order] The supervisor, or the proposer where there is no supervisor, must as soon as reasonably practicable deliver a notice that the order has been made to every person who had received a notice to vote on the matter or who is affected by the order.

2.37(5) [Copy to registrar of companies] The member who applied for the order must, within five business days of the order, deliver a copy to the registrar of companies.

General Note

The procedure for notification of court orders directing that the views of members shall prevail over creditors. Such orders are rare. See Form VAMC.

2.38 Report of consideration of proposal under section 4(6) and (6A) or paragraph 30(3) and (4) of Schedule A1

2.38(1) [Report by meeting convener or chair] A report or reports as the case may be must be prepared of the consideration of a proposal under section 4(6) and (6A) or paragraph 30(3) and (4) of Schedule A1 by the convener or, in the case of a meeting, the chair.

2.38(2) [Content of report] The report must–

(a) state whether the proposal was approved or rejected and whether by the creditors alone or by both the creditors and members and, in either case, whether any approval was with any modifications;

(b) list the creditors and members who voted or attended or who were represented at the meeting or decision procedure (as applicable) used to consider the proposal, setting out (with their respective values) how they voted on each resolution or whether they abstained;

(c) identify which of those creditors were considered to be connected with the company;

(d) if the proposal was approved, state with reasons whether the proceedings are main, territorial or non-EU proceedings; and

(e) include such further information as the nominee or the chair thinks it appropriate to make known to the court.

2.38(3) [Copy report filed in court] A copy of the report must be filed with the court, within four business days of the date of the company meeting.

2.38(4) [Court to endorse copy report] The court must endorse the copy of the report with the date of filing.

2.38(5) [Chair/convener to give notice of result] The chair (in the case of a company meeting) or otherwise the convener must give notice of the result of the consideration of the proposal to everyone who was invited to consider the proposal or to whom notice of a decision procedure or meeting was delivered as soon as reasonably practicable after a copy of the report is filed with the court.

2.38(6) [Copy of convenor/chair's report to registrar of companies after approval] Where the decision approving the CVA has effect under section 4A or paragraph 36 of Schedule A1 with or without modifications, the supervisor must as soon as reasonably practicable deliver a copy of the convener's report or, in the case of a meeting, the chair's report to the registrar of companies.

General Note to rr.2.25–2.38

The detailed procedure for the summoning and conduct of the company meeting is here set out, and the "decision procedure" for creditors is referred to but the detail for the latter is actually contained in IR 2016 Pt 15: see that Part and some specific rules on proposed CVAs are summarised below. A number of points which the Insolvency Act appears to leave in doubt are settled.

A notice to participate in a creditors' meeting must be delivered to every present or former officer of the company whose presence the convener thinks is required and that person's attendance is compulsory (r.15.14(1)).

Rule 2.28 clarifies that although the date for the creditors' decision procedure may be on the same day as company meeting, the creditors' decision on the proposal must be made before the members' decision.

The chair may adjourn a meeting for a proposed CVA for not more than 14 days and if the meeting resolves and where a moratorium is in force must adjourn a meeting under Sch.A1 para.29(1) to no more than 14 days after the moratorium (including any extension) ends.

Every creditor, secured or unsecured, who has notice of the decision procedure is entitled to vote on the debt (r.15.28(5)).

Although a contingent or prospective creditor, or a person who has a claim for an unliquidated amount is not, on a strict view, a "creditor", the cases now make it reasonably clear that they should be treated as creditors for the purposes of Pt I of the Act and for the Rules (see the note to s.1(1) and the cases there cited). Any such person is therefore entitled to be invited and given notice to consider the proposal by way of a decision procedure under r.2.25(2) and (4) or to receive notice of a creditors' physical meeting under r.2.31(3) and in either case (subject to r.15.31(2) and (3), see below) to vote on it. If he has had notice and was entitled to vote on the procedure or at the meeting, he is bound by the voluntary arrangement which was approved, whether or not he voted.

In *Beverley Group plc v McClue* [1995] B.C.C. 751 a person who had a claim for an unliquidated amount (and was accordingly held to have been entitled to vote) had been sent formal notice of the meeting by post but this had never reached him. He had, however, learned of the meeting from another source but chose not to attend it. The court ruled that he had had notice of the meeting and was bound by the arrangement.

Rule 15.31(2) allows a creditor whose debt is for an unliquidated amount or whose value is not ascertained to vote but under r.15.31(3) the debt is to be valued at £1 unless the convener or chair or an appointed person decides to put a higher value on it for the purpose of entitlement to vote and admits the vote for that purpose. The former wording was that the "chairman agrees to put a higher value on it" but "agrees" did not mean "agrees with the creditor" in the sense that there must be a bilateral consent to the estimated value, but rather "expresses a willingness" to put a value: *Re Cancol Ltd* [1995] B.C.C. 1133; *Doorbar v Alltime Securities Ltd* [1995] B.C.C. 1149. The wording from 6 April 2017, states that the person now "decides" to put a higher value and so this issue appears otiose. The earlier case of *Re Cranley Mansions Ltd* [1994] B.C.C. 576, in which the applicant had refused to accept the chairman's estimate of £1 on a claim for £900,000, would not now be followed on this point (note the use of the £1 valuation prescription). If a person declines to attend the creditors' meeting it is not open to him to object that the chairman has not put an estimated valuation on his debt: see *Beverley Group plc v McClue* (above). On voting entitlement see also *Lombard North Central plc v Brook* [1999] B.P.I.R. 701.

A creditor or member may appeal to the court against a decision of the convener or chair but the court may only make an order if there was unfair prejudice or material irregularity: r.15.35(1), (2). An appeal may not be made after 28 beginning with the day of the report of the result of the decision under s.4(6) or (where a moratorium was sought) Sch.A1 para.30(3) was filed in court (see below) (r.15.35(5)(a)). This time limitation was emphasised in *Re Bournemouth & Boscombe AFC Co Ltd* [1998] B.P.I.R. 183 (a case decided under s.6).

Creditors' votes are calculated in a proposed CVA under r.15.31(1)(d) as at the decision date except: if the company is being wound up, then at the date it went into liquidation; if it is in administration, at the date it entered into administration (less any payments made to the creditor after that date in respect of the claim); or where a moratorium has been obtained (less any payments made to the creditor after that date in respect of the claim), at the beginning of the moratorium.

Although every creditor, secured or unsecured, who has notice of the decision procedure is entitled to vote on the debt, for voting purposes a fully secured debt is valued as nil and a partly secured debt is valued only as to the unsecured part. However in a proposed CVA where there is a decision on whether to extend or further extend a moratorium or to bring a moratorium to an end before the end of the period of any extension, the debt is valued at full value without deduction of the value of the security: r.15.31(4), (5), (6)(b).

The requisite majority for a decision is specified in r.15.34(1) normally as a majority in value of the creditors voting in favour but a super majority of three-quarters (in value) is required for a decision: approving a proposal or a modification thereto, extending or further extending a moratorium or bringing a moratorium to an end before the end of the period of any extension (r.15.34(3)). However a decision is not made if more than half of the total value of unconnected creditors whose claims were admitted for voting voted against it (a creditor is unconnected unless the convener or chair decides that the creditor is connected with the company, relying on the information in the statement of affairs or otherwise under the definition in s.249) (r.15.34(4), (5)).

The convener or the chair must report the result of the decision to the court under s.4(6), (6A) or (where a moratorium is sought) Sch.A1 para.30(3), (4) and the procedure is provided by r.2.38 under which the report must also be sent to everyone who was invited to consider the proposal or to whom notice of a decision procedure or meeting was delivered as soon as reasonably practicable after a copy of the report is filed with the court. The supervisor must deliver a copy of the report to the registrar of companies.

On r. 2.38 see Form CVA1.

Rule 2.38(2)(d) amended by the Insolvency (England and Wales) and Insolvency (Scotland) (Miscellaneous and Consequential Amendments) Rules 2017 (SI 2017/1115) rr.1(1), (2), 22, 30(5) as from 8 December 2017.

Chapter 6

Additional matters concerning and following approval of CVA

[Note: a document required by the Act or these Rules must also contain the standard contents set out in Part 1.]

2.39 Hand-over of property etc. to supervisor

2.39(1) [Putting supervisor into possession of assets] Where the decision approving a CVA has effect under section 4A or paragraph 36 of Schedule A1, and the supervisor is not the same person as the proposer, the proposer must, as soon as reasonably practicable, do all that is required to put the supervisor in possession of the assets included in the CVA.

2.39(2) [Discharge balance of insolvency practitioner's remuneration etc.] Where the company is in administration or liquidation and the supervisor is not the same person as the administrator or liquidator, the supervisor must–

(a) before taking possession of the assets included in the CVA, deliver to the administrator or liquidator an undertaking to discharge the balance referred to in paragraph (3) out of the first realisation of assets; or

(b) upon taking possession of the assets included in the CVA, discharge such balance.

2.39(3) [Balance due] The balance is any balance due to the administrator or liquidator, or to the official receiver not acting as liquidator–

(a) by way of fees or expenses properly incurred and payable under the Act or these Rules; and

(b) on account of any advances made in respect of the company together with interest on such advances at the rate specified in section 17 of the Judgments Act 1838 at the date on which the company entered administration or went into liquidation.

2.39(4) [Charge on assets] The administrator or liquidator, or the official receiver not acting as liquidator, has a charge on the assets included in the CVA in respect of any sums comprising such balance, subject only to the deduction from realisations by the supervisor of the proper costs and expenses of such realisations.

2.39(5) [Discharge of guarantees etc.] The supervisor must from time to time out of the realisation of assets–

(a) discharge all guarantees properly given by the administrator or liquidator for the benefit of the company; and

(b) pay all the expenses of the administrator or liquidator or of the official receiver not acting as liquidator.

2.39(6) [Priority of sums due to official receiver] Sums due to the official receiver take priority over those due to any other person under this rule.

GENERAL NOTE

When the CVA has been approved there is a positive duty on the proposer (if not the supervisor) to "do all that is required" to put the supervisor in possession of the assets included in the CVA, subject where the company is in administration or liquidation (and the supervisor is not the administrator or liquidator) to discharge specified rights and duties of those office-holders.

2.40 Revocation or suspension of CVA

2.40(1) [Application] This rule applies where the court makes an order of revocation or suspension under section 6 or paragraph 38 of Schedule A1.

2.40(2) [Sealed copy of order] The applicant for the order must deliver a sealed copy of it to–

(a) the proposer; and

(b) the supervisor (if different).

2.40(3) [Single copy to company] If the directors are the proposer a single copy of the order may be delivered to the company at its registered office.

2.40(4) [Direction of court for further consideration in order] If the order includes a direction by the court under section 6(4)(b) or (c) or under paragraph 38(4)(b) or (c) of Schedule A1 for action to be taken, the applicant for the order must deliver a notice that the order has been made to the person who is directed to take such action.

2.40(5) [Notice of order and any revised proposal] The proposer must–

(a) as soon as reasonably practicable deliver a notice that the order has been made to all of those persons to whom a notice to consider the matter was delivered or who appear to be affected by the order;

(b) within five business days of delivery of a copy of the order (or within such longer period as the court may allow), deliver (if applicable) a notice to the court advising that it is intended to make a revised proposal to the company and its creditors, or to invite re-consideration of the original proposal.

2.40(6) [Copy order to registrar of companies] The applicant for the order must deliver a copy of the order to the registrar of companies within five business days of the making of the order with a notice which must contain the date on which the voluntary arrangement took effect.

GENERAL NOTE

Once approved by the creditors and the company meeting the CVA takes effect under s.5(2)(a) as if made by the company at the creditors' meeting but revocation or suspension of the CVA requires a court order. This rule places duties on the applicant for such an order and on the proposer. See Form CVA2.

2.41 Supervisor's accounts and reports

2.41(1) [Duty of supervisor to keep] The supervisor must keep accounts and records where the CVA authorises or requires the supervisor–

(a) to carry on the business of the company;

(b) to realise assets of the company; or

(c) otherwise to administer or dispose of any of its funds.

2.41(2) [Obligation for accounts and records and receipts and payments] The accounts and records which must be kept are of the supervisor's acts and dealings in, and in connection with, the CVA, including in particular records of all receipts and payments of money.

2.41(3) [Preservation of any other supervisor's accounts etc.] The supervisor must preserve any such accounts and records which were kept by any other person who has acted as supervisor of the CVA and are in the supervisor's possession.

2.41(4) [Progress reports] The supervisor must deliver reports on the progress and prospects for the full implementation of the CVA to–

(a) the registrar of companies;

(b) the company;

(c) the creditors bound by the CVA;

(d) subject to paragraph (10) below, the members; and

(e) if the company is not in liquidation, the company's auditors (if any) for the time being.

2.41(5) [Notice with report to contain date CVA took effect] The notice which accompanies the report when delivered to the registrar of companies must contain the date on which the voluntary arrangement took effect.

2.41(6) [Annual reports] The first report must cover the period of 12 months commencing on the date on which the CVA was approved and a further report must be made for each subsequent period of 12 months.

2.41(7) [Time for delivery of reports] Each report must be delivered within the period of two months after the end of the 12 month period.

2.41(8) [Release from annual report requirement] Such a report is not required if the obligation to deliver a final report under rule 2.44 arises in the two month period.

2.41(9) [Report to include abstract of receipts and payments] Where the supervisor is authorised or required to do any of the things mentioned in paragraph (1), the report must–

(a) include or be accompanied by a summary of receipts and payments required to be recorded by virtue of paragraph (2); or

(b) state that there have been no such receipts and payments.

2.41(10) [Dispensing power of court re members] The court may, on application by the supervisor, dispense with the delivery of such reports or summaries to members, either altogether or on the basis that the availability of the report to members is to be advertised by the supervisor in a specified manner.

(See General Note after r.2.44.) See Form CVA3.

2.42 Production of accounts and records to the Secretary of State

2.42(1) [Power of Secretary of State to require] The Secretary of State may during the CVA, or after its full implementation or termination, require the supervisor to produce for inspection (either at the premises of the supervisor or elsewhere)–

(a) the supervisor's accounts and records in relation to the CVA; and

(b) copies of reports and summaries prepared in compliance with rule 2.41.

2.42(2) [Audit of accounts and records] The Secretary of State may require the supervisor's accounts and records to be audited and, if so, the supervisor must provide such further information and assistance as the Secretary of State requires for the purposes of audit.

(See General Note after r.2.44.)

2.43 Fees and expenses

2.43 The fees and expenses that may be incurred for the purposes of the CVA are–

(a) fees for the nominee's services agreed with the company (or, as the case may be, the administrator or liquidator) and disbursements made by the nominee before the decision approving the CVA takes effect under section 4A or paragraph 36 of Schedule A1;

(b) fees or expenses which–

(i) are sanctioned by the terms of the CVA, or

(ii) where they are not sanctioned by the terms of the CVA would be payable, or correspond to those which would be payable, in an administration or winding up.

(See General Note after r.2.44.)

2.44 Termination or full implementation of CVA

2.44(1) [Supervisor to deliver notice] Not more than 28 days after the full implementation or termination of the CVA the supervisor must deliver a notice that the CVA has been fully implemented or terminated to all the members and those creditors who are bound by the arrangement.

2.44(2) [Notice to be accompanied by copy report by supervisor] The notice must state the date the CVA took effect and must be accompanied by a copy of a report by the supervisor which–

(a) summarises all receipts and payments in relation to the CVA;

(b) explains any departure from the terms of the CVA as it originally had effect;

(c) if the CVA has terminated, sets out the reasons why; and

(d) includes (if applicable) a statement as to the amount paid to any unsecured creditors by virtue of section 176A.

2.44(3) [Copy notice and report to registrar of companies and court] The supervisor must within the 28 days mentioned above send to the registrar of companies and file with the court a copy of the notice to creditors and of the supervisor's report.

2.44(4) [No vacation of supervisor's office until r.2.44(3) complied with] The supervisor must not vacate office until after the copies of the notice and report have been delivered to the registrar of companies and filed with the court.

General Note to rr.2.39–2.44

The scheme takes effect without further formality from the time of the creditors' decision to approve (IA 1986 s.5(2)(a); but compare the "decision date" defined in r.15.2(1)). The creditors' decision must be made before the members' decision (r.2.28(2)).

The detailed procedure for the implementation of the proposal, if approved, is set out here requiring hand-over of property where relevant, revocation and/or suspension of the CVA, accounts and reports, what fees and expenses may be incurred and notice of termination or full implementation of the CVA.

On r.2.44 see Form CVA4.

Chapter 7

Time recording information

[Note: a document required by the Act or these Rules must also contain the standard contents set out in Part 1.]

2.45 Provision of information

2.45(1) [Application] This rule applies where the remuneration of the nominee or the supervisor has been fixed on the basis of the time spent.

2.45(2) [Duty of nominee or supervisor to deliver statement] A person who is acting, or has acted within the previous two years, as–

(a) a nominee in relation to a proposal; or

(b) the supervisor in relation to a CVA;

must, within 28 days of receipt of a request from a person mentioned in paragraph (3), deliver free of charge to that person a statement complying with paragraphs (4) and (5).

2.45(3) [Who may request statement] The persons are–

(a) any director of the company; and

(b) where the proposal has been approved, any creditor or member.

2.45(4) [Period of statement] The statement must cover the period which–

(a) in the case of a person who has ceased to act as nominee or supervisor in relation to a company, begins with the date of appointment as nominee or supervisor and ends with the date of ceasing to act; and

(b) in any other case, consists of one or more complete periods of six months beginning with the date of appointment and ending most nearly before the date of receiving the request.

2.45(5) [Content of statement] The statement must set out–

(a) the total number of hours spent on the matter during that period by the nominee or supervisor, and any staff;

(b) for each grade of staff engaged on the matter, the average hourly rate at which work carried out by staff in that grade is charged; and

(c) the number of hours spent on the matter by each grade of staff during that period.

General Note

The equivalent of this rule was introduced in 2010 to provide greater transparency on the nominee's or supervisor's remuneration based on time spent.

Part 3

Administration

Introductory note to Part 3

The rules which follow apply in the "new" administration regime (Sch.B1, introduced by EA 2002 with effect from 15 September 2003). In those cases where the original regime continues to apply, reference should be made to the original Pt 2 (see Vol.2 of the 19th edition).

Part 3 of the new Rules replaces Pt 2 of IR 1986. The most noticeable changes include the following:

- Forms are no longer prescribed: although a particular rule may require a document to be "in the prescribed form", it is not to be *on* a prescribed form. Instead the rule sets out a check-list of items which must be included in the contents of the document in question. Forms are still required for documents to be filed with the registrar of companies.
- As a general rule, decisions are not to be taken by the participants at physical meetings, convened in the traditional manner. The options available are: electronic voting, "virtual" meetings (e.g. conference calls) and the "deemed consent" procedure (see rr.15.3–15.7). A physical meeting cannot be instigated on the initiative of the administrator, but only at the request of the prescribed number or percentage of the creditors or contributories (IA 1986 s.246ZE(7)).
- Many rules formerly to be found in Pt 2 of the 1986 Rules have been moved to other Parts, where provision is made for the rules relating to several insolvency procedures to be dealt with under a single head, for instance: defined terms and form and contents of documents (Pt 1), court procedure and practice (Pt 12), creditors' claims (Pt 14), proxies and corporate representation (Pt 16), creditors' meetings (Pt 17), reporting and remuneration of office-holders (Pt 18), disclaimer (Pt 19) and service (Sch.4).

Chapter 1

Interpretation for this Part

[Note: a document required by the Act or these Rules must also contain the standard contents set out in Part 1.]

3.1 Interpretation for Part 3

3.1 In this Part–

"pre-administration costs" means fees charged, and expenses incurred by the administrator, or another person qualified to act as an insolvency practitioner in relation to the company, before the company entered administration but with a view to it doing so; and

"unpaid pre-administration costs" means pre-administration costs which had not been paid when the company entered administration.

General Note

The rules in this Part govern administrations where the administrator is appointed under the new IA 1986 Pt II, which is to be found in Sch.B1 to the Act. The appointment may be made by the court under Sch.B1 para.11, by the holder of a "qualifying" floating charge under para.14, or by the company itself or its directors under para.22.

References to paragraph numbers in the notes which follow are to paragraphs of Sch.B1, and those to section numbers are to sections of IA 1986. Cross-references to other rules, if in italics, are to the original Pt 2 of IR 1986; if in roman type, to the new Pt 2.

Rule 3.1 contains two specific definitions relating exclusively to administration costs. For definitions of general terms in the Rules, reference should be made to r.1.2(2)

3.2 Proposed administrator's statement and consent to act

3.2(1) [References to and content of] References in this Part to a consent to act are to a statement by a proposed administrator headed "Proposed administrator's statement and consent to act" which contains the following–

(a) identification details for the company immediately below the heading;

(b) a certificate that the proposed administrator is qualified to act as an insolvency practitioner in relation to the company;

(c) the proposed administrator's IP number;

(d) the name of the relevant recognised professional body which is the source of the proposed administrator's authorisation to act in relation to the company;

(e) a statement that the proposed administrator consents to act as administrator of the company;

(f) a statement whether or not the proposed administrator has had any prior professional relationship with the company and if so a short summary of the relationship;

(g) the name of the person by whom the appointment is to be made or the applicant in the case of an application to the court for an appointment; and

(h) a statement that the proposed administrator is of the opinion that the purpose of administration is reasonably likely to be achieved in the particular case.

3.2(2) [Authentication] The statement and consent to act must be authenticated and dated by the proposed administrator.

3.2(3) [Joint appointments] Where a number of persons are proposed to be appointed to act jointly or concurrently as the administrator of a company, each must make a separate statement and consent to act.

General Note

This rule had no direct counterpart in IR 1986, where the detail of the statement and consent to act was formerly contained in Form 2.2B. IR 2016 do not prescribe forms but rather specify the content of notices, applications etc.

Chapter 2

Appointment of administrator by Court

[Note: a document required by the Act or these Rules must also contain the standard contents set out in Part 1.]

3.3 Administration application (paragraph 12 of Schedule B1)

3.3(1) [Heading of application] An administration application in relation to a company must be headed

"Administration application" and must identify the company immediately below the heading.

3.3(2) [Content of application] The application must contain–

(a) the name of the applicant;

(b) a statement whether the application is being made by–

(i) the company under paragraph 12(1)(a) of Schedule B1,

(ii) the directors of the company under paragraph 12(1)(b) of Schedule B1,

(iii) a single creditor under paragraph 12(1)(c) of Schedule B1,

(iv) a creditor under paragraph 12(1)(c) of Schedule B1 on behalf of that creditor and others,

(v) the holder of a qualifying floating charge under paragraph 35 or 37 of Schedule B1 (specifying which),

(vi) the liquidator of the company under paragraph 38 of Schedule B1,

(vii) the supervisor of a CVA under section 7(4)(b), or

(viii) a designated officer of a magistrates' court under section 87A of the Magistrates' Courts Act 1980;

(c) if the application is made by a creditor on behalf of that creditor and others, the names of the others;

(d) if the application is made by the holder of a qualifying floating charge, details of the charge including the date of the charge, the date on which it was registered and the maximum amount if any secured by the charge;

(e) if the company is registered under the Companies Act–

(i) any issued and called-up capital, the number of shares into which the capital is divided, the nominal value of each share and the amount of capital paid up or treated as paid up; or

(ii) that it is a company limited by guarantee;

(f) particulars of the principal business carried on by the company;

(g) a statement whether the company is an Article 1.2 undertaking;

(h) a statement whether the proceedings flowing from the appointment will be main, secondary, territorial or non-EU proceedings and that the reasons for the statement are set out in the witness statement in support of the application made under rule 3.6;

(i) except where the applicant is the holder of a qualifying floating charge and is making the application under paragraph 35 of Schedule B1, a statement that the applicant believes, for the reasons set out in the witness statement in support of the application that the company is, or is likely to become, unable to pay its debts;

(j) the name and address of the proposed administrator;

(k) the address for service of the applicant;

(l) the statement that the applicant requests the court–

(i) to make an administration order in relation to the company,

(ii) to appoint the proposed person to be administrator, and

(iii) to make such ancillary order as the applicant may request, and such other order as the court thinks appropriate.

3.3(3) [Authentication] The application must be authenticated by the applicant or the applicant's solicitor and dated.

General Note

This rule had no direct counterpart in IR 1986, where the detail of the application was formerly contained in Form 2.1B, but IR 2016 do not prescribe forms but rather specify the content required.

"Article 1.2 undertaking" in r.3.3(2)(f) is defined in r.1.2(2).

Rule 3.3(2)(h) amended by the Insolvency (England and Wales) and Insolvency (Scotland) (Miscellaneous and Consequential Amendments) Rules 2017 (SI 2017/1115) rr.1(1), (2), 22, 30(6) as from 8 December 2017.

(See further General Note after r.3.10.)

3.4 Administration application made by the directors

3.4 After an application by the directors for an administration order is filed it is to be treated for all purposes as an application by the company.

(See General Note after r.3.10.)

3.5 Administration application by the supervisor of a CVA

3.5 After an application by the supervisor of a CVA for an administration order in respect of the company has been served on the company as required by rule 3.8(3)(d) it is to be treated for all purposes as an application by the company.

(See General Note after r.3.10.)

3.6 Witness statement in support of administration application

3.6(1) [Who to be make] If an administration application is to be made by–

(a) the company, a witness statement must be made by one of the following stating that the person making the statement does so on behalf of the company–

(i) one of the directors,

(ii) the secretary of the company, or

(iii) the supervisor of a CVA;

(b) the company's directors, a witness statement must be made by one of the following stating that the person making it does so on behalf of the directors–

(i) one of the directors, or

(ii) the secretary of the company;

(c) a single creditor, a witness statement must be made by–

(i) that creditor, or

(ii) a person acting under that creditor's authority;

(d) two or more creditors, a witness statement must be made by a person acting under the authority of them all, whether or not one of their number.

3.6(2) [Nature of applicant creditor authority] In a case falling within paragraph (1)(c)(ii) or (d), the witness statement must state the nature of the authority of the person making it and the means of that person's knowledge of the matters to which the witness statement relates.

3.6(3) [Content] The witness statement must contain–

(a) a statement of the company's financial position, specifying (to the best of the applicant's knowledge and belief) the company's assets and liabilities, including contingent and prospective liabilities;

(b) details of any security known or believed to be held by creditors of the company, and whether in any case the security is such as to confer power on the holder to appoint an administrative receiver or to appoint an administrator under paragraph 14 of Schedule B1;

(c) a statement that an administrative receiver has been appointed if that is the case;

(d) details of any insolvency proceedings in relation to the company, including any petition that has been presented for the winding up of the company so far as known to the applicant;

(e) where it is intended to appoint a number of persons as administrators, a statement of the matters relating to the exercise of their functions set out in paragraph 100(2) of Schedule B1;

(f) the reasons for the statement that the proceedings will be main, secondary, territorial or non-EU proceedings; and

(g) any other matters which, in the applicant's opinion, will assist the court in deciding whether to make such an order.

3.6(4) [Entitlement of QFC holder] Where the application is made by the holder of a qualifying floating charge under paragraph 35 or 37 of Schedule B1, the witness statement must give sufficient details to satisfy the court that the applicant is entitled to appoint an administrator under paragraph 14 of Schedule B1.

3.6(5) [Further content where company in liquidation] Where the application is made under paragraph 37 or 38 of Schedule B1 in relation to a company in liquidation, the witness statement must also contain–

(a) details of the existing insolvency proceedings, the name and address of the liquidator, the date the liquidator was appointed and by whom;

(b) the reasons why it has subsequently been considered appropriate that an administration application should be made; and

(c) any other matters that would, in the applicant's opinion, assist the court in deciding whether to make provision in relation to matters arising in connection with the liquidation.

(See General Note after r.3.10.)

3.7 Filing of application

3.7(1) [In court] The application must be filed with the court together with the witness statement in support and the proposed administrator's consent to act.

3.7(2) [Court to fix hearing venue] The court must fix a venue for the hearing of the application.

3.7(3) There must also be filed, at the same time as the application or at any time after that, a sufficient number of copies of the application and the statement for service in accordance with rule 3.8.

3.7(4) [Court to seal, endorse and deliver copies to applicant] Each of the copies filed must–

(a) have applied to it the seal of the court;

(b) be endorsed with–

(i) the date and time of filing, and

(ii) the venue fixed by the court; and

(c) be delivered by the court to the applicant.

(See General Note after r.3.10.)

3.8 Service of application

3.8(1) [References to application] In this rule, references to the application are to a copy of the application and witness statement delivered by the court under rule 3.7(4)(c).

3.8(2) [Notification by service] Notification for the purposes of paragraph 12(2) of Schedule B1 must be by service of the application.

3.8(3) [Persons to be served] The applicant must serve the application on the following (in addition to serving it on the persons referred to in paragraph 12(2)(a) to (c) of Schedule B1)–

(a) any administrative receiver of the company;

(b) if there is a petition pending for the winding up of the company on–

(i) the petitioner, and

(ii) any provisional liquidator;

(c) any member State liquidator appointed in main proceedings in relation to the company;

(d) the company, if the application is made by anyone other than the company or its directors;

(e) any supervisor of a CVA in relation to the company; and

(f) the proposed administrator.

3.8(4) [Certificate of service to be filed in court] The certificate of service must be filed with the court as soon as reasonably practicable after service and in any event not later than the business day before the hearing of the application.

(See General Note after r.3.10.)

3.9 Notice to enforcement agents charged with distress or other legal process, etc.

3.9 The applicant must as soon as reasonably practicable after filing the application deliver a notice of its being made to–

(a) any enforcement agent or other officer who to the knowledge of the applicant is charged with distress or other legal process against the company or its property; and

(b) any person who to the knowledge of the applicant has distrained against the company or its property.

(See General Note after r.3.10.)

3.10 Notice of other insolvency proceedings

3.10 After the application has been filed and until an order is made, it is the duty of the applicant to file with the court notice of the existence of any insolvency proceedings in relation to the company, as soon as the applicant becomes aware of them–

(a) anywhere in the world, in the case of a company registered under the Companies Act in England and Wales;

(b) in any EEA State (including the United Kingdom), in the case of a company incorporated in an EEA State other than the United Kingdom; or

(c) in any member State other than Denmark, in the case of a company not incorporated in an EEA State.

General Note to rr.3.3–3.10

The procedure for an administration order is by way of application rather than by petition as under the original Pt II of IA 1986.

R.3.4

An application by the directors must be authorised by all of the directors or by a resolution passed at a duly constituted board meeting: para.105 does not apply in this context: *Minmar (929) Ltd v Khalastchi* [2011] EWHC 1159 (Ch); [2011] B.C.C. 485. Where the company's articles confer exclusive powers of management on the directors, it has been held (obiter) that only the directors can authorise an application by the company: *Re Frontsouth (Witham) Ltd* [2011] EWHC 1668 (Ch); [2011] B.C.C. 635; but this view may be open to challenge. See the notes to Sch.B1 paras 12(1) and 22(1).

The "Rule 2.2 report" required to be made under the original regime has been replaced by the statement described in r.3.2.

R.3.6(3)(f)

On the question whether the EU Regulation applies and the different types of proceedings, see the notes to art.3 of the Regulation and the note to Pt 21 of these Rules.

Rule 3.6(3)(f) amended by the Insolvency (England and Wales) and Insolvency (Scotland) (Miscellaneous and Consequential Amendments) Rules 2017 (SI 2017/1115) rr.1(1), (2), 22, 30(7) as from 8 December 2017.

R.3.8
On *where* service of the application for an administration order is to be effected in relation to the company and any other person, now see Sch.4 para.3 to these Rules. Those provisions do not contain a complete and exhaustive code as to the mode of service on a company: *Re Bezier Acquisitions Ltd* [2011] EWHC 3299 (Ch); [2012] B.C.C. 219, where service on a solicitor authorised to accept delivery was held sufficient.

R.3.10
The applicant's duty to file with the court notice of the existence of any insolvency proceedings in relation to the company is spelt out more widely than previously.

3.11 Intervention by holder of qualifying floating charge (paragraph 36(1)(b) of Schedule B1)

3.11(1) [Production to court by QFC holder] Where the holder of a qualifying floating charge applies to the court under paragraph 36(1)(b) of Schedule B1 to have a specified person appointed as administrator, the holder must produce to the court–

(a) the written consent of the holder of any prior qualifying floating charge;

(b) the proposed administrator's consent to act; and

(c) sufficient evidence to satisfy the court that the holder is entitled to appoint an administrator under paragraph 14 of Schedule B1.

3.11(2) [Costs to be expense of administration] If an administration order is made appointing the specified person, the costs of the person who made the administration application and of the applicant under paragraph 36(1)(b) of Schedule B1 are, unless the court orders otherwise, to be paid as an expense of the administration.

General Note

Where another person has made an application to the court for the appointment of an administrator, para.36 allows the holder of a qualifying floating charge to intervene and request the court to appoint a specified insolvency practitioner as administrator instead of the person nominated in the application. This rule sets out the procedural requirements for such an application.

3.12 The hearing

3.12(1) [Appearances] At the hearing of the administration application, any of the following may appear or be represented–

(a) the applicant;

(b) the company;

(c) one or more of the directors;

(d) any administrative receiver;

(e) any person who has presented a petition for the winding up of the company;

(f) the proposed administrator;

(g) any member State liquidator appointed in main proceedings in relation to the company;

(h) the holder of any qualifying floating charge;

(i) any supervisor of a CVA;

(j) with the permission of the court, any other person who appears to have an interest which justifies appearance.

3.12(2) [Costs to be expense of administration] If the court makes an administration order, the costs of the applicant, and of any other person whose costs are allowed by the court, are payable as an expense of the administration.

(See General Note after r.3.15.)

3.13 The order

3.13(1) [Heading and content] Where the court makes an administration order the court's order must be headed "Administration order" and must contain the following–

(a) identification details for the proceedings;

(b) the name and title of the judge making the order;

(c) the address for service of the applicant;

(d) details of any other parties (including the company) appearing and by whom represented;

(e) an order that during the period the order is in force the affairs, business and property of the company is to be managed by the administrator;

(f) the name of the person appointed as administrator;

(g) an order that that person is appointed as administrator of the company;

(h) a statement that the court is satisfied either that the EU Regulation does not apply or that it does;

(i) where the EU Regulation does apply, a statement whether the proceedings are main, secondary or territorial proceedings;

(j) the date of the order (and if the court so orders the time); and

(k) such other provisions if any as the court thinks just.

3.13(2) [Functions of joint appointees] Where two or more administrators are appointed the order must also specify (as required by paragraph 100(2) of Schedule B1)–

(a) which functions (if any) are to be exercised by those persons acting jointly; and

(b) which functions (if any) are to be exercised by any or all of those persons.

(See General Note after r.3.15.)

3.14 Order on an application under paragraph 37 or 38 of Schedule B1

3.14 Where the court makes an administration order in relation to a company on an application under paragraph 37 or 38 of Schedule B1, the court must also include in the order–

(a) in the case of a liquidator appointed in a voluntary winding up, the removal of that liquidator from office;

(b) provision for payment of the expenses of the winding up;

(c) such provision as the court thinks just relating to–

  (i) any indemnity given to the liquidator,

  (ii) the release of the liquidator,

  (iii) the handling or realisation of any of the company's assets in the hands of or under the control of the liquidator, and

  (iv) other matters arising in connection with the winding up; and

(d) such other provisions if any as the court thinks just.

(See General Note after r.3.15.)

3.15 Notice of administration order

3.15(1) [Court to send two sealed copies to applicant] If the court makes an administration order, it must as soon as reasonably practicable deliver two sealed copies of the order to the applicant.

3.15(2) [Applicant to send copy to administrator] The applicant must as soon as reasonably practicable deliver a sealed copy of the order to the person appointed as administrator.

3.15(3) [Directions as notice of interim or other order] If the court makes an order under sub-paragraph (d) or (f) of paragraph 13(1) of Schedule B1, it must give directions as to the persons to whom, and how, notice of that order is to be delivered.

General Note to rr.3.12–3.15

R.3.12(2)
The court may order the costs of a person who has presented a winding-up petition which is dismissed on the making of an administration order to be paid as an expense of the administration (*Irish Reel Productions Ltd v Capitol Films Ltd* [2010] EWHC 180 (Ch); [2010] B.C.C. 588). But the court declined to exercise its discretion to order that such costs should be paid in priority to the administrator's expenses under what is now r.3.51(2)(a). A creditor who unsuccessfully opposes an application may be allowed his costs, but only (and exceptionally) if the court considers it just in all the circumstances: *Re Professional Computer Group Ltd* [2008] EWHC 1541 (Ch); [2009] B.C.C. 323. In this case it was held that, since the creditor's unsuccessful opposition to the application had significantly increased the company's own costs, he should be ordered under the then CPR r.48.2 to pay its costs to that extent. In *Re Japanese Koi Co Ltd*, unreported, 13 July 2016, faced with two administration applications and a winding-up petition, in making an administration order Snowden J capped the amount of costs that would be treated as an administration expense to reflect the parties' unreasonable behaviour where a director and a creditor each proposed a different administrator and could not agree on a choice, resulting in the court appointing independent administrators.

R.3.13
This rule had no direct counterpart in IR 1986 where the detail of the application was formerly contained in Form 2.4B, but IR 2016 do not prescribe forms but rather specify the content required.

Rule 3.13(1)(h), (i) amended by the Insolvency (England and Wales) and Insolvency (Scotland) (Miscellaneous and Consequential Amendments) Rules 2017 (SI 2017/1115) rr.1(1), (2), 22, 23(7) as from 8 December 2017.

Chapter 3

Appointment of administrator by holder of floating charge

[Note: a document required by the Act or these Rules must also contain the standard contents set out in Part 1.]

3.16 Notice of intention to appoint

3.16(1) [Application of rule] This rule applies where the holder of a qualifying floating charge ("the appointer") gives a notice under paragraph 15(1)(a) of Schedule B1 of intention to appoint an administrator under paragraph 14 and files a copy of the notice with the court under paragraph 44(2).

3.16(2) [Heading and content of notice] The notice filed with the court must be headed "Notice of intention to appoint an administrator by holder of qualifying floating charge" and must contain the following–

(a) identification details for the proceedings;

(b) the name and address of the appointer;

(c) a statement that the appointer intends to appoint an administrator of the company;

(d) the name and address of the proposed administrator;

(e) a statement that the appointer is the holder of the qualifying floating charge in question and that it is now enforceable;

(f) details of the charge, the date upon which it was registered and the maximum amount if any secured by the charge;

(g) a statement that the notice is being given in accordance with paragraph 15(1)(a) of Schedule B1 to the holder of every prior floating charge which satisfies paragraph 14(2) of that Schedule;

(h) the names and addresses of the holders of such prior floating charges and details of the charges;

(i) a statement whether the company is or is not subject to insolvency proceedings at the date of the notice, and details of the proceedings if it is;

(j) a statement whether the company is an Article 1.2 undertaking; and

(k) a statement whether the proceedings flowing from the appointment will be main, secondary, territorial or non-EU proceedings with reasons for the statement.

3.16(3) [Authentication] The notice must be authenticated by the appointer or the appointer's solicitor and dated.

3.16(4) [Filing of copy notice in court; notice to QFC holder] The filing of the copy with the court under paragraph 44(2) of Schedule B1 must be done at the same time as notice is given in accordance with paragraph 15(1)(a).

3.16(5) [Service of notice to QFC holder] The giving of notice under paragraph 15(1)(a) must be by service of the notice.

(See General Note after r.3.19.)

3.17 Notice of appointment

3.17(1) [Heading and content of notice] Notice of an appointment under paragraph 14 of Schedule B1 must be headed "Notice of appointment of an administrator by holder of a qualifying floating charge" and must contain–

(a) identification details for the proceedings;

(b) the name and address of the appointer;

(c) a statement that the appointer has appointed the person named as administrator of the company;

(d) the name and address of the person appointed as administrator;

(e) a statement that a copy of the administrator's consent to act accompanies the notice;

(f) a statement that the appointer is the holder of the qualifying floating charge in question and that it is now enforceable;

(g) details of the charge including the date of the charge, the date on which it was registered and the maximum amount if any secured by the charge;

(h) one of the following statements–

(i) that notice has been given in accordance with paragraph 15(1)(a) of Schedule B1 to the holder of every prior floating charge which satisfies paragraph 14(2) of that Schedule, that two business days have elapsed from the date the last such notice was given (if more than one) and–

(aa) that a copy of every such notice was filed with the court under paragraph 44(2) of Schedule B1, and the date of that filing (or the latest date of filing if more than one), or

(bb) that a copy of every such notice accompanies the notice of appointment but was not filed with the court under paragraph 44(2) of Schedule B1

(ii) that the holder of every such floating charge to whom notice was given has consented in writing to the making of the appointment and that a copy of every consent accompanies the notice of appointment,

(iii) that the holder of every such floating charge has consented in writing to the making of the appointment without notice having been given to all and that a copy of every consent accompanies the notice of appointment, or

(iv) that there is no such floating charge;

(i) a statement whether the company is or is not subject to insolvency proceedings at the date of the notice, and details of the proceedings if it is;

(j) a statement whether the company is an Article 1.2 undertaking;

(k) a statement whether the proceedings flowing from the appointment will be main, secondary, territorial or non-EU proceedings and the reasons for so stating; and

(l) a statement that the appointment is in accordance with Schedule B1.

3.17(2) [Functions of joint appointees] Where two or more administrators are appointed the notice must also specify (as required by paragraph 100(2) of Schedule B1)–

(a) which functions (if any) are to be exercised by those persons acting jointly; and

(b) which functions (if any) are to be exercised by any or all of those persons.

3.17(3) [Statutory declaration] The statutory declaration included in the notice in accordance with paragraph 18(2) of Schedule B1 must be made not more than five business days before the notice is filed with the court.

(See General Note after r.3.19.)

3.18 Filing of notice with the court

3.18(1) [Three copies to be filed in court, etc.] Three copies of the notice of appointment must be filed with the court, accompanied by–

(a) the administrator's consent to act; and

(b) either–

(i) evidence that the appointer has given notice as required by paragraph 15(1)(a) of Schedule B1; or

(ii) copies of the written consent of all those required to give consent in accordance with paragraph 15(1)(b) of Schedule B1.

3.18(2) [Court to seal, endorse and deliver copies] The court must apply the seal of the court to the copies of the notice, endorse them with the date and time of filing and deliver two of the sealed copies to the appointer.

3.18(3) [Appointer to deliver sealed copy to administrator] The appointer must as soon as reasonably practicable deliver one of the sealed copies to the administrator.

3.18(4) [Appointment out of court business hours] This rule is subject to rules 3.20 and 3.21 (appointment made out of court business hours).

(See General Note after r.3.19.)

3.19 Appointment by floating charge holder after administration application made

3.19(1) [Application of rule] This rule applies where the holder of a qualifying floating charge, after receiving notice that an administration application has been made, appoints an administrator under paragraph 14 of Schedule B1.

3.19(2) [QFC holder to deliver copy of notice of appointment] The holder must as soon as reasonably practicable deliver a copy of the notice of appointment to–

(a) the person making the administration application; and

(b) the court in which the application has been made.

General Note to rr.3.16–3.19

The holder of a "qualifying" floating charge (as defined in para.14(2), (3)) may appoint an administrator out of court under para.14. These rules set out the procedural requirements.

Where there is a prior-ranking qualifying floating charge, para.15 will apply, and either two business days' written notice must be given to the holder or his written consent must be obtained. Paragraph 15 does not specify that the notice to the creditor should be in a prescribed form, but Form 2.5B (now discontinued) was formerly used to file a copy with the court under para.44(2) if it was desired to obtain a moratorium. (Note that filing with the court is not obligatory. On the question whether a notice of intention to appoint can be filed in other circumstances, see the notes to paras 15 and 44.) Since 6 April 2017, the form is no longer used but equivalent content is prescribed by r.3.16. Where there is no prior-ranking floating charge, the charge holder may proceed to make an appointment immediately, without the need to give or file any notice.

"Article 1.2 undertaking" in rr.3.16(2)(j) and 3.17(1)(j) is defined in r.1.2(2).

Rules 3.16(2)(k) and 3.17(1)(k) amended by the Insolvency (England and Wales) and Insolvency (Scotland) (Miscellaneous and Consequential Amendments) Rules 2017 (SI 2017/1115) rr.1(1), (2), 22, 30(8), (9) as from 8 December 2017.

3.20 Appointment taking place out of court business hours: procedure

3.20(1) [Notice by fax or email when court closed] When (but only when) the court is closed, the holder of a qualifying floating charge may file a notice of appointment with the court by–

(a) faxing it to a designated telephone number; or

(b) emailing it, or attaching it to an email, to a designated email address.

3.20(2) [Notice to specify court with jurisdiction] The notice must specify the name of the court (and hearing centre if applicable) that has jurisdiction.

3.20(3) [Fax number, email address] The Lord Chancellor must designate the telephone number and email address.

3.20(4) [Publication on Insolvency Service webpages] The Secretary of State must publish the designated telephone number and email address on the Insolvency Service webpages and deliver notice of them to any person requesting them from the Insolvency Service.

3.20(5) [Fax transmission report and hard-copy email created] The appointer must ensure that–

(a) a fax transmission report giving the time and date of the fax transmission and the telephone number to which the notice was faxed and containing a copy of the first page (in part or in full) of the document faxed is created by the fax machine that is used to fax the notice; or

(b) a hard copy of the email is created giving the time and date of the email and the address to which it was sent.

3.20(6) [Fax transmission report and hard-copy email retained] The appointer must retain the fax transmission report or hard copy of the email.

3.20(7) [Notice of appointment to administrator] The appointer must deliver a notice to the administrator of the filing of the notice of appointment as soon as reasonably practicable.

3.20(8) [Copy of faxed notice or email to court and on court file] The copy of the faxed or emailed notice of appointment as received by the Courts Service must be delivered by the Lord Chancellor as soon as reasonably practicable to the court specified in the notice as the court having jurisdiction in the case, to be placed on the relevant court file.

3.20(9) [Copies to court with reasons for out-of-hours filing] The appointer must take to the court on the next occasion that the court is open for business–

(a) three copies of the faxed or emailed notice of appointment;

(b) the fax transmission report or hard copy required by paragraph (5);

(c) all supporting documents referred to in the notice in accordance with rule 3.21(1) which are in the appointer's possession; and

(d) a statement providing reasons for the out-of-hours filing of the notice of appointment, including why it would have been damaging to the company or its creditors not to have so acted.

3.20(10) [Copies sealed and endorsed by court] The copies of the notice must be sealed by the court and endorsed with–

(a) the date and time when, according to the appointer's fax transmission report or hard copy of the email, the notice was faxed or sent; and

(b) the date when the notice and accompanying documents were delivered to the court.

3.20(11) [Two sealed copies to appointer] The court must deliver two of the sealed copies of the notice of appointment to the appointer.

3.20(12) [Sealed copy to administrator] The appointer must, as soon as reasonably practicable, deliver one of the copies to the administrator.

3.20(13) [Insolvency Service, Courts Service] The reference–

(a) to the Insolvency Service in paragraph (4) means the Secretary of State acting by means of the Insolvency Service; and

(b) to the Courts Service in paragraph (8) means the Lord Chancellor acting by means of Her Majesty's Courts and Tribunals Service.

(See General Note after r.3.22.)

3.21 Appointment taking place out of court business hours: content of notice

3.21(1) [Heading and content of notice] Notice of an appointment filed in accordance with rule 3.20 must be headed "Notice of appointment of an administrator by holder of a qualifying floating charge", identify the company immediately below the heading and must contain–

(a) the name and address of the appointer;

(b) a statement that the appointer has appointed the person named as administrator of the company;

(c) the name and address of the person appointed as administrator;

(d) a statement that the appointer is the holder of the qualifying floating charge in question and that it is now enforceable;

(e) details of the charge, the date upon which it was registered and the maximum amount secured by the charge;

(f) one of the following statements–

(i) that notice has been given in accordance with paragraph 15(1)(a) of Schedule B1 to the holder of every prior floating charge which satisfies paragraph 14(2) of that Schedule, that a copy of every such notice was filed with the court under paragraph 44(2) of that Schedule, the date of that filing (or the latest date of filing if more than one) and that two business days have elapsed since notice was given under paragraph 15(1)(a) of Schedule B1,

(ii) that notice has been given in accordance with paragraph 15(1)(a) of Schedule B1 to the holder of every prior floating charge which satisfies paragraph 14(2) of that Schedule and that a copy of every such notice is in the appointer's possession but was not filed with the court under paragraph 44(2) of that Schedule,

(iii) that the holder of every such floating charge to whom notice was given has consented to the making of the appointment and that a copy of every consent in writing is in the appointer's possession,

(iv) that the holder of every such floating charge has consented to the making of the appointment without notice having been given to all and that a copy of every consent in writing is in the appointer's possession, or

(v) that there is no such floating charge;

(g) a statement whether the company is or is not subject to insolvency proceedings at the date of the notice, and details of the proceedings if it is;

(h) a statement whether the company is an Article 1.2 undertaking;

(i) a statement whether the proceedings flowing from the appointment will be main, secondary, territorial or non-EU proceedings and that a statement of the reasons for stating this is in the appointer's possession;

(j) an undertaking that the following will be delivered to the court on the next occasion on which the court is open–

(i) any document referred to in the notice in accordance with rule 3.20 as being in the appointer's possession,

(ii) the fax transmission report or hard copy of the email, and

(iii) the statement of reasons for out-of-hours filing;

(k) a statement that the proposed administrator consents to act; and

(l) a statement that the appointment is in accordance with Schedule B1.

3.21(2) [Functions of joint appointees] Where two or more administrators are appointed the notice must also specify (as required by paragraph 100(2) of Schedule B1)–

(a) which functions (if any) are to be exercised by those persons acting jointly; and

(b) which functions (if any) are to be exercised by any or all of those persons.

3.21(3) [Statutory declaration] The statutory declaration included in the notice in accordance with paragraph 18(2) of Schedule B1 must be made not more than five business days before the notice is filed with the court.

(See General Note after r.3.22.)

3.22 Appointment taking place out of court business hours: legal effect

3.22(1) [Legal effect] The filing of a notice in accordance with rule 3.20 has the same effect for all purposes as the filing of a notice of appointment in accordance with rule 3.18.

3.22(2) [Time of effect; cessation] The appointment–

(a) takes effect from the date and time of the fax transmission or sending of the email; but

(b) ceases to have effect if the requirements of rule 3.20(9) are not completed on the next occasion the court is open for business.

3.22(3) [Presumption as to date and time notice of appointment filed] Where any question arises in relation to the date and time that the notice of appointment was filed with the court, it is a presumption capable of rebuttal that the date and time shown on the appointer's fax transmission report or hard copy of the email is the date and time at which the notice was filed.

General Note to rr.3.20–3.22

There may be occasions when the holder of a floating charge will wish to appoint an administrator at a time when the court office is closed. Since the appointment only takes effect on the filing of a notice of appointment with the court (para.19), it has been necessary to make special provision in this rule, providing for the filing of a notice of appointment by fax or (since 6 April 2010) email, with confirmation by the lodgement of physical documents on the next day that the court is open for business. The requirements, spelt out in this rule, are quite strict; and it should be noted that the option of filing by fax or email is available when, and only when, the court office is closed.

The fax number is published on the Insolvency Service's website (*https://www.gov.uk/government/publications/insolvency-notify-court-of-appointment-of-administrator-outside-court-business-hours/how-to-notify-a-court-in-england-and-wales-or-scotland*) and is currently 0870 761 7716. The email address is *rcjcompanies.orders@hmcts.gsi.gov.uk*. Note the requirement in r.3.20(5), (9)(b) that evidence be preserved in hard copy (in some detail) for filing in court on the first available day.

Rule 3.20(9)(d) carries the implication that a floating charge holder should not use a notice by fax or email, rather than wait for the court office to open on a later date, without good reason. Absurdly, it is suggested that the reason should relate to the interests of the company and/or its creditors, rather than that of the charge holder himself. However, it should not be beyond the wit of man to devise a formula sufficient to deter anyone minded to challenge the appointment.

"Article 1.2 undertaking" in r.3.21(1)(h) is defined in r.1.2(2).

Rule 3.21(1)(i) amended by the Insolvency (England and Wales) and Insolvency (Scotland) (Miscellaneous and Consequential Amendments) Rules 2017 (SI 2017/1115) rr.1(1), (2), 22, 30(10) as from 8 December 2017.

Chapter 4

Appointment of administrator by company or directors

[Note: a document required by the Act or these Rules must also contain the standard contents set out in Part 1.]

3.23 Notice of intention to appoint

3.23(1) [Heading and content] If paragraph 26 of Schedule B1 requires a notice of intention to appoint an administrator under paragraph 22 of that Schedule then the notice must be headed "Notice of intention to appoint an administrator by company or directors" and must contain the following–

(a) identification details for the proceedings;

(b) a statement that the company or the directors, as the case may be, intend to appoint an administrator of the company;

(c) the name and address of the proposed administrator;

(d) the names and addresses of the persons to whom notice is being given in accordance with paragraph 26(1) of Schedule B1;

(e) a statement that each of those persons is or may be entitled to appoint–

(i) an administrative receiver of the company, or

(ii) an administrator of the company under paragraph 14 of Schedule B1;

(f) a statement that the company has not within the preceding 12 months been–

(i) in administration;

(ii) the subject of a moratorium under Schedule A1which ended on a date when no CVA was in force; or

(iii) the subject of a CVA which was made during a moratorium under Schedule A1 and which ended prematurely within the meaning of section 7B;

(g) a statement that in relation to the company there is no–

(i) petition for winding up which has been presented but not yet disposed of,

(ii) administration application which has not yet been disposed of, or

(iii) administrative receiver in office;

(h) a statement whether the company is an Article 1.2 undertaking;

(i) a statement whether the proceedings flowing from the appointment will be main, secondary, territorial or non-EU proceedings and the reasons for so stating;

(j) a statement that the notice is accompanied (as appropriate) by either–

(i) a copy of the resolution of the company to appoint an administrator, or

(ii) a record of the decision of the directors to appoint an administrator; and

(k) a statement that if a recipient of the notice who is named in paragraph (e) wishes to consent in writing to the appointment that person may do so but that after five business days have expired from delivery of the notice the appointer may make the appointment although such a recipient has not replied.

3.23(2) [Copy resolution or record of directors' decision to accompany notice] The notice must be accompanied by–

(a) a copy of the resolution of the company to appoint an administrator, where the company intends to make the appointment, or

(b) a record of the decision of the directors, where the directors intend to make the appointment.

3.23(3) [Notice under IA 1986 Sch.B1 para.26(1) by service] The giving of notice under paragraph 26(1) of Schedule B1 must be by service of the notice.

3.23(4) [To whom copy of notice to be sent] If notice of intention to appoint is given under paragraph 26(1) of Schedule B1, a copy of the notice under paragraph 26(2) must be sent at the same time to–

(a) any enforcement agent or other officer who, to the knowledge of the person giving the notice, is charged with distress or other legal process against the company;

(b) any person who, to the knowledge of the person giving the notice, has distrained against the company or its property;

(c) any supervisor of a CVA; and

(d) the company, if the company is not intending to make the appointment.

3.23(5) [Notice under IA 1986 Sch.B1 para.26(2) by service] The giving of notice under paragraph 26(2) of Schedule B1 must be by service of the notice.

3.23(6) [Statutory declaration under IA 1986 Sch.B1 para.27(2)] The statutory declaration accompanying the notice in accordance with paragraph 27(2) of Schedule B1 must–

(a) if it is not made by the person making the appointment, indicate the capacity in which the person making the declaration does so; and

(b) be made not more than five business days before the notice is filed with the court.

(See General Note after r.3.26.)

3.24 Notice of appointment after notice of intention to appoint

3.24(1) [Heading and content of notice] Notice of an appointment under paragraph 22 of Schedule B1 (when notice of intention to appoint has been given under paragraph 26) must be headed "Notice of appointment of an administrator by a company (where a notice of intention to appoint has been given)" or "Notice of appointment of an administrator by the directors of a company (where a notice of intention to appoint has been given)" and must contain–

(a) identification details for the company immediately below the heading;

(b) a statement that the company has, or the directors have, as the case may be, appointed the person named as administrator of the company;

(c) the name and address of the person appointed as administrator;

(d) a statement that a copy of the administrator's consent to act accompanies the notice;

(e) a statement that the company is, or the directors are, as the case may be, entitled to make an appointment under paragraph 22 of Schedule B1;

(f) a statement that the appointment is in accordance with Schedule B1;

(g) a statement whether the company is an Article 1.2 undertaking;

(h) a statement whether the proceedings flowing from the appointment will be main, secondary, territorial or non-EU proceedings and the reasons for so stating;

(i) a statement that the company has, or the directors have, as the case may be, given notice of their intention to appoint in accordance with paragraph 26(1) of Schedule B1, that a copy of the notice was filed with the court, the date of that filing and either–

    (i) that five business days have elapsed since notice was given under paragraph 26 of Schedule B1, or

    (ii) that each person to whom the notice was given has consented to the appointment; and

(j) the date and time of the appointment.

3.24(2) [Functions of joint appointees] Where two or more administrators are appointed the notice must also specify (as required by paragraph 100(2) of Schedule B1)–

(a) which functions (if any) are to be exercised by those persons acting jointly; and

(b) which functions (if any) are to be exercised by any or all of those persons.

3.24(3) [Statutory declaration under IA 1986 Sch.B1 para.29(2)] The statutory declaration included in the notice in accordance with paragraph 29(2) of Schedule B1 must be made not more than five business days before the notice is filed with the court.

3.24(4) [Capacity of person making statutory declaration if not appointer] If the statutory declaration is not made by the person making the appointment it must indicate the capacity in which the person making the declaration does so.

(See General Note after r.3.26.)

3.25 Notice of appointment without prior notice of intention to appoint

3.25(1) [Heading of notice] Notice of an appointment under paragraph 22 of Schedule B1 (when notice of intention to appoint has not been given under paragraph 26) must be headed "Notice of appointment of an administrator by a company (where a notice of intention to appoint has not been given)" or "Notice of appointment of an administrator by the directors of a company (where a notice of intention to appoint has not been given)" and must identify the company immediately below the heading.

3.25(2) [Content of notice]The notice must state the following–

(a) that the company has, or the directors have, as the case may be, appointed the person specified under sub-paragraph (b) as administrator of the company;

(b) the name and address of the person appointed as administrator;

(c) that a copy of the administrator's consent to act accompanies the notice;

(d) that the company is or the directors are, as the case may be, entitled to make an appointment under paragraph 22 of Schedule B1;

(e) that the appointment is in accordance with Schedule B1;

(f) that the company has not within the preceding 12 months been–

(i) in administration,

(ii) the subject of a moratorium under Schedule A1 which ended on a date when no CVA was in force, or

(iii) the subject of a CVA which was made during a moratorium under Schedule A1 and which ended prematurely within the meaning of section 7B;

(g) that in relation to the company there is no–

(i) petition for winding up which has been presented but not yet disposed of,

(ii) administration application which has not yet been disposed of, or

(iii) administrative receiver in office;

(h) whether the company is an Article 1.2 undertaking;

(i) whether the proceedings flowing from the appointment will be main, secondary, territorial or non-EU proceedings and the reasons for so stating;

(j) that the notice is accompanied by–

(i) a copy of the resolution of the company to appoint an administrator, or

(ii) a record of the decision of the directors to appoint an administrator; and

(k) the date and time of the appointment.

3.25(3) [Functions of joint appointees] Where two or more administrators are appointed the notice must also specify (as required by paragraph 100(2) of Schedule B1)–

(a) which functions (if any) are to be exercised by those persons acting jointly; and

(b) which functions (if any) are to be exercised by any or all of those persons.

3.25(4) [Statutory declaration under IA 1986 Sch.B1 paras 29(2), 30] The statutory declaration included in the notice in accordance with paragraphs 29(2) and 30 of Schedule B1 must–

(a) if the declaration is made on behalf of the person making the appointment, indicate the capacity in which the person making the declaration does so; and

(b) be made not more than five business days before the notice is filed with the court.

(See General Note after r.3.26.)

3.26 Notice of appointment: filing with the court

3.26(1) [Three copies with consents] Three copies of the notice of appointment must be filed with the court, accompanied by–

(a) the administrator's consent to act; and

(b) the written consent of all those persons to whom notice was given in accordance with paragraph 26(1) of Schedule B1 unless the period of notice set out in paragraph 26(1) has expired.

3.26(2) [Copy resolution or record of directors' decision to accompany appointment notice] Where a notice of intention to appoint an administrator has not been given, the copies of the notice of appointment must also be accompanied by–

(a) a copy of the resolution of the company to appoint an administrator, where the company is making the appointment; or

(b) a record of the decision of the directors, where the directors are making the appointment.

3.26(3) [Copies sealed, endorsed and delivered by court] The court must apply to the copies the seal of the court, endorse them with the date and time of filing and deliver two of the sealed copies to the appointer.

3.26(4) [Appointer to deliver sealed copy to administrator] The appointer must as soon as reasonably practicable deliver one of the sealed copies to the administrator.

GENERAL NOTE TO RR.3.23–3.26

These rules apply in the appointment of an administrator by a company or its directors out of court under paras 22 et seq.

Rule 3.23(1) begins by stating: "*If* para.26 requires a notice of intention to appoint an administrator under paragraph 22". It is thus not always necessary that the company or directors should give notice of intention to appoint under para.26. If there is no person to whom such a notice needs to be sent, the appointment can be made directly (in which case there will be no moratorium). Whether a notice of intention to appoint can be filed (so securing a brief moratorium) when there is no person entitled to the statutory notice is open to debate: see the note to para.26.

Notice of intention to appoint must be given to the persons prescribed under para.26(2) (including the company itself) only if there is a floating charge holder entitled to notice under para.26(1). This follows from the amendment made to para.26(2) by SBEEA 2015. Previously that provision applied to "every person who proposes to make an appointment under paragraph 22", but the restriction to "a person who gives notice of intention to appoint under sub-paragraph (1)" limits the obligation to give a para.26(2) notice to cases where there is such a floating charge holder. See further the note to para.26.

The content of the notice of intention to appoint (before 6 April 2017, in Form 2.8B) is now spelt out in r.3.23(1).

The content of the notice of appointment after the notice of intention to appoint (before 6 April 2017, in Form 2.9B) is now spelt out in r.3.24(1), a second statutory declaration in addition to that under r.3.23 is required, and it too must not be more than five business days old.

The content of the notice of appointment without prior notice of intention to appoint (before 6 April 2017, in Form 2.10B) is now spelt out in r.3.25(1), again a statutory declaration in addition to that under r.3.23 is required, and it too must not be more than five business days old.

"Article 1.2 undertaking" in rr.3.23(1)(h), 3.24(1)(g) and 3.25(1)(h) is defined in r.1.2(2).

Rules 3.23(1)(i), 3.24(1)(h), 3.25(2)(i) amended by the Insolvency (England and Wales) and Insolvency (Scotland) (Miscellaneous and Consequential Amendments) Rules 2017 (SI 2017/1115) rr.1(1), (2), 22, 30(11), (12), (13) as from 8 December 2017.

Chapter 5

Notice of administrator's appointment

[Note: a document required by the Act or these Rules must also contain the standard contents set out in Part 1.]

3.27 Publication of administrator's appointment

3.27(1) [Administrator to gazette and advertise appointment] The notice of appointment, to be published by the administrator as soon as reasonably practicable after appointment under paragraph 46(2)(b) of Schedule B1, must be gazetted and may be advertised in such other manner as the administrator thinks fit.

3.27(2) [Content of notice] The notice of appointment must state the following–

(a) that an administrator has been appointed;

(b) the date of the appointment; and

(c) the nature of the business of the company.

3.27(3) [To whom administrator to deliver notice of appointment] The administrator must, as soon as reasonably practicable after the date specified in paragraph 46(6) of Schedule B1, deliver a notice of the appointment–

(a) if a receiver or an administrative receiver has been appointed, to that person;

(b) if there is pending a petition for the winding up of the company, to the petitioner (and also to the provisional liquidator, if any);

(c) to any enforcement officer, enforcement agent or other officer who, to the administrator's knowledge, is charged with distress or other legal process against the company or its property;

(d) to any person who, to the administrator's knowledge, has distrained against the company or its property; and

(e) any supervisor of a CVA.

3.27(4) [Heading and content of notice to registrar of companies] Where, under Schedule B1 or these Rules, the administrator is required to deliver a notice of the appointment to the registrar of companies or any other person, it must be headed "Notice of administrator's appointment" and must contain–

(a) the administrator's name and address and IP number;

(b) identification details for the proceedings; and

(c) a statement that the administrator has been appointed as administrator of the company;

3.27(5) [Authentication] The notice must be authenticated and dated by the administrator.

General Note

This and the succeeding rules in Pt 3 apply whether the administrator is appointed by the court or out of court.

The notice of appointment should be delivered to the registrar using Form AM01.

On the standard contents for gazetted notices, see rr.1.10–1.12.

CHAPTER 6

STATEMENT OF AFFAIRS

[Note: a document required by the Act or these Rules must also contain the standard contents set out in Part 1.]

3.28 Interpretation

3.28 In this Chapter–

"nominated person" means a relevant person who has been required by the administrator to make out and deliver to the administrator a statement of affairs; and

"relevant person" means a person mentioned in paragraph 47(3) of Schedule B1.

GENERAL NOTE

Oddly perhaps the "nominated person" person is defined here rather than in r.1.2 where counterparts are defined for administrative receivership and winding up.

3.29 Statement of affairs: notice requiring and delivery to the administrator (paragraph 47(1) of Schedule B1)

[Note: see section 234(1) and 235(1) for the application of section 235 to administrators.]

3.29(1) [Notice to relevant persons] A requirement under paragraph 47(1) of Schedule B1 for one or more relevant persons to provide the administrator with a statement of the affairs of the company must be made by a notice delivered to each such person.

3.29(2) [Heading and content of notice] The notice must be headed "Notice requiring statement of affairs" and must–

(a) require each nominated person to whom the notice is delivered to prepare and submit to the administrator a statement of the affairs of the company;

(b) inform each nominated person of–

(i) the names and addresses of all others (if any) to whom the same notice has been delivered,

(ii) the requirement to deliver the statement of affairs to the administrator no later than eleven days after receipt of the notice requiring the statement of affairs;

(iii) the effect of paragraph 48(4) of Schedule B1 (penalty for non-compliance) and section 235 (duty to co-operate with the office-holder).

3.29(3) [Request for document for preparation of the statement of affairs] The administrator must inform each nominated person to whom notice is delivered that a document for the preparation of the statement of affairs capable of completion in compliance with rule 3.30 will be supplied if requested.

3.29(4) [Delivery of statement with statement of truth] The nominated person (or one of them, if more than one) must deliver the statement of affairs to the administrator with the statement of truth required by paragraph 47(2)(a) of Schedule B1 and a copy of each statement.

(See General Note after r.3.34.)

3.30 Statement of affairs: content (paragraph 47 of Schedule B1)

[Note: paragraph 47(2)(a) of Schedule B1 requires the statement of affairs to be verified by a statement of truth.]

3.30(1) [Heading and content of statement] The statement of the company's affairs must be headed "Statement of affairs" and must–

(a) identify the company immediately below the heading; and

(b) state that it is a statement of the affairs of the company on a specified date, being the date on which it entered administration.

3.30(2) [Further content] The statement of affairs must contain (in addition to the matters required by paragraph 47(2) of Schedule B1)–

(a) a summary of the assets of the company, setting out the book value and the estimated realisable value of–

(i) any assets subject to a fixed charge,

(ii) any assets subject to a floating charge,

(iii) any uncharged assets, and

(iv) the total value of all the assets available for preferential creditors;

(b) a summary of the liabilities of the company, setting out–

(i) the amount of preferential debts,

(ii) an estimate of the deficiency with respect to preferential debts or the surplus available after paying the preferential debts,

(iii) an estimate of the prescribed part, if applicable,

(iv) an estimate of the total assets available to pay debts secured by floating charges,

(v) the amount of debts secured by floating charges,

(vi) an estimate of the deficiency with respect to debts secured by floating charges or the surplus available after paying the debts secured by fixed or floating charges,

(vii) the amount of unsecured debts (excluding preferential debts),

(viii) an estimate of the deficiency with respect to unsecured debts or the surplus available after paying unsecured debts,

(ix) any issued and called-up capital, and

(x) an estimate of the deficiency with respect to, or surplus available to, members of the company;

(c) a list of the company's creditors with the further particulars required by paragraph (3) indicating–

(i) any creditors under hire-purchase, chattel leasing or conditional sales agreements, and

(ii) any creditors claiming retention of title over property in the company's possession; and

(d) the name and address of each member of the company and the number, nominal value and other details of the shares held by each member.

3.30(3) [List of creditors] The list of creditors required by paragraph 47(2) of Schedule B1 and paragraph (2)(c) of this rule must contain the details required by paragraph (4) except where paragraphs (5) and (6) apply.

3.30(4) [Creditor particulars required] The particulars required by paragraph (3) are as follows–

(a) the name and postal address of the creditor;

(b) the amount of the debt owed to the creditor;

(c) details of any security held by the creditor;

(d) the date on which the security was given; and

(e) the value of any such security.

3.30(5) [Employee and pre-paid consumer creditors] Paragraph (6) applies where the particulars required by paragraph (4) relate to creditors who are either–

(a) employees or former employees of the company; or

(b) consumers claiming amounts paid in advance for the supply of goods or services.

3.30(6) [Particulars re r.3.30(5)] Where this paragraph applies–

(a) the statement of affairs itself must state separately for each of paragraph (5)(a) and (b) the number of such creditors and the total of the debts owed to them; and

(b) the particulars required by paragraph (4) must be set out in separate schedules to the statement of affairs for each of paragraphs (5)(a) and (b).

(See General Note after r.3.34.)

3.31 Statement of affairs: statement of concurrence

3.31(1) [Statement of concurrence from relevant persons] The administrator may require a relevant person to deliver to the administrator a statement of concurrence.

3.31(2) [Meaning of statement of affairs] A statement of concurrence is a statement, verified by a statement of truth, that that person concurs in the statement of affairs submitted by a nominated person.

3.31(3) [Administrator to inform nominated person to deliver statement of concurrence] The administrator must inform the nominated person who has been required to submit a statement of affairs that the relevant person has been required to deliver a statement of concurrence.

3.31(4) [Nominated person to deliver copy statement of affairs to relevant persons] The nominated person must deliver a copy of the statement of affairs to every relevant person who has been required to submit a statement of concurrence.

3.31(5) [Content of statement of concurrence] A statement of concurrence–

(a) must identify the company; and

(b) may be qualified in relation to matters dealt with in the statement of affairs where the relevant person–

(i) is not in agreement with the statement of affairs,

(ii) considers the statement of affairs to be erroneous or misleading, or

(iii) is without the direct knowledge necessary for concurring with it.

3.31(6) [Period for delivery of statement of concurrence] The relevant person must deliver the required statement of concurrence together with a copy to the administrator before the end of the period of five business days (or such other period as the administrator may agree) beginning with the day on which the relevant person receives the statement of affairs.

(See General Note after r.3.34.)

3.32 Statement of affairs: filing

3.32(1) [Duty of administrator to file copy with registrar of companies] The administrator must as soon as reasonably practicable deliver to the registrar of companies a copy of–

(a) the statement of affairs; and

(b) any statement of concurrence.

3.32(2) [Rule 3.30(6)(b) schedules to be omitted from statement] However, the administrator must not deliver to the registrar of companies with the statement of affairs any schedule required by rule 3.30(6)(b).

3.32(3) [Limited disclosure to registrar of companies] The requirement to deliver the statement of affairs is subject to any order of the court made under rule 3.45 that the statement of affairs or a specified part must not be delivered to the registrar of companies.

(See General Note after r.3.34.)

3.33 Statement of affairs: release from requirement and extension of time

3.33(1) [Exercise of power] The power of the administrator under paragraph 48(2) of Schedule B1 to revoke a requirement to provide a statement of affairs or to extend the period within which it must be submitted may be exercised upon the administrator's own initiative or at the request of a nominated person who has been required to provide it.

3.33(2) [Application to court] The nominated person may apply to the court if the administrator refuses that person's request for a revocation or extension.

3.33(3) [Power of court] On receipt of an application, the court may, if it is satisfied that no sufficient cause is shown for it, dismiss it without giving notice to any party other than the applicant.

3.33(4) [Court to fix venue] Unless the application is dismissed, the court must fix a venue for it to be heard.

3.33(5) [Notice of hearing] The applicant must, at least 14 days before any hearing, deliver to the administrator a notice stating the venue with a copy of the application and of any evidence on which the applicant intends to rely.

3.33(6) [Power of administrator to file report or appear] The administrator may do either or both of the following–

(a) file a report of any matters which the administrator thinks ought to be drawn to the court's attention; or

(b) appear and be heard on the application.

3.33(7) [Copy of filed report] If a report is filed, the administrator must deliver a copy of it to the applicant not later than five business days before the hearing.

3.33(8) [Sealed copies of order] Sealed copies of any order made on the application must be delivered by the court to the applicant and the administrator.

3.33(9) [Applicant's costs as administration expense] On an application under this rule, the applicant's costs must be paid by the applicant in any event, but the court may order that an allowance of all or part of them be payable as an expense of the administration.

(See General Note after r.3.34.)

3.34 Statement of affairs: expenses

3.34(1) [Expenses of nominated person] The expenses of a nominated person which the administrator considers to have been reasonably incurred in making a statement of affairs or of a relevant person in making a statement of concurrence must be paid by the administrator as an expense of the administration.

3.34(2) [Expenses not reasonably incurred: appeal to court] A decision by the administrator that expenses were not reasonably incurred (and are therefore not payable as an expense of the administration) may be appealed to the court.

General Note to rr.3.29–3.34

On the statement of affairs generally, see the note to para.47.

The additional detail in rr.3.29–3.31 compared with their counterpart rules in IR 1986 is mainly because IR 2016 do not prescribe forms but rather specify the content required.

R.3.32
Form AM02 should be used, with the statements attached.

Chapter 7

Administrator's proposals

[Note: a document required by the Act or these Rules must also contain the standard contents set out in Part 1.]

3.35 Administrator's proposals: additional content

3.35(1) [Content] The administrator's statement of proposals made under paragraph 49 of Schedule B1 (which is required by paragraph 49(4) to be delivered to the registrar of companies, creditors and members) must identify the proceedings and, in addition to the matters set out in paragraph 49, contain–

- (a) any other trading names of the company;
- (b) details of the administrator's appointment, including–
  - (i) the date of appointment,
  - (ii) the person making the application or appointment, and
  - (iii) where a number of persons have been appointed as administrators, details of the matters set out in paragraph 100(2) of Schedule B1 relating to the exercise of their functions;
- (c) the names of the directors and secretary of the company and details of any shareholdings in the company which they may have;
- (d) an account of the circumstances giving rise to the appointment of the administrator;
- (e) the date the proposals are delivered to the creditors;
- (f) if a statement of the company's affairs has been submitted–
  - (i) a copy or summary of it, except so far as an order under rule 3.45 or 3.46 limits disclosure of it, and excluding any schedule referred to in rule 3.30(6)(b), or the particulars relating to individual creditors contained in any such schedule,
  - (ii) details of who provided the statement of affairs, and
  - (iii) any comments which the administrator may have upon the statement of affairs;
- (g) if an order under rule 3.45 or 3.46 has been made–
  - (i) a statement of that fact, and
  - (ii) the date of the order;
- (h) if no statement of affairs has been submitted–
  - (i) details of the financial position of the company at the latest practicable date (which must, unless the court orders otherwise, be a date not earlier than that on which the company entered administration), and
  - (ii) an explanation as to why there is no statement of affairs;

(i) a full list of the company's creditors in accordance with paragraph (2) if either–

(i) no statement of affairs has been submitted, or

(ii) a statement of affairs has been submitted but it does not include such a list, or the administrator believes the list included is less than full;

(j) a statement of–

(i) how it is envisaged the purpose of the administration will be achieved, and

(ii) how it is proposed that the administration will end, including, where it is proposed that the administration will end by the company moving to a creditors' voluntary winding up–

(aa) details of the proposed liquidator,

(bb) where applicable, the declaration required by section 231, and

(cc) a statement that the creditors may, before the proposals are approved, nominate a different person as liquidator in accordance with paragraph 83(7)(a) of Schedule B1 and rule 3.60(6)(b);

(k) a statement of either–

(i) the method by which the administrator has decided to seek a decision from creditors as to whether they approve the proposals, or

(ii) the administrator's reasons for not seeking a decision from creditors;

(l) the manner in which the affairs and business of the company–

(i) have, since the date of the administrator's appointment, been managed and financed, including, where any assets have been disposed of, the reasons for the disposals and the terms upon which the disposals were made, and

(ii) will, if the administrator's proposals are approved, continue to be managed and financed;

(m) a statement whether the proceedings are main, secondary, territorial or non-EU proceedings; and

(n) any other information that the administrator thinks necessary to enable creditors to decide whether or not to approve the proposals.

3.35(2) [List of creditors] The list of creditors required by paragraph (1)(i) must contain the details required by sub-paragraph (3) except where paragraphs (4) and (5) apply;

3.35(3) [Particulars of list of creditors] The particulars required by paragraph (2) are as follows and must be given in this order–

(a) the name and postal address of the creditor;

(b) the amount of the debt owed to the creditor;

(c) details of any security held by the creditor;

(d) the date on which any such security was given; and

(e) the value of any such security;

3.35(4) [Employee and pre-paid consumer creditors] This paragraph applies where the particulars required by paragraph (3) relate to creditors who are either–

(a) employees or former employees of the company; or

(b) consumers claiming amounts paid in advance for the supply of goods and services.

3.35(5) [Particulars re r.3.35(4)] Where paragraph (4) applies–

(a) the list of creditors required by paragraph (1)(i) must state separately for each of paragraphs (4)(a) and (b) the number of the creditors and the total of the debts owed to them; and

(b) the particulars required by paragraph (3) in respect of such creditors must be set out in separate schedules to the list of creditors for each of sub-paragraphs (4)(a) and (b); and

(c) the administrator must not deliver any such schedule to the registrar of companies with the statement of proposals.

3.35(6) [Details re prescribed part] Except where the administrator proposes a CVA in relation to the company, the statement made by the administrator under paragraph 49 of Schedule B1 must also include–

(a) to the best of the administrator's knowledge and belief, an estimate of the value of–

  (i) the prescribed part (whether or not the administrator might be required under section 176A to make the prescribed part available for the satisfaction of unsecured debts), and

  (ii) the company's net property (as defined by section 176A(6)); and

(b) a statement whether the administrator proposes to make an application to the court under section 176A(5) and if so the reason for the application.

3.35(7) [Exclusion from prescribed part details] The administrator may exclude from an estimate under paragraph (6)(a) information the disclosure of which could seriously prejudice the commercial interests of the company.

3.35(8) [Exclusion affecting calculation of estimate] If the exclusion of such information affects the calculation of an estimate, the report must say so.

3.35(9) [Statement as to fixing basis of administrator's remuneration] The document containing the statement of proposals must include a statement of the basis on which it is proposed that the administrator's remuneration should be fixed by a decision in accordance with Chapter 4 of Part 18 of these Rules.

3.35(10) [Pre-administration costs, unpaid pre-administration costs] Where applicable the document containing the statement of proposals must include–

(a) a statement of any pre-administration costs charged or incurred by the administrator or, to the administrator's knowledge, by any other person qualified to act as an insolvency practitioner in relation to the company;

(b) a statement that the payment of any unpaid pre-administration costs as an expense of the administration is–

  (i) subject to approval under rule 3.52, and

  (ii) not part of the proposals subject to approval under paragraph 53 of Schedule B1.

(See General Note after r.3.37.)

3.36 Administrator's proposals: statement of pre-administration costs

3.36 A statement of pre-administration costs under rule 3.35(10)(a) must include–

(a) details of any agreement under which the fees were charged and expenses incurred, including the parties to the agreement and the date on which the agreement was made;

(b) details of the work done for which the fees were charged and expenses incurred;

(c) an explanation of why the work was done before the company entered administration and how it had been intended to further the achievement of an objective in paragraph 3(1) of Schedule B1 in accordance with sub-paragraphs (2) to (4) of that paragraph;

(d) a statement of the amount of the pre-administration costs, setting out separately–

  (i) the fees charged by the administrator,

  (ii) the expenses incurred by the administrator,

  (iii) the fees charged (to the administrator's knowledge) by any other person qualified to act as an insolvency practitioner in relation to the company (and, if more than one, by each separately), and

  (iv) the expenses incurred (to the administrator's knowledge) by any other person qualified to act as an insolvency practitioner in relation to the company (and, if more than one, by each separately);

(e) a statement of the amounts of pre-administration costs which have already been paid (set out separately as under sub-paragraph (d));

(f) the identity of the person who made the payment or, if more than one person made the payment, the identity of each such person and of the amounts paid by each such person set out separately as under sub-paragraph (d); and

(g) a statement of the amounts of unpaid pre-administration costs (set out separately as under sub-paragraph (d)).

(See General Note after r.3.37.)

3.37 Advertising administrator's proposals and notices of extension of time for delivery of proposals (paragraph 49 of Schedule B1)

3.37(1) [Content of notice] A notice published by the administrator under paragraph 49(6) of Schedule B1 must–

(a) identify the proceedings and contain the registered office of the company;

(b) be advertised in such manner as the administrator thinks fit; and

(c) be published as soon as reasonably practicable after the administrator has delivered the statement of proposals to the company's creditors but no later than eight weeks (or such other period as may be agreed by the creditors or as the court may order) from the date on which the company entered administration.

3.37(2) [Delivery of notice] Where the court orders, on an application by the administrator under paragraph 107 of Schedule B1, an extension of the period in paragraph 49(5) of Schedule B1 for delivering copies of the statement of proposals, the administrator must as soon as reasonably practicable after the making of the order deliver a notice of the extension to–

(a) the creditors of the company;

(b) the members of the company of whose address the administrator is aware; and

(c) the registrar of companies.

3.37(3) [Content of notice] The notice must–

(a) identify the proceedings;

(b) state the date to which the court has ordered an extension; and

(c) contain the registered office of the company.

3.37(4) [Publication] The administrator is taken to comply with paragraph (2)(b) if the administrator publishes a notice complying with paragraph (5).

3.37(5) [Publication notice] The notice must–

(a) contain the information required by paragraph (3);

(b) be advertised in such manner as the administrator thinks fit;

(c) state that members may request in writing a copy of the notice of the extension, and state the address to which to write; and

(d) be published as soon as reasonably practicable after the administrator has delivered the notice of the extension to the company's creditors.

General Note to rr.3.35–3.37

These rules apply to all administrations under Sch.B1, however initiated. The legislators have embraced the philosophy of disclosure with both hands! At least they have provided administrators with a comprehensive check-list.

R.3.35(1)(h), (1)(i).
It does not appear that the administrator has any discretion not to require a statement of affairs to be submitted (see para.47(1)), but these measures could apply if no statement of affairs has been submitted at the time when the proposals are sent out, and conceivably also where nobody formerly connected with the company can be traced.

R.3.35(1)(m)
On this issue, see the note to art.3 of the EU Regulation.

Rule 3.35(1)(m) amended by the Insolvency (England and Wales) and Insolvency (Scotland) (Miscellaneous and Consequential Amendments) Rules 2017 (SI 2017/1115) rr.1(1), (2), 22, 30(14) as from 8 December 2017.

Rr.3.35(10), 3.36
These measures make provision for an administrator (or another qualified insolvency practitioner) to be able to recover remuneration charged and expenses incurred before the formal start of the administration. Where one of the purposes of a decision is to seek approval for the payment of pre-administration costs, the Insolvency Service has directed that this purpose should be identified as a separate resolution in the notice, in order to ensure maximum transparency to creditors: see *Dear IP*, September 2014, p.1.46. The procedure for authorising the payment of pre-administration expenses is set out in r.3.52. In *Re Johnson Machine and Tool Co Ltd* [2010] EWHC 582 (Ch); [2010] B.C.C. 382 HHJ Purle QC discussed the circumstances in which, and the extent to which, such expenses might be treated as expenses of the ensuing administration and, in the case before him, declined to make any order to that effect where the company's assets had been sold under a pre-pack arrangement to the company's existing management.

R.3.37
Form AM03 should be used for the notice of proposals, with the statement attached, and Form AM04 for the notice of extension of time. On the standard contents (for notices other than gazetted notices), see rr.1.15, 1.16, 1.18.

Rule 3.37(4) amended by the Insolvency (England and Wales) and Insolvency (Scotland) (Miscellaneous and Consequential Amendments) Rules 2017 (SI 2017/1115) rr.1(1), (2), 2, 4 as from 8 December 2017.

3.38 Seeking approval of the administrator's proposals

3.38(1) [Application of rule] This rule applies where the administrator is required by paragraph 51 of Schedule B1 to seek approval from the company's creditors of the statement of proposals made under paragraph 49 of that Schedule.

3.38(2) [Statement to be accompanied by notice of decision procedure] The statement of proposals delivered under paragraph 49(4) of Schedule B1 must be accompanied by a notice to the creditors of the decision procedure in accordance with rule 15.8.

3.38(3) [Deemed consent] The administrator may seek a decision using deemed consent in which case the requirements in rule 15.7 also apply to the notice.

3.38(4) [Where administrator does not seek approval] Where the administrator has made a statement under paragraph 52(1) of Schedule B1 and has not sought a decision on approval from creditors, the proposal will be deemed to have been approved unless a decision has been requested under paragraph 52(2) of Schedule B1.

3.38(5) [Notice of date of deemed approval under r.3.38(4)] Where under paragraph (4) the proposal is deemed to have been approved the administrator must, as soon as reasonably practicable after the expiry of the period for requisitioning a decision set out in rule 15.18(2), deliver a notice of the date of deemed approval to the registrar of companies, the court and any creditor to whom the administrator has not previously delivered the proposal.

3.38(6) [Content of notice] The notice must contain–

(a) identification details for the proceedings;

(b) the name of the administrator;

(c) the date the administrator was appointed; and

(d) the date on which the statement of proposals was delivered to the creditors.

3.38(7) [Copies to accompany notice to court and certain creditors] A copy of the statement of proposals, with the statements required by rule 3.35(5), must accompany the notice given to the court and to any creditors to whom a copy of the statement of proposals has not previously been delivered.

General Note

This rule takes us to the new provisions on decision procedures and deemed consent under respectively rr.15.8 and 15.7 (and see s.246ZF) and the procedural rules on decision making in Pt 15 of these Rules. It is now anticipated that decisions will normally be made without meetings (although creditors can requisition a meeting under s.246ZE(3), (7) if they are at least 10 per cent in number or value or simply 10 creditors). See the table in r.15.11 for details of the persons to whom notice must be delivered of decision procedures and deemed consent. There is a minimum notice period of 14 days (although this does not apply to notice of a decision procedure by advertising under a court order: see r.15.12). Where a decision is sought by a meeting, notice of the procedure must be gazetted under r.15.13; on the standard contents for gazetted notices, see rr.1.10–1.12. On the proof required for creditors' voting rights and calculation of voting rights, see rr.15.28 and 15.31 (or r.15.32 in special cases such as hire-purchase creditors). A secured creditor may vote for the full amount of his secured debt only where there is insufficient property to enable a distribution to be made to unsecured creditors (apart from the "prescribed part") (r.15.31(6)(a) and para.52(1)(b)). For the majority required for approval see r.15.34(1), (2). Approval is unnecessary in certain events: that the administrator states in the statement of proposals that he thinks that all creditors will be paid in full, that no prescribed part can be paid to unsecured creditors, or that the objectives in s.3(1)(a) or (b) cannot be achieved (para.52(1)). However a creditor or creditors with debts amounting to at least 10 per cent of the total debts of the company may request the administrator to seek a decision from the creditors as to whether they approve the proposals (para.52(2)).

Reference is made to r.3.38(4) in *Promontoria (Chestnut) Ltd v Craig* [2017] EWHC 2405 (Ch).

R.3.38(5)
Form AM06 should be used.

3.39 Invitation to creditors to form a creditors' committee

3.39(1) [Notice inviting establishment of creditors' committee] Where the administrator is required to seek a decision from the company's creditors under rule 3.38, the administrator must at the same time deliver to the creditors a notice inviting them to decide whether a creditors' committee should be established if sufficient creditors are willing to be members of the committee.

3.39(2) [Notice to invite membership nominations] The notice must also invite nominations for membership of the committee, such nominations to be received by the administrator by a date to be specified in the notice.

3.39(3) [Notice re nominations] The notice must state that any nominations–

(a) must be delivered to the administrator by the specified date; and

(b) can only be accepted if the administrator is satisfied as to the creditor's eligibility under rule 17.4.

3.39(4) [Other times for notice where no committee] A notice under this rule must also be delivered to the creditors at any other time when the administrator seeks a decision from creditors and a creditors' committee has not already been established at that time.

General Note

This rule had no counterpart in IR 1986, although those rules did provide for creditors' committees: it was left to the creditors themselves to take the initiative at the creditors' meeting. On creditors' committees, see Pt 17 of these Rules.

3.40 Notice of extension of time to seek approval

3.40(1) [Delivery of notice of extension ordered] Where the court orders an extension to the period set out in paragraph 51(2) of Schedule B1, the administrator must deliver a notice of the extension as soon as reasonably practicable to each person mentioned in paragraph 49(4) of Schedule B1.

3.40(2) [Content of notice] The notice must contain identification details for the proceedings and the date to which the court has ordered an extension.

3.40(3) [Publication of notice rather than delivery] The administrator is taken to have complied with paragraph (1) as regards members of the company if the administrator publishes a notice complying with paragraph (4).

3.40(4) [Published noticed] The notice must–

(a) be advertised in such manner as the administrator thinks fit;

(b) state that members may request in writing a copy of the notice of the extension, and state the address to which to write; and

(c) be published as soon as reasonably practicable after the administrator has delivered the notice of the extension to the company's creditors.

(See General Note after r.3.43.)

3.41 Notice of the creditors' decision on the administrator's proposals (paragraph 53(2))

3.41(1) [To whom report of decision to be sent] In addition to delivering a report to the court and the registrar of companies (in accordance with paragraph 53(2) of Schedule B1) the administrator must deliver a report to–

(a) the company's creditors (accompanied by a copy of the statement of proposals, with the statement required by rule 3.35(10)(a) and (b), if it has not previously been delivered to the creditor); and

(b) every other person to whom a copy of the statement of proposals was delivered.

3.41(2) [Contents of report] A report mentioned in paragraph (1) must contain–

(a) identification details for the proceedings;

(b) details of decisions taken by the creditors including details of any modifications to the proposals which were approved by the creditors; and

(c) the date such decisions were made.

3.41(3) [Copy statement of proposals to accompany report to court] A copy of the statement of proposals, with any statements required by rule 3.35(9) and (10), must accompany the report to the court.

(See General Note after r.3.43.)

3.42 Administrator's proposals: revision

3.42(1) [Delivery of proposed revised statement with notice of decision procedure] Where paragraph 54(1) of Schedule B1 applies, the statement of the proposed revision which is required to be delivered to the creditors must be delivered with a notice of the decision procedure in accordance with rule 15.8.

3.42(2) [Content of revised statement of proposals] The statement must identify the proceedings and include–

(a) any other trading names of the company;

(b) details of the administrator's appointment, including–

(i) the date of appointment, and

(ii) the person making the application or appointment;

(c) the names of the directors and secretary of the company and details of any shareholdings in the company which they may have;

(d) a summary of the original proposals and the reason or reasons for proposing a revision;

(e) details of the proposed revision, including details of the administrator's assessment of the likely impact of the proposed revision upon creditors generally or upon each class of creditors;

(f) where the proposed revision relates to the ending of the administration by a creditors' voluntary winding up and the nomination of a person to be the proposed liquidator of the company–

(i) details of the proposed liquidator,

(ii) where applicable, the declaration required by section 231, and

(iii) a statement that the creditors may, before the proposals are approved, nominate a different person as liquidator in accordance with paragraph 83(7)(a) of Schedule B1 and rule 3.60(6)(b); and

(g) any other information that the administrator thinks necessary to enable creditors to decide whether or not to vote for the proposed revisions.

3.42(3) [Deemed consent] The administrator may seek a decision using deemed consent in which case the requirements in rule 15.7 also apply to the notice.

3.42(4) [Period for delivery of statement to members] The period within which, subject to paragraph 54(3) of Schedule B1, the administrator must send a copy of the statement to every member of the company of whose address the administrator is aware is five business days after sending the statement of the proposed revision to the creditors.

3.42(5) [Advertisement of notice] Notice under paragraph 54(3) and (4) of Schedule B1 must–

(a) be advertised in such manner as the administrator thinks fit as soon as reasonably practicable after the administrator has sent the statement to the creditors; and

(b) state that members may request in writing a copy of the proposed revision, and state the address to which to write.

3.42(6) [Copy to be registered] A copy of the statement of revised proposals under rule 3.43(3) must be delivered to the registrar of companies not later than five days after the report under rule 3.43(1) is delivered.

(See General Note after r.3.43.)

3.43 Notice of result of creditors' decision on revised proposals (paragraph 54(6))

3.43(1) [Delivery of report] In addition to delivering a report to the court and the registrar of companies (in accordance with paragraph 54(6) of Schedule B1) the administrator must deliver a report to–

(a) the company's creditors (accompanied by a copy of the original statement of proposals and the revised statement of proposals if the administrator had not delivered notice of the decision procedure or deemed consent procedure to the creditor); and

(b) every other person to whom a copy of the original statement of proposals was delivered.

3.43(2) [Content of report] A report mentioned in paragraph (1) must contain–

(a) identification details for the proceedings;

(b) the date of the revised proposals;

(c) details of decisions taken by the creditors including details of any modifications to the revised proposals which were approved by the creditors; and

(d) the date such decisions were made.

3.43(3) [Copy revised proposals to court] A copy of the statement of revised proposals must accompany the notice to the court.

General Note to rr.3.40–3.43

In relation to an extension of time under r.3.40 for seeking approval of the proposals for the creditors, the initial decision date under para.51(2) must be within 10 weeks from the day the company entered administration (the actual decision date will depend on whether the decision is initially sought using the deemed consent procedure or a qualifying decision procedure).

Rr.3.40, 3.41, 3.42, 3.43
Forms AM05, AM07, AM08 and AM09 (respectively) should be used. The detailed contents in the notices in these rules are increased by comparison with the previous forms.

Chapter 8

Limited disclosure of statements of affairs and proposals

[Note: a document required by the Act or these Rules must also contain the standard contents set out in Part 1.]

3.44 Application of Chapter

3.44 This Chapter applies to the disclosure of information which would be likely to prejudice the conduct of the administration or might reasonably be expected to lead to violence against any person.

(See General Note after r.3.48.)

3.45 Orders limiting disclosure of statement of affairs etc.

3.45(1) [Application to court] If the administrator thinks that the circumstances in rule 3.44 apply in relation to the disclosure of–

(a) the whole or part of the statement of the company's affairs;

(b) any of the matters specified in rule 3.35(1)(h) and (i) (administrator's proposals); or

(c) a statement of concurrence,

the administrator may apply to the court for an order in relation to the particular document or a specified part of it.

3.45(2) [Court order] The court may order that the whole of or a specified part of a document referred to in paragraph (1)(a)to (c) must not be delivered to the registrar of companies or, in the case of the statement of proposals, to creditors or members of the company.

3.45(3) [Delivery to registrar of companies] The administrator must as soon as reasonably practicable deliver to the registrar of companies–

(a) a copy of the order;

(b) the statement of affairs, statement of proposals and any statement of concurrence to the extent provided by the order; and

(c) if the order relates to the statement of proposals, an indication of the nature of the matter in relation to which the order was made.

3.45(4) [Order re statement of proposals] If the order relates to the statement of proposals, the administrator must as soon as reasonably practicable also deliver to the creditors and members of the company–

(a) the statement of proposals to the extent provided by the order; and

(b) an indication of the nature of the matter in relation to which the order was made.

(See General Note after r.3.48.)

3.46 Order for disclosure by administrator

3.46(1) [Application by creditor for disclosure] A creditor may apply to the court for an order that the administrator disclose any of the following in relation to which an order has been made under rule 3.45(2)–

(a) a statement of affairs;

(b) a specified part of it;

(c) a part of a statement of proposals; or

(d) statement of concurrence.

3.46(2) [Witness statement] The application must be supported by a witness statement.

3.46(3) [Notice to administrator] The applicant must deliver to the administrator notice of the application at least three business days before the hearing.

3.46(4) [Order subject to conditions] In an order for disclosure, the court may include conditions as to confidentiality, duration, the scope of the order in the event of any change of circumstances or such other matters as it thinks just.

(See General Note after r.3.48.)

3.47 Rescission or amendment of order for limited disclosure

3.47(1) [Material change in circumstances] If there is a material change in circumstances rendering an order for limited disclosure under rule 3.45(2) wholly or partially unnecessary, the administrator must, as soon as reasonably practicable after the change, apply to the court for the order to be rescinded or amended.

3.47(2) [Order rescinded] If the court makes such an order, the administrator must as soon as reasonably practicable deliver to the registrar of companies–

(a) a copy of the order; and

(b) the statement of affairs, the statement of proposals and any statement of concurrence to the extent provided by the order.

3.47(3) [Order re statement of proposals] If the order relates to the statement of proposals, the administrator must as soon as reasonably practicable also deliver to the creditors and members the statement of proposals to the extent allowed by the order.

(See General Note after r.3.48.)

3.48 Publication etc. of statement of affairs or statement of proposals

3.48(1) [CPR Pt 31 not to apply] CPR Part 31 does not apply to an application under rule 3.45, 3.46 or 3.47.

3.48(2) [Delivery of copy/summary of statement of affairs to creditors] If, after the administrator has sent a statement of proposals under paragraph 49(4) of Schedule B1, a statement of affairs is delivered to the registrar of companies in accordance with rule 3.47(2) as the result of the rescission or amendment of an order, the administrator must deliver to the creditors a copy or summary of the statement of affairs as delivered to the registrar of companies.

3.48(3) [Requirements for delivery to members] The administrator is taken to comply with the requirements for delivery to members of the company in rule 3.45(4) or 3.47(3) if the administrator publishes the required notice.

3.48(4) [Required notice] The required notice must–

(a) be advertised in such manner as the administrator thinks fit;

(b) state that members can request in writing–

  (i) a copy of the statement of proposals to the extent provided by the order, and

  (ii) an indication of the nature of the matter in relation to which the order was made;

(c) state the address to which to such a written request is to be made; and

(d) be published as soon as reasonably practicable after the administrator has delivered the statement of proposals to the extent provided by the order to the company's creditors.

GENERAL NOTE TO RR.3.44–3.48

On the statement of affairs generally, see the note to para.47. These rules set out the protection against disclosure of information in the statement of affairs or the other documents specified in r.3.45(1) that would be likely to prejudice the administration or might reasonably be expected to lead to violence against any person, with r.3.48 disapplying the rules on disclosure in CPR Pt 31 in these circumstances. For an example of a limited disclosure order see *Re All Leisure Holidays Ltd* [2017] EWHC 870 (Ch); [2017] B.C.C. 354 where the court accepted that full statements of affairs containing the names and addresses and debts of all identified creditors might prejudice the administrations as competitors might take advantage of disclosure of those details and also of the terms of the sale of the businesses and assets contained confidentiality clauses.

R.3.45
Form AM12 should be used, with the statements and court order attached.

R.3.47
The court's powers may be exercised with retrospective effect, after a document containing information which should not have been disclosed has been delivered to the registrar and filed: see *Registrar of Companies v Swarbrick* [2014] EWHC 1466 (Ch); [2014] Bus. L.R. 625.

Form AM13 should be used, with the statements and court order attached.

CHAPTER 9

DISPOSAL OF CHARGED PROPERTY

[Note: a document required by the Act or these Rules must also contain the standard contents set out in Part 1.]

3.49 Disposal of charged property

3.49(1) [Application of rule] This rule applies where the administrator applies to the court under paragraph 71 or 72 of Schedule B1 for authority to dispose of–

(a) property which is subject to a security other than a floating charge; or

(b) goods in the possession of the company under a hire-purchase agreement.

3.49(2) [Court to fix venue for hearing] The court must fix a venue for the hearing of the application.

3.49(3) [Notice of venue to the security holder, etc.] As soon as reasonably practicable after the court has done so, the administrator must deliver notice of the venue to the holder of the security or the owner of the goods.

3.49(4) [Sealed copies of order re non-floating charge or HP property] If an order is made under paragraph 71 or 72 of Schedule B1, the court must deliver two sealed copies to the administrator.

3.49(5) [Administrator to deliver copies] The administrator must deliver–

(a) one of the sealed copies to the holder of the security or the owner of the goods; and

(b) a copy of the sealed order to the registrar of companies.

GENERAL NOTE

The leave of the court is not required where the administrator wishes to deal with property that is subject to a floating charge.

Form AM14 should be delivered to the registrar, with the order attached.

"Hire purchase agreement" includes a conditional sale agreement, a chattel leasing agreement and a retention of title agreement (para.111(1)).

CHAPTER 10

EXPENSES OF THE ADMINISTRATION

[Note: a document required by the Act or these Rules must also contain the standard contents set out in Part 1.]

3.50 Expenses

3.50(1) [Incidence of costs, etc.] All fees, costs, charges and other expenses incurred in the course of the administration are to be treated as expenses of the administration.

3.50(2) [Prescribed part expenses] The expenses associated with the prescribed part must be paid out of the prescribed part.

3.50(3) [Cost of administrator's security] The cost of the security required by section 390(3) for the proper performance of the administrator's functions is an expense of the administration.

3.50(4) [Former administrator] For the purposes of paragraph 99 of Schedule B1, a former administrator's remuneration and expenses comprise all the items in rule 3.51(2).

General Note

Amendments to the equivalent rule in IR 1986 were made in 2003 to reflect the more expanded role of administration as a distributional regime and the coming into operation of the reserved fund for unsecured creditors (the "prescribed part": see IA 1986 s.176A). Expenses incurred with regard to the latter come exclusively out of that fund. The previous version of r.3.50(2) referred to "costs" rather than "expenses" but meant the same: see HHJ Purle QC in *Re International Sections Ltd* [2009] B.C.C. 574 at [16].

See also the comments of Snowden J in *Re Nortel Networks UK Ltd* [2017] EWHC 1429 (Ch).

3.51 Order of priority

3.51(1) [Former administrator's priority] Where there is a former administrator, the items in paragraph 99 of Schedule B1 are payable in priority to the expenses in this rule.

3.51(2) [Priority of expenses] Subject to paragraph (1) and to any court order under paragraph (3) the expenses of the administration are payable in the following order of priority–

(a) expenses properly incurred by the administrator in performing the administrator's functions;

(b) the cost of any security provided by the administrator in accordance with the Act or these Rules;

(c) where an administration order was made, the costs of the applicant and any person appearing on the hearing of the application whose costs were allowed by the court;

(d) where the administrator was appointed otherwise than by order of the court–

 (i) the costs and expenses of the appointer in connection with the making of the appointment, and

 (ii) the costs and expenses incurred by any other person in giving notice of intention to appoint an administrator;

(e) any amount payable to a person in respect of assistance in the preparation of a statement of affairs or statement of concurrence;

(f) any allowance made by order of the court in respect of the costs on an application for release from the obligation to submit a statement of affairs or deliver a statement of concurrence;

(g) any necessary disbursements by the administrator in the course of the administration (including any costs referred to in Articles 30 or 59 of the EU Regulation and expenses incurred by members of the creditors' committee or their representatives and allowed for by the administrator under rule 17.24, but not including any payment of corporation tax in circumstances referred to in sub-paragraph (j) below);

(h) the remuneration or emoluments of any person who has been employed by the administrator to perform any services for the company, as required or authorised under the Act or these Rules;

(i) the administrator's remuneration the basis of which has been fixed under Part 18 and unpaid pre-administration costs approved under rule 3.52; and

(j) the amount of any corporation tax on chargeable gains accruing on the realisation of any asset of the company (irrespective of the person by whom the realisation is effected).

3.51(3) [Priorities where assets insufficient to satisfy liabilities] If the assets are insufficient to satisfy the liabilities, the court may make an order as to the payment out of the assets of the expenses incurred in the administration in such order of priority as the court thinks just.

General Note

Despite the possibility of this rule being reformulated in 2017 in light of recent case law (on administration and liquidation expenses: for some of which, see below), such has not transpired.

The notes to s.156 and r.7.108 (dealing with the expenses of a compulsory liquidation) may be helpful. However, the drafting of this rule is not as detailed as r.7.108 (to an extent it bears stronger similarity to r.6.42 dealing with priority in creditors' voluntary winding up) and it may be open to a different construction, e.g. in regard to litigation costs: see Lyons and Roberts (2005) Co. L.N. 16 p.1; and Lyons and Birch, (2005) 18 Insolv. Int. 150. In *Re Allders Department Stores Ltd* [2005] EWHC 172 (Ch); [2005] 2 All E.R. 122; [2005] B.C.C. 289 statutory liabilities to make redundancy and unfair dismissal payments were held not to have priority as "expenses properly incurred" by the administrator under what is now r.3.51(2)(a) or "necessary disbursements" under r.3.51(2)(g). Rent of premises occupied wholly or partly by a company in administration were held to be payable as an administration expense by the Court of Appeal in *Pillar Denton Ltd v Jervis, Re Games Station Ltd* [2014] EWCA Civ 180; [2014] B.C.C. 165 (overruling the first instance decisions *Goldacre (Offices) Ltd v Nortel Networks UK Ltd* [2009] EWHC 3389 (Ch); [2010] Ch. 455; [2010] B.C.C. 299 and *Leisure (Norwich) II Ltd v Luminar Lava Ignite Ltd* [2012] EWHC 951 (Ch); [2012] B.C.C. 497). Applying the "salvage" principle laid down in *Re Lundy Granite Co* (1870–71) L.R. 6 Ch. App. 462, the court held that the rule applied irrespective of the question whether the rent day occurred prior to or during the administration: the determining factor was whether the administrator retained possession of the property for the benefit of the administration; the rent was to be treated as accruing from day to day and ranked as an expense of the administration and not simply a provable debt. Moreover, applying the same principle, if the administrator vacated the premises, leaving the landlord free to re-let, rent ceased to be payable, irrespective of the terms of the lease. In *Bloom v Pensions Regulator* [2011] EWCA Civ 1124; [2012] B.C.C. 83 money payable under a financial support direction imposed by the Pensions Regulator on a company in administration was held to be a necessary disbursement (but not a provable debt or administration expense under any other provision of the legislation) and accordingly entitled to super-priority. However, the Supreme Court reversed this ruling (*Re Nortel GmbH, Bloom v Pensions Regulator* [2013] UKSC 52; [2014] A.C. 209; [2013] B.C.C. 624): the liability was a provable debt ranking pari passu with the unsecured creditors. Even if it were found not to be a provable debt, it would not have been an administration expense (as a necessary disbursement under r.3.51(2)(g)) because the liability did not arise out of something done by or on behalf of the administrator in the course of the administration. This case was followed in *Laverty v British Gas Trading Ltd* [2014] EWHC 2721 (Ch); [2014] B.C.C. 701, where the charge for a continued supply of energy to a company in administration (under a deemed contract, after the original supply had been terminated by the provider) was held to be a provable debt, but not an administration expense. (On these cases and subsequent developments, see the note to Sch.B1 para.99(2)–(3).)

Although under r.3.51(3) the court has a discretion to alter the order of priority, it will not do so without good and sufficient reason: *Irish Reel Productions Ltd v Capitol Films Ltd* [2010] EWHC 180 (Ch); [2010] B.C.C. 588. In that case a petition for winding up had been dismissed when the administration order was made. The court allowed the winding-up costs to be paid as an expense of the administration (but not in priority to the administrator's own expenses). Contrast *Re Portsmouth City Football Club Ltd, Neumans LLP v Andronikou* [2013] EWCA Civ 916; [2013] B.C.C. 741, where an administration terminated when the company was put into liquidation. The court ordered that the legal fees and disbursements incurred in relation to the winding-up petition should not be treated as expenses of the administration but should be allowed as an expense of the liquidation under what is now r.7.108.

Sums payable as non-domestic rates in respect of premises occupied by a company in administration were held to be "necessary disbursements" and accordingly entitled to priority under Sch.B1 para.99 in *Exeter City Council v Bairstow* [2007] EWHC 400 (Ch); [2007] B.C.C. 236. The court expressed the view that unoccupied property rates would rank similarly, but the law has since been amended so that such rates are no longer payable where the owner of the relevant property is a company in administration, under either the original or the Sch.B1 regime: see the Non-Domestic Rating (Unoccupied Property) (England) Regulations 2008 (SI 2008/386) regs 3, 4(l); and the Non-Domestic Rating (Unoccupied Property) (Scotland) Regulations 2008 (SSI 2008/83) reg.2, both effective 1 April 2008. In regard to Wales, see the Non-Domestic Rating (Unoccupied Property) (Wales) Regulations 2008 (SI 2008/2499 (W 217)). See further the notes to Sch.B1 para.99(3) and r.7.108.

While r.3.51 may constitute a complete statutory code of administration expenses, the court may in its discretion (e.g. under Sch.B1 para.13(1)(f)) declare that other items shall be treated "as if" they were expenses of the administration (such as the costs of an earlier, abortive, application for an administration order: *Re Bickland Ltd* [2012] EWHC 706 (Ch); [2013] B.C.C. 501).

Rule 3.51(2)(g) amended by the Insolvency Amendment (EU 2015/848) Regulations 2017 (SI 2017/702) regs 1, 2(1), Sch. paras 32, 37 in relation to proceedings opened on or after 26 June 2017 (see reg.3) when the Recast EU Regulation 2015/848 came into force.

3.52 Pre-administration costs

3.52(1) [Creditors' committee may approve for payment] Where the administrator has made a statement of pre-administration costs under rule 3.35(10)(a), the creditors' committee may determine whether and to what extent the unpaid pre-administration costs set out in the statement are approved for payment.

3.52(2) [Application of r.3.52(3)] Paragraph (3) applies where–

(a) there is no creditors' committee;

(b) there is a creditors' committee but it does not make the necessary determination; or

(c) the creditors' committee does make the necessary determination but the administrator or other insolvency practitioner who has charged fees or incurred expenses as pre-administration costs considers the amount determined to be insufficient.

3.52(3) [Approval by creditors, secured or preferential creditors] When this paragraph applies, determination of whether and to what extent the unpaid pre-administration costs are approved for payment must be–

(a) by a decision of the creditors through a decision procedure; or

(b) in a case where the administrator has made a statement under paragraph 52(1)(b) of Schedule B1, by–

  (i) the consent of each of the secured creditors, or

  (ii) if the administrator has made, or intends to make, a distribution to preferential creditors, by–

    (aa) the consent of each of the secured creditors, and

    (bb) a decision of the preferential creditors in a decision procedure.

3.52(4) [Creditors' meeting for approval of expenses of other IP] The administrator must call a meeting of the creditors' committee or seek a decision of creditors by a decision procedure if so requested for the purposes of paragraphs (1) to (3) by another insolvency practitioner who has charged fees or incurred expenses as pre-administration costs; and the administrator must deliver notice of the meeting or decision procedure within 28 days of receipt of the request.

3.52(5) [Application to court by administrator or other IP] The administrator (where the fees were charged or expenses incurred by the administrator) or other insolvency practitioner (where the fees were charged or expenses incurred by that practitioner) may apply to the court for a determination of whether and to what extent the unpaid pre-administration costs are approved for payment if either–

(a) there is no determination under paragraph (1) or (3); or

(b) there is such a determination but the administrator or other insolvency practitioner who has charged fees or incurred expenses as pre-administration costs considers the amount determined to be insufficient.

3.52(6) [Notice to creditors' committee] Where there is a creditors' committee the administrator or other insolvency practitioner must deliver at least 14 days' notice of the hearing to the members of the committee; and the committee may nominate one or more of its members to appear, or be represented, and to be heard on the application.

3.52(7) [Where no creditors' committee] If there is no creditors' committee, notice of the application must be delivered to such one or more of the company's creditors as the court may direct, and those creditors may nominate one or more of their number to appear or be represented, and to be heard on the application.

3.52(8) [Costs of application] The court may, if it appears to be a proper case, order the costs of the application, including the costs of any member of the creditors' committee appearing or being represented on it, or of any creditor so appearing or being represented, to be paid as an expense of the administration.

3.52(9) [Where administrator fails to call a creditors' meeting, etc.] Where the administrator fails to call a meeting of the creditors' committee or seek a decision from creditors in accordance with paragraph (4), the other insolvency practitioner may apply to the court for an order requiring the administrator to do so.

General Note

This rule, first introduced in 2010, sets out the procedure for authorising the payment of pre-administration expenses. On pre-administration costs, see further r.3.36.

Where one of the purposes of a meeting (or other decision procedure) is to seek approval for the payment of pre-administration costs, the Insolvency Service has directed that this purpose should be identified as a separate issue in the relevant notice, in order to ensure maximum transparency to creditors: see *Dear IP*, September 2014, p.1.46.

Ethical questions may arise where an administrator's pre-administration expenses are paid to him directly by the purchaser of the insolvent business. See the note to Sch.B1 para.2.

Chapter 11

Extension and ending of administration

[Note: a document required by the Act or these Rules must also contain the standard contents set out in Part 1.]

3.53 Interpretation

3.53 "Final progress report" means in this Chapter, and in Part 18 in so far as it relates to final progress reports in an administration, a progress report which includes a summary of–

(a) the administrator's proposals;

(b) any major amendments to, or deviations from, those proposals;

(c) the steps taken during the administration; and

(d) the outcome.

(See General Note after r.3.61.)

3.54 Application to extend an administration and extension by consent (paragraph 76(2) of Schedule B1)

3.54(1) [Application of rule] This rule applies where an administrator makes an application to the court for an order, or delivers a notice to the creditors requesting their consent, to extend the administrator's term of office under paragraph 76(2) of Schedule B1.

3.54(2) [Reasons for extension] The application or the notice must state the reasons why the administrator is seeking an extension.

3.54(3) [Extension request to creditors] A request to the creditors may contain or be accompanied by a notice that if the extension is granted a notice of the extension will be made available for viewing and downloading on a website and that no other notice will be delivered to the creditors.

3.54(4) [Request result; use of website] Where the result of a request to the creditors is to be made available for viewing and downloading on a website, the notice must comply with the requirements for use of a website to deliver documents set out in rule 1.49(2)(a) to (c), (3) and (4) with any necessary modifications and rule 1.49(5)(a) applies to determine the time of delivery of the document.

3.54(5) [Notice where extension order by court] Where the court makes an order extending the administrator's term of office, the administrator must as soon as reasonably practicable deliver to the creditors a notice of the order together with the reasons for seeking the extension given in the application to the court.

3.54(6) [Notice where extension by consent of creditors] Where the administrator's term of office has been extended with the consent of creditors, the administrator must as soon as reasonably practicable deliver a notice of the extension to the creditors except where paragraph (3) applies.

3.54(7) [Notice to registrar of companies] The notices which paragraph 78(5)(b) of Schedule B1 require to be delivered to the registrar of companies must also identify the proceedings.

(See General Note after r.3.61.)

3.55 Notice of automatic end of administration (paragraph 76 of Schedule B1)

3.55(1) [Application of rule] This rule applies where–

(a) the appointment of an administrator has ceased to have effect; and

(b) the administrator is not required by any other rule to give notice of that fact.

3.55(2) [Notice to registrar of companies and court with final progress report] The former administrator must, as soon as reasonably practicable, and in any event within five business days of the date on which the appointment has ceased, deliver to the registrar of companies and file with the court a notice accompanied by a final progress report.

3.55(3) [Notice heading] The notice must be headed "Notice of automatic end of administration" and identify the company immediately below the heading.

3.55(4) [Content of notice] The notice must contain–

(a) identification details for the proceedings;

(b) the former administrator's name and address;

(c) a statement that that person had been appointed administrator of the company;

(d) the date of the appointment;

(e) the name of the person who made the appointment or the administration application, as the case may be;

(f) a statement that the appointment has ceased to have effect;

(g) the date on which the appointment ceased to have effect; and

(h) a statement that a copy of the final progress report accompanies the notice.

3.55(5) [Authentication] The notice must be authenticated by the administrator and dated.

3.55(6) [Copy notice etc. to directors and others] A copy of the notice and accompanying final progress report must be delivered as soon as reasonably practicable to–

(a) the directors of the company; and

(b) all other persons to whom notice of the administrator's appointment was delivered.

3.55(7) [Default, penalty] A former administrator who makes default in complying with this rule is guilty of an offence and liable to a fine and, for continued contravention, to a daily default fine.

(See General Note after r.3.61.)

3.56 Notice of end of administration when purposes achieved (paragraph 80(2) of Schedule B1)

3.56(1) [Notice to registrar of companies and court] Where an administrator who was appointed under paragraph 14 or 22 of Schedule B1 thinks that the purpose of administration has been sufficiently achieved, the notice ("notice of end of administration") which the administrator may file with the court and deliver to the registrar of companies under paragraph 80(2) of Schedule B1 must be headed "Notice of end of administration" and identify the company immediately below the heading.

3.56(2) [Content of notice] The notice must contain–

(a) identification details for the proceedings;

(b) the administrator's name and address;

(c) a statement that that person has been appointed administrator of the company;

(d) the date of the appointment;

(e) the name of the person who made the appointment or the administration application, as the case may be;

(f) a statement that the administrator thinks that the purpose of the administration has been sufficiently achieved;

(g) a statement that a copy of the final progress report accompanies the notice; and

(h) a statement that the administrator is filing the notice with the court and delivering a copy to the registrar of companies.

3.56(3) [Authentication] The notice must be authenticated by the administrator and dated.

3.56(4) [Final progress report] The notice must be accompanied by a final progress report.

3.56(5) [Notice in court] The notice filed with the court must also be accompanied by a copy of the notice.

3.56(6) [Court to endorse notice and copy] The court must endorse the notice and the copy with the date and time of filing, seal the copy and deliver it to the administrator.

3.56(7) [Prescribed period for copy notice to creditors] The prescribed period within which the administrator, under paragraph 80(4) of Schedule B1, must send a copy of the notice to the creditors is five business days from the filing of the notice.

3.56(8) [Final progress report] The copy notice sent to creditors must be accompanied by the final progress report.

3.56(9) [Copy notice and final progress report to other persons] The administrator must within the same period deliver a copy of the notice and the final progress report to all other persons (other than the creditors and the registrar of companies) to whom notice of the administrator's appointment was delivered.

3.56(10) [Gazetting of notice to creditors] The administrator is taken to have complied with the requirement in paragraph 80(4) of Schedule B1 to give notice to the creditors if, within five business days of filing the notice with the court, the administrator gazettes a notice which–

(a) states that the administration has ended, and the date on which it ended;

(b) undertakes that the administrator will provide a copy of the notice of end of administration to any creditor of the company who applies in writing; and

(c) specifies the address to which to write.

3.56(11) [Advertisement] The Gazette notice may be advertised in such other manner as the administrator thinks fit.

(See General Note after r.3.61.)

3.57 Administrator's application for order ending administration (paragraph 79 of Schedule B1)

3.57(1) [Further progress report, etc.] An application to court by the administrator under paragraph 79 of Schedule B1 for an order ending an administration must be accompanied by–

(a) a progress report for the period since–

(i) the last progress report (if any), or

(ii) if there has been no previous progress report, the date on which the company entered administration;

(b) a statement indicating what the administrator thinks should be the next steps for the company (if applicable); and

(c) where the administrator makes the application because of a requirement decided by the creditors, a statement indicating with reasons whether or not the administrator agrees with the requirement.

3.57(2) [Application other than creditors' decision] Where the application is made other than because of a requirement by a decision of the creditors–

(a) the administrator must, at least five business days before the application is made, deliver notice of the administrator's intention to apply to court to–

(i) the person who made the administration application or appointment, and

(ii) the creditors; and

(b) the application must be accompanied by–

(i) a statement that notice has been delivered to the creditors, and

(ii) copies of any response from creditors to that notice.

3.57(3) [Application in conjunction with winding-up petition] Where the application is in conjunction with a petition under section 124 for an order to wind up the company, the administrator must, at least five business days before the application is filed, deliver notice to the creditors as to whether the administrator intends to seek appointment as liquidator.

(See General Note after r.3.61.)

3.58 Creditor's application for order ending administration (paragraph 81 of Schedule B1)

3.58(1) [To whom copy application to be delivered] Where a creditor applies to the court under paragraph 81 of Schedule B1 for an order ending an administration, a copy of the application must be delivered, not less than five business days before the date fixed for the hearing, to–

(a) the administrator;

(b) the person who made the administration application or appointment; and

(c) where the appointment was made under paragraph 14 of Schedule B1, the holder of the floating charge by virtue of which the appointment was made (if different to (b)).

3.58(2) [Appearances] Any of those persons may appear at the hearing of the application.

3.58(3) [Court to copy order to administrator] Where the court makes an order under paragraph 81 ending the administration, the court must deliver a copy of the order to the administrator.

(See General Note after r.3.61.)

3.59 Notice by administrator of court order

3.59 Where the court makes an order ending the administration, the administrator must as soon as reasonably practicable deliver a copy of the order and of the final progress report to–

(a) the registrar of companies;

(b) the directors of the company; and

(c) all other persons to whom notice of the administrator's appointment was delivered.

(See General Note after r.3.61.)

3.60 Moving from administration to creditors' voluntary winding up (paragraph 83 of Schedule B1)

[Note: the information referred to in paragraph (5) is required to be included in the first progress report of the liquidator. See rule 18.3(5).]

3.60(1) [Application of rule] This rule applies where the administrator delivers to the registrar of companies a notice under paragraph 83(3) of Schedule B1 of moving from administration to creditors' voluntary winding up.

3.60(2) [Content of notice] The notice must contain–

(a) identification details for the proceedings;

(b) the name of the person who made the appointment or the administration application, as the case may be; and

(c) the name and IP number of the proposed liquidator.

3.60(3) [Notice to registrar of companies with final progress report] The notice to the registrar of companies must be accompanied by a copy of the administrator's final progress report.

3.60(4) [Copies to other persons] A copy of the notice and the final progress report must be sent as soon as reasonably practicable after delivery of the notice to all those persons to whom notice of the administrator's appointment was delivered in addition to the creditors (as required by paragraph 83(5)(b)).

3.60(5) [Former administrator to inform liquidator] The person who ceases to be administrator on the registration of the notice must inform the person who becomes liquidator of anything which happens after the date of the final progress report and before the registration of the notice which the administrator would have included in the final report had it happened before the date of the report.

3.60(6) [Nomination of liquidator by creditors] For the purposes of paragraph 83(7)(a) of Schedule B1, a person is nominated by the creditors as liquidator by–

(a) their approval of the statement of the proposed liquidator in the administrator's proposals or revised proposals; or

(b) their nomination of a different person, through a decision procedure, before their approval of the proposals or revised proposals.

3.60(7) [Different person nominated] Where the creditors nominate a different person, the nomination must, where applicable, include the declaration required by section 231.

(See General Note after r.3.61.)

3.61 Moving from administration to dissolution (paragraph 84 of Schedule B1)

3.61(1) [Application of rule] This rule applies where the administrator delivers to the registrar of companies a notice under paragraph 84(1) of Schedule B1 of moving from administration to dissolution.

3.61(2) [Notice to identify proceedings] The notice must identify the proceedings.

3.61(3) [Copy notice to other persons] As soon as reasonably practicable after sending the notice, the administrator must deliver a copy of the notice to all persons to whom notice of the administrator's appointment was delivered (in addition to the creditors mentioned in paragraph 84(5)(b) but excluding opted-out creditors).

3.61(4) [Final progress report with notice to registrar etc.] A final progress report must accompany the notice to the registrar of companies and every copy filed or otherwise delivered.

3.61(5) [Court to copy order to administrator] Where a court makes an order under paragraph 84(7) of Schedule B1 it must, where the applicant is not the administrator, deliver a copy of the order to the administrator.

3.61(6) [Administrator to copy order to registrar of companies] The administrator must deliver a copy of the order to the registrar of companies with the notice required by paragraph 84(8).

General Note to rr.3.53–3.61

Paragraphs 76 et seq. of Sch.B1 deal with the various ways in which an administration can come to an end (in the words of the draftsman, "the appointment of an administrator shall cease to have effect"). These rules supplement those provisions by spelling out the procedure to be followed and the contents of notices to be used.

R.3.54
The period for which the administrator's term of office may be extended under Sch.B1 para.76(2)(b) was increased from up to six months to up to one year by SBEEA 2015 s.127 as from 26 May 2015.

An application for extension must be made well ahead of time so that it can be heard by the registrar. On 15 October 2008 Mann J issued a warning that administrators who leave applying until a late date will have their costs disallowed by the applications judge. It is understood that in London the Companies Court registrars require notice to be filed six weeks in advance of the expiry date, unless the circumstances are unusual. See also the unreported case *Re Taylor Made Foods plc*, discussed in the note to Sch.B1 paras 76–77.

R.3.54(7)
Form AM19 should be used.

R.3.55(2), (7)
Form AM20 should be used, with the report attached. On penalties see s.430 and Sch.3 to these Rules.

R.3.56
Form AM21 should be used, with the report attached. On the standard contents for gazetted notices (r.3.56(11)), see rr.1.10–1.12.

R.3.59
Form AM25 should be used, with the court order attached.

R.3.60
On the notice to be filed, seethe note to r.3.64. Form AM22 should be used, with the report attached.

R.3.61(1), (6)
Forms AM23(with the report attached) and AM24 (with the court order attached) should respectively be used.

R.3.61(3)
Opted-out creditors are excluded. Rule 3.61(3) amended by the Insolvency (England and Wales) and Insolvency (Scotland) (Miscellaneous and Consequential Amendments) Rules 2017 (SI 2017/1115) rr.1(1), (2), 2, 5 as from 8 December 2017.

Chapter 12

Replacing the administrator

[Note: a document required by the Act or these Rules must also contain the standard contents set out in Part 1.]

3.62 Grounds for resignation

3.62(1) [Grounds] The administrator may resign–

(a) on grounds of ill health;

(b) because of the intention to cease to practise as an insolvency practitioner; or

(c) because the further discharge of the duties of administrator is prevented or made impractical by–

(i) a conflict of interest, or

(ii) a change of personal circumstances.

3.62(2) [Other grounds] The administrator may, with the permission of the court, resign on other grounds.

(See General Note after r.3.70.)

3.63 Notice of intention to resign

3.63(1) [Notice] The administrator must give at least five business days' notice of intention–

(a) to resign in a case falling within rule 3.62(1); or

(b) to apply for the court's permission to resign in a case falling within rule 3.62(2).

3.63(2) [Content of notice] The notice must contain–

(a) identification details for the proceedings;

(b) the date of the appointment of the administrator;

(c) the name of the person who made the appointment or the administration application, as the case may be.

3.63(3) [Further content] The notice must also contain–

(a) the date with effect from which the administrator intends to resign; or

(b) where the administrator was appointed by an administration order, the date on which the administrator intends to file with the court an application for permission to resign.

3.63(4) [To whom notice to be delivered] The notice must be delivered–

(a) to any continuing administrator of the company;

(b) to the creditors' committee (if any);

(c) if there is neither a continuing administrator nor a creditors' committee, to–

(i) the company, and

(ii) the company's creditors;

(d) to the member State liquidator appointed in relation to the company (if there is one);

(e) where the administrator was appointed by the holder of a qualifying floating charge under paragraph 14 of Schedule B1, to–

(i) the person who appointed the administrator, and

(ii) all holders of prior qualifying floating charges;

(f) where the administrator was appointed by the company or the directors of the company under paragraph 22 of Schedule B1, to–

(i) the appointer, and

(ii) all holders of qualifying floating charges.

3.63(5) [Notice with summary receipts and payments] The notice must be accompanied by a summary of the administrator's receipts and payments.

(See General Note after r.3.70.)

3.64 Notice of resignation (paragraph 87 of Schedule B1)

3.64(1) [To whom notice to be delivered] A resigning administrator must, within five business days of delivering the notice under paragraph 87(2) of Schedule B1, deliver a copy of the notice to–

(a) the registrar of companies;

(b) all persons, other than the person who made the appointment, to whom notice of intention to resign was delivered under rule 3.63; and

(c) except where the appointment was by administration order, file a copy of the notice with the court.

3.64(2) [Content of notice] The notice must contain–

(a) identification details for the proceedings;

(b) the date of the appointment of the administrator; and

(c) the name of the person who made the appointment or the administration application, as the case may be.

3.64(3) [Further content] The notice must state–

(a) the date from which the resignation is to have effect; and

(b) where the resignation is with the permission of the court, the date on which permission was given.

3.64(4) [Filing with court] Where an administrator was appointed by an administration order, notice of resignation under paragraph 87(2)(a) of Schedule B1 must be given by filing the notice with the court.

(See General Note after r.3.70.)

3.65 Application to court to remove administrator from office

3.65(1) [Application to state grounds] An application for an order under paragraph 88 of Schedule B1 that the administrator be removed from office must state the grounds on which the order is requested.

3.65(2) [To whom copy of application to be delivered] A copy of the application must be delivered, not less than five business days before the date fixed for the hearing–

(a) to the administrator;

(b) to the person who–

(i) made the application for the administration order, or

(ii) appointed the administrator;

(c) to the creditors' committee (if any);

(d) to any continuing administrator appointed to act jointly or concurrently; and

(e) where there is neither a creditors' committee nor a continuing administrator appointed, to the company and the creditors, including any floating charge holders.

3.65(3) [Court to deliver copy order to applicant] The court must deliver to the applicant a copy of any order removing the administrator.

3.65(4) [To whom applicant to deliver copy order] The applicant must deliver a copy–

(a) as soon as reasonably practicable, and in any event within five business days of the copy order being delivered, to the administrator; and

(b) within five business days of the copy order being delivered, to–

(i) all other persons to whom notice of the application was delivered, and

(ii) the registrar of companies.

(See General Note after r.3.70.)

3.66 Notice of vacation of office when administrator ceases to be qualified to act

3.66 An administrator who has ceased to be qualified to act as an insolvency practitioner in relation to the company and gives notice in accordance with paragraph 89 of Schedule B1 must also deliver notice to the registrar of companies.

(See General Note after r.3.70.)

3.67 Deceased administrator

3.67(1) [Notice filed in court] If the administrator dies a notice of the fact and date of death must be filed with the court.

3.67(2) [Who to file notice] The notice must be filed as soon as reasonably practicable by one of the following–

(a) a surviving administrator;

(b) a member of the deceased administrator's firm (if the deceased was a member or employee of a firm);

(c) an officer of the deceased administrator's company (if the deceased was an officer or employee of a company); or

(d) a personal representative of the deceased administrator.

3.67(3) [No filing within 21 days] If such a notice has not been filed within the 21 days following the administrator's death then any other person may file the notice.

3.67(4) [Delivery notice to registrar of companies] The person who files the notice must also deliver a notice to the registrar of companies which contains–

(a) identification details for the proceedings;

(b) the name of the person who made the appointment or the administration application, as the case may be;

(c) the date of the appointment of the administrator; and

(d) the fact and date of death.

(See General Note after r.3.70.)

3.68 Application to replace

3.68(1) [Replacement administrator's consent to act] Where an application to court is made under paragraph 91(1) or 95 of Schedule B1 to appoint a replacement administrator, the application must be accompanied by the proposed replacement administrator's consent to act.

3.68(2) [To whom copy application to be delivered] Where the application is made under paragraph 91(1), a copy of the application must be delivered–

(a) to the person who made the application for the administration order;

(b) to any person who has appointed an administrative receiver of the company;

(c) to any person who is or may be entitled to appoint an administrative receiver of the company;

(d) to any person who is or may be entitled to appoint an administrator of the company under paragraph 14 of Schedule B1;

(e) to any administrative receiver of the company;

(f) if there is pending a petition for the winding up of the company, to–

(i) the petitioner, and

(ii) any provisional liquidator;

(g) to any member State liquidator appointed in main proceedings in relation to the company;

(h) to the company, if the application is made by anyone other than the company;

(i) to any supervisor of any CVA in relation to the company; and

(j) to the proposed administrator.

3.68(3) [Application under IA 1986 Sch.B1 para.95; witness statement] Where the application is made under paragraph 95, the application must be accompanied by a witness statement setting out the applicant's belief as to the matters set out in that paragraph.

3.68(4) [Application of rr.3.12, 3.13, 3.15(1), (2)] Rules 3.12, 3.13, and 3.15(1) and (2) apply to applications made under paragraph 91(1) and 95 of Schedule B1, with any necessary modifications.

(See General Note after r.3.70.)

3.69 Appointment of replacement or additional administrator

3.69 Where a replacement administrator is appointed or an additional administrator is appointed to act–

(a) the following apply–

(i) rule 3.17 (notice of appointment) the requirement as to the heading in paragraph (1) and paragraphs (1)(a) to (f), and (2),

(ii) rule 3.18 (filing of notice with court) paragraphs (1)(a) and (b)(ii), (2) and (3),

(iii) rule 3.24 (notice of appointment after notice of intention to appoint) paragraphs (1)(a) to (d) and (2),

(iv) rule 3.25 (notice of appointment without prior notice of intention to appoint) paragraphs (1), (2)(a) to (c) and (3),

(v) rule 3.26 (notice of appointment: filing with the court) paragraphs (1)(a), (3) and (4), and

(vi) rule 3.27 (publication of administrator's appointment) paragraphs (1), (2)(a) and (b), (3) and (4);

(b) the replacement or additional administrator must deliver notice of the appointment to the registrar of companies; and

(c) all documents must clearly identify the appointment as of a replacement administrator or an additional administrator.

(See General Note after r.3.70.)

3.70 Administrator's duties on vacating office

3.70(1) [Delivery to successor administrator] An administrator who ceases to be in office as a result of removal, resignation or ceasing to be qualified to act as an insolvency practitioner in relation to the company must as soon as reasonably practicable deliver to the person succeeding as administrator–

(a) the assets (after deduction of any expenses properly incurred and distributions made by the departing administrator);

(b) the records of the administration, including correspondence, proofs and other documents relating to the administration while it was within the responsibility of the departing administrator; and

(c) the company's records.

3.70(2) [Default, penalty] An administrator who makes default in complying with this rule is guilty of an offence and liable to a fine and, for continued contravention, to a daily default fine.

General Note to rr.3.62–3.70

Paragraphs 87 et seq. of Sch.B1 deal with the various circumstances in which an administrator can leave office and be replaced by another, with the appointment of one or more additional administrators, and with matters consequential upon an administrator leaving office. These rules supplement those provisions by spelling out the procedure to be followed and the content of any notice to be used in each case.

R.3.62
The predecessor to r.3.62(2) was considered in *Re Lehman Brothers Ltd,* unreported, 15 March 2016, where in order to exercise its discretion to permit four (out of five) administrators to resign and be replaced, the court had to be satisfied that there was good reason to do so and that the new appointment was appropriate; in the circumstances the replacements were the only practical solution and the administration would be best served by permitting the resignations and the new appointees acting with the continuing lead administrator. For explanation by Registrar Jones of the correct procedure to be followed by an administrator who wishes to resign office under rr.3.62 and 3.63 see *VE Vegas Investors IV LLC v Shinners* [2018] EWHC 186 (Ch).

R.3.64
Form AM15 should be used for the notice of resignation.

On the conversion of an administration to a creditors' voluntary liquidation, various other documents must also be filed with the registrar, including a notice of move from administration to CVA (Form AM22) and a notice of appointment of liquidator (Form 600—unchanged and still in use). The latter must be filed *after* Form AM22 has been registered. However, it is not necessary to file a notice of end of administration (Form AM20, AM21 or AM25, as appropriate) in addition to Form AM22. See the note to Sch.B1 para.83 and the Guidance Note published by Companies House and *Dear IP*, July 2013. Both the termination of the administration and the commencement of the liquidation take effect on the date that Form AM22 is registered.

On "block transfers" (where it is proposed that an insolvency practitioner who holds multiple offices is to vacate them simultaneously and be replaced by another), see the note to IA 1986 s.172(1), (2); and IR rr.12.35 et seq.

Part 4

Receivership

[Note: for the application of this Part see introductory rule 3.]

Introductory note to Part 4
The predecessor to this Part—IR 1986 Pt 3—was headed "Administrative Receivership" whereas we now have a broader description to the current Part, although the very great majority of its provisions (rr.4.2–4.21) do indeed apply only to administrative receivers. The bulk of the rules of Pt 4 deal with the statement of affairs and the administrative receiver's report. It should be noted that the following rules do not apply to Scottish receiverships (see rr.3(3) and 4.2) or receivers in Northern Ireland (see r.3(1)).

Chapter 1

Appointment of joint receivers or managers to whom Part 3 of the Act applies (other than those appointed under section 51 (Scottish receiverships))

[Note: a document required by the Act or these Rules must also contain the standard contents set out in Part 1.]

4.1 Receivers or managers appointed under an instrument: acceptance of appointment (section 33)

4.1(1) [Application of Ch.1] This Chapter applies to all receivers to whom Part 3 of the Act applies (other than those appointed under section 51 (Scottish Receiverships)).

4.1(2) [Two or more persons appointed jointly] Where two or more persons are appointed as joint receivers or managers of a company's property under powers contained in an instrument–

(a) each of them must accept the appointment in accordance with section 33 as if each were a sole appointee;

(b) the joint appointment takes effect only when all of them have accepted; and

(c) the joint appointment is deemed to have been made at the time at which the instrument of appointment was received by or on behalf of all of them.

4.1(3) [Sole or joint receiver or manager] A person who is appointed as the sole or joint receiver or manager of a company's property under powers contained in an instrument and accepts the appointment in accordance with section 33(1)(a), but not in writing, must confirm the acceptance in writing to the person making the appointment within five business days.

4.1(4) [Content of written acceptance or confirmation of acceptance] The written acceptance or confirmation of acceptance must contain–

(a) the name and address of the appointer;

(b) the name and address of the appointee;

(c) the name of the company concerned;

(d) the time and date of receipt of the instrument of appointment; and

(e) the time and date of acceptance.

4.1(5) [Who may accept or confirm] Acceptance or confirmation of acceptance of appointment as a receiver or manager of a company's property, whether under the Act or these Rules, may be given by any person (including, in the case of a joint appointment, any joint appointee) duly authorised for that purpose on behalf of the receiver or manager.

General Note

This rule should be viewed in the light of s.33. It deals with acceptance and confirmation of appointment as receiver or manager (not just an administrative receiver) appointed by an instrument, rather than by the court. It does not apply to Scottish receivers (see r.3(3)) or in Northern Ireland (see r.3(1)).

Chapter 2

Administrative receivers (other than in Scottish receiverships)

[Note: a document required by the Act or these Rules must also contain the standard contents set out in Part 1.]

4.2 Application of Chapter 2

4.2 This Chapter applies to administrative receivers (other than those appointed under section 51 (Scottish receiverships)).

GENERAL NOTE

See s.29(2) for the definition of administrative receiver and the note thereto for a description. The qualification in relation to Scotland appears unnecessary in light of the more generic ambit of r.3(3).

4.3 Interpretation

4.3 In this Chapter–

"nominated person" means a relevant person who has been required by the administrative receiver to make out and deliver to the administrative receiver a statement of affairs; and

"relevant person" means a person mentioned in section 47(3).

GENERAL NOTE

This rule had no counterpart in IR 1986. The definition of "nominated person" duplicates that in r.1.2(2).

4.4 Administrative receiver's security

4.4 The cost of the administrative receiver's security required by section 390(3) for the proper performance of the administrative receiver's functions is an expense of the administrative receivership.

GENERAL NOTE

It is standard practice for the insolvency practitioner's security to be an expense of a corporate insolvency procedure: see also rr.3.50 (administration), 5.5 (members' voluntary winding up), 6.24 (creditors' voluntary winding up) and 7.58 (compulsory winding up).

4.5 Publication of appointment of administrative receiver (section 46(1))

4.5(1) [Content of notice required by IA 1986 s.46(1)] The notice which an administrative receiver is required by section 46(1) to send to the company and the creditors on being appointed must contain–

(a) identification details for the company;

(b) any other registered name of the company in the 12 months before the date of the appointment;

(c) any name under which the company has traded at any time in those 12 months, if substantially different from its then registered name;

(d) the name and address of the person appointed;

(e) the date of the appointment;

(f) the name of the person who made the appointment;

(g) the date of the instrument conferring the power under which the appointment was made;

(h) a brief description of the instrument; and

(i) a brief description of any assets of the company in relation to which the appointment is not made.

4.5(2) [Gazetting and advertisement of notice of appointment] The notice which an administrative receiver is required by section 46(1) to publish–

(a) must be gazetted;

(b) may be advertised in such other manner as the administrative receiver thinks fit; and

(c) must state–

 (i) that an administrative receiver has been appointed,

 (ii) the date of the appointment,

 (iii) the name of the person who made the appointment, and

 (iv) the nature of the business of the company.

General Note

Details of the notices required to be given by an administrative receiver under IA 1986 s.46 to the company and the public at large are here provided. Greater detail of the content of the notice is now required as Form 3.1A is no longer used after 6 April 2017. For the standard contents of gazetted notices see rr.1.10–1.12

4.6 Requirement to provide a statement of affairs (section 47(1))

[Note: see sections 234(1) and 235(1) for the application of section 235 to administrative receivers.]

4.6(1) [Notice re IA 1986 s.47 statement] A requirement under section 47(1) for a nominated person to make out and submit to the administrative receiver a statement of the affairs of the company must be made by a notice delivered to such a person.

4.6(2) [Heading and content of notice] The notice must be headed "Notice requiring statement of affairs" and must–

(a) identify the company immediately below the heading;

(b) require the recipient to prepare and submit to the administrative receiver a statement of the affairs of the company; and

(c) inform each recipient of–

 (i) the name and address of any other nominated person to whom a notice has been delivered,

 (ii) the date by which the statement must be delivered to the administrative receiver, and

 (iii) the effect of sections 47(6) (penalty for non-compliance) and 235 (duty to co-operate with the office-holder).

4.6(3) [Document for preparation of statement of affairs] The administrative receiver must inform each nominated person that a document for the preparation of the statement of affairs capable of completion in compliance with rule 4.7 can be supplied if requested.

General Note

This rule fills out the contents of any notice given by an administrative receiver under IA 1986 s.47 to "nominated persons" who must submit a statement of the company's affairs to him. The penalty for non-compliance under s.47(6) and the duty to co-operate with the administrative receiver under s.235 are spelled out in r.4.6(2)(c)(iii).

The receiver *must* demand a statement from someone: his only discretion is in determining who to "require" it from (see s.47 itself).

Note that although from 6 April 2017, there is no longer a prescribed form (previously Form 3.2) the nominated person(s) may request a document for the preparation of the statement of affairs.

4.7 Statement of affairs: contents and delivery of copy (section 47(2))

[Note: section 47(2) requires the statement of affairs to be verified by a statement of truth.]

4.7(1) [Heading of statement] The statement of affairs must be headed "Statement of affairs" and must state that it is a statement of the affairs of the company on a specified date, being the date on which the administrative receiver was appointed.

4.7(2) [Content of statement] The statement of affairs must contain, in addition to the matters required by section 47(2)–

(a) a summary of the assets of the company, setting out the book value and the estimated realisable value of–

(i) any assets subject to a fixed charge,

(ii) any assets subject to a floating charge,

(iii) any uncharged assets, and

(iv) the total assets available for preferential creditors;

(b) a summary of the liabilities of the company, setting out–

(i) the amount of preferential debts,

(ii) an estimate of the deficiency with respect to preferential debts or the surplus available after paying the preferential debts,

(iii) an estimate of the prescribed part, if applicable,

(iv) an estimate of the total assets available to pay debts secured by floating charges,

(v) the amount of debts secured by floating charges,

(vi) an estimate of the deficiency with respect to debts secured by floating charges or the surplus available after paying the debts secured by floating charges,

(vii) the amount of unsecured debts (excluding preferential debts and any deficiency with respect to debts secured by floating charges),

(viii) an estimate of the deficiency with respect to unsecured debts or the surplus available after paying unsecured debts (excluding preferential debts and any deficiency with respect to debts secured by fixed and floating charges),

(ix) any issued and called-up capital, and

(x) an estimate of the deficiency with respect to, or surplus available to, members of the company;

(c) a list of the company's creditors with the further particulars required by paragraph (3) indicating–

(i) any creditors under hire-purchase, chattel leasing or conditional sale agreements,

(ii) any creditors who are consumers claiming amounts paid in advance for the supply of goods or services, and

(iii) any creditors claiming retention of title over property in the company's possession.

4.7(3) [Particulars re creditors] The particulars required by section 47(2) and paragraph (2)(c) of this rule to be included in the statement of affairs relating to each creditor are as follows–

(a) the name and postal address;

(b) the amount of the debt owed to the creditor;

(c) details of any security held by the creditor;

(d) the date the security was given; and

(e) the value of any such security.

4.7(4) [Application of r.4.7(5)] Paragraph (5) applies where the particulars required by paragraph (3) relate to creditors who are either–

(a) employees or former employees of the company; or

(b) consumers claiming amounts paid in advance for the supply of goods or services.

4.7(5) [Further particulars re creditors] Where this paragraph applies–

(a) the statement of affairs must state separately for each of paragraphs (4)(a) and (b) the number of such creditors and the total of the debts owed to them; and

(b) the particulars required by paragraph (3) must be set out in separate schedules to the statement of affairs for each of paragraphs (4)(a) and (b).

4.7(6) [Deliver of statement of affairs and copy to administrative receiver] The nominated person who makes the statement of truth required by section 47(2) (or, if more than one, by one of them) must deliver the statement of affairs together with a copy to the administrative receiver.

General Note

This relates to the statement of affairs to be submitted under IA 1986 s.47. As mentioned in the note to r.4.6, after 6 April 2017, there is no longer a prescribed form to replace Form 3.2 and so the content of the statement of affairs is now detailed in this rule. It seems likely that practitioners will adapt former Form 3.2, which largely mirrors the required content in r.4.7, to send to nominated persons who request a document under r.4.6 to enable them to comply. The statement is verified by a statement of truth.

4.8 Statement of affairs: statement of concurrence

4.8(1) [Administrative receiver may require statement of concurrence] The administrative receiver may require a relevant person to deliver to the administrative receiver a statement of concurrence.

4.8(2) [Statement of concurrence] A statement of concurrence is a statement, verified by a statement of truth, that that person concurs in the statement of affairs submitted by a nominated person.

4.8(3) [Notice re statement of concurrence] The administrative receiver must inform the nominated person who has been required to submit a statement of affairs that the relevant person has been required to deliver a statement of concurrence.

4.8(4) [Copy statement of affairs] The nominated person must deliver a copy of the statement of affairs to every relevant person who has been required to deliver a statement of concurrence.

4.8(5) [Statement of concurrence may be qualified] A statement of concurrence–

(a) must identify the company; and

(b) may be qualified in relation to matters dealt with in the statement of affairs where the relevant person–

(i) is not in agreement with the statement of affairs,

(ii) considers the statement to be erroneous or misleading, or

(iii) is without the direct knowledge necessary for concurring in it.

4.8(6) [Delivery of statement of concurrence] The relevant person must deliver the required statement of concurrence together with a copy to the administrative receiver before the end of the period of five business days (or such other period as the administrative receiver may agree) beginning with the day on which the relevant person receives the statement of affairs.

General Note

As more than one relevant person may be required to make out a statement of affairs, to avoid confusion and duplication this rule permits the administrative receiver to require a person to concur within five business days, under a statement of truth, with a statement of affairs submitted by a nominated person who must copy the statement to each relevant person required to make a statement on concurrence.

4.9 Statement of affairs: retention by administrative receiver

4.9 The administrative receiver must retain the verified statement of affairs and each statement of concurrence as part of the records of the receivership.

General Note

The administrative receiver's duty to retain the documents in rr.4.7 and 4.8.

4.10 Statement of affairs: release from requirement and extension of time (section 47(5))

4.10(1) [Exercise of IA 1986 s.47(5) power] The administrative receiver may exercise the power in section 47(5) to release a person from an obligation to submit a statement of affairs imposed under section 47(1) or (2), or to grant an extension of time, either on the administrative receiver's own discretion or at the request of a nominated person.

4.10(2) [Application to court] A nominated person may apply to the court if the administrative receiver refuses that person's request.

4.10(3) [Court may dismiss application] On receipt of an application, the court may, if it is satisfied that no sufficient cause is shown for it, dismiss it without giving notice to any party other than the applicant.

4.10(4) [Notice of venue to administrative receiver] The applicant must, at least 14 days before any hearing, deliver to the administrative receiver a notice stating the venue with a copy of the application and of any evidence on which the applicant intends to rely.

4.10(5) [Report or appearance by administrative receiver] The administrative receiver may do either or both of the following–

(a) file a report of any matters which the administrative receiver thinks ought to be drawn to the court's attention; or

(b) appear and be heard on the application.

4.10(6) [Copy report] If a report is filed, the administrative receiver must deliver a copy of it to the applicant not later than five business days before the hearing.

4.10(7) [Sealed copies of order] Sealed copies of any order made on the application must be delivered by the court to the applicant and the administrative receiver.

4.10(8) [Applicant's costs] On any application under this rule, the applicant's costs must be paid by the applicant in any event; but the court may order that an allowance of all or part of them be payable out of the assets under the administrative receiver's control.

General Note

Further details of any release given by an administrative receiver under IA 1986 s.47(5) are provided by this rule.

4.11 Statement of affairs: expenses

4.11(1) [Payment of expenses] The administrative receiver must pay, out of the assets under the administrative receiver's control, the expenses which the administrative receiver considers to have been reasonably incurred by–

(a) a nominated person in making a statement of affairs and statement of truth; or

(b) a relevant person in making a statement of concurrence.

4.11(2) [Appeal to court] Any decision by the administrative receiver under this rule is subject to appeal to the court.

General Note

This allows a "nominated person" (see r.4.6(1)) to recover from the administrative receiver out of the company's assets the former's expenses incurred in producing the statement of affairs. This rule extends such right to any relevant person making a statement of concurrence.

4.12 Limited disclosure

4.12(1) [Application of rule] This rule applies where the administrative receiver thinks that disclosure of the whole or part of a statement of the company's affairs or a statement of concurrence would be likely to prejudice the conduct of the receivership or might reasonably be expected to lead to violence against any person.

4.12(2) [Application to court] The administrative receiver may apply to the court for an order in respect of–

(a) the statement of affairs; or

(b) a statement of concurrence;

and the court may order that the whole or any specified part of the statement of affairs or a statement of concurrence must not be open to inspection except with permission of the court.

4.12(3) [Directions re delivery] The court's order may include directions regarding the delivery of documents to the registrar of companies and the disclosure of relevant information to other persons.

General Note

This allows the administrative receiver to apply to the court to censor the statement of affairs if publication would prejudice his task or endanger persons. Such an application was extended from 6 April 2017, to statements of concurrence.

4.13 Administrative receiver's report to the registrar of companies and secured creditors (section 48(1))

4.13(1) [IA 1986 s.48(1) report with copy statement of affairs] The report which under section 48(1) an administrative receiver is to send to the registrar of companies must be accompanied by a copy of any statement of affairs under section 47 and any statement of concurrence under rule 4.8.

4.13(2) [Schedules re employees and pre-paid consumers excluded from delivery] However the administrative receiver must not deliver to the registrar of companies with the statement of affairs any schedule required by rule 4.7(5)(b).

4.13(3) [Limited disclosure under r.4.12] The duty to send a copy of the report to the registrar of companies is subject to any order for limited disclosure made under rule 4.12.

4.13(4) [Statements to administrative receiver after report sent] If a statement of affairs or statement of concurrence is submitted to the administrative receiver after the report is sent to the registrar of companies, the administrative receiver must deliver a copy of it to the registrar of companies as soon as reasonably practicable after its receipt by the administrative receiver.

4.13(5) [Estimates re prescribed part] The report must contain (in addition to the matters required by section 48(1)) estimates to the best of the administrative receiver's knowledge and belief of–

(a) the value of the prescribed part (whether or not the administrative receiver might be required under section 176A to make the prescribed part available for the satisfaction of unsecured debts); and

(b) the value of the company's net property (as defined by section 176A(6)).

4.13(6) [Non-disclosure of seriously prejudicial information] The administrative receiver may exclude from an estimate under paragraph (5) information the disclosure of which could seriously prejudice the commercial interests of the company.

4.13(7) [Non-disclosure affecting estimate] If the exclusion of such information affects the calculation of an estimate, the report must say so.

4.13(8) [Report to state whether application to court under IA 1986 s.176A(5)] If the administrative receiver proposes to make an application to court under section 176A(5) the report must say so and give the reason for the application.

General Note

This rule deals with various actions of the administrative receiver under IA 1986 s.48(1) in relation to his report. See Forms REC1 and REC4.

4.14 Copy of report for unsecured creditors (section 48(2))

4.14 A notice under section 48(2)(b) stating an address to which unsecured creditors should write for copies of an administrative receiver's report under that section–

(a) must be gazetted;

(b) may be advertised in such other manner as the administrative receiver thinks fit; and

(c) must be accompanied by a notice under rule 4.15.

General Note

If the administrative receiver opts to inform creditors (other than opted-out creditors) under IA 1986 s.48(2)(b) by publishing a notice as to obtaining copies of his report rather than sending them unsolicited copies, then this rule will apply. For the standard contents of gazetted notices see rr.1.10–1.12.

4.15 Invitation to creditors to form a creditors' committee

4.15(1) [Notice re creditors' committee] An administrative receiver must deliver to the creditors with the report under section 48(1) a notice inviting the creditors to decide whether a creditors' committee should be established if sufficient creditors are willing to be members of the committee.

4.15(2) [Notice to invite nominations for membership] The notice must also invite nominations for membership of the committee, such nominations to be received by the administrative receiver by a date to be specified in the notice.

4.15(3) [Notice as to nominations] The notice must state that any nominations–

(a) must be delivered to the administrative receiver by the specified date; and

(b) can only be accepted if the administrative receiver is satisfied as to the creditor's eligibility under rule 17.4.

General Note

This rule had no counterpart in IR 1986 although those rules did provide for creditors' committees. On creditors' committees see Pt 17 of these Rules.

4.16 Disposal of charged property (section 43(1))

4.16(1) [Application of rule] This rule applies where an administrative receiver applies to the court under section 43(1) for authority to dispose of property of the company which is subject to a security.

4.16(2) [Court to fix venue for hearing] The court must fix a venue for the hearing of the application.

4.16(3) [Notice of venue to security holder] As soon as reasonably practicable after the court has fixed the venue, the administrative receiver must deliver notice of the venue to the person who is the holder of the security.

4.16(4) [Copies of IA 1986 s.43(1) order to administrative receiver] If an order is made under section 43(1), the court must deliver two sealed copies to the administrative receiver and the administrative receiver must deliver one of them to the holder of the security.

General Note

This clarifies the position where applications are made by the administrative receiver to the court under IA 1986 s.43(1). For "venue" in r.4.16 see r.1.2(2). See Form REC3.

4.17 Summary of receipts and payments

4.17(1) [Administrative receiver to deliver summary to registrar of companies, etc.] The administrative receiver must deliver a summary of receipts and payments as receiver to the registrar of companies, the company and to the person who made the appointment, and to each member of the creditors' committee.

4.17(2) [Date of appointment in r.1.20 notice] The notice delivered to the registrar of companies under rule 1.20 must contain the date of the appointment of the administrative receiver.

4.17(3) [Period for delivery] The summary must be delivered to those persons within two months after–

(a) the end of the period of 12 months from the date of being appointed;

(b) the end of every subsequent period of 12 months; and

(c) ceasing to act as administrative receiver (unless there is a joint administrative receiver who continues in office).

4.17(4) [Period for summary] The summary must show receipts and payments–

(a) during the relevant period of 12 months; or

(b) where the administrative receiver has ceased to act, during the period–

(i) from the end of the last 12-month period to the time when the administrative receiver so ceased, or

(ii) if there has been no previous summary, since being appointed.

4.17(5) [Other requirement to produce proper accounts] This rule is without prejudice to the administrative receiver's duty to produce proper accounts otherwise than as above.

4.17(6) [Default, penalty] An administrative receiver who makes default in complying with this rule is guilty of an offence and liable to a fine and, for continued contravention, to a daily default fine.

General Note

This imposes accounting requirements on the administrative receiver in the form of a summary (previously an "abstract"). A prescribed form from Companies House is REC2. Compare these requirements with those of IA 1986 s.38. Rule 4.17(5) preserves the common-law duty to account: see *Smiths Ltd v Middleton* [1979] 3 All E.R. 842. For the sanction in r.4.17(6), see IR 2016 Sch.3.

4.18 Resignation

4.18(1) [Delivery of notice of intention] An administrative receiver must deliver notice of intention to resign at least five business days before the date the resignation is intended to take effect to–

(a) the person by whom the appointment was made;

(b) the company or, if it is then in liquidation, the liquidator; and

(c) the members of the creditors' committee.

4.18(2) [Notice of date to take effect] The notice must specify the date on which the administrative receiver intends the resignation to take effect.

General Note

This expands upon the provisions of IA 1986 s.45.

4.19 Deceased administrative receiver

4.19(1) [To whom notice to be delivered] If the administrative receiver dies a notice of the fact and date of death must be delivered as soon as reasonably practicable to–

(a) the person by whom the appointment was made;

(b) the registrar of companies;

(c) the company or, if it is in liquidation, the liquidator; and

(d) the members of the creditors' committee.

4.19(2) [Who to deliver notice] The notice must be delivered by one of the following–

(a) a surviving joint administrative receiver;

(b) a member of the deceased administrative receiver's firm (if the deceased was a member or employee of a firm);

(c) an officer of the deceased administrative receiver's company (if the deceased was an officer or employee of a company); or

(d) a personal representative of the deceased administrative receiver.

4.19(3) [Delivery by other person] If such a notice has not been delivered within 21 days following the administrative receiver's death then any other person may deliver the notice.

General Note

The list of persons who must deliver the notice is no longer restricted just to the person who made the appointment and has been considerably increased. See Form REC5.

4.20 Other vacation of office

4.20 An administrative receiver, on vacating office on completion of the administrative receivership, or in consequence of ceasing to be qualified to act as an insolvency practitioner in relation to the company, must as soon as reasonably practicable deliver a notice of doing so to–

(a) the person by whom the appointment was made;

(b) the company or, if it is then in liquidation, the liquidator; and

(c) the members of the creditors' committee.

General Note

This rule should be viewed in the light of IA 1986 s.45.

4.21 Notice to registrar of companies (section 45(4))

4.21 Where an administrative receiver's office is vacated other than by death, the notice to the registrar of companies required by section 45(4) may be given by delivering to the registrar of companies the notice required by section 859K(3) of the Companies Act.

General Note

The Companies Act 2006 s.859K(3), inserted by the Companies Act 2006 (Amendment of Part 25) Regulations 2013 (SI 2013/600) Sch.1 para.1 as from 6 April 2013, requires a person appointed receiver or manager of a company's property or undertaking under powers contained in an instrument ceasing to act as such to give notice to the registrar of companies of that fact. This rule obviates duplication of notice to the registrar.

Chapter 3

Non-administrative receivers and the prescribed part

[Note: a document required by the Act or these Rules must also contain the standard contents set out in Part 1.]

4.22 Application of Chapter 3

4.22 This Chapter applies where a receiver (other than an administrative receiver) is appointed by the court or otherwise under a charge which was created as a floating charge; and section 176A applies.

(See General Note after r.4.24.)

4.23 Report to creditors

4.23(1) [Notice of appointment and report] Within three months (or such longer period as the court may allow) of the date of the appointment, the receiver must deliver to the creditors–

(a) a notice of the appointment; and

(b) a report.

4.23(2) [Report to contain estimates re prescribed part] The report must contain estimates to the best of the receiver's knowledge and belief of–

(a) the value of the prescribed part (whether or not the receiver might be required under section 176A to make the prescribed part available for the satisfaction of unsecured debts); and

(b) the value of company's net property (as defined by section 176A(6)).

4.23(3) [Non-disclosure of seriously prejudicial information] The receiver may exclude from an estimate under paragraph (2) information the disclosure of which could seriously prejudice the commercial interests of the company.

4.23(4) [Non-disclosure affecting estimate] If the exclusion of such information affects the calculation of an estimate, the report must say so.

4.23(5) [Report to state if application under IA 1986 s.176A(5)] If the receiver proposes to make an application to court under section 176A(5) the report must say so and give the reason for the application.

4.23(6) [Statement re winding-up petition] The report must also state whether, and if so why, the receiver proposes to present a petition for the winding up of the company.

4.23(7) [Gazetting and advertisement of notice re report] The receiver may, instead of delivering the report under paragraph (1), cause a notice to be gazetted and may advertise that notice in such other manner as the receiver thinks fit where–

(a) full details of the unsecured creditors of the company are not available to the receiver; or

(b) the receiver thinks it is otherwise impracticable to deliver such a report.

4.23(8) [Content of r.4.23(7) notice] A notice under paragraph (7) must contain the matters required to be included in the receiver's report.

(See General Note after r.4.24.)

4.24 Receiver to deal with prescribed part

4.24(1) [Winding-up petition and prescribed part] The receiver–

(a) may present a petition for the winding up of the company if the ground of the petition is that in section 122(1)(f); and

(b) must deliver to any administrator or liquidator the sums representing the prescribed part.

4.24(2) [Where no administrator or liquidator] If there is no administrator or liquidator the receiver must–

(a) apply to the court for directions as to the manner in which to discharge the duty under section 176A(2)(a); and

(b) act in accordance with any directions given.

General Note to rr.4.22–4.24

Section 176A(1)(d) makes provision for the prescribed part of the fund for unsecured creditors in cases of receivership and is not restricted to administrative receivership. The application of Ch.3 is defined by r.4.22. With the striking down of "fixed charges" using the *Siebe Gorman* precedent by the House of Lords in *National Westminster Bank v Spectrum Plus Ltd* [2005] UKHL 41; [2005] 3 W.L.R. 58; [2005] B.C.C. 694, the significance of this reserved fund will grow.

R.4.23
This rule requires the receiver to keep unsecured creditors informed of the prospects for them of the reserved fund being operated. Note the options in r.423(7) where individual notification is not feasible.

R.4.24
This allows a receiver to present a winding-up petition or take other specified action in order to facilitate the operation of the reserved fund mechanism.

Part 5

Members' Voluntary Winding Up

Introductory note to Part 5
In contrast to IR 1986, the rules governing a members' voluntary winding up are now contained in a separate Part. The new rules do not make any changes of significance—indeed, the basic understanding is that decisions will continue to be taken by the members at physical meetings (or their equivalent), in accordance with CA 2006 and the company's articles, and the decision-making procedures in Pt 15 do not apply.

Chapter 1

Statutory declaration of solvency (section 89)

[Note: a document required by the Act or these Rules must also contain the standard contents set out in Part 1.]

5.1 Statutory declaration of solvency: requirements additional to those in section 89

[Note: the "official rate" referred to in paragraph (1)(b) is defined in section 251 as being the rate referred to in section 189(4).]

5.1(1) [Content of statutory declaration] The statutory declaration of solvency required by section 89 must identify the company and state–

(a) the name and a postal address for each director making the declaration (which may be the director's service address provided for by section 163 of the Companies Act);

(b) either–

(i) that all of the directors, or

(ii) that a majority of the directors,

have made a full inquiry into the company's affairs and that, having done so, they have formed the opinion that the company will be able to pay its debts in full together with interest at the official rate within a specified period (which must not exceed 12 months) from the commencement of the winding up; and

(c) that the declaration is accompanied by a statement of the company's assets and liabilities as at a date which is stated (being the latest practicable date before the making of the declaration as required by section 89(2)(b)).

5.1(2) [Statement of assets and liabilities] The statement of the company's assets and liabilities must contain–

(a) the date of the statement;

(b) a statement that the statement shows the assets of the company at estimated realisable values and liabilities of the company expected to rank as at the date referred to in sub-paragraph (1)(c);

(c) a summary of the assets of the company, setting out the estimated realisable value of–

(i) any assets subject to a fixed charge,

(ii) any assets subject to a floating charge,

(iii) any uncharged assets; and

(iv) the total value of all the assets available to preferential creditors;

(d) the value of each of the following secured liabilities of the company expected to rank for payment–

(i) liabilities secured on specific assets, and

(ii) liabilities secured by floating charges;

(e) a summary of the unsecured liabilities of the company expected to rank for payment;

(f) the estimated costs of the winding up and other expenses;

(g) the estimated amount of interest accruing until payment of debts in full; and

(h) the estimated value of any surplus after paying debts in full together with interest at the official rate.

General Note

See the note to IA 1986 s.89. The Rules no longer require the use of a prescribed form, but instead list the detailed contents which must be stated. However, a notice of statutory declaration of solvency in Form LIQ01 (with declaration attached) must be sent to the registrar of companies to comply with s.89(3).

Chapter 2

The liquidator

[Note: a document required by the Act or these Rules must also contain the standard contents set out in Part 1.]

5.2 Appointment by the company

5.2(1) [Application of rule] This rule applies where the liquidator is appointed by the company.

5.2(2) [Certification as qualified IP] The chair of the meeting, or a director or the secretary of the company in the case of a written resolution of a private company, must certify the appointment when the appointee has provided to the person certifying the appointment a statement to the effect that the appointee is an insolvency practitioner qualified under the Act to be the liquidator and consents to act.

5.2(3) [Authentication and content of certificate] The certificate must be authenticated and dated by the person who certifies the appointment and must contain–

(a) identification details for the company;

(b) identification and contact details for the person appointed as liquidator;

(c) the date the liquidator was appointed; and

(d) a statement that the appointee–

- (i) provided a statement of being qualified to act as an insolvency practitioner in relation to the company,
- (ii) has consented to act, and
- (iii) was appointed liquidator of the company.

5.2(4) [Two or more liquidators appointed] Where two or more liquidators are appointed the certificate must also specify (as required by section 231) whether any act required or authorised under any enactment to be done by the liquidator is to be done by all or any one or more of them.

5.2(5) [Delivery of certificate to liquidator] The person who certifies the appointment must deliver the certificate as soon as reasonably practicable to the liquidator, who must keep it as part of the records of the winding up.

5.2(6) [Notice of appointment to creditors] Not later than 28 days from the liquidator's appointment, the liquidator must deliver notice of the appointment to the creditors of the company.

(See General Note after r.5.16.)

5.3 Meetings in members' voluntary winding up of authorised deposit-takers

5.3(1) [Application of rule] This rule applies to a meeting of the members of an authorised deposit-taker at which it is intended to propose a resolution for its winding up.

5.3(2) [Notice of meeting to FCA and FSMA 2000 s.212(1) scheme manager] Notice of such a meeting of the company must be delivered by the directors to the Financial Conduct Authority and to the scheme manager established under section 212(1) of the Financial Services and Markets Act 2000.

5.3(3) [Notice under r.5.3(2) must be same as to members] The notice to the Financial Conduct Authority and the scheme manager must be the same as delivered to members of the company.

5.3(4) [Scheme manager may be represented] The scheme manager is entitled to be represented at any meeting of which it is required by this rule to be given notice.

(See General Note after r.5.16.)

5.4 Appointment by the court (section 108)

5.4(1) [Application of rule] This rule applies where the liquidator is appointed by the court under section 108.

5.4(2) [Content of order] The order of the court must contain–

(a) the name of the court (and hearing centre if applicable) in which the order is made;

(b) the name and title of the judge making the order;

(c) identification details for the company;

(d) the name and address of the applicant;

(e) the capacity in which the applicant made the application;

(f) identification details for the proposed liquidator;

(g) a statement that the appointee has filed with the court a statement to the effect that the appointee is an insolvency practitioner qualified to act as the liquidator and consents to act;

(h) an order that the proposed liquidator, having filed a statement of being qualified to act as an insolvency practitioner in relation to the company and having consented to act, is appointed liquidator of the company from the date of the order, or such other date as the court orders; and

(i) the date of the order.

5.4(3) [Two or more liquidators appointed] Where two or more liquidators are appointed the order must also specify (as required by section 231) whether any act required or authorised under any enactment to be done by the liquidator is to be done by all or any one or more of them.

5.4(4) [Sealed copy; effect of appointment] The court must deliver a sealed copy of the order to the liquidator, whose appointment takes effect from the date of the order or from such other date as the court orders.

5.4(5) [Notice to creditors] Not later than 28 days from the liquidator's appointment, the liquidator must deliver notice of the appointment to the creditors of the company.

(See General Note after r.5.16.)

5.5 Cost of liquidator's security (section 390(3))

5.5 The cost of the liquidator's security required by section 390(3) for the proper performance of the liquidator's functions is an expense of the winding up.

(See General Note after r.5.16.)

5.6 Liquidator's resignation

5.6(1) [Grounds for resignation] A liquidator may resign only–

(a) on grounds of ill health;

(b) because of the intention to cease to practise as an insolvency practitioner;

(c) because the further discharge of the duties of liquidator is prevented or made impractical by–

  (i) a conflict of interest, or

  (ii) a change of personal circumstances;

(d) where two or more persons are acting as liquidator jointly and it is the opinion of both or all of them that it is no longer expedient that there should continue to be that number of joint liquidators.

5.6(2) [Notice to members] Before resigning, the liquidator must deliver a notice to the members of the company–

(a) stating the liquidator's intention to resign; and

(b) calling a meeting for the members to consider whether a replacement should be appointed;

except where the resignation is under sub-paragraph (1)(d).

5.6(3) [Summary receipts and payments] The notice must be accompanied by a summary of the liquidator's receipts and payments.

5.6(4) [Suggestion of replacement] The notice may suggest the name of a replacement liquidator.

5.6(5) The date of the meeting must be not more than five business days before the date on which the liquidator intends to give notice of resignation to the registrar of companies under section 171(5).

5.6(6) [Date release effective] The resigning liquidator's release is effective 21 days after the date of delivery of the notice of resignation to the registrar of companies under section 171(5), unless the court orders otherwise.

(See General Note after r.5.16.)

5.7 Removal of liquidator by the court

5.7(1) [Application of rule] This rule applies where an application is made to the court for the removal of the liquidator, or for an order directing the liquidator to summon a company meeting for the purpose of removing the liquidator.

5.7(2) [Court may dismiss application] On receipt of an application, the court may, if it is satisfied that no sufficient cause is shown for it, dismiss it without giving notice to any party other than the applicant.

5.7(3) [Court to fix venue] Unless the application is dismissed, the court must fix a venue for it to be heard.

5.7(4) [Notice of venue to liquidator] The applicant must, at least 14 days before any hearing, deliver to the liquidator a notice stating the venue with a copy of the application and of any evidence on which the applicant intends to rely.

5.7(5) [Security for costs of application] A respondent may apply for security for the costs of the application and the court may make such an order if it is satisfied, having regard to all the circumstances of the case, that it is just to make such an order.

5.7(6) [Power of liquidator to file report and/or appear] The liquidator may do either or both of the following at such a hearing–

(a) file a report of any matters which the liquidator thinks ought to be drawn to the court's attention; or

(b) appear and be heard on the application.

5.7(7) [Content of court order] On a successful application the court's order must contain the following–

(a) the name of the court (and hearing centre if applicable) in which the order is made;

(b) the name and title of the judge making the order;

(c) identification details for the company;

(d) the name and address of the applicant;

(e) the capacity in which the applicant made the application;

(f) identification and contact details for the liquidator (or former liquidator);

(g) an order either–

(i) that the liquidator is removed from office, or

(ii) that the liquidator must summon a company meeting on or before a date which is stated in the order for the purpose of considering the liquidator's removal from office; and

(h) the date of the order.

5.7(8) [Further content] The order of the court may include such provision as the court thinks just relating to matters arising in connection with the removal.

5.7(9) [Costs] The costs of the application are not payable as an expense of the winding up unless the court orders otherwise.

5.7(10) [Court to deliver sealed order] Where the court removes the liquidator–

(a) it must deliver the sealed order of removal to the former liquidator; and

(b) the former liquidator must deliver a copy of the order to the registrar of companies as soon as reasonably practicable.

5.7(11) [New liquidator appointed] If the court appoints a new liquidator, rule 5.4 applies.

(See General Note after r.5.16.)

5.8 Removal of liquidator by company meeting

5.8 A liquidator removed by a meeting of the company must as soon as reasonably practicable deliver notice of the removal to the registrar of companies.

(See General Note after r.5.16.)

5.9 Delivery of proposed final account to members (section 94)

5.9(1) [Notice of final account] The liquidator must deliver a notice to the members accompanied by the proposed final account required by section 94(1) and rule 18.14 giving them a minimum of eight weeks' notice of a specified date on which the liquidator intends to deliver the final account as required by section 94(2).

5.9(2) [Information in notice] The notice must inform the members that when the company's affairs are fully wound up–

(a) the liquidator will make up the final account and deliver it to the members; and

(b) when the final account is delivered to the registrar of companies the liquidator will be released under section 171(6).

5.9(3) [When company affairs fully wound up] The affairs of the company are not fully wound up until the latest of–

(a) the period referred to in paragraph (1) having expired without the liquidator receiving any request for information under rule 18.9 or the filing of any application to court under that rule or under rule 18.34 (application to court on the grounds that the liquidator's remuneration or expenses are excessive);

(b) any request for information under rule 18.9 having been finally determined (including any applications to court under that rule); or

(c) any application to the court under rule 18.34 having been finally determined.

5.9(4) [Earlier date for full winding up] However the liquidator may conclude that the company's affairs are fully wound up before the period referred to in paragraph (1) has expired if every member confirms in writing to the liquidator that they do not intend to make any such request or application.

(See General Note after r.5.16.)

5.10 Final account prior to dissolution (section 94)

5.10(1) [Content of final account] The contents of the final account which the liquidator is required to make up under section 94 must comply with the requirements of rule 18.14.

5.10(2) [Notice with account] When the account is delivered to the members under section 94(2) it must be accompanied by a notice which states that–

(a) the company's affairs are fully wound up;

(b) the liquidator having delivered copies of the account to the members must, within 14 days of the date on which the account is made up, deliver a copy of the account to the registrar of companies; and

(c) the liquidator will vacate office and be released under section 171 on delivering the final account to the registrar of companies.

5.10(3) [Notice with copy account to registrar of companies] The copy of the account which the liquidator must deliver to the registrar of companies under section 94(3) must be accompanied by a notice stating that the liquidator has delivered the final account of the winding up to the members in accordance with section 94(2).

(See General Note after r.5.16.)

5.11 Deceased liquidator

5.11(1) [Delivery of notice to directors and registrar of companies] If the liquidator dies a notice of the fact and date of death must be delivered as soon as reasonably practicable to–

(a) one of the company's directors; and

(b) the registrar of companies.

5.11(2) [Who must deliver notice] One of the following must deliver the notice–

(a) a surviving joint liquidator;

(b) a member of the deceased liquidator's firm (if the deceased was a member or employee of a firm);

(c) an officer of the deceased liquidator's company (if the deceased was an officer or employee of a company); or

(d) a personal representative of the deceased liquidator.

5.11(3) [Any other person to deliver notice] If such notice has not been delivered within the 21 days following the liquidator's death then any other person may deliver the notice.

(See General Note after r.5.16.)

5.12 Loss of qualification as insolvency practitioner

5.12(1) [Application of rule] This rule applies where the liquidator vacates office on ceasing to be qualified to act as an insolvency practitioner in relation to the company.

5.12(2) [Notice to registrar of companies and Secretary of State] A notice of the fact must be delivered as soon as reasonably practicable to the registrar of companies and the Secretary of State by one of the following–

(a) the liquidator who has vacated office;

(b) a continuing joint liquidator; or

(c) the recognised professional body which was the source of the vacating liquidator's authorisation to act in relation to the company.

5.12(3) [Authentication of notice] Each notice must be authenticated and dated by the person delivering the notice.

(See General Note after r.5.16.)

5.13 Liquidator's duties on vacating office

5.13 A liquidator who ceases to be in office as a result of removal, resignation or ceasing to be qualified to act as an insolvency practitioner in relation to the company, must as soon as reasonably practicable deliver to the succeeding liquidator–

(a) the assets (after deduction of any expenses properly incurred, and distributions made, by the former liquidator);

(b) the records of the winding up, including correspondence, proofs and other documents relating to the winding up; and

(c) the company's documents and other records.

(See General Note after r.5.16.)

5.14 Application by former liquidator to the Secretary of State for release (section 173(2)(b))

5.14(1) [Application of rule] This rule applies to a liquidator who–

(a) is removed by the court;

(b) vacates office on ceasing to be qualified to act as an insolvency practitioner in relation to the company; or

(c) vacates office in consequence of the court making a winding-up order against the company.

5.14(2) [Content of application] Where the former liquidator applies to the Secretary of State for release the application must contain–

(a) identification details for the former liquidator;

(b) identification details for the company;

(c) the circumstances under which the former liquidator ceased to act as liquidator; and

(d) a statement that the former liquidator is applying to the Secretary of State for release.

5.14(3) [Authentication of application] The application must be authenticated and dated by the former liquidator.

5.14(4) [Grant of release by Secretary of State] When the Secretary of State gives a release, the Secretary of State must deliver–

(a) a certificate of the release to the former liquidator; and

(b) a notice of the release to the registrar of companies.

5.14(5) [Date release effective] Release is effective from the date of the certificate or such other date as the certificate specifies.

(See General Note after r.5.16.)

5.15 Power of court to set aside certain transactions entered into by liquidator

5.15(1) [Transactions with associated persons] If in dealing with the estate the liquidator enters into any transaction with a person who is an associate of the liquidator, the court may, on the application of any interested person, set the transaction aside and order the liquidator to compensate the company for any loss suffered in consequence of it.

5.15(2) [Non-application of rule] This does not apply if either–

(a) the transaction was entered into with the prior consent of the court; or

(b) it is shown to the court's satisfaction that the transaction was for value, and that it was entered into by the liquidator without knowing, or having any reason to suppose, that the person concerned was an associate.

5.15(3) [Effect of rule] Nothing in this rule is to be taken as prejudicing the operation of any rule of law or equity relating to a liquidator's dealings with trust property, or the fiduciary obligations of any person.

(See General Note after r.5.16.)

5.16 Rule against improper solicitation by or on behalf of the liquidator

5.16(1) [Power of court] Where the court is satisfied that any improper solicitation has been used by or on behalf of the liquidator in obtaining proxies or procuring the liquidator's appointment, it may order that no remuneration be allowed as an expense of the winding up to any person by whom, or on whose behalf, the solicitation was exercised.

5.16(2) [Effect of court order] An order of the court under this Rule overrides any resolution of the members, or any other provision of these Rules relating to the liquidator's remuneration.

General Note to rr.5.2–5.16

These rules, which are largely self-explanatory, vary from their counterparts in IR 1986 mainly in that they set out in detail the required contents of the various documents rather than specifying prescribed forms which must be used. As with all other insolvency proceedings, there is now no provision for a final meeting; instead, the liquidator must deliver a draft final account to the company's members (r.5.9), followed in due course by a final account (r.5.10), after which he vacates office and gains his release. Rules relating to the liquidator's remuneration and expenses are now to be found in Pt 18.

On the appointment of a liquidator a notice of appointment must be delivered to the registrar of companies. Form 600 (which continues unaffected by the new Rules) should be used.

R.5.3
This rule ensures that the FCA, the PRA and the scheme manager are notified of meetings summoned in connection with the winding up of an authorised deposit-taker under the Banking Act 2009.

R.5.6(5)
The notice should be in Form LIQ06.

R.5.7(10)(b)
The notice should be in Form LIQ10, with a copy of the court order attached.

R.5.8
The notice should be in Form LIQ11.

R.5.10
The notice should be in Form LIQ13.

R.5.11(1)(b)
The notice should be in Form LIQ09.

R.5.12(2)
The notice should be in Form LIQ08.

R.5.14
The notice should be in Form LIQ12.

Rr.5.15, 5.16
These rules, which are repeated several times in other Parts, supplement remedies which would in any case be available at common law, particularising in the one case and disallowing in the other a defence which might be pleaded under the general law.

Chapter 3

Special manager

[Note: a document required by the Act or these Rules must also contain the standard contents set out in Part 1.]

5.17 Application for and appointment of special manager (section 177)

5.17(1) [Report in support by liquidator] An application by the liquidator under section 177 for the appointment of a special manager must be supported by a report setting out the reasons for the application.

5.17(2) [Value of business/property re special manager] The report must include the applicant's estimate of the value of the business or property in relation to which the special manager is to be appointed.

5.17(3) [Title and content of court order] The court's order appointing a special manager must have the title "Order of Appointment of Special Manager" and must contain–

(a) the name of the court (and hearing centre if applicable) in which the order is made;

(b) the name and title of the judge making the order;

(c) identification details for the proceedings;

(d) the name and address of the applicant;

(e) the name and address of the proposed special manager;

(f) an order that the proposed special manager is appointed as special manager of the company;

(g) details of the special manager's responsibility over the company's business or property;

(h) the powers to be entrusted to the special manager under section 177(3);

(i) the time allowed for the special manager to give the required security for the appointment;

(j) the duration of the special manager's appointment, being one of the following–

 (i) for a fixed period stated in the order;

 (ii) until the occurrence of a specified event; or

 (iii) until the court makes a further order;

(k) the order that the special manager's remuneration will be fixed from time to time by the court; and

(l) the date of the order and the date on which it takes effect if different.

5.17(4) [Order may be renewed] The appointment of the special manager may be renewed by order of the court.

5.17(5) [Special manager's acts] The acts of the special manager are valid notwithstanding any defect in the special manager's appointment or qualifications.

(See General Note after r.5.21.)

5.18 Security

5.18(1) [Appointment subject to security] The appointment of the special manager does not take effect until the person appointed has given (or, if the court allows, undertaken to give) security to the liquidator for the appointment.

5.18(2) [Specific or general security] A person appointed as special manager may give security either specifically for a particular winding up, or generally for any winding up in relation to which that person may be appointed as special manager.

5.18(3) [Amount of security] The amount of the security must be not less than the value of the business or property in relation to which the special manager is appointed, as estimated in the liquidator's report which accompanied the application for appointment.

5.18(4) [Certificate as to adequacy of security] When the special manager has given security to the liquidator, the liquidator must file with the court a certificate as to the adequacy of the security.

5.18(5) [Cost of providing security] The cost of providing the security must be paid in the first instance by the special manager, but the special manager is entitled to be reimbursed as an expense of the winding up.

(See General Note after r.5.21.)

5.19 Failure to give or keep up security

5.19(1) [Liquidator to report failure to court] If the special manager fails to give the required security within the time stated in the order of appointment, or any extension of that time that may be allowed, the liquidator must report the failure to the court, which may discharge the order appointing the special manager.

5.19(2) [Security to be kept up] If the special manager fails to keep up the security, the liquidator must report the failure to the court, which may remove the special manager, and make such order as it thinks just as to costs.

5.19(3) [Directions as to replacement special manager] If the court discharges the order appointing the special manager, or makes an order removing the special manager, the court must give directions as to whether any, and if so what, steps should be taken for the appointment of another special manager.

(See General Note after r.5.21.)

5.20 Accounting

5.20(1) [Duty of special manager] The special manager must produce accounts, containing details of the special manager's receipts and payments, for the approval of the liquidator.

5.20(2) [Period of accounts] The accounts must be for–

(a) each three month period for the duration of the special manager's appointment; and

(b) any shorter period ending with the termination of the special manager's appointment.

5.20(3) [Receipts and payments added to liquidator's] When the accounts have been approved, the special manager's receipts and payments must be added to those of the liquidator.

(See General Note after r.5.21.)

5.21 Termination of appointment

5.21(1) [Application to court by liquidator] If the liquidator thinks that the appointment of the special manager is no longer necessary or beneficial for the company, the liquidator must apply to the court for directions, and the court may order the special manager's appointment to be terminated.

5.21(2) [Members' request for termination] The liquidator must also make such an application if the members pass a resolution requesting that the appointment be terminated.

General Note To rr.5.17–5.21

On the appointment of a special manager, see IA 1986 s.177 and the notes thereto. A special manager need not be qualified to act as an insolvency practitioner. These rules bring forward virtually identical provisions from IR 1986, the one exception being that the rules as to remuneration are now in Pt 18.

Chapter 4

Conversion to creditors' voluntary winding up

5.22 Statement of affairs (section 95(3))

5.22 The rules in Chapter 2 of Part 6 apply to the statement of affairs made out by the liquidator under section 95(1A) where the liquidator is of the opinion that the company will be unable to pay its debts in full (together with interest at the official rate) within the period stated in the directors' declaration under section 89.

General Note

A statement of affairs is not required in a voluntary liquidation, so long as the company is solvent. But if this proves not to be the case and the winding up is to continue as a creditors' voluntary liquidation, the liquidator must take this step.

Part 6

Creditors' Voluntary Winding Up

Introductory note to Part 6
The rules contained in this Part were formerly to be found in Pt 4 of IR 1986. The most noticeable changes include the following:

- The Rules dealing with creditors' voluntary liquidation are treated separately in this Part instead of being combined with compulsory liquidations as in IR 1986. The practice by which differentiation was effected by the labelling "CVL" and "NO CVL" in the former Rules is discontinued.
- Forms are no longer prescribed: although a particular rule may require a document to be "in the prescribed form", it is not to be *on* a prescribed form. Instead the rule sets out a check-list of items which must be included in the contents of the document in question. Forms are still required for documents to be filed with the registrar of companies: these are listed in App.VII.
- In the main, decisions are not to be taken by the creditors at physical meetings, convened in the traditional manner. The options available are: electronic voting, "virtual" meetings (e.g. conference calls) and the "deemed consent" procedure (see rr.15.3–15.7). A physical meeting cannot be instigated on the initiative of the company or the liquidator, but only at the request of the prescribed number or percentage of the creditors or contributories (IA 1986 s.246ZE(7)).
- Many rules formerly to be found in Pt 4 of the 1986 Rules have been moved to other Parts, where provision is made for the rules relating to several insolvency procedures to be dealt with under a single head, for instance: defined terms and form and contents of documents (Pt 1), court procedure and practice (Pt 12), creditors' claims (Pt 14), proxies and corporate representation (Pt 16), reporting and remuneration of office-

holders (Pt 18), disclaimer (Pt 19) and service (Sch.4). "Liquidation committees" has a separate Part all to itself (Pt 17).

CHAPTER 1

APPLICATION OF PART 6

6.1 Application of Part 6

6.1(1) [Application] This Part applies to a creditors' voluntary winding up.

[Non-application of rules where company moves to CVL under IA 1986 Sch.B1 para.83(3)] However where a company moves from administration to creditors' voluntary winding up by the registration of a notice under paragraph 83(3) of Schedule B1 the following rules do not apply–

6.2 to 6.7 (statement of affairs etc.);

6.11 to 6.15 (information to creditors and contributories and appointment of liquidator);

6.17 (report by directors etc.);

6.18 (decisions on nomination);

6.20 (appointment by creditors or by the company);

6.22 (appointment by the court (section 100(3) or 108), other than in respect of appointments under section 108); and

6.23 (advertisement of appointment).

GENERAL NOTE

The disapplication of the rules listed is designed as a short cut to the procedure where a creditors' voluntary winding up follows directly upon an administration.

CHAPTER 2

STATEMENT OF AFFAIRS AND OTHER INFORMATION

[Note: a document required by the Act or these Rules must also contain the standard contents set out in Part 1.]

6.2 Statement of affairs made out by the liquidator under section 95(1A)

[Note: (1) section 95(4A) requires the statement of affairs to be verified by a statement of truth;

(2) the "official rate" referred to in paragraph (2)(c) is defined in section 251 as being the rate referred to in section 189(4)).]

6.2(1) [Application of rule] This rule applies to the statement of affairs made out by the liquidator under section 95(1A) (effect of company's insolvency in members' voluntary winding up).

6.2(2) [Heading and content of statement] The statement of affairs must be headed "Statement of affairs" and must contain–

(a) identification details for the company;

(b) a statement that it is a statement of the affairs of the company on a date which is specified, being the date of the opinion formed by the liquidator under section 95(1);

(c) a statement that as at that date, the liquidator formed the opinion that the company would be unable to pay its debts in full (together with interest at the official rate) within the period stated in the directors' declaration of solvency made under section 89; and

(d) the date it is made.

6.2(3) [Duty of liquidator to deliver to registrar of companies] The statement of affairs must be delivered by the liquidator to the registrar of companies within five business days after the completion of the decision procedure or deemed consent procedure referred to in rule 6.11 in respect of the appointment of the liquidator.

6.2(4) [Liquidator not to deliver certain schedules to registrar of companies] However the liquidator must not deliver to the registrar of companies with the statement of affairs any schedule required by rule 6.4(4)(b).

(See General Note after r.6.9.)

6.3 Statement of affairs made out by the directors under section 99(1)

[Note: section 99(2A) requires the statement of affairs to be verified by a statement of truth.]

6.3(1) [Application of rule] This rule applies to the statement of affairs made out by the directors under section 99(1).

6.3(2) [Heading and content of statement] The statement of affairs must be headed "Statement of affairs" and must contain–

(a) identification details for the company;

(b) a statement that it is a statement of the affairs of the company on a date which is specified, being a date not more than 14 days before the date of the resolution for winding up; and

(c) the date it is made.

6.3(3) [Duty of directors to deliver copy to requesting creditor] If a creditor requests a copy of the statement of affairs at a time when no liquidator is appointed the directors must deliver a copy to the creditor.

6.3(4) [Duty of directors to deliver copy to liquidator] The directors must deliver the statement of affairs to the liquidator as soon as reasonably practicable after the liquidator is appointed.

6.3(5) [Duty of liquidator to deliver to registrar of companies] The liquidator must deliver the statement of affairs to the registrar of companies within five business days after the completion of the decision procedure or deemed consent procedure referred to in rule 6.14 in respect of the appointment of the liquidator.

6.3(6) [Liquidator not to deliver certain schedules to registrar of companies] However the liquidator must not deliver to the registrar of companies with the statement of affairs any schedule required by rule 6.4(4)(b).

(See General Note after r.6.9.)

6.4 Additional requirements as to statements of affairs

6.4(1) [Additional contents] A statement of affairs under section 95(1A) or 99(1) must also contain–

(a) a list of the company's shareholders, with the following details about each shareholder–

(i) name and postal address,

(ii) the type of shares held,

(iii) the nominal amount of the shares held,

(iv) the number of shares held,

(v) the amount per share called up, and

(vi) the total amount called up;

(b) the total amount of shares called up held by all shareholders;

(c) a summary of the assets of the company, setting out the book value and estimated realisable value of–

(i) any assets subject to a fixed charge,

(ii) any assets subject to a floating charge,

(iii) any uncharged assets, and

(iv) the total value of all the assets available for preferential creditors;

(d) a summary of the liabilities of the company, setting out–

(i) the amount of preferential debts,

(ii) an estimate of the deficiency with respect to preferential debts or the surplus available after paying the preferential debts,

(iii) an estimate of the prescribed part, if applicable,

(iv) an estimate of the total assets available to pay debts secured by floating charges,

(v) the amount of debts secured by floating charges,

(vi) an estimate of the deficiency with respect to debts secured by floating charges or the surplus available after paying the debts secured by fixed or floating charges,

(vii) the amount of unsecured debts (excluding preferential debts),

(viii) an estimate of the deficiency with respect to unsecured debts or the surplus available after paying unsecured debts,

(ix) any issued and called-up capital, and

(x) an estimate of the deficiency with respect to, or surplus available to, members of the company;

(e) a list of the company's creditors with the further particulars required by paragraph (2) indicating–

(i) any creditors under hire-purchase, chattel leasing or conditional sale agreements,

(ii) any creditors who are consumers claiming amounts paid in advance of the supply of goods or services, and

(iii) any creditors claiming retention of title over property in the company's possession.

6.4(2) [Further particulars re each creditor] The further particulars required by this paragraph relating to each creditor are as follows–

(i) the name and postal address,

(ii) amount of the debt owed to the creditor, (as required by section 95(4) or 99(2)),

(iii) details of any security held by the creditor,

(iv) the date the security was given, and

(v) the value of any such security.

6.4(3) [Application of r.6.4(4) where r.6.4(2) particulars re employee/prepaid consumer creditors] Paragraph (4) applies where the particulars required by paragraph (2) relate to creditors who are either–

(a) employees or former employees of the company; or

(b) consumers claiming amounts paid in advance for the supply of goods or services.

6.4(4) [Number of r.6.4(3)(a), (b) creditors; separate schedules required] Where this paragraph applies–

(a) the statement of affairs must state separately for each of paragraphs (3)(a) and (b) the number of such creditors and the total of the debts owed to them; and

(b) the particulars required by paragraph (2) must be set out in separate schedules to the statement of affairs for each of paragraphs (3)(a) and (b).

(See General Note after r.6.9.)

6.5 Statement of affairs: statement of concurrence

6.5(1) [Liquidator may require statement of concurrence from director] The liquidator may require a director ("the relevant person") to deliver to the liquidator a statement of concurrence.

6.5(2) [Nature of statement of concurrence] A statement of concurrence is a statement that the relevant person concurs in the statement of affairs submitted by another director.

6.5(3) [Notification to director submitting statement of affairs] The liquidator must inform the director who has been required to submit a statement of affairs that the relevant person has been required to deliver a statement of concurrence.

6.5(4) [Director to submit copy statement of affairs to relevant person] The director who has been required to submit the statement of affairs must deliver a copy to every relevant person who has been required to submit a statement of concurrence.

6.5(5) [Statement of concurrence may be qualified] A statement of concurrence–

(a) must identify the company; and

(b) may be qualified in relation to matters dealt with in the statement of affairs, where the maker of the statement of concurrence–

  (i) is not in agreement with the statement of affairs,

  (ii) considers the statement of affairs to be erroneous or misleading, or

  (iii) is without the direct knowledge necessary for concurring with it.

6.5(6) [Duty of relevant person to deliver verified statement to liquidator] The relevant person must deliver the required statement of concurrence, verified by a statement of truth, to the liquidator together with a copy before the end of the period of five business days (or such other period as the liquidator may agree) beginning with the day on which the relevant person receives the statement of affairs.

6.5(7) [Liquidator to deliver to registrar of companies] The liquidator must deliver the verified statement of concurrence to the registrar of companies.

(See General Note after r.6.9.)

6.6 Order limiting disclosure of statement of affairs etc.

6.6(1) [Power of liquidator to apply to court] Where the liquidator thinks that disclosure of the whole or part of the statement of affairs or of any statement of concurrence would be likely to prejudice the conduct of the winding up or might reasonably be expected to lead to violence against any person, the liquidator may apply to the court for an order that the statement of affairs, statement of concurrence or any specified part of them must not be delivered to the registrar of companies.

6.6(2) [Powers of court] The court may order that the whole or a specified part of the statement of affairs or a statement of concurrence must not be delivered to the registrar of companies.

6.6(3) [Liquidator to deliver copy order etc. to registrar of companies] The liquidator must as soon as reasonably practicable deliver to the registrar of companies a copy of the order, the statement of affairs and any statement of concurrence to the extent allowed by the order.

(See General Note after r.6.9.)

6.7 Expenses of statement of affairs and decisions sought from creditors

6.7(1) [Payment out of assets as liquidation expense] Any reasonable and necessary expenses of preparing the statement of affairs under section 99 may be paid out of the company's assets, either before or after the commencement of the winding up, as an expense of the winding up.

6.7(2) [Expenses of decision/deemed consent procedure on nomination of liquidator] Any reasonable and necessary expenses of the decision procedure or deemed consent procedure to seek a decision from the creditors on the nomination of a liquidator under rule 6.14 may be paid out of the company's assets, either before or after the commencement of the winding up, as an expense of the winding up.

6.7(3) [Payments before commencement of winding up] Where payment under paragraph (1) or (2) is made before the commencement of the winding up, the directors must deliver to the creditors with the statement of affairs a statement of the amount of the payment and the identity of the person to whom it was made.

6.7(4) [Notice of payment to liquidation committee] The liquidator appointed under section 100 may make such a payment, but if there is a liquidation committee, the liquidator must deliver to the committee at least five business days' notice of the intention to make it.

6.7(5) [Approval of liquidation committee, creditors or court] However such a payment may not be made to the liquidator, or to any associate of the liquidator, otherwise than with the approval of the liquidation committee, the creditors, or the court.

6.7(6) [CVL superseded by winding up by court] This is without prejudice to the court's powers under rule 7.109 (voluntary winding up superseded by winding up by the court).

(See General Note after r.6.9.)

6.8 Delivery of accounts to liquidator (section 235)

6.8(1) [Duty of officers, etc. to deliver] A person who is specified in section 235(3) must deliver to the liquidator accounts of the company of such nature, as at such date, and for such period, as the liquidator requires.

6.8(2) [Period for accounts] The period for which the liquidator may require accounts may begin from a date up to three years before the date of the resolution for winding up, or from an earlier date to which audited accounts of the company were last prepared.

6.8(3) [Accounts to be verified] The accounts must, if the liquidator so requires, be verified by a statement of truth.

6.8(4) [Period for delivery of verified accounts] The accounts (verified by a statement of truth if so required) must be delivered to the liquidator within 21 days from the liquidator's request, or such longer period as the liquidator may allow.

(See General Note after r.6.9.)

6.9 Expenses of assistance in preparing accounts

6.9(1) [Person assisting with deliver of accounts] Where the liquidator requires a person to deliver accounts under rule 6.8 the liquidator may, with the approval of the liquidation committee (if there is one) and as an expense of the winding up, employ a person or firm to assist that person in the preparation of the accounts.

6.9(2) [Allowance toward expenses] The person who is required to deliver accounts may request an allowance of all or part of the expenses to be incurred in employing a person or firm to assist in preparing the accounts.

6.9(3) [Estimate of expenses] A request for an allowance must be accompanied by an estimate of the expenses involved.

6.9(4) [Employment of a named person/ firm approved by liquidator] The liquidator must only authorise the employment of a named person or a named firm approved by the liquidator.

6.9(5) [Authorisation with approval of liquidation committee] The liquidator may, with the approval of the liquidation committee (if there is one), authorise such an allowance, payable as an expense of the winding up.

General Note to rr.6.2–6.9

A statement of affairs is required in every form of winding up where the company is insolvent, but as the detailed content of the statement varies as between one form and another regard must be had to the relevant Part of the Rules in each case. There is no form prescribed for the statement, which must be delivered to the registrar of companies as an attachment to a notice in Companies House Form LIQ02. The rules governing the statement of concurrence, limited disclosure and expenses have close counterparts in other Parts of the Rules.

In an application for directions under IA 1986 s.112 the court concluded in *Re Central A1 Ltd; Rubin v Cohen* [2017] EWHC 220 (Ch); [2017] B.C.C. 69 that it had jurisdiction to determine a dispute as to what were "reasonable and necessary" expenses under what is now r.6.7 regarding fixed fees charged by a firm of accountants for work undertaken in relation to statements of affairs of a vast number of companies.

R.6.6(3)
The notice should be in Form LIQ05, with the statement of affairs and statement of concurrence attached.

Chapter 3

Nomination and appointment of liquidators and information to creditors

[Note: a document required by the Act or these Rules must also contain the standard contents set out in Part 1.]

6.10 Application of the rules in this Chapter

6.10(1) [Application] The rules in this Chapter apply as follows.

6.10(2) [Rules 6.11–6.13: conversion from MVL to CVL] Rules 6.11 to 6.13 only apply to a conversion from a members' voluntary winding up to a creditors' voluntary winding up.

6.10(3) [Rule 6.16: CVL follows administration] Rule 6.16 only applies where the administrator becomes the liquidator in a voluntary winding up which follows an administration.

6.10(4) [Rules 6.14, 6.15, 6.17: CVL not converted] Rules 6.14, 6.15 and 6.17 only apply to a creditors' voluntary winding up which has not been commenced by a conversion from a members' voluntary winding up or an administration.

6.10(5) [Rules 6.18, 6.19: all CVLs] Rules 6.18 and 6.19 apply to all creditors' voluntary windings up.

General Note

Only rr.6.18 and 6.19 are of general application. Otherwise, the relevant rule (depending upon the event which preceded the commencement of the winding up) is specified in the particular title, and the appropriate procedure is described.

6.11 Nomination of liquidator and information to creditors on conversion from members' voluntary winding up (section 96)

6.11(1) [Application of rule] This rule applies in respect of the conversion of a members' voluntary winding up to a creditors' voluntary winding up under section 96.

6.11(2) [Liquidator to seek nomination from creditors] The liquidator must seek a nomination from the creditors for a liquidator in the creditors' voluntary winding up by–

(a) a decision procedure; or

(b) the deemed consent procedure.

6.11(3) [Liquidator to deliver to creditors copy statement, notice re deemed consent/decision procedure] The liquidator must deliver to the creditors a copy of the statement of affairs required by section 95(1A) and Chapter 2 of this Part together with a notice which complies with rules 15.7 or 15.8 so far as are relevant.

6.11(4) [Further content of notice] The notice must also contain–

(a) identification and contact details for the existing liquidator; and

(b) a statement that if no person is nominated by the creditors then the existing liquidator will be the liquidator in the creditors' voluntary winding up.

6.11(5) [Decision date in notice] The decision date in the notice must be not later than 28 days from the date under section 95(1) that the liquidator formed the opinion that the company will be unable to pay its debts in full.

6.11(6) [Notice of decision date] Subject to paragraph (9), the creditors must be given at least 14 days' notice of the decision date.

6.11(7) [Application of r.6.11(8)] Paragraph (8) applies where–

(a) the liquidator has sought a decision from creditors on the nomination of a liquidator by the deemed consent procedure; but

(b) the level of objections to the proposed nomination have meant, under section 246ZF, that no nomination is deemed to have been made.

6.11(8) [Liquidator to seek nomination from creditors by decision procedure] Where this paragraph applies, the liquidator must seek a nomination from creditors by way of a decision procedure in accordance with this rule, the decision date to be as soon as reasonably practicable, but no more than 28 days from the date that the level of objections had the effect that no nomination was deemed to have been made.

6.11(9) [Notice of r.6.11(8) decision date] Where paragraph (8) applies, the creditors must be given at least seven days' notice of the decision date.

6.11(10) [Notice and holding of physical meetings] Where the liquidator is required by rule 15.6 to summon a physical meeting as a result of requests from creditors received in response to a notice delivered under this rule, the physical meeting must be summoned to take place–

(a) within 28 days of the date on which the threshold for requiring a physical meeting was met; and

(b) with at least 14 days' notice.

(See General Note after r.6.17.)

6.12 Creditors' decision on appointment other than at a meeting (conversion from members' voluntary winding up)

6.12(1) [Application of rule] This rule applies where the creditors' decision on the nomination of a liquidator in a conversion of a members' into a creditors' voluntary winding up is intended to be sought otherwise than through a meeting or through the deemed consent procedure, including where the conditions in rule 6.11(7) are met and the liquidator, under rule 6.11(8), goes on to seek a nomination from creditors by way of a decision procedure other than a meeting.

6.12(2) [Notice to creditors to propose nomination of liquidator] Instead of delivering a notice of the decision procedure or deemed consent procedure under rule 6.11, the liquidator must deliver a notice to creditors inviting them to make proposals for the nomination of a liquidator.

6.12(3) [Content of notice] Such a notice must–

(a) identify any liquidator for whom a proposal which is in compliance with paragraph 4 has already been received;

(b) explain that the liquidator is not obliged to seek the creditors' views on any proposal that does not meet the requirements of paragraphs (4) and (5); and

(c) be accompanied by the statement of affairs unless that has previously been delivered to the creditor.

6.12(4) [Details of proposed liquidator] Any proposal must state the name and contact details of the proposed liquidator, and contain a statement that the proposed liquidator is qualified to act as an insolvency practitioner in relation to the company and has consented to act as liquidator of the company.

6.12(5) [Time limit for proposal to liquidator] Any proposal must be received by the liquidator within five business days of the date of the notice under paragraph (2).

6.12(6) [Notice to creditors of decision procedure under r.6.11] Within two business days of the end of the period referred to in paragraph (5), the liquidator must send a notice to creditors of a decision procedure under rule 6.11.

(See General Note after r.6.17.)

6.13 Information to creditors and contributories (conversion of members' voluntary winding up into creditors' voluntary winding up)

6.13(1) [Liquidator's notice to creditors] The liquidator must deliver to the creditors and contributories within 28 days of the conversion of a members' voluntary winding up into a creditors' voluntary winding up under section 96 a notice which must contain–

(a) the date the winding up became a creditors' voluntary winding up;

(b) a report of the decision procedure or deemed consent procedure which took place under rule 6.11; and

(c) the information required by paragraph (3).

6.13(2) [Notice with copy statement of affairs or summary] The notice must be accompanied by a copy of the statement of affairs or a summary except where the notice is being delivered to a creditor to whom a copy of the statement of affairs has previously been delivered under section 95(1A).

6.13(3) [Estimate as to prescribed part] The required information is an estimate to the best of the liquidator's knowledge and belief of–

(a) the value of the prescribed part (whether or not the liquidator might be required under section 176A to make the prescribed part available for the satisfaction of unsecured debts); and

(b) the value of the company's net property (as defined by section 176A(6)).

6.13(4) [Exclusion of seriously prejudicial information] The liquidator may exclude from an estimate under paragraph (3) information the disclosure of which could seriously prejudice the commercial interests of the company.

6.13(5) [Exclusion affecting estimate] If the exclusion of such information affects the calculation of an estimate, the report must say so.

6.13(6) [Report to state if application under IA 1986 s.176(5)] If the liquidator proposes to make an application to court under section 176A(5) the report must say so and give the reason for the application.

(See General Note after r.6.17.)

6.14 Information to creditors and appointment of liquidator

6.14(1) [Application of rule] This rule applies in respect of the appointment of a liquidator under section 100.

6.14(2) [Notice by deemed consent procedure/virtual meeting] The directors of the company must deliver to the creditors a notice seeking their decision on the nomination of a liquidator by–

(a) the deemed consent procedure; or

(b) a virtual meeting.

6.14(3) [Decision date] The decision date for the decision of the creditors on the nomination of a liquidator must be not earlier than three business days after the notice under paragraph (2) is delivered but not later than 14 days after the resolution is passed to wind up the company.

6.14(4) [Physical meeting] Where the directors have sought a decision from the creditors through the deemed consent procedure under paragraph (2)(a) but, pursuant to section 246ZF(5)(a) (deemed consent procedure), more than the specified number of creditors object so that the decision cannot be treated as having been made, the directors must then seek a decision from the creditors on the nomination of a liquidator by holding a physical meeting under rule 15.6 (physical meetings) as if a physical meeting had been required under section 246ZE(4) (decisions by creditors and contributories: general).

6.14(5) [Holding of physical meeting] Where paragraph (4) applies, the meeting must not be held earlier than three business days after the notice under rule 15.6(3) is delivered or later than 14 days after the level of objections reach that described in paragraph (4).

6.14(6) [Physical meeting request under r.15.6, exceptions] A request for a physical meeting under section 246ZE must be made in accordance with rule 15.6 except that–

(a) such a request may be made at any time between the delivery of the notice under paragraph (2) and the decision date under paragraph (3); and

(b) the decision date where this paragraph applies must be not earlier than three business days after the notice under rule 15.6(3) is delivered and not later than 14 days after the level of requests reach that described in section 246ZE.

6.14(7) [Directors to deliver copy statement of affairs to creditors] The directors must deliver to the creditors a copy of the statement of affairs required under section 99 of the Act not later than on the business day before the decision date.

6.14(8) [Content of notice under r.6.14(2)] A notice delivered under paragraph (2), in addition to the information required by rules 15.7 (deemed consent) and 15.8 (notices to creditors of decision procedure), must contain–

(a) the date the resolution to wind up is to be considered or was passed;

(b) identification and contact details of any liquidator nominated by the company;

(c) a statement of either–

(i) the name and address of a person qualified to act as an insolvency practitioner in relation to the company who during the period before the decision date, will furnish creditors free of charge with such information concerning the company's affairs as they may reasonably require, or

(ii) a place in the relevant locality where, on the two business days falling next before the decision date, a list of the names and addresses of the company's creditors will be available for inspection free of charge; and

(d) where the notice is sent to creditors in advance of the copy of the statement of affairs, a statement that the directors, before the decision date and before the end of the period of seven days beginning with the day after the day on which the company passed a resolution for winding up, are required by section 99 of the Insolvency Act 1986–

(i) to make out a statement in the prescribed form as to the affairs of the company, and

(ii) send the statement to the company's creditors.

6.14(9) [Company's principal place of business in different localities at different times] Where the company's principal place of business in England or Wales was situated in different localities at different times during the relevant period, the duty imposed by sub-paragraph (8)(c)(ii) above applies separately in relation to each of those localities.

6.14(10) [Where no place of business in England or Wales in relevant period] Where the company had no place of business in England or Wales during the relevant period, the reference in paragraph (9) to the company's principal place of business in England or Wales are replaced by references to its registered office.

6.14(11) ["The relevant period" in r.6.14(9)] In paragraph (9), "the relevant period" means the period of six months immediately preceding the day on which the notices referred to in paragraph (2) were delivered.

6.14(12) [Meeting held rule and liquidator already nominated by company] Where a virtual or physical meeting is held under this rule and a liquidator has already been nominated by the company, the liquidator or an appointed person must attend any meeting held under this rule and report on any exercise of the liquidator's powers under section 112, 165 or 166 of the Act.

6.14(13) [Director in default, penalty] A director who is in default in seeking a decision on the nomination of a liquidator in accordance with this rule is guilty of an offence and is liable to a fine.

(See General Note after r.6.17.)

6.15 Information to creditors and contributories

6.15(1) [Duty of liquidator to deliver notice to creditors] The liquidator must deliver to the creditors and contributories within 28 days of the appointment of the liquidator under section 100 a notice which must–

(a) be accompanied by a statement of affairs or a summary where the notice is delivered to any contributory or creditor to whom the notice under rule 6.14 was not delivered;

(b) be accompanied by a report on the decision procedure or deemed consent procedure under rule 6.14; and

(c) be accompanied by the information required by paragraph (2).

6.15(2) [Estimate as to prescribed part] The required information is an estimate to the best of the liquidator's knowledge and belief of–

(a) the value of the prescribed part (whether or not the liquidator might be required under section 176A to make the prescribed part available for the satisfaction of unsecured debts); and

(b) the value of the company's net property (as defined by section 176A(6)).

6.15(3) [Exclusion from estimate of seriously prejudicial information] The liquidator may exclude from an estimate under paragraph (2) information the disclosure of which could seriously prejudice the commercial interests of the company.

6.15(4) [Exclusion affecting calculation of estimate] If the exclusion of such information affects the calculation of an estimate, the report must say so.

6.15(5) [Report to state if application under IA 1986 s.176(5)] If the liquidator proposes to make an application to court under section 176A(5) the report must say so and give the reason for the application.

(See General Note after r.6.17.)

6.16 Further information where administrator becomes liquidator (paragraph 83(3) of Schedule B1)

6.16(1) [Creditors not formerly known to liquidator as administrator] This rule applies where an administrator becomes liquidator on the registration of a notice under paragraph 83(3) of Schedule B1, and becomes aware of creditors not formerly known to that person as administrator.

6.16(2) [Copy statement of administrator's proposals to those creditors] The liquidator must deliver to those creditors a copy of any statement delivered by the administrator to creditors in accordance with paragraph 49(4) of Schedule B1 and rule 3.35.

(See General Note after r.6.17.)

6.17 Report by director etc.

6.17(1) [State of company's affairs] Where the statement of affairs sent to creditors under section 99(1) does not, or will not, state the company's affairs at the decision date for the creditors' nomination of a liquidator, the directors of the company must cause a report (written or oral) to be made to the creditors in accordance with this rule on any material transactions relating to the company occurring between the date of the making of the statement and the decision date.

6.17(2) [Decision at meeting] In the case of a decision being taken through a meeting, the report must be made at the meeting by the director chairing the meeting or by another person with knowledge of the relevant matters.

6.17(3) [Deemed consent procedure used] Where the deemed consent procedure is used, the report must be delivered to creditors as soon as reasonably practicable after the material transaction takes place in the same manner as the deemed consent procedure.

6.17(4) [Extension of decision date] Where the decision date is within the period of three business days from the delivery of a report under paragraph (3), this rule extends the decision date until the end of that period notwithstanding the requirement in rule 6.14(3) relating to the timing of the decision date.

6.17(5) [Directors to notify creditors of extension] On delivery of a report under paragraph (3), the directors must notify the creditors of the effects of paragraph (4).

6.17(6) [Report in r.15.40 record of decision] A report under this rule must be recorded in the record of the decision under rule 15.40.

GENERAL NOTE TO RR.6.11–6.17

These rules give details of the procedure to be followed in the nomination and appointment of the liquidator, and the information which must be given to the creditors in the different cases. There is a general trend away from the use of the traditional physical meeting.

The minimum decision date in r.6.14(3) for the decision of the creditors on the appointment of a liquidator is three business days after notice of nomination but for certain Government departments such as HMRC, as the country's largest creditor, this may not be enough time for their staff to engage in the decision process. Thus *Dear IP* Issue 79 (December 2017), Ch.8, art.26 requests that pre-appointment notifications by IPs for the deemed consent or virtual meeting procedures for all CVLs be sent to a designated HMRC email address, "notifications.hmrccvl@hmrc.gsi.gov.uk", the email subject line to contain the company name, registered number and the decision date. Note this is only to be used for pre-appointment notifications under the deemed consent or virtual meeting procedures.

R.6.14(13)
On penalties, see s.430 and Sch.3 to these Rules.

R.6.14(13)
On penalties, see s.430 and Sch.3 to these Rules.

R.6.15
On the scope of this provision see *Hunt v Katz* [2017] EWHC 2756 (Ch).

Rule 6.15(1)(b) amended by the Insolvency (England and Wales) and Insolvency (Scotland) (Miscellaneous and Consequential Amendments) Rules 2017 (SI 2017/1115) rr.1(1), (2), 2, 6 as from 8 December 2017.

R.6.16
Existing creditors should already be in possession of the information.

6.18 Decisions on nomination

6.18(1) [Multiple nominees, etc.] In the case of a decision on the nomination of a liquidator–

(a) if on any vote there are two nominees, the person who obtains the most support is appointed;

(b) if there are three or more nominees, and one of them has a clear majority over both or all the others together, that one is appointed; and

(c) in any other case, the convener or chair must continue to take votes (disregarding at each vote any nominee who has withdrawn and, if no nominee has withdrawn, the nominee who obtained the least support last time) until a clear majority is obtained for any one nominee.

6.18(2) [Joint nomination] In the case of a decision being made at a meeting, the chair may at any time put to the meeting a resolution for the joint nomination of any two or more nominees.

GENERAL NOTE

It is surely not intended that a joint appointment may not be made by a decision procedure other than a resolution at a physical meeting.

6.19 Invitation to creditors to form a liquidation committee

6.19(1) [Convener to deliver invitation notice] Where any decision is sought from the company's creditors–

(a) in a creditors' voluntary winding up; or

(b) where a members' voluntary winding up is converting in a creditors' voluntary winding up;

the convener of the decision must at the same time deliver to the creditors a notice inviting them to decide whether a liquidation committee should be established if sufficient creditors are willing to be members of the committee.

6.19(2) [Invitation for nominations for membership of committee] The notice must also invite nominations for membership of the committee, such nominations to be received by a date specified in the notice.

6.19(3) [Content of notice] The notice must state that nominations–

(a) must be delivered to the convener by the specified date; and

(b) can only be accepted if the convener is satisfied as to the creditor's eligibility under rule 17.4.

GENERAL NOTE

The rules relating to the creditors' committee are to be found in Pt 17.

CHAPTER 4

THE LIQUIDATOR

[Note: a document required by the Act or these Rules must also contain the standard contents set out in Part 1.]

6.20 Appointment by creditors or by the company

6.20(1) [Application of rule] This rule applies where a person is appointed as liquidator by creditors or the company.

6.20(2) [When appointment takes effect] The liquidator's appointment takes effect from the date of the passing of the resolution of the company or, where the creditors decide to appoint a person who is not the person appointed by the company, from the relevant decision date.

6.20(3) [Certification of appointment] Their appointment must be certified by–

(a) the convener or chair of the decision procedure or deemed consent procedure; or

(b) in respect of an appointment by the company the chair of the company meeting or a director or the secretary of the company (in the case of a written resolution).

6.20(4) [Condition for certification] The person who certifies the appointment must not do so unless and until the proposed liquidator ("the appointee") has provided that person with a statement of being an insolvency practitioner qualified under the Act to be the liquidator and of consenting to act.

6.20(5) [Authentication of certificate] The certificate must be authenticated and dated by the person who certifies the appointment and must contain–

(a) identification details for the company;

(b) identification and contact details for the person appointed as liquidator;

(c) the date of the meeting of the company or conclusion of the decision procedure or deemed consent procedure when the liquidator was appointed;

(d) a statement that the appointee–

  (i) has provided a statement of being qualified to act as an insolvency practitioner in relation to the company,

  (ii) has consented to act, and

  (iii) was appointed liquidator of the company.

6.20(6) [Acts by two or more appointees] Where two or more liquidators are appointed the certificate must also specify (as required by section 231) whether any act required or authorised under any enactment to be done by the liquidator is to be done by all or any one or more of them.

6.20(7) [Delivery of certificate to liquidator] The person who certifies the appointment must deliver the certificate as soon as reasonably practicable to the liquidator, who must keep it as part of the records of the winding up.

(See General Note after r.6.24.)

6.21 Power to fill vacancy in office of liquidator

6.21 Where a vacancy in the office of liquidator occurs in the manner mentioned in section 104 a decision procedure to fill the vacancy may be initiated by any creditor or, if there was more than one liquidator, by the continuing liquidator or liquidators.

(See General Note after r.6.24.)

6.22 Appointment by the court (section 100(3) or 108)

6.22(1) [Application of rule] This rule applies where the liquidator is appointed by the court under section 100(3) or 108.

6.22(2) [Court order] The court's order must not be made unless and until the proposed liquidator has filed with the court a statement of being qualified under the Act to act as an insolvency practitioner in relation to the company and of consenting to act.

6.22(3) [Content of order] The order of the court must contain–

(a) the name of the court (and hearing centre if applicable) in which the order is made;

(b) the name and title of the judge making the order;

(c) the date on which it is made;

(d) identification details for the company;

(e) the name and postal address of the applicant;

(f) the capacity in which the applicant made the application;

(g) identification details for the proposed liquidator; and

(h) an order that the proposed liquidator, having filed a statement of being qualified to act as an insolvency practitioner in relation to the company and having consented to act, is appointed liquidator of the company from the date of the order, or such other date as the court orders.

6.22(4) [Acts by two or more appointees] Where two or more liquidators are appointed the order must also specify (as required by section 231) whether any act required or authorised under any enactment to be done by the liquidator is to be done by all or any one or more of them.

6.22(5) [Sealed copy to liquidator] The court must deliver a sealed copy of the order to the liquidator.

6.22(6) [Notice of appointment to creditors; advertisement] Within 28 days from appointment, the liquidator must–

(a) deliver a notice of the appointment to creditors of the company; or

(b) advertise the appointment in accordance with any directions given by the court.

(See General Note after r.6.24.)

6.23 Advertisement of appointment

6.23(1) [Notice may be advertised] A liquidator appointed in a voluntary winding up in addition to delivering a notice of the appointment in accordance with section 109(1) may advertise the notice in such other manner as the liquidator thinks fit.

6.23(2) [Content of notice] The notice must state–

(a) that a liquidator has been appointed; and

(b) the date of the appointment.

6.23(3) [Reimbursement of expense] The liquidator must initially bear the expense of giving notice under this rule but is entitled to be reimbursed for the expenditure as an expense of the winding up.

(See General Note after r.6.24.)

6.24 Cost of liquidator's security (section 390(3))

6.24 The cost of the liquidator's security required by section 390(3) for the proper performance of the liquidator's functions is an expense of the winding up.

General Note to rr.6.20–6.24

These rules give directions concerning the various ways of appointing a liquidator, and specify the date when the appointment takes effect and the notices that must be given. The phrase "from the date" indicates (at least prima facie) that the whole of the day in question is included. On appointment, a notice of appointment of liquidator must be delivered to the registrar, using Form 600 (not affected by the new Rules).

R.6.22(6)
Some discussion of r.6.22(6) is to be found in *Hunt v Katz* [2017] EWHC 2756 (Ch).

6.25 Liquidator's resignation and replacement

6.25(1) [Grounds for resignation] A liquidator may resign only–

(a) on grounds of ill health;

(b) because of the intention to cease to practise as an insolvency practitioner;

(c) because the further discharge of the duties of liquidator is prevented or made impractical by–

(i) a conflict of interest, or

(ii) or a change of personal circumstances; or

(d) where two or more persons are acting as liquidator jointly and it is the opinion of both or all of them that it is no longer expedient that there should continue to be that number of joint liquidators.

6.25(2) [Invitation to creditors to consider replacement] Before resigning the liquidator must invite the creditors by a decision procedure, or by deemed consent, to consider whether a replacement should be appointed except where the resignation is under paragraph (1)(d).

6.25(3) [Notice of decision procedure/deemed consent] The notice of the decision procedure or of deemed consent must–

(a) state the liquidator's intention to resign;

(b) state that under rule 6.25(7) of these Rules the liquidator will be released 21 days after the date of delivery of the notice of resignation to the registrar of companies under section 171(5), unless the court orders otherwise; and

(c) comply with rules 15.7 and 15.8 so far as are relevant.

6.25(4) [Name of replacement] The notice may suggest the name of a replacement liquidator.

6.25(5) [Summary of the liquidator's receipts and payments] The notice must be accompanied by a summary of the liquidator's receipts and payments.

6.25(6) [Decision date] The decision date must be not more than five business days before the date on which the liquidator intends to give notice of resignation to the registrar of companies under section 171(5).

6.25(7) [Date of resigning liquidator's release] The resigning liquidator's release is effective 21 days after the date of delivery of the notice of resignation to the registrar of companies under section 171(5), unless the court orders otherwise.

(See General Note after r.6.33.)

6.26 Removal of liquidator by creditors

6.26(1) [Certificate of removal] Where the creditors decide that the liquidator be removed, the convener of the decision procedure or the chair of the meeting (as the case may be) must as soon as reasonably practicable deliver the certificate of the liquidator's removal to the removed liquidator.

6.26(2) [Notice of removal to registrar of companies] The removed liquidator must deliver a notice of the removal to the registrar of companies as soon as reasonably practicable.

(See General Note after r.6.33.)

6.27 Removal of liquidator by the court

6.27(1) [Application of rule] This rule applies where an application is made to the court for the removal of the liquidator, or for an order directing the liquidator to initiate a decision procedure of creditors for the purpose of removing the liquidator.

6.27(2) [Power of court to dismiss application] On receipt of an application, the court may, if it is satisfied that no sufficient cause is shown for it, dismiss it without giving notice to any party other than the applicant.

6.27(3) [Court to fix venue for hearing] Unless the application is dismissed, the court must fix a venue for it to be heard.

6.27(4) [Notice of venue with copy application to liquidator] The applicant must, at least 14 days before any hearing, deliver to the liquidator a notice stating the venue with a copy of the application and of any evidence on which the applicant intends to rely.

6.27(5) [Security for costs] A respondent may apply for security for the costs of the application and the court may make such an order if it is satisfied, having regard to all the circumstances of the case, that it is just to make such an order.

6.27(6) [Liquidator's report to court; appearance] The liquidator may do either or both of the following–

(a) file a report of any matters which the liquidator thinks ought to be drawn to the court's attention; or

(b) appear and be heard on the application.

6.27(7) [Costs of application] The costs of the application are not payable as an expense of the winding up unless the court orders otherwise.

6.27(8) [Content of court order] On a successful application the court's order must contain the following–

(a) the name of the court (and hearing centre if applicable) in which the order is made;

(b) the name and title of the judge making the order;

(c) identification details for the company;

(d) the name and postal address of the applicant;

(e) the capacity in which the applicant made the application;

(f) identification and contact details for the liquidator;

(g) an order either–

(i) that the liquidator is removed from office from the date of the order (unless the order specifies otherwise), or

(ii) that the liquidator must initiate a decision procedure of the company's creditors (specifying which procedure is to be used) on or before a date stated in the order for the purpose of considering the liquidator's removal from office; and

(h) the date of the order.

6.27(9) [Sealed orders] Where the court removes the liquidator–

(a) it must deliver the sealed order of removal to the former liquidator; and

(b) the former liquidator must deliver a copy of the order to the registrar of companies as soon as reasonably practicable.

6.27(10) [Appointment of replacement] If the court appoints a new liquidator rule 6.22 applies.

(See General Note after r.6.33.)

6.28 Final account prior to dissolution (section 106)

6.28(1) [Account to comply with r.18.14] The final account which the liquidator is required to make up under section 106(1) and deliver to members and creditors must comply with the requirements of rule 18.14.

6.28(2) [Delivery to creditors with notice] When the account is delivered to the creditors it must be accompanied by a notice which states–

(a) that the company's affairs are fully wound up;

(b) that the creditors have the right to request information from the liquidator under rule 18.9;

(c) that the creditors have the right to challenge the liquidator's remuneration and expenses under rule 18.34;

(d) that a creditor may object to the release of the liquidator by giving notice in writing to the liquidator before the end of the prescribed period;

(e) that the prescribed period is the period ending at the later of–

(i) eight weeks after delivery of the notice, or

(ii) if any request for information under rule 18.9 or any application to court under that rule or rule 18.34 is made, when that request or application is finally determined;

(f) that the liquidator will vacate office under section 171 on delivering to the registrar of companies the final account and notice saying whether any creditor has objected to release; and

(g) that the liquidator will be released under section 173 at the same time as vacating office unless any of the company's creditors objected to the liquidator's release.

6.28(3) [Copy account to registrar with any objections to release] The copy of the account which the liquidator delivers to the registrar of companies under section 106(3) must be accompanied by a notice containing the statement required by section 106(3)(a) of whether any creditors have objected to the liquidator's release.

6.28(4) [Objections to release: application of r.6.33] Where a creditor has objected to the liquidator's release rule 6.33 applies to an application by the liquidator to the Secretary of State for release.

6.28(5) [No obligation for final progress report] The liquidator is not obliged to prepare or deliver any progress report which may become due under these Rules in the period between the date to which the final account is made up and the date when the account is delivered to the registrar of companies under section 106(3)(a).

(See General Note after r.6.33.)

6.29 Deceased liquidator

6.29(1) [Notice to liquidation committee and registrar of companies] If the liquidator dies a notice of the fact and date of death must be delivered as soon as reasonably practicable–

(a) where there is a liquidation committee, to the members of that committee; and

(b) to the registrar of companies.

6.29(2) [Who to deliver notice] The notice must be delivered by one of the following–

(a) a surviving joint liquidator;

(b) a member of the deceased liquidator's firm (if the deceased was a member or employee of a firm);

(c) an officer of the deceased liquidator's company (if the deceased was an officer or employee of a company); or

(d) a personal representative of the deceased liquidator.

6.29(3) [Delivery by any other person] If such a notice has not been delivered within the 21 days following the liquidator's death then any other person may deliver the notice.

(See General Note after r.6.33.)

6.30 Loss of qualification as insolvency practitioner

6.30(1) [Application of rule] This rule applies where the liquidator vacates office on ceasing to be qualified to act as an insolvency practitioner in relation to the company.

6.30(2) [Notice to registrar of companies and Secretary of State] A notice of the fact must be delivered as soon as reasonably practicable to the registrar of companies and the Secretary of State by one of the following–

(a) the liquidator who has vacated office;

(b) a continuing joint liquidator;

(c) the recognised professional body which was the source of the vacating liquidator's authorisation to act in relation to the company.

6.30(3) [Authentication of notice] Each notice must be authenticated and dated by the person delivering the notice.

(See General Note after r.6.33.)

6.31 Vacation of office on making of winding-up order

6.31 Where the liquidator vacates office in consequence of the court making a winding-up order against the company, rule 6.33 applies in relation to the application to the Secretary of State for release of the liquidator.

(See General Note after r.6.33.)

6.32 Liquidator's duties on vacating office

6.32 A liquidator who ceases to be in office in consequence of removal, resignation or ceasing to be qualified as an insolvency practitioner in relation to the company, must as soon as reasonably practicable deliver to the succeeding liquidator–

(a) the assets (after deduction of any expenses properly incurred, and distributions made, by the former liquidator);

(b) the records of the winding up, including correspondence, proofs and other documents; and

(c) the company's records.

(See General Note after r.6.33.)

6.33 Application by former liquidator for release (section 173(2)(b))

6.33(1) [Content of application] An application to the Secretary of State by a former liquidator for release under section 173(2)(b) must contain–

(a) identification and contact details for the former liquidator;

(b) identification details for the company;

(c) details of the circumstances under which the liquidator has ceased to act as liquidator;

(d) a statement that the former liquidator of the company is applying to the Secretary of State for a certificate of release as liquidator as a result of the circumstances specified in the application.

6.33(2) [Authentication of application] The application must be authenticated and dated by the former liquidator.

6.33(3) [Release by Secretary of State; certification] When the Secretary of State releases the former liquidator, the Secretary of State must certify the release and deliver the certificate to the former liquidator whose release is effective from the date of the certificate or such other date as the certificate specifies.

6.33(4) [Notice of release to registrar of companies] The Secretary of State must deliver a notice of the release to the registrar of companies.

General Note to rr.6.25–6.33

A liquidator may resign only on the grounds specified in r.6.25. Rules 6.26–6.27 and 6.29–6.31 deal with the other situations in which a liquidator may case to hold office, and the remaining rules cover various incidental points. The requirement of a final meeting has, as in all other procedures, been abolished, and replaced with an obligation to make up and deliver a final account (r.6.28).

R.6.26
The notice should be in Form LIQ07.

R.6.27
The notice should be in Form LIQ10.

R.6.28
The notice should be in Form LIQ14.

R.6.29
The notice should be in Form LIQ09.

R.6.30
The notice should be in Form LIQ08.

6.34 Power of court to set aside certain transactions

6.34(1) [Transactions with liquidator's associates] If in dealing with the insolvent estate the liquidator enters into any transaction with a person who is an associate of the liquidator, the court may, on the application of any interested person, set the transaction aside and order the liquidator to compensate the company for any loss suffered in consequence of it.

6.34(2) [Non-application] This does not apply if either–

(a) the transaction was entered into with the prior consent of the court; or

(b) it is shown to the court's satisfaction that the transaction was for value, and that it was entered into by the liquidator without knowing, or having any reason to suppose, that the person concerned was an associate.

6.34(3) [Liquidator's dealings with trust property, etc.] Nothing in this rule is to be taken as prejudicing the operation of any rule of law or equity relating to a liquidator's dealings with trust property or the fiduciary obligations of any person.

(See General Note after r.6.35.)

6.35 Rule against improper solicitation

6.35(1) [Power of court] Where the court is satisfied that any improper solicitation has been used by or on behalf of the liquidator in obtaining proxies or procuring the liquidator's appointment, it may order that no remuneration be allowed as an expense of the winding up to any person by whom, or on whose behalf, the solicitation was exercised.

6.35(2) [Order of court] An order of the court under this rule overrides any resolution of the liquidation committee or the creditors, or any other provision of these Rules relating to the liquidator's remuneration.

General Note to rr.6.34, 6.35

See the note to r.5.16.

6.36 Permission for exercise of powers by liquidator

6.36(1) [No general permission] Where these Rules require permission for the liquidator to exercise a power any permission given must not be a general permission but must relate to a particular proposed exercise of the liquidator's power.

6.36(2) [Person dealing in good faith for value] A person dealing with the liquidator in good faith and for value is not concerned to enquire whether any such permission has been given.

6.36(3) [Ratification of liquidator acting without permission] Where the liquidator has done anything without such permission, the court or the liquidation committee may, for the purpose of enabling the liquidator to meet the liquidator's expenses out of the assets, ratify what the liquidator has done; but neither may do so unless satisfied that the liquidator has acted in a case of urgency and has sought ratification without undue delay.

6.36(4) ["Permission"] In this rule "permission" includes "sanction".

GENERAL NOTE

This rule qualifies the exercise of a power by the liquidator where he is required to obtain the permission of the creditors' committee.

CHAPTER 5

SPECIAL MANAGER

[Note: a document required by the Act or these Rules must also contain the standard contents set out in Part 1.]

6.37 Application for and appointment of special manager (section 177)

6.37(1) [Report in support of application] An application by the liquidator under section 177 for the appointment of a special manager must be supported by a report setting out the reasons for the application.

6.37(2) [Report to include estimate of value of relevant business] The report must include the applicant's estimate of the value of the business or property in relation to which the special manager is to be appointed.

6.37(3) [Title and content of court order] The court's order appointing a special manager must have the title "Order of Appointment of Special Manager" and must contain–

(a) the name of the court (and hearing centre if applicable) in which the order is made;

(b) the name and title of the judge making the order;

(c) identification details for the proceedings;

(d) the name and address of the applicant;

(e) the name and address of the proposed special manager;

(f) the order that that the proposed special manager is appointed as special manager of the company from the date of the order (or otherwise as the order provides);

(g) details of the special manager's responsibility over the company's business or property;

(h) the powers entrusted to the special manager under section 177(3);

(i) the time allowed for the special manager to give the required security for the appointment;

(j) the duration of the special manager's appointment, being one of the following–

  (i) for a fixed period stated in the order,

  (ii) until the occurrence of a specified event, or

  (iii) until the court makes a further order;

(k) the order that the special manager's remuneration will be fixed from time to time by the court; and

(l) the date of the order.

6.37(4) [Renewal of order] The appointment of the special manager may be renewed by order of the court.

6.37(5) [Validity of acts] The acts of the special manager are valid notwithstanding any defect in the special manager's appointment or qualifications.

(See General Note after r.6.41.)

6.38 Security

6.38(1) [Appointment effective from giving of security] The appointment of the special manager does not take effect until the person appointed has given (or, if the court allows, undertaken to give) security to the applicant for the appointment.

6.38(2) [Specific or general security] A person appointed as special manager may give security either specifically for a particular winding up, or generally for any winding up in relation to which that person may be appointed as special manager.

6.38(3) [Amount of security] The amount of the security must be not less than the value of the business or property in relation to which the special manager is appointed, as estimated in the applicant's report which accompanied the application for appointment.

6.38(4) [Certificate of adequacy of security] When the special manager has given security to the applicant, the applicant must file with the court a certificate as to the adequacy of the security.

6.38(5) [Cost of security may be reimbursed] The cost of providing the security must be paid in the first instance by the special manager; but the special manager is entitled to be reimbursed as an expense of the winding up, in the prescribed order of priority.

(See General Note after r.6.41.)

6.39 Failure to give or keep up security

6.39(1) [Liquidator to report to court failure to give security] If the special manager fails to give the required security within the time stated in the order of appointment, or any extension of that time that may be allowed, the liquidator must report the failure to the court which may discharge the order appointing the special manager.

6.39(2) [Liquidator to report to court failure to keep up security] If the special manager fails to keep up the security, the liquidator must report the failure to the court, which may remove the special manager, and make such order as it thinks just as to costs.

6.39(3) [Directions as to replacement special manager] If the court discharges the order appointing the special manager or makes an order removing the special manager, the court must give directions as to whether any, and if so what, steps should be taken for the appointment of another special manager.

(See General Note after r.6.41.)

6.40 Accounting

6.40(1) [Duty of special manager] The special manager must produce accounts, containing details of the special manager's receipts and payments, for the approval of the liquidator.

6.40(2) [Period of account] The account must be for–

(a) each three month period for the duration of the special manager's appointment;

(b) any shorter period ending with the termination of the special manager's appointment.

6.40(3) [Receipts and payments added to liquidator's] When the accounts have been approved, the special manager's receipts and payments must be added to those of the liquidator.

(See General Note after r.6.41.)

6.41 Termination of appointment

6.41(1) [Liquidator's application for termination] If the liquidator thinks that the employment of the special manager is no longer necessary or beneficial for the company, the liquidator must apply to the court for directions, and the court may order the special manager's appointment to be terminated.

6.41(2) [Liquidator's duty if creditors decide to terminate] The liquidator must also make such an application if the creditors decide that the appointment should be terminated.

General Note to rr.6.37–6.41

On the appointment of a special manager, see IA 1986 s.177 and the notes thereto. A special manager need not be qualified to act as an insolvency practitioner. These rules bring forward virtually identical provisions from IR 1986, the one exception being that the rules as to remuneration are now in Pt 18.

Chapter 6

Priority of payment of costs and expenses, etc.

6.42 General rule as to priority

6.42(1) [Expenses of the liquidation] All fees, costs, charges and other expenses incurred in the course of the winding up are to be treated as expenses of the winding up.

6.42(2) [Assets from which expenses payable] The expenses of the winding up are payable out of–

(a) assets of the company available for the payment of general creditors, including–

   (i) proceeds of any legal action which the liquidator has power to bring in the liquidator's own name or in the name of the company,

   (ii) proceeds arising from any award made under any arbitration or other dispute resolution procedure which the liquidator has power to bring in the liquidator's own name or in the name of the company,

   (iv) any payments made under any compromise or other agreement intended to avoid legal action or recourse to arbitration or to any other dispute resolution procedure, and

   (iv) payments made as a result of an assignment or a settlement of any such action, arbitration or other dispute resolution procedure in lieu of or before any judgment being given or award being made; and

(b) subject as provided in rules 6.44 to 6.48, property comprised in or subject to a floating charge created by the company.

6.42(3) [Prescribed part expenses] The expenses associated with the prescribed part must be paid out of the prescribed part.

6.42(4) [Order of priority] Subject as provided in rules 6.44 to 6.48, the expenses are payable in the following order of priority–

(a) expenses which are properly chargeable or incurred by the liquidator in preserving, realising or getting in any of the assets of the company or otherwise in the preparation, conduct or assignment of any legal proceedings, arbitration or other dispute resolution procedures, which the liquidator has power to bring in the liquidator's own name or bring or defend in the name of the company or in the preparation or conduct of any negotiations intended to lead or leading to a settlement or compromise of any legal action or dispute to which the proceedings or procedures relate;

(b) the cost of any security provided by the liquidator or special manager under the Act or these Rules;

(c) the remuneration of the special manager (if any);

(d) any amount payable to a person employed or authorised, under Chapter 2 of this Part, to assist in the preparation of a statement of affairs or of accounts;

(e) the costs of employing a shorthand writer on the application of the liquidator;

(f) any necessary disbursements by the liquidator in the course of the administration of the winding up (including any costs referred to in Articles 30 or 59 of the EU Regulation and expenses incurred by members of the liquidation committee or their representatives and allowed by the liquidator under rule 17.24, but not including any payment of corporation tax in circumstances referred to in sub-paragraph (i));

(g) the remuneration or emoluments of any person who has been employed by the liquidator to perform any services for the company, as required or authorised by or under the Act or these Rules;

(h) the remuneration of the liquidator, up to an amount not exceeding that which is payable under Schedule 11 (determination of insolvency office-holder's remuneration);

(i) the amount of any corporation tax on chargeable gains accruing on the realisation of any asset of the company (irrespective of the person by whom the realisation is effected);

(j) the balance, after payment of any sums due under sub-paragraph (h) above, of any remuneration due to the liquidator; and

(k) any other expenses properly chargeable by the liquidator in carrying out the liquidator's functions in the winding up.

(See General Note after r.6.43.)

6.43 Saving for powers of the court

6.43 Nothing in these Rules–

(a) applies to or affects the powers of any court, in proceedings by or against the company, to order costs to be paid by the company, or the liquidator; or

(b) affects the rights of any person to whom such costs are ordered to be paid.

General Note to rr.6.42, 6.43

In the new Rules, each Part lists separately the order of priority of payment, as here. For detailed commentary on particular points, see the note to r.7.108.

Rule 6.42(4)(f) amended by the Insolvency Amendment (EU 2015/848) Regulations 2017 (SI 2017/702) regs 1, 2(1), Sch. paras 32, 38 in relation to proceedings opened on or after 26 June 2017 (see reg.3) when the Recast EU Regulation 2015/848 came into force.

Chapter 7

Litigation expenses and property subject to a floating charge

[Note: a document required by the Act or these Rules must also contain the standard contents set out in Part 1.]

6.44 Interpretation

6.44(1) [Definitions] In this Chapter–

"approval" and "authorisation" respectively mean–

(a) where yet to be incurred, the approval; and

(b) where already incurred, the authorisation; of expenses specified in section 176ZA(1);

"the creditor" means–

(a) a preferential creditor of the company; or

(b) a holder of a debenture secured by, or a holder of, a floating charge created by the company;

"legal proceedings" means–

(a) proceedings under sections 212, 213, 214, 238, 239, 244 and 423 and any arbitration or other dispute resolution proceedings invoked for purposes corresponding to those to which the sections relate and any other proceedings, including arbitration or other dispute resolution procedures, which a liquidator has power to bring in the liquidator's own name for the purpose of preserving, realising, or getting in any of the assets of the company;

(b) legal actions and proceedings, arbitration or any other dispute resolution procedures which a liquidator has power to bring or defend in the name of the company; and

(c) negotiations intended to lead or leading to a settlement or compromise of any action, proceeding or procedure to which sub-paragraphs (a) or (b) relate;

"litigation expenses" means expenses of a winding up which–

(a) are properly chargeable or incurred in the preparation or conduct of any legal proceedings; and

(b) as expenses in the winding up, exceed, or in the opinion of the liquidator are likely to exceed (and only in so far as they exceed or are likely to exceed), in the aggregate £5,000; and

"specified creditor" means a creditor identified under rule 6.45(2).

6.44(2) [Litigation expenses] Litigation expenses will not have the priority provided by section 176ZA over any claims to property comprised in or subject to a floating charge created by the company and must not be paid out of any such property unless and until approved or authorised in accordance with rules 6.45 to 6.48.

(See General Note after r.6.48.)

6.45 Requirement for approval or authorisation

6.45(1) [Liquidator's opinion] Subject to rules 6.46 to 6.48, either paragraphs (3) and (4) apply or paragraph (5) applies where, in the course of winding up a company, the liquidator–

(a) ascertains that property is comprised in or subject to a floating charge;

(b) has personally instituted or proposes to institute or continue legal proceedings or is in the process of defending or proposes to defend any legal proceeding brought or likely to be brought against the company; and

(c) before or at any stage in those proceedings, is of the opinion that–

(i) the assets of the company available for payment of general creditors are or will be insufficient to pay litigation expenses; and

(ii) in order to pay litigation expenses the liquidator will have to have recourse to property comprised in or subject to a floating charge created by the company.

6.45(2) [Identification of creditors with claim to property] As soon as reasonably practicable after the date on which the liquidator forms the opinion referred to in paragraph (1), the liquidator must identify the creditor who, in the liquidator's opinion at that time–

(a) has a claim to property comprised in or subject to a floating charge created by the company; and

(b) taking into account the value of that claim and any subsisting property then comprised in or secured by such a charge, appears to the liquidator to be the creditor most immediately likely of any persons having such claims to receive some payment in respect of a claim but whose claim would not be paid in full.

6.45(3) [Request for approval of litigation expenses: specified creditors] The liquidator must request from the specified creditor the approval or authorisation of such amount for litigation expenses as the liquidator thinks fit.

6.45(4) [Request for approval of litigation expenses: multiple creditors] Where the liquidator identifies two or more specified creditors, the liquidator must seek from each of them approval or authorisation of such amount of litigation expenses as the liquidator thinks fit, apportioned between them ("the apportioned amount") according to the value of the property to the extent covered by their charges.

6.45(5) [Further requests for litigation expenses] For so long as the conditions specified in paragraph (1) subsist, the liquidator may, in the course of a winding up, make such further requests to the specified creditor or creditors for approval or authorisation of such further amount for litigation expenses as the liquidator thinks fit to be paid out of property comprised in or subject to a floating charge created by the company, taking into account any amount for litigation expenses previously approved or authorised and the value of the property comprised in or subject to the floating charge.

(See General Note after r.6.48.)

6.46 Request for approval or authorisation

6.46(1) [Details of written requests] All requests made by the liquidator for approval or authorisation must include the following–

(a) a statement describing the nature of the legal proceedings, including, where relevant, the statutory provision under which proceedings are or are to be brought and the grounds upon which the liquidator relies;

(b) a statement specifying the amount or apportioned amount of litigation expenses for which approval or authorisation is sought ("the specified amount");

(c) notice that approval or authorisation or other reply to the request must be made in writing within 28 days from the date of its being received ("the specified time limit"); and

(d) a statement explaining the consequences of a failure to reply within the specified time limit.

6.46(2) [Exclusion/exclusion of seriously prejudicial information] Where anything in paragraph (1) requires the inclusion of any information, the disclosure of which could be seriously prejudicial to the winding up of the company, the liquidator may–

(a) exclude such information from any of the above statements or notices if accompanied by a statement to that effect; or

(b) include it on terms–

(i) that bind the creditor to keep the information confidential; and

(ii) that include an undertaking on the part of the liquidator to apply to the court for an order that so much of the information as may be kept in the files of the court is not to be open to public inspection.

6.46(3) [Creditor's application for further particulars] The creditor may within the specified time limit apply to the liquidator in writing for such further particulars as is reasonable and in such a case, the time limit specified in paragraph (1)(c) will apply from the date of the creditor's receipt of the liquidator's response to any such request.

6.46(4) [Approval from multiple creditors: supplemental details to r.6.46(1) requests] Where the liquidator requires the approval or authorisation of two or more creditors, the liquidator must deliver a request to each creditor, containing the matters listed in paragraph (1) and also giving–

(a) the number of creditors concerned;

(b) the total value of their claims, or if not known, as it is estimated to be by the liquidator immediately before delivering any such request; and

(c) to each preferential creditor, notice that approval or authorisation of the specified amount will be taken to be given where a majority in value of those preferential creditors who respond within the specified time limit are in favour of it; or

(d) where rule 6.45 applies, notice to the specified creditors that the amount of litigation expenses will be apportioned between them in accordance with that rule and notice of the value of the portion allocated to, and the identity of, the specified creditors affected by that apportionment.

(See General Note after r.6.48.)

6.47 Grant of approval or authorisation

6.47(1) [Failure to include matters in liquidator's request] Where the liquidator fails to include in the liquidator's request any one of the matters, statements or notices required to be specified by paragraph (1) or paragraphs (1) and (4), of rule 6.46, the request for approval or authorisation will be treated as not having been made.

6.47(2) [Where approval or authorisation taken to have been given] Subject to paragraphs (3), (4) and (5), approval or authorisation will be taken to have been given where the specified amount has been requested by the liquidator, and–

(a) that amount is approved or authorised within the specified time limit; or

(b) a different amount is approved or authorised within the specified time limit and the liquidator considers it sufficient.

6.47(3) [Approval or authorisation by preferential creditors] Where the liquidator requires the approval or authorisation of two or more preferential creditors, approval or authorisation will be taken to be given where a majority in value of those who respond within the specified time limit approve or authorise–

(a) the specified amount; or

(b) a different amount which the liquidator considers sufficient.

6.47(4) [Proposal of different amount] Where a majority in value of two or more preferential creditors propose an amount other than that specified by the liquidator, they will be taken to have approved or authorised an amount equal to the lowest of the amounts so proposed.

6.47(5) [No written response within specified time limit] In any case in which there is no response in writing within the specified time limit to the liquidator's request–

(a) at all, or

(b) at any time following the liquidator's provision of further particulars under rule 6.46(3), the liquidator's request will be taken to have been approved or authorised from the date of the expiry of that time limit.

(See General Note after r.6.48.)

6.48 Application to the court by the liquidator

6.48(1) [Court approval or authorisation] In the circumstances specified below the court may, on the application of the liquidator, approve or authorise such amount of litigation expenses as it thinks just.

6.48(2) [Circumstances when liquidator can apply to court] Except where paragraph (3) applies, the liquidator may apply to the court for an order approving or authorising an amount for litigation expenses only where the specified creditor (or, if more than one, any one of them)–

(a) is or is intended to be a defendant in the legal proceedings in relation to which the litigation expenses have been or are to be incurred; or

(b) has been requested to approve or authorise the amount specified under rule 6.46(1)(b) and has–

(i) declined to approve or authorise, as the case may be, the specified amount;

(ii) approved or authorised an amount which is less than the specified amount and which lesser amount the liquidator considers insufficient; or

(iii) made such application for further particulars or other response to the liquidator's request as is, in the liquidator's opinion, unreasonable.

6.48(3) [Application for urgent approval or authorisation] Where the liquidator thinks that circumstances are such that the liquidator requires urgent approval or authorisation of litigation expenses, the liquidator may apply to the court for approval or authorisation either–

(a) without seeking approval or authorisation from the specified creditor; or

(b) if sought, before the expiry of the specified time limit.

6.48(4) [Power of court to grant approval/authorisation] The court may grant such application for approval or authorisation–

(a) if the liquidator satisfies the court of the urgency of the case; and

(b) subject to such terms and conditions as the court thinks just.

6.48(5) [Copies of application to specified creditor] The liquidator must, at the same time as making any application to the court under this rule, deliver copies of it to the specified creditor, unless the court orders otherwise.

6.48(6) [Creditor's entitlement to be heard] The specified creditor (or, if more than one, any one of them) is entitled to be heard on any such application unless the court orders otherwise.

6.48(7) [Terms and conditions of grant] The court may grant approval or authorisation subject to such terms and conditions as it may think just, including terms and conditions relating to the amount or nature of the litigation expenses and as to any obligation to make further applications to the court under this rule.

6.48(8) [Costs of liquidator's application] The costs of the liquidator's application under this rule, including the costs of any specified creditor appearing or represented on it, are an expense of the winding up unless the court orders otherwise.

General Note to rr.6.44–6.48

These rules are essentially the same as rr.7.111–7.116, which apply in a compulsory winding up. For commentary, see the notes to those rules.

Part 7

Winding Up by the Court

Introductory note to Part 7

Part 7 of the new Rules replaces Pt 4 of IR 1986. The most noticeable changes include the following:

- Winding up by the court is now in a separate Part.
- Forms are no longer prescribed: although a particular rule may require a document to be "in the prescribed form", it is not to be *on* a prescribed form. Instead the rule sets out a check-list of items which must be

included in the contents of the document in question. Forms are still required for documents to be filed with the registrar of companies. Companies House has in fact provided some forms for compulsory liquidation purposes.

- In the main, decisions are not to be taken by the creditors at physical meetings, convened in the traditional manner. The options available are: electronic voting, "virtual" meetings (e.g. conference calls), and the "deemed consent" procedure (see rr.15.3–15.7). A physical meeting cannot be instigated on the initiative of the liquidator, but only at the request of the prescribed number or percentage of the creditors or contributories (IA 1986 s.246ZE(7)).
- Many rules formerly to be found in Pt 4 of the 1986 Rules have been moved to other Parts, where provision is made for the rules relating to several insolvency procedures to be dealt with under a single head, for instance: defined terms and form and contents of documents (Pt 1), court procedure and practice (Pt 12), creditors' claims (Pt 14), proxies and corporate representation (Pt 16), liquidation committees (Pt 17), reporting and remuneration of office-holders (Pt 18), disclaimer (Pt 17) and service (Sch.4).

This Part covers the winding up of registered companies and "unregistered companies"—a term which includes (inter alia) foreign companies and insolvent partnerships (see the note to IA 1986 s.220). It is not confined to the winding up of companies on the ground of insolvency, but applies also, so far as appropriate, to public interest petitions (IA 1986 s.124A) and petitions on the "just and equitable" ground (s.122(1)(g)).

Chapter 1

Application of Part

7.1 Application of Part 7

7.1 This Part applies to winding up by the court.

General Note

This rule sets the overall application of Pt 7 to compulsory winding up and rr.7.4 and 7.25 should be read in conjunction with it.

Chapter 2

The statutory demand (sections 123(1)(a) and 222(1)(a))

7.2 Interpretation

7.2 A demand served by a creditor on a company under section 123(1)(a) (registered companies) or 222(1)(a) (unregistered companies) is referred to in this Part as "a statutory demand".

(See General Note after r.7.3.)

7.3 The statutory demand

7.3(1) [Heading and content] A statutory demand must be headed either "Statutory Demand under section 123(1)(a) of the Insolvency Act 1986" or "Statutory Demand under section 222(1)(a) of the Insolvency Act 1986" (as applicable) and must contain–

(a) identification details for the company;

(b) the registered office of the company (if any);

(c) the name and address of the creditor;

(d) either a statement that the demand is made under section 123(1)(a) or a statement that it is made under section 222(1)(a);

(e) the amount of the debt and the consideration for it (or, if there is no consideration, the way in which it arises);

(f) if the demand is founded on a judgment or order of a court, details of the judgment or order;

(g) if the creditor is entitled to the debt by way of assignment, details of the original creditor and any intermediary assignees;

(h) a statement that the company must pay the debt claimed in the demand within 21 days of service of the demand on the company after which the creditor may present a winding-up petition unless the company offers security for the debt and the creditor agrees to accept security or the company compounds the debt with the creditor's agreement;

(i) the name of an individual with whom an officer or representative of the company may communicate with a view to securing or compounding the debt to the creditor's satisfaction;

(j) the named individual's address, electronic address and telephone number (if any);

(k) a statement that the company has the right to apply to the court for an injunction restraining the creditor from presenting or advertising a petition for the winding up of the company; and

(l) the name of the court (and hearing centre if applicable) to which, according to the present information, the company must make the application (i.e. the High Court, the County Court at Central London or a named hearing centre of the County Court, as the case may be).

7.3(2) [Separate identification of charged interest/other charge] The following must be separately identified in the demand (if claimed) with the amount or rate of the charge and the grounds on which payment is claimed–

(a) any charge by way of interest of which notice had not previously been delivered to the company as included in its liability; and

(b) any other charge accruing from time to time.

7.3(3) [Charges accrued at date of demand] The amount claimed for such charges must be limited to that which has accrued due at the date of the demand.

7.3(4) [Authentication] The demand must be dated, and authenticated either by the creditor, or a person authorised to make the demand on the creditor's behalf.

7.3(5) [Authentication by authorised person] A demand which is authenticated by a person other than the creditor must state that the person is authorised to make the demand on the creditor's behalf and state the person's relationship to the creditor.

General Note to rr.7.2–7.3

This chapter has no application except in relation to an unpaid creditor of the company satisfying IA 1986 s.123(1)(a) or s.222(1)(a): see r.7.2.

Under IA 1986 s.123, a written demand for the payment of a debt must be "in the prescribed form". These rules deal with the content of the statutory demand, but the form formerly prescribed by IR 1986 (Form 4.1) is not continued in IR 2016 which from 6 April 2017, no longer prescribe forms.

A statutory demand may be effective despite some inaccuracy, e.g. in relation to the sum stated to be due: see the note to s.123.

Chapter 3

Petition for winding-up order

[Notes: (1) for petitions by a contributory or relevant office-holder (an administrator, administrative receiver or supervisor of a CVA) see Chapter 4;

(2) a document required by the Act or these Rules must also contain the standard contents set out in Part 1.]

7.4 Application of this Chapter

7.4(1) [Application of Chapter 3] This Chapter applies subject to rule 7.25 to–

(a) a petition for winding up presented by a contributory; or

(b) a petition for winding up presented by a relevant office-holder of the company.

7.4(2) ["Relevant office-holder"] "Relevant office-holder" in this Part means an administrator, administrative receiver and supervisor of a CVA.

(See General Note after r.7.12.)

7.5 Contents of petition

7.5(1) [Content] The petition must contain–

(a) the name of the court (and hearing centre if applicable);

(b) the name and address of the petitioner;

(c) identification details for the company subject to the petition;

(d) the company's registered office (if any);

(e) the date the company was incorporated and the enactment under which it was incorporated;

(f) the total number of issued shares of the company and the manner in which they are divided up;

(g) the aggregate nominal value of those shares;

(h) the amount of capital paid up or credited as paid up;

(i) a statement of the nature of the company's business if known;

(j) the grounds on which the winding-up order is sought;

(k) where the ground for the winding-up order is section 122(1)(a), a statement that the company has by special resolution resolved that the company be wound up by the court and the date of such resolution;

(l) where the ground for the winding-up order is section 122(1)(f) or 221(5)(b) and a statutory demand has been served on the company, a statement that such a demand has been served and the date of service and that the company is insolvent and unable to pay its debts;

(m) a statement whether the company is an Article 1.2 undertaking;

(n) a statement whether the proceedings will be main, secondary, territorial or non-EU proceedings and that the reasons for so stating are given in a witness statement;

(o) a statement that in the circumstances it is just and equitable that the company should be wound up;

(p) a statement that the petitioner therefore applies for an order that the company may be wound up by the court under the Act, or that such other order may be made as the court thinks just;

(q) the name and address of any person on whom the petitioner intends to serve the petition; and

(r) the contact details of the petitioner's solicitor (if any).

7.5(2) [Blank box for venue] The petition must also contain a blank box for the court to complete with the details of the venue for hearing the petition.

(See General Note after r.7.12.)

7.6 Verification of petition

7.6(1) [Statement of truth] The petition must be verified by a statement of truth.

7.6(2) [Debts due to different creditors] Where the petition is in respect of debts due to different creditors then the debt to each creditor must be verified separately.

7.6(3) [Separate statement of truth] A statement of truth which is not contained in or endorsed upon the petition must identify the petition and must contain–

(a) identification details for the company;

(b) the name of the petitioner; and

(c) the name of the court (and hearing centre if applicable) in which the petition is to be presented.

7.6(4) [Authentication of statement of truth] The statement of truth must be authenticated and dated by or on behalf of the petitioner.

7.6(5) [Person authenticating statement of truth not petitioner] Where the person authenticating the statement of truth is not the petitioner, or one of the petitioners, the statement of truth must state–

(a) the name and postal address of the person making the statement;

(b) the capacity in which, and the authority by which, the person authenticates the statement; and

(c) the means of that person's knowledge of the matters verified in the statement of truth.

7.6(6) [Petition based on statutory demand] If the petition is based on a statutory demand, and more than four months have elapsed between the service of the demand and the presentation of the petition, a witness statement must explain the reasons for the delay.

7.6(7) [Statement of truth verifying multiple petitions] A statement of truth verifying more than one petition must include in its title the names of the companies to which it relates and must set out, in relation to each company, the statements relied on by the petitioner; and a clear and legible photocopy of the statement of truth must be filed with each petition which it verifies.

7.6(8) [Main, secondary, territorial or non-EC proceedings] The witness statement must give the reasons for the statement that the proceedings will be main, secondary, territorial or non-EC proceedings.

(See General Note after r.7.12.)

7.7 Petition: presentation and filing

7.7(1) [Filed in court] The petition must be filed with the court.

7.7(2) [Deposit or notice of alternative arrangements given] A petition may not be filed unless–

(a) a receipt for the deposit payable to the official receiver is produced on presentation of the petition; or

(b) the Secretary of State has given notice to the court that the petitioner has made suitable alternative arrangements for the payment of the deposit and that notice has not been revoked.

7.7(3) [Revocation of alternative arrangements for deposit] A notice of alternative arrangements for the deposit may be revoked by a further notice filed with the court.

7.7(4) [Court to fix venue for hearing] The court must fix a venue for hearing the petition, and this must be endorsed on the petition and the copies.

7.7(5) [Copy petition sealed and delivered to petitioner] Each copy of the petition must have the seal of the court applied to it, and must be delivered to the petitioner.

(See General Note after r.7.12.)

7.8 Court to which petition is to be presented where the company is subject to a CVA or is in administration

7.8(1) [Filing if in CVA or administration] A petition which is filed in relation to a company for which there is in force a CVA must be presented to the court or hearing centre to which the nominee's report under section 2 was submitted or where the documents for a moratorium under section 1A were filed.

7.8(2) [Court where company in administration] A petition which is filed in relation to a company which is in administration must be presented to the court or hearing centre of the court having jurisdiction for the administration.

(See General Note after r.7.12.)

7.9 Copies of petition to be served on company or delivered to other persons

7.9(1) [Additional copies] Where this rule requires the petitioner to serve a copy of the petition on the company or deliver a copy to another person the petitioner must, when filing the petition with the court, file an additional copy with the court for each such person.

7.9(2) [Service on company] Where the petitioner is not the company the petitioner must serve a sealed copy of the petition on the company in accordance with Schedule 4.

7.9(3) [Where other proceedings] If, to the petitioner's knowledge–

(a) the company is in the course of being wound up voluntarily, the petitioner must deliver a copy of the petition to the liquidator;

(b) an administrative receiver has been appointed in relation to the company, or the company is in administration, the petitioner must deliver a copy of the petition to the receiver or the administrator;

(c) there is in force for the company a CVA, the petitioner must deliver a copy of the petition to the supervisor of the CVA; or

(d) there is a member State liquidator appointed in main proceedings in relation to the company, the petitioner must deliver a copy to that person.

7.9(4) [Copy to FCA or PRA] If either the Financial Conduct Authority or Prudential Regulation Authority is entitled to be heard at the hearing of the petition in accordance with section 371 of the Financial Services and Markets Act 2000, the petitioner must deliver a copy of the petition to the Financial Conduct Authority or Prudential Regulation Authority (as appropriate).

7.9(5) [Time for delivery to any other person] Where this rule requires the petitioner to deliver a copy of the petition to any other person that copy must be delivered within three business days after the day on which the petition is served on the company or where the petitioner is the company within three business days of the company receiving the sealed petition.

(See General Note after r.7.12.)

7.10 Notice of petition

7.10(1) [Petitioner to give notice] Unless the court otherwise directs, the petitioner must give notice of the petition.

7.10(2) [Content of notice] The notice must state–

(a) that a petition has been presented for the winding up of the company;

(b) in the case of an overseas company, the address at which service of the petition was effected;

(c) the name and address of the petitioner;

(d) the date on which the petition was presented;

(e) the venue fixed for the hearing of the petition;

(f) the name and address of the petitioner's solicitor (if any); and

(g) that any person intending to appear at the hearing (whether to support or oppose the petition) must give notice of that intention in accordance with rule 7.14.

7.10(3) [Notice in Gazette] The notice must be gazetted.

7.10(4) [Time limit for notice] The notice must be made to appear–

(a) if the petitioner is the company itself, not less than seven business days before the day appointed for the hearing; and

(b) otherwise, not less than seven business days after service of the petition on the company, nor less than seven business days before the day appointed for the hearing.

7.10(5) [Court may dismiss petition if no notice] The court may dismiss the petition if notice of it is not given in accordance with this rule.

(See General Note after r.7.12.)

7.11 Persons entitled to request a copy of petition

7.11 If a director, contributory or creditor requests a hard copy of the petition from the solicitor for the petitioner, or the petitioner, if acting in person, and pays the standard fee for copies the solicitor or petitioner must deliver the copy within two business days.

(See General Note after r.7.12.)

7.12 Certificate of compliance

7.12(1) [Filing in court] The petitioner or the petitioner's solicitor must, at least five business days before the hearing of the petition, file with the court a certificate of compliance with rules 7.9 and 7.10 relating to service and notice of the petition.

7.12(2) [Authentication and content of certificate] The certificate must be authenticated and dated by the petitioner or the petitioner's solicitor and must state–

(a) the date of presentation of the petition;

(b) the date fixed for the hearing; and

(c) the date or dates on which the petition was served and notice of it was given in compliance with rules 7.9 and 7.10.

7.12(3) [Copy notice/statement of content] A copy of or, where that is not reasonably practicable, a statement of the content of, any notice given must be filed with the court with the certificate.

7.12(4) [Court may dismiss petition for no compliance] The court may, if it thinks just, dismiss the petition if this rule is not complied with.

General Note to rr.7.4–7.12

These rules deal with the filing, service, advertisement (now called notice) and verification of the petition.

The deposit referred to in r.7.7(2)(a) is fixed at £1,600 (but £5,000 on a petition based on s.124A) from 21 July 2016. See the Insolvency Proceedings (Fees) Order 2016 (SI 2016/692) art.2. Rule 7.7(2)(b) allows alternative arrangements to be made for the payment of the deposit.

Any director, contributory or creditor of the company is entitled to a copy of the petition on payment of the appropriate fee (r.7.11).

Service of the petition under r.7.9 is now proved by a certificate of compliance rather than an affidavit in all cases (r.7.12). The gazetting of the notice of petition (r.7.10(3)) must now include the standard contents (see rr.1.10–1.12) with the further details set out in r.7.10(2). Service by a petitioner other than the company must be with a sealed copy on the company in accordance with Sch.4

In *Re Oakwood Storage Services Ltd* [2003] EWHC 2807 (Ch); [2004] 2 B.C.L.C. 404 service of a winding-up petition was effected at the company's registered office at a time when its directors were barred from attending the premises as a result of action taken by the Customs and Excise. The court held that the directors could not complain that the service was ineffective since it was up to them to have made suitable arrangements to ensure that such documents came to their notice while the ban continued. In *Re Southbourne Trading Co Ltd* (unreported, 1 December 2017 Ch D (Companies Court)), the court dismissed HMRC's winding-up petition and criticised HMRC for failing to effect valid service under IR 1986 r.4.8(2) (now Sch.4 para.2). HMRC clearly knew that the registered office was on a particular floor of a large building but had not informed the process server who merely left the petition on the ground floor without handing to a person as required by the provision.

The court is given a discretion by r.7.10(5) to dismiss the petition if notice of it has not been duly given. It has been the practice of the court since the ruling in *Re Signland Ltd* [1982] 2 All E.R. 609 to strike out any petition where the petitioning creditor has not observed the provisions as to time set out in r.7.10(4)(b), and in particular where the petition has been advertised without giving the company the prescribed seven days' notice. This is confirmed by para.9.8.1 of the *Practice Direction: Insolvency Proceedings* [2018] B.C.C. 241 (reproduced as App.IV to this *Guide*). If the court, in its discretion, grants an adjournment instead of dismissing the petition, this will be on the condition that the petition is advertised in due time for the adjourned hearing, and no further adjournment for the purpose of gazetting will be granted.

Rule 7.12 must be complied with even if the notice is defective in any way or if the petitioner decides not to pursue the petition (e.g. on receiving payment) (ibid., para.9.8.2).

The heading to r.7.10 refers to "notice" of the petition whereas its predecessor was headed "advertisement" of the petition (although the content of the rule then used the word "notice"). The word "advertised" (and in this context, "notice") has two meanings: (1) a paid announcement in a general publication; and (2) notifying the existence of the matter in question. Where the court has made an order restraining the advertisement of a winding-up petition, the word is to be construed in a wide sense, and any communication to an unauthorised party (e.g. informing the company's bank) of the fact that the petition has been presented will be a breach of the order: see the note to r.7.31(2)(c). However in rr.7.10 and 7.12 the word "notice" refers to publication in the *Gazette*—i.e. is used in the former sense (*SN Group plc v Barclays Bank plc* [1993] B.C.C. 506), and a notification to a third party of the existence of the petition will not in itself be a breach of rr.7.10 or 7.12. The Court of Appeal in *Secretary of State for Trade and Industry v North West Holdings plc* [1998] B.C.C. 997 approved *SN Group v Barclays Bank* and held that press notices by the Department of Trade and Industry stating that a winding-up petition had been presented and provisional liquidator appointed to a company were not in breach of r.7.10, although Chadwick LJ warned the DTI that if it were in any doubt whether it was appropriate to issue a press notice then directions from the court should be sought. A communication to a third party, may, however be open to condemnation as an abuse of the process of the court, if made for an improper purpose such as putting pressure on the company: if so, the petition may be struck out for this reason (*Re Bill Hennessey Associates Ltd* [1992] B.C.C. 386).

The court has a discretion under r.7.10(1) to restrain or dispense altogether with notice, which it may do (e.g.) in order to enable presentation of an application (formerly a petition) for an administration order (*Re a Company (No.001448 of 1989)* [1989] B.C.L.C. 715) but otherwise, unless the petition is held to constitute an abuse of the process of the court, this discretion will be exercised only in exceptional circumstances: *Applied Data Base Ltd v Secretary of State for Trade & Industry* [1995] 1 B.C.L.C. 272. Conduct must be improper, and something more than pressure applied by a creditor, in order to constitute abuse: *Re a Company* [2010] EWHC 3814 (Ch); [2012] B.C.C. 289.

The factors which the court will take into account in considering whether to order a restraint on advertisement/notice were examined in *Re a Company (No.007923 of 1994)* [1995] 1 W.L.R. 953; [1995] B.C.C. 634. In addition to satisfying the court that there was not likely to be any significant damage to the company's creditors, contributories and current trading partners, it was held that company needed to show that advertisement might cause serious damage to its reputation and financial stability. On a without-notice application to restrain advertisement of a petition, the court would normally expect evidence of the company's solvency, but the absence of such evidence was held not to be a bar where the issue was whether the debt was disputed on substantial grounds: *Global Acquirers Ltd v Laycatelcom Lda* (unreported, 2 July 2014). See also *James Dolman & Co Ltd v Pedley* [2003] EWCA Civ 1686; [2004] B.C.C. 504; *Secretary of State for Business, Innovation and Skills v Broomfield Developments Ltd* [2014] EWHC 3925 (Ch) (application refused: customers of the company, as contingent creditors, needed to know the position).

The court is more likely to dispense with the advertisement (now notice) of a s.124A petition than a creditor's petition under s.124 (unless the members might thereby be prejudiced): *Secretary of State for Business, Innovation and Skills v Combined Maintenance Services Ltd* (unreported, 6 November 2014).

By virtue of r.7.4, modifications to the procedure in Ch.3 on a petition presented by contributories or a relevant office-holder (administrator, administrative receiver or CVA supervisor: r.7.4(2)) are set out in Ch.4 (rr.7.25 et seq.).

Service of documents is now covered by IR 2016 Sch.4. Service of the winding-up petition on the company is provided for by Sch.4 para.2, of which para.2(3), (4) enables service to be effected more easily on a company which has ceased trading.

Rule 7.5(1)(n) amended by the Insolvency (England and Wales) and Insolvency (Scotland) (Miscellaneous and Consequential Amendments) Rules 2017 (SI 2017/1115) rr.1(1), (2), 22, 30(15) as from 8 December 2017.

7.13 Permission for the petitioner to withdraw

7.13(1) [Power of court to order] The court may order that the petitioner has permission to withdraw the petition on such terms as to costs as the parties may agree if at least five business days before the first hearing the petitioner, on an application without notice to any other party, satisfies the court that–

(a) notice of the petition has not been given under rule 7.10;

(b) no notices in support or in opposition to the petition have been received by the petitioner; and

(c) the company consents to an order being made under this rule.

7.13(2) [Content of order] The order must contain–

(a) identification details for the company;

(b) the date the winding-up petition was presented;

(c) the name and postal address of the applicant;

(d) a statement that upon the application made without notice to any other party by the applicant named in the order the court is satisfied that notice of the petition has not been given, that no notices in support of or in opposition to the petition have been received by the petitioner and that the company consents to this order; and

(e) an order that, with the permission of the court, the petition is withdrawn.

General Note

The circumstances in which a petition may be withdrawn are limited to those prescribed.

See *Practice Direction: Insolvency Proceedings* [2018] B.C.C. 241 (reproduced in App.IV to this *Guide*).

7.14 Notice by persons intending to appear

7.14(1) [Delivery to petitioner] A creditor or contributory who intends to appear on the hearing of the petition must deliver a notice of intention to appear to the petitioner.

7.14(2) [Content of notice] The notice must contain–

(a) the name and address of the creditor or contributory, and any telephone number and reference which may be required for communication with that person or with any other person (also to be specified in the notice) authorised to speak or act on the creditor's or contributory's behalf;

(b) the date of the presentation of the petition and a statement that the notice relates to the matter of that petition;

(c) the date of the hearing of the petition;

(d) for a creditor, the amount and nature of the debt due from the company to the creditor;

(e) for a contributory, the number of shares held in the company;

(f) a statement whether the creditor or contributory intends to support or oppose the petition;

(g) where the creditor or contributory is represented by a solicitor or other agent, the name, postal address, telephone number and any reference number of that person and details of that person's position with or relationship to the creditor or contributory; and

(h) the name and postal address of the petitioner.

7.14(3) [Authentication of notice] The notice must be authenticated and dated by or on behalf of the creditor or contributory delivering it.

7.14(4) [Person authenticating notice not creditor or contributory] Where the person authenticating the notice is not the creditor or contributory the notice must state the name and postal address of the person making the statement and the capacity in which, and the authority by which, the person authenticates the notice.

7.14(5) [Where notice to be delivered to] The notice must be delivered to the petitioner or the petitioner's solicitor at the address shown in the court records, or in the notice of the petition required by rule 7.10.

7.14(6) [Time limit for notice] The notice must be delivered so as to reach the petitioner (or the petitioner's solicitor) not later than 4pm on the business day before that which is appointed for the hearing (or, where the hearing has been adjourned, for the adjourned hearing).

7.14(7) [Failure to comply] A person who fails to comply with this rule may appear on the hearing of the petition only with the permission of the court.

(See General Note after r.7.24.)

7.15 List of appearances

7.15(1) [Petitioner to prepare list] The petitioner must prepare for the court a list of the creditors and contributories who have given notice under rule 7.14.

7.15(2) [Content of list] The list must contain–

(a) the date of the presentation of the petition;

(b) the date of the hearing of the petition;

(c) a statement that the creditors and contributories listed have delivered notice that they intend to appear at the hearing of the petition;

(d) their names and addresses;

(e) the amount each creditor claims to be owed;

(f) the number of shares claimed to be held by each contributory;

(g) the name and postal address of any solicitor for a person listed; and

(h) whether each person listed intends to support the petition, or to oppose it.

7.15(3) [Copy of list into court on day of hearing] On the day appointed for the hearing of the petition, a copy of the list must be handed to the court before the hearing commences.

7.15(4) [List to person with r.7.14(7) permission] If the court gives a person permission to appear under rule 7.14(7), then the petitioner must add that person to the list with the same particulars.

(See General Note after r.7.24.)

7.16 Witness statement in opposition

7.16(1) [Filed in court; copied to petitioner] If the company intends to oppose the petition, it must not later than five business days before the date fixed for the hearing–

(a) file with the court a witness statement in opposition; and

(b) deliver a copy of the witness statement to the petitioner or the petitioner's solicitor.

7.16(2) [Content] The witness statement must contain–

(a) identification details for the proceedings;

(b) a statement that the company intends to oppose the making of a winding-up order; and

(c) a statement of the grounds on which the company opposes the making of the order.

(See General Note after r.7.24.)

7.17 Substitution of creditor or contributory for petitioner

7.17(1) [Application of rule] This rule applies where the petitioner–

(a) is subsequently found not to have been entitled to present the petition;

(b) fails to give notice of the petition in accordance with rule 7.10;

(c) consents to withdraw the petition, or to allow it to be dismissed, consents to an adjournment, or fails to appear in support of the petition when it is called on in court on the day originally fixed for the hearing, or on a day to which it is adjourned; or

(d) appears, but does not apply for an order in the terms requested in the petition.

7.17(2) [Power of court] The court may, on such terms as it thinks just, substitute as petitioner–

(a) a creditor or contributory who in its opinion would have a right to present a petition and who wishes to prosecute it; or

(b) a member State liquidator who has been appointed in main proceedings in relation to the company, and who wishes to prosecute the petition.

(See General Note after r.7.24.)

7.18 Order for substitution of petitioner

7.18 An order for substitution of a petitioner must contain–

(a) identification details for the proceedings;

(b) the name of the original petitioner;

(c) the name of the creditor, contributory or member State liquidator ("the named person") who is substituted as petitioner;

(d) a statement that the named person has requested to be substituted as petitioner under rule 7.17;

(e) the following orders–

(i) either–

(aa) that the named person must pay the statutory deposit to the court and that, upon such payment being made, the statutory deposit paid by the original petitioner is to be repaid to the original petitioner by the official receiver, or

(bb) where the named person is the subject of a notice to the court by the Secretary of State under rule 7.7(2)(b) (notice of alternative arrangements for the payment of deposit) that the statutory deposit paid by the original petitioner is to be repaid to the original petitioner by the official receiver;

(ii) that the named person be substituted as petitioner in place of the original petitioner and that the named person may amend the petition accordingly,

(iii) that the named person must within a period specified in the order file a statement of truth of the statements in the amended petition,

(iv) that not later than before the adjourned hearing of the petition, by a date specified in the order, the named person must serve a sealed copy of the amended petition on the company and deliver a copy to any other person to whom the original petition was delivered,

(v) that the hearing of the amended petition be adjourned to the venue specified in the order, and

(vi) that the question of the costs of the original petitioner and of the statutory deposit (if appropriate) be reserved until the final determination of the amended petition;

(f) the venue of the adjourned hearing; and

(g) the date of the order.

(See General Note after r.7.24.)

7.19 Notice of adjournment

7.19(1) [Petitioner to notify company, etc.] If the court adjourns the hearing of the petition the petitioner must as soon as reasonably practicable deliver a notice of the making of the order of adjournment and of the venue for the adjourned hearing to–

(a) the company; and

(b) any creditor or contributory who has given notice under rule 7.14 but was not present at the hearing.

7.19(2) [Proceedings identified] The notice must identify the proceedings.

(See General Note after r.7.24.)

7.20 Order for winding up by the court

7.20(1) [Content] An order for winding-up by the court must contain–

(a) identification details for the proceedings;

(b) the name and title of the judge making the order;

(c) the name and postal address of the petitioner;

(d) the nature of the petitioner which entitles that person to present the petition (e.g. the company, a creditor, or a regulator);

(e) the date of presentation of the petition;

(f) an order that the company be wound up by the court under the Act;

(g) a statement whether the proceedings are main, secondary, territorial or non-EU proceedings;

(h) an order that the petitioner's costs of the petition be paid out of the assets of the company (unless the court determines otherwise);

(i) if applicable, an order that the costs of other persons as specified in the order be paid out of the assets of the company;

(j) the date of the order; and

(k) a statement that an official receiver attached to the court is by virtue of the order liquidator of the company, or

7.20(2) [Additional terms] The order may contain such additional terms concerning costs as the court thinks just.

(See General Note after r.7.24.)

7.21 Notice to official receiver of winding-up order

7.21(1) [Duty of court to deliver] When a winding-up order has been made, the court must deliver notice of the fact to the official receiver as soon as reasonably practicable.

7.21(2) [Title and content] The notice must have the title "Notice to Official Receiver of Winding-up Order" and must contain–

(a) identification details for the proceedings;

(b) the company's registered office;

(c) the date of presentation of the petition;

(d) the date of the winding-up order; and

(e) the name and postal address of the petitioner or the petitioner's solicitor.

(See General Note after r.7.24.)

7.22 Delivery and notice of the order

7.22(1) [Sealed copies to official receiver] As soon as reasonably practicable after making a winding-up order, the court must deliver to the official receiver two copies of the order sealed with the seal of the court.

7.22(2) [Official receiver to copy company and registrar of companies] The official receiver must deliver–

(a) a sealed copy of the order to the company; and

(b) a copy of the order to the registrar of companies (in compliance with section 130(1)).

7.22(3) [Alternative to company] As an alternative to delivering a sealed copy of the order to the company, the court may direct that the sealed copy be delivered to such other person or persons, as the court directs.

7.22(4) [Gazetting/advertisement of notice of order] The official receiver–

(a) must cause a notice of the order to be gazetted as soon as reasonably practicable; and

(b) may advertise a notice of the order in such other manner as the official receiver thinks fit.

7.22(5) [Content of notice] The notice must state–

(a) that a winding-up order has been made in relation to the company; and

(b) the date of the order.

(See General Note after r.7.24.)

7.23 Petition dismissed

7.23(1) [Duty of petitioner to give notice of dismissal] Unless the court otherwise directs, when a petition is dismissed the petitioner must give a notice of the dismissal as soon as reasonably practicable.

7.23(2) [Gazetting/advertisement of notice] The notice must be–

(a) gazetted; or

(b) advertised in accordance with any directions of the court.

7.23(3) [Content of notice] The notice must contain–

(a) a statement that a petition for the winding up of the company has been dismissed;

(b) in the case of an overseas company, the address at which service of the petition was effected;

(c) the name and address of the petitioner;

(d) the date on which the petition was presented;

(e) the date on which the petition was gazetted or otherwise advertised; and

(f) the date of the hearing at which the petition was dismissed.

7.23(4) [Power of company to gazette notice of dismissal] The company may itself gazette notice of the dismissal where–

(a) the petitioner is not the company; and

(b) the petitioner has not given notice in accordance with paragraphs (1) to (3) within 21 days of the date of the hearing at which the petition was dismissed.

(See General Note after r.7.24.)

7.24 Injunction to restrain presentation or notice of petition

7.24(1) [Application to restrain petition to court with jurisdiction] An application by a company for an injunction restraining a creditor from presenting a petition for the winding up of the company must be made to a court having jurisdiction to wind up the company.

7.24(2) [Application to restrain notice to court where petition pending] An application by a company for an injunction restraining a creditor from giving notice of a petition for the winding up of a company must be made to the court or hearing centre in which the petition is pending.

General Note to rr.7.14–7.24

These rules deal with the conduct of the hearing and the steps which are to be taken once a winding-up order has been made. This includes the registration of a copy of the winding-up order in the Companies Registry. For petitions by a contributory or a relevant office-holder (administrator, administrative receiver or supervisor of a CVA) see Ch.4 below.

Where the court orders the rescission of a winding-up order under r.12.59, the registrar of companies may be directed to remove the order from his files; but he may, if he thinks it desirable, record the fact that it has been removed in a note: *Re Calmex Ltd* (1988) 4 B.C.C. 761.

For an example of the exercise of the court's discretion under r.7.14(7), see *Re Dollar Land (Feltham) Ltd* [1995] B.C.C. 740. (Note that "appear" in this paragraph and elsewhere in r.7.14 means "have a right of audience": *Re Piccadilly Property Management Ltd* [2000] B.C.C. 44 at 50.)

A petition presented in the name of a non-existent person is a nullity, but this is to be distinguished from the case where the petitioner exists but is merely misnamed, which can be dealt with by an application to amend: *Re Goldthorpe & Lacey Ltd* (1987) 3 B.C.C. 595—a case which also illustrates the exercise of the court's discretion to substitute a petitioner under r.7.17(2).

Where a winding-up order is made against a company which is subject to a CVA, the funds in the hands of the supervisor will in many cases be subject to a trust in favour of the CVA creditors: see the note to IA 1986 s.7(4).

Both the making of the winding-up order and the dismissal of the petition must be gazetted, incorporating the standard contents (see rr.1.10–1.12) and the further information set out in para.7.22(5) or 7.23(3). A copy of the winding-up order must be delivered by the official receiver to Companies House attached to Form WU01 (r.7.22(2)(b)).

R.7.17
See *Practice Direction: Insolvency Proceedings* [2018] B.C.C. 241 (reproduced in App.IV to this *Guide*). Rule 7.17(2)(b) will apply only where the debtor company's centre of main interests is situated in another EU Member State.

R.7.20
Rule 7.20(1)(g) amended by the Insolvency (England and Wales) and Insolvency (Scotland) (Miscellaneous and Consequential Amendments) Rules 2017 (SI 2017/1115) rr.1(1), (2), 22, 30(17) as from 8 December 2017.

R.7.24
The court will grant an injunction to prevent presentation of a winding-up petition where it considers that the petition would be an abuse of process and/or that the petition is bound to fail (to the extent they are different). See the guidance given in *Coilcolour Ltd v Camtrex Ltd* [2015] EWHC 3202 (Ch); [2016] B.P.I.R. 1129 at [32] et seq. On the grounds for applications to restrain a petition based on the commonly pleaded inability to pay the company's debts, see the note to s.123.

Chapter 4

Petition by a contributory or a relevant office-holder

[Note: (1) "relevant office-holder" is defined in rule 7.4(2);

(2) a document required by the Act or these Rules must also contain the standard contents set out in Part 1.]

7.25 Interpretation and application of rules in Chapter 3

7.25(1) [Application subject to modifications to petition by contributory or office-holder] The following rules in Chapter 3 apply subject to paragraph (2), with the necessary modifications, to a petition under this Chapter by a contributory or a relevant office-holder–

rule 7.8 (court to which petition is to be presented where the company is subject to a CVA or is in administration);

rule 7.9(1), (4) and (5) (copies of petition to be served on other persons);

rule 7.11 (persons entitled to request a copy of petition);

rule 7.14 (notice by persons intending to appear);

rule 7.15 (list of appearances);

rule 7.19 (notice of adjournment);

rule 7.20 (order for winding up by the court) except where rule 7.32 applies (petition by administrator or where there is a supervisor);

rule 7.21 (notice to official receiver of winding-up order); and rule 7.22 (delivery and notice of the order).

7.25(2) [Petition by relevant office-holder] The following rules apply to petitions under this Chapter presented by a relevant office-holder–

rule 7.23 (petition dismissed); and

rule 7.24 (injunction to restrain presentation or notice of petition).

General Note

Rule 7.25(1) is poorly drafted. Although it applies various rules in Ch.3, as modified, to a petition by a contributory or a relevant office-holder (administrator, administrative receiver and CVA supervisor: r.7.4(2)), a reader has to imply one's own "necessary modifications".

See also note after r.7.32.

7.26 Contents of petition for winding-up order by a contributory

7.26(1) [Content] A petition presented by a contributory must contain–

(a) the name of the court (and hearing centre if applicable);

(b) the name and postal address of the petitioner;

(c) identification details for the company subject to the petition;

(d) the company's registered office (if any);

(e) the date the company was incorporated and the enactment under which it was incorporated;

(f) the total number of issued shares of the company and the manner in which they are divided up;

(g) the aggregate nominal value of those shares;

(h) the amount of capital paid up or credited as paid up;

(i) a statement of the nature of the company's business if known;

(j) the number and total value of the shares held by the petitioner;

(k) a statement whether the shares held by the petitioner–

  (i) were allotted to the petitioner on the incorporation of the company,

  (ii) have been registered in the name of the petitioner for more than six months in the last 18 months, or

  (iii) devolved upon the petitioner through the death of the former holder of the shares;

(l) the grounds on which the winding-up order is sought;

(m) a statement whether the company is an Article 1.2 undertaking;

(n) a statement whether the proceedings will be main, secondary, territorial or non-EU proceedings and that the reasons for so stating are given in the form of a witness statement;

(o) a statement that in the circumstances it is just and equitable that the company should be wound up;

(p) a statement that the petitioner therefore applies for an order that the company may be wound up by the court under the Act, or that such other order may be made as the court thinks just;

(q) the name and postal address of any person on whom the petitioner intends to serve the petition; and

(r) the contact details of the petitioner's solicitor (if any).

7.26(2) [Blank box for venue] The petition must also contain a blank box for the court to complete with the details of the venue for hearing the petition.

(See General Note after r.7.32.)

7.27 Petition presented by a relevant office-holder

7.27(1) [How petition to be expressed] A petition by a relevant office-holder must be expressed to be the petition of the company by the office-holder.

7.27(2) [Content] The petition must contain the particulars required by rule 7.26 (other than paragraph (1)(j) and (k) and the following (as applicable)–

(a) identification details for the office-holder;

(b) the full name of the court or hearing centre in which the proceedings are being conducted or where documents relating to the proceedings are filed;

(c) the court case number;

(d) the date the insolvency proceedings in respect of which the office-holder holds office commenced; and

(e) where the office-holder is an administrator, an application under paragraph 79 of Schedule B1, requesting that the appointment of the administrator should cease to have effect.

(See General Note after r.7.32.)

7.28 Verification of petition

7.28(1) [Statement of truth] The petition must be verified by a statement of truth.

7.28(2) [Content of statement of truth] A statement of truth which is not contained in or endorsed upon the petition must identify the petition and must contain–

(a) identification details for the company;

(b) the name of the petitioner; and

(c) the name of the court (and hearing centre if applicable) in which the petition is to be presented.

7.28(3) [Authentication of statement of truth] The statement of truth must be authenticated and dated by or on behalf of the petitioner.

7.28(4) [Authentication by other than petitioner] Where the person authenticating the statement of truth is not the petitioner, or one of the petitioners, the statement of truth must state–

(a) the name and postal address of the person making the statement;

(b) the capacity in which, and the authority by which, the person authenticates the statement; and

(c) the means of the person's knowledge of the matters verified in the statement of truth.

7.28(5) [Verification of multiple petitions] A statement of truth verifying more than one petition must include in its title the names of the companies to which it relates and must set out, in relation to each company, the statements relied on by the petitioner; and a clear and legible photocopy of the statement of truth must be filed with each petition which it verifies.

7.28(6) [Main, secondary, territorial or non-EU proceedings] The reasons for the statement that the proceedings will be main, secondary, territorial or non-EU proceedings must be given in a witness statement.

(See General Note after r.7.32.)

7.29 Presentation and service of petition

7.29(1) [Filing with copy in court] The petition with one copy must be filed with the court.

7.29(2) [Deposit receipt to be produced] The petition may not be filed unless a receipt for the deposit payable to the official receiver is produced on presentation of the petition.

7.29(3) [Court to fix return day] The court must fix a hearing for a return day on which, unless the court otherwise directs, the petitioner and the company must attend before the court for–

(a) directions to be given in relation to the procedure on the petition; or

(b) the hearing of the petition where–

(i) it is presented by a relevant office-holder, and

(ii) the court considers it just in all the circumstances.

7.29(4) [Sealed copy of endorsed petition to petitioner] On fixing the return day, the court must deliver to the petitioner a sealed copy of the petition endorsed with the return day and time of hearing.

7.29(5) [Service of sealed copy on company] The petitioner must serve a sealed copy of the petition on the company at least 14 days before the return day.

7.29(6) [Delivery to Member State liquidator] Where a member State liquidator has been appointed in main proceedings in relation to the company, the petitioner must deliver a copy of the petition to the member State liquidator.

(See General Note after r.7.32.)

7.30 Request to appoint former administrator or supervisor as liquidator (section 140)

7.30(1) [Application of rule] This rule applies where a petition requests under section 140 the appointment of a former administrator or supervisor as liquidator.

7.30(2) [Appointee to file report in court] The person whose appointment is sought ("the appointee") must, not less than two business days before the return day fixed under rule 7.29(3), file with the court a report including particulars of–

(a) the date on which the appointee delivered notice to creditors of the company, of the appointee's intention to seek appointment as liquidator, such date to be at least seven business days before the day on which the report is filed; and

(b) details of any response from creditors to that notice, including any objections to the proposed appointment.

(See General Note after r.7.32.)

7.31 Hearing of petition

7.31(1) [Court to give directions or order] On the return day, or at any time after it, the court–

(a) must, where the petition is presented by a person who is not a relevant office-holder, give directions;

(b) may, in any other case, give directions; or

(c) may, in either case, make any such order as it sees fit.

7.31(2) [Particular directions] In particular, the court may give directions relating to the following matters–

(a) service or delivery of the petition, whether in connection with the venue for a further hearing, or for any other purpose;

(b) whether particulars of claim and defence are to be delivered, and generally as to the procedure on the petition;

(c) whether and if so by what means, notice of the petition is to be given;

(d) the manner in which any evidence is to be provided at any hearing before the judge and in particular (but without prejudice to the generality of the above) as to–

(i) the taking of evidence wholly or in part by witness statement or orally,

(ii) the cross-examination of any person who has made a witness statement, and

(iii) the matters to be dealt with in evidence; and

(e) any other matter affecting the procedure on the petition or in connection with the hearing and disposal of the petition.

7.31(3) [Court to consider service of copy petition on r.7.9 persons] In giving directions the court must consider whether a copy of the petition should be served on or delivered to any of the persons specified in rule 7.9.

(See General Note after r.7.32.)

7.32 Order for winding up by the court of a company in administration or where there is a supervisor of a CVA in relation to the company

7.32(1) [Content] An order for winding-up by the court of a company in administration or where there is a supervisor of a CVA in relation to the company must contain–

(a) identification details for the proceedings;

(b) the name and title of the judge making the order;

(c) the name and postal address of the administrator or supervisor of the company;

(d) the date of the administrator's or supervisor's appointment;

(e) the date of presentation of the petition;

(f) where there is an administrator, an order that the administrator's appointment ceases to have effect;

(g) an order that the company be wound up by the court under the Act;

(h) a statement whether the proceedings are main, secondary, territorial or non-EU proceedings; and

(i) the name and address of the person appointed as liquidator of the company (if applicable);

(j) an order that–

(i) an official receiver attached to the court is by virtue of the order liquidator of the company, or

(ii) that the administrator or the supervisor (as the case may be) specified in the order is appointed liquidator of the company; and

(k) the date of the order.

7.32(2) [Additional terms] The order may contain such additional terms as to the costs as the court thinks just.

7.32(3) [Rule 7.56(3)(c), (4), (7), (8), (9)] Where the court appoints the former administrator or the supervisor as liquidator paragraphs (3)(c), (4), (7), (8) and (9) of rule 7.56 apply.

General Note to rr.7.25–7.32

The procedure to be followed on a petition by a contributory or a relevant office-holder (i.e. an administrator, administrative receiver or supervisor of a CVA: see r.7.4(2)) is generally the same as that for other petitions, with the modifications set out here. Directions from the court regarding the service, notice and hearing of the petition must be sought in every case. If notice of the petition is given prematurely the court may order that the petition be struck out and removed from the court file: *Re a Company (No.007020 of 1996)* [1998] 2 B.C.L.C. 54. See further the *Practice Direction: Insolvency Proceedings* [2018] B.C.C. 241 (reproduced as App.IV to this Guide) para.9.8.

IR 2016 r.7.10 refers to "notice" of the petition whereas e.g. IR 1986 r.4.11 was headed "advertisement" of the petition (although the content of the rule then used the word "notice"). The word "advertised" (and in this context, "notice") has two meanings: primarily, a paid announcement in a general publication, but also notifying the existence of the matter in question in any way. Where the court has made an order restraining notice of a winding-up petition under r.7.31(2)(c), the word may be construed in the latter sense, and any communication to an unauthorised party (e.g. informing the company's bank) of the fact that the petition has been presented will be a breach of the order (*Re a Company (No.00687 of 1991)* [1991] B.C.C. 210). It may also be an abuse of the process of the court to engage in premature notice of a contributories' petition, e.g. by telling the company's bank and trading partners that a petition has been or will be presented: *Re Doreen Boards Ltd* [1996] 1 B.C.L.C. 501. (See also the note to r.7.10, above.)

Rule 7.29(6) will apply only where the debtor company's centre of main interests is situated in another EU Member State.

Rule 7.32 had no direct counterpart in IR 1986 but is partly derived from forms prescribed under those Rules.

Rules 7.26(1)(n), 7.28(6), 7.32(1)(h) amended by the Insolvency (England and Wales) and Insolvency (Scotland) (Miscellaneous and Consequential Amendments) Rules 2017 (SI 2017/1115) rr.1(1), (2), 22, 30(18), (19), (20) as from 8 December 2017.

Chapter 5

Provisional liquidator

[Note: a document required by the Act or these Rules must also contain the standard contents set out in Part 1.]

7.33 Application for appointment of provisional liquidator (section 135)

7.33(1) [Who may make application] An application to the court for the appointment of a provisional liquidator under section 135 may be made by–

(a) the petitioner;

(b) a creditor of the company;

(c) a contributory;

(d) the company;

(e) the Secretary of State;

(f) a temporary administrator;

(g) a member State liquidator appointed in main proceedings (including in accordance with Article 37 of the EU Regulation); or

(h) any person who under any enactment would be entitled to present a petition for the winding up of the company.

7.33(2) [Supporting witness statement] The application must be supported by a witness statement stating–

(a) the grounds on which it is proposed that a provisional liquidator should be appointed;

(b) if some person other than the official receiver is proposed to be appointed, that that person has consented to act and, to the best of the applicant's belief, is qualified to act as an insolvency practitioner in relation to the company;

(c) whether or not the official receiver has been informed of the application and, if so, whether a copy of it has been delivered to the official receiver;

(d) whether to the applicant's knowledge–

(i) there has been proposed or is in force for the company a CVA;

(ii) an administrator or administrative receiver is acting in relation to the company; or

(iii) a liquidator has been appointed for its voluntary winding up; and

(e) the applicant's estimate of the value of the assets in relation to which the provisional liquidator is to be appointed;

(f) a statement whether the proceedings will be main, secondary, territorial or non-EU proceedings with the reasons for so stating.

7.33(3) [Copies to official receiver, etc.] The applicant must deliver copies of the application and the witness statement in support to the official receiver, who may attend the hearing and make any representations which the official receiver thinks appropriate.

7.33(4) [Where no copies to official receiver] If for any reason it is not practicable to deliver copies of the application and statement to the official receiver before the hearing, the applicant must inform the official receiver of the application in sufficient time for the official receiver to be able to attend.

7.33(5) [Appointment if sufficient grounds] If satisfied that sufficient grounds are shown for the appointment the court may appoint a provisional liquidator on such terms as it thinks just.

(See General Note after r.7.39.)

7.34 Deposit by applicant

7.34(1) [Security for official receiver's remuneration] An applicant for an order appointing the official receiver as provisional liquidator must, before the order is made, deposit with the official receiver, or otherwise secure to the official receiver's satisfaction, such sum as the court directs to cover the official receiver's remuneration and expenses.

7.34(2) [Insufficiency of deposit, etc.] If the sum deposited or secured proves to be insufficient, the court may, on the application of the official receiver, order the applicant for the appointment to deposit or secure an additional sum.

7.34(3) [Additional sum not deposited] If such additional sum is not deposited or secured within two business days after service of the order on the applicant then the court may discharge the order appointing the official receiver as provisional liquidator.

7.34(4) [Repayment of deposit after winding-up order] If a winding-up order is made after a provisional liquidator has been appointed, any money deposited under this rule must (unless it is required because the assets are insufficient to pay the remuneration and expenses of the provisional liquidator) be repaid to the person depositing it (or as that person may direct) as an expense of the winding up, in the prescribed order of priority.

(See General Note after r.7.39.)

7.35 Order of appointment of provisional liquidator

7.35(1) [Title and content] The order appointing the provisional liquidator must have the title "Order of appointment of Provisional Liquidator" and contain–

(a) the name of the court (and hearing centre if applicable) in which the order is made;

(b) the name and title of the judge making the order;

(c) the name and postal address of the applicant;

(d) identification details for the company;

(e) the statement that the court is satisfied–

(i) that the company is unable to pay its debts (if applicable), and

(ii) that the proceedings are main, secondary, territorial or non-EU proceedings, as the case may be;

(f) an order either that–

(i) upon the sum, which is specified in the order, being deposited by the applicant with the official receiver, the official receiver is appointed provisional liquidator of the company, or

(ii) the person specified in the order is appointed provisional liquidator of the company;

(g) identification and contact details for the provisional liquidator, where the provisional liquidator is not the official receiver;

(h) details of the functions to be carried out by the provisional liquidator in relation to the company's affairs;

(i) a notice to the officers of the company that they are required by section 235 to give the provisional liquidator all the information the provisional liquidator may reasonably require relating to the company's property and affairs and to attend upon the provisional liquidator at such times as the provisional liquidator may reasonably require; and

(j) the date of the order.

7.35(2) [Multiple appointments] Where two or more provisional liquidators are appointed the order must also specify (as required by section 231) whether any act required or authorised under any enactment to be done by the provisional liquidator is to be done by all or any one or more of them.

7.35(3) [Sealed copies to official receiver, etc.] The court must, as soon as reasonably practicable after the order is made, deliver copies of the order as follows–

(a) if the official receiver is the provisional liquidator, two sealed copies to the official receiver;

(b) if another person is appointed as provisional liquidator–

(i) two sealed copies to that person, and

(ii) one copy to the official receiver;

(c) if there is an administrative receiver acting in relation to the company, one sealed copy to the administrative receiver.

7.35(4) [Sealed copy to company or liquidator] The official receiver or other person appointed as provisional liquidator must as soon as reasonably practicable deliver a sealed copy of the order to either–

(a) the company, or

(b) the liquidator, if a liquidator was appointed for the company's voluntary winding-up.

7.35(5) [Copy to registrar of companies] The official receiver or other person appointed as provisional liquidator must as soon as reasonably practicable deliver a copy of the order to the registrar of companies.

(See General Note after r.7.39.)

7.36 Notice of appointment of provisional liquidator

7.36(1) [Duty of provisional liquidator] The provisional liquidator must as soon as reasonably practicable after receipt of the copy of the order of appointment give notice of appointment unless the court directs otherwise.

7.36(2) [Gazetting and advertisement] The notice–

(a) must be gazetted; and

(b) may be advertised in such other manner as the provisional liquidator thinks fit.

7.36(3) [Content of notice] The notice must state–

(a) that a provisional liquidator has been appointed; and

(b) the date of the appointment.

(See General Note after r.7.39.)

7.37 Security

7.37(1) [Application of rule] This rule applies where an insolvency practitioner is appointed as provisional liquidator.

7.37(2) [Cost of providing to be reimbursed] The cost of providing the security required under the Act must be paid in the first instance by the provisional liquidator, however–

(a) if a winding-up order is not made, the person appointed is entitled to be reimbursed out of the property of the company, and the court may make an order on the company accordingly; and

(b) if a winding-up order is made, the person appointed is entitled to be reimbursed as an expense of the winding up in the prescribed order of priority.

7.37(3) [Failure to give or keep up security] If the provisional liquidator fails to give or keep up the required security, the court may remove the provisional liquidator, and make such order as it thinks just as to costs.

7.37(4) [Replacement] If an order is made under this rule removing the provisional liquidator, or discharging the order appointing the provisional liquidator, the court must give directions as to whether any, and if so what, steps should be taken for the appointment of another person in the place of the removed or discharged provisional liquidator.

(See General Note after r.7.39.)

7.38 Remuneration

7.38(1) [Fixed by court] The remuneration of the provisional liquidator (other than the official receiver) is to be fixed by the court from time to time on the application of the provisional liquidator.

7.38(2) [Matters to be taken into account] In fixing the remuneration of the provisional liquidator, the court must take into account–

(a) the time properly given by the provisional liquidator and the staff of the provisional liquidator in attending to the company's affairs;

(b) the complexity of the case;

(c) any respects in which, in connection with the company's affairs, there falls on the provisional liquidator any responsibility of an exceptional kind or degree;

(d) the effectiveness with which the provisional liquidator appears to be carrying out, or to have carried out, the duties of the provisional liquidator; and

(e) the value and nature of the property with which the provisional liquidator has to deal.

7.38(3) [Source of payment of remuneration, expenses] Without prejudice to any order the court may make as to costs, the remuneration of the provisional liquidator (whether the official receiver or another) must be paid to the provisional liquidator, and the amount of any expenses incurred by the provisional liquidator (including the remuneration and expenses of any special manager appointed under section 177) reimbursed–

(a) if a winding-up order is not made, out of the property of the company;

(b) if a winding-up order is made, as an expense of the winding up, in the prescribed order of priority; and

(c) in either case (if the relevant funds are insufficient), out of the deposit under rule 7.34.

7.38(4) [Power of retention where winding-up order not made] Unless the court otherwise directs, where a winding up order is not made, the provisional liquidator may retain out of the company's property such sums or property as are or may be required for meeting the remuneration and expenses of the provisional liquidator.

7.38(5) [Provisional liquidator other than official receiver] Where a person other than the official receiver has been appointed provisional liquidator, and the official receiver has taken any steps for the purpose of obtaining a statement of affairs or has performed any other duty under these Rules, the provisional liquidator must pay the official receiver such sum (if any) as the court may direct.

(See General Note after r.7.39.)

7.39 Termination of appointment

7.39(1) [Power of court] The appointment of the provisional liquidator may be terminated by the court on the application of the provisional liquidator, or a person specified in rule 7.33(1).

7.39(2) [Directions on termination on dismissal of winding-up petition, etc.] If the provisional liquidator's appointment terminates, in consequence of the dismissal of the winding-up petition or otherwise, the court may give such directions as it thinks just relating to the accounts of the provisional liquidator's administration or any other matters which it thinks appropriate.

7.39(3) [Notice of termination except on winding up] The provisional liquidator must give notice of termination of the appointment as provisional liquidator, unless the termination is on the making of a winding-up order or the court directs otherwise.

7.39(4) [Notice to be delivered to registrar, gazetted/advertised] The notice referred to in paragraph (3)–

(a) must be delivered to the registrar of companies as soon as reasonably practicable;

(b) must be gazetted as soon as reasonably practicable; and

(c) may be advertised in such other manner as the provisional liquidator thinks fit.

7.39(5) [Content of notice] The notice under paragraph (3) must state–

(a) that the appointment as provisional liquidator has been terminated;

(b) the date of that termination; and

(c) that the appointment terminated otherwise than on the making of a winding-up order.

General Note to rr.7.33–7.39

These rules set out the procedure governing an application to the court for the appointment of a provisional liquidator under IA 1986 s.135, and the associated questions of furnishing a deposit (where the official receiver is appointed) or security (where the provisional liquidator is an insolvency practitioner), and the liquidator's remuneration.

The order of appointment must be sent to Companies House under r.7.35(5) attached to Form WU02.

The court may in an appropriate case refer the fixing of remuneration under r.7.38 to one or more assessors: *Re Independent Insurance Co Ltd* [2002] EWHC 1577 (Ch); [2003] EWHC 51 (Ch); [2004] B.C.C. 919. In the judgment the principles for the fixing of remuneration and making of interim payments are discussed in detail. The judgment of Peter Smith J in *Jacob v UIC Insurance Co Ltd* [2006] EWHC 2717 (Ch); [2007] B.C.C.167 discusses many issues relating to the review of the remuneration of provisional liquidators, including (i) the procedure for an appeal under r.12.59 against an assessment made by a registrar; (ii) the reasons for disallowing claims for remuneration on the basis of over-management, the use of staff of too high a grade and of consultants; (iii) the justice of re-opening claims settled or agreed in the past; and (iv) the irrelevance of the fact that the provisional liquidation was successful. (For further proceedings, see *Re UIC Insurance Co Ltd (No.2)* [2007] B.P.I.R. 589.) See also the *Practice Direction* [2018] B.C.C. 241 (reproduced as App.IV to this *Guide*) Pt 6.

There is no provision in the rules governing the priority in which the remuneration and expenses of a provisional liquidator should be paid, either vis-à-vis the company's debts or in relation to each other; but in *Re Grey Marlin Ltd* [2000] B.C.C. 410 and *Smith v UIC Insurance Co Ltd* [2001] B.C.C. 11 the rules governing a liquidator's remuneration and expenses were applied by analogy.

In *Re Beppler & Jacobson Ltd* [2016] EWHC 20 (Ch) an agreement to "advance" the funding of a provisional liquidator connoted a loan with a right of recourse out of the assets to reimburse the outlay in accordance with r.7.38(3).

The provisions in rr.7.37 and 7.38 are directory, although subject to the overall discretion conferred by r.7.39(2); and so a court will not normally make an order that an unsuccessful petitioner should pay the remuneration of a provisional liquidator: *Re Walter L Jacob & Co Ltd* (1987) 3 B.C.C. 532. (See, however, *Re Secure & Provide plc* [1992] B.C.C. 405, where such an order was made against the Secretary of State following the failure of a petition under s.124A; and compare *Re Xyllyx plc (No.2)* [1992] B.C.L.C. 378.)

The court has power under r.7.39(2) to direct that a provisional liquidator who has been discharged before the hearing of the petition shall be paid remuneration out of the company's assets: see *Re UOC Corp, Alipour v UOC Corp* [1998] B.C.C. 191.

Rules 7.36(3) and 7.39(3)–(5) prescribe in detail the required contents of the notice of the provisional liquidator's appointment and its termination. On the standard contents for gazetted notices, see rr.1.10–1.12. The notice of termination to be sent to Companies House under r.7.39(3), (4)(a) is in Form WU03.

A provisional liquidator is listed in Annex B to the Recast EU Regulation 2015/848 as an "insolvency practitioner" referred to in art.2(5) of the Regulation.

Rule 7.33(1)(g) amended by the Insolvency (England and Wales) and Insolvency (Scotland) (Miscellaneous and Consequential Amendments) Rules 2017 (SI 2017/1115) rr.1(1), (2), 22, 26 as from 8 December 2017.

Rule 7.33(2)(f) inserted by the Insolvency Amendment (EU 2015/848) Regulations 2017 (SI 2017/702) regs 1, 2(1), Sch. paras 32, 39 in relation to proceedings opened on or after 26 June 2017 (see reg.3) when the Recast EU Regulation 2015/848 came into force.

Rule 7.35(1)(e)(ii) amended by the Insolvency (England and Wales) and Insolvency (Scotland) (Miscellaneous and Consequential Amendments) Rules 2017 (SI 2017/1115) rr.1(1), (2), 22, 30(21) as from 8 December 2017.

Chapter 6

Statement of affairs and other information

[Note: a document required by the Act or these Rules must also contain the standard contents set out in Part 1.]

7.40 Notice requiring statement of affairs (section 131)

7.40(1) [Official receiver to deliver notice to nominated person] Where, under section 131, the official receiver requires a nominated person to provide the official receiver with a statement of the affairs of the company, the official receiver must deliver a notice to that person.

7.40(2) [Heading and content] The notice must be headed "Notice requiring statement of affairs" and must–

(a) identify the company immediately below the heading;

(b) require a nominated person to prepare and submit to the official receiver a statement of affairs of the company;

(c) inform the nominated person–

(i) of the names and addresses of any other nominated person to whom such a notice has been delivered, and

(ii) of the date by which the statement must be delivered; and

(d) state the effect of section 131(7) (penalty for non-compliance) and section 235 (duty to co-operate) as it applies to the official receiver.

7.40(3) [Supply of document] The official receiver must inform the nominated person that a document for the preparation of the statement of affairs capable of completion in compliance with rule 7.41 can be supplied by the official receiver if requested.

(See General Note after r.7.42.)

7.41 Statement of affairs

7.41(1) [Heading and content] The statement of affairs must be headed "Statement of affairs" and must contain–

(a) identification details for the company;

(b) a statement that it is a statement of the affairs of the company on a date which is specified, being–

(i) the date of the winding-up order, or

(ii) the date directed by the official receiver;

(c) a list of the company's shareholders with the following information about each one–

(i) name and postal address,

(ii) the type of shares held,

(iii) the nominal amount of the shares held,

(iv) the number of shares held,

(v) the amount per share called up, and

(vi) the total amount of shares called up;

(d) the total amount of shares called up held by all shareholders;

(e) a summary of the assets of the company, setting out the book value and estimated realisable value of–

(i) any assets subject to a fixed charge,

(ii) any assets subject to a floating charge,

(iii) any uncharged assets, and

(iv) the total value of all the assets available for preferential creditors;

(f) a summary of the liabilities of the company, setting out–

(i) the amount of preferential debts,

(ii) an estimate of the deficiency with respect to preferential debts or the surplus available after paying the preferential debts,

(iii) an estimate of the prescribed part, if applicable,

(iv) an estimate of the total assets available to pay debts secured by floating charges,

(v) the amount of debts secured by floating charges,

(vi) an estimate of the deficiency with respect to debts secured by floating charges or the surplus available after paying the debts secured by fixed or floating charges,

(vii) the amount of unsecured debts (excluding preferential debts),

(viii) an estimate of the deficiency with respect to unsecured debts or the surplus available after paying unsecured debts,

(ix) any issued and called-up capital, and

(x) an estimate of the deficiency with respect to, or surplus available to, members of the company;

(g) a list of the company's creditors (as required by section 131(2)) with the following particulars required by paragraph (2) indicating–

(i) any creditors under hire-purchase, chattel leasing or conditional sale agreements,

(ii) any creditors who are consumers claiming amounts paid in advance of the supply of goods or services, and

(iii) any creditors claiming retention of title over property in the company's possession.

7.41(2) [Particulars required re creditors] The particulars required by this paragraph are as follows–

(i) the name and postal address,

(ii) the amount of the debt owed to the creditor,

(iii) details of any security held by the creditor,

(iv) the date the security was given, and

(v) the value of any such security.

7.41(3) [Particulars re creditors who are employees/prepaid consumers] Paragraph (4) applies where the particulars required by paragraph (2) relate to creditors who are either–

(a) employees or former employees of the company; or

(b) consumers claiming amounts paid in advance for the supply of goods or services.

7.41(4) [Details of r.7.41(3)(a), (b) creditors; schedules] Where this paragraph applies–

(a) the statement of affairs itself must state separately for each of paragraph (3)(a) and (b) the number of such creditors and the total of the debts owed to them; and

(b) the particulars required by paragraph (2) in respect of those creditors must be set out in separate schedules to the statement of affairs for each of paragraph (3)(a) and (b).

7.41(5) [Verification] The statement of affairs must be verified by a statement of truth by the nominated person, or all of them if more than one, making the statement of affairs.

7.41(6) [Delivery of statement to official receiver with copy] The nominated person (or one of them, if more than one) must deliver the statement of affairs verified as required by paragraph (5) to the official receiver together with a copy.

7.41(7) [Official receiver to deliver verified copy to registrar of companies] The official receiver must deliver the verified copy of the statement of affairs and any statements of concurrence delivered under rule 7.42 to the registrar of companies.

7.41(8) [Exclusion of schedules in r.7.41(4)(b)] However the official receiver must not deliver to the registrar of companies with the statement of affairs any schedule required by paragraph (4)(b).

(See General Note after r.7.42.)

7.42 Statement of affairs: statement of concurrence

7.42(1) [Relevant person to deliver statement of concurrence to official receiver] The official receiver may require a person mentioned in section 131(3) ("a relevant person") to deliver to the official receiver a statement of concurrence.

7.42(2) [Nature of statement of concurrence] A statement of concurrence is a statement, verified by a statement of truth, that that person concurs in the statement of affairs submitted by a nominated person.

7.42(3) [Official receiver to inform re statement of affairs/statement of concurrence] The official receiver must inform the nominated person who has been required to submit a statement of affairs that the relevant person has been required to deliver a statement of concurrence.

7.42(4) [Nominated person to deliver copy statement of affairs to relevant persons] The nominated person must deliver a copy of the statement of affairs to every relevant person who has been required to submit a statement of concurrence.

7.42(5) [Statement of concurrence may be qualified] A statement of concurrence–

(a) must identify the company; and

(b) may be qualified in relation to matters dealt with in the statement of affairs, where the relevant person–

 (i) is not in agreement with the statement of affairs,

 (ii) considers the statement of affairs to be erroneous or misleading, or

 (iii) is without the direct knowledge necessary for concurring in it.

7.42(6) [Duty of relevant person to deliver verified statement to official receiver] The relevant person must deliver the required statement of concurrence (with a copy) to the official receiver before the end of the period of five business days (or such other period as the official receiver may agree) beginning with the day on which the relevant person receives the statement of affairs.

General Note to rr.7.40–7.42

The statement of affairs referred to in these rules is that which the official receiver may require when an order for winding up or for the appointment of a provisional liquidator has been made. The detailed content of the statement of affairs in r.7.41 is largely derived from former prescribed forms and doubtless these forms will be adapted by practitioners in the absence of prescribed forms after 6 April 2017. The copy of the statement of affairs and statement of concurrence delivered to Companies House under r.7.41(7) must be attached to Form WU05 unless the court orders limited disclosure: see r.7.43.

7.43 Order limiting disclosure of statement of affairs etc.

7.43(1) [Power of official receiver to apply to court] Where the official receiver thinks that disclosure of the whole or part of the statement of affairs or of any statement of concurrence would be likely to prejudice the conduct of the winding up or might reasonably be expected to lead to violence against any person, the official receiver may apply to the court for an order that the statement of affairs, statement of concurrence or any specified part of them must not be filed with the registrar of companies.

7.43(2) [Powers of court] The court may order that the whole or a specified part of the statement of affairs or of a statement of concurrence must not be delivered to the registrar of companies.

7.43(3) [Official receiver to deliver copy order etc. to registrar of companies] The official receiver must as soon as reasonably practicable deliver to the registrar of companies a copy of the order, and the statement of affairs and any statement of concurrence to the extent allowed by the order.

General Note

See *Practice Direction: Insolvency Proceedings* [2018] B.C.C. 241 (reproduced in App.IV to this *Guide*). The copy of the order of limited disclosure to be delivered to Companies House with (except in the case of total disclosure) copies of the statement of affairs and statement of concurrence must be attached to Form WU06. See also General Note after r.7.45.

7.44 Release from duty to submit statement of affairs: extension of time (section 131)

7.44(1) [Power of official receiver] The official receiver may exercise the power in section 131(5) to release a person from an obligation to submit a statement of affairs imposed under section 131(1) or (2), or to grant an extension of time, either at the official receiver's own discretion, or at the request of a nominated person.

7.44(2) [Nominated person may apply for release/extension of time] A nominated person may apply to the court for a release or an extension of time if the official receiver refuses that person's request.

7.44(3) [Court may dismiss application] On receipt of an application, the court may, if it is satisfied that no sufficient cause is shown for it, dismiss it without giving notice to any party other than the applicant.

7.44(4) [Court to fix venue for hearing of application] Unless the application is dismissed, the court must fix a venue for it to be heard.

7.44(5) [Applicant to deliver notice of venue to official receiver] The applicant must, at least 14 days before any hearing, deliver to the official receiver a notice stating the venue with a copy of the application and of any evidence on which the applicant intends to rely.

7.44(6) [Official receiver may file report and/or appear] The official receiver may do either or both of the following–

(a) file a report of any matters which the official receiver thinks ought to be drawn to the court's attention; or

(b) appear and be heard on the application.

7.44(7) [Copy report to applicant] If a report is filed, the official receiver must deliver a copy of it to the applicant not later than five business days before the hearing.

7.44(8) [Court to deliver sealed copies of order] The court must deliver sealed copies of any order made on the application to the nominated person and the official receiver.

7.44(9) [Costs] The applicant must pay the applicant's own costs in any event and, unless and to the extent that the court orders otherwise those costs will not be an expense of the winding up.

(See General Note after r.7.45.)

7.45 Statement of affairs: expenses

7.45(1) [Person assisting with preparation of statement] If a nominated person cannot personally prepare a proper statement of affairs, the official receiver may, as an expense of the winding up, employ a person or firm to assist in the preparation of the statement.

7.45(2) [Allowance toward expenses] At the request of a nominated person, made on the grounds that the nominated person cannot personally prepare a proper statement, the official receiver may authorise an allowance, payable as an expense of the winding up, of all or part of the expenses to be incurred by the nominated person in employing a person or firm to assist the nominated person in preparing it.

7.45(3) [Estimate of expenses] Any such request by the nominated person must be accompanied by an estimate of the expenses involved; and the official receiver must only authorise the employment of a named person or a named firm, approved by the official receiver.

7.45(4) [Conditions of authorisation to access relevant documents, records] An authorisation given by the official receiver under this rule must be subject to such conditions (if any) as the official receiver thinks fit to impose relating to the manner in which any person may obtain access to relevant documents and other records.

7.45(5) [Obligation re preparation, verification and submission of statement] Nothing in this rule relieves a nominated person from any obligation relating to the preparation, verification and submission of the statement of affairs, or to the provision of information to the official receiver or the liquidator.

7.45(6) [Payment an expense in prescribed order of priority] Any payment made as an expense of the winding up under this rule must be made in the prescribed order of priority.

7.45(7) [Application of r.7.45(2)–(6) to statement of concurrence] Paragraphs (2) to (6) of this rule may be applied, on application to the official receiver by any nominated person, in relation to the making of a statement of concurrence.

General Note to rr.7.44–7.45

These rules are concerned with various discretionary powers conferred on the official receiver in regard to the statement of affairs: to apply to the court for an order authorising limited disclosure in the statement of affairs, to grant a release or an extension of time, and to provide a nominated person with professional help.

7.46 Delivery of accounts to official receiver

7.46(1) [Duty of officers, etc. to deliver] Any of the persons specified in section 235(3) must, at the request of the official receiver, deliver to the official receiver accounts of the company of such nature, as at such date, and for such period, as the official receiver may specify.

7.46(2) [Period for accounts] The period specified may begin from a date up to three years before the date of the presentation of the winding-up petition, or from an earlier date to which audited accounts of the company were last prepared.

7.46(3) [Accounts for earlier period] The court may, on the official receiver's application, require accounts for any earlier period.

7.46(4) [Application of r.7.45] Rule 7.45 applies (with the necessary modifications) in relation to accounts to be delivered under this rule as it applies in relation to the statement of affairs.

7.46(5) [Accounts to be verified and delivered to official receiver] The accounts must, if the official receiver so requires, be verified by a statement of truth and (whether or not so verified) be delivered to the official receiver within 21 days of the request under paragraph (1), or such longer period as the official receiver may allow.

General Note

The official receiver may call for accounts for up to three years past or up to the date of the last audited accounts, or for a longer period on an order of the court.

Professional assistance may be authorised under r.7.45. The official receiver may call for further disclosure under r.7.47.

7.47 Further disclosure

7.47(1) [Official receiver requirement to nominated person] The official receiver may at any time require a nominated person to deliver (in writing) further information amplifying, modifying or explaining any matter contained in the statement of affairs, or in accounts delivered under the Act or these Rules.

7.47(2) [Information to be verified and delivered to official receiver] The information must, if the official receiver so directs, be verified by a statement of truth, and (whether or not so verified) be delivered to the official receiver within 21 days of the requirement under paragraph (1), or such longer period as the official receiver may allow.

General Note

This rule should be read in conjunction with rr.7.41 et seq. (statement of affairs) and r.7.46 (delivery of accounts).

Chapter 7

Reports and information to creditors and contributories

[Note: a document required by the Act or these Rules must also contain the standard contents set out in Part 1.]

7.48 Reports by official receiver

7.48(1) [Duty to report on winding up and state of company's affairs] The official receiver must deliver a report on the winding up and the state of the company's affairs to the creditors and contributories at least once after the making of the winding-up order.

7.48(2) [Content of report] The report must contain–

(a) identification details for the proceedings;

(b) contact details for the official receiver;

(c) a summary of the assets and liabilities of the company as known to the official receiver at the date of the report;

(d) such comments on the summary and the company's affairs as the official receiver thinks fit; and

(e) any other information of relevance to the creditors or contributories.

7.48(3) [Application for relief from duty] The official receiver may apply to the court to be relieved of any duty imposed by this rule or to be authorised to carry out the duty in another way.

7.48(4) [Matters court to have regard to] On such an application the court must have regard to the cost of carrying out the duty, to the amount of the assets available, and to the extent of the interest of creditors or contributories, or any particular class of them.

7.48(5) [Cessation of duty on stay of proceedings] If proceedings in a winding-up are stayed by order of the court any duty of the official receiver to deliver a report under this rule ceases.

General Note

See also General Note after r.7.51.

7.49 Reports by official receiver: estimate of prescribed part

7.49(1) [Prescribed part] The official receiver must include in a report under rule 7.48(1) estimates to the best of the official receiver's knowledge and belief of the value of–

(a) the prescribed part (whether or not the official receiver might be required under section 176A to make the prescribed part available for the satisfaction of unsecured debts); and

(b) the company's net property (as defined by section 176A(6)).

7.49(2) [Report to state if official receiver proposes application under IA 1986 s.176(5)] If the official receiver (as liquidator) proposes to make an application to court under section 176A(5) the report must say so and give the reason for the application.

7.49(3) [Exclusion of seriously prejudicial information] The official receiver may exclude from an estimate under paragraph (1) information the disclosure of which could seriously prejudice the commercial interests of the company.

7.49(4) [Where exclusion affects calculation of estimate] If the exclusion of such information affects the calculation of the estimate, the report must say so.

(See General Note after r.7.51.)

7.50 Further information where winding up follows administration

7.50(1) [Liquidator becomes aware of creditors not formerly known to him as administrator] This rule applies where an administrator is appointed by the court under section 140 as the company's liquidator and becomes aware of creditors not formerly known to that person as administrator.

7.50(2) [Liquidator to deliver statement of administrator's proposals] The liquidator must deliver to those creditors a copy of any statement previously sent by the administrator to creditors in accordance with paragraph 49(4) of Schedule B1 and rule 3.35.

(See General Note after r.7.51.)

7.51 Notice of stay of winding up

7.51 Where the court grants a stay in a winding up it may include in its order such requirements on the company as it thinks just with a view to bringing the stay to the notice of creditors and contributories.

General Note to rr.7.48–7.51

These rules are designed to ensure that creditors and contributories are kept informed of the state of the company's affairs in the various situations referred to.

It has been a rule at common law for over a century that a liquidator is under a duty to find out from the books and papers of the company and the statement of affairs who the creditors of the company are, and that he may be liable in damages to any creditors who have been overlooked: *Pulsford v Devenish* [1903] 2 Ch. 625.

Progress reporting requirements of liquidators appear in Pt 18 (see rr.18.3, 18.7, 18.8 (progress reports to Companies House using Form WU01), 18.10) but these do not apply to the official receiver acting as liquidator (r.18.1).

Chapter 8

The liquidator

[Note: a document required by the Act or these Rules must also contain the standard contents set out in Part 1.]

7.52 Choosing a person to be liquidator

7.52(1) [Application of rule] This rule applies where nominations are sought by the official receiver from the company's creditors and contributories under section 136 for the purpose of choosing a person to be liquidator of the company in place of the official receiver.

7.52(2) [Duty of official receiver] The official receiver must deliver to the creditors and contributories a notice inviting proposals for a liquidator.

7.52(3) [Notice] The notice must explain that the official receiver is not obliged to seek the creditors' views on any proposals that do not meet the requirements of paragraphs (4) and (5).

7.52(4) [Proposal to provide details as to proposed liquidator] A proposal must state the name and contact details of the proposed liquidator, and contain a statement that the proposed liquidator is qualified to act as an insolvency practitioner in relation to the company and has consented to act as liquidator of the company.

7.52(5) [Time limit for proposals] A proposal must be received by the official receiver within five business days of the date of the notice under paragraph (2).

7.52(6) [Official receiver to seek decision from creditors on nomination of liquidator] Following the end of the period for inviting proposals under paragraph (2), where any proposals are received the official receiver must seek a decision on the nomination of a liquidator from the creditors (on any proposals received from creditors) and from the contributories (on any proposals received from contributories) by–

(a) a decision procedure; or

(b) the deemed consent procedure.

7.52(7) [Decision date] Where a decision is sought under paragraph (6) following the official receiver's decision under section 136(5)(a) to seek a nomination, the decision date must be not more than four months from the date of the winding-up order.

7.52(8) [Official receiver to notify creditors as to deemed consent and decision procedure] Where the official receiver is required under section 136(5)(c) to seek such a decision, the official receiver must send a notice to the creditors and contributories which complies with rule 15.7 or 15.8 so far as relevant.

7.52(9) [Further content of notice] The notice must also–

(a) identify any liquidator proposed to be nominated by a creditor (in the case of a notice to creditors) or by a contributory (in the case of a notice to contributories) in accordance with this rule; and

(b) contain a statement explaining the effect of section 137(2) (duty of official receiver to consider referral of need for appointment of liquidator to the Secretary of State where no person is chosen to be liquidator).

7.52(10) [Decision date from date for receiving proposals] The decision date in the notice must be no later than 21 days after the date for receiving proposals has passed.

7.52(11) [Notice of decision date to creditors] The creditors and contributories must be given at least 14 days' notice of the decision date.

7.52(12) [No proposals received under r.7.52(9)] Where no proposal is received by the official receiver under paragraph (2), the official receiver has no obligation to seek a decision from creditors or contributories on a liquidator.

7.52(13) [Official receiver's power to replace himself as liquidator] Nothing in this rule affects the official receiver's ability under section 137(1), at any time when liquidator of the company, to apply to the Secretary of State to appoint a liquidator in place of the official receiver.

(See General Note after r.7.57.)

7.53 Appointment of liquidator by creditors or contributories

7.53(1) [Application of rule] This rule applies where a person is appointed as liquidator by the creditors or contributories.

7.53(2) [Certification of appointment] The convener of the decision procedure or deemed consent procedure, or the chair in the case of a meeting must certify the appointment, but not unless and until the appointee has provided to the convener or the chair a statement to the effect that the appointee is an insolvency practitioner qualified under the Act to be the liquidator and consents to act.

7.53(3) [Authentication of certification] The certificate must be authenticated and dated by the convener or chair and must–

(a) identify the company;

(b) identify and provide contact details for the person appointed as liquidator;

(c) state the date on which the liquidator was appointed;

(d) state that the appointee–

(i) has provided a statement of being qualified to act as an insolvency practitioner in relation to the company,

(ii) has consented to act, and

(iii) was appointed as liquidator of the company.

7.53(4) [Acts by multiple liquidators] Where two or more liquidators are appointed the certificate must also specify (as required by section 231) whether any act required or authorised under any enactment to be done by the liquidator is to be done by all or any one or more of them.

7.53(5) [Date appointment effective] The liquidator's appointment is effective from the date on which the appointment is certified, that date to be endorsed on the certificate.

7.53(6) [Convener/chair to deliver certificate to official receiver] The convener or chair (if that person is not the official receiver) must deliver the certificate to the official receiver.

7.53(7) [Official receiver to deliver certificate to liquidator] The official receiver must in any case deliver the certificate to the liquidator.

(See General Note after r.7.57.)

7.54 Decision on nomination

7.54(1) [Multiple nominees] In the case of a decision on the nomination of a liquidator–

(a) if on any vote there are two nominees, the person who obtains the most support is appointed;

(b) if there are three or more nominees, and one of them has a clear majority over both or all the others together, that one is appointed; and

(c) in any other case, the convener or chair must continue to take votes (disregarding at each vote any nominee who has withdrawn and, if no nominee has withdrawn, the nominee who obtained the least support last time) until a clear majority is obtained for any one nominee.

7.54(2) [Decision at meeting] In the case of a decision being made at a meeting, the chair may at any time put to the meeting a resolution for the joint nomination of any two or more nominees.

(See General Note after r.7.57.)

7.55 Invitation to creditors and contributories to form a liquidation committee

7.55(1) [Convener to deliver invitation notice to and contributories] Where a decision is sought from the company's creditors and contributories on the appointment of a liquidator, the convener of the decision must at the same time deliver to the creditors and contributories a notice inviting them to decide whether a liquidation committee should be established if sufficient creditors are willing to be members of the committee.

7.55(2) [Notice to invite nominations for membership of committee] The notice must also invite nominations for membership of the committee, such nominations to be received by a date specified in the notice.

7.55(3) [Content of notice] The notice must–

(a) state that nominations must be delivered to the convener by the specified date;

(b) state, in the case of creditors, that nominations can only be accepted if the convener is satisfied as to the creditors' eligibility under rule 17.4; and

(c) explain the effect of section 141(2) and (3) on whether a committee is to be established under Part 17.

(See General Note after r.7.57.)

7.56 Appointment by the court

7.56(1) [Application of rule] This rule applies where the liquidator is appointed by the court under section 139(4) (different persons nominated by creditors and contributories) or section 140 (winding up following administration or CVA).

7.56(2) [Statement as to qualification and consent to act] The court must not make the order unless and until the person being appointed has filed with the court a statement to the effect that that person is an insolvency practitioner, duly qualified under the Act to be the liquidator, and consents to act.

7.56(3) [Content of court order] The order of the court must contain–

(a) identification details for the proceedings;

(b) the name and title of the judge making the order;

(c) the name and postal address of the applicant;

(d) the capacity in which the applicant made the application;

(e) identification and contact details for the proposed liquidator;

(f) a statement that the proposed liquidator has filed–

(i) a statement of qualification to act as an insolvency practitioner in relation to the company, and

(ii) a consent to act;

(g) the order that the proposed liquidator is appointed liquidator of the company; and

(h) the date on which the order is made.

7.56(4) [Acts by multiple liquidators] Where two or more liquidators are appointed the order must also specify (as required by section 231) whether any act required or authorised under any enactment to be done by the liquidator is to be done by all or any one or more of them.

7.56(5) [Copies of order to official receiver; one sealed] The court must deliver two copies of the order to the official receiver one of which must be sealed.

7.56(6) [Sealed copy to liquidator] The official receiver must deliver the sealed copy of the order to the person appointed as liquidator.

7.56(7) [Date appointment effective] The liquidator's appointment takes effect from the date of the order or such other date as the court orders.

7.56(8) [Liquidator must to deliver notice of appointment to creditors and advertise] Within 28 days from appointment, the liquidator must–

(a) deliver notice of the appointment to the creditors and to the contributories of the company of whom the liquidator is aware; or

(b) advertise the appointment in accordance with any directions given by the court.

7.56(9) [Content of notice] In the notice under this rule the liquidator must–

(a) state whether the liquidator proposes to seek decisions from creditors and contributories for the purpose of establishing a liquidation committee, or proposes only to seek a decision from creditors for that purpose; and

(b) if the liquidator does not propose to seek any such decision, set out the powers of the creditors under the Act to require the liquidator to seek one.

(See General Note after r.7.57.)

7.57 Appointment by the Secretary of State

7.57(1) [Replacement of official receiver] This rule applies where the official receiver applies to the Secretary of State to appoint a liquidator in place of the official receiver, or refers to the Secretary of State the need for an appointment.

7.57(2) [Copy certificate of appointment to official receiver] If the Secretary of State makes an appointment, the Secretary of State must deliver a copy of the certificate of appointment to the official receiver, who must deliver it to the person appointed.

7.57(3) [Date appointment effective] The certificate must specify the date from which the liquidator's appointment is to be effective.

General Note to rr.7.52–7.57

These rules are concerned with the formalities relating to the appointment of a liquidator by the creditors or contributories (rr.7.52–7.54), whether they wish to form a liquidation committee (r.7.55), and appointment of a liquidator by the court (r.7.56) and by the Secretary of State (r.7.57).

By virtue of his office the official receiver becomes liquidator of the company but has a discretion to seek nominations from the creditors and contributories to nominate another person (who must be fully authorised to act as an insolvency practitioner or partially authorised so to act in relation to companies: IA 1986 s.390A) to act as liquidator: IA 1986 s.136. Rule 7.52 deals with notice from the official receiver where he exercises that discretion to seek nominations, with relevant time limits; if he receives no proposals he is not required to seek a decision from the creditors or contributories. In any event, the official receiver may apply to the Secretary of State to appoint a liquidator in his place.

The invitation in r.7.55 to creditors or contributories to form a liquidation committee is placed here as the convener of their decision to appoint a liquidator must at the same time deliver a notice inviting them to decide whether a liquidation committee should be established. See IA 1986 s.141 and IR 2016 Pt 17 on liquidation committees.

7.58 Cost of liquidator's security (section 390(3))

7.58 The cost of the liquidator's security required by section 390(3) for the proper performance of the liquidator's functions is an expense of the winding up.

General Note

The security is a requirement under IA 1986 s.390(3) of being qualified to act as an insolvency practitioner.

7.59 Appointment to be gazetted and notice given to registrar of companies

7.59(1) [Duty of liquidator] The liquidator–

(a) must gazette a notice of the appointment as soon as reasonably practicable after appointment; and

(b) may advertise the notice in such other manner as the liquidator thinks fit.

7.59(2) [Content of notice] The notice must state–

(a) that a liquidator has been appointed; and

(b) the date of the appointment.

7.59(3) [Notice to registrar of companies] As soon as reasonably practicable the liquidator must deliver notice of the appointment to the registrar of companies.

General Note

The liquidator was formerly required to give notice of his appointment in an appropriate newspaper as well as in the *Gazette*. It is now for him to decide in his discretion whether additional advertisement is needed.

The notice of the liquidator's appointment must include the standard contents and also the details set out in r.7.59(2). On the standard contents for gazetted notices, see rr.1.10–1.12. On the standard contents for notices other than gazetted notices, see rr.1.15, 1.16, 1.18. On the standard contents for notices to be delivered to the registrar of companies, see rr.1.19, 1.21, 1.22. The notice of appointment delivered to Companies House must be in Form WU04.

7.60 Hand-over of assets by official receiver to liquidator

7.60(1) [Application of rule] This rule only applies where the liquidator is appointed in succession to the official receiver acting as liquidator.

7.60(2) [On liquidator's appointment] When the liquidator's appointment takes effect, the official receiver must as soon as reasonably practicable do all that is required for putting the liquidator into possession of the assets.

7.60(3) [Discharge balance due to official receiver] On taking possession of the assets, the liquidator must discharge any balance due to the official receiver on account of–

(a) expenses properly incurred by the official receiver and payable under the Act or these Rules; and

(b) any advances made by the official receiver in respect of the assets, together with interest on such advances at the rate specified in section 17 of the Judgments Act 1838 at the date of the winding-up order.

7.60(4) [Undertaking to discharge balance] Alternatively, the liquidator may (before taking office) give to the official receiver a written undertaking to discharge any such balance out of the first realisation of assets.

7.60(5) [Official receiver's charge on assets] The official receiver has a charge on the assets in respect of any sums due to the official receiver under paragraph (3) until they have been discharged, subject only to the deduction from realisations by the liquidator of the proper costs and expenses of such realisations.

7.60(6) [Discharge of guarantees] The liquidator must from time to time out of the realisation of assets discharge all guarantees properly given by the official receiver for the benefit of the insolvent estate, and must pay all the official receiver's expenses.

7.60(7) [Official receiver to give liquidator information] The official receiver must give to the liquidator all such information relating to the affairs of the company and the course of the winding up as the official receiver considers to be reasonably required for the effective discharge by the liquidator of the liquidator's duties.

7.60(8) [Copy official receiver's report to liquidator] The official receiver must also deliver to the liquidator a copy of any report made by the official receiver under Chapter 7 of Part 7.

General Note

This rule applies following the appointment of a private liquidator under IA 1986 ss.136 and 139, or s.137.

7.61 Liquidator's resignation

7.61(1) [Grounds for resignation] A liquidator may resign only–

(a) on grounds of ill health;

(b) because of the intention to cease to practise as an insolvency practitioner;

(c) because the further discharge of the duties of liquidator is prevented or made impracticable by–

(i) a conflict of interest, or

(ii) a change of personal circumstances;

(d) where two or more persons are acting as liquidator jointly, and it is the opinion of both or all of them that it is no longer expedient that there should continue to be that number of joint liquidators.

7.61(2) [Notice to creditors; invitation for replacement] Before resigning, the liquidator must deliver a notice to creditors, and invite the creditors by a decision procedure, or by deemed consent procedure, to consider whether a replacement should be appointed, except where the resignation is under sub-paragraph (1)(d).

7.61(3) [Content of notice] The notice must–

(a) state the liquidator's intention to resign;

(b) state that under rule 7.61(7) of these Rules the liquidator will be released 21 days after the date of delivery of the notice of resignation to the court under section 172(6), unless the court orders otherwise; and

(c) comply with rule 15.7 or 15.8 so far as applicable.

7.61(4) [Suggested replacement] The notice may suggest the name of a replacement liquidator.

7.61(5) [Summary of receipts and payments] The notice must be accompanied by a summary of the liquidator's receipts and payments.

7.61(6) [Decision date] The decision date must be not more than five business days before the date on which the liquidator intends to give notice under section 172(6).

7.61(7) [Date of release of liquidator] The resigning liquidator's release is effective 21 days after the date on which the notice of resignation under section 172(6) is filed with the court.

(See General Note after r.7.62.)

7.62 Notice to official receiver of intention to vacate office

7.62(1) [Application of rule] This rule applies where the liquidator intends to vacate office, whether by resignation or otherwise, and as a result there will be a vacancy in the office of liquidator (so that by virtue of section 136(3) the official receiver is liquidator until the vacancy is filled).

7.62(2) [Notice of intention to official receiver] The liquidator must deliver notice of that intention to the official receiver at least 21 days before the liquidator intends to vacate office.

7.62(3) [Content of notice] The liquidator must include in the notice to the official receiver the following details of any property of the company which has not been realised, applied, distributed or otherwise fully dealt with in the winding up–

(a) the nature of the property;

(b) its value (or the fact that it has no value);

(c) its location;

(d) any action taken by the liquidator to deal with the property or any reason for the liquidator not dealing with it; and

(e) the current position in relation to it.

General Note to rr.7.61–7.62

The only circumstances in which a liquidator may resign are set out in r.7.61(1) and the rule goes on to detail the procedure to be followed concerning his notice to creditors, their decision and the date of the liquidator's release. Rule 7.62 covers notice by the liquidator to the official receiver of the liquidator's intention to vacate office whether by resignation "or otherwise" if there will then be a vacancy as liquidator.

7.63 Decision of creditors to remove liquidator

7.63(1) [Convener/chair not official receiver; decision procedure] This rule applies where the convener of the decision procedure or chair of the meeting (as the case may be) is other than the official receiver, and a decision is made, using a decision procedure, to remove the liquidator

7.63(2) [Certificate of removal to official receiver] The convener or chair must within three business days of the decision to remove the liquidator deliver a certificate to that effect to the official receiver.

7.63(3) [Certificate of new liquidator's appointment] If the creditors decided to appoint a new liquidator, the certificate of the new liquidator's appointment must also be delivered to the official receiver within that time; and the certificate must comply with the requirements in rule 7.53.

7.63(4) [Content of certificate of removal] The certificate of the liquidator's removal must–

(a) identify the company;

(b) identify and provide contact details for the removed liquidator;

(c) state that the creditors of the company decided on the date specified in the certificate that the liquidator specified in the certificate be removed from office as liquidator of the company;

(d) state the decision procedure used, and the decision date;

(e) state that the creditors either–

(i) did not decide against the liquidator being released, or

(ii) decided that the liquidator should not be released; and

(f) be authenticated and dated by the convener or chair.

7.63(5) [Date removal effective] The liquidator's removal is effective from the date of the certificate of removal.

(See General Note after r.7.66.)

7.64 Procedure on removal by creditors

7.64(1) [Certificate of removal to be filed in court] Where the creditors have decided that the liquidator be removed, the official receiver must file the certificate of removal with the court.

7.64(2) [Copy certificate to liquidator; notice of removal to registrar of companies] The official receiver must deliver a copy of the certificate as soon as reasonably practicable to the removed liquidator and deliver a notice of the removal to the registrar of companies.

(See General Note after r.7.66.)

7.65 Removal of liquidator by the court (section 172(2))

7.65(1) [Application of rule] This rule applies where an application is made to the court under section 172(2) for the removal of the liquidator, or for an order directing the liquidator to initiate a decision procedure of creditors for the purpose of removing the liquidator.

7.65(2) [Court may dismiss application] On receipt of an application, the court may, if it is satisfied that no sufficient cause is shown for it, dismiss it without giving notice to any party other than the applicant.

7.65(3) [Court to fix venue for hearing] Unless the application is dismissed, the court must fix a venue for it to be heard.

7.65(4) [Notice of hearing with copy application, etc.] The applicant must, at least 14 days before any hearing, deliver to the liquidator and the official receiver a notice stating the venue with a copy of the application and of any evidence on which the applicant intends to rely.

7.65(5) [Security of costs] A respondent may apply for security for costs of the application and the court may make such an order if it is satisfied, having regard to all the circumstances of the case, that it is just to make such an order.

7.65(6) [Liquidators and official receiver may file report and/or appear] The liquidator and the official receiver may do either or both of the following–

(a) file a report of any matters which the liquidator or the official receiver thinks ought to be drawn to the court's attention; or

(b) appear and be heard on the application.

7.65(7) [Content of order] On a successful application the court's order must contain–

(a) the name of the court (and hearing centre if applicable) in which the order is made;

(b) the name and title of the judge making the order;

(c) the name and postal address of the applicant;

(d) the capacity in which the applicant made the application;

(e) identification and contact details for the liquidator;

(f) identification details for the company;

(g) an order either–

   (i) that that the liquidator is removed from office; or

   (ii) that the liquidator must initiate a decision procedure of the company's creditors (specifying which procedure is to be used) on or before the date specified in the order for the purpose of considering the liquidator's removal from office; and

(h) the date the order is made.

7.65(8) [Costs] The costs of the application are not payable as an expense of the winding up unless the court orders otherwise.

7.65(9) [Sealed order etc. to former liquidator; copy to registrar of companies] Where the court removes the liquidator–

(a) it must deliver the sealed order of removal to the former liquidator and a copy of the order to the official receiver; and

(b) the former liquidator must deliver a copy of the order to the registrar of companies as soon as reasonably practicable.

7.65(10) [Appointment of replacement, r.7.56] If the court appoints a new liquidator, rule 7.56 applies.

(See General Note after r.7.66.)

7.66 Removal of liquidator by the Secretary of State (section 172(4))

7.66(1) [Application of rule] This rule applies where the Secretary of State decides to direct under section 172(4) the removal of a liquidator appointed by the Secretary of State.

7.66(2) [Notice to liquidator and official receiver] Before doing so the Secretary of State must deliver to the liquidator and the official receiver a notice of the Secretary of State's decision and the grounds for the decision.

7.66(3) [Period for representations] The notice must specify a period within which the liquidator may make representations against implementation of the decision.

7.66(4) [Notice of removal to registrar, liquidator, official receiver, court] If the Secretary of State directs the removal of the liquidator, the Secretary of State must as soon as reasonably practicable–

(a) deliver notice of the Secretary of State's decision to the registrar of companies, the liquidator and the official receiver; and

(b) file notice of the decision with the court.

7.66(5) [Power of court to make order] Where the Secretary of State directs the liquidator be removed the court may make any order that it could have made if the liquidator had been removed by the court.

General Note to rr.7.63–7.66

The removal of a liquidator is dealt with in IA 1986 ss.171, 172, which these rules supplement. The exercise of the court's discretion under what is now restated as r.7.65(5) was discussed, in the context of creditors' voluntary winding up, in *Re Buildlead Ltd* [2003] EWHC 1981 (Ch); [2003] 4 All E.R. 864; [2005] B.C.C. 133; and *Re Buildlead Ltd (No.2)* [2004] EWHC 2443 (Ch); [2005] B.C.C. 138. On the liquidator's release, see r.7.69. Costs on an indemnity basis may be awarded against a liquidator who unreasonably resists an application for his removal: *Shepheard v Lamey* [2001] B.P.I.R. 939. The notice of removal by creditors, the court or the Secretary of State to be delivered under rr.7.64, 7.65 or 7.66 to Companies House must be respectively in Form WU08, WU14 (with a copy of the order) or WU10.

Where an insolvency practitioner holds multiple offices and application is made to the court for a "block transfer" order, to remove him from all the offices and appoint a suitable replacement, the court has jurisdiction to bypass the procedures laid down in these rules (and the corresponding rules for the removal of other office-holders) where it is satisfied that no useful purpose will be served by seeking decisions of creditors (formerly by holding meetings): see *Re Alt Landscapes Ltd* [1999] B.P.I.R. 459; *Re Equity Nominees Ltd* [2000] B.C.C. 84, and the note to s.172(1), (2). For the relevant rules, see rr.12.35–12.38.

7.67 Deceased liquidator

7.67(1) [Notice to official receiver, who by] If the liquidator (not being the official receiver) dies a notice of the fact and date of death must be delivered to the official receiver by one of the following–

(a) a surviving joint liquidator;

(b) a member of the deceased liquidator's firm (if the deceased was a member or employee of a firm);

(c) an officer of the deceased liquidator's company (if the deceased was an officer or employee of a company);

(d) a personal representative of the deceased liquidator.

7.67(2) [Notice by any other person] If no such notice has been delivered within the 21 days following the liquidator's death then any other person may deliver the notice.

7.67(3) [Notice to court, copy to registrar of companies] The official receiver must–

(a) file notice of the death with the court, for the purpose of fixing the date of the deceased liquidator's release under section 174(4)(a); and

(b) deliver a copy of the notice to the registrar of companies.

(See General Note after r.7.68.)

7.68 Loss of qualification as insolvency practitioner

7.68(1) [Application of rule] This rule applies where the liquidator vacates office on ceasing to be qualified to act as an insolvency practitioner in relation to the company.

7.68(2) [Notice to official receiver, who by] A notice of the fact must be delivered as soon as reasonably practicable to the official receiver by one of the following–

(a) the liquidator who has vacated office;

(b) a continuing joint liquidator;

(c) the recognised professional body which was the source of the vacating liquidator's authorisation to act in relation to the company.

7.68(3) [Authentication of notice] The notice must be authenticated and dated by the person delivering the notice.

7.68(4) [Notice to Secretary of State, copy to registrar of company] The official receiver must–

(a) deliver a notice of receiving such a notice to the Secretary of State; and

(b) deliver a copy to the registrar of companies.

General Note to rr.7.67–7.68

Apart from resignation and removal, which are dealt with in rr.7.61–7.66, the office of liquidator may be vacated by death or disqualification. The present rules are concerned with these situations. Notice to Companies House on death of loss of qualification must be respectively in Form WU11 or WU12.

7.69 Application by liquidator for release (section 174(4)(b) or (d))

7.69(1) [Content] An application by a liquidator to the Secretary of State for release under section 174(4)(b) or (d) must contain–

(a) identification details for the proceedings;

(b) identification and contact details for the liquidator;

(c) a statement that the liquidator of the company is applying to the Secretary of State to grant the liquidator with a certificate of the liquidator's release as liquidator as a result of the circumstances specified in the application;

(d) details of the circumstances referred to in sub-paragraph (c) under which the liquidator has ceased to act as liquidator.

7.69(2) [Authentication] The application must be authenticated and dated by the liquidator.

7.69(3) [Certificate of release and certificate to former liquidator] When the Secretary of State releases the former liquidator, the Secretary of State must certify the release and deliver the certificate to the former liquidator whose release is effective from the date of the certificate or such other date as the certificate specifies.

7.69(4) [Notice to registrar of companies] The Secretary of State must deliver notice of the release to the registrar of companies.

(See General Note after r.7.72.)

7.70 Release of official receiver

7.70(1) [Notice of intention] The official receiver must, before giving notice to the Secretary of State under section 174(3) (that the winding up is for practical purposes complete), deliver notice of intention to do so to the creditors.

7.70(2) [Accompanying summary receipts and payments] The notice must be accompanied by a summary of the official receiver's receipts and payments as liquidator.

7.70(3) [Summary to include amount paid under prescribed part] The summary of receipts and payments must also include a statement as to the amount paid to unsecured creditors under section 176A (prescribed part).

7.70(4) [Notice to official receiver, registrar of companies] When the Secretary of State has determined the date from which the official receiver's release is to be effective, the Secretary of State must–

(a) notify the official receiver of the release; and

(b) deliver a notice of the release to the registrar of companies accompanied by the summary of the official receiver's receipts and payments.

(See General Note after r.7.72.)

7.71 Final account prior to dissolution (section 146)

7.71(1) [Account to company with r.18.14] The final account which the liquidator is required to make up under section 146(2) and deliver to creditors must comply with the requirements of rule 18.14.

7.71(2) [Content of notice accompanying account] When the account is delivered to the creditors it must be accompanied by a notice which states–

(a) that the company's affairs are fully wound up;

(b) that the creditor has the right to request information from the liquidator under rule 18.9;

(c) that a creditor has the right to challenge the liquidator's remuneration and expenses under rule 18.34;

(d) that a creditor may object to the release of the liquidator by giving notice in writing to the liquidator before the end of the prescribed period;

(e) that the prescribed period is the period ending at the later of–

(i) eight weeks after delivery of the notice, or

(ii) if any request for information under rule 18.9 or any application to court under that rule or rule 18.34 is made when that request or application is finally determined;

(f) that the liquidator will vacate office under section 172(8) as soon as the liquidator has complied with section 146(4) by filing with the court and delivering to the registrar of companies the final account and notice containing the statement required by section 146(4)(b) of whether any creditors have objected to the liquidator's release; and

(g) that the liquidator will be released under section 174(4)(d)(ii) at the same time as vacating office unless any of the creditors objected to the release.

7.71(3) [Copy notice to Secretary of State] The liquidator must deliver a copy of the notice under section 146(4) to the Secretary of State.

7.71(4) [Application of r.7.69] Rule 7.69 applies to an application by the liquidator to the Secretary of State for release.

(See General Note after r.7.72.)

7.72 Relief from, or variation of, duty to report

7.72(1) [Power of court] The court may, on the application of the liquidator or the official receiver, relieve the liquidator or official receiver of any duty imposed on the liquidator or official receiver by rule

7.70 or rule 7.71, or authorise the liquidator or official receiver to carry out the duty in a way other than required by either of those rules.

7.72(2) [Matters court to have regard to] In considering whether to act under this rule, the court must have regard to the cost of carrying out the duty, to the amount of the assets available, and to the extent of the interest of creditors or contributories, or any particular class of them.

GENERAL NOTE TO RR.7.69–7.72

These rules deal with the liquidator's release following his removal and following the completion of his administration of the estate (r.7.69), release of the official receiver (r.7.70), the liquidator's final account (r.7.71) and relief from certain duties in relation thereto (r.7.72). On the question of the liquidator's release upon his resignation, see r.7.61(7).

Under r.7.69 it is the Secretary of State who must determine the time of the release of a liquidator (other than the official receiver) who has been removed and the creditors have decided against his release, or who has vacated office after sending the final account but the creditors have objected in required time to the release; otherwise, if the liquidator has completed the estate, the release is automatic when he vacates office. Note the extra details in r.7.71 of the final account when the winding up is complete (required by IA 1986 s.146(2)) to be sent to creditors (unless opted out), to the court and to the registrar of companies) in addition to the standard contents in rr.1.19–1.22; the account must also comply with r.18.14. Forms WU09 and WU15 are used for notice of release and final account to Companies House under rr.7.70 and 7.71. Note that r.7.72 allows for dispensation by the court for the liquidator or official receiver from the duties in rr.7.70 and 7.71.

7.73 Liquidator's duties on vacating office

7.73(1) [Duty to deliver up assets, etc., to successor liquidator] A liquidator who ceases to be in office in consequence of removal, resignation or ceasing to be qualified to act as an insolvency practitioner in relation to the company, must as soon as reasonably practicable deliver to the successor as liquidator–

(a) the assets (after deduction of any expenses properly incurred, and distributions made, by the previous liquidator);

(b) the records of the winding up, including correspondence, proofs and other documents relating to the winding up while it was within the former liquidator's responsibility; and

(c) the company's documents and other records.

7.73(2) [Vacation following final account] Where the liquidator vacates office under section 172(8) (final report to creditors), the liquidator must deliver to the official receiver the company's documents and other records which have not already been disposed of in accordance with general regulations in the course of the winding up.

GENERAL NOTE

This ensures that a liquidator who vacated office other than on death or completion of the winding up is required to deliver the net assets, his records (including proofs) of the winding up and the company's records to his successor liquidator—and thereby closes a gap in the former law. If the winding up was completed, only the company's records and other documents not disposed of need be delivered by the liquidator to the official receiver.

7.74 Power of court to set aside certain transactions

7.74(1) [Transactions with associates of liquidator] If in dealing with the insolvent estate the liquidator enters into any transaction with a person who is an associate of the liquidator, the court may, on the application of any interested person, set the transaction aside and order the liquidator to compensate the company for any loss suffered in consequence of it.

7.74(2) [Non-application if with consent, for value, etc.] This does not apply if either–

(a) the transaction was entered into with the prior consent of the court; or

(b) it is shown to the court's satisfaction that the transaction was for value, and that it was entered into by the liquidator without knowing, or having any reason to suppose, that the person concerned was an associate.

7.74(3) [Dealings with trust property, etc.] Nothing in this rule is to be taken as prejudicing the operation of any rule of law or equity relating to a liquidator's dealings with trust property, or the fiduciary obligations of any person.

General Note

This rule imposes statutory duties of a fiduciary character on a liquidator, supplementing the rules of equity and the common law. For the meaning of "associate", see IA 1986 s.435.

7.75 Rule against improper solicitation

7.75(1) [Power of court] Where the court is satisfied that any improper solicitation has been used by or on behalf of the liquidator in obtaining proxies or procuring the liquidator's appointment, it may order that no remuneration be allowed as an expense of the winding up to any person by whom, or on whose behalf, the solicitation was exercised.

7.75(2) [Effect of court order] An order of the court under this rule overrides any resolution of the liquidation committee or the creditors, or any other provision of these Rules relating to the liquidator's remuneration.

General Note

This rule similarly supplements principles of equity and the common law; and see also IA 1986 s.164 (corrupt inducement affecting liquidator's appointment).

Chapter 9

Duties and powers of liquidator

[Note: a document required by the Act or these Rules must also contain the standard contents set out in Part 1.]

7.76 General duties of liquidator

7.76(1) [Officer of the court] The duties which the Act imposes on the court relating to the collection of the company's assets and their application in discharge of the company's liabilities are discharged by the liquidator as an officer of the court subject to its control.

7.76(2) [Same powers a receiver] In the discharge of the liquidator's duties, the liquidator, for the purposes of acquiring and retaining possession of the company's property, has the same powers as a receiver appointed by the High Court, and the court may on the application of the liquidator enforce such acquisition or retention accordingly.

General Note

For the statutory source of this rule, see IA 1986 ss.148(1), 160(1)(b).

7.77 Permission for exercise of powers by liquidator

7.77(1) [Particular, not general, permission] Where the Act or these Rules require permission for the liquidator to exercise a power any permission given must not be a general permission but must relate to a particular proposed exercise of the liquidator's power.

7.77(2) [Person in good faith and for value] A person dealing with the liquidator in good faith and for value is not concerned to enquire whether any such permission has been given.

7.77(3) [Ratification] Where the liquidator has done anything without such permission, the court or the liquidation committee may, for the purpose of enabling the liquidator to meet the liquidator's expenses out of the assets, ratify what the liquidator has done; but neither must do so unless satisfied that the liquidator has acted in a case of urgency and has sought ratification without undue delay.

7.77(4) ["Permission"] In this rule "permission" includes "sanction".

General Note

The powers referred to in IA 1986 are set out in Sch.4 to that Act. Many of these powers formerly required the sanction of the liquidation committee, the creditors or the court, but the requirement of sanction was totally abolished by SBEEA 2015 with effect from 26 May 2015. (See the note to s.167.) This rule will therefore be relevant only to acts of a liquidator prior to that date.

In *Gresham International Ltd v Moonie* [2009] EWHC 1093 (Ch); [2010] Ch. 285 the liquidator, who had commenced proceedings without obtaining sanction, applied to the court to have it granted retrospectively. The court ruled that this would be appropriate in cases of inadvertent failure but declined to make an order with retrospective effect where this was not so and the requirements of r.4.184(2) had not been met. Contrast *Mather & Fry v Bovey* (unreported, 25 June 2014) (mere inadvertence, retrospective sanction granted). Where one of the purposes of a meeting is to seek approval for the payment of pre-administration costs, the Insolvency Service has directed that this purpose should be identified as a separate resolution in the notice of meeting (or equivalent), in order to ensure maximum transparency to creditors: see *Dear IP*, September 2014, p.1.46.

7.78 Enforced delivery up of company's property (section 234)

7.78(1) [Powers of court exercisable by liquidator] The powers conferred on the court by section 234 (enforced delivery of company property) are exercisable by the liquidator or, where a provisional liquidator has been appointed, by the provisional liquidator.

7.78(2) [Duty to comply] Any person on whom a requirement under section 234(2) is imposed by the liquidator or provisional liquidator must, without avoidable delay, comply with it.

General Note

For the statutory source of this rule, see IA 1986 ss.160(1)(c), 234.

Chapter 10

Settlement of list of contributories

[Note: a document required by the Act or these Rules must also contain the standard contents set out in Part 1.]

7.79 Delegation to liquidator of power to settle list of contributories

7.79(1) [Duties of court delegated to liquidator] The duties of the court under section 148 in relation to settling the list of contributories are, by virtue of these Rules and in accordance with section 160, delegated to the liquidator.

7.79(2) [Liquidator's duties as officer of court] The liquidator's duties in settling the list of contributories are performed as an officer of the court subject to the court's control.

(See General Note after r.7.80.)

7.80 Duty of liquidator to settle list (section 148)

7.80 The liquidator must, as soon as reasonably possible after the liquidator's appointment, exercise the court's power to settle a list of the company's contributories for the purposes of section 148 and, with the court's approval, rectify the register of members.

General Note to rr.7.79–7.80

For the statutory source of these rules, see IA 1986 ss.148, 160(1)(b).

7.81 Contents of list

7.81(1) [List to identify]The list must identify–

(a) the several classes of the company's shares (if more than one); and

(b) the several classes of contributories, distinguishing between those who are contributories in their own right and those who are so as representatives of, or liable for the debts of, others.

7.81(2) [Further content] In the case of each contributory the list must state–

(a) the address of the contributory;

(b) the number and class of shares, or the extent of any other interest to be attributed to the contributory; and

(c) if the shares are not fully paid up, the amounts which have been called up and paid in respect of them (and the equivalent, if any, where the interest of the contributory is other than shares).

(See General Note after r.7.85.)

7.82 Procedure for settling list

7.82(1) [Notice to those on list] Having settled the list, the liquidator must as soon as reasonably practicable deliver a notice, to each person included in the list, that this has been done.

7.82(2) [Content of notice] The notice given to each person must state–

(a) in what character, and for what number of shares or what interest, that person is included in the list;

(b) what amounts have been called up and paid up in respect of the shares or interest; and

(c) that in relation to any shares or interest not fully paid up, that person's inclusion in the list may result in the unpaid capital being called.

7.82(3) [Information as to objection] The notice must inform a person to whom it is given that, if that person objects to any entry in, or omission from, the list, that person should so inform the liquidator in writing within 21 days from the date of the notice.

7.82(4) [Notice to objector] On receipt of an objection, the liquidator must within 14 days deliver a notice to the objector either–

(a) that the liquidator has amended the list (specifying the amendment); or

(b) that the liquidator considers the objection to be not well-founded and declines to amend the list.

7.82(5) [Objector may apply to court] The notice must in either case inform the objector of the effect of rule 7.83.

(See General Note after r.7.85.)

7.83 Application to court for variation of the list

7.83(1) [Application by objector] If a person ("the objector") objects to any entry in, or exclusion from, the list of contributories as settled by the liquidator and, notwithstanding notice by the liquidator declining to amend the list, the objector maintains the objection, the objector may apply to the court for an order removing the entry objected to or (as the case may be) otherwise amending the list.

7.83(2) [Time limit for application] The application must be made within 21 days of the delivery to the applicant of the liquidator's notice under rule 7.82(4).

(See General Note after r.7.85.)

7.84 Variation of, or addition to, the list

7.84 The liquidator may from time to time vary or add to the list of contributories as previously settled by the liquidator, but subject in all respects to the preceding rules in this Chapter.

(See General Note after r.7.85.)

7.85 Costs of applications to vary etc. the list of contributories

7.85 Where a person applies to set aside or vary any act or decision of the liquidator in settling the list of contributories then–

(a) the liquidator (if other than the official receiver) is not liable for any costs incurred by that person in relation to the application unless the court makes an order to that effect; and

(b) the official receiver is not personally liable for such costs.

General Note to rr.7.81–7.85

Here are set out the rules prescribing the form of the list of contributories and the procedure for settling it. Note that the power to rectify the register of members may be exercised only with the special leave of the court: IA 1986 s.160(2), r.7.80.

Chapter 11

Calls on contributories

[Note: a document required by the Act or these Rules must also contain the standard contents set out in Part 1.]

7.86 Making of calls by the liquidator (sections 150 and 160)

7.86(1) [Liquidator as officer of court] Subject as follows the powers relating to the making of calls on contributories are exercisable by the liquidator as an officer of the court.

7.86(2) [Sanction of liquidation committee or court permission required] However as provided by section 160(2) the making of a call requires either the sanction of the liquidation committee or the court's special permission.

(See General Note after r.7.91.)

7.87 Sanction of the liquidation committee for making a call

7.87(1) [Liquidator may summon a meeting for sanction] Where the liquidator proposes to make a call, and there is a liquidation committee, the liquidator may summon a meeting of the committee for the purpose of obtaining its sanction.

7.87(2) [Notice of meeting] The liquidator must deliver a notice of the meeting to each member of the committee giving at least five business days' notice of the meeting.

7.87(3) [Content of notice] The notice must state the purpose of making the call and the proposed amount of the call.

(See General Note after r.7.91.)

7.88 Application to court for permission to make a call (sections 150 and 160)

7.88(1) [Application without notice] Where the liquidator proposes to make a call the liquidator may apply to the court without notice to any other party for permission to make a call on any contributories of the company.

7.88(2) [Content of application] The application must state the amount of the proposed call, and the contributories on whom it is to be made.

7.88(3) [Witness statement in support, schedule] The application must be supported by a witness statement accompanied by a schedule.

7.88(4) [Title and content of witness statement] The witness statement must have the title "Witness statement of liquidator in support of application for call" and must contain–

- (a) identification and contact details for the liquidator;
- (b) identification details for the company;
- (c) the number of persons on the list of contributories settled by the liquidator;
- (d) the total number of shares to which the proposed call relates;
- (e) the statement that in addition to the amount of the assets of the company mentioned in the schedule the liquidator believes a further sum will be required to satisfy the debts and liabilities of the company, and pay the expenses of and incidental to the winding up;
- (f) the additional sum required;
- (g) a statement that in order to provide the additional sum it is necessary to make a call upon the persons on the settled list of contributories, and that as it is probable that some of those contributories will partly or wholly fail to pay the amount of the call, the liquidator believes that it is necessary that a call of a specified amount per share be made in order to realise the amount required;
- (h) the specified amount per share.

7.88(5) [Content of accompanying schedule] The accompanying schedule must show–

- (a) the amount due in respect of debts already proved;
- (b) the estimated amount of–
  - (i) further liabilities of the company, and
  - (ii) the expenses of the winding up;
- (c) the total of the amounts referred to in sub-paragraphs (a) and (b); and
- (d) a list of the assets in hand belonging to the company with their total value.

7.88(6) [Verification of schedule] The schedule must be verified by a statement of truth made by the liquidator.

(See General Note after r.7.91.)

7.89 Order giving permission to make a call

7.89(1) [Title and content of order] The court's order giving permission to make a call must have the title "Order giving permission to make a call" and must contain–

(a) the name of the court (and hearing centre if applicable) in which the order is made;

(b) the name and title of the judge making the order;

(c) identification and contact details for the liquidator;

(d) identification details for the company;

(e) an order that the liquidator may make a call of the amount per share specified in the order on the contributories who are specified in the order;

(f) the amount per share of the call;

(g) the names of the contributories of the company on whom the liquidator is to make the call;

(h) an order that each such contributory must on or before the date specified in the order pay to the liquidator of the company the amount due from that contributory in respect of the call; and

(i) the date of the order.

7.89(2) [Power of court re notice of order] The court may direct that notice of the order be delivered to the contributories concerned, or to other contributories, or may direct that the notice be publicly advertised.

(See General Note after r.7.91.)

7.90 Making and enforcement of the call

7.90(1) [Notice of call] The liquidator must deliver a notice of the call to each of the contributories concerned.

7.90(2) [Content of notice] The notice must contain–

(a) identification details for the company;

(b) identification and contact details for the liquidator;

(c) a statement that a call on the contributories specified in the notice of the amount per share stated in the notice was sanctioned by–

  (i) a resolution of the liquidation committee of the company passed on the date which is stated in the notice, or

  (ii) an order of the court named in the notice on the date which is stated in the notice;

(d) the amount per share of the call;

(e) the amount or balance due from the contributory to whom the notice is addressed in respect of the call;

(f) the date by which the sum must be paid;

(g) a warning to the contributory that, if the required sum is not paid by the date specified in the notice, interest at the rate specified in the notice will be charged on the unpaid amount from that date until payment; and

(h) the specified annual interest rate.

7.90(3) [Notice accompanied by liquidation committee's copy resolution] The notice must be accompanied by a copy of the resolution of the liquidation committee sanctioning the call or of the court's order giving permission as the case may be.

(See General Note after r.7.91.)

7.91 Court order to enforce payment of call by a contributory

7.91(1) [Power of court] The court may make an order to enforce payment of the amount due from a contributory.

7.91(2) [Title and content of order] The order must have the title "Order for payment of call due from contributory" and must contain–

(a) the name of the court (and hearing centre if applicable) in which the order is made;

(b) identification and contact details for the liquidator who made the application;

(c) the name and title of the judge making the order;

(d) identification details for the company;

(e) the name and postal address of the contributory who is the subject of the order;

(f) the amount per share of the call;

(g) an order that the contributory pay the liquidator the sum stated in the order in respect of the call on or before the date stated in the order or within four business days after service of the order whichever is the later;

(h) an order that the contributory pay the liquidator interest at the rate stated in the order for the period commencing from the date specified in the order to the date of payment;

(i) an order that the contributory pay the liquidator a stated sum in respect of the liquidator's costs of the application within the same period as the amount of the call must be paid;

(j) a warning to the contributory that if the required sums are not paid within the time specified in the order further steps will be taken to compel the contributory to comply with the order; and

(k) the date of the order.

General Note to rr.7.86–7.91

For the statutory source of these rules, see IA 1986 ss.150, 160(1)(d). The exercise of the power of the liquidator to make a call requires the special leave of the court or the sanction of the liquidation committee (s.160(2), rr.7.87, 7.88). Rule 7.89 had no direct counterpart in IR 1986 but is derived from the content in former Form 4.57, whilst parts of rr.7.88, 7.90 and 7.91 are also derived from previously prescribed Forms 4.56, 4.58 and 4.59.
On the procedures in relation to the liquidation committee referred to in rr.7.86, 7.87 and 7.90, see Pt 17. For the standard content of an application to court under r.7.88, see r.1.35.

Chapter 12

Special manager

[Note: a document required by the Act or these Rules must also contain the standard contents set out in Part 1.]

7.92 Application of this Chapter and interpretation

7.92 This Chapter applies to applications for the appointment of a special manager by a liquidator and by a provisional liquidator (where one has been appointed), and so references to the liquidator are to be read as including a provisional liquidator.

(See General Note after r.7.97.)

7.93 Appointment and remuneration of special manager (section 177)

7.93(1) [Liquidator's report in support] An application made by the liquidator under section 177 for the appointment of a special manager must be supported by a report setting out the reasons for the application.

7.93(2) [Report to include value of business etc.] The report must include the applicant's estimate of the value of the business or property in relation to which the special manager is to be appointed.

7.93(3) [Title and content of order] The court's order appointing the special manager must have the title "Order of appointment of special manager" and must contain–

(a) identification details for the proceedings;

(b) the name and address of the person who made the application;

(c) the name and title of the judge making the order;

(d) the name and address of the proposed special manager;

(e) the order that the proposed special manager is appointed as special manager of the company;

(f) details of the special manager's responsibility over the company's business or property;

(g) the powers to be entrusted to the special manager under section 177(3);

(h) the time allowed for the special manager to give the required security for the appointment;

(i) the duration of the special manager's appointment being one of the following–

  (i) for a fixed period stated in the order,

  (ii) until the occurrence of a specified event, or

  (iii) until the court makes a further order;

(j) an order that the special manager's remuneration will be fixed from time to time by the court; and

(k) the date of the order.

7.93(4) [Renewal of appointment] The appointment of a special manager may be renewed by order of the court.

7.93(5) [Remuneration] The special manager's remuneration will be fixed from time to time by the court.

7.93(6) [Validation of special manager's acts] The acts of the special manager are valid notwithstanding any defect in the special manager's appointment or qualifications.

(See General Note after r.7.97.)

7.94 Security

7.94(1) [Effect of giving security] The appointment of the special manager does not take effect until the person appointed has given (or, if the court allows, undertaken to give) security to the applicant for the appointment.

7.94(2) [Specific or general security] A person appointed as a special manager may give security either specifically for a particular winding up, or generally for any winding up in relation to which that person may be employed as special manager.

7.94(3) [Amount of security] The amount of the security must be not less than the value of the business or property in relation to which the special manager is appointed, as estimated in the applicant's report which accompanied the application for appointment.

7.94(4) [Certificate of adequacy] When the special manager has given security to the applicant that person must file with the court a certificate as to the adequacy of the security.

7.94(5) [Cost of security] The cost of providing the security must be paid in the first instance by the special manager; but–

(a) where a winding-up order is not made, the special manager is entitled to be reimbursed out of the property of the company, and the court may order accordingly; and

(b) where a winding-up order is made, the special manager is entitled to be reimbursed as an expense of the winding up in the prescribed order of priority.

(See General Note after r.7.97.)

7.95 Failure to give or keep up security

7.95(1) [Effect of failure to give required security] If the special manager fails to give the required security within the time allowed for that purpose by the order of appointment, or any extension of that time that may be allowed, the liquidator must report the failure to the court, which may discharge the order appointing the special manager.

7.95(2) Effect of failure to keep up required security If the special manager fails to keep up the security, the liquidator must report the failure to the court, which may remove the special manager, and make such order as it thinks just as to costs.

7.95(3) [Court directions on removal] If the court discharges the order appointing the special manager or makes an order removing the special manager, the court must give directions as to whether any, and if so what, steps should be taken for the appointment of another special manager.

(See General Note after r.7.97.)

7.96 Accounting

7.96(1) [Contents of accounts for approval] The special manager must produce accounts, containing details of the special manager's receipts and payments, for the approval of the liquidator.

7.96(2) [Period of accounts] The accounts must be for–

(a) each three month period for the duration of the special manager's appointment; or

(b) any shorter period ending with the termination of the special manager's appointment.

7.96(3) [When approved receipts and payments added to liquidator's] When the accounts have been approved, the special manager's receipts and payments must be added to those of the liquidator.

(See General Note after r.7.97.)

7.97 Termination of appointment

7.97(1) [Automatic termination] The special manager's appointment terminates–

(a) if the winding-up petition is dismissed; or

(b) in a case where a provisional liquidator was appointed under section 135, if the appointment is discharged without a winding-up order having been made.

7.97(2) [Liquidator's application for directions] If the liquidator is of the opinion that the employment of the special manager is no longer necessary or beneficial for the company, the liquidator must apply to the court for directions, and the court may order the special manager's appointment to be terminated.

7.97(3) [Application if creditors decide] The liquidator must make the same application if the creditors decide that the appointment should be terminated.

General Note to rr.7.92–7.97

On the appointment of a special manager, see IA 1986 s.177 and the notes thereto. A special manager need not be qualified to act as an insolvency practitioner. These rules deal with the appointment and remuneration, the furnishing of security and failure to do so, obligation to keep accounts and the termination of the appointment.

The content of the court order in r.7.93 is derived from former Form 4.60.

Chapter 13

Public examination of company officers and others (section 133)

[Note: a document required by the Act or these Rules must also contain the standard contents set out in Part 1.]

7.98 Applications relating to promoters, past managers etc. (section 133(1)(c))

7.98(1) [Official receiver's report] An application under section 133(1) for the public examination of a person falling within paragraph (c) of subsection (1) (promoters, past managers, etc.) must be accompanied by a report by the official receiver indicating–

(a) the grounds on which the official receiver thinks the person is within that paragraph; and

(b) whether the official receiver thinks it is likely that the order can be served on the person at a known address and, if so, by what means.

7.98(2) [Means of service] If the official receiver thinks that there is no reasonable certainty that service at a known address will be effective, the court may direct that the order be served by some means other than, or in addition to, service in such manner.

(See General Note after r.7.107.)

7.99 Request by a creditor for a public examination (section 133(2))

7.99(1) [Content of request] A request made under section 133(2) by a creditor to the official receiver for the public examination of a person must contain–

(a) identification details for the company;

(b) the name and postal address of the creditor;

(c) the name and postal address of the proposed examinee;

(d) a description of the relationship which the proposed examinee has, or has had, with the company;

(e) a request by the creditor to the official receiver to apply to the court for a public examination of the proposed examinee under section 133(2);

(f) the amount of the creditor's claim in the winding up;

(g) a statement that the total amount of the creditor's and any concurring creditors' claims is believed to represent not less than one-half in value of the debts of the company;

(h) a statement that the creditor understands the requirement to deposit with the official receiver such sum as the official receiver may determine to be appropriate by way of security for the expenses of holding a public examination; and

(i) a statement that the creditor believes that a public examination is required for the reason stated in the request.

7.99(2) [Authentication of request] The request must be authenticated and dated by the creditor.

7.99(3) [List of concurring creditors, etc. and conformation of concurrence] The request must be accompanied by–

(a) a list of the creditors concurring with the request and the amounts of their respective claims in the winding up, with their respective values; and

(b) from each concurring creditor, confirmation of the creditor's concurrence.

(See General Note after r.7.107.)

7.100 Request by a contributory for a public examination

7.100(1) [Content of request] A request made under section 133(2) by a contributory to the official receiver for the public examination of a person must contain–

(a) identification details for the company;

(b) the name and postal address of the contributory;

(c) the name and postal address of the proposed examinee;

(d) a description of the relationship which the proposed examinee has, or has had, with the company;

(e) a request by the contributory to the official receiver to apply to the court for a public examination of the proposed examinee under section 133(2);

(f) the number of shares held in the company by the contributory;

(g) the number of votes to which the contributory is entitled;

(h) a statement that the total amount of the contributory's and any concurring contributories' shares and votes is believed to represent not less than three-quarters in value of the company's contributories;

(i) a statement that the contributory understands the requirement to deposit with the official receiver such sum as the official receiver may determine to be appropriate by way of security for the expenses of holding a public examination; and

(j) a statement that the contributory believes that a public examination is required for the reason specified in the request.

7.100(2) [Authentication of request] The request must be authenticated and dated by the contributory.

7.100(3) [List of concurring contributories, confirmation of concurrence, etc.] The request must be accompanied by–

(a) a list of the contributories concurring with the request and the number of shares and votes each holds in the company; and

(b) from each concurring contributory, confirmation of the concurrence and of the number of shares and votes held in the company.

(See General Note after r.7.107.)

7.101 Further provisions about requests by a creditor or contributory for a public examination

7.101(1) [Support of concurring creditors/contributories not required] A request by a creditor or contributory for a public examination does not require the support of concurring creditors or contributories if the requisitioning creditor's debt or, as the case may be, requisitioning contributory's shares, is sufficient alone under section 133(2).

7.101(2) [Security for expenses of examination] Before the official receiver makes the requested application, the creditor or contributory requesting the examination must deposit with the official receiver such sum (if any) as the official receiver determines is appropriate as security for the expenses of the public examination (if ordered).

7.101(3) [Time limit for application] The official receiver must make the application for the examination–

(a) within 28 days of receiving the creditor's or contributory's request (if no security is required under paragraph (2); or

(b) within 28 days of the creditor or contributory (as the case may be) depositing the required security.

7.101(4) [Relief from unreasonable request] However if the official receiver thinks the request is unreasonable, the official receiver may apply to the court for an order to be relieved from making the application.

7.101(5) [Application for relief under r.7.101(4) made without notice, notice of order] If the application for an order under paragraph (4) is made without notice to any other party and the court makes such an order then the official receiver must deliver a notice of the order as soon as reasonably practicable to the creditors or contributories who requested the examination.

7.101(6) [Application for relief under r.7.101(4) dismissed] If the court dismisses the official receiver's application under paragraph (4), the official receiver must make the application under section 133(2) as soon as reasonably practicable.

(See General Note after r.7.107.)

7.102 Order for public examination

7.102(1) [Title and content of order] An order for a public examination must have the title "Order for Public Examination" and must contain the following–

(a) identification details for the proceedings;

(b) the name and title of the judge making the order;

(c) the name and postal address of the person to be examined;

(d) the venue for the public examination;

(e) the order that the person named in the order must attend the specified venue for the purpose of being publicly examined;

(f) the date of the order; and

(g) a warning to the person to be examined that failure without reasonable excuse to attend the public examination at the time and place specified in the order will make the person liable to be arrested without further notice under section 134(2); and that the person will also be guilty of contempt of court under section 134(1) and be liable to be committed to prison or fined.

7.102(2) [Copy order served on examinee] The official receiver must serve a copy of the order on the person to be examined as soon as reasonably practicable after the order is made.

7.102(3) [Rescission of order re IA 1986 s.133(1)(c) person] The court must rescind an order for the public examination of a person who was said to fall within section 133(1)(c) if that person satisfies the court that it is not so.

[Note: rule 81.9 (as amended) of the CPR requires a warning as mentioned in paragraph (1)(g) to be displayed prominently on the front of the order.]

(See General Note after r.7.107.)

7.103 Notice of the public examination

7.103(1) [To whom notice to be given] The official receiver must give at least 14 days' notice of the public examination to–

(a) the liquidator (if a liquidator has been nominated or appointed);

(b) the special manager (if a special manager has been appointed); and

(c) the creditors and all the contributories of the company who are known to the official receiver (subject to any contrary direction of the court).

7.103(2) [Additional notice by gazetting] Where the official receiver thinks fit additional notice of the order may be given by gazetting the notice.

7.103(3) [Advertisement of notice] The official receiver may in addition to gazetting the notice advertise it in such other manner as the official receiver thinks fit;

7.103(4) [Content of notice] The notice must state–

(a) the purpose of the public examination; and

(b) the venue.

7.103(5) [Delayed gazetting re IA 1986 s.133(1)(c) person] Unless the court directs otherwise, the official receiver must not give notice under paragraph (2) of an order relating to a person falling within section 133(1)(c) until at least five business days have elapsed since the examinee was served with the order.

(See General Note after r.7.107.)

7.104 Examinee unfit for examination

7.104(1) [Stay, etc.] Where the examinee is a person who lacks capacity within the meaning of the Mental Capacity Act 2005 or is unfit to undergo or attend for public examination, the court may–

(a) stay the order for the examinee's public examination; or

(b) order that it is to be conducted in such manner and at such place as it thinks just.

7.104(2) [Who may apply] The applicant for an order under paragraph (1) must be–

(a) a person who has been appointed by a court in the United Kingdom or elsewhere to manage the affairs of, or to represent, the examinee;

(b) a person who appears to the court to be a suitable person to make the application; or

(c) the official receiver.

7.104(3) [Application not by official receiver] Where the application is made by a person other than the official receiver, then–

(a) the application must, unless the examinee is a person who lacks capacity within the meaning of the Mental Capacity Act 2005, be supported by the witness statement of a registered medical practitioner as to the examinee's mental and physical condition;

(b) at least five business days' notice of the application must be given to the official receiver and the liquidator (if other than the official receiver); and

(c) before any order is made on the application, the applicant must deposit with the official receiver such sum as the latter certifies to be necessary for the additional expenses of an examination.

7.104(4) [Content of order] An order must contain–

(a) identification details for the proceedings;

(b) the name and postal address of the applicant;

(c) the name and title of the judge making the order;

(d) the capacity in which the applicant (other than the official receiver) made the application;

(e) the name and postal address of the examinee;

(f) the date of the order for the examinee's public examination ("the original order");

(g) a statement that the court is satisfied that the examinee specified in the order lacks capacity within the meaning of the Mental Capacity Act 2005 to manage and administer the examinee's property and affairs or is unfit to undergo a public examination;

(h) an order that–

  (i) the original order is to be stayed on the grounds that the examinee is unfit to undergo a public examination, or

  (ii) the original order is varied (as specified in this order) on the grounds that the examinee is unfit to attend the public examination fixed by the original order; and

(i) the date of the order.

7.104(5) [Expenses out of r.7.104(3)(c) deposit] Where a person other than the official receiver makes the application, the court may order that some or all of the expenses of the examination are to be payable out of the deposit under paragraph (3)(c), instead of as an expense of the winding up.

7.104(6) [Application by official receiver without notice] Where the application is made by the official receiver it may be made without notice to any other party, and may be supported by evidence set out in a report by the official receiver to the court.

(See General Note after r.7.107.)

7.105 Procedure at public examination

7.105(1) [Examination on oath and answer all questions] At the public examination the examinee must–

(a) be examined on oath; and

(b) answer all the questions which the court puts, or allows to be put.

7.105(2) [Appearances etc.] A person allowed by section 133(4) to question the examinee may–

(a) with the approval of the court appear by an appropriately qualified legal representative; or

(b) in writing authorise another person to question the examinee on that person's behalf.

7.105(3) [Representation of examinee] The examinee may at the examinee's own expense employ an appropriately qualified legal representative, who may put to the examinee such questions as the court may allow for the purpose of enabling the examinee to explain or qualify any answers given by the examinee, and may make representations on behalf of the examinee.

7.105(4) [Record of examination] The court must have such record made of the examination as the court thinks proper.

7.105(5) [Record used in evidence] The record may, in any proceedings (whether under the Act or otherwise) be used as evidence of any statement made by the examinee in the course of the public examination.

7.105(6) [Adjournment if criminal proceedings prejudiced] If criminal proceedings have been instituted against the examinee, and the court is of the opinion that continuing the hearing might prejudice a fair trial of those proceedings, the hearing may be adjourned.

(See General Note after r.7.107.)

7.106 Adjournment

[Note: rule 81.9 (as amended) of the CPR requires a warning as mentioned in paragraph (3) to be displayed prominently on the front of the order.]

7.106(1) [Power of court] The court may adjourn the public examination from time to time, either to a fixed date or generally.

7.106(2) [Resumption] Where the examination has been adjourned generally, the court may at any time on the application of the official receiver or of the examinee–

(a) fix a venue for the resumption of the examination; and

(b) give directions as to the manner in which, and the time within which, notice of the resumed public examination is to be given to persons entitled to take part in it.

7.106(3) [Warning to examinee re attending resumption] An order adjourning the public examination to a fixed date must contain a warning to the examinee that failure without reasonable excuse to attend the public examination at the time and place specified in the order will make the examinee liable to be arrested without further notice under section 134(2); and that the examinee will also be guilty of contempt of court under section 134(1) and be liable to be committed to prison or fined.

7.106(4) [Court's power on application to resume] Where an application to resume an examination is made by the examinee, the court may grant it on terms that the examinee must pay the expenses of giving the notices required by paragraph (2) and that, before a venue for the resumed public examination is fixed, the examinee must deposit with the official receiver such sum as the official receiver considers necessary to cover those expenses.

(See General Note after r.7.107.)

7.107 Expenses of examination

7.107(1) [Payable out of deposit under rr.7.99, 7.100] Where a public examination of the examinee has been ordered by the court on a request by a creditor under rule 7.99 or by a contributory under rule 7.100, the court may order that some or all of the expenses of the examination are to be paid out of the deposit required under those rules, instead of as an expense of the winding up.

7.107(2) [No liability of official receiver] The costs and expenses of a public examination do not fall on the official receiver personally.

GENERAL NOTE TO RR.7.98–7.107

On the standard contents for gazetted notices (r.7.103(2)), see rr.1.10–1.12. On the standard contents for notices other than gazetted notices (r.7.103(1), (3), (4)), see rr.1.15, 1.16, 1.18.

The power conferred on the official receiver to have company officers and others attend for public examination is conferred by the 1986 Act in more broadly drawn terms than under the former law: see the note to IA 1986 s.133. If the preconditions of s.133 are satisfied, the court should make an order for the examination except where no useful purpose would be served by it: *Jeeves v Official Receiver* [2003] EWCA Civ 1246; [2004] 1 W.L.R. 602; [2003] B.C.C. 912. The court has power under r.7.105 to control the form of the examination and to give directions, or at least guidance, as to the hearing, but will not pre-empt questions which are a matter for the judge presiding at the hearing, e.g. as to the admissibility of questions and whether a particular question would be oppressive: *Re Richbell Strategic Holdings Ltd* [2001] B.C.C. 409. However, it was said in *Jeeves v Official Receiver* (above) that if the court was hearing an application under r.12.59 to rescind an order for examination, it was appropriate for that court to consider whether some sanction in a foreign jurisdiction might make it difficult or oppressive to require the proposed examinee to answer questions.

On the *private* examination of persons connected with an insolvent company, see IA 1986 s.236, and rr.12.17 et seq., and the notes thereto.

Subject to rr.7.98(1)(a), 7.102(3), the official receiver is entitled to an order ipso facto, i.e. he need not make out any case to the court.

Rule 7.102(1) has no direct counterpart in IR 1986 but the content of the order is derived from former Form 4.61. Similarly the content of a request by a creditor or contributory for public examination in r.7.99(1) and r.7.100(1) is derived from former Forms 4.62 and 4.63.

A note to r.7.102(1)(g) and r.7.106(3) reiterates the requirement of CPR r.81.9 of the requirement for *prominent* display in the order for attendance that failure to attend the examination (or an adjourned examination) will render the examinee liable to arrest and be guilty of criminal contempt of court under IA 1986 s.134.

Chapter 14

Priority of payment of costs and expenses, etc.

7.108 General rule as to priority

7.108(1) [Expenses of winding up] All fees, costs, charges and other expenses incurred in the course of the winding up are to be treated as expenses of the winding up.

7.108(2) [Assets from which expenses payable] The expenses of the winding up are payable out of–

(a) assets of the company available for the payment of general creditors, including–

  (i) proceeds of any legal action which the liquidator has power to bring in the liquidator's own name or in the name of the company;

  (ii) proceeds arising from any award made under any arbitration or other dispute resolution procedure which the liquidator has power to bring in the liquidator's own name or in the name of the company;

  (iii) any payments made under any compromise or other agreement intended to avoid legal action or recourse to arbitration or to any other dispute resolution procedure;

  (iv) payments made as a result of an assignment or a settlement of any such action, arrangement or procedure in lieu of or before any judgment being given or award being made; and

(b) subject as provided in rules 7.111 to 7.116, property comprised in or subject to a floating charge created by the company.

7.108(3) [Prescribed part expenses] The expenses associated with the prescribed part must be paid out of the prescribed part.

7.108(4) [Order of priority] Subject as provided in rules 7.112 to 7.116, the expenses are payable in the following order of priority–

(a) the following expenses, which rank equally in order of priority–

  (i) expenses that are properly chargeable or incurred by the provisional liquidator in carrying out the functions conferred on the provisional liquidator by the court,

(ii) expenses that are properly chargeable or incurred by the official receiver or the liquidator in preserving, realising or getting in any of the assets of the company or otherwise in the preparation, conduct or assignment of any legal proceedings, arbitration or other dispute resolution procedures, which the official receiver or liquidator has power to bring in the official receiver's or liquidator's own name or bring or defend in the name of the company or in the preparation or conduct of any negotiations intended to lead or leading to a settlement or compromise of any legal action or dispute to which the proceedings or procedures relate,

(iii) expenses that relate to the employment of a shorthand writer, if appointed by an order of the court made at the instance of the official receiver in connection with an examination, and

(iv) expenses that are incurred in holding a hearing under rule 7.104 (examinee unfit) where the application for it was made by the official receiver;

(b) any other expenses incurred or disbursements made by the official receiver or under the official receiver's authority, including those incurred or made in carrying on the business of the company;

(c) the fees payable under any order made under section 414 or section 415A, including those payable to the official receiver (other than the fee referred to in sub-paragraph (d)), and any remuneration payable to the official receiver under general regulations;

(d) the fee payable under any order made under section 414 for the performance by the official receiver of the general duties of the official receiver and any repayable sum deposited under any such order as security for the fee;

(e) the cost of any security provided by a provisional liquidator, liquidator or special manager in accordance with the Act or these Rules;

(f) the remuneration of the provisional liquidator (if any);

(g) any sum deposited on an application for the appointment of a provisional liquidator;

(h) the costs of the petitioner, and of any person appearing on the petition whose costs are allowed by the court;

(i) the remuneration of the special manager (if any);

(j) any amount payable to a person employed or authorised, under Chapter 6 of this Part, to assist in the preparation of a statement of affairs or of accounts;

(k) any allowance made, by order of the court, in respect of costs on an application for release from the obligation to submit a statement of affairs, or for an extension of time for submitting such a statement;

(l) the costs of employing a shorthand writer in any case other than one appointed by an order of the court at the instance of the official receiver in connection with an examination;

(m) any necessary disbursements by the liquidator in the course of the administration of the winding up (including any costs referred to in Articles 30 or 59 of the EU Regulation and expenses incurred by members of the liquidation committee or their representatives and allowed by the liquidator under rule 17.24, but not including any payment of corporation tax in circumstances referred to in sub-paragraph (p));

(n) the remuneration or emoluments of any person who has been employed by the liquidator to perform any services for the company, as required or authorised by or under the Act or these Rules;

(o) the remuneration of the liquidator, up to an amount not exceeding that which is payable under Schedule 11 (determination of insolvency office-holder's remuneration);

(p) the amount of any corporation tax on chargeable gains accruing on the realisation of any asset of the company (irrespective of the person by whom the realisation is effected);

(q) the balance, after payment of any sums due under sub-paragraph (o) above, of any remuneration due to the liquidator; and

(r) any other expenses properly chargeable by the liquidator in carrying out the liquidator's functions in the winding up.

(See General Note after r.7.110.)

7.109 Winding up commencing as voluntary

7.109 Where the winding up by the court immediately follows a voluntary winding up (whether members' voluntary or creditors' voluntary), such remuneration of the voluntary liquidator and costs and expenses of the voluntary winding up as the court may allow are to rank in priority with the expenses specified in rule 7.108(4)(a).

(See General Note after r.7.110.)

7.110 Saving for powers of the court (section 156)

7.110(1) [Powers of court under IA 1986 s.156] The priorities laid down by rules 7.108 and 7.109 are subject to the power of the court to make orders under section 156, where the assets are insufficient to satisfy the liabilities.

7.110(2) [Powers of court re costs, etc.] Nothing in those rules–

(a) applies to or affects the power of any court, in proceedings by or against the company, to order costs to be paid by the company, or the liquidator; or

(b) affects the rights of any person to whom such costs are ordered to be paid.

General Note to rr.7.108–7.110

These rules deal with the expenses of the liquidation, and define the order of priority as between the various heads of expenditure incurred by the liquidator. The provisions governing expenses in an administration (r.3.51) are very similar to r.7.108 and the case-law commonly considers both (indeed the Insolvency Service at one stage intimated that the consolidated rules might be amended in light of some recent case-law decisions, but this has not materialised in IR 2016). It may be helpful to refer to the note to r.3.51.

The rules in relation to IA 1986 s.176ZA regarding litigation expenses and claims to assets covered by a floating charge appear in Ch.15 (rr.7.111–r.7.116) below and r.7.108(4) makes clear that the order of priority in that sub-rule is subject to rr.7.112–7.116 as relevant.

R.7.108

The rule as now worded makes it plain that the line of cases, from *Re MC Bacon Ltd (No.2)* [1991] Ch. 127; [1990] B.C.C. 430 to *Re Floor Fourteen Ltd, Lewis v Inland Revenue Commissioners* [2001] 3 All E.R. 499; [2002] B.C.C. 198 (in which it was held that the expenses incurred by a liquidator in pursuing claims for wrongful trading and to recover preferences, etc. were not "expenses of the liquidation"), are no longer good law.

An application for the interim reimbursement of costs in proceedings brought by the liquidator against the company's former directors was held to be premature in *Re Romar Engineering Co Ltd* [2003] B.C.C. 535.

The order of priority of expenses in a creditors' voluntary winding up, and from what assets payable, is provided by r.6.42 (which is similar to but necessarily shorter than r.7.108).

R.7.108(1)–(4)

Rule 7.108(1) and (2) elaborate the terms "expenses of the winding up" and the "assets" out of which the expenses are to be paid. In particular, it is expressly provided that the expenses of the liquidation may be paid out of the fruits of any litigation which the liquidator has power to bring or defend in his own name or of any corresponding arbitration or dispute resolution procedures, and any settlement or compromise of a claim or dispute.

Rule 7.108(3) states that expenses in relation to the prescribed part under r.176A are payable out of that reserved fund for unsecured creditors, a principle reiterated in rr.3.50(2), 6.42(3). See the note to s.176A.

Rule 7.108(4)(m) amended by the Insolvency Amendment (EU 2015/848) Regulations 2017 (SI 2017/702) regs 1, 2(1), Sch. paras 32, 40 in relation to proceedings opened on or after 26 June 2017 (see reg.3) when the Recast EU Regulation 2015/848 came into force.

The ruling in *Re Barleycorn Enterprises Ltd* [1970] Ch. 465 (which was followed in a number of cases including *Re Portbase Clothing Ltd, Mond v Taylor* [1993] Ch. 388; [1993] B.C.C. 96), that for the purposes of the former r.4.218(1) the company's "assets" include assets covered by a floating charge, was overruled by the House of Lords in *Re Leyland DAF Ltd, Buchler v Talbot* [2004] UKHL 9; [2004] 2 A.C. 298; [2004] B.C.C. 214: see the note to s.107. It followed that the liquidator's claims for expenses ranked behind those of the holder of a floating charge and the preferential creditors.

However, this ruling was considered by government to run contrary to the current philosophy and objectives of insolvency law and a clause was inserted into the then Companies Bill to reverse the decision, which in due course became CA 2006 s.1282. This provision has inserted new s.176ZA into IA 1986, which provides that the expenses of a winding up should, so far as necessary, have priority over any claims to property comprised in or subject to a floating charge. There is power in s.176ZA(3) to make rules restricting the application of this rule and rr.7.111–7.116 are the modern version of these. See further the notes to s.176ZA and rr.7.111–7.116.

In *Kahn v Inland Revenue Commissioners, Re Toshoku Finance (UK) plc* [2002] UKHL 6; [2002] 1 W.L.R. 671; [2002] B.C.C. 110 the House of Lords held that corporation tax was payable out of the assets in priority to other claims as an expense of the liquidation even though the "income" in respect of which the tax was assessed had not been (and never would be) received by the company, and the tax debt had not arisen as a result of something done for the purposes of or with a view to obtaining a benefit for the estate. On this case, see Lyons and Birch, (2005) 18 Insolv. Int. 150. Rent payable in respect of premises occupied by a company in administration was held to be an expense of the administration on the same principle as in *Toshoku Finance* in *Pillar Denton Ltd v Jervis, Re Games Station Ltd* [2014] EWCA Civ 180; [2014] B.C.C. 165: see the notes to Sch.B1 para.99(2)–(3) and r.2.67. This principle, derived from *Re Lundy Granite Co* (1870–71) L.R. 6 Ch. App. 462, also applies in a provisional liquidation: *Re MK Airlines Ltd (No.2)* [2014] B.C.C. 101.

In *Re WF Fearman Ltd (No.2)* (1988) 4 B.C.C. 141 it was held that the costs of an administration petition (although bona fide presented and proving in the event to have been in the interests of the creditors) could not be allowed as a liquidation expense when the administration proceedings were terminated and a winding-up order was made. However, in the later case of *Re Gosscott (Groundworks) Ltd* (1988) 4 B.C.C. 372, an order was made in such circumstances (this decision in relation to jurisdiction under s.51 of the Senior Courts Act 1981 was doubted in *Re Broomfield Developments Ltd* (unreported, 19 June 2017)). See also *Re Portsmouth City Football Club Ltd* [2012] EWHC 3088 (Ch); [2013] 1 B.C.L.C. 572, upheld on appeal *Neumans LLP v Andronikou* [2013] EWCA Civ 916; [2013] B.C.C. 741. In the Court of Appeal, Mummery LJ sets out in detail a summary of the legal position on whether and when solicitors' fees rank as expenses in a liquidation or administration "as an aid to practitioners and courts in future cases", where a winding-up petition was suspended on the making of an administration order but the administration was later terminated and a winding-up order made. The applicant claimed payment of fees and disbursements incurred in relation to the winding-up petition and sought a ruling that they were an expense of the administration. This request was declined by the court, but the sums were allowed as an expense of the liquidation.

In *Re Movitex Ltd* [1990] B.C.C. 491 the liquidators had continued an action, which had been commenced by the company before the winding up, to have certain property transactions set aside on the ground that they had been entered into without authority or in breach of directors' duty. Judgment had been given for the defendants with costs against the company, but the company's assets were insufficient to pay the costs order. It was held that the litigation costs were payable in full to the extent of the company's assets, but only after allowing the liquidators a deduction in respect of their costs in realising those assets. See also *Re MT Realisations Ltd* [2003] EWHC 2895 (Ch); [2004] 1 W.L.R. 678, where the court not only confirmed that costs which had been awarded against the liquidator in litigation were payable in priority to the general expenses of the liquidation but also held that they were not "expenses of the liquidation" within r.4.218 at all, so that the court had no power under IA 1986 s.156 to accord them a lower priority. In *RBG Resources plc v Rastogi* [2005] EWHC 994 (Ch); [2005] 2 B.C.L.C. 592 Lightman J warned that liquidators should think very carefully before making decisions to bring or continue expensive proceedings against impecunious defendants. The liquidator in that case had been obliged to discontinue an action for want of funds; the normal rule was applied that the claimant should be liable for the defendant's costs on the standard basis, which in the circumstances had to be funded at the expense of the liquidator's remuneration. In *Unadkat & Co (Accountants) Ltd v Bhardwaj* [2006] EWHC 2785 (Ch); [2007] B.C.C. 452 the company had been dissolved, but a creditor had put up funds to have it restored to the register and a new liquidator appointed, so that misfeasance proceedings (which were successfully settled) could be brought against a former director. The judgment contains an interesting discussion of the court's discretionary power to award costs in the restoration proceedings and the status of those costs (as liquidation expenses) under what is now r.7.108.

A company's liability under a protective award made after the commencement of liquidation was considered not to be a necessary disbursement under what is now r.7.108(4)(m) in *Day v Haine* [2007] EWHC 2691 (Ch); [2008] B.C.C. 199, on the basis that there was no certainty that the employees would ever have an enforceable claim against the company; but this decision was reversed by the Court of Appeal: *Haine v Day* [2008] EWCA Civ 626, and approved by the Supreme Court in *Re Nortel GmbH, Bloom v Pensions Regulator* [2013] UKSC 52; [2014] A.C. 209; [2013] B.C.C. 624 (distinguishing *Re Toshoku Finance* (above)). See the note to r.14.1.

A liquidator may seek guidance from the court in anticipation of making any particular expenditure in order to determine whether it will be treated as an expense of the liquidation: *Re Demaglass Ltd* (above). Liquidators in *Re Central A1 Ltd; Rubin v Cohen* [2017] EWHC 220 (Ch); [2017] B.C.C. 69 applied for directions under IA 1986 s.112 to determine a dispute as to what were "reasonable and necessary" expenses under what are now r.6.7 and r.7.45 regarding fixed fees charged by a firm of accountants for work undertaken in relation to preparation of statements of affairs (and creditors' meetings) to enable 1,796 companies to be placed into creditors' voluntary liquidation. Registrar Jones noted that what are now r.6.42(4)(d) and r.7.108(4)(j) identified as an expense any amount payable to a person employed to assist in the preparation of a statement of affairs or of accounts and that, to the extent that those provisions did not apply to the instant case, what are now r.6.42(4)(f) and r.7.108(4)(m) would apply because the expenses would be paid by the liquidators as a necessary disbursement in the course of the administration. That conclusion was not affected by the fact that payment might be made before the liquidation commenced.

Where a winding up by the court immediately follows a voluntary winding up the court has power under r.7.109 to allow, review or disallow in whole or in part the voluntary liquidator's remuneration, costs and expenses. However, if the voluntary liquidator seeks an increase of remuneration it is more appropriate to proceed under r.18.23 than r.7.109: *Re Tony Rowse NMC Ltd* [1996] B.C.C. 196.

Where the liquidator administers assets which are outside the scope of the liquidation (e.g. assets held by the company on trust), the court has jurisdiction to allow him access to those funds to recoup his remuneration and expenses: *Re Berkeley Applegate (Investment Consultants) Ltd (No.2)* [1989] Ch. 32; (1988) B.C.C. 279. But it will not do so in relation to assets which are in dispute: *Re London Local Residential Ltd* [2004] EWHC 114 (Ch); [2004] 2 B.C.L.C. 72; or where it was not necessary to incur the costs (*Re Birchall* [2015] EWHC 1541 (Ch)); and it may be limited to circumstances where the beneficiaries needed the assistance of the court to secure their rights (ibid.).

Chapter 15

Litigation expenses and property subject to a floating charge

[Note: a document required by the Act or these Rules must also contain the standard contents set out in Part 1.]

7.111 Interpretation

7.111 In this Chapter–

"approval" and "authorisation" respectively mean–

(a) where yet to be incurred, the approval, and

(b) where already incurred, the authorisation, of expenses specified in section 176ZA(3);

"the creditor" means–

(a) a preferential creditor of the company; or

(b) a holder of a debenture secured by, or a holder of, a floating charge created by the company;

"legal proceedings" means–

(a) proceedings under sections 212, 213, 214, 238, 239, 244 and 423 and any arbitration or other dispute resolution proceedings invoked for purposes corresponding to those to which the sections relate and any other proceedings, including arbitration or other dispute resolution procedures, which a liquidator has power to bring in the liquidator's own name for the purpose of preserving, realising, or getting in any of the assets of the company;

(b) legal actions and proceedings, arbitration or any other dispute resolution procedures which a liquidator has power to bring or defend in the name of the company; and

(c) negotiations intended to lead or leading to a settlement or compromise of any action, proceeding or procedure to which sub-paragraphs (a) or (b) relate;

"litigation expenses" means expenses of a winding up which–

(a) are properly chargeable or incurred in the preparation or conduct of any legal proceedings; and

(b) as expenses in the winding up, exceed, or in the opinion of the liquidator are likely to exceed (and only in so far as they exceed or are likely to exceed), in the aggregate £5,000; and

"specified creditor" means a creditor identified under rule 7.113(2).

(See General Note after r.7.116.)

7.112 Priority of litigation expenses

7.112 Litigation expenses will not have the priority provided by section 176ZA over any claims to property comprised in or subject to a floating charge created by the company and must not be paid out of any such property unless and until approved or authorised in accordance with rules 7.113 to 7.116.

(See General Note after r.7.116.)

7.113 Requirement for approval or authorisation of litigation expenses

7.113(1) [Liquidator's opinion] Subject to rules 7.114 to 7.116 either paragraphs (3) and (4) apply or paragraph (5) applies where, in the course of winding up a company, the liquidator–

(a) ascertains that property is comprised in or subject to a floating charge;

(b) has personally instituted or proposes to institute or continue legal proceedings or is in the process of defending or proposes to defend any legal proceeding brought or likely to be brought against the company; and

(c) before or at any stage in those proceedings, is of the opinion that–

(i) the assets of the company available for payment of general creditors are or will be insufficient to pay litigation expenses, and

(ii) in order to pay litigation expenses the liquidator will have to have recourse to property comprised in or subject to a floating charge created by the company.

7.113(2) [Identification of creditors with claim to property] As soon as reasonably practicable after the date on which the liquidator forms the opinion referred to in paragraph (1), the liquidator must identify the creditor who, in the liquidator's opinion at that time–

(a) has a claim to property comprised in or subject to a floating charge created by the company; and

(b) taking into account the value of that claim and any subsisting property then comprised in or secured by such a charge, appears to the liquidator to be the creditor most immediately likely of any persons having such claims to receive some payment in respect of a claim but whose claim would not be paid in full.

7.113(3) [Request for approval of litigation expenses: specified creditor] The liquidator must request from the specified creditor the approval or authorisation of such amount for litigation expenses as the liquidator thinks fit.

7.113(4) [Multiple creditors identified; litigation expenses apportioned] Where the liquidator identifies two or more specified creditors, the liquidator must seek from each of them approval or authorisation of such amount of litigation expenses as the liquidator thinks fit, apportioned between them ("the apportioned amount") according to the value of the property to the extent covered by their charges.

7.113(5) [Further requests for litigation expenses] For so long as the conditions specified in paragraph (1) subsist, the liquidator may, in the course of a winding up, make such further requests to the specified creditor or creditors for approval or authorisation of such further amount for litigation expenses as the liquidator thinks fit to be paid out of property comprised in or subject to a floating charge created by the company, taking into account any amount for litigation expenses previously approved or authorised and the value of the property comprised in or subject to the floating charge.

(See General Note after r.7.116.)

7.114 Requests for approval or authorisation

7.114(1) [Statements, etc. required] All requests made by the liquidator for approval or authorisation must include the following–

(a) a statement describing the nature of the legal proceedings, including, where relevant, the statutory provision under which proceedings are or are to be brought and the grounds upon which the liquidator relies;

(b) a statement specifying the amount or apportioned amount of litigation expenses for which approval or authorisation is sought ("the specified amount");

(c) notice that approval or authorisation or other reply to the request must be made in writing within 28 days from the date of its being received ("the specified time limit"); and

(d) a statement explaining the consequences of a failure to reply within the specified time limit.

7.114(2) [Exclusion of seriously prejudicial information from r.7.114(1) statements, notices] Where anything in paragraph (1) requires the inclusion of any information, the disclosure of which could be seriously prejudicial to the winding up of the company, the liquidator may–

(a) exclude such information from any of the above statements or notices if accompanied by a statement to that effect; or

(b) include it on terms–

  (i) that bind the creditor to keep the information confidential, and

  (ii) that include an undertaking on the part of the liquidator to apply to the court for an order that so much of the information as may be kept in the files of the court, is not be open to public inspection.

7.114(3) [Creditor's application for further particulars] The creditor may within the specified time limit apply to the liquidator in writing for such further particulars as is reasonable and in such a case, the time limit specified in paragraph (1)(c) will apply from the date of the creditor's receipt of the liquidator's response to any such request.

7.114(4) [Supplemental details to r.7.114(1) requests] Where the liquidator requires the approval or authorisation of two or more creditors, the liquidator must deliver a request to each creditor, containing the matters listed in paragraph (1) and also giving–

(a) the number of creditors concerned;

(b) the total value of their claims, or if not known, as it is estimated to be by the liquidator immediately before delivering any such request; and

(c) to each preferential creditor, notice that approval or authorisation of the specified amount will be taken to be given where a majority in value of those preferential creditors who respond within the specified time limit are in favour of it; or

(d) where rule 7.113 applies, notice to the specified creditors that the amount of litigation expenses will be apportioned between them in accordance with that rule and notice of the value of the portion allocated to, and the identity of, the specified creditors affected by that apportionment.

(See General Note after r.7.116.)

7.115 Grant of approval or authorisation

7.115(1) [Failure to include matters in liquidator's request] Where the liquidator fails to include in the liquidator's request any one of the matters, statements or notices required by paragraph (1) or paragraphs (1) and (4), of rule 7.114, the request for approval or authorisation will be treated as not having been made.

7.115(2) [Approval or authorisation taken to have been given] Subject to paragraphs (3), (4) and (5), approval or authorisation will be taken to have been given where the specified amount has been requested by the liquidator, and–

(a) that amount is approved or authorised within the specified time limit; or

(b) a different amount is approved or authorised within the specified time limit and the liquidator considers it sufficient.

7.115(3) [Approval or authorisation of multiple preferential creditors] Where the liquidator requires the approval or authorisation of two or more preferential creditors, approval or authorisation will be taken to be given where a majority in value of those who respond within the specified time limit approve or authorise–

(a) the specified amount; or

(b) a different amount which the liquidator considers sufficient.

7.115(4) [Proposal of different amount] Where a majority in value of two or more preferential creditors propose an amount other than that specified by the liquidator, they will be taken to have approved or authorised an amount equal to the lowest of the amounts so proposed.

7.115(5) [Where no written response within time limits] In any case in which there is no response in writing within the specified time limit to the liquidator's request–

(a) at all; or

(b) at any time following the liquidator's provision of further particulars under rule 7.114(3); the liquidator's request will be taken to have been approved or authorised from the date of the expiry of that time limit.

(See General Note after r.7.116.)

7.116 Application to the court by the liquidator

7.116(1) [Court approval or authorisation] In the circumstances specified below the court may, upon the application of the liquidator, approve or authorise such amount of litigation expenses as it thinks just.

7.116(2) [Circumstances where application can be made] Except where paragraph (3) applies, the liquidator may apply to the court for an order approving or authorising an amount for litigation expenses only where the specified creditor (or, if more than one, any of them)–

(a) is or is intended to be a defendant in the legal proceedings in relation to which the litigation expenses have been or are to be incurred; or

(b) has been requested to approve or authorise the amount specified under rule 7.114(1)(b) and has–

(i) declined to approve or authorise, as the case may be, the specified amount,

(ii) approved or authorised an amount which is less than the specified amount and which lesser amount the liquidator considers insufficient, or

(iii) made such application for further particulars or other response to the liquidator's request as is, in the liquidator's opinion, unreasonable.

7.116(3) [Application for urgent approval or authorisation] Where the liquidator thinks that circumstances are such that the liquidator requires urgent approval or authorisation of litigation expenses, the liquidator may apply to the court for approval or authorisation either–

(a) without seeking approval or authorisation from the specified creditor; or

(b) if sought, before the expiry of the specified time limit.

7.116(4) [Conditions for granting urgent applications] The court may grant such application for approval or authorisation–

(a) if the liquidator satisfies the court of the urgency of the case; and

(b) subject to such terms and conditions as the court thinks just.

7.116(5) [Liquidator to copy application to specified creditor] The liquidator must, at the same time as making any application to the court under this rule, deliver copies of it to the specified creditor, unless the court orders otherwise.

7.116(6) [Creditor's entitlement to be heard] The specified creditor (or, if more than one, any of them) is entitled to be heard on any such application unless the court orders otherwise.

7.116(7) [Terms and conditions of grant] The court may grant approval or authorisation subject to such terms and conditions as it may think just, including terms and conditions relating to the amount or nature of the litigation expenses and as to any obligation to make further applications to the court under this rule.

7.116(8) [Costs of liquidator's application] The costs of the liquidator's application under this rule, including the costs of any specified creditor appearing or represented on it, will be an expense of the winding up unless the court orders otherwise.

General Note to rr.7.111–7.116

Section 176ZA, inserted by CA 2006 s.1282 with effect from 6 April 2008 (reversing the effect of *Re Leyland DAF Ltd, Buchler v Talbot* [2004] UKHL 9; [2004] 2 A.C. 298; [2004] B.C.C. 214), is expressly made subject to any rules restricting its application in certain circumstances to expenses authorised or approved by (a) floating charge holders; (b) preferential creditors; or (c) the court. These are the relevant rules.

They provide that the litigation expenses incurred in any of the legal proceedings described in r.7.111 (or corresponding arbitration or dispute resolution proceedings) may not be paid out of property subject to a floating charge without the approval or authorisation of the preferential creditors and charge holders who have claims on it (or, failing such approval or authorisation, of the court) (r.7.112). The rules set out the conditions with which the liquidator and the creditors and charge holders must comply. The rules recognise the interest that these parties have in the asset realisations because they are effectively funding the liquidator's litigation. In all other types of litigation the liquidator is free to make his own decisions.

In an explanatory memorandum issued by the Insolvency Service it is acknowledged that insolvency practitioners may be inclined to favour administration (where there are no provisions corresponding to these rules) rather than liquidation because of the relative certainty of recovering their expenses. The rules also impact upon the returns floating charge holders may receive, depending on which insolvency procedure is employed.

Note that authorisation or approval is not required where the litigation expenses do not exceed (or in the liquidator's opinion are not likely to exceed) in aggregate £5,000 (r.7.111)).

R.7.111

Compared with its predecessor (IR 1986 r.4.218A) this rule is poorly drafted. Several of the definitions contain paras (a), (b) etc. and so one cannot just refer to r.7.111(a) as there is more than one. The first definitions, "approval" and "authorisation" confusingly begin to be described under paras "(c)" and "(d)": it may be assumed that this is just a slip for the more traditional "(a)" and "(b)" (cf. r.6.44(1), the equivalent in creditors' voluntary liquidation).

R.7.113(2)
The "specified creditor" (now defined in r.7.111) may be a preferential creditor or a floating charge holder but must be one whose claim will not be paid in full. If all preferential creditors' claims will be paid in full, the next in line will be the floating charge holder or holders. This rule deals expressly with the case where there are two or more floating charge holders, but not with a plurality of preferential creditors. However, it is to be assumed that, following the usual rules of statutory interpretation, it is intended that the singular includes the plural and that where there are several preferential creditors the authorisation of all must be sought. (This is confirmed by rr.7.114(4)(c) and 7.115.)

There must needs be a further assumption, namely that the actual or anticipated expenses are to be brought into account by the liquidator in determining whether a creditor's debt is likely to be paid in full. The scenario could be more complex if, having initially secured the necessary authorisation for a specified amount under r.7.113(3), the liquidator seeks approval for an additional sum under r.7.113(5). If the new sum is expected to eat into the assets to an extent that a prior-ranking creditor will no longer be paid less than his full claim, he will become the specified creditor under r.7.113(2), (3) and a new round of authorisation will be necessary, superseding and supplementing the existing one.

If the specified creditor is, or is intended to be, a defendant in the proceedings, application may be made to the court for approval under r.7.116.

R.7.113(4)
The assumption is that any preferential creditors will be paid in full. If the floating charges relate to the same property, it must be assumed that the charge holders rank equally: if not, the "specified creditor" will be the first in the priority ranking whose debt will not be fully paid. If, on the other hand, one has a charge over (for instance) the company's book debts and another over other assets, it appears that the apportioned amount will depend on either or both of the value of the respective properties and the amount covered by each charge. The former would be more appropriate where the charge is insufficient to cover all the secured debt; the latter if the debt is fully secured.

R.7.114
Note the provision in para.(2) for information thought by the liquidator to be confidential.

R.7.115
This rule contains various default provisions on the basis of which approval will be deemed either to have been made or refused.

R.7.116
Standing is given to the liquidator by this rule to seek authorisation or approval from the court in the circumstances specified, which include, in effect, an appeal to the court where the specified creditor has declined to approve the requested amount. The specified creditor is entitled to be served and to be heard unless the circumstances justify an order that he be excluded: *Re Premier Motor Auctions Leeds Ltd* [2015] EWHC 3568 (Ch); [2016] B.C.C. 463. There is no corresponding right expressly given to a creditor—say a minority creditor who wishes to challenge a decision of the majority—but this would not rule out the court having jurisdiction in an appropriate case.

Chapter 16

Miscellaneous Rules

[Note: a document required by the Act or these Rules must also contain the standard contents set out in Part 1.]

Sub-division A: Return of capital

7.117 Application to court for order authorising return of capital

7.117(1) [Application of rule] This rule applies where the liquidator intends to apply to the court for an order authorising a return of capital.

7.117(2) [Accompanying list] The application must be accompanied by a list of the persons to whom the return is to be made.

7.117(3) [Details of list] The list must include the same details of those persons as appears in the settled list of contributories, with any necessary alterations to take account of matters after settlement of the list, and the amount to be paid to each person.

7.117(4) [Court to deliver sealed copy order to liquidator] Where the court makes an order authorising the return, it must deliver a sealed copy of the order to the liquidator.

(See General Note after r.7.118.)

7.118 Procedure for return

7.118(1) [Rate of return, etc.] The liquidator must inform each person to whom a return is made of the rate of return per share, and whether it is expected that any further return will be made.

7.118(2) [Method of payment] Any payments made by the liquidator by way of the return may be delivered by post, unless for any reason another method of making the payment has been agreed with the payee.

GENERAL NOTE TO RR.7.117–7.118

In a winding up by the court, the court must "adjust the rights of the contributories among themselves and distribute any surplus among the persons entitled to it" (IA 1986 s.154). Although it might have been thought from the language of IA 1986 ss.143(1) and 160(1)(b), (2) that capital could be returned to contributories on the liquidator's own authority, these rules confirm that he must have the sanction of the court.

Sub-division B: Dissolution after winding up

7.119 Secretary of State's directions under sections 203 and 205 and appeal

7.119(1) [Application of rule] This rule applies where the Secretary of State gives a direction under–

(a) section 203 (where official receiver applies to the registrar of companies for a company's early dissolution); or

(b) section 205 (application by interested person for postponement of dissolution).

7.119(2) [Duty of Secretary of State] The Secretary of State must deliver the direction to the applicant for it.

7.119(3) [Copy direction to registrar of companies] The applicant must deliver a copy of the direction to the registrar of companies, to comply with section 203(5) or, as the case may be, section 205(6).

7.119(4) [Appeals; copy of sealed order] Following an appeal under section 203(4) or 205(4) (against a decision of the Secretary of State under the applicable section) the court must deliver a sealed copy of its order to the person in whose favour the appeal was determined.

7.119(5) [Copy to registrar of companies] That person must deliver a copy to the registrar of companies to comply with section 203(5) or, as the case may be, section 205(6).

GENERAL NOTE

This rule provides machinery for the exercise of the official receiver's power under IA 1986 ss.202 et seq., to apply to the registrar of companies for the early dissolution of the company where the assets are not worth the expense of administration. Notice with the copy of the court order to Companies House under r.7.119(5) must be in Form WU13.

Part 8

Individual Voluntary Arrangements (IVA)

Introductory note to Part 8
This Part replaces Pt 5 of IR 1986 which was itself inserted by the Insolvency (Amendment) (No.2) Rules 2002 (SI 2002/2712) with effect from 1 January 2003 to cater for the significant changes in the IVA regime brought about by IA 2000. The new Pt 5 only applied to IVAs agreed after 1 January 2003. Note that there is now no provision of official Forms—the required details are delineated in the appropriate Rules.

Chapter 1

Preliminary

8.1 Interpretation

8.1 In this Part–

"authorised person" means the official receiver where the official receiver is authorised to act as nominee or supervisor under section 389B(1) of the Act;

"nominee" and "supervisor" include the proposed nominee or supervisor in relation to a proposal for an IVA; and

"proposal" means a proposal for an IVA.

Chapter 2

Preparation of the debtor's proposal for an IVA

[Note: a document required by the Act or these Rules must also contain the standard contents set out in Part 1.]

8.2 Proposal for an IVA: general principles and amendment

8.2(1) [Explanation why voluntary arrangement desirable] A proposal must–

(a) identify the debtor;

(b) explain why the debtor thinks an IVA is desirable;

(c) explain why the creditors are expected to agree to an IVA; and

(d) be authenticated and dated by the debtor.

8.2(2) [Amendment of the proposal] The proposal may be amended with the nominee's agreement in writing at any time up to the filing of the nominee's report with the court under section 256, or the submission of the nominee's report to the creditors under section 256A.

General Note

See the introductory note to Pt 8. This rule explains the debtor's responsibilities with regard to the preparation of the IVA proposal.

8.3 Proposal: contents

8.3 The proposal must set out the following so far as known to the debtor–

Assets	(a) the debtor's assets, with an estimate of their respective values; (b) which assets are charged and the extent of the charge; (c) which assets are to be excluded from the IVA; and (d) particulars of any property to be included in the IVA which is not owned by the debtor including details of who owns such property and the terms on which it will be available for inclusion;
Liabilities	(e) the nature and amount of the debtor's liabilities; (f) how the debtor's liabilities will be met, modified, postponed or otherwise dealt with by means of the IVA and, in particular– (i) how preferential creditors and creditors who are, or claim to be, secured will be dealt with, (ii) how creditors who are associates of the debtor will be dealt with, (iii) if the debtor is an undischarged bankrupt, whether any claim has been made under section 339 (transactions at an undervalue), section 340 (preferences), or section 343 (extortionate credit transactions) and, if it has, whether, and if so what, provision is being made to indemnify the bankrupt's estate in respect of such a claim; and (iv) if the debtor is not an undischarged bankrupt whether there are circumstances which might give rise to a claim as referred to in sub-paragraph (iii) if the debtor were made bankrupt and, where there are such circumstances, whether and, if so what, provision will be made to indemnify the bankrupt's estate in respect of such a claim;
Nominee's fees and expenses	(g) the amount proposed to be paid to the nominee by way of fees and expenses;
Supervisor	(h) identification and contact details for the supervisor; (i) confirmation that the supervisor is qualified to act as an insolvency practitioner (or is an authorised person) in relation to the debtor and the name of the relevant recognised professional body which is the source of the supervisor's authorisation; (j) how the fees and expenses of the supervisor will be determined and paid; (k) the functions to be undertaken by the supervisor; (l) where it is proposed that two or more supervisors be appointed, a statement whether acts done in connection with the IVA may be done by any one or more of them or must be done by all of them;
Guarantees and proposed guarantees	(m) whether any, and if so what, guarantees have been given in respect of the debtor's debts, specifying which of the guarantors are associates of the debtor; (n) whether any guarantees are proposed to be offered for the purposes of the IVA, and if so what, by whom and whether security is to be given or sought;
Timing	(o) the proposed duration of the IVA;
	(p) the proposed dates of distributions to creditors, with estimates of their amounts;
Type of proceedings	(q) whether the proceedings will be main, territorial or non-EU proceedings with reasons;
Conduct of business	(r) if the debtor has any business, how that business will be conducted during the IVA;

Further credit facilities	(s) details of any further proposed credit facilities for the debtor and how the debts so arising are to be paid;
Handling of funds arising	(t) the manner in which funds held for the purposes of the IVA are to be banked, invested or otherwise dealt with pending distribution to creditors; (u) how funds held for the purpose of payment to creditors, and not so paid on the termination of the IVA, will be dealt with; (v) how the claim of any person bound by the IVA by virtue of section 260(2)(b)(ii) will be dealt with;
Other proposals	(w) whether another proposal in relation to the debtor has been submitted within the 24 months before the date of the submission of the proposal to the nominee– (i) for approval by the creditors and, if so, (aa) whether that proposal was approved or rejected, (bb) whether, if approved, the IVA was completed or was terminated, and (cc) in what respects such a proposal, where rejected, differs from the current proposal; (ii) to the court in connection with an application for an interim order under section 253 and, if so, whether the interim order was made;
Other matters	(x) any other matters which the debtor considers appropriate to enable creditors to reach an informed decision on the proposal.

General Note

See the introductory note to Pt 8. Rule 8.3 details the required contents of the proposal in tabular form—e.g. information on assets, liabilities, duration of IVA, proposed dividends, supervisor's remuneration, etc.

In the table, entry for "Type of proceedings" amended by the Insolvency (England and Wales) and Insolvency (Scotland) (Miscellaneous and Consequential Amendments) Rules 2017 (SI 2017/1115) rr.1(1), (2), 22, 30(22) as from 8 December 2017.

8.4 Notice of nominee's consent

8.4(1) [Delivery of notice of consent] A nominee who consents to act must deliver a notice of that consent to the debtor as soon as reasonably practicable after the proposal has been submitted to the nominee under section 256(2) or 256A(2).

8.4(2) [Statement of receipt of notice] The notice must state the date the nominee received the proposal.

General Note

This deals with the giving of formal consent to act as nominee for the proposal by the nominee. Unlike the previous IR 1986 r.5.4 there are no specific requirements as to how the debtor communicates the nomination to the nominee.

8.5 Statement of affairs (section 256 and 256A)

8.5(1) [Contents of the statement of affairs] The statement of affairs which the debtor is required to submit to the nominee under either section 256(2) or 256A(2) must contain–

(a) a list of the debtor's assets, divided into such categories as are appropriate for easy identification, and with each category given an estimated value;

(b) in the case of any property on which a claim against the debtor is wholly or partly secured, particulars of the claim and of how and when the security was created;

(c) the names and addresses of the preferential creditors with the amounts of their respective claims;

(d) the names and addresses of the unsecured creditors, with the amounts of their respective claims;

(e) particulars of any debts owed by the debtor to persons who are associates of the debtor;

(f) particulars of any debts owed to the debtor by persons who are associates of the debtor; and

(g) any other particulars that the nominee in writing requires to be provided for the purposes of making the nominee's report on the proposal to the court or to the creditors (as the case may be).

8.5(2) [Relevant date] The statement must be made up to a date not earlier than two weeks before the date of the proposal.

8.5(3) [Exception for earlier statement date] However the nominee may allow the statement to be made up to a date that is earlier than two weeks (but no earlier than two months) before the date of the proposal where that is more practicable.

8.5(4) [Explanation of earlier date] If the statement is made up to an earlier date the nominee's report must explain why an earlier date was allowed.

8.5(5) [Statement verified by statement of truth] The statement must be verified by a statement of truth made by the debtor.

8.5(6) [Exception for undischarged bankrupt] Where the debtor is an undischarged bankrupt and has already delivered a statement of affairs under section 288 the debtor need not submit a statement of affairs to the nominee under section 256(2) or 256A(2) unless the nominee requires a further statement of affairs to supplement or amplify the earlier one.

General Note

See the introductory note to Pt 8. The debtor must furnish the nominee with a formal statement of affairs along with the proposal in order for the nominee to prepare their report under s.256 or 256A. Rule 8.5 details the contents of this statement.

8.6 Application to omit information from statement of affairs delivered to creditors

8.6 The nominee, the debtor or any person appearing to the court to have an interest may, if any information in the statement of affairs would be likely to prejudice the conduct of the IVA or might reasonably be expected to lead to violence against any person, apply to the court for an order that specified information be omitted from any statement of affairs required to be delivered to the creditors.

General Note

This provision is based upon IR 1986 r.5.68. It is a new safety-conscious provision first inserted by I(A)R 2010 (SI 2010/686).

8.7 Additional disclosure for assistance of nominee

8.7(1) [Nominee may request further information] If it appears to the nominee that the report to the court under section 256(1) or to the creditors under section 256A(3) cannot properly be prepared on the basis of information in the proposal and statement of affairs, the nominee may require the debtor to provide–

(a) more information about the circumstances in which, and the reasons why, an IVA is being proposed;

(b) more information about any proposals of the kind referred to in rule 8.3(w);

(c) information about any proposals which have at any time been made by the debtor under Part 8 of the Act; and

(d) any further information relating to the debtor's affairs which the nominee thinks necessary for the purposes of the report.

8.7(2) [Whether debtor concerned with insolvent company, bankrupt etc] The nominee may require the debtor to inform the nominee whether and in what circumstances the debtor has at any time–

(a) been concerned in the affairs of a company wherever incorporated or limited liability partnership which has become the subject of insolvency proceedings;

(b) been made bankrupt;

(c) been the subject of a debt relief order; or

(d) entered into an arrangement with creditors.

8.7(3) [Access to accounts and records] The debtor must give the nominee such access to the debtor's accounts and records as the nominee requires to enable the nominee to consider the debtor's proposal and prepare the report on it.

General Note

See the introductory note to Pt 8. This allows the nominee to call for further information from the debtor.

Chapter 3

Cases in which an application for an interim order is made

[Note: a document required by the Act or these Rules must also contain the standard contents set out in Part 1.]

8.8 Application for interim order

8.8(1) [Accompanying witness statement] An application to the court for an interim order under Part 8 of the Act must be accompanied by a witness statement containing–

(a) the reasons for making the application;

(b) information about any action, execution, other legal process or the levying of any distress which, to the debtor's knowledge, has been commenced against the debtor or the debtor's property;

(c) a statement that the debtor is an undischarged bankrupt or is able to make a bankruptcy application;

(d) a statement that no previous application for an interim order has been made by or in relation to the debtor in the period of 12 months ending with the date of the witness statement; and

(e) a statement that a person named in the witness statement is willing to act as nominee in relation to the proposal and is qualified to act as an insolvency practitioner (or is an authorised person) in relation to the debtor.

8.8(2) [Copies proposal and consent to be attached to witness statement] The witness statement must be accompanied by a copy of–

(a) the proposal; and

(b) the notice of the nominee's consent to act.

8.8(3) [Court to fix venue] When the application and the witness statement have been filed, the court must fix a venue for the hearing of the application.

8.8(4) [Notice of hearing] The applicant must deliver a notice of the hearing and the venue at least two business days before the hearing to–

(a) the nominee;

(b) the debtor, the official receiver or the trustee (whichever is not the applicant) where the debtor is an undischarged bankrupt; and

(c) any creditor who (to the debtor's knowledge) has presented a bankruptcy petition against the debtor where the debtor is not an undischarged bankrupt.

8.8(5) [Detail to be contained in notice] A notice under section 253(4) must contain the name and address of the nominee.

General Note

See the introductory note to Pt 8. This explains the procedure to be followed on an application for an interim order.

8.9 Court in which application is to be made

8.9(1) [Court for application] An application must be made–

(a) to the court (and hearing centre if applicable), if any, which has the conduct of the bankruptcy, where the debtor is an undischarged bankrupt; or

(b) to the court (and hearing centre if applicable) determined in accordance with rule 10.48.

8.9(2) [Information in application] The application must contain sufficient information to establish that it is made to the appropriate court or hearing centre.

General Note

See the introductory note to Pt 8. This identifies the appropriate court where an application for an interim order is made. See the former I(A)R 2010 (SI 2010/686) for background.

8.10 Order granting a stay

8.10 A court order under section 254(1)(b) granting a stay pending hearing of an application must identify the proceedings and contain–

(a) the section number of the Act under which it is made;

(b) details of the action, execution or other legal process which is stayed;

(c) the date on which the application for an interim order will be heard; and

(d) the date that the order granting the stay is made.

General Note

This is a new provision added in the 2016 Rules which is derived from Form 5.1 of the 1986 Rules.

8.11 Hearing of the application

8.11(1) [Persons who may appear or be represented] A person to whom a notice of the hearing of the application for an interim order was (or should have been) delivered under rule 8.8(4) may appear or be represented at the hearing.

8.11(2) [Representations to be taken into account] The court must take into account any representations made by or on behalf of such a person (in particular, as to whether an order should contain such provision as is referred to in section 255(3) (provisions as to the conduct of the bankruptcy etc.) and (4) (provisions staying proceedings in bankruptcy etc.).

8.11(3) [Consideration of report where interim order made] If the court makes an interim order, it must fix a venue for consideration of the nominee's report for a date no later than the date on which the order ceases to have effect.

General Note

See the introductory note to Pt 8. This explains the procedure to be followed on hearing an application for an interim order.

8.12 The interim order

8.12 An interim order must contain–

(a) identification details for the proceedings;

(b) the section number of the Act under which it is made;

(c) a statement that the order has effect from its making until the end of the period of 14 days beginning on the day after the date on which it is made;

(d) particulars of the effect of the order (as set out in section 252(2));

(e) an order that the report of the nominee be delivered to the court no later than two business days before the date fixed for the court's consideration of the report;

(f) particulars of any orders made under section 255(3) and (4);

(g) where the debtor is an undischarged bankrupt and the applicant is not the official receiver, an order that the applicant delivers, as soon as reasonably practicable, a copy of the interim order to the official receiver;

(h) the venue for the court's consideration of the nominee's report; and

(i) the date of the order.

General Note

This is a new provision added in the 2016 Rules which is derived from Form 5.2 of the 1986 Rules.

8.13 Action to follow making of an interim order

8.13(1) [Sealed copies of interim order] The court must deliver at least two sealed copies of the interim order to the applicant.

8.13(2) [Delivery of copy order and notices] As soon as reasonably practicable, the applicant must deliver–

(a) one copy to the nominee and, where the debtor is an undischarged bankrupt, another copy to the official receiver (unless the official receiver was the applicant); and

(b) a notice that the order has been made to any other person to whom a notice of the hearing of the application for an interim order was (or should have been) delivered under rule 8.8(4) and who was not in attendance or represented at the hearing.

General Note

See the introductory note to Pt 8. This rule deals with the dissemination of the fact that an interim order has been made.

8.14 Order extending period of an interim order (section 256(4))

8.14 An order under section 256(4) extending the period for which an interim order has effect must contain–

(a) identification details for the proceedings;

(b) a statement that the application is that of the nominee for an extension of the period under section 256(4) for which an interim order is to have effect;

(c) an order that the period for which the interim order has effect is extended to a specified date;

(d) particulars of the effect (as set out in section 252(2)) of the interim order;

(e) an order that the report of the nominee be delivered to the court no later two business days before the date fixed for the court's consideration of the nominee's report;

(f) particulars of any orders made under section 255(3) or (4);

(g) where the debtor is an undischarged bankrupt and the applicant is not the official receiver, an order that the applicant deliver, as soon as reasonably practicable, a copy of the order to the official receiver;

(h) the venue for the court's consideration of the report; and

(i) the date of the order.

General Note

This is a new provision added in the 2016 Rules which is derived from Form 5.3 of the 1986 Rules.

8.15 Nominee's report on the proposal

8.15(1) [Time for delivery] The nominee's report under section 256 must be filed with the court not less than two business days before the interim order ceases to have effect, accompanied by–

(a) a copy of the report;

(b) a copy of the proposal (as amended, if applicable, under rule 8.2(2); and

(c) a copy of any statement of affairs or a summary of such a statement.

8.15(2) [Delivery to the debtor] The nominee must also deliver a copy of the report to the debtor.

8.15(3) [Nominee's explanation] The nominee's report must explain whether or not the nominee considers that the proposal has a reasonable prospect of being approved and implemented and whether or not creditors should be invited to consider the proposal.

8.15(4) [Endorsement of filing date] The court must endorse the nominee's report and the copy of it with the date on which they were filed and return the copy to the nominee.

8.15(5) [Where debtor undischarged bankrupt] Where the debtor is an undischarged bankrupt, the nominee must deliver to the official receiver and any trustee, a copy of–

(a) the proposal;

(b) the nominee's report; and

(c) any statement of affairs or summary of such a statement.

8.15(6) [Where debtor not undischarged bankrupt] Where the debtor is not an undischarged bankrupt, the nominee must deliver a copy of each of those documents to any person who has presented a bankruptcy petition against the debtor.

General Note

See the introductory note to Pt 8. This regulates the nominee's report on the debtor's proposal and the communication of his views to the court. Note the right of creditors to inspect the court file.

8.16 Order extending period of interim order to enable the creditors to consider the proposal (section 256(5))

8.16 An order under section 256(5) extending the period for which an interim order has effect to enable creditors to consider the proposal must contain–

(a) identification details for the proceedings;

(b) the section number of the Act under which it is made;

(c) the date that the nominee's report was filed;

(d) a statement that for the purpose of enabling the creditors to consider the proposal, the period for which the interim order has effect is extended to a specified date;

(e) a statement that the nominee will be inviting the creditors to consider the proposal and details of the decision procedure the nominee intends to use;

(f) where the debtor is an undischarged bankrupt and the nominee is not the official receiver, an order that the nominee deliver, as soon as reasonably practicable, a copy of the order to the official receiver; and

(g) the date of the order.

General Note

This is a new provision added in the 2016 Rules which is derived from Form 5.3 of the 1986 Rules.

8.17 Replacement of the nominee (section 256(3))

8.17(1) [Notice of application] A debtor who intends to apply under section 256(3)(a) or (b) for the nominee to be replaced must deliver a notice to the nominee that such an application is intended to be made at least five business days before filing the application with the court.

8.17(2) [Delivery of notice] A nominee who intends to apply under section 256(3)(b) to be replaced must deliver a notice to the debtor that such an application is intended to be made at least five business days before filing the application with the court.

8.17(3) [Replacement nominee to file consent and qualification to act] The court must not appoint a replacement nominee unless the replacement nominee has filed with the court a statement confirming–

(a) that person is qualified to act as an insolvency practitioner (or is an authorised person) in relation to the debtor; and

(b) that person's consent to act.

General Note

See the introductory note to Pt 8. This provision supplements s.256(3) on replacement of nominees. The now superseded I(A)R 2010 (SI 2010/686) which made the change from seven days to five business days.

8.18 Consideration of the nominee's report

8.18(1) [Persons who may appear or be represented] A person to whom a notice was (or should have been) delivered under rule 8.8(4) may appear or be represented at the court's hearing to consider the nominee's report.

8.18(2) [Application of r.8.13] Rule 8.13 applies to any order made by the court at the hearing.

GENERAL NOTE

See the introductory note to Pt 8. This deals with procedural matters where the nominee's report is being considered.

CHAPTER 4

CASES WHERE NO INTERIM ORDER IS TO BE OBTAINED

[Note: a document required by the Act or these Rules must also contain the standard contents set out in Part 1.]

8.19 Nominee's report (section 256A)

8.19(1) [Report to explain likelihood of approval] The nominee's report under section 256A(3) must explain whether or not the nominee considers that the proposal has a reasonable prospect of being approved and implemented and whether or not creditors should be invited to consider the proposal.

8.19(1A) [Jurisdiction to open proceedings] The nominee must examine whether there is jurisdiction to open the proceedings and must specify in the nominee's report whether the proceedings will be main, secondary, territorial on non-EU proceedings with the reasons for so stating.

8.19(2) [Information to be contained in report] The report must contain sufficient information to enable a person to identify (in accordance with rule 8.20) the appropriate court or hearing centre in which to file an application relating to the proposal or the IVA.

8.19(3) [Delivery of report to debtor] The nominee must also deliver a copy of the report to the debtor.

8.19(4) [Documents to be delivered where opinion affirmative] Where the nominee gives an opinion in the affirmative on the matters referred to in section 256A(3)(a) and (b), the copy of the report delivered by the nominee to each of the creditors must be accompanied by–

(a) a statement that an application for an interim order under section 253 is not being made;

(b) a copy of the proposal (as amended, if applicable, under rule 8.2(2));

(c) a copy of any statement of affairs or a summary of such a statement; and

(d) a copy of the notice of the nominee's consent to act.

8.19(5) [Delivery to other persons] In such a case the nominee must also deliver those documents within 14 days (or such longer period as the court may allow) of receipt of the document and statement referred to in section 256A(2) to–

(a) the official receiver and any trustee, where the debtor is an undischarged bankrupt; and

(b) any person who has presented a bankruptcy petition against the debtor.

8.19(6) [Delivery of report where opinion is negative] Where the nominee gives an opinion in the negative on the matters referred to in section 256A(3)(a) and (b) the nominee must within 14 days (or such longer period as the court may allow) of receipt of the document and statement referred to in section 256A(2)–

(a) deliver a copy of the report to the creditors; and

(b) give the reasons for that opinion to the debtor.

General Note

This reflects the previous r.5.14A which had been inserted by I(A)R 2010 (SI 2010/686).

Rule 8.19(1A) inserted by the Insolvency Amendment (EU 2015/848) Regulations 2017 (SI 2017/702) regs 1, 2(1), Sch. paras 32, 41 in relation to proceedings opened on or after 26 June 2017 (see reg.3) when the Recast EU Regulation 2015/848 came into force.

8.20 Court or hearing centre to which applications must be made where no interim order

8.20(1) [Application of this rule] This rule applies where the nominee has made a report under section 256A(3).

8.20(2) [Venue to which application must be made] Any application relating to a proposal or an IVA must be made–

(a) to the court or hearing centre, if any, which has the conduct of the bankruptcy, where the debtor is an undischarged bankrupt; or

(b) to the court or hearing centre determined in accordance with rule 10.48.

8.20(3) [Content of application] The application must contain sufficient information to establish that it is made to the appropriate court or hearing centre.

8.20(4) [Documents to be delivered] The applicant must file with the court (in addition to the documents in support of the application) such other documents required by this Part as the applicant considers may assist the court in determining the application.

General Note

This reflects the previous r.5.14B(1)–(4) as inserted by I(A)R 2010 (SI 2010/686). But see *Revenue and Customs Commissioners v Earley* [2011] EWHC 1783 (Ch) in which Morritt C permitted an application to be made to the High Court in spite of that previous provision restricting jurisdiction to the Bankruptcy Court.

8.21 Replacement of the nominee (section 256A(4))

8.21(1) [Delivery of application by debtor] A debtor who intends to apply under section 256A(4)(a) or (b) for the nominee to be replaced must deliver a notice of the intention to make the application to the nominee at least five business days before filing the application with the court.

8.21(2) [Debtor of application by nominee] A nominee who intends to apply under section 256A(4)(b) to be replaced must deliver a notice of the intention to make such an application to the debtor at least five business days before filing the application with the court.

8.21(3) [Replacement nominee to file consent and qualification to act] The court must not appoint a replacement nominee unless the replacement nominee has filed with the court a statement confirming–

(a) that person is qualified to act as an insolvency practitioner (or is an authorised person) in relation to the debtor; and

(b) that person's consent to act.

General Note

This reflects the previous r 5.14B(5)–(7) as had been inserted by the now superseded I(A)R 2010 (SI 2010/686).

Chapter 5

Consideration of the proposal by the creditors

[Note: a document required by the Act or these Rules must also contain the standard contents set out in Part 1.]

8.22 Consideration of the proposal

8.22(1) [Application of rule] This rule applies where the nominee is required to seek a decision from the debtor's creditors as to whether they approve the debtor's proposal.

8.22(2) [Nominee to deliver notice] The nominee must deliver to each creditor a notice which complies with rule 15.8 so far as is relevant.

8.22(3) [Content of notice] The notice must also contain–

(a) identification details for the proceedings;

(b) where an interim order has not been obtained, details of the court or hearing centre to which an application relating to the proposal or the IVA must be made under rule 8.20(2);

(c) where an interim order is in force, details of the court or hearing centre in which the nominee's report on the debtor's proposal has been filed under section 256;

(d) a statement as to how a person entitled to vote for the proposal may propose a modification to it, and how the nominee will deal with such a proposal for a modification.

8.22(4) [Notification by website] The notice may contain or be accompanied by a notice that the results of the consideration of the proposal will be made available for viewing and downloading on a website and that no other notice will be delivered to the creditors to whom the notice under this rule was sent.

8.22(5) [Requirements for use of website] Where the results of the consideration of the proposal are to be made available for viewing and downloading on a website the nominee must comply with the requirements for use of a website to deliver a document set out in rule 1.49(2)(a) to (c), (3) and (4) with any necessary adaptations and rule 1.49(5)(a) applies to determine the time of delivery of the document.

8.22(6) [Documents to accompany notice] The notice must be accompanied by the following (unless they have been delivered already under rule 8.19)–

(a) a copy of the proposal;

(b) a copy of the statement of affairs, or a summary including a list of creditors with the amounts of their debts; and

(c) a copy of the nominee's report on the proposal.

8.22(7) [Decision date] The decision date must be not less than 14 days from the date of delivery of the notice and not more than 28 days from the date on which–

(a) the nominee received the document and statement of affairs referred to in section 256A(2) in a case where an interim order has not been obtained; or

(b) the nominee's report was considered by the court in a case where an interim order is in force.

General Note

See the introductory note to Pt 8. Chapter 5 is devoted to the consideration of the proposals by the creditors either with or without creditor meetings being held.

8.23 Proposals for an alternative supervisor

8.23(1) [Details of alternative supervisor to be given] If in response to a notice of a decision procedure to consider the proposal other than at a meeting, a creditor proposes that a person other than the nominee be appointed as supervisor, that person's consent to act and confirmation of being qualified to act as an insolvency practitioner (or being an authorised person) in relation to the debtor must be delivered to the nominee by the creditor.

8.23(2) [Documents to be supplied at creditors' meeting] If at a creditors' meeting to consider the proposal a resolution is moved for the appointment of a person other than the nominee to be supervisor, that person must produce to the chair at or before the meeting–

(a) confirmation of being qualified to act as an insolvency practitioner (or being an authorised person) in relation to the debtor; and

(b) written consent to act (unless the person is present at the meeting and signifies consent).

GENERAL NOTE

See the introductory note to Pt 8. This rule covers the situation where a creditor wishes to change the supervisor whether at a meeting or through a creditor decision procedure.

8.24 Report of the creditors' consideration of a proposal

8.24(1) [Person to prepare report] A report of the creditors' consideration of a proposal must be prepared by the convener or, if the proposal is considered at a meeting, by the chair.

8.24(2) [Content of report] The report must–

(a) state whether the proposal was approved or rejected and, if approved, with what (if any) modifications;

(b) list the creditors who voted or attended or who were represented at the meeting or decision procedure (as applicable) used to consider the proposal, setting out (with their respective values) how they voted on each resolution or whether they abstained;

(c) if the proposal was approved, state whether the proceedings are main, territorial or non-EU proceedings and the reasons for so stating; and

(d) include such further information as the nominee or the chair thinks appropriate.

8.24(3) [Filing date where interim order granted] Where an interim order was obtained a copy of the report must be filed with the court, within four business days of the decision date.

8.24(4) [Endorsement by court] The court must endorse the copy of the report with the date of filing.

8.24(5) [Notification of result of consideration] The nominee must give notice of the result of the consideration to–

(a) everyone who was invited to consider the proposal and to whom notice of the decision procedure was delivered;

(b) any other creditor; and

(c) where the debtor is an undischarged bankrupt, the official receiver and any trustee.

8.24(6) [Timing of notification] The notice must be given–

(a) where an interim order was obtained, as soon as reasonably practicable after a copy of the report is filed with the court; or

(b) where an interim order was not obtained, within four business days of the decision date.

GENERAL NOTE

See the introductory note to Pt 8. This rule explains the contents of the report to be given to creditors prepared by either the convenor of the proposal or the chairman of the creditors' meeting (if one is held)—this report, which has become more fulsome with successive reforms, must be filed in court within four business days.

Rule 8.24(2)(c) amended by the Insolvency (England and Wales) and Insolvency (Scotland) (Miscellaneous and Consequential Amendments) Rules 2017 (SI 2017/1115) rr.1(1), (2), 22, 30(23) as from 8 December 2017.

Chapter 6

Action following approval of an IVA

[Note: a document required by the Act or these Rules must also contain the standard contents set out in Part 1.]

8.25 Hand-over of property, etc. to supervisor

8.25(1) [Putting supervisor into possession of assets] As soon as reasonably practicable after the IVA is approved, the debtor or, where the debtor is an undischarged bankrupt, the official receiver or any trustee must do all that is required to put the supervisor in possession of the assets included in the IVA.

8.25(2) [Discharge of official receiver's remuneration] Where the debtor is an undischarged bankrupt, the supervisor must–

(a) before taking possession of the assets included in the IVA, deliver to the official receiver or any trustee an undertaking to discharge the balance due to the official receiver or trustee out of the first realisation of the assets; or

(b) upon taking possession of the assets included in the IVA, discharge such balance.

8.25(3) [Balance due] The balance is any balance due to the official receiver or any trustee–

(a) by way of fees or expenses properly incurred and payable under the Act or these Rules; and

(b) on account of any advances made in respect of the bankrupt's estate, together with interest on such advances at the rate specified in section 17 of the Judgments Act 1838 at the date of the bankruptcy order.

8.25(4) [Charge on assets of undischarged bankrupt] Where the debtor is an undischarged bankrupt, the official receiver and any trustee have a charge on the assets included in the IVA in respect of any sums comprising such balance, subject only to the deduction by the supervisor from realisations of the proper costs and expenses of realisation.

8.25(5) [Official receiver's priority] Any sums due to the official receiver take priority over those due to any trustee.

8.25(6) [Discharge of guarantees; payment of expenses] The supervisor must from time to time out of the realisation of assets–

(a) discharge all guarantees properly given by the official receiver or any trustee for the benefit of the bankrupt's estate; and

(b) pay the expenses of the official receiver and any trustee.

General Note

See the introductory note to Pt 8. Chapter 6 deals with the implementation of the approved arrangement. Rule 8.25 addresses various matters consequential to approval, including the handing over of property to the supervisor. A properly drafted arrangement should carefully identify such property in order for it to become a trust asset protected from the claims of creditors outside the IVA.

8.26 Report to the Secretary of State of the approval of an IVA

8.26(1) [Chair to deliver report] After the creditors approve an IVA the nominee, appointed person or the chair must deliver a report containing the required information to the Secretary of State.

8.26(2) [Time limit for delivery] The report must be delivered as soon as reasonably practicable, and in any event within 14 days after the report that the creditors have approved the IVA has been filed with the court under rule 8.24(3) or the notice that the creditors have approved the IVA has been sent to the creditors under rule 8.24(5) as the case may be.

8.26(3) [Required information] The required information is–

(a) identification details for the debtor;

(b) the debtor's gender;

(c) the debtor's date of birth;

(d) any name by which the debtor was or is known, not being the name in which the debtor has entered into the IVA;

(e) the date on which the IVA was approved by the creditors; and

(f) the name and address of the supervisor.

8.26(4) [Notice of change of supervisor] A person who is appointed to act as a supervisor as a replacement of another person, or who vacates that office must deliver a notice of that fact to the Secretary of State as soon as reasonably practicable.

General Note

See the introductory note to Pt 8. In addition to notifying the court the nominee, appointed person or chair (as appropriate) must notify approved voluntary arrangements to the Secretary of State. This is necessary to enable the latter to maintain the public register. The supervisor must also notify his appointment to the Secretary of State.

8.27 Revocation or suspension of an IVA (section 262)

8.27(1) [Application of rule] This rule applies where the court makes an order of revocation or suspension under section 262.

8.27(2) [Delivery of sealed copy order] The applicant for the order must deliver a sealed copy of it to–

(a) the debtor (if different from the applicant);

(b) the supervisor; and

(c) where the debtor is an undischarged bankrupt, the official receiver and any trustee (in either case, if different from the applicant).

8.27(3) [Delivery to person required to manage decision procedure] If the order includes a direction by the court under section 262(4)(b) for a matter to be considered further by a decision procedure, the applicant for the order must deliver a notice that the order has been made to the person who is directed to take such action.

8.27(4) [Delivery by debtor or trustee] The debtor, or the trustee (if the debtor is an undischarged bankrupt) must–

(a) as soon as reasonably practicable deliver a notice that the order has been made to everyone to whom a notice to consider the matter by a decision procedure was delivered or who appears to be affected by the order; and

(b) within five business days of delivery of a copy of the order (or within such longer period as the court may allow), deliver, if applicable, a notice to the court advising that it is intended to make a revised proposal to the creditors, or to invite re-consideration of the original proposal.

8.27(5) [Delivery of notice of order to Secretary of State] The applicant for the order must, within five business days of the making of the order deliver a notice of the order to the Secretary of State.

8.27(6) [Delivery of notice of expiry to Secretary of State] The applicant for the order must, within five business days of the expiry of any order of suspension, deliver a notice of the expiry to the Secretary of State.

GENERAL NOTE

See the introductory note to Pt 8. This particular rule deals with revocation or suspension of the IVA under the terms of s.262. Various consequential matters are addressed including the requirement imposed on the successful applicant to notify the Secretary of State.

8.28 Supervisor's accounts and reports

8.28(1) [Duty of supervisor to keep] The supervisor must keep accounts and records where the IVA authorises or requires the supervisor–

(a) to carry on the business of the debtor or trade on behalf of or in the name of the debtor;

(b) to realise assets of the debtor or, where the debtor is an undischarged bankrupt, belonging to the bankrupt's estate; or

(c) otherwise to administer or dispose of any funds of the debtor or the bankrupt's estate.

8.28(2) [Accounts and records to be kept] The accounts and records which must be kept are of the supervisor's acts and dealings in, and in connection with, the IVA, including in particular records of all receipts and payments of money.

8.28(3) [Preservation of accounts of past supervisor] The supervisor must preserve any such accounts and records which were kept by any other person who has acted as supervisor of the IVA and are in the supervisor's possession.

8.28(4) [Delivery of report of progress and prospects] The supervisor must deliver reports on the progress and prospects for the full implementation of the IVA to–

(a) the debtor; and

(b) the creditors bound by the IVA.

8.28(5) [Periods covered by reports] The first report must cover the period of 12 months commencing on the date on which the IVA was approved and a further report must be made for each subsequent period of 12 months.

8.28(6) [Delivery of reports] Each report must be delivered within the period of two months after the end of the 12 month period.

8.28(7) [Exemption where r.8.31 applies] Such a report is not required if an obligation to deliver a report under rule 8.31 arises in the two months after the end of the period.

8.28(8) [Additional detail required in reports] Where the supervisor is authorised or required to do any of the things mentioned in paragraph (1), the report–

(a) must include or be accompanied by a summary of receipts and payments which paragraph (2) requires to be recorded; or

(b) where there have been no such receipts and payments, must say so.

GENERAL NOTE

This reflects the new rule originally inserted by the now superseded I(A)R 2010 (SI 2010/686) to replace the former IR 1986 r.5.31.

8.29 Production of accounts and records to the Secretary of State

8.29(1) [Right to require production of accounts and records] The Secretary of State may during the IVA or after its full implementation or termination require the supervisor to produce for inspection (either at the supervisor's premises or elsewhere)–

(a) the supervisor's accounts and records in relation to the IVA; and

(b) copies of reports and summaries prepared in compliance with rule 8.28.

8.29(2) [Right to require accounts and records to be audited] The Secretary of State may require any accounts and records produced under this rule to be audited and, if so, the supervisor must provide such further information and assistance as the Secretary of State requires for the purposes of the audit.

General Note

See the introductory note to Pt 8. In addition to the general accounting requirements imposed by r.8.28, the Secretary of State can at any time require further accounts and reports from the supervisor.

8.30 Fees and expenses

8.30 The fees and expenses that may be incurred for the purposes of the IVA are–

(a) fees for the nominee's services agreed with the debtor, the official receiver or any trustee;

(b) disbursements made by the nominee before the approval of the IVA; and

(c) fees or expenses which–

(i) are sanctioned by the terms of the IVA, or

(ii) where they are not sanctioned by the terms of the IVA, would be payable, or correspond to those which would be payable, in the debtor's bankruptcy.

General Note

See the introductory note to Pt 8. This identifies the fees and expenses, etc. of an IVA.

8.31 Termination or full implementation of the IVA

8.31(1) [Supervisor to send notice] Not more than 28 days after the full implementation or termination of the IVA the supervisor must deliver a notice that the IVA has been fully implemented or terminated to the debtor and the creditors bound by the IVA.

8.31(2) [Statement IVA took effect] The notice must state the date the IVA took effect.

8.31(3) [Report accompanying notice] The notice must be accompanied by a copy of a report by the supervisor which–

(a) summarises all receipts and payments in relation to the IVA;

(b) explains any departure from the terms of the IVA as approved by the creditors; and

(c) if the IVA has terminated, sets out the reasons why.

8.31(4) [Delivery and filing] The supervisor must within the 28 days mentioned above–

(a) deliver a copy of the notice and report to the Secretary of State; and

(b) if the creditors were invited to consider the proposal following a report under section 256(1)(aa), file a copy of the notice and report with the court.

8.31(5) [Delivery to be made before vacation of office] The supervisor must not vacate office until the notice and report have been delivered to the Secretary of State.

General Note

See the introductory note to Pt 8. The supervisor must notify the debtor and all creditors of completion or termination and also must furnish them with a summary of receipts and payments. The Secretary of State must in addition be notified. The time limit for such notifications is fixed at 28 days.

Chapter 7

Applications to annul bankruptcy orders under sections 261(2)(a) and (b)

[Note: a document required by the Act or these Rules must also contain the standard contents set out in Part 1.]

8.32 Application by the bankrupt to annul the bankruptcy order (section 261(2)(a))

8.32(1) [Witness statement in support of application] An application by bankrupt to the court under section 261(2)(a) must be supported by a witness statement stating–

(a) that the IVA has been approved by the creditors;

(b) the date of the approval; and

(c) that the 28 day period in section 262(3)(a) for applications to be made under section 262(1) has expired and no applications or appeals remain to be disposed of.

8.32(2) [Filing in court] The application and witness statement must be filed with the court and the court must deliver a notice of the venue for the hearing to the bankrupt.

8.32(3) [Delivery of notice of venue] Not less than five business days before the date of the hearing, the bankrupt must deliver a notice of the venue, with a copy of the application and witness statement, to–

(a) the official receiver;

(b) any trustee (if different to the official receiver); and

(c) the supervisor.

8.32(4) [Attendance and representation at hearing] The official receiver, any such trustee and the supervisor may attend the hearing or be represented and bring to the court's attention any matters which seem to them to be relevant.

General Note

This Chapter was inserted into the IR 1986 as Chs 8 and 9 by I(A)R 2003 (SI 2003/1730). It dealt with applications to annul a bankruptcy order pursuant to s.261(2)(a) in order to allow an IVA to be promoted. This was then modernised by I(A)R 2010 (SI 2010/686). This rule describes the manner of application and the procedure relating to the hearing of such application.

8.33 Application by the official receiver to annul the bankruptcy order (section 261(2)(b))

8.33(1) [Content of report supporting application] An application by the official receiver to the court under section 261(2)(b) to annul a bankruptcy order must be supported by a report stating–

(a) the grounds on which it is made;

(b) that the time period in paragraph (2) has expired; and

(c) that the official receiver is not aware that any application under section 262 or appeal remains to be disposed of.

8.33(2) [Time restriction on making of application] The official receiver must not make such an application before the expiry of the period of 42 days beginning with the day on which–

(a) the nominee filed the report of the creditors' consideration with the court, where the creditors considered the proposal under section 257 following a report to a court under section 256(1)(aa); or

(b) the nominee delivered a notice to the creditors of the result of their consideration, where the creditors considered the proposal under section 257 following a report to the creditors under section 256A(3).

8.33(3) [Filing in court] The application and the report must be filed with the court and the court must deliver a notice of the venue for the hearing to the official receiver.

8.33(4) [Delivery of notice of venue] Not less than five business days before the date of the hearing, the official receiver must deliver a notice of the venue, with a copy of the application and the report, to the bankrupt.

General Note

This rule deals with applications to annul bankruptcy orders in cases covered by s.261(2)(b) and details the application procedure.

8.34 Order annulling bankruptcy

8.34(1) [Contents of order] An order under section 261(2) annulling a bankruptcy order must contain–

(a) identification details the proceedings;

(b) the section number of the Act under which the order is made;

(c) the name and address of the applicant;

(d) a statement that it appears that an IVA under section 258 has been approved and implemented and the date of approval;

(e) a statement that there has been no application under section 262 for the revocation or suspension of the IVA and that the time period for making such an application has expired;

(f) where the applicant is the official receiver under section 261(2)(b) that the time period in rule 8.33(2) has expired;

(g) the order that the relevant bankruptcy order, identified by its date and the name of the bankrupt as set out in the bankruptcy order, be annulled;

(h) if appropriate, an order that the relevant bankruptcy petition (identified by the date of its presentation) or the relevant bankruptcy application (identified by the date it was made) (as the case may be) be dismissed;

(i) where there is a trustee, an order in respect of the trustee's release, having regard to rule 8.37;

(j) an order that the registration of the bankruptcy petition or bankruptcy application as a pending action at the Land Charges Department of HM Land Registry be vacated (identified by the date of registration and reference number);

(k) an order that the registration of the bankruptcy order on the register of writs and orders affecting land at the Land Charges Department of HM Land Registry be vacated (identified by date of registration and reference number);

(l) the date the order is made;

(m) a notice to the effect that if the former bankrupt requires notice of the order to be gazetted and advertised in the same manner as the bankruptcy order was advertised, the bankrupt must deliver a notice to the official receiver within 28 days; and

(n) a notice to the effect that it is the responsibility of the former bankrupt and in the former bankrupt's interest to ensure that any registration of the petition or bankruptcy application and of the bankruptcy order at the Land Charges Department of HM Land Registry and any entries relating to the petition or bankruptcy application and bankruptcy order in any registered titles at

HM Land Registry are cancelled (such a notice giving relevant HM Land Registry contact details and referring to relevant Registry guidance).

8.34(2) [Sealed copy order] The court must deliver a sealed copy of the order to–

(a) the former bankrupt;

(b) the official receiver;

(c) any trustee (if different to the official receiver); and

(d) the supervisor.

GENERAL NOTE

This is a new provision added in the 2016 Rules which is derived from Form 5.7 of the 1986 Rules.

8.35 Notice of order

8.35(1) [Delivery of notice of annulment] An official receiver, who has delivered a notice of the debtor's bankruptcy to the creditors, must, as soon as reasonably practicable, deliver a notice of an annulment under section 261(2) to them.

8.35(2) [Official receiver's expenses a charge over property] Expenses incurred by the official receiver in delivering a notice under this rule are a charge in the official receiver's favour on the property of the former bankrupt, whether or not actually in the hands of the former bankrupt.

8.35(3) [Validity of charge over property held by another] Where any such property is in the hands of any person other than the former bankrupt, the official receiver's charge is valid subject only to any costs that may be incurred by that person in effecting realisation of the property for the purpose of satisfying the charge.

GENERAL NOTE

This deals with various matters, including notification of the change of situation and expenses thereby incurred. This rule also explains the consequences of an annulment order made pursuant to the aforementioned procedure.

8.36 Advertisement of order

8.36(1) [Bankrupt's right to require advertisement] The former bankrupt may in writing within 28 days of the date of an order for annulment under section 261(2) require the official receiver–

(a) to cause a notice of the order to be gazetted; and

(b) to advertise the order in the same manner as the bankruptcy order was advertised.

8.36(2) [Duty to comply as soon as reasonably practicable] The official receiver must comply with any such requirement as soon as reasonably practicable.

8.36(3) [Contents of notice] The notice must state–

(a) the name of the former bankrupt;

(b) the date on which the bankruptcy order was made;

(c) that the bankruptcy order has been annulled;

(d) the date of the annulment order; and

(e) the grounds of the annulment.

8.36(4) [Representative's right to stand in bankrupt's stead] Where the former bankrupt has died, or is a person lacking capacity to manage the person's own affairs (within the meaning of the Mental Capacity Act 2005), the references to the former bankrupt in paragraph (1) are to be read as references to the personal representative of the same or, as the case may be, a person appointed by the court to represent or act for the former bankrupt.

General Note

This provision was inserted into IR 1986 as Ch.11 by I(A)R 2003 (SI 2003/1730). It dealt with general matters relevant to applications made under what are now IR 2016 rr.8.32–8.35. It tidies up various loose ends attendant upon this change.

8.37 Trustee's final account

8.37(1) [Trustee liable to account] The making of an order under section 261(2) does not of itself release the trustee from any duty or obligation imposed by or under the Act or these Rules to account for all of the trustee's transactions in connection with the former bankrupt's estate.

8.37(2) [Duty of trustee to deliver and file final account] As soon as reasonably practicable after the making of an order, the trustee must–

(a) deliver a copy of the final account of the trustee to the Secretary of State; and

(b) file a copy of that account with the court.

8.37(3) [Content of final account] The final account must include a summary of the trustee's receipts and payments.

8.37(4) [Release of trustee] The trustee is released from such time as the court may determine, having regard to whether paragraph (2) of this rule has been complied with.

General Note

The obligation of the trustee to produce a final account is not removed by the fact of annulment.

Chapter 8

Time recording information

[Note: a document required by the Act or these Rules must also contain the standard contents set out in Part 1.]

8.38 Provision of information

8.38(1) [Application of rule] This rule applies where the remuneration of the nominee or the supervisor has been fixed on the basis of time spent.

8.38(2) [Duty of nominee or supervisor to supply statement] A person who is acting, or has acted within the previous two years as–

(a) a nominee in relation to a proposal; or

(b) the supervisor in relation to an IVA;

must, within 28 days of receipt of a request from a person mentioned in paragraph (3), deliver free of charge to that person a statement complying with paragraph (4) and (5).

8.38(3) [Who may request statement] The persons are–

(a) the debtor; and

(b) where the proposal has been approved, a creditor bound by the IVA.

8.38(4) [Period covered by statement] The statement must cover the period which–

(a) in the case of a person who has ceased to act as nominee or supervisor in relation to an IVA, begins with the date of that person's appointment as nominee or supervisor and ends with the date of ceasing to act; and

(b) in any other case, consists of one or more complete periods of six months beginning with the date of appointment and ending most nearly before the date of receiving the request.

8.38(5) [Details contained in statement] The statement must set out–

(i) the total number of hours spent on the matter during that period by the nominee or supervisor, and by any staff,

(ii) for each grade of staff engaged on the matter, the average hourly rate at which work carried out by staff in that grade is charged, and

(iii) the number of hours spent on the matter by each grade of staff during that period.

General Note

This provision was originally introduced into the 1986 Rules by I(A)R 2010 (SI 2010/686) in order to promote transparency. Note the time limit for requests imposed by para.(2).

Part 9

Debt Relief Orders

Introductory note to Part 9

Part 9 brings forward Pt 5A of the IR 1986 which was introduced by I(A)R 2009 (SI 2009/642) with effect from 6 April 2009. These rules deal with the process by which a debtor may seek a debt relief order, the consequences of such an order, the rights of creditors and the responsibilities of the debtor and official receiver. In order to obtain a debt relief order a debtor must apply via an approved intermediary to the official receiver. On debt relief orders note also Sch.4ZA of the Act. Schedule 4ZB deals with debt relief restriction orders, etc. A detailed review of the DRO regime is to be found in the judgment of Stadlen J in *R. (Howard) v Official Receiver* [2013] EWHC 1839 (Admin); [2014] B.P.I.R. 204. A creditor can challenge a DRO and has 30 days from notification to do so under r.9.15 (previously it was 28 days).

Chapter 1

Interpretation

[Notes: (1) a debt relief order under Part 7A of the Act may be made in respect of "qualifying debts" (as defined in section 251A(2)); these do not include "excluded debts" which are prescribed by rule 9.2 for the purposes of section 251A(4).

(2) "approved intermediaries" and "competent authority" are defined in section 251U of the Act for purposes of Part 7A of the Act.]

9.1 Debtor's family

9.1 In this Part the expression "debtor's family" has the same meaning in relation to a debtor as it has in section 385(1) in relation to a bankrupt.

9.2 Excluded debts

9.2(1) ["Excluded debts"] For the purposes of Part 7A of the Act debts of the following descriptions are prescribed under section 251A(4) as "excluded debts"–

(a) any fine imposed for an offence and any obligation (including an obligation to pay a lump sum or to pay costs) arising under an order made in family proceedings or any obligation arising under a maintenance assessment or maintenance calculation made under the Child Support Act 1991;

(b) any debt or liability to which a debtor is or may become subject in respect of any sum paid or payable to the debtor as a student by way of a loan and which the debtor receives whether before or after the debt relief order is made;

(c) any obligation arising under a confiscation order made under section 1 of the Drug Trafficking Offences Act 1986, section 1 of the Criminal Justice (Scotland) Act 1987, section 71 of the Criminal Justice Act 1988, or Parts 2, 3 or 4 of the Proceeds of Crime Act 2002;

(d) any debt which consists of a liability to pay damages for negligence, nuisance or breach of a statutory, contractual or other duty, or to pay damages by virtue of Part 1 of the Consumer Protection Act 1987, being in either case damages in respect of the death of or personal injury (including any disease or other impairment of physical or mental condition) to any person; and

(e) any obligation arising from a payment out of the social fund under section 138(1)(b) of the Social Security Contributions and Benefits Act 1992 by way of crisis loan or budgeting loan.

9.2(2) ["Family proceedings", "fine"] In paragraph (1)(a) "family proceedings" and "fine" have the meanings given by section 281(8) (which applies the Magistrates' Courts Act 1980 and the Matrimonial and Family Proceedings Act 1984).

9.2(3) ["Loan"] In paragraph (1)(b) "loan" means a loan made under–

(a) regulations made under section 22(1) of the Teaching and Higher Education Act 1998; or

(b) the Education (Student Loans) Act 1990, or that Act as it continues in force by virtue of any savings made, in connection with its repeal by the Teaching and Higher Education Act 1998, by an order made under section 46(4) of that Act;

(c) and includes any interest on the loan and any penalties or charges incurred in connection with it.

General Note

This rule includes the amendments made by I(A)R 2010 (SI 2010/686) and I(A)R 2012 (SI 2012/469) to protect the Social Fund from bad debts in the wake of the Supreme Court ruling in *Secretary of State for Work and Pensions v Payne* [2011] UKSC 60 as well as the amendment made by the Crime and Courts Act 2013 (Family Court: Consequential Provision) (No.2) Order 2014 (SI 2014/879) with effect from April 22, 2014.

Chapter 2

Application for a debt relief order

[Note: a document required by the Act or these Rules must also contain the standard contents set out in Part 1.]

9.3 Application for a debt relief order: information required in the application

9.3(1) [Matters to be stated in application] An application for a debt relief order under section 251A must state the matters set out in paragraphs (2) to (9) (which are prescribed for the purposes of section 251B(2)(c)) as they are at the date of the application as well as the matters referred to in section 251B(2)(a) (list of the debtor's debts at the date of the application) and 251B(2)(b) (details of any security held in respect of those debts).

9.3(2) [Details of the debtor in the application] The application must identify the debtor and state–

(a) the debtor's occupation (if any);

(b) the debtor's gender;

(c) the debtor's date of birth;

(d) the debtor's places of residence during the three years before the date of the application;

(e) any other name used by the debtor for any purpose;

(f) the name, address and nature of any business carried on by the debtor, including any business carried on by–

(i) a firm or partnership of which the debtor is a member;

(ii) an agent or manager for the debtor or for such firm or partnership;

(g) any other liabilities (including those imposed by an order of the court) to which the debtor is subject;

(h) the address of the creditor to whom each debt is owed;

(i) the total amount of the debtor's monthly income from all sources (see rule 9.7(1));

(j) the sources of that income and the amount from each source;

(k) particulars of the expenditure which the debtor claims is necessary to meet the monthly reasonable domestic needs of the debtor and the debtor's family, including the purpose and the amount of that expenditure;

(l) the total amount available from any source to meet the claimed monthly reasonable domestic needs of the debtor and the debtor's family (see rule 9.7(2)); and

(m) particulars of the debtor's property and its total estimated value (see rules 9.8 and 9.9).

9.3(3) [Debtor's statement of facts] The debtor must also state in the application–

(a) whether or not at the date of the application the debtor–

(i) has given a preference to any person during the period of two years ending with the application date,

(ii) has entered into a transaction with any person at an undervalue during the period of two years ending with the application date,

(iii) is domiciled in England and Wales,

(iv) at any time during the period of three years ending with the application date–

(aa) was resident,

(bb) had a place of residence, or

(cc) carried on business, in England and Wales,

(v) is an undischarged bankrupt,

(vi) is subject to a debt relief order,

(vii) has been subject to a debt relief order in the six years ending with the application date,

(viii) is subject to an interim order or an IVA under Part 8 of the Act, or

(ix) is subject to a bankruptcy restrictions order or undertaking or debt relief restrictions order or undertaking; and

(b) whether at the date of the application–

(i) a bankruptcy petition has been presented against the debtor,

(ii) a bankruptcy application has been made by the debtor,

(iii) any debt management arrangements (see section 251F) are in force in relation to the debtor, and

(iv) any other legal action has been taken against the debtor in relation to any of the debtor's existing debts.

9.3(4) [Deduction of discounts] In the application, the debtor must deduct from each debt all trade and other discounts which are available to the debtor, except any discount for immediate or early settlement.

9.3(5) [Debts in foreign currency] Where any debts were incurred or are payable in a foreign currency, the amount of those debts must be converted into sterling at a single exchange rate for that currency prevailing on the relevant date.

9.3(6) [Appeal against unreasonable rate] A creditor who considers that the rate is unreasonable may apply to the court.

9.3(7) [Determination of rate by court] If the court finds that the rate is unreasonable it may itself determine the rate.

9.3(8) [Calculation of periodic debts] Where a debt consists of unpaid payments of a periodical nature, the amount of the debt will consist of any amounts due and unpaid up to the application date.

9.3(9) [Debts to accrue on a daily basis] Where at the application date any payment was accruing due, the amount of the debt will be so much as would have fallen due at that date, if accruing from day to day.

9.3(10) [Treatment of future debts] A debtor may include a debt of which payment is not yet due at the date of the application if it is for a liquidated sum payable at some certain future time.

9.3(11) [Debtor's statement and confirmation] In the application, the debtor must also–

(a) consent to the official receiver making checks for the purpose of verifying that the debtor complies with the conditions to which the making of a debt relief order is subject;

(b) state that the debtor is unable to pay the debts;

(c) request a debt relief order; and

(d) indicate the date on which the application is completed.

9.3(12) [Delivery to approved intermediary] The debtor must deliver to the approved intermediary such information and such documents as will enable the intermediary to substantiate the information in the application, including information about each debt, the amount of the debt and the name and address of the creditor.

9.4 Delivery of application

9.4(1) [Delivery to official receiver] An application for a debt relief order must be completed and delivered to the official receiver in electronic form and by electronic means.

9.4(2) [Non-application of r.1.45(2) conditions] The preconditions for delivering a document electronically set out in rule 1.45(2) do not apply to applications for debt relief orders.

9.4(3) [Failure of electronic delivery system] In the event of any malfunction or error in the operation of the electronic form or means of delivery, the official receiver must inform the competent authorities and approved intermediaries–

(a) that approved intermediaries may complete and deliver applications in hard copy for a specified period; and

(b) of the postal address to which such applications are to be delivered and of any terms or conditions to which the use of the address is subject.

9.4(4) [Restriction on use of fax delivery] Such an application completed in hard copy may not be delivered by fax.

9.5 Role of approved intermediary

9.5(1) [Intermediary to act as soon as possible] The approved intermediary, through whom the application for a debt relief order is to be made, must create an application for a debt relief order in the name of the debtor as soon as reasonably practicable after being asked by the debtor to do so.

9.5(2) [Assistance provided by intermediary] The approved intermediary may assist the debtor–

(a) to identify what information is required to complete the application;

(b) based upon the documentation and information supplied by the debtor, to ascertain whether–

(i) the debtor appears to have debts not exceeding the prescribed amount,

(ii) the debtor's surplus income does not exceed the prescribed amount, and

(iii) the value of the debtor's property does not exceed the prescribed amount; and

(c) to ensure that the application (if made) is completed in full.

9.5(3) [Intermediary to advise debtor] The approved intermediary must draw the debtor's attention to–

(a) all the conditions to which an application for, and the making of, a debt relief order is subject;

(b) the possible consequences of the debtor making any false representation or omission in the application; and

(c) the fact that verification checks will be made for the purpose of verifying that the debtor complies with the conditions to which the making of a debt relief order is subject and the requirement for the debtor to consent to such checks being made.

9.5(4) [Intermediary's duty to deliver application] The approved intermediary must deliver the application to the official receiver as soon as reasonably practicable after being instructed by the debtor to do so.

CHAPTER 3

VERIFYING THE APPLICATION AND DETERMINING THE DEBTOR'S INCOME AND PROPERTY

9.6 Prescribed verification checks: conditions in paragraphs 1 to 8 of Schedule 4ZA of the Act

9.6(1) [Definition of verification checks] For the purposes of section 251D(4) and (5) and the conditions in paragraphs 1 to 8 of Schedule 4ZA of the Act, the prescribed verification checks are those searches or enquiries specified in this rule.

9.6(2) [Debtor's connection with England and Wales] For the purpose of verifying a debtor's connection with England and Wales on the application date, verification checks made in, or with, one or more of the following–

(a) the electoral registers for the areas in England and Wales in which the debtor claims to reside or to carry on business or to have resided or carried on business at the date of the application;

(b) the individual insolvency register;

(c) the bankruptcy restrictions register;

(d) the debt relief restrictions register;

(e) a credit reference agency.

9.6(3) [Checks in registers for personal insolvency] Verification checks made in one or more of the registers specified in paragraph (4), for the purpose of verifying that a debtor–

(a) is not, on the determination date–

(i) an undischarged bankrupt,

(ii) subject to a bankruptcy restrictions order or undertaking,

(iii) subject to a debt relief restrictions order or undertaking, (iv) subject to an IVA; or

(b) has not been the subject of a debt relief order in the period of six years ending with the determination date.

9.6(4) [Registers to be checked] The registers referred to in paragraph (3) are–

(a) the individual insolvency register;

(b) the bankruptcy restrictions register; and

(c) the debt relief restrictions register.

9.6(5) [Verification of bankruptcy] Verification checks made in, or with, one or more of the sources specified in paragraph (6) for the purpose of verifying–

(a) that the debtor is not subject to an interim order on the determination date;

(b) whether a creditor's bankruptcy petition has been presented against the debtor before the determination date;

(c) whether the debtor has made a bankruptcy application before the determination date;

(d) whether proceedings in relation to any such bankruptcy application have finally been disposed of before the determination date;

(e) where a creditor's bankruptcy petition has been presented against the debtor before the determination date, the status of the proceedings in relation to the petition and whether the person who presented the petition has consented to the making of the application for a debt relief order.

9.6(6) [Sources to be checked] The sources are–

(a) the individual insolvency register;

(b) county or other court records;

(c) a credit reference agency.

9.6(7) [Checks with credit reference agency] Verification checks made with a credit reference agency, for the purpose of verifying that each of the following does not exceed the prescribed amount–

(a) the amount of the debtor's overall indebtedness;

(b) the amount of the debtor's monthly surplus income; or

(c) the total value of the debtor's property.

9.7 Determination of debtor's monthly surplus income

9.7(1) [Income from business, office, employment or pension] For the purposes of this Part, the income of a debtor comprises every payment in the nature of income which is from time to time made to the debtor or to which the debtor from time to time becomes entitled, including any payment in respect of the carrying on of a business or in respect of an office or employment and any payment under a pension scheme.

9.7(2) [Contributions from debtor's family] In determining the monthly surplus income of a debtor, the official receiver must take into account any contribution made by a member of the debtor's family to the amount necessary for the reasonable domestic needs of the debtor and the debtor's family.

9.8 Determination of value of the debtor's property (paragraph 8 of Schedule 4ZA)

9.8(1) [Relevant property] The official receiver in determining the total value of the debtor's property for the purposes of determining whether the condition in paragraph 8 of Schedule 4ZA is met must treat as a debtor's property for the purposes of this Part–

(a) all property belonging to or vested in the debtor on the determination date; and

(b) any property which by virtue of any of the following provisions of this Part is comprised in or is treated as falling within the preceding sub-paragraph.

9.8(2) [Property includes power over property] For the purposes of this Part–

(a) property, in relation to a debtor, includes references to any power exercisable by the debtor over or in relation to property except in so far as the power is exercisable over or in relation to property which is not or is deemed not for the time being to be the property of the debtor and cannot be exercised for the benefit of the debtor;

(b) a power exercisable over or in relation to property is deemed for the purposes of this Part to vest in the person entitled to exercise it at the time of the transaction or event by virtue of which it is exercisable by that person (whether or not it becomes so exercisable at that time);

(c) property belonging to or vested in the debtor so belongs or vests in the debtor subject to the rights of any person other than the debtor (whether as a secured creditor of the debtor or otherwise).

9.8(3) [Exclusion of property listed in r.9.9] In determining the value of the debtor's property the descriptions of property set out in rule 9.9 must be excluded.

9.9 Property to be excluded in determining the value of a debtor's property

9.9(1) [Property to be disregarded from r.9.8] For the purposes of determining the value of a person's property under rule 9.8, the official receiver must disregard–

(a) a single domestic motor vehicle belonging to or vested in the debtor if–

(i) it has been especially adapted for use by the debtor because of a physical impairment that has a substantial and long-term adverse effect on the debtor's ability to carry out normal day-to-day activities, subject to paragraph (2), or

(ii) the maximum potential realisable value of the vehicle is less than £1,000 (the prescribed amount);

(b) subject to paragraph (3), such tools, books and other items of equipment as are necessary to the debtor for use personally in the debtor's employment, business or vocation;

(c) subject to paragraph (3), such clothing, bedding, furniture, household equipment and provisions as are necessary for satisfying the basic domestic needs of the debtor and the debtor's family;

(d) property held by the debtor on trust for any other person;

(e) the right of nomination to a vacant ecclesiastical benefice;

(f) a tenancy which is an assured tenancy or an assured agricultural occupancy, within the meaning of Part 1 of the Housing Act 1988, and the terms of which inhibit an assignment as mentioned in section 127(5) of the Rent Act 1977;

(g) a protected tenancy, within the meaning of the Rent Act 1977, in relation to which, by virtue of any provision of Part 9 of that Act, no premium can lawfully be required as a condition of assignment;

(h) a tenancy of a dwelling-house by virtue of which the debtor is, within the meaning of the Rent (Agriculture) Act 1976, a protected occupier of the dwelling-house, and the terms of which inhibit an assignment as mentioned in section 127(5) of the Rent Act 1977;

(i) a secure tenancy, within the meaning of Part 4 of the Housing Act 1985, which is not capable of being assigned, except in the cases mentioned in section 91(3) of that Act; and

(j) any right of the debtor under an approved pension arrangement (as defined by section 11 of the Welfare Reform and Pensions Act 1999).

9.9(2) [Vehicle where realisable value exceeds replacement cost] The amount the official receiver must disregard under paragraph (1)(a)(i) is limited to the value of a reasonable replacement where it appears to the official receiver that the realisable value of the vehicle to be disregarded exceeds the cost of a reasonable replacement for it.

9.9(3) [Tools, household effects where realisable value exceeds replacement cost] The amount the official receiver must disregard under paragraph (1)(b) or (c) is limited to the value of a reasonable replacement where it appears to the official receiver that the realisable value of the whole or a part of the property to be disregarded exceeds the cost of a reasonable replacement for that property or that part.

9.9(4) [Reasonable replacement A vehicle or other property is a reasonable replacement if it is reasonably adequate for meeting the needs met by the other vehicle or other property.

Chapter 4

Making or refusal of a debt relief order

[Note: a document required by the Act or these Rules must also contain the standard contents set out in Part 1.]

9.10 Contents of debt relief order

9.10 A debt relief order must contain–

(a) the debtor's identification details;

(b) the date of, and the reference number allocated to, the debtor's application;

(c) a list of the debtor's qualifying debts as at the application date, specifying the amount owed and the creditor's name, address and reference (if any); and

(d) the date on which the order was made.

9.11 Other steps to be taken by official receiver or debtor upon making of the order

9.11(1) [Notification to approved intermediary; entry in register] In addition to delivering a copy of the order to the debtor under section 251E, the official receiver must–

(a) deliver a notice of the making and date of the order to the approved intermediary through whom the debtor's application was made; and

(b) cause an entry to be made in the individual insolvency register in accordance with rule 11.18.

9.11(2) [Notification of other debt management arrangements] If there are other debt management arrangements or an attachment of earnings order in force in relation to the debtor, the official receiver must deliver a notice of the making of the debt relief order to the court, or the body, as the case may be, responsible for making the debt management arrangements or order.

9.12 Prescribed information for creditors on making of debt relief order

9.12 The official receiver must deliver a notice to each creditor to whom a qualifying debt specified in the order is owed, of–

(a) the making, the date and the reference number of the order;

(b) the effect of the order;

(c) the matters to which a creditor may object under section 251K; and

(d) the name, address and telephone number of the official receiver delivering the notice and the address to which any objection under that section may or must be delivered.

9.13 Refusal of application for debt relief order

9.13 If the official receiver refuses an application for a debt relief order, the official receiver must deliver a notice to the debtor stating that the official receiver refused the application, and the reason why it has been refused.

Chapter 5

Objection and revocation

[Note: a document required by the Act or these Rules must also contain the standard contents set out in Part 1.]

9.14 Meaning of "creditor"

9.14 In this Chapter, "creditor" means a person specified in a debt relief order as a creditor to whom a qualifying debt is owed.

9.15 Creditor's objection to a debt relief order (section 251K)

9.15(1) [Prescribed period during moratorium] The prescribed period under section 251K(2)(a) for a creditor to object to a debt relief order during the moratorium period is within 30 days of the date on which a notice of the making of the order was delivered to the creditor.

9.15(2) [Content of objection] The objection must be made in writing to the official receiver and must contain–

(a) the name and address of the creditor;

(b) the name of the debtor and the reference number of the order;

(c) the matters under section 251K to which the creditor objects;

(d) a statement of which of the prescribed grounds for objection the creditor relies upon;

(e) a statement of the facts on which the creditor relies; and

(f) information and documents in support of the grounds and the facts on which the creditor relies.

9.15(3) [Grounds for objection] The prescribed grounds for objection are that–

(a) there is an error in, or an omission from, something specified in the debt relief order;

(b) a bankruptcy order has been made in relation to the debtor;

(c) the debtor has made a proposal under Part 8 of the Act;

(d) the official receiver should not have been satisfied that–

(i) the debts specified in the order were qualifying debts of the debtor as at the application date,

(ii) the conditions specified in Part 1 of Schedule 4ZA were met, or

(iii) the conditions specified in Part 2 of that Schedule were met; or

(e) the official receiver should have been satisfied that the official receiver was permitted to make an order in spite of any failure to meet the conditions referred to in sub-paragraphs (d)(ii) and (iii).

9.16 Official receiver's response to objection under section 251K

9.16(1) [Particulars to debtor] After considering a creditor's objection to a debt relief order in accordance with section 251K, the official receiver, if minded to revoke or amend the debt relief order, must deliver to the debtor–

(a) particulars of the objection;

(b) the grounds and facts upon which the creditor relies;

(c) an invitation to the debtor to deliver any comments on them to the official receiver within 21 days of delivery of the particulars; and

(d) the address to which the debtor's comments must be delivered.

9.16(2) [Official receiver to consider comments of debtor] Before deciding whether to revoke or amend the debt relief order, the official receiver must consider any comments made by the debtor provided they are received within the 21 day period.

9.16(3) [Official receiver to notify decision to creditor] After coming to a decision on the objection the official receiver must deliver a notice of the decision to the creditor within 14 days.

9.16(4) [Creditor to be treated as person interested] If the official receiver has decided to make an application under section 251M(2) then the official receiver must treat the creditor as a person interested in the application under rule 9.21(3)(b) (if the creditor would not otherwise be such).

9.17 Creditor's request that a debt relief order be revoked (section 251L(4))

9.17(1) [Creditor's right to request revocation] A creditor may request that the official receiver revoke a debt relief order under section 251L(4) because either or both of the conditions in paragraphs 7 and 8 of Schedule 4ZA are not met at any time after the debt relief order was made.

9.17(2) [Content of request] The request must contain–

(a) the name and address of the creditor;

(b) the name of the debtor and the reference number of the order;

(c) which of the conditions under paragraph 7 and 8 of Schedule 4ZA are not met;

(d) a statement of the facts on which the creditor relies; and

(e) information and documents supporting the facts which are relied upon.

9.17(3) [Official receiver to notify decision to creditor] After coming to a decision on the request the official receiver must deliver a notice of the decision to the creditor within 14 days.

9.17(4) [Creditor to be treated as person interested If the official receiver has decided to make an application under section 251M(2) then the official receiver must treat the creditor as a person interested in the application under rule 9.21(3)(b) (if the creditor would not otherwise be such).

9.18 Procedure in revoking or amending a debt relief order (section 251L)

9.18(1) [Official receiver to notify debtor and creditors] The official receiver must as soon as reasonably practicable after deciding to revoke a debt relief order under section 251L deliver notice of the decision to the debtor and the creditors.

9.18(2) [Content of notice] The notice must contain–

(a) identification details for the debtor;

(b) the date and reference number of the debt relief order;

(c) the reasons for revocation; and

(d) the date (under subsection (5) or (7) of section 251L) on or from which the revocation has effect.

9.18(3) [Notice of early revocation] Where the official receiver–

(a) has delivered notices under paragraph (1) of the revocation of a debt relief order from a specified date; and

(b) thinks it appropriate under section 251L(7) to revoke the debt relief order with immediate effect before the specified date;

the official receiver must deliver a notice of the new date to anyone who previously received a notice under paragraph (1).

9.18(4) [Amending the individual insolvency register] The official receiver must cause the entry in the individual insolvency register relating to the order to be amended so far as information concerning the order has not already been deleted under rule 11.19.

9.18(5) [Death of debtor during moratorium] Where the debtor has died during the moratorium period rule 9.20 applies.

9.18(6) [Notice of amendment] The official receiver must as soon as reasonably practicable after amending a debt relief order deliver a notice of the amendment to the debtor and the creditors.

9.18(7) [Content of notice of amendment] The notice must contain–

(a) identification details for the debtor and the date and reference number of the debt relief order;

(b) the amendment;

(c) the date on which the amendment was made; and

(d) the reasons for it.

9.18(8) [Amendment of individual insolvency register] The official receiver must as soon as reasonably practicable cause the entry in the individual insolvency register relating to the amended debt relief order to be amended accordingly.

9.19 Debtor's notification of official receiver of matters in section 251J(3) or (5)

9.19(1) [Duty of debtor to notify error, omission etc. in information] The debtor must deliver a notice to the official receiver as soon as reasonably practicable after the debtor becomes aware of an error in, or omission from, the information supplied to the official receiver in, or in support of, the application.

9.19(2) [Notice to state the error or omission] The notice must state the nature of the error or omission and the reason for it.

9.19(3) [Notice to be give as soon as practicable] The debtor must deliver a notice to the official receiver as soon as reasonably practicable after the debtor becomes aware of a change in the debtor's circumstances between the application date and the determination date that would affect (or would have affected) the determination of the application.

9.19(4) [Notice to state nature and date of change] The notice must state the nature of the change and the date of the change.

9.19(5) [Duty where debt relief order made] Where a debt relief order is made and–

(a) the debtor's income increases during the moratorium period applicable to the order, the debtor must as soon as reasonably practicable after the date of the increase deliver a notice to the official receiver stating–

(i) the amount of the increase,

(ii) the reason for it,

(iii) the date of the increase, and

(iv) its expected duration;

(b) the debtor acquires property or property is devolved upon the debtor during that period, the debtor must as soon as reasonably practicable after the date of the acquisition or devolution deliver a notice to the official receiver stating–

(i) the nature of the acquisition or devolution,

(ii) the date of the acquisition or devolution,

(iii) the reason for it, and

(iv) its value;

(c) the debtor becomes aware of any error in or omission from any information supplied by the debtor to the official receiver after the determination date, the debtor must as soon as reasonably practicable after the date on which the debtor becomes aware of it deliver a notice to the official receiver, stating–

(i) the nature of the error or omission,

(ii) the reason for it, and

(iii) the date on which the debtor became aware of it.

9.20 Death of debtor during a moratorium period under a debt relief order

9.20(1) [Application of rule] This rule applies where a debtor dies during a moratorium period under a debt relief order.

9.20(2) [Duty of official receiver on notification] The official receiver must, as soon as reasonably practicable after being informed of the death of the debtor–

(a) cause a note of the fact and the date of the death to be entered on the individual insolvency register under rule 11.23;

(b) revoke the debt relief order; and

(c) deliver a notice of the revocation to–

(i) the creditors, and

(ii) the personal representatives of the debtor.

9.20(3) [Content of notice of revocation] The notice of revocation must–

(a) state the reason for the revocation; and

(b) specify the date on which the revocation took effect.

Chapter 6

Applications to the court

[Note: a document required by the Act or these Rules must also contain the standard contents set out in Part 1.]

9.21 Notice of application to court under section 251M

9.21(1) [Application of rule] This rule applies to applications to the court under section 251M.

9.21(2) [Delivery of notice by dissatisfied person] Where the application is made by a person who is dissatisfied by an act, omission or decision of the official receiver in connection with a debt relief order or an application for a debt relief order the applicant must deliver a notice–

(a) if the applicant is the debtor, to the official receiver and any creditor specified in the debt relief order or in the application for the debt relief order; or

(b) if the applicant is a person other than the debtor, to the official receiver and the debtor.

9.21(3) [Delivery of notice by official receiver] Where the application is made by the official receiver for directions or an order in relation to a matter arising in connection with a debt relief order or an application for such an order, the official receiver must deliver notice to–

(a) the debtor; and

(b) any person appearing to the official receiver to have an interest in the application.

9.22 Court in which applications under sections 251M or 251N are to be made

9.22(1) [Venue for application] An application to the court under section 251M or 251N must be made to–

(a) the County Court at Central London, where the proceedings are allocated to the London Insolvency District under rule 12.5(a)(i) to (iv);

(b) the High Court, where the proceedings are allocated to the London Insolvency District under rule 12.5(a)(v);

(c) the debtor's own hearing centre as determined under paragraph (3) (subject to paragraph (4)), in any other case where the debtor is resident in England and Wales.

9.22(2) [Debtor no longer resident in England and Wales] The application may be filed either with the debtor's own hearing centre or with the High Court if–

(a) the debtor is not resident in England and Wales but was resident or carried on business in England and Wales within the six months immediately before the application is filed with the court; and

(b) the proceedings are not allocated to the London Insolvency District.

9.22(3) [Debtor's own hearing centre] In this rule the debtor's own hearing centre is–

(a) where the debtor has carried on business in England and Wales within the six months immediately before the application is filed with the court, the hearing centre which serves the insolvency district where for the longest period during those six months–

(i) the debtor carried on business, or

- (ii) the principal place of business was located, if business was carried on in more than one insolvency district; or

(b) where the debtor has not carried on business in England and Wales within the six months immediately before the application is filed with the court, the hearing centre which serves the insolvency district where the debtor resided for the longest period during those six months.

9.22(4) [Expediting application where not possible in debtor's own hearing centre] Where, for whatever reason, it is not possible for the application to be filed with the debtor's own hearing centre, the applicant may, with a view to expediting the application, file the application–

(a) where paragraph (3)(a) applies, with–

- (i) the hearing centre for the insolvency district in which the debtor resides, or
- (ii) the hearing centre specified in Schedule 6 as the nearest full-time hearing centre to the hearing centre specified in paragraph (3)(a), or paragraph (i) as the case may be; or

(b) where paragraph (3)(b) applies, with the hearing centre specified in Schedule 6 as being the nearest full-time hearing centre to that specified in paragraph (3)(b).

9.22(5) [Application to contain sufficient information to determine court] The application must contain sufficient information to establish that it is brought in the appropriate court, and where the application is made to the County Court, the appropriate hearing centre.

9.23 Creditor's bankruptcy petition: creditor consents to making application for a debt relief order

9.23(1) [Application of rule] This rule applies where before the determination of an application for a debt relief order, a creditor's petition for bankruptcy has been presented against a debtor and the proceedings in relation to the petition remain before the court.

9.23(2) ["The debt"] In this rule "the debt" means the debt to which the creditor's bankruptcy petition relates.

9.23(3) [Duty of court] If, on the hearing of the petition, the petitioner consents to the debtor making an application for a debt relief order in relation to the debt the court must–

(a) refer the debtor to an approved intermediary for the purpose of making an application for a debt relief order in relation to the debtor and the debt noting the consent of the creditor on the order for referral; and

(b) stay the proceedings on the petition in relation to the debt on such terms and conditions as it thinks just.

9.23(4) [Duty of debtor] The debtor must deliver to the approved intermediary as soon as reasonably practicable after the making of the order of referral–

(a) a sealed copy of the order; and

(b) copies of the petition and the creditor's statutory demand (if there was one).

9.23(5) [Duty of approved intermediary] The approved intermediary must, on receipt of the order and the copies, as soon as reasonably practicable after the application for a debt relief order has been made, deliver them to the official receiver endorsed with the name of the debtor and the number of the application to which they relate.

9.23(6) [Petition dismissed if debt relief order made] If, following the reference by the court, a debt relief order is made in relation to the debt, the petition must be dismissed in relation to it unless the court otherwise directs.

9.24 Extension of moratorium period

9.24 Where the moratorium period applicable to a debt relief order is extended–

(a) notice of the extension, and the period of extension must be delivered–

(i) where extended by the court, to the official receiver, who must deliver a copy to the debtor and to the creditors specified in the debt relief order,

(ii) where extended by the official receiver, to the debtor and to the creditors specified in the debt relief order; and

(b) the official receiver must cause to be entered in the individual insolvency register–

(i) that such an extension has been made in relation to the debtor,

(ii) the date on which the extension was made,

(iii) its duration, and

(iv) the date of the anticipated end of the moratorium period.

Chapter 7

Permission to act as a director, etc.

[Note: a document required by the Act or these Rules must also contain the standard contents set out in Part 1.]

9.25 Application for permission under the Company Directors Disqualification Act 1986

9.25(1) [Application of rule] This rule relates to an application for permission under section 11 of the Company Directors Disqualification Act 1986, to act as director of, or to take part or be concerned in the promotion, formation or management of a company by a person–

(a) in relation to whom a moratorium period under a debt relief order applies; or

(b) in relation to whom a debt relief restrictions order or undertaking is in force.

9.25(2) [Witness statement in report] The application must be supported by a witness statement which must contain identification details for the company and specify–

(a) the nature of its business or intended business, and the place or places where that business is, or is to be, carried on;

(b) in the case of a company which has not yet been incorporated, whether it is, or is to be, a private or a public company;

(c) the persons who are, or are to be, principally responsible for the conduct of its affairs (whether as directors, shadow directors, managers or otherwise);

(d) the manner and capacity in which the applicant for permission proposes to take part or be concerned in the promotion or formation of the company or, as the case may be, its management; and

(e) the emoluments and other benefits to be obtained by virtue of the matters referred to in paragraph (d).

9.25(3) [Court to fix venue, notice] The court must fix a venue for the hearing of the application, and must deliver a notice to the applicant for permission accordingly.

9.26 Report of official receiver

9.26(1) [Applicant to deliver notice and witness statement] The applicant for permission must, not less than 28 days before the date fixed for the hearing, deliver to the official receiver, notice of the venue, accompanied by copies of the application and the witness statement under rule 9.25.

9.26(2) [Official receiver may file report] The official receiver may, not less than 14 days before the date fixed for the hearing, file with the court a report of any matters which the official receiver considers ought to be drawn to the court's attention.

9.26(3) [Delivery of report to applicant] A copy of the report must be delivered by the official receiver, as soon as reasonably practicable after it is filed, to the applicant for permission.

9.26(4) [Applicant's notice denying or disputing report] The applicant for permission may, not later than five business days before the date of the hearing, file with the court a notice specifying any statements in the official receiver's report which are to be denied or disputed.

9.26(5) [Delivery of notice of denial or dispute] If a notice is filed under paragraph (4), the applicant for permission must deliver copies of it, not less than three business days before the date of the hearing, to the official receiver.

9.26(6) [Right of official receiver to appear at hearing] The official receiver may appear on the hearing of the application, and may make representations and put to the applicant for permission such questions as the court may allow.

9.27 Court's order on application

9.27(1) [Court order to specify extent of permission granted] If the court grants the application for permission under section 11 of the Company Directors Disqualification Act 1986, its order must specify that which by virtue of the order the applicant has permission to do.

9.27(2) [Court's power under IA 1986 s.251M] The court may at the same time, having regard to any representations made by the official receiver on the hearing of the application, exercise in relation to the moratorium period or the debt relief order to which the applicant for permission is subject, any power which it has under section 251M.

9.27(3) [Court to deliver order to applicant and official receiver] Whether or not the application is granted, copies of the order must be delivered by the court to the applicant and the official receiver.

Part 10

Bankruptcy

Introductory note to Part 10
This Part deals with bankruptcy and should be set against the background of Pt 9 of the Act. It is a truncated version of its predecessor in IR 1986 (Pt 6) because a number of discrete bankruptcy elements have been hived off into new Parts (for example Pt 11, which deals with bankruptcy restrictions). In order to understand the operation of this Part it is also necessary to refer to other "common" Parts, such as Pts 14 and 15.

Chapter 1

The statutory demand

[Note: a document required by the Act or these Rules must also contain the standard contents set out in Part 1.]

10.1 The statutory demand (section 268)

10.1(1) [Heading and content of statutory declaration] A statutory demand under section 268 must contain–

(a) the heading either "Statutory demand under section 268(1) (debt payable immediately) of the Insolvency Act 1986" or "Statutory demand under section 268(2) (debt not immediately payable)";

(b) identification details for the debtor;

(c) the name and address of the creditor;

(d) a statement of the amount of the debt, and the consideration for it (or, if there is no consideration, the way in which it arises);

(e) if the demand is made under section 268(1) and founded on a judgment or order of a court, the date of the judgment or order and the court in which it was obtained;

(f) if the demand is made under section 268(2), a statement of the grounds on which it is alleged that the debtor appears to have no reasonable prospect of paying the debt;

(g) if the creditor is entitled to the debt by way of assignment, details of the original creditor and any intermediary assignees;

(h) a statement that if the debtor does not comply with the demand bankruptcy proceedings may be commenced;

(i) the date by which the debtor must comply with the demand, if bankruptcy proceedings are to be avoided;

(j) a statement of the methods of compliance which are open to the debtor;

(k) a statement that the debtor has the right to apply to the court to have the demand set aside;

(l) a statement that rule 10.4(4) of the Insolvency (England and Wales) Rules 2016 states to which court such an application must be made; and name the court or hearing centre of the County Court to which, according to the present information, the debtor must make the application (i.e. the High Court, the County Court at Central London or a named hearing centre of the County Court as the case may be);

(m) a statement that any application to set aside the demand must be made within 18 days of service on the debtor; and

(n) a statement that if the debtor does not apply to set aside the demand within 18 days or otherwise deal with this demand within 21 days after its service the debtor could be made bankrupt and the debtor's property and goods taken away.

10.1(2) [Service by Minister or Government Department] Where the statutory demand is served by a Minister of the Crown or a Government Department the statutory demand must explain that the debtor may alternatively apply to set aside the demand to the High Court or the County Court at Central London (as the case may be) if the Minister or Department intends to present a bankruptcy petition to one of them.

10.1(3) [Demand to name individuals to communicate with] A demand must name one or more individuals with whom the debtor may communicate with a view to–

(a) securing or compounding the debt to the satisfaction of the creditor; or

(b) establishing to the creditor's satisfaction that there is a reasonable prospect that the debt will be paid when it falls due.

10.1(4) [Contact details to be given] The postal address, electronic address and telephone number (if any) of the named individual must be given.

10.1(5) [Authentication of demand] A demand must be dated and authenticated either by the creditor or by a person who is authorised to make the demand on the creditor's behalf.

10.1(6) [Statement of authorisation for non-creditor] A demand which is authenticated by a person other than the creditor must state that the person is authorised to make the demand on the creditor's behalf and state the person's relationship to the creditor.

10.1(7) [Interest and accruing charges] If the amount claimed in the demand includes–

(a) any charge by way of interest of which notice had not previously been delivered to the debtor as a liability of the debtor's; or

(b) any other charge accruing from time to time,

the amount or rate of the charge must be separately identified, and the grounds on which payment of it is claimed must be stated.

10.1(8) [Limitation of charges] The amount claimed for such charges must be limited to that which has accrued at the date of the demand.

10.1(9) [Security held by creditor] If the creditor holds any security in respect of the debt, the full amount of the debt must be specified, but–

(a) the demand must specify the nature of the security, and the value which the creditor puts upon it at the date of the demand; and

(b) the demand must claim payment of the full amount of the debt, less the specified value of the security.

10.1(10) [Time limits where service out of jurisdiction] When the statutory demand is to be served out of the jurisdiction, the time limits of 18 days and 21 days referred to in sub-paragraphs 10.1(1)(m) and (n) above must be amended as follows–

(a) for any reference to 18 days there must be substituted the number of days which is the appropriate number of days set out in the table accompanying the Practice Direction supplementing Section IV of CPR Part 6 plus 4 days; and

(b) for any reference to 21 days there must be substituted the number of days which is the appropriate number of days set out in the table accompanying the Practice Direction supplementing Section IV of CPR Part 6 plus 7 days.

General Note

This rule describes the statutory demand mentioned in IA 1986 s.268(1)(a) and (2)(a). The form and contents are detailed. Where the demand is made under FSMA 2000 s.372(4)(a) IR 1986 r.6.1 (now IR 2016 r.10.1) is disapplied (and substitute rules provided) by the Bankruptcy (Financial Services and Markets Act 2000) Rules 2001 (SI 2001/3634).

For practical guidance see Baister (2006) 22 I.L. & P. 55. On who is an authorised signatory for the purposes of r.10.1(1) see *Horne v Dacorum BC* [2000] B.P.I.R. 1047.

On valuation of security and r.10.1 see the comments of HHJ Pelling QC in *Cahillane v NALM Ltd* [2014] EWHC 1992 (Ch); [2014] B.P.I.R. 1093.

For judicial consideration of this provision see *Re a Debtor (No.310 of 1988)* [1989] 1 W.L.R. 452. Here Knox J held that the phrase "any security in respect of the debt" when used in the former 1986 r.6.1(5) (now IR 2016 r.10.1(9)) must have the same meaning as when used in IA 1986 ss.383 and 385(1). Therefore the security that had to be referred to in the statutory demand was security over any property of the alleged debtor and not security provided by a third party. Failure to specify the security held as required under former IR 1986 r.6.1(5) (now IR 2016 r.10.1(9)) may not always be fatal for the creditor, as the court now tends to consider whether the debtor has suffered any real injustice: see *Re a Debtor (No.106 of 1992), The Independent*, 20 April 1992 and the comments on s.268. For the position where the incorrect form is used see *Cartwright v Staffordshire and Moorlands DC* [1998] B.P.I.R. 328.

Canning v Irwin Mitchell LLP [2017] EWHC 718 (Ch); [2017] B.P.I.R. 934 stresses the importance of proper service of the statutory demand or else the subsequent petition will be undermined.

Rule 10.1(10) inserted by the Insolvency (England and Wales) and Insolvency (Scotland) (Miscellaneous and Consequential Amendments) Rules 2017 (SI 2017/1115) rr.1(1), (2), 2, 7 as from 8 December 2017.

10.2 Service of statutory demand

10.2 A creditor must do all that is reasonable to bring the statutory demand to the debtor's attention and, if practicable in the particular circumstances, serve the demand personally.

General Note

The rules as to service of the statutory demand are hereby prescribed. Personal service is the preferred method unless impracticable. See also *Practice Direction: Insolvency Proceedings* [2018] B.C.C. 241 (included as App.IV of this *Guide*).

In *Re a Debtor (No.234 and 236 of 1991), The Independent*, 29 June 1992 it was confirmed by Blackett-Ord QC (sitting as a judge of the High Court) that in some cases it may be appropriate to serve the statutory demand upon the solicitors of the debtor. In *Regional Collection Services Ltd v Heald* [2000] B.P.I.R. 641 it was held that a creditor had failed to take all reasonable steps to bring the demand to the debtor's attention because it had failed to visit the debtor's business premises. For a case where substituted service was found to be sufficient compliance with IR 1986 r.6.3 (now IR 2016 r.10.2) see *Takavarasha v Newham Borough Council* [2004] EWHC 3232 (Ch); [2006] B.P.I.R. 311 (statutory demand pushed through letter box where debtor had refused to meet process server). See *Bush v Bank Mandiri (Europe) Ltd* [2011] B.P.I.R. 19 where the point was made by Registrar Barber that failure to comply with the requirements of IR 1986 r.6.3 (now IR 2016 r.10.2) is not necessarily fatal to the procedure.

For the obligations of the creditor under r.10.2 see *Omokwe v HFC Bank Ltd* [2007] B.P.I.R. 1157 and HHJ Hodge QC judgment in *Yang v Official Receiver* [2013] EWHC 3577 (Ch); [2014] B.P.I.R. 826.

In *Canning v Irwin Mitchell LLP* [2017] EWHC 718 (Ch); [2017] B.P.I.R. 934 there was a fundamental failure to serve the statutory demand and this undermined the resulting petition. The court expressed some doubts about comments made in *Bush v Bank Mandiri (Europe) Ltd* [2011] B.P.I.R. 19.

On service of a statutory demand see *Emmanuel v Revenue and Customs Commissioners* [2017] EWHC 1253 (Ch); [2017] B.P.I.R. 1182.

10.3 Proof of service of statutory demand

10.3(1) [Certificate of service] Where section 268 requires a statutory demand to be served before the petition, a certificate of service of the demand must be filed with the court with the petition.

10.3(2) [Certificate accompanied by statement of truth] The certificate must be verified by a statement of truth and be accompanied by a copy of the demand served.

10.3(3) [Statement of truth made by actual server] If the demand has been served personally on the debtor, the statement of truth must be made by the person who served the demand unless service has been acknowledged in writing by the debtor or a person authorised to accept service.

10.3(4) [Service acknowledged in writing] If service has been acknowledged in writing either by–

(a) the debtor; or

(b) a person who is authorised to accept service on the debtor's behalf and who has stated that this is the case in the acknowledgement of service;

then the certificate of service must be authenticated either by the creditor or by a person acting on the creditor's behalf, and the acknowledgement of service must accompany the certificate.

10.3(5) [Statement of truth where personal service not possible] If the demand has been served other than personally and there is no acknowledgement of service, the certificate must be authenticated by a person or persons having direct personal knowledge of the means adopted for serving the statutory demand, and must contain the following information–

(a) the steps taken to serve the demand; and

(b) a date by which, to the best of the knowledge, information and belief of the person authenticating the certificate, the demand will have come to the debtor's attention.

10.3(6) [Effective date of service for non-personal service] Where paragraph (5) applies the statutory demand is deemed to have been served on the debtor on the date referred to in paragraph (5)(b) unless the court determines otherwise.

General Note

See *Practice Direction: Insolvency Proceedings* [2018] B.C.C. 241 (reproduced as App.IV of this *Guide*). IR 1986 r.6.11 (now IR 2016 r.10.3) was noted in passing in *Revenue and Customs Commissioners v Soor* [2005] EWHC 3080 (Ch); [2006] B.P.I.R. 429.

10.4 Application to set aside statutory demand

10.4(1) [Debtor's right to apply to set aside] The debtor may apply to the court for an order setting aside the statutory demand.

10.4(2) [Time limit for application] The application must be made within 18 days from the date of the service of the statutory demand.

10.4(3) [Content of application] The application must–

(a) identify the debtor;

(b) state that the application is for an order that the statutory demand be set aside;

(c) state the date of the statutory demand; and

(d) be dated and authenticated by the debtor, or by a person authorised to act on the debtor's behalf.

10.4(4) [Venue to be applied to] The application must be made to the court or hearing centre–

(a) determined in accordance with rule 10.48; or

(b) to which rule 10.11(1) requires a petition to be presented if–

(i) the creditor serving the statutory demand is a Minister of the Crown or a government Department,

(ii) the debt in respect of which the statutory demand is made, or part of it equal to or exceeding the bankruptcy level (within the meaning of section 267), is the subject of a judgment or order of a court, and

(iii) the statutory demand–

(aa) specifies the date of the judgment or order and the court in which it was obtained, and

(bb) indicates the creditor's intention to present a bankruptcy petition against the debtor in the High Court or the County Court at Central London as the case may be.

10.4(5) [Effect of filing application] The time within which the debtor must comply with the statutory demand ceases to run on the date the application is filed with the court, subject to any order of the court under rule 10.5.

10.4(6) [Documents supporting application] The debtor's application must be accompanied by a copy of the statutory demand, where it is in the debtor's possession, and supported by a witness statement containing the following–

(a) the date on which the debtor became aware of the statutory demand;

(b) the grounds on which the debtor claims that it should be set aside; and (c) any evidence in support of the application.

General Note

The debtor can apply to the court to have the statutory demand set aside. He has 18 days after service to make such an application. If an application is made, the three weeks' deadline for compliance with the demand ceases to run. In

Revenue and Customs v Soor [2005] EWHC 3080 (Ch); [2006] B.P.I.R. 429 Warren J rejected a later application to set aside a statutory demand. There were no grounds for allowing an application for the late setting aside of the statutory demand. The liability, established by court judgment, could not be disputed.

See also *Practice Direction: Insolvency Proceedings* [2018] B.C.C. 241 reproduced as App.IV of this *Guide*); and *Morley v Inland Revenue Commissioners* [1996] B.P.I.R. 452. On the need for proper formal requirements to be satisfied see *Ariyo v Sovereign Leasing* [1998] B.P.I.R. 177.

10.5 Hearing of application to set aside

10.5(1) [Power of court to dismiss if no sufficient cause] On receipt of an application to set aside a statutory demand, the court may, if satisfied that no sufficient cause is shown for it, dismiss it without giving notice of the application to the creditor.

10.5(2) [Dismissal of application restarts time for compliance] The time for complying with the statutory demand runs again from the date the application is dismissed under paragraph (1).

10.5(3) [Court to fix venue, notice] Unless the application is dismissed under paragraph (1), the court must fix a venue for it to be heard, and must give at least five business days' notice to–

(a) the debtor or, if the debtor's application was made by a solicitor acting for the debtor, to the solicitor;

(b) the creditor; and

(c) whoever is named in the statutory demand as the person with whom the debtor may communicate about the demand (or the first such if more than one).

10.5(4) [Summary determination or adjournment] On the hearing of the application, the court must consider the evidence then available to it, and may either determine the application or adjourn it, giving such directions as it thinks appropriate.

10.5(5) [Setting aside demand] The court may grant the application if–

(a) the debtor appears to have a counterclaim, set-off or cross demand which equals or exceeds the amount of the debt specified in the statutory demand;

(b) the debt is disputed on grounds which appear to the court to be substantial;

(c) it appears that the creditor holds some security in relation to the debt claimed by the demand, and either rule 10.1(9) is not complied with in relation to it, or the court is satisfied that the value of the security equals or exceeds the full amount of the debt; or

(d) the court is satisfied, on other grounds, that the demand ought to be set aside.

10.5(6) [Content of order] An order setting aside a statutory demand must contain–

(a) identification details for the debtor;

(b) the date of the hearing of the application;

(c) the date of the statutory demand;

(d) an order that the statutory demand be set aside;

(e) details of any further order in the matter; and

(f) the date of the order.

10.5(7) [Under-valued security] Where the creditor holds some security in relation to the debt and has complied with rule 10.1(9) but the court is satisfied that the statutory demand undervalues the security, the court may order the creditor to amend the demand (but without prejudice to the creditor's right to present a bankruptcy petition by reference to the original demand as so amended).

10.5(8) [On dismissal of application] If the court dismisses the application, it must make an order authorising the creditor to present a bankruptcy petition either as soon as reasonably practicable, or on or after a date specified in the order.

10.5(9) [Delivery of copy order to creditor] The court must deliver a copy of any order under paragraphs (6) to (8) to the creditor as soon as reasonably practicable.

General Note

This rule outlines the hearing procedure for an application made under r.10.4. If the application succeeds, the court's order should contain the details in r.10.5(6). If the application fails the court can permit the immediate presentation of the bankruptcy petition. The leading case on former IR 1986 r.6.5(4) (now IR 2016 r.10.5(5)) is *Re a Debtor (No.1 of 1987)* [1989] 1 W.L.R. 271 where the Court of Appeal held that a document purporting to be a statutory demand was to be treated as such until set aside. In cases of setting aside under r.10.5(4)(d) the debtor must not merely convince the court that the demand was perplexing but also prove what the true position was between himself and the creditor. See the general note after s.268. For a useful comparison between the rules relating to set aside of statutory demands in corporate and personal insolvency law see *Re A Debtor (544/SD/98)* [2001] 1 B.C.L.C. 103 (also reported as *Garrow v The Society of Lloyds* [1999] B.P.I.R. 885).

A set aside is most likely to succeed where the statutory demand was served by a person who was neither a creditor nor appointed agent of the creditor—*Agilo Ltd v Henry* [2010] EWHC 2717 (Ch).

For the purposes of r.10.5 it is not necessary to state the date of the petition—*Vaidya v Wijayawardhana* [2010] B.P.I.R. 1016.

A set-aside application is not a trial on the merits and fresh evidence can be adduced: *Royal Bank of Scotland v Binnell* [1996] B.P.I.R. 352; *Norman Laurier v United Overseas Bank* [1996] B.P.I.R. 635; *Salvidge v Hussein* [1999] B.P.I.R. 410. These cases confirm that the rule in *Ladd v Marshall* [1954] 1 W.L.R. 1489 does not apply. For further discussion in the context of appeals from decisions on set-aside applications see *AIB Finance Ltd v Alsop* [1998] B.C.C. 780. Such appeals are true appeals and subsequent events should not be taken into account—*Cozens v Customs and Excise Commissioners* [2000] B.P.I.R. 252.

The jurisdiction to set aside statutory demands is permissive; the court is under no obligation to act, as was stressed in *Re a Debtor (No.106 of 1992), The Independent*, 20 April 1992. See also *Khan v Breezevale SARL* [1996] B.P.I.R. 190 (failure to refer to security). The fact that a statutory demand may be defective does not guarantee that it will be set aside under r.10.5(4)—*Coulter v Chief of Dorset Police* [2004] EWCA Civ 1259; [2005] B.P.I.R. 62. For a continuation of this saga see *Coulter v Dorset Police (No.2)* [2005] EWCA Civ 1113; [2006] B.P.I.R. 10. *Coulter (No.2)* was followed in *Vaidya v Wijayawardhana* [2010] B.P.I.R. 1016.

The court cannot make a conditional order on a set-aside application. Either the demand must be set aside or the application rejected: *Re a Debtor (No.90 of 1992)* [1993] T.L.R. 387; and *Re Debtor (No.32 of 1991) (No.2)* [1994] B.C.C. 524. Equally the courts will not allow a petition to be presented and then adjourned simply in order to trigger time periods for transactional avoidance. Thus if the debtor has an arguable cross claim the proper course of action is to set aside the demand and not to allow this issue to be reserved for trial of the petition—*Garrow v The Society of Lloyds* [1999] B.P.I.R. 885. If a set-aside application fails the same issues cannot normally be relitigated on the hearing of the petition—*Turner v Royal Bank of Scotland* [2000] B.P.I.R. 683; *Atherton v Ogunlende* [2003] B.P.I.R. 21. See also *Coulter v Dorset Police (No.2)* [2005] EWCA Civ 1113; [2006] B.P.I.R. 10. See also *Roseoak Investment Ltd v Network Rail* [2010] B.P.I.R. 646, where the point was re-emphasised that failed arguments on a set aside application cannot be reopened.

An application to set aside a statutory demand based upon former IR 1986 r.6.5(4)(a) failed in *Ghadami v Donegan* [2014] EWHC 4448 (Ch).

A statutory demand was set aside by Registrar Barber in *Dowling v Promontoria (Arrow) Ltd* [2017] EWHC B25 (Ch); [2017] B.P.I.R. 1477. Multiple reasons were given for the setting aside of this large demand which was based upon an alleged guarantee liability.

On r.10.5(5)(a) see *Hofer v Strawson* [1999] B.P.I.R. 501; and *Re A Debtor (No.87 of 1999)* [2000] B.P.I.R. 589, which offer guidance on cross claims. The requirements of former IR 1986 r.6.5(4)(a) (now IR 2016 r.10.5(5)(a)) were found to be satisfied in *Stone v Vallance* [2008] B.P.I.R. 236. For the meaning of a cross demand within r.10.5(5)(a) see *Popely v Popely* [2004] EWCA Civ 463; [2004] B.P.I.R. 778. In determining whether to set aside a statutory demand because of the existence of a potential cross claim the court should ask itself whether there was a "genuinely triable issue" as to the existence of the cross claim. That test was, in effect, the same as that used in the Civil Procedure Rules, where the requirement was for a "real prospect of success"—*Ashworth v Newnote Ltd* [2007] EWCA Civ 793; [2007] B.P.I.R. 1012. See *Abernethy v Hotbed Ltd* [2011] EWHC 1476 (Ch); [2011] B.P.I.R. 1547 where Newey J equates the genuinely triable issue with the test applied to summary judgment applications. In *Darjan Estate Co plc v Hurley* [2012] EWHC 189 (Ch); [2012] 1 W.L.R. 1782 the High Court confirmed a decision of the deputy district judge that there were no substantial grounds for disputing the debt (which consisted of rent arrears) featured in the statutory demand. The court refused to extend the full protective rules embodied in cases such as *RBS v Etridge (No.2)* [2002] 2 A.C. 773 to wives signing standard contracts, as opposed to contracts of surety. A set aside was granted in *Welsh v Bank of Ireland* [2013] NIMaster 6 as the debt was disputed on *Etridge* grounds. The court made the point that the test to be applied was whether the debtor had raised a good arguable case in respect of the dispute. See also *Logue v Bank of Ireland* [2012] NIMaster 10 for a similar approach. An attempt to seek a set aside on the basis of a dubious cross claim failed in *Gustavi v Moore* [2004] B.P.I.R. 268. Any counterclaim must be legally enforceable—*Re A Debtor (No.35 of 2000)* [2002] B.P.I.R. 75. Where there is a counterclaim within r.10.5(5)(a) there appears to be a mutuality requirement—*Hurst v Bennett* [2001] EWCA Civ 182; [2001] B.P.I.R. 287; *Southward v Banham* [2002] B.P.I.R. 1253. In *Chan Sui v Appasamy* [2005] EWHC 3519 (Ch); [2008] B.P.I.R. 18 the court set aside a statutory demand under IR 1986 r.6.5(4)(a) where there were a series of interlocking cross claims producing a situation that could not be resolved by the court on a summary set aside application. HHJ Weeks QC in this case explains the residual role played by r.10.5(5)(d). In *Vaidya v Wijayawardhana* [2010] B.P.I.R. 1016 the court was quite liberal on the background to the cross claim which was being raised—it need not relate to the debt featured in the statutory demand. On cross claims see also *Bush v Bank Mandiri (Europe) Ltd* [2011] B.P.I.R. 19. In *Ahmed v Landstone Leisure Ltd* [2009] B.P.I.R. 227 the statutory demand was set aside under IR 1986 r.6.5(4)(a) (now IR 2016 r.10.5.(5)(a)) by HHJ Purle QC because the debtor may have had a counterclaim. For comment see V. Cocks (2009) 22 Insolv. Int. 108. An appellate court is unlikely to overturn a finding at first instance that a debt is not disputed on substantial grounds—*Macpherson v Wise* [2011] EWHC 141 (Ch); [2011] B.P.I.R. 472.

Note also *Hayes v Hayes* [2014] EWHC 2694 (Ch); [2014] B.P.I.R. 1212 where Nugee J undertook an in depth review of the position on disputed debts and cross claims. In upholding the decision of the Registrar to dismiss the creditor's petition the point was made that in some situations the court hearing the petition could revisit arguments made on an abortive set aside application if new evidence had come to light.

A statutory demand was set aside by Registrar Jones in *Ryan v Tiuta International Ltd* [2015] B.P.I.R. 123 in view of a dispute as to the alleged underlying liability on a guarantee. See also *Baker v LSREF III Wight Ltd* [2016] B.P.I.R. 509 on the test to be applied as to whether there is a bona fide dispute on substantial grounds.

In *Inbakumar v United Trust Bank Ltd* [2012] EWHC 845 (Ch); [2012] B.P.I.R. 758 the court indicated that the fact that a debtor may have a claim against a third party in connection with the transaction from which the debt arose was no justification in itself for setting aside a statutory demand served by a creditor. In [41] of his judgment Vos J confined his observations to the facts of the present case.

An attempt to rely on former IR 1986 r.6.5(4)(b) (now IR 2016 r.10.5.(5)(b)) was rejected by Nugee J in *Knight v APS Recycling Ltd* [2014] EWHC 4620 (Ch).

In *Re a Debtor (No.960/SD/1992)* [1993] S.T.C. 218 Mummery J refused to set aside a statutory demand under former IR 1986 r.6.5(4)(c) (now IR 2016 r.10.5(5)(c)) in a case where a tax assessment was being challenged by the taxpayer; the case did not appear to be covered by this provision. See *Fagg v Rushton* [2007] EWHC 657 (Ch); [2007] B.P.I.R. 1059 for the meaning of "security" in r.10.5(5)(c). On the valuation of security see *Ludsin Overseas Ltd v Maggs* [2014] EWHC 3566 (Ch). On the interpretation of r.10.5(5)(c) see the ruling of Floyd J in *White v Davenham Trust* [2010] EWHC 2748 (Ch); [2011] B.P.I.R. 280. Note also *1st Credit (Finance) Ltd v Bartram* [2010] EWHC 2910 (Ch); [2011] B.P.I.R. 1. The fact that a creditor enjoys security *granted by a third party* does not preclude a creditor from pursuing bankruptcy proceedings against a person properly determined as a debtor—*White v Davenham Trust Ltd* [2011] EWCA Civ 747; [2011] B.P.I.R. 1193. This ruling is important in the context of guarantees given by company directors where the lender has security over the company's assets. On r.10.5(5)(c) see *Cahillane v National Asset Management Ltd* [2014] EWHC 1992 (Ch); [2014] B.P.I.R. 1093.

A set-aside application also proved unsuccessful in *Re a Debtor (No.415/SD/1993)* [1994] 1 W.L.R. 917. Here the debtor was seeking to set aside the demand by arguing that he had made a reasonable offer of security to the creditor. In discussing the meaning of "other grounds" in IR 1986 r.6.5(4)(d) Jacob J made it clear that set-aside applications were designed to deal with procedural flaws in the demand and were not meant to raise substantive issues of reasonableness—these issues could be considered when the petition was heard. Equally in *Platts v Western Trust and Savings Ltd* [1996] B.P.I.R. 339 the court indicated that it would not investigate such questions as whether the creditor was secured or not as these were issues best dealt with when the petition was heard. However see the comments of the Court of Appeal on IR 1986 r.6.5(4)(d) (now IR 2016 r.10.5(5)(d)) in *Budge v Budge (Contractors) Ltd* [1997] B.P.I.R. 366. *Budge* (above) was followed in *Mahon and Mahon v FBN Bank (UK) Ltd* [2011] EWHC 1432 (Ch); [2011] B.P.I.R. 1035. In *Re a Debtor (No.90 of 1997), The Times*, 1 July 1998, the High Court considered the position with regard to setting aside under IR 1986 r.6.5(4)(d) (now IR 2016 r.10.5(5)(d)) when there were parallel bankruptcy and civil proceedings afoot. The importance of the general discretion vested in the court by r.10.5(5)(d) was clearly illustrated in *City Electrical Factors v Hardingham* [1996] B.P.I.R. 541 where a statutory demand based upon a debt slightly in excess of £750 was set aside. In *Turner v Turner* [2006] EWHC 2023 (Ch); [2006] B.P.I.R. 1531 the court dealt with the factors relevant to the exercise of discretion under r.10.5(5)(d). The factors taken into account should have some relevance/proximity to the statutory demand.

Note *Howell v Lerwick Commercial Mortgage Corp Ltd* [2015] EWHC 1177 (Ch); [2015] B.P.I.R. 821. This case features a valuable analysis by Nugee J of the situation where the debtor seeking set aside has a cross claim or counterclaim that might reduce the amount of the debt to below the prescribed amount (then £750). According to Nugee J this would not require the court to accede to the set aside application; this conclusion was arrived at by examination of the statutory provision and after taking soundings from the bankruptcy registrars. Nugee J noted that the position might be different where there was a disputed element in the debt—r.10.5(5)(d) might then be engaged. Nugee J did note that if a bankruptcy petition did proceed where the debt was less than the minimum amount then the petition would be likely to fail.

Harvey v Dunbar Assets [2013] EWCA Civ 952; [2013] B.P.I.R. 722 is a case on guarantee liability that bucks the trend. The statutory demand here was set aside because the alleged guarantee liability did not arise. The guarantee was a composite guarantee and as there was not a valid signature from each of the guarantors, no liability arose. *Josife v Summertrot Holdings Ltd* [2014] EWHC 996 (Ch); [2014] B.P.I.R. 1250 featured an abortive attempt to set aside a statutory demand on the basis of an allegation that the debtor lacked mental capacity when signing up to the guarantee producing the underlying debt. The court also made the general point that set aside will not be granted simply because the debtor might come up with a defence before any bankruptcy petition is heard. In *Harvey v Dunbar Assets plc* [2015] EWHC 3355 (Ch) HHJ Kaye QC warned about allowing arguments to be rerun by a debtor on a set aside application where these same arguments had been unsuccessful at an earlier hearing. This point was stressed even though the doctrine of res judicata might not apply.

Some further consideration was given to the criteria governing the exercise of discretion under former IR 1986 r.6.5(4)(d) (now IR 2016 r.10.5(5)(d)) in *TS&S Global Ltd v Fithian-Franks* [2007] EWHC 1401 (Ch). For an interesting discussion on whether it was appropriate to set aside a statutory demand served on a guarantor of a tenant see *Octagon Assets Ltd v Remblance* [2009] B.P.I.R. 1129.

For the utility of the "other grounds" basis for set aside which is located in r.10.5(5)(d) see *Maud v Libyan Investment Authority* [2015] EWHC 1625 (Ch); [2015] B.P.I.R. 858. The set aside decision in this case was set aside on appeal in *Libyan Investment Authority v Maud* [2016] EWCA Civ 788 with the Court of Appeal basing its decision on its interpretation of a range of grounds in the former IR 1986 r.6.5(4).

If the creditor bases his petition upon a judgment debt the court will not on a set-aside application look behind the earlier judgment: see Ferris J in *Re a Debtor (657/SD/1991)* [1993] B.C.L.C. 1280 applying *Practice Direction* [1987] 1 W.L.R. 119. Note also *Neely v Inland Revenue Commissioners* [1996] B.P.I.R. 473; and *Practice Direction: Insolvency Proceedings* [2018] B.C.C. 241, para.11.4.4 in App.IV of this *Guide*.

For the position where the debt is disputed within the context of r.10.5(5)(b), see *Re a Debtor (No.11 of 1987), The Independent*, 28 March 1988; *Re a Debtor (No.10 of 1988)* [1989] 1 W.L.R. 405; and *Cale v Assiudoman KPS (Harrow) Ltd* [1996] B.P.I.R. 245. On the standard of proof see *Kellar v BBR Graphic Engineers Ltd* [2002] B.P.I.R. 544. Another interesting case involving a disputed debt was *Re a Debtor (No.49 and 50 of 1992)* [1995] Ch. 66. Here part of the debt upon which the statutory demand was based was disputed by the debtor. The undisputed element was for an amount less than the statutory minimum upon which a creditor could petition for bankruptcy. In those circumstances the Court of Appeal held that although the demand could not be set aside in its entirety under former IR 1986 r.6.5(4)(b) (now IR 2016 r.10.5(5)(b)) the court could set aside the whole demand using its residual discretion under the previous IR 1986 r.6.5(4)(d) (now IR 2016 r.10.5(5)(d)). In *Interframe Ltd v Brown* [2005] EWHC 3527 (Ch); [2008] B.P.I.R. 49 Lawrence Collins J indicated that an overstated debt will not normally justify the setting aside of a statutory demand. For the dangers as to costs of a creditor using a statutory demand in cases where a trial of the action is pending see *Re a Debtor (No. 620 of 1997), The Times*, 18 June 1998.

In *Feldman v Nissim* [2010] B.P.I.R. 815 the court discussed the requirements of success under former IR 1986 r.6.5(4)(b) (now IR 2016 r.10.5(5)(b))—substantial grounds must be established in order to show that a debt was disputed. Note also *Crossley-Cooke v Europanel (UK) Ltd* [2010] B.P.I.R. 561 for discussion of the appropriate test to be applied where a debt is said to be disputed within the meaning of r.10.5(5)(b). On the test as to whether a debt is to be treated as disputed see the latest authority of *Alexander-Theodotou v Michael Kyprianou & Co LLC* [2016] B.P.I.R. 1114

See *MFP Foundations v Shaw* [2010] B.P.I.R. 397 where the point was reiterated that the fact a debtor could have afforded to pay the statutory demand was not in itself grounds for dismissing the debtor's set aside application.

On the exercise of discretion under r.10.5(8) see *Everard v Lloyds* [2003] B.P.I.R. 1286. In *Davies v Barnes Webster & Sons Ltd* [2011] EWHC 2560 (Ch); [2012] B.P.I.R. 97 the court deferred the earliest date before which a petition could be presented.

On the predecessor IR 1986 r.6.5(6) (now IR 2016 r.10.5(8)) see *Darbyshire v Turpin* [2013] EWHC 954 (Ch); [2013] B.P.I.R. 558—if a set aside application is dismissed, the creditor can present a petition immediately unless court has set a date for presentation.

Note the unusual case of *Pace (Europe) Ltd v Dunham* [2012] EWHC 852 (Ch); [2012] B.P.I.R. 836 where the court allowed an appeal against a decision to set aside a statutory demand based upon a foreign judgment debt. In his judgment HHJ Purle undertakes a comprehensive analysis of the enforcement of foreign judgment debts.

An appeal against a decision to set aside a statutory demand where *Etridge* issues had been raised by the debtor was unsuccessful in *O'Neill v Ulster Bank Ltd* [2015] NICA 64.

There is authority that the remedial IR 1986 r.7.55 (now IR 2016 r.10.64) cannot apply in the context of defects in the statutory demand: *Re a Debtor (No.190 of 1987), The Times*, 21 May 1988.

See *Woolsey v Payne* [2015] EWHC 968 (Ch); [2015] B.P.I.R. 933 where the court made the point that the same test is to be applied on both a set aside application and an annulment application as to whether a debt is to be regarded as disputed.

A set aside application was dismissed in *Maud v Aabar Block SARL* [2015] EWHC 1626 (Ch); [2015] B.P.I.R. 845 as there were no arguable grounds for disputing the underlying liability. For later proceedings as to whether the bankruptcy petition should be adjourned for a second time—see the ruling of Registrar Briggs reported in [2015] EWHC 3681 (Ch). Eventually Registrar Briggs made a bankruptcy order (see [2016] EWHC 1016 (Ch) but the appeal to Snowden J succeeded [2016] EWHC 2175 (Ch) and the issue is therefore still unresolved. Note also S. Najib [2016] 9 CRI 214 for an account of the latest state of play.

See *Blavo v Law Society* [2017] EWHC 561 (Ch); [2017] B.P.I.R. 909.

Note also *Diamond v Holding* (unreported, 2 November 2017). See also the views of Barling J in *Dunhill v Hughmans (a firm)* [2017] EWHC 2073 (Ch).

Chapter 2

Creditors' Bankruptcy Petitions

Preliminary

[Note: a document required by the Act or these Rules must also contain the standard contents set out in Part 1.]

10.6 Application and interpretation

10.6(1) [Application of Ch.2] This Chapter relates to a creditor's petition and making a bankruptcy order on such a petition.

10.6(2) ["The debt"] In this Chapter "the debt" means the debt in relation to which the petition is presented.

10.6(3) [Application to IVA supervisor, etc.] This Chapter also applies to a petition under section 264(1)(c) by a supervisor of, or person bound by, an IVA, with any necessary modifications.

General Note

See the guidance in *Practice Direction: Insolvency Proceedings* [2018] B.C.C. 241.

10.7 Contents of petition

10.7(1) [Content of petition] The petition must state–

(a) the name and postal address of the petitioner;

(b) where the petitioner is represented by a solicitor, the name, postal address and telephone number of the solicitor;

(c) that the petitioner requests that the court make a bankruptcy order against the debtor;

(d) whether–

(i) the debtor's centre of main interests is within a member State,

(ii) the debtor's centre of main interests is not within a member State, or

(iii) the debtor carries on business as an Article 1.2 undertaking;

(e) whether the debtor–

(i) is resident in England and Wales, or

(ii) is not resident in England and Wales;

(f) whether the petition is presented to–

(i) the High Court,

(ii) the County Court at Central London, or

(iii) a specified hearing centre; and

(g) the reasons why the court or hearing centre to which the petition is presented is the correct court or hearing centre under rule 10.11.

10.7(2) [Petition to explain any delay over four months] If the petition is based on a statutory demand, and more than four months have elapsed between the service of the demand and the presentation of the petition, the petition must explain the reasons for the delay.

10.7(3) [Petition to leave venue blank] The petition must also contain a blank box for the court to complete with the details of the venue for hearing the petition.

GENERAL NOTE

This rule is new for the IR 2016 and covers the information required in the petition previously contained in prescribed Forms 6.7–6.10.

10.8 Identification of debtor

10.8(1) [Details of debtor] The petition must state the following matters about the debtor, so far as they are within the petitioner's knowledge–

(a) the debtor's identification details;

(b) the occupation (if any) of the debtor;

(c) the name or names in which the debtor carries on business, if other than the name of the debtor, and whether, in the case of any business of a specified nature, the debtor carries it on alone or with others;

(d) the nature of the debtor's business, and the address or addresses at which it is carried on;

(e) any name or names, other than the name of the debtor, in which the debtor has carried on business at or after the time when the debt was incurred, and whether the debtor has done so alone or with others;

(f) any address or addresses at which the debtor has resided or carried on business at or after that time, and the nature of that business; and

(g) whether the centre of main interests or an establishment of the debtor (as defined in Article 2(10) of the EU Regulation) is in another member State.

10.8(2) [Title of proceedings] The particulars of the debtor given under this rule determine the title of the proceedings.

10.8(3) [Debtor's other names] If to the petitioner's knowledge the debtor has used any name other than the one specified under paragraph (1)(a), that fact must be stated in the petition.

(See General Note after r.10.9)

10.9 Identification of debt

10.9(1) [Details of debt] The petition must state for each debt in relation to which it is presented–

(a) the amount of the debt, the consideration for it (or, if there is no consideration, the way in which it arises) and the fact that it is owed to the petitioner;

(b) when the debt was incurred or became due;

(c) if the amount of the debt includes any charge by way of interest not previously notified to the debtor as a liability of the debtor's, the amount or rate of the charge (separately identified);

(d) if the amount of the debt includes any other charge accruing from time to time, the amount or rate of the charge (separately identified);

(e) the grounds on which any such a charge is claimed to form part of the debt, provided that the amount or rate must, in the case of a petition based on a statutory demand, be limited to that claimed in the demand;

(f) that the debt is unsecured (subject to section 269); and

(g) either–

(i) that the debt is for a liquidated sum payable immediately, and the debtor appears to be unable to pay it, or

(ii) that the debt is for a liquidated sum payable at some certain, future time (that time to be specified), and the debtor appears to have no reasonable prospect of being able to pay it.

10.9(2) [Petition to detail prior statutory demand] Where the debt is one for which, under section 268, a statutory demand must have been served on the debtor, the petition must–

(a) specify the date and manner of service of the statutory demand; and

(b) state that, to the best of the creditor's knowledge and belief–

(i) the demand has been neither complied with nor set aside in accordance with these Rules, and

(ii) that no application to set it aside is outstanding.

10.9(3) [If case within IA 1986 s.268(1)(b)] If the case is within section 268(1)(b) (unsatisfied execution or process in respect of judgment debt, etc.) the petition must state which court issued the execution or other process and give particulars of the return.

10.9(4) [Court power if statutory demand not served] The court may decline to file the petition if not satisfied that the creditor has discharged the obligation imposed by rule 10.2.

General Note to rr.10.8–10.9

These rules outline the contents of a creditor's petition.

See *Practice Direction: Insolvency Proceedings* [2018] B.C.C. 241 (reproduced as App.IV of this *Guide*). See *Lambeth LBC v Simon* [2007] B.P.I.R. 1629 for a stern reminder of the need to comply with the requirements of this rule. For the remedial effect of r.12.64 in cases where the requirements of r.10.9 have not been met see *Re a Debtor (No.510 of 1997), The Times*, 18 June 1998.

Rule 10.8(1)(g) amended, and r.10.9(4) inserted, by the Insolvency (England and Wales) and Insolvency (Scotland) (Miscellaneous and Consequential Amendments) Rules 2017 (SI 2017/1115) rr.1(1), (2), 2, 8, 22, 27 as from 8 December 2017.

10.10 Verification of petition

10.10(1) [Requirement for statement of truth] The petition must be verified by a statement of truth.

10.10(2) [Verification of multiple debts] If the petition relates to debts to different creditors, the debt to each creditor must be separately verified.

10.10(3) [Statement to identify petition] A statement of truth which is not contained in or endorsed upon the petition which it verifies must be sufficient to identify the petition and must contain–

(a) the name of the debtor;

(b) the name of the petitioner; and

(c) the court or hearing centre in which the petition is to be presented.

10.10(4) [Authentication of statement] The statement of truth must be authenticated and dated by or on behalf of the petitioner.

10.10(5) [Identification where statement not made by petitioner] Where the person authenticating the statement of truth is not the petitioner, or one of the petitioners, the statement of truth must state–

(a) the name and postal address of the authenticating person;

(b) the capacity in which, and the authority by which, that person authenticates the statement of truth; and

(c) the means of the authenticating person's knowledge of the matters verified.

(See General Note after r.10.14.)

10.11 Court in which petition is to be presented

10.11(1) [London Insolvency District] Where the proceedings are allocated to the London Insolvency District under rule 12.5(a)(i) to (iv) or (b), the creditor must present the petition to–

(a) the High Court where the debt is £50,000 or more; or

(b) the County Court at Central London where the debt is less than £50,000.

10.11(2) [Petition to High Court] Where the proceedings are allocated to the London Insolvency District under rule 12.5(a)(v), (c) or (d), the creditor must present the petition to the High Court.

10.11(3) [Petitions outside London] Where the debtor is resident in England and Wales and the proceedings are not allocated to the London Insolvency District, the creditor must present the petition to the debtor's own hearing centre.

10.11(4) [Hearing centres] The debtor's own hearing centre is–

(a) where the debtor has carried on business in England and Wales within the six months immediately preceding the presentation of the petition, the hearing centre for the insolvency district where for the longest period during those six months–

  (i) the debtor carried on business, or

  (ii) the principal place of business was located, if business was carried on in more than one insolvency district; or

(b) where the debtor has not carried on business in England and Wales within the six months immediately preceding the presentation of the petition, the hearing centre for the insolvency district where the debtor resided for the longest period during those six months.

10.11(5) [Debtor not resident in England and Wales] If the debtor is not resident in England and Wales but was resident or carried on business in England and Wales within the six months immediately preceding the presentation of the petition and the proceedings are not allocated to the London Insolvency District, the petition may be presented either to the debtor's own hearing centre or to the High Court.

10.11(6) [Where IVA in force] Unless paragraph (2) applies, where to the petitioner's knowledge there is in force for the debtor an IVA under Part 8 of the Act, the petition must be presented to the court or hearing centre–

(a) to which the nominee's report under section 256 was submitted;

(b) to which an application has been made, where a nominee has made a report under section 256A(3); or

(c) as determined under paragraphs (1) to (5) in any other case.

10.11(7) [Information in petition must support choice of venue] The petition must contain sufficient information to establish that it is presented in the appropriate court and, where the court is the County Court, the appropriate hearing centre.

(See General Note after r.10.14.)

10.12 Procedure for presentation and filing of petition

10.12(1) [Filing in court] The petition must be filed with the court.

10.12(2) [When petition may not be filed] A petition may not be filed unless–

(a) a receipt for the deposit payable to the official receiver is produced on presentation of the petition; or

(b) the Secretary of State has given notice to the court that the petitioner has made suitable alternative arrangements in accordance with an order made under section 415(3) for the payment of the deposit and that notice has not been revoked.

10.12(3) [Court may revoke alternative arrangements] A notice of alternative arrangements for the deposit may be revoked by a further notice filed with the court.

10.12(4) [Copies to be filed] The following copies of the petition must also be filed with the court with the petition–

(a) one for service on the debtor;

(b) one copy for the supervisor, if to the petitioner's knowledge there is in force for the debtor an IVA under Part 8 of the Act, and the petitioner is not the supervisor of the IVA; and

(c) one copy for the liquidator, if to the petitioner's knowledge there is a member State liquidator appointed in main proceedings in relation to the debtor.

10.12(5) [Endorsement of petition] The date and time of filing the petition must be endorsed on the petition and on the copies.

10.12(6) [Court to endorse venue on petition] The court must fix a venue for hearing the petition, and this must also be endorsed on the petition and the copies.

10.12(7) [Petition sealed by court] Each copy of the petition must have the seal of the court applied to it and must be delivered to the petitioner.

(See General Note after r.10.14.)

10.13 Application to Chief Land Registrar to register petition

10.13(1) [Delivery to Chief Land Registrar] When the petition is filed, the court must as soon as reasonably practicable deliver to the Chief Land Registrar an application for registration of the petition in the register of pending actions.

10.13(2) [Content of application] The application must contain–

(a) a statement that the court is applying for registration of a petition in bankruptcy proceedings as a pending action with the Chief Land Registrar under section 5 of the Land Charges Act 1972;

(b) the debtor's name;

(c) the debtor's gender, if known;

(d) details of the debtor's trade, profession or occupation, including any trading name and, in the case of a partnership, the name and gender, if known, of each of the other partners;

(e) the postal address for each known place of residence of the debtor, including the debtor's business address where the court considers it to be appropriate for the purpose of the notice;

(f) the relevant key number allocated by the Land Charges Department;

(g) the name of the court (and hearing centre if applicable);

(h) the number and date of the petition; and

(i) the name and postal address of the petitioner.

10.13(3) [Court to seal and date application] The application must be sealed and dated by the court.

10.13(4) [Separate applications for each debtor] A separate application must be completed for each debtor and for any alternative name by which the debtor has been or is known (other than any trading name).

(See General Note after r.10.14.)

10.14 Service of petition and delivery of copies

10.14(1) [Petitioner to serve under Sch.4] The petitioner must serve the petition on the debtor in accordance with Schedule 4 (Service of documents).

10.14(2) [Service on any IVA supervisor] If to the petitioner's knowledge there is in force for the debtor an IVA, and the petitioner is not the supervisor of the IVA, a copy of the petition must be delivered by the petitioner to the supervisor.

10.14(3) [Service on any Member State liquidator] If to the petitioner's knowledge, there is a member State liquidator appointed in main proceedings in relation to the debtor, a copy of the petition must be delivered by the petitioner to the member State liquidator.

General Note to rr.10.10–10.14

The procedure for filing a creditor's petition is described in these rules. The petition should be accompanied by a statement of truth.

R.10.9

Personal service of a creditor's petition is required unless it is a case where substituted service may be appropriate: see *Re a Debtor (No.234 and 236 of 1991), The Independent*, 29 June 1992 (Blackett-Ord QC sitting as a judge of the High Court).

On personal service and substituted service under this rule see the approach of Registrar Briggs in *Gate Gourmet Luxembourg IV SARL v Morby* [2015] EWHC 1203 (Ch); [2015] B.P.I.R. 787—confirmed on appeal by Edward Murray (sitting as a Deputy Judge of the High Court) and reported in [2016] EWHC 74 (Ch).

See *Practice Direction: Insolvency Proceedings* [2018] B.C.C. 241 (see App.IV of this *Guide*). For service outside the jurisdiction see Sch.4 para.4.

R.10.13

In *Trustee in Bankruptcy of St John Poulton v Ministry of Justice* [2010] EWCA Civ 392; [2010] B.P.I.R. 775 the Court of Appeal, rejecting the approach taken at first instance, held that no claim for breach a statutory duty lay in respect of any failure by the court service to comply with obligations under this provision. This judgment is very much policy driven and typifies the uncertainty inherent in the law relating to the acceptance of private causes of action for breach of statutory duty. For discussion of the case see H. Phillips (2010) 23 Insolv. Int. 155. Further guidance on the legal position in this broad area may be gleaned from the judgment of Edis J in *Sebry v Companies House* [2015] EWHC 115 (QB)—note in particular [116].

Further consideration of the interface between bankruptcy law and the land registration system as operated under the Land Registration Act 2002 was undertaken by Proudman J in *Pick v Chief Land Registrar* [2011] EWHC 206 (Ch); [2012] 3 W.L.R. 3, which was concerned with disposals of land completed by a bankrupt in favour of a bona fide purchaser without notice of the bankruptcy in circumstances where the register did not disclose the bankruptcy. As had been the position under the 1925 legislation, the rights of the innocent purchaser under s.86 of the 2002 Act prevailed over the interests of the estate.

R.10.14

On service of statutory demand and petition see *Emmanuel v Revenue and Customs Commissioners* [2017] EWHC 1253 (Ch); [2017] B.P.I.R. 1182. Here HHJ Walden-Smith found that the creditor had done all that was reasonable to bring these documents to the attention of the debtor.

10.15 Death of debtor before service

10.15 If the debtor dies before service of the petition, the court may order service to be effected on the debtor's personal representative, or on such other person as it thinks just.

10.16 Amendment of petition

10.16 The petition may be amended at any time after presentation with the court's permission.

General Note

For rationale see s.271(5). On the general rules on amendments to petitions laid down by the former RSC Ord.20 r.8: see *Aspinalls Club Ltd v Simone Halabi* [1998] B.P.I.R. 322. See CPR r.17.1.

10.17 Security for costs

10.17(1) [Application of rule] This rule applies where the debt is a liquidated sum payable at some future time, it being claimed in the petition that the debtor appears to have no reasonable prospect of being able to pay it.

10.17(2) [Application for petitioner to give security] The debtor may apply for an order that the petitioning creditor give security for the debtor's costs.

10.17(3) [Court's discretion over amount and nature of security] The nature and amount of the security to be ordered is in the court's discretion.

10.17(4) [Security to be given before petition heard] If an order for security is made then the petition may not be heard until the whole amount of the security has been given.

General Note

This imposes additional financial requirements for petitions based on IA 1986 s.268(2).

10.18 Debtor's notice of opposition to petition

10.18(1) [Time for filing and delivery of opposition] A debtor who intends to oppose the making of a bankruptcy order must not less than five business days before the day fixed for the hearing–

(a) file a notice with the court; and

(b) deliver a copy of the notice to the petitioning creditor or the petitioner's solicitor.

10.18(2) [Contents of notice] The notice must–

(a) identify the proceedings;

(b) state that the debtor intends to oppose the making of a bankruptcy order; and

(c) state the grounds on which the debtor opposes the making of the order.

General Note

On the relevance of r.10.18 see *Darbyshire v Turpin* [2013] EWHC 954 (Ch); [2013] B.P.I.R. 558.

10.19 Notice by persons intending to appear

10.19(1) [Delivery of notice of intention to appear] A creditor or a member State liquidator appointed in main proceedings in relation to the debtor who intends to appear on the hearing of the petition must deliver a notice of intention to appear to the petitioner.

10.19(2) [Content of notice] The notice must contain the following–

(a) the name and address of the person, and any telephone number and reference which may be required for communication with that creditor or with any other person (also to be specified in the notice) authorised to speak or act on the person's behalf;

(b) the date of the presentation of the bankruptcy petition and a statement that the notice relates to the matter of that petition;

(c) the date of the hearing of the petition;

(d) in the case of a creditor, the amount and nature of the debt due from the debtor to the creditor;

(e) whether the person intends to support or oppose the petition;

(f) where the person is represented by a solicitor or other agent, the name, postal address, telephone number and reference number (if any) of that person and details of that person's position with or relationship to the creditor or member State liquidator; and

(g) the name and postal address of the petitioner.

10.19(3) [Authentication of notice] The notice must be authenticated and dated by the person delivering it.

10.19(4) [Address for delivery] The notice must be delivered to the petitioner or the petitioner's solicitor at the address shown in the court records.

10.19(5) [Time limit for delivery] The notice must be delivered so as to reach the petitioner (or the petitioner's solicitor) not later than 4pm on the business day before that which is appointed for the hearing (or, where the hearing has been adjourned, for the adjourned hearing).

10.19(6) [Consequence of failure to notify] A person who fails to comply with this rule may appear and be heard on the hearing of the petition only with the permission of the court.

(See General Note after r.10.20.)

10.20 List of appearances

10.20(1) [Petitioner to prepare list] The petitioner must prepare for the court a list of the persons who have delivered a notice under rule 10.19 of their intention to appear.

10.20(2) [Content of the list] The list must contain–

(a) the date of the presentation of the bankruptcy petition;

(b) the date of the hearing of the petition;

(c) a statement that the persons listed have delivered notice that they intend to appear at the hearing of the petition;

(d) the name and address of each person who has delivered notice of intention to appear;

(e) in the case of creditors, the amount owed to each such creditor;

(f) the name and postal address of any solicitor for a person listed; and

(g) whether each person listed intends to support the petition, or to oppose it.

10.20(3) [List to be given to court on hearing day] On the day appointed for hearing the petition, a copy of the list must be handed to the court before the hearing commences.

10.20(4) [Court may permit persons to be added] If the court gives a person permission to appear under rule 10.19(6) then the petitioner must add that person to the list with the same particulars.

General Note to rr.10.19–10.20

Creditors who wish to attend the hearing must notify the petitioning creditor, informing him of their intention to support or oppose the petition. The petitioning creditor must draw up a list of such persons, and hand it to the court before the start of the hearing.

10.21 Hearing of petition

10.21(1) [Time for hearing] The petition may not be heard until at least 14 days have elapsed since it was served on the debtor.

10.21(2) [Expedited hearing] However the court may, on such terms as it thinks just, hear the petition at an earlier date, if–

(a) it appears that the debtor has absconded;

(b) the court is satisfied that it is a proper case for an expedited hearing; or

(c) the debtor consents to a hearing within the 14 days.

10.21(3) [Appearances] The following persons may appear and be heard–

(a) the petitioning creditor;

(b) the debtor;

(c) the supervisor of any IVA in force for the debtor; and

(d) any person who has delivered a notice under rule 10.19.

10.22 Postponement of hearing

10.22(1) [Petitioner may apply for another date] The petitioner may, if the petition has not been served, apply to the court to appoint another day for the hearing.

10.22(2) [Petitioner to explain late service] The application must state the reasons why the petition has not been served.

10.22(3) [Costs only at court's discretion] Costs of the application may not be allowed in the proceedings except by order of the court.

10.22(4) [Delivery of notice of postponement] If the court appoints another day for the hearing, the petitioner must as soon as reasonably practicable deliver notice of that day to any person who delivered notice of intention to appear under rule 10.19 and to any person who must be served with a copy of the petition under rule 10.14.

10.23 Adjournment of the hearing

10.23(1) [Application of this rule] This rule applies if the court adjourns the hearing of a bankruptcy petition.

10.23(2) [Contents of order] The order of adjournment must identify the proceedings and contain–

(a) the date of the presentation of the petition;

(b) the order that the further hearing of the petition be adjourned to the venue specified in the order;

(c) the venue of the adjourned hearing; and

(d) the date of the order.

10.23(3) [Delivery of notice] Unless the court otherwise directs, the petitioner must as soon as reasonably practicable deliver a notice of the order of adjournment to–

(a) the debtor; and

(b) any person who has delivered a notice of intention to appear under rule 10.19 but was not present at the hearing.

10.23(4) [Contents of notice] The notice of the order of adjournment must identify the proceedings and–

(a) contain–

   (i) the date of the presentation of the petition,

   (ii) the date the order of adjournment was made, and

   (iii) the venue for the adjourned hearing; and

(b) be authenticated and dated by the petitioner or the petitioner's solicitor.

General Note

On this rule see *Johnson v Tandrige DC* [2008] B.P.I.R. 405. See also *Sekhon v Edginton* [2015] EWCA Civ 816; [2015] 1 W.L.R. 4435.

10.24 Decision on the hearing

10.24(1) [Bankruptcy order] On the hearing of the petition, the court may make a bankruptcy order if satisfied that the statements in the petition are true, and that the debt on which it is founded has not been paid, or secured or compounded.

10.24(2) [Stay or dismissal] If the petition is brought in relation to a judgment debt, or a sum ordered by any court to be paid, the court may stay or dismiss the petition on the ground that an appeal is pending from the judgment or order, or that execution of the judgment has been stayed.

10.24(3) [Content of order] An order dismissing or giving permission to withdraw a bankruptcy petition must contain–

(a) identification details for the proceedings;

(b) the date of the presentation of the bankruptcy petition;

(c) the name, postal address and description of the applicant;

(d) a statement that the petition has been heard;

(e) the order that the petition be dismissed or that, with the permission of the court, the petition is withdrawn;

(f) details of any further terms of the order;

(g) the date and reference number of the registration of the petition as a pending action with the Chief Land Registrar;

(h) an order that the entry relating to the petition in the register of pending actions be vacated on the debtor's application; and

(i) the date of the order.

10.24(4) [Order to state debtor's responsibility for land registry entry] The order must notify the debtor that it is the debtor's responsibility and in the debtor's interest to ensure that the registration of the petition as an entry, both with the Chief Land Registrar and in the title register of any property owned by the debtor, is cancelled.

10.24(5) [Debt overstated in statutory demand] In the case of a petition preceded by a statutory demand, the petition will not be dismissed on the ground only that the amount of the debt was over-stated in the demand, unless the debtor, within the time allowed for complying with the demand, delivered a notice to the creditor disputing the validity of the demand on that ground; but, in the absence of such notice, the debtor is deemed to have complied with the demand if the correct amount is paid within the time allowed.

General Note

This rule and r.10.26 supplement IA 1986 s.271, see *Eberhardt v Mair* [1995] B.C.C. 845 and *Legal Services Commission v Leonard* [2002] EWCA Civ 744; [2002] B.P.I.R. 994. On the power of the court to go behind a judgment debt see *Dawodu v American Express Bank* [2001] B.P.I.R. 983. For the role of the court under r.10.24(1) in satisfying itself that the statements in the petition are true see *Barnes v Whitehead* [2004] B.P.I.R. 693. See *Lambeth LBC v Simon* [2007] B.P.I.R. 1629 for the latitude given to the court by this particular rule when considering whether to accede to a bankruptcy petition. For a review of IR 1986 r.6.25(2) (now IR 2016 r.10.24(2)) see *Rehman v Boardman* [2004] EWHC 505 (Ch); [2004] B.P.I.R. 820. On overstated demands and IR 1986 r.6.25(3) (now IR 2016 r.10.24(3)) see *Mohammed v London Borough of Southwark* [2006] EWHC 305 (Ch); [2006] B.P.I.R. 782. This Rule was mentioned in passing in *Governor of the Bank of Ireland v Gill* [2013] EWHC 2996 (Ch). See also *Rightmatch Ltd (Acting by its LPA Receiver) v Meisels* [2014] B.P.I.R. 733.

The court refused to go behind a judgment in *Barclays Bank v Atay* [2015] EWHC 3198 (Ch). Registrar Briggs undertook a detailed review of the underlying jurisprudence.

This provision often comes into play when the petition of a foreign debtor to secure an English bankruptcy is before the court, as the statement in the petition that the debtor's COMI is within the jurisdiction may be open to question. Readers should cross reference the "COMI cases" on the former regime of debtor petitions in bankruptcy, especially *O'Mahony v National Irish Bank* [2012] B.P.I.R. 1174 where the statements in the petition were held by Deputy Registrar Nicholas Briggs to comply with IR 1986 r.6.25 (now IR 2016 r.10.24).

10.25 Vacating registration on withdrawal of petition

10.25 If the petition is withdrawn by permission of the court, the court must deliver to the debtor two sealed copies of the order (one for the Chief Land Registrar).

General Note

This should be viewed in the light of r.10.13.

10.26 Non-appearance of petitioning creditor

10.26 A petitioning creditor who fails to appear on the hearing of the petition may not present a petition either alone or jointly with any other person against the same debtor in respect of the same debt without the permission of the court to which the previous petition was presented.

General Note

This rule and r.10.24 supplement IA 1986 s.271. Note the sanction against non-appearance by a petitioning creditor. For guidance on the exercise of discretion under former IR 1986 r.6.26 (now IR 2016 r.10.26) see *Omgate Ltd v Gordon* [2001] B.P.I.R. 909. In *Kasumu v Arrow Global (Guernsey) Ltd* [2013] EWHC 789 (Ch); [2013] B.P.I.R 1047 there had been a failure to comply with the requirements of former IR 1986 r.6.26 but Asplin J indicated that this was the sort of irregularity that could be cured by the application of the previous IR 1986 r.7.55. Failure to comply with the former IR 1986 r.6.26 did not render the petition a complete nullity.

10.27 Substitution of petitioner

10.27(1) [Application of rule] This rule applies where the petitioner–

- (a) is subsequently found not to have been entitled to present the petition;
- (b) consents to withdraw the petition or to allow it to be dismissed;
- (c) consents to an adjournment;
- (d) fails to appear in support of the petition when it is called on in court on the day originally fixed for the hearing, or on a day to which it is adjourned; or
- (e) appears, but does not apply for an order in the terms of the petition.

10.27(2) [Persons who may be substituted] The court may, on such terms as it thinks just, substitute as petitioner a person who–

- (a) has delivered a notice under rule 10.19 of intention to appear at the hearing;
- (b) is willing to prosecute the petition; and
- (c) was, in the case of a creditor, at the date on which the petition was presented, in such a position in relation to the debtor as would have enabled the creditor on that date to present a bankruptcy petition in relation to a debt or debts owed to that creditor by the debtor, paragraphs (a) to (d) of section 267(2) being satisfied in relation to that debt or those debts.

General Note

This allows the court to substitute petitioners in appropriate circumstances. See *Flett v Revenue and Customs Commissioners* [2010] B.P.I.R. 1075.

10.28 Order for substitution of petitioner

10.28 The order for substitution of a petitioner must contain–

- (a) identification details for the proceedings;
- (b) the date of the hearing of the petition;
- (c) the name of the original petitioner;
- (d) the name of the person who is willing to prosecute the petition ("the named person");
- (e) a statement that the named person meets the requirements of rule 10.27(2);
- (f) details of the statutory demand or return of the enforcement officer or enforcement agent;
- (g) the following orders–
  - (i) that upon payment by the named person of the statutory deposit to the court the statutory deposit paid by the original petitioner to the court be repaid to the original petitioner by the official receiver,
  - (ii) that the named person be substituted as petitioner in place of the original petitioner and that the relevant person may amend the petition accordingly,
  - (iii) that the named person must within five business days from the date of the order file a copy of the amended petition together with a statement of truth verifying the amended petition,
  - (iv) that at least 14 days before the date of the adjourned hearing of the petition the named person must serve upon the debtor a sealed copy of the amended petition,

(v) that the hearing of the amended petition be adjourned to the venue specified in the order, and

(vi) that the question of the costs of the original petitioner and of the statutory deposit (if appropriate) be reserved until the final determination of the amended petition;

(h) the venue of the adjourned hearing; and

(i) the date of the order.

General Note

This is a new rule for the IR 2016 and covers the detail previously set out in prescribed form 6.24A.

10.29 Change of carriage of petition

10.29(1) [Application by person intending to appear] On the hearing of the petition, a person who has delivered notice under rule 10.19 of intention to appear at the hearing, may apply to the court for an order giving that person carriage of the petition in place of the petitioner, but without requiring any amendment of the petition.

10.29(2) [Powers of court] The court may, on such terms as it thinks just, make a change of carriage order if satisfied that–

(a) the applicant is an unpaid and unsecured creditor of the debtor or a member State liquidator appointed in main proceedings in relation to the debtor; and

(b) the petitioner either–

(i) intends by any means to secure the postponement, adjournment, dismissal or withdrawal of the petition, or

(ii) does not intend to prosecute the petition, either diligently or at all.

10.29(3) [Limit on court's power] The court must not make such an order if satisfied that the petitioner's debt has been paid, secured or compounded by means of–

(a) a disposition of property made by some person other than the debtor; or

(b) a disposition of the debtor's own property made with the approval of, or ratified by, the court.

10.29(4) [Appearance by petitioning creditor] A change of carriage order may be made whether or not the petitioner appears at the hearing.

10.29(5) [If order made prior evidence stands] If the order is made, the person given the carriage of the petition is entitled to rely on all evidence previously provided in the proceedings.

10.29(6) [Content of order] The change of carriage order will contain–

(a) identification details for the proceedings;

(b) the date of the hearing of the petition;

(c) the name of the person who is willing to be given carriage of the petition ("the relevant person");

(d) a statement that the relevant person is a creditor of the debtor or a member State liquidator appointed in main proceedings in relation to the debtor;

(e) the name of the original petitioner;

(f) a statement that the relevant person has applied for an order under this rule to have carriage of the petition in place of the original petitioner;

(g) the order that the relevant person must within a period which is specified in the order serve upon the debtor and the original petitioner a sealed copy of the order;

(h) the order that the further hearing of the petition be adjourned to the venue specified in the order;

(i) the venue of the adjourned hearing;

(j) the order that the question of the costs of the original petitioner be reserved until the final determination of the petition; and

(k) the date of the order.

General Note

Other creditors can apply to the court for carriage of the petition. A formal amendment of the petition is not required. See *Re Purvis* [1998] B.P.I.R. 153.

10.30 Petitioner seeking dismissal or permission to withdraw

[Note. See rule 10.24 for the contents of an order dismissing or giving permission to withdraw a petition.]

10.30(1) [Witness statement specifying grounds of application] Where the petitioner applies to the court for the petition to be dismissed, or for permission to withdraw it, the petitioner must file with the court a witness statement specifying the grounds of the application and the circumstances in which it is made if–

(a) a person has delivered notice under rule 10.19 of intention to appear at the hearing of the petition; or

(b) the court so orders.

10.30(2) [If payment made since petition filed] If any payment has been made to the petitioner since the petition was filed by way of settlement (in whole or in part) of the debt or any arrangement has been entered into for securing or compounding the debt, the witness statement must also state–

(a) what dispositions of property have been made for the purposes of the settlement or arrangement;

(b) whether, in the case of any disposition, it was property of the debtor, or of some other person; and

(c) whether, if it was property of the debtor, the disposition was made with the approval of, or has been ratified by, the court (if so, specifying the relevant court order).

10.30(3) [No order before hearing] An order giving permission to withdraw a petition must not be made before the petition is heard.

10.30(4) [Content of the order] The order of dismissal or granting permission to withdraw a bankruptcy petition must contain–

(a) identification details for the proceedings;

(b) the date of the filing of the bankruptcy petition;

(c) the name, postal address and description of the applicant;

(d) a statement that the petition has been heard;

(e) the order that the petition be dismissed or that, with the permission of the court, the petition is withdrawn;

(f) details of any further terms of the order;

(g) the date and reference number of the registration of the petition as a pending action with the Chief Land Registrar;

(h) an order that the entry relating to the petition in the register of pending actions be vacated on the debtor's application; and

(i) the date of the order.

General Note

This restricts the right of a petitioner to change his mind, so to speak. Bankruptcy proceedings are essentially a class remedy for the benefit of all creditors.

10.31 Contents of bankruptcy order

10.31(1) [Contents of the order] The bankruptcy order must identify the proceedings and contain–

(a) the name and address of the petitioner;

(b) the date of the presentation of the petition;

(c) the details of the debtor as provided under rule 10.8(1)(a) to (g);

(d) the order that the person named is made bankrupt;

(e) the order either–

  (i) that the court being satisfied that the EU Regulation applies declares that the proceedings are main, secondary or territorial proceedings (as the case may be) as defined in Article 3 of the EU Regulation, or

  (ii) that the court is satisfied that the EU Regulation does not apply in relation to the proceedings;

(f) a statement that the official receiver (or one of them) attached to the court is by virtue of the order trustee of the bankrupt's estate;

(g) a notice of the bankrupt's duties in relation to the official receiver under section 291, and in particular to the bankrupt's duty to give the official receiver such inventory of the bankrupt's estate and such other information, and to attend on the official receiver at such times, as the official receiver may reasonably require; and

(h) the date and time of the order.

10.31(2) [Solicitor's details] If the petitioner is represented by a solicitor the order is to be endorsed with the name, address, telephone number and reference of the solicitor.

10.31(3) [Order staying proceedings] Subject to section 346 (effect of bankruptcy on enforcement procedures), the order may include provision staying any action or proceeding against the bankrupt.

General Note

This regulates the form of any bankruptcy order made under IA 1986 s.271.

Rule 10.31(1)(e) amended by the Insolvency (England and Wales) and Insolvency (Scotland) (Miscellaneous and Consequential Amendments) Rules 2017 (SI 2017/1115) rr.1(1), (2), 22, 23(8) as from 8 December 2017.

10.32 Delivery and notice of the order

10.32(1) [Delivery to official receiver] As soon as reasonably practicable after making a bankruptcy order the court must deliver two sealed copies of the order to the official receiver.

10.32(2) [Delivery to bankrupt] The official receiver must as soon as reasonably practicable deliver a sealed copy of the order to the bankrupt.

10.32(3) [Duties of official receiver] On receipt of the sealed copies of the bankruptcy order the official receiver–

(a) must as soon as reasonably practicable–

(i) deliver an application for registration of the order containing the particulars specified in rule 10.33 to the Chief Land Registrar, for registration in the register of writs and orders affecting land, and

(ii) cause notice of the order to be gazetted;

(b) must cause an entry to be made in the individual insolvency register in accordance with rule 11.16; and

(c) may cause notice of the order to be advertised in such other manner as the official receiver thinks fit.

10.32(4) [Content of Gazette notice] The notice to be gazetted and any notice to be advertised must state–

(a) that a bankruptcy order has been made against the bankrupt;

(b) the date and time of the making of the bankruptcy order;

(c) the name and address of the petitioning creditor; and

(d) the date of presentation of the petition.

10.32(5) [Order for suspension] The court may, on the application of the bankrupt or a creditor, order the official receiver to suspend action under paragraph (3) and rule 11.16, pending a further order of the court.

10.32(6) [Witness statement in support of application for suspension] An application for such action to be suspended must be supported by a witness statement stating the grounds on which it is made.

10.32(7) [Delivery of order for suspension] Where an order to suspend such action is made, the applicant must deliver a copy of the order to the official receiver as soon as reasonably practicable.

General Note

This provides for the dissemination, advertisement and gazetting of the bankruptcy order. Although the OR must gazette notice of the order, there is no requirement to gazette notice of a stay, rescission or annulment of a bankruptcy order—for the consequences of this apparent lacuna see the discussion in *Smeaton v Equifax plc* [2013] EWCA Civ 108.

10.33 Application to Chief Land Registrar to register bankruptcy order

10.33(1) [Content of application] The application for registration of the bankruptcy order delivered to the Chief Land Registrar under rule 10.32 must contain–

(a) identification details for the proceedings;

(b) a statement that the official receiver is applying for registration of a bankruptcy order in the register of writs and orders under section 6 of the Land Charges Act 1972;

(c) the name of the bankrupt;

(d) the bankrupt's gender, if known;

(e) details of the bankrupt's trade, profession or occupation, including any trading name and, in the case of a partnership, the name and gender, if known, of each of the other partners;

(f) the postal address for each known place of residence of the bankrupt, including the bankrupt's business address where the official receiver considers it to be appropriate for the purpose of the notice;

(g) the relevant key number allocated by the Chief Land Registrar;

(h) the date of the bankruptcy order; and

(i) the name and postal address of the petitioner.

10.33(2) [Authentication] The application must be authenticated and dated by the official receiver.

10.33(3) [Separate applications for each name and address] A separate application must be completed for each address and for any alternative name by which the bankrupt has been or is known (other than any trading name).

General Note

This is a new rule for the IR 2016 and covers the detail previously set out in prescribed Form 6.26.

Chapter 3

Debtors' bankruptcy applications

[Note: a document required by the Act or these Rules must also contain the standard contents set out in Part 1.]

10.34 Preliminary

10.34 This Chapter relates to a debtor's bankruptcy application and the making of a bankruptcy order on the application of a debtor.

(See General Note after r.10.48.)

10.35 Bankruptcy application for a bankruptcy order

10.35(1) [Content of application] In the bankruptcy application the debtor must–

(a) state that the debtor is unable to pay the debtor's debts;

(b) request that the adjudicator make a bankruptcy order against the debtor;

(c) state that the debtor is not aware of any pending bankruptcy petition;

(d) state whether a bankruptcy order has been made in respect of any of the debts which are the subject of the bankruptcy application;

(e) state whether the debtor has taken debt advice before completing the bankruptcy application;

(f) consent to verification checks being made by the adjudicator;

(g) provide the information set out in Schedule 7;

(h) provide the additional information set out in Schedule 8;

(i) state that the information provided in accordance with this rule is accurate and up-to-date at the date of the bankruptcy application; and

(j) state that the prescribed fee and deposit have been paid in full.

10.35(2) [Authentication] The bankruptcy application must be authenticated by the debtor.

(See General Note after r.10.48.)

10.36 Procedure for making a bankruptcy application and communication with the adjudicator

10.36(1) [Application to be in electronic form] The bankruptcy application must be completed in accordance with these Rules in electronic form and delivered to the adjudicator by electronic means unless otherwise agreed with the adjudicator in accordance with paragraph (4).

10.36(2) [Date of application] For the purposes of rule 10.35(1)(i) the date of the bankruptcy application is the date that the debtor submits the bankruptcy application to the adjudicator under these Rules.

10.36(3) [Effective date] A bankruptcy application is made when its receipt has been acknowledged by the adjudicator by electronic or other means.

10.36(4) [Procedure upon malfunction of electronic systems] In the event of any malfunction or error in the operation of the electronic form or means of delivery, the adjudicator must–

(a) agree that debtors may, for a specified period, complete and deliver bankruptcy applications in another format; and

(b) provide an alternative means of delivery for the bankruptcy application and details of any terms or conditions to which their use is subject.

10.36(5) [Exclusion of fax delivery] If a bankruptcy application is completed in hard copy, it may not be delivered by fax.

10.36(6) [Communication by electronic means] Where the debtor has given an electronic address in the bankruptcy application, the adjudicator must so far as reasonably practicable communicate with the debtor by electronic means.

10.36(7) [Evidence of electronic delivery] Unless the contrary is shown, a document (other than a bankruptcy application) is to be treated as delivered by electronic means to an electronic address where the sender can produce a copy of the electronic communication which–

(a) contains the document; and

(b) shows the time and date the communication was sent and the electronic address to which it was sent.

10.36(8) [Default time of delivery] Unless the contrary is shown, a document (other than a bankruptcy application) is to be treated as delivered to the electronic address to which it is sent at 9.00am on the next business day after it was sent.

10.36(9) [Non-application of r.1.45] Rule 1.45 does not apply to electronic delivery of documents between a debtor and the adjudicator.

(See General Note after r.10.48.)

10.37 Application to the Chief Land Registrar to register a bankruptcy application

10.37(1) [Delivery to Chief Land Registrar] When a bankruptcy application is made, the adjudicator must as soon as reasonably practicable deliver to the Chief Land Registrar an application for registration of the bankruptcy application, in the register of pending actions.

10.37(2) [Content of application] The application must contain–

(a) a statement that the adjudicator is applying for registration of a bankruptcy application as a pending action under section 5 of the Land Charges Act 1972;

(b) the debtor's name and any alternative name by which the debtor has been or is known;

(c) the debtor's date of birth;

(d) the debtor's gender, if known;

(e) the debtor's occupation, including any trading name;

(f) the postal address for each known place of residence of the debtor;

(g) the debtor's business address where the adjudicator considers it appropriate for the purpose of the application;

(h) the relevant key number allocated by the Chief Land Registrar;

(i) the reference allocated to the bankruptcy application; and

(j) the date of the bankruptcy application.

10.37(3) [Authentication] The application must be authenticated and dated by the adjudicator.

(See General Note after r.10.48.)

10.38 Verification checks

10.38 For the purpose of determining whether the adjudicator can make a bankruptcy order, verification checks may be made in, or with, one or more of the following–

(a) the electoral registers for such districts in England and Wales as the adjudicator considers appropriate to determine the identity and residence of the debtor;

(b) the individual insolvency register;

(c) the official receiver; or

(d) a credit reference agency.

(See General Note after r.10.48.)

10.39 Determination of the bankruptcy application

10.39(1) [Period for determination] The adjudicator must determine whether to make a bankruptcy order within the determination period referred to in rule 10.40.

10.39(2) [Requirements of IA 1986 s.263K] In reaching a determination, the adjudicator must have regard to whether the requirements of section 263K of the Act are met.

10.39(3) [Adjudicator's right to request information] During the determination period the adjudicator may request such further information from the debtor as the adjudicator considers is necessary in order to make the determination, such information to be provided in writing or at the request of the adjudicator, to be provided orally.

10.39(4) [Adjudicator to determine on basis of information given] Subject to paragraph (5), the adjudicator must make a determination from the information provided under rule 10.35(1)(g), any further information provided under paragraph (3) and from the verification checks.

10.39(5) [Consideration of information supplied under r.10.35(1)(h)] Before determining that the requirements of section 263K are not met, the adjudicator must have regard to the additional information provided under rule 10.35(1)(h).

(See General Note after r.10.48.)

10.40 The determination period

10.40(1) [Time limit for determination] The determination period is 28 days from the date the bankruptcy application is made.

10.40(2) [Extension where further information requested after 14 days] Where the adjudicator requests further information from the debtor more than 14 days after the date the bankruptcy application is made, the determination period is extended by 14 days.

10.40(3) [Refusal by default of determination] A failure to make a determination within the determination period is a refusal.

(See General Note after r.10.48.)

10.41 Settlement and contents of bankruptcy order

10.41(1) [Order settled by adjudicator] The bankruptcy order must be settled by the adjudicator.

10.41(2) [Contents of order] The bankruptcy order must contain–

(a) the information set out in Part 1 of Schedule 7;

(b) the date of delivery of the bankruptcy application on which the order is made;

(c) the order that upon reading the application it is ordered that person named be made bankrupt;

(d) the order either–

- (i) that the adjudicator being satisfied that the EU Regulation applies declares that the proceedings are main, secondary or territorial proceedings (as the case may be) as defined in Article 3 of the EU Regulation, or
- (ii) that the adjudicator is satisfied that the EU Regulation does not apply in relation to the proceedings;

(e) a statement that the official receiver (or one of them) attached to the court is, by virtue of the order, trustee of the bankrupt's estate; and

(f) a notice of the bankrupt's duties in relation to the official receiver under section 291(4) (duties of bankrupt in relation to the official receiver), and in particular to the bankrupt's duty to give the official receiver such inventory of the bankrupt's estate and such other information, and to attend on the official receiver at such times, as the official receiver may reasonably require.

(See General Note after r.10.48.)

10.42 Refusal to make a bankruptcy order and contents of notice of refusal

10.42(1) [Refusal where requirements of s.263K not met] Where the adjudicator determines that the requirements of section 263K are not met, the adjudicator must refuse to make a bankruptcy order.

10.42(2) [Delivery of notice of refusal] The adjudicator must deliver notice of the refusal to make a bankruptcy order to the debtor as soon as reasonably practicable after the refusal to make the bankruptcy order under paragraph (1) or under rule 10.40(3).

10.42(3) [Content of notice of refusal] The notice of refusal must state–

(a) the reason or reasons for the refusal to make a bankruptcy order;

(b) that the debtor may request that the adjudicator review the decision to refuse to make a bankruptcy order within 14 days from the date of delivery of the notice of refusal;

(c) that where a review is requested it will be a review of the information that was available to the adjudicator at the date when the adjudicator refused to make a bankruptcy order;

(d) that following a review, the adjudicator must either–

- (i) confirm the refusal to make a bankruptcy order; or
- (ii) make a bankruptcy order against the debtor; and

(e) where the adjudicator confirms the refusal following a review, that the debtor may appeal to the court against the decision within 28 days from the date of delivery of the notice of confirmation of the refusal.

(See General Note after r.10.48.)

10.43 Review of refusal to make a bankruptcy order

10.43(1) [Debtor's right to request review] The debtor may request the adjudicator to review the decision to refuse to make a bankruptcy order within 14 days from the date of delivery of the notice of refusal.

10.43(2) [Reasons for review request] The debtor must give reasons for requesting a review but the request may not include additional information that was not available to the adjudicator when the determination was made.

10.43(3) [Settlement of bankruptcy order on review] Where the adjudicator makes a bankruptcy order following a review, the bankruptcy order must be settled by the adjudicator in accordance with rule 10.41.

10.43(4) [Notice of confirmation of refusal to make bankruptcy order] Where the adjudicator confirms the refusal to make a bankruptcy order, the adjudicator must deliver notice to the debtor as soon as reasonably practicable.

10.43(5) [Contents of notice of refusal] The notice will state–

(a) the reason or reasons for confirming the refusal to make the bankruptcy order; and

(b) that the debtor may appeal to the court against the decision within 28 days from the date of delivery of the confirmation of the notice of refusal.

(See General Note after r.10.48.)

10.44 Appeal to the court following a review of refusal to make a bankruptcy order

10.44(1) [Debtor's right of appeal to court] Following a decision by the adjudicator to confirm the refusal to make a bankruptcy order, a debtor may appeal the decision to the court.

10.44(2) [Time limit for appeal] An appeal under this rule must be made within 28 days from the date of delivery of the confirmation of the notice of refusal.

10.44(3) [Appeal to set out grounds] The appeal must set out the grounds for the appeal.

10.44(4) [Duty of court] The court must either–

(a) dismiss the application; or

(b) make a bankruptcy order against the debtor.

10.44(5) [Content of bankruptcy order] The bankruptcy order must contain–

(a) the information set out in Part 1 of Schedule 7;

(b) the date of delivery of the bankruptcy application on which the order is made;

(c) the date and time of the making of the order; and

(d) a statement that the order has been made following an appeal to the court under this rule.

10.44(6) [Liability for costs of appeal] The adjudicator is not personally liable for costs incurred by any person in respect of an application under this rule.

10.44(7) [Delivery of sealed copies] As soon as reasonably practicable after the making of the bankruptcy order the court must deliver sealed copies of the order to the debtor and the official receiver.

(See General Note after r.10.48.)

10.45 Action to follow making of order

10.45(1) [Delivery of order to debtor and official receiver. As soon as reasonably practicable following the making of the bankruptcy order the adjudicator must deliver copies of the bankruptcy order to the debtor and the official receiver.

10.45(2) [Delivery of hard copy] On the application of the bankrupt to the official receiver, the official receiver must deliver to the bankrupt a hard copy of the bankruptcy order.

10.45(3) [Duty etc. of official receiver on receipt of order] Subject to paragraph (5), on receipt of the bankruptcy order, the official receiver–

- (a) must as soon as reasonably practicable–
  - (i) deliver an application to the Chief Land Registrar for registration of the bankruptcy order in the register of writs and orders affecting land, and
  - (ii) must cause notice of the bankruptcy order to be gazetted;
- (b) may cause notice of the bankruptcy order to be advertised in such other manner as the official receiver thinks fit; and
- (c) must cause an entry to be made in the individual insolvency register in accordance with rule 11.16.

10.45(4) [Content of gazetting and advertisement] The notice to be gazetted under paragraph (3)(a)(ii) and any notice to be advertised under paragraph (3)(b) must state–

- (a) that a bankruptcy order has been made against the bankrupt;
- (b) the date of the bankruptcy order;
- (c) that the bankruptcy order was made on the debtor's own bankruptcy application; and
- (d) the date of delivery of the bankruptcy application.

10.45(5) [Application to suspend action] The court may, on the application of the bankrupt or a creditor, order the official receiver to suspend action under paragraph (3), pending a further order of the court.

10.45(6) [Witness statement to support application] An application for such action to be suspended must be supported by a witness statement stating the grounds on which it is made.

10.45(7) [Delivery of order to suspend] Where an order is made to suspend such action, the applicant must deliver a copy of it to the official receiver as soon as reasonably practicable.

(See General Note after r.10.48.)

10.46 Application to the Chief Land Registrar

10.46(1) [Contents of application for registration] The application to the Chief Land Registrar for registration of the bankruptcy order under rule 10.45 must contain–

- (a) a statement that the official receiver is applying for registration of a bankruptcy order made by the adjudicator in the register of writs and orders under section 6 of the Land Charges Act 1972;
- (b) the bankrupt's name and any alternative names by which the bankrupt has been or is known;
- (c) the bankrupt's date of birth;

(d) the bankrupt's gender, if known;

(e) the bankrupt's occupation including any trading name;

(f) the postal address for each known place of residence of the bankrupt;

(g) the bankrupt's business address where the official receiver considers it appropriate for the purpose of the application;

(h) the relevant key number allocated by the Chief Land Registrar;

(i) the reference allocated to the bankruptcy order; and

(j) the date of the bankruptcy order.

10.46(2) [Authentication] The application must be authenticated and dated by the official receiver.

(See General Note after r.10.48.)

10.47 The bankruptcy file

10.47(1) [Duty of adjudicator to open file on receipt of application] On receipt of a bankruptcy application, the adjudicator must open a file on which the adjudicator must place the bankruptcy application and any documents which are filed with the adjudicator under this Chapter.

10.47(2) [Adjudicator to deliver file to official receiver on making of order] As soon as reasonably practicable following the making of the bankruptcy order the adjudicator must deliver the bankruptcy file to the official receiver.

10.47(3) [What official receiver must place on file] The official receiver must place on the bankruptcy file–

(a) any documents delivered to the official receiver by the court; and

(b) any notices delivered to the official receiver under these Rules.

10.47(4) [Who may inspect file] The following persons may inspect the bankruptcy file–

(a) the court;

(b) the trustee;

(c) the Secretary of State; and

(d) the bankrupt.

10.47(5) [Creditor's right of inspection] Following the making of a bankruptcy order, a creditor may inspect the following information and documents filed on the bankruptcy file–

(a) the information provided to the adjudicator and set out in Schedule 9;

(b) the bankruptcy order; and

(c) directions and orders of the court, if any.

10.47(6) [Inspection by authorised person] The right to inspect the bankruptcy file may be exercised on that person's behalf by a person authorised to do so by that person.

10.47(7) [Inspection with court's permission] Any person who is not otherwise entitled to inspect the bankruptcy file (or any part of it) may do so if the court gives permission.

10.47(8) [Court direction that availability requires court permission] The court may direct that the bankruptcy file, a document (or part of it) must not be made available under this rule without the permission of the court.

10.47(9) [Application to withhold bankruptcy file, documents etc] An application for a direction to withhold the bankruptcy file, a document (or part of it) may be made by–

(a) the official receiver;

(b) the trustee; or

(c) any person appearing to the court to have an interest.

10.47(10) [Notice for permission to inspect or withhold file] An application under this rule for–

(a) permission to inspect the bankruptcy file; or

(b) a direction to withhold the bankruptcy file, a document (or part of it),

may be made without notice to any other party, but the court may direct that notice must be delivered to any person who would be affected by its decision.

(See General Note after r.10.48.)

10.48 Court to which applications are to be made

10.48(1) [Application to debtor's own hearing centre] An application to the court under this Chapter must be made to the debtor's own hearing centre where the debtor is resident in England and Wales.

10.48(2) [Where debtor not resident in England and Wales] If the debtor is not resident in England and Wales but was resident or carried on business in England and Wales within the six months immediately preceding the making of the bankruptcy application, an application may be made to the debtor's own hearing centre or to the High Court.

10.48(3) [Location of debtor's hearing centre] In this rule the debtor's own hearing centre is–

(a) where the debtor has carried on business in England and Wales within the six months immediately preceding the filing with the court of the application, the hearing centre for the insolvency district where for the longest period during those six months–

  (i) the debtor carried on business, or

  (ii) the principal place of business was located, if business was carried on in more than one insolvency district; or

(b) where the debtor has not carried on business in England and Wales within the six months immediately before making the application to the court, the hearing centre for the insolvency district where the debtor resided for the longest period during those six months.

10.48(4) [Where application to own hearing centre not possible] Where, for whatever reason, it is not possible for the application to be made to the debtor's own hearing centre, the applicant may, with a view to expediting the application, make the application–

(a) where paragraph (3)(a) applies, to–

  (i) the hearing centre for the insolvency district in which the debtor resides, or

  (ii) whichever court or hearing centre is specified in Schedule 6 as being the nearest full-time court or hearing centre in relation to–

    (aa) the hearing centre in paragraph (3)(a), or

    (bb) the hearing centre in paragraph (4)(a)(i); or

(b) where paragraph (3)(b) applies, whichever court or hearing centre is specified in Schedule 6 as being the nearest full-time court or hearing centre in relation to the court in that paragraph.

10.48(5) [Information in application] The application must contain sufficient information to establish that it is brought in the appropriate court or hearing centre.

GENERAL NOTE TO RR.10.34–10.48

Further detail on the new bankruptcy application procedure is to be found in I(A)R 2016 (SI 2016/187), which came into effect in April 2016. The key provisions on the new bankruptcy adjudication procedure are located in Sch.1, which inserted former IR 1986 rr.6.37–6.50B (now IR 2016 rr.10.34–10.48). These explain the form and contents of the application. Note that electronic means will normally be used in order to access this procedure, though hard copy format may be adopted provided the documents are signed. With regard to r.10.36, doubts have been raised as to whether this is ultra vires in that it appears to dismiss the possibility of a hard copy application. This observation was made by the Parliamentary Joint Committee on Statutory Instruments, Sixteenth Report of session 2016/17, HL Paper 80, HC 93-xvi. The Committee was concerned (see para.1.13) that not all citizens are able to make electronic applications because of a lack of access to the technology.

If hard copy is to be used this must be cleared in advance with the adjudicator—r.10.36. Provision is made for the Chief Land Registrar to be alerted—r.10.37.

The application is determined by the adjudicator within 28 days—r.10.40. Details of required verification checks are spelled out. Where the adjudicator agrees to make a bankruptcy order the contents of said order are specified. If an order is refused the adjudicator must notify the debtor as soon as reasonably practicable and must give reasons. The notification should also alert the debtor of the right to seek a review. The debtor can ask the adjudicator to review any such refusal: this review must be carried out within 14 days—r.10.43. The debtor can in the event of an unsuccessful review appeal to the court (as defined by r.10.48) within 28 days. On an appeal the court must either make the bankruptcy order of dismiss the appeal.

Where a bankruptcy order is made under this procedure the Chief Land Registrar must be notified—r.10.46. The adjudicator must open a file on the case when the application is made and then deliver the file to the official receiver as soon as is reasonably practicable. This file is open to inspection by various parties.

Further details on the information to be contained in the application is to be found in Schs 7, 8 and 9 of these Rules.

Rule 10.41(2)(d) amended by the Insolvency (England and Wales) and Insolvency (Scotland) (Miscellaneous and Consequential Amendments) Rules 2017 (SI 2017/1115) rr.1(1), (2), 22, 23(9) as from 8 December 2017.

CHAPTER 4

THE INTERIM RECEIVER

[Note: a document required by the Act or these Rules must also contain the standard contents set out in Part 1.]

10.49 Application for appointment of interim receiver (section 286)

10.49(1) [Who may apply for interim receivership] An application to the court under section 286 for the appointment of the official receiver or an insolvency practitioner as interim receiver may be made by–

(a) a creditor;

(b) the debtor;

(c) a temporary administrator; or

(d) a member State liquidator appointed in main proceedings (including in accordance with Article 37 of the EU Regulation).

10.49(2) [Witness statement supporting application] The application must be supported by a witness statement stating–

(a) the grounds on which it is proposed that the interim receiver should be appointed;

(b) whether or not the official receiver has been informed of the application and, if so, whether a copy of it has been delivered to that person;

(c) if the proposed interim receiver is an insolvency practitioner, that the insolvency practitioner has consented to act;

(d) whether to the applicant's knowledge there has been proposed or is in force an IVA; and

(e) the applicant's estimate of the value of the property or business in relation to which the interim receiver is to be appointed;

(f) a statement whether the proceedings will be main, secondary, territorial or non-EU proceedings with the reason for so stating.

10.49(3) [Delivery of application to receivers] The applicant must deliver copies of the application and the witness statement to the proposed interim receiver and to the official receiver.

10.49(4) [Interim receiver to be informed if delivery not possible] If for any reason it is not practicable to deliver a copy of the application to the proposed interim receiver that person must be informed of the application in sufficient time to be able to be present at the hearing.

10.49(5) [Official receivers right to appear] The official receiver may attend the hearing of the application and make representations.

10.49(6) [Courts power to appoint interim receiver] If satisfied that sufficient grounds are shown for the appointment, the court may appoint an interim receiver on such terms as it thinks just.

(See General Note after r.10.54.)

10.50 Deposit

10.50(1) [Applicant to deposit security for receiver's cost] An applicant for an order appointing the official receiver as interim receiver must, before the order is made, deposit with the official receiver, or otherwise secure to the official receiver's satisfaction, such sum as the court directs to cover the official receiver's remuneration and expenses.

10.50(2) [Court may order extra security] If the sum proves to be insufficient, the court may, on the application of the official receiver, order the applicant to deposit or secure an additional sum.

10.50(3) [Power to discharge if additional security not given] If such additional sum is not deposited or secured within two business days after service of the order on the applicant the court may discharge the order appointing the official receiver as interim receiver.

10.50(4) [Security to be repaid out of bankrupt's estate] If a bankruptcy order is made after an interim receiver has been appointed, any money deposited under this rule must (unless it is required because the assets are insufficient to pay the remuneration and expenses of the interim receiver, or the deposit was made by the debtor out of the debtor's own property) be repaid to the person depositing it (or as that person may direct) out of the bankrupt's estate, in the prescribed order of priority.

(See General Note after r.10.54.)

10.51 Order of appointment

10.51(1) [Content of order] The order appointing the interim receiver must contain–

(a) identification details for the proceedings;

(b) the name and title of the judge making the order;

(c) the name and postal address of the applicant;

(d) identification details for the debtor;

(e) the statement that the court is satisfied–

  (i) that the debtor is unable to pay the debtor's debts, and

  (ii) that the proceedings are main, secondary, territorial or non-EU proceedings (as the case may be);

(f) the order either that–

(i) upon the applicant depositing the sum specified in the order with the official receiver, the official receiver is appointed interim receiver of the property of the debtor, or

(ii) the person specified in the order is appointed interim receiver of the property of the debtor;

(g) identification and contact details for the interim receiver, where the interim receiver is not the official receiver;

(h) details of the nature, together with a short description, of the property of which the interim receiver is to take possession;

(i) details of the duties to be carried out by the interim receiver in relation to the debtor's affairs;

(j) a notice to the debtor stating that the debtor must give the interim receiver all the information about the debtor's property that the interim receiver may require in order to carry out the functions imposed on the interim receiver by the order; and

(k) the date of the order.

10.51(2) [Court to deliver copies to interim receiver] The court must, as soon as reasonably practicable after the order is made, deliver two sealed copies of the order to the person appointed interim receiver.

10.51(3) [Interim receiver to deliver order to debtor] The interim receiver must as soon as reasonably practicable deliver a sealed copy of the order to the debtor.

(See General Note after r.10.54.)

10.52 Security

10.52(1) [Application of this rule] This rule applies where an insolvency practitioner is appointed as interim receiver under section 286.

10.52(2) [Cost of security to be paid by interim receiver] The cost of providing the security required under the Act must be paid in the first instance by the interim receiver.

10.52(3) [Reimbursement of costs where no order made] If a bankruptcy order is not made, the person so appointed is entitled to be reimbursed out of the property of the debtor, and the court may make an order on the debtor accordingly.

10.52(4) [Reimbursement of costs where an order is made] If a bankruptcy order is made, the person so appointed is entitled to be reimbursed out of the bankrupt's estate in the prescribed order of priority.

10.52(5) [Failure to give or keep up security] If the interim receiver fails to give or keep up the required security, the court may remove the interim receiver, and make such order as it thinks just as to costs.

10.52(6) [Directions on removal] If an order is made under this rule removing the interim receiver, or discharging the order appointing the interim receiver, the court must give directions as to whether any, and if so what, steps should be taken for the appointment of another person as interim receiver.

(See General Note after r.10.54.)

10.53 Remuneration

10.53(1) [Remuneration fixed by the court] The remuneration of an interim receiver (other than the official receiver) must be fixed by the court from time to time on application of the interim receiver.

10.53(2) [Matters to be taken into account] In fixing the remuneration of the interim receiver, the court must take into account–

(a) the time properly given by the interim receiver and staff of the interim receiver in attending to the debtor's affairs;

(b) the complexity of the case;

(c) any respects in which, in connection with the debtor's affairs, there falls on the interim receiver any responsibility of an exceptional kind or degree;

(d) the effectiveness with which the interim receiver appears to be carrying out, or to have carried out, the duties of the interim receiver; and

(e) the value and nature of the property with which the interim receiver has to deal.

10.53(3) [Source of payment of remuneration etc] Without prejudice to any order the court may make as to costs, the interim receiver's remuneration (whether the official receiver or another) must be paid to the interim receiver, and the amount of any expenses incurred by the interim receiver (including the remuneration and expenses of any special manager appointed under section 370) reimbursed–

(a) if a bankruptcy order is not made, out of the property of the debtor; and

(b) if a bankruptcy order is made, out of the bankrupt's estate in the prescribed order of priority; or

(c) in either case (the relevant funds being insufficient), out of any deposit under rule 10.50.

10.53(4) [Power of retention] Unless the court otherwise directs, if a bankruptcy order is not made, the interim receiver may retain out of the debtor's property such sums or property as are or may be required for meeting the remuneration and expenses of the interim receiver.

10.53(5) [Interim receiver to reimburse official receiver] Where a person other than the official receiver has been appointed interim receiver, and the official receiver has taken any steps for the purpose of obtaining a statement of affairs or has performed any other duty under these Rules, the interim receiver must pay the official receiver such sum (if any) as the court may direct.

(See General Note after r.10.54.)

10.54 Termination of appointment

10.54(1) [Power of court to terminate appointment] The appointment of the interim receiver may be terminated by the court on the application of the interim receiver, or a person specified in rule 10.49(1).

10.54(2) [Directions on termination] If the interim receiver's appointment terminates, in consequence of the dismissal of the bankruptcy petition or otherwise, the court may give such directions as it thinks just relating to the accounts of the interim receiver's administration and any other matters which it thinks appropriate.

General Note to rr.10.49–10.54

These rules all deal with the appointment of an interim receiver to protect the debtor's assets under IA 1986 s.286. Note the major changes made to that provision by SBEEA 2015 by allowing private practitioners to occupy that role. The application procedure is detailed. The details for the order of appointment are set out in r.10.51. A deposit may be required from the applicant. The interim receiver may be required to give security; failure to do so could result in his removal by the court. The court is to determine the remuneration of an interim receiver. The question of the termination of his appointment is governed by r.10.54, which should be cross-referenced to IA 1986 s.286(7).

Rule 10.49(1)(d) was amended and r.10.49(2)(f) inserted by the Insolvency Amendment (EU 2015/848) Regulations 2017 (SI 2017/702) regs 1, 2(1), Sch. paras 32, 42 in relation to proceedings opened on or after 26 June 2017 (see reg.3) when the Recast EU Regulation 2015/848 came into force.

Rule 10.51(e)(ii) amended by the Insolvency (England and Wales) and Insolvency (Scotland) (Miscellaneous and Consequential Amendments) Rules 2017 (SI 2017/1115) rr.1(1), (2), 22, 30(24) as from 8 December 2017.

CHAPTER 5

DISCLOSURE OF THE BANKRUPT'S AFFAIRS

[Note: a document required by the Act or these Rules must also contain the standard contents set out in Part 1.]

Sub-division A: creditor's petition

10.55 Notice requiring statement of affairs (section 288)

10.55(1) [Delivery of notice to bankrupt] Where, under section 288, the official receiver requires a bankrupt to provide the official receiver with a statement of affairs, the official receiver must deliver a notice to the bankrupt.

10.55(2) [Heading and content of notice] The notice must be headed "Notice requiring statement of affairs" and must–

(a) require the bankrupt to prepare and submit to the official receiver a statement of affairs;

(b) inform the bankrupt of the date by which the statement must be delivered; and

(c) state the effect of section 288(4) (penalty for non-compliance) and section 291 (duty to co-operate).

10.55(3) [Instructions to accompany notice] The official receiver must deliver instructions for the preparation of the statement of affairs with the notice.

(See General Note after r.10.56.)

10.56 Statement of affairs

10.56(1) [Content of statement] The statement of affairs must contain–

(a) identification details for the proceedings;

(b) identification details for the bankrupt;

(c) the date of the bankruptcy order;

(d) a list of the bankrupt's secured creditors giving in relation to each–

(i) the name and postal address,

(ii) the amount owed to the creditor, and

(iii) particulars of the property of the bankrupt which is claimed by the creditor to clear or reduce the creditor's debt and the value of that property;

(e) a list of unsecured creditors giving in relation to each–

(i) the name and postal address of the creditor,

(ii) the amount the creditor claims the bankrupt owes to that creditor, and

(iii) the amount the bankrupt thinks is owed by the bankrupt to that creditor;

(f) a list of the bankrupt's total assets (which must include anything not previously mentioned in the statement of affairs which may be of value) divided into the following categories and giving the value of each asset listed–

(i) cash at the bank or building society,

(ii) household furniture and belongings,

(iii) life policies,

(iv) money owed to the bankrupt,

(v) stock in trade,

(vi) motor vehicles, and

(vii) other property; and

(g) the total value of the assets listed under paragraph (f).

10.56(2) [Authentication] The bankrupt must authenticate and date each page of the statement of affairs.

10.56(3) [Verification] The statement of affairs must be verified by a statement of truth and delivered to the official receiver, together with one copy.

10.56(4) [Filing of verified statement] The official receiver must file the verified statement with the court.

General Note to rr.10.55–10.56

These rules expand upon the provisions of IA 1986 s.288.

R.10.56
This rule now contains the details previously set out in prescribed Form 6.33A.

10.57 Limited disclosure

10.57 Where the official receiver thinks that disclosure of the whole or part of the statement of affairs would be likely to prejudice the conduct of the bankruptcy or might reasonably be expected to lead to violence against any person, the official receiver may apply to the court for an order that the statement of affairs or any specified part of it either–

(a) must not be filed with the court; or

(b) must be filed separately and not open to inspection otherwise than with permission of the court.

General Note

This is the standard provision in the rules enabling the court to censor sensitive information. It was extended by I(A)R 2010 (SI 2010/686) to protect personal safety.

10.58 Requirement to submit statement of affairs and extension of time (section 288(3))

10.58(1) [Power to require submission of statement of affairs] The official receiver may exercise the power in section 288(3) to require the bankrupt to submit a statement of affairs under section 288(3) and to grant an extension of time, either on the official receiver's own initiative, or at the bankrupt's request.

10.58(2) [Application for release or extension] A bankrupt required to submit a statement of affairs under paragraph (1) may apply to the court for a release or extension of time, if the official receiver has refused to release the bankrupt from that requirement or grant an extension.

10.58(3) [Courts power of summary dismissal] On receipt of an application, the court may, if it is satisfied that no sufficient cause is shown for it, dismiss it without giving notice to any party other than the applicant.

10.58(4) [Court to fix venue for hearing] Unless the application is dismissed, the court must fix a venue for it to be heard.

10.58(5) [Delivery of notice to official receiver] The applicant must, at least 14 days before any hearing, deliver to the official receiver a notice stating the venue with a copy of the application and any evidence on which the applicant intends to rely.

10.58(6) [Action to be taken by official receiver] The official receiver may do either or both of the following–

(a) file a report of any matters which the official receiver thinks ought to be drawn to the court's attention; or

(b) appear and be heard on the application.

10.58(7) [Delivery of report to bankrupt] If such a report is filed, the official receiver must deliver a copy of it to the bankrupt not later than five business days before the hearing.

10.58(8) [Delivery of order to official receiver and bankrupt] The court must deliver sealed copies of any order made on the application to the bankrupt and the official receiver.

10.58(9) [Bankrupt to pay own expenses] The bankrupt must pay the bankrupt's costs of the application in any event and, unless and to the extent the court orders otherwise, no allowance in respect of them will be made out of the bankrupt's estate.

General Note

This builds upon IA 1986 s.288(3). The references to ex parte hearings were removed by I(A)R 2010 (SI 2010/686).

10.59 Expenses of assisting bankrupt to prepare statement of affairs

10.59(1) [Persons assisting in preparation of the statement] If the bankrupt cannot personally prepare a proper statement of affairs, the official receiver may, at the expense of the bankrupt's estate, employ a person or firm to assist in the preparation of the statement.

10.59(2) [Allowance of expenses] At the request of the bankrupt, made on the grounds that the bankrupt cannot personally prepare a proper statement, the official receiver may authorise an allowance payable out of the bankrupt's estate (in accordance with the prescribed order of priority) of all or part of the expenses to be incurred by the bankrupt in employing a person or firm to assist the bankrupt in preparing it.

10.59(3) [Estimate of expenses] The bankrupt's request must be accompanied by an estimate of the expenses involved, and the official receiver must only authorise the employment of a named person or named firm approved by the official receiver.

10.59(4) [Authorisation subject to conditions] The official receiver may make the authorisation subject to such conditions (if any) as the official receiver thinks fit relating to the manner in which any person may obtain access to relevant documents and other records.

10.59(5) [Effect of rule] Nothing in this rule relieves the bankrupt from any obligation relating to the preparation, verification and submission of a statement of affairs, or to the provision of information to the official receiver or the trustee.

General Note

This deals with the funding of the statement of affairs where the bankrupt is unable to prepare it himself.

10.60 Delivery of accounts to official receiver

10.60(1) [Request of official receiver] The bankrupt must, at the request of the official receiver, deliver to the official receiver accounts relating to the bankrupt's affairs of such nature, as at such date and for such period as the official receiver may specify.

10.60(2) [Beginning of specified period] The period specified may begin from a date up to three years before the date of the presentation of the bankruptcy petition.

10.60(3) [Accounts for earlier period] The court may, on the official receiver's application, require accounts for any earlier period.

10.60(4) [Application of r.10.59] Rule 10.59 (expenses of assisting bankrupt to prepare statement of affairs) applies to accounts to be delivered under this rule as it applies to the statement of affairs.

10.60(5) [Verification by statement of truth] The accounts must, if the official receiver so requires, be verified by a statement of truth, and (whether or not so verified) delivered to the official receiver within 21 days of the request, or such longer period as the official receiver may allow.

(See General Note after r.10.61.)

10.61 Further disclosure

10.61(1) [Official receiver may require further information] The official receiver may at any time require the bankrupt to deliver in writing further information amplifying, modifying or explaining any matter contained in the bankrupt's statement of affairs, or in accounts delivered under the Act or these Rules.

10.61(2) [Verification and delivery] The information must, if the official receiver directs, be verified by a statement of truth, and (whether or not verified) delivered to the official receiver within 21 days from the date of the requirement, or such longer period as the official receiver may allow.

General Note to rr.10.60–10.61

These provisions clarify IA 1986 s.288(2)(b). Note how far back the official receiver can request accounts for under r.10.60(2).

Sub-division B: Bankruptcy application

10.62 Preliminary

10.62 The rules in this sub-division apply in relation to further disclosure which is required of a bankrupt where the bankruptcy order was made on a bankruptcy application.

General Note

This provision was updated by I(A)R 2016 (SI 2016/187) prior to being consolidated in the 2016 Rules.

10.63 Delivery of accounts to official receiver

10.63(1) [Official receiver's request] The bankrupt must, at the request of the official receiver, deliver to the official receiver accounts relating to the bankrupt's affairs of such nature, as at such date and for such period as the official receiver may specify.

10.63(2) [Specified period] The specified period may begin from a date up to three years preceding the date of the bankruptcy application.

10.63(3) [Verification by statement of truth] The accounts must, if the official receiver so requires, be verified by a statement of truth, and (whether or not so verified) be delivered to the official receiver within 21 days of the request or such longer period as the official receiver may allow.

10.63(4) [Accounts for earlier periods] The court may, on the official receiver's application, require accounts in respect of any earlier period.

(See General Note after r.10.65.)

10.64 Expenses of preparing accounts

10.64(1) [Persons assisting in the preparation of accounts] If the bankrupt cannot personally prepare adequate accounts under rule 10.63, the official receiver may, at the expense of the bankrupt's estate, employ a person or firm to assist in their preparation.

10.64(2) [Allowance towards expenses] At the request of the bankrupt, made on the grounds that the bankrupt cannot personally prepare the accounts, the official receiver may authorise an allowance payable out of the bankrupt's estate (in accordance with the prescribed order of priority) of all or part of the expenses to be incurred by the bankrupt in employing a person or firm to assist the bankrupt in their preparation.

10.64(3) [Estimate of expenses] The bankrupt's request must be accompanied by an estimate of the expenses involved; and the official receiver must only authorise the employment of a named person or a named firm, being in either case approved by the official receiver.

10.64(4) [Authorisation subject to conditions] The official receiver may make the authorisation subject to such conditions (if any) as the official receiver thinks fit relating to the manner in which any person may obtain access to relevant documents and other records.

10.64(5) [Effect of rule] Nothing in this rule relieves the bankrupt from any obligation relating to the preparation and delivery of accounts, or to the provision of information to the official receiver or the trustee.

(See General Note after r.10.65.)

10.65 Further disclosure

10.65(1) [Official receiver may require further information] The official receiver may at any time require the bankrupt to deliver in writing further information amplifying, modifying or explaining any matter contained in the bankruptcy application, or in accounts delivered under the Act or these Rules.

10.65(2) [Verification and delivery] The information must, if the official receiver so directs, be verified by a statement of truth, and (whether or not so verified) delivered to the official receiver within 21 days from the date of the requirement, or such longer period as the official receiver may allow.

General Note to rr.10.63–10.65

These provisions largely mirror rr.10.59–10.61.

Sub-division C: Reports by the official receiver

10.66 Reports by the official receiver

10.66(1) [Reports to creditors] The official receiver must deliver a report on the bankruptcy and the bankrupt's affairs to the creditors at least once after the making of the bankruptcy order.

10.66(2) [Content of report] The report must contain–

(a) identification details for the proceedings;

(b) contact details for the official receiver;

(c) a summary of the assets and liabilities of the bankrupt as known to the official receiver at the date of the report;

(d) such comments on the summary and the bankrupt's affairs as the official receiver thinks fit; and

(e) any other information of relevance to the creditors.

10.66(3) [Application to be relieved of or to vary duty to report] The official receiver may apply to the court to be relieved of any duty imposed by this rule or to be authorised to carry out the duty in another way.

10.66(4) [Court to have regard to costs of duty] On such an application the court must have regard to the cost of carrying out the duty, to the amount of the assets available, and to the extent of the interest of creditors or any particular class of them.

10.66(5) [Cessation of duty if order annulled] If a bankruptcy order is annulled, any duty of the official receiver to deliver a report under this rule ceases.

General Note

The rules in Ch.5 impose additional duties upon the official receiver to keep creditors informed. This rule develops IA 1986 s.288 and relates to the dissemination of the statement of affairs. If IA 1986 s.288(3)(a) has been activated, the official receiver must supply a report to the creditors dealing with the financial position of the bankrupt. Note the court's power of waiver under r.10.66(3).

Chapter 6

The Trustee in Bankruptcy

[Note: a document required by the Act or these Rules must also contain the standard contents set out in Part 1.]

Sub-division A: appointment and associated formalities

10.67 Appointment by creditors of new trustee

10.67(1) [Application of rule] This rule applies where the bankrupt's creditors decide to remove a trustee in bankruptcy under section 298 but do not, as part of the decision procedure to remove the trustee, appoint a new trustee.

10.67(2) [Invitation to propose new trustee] The existing trustee must send the creditors a notice inviting proposals for a new trustee.

10.67(3) [Notice to explain effect of IA 1986 s.298(4B)] The notice must contain a statement explaining the effect of section 298(4B) (decision of creditors to remove a trustee does not take effect until creditors appoint another trustee).

10.67(4) [Notice to state proposals must comply with r.10.67(5), (6)] The notice must also explain that the existing trustee is not obliged to seek the creditors' views on any proposals that do not meet the requirements of paragraphs (5) and (6).

10.67(5) [Proposal must state contact details and qualification of nominee] Any proposal must state the name and contact details of the proposed trustee, and contain a statement that the proposed trustee is qualified to act as an insolvency practitioner in relation to the bankrupt and has consented to act as trustee.

10.67(6) [Time limit for proposals] Any proposal must be received by the existing trustee within five business days of the date of the notice.

10.67(7) [Choice of decision procedure to be followed] Following the end of the period for inviting proposals under paragraph (2) of this rule, where any proposals are received the existing trustee must seek a decision from the creditors on the appointment of a replacement trustee by–

(a) a decision procedure; or

(b) the deemed consent procedure.

10.67(8) [Notice of decision procedure] Where paragraph (7) applies, the existing trustee must send the creditors a notice which complies with rules 15.7 and 15.8 so far as are relevant.

10.67(9) [Notice to identify nominee] The notice must also identify any person proposed to be nominated as trustee in accordance with this rule.

10.67(10) [Time limit for decision] The decision date in the notice must be no later than 14 days after the date for receiving proposals has passed.

10.67(11) [Period of notice for decision date] The creditors must be given at least seven days' notice of the decision date.

10.67(12) [Timing of invitation notice] A notice inviting proposals for a new trustee under paragraph (2) may be sent before or after the date of the decision to remove the trustee.

10.67(13) [Official receiver's right to apply to appoint trustee] Nothing in this rule affects the official receiver's ability under section 296(1), at any time when trustee, to apply to the Secretary of State to appoint a trustee instead of the official receiver.

General Note

This supplements IA 1986 s.293. See the impact of the now repealed I(A)R 2010 (SI 2010/686)—filing in court was no longer required.

10.68 Certification of appointment

10.68(1) [Application of rule] This rule applies where a person has been appointed as trustee by a decision of the creditors.

10.68(2) [Certification of appointment] The convener or the chair (as the case may be) must certify the appointment, but not unless and until the appointee has delivered to the convener or chair a statement that the appointee is an insolvency practitioner qualified to act as trustee in relation to the bankrupt and consents to act.

10.68(3) [Date appointment takes effect] The trustee's appointment takes effect from the date on which the appointment is certified, that date to be endorsed on the certificate.

10.68(4) [Content of certificate] The certificate must contain–

(a) identification details for the proceedings;

(b) identification details for the bankrupt;

(c) identification and contact details for the person appointed as trustee;

(d) the date on which the creditors made the appointment; and

(e) the statement that the appointee–

  (i) has provided a statement of being qualified to act as an insolvency practitioner in relation to the bankrupt,

  (ii) has consented to act, and

  (iii) was appointed trustee of the bankrupt's estate.

10.68(5) [Authentication] The certificate must be authenticated and dated by the person who certifies the appointment.

10.68(6) [Certification where two or more trustees] Where two or more trustees are appointed the certificate must also specify (as required by section 292(3)) the circumstances in which the trustees must act together and the circumstances in which one or more of them may act for the others.

10.68(7) [Delivery of certificate to official receiver] The convener or chair (if that person is not the official receiver) must deliver the certificate to the official receiver.

10.68(8) [Delivery to the trustee] The official receiver must in any case deliver the certificate to the trustee.

General Note

This new rule for IR 2016 covers the detail previously set out in prescribed Forms 6.40 and 6.41.

10.69 Cost of the trustee's security (section 390(3))

10.69 The cost of the trustee's security required by section 390(3) for the proper performance of the trustee's functions is an expense of the bankruptcy.

General Note

This deals with the security required of insolvency practitioners.

10.70 Creditors' decision to appoint a trustee

10.70(1) [Clear majority required for appointment] In the case of a decision on the appointment of a trustee–

(a) if on any vote there are two nominees for appointment, the person who obtains the most support is appointed;

(b) if there are three or more nominees, and one of them has a clear majority over both or all the others together, that one is appointed; and

(c) in any other case the convener or chair must continue to take votes (disregarding at each vote any nominee who has withdrawn and, if no nominee has withdrawn, the nominee who obtained the least support last time) until a clear majority is obtained for any one nominee.

10.70(2) [Resolution to appoint joint trustees] In the case of a decision being made at a meeting, the chair may at any time put to the meeting a resolution for the joint appointment of any two or more nominees.

General Note

Simple majorities are required to pass resolutions.

10.71 Appointment by the court (section 291A(2))

10.71(1) [Application of rule] This rule applies where the court appoints the trustee under section 291A(2).

10.71(2) [No order until statement of appointee's qualification filed] The court's order must not be made unless and until the proposed appointee has filed with the court a statement that the proposed appointee is an insolvency practitioner, qualified to act as the trustee in relation to the bankrupt and consents to act.

10.71(3) [Content of order] The order of the court must contain–

(a) identification details the proceedings;

(b) the name and title of the judge making the order;

(c) the name and postal address of the applicant;

(d) the capacity in which the applicant made the application;

(e) identification and contact details for the person appointed as trustee;

(f) a statement that that the appointee has filed a statement of qualification to act as an insolvency practitioner in relation to the bankrupt and of consent to act;

(g) the order that the appointee is appointed trustee of the bankrupt's estate; and

(h) the date of the order.

10.71(4) [Order to specify how joint trustees to act] Where two or more trustees are appointed the order must also specify (as required by section 292(3)) the circumstances in which the trustees must act together and the circumstances in which one or more of them may act for the others.

10.71(5) [Delivery to official receiver] The court must deliver two copies of the order, one of which must be sealed, to the official receiver.

10.71(6) [Delivery to trustee] The official receiver must deliver the sealed copy of the order to the person appointed as trustee.

10.71(7) [Effective date of trustee's appointment] The trustee's appointment takes effect from the date of the order.

General Note

This rule should be viewed in the light of IA 1986 s.297(3), (4), (5). If the court appoints a trustee under these provisions, The detail previously contained in prescribed Forms 6.42 and 6.43 have been incorporated into this rule.

10.72 Appointment by the Secretary of State

10.72(1) [Application of rule] This rule applies where the official receiver–

(a) refers the need for an appointment of a trustee to the Secretary of State under section 300(4); or

(b) applies to the Secretary of State under section 296 to make the appointment.

10.72(2) [Delivery of certificate to official receiver] If the Secretary of State makes an appointment the Secretary of State must deliver a copy of the certificate of appointment to the official receiver, who must deliver it to the person appointed.

10.72(3) [Effective date of trustee's appointment] The certificate must specify the date from which the trustee's appointment is to be effective.

General Note

This rule clarifies the provisions of IA 1986 ss.295, 296 and 300.

10.73 Authentication of trustee's appointment

10.73 Where a trustee is appointed under any of rules 10.70, 10.71 or 10.72, a sealed copy of the order of appointment or (as the case may be) a copy of the certificate of the trustee's appointment may in any proceedings be adduced as proof that the trustee is duly authorised to exercise the powers and perform the duties of trustee of the bankrupt's estate.

General Note

This relates to rr.10.70–10.72 by providing for the authentication of the trustee's appointment.

10.74 Appointment to be gazetted

10.74(1) [Action to be taken by trustee] As soon as reasonably practicable after appointment a trustee appointed by a decision of the bankrupt's creditors–

(a) must gazette a notice of the appointment; and

(b) may advertise the notice in other such manner as the trustee thinks fit.

10.74(2) [Content of notice] The notice must state–

(a) that a trustee has been appointed by a decision of creditors; and

(b) the date of the appointment.

General Note

The onus is on the trustee to ensure that his appointment is advertised as appropriate and gazetted.

10.75 Hand-over of bankrupt's estate by official receiver to trustee

10.75(1) [Application of rule] This rule applies where a trustee is appointed in succession to the official receiver acting as trustee.

10.75(2) [Trustee to take possession of bankrupt's estate] When the trustee's appointment takes effect, the official receiver must as soon as reasonably practicable do all that is required for putting the trustee into possession of the bankrupt's estate.

10.75(3) [Trustee to discharge balance due to official receiver] On taking possession of the bankrupt's estate, the trustee must discharge any balance due to the official receiver on account of–

(a) expenses properly incurred by the official receiver and payable under the Act or these Rules; and

(b) any advances made by the official receiver in respect of the bankrupt's estate, together with interest on such advances at the rate specified in section 17 of the Judgments Act 1838 on the date of the bankruptcy order.

10.75(4) [Undertaking in place of immediate discharge] Alternatively, the trustee may (before taking office) deliver to the official receiver a written undertaking to discharge any such balance out of the first realisation of assets.

10.75(5) [Official receiver's charge over estate] The official receiver has a charge on the bankrupt's estate in respect of any sums due under paragraph (3) until they have been discharged, subject only to the deduction from realisations by the trustee of the costs and expenses of such realisations.

10.75(6) [Trustee to discharge guarantees and expenses of official receiver] The trustee must from time to time out of the realisation of assets discharge all guarantees properly given by the official receiver for the benefit of the bankrupt's estate, and must pay all the official receiver's expenses.

10.75(7) [Official receiver to provide information to trustee] The official receiver must give to the trustee all the information relating to the affairs of the bankrupt and the course of the bankruptcy which the official receiver considers to be reasonably required for the effective discharge by the trustee of the trustee's duties in relation to the bankrupt's estate.

10.75(8) [Trustee to be given any report under r.10.66] The official receiver must also deliver to the trustee any report of the official receiver under rule 10.66.

General Note

See IA 1986 ss.287 and 306 for the relevant statutory provisions here.

10.76 Invitation to creditors to form a creditors' committee

10.76(1) [Trustee to invite creditors to form committee] Where the trustee seeks any decision from the bankrupt's creditors, the trustee must at the same time deliver to the creditors a notice inviting them to decide whether a creditors' committee should be established if sufficient creditors are willing to be members of the committee.

10.76(2) [Notice to invite nominations to the committee] The notice must also invite nominations for membership of the committee, such nominations to be received by a date specified in the notice.

10.76(3) [Other content of notice] The notice must state that nominations–

(a) must be delivered to the trustee by the specified date; and

(b) can only be accepted if the convener is satisfied as to the creditors' eligibility under rule 17.4.

GENERAL NOTE

This is a new rule for IR 2016 with no corresponding rule in IR 1986.

Sub-division B: resignation and removal

10.77 Trustee's resignation and appointment of replacement (section 298(7))

10.77(1) [Grounds for resignation] A trustee may resign under section 298(7) only–

(a) on grounds of ill health;

(b) because of the intention to cease to practise as an insolvency practitioner;

(c) because the further discharge of the duties of trustee is prevented or made impracticable by–

(i) a conflict of interest, or

(ii) a change of personal circumstances; or

(d) where two or more persons are acting as trustee jointly, and it is the opinion of both or all of them that it is no longer expedient that there should continue to be that number of joint trustees.

10.77(2) [Invitation to creditors to replace trustee] Before resigning, the trustee must invite the creditors to consider, either by a decision procedure or by the deemed consent procedure, whether a replacement should be appointed except where the resignation is under sub-paragraph (1)(d).

10.77(3) [Content of notice] The notice to the creditors must–

(a) state the trustee's intention to resign;

(b) state that under rule 10.77(8) of the Insolvency (England and Wales) Rules 2016, the trustee will be released 21 days after the date of delivery of the notice of resignation to the prescribed person under section 298(7), unless the court orders otherwise; and

(c) comply with rule 15.7 or 15.8 so far as applicable.

10.77(4) [Notice may include suggested replacement] The notice may suggest the name of a replacement trustee.

10.77(5) [Notice accompanied by receipts and payments summary] The notice must be accompanied by a summary of the trustee's receipts and payments.

10.77(6) [Timing of decision date] The decision date must be not more than five business days before the date on which the trustee intends to give notice under section 298(7).

10.77(7) [Delivery of notice] The trustee must deliver a copy of the notice to the official receiver and the bankrupt.

10.77(8) [Effective date of release] The resigning trustee's release is effective 21 days after the date on which the notice of resignation under section 298(7) is filed with the court in a bankruptcy based on a petition or, delivered to the official receiver in a bankruptcy based on a debtor's application.

GENERAL NOTE

The relevant statutory provision here is IA 1986 s.298(7). Note the restriction in r.10.77(1) on the grounds for resignation. The concept of impracticability in r.10.77(1)(c) has been construed narrowly—*Re Alt Landscapes Ltd* [1999] B.P.I.R. 459 where the court rejected *Re Sankey Furniture Ltd Ex p. Harding* [1995] 2 B.C.L.C. 594. For the facilitation of multiple resignations see *Re Equity Nominees Ltd* [2000] B.C.C. 84. Further explanation is provided by *Customs and Excise Commissioners v Allen* [2003] B.P.I.R. 830.

10.78 Decision of creditors to remove trustee (section 298(1))

10.78(1) [Certificate of decision to remove] Where the convener of the decision procedure or chair of a meeting of creditors is other than the official receiver, and a decision is taken to remove the trustee, the convener or chair must, within three business days, deliver a certificate to that effect to the official receiver.

10.78(2) [Certificate of appointment of new trustee] If the creditors have decided to appoint a new trustee, the certificate of the new trustee's appointment must also be delivered to the official receiver within three business days from the date of that decision and rule 10.68 must be complied with in relation to it.

10.78(3) [Content and authentication of certificate] The certificate of the trustee's removal must be authenticated and dated by the convener or chair and–

(a) identify the bankrupt;

(b) identify and provide contact details for the removed trustee;

(c) state that the creditors decided that the trustee specified in the certificate be removed from office as trustee of the bankrupt's estate;

(d) state the decision date and the decision procedure used; and

(e) state that the creditors either–

  (i) did not decide against the trustee being released, or

  (ii) decided that the trustee should not be released.

10.78(4) [Effective date of removal] The trustee's removal is effective from the date of the certificate of removal.

General Note

This develops IA 1986 s.298(1).

10.79 Procedure on removal by creditors

10.79(1) [Certificate of removal filed with court] Where the creditors have decided that the trustee be removed, the official receiver must in a bankruptcy based on a petition file the certificate of removal with the court.

10.79(2) [Delivery of copy certificate to removed trustee] The official receiver must deliver a copy of the certificate to the removed trustee.

10.80 Removal of trustee by the court (section 298(1))

10.80(1) [Application of rule] This rule applies where an application is made to the court under section 298(1) for the removal of the trustee, or for an order directing the trustee to initiate a creditors' decision procedure for the purpose of removing the trustee.

10.80(2) [Summary dismissal by court] On receipt of an application, the court may, if it is satisfied that no sufficient cause is shown for it, dismiss it without giving notice to any party other than the applicant.

10.80(3) [Court to fix venue for hearing] Unless the application is dismissed, the court must fix a venue for it to be heard.

10.80(4) [Delivery of notice to trustee and official receiver] The applicant must, at least 14 days before any hearing, deliver to the trustee and the official receiver a notice stating the venue with a copy of the application and of any evidence on which the applicant intends to rely.

10.80(5) [Security for costs] A respondent may apply for security for the costs of the application and the court may make such an order if it is satisfied, having regard to all the circumstances of the case, that it is just to make such an order.

10.80(6) [Choice of action by trustee and official receiver] The trustee and the official receiver may do either or both of the following–

(a) file a report of any matters which the trustee or the official receiver thinks ought to be drawn to the court's attention; or

(b) appear and be heard on the application.

10.80(7) [Costs of application not expense of bankruptcy] The costs of the application are not payable as an expense of the bankruptcy unless the court orders otherwise.

10.80(8) [Content of order] On a successful application the court's order must contain–

(a) identification details for the proceedings;

(b) the name and title of the judge making the order;

(c) the name and postal address of the applicant;

(d) a statement as to the capacity in which the applicant made the application;

(e) identification and contact details for the trustee;

(f) an order that either–

 (i) the trustee is removed from office, or

 (ii) the trustee must instigate a creditors' decision procedure on or before the date specified in the order for the purpose of considering the trustee's removal from office;

(g) details of any further order in the matter; and

(h) the date of the order.

10.80(9) [Delivery of copies to official receiver and trustee] Where the court removes the trustee it must deliver a sealed copy of the order of removal to the trustee and a copy to the official receiver.

10.80(10) [Application of r.10.71 if new trustee appointed] If the court appoints a new trustee, rule 10.71 applies.

General Note

The court enjoys power to remove trustees under IA 1986 s.298(1). For the meaning of "venue" in r.10.80(3) and (4), see r.1.2. Rule 10.80(10) does not confer jurisdiction to appoint a trustee in bankruptcy—*Donaldson v O'Sullivan* [2008] EWHC 387 (Ch); [2008] B.P.I.R. 288—confirmed in [2008] EWCA Civ 879.

10.81 Removal of trustee by the Secretary of State (section 298(5))

10.81(1) [Application of rule] This rule applies where the Secretary of State decides to remove a trustee appointed by the Secretary of State.

10.81(2) [Delivery of notice of decision] Before doing so the Secretary of State must deliver to the trustee and the official receiver a notice of the Secretary of State's decision and the grounds for the decision.

10.81(3) [Notice to give period for representations] The notice must specify a period within which the trustee may make representations against implementation of the decision.

10.81(4) [Actions on removal of trustee] If the Secretary of State directs the removal of the trustee, the Secretary of State must as soon as reasonably practicable–

(a) deliver the notice to the trustee and the official receiver; and

(b) where the bankruptcy was based upon a petition, file a notice of the decision with the court.

10.81(5) [Court's power to make order] Where the Secretary of State directs the trustee be removed, the court may make any order that it could have made if the trustee had been removed by the court.

10.82 Notice of resignation or removal

10.82 Where a new trustee is appointed in place of one who has resigned or been removed, the new trustee must, in the notice of appointment, state that the predecessor trustee has resigned or, as the case may be, been removed and (if it be the case) has been given release.

General Note

Note I(A)R 2009 (SI 2009/642) (effective from 6 April 2009). Under these amendment rules the word "advertisement" was removed from the heading and the rule itself to be replaced by "notice".

10.83 Release of removed trustee (section 299)

10.83(1) [Certificate of removal to state if trustee released] Where the trustee is removed by a creditors' decision procedure the certificate of removal must state whether or not the creditors decided against the trustee's release.

10.83(2) [Content of application for release] Where the creditors decided against release, the trustee's application to the Secretary of State for release under subsection 299(3)(b) must–

(a) identify the proceedings;

(b) identify the bankrupt;

(c) identify and provide contact details for the trustee;

(d) provide details of the circumstances under which the trustee has ceased to act as trustee;

(e) state that the trustee is applying to the Secretary of State for a certificate of the trustee's release as a trustee as a result of the circumstances specified in the application; and

(f) be authenticated and dated by the trustee.

10.83(3) [Certification and filing of release] When the Secretary of State gives the release, the Secretary of State must certify it accordingly and file the certificate with the court in a bankruptcy based on a creditor's petition.

10.83(4) [Delivery of certificate to official receiver and trustee] The Secretary of State must deliver a copy of the certificate to the official receiver and former trustee whose release is effective from the date of the certificate or such other date as the certificate specifies.

General Note

This supplements IA 1986 s.299 (release of trustees).

10.84 Deceased trustee

10.84(1) [Content of notice of death of trustee] If the trustee (not being the official receiver) dies, notice of the fact and date of death must be delivered to the official receiver by one of the following–

(a) a surviving joint trustee;

(b) a member or partner in the deceased trustee's firm (if the deceased was a member, partner or employee of a firm);

(c) an officer of the deceased trustee's company (if the deceased was an officer or employee of a company); or

(d) a personal representative of the deceased trustee.

10.84(2) [Delivery of notice in default of trustee notice] If no such notice has been delivered within 21 days following the trustee's death then any other person may deliver the notice.

10.84(3) [Filing of notice with court] In a bankruptcy based on a creditor's petition the official receiver must file notice of the death with the court.

10.84(4) [Effective date deceased trustee's release] The date of the deceased trustee's release under section 299(3)(a) is–

(a) the date of the filing of the notice with the court where the bankruptcy is based on a creditor's petition; or

(b) the date of delivery of the notice under paragraph (1) to the official receiver where the bankruptcy is based on a debtor's application.

10.85 Loss of qualification as insolvency practitioner (section 298(6))

10.85(1) [Application of rule] This rule applies where the trustee vacates office under section 298(6), on ceasing to be qualified to act as an insolvency practitioner in relation to the bankrupt.

10.85(2) [Delivery of notice to official receiver] A notice of the fact must be delivered as soon as reasonably practicable to the official receiver by one of the following–

(a) the trustee who has vacated office;

(b) a continuing joint trustee;

(c) the recognised professional body which was the source of the vacating trustee's authorisation to act in relation to the bankrupt.

10.85(3) [Authentication and date of notice] The notice must be authenticated and dated by the person delivering the notice.

10.85(4) [Duty of official receiver] On receiving such a notice the official receiver must–

(a) deliver a copy of the notice to the Secretary of State; and

(b) file a copy of the notice with the court where the bankruptcy was based on a creditor's petition.

10.85(5) [Application for release] Rule 10.83(2) to (4) applies in relation to the trustee's application for release under section 299(3)(b).

General Note

On qualification, see IA 1986 Pt XIII.

Sub-division C: release on completion of administration of bankrupt's estate

10.86 Release of official receiver on completion of administration (section 299)

10.86(1) [Notice of intention] Before giving a notice that the administration of the bankrupt's estate is for practical purposes complete to the Secretary of State under section 299(2), the official receiver must deliver a notice of intention to do so to the creditors and to the bankrupt.

10.86(2) [Accompanying summary to notice] The notice must be accompanied by a summary of the official receiver's receipts and payments as trustee.

10.86(3) [Notice to court of date of release] When the Secretary of State has determined the date from which the official receiver's release is effective, the Secretary of State must–

(a) where the bankruptcy was based on a bankruptcy application, deliver a notice of release to the official receiver; or

(b) in all other cases, file a notice of the release with the court.

10.86(4) [Accompanying summary to notice] The Secretary of State's notice to the court must be accompanied by the summary of the official receiver's receipts and payments.

General Note

These supplement IA 1986 s.299 (release of trustees).

10.87 Vacation of office on completion of bankruptcy (sections 298(8) and 331)

10.87(1) [Report under IA 1986 s.331(2A)(a) to comply with r.18.14] The report which the trustee is required to make under section 331(2A)(a) must comply with the requirements of rule 18.14.

10.87(2) [Copy notice and report to bankrupt] A copy of the notice and report that is sent to creditors under section 331(2) and (2A) must be sent to the bankrupt as soon as is reasonably practicable after notice is given to creditors under that provision.

10.87(3) [Content of notice] The notice under section 331(2) must also state–

(a) that the creditors have the right to request information from the trustee under rule 18.9;

(b) that the creditors have the right to challenge the trustee's remuneration and expenses under rule 18.34;

(c) that the bankrupt has a right to challenge the trustee's remuneration and expenses under rule 18.35;

(d) that the creditors may object to the trustee's release by giving notice in writing to the trustee before the end of the prescribed period;

(e) that the prescribed period is the period ending at the later of–

  (i) eight weeks after delivery of the notice; or

  (ii) if any request for information under rule 18.9 or any application to the court under that rule, rule 18.34 or rule 18.35 is made when that request or application is finally determined;

(f) that the trustee will vacate office under section 298(8) when, after the end of the prescribed period, the trustee files with the court a notice that the trustee has given notice to the creditors under section 331; and

(g) that the trustee will be released under section 299(3)(d) at the same time as vacating office unless any of the creditors objected to the trustee's release.

10.87(4) [Authentication of notice under s.298(8)] The notice under section 298(8) must be authenticated and dated by the trustee.

10.87(5) [Notice accompanied copy final report] The notice must be accompanied by a copy of the final report.

10.87(6) [Copy notice under s.298(8) to Secretary of State, official receiver] The trustee must deliver a copy of the notice under section 298(8) to–

(a) the Secretary of State; and

(b) the official receiver.

10.87(7) [Application of r.10.83(2)–(4)] Rule 10.83(2) to (4) applies to an application by the trustee to the Secretary of State for release.

General Note

See IA 1986 s.331. 28 days' notice of the final meeting must be given.

10.88 Rule as to reporting

10.88(1) [Power of court] The court may, on the application of the trustee or official receiver, relieve the applicant of any duty imposed on the applicant by rule 10.86 and 10.87 and rule 18.14 (contents of final report), or authorise the applicant to carry out the duty in any other way.

10.88(2) [Matters court to have regard to] In considering whether to relieve the applicant, the court must have regard to the cost of carrying out the duty, to the amount of the funds available in the bankrupt's estate, and to the extent of the interest of creditors or any particular class of them.

General Note

This new rule was added (as IR 1986 r.6.137A) by I(A)R 2004 (SI 2004/584) with effect from 1 April 2004. It shows an awareness of the need for cost efficiencies by removing the automatic requirement to send out certain notices.

10.89 Notice to official receiver of intention to vacate office

10.89(1) [Application of rule] This rule applies where the trustee intends to vacate office, whether by resignation or otherwise, and as a result there will be a vacancy in the office of trustee (so that by virtue of section 300 the official receiver is trustee until the vacancy is filled).

10.89(2) [Notice of intention to official receiver] The trustee must deliver notice of that intention to the official receiver at least 21 days before the trustee intends to vacate office.

10.89(3) [Details of property] The notice must include the following details of any property which has not been realised, applied, distributed or otherwise fully dealt with in the bankruptcy–

(a) the nature of the property;

(b) its value (or that it has no value);

(c) its location;

(d) any action taken by the trustee to deal with the property or any reason for the trustee not dealing with it; and

(e) the current position in relation to it.

General Note

Rule 10.89(3) makes it clear that valueless property must now be detailed in the report to the official receiver. The word "assets" used in the previous version (IR 1986 r.6.145) has now been dropped to clarify matters. See also *Dear IP* Issue 25 (December 2005).

10.90 Trustee's duties on vacating office

10.90 A trustee who ceases to be in office in consequence of removal, resignation or ceasing to be qualified to act as an insolvency practitioner in relation to the bankrupt, must as soon as reasonably practicable deliver to the successor as trustee–

(a) the assets of the bankrupt's estate (after deduction of any expenses properly incurred, and distributions made, by the trustee);

(b) the records of the bankruptcy, including correspondence, proofs and other documents relating to the bankruptcy while it was within the trustee's responsibility, and

(c) the bankrupt's documents and other records.

General Note

This ties up matters left unresolved by IA 1986 s.298.

10.91 Power of the court to set aside certain transactions

10.91(1) [Trustee's transactions with associates] If in dealing with the bankrupt's estate the trustee enters into any transaction with a person who is an associate of the trustee, the court may, on the application of any interested person, set the transaction aside and order the trustee to compensate the bankrupt's estate for any loss suffered in consequence of it.

10.91(2) [Non-application if with prior consent or for value without knowledge] This does not apply if either–

(a) the transaction was entered into with the prior consent of the court; or

(b) it is shown to the court's satisfaction that the transaction was for value, and that it was entered into by the trustee without knowing, or having any reason to suppose, that the person concerned was an associate.

10.91(3) [Dealings with trust property, etc.] Nothing in this rule is to be taken as prejudicing the operation of any rule of law or equity relating to a trustee's dealings with trust property, or the fiduciary obligations of any person.

General Note

This power is sufficiently important to have been located within the text of IA 1986. For "associate" see IA 1986 s.435.

10.92 Rule against improper solicitation

10.92(1) [Power of court] Where the court is satisfied that any improper solicitation has been used by or on behalf of the trustee in obtaining proxies or procuring the trustee's appointment, it may order that no remuneration be allowed out of the bankrupt's estate to any person by whom, or on whose behalf, the solicitation was exercised.

10.92(2) [Effect of court order] An order of the court under this rule overrides any decision of the creditors' committee or the creditors, or any other provision of these Rules relating to the trustee's remuneration.

10.93 Enforcement of trustee's obligations to official receiver (section 305(3))

10.93(1) [Power of court] On the application of the official receiver, the court may make such orders as it thinks necessary to enforce the duties of the trustee under section 305(3).

10.93(2) [Costs] An order of the court under this rule may provide that all costs of and incidental to the official receiver's application must be borne by the trustee.

Chapter 7

Special manager

[Note: a document required by the Act or these Rules must also contain the standard contents set out in Part 1.]

10.94 Application for and order of appointment of special manager (section 370)

[Note: section 377 provides that the acts of the special manager are valid notwithstanding any defect in the special manager's appointment or qualifications.]

10.94(1) [Application to be supported by report] An application by the interim receiver or trustee under section 370 for the appointment of a special manager must be supported by a report setting out the reasons for the application. The report must include the applicant's estimate of the value of the bankrupt's estate, property or business in relation to which the special manager is to be appointed.

10.94(2) [Content of order] The court's order appointing the special manager must contain–

- (a) identification details for the proceedings;
- (b) the name and title of the judge making the order;
- (c) the name and postal address of the applicant;
- (d) the name and postal address of the proposed special manager;
- (e) an order that the proposed special manager is appointed as special manager;
- (f) details of the special manager's responsibility over the debtor's property or the bankrupt's estate;
- (g) the powers entrusted to the special manager under section 370(4);
- (h) the time allowed for the special manager to give the required security for the appointment;
- (i) the duration of the special manager's appointment, being one of the following–
    - (i) for a fixed period stated in the order,
    - (ii) until the occurrence of a specified event, or
    - (iii) until the court makes a further order;
- (j) an order that the special manager's remuneration will be fixed from time to time by the court; and
- (k) the date of the order.

10.94(3) [Renewal by order] The appointment of a special manager may be renewed by order of the court.

(See General Note after r.10.98.)

10.95 Security

10.95(1) [Appointment effective from when security given or undertaken] The appointment of the special manager does not take effect until the person appointed has given (or, if the court allows, undertaken to give) security to the applicant for the appointment.

10.95(2) [Specific or general security] A person appointed as special manager may give security either specifically for a particular bankruptcy, or generally for any bankruptcy in relation to which that person may be appointed as special manager.

10.95(3) [Amount of security] The amount of the security must be not less than the value of the bankrupt's estate, property or business in relation to which the special manager is appointed, as estimated in the applicant's report which accompanied the application for appointment.

10.95(4) [Certificate of adequacy] When the special manager has given security to the applicant, the applicant must file with the court a certificate as to the adequacy of the security.

10.95(5) [Cost of providing security] The cost of providing the security must be paid in the first instance by the special manager; but–

(a) where a bankruptcy order is not made, the special manager is entitled to be reimbursed out of the property of the debtor, and the court may order accordingly; and

(b) where a bankruptcy order is made, the special manager is entitled to be reimbursed out of the bankrupt's estate in the prescribed order of priority.

(See General Note after r.10.98.)

10.96 Failure to give or keep up security

10.96(1) [Failure to give security] If the special manager fails to give the required security within the time stated for that purpose by the order of appointment, or any extension of that time that may be allowed, the interim receiver or trustee (as the case may be) must report the failure to the court, which may discharge the order appointing the special manager.

10.96(2) [Failure to keep up security] If the special manager fails to keep up the security, the interim receiver or trustee must report the failure to the court, which may remove the special manager, and make such order as it thinks just as to costs.

10.96(3) [Discharge of appointment order; directions] If the court discharges the order appointing the special manager or makes an order removing the special manager, the court must give directions as to whether any, and if so what, steps should be taken for the appointment of another special manager.

(See General Note after r.10.98.)

10.97 Accounting

10.97(1) [Receipts and payments; approval] The special manager must produce accounts, containing details of the special manager's receipts and payments, for the approval of the trustee.

10.97(2) [Period of accounts] The accounts must be for–

(a) each three month period for the duration of the special manager's appointment; or

(b) any shorter period ending with the termination of the special manager's appointment.

10.97(3) [Approved receipts and payments added trustee's] When the accounts have been approved, the special manager's receipts and payments must be added to those of the trustee.

(See General Note after r.10.98.)

10.98 Termination of appointment

10.98(1) [Automatic termination] The special manager's appointment terminates if–

(a) the bankruptcy petition is dismissed; or

(b) in a case where an interim receiver was appointed under section 286, the appointment is discharged without a bankruptcy order having been made.

10.98(2) [Application to court for directions] If the interim receiver or the trustee thinks that the appointment of the special manager is no longer necessary or beneficial to the bankrupt's estate, the interim receiver or the trustee must apply to the court for directions, and the court may order the special manager's appointment to be terminated.

10.98(3) [Application if creditors decide on termination] The interim receiver or the trustee must make such an application if the creditors decide that the appointment should be terminated.

General Note to rr.10.94–10.98

These rules develop the provisions of IA 1986 s.370. If the court appoints a special manager it must contain the details in r.10.94(2) (previously contained in prescribed Form 6.54). The court fixes his remuneration. Security is required. The special manager must provide three-monthly accounts for the trustee. The circumstances leading to the termination of the appointment of the special manager are mapped out.

Chapter 8

Public examination of bankrupt

[Note: a document required by the Act or these Rules must also contain the standard contents set out in Part 1.]

10.99 Order for public examination of bankrupt

[Note: rule 81.9 (as amended) of the CPR requires a warning as mentioned in paragraph (2)(f) to be displayed prominently on the front of the order.]

10.99(1) [Application of rule] This rule applies to a court order for the public examination of a bankrupt made on an application by the official receiver under section 290.

10.99(2) [Title and content of order] The order must have the title "Order for public examination" and contain–

(a) identification details for the proceedings;

(b) the name and the title of the judge making the order;

(c) an order that the bankrupt must attend the venue specified in the order for the purpose of being publicly examined;

(d) the venue for the public examination;

(e) the date of the order; and

(f) a warning that if the bankrupt fails without reasonable excuse to attend the public examination at the time and place specified in the order the bankrupt will be liable to be arrested without further notice under section 364(1) and may be held to be in contempt of court under section 290(5) and imprisoned or fined.

10.99(3) [Copy order to bankrupt] The official receiver must serve a copy of the court's order on the bankrupt as soon as reasonably practicable after the order is made.

(See General Note after r.10.105.)

10.100 Notice of public examination

10.100(1) [To whom delivery of notice required] The official receiver must deliver at least 14 days' notice of the public examination to–

(a) any trustee or special manager; and

(b) subject to any contrary direction of the court, every creditor of the bankrupt who is known to the official receiver.

10.100(2) [Gazetting of notice] Where the official receiver thinks fit, a notice of the order must be gazetted not less than 14 days before the day fixed for the hearing.

10.100(3) [Advertisement of notice] The official receiver may advertise the notice in such other manner as the official receiver thinks fit.

10.100(4) [Notice to state purpose, venue] The notice must state the purpose of the examination hearing and the venue.

(See General Note after r.10.105.)

10.101 Order for public examination requested by creditors

10.101(1) [Accompanying documents with request] A notice by a creditor to the official receiver, under section 290(2), requesting the bankrupt to be publicly examined must be accompanied by–

(a) a list of the creditors concurring with the request with the name and postal address of each and the amount of their respective claims; and

(b) confirmation by each creditor of that creditor's concurrence; and

(c) a statement of the reasons why the public examination is requested.

10.101(2) [Authentication of request] The request must be authenticated and dated by the creditor giving the notice.

10.101(3) [When list of concurring creditors not required] A list of concurring creditors is not required if the requisitioning creditor's debt alone is at least one half in value of the bankrupt's creditors.

10.101(4) [Security for expenses of examination] Before the official receiver makes the requested application, the creditor requesting the examination must deposit with the official receiver such sum (if any) as the official receiver determines is appropriate as security for the expenses of the public examination, if ordered.

10.101(5) [Time limit for application] The official receiver must make the application for the examination–

(a) within 28 days of receiving the creditor's request (if no security is required under paragraph (4)); or

(b) within 28 days of the creditor depositing such security if security is requested.

10.101(6) [Relief from unreasonable request] However, if the official receiver thinks the request is unreasonable, the official receiver may apply to the court for an order to be relieved from making the application.

10.101(7) [Copy of without notice relief order] If the court so orders, and the application for the order was made without notice to any other party, the official receiver must deliver a copy of the order as soon as reasonably practicable to the requisitionist.

10.101(8) [Application dismissed] If such an application is dismissed, the official receiver's application under section 290(2) must be made as soon as reasonably practicable on conclusion of the hearing of the application first mentioned.

(See General Note after r.10.105.)

10.102 Bankrupt unfit for examination

[Note: rule 81.9 (as amended) of the CPR requires a warning as mentioned in paragraph (6) to be displayed prominently on the front of the order.]

10.102(1) [Stay of order or court direction] Where the bankrupt is a person who lacks capacity within the meaning of the Mental Capacity Act 2005 or is unfit to undergo or attend for public examination, the court may–

(a) stay the order for the bankrupt's public examination; or

(b) direct that it will be conducted in a manner and place the court thinks just.

10.102(2) [Who way make application] An application for an order under paragraph (1) must be made–

(a) by a person who has been appointed by a court in the United Kingdom or elsewhere to manage the affairs of, or to represent, the bankrupt;

(b) by a person who appears to the court to be a suitable person to make the application; or

(c) by the official receiver.

10.102(3) [Application not by official receiver] Where an application is made by a person other than the official receiver, then–

(a) the application must, unless the bankrupt is a person who lacks capacity within the meaning of the Mental Capacity Act 2005, be supported by a witness statement by a registered medical practitioner as to the bankrupt's mental and physical condition;

(b) at least five business days' notice of the application must be delivered to the official receiver and the trustee (if one is appointed); and

(c) before any order is made on the application, the applicant must deposit with the official receiver such sum as the official receiver determines is necessary for the additional expenses of an examination.

10.102(4) [Expenses of examination] The court may order that some or all of the expenses of the examination are to be payable out of the deposit under paragraph (3)(c), instead of out of the bankrupt's estate.

10.102(5) [Content of order] The order must contain–

(a) identification details for the proceedings;

(b) the name and title of the judge making the order;

(c) the date of the original order for the public examination of the bankrupt;

(d) the name and postal address of the applicant;

(e) a statement as to the capacity in which the applicant (other than the official receiver) made the application;

(f) a statement that the court is satisfied that the bankrupt is a person who lacks capacity within the meaning of the Mental Capacity Act 2005 to manage and administer the bankrupt's property and affairs or is unfit to undergo a public examination;

(g) an order either that–

(i) the original order is stayed on the grounds that the bankrupt is unfit to undergo a public examination, or

(ii) the original order is varied (as specified in this order) on the grounds that the bankrupt is unfit to attend the public examination fixed by the original order; and

(h) the date of the order.

10.102(6) [Warning to bankrupt where order varied] If the original order is varied, the order must also contain a warning to the bankrupt, which must be displayed prominently on the front page of the order, stating that if the bankrupt fails without reasonable excuse to attend the public examination at the time and place set out in the order the bankrupt–

(a) may be arrested without further notice under section 364(1); and

(b) may be held to be in contempt of court under section 290(5) and imprisoned or fined.

10.102(7) [Application by official recover without notice] Where the application is made by the official receiver, it may be made without notice to any other party, and may be supported by evidence set out in a report by the official receiver to the court.

(See General Note after r.10.105.)

10.103 Procedure at public examination

10.103(1) [Examination on oath to answer all questions] At the public examination the bankrupt must–

(a) be examined on oath; and

(b) answer all the questions the court puts, or allows to be put.

10.103(2) [Questions by legal representative or other authorised person] A person allowed by section 290(4) to question the bankrupt may–

(a) with the approval of the court be represented by an appropriately qualified legal representative;

(b) in writing authorise another person to question the bankrupt on that person's behalf.

10.103(3) [Representation of bankrupt] The bankrupt may at the bankrupt's own expense instruct an appropriately qualified legal representative, who may put such questions as the court may allow to the bankrupt for the purpose of enabling the bankrupt to explain or qualify any answers given by the bankrupt, and may make representations on the bankrupt's behalf.

10.103(4) [Record of examination] The court must have such record made of the examination as the court thinks proper.

10.103(5) [Record as evidence] The record may, in any proceedings (whether under the Act or otherwise) be used as evidence of any statement made by the bankrupt in the course of the bankrupt's public examination.

10.103(6) [Adjournment if criminal proceedings instituted] If criminal proceedings have been instituted against the bankrupt, and the court is of the opinion that the continuance of the hearing might prejudice a fair trial of those proceedings, the hearing may be adjourned.

(See General Note after r.10.105.)

10.104 Adjournment

[Note: rule 81.9 (as amended) of the CPR requires a warning as mentioned in paragraph (2) to be displayed prominently on the front of the order.]

10.104(1) [By court] The court may adjourn the public examination from time to time, either to a fixed date or generally.

10.104(2) [Warning to creditor to attend fixed date for resumption] The order of adjournment of the public examination to a fixed date must contain a warning to the bankrupt, which must be displayed prominently on the front page of the order, stating that if the bankrupt fails without reasonable excuse to attend the public examination at the time and place set out in the order the bankrupt–

(a) may be arrested without further notice under section 364(1); and

(b) may be held to be in contempt of court under section 290(5) and imprisoned or fined.

10.104(3) [Examination adjourned generally] Where the examination has been adjourned generally, the court may at any time on the application of the official receiver or of the bankrupt–

(a) fix a venue for the resumption of the examination; and

(b) give directions as to the manner in which, and the time within which, notice of the resumed public examination is to be given to persons entitled to take part in it.

10.104(4) [Application for resumption by bankrupt, expenses] Where such an application is made by the bankrupt, the court may grant it on terms that the expenses of giving the notices required by that paragraph must be paid by the bankrupt and that, before a venue for the resumed public examination is fixed, the bankrupt must deposit with the official receiver such sum as the official receiver considers necessary to cover those expenses.

10.104(5) [Official receiver may apply for suspension of automatic discharge] Where the examination is adjourned, the official receiver may, there and then, make an application under section 279(3) (suspension of automatic discharge).

10.104(6) [Copies of order of suspension of discharge] If the court makes such an order suspending the bankrupt's discharge, then the court must deliver copies of the order to the official receiver, the trustee and the bankrupt.

(See General Note after r.10.105.)

10.105 Expenses of examination

10.105(1) [Order for examination expenses out of r.10.101 deposit] Where a public examination of the bankrupt has been ordered by the court on a creditor's request under rule 10.101, the court may order that some or all of the expenses of the examination are to be paid out of the deposit under rule 10.101, instead of out of the bankrupt's estate.

10.105(2) [Official receiver not liable for expenses] The costs and expenses of a public examination do not fall on the official receiver personally.

General Note to rr.10.99–10.105

These rules provide detailed guidance on the conduct of a public examination of a bankrupt under IA 1986 s.290. A creditor seeking a public examination must provide security. If the bankrupt is not fit to be publicly examined, the court can excuse him. The hearing procedure is mapped out by rr.10.103 and 10.104. For an application under the predecessor to IR 2016 r.10.103(6) see *Rottmann v OR* [2009] B.P.I.R. 617 (which is discussed in the note to s.433). The solution of a private examination to be conducted before a judge was endorsed in [2009] EWCA Civ 473. The public examination is normally to be funded out of the estate, unless the deposit furnished by a requisitioning creditor is made use of. The fee on public examination was abolished in 1995.

Chapter 9

Replacement of exempt property

10.106 Purchase of replacement property

10.106(1) [Time for purchase] A purchase of replacement property under section 308(3) may be made either before or after the realisation by the trustee of the value of the property vesting in the trustee under the section.

10.106(2) [No obligation on trustee to repurchase without sufficient funds] The trustee is under no obligation to apply funds to the purchase of a replacement for property vested in the trustee, unless and until the trustee has sufficient funds in the bankrupt's estate for that purpose.

(See General Note after r.10.107.)

10.107 Money provided in lieu of sale

10.107(1) [Third party proposal to supply money] The following applies where a third party proposes to the trustee that the third party should provide the bankrupt's estate with a sum of money enabling the bankrupt to be left in possession of property which would otherwise be made to vest in the trustee under section 308.

10.107(2) [Power of trustee where proposal reasonable, etc.] The trustee may accept that proposal, if satisfied that it is a reasonable one, and that the bankrupt's estate will benefit to the extent of the value of the property in question less the cost of a reasonable replacement.

General Note to rr.10.106–10.107

These rules provide further guidance on the operation of IA 1986 s.308, which was a novel provision in the 1986 Act. A third party can provide funds for the estate to prevent a sale and replacement of assets.

Chapter 10

Income payments orders

[Note: a document required by the Act or these Rules must also contain the standard contents set out in Part 1.]

10.108 Interpretation

10.108 In this Chapter the "permitted fee" means the amount which is prescribed for the purposes of section 7(4)(a) of the Attachment of Earnings Act 1971.

General Note

This rule was introduced for IR 2016 and has no equivalent in IR 1986.

10.109 Application for income payments order (section 310)

10.109(1) [Court to fix venue for hearing application] Where the trustee applies for an income payments order under section 310, the court must fix a venue for the hearing of the application.

10.109(2) [Time limit for notice to bankrupt] Notice of the application and the venue must be delivered by the trustee to the bankrupt at least 28 days before the day fixed for the hearing, together with a copy of the trustee's application and a short statement of the grounds on which it is made.

10.109(3) [Content of notice] The notice must inform the bankrupt that–

(a) the bankrupt is required to attend the hearing unless at least five business days before the date fixed for the hearing the bankrupt files with the court and delivers to the trustee, consent to an order being made in the terms of the application; and

(b) if the bankrupt attends, the bankrupt will be given an opportunity to show cause why the order should not be made, or why a different order should be made to that applied for by the trustee.

10.109(4) [Authentication of notice] The notice must be authenticated and dated by the trustee.

(See General Note after r.10.114.)

10.110 Order for income payments order

10.110 An order under section 310 must have the title "Income Payments Order" and must contain–

(a) identification details for the proceedings;

(b) identification and contact details for the trustee;

(c) a statement that the bankrupt has or has not consented to the order (as the case may be);

(d) the order that it appears to the court that the sum which is specified in the order should be paid to the trustee in accordance with the payments schedule detailed in the order until the date specified in the order;

(e) the order that the bankrupt must pay to the trustee the sum referred to in paragraph (e) in accordance with the payments schedule out of the bankrupt's income, the first of such instalments to be made on or before the date specified in the order; and

(f) the date of the order.

(See General Note after r.10.114.)

10.111 Action to follow making of order

10.111(1) [Sealed copy order to bankrupt] Where the court makes an income payments order, the trustee must deliver a sealed copy of the order to the bankrupt as soon as reasonably practicable after it is made.

10.111(2) [Copy order under IA 1986 s.310(3)(b)] If the order is made under section 310(3)(b), a sealed copy of the order must also be delivered by the trustee to the person to whom the order is directed.

(See General Note after r.10.114.)

10.112 Variation of order

10.112(1) [Non-compliance with IA 1986 s.310(3)(a) order] If an income payments order is made under section 310(3)(a), and the bankrupt does not comply with it, the trustee may apply to the court for the order to be varied, so as to take effect under section 310(3)(b) as an order to the payer of the relevant income.

10.112(2) [Application without notice] The trustee's application under this rule may be made without notice to any other party.

10.112(3) [Content of order] The order must contain–

(a) identification details for the proceedings;

(b) identification and contact details for the trustee who made the application;

(c) the name and address of the payer;

(d) a statement that the applicant is the trustee of the bankrupt;

(e) the date of the income payments order;

(f) a statement that it appears to the court that the bankrupt has failed to comply with the income payments order;

(g) the order that the income payments order be varied to the effect that the payer specified in this order do take payment in accordance with the payments schedule detailed in this order out of the bankrupt's income and that the first instalment must be paid on the date specified in the order; and that the payer must deliver the sums deducted to the trustee; and

(h) the date of the order.

10.112(4) [Sealed copies to trustee and bankrupt] The court must deliver sealed copies of any order made on the application to the trustee and the bankrupt as soon as reasonably practicable after the order is made.

10.112(5) [Order varying etc. s.310(3)(b) order] In the case of an order varying or discharging an income payments order made under section 310(3)(b), the court must deliver an additional sealed copy of the order to the trustee, for delivery as soon as reasonably practicable to the payer of the relevant income.

(See General Note after r.10.114.)

10.113 Order to payer of income: administration

10.113(1) [Compliance by payer] Where a person receives notice of an income payments order under section 310(3)(b), with reference to income otherwise payable by that person to the bankrupt, that person ("the payer") must make the necessary arrangements for compliance with the order as soon as reasonably practicable.

10.113(2) [Costs of compliance] When making any payment to the trustee, the payer may deduct the permitted fee towards the clerical and administrative costs of compliance with the income payments order.

10.113(3) [Statement of amount deducted under r.10.113(2)] The payer must give to the bankrupt a statement of any amount deducted by the payer under paragraph (2).

10.113(4) [Where payer no longer liable, etc.] Where a payer receives notice of an income payments order imposing on the payer a requirement under section 310(3)(b), and either–

(a) the payer is then no longer liable to make to the bankrupt any payment of income; or

(b) having made payments in compliance with the order, the payer ceases to be so liable;

the payer must as soon as reasonably practicable deliver notice of that fact to the trustee.

(See General Note after r.10.114.)

10.114 Review of order

10.114(1) [Application for variation or discharge of IPO] Where an income payments order is in force, either the trustee or the bankrupt may apply to the court for the order to be varied or discharged.

10.114(2) [Application by trustee] If the application is made by the trustee, rule 10.109 applies (with any necessary modification) as in the case of an application for an income payments order.

10.114(3) [Application by bankrupt] If the application is made by the bankrupt, it must be accompanied by a short statement of the grounds on which it is made.

10.114(4) [Power of court to dismiss application] On receipt of an application, the court may, if it is satisfied that no sufficient cause is shown for it, dismiss it without giving notice to any party other than the applicant.

10.114(5) [Court to fix venue for hearing] Unless the application is dismissed, the court must fix a venue for it to be heard.

10.114(6) [Time limit for notice to trustee or bankrupt] The applicant must, at least 28 days before any hearing, deliver to the trustee or the bankrupt (whichever of them is not the applicant) a notice stating the venue with–

(a) a copy of the application; and

(b) where the applicant is the bankrupt, a copy of the statement of the grounds for the application referred to in paragraph (3).

10.114(7) [Power of trustee to file report or appear] The trustee may do either or both of the following–

(a) file a report of any matters which the trustee thinks ought to be drawn to the court's attention; or

(b) appear and be heard on the application.

10.114(8) [Trustee to file copy report] The trustee must file a copy of a report under paragraph (7)(a) with the court not less than five business days before the date fixed for the hearing and must deliver a copy of it to the bankrupt.

10.114(9) [Content of court order] The court order must contain–

(a) identification details for the proceedings;

(b) the name and title of the judge making the order;

(c) the name and postal address of the applicant;

(d) an order that the income payments order specified is varied as specified;

(e) the date of the income payments order referred to in paragraph (d);

(f) details of how the income payments order is varied by this order; and

(g) the date of the order.

10.114(10) [Sealed copies of order to trustee, bankrupt, payer] Sealed copies of any order made on the application must be delivered by the court to the trustee, the bankrupt and the payer (if other than the bankrupt) as soon as reasonably practicable after the order is made.

General Note to rr.10.109–10.114

These rules develop an innovation introduced by IA 1986 s.310, the income payments order. The details previously set out in prescribed Forms 6.64 to 6.67 have been set out within the rules themselves and the forms dispensed with.

R.10.110
This rules replaces prescribed Forms 6.65 and 6.66.

R.10.112
This rule contains the detail previously set out in prescribed Form 6.67.

R.10.114
This rule contains the detail previously set out in prescribed Form 6.68.

Chapter 11

Income payments agreements

[Note: a document required by the Act or these Rules must also contain the standard contents set out in Part 1.]

10.114A Interpretation

10.114A In this Chapter, the "permitted fee" means the amount which is prescribed for the purposes of section 7(4)(a) of the Attachment of Earnings Act 1971.

General Note

This clarification was inserted by the Insolvency (England and Wales) (Amendment) Rules 2017 (SI 2017/366).

10.115 Approval of income payments agreements

10.115(1) [Entry prior to bankrupt's discharge] An income payments agreement can only be entered into before the bankrupt's discharge.

10.115(2) [Draft agreement for bankrupt's approval] The official receiver or trustee must provide a draft of the agreement to the bankrupt for the bankrupt's approval.

10.115(3) [Period for approval or not] Within 14 days or such longer period as may be specified by the official receiver or trustee from the date on which the income payments agreement was delivered, the bankrupt must–

(a) if the bankrupt decides to approve the agreement, authenticate the agreement and return it to the official receiver or trustee; or

(b) if the bankrupt decides not to approve the agreement, deliver a notice of that decision specifying the bankrupt's reasons for not approving the agreement to the official receiver or trustee.

(See General Note after r.10.117.)

10.116 Acceptance of income payments agreements

10.116(1) [Official receiver or trustee to authenticate and date] On receipt by the official receiver or trustee of the authenticated income payments agreement, the official receiver or trustee must authenticate and date it at which time it will come into force and a copy must be delivered to the bankrupt.

10.116(2) [Notice where payments by third person under IA 1986 s.310A(1)(b)] Where the agreement provides for payments by a third person in accordance with section 310A(1)(b), a notice of the agreement must be delivered by the official receiver or trustee to that person.

10.116(3) [Content of notice] The notice must–

(a) identify the bankrupt;

(b) state that an income payments agreement has been made, the date of it, and that it provides for the payment by the third person of sums owed to the bankrupt (or a part of those sums) to be paid to the official receiver or trustee;

(c) state the name and address of the third person;

(d) state the amount of money to be paid to the official receiver or trustee from the bankrupt's income, the period over which the payments are to be made, and the intervals at which the sums are to be paid; and

(e) identify and provide contact details for the official receiver or trustee and details of how and where the sums are to be paid.

10.116(4) [Deduction for clerical and administrative costs of IPA compliance] When making any payment to the official receiver or the trustee a person who has received notice of an income payments agreement with reference to income otherwise payable by that person to the bankrupt may deduct the permitted fee towards the clerical and administrative costs of compliance with the income payments agreement.

10.116(5) [Statement to bankrupt of deduction under r.10.116(4)] The payer must give to the bankrupt a statement of any amount deducted by the payer under paragraph (4).

(See General Note after r.10.117.)

10.117 Variation of income payments agreements

10.117(1) [Application with accompanying copy of IPA] Where an application is made to court for variation of an income payments agreement, the application must be accompanied by a copy of the agreement.

10.117(2) [Application by bankruptcy: copy and notice of venue] Where the bankrupt applies to the court for variation of an income payments agreement under section 310A(6)(b), the bankrupt must deliver a copy of the application and notice of the venue to the official receiver or trustee (whichever is appropriate) at least 28 days before the date fixed for the hearing.

10.117(3) [Application by trustee or bankrupt: copy and notice of venue] When the official receiver or trustee applies to the court for variation of an income payments agreement under section 310A(6)(b), the official receiver or trustee must deliver a copy of the application and notice of the venue to the bankrupt at least 28 days before the date fixed for the hearing.

10.117(4) [Power of court] The court may order the variation of an income payments agreement under section 310A.

10.117(5) [Content of court order] The court order must contain–

(a) identification details for the proceedings;

(b) the name and title of the judge making the order;

(c) the name and postal address of the applicant

(d) the order that the income payments agreement be varied as specified;

(e) the date of the income payments agreement referred to in paragraph (d);

(f) details of how the income payments agreement is varied by the order; and

(g) the date of the order.

10.117(6) [Order where third party to make payments] Where the court orders an income payments agreement under section 310A(1)(a) to be varied, so as to be an agreement under section 310A(1)(b) providing that a third person is to make payments to the trustee or the official receiver, the official receiver or trustee must deliver a notice of the agreement to that person in accordance with rule 10.116(2).

10.117(7) [Deduction of fee for clerical and administrative costs of compliance with the IPA] A person who has received notice of an income payments agreement relating to income otherwise payable by that person to the bankrupt may deduct the permitted fee towards the clerical and administrative costs of compliance with the agreement when making any payment to the official receiver or the trustee.

10.117(8) [Statement to bankrupt of deduction under r.10.117(7)] The payer must give the bankrupt a statement of any amount deducted under paragraph (7).

General Note to rr.10.115–10.117

This chapter was introduced by I(A)R 2003 (SI 2003/1730) to provide further regulations for the income payments agreements regime, which was introduced by EA 2002. See the note to s.310A. In *Re Hargreaves (Booth v Mond)* [2010] B.P.I.R. 1111 the enforceability under IR 1986 r.6.193B(2) (now IR 2016 r.10.116(1)) of an income payments agreement under which arrears were due was stressed.

Chapter 12

Applications for production of documents by Her Majesty's Revenue and Customs (section 369)

[Note: a document required by the Act or these Rules must also contain the standard contents set out in Part 1.]

10.118 Application for order

10.118(1) [Application to specify documents etc.] An application by the official receiver or the trustee for an order under section 369 (order for production of documents) must specify (with such details as will enable the order, if made, to be most easily complied with) the documents the production of which is sought, naming the official to whom the order is to be addressed.

10.118(2) [Court to fix venue] The court must fix a venue for the hearing of the application.

10.118(3) [Notice of venue etc. to Commissioners] The applicant must deliver notice of the venue, accompanied by a copy of the application to the Commissioners for Her Majesty's Revenue and Customs ("the Commissioners") at least 28 days before the hearing.

10.118(4) [Whether Commissioners consent or object] The notice must require the Commissioners, not later than five business days before the date fixed for the hearing of the application, to inform the court whether they consent or object to the making of an order.

10.118(5) [If Commissioners consent] If the Commissioners consent to the making of an order, the statement must include the name of the official to whom the order should be addressed, if other than the one named in the application.

10.118(6) [If Commissioners object] If the Commissioners object to the making of an order, they must file with the court a statement of their grounds of objection not less than five business days before the hearing of the application and must ensure that an official of theirs attends the hearing.

10.118(7) [Commissioners to deliver copy statement of objections to applicant] The Commissioners must deliver a copy of the statement of objections to the applicant as soon as reasonably practicable.

(See General Note after r.10.120.)

10.119 Making and service of the order

10.119(1) [Powers of court] The court may make the order applied for, with any modifications which appear appropriate, having regard to any representations made on behalf of the Commissioners.

10.119(2) [Content of order] The order–

(a) may be addressed to an official of Her Majesty's Revenue and Customs other than the one named in the application;

(b) must specify a time, not less than 28 days after service on the official to whom the order is addressed, within which compliance is required; and

(c) may include requirements as to the manner in which documents to which the order relates are to be produced.

10.119(3) [Service of sealed copy of order] A sealed copy of the order must be served by the applicant on the official to whom it is addressed.

10.119(4) [If official unable to comply] If the official is unable to comply with the order because the relevant documents are not in the possession of the official, and the official has been unable to obtain possession of them, the official must file with the court a statement as to the reasons for the official's non-compliance.

10.119(5) [Official to deliver copy statement under r.10.119(4) to applicant] The official must deliver a copy of the statement referred to in paragraph (4) to the applicant as soon as reasonably practicable.

(See General Note after r.10.120.)

10.120 Custody of documents

10.120 When, in compliance with an order under section 369, original documents are produced, any person who, by order of the court under section 369(2), has possession or custody of those documents is responsible to the court for their safe keeping as, and return when, directed.

General Note to rr.10.118–10.120

These rules provide further details on orders made under IA 1986 s.369. A maximum of 28 days after service is fixed for compliance with a s.369 order.

CHAPTER 13

MORTGAGED PROPERTY

[Note: a document required by the Act or these Rules must also contain the standard contents set out in Part 1.]

10.121 Interpretation

10.121 For the purposes of this Chapter "land" includes any interest in, or right over, land.

(See General Note after r.10.124.)

10.122 Claim by mortgagee of land

10.122(1) [Application for order for sale of land] Any person claiming to be the legal or equitable mortgagee of land belonging to the bankrupt may apply to the court for an order directing that the land be sold.

10.122(2) [Court may direct accounts to be taken, etc.] The court, if satisfied as to the applicant's title, may direct accounts to be taken and enquiries made to ascertain–

(a) the principal, interest and costs due under the mortgage; and

(b) where the mortgagee has been in possession of the land or any part of it, the rents and profits, dividends, interest, or other proceeds received by the mortgagee or on the mortgagee's behalf.

10.122(3) [Directions re other mortgage on property] The court may also give directions in relation to any mortgage (whether prior or subsequent) on the same property, other than that of the applicant.

10.122(4) [Powers of examination by court] For the purpose of those accounts and enquiries, and of making title to the purchaser, any of the parties may be examined by the court, and must produce on oath before the court all such documents in their custody or under their control relating to the bankrupt's estate as the court may direct.

10.122(5) [Clarification of disputed matters, etc.] The court may under paragraph (4) order any of the parties to clarify any matter which is in dispute in the proceedings or give additional information in relation to any such matter and CPR Part 18 (further information) applies to any such order.

10.122(6) [In like manner as in High Court] In any proceedings between a mortgagor and mortgagee, or the trustee of either of them, the court may order accounts to be taken and enquiries made in like manner as in the Chancery Division of the High Court.

(See General Note after r.10.124.)

10.123 Power of court to order sale

10.123(1) [Order for sale, possession etc.] The court may order that the land, or any specified part of it, be sold and any party bound by the order and in possession of the land or part, or in receipt of the rents and profits from it, may be ordered to deliver possession or receipt to the purchaser or to such other person as the court may direct.

10.123(2) [Directions re sale] The court may–

(a) permit the person having the conduct of the sale to sell the land in such manner as that person thinks fit; or

(b) direct that the land be sold as directed by the order.

10.123(3) [Order directions] The court's order may contain directions–

(a) appointing the person to have the conduct of the sale;

(b) fixing the manner of sale (whether by contract conditional on the court's approval, private treaty, public auction, or otherwise);

(c) settling the particulars and conditions of sale;

(d) for obtaining evidence of the value of the property and for fixing a reserve or minimum price;

(e) requiring particular persons to join in the sale and conveyance;

(f) requiring the payment of the purchase money into court, or to trustees or others; or

(g) if the sale is to be by public auction, fixing the security (if any) to be given by the auctioneer, and the auctioneer's remuneration.

10.123(4) [Sale by auction, mortgagee may bid] The court may direct that, if the sale is to be by public auction, the mortgagee may bid on the mortgagee's own behalf.

10.123(5) [Rights in rem] Nothing in this rule or rule 10.124 affects the rights in rem of creditors or third parties protected under Article 8 of the EU Regulation.

(See General Note after r.10.124.)

10.124 Proceeds of sale

10.124(1) [Application of proceeds] The proceeds of sale must be applied as follows–

(a) first in payment of–

(i) the trustee's expenses in relation to the application to the court,

(ii) the trustee's expenses of the sale and attendance at it, and

(iii) any costs of the trustee arising from the taking of accounts, and making of enquiries, as directed by the court under rule 10.122;

(b) secondly, in payment of the amount found due to any mortgagee, for principal, interest and costs; and

(c) the balance must be retained by or paid to the trustee.

10.124(2) [Where proceeds insufficient] Where the proceeds of the sale are insufficient to pay in full the amount found due to any mortgagee, the mortgagee is entitled to prove as a creditor for any deficiency, and to receive dividends rateably with other creditors, but not so as to disturb any dividend already declared.

General Note to rr.10.121–10.124

These provisions regulate the rights of mortgagees of the bankrupt's land. The court can order the sale of the mortgage property. Note the priority of claims against the proceeds of sale (r.10.124).

Rule 10.123(5) amended by the Insolvency (England and Wales) and Insolvency (Scotland) (Miscellaneous and Consequential Amendments) Rules 2017 (SI 2017/1115) rr.1(1), (2), 22, 25(1) as from 8 December 2017.

Chapter 14

After-acquired property

10.125 Duties of bankrupt in relation to after-acquired property

10.125(1) [Time limit for bankrupt to give notice] The notice to be given by the bankrupt to the trustee, under section 333(2), of property acquired by, or devolving upon, the bankrupt, or of any increase of the bankrupt's income, must be given within 21 days of the bankrupt becoming aware of the relevant facts.

10.125(2) [Bankrupt not to dispose of property without consent] The bankrupt must not, without the trustee's consent in writing, dispose of such property or income within the period of 42 days beginning with the date of giving the notice.

10.125(3) [Disposal of property, bankrupt to identify, etc. person disposed to] If the bankrupt disposes of property before giving the notice required by this rule or contrary to paragraph (2), it is the bankrupt's duty as soon as reasonably practicable to disclose to the trustee the name and address of the person to whom the property was disposed, and to provide any other information which may be necessary to enable the trustee to trace the property and recover it for the bankrupt's estate.

10.125(4) [Property to which r.19.125(1)–(3) do not apply] Paragraphs (1) to (3) do not apply to property acquired by the bankrupt in the ordinary course of a business carried on by the bankrupt.

10.125(5) [Bankrupt carries on business] A bankrupt who carries on a business must, when required by the trustee, deliver to the trustee–

(a) information about the business, showing the total of goods bought and sold and services supplied and the profit or loss arising from the business; and

(b) fuller details including accounts of the business.

(See General Note after r.10.126.)

10.126 Trustee's recourse to person to whom property disposed

10.126(1) [Trustee may serve notice on person property disposed to] Where property has been disposed of by the bankrupt, before giving the notice required by section 333(2) or otherwise in contravention of rule 10.125, the trustee may serve notice on the person to whom the property was disposed, claiming the property as part of the bankrupt's estate by virtue of section 307.

10.126(2) [Time limit for serving notice] The trustee's notice must be served within 28 days of the trustee becoming aware of the identity of the person to whom the property was disposed and an address at which that person can be served.

General Note to rr.10.125–10.126

The key provision on after-acquired property is IA 1986 s.307, which represents a new departure in bankruptcy law. Section 333(2) is also relevant. The bankrupt has 21 days after becoming aware that after-acquired property has become vested in him to notify the trustee. The bankrupt must then wait 42 days before disposing of that property. If property is wrongfully disposed of, it may be traced by the trustee at the expense of the estate.

Chapter 15

Permission to act as director, etc.

[Note: a document required by the Act or these Rules must also contain the standard contents set out in Part 1.]

10.127 Interpretation

10.127 In this Chapter a bankrupt includes a person in relation to whom a bankruptcy restrictions order is in force.

(See General Note after r.10.131.)

10.128 Application for permission

10.128(1) [Application supported by witness statement] An application under section 11 of the Company Directors Disqualification Act 1986 by the bankrupt for permission to act as director of, or to take part or be concerned in the promotion, formation or management of a company, must be supported by a witness statement.

10.128(2) [Content of witness statement] The witness statement must identify the company and specify–

(a) the nature of its business or intended business, and the place or places where that business is, or is to be, carried on;

(b) whether it is, or in the case of a company which has not yet been incorporated is to be, a private or a public company;

(c) the persons who are, or are to be, principally responsible for the conduct of its affairs (whether as directors, shadow directors, managers or otherwise);

(d) the manner and capacity in which the applicant proposes to take part or be concerned in the promotion or formation of the company or, as the case may be, its management; and

(e) the emoluments and other benefits to be obtained from the directorship.

10.128(3) [Court to fix venue for hearing; notice] The court must fix a venue for hearing the bankrupt's application and deliver notice of the hearing to the bankrupt.

(See General Note after r.10.131.)

10.129 Report of official receiver

10.129(1) [Time limit for notice of venue, etc.] The bankrupt must, not less than 28 days before the date fixed for the hearing, deliver to the official receiver and the trustee (if different) notice of the venue, accompanied by copies of the application and the witness statement under rule 10.128.

10.129(2) [Official receiver's report filed in court] The official receiver may, not less than 14 days before the date fixed for the hearing, file with the court a report of any matters which the official receiver considers ought to be drawn to the court's attention.

10.129(3) [Copy report to bankrupt] The official receiver must deliver a copy of the report to the bankrupt and to the trustee (if not the official receiver) as soon as reasonably practicable after it is filed.

10.129(4) [Report delivered by post] Where a copy of the report is delivered by post under paragraph (3) it must be delivered by first class post.

10.129(5) [Bankrupt's notice denying or disputing statements in report] The bankrupt may, not later than five business days before the date of the hearing, file with the court a notice specifying any statements in the official receiver's report which the bankrupt intends to deny or dispute.

10.129(6) [Delivery of notice copies] If the bankrupt files such a notice, the bankrupt must deliver copies of it, not less than three business days before the date of the hearing, to the official receiver and the trustee.

10.129(7) [Appearances, representations, questions] The official receiver and the trustee may appear on the hearing of the application, and may make representations and put to the bankrupt such questions as the court may allow.

(See General Note after r.10.131.)

10.130 Court's order on application

10.130(1) [If court grants application] A court order granting the bankrupt permission under section 11 of the Company Directors Disqualification Act 1986 must specify what the bankrupt has permission to do.

10.130(2) [Powers of court] The court, having regard to any representations made by the trustee on the hearing of the application, may–

(a) include in the order provision varying an income payments order or an income payments agreement already in force in relation to the bankrupt; or

(b) if no income payments order is in force, make one.

10.130(3) [Copies of order] Whether or not the application is granted, copies of the order must be delivered by the court to the bankrupt, the official receiver and the trustee (if different).

(See General Note after r.10.131.)

10.131 Costs under this Chapter

10.131 In no case do any costs or expenses arising under this Chapter fall on the official receiver personally.

General Note to rr.10.127–10.131

This was originally inserted by I(A)R 2003 (SI 2003/1730) to widen the definition of a bankrupt to include those against whom a BRO or BRU is in force. A person may thus be discharged from bankruptcy but still be regarded as a bankrupt for the purposes of Ch.15 if a BRO or BRU remains in force.

The placement of these provisions within the Insolvency Rules is puzzling. These rules relate to applications by a bankrupt for leave to participate in company management under CDDA 1986 s.11. The official receiver is to be notified to give him a chance to put his views to the court.

Chapter 16

Annulment of bankruptcy order

[Note: a document required by the Act or these Rules must also contain the standard contents set out in Part 1.]

10.132 Application for annulment

10.132(1) [Application to specify in made under IA 1986 s.282(1)(a) or (b)] An application to the court under section 282(1) for the annulment of a bankruptcy order must specify whether it is made–

(a) under subsection (1)(a) (claim that the order ought not to have been made); or

(b) under subsection (1)(b) (debts and expenses of the bankruptcy all paid or secured).

10.132(2) [Application supported by witness statement stating grounds] The application must be supported by a witness statement stating the grounds on which it is made.

10.132(3) [Witness statement where application under s.282(1)(a)] Where the application is made under section 282(1)(b), the witness statement must contain all the facts by reference to which, under the Act and these Rules, the court may be satisfied that the condition in section 282(1)(b) applies before annulling the bankruptcy order.

10.132(4) [Copy application, witness statement into court] A copy of the application and the witness statement in support must be filed with the court.

10.132(5) [Notice of venue fixed for hearing] The court must deliver notice of the venue fixed for the hearing to the applicant.

10.132(6) [Where application under s.282(1)(a) notice of venue, etc.] Where the application is made under section 282(1)(a) the applicant must deliver notice of the venue, accompanied by copies of the application and the supporting witness statement, to the official receiver, the trustee (if different), and the person on whose petition the bankruptcy order was made in sufficient time to enable them to be present at the hearing.

10.132(7) [Where application under s.282(1)(b) notice of venue, etc.] Where the application is made under section 282(1)(b) the applicant must deliver notice of the venue, accompanied by copies of the application and the supporting witness statement, to the official receiver and the trustee (if different) not less than 28 days before the hearing.

10.132(8) [Where applicant not bankrupt] Where the applicant is not the bankrupt, all notices, documents and evidence required by this Chapter to be delivered to another party by the applicant must also be delivered to the bankrupt.

(See General Note after r.10.141.)

10.133 Report by trustee

10.133(1) [Application of rule, application under IA 1986 s.282(1)(b)] The following applies where the application is made under section 282(1)(b) (debts and expenses of the bankruptcy all paid or secured).

10.133(2) [Trustee to file report in court; matters] Not less than 21 days before the date fixed for the hearing, the trustee must file with the court a report relating to the following matters–

(a) the circumstances leading to the bankruptcy;

(b) a summary of the bankrupt's assets and liabilities at the date of the bankruptcy order and at the date of the application;

(c) details of any creditors who are known to the trustee to have claims, but have not proved; and

(d) such other matters as the person making the report considers to be, in the circumstances, necessary for the information of the court.

10.133(3) [Additional contents of report where trustee not official receiver] Where the trustee is other than the official receiver, the report must also include a statement of–

(a) the trustee's remuneration;

(b) the basis fixed for the trustee's remuneration under rule 18.16; and

(c) the expenses incurred by the trustee.

10.133(4) [Particulars of debts etc. paid or secured] The report must include particulars of the extent to which, and the manner in which, the debts and expenses of the bankruptcy have been paid or secured.

10.133(5) [Whether security satisfactory] In so far as debts and expenses are unpaid but secured, the person making the report must state in it whether and to what extent that person considers the security to be satisfactory.

10.133(6) [Copy of report to applicant; witness statement] A copy of the report must be delivered to the applicant as soon as reasonably practicable after it is filed with the court and the applicant may file a further witness statement in answer to statements made in the report.

10.133(7) [Copies of witness statement to official receiver/trustee] Copies of any such witness statement must be delivered by the applicant to the official receiver and the trustee (if different).

10.133(8) [If trustee not official receiver] If the trustee is other than the official receiver, a copy of the trustee's report must be delivered to the official receiver at least 21 days before the hearing.

10.133(9) [Official receiver's additional report] The official receiver may then file an additional report, a copy of which must be delivered to the applicant and the trustee (if not the official receiver) at least five business days before the hearing.

(See General Note after r.10.141.)

10.134 Applicant's claim that remuneration or expenses are excessive

10.134(1) [Application for order where application for annulment] Where the trustee is other than the official receiver and application for annulment is made under section 282(1)(b), the applicant may also apply to the court for one or more of the orders in paragraph (4) on the ground that the remuneration charged, or expenses incurred, by the trustee are in all the circumstances excessive.

10.134(2) [Time limit for application] Application for such an order must be made no later than five business days before the date fixed for the hearing of the application for annulment and be accompanied by a copy of any evidence which the applicant intends to provide in support.

10.134(3) [Copy of application and accompanying evidence to trustee] The applicant must deliver a copy of the application and of any evidence accompanying it to the trustee as soon as reasonably practicable after the application is made.

10.134(4) [Court order if application well-founded] If the court annuls the bankruptcy order under section 282(1)(b) and considers the application to be well-founded, it must also make one or more of the following orders–

(a) an order reducing the amount of remuneration which the trustee was entitled to charge;

(b) an order that some or all of the remuneration or expenses in question be treated as not being bankruptcy expenses;

(c) an order that the trustee or the trustee's personal representative pay to the applicant the amount of the excess of remuneration or expenses or such part of the excess as the court may specify; and

(d) any other order that the court thinks just.

(See General Note after r.10.141.)

10.135 Power of court to stay proceedings

10.135(1) [Order in advance of hearing] The court may, in advance of the hearing, make an order staying any proceedings which it thinks ought, in the circumstances of the application, to be stayed.

10.135(2) [Application without notice] Except in relation to an application for an order staying all or any part of the proceedings in the bankruptcy, application for an order under this rule may be made without notice to any other party.

10.135(3) [Copies of application to official receiver and trustee] Where an application is made under this rule for an order staying all or any part of the proceedings in the bankruptcy, the applicant must deliver copies of the application to the official receiver and the trustee, if other than the official receiver, in sufficient time to enable them to be present at the hearing and make representations.

10.135(4) [Effect of staying order on annulment] Where the court makes an order under this rule staying all or any part of the proceedings in the bankruptcy, the rules in this Chapter nevertheless continue to apply to any application for, or other matters in connection with, the annulment of the bankruptcy order.

10.135(5) [Copies of staying order] If the court makes an order under this rule, it must deliver copies of the order to the applicant, the official receiver and the trustee (if different).

(See General Note after r.10.141.)

10.136 Notice to creditors who have not proved

10.136 Where the application for annulment is made under section 282(1)(b) and it has been reported to the court under rule 10.133(2)(c) that there are known creditors of the bankrupt who have not proved, the court may–

(a) direct the trustee or, if no trustee has been appointed, the official receiver to deliver notice of the application to such of those creditors as the court thinks ought to be informed of it, with a view to their proving for their debts within 21 days;

(b) direct the trustee or, if no trustee has been appointed, the official receiver to advertise the fact that the application has been made, so that creditors who have not proved may do so within a specified time; and

(c) adjourn the application meanwhile, for any period not less than 35 days.

(See General Note after r.10.141.)

10.137 The hearing

10.137(1) [Trustee to attend] The trustee must attend the hearing of the application under section 282 unless the court directs otherwise.

10.137(2) [Attendance of official receiver] The official receiver, if not the trustee, may attend, but is not required to do so unless the official receiver has filed a report under rule 10.133.

10.137(3) [Copies of order] If the court makes an order on the application or on an application under rule 10.134, it must deliver copies of the order to the applicant, the official receiver and (if other) the trustee.

10.137(4) [Content of order] An order of annulment under section 282 must contain–

(a) identification details for the proceedings;

(b) the name and address of the applicant;

(c) the date of the bankruptcy order;

(d) the date of the filing of the bankruptcy petition or the making of the bankruptcy application;

(e) the date and reference number of the registration of the bankruptcy petition or bankruptcy application as a pending action with the Chief Land Registrar;

(f) the date and reference number of the registration of the bankruptcy order on the register of writs and orders affecting land with the Chief Land Registrar;

(g) a statement that it appears to the court that–

  (i) the bankruptcy order ought not to have been made, or

  (ii) the bankruptcy debts and expenses of the bankruptcy have all been paid or secured to the satisfaction of the court;

  and that under section 282(2) the bankruptcy order ought to be annulled;

(h) an order–

  (i) that the bankruptcy order specified in the order is annulled,

(ii) that the bankruptcy petition or bankruptcy application specified in the order be dismissed, and

(iii) that the registration of the petition or the bankruptcy application as a pending action with the Chief Land Registrar and of the bankruptcy order with the Chief Land Registrar specified in the order be vacated upon application made by the bankrupt; and

(i) the date of the order.

10.137(5) [Order to contain notice to bankrupt] The order must contain a notice to the bankrupt stating–

(a) should the bankrupt require notice of the order to be gazetted and to be advertised in the same manner as the bankruptcy order was advertised, the bankrupt must within 28 days deliver notice of that requirement to the official receiver; and

(b) it is the bankrupt's responsibility and in the bankrupt's interest to ensure that the registration of the petition or bankruptcy application and of the bankruptcy order with the Chief Land Registrar are cancelled.

10.137(6) [Costs] The adjudicator is not in any event to be liable for costs arising on an application under section 282.

(See General Note after r.10.141.)

10.138 Matters to be proved under section 282(1)(b)

10.138(1) [Application of Rule] This rule applies in relation to the matters which–

(a) must, in an application under section 282(1)(b), be proved to the satisfaction of the court; and

(b) may be taken into account by the court on hearing such an application.

10.138(2) [Debts paid in full or secured] Subject to the following paragraph, all bankruptcy debts which have been proved must have been–

(a) paid in full; or

(b) secured in full to the satisfaction of the court.

10.138(3) [If debt disputed, etc., security to be given] If a debt is disputed, or a creditor who has proved can no longer be traced, the bankrupt must have given such security (in the form of money paid into court, or a bond entered into with approved sureties) as the court considers adequate to satisfy any sum that may subsequently be proved to be due to the creditor concerned and (if the court thinks just) costs.

10.138(4) [Advertisement in case of untraced creditor] Where such security has been given in the case of an untraced creditor, the court may direct that particulars of the alleged debt, and the security, be advertised in such manner as it thinks just.

10.138(5) [Advertisement results in no claim] If the court directs such advertisement and no claim on the security is made within 12 months from the date of the advertisement (or the first advertisement, if more than one), the court must, on application, order the security to be released.

10.138(6) [Payments court may take into account] In determining whether to annul a bankruptcy order under section 282(1)(b), the court may, if it thinks just and without prejudice to the generality of its discretion under section 282(1), take into account whether any sums have been paid or payment of any sums has been secured in respect of post-commencement interest on the bankruptcy debts which have been proved.

10.138(7) [Security in r.10.138(2), (6)] For the purposes of paragraphs (2) and (6), security includes an undertaking given by a solicitor and accepted by the court.

10.138(8) ["Post-commencement interest" in r.10.138(6)] For the purposes of paragraph (6), "post-commencement interest" means interest on the bankruptcy debts at the rate specified in section 328(5) in relation to periods during which those debts have been outstanding since the commencement of the bankruptcy.

(See General Note after r.10.141.)

10.139 Notice to creditors

10.139(1) [Notice of annulment] Where the official receiver has delivered notice of the debtor's bankruptcy to the creditors and the bankruptcy order is annulled, the official receiver must as soon as reasonably practicable deliver notice of the annulment to them.

10.139(2) [Expenses of giving notice] Expenses incurred by the official receiver in delivering such notice are a charge in the official receiver's favour on the property of the former bankrupt, whether or not the property is actually in the official receiver's hands.

10.139(3) [Property in hands of trustee, etc.] Where any property is in the hands of a trustee or any person other than the former bankrupt, the official receiver's charge is subject to any costs that may be incurred by the trustee or that other person in effecting realisation of the property for the purpose of satisfying the charge.

(See General Note after r.10.141.)

10.140 Other matters arising on annulment

10.140(1) [Former bankrupt may require official receiver to publish notice of order] Within 28 days of the making of an order under section 282, the former bankrupt may require the official receiver to publish a notice of the making of the order in accordance with paragraphs (2) and (3).

10.140(2) [Gazetting/advertisement of notice of order] As soon as reasonably practicable the notice must be–

(a) gazetted; and

(b) advertised in the same manner as the bankruptcy order to which it relates was advertised.

10.140(3) [Content of notice] The notice must state–

(a) the name of the former bankrupt;

(b) the date on which the bankruptcy order was made;

(c) that the bankruptcy order against the former bankrupt has been annulled under section 282(1); and

(d) the date of the annulment.

10.140(4) [Former bankrupt deceased or lacking capacity] Where the former bankrupt–

(a) has died; or

(b) is a person lacking capacity to manage the person's own affairs (within the meaning of the Mental Capacity Act 2005);

the reference to the former bankrupt in paragraph (1) is to be read as referring to the former bankrupt's personal representative or, as the case may be, a person appointed by the court to represent or act for the former bankrupt.

(See General Note after r.10.141.)

10.141 Trustee's final account

10.141(1) [Duty to account for all transactions] Where a bankruptcy order is annulled under section 282, this does not of itself release the trustee from any duty or obligation, imposed on the trustee by or under the Act or these Rules, to account for all of the trustee's transactions in connection with the former bankrupt's estate.

10.141(2) [Final account to Secretary of State etc.] The trustee must deliver a copy of the trustee's final account to the Secretary of State as soon as practicable after the court's order annulling the bankruptcy order.

10.141(3) [Final account filed in court] The trustee must file a copy of the final account with the court.

10.141(4) [Content of final account] The final account must include a summary of the trustee's receipts and payments in the administration, and contain a statement to the effect that the trustee has reconciled the account with that which is held by the Secretary of State in respect of the bankruptcy.

10.141(5) [Release of trustee] The trustee is released from such time as the court may determine, having regard to whether–

(a) the trustee has delivered the final accounts under paragraph (2); and

(b) any security given under rule 10.138 has been, or will be, released.

General Note to rr.10.132–10.141

The key provisions on annulment of bankruptcy orders, IA 1986 ss.261 and 282, leave many questions unanswered. These rules provide the necessary answers. The details for the application to the court are set out and if the application is under s.282(1)(b), a full report from the trustee is required. Proceedings can be stayed where an annulment application is pending. Notice of the application may have to be sent to known creditors who have not proved. Public advertisements may also be required. Rule 10.138 explains further s.282(1)(b). Creditors must be notified of the annulment, entries in the Land Register, etc. will have to be vacated, the Secretary of State must be told and the former bankrupt can demand that the annulment be publicly advertised. Rule 10.141 is a necessary saving provision relating to the trustee's accounts. On the right of the trustee to be present see *Oraki v Dean & Dean* [2017] EWHC 11 (Ch).

R.10.132
The general 28-day limit originally fixed by IR 1986 r.6.206(4) was modified to deal with applications under s.282(1)(a) and in IR 2016 has been split into two separate paragraphs r.10.132(6) and (7). Sub-paragraph (8) results from I(A)R 2003 (SI 2003/1730).

R.10.133
This rule and its relationship with what is now r.10.136 was considered by Lewison J in *Howard v Savage* [2006] EWHC 3693 (Ch); [2007] B.P.I.R. 1097.

R.10.134
This provision was introduced by the former I(A)R 2010 (SI 2010/686). This was intended to assist the court if the circumstances such as found in *Engel v Peri* [2002] B.P.I.R. 961 repeat themselves. The fact that this provision was not retrospective was highlighted in *Secondus v Atkinson* [2013] B.P.I.R. 632.

R.10.135
This rule was substantially expanded in 1988 to enable the official receiver to have an early warning of an application to stay. There is also provision for annulment proceedings.

R.10.136
For the significance of the predecessor of this rule see the comments of Warner J in *Re Robertson (a Bankrupt)* [1989] 1 W.L.R. 1139. In *Howard v Savage* [2006] EWHC 3693 (Ch); [2007] B.P.I.R. 1097 the link between the predecessor of this rule and what is now r.10.137 was considered by Lewison J.

R.10.137
This IR 2016 rule now contains the detail previously set out in prescribed Form 6.71 under IR 1986.

R 10.138
For the significance of this rule see *Re Robertson (a Bankrupt)* [1989] 1 W.L.R. 1139. Also see the comments of Lewison J in *Howard v Savage* [2006] EWHC 3693 (Ch); [2007] B.P.I.R. 1097. For the consequences of non-compliance with r.10.138 see *Inland Revenue Commissioners v Khan* [2005] B.P.I.R. 409. Significant changes were made by I(A)R 2010 (SI 2010/686). These amendments, particularly the introduction of r.10.138(7) have the effect of neutralising the difficulties arising from *Halabi v Camden LBC* [2008] B.P.I.R. 370. The rule was intended to ease some of the difficulties that have confronted the courts in annulment cases by making it clear that payment of statutory interest is a relevant consideration when exercising discretion to annul under s.282(1)(b).

R.10.140
The 28-day limit was inserted by the former I(A)R 2004 (SI 2004/584).

Chapter 17

Discharge

[Note: a document required by the Act or these Rules must also contain the standard contents set out in Part 1.]

10.142 Application for suspension of discharge

10.142(1) [Application of rule] The following applies where the official receiver or trustee (if different) applies to the court for an order under section 279(3) (suspension of automatic discharge), but not where the official receiver makes that application under rule 10.104 on the adjournment of the bankrupt's public examination.

10.142(2) [Evidence in support] The official receiver or trustee must file, with the application, evidence in support setting out the reasons why it appears that such an order should be made.

10.142(3) [Court to fix venue for hearing, etc.] The court must fix a venue for the hearing of the application, and deliver notice of it to the official receiver, the trustee, and the bankrupt.

10.142(4) [Copies of official receiver's report] Copies of the official receiver's report under this rule must be delivered by the official receiver to the bankrupt and any trustee who is not the official receiver, so as to reach them at least 21 days before the date fixed for the hearing.

10.142(5) [Copies of the trustee's evidence in support] Copies of the trustee's evidence in support of the application must be delivered by the trustee to the official receiver and the bankrupt at least 21 days before the date fixed for the hearing.

10.142(6) [Where bankrupt intends to deny or dispute evidence] If the bankrupt intends to deny or dispute any statements in the official receiver's or trustee's evidence in support then the bankrupt must not later than five business days before the date of the hearing, file with the court a notice specifying the statements which the bankrupt intends to deny or dispute.

10.142(7) [Copies of notice] If the bankrupt files such a notice under paragraph (6), the bankrupt must deliver copies of it, not less than three business days before the date of the hearing, to the official receiver and any trustee.

10.142(8) [Copies of order] If the court makes an order suspending the bankrupt's discharge, copies of the order must be delivered by the court to the official receiver, any trustee and the bankrupt.

10.142(9) [Heading and content of order] An order of suspension of discharge under section 279(3) must be headed "Suspension of Discharge" and must contain–

(a) identification details for the proceedings;

(b) the name and title of the judge making the order;

(c) identification and contact details for the applicant who will be the official receiver or the trustee;

(d) the date of the bankruptcy order;

(e) a statement that it appears to the court that the bankrupt has failed or is failing to comply with the bankrupt's obligations under the Act for the reasons specified in the order;

(f) a statement in what respect the bankrupt has failed to comply with the bankrupt's obligations under the Act;

(g) an order that the relevant period for the purpose of section 279 will cease to run for either–

(i) a specified period, or

(ii) until specified conditions have been fulfilled;

(h) the period or conditions referred to in paragraph (g); and

(i) the date of the order.

(See General Note after r.10.143.)

10.143 Lifting of suspension of discharge

10.143(1) [Bankrupt may apply for suspension order to be discharged] Where the court has made an order under section 279(3) that the period specified in section 279(1) will cease to run, the bankrupt may apply to it for the order to be discharged.

10.143(2) [Court to fix venue for hearing] The court must fix a venue for the hearing of the application and deliver notice of it to the bankrupt.

10.143(3) [Notice of venue etc. to official receiver and trustee] The bankrupt must, not less than 28 days before the date fixed for the hearing, deliver notice of the venue with a copy of the application to the official receiver and any trustee.

10.143(4) [Appearances] The official receiver and the trustee may appear and be heard on the bankrupt's application.

10.143(5) [Official receiver and trustee may file report of evidence in support] Whether or not they appear, the official receiver and trustee may file with the court a report containing evidence in support of any matters which either of them considers ought to be drawn to the court's attention.

10.143(6) [Official receiver or trustee report on condition in order] If the court made an order under section 279(3)(b), the court may request a report from the official receiver or the trustee as to whether or not the condition specified in the order has been fulfilled.

10.143(7) [Copies of report] Copies of a report filed under paragraph (5) or requested by the court under paragraph (6) must be delivered by the official receiver or trustee to the bankrupt and to either the official receiver or trustee (depending on which has filed the report), not later than 14 days before the hearing.

10.143(8) [Where bankrupt intends to deny or dispute statements in report] The bankrupt may, not later than five business days before the date of the hearing, file with the court a notice specifying any statements in the official receiver's or trustee's report which the bankrupt intends to deny or dispute.

10.143(9) [Copies of notice to official receiver and trustee] If the bankrupt files such a notice, the bankrupt must deliver copies of it to the official receiver and the trustee not less than three business days before the date of the hearing.

10.143(10) [If court discharges order] If on the bankrupt's application the court discharges the order under section 279(3) (being satisfied that the period specified in section 279(1) should begin to run again), it must deliver to the bankrupt a certificate that it has done so, and must deliver copies of the certificate to the official receiver and the trustee (if different).

10.143(11) [Content of order] The court's order lifting the suspension of discharge must contain–

(a) identification details for the proceedings;

(b) the name and title of the judge making the order;

(c) the date and terms of the order made under section 279;

(d) a statement that the bankrupt specified in the order has made the application;

(e) a statement whether or not the court has taken into consideration the report of the official receiver or of the trustee or both in this matter;

(f) an order discharging the order suspending discharge; and

(g) state the date of the order.

10.143(12) [Content of certificate that order has been lifted] The certificate that the order suspending discharge has been lifted must contain–

(a) identification details for the proceedings;

(b) the date of the bankruptcy order;

(c) the date of the order suspending discharge;

(d) a statement that the court has made–

   (i) the bankruptcy order specified in this order against the bankrupt specified in this order, and

   (ii) the order suspending the bankrupt's discharge specified in this order;

(e) a statement that it is certified that the order of suspension of discharge was lifted on the date specified in this order; and

(f) the date of the certificate.

General note to rr.10.142–10.143

The reference to "report" in r.10.142(4) is unclear. The possibility of a bankrupt using this provision to seek a discharge from bankruptcy where discharge had been suspended was flagged up by Rose J in *Mawer v Bland* [2013] EWHC 3122 (Ch). It deals with the scenario where discharge has been suspended and the bankrupt seeks to have that suspension lifted. See also *Wilson v Williams* [2015] EWHC 1841 (Ch); [2015] B.P.I.R. 1319. For discussion see Patterson [2016] 29 Insolv. Int. 22. For the meaning of "venue" in r.10.142(3) see r.1.2. On alternative avenues open to the bankrupt see *Holmes v Official Receiver (Re a Debtor (No.26 of 1991))* [1996] B.C.C. 246.

R.10.142
Insolvency practitioners have been reminded of their obligations under the former IR 1986 r.6.215(5) (now IR 2016 r.10.142(5))—see *Dear IP*, December 2007. On the need for timely suspension applications see *Chadwick v Nash* [2012] B.P.I.R. 70. See also *Hafiz v Ingram* [2012] EWHC 274 (Ch); [2012] B.P.I.R. 1116 where the requirements for strict procedural compliance were once again reinforced. At the end of the day Roth J felt justified in making an interim order suspending discharge pending the hearing of the application for a suspension. The equivalent provision in Northern Ireland was examined in *OR v McWilliams* [2012] NICh 28.

10.144 Certificate of discharge from bankruptcy order made otherwise than on a bankruptcy application

10.144(1) [Application to court] A bankrupt may apply to the court for a certificate of discharge where the bankruptcy order was made otherwise than on a bankruptcy application.

10.144(2) [Court to deliver certificate of discharge to former bankrupt] Where it appears to the court that the bankrupt is discharged, whether by expiration of time or otherwise, the court must deliver a certificate of discharge to the former bankrupt.

10.144(3) [Heading and content of order] The certificate of discharge must be headed "Certificate of Discharge" and must contain–

(a) identification details for the proceedings;

(b) the date of the bankruptcy order;

(c) the statement that the former bankrupt was discharged from bankruptcy;

(d) the date of discharge from bankruptcy; and

(e) the date of the certificate.

10.144(4) [Certificate also to state] The certificate must also state–

(a) that the former bankrupt may request in writing notice of the discharge to be gazetted and advertised in the same manner as the bankruptcy order; and

(b) that such a request must be delivered to the official receiver within 28 days of the making of the certificate of discharge.

10.144(5) [Notice of discharge to be gazetted and advertised] As soon as reasonably practicable after delivery of such a request to the official receiver the notice of discharge must be gazetted, and advertised in the same manner as the bankruptcy order.

10.144(6) [Content of notice] The notice must contain–

(a) the name of the former bankrupt;

(b) the date of the bankruptcy order;

(c) the statement that a certificate of discharge has been delivered to the former bankrupt;

(d) the date of the certificate; and

(e) the date from which the discharge is effective.

10.144(7) [Application etc. by former bankrupt's personal representative, etc.] An application for a notice of discharge and a request in writing that the notice be gazetted and advertised may be made by the former bankrupt's personal representative or, as the case may be, a person appointed by the court to represent or act for the former bankrupt where the former bankrupt–

(a) has died; or

(b) is a person lacking capacity to manage the person's own affairs (within the meaning of the Mental Capacity Act 2005).

(See General Note after r.10.147.)

10.145 Certificate of discharge from bankruptcy order made on a bankruptcy application

10.145(1) [Application to official receiver] A bankrupt may apply to the official receiver for a certificate of discharge where the bankruptcy order was made on a bankruptcy application.

10.145(2) [Prescribed fee] The bankrupt must send the application to the official receiver with the prescribed fee.

10.145(3) [Delivery of certificate of discharge to former bankrupt by electronic means] Where it appears to the official receiver that the bankrupt is discharged, the official receiver must deliver a certificate of discharge to the former bankrupt by electronic means.

10.145(4) [Heading and content of certificate] The certificate of discharge must be headed "Certificate of Discharge" and must contain–

(a) identification details for the former bankrupt;

(b) the date of the bankruptcy order;

(c) a statement that the former bankrupt was discharged from bankruptcy;

(d) the date of discharge from the bankruptcy; and

(e) the date of the certificate.

10.145(5) [Certificate also to state] The certificate must also state–

(a) that the former bankrupt may request in writing notice of the discharge to be gazetted and advertised in the same manner as the bankruptcy order; and

(b) that such a request must be delivered to the official receiver within 28 days of the making of the certificate of discharge.

10.145(6) [Notice of discharge to be gazetted and advertised] As soon as reasonably practicable after delivery of such a request to the official receiver the notice of discharge must be gazetted, and advertised in the same manner as the bankruptcy order.

10.145(7) [Content of notice] The notice must contain–

(a) the name of the former bankrupt;

(b) the date of the bankruptcy order;

(c) the statement that a certificate of discharge has been delivered to the former bankrupt;

(d) the date of the certificate; and

(e) the date from which the discharge is effective.

10.145(8) [Application etc. by former bankrupt's personal representative, etc.] An application for a notice of discharge and a request in writing that the notice be gazetted and advertised may be made by the former bankrupt's personal representative or, as the case may be, a person appointed by the court to represent or act for the former bankrupt where the former bankrupt–

(a) has died; or

(b) is a person lacking capacity to manage the person's own affairs (within the meaning of the Mental Capacity Act 2005).

(See General Note after r.10.147.)

10.146 Bankrupt's debts surviving discharge

[Note: see also section 281 (effect of discharge).]

10.146 Discharge does not release the bankrupt from any obligation arising–

(a) under a confiscation order made under section 1 of the Drug Trafficking Offences Act 1986;

(b) under a confiscation order made under section 1 of the Criminal Justice (Scotland) Act 1987;

(c) under a confiscation order made under section 71 of the Criminal Justice Act 1988;

(d) under a confiscation order made under Parts 2, 3 or 4 of the Proceeds of Crime Act 2002; or

(e) from a payment out of the social fund under section 138(1)(b) of the Social Security Contributions and Benefits Act 1992 by way of crisis loan or budgeting loan.

(See General Note after r.10.147.)

10.147 Costs under this Chapter

10.147 In no case do any costs or expenses arising under this Chapter fall on the official receiver personally.

GENERAL NOTE TO RR.10.144–10.147

These rules provide additional information on the effect of IA 1986 ss.279–281. Applications for suspension of automatic discharge under s.279(3) are explained. Suspension orders can be varied by the court. Rules 10.160 and 10.161 are specially referable to applications by the bankrupt to the court for discharge under IA 1986 s.280. The official receiver must be notified and he must file a report on the bankrupt's conduct. Rule 10.146 is a specialised provision dealing with the enforcement of sanctions against drug dealers, etc.: compare s.281(4).

CHAPTER 18

PRIORITY OF PAYMENT OF COSTS ETC. OUT OF THE BANKRUPT'S ESTATE

[Note: a document required by the Act or these Rules must also contain the standard contents set out in Part 1.]

10.148 Expenses

10.148 All fees, costs, charges and other expenses incurred in the course of the bankruptcy are to be treated as expenses of the bankruptcy.

GENERAL NOTE

Instalments of rates on non-domestic property which fell due for payment after the liquidation date were held to be liquidation expenses in *Re Nolton Business Centres Ltd* [1996] B.C.C. 500, even though the local authority had fixed the rates prior to that date. Amendments were made by I(A)R 2003 (SI 2003/1730) to reflect the more expanded role of administration as a distributional regime and the coming into operation of the reserved fund for unsecured creditors (see IA 1986 s.176A). Costs incurred with regard to the latter come exclusively out of that fund. For the meaning of "costs" in r.10.148 see HHJ Purle QC in *Re International Sections Ltd* [2009] B.P.I.R. 297 at [16].

10.149 General rule as to priority

10.149 The expenses of the bankruptcy are payable out of the bankrupt's estate in the following order of priority–

(a) expenses or costs which–

   (i) are properly chargeable or incurred by the official receiver or the trustee in preserving, realising or getting in any of the assets of the bankrupt or otherwise relating to the conduct of any legal proceedings which the official receiver or the trustee has power to bring (whether the claim on which the proceedings are based forms part of the bankrupt's estate or otherwise) or defend,

   (ii) relate to the employment of a shorthand writer, if appointed by an order of the court made at the instance of the official receiver in connection with an examination, or

   (iii) are incurred in holding an examination under rule 10.102 (examinee unfit) where the application was made by the official receiver;

(b) any other expenses incurred or disbursements made by the official receiver or under the official receiver's authority, including those incurred or made in carrying on the business of a debtor or bankrupt;

(c) the fees payable under any order made under section 415 or 415A, including those payable to the official receiver (other than the fee referred to in sub-paragraph (d)), and any remuneration payable to the official receiver under general regulations;

(d) the fee payable under any order made under section 415 for the performance by the official receiver of the general duties of the official receiver and any repayable sum deposited under any such order as security for the fee;

(e) [Omitted]

(f) the cost of any security provided by an interim receiver, trustee or special manager in accordance with the Act or these Rules;

(g) the remuneration of the interim receiver (if any);

(h) any sum deposited on an application for the appointment of an interim receiver;

(i) the costs of the petitioner, and of any person appearing on the petition whose costs are allowed by the court;

(j) the remuneration of the special manager (if any);

(k) any amount payable to a person or firm employed or authorised, under rules 10.59, 10.60 or 10.64, to assist in the preparation of a statement of affairs or of accounts;

(l) any allowance made, by order of the court, in respect of costs on an application for release from the obligation to submit a statement of affairs, or for an extension of time for submitting such a statement;

(m) the costs of employing a shorthand writer in any case other than one appointed by an order of the court at the instance of the official receiver in connection with an examination;

(n) any necessary disbursements by the trustee in the course of the trustee's administration (including any costs referred to in Article 30 of the EU Regulation and expenses incurred by members of the creditors' committee or their representatives and allowed by the trustee under rule 17.24, but not including any payment of capital gains tax in circumstances referred to in sub-paragraph (q));

(o) the remuneration or emoluments of any person (including the bankrupt) who has been employed by the trustee to perform any services for the bankrupt's estate, as required or authorised by or under the Act or these Rules;

(p) the remuneration of the trustee, up to any amount not exceeding that which is payable under Schedule 11;

(q) the amount of any capital gains tax on chargeable gains accruing on the realisation of any asset of the bankrupt (irrespective of the person by whom the realisation is effected);

(r) the balance, after payment of any sums due under sub-paragraph (p), of any remuneration due to the trustee; and

(s) any other expenses properly chargeable by the trustee in carrying out the trustee's functions in the bankruptcy.

General Note

This is the normal priority regime though it is described in great detail here. Link this list with IA 1986 s.328. For "general regulations" see r.1.2.

The potential application of r.10.149(1)(a) to the possibility of a trustee's personal liability in costs was considered by Etherton LJ in the Court of Appeal in *Nutting v Khaliq* [2012] EWCA Civ 1726; [2013] B.P.I.R. 340 at [32].

Rule 10.149(n) amended by the Insolvency Amendment (EU 2015/848) Regulations 2017 (SI 2017/702) regs 1, 2(1), Sch. paras 32, 43 in relation to proceedings opened on or after 26 June 2017 (see reg.3) when the Recast EU Regulation 2015/848 came into force.

Rule 10.149(d) substituted and para.(e) omitted by the Insolvency (England and Wales) and Insolvency (Scotland) (Miscellaneous and Consequential Amendments) Rules 2017 (SI 2017/1115) rr.1(1), (2), 2, 9 as from 8 December 2017.

Chapter 19

Second bankruptcy

[Note: a document required by the Act or these Rules must also contain the standard contents set out in Part 1.]

10.150 Scope of this Chapter

[Note: "the earlier bankruptcy", "the existing trustee" and "the later bankruptcy" are defined in section 334(1).]

10.150 The rules in this Chapter relate to the manner in which, in the case of a second bankruptcy, the existing trustee is to deal with property and money to which section 334(3) applies until there is a trustee of the bankrupt's estate in the later bankruptcy.

(See General Note after r.10.153.)

10.151 General duty of existing trustee

10.151(1) [Official receiver's duty to get in property, money] The existing trustee must take into custody or under control the property and money to which section 334(3) applies so far as this has not already been done in the earlier bankruptcy.

10.151(2) [Power to sell perishable goods, etc.] Where any of that property consists of perishable goods, or goods the value of which is likely to diminish if they are not disposed of, the existing trustee has power to sell or otherwise dispose of those goods.

10.151(3) [Proceeds of sale] The proceeds of such a sale or disposal must be held, under the existing trustee's control, with the other property and money comprised in the bankrupt's estate.

(See General Note after r.10.153.)

10.152 Delivery up to later trustee

10.152 The existing trustee must, if requested by the later trustee for the purposes of the later bankruptcy, deliver to the later trustee as soon as reasonably practicable all the property and money in the existing trustee's custody or under the existing trustee's control under rule 10.151.

(See General Note after r.10.153.)

10.153 Existing trustee's expenses

10.153 Any expenses incurred by the existing trustee in compliance with section 335(1) and this Chapter must be paid out of, and are a charge on, all of the property and money referred to in section 334(3), whether in the hands of the existing trustee or of the later trustee for the purposes of the later bankruptcy.

General Note to rr.10.150–10.153

These rules supplement IA 1986 s.334 and deal with the complex relationship between the two successive bankruptcy regimes.

CHAPTER 20

CRIMINAL BANKRUPTCY

Introductory note to Chapter 20
There may be an issue of defective drafting in the original version of the 2016 Rules—The Parliamentary Joint Committee of Statutory Instruments (Sixteenth Report of Session 2016/17) HL Paper 80, HC 93-xvi) has indicated that should there have been an application provision at the start of this Chapter—see para.1.14. See now r.10.153A.

[Note: a document required by the Act or these Rules must also contain the standard contents set out in Part 1.]

10.153A Application

10.153A The rules in this chapter apply to proceedings arising out of criminal bankruptcy orders.

10.154 Contents of petition

10.154 The petition must contain–

(a) identification details for the debtor;

(b) the name and postal address of the petitioner if other than the Official Petitioner;

(c) the occupation (if any) of the debtor;

(d) any other address at which the debtor has resided at or after the time the petition debt was incurred;

(e) any other name by which the debtor is or has been known;

(f) the trading name, business address and nature of the business of any business carried on by the debtor;

(g) details of any other businesses which have been carried on by the debtor at or after the time the petition debt was incurred;

(h) a statement that the petitioner requests that court make a bankruptcy order against the debtor;

(i) a statement that a criminal bankruptcy order was made against the debtor at the court specified in this petition and that an office copy of the order accompanies the petition;

(j) the name of the court that made the criminal bankruptcy order;

(k) a statement that the criminal bankruptcy order–

  (i) remains in force, or

  (ii) was amended by the Court of Appeal on the date specified in this petition, that an office copy of the order of the Court of Appeal accompanies the petition and that the order as amended by the Court of Appeal remains in force;

(l) a statement that according to the criminal bankruptcy order the debtor is indebted to the persons specified in this petition as having suffered loss or damage in the aggregate sum of the amount of loss or damage suffered specified in this petition;

(m) the names and addresses of the persons referred to in paragraph (k); and

(n) the amount of loss or damage suffered referred to in paragraph (k).

(See General Note after r.10.163.)

10.155 Status and functions of Official Petitioner

10.155(1) [Treatment as creditor] The Official Petitioner is to be treated for all purposes of the Act and these Rules as a creditor of the bankrupt.

10.155(2) [Power to attend meetings, etc.] The Official Petitioner may attend or be represented at any meeting of creditors, and is to be given any notice under the Act or these Rules which is required or authorised to be delivered to creditors; and the requirements of these Rules as to the delivery and use of proxies do not apply to the Official Petitioner.

(See General Note after r.10.163.)

10.156 Interim receivership

10.156 The rules in Chapter 4 of this Part about the appointment of an interim receiver apply in criminal bankruptcy only in so far as they provide for the appointment of the official receiver as interim receiver.

(See General Note after r.10.163.)

10.157 Proof of bankruptcy debts and notice of order

10.157(1) [Effect of bankruptcy order] The making of a bankruptcy order on a criminal bankruptcy petition does not affect the right of creditors to prove for their debts arising otherwise than in consequence of the criminal proceedings.

10.157(2) [Person suffering loss, etc.] A person specified in a criminal bankruptcy order as having suffered loss or damage must be treated as a creditor of the bankrupt; and a copy of the order is sufficient evidence of that person's claim, subject to its being shown by any party to the bankruptcy proceedings that the loss or damage actually suffered was more or (as the case may be) less than the amount specified in the order.

10.157(3) [Non-application of rules on proofs] The requirements of these Rules about proofs do not apply to the Official Petitioner.

10.157(4) [Notice of order, blank proofs to creditors] In criminal bankruptcy, notice of the making of the bankruptcy order and blank proofs must be delivered by the official receiver to every creditor who is known to the official receiver within 12 weeks from the making of the bankruptcy order.

(See General Note after r.10.163.)

10.158 Rules not applying in criminal bankruptcy

10.158 The following rules do not apply in criminal bankruptcy–

(a) [Omitted]

(b) Chapter 6 of this Part, except rules 10.86 (release of official receiver) and 10.91 (power of court to set aside transactions);

(c) rule 15.21(a) and (b) (chair at meetings); and

(d) Part 17 (creditors' and liquidation committees).

(See General Note after r.10.163.)

10.159 Annulment of criminal bankruptcy order

10.159 Chapter 16 of this Part (annulment of bankruptcy order) applies to an application to the court under section 282(2) as it applies to an application under section 282(1), with any necessary modifications.

(See General Note after r.10.163.)

10.160 Application by bankrupt for discharge

10.160(1) If bankrupt makes IA 1986 s.280 application A bankrupt who applies under section 280 for an order of discharge must deliver notice of the application to the official receiver, and deposit with the official receiver such sum as the official receiver may require for the purpose of covering the costs of the application.

10.160(2) [Court to fix venue, give notice] The court, if satisfied that the bankrupt has complied with paragraph (1), must fix a venue for the hearing of the application, and give at least 42 days' notice of it to the official receiver and the bankrupt.

10.160(3) Notice by official receiver The official receiver must deliver notice of the application and venue to–

(a) the trustee; and

(b) every creditor who, to the official receiver's knowledge, has a claim outstanding against the bankrupt's estate which has not been satisfied.

10.160(4) [Time limit for notices] These notices must be delivered not later than 14 days before the date fixed for the hearing of the bankrupt's application.

(See General Note after r.10.163.)

10.161 Report of official receiver

10.161(1) [Content of report filed in court] Where the bankrupt makes an application under section 280, the official receiver must, at least 21 days before the date fixed for the hearing of the application, file with the court a report containing–

(a) particulars of any failure by the bankrupt to comply with the bankrupt's obligations under Parts 8 to 11 of the Act;

(b) the circumstances surrounding the present bankruptcy, and those surrounding any previous bankruptcy of the bankrupt;

(c) the extent to which, in the present and in any previous bankruptcy, the bankrupt's liabilities have exceeded the bankrupt's assets; and

(d) particulars of any distribution which has been, or is expected to be, made to creditors in the present bankruptcy or, if such is the case, that there has been and is to be no distribution; and

(e) any other matters which in the official receiver's opinion ought to be brought to the court's attention.

10.161(2) [Copy report to bankrupt and trustee] The official receiver must deliver a copy of the report to the bankrupt and the trustee, so as to reach them at least 14 days before the date of the hearing of the application under section 280.

10.161(3) [Bankrupt notice in court denying/disputing statements in report] The bankrupt may, not later than five business days before the date of the hearing, file with the court a notice specifying any statements in the official receiver's report which the bankrupt intends to deny or dispute.

10.161(4) [Authentication of notice] Such a notice must be authenticated and dated by the bankrupt and must contain the bankrupt's name and postal address.

10.161(5) [Copies to trustee and official receiver] The bankrupt must deliver copies of such a notice to the official receiver and the trustee not less than three business days before the date of the hearing.

10.161(6) [Appearances at hearing] The official receiver, the trustee and any creditor may appear on the hearing of the bankrupt's application, and may make representations and put to the bankrupt such questions as the court allows.

(See General Note after r.10.163.)

10.162 Order of discharge

10.162(1) [Content of order] An order of the court under section 280(2)(b) (discharge absolutely) or (c) (discharge subject to conditions relating to income or property) must contain–

(a) the name of the court;

(b) identification details for the bankrupt;

(c) the date of the bankruptcy order;

(d) the date of the report of the official receiver in the matter;

(e) the statement that the court has taken into consideration the report of the official receiver specified in the order as to the bankrupt's conduct and affairs, including the bankrupt's conduct during the bankruptcy;

(f) an order–

  (i) that the bankrupt be discharged absolutely, or

  (ii) that the bankrupt be discharged but that the bankrupt's discharge be suspended until the conditions specified in the order are fulfilled;

(g) the date on which the order is made;

(h) the date on which the order takes effect; and

(i) any conditions required to be fulfilled for discharge.

10.162(2) [Copy order to bankrupt, trustee, official receiver] Copies of any order made on an application by the bankrupt for discharge under section 280 must be delivered by the court to the bankrupt, the trustee and the official receiver.

10.162(3) [Notice re gazetting, advertisement] The order must contain a notice to the bankrupt stating that should the bankrupt require notice of the order to be gazetted and to be advertised in the same manner as the bankruptcy order was advertised, then the bankrupt must within 28 days deliver a notice of that requirement to the official receiver

(See General Note after r.10.163.)

10.163 Deferment of issue of order pending appeal

10.163 An order made by the court on an application by the bankrupt for discharge under section 280 must not be drawn up or gazetted until the time allowed for appealing has expired or, if an appeal is entered, until the appeal has been determined.

General Note to rr.10.154–10.163

The criminal bankruptcy regime (see IA 1986 s.277) sits uneasily alongside the other facets of bankruptcy law. Further details of its operation are hereby provided. The role of the official petitioner (see IA 1986 s.402) is described. Proof of debts, meetings or creditors, etc. are also regulated by these rules.

R.10.154
This new rule for IR 2016 sets out the detail previously contained in prescribed Form 6.79 to the IR 1986.

R.10.158
Again there may be an issue of defective drafting—see Joint Parliamentary Committee on Statutory Instruments, Sixteenth Report of Session 2016/17, HL Paper 80, HC 93-xvi at para.1.15.

10.164 Costs under this Chapter

10.164 In no case do any costs or expenses arising under this Chapter fall on the official receiver personally.

Chapter 21

Miscellaneous rules in bankruptcy

[Note: a document required by the Act or these Rules must also contain the standard contents set out in Part 1.]

10.165 Amendment of title of proceedings

10.165(1) [Power of official receiver to amend] At any time after the making of a bankruptcy order, the official receiver may amend the title of the proceedings.

10.165(2) [Duty of official receiver; application to Chief Land Registrar] An official receiver who amends the title of proceedings must as soon as reasonably practicable–

(a) where the bankruptcy is on the petition of a creditor, file a notice of the amendment with the court;

(b) where the bankruptcy is on the application of a debtor, file a notice of the amendment on the bankruptcy file; and

(c) make an application to the Chief Land Registrar to amend the register of writs and orders.

10.165(3) [Gazetting and advertisement of amendment] If the official receiver thinks fit to gazette the amendment then it must be gazetted as soon as reasonably practicable, and may be advertised in such other manner as the official receiver thinks fit.

10.165(4) [Content of notice] The notice must–

(a) state that the title of the proceedings has been amended; and

(b) specify the amendment.

General Note

For comment on the former IR 1986 r.6.35(1) (now IR 2016 r.10.165) in an unusual case see *Michael Yee Fun Chu v Price* [2003] EWCA Civ 1744; [2004] B.P.I.R. 603.

10.166 Application for redirection order

10.166(1) [Application of rule] This rule applies where the official receiver or trustee other than the official receiver makes an application to the court under section 371(1) (re-direction of bankrupt's letters etc.).

10.166(2) [Application without notice] The application must be made without notice to the bankrupt or any other person, unless the court directs otherwise.

10.166(3) [Official receiver applicant] Where the applicant is the official receiver the applicant must file with the court with the application a report setting out the reasons why the order is sought.

10.166(4) [Trustee in bankruptcy applicant] Where the applicant is the trustee the applicant must file with the court a witness statement setting out the reasons why the order is sought.

10.166(5) [Court to fix venue, notice] The court must fix a venue for the hearing of the application if the court thinks just and deliver notice to the applicant.

10.166(6) [Power of court to make any order] The court may make an order on such conditions as it thinks just.

10.166(7) [Service of order] The order must identify the person on whom it is to be served, and need not be served on the bankrupt unless the court so directs.

General Note

Former IR 1986 r.6.235A (now IR 2016 r.10.166) was inserted by I(A)R 2005 (SI 2005/527) in order to clarify procedures on redirection orders under s.371.

10.167 Bankrupt's home: property falling within section 283A

10.167(1) [Notice by trustee where IA 1986 s.283A applies] Where it appears to a trustee that section 283A(1) applies, the trustee must deliver notice as soon as reasonably practicable to–

(a) the bankrupt;

(b) the bankrupt's spouse or civil partner (in a case falling within section 283A(1)(b)); and

(c) the former spouse or former civil partner of the bankrupt (in a case falling within section 283A(1)(c)).

10.167(2) [Content of notice] Such a notice must contain–

(a) the name of the bankrupt;

(b) the address of the dwelling-house;

(c) if the dwelling-house is registered land, the title number; and

(d) the date by which the trustee must have delivered the notice.

10.167(3) [Time limit for delivery of notice] A trustee must not deliver such a notice any later than 14 days before the third anniversary of the bankruptcy order or, 14 days before the third anniversary of when the official receiver or trustee became aware of the property.

10.168 Application in relation to the vesting of an interest in a dwelling-house (registered land)

10.168(1) [Application of rule] This rule applies where–

(a) the bankrupt's estate includes an interest in a dwelling-house which at the date of bankruptcy was the sole or principal residence of–

  (i) the bankrupt,

  (ii) the bankrupt's spouse or civil partner, or

  (iii) a former spouse or former civil partner of the bankrupt; and

(b) the dwelling-house is registered land; and

(c) an entry has been made relating to the bankruptcy in the individual register of the dwelling-house or the register has been altered to reflect the vesting of the bankrupt's interest in a trustee in bankruptcy.

10.168(2) [Interest vests back in bankrupt] Where such an interest ceases to be comprised in the bankrupt's estate and vests in the bankrupt under either section 283A(2) or 283A(4) of the Act, or under section 261(8) of the Enterprise Act 2002, the trustee must, within five business days of the vesting, make such application to the Chief Land Registrar as is necessary to show in the individual register of the dwelling-house that the interest has vested in the bankrupt.

10.168(3) [Trustee's application in accordance with the Land Registration Act 2002, etc.] The trustee's application must be made in accordance with the Land Registration Act 2002 and must be accompanied by–

(a) evidence of the trustee's appointment (where not previously provided to the Chief Land Registrar); and

(b) a certificate from the trustee stating that the interest has vested in the bankrupt under section 283A(2) or 283A(4) of the Act or section 261(8) of the Enterprise Act 2002 (whichever is appropriate).

10.168(4) [Notice of application to bankrupt, etc.] As soon as reasonably practicable after making such an application, the trustee must deliver notice of the application–

(a) to the bankrupt; and

(b) to the bankrupt's spouse, former spouse, civil partner or former civil partner if the dwelling-house was the sole or principal residence of that person.

10.168(5) [Notice to others] The trustee must deliver notice of the application to every person who (to the trustee's knowledge) claims an interest in, or is under any liability in relation to, the dwelling-house.

General Note

This deals with applications in respect of the vesting of an interest in a dwelling-house where the land is registered.

10.169 Vesting of bankrupt's interest (unregistered land)

10.169(1) [Certificate as to vesting] Where an interest in a dwelling-house which at the date of the bankruptcy was the sole or principal residence of–

(a) the bankrupt;

(b) the bankrupt's spouse or civil partner; or

(c) a former spouse or former civil partner of the bankrupt;

ceases to be comprised in the bankrupt's estate and vests in the bankrupt under either section 283A(2) or 283A(4) of the Act or section 261(8) of the Enterprise Act 2002 and the dwelling-house is unregistered land, the trustee must as soon as reasonably practicable deliver to the bankrupt a certificate as to the vesting.

10.169(2) [Certificate conclusive proof of interest] Such a certificate is conclusive proof that the interest mentioned in paragraph (1) has vested in the bankrupt.

10.169(3) [Copy certificate to bankrupt, etc.] As soon as reasonably practicable after delivering the certificate, the trustee must deliver a copy of the certificate to the bankrupt's spouse, former spouse, civil partner or former civil partner if the dwelling-house was the sole or principal residence of that person.

10.169(4) [Copy certificate to others] The trustee must deliver a copy of the certificate to every person who (to the trustee's knowledge) claims an interest in, or is under any liability relating to, the dwelling-house.

General Note

This covers the same matters as r.10.168 but the land here is unregistered.

10.170 Vesting of bankrupt's estate: substituted period

[Note: section 283A(6)(b) gives the court the power to impose a longer period than the three years mentioned in section 283A(2) in such circumstances as the court thinks appropriate.]

10.170(1) [Substituted period for IA 1986 s.283A(2)] For the purposes of section 283A(2) the period of one month is substituted for the period of three years set out in that section where the trustee has delivered notice to the bankrupt that the trustee considers–

(a) the continued vesting of the property in the bankrupt's estate to be of no benefit to creditors; or

(b) the re-vesting to the bankrupt will make dealing with the bankrupt's estate more efficient.

10.170(2) [Commencement of one-month period] The one month period starts from the date of the notice.

General Note

This rule was inserted by the former I(A)R 2004 (SI 2004/584) with effect from 1 April 2004. It provides further fine tuning for this new regime in dealing with the family home.

10.171 Charging order

10.171(1) [Application of rule] This rule applies where the trustee applies to the court under section 313 for an order imposing a charge on property consisting of an interest in a dwelling-house.

10.171(2) [Respondents to application]The respondents to the application must be–

(a) any spouse or former spouse or civil partner or former civil partner of the bankrupt having or claiming to have an interest in the property;

(b) any other person appearing to have an interest in the property; and

(c) such other persons as the court may direct.

10.171(3) [Trustee's report to court] The trustee must make a report to the court, containing the following particulars–

(a) the extent of the bankrupt's interest in the property;

(b) the amount which, at the date of the application, remains owing to unsecured creditors of the bankrupt; and

(c) an estimate of the cost of realising the interest.

10.171(4) [Terms of charge] The terms of the charge to be imposed must be agreed between the trustee and the bankrupt or in the absence of an agreement must be settled by the court.

10.171(5) [Rate of interest] The rate of interest applicable under section 313(2) is the rate specified in section 17 of the Judgments Act 1838 on the day on which the charge is imposed, and the rate must be stated in the court's order imposing the charge.

10.171(6) [Content of court order] The court's order must also–

(a) describe the property to be charged;

(b) state whether the title to the property is registered and, if it is, specify the title number;

(c) set out the extent of the bankrupt's interest in the property which has vested in the trustee;

(d) indicate by reference to any, or the total, amount which is payable otherwise than to the bankrupt out of the bankrupt's estate and of interest on that amount, how the amount of the charge to be imposed is to be ascertained;

(e) set out the conditions (if any) imposed by the court under section 3(1) of the Charging Orders Act 1979; and

(f) identify the date any property charged under section 313 will cease to be comprised in the bankrupt's estate and will, subject to the charge (and any prior charge), vest in the bankrupt.

10.171(7) [Date in r.10.171(6)(f)] The date referred to in paragraph (6)(f) must be that of the registration of the charge in accordance with section 3(2) of the Charging Orders Act 1979 unless the court is of the opinion that a different date is appropriate.

10.171(8) [Application to Chief Land Registrar re LCA 1972/LRA 2002] Where the court order is capable of giving rise to an application under the Land Charges Act 1972 or the Land Registration Act 2002 the trustee must, as soon as reasonably practicable after the making of the court order or at the appropriate time, make the appropriate application to the Chief Land Registrar.

10.171(9) [Appropriate application] The appropriate application is–

(a) an application under section 6(1)(a) of the Land Charges Act 1972 (application for registration in the register of writs and orders affecting land); or

(b) an application under the Land Registration Act 2002 for an entry in the register in relation to the charge imposed by the order; and such application under that Act as is necessary to show in the individual register or registers of the dwelling-house that the interest has vested in the bankrupt.

10.171(10) [Determining value of bankrupt's interest in r.10.171(6)(c)] In determining the value of the bankrupt's interest for the purposes of paragraph (6)(c), the court must disregard that part of the value of the property in which the bankrupt's interest subsists which is equal to the value of–

(a) any loans secured by mortgage or other charge against the property;

(b) any other third party interest; and

(c) the reasonable costs of sale.

General Note

This deals with applications for charging orders pursuant to s.313. The IR 2016 rule incorporates the detail previously contained in prescribed Form 6.79A under the IR 1986.

Part 11

Bankruptcy and Debt Relief Restrictions Orders and Undertakings and the Insolvency Registers

Introductory note to Part 11
This is a new Part that combines together elements of Pts 6 and 6A of IR 1986.

Chapter 1

Interpretation

11.1 References to the Secretary of State

11.1 References to the Secretary of State in Chapters 2 and 3 include the official receiver acting on the direction of the Secretary of State in making an application for–

(a) a bankruptcy restrictions order or an interim bankruptcy restrictions order in accordance with paragraph 1(2)(b) or 5(3)(b) respectively of Schedule 4A; or

(b) a debt relief restrictions order or an interim debt relief restrictions order in accordance with paragraph 1(2)(b) or 5(3)(b) respectively of Schedule 4ZB.

General Note

This Chapter was originally inserted by I(A)R 2003 (SI 2003/1730) to support the legislation on bankruptcy restriction orders, which were an innovation in EA 2002. Rule 11.1 is a curiously located interpretation provision.

Chapter 2

Bankruptcy and debt relief restrictions orders (Schedules 4ZB and 4A)

[Note: a document required by the Act or these Rules must also contain the standard contents set out in Part 1.]

11.2 Application for a bankruptcy or debt relief restrictions order

11.2(1) [Application to be supported by report by Secretary of State] An application by the Secretary of State to the court for a bankruptcy restrictions order under paragraph 1 of Schedule 4A, or for a debt relief restrictions order under paragraph 1 of Schedule 4ZB, must be supported by a report by the Secretary of State.

11.2(2) [Content of report] The report must–

(a) set out the conduct which the Secretary of State thinks justifies making a bankruptcy restrictions order or a debt relief restrictions order; and

(b) contain the evidence on which the Secretary of State relies in support of the application.

11.2(3) [Evidence in support in witness statement] Any evidence in support of the application provided by a person other than the Secretary of State must be given in a witness statement.

11.2(4) [Date and venue for hearing] The date for the hearing must be at least eight weeks after the date when the court fixes the venue for the hearing.

General Note

This outlines the procedure where an application is made for a BRO.

11.3 Service of the application on the bankrupt or debtor

11.3(1) [Time limit] The Secretary of State must serve a notice of the application and the venue on the bankrupt or debtor not more than 14 days after the application is filed with the court.

11.3(2) [Documents to accompany notice] The notice must be accompanied by–

(a) a copy of the application;

(b) a copy of the Secretary of State's report;

(c) a copy of any other evidence filed in support of the application; and

(d) a document for completion as an acknowledgement of service.

11.3(3) [Acknowledgement of service] The bankrupt or debtor must file the acknowledgement of service, indicating whether or not the application is contested, not more than 14 days after service of the application.

11.3(4) [Failure to file acknowledgement] A bankrupt or debtor who fails to file an acknowledgement of service within that time may attend the hearing of the application but may not take part in the hearing unless the court gives permission.

General Note

Notice of the application must be served on the bankrupt within 14 days of the application being lodged.

11.4 The bankrupt's or debtor's evidence opposing an application

11.4(1) [Time limit etc.] A bankrupt or debtor who wishes to oppose the application must–

(a) file with the court any evidence for the court to take into consideration within 28 days of service of the application; and

(b) serve a copy of it on the Secretary of State within three business days of filing the evidence with the court.

11.4(2) [Time limit for Secretary of State filing evidence in reply, etc.] The Secretary of State must file with the court any evidence in reply within 14 days from receiving the copy of the bankrupt's or debtor's evidence, and must serve a copy of that evidence on the bankrupt or debtor as soon as reasonably practicable.

General Note

This outlines the responsibilities of the bankrupt if he wishes to oppose the application for a BRO.

11.5 Making a bankruptcy or debt relief restrictions order

11.5(1) [Power of court to make order] The court may make a bankruptcy restrictions order or a debt relief restrictions order whether or not the bankrupt or debtor appears or has filed evidence.

11.5(2) [Sealed copies to Secretary of State] Where the court makes such an order, it must deliver two sealed copies to the Secretary of State as soon as reasonably practicable.

11.5(3) [Sealed copy to bankrupt or debtor] As soon as reasonably practicable after receiving the sealed copies, the Secretary of State must deliver one of them to the bankrupt or debtor.

General Note

This deals with the making of the BRO and dissemination of the fact that it has been made.

Chapter 3

Interim bankruptcy and debt relief restrictions orders

[Note: a document required by the Act or these Rules must also contain the standard contents set out in Part 1.]

11.6 Application for an interim bankruptcy or debt relief restrictions order

11.6(1) [Application to be supported by report by Secretary of State] An application by the Secretary of State to the court for an interim bankruptcy restrictions order under paragraph 5 of Schedule 4A or an interim debt relief restrictions order under paragraph 5 of Schedule 4ZB, must be supported by a report by the Secretary of State.

11.6(2) [Content of report] The report must–

(a) set out the conduct which the Secretary of State thinks justifies making an interim bankruptcy restrictions order or an interim debt relief restrictions order; and

(b) contain the evidence on which the Secretary of State relies in support of the application including evidence of why it would be in the public interest to make such an order.

11.6(3) [Evidence in support in witness statement Any evidence in support of the application provided by a person other than the Secretary of State must be given in a witness statement.

11.6(4) [Time limit for notice of application] The Secretary of State must deliver a notice of the application to the bankrupt or debtor at least two business days before the date set for the hearing unless the court directs otherwise.

11.6(5) [Documents to accompany notice] The notice must be accompanied by–

(a) a copy of the application;

(b) a copy of the Secretary of State's report;

(c) a copy of any other evidence filed in support of the application; and

(d) a document for completion as an acknowledgement of service.

11.6(6) [Power of bankrupt or debtor to file evidence and appear] The bankrupt or debtor may file with the court evidence for the court to take into consideration and may appear at the hearing.

General Note

This Chapter was originally inserted by Insolvency (Amendment) Rules 2003 (SI 2003/1730) to regulate interim BROs granted in cases of urgency before a full BRO hearing can be held. Rule 11.6 explains the mode of application.

11.7 Making an interim bankruptcy or debt relief restrictions order

11.7(1) [Power of court to make order] The court may make an interim bankruptcy restrictions order or interim debt relief restrictions order whether or not the bankrupt or debtor appears or has filed evidence.

11.7(2) [Sealed copies to Secretary of State] Where the court makes such an order, it must deliver two sealed copies of the order to the Secretary of State as soon as reasonably practicable.

11.7(3) [Sealed copy to bankrupt or debtor] As soon as reasonably practicable after receiving the sealed copies, the Secretary of State must deliver one of them to the bankrupt or debtor.

General Note

This explains the approach of the court to an application made under r.11.6 and the consequences of any order being made.

11.8 Application to set aside an interim order

11.8(1) [Power of bankrupt or debtor to apply to court] A bankrupt subject to an interim bankruptcy restrictions order or a debtor subject to an interim debt relief restrictions order may apply to the court to set the order aside.

11.8(2) [Application supported by witness statement stating grounds] The application must be supported by a witness statement stating the grounds on which it is made.

11.8(3) [Notice etc. to Secretary of State] The bankrupt or debtor must deliver to the Secretary of State, not less than five business days before the hearing–

(a) a notice of the venue;

(b) a copy of the application; and

(c) a copy of the supporting witness statement.

11.8(4) [Power of Secretary of State to attend, etc.] The Secretary of State may attend the hearing and call the attention of the court to any matter which seems to be relevant, and may give evidence or call witnesses.

GENERAL NOTE

A bankrupt wishing to have the interim BRO set aside must follow this procedure.

11.9 Order setting aside an interim order

11.9(1) [Sealed copies to Secretary of State] Where the court sets aside an interim bankruptcy restrictions order or an interim debt relief restrictions order, it must deliver two sealed copies of the order to the Secretary of State as soon as reasonably practicable.

11.9(2) [Sealed copy to bankrupt or debtor] As soon as reasonably practicable after receiving the sealed copies, the Secretary of State must deliver one of them to the bankrupt or debtor.

CHAPTER 4

BANKRUPTCY RESTRICTIONS AND DEBT RELIEF RESTRICTIONS UNDERTAKINGS

[Note: a document required by the Act or these Rules must also contain the standard contents set out in Part 1.]

11.10 Acceptance of a bankruptcy restrictions or a debt relief restrictions undertaking

11.10(1) [BRU accepted when Secretary of State authenticates undertaking] A bankruptcy restrictions undertaking authenticated by the bankrupt is accepted by the Secretary of State for the purposes of paragraph 9 of Schedule 4A when the Secretary of State authenticates the undertaking.

11.10(2) [DRRU accepted when Secretary of State authenticates undertaking] A debt relief restrictions undertaking authenticated by a person in relation to whom a debt relief order has been made is accepted by the Secretary of State for the purposes of paragraph 9 of Schedule 4ZB when the Secretary of State authenticates the undertaking.

GENERAL NOTE

This Chapter was originally inserted by I(A)R 2003 (SI 2003/1730) to permit bankruptcy restrictions to be established consensually by an undertakings procedure. This procedure bears many of the features of the director disqualification undertakings regime, which was introduced by IA 2000. Rule 11.10 explains when a BRU is deemed to have been agreed.

11.11 Notification

11.11(1) [Delivery of copies] The Secretary of State must, as soon as reasonably practicable after accepting a bankruptcy restrictions undertaking or a debt relief restrictions undertaking, deliver copies to the person who offered the undertaking and to the official receiver.

11.11(2) [BRU filed in court or on bankruptcy file] In the case of a bankruptcy restrictions undertaking the Secretary of State must also file a copy with the court in the case of a creditor's bankruptcy petition or on the bankruptcy file in the case of a debtor's bankruptcy application.

GENERAL NOTE

The court and the OR must be told of any BRU.

11.12 Application to annul a bankruptcy restrictions or a debt relief restrictions undertaking

11.12(1) [Application supported by witness statement stating grounds] An application by a bankrupt or debtor to annul or vary an undertaking under paragraph 9(3)(a) or (b) of Schedule 4A or paragraph 9(3)(a) or (b) of Schedule 4ZB must be supported by a witness statement stating the grounds on which the application is made.

11.12(2) [Notice etc. to Secretary of State] The bankrupt or debtor must, at least 28 days before the date fixed for the hearing, deliver to the Secretary of State–

(a) a notice of the venue;

(b) a copy of the application; and

(c) a copy of the supporting witness statement.

11.12(3) [Power of Secretary of State to attend, etc.] The Secretary of State may attend the hearing and call the attention of the court to any matter which seems to be relevant, and may give evidence or call witnesses.

11.12(4) [Sealed copies to Secretary of State] Where the court annuls or varies a bankruptcy restrictions undertaking or debt relief restrictions undertaking, it must deliver two sealed copies of the order to the Secretary of State as soon as reasonably practicable.

11.12(5) [Sealed copy to bankrupt or debtor] As soon as reasonably practicable after receiving the sealed copies, the Secretary of State must deliver one of them to the bankrupt or debtor.

General Note

This explains how and when a BRU may be annulled.

Chapter 5

Insolvency Registers: General

Introductory note to Chapter 5

This chapter was originally inserted as Pt 6A into the Insolvency Rules 1986 through the Insolvency (Amendment) Rules 2003 (SI 2003/1730). It brings together previously scattered provisions in previous formulations of the rules and to enhance them in the light of the information that now needs to be lodged on public registers.

11.13 Maintenance of the registers and inspection

11.13(1) [Duty of Secretary of State re individual insolvency register] The Secretary of State must maintain the individual insolvency register of matters relating to bankruptcies, debt relief orders and IVAs in accordance with Chapter 6.

11.13(2) [Duty of Secretary of State re bankruptcy restrictions and debt relief restrictions registers] The Secretary of State must maintain the bankruptcy restrictions register and the debt relief restrictions register in accordance with Chapter 7.

11.13(3) [Registers open for electronic public search] The registers must be available to be searched electronically by members of the public at any time unless there is malfunction or error in the electronic operation of the registers.

11.13(4) [Times available for search] Any person may request the official receiver to make a search of the registers on any business day between 9am and 5pm.

11.13(5) [Amendment of register] An obligation under this Part to enter information on, or delete information from, a register, must be performed as soon as is reasonably practicable after it arises.

General Note

This explains the obligations of the Secretary of State with regard to the register of individual insolvencies. Changes were introduced by I(A)R 2009 (SI 2009/642) (in operation from 6 April 2009). These changes cater for the arrival of debt relief orders.

Note that Companies House now automatically checks the Individual Insolvency Register when receiving notices of appointment of new company directors and will issue a rejection letter if a name appears on that Register—see R3 Technical Bulletin 107.5

Chapter 6

Individual insolvency register

Introductory note to Chapter 6
This chapter was originally introduced by I(A)R 2009 (SI 2009/642), which took effect on 6 April 2009. It deals with entry on the register of information with regard to debt relief orders (IR 2016 r.11.18). The position on deletion is governed by IR 2016 r.11.19.

11.14 Entry of information on the individual insolvency register: IVAs

11.14(1) [Application of rule] This rule applies where–

(a) an IVA has been accepted by the debtor's creditors; and

(b) the Secretary of State receives any of the following–

(i) a report under rule 8.26 (report on approval of IVA), or

(ii) a notice under rules 8.27(5) (notice of revocation or suspension of IVA), 8.27(6) (notice of expiry of suspension) or 8.31 (notice that the IVA has been terminated or fully implemented).

11.14(2) [Details for Secretary of State to register] The Secretary of State must enter the following on the individual insolvency register–

(a) the debtor's identification details;

(b) the debtor's date of birth;

(c) the date on which the IVA was approved by the creditors;

(d) the debtor's gender;

(e) any name other than the name in which the debtor entered into IVA by which the debtor was or is known;

(f) a statement as to whether the IVA has been–

(i) completed in accordance with its terms,

(ii) terminated, or

(iii) revoked; and

(g) the name and address of the supervisor.

11.14(3) [Rule subject to orders under rr.20.2, 20.3] This rule is subject to any court order for the non-disclosure of the debtor's current address made under rule 20.2 (debtors at risk of violence: proposed IVA) or 20.3 (debtors at risk of violence: IVA).

11.15 Deletion of information from the individual insolvency register: IVAs

11.15 The Secretary of State must delete from the individual insolvency register all information concerning an IVA three months after receiving one of the following–

(a) a notice under rule 8.27(5) of the making of a revocation order in relation to the IVA; or

(b) a notice under rule 8.31(3) of the termination or full implementation of the IVA.

GENERAL NOTE

This covers deletion of entries with regard to IVAs.

11.16 Entry of information on to the individual insolvency register: bankruptcy orders

11.16(1) [Duty of official receiver] Where the official receiver receives a copy of a bankruptcy order from the court under rule 10.32, or from the adjudicator under rule 10.45, the official receiver must cause the following to be entered on the individual insolvency register–

(a) the matters listed in rules 10.8 or the information set out in Part 1 of Schedule 7, relating to the debtor as they are stated in the bankruptcy petition or bankruptcy application;

(b) the date of the bankruptcy order; and

(c) identification details for the proceedings.

11.16(2) [Official receiver to enter information] The official receiver must cause to be entered on to the individual insolvency register the following information–

(a) the bankrupt's identification details and date of birth;

(b) the bankrupt's gender and occupation (if any);

(c) the date of a previous bankruptcy order or debt relief order (if any) made against the bankrupt in the period of six years before the latest bankruptcy order (if there is more than one such previous order only the latest and excluding any bankruptcy order that was annulled or any debt relief order that was revoked);

(d) any name by which the bankrupt was known, not being the name in which the individual was made bankrupt;

(e) the address of any business carried on by the bankrupt and the name in which that business was carried on if carried on in a name other than the name in which the individual was made bankrupt;

(f) the name and address of any insolvency practitioner appointed to act as trustee in bankruptcy;

(g) the address at which the official receiver may be contacted;

(h) the automatic discharge date under section 279; and

(i) where a bankruptcy order is annulled or rescinded by the court, the fact that such an order has been made, the date on which it is made and (if different) the date on which it has effect.

11.16(3) [Duty of official receiver when discharge of bankrupt suspended] Where the official receiver receives a copy of an order under rule 10.104(6) or 10.142(8) suspending the bankrupt's discharge the official receiver must cause to be entered on to the individual insolvency register–

(a) the fact that such an order has been made; and

(b) the period for which the discharge has been suspended or that the relevant period has ceased to run until the fulfilment of conditions specified in the order.

11.16(4) [Duty of official receiver re certificate of discharge of IA 1986 s.279(3) order] Where the official receiver receives under rule 10.143(10) a copy of a certificate of the discharge of an order under section 279(3) the official receiver must cause the following to be entered on the individual insolvency register–

(a) that the court has discharged the order made under section 279(3); and

(b) the new date of discharge of the bankrupt.

11.16(5) [Amendment of register if s.279(3) discharge order rescinded] Where the order discharging the order under section 279(3) is subsequently rescinded by the court, the official receiver must cause the register to be amended accordingly.

11.16(6) [Duty re discharge from bankruptcy] Where a bankrupt is discharged from bankruptcy under section 279(1), the official receiver must cause the fact and date of such discharge to be entered in the individual insolvency register.

11.16(7) [Rule subject to orders under rr.20.5, 20.6] This rule is subject to any court order for the non-disclosure of the debtor's current address made under rule 20.5 (persons at risk of violence: bankruptcy application) or 20.6 (debtors at risk of violence: bankruptcy and debt relief proceedings).

General Note

Registration of bankruptcy details is described.

11.17 Deletion of information from the individual insolvency register: bankruptcy orders

11.17 The Secretary of State must delete from the individual insolvency register all information concerning a bankruptcy where–

(a) the bankruptcy order has been annulled under section 261(2)(a), 261(2)(b) or section 282(1)(b) and a period of three months has elapsed since a notice of the annulment was delivered to the official receiver;

(b) the bankrupt has been discharged from the bankruptcy and a period of three months has elapsed from the date of discharge;

(c) the bankruptcy order is annulled under section 282(1)(a) and 28 days have elapsed since a notice of the annulment was delivered to the official receiver under rule 10.137(3); or

(d) an order has been made by the court under section 375 rescinding the bankruptcy order and 28 days have elapsed since receipt by the official receiver.

General Note

Deletion of information on bankruptcies is dealt with here.

11.18 Entry of information on to the individual insolvency register: debt relief orders

11.18(1) [Duty of official receiver] The official receiver must cause to be entered on to the individual insolvency register after the making of a debt relief order the following information relating to the order or the debtor–

(a) as they are stated in the debtor's application–

(i) the debtor's identification details and date of birth,

(ii) the debtor's gender and occupation (if any),

(iii) the name or names in which the debtor has carried on business, if other than the debtor's true name, and

(iv) the nature of the debtor's business and the address or addresses at which the debtor carries or has carried it on and whether alone or with others;

(b) the date of the debt relief order;

(c) the reference number of the order;

(d) the date of the end of the moratorium period; and

(e) the date of a previous bankruptcy order or a debt relief order (if any) made against the debtor in the period of six years before the latest debt relief order (if there is more than one such order only the latest and excluding any bankruptcy order that was annulled or debt relief order that was revoked).

11.18(2) [Further duty of official receiver] Except where information concerning a debt relief order has been deleted under rule 11.19, the official receiver must also cause to be entered on the register in relation to the order–

(a) where the moratorium period is terminated early, the fact that such has happened, the date of early termination and whether the early termination is on revocation of the debt relief order or by virtue of any other enactment;

(b) where the moratorium period is extended, the fact that such has happened, the date on which the extension was made, its duration and the date of the new anticipated end of the moratorium period; or

(c) where the debtor is discharged from all qualifying debts, the date of such discharge.

11.18(3) [Rule subject to orders under rr.20.5, 20.6] This rule is subject to any court order for the non-disclosure of the debtor's current address made under rule 20.4 (debtors at risk of violence: debt relief application) or 20.6 (debtors at risk of violence: bankruptcy and debt relief proceedings).

11.19 Deletion of information from the individual insolvency register: debt relief orders

11.19 The Secretary of State must delete from the individual insolvency register all information concerning a debt relief order where three months have elapsed from the date on which–

(a) the debt relief order has been revoked; or

(b) the debtor has been discharged from the qualifying debts.

Chapter 7

Bankruptcy and debt relief restrictions register

11.20 Bankruptcy restrictions and debt relief restrictions orders and undertakings: entry of information on the registers

11.20(1) [Duty of Secretary of State re orders] Where any of the following orders are made against a bankrupt or a debtor the Secretary of State must enter on the bankruptcy restrictions register or debt relief restrictions register as appropriate the specified information–

(a) an interim bankruptcy restrictions order;

(b) a bankruptcy restrictions order;

(c) an interim debt relief restrictions order; or

(d) a debt relief restrictions order.

11.20(2) [Specified information] The specified information is–

(a) the bankrupt's or debtor's identification details;

(b) the bankrupt's or debtor's gender;

(c) the bankrupt's or debtor's occupation (if any);

(d) a statement that an interim bankruptcy restrictions order, a bankruptcy restrictions order, an interim debt relief restrictions order or a debt relief restrictions order has been made against the bankrupt or debtor;

(e) the date of the order;

(f) the court in which the order was made and the court or order reference number; and

(g) the duration of the order.

11.20(3) [Duty of Secretary of State re BRU, DRRU] Where a bankruptcy restrictions undertaking is given by a bankrupt or a debt relief restrictions undertaking is given by a debtor, the Secretary of State must enter on to the bankruptcy restrictions or debt relief restrictions register–

(a) the bankrupt's or debtor's identification details;

(b) the bankrupt's or debtor's gender;

(c) the bankrupt's or debtor's occupation (if any);

(d) a statement that a bankruptcy restrictions undertaking or debt relief restrictions undertaking has been given;

(e) the date of the acceptance of the bankruptcy restrictions undertaking or debt relief restrictions undertaking by the Secretary of State; and

(f) the duration of the bankruptcy restrictions undertaking or debt relief restrictions undertaking.

11.20(4) [Rule subject to orders under rr.20.6, 20.7] This rule is subject to any court order for the non-disclosure of the debtor's current address made under rules 20.6 (debtors at risk of violence: bankruptcy and debt relief proceedings) or 20.7 (additional provisions in respect of order under rule 20.6(4)).

General Note

Entry of details of BROs and BRUs is outlined. Amendments to were made to the IR 1986 provision (r.6A.6) by I(A)R 2004 (SI 2004/584) with effect from 1 April 2004. The purpose of the change was to provide more information on the public register of the background of the bankrupt made subject to a BRO or BRU. See I(A)R 2010 (SI 2010/686). This rule also deals with the registration of debt relief restriction orders and undertakings.

11.21 Deletion of information from the registers

11.21 The Secretary of State must delete from the bankruptcy restrictions register or debt relief restrictions register all information relating to an interim bankruptcy restrictions order, bankruptcy restrictions order, interim debt relief restrictions order, debt relief restrictions order, bankruptcy restrictions undertaking or debt relief restrictions undertaking after–

(a) receipt of notice that the order or undertaking has ceased to have effect; or

(b) the expiry of the order or undertaking.

General Note

Deletion of information about BROs and BRUs is regulated by this rule. This rule also deals with deletion of entries with regard to DRRO and DRRU

CHAPTER 8

RECTIFICATION OF REGISTERS AND DEATH OF PERSONS ON REGISTER

11.22 Rectification of the registers

11.22 Where the Secretary of State becomes aware of an inaccuracy in information on the individual insolvency register, the bankruptcy restrictions register or the debt relief restrictions register, the Secretary of State must rectify the inaccuracy as soon as reasonably practicable.

GENERAL NOTE

This explains rectification procedures where there are errors on the register.

11.23 Death of a person about whom information is held on a register

11.23 Where the Secretary of State receives notice of the date of the death of a person in relation to whom information is held on any of the registers, the Secretary of State must cause the fact and date of the person's death to be entered on to the register.

GENERAL NOTE

This rule was added (as IR 1986 r.6A.8(2)) by I(A)R 2009 (SI 2009/642) with effect from 6 April 2009.

PART 12

COURT PROCEDURE AND PRACTICE

CHAPTER 1

GENERAL APPLICATION OF THE CIVIL PROCEDURE RULES 1998

Introductory note to Part 12
Part 12 deals with the practice and procedure on all applications to the court, whether in corporate insolvency or individual bankruptcy, except for the three categories of petition listed in r.12.6. Part 12 carries over many provisions from the former Pt 7 of the 1986 Rules. Rules 12.35–12.38 deal with block transfer orders. The growing problem of debtors who lack capacity to handle their affairs is governed by IR 2016 rr.12.23–12.26. Of particular importance is r.12.59, which replicates IR 1986 r.7.47 and deals with appeals in winding up. We are reminded by r.12.1 that the CPR apply unless inconsistent with the Insolvency Rules. The frequently resorted to curative power formerly located in IR 1986 r.7.55 is now located in r.12.64. Special provision is made for applications to court by office holders to disapply the prescribed part—rr.12.14–12.16.

Note Companies House Form NCOP (r.12.16).

12.1 Court rules and practice to apply

12.1(1) [Application of CPR to Pts 1–11] The provisions of the CPR (including any related Practice Directions) apply for the purposes of proceedings under Parts 1 to 11 of the Act with any necessary modifications, except so far as disapplied by or inconsistent with these Rules.

12.1(2) [Allocation to CPR multi-track] All insolvency proceedings must be allocated to the multi-track for which CPR Part 29 makes provision, and accordingly those provisions of the CPR which provide for directions questionnaires and track allocation do not apply.

12.1(3) [Application of CPR Pt 32 to verified documents] CPR Part 32 applies to a false statement in a document verified by a statement of truth made under these Rules as it applies to a false statement in a document verified by a statement of truth made under CPR Part 22.

General Note

For the significance of the nexus between IR and the CPR see *Thakerar v Lynch Hall & Hornby (No.2) (Practice Note)* [2005] EWHC 2752 (Ch); [2006] 1 W.L.R. 1513 where Lewison J ruled that a bankruptcy registrar enjoyed jurisdiction to make a third party debt order in relation to an order for costs made in insolvency proceedings in the High Court.

See *Hayes v Hayes* [2014] EWHC 2694 (Ch); [2014] B.P.I.R. 1212 where Nugee J confirmed that CPR practice must yield to specific provision in the Insolvency Rules if an inconsistency arises.

On the linkage with the CPR and the ability of the court to revisit its own judgment see *Paulin v Paulin* [2009] EWCA Civ 221. In *Re Beloit Walmsley Ltd* [2008] B.P.I.R. 1445 the court made the point that although r.7.51 incorporated the CPR regime, that procedural regime cannot be used to undermine time limits imposed by primary legislation in IA 1986.

In *Arif v Zar* [2012] EWCA Civ 986; [2012] B.P.I.R. 948 a number of procedural issues tied up with the interface between the bankruptcy jurisdiction (particularly annulment applications) and proceedings for ancillary relief were considered. The linkage with the CPR was emphasised.

In *Nutting v Khaliq* [2012] EWCA Civ 1726 the linkage with CPR which is made by this provision was again explained. In *Re Lehman Bros International (Europe)* [2014] EWHC 1687 (Ch); [2014] B.P.I.R. 1259 David Richards J stresses the common links between application of the Rules and the CPR in terms of the policy of efficient case management and estate management. This is particularly relevant when considering whether time periods should be extended.

Proudman J held in *Bishop v Fox* (unreported, 9 February 2016) that CPR Pt 44 could be applied to insolvency proceedings by virtue of this connecting provision.

12.2 Performance of functions by the Court

12.2(1) [Proceedings before judge, district judge, registrar] Anything to be done under or by virtue of the Act or these Rules by, to or before the court may be done by, to or before a judge, District Judge or a registrar.

12.2(2) [Registrar or district judge may authorise any formal or administrative act] The registrar or District Judge may authorise any act of a formal or administrative character which is not by statute that person's responsibility to be carried out by the chief clerk or any other officer of the court acting on that person's behalf, in accordance with directions given by the Lord Chancellor.

12.2(3) [Hearing in open court] The hearing of an application must be in open court unless the court directs otherwise.

Chapter 2

Commencement of insolvency proceedings in the County Court

[A document required by the Act or these Rules must also contain the standard contents set out in Part 1.]

12.3 Commencement of insolvency proceedings under Parts 1 to 7 of the Act (corporate insolvency proceedings)

12.3(1) [County Court Hearing Centre for area of company's registered office] Where section 117 of the Act, as extended in its application by section 251, gives jurisdiction to the County Court in respect of proceedings under Parts 1 to 7 of the Act any such proceedings when they are commenced in the County Court may only be commenced in the hearing centre which serves the area in which the company's registered office is situated.

12.3(2) [Alternative court or hearing centre in IR 2016 Sch.6] However if the registered office is situated in an area served by a hearing centre for which Schedule 6 lists an alternative court or hearing centre then any such proceedings in the County Court may only be commenced in that alternative court or hearing centre.

12.4 Commencement of insolvency proceedings under Parts 7A to 11 of the Act (personal insolvency proceedings; bankruptcy)

12.4(1) [London Insolvency District proceedings in County Court at Central London] Proceedings under Parts 7A to 11 of the Act that are allocated in accordance with rule 12.5 to the London Insolvency District when they are commenced in the County Court may only be commenced in the County Court at Central London.

12.4(2) [Other proceedings commenced in County Court in the hearing centre under IR 2016] Elsewhere such proceedings when they are commenced in the County Court may only be commenced in the hearing centre determined in accordance with these Rules.

12.4(3) [Alternative hearing centre in IR 2016 Sch.6] However if the hearing centre so determined is one for which Schedule 6 lists an alternative hearing centre then such proceedings when they are commenced in the County Court may only be commenced in that alternative hearing centre.

General Note

This rule reflects r.3 of the Insolvency (Commencement of Proceedings) and Insolvency Rules 1986 (Amendment) Rules 2014 (SI 2014/817).

12.5 Allocation of proceedings to the London Insolvency District

12.5 The following proceedings are allocated to the London Insolvency District–

(a) bankruptcy petitions or applications in relation to a debt relief order under section 251M (powers of court in relation to debt relief orders) or 251N (inquiry into debtor's dealings and property) where–

(i) the debtor is resident in England and Wales and within the six months immediately preceding the presentation of the petition or the making of the application the debtor carried on business within the area of the London Insolvency District–

(aa) for the greater part of those six months, or

(bb) for a longer period in those six months than in any other insolvency district,

(ii) the debtor is resident in England and Wales and within the six months immediately preceding the presentation of the petition or the making of the application the debtor did not carry on business in England and Wales but resided within the area of the London Insolvency District for–

(aa) the greater part of those six months, or

(bb) a longer period in those six months than in any other insolvency district,

(iii) the debtor is not resident in England and Wales but within the six months immediately preceding the presentation of the petition or the making of the application carried on business within the area of the London Insolvency District,

(iv) the debtor is not resident in England and Wales and within the 6 months immediately preceding the presentation of the petition or the making of the application did not carry on business in England and Wales but resided within the area of the London Insolvency District, or

(v) the debtor is not resident in England and Wales and within the 6 months immediately preceding the presentation of the petition or the making of the application the debtor neither carried on business nor resided in England and Wales;

(b) creditors' bankruptcy petitions presented by a Minister of the Crown or a Government Department, where either–

(i) in any statutory demand on which the petition is based the creditor has indicated the intention to present a bankruptcy petition to a court exercising jurisdiction in relation to the London Insolvency District, or

(ii) the petition is presented under section 267(2)(c) on the grounds specified in section 268(1)(b);

(c) bankruptcy petitions–

(i) where the petitioner is unable to ascertain the place where the debtor resides or, if the debtor carries on business in England and Wales, both where the debtor resides and where the debtor carries on business, or

(ii) where the debtor is a member of a partnership and–

(aa) the partnership is being wound up by the High Court sitting in London; or

(bb) a petition for the winding up of the partnership has been presented to the High Court sitting in London and at the time of the presentation of the bankruptcy petition, the petition for the winding up of the partnership has not been fully disposed of; and

(d) bankruptcy petitions based on criminal bankruptcy orders under section 264(1)(d).

General Note

This rule was originally introduced by I(A)R 2011 (SI 2011/785).

Chapter 3

Making applications to court: general

[Note: (1) a document required by the Act or these Rules must also contain the standard contents set out in Part 1 and an application to court must also contain the standard contents set out in rule 1.35;

(2) Paragraphs 3 and 4 of Schedule 5 make provision in relation to the court's power to extend the time for doing anything required by these Rules;

(3) the rules about the applications referred to in rule 12.6 are found in Chapter 2 of Part 3 (administration applications); Chapter 3 of Part 7 (petition for winding up order by creditor) and Chapter 4 of Part 7 (petition for winding up by contributory or office-holder) and Chapter 2 of Part 10 (creditor's bankruptcy petitions).]

12.6 Preliminary

12.6 This Chapter applies to an application made to the court except–

(a) an administration application under Part 2 of the Act;

(b) a petition for a winding-up order under Part 4 of the Act; and

(c) a creditor's petition for a bankruptcy order under Part 9 of the Act.

General Note

Note *Hayes v Hayes* [2014] EWHC 2694 (Ch); [2014] B.P.I.R. 1212 on the significance of r.12.6(c).

12.7 Filing of application

[Note: see rule 1.46 for electronic delivery of documents to the court.]

12.7 An application filed with the court in hard-copy form must be accompanied by one copy and a number of additional copies equal to the number of persons who are to be served with the application.

12.8 Fixing the venue

12.8 When an application is filed the court must fix a venue for it to be heard unless–

(a) it considers it is not appropriate to do so;

(b) the rule under which the application is brought provides otherwise; or

(c) the case is one to which rule 12.12 applies.

12.9 Service or delivery of application

12.9(1) [Sealed copy endorsed with venue] The applicant must serve a sealed copy of the application, endorsed with the venue for the hearing, on the respondent named in the application unless the court directs or these Rules provide otherwise.

12.9(2) [Court directions] The court may also give one or more of the following directions–

(a) that the application be served upon persons other than those specified by the relevant provision of the Act or these Rules;

(b) that service upon, or the delivery of a notice to any person may be dispensed with;

(c) that such persons be notified of the application and venue in such other a way as the court specifies; or

(d) such other directions as the court sees fit.

12.9(3) [Time limit for service] A sealed copy of the application must be served, or notice of the application and venue must be delivered, at least 14 days before the date fixed for its hearing unless–

(a) the provision of the Act or these Rules under which the application is made makes different provision;

(b) the case is urgent and the court acts under rule 12.10; or

(c) the court extends or abridges the time limit.

12.10 Hearing in urgent case

12.10(1) [Immediate hearing without notice] Where the case is urgent, the court may (without prejudice to its general power to extend or abridge time limits) hear the application immediately with or without notification to, or the attendance of, other parties.

12.10(2) [Hearing on terms] The application may be heard on terms providing for the filing or service of documents, notification, or the carrying out of other formalities as the court thinks just.

General Note

See also *Bagnall v Official Receiver* [2003] EWCA Civ 1925; [2004] B.P.I.R. 445.

12.11 Directions

12.11 The court may at any time give such directions as it thinks just as to–

(a) service or notice of the application on or to any person;

(b) whether particulars of claim and defence are to be delivered and generally as to the procedure on the application including whether a hearing is necessary;

(c) the matters to be dealt with in evidence; and

(d) the manner in which any evidence is to be provided and in particular as to–

(i) the taking of evidence wholly or partly by witness statement or orally,

(ii) any report to be made by an office-holder, and

(iii) the cross-examination of the maker of a witness statement or of a report.

12.12 Hearing and determination without notice

12.12(1) [Power of court] Where the Act and these Rules do not require service of a sealed copy of the application on, or notice of it to be delivered to, any person, the court may–

(a) hear the application as soon as reasonably practicable;

(b) fix a venue for the application to be heard, in which case rule 12.9 applies to the extent that it is relevant; or

(c) determine the application without a hearing.

12.12(2) [No prohibition on applicant giving notice] However nothing in the Act or these Rules is to be taken as prohibiting the applicant from giving notice.

12.13 Adjournment of the hearing of an application

12.13(1) [Power of court] The court may adjourn the hearing of an application on such terms as it thinks just.

12.13(2) [Directions as to evidence] The court may give directions as to the manner in which any evidence is to be provided at a resumed hearing and in particular as to–

(a) the taking of evidence wholly or partly by witness statement or orally;

(b) the cross-examination of the maker of a witness statement; or

(c) any report to be made by an office-holder.

General Note

On r.12.13(2) see *Re Gunningham* [2002] B.P.I.R. 302.

Chapter 4

Making applications to court: specific applications

[Note: a document required by the Act or these Rules must also contain the standard contents set out in Part 1.]

Sub-division A: Applications in connection with section 176A (prescribed part)

12.14 Applications under section 176A(5) to disapply section 176A

12.14(1) [Application accompanied by witness statement] An application under section 176A(5) must be accompanied by a witness statement of the liquidator, administrator or receiver.

12.14(2) [Content of witness statement] The witness statement must state–

(a) the type of insolvency proceedings in which the application arises;

(b) a summary of the financial position of the company;

(c) the information substantiating the applicant's view that the cost of making a distribution to unsecured creditors would be disproportionate to the benefits; and

(d) whether any other office-holder is acting in relation to the company and, if so, that office-holder's address.

General Note

This rule was deals with the obligations of the insolvency practitioner when seeking an order to disapply the special reserve fund for unsecured creditors—see the comment on s.176A.

12.15 Notice of application under section 176A(5)

12.15(1) [No service of notice] An application under section 176A(5) may be made without the application being served upon, or notification to any other party.

12.15(2) [Applicant office-holder to notify any other office-holder acting] However the office-holder making the application must notify any other office-holder who is acting in relation to the company including any member State liquidator.

General Note

This covers notice requirements where an application is made pursuant to s.176A to disapply the reserve fund for unsecured creditors.

12.16 Notice of an order under section 176A(5)

12.16(1) [Sealed copies to applicant and any other office-holder] Where the court makes an order under section 176A(5), the court must, as soon as reasonably practicable, deliver the sealed order to the applicant and a sealed copy to any other office-holder.

12.16(2) [Office-holder to give notice to creditors] The liquidator, administrator or receiver must, as soon as reasonably practicable, deliver notice of the order to each creditor unless the court directs otherwise.

12.16(3) [Publication of disapplication of r.12.16(2) requirement] The court may direct that the requirement in paragraph (2) is complied with if a notice is published by the liquidator, administrator or receiver which states that the court has made an order disapplying the requirement to set aside the prescribed part.

12.16(4) [Gazetting and advertisement of notice] As soon as reasonably practicable the notice–

(a) must be gazetted; and

(b) may be advertised in such other manner as the liquidator, administrator, or receiver thinks fit.

12.16(5) [Copy of order to registrar of companies] The liquidator, administrator or receiver must deliver a copy of the order to the registrar of companies as soon as reasonably practicable after the making of the order.

General Note

This is a specific provision linked to applications/notifications under s.176A(5) of the Act (reserved fund for unsecured creditors).

Sub-division B: Applications for private examination (sections 236, 251N and 366)

Introductory note to Chapter 4, Sub-division B

The examinations authorised by IA 1986 ss.236, 366, to which this Part refers, are private examinations, in contrast to the public examinations which may be ordered under IA 1986 ss.133, 134 and 290. For further discussion, see notes to those sections, and for the rules applicable in the latter case, see rr.7.98 et seq. and 10.99 et seq. for example. In addition, ss.237 and 367, referred to in r.12.22 empower the court to order a person to deliver up property to the liquidator or other office holder, or to pay money in discharge of a debt.

[Note: for rules about public examinations see Chapter 13 of Part 7 and Chapter 8 of Part 10.]

12.17 Application of this sub-division and interpretation

12.17(1) [Application of sub-division B rules re IA 1986 ss.235, 251N, 366 orders]The rules in his sub-division apply to applications to the court for an order under–

(a) section 236 (inquiry into company's dealings);

(b) section 251N (debt relief orders – inquiry into dealings and property of debtor); and

(c) section 366 (inquiry into bankrupt's dealings and property) including section 366 as it applies by virtue of section 368.

12.17(2) ["Applicable section", "the insolvent"] In this sub-division–

"applicable section" means section 236, 251N or 366; and

"the insolvent" means the company, the debtor or the bankrupt as the case may be.

12.18 Contents of application

12.18(1) [Grounds and orders sought] An application to the court under section 236, 251N or 366 must state–

(a) the grounds on which it is made; and

(b) which one or more of the following orders is sought–

(i) for the respondent to appear before the court,

(ii) for the respondent to clarify any matter which is in dispute in the proceedings or to give additional information in relation to any such matter (if so Part 18 CPR (further information) applies to any such order),

(iii) for the respondent to submit witness statements (if so, particulars must be given of the matters to be included), or

(iv) for the respondent to produce books, papers or other records (if so, the items in question to be specified).

12.18(2) [Application without notice] An application under an applicable section may be made without notice to any other party.

12.18(3) [Power of court] The court may, whatever the order sought in the application, make any order which it has power to make under the applicable section.

General Note

The previous version of this rule (IR 1986 r.9.2) was considered in *Re Comet Group Ltd, Kahn v Whirlpool UK Ltd* [2014] EWHC 3477 (Ch), where John Baldwin QC (sitting as a Deputy Judge of the High Court) stressed the importance of compliance with this rule. The judgment considers the relationship between this rule and the information gathering provisions in s.236. The circumstances under which an order can be made under r.12.18(2) are determined by case law—*Hill v Van der Merwe* [2007] EWHC 1613 (Ch); [2007] B.P.I.R. 1562.

12.19 Order for examination etc.

12.19(1) [Court to specify venue for appearance] Where the court orders the respondent to appear before it, it must specify the venue for the appearance.

12.19(2) [Time limit] The date must not be less than 14 days from the date of the order.

12.19(3) [Order re filing witness statement, written account] If the respondent is ordered to file with the court a witness statement or a written account, the order must specify–

(a) the matters which are to be dealt with in it; and

(b) the time within which it is to be delivered.

12.19(4) [Order to produce books, etc.] If the order is to produce documents or other records, the time and manner of compliance must be specified.

12.19(5) [Service of copy order] The applicant must serve a copy of the order on the respondent as soon as reasonably practicable.

General Note

For the meaning of "venue" see r.1.2.

12.20 Procedure for examination

12.20(1) [Applicant may attend] The applicant may attend an examination of the respondent, in person, or be represented by an appropriately qualified legal representative, and may put such questions to the respondent as the court may allow.

12.20(2) [Other attendees, etc.] Unless the applicant objects, the following persons may attend the examination with the permission of the court and may put questions to the respondent (but only through the applicant)–

(a) any person who could have applied for an order under the applicable section; and

(b) any creditor who has provided information on which the application was made under section 236 or 366.

12.20(3) [Clarification, additional information] If the respondent is ordered to clarify any matter or to give additional information, the court must direct the respondent as to the questions which the respondent is required to answer, and as to whether the respondent's answers (if any) are to be made in a witness statement.

12.20(4) [Legal representation of respondent] The respondent may employ an appropriately qualified legal representative at the respondent's own expense, who may–

(a) put to the respondent such questions as the court may allow for the purpose of enabling the respondent to explain or qualify any answers given by the respondent; and

(b) make representations on the respondent's behalf.

12.20(5) [Written record of examination] Such written record of the examination must be made as the court thinks proper and such record must be read either to or by the respondent and authenticated by the respondent at a venue fixed by the court.

12.20(6) [Record as evidence] The record may, in any proceedings (whether under the Act or otherwise), be used as evidence against the respondent of any statement made by the respondent in the course of the respondent's examination.

General Note

Note *Re Harvest Finance Ltd (in liq.)* [2014] EWHC 4237 (Ch).

12.21 Record of examination

12.21(1) [Record, witness statement, written account not to be filed] Unless the court otherwise directs, the record of questions put to the respondent, the respondent's answers and any witness statement or written account delivered to the court by the respondent in compliance with an order of the court under the applicable section are not to be filed with the court.

12.21(2) [Inspection of documents] The documents listed in paragraph (3) may not be inspected without the permission of the court, except by–

(a) the applicant for an order under the applicable section; or

(b) any person who could have applied for such an order in relation to the affairs of the same insolvent.

12.21(3) [Relevant documents] The documents are–

(a) the record of the respondent's examination;

(b) copies of questions put to the respondent or proposed to be put to the respondent and answers to questions given by the respondent;

(c) any witness statement by the respondent; and

(d) any document on the court file that shows the grounds for the application for the order.

12.21(4) [Directions by court] The court may from time to time give directions as to the custody and inspection of any documents to which this rule applies, and as to the provision of copies of, or extracts from, such documents.

12.22 Costs of proceedings under sections 236, 251N and 366

12.22(1) [Power of court] Where the court has ordered an examination of a person under an applicable section, and it appears to it that the examination was made necessary because information had been unjustifiably refused by the respondent, it may order that the respondent pay the costs of the examination.

12.22(2) [Order under IA 1986 ss.237(1), (2), 367(1), (2)] Where the court makes an order against a person under–

(a) section 237(1) or 367(1) (to deliver up property in any person's possession which belongs to the insolvent estate); or

(b) section 237(2) or 367(2) (to pay any amount in discharge of a debt due to the insolvent); the costs of the application for the order may be ordered by the court to be paid by the respondent.

12.22(3) [Applicant's cost otherwise] Subject to paragraphs (1) and (2), the applicant's costs must, unless the court orders otherwise, be paid–

(a) in relation to a company insolvency, as an expense of the insolvency proceedings; and

(b) in relation to an individual insolvency, but not in proceedings relating to debt relief orders or applications for debt relief orders, out of the bankrupt's estate or (as the case may be) the debtor's property.

12.22(4) [Travelling expenses, etc.] A person summoned to attend for examination must be tendered a reasonable sum for travelling expenses incurred in connection with that person's attendance but any other costs falling on that person are at the court's discretion.

12.22(5) [Official receiver applicant] Where the examination is on the application of the official receiver otherwise than in the capacity of liquidator or trustee, no order may be made for the payment of costs by the official receiver.

General Note

Under the former winding-up rules, it was the practice for an applicant seeking an order to support his application by a memorandum which was required to be verified by affidavit in every case except where the applicant, as a liquidator, was an officer of the court. The IR 1986 r.9.2(1) (now replaced by r.12.18(1)) abolished this distinction, so that an unsworn statement is now sufficient in all cases. The statement is confidential: *Re Aveling Barford Ltd* [1989] 1 W.L.R. 360; (1988) 4 B.C.C. 548; but (in a departure from the previous practice) the court may order that it be disclosed in whole or in part to the person against whom the order is sought in a proper case: see the note to s.236.

An order requiring a person to give "an account of full particulars of all dealings" by him with the company may be open to objection on the grounds that it lacks the particularity called for by r.12.18(1)(b)(i) and (iii): *Re Aveling Barford Ltd* (above). It was held in the same case that the phrase "a person summoned to attend for examination under this Chapter" in r.12.22(4) includes a person required to give information by the alternative methods permitted under s.236. On the question of the examinee's costs, Hoffmann J declined to make an order in advance or to say that there should be a presumption in favour of allowing costs, over and above the travelling expenses mentioned in r.9.6(4). It is clear that the words "other costs falling on him are at the court's discretion" when used in IR 2016 r.12.22(4) are to be widely interpreted and are not limited to travelling expenses incurred for the purpose of attending an examination but might cover costs incurred in complying with an order under s.236(2) to produce documents. On this see *Re Harvest Finance Ltd, Jackson v Cannons Law Practice LLP* [2014] EWHC 4237 (Ch).

For comments on the exercise of the discretion conferred on the court by r.12.21(4), see *Hamilton v Naviede, Re Arrows Ltd (No.4)* [1995] 2 A.C. 75; [1994] B.C.C. 641.

See *Akers v Hayley* [2017] B.P.I.R. 1700, a case decided under IR 1986 r.9.6(4). Chief Registrar Baister dealt with the issue of costs and expenses arising from an examination and who bears said costs. The provision does *not* apply to costs run up through some alternative form of information gathering. The discretion of the court is therefore limited.

There was an amendment made to IR 1986 r.9.6(3) (now r.12.22(3)) by the Insolvency (Amendment) Rules 2008 (SI 2008/737) with effect from 6 April 2008 to cater for the insertion of new rr.4.218A–4.218E.

For determination of costs under r.12.22 see Registrar Jaques in *Hunt v Renzland* [2008] B.P.I.R. 1380, where the point was made that there was a need to distinguish between the treatment of the costs of obtaining the order for the private examination and the costs of the examination itself.

The Insolvency (Amendment) Rules 2009 (SI 2009/642) (effective 6 April 2009) made changes to this rule by inserting specific mention to s.251N and by including reference to debt relief orders.

See also I(A)R 2010 (SI 2010/686).

Sub-division C – persons unable to manage own property or affairs

Introductory note to Chapter 4, Sub-division C

The court is empowered by these rules to make special provision for any person subject to a disability who is affected by insolvency proceedings. In *Hunt v Fylde BC* [2008] B.P.I.R. 1368 Ashton D.J. indicated that the court can invoke r.12.23 on its own initiative.

12.23 Application and interpretation

12.23(1) [Application of rr.12.23–12.26] This sub-division applies where it appears to the court in insolvency proceedings that a person affected by the proceedings is unable to manage and administer that person's own property and affairs by reason of–

(a) lacking capacity within the meaning of the Mental Capacity Act 2005;

(b) suffering from a physical affliction; or

(c) disability.

12.23(2) ["The incapacitated person"] Such a person is referred to in this sub-division as "the incapacitated person".

12.24 Appointment of another person to act

12.24(1) [Power of court re incapacitated person] The court may appoint such person as it thinks just to appear for, represent or act for the incapacitated person.

12.24(2) [General or particular appointment] The appointment may be made either generally or for the purpose of a particular application or proceeding, or for the exercise of particular rights or powers which the incapacitated person might have exercised but for that person's incapacity.

12.24(3) [Appointment on court's own motion or on application] The court may make the appointment either of its own motion or on application by–

(a) a person who has been appointed by a court in the United Kingdom or elsewhere to manage the affairs of, or to represent, the incapacitated person;

(b) any person who appears to the court to be a suitable person to make the application;

(c) the official receiver; or

(d) the office-holder.

12.24(4) [Without notice application] An application may be made without notice to any other party.

12.24(5) [Notice to incapacitated person, etc.] However the court may require such notice of the application as it thinks necessary to be delivered to the incapacitated person, or any other person, and may adjourn the hearing of the application to enable the notice to be delivered.

General Note

Minor changes of terminology were made by I(A)R 2010 (SI 2010/686). See also *Marquis De Toucy v Bonhams 1793 Ltd* [2011] EWHC 3809 (Ch); [2012] B.P.I.R. 793 where Vos J indicated that it was not appropriate to make a bankruptcy order against a person known to have mental capacity problems without first considering whether a representative should be appointed under IR 2016 r.12.24. It was not good enough to proceed with the bankruptcy and then expect the trustee to deal with any issues of lack of capacity. The judgment also deals with the interface with provisions in the CPR and makes the point that the particular rules in the Insolvency Rules are to be applied. See also *Levy v Ellis-Carr* [2012] EWHC 63 (Ch). See also the judicial comment of Ashton DJ in *Hunt v Fylde BC* [2008] B.P.I.R. 1368.

12.25 Witness statement in support of application

12.25 An application under rule 12.24(3) must be supported by a witness statement made by a registered medical practitioner as to the mental or physical condition of the incapacitated person.

12.26 Service of notices following appointment

12.26 Any notice served on, or sent to, a person appointed under rule 12.24 has the same effect as if it had been served on, or delivered to, the incapacitated person.

Chapter 5

Obtaining information and evidence

[Note: a document required by the Act or these Rules must also contain the standard contents set out in Part 1.]

12.27 Further information and disclosure

12.27(1) [Clarification, additional information, etc.] A party to insolvency proceedings in court may apply to court for an order–

(a) that in accordance with CPR Part 18 (further information) another party–

(i) clarify a matter that is in dispute in the proceedings, or

(ii) give additional information in relation to such a matter; or

(b) for disclosure from any person in accordance with CPR Part 31 (disclosure and inspection of documents).

12.27(2) [Without notice application] An application under this rule may be made without notice to any other party.

General Note

See *Highberry Ltd v Colt Telecom Group plc* [2002] EWHC 2503 (Ch); [2003] B.P.I.R. 311. The situation prior to the introduction of IR 1986 was considered in detail by Harman J in *Re Primlaks (UK) Ltd (No.2)* [1990] B.C.L.C. 234. There it was held that in an unfair prejudice application under s.6 of the Act arising out of a corporate voluntary arrangement, discovery [disclosure] should be ordered if it was in the interests of justice to do so; and clearly if a particular creditor was making an application under s.6 it was necessary for him to know the full facts of the transactions which he alleged were unfair.

12.28 Witness statements and reports

12.28(1) [Evidence in witness statements; exceptions] Where the Act or these Rules require evidence as to a matter, such evidence may be given by witness statement unless–

(a) in a specific case a rule or the Act makes different provision; or

(b) the court otherwise directs.

12.28(2) [Filing in court if relying on evidence] Unless either the provision of the Act or rule under which the application is made provides otherwise, or the court directs otherwise–

(a) if the applicant intends to rely at the first hearing on evidence in a witness statement or report, the applicant must file the witness statement or report with the court and serve a copy of it on the respondent not less than 14 days before the date fixed for the hearing; and

(b) where the respondent intends to oppose the application and rely for that purpose on evidence contained in a witness statement or report, the respondent must file the witness statement or report with the court and serve a copy on the applicant not less than five business days before the date fixed for the hearing.

12.28(3) [Cross-examination] The court may order a person who has made a witness statement or report to attend for cross-examination.

12.28(4) [Failure to attend] Where a person who has been ordered to attend fails to do so the witness statement or report must not be used in evidence without the court's permission.

General Note

On statements of truth and applications for BROs see *OR v Bayliss* (unreported, 26 July 2017, E. Johnson QC) (decided under IR 1986 r.7.9).

12.29 Evidence provided by the official receiver, an insolvency practitioner or a special manager

12.29(1) [Witness statement by office-holder] Where in insolvency proceedings a witness statement is made by an office-holder, the office-holder must state–

(a) the capacity in which the office-holder is acting; and

(b) the office-holder's address.

12.29(2) [Who may file report instead of witness statement in all proceedings] The following may file a report with the court instead of a witness statement in all insolvency proceedings–

(a) the official receiver; and

(b) the adjudicator.

12.29(3) [Who may file report instead of witness statement where no other parties] The following may file a report with the court instead of a witness statement unless the application involves other parties or the court otherwise directs–

(a) an administrator;

(b) a provisional liquidator;

(c) a liquidator;

(d) an interim receiver;

(e) a trustee; and

(f) a special manager.

12.29(4) [Report treated as witness statement] Where a report is filed instead of a witness statement, the report must be treated for the purpose of rule 12.28 and any hearing before the court as if it were a witness statement.

General Note

In *OR v Bayliss* (unreported, 26 July 2017) applications for bankruptcy restrictions orders and supporting reports by the official receiver were not required by the relevant rules to be verified by statements of truth, and the absence of such statements did not unduly disadvantage the bankrupts and breach their rights under art.6 of the European Convention on Human Rights.

Chapter 6

Transfer of proceedings

[Note: a document required by the Act or these Rules must also contain the standard contents set out in Part 1.]

Sub-division A: General

12.30 General power of transfer

12.30(1) [High Court to hearing centre] The High Court may order insolvency proceedings which are pending in that court to be transferred to a specified hearing centre.

12.30(2) [County Court to High Court] The County Court may order insolvency proceedings which are pending in a hearing centre to be transferred either to the High Court or another hearing centre.

12.30(3) [High Court judge may order from County Court to High Court] A judge of the High Court may order insolvency proceedings which are pending in the County Court to be transferred to the High Court.

12.30(4) [Order for transfer] The court may order a transfer of proceedings–

(a) of its own motion;

(b) on the application of the official receiver; or

(c) on the application of a person appearing to the court to have an interest in the proceedings.

12.30(5) [Winding-up proceedings: jurisdiction] Winding-up proceedings may only be transferred to a hearing centre in which proceedings to wind up companies may be commenced under the Act or to the County Court at Central London.

12.30(6) [Bankruptcy or DRO proceedings: jurisdiction] Bankruptcy proceedings or proceedings relating to a debt relief order may only be transferred to a hearing centre in which bankruptcy proceedings may be commenced under the Act.

12.30(7) [Block transfer order schedule] A case in a schedule under rule 12.37(8) may be transferred solely for the purposes of rule 12.38 (action following application for a block transfer order) by–

(a) the registrar to or from the High Court; and

(b) the District Judge of the hearing centre to which the application is made, to or from that hearing centre.

General Note

See the *Practice Direction: Insolvency Proceedings* [2018] B.C.C. 241 (reproduced as App.IV to this *Guide*). See *Hall and Shivers v Van Der Heiden* [2010] B.P.I.R. 585. Various amendments were made to the IR 1986 version of this rule (r.7.11) by the Insolvency (Amendment) Rules 2009 (SI 2009/642) with effect from 6 April 2009. These catered for the introduction of debt relief orders. Further amendments were made by I(A)R 2010 (SI 2010/686) and the Insolvency (Amendment) Rules 2015 (SI 2015/443).

In *Forster v Bleasdale* (unreported, 15 January 2015) proceedings were transferred under IR 1986 r.7.11 (now r.12.30) from the county court to the High Court in view of their potential complexity.

12.31 Proceedings commenced in the wrong court

12.31 Where insolvency proceedings are commenced in the wrong court or hearing centre, that court may order–

(a) the proceedings be transferred to the court or hearing centre in which they ought to have been commenced;

(b) the proceedings be continued in the court in which they have been commenced; or

(c) the proceedings be struck out.

12.32 Applications for transfer

12.32(1) [Official receiver's report] An application by the official receiver for proceedings to be transferred must be accompanied by a report by the official receiver.

12.32(2) [Report to include reasons for transfer, etc.] The report must set out the reasons for the transfer, and include a statement either that–

(a) the petitioner, or the debtor in proceedings relating to a debt relief order, consents to the transfer; or

(b) the petitioner or such a debtor has been given at least 14 days' notice of the official receiver's application.

12.32(3) [More convenient conduct of proceedings] If the court is satisfied from the report that the proceedings can be conducted more conveniently in another court or hearing centre, it must order that the proceedings be transferred to that court or hearing centre.

12.32(4) [Application not by official receiver] A person other than the official receiver who applies for the transfer of winding up or bankruptcy proceedings or proceedings relating to a debt relief order must deliver a notice that such an application is intended to be made at least 14 days' before filing the application with the court to–

(a) the official receiver attached to the court or hearing centre in which the proceedings are pending; and

(b) the official receiver attached to the court or hearing centre to which it is proposed that they should be transferred.

12.33 Procedure following order for transfer

12.33(1) [Sealed copy of order to transferee court or hearing centre] Where a court makes an order for the transfer of proceedings under rule 12.30 (other than paragraph (7) of that rule), it must as soon as reasonably practicable deliver to the transferee court or hearing centre a sealed copy of the order, and the file of the proceedings.

12.33(2) [Transferee court to notify official receiver at that court] A transferee court (or hearing centre) which receives such an order and the file in winding up or bankruptcy proceedings or proceedings relating to a debt relief order must, as soon as reasonably practicable, deliver notice of the transfer to the official receiver attached to that court or hearing centre and the transferor court respectively.

12.33(3) [High Court transfer order under r.12.30(7)] Where the High Court makes a transfer order under rule 12.30(7)–

(a) it must deliver sealed copies of the order–

  (i) to the hearing centre from which the proceedings are transferred, and

  (ii) in winding up or bankruptcy proceedings or proceedings relating to a debt relief order, to the official receiver attached to that hearing centre and the High Court respectively; and

(b) the hearing centre must deliver the file of the proceedings to the High Court.

12.34 Consequential transfer of other proceedings

12.34(1) [Application of rule] This rule applies where–

(a) the High Court has–

  (i) made a winding-up order,

  (ii) appointed a provisional liquidator,

  (iii) made a bankruptcy order, or

  (iv) appointed an interim receiver; or

(b) winding-up or bankruptcy proceedings have been transferred to the High Court from the County Court.

12.34(2) [Power of High Court judge] A judge of any division of the High Court may, of that judge's own motion, order the transfer to that division of any such proceedings as are mentioned below and are pending against the company or individual concerned ("the insolvent") either in another division of the High Court or in a court in England and Wales other than the High Court.

12.34(3) [Rule 12.34(2) subject to CPR r.30.5(4)] Paragraph (2) is subject to rule 30.5(4) CPR (transfer between divisions and to and from a specialist list).

12.34(4) [Proceedings which may be transferred] The proceedings which may be transferred are those brought by or against the insolvent for the purpose of enforcing a claim against the insolvent estate, or brought by a person other than the insolvent for the purpose of enforcing any such claim (including in either case proceedings of any description by a debenture-holder or mortgagee).

12.34(5) [Listing of transferred proceedings] Where any such proceedings are transferred, they must be listed before a registrar for directions or final disposal as the registrar sees fit.

General Note

See *Arif v Zar* [2012] EWCA Civ 986; [2012] B.P.I.R. 948 on the limitations imposed by IR 2016 r.12.34(3) on the transfer of proceedings within the High Court.

Sub-division B: Block transfer of cases where insolvency practitioner has died etc.

Introductory note to Chapter 6, Sub-division B

These rules, originally inserted by I(A)R 2010 (SI 2010/686), were a welcome addition to the Insolvency Rules. They regularise the position where an office-holder leaves office with regard to multiple insolvencies. The underlying problem here is the position taken by English law that appointments are held by named individuals, rather than by the firms of which they are members. Thus an individual insolvency practitioner may hold scores of appointments and there is significant disruption when that individual leaves the firm, which is effectively managing the insolvency. Under the former law, the courts, drawing upon the inherent jurisdiction of the court as recognised by various provisions in the Act, were able to construct a set of working rules to deal with this scenario. The Insolvency Rules themselves did not offer any assistance. These judicial innovations were only finally free from doubt as a result of *Donaldson v O'Sullivan* [2008] EWCA Civ 879. The position for the future is much more secure.

Where a block transfer is made this cannot be used to increase levels of fee and disbursement on existing insolvencies—see *Re a Block Transfer by Kaye and Morgan* [2010] B.P.I.R. 602. Where a transfer of insolvency offices is being considered, it is clear that the court does not simply act as a rubber stamp of the nomination put forward by the outgoing office holder—on this see *ICAEW v Webb* [2009] EWHC 3461 (Ch) and *ACCA v Koumettou* [2012] EWHC 1265 (Ch).

12.35 Interpretation

12.35 In this Sub-division–

"outgoing office-holder" has the meaning given in rule 12.36(1);

"replacement office-holder" has the meaning given in rule 12.36(1);

"block transfer order" has the meaning given in rule 12.36(2);

"substantive application" is that part of the application in rule 12.37(1)(c) and (d).

12.36 Power to make a block transfer order

12.36(1) [Application of rule] This rule applies where an office-holder ('the outgoing office-holder')–

(a) dies;

(b) retires from practice; or

(c) is otherwise unable or unwilling to continue in office;

and it is expedient to transfer some or all of the cases in which the outgoing office-holder holds office to one or more office-holders ('the replacement office-holder') in a single transaction.

12.36(2) ["Block transfer order"] In a case to which this rule applies the court has the power to make an order ('a block transfer order') appointing a replacement office-holder in the place of the outgoing office-holder to be–

(a) liquidator in any winding up (including a case where the official receiver is the liquidator by virtue of section 136);

(b) administrator in any administration;

(c) trustee in a bankruptcy (including a case where the official receiver is the trustee by virtue of section 300); or

(d) supervisor of a CVA or an IVA.

12.36(3) [Replacement office-holder to be qualified to act] The replacement office-holder must be–

(a) qualified to act as an insolvency practitioner in relation to the company or bankrupt; or

(b) where the replacement office-holder is to be appointed supervisor of an IVA–

(i) qualified to act as an insolvency practitioner in relation to the debtor, or

(ii) a person authorised so to act.

General Note

This provision explains when an application for a block transfer order can be made.

12.37 Application for a block transfer order

12.37(1) [Scope of order] An application for a block transfer order may be made to the registrar or District Judge for–

(a) the transfer to the High Court of the cases specified in the schedule to the application under paragraph (8);

(b) the transfer of the cases back to the court or hearing centre from which they were transferred when a replacement office-holder has been appointed;

(c) the removal of the outgoing office-holder by the exercise of any of the powers in paragraph (2);

(d) the appointment of a replacement office-holder by the exercise of any of the powers in paragraph (3); or

(e) such other order or direction as may be necessary or expedient in connection with any of the matters referred to above.

12.37(2) [Powers of removal in r.12.37(1)(c)] The powers referred to in paragraph (1)(c) are those in–

(a) section 7(5) and paragraph 39(6) of Schedule A1 (CVA);

(b) section 19, paragraph 88 of Schedule B1 and rule 12.36(2) (administration);

(c) section 108 (voluntary winding up);

(d) section 172(2) and rule 12.36(2) (winding up by the court);

(e) section 263(5) (IVA); and

(f) section 298 and rule 12.36(2) (bankruptcy).

12.37(3) [Powers of replacement in r.12.37(1)(d)] The powers referred to in paragraph (1)(d) are those in–

(a) section 7(5) and paragraph 39(6) of Schedule A1 (CVA);

(b) section 13, paragraphs 63, 91 and 95 of Schedule B1 and rule 12.36(2) (administration);

(c) section 108 (voluntary winding up);

(d) section 168(3) and (5) and rule 12.36(2) (winding up by the court);

(e) section 263(5) (IVA); and

(f) sections 298 and 303(2) and rule 12.36(2) (bankruptcy).

12.37(4) [Who may make application] Subject to paragraph (5), the application may be made by any of the following–

(a) the outgoing office-holder (if able and willing to do so);

(b) any person who holds office jointly with the outgoing office-holder;

(c) any person who is proposed to be appointed as the replacement office-holder;

(d) any creditor in a case subject to the application;

(e) the recognised professional body which was the source of the outgoing office-holder's authorisation; or

(f) the Secretary of State.

12.37(5) [Where outgoing office-holder in r.12.37(8) schedule an administrator] Where one or more outgoing office-holder in the schedule under paragraph (8) is an administrator, an application may not be made unless the applicant is a person permitted to apply to replace that office-holder under section 13 or paragraph 63, 91 or 95 of Schedule B1 or such a person is joined as applicant in relation to the replacement of that office-holder.

12.37(6) [Notice of intended application to Secretary of State] An applicant (other than the Secretary of State) must deliver a notice of the intended application to the Secretary of State on or before the date the application is made.

12.37(7) [Respondents] The following must be made a respondent to the application and served with it–

(a) the outgoing office-holder (if not the applicant or deceased);

(b) any person who holds office jointly with the outgoing office-holder; and

(c) such other person as the registrar or District Judge directs.

12.37(8) [Schedule of application]The application must contain a schedule setting out–

(a) identification details for the proceedings; and

(b) the capacity in which the outgoing office-holder was appointed.

12.37(9) [Supporting evidence] The application must be supported by evidence–

(a) setting out the circumstances as a result of which it is expedient to appoint a replacement office-holder; and

(b) exhibiting the consent to act of each person who is proposed to be appointed as replacement office-holder.

12.37(10) [Application to district judge where all cases in schedule in County Court] Where all the cases in the schedule under paragraph (8) are in the County Court–

(a) the application may be made to a District Judge of a convenient hearing centre in which insolvency proceedings of such type may be commenced; and

(b) this rule applies with appropriate modifications.

GENERAL NOTE

This rule outlines the procedure to be followed to obtain a block transfer order.

12.38 Action following application for a block transfer order

12.38(1) [Consideration without hearing] The registrar or District Judge may in the first instance consider the application without a hearing and make such order as the registrar or District Judge thinks just.

12.38(2) [Power of registrar or district judge] In the first instance, the registrar or District Judge may do any of the following–

(a) make an order directing the transfer to the High Court of those cases not already within its jurisdiction for the purpose only of the substantive application;

(b) if the documents are considered to be in order and the matter is considered straightforward, make an order on the substantive application;

(c) give any directions which are considered to be necessary including (if appropriate) directions for the joinder of any additional respondents or requiring the service of the application on any person or requiring additional evidence to be provided; or

(d) if an order is not made on the substantive application, give directions for the further consideration of the substantive application by the registrar or District Judge or a judge of the Chancery Division.

12.38(3) [Sealed copies of order to court with jurisdiction] The applicant must ensure that a sealed copy of every order transferring any case to the High Court and of every order which is made on a substantive application is filed with the court having jurisdiction over each case affected by such order.

12.38(4) [Incidence of costs except in administration] In any case other than an application relating to the appointment of an administrator, in deciding to what extent (if any) the costs of making an application under this rule should be paid as an expense of the insolvency proceedings to which the application relates, the factors to which the court must have regard include–

(a) the reasons for the making of the application;

(b) the number of cases to which the application relates;

(c) the value of assets comprised in those cases; and

(d) the nature and extent of the costs involved.

12.38(5) [Incidence of costs re appointment of administrator] Where an application relates to the appointment of an administrator and is made by a person under section 13 or paragraph 63, 91 or 95 of Schedule B1, the costs of making that application are to be paid as an expense of the administration to which the application relates unless the court directs otherwise.

12.38(6) [Notice of appointment] Notice of any appointment made under this rule must be delivered–

(a) to the Secretary of State as soon as reasonably practicable; and

(b) to–

(i) the creditors, and

(ii) such other persons as the court may direct, in such manner as the court may direct.

12.38(7) [Application to district judge under r.12.37(10)] Where the application was made to the District Judge under rule 12.37(10) this rule applies with appropriate modifications.

General Note

This rule is a consequential provision that deals with a range of pragmatic issues, including the thorny issue of who foots the bill for the replacement of an insolvency practitioner via block transfer.

Chapter 7

The court file

[Note: a document required by the Act or these Rules must also contain the standard contents set out in Part 1.]

12.39 The court file

12.39(1) [Duty of court to open and maintain file] Where documents are filed with the court under the Act or these Rules, the court must open and maintain a court file and place those documents on the file.

12.39(2) [Bankruptcy file under r.10.47] However where a bankruptcy file has been opened under rule 10.47, documents filed with the court under the Act or these Rules must be placed on the bankruptcy file.

12.39(3) [Who may inspect file or obtain copy] The following may inspect the court file, or obtain from the court a copy of the court file, or of any document in the court file–

(a) the office-holder in the proceedings;

(b) the Secretary of State; and

(c) a creditor who provides the court with a statement confirming that that person is a creditor of the company or the individual to whom the proceedings relate.

12.39(4) [Proceedings where right to inspect and obtain copies exercisable] The same right to inspect and obtain copies is exercisable–

(a) in proceedings under Parts 1 to 7 of the Act, by–

(i) an officer or former officer of the company to which the proceedings relate, or

(ii) a member of the company or a contributory in its winding up;

(b) in proceedings relating to an IVA, by the debtor;

(c) in bankruptcy proceedings, by–

(i) the bankrupt,

(ii) a person against whom a bankruptcy petition has been presented, or

(iii) a person who has been served with a statutory demand under section 268;

(d) in proceedings relating to a debt relief order, by the debtor.

12.39(5) [Right exercisable by authorised person] The right to inspect and obtain copies may be exercised on a person's behalf by someone authorised to do so by that person.

12.39(6) [Right of other persons with court permission] Other persons may inspect the file or obtain copies if the court gives permission.

12.39(7) [Fee chargeable under Courts Act 2003 s.92] The right to a copy of a document is subject to payment of the fee chargeable under an order made under section 92 of the Courts Act 2003.

12.39(8) [Inspection of file at reasonable time] Inspection of the file, with permission if required, may be at any reasonable time.

12.39(9) [Court may direct that permission required under r.12.39(3)–(5)] The court may direct that the file, a document (or part of it) or a copy of a document (or part of it) must not be made available under paragraph (3), (4) or (5) without the permission of the court.

12.39(10) [Application for r.12.39(9) direction] An application for a direction under paragraph (9) may be made by–

(a) the official receiver;

(b) the office-holder in the proceedings; or

(c) any person appearing to the court to have an interest.

12.39(11) [Applications without notice under r.12.39(6), (9)] The following applications may be made without notice to any other party, but the court may direct that notice must be delivered to any person who would be affected by its decision–

(a) an application for permission to inspect the file or obtain a copy of a document under paragraph (6); and

(b) an application for a direction under paragraph (9).

12.39(12) [Request by Secretary of State or official receiver to be complied with] If, for the purposes of powers conferred by the Act or these Rules, the Secretary of State or the official receiver makes a request to inspect or requests the transmission of the file of insolvency proceedings, the court must comply with the request (unless the file is for the time being in use for the court's own purposes).

General Note

See *Times Newspapers v McNamara* [2013] B.P.I.R. 1092 where Chief Registrar Baister in dealing with a test case under this rule allowed a reputable journalist engaged in a legitimate public interest story on the phenomenon of Irish bankruptcy tourism access to court papers which had been read by a judge, who had granted a bankruptcy order on the petition of an Irish public figure. The bankrupt had not sought to seal the file under IR 1986 r.7.31A(8) (now r.12.39(10)). As this was the first recorded application of this right of access under IR 1986 r.7.31A(6) (now IR 2016 r.12.39(6)) Chief Registrar Baister gave permission under the *Practice Direction (Citation of Authorities)* [2001] 1 W.L.R. 1001 for the decision to be reported, notwithstanding the fact that the bankrupt had not appeared on the application for access.

The court granted an order under r.12.39(9) in *Re LB Holdings Intermediate 2 Ltd (in admin.)* [2017] EWHC 2032 (Ch) that an exhibit should not be open for inspection without the permission of the court where the other parties supported the administrators' application for the order as all had agreed to confidentiality in respect of at least a substantial part of the exhibit.

12.40 Office copies of documents

12.40(1) [Duty of court to provide] The court must provide an office copy of a document from the court file to a person who has under these Rules the right to inspect the court file where that person has requested such a copy and paid the appropriate fee under rule 12.39(7).

12.40(2) [Right exercisable by authorised person] A person's right under this rule may be exercised on that person's behalf by someone authorised to do so by that person.

12.40(3) [Form of office copy] An office copy must be in such form as the registrar or District Judge thinks appropriate, and must bear the court's seal.

Chapter 8

Costs

[Note: a document required by the Act or these Rules must also contain the standard contents set out in Part 1.]

12.41 Application of Chapter and interpretation

12.41(1) [Application] This Chapter applies to costs of and in connection with insolvency proceedings.

12.41(2) ["Costs"] In this Chapter "costs" includes charges and expenses.

12.41(3) [Application of CPR Pts 44, 47] CPR Parts 44 and 47 (which relate to costs) apply to such costs.

General Note

See *Bannai v Erez* [2013] EWHC 4287 (Comm); [2014] B.P.I.R. 1369.

12.42 Requirement to assess costs by the detailed procedure

12.42(1) [Where costs payable as insolvency expense] Where the costs of any person are payable as an expense out of the insolvent estate, the amount payable must be decided by detailed assessment unless agreed between the office-holder and the person entitled to payment.

12.42(2) [Service by office-holder] In the absence of agreement, the office-holder–

(a) may serve notice requiring the person entitled to payment to commence detailed assessment proceedings in accordance with CPR Part 47; and

(b) must serve such notice (except in an administrative receivership) where a liquidation or creditors' committee formed in relation to the insolvency proceedings resolves that the amount of the costs must be decided by detailed assessment.

12.42(3) [Detailed assessment in court with insolvency proceedings] Detailed assessment proceedings must be commenced in the court to which the insolvency proceedings are allocated or, where in relation to a company there is no such court, any court having jurisdiction to wind up the company.

12.42(4) [Payments on accounts of person employed by office-holder] Where the costs of any person employed by an office-holder in insolvency proceedings are required to be decided by detailed assessment or fixed by order of the court, the office-holder may make payments on account to such person in respect of those costs if that person undertakes in writing–

(a) to repay as soon as reasonably practicable any money which may, when detailed assessment is made, prove to have been overpaid; and

(b) to pay interest on any such sum as is mentioned in sub-paragraph (a) at the rate specified in section 17 of the Judgments Act 1838 on the date payment was made and for the period beginning with the date of payment and ending with the date of repayment.

12.42(5) [Detailed assessment in any proceedings] In any proceedings before the court (including proceedings on a petition), the court may order costs to be decided by detailed assessment.

12.42(6) [Costs of trustee in bankruptcy or liquidator on standard basis] Unless otherwise directed or authorised, the costs of a trustee in bankruptcy or a liquidator are to be allowed on the standard basis for which provision is made in–

(a) CPR rule 44.3 (basis of assessment); and

(b) CPR rule 44.4 (factors to be taken into account when deciding the amount of costs).

General Note

The original 1986 rule (IR 1986 r.7.34) was subjected to detailed scrutiny by Registrar Jones in *Hosking v Slaughter and May (a firm)* (sub nom. *Re Hellas Telecommunications (Luxembourg) II SCA* (unreported, 12 November 2013). The history of this provision and its ambit were fully explained. Particular attention was paid to IR 1986 r.7.34(4). The importance of the residual inherent jurisdiction of the court to deal with the assessment of costs was reiterated. The ruling of Registrar Jones is of value in the context of challenges to the costs incurred in an insolvency process. Presumably this ruling will be of assistance when construing r.12.42 in the future. This ruling of Registrar Jones ([2014] B.P.I.R. 179) was largely upheld by HHJ David Cooke QC in his judgment reported in [2014] EWHC 1390 (Ch).

12.43 Procedure where detailed assessment is required

12.43(1) [Costs officer to require certificate of employment] The costs officer must require a certificate of employment before making a detailed assessment of the costs of a person employed in insolvency proceedings by the office-holder.

12.43(2) [Content of certificate] The certificate must be endorsed on the bill and signed by the office-holder and must include–

(a) the name and address of the person employed;

(b) details of the functions to be carried out under the employment; and

(c) a note of any special terms of remuneration which have been agreed.

12.43(3) [Commencement of detailed assessment proceedings under CPR Pt 47] A person whose costs in insolvency proceedings are required to be decided by detailed assessment must, on being required in writing to do so by the office-holder, commence detailed assessment proceedings in accordance with CPR Part 47 (procedure for detailed assessment of costs and default provisions).

12.43(4) [Proceedings to commence within three months or forfeited] If that person does not commence such proceedings within 3 months of being required to do so under paragraph (3), or within such further time as the court, on application, may permit, the office-holder may deal with the insolvent estate without regard to any claim for costs by that person, whose claim is forfeited by such failure to commence proceedings.

12.43(5) [Additional costs against office-holder] Where in any such case such a claim for costs lies additionally against an office-holder in the office-holder's personal capacity, that claim is also forfeited by such failure to commence proceedings.

12.43(6) [Assessment of costs by High Court] Where costs have been incurred in insolvency proceedings in the High Court and those proceedings are subsequently transferred to the County Court, all costs of those proceedings directed by the court or otherwise required to be assessed may nevertheless, on the application of the person who incurred the costs, be ordered to be decided by detailed assessment in the High Court.

12.44 Costs of officers charged with execution of writs or other process

12.44(1) [Application of rule] This rule applies where an enforcement officer, or other officer charged with execution of the writ or other process–

(a) is required under section 184(2) or 346(2) to deliver up goods or money; or

(b) has under section 184(3) or 346(3) deducted costs from the proceeds of an execution or money paid to that officer.

12.44(2) [Enforcement or other officer's bill of costs] The office-holder may require in writing that the amount of the enforcement officer's or other officer's bill of costs be decided by detailed assessment and where such a requirement is made rule 12.43 (procedure where detailed assessment is required) applies.

12.44(3) [In case of r.12.44(1)(b) deduction] Where, in the case of a deduction of the kind mentioned in paragraph (1)(b), any amount deducted is disallowed at the conclusion of the detailed assessment proceedings, the enforcement officer must as soon as reasonably practicable pay a sum equal to that disallowed to the office-holder for the benefit of the insolvent estate.

General Note

The former references to "sheriff" were replaced by the more anodyne "enforcement officer" by I(A)R 2005 (SI 2005/527). This reflected changes in the Courts Act 2003.

12.45 Petitions presented by insolvent companies

12.45(1) [Company's own winding-up petition] This rule applies where a winding-up petition is presented by a company against itself.

12.45(2) [Solicitor to give credit for any deposit from company] A solicitor acting for the company must in the solicitor's bill of costs give credit for any sum or security received by the solicitor as a deposit from the company on account of the costs and expenses to be incurred in respect of the filing and prosecution of the petition and the deposit must be noted by the costs officer on the final costs certificate.

12.45(3) [Intervening creditor petition] Where an order is made on a petition presented by the company and before the presentation of that petition a petition had been presented by a creditor, no costs are to be allowed to the company or that company's solicitor out of the insolvent estate unless the court considers that–

(a) the insolvent estate has benefited by the company's conduct; or

(b) there are otherwise special circumstances justifying the allowance of costs.

12.46 Costs paid otherwise than out of the insolvent estate

12.46 Where the amount of costs is decided by detailed assessment under an order of the court directing that those costs are to be paid otherwise than out of the insolvent estate, the costs officer must note on the final costs certificate by whom, or the manner in which, the costs are to be paid.

12.47 Awards of costs against an office-holder, the adjudicator or the official receiver

12.47 Without prejudice to any provision of the Act or Rules by virtue of which the official receiver or the adjudicator is not in any event to be liable for costs and expenses, where an office-holder, the adjudicator or the official receiver (where the official receiver is not acting as an office-holder) is made a party to any proceedings on the application of another party to the proceedings, the office-holder, the adjudicator or official receiver is not to be personally liable for the costs unless the court otherwise directs.

General Note

Note *Bannai v Erez* [2013] EWHC 4287 (Comm); [2014] B.P.I.R. 1369. On costs under this rule see the comments of Lewison J in *Appleyard v Ritecrown Ltd* [2009] B.P.I.R. 235 at [55].

12.48 Applications for costs

12.48(1) [Application of rule] This rule applies where a party to, or person affected by, any proceedings in an insolvency applies to the court for an order allowing their costs, or part of them, of or incidental to the proceedings, and that application is not made at the time of the proceedings.

12.48(2) [Applicant to serve sealed copy] The applicant must serve a sealed copy of the application–

(a) in proceedings other than proceedings relating to a debt relief order–

  (i) on the office-holder, and

  (ii) in a winding up by the court or a bankruptcy, on the official receiver; or

(b) in proceedings relating to a debt relief order, on the official receiver.

12.48(3) [Appearances by office-holder, official receiver in r.12.48(2)(a) application] The office-holder and, where appropriate, the official receiver may appear on an application to which paragraph (2)(a) applies.

12.48(4) [Appearance by official receiver in r.12.48(2)(b) application] The official receiver may appear on an application to which paragraph (2)(b) applies.

12.48(5) [When costs to be disallowed] No costs of or incidental to the application are to be allowed to the applicant unless the court is satisfied that the application could not have been made at the time of the proceedings.

12.49 Costs and expenses of petitioners and other specified persons

12.49(1) [No allowance to petitioner as witness for attending hearing] The petitioner is not to receive an allowance as a witness for attending the hearing of the petition.

12.49(2) [Travelling and subsistence expenses for attending] However the costs officer may allow that person's expenses of travelling and subsistence in attending the hearing.

12.49(3) [No other costs as witness unless court directs] The bankrupt, the debtor or an officer of the insolvent company to which the proceedings relate is not to receive an allowance as a witness in an examination or other proceedings before the court except as directed by the court.

12.50 Final costs certificate

12.50(1) [Certificate final and conclusive] A final costs certificate of the costs officer is final and conclusive as to all matters which have not been objected to in the manner provided for under the rules of the court.

12.50(2) [Duplicate if certificate lost or destroyed] Where it is proved to the satisfaction of a costs officer that a final costs certificate has been lost or destroyed, the costs officer may issue a duplicate.

Chapter 9

Enforcement procedures

Introductory note to Chapter 9

Chapter 9, as the title indicates, deals with the procedures for the enforcement of court orders, of statutory duties and of warrants issued under IA 2016. In particular, r.12.52 sanctions with the backing of the court the general duty of corporate officers and others to co-operate with the official receiver and with insolvency practitioners holding office as liquidator, etc.

[Note: a document required by the Act or these Rules must also contain the standard contents set out in Part 1.]

12.51 Enforcement of court orders

12.51(1) [Orders enforced as judgments] In any insolvency proceedings, orders of the court may be enforced in the same manner as a judgment to the same effect.

12.51(2) [County Court order enforceable in any hearing centre] Where an order in insolvency proceedings is made, or any process is issued, by the County Court, the order or process may be enforced, executed and dealt with by any hearing centre, as if it had been made or issued for the enforcement of a judgment or order to the same effect made by that hearing centre.

12.51(3) [Application of r.12.51(2)] Paragraph (2) applies whether or not the other hearing centre is one in which such insolvency proceedings may be commenced.

12.51(4) [Discharge of arrest warrant] Where a warrant for the arrest of a person is issued by the High Court, the warrant may be discharged by the County Court where the person who is the subject of the warrant–

(a) has been brought before a hearing centre in which insolvency proceedings may be commenced; and

(b) has given to the County Court a satisfactory undertaking to comply with the obligations that apply to that person under the Act or these Rules.

12.52 Orders enforcing compliance

12.52(1) [Power of court on application by competent person] The court may, on application by the competent person, make such orders as it thinks necessary for the enforcement of obligations falling on any person in accordance with–

(a) paragraph 47 of Schedule B1 (duty to submit statement of affairs in administration);

(b) section 47(duty to submit statement of affairs in administrative receivership);

(c) section 131 (duty to submit statement of affairs in a winding up);

(d) section 143(2) (liquidator to furnish information, books, papers, etc.); or

(e) section 235 (duty of various persons to co-operate with office-holder).

12.52(2) [Competent person] The competent person for this purpose is–

(a) under paragraph 47 of Schedule B1, the administrator;

(b) under section 47, the administrative receiver;

(c) under section 131 or 143(2), the official receiver; and

(d) under section 235, the official receiver, the administrator, the administrative receiver, the liquidator or the provisional liquidator, as the case may be.

12.52(3) [Costs] An order of the court under this rule may provide that all costs of and incidental to the application for it are to be borne by the person against whom the order is made.

12.53 Warrants (general provisions)

12.53(1) [Address for warrant] A warrant issued by the court under any provision of the Act must be addressed to such officer of the High Court or of the County Court as the warrant specifies, or to any constable.

12.53(2) [Prescribed officers of the court] The persons referred to in sections 134(2), 236(5), 251N(5), 364(1), 365(3) and 366(3) (court's powers of enforcement) as the prescribed officer of the court are–

(a) in the case of the High Court, the tipstaff and the tipstaff's assistants of the court; and

(b) in the case of the County Court, a bailiff.

12.53(3) [References to property in Ch.9] In this Chapter references to property include books, papers and other documents and records.

12.54 Warrants under sections 134 and 364

12.54 When a person ("the arrested person") is arrested under a warrant issued by the court under section 134 (officer of company failing to attend for public examination), or section 364 (arrest of debtor or bankrupt)–

(a) the arresting officer must give the arrested person into the custody of–

  (i) the court in a case where the court is ready and able to deal with the arrested person, or

  (ii) where the court is not ready and able, the governor of the prison named in the warrant (or where that prison is not able to accommodate the arrested person, the governor of such other prison with appropriate facilities which is able to accommodate the arrested person), who must keep the arrested person in custody until such time as the court orders otherwise and must produce that person before the court at its next sitting; and

(b) any property in the arrested person's possession which may be seized must, as directed by the warrant, be–

(i) delivered to whoever is specified in the warrant as authorised to receive it, or otherwise dealt with in accordance with the directions in the warrant, or

(ii) kept by the officer seizing it pending the receipt of written orders from the court as to its disposal.

12.55 Warrants under sections 236, 251N and 366

12.55(1) [Arresting officer to bring arrested person before court for examination] When a person is arrested under a warrant issued under section 236 (inquiry into insolvent company's dealings), 251N (the equivalent in relation to debt relief orders) or 366 (the equivalent in bankruptcy), the arresting officer must as soon as reasonably practicable bring the arrested person before the court issuing the warrant in order that the arrested person may be examined.

12.55(2) [Custody of arrested person if immediate examination not possible] If the arrested person cannot immediately be brought up for examination, the officer must deliver that person into the custody of the governor of the prison named in the warrant (or where that prison is not able to accommodate the arrested person, the governor of such other prison with appropriate facilities which is able to accommodate the arrested person), who must keep the arrested person in custody and produce that person before the court as it may from time to time direct.

12.55(3) [Application to fix venue for arrested person's examination] After arresting the person named in the warrant, the officer must as soon as reasonably practicable report to the court the arrest or delivery into custody (as the case may be) and apply to the court to fix a venue for the arrested person's examination.

12.55(4) [Duty of court] The court must appoint the earliest practicable time for the examination, and must–

(a) direct the governor of the prison to produce the arrested person for examination at the time and place appointed; and

(b) as soon as reasonably practicable deliver notice of the venue to the applicant for the warrant.

12.55(5) [Property in arrested person's possession] Where any property in the arrested person's possession is seized, the property must, as directed by the warrant, be–

(a) delivered to whoever is specified in the warrant as authorised to receive it, or otherwise dealt with in accordance with the directions in the warrant; or

(b) kept by the officer seizing it pending the receipt of written orders from the court as to its disposal.

12.56 Warrants under section 365

12.56(1) [Seizure of property] A warrant issued under section 365(3) (search of premises not belonging to the bankrupt) must authorise any person executing it to seize any property of the bankrupt found as a result of the execution of the warrant.

12.56(2) [Seized property] Any property seized under a warrant issued under section 365(2) or (3) must, as directed by the warrant, be–

(a) delivered to whoever is specified in the warrant as authorised to receive it, or otherwise dealt with in accordance with the directions in the warrant; or

(b) kept by the officer seizing it pending the receipt of written orders from the court as to its disposal.

12.57 Execution overtaken by judgment debtor's insolvency

12.57(1) [Application of rule] This rule applies where execution has been taken out against property of a judgment debtor, and notice is delivered to the enforcement officer or other officer charged with the execution–

(a) under section 184(1) (that a winding-up order has been made against the debtor, or that a provisional liquidator has been appointed, or that a resolution for voluntary winding up has been passed);

(b) under section 184(4) (that a winding-up petition has been presented, or a winding-up order made, or that a meeting has been called at which there is to be proposed a resolution for voluntary winding up, or that such a resolution has been passed);

(c) under section 346(2) (that a judgment debtor has been made bankrupt); or

(d) under section 346(3)(b) (that a bankruptcy petition has been presented or a bankruptcy application has been made in relation to the debtor).

12.57(2) [Notice to be delivered to enforcement or other officer] Subject to paragraph (3) and rule 1.47, the notice must be delivered to the office of the enforcement officer or of the officer charged with the execution–

(a) by hand; or

(b) by any other means of delivery which enables proof of receipt of the document at the relevant address.

12.57(3) [Execution in County Court] Where the execution is in the County Court then if–

(a) there is filed with the hearing centre in charge of such execution in relation to the judgment debtor a winding-up or bankruptcy petition; or

(b) there is made by the hearing centre in charge of such execution in relation to the judgment debtor a winding-up order or an order appointing a provisional liquidator, or a bankruptcy order or an order appointing an interim receiver;

section 184 or 346 is deemed satisfied in relation to the requirement of a notice to be served on, or delivered to, the officer in charge of the execution.

General Note

This deals with substantive issues concerned with executions—see IA 1986 ss.184 and 346.

Chapter 10

Appeals

[Note: a document required by the Act or these Rules must also contain the standard contents set out in Part 1.]

12.58 Application of Chapter

12.58 CPR Part 52 (appeals) applies to appeals under this Chapter as varied by any applicable Practice Direction.

General Note

In *Raguz v Scottish & Newcastle Ltd* [2010] B.P.I.R. 945 the differences between an appeal under this chapter and a s.375 review were explained. This rule was noted in *Michael v Official Receiver* [2013] EWHC 4286 (Ch); [2014] B.P.I.R. 666—the earlier ruling of Chief Registrar Baister was appealed and, although the BRO was upheld by Roth J, the period for which it was scheduled to run was reduced from 8 to 6.5 years.

Note here *Sykes v Shillito* [2017] EWHC 3588 (Ch).

See for further detail on the routes of appeal, *Practice Direction: Insolvency Proceedings* [2018] B.C.C. 241, para.17.

12.59 Appeals and reviews of court orders in corporate insolvency

12.59(1) [Powers of court] Every court having jurisdiction for the purposes of Parts 1 to 7 of the Act and the corresponding Parts of these Rules, may review, rescind or vary any order made by it in the exercise of that jurisdiction.

12.59(2) [Where appeals lie from single judge or registrar] Appeals in civil matters in proceedings under Parts 1 to 7 of the Act and the corresponding Parts of these Rules lie as follows–

(a) where the decision appealed against is made by a District Judge sitting in a hearing centre specified in the first column of the table in Schedule 10–

(i) to a High Court Judge sitting in a district registry, or

(ii) to an Insolvency and Companies Court Judge;

as specified in the second column of the table;

(b) to a High Court Judge where the decision appealed against is made by–

(i) a Circuit Judge sitting in the County Court,

(ii) a Master,

(iii) an Insolvency and Companies Court Judge, if that decision is made at first instance, or

(iv) a District Judge sitting in a district registry;

(c) to the Civil Division of the Court of Appeal where the decision appealed against is made by a Registrar in Bankruptcy of the High Court, if that decision is an appeal from a decision made by a District Judge; and

(d) to the Civil Division of the Court of Appeal where the decision is made by a High Court Judge.

12.59(3) [Time limit for application for rescission of winding-up order] Any application for the rescission of a winding-up order must be made within five business days after the date on which the order was made.

12.59(4) [Definitions] In this rule–

"Circuit Judge sitting in the county court" means a judge sitting pursuant to section 5(1)(a) of the County Courts Act 1984;

"Civil Division of the Court of Appeal" means the division of the Court of Appeal established by section 3(1) of the Senior Courts Act 1981;

"county court" means the court established by section A1 of the County Courts Act 1984; "District Judge" means a person appointed a District Judge under section 6(1) of the County Courts Act 1984;

"District Judge sitting in a district registry" means a District Judge sitting in an assigned district registry as a District Judge of the High Court under section 100 of the Senior Courts Act 1981;

"district registry" means a district registry of the High Court under section 99 of the Senior Courts Act 1981;

"High Court Judge" means a judge listed in section 4(1) of the Senior Courts Act 1981; "Master" means a person appointed to the office of Master, Chancery Division under section 89(1) of the Senior Courts Act 1981;

"Insolvency and Companies Court Judge" means a person appointed to the office of Insolvency and Companies Court Judge under section 89(1) of the Senior Courts Act 1981;

and for the purposes of each definition a person appointed to act as a deputy for any person holding that office is included.

General Note

Appeals from a registrar's winding-up order go to the High Court, not the Court of Appeal: *Re Calahurst Ltd* (1989) 5 B.C.C. 318. This point was confirmed by the Court of Appeal in *Re Tasbian Ltd (No.2)* [1990] B.C.C. 322. This is also true in relation to an order made by a district judge in the county court: *Re Langley Marketing Services Ltd* [1992] B.C.C. 585; and the rule applies to an order made under CDDA 1986. It applies also to administration orders: *Cornhill Insurance plc v Cornhill Financial Services Ltd* [1992] B.C.C. 818. The appeal may take the form either of an appeal against the original decision of the registrar, or of an appeal from the registrar's refusal to review his original decision (*Re S N Group plc* [1993] B.C.C. 808). The jurisdiction under this rule is very wide, and extends even to the review, rescission or variation by a High Court judge of a decision of any judge of that court: *Re W&A Glaser Ltd* [1994] B.C.C. 199 at 208, per Harman J. A judge can review his or her own decisions under r.12.59(1)—*Re Thirty Eight Building Ltd (No.2)* [2000] B.P.I.R. 158. The court has power to make retrospective orders under IR 2016 r.12.59(1)—see *Re Roches Leisure Services Ltd* [2005] EWHC 3148 (Ch); [2006] B.P.I.R. 453 (retrospectively extending date for expiry of administration). Leave is not required for an appeal to the High Court (*Re Busytoday Ltd* [1992] B.C.C. 480), but is necessary for a further appeal to the Court of Appeal (*Midrome Ltd v Shaw* [1993] B.C.C. 659). In spite of the wording of r.12.59(2) second appeals to the Court of Appeal require the leave of the Court of Appeal—Access to Justice Act 1999 s.55.

Appeals under r.12.59(2) are true appeals and do not require a hearing *de novo*. Thus a decision of the registrar will only be overturned if it was based on an error of law or wrongful exercise of discretion: *Re Probe Data Systems Ltd (No.3)* [1991] B.C.C. 428; and *Re Tasbian Ltd (No.3)* [1991] B.C.C. 435. See also *Re Industrial & Commercial Securities plc* (1989) 5 B.C.C. 320. The court will review an exercise of discretion only if it is satisfied that no judge, properly instructed as to the law with regard to the relevant facts, could have reached the conclusion that was reached in the court below: *Re MTI Trading Systems Ltd* [1998] B.C.C. 400. However, the court may rescind a winding-up order made by the registrar notwithstanding the fact that there is no ground to allow an appeal from his decision: *Re Dollar Land (Feltham) Ltd* [1995] B.C.C. 740. The High Court can hear both an appeal from and a request to review a registrar's order—*Re Piccadilly Property Management Ltd* [1999] B.P.I.R. 260.

The jurisdiction of the court under r.12.59 is not inconsistent with CPR r.40.12 (the "slip rule"); and an error in an order may be corrected under either provision, or under the court's inherent jurisdiction: *Re Brian Sheridan Cars Ltd* [1995] B.C.C. 1,035.

For limitations on the jurisdiction under IR 2016 r.12.59 see *Wilson v The Specter Partnership* [2007] EWHC 133 (Ch); [2007] B.P.I.R. 649 at [25]. Again, in *Eastaway v Secretary of State for Trade and Industry* [2007] B.C.C. 550 the Court of Appeal indicated that IR 2016 r.12.59(1) does not confer jurisdiction on the court to discharge a director disqualification *undertaking* because that rule applies only to court orders.

A full consideration of how the exercise of discretion is to be carried out is to be found in *Re Metrocab Ltd* [2010] B.P.I.R. 1368. Here the application was brought out of time and the court, following *Sayers v Clarke Walker (a Firm)* [2002] 1 W.L.R. 3095, held that CPR r.3.9 was engaged. The commonality of principles developed under IA 1986 s.375 was also stressed. The application proved unsuccessful. This provision came into play in *Re Broadside Colours and Chemicals Ltd (No.2)* [2012] EWHC 195 (Ch) where the linkage with the principles in CPR r.39.3 was emphasised. IR 2016 r.12.59(1) was also considered in *Re Switch Services Ltd* [2012] Bus. L.R. D91. For the latest review of the principles governing the exercise of discretion under IR r.12.59(1) see the judgment of Barling J in *Credit Lucky Ltd and Gui Hui Dong v National Crime Agency* [2014] EWHC 83 (Ch) where the court refused either to rescind or even stay a winding-up order.

Paragraph (3) was considered by Mann J in *Wilson v The Specter Partnership* (above) in which the point was made that the court enjoys discretion to extend the seven day period where the delay was justified and can be explained.

The procedure for appeals against orders under IR 2016 r.12.59 is governed by CPR r.52.11—*Jacob v UIC Insurance Co Ltd* [2007] B.C.C. 167.

Rule 12.59(2)(a)(ii), (b)(iii), (c), (4) amended by the Alteration of Judicial Titles (Registrar in Bankruptcy of the High Court) Order 2018 (SI 2018/130) arts 1, 3 Sch. para.14(a)(ii), (b) as from 26 February 2018.

See further the General Note to IA 1986 s.375.

12.60 Appeals in bankruptcy by the Secretary of State

12.60 In bankruptcy proceedings, an appeal lies at the instance of the Secretary of State from any order of the court made on an application for the rescission or annulment of a bankruptcy order, or for the bankrupt's discharge.

12.61 Procedure on appeal

12.61(1) [Permission of first instance or appeal court required] An appeal against a decision at first instance may be brought only with the permission of the court which made the decision or of the court that has jurisdiction to hear the appeal.

12.61(2) [Time limit for appellant's notice] An appellant must file an appellant's notice within 21 days after the date of the decision of the court that the appellant wishes to appeal.

General Note

See note to r.12.58.

12.62 Appeals against decisions of the Secretary of State or official receiver

12.62 An appeal under the Act or these Rules against a decision of the Secretary of State or the official receiver must be brought within 28 days of delivery of notice of the decision.

Chapter 11

Court orders, formal defects and shorthand writers

[Note: a document required by the Act or these Rules must also contain the standard contents set out in Part 1.]

12.63 Court orders

12.63 Notwithstanding any requirement in these Rules as to the contents of a court order the court may make such other order or in such form as the court thinks just.

12.64 Formal defects

12.64 No insolvency proceedings will be invalidated by any formal defect or any irregularity unless the court before which objection is made considers that substantial injustice has been caused by the defect or irregularity and that the injustice cannot be remedied by any order of the court.

General Note

This rule appears to have been based on BA 1914 s.147(1), but is made to apply to all forms of insolvency proceedings. For its relevance in the context of setting aside a statutory demand, see *Re a Debtor (No.1 of 1987)* [1988] 1 W.L.R. 419. In the later case of *Re a Debtor (No.190 of 1987), The Times*, May 21, 1988, Vinelott J held that IR 1986 r.7.55 (now IR 2016 r.12.64) did not apply to cure defects in the statutory demand. He thereby followed *Re Cartwright* [1975] 1 W.L.R. 573, which was decided under the old law. In *Re Awan* [2000] B.P.I.R. 241 Boggis J refused to allow IR 1986 r.7.55 to be invoked to justify failure to provide proof of service of petition as this was regarded as such a fundamental flaw. The courts have stated repeatedly that this provision cannot be used to validate the defective appointment of an administrator out of court where there has been a significant procedural defect—see

Henderson J in *Re Frontsouth (Witham) Ltd* [2011] EWHC 1668 (Ch); [2011] B.P.I.R. 1382. But the test today is to ask whether the flaw is so fundamental as to render the appointment a nullity. The law is evolving here (see Norris J in *Re Euromaster Ltd* [2012] EWHC 2356 (Ch); [2012] B.C.C. 754) and there is therefore a question of degree engaged depending upon the procedural defect in each case under scrutiny. In *Re Anderson Owen Ltd* [2009] EWHC 2837 (Ch); [2010] B.P.I.R. 37 it was held by Norris J that IR 1986 r.7.55 (now IR 2016 r.12.64) could be invoked to cure any defective service of proceedings instituted under IA 1986 s.212.

Rule 12.64 only applies in the context of "insolvency proceedings"—this phrase had in the past been somewhat narrowly defined by the courts so as to exclude the appointment of an administrator out of court pursuant to Sch.B1 para.22—*Re Blights Builders Ltd* [2006] EWHC 3549 (Ch); [2007] B.C.C. 712. This provision can only come into play if there are insolvency proceedings afoot—see *Pui-Kwan v Kam-Ho* [2015] EWHC 621 (Ch). Here the Chancellor refused to apply it to the appointment of an administrator where there was no decision ever taken by the directors to make such an appointment—see [75] per Sir Terence Etherton. IR 1986 r.7.55 (now IR 2016 r.12.64) was also held not to be applicable in exactly the same circumstances in *Re G-Tech Construction Ltd* [2007] B.P.I.R. 1275. However, later decisions have adopted a more expansive approach—see *Re Frontsouth (Witham) Ltd* [2011] EWHC 1668 (Ch); [2011] B.C.C. 635 and *Re Euromaster Ltd* [2012] EWHC 2356 (Ch); [2012] B.C.C. 754 at [37] per Norris J. This view that administration activated outside court is a form of insolvency proceeding reflects reality and is consistent with its treatment under the Recast EU Insolvency Regulation 2015/848. But on the specific point of determining the appropriate relief to excuse the defective appointment out of court of administrators the observations of Norris J in *Euromaster* (above) were not followed by Andrew Hochhauser QC (sitting in the High Court) in *Re Eiffel Steelworks Ltd* [2015] EWHC 511 (Ch); [2015] 2 B.C.L.C. 57. Although the irregularity was excused because no one was prejudiced, the court also flatly refused to make a retrospective order validating the appointment. The Northern Irish decision of Deeny J in *Cavanagh v Dolan* [2015] NICh 14 adds weight to the uncertainty as to the applicability of IR 1986 r.7.55 to defective out of court appointments of administrators.

In *Re a Debtor (No.340 of 1992)* [1996] 2 All E.R. 211 it was held that IR 1986 r.7.55 did not validate an improperly executed writ of *fieri facias* as in the circumstances of the case the irregularity was so serious as to mean that the writ could not be said to have been served at all. Here apart from knocking on a debtor's door the bailiff had left the premises without any serious attempt to gain access.

IR 1986 r.7.55 did, however, come into play in *Re a Debtor (No.22 of 1993)* [1994] 1 W.L.R. 46 (sometimes cited as *Focus Insurance v a Debtor*) where an omission by a creditor to state in his petition that there was an extant set-aside application by the debtor was waved through by Mummery J. See also *Re Continental Assurance Co of London plc (in liq.) (No.2)* [1998] 1 B.C.L.C. 583, where an application had been made in the wrong form but no prejudice had occurred. See also *Oben v Blackman* [2000] B.P.I.R. 302.

In *Foenander v Allan* [2006] B.P.I.R. 1392 the potential usage of this rule in addressing complaints about the constitution of the creditors' committee was noted.

Rule 12.64 could be used to correct a slip in a block transfer order that had incorrectly suggested that there was jurisdiction under IR 1986 r.6.132(5) (now IR 2016 r.10.80) to make an appointment of a trustee in bankruptcy—*Donaldson v O'Sullivan* [2008] EWHC 387 (Ch); [2008] B.P.I.R. 288 which was confirmed on other grounds—see [2008] EWCA Civ 879. But see now IR 2016 rr.12.35–12.39.

This provision was deployed to excuse a possible defect in the service of a bankruptcy petition in *Gate Gourmet Luxembourg IV SARL v Morby* [2015] EWHC 1203 (Ch); [2015] B.P.I.R. 787. On whether that was necessary on the facts of the case see the appeal before Edward Murray in [2016] EWHC 74 (Ch), where useful observations are made on when IR 2016 r.12.64 should come into play. In *Canning v Irwin Mitchell LLP* [2017] EWHC 718 (Ch); [2017] B.P.I.R. 934, however, improper service of a statutory demand was found not to be a defect that could be cured and the *Gate Gourmet* case (above) was distinguished.

The potential application of this remedial rule to errors in a bankruptcy order relating to the application of what is now EU Insolvency Regulation 2015/848 was also confirmed in *Loy v O'Sullivan* [2010] EWHC 3583 (Ch); [2011] B.P.I.R. 181. There was no evidence that such errors had caused prejudice to the debtor.

IR 1986 r.7.55 (now IR 2016 r.12.64) was used by Norris J to cure the procedural defect in the appointment of administrators in *Re Euromaster Ltd* [2012] EWHC 2356 (Ch); [2012] B.C.C. 754 (appointment made one day after notice of intention to appoint had expired). But compare *Re Eco Link Resources Ltd* [2012] B.C.C. 731 where the court refused to deploy this provision to cure the defect (failure to notify prior charge holder). See also *Re MTB Motors Ltd* [2010] EWHC 3751 (Ch); [2012] B.C.C. 601 (IR 1986 r.7.55 validation refused where appointment of administrator was defective).

In *Re Baillies Ltd* [2012] EWHC 285 (Ch); [2012] B.P.I.R. 665 HHJ Purle QC discussed this provision in the context of a failure to comply with the requirements of the EC Service Regulation (1393/2007) and doubted whether IR 1986 r.7.55 could operate in this context to override the Regulation.

In *Re Care People Ltd* [2013] EWHC 1734 (Ch); [2013] B.C.C. 466 HHJ Purle QC used this provision to validate an irregular appointment of an administrator made under Sch.B1 para.14. The qualifying floating charge holder had not allowed the debtor company adequate time to meet the demand but it was crystal clear that the company could not have met the repayment even if such time had been granted. The interests of creditors generally dictated the validation of the appointment of the administrator. The potential utility of this provision was raised in *Kasumu v Arrow Global (Guernsey) Ltd* [2013] EWHC 789 (Ch); [2013] B.P.I.R. 1047 where there had been a failure to comply with the requirements of IR 1986 r.6.26 (now IR 2016 r.10.26).

For a lucid account of the rationale behind this provision and comparison with IR 1986 r.7.55 see Baister [2018] 31 Insolv. Int. 3.

12.65 Shorthand writers: nomination etc.

12.65(1) [Nomination in writing] The court may in writing nominate a person to be official shorthand writer to the court.

12.65(2) [Appointment re evidence in examination under IA 1986 ss.133, 236, 251N, 290, 366] The court may, at any time in the course of insolvency proceedings, appoint a shorthand writer to take down evidence of a person examined under section 133, 236, 251N, 290 or 366.

12.65(3) [Application by official receiver] Where the official receiver applies to the court for an order appointing a shorthand writer, the official receiver must name the person the official receiver proposes for the appointment.

12.65(4) [Liability for remuneration] The remuneration of a shorthand writer appointed in insolvency proceedings must be paid by the party at whose instance the appointment was made, or out of the insolvent estate, or otherwise, as the court may direct.

12.65(5) [Remuneration rate determined by court] Any question arising as to the rates of remuneration payable under this rule must be determined by the court.

Part 13

Official Receivers

Introductory note to Part 13

This commendably short Part of IR 2016 provides detail on the role of Official Receivers. It mirrors Pt 10 of IR 1986. Note that private stakeholders cannot appoint the official receiver to insolvency office (r.13.5).

The rules in this Part supplement IA 1986 ss.399–401.

13.1 Official receivers in court

13.1(1) [Judicial notice of appointment under IA 1986 ss.399–401] Judicial notice must be taken of the appointment under sections 399 to 401 of official receivers and deputy official receivers.

13.1(2) [Right of audience] Official receivers and deputy official receivers have a right of audience in insolvency proceedings, whether in the High Court or the County Court.

General Note

Court involvement for the OR.

13.2 Persons entitled to act on official receiver's behalf

13.2(1) [In absence of official receiver] In the absence of the official receiver authorised to act in a particular case, an officer authorised in writing for the purpose by the Secretary of State, or by the official receiver, may with the permission of the court, act on the official receiver's behalf and in the official receiver's place–

(a) in any examination under section 133, 236, 251N, 290 or 366; and

(b) in relation to any application to the court.

13.2(2) [In case of emergency] In case of emergency, where there is no official receiver capable of acting, anything to be done by, to or before the official receiver may be done by, to or before the registrar or District Judge.

General Note

The possibility of a person acting on behalf of the official receiver would appear to be in addition to the appointment of a deputy under IA 1986 s.401.

13.3 Application for directions

13.3 The official receiver may apply to the court for directions in relation to any matter arising in insolvency proceedings.

General Note

This is a standard facility for all insolvency practitioners.

13.4 Official receiver's expenses

13.4(1) [Proceedings against official receiver] Any expenses (including damages) incurred by the official receiver (in whatever capacity the official receiver may be acting) in connection with proceedings taken against the official receiver in insolvency proceedings are to be treated as expenses of the insolvency proceedings.

13.4(2) [Official receiver's charge except re DRO proceedings] The official receiver has a charge on the insolvent estate in respect of any sums due to the official receiver under paragraph (1) in connection with insolvency proceedings other than proceedings relating to debt relief orders or applications for debt relief orders.

General Note

Note the wide definition of "expenses".

13.5 Official receiver not to be appointed liquidator or trustee

13.5 The official receiver may not be appointed as liquidator or trustee by any decision of creditors or (in a winding up) contributories or the company.

General Note

The OR cannot be privately appointed.

Part 14

Claims by and Distributions to Creditors in Administration, Winding Up and Bankruptcy

Introductory note to Part 14

This is one of the co-ordinated Parts of IR 2016 that is relevant to a wide range of insolvency regimes. Its provisions on claims and distributions contain much that was in the former IR 1986 Pt 11.

Rule 14.1(3) introduces from 6 April 2017 the novel concept of a "small debt" (not exceeding £1,000), which under r.14.3(3) in administration, winding up and bankruptcy is deemed to have been proved—but only for the purposes of determination and payment of a dividend. The provision was prescribed by IA 1986 Sch.8 para.13A (corporate insolvency) and Sch.9 para.18A (personal insolvency) as inserted by SBEEA 2015 ss.131 and 132.

Rule 14.2 identifies provable debts. Reference should be made to r.14.1 to see what constitutes a "debt" while "bankruptcy debt" is defined in s.382 illustrating an inconsistency in materials between IA 1986 and IR 2016.

Procedures relating to proof of debt are spelled out. On rejection of proof see r.14.8. The position of secured creditors is also addressed with r.14.5 addressing valuation of security.

The procedures for proving small debts are deregulated by r.14.31. This is a change brought about by SBEEA 2015 s.121 which inserted a new para.18A into Sch.9 to IA 1986. A small debt is defined by r.14.1 as a debt worth less than £1,000.

The rules on set-off for cases of administration and winding up are now located in IR 2016 rr.14.24 and 14.25 respectively.

Chapter 1

Application and interpretation

14.1 Application of Part 14 and interpretation

[Note: "bankruptcy debt" and related expressions are defined in relation to bankruptcy in section 382.]

14.1(1) [Application] This Part applies to administration, winding up and bankruptcy proceedings.

14.1(2) [Application of definitions] The definitions in this rule apply to administration, winding up and bankruptcy proceedings except as otherwise stated.

14.1(3) [Definitions] "Debt", in relation to winding up and administration, means (subject to the next paragraph) any of the following–

(a) any debt or liability to which the company is subject at the relevant date;

(b) any debt or liability to which the company may become subject after the relevant date by reason of any obligation incurred before that date;

(c) any interest provable as mentioned in rule 14.23;

"small debt" means a debt (being the total amount owed to a creditor) which does not exceed £1,000 (which amount is prescribed for the purposes of paragraph 13A of Schedule 8 to the Act and paragraph 18A of Schedule 9 to the Act);

"dividend", in relation to a members' voluntary winding up, includes a distribution; "provable debt" has the meaning given in rule 14.2; and

"relevant date" means–

(a) in the case of an administration which was not immediately preceded by a winding up, the date on which the company entered administration,

(b) in the case of an administration which was immediately preceded by a winding up, the date on which the company went into liquidation,

(c) in the case of a winding up which was not immediately preceded by an administration, the date on which the company went into liquidation,

(d) in the case of a winding up which was immediately preceded by an administration, the date on which the company entered administration, and

(e) in the case of a bankruptcy, the date of the bankruptcy order.

14.1(4) [Liability in tort] For the purposes of any provision of the Act or these Rules about winding up or administration, any liability in tort is a debt provable in the winding up or administration, if either–

(a) the cause of action has accrued at the relevant date; or

(b) all the elements necessary to establish the cause of action exist at that date except for actionable damage.

14.1(5) [Debt or liability] For the purposes of references in any provision of the Act or these Rules about winding up or administration to a debt or liability, it is immaterial whether the debt or liability is present or future, whether it is certain or contingent, or whether its amount is fixed or liquidated, or is capable of being ascertained by fixed rules or as a matter of opinion; and references in any such provision to owing a debt are to be read accordingly.

14.1(6) ["Liability"] In any provision of the Act or these Rules about winding up or administration, except in so far as the context otherwise requires, "liability" means (subject to paragraph (4)) a liability to pay money or money's worth, including any liability under an enactment, a liability for breach of trust, any liability in contract, tort or bailment, and any liability arising out of an obligation to make restitution.

General Note

This important provision, the predecessor of which in IR 1986 which had been remodelled in 2006 and 2010, would have been better located in the Act itself. Compare IA 1986 s.382 ("debt" in bankruptcy cases), and see also r.14.2 (provable debts); and note that although unlike IR 1986 this Part now applies to administration as well as to winding up there are no corresponding definitions for company voluntary arrangements—a somewhat surprising omission in view of the reference to "a debt of an unliquidated or ascertained amount" in r.15.31(3). These omissions have had to be made good by the case law. For references to the relevant cases and a general discussion of the terms "debt" and "creditor", see the note to IA 1986 s.1(1), and also the notes to IA 1986 Sch.8 paras 12 and 14. In *Re T&N Ltd* [2005] EWHC 2870 (Ch); [2006] B.P.I.R. 532 David Richards J held that future tort claimants could not be regarded as creditors with provable debts under what was then IR 1986 r.13.12. In so deciding David Richards J rejected the suggestion that such an exclusionary approach contravened either art.14 or the First Protocol of ECHR. In response to that decision the rule was modified so as specifically to include such claimants within the concept of "creditor": now in r.14.1(4). The original wording of this rule was considered in *Re Beloit Walmsley Ltd* [2008] B.P.I.R. 1445.

In *Re Kentish Homes Ltd* [1993] B.C.C. 212 a rare example of non-provable debt arose. In this case a Law of Property Act receiver had incurred community charges in respect of premises which had been constructed by the receiver in order to fulfil contractual obligations of the insolvent company, but which had remained unoccupied until they were sold. This property development company had gone into liquidation after the commencement of a Law of Property Act receivership but the liquidator had not been allowed into possession. On the subsequent liquidation of the company it was held by Nicholls VC that the conditions laid down in what is now r.14.1(3) had not been satisfied in respect of this sum and the local authority could not prove in respect of it. The liability to pay the community charge did not exist at the date of entry into liquidation nor did it arise in respect of a pre-liquidation obligation. The receiver was empowered to settle this debt but he had no legal obligation under LPA 1925 s.109(8)(i) to do so nor would the court require him to do so. His Lordship made the point that the position would be the same in respect of the new council tax. These comments should be viewed with caution in view of *Re Toshoku Finance (UK) plc* [2002] UKHL 6; [2002] 1 W.L.R. 671.

By way of contrast it was held in *Tottenham Hotspur plc v Edennote plc* [1994] B.C.C. 681 that an order for costs was a debt for the purposes of what are now r.14.1(3)(b) and (5) and so could form the basis of a winding-up petition.

In *Haine and Secretary of State v Day* [2008] EWCA Civ 626; [2008] B.C.C. 845 the Court of Appeal, allowing an appeal from Sir Donald Rattee, held that a protective award made against an employer pursuant to the Trade Union and Labour Relations (Consolidation) Act 1992 s.189(2) but after the entry into liquidation of that employer was a provable debt. Although the quantum of the award was a matter of judicial discretion which was exercised by the tribunal after the liquidation date, the underlying liability itself was triggered by the failure to consult about the job losses prior to liquidation. This interpretation was necessary to give effect to EC Council Directive 98/59. Also where there had been no attempt to consult the assumption would be that the full award would be made unless there were mitigating circumstances.

On contingent liabilities see *Re Nortel Networks (UK) Ltd* [2010] EWHC 826 (Ch); [2010] B.C.C. 706 (Norris J).

Further consideration of the issue of what is a contingent liability for the purposes of r.14.1 was given by Briggs J in the test case of *Bloom v Pensions Regulator* [2010] EWHC 3010 (Ch); [2011] B.C.C. 277. Here one question was whether a financial support direction and/or a contribution notice given under the moral hazard provisions in the Pensions Act 2004 when issued against a company in administration constituted a provable debt or not. This may depend upon issues of timing and whether the company subsequently enters liquidation. Briggs J offered a detailed analysis of the history of this rule and made the point that authorities dealing with it are not entirely consistent. The ruling of Briggs J was upheld by the Court of Appeal—*Bloom v Pensions Regulator* [2011] EWCA Civ 1124; [2012] B.C.C. 83—but the Supreme Court differed: [2013] UKSC 52; [2014] A.C. 209; [2013] B.C.C. 624. Cases suggesting a restrictive view of risk and contingent liability (i.e. *Glenister v Rowe* [2000] Ch. 76 and *R. (Steele) v*

Birmingham City Council [2005] EWCA Civ 1824) were overruled by the Supreme Court in *Re Nortel Companies; Bloom v Pensions Regulator* [2013] UKSC 52; [2014] A.C. 209; [2013] B.C.C. 624. It is clear that we now have a wider, more flexible concept of provable debt—that is a welcome development that reflects commercial reality. For discussion see Moss [2013] 26 Insolv. Int. 108. Note also *Laverty v British Gas Trading Ltd* [2014] EWHC 2721 (Ch); [2014] B.C.C. 701 where Etherton C applied the wide *Nortel* view of provable debts to rule that sums arising in respect of deemed utility contracts for the supply of gas and electricity during administration were provable debts within the meaning of what is now r.14.1(3)(b).

See also *Liquidator of Ben Line Steamers, Noter* [2010] CSOH 174. See also the discussion by HHJ Hodge QC in *Kaye v South Oxfordshire District Council* [2013] EWHC 4165 (Ch); [2014] B.C.C. 143.

Note that a "small debt" (r.14.1(3): not exceeding £1,000) does not need to be proved but is treated as having been so under r.14.3(3) for the purpose of dividend provided proper notice has been given (see rr.14.29 and 14.31) and note that creditors cannot opt out of receiving distribution notices: IA 1986 ss.246C(1), (2), 379C(1), (2).

R.14.1(4)
This rule would appear to settle the inconsistency between *Re Berkeley Securities (Property) Ltd* [1980] 1 W.L.R. 1589; and *Re Islington Metal and Plating Works Ltd* [1984] 1 W.L.R. 14; (1983) 1 B.C.C. 98933. The Cork Committee (*Report*, para.1310) favoured the former decision. This new rule is not ultra vires but is authorised by IA 1986 Sch.8 para.12.

Chapter 2

Creditors' claims in administration, winding up and bankruptcy

[Note: a document required by the Act or these Rules must also contain the standard contents set out in Part 1.]

14.2 Provable debts

14.2(1) [All claims provable subject to exceptions] All claims by creditors except as provided in this rule, are provable as debts against the company or bankrupt, whether they are present or future, certain or contingent, ascertained or sounding only in damages.

14.2(2) [Claims not provable] The following are not provable–

(a) an obligation arising under a confiscation order made under–

  (i) section 1 of the Drug Trafficking Offences Act 1986,

  (ii) section 1 of the Criminal Justice (Scotland) Act 1987,

  (iii) section 71 of the Criminal Justice Act 1988, or

  (iv) Parts 2, 3 or 4 of the Proceeds of Crime Act 2002;

(b) an obligation arising from a payment out of the social fund under section 138(1)(b) of the Social Security Contributions and Benefits Act 1992 by way of crisis loan or budgeting loan.

(c) in bankruptcy–

  (i) a fine imposed for an offence,

  (ii) an obligation (other than an obligation to pay a lump sum or to pay costs) arising under an order made in family proceedings, or

  (iii) an obligation arising under a maintenance assessment made under the Child Support Act 1991.

14.2(3) ["Fine" and "family proceedings" in r.14.2(2)(c)] In paragraph (2)(c), "fine" and "family proceedings" have the meanings given by section 281(8) (which applies the Magistrates Courts Act 1980 and the Matrimonial and Family Proceedings Act 1984).

14.2(4) [Postponed debts] The following claims are not provable until after all other claims of creditors have been paid in full with interest under sections 189(2) (winding up), section 328(4) (bankruptcy) and rule 14.23 (payment of interest)–

(a) a claim arising by virtue of section 382(1)(a) of the Financial Services and Markets Act 2000 (restitution orders), unless it is also a claim arising by virtue of sub-paragraph (b) of that section (a person who has suffered loss etc.); or

(b) in administration and winding up, a claim which by virtue of the Act or any other enactment is a claim the payment of which in a bankruptcy, an administration or a winding up is to be postponed.

14.2(5) [Debt not provable under other law] Nothing in this rule prejudices any enactment or rule of law under which a particular kind of debt is not provable, whether on grounds of public policy or otherwise.

General Note

This provision complements IA 1986 ss.322 and 382. It must be read in the light of r.14.1. Its predecessor in IR 1986 was amended to reflect the wider role of administration in 2003 where issues of proof of debt became relevant. Note also the changes necessitated by POCA 2002. Not all debts are provable debts: see the discussion in *Woodley v Woodley (No.2)* [1994] 1 W.L.R. 1167 at 1175. Note that fines are now regarded as not provable in a bankruptcy (reversing the former position as declared in *Re Pascoe* [1944] Ch. 310). The Cork Committee (Cmnd.8558, para.1330) recommended that the law should be changed for all insolvency proceedings, but the legislators have done so only for bankruptcies.

Criminal compensation orders are viewed in like fashion and are non-provable—*R. v Barnet JJ Ex p. Phillippou* [1997] B.P.I.R. 134. Confiscation order liabilities are treated in similar fashion. On the other hand, tax penalties are provable—*Re Hurren* [1983] 1 W.L.R. 183; *Count Artsrunik v Waller* [2005] B.P.I.R. 82—as are penalties imposed by professional associations which may be characterised as contractual debts (*Marcus v Institute of Chartered Accountants* [2004] EWHC 3010 (Ch); [2005] B.P.I.R. 413).

Rule 14.2(4) further restricts the categories of provable debt.

The legal status of r.14.2 came under consideration in the Court of Appeal in *Woodley v Woodley (No.2)* [1994] 1 W.L.R. 1167. Here the suggestion that r.14.2 might be ultra vires the 1986 Act was considered and then dismissed. Authority for it was based upon IA 1986 Sch.9 para.17 and ultimately upon s.412(2)(a). In spite of this reassuring finding the Court of Appeal suggested that the Insolvency Rules Committee should look at the question of whether lump-sum orders made in family proceedings should be restored as provable debts, which was the position before the 1986 Rules came into effect. Costs orders in matrimonial proceedings fall within r.14.2(2)(c)—*Levy v Legal Services Commission* [2000] B.P.I.R. 1065. Note also *Wehmeyer v Wehmeyer* [2001] B.P.I.R. 548. Compare *Cadwell v Jackson* [2001] B.P.I.R. 966. On r.14.2 and foreign family proceedings see *Cartwright v Cartwright* [2002] EWCA Civ 931; [2002] B.P.I.R. 895. The Court of Appeal restated its criticism of the fact that lump sums were not provable in *Ram v Ram* [2004] EWCA Civ 1452; [2005] B.P.I.R. 616. As a result of the intervention of the Insolvency Rules Committee the position on proving for lump sums and costs in family proceedings was finally changed in 2005. For background see C. Brougham [2005] 18 Insolv. Int. 106. Note *Re Hargreaves (Booth v Mond)* [2010] B.P.I.R. 1111 where HHJ Hodge QC made the point that the exception from provability of a debt under r.14.2(5) did not apply to arrears due under an income payments order or agreement. Such arrears were provable. *Hayes v Hayes* [2012] EWHC 1240 (Ch); [2012] B.P.I.R. 739 considers the linkage between this rule and s.281 and also the impact of the 2005 amendments to this provision. On r.14.2(2)(c) and a child support debt in the context of a deceased's insolvent estate, see *Berry v Child Support Agency* [2016] EWHC 1418 (Ch); [2016] B.P.I.R. 1256 where the court found that the Child Support Act 1991 s.43A enabled the recovery of arrears as a debt payable from a deceased's estate as a different concept from an obligation arising under a child support maintenance assessment under r.14.2(2)(c); the arrears were a provable debt which could be recovered from the estate and it made no difference that the estate was insolvent.

Historically tax debts were non-provable on policy grounds: see *Government of India, Ministry of Finance (Revenue Division) v Taylor* [1955] A.C. 491 which is discussed by Miller in [1991] J.B.L. 144. See also *QRS 1 Aps v Frandsen* [1999] 1 W.L.R. 2169. However this common law bar has been supplanted by a more comity-based approach, as reflected by the EC Regulation on Insolvency Proceedings 1346/2000 art.39 (from June 26, 2017 EU Regulation on Insolvency Proceedings 2015/848 art.53 read in light of art.2(12) (and note recital 63)) and the Cross Border Insolvency Regulations (SI 2006/1030) Sch.1 art.13.3.

On future tort claimants see *Re T&N Ltd* [2005] EWHC 2870 (Ch); [2006] B.P.I.R. 532 and the subsequent legislative reforms introduced by SI 2006/1272 to r.14.1.

For consideration of the possibility of protective awards ranking as provable debts see the Court of Appeal judgment in *Haine v Day* [2008] B.P.I.R. 1343.

In *Re Nortel Networks UK Ltd* [2010] EWHC 826 (Ch); [2010] B.C.C. 706 Norris J reviewed the authorities on contingent liabilities for the purpose of this rule.

It is now clear from *Re Nortel Companies* [2013] UKSC 52; [2013] B.C.C. 624 that an expansive view of what is a provable debt is now favoured. This rule was discussed in *Re Mireskandari* [2014] B.P.I.R. 163 (Registrar Barber) and it was held that a transactional avoidance claim could be a provable debt—but see the appeal to the High Court (Charles Hollander QC sitting as a Deputy Judge) reported sub nomine *Hellard v Chadwick* in [2014] EWHC 2158 (Ch); [2014] B.P.I.R. 1234 where, in dismissing the appeal, this point was upheld and no further comment was made on this particular rule.

See the comments of Registrar Briggs in *Ecology Support Services v Hellard* [2017] EWHC 160 (Ch). See also the comments of Snowden J at [52] in *Re Nortel Networks UK Ltd* [2017] EWHC 1429 (Ch).

This rule was also noted in passing in *Laverty v British Gas Trading Ltd* [2014] EWHC 2721 (Ch); [2014] B.C.C. 701—see the note to r.14.1.

A Scottish perspective on what is a contingent debt can be found in *Liquidator of Ben Line Steamers Ltd, Noter* [2010] CSOH 174.

14.3 Proving a debt

14.3(1) [Creditor to submit proof to office-holder] A creditor wishing to recover a debt must submit a proof to the office-holder unless–

(a) this rule or an order of the court provides otherwise; or

(b) it is a members' voluntary winding up in which case the creditor is not required to submit a proof unless the liquidator requires one to be submitted.

14.3(2) [Deemed proof in administration/winding up] A creditor is deemed to have proved–

(a) in a winding up immediately preceded by an administration, where the creditor has already proved in the administration; or

(b) in an administration immediately preceded by a winding up, where the creditor has already proved in the winding up.

14.3(3) [Deemed proof of small debts for dividend] A creditor is deemed to have proved for the purposes of determination and payment of a dividend but not otherwise where–

(a) the debt is a small debt;

(b) a notice has been delivered to the creditor of intention to declare a dividend or make a distribution under rule 14.29 which complies with rule 14.31 (further contents of notice to creditors owed small debts); and

(c) the creditor has not advised the office-holder that the debt is incorrect or not owed in response to the notice.

(See General Note after r.14.11.)

14.4 Requirements for proof

14.4(1) [Authentication and content] A proof must–

(a) be made out by, or under the direction of, the creditor and authenticated by the creditor or a person authorised on the creditor's behalf;

(b) state the creditor's name and address;

(c) if the creditor is a company, identify the company;

(d) state the total amount of the creditor's claim (including any value added tax) as at the relevant date, less any payments made after that date in relation to the claim, any deduction under rule 14.20 and any adjustment by way of set-off in accordance with rules 14.24 and 14.25;

(e) state whether or not the claim includes any outstanding uncapitalised interest;

(f) contain particulars of how and when the debt was incurred by the company or the bankrupt;

(g) contain particulars of any security held, the date on which it was given and the value which the creditor puts on it;

(h) provide details of any reservation of title in relation to goods to which the debt relates;

(i) provide details of any document by reference to which the debt can be substantiated;

(j) be dated and authenticated; and

(k) state the name, postal address and authority of the person authenticating the proof (if someone other than the creditor).

14.4(2) [Substantiating document] Where sub-paragraph (i) applies the document need not be delivered with the proof unless the office-holder has requested it.

14.4(3) [Office-holder may require other evidence] The office-holder may call for the creditor to produce any document or other evidence which the office-holder considers is necessary to substantiate the whole or any part of a claim.

(See General Note after r.14.11.)

14.5 Costs of proving

14.5 Unless the court orders otherwise–

(a) each creditor bears the cost of proving for that creditor's own debt, including costs incurred in providing documents or evidence under rule 14.4 (3);

(b) in an administration or winding up, costs incurred by the office-holder in estimating the value of a debt under rule 14.14 are payable out of the assets as an expense of the administration or winding up; and

(c) in a bankruptcy, costs incurred by the office-holder in estimating the value of a debt under section 322(3) fall on the bankrupt's estate as an expense of the bankruptcy.

(See General Note after r.14.11.)

14.6 Allowing inspection of proofs

14.6 The office-holder must, so long as proofs delivered to the office-holder are in the possession of the office-holder, allow them to be inspected, at all reasonable times on any business day, by the following–

(a) a creditor who has delivered a proof (unless the proof has been wholly rejected for purposes of dividend or otherwise, or withdrawn);

(b) a member or contributory of the company or, in the case of a bankruptcy, the bankrupt; and

(c) a person acting on behalf of any of the above.

(See General Note after r.14.11.)

14.7 Admission and rejection of proofs for dividend

14.7(1) [Power of office-holder] The office-holder may admit or reject a proof for dividend (in whole or in part).

14.7(2) [Reasons for rejection] If the office-holder rejects a proof in whole or in part, the office-holder must deliver to the creditor a statement of the office-holder's reasons for doing so, as soon as reasonably practicable.

(See General Note after r.14.11.)

14.8 Appeal against decision on proof

14.8(1) [Creditor's right to appeal to court] If a creditor is dissatisfied with the office-holder's decision under rule 14.7 in relation to the creditor's own proof (including a decision whether the debt is preferential), the creditor may apply to the court for the decision to be reversed or varied.

14.8(2) [Time limit for appeal] The application must be made within 21 days of the creditor receiving the statement delivered under rule 14.7(2).

14.8(3) [Application by other parties] A member, a contributory, any other creditor or, in a bankruptcy, the bankrupt, if dissatisfied with the office-holder's decision admitting, or rejecting the whole or any part of, a proof or agreeing to revalue a creditor's security under rule 14.15, may make such an application within 21 days of becoming aware of the office-holder's decision.

14.8(4) [Court to fix venue for hearing] The court must fix a venue for the application to be heard.

14.8(5) [Notice of venue] The applicant must deliver notice of the venue to the creditor who delivered the proof in question (unless it is the applicant's own proof) and the office-holder.

14.8(6) [Office-holder to file proof in court with rejection reasons] The office-holder must, on receipt of the notice, file the relevant proof with the court, together (if appropriate) with a copy of the statement sent under rule 14.7(2).

(See General Note after r.14.11.)

14.9 Office-holder not liable for costs under rule 14.8

14.9(1) [No liability on official receiver] The official receiver is not personally liable for costs incurred by any person in respect of an application under rule 14.8.

14.9(2) [No liability on other office-holder subject to court order] An office-holder other than the official receiver is not personally liable for costs incurred by any person in respect of an application under rule 14.8 unless the court orders otherwise.

(See General Note after r.14.11.)

14.10 Withdrawal or variation of proof

14.10(1) [Withdrawal by written notice] A creditor may withdraw a proof at any time by delivering a written notice to the office-holder.

14.10(2) [Variation of amount by agreement] The amount claimed by a creditor's proof may be varied at any time by agreement between the creditor and the office-holder.

(See General Note after r.14.11.)

14.11 Exclusion of proof by the court

14.11(1) [Power of court] The court may exclude a proof or reduce the amount claimed–

(a) on the office-holder's application, where the office-holder thinks that the proof has been improperly admitted, or ought to be reduced; or

(b) on the application of a creditor, a member, a contributory or a bankrupt, if the office-holder declines to interfere in the matter.

14.11(2) [Court to fix venue for hearing] Where application is made under paragraph (1), the court must fix a venue for the application to be heard.

14.11(3) [Applicant to deliver notice of venue] The applicant must deliver notice of the venue–

(a) in the case of an application by the office-holder, to the creditor who submitted the proof; and

(b) in the case of an application by a creditor, a member, a contributory or a bankrupt, to the office-holder and to the creditor who made the proof (if not the applicant).

General Note to rr.14.3–14.11

These rules bring together under one roof as it were the provisions on proof of debt that were previously scattered in a repetitive fashion throughout IR 1986 in relation to the relevant insolvency procedure (administration, winding up (creditors' voluntary and compulsory liquidation), bankruptcy).

The rules govern the proof of debts, the rights of inspection of proofs, appeals against a liquidator's decision with respect to a proof, etc. See generally the comment preceding s.175.

"Small debt" in r.14.3(3) is quantified by r.14.1(3) as the total amount owing a creditor not exceeding £1,000: see notes to r.14.1 and for the required notice, r.14.31.

On the meaning of "debt", see r.14.1(3) (winding up and administration) and IA 1986 s.382 (bankruptcy). On "provable debt" see r.14.2 (winding up, administration and bankruptcy).

As long ago as 2004 a liquidator in compulsory winding up and official receiver or trustee in bankruptcy was no longer obliged to send a form of proof to every creditor, but only to do so for a particular creditor if requested, but the removal of prescribed insolvency forms under IR 2016 has rendered this redundant. The contents required to be stated in the creditor's proof of debt are provided in r.14.4(1). Where an insolvency practitioner holds a blanket authority from a creditor to act under r.14.4(1)(k), an approved form of authority acceptable to official receivers is to be found in *Dear IP*, October 2008, Ch.3.15.

On the meaning of "relevant date " in r.14.4(1)(d), see r.14.1(3).

Rule 14.4(1)(g) was considered in the bankruptcy case of *Evans v Finance-U-Ltd* [2013] EWCA Civ 869; [2013] B.P.I.R. 1001 where Patten LJ explained that the provision required the secured creditor to provide details of the security and to place its valuation upon it. Valuation and consideration of the amount that could be admitted to proof was then a matter for the trustee in bankruptcy.

The "rule against double proof" forbids more than one proof to be admitted in respect of the same debt (e.g. by a guarantor as well as a principal creditor). See *Re Oriental Commercial Bank* (1871) 7 Ch. App. 99; and the discussion in *Re Polly Peck International plc* [1996] B.C.C. 486; and contrast *Re Parkfield Group plc* [1997] B.C.C. 778. A debt which would be excluded by the rule against double proof cannot be set off against a reciprocal obligation: *Re Kaupthing Singer & Friedlander Ltd, Mills v HSBC Trustee (CI) Ltd* [2011] UKSC 48; [2012] 1 A.C. 104; [2012] B.C.C. 1.

On contingent debts, see the notes to IA 1986 s.382 and to IR 2016 r.14.1. It is normally for the office-holder, rather than the court, to fix the value of the debt: *Re Legal and Equitable Securities plc* [2012] EWHC 910 (Ch).

The right of inspection conferred by r.14.6 on creditors who have delivered their proof (which has not been rejected or withdrawn), a member or contributory of the debtor company or the bankrupt and their representatives is restricted to the proof itself, and does not extend to documentation submitted in support: *MG Rover Dealer Properties Ltd v Hunt* [2012] B.P.I.R. 590.

The office-holder may admit or reject a proof in whole or in part (r.14.7) and the creditor may appeal against that decision (r.14.8). This is not a true appeal—*Cadwell v Jackson* [2001] B.P.I.R. 966. For the meaning of "venue" in r.14.8(4) see r.1.2. Registrar Briggs upheld an appeal against the rejection by liquidators of a proof in *Ecology Support Services Ltd v Hellard* [2017] EWHC 160 (Ch). For the potential utility of r.14.8 see *Barclays Bank v Henson* [2000] B.P.I.R. 941. For guidance on the court using its discretion to extend the 21-day period in r.14.8(2) for a creditor appealing against a decision with respect to his proof, see *McCarthy v Tann* [2016] EWHC 542 (Ch): relief would usually be granted if the breach was not a serious or significant violation impeding or disrupting the proper conduct of the liquidation or the litigation. In a creditors' appeal (*Re Burnden Group Ltd; Fielding v Hunt* [2017] EWHC 247 (Ch); [2017] B.P.I.R. 554) under r.14.8 against a liquidator's rejection of their proof owing to a dispute of fact, the court would not make adverse findings against the creditors that would involve rejecting their witness evidence without it being tested in cross-examination, but cross-examination requests should not be made every time there was a dispute of fact. In general, the benefit of the doubt should be given to the witness whose evidence should only be disbelieved if it could properly be regarded as incredible. (In later proceedings on costs, see [2017] EWHC 406 (Ch); [2017] B.P.I.R. 585.)

On the approach towards a r.14.8(3) application see the decision of Hildyard J in *Wentworth Sons Sub-Debt SARL v Lomas* [2017] EWHC 3158 (Ch).

Claims by employees who had been made redundant for breach of contract, unfair dismissal and discrimination were held to be provable debts (without the need to obtain any judgment) in *Re Nortel Networks UK Ltd, Unite the Union v Nortel Networks UK Ltd* [2010] EWHC 826 (Ch); [2010] B.C.C. 706. The court may extend the time for an application to challenge the rejection of a proof, under Sch.5 para.3 (applying CPR r.3.1(2)(a)), but the applicant in *Re Contrarian Funds LLC, Re Lehman Bros International (Europe)* [2014] EWHC 1687 (Ch); [2014] 2 B.C.L.C. 651 was unsuccessful.

Where a proof has been withdrawn or varied under r.14.10 see *Official Receiver v McKay* [2009] B.P.I.R. 1061.

The words "improperly admitted" in r.14.11(1)(a) on exclusion of proof by the court carry no connotation of impropriety. It is sufficient that the proof was admitted in error, and the burden of proof in establishing this is the balance of probabilities: see *Re Globe Legal Services Ltd* [2002] B.C.C. 858; *Re Allard Holdings Ltd* [2001] 1 B.C.L.C. 404 (in which the relevance of delay is also discussed); *McCarthy v Tann* [2015] EWHC 2049 (Ch); [2015] B.P.I.R. 1224. If a proof has been improperly rejected, the court may, of course, direct the office-holder to accept it under r.14.8. For an example, see *Re Shruth Ltd* (above).

For the meaning of "venue" in r.14.11(2) see r.1.2. See *Official Receiver v McKay* [2009] B.P.I.R. 1061.

Only the office-holder or a creditor has standing to apply to exclude a proof under r.14.11: in *Re Mama Milla Ltd; Sharma v Top Brands Ltd* [2015] EWCA Civ 1140; [2016] B.C.C. 1 a former liquidator was held ineligible to apply.

In a proper case, an office-holder or the court may disallow a proof (rr.14.7, 14.11) notwithstanding the fact that a judgment has been obtained in respect of the debt in question; but only if it appears that there was some fraud, collusion or miscarriage of justice: *Re Menastar Finance Ltd* [2002] EWHC 2610 (Ch); [2003] B.C.C. 404; *Re Shruth Ltd* [2005] EWHC 1293 (Ch); [2007] B.C.C. 960.

Where a single claim has been submitted, it is probably correct that that claim can only be increased by variation of the original proof and not by submission of a new proof: *Meisels v Martin* [2005] EWHC 845 (Ch); [2005] B.P.I.R. 1151.

On the application of the Limitation Act 1980 to claims in compulsory winding up, see the note to s.129.

The proper law of a debt is determined by its *lex situs*, and is not affected by the fact that the debtor is subsequently wound up in another jurisdiction. But if the debt has been discharged under its proper law, it may not be proved in the liquidation: *Wight v Eckhardt Marine GmbH* [2003] UKPC 37; [2004] 1 A.C. 147; [2003] B.C.C. 702. It is not an abuse of process for a creditor to submit a proof of debt in this country when he has also submitted a proof for the same debt in foreign proceedings: *Rawlinson & Hunter Trustees SA v Kaupthing Bank HF* [2011] EWHC 566 (Comm); [2012] B.C.C. 441; *Lornamead Acquisitions Ltd v Kaupthing Bank HF* [2011] EWHC 2611 (Comm); [2013] 1 B.C.L.C. 73.

If a foreign creditor submits a proof of debt in an English winding up, he thereby submits to the jurisdiction of the court which is administering the proceedings, with the consequence that the office-holder may obtain an anti-suit injunction to prevent him from opening proceedings abroad to enforce his claim: *Stichting Shell Pensioenfonds v Krys* [2014] UKPC 41; [2015] A.C. 616; [2015] B.C.C. 20.

14.12 Administration and winding up by the court: debts of insolvent company to rank equally

[Note: for the equivalent rule for voluntary liquidation see section 107 of the Act and for bankruptcy section 328 of the Act.]

14.12(1) [Application of rule] This rule applies in an administration and a winding up by the court.

14.12(2) [Ranking, abatement] Debts other than preferential debts rank equally between themselves and, after the preferential debts, must be paid in full unless the assets are insufficient for meeting them, in which case they abate in equal proportions between themselves.

General Note

The *pari passu* principle applies, but there can hardly be any question of the "ranking" of debts that are all to be paid in full. See also s.107 (voluntary winding up) and s.328 (bankruptcy). On preferential debts see IA 1986 s.386 and Sch.6.

14.13 Administration and winding up: division of unsold assets

[Note: in respect of bankruptcy see section 326 (distribution of property in specie).]

14.13(1) [Application of rule] This rule applies in an administration or in a winding up of a company (other than a members' voluntary winding up) to any property which from its peculiar nature or other special circumstances cannot be readily or advantageously sold.

14.13(2) [Power of office-holder with permission] The office-holder may with the required permission divide the property in its existing form among the company's creditors according to its estimated value.

14.13(3) [Permission] The required permission is–

(a) the permission of the creditors' committee in an administration or, if there is no creditors' committee, the creditors; and

(b) the permission of the liquidation committee in a winding up, or, if there is no liquidation committee, the creditors (without prejudice to provisions of the Act about disclaimer).

General Note

Where any assets have been distributed in specie, there is no longer the previous requirement for liquidator's report including details of the valuation of the property concerned (and compare s.326 in bankruptcy).

14.14 Administration and winding up: estimate of value of debt

14.14(1) [Estimating value of debt] In an administration or in a winding up, the office-holder must estimate the value of a debt that does not have a certain value because it is subject to a contingency or for any other reason.

14.14(2) [Revision of estimate] The office-holder may revise such an estimate by reference to a change of circumstances or to information becoming available to the office-holder.

14.14(3) [Information to creditor] The office-holder must inform the creditor of the office-holder's estimate and any revision.

14.14(4) [Amount provable] Where the value of a debt is estimated under this rule or by the court under section 168(3) or (5), the amount provable in the case of that debt is that of the estimate for the time being.

General Note

This is the rule for assessing a debt for the purposes of proof in the special cases of contingent and secured debts, etc. Questions of valuation are reckoned as at the date when the company went into liquidation or administration: *Re Global Trader Europe Ltd* [2009] EWHC 699 (Ch); [2010] B.C.C. 729. On the question of valuation where mutual claims or set-off are involved, see rr.14.24 and 14.25.

An estimated value put on a contingent debt may be revised in the light of changed circumstances (r.14.14(2)), but this rule does not apply where the valuation is not an estimate made by the liquidator but is the notional valuation of an open position under rules such as those contained in the Client Assets Sourcebook: *Re MF Global Trader UK Ltd* [2013] EWHC 92 (Ch); see further *Re MF Global UK Ltd, Heis v Attestor Value Master Fund LP* [2013] EWHC 2556 (Ch); [2014] 1 W.L.R. 1558 (rule against double proof applied).

The provision is mandatory and applies in all forms of liquidation and in administration. No alternative mechanism is permitted (e.g. holding a sum in reserve pending the outcome of contingencies: *Re Danka Business Systems plc* [2013] EWCA Civ 92; [2013] B.C.C. 450).

14.15 Secured creditor: value of security

14.15(1) [Alteration of value] A secured creditor may, with the agreement of the office-holder or the permission of the court, at any time alter the value which that creditor has put upon a security in a proof.

14.15(2) [Application of r.14.15(3)] Paragraph (3) applies where a secured creditor–

(a) being the applicant for the administration order or the appointer of the administrator, has in the application or the notice of appointment put a value on the security;

(b) being the petitioner in winding-up or bankruptcy proceedings, has put a value on the security in the petition; or

(c) has voted in respect of the unsecured balance of the debt.

14.15(3) [Revaluation] Where this paragraph applies–

(a) the secured creditor may re-value the security only with the agreement of the office-holder or the permission of the court; and

(b) where the revaluation was by agreement, the office-holder must deliver a notice of the revaluation to the creditors within five business days after the office-holder's agreement.

(See General Note after r.14.19.)

14.16 Secured creditor: surrender for non-disclosure

14.16(1) [Failure to disclose security] If a secured creditor fails to disclose a security in a proof, the secured creditor must surrender that security for the general benefit of creditors, unless the court, on application by the secured creditor, relieves the secured creditor from the effect of this rule on the grounds that the omission was inadvertent or the result of honest mistake.

14.16(2) [Amendment of proof] If the court grants that relief, it may require or allow the creditor's proof to be amended, on such terms as may be just.

14.16(3) [Rights in rem] Nothing in this rule or in rules 14.17 or 14.18 affects the rights in rem of creditors or third parties protected under Article 8 of the EU Regulation.

(See General Note after r.14.19.)

14.17 Secured creditor: redemption by office-holder

14.17(1) [Notice of proposed redemption] The office-holder may at any time deliver a notice to a creditor whose debt is secured that the office-holder proposes, at the expiration of 28 days from the date of the notice, to redeem the security at the value put upon it in the creditor's proof.

14.17(2) [Time limit for revaluation] The creditor then has 21 days (or such longer period as the office-holder may allow) in which to alter the value of the security in accordance with rule 14.15.

14.17(3) [Redemption at new value] If the creditor alters the value of the security with the permission of the office-holder or the court then the office-holder may only redeem at the new value.

14.17(4) [Cost of redemption] If the office-holder redeems the security the cost of transferring it is payable as an expense out of the insolvent estate.

14.17(5) [Notice to office-holder to elect] A creditor whose debt is secured may at any time deliver a notice to the office-holder requiring the office-holder to elect whether or not to redeem the security at the value then placed on it.

14.17(6) [Time limit for redemption] The office-holder then has three months in which to redeem the security or elect not to redeem the security.

(See General Note after r.14.19.)

14.18 Secured creditor: test of security's value

14.18(1) [Offer for sale] If the office-holder is dissatisfied with the value which a secured creditor puts on a security in the creditor's proof the office-holder may require any property comprised in the security to be offered for sale.

14.18(2) [Terms of sale] The terms of sale will be as agreed between the office-holder and the secured creditor, or as the court may direct.

14.18(3) [Sale by auction] If the sale is by auction, the office-holder on behalf of the company or the insolvent estate and the creditor may bid.

14.18(4) [Value of security altered] This rule does not apply if the value of the security has been altered with the court's permission.

(See General Note after r.14.19.)

14.19 Realisation or surrender of security by creditor

14.19(1) [Net realisation as amended valuation and proof for balance] If a creditor who has valued a security subsequently realises the security (whether or not at the instance of the office-holder)–

(a) the net amount realised must be treated in all respects (including in relation to any valuation in a proof) as an amended valuation made by the creditor; and

(b) the creditor may prove for the balance of the creditor's debt.

14.19(2) [Voluntary surrender of security] A creditor who voluntarily surrenders a security may prove for the whole of the creditor's debt as if it were unsecured.

General Note to rr.14.15–14.19

These rules deal with the valuation of his security by a secured creditor, surrender due to the creditor's failure to disclose the security, the office-holder's right to redeem the security, the consequences of the realisation of a security, and various related matters.

Rule 14.15 was considered in the bankruptcy context by Lightman J in *Rey v FNCB* [2006] B.P.I.R. 1260 where it was held that the fact that a secured creditor was party to an IVA which made reference to what is now r.14.15 did not prevent it from relying on its enforcement rights as secured creditor because there was no explicit prohibitory provision to that effect in the IVA. In *Webb v Macdonald* [2010] B.P.I.R. 503 the protection of secured creditors was stressed. See also s.383(2).

A landlord who had submitted a proof without mentioning his right of distress was ruled to be a secured creditor who had abandoned his security under r.14.16(1) in *LCP Retail Ltd v Segal* [2006] EWHC 2087 (Ch); [2007] B.C.C. 584.

The rights in rem referred to in r.14.16(3) are those in respect of assets belonging to the debtor company which are situated within the territory of another Member State at the time of the opening of proceedings. See further the note to EU Recast Regulation 2015/848 art.8.

The period of time within which the liquidator must make his election under r.14.17(6) was reduced as from 6 April 2010, from six months to three.

A secured creditor who has been paid part of his debt as a result of realising his security after previously valuing it may prove for the balance without bringing what he has received into hotchpot: r.14.19 and see *Cleaver v Delta American Reinsurance Co* [2001] UKPC 6; [2001] 1 B.C.L.C. 482. If he surrenders the security he can prove for the entire debt as an unsecured creditor. This must be read in light of IA 1986 s.269 in bankruptcy. The debt of a secured creditor who has surrendered his entire security is to be treated as an unsecured debt for all purposes so that (e.g.) in administration and insolvent liquidation he may share in the "prescribed part" under s.176A: *Re PAL SC Realisations 2007 Ltd* [2010] EWHC 2850 (Ch); [2011] B.C.C. 93.

Note *Cahillane v NALM Ltd* [2014] EWHC 1992 (Ch); [2014] B.P.I.R. 1093 where HHJ Pelling QC explains the consequences of a secured creditor receiving more than the value it placed on the security.

See r.14.41 for the position where a creditor alters the value of a security after a dividend has been declared.

Rule 14.16(3) amended by the Insolvency (England and Wales) and Insolvency (Scotland) (Miscellaneous and Consequential Amendments) Rules 2017 (SI 2017/1115) rr.1(1), (2), 22, 25(2) as from 8 December 2017.

14.20 Discounts

14.20 All trade and other discounts (except a discount for immediate or early settlement) which would have been available to the company or the debtor but for the insolvency proceedings must be deducted from the claim.

(See General Note after r.14.23.)

14.21 Debts in foreign currency

14.21(1) [Amount of debt in foreign currency] A proof for a debt incurred or payable in a foreign currency must state the amount of the debt in that currency.

14.21(2) [Conversion into sterling] The office-holder must convert all such debts into sterling at a single rate for each currency determined by the office-holder by reference to the exchange rates prevailing on the relevant date.

14.21(3) [Rate determined] On the next occasion when the office-holder communicates with the creditors the office-holder must advise them of any rate so determined.

14.21(4) [Application by creditor] A creditor who considers that the rate determined by the office-holder is unreasonable may apply to the court.

14.21(5) [Power of court to determine rate] If on hearing the application the court finds that the rate is unreasonable it may itself determine the rate.

14.21(6) [Non-application to DRO applications] This rule does not apply to the conversion of foreign currency debts in an application for a debt relief order.

(See General Note after r.14.23.)

14.22 Payments of a periodical nature

14.22(1) [Rent, etc., unpaid to relevant date] In the case of rent and other payments of a periodical nature, the creditor may prove for any amounts due and unpaid up to the relevant date.

14.22(2) [If accruing for day to day] Where at that date any payment was accruing due, the creditor may prove for so much as would have been due at that date, if accruing from day to day.

(See General Note after r.14.23.)

14.23 Interest

[Note: provision for the payment of interest out of a surplus remaining after payment of the debts is made by section 189(2) in respect of winding up and section 328(4) in respect of bankruptcy.]

14.23(1) [Debt bearing interest] Where a debt proved in insolvency proceedings bears interest, that interest is provable as part of the debt except in so far as it is payable in respect of any period after the relevant date.

14.23(2) [When claim may include interest not agreed] In the circumstances set out below the creditor's claim may include interest on the debt for periods before the relevant date although not previously reserved or agreed.

14.23(3) [Debt due by written instrument] If the debt is due by virtue of a written instrument and payable at a certain time, interest may be claimed for the period from that time to the relevant date.

14.23(4) [Debt due otherwise] If the debt is due otherwise, interest may only be claimed if demand for payment of the debt was made in writing by or on behalf of the creditor, and notice was delivered that interest would be payable from the date of the demand to the date of the payment, before–

(a) the relevant date, in respect of administration or winding up; or

(b) the presentation of the bankruptcy petition or the bankruptcy application.

14.23(5) [Interest under r.14.23(4)] Interest under paragraph (4) may only be claimed for the period from the date of the demand to the relevant date and, for the purposes of the Act and these Rules, must be charged at a rate not exceeding that mentioned in paragraph (6).

14.23(6) [Rate of interest under r.14.23(3), (4)] The rate of interest to be claimed under paragraphs (3) and (4) is the rate specified in section 17 of the Judgments Act 1838 on the relevant date.

14.23(7) [Surplus in administration] In an administration–

(a) any surplus remaining after payment of the debts proved must, before being applied for any other purpose, be applied in paying interest on those debts in respect of the periods during which they have been outstanding since the relevant date;

(b) all interest payable under sub-paragraph (a) ranks equally whether or not the debts on which it is payable rank equally; and

(c) the rate of interest payable under sub-paragraph (a) is whichever is the greater of the rate specified under paragraph (6) and the rate applicable to the debt apart from the administration.

GENERAL NOTE TO RR.14.20–14.23

R.14.21

This confirms the ruling in *Re Lines Bros Ltd* [1983] Ch. 1 in which comments made (obiter) in the earlier decision of the House of Lords in *Miliangos v George Frank (Textiles) Ltd* [1976] A.C. 443 were not followed. For the meaning of "went into liquidation", see s.247(2). Note that the rule refers to the *date*, rather than the *time* (see *Re Dynamics Corp of America (No.2)* [1976] 1 W.L.R. 757). (On the commencement of winding up, see the note to s.86.) For Supreme Court comments on other aspects of these three cases, see below.

Creditors whose claims were denominated in a foreign currency were held to be entitled to claim in the liquidation for any losses suffered by them as a result of a fall in the value of sterling between the date of the liquidation (or preceding administration) and the date of the distribution, but such claims were payable only after the payment in full of all proved debts and statutory interest: *Re Lehman Bros International (Europe)* [2014] EWHC 704 (Ch); [2014] B.C.C. 193 (affirmed on appeal (*Joint Administrators of LB Holdings Intermediate 2 Ltd v Lomas* [2015] EWCA Civ 485; [2016] Ch. 50; [2015] B.C.C. 431)). However on further appeal the Supreme Court has overturned this point in *Joint Administrators of LB Holdings Intermediate 2 Ltd v Joint Administrators of Lehman Bros International (Europe)* [2017] UKSC 38; [2017] 2 W.L.R. 1497; [2017] B.C.C. 235. According to Lord Neuberger (Lord Clarke dissenting on this point), the predecessor of r.14.21—IR 1986 r.2.86—for the first time in legislation expressly dealt with foreign currency creditors and accordingly there had to be a presumption that the provision was intended to spell out the full extent of a foreign currency creditor's rights (especially as the purpose of the 1986 legislation was to simplify and clarify the law). If it were otherwise, what is now r.14.21 would operate as a one-way option on the currency markets in a foreign currency creditor's favour. (This approach has been criticised: see Moss, "Waterfall 1 and erroneous coding for currency conversions" (2017) 30 (7) Insolv. Int. 103–106.) The Supreme Court distinguished the above case of *Miliangos v George Frank (Textiles) Ltd* and declined to apply *Re Lines Bros Ltd* and *Re Dynamics Corp of America*. In further proceedings (*Re Lehman Bros International (Europe); Lomas v Burlington Loan Management Ltd* [2016] EWHC 2131 (Ch); [2017] B.C.C. 1), it was held that no currency conversion claim arose as a result of set-off under what is now r.14.24.

Conversion into sterling is not required at the stage when a statutory demand is presented: see the ruling of Morritt J in *Re a Debtor (51/SD/1991)* [1992] 1 W.L.R. 1294.

R.14.23

In the note to s.189 there is a discussion of the judgments of David Richards J and the Court of Appeal in *Re Lehman Bros International (Europe)* [2014] EWHC 704 (Ch); [2015] Ch. 1; [2014] B.C.C. 193, on appeal sub nom. *Joint Administrators of LB Holdings Intermediate 2 Ltd v Lomas* [2015] EWCA Civ 485; [2015] 3 W.L.R. 1205; [2015] B.C.C. 431, which dealt with the rankings in the liquidation of a solvent company of statutory and other interest, losses incurred on the conversion of foreign debts and subordinated debt claims (now superseded by the Supreme Court decision in *Joint Administrators of LB Holdings Intermediate 2 Ltd v Joint Administrators of Lehman Bros International (Europe)* [2017] UKSC 38; [2017] 2 W.L.R. 1497; [2017] B.C.C. 235). The topic was explored further in a later judgment of David Richards J (*Re Lehman Bros International (Europe); Lomas v Burlington Loan*

Management Ltd [2015] EWHC 2269 (Ch); [2016] B.C.C. 239). This series of rulings has come to be known as the "Waterfall" proceedings. The second hearing before David Richards J was concerned with a detailed examination of the rules relating to statutory and other interest in an administration (and, by inference, in a winding up) and was upheld by the Court of Appeal in *Burlington Loan Management Ltd v Lomas* [2017] EWCA Civ 1462; [2017] B.C.C. 759. Among other points it was decided that:

- the common-law "rule in *Bower v Marris* (1841) Cr. & P. 351" (that sums paid by a debtor must be appropriated first to payment of interest, ahead of repayment of capital) does not apply to post-administration interest under what is now r.14.23(7);
- r.14.23 represents a complete code for the payment of interest on proved debts;
- interest is not payable on statutory interest in respect of the period between the payment in full of the debts proved and the date or dates on which statutory interest was paid;
- the "rate payable" under r.14.23(7)(c) does not include the judgment rate (8 per cent) on a judgment obtained after the commencement of the administration (or which would have applied had the creditor obtained such a judgment);
- statutory interest is payable on future and contingent debts from the date of the commencement of the administration;
- the calculation of the currency conversion claims should not take into account the statutory interest paid to the creditor.

It was also held that the rights due to the creditors under these rulings were not displaced by a claims resolution agreement made by the administrators with certain creditors at an early stage to accelerate the return of trust assets.

In further "Waterfall" proceedings (*Re Lehman Bros International (Europe); Lomas v Burlington Loan Management Ltd* [2016] EWHC 2131 (Ch); [2017] B.C.C. 1), David Richards LJ determined further issues on the position of post-administration interest (again upheld by the Court of Appeal [2017] EWCA Civ 1462; [2017] B.C.C. 759) holding that:

- where contractual interest first started to run on a provable debt at some point after the date of administration, the "rate applicable" for the period from the date of administration to the date when contractual interest first started to run was zero; moreover, statutory interest under r.14.12(7)(c) was to be calculated by comparing the two alternative rates for the whole period from the date of administration to the date(s) of dividend payments (the Court of Appeal (above) agreed that the judge had been correct to hold that the phrase "the rate applicable to the debt apart from the administration" in what is now r.14.23(7)(c) related to actual rather than hypothetical rates of interest: the inclusion of hypothetical judgment debts had to be rejected as that would lead to speculative uncertainty in a relatively simple and straight forward code); and
- a non-provable claim to interest on a currency conversion claim should not be reduced by interest received by the creditor pursuant to r.14.23 on its proved debt: statutory interest was payable by law on the proved debt and was referable only to the proved debt.

Yet a further point made in Waterfall proceedings (this time on appeal from Hildyard J at [2016] EWHC 2417 (Ch) by the Court of Appeal ([2017] EWCA Civ 1462; [2017] B.C.C. 759)) concerned a contractual interest rate due only after a close-out position. Wherever, after the onset of administration, the creditor triggered a contractual right contained in a pre-administration contract giving rise to an interest entitlement at a particular rate, higher than the Judgments Act 1838 s.17 rate, an interpretation of r.14.23(7)(c) was required: the starting point was to examine what contractual rights to interest existed at the administration date, by reference to the rate of interest which each creditor would have enjoyed between the cut-off date and the distribution date. That rate could be established for current, future, or contingent rights with the benefit of hindsight to see what rate of interest they would have generated had they not been extinguished by the administration.

Statutory interest payable in an administration under r.14.23(7)(a) was held in *Lomas v Revenue and Customs Commissioners* [2016] EWHC 2492 (Ch); [2017] Bus. L.R. 520 not to be "yearly interest" from which tax should be first be deducted under the Income Tax Act 2007 s.874, but HMRC's appeal was successful ([2017] EWCA Civ 2124) so that statutory interest payable on proven debts in an administration under r.14.23(7) is "yearly interest" and thus subject to deductions of basic rate income tax.

There is a good discussion of the predecessor to the rule and its legislative antecedents in relation to bankruptcy in *El Ajou v Stern* [2006] EWHC 3067 (Ch); [2007] B.P.I.R. 693 (which ironically is an IVA case). For further guidance on claims in respect of interest in bankruptcy, see IA 1986 s.328(4), (5).

14.24 Administration: mutual dealings and set-off

14.24(1) [Application of rule] This rule applies in an administration where the administrator intends to make a distribution and has delivered a notice under rule 14.29.

14.24(2) [Account of mutual dealings and set off] An account must be taken as at the date of the notice of what is due from the company and a creditor to each other in respect of their mutual dealings and the sums due from the one must be set off against the sums due from the other.

14.24(3) [Balance owed to creditor provable] If there is a balance owed to the creditor then only that balance is provable in the administration.

14.24(4) [Balance owed to company] If there is a balance owed to the company that must be paid to the administrator as part of the assets.

14.24(5) [Balance owed to company from contingent or prospective debt owed by creditor] However if all or part of the balance owed to the company results from a contingent or prospective debt owed by the creditor then the balance (or that part of it which results from the contingent or prospective debt) must be paid in full (without being discounted under rule 14.44) if and when that debt becomes due and payable.

14.24(6) ["Obligation", "mutual dealings"] In this rule–

"obligation" means an obligation however arising, whether by virtue of an agreement, rule of law or otherwise; and

"mutual dealings" means mutual credits, mutual debts or other mutual dealings between the company and a creditor proving or claiming to prove for a debt in the administration but does not include any of the following–

(a) a debt arising out of an obligation incurred after the company entered administration;

(b) a debt arising out of an obligation incurred at a time when the creditor had notice that–

(i) an application for an administration order was pending, or

(ii) any person had delivered notice of intention to appoint an administrator;

(c) a debt arising out of an obligation where–

(i) the administration was immediately preceded by a winding up, and

(ii) at the time when the obligation was incurred the creditor had notice that a decision had been sought from creditors under section 100 on the nomination of a liquidator or that a winding-up petition was pending;

(d) a debt arising out of an obligation incurred during a winding up which immediately preceded the administration; or

(e) a debt which has been acquired by a creditor by assignment or otherwise, under an agreement between the creditor and another party where that agreement was entered into–

(i) after the company entered administration,

(ii) at a time when the creditor had notice that an application for an administration order was pending,

(iii) at a time when the creditor had notice that any person had given notice of intention to appoint an administrator,

(iv) where the administration was immediately preceded by a winding up, at a time when the creditor had notice that a decision had been sought from creditors under section 100 on the nomination of a liquidator or that a winding-up petition was pending, or

(v) during a winding up which immediately preceded the administration.

14.24(7) [Sum treated as being due in r.14.24(2)] A sum must be treated as being due to or from the company for the purposes of paragraph (2) whether–

(a) it is payable at present or in the future;

(b) the obligation by virtue of which it is payable is certain or contingent; or

(c) its amount is fixed or liquidated, or is capable of being ascertained by fixed rules or as a matter of opinion.

14.24(8) [Application of rr.14.14, 14.21–14.23, 14.44] For the purposes of this rule–

(a) rule 14.14 applies to an obligation which, by reason of its being subject to a contingency or for any other reason, does not bear a certain value;

(b) rules 14.21 to 14.23 apply to sums due to the company which–

(i) are payable in a currency other than sterling,

(ii) are of a periodical nature, or

(iii) bear interest; and

(c) rule 14.44 applies to a sum due to or from the company which is payable in the future.

General Note

The corresponding provision in a liquidation is r.14.25 below. See the note to that rule. In *Re Kaupthing Singer & Friedlander Ltd* [2010] EWCA Civ 518; [2011] B.C.C. 555 Etherton LJ laid down the following propositions regarding the set-off of debts owed to the company and repayable in the future: that the debts owed by and to the company should be set off against each other at their present value at the time of distribution and that, to the extent that a future debt owed to the company is not extinguished by the set-off, it remains payable at its full non-discounted amount when it falls due.

Rule 14.24(7)(a) and (c) does not apply to a close-out netting provision under a financial collateral arrangement unless the party concerned was aware at the time he entered into the arrangement that winding-up proceedings or re-organisation measures in relation to the other party had commenced: Financial Collateral Arrangements (No.2) Regulations 2003 (SI 2003/3226) reg.12(4).

The principle of insolvency set-off was not applicable under the original administration regime, which had no provision corresponding to r.14.24: *Isovel Contracts Ltd v ABB Building Technologies Ltd* [2002] 1 B.C.L.C. 390.

14.25 Winding up: mutual dealings and set-off

14.25(1) [Application of rule] This rule applies in a winding up where, before the company goes into liquidation, there have been mutual dealings between the company and a creditor of the company proving or claiming to prove for a debt in the liquidation.

14.25(2) [Account of mutual dealings and set off] An account must be taken of what is due from the company and the creditor to each other in respect of their mutual dealings and the sums due from the one must be set off against the sums due from the other.

14.25(3) [Balance owed to creditor provable] If there is a balance owed to the creditor then only that balance is provable in the winding up.

14.25(4) [Balance owed to company] If there is a balance owed to the company then that must be paid to the liquidator as part of the assets.

14.25(5) [Balance owed to company from contingent or prospective debt owed by creditor] However if all or part of the balance owed to the company results from a contingent or prospective debt owed by the creditor then the balance (or that part of it which results from the contingent or prospective debt) must be paid in full (without being discounted under rule 14.44) if and when that debt becomes due and payable.

14.25(6) [“Obligation”, “mutual dealings”] In this rule–

“obligation” means an obligation however arising, whether by virtue of an agreement, rule of law or otherwise; and

“mutual dealings” means mutual credits, mutual debts or other mutual dealings between the company and a creditor proving or claiming to prove for a debt in the winding up but does not include any of the following–

(a) a debt arising out of an obligation incurred at a time when the creditor had notice that–

(i) a decision had been sought from creditors on the nomination of a liquidator under section 100, or

(ii) a petition for the winding up of the company was pending;

(b) a debt arising out of an obligation where–

(i) the liquidation was immediately preceded by an administration, and

(ii) at the time the obligation was incurred the creditor had notice that an application for an administration order was pending or a person had delivered notice of intention to appoint an administrator; and

(c) a debt arising out of an obligation incurred during an administration which immediately preceded the liquidation;

(d) a debt which has been acquired by a creditor by assignment or otherwise, under an agreement between the creditor and another party where that agreement was entered into–

(i) after the company went into liquidation,

(ii) at a time when the creditor had notice that a decision had been sought from creditors under section 100 on the nomination of a liquidator,

(iii) at a time when the creditor had notice that a winding-up petition was pending,

(iv) where the winding up was immediately preceded by an administration at a time when the creditor had notice that an application for an administration order was pending or a person had delivered notice of intention to appoint an administrator, or

(v) during an administration which immediately preceded the winding up.

14.25(7) [Sum treated as being due in r.14.25(2)] A sum must be treated as being due to or from the company for the purposes of paragraph (2) whether–

(a) it is payable at present or in the future;

(b) the obligation by virtue of which it is payable is certain or contingent; or

(c) its amount is fixed or liquidated, or is capable of being ascertained by fixed rules or as a matter of opinion.

14.25(8) [Application of rr.14.14, 14.21–14.23, 14.44] For the purposes of this rule–

(a) rule 14.14 applies to an obligation which, by reason of its being subject to a contingency or for any other reason, does not bear a certain value;

(b) rules 14.21 to 14.23 apply to sums due to the company which–

(i) are payable in a currency other than sterling,

(ii) are of a periodical nature, or

(iii) bear interest; and

(c) rule 14.44 applies to a sum due to or from the company which is payable in the future.

General Note

There is no provision in the Insolvency Act itself for the case of mutual credits and set-off in company insolvency corresponding to IA 1986 s.323, which deals with individual bankruptcy. The present rule (and r.14.24 on administration) make good this shortcoming on the corporate side. See the Introductory note to Part IV, Chapter VIII preceding IA 1986 s.175.

The predecessor to r.14.25 (and with it r.14.24) were totally recast as from 1 April 2005, designed to provide greater detail and clarity of meaning, to reflect the applicable case law, to remove certain anomalies and to bring the set-off rules for liquidation and administration into line.

The predecessor rule, as originally drafted, removed some uncertainties that were not fully resolved previously. First, it was made clear that the rules as to mutual credits and set-off applied to all liquidations, irrespective of the solvency or otherwise of the company and whether the liquidation was voluntary or compulsory. Secondly, it was also made clear that the relevant date (or time: see the note to s.86) for all purposes of proof and set-off is that when the company went into liquidation. (For the meaning of this expression, see s.247(2).) On the other hand, some difficult questions remained to be resolved. The reforms introduced in 2005 were intended to deal with the most important of these.

First, the former rule gave inadequate guidance as to the set-off of contingent liabilities, and in particular how such liabilities when owed *to* the company should be quantified. (On this point see Wood, (1987) 8 Co. Law. 262; Roy Goode, *Principles of Corporate Insolvency Law* 4th edn (2011), Ch.9; *MS Fashions Ltd v Bank of Credit & Commerce International SA (No.2)* [1993] Ch. 425 at 435; [1993] B.C.C. 70 at 75; and, especially, *Stein v Blake* [1996] A.C. 243 at 251 et seq., per Lord Hoffmann. In contrast, the rules did contain provisions dealing with contingent liabilities owed *by* the company.

The revised r.14.25 now puts all contingent liabilities on the same footing, and the new rules assimilate the position for both liquidations and administrations (or, at least, those established under Sch.B1). Those rules which relate to the quantification of debts (i.e. rr.14.14, 14.21–14.23 and 14.44) are extended to cover debts owed *to* a company, as well as those owed *by* a company. Accordingly, debts owed to the company that are contingent or payable at a future time are to be included in the set-off account, and liquidators and administrators will be able to put a value on such debts.

Other innovations introduced by what is now r.14.25 are:

- "Mutual debts" that are not to be included in the set-off account are defined. These include any debt acquired by a creditor by assignment or otherwise, pursuant to an agreement entered into after one of the dates set out in rr.14.24(6)(e) and 14.25(6)(d). But if a creditor acquires or re-acquires a debt after one of those dates as a result of an agreement entered into at an earlier date, it is to be considered a "mutual dealing" for the purposes of the set-off account.
- Rule 14.25(7) now clarifies the question when a sum becomes "due" for set-off purposes, drawing on the definition of "debt or liability" in r.14.1(5). (Note also r.14.25(8)(c).)
- Where, after the calculation of the set-off account, an amount is owed to the company arising from a contingent debt or a sum payable at a future time, that amount only has to be paid to the liquidator if and when it becomes due and payable.

A creditor whose proof has been rejected cannot reassert the debt by claiming to rely on it as a set-off: *Bank of Credit & Commerce International (Overseas) Ltd v Habib Bank Ltd* [1998] 2 B.C.L.C. 459. On similar reasoning, a claim that would be open to objection on the grounds of double proof cannot be set off: *Re Glen Express Ltd* [2000] B.P.I.R. 456. In the *Habib Bank* case it was also held that under r.4.90 the court had to take account of the fact that debts owed to the creditor at the date of the liquidation had subsequently been paid by third parties.

Under the equitable principle traditionally known as the rule in *Cherry v Boultbee* (1839) 4 My. & C. 442 a person who is entitled to a share in a fund and also owes money to that fund may not participate in the fund without first paying into it the whole of what he owes. The Supreme Court has held in *Re Kaupthing Singer & Friedlander Ltd, Mills v HSBC Trustee (CI) Ltd* [2011] UKSC 48; [2012] B.C.C. 1 that this principle is excluded by the rule against double proof, for the same reasons as the latter has been held to oust the rules of insolvency set-off. The contrary view, expressed obiter in *Re SSSL Realisations (2002) Ltd* [2006] EWCA Civ 7; [2006] Ch. 610; [2006] B.C.C. 233, was disapproved. A similar but distinct rule, commonly known as the "contributory rule", which applies in a winding up, forbids a contributory from participating in a distribution until he has discharged all liabilities owed by him to the company (*Re Overend Gurney & Co, Grissell's Case* (1865-66) L.R. 1 Ch. App. 528; *Re West Coast Gold Fields Ltd* [1905] 1 Ch. 597; [1906] 1 Ch. 1). The rule is discussed by David Richards J in *Re Lehman Bros International (Europe)* [2014] EWHC 704 (Ch); [2014] B.C.C. 193 at [179] et seq. (where it was held not to apply in an administration) and this was confirmed on appeal (*Joint Administrators of LB Holdings Intermediate 2 Ltd v Lomas* [2015] EWCA Civ 485; [2016] Ch. 50; [2015] B.C.C. 431) but on further appeal the Supreme Court in *Joint Administrators of LB Holdings Intermediate 2 Ltd v Joint Administrators of Lehman Bros International (Europe)* [2017] UKSC 38; [2017] 2 W.L.R. 1497; [2017] B.C.C. 235 has, surprisingly, overruled this point to hold that the contributory rule can apply in a distributing administration—despite the fact that, unlike a liquidator (under IA 1986 s.74), an administrator has no power to call on contributories to contribute to the company's assets. Lord Neuberger was very conscious (at [176]) that a judge should think long and hard before laying down a new judge-made rule on liquidations, but considered that he was extending an existing rule rather than inventing an entirely new one. The existing rule he described ([178]) as an aspect of a "general equitable principle" which operated as a qualification to the Insolvency Rules needed to ensure compliance with the overall purpose of those rules. He believed that the contributory rule could be applied to distributing administrations subject to minor procedural modifications, which he described in [180]. See also *Re MK Airlines Ltd (No.2)* [2014] B.C.C. 103.

The rules as to set-off in insolvency proceedings apply in both solvent and insolvent liquidations (*Rayden v Edwardo Ltd* [2008] EWHC 2689 (Comm); [2009] B.P.I.R. 892, but are different from those which apply in other contexts (or before such proceedings take effect): see the subject discussed by Lord Hoffmann in *Stein v Blake* (above). The object of the latter is to avoid cross-actions, and their scope is restricted. The former, in contrast, are intended to do substantial justice between the parties, and their application is not limited to particular categories of claim, but apply to all cross-claims provided that they are mutual and measurable in money terms (*Stein v Blake* [1993] B.C.C. 587 at 590, per Balcombe LJ). Claims are only "mutual" if they are due between the same parties and in the same right—e.g. a debt owed by A to B as trustee for C and a debt owed to A by B personally cannot be set off: *Re ILG Travel Ltd* [1996] B.C.C. 21; *Re Griffin Trading Co* [1999] B.P.I.R. 256; *Simpson and Spratt v Kaupthing Singer & Friedlander (Isle of Man) Ltd* (31 October 2011, App. Div. Isle of Man). In the converse case, where B alleges that a debt owed by A to C is in fact held by C as trustee for B, the court will allow set-off only where it is satisfied that the debt is clear and ascertained and that B is the sole beneficiary and entitled without further inquiry to demand that the debt be transferred to him: *Ex p. Morier* (1879) 12 Ch. D. 491; *Bank of Credit and Commercial International SA (in liq.) v Prince Fahd Bin Salman Abdul Aziz Al-Saud* [1997] B.C.C. 63. The fact that one debt is secured and the other unsecured is not inconsistent with mutuality: *Re ILG Travel Ltd* (above). But there must have been "dealing" between the parties; and so (for instance) a debt cannot be set off against the creditor's liability to the company in damages for conversion: *Re Cosslett (Contractors) Ltd (No.2), Smith v Bridgend County Borough Council* [2001] UKHL 58; [2002] 1 A.C. 336; [2001] B.C.C. 740; *Goldtrail Travel Ltd v Aydin* [2014] EWHC 1587 (Ch); [2015] 1 B.C.L.C. 89. (Contrast *Myles J. Callaghan Ltd (in rec.) v City of Glasgow District Council* (1987) 3 B.C.C. 337, where it was held competent in Scots law for a creditor in a liquidation to set off a claim for damages for breach of a building contract against a claim by the company for the return of its plant and equipment or payment of its value, and to do so notwithstanding the appointment of a receiver.) The rules as to set-off are mandatory and cannot be excluded by agreement between the parties (*National Westminster Bank Ltd v Halesowen Presswork & Assemblies Ltd* [1972] A.C. 785); nor can they be disapplied by the court in the exercise of its discretion: *Re Bank of Credit & Commerce International SA (No.10)* [1997] Ch. 213; [1996] B.C.C. 980. In the *M S Fashions* case (above, affirmed [1993] Ch. 425 at 439, sub nom. *High Street Services Ltd v Bank of Credit & Commerce International SA* [1993] B.C.C. 360), it was held that where several persons were each liable to the company as principal debtors in respect of the same debt, a set-off available against one of them operated automatically to reduce the debt for the benefit of them all. It was not open to a liquidator to seek to avoid this consequence by electing to claim the full amount in the first instance from the other debtors. (For earlier proceedings in the same case, see *MS Fashions Ltd v Bank of Credit & Commerce International SA* [1992] B.C.C. 571.) In contrast, in *Re Bank of Credit & Commerce International SA (No.8), Morris v Rayners Enterprises Inc* [1988] A.C. 214; [1997] B.C.C. 965, the House of Lords held that the bank's liquidators could proceed first against the principal debtors concerned, without bringing into account the amounts of certain deposits made with the bank by other persons and allegedly charged to secure the debts. In this case the depositors had no personal liability for the principal debts, and accordingly there was no sum "due" from them on which a set-off could operate. It was observed that to permit the set-off of claims by third parties, even with their consent, would be to allow the parties by agreement to subvert the fundamental principle of pari passu distribution of assets in an insolvency. Other cases on r.14.25 include *Re a Company (No.1641 of 2003)* [2003] EWHC 2652 (Ch); [2004] 1 B.C.L.C. 211 (debt arising out of unlawful transaction cannot be set off); and *Re*

Greenport Ltd [2004] 1 B.C.L.C. 555 (no question of set-off under r.14.25 arises where creditor has a contractual right to make deductions from a deposit and that suffices to determine the rights of the parties).

A right of set-off arising under the general law (e.g. under a contract) which has not been exercised prior to the commencement of the liquidation is displaced by the rules of insolvency set-off under r.14.25: otherwise, to allow reliance on it would infringe the pari passu principle (*Larsen v Navios International Inc* [2011] EWHC 878 (Ch); [2012] B.C.C. 353). In contrast, the set-off rule under r.14.25 cannot be applied in regard to mutual debts before the company goes into liquidation, even though it may be insolvent: *FG Skerritt Ltd v Caledonian Building Systems Ltd* [2013] EWHC 1898 (TCC).

A debt owed to a company by the Crown for overpaid VAT and a sum which became payable by the company in its liquidation to the Crown for redundancy payments made after the commencement of the liquidation were held to arise out of "mutual dealings" in *Secretary of State for Trade and Industry v Frid, Re West End Networks Ltd* [2004] UKHL 24; [2004] 2 A.C. 506; [2004] B.C.C. 525. It was not necessary that the latter sums should have become due and payable at the date of the liquidation, so long as there was an obligation arising out of a contract, or the commission of a tort, or (as in this case) a statutory provision, by which a debt sounding in money would become payable on the occurrence of some future event. The Crown for this purpose was to be regarded as indivisible. However, where the obligation has arisen after the date of liquidation and the company had no claim at all before that date, set-off is not available: *Revenue and Customs Commissioners v Millichap* [2011] B.P.I.R. 145.

Rule 14.8 provides the means of appeal if a third party disagrees with the valuation that has been placed on a debt that he owes to the company.

Although r.14.25(2) states that "account must be taken" of what is due as between the parties, the rule is silent as to the procedure to be adopted in taking the account. In *Philpott v Lycée Français Charles de Gaulle School* [2015] EWHC 1065 (Ch) an arbitration clause was held to be binding on the parties and that a stay could be granted to enforce this.

A contributory's liability for calls cannot be set off in a liquidation against any liability of the company to him: *Re Overend Gurney, Grissell's case* (1864) 1 Ch. App. 528; *Re Pinecord Ltd* [1995] B.C.C. 483.

The holder of a secured debt is not required by r.14.25 to set off money owed by the company to him against that debt, unless he elects to give up his security and prove his debt in the liquidation: *Re Norman Holding Co Ltd (in liq.)* [1991] 1 W.L.R. 10; [1991] B.C.C. 11.

For a case where a creditor acquired a debt by assignment shortly before the debtor company entered administration and successfully avoided the statutory exclusion corresponding to r.14.25(6)(b)(ii), see *Re Parkside International Ltd* [2008] EWHC 3554 (Ch); [2010] B.C.C. 309.

In *Swissport (UK) Ltd v Aer Lingus Ltd* [2007] EWHC 1089 (Ch); [2009] B.C.C. 113 an insolvent company applied for summary judgment in respect of charges for services performed for the defendant, but the latter contended that it had a possible cross-claim which might be set off against that debt and that in such circumstances summary judgment was inappropriate and leave to defend should always be given, even where the debt was undisputed. The court held that this was not the case and gave summary judgment.

For consideration of the application of this provision see the approach of Registrar Jones in *Re Bowe Watts Clargo Ltd* [2017] EWHC 7879 (Ch).

For the exclusion of set-off in respect of post-insolvency VAT credits, see Value Added Tax Act 1994 s.81(4A)–(5).

On the application of r.14.25 in the context of payment and securities settlement systems, see the Finality Regulations reg.15. Rule 14.25(7)(b) does not apply to a close-out netting provision under a financial collateral arrangement unless the party concerned was aware at the time he entered into the arrangement that winding-up proceedings or re-organisation measures in relation to the other party had commenced: Financial Collateral Arrangements (No.2) Regulations 2003 (SI 2003/3226) reg.12(4).

Note that r.14.25 (like IR 2016 generally) does not apply to bodies other than companies (e.g. building societies), and it applies only in England and Wales. In Scotland set-off is determined by the rules of the common law. (See Lord Hope in *Secretary of State for Trade and Industry v Frid* (above), at [31]).

Chapter 3

Distribution to creditors in administration, winding up and bankruptcy

[Note: a document required by the Act or these Rules must also contain the standard contents set out in Part 1.]

14.26 Application of Chapter to a particular class of creditors and to distributions

14.26(1) [Application of Ch.3] This Chapter applies where the office-holder makes, or proposes to make, a distribution to any class of creditors other than secured creditors.

14.26(2) [Distribution to particular class of creditors in administration] Where the distribution is to a particular class of creditors in an administration, a reference in this Chapter to creditors is a reference to that class of creditors only.

(See General Note after r.14.31.)

14.27 Declaration and distribution of dividends in a winding up

[Note: section 324 makes provision in respect of such a declaration and distribution in a bankruptcy.]

14.27 Whenever a liquidator in a creditors' voluntary winding up or a winding up by the court has sufficient funds in hand for the purpose the liquidator must, while retaining such sums as may be necessary for the expenses of the winding up, declare and distribute dividends among the creditors in respect of the debts which they have proved.

(See General Note after r.14.31.)

14.28 Gazette notice of intended first dividend or distribution

14.28(1) [Gazetting notice of intended first dividend] Subject to paragraphs (2) and (4) where the office-holder intends to declare a first dividend or distribution the office-holder must gazette a notice containing–

(a) a statement that the office-holder intends to declare a first dividend or distribution;

(b) the date by which and place to which proofs must be delivered; and

(c) in the case of a members' voluntary winding up, where the dividend or distribution is to be a sole or final distribution, a statement that the distribution may be made without regard to the claim of any person in respect of a debt not proved.

14.28(2) [Intended dividend to preferential creditors only] Where the intended dividend is only to preferential creditors the office-holder need only gazette a notice if the office-holder thinks fit.

14.28(3) [Additional advertisement] The office-holder may in addition advertise such a notice in such other manner (if any) as the office-holder thinks fit.

14.28(4) [Non-application of r.14.28(1)] Paragraph (1) does not apply where the office-holder has previously, by a notice which has been gazetted, invited creditors to prove their debts.

(See General Note after r.14.31.)

14.29 Individual notices to creditors etc. of intended dividend or distribution

14.29(1) [To whom notices to be delivered] The office-holder must deliver a notice of the intention to make a distribution to creditors or declare a dividend–

(a) to the creditors in an administration; and

(b) to all creditors in a winding up or a bankruptcy who have not proved (including any creditors who are owed small debts and are not deemed under rule 14.3(3) to have proved as a result of a previous notice under rule 14.29).

14.29(2) [Intended dividend to preferential creditors only] Where the intended dividend is only for preferential creditors, the office-holder is only required to deliver such a notice to the preferential creditors.

14.29(3) [Notice re prescribed part] Where the office-holder intends to declare a dividend to unsecured creditors in an administration or winding-up the notice must also state the value of the prescribed part unless there is no prescribed part or the court has made an order under section 176A(5).

(See General Note after r.14.31.)

14.30 Contents of notice of intention to declare a dividend or make a distribution

14.30 A notice under rule 14.29 must contain the following–

(a) a statement that the office-holder intends to make a distribution to creditors or declare a dividend (as the case may be) within the period of two months from the last date for proving;

(b) a statement whether the proposed distribution or dividend is interim or final;

(c) the last date by which proofs may be delivered which must be–

(i) the same date for all creditors who prove, and

(ii) not less than 21 days from the date of notice;

(d) a statement of the place to which proofs must be delivered;

(e) the additional information required by rule 14.31 where the office-holder intends to treat a small debt as proved for the purposes of paying a dividend; and

(f) in the case of a members' voluntary winding up, where the distribution is to be a sole or final distribution, a statement that the distribution may be made without regard to the claim of any person in respect of a debt not proved.

(See General Note after r.14.31.)

14.31 Further contents of notice to creditors owed small debts etc.

14.31(1) [Treatment of small debts as proved] The office-holder may treat a debt, which is a small debt according to the accounting records or the statement of affairs of the company or bankrupt, as if it were proved for the purpose of paying a dividend.

14.31(2) [Notice under r.14.29 where debt treated as proved] Where the office-holder intends to treat such a debt as if it were proved the notice delivered under rule 14.29 must–

(a) state the amount of the debt which the office-holder believes to be owed to the creditor according to the accounting records or statement of affairs of the company or the bankrupt (as the case may be);

(b) state that the office-holder will treat the debt which is stated in notice, being for £1,000 or less, as proved for the purposes of paying a dividend unless the creditor advises the office-holder that the amount of the debt is incorrect or that no debt is owed;

(c) require the creditor to notify the office-holder by the last date for proving if the amount of the debt is incorrect or if no debt is owed; and

(d) inform the creditor that where the creditor advises the office-holder that the amount of the debt is incorrect the creditor must also submit a proof in order to receive a dividend.

14.31(3) [Information in r.14.31(2)(a)] The information required by paragraph (2)(a) may take the form of a list of small debts which the office-holder intends to treat as proved which includes that owed to the particular creditor to whom the notice is being delivered.

General Note to rr.14.26–14.31

These rules relate to publicity in advance of an office-holder paying a dividend or making a distribution to creditors (except secured creditors). Note under r.14.27 the positive duty on a liquidator in insolvent winding up to declare and distribute dividends to creditors when he has sufficient net assets (subject to retention to pay winding-up expenses) to do so. The equivalent duty on trustees in bankruptcy is in IA 1986 s.324. Note that an administrator may not make a distribution to unsecured, non-preferential creditors (except in relation to the prescribed part under IA 1986 s.176A) without the permission of the court (Sch.B1 para.65(3)).

A sum due to a member qua member is not deemed to be a debt, and ranks after the claims of the company's creditors: IA 1986 s.74(2)(f).

See rr.14.28–14.30 on gazetting and individual notices to creditors. For the standard contents of gazette and non-gazette notices see rr.1.10–1.18.

Note the last date for proving in r.14.30.

The innovation from 6 April 2017, is r.14.31(1) on treating small debts as having been proved in light of the reforms in ss.131 (company insolvency) and 132 (individual insolvency) of SBEEA 2015. A debt is "small" if not more than £1,000 (r.14.1(3), IA 1986 Sch.8 para.13A, Sch.9 para.18A) in the accounting records or the statement of affairs of the company or bankrupt. See r.14.31(2), (3) on individual notices to creditors regarding small debts.

14.32 Admission or rejection of proofs following last date for proving

14.32(1) [Treatment of proofs after last date for proving] Unless the office-holder has already dealt with them, the office-holder must within 14 days of the last date for proving set out in the notice under rule 14.29–

(a) admit or reject (in whole or in part) proofs delivered to the office-holder; or

(b) make such provision in relation to them as the office-holder thinks fit.

14.32(2) [No obligation to deal with late proofs] The office-holder is not obliged to deal with a proof delivered after the last date for proving, but the office-holder may do so if the office-holder thinks fit.

14.32(3) [Single payment only of debts] In the declaration of a dividend a payment must not be made more than once in respect of the same debt.

14.32(4) [Creditor and Member State liquidator proved] Subject to rule 14.43 (assignment of right to dividend), payment must only be made to the creditor in a case where both the creditor and a member State liquidator have proved in relation to the same debt.

General Note

For the "last date for proving" see r.14.30. Late proofs may be accepted at the discretion of the office-holder. With regard to late proof of debts see *Painter v Hutchison* [2007] EWHC 758 (Ch); [2008] B.P.I.R. 170.

14.33 Postponement or cancellation of dividend

14.33(1) [Application court for decision on proof to be reversed, varied, etc.] The office-holder may postpone or cancel the dividend in the period of two months from the last date for proving if an application is made to the court for the office-holder's decision on a proof to be reversed or varied, or for a proof to be excluded, or for a reduction of the amount claimed.

14.33(2) [Real complexity in admitting or rejecting proofs] The office-holder may postpone a dividend if the office-holder considers that due to the nature of the affairs of the person to whom the proceedings relate there is real complexity in admitting or rejecting proofs of claims submitted.

14.33(3) [New notice under r.14.29 required] Where the dividend is postponed or cancelled a new notice under rule 14.29 will be required if the dividend is paid subsequently.

General Note

An application to the court to have the decision of the office-holder on the admission or rejection of proofs varied is made under r.14.8. There is a time-limit of 21 days in each case. If such an application has been made, the office-holder may postpone or cancel the dividend under this rule; but, if he proposes to pay a dividend, r.14.34(2) applies.

14.34 Declaration of dividend

14.34(1) [Declaration in two months of last date for proving] The office-holder must declare the dividend in the two month period referred to in rule 14.30(a) in accordance with the notice of intention to declare a dividend unless the office-holder has had cause to postpone or cancel the dividend.

14.34(2) [No declaration if pending application to reverse, vary, etc. proof] The office-holder must not declare a dividend so long as there is pending an application to the court to reverse or vary a decision of the office-holder on a proof, or to exclude a proof or to reduce the amount claimed unless the court gives permission.

14.34(3) [Court direction] If the court gives such permission, the office-holder must make such provision in relation to the proof as the court directs.

General Note

If no application has been made to the court to challenge a decision on the admission or rejection of a proof, the dividend must be declared within the two-month period. If the office-holder wishes to declare an interim dividend pending the outcome of such an application, the leave of the court is required under r.14.34(3). Where this rule applies, the normal rules as to the payment of interim dividends (IA 1986 s.324, IR 2016 rr.14.27, 14.39, 14.40) are displaced. For discussion see *Lomax Leisure Ltd v Miller* [2008] EWCA Civ 525; [2008] B.C.C. 686 where the point was made that the liquidator's obligations under r.14.34 with regard to payment of a declared dividend must be taken as being subject to his overriding duties under r.14.27 to ensure a proper distribution of assets (IA 1986 s.324 in bankruptcy).

14.35 Notice of declaration of a dividend

14.35(1) [Notice of declaration to all creditors who have proved] Where the office-holder declares a dividend the office-holder must deliver notice of that fact to all creditors who have proved for their debts (subject to paragraph (5)).

14.35(2) [Notice may be simultaneous with declaration] The notice declaring a dividend may be delivered at the same time as the dividend is distributed.

14.35(3) [Content of notice] The notice must include the following in relation to the insolvency proceedings–

(a) the amounts raised from the sale of assets, indicating (so far as practicable) amounts raised by the sale of particular assets;

(b) the payments made by the office-holder in carrying out the office-holder's functions;

(c) the provision (if any) made for unsettled claims, and funds (if any) retained for particular purposes;

(d) the total amount to be distributed and the rate of dividend; and

(e) whether, and if so when, any further dividend is expected to be declared.

14.35(4) [Distribution to unsecured creditors: value of prescribed part] In an administration, a creditors' voluntary winding-up or a winding up by the court, where the administrator or liquidator intends to make a distribution to unsecured creditors, the notice must also state the value of the prescribed part unless there is no prescribed part or the court has made an order under section 176A(5).

14.35(5) [Notice where dividend to preferential creditors only] Where the office-holder declares a dividend for preferential creditors only, the notice under paragraph (1) need only be delivered to those preferential creditors who have proved for their debts.

General Note

Creditors are to receive full information relating to the payment of dividends, including the value of any prescribed part in a corporate insolvency unless the court orders that the cost of distribution would be disproportionate to the benefit under IA 1986 s.176A(5).

14.36 Last notice about dividend in a winding up

[Note: section 330 contains the requirement to deliver such a notice in a bankruptcy.]

14.36(1) [Notice as to final or no dividend] When the liquidator in a winding up has realised all the company's assets or so much of them as can, in the liquidator's opinion, be realised without needlessly prolonging the winding up, the liquidator must deliver a notice as provided for in this Chapter, either–

(a) of intention to declare a final dividend; or

(b) that no dividend, or further dividend, will be declared.

14.36(2) [Particulars of notice] The notice must contain the particulars required by rule 14.30, 14.31, 14.37 or 14.38 as the case may be and must require claims against the assets to be established by a date set out in the notice.

(See General Note after r.14.38.)

14.37 Contents of last notice about dividend (administration, winding up and bankruptcy)

14.37(1) [Application of rule] This rule applies in an administration, winding up or bankruptcy.

14.37(2) [Notice re no or no further dividend] If the office-holder delivers notice to creditors that the office-holder is unable to declare any dividend or (as the case may be) any further dividend, the notice must contain a statement to the effect either–

(a) that no funds have been realised; or

(b) that the funds realised have already been distributed or used or allocated for paying the expenses of the insolvency proceedings.

14.37(3) [Rule 14.37(2) in progress report] The information required by paragraph (2) may be included in a progress report.

(See General Note after r.14.38.)

14.38 Sole or final dividend

[Note: see section 330 in respect of a dividend in a bankruptcy.]

14.38(1) [Payments] Where, in an administration or winding up, it is intended that the distribution is to be a sole or final dividend, after the date specified as the last date for proving in the notice under rule 14.29, the office-holder–

(a) in a winding up, must pay any outstanding expenses of the winding up out of the assets;

(b) in an administration, must–

  (i) pay any outstanding expenses of a winding up (including any of the items mentioned in rule 6.42 or 7.108 (as appropriate)) or provisional winding up that immediately preceded the administration,

  (ii) pay any items payable in accordance with the provisions of paragraph 99 of Schedule B1,

  (iii) pay any amount outstanding (including debts or liabilities and the administrator's own remuneration and expenses) which would, if the administrator were to cease to be the administrator of the company, be payable out of the property of which he had custody or control in accordance with the provisions of paragraph 99, and

  (iv) declare and distribute that dividend without regard to the claim of any person in respect of a debt not already proved; or

(c) in a members' voluntary winding up may, and in every other case must, declare and distribute that dividend without regard to the claim of any person in respect of a debt not already proved.

14.38(2) [Small debts excluded from debts that have not been proved] The reference in paragraph (1)(b)(iv) and (c) to debts that have not been proved does not include small debts treated as proved by the office-holder.

14.38(3) [Postponement of date in notice] The court may, on the application of any person, postpone the date specified in the notice.

General Note to rr.14.36–14.38

The rules on no, no further, sole or final dividend. Reference to s.330 is required in bankruptcy.

In *Lomax Leisure Ltd* [2007] EWHC 2508 (Ch); [2008] B.C.C. 686 a final dividend had been declared and cheques had been posted to all the creditors who had been admitted to proof. Meantime, a creditor whose proof had been rejected had applied to the court appealing against the rejection of his proof, but notice of his application was not served on the liquidators until after the cheques had been sent out. The liquidators immediately stopped payment on the cheques. It was held that the creditors had no right to enforce payment of the cheques under the Bills of Exchange Act 1882 s.27, since they had given no consideration sufficient to support the cheques. The court also confirmed that the only remedy of a creditor who wished to enforce payment of a dividend was to apply under what is now r.14.45: he could not sue the liquidator directly.

14.39 Administration and winding up: provisions as to dividends

[Note: see section 324(4) in respect of such provisions in bankruptcy.]

14.39 In an administration or winding up, in the calculation and distribution of a dividend the office-holder must make provision for–

(a) any debts which are the subject of claims which have not yet been determined; and

(b) disputed proofs and claims.

General Note

This is a sensible provision, echoing s.324(4) except that the latter (as did the predecessor of this rule) includes provision to be made for debts due to persons who by reason of their place of residence may not have had sufficient time to tender and establish their proofs: it seems likely that this may now be regarded s falling within para.(a).

If the office-holder wishes to declare an interim dividend pending the outcome of an application on disputed proofs and claims, the permission of the court is required under r.14.34(2).

14.40 Supplementary provisions as to dividends and distributions

14.40(1) [Creditor may not disturb payment of dividend] A creditor is not entitled to disturb the payment of any dividend or making of any distribution because–

(a) the amount claimed in the creditor's proof is increased after payment of the dividend;

(b) in an administration, a creditors' voluntary winding up or a winding up by the court the creditor did not prove for a debt before the declaration of the dividend; or

(c) in a members' voluntary winding up, the creditor did not prove for a debt before the last date for proving or increases the claim in proof after that date.

14.40(2) [Entitlement out of further dividend] However the creditor is entitled to be paid a dividend or receive a distribution which the creditor has failed to receive out of any money for the time being available for the payment of a further dividend or making a further distribution.

14.40(3) [Payment before further dividend] Such a dividend must be paid or distribution made before that money is applied to the payment of any further dividend or making of any further distribution.

14.40(4) [Repayment of amount overpaid] If, after a creditor's proof has been admitted, the proof is withdrawn or excluded, or the amount of it is reduced, the creditor is liable to repay to the office-holder, for the credit of the insolvency proceedings, any amount overpaid by way of dividend.

General Note

Here we have a "heads I win, tails you lose" situation.

14.41 Secured creditors

14.41(1) [Value of security altered after dividend paid] The following applies where a creditor alters the value of a security after a dividend has been declared.

14.41(2) [Alteration reduces creditor's unsecured claim] If the alteration reduces the creditor's unsecured claim ranking for dividend, the creditor must as soon as reasonably practicable repay to the office-holder, for the credit of the administration or of the insolvent estate, any amount received by the creditor as dividend in excess of that to which the creditor would be entitled, having regard to the alteration of the value of the security.

14.41(3) [Alteration increases creditor's unsecured claim] If the alteration increases the creditor's unsecured claim, the creditor is entitled to receive from the office-holder, out of any money for the time being available for the payment of a further dividend, before any such further dividend is paid, any dividend or dividends which the creditor has failed to receive, having regard to the alteration of the value of the security.

14.41(4) [No disturbance of dividend already declared] The creditor is not entitled to disturb any dividend declared (whether or not distributed) before the date of the alteration.

General Note

This again shows that the law will not disturb dividends that have already been declared.

On this rule see *Webb v Macdonald* [2010] B.P.I.R. 503, which highlights the protection afforded to secured creditors.

On r.14.41(2) see *Cahillane v NALM Ltd* [2014] EWHC 1992 (Ch); [2014] B.P.I.R. 1093.

14.42 Disqualification from dividend

14.42 If a creditor contravenes any provision of the Act or these Rules relating to the valuation of securities, the court may, on the application of the office-holder, order that the creditor be wholly or partly disqualified from participation in any dividend.

General Note

This is a useful sanction.

14.43 Assignment of right to dividend

14.43(1) [Payment to other person] If a person entitled to a dividend ("the entitled person") delivers notice to the office-holder that the entitled person wishes the dividend to be paid to another person, or that the entitled person has assigned the entitlement to another person, the office-holder must pay the dividend to that other person accordingly.

14.43(2) [Notice to specify name and address of other person] A notice delivered under this rule must specify the name and address of the person to whom payment is to be made.

General Note

The right to receive a dividend can be assigned.

14.44 Debt payable at future time

14.44(1) [Entitlement to dividend] Where a creditor has proved for a debt of which payment is not due at the date of the declaration of a dividend, the creditor is entitled to the dividend equally with other creditors, but subject as follows.

14.44(2) [Calculation of discount of proof] For the purpose of dividend (and no other purpose) the amount of the creditor's admitted proof must be discounted by applying the following formula–

$$\frac{X}{1.05^n}$$

where–

(a) "X" is the value of the admitted proof; and

(b) "n" is the period beginning with the relevant date and ending with the date on which the payment of the creditor's debt would otherwise be due, expressed in years (part of a year being expressed as a decimal fraction of a year).

General Note

A predecessor to r.14.44(2) was amended from 1 April 2005, to meet the criticisms made of the former wording by Lord Millett in *Re Park Air Services plc* [2000] 2 A.C. 172 at 188. The discount is now to be applied to the reducing amount of the debt rather than to the full amount of the admitted proof.

On the valuation of future debts for the purposes of set-off, see the notes to r.14.24 (administration) and r.14.25 (winding up).

14.45 Administration and winding up: non-payment of dividend

[Note: see section 325(2) for equivalent provisions in respect of bankruptcy.]

14.45(1) [No action against office-holder] No action lies against the office-holder in an administration or winding up for payment of a dividend.

14.45(2) [Order for payment if officer-holder refuses] However, if the office-holder refuses to pay a dividend the court may, if it thinks just, order the office-holder to pay it and also to pay, out of the office-holder's own money–

(a) interest on the dividend, at the rate for the time being specified in section 17 of the Judgments Act 1838, from the time when it was withheld; and

(b) the costs of the proceedings in which the order to pay is made.

General Note

This rule reiterates that no action lies against a corporate office-holder for payment of a dividend, but then rather oddly empowers the court to order him to pay it with interest and costs from his own pocket. See IA 1986 s.325(2) in relation to bankruptcy.

Part 15

Decision Making

Introduction note to Part 15

This is one of the so-called common parts of the new IR 2016 regime. It tries to bring together similar rules scattered around IR 1986 into a common grouping. It does not totally succeed in that goal because differences will remain. Part 15 also seeks to add flesh to significant reforms introduced by SBEEA 2015 with regard to creditor decision procedures. These procedures seek to move away from the use of creditor meetings as a means to determine creditor views. The new regime fully embraces new technology and recognises that many creditor meetings have become pointless affairs due to creditor apathy. Red tape is further reduced via the so-called "deemed consent procedure" (see IA 1986 ss.246ZF and 379ZB, inserted by SBEEA 2015 ss.122, 123). There is less flexibility on offer for company meetings. For a valuable explanation of Pt 15 see Morgan [2017] 30 Insolv. Int. 17. For definitions note in particular IR 2016 r.1.2. A new Statement of Insolvency Practice (SIP 6, replacing SIPs 8, 10 and 12) provides guidance for IPs intended so that they may ensure that persons entitled to participate in decision making are able to make informed decisions and are aware of the deemed consent procedure. SIP 6 was effective from 6 April 2017 with interim status and subsequently republished and expanded in a new version (SIP 6, *Deemed consent and decision procedures in insolvency proceedings*) containing extra disclosure requirements with effect from 1 January 2018.

Chapter 1

Application of Part

15.1 Application of Part

15.1 In this Part–

(a) Chapters 2 to 11 apply where the Act or these Rules require a decision to be made by a qualifying decision procedure, or by a creditors' decision procedure or permit a decision to be made by the deemed consent procedure; and

(b) Chapter 12 applies to company meetings.

General Note

Since IA 1986 deals with solvent as well as insolvent liquidations, the company in the former case (e.g. in a members' voluntary liquidation) will continue to function as a company governed by CA 2006 and meetings will be conducted in accordance with that Act and the company's articles, supplemented by Ch.12 of this Part. The same will apply in some other situations, e.g. if it is proposed to exit an administration via a reorganisation under CA 2006 Pt 26 which involves shareholders as well as creditors. In such a case the administrator is empowered by CA 2006 s.896(2)(d) to summon a meeting of the company and r.15.41(3) with apply.

In an insolvent liquidation, if the company's members are involved, they will do so qua contributories and Chs 2–11 of the Rules will apply.

For definitions see IR 2016 rr.1.2(2), 15.2(1), 15.3.

The meaning of the phrase "qualifying decision procedure" has to be tracked down through IA 1986 ss.246ZE, Sch.8 para.8A (and see also s.379ZA, Sch.9 para.11A) to IR 2016 Pt 15. Essentially it refers to a decision reached by the company's contributories or creditors by correspondence, electronic voting, virtual meeting, physical meeting or any other decision making procedure which enables all creditors who are entitled to participate in the making of the decision to participate equally (as appropriate in the circumstances) and achieved by whatever majority (and in accordance with any conditions as to notice, eligibility to vote, etc.) that is prescribed by the remaining rules of Pt 15. If the procedure ticks all the boxes in that Part, it "qualifies".

Chapter 2

Decision procedures

[Note: a document required by the Act or these Rules must also contain the standard contents set out in Part 1.]

15.2 Interpretation

15.2(1) [Definitions] In these Rules–

"decision date" means–

(a) in the case of a decision to be made at a meeting, the date of the meeting;

(b) in the case of a decision to be made either by a decision procedure other than a meeting or by the deemed consent procedure, the date the decision is to be made or deemed to have been made;

and a decision falling within paragraph (b) is to be treated as made at 23:59 on the decision date;

"decision procedure" means a qualifying decision procedure or a creditors' decision procedure as prescribed by rule 15.3;

"electronic voting" includes any electronic system which enables a person to vote without the need to attend at a particular location to do so;

"physical meeting" means a meeting as described in section 246ZE(9) or 379ZA(9);

"virtual meeting" means a meeting where persons who are not invited to be physically present together may participate in the meeting including communicating directly with all the other participants in the meeting and voting (either directly or via a proxy-holder);

15.2(2) **[Decision date]** The decision date is to be set at the discretion of the convener, but must be not less than 14 days from the date of delivery of the notice, except where the table in rule 15.11 requires a different period or the court directs otherwise.

15.2(3) **[Rules on decision procedures modified re contributories]** The rules in Chapters 2 to 11 about decision procedures of creditors apply with any necessary modifications to decision making by contributories.

15.2(4) **[Percentages re contributories]** In particular, in place of the requirement for percentages or majorities in decision making by creditors to be determined by value, where the procedure seeks a decision from contributories value must be determined on the percentage of voting rights in accordance with rule 15.39.

General Note

This is an interpretation provision. Precise timing is of some significance in determining whether specified actions are taken within required timescales.

15.3 The prescribed decision procedures

[Note: under sections 246ZE and 379ZA a decision may not be made by a creditors' meeting (a physical meeting) unless the prescribed proportion of the creditors request in writing that the decision be made by such a meeting.]

15.3 The following decision procedures are prescribed as decision procedures under sections 246ZE and 379ZA by which a convener may seek a decision under the Act or these Rules from creditors–

(a) correspondence;

(b) electronic voting;

(c) virtual meeting;

(d) physical meeting;

(e) any other decision making procedure which enables all creditors who are entitled to participate in the making of the decision to participate equally.

General Note

The variety of creditor decision procedures in both corporate and personal insolvency situations is thus outlined. There are five alternatives. Note the restriction on physical meetings imposed by IA 1986 ss.246ZE and 379ZA.

15.4 Electronic voting

15.4 Where the decision procedure uses electronic voting–

(a) the notice delivered to creditors must give them any necessary information as to how to access the voting system including any password required;

(b) except where electronic voting is being used at a meeting, the voting system must be a system capable of enabling a creditor to vote at any time between the notice being delivered and the decision date; and

(c) in the course of a vote the voting system must not provide any creditor with information concerning the vote cast by any other creditor.

General Note

New technology is to the fore, though the dangers of new technology are highlighted by the terms of r.15.4(c).

15.5 Virtual meetings

15.5 Where the decision procedure uses a virtual meeting the notice delivered to creditors must contain–

(a) any necessary information as to how to access the virtual meeting including any telephone number, access code or password required; and

(b) a statement that the meeting may be suspended or adjourned by the chair of the meeting (and must be adjourned if it is so resolved at the meeting).

General Note

This is purely pragmatic detail. Although the meeting is virtual many of the basic rules of meetings continue to apply.

15.6 Physical meetings

15.6(1) [Timing for requests for] A request for a physical meeting may be made before or after the notice of the decision procedure or deemed consent procedure has been delivered, but must be made not later than five business days after the date on which the convener delivered the notice of the decision procedure or deemed consent procedure unless these Rules provide to the contrary.

15.6(2) [Responsibility of convener to check for requests] It is the convener's responsibility to check whether any requests for a physical meeting are submitted before the deadline and if so whether in aggregate they meet or surpass one of the thresholds requiring a physical meeting under sections 246ZE(7) or 379ZA(7).

15.6(3) [Convener to give notice summoning meeting] Where the prescribed proportion of creditors require a physical meeting the convener must summon the meeting by giving notice which complies with rule 15.8 so far as applicable and which must also contain a statement that the meeting may be suspended or adjourned by the chair of the meeting (and must be adjourned if it is so resolved at the meeting).

15.6(4) [Notice under r.15.6(3)] In addition, the notice under paragraph (3) must inform the creditors that as a result of the requirement to hold a physical meeting the original decision procedure or the deemed consent procedure is superseded.

15.6(5) [Time limit for notice] The convener must send the notice under paragraph (3) not later than three business days after one of the thresholds requiring a physical meeting has been met or surpassed.

15.6(6) [Remote attendance] The convener–

(a) may permit a creditor to attend a physical meeting remotely if the convener receives a request to do so in advance of the meeting; and

(b) must include in the notice of the meeting a statement explaining the convener's discretion to permit remote attendance.

15.6(7) ["Remotely"] In this rule, attending a physical meeting "remotely" means attending and being able to participate in the meeting without being in the place where the meeting is being held.

15.6(8) [Calculation of value of creditor's debt] For the purpose of determining whether the thresholds under section 246ZE(7) or 379ZA(7) are met, the convener must calculate the value of the creditor's debt by reference to rule 15.31.

General Note

The tenor of this provision indicates that physical meetings are to be seen as a last resort. Note the various deadlines specified. Remote attendance at such a physical meeting is possible. See annotations to IA 1986 ss.246ZE and 379ZA.

15.7 Deemed consent (sections 246ZF and 379ZB)

[Note: the deemed consent procedure cannot be used to make a decision on remuneration of any person, or where the Act, these Rules or any other legislation requires a decision to be made by a decision procedure.]

15.7(1) [Further provision to IA 1986 ss.246ZF, 379ZB] This rule makes further provision about the deemed consent procedure to that set out in sections 246ZF and 379ZB.

15.7(2) [Notice seeking deemed consent to comply with r.15.8] A notice seeking deemed consent must, in addition to the requirements of section 246ZF or 379ZB (as applicable) comply with the requirements of rule 15.8 so far as applicable and must also contain–

(a) a statement that in order to object to the proposed decision a creditor must have delivered a notice, stating that the creditor so objects, to the convener not later than the decision date together with a proof in respect of the creditor's claim in accordance with these Rules failing which the objection will be disregarded;

(b) a statement that it is the convener's responsibility to aggregate any objections to see if the threshold is met for the decision to be taken as not having been made; and

(c) a statement that if the threshold is met the deemed consent procedure will terminate without a decision being made and if a decision is sought again on the same matter it will be sought by a decision procedure.

15.7(3) [Threshold for objection to proposed decision] In this rule, the threshold is met where the appropriate number of relevant creditors (as defined in sections 246ZF and 379ZB) have objected to the proposed decision.

15.7(4) [Aggregating objections] For the purpose of aggregating objections, the convener may presume the value of relevant creditors' claims to be the value of claims by those creditors who, in the convener's view, would have been entitled to vote had the decision been sought by a decision procedure in accordance with this Part, even where those creditors had not already met the criteria for such entitlement to vote.

15.7(5) [Application of rr.15.31(2), 15.32, 15.33 re calculating objections] The provisions of rules 15.31(2) (calculation of voting rights), 15.32 (calculation of voting rights: special cases) and 15.33 (procedure for admitting creditors' claims for voting) apply to the admission or rejection of a claim for the purpose of the convener deciding whether or not an objection should count towards the total aggregated objections.

15.7(6) [Appeal from decision on aggregation of objections] A decision of the convener on the aggregation of objections under this rule is subject to appeal under rule 15.35 as if it were a decision under Chapter 8 of this Part.

General Note

This adds flesh to the provisions on deemed consent in IA 1986 (ss.246ZF and 379ZB). Guidance is provided on how the weight of objections to this procedure are to be calculated.

CHAPTER 3

NOTICES, VOTING AND VENUES FOR DECISIONS

[Note: a document required by the Act or these Rules must also contain the standard contents set out in Part 1.]

15.8 Notices to creditors of decision procedure

15.8(1) [Requirements for notices] This rule sets out the requirements for notices to creditors where a decision is sought by a decision procedure.

15.8(2) [Duty of convener to deliver notice] The convener must deliver a notice to every creditor who is entitled to notice of the procedure.

15.8(3) [Content of notice] The notice must contain the following–

(a) identification details for the proceedings;

(b) details of the decision to be made or of any resolution on which a decision is sought;

(c) a description of the decision procedure which the convener is using, and arrangements, including the venue, for the decision procedure;

(d) a statement of the decision date;

(e) a statement of by when the creditor must have delivered a proof in respect of the creditor's claim in accordance with these Rules failing which a vote by the creditor will be disregarded;

(f) a statement that a creditor whose debt is treated as a small debt in accordance with rule 14.31(1) must still deliver a proof if that creditor wishes to vote;

(g) a statement that a creditor who has opted out from receiving notices may nevertheless vote if the creditor provides a proof in accordance with paragraph (e);

(h) in the case of a decision to remove a liquidator in a creditors' voluntary winding-up or a winding up by the court, a statement drawing the attention of creditors to section 173(2), 174(2) or 174(4) (which relate to the release of the liquidator), as appropriate;

(i) in the case of a decision to remove a trustee in a bankruptcy, a statement drawing the attention of creditors to section 299(1) or 299(3) (which relates to the release of the trustee);

(j) in the case of a decision in relation to a proposed CVA or IVA, a statement of the effects of the relevant provisions of the following–

  (i) rule 15.28 about creditors' voting rights,

  (ii) rule 15.31 about the calculation of creditors' voting rights, and

  (iii) rule 15.34 about the requisite majority of creditors for making decisions;

(k) except in the case of a physical meeting, a statement that creditors who meet the thresholds in sections 246ZE(7) or 379ZA(7) may, within five business days from the date of delivery of the notice, require a physical meeting to be held to consider the matter;

(l) in the case of a meeting, a statement that any proxy must be delivered to the convener or chair before it may be used at the meeting;

(m) in the case of a meeting, a statement that, where applicable, a complaint may be made in accordance with rule 15.38 and the period within which such a complaint may be made; and

(n) a statement that a creditor may appeal a decision in accordance with rule 15.35, and the relevant period under rule 15.35 within which such an appeal may be made.

15.8(4) [Authentication of notice] The notice must be authenticated and dated by the convener.

15.8(5) [Proxy where decision procedure a meeting] Where the decision procedure is a meeting the notice must be accompanied by a blank proxy complying with rule 16.3.

15.8(6) [Non-application where court orders advertisement only] This rule does not apply if the court orders under rule 15.12 that notice of a decision procedure be given by advertisement only.

General Note

This delineates in great detail various notice requirements for the full range of insolvency procedures. This rule is drawn from numerous predecessors in IR 1986. Note the special provision made in r.15.8(3)(f), (g) for opted-out creditors and creditors with small debts (instances not covered under the former regime). A "blank proxy" (see r.16.3) must accompany the notice where the decision procedure is a meeting (r.15.8(5)). Giving of notices is not required where the court allows notice of decision procedures by advertisement under r.15.12 (r.15.8(6)).

15.9 Voting in a decision procedure

15.9(1) [Requirements for votes to be counted] In order to be counted in a decision procedure other than where votes are cast at a meeting, votes must–

(a) be received by the convener on or before the decision date; and

(b) in the case of a vote cast by a creditor, be accompanied by a proof in respect of the creditor's claim unless it has already been given to the convener.

15.9(2) [When vote to be disregarded] In an administration, an administrative receivership, a creditors' voluntary winding up, a winding up by the court or a bankruptcy a vote must be disregarded if–

(a) a proof in respect of the claim is not received by the convener on or before the decision date or, in the case of a meeting, 4pm on the business day before the decision date unless under rule 15.26 or 15.28(1)(b)(ii) (as applicable) the chair is content to accept the proof later; or

(b) the convener decides, in the application of Chapter 8 of this Part, that the creditor is not entitled to cast the vote.

15.9(3) [Minimum of one valid vote for decision] For the decision to be made, the convener must receive at least one valid vote on or before the decision date.

General Note

IR 2016 r.15.9(2) does not have general application. Again this rule draws inspiration from a range of provisions in IR 1986.

15.10 Venue for decision procedure

15.10 The convener must have regard to the convenience of those invited to participate when fixing the venue for a decision procedure (including the resumption of an adjourned meeting).

General Note

This goes beyond courtesy, but the phrase "have regard to" imposes only a minimum obligation (see the discourse on CA 2006 s.172).

15.11 Notice of decision procedures or of seeking deemed consent: when and to whom delivered

[Note: when an office-holder is obliged to give notice to "the creditors", this is subject to rule 1.37, which limits the obligation to giving notice to those creditors of whose address the office-holder is aware.]

15.11(1) [Requirements for delivery of notices] Notices of decision procedures, and notices seeking deemed consent, must be delivered in accordance with the following table.

Proceedings	*Decisions*	*Persons to whom notice must be delivered*	*Minimum notice required*
administration	decisions of creditors	the creditors who had claims against the company at the date when the company entered administration (except for those who have subsequently been paid in full)	14 days
administrative receivership	decisions of creditors	the creditors	14 days
creditors' voluntary winding up	decisions of creditors for appointment of liquidator (including any decision made at the same time on the liquidator's remuneration or the establishment of a liquidation committee)	the creditors	14 days on conversion from members' voluntary liquidation, 7 days on conversion from member's voluntary liquidation where deemed consent has been objected to and in other cases, 3 business days
creditors' voluntary winding up or a winding up by the court	decisions of creditors to consider whether a replacement should be appointed after a liquidator's resignation	the creditors	28 days
winding up by the court	decisions of creditors to consider whether to remove or replace the liquidator (other than after a liquidator's resignation)	the creditors and the official receiver	14 days
creditors' voluntary winding up or a winding up by the court	other decisions of creditors	the creditors	14 days
winding up by the court	decisions of contributories	every person appearing (by the company's records or otherwise) to be a contributory	14 days

Proceedings	*Decisions*	*Persons to whom notice must be delivered*	*Minimum notice required*
proposed CVA	decisions of creditors	the creditors	7 days for a decision on proposed modifications to the proposal from the company's directors under paragraph 31(7) of Schedule A1; 7 days for consideration of proposal where physical meeting requisitioned; in other cases, 14 days
proposed IVA	decisions of creditors	the creditors	14 days
bankruptcy	decisions of creditors to consider whether a replacement should be appointed after the resignation of a trustee	the creditors and the official receiver	28 days
bankruptcy	decisions of creditors to consider removing the trustee	the creditors and the official receiver	14 days
bankruptcy	decisions of creditors on appointment of new trustee following removal of previous trustee (including any decision made at the same time on the establishment of a creditors' committee)	the creditors	7 days
bankruptcy	other decisions of creditors	the creditors	14 days
Main proceedings in another member State	Approval under Article 36(5) of the EU Regulation of proposed undertaking offered by a member State liquidator	all the local creditors in the United Kingdom	14 days

15.11(2) [Non-application where court orders advertisement only] This rule does not apply where the court orders under rule 15.12 that notice of a decision procedure be given by advertisement only.

General Note

The use of a table here is innovative and constructive. It might have been improved upon by linkage to specific provisions in IA 1986.

The final entry relating to "main proceedings in another member State" inserted by the Insolvency Amendment (EU 2015/848) Regulations 2017 (SI 2017/702) regs 1, 2(1), Sch. paras 32, 44 in relation to proceedings opened on or after 26 June 2017 (see reg.3) when the Recast EU Regulation 2015/848 came into force.

15.12 Notice of decision procedure by advertisement only

15.12(1) [Court order for advertisement of notice only] The court may order that notice of a decision procedure is to be given by advertisement only and not by individual notice to the persons concerned.

15.12(2) [Matters court to have regard to] In considering whether to make such an order, the court must have regard to the relative cost of advertisement as against the giving of individual notices, the amount of assets available and the extent of the interest of creditors, members and contributories or any particular class of them.

15.12(3) [Additional content for advertisement to r.15.8(3) requirements] The advertisement must meet the requirements for a notice under rule 15.8(3), and must also state–

(a) that the court ordered that notice of the decision procedure be given by advertisement only; and

(b) the date of the court's order.

General Note

The advantages of general advertisement over personal notices are obvious, but, as there are dangers of a democratic deficit, only the court can order that this method be exploited.

15.13 Gazetting and advertisement of meeting

15.13(1) [Content of Gazette notice] In an administration, a creditors' voluntary winding up, a winding up by the court, or a bankruptcy, where a decision is being sought by a meeting the convener must gazette a notice of the procedure stating–

(a) that a meeting of creditors or contributories is to take place;

(b) the venue for the meeting;

(c) the purpose of the meeting; and

(d) the time and date by which, and place at which, those attending must deliver proxies and proofs (if not already delivered) in order to be entitled to vote.

15.13(2) [Further content] The notice must also state–

(a) who is the convener in respect of the decision procedure; and

(b) if the procedure results from a request of one or more creditors, the fact that it was so summoned and the section of the Act under which it was summoned.

15.13(3) [When notice to be gazetted] The notice must be gazetted before or as soon as reasonably practicable after notice of the meeting is delivered in accordance with these Rules.

15.13(4) [Advertisement] Information to be gazetted under this rule may also be advertised in such other manner as the convener thinks fit.

15.13(5) [Gazetting of other decision procedures or deemed consent procedure] The convener may gazette other decision procedures or the deemed consent procedure in which case the equivalent information to that required by this rule must be stated in the notice.

General Note

This transparency procedure does not apply to voluntary arrangements. Indeed one attraction in voluntary arrangements is that they are relatively discreet. For definitions see IR 2016 r.1.2. On the standard content of Gazette notices see rr.1.10–1.13.

15.14 Notice to company officers, bankrupts etc. in respect of meetings

15.14(1) [Notice to company officers] In a proposal for a CVA, an administration, a creditors' voluntary winding up or a winding up by the court notice to participate in a creditors' meeting must be delivered to every present or former officer of the company whose presence the convener thinks is required and that person is required to attend the meeting.

15.14(2) [Notice to bankrupt] In a bankruptcy, notice of a meeting must be delivered to the bankrupt who is required to attend the meeting unless paragraph (3) applies.

15.14(3) [Notice where bankrupt not required] In a bankruptcy, where the bankrupt is not required to attend the meeting, the notice must state–

(a) that the bankrupt is not required to attend the meeting;

(b) that if the bankrupt wishes to attend, the bankrupt should tell the convener as soon as reasonably practicable;

(c) that whether the bankrupt will be allowed to participate in the meeting is at the discretion of the chair; and

(d) that the decision of the chair as to what intervention, if any, the bankrupt may make is final.

15.14(4) [Minimum notice requirements] Notices under this rule must be delivered in compliance with the minimum notice requirements set out in rule 15.2(2) or in compliance with an order of the court under rule 15.12.

General Note

Persons or firms facing insolvency proceedings clearly have a right to know the position. IVAs appear to be excluded from the ambit of this section but the debtor should be aware of what is going on as he/she will be making the proposal to creditors.

15.15 Non-receipt of notice of decision

15.15 Where a decision is sought by a notice in accordance with the Act or these Rules, the decision procedure or deemed consent procedure is presumed to have been duly initiated and conducted, even if not everyone to whom the notice is to be delivered has received it.

General Note

It would be folly to invalidate a procedure simply because not all notices have been received. There are adequate safeguards to prevent abuse, such as material irregularity in voluntary arrangements (IA 1986 ss.6, 262), unfair harm in administration (IA 1986 Sch.B1 para.74), etc.

15.16 Decisions on remuneration and conduct

15.16(1) [Application of rule] This rule applies in relation to a decision or resolution which is proposed in an administration, a creditors' voluntary winding up, a winding up by the court or a bankruptcy and which affects a person in relation to that person's remuneration or conduct as administrator, liquidator or trustee (actual, proposed or former).

15.16(2) [Who may not vote on decision re office-holder remuneration] The following may not vote on such a decision or resolution whether as a creditor, contributory, proxy-holder or corporate representative, except so far as permitted by rule 16.7 (proxy-holder with financial interest)–

(a) that person;

(b) the partners and employees of that person; and

(c) the officers and employees of the company of which that person is a director, officer or employee.

General Note

This imposes important voting restrictions on those who may be said to have self interest in remuneration/conduct decisions. It mirrors IR 1986 rr.4.63(4) and 6.88(4)

Chapter 4

Decision making in particular proceedings

[Note: a document required by the Act or these Rules must also contain the standard contents set out in Part 1.]

15.17 Decisions in winding up of authorised deposit-takers

15.17(1) [Application of rule] This rule applies in a creditors' voluntary winding up or a winding up by the court of an authorised deposit-taker.

15.17(2) [Directors to deliver notice of meeting to FCA and scheme manager] The directors of a company must deliver a notice of a meeting of the company at which it is intended to propose a resolution for its winding up to the Financial Conduct Authority and to the scheme manager established under section 212(1) of the Financial Services and Markets Act 2000.

15.17(3) [Notices same as for members] These notices must be the same as those delivered to members of the company.

15.17(4) [Copy notice to FCA and scheme manager re replacement or new liquidator] Where any decision is sought for the purpose of considering whether a replacement should be appointed after the liquidator's resignation, removing the liquidator or appointing a new liquidator, the convener must also deliver a copy of the notice by which such a decision is sought to the Financial Conduct Authority and the scheme manager.

15.17(5) [Scheme manager represented at meeting] A scheme manager who is required by this rule to be given notice of a meeting is entitled to be represented at the meeting.

General Note

Clearly, this provision applies only in special situations. It is derived from IR 1986 r.4.72 subject to a change that notice to the Prudential Regulation Authority no longer appears. For definition of "authorised deposit-taker" see IR 2016 r.1.2(2).

Chapter 5

Requisitioned decisions

[Note: a document required by the Act or these Rules must also contain the standard contents set out in Part 1.]

15.18 Requisitions of decision

[Note: this rule is concerned with requests by creditors or contributories for a decision, rather than requests for decisions to be made by way of a physical meeting under sections 246ZE(3) or 379ZA(3).]

15.18(1) ["Requisitioned decision"] In this Chapter, "requisitioned decision" means a decision on nominations requested to be sought under section 136(5)(c) or a decision requested to be sought under section 168(2), 171(2)(b), 171(3A), 172(3), 298(4)(c) or 314(7) or paragraph 52(2) or 56(1) of Schedule B1.

15.18(2) [Request for decision under IA 1986 Sch.B1 para.52(2)] A request for a decision to be sought under paragraph 52(2) of Schedule B1 must be delivered within 8 business days of the date on which the administrator's statement of proposals is delivered.

15.18(3) [Statement of purpose, etc.] The request for a requisitioned decision must include a statement of the purpose of the proposed decision and either–

(a) a statement of the requesting creditor's claim or contributory's value, together with–

 (i) a list of the creditors or contributories concurring with the request and of the amounts of their respective claims or values, and

 (ii) confirmation of concurrence from each creditor or contributory concurring; or

(b) a statement of the requesting creditor's debt or contributory's value and that that alone is sufficient without the concurrence of other creditors or contributories.

15.18(4) [Decision procedure under IA 1986 s.171(2)(b) for the removal of liquidator] A decision procedure must be instigated under section 171(2)(b) for the removal of the liquidator, other than a liquidator appointed by the court under section 108, if 25% in value of the company's creditors, excluding those who are connected with the company, request it.

15.18(5) [Where decision procedure under IA 1986 ss.171(2)(b), (3), (3A), 298(4)(c)] Where a decision procedure under section 171(2)(b), 171(3), 171(3A) or 298(4)(c) is to be instigated, or is proposed to be instigated, the court may, on the application of any creditor, give directions as to the decision procedure to be used and any other matter which appears to the court to require regulation or control.

15.18(6) [Official receiver request under IA 1986 s.136(5)(c)] Where the official receiver receives a request under section 136(5)(c) and it appears that it is properly made, the official receiver must withdraw any notices previously given under section 136(5)(b) and act in accordance with Chapter 2 as if the official receiver had decided under section 136 to seek nominations.

General Note

There is a wide potential ambit to this provision on requisitioned decisions. As the matter is likely to be contentious faithful compliance with this provision is doubly important. The Note to this rule qualifies its application.

15.19 Expenses and timing of requisitioned decision

15.19(1) [Details as to sum for security for expenses of procedure] The convener must, not later than 14 days from receipt of a request for a requisitioned decision, provide the requesting creditor with itemised details of the sum to be deposited as security for payment of the expenses of such procedure.

15.19(2) [No obligation to initiate decision procedure without required sum, etc.] The convener is not obliged to initiate the decision procedure or deemed consent procedure (where applicable) until either–

(a) the convener has received the required sum; or

(b) the period of 14 days has expired without the convener having informed the requesting creditor or contributory of the sum required to be deposited as security.

15.19(3) [Time limit for requisitioned decision] A requisitioned decision must be made–

(a) where requested under section 136(5)(c), within three months; or

(b) in any other case, within 28 days;

of the date on which the earlier of the events specified in paragraph (2) of this rule occurs.

15.19(4) [Expenses of requisitioned decision] The expenses of a requisitioned decision must be paid out of the deposit (if any) unless–

(a) the creditors decide that they are to be payable as an expense of the administration, winding up or bankruptcy, as the case may be; and

(b) in the case of a decision of contributories, the creditors are first paid in full, with interest.

15.19(5) [Statement in notice of a requisitioned decision] The notice of a requisitioned decision of creditors must contain a statement that the creditors may make a decision as in paragraph (4)(a) of this rule.

15.19(6) [Expenses where no decision under r.15.19(4)(a)] Where the creditors do not so decide, the expenses must be paid by the requesting creditor or contributory to the extent that the deposit (if any) is not sufficient.

15.19(7) [Repayment of deposit not required] To the extent that the deposit (if any) is not required for payment of the expenses, it must be repaid to the requesting creditor or contributory.

General Note

There is a potential cost involved as far as the requisitioning creditor is concerned. Note the precise deadlines/ timescale specified in this provision.

Chapter 6

Constitution of meetings

15.20 Quorum at meetings

15.20(1) [Quorum to be in attendance] A meeting is not competent to act unless a quorum is in attendance.

15.20(2) [Number for quorum] A quorum is–

(a) in the case of a meeting of creditors, at least one creditor entitled to vote; and

(b) in the case of a meeting of contributories, at least two contributories entitled to vote, or all the contributories, if their number does not exceed two.

15.20(3) [Chair may delay start of meeting] Where the provisions of this rule as to quorum are satisfied by the attendance of the chair alone or the chair and one additional person, but the chair is aware, either by virtue of proofs and proxies received or otherwise, that one or more additional persons would, if attending, be entitled to vote, the chair must delay the start of the meeting by at least 15 minutes after the appointed time.

General Note

These are fairly standard rules on quorum—based upon IR 1986 r.12A.21. In practice, the rules have to be flexible because attendance at such meetings tends to be sparse.

15.21 Chair at meetings

15.21(1) [Who to be chair] The chair of a meeting must be–

(a) the convener;

(b) an appointed person; or

(c) in cases where the convener is the official receiver, a person appointed by the official receiver.

15.21(2) [Chair at physical/virtual meeting to appoint liquidator in CVL] However, where a decision on the appointment of a liquidator under rule 6.14(2)(b), 6.14(4) or 6.14(6) is made by a meeting or a virtual meeting, the chair of the meeting must be convener.

General Note

Rule 15.21(1) draws upon a range of provisions in the former IR 1986 and uses the modern drafting nomenclature rather than "chairman". For "convener" see IR 2016 r.1.2. On an "appointed person" see IR 2016 r.1.2(3). Note the special rule for the chair at meetings to appoint a liquidator in a CVL.

15.22 The chair – attendance, interventions and questions

15.22 The chair of a meeting may–

(a) allow any person who has given reasonable notice of wishing to attend to participate in a virtual meeting or to be admitted to a physical meeting;

(b) decide what intervention, if any, may be made at–

(i) a meeting of creditors by any person attending who is not a creditor, or

(ii) a meeting of contributories by any person attending who is not a contributory; and

(c) decide what questions may be put to–

(i) any present or former officer of the company, or

(ii) the bankrupt or debtor.

General Note

Considerable discretion is vested in the chair—but note the complaint procedure for excluded parties in IR 2016 rr.15.36 and 15.46.

Chapter 7

Adjournment and suspension of meetings

15.23 Adjournment by chair

15.23(1) [Power to adjourn] The chair may (and must if it is so resolved) adjourn a meeting for not more than 14 days, but subject to any direction of the court and to rule 15.24.

15.23(2) [Further adjournment] Further adjournment under this rule must not be to a day later than 14 days after the date on which the meeting was originally held (subject to any direction by the court).

15.23(3) [Adjournment under IA 1986 Sch.A1 para.29(1) re proposed CVA] But in a case relating to a proposed CVA, the chair may, and must if the meeting so resolves, adjourn a meeting held under paragraph 29(1) of Schedule A1 to a day which is not more than 14 days after the date on which the moratorium (including any extension) ends.

General Note

Here we have general rules on adjournment, coupled with a special rule in the case of a IA 1986 Sch.A1 proposed CVA. On adjournment generally see *Tradition (UK) Ltd v Ahmed* [2009] B.P.I.R. 626. The rule is subject to any direction of the court and to IR 2016 r.15.24.

15.24 Adjournment of meetings to remove a liquidator or trustee

15.24 If the chair of a meeting to remove the liquidator or trustee in a creditors' voluntary winding up, a winding up by the court or a bankruptcy is the liquidator or trustee or the liquidator's or trustee's nominee and a resolution has been proposed for the liquidator's or trustee's removal, the chair must not adjourn the meeting without the consent of at least one-half (in value) of the creditors attending and entitled to vote.

General Note

This is a special adjournment procedure where a decision is sought about the removal of such an office-holder.

15.25 Adjournment in absence of chair

15.25(1) [No chair within 30 minutes of start time] In an administration, administrative receivership, a creditors' voluntary winding up, a winding up by the court or a bankruptcy, if no one attends to act as chair within 30 minutes of the time fixed for a meeting to start, then the meeting is adjourned to the same time and place the following week or, if that is not a business day, to the business day immediately following.

15.25(2) [Meting to end after second adjournment on same ground] If no one attends to act as chair within 30 minutes of the time fixed for the meeting after a second adjournment under this rule, then the meeting comes to an end.

General Note

This encompasses a situation that should not happen in an ideal world. This draws upon amendments to the IR 1986 made in 2010. It seems unlikely that such a scenario does happen often in practice

15.26 Proofs in adjournment

15.26 Where a meeting in an administration, an administrative receivership, a creditors' voluntary winding-up, a winding up by the court or a bankruptcy is adjourned, proofs may be used if delivered not later than 4pm on the business day immediately before resumption of the adjourned meeting, or later than that time where the chair is content to accept the proof.

General Note

Late delivery of proofs may be a permitted consequence of an adjournment.

15.27 Suspension

15.27 The chair of a meeting may, without an adjournment, declare the meeting suspended for one or more periods not exceeding one hour in total (or, in exceptional circumstances, such longer total period during the same day at the chair's discretion).

General Note

Suspension is not adjournment. But suspension can only be for very short periods. The IR 1986 after amendments in 2010 recognised the possibility of suspension of meetings in a number of its provisions. See *Re Forstater* [2015] B.P.I.R. 21 and *Rowbury v OR* [2015] EWHC 2276 (Ch).

Chapter 8

Creditors' voting rights and majorities

[Note: a document required by the Act or these Rules must also contain the standard contents set out in Part 1.]

15.28 Creditors' voting rights

15.28(1) [Conditions for voting] In an administration, an administrative receivership, a creditors' voluntary winding up, a winding up by the court and a bankruptcy, a creditor is entitled to vote in a decision procedure or to object to a decision proposed using the deemed consent procedure only if–

(a) the creditor has, subject to rule 15.29, delivered to the convener a proof of the debt claimed in accordance with paragraph (3), including any calculation for the purposes of rule 15.31 or 15.32, and

(b) the proof was received by the convener–

(i) not later than the decision date, or in the case of a meeting, 4pm on the business day before the meeting, or

(ii) in the case of a meeting, later than the time given in sub-paragraph (i) where the chair is content to accept the proof; and

(c) the proof has been admitted for the purposes of entitlement to vote.

15.28(2) [Proxy vote] In the case of a meeting, a proxy-holder is not entitled to vote on behalf of a creditor unless the convener or chair has received the proxy intended to be used on behalf of that creditor.

15.28(3) [Debt claimed] A debt is claimed in accordance with this paragraph if it is–

(a) claimed as due from the company or bankrupt to the person seeking to be entitled to vote; or

(b) in relation to a member State liquidator, claimed to be due to creditors in proceedings in relation to which that liquidator holds office.

15.28(4) [Evidence substantiating claim] The convener or chair may call for any document or other evidence to be produced if the convener or chair thinks it necessary for the purpose of substantiating the whole or any part of a claim.

15.28(5) [Voting entitlement in CVA, IVA] In a decision relating to a proposed CVA or IVA every creditor, secured or unsecured, who has notice of the decision procedure is entitled to vote in respect of that creditor's debt.

15.28(6) [Creditor participation in administration under rr.3.52(3)(b), 18.18(4), 18.26(2)] Where a decision is sought in an administration under rule 3.52(3)(b) (pre-administration costs), rule 18.18(4) (remuneration: procedure for initial determination in an administration) or rule 18.26(2) (first exception: administrator has made statement under paragraph 52(1)(b) of Schedule B1), creditors are entitled to participate to the extent stated in those paragraphs.

General Note

This is an important provision. It determines who has the right to vote and the degree of voting power is then dealt with by r.15.31. Note sub-para.(5) for voting on a voluntary arrangement.

The primacy of the predecessor to the rule in determining voting rights was emphasised by David Richards J in *Davis v Price* [2013] EWHC 323 (Ch); [2013] B.P.I.R. 200 and this interpretation was confirmed on appeal by the Court of Appeal in *Price v Davis* [2014] EWCA Civ 26; [2014] 1 W.L.R. 2129; [2014] B.P.I.R. 494. In *Kapoor v National Westminster Bank plc* [2011] EWCA Civ 1083; [2011] B.P.I.R. 1680 the Court of Appeal indicated that in principle an equitable assignee of a debt could exercise voting rights.

15.29 Scheme manager's voting rights

15.29(1) [Statement instead of proof] For the purpose of voting in a creditors' voluntary winding up or a winding up by the court of an authorised deposit-taker at which the scheme manager established under section 212(1) of the Financial Services and Markets Act 2000 is entitled to be represented under rule 15.17 (but not for any other purpose), the manager may deliver, instead of a proof, a statement containing–

(a) the names of the creditors of the company in relation to whom an obligation of the scheme manager has arisen or may reasonably be expected to arise;

(b) the amount of each such obligation; and

(c) the total amount of all such obligations.

15.29(2) [Further superseding statements] The manager may from time to time deliver a further statement; and each such statement supersedes any previous statement.

GENERAL NOTE

This is a specialist provision that was previously tucked away in IR 1986 Sch.1.

15.30 Claim made in proceedings in other member States

15.30(1) [Creditor's vote counts over Member State liquidator's vote on same claim] Where a creditor in an administration, a creditors' voluntary winding up, a winding up by the court or a bankruptcy–

(a) is entitled to vote under rule 15.28(1) (as determined, where that be the case, in accordance with rule 15.35);

(b) has made the claim in other proceedings; and

(c) votes on a resolution in a decision procedure;

and a member State liquidator casts a vote in respect of the same claim, only the creditor's vote is to be counted.

15.30(2) [Member State liquidator, multiple other proceedings] Where in an administration, a creditors' voluntary winding up, a winding up by the court or a bankruptcy–

(a) a creditor has made a claim in more than one set of other proceedings; and

(b) more than one member State liquidator seeks to vote in respect of that claim;

the entitlement to vote in respect of that claim is exercisable by the member State liquidator in the main proceedings, whether or not the creditor has made the claim in the main proceedings.

15.30(3) ["Other proceedings"] In this rule, "other proceedings" mean main, secondary or territorial proceedings in another member State.

GENERAL NOTE

This deals with a cross-border scenario.

15.31 Calculation of voting rights

15.31(1) [Date of calculation] Votes are calculated according to the amount of each creditor's claim–

(a) in an administration, as at the date on which the company entered administration, less–

(i) any payments that have been made to the creditor after that date in respect of the claim, and

(ii) any adjustment by way of set-off which has been made in accordance with rule 14.24 or would have been made if that rule were applied on the date on which the votes are counted;

(b) in an administrative receivership, as at the date of the appointment of the receiver, less any payments that have been made to the creditor after that date in respect of the claim;

(c) in a creditors' voluntary winding up, a winding up by the court or a bankruptcy, as set out in the creditor's proof to the extent that it has been admitted;

(d) in a proposed CVA–

(i) at the date the company went into liquidation where the company is being wound up,

(ii) at the date the company entered into administration (less any payments made to the creditor after that date in respect of the claim) where it is in administration,

(iii) at the beginning of the moratorium where a moratorium has been obtained (less any payments made to the creditor after that date in respect of the claim), or

(iv) where (i) to (iii) do not apply, at the decision date;

(e) in a proposed IVA–

(i) where the debtor is not an undischarged bankrupt–

(aa) at the date of the interim order, where there is an interim order in force,

(bb) otherwise, at the decision date,

(ii) where the debtor is an undischarged bankrupt, at the date of the bankruptcy order.

15.31(2) [Debt of unliquidated or unascertained amount] A creditor may vote in respect of a debt of an unliquidated or unascertained amount if the convener or chair decides to put upon it an estimated minimum value for the purpose of entitlement to vote and admits the claim for that purpose.

15.31(3) [Proposed CVA, IVA: debt of unliquidated or unascertained amount] But in relation to a proposed CVA or IVA, a debt of an unliquidated or unascertained amount is to be valued at £1 for the purposes of voting unless the convener or chair or an appointed person decides to put a higher value on it.

15.31(4) [Wholly secured debt] Where a debt is wholly secured its value for voting purposes is nil.

15.31(5) [Partly secured debt] Where a debt is partly secured its value for voting purposes is the value of the unsecured part.

15.31(6) [Where full value without deduction of value of security] However, the value of the debt for voting purposes is its full value without deduction of the value of the security in the following cases–

(a) where the administrator has made a statement under paragraph 52(1)(b) of Schedule B1 and the administrator has been requested to seek a decision under paragraph 52(2); and

(b) where, in a proposed CVA, there is a decision on whether to extend or further extend a moratorium or to bring a moratorium to an end before the end of the period of any extension.

15.31(7) [Single vote on claim; Member State liquidator] No vote may be cast in respect of a claim more than once on any resolution put to the meeting; and for this purpose (where relevant), the claim of a creditor and of any member State liquidator in relation to the same debt are a single claim.

15.31(8) [Vote cast not in meeting not changeable] A vote cast in a decision procedure which is not a meeting may not be changed.

15.31(9) [Creditor and Member State liquidator voting] Paragraph (7) does not prevent a creditor or member State liquidator from–

(a) voting in respect of less than the full value of an entitlement to vote; or

(b) casting a vote one way in respect of part of the value of an entitlement and another way in respect of some or all of the balance of that value.

General Note

This needs to be read in the light of IR 2016 r.15.28. There are several special provisions applicable to quantifying voting rights in the different types of voluntary arrangement. Note r.15.31(3) on attaching a £1 nominal value to unliquidated or unascertained claims in a voluntary arrangement. Cases of interest under the former regime which might continue to have relevance include: *Re Newland (Seaford) Educational Trust* [2007] B.C.C. 195, *Leighton Contracting (Qatar) WLL v Simms* [2011] B.P.I.R. 1395, *Cahillane v NALM* [2014] B.P.I.R. 1093 and *Rowbury v OR* [2015] EWHC 2591 (Ch). See also *Sofaer v Anglo Irish Finance plc* [2011] EWHC 1480 (Ch); [2011] B.P.I.R. 1736. Note also *National Westminster Bank v Yadgaroff* [2011] EWHC 3711 (Ch) where Norris J made the point that if a claim is unascertained then the chairman must pursuant what is now r.15.31(3) seek to place a value on it, but note that the word "shall" (in IR 1986 r.5.21(3)) or its modern equivalent, "must", does not appear in r.15.31(3). In *AB*

Agri Ltd v Curtis [2016] B.P.I.R. 1297 where a claim under a personal guarantee was valued at £1 but the chairman had not had power to ascribe that value as the claim was not unliquidated or unascertained, failure to follow the correct procedure was a material irregularity and approval of the IVA was revoked. A debt allowed in full but marked as objected to does not have to be valued.

See also *Revenue and Customs Commissioners v Earley* [2011] EWHC 1783 (Ch); [2011] B.P.I.R. 1590.

On entitlement to vote see *Price v Davis* [2014] EWCA Civ 26; [2014] 1 W.L.R. 2129; [2014] B.P.I.R. 494.

15.32 Calculation of voting rights: special cases

15.32(1) [Administration: HP agreement] In an administration, a creditor under a hire-purchase agreement is entitled to vote in respect of the amount of the debt due and payable by the company on the date on which the company entered administration.

15.32(2) [Calculation of debt in r.15.32(1)] In calculating the amount of any debt for the purpose of paragraph (1), no account is to be taken of any amount attributable to the exercise of any right under the relevant agreement so far as the right has become exercisable solely by virtue of–

(a) the making of an administration application;

(b) a notice of intention to appoint an administrator or any matter arising as a consequence of the notice; or

(c) the company entering administration.

15.32(3) [CVL or compulsory winding up of authorised deposit-taker] Any voting rights which a creditor might otherwise exercise in respect of a claim in a creditors' voluntary winding up or a winding up by the court of an authorised deposit-taker are reduced by a sum equal to the amount of that claim in relation to which the scheme manager, by virtue of its having delivered a statement under rule 15.29, is entitled to exercise voting rights.

General Note

As the heading indicates, we are looking at special cases within the corporate insolvency field. On hire-purchase agreement see IR 2016 r.1.2(2) referring to IA 1986 s.436(1).

15.33 Procedure for admitting creditors' claims for voting

15.33(1) [Convener or chair to admit or reject claims] The convener or chair in respect of a decision procedure must ascertain entitlement to vote and admit or reject claims accordingly.

15.33(2) [May admit or reject in whole or part] The convener or chair may admit or reject a claim in whole or in part.

15.33(3) [Doubtful claim allowed as objected to] If the convener or chair is in any doubt whether a claim should be admitted or rejected, the convener or chair must mark it as objected to and allow votes to be cast in respect of it, subject to such votes being subsequently declared invalid if the objection to the claim is sustained.

General Note

This offers guidance to conveners/chairs. There of course is a right to appeal against any decision by the convener/chair—see IR 2016 r.15.35.

15.34 Requisite majorities

15.34(1) [Decision by creditors by majority in value] A decision is made by creditors when a majority (in value) of those voting have voted in favour of the proposed decision, except where this rule provides otherwise.

15.34(2) [Administration] In the case of an administration, a decision is not made if those voting against it include more than half in value of the creditors to whom notice of the decision procedure was delivered who are not, to the best of the convener's or chair's belief, persons connected with the company.

15.34(3) [CVA proposal] Each of the following decisions in a proposed CVA is made when three-quarters or more (in value) of those responding vote in favour of it–

(a) a decision approving a proposal or a modification;

(b) a decision extending or further extending a moratorium; or

(c) a decision bringing a moratorium to an end before the end of the period of any extension.

15.34(4) [CVA proposal where majority unconnected creditors vote against] In a proposed CVA a decision is not made if more than half of the total value of the unconnected creditors vote against it.

15.34(5) [Unconnected creditors in r.15.34(4)] For the purposes of paragraph (4)–

(a) a creditor is unconnected unless the convener or chair decides that the creditor is connected with the company;

(b) in deciding whether a creditor is connected reliance may be placed on the information provided by the company's statement of affairs or otherwise in accordance with these Rules; and

(c) the total value of the unconnected creditors is the total value of those unconnected creditors whose claims have been admitted for voting.

15.34(6) [Proposed IVA] In a case relating to a proposed IVA–

(a) a decision approving a proposal or a modification is made when three-quarters or more (in value) of those responding vote in favour of it;

(b) a decision is not made if more than half of the total value of creditors who are not associates of the debtor vote against it.

15.34(7) [Associate in r.15.34(6)] For the purposes of paragraph (6)–

(a) a creditor is not an associate of the debtor unless the convener or chair decides that the creditor is an associate of the debtor;

(b) in deciding whether a creditor is an associate of the debtor, reliance may be placed on the information provided by the debtor's statement of affairs or otherwise in accordance with these Rules; and

(c) the total value of the creditors who are not associates of the debtor is the total value of the creditors who are not associates of the debtor whose claims have been admitted for voting.

General Note

The starting point favours simple majorities in value—but this is then supplemented by rules providing for special majorities. In voluntary arrangements 75 per cent support in value of creditors is required including more than half in value of the independent creditors. This merely reflects the position under IR 1986. For the meaning of "associate" in IR 2016 r.15.34(6), (7) see IR 2016 r.1.2(2) and IA 1986 s.435.

15.35 Appeals against decisions under this Chapter

15.35(1) [Right of appeal] A decision of the convener or chair under this Chapter is subject to appeal to the court by a creditor, by a contributory, or by the bankrupt or debtor (as applicable).

15.35(2) [Proposed CVA: appeal also by member] In a proposed CVA, an appeal against a decision under this Chapter may also be made by a member of the company.

15.35(3) [Another decision procedure if decision reversed or varied] If the decision is reversed or varied, or votes are declared invalid, the court may order another decision procedure to be initiated or make such order as it thinks just but, in a CVA or IVA, the court may only make an order if it considers that the circumstances which led to the appeal give rise to unfair prejudice or material irregularity.

15.35(4) [Time limit for appeal] An appeal under this rule may not be made later than 21 days after the decision date.

15.35(5) [Non-application of r.15.35(4) to proposed CVA, IVA] However, the previous paragraph does not apply in a proposed CVA or IVA, where an appeal may not be made after the end of the period of 28 days beginning with the day–

(a) in a proposed CVA, on which the first of the reports required by section 4(6) or paragraph 30(3) of Schedule A1 was filed with the court; or

(b) in a proposed IVA–

(i) where an interim order has not been obtained, on which the notice of the result of the consideration of the proposal required by section 259(1)(a) has been given, or

(ii) otherwise, on which the report required by section 259(1)(b) is made to the court.

15.35(6) [Costs of appeal] The person who made the decision is not personally liable for costs incurred by any person in relation to an appeal under this rule unless the court makes an order to that effect.

15.35(7) [No court order against official receiver etc. in compulsory winding up, bankruptcy] The court may not make an order under paragraph (6) if the person who made the decision in a winding up by the court or a bankruptcy is the official receiver or a person nominated by the official receiver.

General Note

This right to appeal applies to matters covered by IR 2016 rr.15.28–15.35 above. Similar provisions existed under IR 1986. Note the longer leeway for appeals in the case of proposed voluntary arrangements.

A judge hearing an appeal under r.15.35(1) should form his or her own view, based on the evidence and arguments advanced in court, and not merely review the decision of the convenor or chair of the decision procedure: *Revenue and Customs Commissioners v Maxwell* [2010] EWCA Civ 1379; [2012] B.C.C. 30. In this administration case under IR 1986, the Court of Appeal stated that the characterisation and quantification of a debt under what is now r.15.31 should be effected at the date when the company went into administration rather than the date of the meeting (now decision procedure: see r.15.31(1)), but the chair's powers of quantification under what are now rr.15.31(2) and 15.35 should be exercised taking into account events which had occurred since the date of the administration.

Chapter 9

Exclusions from meetings

[Note: a document required by the Act or these Rules must also contain the standard contents set out in Part 1.]

15.36 Action where person excluded

15.36(1) ["Excluded person" in rr.15.36–15.38] In this rule and rules 15.37 and 15.38, an "excluded person" means a person who has taken all steps necessary to attend a virtual meeting or has been permitted by the convener to attend a physical meeting remotely under the arrangements which–

(a) have been put in place by the convener of the meeting; but

(b) do not enable that person to attend the whole or part of that meeting.

15.36(2) [Power of chair aware of excluded person] Where the chair becomes aware during the course of the meeting that there is an excluded person, the chair may–

(a) continue the meeting;

(b) declare the meeting void and convene the meeting again; or

(c) declare the meeting valid up to the point where the person was excluded and adjourn the meeting.

15.36(3) [Validity of continued meeting] Where the chair continues the meeting, the meeting is valid unless–

(a) the chair decides in consequence of a complaint under rule 15.38 to declare the meeting void and hold the meeting again; or

(b) the court directs otherwise.

15.36(4) [Suspension of meeting without adjournment] Without prejudice to paragraph (2), where the chair becomes aware during the course of the meeting that there is an excluded person, the chair may, at the chair's discretion and without an adjournment, declare the meeting suspended for any period up to 1 hour.

General Note

Based upon IR 1986 r.12A.23 this maps out the position where a person entitled to attend a virtual meeting (or a physical meeting remotely) is unable to do so. It provides a good reason for the use of other decision-taking procedures.

15.37 Indication to excluded person

15.37(1) [Request for indication by excluded person] A creditor who claims to be an excluded person may request an indication of what occurred during the period of that person's claimed exclusion.

15.37(2) [Time limit for request] A request under paragraph (1) must be made in accordance with paragraph (3) as soon as reasonably practicable, and in any event, not later than 4pm on the business day following the day on which the exclusion is claimed to have occurred.

15.37(3) [To whom request to be made] A request under paragraph (1) must be made to–

(a) the chair where it is made during the course of the business of the meeting; or

(b) the convener where it is made after the conclusion of the business of the meeting.

15.37(4) [Time limit for indication] Where satisfied that the person making the request is an excluded person, the person to whom the request is made under paragraph (3) must deliver the requested indication to the excluded person as soon as reasonably practicable, and in any event, not later than 4pm on the business day following the day on which the request was made under paragraph (1).

General Note

This outlines what a person claiming to be an excluded person must do to protect his/her position. See former IR 1986 r.12A.24.

15.38 Complaint

15.38(1) [Person who may make complaint] A person may make a complaint who–

(a) is, or claims to be, an excluded person; or

(b) attends the meeting and claims to have been adversely affected by the actual, apparent or claimed exclusion of another person.

15.38(2) [Appropriate person to whom complaint to be made] The complaint must be made to the appropriate person who is–

(a) the chair, where the complaint is made during the course of the meeting; or

(b) the convener, where it is made after the meeting.

15.38(3) [Time limit for complaint] The complaint must be made as soon as reasonably practicable and, in any event, no later than 4pm on the business day following–

(a) the day on which the person was, appeared or claimed to be excluded; or

(b) where an indication is sought under rule 15.37, the day on which the complainant received the indication.

15.38(4) [Duty of appropriate person] The appropriate person must, as soon as reasonably practicable following receipt of the complaint,–

(a) consider whether there is an excluded person;

(b) where satisfied that there is an excluded person, consider the complaint; and

(c) where satisfied that there has been prejudice, take such action as the appropriate person considers fit to remedy the prejudice.

15.38(5) [Application of r.15.38(6)] Paragraph (6) applies where the appropriate person is satisfied that the complainant is an excluded person and–

(a) a resolution was voted on at the meeting during the period of the person's exclusion; and

(b) the excluded person asserts how the excluded person intended to vote on the resolution.

15.38(6) [Excluded person's vote would have changed resolution result] Where the appropriate person is satisfied that if the excluded person had voted as that person intended it would have changed the result of the resolution, then the appropriate person must, as soon as reasonably practicable,–

(a) count the intended vote as having been cast in that way;

(b) amend the record of the result of the resolution;

(c) where notice of the result of the resolution has been delivered to those entitled to attend the meeting, deliver notice to them of the change and the reason for it; and

(d) where notice of the result of the resolution has yet to be delivered to those entitled to attend the meeting, the notice must include details of the change and the reason for it.

15.38(7) [Intended votes of more than one excluded person complainants] Where satisfied that more than one complainant is an excluded person, the appropriate person must have regard to the combined effect of the intended votes.

15.38(8) [Notice to complainant] The appropriate person must deliver notice to the complainant of any decision as soon as reasonably practicable.

15.38(9) [Unsatisfied complainant right to apply to court] A complainant who is not satisfied by the action of the appropriate person may apply to the court for directions and any application must be made no more than two business days from the date of receiving the decision of the appropriate person.

General Note

This deals with consequential issues in the wake of an exclusion having an adverse effect on any aggrieved party. For former provision see IR 1986 r.12A.25.

Chapter 10

Contributories' voting rights and majorities

15.39 Contributories' voting rights and requisite majorities

15.39 In a decision procedure for contributories–

(a) voting rights are as at a general meeting of the company, subject to any provision of the articles affecting entitlement to vote, either generally or at a time when the company is in liquidation; and

(b) a decision is made if more than one half of the votes cast by contributories are in favour.

General Note

This imports basic shareholder voting rules into company meetings in cases covered by Pt 15. Contributories may be under a potential liability in the case of a corporate insolvency, so arguably they have a stake in what transpires.

Chapter 11

Records

15.40 Record of a decision

15.40(1) [Duty of convener] The convener or chair must cause a record of the decision procedure to be kept.

15.40(2) [Minute of meeting] In the case of a meeting, the record must be in the form of a minute of the meeting.

15.40(3) [Authentication and retention of record] The record must be authenticated by the convener or chair and be retained by the office-holder as part of the records of the insolvency proceedings in question.

15.40(4) [Content of record] The record must identify the proceedings, and must include–

(a) in the case of a decision procedure of creditors, a list of the names of the creditors who participated and their claims;

(b) in the case of a decision procedure of contributories, a list of the names of the contributories who participated;

(c) where a decision is taken on the election of members of a creditors' committee or liquidation committee, the names and addresses of those elected;

(d) a record of any change to the result of the resolution made under rule 15.38(6) and the reason for any such change; and

(e) in any case, a record of every decision made and how creditors voted.

15.40(5) [Record using deemed consent procedure] Where a decision is sought using the deemed consent procedure, a record must be made of the procedure, authenticated by the convener, and must be retained by the office-holder as part of the records of the insolvency proceedings in question.

15.40(6) [Record in r.15.40(5)] The record under paragraph (5) must–

(a) identify the proceedings;

(b) state whether or not the decision was taken; and

(c) contain a list of the creditors or contributories who objected to the decision, and in the case of creditors, their claims.

15.40(7) [Record to identify decision procedure where decision previously sought] A record under this rule must also identify any decision procedure (or the deemed consent procedure) by which the decision had previously been sought.

General Note

This maps out good practice in terms of minute-keeping. This bundles together a number of similar provisions in IR 1986.

Chapter 12

Company meetings

15.41 Company meetings

15.41(1) [Law of state applicable] Unless the Act or these Rules provide otherwise, a company meeting must be called and conducted, and records of the meeting must be kept–

(a) in accordance with the law of England and Wales, including any applicable provision in or made under the Companies Act, in the case of a company incorporated–

(i) in England and Wales, or

(ii) outside the United Kingdom other than in an EEA state;

(b) in accordance with the law of that state applicable to meetings of the company in the case of a company incorporated in an EEA state other than the United Kingdom.

15.41(2) [Written resolution under CA 2006 s.288] For the purpose of this rule, reference to a company meeting called and conducted to resolve, decide or determine a particular matter includes a reference to that matter being resolved, decided or determined by written resolution of a private company passed in accordance with section 288 of the Companies Act.

15.41(3) [Administration] In an administration–

(a) in summoning any company meeting the administrator must have regard to the convenience of the members when fixing the venue; and

(b) the chair of the meeting must be either the administrator or an appointed person.

General Note

Basic rules of company law operate here. See former IR 1986 r.2.49(5A).

15.42 Remote attendance: notification requirements

15.42 When a meeting is to be summoned and held in accordance with section 246A(3), the convener must notify all those to whom notice of the meeting is being given of–

(a) the ability of a person claiming to be an excluded person to request an indication in accordance with rule 15.45;

(b) the ability of a person within rule 15.46(1) to make a complaint in accordance with that rule; and

(c) in either case, the period within which a request or complaint must be made.

General Note

See the note to s.246A.

15.43 Location of company meetings

15.43(1) [Remote attendance: request to convener to specify place for meeting] This rule applies to a request to the convener of a meeting under section 246A(9) to specify a place for the meeting.

15.43(2) [Request to be accompanied by concurrence] The request must be accompanied by

(a) a list of the members making or concurring with the request and their voting rights, and

(b) from each person concurring, confirmation of that person's concurrence.

15.43(3) [Time limit for delivery of request] The request must be delivered to the convener within seven business days of the date on which the convener delivered the notice of the meeting in question.

15.43(4) [Notice by convener for attendance] Where the convener considers that the request has been properly made in accordance with the Act and this rule, the convener must–

(a) deliver notice to all those previously given notice of the meeting–

(i) that it is to be held at a specified place, and

(ii) as to whether the date and time are to remain the same or not;

(b) set a venue (including specification of a place) for the meeting, the date of which must be not later than 28 days after the original date for the meeting; and

(c) deliver at least 14 days' notice of that venue to all those previously given notice of the meeting;

and the notices required by sub-paragraphs (a) and (c) may be delivered at the same or different times.

15.43(5) [Chair to attend at place of meeting] Where the convener has specified a place for the meeting in response to a request to which this rule applies, the chair of the meeting must attend the meeting by being present in person at that place.

General Note

This deals with matters of location. For the previous provision see IR 1986 r.12A.22 and note IA 1986 ss.246A and 379A.

15.44 Action where person excluded

15.44(1) ["Excluded person"] In this rule and rules 15.45 and 15.46, an "excluded person" means a person who has taken all steps necessary to attend a company meeting under the arrangements which–

(a) have been put in place by the convener of the meeting under section 246A(6); but

(b) do not enable that person to attend the whole or part of that meeting.

15.44(2) [Power of chair becoming aware of excluded person] Where the chair becomes aware during the course of the meeting that there is an excluded person, the chair may–

(a) continue the meeting;

(b) declare the meeting void and convene the meeting again; or

(c) declare the meeting valid up to the point where the person was excluded and adjourn the meeting.

15.44(3) [Validity of meeting] Where the chair continues the meeting, the meeting is valid unless–

(a) the chair decides in consequence of a complaint under rule 15.46 to declare the meeting void and hold the meeting again; or

(b) the court directs otherwise.

15.44(4) [Power of chair to suspend meeting without adjournment] Without prejudice to paragraph (2), where the chair becomes aware during the course of the meeting that there is an excluded person, the chair may, in the chair's discretion and without an adjournment, declare the meeting suspended for any period up to 1 hour.

General Note

These are the equivalent to the rules where it is a creditor who has been excluded from a meeting (see IR 2016 r.15.36). Note IR 1986 r.12A.23 for the previous provision.

15.45 Indication to excluded person

15.45(1) [Request for indication by excluded person] A person who claims to be an excluded person may request an indication of what occurred during the period of that person's claimed exclusion.

15.45(2) [Time limit for request] A request under paragraph (1) must be made in accordance with paragraph (3) as soon as reasonably practicable, and in any event, not later than 4pm on the business day following the day on which the exclusion is claimed to have occurred.

15.45(3) [To who request for indication to be made] A request under paragraph (1) must be made to–

(a) the chair where it is made during the course of the business of the meeting; or

(b) the convener where it is made after the conclusion of the business of the meeting.

15.45(4) [Time limit for indication] Where satisfied that the person making the request is an excluded person, the person to whom the request is made under paragraph (3) must deliver the requested indication to the excluded person as soon as reasonably practicable, and in any event, not later than 4pm on the business day following the day on which the request was made under paragraph (1).

General Note

See the annotation to IR 2016 r.15.37 above. For predecessor see IR 1986 r.12A.24.

15.46 Complaint

15.46(1) [Person who may make complaint] A person may make a complaint who–

(a) is, or claims to be, an excluded person; or

(b) attends the meeting and claims to have been adversely affected by the actual, apparent or claimed exclusion of another person.

15.46(2) [Appropriate person to whom complaint to be made] The complaint must be made to the appropriate person who is–

(a) the chair, where the complaint is made during the course of the meeting; or

(b) the convener, where it is made after the meeting.

15.46(3) [Time limit for complaint] The complaint must be made as soon as reasonably practicable and, in any event, no later than 4pm on the business day following–

(a) the day on which the person was, appeared or claimed to be excluded; or

(b) where an indication is sought under rule 15.45, the day on which the complainant received the indication.

15.46(4) [Duty of appropriate person The appropriate person must, as soon as reasonably practicable following receipt of the complaint,–

(a) consider whether there is an excluded person;

(b) where satisfied that there is an excluded person, consider the complaint; and

(c) where satisfied that there has been prejudice, take such action as the appropriate person considers fit to remedy the prejudice.

15.46(5) [Application of r.15.46(6)] Paragraph (6) applies where the appropriate person is satisfied that the complainant is an excluded person and–

(a) a resolution was voted on at the meeting during the period of the person's exclusion; and

(b) the excluded person asserts how the excluded person intended to vote on the resolution.

15.46(6) [Excluded person's vote would have changed resolution result] Where the appropriate person is satisfied that if the excluded person had voted as that person intended it would have changed the result of the resolution, then the appropriate person must, as soon as reasonably practicable,–

(a) count the intended vote as having been cast in that way;

(b) amend the record of the result of the resolution;

(c) where notice of the result of the resolution has been delivered to those entitled to attend the meeting, deliver notice to them of the change and the reason for it; and

(d) where notice of the result of the resolution has yet to be delivered to those entitled to attend the meeting, the notice must include details of the change and the reason for it.

15.46(7) [Intended votes of more than one excluded person complainants] Where satisfied that more than one complainant is an excluded person, the appropriate person must have regard to the combined effect of the intended votes.

15.46(8) [Notice to complainant] The appropriate person must deliver notice to the complainant of any decision as soon as reasonably practicable.

15.46(9) [Unsatisfied complainant right to apply to court] A complainant who is not satisfied by the action of the appropriate person may apply to the court for directions and any application must be made no more than two business days from the date of receiving the decision of the appropriate person.

General Note

This mirrors IR 2016 r.15.38. See IR r.12A.25 for the previous provision.

Part 16

Proxies and Corporate Representation

Introductory note to Part 16

What we have here is a loose recasting of Pt 8 of IR 1986 but with in particular some interesting new nomenclature for types of proxy and some innovations, e.g. appointment of more than one person to be proxy-holder (r.16.2(7)); a proxy must be an individual (r.16.2(8)).

[Note: a document required by the Act or these Rules must also contain the standard contents set out in Part 1.]

16.1 Application and interpretation

16.1(1) [Application] This Part applies in any case where a proxy is given in relation to a meeting or proceedings under the Act or these Rules, or where a corporation authorises a person to represent it.

16.1(2) ["The chair"] References in this Part to "the chair" are to the chair of the meeting for which a specific proxy is given or at which a continuing proxy is exercised.

General Note

This introductory rule has no counterpart in IR 1986.

Use of "the chair" in r.16.1(2) reflects the modern drafting of IR 2016 compared to the previous "chairman" in IR 1986 and earlier rules.

See note after r.16.7.

16.2 Specific and continuing proxies

16.2(1) ["Proxy", "the proxy-holder"] A "proxy" is a document made by a creditor, member or contributory which directs or authorises another person ("the proxy-holder") to act as the representative of the creditor, member or contributory at a meeting or meetings by speaking, voting, abstaining, or proposing resolutions.

16.2(2) [Specific or continuing proxies] A proxy may be either–

(a) a specific proxy which relates to a specific meeting; or

(b) a continuing proxy for the insolvency proceedings.

16.2(3) [Specific proxy] A specific proxy must–

(a) direct the proxy-holder how to act at the meeting by giving specific instructions;

(b) authorise the proxy-holder to act at the meeting without specific instructions; or

(c) contain both direction and authorisation.

16.2(4) [Treatment as a specific proxy] A proxy is to be treated as a specific proxy for the meeting which is identified in the proxy unless it states that it is a continuing proxy for the insolvency proceedings.

16.2(5) [Continuing proxy] A continuing proxy must authorise the proxy-holder to attend, speak, vote or abstain, or to propose resolutions without giving the proxy-holder any specific instructions how to do so.

16.2(6) [Continuing proxy being superseded or withdrawn] A continuing proxy may be superseded by a proxy for a specific meeting or withdrawn by a written notice to the office-holder.

16.2(7) [Appointment of one person as proxy] A creditor, member or contributory may appoint more than one person to be proxy-holder but if so–

(a) their appointment is as alternates; and

(b) only one of them may act as proxy-holder at a meeting.

16.2(8) [Proxy-holder to be individual] The proxy-holder must be an individual.

General Note

This rule interestingly appears to take a different approach to "proxy" and types of proxy than its predecessor rules on definitions and descriptions. So a proxy has become a "document" which authorises the proxy-holder to act as a representative of a creditor, member or contributory (compared to an "authority" in IR 1986). The expressions "specific proxy" and "continuing proxy" did not appear in IR 1986 and are not as such legal terms of art but more descriptive in character; a "continuing proxy" may be thought of as what is often called a "general proxy". Rule 16.2(8) is mandatory that, like an insolvency office-holder, only an individual can be a proxy-holder.

See *Horler v Rubin* [2012] EWCA Civ 4; [2012] B.P.I.R. 749 for a detailed consideration by Lewison LJ of the position of proxies under a differently worded predecessor to this rule.

See note after r.16.7.

16.3 Blank proxy

16.3(1) ["Blank proxy"] A "blank proxy" is a document which–

(a) complies with the requirements in this rule; and

(b) when completed with the details specified in paragraph (3) will be a proxy as described in rule 16.2.

16.3(2) [What blank proxy to state] A blank proxy must state that the creditor, member or contributory named in the document (when completed) appoints a person who is named or identified as the proxy-holder of the creditor, member or contributory.

16.3(3) [Specified details] The specified details are–

(a) the name and address of the creditor, member or contributory;

(b) either the name of the proxy-holder or the identification of the proxy-holder (e.g. the chair of the meeting or the official receiver);

(c) a statement that the proxy is either–

(i) for a specific meeting, which is identified in the proxy, or

(ii) a continuing proxy for the proceedings; and

(d) if the proxy is for a specific meeting, instructions as to the extent to which the proxy holder is directed to vote in a particular way, to abstain or to propose any resolution.

16.3(4) [No name, description or instructions how to act] When it is delivered, a blank proxy must not have inserted into it the name or description of any person as proxy-holder or as a nominee for the office-holder, or instructions as to how a person appointed as proxy-holder is to act.

16.3(5) [Note to blank proxy] A blank proxy must have a note to the effect that the proxy may be completed with the name of the person or the chair of the meeting who is to be proxy-holder.

General Note

Another first here is the "blank proxy", also mentioned in r.1.2(2) by reference to Pt 16, where the name or description of the proxy-holder must not appear in the document of authority, nor must there be instructions how the person appointed is to act (and to the latter extent appears as a sub-species of continuing proxy), but that document must have a "note" to the effect that it may be completed (i.e. it is discretionary) with the name of the person or the chair to be proxy holder.

Rule 16.3(4) substituted by the Insolvency (England and Wales) and Insolvency (Scotland) (Miscellaneous and Consequential Amendments) Rules 2017 (SI 2017/1115) rr.1(1), (2), 2, 10 as from 8 December 2017.

See note after r.16.7.

16.4 Use of proxies

16.4(1) [Delivered to chair for specific meeting] A proxy for a specific meeting must be delivered to the chair before the meeting.

16.4(2) [Continuing proxy delivered to office-holder] A continuing proxy must be delivered to the office-holder and may be exercised at any meeting which begins after the proxy is delivered.

16.4(3) [Different proxy for use at resumed meeting] A proxy may be used at the resumption of the meeting after an adjournment, but if a different proxy is given for use at a resumed meeting, that proxy must be delivered to the chair before the start of the resumed meeting.

16.4(4) [Joint appointments as insolvency office-holder] Where a specific proxy directs a proxy-holder to vote for or against a resolution for the nomination or appointment of a person as office-holder, the proxy-holder may, unless the proxy states otherwise, vote for or against (as the proxy-holder thinks fit) a resolution for the nomination or appointment of that person jointly with another or others.

16.4(5) [Proposal of resolution] A proxy-holder may propose a resolution which is one on which the proxy-holder could vote if someone else proposed it.

16.4(6) [Proxy-holder discretion to vote on resolution not dealt with by proxy] Where a proxy gives specific directions as to voting, this does not, unless the proxy states otherwise, prohibit the proxy-holder from exercising discretion how to vote on a resolution which is not dealt with by the proxy.

16.4(7) [Power of chair re blank proxy] The chair may require a proxy used at a meeting to be the same as or substantially similar to the blank proxy delivered for that meeting or to a blank proxy previously delivered which has been completed as a continuing proxy.

General Note

See *Horler v Rubin* [2012] EWCA Civ 4; [2012] B.P.I.R. 749 where Lewison LJ considered what is now r.16.4(6). See note after r.16.7.

16.5 Use of proxies by the chair

16.5(1) [Chair may not refuse appointment as proxy-holder] Where a proxy appoints the chair (however described in the proxy) as proxy-holder the chair may not refuse to be the proxy-holder.

16.5(2) [Office-holder appointed as proxy-holder but other person as chair] Where the office-holder is appointed as proxy-holder but another person acts as chair of the meeting, that other person may use the proxies as if that person were the proxy-holder.

16.5(3) [Where resolution to be voted by proxy-holder not proposed] Where, in a meeting of creditors in an administration, creditors' voluntary winding up, winding up by the court or a bankruptcy, the chair holds a proxy which requires the proxy-holder to vote for a particular resolution and no other person proposes that resolution the chair must propose it unless the chair considers that there is good reason for not doing so.

16.5(4) [Chair to deliver notice why did not propose resolution in r.16.5(3)] If the chair does not propose such a resolution, the chair must as soon as reasonably practicable after the meeting deliver a notice of the reason why that was not done to the creditor, member or contributory.

General Note

Note in the winding-up case of *Re Shruth Ltd* [2005] EWHC 1293 (Ch); [2007] B.C.C. 960 it was stated that the identity of a person named as proxy is a procedural matter "of absolutely no significance" and if another person attends the meeting in his place and no objection is taken the requirement may be treated as waived, or the company and the liquidator may be estopped from relying on the point.

See note after r.16.7.

16.6 Right of inspection and retention of proxies

16.6(1) [Inspection of proxies by person entitled to attend meeting] A person attending a meeting is entitled, immediately before or in the course of the meeting, to inspect proxies and associated documents delivered to the chair or to any other person in accordance with the notice convening the meeting.

16.6(2) [Office-holder as chair to retain used proxies] The chair must–

(a) retain the proxies used for voting at a meeting where the chair is the office-holder, or

(b) deliver them as soon as reasonably practicable after the meeting to the office-holder.

16.6(3) [Who may inspect proxies] The office-holder must allow proxies, so long as they remain in the office-holder's hands, to be inspected at all reasonable times on any business day by–

(a) a creditor, in the case of proxies used at a meeting of creditors;

(b) a member of the company or a contributory, in the case of proxies used at a meeting of the company, or a meeting of contributories;

(c) a director of the company in the case of corporate insolvency proceedings; or

(d) the debtor or the bankrupt in the case of personal insolvency proceedings.

16.6(4) [Creditor in r.16.6(3)(a)] A creditor in paragraph (3)(a) is a person who has delivered a proof in the proceedings, but does not include a person whose claim has been wholly rejected.

16.6(5) [Right of inspection subject to confidentiality under r.1.58] However the right of inspection is subject to rule 1.58 (confidentiality of documents – grounds for refusing inspection).

(See General Note after r.16.7.)

16.7 Proxy-holder with financial interest

16.7(1) [Limitation on voting by proxy-holder] A proxy-holder must not vote for a resolution which would–

(a) directly or indirectly place the proxy-holder or any associate of the proxy-holder in a position to receive any remuneration, fees or expenses from the insolvent estate; or

(b) fix or change the amount of or the basis of any remuneration, fees or expenses receivable by the proxy-holder or any associate of the proxy-holder out of the insolvent estate.

16.7(2) [Voting for r.16.7(1) resolution if specifically directed to] However a proxy-holder may vote for such a resolution if the proxy specifically directs the proxy-holder to vote in that way.

16.7(3) [Office-holder deemed associate of other person as chair] Where an office-holder is appointed as proxy-holder and that proxy is used under rule 16.5(2) by another person acting as chair, the office-holder is deemed to be an associate of the person acting as chair.

General Note to rr.16.1–16.7

The use of proxies in insolvency proceedings is fairly strictly controlled by these rules.

For the meaning of "associate" in r.16.7, see r.1.2(2) and IA 1986 s.435.

A faxed form of proxy may be accepted for the purposes of these rules: *Inland Revenue Commissioners v Conbeer* [1996] B.C.C. 189.

In accordance with general principles, a proxy may be varied or revoked by the party who has given it at any time prior to the relevant meeting or decision: *Re Cardona, Inland Revenue Commissioners v Cardona* [1997] B.C.C. 697.

16.8 Corporate representation: bankruptcy and IVA

[Note: section 434B makes similar provision for corporate representation in company insolvency proceedings.]

16.8(1) [Authorisation of representative by directors or other governing body] If a corporation is a creditor in a bankruptcy or an IVA, it may by resolution of its directors or other governing body authorise a person or persons to act as its representative or representatives in relation to any decision procedure of the bankrupt or debtor's creditors held in pursuance of the Act or of these Rules.

16.8(2) [Only one person authorised] Where the corporation authorises only one person, that person is entitled to exercise the same powers on behalf of the corporation as the corporation could exercise if it were an individual creditor.

16.8(3) [Multiple persons authorised] Where the corporation authorises more than one person, any one of them is entitled to exercise the same powers on behalf of the corporation as the corporation could exercise if it were an individual creditor.

16.8(4) [Multiple authorisations who purport to act] Where the corporation authorises more than one person and more than one of them purport to exercise a power under paragraph (3)–

(a) if they purport to exercise the power in the same way, the power is treated as exercised in that way; but

(b) if they do not purport to exercise the power in the same way, the power is treated as not exercised.

(See General Note after r.16.9.)

16.9 Instrument conferring authorisation to represent corporation

16.9(1) [Copy of instrument of authorisation] A person authorised to represent a corporation (other than as a proxy-holder) at a meeting of creditors or contributories must produce to the chair–

(a) the instrument conferring the authority; or

(b) a copy of it certified as a true copy by–

(i) two directors,

(ii) a director and the secretary, or

(iii) a director in the presence of a witness who attests the director's signature.

16.9(2) [Instrument to be executed under CA 2006 s.44(1)–(3)] The instrument conferring the authority must have been executed in accordance with section 44(1) to (3) of the Companies Act unless the instrument is the constitution of the corporation.

General Note to rr.16.8–16.9

These rules provide formalities for corporate representation with r.16.8 restricting application to where a corporation is a creditor in bankruptcy or IVA proceedings: the equivalent provision in corporate insolvency proceedings is IA 1986 s.434B.

Rule 16.9(1) does not distinguish between public and private company authentication whereas CA 2006 s.44(1)–(3) on execution of company documents, referred to in r.16.9(2) does so. Rule 16.9(1)(b)(iii) caters for the position of a private company or one-person company.

Part 17

Creditors' and Liquidation Committees

Introductory note to Part 17

This Part deals with creditors' committees in administration, administrative receivership and bankruptcy and liquidation committees in creditors' voluntary winding up and winding up by the court. It brings together a mixture of provisions that were previously scattered around IR 1986. As such committees are less frequently used these days, the significance of this Part is diminished. Any committee must comprise of between three and five members (r.17.3) and has a quorum of two (r.17.6). The restrictions on committee members dealing with the estate are now found in rr.17.25 and 17.26.

Chapter 1

Introductory

17.1 Scope and interpretation

17.1(1) [Application of Pt 17] This Part applies to the establishment and operation of–

(a) a creditors' committee in an administration;

(b) a creditors' committee in an administrative receivership;

(c) a liquidation committee in a creditors' voluntary winding up;

(d) a liquidation committee in a winding up by the court; and

(e) a creditors' committee in a bankruptcy.

17.1(2) ["Contributory member", "creditor member"] In this Part–

"contributory member" means a member of a liquidation committee appointed by the contributories; and

"creditor member" means a member of a liquidation committee appointed by the creditors.

GENERAL NOTE

The introductory rule establishes that Pt 17 applies to creditors' committees in administration, administrative receivership and bankruptcy and liquidation committees in creditors' voluntary winding up and winding up by the court and provides definitions for the two types members of liquidation committees.

CHAPTER 2

FUNCTIONS OF A COMMITTEE

17.2 Functions of a committee

17.2 In addition to any functions conferred on a committee by any provision of the Act, the committee is to–

(a) assist the office-holder in discharging the office-holder's functions; and

(b) act in relation to the office-holder in such manner as may from time to time be agreed.

GENERAL NOTE

This outlines the role of creditors' and liquidation committees and one needs to consult provisions of IA 1986 for direction, although some of these are also generic (e.g. ss.49(1), 101(1), 141(3A), 301(1) and Sch.B1 para.57(2) provide that a liquidation committee or creditors' committee has such functions "as are conferred on it by or under this Act"). Other provisions do give greater direction: see e.g. ss.103, 110, 160, 165, 167, 314, 326, 349A, Sch.B1 paras 83, 91, 98, Sch.5 para.3.

CHAPTER 3

MEMBERSHIP AND FORMALITIES OF FORMATION OF A COMMITTEE

[Note: (1) a document required by the Act or these Rules must also contain the standard contents set out in Part 1;

(2) see sections 215, 362, 363, 365, 371 and 374 of the Financial Services and Markets Act 2000 (c.8) for the rights of persons appointed by a scheme manager, the Financial Conduct Authority and the Prudential Regulation Authority to attend committees and make representations.]

17.3 Number of members of a committee

[Note: section 101(1) provides that a liquidation committee in a creditors' voluntary winding up may not have more than five members.]

17.3(1) [Constitution in administration, administrative receivership, bankruptcy] A committee in an administration, administrative receivership or a bankruptcy must have at least three members but not more than five members.

17.3(2) [Constitution in CVL] A liquidation committee in a creditors' voluntary winding up appointed pursuant to section 101 must have at least three members.

17.3(3) [Constitution in compulsory winding up] A liquidation committee in a winding up by the court established under section 141 must have–

(a) at least three and not more than five members elected by the creditors; and

(b) where the grounds on which the company was wound up do not include inability to pay its debts, and where the contributories so decide, up to three contributory members elected by the contributories.

GENERAL NOTE

This details the constitution and size of any committee as between three and five creditor members and, only in r.17.3(b), a maximum of three contributories.

17.4 Eligibility for membership of creditors' or liquidation committee

17.4(1) [Application of rule] This rule applies to a creditors' committee in an administration, an administrative receivership, and a bankruptcy and to a liquidation committee in a creditors' voluntary winding up and a winding up by the court.

17.4(2) [Eligibility of creditor] A creditor is eligible to be a member of such a committee if–

(a) the person has proved for a debt;

(b) the debt is not fully secured; and

(c) neither of the following apply–

(i) the proof has been wholly disallowed for voting purposes, or

(ii) the proof has been wholly rejected for the purpose of distribution or dividend.

17.4(3) [No member as creditor and contributory] No person can be a member as both a creditor and a contributory.

17.4(4) [Body corporate as member acting under r.17.17] A body corporate may be a member of a creditors' committee, but it cannot act otherwise than by a representative appointed under rule 17.17.

GENERAL NOTE

The bankruptcy case of *Foenander v Allan* [2006] B.P.I.R. 1392 indicates that for the purposes of what is now r.17.4(2) eligibility is to be determined by proof of debt and not by other unproved claims. Corporate members are allowed (r.17.4(4)) and see r.17.7 on their representation.

17.5 Establishment of committees

17.5(1) [Decision of creditors or contributories] Where the creditors, or where applicable, contributories, decide that a creditors' or liquidation committee should be established, the convener or chair of the decision procedure or convener of the deemed consent process (if not the office-holder) must–

(a) as soon as reasonably practicable deliver a notice of the decision to the office-holder (or to the person appointed as office-holder); and

(b) where a decision has also been made as to membership of the committee, inform the office-holder of the names and addresses of the persons elected to be members of the committee.

17.5(2) [Person's agreement to act] Before a person may act as a member of the committee that person must agree to do so.

17.5(3) [Agreement by proxy-holder] A person's proxy-holder attending a meeting establishing the committee or, in the case of a corporation, its duly appointed representative, may give such agreement (unless the proxy or instrument conferring authority contains a statement to the contrary).

17.5(4) [Office-holder to seek decision as to members] Where a decision has been made to establish a committee but not as to its membership, the office-holder must seek a decision from the creditors (about creditor members of the committee) and, where appropriate in a winding up by the court, a decision from contributories (about contributory members of the committee).

17.5(5) [Establishment when office-holder sends notice of membership] The committee is not established (and accordingly cannot act) until the office-holder has sent a notice of its membership in order to comply with paragraph (9) or (10).

17.5(6) [Content of notice] The notice must contain the following–

(a) a statement that the committee has been duly constituted;

(b) identification details for any company that is a member of the committee;

(c) the full name and address of each member that is not a company.

17.5(7) [Authentication of notice]The notice must be authenticated and dated by the office-holder.

17.5(8) [Delivery of notice] The notice must be delivered as soon as reasonably practicable after the minimum number of persons required by rule 17.3 have agreed to act as members and been elected.

17.5(9) [Notice in corporate insolvency to registrar of companies] Where the notice relates to a liquidation committee or a creditors' committee other than in a bankruptcy the office-holder must, as soon as reasonably practicable, deliver the notice to the registrar of companies.

17.5(10) [Notice in bankruptcy to court or official receiver] Where the notice relates to a creditors' committee in a bankruptcy the office-holder must, as soon as reasonably practicable–

(a) in bankruptcy proceedings based on a petition file the notice with the court; and

(b) in bankruptcy proceedings based on a bankruptcy application deliver the notice to the official receiver.

General Note

This rule provides the formalities for establishing a creditors' or liquidation committee (and see the special circumstances in r.17.6 where no liquidation committee). The predecessor to r.17.5(3) was amended to facilitate immediate committee meetings after the creditors' meeting. The former requirement in IR 1986 for a certificate of due constitution (formerly Form 4.47) is no longer required with the demise of prescribed forms in IR 2016, but except in bankruptcy a notice of establishment of a liquidation or a creditors' committee must be delivered by the administrator, administrative receiver or liquidator to the registrar of companies using form COM1.

Rule 17.5(1) amended and r.17.5(5) substituted by the Insolvency (England and Wales) and Insolvency (Scotland) (Miscellaneous and Consequential Amendments) Rules 2017 (SI 2017/1115) rr.1(1), (2), 2, 11 as from 8 December 2017.

17.6 Liquidation committee established by contributories

17.6(1) [Application of rule] This rule applies where, under section 141, the creditors do not decide that a liquidation committee should be established, or decide that a committee should not be established.

17.6(2) [Application to court to order further decision of creditors] The contributories may decide to appoint one of their number to make application to the court for an order requiring the liquidator to seek a further decision from the creditors on whether to establish a liquidation committee; and–

(a) the court may, if it thinks that there are special circumstances to justify it, make such an order; and

(b) the creditors' decision sought by the liquidator in compliance with the order is deemed to have been a decision under section 141.

17.6(3) [Contributories may establish committee if creditors do not] If the creditors decide under paragraph (2)(b) not to establish a liquidation committee, the contributories may establish a committee.

17.6(4) [Constitution of committee] The committee must then consist of at least three, and not more than five, contributories elected by the contributories; and rule 17.5 applies, substituting for the reference to rule 17.3 in rule 17.5(8) a reference to this paragraph.

General Note

This rule applies in the special circumstances under IA 1986 s.141(3) where creditors and contributories disagree on establishing a liquidation committee but contributories desire one.

17.7 Notice of change of membership of a committee

17.7(1) [Office-holder to deliver/file notice of change] The office-holder must deliver or file a notice if there is a change in membership of the committee.

17.7(2) [Content of notice] The notice must contain the following–

(a) the date of the original notice in respect of the constitution of the committee and the date of the last notice of membership given under this rule (if any);

(b) a statement that this notice of membership replaces the previous notice;

(c) identification details for any company that is a member of the committee;

(d) the full name and address of any member that is not a company;

(e) a statement whether any member has become a member since the issue of the previous notice;

(f) the identification details for a company or otherwise the full name of any member named in the previous notice who is no longer a member and the date the membership ended.

17.7(3) [Authentication of notice] The notice must be authenticated and dated by the office-holder.

17.7(4) [Notice in corporate insolvency to registrar of companies] Where the notice relates to a liquidation committee or a creditors' committee other than in a bankruptcy the office-holder must, as soon as reasonably practicable, deliver the notice to the registrar of companies.

17.7(5) [Notice in bankruptcy to court or official receiver] Where the notice relates to a creditors' committee in a bankruptcy the office-holder must, as soon as reasonably practicable–

(a) in bankruptcy proceedings based on a petition file the notice with the court; and

(b) in bankruptcy proceedings based on a bankruptcy application deliver the notice to the official receiver.

General Note

The form to be filed with the registrar of companies of notice of change in membership of a committee is COM2. Note the separate arrangements in bankruptcy in r.17.7(5).

17.8 Vacancies: creditor members of creditors' or liquidation committee

17.8(1) [Application of rule] This rule applies if there is a vacancy among the creditor members of a creditors' or liquidation committee or where the number of creditor members of the committee is fewer than the maximum allowed.

17.8(2) [Vacancy need not be filled] A vacancy need not be filled if–

(a) the office-holder and a majority of the remaining creditor members agree; and

(b) the total number of creditor members does not fall below three.

17.8(3) [Power of office-holder may appoint a creditor] The office-holder may appoint a creditor, who is qualified under rule 17.4 to be a member of the committee, to fill a vacancy or as an additional member of the committee, if–

(a) a majority of the remaining creditor members of the committee (provided there are at least two) agree to the appointment; and

(b) the creditor agrees to act.

17.8(4) [Office-holder may seek decision from creditors] Alternatively, the office-holder may seek a decision from creditors to appoint a creditor (with that creditor's consent) to fill the vacancy.

17.8(5) [Appointment to be reported to office-holder] Where the vacancy is filled by an appointment made by a decision of creditors which is not convened or chaired by the office-holder, the convener or chair must report the appointment to the office-holder.

(See General Note after r.17.9.)

17.9 Vacancies: contributory members of liquidation committee

17.9(1) [Application of rule] This rule applies if there is a vacancy among the contributory members of a liquidation committee or where the number of contributory members of the committee is fewer than the maximum allowed under rule 17.3(3)(b) or 17.6(4) as the case may be.

17.9(2) [Vacancy need not be filled] A vacancy need not be filled if–

(a) the liquidator and a majority of the remaining contributory members agree; and

(b) in the case of a committee of contributories only, the number of members does not fall below three.

17.9(3) [Power of liquidator to appoint a contributory] The liquidator may appoint a contributory to be a member of the committee, to fill a vacancy or as an additional member of the committee, if–

(a) a majority of the remaining contributory members of the committee (provided there are at least two) agree to the appointment; and

(b) the contributory agrees to act.

17.9(4) [Liquidator may seek decision from contributories] Alternatively, the office-holder may seek a decision from contributories to appoint a contributory (with that contributory's consent) to fill the vacancy.

17.9(5) [Appointment to be reported to liquidator] Where the vacancy is filled by an appointment made by a decision of contributories which is not convened or chaired by the office-holder, the convener or chair must report the appointment to the office-holder.

General Note to rr.17.8–17.9

As long as the office-holders and a majority of remaining members agree, a vacancy need not be filled provided the number of creditor members (r.17.8) and contributory members (r.17.9) is three or more. Committee resolutions are to be passed by simple majority and there is to be no weighting of votes (see r.17.18).

17.10 Resignation

17.10 A member of a committee may resign by informing the office-holder in writing.

(See General Note after r.17.13.)

17.11 Termination of membership

17.11 A person's membership of a committee is automatically terminated if that person–

(a) becomes bankrupt, in which case the person's trustee in bankruptcy replaces the bankrupt as a member of the committee;

(b) is a person to whom a moratorium period under a debt relief order applies;

(c) neither attends nor is represented at three consecutive meetings (unless it is resolved at the third of those meetings that this rule is not to apply in that person's case);

(d) has ceased to be eligible to be a member of the committee under rule 17.4;

(e) ceases to be a creditor or is found never to have been a creditor;

(f) ceases to be a contributory or is found never to have been a contributory.

(See General Note after r.17.13.)

17.12 Removal

17.12(1) [Removal of creditor member by creditors, contributory member by contributories] A creditor member of a committee may be removed by a decision of the creditors through a decision procedure and in the case of a liquidation committee a contributory member of the committee may be removed by a decision of contributories through a decision procedure.

17.12(2) [Notice of decision procedure] At least 14 days' notice must be given of a decision procedure under this rule.

(See General Note after r.17.13.)

17.13 Cessation of liquidation committee in a winding up when creditors are paid in full

17.13(1) [Liquidator to deliver notice of circumstances to registrar of companies] Where the creditors have been paid in full together with interest in accordance with section 189, the liquidator must deliver to the registrar of companies a notice to that effect.

17.13(2) [Cessation of committee] On the delivery of the notice the liquidation committee ceases to exist.

17.13(3) [Content of notice] The notice must–

(a) identify the liquidator;

(b) contain a statement by the liquidator certifying that the creditors of the company have been paid in full with interest in accordance with section 189; and

(c) be authenticated and dated by the liquidator.

General Note to rr.17.10–17.13

Termination of membership is automatic under r.7.11, which contains fairly standard grounds but note in particular absenteeism in r.17.11(c) subject to a saving resolution (passed by simple majority with no weighting of votes), and under r.17.13 in relation to the liquidation committee in winding up in the unusual event in insolvent liquidation that creditors have been paid in full with interest once notice to Companies House has been filed, for which form COM4 has been prescribed.

Termination by resignation and removal (note the use of decision procedures) are standard methodologies.

Chapter 4

Meetings of Committee

[Note: a document required by the Act or these Rules must also contain the standard contents set out in Part 1.]

17.14 Meetings of committee

17.14(1) [Office-holder to determine] Meetings of the committee must be held when and where determined by the office-holder.

17.14(2) [First meeting] The office-holder must call a first meeting of the committee to take place within six weeks of the committee's establishment.

17.14(3) [Subsequent meetings] After the calling of the first meeting, the office-holder must call a meeting–

(a) if so requested by a member of the committee or a member's representative (the meeting then to be held within 21 days of the request being received by the office-holder); and

(b) for a specified date, if the committee has previously resolved that a meeting be held on that date.

17.14(4) [Notice of venue] The office-holder must give five business days' notice of the venue of a meeting to each member of the committee (or a member's representative, if designated for that purpose), except where the requirement for notice has been waived by or on behalf of a member.

17.14(5) [Waiver] Waiver may be signified either at or before the meeting.

General Note

See r.17.2 for the functions of a committee: it may be implied that meetings are only held for the purpose of those functions.

The first meeting must be called by the office-holder within six weeks of the establishment of the committee (and not as formerly six weeks from the date of his appointment or establishment of the committee if later).

The office-holder determines where and when meetings are to be held and, if deemed appropriate, may allow remote attendance (see r.17.20). If the office-holder does not specify a venue for the meeting, any committee member may request him to do so (see rr.17.20(8), 17.21).

A committee member may appoint a representative by letter of authority (see r.17.17).

17.15 The chair at meetings

17.15 The chair at a meeting of a committee must be the office-holder or an appointed person.

(See General Note after r.17.16.)

17.16 Quorum

17.16 A meeting of a committee is duly constituted if due notice of it has been delivered to all the members, and at least two of the members are in attendance or represented.

General Note to rr.17.15–17.16

These are standard provisions in insolvency.

17.17 Committee-members' representatives

17.17(1) [Representation] A member of the committee may, in relation to the business of the committee, be represented by another person duly authorised by the member for that purpose.

17.17(2) [Letter of authority] A person acting as a committee-member's representative must hold a letter of authority entitling that person to act (either generally or specifically) and authenticated by or on behalf of the committee-member.

17.17(3) [Proxy or instrument of authority confers general authority] A proxy or an instrument conferring authority (in respect of a person authorised to represent a corporation) is to be treated as a letter of authority to act generally (unless the proxy or instrument conferring authority contains a statement to the contrary).

17.17(4) [Production of letter of authority to chair] The chair at a meeting of the committee may call on a person claiming to act as a committee-member's representative to produce a letter of authority, and may exclude that person if no letter of authority is produced at or by the time of the meeting or if it appears to the chair that the authority is deficient.

17.17(5) [Who may not be representative] A committee member may not be represented by–

(a) another member of the committee;

(b) a person who is at the same time representing another committee-member;

(c) a body corporate;

(d) an undischarged bankrupt;

(e) a person whose estate has been sequestrated and who has not been discharged;

(f) a person to whom a moratorium period under a debt relief order applies;

(g) a person who is subject to a company directors disqualification order or a company directors disqualification undertaking; or

(h) a person who is subject to a bankruptcy restrictions order (including an interim order), a bankruptcy restrictions undertaking, a debt relief restrictions order (including an interim order) or a debt relief restrictions undertaking.

17.17(6) [Authentication as representative] Where a representative authenticates any document on behalf of a committee-member the fact that the representative authenticates as a representative must be stated below the authentication.

General Note

Committee members may appoint representatives to act for them, subject to safeguards in this rule. On the role of representatives, see *Re W&A Glaser Ltd* [1994] B.C.C. 199 at 208.

17.18 Voting rights and resolutions

17.18(1) [One vote per member] At a meeting of the committee, each member (whether the member is in attendance or is represented by a representative) has one vote.

17.18(2) [Resolution passed by majority votes in favour] A resolution is passed when a majority of the members attending or represented have voted in favour of it.

17.18(3) [Record of resolutions] Every resolution passed must be recorded in writing and authenticated by the chair, either separately or as part of the minutes of the meeting, and the record must be kept with the records of the proceedings.

General Note

Votes at committee meetings are passed by a simple majority. There is no weighting of votes here.

17.19 Resolutions by correspondence

17.19(1) [Details of proposed resolution to committee members] The office-holder may seek to obtain the agreement of the committee to a resolution by delivering to every member (or the member's representative designated for the purpose) details of the proposed resolution.

17.19(2) [Details to allow recipient to indicate agreement or dissent] The details must be set out in such a way that the recipient may indicate agreement or dissent and where there is more than one resolution may indicate agreement to or dissent from each one separately.

17.19(3) [Member may request meeting] A member of the committee may, within five business days from the delivery of details of the proposed resolution, require the office-holder to summon a meeting of the committee to consider the matters raised by the proposed resolution.

17.19(4) [Resolution by agreement in absence of request] In the absence of such a request, the resolution is passed by the committee if a majority of the members (excluding any who are not permitted to vote by reason of rule 17.25(4)) deliver notice to the office-holder that they agree with the resolution.

17.19(5) [Copy of resolution] A copy of every resolution passed under this rule, and a note that the agreement of the committee was obtained, must be kept with the records of the proceedings.

General Note

This rule makes life easy for committee members (and for the office-holder) by allowing committee resolutions to be obtained by simple majority without a meeting, but subject to any member requisitioning a meeting.

17.20 Remote attendance at meetings of committee

17.20(1) [Remote attendance when office-holder considers it appropriate] Where the office-holder considers it appropriate, a meeting may be conducted and held in such a way that persons who are not present together at the same place may attend it.

17.20(2) [Attendance by right to speak and vote] A person attends such a meeting who is able to exercise that person's right to speak and vote at the meeting.

17.20(3) [Person to be in position to communicate during the meeting to all attending] A person is able to exercise the right to speak at a meeting when that person is in a position to communicate during the meeting to all those attending the meeting any information or opinions which that person has on the business of the meeting.

17.20(4) [How right to speak and vote exercisable] A person is able to exercise the right to vote at a meeting when–

(i) that person is able to vote, during the meeting, on resolutions or determinations put to the vote at the meeting, and

(ii) that person's vote can be taken into account in determining whether or not such resolutions or determinations are passed at the same time as the votes of all the other persons attending the meeting.

17.20(5) [Office-holder to make appropriate arrangements] Where such a meeting is to be held the office-holder must make whatever arrangements the office-holder considers appropriate to–

(a) enable those attending the meeting to exercise their rights to speak or vote; and

(b) verify the identity of those attending the meeting and to ensure the security of any electronic means used to enable attendance.

17.20(6) [Satisfaction of requirement in to specify place for meeting] A requirement in these Rules to specify a place for the meeting may be satisfied by specifying the arrangements the office-holder proposes to enable persons to exercise their rights to speak or vote where in the reasonable opinion of the office-holder–

(a) a meeting will be attended by persons who will not be present together at the same place; and

(b) it is unnecessary or inexpedient to specify a place for the meeting.

17.20(7) [Office-holder to have regard to legitimate interests of committee members] In making the arrangements referred to in paragraph (6) and in forming the opinion referred to in paragraph (6)(b), the office-holder must have regard to the legitimate interests of the committee members or their representatives attending the meeting in the efficient despatch of the business of the meeting.

17.20(8) [When office-holder to specify place for meeting] Where the notice of a meeting does not specify a place for the meeting the office-holder must specify a place for the meeting if at least one member of the committee requests the office-holder to do so in accordance with rule 17.21.

General Note

Remote attendance of committee meetings is only allowed if the office-holder considers it appropriate and he then has a duty to make necessary arrangements. A single member may request a place for the meeting to be specified if no place was notified (and see r.17.21).

17.21 Procedure for requests that a place for a meeting should be specified

17.21(1) [Application of rule] This rule applies to a request to the office-holder under rule 17.20(8) to specify a place for the meeting.

17.21(2) [Time limit for request] The request must be made within three business days of the date on which the office-holder delivered the notice of the meeting in question.

17.21(3) [Duty of office-holder where request properly made] Where the office-holder considers that the request has been properly made in accordance with this rule, the office-holder must–

(a) deliver notice to all those previously given notice of the meeting–

(i) that it is to be held at a specified place, and

(ii) as to whether the date and time are to remain the same or not;

(b) fix a venue for the meeting, the date of which must be not later than seven business days after the original date for the meeting; and

(c) give three business days' notice of the venue to all those previously given notice of the meeting.

17.21(4) [Notices in r.17.21(3)(a), (c)] The notices required by sub-paragraphs (a) and (c) may be delivered at the same or different times.

17.21(5) [Chair to be present in person] Where the office-holder has specified a place for the meeting in response to a request under rule 17.20(8), the chair of the meeting must attend the meeting by being present in person at that place.

General Note

This rule is consequential on r.17.20.

Chapter 5

Supply of information by the office-holder to the committee

[Note: a document required by the Act or these Rules must also contain the standard contents set out in Part 1.]

17.22 Notice requiring office-holder to attend the creditors' committee (administration and administrative receivership) (paragraph 57(3)(a) of Schedule B1 and section 49(2))

[Note: in an administration paragraph 57(3) of Schedule B1 enables the creditors' committee to require the administrator to provide the committee with information: section 49(2) makes similar provision in an administrative receivership.]

17.22(1) [Application of rule] This rule applies where–

(a) a committee in an administration resolves under paragraph 57(3)(a) of Schedule B1 to require the attendance of an administrator; or

(b) a committee in an administrative receivership resolves under section 49(2) to require the attendance of the administrative receiver.

17.22(2) [Notice authenticated and accompanies by copy resolution] The notice delivered to the office-holder requiring the office-holder's attendance must be–

(a) accompanied by a copy of the resolution; and

(b) authenticated by a member of the committee.

17.22(3) [Authentication by member's representative] A member's representative may authenticate the notice for the member.

17.22(4) [Meeting on business day] The meeting at which the office-holder's attendance is required must be fixed by the committee for a business day, and must be held at such time and place as the office-holder determines.

17.22(5) [Committee may elect chair for meeting] Where the office-holder so attends, the committee may elect one of their number to be chair of the meeting in place of the office-holder or an appointed person.

General Note

This provides essential procedural guidance on the operation of IA 1986 s.49(2) and Sch.B1 para.57(3)(a). "Business day" in r.17.22(4)) is defined in r.1.2(2).

17.23 Office-holder's obligation to supply information to the committee (winding up and bankruptcy)

[Note: see section 49(2) and paragraph 57(3) of Schedule B1 for the office-holder's duty in an administrative receivership and an administration to supply information to the creditors' committee.]

17.23(1) [Application of rule] This rule applies in relation to a creditors' voluntary winding up, a winding up by the court and a bankruptcy.

17.23(2) [Office-holder to deliver report] The office-holder must deliver a report to every member of the liquidation committee or the creditors' committee (as appropriate) containing the information required by paragraph (3)–

(a) not less than once in every period of six months (unless the committee agrees otherwise); and

(b) when directed to do so by the committee.

17.23(3) [Information in report] The required information is a report setting out–

(a) the position generally in relation to the progress of the proceedings; and

(b) any matters arising in connection with them to which the office-holder considers the committee's attention should be drawn.

17.23(4) [Delivery of report, etc.] The office-holder must, as soon as reasonably practicable after being directed by the committee–

(a) deliver any report directed under paragraph (2)(b);

(b) comply with a request by the committee for information.

17.23(5) [Where office-holder need comply with r.17.23(4)] However the office-holder need not comply with such a direction where it appears to the office-holder that–

(a) the direction is frivolous or unreasonable;

(b) the cost of complying would be excessive, having regard to the relative importance of the information; or

(c) there are insufficient assets to enable the office-holder to comply.

17.23(6) [Summary report; questions on conduct so far] Where the committee has come into being more than 28 days after the appointment of the office-holder, the office-holder must make a summary report to the members of the committee of what actions the office-holder has taken since the office-holder's appointment, and must answer such questions as they may put to the office-holder relating to the office-holder's conduct of the proceedings so far.

17.23(7) [Member of committee after first establishment may not require full report] A person who becomes a member of the committee at any time after its first establishment is not entitled to require a report under this rule by the office-holder of any matters previously arising, other than a summary report.

17.23(8) [Members' access to office-holder's record of proceedings, etc.] Nothing in this rule disentitles the committee, or any member of it, from having access to the office-holder's record of the proceedings, or from seeking an explanation of any matter within the committee's responsibility.

General Note

This rule only applies in insolvent winding up and bankruptcy to impose a duty of reporting obligations on liquidators and trustees in bankruptcy to keep the liquidation/creditors' committee informed.

Documents passing between a liquidator and the Insolvency Service concerning possible disqualification of directors are not documents which are within any of the statutory rights of the liquidation committee to inspect, or in respect of which the committee can properly put questions to the liquidator and ask him to report to them: *Re W&A Glaser Ltd* [1994] B.C.C. 199.

In *Re Buildlead Ltd (No.2)* [2004] EWHC 2443 (Ch); [2005] B.C.C. 138 liquidators had not made the reports required by what is now r.17.23(2) for several years and had used the method of postal ballots permitted by what is now r.17.19 to sanction payment of their fees when, in the view of the court, it would have been more in keeping with the spirit of professional guidance to have held a meeting of the committee and held a full and frank discussion about the level of their fees. This was a material factor influencing the court in its decision to order that the liquidators be removed.

Chapter 6

Miscellaneous

[Note: a document required by the Act or these Rules must also contain the standard contents set out in Part 1.]

17.24 Expenses of members etc.

17.24(1) [Travelling expenses, etc.] The office-holder must pay, as an expense of the insolvency proceedings, the reasonable travelling expenses directly incurred by members of the committee or their representatives in attending the committee's meetings or otherwise on the committee's business.

17.24(2) [Where require to pay does not apply] The requirement for the office-holder to pay the expenses does not apply to a meeting of the committee held within six weeks of a previous meeting, unless the meeting is summoned by the office-holder.

General Note

The main expense here will be travelling expenses but remote attendance of meetings may help keep these down.

On priority see r.3.51(2)(g) (administration), rr.6.42(4)(f) and 7.108(4)(m) (winding up), r.10.149(n).

17.25 Dealings by committee members and others

17.25(1) [Application of rule] This rule applies in a creditors' voluntary winding up, a winding up by the court and a bankruptcy to a person who is, or has been in the preceding 12 months–

(a) a member of the committee;

(b) a member's representative; or

(c) an associate of a member, or of a member's representative.

17.25(2) [Prohibited transactions] Such a person must not enter into a transaction as a result of which that person would–

(a) receive as an expense of the insolvency proceedings a payment for services given or goods supplied in connection with the administration of the insolvent estate;

(b) obtain a profit from the administration of the insolvent estate; or

(c) acquire an asset forming part of the insolvent estate.

17.25(3) [Permission or sanction for otherwise prohibited transaction] However such a transaction may be entered into–

(a) with the prior sanction of the committee, where it is satisfied (after full disclosure of the circumstances) that the person will be giving full value in the transaction;

(b) with the prior permission of the court; or

(c) if that person does so as a matter of urgency, or by way of performance of a contract in force before the start of the insolvency proceedings, and that person obtains the court's permission for the transaction, having applied for it without undue delay.

17.25(4) [Interested member etc. not to vote to sanction] Neither a member nor a representative of a member who is to participate directly or indirectly in a transaction may vote on a resolution to sanction that transaction.

17.25(5) [Power of court on application] The court may, on the application of an interested person–

(a) set aside a transaction on the ground that it has been entered into in contravention of this rule; and

(b) make such other order about the transaction as it thinks just, including an order requiring a person to whom this rule applies to account for any profit obtained from the transaction and compensate the insolvent estate for any resultant loss.

17.25(6) [No order re member or representative's associates] The court will not make an order under the previous paragraph in respect of an associate of a member of the committee or an associate of a member's representative, if satisfied that the associate or representative entered into the relevant transaction without having any reason to suppose that in doing so the associate or representative would contravene this rule.

17.25(7) [Costs on application] The costs of the application are not payable as an expense of the insolvency proceedings unless the court orders otherwise.

General Note

This rule imposes strict controls in winding up and bankruptcy to guard against the risks of conflicts of interest on the part of committee members and their associates (for the meaning of "associate" see r.1.2(2) and IA 1986 s.435.)

The committee or the court may sanction the transaction otherwise the court may set it aside on an application by an interested person.

See the bankruptcy cases of *Re Gallard* [1896] 1 Q.B. 68 and *Re Bulmer Ex p. Greaves* [1937] Ch. 499.

An important substantive provision like this would have been more appropriately placed in IA 1986 itself.

Compare the less strict r.17.26 below in administration and administrative receivership.

17.26 Dealings by committee members and others: administration and administrative receivership

17.26(1) [Application of rule] This rule applies in an administration and administrative receivership.

17.26(2) [Dealings to be in good faith and for value] Membership of the committee does not prevent a person from dealing with the company provided that a transaction is in good faith and for value.

17.26(3) [Power of court on application] The court may, on the application of an interested person–

(a) set aside a transaction which appears to it to be contrary to this rule; and

(b) make such other order about the transaction as it thinks just including an order requiring a person to whom this rule applies to account for any profit obtained from the transaction and compensate the company for any resultant loss.

General Note

Compared with the more strict r.17.25 in winding up and bankruptcy, this rule allows committee members in administration and administrative receivership to deal with the company in good faith and for value. However the court can invalidate transactions entered into in breach of this provision. Again, this power of invalidation would have been better located within the Insolvency Act itself.

17.27 Formal defects

[Note: section 377 makes similar provision to paragraph (1) for the validity of acts of the creditors' committee in a bankruptcy.]

17.27(1) [Validity of acts notwithstanding defect] The acts of a creditors' committee or a liquidation committee are valid notwithstanding any defect in the appointment, election or qualifications of a member of the committee or a committee-member's representative or in the formalities of its establishment.

17.27(2) [No application in bankruptcy] This rule does not apply to the creditors' committee in a bankruptcy.

General Note

This reflects a common philosophy in insolvency legislation: see also IA 1986 s.377 in bankruptcy.

The standard-form provision is designed to prevent technical objections to the constitution of the committee. (See, however, *Re W&A Glaser Ltd* [1994] B.C.C. 199, which makes it clear that the court itself is free to go into this question.)

17.28 Special rule for winding up by the court and bankruptcy: functions vested in the Secretary of State

17.28(1) [Office-holder's notices and reports] At any time when the functions of a committee in a winding up by the court or a bankruptcy are vested in the Secretary of State under section 141(4) or (5) or section 302(1) or (2), requirements of the Act or these Rules about notices to be delivered, or reports to be made, to the committee by the office-holder do not apply, otherwise than as enabling the committee to require a report as to any matter.

17.28(2) [Exercise by official receiver] Where the committee's functions are so vested under section 141(5) or 302(2), they may be exercised by the official receiver.

General Note

IA 1986 s.141(4) applies when the official receiver is liquidator, and s.141(5) where there is for the time being no liquidation committee. The same applies *mutatis mutandis* in bankruptcy in s.303(1) and (2).

Chapter 7

Winding up by the court following an administration

[Note: a document required by the Act or these Rules must also contain the standard contents set out in Part 1.]

17.29 Continuation of creditors' committee

[Note: paragraph 83(8)(f) of Schedule B1 makes similar provision to this rule for the liquidation committee to continue where the administration is followed by a creditors' voluntary winding up.]

17.29(1) [Application of rule] This rule applies where–

(a) a winding-up order has been made by the court on the application of the administrator under paragraph 79 of Schedule B1;

(b) the court makes an order under section 140(1) appointing the administrator as the liquidator; and

(c) a creditors' committee was in existence immediately before the winding-up order was made.

17.29(2) [Creditors' committee to continue as liquidation committee] The creditors' committee shall continue in existence after the date of the order as if appointed as a liquidation committee under section 141.

17.29(3) [Conditions for committee to act] However, subject to rule 17.8(3)(a), the committee cannot act until–

(a) the minimum number of persons required by rule 17.3 have agreed to act as members of the liquidation committee (including members of the former creditors' committee and any other who may be appointed under rule 17.8); and

(b) the liquidator has delivered a notice of continuance of the committee to the registrar of companies.

17.29(4) [When notice of continuation to be delivered to registrar] The notice must be delivered as soon as reasonably practicable after the minimum number of persons required have agreed to act as members or, if applicable, been appointed.

17.29(5) [Content of notice] The notice must contain–

(a) a statement that the former creditors' committee is continuing in existence;

(b) identification details for any company that is a member of the committee;

(c) the full name and address of each member that is not a company.

17.29(6) [Authentication of notice] The notice must be authenticated and dated by the office-holder.

General Note

This rule applies exclusively on winding up by the court following administration on the application of the administrator under IA 1986 Sch.B1 para.79 and the court appoints the administrator as liquidator under s.140(1) where there was a creditors' committee in existence immediately before the winding-up order was made. The creditors' committee appointed for the purpose of the administration continues in being as the liquidation committee.

The notice of continuance to Companies House required by r.17.29(3)(b) must be in form COM3.

The rule is more simply drafted then its counterparts in IR 1986 rr.4.173–4.178 and no longer states that the preceding rules apply to the liquidation committee, but that must be implied.

Part 18

Reporting and Remuneration of Office-Holders

Introductory note to Part 18

This Part deals with reporting by and remuneration of office-holders (not the official receiver). On progress reports see r.18.3 et seq. The component dealing with office-holder fees is high profile and it is vital that the rules are seen to work effectively in practice. Again we see an attempt to coordinate provisions that were previously spread around various Parts of IR 1986. Note the fairly new provisions on binding fee estimates (rr.18.16 and 18.30). A creditor can apply to the court to challenge fee claims that appear excessive (r.18.34). A bankrupt enjoys a similar right of challenge pursuant to r.18.35.

The provisions on remuneration need to be read alongside Pt 6 of the *Practice Direction: Insolvency Proceedings* [2018] B.C.C. 241.

[Note: this Part does not apply to the official receiver acting as an office-holder.]

Chapter 1

Introductory

18.1 Scope of Part 18 and interpretation

18.1(1) [Application of Pt 18] This Part applies to administration, winding up and bankruptcy.

18.1(2) [No application to official receiver as office-holder] However this Part does not apply to the official receiver as office-holder or in respect of any period for which the official receiver is the office-holder.

18.1(3) [Particular non-application] In particular an office-holder other than the official receiver is not required to make any report in respect of a period during which the official receiver was office-holder.

18.1(4) ["Committee"] In this Part "committee" means either or both of a creditors' committee and a liquidation committee as the context requires.

General Note

This rule sets out which insolvency procedures Pt 18 applies to—administration, winding up and bankruptcy only—and stresses that it does not apply to the official receiver as office-holder.

Chapter 2

Progress reports

[Note: a document required by the Act or these Rules must also contain the standard contents set out in Part 1.]

18.2 Reporting by the office-holder

18.2 The office-holder in an administration, winding up or bankruptcy must prepare and deliver reports in accordance with this Chapter.

General Note

On the relevant reports see rr.18.3–18.13 (the liquidator's final account in winding up and trustee in bankruptcy's final report are covered in Ch.3 (r.18.14)).

Progress reports, already a feature of administrations, were introduced in winding up by LRO 2010 (SI 2010/18) art.6 inserting IA 1986 s.92A and 104A.

18.3 Contents of progress reports in administration, winding up and bankruptcy

[Note: see rule 3.53 for provisions about the contents of a final progress report in an administration.]

18.3(1) [Content] The office-holder's progress report in an administration, winding up and bankruptcy must contain the following–

(a) identification details for the proceedings;

(b) identification details for the bankrupt;

(c) identification and contact details for the office-holder;

(d) the date of appointment of the office-holder and any changes in the office-holder in accordance with paragraphs (3) and (4);

(e) details of progress during the period of the report, including a summary account of receipts and payments during the period of the report;

(f) the information relating to remuneration and expenses required by rule 18.4;

(g) the information relating to distributions required by rules 18.10 to 18.13 as applicable;

(h) details of what remains to be done; and

(i) any other information of relevance to the creditors.

18.3(2) [Prescribed part in receipts and payments account in final progress report] The receipts and payments account in a final progress report must state the amount paid to unsecured creditors by virtue of the application of section 176A.

18.3(3) [Change in office-holder] A change in the office-holder is only required to be shown in the next report after the change.

18.3(4) [Repayment of pre-administration expenses from former office-holder] However if the current office-holder is seeking the repayment of pre-administration expenses from a former office-holder the change in office-holder must continue to be shown until the next report after the claim is settled.

18.3(5) [Extension of administrator's appointment] Where the period of an administrator's appointment is extended the next progress report after the date the extension is granted must contain details of the extension.

18.3(6) [Administration converted to CVL: first progress report] Where an administration has converted to a voluntary winding up the first progress report by the liquidator must include a note of any information received by the liquidator from the former administrator under rule 3.60(5) (matters occurring after the date of the administrator's final progress report).

General Note

For further content of the final progress report in administration, see r.3.53 (the official "Note" to r.18.3 states "r.3.52" but this must be a drafting error).

See General Note after r.18.13.

18.4 Information about remuneration

18.4(1) [Information on remuneration and expenses in r.18.3(1)(f)] The information relating to remuneration and expenses referred to in rule 18.3(1)(f) is as follows–

(a) the basis fixed for the remuneration of the office-holder under rules 18.16 and 18.18 to 18.21 as applicable, (or, if not fixed at the date of the report, the steps taken during the period of the report to fix it);

(b) if the basis of remuneration has been fixed, a statement of–

(i) the remuneration charged by the office-holder during the period of the report, and

(ii) where the report is the first to be made after the basis has been fixed, the remuneration charged by the office-holder during the periods covered by the previous reports, together with a description of the things done by the office-holder during those periods in respect of which the remuneration was charged;

(c) where the basis of the remuneration is fixed as a set amount under rule 18.16(2)(c), it may be shown as that amount without any apportionment to the period of the report;

(d) a statement of the expenses incurred by the office-holder during the period of the report;

(e) a statement setting out whether at the date of the report–

(i) in a case other than a members' voluntary winding up, the remuneration expected to be charged by the office-holder is likely to exceed the fees estimate under rule 18.16(4) or any approval given,

(ii) the expenses incurred or expected to be incurred are likely to exceed, or have exceeded, the details given to the creditors prior to the determination of the basis of remuneration, and

(iii) the reasons for that excess; and

(f) a statement of the rights of creditors or, in a members' voluntary winding up, of members–

(i) to request information about remuneration or expenses under rule 18.9, and

(ii) to challenge the office-holder's remuneration and expenses under rule 18.34.

18.4(2) [Information required irrespective of whether payment during period of report] The information about remuneration and expenses is required irrespective of whether payment was made in respect of them during the period of the report.

(See General Note after r.18.13.)

18.5 Information about pre-administration costs

18.5(1) [Progress reports] Where the administrator has made a statement of pre-administration costs under rule 3.35(10)(a)–

(a) if they are approved under rule 3.52, the first progress report after the approval must include a statement setting out the date of the approval and the amounts approved;

(b) while any of the costs remain unapproved each successive report must include a statement of any steps taken to get approval.

18.5(2) [Where no approval] However if either the administrator has decided not to seek approval, or another insolvency practitioner entitled to seek approval has told the administrator of that practitioner's decision not to seek approval then–

(a) the next report after that must include a statement of whichever is the case; and

(b) no statement under paragraph (1)(b) is required in subsequent reports.

(See General Note after r.18.13.)

18.6 Progress reports in administration: timing

18.6(1) [Six-month periods] The administrator's progress report in an administration must cover the periods of–

(a) six months starting on the date the company entered administration; and

(b) each subsequent period of six months.

18.6(2) [Periods unaffected by change in administrator] The periods for which progress reports are required under paragraph (1) are unaffected by any change in the administrator.

18.6(3) [Notice by succeeding administrator] However where an administrator ceases to act the succeeding administrator must, as soon as reasonably practicable after being appointed, deliver a notice to the creditors of any matters about which the succeeding administrator thinks the creditors should be informed.

18.6(4) [Copy progress to registrar of companies and creditors] The administrator must deliver a copy of a report to the registrar of companies and the creditors within one month of the end of the period covered by the report unless the report is a final progress report under rule 3.55.

18.6(5) [Default, penalty] An administrator who makes default in delivering a progress report within the time limit in paragraph (4) is guilty of on offence and liable to a fine and, for continued contravention, to a daily default fine.

(See General Note after r.18.13.)

18.7 Progress reports in voluntary winding up: timing

18.7(1) [Application of rule] This rule applies for the purposes of sections 92A and 104A and prescribes the periods for which reports must be made.

18.7(2) [12-month periods] The liquidator's progress reports in a voluntary winding up must cover the periods of–

(a) 12 months starting on the date the liquidator is appointed; and

(b) each subsequent period of 12 months.

18.7(3) [Periods unaffected by change in liquidator] The periods for which progress reports are required under paragraph (2) are unaffected by any change in the liquidator.

18.7(4) [Notice by succeeding liquidator] However where a liquidator ceases to act the succeeding liquidator must, as soon as reasonably practicable after being appointed, deliver a notice to the members (in a members' voluntary winding up) or to members and creditors (in a creditors' voluntary winding up) of any matters about which the succeeding liquidator thinks the members or creditors should be informed.

18.7(5) [No progress report after final account] A progress report is not required for any period which ends after a notice is delivered under rule 5.9(1) (members' voluntary winding up) or after the date to which a final account is made up under section 106 and is delivered by the liquidator to members and creditors (creditors' voluntary winding up).

18.7(6) [Copy progress to registrar of companies, etc.] The liquidator must deliver a copy of each progress report within two months after the end of the period covered by the report to–

(a) the registrar of companies (who is a prescribed person for the purposes of sections 92A and 104A);

(b) the members; and

(c) in a creditors' voluntary liquidation, the creditors.

(See General Note after r.18.13.)

18.8 Progress reports in winding up by the court and bankruptcy: timing

18.8(1) [12-month periods] The liquidator or trustee's progress report in a winding up by the court or bankruptcy must cover the periods of–

(a) 12 months starting on the date a person other than the official receiver is appointed liquidator or trustee; and

(b) each subsequent period of 12 months.

18.8(2) [Periods unaffected by change in liquidator/trustee; exceptions] The periods for which progress reports are required under paragraph (1) are unaffected by any change in the liquidator or trustee unless at any time the official receiver becomes liquidator or trustee in succession to another person in which case–

(a) the current reporting period under paragraph (1) ends; and

(b) if a person other than the official receiver is subsequently appointed as liquidator or trustee a new period begins under paragraph (1)(a).

18.8(3) [Notice by succeeding liquidator/trustee] Where a liquidator or trustee ceases to act the succeeding liquidator or trustee must as soon as reasonably practicable after being appointed, deliver a notice to the creditors of any matters about which the succeeding liquidator or trustee thinks the creditors should be informed.

18.8(4) [No progress report after final account] A progress report is not required for any period which ends after the date to which a final account or report is made up under section 146 (winding up by the court) or section 331 (bankruptcy) and is delivered by the liquidator or the trustee to the creditors.

18.8(5) [Winding up: copy progress to registrar of companies, etc.] In a winding up by the court, the liquidator must deliver a copy of the progress report to the registrar of companies, the members of the company and the creditors within two months of the end of the period covered by the report.

18.8(6) [Bankruptcy: copy progress to creditors] In a bankruptcy, the trustee must deliver a copy of the progress report to the creditors within two months of the end of the period covered by the report.

(See General Note after r.18.13.)

18.9 Creditors' and members' requests for further information in administration, winding up and bankruptcy

18.9(1) [Who may make written request] The following may make a written request to the office-holder for further information about remuneration or expenses (other than pre-administration costs in an administration) set out in a progress report under rule 18.4(1)(b), (c) or (d) or a final report or account under rule 18.14–

(a) a secured creditor;

(b) an unsecured creditor with the concurrence of at least 5% in value of the unsecured creditors (including the creditor in question);

(c) members of the company in a members' voluntary winding up with at least 5% of the total voting rights of all the members having the right to vote at general meetings of the company;

(d) any unsecured creditor with the permission of the court; or

(e) any member of the company in a members' voluntary winding up with the permission of the court.

18.9(2) [Request or application court for permission filed in court] A request, or an application to the court for permission, by such a person or persons must be made or filed with the court (as applicable) within 21 days of receipt of the report or account by the person, or by the last of them in the case of an application by more than one member or creditor.

18.9(3) [Duty of office-holder to respond to request] The office-holder must, within 14 days of receipt of such a request respond to the person or persons who requested the information by–

(a) providing all of the information requested;

(b) providing some of the information requested; or

(c) declining to provide the information requested.

18.9(4) [Office-holder may provide partial information or decline request] The office-holder may respond by providing only some of the information requested or decline to provide the information if–

(a) the time or cost of preparation of the information would be excessive; or

(b) disclosure of the information would be prejudicial to the conduct of the proceedings;

(c) disclosure of the information might reasonably be expected to lead to violence against any person; or

(d) the office-holder is subject to an obligation of confidentiality in relation to the information.

18.9(5) [Reasons in r.18.9(4)] An office-holder who does not provide all the information or declines to provide the information must inform the person or persons who requested the information of the reasons for so doing.

18.9(6) [Application to court] A creditor, and a member of the company in a members' voluntary winding up, who need not be the same as the creditor or members who requested the information, may apply to the court within 21 days of–

(a) the office-holder giving reasons for not providing all of the information requested; or

(b) the expiry of the 14 days within which an office-holder must respond to a request.

18.9(7) [Court order] The court may make such order as it thinks just on an application under paragraph (6).

(See General Note after r.18.13.)

18.10 Administration, creditors' voluntary liquidation and compulsory winding up: reporting distribution of property to creditors under rule 14.13

18.10(1) [Application of rule] This rule applies where in an administration, creditors' voluntary liquidation or compulsory winding up there has been a distribution of property to creditors under rule 14.13.

18.10(2) [Content of account or summary of receipts and payments] In any account or summary of receipts and payments which is required to be included in an account or report prepared under a rule listed in paragraph (3) the office-holder must–

(a) state the estimated value of the property divided among the creditors of the company during the period to which the account or summary relates; and

(b) provide details of the basis of the valuation as a note to the account or summary of receipts and payments.

18.10(3) [Application of r.18.10(2) to rr.3.63, 6.25, 18.3, 18.14] Paragraph (2) applies to the following–

(a) rule 3.63 (administrator's intention to resign);

(b) rule 6.25 (liquidator's resignation and replacement);

(c) rule 7.61 (liquidator's resignation);

(d) rule 18.3 (contents of progress report); and

(e) rule 18.14 (contents of final account (winding up) and final report (bankruptcy)).

(See General Note after r.18.13.)

18.11 Voluntary winding up: reporting arrangement under section 110

18.11(1) [Application of rule] This rule applies where in a voluntary winding up there has been an arrangement under section 110 and a distribution to members has taken place under section 110(2) or (4).

18.11(2) [Content of account or summary of receipts and payments] In any account or summary of receipts and payments which is required to be included in an account or report prepared under a section or rule listed in paragraph (3) the liquidator must–

(a) state the estimated value during the period to which the account or report relates of–

(i) the property transferred to the transferee,

(ii) the property received from the transferee, and

(iii) the property distributed to members under section 110(2) or (4); and

(b) provide details of the basis of the valuation as a note to the account or summary of receipts and payments.

18.11(3) [Application of r.18.11(2) to provisions of IA 1986 and to IR 2016] Paragraph (2) applies to the following–

(a) section 92A and rule 18.7 (members' voluntary winding up: progress report to company at year's end);

(b) section 94 and rule 18.14 (members' voluntary winding up: final account prior to dissolution);

(c) section 104A (creditors' voluntary winding up: progress report to company and creditors at year's end);

(d) section 106 and rules 6.28 and 18.14 (creditors' voluntary winding up: final account prior to dissolution).

(See General Note after r.18.13.)

18.12 Members' voluntary winding up: reporting distribution to members other than under section 110

18.12(1) [Application of rule] This rule applies where in a members' voluntary winding up there has been a distribution of property to members in its existing form other than under an arrangement under section 110.

18.12(2) [Content of account or summary of receipts and payments] In any account or summary of receipts and payments which is required to be included in an account or report prepared under a section or rule listed in paragraph (3) the liquidator must–

(a) state the estimated value of the property distributed to the members of the company during the period to which the account or report relates; and

(b) provide details of the basis of the valuation as a note to the account or summary of receipts and payments.

18.12(3) [Application of r.18.12(2) to IA 1986 ss.92A, 94, IR 2016 r.5.6] Paragraph (2) applies to the following–

(a) section 92A (progress report);

(b) section 94 (final account prior to dissolution);

(c) rule 5.6 (liquidator's resignation).

(See General Note after r.18.13.)

18.13 Bankruptcy proceedings: reporting distribution of property to creditors under section 326

18.13(1) [Application of rule] This rule applies in bankruptcy where there has been a distribution of property to creditors under section 326.

18.13(2) [Content of account or report] In an account or report which the trustee is required to prepare under a section or rule listed in paragraph (3) the trustee must–

(a) state the estimated value of the property distributed among the creditors during the period to which the account or report relates; and

(b) provide details of the basis of the valuation in a note to the account or report.

18.13(3) [Application of r.18.13(2) to IA 1986 s.331, IR 2016 r.10.77, Pt 18 Ch.2, 3] Paragraph (2) applies to the following–

(a) section 331 (final report to creditors in bankruptcy);

(b) rule 10.77 (consideration of appointment of replacement trustee); and

(c) Chapters 2 and 3 of this Part.

General Note to rr.18.3–18.13

These rules are designed to ensure that creditors and others (in the case of corporate insolvency, the members of the company and the registrar of companies) are kept informed of the state of the company's or bankrupt's affairs in the various situations referred to.

The timing of progress reports depends on the insolvency procedure concerned: every six months from first *entry into administration* (r.18.6 and note about extensions in r.18.3(5)) but every 12 months from *appointment of a liquidator or trustee in bankruptcy* and the timing in each case is unaffected by a change in office-holder (rr.18.7, 18.8). Rule 18.7(4) makes clear that when a liquidator ceases to act the succeeding liquidator must notify members (in either voluntary winding up) and creditors (in a creditors' voluntary winding up) of matters which he thinks they should be informed. A progress report is not required in winding up or bankruptcy for any period ending after the date to which a liquidator's final account or trustee in bankruptcy's final report is made up provided the final account or report has been delivered to the creditors as required by r.18.14 (r.18.8(4)). In compulsory winding up the liquidator must deliver a copy of the progress report to the registrar of companies under r.18.8(5) using Form "WU07".

Rule 18.9 empowers creditors or (in liquidation) members with the necessary authority in r.18.9(1) to seek further information relating to the office-holder's remuneration and expenses. If the office-holder is unwilling to comply on any of the grounds listed in r.18.9(4) the matter may be resolved by the court under r.18.9(7).

Rule 18.11 requires a liquidator who makes a distribution in specie to members in a reconstruction under IA 1986 s.110 to give details of the basis of the valuation of the property concerned, and this is also a requirement when the liquidator in a voluntary winding up makes a distribution in specie otherwise than under s.110 (r.18.12). The equivalent in bankruptcy is r.18.13.

For a liquidator's final account or trustee in bankruptcy's final report, see r.18.14 below.

On the standard contents (for notices other than gazetted notices) in rr.18.6–18.8 see rr.1.11, 1.15–1.18 and on delivery of documents to Companies House in those rules see rr.1.19–1.22.

Chapter 3

Final accounts in winding up and final reports in bankruptcy

[Note: a document required by the Act or these Rules must also contain the standard contents set out in Part 1.]

18.14 Contents of final account (winding up) and final report (bankruptcy)

18.14(1) [Content of account] The liquidator's final account under section 94, 106 or 146 or the trustee's final report under section 331 must contain an account of the liquidator's administration of the winding up or of the trustee's administration of the bankruptcy including–

(a) a summary of the office-holder's receipts and payments, including details of the office-holder's remuneration and expenses; and

(b) details of the basis fixed for the office-holder's remuneration.

18.14(2) [Statement as to prescribed part] The liquidator's final account under section 106 or 146(1)(a) must also include a statement as to the amount paid to unsecured creditors by virtue of section 176A.

18.14(3) [Further details of account] The final account or report to creditors or members must also contain–

(a) details of the remuneration charged and expenses incurred by the office-holder during the period since the last progress report (if any);

(b) a description of the things done by the office-holder in that period in respect of which the remuneration was charged and the expenses incurred; and

(c) a summary of the receipts and payments during that period.

18.14(4) [Basis of office-holder's remuneration if not previously fixed] If the basis of the office-holder's remuneration had not been fixed by the date to which the last progress report was made up, the final account or report must also include details of the remuneration charged in the period of any preceding progress report in which details of remuneration were not included.

18.14(5) [Where basis of remuneration fixed as set amount] Where the basis of remuneration has been fixed as a set amount, it is sufficient for the office-holder to state that amount and to give details of the expenses charged within the period in question.

General Note

With the demise of meetings in general and final meetings in particular as from 6 April 2017 (ss.94, 106, 146 are substituted, and s.331 heavily amended, by SBEEA 2015) the office-holder must now only prepare a final account and send copies to creditors (unless opted-out), members and the registrar of companies in winding up (using Form LIQ113 (in MVL), Form LIQ14 (in CVL) or Form WU15 (in compulsory winding up)) and just to creditors (unless opted-out) in bankruptcy containing the requirements of those sections and this rule, which does not apply in administration (for which see r.3.56).

Chapter 4

Remuneration and expenses in administration, winding up and bankruptcy

[Note: a document required by the Act or these Rules must also contain the standard contents set out in Part 1.]

18.15 Application of Chapter

18.15(1) [Application of Ch.4] This Chapter applies to the remuneration of–

(a) an administrator;

(a) a liquidator; and

(b) a trustee in bankruptcy.

18.15(2) [No application to remuneration of provisional liquidator or interim receiver] This Chapter does not apply to the remuneration of a provisional liquidator or an interim receiver.

General Note

As with the rest of Pt 18, rr.18.15–18.38 on remuneration applies only in administration, winding up and bankruptcy. These rules do not apply to a provisional liquidator, an interim receiver (r.18.15(2) or, of course, to the official receiver (r.18.1(2)).

For the rules relating to the payment of pre-administration remuneration and expenses, see r.3.52.

18.16 Remuneration: principles

18.16(1) [Entitlement to remuneration] An administrator, liquidator or trustee in bankruptcy is entitled to receive remuneration for services as office-holder.

18.16(2) [Basis of remuneration to be fixed] The basis of remuneration must be fixed–

(a) as a percentage of the value of–

(i) the property with which the administrator has to deal, or

(ii) the assets which are realised, distributed or both realised and distributed by the liquidator or trustee;

(b) by reference to the time properly given by the office-holder and the office-holder's staff in attending to matters arising in the administration, winding up or bankruptcy; or

(c) as a set amount.

18.16(3) [Combination of bases] The basis of remuneration may be one or a combination of the bases set out in paragraph (2) and different bases or percentages may be fixed in respect of different things done by the office-holder.

18.16(4) [Fees estimate and expenses where time basis proposed] Where an office-holder, other than in a members' voluntary winding up, proposes to take all or any part of the remuneration on the basis set out in paragraph (2)(b), the office-holder must, prior to the determination of which of the bases set out in paragraph (2) are to be fixed, deliver to the creditors–

(a) a fees estimate; and

(b) details of the expenses the office-holder considers will be, or are likely to be, incurred.

18.16(5) [Fees estimate etc. expected if administrator to become liquidator] The fees estimate and details of expenses given under paragraph (4) may include remuneration expected to be charged and expenses expected to be incurred if the administrator becomes the liquidator where the administration moves into winding up.

18.16(6) [Information before determination of bases] An office-holder, other than in a members' voluntary winding up, must deliver to the creditors the information required under paragraph (7) before the determination of which of the bases set out in paragraph (2) is or are to be fixed, unless the information has already been delivered under paragraph (4).

18.16(7) [Information under r.18.16(6)] The information the office-holder is required to give under this paragraph is–

(a) the work the office-holder proposes to undertake; and

(b) details of the expenses the office-holder considers will be, or are likely to be, incurred.

18.16(8) [Matters to be determined in fixing basis of remuneration] The matters to be determined in fixing the basis of remuneration are–

(a) which of the bases set out in paragraph (2) is or are to be fixed and (where appropriate) in what combination;

(b) the percentage or percentages (if any) to be fixed under paragraphs (2)(a) and (3);

(c) the amount (if any) to be set under paragraph (2)(c).

18.16(9) [Matters for regard in determination] In arriving at that determination, regard must be had to the following–

(a) the complexity (or otherwise) of the case;

(b) any respects in which, in connection with the company's or bankrupt's affairs, there falls on the office-holder, any responsibility of an exceptional kind or degree;

(c) the effectiveness with which the office-holder appears to be carrying out, or to have carried out, the office-holder's duties; and

(d) the value and nature of the property with which the office-holder has to deal.

18.16(10) [Proposed liquidator in CVL] A proposed liquidator in respect of a creditors' voluntary winding up may deliver to the creditors the information required by paragraphs (4) or (6) before becoming liquidator in which case that person is not required to deliver that information again if that person is appointed as liquidator.

General Note

The IA 1986 is silent on the fixing of the insolvency office-holders' remuneration.

Although the courts may be adopting a more circumspect approach to the quantum of remuneration they are still supportive of the right to be remunerated for work properly completed—on this see *Oraki v Dean & Dean (a firm)* [2013] EWCA Civ 1629. The right of a trustee in bankruptcy to be properly remunerated was upheld in *Green v Austin* [2014] B.P.I.R. 1176 where the court indicated that it is no justification to refuse to set aside a transfer at an undervalue simply because the main beneficiary would be the insolvency practitioner in respect of his legitimate claim for fees and expenses.

The wording of r.18.16(1) provides that an administrator, liquidator or trustee in bankruptcy is entitled to receive remuneration for services as "office-holder": this contrasts with the wording in IR 1986 where each type of office-holder was provided for in different Parts of the rules and was entitled to be remunerated "as such" (see IR 1986 rr.2.106(1), 4.148A(1), 4.127(1), 6.138A(1)). In *Brilliant Independent Media Specialists Ltd; Maxwell v Brookes* [2015] B.C.C. 113, where the creditors' committee had refused to sanction further remuneration, the court fixed a fair reasonable and proportionate sum, stressing that IR 1986 r.2.106(1) (now IR 2016 r.18.16(1)) applied to remuneration only while administrators were in office for services "as such", so that the remuneration for work done after termination of the administrators' appointment when the company was placed into winding up with new office-holders as liquidators was a matter between the administrators and the liquidators. The court referred to the need under what is now *Practice Direction: Insolvency Proceedings* [2018] B.C.C. 241 para.21.4 for a succinct narrative of the work done, which had not been available in the instant case.

Rule 18.16(2) provides the three methods for fixing the "basis of remuneration" by: (i) a percentage (or percentages) of the value of the property which an administrator has to deal with or of the assets which are realised and/or distributed by a liquidator or trustee in bankruptcy, (ii) time spent by the office-holder and his staff on the insolvency procedure (for which a pre-estimate must be given), or (iii) a set amount. It may be a combination of more than one of these. On time properly spent in r.18.16(2)(b) see *Salliss v Hunt* [2014] EWHC 229 (Ch); [2014] B.P.I.R. 754 and *Re Borodzicz* [2016] B.P.I.R. 24 (Chief Registrar Baister).

Capping does not amount to the fixing of remuneration "as a set amount" under what is now r.18.16(2)(c): *Re Pudsey Steel Services Ltd* [2015] B.P.I.R. 1459.

On the determining factors on fixing the basis of remuneration in r.18.16(9) see the bankruptcy case of *Freeburn v Hunt* [2010] B.P.I.R. 325.

An office-holder may, in an appropriate case, also be paid remuneration and allowed expenses for work done in relation to property which does not form part of the assets in the insolvency procedure, for instance property held by the company on trust, or property subject to a fixed or floating charge where the chargee has not appointed a receiver (see *Re Leyland DAF Ltd, Buchler v Talbot* [2004] UKHL 9; [2004] 2 A.C. 298; [2004] B.C.C. 214 at [63]). In *Re Berkeley Applegate (Investment Consultants) Ltd (No.2)* (1988) 4 B.C.C. 279 the liquidator in a creditors' voluntary winding up discovered, after extensive investigations, that certain assets standing in the name of the company were held by it on trust for people who had paid money to the company for investment. Although there was no statutory authority for payment, the court held that fair compensation could be awarded to the liquidator on general equitable principles. In later proceedings (*Re Berkeley Applegate (Investment Consultants) Ltd (No.3)* (1989) 5 B.C.C. 803), it was held that this remuneration could not properly be charged on the company's assets in the liquidation but only on the trust funds themselves. For a modern example of the latter principle see *Gillan v HEC Enterprises Ltd* [2016] EWHC 3179 (Ch).

For comment on assessment of a trustee's remuneration see *Mirror Group Newspapers v Maxwell* [1998] B.C.C. 324 at 336, per Ferris J. On taxation the claim for fees and disbursements was largely upheld—see the note in [1999] B.C.C. 684 (a rare instance of a determination on a matter of taxation of costs being reported). Matters in this area were reviewed by the Ferris Working Party in 1998. A revised SIP 9, *Payments to Insolvency Office-holders and their Associates*, is in effect from December 2015.

18.17 Remuneration of joint office-holders

18.17 Where there are joint office-holders it is for them to agree between themselves how the remuneration payable should be apportioned; and any dispute arising between them may be referred–

(a) to the committee, to the creditors (by a decision procedure) or (in a members' voluntary winding up) the company in general meeting, for settlement by resolution; or

(b) to the court, for settlement by order.

General Note

Should joint appointees not agree on remuneration apportionment, this dictates how the matter should be resolved with any liquidation or creditors' committee the first port of call. The court will be the last resort.

18.18 Remuneration: procedure for initial determination in an administration

18.18(1) [Application of rule] This rule applies to the determination of the officer-holder's remuneration in an administration.

18.18(2) [Duty of committee] It is for the committee to determine the basis of remuneration.

18.18(3) [Committee fails to determine basis or no committee] If the committee fails to determine the basis of the remuneration or there is no committee then the basis of remuneration must be fixed by a decision of the creditors by a decision procedure except in a case under paragraph (4).

18.18(4) [Where administrator statement of insufficient funds to pay secured creditors] Where the administrator has made a statement under paragraph 52(1)(b) of Schedule B1 that there are insufficient funds for distribution to unsecured creditors other than out of the prescribed part and either there is no committee, or the committee fails to determine the basis of remuneration, the basis of the administrator's remuneration may be fixed by–

(a) the consent of each of the secured creditors; or

(b) if the administrator has made or intends to make a distribution to preferential creditors–

(i) the consent of each of the secured creditors, and

(ii) a decision of the preferential creditors in a decision procedure.

(See General Note after r.18.21.)

18.19 Remuneration: procedure for initial determination in a members' voluntary winding up

18.19 In a members' voluntary winding up, it is for the company in general meeting to determine the basis of remuneration.

(See General Note after r.18.21.)

18.20 Remuneration: procedure for initial determination in a creditors' voluntary winding up or a winding up by the court

18.20(1) [Application of rule] This rule applies to the determination of the office-holder's remuneration in a creditors' voluntary winding up or a winding up by the court.

18.20(2) [Duty of committee] It is for the committee to determine the basis of remuneration.

18.20(3) [Committee fails to determine basis or no committee] If the committee fails to determine the basis of remuneration or there is no committee then the basis of remuneration may be fixed by a decision of the creditors by a decision procedure.

18.20(4) [Basis of remuneration fixed under r.18.18] However where an administrator becomes liquidator in either of the following two cases the basis of remuneration fixed under rule 18.18 for the administrator is treated as having been fixed for the liquidator, and paragraphs (2) and (3) do not apply.

18.20(5) [Cases when r.18.20(4) applies] The two cases are where–

(a) a company which is in administration moves into winding up under paragraph 83 of Schedule B1 and the administrator becomes the liquidator; and

(b) a winding-up order is made immediately upon the appointment of an administrator ceasing to have effect and the court under section 140(1) appoints as liquidator the person whose appointment as administrator has ceased to have effect.

(See General Note after r.18.21.)

18.21 Remuneration: procedure for initial determination in a bankruptcy

18.21(1) [Application of rule] This rule applies to the determination of the office-holder's remuneration in a bankruptcy.

18.21(2) [Duty of committee] It is for the committee to determine the basis of remuneration.

18.21(3) [Committee fails to determine basis or no committee] If the committee fails to determine the basis of the remuneration or there is no committee then the basis of the remuneration may be fixed by a decision of the creditors by a decision procedure.

General Note

Although an office-holder is entitled to receive remuneration for his services, he may not fix his own remuneration, and has no right to retain remuneration out of the assets if they are insufficient to pay other expenses of the liquidation ranking no lower than the remuneration in question: *Re Salters Hall School Ltd (in liq.)* [1998] B.C.C. 503.

Not surprisingly the company determines the basis of remuneration in a members' voluntary liquidation. It is the liquidation committee who decides in compulsory and creditors' voluntary liquidation and the creditors' committee in administration and bankruptcy and, failing these, the creditors by a decision procedure, subject to rr.18.18(4) and 18.20(4) following administration.

18.22 Application of scale fees where creditors fail to fix the basis of the office-holder's remuneration

18.22(1) [Application of rule] This rule applies where in a winding up by the court or bankruptcy, the liquidator or trustee–

(a) has requested the creditors to fix the basis of remuneration under rule 18.20(3) or 18.21(3) as applicable and the creditors have not done so; or

(b) in any event if the basis of remuneration is not fixed by the creditors within 18 months after the date of the liquidator's or trustee's appointment.

18.22(2) [Realisation scale in Sch.11] The liquidator or trustee is entitled to such sum as is arrived at (subject to paragraph (3)) by–

(a) applying the realisation scale set out in Schedule 11 to the moneys received by the liquidator or trustee from the realisation of the assets of the company or bankrupt (including any Value Added Tax on the realisation but after deducting any sums paid to secured creditors in respect of their securities and any sums spent out of money received in carrying on the business of the company or bankrupt); and

(b) adding to the sum arrived at under sub-paragraph (a) such sum as is arrived at by applying the distribution scale set out in Schedule 11 to the value of assets distributed to creditors of the company or bankrupt (including payments made in respect of preferential debts) and to contributories.

18.22(3) [Realisation scale not to exceed bankruptcy debts, expenses etc.] In a bankruptcy that part of the trustee's remuneration calculated under paragraph (2) by reference to the realisation scale must not exceed such sum as is arrived at by applying the realisation scale to such part of the bankrupt's assets as are required to pay–

(a) the bankruptcy debts (including any interest payable by virtue of section 328(4)) to the extent required to be paid by these Rules (ignoring those debts paid otherwise than out of the proceeds of the realisation of the bankrupt's assets or which have been secured to the satisfaction of the court);

(b) the expenses of the bankruptcy other than–

  (i) fees or the remuneration of the official receiver, and

  (ii) any sums spent out of money received in carrying on the business of the bankrupt;

(c) fees payable by virtue of any order made under section 415; and

(d) the remuneration of the official receiver.

General Note

This rule introduces Sch.11 scale fees utilising realisations and distributions in insolvent liquidation and bankruptcy where the creditors have failed to fix the liquidator's or trustee's fees within 18 months of appointment: it does not apply in administration. Schedule 11 is identical to IR 1986 Sch.6 and the figures therein have not changed since the latter was introduced in 2004. (Before then, in a case decided under BA 1914 the court decided that the use of the official receiver's scale was not suitable to be applied to value the work of a private practitioner: *Upton v Taylor and Colley* [1999] B.P.I.R. 168.)

18.23 Remuneration: application to the court to fix the basis

18.23(1) [Application if basis not fixed] If the basis of the administrator's remuneration or the liquidator's remuneration in a voluntary winding up is not fixed under rules 18.18 to 18.20 (as applicable) then the administrator or liquidator must apply to the court for it to be fixed.

18.23(2) [Attempt to fix before application] Before making such an application the liquidator or administrator must attempt to fix the basis in accordance with rules 18.18 to 18.20.

18.23(3) [Time limit for application] An application under this rule may not be made more than 18 months after the date of the administrator's or liquidator's appointment.

18.23(4) [Notice to creditors in MVL] In a members' voluntary winding up–

(a) the liquidator must deliver at least 14 days' notice of such an application to the company's contributories, or such one or more of them as the court may direct; and

(b) the contributories may nominate one or more of their number to appear, or be represented, and to be heard on the application.

GENERAL NOTE

Where no rate was fixed under rr.18.18 or 18.20 an administrator or members' voluntary liquidator *must* apply to court within 18 months of appointment to fix it. In *Re Super Aguri F1 Ltd, Long v Turner* [2011] B.C.C. 452 administrators were held entitled to claim remuneration on a time cost basis for additional work necessitated by threats of litigation made by a majority creditor opposed to their appointment.

For an example of the exercise by the court of its jurisdiction under r.18.23, see *Re Tony Rowse NMC Ltd* [1996] B.C.C. 196.

18.24 Remuneration: administrator, liquidator or trustee seeking increase etc.

18.24 An office-holder who considers the rate or amount of remuneration fixed to be insufficient or the basis fixed to be inappropriate may–

(a) request the creditors to increase the rate or amount or change the basis in accordance with rules 18.25 to 18.27;

(b) apply to the court for an order increasing the rate or amount or changing the basis in accordance with rule 18.28.

(See General Note after r.18.27.)

18.25 Application for an increase etc. in remuneration: the general rule

18.25(1) [Application of rule] This rule applies to a request by an office-holder in accordance with rule 18.24 for an increase in the rate or amount of remuneration or a change in the basis.

18.25(2) [Request to creditors] Subject to the exceptions set out in rules 18.26 and 18.27, where the basis of the office-holder's remuneration has been fixed by the committee an administrator, liquidator or trustee may make such a request to the creditors for approval by a decision procedure.

(See General Note after r.18.27.)

18.26 First exception: administrator has made a statement under paragraph 52(1)(b) of Schedule B1

18.26(1) [Application of exception] This exception applies in an administration where–

(a) the basis of the administrator's remuneration has been fixed by the committee; and

(b) the administrator has made a statement under paragraph 52(1)(b) of Schedule B1.

18.26(2) [Approve by secured creditors, preferential creditors] A request by the administrator for an increase in the rate or amount of remuneration or a change in the basis must be approved by–

(a) the consent of each of the secured creditors; or

(b) if the administrator has made or intends to make a distribution to preferential creditors–

(i) the consent of each of the secured creditors, and

(ii) a decision of the preferential creditors in a decision procedure.

(See General Note after r.18.27.)

18.27 Second exception: administrator who had applied for increase etc. under rule 18.24 becomes liquidator

18.27(1) [Application of exception] This exception applies in a liquidation where–

(a) an administrator has become the liquidator;

(b) the remuneration had been determined by the committee in the preceding administration;

(c) the basis of the liquidator's remuneration is treated under rule 18.20(4) and (5) as being that which was fixed in the administration; and

(d) the administrator had subsequently requested an increase under rule 18.24.

18.27(2) [Application to court] A request by the liquidator for an increase in the rate or amount of remuneration or a change in the basis may only be made by application to the court.

18.27(3) [Rule 18.28(6)–(8) apply] Rule 18.28(6) to (8) apply to such an application.

GENERAL NOTE TO RR.18.24–18.27

These important technical rules apply in administration, winding up and bankruptcy where the office-holder seeks an increase of the fixed remuneration rate which he considers to be insufficient or the basis to be inappropriate. Generally the first recourse is to the creditors (where a liquidation/creditors' committee fixed the initial rate) by a decision procedure (rr.18.24, 18.25). This is subject to the exceptions for an administrator where the creditors' committee set the remuneration and the administrator's proposals stated under IA 1986 Sch.B1 para.52(1)(b) that there were only funds to pay unsecured creditors out of the prescribed part under s.176A and not otherwise, in which event the secured and preferential creditors become involved, and where an administrator becomes liquidator remaining subject to the administration rate, in which event only the court can decide (rr.18.26, 18.27). On the meaning of "decision procedure" see rr.15.2, 15.3. Otherwise the application is to the court, on which see r.18.28.

18.28 Remuneration: recourse by administrator, liquidator or trustee to the court

18.28(1) [Application of rule] This rule applies to an application by an office-holder to the court in accordance with rule 18.24 for an increase in the rate or amount of remuneration or change in the basis.

18.28(2) [Application by administrator] An administrator may make such an application where the basis of the administrator's remuneration has been fixed–

(a) by the committee and the administrator has requested that the rate or amount be increased or the basis changed by decision of the creditors (by a decision procedure), but the creditors have not changed it;

(b) by decision of the creditors (by decision procedure); or

(c) by the approval of either the secured creditors or the preferential creditors or both in a case where the administrator has made a statement under paragraph 52(1)(b) of Schedule B1.

18.28(3) [Application by liquidator] A liquidator may make such an application where the basis of the liquidator's remuneration has been fixed–

(a) by the committee, and the liquidator has requested that the rate or amount be increased or the basis changed by decision of the creditors (by a decision procedure), but the creditors have not changed it;

(b) by decision of the creditors (by a decision procedure);

(c) under rule 18.20(4) and (5) or 18.22; or

(d) in a members' voluntary winding up, by the company in general meeting.

18.28(4) [Application by trustee in bankruptcy] A trustee may make such an application where the trustee's remuneration has been fixed–

(a) by the committee and the trustee has requested that the amount be increased or the basis changed by decision of the creditors (by a decision procedure), but the creditors have not changed it;

(b) by decision of the creditors (by a decision procedure); or

(c) under rule 18.22.

18.28(5) [Administrator's notice to creditors] Where an application is made under paragraph (2)(c), the administrator must deliver notice to each of the creditors whose approval was sought under rule 18.18(4).

18.28(6) [Deliver of notice by office-holder] The office-holder must deliver a notice of the application at least 14 days before the hearing as follows–

(a) in an administration, a creditors' voluntary winding up, a winding up by the court or a bankruptcy–

(i) to the members of the committee, or

(ii) if there is no committee to such one or more of the creditors as the court may direct;

(b) in a members' voluntary winding up, to the company's contributories, or such one or more of them as the court may direct.

18.28(7) [Nomination of person to appear or be represented on application] The committee, the creditors or the contributories (as the case may be) may nominate one or more of their number to appear or be represented and to be heard on the application.

18.28(8) [Costs] The court may, if it appears to be a proper case (including in a members' voluntary winding up), order the costs of the office-holder's application, including the costs of any member of the committee appearing or being represented on it, or of any creditor or contributory so appearing or being represented on it, to be paid as an expense of the estate.

General Note

The court will always have the final say on issues of office-holders' remuneration. For governing principles note *Practice Statement: The Fixing and Approval of Remuneration of Appointees* [2004] B.C.C. 912, replaced by *Practice Direction: Insolvency Proceedings* [2012] B.C.C. 265 Pt 5 and, from 29 July 2014, *Practice Direction: Insolvency Proceedings* [2018] B.C.C. 241 Pt 6, reproduced in App.IV to this *Guide*, and containing nine guiding principles by which the court will consider remuneration applications. Remuneration fixed and approved by the court will be "fair, reasonable and commensurate with the nature and extent of the work properly undertaken or to be undertaken by the office-holder ... by a process which is consistent and predictable" (*Practice Direction*, para.21.1). The then *Practice Statement* was considered by David Richards J in *Simion v Brown* [2007] B.P.I.R. 412 where a creditor challenged the remuneration claimed by the trustee. The judge made a number of important points. In small bankruptcies the amount of remuneration/expenses will be inevitably appear disproportionately large. A trustee has to carry out certain statutory functions and this has cost implications. The guiding principle under the *Practice Statement* was whether the work undertaken provided value for money. Itemisation of all expenses was to be recommended rather than a general claim for overheads. The *Practice Statement* was also considered in *Hunt v Yearwood-Grazette* [2009] B.P.I.R. 810 on an application a trustee and by Lord Malcolm in the Court of Session (Outer House) at para.[32] in *Re Blair Carnegie Nimmo (as Liquidator of St Margaret's School Edinburgh Ltd)* [2013] CSOH 4; [2013] B.P.I.R. 188.

The Court of Appeal reviewed the status of the former *Practice Statement* in *Brook v Reed* [2011] EWCA Civ 331; [2011] B.C.C. 423; [2012] 1 W.L.R. 419. In issuing what was in effect a *Practice Note* it was emphasised by David Richards J that the 2004 *Practice Statement* was meant to provide a set of guiding principles rather than to create new substantive law. That said, the general utility of these guidelines in all situations where the remuneration of an appointee was at issue was stressed. See the illuminating piece by Tribe and Hunt [2010] 23 Insolv. Int. 139.

For an account of a disputed case (*Re Cabletel Installations Ltd* (unreported, 20 April 2004)), see Moss (2005) 18 Insolv. Int. 61. For another disputed case see *Re Brilliant Independent Media Specialists Ltd; Maxwell v Brookes*. In *Re Super Aguri F1 Ltd, Long v Turner* [2011] B.C.C. 452 administrators were held entitled to claim remuneration on a time cost basis for additional work necessitated by threats of litigation made by a majority creditor opposed to their appointment. See also *Hyndman v Readman*, 2004 S.L.T. 959. The provisional liquidator case of *Jacob v UIC Insurance Co Ltd* [2006] EWHC 2717 (Ch); [2007] B.C.C.167, discussed in the note to r.7.38, is also relevant. For an example of an application by a trustee in bankruptcy see *Barker v Bajjon* [2008] B.P.I.R. 771.

In *Secondus v Atkinson* [2013] B.P.I.R. 632 Registrar Jones adopted a challenging approach towards a claim for remuneration and expenses where the case in question could not be characterised as a challenging one. Items in the claim put forward for approval were tested on a line by line basis and often scaled back. The strict vetting of remuneration claims is apparent in *Re Brilliant Independent Media Specialists Ltd* [2015] B.C.C. 113 where the creditors' committee had refused to sanction further remuneration and Registrar Jones, after detailed line by line scrutiny, culled back a remuneration/expenses claim presented by administrators to fix a fair reasonable and proportionate sum.

18.29 Remuneration: review at request of administrator, liquidator or trustee

18.29(1) [Office-holder request to change basis] Where, after the basis of the office-holder's remuneration has been fixed, there is a material and substantial change in the circumstances which were taken into account in fixing it, the office-holder may request that the basis be changed.

18.29(2) [To whom request must be made] The request must be made–

(a) to the company, where in a members' voluntary liquidation the company fixed the basis in general meeting;

(b) to the committee, where the committee fixed the basis;

(c) to the creditors or a particular class of creditors where the creditors or that class of creditors fixed the basis;

(d) by application to the court, where the court fixed the basis;

(e) to the committee if there is one and otherwise to the creditors where, in a winding up or bankruptcy, the remuneration was determined under rule 18.22.

18.29(3) [Preceding provisions of Ch.4 apply to request] The preceding provisions of this Chapter which apply to the fixing of the office-holder's remuneration apply to a request for a change as appropriate.

18.29(4) [Non-application of r.18.27] However the exception in rule 18.27 which would require such an application to be made to the court in the circumstances there set out does not apply.

18.29(5) [Date of change of basis] Any change in the basis of remuneration applies from the date of the request under paragraph (2) and not for any earlier period.

General Note

This rule was originally added on 6 April 2010, to allow an office-holder to seek a review of his remuneration if there has been a "material and substantial change in the circumstances" on which the remuneration was based.

18.30 Remuneration: exceeding the fee estimate

18.30(1) [Duty not to exceed estimate without approval] The office-holder must not draw remuneration in excess of the total amount set out in the fees estimate without approval.

18.30(2) [To whom approval must be made] The request for approval must be made–

(a) where the committee fixed the basis, to that committee;

(b) where the creditors or a class of creditors fixed the basis, to the creditors or that class of creditors;

(c) where the court fixed the basis, to the court;

and rules 18.16 to 18.23 apply as appropriate.

18.30(3) [Matters request for approval to specify] The request for approval must specify–

(a) the reasons why the office-holder has exceeded, or is likely to exceed, the fees estimate;

(b) the additional work the office-holder has undertaken or proposes to undertake;

(c) the hourly rate or rates the office-holder proposes to charge for each part of that additional work;

(d) the time that additional work has taken or the office-holder expects that work will take;

(e) whether the office-holder anticipates that it will be necessary to seek further approval; and

(f) the reasons it will be necessary to seek further approval.

General Note

Fee estimates were first introduced on 1 October 2015. The duty on office-holders in this rule is not that they must not exceed the estimate; rather that they must not do so without approval of either the liquidation/creditors' committee, the creditors or the court, depending on who fixed the basis.

18.31 Remuneration: new administrator, liquidator or trustee

18.31(1) [Application of rule] This rule applies where a new administrator, liquidator or trustee is appointed in place of another.

18.31(2) [Previous basis continues until new decision, determination, resolution or court order] Any decision, determination, resolution or court order in effect under the preceding provisions of this Chapter immediately before the former office-holder ceased to hold office (including any application of scale fees under rule 18.22) continues to apply in relation to the remuneration of the new office-holder until a further decision, determination, resolution or court order is made in accordance with those provisions.

General Note

This maintains the status quo in relation to fees on replacement of an office-holder unless and until it is properly changed.

18.32 Remuneration: apportionment of set fees

18.32(1) [Application of rule] This rule applies where the basis of the office-holder's remuneration is a set amount under rule 18.16(2)(c) and the office-holder ceases (for whatever reason) to hold office before the time has elapsed or the work has been completed in respect of which the amount was set.

18.32(2) [Request or application] A request or application may be made to determine what portion of the amount should be paid to the former office-holder or the former office-holder's personal representative in respect of the time which has actually elapsed or the work which has actually been done.

18.32(3) [Who may make request or application] The request or application may be made by–

(a) the former office-holder or the former office-holder's personal representative within the period of 28 days beginning with the date upon which the former office-holder ceased to hold office; or

(b) the office-holder for the time being in office, if the former office-holder or the former office-holder's personal representative has not applied by the end of that period.

18.32(4) [To whom application to be made] The request or application to determine the portion must be made to the relevant person being–

(a) the company, where the company is in members' voluntary liquidation and it fixed the basis in general meeting;

(b) the committee, where the committee fixed the basis;

(c) the creditors or a class of creditors where the creditors or that class fixed the basis;

(d) the court where the court fixed the basis.

18.32(5) [Administration] In an administration where the circumstances set out in rule 18.18(4) apply the relevant person is to be determined under that paragraph.

18.32(6) [Copy request or application to "recipient"] The person making the request or application must deliver a copy of it to the office-holder for the time being or to the former office-holder or the former office-holder's personal representative, as the case may be ("the recipient").

18.32(7) [Notice of recipient's intention to make representations] The recipient may, within 21 days of receipt of the copy of the request or application, deliver notice of intent to make representations to the relevant person or to appear or be represented before the court on an application to the court.

18.32(8) [Period for determination] No determination may be made upon the request or application until either–

(a) the expiry of the 21 days, or

(b) if the recipient delivers a notice of intent, the recipient has been given the opportunity to make representations or to appear or be represented.

18.32(9) [Application to increase portion] Where the former office-holder or the former office-holder's personal representative (whether or not the original person making the request or application) considers that the portion so determined is insufficient that person may apply–

(a) to the creditors for a decision increasing the portion, in the case of a determination by the committee;

(b) to the court, in the case of a decision or resolution (as the case may be) of–

(i) the creditors (whether under paragraph (4)(c) or under sub-paragraph (a)), or

(ii) the company in general meeting.

18.32(10) [Rule 18.32(6)–(8) apply to application] Paragraphs (6) to (8) apply to an application under paragraph (9) as appropriate.

General Note

Set fees were introduced from 6 April 2010. This rule allows apportionment of set fees if the office-holder ceases to hold office before the time or work has been completed for which the fee was set so that the former office-holder can be paid the portion for the work actually done.

18.33 Remuneration: variation of the application of rules 18.29, 18.30 and 18.32

18.33(1) [Application of rule] This rule applies where the basis of remuneration has been fixed in accordance with rule 18.18(4) and all of the following apply–

(a) there is now, or is likely to be, sufficient property to enable a distribution to be made to unsecured creditors other than by virtue of section 176A(2)(a); and

(b) the administrator or liquidator in a winding up which immediately follows an administration makes a request under rule 18.29, 18.30 or 18.32.

18.33(2) [To whom request under rr.18.29, 18.30, 18.32 to be made] A request under 18.29, 18.30 or 18.32, must be made–

(a) where there is a committee, to the committee; or

(b) where there is no committee, to the creditors for a decision by decision procedure.

General Note

This rule states to whom a request must be made under rr.18.29, 18.30 or 18.32 where the administrator's proposals stated under IA 1986 Sch.B1 para.52(1)(b) that there were only funds to pay unsecured creditors out of the prescribed part under IA 1986 s.176A, but there is now or likely to be sufficient property to enable a distribution to unsecured creditors without recourse to the prescribed part.

18.34 Remuneration and expenses: application to court by a creditor or member on grounds that remuneration or expenses are excessive

18.34(1) [Application of rule] This rule applies to an application in an administration, a winding-up or a bankruptcy made by a person mentioned in paragraph (2) on the grounds that–

(a) the remuneration charged by the office-holder is in all the circumstances excessive;

(b) the basis fixed for the office-holder's remuneration under rules 18.16, 18.18, 18.19, 18.20 and 18.21 (as applicable) is inappropriate; or

(c) the expenses incurred by the office-holder are in all the circumstances excessive.

18.34(2) [Who may make application] The following may make such an application for one or more of the orders set out in rule 18.36 or 18.37 as applicable–

(a) a secured creditor,

(b) an unsecured creditor with either–

(i) the concurrence of at least 10% in value of the unsecured creditors (including that creditor), or

(ii) the permission of the court, or

(c) in a members' voluntary winding up–

(i) members of the company with at least 10% of the total voting rights of all the members having the right to vote at general meetings of the company, or

(ii) a member of the company with the permission of the court.

18.34(3) [Time limit for application] The application by a creditor or member must be made no later than eight weeks after receipt by the applicant of the progress report under rule 18.3, or final report or account under rule 18.14 which first reports the charging of the remuneration or the incurring of the expenses in question ("the relevant report").

General Note

If an unsecured creditor wishes to challenge the trustee's remuneration as excessive he must have the support of 10 per cent in value of the creditors or permission of the court. There is a similar requirement for members in members' voluntary winding up.

Creditors may only challenge under r.18.34 an office-holder's remuneration and expenses already incurred, and not future sums: *Re Calibre Solicitors Ltd, Justice Capital Ltd v Murphy* [2015] B.P.I.R. 435. The procedure under r.18.34 is not the only mechanism for creditors challenging the liquidator's remuneration: in *Autobrokers Ltd v Dymond* [2015] EWHC 2691 (Ch) creditors sought a court order under IA 1986 s.112 directing the liquidators to summon a creditors' meeting for the purpose.

See also General Note after r.18.37.

18.35 Remuneration and expenses: application to court by a bankrupt on grounds that remuneration or expenses are excessive

[Note: where a bankrupt is applying for an annulment under section 282(1)(b) the bankrupt may also make an application in respect of the trustee's remuneration or expenses. See rule 10.134.]

18.35(1) [Application to court for permission to apply] A bankrupt may, with the permission of the court, make an application on the grounds that–

(a) the remuneration charged by the office-holder is in all the circumstances excessive;

(b) the expenses incurred by the office-holder are in all the circumstances excessive.

18.35(2) [Orders in r.18.36(4)] The bankrupt may make such an application for one or more of the orders set out in rule 18.36(4).

18.35(3) [Time limit for application] The application must be made no later than eight weeks after receipt by the bankrupt of the report under rule 10.87.

18.35(4) [Surplus of assets required] The court must not give the bankrupt permission to make an application unless the bankrupt shows that–

(a) there is (or would be but for the remuneration or expenses in question); or

(b) it is likely that there will be (or would be but for the remuneration or expenses in question),

a surplus of assets to which the bankrupt would be entitled.

18.35(5) [Other matters court to have regard] Paragraph (4) is without prejudice to the generality of the matters which the court may take into account in determining whether to give the bankrupt permission.

(See General Note after r.18.37.)

18.36 Applications under rules 18.34 and 18.35 where the court has given permission for the application

18.36(1) [Application of rule] This rule applies to applications made with permission under rules 18.34 and 18.35.

18.36(2) [Court to fix venue for hearing] Where the court has given permission, it must fix a venue for the application to be heard.

18.36(3) [Notice to office-holder of venue etc.] The applicant must, at least 14 days before the hearing, deliver to the office-holder a notice stating the venue and accompanied by a copy of the application and of any evidence on which the applicant intends to rely.

18.36(4) [Court order if application well-founded] If the court considers the application to be well-founded, it must make one or more of the following orders–

(a) an order reducing the amount of remuneration which the office-holder is entitled to charge;

(b) an order reducing any fixed rate or amount;

(c) an order changing the basis of remuneration;

(d) an order that some or all of the remuneration or expenses in question is not to be treated as expenses of the administration, winding up or bankruptcy;

(e) an order for the payment of the amount of the excess of remuneration or expenses or such part of the excess as the court may specify by–

(i) the administrator or liquidator or the administrator's or liquidator's personal representative to the company, or

(ii) the trustee or the trustee's personal representative to such person as the court may specify as property comprised in the bankrupt's estate;

(f) any other order that it thinks just.

18.36(5) [Order under r.18.36(4)(b), (c)] An order under paragraph (4)(b) or (c) may only be made in respect of periods after the period covered by the relevant report.

18.36(6) [Costs of application] Unless the court orders otherwise the costs of the application must be paid by the applicant, and are not payable as an expense of the administration, winding up or bankruptcy.

(See General Note after r.18.37.)

18.37 Applications under rule 18.34 where the court's permission is not required for the application

18.37(1) [Power of court to dismiss application] On receipt of an application under rule 18.34 for which the court's permission is not required, the court may, if it is satisfied that no sufficient cause is shown for the application, dismiss it without giving notice to any party other than the applicant.

18.37(2) [Otherwise court to fix venue] Unless the application is dismissed, the court must fix a venue for it to be heard.

18.37(3) [Notice to office-holder of venue, etc.] The applicant must, at least 14 days before any hearing, deliver to the office-holder a notice stating the venue with a copy of the application and of any evidence on which the applicant intends to rely.

18.37(4) [Court order if application well-founded] If the court considers the application to be well-founded, it must make one or more of the following orders–

(a) an order reducing the amount of remuneration which the office-holder is entitled to charge;

(b) an order reducing any fixed rate or amount;

(c) an order changing the basis of remuneration;

(d) an order that some or all of the remuneration or expenses in question be treated as not being expenses of the administration or winding up or bankruptcy;

(e) an order for the payment of the amount of the excess of remuneration or expenses or such part of the excess as the court may specify by–

(i) the administrator or liquidator or the administrator's or liquidator's personal representative to the company, or

(ii) the trustee or the trustee's personal representative to such person as the court may specify as property comprised in the bankrupt's estate;

(f) any other order that it thinks just.

18.37(5) [Order under r.18.37(4)(b), (c)] An order under paragraph (4)(b) or (c) may only be made in respect of periods after the period covered by the relevant report.

18.37(6) [Costs of application] Unless the court orders otherwise the costs of the application must be paid by the applicant, and are not payable as an expense of the administration or as winding up or bankruptcy.

General Note to rr.18.35–18.37

An application under r.18.35 is not necessary if a bankrupt successfully applies for an annulment under IA 1986 s.282(1)(b) as the debts have been paid or secured since the bankruptcy order, he may also make an application in respect of the trustee's remuneration or expenses which if well founded, must result in the court reducing the trustee in bankruptcy's remuneration under r.10.134.

For a consideration of what is now r.18.35(4) where the issue of whether permission to challenge remuneration arose see the ruling of Snowden J in *Mattu v Toone* [2015] EWHC 3506 (Ch); [2016] B.P.I.R. 408.

Rules 18.36 and 18.37 provide greater procedural detail to applications under rr.18.35 and 18.36 depending on whether court permission for such an application has been granted or is not necessary.

18.38 Remuneration of a liquidator or trustee who realises assets on behalf of a secured creditor

18.38(1) [Calculation unless otherwise agreed] A liquidator or trustee who realises assets on behalf of a secured creditor is entitled to such sum by way of remuneration as is arrived at as follows, unless the liquidator or trustee has agreed otherwise with the secured creditor–

(a) in a winding up–

(i) where the assets are subject to a charge which when created was a mortgage or a fixed charge, such sum as is arrived at by applying the realisation scale in Schedule 11 to the monies received in respect of the assets realised (including any sums received in respect of Value Added Tax on them but after deducting any sums spent out of money received in carrying on the business of the company),

(ii) where the assets are subject to a charge which when created was a floating charge such sum as is arrived at by–

(aa) first applying the realisation scale in Schedule 11 to monies received by the liquidator from the realisation of the assets (including any Value Added Tax on the realisation but ignoring any sums received which are spent in carrying on the business of the company),

(bb) then by adding to the sum arrived at under sub-paragraph (a)(ii)(aa) such sum as is arrived at by applying the distribution scale in Schedule 11 to the value of the assets distributed to the holder of the charge and payments made in respect of preferential debts; or

(b) in a bankruptcy such sum as is arrived at by applying the realisation scale in Schedule 11 to the monies received in respect of the assets realised (including any Value Added Tax on them).

18.38(2) [Remuneration from proceeds realised] The sum to which the liquidator or trustee is entitled must be taken out of the proceeds of the realisation.

General Note

This relates to remuneration where the liquidator or trustee in bankruptcy is really acting for the benefit of a secured creditor and the parties have not agreed on remuneration: the Sch.11 realisation scale (and distribution scale in winding up) is utilised. Note that the sum due is taken from the realisation proceeds. Schedule 11 is identical to IR 1986 Sch.6.

Part 19

Disclaimer in Winding Up and Bankruptcy

Introductory note to Part 19

This new Part combines the provisions on disclaimer previously located separately in IR 1986 Pts 4 and 6 dealing with liquidation and bankruptcy. Note the presumption of validity stated in r.19.10.

[Note: a document required by the Act or these Rules must also contain the standard contents set out in Part 1.]

19.1 Application of this Part

19.1 This Part applies to disclaimer by a liquidator under section 178 (winding up) and by a trustee under section 315 (bankruptcy).

(See General Note after r.19.11.)

19.2 Notice of disclaimer (sections 178 and 315)

19.2(1) [Title and content of notice] An office-holder's notice of disclaimer of property under section 178 (winding up) or section 315 (bankruptcy) must (as appropriate)–

(a) have the title–

(i) "Notice of disclaimer under section 178 of the Insolvency Act 1986" (in the case of a winding up), or

(ii) "Notice of disclaimer under section 315 of the Insolvency Act 1986" (in the case of a bankruptcy);

(b) identify the company or the bankrupt;

(c) identify and provide contact details for the office-holder;

(d) contain such particulars of the property disclaimed as will enable it to be easily identified;

(e) state–

(i) that the liquidator of the company disclaims all the company's interest in the property, or

(ii) that the trustee of the bankrupt's estate disclaims all the bankrupt's interest in the property.

19.2(2) [Authentication] The notice must be authenticated and dated by the office-holder.

19.2(3) [Registered land] If the property consists of registered land–

(a) the notice must state the registered title number; and

(b) the office-holder must deliver a copy of the notice to the Chief Land Registrar as soon as reasonably practicable after authenticating the notice.

19.2(4) [Liquidator to deliver copy notice to registrar of companies] The liquidator must, as soon as reasonably practicable after authenticating the notice, deliver a copy of the notice to the registrar of companies.

19.2(5) [Trustee in bankruptcy to file copy notice in court or on bankruptcy file] The trustee must, as soon as reasonably practicable after authenticating the notice, file a copy of the notice–

(a) with the court; or

(b) where the bankruptcy is based on a bankruptcy application, on the bankruptcy file.

19.2(6) [Interest in land or building] If the property consists of land or buildings the nature of the interest must be stated in the notice.

19.2(7) [Date of disclaimer] The date of disclaimer for the purposes of section 178(4)(a) (winding up) or section 315(3)(a) (bankruptcy) is the date on which the liquidator or trustee authenticated the notice.

(See General Note after r.19.11.)

19.3 Notice of disclaimer to interested persons (sections 178 and 315)

19.3(1) [Time limit for delivery of copy notice] The office-holder must deliver a copy of the notice of disclaimer within seven business days after the date of the notice to every person who (to the office-holder's knowledge)–

(a) claims an interest in the disclaimed property;

(b) is under any liability in relation to the property, not being a liability discharged by the disclaimer; and

(c) if the disclaimer is of an unprofitable contract, is a party to the contract or has an interest under it.

19.3(2) [Subsequent knowledge] If it subsequently comes to the office-holder's knowledge that a person has an interest in the disclaimed property which would have entitled that person to receive a copy of the notice under paragraph (1) then the office-holder must deliver a copy to that person as soon as reasonably practicable.

19.3(3) [Subsequent knowledge of leasehold or dwelling house] If it subsequently comes to the office-holder's knowledge that a person has an interest in the disclaimed property which would have entitled that person to receive a copy of the notice under rule 19.4 or 19.5 then the office-holder must serve a copy on that person as soon as reasonably practicable.

19.3(4) [No duty under r.19.3(2), (3)] The office-holder is not required to deliver or serve a copy of a notice under paragraph (2) or (3) if–

(a) the office-holder is satisfied that the person has already been made aware of the disclaimer and its date, or

(b) the court, on the office-holder's application, orders that delivery or service of a copy is not required in the particular case.

(See General Note after r.19.11.)

19.4 Notice of disclaimer of leasehold property (sections 179 and 317)

19.4 Where a notice of disclaimer relates to leasehold property the office-holder must serve any copies of the notice of disclaimer which are required by either section 179 (winding up) or section 317 (bankruptcy) within seven business days after the date of the notice of disclaimer.

(See General Note after r.19.11.)

19.5 Notice of disclaimer in respect of a dwelling house (bankruptcy) (section 318)

19.5(1) [Application of rule] This rule applies in a bankruptcy where the disclaimer is of property in a dwelling house.

19.5(2) [Time limit for service] The trustee must serve any copies of the notice of disclaimer which are required by section 318 within seven business days after the date of the notice of disclaimer.

19.5(3) [Service on person aged under 18] A notice, or copy notice in relation to the disclaimer by a trustee of property in a dwelling house which is to be served on a person under the age of 18 may be served on the person's parent or guardian.

(See General Note after r.19.11.)

19.6 Additional notices of disclaimer

19.6 An office-holder who is disclaiming property may at any time deliver a copy of the notice of the disclaimer to any other person whom the office-holder thinks ought, in the public interest or otherwise, to be informed of the disclaimer.

(See General Note after r.19.11.)

19.7 Records

19.7 The office-holder must include in the records of the insolvency a record of–

(a) the name and address of each person to whom a copy of the notice of disclaimer has been delivered or served under rules 19.3 to 19.6, with the nature of the person's interest;

(b) the date on which the copy of the notice was delivered to or served on that person;

(c) the date on which the liquidator delivered a copy of the notice to the registrar of companies;

(d) the date on which the trustee filed a copy of the notice with the court or on the bankruptcy file; and

(e) if applicable, the date on which a copy of the notice was delivered to the Chief Land Registrar.

(See General Note after r.19.11.)

19.8 Application for permission to disclaim in bankruptcy (section 315(4))

19.8(1) [Application of rule] This rule applies where section 315(4) requires the trustee to obtain the court's permission to disclaim property claimed for the bankrupt's estate under section 307 or 308.

19.8(2) [Application without notice] The trustee may apply for permission without notice to any other party.

19.8(3) [Accompanying report] The application must be accompanied by a report–

(a) containing such particulars of the property as will enable it to be easily identified;

(b) setting out the reasons why, the property having been claimed for the bankrupt's estate, the trustee is now applying for the court's permission to disclaim it; and

(c) stating the persons (if any) who have been informed of the trustee's intention to make the application.

19.8(4) [Copy of consent to disclaimer] If the report says that any person has consented to the disclaimer, a copy of that consent must accompany the report.

19.8(5) [Power of court to grant permission, etc.] The court may grant the permission, and may, before doing so–

(a) order that notice of the application be delivered to all such persons who, if the property is disclaimed, will be entitled to apply for a vesting or other order under section 320; and

(b) fix a venue for the hearing of the application.

(See General Note after r.19.11.)

19.9 Application by interested party for decision on disclaimer (sections 178(5) and 316)

19.9(1) [Application of rule] This rule applies where an interested party makes an application under section 178(5) (winding up) or section 316 (bankruptcy) to the office-holder in respect of any property.

19.9(2) [Delivery of application to office-holder] The applicant must deliver the application to the office-holder and must provide proof of delivery in accordance with rule 1.52 if requested.

19.9(3) [Where property cannot be disclaimed without court's permission] If in a bankruptcy the trustee cannot disclaim the property concerned without the court's permission and the trustee applies for permission within the period of 28 days mentioned in section 316(1)(b), then the court must extend the time allowed for giving notice of disclaimer to a date not earlier than the date fixed for hearing the application.

(See General Note after r.19.11.)

19.10 Disclaimer presumed valid and effective

19.10 Any disclaimer of property by the office-holder is presumed valid and effective, unless it is proved that the office-holder has been in breach of the office-holder's duties relating to the giving of notice of disclaimer or otherwise under sections 178 to 180 (winding up) or sections 315 to 319 (bankruptcy), or under this Part.

(See General Note after r.19.11.)

19.11 Application for exercise of court's powers under section 181 (winding up) or section 320 (bankruptcy)

19.11(1) [Application of rule] This rule applies to an application under section 181 (winding up) or section 320 (bankruptcy) for a court order to vest or deliver disclaimed property.

19.11(2) [Time limit for application] The application must be made within three months of the applicant becoming aware of the disclaimer, or of the applicant receiving a copy of the office-holder's notice of disclaimer delivered under rule 19.3 to 19.6, whichever is the earlier.

19.11(3) [Witness statement] The applicant must file with the application a witness statement stating–

(a) whether the application is made under–

- (i) section 181(2)(a) (claim of interest in the property),
- (ii) section 181(2)(b) (liability not discharged),
- (iii) section 320(2)(a) (claim of interest in the property),
- (iv) section 320(2)(b) (liability not discharged), or
- (v) section 320(2)(c) (occupation of a dwelling-house);

(b) the date on which the applicant received a copy of the office-holder's notice of disclaimer, or otherwise became aware of the disclaimer; and

(c) the grounds of the application and the order sought.

19.11(4) [Court to fix venue for hearing] The court must fix a venue for hearing the application.

19.11(5) [Applicant to deliver notice of venue, etc. to office-holder] The applicant must, not later than five business days before the date fixed, deliver to the office-holder notice of the venue, accompanied by copies of the application and the filed witness statement.

19.11(6) [Power of court to give directions] On hearing the application, the court may give directions as to any other persons to whom notice of the application and the grounds on which it is made should be delivered.

19.11(7) [Sealed copies of order] The court must deliver sealed copies of any order made on the application to the applicant and the office-holder.

19.11(8) [Leasehold or property in dwelling house] If the property disclaimed is of a leasehold nature, or in a bankruptcy is property in a dwelling house, and section 179 (winding up), 317 or 318 (bankruptcy) applies to suspend the effect of the disclaimer, the court's order must include a direction giving effect to the disclaimer.

19.11(9) [Non-application of r.19.11(8)] However, paragraph (8) does not apply if, before the order is drawn up, other applications under section 181 (winding up) or section 320 (bankruptcy) are pending in relation to the same property.

General Note to rr.19.1–19.11

The statutory powers of disclaimer are contained in IA 1986 ss.178–182 (winding up) and ss.315–321 (bankruptcy). These rules supplement those provisions. On property "of a leasehold nature", see IA 1986 ss.179, 182, 317 and 321, on land "subject to a rentcharge" see ss.180 and 319 and on property "in a dwelling house", see s.318.

In both liquidation and bankruptcy the liquidator and trustee in bankruptcy must under r.19.2 date and authenticate the notice of disclaimer and, if the property consists of registered land, deliver a copy of the authenticated notice of disclaimer to the Chief Land Registrar. (In relation to the liquidator's or trustee in bankruptcy's dealings with the Chief Land Registrar under r.19.2, see the Land Registry Practice Guide 35 (PG 35 Corporate Insolvency), available at *http://www.landregistry.gov.uk/professional/guides/practice-guide-35* and Practice Guide 34 (PG 34 Personal insolvency) available at *https://www.gov.uk/government/publications/personal-insolvency*). Since 6 April 2010, it is no longer a requirement that a liquidator must file a copy of the disclaimer in court and in due course this be returned to the liquidator endorsed by the court. Instead, a copy must be sent to Companies House (and where appropriate to the Chief Land Registrar). There is no longer a prescribed form of disclaimer but the content of the notice is prescribed by r.19.2 and Form NDISC must be used for notice to Companies House. In bankruptcy, the trustee must file a copy of the disclaimer notice in court (or on the bankruptcy file in an out-of-court bankruptcy).

Rules 19.3–19.6 relate to the dissemination of the notice of disclaimer.

There is no requirement in IR 2016 comparable to IR 1986 rr.4.192, 6.184, for a liquidator or trustee in bankruptcy to require persons to declare their interest in any property which he is considering disclaiming.

The former rules prior to 6 April 2010, which required the office-holder to keep the court informed regarding the disclaimer, have been replaced by an obligation to keep certain records (r.19.7).

Rule 19.8 develops IA 1986 s.315(4) (leave of court for certain notices of disclaimer). Sections 178(5) and 316 must be read in the light of r.19.9.

The onus of proving that a disclaimer has been exercised improperly is naturally cast upon the person challenging it (r.19.10). Sections 181 and 320 are to be viewed in the light of r.19.11. Note especially the time limitation upon applications: the period of three months specified in r.19.11(2) may be extended at the discretion of the court: *WH Smith Ltd v Wyndham Investments Ltd* [1994] B.C.C. 699. In the same case it was held that, although a lease becomes ownerless following a disclaimer, it does not disappear, but ceases to exist only on the occurrence of one of the normal means of termination—effluxion of time, surrender or retaking of possession by the landlord.

For interpretation of what are now IR 2016 rr.19.2 and 19.10 see *Hunt v Conwy CBC* [2013] EWHC 1154 (Ch); [2013] B.P.I.R. 790. With regard to a failure to comply with the procedure laid down in r.19.2 Sir William Blackburne concluded that the notice of disclaimer was not invalid but merely that the presumption of validity had been removed.

Part 20

Debtors and their Families at Risk of Violence: Orders not to Disclose Current Address

Introductory note to Part 20

This Part has a protective aim by ensuring that personal and residential details of potential victims of violence do not become freely available through standard and transparent insolvency procedures. Thus, there are mechanisms by which IVA debtor, bankrupts and those seeking DROs can apply to keep addresses confidential.

[Note: a document required by the Act or these Rules must also contain the standard contents set out in Part 1.]

20.1 Application of this Part and interpretation

20.1(1) [Application of Pt 20] The rules in this Part apply where disclosure or continuing disclosure of the current address or whereabouts of a debtor to other persons (whether to the public generally or to specific persons) might reasonably be expected to lead to violence against the debtor or against a person who normally resides with the debtor as a member of the debtor's family.

20.1(2) ["Current address", "family"] In this Part–

"current address" means the debtor's residential address and any address at which the debtor currently carries on business; and "family" in the expression "debtor's family" has the same meaning in relation to a debtor other than a bankrupt as is provided by section 385(1) in respect of a bankrupt.

(See General Note after r.20.7.)

20.2 Proposed IVA (order for non-disclosure of current address)

20.2(1) [Application of rule] This rule applies where a debtor intends to make a proposal for an IVA and has received notice of consent to act from the nominee.

20.2(2) [Application by debtor] The debtor may make an application for an order as set out in paragraph (4) for the non-disclosure of the debtor's current address.

20.2(3) [Accompanying witness statement] The application must be accompanied by a witness statement referring to this rule and containing sufficient evidence to satisfy the court that rule 20.1(1) applies.

20.2(4) [Power of court to make order] If the court is satisfied that the circumstances set out in rule 20.1(1) apply, the court may order that if the IVA is approved–

(a) the debtor's current address must be omitted from–

(i) any part of the court file of the proceedings in relation to the debtor's IVA which is open to inspection,

(ii) the debtor's identification details required to be entered on the individual insolvency register under rule 11.14,

(iii) any notice or advertisement under rule 8.36 of an order under section 261 to annul the bankruptcy order where an IVA is approved; and

(b) where there is a requirement in these Rules to identify the debtor, the debtor's identification details must not include details of the debtor's current address.

20.2(5) [Further order of court] Where the court makes such an order, it may further order that the details to be entered on the individual insolvency register must include instead such other details of the debtor's addresses or whereabouts as the court thinks just, including details of any address at which the debtor has previously resided or carried on business.

(See General Note after r.20.7.)

20.3 IVA (order for non-disclosure of current address)

20.3(1) [Application of rule] This rule applies where a debtor has entered into an IVA.

20.3(2) [Who may make application] The following may make an application for an order as set out in paragraph (4) for the non-disclosure of the debtor's current address–

(a) the debtor;

(b) the supervisor;

(c) the official receiver (whether acting as a supervisor or otherwise); and

(d) the Secretary of State.

20.3(3) [Accompanying witness statement] The application must be accompanied by a witness statement referring to this rule and containing sufficient evidence to satisfy the court that rule 20.1(1) applies.

20.3(4) [Power of court to make order] If the court is satisfied that the circumstances set out in rule 20.1(1) apply, the court may order that–

(a) the debtor's current address must be omitted from–

(i) any part of the court file of the proceedings in relation to the debtor which is open to inspection,

(ii) the debtor's identification details entered or required to be entered on the individual insolvency register under rule 11.14, and

(iii) any notice or advertisement under rule 8.35 of an order under section 261 to annul the bankruptcy order where an IVA is approved; and

(b) where there is a requirement in these Rules to identify the debtor, the debtor's identification details must not include the debtor's current address.

20.3(5) [Further order of court] Where the court makes such an order, it may further order that the details to be entered on the individual insolvency register must include instead such other details of the debtor's addresses or whereabouts as the court thinks just, including details of any address at which the debtor has previously resided or carried on business.

(See General Note after r.20.7.)

20.4 Debt relief application (order for non-disclosure of current address)

20.4(1) [Application of rule] This rule applies where a debtor intends to make a debt relief application and has been issued with a unique identifier for the application.

20.4(2) [Application by debtor] The debtor may make an application for an order as set out in paragraph (4) for the non-disclosure of the debtor's current address.

20.4(3) [Accompanying witness statement] The application must be accompanied by a witness statement referring to this rule and containing sufficient evidence to satisfy the court that rule 20.1(1) applies.

20.4(4) [Power of court to make order] If the court is satisfied that the circumstances set out in rule 20.1(1) apply, the court may order that if a debt relief order is made–

(a) the debtor's current address must be omitted from–

(i) any part of the court file of the proceedings in relation to the debtor which is open to inspection, and

(ii) the debtor's identification details required to be entered on the individual insolvency register under rule 11.18; and

(b) where there is a requirement in these Rules to identify the debtor, the debtor's identification must not include the debtor's current address.

20.4(5) [Further order of court] Where the court makes such an order, it may further order that the details to be entered on the individual insolvency register must include instead such other details of the debtor's addresses or whereabouts as the court thinks just, including details of any address at which the debtor has previously resided or carried on business.

(See General Note after r.20.7.)

20.5 Bankruptcy application (order for non-disclosure of current address)

20.5(1) [Application of rule] This rule applies where a debtor intends to make a bankruptcy application and has been issued with a unique identifier for the application.

20.5(2) [Application by debtor] The debtor may make an application for an order as set out in paragraph (4) for the non-disclosure of the debtor's current address.

20.5(3) [Accompanying witness statement] The application must be accompanied by a witness statement referring to this rule and containing sufficient evidence to satisfy the court that rule 20.1(1) applies.

20.5(4) [Power of court to make order] If the court is satisfied that the circumstances set out in rule 20.1(1) apply, the court may order that if a bankruptcy order is made–

(a) the debtor's current address must be omitted from–

(i) any part of the bankruptcy file which is open to inspection,

(ii) the details in respect of the debtor to be entered on the individual insolvency register under rule 11.16,

(iii) the details in respect of the debtor to be entered in the bankruptcy order; and

(b) where there is a requirement in these Rules to identify the debtor, the debtor's identification details must not include the debtor's current address.

20.5(5) [Further order of court] Where the court makes an order under paragraph (4), it may further order that such other details of the debtor's addresses or whereabouts as the court thinks just, including details of any address at which the debtor has previously resided or carried on business, are to be included in–

(a) the details in respect of the debtor kept on or to be entered on the individual insolvency register under rule 11.16;

(b) the details in respect of the debtor included on the bankruptcy file; or

(c) the description of the debtor to be inserted in the bankruptcy order.

(See General Note after r.20.7.)

20.6 Bankruptcy and debt relief proceedings (order for non-disclosure of current address)

20.6(1) ["Debtor" in r.20.6] For the purposes of this rule, "debtor" means a person subject to a bankruptcy order, a debt relief order, a bankruptcy restrictions order, a debt relief restrictions order, a bankruptcy restrictions undertaking or a debt relief restrictions undertaking.

20.6(2) [Who may make application] The following may make an application for an order as set out in paragraph (4) for the non-disclosure of the debtor's current address–

(a) the debtor;

(b) the official receiver; or

(c) in respect of a bankruptcy order, a bankruptcy restrictions order or a bankruptcy restrictions undertaking, the trustee or the Secretary of State.

20.6(3) [Accompanying witness statement] The application must be accompanied by a witness statement referring to this rule and containing sufficient evidence to satisfy the court that rule 20.1(1) applies.

20.6(4) [Power of court to make order] If the court is satisfied that the circumstances set out in rule 20.1(1) apply, the court may order that–

(a) the debtor's current address must be omitted from–

(i) any part of the court file or bankruptcy file of the proceedings in relation to the debtor which is open to inspection,

(ii) the debtor's identification details entered or required to be entered on the individual insolvency register under rule 11.16 (bankruptcy orders), rule 11.18 (debt relief orders), or the bankruptcy restrictions register or the debt relief restrictions register under 11.20 (as the case may be), and

(iii) the details in respect of the debtor to be entered in the bankruptcy order or debt relief order;

(b) the full title of the proceedings must be amended by the omission of the debtor's current address; and

(c) where there is a requirement in these Rules to identify the debtor, the debtor's identification details must not include the debtor's current address.

20.6(5) [Further order of court] Where the court makes an order under paragraph (4), it may further order that such other details of the debtor's addresses or whereabouts as the court thinks just, including details of any address at which the debtor has previously resided or carried on business, are to be included in–

(a) the full title of any proceedings;

(b) the details in respect of the debtor kept on or to be entered on the relevant register; or

(c) the description of the debtor to be inserted in the bankruptcy order or the debt relief order.

(See General Note after r.20.7.)

20.7 Additional provisions in respect of orders under rule 20.6(4)

20.7(1) [Application of rule] This rule applies where the court is making an order under rule 20.6(4) in respect of a debtor who is subject to a bankruptcy order, a bankruptcy restrictions order or a bankruptcy restrictions undertaking.

20.7(2) [Power of court to make order] The court may make either or both of the following further orders–

(a) that the details of the debtor required to be included in any notice to be gazetted or otherwise advertised must not include the debtor's current address; and.

(b) that the details of the debtor required to be included in any such notice to be gazetted or otherwise advertised must instead of the debtor's current address include such other details of the debtor's addresses or whereabouts as the court thinks just, including details of any address at which the debtor has previously resided or carried on business.

20.7(3) [Delivery and publication of notice of order under r.20.6(4)] Where the court makes an order under rule 20.6(4) amending the full title of the proceedings by the omission of the debtor's current address from the description of the debtor, the official receiver–

(a) must as soon as reasonably practicable deliver notice of it to the Chief Land Registrar, for corresponding amendment of the register; and

(b) may cause notice of the order to be–

(i) gazetted, or

(ii) both gazetted and delivered in such other manner as the official receiver thinks fit.

20.7(4) [Publication of notice under r.20.7(3)] A notice of the amendment of the title of the proceedings which is published in accordance with paragraph (3)–

(a) must omit the current address of the debtor;

(b) must contain the amended title of the proceedings, and the date of the bankruptcy order; and

(c) must not include the description under which the proceedings were previously published.

General Note to rr.20.1–20.7

This Part applies only in personal insolvency and is not relevant to corporate insolvency. Its predecessor provisions (certainly to rr.20.1–20.6) were first introduced into IR 1986 as recently as 6 April 2010. Rule 20.7 is the only rule in this Part that had no counterpart in IR 1986.

Rules 20.2–20.6 relate to non-disclosure of the current address of the debtor in a proposal for an IVA (r.20.2), the IVA itself (r.20.3), debt relief applications (r.20.4), bankruptcy out-of-court applications (r.20.5) and proceedings in relation to debtors subject to a bankruptcy order, a debt relief order (DRO), a bankruptcy restrictions order (BRO), a debt relief restrictions order, a bankruptcy restrictions undertaking (BRU) or a debt relief restrictions undertaking (r.20.6). "Debtor" is defined only in relation to r.20.6 (see r.20.6(1)). "Unique identifier" in r.20.4(1) and r.20.5(1) is not defined. The court may order that the debtor's current address (defined in r.20.1(2)) be omitted from the court file or bankruptcy file open to inspection, from identification details on the individual insolvency register, relevant notices and advertisements, titles of proceedings, etc. In each case if the court makes a non-disclosure order it may further order, e.g. that former residential addresses of the debtor are disclosed instead.

Also see r.20.7 which empowers the court to make further orders, in relation to a non-disclosure order re a debtor subject to a bankruptcy order, a BRO or a BRU, concerning gazetting, advertising, etc. so as to impose duties on the official receiver. For the standard content of Gazette and other notices see rr.1.10, 1.11, 1.13.

A new template for r.20.4 was provided by the Insolvency Service in April 2017.

Part 21

The EU Regulation

Introductory note to Part 21

The references in this Part are to the Recast EU Regulation on Insolvency Proceedings 2015/848 (EURIP) which as from 26 June 2017 superseded the EC Regulation on Insolvency Proceedings 1346/2000. This has required amendments to Pt 21 by the Insolvency Amendment (EU 2015/848) Regulations 2017 (SI 2017/702) regs 1, 2(1), Sch. paras 32, 45–52 in relation to proceedings opened on or after 26 June 2017 (see reg.3) when the Recast EU Regulation 2015/848 came into force.

[Note: a document required by the Act or these Rules must also contain the standard contents set out in Part 1.]

21.1 Interpretation for this Part

21.1 In this Part–

"winding-up proceedings" means insolvency proceedings listed in the United Kingdom entry in Annex A to the EU Regulation other than voluntary arrangements where they relate to individuals, bankruptcy or sequestration; and

"conversion into winding-up proceedings" refers to an order under Article 51 of the EU Regulation (conversion of secondary insolvency proceedings) that winding-up proceedings of one kind are converted into winding-up proceedings of another kind.

(See General Note after r.21.3.)

21.1A Where an application is made to the court under the EU Regulation the standard contents set out in rule 1.35 apply to the application with any necessary adaptations except in so far as these Rules make specific provision for such an application.

(See General Note after r.21.3.)

21.2 Conversion into winding up proceedings or bankruptcy: application

[Note: "Local creditor" is defined in Article 2(11) of the EU Regulation.]

21.2(1) [Application of rule] This rule applies where a member State liquidator in main proceedings applies to the court under Article 51 of the EU Regulation for–

(a) conversion of winding-up proceedings of one kind into winding-up proceedings of another kind; or

(b) conversion of an IVA into bankruptcy or of bankruptcy into an IVA.

21.2(2) [Witness statement] A witness statement made by or on behalf of the member State liquidator must be filed with the court in support of the application.

21.2(3) [Content of witness statement] The witness statement must state–

(a) that main proceedings have been opened in relation to the company or, as the case may be, the debtor in a member State other than the United Kingdom;

(b) the belief of the person making the statement that the conversion of the CVA or administration into winding-up proceedings or the IVA into a bankruptcy would be most appropriate as regards the interests of the local creditors and coherence between the main and secondary insolvency proceedings;

(c) where the application is for conversion into winding-up proceedings of a CVA or an administration, in the opinion of the person making the statement, into which proceedings the CVA or administration should be converted; and

(d) all other matters that, in the opinion of the member State liquidator, would assist the court in–

  (i) deciding whether to make such an order, and

  (ii) considering whether and, if so, what consequential provision to include.

21.2(4) [Service of application and witness statement] The application and the witness statement must be served upon–

(a) the company or the debtor, as the case may be; and

(b) the supervisor or the administrator, as the case may be.

(See General Note after r.21.3.)

21.3 Conversion into winding up proceedings or bankruptcy: court order

21.3(1) [Power of court to make order] On hearing an application for conversion into winding-up proceedings, or conversion of an IVA into a bankruptcy the court may, subject to Article 51 of the EU Regulation, make such order as it thinks just.

21.3(2) [Order for conversion of CVA or administration into winding-up proceedings] An order for conversion into winding-up proceedings may–

(a) provide that the company be wound up as if a resolution for voluntary winding up under section 84 were passed on the day on which the order is made; and

(b) contain such consequential provisions as the court thinks just.

21.3(3) [Order for conversion of IVA into bankruptcy] An order for the conversion of an IVA into a bankruptcy may contain such consequential provisions as the court thinks just.

General Note to rr.21.1–21.3

Under the original Regulation of 2000 (ECRIP) it was not permitted for secondary proceedings to have any purpose other than winding up or bankruptcy. Other procedures such as an IVA, CVA or administration which had been commenced (as territorial proceedings) could not continue as such after main proceedings had been opened in another Member State (and they consequentially became secondary proceedings). They were obliged to convert to winding up or bankruptcy proceedings. Rules 21.1–21.3 make provision for this conversion.

Under the 2015 Regulation (EURIP), however, there is no such limitation on the purpose of secondary proceedings, no reason why an IVA, CVA or administration should not continue as such. The old Annex B has no equivalent in EURIP.

"Liquidator" had an extended meaning in ECRIP and included a trustee in bankruptcy and any other office-holder in an insolvency proceeding. In EURIP however "insolvency practitioner" is used now more generally and "member

State liquidator" is defined in IR 2016 r.1.2 to mean a person falling within the definition of "insolvency practitioner" in art.2(5) of EURIP appointed in proceedings to which the EU Regulation applies in a Member State other than the United Kingdom (and see rr.21.6 et seq. below).

Rule 21.1A inserted and r.21.2(1), (3)(b) amended by the Insolvency Amendment (EU 2015/848) Regulations 2017 (SI 2017/702) regs 1, 2(1), Sch. paras 32, 47, 48 in relation to proceedings opened on or after 26 June 2017 (see reg.3) when the Recast EU Regulation 2015/848 came into force.

Rule 21.3(1) amended by the Insolvency (England and Wales) and Insolvency (Scotland) (Miscellaneous and Consequential Amendments) Rules 2017 (SI 2017/1115) rr.1(1), (2), 22, 28 as from 8 December 2017.

21.4 Confirmation of creditors' voluntary winding up: application

21.4(1) [Application of rule] This rule applies where–

(a) a company has passed a resolution for voluntary winding up, and either–

(i) no declaration of solvency has been made in accordance with section 89, or

(ii) a declaration made under section 89–

(aa) has no effect by virtue of section 89(2), or

(bb) is treated as not having been made by virtue of section 96; or

(b) a company has moved from administration to creditors' voluntary winding up in accordance with paragraph 83 of Schedule B1.

21.4(2) [Power of liquidator to apply to court] The liquidator may apply to court for an order confirming the winding up as a creditors' voluntary winding up for the purposes of the EU Regulation.

21.4(3) [Witness statement] The application must be supported by a witness statement made by the liquidator which must contain–

(a) identification details for the liquidator and the company;

(b) the date on which the resolution for voluntary winding up was passed;

(c) a statement that the application is accompanied by the documents required by paragraph (4);

(d) a statement that the documents required by paragraph (4)(c) and (d) are true copies of the originals; and

(e) a statement whether the proceedings will be main proceedings, secondary proceedings or territorial proceedings and the reasons for so stating.

21.4(4) [Duty of liquidator to file in court] The liquidator must file with the court–

(a) two copies of the application;

(b) evidence of having been appointed liquidator of the company;

(c) a copy of–

(i) the resolution for voluntary winding up, or

(ii) the notice of moving from administration to creditors' voluntary winding up sent by the administrator to the registrar of companies under paragraph 83(3) of Schedule B1; and

(d) a copy of–

(i) the statement of affairs required by section 99(a) or under paragraph 47 of Schedule B1, or

(ii) the information included in the administrator's statement of proposals under rule 3.35(1)(h).

(See General Note after r.21.8.)

21.5 Confirmation of creditors' voluntary winding up: court order

21.5(1) [Power of court to make order] On an application under the preceding rule, the court may make an order confirming the creditors' voluntary winding up.

21.5(2) [No hearing required] It may do so without a hearing.

21.5(3) [Seal to application] If the court makes an order confirming the creditors' voluntary winding up, it must affix its seal to the application.

21.5(4) [Member of court staff may deal with application] A member of the court staff may deal with an application under this rule.

(See General Note after r.21.8.)

21.6 Confirmation of creditors' voluntary winding up: notice to member State liquidator

21.6(1) [Notice to Member State liquidator] Where the court has confirmed the creditors' voluntary winding up, the liquidator must as soon as reasonably practicable give notice to any member State liquidator appointed in relation to the company.

21.6(2) [Liquidator's obligation in EU Regulation art.40 continues] Paragraph (1) is without prejudice to the liquidator's obligation in Article 54 of the EU Regulation (duty to inform creditors in other member States) in relation to the creditors' voluntary winding up.

(See General Note after r.21.8.)

21.7 Proceedings in another member State: duty to give notice

21.7(1) [Application of rule] This rule applies where–

(a) the supervisor of a CVA or an IVA, an administrator, a liquidator, provisional liquidator, interim receiver or a trustee in bankruptcy is required to give notice, or provide a copy of a document (including an order of court), to the court, the registrar of companies or the official receiver.

21.7(2) [Notice or copy to Member State liquidator etc.] Where not already required to do so by Article 41 of the EU Regulation, the supervisor, administrator, liquidator, provisional liquidator, interim receiver or trustee must also give notice or provide a copy to–

(a) any member State liquidator; or

(b) where the supervisor, administrator, liquidator, provisional liquidator, interim receiver or trustee knows that an application has been made to commence insolvency proceedings in another member State but a member State liquidator has not yet been appointed to the court to which that application has been made.

(See General Note after r.21.8.)

21.8 Member State liquidator: rules on creditors' participation in proceedings

21.8(1) [Participation in EU Regulation art.45 proceedings] The provisions in these Rules apply to a member State liquidator's participation in proceedings in accordance with Article 45 of the EU Regulation (exercise of creditors' rights) in the same manner as they do to creditors' participation in those proceedings.

21.8(2) ["Creditors' participation"] In this rule, "creditors' participation"–

(a) includes the following matters–

(i) requesting and being provided with information, including inspecting or obtaining copies of documents or files,

(ii) being provided with notices or other documents,

(iii) participating and voting in decision procedures,

(iv) the establishment and operation of creditor committees,

(v) proving in respect of debts and receipt of dividends, and

(vi) applying to the court and appearing at hearings; and

(b) is limited to creditors' participation from the time of the opening of proceedings in accordance with Article 2(8) of the EU Regulation.

General Note to rr.21.4–21.8

Under Annex A of EURIP a creditors' voluntary winding up is recognised as an insolvency proceeding for the purposes of the Regulation throughout the EU (except Denmark, which has an opt-out), if it has been confirmed by the court. These rules set out the procedure to be followed to obtain confirmation.

Rules 21.4(3)(e), 21.7, 21.8(1), (2)(b) amended by the Insolvency Amendment (EU 2015/848) Regulations 2017 (SI 2017/702) regs 1, 2(1), Sch. paras 32, 49–51 in relation to proceedings opened on or after 26 June 2017 (see reg.3) when the Recast EU Regulation 2015/848 came into force.

Rules 21.4(2), 21.6(2) amended by the Insolvency (England and Wales) and Insolvency (Scotland) (Miscellaneous and Consequential Amendments) Rules 2017 (SI 2017/1115) rr.1(1), (2), 22, 23(10), 29 as from 8 December 2017.

[Note: "local creditor" is defined in Article 2(11) of the EU Regulation.]

21.9 Main proceedings in England and Wales: undertaking by office-holder in respect of assets in another member State (Article 36 of the EU Regulation)

21.9(1) [Application of rule] This rule applies where an office-holder in main proceedings proposes to give an undertaking under Article 36 of the EU Regulation in respect of assets located in another member State.

21.9(2) [Requirements re proposed undertaking] The following requirements apply in respect of the proposed undertaking.

21.9(3) [Contents of undertaking] In addition to the requirements as to form and content set out in Article 36 the undertaking must contain–

(a) the heading "Proposed Undertaking under Article 36 of the EU Insolvency Regulation (2015/848)";

(b) identification details for the main proceedings;

(c) identification and contact details for the office-holder; and

(d) a description of the effect of the undertaking if approved.

21.9(4) [Undertaking to all local creditors] The proposed undertaking must be delivered to all the local creditors in the member State concerned of whose address the office-holder is aware.

21.9(5) [Where undertaking rejected] Where the undertaking is rejected the office-holder must inform all the creditors of the company of the rejection of the undertaking as soon as reasonably practicable.

21.9(6) [Where undertaking approved] Where the undertaking is approved the office-holder must as soon as reasonably practicable–

(a) send a copy of the undertaking to all the creditors with a notice informing them of the approval of the undertaking and of its effect (so far as they have not already been given this information under paragraph (3)(d));

(b) in the case of a bankruptcy file the undertaking on the court file or the bankruptcy file as the case may be;

(c) where the insolvency proceedings relate to a registered company deliver a copy of the undertaking to the registrar of companies.

21.9(7) [Advertisement of undertaking details] The office-holder may advertise details of the undertaking in the other member State in such manner as the office-holder thinks fit.

(See General Note after r.21.17.)

21.10 Main proceedings in another member State: approval of undertaking offered by the member State liquidator to local creditors in the UK

21.10(1) [Application of rule] This rule applies where a member State liquidator proposes an undertaking under Article 36 and the secondary proceedings which the undertaking is intended to avoid would be insolvency proceedings to which these Rules apply.

21.10(2) [Local creditors' decision by decision procedure] The decision by the local creditors whether to approve the undertaking must be made by a decision procedure subject to the rules which apply to the approval of a CVA (with any necessary modifications) and subject as follows.

21.10(3) [Decision procedure applicable rules] In Part 15 the rules in Chapters 1 to 9 and 11 apply to the decision procedure (with any necessary modifications) except for the following–

15.7, 15.12, 15.14, 15.16–15.19, 15.24, 15.29 to 15.30.

21.10(4) [Company: copy to registrar of companies] Where the main proceedings relate to a registered company the member State liquidator must deliver a copy of the approved undertaking to the registrar of companies.

21.10(5) [Individual: gazette notice] Where the main proceedings relate to an individual the member State liquidator must gazette a notice of the undertaking containing–

(a) the fact that the undertaking was approved;

(b) the date the undertaking was approved; and

(c) a description of the effect of the undertaking.

(See General Note after r.21.17.)

21.11 Powers of an office-holder or member State liquidator in proceedings concerning members of a group of companies (Article 60 of the EU Regulation)

21.11 Where an office-holder or a member State liquidator makes an application in accordance with paragraph (1)(b) of Article 60 of the EU Regulation the application must state with reasons why the applicant thinks the matters set out in points (i) to (iv) of that paragraph apply.

(See General Note after r.21.17.)

21.12 Group coordination proceedings (Section 2 of Chapter 5 of the EU Regulation)

21.12(1) [Contents of application] An application to open group coordination proceedings must be headed "Application under Article 61 of Regulation (EU) 2015/848 to open group coordination proceedings" and must, in addition to the requirements in Article 61 contain–

(a) identification and contact details for the office-holder making the application;

(b) identification details for the insolvency proceedings by virtue of which the office-holder is making the application;

(c) identification details for the insolvency proceedings in respect of each company which is a member of the group;

(d) contact details for the office-holders and member state liquidators appointed in those proceedings;

(e) identification details for any insolvency proceedings in respect of a member of the group which are not to be subject to the coordination because of an objection to being included; and

(f) if relevant, a copy of any such agreement as is mentioned in Article 66 of the EU Regulation.

21.12(2) ["Office-holder"] "Office-holder" in this rule includes as the context requires a person holding office in insolvency proceedings in relation to the company in Scotland or Northern Ireland, and a member State liquidator.

(See General Note after r.21.17.)

[Note: an order opening group coordination proceedings must also contain the matters set out in Article 68(1)(a) to (c).]

21.13 Group coordination order (Article 68 EU Regulation)

21.13(1) [Contents of order] An order opening group coordination proceedings must also contain–

(a) identification details for the insolvency proceedings by virtue of which the office-holder is making the application;

(b) identification and contact details for the office-holder making the application;

(c) identification details for the insolvency proceedings which are subject to the coordination;

(d) identification details for any insolvency proceedings for a member of the group which are not subject to the coordination because of an objection to being included.

21.13(2) [Duty to office-holder to deliver copy orders] The office-holder who made the application must deliver a copy of the order to the coordinator and to any person who is, in respect of proceedings subject to the coordination–

(a) an office-holder,

(b) a person holding office in insolvency proceedings in relation to the company in Scotland or Northern Ireland, and

(c) a member State liquidator.

(See General Note after r.21.17.)

21.14 Delivery of group coordination order to registrar of companies

21.14 An office-holder in respect of insolvency proceedings subject to coordination must deliver a copy of the group coordination order to the registrar of companies.

(See General Note after r.21.17.)

21.15 Office-holder's report

21.15(1) [Application of rule] This rule applies where, under the second paragraph of Article 70(2) of the EU Regulation, an office-holder is required to give reasons for not following the coordinator's recommendations or the group coordination plan.

21.15(2) [Reasons by notice to creditors] Those reasons must be given as soon as reasonably practicable by a notice to all the creditors.

21.15(3) [Reasons in next progress report] Those reasons may be given in the next progress report where doing so satisfies the requirement to give the reasons as soon as reasonably practicable.

(See General Note after r.21.17.)

21.16 Publication of opening of proceedings by a member State liquidator

21.16(1) [Application of rule] This rule applies where–

(a) a company subject to insolvency proceedings has an establishment in England and Wales; and

(b) a member State liquidator is required or authorised under Article 28 of the EU Regulation to publish a notice.

21.16(2) [Duty to publish in the Gazette] The notice must be published in the Gazette.

(See General Note after r.21.17.)

21.17 Statement by member State liquidator that insolvency proceedings in another member State are closed etc

21.17 A statement by a member State liquidator under any of sections 201, 202, 205 or paragraph 84 of Schedule B1 informing the registrar of companies that the insolvency proceedings in another member State are closed or that the member State liquidator consents to the dissolution must contain–

(a) identification details for the company; and

(b) identification details for the member State liquidator.

General Note to rr.21.9–21.17

Rules 21.9–21.17 inserted by the Insolvency Amendment (EU 2015/848) Regulations 2017 (SI 2017/702) regs 1, 2(1), Sch. paras 32, 52 in relation to proceedings opened on or after 26 June 2017 (see reg.3) when the Recast EU Regulation 2015/848 came into force. The inserted rules provide further procedure in relation to undertakings as to assets by an office-holder/Member State liquidator in order to avoid secondary proceedings; group proceedings; and certain report/notice requirements.

Part 22

Permission to Act as Director etc. of Company with a Prohibited Name (section 216)

Introductory note to Part 22
These rules are essentially the same as IR 1986 rr.4.226–4.230.

[Note: a document required by the Act or these Rules must also contain the standard contents set out in Part 1.]

22.1 Preliminary

22.1(1) [Application of rules in Pt 22] The rules in this Part–

(a) relate to permission required under section 216 (restriction on re-use of name of company in insolvent liquidation) for a person to act as mentioned in section 216(3) in relation to a company with a prohibited name;

(b) prescribe the cases excepted from that provision, that is to say, in which a person to whom the section applies may so act without that permission; and

(c) apply to all windings up to which section 216 applies.

(See General Note after r.22.3.)

22.2 Application for permission under section 216(3)

22.2(1) [Notice of application] At least 14 days' notice of any application for permission to act in any of the circumstances which would otherwise be prohibited by section 216(3) must be given by the applicant to the Secretary of State, who may–

(a) appear at the hearing of the application; and

(b) whether or not appearing at the hearing, make representations.

(See General Note after r.22.3.)

22.3 Power of court to call for liquidator's report

22.3 When considering an application for permission under section 216, the court may call on the liquidator, or any former liquidator, of the liquidating company for a report of the circumstances in which the company became insolvent and the extent (if any) of the applicant's apparent responsibility for its doing so.

General Note to rr.22.1–22.3

A former director or shadow director may not reuse a prohibited company name "except with the leave of the court or in such circumstances as may be prescribed" (IA 1986 s.216(3)). Rules 22.2 and 22.3 deal with an application for such permission, while rr.22.4–22.7 specify three sets of circumstances which are to be treated as excepted cases. Rule 22.1(c) makes this chapter co-extensive with s.216

Notice of an application for permission to act must be given to the Secretary of State, who may appear at the hearing and/or make representations to the court, which may call on the liquidator to report on the company's insolvency and the applicant's responsibility therefor.

22.4 First excepted case

22.4(1) [Application of rule] This rule applies where–

(a) a person ("the person") was within the period mentioned in section 216(1) a director, or shadow director, of an insolvent company that has gone into insolvent liquidation; and

(b) the person acts in all or any of the ways specified in section 216(3) in connection with, or for the purposes of, the carrying on (or proposed carrying on) of the whole or substantially the whole of the business of the insolvent company where that business (or substantially the whole of it) is (or is to be) acquired from the insolvent company under arrangements–

(i) made by its liquidator, or

(ii) made before the insolvent company entered into insolvent liquidation by an office-holder acting in relation to it as administrator, administrative receiver or supervisor of a CVA.

22.4(2) [Circumstances not contravening IA 1986 s.216] The person will not be taken to have contravened section 216 if prior to that person acting in the circumstances set out in paragraph (1) a notice is, in accordance with the requirements of paragraph (3),–

(a) given by the person, to every creditor of the insolvent company whose name and address–

(i) is known by that person, or

(ii) is ascertainable by that person on the making of such enquiries as are reasonable in the circumstances; and

(b) published in the Gazette.

22.4(3) [Notice in r.22.4(2)] The notice referred to in paragraph (2)–

(a) may be given and published before the completion of the arrangements referred to in paragraph (1)(b) but must be given and published no later than 28 days after their completion;

(b) must contain–

(i) identification details for the company,

(ii) the name and address of the person,

(iii) a statement that it is the person's intention to act (or, where the insolvent company has not entered insolvent liquidation, to act or continue to act) in all or any of the ways specified in section 216(3) in connection with, or for the purposes of, the carrying on of the whole or substantially the whole of the business of the insolvent company,

(iv) the prohibited name or, where the company has not entered into insolvent liquidation, the name under which the business is being, or is to be, carried on which would be a prohibited name in respect of the person in the event of the insolvent company entering insolvent liquidation,

(v) a statement that the person would not otherwise be permitted to undertake those activities without the leave of the court or the application of an exception created by Rules made under the Insolvency Act 1986,

(vi) a statement that breach of the prohibition created by section 216 is a criminal offence, and

(vii) a statement as set out in rule 22.5 of the effect of issuing the notice under rule 22.4(2);

(c) where the company is in administration, has an administrative receiver appointed or is subject to a CVA, must contain–

(i) the date that the company entered administration, had an administrative receiver appointed or a CVA approved (whichever is the earliest), and

(ii) a statement that the person was a director of the company on that date; and

(d) where the company is in insolvent liquidation, must contain–

(i) the date that the company entered insolvent liquidation, and

(ii) a statement that the person was a director of the company during the 12 months ending with that date.

22.4(4) [Timing of r.22.4(2) notice] Notice may in particular be given under this rule–

(a) prior to the insolvent company entering insolvent liquidation where the business (or substantially the whole of the business) is, or is to be, acquired by another company under arrangements made by an office-holder acting in relation to the insolvent company as administrator, administrative receiver or supervisor of a CVA (whether or not at the time of the giving of the notice the person is a director of that other company); or

(b) at a time when the person is a director of another company where–

(i) the other company has acquired, or is to acquire, the whole, or substantially the whole, of the business of the insolvent company under arrangements made by its liquidator, and

(ii) it is proposed that after the giving of the notice a prohibited name should be adopted by the other company.

22.4(5) [Whom may not give notice] Notice may not be given under this rule by a person who has already acted in breach of section 216.

(See General Note after r.22.5.)

22.5 Statement as to the effect of the notice under rule 22.4(2)

22.5 The statement as to the effect of the notice under rule 22.4(2) must be as set out below–

"Section 216(3) of the Insolvency Act 1986 lists the activities that a director of a company that has gone into insolvent liquidation may not undertake unless the court gives permission or there is an exception in the Insolvency Rules made under the Insolvency Act 1986. (This includes the exceptions in Part 22 of the Insolvency (England and Wales) Rules 2016.) These activities are–

(a) acting as a director of another company that is known by a name which is either the same as a name used by the company in insolvent liquidation in the 12 months before it entered liquidation or is so similar as to suggest an association with that company;

(b) directly or indirectly being concerned or taking part in the promotion, formation or management of any such company; or

(c) directly or indirectly being concerned in the carrying on of a business otherwise than through a company under a name of the kind mentioned in (a) above.

This notice is given under rule 22.4 of the Insolvency (England and Wales) Rules 2016 where the business of a company which is in, or may go into, insolvent liquidation is, or is to be, carried on otherwise than by the company in liquidation with the involvement of a director of that company and under the same or a similar name to that of that company.

The purpose of giving this notice is to permit the director to act in these circumstances where the company enters (or has entered) insolvent liquidation without the director committing a criminal offence and in the case of the carrying on of the business through another company, being personally liable for that company's debts.

Notice may be given where the person giving the notice is already the director of a company which proposes to adopt a prohibited name."

General Note to rr.22.4, 22.5

The predecessor of r.22.4 was unsatisfactory as it was interpreted in some county court judgments in a way which made it virtually impossible to apply in any case where the director was already working in the management of the successor company (e.g. in a management buy-out situation); and this construction was upheld by the Court of Appeal in *Churchill v First Independent Factors and Finance Ltd* [2006] EWCA Civ 1623; [2007] B.C.C. 45. The wording was amended in 2007 so that a director could bring himself within the first excepted case (and so not require the leave of the court) if the prescribed notice is given in accordance with r.22.4(2)–(4). Such a notice may be given before the company enters into insolvent liquidation (e.g. where the company is in administration and it is likely or possible that it will subsequently go into liquidation), or in cases where the successor company has not yet adopted a prohibited name. There is no longer a prescribed form but the detail of the content of the notice is provided in r.22.4(3) together with the statement in r.2.25. For the standard content of gazetted notices see rr.1.10–1.12.

22.6 Second excepted case

22.6(1) [Where director applies or permission] Where a person to whom section 216 applies as having been a director or shadow director of the liquidating company applies for permission of the court under that section not later than seven business days from the date on which the company went into liquidation, the person may, during the period specified in paragraph (2) below, act in any of the ways mentioned in section 216(3), notwithstanding that the person does not have the permission of the court under that section.

22.6(2) [Period in r.22.6(1)] The period referred to in paragraph (1) begins with the day on which the company goes into liquidation and ends either on the day falling six weeks after that date or on the day on which the court disposes of the application for permission under section 216, whichever of those days occurs first.

General Note

This exception enables a person who is seeking the leave of the court to act as a director, etc. of a company with a prohibited name for a brief period while his application is awaiting a hearing. Note the strict time limits. The six-week period in r.22.6(2) is intended to avoid the risk that an applicant who is unsuccessful would have unwittingly committed an offence while the hearing of his case was pending.

22.7 Third excepted case

22.7 The court's permission under section 216(3) is not required where the company there referred to though known by a prohibited name within the meaning of the section–

(a) has been known by that name for the whole of the period of 12 months ending with the day before the liquidating company went into liquidation; and

(b) has not at any time in those 12 months been dormant within the meaning of section 1169(1), (2) and (3)(a) of the Companies Act.

General Note

This exception allows a former director to continue to act in the affairs of an established company even though it is known by a prohibited name, provided that it has been using that name for at least a year before his other company went into liquidation. See *ESS Production Ltd v Sully* [2005] EWCA Civ 554; [2005] B.C.C. 435. But the exception applies only where there was a previously established and active business trading with limited liability. It was held not to apply in *First Independent Factors & Finance Ltd v Mountford* [2008] EWHC 835 (Ch); [2008] B.C.C. 598, where the business in question had been carried on by the defendant personally and was then transferred to a dormant company controlled by him.

R.22.7(b)
CA 2006 s.1169(1), (2) defines a company as dormant during any period in which it has no significant accounting transaction (i.e. a transaction that is required by CA 2006 s.386 to be entered in its accounting records).

Schedule 1

Introductory rule 2

Revocations

The Insolvency Rules 1986	1986/1925
The Insolvency (Amendment) Rules 1987	1987/1919
The Insolvency (Amendment) Rules 1989	1989/397
The Insolvency (Amendment) Rules 1991	1991/495
The Insolvency (Amendment) Rules 1993	1993/602
The Insolvency (Amendment) Rules 1995	1995/586
The Insolvency (Amendment) Rules 1999	1999/359
The Insolvency (Amendment) (No. 2) Rules 1999	1999/1022
The Insolvency (Amendment) Rules 2001	2001/763
The Insolvency (Amendment) Rules 2002	2002/1307
The Insolvency (Amendment) (No. 2) Rules 2002	2002/2712
The Insolvency (Amendment) Rules 2003	2003/1730
The Insolvency (Amendment) Rules 2004	2004/584
The Insolvency (Amendment) (No. 2) Rules 2004	2004/1070
The Insolvency (Amendment) Rules 2005	2005/527
The Insolvency (Amendment) Rules 2006	2006/1272
The Insolvency (Amendment) Rules 2007	2007/1974
The Insolvency (Amendment) Rules 2008	2008/737
The Insolvency (Amendment) Rules 2009	2009/642
The Insolvency (Amendment No. 2) Rules 2009	2009/2472
The Insolvency (Amendment) Rules 2010	2010/686

The Insolvency (Amendment) (No. 2) Rules 2010	2010/734
The Insolvency (Amendment) Rules 2011	2011/785
The Insolvency (Amendment) Rules 2012	2012/469
The Insolvency (Amendment) Rules 2013	2013/2135
The Insolvency (Commencement of Proceedings) and Insolvency Rules 1986 (Amendment) Rules 2014	2014/817
The Insolvency (Amendment) Rules 2015	2015/443
The Insolvency (Amendment) Rules 2016	2016/187
The Insolvency (Amendment) (No. 2) Rules 2016	2016/903

General Note

This provides the raison d'être for the 2016 Rules. The scale of the amendments to IR 1986 is laid bare by this table of revocations. Obviously it had no counterpart in IR 1986.

Schedule 2

Transitional and savings provisions

Introductory rule 4

1 General

1 In this Schedule–

"the 1986 Rules" means the Insolvency Rules 1986 as they had effect immediately before the commencement date and a reference to "1986 rule" followed by a rule number is a reference to a rule in the 1986 Rules; and

"the commencement date" means the date these Rules come into force.

2 Requirement for office-holder to provide information to creditors on opting out

2(1) Rule 1.39, which requires an office-holder to provide information to a creditor on the right to opt out under rule 1.38 in the first communication to the creditor, does not apply to an office-holder who has delivered the first communication before the commencement date.

2(2) However, such an office-holder may choose to deliver information on the right to opt out in which case the communication to the creditor must contain the information required by rule 1.39(2).

3 Electronic communication

3(1) Rule 1.45(4) does not apply where the relevant proceedings commenced before the commencement date.

3(2) In this paragraph "commenced" means–

(a) the delivery of a proposal for a voluntary arrangement to the intended nominee;

(b) the appointment of an administrator under paragraph 14 or 22 of Schedule B1;

(c) the making of an administration order;

(d) the appointment of an administrative receiver;

(e) the passing or deemed passing of a resolution to wind up a company;

(f) the making of a winding-up order; or

(g) the making of a bankruptcy order.

4 Statements of affairs

4(1) The provisions of these Rules relating to statements of affairs in administration, administrative receivership, company winding up and bankruptcy do not apply and the following rules in the 1986 Rules continue to apply where relevant proceedings commenced before the commencement date and a person is required to provide a statement of affairs–

(a) 1986 rules 2.28 to 2.32 (administration);

(b) 1986 rules 3.3 to 3.8 (administrative receivership);

(c) 1986 rules 4.32 to 4.42 (company winding up); and

(d) 1986 rules 6.58 to 6.72 (bankruptcy).

4(2) In this paragraph "commenced" means–

(a) the appointment of an administrator under paragraph 14 or 22 of Schedule B1;

(b) the making of an administration order;

(c) the appointment of an administrative receiver

(d) the passing or deemed passing of a resolution to wind up a company;

(e) the making of a winding-up order; or

(f) the making of a bankruptcy order.

5 Savings in respect of meetings taking place on or after the commencement date and resolutions by correspondence

5(1) This paragraph applies where on or after the commencement date–

(a) a creditors' or contributories' meeting is to be held as a result of a notice issued before that date in relation to a meeting for which provision is made by the 1986 Rules or the 1986 Act;

(b) a meeting is to be held as a result of a requisition by a creditor or contributory made before that date;

(c) a meeting is to be held as a result of a statement made under paragraph 52(1)(b) of Schedule B1 and a request is made before that date which obliges the administrator to summon an initial creditors' meeting;

(d) a meeting is required by sections 93 or 105 of the 1986 Act in the winding up of a company where the resolution to wind up was passed before 6th April 2010.

5(2) Where a meeting is to be held under sub-paragraph (1)(a) to (1)(d), Part 15 of these Rules does not apply and the 1986 Rules relating to the following continue to apply–

(a) the requirement to hold the meeting;

(b) notice and advertisement of the meeting;

(c) governance of the meeting;

(d) recording and taking minutes of the meeting;

(e) the report or return of the meeting;

(f) membership and formalities of establishment of liquidation and creditors' committees where the resolution to form the committee is passed at the meeting;

(g) the office-holder's resignation or removal at the meeting;

(h) the office-holder's release;

(i) fixing the office-holder's remuneration;

(j) [Omitted]

(k) hand-over of assets to a supervisor of a voluntary arrangement where the proposal is approved at the meeting;

(l) the notice of the appointment of a supervisor of a voluntary arrangement where the appointment is made at the meeting;

(m) the advertisement of appointment of a trustee in bankruptcy where the appointment is made at the meeting;

(n) claims that remuneration is or that other expenses are excessive; and

(o) complaints about exclusion at the meeting.

5(3) Where, before the commencement date, the office-holder sought to obtain a resolution by correspondence under 1986 rule 2.48, 4.63A or 6.88A, the 1986 Rules relating to resolutions by correspondence continue to apply and sub-paragraph (2) applies to any meeting that those rules require the office-holder to summon.

5(4) However, any application to the court in respect of such a meeting or vote is to be made in accordance with Part 12 of these Rules.

6 Savings in respect of final meetings taking place on or after the commencement date

6(1) This paragraph applies where–

(a) before the commencement date–

  (i) a final report to creditors has been sent under 1986 rule 4.49D (final report to creditors in liquidation),

  (ii) a final report to creditors and bankrupt has been sent under 1986 rule 6.78B (final report to creditors and bankrupt), or

  (iii) a meeting has been called under sections 94, 106, 146 or 331 of the 1986 Act (final meeting); and

(b) a meeting under section 94, 106, 146 or 331 of the 1986 Act is held on or after the commencement date.

6(2) Where a meeting is held to which this paragraph applies, Part 15 of these Rules does not apply and the 1986 Rules relating to the following continue to apply–

(a) the requirement to hold the meeting;

(b) notice and advertisement of the meeting;

(c) governance of the meeting;

(d) recording and taking minutes of the meeting;

(e) the form and content of the final report;

(f) the office-holder's resignation or removal;

(g) the office-holder's release;

(h) fixing the office-holder's remuneration;

(i) requests for further information from creditors;

(j) claims that remuneration is or other expenses are excessive; and

(k) complaints about exclusion at the meeting.

6(3) However, any application to the court in respect of such a meeting is to be made in accordance with Part 12 of these Rules.

7 Progress reports and statements to the registrar of companies

7(1) Where an obligation to prepare a progress report arises before the commencement date but has not yet been fulfilled the following provisions of the 1986 Rules continue to apply–

(a) 1986 rule 2.47 (reports to creditors in administration;

(b) 1986 rules 4.49B and 4.49C (progress reports–winding up); and

(c) 1986 rule 6.78A (reports to creditors in bankruptcy).

7(2) Where before the commencement date, a conversion notice under paragraph 83 of Schedule B1 was sent to the registrar of companies, 1986 rule 2.117A(1) continues to apply.

7(3) The provisions of these Rules relating to progress reporting do not apply–

(a) in the case of a bankruptcy, where the bankruptcy order was made on a petition presented before 6th April 2010; or

(b) in the case of a winding up, where the winding-up order was made on a petition presented before 6th April 2010.

7(4) Where a voluntary winding up commenced before 6th April 2010, 1986 rule 4.223-CVL as it had effect immediately before that date, continues to apply.

7(5) Where rules 18.6, 18.7 or 18.8 prescribe the periods for which progress reports must be made but before the commencement date an office-holder has ceased to act, or an administrator has sent a progress report to creditors in support of a request for their consent to an extension of the administration, resulting in a change in reporting period under 1986 rule 2.47(3A), 2.47(3B) 4.49B(5), 4.49C(3), or 6.78A(4), the period for which reports must be made is the period for which reports were required to be made under the 1986 Rules immediately before the commencement date.

8 Foreign currency

8(1) Where, before the commencement date an amount stated in a foreign currency on an application, claim or proof of debt is converted into sterling by the office-holder under 1986 rule 2.86, 1986 rule 4.91, 1986 rule 5A.3 or 1986 rule 6.111, the office-holder and any successor to the office-holder must continue to use that exchange rate for subsequent conversions of that currency into sterling for the purpose of distributing any assets of the insolvent estate.

8(2) However when an office-holder, convener, appointed person or chair uses an exchange rate to convert an application, claim or proof in a foreign currency into sterling solely for voting purposes before the commencement date, it does not prevent the office-holder from using an alternative rate for subsequent conversions.

9 CVA moratoria

9 Where, before the commencement date, the directors of a company submit to the nominee the documents required under paragraph 6(1) of Schedule A1, the 1986 Rules relating to moratoria continue to apply to that proposed voluntary arrangement.

10 Priority of expenses of voluntary arrangements

10 1986 rule 4.21A (expenses of CVA in a liquidation) and 1986 rule 6.46A (expenses of IVA in a bankruptcy) continue to apply where a winding up or bankruptcy petition is presented or a bankruptcy application is made (as the case may be) before the commencement date.

11 General powers of liquidator

11 1986 rule 4.184 (General powers of liquidator) continues to apply as regards a person dealing in good faith and for value with a liquidator and in respect of the power of the court or the liquidation committee to ratify anything done by the liquidator without permission before the amendments made to sections 165 and 167 of the Act by section 120(2) and (3) of the Small Business, Enterprise and Employment Act 2015 (which removed the requirements for the liquidator to obtain such permission) came into force.

12 Fast-track voluntary arrangements

12 Where a fast-track voluntary arrangement is in effect on the commencement date the following 1986 Rules continue to apply to it after the commencement date–

(a) 1986 rules 5.35 to 5.50 (fast-track voluntary arrangement);

(b) 1986 rules 5.57 to 5.59 (application by official receiver to annul a bankruptcy order under section 263D(3)); and

(c) 1986 rules 5.60 to 5.61 (other matters arising on annulments under sections 261(2)(a), 261(2)(b) or 263D(3)).

13 First trustee in bankruptcy

13 On the commencement date the official receiver becomes trustee of the bankrupt's estate where–

(a) a bankruptcy order was made before the commencement date; and

(b) no trustee has yet been appointed.

14 Applications before the court

14(1) Subject to paragraph (1A), where an application to court is filed or a petition is presented under the Act or under the 1986 Rules before the commencement date and the court remains seised of that application or petition on the commencement date, the 1986 rules continue to apply to that application or petition.

14(1A) Where the 1986 Rules apply by virtue of paragraph (1) they are to apply as though–

(a) in rules 7.47(2)(a)(ii), (b)(iii) and (c) and 13.2(3A)(a) for "a Registrar in Bankruptcy of the High Court" there were substituted "an Insolvency and Companies Court Judge", and

(b) in rule 7.47(5), for the words "Registrar in Bankruptcy of the High Court" both times they appear there were substituted "Insolvency and Companies Court Judge.

14(2) For the purpose of paragraph (1), the court is no longer seised of an application when–

(a) it makes an order having the effect of determining of the application; or

(b) in relation to a petition for bankruptcy or winding up when–

  (i) the court makes a bankruptcy order or a winding up order,

  (ii) the court dismisses the petition, or

  (iii) the petition is withdrawn.

14(3) Any application to the court to review, rescind, vary or appeal an order made under paragraph 14(2) is to be made in accordance with Part 12 of these Rules.

15 Forms

15 A form contained in Schedule 4 to the 1986 Rules may be used on or after the commencement date if–

(a) the form is used to provide a statement of affairs pursuant to paragraph 4 of this Schedule;

(b) the form relates to a meeting held under the 1986 Rules as described in paragraph 5(1) of this Schedule;

(c) the form is required for the administration of a fast-track voluntary arrangement pursuant to paragraph 12 of this Schedule;

(d) the form is required because before the commencement date, the office-holder sought to obtain the passing of a resolution by correspondence; or

(e) the form relates to any application to the court or petition presented before the commencement date.

16 Registers

16(1) The Secretary of State must maintain on the individual insolvency register, the bankruptcy restrictions register and the debt relief restrictions register information which is on the registers immediately before the commencement date.

16(2) The Secretary of State must also enter on the appropriate register referred to in paragraph (1) information received (but not yet entered on the register) before the commencement date.

16(3) The Court's power under Part 20 to order that information must not be entered in those registers where there is a risk of violence applies equally to information received by the Secretary of State before the commencement date but not yet entered on a register.

16(4) Any obligation in Part 11 to delete information from a register or to rectify a register applies equally to information entered on the register before these rules come into force.

17 Administrations commenced before 15th September 2003

17 The 1986 Rules continue to apply to administrations where the petition for an administration order was presented before 15th September 2003.

18 Set-off in insolvency proceedings commenced before 1st April 2005

18 Where before 1st April 2005 a company has entered administration or gone into liquidation, the office-holder, when calculating any set-off must apply the 1986 Rules as they had effect immediately before 1st April 2005.

19 Calculating the value of future debts in insolvency proceedings commenced before 1st April 2005

19 Where before 1st April 2005 a company has entered administration or gone into liquidation or a bankruptcy order has been made, the office-holder, when calculating the value of a future debt for the purpose of dividend (and no other purpose) must apply the 1986 Rules as they had effect immediately before 1st April 2005.

20 Obligations arising under family proceedings where bankruptcy order is made on or before 31 March 2005

20 Rule 12.3 of the 1986 Rules applies, without the amendments made by rule 44 of the Insolvency (Amendment) Rules 2005 to an obligation arising under an order made in family proceedings in any case where a bankruptcy order was made on or before 31 March 2005.

21 Insolvency practitioner fees and expenses estimates

21(1) Rules 18.4(1)(e), 18.16(4) to (10), and 18.30 do not apply in a case where before 1st October 2015–

(a) the appointment of an administrator took effect;

(b) a liquidator was nominated under section 100(2), or 139(3) of the Act;

(c) a liquidator was appointed under section 139(4) or 140 of the Act;

(d) a person was directed by the court or appointed to be a liquidator under section 100(3) of the Act;

(e) a liquidator was nominated or the administrator became the liquidator under paragraph 83(7) of Schedule B1 to the Act; or

(f) a trustee of a bankrupt's estate was appointed.

21(2) Paragraphs (4) and (5) of rule 18.20 do not apply where an administrator was appointed before 1st October 2015 and–

(a) the company is wound up under paragraph 83 of Schedule B1 on or after the commencement date and the administrator becomes the liquidator; or

(b) a winding-up order is made upon the appointment of an administrator ceasing to have effect on or after the commencement date and the court under section 140(1) appoints as liquidator the person whose appointment as administrator has ceased to have effect.

22 Transitional provision for companies entering administration before 6th April 2010 and moving to voluntary liquidation between 6th April 2010 and 8th December 2017 inclusive of those dates

22 Where–

(a) a company goes into administration before 6th April 2010; and

(b) the company goes into voluntary liquidation under paragraph 83 of Schedule B1 between 6th April 2010 and 8th December 2017 inclusive of those dates;

the 1986 Rules as amended by the Insolvency (Amendment) Rules 2010 apply to the extent necessary to give effect to section 104A of the Act notwithstanding that by virtue of paragraph 1(6)(a) or (b) of Schedule 4 to the Insolvency (Amendment) Rules 2010 those amendments to the Insolvency Rules 1986 would otherwise not apply.

General Note

These are important transitional provisions. The commencement date is 6 April 2017 and the intention behind this Schedule is not to disturb the conduct of ongoing insolvency proceedings by introducing change in mid-stream. Specific areas of activity/practice are addressed to provide an optimum transitional solution. Note in particular para.14 which deals with ongoing litigation. On para.14 see *Re Nortel Networks UK Ltd* [2017] EWHC 1429 (Ch). The Schedule also deals with transitional issues linked to previous changes in the Insolvency Rules. This Schedule merely reinforces the need to retain the 19th edition of this *Guide*.

For in depth analysis of Sch.2 see Clench [2017] 30 Insolv. Int. 37.

Paragraphs 7(5), 14(3) and para.21 amended, and para.22 substituted, by the Insolvency (England and Wales) and Insolvency (Scotland) (Miscellaneous and Consequential Amendments) Rules 2017 (SI 2017/1115) rr.1(1), (2), 2, 13 as from 8 December 2017.

Paragraph 14(1) amended and para.14(1A) inserted by the Alteration of Judicial Titles (Registrar in Bankruptcy of the High Court) Order 2018 (SI 2018/130) arts 1, 3 Sch. para.14(c) as from 26 February 2018.

SCHEDULE 3

PUNISHMENT OF OFFENCES UNDER THESE RULES

Introductory rule 6

Rule creating offence	General nature of the offence	Mode of prosecution	Punishment	Daily default fine (if applicable)
1.56(3)	Falsely claiming to be a person entitled to inspect a document with the intention of gaining sight of it.	1. On indictment. 2. Summary.	2 years, or a fine, or both. 6 months, or a fine, or both.	Not applicable.
3.55(7)	Former administrator failing to file a notice of automatic end of administration and progress report.	Summary.	Level 3 on the standard scale.	One tenth of level 3 on the standard scale.
3.70(2)	Failing to comply with administrator's duties on vacating office.	Summary.	Level 3 on the standard scale.	One tenth of level 3 on the standard scale.
4.17(6)	Administrative receiver failing to deliver required accounts of receipts and payments.	Summary.	Level 3 on the standard scale.	One tenth of level 3 on the standard scale.
6.14(13)	Directors failing to seek a decision on the nomination of a liquidator.	1. On indictment. 2. Summary.	1. A fine. 2. A fine.	Not applicable.
18.6(5)	Administrator failing to deliver required progress reports in accordance with rule 18.6.	Summary.	Level 3 on the standard scale.	One tenth of level 3 on the standard scale.

GENERAL NOTE

This details certain offences under the particular Rules and prescribed punishments. Some of the content is derived from IR 1986 Sch.5. Note the relatively heavy penalty imposed on those persons seeking unauthorised access to documents under IR 2016 r.1.56(3). The only new punishment post-IR 1986 under IR 2016 is r.6.14(13), directors failing to seek a decision on the nomination of a liquidator.

For the standard scale of fines for summary offences see the Criminal Justice Act 1982 s.37. As at 6 April 2017 Level 3 of the standard scale was £1,000.

Schedule 4

Service of documents

Rule 1.2(2)

1(1) This Schedule sets out the requirements for service where a document is required to be served.

1(2) Service is to be carried out in accordance with Part 6 of the CPR as that Part applies to either a "claim form" or a "document other than the claim form" except where this Schedule provides otherwise or the court otherwise approves or directs.

1(3) However, where a document is required or permitted to be served at a company's registered office service may be effected at a previous registered office in accordance with section 87(2) of the Companies Act.

1(4) In the case of an overseas company service may be effected in any manner provided for by section 1139(2) of the Companies Act.

1(5) If for any reason it is impracticable to effect service as provided for in paragraphs (2) to (4) then service may be effected in such other manner as the court may approve or direct.

1(6) The third column of the table below sets out which documents are treated as "claim forms" for the purposes of applying Part 6 of the CPR and which are "documents other than the claim form" (called in this Schedule "other documents").

1(7) The fourth column of the table sets out modifications to Part 6 of the CPR which apply to the service of documents listed in the first and second columns.

1(8) Part 6 of the CPR applies to the service of documents outside the jurisdiction with such modifications as the court may approve or direct.

2 Service of winding-up petitions

2(1) A winding-up petition must be served at a company's registered office by handing it to a person at that address who–

(a) at the time of service acknowledges being a director, other officer or employee of the company;

(b) is, to the best of the knowledge and belief of the person serving the petition, a director, other officer or employee of the company; or

(c) acknowledges being authorised to accept service of documents on the company's behalf.

2(2) However if there is no one of the kind mentioned in sub-paragraph (1) at the registered office, the petition may be served by depositing it at or about the registered office in such a way that it is likely to come to the notice of a person attending the office.

2(3) Sub-paragraph (4) applies if–

(a) for any reason it is not practicable to serve a petition at a company's registered office;

(b) the company has no registered office; or

(c) the company is an unregistered company.

2(4) Where this paragraph applies the petition may be served–

(a) by leaving it at the company's last known principal place of business in England and Wales in such a way that it is likely to come to the attention of a person attending there; or

(b) on the secretary or a director, manager or principal officer of the company, wherever that person may be found.

3 Service of administration application (paragraph 12 of Schedule B1)

3(1) An application to the court for an administration order must be served by delivering the documents as follows–

(a) on the company at its registered office or if service at its registered office is not practicable at its last known principal place of business in England and Wales;

(b) on any other person at that person's proper address.

3(2) A person's proper address is any which he has previously notified as the address for service, but if the person has not notified such an address then the documents may be served at that person's usual or last known address.

3(3) Paragraph (4) sets out the proper address for service for an authorised deposit-taker who–

(a) has appointed, or is or may be entitled to appoint, an administrative receiver of the company; or

(b) is, or may be, entitled to appoint an administrative receiver of the company under paragraph 14 of Schedule B1; and

(c) has not notified an address for service.

3(4) The proper address for service is–

(a) that of an office of the authorised-deposit taker where the applicant knows the company maintains a bank account; or

(b) where the applicant doesn't know of any such office, the registered office; or

(c) if there is no such registered office the usual or last known address.

4 Service on joint office-holders

4 Service of a document on one of joint office-holders is to be treated as service on all of them.

5 Service of orders staying proceedings

5(1) This paragraph applies where the court makes an order staying an action, execution or other legal process against–

(a) the property of a company; or

(b) the property or person of an individual debtor or bankrupt.

5(2) The order may be served within the jurisdiction by serving a sealed copy at the address for service of–

(a) the claimant; or

(b) another party having the carriage of the proceedings to be stayed.

6 Certificate of service

6(1) The service of an application or petition must be verified by a certificate of service.

6(2) The certificate of service must–

(a) identify the application or petition;

(b) identify the company, where the application or petition relates to a company;

(c) identify the debtor, where the application relates to an individual;

(d) identify the applicant or petitioner;

(e) specify–

(i) the court or hearing centre in which the application was made or at which the petition was filed, and the court reference number,

(ii) the date of the application or petition,

(iii) whether the copy served was a sealed copy,

(iv) the person(s) served, and

(v) the manner of service and the date of service; and

(f) be verified by a statement of truth.

6(3) Where the court has directed that service be effected in a particular manner, the certificate must be accompanied by a sealed copy of the order directing such manner of service.

Table of requirements for service

Rule (or section)	*Document*	*Whether treated as claim form or other document*	*Modifications to Part 6 of the CPR which apply unless the court directs otherwise*
3.8	Administration application	Claim form	Service in accordance with paragraph 3 of this Schedule. The applicant must serve the application.
3.16 (& Para 15 of Sch B1)	Notice of intention to appoint administrator by a floating charge holder	Other document	The appointer must serve the notice.
3.23 (& para 26 of Sch B1)	Notice of intention to appoint administrator by company or directors	Other document	Service on the company at its registered office or if that is not practicable, at its last known principal place of business in England and Wales.
7.3	Statutory demand on a company under section 123(1) or 222(1)(a) (unregistered companies)		[Note: the requirements for service of a statutory demand are set out in sections 123(1) and 222(1)(a) respectively.]
7.9 and 7.29	Winding-up petition	Claim form	Service in accordance with paragraph 2 of this Schedule. The petitioner must serve the petition.

Rule (or section)	*Document*	*Whether treated as claim form or other document*	*Modifications to Part 6 of the CPR which apply unless the court directs otherwise*
7.34	Court order for additional deposit to be paid – provisional liquidator	Other document	
7.99	Court order to enforce payment of a call	Other document	
7.102	Court order for public examination served on examinee	Other document	
10.2	Statutory demand (bankruptcy)	Other document	Service in accordance with rule 10.2.
10.14	Bankruptcy petition (creditor's)	Claim form	Personal service. The petitioner must serve the petition.
10.29	Court order – change of carriage of petition	Other document	
10.50	Court order for additional deposit to be paid – interim receiver	Other document	
10.99	Court order for public examination served on bankrupt	Other document	
10.119	Court order for disclosure by HMRC	Other document	
10.126	Notice to recipient of after acquired property	Other document	
10.166	Court order for post redirection	Other document	
11.3	Application for debt relief restrictions order (DRRO) or bankruptcy restrictions order (BRO)	Claim form	The applicant must serve the application.
11.4	Service of evidence for DRRO or BRO	Other document	
12.9	Applications to court generally (where service required)	Claim form	The applicant must serve the application.
12.19	Court order for private examination	Other document	Personal service. The applicant must serve the order.

Rule (or section)	*Document*	*Whether treated as claim form or other document*	*Modifications to Part 6 of the CPR which apply unless the court directs otherwise*
12.28(2)	Witness statement of evidence	Other document	
12.37(7)	Application for block transfer order	Claim form	The applicant must serve the application.
12.42	Notice requiring person to assess costs by detailed assessment	Other document	
12.48	Application for costs	Claim form	The applicant must serve the application.
19.4 (& sections 179 and 317)	Notice of disclaimer (leasehold property)	Other document	
19.5 (& section 318)	Notice of disclaimer (dwelling house)	Other document	
21.2	Application for conversion into winding up /bankruptcy under EU Regulation	Claim form	The applicant must serve the application.
Paragraph 5(1) of this Schedule	Order staying proceedings	Other document	The applicant must serve the order.

General Note

These are important provisions on service of documents in insolvency proceedings. They draw upon the CPR but make dedicated provision in a number of cases. The Table of requirements for service is innovative and useful.

For a lucid review of the modern position on service out of the jurisdiction see G. Davis (2010) 23 Insolv. Int. 145. See also *Re Baillies Ltd* [2012] EWHC 285 (Ch); [2012] B.C.C. 554 where HHJ Purle QC reviews the linkage with the EC Service Regulation (1393/2007). In *Hosking v Apax Partners LLP* [2016] EWHC 558 (Ch); [2016] B.P.I.R. 903 the court concluded that paras 6.4–6.6 of *Practice Direction: Insolvency Proceedings* [2014] B.C.C. 502 applied to service out of the jurisdiction in insolvency proceedings rather than CPR rr.6.30–6.51, and went on to set out the requirements necessary to satisfy para.6.6 of the *Practice Direction* in relation to service out. These paragraphs are not repeated in *Practice Direction: Insolvency Proceedings* [2018] B.C.C. 241, which (para.5.2) merely provides that, subject to the court directing otherwise, CPR Pt 6 applies to service both within and outside the jurisdiction.

See also r.7.9 and the note after r.7.12.

Paragraph 6(3) substituted, and in the table the entry in relation to r.21.2 amended, by the Insolvency (England and Wales) and Insolvency (Scotland) (Miscellaneous and Consequential Amendments) Rules 2017 (SI 2017/1115) rr.1(1), (2), 2, 14, 22, 23(11) as from 8 December 2017.

Schedule 5

Calculation of time periods

Rule 1.3

[Note: section 376 of the Act contains a power for the court to extend the time for doing anything required by the Act or these Rules under the Second Group of Parts (Insolvency of Individuals; bankruptcy).]

1 The rules in CPR 2.8 with the exception of paragraph (4) apply for the calculation of periods expressed in days in the Act and these Rules.

2(1) This paragraph applies for the calculation of periods expressed in months.

2(2) The beginning and the end of a period expressed in months is to be determined as follows–

(a) if the beginning of the period is specified–

(i) the month in which the period ends is the specified number of months after the month in which it begins, and

(ii) the date in the month on which the period ends is–

(aa) the day before the date corresponding to the date in the month on which it begins, or

(bb) if there is no such date in the month in which it ends, the last day of that month;

(b) if the end of the period is specified–

(i) the month in which the period begins is the specified number of months before the month in which it ends, and

(ii) the date in the month on which the period begins is–

(aa) the day after the date corresponding to the date in the month on which it ends, or

(bb) if there is no such date in the month in which it begins, the last day of that month.

3 The provisions of CPR rule 3.1(2)(a) (the court's general powers of management) apply so as to enable the court to extend or shorten the time for compliance with anything required or authorised to be done by these Rules.

4 Paragraph 3 is subject to any time limits expressly stated in the Act and to any specific powers in the Act or these Rules to extend or shorten the time for compliance.

GENERAL NOTE

This details the formulae used to calculate time periods. Again it draws upon standard CPR rules but with a degree of insolvency-related customisation. Note the flexibility offered by IA 1986 s.376 for personal insolvency situations.

Paragraph 3 engages CPR r.3.1(2)(a) to extend or shorten time limits for compliance with IR 2016 requirements: see in relation to the predecessor provision *Re Legal and Equitable Securities plc* [2011] B.C.C. 354 and the judgment of David Richards J in *Re Lehman Bros International (Europe)* [2014] EWHC 1687 (Ch); [2014] B.P.I.R. 1259. *Re Calibre Solicitors Ltd* [2014] All E.R. (D) 187. reaffirmed the ability of the court to extend time and the linkage with CPR jurisprudence was stressed.

For general discussion of time-related issues in the insolvency context see Milman [2014] 2 NIBLeJ 5.

Schedule 6

Insolvency jurisdiction of county court hearing centres

Rule 9.22

[Note: where the entry "London Insolvency District" appears in this table, jurisdiction under Parts 1 to 7 of the Act is conferred on the High Court as a result of article 6B of the High Court and County Courts Jurisdiction Order 1991 (S.I. 1991/724) which was inserted by the High Court and County Courts Jurisdiction (Amendment) Order 2014 (S.I. 2014/821).]

Name of county court hearing centre	**Parts of the Insolvency Act under which proceedings may be commenced at a county court hearing centre or the alternative court or county court hearing centre where proceedings may be commenced**	**Nearest full time court or hearing centre**
Aberystwyth	Parts 1 to 11	Cardiff
Aldershot & Farnham	Guildford	
Banbury	Parts 1 to 11	Luton, Gloucester or Reading
Barnet	London Insolvency District - High Court for Parts 1 to 7 (see head note); County Court at Central London for Parts 7A to 11	
Barnsley	Parts 1 to 11	Sheffield
Barnstaple	Parts 1 to 11	Exeter
Barrow-in-Furness	Parts 1 to 11	Blackpool or Preston
Basildon	Southend-on-Sea	
Basingstoke	Reading	
Bath	Parts 1 to 11	Bristol
Bedford	Parts 1 to 11	Luton
Birkenhead	Parts 1 to 11	
Birmingham	Parts 1 to 11	
Blackburn	Parts 1 to 11	Preston
Blackpool	Parts 1 to 11	
Blackwood	Parts 1 to 11	Cardiff
Bodmin	Truro	
Bolton	Parts 1 to 11	
Boston	Parts 1 to 11	Nottingham
Bournemouth and Poole	Parts 1 to 11	
Bow	London Insolvency District - High Court for Parts 1 to 7 (see head note); County Court at Central London for Parts 7A to 11	

Name of county court hearing centre	Parts of the Insolvency Act under which proceedings may be commenced at a county court hearing centre or the alternative court or county court hearing centre where proceedings may be commenced	Nearest full time court or hearing centre
Bradford	Parts 1 to 11	
Brentford	London Insolvency District - High Court for Parts 1 to 7 (see head note); County Court at Central London for Parts 7A to 11	
Brighton	Parts 1 to 11	
Bristol	Parts 1 to 11	
Bromley	Croydon	
Burnley	Parts 1 to 11	Bolton or Preston
Bury	Parts 1 to 11	Bolton
Bury St. Edmunds	Parts 1 to 11	Cambridge
Caernarfon	Parts 1 to 11	
Cambridge	Parts 1 to 11	
Canterbury	Parts 1 to 11	Croydon or the High Court (London)
Cardiff	Parts 1 to 11	
Carlisle	Parts 1 to 11	Preston or Blackpool
Carmarthen	Parts 1 to 11	Cardiff
County Court at Central London	London Insolvency District - High Court for Parts 1 to 7 (see head note); County Court at Central London for Parts 7A to 11	
Chelmsford	Parts 1 to 11	Southend or the High Court (London)
Chester	Parts 1 to 11	
Chesterfield	Parts 1 to 11	Sheffield
Chichester	Brighton	
Chippenham and Trowbridge	Bath	
Clerkenwell and Shoreditch	London Insolvency District - High Court for Parts 1 to 7 (see head note); County Court at Central London for Parts 7A to 11	
Colchester	Parts 1 to 11	Southend or the High Court (London)
Conwy and Colwyn	Caernarfon	
Coventry	Parts 1 to 11	Birmingham
Crewe	Parts 1 to 11	Stoke or Chester
Croydon	Parts 1 to 11	

Name of county court hearing centre	**Parts of the Insolvency Act under which proceedings may be commenced at a county court hearing centre or the alternative court or county court hearing centre where proceedings may be commenced**	**Nearest full time court or hearing centre**
Croydon	Parts 1 to 11	
Darlington	Parts 1 to 11	Middlesbrough
Dartford	Medway	
Derby	Parts 1 to 11	
Doncaster	Parts 1 to 11	Sheffield
Dudley	Parts 1 to 11	Birmingham
Durham	Parts 1 to 11	Newcastle
Eastbourne	Parts 1 to 11	Brighton
Edmonton	London Insolvency District - High Court for Parts 1 to 7 (see head note); County Court at Central London for Parts 7A to 11	
Exeter	Parts 1 to 11	
Gateshead	Newcastle upon Tyne	
Gloucester and Cheltenham	Parts 1 to 11	
Great Grimsby	Parts 1 to 11	Hull
Guildford	Parts 1 to 11	Croydon
Halifax	Parts 1 to 11	Leeds
Harrogate	Parts 1 to 11	Leeds
Hartlepool	Middlesbrough	
Hastings	Parts 1 to 11	Brighton
Haverfordwest	Parts 1 to 11	Cardiff
Hereford	Parts 1 to 11	Gloucester
Hertford	Parts 1 to 11	Luton
High Wycombe	Aylesbury	
Horsham	Brighton	
Huddersfield	Parts 1 to 11	Leeds
Ipswich	Parts 1 to 11	Norwich or Southend
Kendal	Parts 1 to 11	Blackpool or Preston
Kettering	Northampton	
Kings Lynn	Norwich or Peterborough	
Kingston-upon-Hull	Parts 1 to 11	
Kingston-upon-Thames	Parts 1 to 11	

Name of county court hearing centre	Parts of the Insolvency Act under which proceedings may be commenced at a county court hearing centre or the alternative court or county court hearing centre where proceedings may be commenced	Nearest full time court or hearing centre
Lambeth	London Insolvency District - High Court for Parts 1 to 7 (see head note); County Court at Central London for Parts 7A to 11	
Lancaster	Parts 1 to 11	Blackpool or Preston
Leeds	Parts 1 to 11	
Leicester	Parts 1 to 11	
Lewes	Brighton	
Lincoln	Parts 1 to 11	Nottingham
Liverpool	Parts 1 to 11	
Llanelli	Swansea	
Llangefni	Parts 1 to 11	
Luton	Parts 1 to 11	
Maidstone	Parts 1 to 11	Croydon or the High Court (London)
Manchester	Parts 1 to 11	
Mansfield	Nottingham	
Mayor's and City of London	London Insolvency District - High Court for Parts 1 to 7 (see head note); County Court at Central London for Parts 7A to 11	
Medway	Canterbury	Croydon or the High Court (London)
Merthyr Tydfil	Parts 1 to 11	Cardiff
Middlesbrough	Parts 1 to 11	
Milton Keynes	Parts 1 to 11	Luton
Mold	Wrexham	Wrexham
Newcastle upon Tyne	Parts 1 to 11	
Newport (Gwent)	Parts 1 to 11	Cardiff
Newport (Isle of Wight)	Parts 1 to 11	Southampton or Portsmouth
Northampton	Parts 1 to 11	Luton
North Shields	Newcastle upon Tyne	
Norwich	Parts 1 to 11	
Nottingham	Parts 1 to 11	
Nuneaton	Coventry	

Name of county court hearing centre	**Parts of the Insolvency Act under which proceedings may be commenced at a county court hearing centre or the alternative court or county court hearing centre where proceedings may be commenced**	**Nearest full time court or hearing centre**
Oldham	Parts 1 to 11	
Oxford	Parts 1 to 11	Reading
Peterborough	Parts 1 to 11	Cambridge
Plymouth	Parts 1 to 11	
Pontypridd	Parts 1 to 11	Cardiff
Portsmouth	Parts 1 to 11	
Port Talbot	Parts 1 to 11	
Prestatyn	Parts 1 to 11	
Preston	Parts 1 to 11	
Reading	Parts 1 to 11	
Reigate	Guildford	
Rhyl	Parts 1 to 11	Birkenhead or Chester
Romford	Parts 1 to 11	
Salisbury	Parts 1 to 11	Bournemouth or Southampton
Scarborough	Parts 1 to 11	York, Hull or Middlesbrough
Scunthorpe	Parts 1 to 11	Hull or Sheffield
Sheffield	Parts 1 to 11	
Skipton	Bradford	
Slough	Parts 1 to 11	
Southampton	Parts 1 to 11	
Southend-on-Sea	Parts 1 to 11	
South Shields	Newcastle upon Tyne	
Stafford	Parts 1 to 11	Stoke
Staines	Guildford	
St Albans	Parts 1 to 11	Luton
St Helens	Liverpool	
Stockport	Parts 1 to 11	Manchester
Stoke-on-Trent	Parts 1 to 11	
Sunderland	Parts 1 to 11	Newcastle
Swansea	Parts 1 to 11	Cardiff
Swindon	Parts 1 to 11	Gloucester or Reading
Taunton	Parts 1 to 11	Exeter or Bristol
Telford	Parts 1 to 11	

Name of county court hearing centre	**Parts of the Insolvency Act under which proceedings may be commenced at a county court hearing centre or the alternative court or county court hearing centre where proceedings may be commenced**	**Nearest full time court or hearing centre**
Thanet	Canterbury	
Torquay & Newton Abbot	Parts 1 to 11	Exeter
Truro	Parts 1 to 11	Plymouth
Tunbridge Wells	Parts 1 to 11	Croydon
Uxbridge	The County Court at Central London	
Wakefield	Parts 1 to 11	Leeds
Walsall	Parts 1 to 11	
Wandsworth	London Insolvency District - High Court for Parts 1 to 7 (see head note); County Court at Central London for Parts 7A to 11	
Warwick	Parts 1 to 11	Birmingham
Watford	Luton	
Welshpool & Newton	Parts 1 to 11	Stoke or Chester
West Cumbria	Parts 1 to 11	
Weston Super Mare	Bristol	
Weymouth	Bournemouth	Bournemouth
Wigan	Parts 1 to 11	Bolton, Manchester or Preston
Willesden	London Insolvency District - High Court for Parts 1 to 7 (see head note); County Court at Central London for Parts 7A to 11	
Winchester	Parts 1 to 11	Southampton
Wolverhampton	Parts 1 to 11	
Woolwich	Croydon	
Worcester	Parts 1 to 11	Gloucester
Worthing	Brighton	
Wrexham	Parts 1 to 11	Birkenhead, Stoke or Chester
Yeovil	Parts 1 to 11	Exeter or Bristol
York	Parts 1 to 11	

General Note

This maps out in tabular form the insolvency jurisdiction of county court hearing centres.

See the official "[Note]" in relation to the "London Insolvency District".

Schedule 7

Information to be provided in the bankruptcy application

Rule 10.35

Part 1

Debtor's personal information

1 Debtor's title.

2 Debtor's identification details.

3 Any previous name or other names by which the debtor is known or has been known during the last five years immediately before the date of the bankruptcy application.

Part 2

Additional personal information

4 Debtor's contact telephone number.

5 Debtor's email address (if any).

6 Debtor's date of birth.

7 Debtor's National Insurance number.

8 Debtor's gender.

9 Any previous address at which the debtor has resided during the three years immediately before the date of the bankruptcy application.

10 Whether the debtor is–

(a) single;

(b) married;

(c) divorced;

(d) co-habiting;

(e) separated;

(f) widowed;

(g) a civil partner;

(h) a former civil partner; or

(i) a surviving civil partner.

11 All occupants of the debtor's household and in relation to each person–

(a) name;

(b) age;

(c) relationship to the debtor; and

(d) whether or not that person is dependent on the debtor.

12 Any other person dependent on the debtor and in relation to each person–

(a) name;

(b) age;

(c) postal address; and

(d) reason for that person's dependency on the debtor.

Occupation and employment details

13 Debtor's occupation (if any).

14 Debtor's employment status.

15 Where the debtor is employed–

(a) date when the debtor commenced the employment; and

(b) name and address of the employer.

16 Where the debtor is unemployed–

(a) date when the debtor was last employed;

(b) date when the debtor commenced the employment; and

(c) name and address of the last employer.

17 Where the debtor has worked for any previous employers during the 12 months immediately before the date of the bankruptcy application–

(a) dates of that employment; and

(b) name and address of those employers.

18 Where the debtor is, or has been, self-employed other than as a partner in a partnership, during the three years preceding the date of the bankruptcy application, in respect of each business–

(a) date when the business commenced trading;

(b) name and trading address of the business;

(c) name or names, other than the debtor's name, in which the debtor carried on business;

(d) nature of the business;

(e) trading address or addresses of the business and any address or addresses at which the debtor has carried on business during the period in which any of the debtor's bankruptcy debts were incurred; and

(f) the date the business ceased trading, if applicable.

19 Where the debtor traded in a partnership at any time in the three years immediately preceding the date of the bankruptcy application, in respect of each partnership–

(a) date the partnership commenced;

(b) name and trading address of the partnership;

(c) trading address or addresses of the partnership and any address or addresses at which the partnership has carried on business during or after the time when any of the debtor's bankruptcy debts were incurred; and

(d) date the partnership ceased, if applicable.

20 Where the debtor is, or has been, a director or involved in the management of a company during the 12 months immediately preceding the date of the bankruptcy application–

(a) name and contact details for each company; and

(b) in the case of any company mentioned in accordance with sub paragraph (a) that is subject to any insolvency proceedings, the office-holder and contact details for that office-holder.

Creditors

21 In respect of each creditor–

(a) name and address;

(b) account number or reference (if known);

(c) date the debt was incurred;

(d) the amount the creditor claims the debtor owes the creditor; and

(e) where the debt is secured, the property of the debtor which is claimed by the creditor to clear or reduce the creditor's debt.

22 Where the debtor has an interest in a property, in relation to each property, its address.

Legal proceedings

23 Where the debtor is, or has been in the five years immediately preceding the date of the bankruptcy application, involved in proceedings for divorce, separation or the dissolution of a civil partnership–

(a) identity of the proceedings;

(b) nature of the proceedings; and

(c) date and details of any resolution of those proceedings and any agreed settlement, whether formal or informal, and any gifts or transfers of property that occurred in, or as a result, of those proceedings.

24 Where the debtor is involved in proceedings, other than proceedings for divorce, separation or the dissolution of a civil partnership–

(a) identity of the proceedings;

(b) nature of the proceedings; and

(c) date and details of any interim settlement, whether formal or informal, and any interim orders.

Assets and liabilities

25 Total value of assets.

26 Total value of liabilities.

27 Debtor's net monthly income from all sources.

28 Debtor's monthly surplus income calculated by reference to paragraphs 23 to 30 of Schedule 8 (additional information to be provided in the bankruptcy application).

General Note

This prescribes the content of the bankruptcy application where a debtor seeks to bankrupt himself/herself under IR 2016 r.10.35. It is copied over from Sch.2A to IR 1986. It is not exhaustive as additional information is required by Sch.8.

See also General Note to Sch.9.

Schedule 8

Additional information to be provided in the bankruptcy application

Rule 10.35

Disposal of assets

1 Where in the five years preceding the date on which the bankruptcy application is made the debtor has entered into a transaction at an undervalue within the meaning of section 339(1), given a preference within the meaning of section 340(2), has rights or excluded rights under section 342A(3) of the Act or placed an asset into a trust for the benefit of any person, including the surrender of life, endowment and pension policies, in respect of each asset–

(a) description of the asset;

(b) date the debtor gave away, transferred or sold the asset;

(c) consideration given, if any;

(d) name and address of the person to whom the debtor sold, transferred or gave away the asset;

(e) relationship of that person to the debtor;

(f) if relevant, name of the trustees and beneficiaries or class of beneficiaries;

(g) estimated market value of the asset at the date of the bankruptcy application;

(h) net proceeds (if any) (less any charges and legal fees).

2 Where in the five years preceding the date on which the bankruptcy application is made the debtor has disposed of or sold any property at market value or disposed of, sold at market value or realised any life, endowment and pension policies in respect of each asset–

(a) description of the asset;

(b) date the debtor disposed of, sold at market value or realised the asset; and

(c) net proceeds (if any) (less any charges and legal fees).

Financial arrangements with creditors

3 Where the debtor has been made bankrupt in the two years immediately preceding the date of the bankruptcy application–

(a) date of the bankruptcy order; and

(b) reference allocated by the official receiver.

4 Where the debtor has entered into a debt relief order in the two years immediately preceding the date of the bankruptcy application–

(a) date of the debt relief order; and

(b) reference allocated by the official receiver.

5 Where the debtor has, or has had, an IVA in the two years immediately preceding the date of the bankruptcy application, the date of the arrangement.

6 Where the debtor has, or has had, an arrangement in force with creditors, other than an IVA in the two years immediately preceding the date of the bankruptcy application, the date and nature of the arrangement.

Legal and financial advisers

7 Where a solicitor has acted for or on behalf of the debtor in the five years immediately preceding the date of the bankruptcy application, in relation to each solicitor–

(a) name, address and reference of the solicitor; and

(b) nature and date of the transaction or transactions on which the solicitor advised or acted.

8 Where an accountant, book keeper or other financial adviser has acted for or on behalf of the debtor in the five years immediately preceding the date of the bankruptcy application, in relation to each accountant, book keeper and financial adviser–

(a) name, address and reference; and

(b) dates of acting for the debtor.

Business affairs of a self-employed debtor

9 Where the debtor traded in a partnership at any time in the three years immediately preceding the date of the bankruptcy application, in respect of each partnership–

(a) names and addresses of each of the partners;

(b) name or names, other than the partners' names, in which the partnership carried on business; and

(c) the nature of the partnership business.

10 Where the debtor is or has been self-employed (other than as a partner in a partnership) at any time in the three years immediately preceding the date of the bankruptcy application–

(a) Value Added Tax number, where the business was registered for Value Added Tax;

(b) address where the debtor's books of account and other accounting records are kept; and

(c) where the debtor holds records on a computer, details of which records are held, what software is used (including any passwords) and where the computer is located.

11 Where the debtor is or has been self-employed (including a partner in a partnership) at any time in the three years immediately preceding the date of the bankruptcy application–

(a) name and address of any person employed by the debtor immediately preceding the bankruptcy application; and

(b) whether–

(i) the debtor owes any employee or former employee any money, and

(ii) any employee or former employee has or may claim that the debtor owes that person some money.

Financial affairs – assets

12 The nature and value of each asset belonging to the debtor.

13 Where any asset is owned jointly with another person–

(a) name and address of that joint owner; and

(b) relationship of that person to the debtor.

14 Where any asset is subject to the rights of any person (other than a joint owner), whether as a secured creditor of the debtor or otherwise, in respect of each asset–

(a) nature of third party rights;

(b) account number or reference of that creditor or creditors; and

(c) amount each creditor claims is owed to them.

15 Where the debtor holds or has held in the last two years any bank, building society, credit union or national savings account including any joint, business or dormant accounts, in respect of each account–

(a) name, address and sort code of the bank or supplier;

(b) account number; and

(c) whether or not the debtor's regular income is paid into the account.

16 Where the debtor owns a motor vehicle or has disposed of any vehicle during the 12 months immediately preceding the date of the bankruptcy application, in respect of each motor vehicle–

(a) make and model;

(b) registration number;

(c) what the motor vehicle is or was used for by the debtor

(d) save where the motor vehicle has been disposed of, the location of the motor vehicle; and

(e) where the motor vehicle has been disposed of, the date of disposal and any proceeds from that disposal.

17 Where the debtor regularly uses a motor vehicle that the debtor does not own, in respect of each motor vehicle–

(a) make and model;

(b) registration number;

(c) name and address of the owner; and

(d) debtor's relationship to the vehicle's owner.

18 Where the debtor owns any property consisting of land or buildings, in respect of each property–

(a) type of and description of the property;

(b) who lives at the property and their relationship to the debtor; (c) any income received by the debtor from the property; and

(d) nature of the insurance policy currently in force in relation to the property and the expiry date of that insurance policy.

19 Where the debtor rents or leases a property, in respect of each property–

(a) who lives at the property and their relationship to the debtor;

(b) monthly rent;

(c) name and address of the landlord and any managing agent.

20 Where the debtor has an interest in any other property, in respect of each property–

(a) nature of the interest;

(b) type of and description of the property;

(c) who lives at the property and their relationship to the debtor;

(d) name and address of the person who permits the debtor to use the property;

(e) amount paid by the debtor to the person who permits the debtor to use the property;

(f) any income received by the debtor from the property; and

(g) whether or not there is a written agreement.

21 Where the debtor resides at a property in which the debtor has no interest, the basis on which the debtor resides at that property.

22 Where the debtor has or has held within the five years immediately before the date of the bankruptcy application any occupational pension, personal pension, endowment or other life policy in relation to each policy–

(a) type of policy;

(b) name and address of the pension, endowment or life assurance company or broker;

(c) policy number;

(d) approximate date when the policy was taken out;

(e) estimated value of policy;

(f) amount (if any) being received now by the debtor and the frequency of those payments; and

(g) name of the beneficiary or beneficiaries of the policy.

Financial affairs – income and expenditure

23 Debtor's total annual income from all sources, the sources of that income and the amount from each source.

24 Total annual household income from all sources, the sources of that income and the amount from each source.

25 Current (or last) income tax reference number.

26 Monthly national insurance.

27 Mean monthly tax.

28 Where the debtor has any current attachment of earnings orders in force, in respect of each attachment of earnings order–

(a) name of creditor;

(b) name of the court that made the attachment of earnings order.

29 Particulars of the debtor's mean monthly expenditure which the debtor claims is necessary to meet the monthly reasonable domestic needs of the debtor's family, including the objective and the amount of that expenditure.

30 Particulars of the debtor's monthly expenditure not otherwise provided under this Schedule.

Enforcement officers and enforcement agents

31 Where an enforcement officer or enforcement agent has visited the debtor in the last six months–

(a) name of the creditor by whom the relevant debt is claimed;

(b) date of initial visit;

(c) description and estimated value of property seized.

Cause of insolvency

32 Why the debt was incurred.

33 Date when the debtor first experienced difficulty in paying some or all of the debtor's debts.

34 Reasons for the debtor not having enough money to pay some or all of the debtor's debts.

35 Where the debtor has gambled any money through betting or gambling during the last two years, how much the debtor has gambled.

General Note

This details further information required on a bankruptcy application. It mirrors Sch.2B to IR 1986.

See also General Note to Sch.9.

Schedule 9

Information to be given to creditors

Rule 10.47

1 Title of the debtor.

2 Debtor's identification details.

3 Any previous name or other names by which the debtor is known or has been known during the last five years immediately before the date of the bankruptcy application.

4 Any previous address at which the debtor has resided at during the three years immediately before the date of the bankruptcy application.

5 Name and address for each creditor.

6 Amount each creditor claims is due.

7 Debtor's occupation (if any).

8 Debtor's employment status.

9 Where the debtor is, or has been, self-employed other than as a partner in a partnership, during the three years preceding the date of the bankruptcy application, in respect of each business–

(a) name and trading address of the business;

(b) name or names, other than the debtor's name, in which the debtor carried on business;

(c) nature of the business;

(d) trading address or addresses of the business and any address or addresses at which the debtor has carried on business during the period in which any of the debtor's bankruptcy debts were incurred; and

(e) where the business has ceased trading, the date when the business ceased trading.

10 Total value of assets.

11 Total value of liabilities.

12 Where in the five years preceding the date of the bankruptcy application the debtor has given away, placed into a trust for the benefit of any person, given a preference within the meaning of section 340 of the Act, has rights or excluded rights under section 342A of the Act or has transferred or sold for less than its true value any assets that the debtor owned, either alone or jointly, including the surrender of life, endowment and pension policies in relation to each asset–

(a) description of the asset;

(b) date the debtor gave away, transferred or sold the asset;

(c) relationship of that person to the debtor;

(d) estimated market value or true value of the asset at the date of the bankruptcy application;

(e) value at which the asset was given away, transferred or sold; and

(f) net proceeds (if any) (less any charges and legal fees).

13 Where any asset is owned jointly with another person, the nature of the asset.

14 Where any asset is subject to the rights of any person (other than a joint owner), whether as a secured creditor of the debtor or otherwise, in respect of each asset, the nature of third party rights.

15 Where the debtor owns a motor vehicle or has disposed of any vehicle during the 12 months immediately preceding the date of the bankruptcy application, in respect of each motor vehicle

(a) make, model and year of manufacture;

(b) what the motor vehicle is or was used for by the debtor;

(c) save where the motor vehicle has been disposed of, the location of the motor vehicle;

(d) where the motor vehicle has been disposed of, the date of disposal and any proceeds from that disposal.

16 Where the debtor regularly uses a motor vehicle that the debtor does not own, in relation to each motor vehicle–

(a) make and model; and

(b) debtor's relationship to the vehicle's owner.

17 Where the debtor owns or has an interest in any property, in respect of each property–

(a) address;

(b) type of and description of the property;

(c) nature of the interest

(d) value of that interest; and

(e) any income received by the debtor from the property.

18 Where the debtor holds or has held within the five years immediately before the date of the bankruptcy application any occupational pension, personal pension, endowment or other life policy in respect of each policy–

(a) type of policy;

(b) approximate date when the policy was taken out; and

(c) estimated value of policy.

19 Debtor's net monthly income from all sources.

20 Debtor's monthly surplus income after taking into account any contribution made by a member of the debtor's family to the amount necessary for the reasonable domestic needs of the debtor and the debtor's family.

21 Current (or last) income tax reference number.

22 In respect of each creditor–

(a) name and address;

(b) date the debt was incurred;

(c) the amount the creditor claims the debtor owes the creditor;

(d) where the debt is secured, the property of the debtor which is claimed by the creditor to clear of reduce the creditor's debt.

General Note

This replicates Sch.2C to IR 1986. Former Schs 2A–2C to IR 1986 (now IR 2016 Schs 7–9) were inserted by the Insolvency (Amendment) Rules 2016 (SI 2016/187) with effect from 6 April 2016 to provide further detail on the operation of the new bankruptcy adjudication procedure in force from the latter date. Essentially they are information checklists.

Schedule 10

Destination of appeals from decisions of District Judges in corporate insolvency matters

Rule 12.59

Country court hearing centre	*Destination of Appeal*
Aberystwyth	Cardiff or Caernarfon District Registry
Banbury	Birmingham District Registry
Barnsley	Leeds District Registry
Barnstaple	Bristol District Registry
Barrow-in-Furness	Liverpool District Registry or Manchester District Registry
Bath	Bristol District Registry
Bedford	Birmingham District Registry
Birkenhead	Liverpool District Registry or Manchester District Registry
Birmingham	Birmingham District Registry
Blackburn	Liverpool District Registry or Manchester District Registry
Blackpool	Liverpool District Registry or Manchester District Registry
Blackwood	Cardiff District Registry
Bolton	Liverpool District Registry or Manchester District Registry
Boston	Birmingham District Registry
Bournemouth and Poole	Registrar in Bankruptcy
Bradford	Leeds District Registry

Country court hearing centre	*Destination of Appeal*
Brighton	Registrar in Bankruptcy
Bristol	Bristol District Registry
Burnley	Liverpool District Registry or Manchester District Registry
Bury	Liverpool District Registry or Manchester District Registry
Bury St. Edmunds	Registrar in Bankruptcy
Caernarfon	Cardiff District Registry
Cambridge	Registrar in Bankruptcy
Canterbury	Registrar in Bankruptcy
Cardiff	Cardiff District Registry
Carlisle	Liverpool District Registry or Manchester District Registry
Caernarfon	Cardiff District Registry or Caernarfon District Registry
County Court at Central London	Registrar in Bankruptcy
Chelmsford	Registrar in Bankruptcy
Chester	Liverpool District Registry or Manchester District Registry
Chesterfield	Leeds District Registry
Colchester	Registrar in Bankruptcy
Coventry	Birmingham District Registry
Crewe	Liverpool District Registry or Manchester District Registry
Croydon	Registrar in Bankruptcy
Darlington	Newcastle District Registry
Derby	Birmingham District Registry
Doncaster	Leeds District Registry
Dudley	Birmingham District Registry
Durham	Leeds District Registry or Newcastle District Registry
Eastbourne	Registrar in Bankruptcy
Exeter	Bristol District Registry
Gloucester and Cheltenham	Bristol District Registry
Great Grimsby	Leeds District Registry
Guildford	Registrar in Bankruptcy
Halifax	Leeds District Registry
Harrogate	Leeds District Registry
Hastings	Registrar in Bankruptcy
Haverfordwest	Cardiff District Registry
Hereford	Bristol District Registry
Hertford	Registrar in Bankruptcy
Huddersfield	Leeds District Registry
Ipswich	Registrar in Bankruptcy
Kendal	Liverpool District Registry or Manchester District Registry
Kingston-upon-Hull	Leeds District Registry

Country court hearing centre	*Destination of Appeal*
Kingston-upon-Thames	Registrar in Bankruptcy
Lancaster	Liverpool District Registry or Manchester District Registry
Leeds	Leeds District Registry
Leicester	Birmingham District Registry
Lincoln	Leeds District Registry or Birmingham District Registry
Liverpool	Liverpool District Registry or Manchester District Registry
Llangefni	Cardiff District Registry or Caernarfon District Registry
Luton	Registrar in Bankruptcy
Maidstone	Registrar in Bankruptcy
Manchester	Manchester District Registry
Merthyr Tydfil	Cardiff District Registry
Middlesbrough	Newcastle District Registry
Milton Keynes	Birmingham District Registry
Newcastle upon Tyne	Newcastle District Registry
Newport (Gwent)	Cardiff District Registry
Newport (Isle of Wight)	Registrar in Bankruptcy
Northampton	Birmingham District Registry
Norwich	Registrar in Bankruptcy
Nottingham	Birmingham District Registry
Oldham	Liverpool District Registry or Manchester District Registry
Oxford	Registrar in Bankruptcy
Peterborough	Registrar in Bankruptcy
Plymouth	Bristol District Registry
Pontypridd	Cardiff District Registry
Portsmouth	Registrar in Bankruptcy
Port Talbot	Cardiff District Registry
Prestatyn	Cardiff District Registry or Caernarfon District Registry
Preston	Liverpool District Registry or Manchester District Registry
Reading	Registrar in Bankruptcy
Rhyl	Cardiff District Registry or Caernarfon District Registry
Romford	Registrar in Bankruptcy
Salisbury	Registrar in Bankruptcy
Scarborough	Leeds District Registry
Scunthorpe	Leeds District Registry
Sheffield	Leeds District Registry
Slough	Registrar in Bankruptcy
Southampton	Registrar in Bankruptcy
Southend-on-Sea	Registrar in Bankruptcy
Stafford	Birmingham District Registry

Country court hearing centre	*Destination of Appeal*
St Albans	Registrar in Bankruptcy
Stockport	Liverpool District Registry or Manchester District Registry
Stoke-on-Trent	Manchester District Registry
Sunderland	Newcastle District Registry
Swansea	Cardiff District Registry
Swindon	Bristol District Registry
Taunton	Bristol District Registry
Telford	Birmingham District Registry
Torquay & Newton Abbot	Bristol District Registry
Truro	Bristol District Registry
Tunbridge Wells	Registrar in Bankruptcy
Wakefield	Leeds District Registry
Walsall	Birmingham District Registry
Warwick	Birmingham District Registry
Welshpool & Newton	Cardiff District Registry
West Cumbria	Liverpool District Registry or Manchester District Registry
Wigan	Liverpool District Registry or Manchester District Registry
Winchester	Registrar in Bankruptcy
Wolverhampton	Birmingham District Registry
Worcester	Birmingham District Registry
Wrexham	Cardiff District Registry or Caernarfon District Registry
Yeovil	Bristol District Registry
York	Leeds District Registry

General Note

This Schedule, which had no counterpart in IR 1986, must be read alongside IR 2016 r.12.59. It only applies to appeals in corporate insolvency cases and should remove any doubt on its subject matter.

Schedule 11

Determination of insolvency office-holder's remuneration

Rule 18.22

This table sets out the realisation and distribution scales for determining the remuneration of trustees and liquidators.

The realisation scale

on the first £5,000	20%
on the next £5,000	15%
on the next £90,000	10%
on all further sums realised	5%

The distribution scale

on the first £5,000	10%
on the next £5,000	7.5%
on the next £90,000	5%
on all further sums distributed	2.5%.

General Note

This provides important information for determining the remuneration scales to be applied to trustees in bankruptcy and liquidators. See IR 2016 r.18.22. The scale is copied from Sch.6 to IR 1986 and the figures therein have not changed since the latter was introduced in 2004.

Appendix I

Table of Destinations of the Insolvency Rules 1986

Guide to the destination of the Insolvency Rules 1986 (SI 1986/1925) in the Insolvency Rules (England and Wales) 2016 (SI 2016/1024)

[**Note**: This table is reproduced directly from that prepared by the Insolvency Service. Caution should be taken when using it as it is rather generic and mainly relates rule to rule (rather than sub-rule to sub-rule) and contains inaccuracies.

This Table has not been officially updated to reflect changes post-April 2017 (and in particular still refers to the "EC Regulation").]

This table indicates the destination of provisions in the 1986 Rules. The 2016 Rules broadly derive from the 1986 Rules. However there is rarely an exact match as the structure of the 2016 Rules is different, the language has been modernised and there have been significant changes, in particular as a result of amendments to the primary legislation made by the Enterprise and Regulatory Reform Act 2013, the Deregulation Act 2015, and the Small Business, Enterprise and Employment Act 2015. Furthermore the information requirements previously contained in forms have now been imported into the relevant rule as specified content. Finally the new Rules try to avoid copying out of the primary legislation. Instead they contain many references to the Insolvency Act 1986 to enable the user to connect individual rules with the relevant provisions of the Act that the Rules supplement.

1986 Rule heading	1986 rule	2016 rule
Citation and commencement	0.1	1
Construction and interpretation	0.2	2
Extent	0.3	3
THE FIRST GROUP OF PARTS		
PART 1 COMPANY VOLUNTARY ARRANGEMENTS		
CHAPTER 1 PRELIMINARY		
Scope of this Part; interpretation	1.1	
CHAPTER 2 PROPOSAL BY DIRECTORS		
Preparation of proposal	1.2	
Contents of proposal	1.3	2.2, 2.3
Notice to intended nominee	1.4	
Statement of affairs	1.5	2.6
Additional disclosure for assistance of nominee	1.6	2.8
Nominee's report on the proposal	1.7	2.9
Replacement of nominee	1.8	2.10
Summoning of meetings under s. 3	1.9	2.25 to 2.28
CHAPTER 3 PROPOSAL BY ADMINISTRATOR OR LIQUIDATOR (HIMSELF THE NOMINEE)		
Preparation of proposal	1.10	2.3, 2.5
Summoning of meetings under s. 3	1.11	2.25 to 2.29, 2.31

1986 Rule heading	1986 rule	2016 rule
CHAPTER 4 PROPOSAL BY ADMINISTRATOR OR LIQUIDATOR (ANOTHER INSOLVENCY PRACTITIONER THE NOMINEE)		
Preparation of proposal and notice to nominee	1.12	2.3
CHAPTER 5 PROCEEDINGS ON A PROPOSAL MADE BY THE DIRECTORS, OR BY THE ADMINISTRATOR, OR BY THE LIQUIDATOR		
SECTION A: MEETINGS OF COMPANY'S CREDITORS AND MEMBERS		
Summoning of meetings	1.13	2.29, 15.8, 15.29
The chairman at meetings	1.14	15.21
The chairman as proxy-holder	1.15	16.5
Attendance by company officers	1.16	2.30, 15.14
SECTION B: VOTING RIGHTS AND MAJORITIES		
Voting rights (creditors)	1.17	15.7, 15.29
Procedure for admission of creditors' claims for voting purposes	1.17A	15.33
Voting rights (members)	1.18	2.35
Requisite majorities (creditors)	1.19	15.31
Requisite majorities (members)	1.20	2.36
Proceedings to obtain agreement on the proposal	1.21	Part 15
SECTION C: IMPLEMENTATION OF THE ARRANGEMENT		
Resolutions to follow approval	1.22	2.33
Notice of order made under section 4A(6)	1.22A	2.37
Hand-over of property etc. to supervisor	1.23	2.39
Report of meetings	1.24	2.38
Revocation or suspension of the arrangement	1.25	2.40
Supervisor's accounts and reports	1.26A	2.41
Production of accounts and records to Secretary of State	1.27	2.42
Fees, costs, charges and expenses	1.28	2.43
Completion of the arrangement	1.29	2.44
EC REGULATION—CONVERSION OF VOLUNTARY ARRANGEMENT INTO WINDING UP		
Application for conversion into winding up	1.31	21.2
Contents of witness statement	1.32	21.2
Power of court	1.33	21.3
EC REGULATION—MEMBER STATE LIQUIDATOR		
Interpretation of creditor and notice to member State liquidator	1.34	21.7, 21.8

1986 Rule heading	1986 rule	2016 rule
OBTAINING A MORATORIUM—PROCEEDINGS DURING A MORATORIUM—NOMINEES—CONSIDERATION OF PROPOSALS WHERE MORATORIUM OBTAINED		
SECTION A: OBTAINING A MORATORIUM		
Preparation of proposal by directors and submission to nominee	1.35	
Delivery of documents to the intended nominee etc	1.36	
Statement of affairs	1.37	2.11
The nominee's statement	1.38	2.13
Documents submitted to the court to obtain moratorium	1.39	2.14
Notice and advertisement of beginning of a moratorium	1.40	2.15
Notice of extension of moratorium	1.41	2.16, 2.17
Notice and advertisement of end of moratorium	1.42	2.18, 2.19
SECTION B: PROCEEDINGS DURING A MORATORIUM		
Disposal of charged property etc during a moratorium	1.43	2.18, 2.19
SECTION C: NOMINEES		
Withdrawal of nominee's consent to act	1.44	2.20
Replacement of nominee by the court	1.45	2.22
Notification of appointment of a replacement nominee	1.46	2.23
Applications to court under paragraphs 26 or 27 of Schedule A1 to the Act	1.47	2.24
SECTION D: CONSIDERATION OF PROPOSALS WHERE MORATORIUM OBTAINED		
Summoning of meetings; procedure at meetings etc	1.48	2.25 to 2.28, 2.30, Part 15
Entitlement to vote (creditors)	1.49	15.28
Procedure for admission of creditors' claims for voting purposes	1.50	15.33
Voting rights (members)	1.51	2.35
Requisite majorities (creditors)	1.52	15.31
Requisite majorities (members) and proceedings to obtain agreement	1.53	2.36, 15.21, 15.25
Implementation of the arrangement	1.54	2.39
TIME RECORDING INFORMATION		
Provision by nominee or supervisor of information about time spent	1.55	2.45
OMISSION OF INFORMATION FROM STATEMENT OF AFFAIRS		
Omission of Information from Statement of Affairs	1.56	2.7, 2.12

1986 Rule heading	1986 rule	2016 rule
PART 2 ADMINISTRATION PROCEDURE		
CHAPTER 1 APPLICATION FOR, AND MAKING OF, THE ORDER		
Introductory and interpretation	2.1	N/A
CHAPTER 2 APPOINTMENT OF ADMINISTRATOR BY COURT		
Witness statement in support of administration application	2.2	3.6
Form of application	2.3	3.3, 3.4, 3.5
Contents of application and witness statement in support	2.4	3.6
Filing of application	2.5	3.7, 3.10
Service of application	2.6	3.7, Sch 4 para 3
Notice to officers charged with execution of writs or other process, etc	2.7	3.9
Manner in which service to be effected	2.8	Sch 4
Proof of service	2.9	Sch 4 para 6
Application to appoint specified person as administrator by holder of qualifying floating charge	2.10	3.11
Application where company in liquidation	2.11	3.5
The hearing	2.12	3.11
Contents of court order	2.13	3.13, 3.14
Notice of administration order	2.14	3.15
CHAPTER 3 APPOINTMENT OF ADMINISTRATOR BY HOLDER OF FLOATING CHARGE		
Notice of intention to appoint	2.15	3.16
Notice of appointment	2.16	3.17
Filing notice with court	2.17	3.18
Appointment by floating charge holder	2.18	3.19
Appointment taking place out of court business hours	2.19	3.20, 3.21, 3.22
CHAPTER 4 APPOINTMENT OF ADMINISTRATOR BY COMPANY OR DIRECTORS		
Notice of intention to appoint	2.20	3.23
Statutory declaration	2.21	3.23
Notice of intention to appoint	2.22	3.23
Notice of appointment	2.23	3.24
Statutory declaration	2.24	3.24
Accompanying documents	2.25	3.252.263.27
CHAPTER 5 PROCESS OF ADMINISTRATION		
Notification and advertisement of administrator's appointment	2.27	3.29
Notice requiring statement of affairs	2.28	3.27
Verification and filing	2.29	3.30, 3.31, 3.32
Limited disclosure	2.30	3.44, 3.45, 3.47
Release from duty to submit statement of affairs; extension of time	2.31	3.33, 3.37

1986 Rule heading	1986 rule	2016 rule
Expenses of statement of affairs	2.32	3.34
Administrator's proposals	2.33	3.35, 3.36
Limited disclosure of para 49 statement 15	2.33A	3.45

CHAPTER 6 MEETINGS AND REPORTS

SECTION A: CREDITORS' MEETINGS

Meetings to consider administrator's proposals	2.34	3.38, 15.7, 15.12, 15.13
Creditors' meetings generally	2.35	15.8, 15.9, 15.10, 15.23, 15.24, 15.25
The chairman at meetings	2.36	15.21, 16.5
Meeting requisitioned by creditors	2.37	15.18, 15.19
Notice of meetings by advertisement only	2.37A	15.12
Entitlement to vote	2.38	15.28, 15.31, 15.34
Admission and rejection of claims	2.39	15.33, 15.35
Secured creditors	2.40	15.31
Holders of negotiable instruments	2.41	N/A
Hire-purchase, conditional sale and chattel leasing agreements	2.42	15.32
Resolutions	2.43	15.34
Minutes	2.44A	15.40
Revision of the administrator's proposals	2.45	3.42
Notice to creditors	2.46	3.43
Reports to creditors	2.47	18.6 – 18.10
Correspondence instead of creditors' meetings	2.48	N/A
Creditors' request for further information	2.48A	18.9

SECTION B: COMPANY MEETINGS

Venue and conduct of company meeting	2.49	15.21, 15.25, 15.40, 15.41

CHAPTER 7 THE CREDITORS' COMMITTEE

Constitution of committee	2.50	17.3, 17.4
Formalities of establishment	2.51	17.5
Functions and meetings of the committee	2.52	17.2, 17.14
The chairman at meetings	2.53	17.15
Quorum	2.54	17.16
Committee-members' representatives	2.55	17.17
Resignation	2.56	17.10
Termination of membership	2.57	17.11
Removal	2.58	17.12
Vacancies	2.59	17.8
Procedure at meetings	2.60	17.18
Resolutions of creditors' committee otherwise than at a meeting	2.61	17.19

1986 Rule heading	1986 rule	2016 rule
Information from administrator	2.62	17.22
Expenses of members	2.63	17.24
Members' dealing with the company	2.64	17.25
Formal defects	2.65	17.27

CHAPTER 8 DISPOSAL OF CHARGED PROPERTY

	2.66	3.49

CHAPTER 9 EXPENSES OF THE ADMINISTRATION

	2.67	3.51
Pre-administration costs	2.67A	3.52

CHAPTER 10 DISTRIBUTIONS TO CREDITORS

SECTION A: APPLICATION OF CHAPTER AND GENERAL

	2.68	14.28, 14.27, 14.38
Debts of insolvent company to rank equally	2.69	14.12
Supplementary provisions as to dividend	2.70	14.39
Division of unsold assets	2.71	14.13

SECTION B: MACHINERY OF PROVING A DEBT

Proving a debt	2.72	14.3, 14.4
Costs of proving	2.74	14.5
Administrator to allow inspection of proofs	2.75	14.6
New administrator appointed	2.76	3.70
Admission and rejection of proofs for dividend	2.77	14.7
Appeal against decision on proof	2.78	14.8, 14.9
Withdrawal or variation of proof	2.79	14.10
Expunging of proof by the court	2.80	14.11

SECTION C: QUANTIFICATION OF CLAIMS

Estimate of quantum	2.81	14.14
Negotiable instruments, etc	2.82	N/A
Secured creditors	2.83	14.19
Discounts	2.84	14.20
Mutual credits and set-off	2.85	14.24
Debt in foreign currency	2.86	14.21
Payments of a periodical nature	2.87	14.22
Interest	2.88	14.23
Debt payable at future time	2.89	14.44
Value of security	2.90	14.15

1986 Rule heading	1986 rule	2016 rule
Surrender for non-disclosure	2.91	14.16
Redemption by administrator	2.92	14.17
Test of security's value	2.93	14.18
Realisation of security by creditor	2.94	14.19
Notice of proposed distribution	2.95	14.26, 14.28, 14.29, 14.30
Admission or rejection of proofs	2.96	14.32
Postponement or cancellation of dividend	2.96A	14.33
Declaration of dividend	2.97	14.34
Notice of declaration of a dividend	2.98	14.35
Payments of dividends and related matters	2.99	14.35
Notice of no dividend, or no further dividend	2.100	14.37
Proof altered after payment of dividend	2.101	14.40
rule 2102 Secured creditors	2.1021	4.41
Disqualification from dividend	2.103	14.42
Assignment of right to dividend	2.104	14.43
Debt payable at future time	2.105	14.44
CHAPTER 11 THE ADMINISTRATOR		
Fixing of remuneration	2.106	18.16, 18.17, 18.18, 18.23
Recourse to meeting of creditors	2.107	18.24, 18.25
Recourse to the court	2.108	18.24 to 18.29
Creditors' claim that remuneration is or other expenses are excessive	2.109	18.34, 18.36, 18.37
Review of remuneration	2.109A	18.29
Remuneration of new administrator	2.109B	18.31
Apportionment of set fee remuneration	2.109C	18.32
CHAPTER 12 ENDING ADMINISTRATION		
Final progress reports	2.110	3.56, 18.3
Notice of automatic end of administration	2.111	3.55
Applications for extension of administration	2.112	3.54
Notice of end of administration	2.113	3.56
Application to court by administrator	2.114	3.57
Application to court by creditor	2.115	3.58
Notification by administrator of court order	2.116	3.59
Moving from administration to creditors' voluntary liquidation	2.117A	3.60
Moving from administration to dissolution	2.118	3.61
CHAPTER 13 REPLACING ADMINISTRATOR		
Grounds for resignation	2.119	3.62
Notice of intention to resign	2.120	3.63
Notice of resignation	2.121	3.64
Application to court to remove administrator from office	2.122	3.65
Notice of vacation of office when administrator ceases to be qualified to act	2.123	3.66

1986 Rule heading	**1986 rule**	**2016 rule**
Administrator deceased	2.124	3.67
Application to replace	2.125	3.68
Notification and advertisement of appointment of replacement administrator	2.126	3.69
Notification and advertisement of appointment of joint administrator	2.127	3.69
	2.128	3.69
Administrator's duties on vacating office	2.129	3.70
CHAPTER 14 EC REGULATION: CONVERSION OF ADMINISTRATION INTO WINDING UP		
Application for conversion into winding up	2.130	21.2
Contents of witness statement	2.131	21.2
Power of court	2.132	21.3
CHAPTER 15 EC REGULATION: MEMBER STATE LIQUIDATOR		
Interpretation of creditor and notice to member State liquidator	2.133	21.8
PART 3 ADMINISTRATIVE RECEIVERSHIP		
CHAPTER 1 APPOINTMENT OF ADMINISTRATIVE RECEIVER		
Acceptance of appointment	3.1	4.1
Notice and advertisement of appointment	3.2	4.5
CHAPTER 2 STATEMENT OF AFFAIRS AND REPORT TO CREDITORS		
Notice requiring statement of affairs	3.3	4.6
Verification and filing	3.4	4.7, 4.8, 4.9
Limited disclosure	3.5	4.12
Release from duty to submit statement of affairs; extension of time	3.6	4.10
Expenses of statement of affairs	3.7	4.11
Report to creditors	3.8	4.13, 4.14
CHAPTER 3 CREDITORS' MEETING		
Procedure for summoning meeting under s.48(2)	3.9	15.8, 15.9, 15.10
The chairman at the meeting	3.10	15.21
Voting rights	3.11	15.8, 15.28
Contents of claim	3.11A	1.2
Admission and rejection of claim	3.12	15.31, 15.33
Adjournment	3.14	15.23
Resolutions and minutes	3.15	15.34, 15.40
CHAPTER 4 THE CREDITORS' COMMITTEE		
Constitution of committee	3.16	17.3, 17.4
Formalities of establishment	3.17	17.5

1986 Rule heading	**1986 rule**	**2016 rule**
Functions and meetings of the committee	3.18	17.14
The chairman at meetings	3.19	17.15
Quorum	3.20	17.16
Committee-members' representatives	3.21	17.17
Resignation	3.22	17.10
Termination of membership	3.23	17.11
Removal	3.24	17.12
Vacancies	3.25	17.8
Procedure at meetings	3.26	17.18
Resolutions by post	3.27	17.19
Information from receiver	3.28	17.22
Expenses of members	3.29	17.24
Members' dealings with the company	3.30	17.26
Formal defects	3.30A	17.27

CHAPTER 5 THE ADMINISTRATIVE RECEIVER (MISCELLANEOUS)

Disposal of charged property	3.31	4.16
Abstract of receipts and payments	3.32	4.17
Resignation	3.33	4.18
Receiver deceased	3.34	4.19
Vacation of office	3.35	4.20, 4.21

CHAPTER 7 SECTION 176A THE REVISED PART

Report for creditors	3.39	4.22, 4.23
Receiver to deal with prescribed part	3.40	4.24

PART 4 COMPANIES WINDING UP

CHAPTER 1 THE SCHEME OF THIS PART OF THE RULES

Voluntary winding up; winding up by the court	4.1	6.1
Winding up by the court: the various forms of petition	4.2	
Time-limits	4.3	

CHAPTER 2 THE STATUTORY DEMAND (NO CVL APPLICATION)

Preliminary	4.4	7.2
Form and content of statutory demand	4.5	7.3
Information to be given in statutory demand	4.6	7.3

CHAPTER 3 PETITION TO WINDING-UP ORDER (NO CVL APPLICATION) (NO APPLICATIONTO PETITION BY CONTRIBUTORIES)

Injunction to restrain presentation or advertisement of petition	4.6A	7.24
Presentation and filing of petition	4.7	7.7
Service of petition	4.8	Sch 4 para 2

1986 Rule heading	1986 rule	2016 rule
Proof of service	4.9A	Sch 4 para 6
Other persons to receive copies of petition	4.10	7.9
Advertisement of petition	4.11	7.10
Verification of petition	4.12	7.6
Persons entitled to copy of petition	4.13	7.11
Certificate of compliance	4.14	7.12
Leave for petitioner to withdraw	4.15	7.13
Notice of appearance	4.16	7.14
List of appearances	4.17	7.15
Affidavit in opposition	4.18	7.16
Adjournment	4.18A	7.19
Substitution of creditor or contributory for petitioner	4.19	7.17
Notice and settling of winding-up order	4.20	7.21
Transmission and advertisement of order	4.21	7.22
Expenses of voluntary arrangement	4.21A	N/A
Petition dismissed	4.21B	7.23
CHAPTER 4 PETITION BY CONTRIBUTORIES (NO CVL APPLICATION)		
Presentation and service of petition	4.22	7.29, Sch 4 para 2
Return of petition	4.23	7.31
Application of Rules in Chapter 3	4.24	N/A
CHAPTER 5 PROVISIONAL LIQUIDATOR (NO CVL APPLICATION)		
Appointment of provisional liquidator	4.25	7.33
Notice of appointment	4.25A	7.36
Order of appointment	4.26	7.35
Deposit	4.27	7.34
Security	4.28	7.37
Failure to give or keep up security	4.29	7.37
Remuneration	4.30	7.38, 18.16, 18.20
Termination of appointment	4.31	7.39
CHAPTER 6 STATEMENT OF AFFAIRS AND OTHER INFORMATION		
Notice requiring statement of affairs	4.32	7.40
Verification and filing	4.33	7.41
Statement of affairs	4.34	6.2, 6.3, 6.4, 6.5
Copy statement of affairs	4.34A	N/A
Limited disclosure	4.35	6.6, 7.43
Release from duty to submit statement of affairs; extension of time	4.36	7.44
Expenses of statement of affairs	4.37	7.45
Expenses of statement of affairs	4.38	6.7
Submission of accounts	4.39	7.46
Submission of accounts	4.40	6.8
Expenses of preparing accounts	4.41	6.9
Further disclosure	4.42	7.47

1986 Rule heading	1986 rule	2016 rule
CHAPTER 7 INFORMATION TO CREDITORS AND CONTRIBUTORIES		
Reports by official receiver	4.43	7.48
Meaning of "creditors"	4.44	1.37
Report where statement of affairs lodged	4.45	7.48
Statement of affairs dispensed with	4.46	7.48
General rule as to reporting	4.47	7.48
Winding up stayed	4.48	7.51, 7.52
Information to creditors and contributories	4.49	6.15
Further information where liquidation follows administration	4.49A	6.16, 7.50
Reports to creditors and members — winding up by the court	4.49B	18.3, 18.8
CVL Progress reports — voluntary winding up	4.49C	18.3, 18.7
Final report to creditors	4.49D	18.14
Creditors' and members' request for further information	4.49E	18.9
Arrangements under s 110 (acceptance of shares, etc, as consideration	4.49F	18.11
Other distributions to members in specie	4.49G	18.12
CHAPTER 8 MEETINGS OF CREDITORS AND CONTRIBUTORIES		
SECTION A: RULES OF GENERAL APPLICATION		
First meetings	4.50	7.52, 15.8, 15.11
First meeting of creditors	4.51	15.8
Business at first meetings in the liquidation	4.52	15.9
Business at meeting under s. 95 or 98	4.53	N/A
Effect of adjournment on company meeting	4.53A	N/A
Report by director, etc.	4.53B	6.17
Additional contents of notices gazetted or advertised under s. 95	4.53C	15.8
Additional contents of notices gazetted or advertised under s. 98	4.53D	15.8
General power to call meetings	4.54	1.51, 15.3, 15.6
The chairman at meetings	4.55	15.21, 15.22
The chairman at meeting	4.56	15.21, 15.22
Requisitioned meetings	4.57	15.18, 15.1
Attendance at meetings of company's personnel	4.58	15.14, 15.22
Notice of meetings by advertisement only	4.59	15.12
Venue	4.60	15.10
Expenses of summoning meetings	4.61	15.19
Expenses of meeting under s. 98	4.62	N/A
Resolutions	4.63	6.18, 15.34, 15.39
Resolutions by correspondence	4.63A	15.3
Chairman of meeting as proxy-holder	4.64	16.5
Suspension and adjournment	4.65	15.23, 15.25, 15.26
Entitlement to vote (creditors)	4.67	15.28
Chairman's discretion to allow vote	4.68	15.28
Entitlement to vote (contributories)	4.69	15.39

1986 Rule heading	1986 rule	2016 rule
Admission and rejection of proof (creditors' meeting)	4.70	15.33
Record of proceedings	4.71	15.40

SECTION B: WINDING UP OF RECOGNISED BANKS, ETC

Additional provisions as regards certain meetings	4.72	5.3, 15.17

CHAPTER 9 PROOF OF DEBTS IN A LIQUIDATION

SECTION A: PROCEDURE FOR PROVING

Meaning of "prove"	4.73	1.2, 14.3
Supply of forms	4.74	N/A
Contents of proof	4.75	14.4
Particulars of creditor's claim	4.76	N/A
Cost of proving	4.78	14.5
Liquidator to allow inspection of proofs	4.79	14.6
Transmission of proofs to liquidator	4.80	7.60
New liquidator appointed	4.81	7.73
Admission and rejection of proofs for dividend	4.8214.7	
Appeal against decision on proof	4.83	14.8, 14.9
Withdrawal or variation of proof	4.84	14.10
Expunging of proof by the court	4.85	14.11

SECTION B: QUANTIFICATION OF CLAIM

Estimate of quantum	4.86	14.14
Negotiable instruments, etc	4.87	N/A
Secured creditors	4.88	14.19
Discounts	4.89	14.20
Mutual credit and set-off	4.90	14.25
Debt in foreign currency	4.91	14.21
Payments of a periodical nature	4.92	14.22
Interest	4.93	14.23
Debt payable at future time	4.94	14.44

CHAPTER 10 SECURED CREDITORS

Value of security	4.95	14.15
Surrender for non-disclosure	4.96	14.16
Redemption by liquidator	4.97	14.17
Test of security's value	4.98	14.18
Realisation of security by creditor	4.99	14.19

CHAPTER 11 THE LIQUIDATOR

SECTION A: APPOINTMENT AND ASSOCIATED FORMALITIES

Appointment by creditors or contributories	4.100	7.53
Appointment by creditors or by the company	4.101	6.20

1986 Rule heading	1986 rule	2016 rule
Power to fill vacancy in office of liquidator	4.101A	6.21
Official Receiver not to be appointed liquidator	4.101B	N/A
Appointment by the court	4.102	7.56
Appointment by the court	4.103	6.22
Appointment by Secretary of State	4.104	7.57
Authentication of liquidator's appointment	4.105	N/A
Appointment to be gazetted and registered	4.106A	7.59
Hand-over of assets to liquidator	4.107	7.60
SECTION B: RESIGNATION AND REMOVAL; VACATION OF OFFICE		
Creditors' meeting to receive liquidator's resignation	4.108	6.25, 7.61
Resignation (application under Rule 4.131)	4.108A	N/A
Action following acceptance of resignation	4.109	N/A
Action following acceptance of resignation	4.110	N/A
Leave to resign granted by the court	4.111	N/A
Advertisement of resignation	4.112	N/A
Meeting of creditors to remove liquidator	4.113	7.63
Meeting of creditors to remove liquidator	4.114	15.7(3)
Court's power to regulate meetings under Rules 4.113, 4.114-CVL	4.115	N/A
Procedure on removal	4.116	7.64
Procedure on removal	4.117	6.26
Advertisement of removal	4.118	N/A
Removal of liquidator by the court	4.119	7.65
Removal of liquidator by the court	4.120	6.27
Release of resigning or removed liquidator	4.121	7.69
Release of resigning or removed liquidator	4.122	6.33
Removal of liquidator by Secretary of State	4.123	7.66
SECTION C: RELEASE ON COMPLETION OF ADMINISTRATION		
Release of official receiver	4.124	7.70
Final meeting	4.125	7.69, 7.71, 18.14
Rule as to reporting	4.125A	7.72
Final meeting	4.126	6.28. 18.14
Final meeting	4.126A	5.9, 5.10, 18.14
SECTION D: REMUNERATION		
Fixing of remuneration	4.127	18.16, 18.19, 18.20
Liquidator's entitlement to remuneration where it is not fixed under Rule 4.127	4.127A	18.22
Liquidator's remuneration where he realises assets on behalf of chargeholder	4.127B	18.38
Other matters affecting remuneration	4.128	18.17
Recourse of liquidator to meeting of creditors	4.129A	18.24
Recourse to the court	4.130	18.23

1986 Rule heading	1986 rule	2016 rule
Creditors' claim that remuneration is excessive	4.131	18.28, 18.34
Review of remuneration	4.131A	18.29
Remuneration of new liquidator	4.131B	18.31
Apportionment of set fee remuneration	4.131C	18.32

SECTION E: SUPPLEMENTARY PROVISIONS

Liquidator deceased	4.132	7.67
Liquidator deceased	4.133	6.29
Loss of qualification as insolvency practitioner	4.134	7.68
Loss of qualification as insolvency practitioner	4.135	6.30
Vacation of office on making of winding-up order	4.136	6.31
Notice to official receiver of intention to vacate office	4.137	7.62
Liquidator's duties on vacating office	4.138	6.32, 7.73

SECTION F: THE LIQUIDATOR IN A MEMBERS' VOLUNTARY WINDING UP

Appointment by the company	4.139	5.2
Appointment by the court	4.140	5.4
Authentication of liquidator's appointment	4.141	N/A
Company meeting to receive liquidator's resignation	4.142	5.6, 5.8
Removal of liquidator by the court	4.143	5.7
Release of resigning or removed liquidator	4.144	5.14
Liquidator deceased	4.145	5.11
Loss of qualification as insolvency practitioner	4.146	5.12
Vacation of office on making of winding-up order	4.147	5.14
Liquidator's duties on vacating office	4.148	5.13
Remuneration of liquidator in members' voluntary winding up	4.148A	18.16, 18.19
Members' claim that remuneration is excessive	4.148C	18.34
Remuneration of new liquidator	4.148D	18.31
Apportionment of fixed fee remuneration	4.148E	18.32

SECTION G: RULES APPLYING IN EVERY WINDING UP, WHETHER VOLUNTARY OR BY THE COURT

Power of court to set aside certain transactions	4.149	5.15, 6.34, 7.74
Rule against solicitation	4.150	5.16, 6.35, 7.75

CHAPTER 12 THE LIQUIDATION COMMITTEE

Preliminary	4.151	N/A
Membership of committee	4.152	17.3
Formalities of establishment	4.153	17.5
Committee established by contributories	4.154	17.6
Obligations of liquidator to committee	4.155	17.21
Meetings of the committee	4.156	17.12
The chairman at meetings	4.157	17.13
Quorum	4.158	17.14

1986 Rule heading	1986 rule	2016 rule
Committee-members' representatives	4.159	17.15
Resignation	4.160	17.8
Termination of membership	4.161	17.9
Removal	4.162	17.10
Vacancy (creditor members)	4.163	17.8
Vacancy (contributory members)	4.164	17.9
Voting rights and resolutions	4.165	17.18
Voting rights and resolutions	4.166	17.18
Resolutions by post	4.167	17.19
Liquidator's reports	4.168	17.21
Expenses of members, etc	4.169	17.24
Dealings by committee-members and others	4.170	17.25
Composition of committee when creditors paid in full	4.171A	17.13
Committee's functions vested in Secretary of State	4.172	17.28
Formal defects	4.172A1	7.27

CHAPTER 13 THE LIQUIDATION COMMITTEE WHERE WINDING UP FOLLOWS IMMEDIATELY ON ADMINISTRATION (NO CVL APPLICATION)

Preliminary	4.173	17.29
Continuation of creditors' committee	4.174A	17.29
Liquidator's certificate	4.176	17.29
Obligations of liquidator to committee	4.177	17.23
Application of Chapter 12	4.178	17.29

CHAPTER 14 COLLECTION AND DISTRIBUTION OF COMPANY'S ASSETS BY LIQUIDATOR

General duties of liquidator	4.179	7.76
Manner of distributing assets	4.180	14.27
Debts of insolvent company to rank equally	4.181	14.12
Supplementary provisions as to dividend	4.182	14.39, 14.40, 14.45
Distribution in members' voluntary winding up	4.182A	14.28
Division of unsold assets	4.183	14.13
General powers of liquidator	4.184	6.36, 7.77
Enforced delivery up of company's property	4.185	7.78
Final distribution	4.186	14.36, 14.37, 14.38

CHAPTER 15 DISCLAIMER

Liquidator's notice of disclaimer	4.187	19.1, 19.2
Communication of disclaimer to persons interested	4.188	19.3, 19.4
Additional notices	4.189	19.6
Records	4.190A	19.7
Application to interested party under s 178(5)	4.191A	19.9
Interest in property to be declared on request	4.192	N/A
Disclaimer presumed valid and effective	4.193	19.10
Application for exercise of court's powers under s. 181	4.194	19.11

1986 Rule heading	1986 rule	2016 rule
CHAPTER 16 SETTLEMENT OF LIST OF CONTRIBUTORIES (NO CVL APPLICATION)		
Preliminary	4.195	7.79
Duty of liquidator to settle list	4.196	7.79, 7.80
Form of list	4.197	7.81
Procedure for settling list	4.198	7.82
Application to court for variation of the list	4.199	7.83
Variation of, or addition to, the list	4.200	7.84
Costs not to fall on official receiver	4.201	7.85
CHAPTER 17 CALLS (NO CVL APPLICATION)		
Calls by liquidator	4.202	7.86
Control by liquidation committee	4.203	7.87
Application to court for leave to make a call	4.204	7.88, 7.99
Making and enforcement of the call	4.205	7.90, 7.91
CHAPTER 18 SPECIAL MANAGER		
Appointment and remuneration	4.206	5.17, 6.37, 7.93
Security	4.207	5.18, 6.38, 7.94
Failure to give or keep up security	4.208	5.19, 6.39, 7.95
Accounting	4.209	5.20, 6.40, 7.96
Termination of appointment	4.210	5.21, 6.41, 7.97
CHAPTER 19 PUBLIC EXAMINATION OF COMPANY OFFICERS AND OTHERS		
Order for public examination	4.211	7.98, 7.102
Notice of hearing	4.212	7.103
Order on request by creditors or contributories	4.213	7.99, 7.100. 7.101
Witness unfit for examination	4.214	7.104
Procedure at hearing	4.215	7.105
Adjournment	4.216	7.106
Expenses of examination	4.217	7.107
CHAPTER 20 ORDER OF PAYMENT OF COSTS, ETC., OUT OF ASSETS		
General rule as to priority	4.218	6.42, 7.108
Litigation expenses and property subject to a floating charge — general provisions	4.218A	6.44, 7.111, 7.112
Litigation expenses and property subject to a floating charge — requirement for approval or authorisation	4.218B	6.45, 7.113
Litigation expenses and property subject to a floating charge — request for approval or authorisation	4.218C	6.46, 7.114
Litigation expenses and property subject to a floating charge — grant of approval or authorisation	4.218D	6.47, 7.115
Litigation expenses and property subject to a floating charge — application to court by the liquidator	4.218E	6.48, 7.116
Winding up commencing as voluntary	4.219	7.109
Saving for powers of the court	4.220	6.43, 7.110

1986 Rule heading	1986 rule	2016 rule
CHAPTER 21 MISCELLANEOUS RULES		
SECTION A: RETURN OF CAPITAL (NO CVL APPLICATION)		
Application to court for order authorising return	4.221	7.117
Procedure for return	4.222	7.118
SECTION C: DISSOLUTION AFTER WINDING UP		
Secretary of State's directions under ss.203, 205	4.224	7.119
Procedure following appeal under s.203(4) or 205(4)	4.225	7.119
CHAPTER 22 LEAVE TO ACT AS DIRECTOR, ETC., OF COMPANY WITH PROHIBITED NAME (SECTION 216 OF THE ACT)		
Preliminary	4.226	22.1
Application for leave under s.216(3)	4.227A	22.3
First excepted case	4.228	22.4, 22.5
Second excepted case	4.229	22.6
Third excepted case	4.230	22.7
CHAPTER 23 EC REGULATION – MEMBER STATE LIQUIDATOR		
Interpretation of creditor and notice to member State liquidator	4.231	21.9, 21.10
THE SECOND GROUP OF PARTS		
PART 5 INDIVIDUAL VOLUNTARY ARRANGEMENTS		
Introductory	5.1	N/A
PREPARATION OF THE DEBTOR'S PROPOSAL		
Preparation of proposal	5.2	N/A
Contents of proposal	5.3	8.3
Notice to the intended nominee	5.4	8.4
Statement of Affairs	5.5	8.5
Additional disclosure for assistance of nominee	5.6	8.7
CASES IN WHICH AN APPLICATION FOR AN INTERIM ORDER IS MADE		
Application for interim order	5.7	8.8
Court in which application to be made	5.8	8.9
Hearing of the application	5.9	8.11
Action to follow making of order	5.10	8.13
Nominee's report on the proposal	5.11	8.15
Replacement of nominee	5.12	8.17
Consideration of nominee's report	5.13	8.18

1986 Rule heading	1986 rule	2016 rule
CASES WHERE NO INTERIM ORDER IS TO BE OBTAINED		
Nominee's report	5.14A	8.19
Applications to the court	5.14B	8.20, 8.21
CREDITORS' MEETINGS		
Summoning of creditors' meeting	5.17	8.22, 15.7, 15.8
Creditors' meeting: supplementary	5.18	15.10
The chairman at the meeting	5.19	15.21
The chairman as proxy-holder	5.20	15.15, 16.7
Entitlement to vote	5.21	15.28, 15.31
Procedure for admission of creditors' claims for voting purposes	5.22	15.31, 15.33
Requisite majorities	5.23	15.34
Proceedings to obtain agreement on the proposal	5.24	15.23
IMPLEMENTATION OF THE ARRANGEMENT		
Resolutions to follow approval	5.25	8.23
Hand-over of property, etc to supervisor	5.26	8.25
Report of creditors' meeting	5.27	8.24
Reports to Secretary of State	5.29	8.26
Revocation or suspension of the arrangement	5.30	8.27
Supervisor's accounts and reports	5.31A	8.28
Production of accounts and records to Secretary of State	5.32	8.29
Fees, costs, charges and expenses	5.33	8.30
Completion or termination of the arrangement	5.34	8.31
FAST-TRACK VOLUNTARY ARRANGEMENT		
Application of Chapter	5.35	N/A
Interpretation	5.36	N/A
Contents of proposal	5.37	N/A
Requirement for the official receiver's decision	5.38	N/A
Arrangements for approval of fast-track voluntary arrangement	5.39	N/A
Approval by creditors	5.40	N/A
Entitlement to vote	5.41	N/A
Procedure for admission of creditors' claims for voting purposes	5.42	N/A
Requisite majorities	5.43	N/A
Notification to the court	5.44	N/A
Notice of appointment as supervisor etc	5.45	N/A
Revocation of the fast-track voluntary arrangement	5.46	N/A
Supervisor's accounts and reports	5.47	N/A
Supervisor's accounts and reports	5.47A	N/A
Fees, costs and expenses in respect of the performance of the functions of the official receiver	5.48	N/A

1986 Rule heading	1986 rule	2016 rule
PART 6 BANKRUPTCY		
CHAPTER 1 THE STATUTORY DEMAND		
Form and content of statutory demand	6.1	10.1
Information to be given in statutory demand	6.2	10.1
Requirements as to service	6.3	10.2
Application to set aside statutory demand	6.4	10.4
Hearing of application to set aside	6.5	10.5
CHAPTER 2 BANKRUPTCY PETITION (CREDITOR'S)		
Preliminary	6.6	10.6
Identification of debtor	6.7	10.8
Identification of debt	6.8	10.9
Court in which petition to be presented	6.9A	10.11
Procedure for presentation and filing	6.10	10.12
Proof of service of statutory demand	6.11	10.3
Verification of petition	6.12	10.10
Notice to Chief Land Registrar	6.13	10.13
Service of petition	6.14	10.14
Proof of service	6.15A	Sch 4 para 6
Death of debtor before service	6.16	10.15
Security for costs (s. 268(2) only)	6.17	10.17
Hearing of petition	6.18	10.21
Petition opposed by debtor	6.21	10.18
Amendment of petition	6.22	10.16
Notice by persons intending to appear	6.23	10.19
List of appearances	6.24	10.20
Decision on the hearing	6.25	10.24
Non-appearance of creditor	6.26	10.26
Vacating registration on dismissal of petition	6.27	10.25
Extension of time for hearing	6.28	10.22
Adjournment	6.29	10.23
Substitution of petitioner	6.30	10.27, 10.28
Change of carriage of petition	6.31	10.29
Petitioner seeking dismissal or leave to withdraw	6.32	10.30
Settlement and content of bankruptcy order	6.33	10.31
Action to follow making of order	6.34	10.32
Amendment of title of proceedings	6.35	10.165
CHAPTER 3 DEBTOR'S BANKRUPTCY APPLICATION		
Preliminary	6.37	10.34
Bankruptcy application for a bankruptcy order	6.38	10.35
Procedure for making the bankruptcy application and electronic communications with the adjudicator	6.39	10.36
Application to the Chief Land Registrar to register a bankruptcy application	6.40	10.37

1986 Rule heading	1986 rule	2016 rule
Verification checks	6.41	10.38
Determination of the bankruptcy application	6.42	10.39
The determination period	6.43	10.40
Settlement and content of bankruptcy order	6.44	10.41
Refusal to make a bankruptcy order and contents of the notice of refusal	6.45	10.42
Review of the refusal to make a bankruptcy order	6.46	10.43
Appeal to the court following a review of the refusal to make a bankruptcy order	6.47	10.44
Action to follow making of the order	6.48	10.45
Application to the Chief Land Registrar	6.49	10.46
The bankruptcy file	6.50	10.47
Court in which applications are to be made	6.50A	10.48

CHAPTER 4 THE INTERIM RECEIVER

Application for appointment of interim receiver	6.51	10.49
Order of appointment	6.52	10.51
Deposit	6.53	10.50
Security	6.54	10.52
Failure to give or keep up security	6.55	10.52
Remuneration	6.56	10.54
Termination of appointment	6.57	10.56

CHAPTER 5 DISCLOSURE BY BANKRUPT WITH RESPECT TO THE STATE OF HIS AFFAIRS

SECTION A: CREDITOR'S PETITION

Preliminary	6.58	10.55
The statement of affairs	6.59	10.56
Verification and filing	6.60	10.56
Limited disclosure	6.61	10.57
Release from duty to submit statement of affairs; extension of time	6.62	10.58
Expenses of statement of affairs	6.63	10.59
Requirement to submit accounts	6.64	10.60
Submission and filing of accounts	6.65	10.60
Further disclosure	6.66	10.61

SECTION B: DEBTOR'S PETITION

Preliminary	6.67	10.62
Contents of statement	6.68	N/A
Requirement to submit accounts	6.69	10.63
Submission and filing of accounts	6.70	10.63
Expenses of preparing accounts	6.71	10.64
Further disclosure	6.72	10.65

1986 Rule heading	1986 rule	2016 rule

CHAPTER 6 INFORMATION TO CREDITORS

General duty of official receiver	6.73	10.66
Those entitled to be informed	6.74	1.37
Report where statement of affairs lodged	6.75	10.66
Statement of affairs dispensed with	6.76	10.66
General rule as to reporting	6.77	10.66
Bankruptcy order annulled	6.78	10.66
Reports to creditor	6.78A	18.3, 18.4, 18.8, 18.9
Final report to creditors and bankrupt	6.78B	18.14
Creditors' request for further information	6.78C	18.9
Distribution of property in specie	6.78D	18.13

CHAPTER 7 CREDITORS' MEETINGS

First meeting of creditors	6.79	15.8, 15.10. 15.11
Business at first meeting	6.80	N/A
General power to call meetings	6.81	15.8, 15.11
The chairman at a meeting	6.82	15.21
Requisitioned meetings	6.83	15.18
Attendance at meeting of bankrupt, etc	6.84	15.14, 15.22
Notice of meetings by advertisement only	6.85	15.12
Venue of meetings	6.86	15.10
Expenses of summoning meetings	6.87	15.19
Resolutions	6.88	10.78, 15.16, 15.34
Resolutions by Correspondence	6.88A	15.3
Chairman of meeting as proxy-holder	6.89	16.5
Suspension of meeting	6.90	15.27
Adjournment	6.91	15.23, 15.25, 15.26
Entitlement to vote	6.93	15.28
Chairman's discretion to allow vote	6.93A	15.28
Admission and rejection of proof	6.94	15.33
Record of proceedings	6.95	15.40

CHAPTER 8 PROOF OF BANKRUPTCY DEBTS

SECTION A: PROCEDURE FOR PROVING

Meaning of "prove"	6.96	1.2, 14.3, 14.4
Supply of forms	6.97	N/A
Contents of proof	6.98	14.4
Cost of proving	6.100	14.5
Trustee to allow inspection of proofs	6.101	14.6
Transmission of proofs to trustee	6.103	10.76(7)
Admission and rejection of proofs for dividend	6.104	14.7
Appeal against decision on proof	6.105	14.8, 14.9

1986 Rule heading	1986 rule	2016 rule
Withdrawal or variation of proof	6.106	14.10
Expunging of proof by the court	6.107	14.11

SECTION B: QUANTIFICATION OF CLAIM

Negotiable instruments, etc	6.108	N/A
Secured creditors	6.109	14.41
Discounts	6.110	14.20
Debt in foreign currency	6.111	14.21
Payments of a periodical nature	6.112	14.22
Interest	6.113	14.23
Debt payable at future time	6.114	14.44

CHAPTER 9 SECURED CREDITORS

Value of security	6.115	14.15
Surrender for non-disclosure	6.116	14.16
Redemption by trustee	6.117	14.17
Test of security's value	6.118	14.18
Realisation of security by creditor	6.119	14.19

CHAPTER 10 THE TRUSTEE IN BANKRUPTCY

SECTION A: APPOINTMENT AND ASSOCIATED FORMALITIES

Appointment by creditors' meeting	6.120	10.67, 10.68, 10.70
Official Receiver not to be appointed trustee	6.120A	N/A
Appointment by the court	6.121	10.71
Appointment by Secretary of State	6.122	10.72
Authentication of trustee's appointment	6.123	10.73
Advertisement of appointment	6.124	10.74
Hand-over of estate to trustee	6.125	10.75

SECTION B: RESIGNATION AND REMOVAL; VACATION OF OFFICE

Creditors' meeting to receive trustee's resignation	6.126	10.77
Action following acceptance of resignation	6.127	10.77
Leave to resign granted by the court	6.128	N/A
Meeting of creditors to remove trustee	6.129	10.78
Court's power to regulate meeting under Rule 6.129	6.130	N/A
Procedure on removal	6.131	10.79
Removal of trustee by the court	6.132	10.80
Removal of trustee by Secretary of State	6.133	10.81
Advertisement of resignation or removal	6.134	10.82
Release of resigning or removed trustee	6.135	10.83

SECTION C: RELEASE ON COMPLETION OF ADMINISTRATION

Release of official receiver	6.136	10.86

1986 Rule heading	**1986 rule**	**2016 rule**
Final meeting of creditors	6.137	10.87
Rule as to reporting	6.137A	10.88
SECTION D: REMUNERATION		
Fixing of remuneration	6.138	18.16, 18.21
Trustee's remuneration where it is not fixed in accordance with Rule 6.13	6.138A	18.22
Other matters affecting remuneration	6.139	18.17, 18.38
Recourse of trustee to meeting of creditors	6.140A	18.24
Recourse to the court	6.141	18.23
Creditor's claim that remuneration is excessive	6.142	18.34
Review of remuneration	6.142A	18.29
Remuneration of new trustee	6.142B	18.31
Apportionment of set fee remuneration	6.142C	18.32
SECTION E: SUPPLEMENTARY PROVISIONS		
Trustee deceased	6.143	10.84
Loss of qualification as insolvency practitioner	6.144	10.85
Notice to official receiver of intention to vacate office	6.145	10.89
Trustee's duties on vacating office	6.146	10.90
Power of court to set aside certain transactions	6.147	10.91
Rule against solicitation	6.148	10.92
Enforcement of trustee's obligations to official receiver	6.149	10.93
CHAPTER 11 THE CREDITORS' COMMITTEE		
Membership of creditors' committee	6.150	17.3, 17.4
Formalities of establishment	6.151	17.5
Obligations of trustee to committee	6.152	17.22
Meetings of the committee	6.153	17.14
The chairman at meetings	6.154	17.15
Quorum	6.155	17.16
Committee-members' representatives	6.156	17.17
Resignation	6.157	17.10
Termination of membership	6.158	17.11
Removal	6.159	17.12
Vacancies	6.160	17.9
Voting rights and resolutions	6.161	17.18
Resolutions by post	6.162	17.19
Trustee's reports	6.163	17.23
Expenses of members etc	6.164	17.24
Dealings by committee-members and others	6.165	17.25
Committee's functions vested in Secretary of State	6.166	17.26
CHAPTER 12 SPECIAL MANAGER		
Appointment and remuneration	6.167	10.94

1986 Rule heading	1986 rule	2016 rule
Security	6.168	10.95
Failure to give or keep up security	6.169	10.96
Accounting	6.170	10.97
Termination of appointment	6.171	10.98

CHAPTER 13 PUBLIC EXAMINATION OF BANKRUPT

Order for public examination	6.172	10.100
Order on request by creditors	6.173	10.101
Bankrupt unfit for examination	6.174	10.102
Procedure at hearing	6.175	10.103
Adjournment	6.176	10.104
Expenses of examination	6.177	10.105

CHAPTER 14 DISCLAIMER

Trustee's notice of disclaimer	6.178	19.1, 19.2
Communication of disclaimer to persons interested	6.179	19.3, 19.4, 19.5
Additional notices	6.180	19.6
Records	6.181A	19.7
Application for leave to disclaim	6.182	19.8
Application by interested party under s. 316	6.183	19.9
Interest in property to be declared on request	6.184	N/A
Disclaimer presumed valid and effective	6.185	19.10
Application for exercise of court's powers under s.320	6.186	19.11

CHAPTER 15 REPLACEMENT OF EXEMPT PROPERTY

Purchase of replacement property	6.187	10.106
Money provided in lieu of sale	6.188	10.105

CHAPTER 16 INCOME PAYMENTS ORDERS

Application for order	6.189	10.109
Action to follow making of order	6.190	10.111
Variation of order	6.191	10.11
Order to payor of income: administration	6.192	10.113
Review of order	6.193	10.114

CHAPTER 16A INCOME PAYMENTS AGREEEMENTS

Approval of income payments agreements	6.193A	10.115
Acceptance of income payments agreements	6.193B	10.116
Variation of income payments order	6.193C	10.117

CHAPTER 17 ACTION BY COURT UNDER SECTION 369 ORDER TO INLAND REVENUE OFFICIAL

Application for order	6.194	10.118
Making and service of the order	6.195	10.119
Custody of documents	6.196	10.120

1986 Rule heading	1986 rule	2016 rule
CHAPTER 18 MORTGAGED PROPERTY		
Claim by mortgagee of land	6.197	10.122
Power of court to order sale	6.198	10.123
Proceeds of sale	6.199	10.124
CHAPTER 19 AFTER-ACQUIRED PROPERTY		
Duties of bankrupt in respect of after-acquired property	6.200	10.125
Trustee's recourse to disponee of property	6.201	10.126
Expenses of getting in property for the estate	6.202	N/A
CHAPTER 20 LEAVE TO ACT AS DIRECTOR, ETC		
	6.202A	10.127
Application for leave	6.203	10.128
Report of official receiver	6.204	10.129
Court's order on application	6.205	10.130
CHAPTER 21 ANNULMENT OF BANKRUPTCY ORDER		
Application for annulment	6.206	10.132
Report by trustee	6.207	10.133, 18.35
Applicant's claim that remuneration is or expenses are excessive	6.207A	10.143, 18.35
Power of court to stay proceedings	6.208	10.135
Notice to creditors who have not proved	6.209	10.136
The hearing	6.210	10.137
Matters to be proved under s.282(1)(b)	6.211	10.138
Notice to creditors	6.212	10.139
Other matters arising on annulment	6.213	10.140
Trustee's final account	6.214	10.1401
CHAPTER 22 DISCHARGE		
Application for suspension of discharge	6.215	10.142
Lifting of suspension of discharge	6.216	10.143
Application by bankrupt for discharge	6.217	10.160
Report of official receiver	6.218	10.160
Order of discharge on application	6.219	10.144, 10.145 10.16
Certificate of discharge	6.220	10.144, 10.145
Deferment of issue of order pending appeal	6.221	10.163
Costs under this Chapter	6.222	10.164
Bankrupt's debts surviving discharge	6.223	10.146
CHAPTER 23 ORDER OF PAYMENT OF COSTS, ETC., OUT OF ESTATE		
General rule as to priority	6.224	10.149

1986 Rule heading	1986 rule	2016 rule
CHAPTER 24 SECOND BANKRUPTCY		
Scope of this Chapter	6.225	10.150
General duty of existing trustee	6.226	10.151
Delivery up to later trustee	6.227	10.152
Existing trustee's expenses	6.228	10.153
CHAPTER 25 CRIMINAL BANKRUPTCY		
Status and functions of Official Petitioner	6.230	10.155
Interim receivership	6.231	10.156
Proof of bankruptcy debts and notice of order	6.232	10.157
Meetings under the Rules	6.233	N/A
Trustee in bankruptcy; creditors' committee; annulment of bankruptcy order	6.234	10.158, 10.159
CHAPTER 26 MISCELLANEOUS RULES IN BANKRUPTCY		
Application for redirection order	6.235A	10.166
Persons at risk of violence	6.235B	20.1, 20.5, 20.6
Consolidation of petitions	6.236	N/A
Bankrupt's home – notification of property falling within section 283A	6.237	10.167
Application in respect of the vesting of an interest in a dwelling house	6.237A	10.168
Vesting of bankrupt's interest (unregistered land)	6.237B	10.169
	6.237C	Note above 10.170
Vesting of bankrupt's estate – substituted period	6.237CA	10.170
Charging Order	6.237D	10.171
Interpretation	6.237E	1.2(2)
EC REGULATION—MEMBER STATE LIQUIDATOR		
Interpretation of creditor and notice to member State liquidator	6.238	21.7, 21.8
Interpretation of creditor and notice to member State liquidator appointed in main proceedings	6.239	21.7, 21.8
BANKRUPTCY RESTRICTIONS ORDER		
	6.2401	1.1
Application for bankruptcy restrictions order	6.241	11.2
Service on the defendant	6.242	11.3
The bankrupt's evidence	6.243	11.4
Making a bankruptcy restrictions order	6.244	11.5
INTERIM BANKRUPTCY RESTRICTIONS ORDER		
Application for interim bankruptcy restrictions order	6.245	11.6
The case against the defendant	6.246	11.6

1986 Rule heading	1986 rule	2016 rule
Making an interim bankruptcy restrictions order	6.247	11.7
Application to set aside an interim bankruptcy restrictions order	6.248	11.8, 11.9
BANKRUPTCY RESTRICTIONS UNDERTAKING		
Acceptance of the bankruptcy restrictions undertaking	6.249	11.10
Notification to the court	6.250	11.11
Application under paragraph 9(3) of Schedule 4A to the Act to annul	6.251	11.12
DEBT RELIEF RESTRICTIONS ORDER		
Interpretation	6.252	11.1
Application for debt relief restrictions order	6.253	11.2
Service on the defendant	6.254	11.3
The debtor's evidence	6.255	11.4
Making a debt relief restrictions order	6.256	11.5
INTERIM DEBT RELIEF RESTRICTIONS ORDER		
Application for interim debt relief restrictions order	6.257	11.6
The case against the debtor	6.258	11.6
Making an interim debt relief restrictions order	6.259	11.7
Application to set aside an interim debt relief restrictions order	6.260	11.8
DEBT RELIEF RESTRICTIONS UNDERTAKING		
Acceptance of debt relief restrictions undertaking	6.261	11.10
Notification	6.2621	1.11
Application under paragraph 9(3) of Schedule 4ZB to the Act to annul	6.263	11.12
PART 6A GENERAL		
The individual insolvency register; the bankruptcy restrictions register	6A.1	11.13
INDIVIDUAL INSOLVENCY REGISTER		
Entry of information onto the individual insolvency register — individual voluntary arrangements	6A.2A	11.14
Deletion of information from the individual insolvency register	6A.3	11.15
Entry of information onto the individual insolvency register — bankruptcy orders	6A.4	11.16
Deletion of information from the individual insolvency register — bankruptcy orders	6A.5	11.17
Entry of information onto the individual insolvency register — debt relief orders	6A.5A	11.18

1986 Rule heading	1986 rule	2016 rule
Deletion of information from the individual insolvency register — debt relief orders	6A.5B	11.19

BANKRUPTCY RESTRICTIONS REGISTER

Bankruptcy restrictions orders and undertakings — entry of information	6A.6	11.20
Deletion of information from the bankruptcy restrictions register — bankruptcy restrictions order and undertakings	6A.7	11.21

DEBT RELIEF RESTRICTIONS REGISTER

Debt relief restrictions orders and undertakings — entries of information onto the debt relief restrictions register	6A.7A	11.20
Deletion of information from the debt relief restrictions register — debt relief restrictions order and undertakings	6A.7B	11.21

RECTIFICATION OF REGISTERS

Rectification of the registers	6A.8	11.22, 11.23

THE THIRD GROUP OF PARTS

PART 7 COURT PROCEDURE AND PRACTICE

CHAPTER 1 APPLICATIONS

Preliminary	7.1	12.5
Form and contents of application	7.3	1.35
Application under section 176A(5) to disapply section 176A	7.3A	12.14
Filing and service of application	7.4	12.7 12.9, 12.10
Notice of application under section 176A(5)	7.4A	12.15
Hearings without notice	7.5A	12.12
Hearing of application	7.6A	12.2(3)
Witness statements – general	7.7A	12.28
Filing and service of witness statements	7.8	12.28
Use of reports	7.9	12.28
Adjournment of hearing; directions	7.10	12.9, 12.13

CHAPTER 1ZA THE LONDON INSOLVENCY DISTRICT

Allocation of proceedings to the London insolvency district	7.10ZA	12.5

CHAPTER 1A BLOCK TRANSFER OF CASES WHERE INSOLVENCY PRACTITIONER

Preliminary and interpretation	7.10A	12.35
Power to make a block transfer order	7.10B	12.36
Application for a block transfer order	7.10C	12.37
Action following application for a block transfer order	7.10D	12.38

1986 Rule heading	1986 rule	2016 rule
CHAPTER 2 TRANSFER OF PROCEEDINGS BETWEEN COURTS		
General power of transfer	7.11	12.30
Proceedings commenced in wrong court	7.12	12.31
Applications for transfer	7.13	12.32
Procedure following order for transfer	7.14	12.33
Consequential transfer of other proceedings	7.15	12.34
CHAPTER 3 SHORTHAND WRITERS		
Nomination and appointment of shorthand writers	7.16	12.65
Remuneration	7.17	12.65
CHAPTER 4 ENFORCEMENT PROCEDURES		
Enforcement of court orders	7.19	12.51
Orders enforcing compliance with the Rules	7.20	12.52
Warrants (general provisions)	7.21	12.53
Warrants under ss.134, 364	7.22	12.54
Warrants under ss.236, 366	7.23	12.55
Warrants under s.365	7.25	12.56
CHAPTER 5 COURT RECORDS AND RETURNS		
Court file	7.31A	12.39
CHAPTER 6 COSTS AND TAXATION		
Application of Chapter	7.33A	12.41
Requirement to assess costs by the detailed procedure	7.34A	12.42
Procedure where detailed assessment required	7.35	12.43
Costs of officers charged with execution of writs or other process	7.36	12.44
Petitions presented by insolvents	7.37A	12.45
Costs paid otherwise than out of the insolvent estate	7.38	12.46
Award of costs against official receiver or responsible insolvency practitioner	7.39	12.47
Applications for costs	7.40	12.48
Costs and expenses of witnesses	7.41	12.49
Final costs certificate	7.42	12.50
CHAPTER 7 PERSONS WHO LACK CAPACITY TO MANAGE THEIR AFFAIRS		
Introductory	7.43	12.23
Appointment of another person to act	7.44	12.24
Witness statement in support of application	7.45A	12.25
Service of notices following appointment	7.46	12.26

1986 Rule heading	1986 rule	2016 rule
CHAPTER 8 APPEALS IN INSOLVENCY PROCEEDINGS		
Appeals and reviews of court orders (winding up)	7.47	12.59
Appeals in bankruptcy	7.48	12.60
Procedure on appeal	7.49A	12.58, 12.61
Appeal against decision of Secretary of State or official receiver	7.50	12.62
CHAPTER 9 GENERAL		
Principal court rules and practice to apply	7.51A	12.1
Right of audience	7.52	13.1(2)
Formal defects	7.55	12.65
Service of orders staying proceedings	7.56	Sch 4 para 5
Payment into court	7.59	N/A
Further information and disclosure	7.60	12.27
Office copies of documents	7.61	12.40
EC REGULATION – CREDITORS' VOLUNTARY WINDING UP – CONFIRMATION BY THE COURT		
Application for confirmation	7.62	21.4, 21.5
Notice to Member State liquidator and creditors in member states	7.63	21.6
EC REGULATION – MEMBER STATE LIQUIDATOR		
Interpretation of creditor	7.64	N/A
PART 8 PROXIES AND COMPANY REPRESENTATION		
Definition of "proxy"	8.1	16.2
Issue and use of forms	8.2	16.3, 16.4
Use of proxies at meeting	8.3	16.4, 16.5
Retention of proxies	8.4	16.6
Right of inspection	8.5	16.6
Proxy-holder with financial interest	8.6	16.7
Company representation	8.7	16.8
Interpretation of creditor	8.8	N/A
PART 9 EXAMINATION OF PERSONS CONCERNED IN COMPANY AND INDIVIDUAL INSOLVENCY		
Preliminary	9.1	12.17
Form and contents of application	9.2	12.18
Order for examination, etc	9.3	12.19
Procedure for examination	9.4	12.20
Record of examination	9.5	12.21
Costs of proceedings under ss.236, 366	9.6	12.22

1986 Rule heading	1986 rule	2016 rule
PART 10 OFFICIAL RECEIVERS		
Appointment of official receivers	10.1	13.1
Persons entitled to act on official receiver's behalf	10.2	13.3
Application for directions	10.3	13.4
Official receiver's expenses	10.4	13.5
PART 11 DECLARATION AND PAYMENT OF DIVIDEND (WINDING UP AND BANKRUPTCY)		
Preliminary		N/A
Notice of intended dividend	11.2	14.28
Final admission/rejection of proofs	11.3	14.32
Postponement or cancellation of dividend	11.4	14.33
Decision to declare dividend	11.5	14.34
Notice of declaration	11.6	14.35
Notice of no, or no further, dividend	11.7	14.37
Proof altered after payment of dividend	11.8	14.40
Secured creditors	11.9	14.41
Disqualification from dividend	11.10	14.42
Assignment of right to dividend	11.11	14.43
Preferential creditors	11.12	14.28(2), 14.29(2)
Debt payable at future time	11.13	14.44
PART 12 MISCELLANEOUS AND GENERAL		
Power of Secretary of State to regulate certain matters	12.1	0.5
Costs, expenses, etc	12.2	3.50, 6.42, 7.108, 10.147
Provable debts	12.3	14.2
False claim of status as creditor, etc.	12.18	1.56
Punishment of offences	12.21	0.6
PART 12A PROVISIONS OF GENERAL EFFECT THE GIVING OF NOTICE AND THE SUPPLY OF DOCUMENTS — GENERAL		
Application	12A.1	N/A
Personal delivery of documents	12A.2	1.44
Postal delivery of documents	12A.3	1.42
Non-receipt of notice of meeting	12A.4	N/A
Notice etc to solicitors	12A.5	1.40
THE GIVING OF NOTICE AND THE SUPPLY OF DOCUMENTS BY OR TO OFFICE-HOLDERS		
Application	12A.6	N/A
The form of notices and other documents	12A.7	1.4
Proof of sending etc	12A.8	1.52
Authentication	12A.9	1.5
Electronic delivery in insolvency proceedings — general	12A.10	1.45

1986 Rule heading	1986 rule	2016 rule
Electronic delivery by office-holders	12A.11	1.48
Use of websites by office-holder	12A.12	1.47, 1.49
Special provision on account of expense as to website use	12A.13	1.49, 1.50
Electronic delivery of insolvency proceedings to courts	12A.14	1.46
Notice etc to joint office-holders	12A.15	1.41
SERVICE OF COURT DOCUMENTS		
Application	12A.16	N/A
Application of CPR Part 6 to service of court documents within the jurisdiction	12A.17	Sch 4, para 1
Service of orders staying proceedings	12A.18	Sch 4, para 5
Service on joint office-holders	12A.19	Sch 4 para 4
Application of CPR Part 6 to service of court documents outside the jurisdiction	12A.20	Sch 4, para 1
MEETINGS		
Quorum at meeting of creditors or contributories	12A.21	15.20
Remote attendance at meetings of creditors	12A.22	15.6(6)
Action where person excluded	12A.23	15.36, 15.44
Indication to excluded person	12A.24	15.37, 15.45
Complaint	12A.25	15.38, 15.46
Remote attendance at meetings of creditors' committees and liquidation	12A.26	17.20
Procedure for requests that a place for a meeting should be specified 794	12A.27	17.21
EFFECT OF INSOLVENCY ON EXECUTION — SPECIFIC PROVISIONS FOR NOTICES TO ENFORCEMENT OFFICERS ETC		
Execution overtaken by judgment debtor's insolvency	12A.28	12.57
Notice to enforcement officers	12A.29	1.47
FORMS		
Forms for use in insolvency proceedings	12A.30	N/A
Electronic submission of information instead of submission of forms	12A.31	N/A
Electronic submission of information instead of submission of forms	12A.32	N/A
GAZETTE NOTICES		
Contents of notices to be gazetted under the Act or Rules	12A.33	1.10
Gazette notices relating to companies	12A.34	1.12
Gazette notices relating to bankrupts	12A.35	1.13
Omission of unobtainable information	12A.36	1.10(2)
The Gazette — general	12A.37	1.14

1986 Rule heading	1986 rule	2016 rule
NOTICES ADVERTISED OTHERWISE THAN IN THE GAZETTE		
Notices otherwise advertised under the Act or Rules	12A.38	1.15
Non-Gazette notices relating to companies	12A.39	1.16
Non-Gazette notices relating to bankrupts	12A.40	1.17
Non-Gazette notices — other provisions	12A.41	1.18
NOTIFICATIONS TO THE REGISTRAR OF COMPANIES		
Application of this Chapter	12A.42	1.19
Information to be contained in all notifications to the registrar	12A.43	1.20, 1.21
Notifications relating to the office of office-holders	12A.44	1.22
Notifications relating to documents	12A.45	1.23
Notifications relating to court orders	12A.46	1.24
Returns or reports of meetings	12A.47	1.25, 1.26
Notifications relating to other events	12A.48	1.27
Notifications of more than one nature	12A.49	1.19
Notifications made to other persons at the same time	12A.50	1.19
INSPECTION OF DOCUMENTS AND THE PROVISION OF INFORMATION		
Confidentiality of documents — grounds for refusing inspection	12A.51	1.58
Right to copy documents	12A.52	12.39, 12.40, 12.54
Charges for copy documents	12A.53	1.55
Right to have list of creditors	12A.54	1.57
COMPUTATION OF TIME AND TIME LIMITS		
Time limits	12A.55	1.3, Sch. 5
SECURITY		
Insolvency practitioners' security	12A.56	4.4, 5.5, 6.24, 7.37, 7.58, 10.52, 10.69
NOTICE OF ORDER UNDER SECTION 176A(5)		
Notice of order under section 176A(5)	12A.57	12.15
PART 13 INTERPRETATION AND APPLICATION		
Introductory	13.1	N/A
"The court"; "the registrar"	13.2	1.2
"Give notice", etc.	13.3	N/A
Notice, etc. to solicitors	13.4	N/A
Notice to joint liquidators, joint trustees, etc.	13.5	N/A

1986 Rule heading	**1986 rule**	**2016 rule**
"Venue".13.61.2"Insolvency proceedings"	13.7	N/A
Insolvent estate"	13.8	1.2
"Responsible insolvency practitioner", etc.	13.9	N/A
"Office holder"	13.9A	1.2
"Petitioner"	13.10	1.2
"The appropriate fee"	13.11	N/A
"Debt", "liability" (winding up)	13.12	14.1
"Authorised deposit-taker and former authorised deposit-taker"	13.12A	1.2
Expressions used generally	13.13	1.2
Application	13.14	0.3
Application of Insolvency Act 1986 and Company Directors Disqualification Act 1986	13.15	N/A
Schedule 1 SCHEME MANAGER'S VOTING RIGHTS		15.29, 15.30, 15.31, 15.32
Schedule 2 ALTERNATIVE COUNTY COURT HEARING CENTRES		Sch 6
Schedule 4 FORMS		N/A
Schedule 5 PUNISHMENT OF OFFENCES UNDER THE RULES		Sch 3
Schedule 6 DETERMINATION OF INSOLVENCY OFFICE HOLDER'S REMUNERATION		Sch 11

Appendix II

Table of Derivations of the Insolvency (England and Wales) Rules 2016

Guide to the derivation of the Insolvency (England and Wales) Rules 2016 (SI 2016/1024)

[**Note**: This table is reproduced directly from that prepared by the Insolvency Service. Caution should be taken when using it as it is rather generic and mainly relates rule to rule (rather than sub-rule to sub-rule) and contains inaccuracies.
This Table has not been officially updated to reflect changes post-April 2017 (and in particular still refers to the "EC Regulation").]

This table indicates the derivation of provisions in the 2016 Rules. The 2016 Rules broadly derive from the 1986 Rules and forms. However there is rarely an exact match as the structure of the 2016 Rules is different, the language has been modernised and there have been significant changes, in particular as a result of amendments to the primary legislation made by the Enterprise and Regulatory Reform Act 2013, the Deregulation Act 2015, and the Small Business, Enterprise and Employment Act 2015. Furthermore the information requirements previously contained in forms have now been imported into the relevant rule as specified content. Finally the new Rules try to avoid copying out of the primary legislation. Instead they contain many references to Insolvency Act 1986 to enable the user to connect individual rules with the relevant provisions of the Act that the Rules supplement.

2016 Rule heading	**2016 Rule**	**1986 Rule**
Introductory rules		
Citation and commencement	1	0.1
Revocations	2	N/A
Extent and application	3	0.3
Transitional and savings provisions	4	13.14
Power of Secretary of State to regulate certain matters	5	12.1
Punishment of offences	6	12.21, Sch.5
Review	7	N/A
Part 1: Scope, interpretation, time and rules about documents		
Chapter 1: Scope of these Rules		
Scope	1.1	13.7
Chapter 2: Interpretation		
Defined terms	1.2	0.2, Part 13
Calculation of time periods	1.3	12A.55
Chapter 3: Form and contents of documents		
Requirement for writing and form of documents	1.4	12A.7
Authentication	1.5	12A.9
Information required to identify persons and proceedings etc.	1.6	N/A
Reasons for stating that proceedings are or will be main, secondary etc. under the EC Regulation	1.7	N/A

2016 Rule heading	2016 Rule	1986 Rule
Prescribed format of documents	1.8	N/A
Variation from prescribed contents	1.9	N/A
Chapter 4: Standard contents of Gazette notices and the Gazette as evidence etc.		
Contents of notices to be gazetted under the Act or Rules	1.10	12A.33, 12A.36
Standard contents of all notices	1.11	12A.33, 12A.36
Gazette notices relating to a company	1.12	12A.34, 12A.36
Gazette notices relating to a bankruptcy	1.13	12A.35, 12A.36
The Gazette: evidence, variations and errors	1.14	12A.37
Chapter 5: Standard contents of notices advertised otherwise than in the Gazette		
Standard contents of notices advertised other than in the Gazette	1.15	12A.38, 12A.41
Non-Gazette notices relating to a company	1.16	12A.39, 12A.41
Non-Gazette notices relating to a bankruptcy	1.17	12A.40, 12A.41
Non-Gazette notices: other provisions	1.18	12A.41
Chapter 6: Standard contents of documents to be delivered to the registrar of companies		
Standard contents of documents delivered to the registrar	1.19	12A.42, 12A.43
Registrar of companies: covering notices	1.20	
Standard contents of all documents	1.21	12A.43
Standard contents of documents relating to the office of office-holders	1.22	12A.44
Standard contents of documents relating to other documents	1.23	12A.45
Standard contents of documents relating to court orders	1.24	12A.46
Standard contents of returns or reports of decisions	1.25	12A.47
Standard contents of returns or reports of matters considered by company members by correspondence	1.26	12A.47
Documents relating to other events	1.27	12A.48
Chapter 7: Standard contents of notices for delivery to other persons etc.		
Standard contents of notices to be delivered to persons other than the registrar of companies	1.28	N/A
Standard contents of all notices	1.29	N/A
Standard contents of notices relating to the office of office-holders	1.30	N/A
Standard contents of notices relating to documents	1.31	N/A
Standard contents of notices relating to court proceedings or orders	1.32	N/A
Standard contents of notices of the results of decisions	1.33	N/A
Standard contents of returns or reports of matters considered by company members by correspondence	1.34	N/A
Chapter 8: Applications to the court		
Standard contents and authentication of applications to the court under Parts 1 to 11 of the Act	1.35	7.3

2016 Rule heading	2016 Rule	1986 Rule
Chapter 9: Delivery of documents and opting out (sections 246C, 248A, 379C and 383A		
Application of this Chapter	1.36	N/A
Delivery to the creditors and opting out	1.37	4.44, 6.74. (but not opt-out)
Creditor's election to opt out	1.38	N/A
Office-holder to provide information to creditors on opting-out	1.39	N/A
Delivery of documents to authorised recipients	1.40	12A.5
Delivery of documents to joint office-holders	1.41	12A.15
Postal delivery of documents	1.42	12A.3
Delivery by document exchange	1.43	N/A
Personal delivery of documents	1.44	12A.2
Electronic delivery of documents	1.45	12A.10
Electronic delivery of documents to the court	1.46	12A.14
Electronic delivery of notices to enforcement officers	1.47	12A.29
Electronic delivery by office-holders	1.46	12A.11
Use of website by office-holder to deliver a particular document (section 246B and 379B)	1.49	12A.12
General use of website to deliver documents	1.50	12A.13
Retention period for documents made available on websites	1.51	12A.12, 12A.13
Proof of delivery of documents	1.52	12A.8
Delivery of proofs and details of claims	1.53	4.54, 6.81
Chapter 10: Inspection of documents, copies and provision of information		
Right to copies of documents	1.54	12A.52
Charges for copies of documents provided by the office-holder	1.55	12A.53
Offence in relation to inspection of documents	1.56	12.18
Right to list of creditors	1.57	12A.54
Confidentiality of documents – grounds for refusing inspection	1.58	12A.51
Part 2: Company Voluntary Arrangements under Part 1 of the Act		
Chapter 1: Preliminary		
Interpretation	2.1	N/A
Chapter 2: the proposal for a CVA (section 1)		
Proposal for a CVA: general principles and amendment	2.2	1.3
Proposal: contents	2.3	1.3
Chapter 3: Procedure for a CVA without a moratorium		
Procedure for proposal where the nominee is not the liquidator or the administrator (section 2)	2.4	1.4
Information for the official receiver	2.5	1.10
Statement of affairs (section 2(3))	2.6	1.5
Application to omit information from statement of affairs delivered to creditors	2.7	1.56

2016 Rule heading	2016 Rule	1986 Rule
Additional disclosure for assistance of nominee where the nominee is not the liquidator or administrator	2.8	1.6
Nominee's report on proposal where the nominee is not the liquidator or administrator (section 2(2))	2.9	1.7
Replacement of nominee (section 2(4))	2.10	1.8
Chapter 4: Procedure for a CVA with a moratorium		
Statement of affairs (paragraph 6(1)(b) of Schedule A1)	2.11	1.37
Application to omit information from a statement of affairs	2.12	1.56
The nominee's statement (para 6(2)(a) of Schedule A1)	2.13	1.38
Documents filed with the court to obtain a moratorium (paragraph 7(1) of Schedule A1)	2.14	1.39
Notice and advert of beginning of a moratorium	2.15	1.40
Notice of continuation of a moratorium where physical meeting of creditors is summoned (paragraph 8(3B) of Schedule A1)	2.16	N/A
Notice of decision extending or further extending a moratorium (paragraph 36 of Schedule A1)	2.17	1.41
Notice of court order extending or further extending or continuing or renewing a moratorium (paragraph 34(2) of Schedule A1)	2.18	1.41
Advertisement of end of a moratorium (paragraph 11(1) of Schedule A1)	2.19	1.42
Disposal of charged property etc. during a moratorium	2.20	1.43
Withdrawal of nominee's consent to act (paragraph 25(5) of Schedule A1))	2.21	1.44
Application to the court to replace the nominee (paragraph 28(a) of Schedule A1)	2.22	1.45
Notice of appointment of replacement nominee	2.23	1.46
Applications to court to challenge nominee's actions etc. (paragraphs 26 and 27 of Schedule A1)	2.24	1.47
Chapter 5 Consideration of the proposal by the company members and creditors		
Consideration of proposal – common requirements (section 3)	2.25	1.9, 1.11, 1.48
Members' consideration at a meeting	2.26	
Creditors' consideration by a decision procedure	2.27	
Timing of decisions on proposal	2.28	1.13
Creditors' approval of modified proposal	2.29	N/A
Notice of members' meeting and attendance of officers	2.30	1.9, 1.11, 1.48
Requisition of physical meeting by creditors	2.31	N/A
Non-receipt of notice by members	2.32	12A.4
Proposal for alternative supervisor	2.33	1.22
Chair at meetings	2.34	1.14
Members' voting rights	2.35	1.18, 1.51

2016 Rule heading	2016 Rule	1986 Rule
Requisite majorities of members	2.36	1.20, 1.53
Notice of order made under section 4A(6) or paragraph 36(5) of Schedule A1	2.37	1.22A
Report of consideration of proposal under section 4(6) and (6A)(a) or paragraph 30(3)(b) and (4) of Schedule A1	2.38	1.24
Chapter 6: additional matters concerning and following approval of CVA		
Hand-over of property etc. to supervisor	2.39	1.23, 1.54
Revocation or suspension of CVA	2.40	1.25
Supervisor's accounts and reports	2.41	1.26A
Production of accounts and records to Secretary of State	2.42	1.27
Fees and expenses	2.43	1.28
Termination or full implementation of CVA	2.44	1.29
Chapter 10 Time recording information		
Provision of information	2.45	1.55
Part 3: Administration		
Chapter 1 Interpretation		
Interpretation for Part 3	3.1	2.33(2A)
Proposed administrator's statement and consent to act	3.2	Form 2.2
Chapter 2 Appointment of Administrator by court		
Administration application (paragraph 12 of Schedule B1)	3.3	Form 2.1
Administration application made by the directors	3.4	2.3(2)
Administration application by the supervisor of a CVA	3.5	2.2(4)
Witness statement in support of administration application	3.6	2.2, 2.3, 2.4, 2.11
Filing of application	3.7	2.5
Service of application	3.8	2.6
Notice to enforcement agents charged with distress or other legal process, etc.	3.9	2.7
Notice of other insolvency proceedings	3.10	2.5
Intervention by holder of qualifying floating charge (paragraph 36(1)(b) of Schedule B1)	3.11	2.10
The hearing	3.12	2.12
The order	3.13	2.13, Form 2.4B
Order on an application under paragraph 37 of Schedule B1	3.14	2.13
Notice of administration order	3.15	2.14
Chapter 3 Appointment of administrator by holder of floating charge		
Notice of intention to appoint	3.16	2.15, Form 2.5B
Notice of appointment	3.17	2.16, Form 2.6B
Filing of notice with court	3.18	2.17
Appointment by floating charge holder after administration application made	3.19	2.18

2016 Rule heading	2016 Rule	1986 Rule
Appointment taking place out of court business hours: procedure	3.20	2.19
Appointment taking place out of court business hours: content of notice	3.21	2.19(1) and Form 2.7B
Appointment taking place out of court business hours: legal effect	3.22	2.19(2)
Chapter 4 Appointment of administrator by company or directors		
Notice of intention to appoint	3.23	2.20 form 2.8B
Notice of appointment after notice of intention to appoint	3.24	2.23, 2.24 and Form 2.9B
Notice of appointment without prior notice of intention to appoint	3.25	2.25 and Form 2.8B
Notice of appointment: filing with the court	3.26	2.26
Chapter 5: Notice of administrator's appointment		
Publication of administrator's appointment	3.27	2.27
Chapter 6 Statement of affairs		
Interpretation	3.28	2.28(1)
Statement of affairs: notice requiring and delivery to the administrator (paragraph 47(1) of Schedule B1)	3.29	2.28 and form 2.13B
Statement of affairs: content (paragraph 47 of Schedule B1)	3.30	2.29 and form 2.14B
Statement of affairs: statement of concurrence	3.31	2.29(2) et seq
Statement of affairs: filing	3.32	2.29(7)
Statement of affairs: release from requirement and extension of time	3.33	2.31
Statement of affairs expenses	3.34	2.32
Chapter 7: administrator's proposals		
Administrator's proposals: additional content	3.35	2.33
Administrator's proposals: statement of pre-administration costs	3.36	2.33(2A), (2B)
Administrator's proposals: ancillary provisions about delivery	3.37	2.33
Seeking approval of the administrator's proposals	3.38	2.34
Invitation to creditors to form a creditors' committee	3.39	N/A
Notice of extension of time to seek approval	3.40	2.34
Notice of the creditors' decision on the administrator's proposals (paragraph 53(2))	3.41	2.46
Administrator's proposals: revision	3.42	2.45
Notice of result of creditors' decision on revised proposals (paragraph 54(6))	3.43	2.46
Chapter 8: Limited disclosure of statement of affairs and proposals		
Application of Chapter	3.44	2.30

2016 Rule heading	2016 Rule	1986 Rule
Orders limiting disclosure of statement of affairs etc.	3.45	2.30, 2.33A
Order for disclosure by administrator	3.46	2.30(4)
Rescission or amendment of order for limited disclosure	3.47	2.30(7)
Publication etc. of statement of affairs or statement of proposals	3.48	2.30(8),(9) and (10)
Chapter 9: disposal of charged property		
Disposal of charged property	3.49	2.66
Chapter 10 Expenses of the Administration		
Expenses	3.50	2.67, 12.2
Order of priority	3.51	2.67
Pre-administration costs	3.52	2.67A
Chapter 11: extension and ending of administration		
Interpretation	3.53	2.110
Application to extend an administration and extension by consent (paragraph 76(2)(a) of Schedule B1)	3.54	2.112
Notice of automatic end of administration (paragraph 76 of Schedule B1)	3.55	2.111
Notice of end of administration when purposes achieved (paragraph 80(2) of Schedule B1)	3.56	2.113
Administrator's application for order ending administration (paragraph 79 of Schedule B1)	3.57	2.114
Creditor's application for order ending administration (paragraph 81 of Schedule B1)	3.58	2.115
Notice by administrator of court order	3.59	2.116
Moving from administration to creditors' voluntary winding up (paragraph 83 of Schedule B1)	3.60	2.117A
Moving from administration to dissolution (paragraph 84 of Schedule B1)	3.61	2.118
Chapter 12: Replacing the administrator		
Grounds for resignation	3.62	2.119
Notice of intention to resign	3.63	2.120
Notice of resignation (paragraph 87 of Schedule B1)	3.64	2.12
Application to court to remove administrator from office	3.65	2.122
Notice of vacation of office when administrator ceases to be qualified to act	3.66	2.123
Deceased administrator	3.67	2.124
Application to replace	3.68	2.125
Appointment of replacement or additional administrator	3.69	2.126, 2.127, 2.128
Administrator's duties on vacating office	3.70	2.129

2016 Rule heading	2016 Rule	1986 Rule
Part 4: Receivership		
Chapter 1: Appointment of joint receivers or managers to whom Part 3 of the Act applies (other than those appointed under section 51 (Scottish receiverships))		
Receivers or managers appointed under an instrument: acceptance of appointment (section 33)	4.1	3.1
Chapter 2: Administrative receivers (other than in Scottish receiverships)		
Application of Chapter 2	4.2	N/A
Interpretation	4.3	N/A
Administrative receiver's security	4.4	12A.56
Publication of appointment of administrative receiver (section 46(1))	4.5	3.2
Requirement to provide a statement of affairs (section 47(1))	4.6	3.3
Statement of affairs: contents and delivery of copy (section 47(2))	4.7	3.4(1) form 3.2
Statement of affairs: statement of concurrence	4.8	3.4(2)–(5)
Statement of affairs: retention by administrative receiver	4.9	3.4(6)
Statement of affairs: release from requirement and extension of time (section 47(5))	4.10	3.6
Statement of affairs: expenses	4.11	3.7
Limited disclosure	4.12	3.5
Administrative receiver's report to the registrar of companies and secured creditors (section 48(1))	4.13	3.8
Copy of report for unsecured creditors (section 48(2)(a))	4.14	3.8
Invitation to creditors to form a creditors' committee	4.15	N/A
Disposal of charged property (section 43(1))	4.16	3.31
Summary of receipts and payments	4.17	3.32
Resignation	4.18	3.33
Deceased administrative receiver	4.19	3.34
Other vacation of office	4.20	3.35
Notice to registrar of companies (section 45(4))	4.21	3.35(2)
Chapter 3: Non-administrative receivers and the prescribed part		
Application of Chapter 3	4.22	3.39
Report to creditors	4.23	3.39
Receiver to deal with prescribed part	4.24	3.40
Part 5: Members' voluntary winding up		
Chapter 1 Statutory declaration of solvency (section 89)		
Statutory declaration of solvency: requirements additional to those in section 89	5.1	Form 4.70
Chapter 2: The liquidator		
Appointment by the company	5.2	4.139

2016 Rule heading	2016 Rule	1986 Rule
Meetings in members' voluntary winding up of authorised deposit-takers	5.3	4.72
Appointment by the court (section 108)	5.4	4.140
Cost of liquidator's security	5.5	12A.56
Liquidator's resignation	5.6	4.142(3)
Removal of liquidator by the court	5.7	4.143
Removal of liquidator by company meeting	5.8	4.142
Delivery of draft final account to members (section 94)	5.9	4.126A
Final account prior to dissolution (section 94)	5.10	4.126A
Deceased liquidator	5.11	4.145
Loss of qualification as insolvency practitioner	5.12	4.146
Liquidator's duties on vacating office	5.13	4.148
Application by former liquidator to the Secretary of State for release (section 173(2)(b)(a))	5.14	4.144(3), 4.147
Power of court to set aside certain transactions entered into by liquidator	5.15	4.149
Rule against improper solicitation on or behalf of the liquidator	5.16	4.150
Chapter 3: Special manager		
Application for and appointment of special manager (section 177)	5.17	4.206
Security	5.18	4.207
Failure to give or keep up security	5.19	4.208
Accounting	5.20	4.209
Termination of appointment	5.21	4.210
Chapter 4: Conversion to creditors' voluntary winding up		
Statement of affairs (section 95(3))	5.22	4.34
Part 6: Creditors' voluntary winding up		
Chapter 1: Application of Part 6		
Application of Part 6	6.1	4.1(6)
Chapter 2: Statement of affairs and other information		
Statement of affairs made out by the liquidator under section 95(1A)	6.2	4.34, Form 4.18
Statement of affairs made out by the directors under section 99(1)	6.3	4.34, Form 4.19
Additional requirements as to statement of affairs	6.4	Form 4.18, Form 4.19
Statement of affairs: statement of concurrence	6.5	4.34(5)
Order limiting disclosure of statement of affairs etc.	6.6	4.35
Expenses of statement of affairs and decisions sought from creditors	6.7	4.38

2016 Rule heading	2016 Rule	1986 Rule
Delivery of accounts to liquidator (section 235)	6.8	4.40
Expenses of assistance in preparing accounts	6.9	4.41
Chapter 3: Nomination and appointment of liquidators and information to creditors		
Application of the rules in this Chapter	6.10	N/A
Nomination of liquidator and information to creditors on conversion from members' voluntary winding up (section 96)	6.11	N/A
Creditors' decision on appointment other than at a meeting (conversion from members' voluntary winding up)	6.12	N/A
Information to creditors and contributories (conversion of members' voluntary winding up into creditors' voluntary winding up)	6.13	4.49
Information to creditors and appointment of liquidator	6.14	
Information to creditors and contributories (conversion from MVL)	6.14	4.49
Information to creditors and contributories	6.15	4.49-CVL
Further information where administrator becomes liquidator (paragraph 83(3) of Schedule B1))	6.16	4.49A
Report by director etc.	6.17	4.53B
Decisions on nomination	6.18	4.63
Invitation to creditors to form a liquidation committee	6.19	N/A
Chapter 4: The liquidator		
Appointment by creditors or by the company	6.20	4.101
Power to fill vacancy in office of liquidator	6.21	4.101A
Appointment by the court (section 100(3) or 108)	6.22	4.103
Appointment to be gazetted and registered	6.23	4.106A
Cost of liquidator's security (section 390(3))	6.24	12A.56
Liquidator's resignation and replacement	6.25	4.108
Removal of liquidator by creditors	6.26	4.117
Removal of liquidator by the court	6.27	4.120
Final account prior to dissolution (section 106)	6.28	4.126
Deceased liquidator	6.29	4.133
Loss of qualification as insolvency practitioner	6.30	4.135
Vacation of office on making of winding-up order	6.31	4.136
Liquidator's duties on leaving office	6.32	4.138
Application by former liquidator for release (section 173(2)(b))	6.33	4.122(3), Form 4.41
Power of court to set aside certain transactions	6.34	4.149
Rule against improper solicitation	6.35	4.150
Permission for exercise of powers by liquidator	6.36	4.184

2016 Rule heading	2016 Rule	1986 Rule
Chapter 5: Special manager		
Application for and appointment of special manager (section 177)	6.37	4.206
Security	6.38	4.207
Failure to give or keep up security	6.39	4.208
Accounting	6.40	4.209
Termination of appointment	6.41	4.210
Chapter 6: Priority of payment of costs and expenses, etc.		
General rule as to priority	6.42	4.218, 12.2
Saving for powers of the court	6.43	4.220
Chapter 7: Litigation expenses and property subject to a floating charge		
Interpretation	6.44	4.218A
Requirement for approval or authorisation	6.45	4.218B
Request for approval or authorisation	6.46	4.218C
Grant of approval or authorisation	6.47	4.218D
Application to the court by the liquidator	6.48	4.218E
Part 7: Winding up by the court		
Chapter 1: Application of part		
Application of Part	7.1	N/A
Chapter 2: The statutory demand (sections 123(1)(a) and 222(1)(a))		
Interpretation	7.2	4.4
The statutory demand	7.3	4.5, 4.6 and Form 4.1
Chapter 3: Petition for winding-up order		
Application of this Chapter	7.4	N/A
Contents of petition	7.5	Form 4.2
Verification of petition	7.6	4.12
Petition: presentation and filing	7.7	4.7
Court to which petition is to be presented where the company is subject to a CVA or is in administration	7.8	4.7
Copies of petition to be served on company or delivered to other persons	7.9	4.10
Notice of petition	7.10	4.11
Persons entitled to request a copy of petition	7.11	4.13
Certificate of compliance	7.12	4.14
Permission for the petitioner to withdraw	7.13	4.15
Notice by persons intending to appear	7.14	4.16
List of appearances	7.15	4.17

2016 Rule heading	2016 Rule	1986 Rule
Witness statement in opposition	7.16	4.18
Substitution of creditor or contributory for petitioner	7.17	4.19
Order for substitution of petitioner	7.18	N/A
Notice of adjournment	7.19	4.18A
Order for winding up by the court	7.20	N/A
Notice to official receiver of winding-up order	7.21	4.20 and form 4.13
Delivery and notice of the order	7.22	4.21
Petition dismissed	7.23	4.21B
Injunction to restrain presentation or notice of petition	7.24	4.6A
Chapter 4: Petition by a contributory or a relevant office-holder		
Interpretation and application of rules in Chapter 3	7.25	4.24
Contents of petition for winding-up order by a contributory	7.26	Form 4.14
Petition presented by a relevant office-holder	7.27	4.7
Verification of petition	7.28	Form 4.14
Presentation and service of petition	7.29	4.22
Request to appoint former administrator or supervisor as liquidator (section 140)	7.30	4.7
Hearing of petition	7.31	4.23
Order for winding up by the court of a company in administration or where there is a supervisor of a CVA in relation to the company	7.32	4.20 and form 4.12
Chapter 5: Provisional liquidator		
Application for appointment of provisional liquidator (section 135)	7.33	4.25
Deposit by applicant	7.34	4.27
Order of appointment of provisional liquidator	7.35	4.26, form 4.15
Notice of appointment of provisional liquidator	7.36	4.25A
Security	7.37	4.28, 4.29
Remuneration	7.38	4.30
Termination of appointment	7.39	4.31
Chapter 6: statement of affairs and other information		
Notice requiring statement of affairs (section 131)	7.40	4.32
Statement of affairs	7.41	Form 4.17
Statement of affairs: statement of concurrence	7.42	4.33
Order limiting disclosure of statement of affairs etc.	7.43	4.35
Release from duty to submit statement of affairs: extension of time (section 131)	7.44	4.36
Statement of affairs: expenses	7.45	4.37
Delivery of accounts to official receiver	7.46	4.39

2016 Rule heading	2016 Rule	1986 Rule
Further disclosure	7.47	4.42
Chapter 7: Reports and information to creditors and contributories		
Reports by official receiver	7.48	4.43, 4.45, 4.46
Reports by official receiver: estimate of prescribed part	7.49	4.43
Further information where winding up follows administration	7.50	4.49A
Notice of stay of winding up	7.51	4.48(2)
Chapter 8: The liquidator		
Choosing a person to be liquidator	7.52	4.50
Appointment of liquidator by creditors or contributories	7.53	4.100
Decisions on nomination	7.54	4.63
Invitation to creditors and contributories to form a liquidation committee	7.55	
Appointment by the court	7.56	4.102
Appointment by Secretary of State	7.57	4.104
Cost of liquidator's security (section 390(3))	7.58	12A.56
Appointment to be gazetted and notice given to registrar of companies	7.59	4.106A
Hand-over of assets by official receiver to liquidator	7.60	4.107
Liquidator's resignation	7.61	4.108(4)
Notice to official receiver of intention to vacate office	7.62	4.137
Decision of creditors to remove liquidator	7.63	7.113
Procedure on removal by creditors	7.64	4.116,
Removal of liquidator by the court (section 172(2))	7.65	4.119
Removal of liquidator by the Secretary of State	7.66	4.123
Deceased liquidator	7.67	4.132,
Loss of qualification as insolvency practitioner	7.68	4.134,
Application by liquidator for release (section 174(4)(b) or (d))	7.69	4.121
Release of official receiver	7.70	4.124
Final account prior to dissolution (section 146)	7.71	4.125
Relief from, or variation of, duty to report	7.72	4.125A
Liquidator's duties on vacating office	7.73	4.138
Power of court to set aside certain transactions	7.74	4.149
Rule against improper solicitation	7.75	4.150
Chapter 9: Duties and powers of liquidator		
General duties of liquidator	7.76	4.179
Permission for exercise of powers by liquidator	7.77	4.184
Enforced delivery up of company's property (section 234)	7.78	4.185
Chapter 10: Settlement of list of contributories		
Delegation to liquidator of power to settle list of contributories	7.79	4.195

2016 Rule heading	2016 Rule	1986 Rule
Duty of liquidator to settle list (section 148)	7.80	4.196
Contents of list	7.81	4.197
Procedure for settling list	7.82	4.198
Application to court for variation of the list	7.83	4.199
Variation of, or addition to, the list	7.84	4.200
Costs of applications to vary etc. the list of contributories	7.85	4.201
Chapter 11: Calls on contributories		
Making of calls by the liquidator (sections 150 and 160)	7.86	4.202
Sanction of the liquidation committee for making a call	7.87	4.203
Application to court for permission to make a call (sections 150 and 160)	7.88	4.204, form 4.56
Order giving permission to make a call	7.89	Form 4.57
Making and enforcement of the call	7.90	4.205, form 4.58
Court order to enforce payment of call by a contributory	7.91	4.205, form 4.59
Chapter 12: Special manager		
Application of this Chapter and interpretation	7.92	
Appointment and remuneration of special manager (section 177)	7.93	4.206
Security	7.94	4.207
Failure to give or keep up security	7.95	4.208
Accounting	7.96	4.209
Termination of appointment	7.97	4.210
Chapter 13: public examination of company officers and others (section 133)		
Applications relating to promoters, past managers etc. (section 133(1)(c)	7.98	4.211
Request for a creditor for a public examination (section 133(2))	7.99	4.213
Request by a contributory for a public examination	7.100	4.213
Further provisions about requests by a creditor or contributory for a public examination	7.101	4.213(3), 4.213(4). 4.214(5)
Order for public examination	7.102	Form 4.61
Notice of the public examination	7.103	4.212
Examinee unfit for examination	7.104	4.214
Procedure at public examination	7.105	4.215
Adjournment	7.106	4.216
Expenses of examination	7.107	4.217
Chapter 14: Priority of payment of costs and expenses, etc.		
General rule as to priority	7.108	4.218, 12.2
Winding up commencing as voluntary	7.109	4.219
Saving for powers of the court (section 156)	7.110	4.220

2016 Rule heading	2016 Rule	1986 Rule
Chapter 15: litigation expenses and property subject to a floating charge		
Interpretation	7.111	4.218A
Priority of litigation expenses	7.112	4.218A(2)
Requirement for approval or authorisation of litigation expenses	7.113	4.218B
Requests for approval or authorisation	7.114	4.218C
Grant of approval or authorisation	7.115	4.218D
Application to the court by the liquidator	7.116	4.218E
Chapter 16: Miscellaneous rules		
Sub-division A: Return of capital		
Application to court for order authorising return of capital	7.117	4.221
Procedure for return	7.118	4.222
Sub-division B: Dissolution after winding up		
Secretary of State's directions under sections 203 and 205 and appeal	7.119	4.224, 4.225
Part 8: Individual Voluntary Arrangements		
Chapter 1: Preliminary		
Interpretation	8.1	N/A
Chapter 2: Preparation of the debtor's proposal for an IVA		
Proposal for an IVA: general principles and amendment	8.2	5.3
Proposal: contents	8.3	5.3
Notice of nominee's consent	8.4	5.4
Statement of affairs (section 256 and 256A)	8.5	5.5
Application to omit information from statement of affairs delivered to creditors	8.6	5.68
Additional disclosure for assistance of nominee	8.7	5.6
Chapter 3: Cases in which an application for an interim order is made		
Application for interim order	8.8	5.7
Court in which application to be made	8.9	5.8
Order granting a stay	8.10	Form 5.1
Hearing of the application	8.11	5.9
The interim order	8.12	Form 5.2
Action to follow making of an interim order	8.13	5.10
Order extending period of an interim order (section 256(4))	8.14	Form 5.3
Nominee's report on the proposal	8.15	5.11
Order extending period of interim order to enable the creditors to consider the proposal (section 256(5))	8.16	Form 5.3
Replacement of the nominee (section 256(3))	8.17	5.12

2016 Rule heading	2016 Rule	1986 Rule
Consideration of the nominee's report	8.18	5.13
Chapter 4: Cases where no interim order is to be obtained		
Nominee's report (section 256A)	8.19	5.14A
Court or hearing centre to which applications must be made where no interim order	8.20	5.14B
Replacement of the nominee (section 256A(4))	8.21	5.14B
Chapter 5: Consideration of the proposal by the creditors		
Consideration of the proposal	8.22	5.17
Proposals for an alternative supervisor	8.23	5.25
Report of the creditors' consideration of a proposal	8.24	5.27
Chapter 6: Action following approval of an IVA		
Hand-over of property, etc. to supervisor	8.25	5.26
Report to the Secretary of State of the approval of an IVA	8.26	5.29
Revocation or suspension of an IVA (section 262)	8.27	5.30
Supervisor's accounts and reports	8.28	5.31A
Production of accounts and records to the Secretary of State	8.29	5.32
Fees and expenses	8.30	5.33
Termination or full implementation of the IVA	8.31	5.34
Chapter 7: Applications to annul the bankruptcy order (section 261(2)(a)		
Application by the bankrupt to annul the bankruptcy order (section 261(2)(a))	8.32	5.51, 5.52
Application by the official receiver to annul the bankruptcy order (section 261(2)(b))	8.33	5.54, 5.55
Order annulling bankruptcy	8.34	Form 5.7
Notice of order	8.35	5.53, 5.56
Advertisement of order	8.36	5.60
Trustee's final account	8.37	5.61
Chapter 8: Time recording information		
Provision of information	8.38	5.66
Part 9: Debt relief orders		
Chapter 1: Interpretation		
Debtor's family	9.1	N/A
Excluded debts	9.2	5A.2
Chapter 2: Application for a debt relief order		
Application for a debt relief order: information required in the application	9.3	5A.3
Delivery of application	9.4	5A.4
Role of approved intermediary	9.5	5A.5

2016 Rule heading	2016 Rule	1986 Rule
Chapter 3: Verifying the application and determining the debtor's income and property		
Prescribed verification checks: conditions in paragraphs 1 to 8 of Schedule 4ZA of the Act	9.6	5A.7
Determination of debtor's monthly surplus income	9.7	5A.8
Determination of value of the debtor's property (paragraph 8 of Schedule 4ZA)	9.8	5A.9
Property to be excluded in determining the value of a debtor's property	9.9	5A.10
Chapter 4: making or refusal of a debt relief order		
Content of debt relief order	9.10	5A.11
Other steps to be taken by official receiver or debtor upon making of the order	9.11	5A.12
Prescribed information for creditors on making of debt relief order	9.12	5A.13
Refusal of application for debt relief order	9.13	5A.6
Chapter 5: Objection and revocation		
Meaning of "creditor"	9.14	5A.14
Creditor's objection to a debt relief order (section 251K)	9.15	5A.14
Official receiver's response to objection under section 251K	9.16	5A.15
Creditor's request that a debt relief order be revoked (section 251L(4))	9.17	5A.16
Procedure in revoking or amending a debt relief order (section 251L)	9.18	5A.16
Debtor's notification of official receiver of matters in section 251J(3) or (5)	9.19	5A.17
Death of debtor during a moratorium period under a debt relief order	9.20	5A.27
Chapter 6: Applications to the court		
Notice of application to court under section 251M	9.21	5A.19
Court in which applications under section 251M or 251N to be made	9.22	5A.21
Creditor's bankruptcy petition: creditor consents to making application for a debt relief order	9.23	5A.23
Extension of moratorium period	9.24	5A.20
Chapter 7: Permission to act as a director, etc.		
Application for permission under the Company Directors Disqualification Act 1986(a)	9.25	5A.24
Report of official receiver	9.26	5A.25
Court's order on application	9.27	5A.26

2016 Rule heading	2016 Rule	1986 Rule
Part 10: Bankruptcy		
Chapter 1: The statutory demand		
The statutory demand (section 268)	10.1	6.1 and 6.2
Service of statutory demand	10.2	6.3
Proof of service of statutory demand	10.3	6.11
Application to set aside statutory demand	10.4	6.4
Hearing of application to set aside	10.5	6.5
Chapter 2: Creditors' bankruptcy petitions		
Application and interpretation	10.6	6.6
Contents of petition	10.7	Forms 6.7 to 6.10
Identification of debtor	10.8	6.7
Identification of debt	10.9	6.8
Verification of petition	10.10	6.12
Court in which petition is to be presented	10.11	6.9A
Procedure for presentation and filing of petition	10.12	6.10
Application to Chief Land Registrar to register petition	10.13	6.13
Service of petition and delivery of copies	10.14	6.14
Death of debtor before service	10.15	6.16
Amendment of petition	10.16	6.22
Security for costs	10.17	6.17
Debtor's notice of opposition to petition	10.18	6.21
Notice by persons intending to appear	10.19	6.23
List of appearances	10.20	6.24
Hearing of petition	10.21	6.18
Postponement of hearing	10.22	6.28
Adjournment of the hearing	10.23	6.29
Decision on hearing	10.24	6.25
Vacating registration on withdrawal of petition	10.25	6.27
Non-appearance of petitioning creditor	10.26	6.26
Substitution of petitioner	10.27	6.30
Order for substitution of petitioner	10.28	Form 6.24A
Change of carriage of petition	10.29	6.31
Petitioner seeking dismissal or permission to withdraw	10.30	6.32
Contents of bankruptcy order	10.31	6.33
Delivery and notice of the order	10.32	6.34
Application to Chief Land Registrar to register bankruptcy order	10.33	Form 6.26
Chapter 3: Debtor's bankruptcy applications		
Preliminary	10.34	6.37

2016 Rule heading	2016 Rule	1986 Rule
Bankruptcy application for a bankruptcy order	10.35 and Schedules 7 and 8	6.38 and Schedules 2A and 2B
Procedure for making a bankruptcy application and communication with the adjudicator	10.36	6.39
Application to the Chief Land Registrar to register a bankruptcy	10.37	6.40,
Verification checks	10.38	6.41
Determination of the bankruptcy application	10.39	6.42
The determination period	10.40	6.43
Settlement and contents of bankruptcy order	10.41	6.44
Refusal to make a bankruptcy order and contents of notice of refusal	10.42	6.45
Review of refusal to make a bankruptcy order	10.43	6.46
Appeal to the court following a review of refusal to make a bankruptcy order	10.44	6.47
Action to follow making of order	10.45	6.48
Application to the Chief Land Registrar	10.46	6.49
The bankruptcy file	10.47	6.50
Court to which applications are to be made	10.48	6.50A
Chapter 4: The interim receiver		
Application for appointment of interim receiver (section 286)	10.49	6.51
Deposit	10.50	6.53
Order of appointment	10.51	6.52, Form 6.32
Security	10.52	6.54
Remuneration	10.53	6.56
Termination of appointment	10.54	6.57
Chapter 5: Disclosure of the bankrupt's affairs		
Sub-division A: creditor's petition		
Notice requiring statement of affairs (section 288)	10.55	6.58
Statement of affairs	10.56	6.59, 6.60, Form 6.33A
Limited disclosure	10.57	6.61
Requirement to submit statement of affairs and extension of time (section 288(3))	10.58	6.62
Expenses of assisting bankrupt to prepare statement of affairs	10.59	6.63
Delivery of accounts to official receiver	10.60	6.64, 6.65
Further disclosure	10.61	6.66
Sub-division B: Bankruptcy application		
Preliminary	10.62	6.67
Delivery of accounts to official receiver	10.63	6.69, 6.70

2016 Rule heading	2016 Rule	1986 Rule
Expenses of preparing accounts	10.64	6.71
Further disclosure	10.65	6.72
Sub-division C: Reports by the official receiver		
Reports by the official receiver	10.66	6.73, 6.75, 6.76, 6.77, 6.78
Chapter 6: The Trustee in Bankruptcy		
Appointment by creditors of new trustee	10.67	6.120
Certification of appointment	10.68	6.120, Form 6.40, Form 6.41
Cost of the trustee's security (section 390(3))	10.69	12A.56
Creditors' decision to appoint a trustee	10.70	6.88
Appointment by the court (section 291A(2))	10.71	6.121, forms 6.42, 6.43
Appointment by Secretary of State	10.72	6.122
Authentication of trustee's appointment	10.73	6.123
Appointment to be gazetted	10.74	6.124
Hand-over of estate by official receiver to trustee	10.75	6.125
Invitation to creditors to form a creditors' committee	10.76	N/A
Sub-division B: Resignation and removal		
Trustee's resignation and appointment of replacement (section 298(7))	10.77	6.126
Decision of creditors to remove trustee (section 298(1))	10.78	6.127, 6.129
Procedure on removal by creditors	10.79	6.131
Removal of trustee by the court (section 298(1))	10.80	6.132
Removal of trustee by Secretary of State (section 298(5))	10.81	6.133
Notice of resignation or removal	10.82	6.134
Release of removed trustee (section 299)	10.83	6.135
Deceased trustee	10.84	6.143
Loss of qualification as insolvency practitioner (section 298(6))	10.85	6.144
Sub-division C: Release of official receiver on completion of administration (section 299)		
Release of official receiver on completion of administration	10.86	6.136
Vacation of office on completion of bankruptcy (sections 298(8) and 331)	10.87	6.137
Rule as to reporting	10.88	6.137A
Notice to official receiver of intention to vacate office	10.89	6.145
Trustee's duties on vacating office	10.90	6.146
Power of the court to set aside certain transactions	10.91	6.147
Rule against improper solicitation	10.92	6.148
Enforcement of trustee's obligations to official receiver (section 305(3))	10.93	6.149

2016 Rule heading	2016 Rule	1986 Rule
Chapter 7: Special Manager		
Application for and order of appointment of special manager (section 370)	10.94	6.167, form 6.54
Security	10.95	6.168
Failure to give or keep up security	10.96	6.169
Accounting	10.97	6.170
Termination of appointment	10.98	6.171
Chapter 8: Public examination of bankrupt		
Order for public examination of bankrupt	10.99	6.172, Form 6.55
Notice of public examination	10.100	6.172
Order for public examination requested by creditors	10.101	6.173
Bankrupt unfit for examination	10.102	6.174
Procedure at public examination	10.103	6.175
Adjournment	10.104	6.176
Expenses of examination	10.105	6.177
Chapter 9: Replacement of exempt property		
Purchase of replacement property	10.106	6.187
Money provided in lieu of sale	10.107	6.188
Chapter 10: Income payments orders		
Interpretation	10.108	N/A
Application for income payments order (section 310)	10.109	6.189
Order for income payments order	10.110	Form 6.65, Form 6.66
Action to follow making of order	10.111	6.190
Variation of order	10.112	6.191, Form 6.67
Order to payer of income: administration	10.113	6.192
Review of order	10.114	6.193, Form 6.68
Chapter 11: Income Payments Agreements		
Approval of income payments agreements	10.115	6.193A
Acceptance of income payments agreements	10.116	6.193B
Variation of income payments agreements	10.117	6.193C, Form 6.81
Chapter 12: Applications for production of documents by Her Majesty's Revenue and Customs (section 369)		
Application for order	10.118	6.194
Making and service of the order	10.119	6.195
Custody of documents	10.120	6.196
Chapter 13: Mortgaged property		
Interpretation	10.121	6.197
Claim by mortgagee of land	10.122	6.197

2016 Rule heading	2016 Rule	1986 Rule
Power of court to order sale	10.123	6.198
Proceeds of sale	10.124	6.199
Chapter 14: After-acquired property		
Duties of bankrupt in relation to after-acquired property	10.125	6.200
Trustee's recourse to person to whom property disposed	10.126	6.201
Chapter 15: Permission to act as director, etc.		
Interpretation	10.127	6.202A
Application for permission	10.128	6.203
Report of official receiver	10.129	6.204
Court's order on application	10.130	6.205
Costs under this Chapter	10.131	6.222
Chapter 16: Annulment of bankruptcy order		
Application for annulment	10.132	6.206
Report by trustee	10.133	6.207
Applicant's claim that remuneration of expenses are excessive	10.134	6.207A
Power of court to stay proceedings	10.135	6.208
Notice to creditors who have not proved	10.136	6.209
The hearing	10.137	6.210
Matters to be proved under section 282(1)(b)	10.138	6.211
Notice to creditors	10.139	6.212
Other matters arising on annulment	10.140	6.213
Trustee's final account	10.141	6.214
Chapter 17: Discharge		
Application for suspension of discharge	10.142	6.215
Lifting of suspension of discharge	10.143	6.216
Certificate of discharge from bankruptcy order made otherwise than on a bankruptcy application	10.144	6.219(3), 6220
Certificate of discharge from bankruptcy order made on a bankruptcy application	10.145	6.219(3), 6220
Bankrupt's debts surviving discharge	10.146	6.223
Costs under this Chapter	10.147	6.222
Chapter 18: Priority of payment of costs etc. out of the bankrupt's estate		
Expenses	10.148	12.2
General rule as to priority	10.149	6.224
Chapter 19: Second bankruptcy		
Scope of this Chapter	10.150	6.225
General duty of existing trustee	10.151	6.226
Delivery up to later trustee	10.152	6.227
Existing trustee's expenses	10.153	6.228

2016 Rule heading	2016 Rule	1986 Rule
Chapter 20: Criminal bankruptcy		
Contents of petition	10.154	Form 6.79
Status and functions of Official Petitioner	10.155	6.230
Interim receivership	10.156	6.231
Proof of bankruptcy debts and notice of order	10.157	6.232
Rules not applying in criminal bankruptcy	10.158	6.234
Annulment of criminal bankruptcy order	10.159	6.234(3)
Application by bankrupt for discharge	10.160	6.217
Report of official receiver	10.161	6.218
Order of discharge	10.162	6.219
Deferment of issue of order pending appeal	10.163	6.221
Chapter 21: Miscellaneous rules in bankruptcy		
Amendment of title of proceedings	10.165	6.35
Application for redirection order	10.166	6.235A
Bankrupt's home: property falling within section 283A	10.167	6.237
Application in relation to the vesting of an interest in a dwelling-house (registered land)	10.168	6.237A
Vesting of bankrupt's interest (unregistered land)	10.169	6.237B
Vesting of bankrupt's estate: substituted period	10.170	6.237C, 6.237CA
Charging order	10.171	6.237D, form 6.79A
Part 11: Bankruptcy and debt relief restrictions orders and undertakings and the insolvency registers		
Chapter 1: Interpretation		
References to the Secretary of State	11.1	6.240, 6.252
Chapter 2: Bankruptcy and debt relief restrictions orders (schedules 4ZB and 4A of the Act)		
Applications for a bankruptcy or debt relief restrictions order	11.2	6.241, 6.253,
Service of the application on the bankrupt or debtor	11.3	6.242, 6.254
The bankrupt's or debtor's evidence opposing an application	11.4	6.243, 6.255
Making a bankruptcy restrictions order or debt relief restrictions order	11.5	6.244, 6.256
Chapter 3: Interim bankruptcy and debt relief restrictions orders		
Application for an interim bankruptcy or debt relief restrictions order	11.6	6.245, 6.257, 6.246, 6.258
Making an interim bankruptcy restrictions order or an interim debt relief restrictions order	11.7	6.247, 6.259
Application to set aside an interim order	11.8	6.248, 6.260
Order setting aside an interim order	11.9	6.248(5–6), 6.260(5–6)

2016 Rule heading	2016 Rule	1986 Rule
Chapter 4: Bankruptcy restrictions and debt relief restrictions undertakings		
Acceptance of a bankruptcy restrictions or a debt relief restrictions undertaking	11.10	6.249, 6.261
Notification	11.11	6.250, 6.262
Application to annul a bankruptcy restrictions or a debt relief restrictions undertaking	11.12	6.251, 6.263
Chapter 5: Insolvency Registers: general		
Maintenance of the registers and inspection	11.13	6A.1
Chapter 6: Individual insolvency register		
Entry of information on the individual insolvency register: IVAs	11.14	6A.2A
Deletion of information from the individual insolvency register: IVAs	11.15	6A.3
Entry of information on to the individual insolvency register: bankruptcy orders	11.16	6A.4
Deletion of information from the individual insolvency register: bankruptcy orders	11.17	6A.5
Entry of information on to the individual insolvency register: debt relief orders	11.18	6A.5A
Deletion of information from the individual insolvency register: debt relief orders	11.19	6A.5B
Chapter 7: Bankruptcy and debt relief restrictions register		
Bankruptcy restrictions and debt relief restrictions orders and undertakings: entry of information on the registers	11.20	6A.6, 6A.7A
Deletion of information from the registers	11.21	6A.7, 6A.7B
Chapter 8: Rectification of registers and death of persons on register		
Rectification of the registers	11.22	6A.8
Death of a person about whom information is held on a register	11.23	6A.8(2)
Part 12: Court procedure and practice		
Chapter 1: General, Application of the Civil Procedure Rules 1998		
Court rules and practice to apply	12.1	7.51A
Performance of functions by the Court	12.2	7.6A
Chapter 2: Commencement of insolvency proceedings in the county court		
Commencement of insolvency proceedings under Parts 1 to 7 of the Act (corporate insolvency proceedings)	12.3	Rule 2 of SI 2014/817
Commencement of insolvency proceedings under Parts 7A to 11 of the Act (personal insolvency proceedings; bankruptcy)	12.4	Rule 3 of SI 2014/817
Allocation of proceedings to the London Insolvency District	12.5	7.10ZA
Chapter 3: Making applications to court: general		
Preliminary	12.6	7.1
Filing of application	12.7	7.4(1)

2016 Rule heading	2016 Rule	1986 Rule
Fixing the venue	12.8	7.4(2)
Service or delivery of application	12.9	7.4(3–5)
Hearing in urgent case	12.10	7.4(6)
Directions	12.11	7.10(3)
Hearing and determination without notice	12.12	7.5A
Adjournment of the hearing of an application	12.13	7.10(1–2)
Chapter 4: Making applications to court: specific applications		
Sub-division A: Applications in connection with section 176A (prescribed part)		
Applications under section 176A(5) to disapply section 176A	12.14	7.3A
Notice of application under section 176A(5)	12.15	7.4A
Notice of an order under section 176A(5)	12.16	12A.57
Sub-division B: Applications for private examination (sections 236, 251N and 366)		
Application of this sub-division and interpretation	12.17	9.1
Contents of application	12.18	9.2
Order for examination etc.	12.19	9.3
Procedure for examination	12.20	9.4
Record of examination	12.21	9.5
Costs of proceedings under sections 236, 251N and 366	12.22	9.6
Sub-division C: persons unable to manage own property or affairs		
Application and interpretation	12.23	7.43
Appointment of another person to act	12.24	7.44
Witness statement in support of application	12.25	7.45A
Service of notices following appointment	12.26	7.46
Chapter 5: Obtaining information and evidence		
Further information and disclosure	12.27	7.60
Witness statements and reports	12.28	7.7A, 7.8
Evidence provided by the official receive, an insolvency practitioner or a special manager	12.29	7.9
Chapter 6: Transfer of proceedings		
Sub-division A: General		
General power of transfer	12.30	7.11
Proceedings commenced in the wrong court	12.31	7.12
Applications for transfer	12.32	7.13
Procedure following order for transfer	12.33	7.14
Consequential transfer of other proceedings	12.34	7.15
Sub-division B: Block transfer of cases where insolvency practitioner has died etc.		
Interpretation	12.35	7.10A
Power to make a block transfer order	12.36	7.10B
Application for a block transfer order	12.37	7.10C

2016 Rule heading	2016 Rule	1986 Rule
Action following application for a block transfer order	12.38	7.10D
Chapter 7: The court file		
The court file	12.39	7.31A
Office copies of documents	12.40	7.61
Chapter 8: Costs		
Application of Chapter and interpretation	12.41	7.33A
Requirement to assess costs by the detailed procedure	12.42	7.34A
Procedure where detailed assessment is required	12.43	7.35
Costs of officers charged with execution of writs or other process	12.44	7.36
Petitions presented by insolvent companies	12.45	7.37A
Costs paid otherwise than out of the insolvent estate	12.46	7.38
Awards of costs against an office-holder, the adjudicator or the official receiver	12.47	7.39
Applications for costs	12.48	7.40
Costs and expenses of petitioners and other specified persons	12.49	7.41
Final costs certificate	12.50	7.42
Chapter 9: Enforcement procedures		
Enforcement of court orders	12.51	7.19
Orders enforcing compliance	12.52	7.20
Warrants (general provisions)	12.53	7.21
Warrants under sections 134 and 364	12.54	7.22
Warrants under sections 236, 251N and 366	12.55	7.23
Warrants under section 365	12.56	7.25
Execution overtaken by judgment debtor's insolvency	12.57	12A.28
Chapter 10: Appeals		
Application of Chapter	12.58	7.49A
Appeals and reviews of court orders in corporate insolvency	12.59	7.47
Appeals in bankruptcy by the Secretary of State	12.60	7.48
Procedure on appeal	12.61	7.49A
Appeal against decisions of the Secretary of State or official receiver	12.62	7.50
Chapter 11: Court orders, formal defects and shorthand writers		
Court orders	12.63	N/A
Formal defects	12.64	7.55
Shorthand writers: nomination etc.	12.65	7.16, 7.17
Part 13: Official receivers		
Official receivers in court	13.1	10.1
Persons entitled to act on official receiver's behalf	13.2	10.2

2016 Rule heading	2016 Rule	1986 Rule
Application for directions	13.3	10.3
Official receiver's expenses	13.4	10.4
Official receiver not to be appointed liquidator or trustee	13.5	4.101B
Part 14: Claims by and distributions to creditors in administration, winding up and bankruptcy		
Chapter 1: Application and interpretation		
Application of Part 14 and interpretation	14.1	13.12
Chapter 2: Creditors' claims in administration, winding up and bankruptcy		
Provable debts	14.2	12.3
Proving a debt	14.3	2.72, 4.73, 6.96
Requirements for proof	14.4	2.72(3), 4.73, 4.75, 6.98
Costs of proving	14.5	2.74, 4.78, 6.100
Allowing inspection of proofs	14.6	2.75, 4.79, 6.101
Admission and rejection of proofs for dividend	14.7	2.77, 4.82, 6.104
Appeal against decision on proof	14.8	2.78, 4.83, 6.105
Office-holder not liable for costs under rule 14.8	14.9	2.78(6), 4.83(6), 6.105(6)
Withdrawal or variation of proof	14.10	2.79, 4.84, 6.106
Exclusion of proof by the court	14.11	2.80, 4.85, 6.107
Administration and winding up by the court: debts of insolvent company to rank equally	14.12	2.69, 4.181
Administration and winding up: division of unsold assets	14.13	2.71, 4.183
Administration and winding up: estimate of value of debt	14.14	2.81, 4.86
Secured creditor: value of security	14.15	2.90, 4.95, 6.115
Secured creditor: surrender for non-disclosure	14.16	2.91, 4.96, 6.116
Secured creditor: redemption by office-holder	14.17	2.92, 4.97, 6.117
Secured creditor: test of security's value	14.18	2.93, 4.98, 6.118
Realisation or surrender of security by creditor	14.19	2.83, 2.94, 4.88, 4.99, 6.119
Discounts	14.20	2.84, 4.89, 6.110
Debts in foreign currency	14.21	2.86, 4.91, 6.111
Payments of a periodical nature	14.22	2.87, 4.92, 6.112
Interest	14.23	2.88, 4.93, 6.113
Administration: mutual dealings and set-off	14.24	2.85
Winding up: mutual dealings and set-off	14.25	4.90
Chapter 3: Distributions to creditors in administration, winding up and bankruptcy		
Application of Chapter to particular class of creditors and to distributions	14.26	2.95(5)
Declaration and distribution of dividends in a winding up	14.27	4.180

2016 Rule heading	2016 Rule	1986 Rule
Gazette notice of intended first dividend or distribution	14.28	11.2, 2.95, 4.182A
Individual notices to creditors etc. of intended dividend or distribution	14.29	2.95, 11.2
Contents of notice of intention to declare dividend or make a distribution	14.30	2.95(4), 11.2
Further contents of notice to creditors owed small debts etc.	14.31	
Admission or rejection of proofs following last date for proving	14.32	2.96, 11.3
Postponement or cancellation of dividend	14.33	2.96A, 11.4
Declaration of dividend	14.34	2.97, 11.5
Notice of declaration of a dividend	14.35	2.98, 2.99, 11.6
Last notice about dividend in a winding up	14.36	4.186,
Contents of last notice about dividend (administration, winding up and bankruptcy)	14.37	2.100, 11.7
Sole or final dividend	14.38	2.68, 4.186
Administration and winding up: provisions as to dividends	14.39	4.182(1)
Supplementary provisions as to dividends and distributions	14.40	2.101, 4.182(2), 11.8
Secured creditors	14.41	2.102, 6.109, 11.9
Disqualification from dividend	14.42	2.103, 11.10
Assignment of right to dividend	14.43	2.104, 11.11
Debt payable at future time	14.44	2.89, 2.105, 4.94, 6.114, 11.13
Administration and winding up: non-payment of dividend	14.45	2.70(3), 4.182(3)
Part 15: Decision making		
Chapter 1: Application of Part		
	15.1	N/A
Chapter 2: Decision procedures		
Interpretation	15.2	N/A
The prescribed decision procedures	15.3	N/A
Electronic voting	15.4	N/A
Virtual meetings	15.5	N/A
Physical meetings	15.6	N/A
Deemed consent (sections 246ZF and 379ZB)	15.7	N/A
Chapter 3: Notices, voting and venues for decisions		
Notices to creditors of decision procedure	15.8	1.9, 1.48, 2.34, 4.50, 4.51, 4.54, 5.17, 6.79, 6.81
Voting in a decision procedure	15.9	2.38, 3.11, 4.50, 4.51, 4.54, 6.79, 6.81

2016 Rule heading	2016 Rule	1986 Rule
Venue for decision procedure	15.10	1.13, 2.35, 3.9, 4.60, 5.18, 6.86
Notice of decision procedures or seeking deemed consent: when and to whom delivered	15.11	1.9, 1.48, 2.35, 3.9, 4.50, 4.54, 5.17, 6.79, 6.81
Notice of decision procedure by advertisement only	15.12	2.37A, 4.59, 6.85
Gazetting and advertising of meeting	15.13	2.34, 4.50, 4.53C and D, 6.79
Notice to company officers, bankrupts etc. in respect of meetings	15.14	1.16, 2.34(2), 4.58, 6.84
Non-receipt of notice of decision	15.15	12A.4
Decisions on remuneration and conduct	15.16	4.63, 6.88
Chapter 4: Decision making in particular proceedings		
Decisions in winding up of authorised deposit-takers	15.17	4.72
Chapter 5: Requisitioned decisions		
Requisitions of decision	15.18	2.37, 4.57, 6.83
Expenses and timing of requisitioned decision	15.19	2.37, 4.57(2), 4.61(3, 5) 6.83(2), 6.87
Chapter 6: Constitution of meetings		
Quorum at meetings	15.20	12A.21
Chair at meetings	15.21	2.36, 3.10, 4.55, 4.56, 5.19, 6.82
The chair – attendance, interventions and questions	15.22	4.58, 6.84
Chapter 7: Adjournment and suspension of meetings		
Adjournment by chair	15.23	1.21, 1.53, 2.35, 3.14, 4.65(3), 5.24, 6.91
Adjournment of meetings to remove a liquidator or trustee	15.24	4.113, 4.114, 6.129
Adjournment in absence of chair	15.25	2.35(5), 4.65(6A), 6.91(4A)
Proofs in adjournment	15.26	2.35, 4.65(7), 6.91(5)
Suspension	15.27	1.21, 1.53, 2.35, 3.14, 4.65, 5.24, 6.90
Chapter 8: Creditors' voting rights and majorities		
Creditors' voting rights	15.28	1.17,1.49, 2.38, 3.11, 4.67, 4.68, 5.21, 6.93, 6.93A
Scheme manager's voting rights	15.29	Sch 1, paras 2–4 & 6

2016 Rule heading	2016 Rule	1986 Rule
Claim made in proceedings in other member States	15.30	2.38, 4.67, 6.93
Calculation of voting rights	15.31	1.17(2–3), 1.49(3) 1.52(3), 2.38(4), 2.40(2), 3.11(4), 5.21(2–3), 5.41(2), 6.93
Calculation of voting rights: special cases	15.32	2.42, Sch 1
Procedure for admitting creditors' claims for voting	15.33	1.17A, 1.50, 2.39, 4.70, 5.21(1–4), 5.22, 6.94(1)&(3)
Requisite majorities	15.34	1.19, 1.52, 2.43, 3.15, 4.63, 5.23. 6.88
Appeals against decisions under this Chapter	15.35	1.17A, 1.50, 1.52, 2.39, 3.12, 4.70, 5.22, 5.23, 5.42, 6.94,
Chapter 9: Exclusions from meetings		
Action where person excluded	15.36	12A.23
Indication to excluded persons	15.37	12A.24
Complaint	15.38	12A.25
Chapter 10: Contributories' voting rights and majorities		
Contributories' voting rights and requisite majorities	15.39	4.63, 4.69
Chapter 10: Records		
Record of a decision	15.40	2.44A, 3.15, 4.71, 6.95
Chapter 12: Company meetings		
	15.41	2.49(5A)
Remote attendance: notification requirements	15.42	
Location of company meetings	15.43	12A.22
Action where person excluded	15.44	12A.23
Indication to excluded person	15.45	12A.24
Complaint	15.46	12A.25
Part 16: Proxies and corporate representation		
Application and interpretation	16.1	N/A
Specific and continuing proxies	16.2	8.1
Blank proxy	16.3	8.2
Use of proxies	16.4	8.2, 8.3
Use of proxies by the chair	16.5	1.15,, 2.36, 4.64, 5.20, 6.89, 8.3(3)
Right of inspection and retention of proxies	16.6	8.4, 8.5

2016 Rule heading	2016 Rule	1986 Rule
Proxy-holder with financial interest	16.7	8.6
Corporate representation: bankruptcy and IVA	16.8	8.7
Instrument conferring authorisation to represent corporation	16.9	8.7
Part 17: Creditors' and liquidation committees		
Chapter 1: Introductory		
Scope and interpretation	17.1	N/A
Chapter 2: Functions of a committee		
Functions of a committee	17.2	2.52, 3.18
Chapter 3: Membership and formalities of formation of a committee		
Number of members of a committee	17.3	2.50, 3.16, 4.152, 6.150
Eligibility for membership of creditors' or liquidation committee	17.4	2.50, 3.16, 4.152, 6.150
Establishment of committees	17.5	2.51, 3.17, 4.153, 6.151
Liquidation committee established by contributories	17.6	4.154
Notice of change of membership of a committee	17.7	2.51, 3.17, 4.153, 6.151
Vacancies: creditor members of creditors' or liquidation committee	17.8	2.59, 3.25, 4.163, 6.160
Vacancies: contributory members of liquidation committee	17.9	4.164
Resignation	17.10	2.56, 3.22, 4.160, 6.157
Termination of membership	17.11	2.57, 3.23, 4.161, 6.158
Removal	17.12	2.58, 3.24, 4.162, 6.159
Cessation of liquidation committee in a winding up when creditors are paid in full	17.13	4.171A
Chapter 4: Meetings of committee		
Meetings of committee	17.14	2.52, 3.18, 4.156, 6.153
The chair at meetings	17.15	2.53, 3.19, 4.157, 6.154
Quorum	17.16	2.54, 3.20, 4.158, 6.155
Committee-members' representatives	17.17	2.55, 3.21, 4.159, 6.156
Voting rights and resolutions	17.18	2.60, 3.26, 4.165, 4.166, 6.161
Resolutions by correspondence	17.19	2.61, 3.27, 4.167, 6.162

2016 Rule heading	2016 Rule	1986 Rule
Remote attendance at meetings of committee	17.20	12A.26
Procedure for requests that a place for a meeting should be specified	17.21	12A.27
Chapter 5: Supply of information by the office-holder to the committee		
Notice requiring office-holder to attend the creditors' committee (administration and administrative receivership) (paragraph 57(3)(a) of Schedule B1 and section 49(2))	17.22	2.62, 3.28
Office-holder's obligation to supply information to the committee (winding up and bankruptcy)	17.23	4.155, 4.168, 6.152, 6.163
Chapter 6: Miscellaneous		
Expenses of members etc.	17.24	2.63, 3.29, 4.169, 6.164
Dealings by committee members and others	17.25	4.170, 6.165
Dealings by committee members and others: administration and administrative receivership	17.26	2.64, 3.30
Formal defects	17.27	2.65, 3.30A, 4.172A
Special rule for winding up by the court and bankruptcy: functions vested in the Secretary of State	17.28	4.172, 6.166
Chapter 7: Winding up by the court following an administration		
Continuation of creditors' committee	17.29	4.173, 4.174A, 4.176, 4.178
Part 18: Reporting and remuneration of office-holders		
Chapter 1: Introductory		
Scope of Part 18 and interpretation	18.1	N/A
Chapter 2: Progress reports		
Reporting by the office-holder	18.2	N/A
Contents of progress reports in administration, winding up and bankruptcy	18.3	2.47, 4.49B, 4.49C, 6.78A,
Information about remuneration	18.4	2.47, 4.49B, 4.49C, 6.78A,
Information about pre-administration costs	18.5	2.67A
Progress reports in administration: timing	18.6	2.47(3) and (6)
Progress reports in voluntary winding up: timing	18.7	4.49C
Progress reports in winding up by the court and bankruptcy: timing	18.8	4.49B, 6.78A(3)
Creditors' and members' requests for further information in administration, winding up and bankruptcy	18.9	2.48A, 4.49E, 6.78C
Administration, creditors' voluntary liquidation and compulsory winding up: reporting distribution of property to creditors under rule 14.13	18.10	4.49F

2016 Rule heading	2016 Rule	1986 Rule
Voluntary winding up: reporting arrangements under section 110	18.11	4.49F
Members' voluntary winding up: reporting distribution to members other than under section 110	18.12	4.49G
Bankruptcy proceedings: reporting distribution of property to creditors under section 326	18.13	6.78D
Chapter 3: Final accounts in winding up and bankruptcy		
Contents of final account (winding up) and final report (bankruptcy)	18.14	4.125, 4.126, 4.126A 4.49D, 6.78B
Chapter 4: Remuneration and expenses in administration, winding up and bankruptcy		
Application of Chapter	18.15	
Remuneration: principles	18.16	2.106, 4.127, 4.148A, 6.138
Remuneration of joint office-holders	18.17	2.106(7), 4.128(2), 6.139(2)
Remuneration: procedure for initial determination in an administration	18.18	2.106, 2.106(5A),
Remuneration: procedure for initial determination in a members' voluntary winding up	18.19	4.148A
Remuneration: procedure for initial determination in a creditors' voluntary winding up or a winding up by the court	18.20	4.127
Remuneration: procedure for initial determination in a bankruptcy	18.21	6.138
Application for scale fees where creditors fail to fix the basis for the office-holder's remuneration	18.22	4.127A, 6.138A
Remuneration: application to the court to fix the basis	18.23	2.106(6), 4.127(7), 4.148A(6)
Remuneration: administrator, liquidator or trustee seeking increase etc.	18.24	2.107, 4.129A, 6.140A
Application for an increase etc. in remuneration: the general rule	18.25	2.107(1), 4.129A, 6.140A
First exception: administrator has made a statement under paragraph 52(1)(b) of Schedule B1	18.26	2.107(2)
Second exception: administrator who had applied for increase etc. under rule 18.24 becomes liquidator	18.27	4.127(5A)
Remuneration: recourse by administrator, liquidator or trustee to the court	18.28	2.108 4.130 6.141
Remuneration: review at request of administrator, liquidator or trustee	18.29	2.109A, 4.131A, 6.142A

2016 Rule heading	2016 Rule	1986 Rule
Remuneration: exceeding the fee estimate	18.30	2.109AB, 4.131AB, 6.142AB[1]
Remuneration: new administrator, liquidator or trustee	18.31	2.109B, 4.131B, 4.148D, 6.142B
Remuneration: apportionment of set fees	18.32	2.109C, 4.131C, 4.148E, 6.142C
Remuneration: variation of the application of rules 18.29, 18.30 and 18.32	18.33	2.109D, 4.131D[2]
Remuneration and expenses: application to court by a creditor or member on grounds that remuneration or expenses are excessive	18.34	2.109, 4.131, 4.148C, 6.142
Remuneration and expenses: application to court by a bankrupt on grounds that remuneration or expenses are excessive	18.35	6.142
Applications under rules 18.34 and 18.35 where the court has given permission for the application	18.36	2.109, 4.131, 4.148C, 6.142
Applications under rule 18.34 where the court's permission is not required for the application	18.37	2.109, 4.131, 4.148C 6.142
Remuneration in winding up and bankruptcy where assets are realised on behalf of charge holder	18.38	4.127B, 6.139
Part 19: Disclaimer in winding up and bankruptcy		
Application of this Part	19.1	4.187, 6.178
Notice of disclaimer (sections 178 and 315)	19.2	4.187, 6.178
Notice of disclaimer to interested persons (sections 178 and 315)	19.3	4.188, 6.179
Notice to disclaimer of leasehold property (sections 179 and 317)	19.4	4.188(2), 6.179(2)
Notice of disclaimer in respect of a dwelling house (bankruptcy) (section 318)	19.5	6.179(3)–(4)
Additional notices of disclaimer	19.6	4.189, 6.180
Records	19.7	4.190A, 6.181A
Application for permission to disclaim in bankruptcy (section 315(4))	19.8	6.182
Application by interested party for decision on disclaimer (sections 178(5) and 316)	19.9	4.191A, 6.183
Disclaimer presumed valid and effective	19.10	4.193, 6.185
Application for exercise of court's powers under section 181 (winding up) or section 320 (bankruptcy)	19.11	4.194, 6.186

[1] Inserted into the Insolvency Rules 1986 by the Insolvency (Amendment) Rules 2015, to commence 1/10/15
[2] Inserted into the Insolvency Rules 1986 by the Insolvency (Amendment) Rules 2015, to commence 1/10/15

2016 Rule heading	2016 Rule	1986 Rule
Part 20: Debtors and their families at risk of violence: orders not to disclose current address		
Application of this Part and interpretation	20.1	5.67(2), 5A.18(1), 6.235B(2)
Proposed IVA (order for non-disclosure of current address)	20.2	5.67
IVA (order for non-disclosure of current address)	20.3	5.67
Debt relief application (order for non-disclosure of current address)	20.4	5A.18
Bankruptcy application (order for non-disclosure of current address)	20.5	6.50B
Bankruptcy and debt relief proceedings (order for non-disclosure of current address)	20.6	5A.18, 6.235B
Additional provisions in respect of order under Rule 20.6(4)	20.7	N/A
Part 21: The EC Regulation		
Interpretation for this Part	21.1	N/A
Conversion into winding up proceedings or bankruptcy: application	21.2	1.31,1.32, 2.130, 2.131, 5.62, 5.63
Conversion into winding up proceedings or bankruptcy: court order	21.3	1.33, 2.132, 5.64
Confirmation of creditors' voluntary winding up: application	21.4	7.62(1)–(3)
Confirmation of creditors' voluntary winding up: court order	21.5	7.62(5)–(8)
Confirmation of creditors' voluntary winding up: notice to member State liquidator	21.6	7.63
Member state liquidator: duty to give notice	21.7	1.34, 2.133, 4.231, 5.65, 6.238, 6.239
Member state liquidator: rules on creditors' participation in proceedings	21.8	2.133, 4.231, 6.238, 6.239, 7.64, 8.8
Part 22: Permission to act as director etc. of company with a prohibited name (section 216)		
Preliminary	22.1	4.226
Application for permission under section 216(3)	22.2	4.227A
Power of court to call for liquidator's report	22.3	4.227A(2)
First excepted case: business of insolvent company acquired under specified arrangements	22.4	4.228
	22.5	
Second excepted case	22.6	4.229
Third excepted case	22.7	4.230
Revocations	Sch. 1	N/A
Transitional and Savings Provisions	Sch. 2	N/A

2016 Rule heading	**2016 Rule**	**1986 Rule**
Punishment of Offences under these Rules	Sch. 3	Sch. 5
Service of documents	Sch. 4	
• Service of documents	Para. 1	12A.17, 12A.20
• Service of winding-up petitions	Para. 2	4.8, 4.22
• Service of administration application (paragraph 12 of Schedule B1)	Para. 3	N/A
• Service on joint office-holders	Para. 3	12A.19
• Service of orders staying proceedings	Para. 4	7.56, 12A.18
• Certificate of service	Para. 5	2.8, 2.9, 4.9A, 6.15A
Calculation of time periods	Sch. 5	12.55
Insolvency jurisdiction of county court hearing centres	Sch. 6	Sch. 2 and SI 2014/817
Information to be provided in the bankruptcy application	Sch. 7	Sch. 2A
Part 1: Debtor's personal information		
Part 2: Additional personal information		
Additional information to be provided in the bankruptcy application	Sch. 8	Sch. 2B
Information to be given to creditors	Sch. 9	Sch. 2C
Destination of appeals from decisions of District Judges in corporate insolvency matters	Sch. 10	N/A
Determination of insolvency office-holder's remuneration	Sch. 11	Sch. 6

Index

LEGAL TAXONOMY
FROM SWEET & MAXWELL

This index has been prepared using Sweet & Maxwell's Legal Taxonomy. Main index entries conform to keywords provided by the Legal Taxonomy except where references to specific documents or non-standard terms (denoted by quotation marks) have been included. These keywords provide a means of identifying similar concepts in other Sweet & Maxwell publications and online services to which keywords from the Legal Taxonomy have been applied. Readers may find some minor differences between terms used in the text and those which appear in the index. Suggestions to *sweet&maxwell.taxonomy@thomson.com.*

References within square brackets are located in Volume 2.

Ancillary statutes and statutory instruments are not indexed, though references are set out within the Tables.

The following abbreviations are used to denote the location of entries:

[CBIR]	Cross-Border Insolvency Regulations 2006
[CDDA]	Company Directors Disqualification Act 1986
[EURIP]	EU Regulation on Insolvency Proceedings 2015/848
IA	Insolvency Act 1986
IR	Insolvency (England and Wales) Rules 2016
[UML]	UNCITRAL Model Law on Cross-Border Insolvency

Provision

Debt relief orders—continued **Provision**

Provision

Liquidators—continued **Provision** **Provision**